D1491931

EU STATE AIDS

EU STATE AIDS

EU STATE AIDS

FOURTH EDITION

LEIGH HANCHER
Professor of European Law
University of Tilburg
Of Counseil, Allen & Overy, Amsterdam

TOM OTTERVANGER
Member of the Amsterdam Bar,
Allen & Overy LLP
Professor of European & Competition Law
University of Leiden

PIET JAN SLOT
Professor of Economic Law
University of Leiden

SWEET & MAXWELL   THOMSON REUTERS

Published in 2012 by Sweet & Maxwell, 100 Avenue Road, London NW3 3PF
Part of Thomson Reuters (Professional) UK Limited
(Registered in England & Wales, Company No 1679046.
Registered Office and address for service:
Aldgate House, 33 Aldgate High Street, London EC3N 1DL)

Typeset by Interactive Sciences Ltd, Gloucester
Printed and bound by CPI Group (UK) Ltd,
Croydon, CR0 4YY

For further information on our products and services, visit
www.sweetandmaxwell.co.uk

No natural forests were destroyed to make this product; only farmed
timber was used and re-planted.

A CIP catalogue record for this book is available from the British Library
ISBN 978 0 414 04656 6

Thomson Reuters and the Thomson Reuters logo are
trademarks of Thomson Reuters.
Sweet & Maxwell ® is a registered trademark of Thomson Reuters (Legal) Limited.

Crown copyright material is reproduced with the permission of the Controller of HMSO
and the Queen's Printer for Scotland.

LIST OF CONTRIBUTIONS

Chapters 1, 3, 4, 8, 20
Leigh Hancher

Chapter 2
Phedon Nicolaides Professor European Institute of Public Administration, Maastricht, The Netherlands

Chapter 5
Julia Rapp The author is an official of the European Commission. The views expressed are purely those of the author and may not in any circumstances be regarded as stating an official position of the European Commission.

Chapter 6
Marco Bronckers Professor of Law, University of Leiden; Partner, VVGB Advocaten/Avocats, Brussels; former member of the WTO Permanent Group of Experts on Subsidies. Former Partner at WilmerHale.

Gary Horlick Partner, WilmerHale, Washington DC; former chairman of the WTO Permanent Group of Experts on Subsidies; former head of Import Administration, US Department of Commerce

Ravi Soopramanien Procurement Policy Officer, African Development Bank. Formerly Associate at Vermulst Verhaeghe Graafsma & Bronckers.

Chapters 7, 11
Koen Van de Casteele The author is an official of the European Commission. The views expressed are purely those of the author and may not in any circumstances be regarded as stating an official position of the European Commission.

Chapter 9
Mark Friend Partner, Allen & Overy LLP. The author gratefully acknowledges the valuable contributions of Alison Berridge of Monckton Chambers, and Emily Bourne of Allen & Overy LLP.

Chapter 10

Wolfgang Schön

Dr jur, Director, Max Planck Institute for Intellectual Property, Competition and Tax Law, Munich; Honorary Professor, Ludwig Maximilian University, Munich.

Chapters 12, 24, 25

Piet Jan Slot

Chapter 13

Agnieszka
Stobiecka-Kuik

The author is an official of the European Commission. The views expressed are purely those of the author and may not in any circumstances be regarded as stating an official position of the European Commission.

Chapters 14, 23, 26, 27

Tom Ottervanger

Chapter 15

Klaus-Otto
Junginger-Dittel

The author is an official of the European Commission. The views expressed are purely those of the author and may not in any circumstances be regarded as stating an official position of the European Commission.

Chapter 16

Michael Schütte

Dr. iur., attorney-at-law, Berlin and Brussels. Honorary Chairman of the Berlin Round Table on European State aid law.

Chapter 17

Tibor Scharf

The author is an official of the European Commission. The views expressed are purely those of the author and may not in any circumstances be regarded as stating an official position of the European Commission.

Chapter 18

Antonio Bravasso

Partner, Allen & Overy LLP; Visiting Professor of EU Competition Law, Faculty of Laws, University College London; Director, Jevons Institute for Competition Law and Economics at UCL.

Chapter 19

Christoph Arhold

Counsel at White & Case LLP, Berlin and Brussels.

Chapter 21
Thomas Jestaedt

Partner, Jones Day. The author is one of the coordinators and authors of a study on the application of EU State Aid law by the member States which was prepared for the European Commission in 2006. The author gratefully acknowledges the valuable contribution of Alexandra Deege of Jones Day.

Chapter 22
Melvin Könings

Senior consultant at the Lysias Consulting Group in The Netherlands. Previously he was a detached national expert at the Competition Directorate-General of the European Commission (Directorate State Aid I), seconded by the Dutch Ministry of Economic Affairs.

Ilze Jozepa

Independent consultant, associate at the Lysias Consulting Group in The Netherlands. Previously she was an advisor on state aid at Europa Decentraal, the Netherlands' local and regional authorities' knowledge centre for European law and policy.

Chapter 23
Thibault Kleiner and
Tom Ottervanger

PhD: The author is an official of the European Commission. The views expressed are purely those of the author and may not in any circumstances be regarded as stating an official position of the European Commission. The author would also like to thank Almoro Rubin de Cervin for providing some background analysis.

Chapter 26
Tom Ottervanger and
Paul Adriaanse

Associate Professor in Constitutional and Administrative law at Leiden University.

Chapter 27
Tom Ottervanger and
Leo Flynn

The author is an official of the European Commission. The views expressed are purely those of the author and may not in any circumstances be regarded as stating an official position of the European Commission.

PREFACE TO THE FOURTH EDITION

Almost six years have elapsed since we published the third edition of *EC State Aids*. In the intervening period this area of European law has again grown in importance and also in complexity. We have therefore been very fortunate to have found a number of new contributors who have been willing to write on special topics, thus extending the scope of the book. Among these contributors are a number of Commission officials who have kindly agreed to provide chapters on a personal basis. Their contributions do not in any way reflect the official standpoint of the European Commission.

In completing the fourth edition of this work we have greatly benefitted from the know how and editorial assistance of Euan Peebles and Lyndsey Thomsin. We are very grateful to them for their efforts in ensuring consistency between the chapters, and in co-ordinating the completion of the appendices. As always, responsibility for the final product remains with the authors.

Leigh Hancher
Tom Ottervanger
Piet Jan Slot

January 2012

CONTENTS

PAGE

List of Contributions   v
Preface   ix
Table of Cases   xix
Table of Commission and Council Decisions
  By case number   xliii
  By decision number   lviii
Table of Decisions of the EFTA   lxxiii
Table of European Regulations and Directives   lxxiv
Table of Guidelines and Notices   lxxxv
Table of Treaties and Conventions   xc

PART I   GENERAL

1. EU State Aid Law—Now a Truly Ugly Sister?

PARA

1. Introduction   1–001
2. Aims   1–008
3. Major Developments and Future Trends   1–010
4. Beneficiaries of Aid   1–033
5. Block Exemptions and Guidelines   1–038
6. Conclusion—Towards a Reorientation?   1–043

2. The Economics of State Aid and the Balancing Test

1. Introduction   2–001
2. Subsidies as a Policy Instrument   2–004
3. Why Supranational Rules on Subsidies?   2–008
4. Assessing Cross-border Effects of State Aid: Balancing Effects or
     Coordination of Aid?   2–017
5. The Problem of Defining Optimum Subsidies   2–024
6. The Main Features of the Commission's Refined Economic
     Approach   2–033
7. Conclusions   2–041

3. THE GENERAL FRAMEWORK

1. General	3–001
2. The Attributes	3–015
3. The Selectivity Criteria	3–040
4. Effect on Trade	3–076
5. State Participation and the Market Economy Investor Test	3–081
6. The Relationship Between Articles 107 to 109 TFEU and Other Provisions of the EU Treaty	3–108

4. ARTICLE 107(2) AND ARTICLE 107(3)

1. Introduction	4–001
2. Automatic Exemptions: Article 107(2)	4–003
3. Article 107(3)	4–012
4. The Specific Provisions	4–018
5. The Regulation of Certain Categories and Types of Aid	4–043

5. STATE AID IN THE ACCESSION COUNTRIES

1. Introduction	5–001
2. The State Aid Regime Under the Europe/Association Agreements	5–002
3. The State Aid Regime Under the 2003 Accession Treaty	5–004
4. Aid Measure "Put Into Effect Before Accession"	5–007
5. Aid Measure "Applicable After Accession"	5–009
6. Aid Measures Subject to Specific Transitional Arrangements in the Steel Sector	5–014
7. Aid Measures Granted in the Agricultural and Transport Sectors	5–018
8. The Accession of Bulgaria and Romania	5–020
9. Special Provisions Regarding the Steel Sector in Bulgaria and Romania	5–022
10. Accession Negotiations with Croatia and Ireland	5–024
11. Conclusion	5–029

6. WTO REGULATION OF SUBSIDIES

1. Introduction	6–001
2. The WTO Agreement on Subsidies and Countervailing Measures	6–004
3. The WTO Agreement on Agriculture	6–022
4. The WTO General Agreement on Trade in Services	6–026
5. European Regulation of Countervailing Duties	6–027
6. WTO Subsidy and EU State Aid Control	6–029

7. DE MINIMIS AID

1. Introduction 7–001
2. Enabling Regulation 7–002
3. De Minimis Regulation 7–003
4. Controversy on the Nature of the De Minimis Rule 7–011
5. Crisis Measures: Temporary Framework—Link with De Minimis 7–013

PART II SPECIFIC ISSUES

8. PUBLIC SECTOR AID

1. General 8–001
2. Suveillance: Rules Concerning Transparency 8–015
3. Concept of State Aid: The Market Economy Investor Principle 8–018
4. Compatibility of Aid to Public Undertakings and Undertakings
   Entrusted with the Performance of an SGEI 8–024
5. Cross-subsidisation 8–051
6. Privatisation 8–067

9. GUARANTEES

1. Summary of the Commission's Current Position 9–001
2. Types of Guarantees Covered 9–006
3. General Considerations in Identifying Whether a State Guarantee
   Constitutes Aid 9–011
4. Safe Harbours in the Notice on Guarantees 9–013
5. Practical Difficulties in Applying the Safe Harbours in the Notice
   on Guarantees 9–019
6. Aid to the Lender 9–021
7. Amount of the Aid 9–022
8. Assessing the Compatibility of Aid in the Form of Guarantees 9–025
9. Consequences of Non-notification 9–026
10. The Temporary Framework 9–029

10. STATE AID IN THE AREA OF TAXATION

1. Introduction 10–001
2. General Aspects of Tax Competition and State Aid Law 10–003
3. The Application of Article 107(1) TFEU in Tax Matters: The
   Notion of "Aid" with Respect to Tax 10–006

11. GENERAL BLOCK EXEMPTION REGULATION

1. Introduction   11–001
2. General Block Exemption Regulation   11–004
3. Experience   11–028
4. Why Does the Commission Not Block Exempt More Measures?   11–029

PART III SECTORAL AID

12. SECTORAL AID INTRODUCTION

1. General   12–001
2. The Period Prior to Publication of the Commission's
   Communication   12–003
3. The Commission's Communication on Sectoral Aid   12–004
4. The Application of the General Sectoral Principles   12–008
5. Conclusion   12–021

13. AGRICULTURE

1. Introduction   13–001
2. Common Market Organisation   13–003
3. Rural Development   13–006
4. Accession Treaties   13–009
5. Material State Aid Rules on Compatibility   13–012
6. Fisheries and Aquaculture   13–042

14. STATE AID TO THE COAL AND STEEL SECTORS

1. Introduction   14–001
2. The ECSC Treaty Regime   14–002
3. State Aid in the Coal Industry   14–008
4. State Aid in the Steel Industry   14–052
5. State Aid for Coal and Steel in the New Member States   14–065
6. Concluding Remarks   14–080

15. REGIONAL INVESTMENT AID TO LARGE INVESTMENT PROJECTS: THE RULES UNDER THE STATE AID ARCHITECTURE FOR 2007–2013

1. Introduction   15–001
2. The Definitions and Procedural and Compatibility Assessment
   Rules Applicable to Regional Aid for Large Investment
   Projects   15–004

Contents

3. The Commission's Experience in the Application of the Rules
   Regarding Regional Aid to Large Investment Projects Under the
   Regional Aid Guidelines 2007–2013   15–025
4. Conclusions and Outlook   15–033

16. SHIPBUILDING

1. Introduction   16–001
2. New Framework for State Aid for Shipbuilding   16–005
3. The External Aspect   16–011

17. TRANSPORT

1. Introduction   17–001
2. Secondary Legislation on State Aid for the Inland Transport
   Sector   17–006
3. The Application of the Rules   17–034
4. Conclusion   17–086

18. BROADCASTING

1. Introduction   18–001
2. Public Service Broadcasting   18–002
3. Financing Digital Switchover   18–012

PART IV   HORIZONTAL AID

19. FINANCIAL SECTOR

1. Introduction   19–001
2. Banks and their Position as Grantors or Transmitters of State Aid 19–002
3. Article 107(1) TFEU—State Aid Measures in Favour of Banks   19–005
4. Approval of Rescue and Restructuring Under Article 107(3)(c)
   TFEU   19–018
5. Rescue (Emergency) and Restructuring Cases During the Financial
   Crisis Under Article 107(3)(b) TFEU   19–031
6. Foresights: State Aid to Financial Institutions—Current and Future
   Challenges   19–078

20. THE ENERGY SECTOR

1. General Introduction   20–001
2. The EURATOM Treaty   20–002
3. The EU Treaty Framework   20–014
4. Article 107(2) and (3)—the Exemptions   20–041
5. Rescue and Restructuring Aid   20–054
6. The Methodology on Stranded Costs   20–057
7. The Energy Sector and Article 106(2) TFEU   20–076
8. Aid Through Energy Companies   20–088

21. REGIONAL AID

1. Introduction   21–001
2. First Steps to Co-ordinate National Regional Aid Systems in the 1970s and 1980s   21–005
3. The 1998 Regional Aid Guidelines   21–006
4. Rules Applicable to New Member States Prior to Adoption of the Regional Aid Guidelines 2007–2013   21–012
5. Multisectoral Frameworks 1997 and 2002   21–013
6. The Regional Aid Guidelines 2007–2013   21–014

22. ENVIRONMENTAL AID

1. Summary   22–001
2. The EU Environmental Policy and State Aid Law   22–002
3. Key Priorities in EU Environmental Policy   22–008
4. Market Failure and Justification of Environmental State Aid   22–012
5. Environmental Measures—When Do They Constitute State Aid?   22–017
6. Compatibility of Environmental Aid with the TFEU   22–026
7. Application of the Environmental Guidelines and the GBER   22–030
8. Calculating Eligible Investment Costs—the Method   22–034
9. Aid to Go Beyond Community Standards or in Absence of Such Standards   22–041
10. Aid for the Acquisition of New Transport Vehicles   22–047
11. Aid for Early Adaptation to Future Community Standards   22–049
12. Aid for Environmental Studies   22–050
13. Aid for Energy Saving (Investment/Operating Aid)   22–051
14. Aid for Renewable Energy Sources (Investment/Operating Aid)   22–053
15. Aid for Cogeneration (Investment/Operating Aid)   22–072
16. Aid for Energy Efficient District Heating (Investment/Operating Aid)   22–074

17. Aid for Waste Management ... 22–075
18. Aid for the Remediation of Contaminated Sites ... 22–077
19. Aid for the Relocation of Undertakings ... 22–079
20. Aid Involved in Tradable Permit Schemes/Emission Trading Systems ... 22–081
21. Aid in the Form of Environmental Tax Exemptions or Reductions ... 22–090
22. Compatibility of Aid Under Article 107(3)(b) TFEU ... 22–096
23. State Aid Expenditure on Environmental Aid ... 22–097
24. Outlook to Further Development ... 22–099

23. RESEARCH, DEVELOPMENT AND INNOVATION AID

1. Introduction ... 23–001
2. Notion of Aid for R&D ... 23–008
3. Standard Assessment ... 23–012
4. Detailed Assessment ... 23–022
5. Conclusion ... 23–030

24. RESCUE AND RESTRUCTURING AID

1. General Comments ... 24–001
2. The Main Elements of the Guidelines ... 24–013
3. Conditions for Authorisation for Individual Aid: Rescue Aid ... 24–020
4. Conditions for Authorisation for Individual Aid: Restructuring Aid ... 24–027
5. Aid Schemes for SMEs ... 24–045
6. Miscellaneous ... 24–048
7. Conclusion ... 24–053

PART V PROCEDURE AND REMEDIES

25. ADMINISTRATIVE PROCEDURE

1. Introduction ... 25–001
2. Direct Effect ... 25–004
3. The System of Procedural Rules ... 25–007
4. The Procedural Regime ... 25–013
5. Rights of Interested Parties ... 25–053
6. Monitoring ... 25–057
7. Common Provisions ... 25–060

8. Handling of State Aid Cases within the Commission   25–063
9. Interim Orders and Final Decisions   25–067
10. Procedures Under the EEA Agreement   25–068

26. RECOVERY OF UNLAWFUL AID

1. Introduction   26–001
2. The Concept of Unlawful Aid   26–003
3. The Rules on Recovery of Unlawful Aid   26–005
4. Commission's Power to Demand Recovery   26–009
5. Positions of Member States and Recipients Concerned   26–013
6. Actions by Third Parties before the National Courts   26–021

27. JUDICIAL PROTECTION

1. Introduction   27–001
2. Enforcement by the Commission Before the ECJ   27–003
3. Action Against the Commission   27–012
4. The Role of National Courts   27–050

APPENDICES

    PAGE

1. EU Competition Law Rules Applicable to State Aid   1067
2. European Court of Justice Judgments and Orders   1075
3. General Court Judgments and Orders   1106

Index   1151

TABLE OF CASES

3F (formerly Specialarbejderforbundet i Danmark (SID)) v Commission of the European
  Communities (C–319/07 P) [2009] E.C.R. I–5963; [2009] 3 C.M.L.R. 40 ECJ (3rd
  Chamber) 1–029, 10–034, 25–031, 25–032, 27–019, 27–020, 27–027
ABN-Amro Group (T–319/11) [2011] OJ C252/35 1–025
ACEA v Commission of the European Communities (T–292/02) [2009] E.C.R. II–1659 ... 25–014
ACEA Electrabel v Commission of the European Communities (T–303/05) [2009] E.C.R.
  II–137; upheld (C–480/09 P) 20–039, 20–068, 22–025
AceaElectrabel Produzione SpA v Commission of the European Communities (C–480/09 P)
  Unreported December 16, 2010 .... 3–041, 3–079
Acegas–APS v Commission of the European Communities (T–300/02) [2009 E.C.R.
  II–1737 27–018
Administracion del Estado v Xunta de Galicia (C–71/04) [2005] E.C.R. I–7419; [2006] 2
  C.M.L.R. 6 ECJ (3rd Chamber) 3–015
Adria Wien Pipeline GmbH v Finanzlandesdirektion fur Karnten (C–143/99) [2002] All E.R.
  (EC) 306; [2001] E.C.R. I–8365; [2002] 1 C.M.L.R. 38 ECJ (5th Chamber) 3–044, 3–046,
              3–047, 10–003, 10–011, 10–019, 10–024, 10–026, 10–032, 10–035, 10–036,
                        20–030, 22–024, 22–091, 22–092, 26–020
AEESCAM v Commission (T–95/03). See Asociacion de Empresarios de Estaciones de
  Servicio de la Comunidad Autonoma de Madrid v Commission of the European
  Communities (T95/03)
AEM v Commission of the European Communities (T–301/02) [2009] E.C.R. II–1757 25–014
AEM Brescia SpA v Commission (T–189/03) [2009] E.C.R. II–1831 20–032
AEM SpA v Autorita per l'Energia Elettrica e per il Gas (C–128/03) [2005] E.C.R. I–2861;
  [2005] 2 C.M.L.R. 60 ECJ (3rd Chamber) 3–008, 10–011, 10–013, 10–026, 10–040, 20–032
Aeroports de Paris v Commission of the European Communities (T–128/98) [2000] E.C.R.
  II–3929; [2001] 4 C.M.L.R. 38 CFI (3rd Chamber) 3–087, 17–057, 17–074
AES Tisza v Commission of the European Communities (T–468/08 R) [2008] ECR II–346 ... 27–045
Agrana Zucker und Starke AG v Commission of the European Communities (C–321/01 P)
  [2002] E.C.R. I–10027 ECJ 5–014
Agrana Zucker und Stärke AG v Commission of the European Communities (T–187/99)
  [2001] E.C.R. II–1587 CFI 25–029
Air France v Commission. See Compagnie Nationale Air France v Commission of the
  European Communities (T–358/94)
Air Liquide Industries Belgium SA v Ville de Seraing (C–393/04); Air Liquide Industries
  Belgium SA v Province de Liege (C–41/05) [2006] E.C.R. I–5293; [2006] 3 C.M.L.R.
  23 ECJ (2nd Chamber) 3–131, 3–132, 10–005, 10–011, 10–032, 10–040, 25–006, 27–054
Air One v Commission of the European Communities (T–395/04) [2006] ECR II–1343 27–038,
                                                                                                    27–041
AITEC v Commission of the European Communities (T–277/94). See Associazione Italiana
  Tecnico Economica del Cemento (AITEC) v Commission of the European Commu-
  nities (T–277/94)
AIUFFASS v Commission of the European Communities. See Association Internationale des
  Utilisateurs de Fils de Filaments Artificiels et Synthetiques et de Soie Naturelle (AIUF-
  FASS) v Commission of the European Communities (T–380/94)
Aktionsgemeinschaft Recht und Eigentum v Commission of the European Communities
  (T–114/00) 27–023

Table of Cases

Alcoa Trasformazioni v Commission of the European Communities (T–332/06) [2009]
E.C.R. II–29 .... 20–018, 20–022, 20–091, 25–015, 27–013
Alcoa Trasformazioni v Commission of the European Communities (C–194/09 P), July 21,
2011 ....20–018, 20–091, 27–013
Alitalia Linee Aeree Italiane SpA v Commission of the European Communities (T–296/97)
[2001] All E.R. (EC) 193; [2000] E.C.R. II–3871 CFI (3rd Chamber) 3–083, 3–084, 19–007
Alitalia v Commission of the European Communities (T–96/97) [2000] E.C.R. II–3871 19–007
Alitalia v Commission of the European Communities (T–301/01) [2008] E.C.R. II–1753 ...19–007,
19–071, 25–036
Altmark Trans GmbH v Nahverkehrsgesellschaft Altmark GmbH (C–280/00) [2005] All
E.R. (EC) 610; [2003] E.C.R. I–7747; [2003] 3 C.M.L.R. 12 ECJ 1–017, 3–026, 3–067,
3–068, 3–071, 3–076, 3–077, 3–104, 8–025, 8–028, 8–029, 8–030, 8–031,
8–032, 8–033, 8–034, 8–035, 8–036, 8–037, 8–039, 8–042, 8–044, 8–045,
8–046, 8–047, 8–049, 8–055, 8–056, 8–065, 8–066, 17–002, 17–003,
17–006, 17–010, 17–011, 17–012, 17–013, 17–014, 17–015, 17–016,
17–021, 17–023, 17–034, 17–044, 17–079, 18–002, 18–004, 18–010,
20–040, 20–077, 20–078, 20–095, 22–022, 24–010, 24–043, 25–021
Amministrazione delle Finanze dello Stato v Denkavit Italiana Srl (61/79) [1980] E.C.R.
1205; [1981] 3 C.M.L.R. 694 ECJ 3–004, 3–005, 10–014
Amministrazione Delle Finanze Dello Stato v Essevi Spa and Carlo Salengo (142/80) [1981]
E.C.R. 1413 ECJ 10–003, 10–005, 10–013
Anderson v Commission of the European Communities (T–87/09 [2009] E.C.R. II–225 27–013
ARAP v Commission of the European Communities. See Associacao dos Refinadores de
Acucar Portugueses (ARAP) v Commission of the European Communities (C–321/99
P)
Arbeitsgemeinschaft Deutscher Luftfahrt-Unternehmen v Commission of the European
Communities (T–86/96) [1998] E.C.R. II–641 CFI 10–023, 27–044
Asklepios Kliniken v Commission of the European Communities (T–167/04) [2007] ECR
II–2379 ....27–039, 27–041
Asociacion de Empresarios de Estaciones de Servicio de la Comunidad Autonoma de Madrid
v Commission of the European Communities (T–95/03) [2006] E.C.R. II–4739 CFI 1–023,
3–023
Asociacion de Estaciones de Servicio de Madrid et Federacion Catalana de Estaciones de
Servicio v Commission (T–146/03) [2003] E.C.R. II–98 13–041
Asociacion Telefonica de Mutualistas (ATM) v Commission of the European Communities
(T–178/94) [1997] E.C.R. II–2529 CFI 27–020
Associacao dos Refinadores de Acucar Portugueses (ARAP) v Commission of the European
Communities (C–321/99 P) [2002] E.C.R. I–4287; [2002] 2 C.M.L.R. 38 ECJ (6th
Chamber) 3–039, 25–051
Association des Acieries Europeennes Independantes v Commission of the European Com-
munities (T–239/94) [1994] E.C.R. II–0703 27–044
Association Internationale des Utilisateurs de Fils de Filaments Artificiels et Synthetiques et
de Soie Naturelle (AIUFFASS) v Commission of the European Communities
(T–380/94) [1996] E.C.R. II–2169; [1997] 3 C.M.L.R. 542 CFI (5th Chamber) ...4–021, 21–003,
27–019
Associazione italiana del risparmio gestito and Fineco Asset Management v Commission of
the European Communities (T–455/05)[2009] E.C.R. II–289 ....10–034, 10–037, 27–019
Associazione Italiana Tecnico Economica del Cemento (AITEC) v Commission of the
European Communities (T–447/93) [1995] E.C.R. II–1971 CFI 4–025, 25–010, 27–019
Associazione Italiana Tecnico Economica del Cemento (AITEC) v Commission of the
European Communities (T–277/94) [1996] E.C.R. II–351; [1997] 2 C.M.L.R. 855
CFI 26–005, 27–005
Asteris AE v Greece (106/87) [1988] E.C.R. 5515; [1990] 1 C.M.L.R. 575 ECJ (5th
Chamber) 3–012, 3–013
Athinaiki Techniki AE v Commission of the European Communities (C–521/06 P) [2008]
E.C.R. I–5829; [2008] 3 C.M.L.R. 34 ECJ (4th Chamber) 27–029, 27–030
Atlanta Fruchthandelsgesellschaft mbH v Bundesamt fur Ernahrung und Forstwirtschaft
(C–465/93) [1996] All E.R. (E.C.) 31; [1995] E.C.R. I–3761; [1996] 1 C.M.L.R. 575
ECJ 27–004
Atzeni v Commission of the European Communities (T–21/02) May 29, 2002 27–059

Table of Cases

Atzori v Sardinia (C–346/03) [2006] E.C.R. I–1875 ECJ 3–076, 13–002, 13–003, 3–035, 17–007, 26–019, 27–018, 27–059

Austria v Commission of the European Communities (C–99/98) [2001] E.C.R. I–1101 ECJ ...25–015, 25–023, 25–037

Austria v Scheucher-Fleisch GmbH (C–47/10 P) Unreported October 27, 2010 13–041

Automec Srl v Commission of the European Communities (T–24/90) [1992] E.C.R. II–2223; [1992] 5 C.M.L.R. 431 CFI 25–055

Azores Judgment. *See* Portugal v Commission of the European Communities (C–88/03)

Babyliss SA v Commission of the European Communities (T–114/02) [2003] E.C.R. II–1279; [2004] 5 C.M.L.R. 1 CFI (3rd Chamber) 3–121

BAI v Commission of the European Communities (T–14/96). *See* Bretagne Angleterre Irlande (BAI) v Commission of the European Communities (T14/96)

Banco Comercial dos Açores, SA v Commission of the European Communities (T–75/03) 10–008

Banco Exterior de Espana SA v Ayuntamiento de Valencia (C–387/92); sub nom, Banco de Credito Industrial SA v Ayuntamiento de Valencia (C–387/92) [1994] E.C.R. I–877; [1994] 3 C.M.L.R. 473 ECJ 3–005, 3–029, 3–128, 8–026, 8–027, 10–011, 10–017, 10–036

Banks v British Coal. *See* HJ Banks & Co Ltd v Coal Authority

Belgische Radio en Televisie v SABAM SV (127/73) (No.2) [1974] E.C.R. 313; [1974] 2 C.M.L.R. 238 ECJ 18–004

Belgium v Commission of the European Communities (C–110/03); sub nom. Legality of Regulation 2204/2002, Re (C–110/03) [2005] E.C.R. I–2801; [2006] 2 C.M.L.R. 5 ECJ (3rd Chamber) 1–038, 4–001

Belgium v Commission of the European Communities (C–234/84) [1986] E.C.R. 2263; [1988] 2 C.M.L.R. 331 ECJ 8–067

Belgium v Commission of the European Communities (C–40/85); sub nom. Aid to Boch SA, Re (C–40/85) [1986] E.C.R. 2321; [1988] 2 C.M.L.R. 301 ECJ 19–006

Belgium v Commission of the European Communities (C–142/87); sub nom. Aid to Tube-meuse, Re (C–142/87) [1990] E.C.R. I–959; [1991] 3 C.M.L.R. 213 ECJ 4–045, 7–001, 25–023, 25–039, 25–067, 26–009

Belgium v Commission of the European Communities (C–56/93) [1996] E.C.R. I–723 ECJ 3–015, 3–028, 3–055, 3–086, 19–005, 20–025, 20–089, 20–090

Belgium v Commission of the European Communities (C–53/96) [1998] E.C.R. 1 8–014

Belgium v Commission of the European Communities (C–75/97) [1999] E.C.R. I–3671; [2000] 1 C.M.L.R. 791 ECJ (6th Chamber) 3–048, 10–011, 10–035, 10–036, 19–017

Belgium v Commission of the European Communities (C–457/00) [2003] E.C.R. I–6931 ECJ 8–021

Belgium v Commission of the European Communities (C–5/01) [2002] E.C.R. I–11991 ECJ 10–011, 10–034

Belgium v Commission of the European Communities (C–182/03 R) [2003] E.C.R. I–5479 ECJ 4–002, 4–042, 10–005, 10–006, 10–009, 10–011, 10–018, 10–030, 10–037, 10–041, 10–032, 25–016, 27–047

Belgium v Deutsche Post AG (C–148/09 P) Unreported September 22, 2011 ..8–031 27–024, 27–027

Belgium v Van Calster (C–261/01) [2003] E.C.R. I–12249; [2004] 1 C.M.L.R. 18 ECJ 3–130, 10–028, 10–039, 10–040, 13–041, 25–006, 25–024, 25–055

Bethell (Lord) v Commission of the European Communities (C–246/81) [1982] E.C.R. 2277; [1982] 3 C.M.L.R. 300 ECJ 27–037

BNP Paribas and Banca Nazionale del Lavoro SpA (BNL) v Commission of the European Communities (T–335/08) Unreported July 1, 2010 ....10–018, 10–019, 10–032, 27–018

Bouygues and Bouygues Telecom v Commission of the European Communities (C–399/10 P), (C–401/10 P) [2010] OJ C317/14 3–010

Bouygues SA v Commission of the European Communities (C–431/07 P) [2009] E.C.R. I–2665; [2009] 3 C.M.L.R. 13 ECJ (1st Chamber) 3–008

Bouygues SA v Commission of the European Communities (T–475/04) [2007] E.C.R. II–2097 CFI 3–008, 27–027

Boychou v Commission of the European Communities (T–344/04 [2007] ECR II–92 27–049

BP Chemicals Ltd v Commission of the European Communities (T–11/95) [1998] E.C.R. II–3235; [1998] 3 C.M.L.R. 693 CFI 24–006, 27–022, 27–026, 27–0

BP Chemicals Ltd v Commission of the European Communities (T–184/97) [2000] E.C.R. II–3145; [2000] 3 C.M.L.R. 1076 CFI (2nd Chamber) 4–022, 25–010, 27–036

Table of Cases

BP Nederland and others v Commission of the European Communities (T–237/99) [2000]
E.C.R. II–3849 27–044

Breda Fucine Meridionali SpA (BFM) v Commission of the European Communities
(T–126/96); Ente Partecipazioni e Finanziamento Industria Manifatturiera (EFIM) v
Commission of the European Communities (T–127/96) [1998] E.C.R. II–3437; [1999]
1 C.M.L.R. 997 CFI .... 24–027, 25–031, 25–065, 27–013, 27–035Freistaat Sachsen

Bretagne Angleterre Irlande (BAI) v Commission of the European Communities (T–230/95)
[1999] E.C.R. II–123, CFI 27–048

Bretagne Angleterre Irlande (BAI) v Commission of the European Communities (T14/96)
[1999] E.C.R. II–139; [1999] 3 C.M.L.R. 245 CFI (1st Chamber) 3–006, 3–102, 4–004,
25–010, 25–062

British Aerospace Plc v Commission of the European Communities (C–294/90); Rover
Group Plc v Commission of the European Communities (C–292/90) [1992] E.C.R.
I–493; [1992] 1 C.M.L.R. 853 ECJ 25–018, 25–041, 26–011, 27–006, 27–050

British Aggregates Association v Commission of the European Communities (C–487/06 P)
[2008] E.C.R. I–10505; [2009] 2 C.M.L.R. 10; [2009] Env. L.R. 24 ECJ (3rd Chamber) ...1–025,
3–015, 3–047, 10–024, 10–032, 20–032, 27–033

British Aggregates Association v Commission of the European Communities (T–210/02)
[2006] E.C.R. II–2789; [2007] Env. L.R. 11 CFI (2nd Chamber) 1–043, 3–047, 10–012,
10–024, 20–032, 25–045

British Aggregates Association v Commission of the European Communities (T–359/04)
Unreported July 9, 2010 .... 3–115, 10–005

British Airways Plc v Commission of the European Communities (T–371/94) [1998] E.C.R.
II–2405; [1998] 3 C.M.L.R. 429; [1998] C.E.C. 731 CFI (2nd Chamber) 17–067, 27–006,
27–021, 27–035

British United Provident Association Ltd (BUPA) v Commission of the European Communities (T–289/03) [2008] E.C.R. II–741 ....8–025, 8–034, 8–036, 8–043

British United Provident Association Ltd (BUPA) v Commission of the European Commu-
nities (T–293/03) 8–029

BTR v SABAM. See Belgische Radio en Televisie v SABAM SV (127/73) (No.2)

Buczek Automotive v Commission of the European Communities (T–1/08 R) [2008] ECR
II–42 27–045

Budapsti Eromu v Commission of the European Communities (T–80/06) [2006] OJ
C108/25 20–065

Buy Irish Campaign, Re (C249/81); sub nom. Commission of the European Communities v
Ireland (C–249/81) [1982] E.C.R. 4005; [1983] E.C.R. 4005; [1983] 2 C.M.L.R. 104
ECJ 3–112

Capolongo v Azienda Agricola Maya (77/72) [1973] E.C.R. 611; [1974] 1 C.M.L.R. 230
ECJ 10–005, 12–019, 25–004, 27–057

CDA Datentraeger Albrechts v Commission of the European Communities (T–324/00)
[2005] E.C.R. II–4309 26–015

CELEBI. See Celulose Beira Industrial (Celbi) SA v Fazenda Publica (C–266/91)

CELF v Ministre de la Culture et de la Communication. See Centre d'Exportation du Livre
Francais (CELF) v Societe Internationale de Diffusion et d'Edition (SIDE)
(C–199/06)

CELF. See France v Commission of the European Communities (C–332/98)

Celulose Beira Industrial (Celbi) SA v Fazenda Publica (C–266/91) [1993] E.C.R. I–4337
ECJ 10–005

Centre de coordination Carrefour SNC v Commission of the European Communities
(T–94/08) March 18, 2010 27–015

Centre d'Exportation du Livre Francais (CELF) v Societe Internationale de Diffusion et
d'Edition (SIDE) (C–199/06) [2008] E.C.R. I–469; [2008] 2 C.M.L.R. 20 ECJ (Grand
Chamber) 11–008, 25–005, 25–038, 26–003, 26–006, 26–020, 26–021, 26–022, 27–054

Centre d'Exportation du Livre Francais (CELF) v Societe Internationale de Diffusion et
d'Edition (SIDE) (C–1/09) [2010] E.C.R. 1–2099 ....4–035, 25–005, 25–038

Chambre Syndicale Nationale des Entreprises de Transport de Fonds et Valeurs (Sytraval) v
Commission of the European Communities (T–95/94) [1995] E.C.R. II–2651 CFI (4th
Chamber) 3–006, 3–055, 8–053, 25–002, 25–008, 25–030

Cheap Gas for Dutch Horticulturalists, Re (C213/85); sub nom. Commission of the European
  Communities v Netherlands (C–213/85) [1988] E.C.R. 281; [1988] 2 C.M.L.R. 287
  ECJ 26–010
Chronopost SA v Union Francaise de l'Express (UFEX) (C–83/01 P); La Poste v Union
  Francaise de l'Express (UFEX) (C–93/01 P); France v Union Francaise de l'Express
  (UFEX) (C–94/01 P) [2003] E.C.R. I–6993; [2003] 3 C.M.L.R. 11 ECJ 1–020, 3–084, 3–103,
                                                                    8–041, 8–049, 8–055, 8–056, 20–095
Chronopost SA v Union Francaise de l'Express (UFEX) (C–341/06 P); La Poste v Union
  Francaise de l'Express (UFEX) (C–342/06 P) [2008] E.C.R. I–4777; [2008] 3 C.M.L.R.
  19 ECJ (Grand Chamber) 1–020, 3–055, 3–084, 3–103
Cipeke-Comercio Industria de Papel Lda v Commission of the European Communities
  (T–84/96) [1996] E.C.R. II–1313 27–042
City of Mainz (Germany) v Commission of the European Communities (T–155/96) [1996]
  E.C.R. II–1655 CFI 3–093, 27–020, 27–044
Cofaz II v Commission of the European Communities. *See* Societe CdF Chimie Azote et
  Fertilisants SA v Commission of the European Communities (C–169/84)
Colt Telecommunications France v Commission of the European Communities (T–79/10) 3–072
Comite d'Entreprise de la Societe Francaise de Production v Commission of the European
  Communities (T–189/97) [2000] E.C.R. I–3659 ECJ 27–020
Comite d'Entreprise de la Societe Francaise de Production v Commission of the European
  Communities (C–106/98 P); sub nom. Comite d'Entreprise de la Societe Francaise de
  Production v Commission of the European Communities (T–189/97) [2000] E.C.R.
  I–3659 ECJ 27–020, 27–032
Comite International de la Rayonne et des Fibres Synthetiques (CIRFS) v Commission of the
  European Communities (C–313/90) [1993] E.C.R. I–1125 ECJ (5th Chamber) 25–017,
                                                                    25–027, 25–029, 26–003, 27–019
Commission of the European Communities v Aktionsgemeinschaft Recht und Eigentum
  (ARE) (C–78/03 P) [2005] E.C.R. I–10737 [2006] 2 C.M.L.R. 48 ECJ 27–019, 27–023,
                                                                    27–024, 27–031, 27–033
Commission of the European Communities v Belgium (90 & 91/63) [1964] E.C.R. 1217;
  [1965] C.M.L.R. 58 ECJ 13–041
Commission of the European Communities v Belgium (156/77) [1978] E.C.R. 1881 ECJ 17–001,
                                                                    17–002, 27–058
Commission of the European Communities v Belgium (C–375/89) [1991] E.C.R. 367 27–008
Commission of the European Communities v Belgium (C–378/98) [2001] E.C.R. I–5107
  ECJ 10–006, 26–013
Commission of the European Communities v Belgium (C–221/03) [2005] E.C.R. I–8307;
  [2006] Env. L.R. D4 ECJ (3rd Chamber) 13–017
Commission of the European Communities v Belgium (C–255/03) Unreported, June 17,
  2004 ECJ 13–032
Commission of the European Communities v Belgium Unreported July 28, 2011 8–018
Commission of the European Communities v Belgium; sub nom. State Shareholding in
  Synthetic Fibres, Re (C–74/89) [1990] E.C.R. I–491; [1990] 2 C.M.L.R. 393, ECJ 26–013
Commission of the European Communities v Chambre Syndicale Nationale des Entreprises
  de Transport de Fonds et Valeurs (Sytraval) (C–367/95 P) [1998] E.C.R. I–1719 ECJ 3–006,
               8–053, 25–002, 25–008, 25–027, 25–030, 25–054, 27–022, 27–026, 27–028,
                                                                    27–029, 27–030, 27–036
Commission of the European Communities v Council of Ministers of the European Commu-
  nities (C–309/95) [1998] E.C.R. I–655; [1998] 2 C.M.L.R. 1265 ECJ (6th Chamber) 13–005
Commission of the European Communities v Council of the European Communities
  (C–111/10, C–118/10, C–1221/1 [2010] OJ C113 13–016
Commission of the European Communities v Council of the European Union (C–122/94)
  [1996] E.C.R. I–881 ECJ 4–041, 13–005
Commission of the European Communities v Council of the European Union (C–29/99)
  [2002] ECR I–1121, ECJ 20–004
Commission of the European Communities v Council of the European Union (C–110/02);
  sub nom. Aid to Pig Farmers, Re (C–110/02) [2005] All E.R. (EC) 397; [2004] E.C.R.
  I–6333; [2004] 2 C.M.L.R. 58 ECJ 4–040, 4–042, 13–005; 25–035, 26–008
Commission of the European Communities v Council of the European Union (C–399/03)
  [2006] E.C.R. I–5629 ECJ 4–042, 13–005, 25–035

Commission of the European Communities v EDF (C–124/10 P) [2010] OJ C161/16 3–082
Commission of the European Communities v European Parliament (C–122/04) [2006]
 E.C.R. I–2001 ECJ 4–041
Commission of the European Communities v Feilhauer (C–209/90) [1992] E.C.R. I–2613;
 [1996] 1 C.M.L.R. 26 ECJ 26–010
Commission of the European Communities v France (167/73); sub nom. French Merchant
 Seamen, Re (167/73) [1974] E.C.R. 359; [1974] 2 C.M.L.R. 216 ECJ ...17–002, 17–003, 17–062
Commission of the European Communities v France (171/83R) [1983] E.C.R. 2621 ECJ 27–003
Commission of the European Communities v France (18/84); sub nom. Aid to French
 Newspapers, Re (18/84) [1985] E.C.R. 1339; [1986] 1 C.M.L.R. 605 ECJ 3–112, 10–005
Commission of the European Communities v France (6/69); sub nom. Export Credits, Re
 (6/69) [1969] E.C.R. 523; [1970] C.M.L.R. 43 ECJ 3–043
Commission of the European Communities v France (C–290/83). *See* Grants to Poor
 Farmers, Re (C–290/83)
Commission of the European Communities v France (C–216/84) [1988] E.C.R. 793 ECJ 13–004
Commission of the European Communities v France (C–57/97) 3–044
Commission of the European Communities v France (C–258/00) [2002] E.C.R. I–5959
 AGO 13–017
Commission of the European Communities v France (C–232/05) [2006] E.C.R. I–10071;
 [2007] 3 C.M.L.R. 3 ECJ (1st Chamber) 26–013, 27–057
Commission of the European Communities v France (C–214/07); sub nom. Decision
 2004/343, Re (C–214/07) [2008] E.C.R. I–8357; [2009] 1 C.M.L.R. 27 ECJ (2nd
 Chamber) 1–022, 27–004
Commission of the European Communities v France; sub nom. Tax Credits, Re (270/83)
 [1986] E.C.R. 273; [1987] 1 C.M.L.R. 401 ECJ 10–004
Commission of the European Communities v Freistaat Sachsen (C–334/07 P) [2008] E.C.R.
 I–9465; [2009] 1 C.M.L.R. 42 ECJ 15–031
Commission of the European Communities v French Republic (C–441/06) [2007] E.C.R.
 I–8887 26–010
Commission of the European Communities v Germany (70/72) (Kohlnegesetz); sub nom.
 Investment Grants for Mining, Re (70/72) [1973] E.C.R. 813; [1973] C.M.L.R. 741
 ECJ 3–045, 4–040, 10–011, 26–009, 27–003
Commission of the European Communities v Germany (C–94/87); sub nom. Alcan Alumi-
 niumhutte, Re [1989] E.C.R. 175; [1989] 2 C.M.L.R. 425 ECJ 26–013, 26–018
Commission of the European Communities v Germany (C–161/00) [2002] E.C.R. I–2753
 ECJ (6th Chamber) 13–017
Commission of the European Communities v Germany (C–325/00); sub nom. Quality Label
 Scheme, Re (C–325/00) [2002] E.C.R. I–9977; [2003] 1 C.M.L.R. 1; [2003] E.T.M.R.
 33 ECJ 13–032
Commission of the European Communities v Germany; sub nom. State Aid to Bug-
 Alutechnik GmbH, Re (C–5/89) 1990] E.C.R. I–3437; [1992] 1 C.M.L.R. 117 ECJ ... 26–018
Commission of the European Communities v Gibralter (C–106/09) Unreported November
 15, 2011 ....10–003, 10–012, 10–032
Commission of the European Communities v Gibralter (C–106/09); Spain v Gibralter
 (C–107/09) Unreported April 7, 2011 ....3–053, 10–005, 10–008, 10–011, 10–016, 10–018,
                                                                           10–026, 10–037, 10–041
Commission of the European Communities v Greece (C–61/90); sub nom. Wheat Exports,
 Re [1992] E.C.R. I–2407; [1994] 3 C.M.L.R. 213 ECJ 27–003
Commission of the European Communities v Greece (C–183/91) [1993] E.C.R. I–3131
 ECJ 9–027
Commission of the European Communities v Greece (C–193/91) [1991] E.C.R. I–3131,
 ECJ 26–012
Commission of the European Communities v Greece (C–415/03); sub nom. Aid to Olympic
 Airways, Re (C–415/03) [2005] E.C.R. I–3875; [2005] 3 C.M.L.R. 10 ECJ (2nd
 Chamber) 17–070, 26–016, 27–009
Commission of the European Communities v Greece (C–63/87); sub nom. State Aid to
 Exports, Re [1988] E.C.R. 2875; [1989] 3 C.M.L.R. 677 ECJ 26–008
Commission of the European Communities v Greece (C–369/07) [2009] E.C.R. I–5703 1–035,
                                                                                                                                     27–009

Table of Cases

Commission of the European Communities v Hellenic Republic (C–419/06) [2008] E.C.R. I–27 26–009

Commission of the European Communities v Ireland (C–396/01) [2004] E.C.R. I–2315; [2004] Env. L.R. 46 ECJ 13–017

Commission of the European Communities v Ireland (C–89/08 P) [2009] E.C.R. I–11245; [2010] 2 C.M.L.R. 17 ECJ (Grand Chamber) 1–031, 20–029, 25–016, 25–017

Commission of the European Communities v Italy (169/82); sub nom. State Aids to Agriculture, Re (169/82) [1984] E.C.R. 1603; [1985] 3 C.M.L.R. 30 ECJ 3–125

Commission of the European Communities v Italy (203/82); sub nom. Employers Social Security Contributions, Re (C203/82) [1983] E.C.R. 2525; [1985] 1 C.M.L.R. 653 ECJ 3–043

Commission of the European Communities v Italy (C–277/83); sub nom. Marsala Liqueur Wine, Re [1985] E.C.R. 2049; [1987] 3 C.M.L.R. 324 ECJ 3–128

Commission of the European Communities v Italy (103/84); sub nom. Subsidy for Italian Motor Vehicles, Re [1986] E.C.R. 1759; [1987] 2 C.M.L.R. 825 ECJ 3–112, 3–113

Commission of the European Communities v Italy (C–118/85); sub nom. Amministrazione Autonoma dei Monopoli di Stato, Re (C–118/85) [1987] E.C.R. 2599; [1988] 3 C.M.L.R. 255 ECJ 8–005

Commission of the European Communities v Italy [1987] E.C.R. 2599 3–041

Commission of the European Communities v Italy (C–280/95) [1998] E.C.R. I–259 ECJ 27–004

Commission of the European Communities v Italy (C–35/96); sub nom. Customs Agents, Re (C–35/96) [1998] E.C.R. I–3851; [1998] 5 C.M.L.R. 889 ECJ (5th Chamber) 3–041

Commission of the European Communities v Italy (C–127/99) [2001] E.C.R. I–8305 ECJ (6th Chamber) 13–017

Commission of the European Communities v Italy (C–494/06 P); sub nom. Loans for Foreign Investment, Re (C–494/06 P) [2009] E.C.R. I–3639; [2009] 3 C.M.L.R. 25 ECJ (1st Chamber) 4–046

Commission of the European Communities v Italy (C–302/09) October 6, 2011 27–004

Commission of the European Communities v Italy (C–304/09) Unreported, December 22, 2010 .... 10–037, 27–004

Commission of the European Communities v Koninklijke Friesland Campina NV (C–519/07 P) [2009] E.C.R. I–8495; [2010] 1 C.M.L.R. 13 ECJ (3rd Chamber) 10–041, 27–016, 27–018

Commission of the European Communities v Kvaerner Warnow Werft GmbH (C–181/02 P) [2004] E.C.R. I–5703; [2004] 2 C.M.L.R. 19 ECJ (5th Chamber) 1–026

Commission of the European Communities v Luxembourg (C–266/00) [2001] E.C.R. I–2073; [2001] Env. L.R. D15 ECJ 13–017

Commission of the European Communities v Netherlands (C–213/85). See Cheap Gas for Dutch Horticulturalists, Re (C213/85)

Commission of the European Communities v Poland (C–331/09) Unreported April 14, 2011 26–014

Commission of the European Communities v Portugal (EPAC) (C–404/97) [2000] E.C.R. I–4897, ECJ 9–027, 9–028, 27–004

Commission of the European Communities v Salzgitter AG (C–408/04 P) [2008] E.C.R. I–2767; [2008] 2 C.M.L.R. 52 ECJ (Grand Chamber) 14–057

Commission of the European Communities v Slovak Republic Unreported, 2010 10–016

Commission of the European Communities v Spain (C–499/99) [2002] E.C.R. I–6031, ECJ 26–014

Commission of the European Communities v Spain (C–416/02) [2005] E.C.R. I–7487 ECJ ... 13–017

Commission of the European Communities v Spain (C–485/03) [2006] E.C.R. I–11887 ECJ 27–004

Commission of the European Communities v Tetra Laval BV (C–12/03 P) [2005] All E.R. (EC) 1059; [2005] E.C.R. I–987; [2005] 4 C.M.L.R. 8 ECJ 1–026

Commission of the European Communities v United Kingdom (C–69/99) [2000] E.C.R. I–10979 ECJ (3rd Chamber) 13–017

Compagnie commerciale de l'Ouest (C–78/82) [1992] E.C.R. I–1847 10–005

Compagnie Nationale Air France v Commission of the European Communities (T–358/94) [1996] E.C.R. II–2019 ....3–018, 3–019, 3–028, 3–029, 3–033, 3–034, 8–006, 8–013, 17–067, 19–007, 19–009

Compassion in World Farming Ltd. See R. v Ministry of Agriculture, Fisheries and Food

Comunidad Autonoma de Cantabria v Council of the European Union (T–238/97) [1998]
   E.C.R. II–2271; [1999] 3 C.M.L.R. 656 CFI 27–020
Confederacion Espanola de Transporte de Mercancias (CETM) v Commission of the Euro-
   pean Communities (T–55/99) [2000] E.C.R. II–3207 CFI ...17–043, 17–063, 26–011, 26–019,
                                                                     26–019, 27–012, 27–018, 27–019
Confederation Nationale du Credit Mutuel v Commission of the European Communities
   (T93/02) [2005] E.C.R. II–143 CFI 8–060
Confservizi v Commission of the European Communities (T–292/02) [2009] E.C.R.
   II–1659 27–019
Cook v Commission of the European Communities (C–181/91) [1993] E.C.R. I–2478 27–022,
                                                                                          27–023, 27–024
Cook v Commission of the European Communities (C–198/91). *See* William Cook Plc v
   Commission of the European Communities (C–198/91)
Corbeau, Criminal Proceedings against (C–320/91) [1993] E.C.R. I–2533; [1995] 4
   C.M.L.R. 621 ECJ 18–004
Corsica Ferries France SA v Direction Generale des Douanes Francaises (C–49/89) [1989]
   E.C.R. 4441; [1991] 2 C.M.L.R. 227 ECJ (2nd Chamber) 17–062
Corsica Ferries France SAS v Commission of the European Communities (T–349/03) [2005]
   E.C.R. II–2197 CFI 1–040, 4–015, 27–035
Cuno v Daimler Chrysler, Supreme Court, 386 F.3d 738 (6th Cir. 2004) 19–044
Daewoo Electronics Manufacturing Espana SA (DEMESA) v Commission of the European
   Communities (C183/02 P) [2004] E.C.R. I–10609; [2005] 1 C.M.L.R. 31 ECJ (2nd
   Chamber) 10–002
Danish Buses v Commission of the European Communities (T–157/01) [2004] E.C.R.
   II–917; [2004] 2 C.M.L.R. 29 CFI (2nd Chamber) 5–126, 8–032, 8–065, 17–034, 25–010
De Gezamenlijke Steenkolenmijnen in Limburg v High Authority of the European Coal and
   Steel Community (30/59) [1961] E.C.R. 50; [1961] E.C.R. 95 ECJ ...3–002, 10–001, 10–017,
                                                                                                   10–034
Delimitis v Henninger Brau AG (C–234/89) [1991] E.C.R. I–935; [1992] 5 C.M.L.R. 210
   ECJ 25–038
Deltalinqs and SVW v Commission of the European Communities (T–481/07) Order of
   December 9 2009 27–023
Demenagements-Manutention Transport SA (DMT), Re (C–256/97) [1999] All E.R. (EC)
   601; [1999] E.C.R. I–3913; [1999] 3 C.M.L.R. 1; [1999] C.E.C. 299 ECJ (6th
   Chamber) 10–006, 10–016, 10–035, 10–036
Denkavit. *See* Amministrazione delle Finanze dello Stato v Denkavit Italiana Srl
Departement du Loiret v Commission of the European Communities (T–369/00) [2003]
   E.C.R. II–1789 CFI 26–007
Deufil GmbH & Co KG v Commission of the European Communities (310/85) [1987]
   E.C.R. 901; [1988] 1 C.M.L.R. 553 ECJ (6th Chamber) 3–054, 17–067, 18–014, 26–009,
                                                                                                   26–019
Deutsche Babcock Handels GmbH v Hauptzollamt Lubeck-Ost (C–328/85) [1987] E.C.R.
   5119 ECJ 14–004
Deutsche Bahn AG v Commission of the European Communities (T–351/02) [2006] E.C.R.
   II–1047; [2006] 2 C.M.L.R. 54 CFI (1st Chamber) 3–035, 10–018, 13–033, 20–028, 27–029,
                                                                                                   27–030
Deutsche Post AG v Commission of the European Communities (T–266/02) [2008] E.C.R.
   II–1233 ....8–030, 8–036, 8–063
Deutsche Post AG v Commission of the European Communities (T–388/03) [2009] E.C.R.
   II–199; [2009] 2 C.M.L.R. 35 CFI (2nd Chamber) 8–031, 25–029, 27–033
Deutsche Post AG v Commission of the European Communities (C–367/04) [2006] E.C.R.
   I–26 ECJ 27–033
Deutsche Post and Germany v Commission of the European Communities (C–463/10 P and
   C–475/10 P), October 13, 2011 .... 1–033, 27–013
Deutsche Post v Commission of the European Communities (T–388/11) 8–065
Diputacion Foral de Alava and Gobierno Vasco v Commission of the European Communities
   [2009] E.C.R. II–3029 27–018
Diputacion foral de Alava v Commission of the European Communities (T–127/99) [2002]
   E.C.R. II–1275 CFI 3–097, 10–007, 10–008, 10–011, 10–026, 10–028, 10–035, 10–036,
                                                                                          10–037, 25–031

Table of Cases

DIR International Film Srl v Commission of the European Communities (C–164/98 P) [2000] E.C.R. I–447; [2000] 1 C.M.L.R. 619 ECJ (6th Chamber) 3–021

Distribution Casino France SAS and Others v Caisse nationale de l'organisation autonome d'assurance vieillesse des travailleurs non salariés des professions industrielles et commerciales (Organic) (C–266/04 , C–276/04 and C–321/04—C–325/04) [2005] E.C.R. I1–09481 10–040

Distribution Casino France SAS v Caisse Nationale de l'Organisation Autonome d'Assurance Vieillesse des Travailleurs Non Salaries des Professions Industrielles et Commerciales (ORGANIC) (C–270/04) Unreported, July 14, 2005 AGO 3–132

DMT. See Demenagements-Manutention Transport SA (DMT), Re (C–256/97)

Draft Convention on the Physical Protection of Nuclear Materials, Facilities and Transport, Re (Opinion 1/78) [1978] E.C.R. 2151; [1979] 1 C.M.L.R. 131 ECJ 20–004

EARL Salvat pere & fils, Comite interprofessionnel des vins doux naturels et vins de liqueur a appellations controlees (CIVDN) and Comite national des interprofessions des vins a appellation d'origine (CNIV) v Commission (T–136/05) [2007] E.C.R II–04063 13–030

Ecotrade Srl v Altiforni e Ferriere di Servola SpA (AFS) (C–200/97) [1998] E.C.R. I–7907; [1999] 2 C.M.L.R. 804 ECJ 3–022, 3–023, 3–054, 10–010, 10–011, 25–011

EEC Seed Crushers and Oil Processors Federation (FEDIOL) v Commission of the European Communities (187/85) [1988] E.C.R. 4155; [1988] E.C.R. 4193 ECJ 10–017

EI Du Pont de Nemours Italiana SpA v Unita Sanitaria Locale No.2 di Carrara (C–21/88) [1990] E.C.R. I–889; [1991] 3 C.M.L.R. 25 ECJ 3–110, 3–113, 3–114

Electricite de France (EDF) v Commission (T–156/04) [2009] E.C.R. II–4503 .... 1–003, 1–025, 3–026, 8–023, 3–082, 8–007, 8–023, 10–016, 20–035, 25–031

Ellilnika Nafpigeia v Commission of the European Communities (T–391/08) [2008] OJ 327/29) 3–134

Endesa and Endesa Generacion v Commission of the European Communities (T–490/10 R), November 3, 2010; February 17, 2011 27–047

Enirisorse SpA v Ministero delle Finanze (C–34/01) [2003] E.C.R. I–14243; [2004] 1 C.M.L.R. 10 ECJ (5th Chamber) 3–131, 8–033, 8–045

Enirisorse SpA v Sotacarbo SpA (C–237/04) [2006] E.C.R. I–2843 ECJ 8–010

EPAC Empresa para a Agroalimentacao e Cereais SA v Commission of the European Communities (T–204/97) [2000] E.C.R. II–2267 CFI 3–023, 26–010

EREF v Commission of the European Communities (T–94/07) [2009] ECR II–220 27–034

EREF v Commission of the European Communities (T–40/08) [2009] ECR II–222 27–034

EREF v Commission of the European Communities (C–74/10 and C–75/10) September 29, 2010 27–034

Essent Netwerk Noord BV v Aluminium Delfzijl BV (C–206/06) [2008] E.C.R. I–5497; [2008] 3 C.M.L.R. 32 ECJ (3rd Chamber) 3–027, 3–031, 8–029, 10–005, 10–010, 20–021

EU v Korea, WTO Case DS 273 16–013

EU v Korea, WTO Cases DS 301 16–013

Eurl Le Levant 001 v Commission of the European Communities (T–34/02) [2006] E.C.R. II–267 CFI 3–041

European Commission v Deutsche Post AG (C–399/08 P) Unreported September 2, 2010 ...8–030, 8–035, 8–036, 27–035

European Commission v Kronoply GmbH & Co. KG and Kronotex GmbH & Co. KG (C–83/09 P) [2010] E.C.R. Unreported 1–030, 27–024, 27–027

European Commission v Scott SA (C–290/07 P) September 2, 2010 [2010] OJ C288/6 ....1–026, 1–033, 3–015, 3–094, 25–032, 27–035

European Commission v Technische Glaswerke Ilmenau GmbH (C–139/07 P); sub nom. Commission of the European Communities v Technische Glaswerke Ilmenau GmbH (C–139/07 P) [2011] 1 C.M.L.R. 3; [2011] Bus. L.R. D81 ECJ (Grand Chamber) 1–034, 25–032

Executif Regional Wallon v Commission of the European Communities (62/87); Gaverbel SA v Commission of the European Communities (72/87) [1988] E.C.R. 1573; [1989] 2 C.M.L.R. 771 ECJ (6th Chamber) 4–024, 17–067, 27–020

FAB Fernsehen aus Berlin GmbH v Commission of the European Communities (T–8/06) [2009] E.C.R. II–00196 4–016

Falck SpA v Commission of the European Communities (C–74/00 P); Acciaierie di Bolzano SpA v Commission of the European Communities (C–75/00 P) [2002] E.C.R. I–7869 ECJ 25–031

Federacion Espanola de Empresas de Tecnologia Sanitaria (FENIN) v Commission of the
European Communities (C–205/03 P) [2006] E.C.R. I–6295; [2006] 5 C.M.L.R. 7
ECJ 8–010
Federacion Nacional de Empresas de Instrumentacion Cientifica Medica Tecnica y Dental
(FENIN) v Commission of the European Communities (T–319/99) [2004] All E.R. (EC)
300; [2003] E.C.R. II–357; [2003] 5 C.M.L.R. 1; (2003) 72 B.M.L.R. 128 CFI (1st
Chamber) 8–010
Federal Republic of Germany v Commission of the European Communities (C–399/95R)
[1996] E.C.R. I–2441, ECJ 27–043
Federation Francaise des Societies d'Assurance (FFSA) v Commission of the European
Communities (T–106/95) [1997] E.C.R. II–229; [1997] 2 C.M.L.R. 78 CFI (3rd
Chamber) 8–027, 8–028, 8–032, 8–035, 10–011, 10–036, 20–095, 27–035
Federation Nationale du Commerce Exterieur des Produits Alimentaires v France
(C–354/90) [1991] E.C.R. I–5505 ECJ 11–008, 13–005, 19–004, 25–005, 26–003, 26–021,
27–013, 27–054
Federutility v Autorita per l'energia elettrica e il gas (C–265/08) [2010] E.C.R. I–3377 20–085
FENIN. *See* Federacion Espanola de Empresas de Tecnologia Sanitaria (FENIN) v Commis-
sion of the European Communities (C–205/03 P)
FENIN. *See* Federacion Nacional de Empresas de Instrumentacion Cientifica Medica Tecnica
y Dental (FENIN) v Commission of the European Communities (T–319/99)
Ferriere Nord SpA v Commission of the European Communities (T–176/01) [2004] E.C.R.
II–3931 .... 25–017, 25–029
Ferriere Nord SpA v Commission of the European Communites (C–49/05) [2008] E.C.R.
I–68 25–036
Ferring SA v Agence Centrale des Organismes de Securite Sociale (ACOSS) (C–53/00)
[2001] E.C.R. I–9067; [2003] 1 C.M.L.R. 34 ECJ (6th Chamber) ...3–103, 3–104, 8–025, 8–028,
8–029, 8–034, 8–041, 10–011, 10–013, 10–015, 10–019, 10–020, 10–026,
17–011, 18–002, 20–077
FFSA Case. *See* Federation Francaise des Societies d'Assurance (FFSA) v Commission of
the European Communities (T–106/95)
FG Marine v Commission of the European Communities (T–360/04) [2007] ECR II–91 ... 27–049
Finanzamt Koln-Altstadt v Schumacker (C–279/93) [1996] Q.B. 28; [1995] 3 W.L.R. 498;
[1995] E.C.R. I–225, ECJ 10–004
Fiocchi Munizioni SpA v Commission of the European Communities (T–26/01) [2003]
E.C.R. II–3951 CFI 3–133, 27–037
Firma Foto Frost v Hauptzollamt Lubeck-Ost (314/85) [1987] E.C.R. 4199; [1988] 3
C.M.L.R. 57 ECJ 27–050
Firma Herbert Scharbatke Gmbh v Germany (C–72/92) [1993] E.C.R. I–5509 ECJ 3–128
Firma Sloman Neptun Schiffahrts AG v Seebetriebsrat Bodo Ziesemer (C–72/91 and
C–73/91) [1993] E.C.R. I–887; [1995] 2 C.M.L.R. 97 ECJ 3–017, 3–025, 3–026, 3–050,
3–056, 3–106, 10–010, 10–017
Fleuren Compost BV v Commission of the European Communities (T–109/01) [2004]
E.C.R. II–127 CFI 1–032, 5–007, 25–019, 25–054, 26–017, 26–018
Foreningen af Jernskibs– og Maskinbyggerier i Danmark v Commission of the European
Communities (T–266/94) [1996] E.C.R. II–1399 CFI 27–023
Forum 187 ASBL v Commission of the European Communities (T–189/08) March 18,
2010 .... 25–051, 27–015
France Telecom v Commission [2009] E.C.R. II–4315 1–003
France Telecom v Commission [2010] E.C.R. Unreported 1–003
France v Commission of the European Communities (47/69); sub nom. Aids to the Textile
Industry, Re (47/69) [1970] E.C.R. 487; [1970] C.M.L.R. 351 ECJ 3–128, 3–129, 4–031,
4–032, 10–005
France v Commission of the European Communities (188/80); sub nom. Public Under-
takings, Re (188/80) [1982] E.C.R. 2545; [1982] 3 C.M.L.R. 144 ECJ 8–005, 8–007, 8–017,
14–004, 20–003
France v Commission of the European Communities (102/87); sub nom. Brewery Loan, Re
[1988] E.C.R. 4067; [1989] 3 C.M.L.R. 713 ECJ 10–034
France v Commission of the European Communities (C–301/87) [1990] E.C.R. I–307 ECJ 19–007,
24–011, 25–001, 25–009, 25–023, 25–031, 25–038, 25–039, 25–055,
25–065, 25–067, 27–003

France v Commission of the European Communities (C–325/91) [1993] E.C.R. I–3283 8–017
France v Commission of the European Communities (C–68/94); Societe Commerciale des
    Potasses et de l'Azote (SCPA) v Commission of the European Communities (C–30/95)
    [1998] E.C.R. I–1375; [1998] 4 C.M.L.R. 829, ECJ 24–007
France v Commission of the European Communities (C–241/94); sub nom. Kimberly Clark,
    Re (C–241/94) [1996] E.C.R. I–4551; [1997] 1 C.M.L.R. 983; [1997] I.R.L.R. 415 ECJ ...3–004,
                                            3–005, 3–042, 3–043, 10–017, 10–017, 24–033
France v Commission of the European Communities (C–251/97) [1999] E.C.R. I–6639
    ECJ 10–006, 10–011, 10–015
France v Commission of the European Communities (C–332/98) [2000] E.C.R. I–4833
    ECJ 8–025
France v Commission of the European Communities (C–17/99) [2001] E.C.R. I–2481 ECJ ... 25–023
France v Commission of the European Communities (C–482/99); sub nom. Aid to Stardust
    Marine, Re (C–482/99) [2003] All E.R. (EC) 330; [2002] E.C.R. I–4397; [2002] 2
    C.M.L.R. 41; [2002] C.E.C. 463 ECJ 1–003, 1–025, 3–019, 3–021, 3–028, 3–029, 3–030,
                            3–031, 3–032, 3–033, 8–006, 8–014, 9–010, 19–009, 20–025, 20–054,
                                                            20–089, 20–090, 24–009
France v Commission of the European Communities (C–456/00) [2002] E.C.R. I–11949
    ECJ 3–015, 13–002
France v Commission of the European Communities (CELF) (C–332/98) [2000] E.C.R.
    I–4833 ECJ 8–028
France v Commission of the European Communities (Stardust Marine) (C–437/98) 8–006
France v Commission of the European Communities (T–425/04); France Telecom SA v
    Commission of the European Communities (T–444/04), Bouygues SA and Bouygues
    Telecom SA v Commission of the European Communities (T–450/04) and AFORS
    Telecom v Commission of the European Communities (T–456/04) [2010] E.C.R.
    II–2099 ....3–010, 3–025, 8–020, 9–009, 20–024, 27–014, 27–016
France v Commission of the European Communities (T–427/04); France Telecom SA v
    Commission of the European Communities (T–17/05) [2009] E.C.R. II–4315 ...10–022, 10–026,
                                                            10–036, 25–031
France v Ladbroke Racing Ltd (T–67/94) [1998] E.C.R. II–1; [2000] 3 C.M.L.R. 611; [1998]
    C.E.C. 172 CFI (2nd Chamber) 4–035, 10–003, 10–011, 10–017, 10–020, 10–027, 18–014,
                                                            27–035
France v Ladbroke Racing Ltd (C–83/98 P) [2000] E.C.R. I–3271; [2000] 3 C.M.L.R. 555
    ECJ 3–015, 3–019, 3–029, 10–020
Francovich v Italy (C–6/90); Bonifacti v Italy (C–9/90) [1991] E.C.R. I–5357; [1993] 2
    C.M.L.R. 66 ECJ 26–021
Fred Olsen SA v Commission of the European Communities (T–17/02) [2005] E.C.R.
    II–2031 CFI 8–006, 8–029, 8–035, 25–062
Freistaat Sachsen and Land Sachsen-Anhalt v Commission of the European Communities
    (T–443/08); Leipzig-Halle GbmH v Commission of the European Communities
    (T–455/08); on appeal C–288/11 P), June 8, 2011 .... 8–010, 27–015
Freistaat Sachsen v Commission of the European Communities (C–57/00 P); Volkswagen
    AG v Commission of the European Communities (C–61/00 P) [2003] E.C.R. I–9975 4–009
Freistaat Sachsen v Commission of the European Communities (T–102/07) Unreported
    March 3, 2010 .... 24–015, 27–045
Freistaat Sachsen v Commission of the European Communities (C–459/10 P) Unreported
    July 21, 2011 24–015
Freistaat Thuringen v Commission of the European Communities (T–318/00) [2005] E.C.R.
    II–4179 CFI 25–036
Fresenius Case [1994] OJ C321/4 12–020
Fresistaat Sachsen v Commission of the European Communities (T–132/96); Volkswagen
    AG v Commission of the European Communities (T–143/96) [1999] E.C.R. II–3663;
    [2000] 3 C.M.L.R. 485 CFI (2nd Chamber) 4–025, 27–020
Freskot AE v Elliniko Dimosio (C–355/00); sub nom. Freskot AE v Greece (C–355/00)
    [2003] E.C.R. I–5263; [2003] 2 C.M.L.R. 30 ECJ (5th Chamber) 13–032
Fri-El Acerra Srl v Commission (T–551/10) [2011] OJ C30/52 20–048
Frucona Kosice v Commission of the European Communities (T–11/07) Unreported Decem-
    ber 7, 2010 .... 3–092, 10–016
Frucona Kosice v Commission of the European Communities (C–73/11 P) 3–092

GAARM. v Commission. *See* Groupement des Associations Agricoles pour l'Organisation de la Production et de la Commercialisation des Pommes de Terre et Legumes de la Region Malouine (GAARM) v Commission of the European Communities (C289/83) (No.2)

Gankema v Commission of the European Communities (T–210/99) [2004] ECR II–781 27–034

Gaverbel SA v Commission of the European Communities (72/87). *See* Executif Regional Wallon v Commission of the European Communities (62/87)

Gebroeders van der Kooy BV v Commission of the European Communities. *See* Kwekerij Gebroeders van der Kooy BV v Commission of the European Communities (67/85)

Gemeente Almelo v Energiebedrijf Ijssellmij NV (C–393/92); sub nom. Commune d'Almelo ea v NV Energiebedrijf Ijsselmij (C–393/92); Municipality of Almelo v NV Energiebedrijf Ijsselmij (C–393/92) [1994] E.C.R. I–1477; [1994] 2 C.E.C. 281 ECJ (5th Chamber) 18–004

GEMO. *See* Ministre de l'Economie, des Finances et de l'Industrie v Gemo SA (C–126/01)

Germany v Commission of the European Communities (84/82); sub nom. State Aids to the Belgian Textile Industry, Re (84/82) [1984] E.C.R. 1451; [1985] 1 C.M.L.R. 153 ECJ 3–006, 4–032, 25–001, 25–023, 25–031, 25–033

Germany v Commission of the European Communities (C–248/84); sub nom. Regional Aid Plans, Re (C248/84) [1987] E.C.R. 4013; [1989] 1 C.M.L.R. 591 ECJ 4–030, 21–003, 21–005

Germany v Commission of the European Communities (C–324/90); Pleuger Worthington GmbH v Commission of the European Communities (C342/90) [1994] E.C.R. I–1173; [1994] 3 C.M.L.R. 521 ECJ 3–043

Germany v Commission of the European Communities (C–329/93); Hanseatische Industrie-Beteiligungen GmbH v Commission of the European Communities (C–62/95); Bremer Vulkan Verbund AG v Commission of the European Communities (C–63/95) [1996] E.C.R. I–5151; [1998] 1 C.M.L.R. 591, ECJ 3–100, 25–010, 26–011

Germany v Commission of the European Communities (C–288/96) [2000] E.C.R. I–8237 ECJ 25–031

Germany v Commission of the European Communities (C–301/96) [2003] E.C.R. I–9919 ECJ 4–009, 4–025

Germany v Commission of the European Communities (C–156/98) [2000] E.C.R. I–6857; 3 I.T.L. Rep. 159 ECJ 3–080, 4–009, 10–005, 10–011, 10–034, 10–036, 18–014, 24–044

Germany v Commission of the European Communities (C–334/99) [2003] E.C.R. I–1139 ECJ 4–009, 8–023, 8–070

Germany v Commission of the European Communities (C–242/00) [2002] E.C.R. I–5603 ECJ 4–008

Germany v Commission of the European Communities (C–277/00) [2004] E.C.R. I–3925 .....26–015, 26–016

Germany v Commission of the European Communities (T–21/06) [2009] E.C.R. II–197 ......3–034, 4–016

Germany v Commission of the European Communities (T–376/07) 11–015

Germany v Commission of the European Communities (T–347/09) [2009] OJ C267/75 13–036

Germany v Commission of the European Communities (C–544/09 P) Unreported, September 15, 2011 .... 3–034, 18–012

Germany v Kronofrance SA (C–75/05 P) [2008] E.C.R. I–6619; [2009] 1 C.M.L.R. 3 ECJ (1st Chamber) 1–039, 4–022, 4–031, 27–023

Gestevision Telecinco SA v Commission of the European Communities (T–95/96) [1998] All E.R. (EC) 918; [1998] E.C.R. II–3407; [1998] 3 C.M.L.R. 1112 CFI (3rd Chamber) 25–044, 27–039, 27–040, 27–041

Gezamenlijke Steenkolenmijnen in Limburg v High Authority of the European Coal and Steel Community (17/57) [1959] E.C.R. 1 ECJ 3–107

Gibraltar v Commission of the European Communities (T195/01 R) [2001] E.C.R. II–3915 CFI 27–013, 27–046

Gibraltar v Commission of the European Communities (T–195/01) [2002] All E.R. (EC) 838; [2002] E.C.R. II–2309; [2002] 2 C.M.L.R. 33 CFI (2nd Chamber) 10–011, 25–015, 25–016, 25–019

Gibralter v Commission of the European Communities (T–211/04); United Kingdom, and Northern Ireland v Commission of the European Communities (T–215/04) [2008] E.C.R. II–3745 ....10–003, 10–005, 10–008, 10–012

Table of Cases

GIL Insurance Ltd v Customs and Excise Commissioners (C–308/01) [2004] All E.R. (EC)
954; [2004] S.T.C. 961; [2004] E.C.R. I–4777; [2004] 2 C.M.L.R. 22; [2004] C.E.C.
352; [2005] B.T.C. 5760; [2006] B.V.C. 3; [2004] S.T.I. 1119 ECJ (5th Chamber) 3–020,
3–046, 3–048, 3–049, 3–050, 3–106, 10–005, 10–011, 10–013, 10–021,
10–022, 10–026, 20–032

GlaxoSmithKline Services Unlimited v Commission of the European Communities
(C–501/06 P) [2009] E.C.R. I–9291; [2010] 4 C.M.L.R. 2; [2010] C.E.C. 885; (2010)
11 B.M.L.R. 95 ECJ (3rd Chamber) 1–026

Gonzalez y Diez SA v Commission of the European Communities (T–25/04) [2007] E.C.R.
II–3121 CFI 14–032, 25–041

Grafischer Maschinenbau v Commission of the European Communities (T–126/99) [2002]
E.C.R. II–2427 ....4–016, 20–054, 24–034, 24–037

Grants to Poor Farmers, Re (C–290/83); sub nom. Commission of the European Communities v France (C290/83) [1985] E.C.R. 439; [1986] 2 C.M.L.R. 546 ECJ 3–006, 27–003

Greece v Commission of the European Communities (57/86); sub nom. Export Interest
Rebates, Re (57/86) [1988] E.C.R. 2855; [1990] 1 C.M.L.R. 65 ECJ 19–012

Greece v Commission of the European Communities (C–278/00) [2004] E.C.R. I–3997
ECJ 4–006

Greece v Commission of the European Communities (T–415/05), (T–416/05) and
(T–423/05) (Olympic Airways) Unreported September 13, 2010 .... 1–026, 3–011, 3–034,
17–070, 17–072

Groupement des Associations Agricoles pour l'Organisation de la Production et de la
Commercialisation des Pommes de Terre et Legumes de la Region Malouine (GAARM)
v Commission of the European Communities (C289/83) (No.2) ECJ (1st Chamber) ... 13–003

GT Link A/S v De Danske Statsbaner (DSB) (C242/95) [1997] E.C.R. I–4449; [1997] 5
C.M.L.R. 601; [1998] C.E.C. 19 ECJ (6th Chamber) 8–033

H van den Bor BV v Voedselvoorzieningsin- en Verkoopbureau (C–428/99); sub nom. Van
den Bor BV v Voedselvoorzieningsin- en Verkoopbureau (C–428/99) [2002] E.C.R.
I–127; [2002] 1 C.M.L.R. 34 ECJ (5th Chamber) 13–003, 13–004

HAMSA. See Hijos de Andres Molina SA v Commission of the European Communities
(T–152/99)

Hansen GmbH & Co v Hauptzollamt Flensburg (91/78) [1979] E.C.R. 935; [1980] 1
C.M.L.R. 162 ECJ 3–116

Heineken Brouwerijen BV v Inspecteur der Vennootschapsbelasting (91/83) [1984] E.C.R.
3435; [1985] 1 C.M.L.R. 389 ECJ 25–039

Heiser v Finanzamt Innsbruck (C–172/03); sub nom. Heiser v Finanzlandesdirektion fur
Tirol (C172/03) [2005] E.C.R. I–1627; [2005] 2 C.M.L.R. 18; [2005] C.E.C. 687 ECJ
(2nd Chamber) 3–046, 3–077, 3–080, 10–011, 10–018, 10–034

Hijos de Andres Molina SA v Commission of the European Communities (T–152/99) [2002]
E.C.R. II–3049 CFI .. 1–020, 3–089, 3–091, 3–092, 4–019, 20–024, 24–045 ,20–046, 24–020,
24–022, 24–024

HJ Banks & Co Ltd v Coal Authority (C–390/98) [2001] E.C.R. I–6117; [2001] 3 C.M.L.R.
51 ECJ 3–002, 10–006, 10–011, 10–013, 10–016, 10–018, 10–039

Holland Malt BV v Commission of the European Communities (T–369/06) [2009] E.C.R.
II–3313 4–002

Holland Mlt BV v Commission of the European Communities (C–464/09 P) Unreported
December 2, 2010 ....4–002, 13–016, 27–036

Hotel Cipriani SpA v Commission of the European Communities (T–254/00); Societa
Italiana per il Gas SpA (Italgas) v Commission of the European Communities
(T–270/00); Comitato Venezia Vuole Vivere v Commission of the European Commu-
nities (T–277/00) [2008] E.C.R. II–3269; [2009] 1 C.M.L.R. 39 CFI (6th Chamber) 10–006

Hotel Cipriani SpA v Commission of the European Communities (C–71/09), (C–73/09 P)
and (C–76/09 P) Unreported, 2011 27–018

Huta Buczek v Commission of the European Communities (T–440/07 R) [2008] ECR
II–39 27–045

Huta Czstochowa SA v Commission of the European Communities (T–288/06) [2006]
E.C.R. II–101 CFI 5–016

Iannelli & Volpi SpA v Ditta Paolo Meroni (74/76); Firma Steinike und Weinlig v Bundesamt
fur Ernahrung und Forstwirtschaft (78/76) [1977] E.C.R. 557; [1977] E.C.R. 595;
[1977] 2 C.M.L.R. 688 ECJ 3–110, 3–111

IGAV/ENCC. *See* Industria Gomma Articoli Vari (IGAV) v Ente Nazionale per la Cellulosa
e per la Carta (ENCC) (94/74)

Ijssel-Vliet Combinatie BV v Minister van Economische Zaken (C–311/94) [1996] E.C.R.
I–5023; [1997] 3 C.M.L.R. 373 ECJ 4–038, 13–044, 25–052

Industria Gomma Articoli Vari (IGAV) v Ente Nazionale per la Cellulosa e per la Carta
(ENCC) (94/74) [1975] E.C.R. 699; [1976] 2 C.M.L.R. 37 ECJ 10–005

Industrie Aeronautiche e Meccaniche Rinaldo Piaggio SpA v International Factors Italia SpA
(IFITALIA) (C–295/97) 1999] E.C.R. I–3735; [2000] 3 C.M.L.R. 825 ECJ (5th Cham-
ber) 3–019, 3–022, 10–010, 10–011, 10–016, 25–011, 25–017

ING v Commission (T–33/10) [2010] OJ C 80/40 ....1–025, 19–069, 25–012

Intermills SA v Commission of the European Communities (323/82) [1984] E.C.R. 3809;
[1986] 1 C.M.L.R. 614 ECJ 25–003

Interzuccheri SpA v Ditta Rezzano E Cavassa (C–105/76) [1977] E.C.R. 1029 ECJ 10–005

Ireland v Commission of the European Communities (TT–56/06, TT–62/06 and T–69/06)
[2007] E.C.R. II–172 ....20–029, 25–016, 25–017

Iride SpA and Iride Energia SpA v Commission of the European Communities (T–25/07)
[2009] E.C.R. II–245; set for appeal as C–150/09 P 3–027, 20–022, 22–019

Itainvest v Commission of the European Communities (T–523/99) [2002] E.C.R. II–5645 19–007

Italy v Commission of the European Communities (1/69); sub nom. Preferential Freight
Rates, Re (1/69) [1969] E.C.R. 277; [1970] C.M.L.R. 17 ECJ 17–002

Italy v Commission of the European Communities (173/73); sub nom. Aids to the Textile
Industry, Re (173/73) [1974] E.C.R. 709; [1974] 2 C.M.L.R. 593 ECJ 3–106, 10–017, 10–018

Italy v Commission of the European Communities (41/83); sub nom. British Telecommunications Plc, Re (C41/83) [1985] E.C.R. 873; [1985] 2 C.M.L.R. 368; [1985] F.S.R. 510
ECJ 18–004

Italy v Commission of the European Communities (303/88); sub nom. Aid to Eni-Lanerossi,
Re (303/88) [1991] E.C.R. I–1433; [1993] 2 C.M.L.R. 1ECJ 17–065

Italy v Commission of the European Communities (C–86/89) [1990] E.C.R. I–3891 ECJ 13–004

Italy v Commission of the European Communities (C–261/89) [1991] E.C.R. I–4437 ECJ 25–018

Italy v Commission of the European Communities (C–305/89) [1991] E.C.R. I–1603 8–053

Italy v Commission of the European Communities (C–47/91) [1992] E.C.R. I–4145 ECJ 25–018,
25–029, 25–049, 27–013

Italy v Commission of the European Communities (C–6/97) [1999] E.C.R. I–2981; [2000] 2
C.M.L.R. 919 ECJ (6th Chamber) 3–029, 10–005, 10–017, 10–021

Italy v Commission of the European Communities (C–372/97) [2004] E.C.R. I–3679 ECJ 25–045

Italy v Commission of the European Communities (C–15/98); Sardegna Lines—Servizi
Marittimi della Sardegna SpA v Commission of the European Communities (C–105/99)
[2000] E.C.R. I–8855; [2001] 1 C.M.L.R. 10 ECJ (6th Chamber) 25–036, 27–018

Italy v Commission of the European Communities (C–310/99) [2002] E.C.R. I–2289 ECJ 3–015,
3–020

Italy v Commission of the European Communities (C–328/99); sub nom Aid to Seleco, Re
(C–328/99) [2003] E.C.R. I–4035; [2005] 2 C.M.L.R. 48 ECJ (6th Chamber) 3–015, 3–084,
19–007

Italy v Commission of the European Communities (C–400/99) [2001] E.C.R. I–7303 ECJ 25–005,
25–017, 25–029, 25–031, 25–045, 25–051

Italy v Commission of the European Communities (C–298/00 P) [2004] E.C.R. I–4087
ECJ 25–016, 25–045, 26–019

Italy v Commission of the European Communities (Solar Tech) (C–91/01) [2004] E.C.R.
I–355 ECJ 1–040, 26–020, 27–036

Italy v Commission of the European Communities (C–66/02) [2005] E.C.R. I–10901 ECJ 3–015,
3–041, 10–011, 10–018, 10–021, 10–024, 10–036

Italy v Commission of the European Communities (T–222/04) [2009 E.C.R. II–1877 25–014

Italy v Commission of the European Communities (T–239 and 323/04) [2007] E.C.R.
II–3265 25–015

Italy v Commission of the European Communities (T–244/04) [2009] E.C.R. II14B–1877 10–037

Italy v Commission of the European Communities (T–304/04) [2006] E.C.R. II–64 CFI ... 4–046

Italy v Commission of the European Communities (T–211/05) [2009] E.C.R. II–2777 10–023,
10–026, 10–037

Table of Cases

Italy v Commission of the European Communities (T–53/08); Terni v Commission of the
European Communities (T–62/08) Unreported July 1, 2010; under appeal (C–488/10
P) 3–013, 20–092
Italy v Commission of the European Communities; sub nom. Aid to Eni-Lanerossi, Re
(C–303/88) [1991] E.C.R. I–1433; [1993] 2 C.M.L.R. 1 ECJ 8–053, 26–009, 26–013
Italy v Commission of the European Communities; sub nom. Aid to Tirrenia Group, Re
(C–400/99) [2005] E.C.R. I–3657; [2005] 3 C.M.L.R. 22 ECJ 25–016
Italy v Commission of the European Communities; sub nom. Aids to the Textile Industry, Re
(173/73) [1974] E.C.R. 709; [1974] 2 C.M.L.R. 593, ECJ 3–003, 3–054, 18–014, 22–056,
22–067
Italy v Sacchi (155/73) [1974] E.C.R. 409; [1974] 2 C.M.L.R. 177 ECJ 18–004
Jongeneel Kaas v Netherlands and Stichting Centraal Orgaan Zuivelcontrole (C–237/82)
[1984] E.C.R. 483; [1985] 2 C.M.L.R. 53 ECJ 13–004
Kahla Thuringen Porzellan v Comission of the European Communities (T–20/03 [2008]
E.C.R. II- 2305, upheld on appeal C–537/08P, 16 December 2010 ....4–015, 12–001, 19–007,
24–016, 24–028
Kahn Scheepvaart BV v Commission of the European Communities (T–398/94) [1996]
E.C.R. II–477; [1997] 3 C.M.L.R. 63 CFI 27–025, 27–039
Kainuun Liikenne Oy, Re (C–412/96) [1998] E.C.R. I–5141 ECJ 17–010
Keller SpA v Commission of the European Communities (T–35/99); sub nom. Aid for
Railway Rolling Stock, Re (T35/99) [2002] E.C.R. II–261; [2003] 1 C.M.L.R. 9 CFI
(2nd Chamber) 4–015, 20–054
Kirsammer-Hack v Sidal (C–189/91) [1993] E.C.R. I–6185; [1994] I.R.L.R. 185 ECJ 3–056
Kneissl Dachstein Sportartikel AG v Commission of the European Communities (T110/97)
[1999] E.C.R. II–2881 CFI 4–015
Kronofrance SA v Commission of the European Communities (T–27/02) [2004] E.C.R.
II–4177 CFI 1–039, 4–002, 4–022, 25–010
Kronoply GmbH & Co KG v Commission of the European Communities (T–126/06) [2009]
2 C.M.L.R. 25 CFI (5th Chamber); appeal dismissed in (C–117/09) June 24, 2010 1–041,
4–016, 4–017, 4–031, 4–050
Kronoply. See European Commission v Kronoply GmbH & Co. KG and Kronotex GmbH &
Co. KG (C–83/09 P)
Kuipers v Productschap Zuivel (C–283/03) Kuipers, Re (C–283/03) [2005] E.C.R. I–4255
ECJ 13–004
Kuwait Petroleum (Nederland) BV v Commission of the European Communities (T–354/99)
[2006] E.C.R. II–1475 CFI 1–033
Kvaerner Warnow Werft GmbH v Commission of the European Communities (T–227/99)
[2002] E.C.R. II–1205; [2003] 2 C.M.L.R. 17 CFI (4th Chamber) 16–018
Kwekerij Gebroeders van der Kooy BV v Commission of the European Communities (67/85)
[1988] E.C.R. 219; [1989] 2 C.M.L.R. 804 ECJ 3–030, 3–055, 8–014, 20–025, 20–089,
20–091, 24–019, 27–018, 27–019
Kwekerij Gebroeders Van Der Kooy BV v Commission of the European Communities
(67/85) [1985] E.C.R. 1315 12–020
Laboratoires Boiron SA v Union de Recouvrement des Cotisations de Securite Sociale et
d'Allocations Familiales (URSSAF) de Lyon (C–526/04); sub nom. Laboratoires
Boiron SA v Agence Centrale des Organismes de Securite Sociale (ACOSS)
(C–526/04) [2006] E.C.R. I–7529; [2006] 3 C.M.L.R. 50; [2007] C.E.C. 77 ECJ (2nd
Chamber) 1–037, 3–129, 3–132, 10–040, 25–006
Ladbroke. See Tierce Ladbroke SA v Commission of the European Communities (C–353/95
P)
Land Rheinland-Pfalz v Alcan Deutschland GmbH (C–24/95) [1997] All E.R. (EC) 427;
[1997] E.C.R. I–1591 ECJ 9–026, 26–009, 26–018, 26–019
Landesanstalt fur Medien Nordrhein-Westfalen v Commission of the European Communities
[2009] E.C.R. II–195 27–020
Le Levant v Commission of the European Communities (T–34/02) [2006] E.C.R. II–267 1–031,
4–046, 10–034, 25–031
Lenzing AG v Commission of the European Communities (T–36/99) [2004] E.C.R. II–3597;
[2006] 1 C.M.L.R. 46 CFI (5th Chamber) 1–020, 3–089
Linde AG v Commission of the European Communities (T–98/00) [2002] E.C.R. II–3961;
[2003] 2 C.M.L.R. 7 CFI (5th Chamber) 3–085, 19–005

Lorenz (Gebr) GmbH v Germany (120/70) [1973] E.C.R. 1471 ECJ 3–113, 25–004, 25–015, 25–037, 25–044, 25–064
Lornoy v Belgium (C17/91) [1992] E.C.R. I–6523 ECJ (6th Chamber) 10–005
Lucchini SpA. *See* Ministero dell'Industria del Commercio e dell'Artigianato v Lucchini SpA (C–119/05)
Luxem v Commission of the European Communities (T–306/04) Unreported, September 15, 2005 CFI 4–046
M Alzetta v Commission of the European Communities (T–298/97, T–312/97, T–313/97, T–315/97, T–600/97 to T–607/97, T–1/97, T–3/98 to T–6/98 and T–23/98) [2000] E.C.R. II–2319 CFI 3–080, 21–022, 25–016
M6 and TFI v Commission of the European Communities (T–568/08 and T–573/08) Unreported, 2010; under appeal in (C–451/10 P) [2010] OJ C328/15 1–032
M6 v Commission of the European Communities (T185/00). *See* Metropole Television SA (M6) v Commission of the European Communities (T–185/00)
MABB v Commission of the European Communities (T–24/06) [2009] E.C.R. II–198 27–020
Maizena GmbH v Council of Ministers of the European Communities (139/79) [1980] E.C.R. 3393 ECJ 13–002
Mana Messina v Commission of the European Communities (T–76/02) [2003] E.C.R. II–3203 1–034
Marks & Spencer Plc v Halsey (Inspector of Taxes) (C–446/03) [2006] Ch. 184; [2006] 2 W.L.R. 250, ECJ 10–004
Matra Hachette SA v Commission of the European Communities (T–17/93) [1994] E.C.R. II–595 CFI 3–120
Matra SA v Commission of the European Communities (C–225/91) [1993] E.C.R. I–3203 ECJ 3–061, 25–027, 27–022, 27–023, 27–024
Matra SA v Commission of the European Communities (C–225/91) [1993] E.C.R. I–3203 ECJ 3–120, 3–121
Mediaset SpA v Commission of the European Communities (C–403/10 P) Unreported July 28, 2011 .... 1–037, 3–011, 4–005, 18–012, 18–015
Mediaset SpA v Commission of the European Communities (T–177/07) [2010] E.C.R. II–02341 ....1–037, 3–011, 4–005, 18–015
Meridiana and Meridiana fly v Commission of the European Communities (T–128/09) October 3, 2011 27–034
Metropole Television SA (M6) v Commission of the European Communities (T–185/00); Antena 3 de Television SA v Commission of the European Communities (T–216/00); Gestevision Telecinco SA v Commission of the European Communities (T299/00); Sociedade Independente de Comunicacao SA v Commission of the European Communities (T–300/00) [2002] E.C.R. II–3805; [2003] 4 C.M.L.R. 14; [2003] E.C.D.R. 25 CFI (2nd Chamber) 18–002
MHZ (1735/2010) May 3, 2011 (Ombudsman) 1–034
Ministere Public v Asjes (209–213/84) [1986] E.C.R. 1425; [1986] 3 C.M.L.R. 173 ECJ 17–002, 25–016
Ministero dell'Economia e delle Finanze and Agenzia delle Entrate v Paint Graphos Soc. coop. arl (C–78/08) Unreported, 2011 ....10–021, 10–024, 10–027, 10–037
Ministero dell'Economia e delle Finanze v Cassa di Risparmio di Firenze SpA (C–222/04) [2006] E.C.R. I–289; [2008] 1 C.M.L.R. 28 ECJ (2nd Chamber) 3–048, 8–012, 10–027, 10–037
Ministero dell'Industria del Commercio e dell'Artigianato v Lucchini SpA (C–119/05) [2007] E.C.R. I–6199; [2009] 1 C.M.L.R. 18 ECJ (Grand Chamber) 26–013, 27–059
Ministerul Administratiei si Internelor—Directia Generala de Pasapoarte Bucuresti v Jipa (C–33/07) [2008] E.C.R. I–5157; [2008] 3 C.M.L.R. 23 ECJ (1st Chamber) 3–132
Ministre de l'Economie, des Finances et de l'Industrie v Gemo SA (C–126/01) [2003] E.C.R. I–13769; [2004] 1 C.M.L.R. 9; [2004] C.E.C. 61 ECJ (6th Chamber) ...3–017, 3–020, 8–028, 8–046, 13–025, 19–015, 25–021
MMT v Commission of the European Communities [2006] ECR II–97 (T–392/05) 27–034
MOL v Commission of the European Communities (T–499/10) [2010] OJ C346/52) 20–046
MTU Friedrichshafen v Commission of the European Communities (T–196/02) [2007] E.C.R. II–2889 25–045
Municipality of Almelo v NV Energibedrijf Ijsselmij. *See* Gemeente Almelo v Energiebedrijf Ijssellmij NV (C393/92)

Table of Cases

MyTravel v Commission of the European Communities (T–403/05) [2008] E.C.R. II–2027
and on appeal C–506/08 P Unreported, 2011 1–034
Namur-Les Assurances du Credit SA v Office National du Ducroire and Belgium (C–44/93)
[1994] E.C.R. I–3829 ECJ 4–046, 25–014, 25–017, 25–018
Nazairdis SAS v Caisse Nationale de L'Organisation Autonome d'Assurance Vieillesse des
Travailleurs Non Salaries des Professions Industrielles et Commerciales (ORGANIC)
(C266/04) [2005] E.C.R. I–9481 ECJ 3–132, 10–039, 10–040, 27–055
NDSHT Nya Destination Stockholm Hotell & Teaterpaket AB v European Commission
(C–322/09 P) [2011] 2 C.M.L.R. 8 ECJ (3rd Chamber) 27–029, 27–030
Netherlands v Commission of the European Communities (C–105/11 P) 18–012
Netherlands v Commission of the European Communities (C–159/01) [2004] E.C.R. I–4461
ECJ 10–006, 10–009, 10–024, 10–024, 10–026, 13–037
Netherlands v Commission of the European Communities (C–279/08) [2011] E.C.R. Unre-
ported December 22, 2010 ; on appeal, judgment of September 8 2011 ECJ ... 3–009, 20–034
Netherlands v Commission of the European Communities (C–382/99) [2002] E.C.R. I–5163
ECJ 1–039, 3–079, 7–004, 7–011, 10–034, 25–029
Netherlands v Commission of the European Communities (T–231/06); Nederlandse Omroep
Stichting v Commission of the European Communities (T–237/06) [2011] O.J.C38/54.;
now on appeal C–104/11P, 13 August 2011 ..... 1–033, 8–010, 8–036, 8–062, 18–012, 25–015
Netherlands v Commission of the European Communities (T–233/04) [2008] E.C.R. II–591;
[2008] Env. L.R. 42 CFI (5th Chamber) 3–009, 20–034, 27–014
Netherlands v Commission of the European Communities (C–279/08 P) Unreported, 2011 1–025,
3–017
Neue Erba Lautex v Commission of the European Communities (T–181/02 R) [2002] ECR
II–5081 27–045
Neue Maxhutte Stahlwerke GmbH v Commission of the European Communities (T–129/95)
[1999] E.C.R. II–17; [1999] 3 C.M.L.R. 366 CFI (5th Chamber) 19–007
Nomura Principal Investment Plc v Commission (T–430/2004) 5–013
Noord-West Brabant (T–188/95) [1998] E.C.R. II–3713 CFI 27–017, 27–021, 27–022, 27–025
Norddeutsches Vieh- und Fleischkontor Herbert Will, Trawako, Transit-Warenhandels-Kontor
Gmbh & Co, and Gedelfi Grossein Kauf Gmbh & Co v Bundesanstalt fur Land-
wirtschaftliche Marktordnung (C213/81, C214/81, C215/81) [1982] E.C.R. 3583 ECJ 3–036,
11–012
Nuova Agricast v Commission of the European Communities (T–98/04) Unreported June 15,
2005 27–049
Nuova Agricast and Cofra v Commission of the European Communities (T–362/05 and
T–363/05) [2008] ECR II–297 27–049
Nuova Agricast and Cofra v Commission of the European Communities (C–67/09 P)
October 14, 2010 27–049
Nuova Agricast Srl v Ministero delle Attivita Produttive (C–390/06) [2008] E.C.R. I–2577
ECJ 4–017, 25–030, 27–049
Nygard v Svineafgiftsfonden (C–234/99) [2002] E.C.R. I–3657 ECJ 3–129, 13–041
Olsen SA v Commission of the European Communities. See Fred Olsen SA v Commission
of the European Communities (T–17/02)
Olympic Airways v Commission of the European Communities (T–68/03) [2007] E.C.R.
II–2911 CFI (2nd Chamber) 3–021, 17–070, 20–025, 24–042, 24–049
Olympic Airways. See Greece v Commission of the European Communities (T–415/05),
(T–416/05) and (T–423/05)
Opel Austria GmbH v Council of Ministers of the European Communities (T–115/94) [1997]
All E.R. (E.C.) 97; [1997] E.C.R. II–39 CFI 25–072
Openbaar Ministerie v Van Tiggele (C–82/77) [1978] E.C.R. 25; [1978] 2 C.M.L.R. 528
ECJ 3–017
Operator ARP v Commission of the European Communities (T–291/06) [2009] E.C.R.
II–2275 27–016
P&O European Ferries (Vizcaya) SA v Commission of the European Communities
(T–116/01) [2003] E.C.R. II–2957; [2003] 3 C.M.L.R. 14 CFI (1st Chamber) 3–102, 4–004,
20–042, 26–020, 27–035
P&O European Ferries (Vizcaya) SA v Commission of the European Communities
(C–442/03 P) [2006] E.C.R. I–4845 ECJ 3–102, 4–004, 25–023

Pabst & Richarz KG v Hauptzollamt Oldenburg (17/81) [1982] E.C.R. 1331; [1983] 3 C.M.L.R. 11 ECJ (1st Chamber) 3–128

Pannon Hoeromu v Commission of the European Communities (T–352/08 R) [2009] ECR II–9 27–045

Pantochim SA v Commission of the European Communities (T–107/96) [1998] E.C.R. II–311 CFI 25–045, 27–044

Pape v Minister van Landbouw, Natuurbeheer en Visserij (C–175/02) [2007] S.T.C. 715; [2005] E.C.R. I–127; [2005] S.T.I. 136 ECJ (1st Chamber) 3–132, 10–040, 13–041, 27–055

Pavlov v Stichting Pensioenfonds Medische Specialisten (C–180/98) [2000] E.C.R. I–6451; [2001] 4 C.M.L.R. 1 ECJ 3–041

Pearle BV v Hoofdbedrijfschap Ambachten (C–345/02); sub nom. Peale BV, Re (C–345/02) [2004] E.C.R. I–7139; [2004] 3 C.M.L.R. 9 ECJ (1st Chamber) 1–003, 1–025, 3–015, 3–016, 3–018, 3–027, 3–031, 20–020, 20–021, 20–023, 25–024, 27–054

Perez Escolar v Commission (C379/03 P) (Unreported, October 1, 2004 ECJ 19–014, 27–038

Perez Escolar v Commission of the European Communities (T–41/01) [2003] E.C.R. II–2157 CFI 19–014, 27–038

Pfeifer & Langen, Ogilvie Aquitaine Sa, Cargill BV and Latenstein Zetmeel BV v Commission of the European Communities (T–442/93) [1995] E.C.R. II–1329 27–031

Philip Morris Holland BV v Commission of the European Communities (730/79) [1980] E.C.R. 2671; [1981] 2 C.M.L.R. 321 ECJ 4–002, 4–014, 4–019, 4–025, 27–017

Piaggio. *See* Industrie Aeronautiche e Meccaniche Rinaldo Piaggio SpA v International Factors Italia SpA (IFITALIA) (C–295/97)

Pig Production Subsidies, Re; sub nom. Commission of the European Communities v United Kingdom (C–31/77) [1977] E.C.R. 921; [1977] 2 C.M.L.R. 359, ECJ 27–003

Pigs and Bacon Commission v McCarren & Co Ltd (177/78) [1979] E.C.R. 2161; [1979] 3 C.M.L.R. 389 ECJ 3–124, 13–002, 13–003

Pigs Marketing Board (Northern Ireland) v Redmond (83/78) [1978] E.C.R. 2347; [1979] 1 C.M.L.R. 177 ECJ 3–124, 13–003

PJ van der Hulst's Zonen CV v Produktschap voor Siergewassen (51/74) [1975] E.C.R. 79; [1975] 1 C.M.L.R. 236 ECJ 13–003

Plaumann & Co v Commission of the European Economic Community (25/62) [1963] E.C.R. 95; [1964] C.M.L.R. 29 ECJ 27–023, 27–043

Pollmeier Malchow GmbH & Co KG v Commission of the European Communities (T–137/02)] E.C.R. II–3541 CFI 1–040

Polska sp. z.o.o. v Commission of the European Communities (T–273/06) [2009] E.C.R. II–2181 .... 5–016, 14–072

Polska sp. z.o.o. v Commission of the European Communities (C–369/09) Unreported March 24, 2011 .... 5–016, 14–072

Portugal v Commission of the European Communities (C–204/97) [2001] E.C.R. I–3175 ECJ 10–005, 10–039, 10–040, 13–041, 25–027, 25–029

Portugal v Commission of the European Communities (C–88/03) (Azores Judgment); sub nom. Income Tax Reductions in the Azores, Re (C–88/03) [2007] S.T.C. 1032; [2006] E.C.R. I–7115; [2006] 3 C.M.L.R. 45; [2006] S.T.I. 2179 ECJ 1–043, 3–015, 3–048, 3–052, 10–005, 10–008, 10–013, 10–036, 21–002

Portugal v Commission of the European Communities [2010] OJ C328/49 .... 13–032, 13–041

Portugal v Council of the European Union (C–149/96) [1999] E.C.R. I–8395 ECJ 6–030

Prayon v Commission of the European Communities (T–73/98). *See* Societe Chimique Prayon-Rupel SA v Commission of the European Communities (T–73/98)

Presidente del Consiglio dei Ministri v Regione Sardegna (C–169/08) [2010] All E.R. (EC) 1037; [2009] E.C.R. I–10821; [2010] 2 C.M.L.R. 8; [2010] C.E.C. 1085 ECJ (Grand Chamber) 3–118, 10–005, 10–008, 10–032

PreussenElektra AG v Schleswag AG (C–379/98) [2001] All E.R. (EC) 330; [2001] E.C.R. I–2099; [2001] 2 C.M.L.R. 36; [2001] C.E.C. 217; [2002] Env. L.R. 3 ECJ 1–003, 1–025, 3–017, 3–018, 3–019, 3–021, 3–022, 3–030, 10–010, 20–020, 20–021, 20–022, 20–063, 22–018, 22–019, 22–020, 22–069

Procureur de la Republique v Association de Defense des Bruleurs d'Huiles Usagees (ADBHU) (240/83) [1985] E.C.R. 531 ECJ 8–026

Puffer v Unabhangiger Finanzsenat, Aussenstelle Linz (C–460/07) [2009] S.T.C. 1693; [2009] E.C.R. I–3251; [2009] 3 C.M.L.R. 19; [2009] B.T.C. 5348; [2009] B.V.C. 347; [2009] S.T.I. 1598 ECJ (3rd Chamber) 3–035

Table of Cases

R. v Attorney General Ex p. ICI Plc [1987] 1 C.M.L.R. 72; 60 T.C. 1 CA (Civ Div) 3–004, 10–014
R. v Customs and Excise Commissioners Ex p. Lunn Poly Ltd [1999] S.T.C. 350; [1999] 1
   C.M.L.R. 1357; [1999] Eu. L.R. 653; (1999) 96(13) L.S.G. 32; (1999) 143 S.J.L.B. 104
   CA (Civ Div) 3–046, 3–050
R. v Ministry of Agriculture, Fisheries and Food Ex p. Compassion in World Farming Ltd
   (CWIF) (C1/96) [1998] All E.R. (EC) 302; [1998] E.C.R. I–1251; [1998] 2 C.M.L.R.
   661 ECJ 13–003
R. v Secretary of State for Transport Ex p. Factortame Ltd (C–213/89) [1990] 2 Lloyd's Rep.
   351; [1990] E.C.R. I–24 ECJ 26–021
Regie Networks. See Ministerul Administratiei si Internelor—Directia Generala de Pasa-
   poarte Bucuresti v Jipa (C–33/07)
Region Nord-Pas-De-Calais v Commission of the European Communities (T–267/08 and
   (T–279/08) Unreported May 12, 2011 ....24–015, 25–031
Region Wallone v Commission of the European Communities (T–70/97) [1997] ECR
   II–1513 CFI 27–020
Regione autonoma della Sardegna v Commission [2006] E.C.R. 1–1875 13–025
Regione autonoma della Sardegna v Commission of the European Communities (T–171/02)
   [2005] E.C.R. II–2123 24–016
Reimbursement of Sugar Storage Costs, Re (C–72/79); Reimbusement of Sugar Storage
   Costs, Re (73/79); sub nom. Commission of the European Communites v Italy (73/79);
   Commission of the European Communities v Italy (C72/79) [1980] E.C.R. 1411; [1980]
   E.C.R. 1533; [1982] 1 C.M.L.R. 1 ECJ 3–125, 3–128, 10–005
RENV 3F v Commission of the European Communities (T–30/03) September 27, 2011 27–027
Residex Capital IV CV v Gemeente Rotterdam (C–275/10) Unreported May 26, 2011 9–028,
                                                                                             19–004, 26–010
Rijn-Schelde-Verolme Machinefabrieken en Sheepswerven NV v Commission of the Euro-
   pean Communities (223/85) [1987] E.C.R. 4617; [1989] 2 C.M.L.R. 259 ECJ ...25–036, 26–012,
                                                                                             26–019
RJB Mining Plc v Commission of the European Communities (T–156/98) [2001] E.C.R.
   II–337; [2001] 3 C.M.L.R. 15 CFI (1st Chamber) 3–021
RJB Mining Plc v Commission of the European Communities (C–427/99 P and C–371/00
   P)) 3–122
RSV v Commission of the European Communities. See Rijn-Schelde-Verolme Machinefab-
   rieken en Sheepswerven NV v Commission of the European Communities (223/85)
Ryanair Ltd v Commission of the European Communities (T–140/95) [1998] E.C.R. II–
   3327; [1998] 3 C.M.L.R. 1022 CFI 17–068, 19–082, 19–083, 25–033, 25–047, 25–057
Ryanair Ltd v Commission of the European Communities (T–196/04) [2008] E.C.R. II–
   3643; [2009] 2 C.M.L.R. 7 CFI (8th Chamber) 3–060, 3–063, 3–082, 3–088, 17–077, 20–035
Ryanair Ltd v Commission of the European Communities (T–494/08—T–500/08) Unre-
   ported, 2010 1–034
Ryanair Ltd v Commission of the European Communities (T–423/07) Unreported May 19,
   2011 3–020
Ryanair v Commission of the European Communities (T–442/07) September 29, 2011 27–040
Salengo. See Amministrazione Delle Finanze Dello Stato v Essevi Spa and Carlo Salengo
   (142/80)
Salomon v Commission of the European Communities (T–123/97) [1999] E.C.R. II–2925 25–062,
                                                                                             27–013, 27–025, 27–034
Salt Union Ltd v Commission of the European Communities (T–330/94) [1996] E.C.R.
   II–1475
Salvat v Commission of the European Communities (T–136/05) [2007] E.C.R. II–1933 3–015
Salvat v Commission of the European Communities (T–136/05) [2007] E.C.R. II–4063 3–027,
                                                                                             3–031, 13–041
Salzgitter v Commission of the European Communities (T–308/00) [2004] E.C.R. II–1933
   CFI 3–042
Sanders Adour SNC et Guyomarc'h Orthez Nutrition Animale SA v Director of Tax Services
   for Pyrenees-Atlantique (C149/91) [1992] E.C.R. I–3899 ECJ (6th Chamber) 10–005
Saxonia Edelmetalle GmbH v Commission of the European Communities (T–111/01 and
   T–133/01) [2005] E.C.R. II–1579 ....25–031, 25–046
Scheucher-Fleisch GmbH v Commission of the European Communities (T–375/04) [2009]
   E.C.R. II–199; [2010] OJ C80/21 .... 13–041, 27–033

Table of Cases

Schmitz-Gotha Fahrzeugwerke GmbH v Commission of the European Communities
(T–17/03) [2006] E.C.R. II–1139 CFI 1–026, 24–012, 24–035
Scott and Kimberly Clark v Commission of the European Communities (C–210/09) May 20,
2010 27–057
Scott SA v Commission of the European Communities (T–366/00) [2004] All E.R. (EC) 473;
[2003] E.C.R. II–1763; [2004] 1 C.M.L.R. 6 CFI (5th Chamber) 3–094, 25–031, 25–042,
26–007
Scott SA v Commission of the European Communities (C–276/03) [2005] E.C.R. I–8437
ECJ 25–042, 26–007
Seleco (C–328/99 & 399/00). See Italy v Commission of the European Communities; sub
nom. Aid to Seleco, Re (C–328/99)
Servizi Ausiliari Dottori Commercialisti Srl v Calafiori (C–451/03) [2006] E.C.R. I–2941;
[2006] 2 C.M.L.R. 45 ECJ (3rd Chamber) 3–104, 3–117
SFEI. See Syndicat Francais de l'Express International (SFEI) v La Poste (C–39/94)
SIC—Sociedade Independente de Comunicacao, SA v Commission of the European Com-
munities (T–442/03) 20–024
SIC (T–46/97). See Sociedade Independente de Comunicacao SA (SIC) v Commission of the
European Communities (T–46/97)
Sicilcassa SpA v IRA Costruzioni SpA (C–297/01) [2003] E.C.R. I–7849 ECJ 27–050
Sicily v Commission of the European Communities (T–190/00); sub nom. Regione Siciliana
v Commission of the European Communities (T190/00) [2003] E.C.R. II–5015 CFI 13–041,
25–017
SIDE v Commission of the European Communities (T–348/04). See Commission of the
European Communities
SIDE v Commission of the European Communities (T–49/93). See Societe Internationale de
Diffusion et d'edition (Side) v Commission of the European Communities (T–49/93)
Siemens SA v Commission of the European Communities (T–459/93) [1995] E.C.R.
II–1675 ....26–006, 26–009, 26–012
Siemens SA v Commission of the European Communities (C–278/95 P) [1997] E.C.R.
I–2507; [1997] C.E.C. 1267 ECJ (4th Chamber) 25–049
Skibsvaerftsforeningen v Commission of the European Economic Community (T–266/94).
See Foreningen af Jernskibs– og Maskinbyggerier i Danmark v Commission of the
European Communities (T–266/94)
Sloman. See Firma Sloman Neptun Schiffahrts AG v Seebetriebsrat Bodo Ziesemer
(C–72/91 and C–73/91)
Snaice SAv Commission of the European Communities (T–238/09) [2009] E.C.R. II–125 ...3–090,
3–092, 27–045
Sniace SA v Commission of the European Communities (T–141/03) [2005] E.C.R. II–1197;
[2006] 2 C.M.L.R. 22 CFI (3rd Chamber) 27–015, 27–059
SNIV v Commission (T–327/04) [2008] ECR II–72 27–034
Sociedade Independente de Comunicacao SA (SIC) v Commission of the European Commu-
nities (T–46/97) [2000] E.C.R. II–2125; [2000] 3 C.M.L.R. 987 CFI (1st Chamber) 8–027,
27–027
Societe Baxter v Premier Ministre (C–254/97) [2000] All E.R. (EC) 945; [1999] E.C.R.
I–4809; [2000] 2 C.M.L.R. 899; [2000] C.E.C. 707 ECJ 10–005
Societe CdF Chimie Azote et Fertilisants SA v Commission of the European Communities
(C–169/84) [1990] E.C.R. I–3083; [1992] 1 C.M.L.R. 177, ECJ 12–020, 25–038, 25–064,
26–019, 27–031
Societe Chimique Prayon-Rupel SA v Commission of the European Communities (T–73/98)
[2001] E.C.R. II–867 CFI 20–054, 25–010, 25–029, 25–057, 25–060, 27–027
Societe Chimique Prayon-Rupel SA v Commission of the European Communities (T–73/98)
[1998] E.C.R. II–2769 27–045
Societe de Gestion Industrielle SA (SGI) v Belgium (C–311/08) [2010] 2 C.M.L.R. 38;
[2010] C.E.C. 1130; [2011] B.T.C. 123 ECJ (3rd Chamber) 10–004
Societe des Produits Bertrand SA v Commission of the European Communities (40/75)
[1976] E.C.R. 1; [1976] 1 C.M.L.R. 220 ECJ 27–048
Societe d'Initiatives et de Cooperation Agricoles v Commission of the European Communities (114/83) [1984] E.C.R. 2589; [1985] 2 C.M.L.R. 767 ECJ (1st Chamber) ...3–003, 3–124,
13–003, 27–048

Table of Cases

Societe Internationale de Diffusion et d'edition (Side) v Commission of the European
Communities (T–49/93) [1995] E.C.R. II–2501 CFI 3–120, 4–034, 25–029, 25–038
Societe Internationale de Diffusion et d'Edition (SIDE) v Commission of the European
Communities (T–155/98) [2002] E.C.R. II–1179; [2002] 1 C.M.L.R. 55 CFI (4th
Chamber) 4–034
Societe Internationale de Diffusion et d'edition (Side) v Commission of the European
Communities (T–348/04) [2008] E.C.R. II–625 .... 4–035, 25–038
Societe Nationale Interprofessionnelle de la Tomate (SONITO) v Commission of the Euro-
pean Communities (C–87/89) [1990] E.C.R. I–1981; [1991] 3 C.M.L.R. 439 ECJ 27–037
Societe Regie Networks v Direction de Controle Fiscal Rhone-Alpes Bourgogne (C–333/07)
[2008] E.C.R. I–10807; [2009] 2 C.M.L.R. 20 ECJ (Grand Chamber) 10–040
SP Entertainment Development v Commission (T–44/05) [2007] E.C.R. II–19 27–013
Spain v Commission of the European Communities (C–312/90) [1992] E.C.R. I–4117 ECJ ...25–018,
27–013
Spain v Commission of the European Communities (C–278/92) [1994] E.C.R. I–4103 ECJ 3–083,
4–015, 8–023, 8–067, 8–070, 21–018
Spain v Commission of the European Communities (C–42/93); sub nom. State Aid to Merco
Co, Re (C–42/93) [1994] E.C.R. I–4175; [1995] 2 C.M.L.R. 702 ECJ 3–006, 21–003, 26–014
Spain v Commission of the European Communities (C–135/93) [1995] E.C.R. I–1651 ECJ ... 25–052
Spain v Commission of the European Communities (C–169/95) [1997] E.C.R. I–135 ECJ 26–019
Spain v Commission of the European Communities (C–292/95) [1997] E.C.R. I–1931 25–052
Spain v Commission of the European Communities (C–415/96) [1998] E.C.R. I–6993;
[1999] 1 C.M.L.R. 304 ECJ (6th Chamber) 25–010, 27–007
Spain v Commission of the European Communities (C–342/96) (Tubacex) [1999] E.C.R.
I–2459; [2000] 2 C.M.L.R. 415 ECJ (6th Chamber) 1–020, 3–089, 3–092, 19–005, 25–010
Spain v Commission of the European Communities (C–351/98) [2002] E.C.R. I–8031 ECJ
(6th Chamber) 3–117, 7–011
Spain v Commission of the European Communities (C–480/98) [2000] E.C.R. I–8717 ECJ
(6th Chamber) 10–010, 10–016, 10–036, 26–006, 26–010
Spain v Commission of the European Communities (C–36/00) [2002] E.C.R. I–3243 ECJ
(6th Chamber) 25–052, 27–006
Spain v Commission of the European Communities (C–113/00); sub nom. Aid for Horti-
cultural Products, Re (C–113/00) [2002] E.C.R. I–7601; [2003] 1 C.M.L.R. 16 ECJ (5th
Chamber) 3–076, 4–019, 13–003
Spain v Commission of the European Communities (C–114/00) [2002] E.C.R. I–7657 ECJ
(5th Chamber) 4–019
Spain v Commission of the European Communities (C–398/00) [2002] E.C.R. I–5643 ECJ
(6th Chamber) 25–029
Spain v Commission of the European Communities (C–173/02) [2004] E.C.R. I–9735 ECJ ... 13–004
Spain v Commission of the European Communities (C–276/02) [2004] 3 C.M.L.R. 47;
[2004] E.C.R. I–8091 ECJ (2nd Chamber) 1–020, 3–089, 3–091, 10–011, 10–016
Spain v Commission of the European Communities (C–73/03) Unreported, November 11,
2004 ECJ 4–006
Spain v Commission of the European Communities (C–525/04 P); sub nom. Spain v Lenzing
AG (C–525/04 P) [2007] E.C.R. I–9947; [2008] 1 C.M.L.R. 40 ECJ (1st Chamber) 1–020,
1–026, 3–015, 3–089
Spain v Lenzing AG (C–525/04 P). See Spain v Commission of the European Communities
(C–525/04 P)
Stadtwerke Schwabisch Hall GmbH v Commission of the European Communities (T–92/02)
[2006] E.C.R. II–11 CFI 10–023, 20–008
Stadtwerke Schwabisch Hall GmbH v Commission of the European Communities
(C–176/06) [2007] E.C.R. I–170 10–023
Star Fruit Co SA v Commission of the European Communities (C–247/87) [1989] E.C.R.
291; [1990] 1 C.M.L.R. 733, ECJ 27–037
State Equity Holding, Re; sub nom. Commission of the European Communities v Belgium
(C–52/84) [1986] E.C.R. 89; [1987] 1 C.M.L.R. 710 ECJ 26–008, 26–009
Steenkolenmijnen in Limburg v High Authority. See De Gezamenlijke Steenkolenmijnen in
Limburg v High Authority of the European Coal and Steel Community
Steinike & Weinlig v Germany (78/76) [1977] E.C.R. 595 ECJ .. 3–006, 3–016, 10–005, , 22–056,
22–067, 25–004

Table of Cases

Streekgewest Westelijk Noord-Brabant v Staatssecretaris van Financien (C–174/02) [2007]
   S.T.C. 692; [2005] E.C.R. I–85; [2005] S.T.I. 136 ECJ (1st Chamber) 3–048, 3–132, 10–005,
                                                   10–039, 10–040, 13–041, 27–055
Surul v Bundesanstalt fur Arbeit (C–262/96) [1999] E.C.R. I–2685; [2001] 1 C.M.L.R. 4
   ECJ 5–003
Sweden v Council of the European Union (C–39/05 P); Turco v Council of the European
   Union (C–52/05 P); [2008] E.C.R. I–1429 1–034
Syndicat Francais de l'Express International (SFEI) v La Poste (C–39/94) [1996] All E.R.
   (EC) 685; [1996] E.C.R. I–3547; [1996] 3 C.M.L.R. 369 ECJ ...3–055, 3–092, 3–131, 8–054,
                  8–055, 19–005, 20–095, 25–005, 25–043, 25–044, 26–022, 27–044, 27–053,
                                                                        27–055
Syndicat National de l'Industrie des Viandes (SNIV) v Commission of the European
   Communities (T–327/04) [2004] 13–025, 25–066
Sytraval v Commission of the European Communities (T–95/94). *See* Chambre Syndicale
   Nationale des Entreprises de Transport de Fonds et Valeurs (Sytraval) v Commission of
   the European Communities (T–95/94)
T Port GmbH & Co KG v Bundesanstalt fur Landwirtschaft und Ernahrung (C–68/95) [1996]
   E.C.R. I–6065; [1997 27–038
T–1/08 Unreported; set for appeal as C–405/11 P 14–073
Technische Glaswerke Ilmenau GmbH v Commission of the European Communities
   (T–198/01) [2004] E.C.R. II–2717 .... 3–084, 25–031, 25–054, 25–060, 27–035, 27–036, 27–047
Technische Glaswerke Ilmenau GmbH v Commission of the European Communities
   (T–378/02 R) [2003] E.C.R. II–2921 CFI 3–084
Telaustria Verlags GmbH v Telekom Austria AG (C–324/98) [2000] E.C.R. I–10745 ECJ
   (6th Chamber) 4–005, 8–008
Television Francaise 1 SA (TFI) v Commission of the European Communities (T–354/05)
   E.C.R. II–471; under appeal (C–451/10 P) September 15, 2010 ....8–049, 25–017, 25–019,
                                                                25–049, 27–016, 27–034
Ter Huurne's handelsmaatschappij v Commission of the European Communities (T–216/99)
   March 23, 2004 27–034
Territoria Historico de Alava v Commission of the European Communities (T–92/00) [2002]
   E.C.R. II–1385 CFI 3–052, 10–007, 10–008, 10–009, 10–011, 10–026, 10–028, 10–035,
                                                                10–036, 10–037
Teritorio Historico de Alava v Commission of the European Communities (T–227–229/01,
   265–266/01 and 270/01) [2009] E.C.R. II–3029 25–015
Territoria Historico de Alava v Commission of the European Communities (C–186/02)
   [2006] E.C.R. I–91 3–052
Territorio Historico v Commission of the European Communities (T–230–232/01, 267–
   269/01) [2009] E.C.R. II–139 25–016
Territorio Historico de Alava—Diputacion Foral de Alava v Commission of the European
   Communities (T–346/99) [2002] E.C.R. II–4259 CFI 10–007, 10–008, 10–011, 10–026,
                                                                10–035, 10–037, 25–016
Territorio Historico de Alava—Diputacion foral de Alava v Commission of the European
   Communities (T–227/01) Unreported, January 10, 2006 CFI 10–007, 10–009, 10–035
Territorio Historico de Álava v Commission of the European Communities (T–30/01) [2009]
   E.C.R.II–2919 .... 25–029, 25–031
Territorio Historico de Guipuzcoa (Diputacion Foral de Guipuzcoa) v Commission of the
   European Communities (T–269/99); Territorio Historico de Alava (Diputacion Foral de
   Alava) v Commission of the European Communities (T–271/99); Territorio Historico de
   Vizcaya (Diputacion Foral de Vizcaya) v Commission of the European Communities
   (T–272/99) [2002] E.C.R. II–4217; [2003] 1 C.M.L.R. 10 CFI (3rd Chamber) 10–008,
                                                                10–009, 10–011, 10–035, 10–037, 25–005
Tetra Pak Rausing SA v Commission of the European Communities (T–51/89) [1990] E.C.R.
   II–309 CFI 25–038
Textilwerke Deggendorg GmbH (TWD) v Commission of the European Communities
   (T–244/93) [1995] E.C.R. II–2265; [1996] 1 C.M.L.R. 332 CFI (3rd Chamber) 24–024,
                                                                26–011, 27–007
Textilwerke Deggendorg GmbH (TWD) v Commission of the European Communities
   (C–355/95 P) [1997] E.C.R. I–2549; [1998] 1 C.M.L.R. 234 ECJ ...11–006, 17–065, 20–068,
                                                                24–050, 26–008, 26–011, 27–007

Table of Cases

TF1 v Commission of the European Communities (T–17/96) [1999] ECR II–1757 ....27–038, 27–041

TF1 v Commission of the European Communities (T–193/06) September 13, 2010 ...27–023, 27–033

Thermenhotel Stoiser Franz Gesellschaft mbH & Co KG v Commission of the European
Communities (T–158/99) [2004] E.C.R. II–1 CFI 3–109, 8–068

Tierce Ladbroke SA v Commission of the European Communities (T–471/93) [1995] E.C.R.
II–2537 CFI 3–005

Tierce Ladbroke SA v Commission of the European Communities (C–353/95 P) [1997]
E.C.R. I–7007; [1998] C.E.C. 338 ECJ 3–004, 3–005, 3–015, 3–050

Tirrenia di Navigazione v Commission of the European Communities (T–246/99) [2007]
E.C.R. II–65 25–016

Tirrenia de Navigazione v Commission of the European Communities (T–265, 292 and
504/04) [2009] E.C.R. II–21 .... 25–017, 27–016

Transalpine Olleitung in Osterreich GmbH v Finanzlandesdirektion fur Tirol (C–368/04)
[2006] E.C.R. I–9957; [2007] 1 C.M.L.R. 19 ECJ 3–044, 10–040, 20–030

TV 2/Danmark v Commission of the European Communities (T–309/04, T–317/04,
T–329/04 and T–336/04) [2008] E.C.R. II–2935 .... 8–036, 8–048, 8–059, 8–060, 27–014,
27–016

TWD Textilwerke Deggendorf GmbH v Germany (C–188/92) [1994] E.C.R. I–833; [1995]
2 C.M.L.R. 145 ECJ 27–057

Ufex v Commission of the European Communities (T–613/97). See Union Francaise de
l'Express (UFEX) v Commission of the European Communities (T–613/97)

UGT-Rioja Case. See Union General de Trabajadores de La Rioja (UGT-Rioja) v Juntas
Generales del Territorio Historico de Vizcaya (C–428/06)

Unicredito Italiano SpA v Agenzia delle Entrate Ufficio Genova 1 (C–148/04) [2005] E.C.R.
I–11137 ECJ 3–079, 4–024, 8–067, 10–026, 10–036, 19–017

Union de Televisiones Comerciales Asociadas (UTECA) v Administracion General del
Estado (C–222/07) [2009] E.C.R. I–1407; [2009] 3 C.M.L.R. 2 ECJ (2nd Chamber) 3–027

Union Francaise de l'Express (UFEX II) v Commission of the European Communities
(T–613/97) [2006] E.C.R. II–1531; [2006] 3 C.M.L.R. 17 CFI (3rd Chamber) 1–020, 3–084,
3–103

Union Francaise de l'Express (UFEX) v Commission of the European Communities
(T–613/97) [2000] E.C.R. II–4055 CFI 1–020, 3–002, 3–055, 3–084, 3–103, 5–055, 25–054,
25–060

Union Francaise de l'Express (UFEX) v Commission of the European Communities
(C–119/97 P) [1999] E.C.R. I–1341; [2000] 4 C.M.L.R. 268 ECJ (5th Chamber) 27–027

Union General de Trabajadores de La Rioja (UGT-Rioja) v Juntas Generales del Territorio
Historico de Vizcaya (C–428/06) [2008] E.C.R. I–6747; [2008] 3 C.M.L.R. 46 ECJ (3rd
Chamber) 3–052, 10–008

Universitat Hamburg v Hauptzollamt Hamburg-Kehrwieder (216/82) [1983] E.C.R. 2771
ECJ 27–058

UPS Europe SA v Commission of the European Communities (T–175/99) [2002] E.C.R.
II–1915; [2002] 5 C.M.L.R. 2 CFI (4th Chamber) 3–021

US Steel Kosice v Commission of the European Communities (T–22/07) [2009] E.C.R.
II–61 5–017

UTEC. See Union de Televisiones Comerciales Asociadas (UTECA) v Administracion
General del Estado (C–222/07) [

Valmont Nederland BV v Commission of the European Communities (T–274/01) [2005] All
E.R. (EC) 880; [2004] E.C.R. II–3145; [2005] 3 C.M.L.R. 25 CFI (4th Chamber) 1–025,
3–097, 8–068, 25–056

Van Calester, Cleeren and Openbaar Slachthuis NV. See Belgium v Van Calster
(C–261/01) 3–130

Van den Bor BV v Voedselvoorzieningsin- en Verkoopbureau. See H van den Bor BV v
Voedselvoorzieningsin- en Verkoopbureau

Van der Hulst v Productschap voor Siergewassen. See PJ van der Hulst's Zonen CV v
Produktschap voor Siergewassen (51/74)

Van der Kooy BV v Commission of the European Communities (67/85). See Kwekerij
Gebroeders van der Kooy BV v Commission of the European Communities (67/85)

Van Der Kooy v Staatssecretaris Van Financiën (C–181/97) [1999] E.C.R. I–483 ECJ (5th
Chamber) 3–028

Van Tiggele. See Openbaar Ministerie v Van Tiggele

Table of Cases

VEMW (C–17/03). *See* Vereniging voor Energie Milieu en Water v Directeur van de Dienst
Uitvoering en Toezicht Energie (C–17/03) 20–057
Viscido v Ente Poste Italiane (C–52/97) [1998] All E.R. (EC) 857; [1998] E.C.R. I–2629;
[1998] 3 C.M.L.R. 184 ECJ (4th Chamber) 3–019
Viscido v Ente Poste Italiane (C–52/97) [1998] All E.R. (EC) 857; [1998] E.C.R. I–2629;
[1998] 3 C.M.L.R. 184 ECJ (4th Chamber) 3–057
Visserijbedrijf DJ Koornstra & Zn.vof v Productschap Vis (C–517/04), June 6, 2006 ECJ 13–041
Vlaams Gewest (Flemish Region) v Commission of the European Communities (T–214/95)
[1998] E.C.R. II–717 CFI (5th Chamber) 4–031, 8–020
VOF Josanne v Commission of the European Communities (T–82/01) [2003] E.C.R. II–2013
CFI 17–031
Vtesse Networks v Commission of the European Communities (T–54/07) January 21,
2011 27–033
Werkgroep Commerciële Jachtshaven Zuidelijke Randmeren and Others v Commission of
the European Communities (T–117/04) [2006] ECR II–3861 27–033
Westdeutsche Landesbank Girozentrale v Commission of the European Communities
(T–228/99) [2003] E.C.R. II–435; [2004] 1 C.M.L.R. 17 CFI 1–032, 3–023, 3–025, 3–083,
3–084, 3–085, 19–006, 19–007, 24–009, 25–03125–032
Westfalisch-Lippischer Sparkassen v Commission (T–457/09) January 31, 2011; March 8,
2011 .... 1–025, 19–059, 27–047
Weyl Beef Products BV v Commission of the European Communities (T197/97); Groninger
Vleeshandel BV v Commission of the European Communities (T198/97) [2001] E.C.R.
II–303; [2001] 2 C.M.L.R. 22 CFI (4th Chamber) 3–120
Wheyco GmbH v Commission of the European Communities (T–6/06) [2007] E.C.R.
II–72 .... 19–071, 27–015
William Cook Plc v Commission of the European Communities (C–198/91) [1993] E.C.R.
I–2487; [1993] 3 C.M.L.R. 206 ECJ .... 4–021, 21–003, 25–012 , 25–017
Zoni, Criminal proceedings against (90/86) [1988] E.C.R. 4285 ECJ 13–004
Zuckerfabrik Suderdithmarschen AG v Hauptzollamt Itzehoe (C–143/88); Zuckerfabrik
Soest GmbH v Hauptzollamt Paderborn (C–92/89) [1991] E.C.R. I–415; [1993] 3
C.M.L.R. 1, ECJ 27–004, 27–050

TABLE OF COMMISSION DECISIONS

(by case number)

89/93 [1993] OJ C256/9 25–050

BB 49/99 Spain [2001] OJ C7 20–074

C 50/83 Netherlands, State aid for the Dutch fertiliser industry [1992] OJ C344/4 12–020
C 26/86 and C 43/87 CdF Chimie [1990] OJ C198/2 24–004
C 25/89 Quimigal [1990] OJ C188/3 24–004
C 47/91 CNP and EPSI [1992] OJ C1/5 24–004
C 38/92 (ex NN 128/92) Italy, EFIM [1993] OJ C349/2 9–008
C 98/92 State aid for Esmaltaciones San Ignacio [1993] OJ C277/05 12–009
C 10/94 3–134
C 12/94 Enichem Agricultura [1994] OJ C330/7; [1996] L28/18 24–006
C 20/94 France, Aid for the development of the site occupied by Kimberley Clark Industries
    [1994] OJ C170/8 .... 3–061, 3–065
C 26/97 Spain, State Aid (ex NN 72/96) (Andalusia) 3–054
C 42/97 Everts Erfurt [1998] OJ C37/8 .... 24–007, 24–024
C 47/97 Leuna 2000 refinery [1997] OJ C394/14 24–007
C 74/97 Kali und Salz [1998] OJ C197/7 24–007
C 16/98 (NN 10/98) Italy, Banco di Sicilia and Sicilcassa [1998] OJ C297/3; final decision
    [2000] OJ 2000 L256/21 19–015
C 32/1999 Germany, Aid for a meat processing company, Greussener Salamifabriek
    GmbH 13–039
C 67/99 Dampfkessel [2000] OJ C379/4 24–010
C 1/2000 Holzmann [2000] OJ C110/2 24–003
C 43/2000 Luxembourg [2009] OJ L159/11 .... 3–027, 20–021
C 54/2000 August 23, 2002 .... 8–011, 8–012
C 65/2000 (ex N 679/2000) [2002] OJ L196 17–055
C(2001) 403 Kataleuna [2001] OJ L245/26 24–003
C 3/2001 Belgium, Subsidies loans for fishermen 13–048
C 5/2001 (ex N 775/2000) Italy, Blue tongue compensation 13–025
C 11/2001 (ex N 629/2000) Netherlands, Waste disposal system for car wrecks, [2002] OJ
    L68/18 .... 22–021, 22–022
C 18/2001 (ex N 123/2001) United Kingdom, Climate Change Levy [2002]
    C185/223–037, ... 22–023, 22–024, 22–062, 22–084, 22–092, 22–094
C 22/2001 ES, Mesures d'appui au secteur agricole suite de la hausse du cout du carburant 13–033
C 27/2001 France, Programme to control pollution of agricultural origin "PMPOA" 13–017
C 87/2001 [2002] OJ C38/2 (United Kingdom, Orkney) 13–044
C 56/2001 [2002] OJ L314/97 17–052
C 97/2001 (ex N 93/2001) Maritime transport safety [2002] OJ C50/7 17–055
C 11/2002 (ex N 382/01) Italy (Piedmont), Reduction of tolls for certain heavy goods
    vehicles in order to divert them from the Lake Maggiore State road 33 to the A/26
    motorway [2002] OJ C87 17–043

C 14/2002 (ex NN 72/01) Portugal, Reduction of tolls for certain heavy goods vehicles, coaches and buses adopted following the rise in oil prices in summer/autumn 2000 [2002] OJ C88 17–043

C 31/2002 Belgium, Transitional regime for the Belgian electricity market [2002] OJ C222/2 20–006

C 42/2002 (ex N 286/2002) [2003] OJ L77/61 17–073

C 43/2002 Luxembourg, Compensation fund [2002] OJ C255/15 ....20–021, 20–023, 20–032

C 49/2002 France, Aid to finance a public rendering service 13–025

C 50/2002 Spain, Aid for producer organisations of olive oil 13–021

C 60/2002 Italy, Reduction of the greenhouse gases emissions, [2004] OJ L81/72 22–063

C 61/2002 United Kingdom, Newsprint reprocessing WRAP program and N 443/2003 Belgium, Second Circuit Water [2002] OJ C283/7 ....22–005, 24–027, 22–075

C 76/2002 [2004] OJ L137/1 .... 17–076, 17–077

C(2003) 1329 final [2003] OJ C175 19–009

C 2/2003 (ex NN 22/02) Denmark, State funding of TV2/Danmark [2005] OJ C69/42 (T-V2/Danmark(I) 3–034, 18–002, 18–003, 18–008, 18–011

C 6/2003 France, Plan Rivesaltes and parafiscal taxes CIVDN 13–030

C 9/A/2003 and C B/2003 Germany, Aid for Bavarian machinery rings 13–021

C 13/2003 Measures to support France Telecom [2003] OJ C57; [2005] OJ L269/30 ....3–025, 3–033, 3–085

C 17/2003 Spain 14–016

C 20/2003 (ex. N 433/2002) [2003] OJ L150/1 17–055

C 39/2003 (ex. NN 119/2002) [2003] OJ C199/3 17–073

C 43/2003 Aid in favour of AVR [2006] OJ L84/37 4–050

C 44/2003 (ex NN 158/01) Aid which Austria is planning to implement for Bank Burgenland AG [2005] OJ L263/8 .... 19–007, 19–025

C 46/2003 France, Cotisations au profit d'INTERBEV 13–021

C 50/03 (ex. NN 163/02) Financial compensation for the temporary cessation of fishing for common spiny lobster in Corsica [2003] OJ C211/63 13–047

C 52/2003 Restructuring aid granted by the UK government to British Energy (BE) [2003] OJ C180/5 20–009

C 54/2003 (ex N 194/02) [2009] OJ L50/30 17–043

C 60/2003 Germany, Aid which Germany has granted in favour of the acquisition of business shares in winegrowers' co-operatives 13–021

C 67/2003, C 69/2003 Decision of June 16, 2004 20–040

C 75/2003 Italy, Interventions en faveur des cooperatives et exploitations agricoles—consolidation des dettes couteuses (Lazio) 13–021

C 187/2003 Netherlands, Rehabilitation of polluted gas works sites 22–078

C 6/2004 (ex NN 70/2001) Italy, Exoeration d'accises sur les carburants agricoles 13–033

C 2/2004/ (ex NN 170/2003) on the ad hoc financing of Dutch public service broadcasters [2004] OJ L/49/2008 .... 18–002, 18–012

C 5/2004 Aid in favour of Kronoply GmbH 4–031

C 10/2004 Bull [2004] OJ C102/12 24–003

C 11/2004 Olympic Airways—Restucturing and privatisation [2004] OJ C192/02 .. 8–070, 17–070

C 16/2004 Greece, Hellenic Shipyards [2009] OJ L225 .... 3–134, 8–073

C 17/2004 United Kingdom, Enterprise Capital Funds [2006] OJ C91 4–056

C 20/2004 on restructuring aid to steel producer Huta Czestochowa [2004] OJ C204 5–016

C 20/2004 Huta Czestochowa [2006] OJ L 366/1 14–073

C 24/2004 (ex NN 35/04) [2004] OJ C238/04 (Swedish DVB-T) 3–034, 18–012, 18–013, 18–014, 18–015, 18–017

C 25/2004 (ex NN 36/04) concerning State aid for the introduction of digital terrestrial television in Berlin (German DVB-T) 3–034, 18–012, 18–013, 18–014, 18–015, 18–016, 18–017

C 27/2004 on State aid granted by the Czech Republic to Agrobanka Praha, a.s. and GE Capital Bank, [2004] OJ C292, and Corrigenda [2005] OJ C10 ....5–005, 5–010, 5–011, 5–013

C 32/2004 [2005] OJ C30/12 16–023

C 35/2004 aid granted by Hungary to Postabank es Takarekpenztar Rt./Erste Bank Hungary Rt. [2005] OJ C68/12 .... 5–011, 5–013

C 36/2004 Cordex [2007] OJ L156/23 4–047

C 41/2004 Orfama [2007] OJ L183/46 4–047

C 43/2004 Tax parafiscal a la promotion du vin 13–041
C 45/2004 (ex NN 62/04) on restructuring aid to the Czech steel producer Trinecke Zelezarny
  [2005] OJ C22/2 .... 5–016, 14–068
C 3/2005 on aid granted by Poland to Fabryka Samochodow Osobowych SA [2007] OJ
  L187, Corrigendum [2010] OJ L32 5–008
C 5/2005, Italy, Exoneration d'accises sur les carburants agricoles 13–033
C 7/2005 [2007] OJ L219/9 .... 14–046, 20–078
C 11/2005 Germany, Aid for and ethylene pipeline—Bavaria 3–062
C 13/2005 loans for the purchase of fishing quotas in the Shetland Islands [2003] OJ
  L211/3 13–044
C 14/2005 Netherlands, Holland Malt 13–016
C 19/2005 Poland, State aid granted to Stocnzia Szczecin (Poland) [2005] OJ C222 5–008
C 23/2005, France, Aides dans le secteur de l'equarrissage en 2003 .... 13–024, 13–025
C 24/2005 State aid implemented by France for the Laboratoire Nationale d'essais [2007] OJ
  L95/25 8–040
C 35/2005 (ex N 59/2005) on Netherlands plans to implement concerning broadband
  infrastructure in Appingedam [2005] OJ L/86/2007 18–018
C 40/2005 Ford Genk [2006] OJ L366/32 4–017
C 41/2005 Hungary [2009] OJ L225/53 20–038
C 43/2005 Poland, State aid awarded by Poland as part of Power Purchase Agreements
  [2009] OJ L83/1 .... 20–026, 20–038, 24–032
C 44/2005 Poland, Restructuring aid in favour of Huta Stalowa Wola S.A. [2010] OJ L81 5–008
C 45/2005 [2009] OJ L225/53 20–065
C 46/2005 InterFerryBoats [2009] OJ L225/1 17–039
C 52/2005 (ex. NN 88/2005, ex. CP 101/2004), Italy, Subsidy to digital decoders [2005] OJ
  L/147/2007 18–015
C 1/2006 Chupa Chups [2006] OJ C97/2 24–003
C 4/2006 Djebel [2007] OJ L219/30 4–017
C 9/2006, France, Fonds de prevention des aleas a la peche 13–047
C 10/2006 Cyprus Airways [2006] OJ C113/2 24–003
C 12/2006 (ex. N 132/05) 17–036
C 14/2006 General Motors Antwerp, [2007] OJ L243/71 4–017
C 23/2006 (ex. NN 35/06) on state aid which Poland has implemented for steel producer
  Technologie Buczek Group [2008] OJ L116/26 14–073
C 24/2006, Germany, Animal Health Service (Bayern); C44/2008, Belgium, Arrete royal
  concernant le financement du depistage des enc'ephalopathies spongiformes transmis-
  sibles chez les animaux 13–028
C 29/2006, Italy, Restructuring of enterprises 13–048
C 31/2006, Italy, Mesures urgentes pour la prevention de l'influenza aviaire 13–028
C 34/2006 Introduction of DVB-T in North Rhine-Westphalia 2–039
C 36/2006 on tariffs for certain enregy intensive users in Italy [2010] OJ L227/62 20–018
C 36/b/2006 and C 38/a/2004 Aid granted by Italy subsidizing elecricity prices 20–093
C 40/2006, United Kingdom, Loan assistence schemes 13–047
C 41/2006 on CO2 exemptions (Denmark) [2006] OJ C274/25 20–031
C 45/2006 France, Construction of a nuclear power station [2008] OJ L89/15 4–048
C 46/2006 Sweden, CO2 tax reductions [2006] OJ C297/27 20–031
C 48/2006 [2008] OJ L346/1 17–082
C 50/2006 (ex NN 68/2006, CP 102/2006) implemented by Austria for BAWAG-PSK [2008]
  OJ L83/7 .... 19–026, 19–035
C 53/2006 (ex N 262/05, ex CP 127/04) Citynet Amsterdam [2008] OJ L247/27 19–007
C 55/2006 PT, Bonifications de taux d'interet relatifs a des prets pour des activites dans le
  secteur de la peche 13–047
C 56/2006 (ex NN 77/06) implemented by Austria for the privatisation of Bank Burgenland
  [2008] OJ L 239/32 .... 8–071, 19–009, 19–025
C 3/2007 on regulated tariffs in Spain [2007] OJ C43/9 20–018
C 9/2007 Spain, R&D aid to ITP for the Trent 1000 project (IP/07/395) [2007] OJ C108/18 ... 23–029
C 11/2007 [2009] OJ L259/22 20–56
C 16/2007 Austria 17–044
C 17/2007 on regulated supply tariffs in France [2007] OJ C164/9; [2009] OJ C96/18 20–018,
  20–026

Table of Commission Decisions

C 22/2007 [2009] OJ L119/23 17–056

C 23/2007 United Kingdom, Training aid for Vauxhall at Ellesmere Port 2–039

C 28/2007 Germany, Training aid for DHL Leipzig 2–039

C 29/2007 [2007] OJ L239/51 4–048

C 35/2007 Belgium, Training aid for Volvo Cars in Gent 2–039

C 38/2007 Arbel Fauvet Rail [2010] C(20100 4112 final 24–028

C 41/2007 Privatisation of Tractorul 2008 L263/2008 8–071

C 46/2007 8–071

C 61/2007 [2010] OJ L222/62 .... 17–070, 17–071

C 1/2008, France, Industries de transformation et de commercialisation du secteur de la
peche et de l'aquaculture 13–047

C 9/2008 (ex NN 8/08, CP 244/07) implemented by Germany for Sachsen LB [2009] OJ
L104/34 .... 4–025, 19–007, 19–008, 19–009, 19–027, 19–054

C 10/2008 (ex NN 7/08) implemented by Germany for the restructuring of IKB Deutsche
Industriebank AG [2009] OJ L278/32 ...... 19–007, 19–010, 19–027, 19–028, 19–054, 19–070,
19–073

C 12/2008 Agreement between Bratislava Airport and Ryanair 17–083

C 14/2008 (ex NN 1/2008) implemented by the United Kingdom for Northern Rock [2010]
OJ L112/38 .... 19–029, 19–042, 19–054, 19–057, 19–073, 19–075

C 18/2008 Hungary, Dunaferr 15–025

C 22/2008 Aides a El Pozo de Alimentacion [2010] OJ C217/6. S.A., ES 13–019, 13–034

C 23/2008 Aide a J Garcia Carrion (Castilla la Mancha), ES [2010] O.J C217/6 .. 13–019, 13–034

C 30/2008 Belgium, Steunverlening aan de visafslag van Oostende 13–047

C 31/2008 France, Sauvetage de la societe "Volailles du Perigord" 13–039

C 33/2008 Sweden, State loan for R&D to Volvo Aero/Genx [2008] OJ C253/31 23–029

C 34/2008 Germany, Deutsche Solar AG [2008] OJ 217/51 ....15–004, 15–026, 15–028, 15–030,
15–031

C 41/2008 Public service contracts between the Danish Government and Dankse Statbaner
[2008] OJ C309/14 17–039

C 42/2008 France, aides aux marins-pecheurs salaries 13–047

C 43/2008 (ex N 390/08) on State aid which Germany proposes to grant towards the
restructuring of WestLB AG [2009] OJ L345/1 .... 19–029, 19–054, 19–059, 19–061, 19–067,
19–068, 19–073, 19–075

C 46/2008 Poland, Dell [2010] OJ L29/53 ....15–026, 15–030, 15–031

C 1/2009 on state aid C 1/09 (ex NN 69/08) granted by Hungary to MOL Nyrt [2011] OJ
L34/55. .... 4–050, 20–019, 20–030, 20–046, 20–047

C 2/2009 on the German Law to Modernise the General Conditions for Capital Investments,
[2010] OJ L6/32 4–056

C 3/2009 PT, Financement de la collecte, le transport et la destruction des sous-produits
obtenus de l'abattage des ruminants et des volailles 13–024

C 8/2009 Fri-El Acerra [2009] OJ C95/20 20–048

C 9/2009 (ex NN 49/08, NN 50/08 and NN 45/08) Aid implemented by the Kingdom of
Belgium, the French Republic and the Grand Duchy of Luxembourg for Dexia SA
[2010] OJ L274/54 .... 8–010, 19–007, 19–008, 19–009, 19–013, 19–055, 19–057, 19–061,
19–063, 19–073, 19–074, 19–075

C 10/2009 (ex N 138/09) State aid implemented by the Netherlands for ING's Liquid assets
back facility and restructuring plan [2010] OJ L274/139 .....19–038, 19–048, 19–055, 19–062,
19–065, 19–069, 19–073, 19–074, 19–075

C 11/2009 (ex NN 53b/2008, NN 2/2010 and N 19/2010) Aid implemented by Dutch State
for ABN AMRO Group NV 19–007, 19–030, 19–036, 19–052, 19–059, 19–064, 19–069,
19–070, 19–073, 19–074, 19–075

C 15/2009 (ex N 196/2009) State aid which Germany intends to grant to Hypo Real Estate 19–042,
19–052, 19–055, 19–057, 19–059, 19–072, 19–073, 19–075

C 17/2009 (ex N 265/09) State aid by Germany for the restructuring of Landesbank Baden
Wurttemberg [2010] OJ L188/1 .... 19–056, 19–057, 19–059, 19–073, 19–074, 19–075

C 18/2009 (ex N 360/09) State aid implemented by Belgium for KBC [2010] OJ L188/24 19–063,
19–069, 19–073, 19–074, 19–075

C 21/2009 Greece Port of Pireaus [2009] OJ C245/21 3–064

xlvi

C 24/2009 (ex N 446/2008) State aid for energy-intensive businesses under the Green Electricity Act in Austria, Brussels, 8 March 2011 C(2011) 1363 final. [2011] OJ L235/42 ....3–034, 4–050, 20–032, 20–023

C 27/2009 (ex N 34/B/09) France, Budgetary grant for France Televisions which the French Republic plans to implement in favour of France Televisions (France III) [2009] OJ L/59/2011 18–007

C 29/2009 (ex N 264/2009) State aid granted by Germany to HSH Nordbank, September 20, 2011 19–009

C 30/2009 22–091

C 31/2009 Hungary, Audi Hungaria 2010 OJ C64/53 .... 15–026, 15–028, 15–030

C 32/2009 (ex NN 50/09) State aid implemented by Germany for the restructuring of Sparkasse KolnBonn [2011] OJ L235/1 ....19–058, 19–059, 19–067, 19–073, 19–074, 19–075

C 34/2009 Portugal, Petrogal [2010] OJ C23/53. .... 15–026, 15–028, 15–030

C 35/2009 Italy, Region Sardaigne—mesures urgentes en faveur de l'emploi (loi regionale n. 28/1984) 13–047

C 38/2009 (ex NN 58/2009) on new tax-based funding system for public broadcasting in Spain (RTVE Spain) [2009] OJ L/1/11 ....18–002, 18–004, 18–005, 18–006

C 39/2009 (ex. N 385/2008) Public financing of port infrastructure in Ventspils port [2010] OJ C62/7 17–060

C 61/2009 Change of ownership of Anglo-Irish Bank [2009] OJ C 177/2 .... 19–042, 19–054

C(2010) 2532,April 27, 2010, Stranded Costs legislation (Hungary) [2010] OJ C213 20–058

C 1/2010, Belgium, Aide a l'enlevement et a la destruction des animaux trouves morts 13–028

C 3/2010 Paiemenents de compensation verses par l'Organisme grec d'assurances (ELGA) pendant l'annee 2008 et 2009 13–029

C 4/2010 France, Suspected aid to Treves [2010] OJ C133 19–009

C 9/2010 Temporary capital tax gains tax relief on sales of cultivated land, FI 13–016

C 21/2010 Guidelines for the examination of State Aid to fisheries and aquaculture—Non acceptance of the appropriate measures for the Fisheries 13–047

C 32/2010 [2011] OJ C52/3 20–087

C 36/2010—Greece, Aid to cereal producing farmers and cereal collecting cooperatives ... 13–021

C 178/2010 [2010] OJ C31/2 20–087

CPN 3/2001 on the UK's Regional Venture Capital Funds in England 4–057

CZ 14/2003 on State Aid granted by the Czech Republic to Ceska spo ritelna, a.s., C(2004)11fin. COR, January 28, 2004 5–009

CZ 46/2003 Investicní a postovní banka, a.s., OJ 2005 C 137/4 .... 5–012, 5–013

E 10/2000 Germany, Anstaltslast and Gewahrtragerhaftung 19–003

E 45/2000 [2004] OJ C37/13. 17–075

E 50/2001 France, CDC IXIS 19–009

E 4/2005 Ireland, State aid financing of RTE and TNAG (TG4) [2005] OJ C121 18–003

E 2/2005 Dutch social housing [2010] OJ C31/53 8–038

E 3/2005, March 3, 2005 8–059

E 3/2005, April 24, 2007 8–047

E 5/2005 Netherlands, Annual financing of the Dutch public service broadcasters [2005] O.J C/74/2010 18–003

E 8/2005 RTVE, April 20, 2005 8–049

E 8/2006, State funding for Flemish public broadcaster VRT [2008] OJ C143 18–003

E 2/2008 Austria, October 28, 2008 8–047

N 464/1993 Germany—New demarcation of assisted regions for the period 1994 to 1996— former GDR [1994] OJ C373/3 8–080

N 262/94 VAMIL regime [1994] OJ C267 22–055

N 750/1996 13–035

N 752/1996 13–035

N 660/1996 13–035

N 132/1997 Maribel Quarter [1997] OJ C201/6 3–054

N 286/1998 13–035

N 433/1998 Recovery of the economic activities affected by the earthquake in Umbria [1999] OJ C56 3–014

N 597/1998 Netherlands, Stranded costs [2006] OJ C178 24–032

N 34/1999 Austria, Stranded costs [2002] OJ C5 .... 20–078, 24–032

N 223/1999 13–035

N 416/1999 Denmark, CO2 Quotas [2000] OJ C354 22–083

N 640/2009 (ex PN 119/2009) Austria rescue aid (capital injection and asst guarantee) to
    BAWAG-PSK [2009] OJ C55/3 ....19–036, 19–048, 19–051

N 646/1999 13–035

N 653/1999 Denmark, CO2 Quotas [2000] OJ C322/9 ....22–083, 22–084, 22–088

N 790/1999 [2000] OJ C58/3 17–055

N 58/2000 [2004] OJ C64/12 17–075

N 120/2000 13–035

N 304/2000 Netherlands, CO2 Reduction Plan [2000] OJ C328/32 22–062

N 504/2000 United Kingdom, Renewable Obligation and Capital Grants for Renewable
    Technologies [2002] OJ C30/12 ....22–020, 20–021, 22–055, 22–070

N 550/2000 Belgium, Green Electricity Certificates (Flanders) [2001] OJ C330/3 .....22–020, 22–062,
                                                                              22–068, 22–088

N 597/2000 Netherlands [2001] OJ C102/8 .... 17–032, 17–041

N 645/2000 Austria, Grants for Biomass [2001] OJ C234/12 22–063

N 797/2000 United Kingdom, Enhanced capital allowances for energy efficient investments
    [2001] OJ C160 22–094

N 841/A/2000 [2002] OJ C238/13 20–030

N 842/2000 Luxembourg, Electricity Reforms, New RE-based Power Plants (Prime
    d'encouragement ecologique) 22–065

N 6/A/2001 [2002] OJ C77/25 20–078

N 133/2001 Greece, Stranded costs [2003] OJ C9/6 24–032

N 168/A/2001 Netherlands, Modifications energy tax [2002] OJ C30 ....22–062, 22–071, 22–093

N 209/2001 Decision concerning a state guarantee to the Irish Housing Finance Authority
    [2002] OJ C67/33 8–010

N 239/2001 Netherlands, Partial exemption energy tax for waste incineration units [2002] OJ
    C32 22–065

N 278/2001 Denmark, Electricity Reforms, New RE-based Power Plants [2001] OJ
    C263/6 22–065

N 299/2001 [2001] OJ C342/ 17–041

N 323/2001 Greece, Aid for investment in sustainable energy [2002] OJ C98/32 22–055

N 354/2001 France, FIDEME (Fonds d'investissement de l'environnement et de la maitrise
    de l'energie) 24–046

N 358/2001 SIKB (Netherlands) [2001] [2002] OJ C146 8–011

N 415/A/2001 Belgium, Green certificate mechanism (Wallonia) [2002] OJ C30/14 20–021,
                                                                              22–062, 22–068

N 416/2001 United Kingdom, Emission trading scheme [2002] OJ C88/16 ..24–027, 22–083, 22–088

N 449/2001 Germany, Continuation of the ecological tax reform after March 31, 2002 [2002]
    OJ C137/24 22–023

N 459/2001 Spain, Aide en faveur de l'energie solaire thermique 22–064

N 460/2001 22–064

N 497/2001 Grants for Owner Occupation in Scotland [2002] OJ C32/18 4–058

N 509/2001 Salmon net licences buy-out scheme (United Kingdom) [2002] OJ C252/45 3–014

N 513/2001 Aid to Hellenic shipyards [2002] OJ C186 3–134

N 520/2001 Netherlands, Soil protection agreement [2002] OJ C146 22–078

N 550/2001 [2002] OJ C24/2, extended by N 344/2004 ....17–041, 17–058

N 553/2001 Ireland, Alternative Energy Requirements V [2002] OJ C54 22–070

N 706/2001 Channel Tunnel Rail Link (United Kingdom), C(2002)1446fin of April 24,
    2002 9–020

N 711/2001 Community Investment Tax Credit (United Kingdom) [2003] OJ C18/38 4–055

N 863/2001 Aggregates Levy (Northern Ireland) (United Kingdom) C(2002) 1478 3–047

N 854/2001 [2002] OJ C98/5 United Kingdom 17–073

N 806/2001 France [2002] OJ C59 17–073

N 826/2001 Ireland, Alternative Energy Requirements I to IV [2002] OJ C59 22–070

N 649/2001 17–057

N 651/2001 Netherlands, Special provision in the energy tax for producers of sustainable
    heat [2002] OJ C77 ....22–062, 22–065, 22–094

N 631/2001 United Kingdom, BBC Licence fee at [2003] OJ C23/03 18–002

Table of Commission Decisions

N 644i/2002 Germany [2005] OJ C126/12 17–081

N 671/2001 and 672/2001 France, OFIVAL, Contrats Plan Etat-regions. Production equine et desaisonnnalisation de la production de poulains lourds 13–003

N 158/2002 United Kingdom, First Phase Major Photovoltaic Demonstration Programme, [2002] OJ C238/12 22–063

N 198/2002 [2003] OJ C/23 22–064

N 217/2002 Enschede fireworks disaster [2002] OJ L164/45 3–014

N 264/2002 [2002] OJ C319/15 17–013

N 269/2002 Germany [2003] OJ C23/5 17–073

N 308/2002, Promotion of investments for railway infrastructure [2002] OJ C277 17–036

N 338/2002 13–011

N 339/2002 13–011

N 340/2002 13–011

N 356/2002 United Kingdom, Network Rail July 17, 2002 ....3–067, 3–080, 20–040

N 385/2002 prolonged by State aid N 221.2006 United Kingdom, Support for land remediation [2006] OJ C222 .... 22–078, 22–080

N 403/2002 Austria [2003] OJ C138/4 4–054

N 441/2002 13–035

N 472/2002 Denmark, Permanent ceiling on land taxes for productive land. 13–037

N 496/2002 France, Aides a l'elimination des dechets dangereux pour l'eau [2003] OJ C108/5 22–076

N 511/2002 Sardinia, September 17, 2003 4–060

N 527/2002 Aviation fuel pipeline to Athens Airport [2003] OJ C148/11 3–062

N 550/2002 Germany 14–016

N 551/2002 France 14–016

N 559/2002 [2003] OJ C76/27 24–046

N 588/2002 [2003] OJ C76/28 17–044

N 652/2002 Fiscal reforms energy tax 2003 [2003] OJ C104 22–093

N 677/2002 Austria [2003] OJ C148/8 4–054

N 692/2002 Italy—Honey, project U.N.A.A.P.I 13–003

N 693/2002, United Kindgom, Changes to the Farm Waste Grant Scheme 13–017

N 698/2002 Interest-free loan with proportionate loss compensation by Hamburg to the BTG Beteiligungsgesellschaft mbH (Germany) [2004] OJ C78/31 4–055

N 707/2002 Netherlands, MEP Stimulating Renewable Energy, March 19, 2003; [2003] OJ C148/11 ....22–018, 22–056, 22–067

N 740/2002 United Kingdom 14–016

N 789/2002 on green certificates in Sweden [2003] OJ C120/8 20–021

N 814/2002 [2004] OJ C38/4. 14–023

N 800/2002 United Kingdom, Nitrate Vulnerable Zones Grants Scheme 13–017

N 863/2002 United Kingdom , Aggregates Levy, April 24, 2002 20–032

N 35/2003 Netherlands, Nox Trading Scheme [2003] OJ C227/8 22–083

N 37/2003 United Kingdom, BBC Digital Curriculum [2003] OJ C271/06 ......3–016, 8–053, 18–002, 18–003

N 46/2003 Irish health insurance N 46/2003 [2003] OJ C186/46 8–028

N 159/2003 Netherlands, Promotion and research for the fishery 13–045

N 195/2003 AMA Biosiegel and AMA Gütesiegel (Austria) [2000] OJ L382/2 13–032

N 266/2003 Netherlands, Q7 Offshore Windpark [2003] OJ C266 ..22–023, 24–038, 22–059, 22–099

N 267/2003 Aides au secteur des produteurs et negociants de vins de liqueur France 13–041

N 277/2003 Transfer of nature protection land 13–035, 13–036

N 282/2003 United Kingdom, Cumbria Broadband-Project Access 8–045

N 295/2003 United Kingdom, Bio-Energy Infrastructure scheme [2005] OJ C–316/22 ....20–051, 20–052

N 304/2003 Netherlands, AKZO Nobel (relocation aid for matters of external safety) [2005] OJ C81/5 ....22–005, 24–027, 22–079

N 318/2003 Germany [2004] OJ C67/9 4–058

N 322/2003, Fiat Auto [2003] OJ C284/36 4–017

N 335/2003 [2004] OJ C22 17–046

N 443/2003 Belgium, Second Circuit Water, June 2, 2004; [2006] OJ C21/4 .... 22–022, 24–027, 22–075

N 464/2003 United Kingdom, Company neutral revenue scheme (CNRS) [2003] OJ
  C16/25 17–036
N 475/2003 December 16, 2003 [2004] OJ C34/7 20–078
N 515/B/2003, France, Slaughter tax 13–025
N 520/2003 [2005] OJ C176/12 17–058
N 536/2003 Italy, Regional intervention for the development of Confidi in the agricultural
  sector 13–021
N 539/2003 Germany, Aid for conversion of fisheries resources 13–045
N 551/2003 [2005] OJ C125/8. 17–046
N 592/2003 Determination of the terms and conditions for the granting of contributions for
  the purchase of used vessels (Italy) 13–047
N 603/2003 C(2004) 1375, April 2004 3–051
N 617/2003 [2005] OJ C24/04 16–025
N 622/2003 Austria, Fund for Digitalisation, C(2005) 586 [2004] OJ C216/03 ...... 18–002, 18–016
N 632/2003 Belgium [2005] OJ C223/2 4–056
N 662/2003, Austria, Digitalisierungfonds (Austrian Digital) [2005] OJ C228 18–012
N 4/2004 [2005] OJ C125/6 17–041
N 14/2004 13–035
N 38/2004 [2005] OJ C136/41 17–016
N 53/2004 United Kingdom, Farm Waste Management 13–017
N 57/2004 Denmark, Reduction of land taxes 13–037
N 75/2004 Italy, Rescue aid in favour of Parmalat suppliers Lombardy 13–039
N 88/2004 [2005] OJ C77/29 17–047
N 161/2004 Portugal, Portuguese stranded costs [2005] OJ C250/9 24–032
N 156/2004 [2005] OJ C137/5 22–095
N 159/2004 and N136/2003 Salmon net licences buyout scheme (United Kingdom) [2006]
  OJ C42/29 3–014
N 171/2004 [2005] OJ C136/42 17–055
N 179/2004 Finish municipal guarantees 19–003
N 199/2004 Broadband Business Fund (United Kingdom) 2005] OJ C96 3–071
N 212/2004 ERDF Venture Capital Funds (Germany) [2005] OJ C95/8 4–055
N 233/2004 13–035
N 234/2004 13–035
N 241/2004 Austria, Viennese Aid Programme, September 9, 2004 20–042
N 249/2004 [2005] OJ C280/9 17–016
N 253/2004 [2005] OJ C136/43 22–095
N 306/2004 Ireland [2005] OJ C37/48 4–055
N 313/2004 Denmark, Recapitalisation of TV2/Danmark A/S (T-V2/Danmark (II)) [2005]
  OJ C172/03 .... 18–002, 18–003, 18–004, 18–008
N 320/2004, June 22, 2005 2005] OJ C228/11 14–027
N 323/2004 [2006] OJ C83/10 17–035
N 343/2004 Denmark, Tax on mineral phosphorous in feed phosphates 13–037
N 355/2004 Belgium [2005] OJ C176/11 17–081
N 381/2004 Haut débit en Pyrénées-Atlantiques(France) 3–071
N 384/2004 France, restructuring aid to SNCF [2005] OJ C172/3 17–001
N 389/2004 [2005] OJ C172/3 17–037
N 440/2004, January 27, 2005 on Research and development aid for the vegetative reproduc-
  tion of the Nordmanns-fir (Nordrhein-Westfalen [2005] OJ C258/04 13–035
N 478/2004 Ireland, "Irish Rail" June 7, 2006 3–065
N 492/2004 Regional development aid in favour of SABIC [2005] OJ C176 4–032
N 524/2004 Sweden, Investment aid for energy efficiency and conversion to renewable
  source in public premises, March 16, 2005, [2005] OJ C226/6 22–063
N 568/2004 DN 13–015
N 597/2004 [2005] O.J.C250/11 14–031
N 604/b/2004 Denmark, Fiscal treatment of quotas and payments entitlements 13–037
N 5/2005 Tax Reduction of donations to cultural institutions (Denmark) 3–035
N 43/2005 Stranded Costs in Poland [2006] OJ C52/8 3–120
N 54/2005 Chaine francaise d'information internationale C(2005) 1479 Fin 8–049
N 57/2005 Regional Innovative Broadband Support (Wales) 2–038
N 85/2005 Netherlands, Sbil rehabilitation of polluted industrial sites [2005] OJ C228 22–078

Table of Commission Decisions

N 103/2005 United Kingdom, Amendment to the farm Nutrient management 13–017
N 188/2005 Spain, Modification of aid schemes for renewable energy and energy efficiency, [2005] OJ C307/4 22–064
N 190A/2005 United Kingdom, Modification of the Climate Change Levy [2006] OJ C 146/05 20–029
N 192/2005 [2006] OJ C79/23 8–022
N 251/2005 Netherlands, Aid for reduction of fishing capacities in Ijsselmeer 13–047
N 253/2005 [2005] C228/04 16–026
N 278/2005, N281/2004; N9/2010 Italy—Dispositions regionales en matiere de reglementation et de promotion de l'apiculture (Friuli-Venezia-Giulia) 13–003
N 283/2005 Portugal, Fonds d'Investissement Immobilier Forestier 13–035, 13–036
N 284/2005 Metropolitan Area Networks (Ireland) 2–038, 2–076
N 304/2005 Aid in favour of Akzo-Nobel in order to minimise chlorine transports (Netherlands) [2005] OJ C81/48 3–013
N 344/2005 Spain [2006] OJ C14/12 4–054
N 355/2005 Aid in favour of a periodical, C(2005) 4457 (Slovak Republic) 4–033
N 368/2005 Spain, Aid for the promotion of audiovisual works in Andalucia 4–036
N 416/2005 DE, Aid for consultancy services in the potato sector [2005] OJ L66/10 13–023
N 420/2005 France, Mont Blanc Tunnel [2007] OJ C90 3–075
N 486/2005 Ireland 13–017
N 501/2005 Netherlands, Financial strength support soil rehabilitation [2006] OJ C313/13 22–078
N 503/2005 United Kingdom, Great Yarmouth Outer Harbour COM(2005) 5440 final [2009] OJ L83/1 .... 17–059, 20–040
N 531/2005 France, Creation de la banque postale—measures relating to banking subsidiary of La Poste C(2005) 5412 final, December 21, 2005 .... 8–019, 8–043, 8–056
N 575/2005 Netherlands, Relocation car dismantling company Steenbergen [2007] OJ C80 ...22–021, 22–080
N 604/2005 [2006] OJ C207/2 17–044
N 642/2005 Sweden [2007] OJ C2941 8–066
N 38b/2006 GR, Programme ZEUS (mesures en faveur des pisciculteurs dont les exploitations ont ete touchees par des calamites naturelles ou des conditions climatique defavorables 13–047
N 68/2006, Sweden, Replanting of trees in stormfelled forest 13–035
N 92/2006 on Poland's excise tax refund on diesel used in agriculture 13–033
N 149/2006 Irish Ring Road (Ireland) [2006] OJ C207 3–076
N 183/06 Poland [2006] OJ C 141, C21/2006 8–066
N 194/2006 Screen East Investment Fund (United Kingdom) June 7, 2006 4–060
N 254/2006 Belgium, Panneaux photovoltaiques [2006] OJ C314/80 22–020
N 315/2006, October 29, 2007 on the refund of energy tax on certain energy products to agricultural producers (Case), summary note [2007] OJ C296/2 13–033
N 330/2006 Berlin Kapital Fonds 4–060
N 383/2006 CY, Regime national 2006–2008 pour les producteurs de pommes de terre 13–003
N 588/2006 Netherlands, Subsidy measure vital Gelderland [2007] OJ C107/1 22–025
N 613/2006, October 1, 2007 on aid for the voluntary or partial suspension of breeding of pigeons following perturbations caused by the avian influenza crisis 13–030
N 674/2006, France, R&D NeoVal for the development of a new automatic metro system on rubber tyres [2007] OJ C120/1 .... 2–038, 4–017, 23–026
N 679/2006 PR 13–015
N 692/2006 German Film Fund December 20, 2006 4–036
N 715/2006 Finland, Tax exemption to Finnvera Oyj 19–003
N 725/2006, January 29, 2007 on Contrat de programme en faveur du Consortium pour la protection de l'ASTI, pour des investissements en matiere de publicite (Piemonte) 13–032
N 770/06, State guarantee for the purpose of financing the purchase of railway rolling stock by Ceske Drahy (Czech Railways) [2007] OJ C227/4 17–036
N 810/2006, Germany 15–028
N 854/2006 France, TVMSL—Alcatel Lucent for the developing of a satellite based solution for TV broadcasting on 3G mobile phones [2007] OJ C182/50 ...2–038, 4–017, 23–026, 23–028
N 887/2006, Bernin 2010 [2007] OJ C200/50 4–017
N 911/2006 France C(2007) 2198 4–005

Table of Commission Decisions

N 17/2007 Premium subsidies for insurance of tobacco and partial compensation for damage
    caused by draught), summary notice published in [2007] OJ C308/07 13–029
N 46/2007 Welsh public sector network scheme (United Kingdom) [2007] OJ C157 8–008
N 130b/2007 Finland, Prolongation of N469/2002: Aid for Chipping of Energy Wood 13–033
N 219/2007 IE, Conservation of Plant and Animal Genetic Resources Scheme 13–024
N 340/2007 Aid for theatre etc in the Basque country July 18, 2007 4–036
N 349/2007 France, OSIRIS—Soufflet for a new industrial process for the production of
    enzymes [2007] OJ C304/5 23–026
N 354/2007 France, Aide d'etat accord'ee pour la construction de navires dans le cadre du
    plan de developpement de la flotte de peche des departements d'Outre-Mer 13–047
N 419/2007 ES, developpement technologique du secteur de la peche 13–049
N 478/2007 Netherlands, Stimulating renewable energy, modification and prolongation of
    the MEP [2008] OJ C39/3 22–018
N 480/2007 Spain, Reduction of tax from intangible assets [2008] OJ C80/1 23–011
N 500/2007 Technology Sectors Fund, Berlin December 12, 2007 4–060
N 524/2007 Netherlands, Aid for investments in pulse trawl gear 13–047
N 529/2007 on the Agricultural and Horticulture Development Board—Advertising and
    Promotion Scheme 13–032
N 530/2007 France, Opening of formal investigation on R&D aid to Peugeot-Citroen 2–038,
                                                                                                                23–029
N 582/2007 Germany, Propapier 15–026
N 597/2004 [2005] O.J.C250/11 14–031
N 604/b/2004, Denmark, Fiscal treatment of quotas and payments entitlements 13–037
N 632/2007 Italy, Deliberazione della Giunta regionale n. 80–7203 del 22.10.2007, D.lgs.
    143/1997. Misura Campagne di promozione in materia di pesca e acquacoltura. Appro-
    vazione bando 13–047
N 693/2007 France, Programme d'aides a la collecte et a l'allotement des poulains lourds.
    [2008] OJ C101/7 13–003
N 1/2008 France, H2E for the development of hydrogen-powered batteries and applications
    [2009] OJ C38/5 23–028
N 9/2008 France, Notification PSR LRP AGRAP 28/08. Plan de sauvetage et de
    restructuration 13–048
N 11/2008 and NN 34/2008 [2009] OJ C38/3 17–047
N 31/2008 Austria 17–032
N 415/2008 [2009] OJ C53/ 1 17–046
N 110/2008 [2009] OJ C137/1 17–060
N 159/2008 [2008] OJ C202/1 17–046
N 195/2008 [2008] OJ C329/3 17–046
N 234/2008 Sweden, investment aid project for heating installations and solar panels 22–055
N 275/2008 Italy, Refuelling infrastructure for natural gas powered vehicles (Bolzano)
    [2008] OJ C256/1 22–025
N 295/2008 Austria, Investment aid for co-generation of electricity and heat [2010] OJ
    C154/1 ....20–052, 24–039
N 304/2008 [2009] OJ C106/17 17–046
N 316/2008 [2009] OJ C232/2 17–046
N 321/2008, N 322/2008 and N 323/2008 [2010] OJ C18/9 17–071
N 331/2008 Hauts d Seine (France) IP/09/1391 3–072
N 352/2008 [2008] OJ C7/1 17–046
N 383/2008 Austria, 2008 Guidelines for remediation of inherited waste [2009] OJ C50 ... 22–078
N 395/2008 [2009] OJ C125/1 17–043
N 449/2008 [2009] OJ C196/1. 17–041
N 485/2008 Austria, Aid Scheme for District Heating and Cooling Infrastructure and
    Cooling Installations [2009] OJ C191/1 24–029
N 507/2008 Financial support measures to banking sector in the UK [2008] OJ C290/1 19–029
N 512/2008, Support measures for financial institutions in Germany 19–048
N 521/2008 Germany, Aid to Offshore Wind Park Borkum " Alpha Ventus", October 27,
    2010 24–036
N 528/2008 Netherlands, Aid to ING Group NV, November 12, 2008 .... 19–048, 19–070
N 538/2008 Germany, Ersol Thin Film Erfurt [2009] OJ C63/52 15–028
N 539/2008 Germany, ASI Industries/Ersol Solar Energy [2010] OJ C12/53 15–028

N 561/2008 Actions conduites par les interprofessions, FR, under appeal, Case T–302/09 to
T–306/09 [2009] O.J C 244 13–041
N 574/2008 Belgium State guarantees for Fortis Bank [2008] OJ C38/2 .... 19–046, 19–070
N 584/2008 France, ADEME Aid scheme for renewables 2009/2013 [2009] OJ C195 24–029
N 615/2008, Bayern LB [2009] O C80/4 19–062
N 625/2008 Rettungspaket fur Finanzinstitute in Deutschland [2009] OJ C 143/1 19–029
N 629/2008 United Kingdom, Carbon Reduction Commitment [2009] C238/1 24–026
N 635/2008, Italy, LIP Fiat Sicily OJ [2009] C219/52 15–008
N 639/2008Germany, Liquidity guarantee to IKB 19–028, 19–039
N 650/2008 Notification of modification to the financial support measures to the banking
industry in the UK [2009] OJ C054/3 19–029
N 5/2009 France, CARMAT where the beneficiaries were SMEs or spin-off from a research
center, competing with large multinationals like Siemens or GE [2009] OJ C176/1 23–023
N 6/2009 Italy, Incentives for investments in solar energy on decommissioned landfills
(Piedmont Region), May 29, 2009 24–039
N 11/2009, France 22–007
N 60/2009 [2009] OJ C125/1. 17–041
N 54/2009 Poland, Modernisation of heating distribution networks in Poland [2009] OJ
C204/2 24–029
N 55/2009 Poland, Constructing and modernisation of electricity connection networks for
renewable energies in Poland [2006]OJ C206/3 24–029
N 66/2009 Sweden, State aid scheme for solar cells 22–055
N 72/2009, United Kingdom 22–007
N 74/2009 United Kingdom, CCS Demonstration Competition, FEED [2009] OJ C203/2 14–080,
24–028
N 83/2009 Sale of assets of Olympic Airlines/Olympic Airways Services [2010] OJ
C25/53 8–077
N 83/2009 [2010] OJ C25/15 17–071
N 140/2009 Spain 22–007
N 190/2009 Netherlands, CO2 Catch-up pilot project at Nuon Buggenum plant [2010] OJ
C238 24–028
N 193/2009 Extension of credit guarantee scheme (CGS [2009] OJ C145/3 19–029
N 221/2009 Germany, Wacker Chemie [2010] OJ C312/53 15–028
N 244/2009 Germany, Commerzbank [2009] OJ C147/4 ...19–008, 19–069, 19–073, 19–074, 19–075
N 247/2009 [2009] OJ C255/4 17–046
N 255/2009 Belgium and N 274/2009 Luxembourg, Additional aid for Fortis Banque, Fortis
Bank Luxembourg and Fortis Holding [2009] OJ C 178/2 .... 19–056, 19–074, 19–075
N 256/2009 Belgium, Restructuring aid to Ethias [2010] OJ C252/5 ......19–015, 19–038, 19–048,
19–067, 19–069, 19–075, 19–076
N 261/2009 Germany, Liebherr Unreported. Press release IP/10/900 15–028
N 264/2009 Rescue aid to HSH NOrdbank AG [2009] OJ C179 19–008
N 284/2009, The Netherlands, Fonds voor scholpromotie 13–047
N 296&297/2009 Germany, Diehl Air cabin [2010] OJ C70/21 23–025
N 314/2009, German asset relief scheme [2009] OJ C199/3 19–057
N 324/2009 [2009] OJ C299/5 17–036
N 332/2009 Belgium, Indemnisation des pertes subies par les producteurs de pommes de
terre suite aux mesures prises contre des organismes nuisibles 13–003
N 356/2009 Recapitalisation of Anglo Irish Bank by the Irish State [2009] OJ C 235/3 19–045
N 364/2009 Italy, State aid for the creation of a cogeneration power plant (Valle d'Aosta) 22–074
N 368/2009 (Germany) 3–072
N 371/2009 Netherlands, Viability plan SNS REAAL [2010] OJ C93/2 19–037
N 372/2009 Netherlands, Restructuring aid to AEGON [2010] OJ C290/1 19–037
N 383/2009 Broadband in rural areas of Saxony (Germany) IP/10/141 3–072
N 388/2009 Finalnad, High Speed Broadband pilot projects 3–072
N 400/2009 Germany, Liquidity guarantee for IKB, August 17, 2009 .... 19–028, 19–046
N 414/2009 France, Aides de l'Agence de l'eau Artois-Picardie aux engagements agro
environnementaux dans le bassin Artois Picardie (EAEAP) 13–027
N 419/2009 Malta—Investments on electricity and interconnector infrastructure [2010] OJ
C57 20–037

Table of Commission Decisions

N 422/2009, RBS [2010] OJ C119/1 ...... 19–036, 19–045, 19–049, 19–050, 19–051, 19–052, 19–054, 19–055, 19–057, 19–062, 19–065, 19–067, 19–068, 19–073, 19–074, 19–075

N 426/2009 Germany 22–007

N 434, N 435 and N 436 gas distribution networks (Poland) [2009] OJ C234/1 20–044

N 442/2009 Netherlands, Guarantee facility for geothermal energy [2009] OJ C284 24–039

N 450/2009 Germany, Top Gas Recycling (TGR) Project-Aid to ArcelorMittal Eisenhutten-
stadt GmbH [2010] OJ C94 .... 24–039, 24–045

N 451/2009, Energy saving by strip casting technology for light steels of Salzgitter Flachstahl GmbH [2010] OJ C154/2 14–056

N 456/2009, Recapitalisation of Bank of Ireland [2011] OJ C40/9 19–070

N 457/2009 [2010] OJ C25/15 17–043

N 462/2009 Aid for transport infrastructure (Poland) 3–074

N 487/2009 [2010] OJ C29/2 17–071

N 493/2009 France, Aid to the Project GAYA [2010] OJ C213/9 23–029

N 517/2009 [2010] OJ C74/3 17–043

N 542/2009 Italy 22–007

N 546/2009, Recapitalisation of Bank of Ireland [2011] OJ C40/9 ....19–073, 19–074, 19–075

N 573/2009 and N 647/2009 France, Aide a la mise en oeuvre et a l'exploitation de
l'autoroute de la mer entre le port de Nantes-Saint-Nazaire et le port de Gijon (Espagne)
operee par GLD Atlantique [2010] OJ C74/5 17–056

N 592/2009 Financing the completion of the subsidized coal industry for the year 2018 (aid
for 2010) [2010] OJ C94/7 14–028

N 601/2009 LU, Regime d'aides pour la sauvegarde de la diversite biologique 13–020

N 630/2009 France, Project T3 East Paris. Constructing of a district heating network in the
North East of Paris 24–029

N 635/2009 PL, Aid to the State Forest Holding for recultivation 13–035

N 653/2009 Poland, Investment aid for hard coal mining sector C (2010) 3063 14–021

N 660/2009 Aid to PGNiG for underground gas storage in Poland [2010] OJ C213/9 20–049,
20–082

N 675/2009 [2010] OJ C213/9 20–080

N 714/2009 Extension of the tonnage tax scheme to cable layers, pipeline layers, research
vessels and crane vessels [2010] OJ C158/2 17–056

N 718/2009, February 20, 2010 20–081

N 726/2009 Aide a la restructuration des activites "fret" de la SA de droit public SNCB
[2010] OJ C327/6 .... 17–039, 17–040

N 42/2010, Finland, Aid for the cessation of agricultural production 13–030

N 43/2010, Finland, Investointituki Carelian Caviar Oylle 13–047

N 49/2010, N295/2010 Spain, Aides contre la peste de la mouche d'olivier (Andalucia) ... 13–028

N 79/2010—ES, Aides a l'application des mesures agroenvironemmentales a la vigne 13–020

N 83/2010, Italy, Interventions in favour of agriculture enterprises in difficulty. Aid in favour
of "Unione pastori societa cooperativa agricola" registered in Z.I Taccu, Nurri,
Cagliari 13–039

N 93/2010—PL, Restoration of forests damaged by adverse weather conditions and preven-
tion measures 13–036

N 107/2010, Italy, Measure 6.1.14: Containment of animal diseases 13–028

N 119/2010—FR, Plan de soutien exceptionnel aux conchyliculteurs et pisciculteurs des
d'epartements touches par la tempete Xynthia dans le nuit du 27 au 28 Fevrier 2010 13–047

N 131/2010—BG, Compensation of losses incurred by agricultural producers for totally
devasted areas as a result of natural disasters or adverse weather conditions 13–026

N 133/2010, Italy, Aides dans le domaine des forets 13–036

N 135/2010 Austria, Aid for the remediation of a contamintated site in Linz [2010] C312 22–078

N 175/2010 Postponement of the closure of mine Trbovlje Hrastnik Ltd [2011] OJ C294/4 14–051

N 178/2010 [2010] OJ C312/6 ....14–043, 14–044, 20–079

N 191/2010 CZ, Zmırnenı skod zpusobenych povodnemi na rybach v letnıch mesıcıch roku
2009 13–047

N 197/2010 Austria, individual aid for the remediation of the contaminated site in Unterkarn-
ten [2010] OJ C265 22–078

N 208/2010 Netherlands, Aid for CO2 delivery to Zuidplaspolder 24–028, 24–029

Table of Commission Decisions

N 209/2010 France, Ides aux exploitants agricoles de Charente- Maritime, de Vendee et du nord de la Gironde victimes des inondations marines causees par la tempete Xynthia du 28 Fevrier 2010 13–026

N 210/2010 BG, Measure 223 "First afforestation of non-agricultural land" and measure 226 "Restoring forestry potential and introducing prevention actions" of the Bulgarian Rural Development programme (2007–2013) 13–035

N 213/2010 EE, Measure 2.7 of the Estonian Rural Development Programme 2007–2013 "Natura 2000 support to private forest owners" 13–016

N 226/2010 LV, tax exemption for primary producers 13–033

N 251/2010 Mesure 221—Boisement de terres agricoles 13–035

N 253/2010 Italy, Mesure 225—Paiements sylvoenvironnementaux 13–036

N 261/2010 (ex PN 9/2010) Austria, Second restructuring aid for BAWAG PSK [2010] OJ C 250/5 ....19–026, 19–049, 19–050, 19–057, 19–058, 19–061, 19–064, 19–066, 19–072, 19–073, 19–074, 19–075

N 265/2010 Italy, Aid scheme for advertising of food and agricultural products in third countries 13–032

N 300/2010, Spain, Aid for combating the Mediterranean fruit fly and insect vectors causing viral plant diseases (notificaion of amendment) 13–028

N 323/2010 (Amendment of N 577/2006) The Netherlands, Catalogue Green and Blue Services 13–023

N 341/2010 RO, R'ealisation d'engagements pris en faveur du bien-etre et de la protection des porcs 13–016

N 352/2010 ES, Aides aux investissements non productifs dans les bois priv'es du r'eseau Natura 2000 dans la region de Murcia 13–016

N 360/2010 DE, Mecklenburg-Western Pomerania: Forestry aid in the framework of the EAFRD; disaster prevention / construction of a main wet storage area 13–036

N 361/2010 ES, Modernisation et augmentation de l'efficacité energetique des serres orientes a la production du tomate 13–020

N 362/2010 ES, Aides destinees a la promotion de systèmes de production qui reduisent l'impact environnemental de la culture du petit pois dans la province de Teruel 13–016

N 366/2010, France, Aide aux investissements realises dans les elevages de poules pondeuses en vue de se conformer aux normes de la directive 1999/74/CE 13–016

N 369/2000 13–035

N 372/2010 RO, Aide d'Etat temporaire destinee a assurer l'acces au financement en agriculture 13–040

N 374/2010 DE, staatliche Beihilfen im Fischerei und Aquakultursektor im Zusammenhang mit Naturkatastrophen 13–047

N 379/2010 DE, Guidelines for a national framework directive on state subsidies for compensation of losses caused by natural disasters in the agricultural sector 13–026

N 381/2010 Netherlands, Aid for a CCS-project in the Rotterdam harbour area 24–028

N 384/2010 Germany, Les investissements non productifs dans les terres forestieres, ES ... 13–036

N 386/2010 Denmark, Pilot scheme for purchase of electric vehicles, March 8, 2011 24–047

N 396/2010 SI, Regime temporaire d'aides d'un montant limite dans le secteur agricole, dans le contexte de la crise economique et financiere de 2009 13–040

N 434/2010, Italy, Premiere installation de syst'emes agroforestiers sur des terres agricoles (Mesure 222 du Developement Rural), ES 13–035

N 494/2010 Italy, Aid scheme for district heating installations and infrastructure in Veneto [2011] C(2011) 1619 24–029

N 546/2010 BG, Aid for investment in agricultural holdings in the form of corporate tax relief 13–016

NN 70/88 Kinderkanal and Phoenix [1999] OJ C238/3 3–022

NN 11/91 Greece 4–025

NN 131/96 Germany, GMB Magnete Bitterfeld GmbH [1998] OJ C50/6 24–037

NN 11/98 13–035

NN 61/98 (ex NN 173/97) Germany, Stahl– und Maschinenbau [1999] OJ C365/9 24–037

NN 70/98, Kinderkanal and Phoenix [1999] OJ C238/3 (Kinderkanal) 18–003

NN 88/98 BBC News 24 [2000] OJ C78/6 ....18–002, 18–003, 18–006, 18–011

NN109/98, Manchester Airport 17–074

NN 49/99 Spain, Competition transition costs scheme [2001] OJ C268/7 .... 24–032, 20–078

NN 27/2000 Germany, Act on Granting Priority To Renewable Energy Sources, May 23, 2002; [2002] OJ C164/3 .... 22–019, 22–062

NN 30/A/2000 Netherlands, Tax Rate Increases In Relation to the Rinse Water Exemption, The Exemption for De-Inking Residue, The Green Electricity Zero Tariff And The Exemption forWaste Incineration Plants [2001] OJ C117/14 22–065

NN 30/b/2000 The Netherlands, Tax rate increase in relation to the green electricity zero tariff [2002] OJ C30 .... 22–023, 22–062, 22–066, 22–070, 22–093

NN 68/2000 Germany, Law on the protection of electricity generated from combined heat and power [2002] OJ C164/3 .... 22–019, 22–062

NN 139/2001 and NN 141/2001 [2002] OJ C24/2 17–061

NN 170/2001 London underground, C(2002) 438 (United Kingdom) 3–064

NN 3/B/2002 Sweden, Eco-tax and energy tax system 3–035, 20–028

NN 75/2002 [2002] OJ C309/17, NN 3/A/2001 and NN 4/A/2001 20–031

NN 106/2002, Portugal, Mesures a caractere socio-economiques- secteur de la peche (Madere) 13–047

NN 153/2003 Aid for enterprises of Kastoria and Eubee departments, opening 13–039

NN 162/a/2003 Austria, Support of electricity production from renewable sources under the Green Electricity Act (Feed in tariffs) [2006] OJ C221/8 22–020

NN 35/2004 Digital Terrestrial Television (Sweden) 3–034

NN 36/2004 DVB-T Berlin-Brandenburg (Germany) C(2004) 2672 3–034

NN 40/2004 Banana producer groups support (Guadeloupe and Martinique) 13–011

NN 71/2004 Italy, Excise duty exemption on fuels in agriculture 13–033

NN 37/2005 Italy, Construction of fishing vessels 13–047

NN 38/2005 and NN 39/2005, Ireland, Aid for development of salmon farming 13–048

NN 64/2005 Digital Replacement Licences (United Kingdom) 3–007

NN 71/2005 HSH Nordbank 19–007

NN 72/2005 BayernLB 19–007

NN 429/2005 13–035

NN 12a, b, c, d/2006, Belgium, Promotion of different agricultural products 13–032

NN 46/A/06 (ex. N 361/A/06), April 4, 2007 on the reduction of excise duty on mineral oils summary notice [2007] OJ C132/1 13–033

NN 75/2006 Germany, Aid for Bavarian Animal Health Service [2006] OJ C244/15 13–020

NN 7/2007 Support for the eco-label NT 13–032

NN 24/2007 Prague Municipal Network (Czech Republic) [2007] OJ C414 8–008

NN 34/2007 Nord/LB 19–007

NN 53/2007 Measures in favour of Munich airport terminal 2 (Germany) 3–120

NN 70/2007 (ex CP 269/07) United Kingdom, Rescue aid to Northern Rock [2008] OJ C43/1 .... 4–025, 19–013, 19–018, 19–027, 19–029

NN 24/2008 Italy Com (2008) 1606 fin 8–066

NN 25/2008 (ex CP 15/08) Germany, WestLB riskshield, April 30, 2008 .... 4–025, 19–018, 19–027, 19–029

NN 38/2008 State aid which Denmark grants to Roskilde Bank [2009] OJ C 12/3 19–055

NN 41/2008 State aid which United Kingdom grants to Bradford and Bingley [2008] OJ C290/2 .... 19–034, 19–055

NN 42/2008 Belgium; NN 46/2008 Luxembourg; NN 53/A/2008 Netherlands, Restructuring aid to Fortis Bank and Fortis Bank Luxembourg [2009] OJ C80/7 ...19–007, 19–013, 19–035, 19–036, 19–064, 19–070, 19–073, 19–075

NN 49/2008, NN 50/2008 and NN 45/2006, Guarantees to Dexia 19–070

NN 57/2008 Belgium, Emergency aid for Ethias [2009] OJ C176/1 19–015

NN 8/2009 GE, Conservation areas 13–036

NN 20/2009 Aides a l'industrie charbonniere pour la periode 2008–2010 [2009] OJ C234/5 14–025

NN 40/2009 Hypo Steiermarkt [2009] OJ C206/02 19–007

NN 54/2009 Belgian hospitals [2010] OJ C74/53 8–038

NN 60/2009 Latvia, Recapitalization of "The Mortgage and Land Bank of Latvia" 19–003

NN 12/2010 and C 11/2010 (ex N 667/2009) Second rescue in favour of Anglo Irish Bank [2010] OJ C 214/3 19–45

NN16/2010 FR, Mesures de soutien accordees aux entreprises conchylicoles et piscicoles touchees par la tempete Klaus du 24 Janvier 2009 13–047

NN 26/2010 CZ, Partial refund of excise duties 13–033

NN 35/2010 (ex N 279/2010) Ireland, Temporary approval of the third recapitalisation in favour of Anglo Irish Bank [2010] OJ C290/4 19–045

SA 29338 (C 29/2009, ex N 264/2009) State aid granted by Germany to HSH Nordbank 19–007, 19–016, 19–048, 19–052, 19–054, 19–057, 19–061, 19–069, 19–072, 19–073, 19–075, 19–076
SA 30340 (2011/C) Poland, Fiat Powertrain 15–026, 15–028, 15–030
SA 31083 (N 240/2010) Sweden, Aid for the Domsjö project [2011] OJ C180/1 23–028
SA 31390 (N 344/2010) Training aid to De Tomaso Automobile SpA approved [2011] OJ C149/54 11–011
SA 32057 (2010/NN) Ireland, Temporary approval of the fourth recapitalisation and guarantee in respect of certain liabilities in favour of Anglo Irish Bank [2011] OJ C 76/4 ... 19–045
SA 32173 FR, Regime temporaire d'aides d'Etat a montant limite adaptees, pour le secteur agricole, au contexte de la crise economique et financiere 13–040
SA 32185 SE, Support for marketing measures of organic products 13–032
SA 32504 (2011/N) and C 11/2010 (ex N 667/2009) implemented by Ireland fo Anglo Irish Bank and Irish Nationwide Building Society 19–007, 19–054, 19–059, 19–077
SA 32713 Netherlands, State aid notification Product board horticulture, vegetables and fruits sector 13–021, 13–032
SA 32745 (2011/NN) Austria, restructuring of Kommunal Austria AG [2011] OJ C239/2 ......19–042, 19–057, 19–073, 19–074, 19–075
SA 33216 (2011/N) Ireland, Second rescue of Bank of Ireland [2011] OJ C274/2 ......19–045, 19–075
SA 33751, Dexia Banque Belgique, October 17, 2011 .... 19–045, 19–075
SG (2000) D/103729 on a Belgian fiscal measure in relation to night and team labour 3–051
SI 7/2003 Slovenian stranded costs, C(2005) 172 fin 8–046
SK 4/2004 on State aid granted by the Slovak Republic to OTP Banka Slovensko, a.s., C(2004)2625 5–010
SK 5/2004 on a reduction of tax concession granted by Slovakia to U.S. Steel Kosice, Slovakia, C(2004)3496fin 5–017

X 411/2009 [2010] OJ C20/2002 24–045
X 491/2009 United Kingdom, One North East and Yorkshire Forward Environmental Action Scheme 2009—2013 24–050
X 760/2009 Welsh Assembly Government Environmental Protection Scheme 24–050
X 97/2010 South East England Development Agency, General Block Exemption Scheme 2010–2013 24–050

TABLE OF COMMISSION AND COUNCIL DECISIONS

(by number)

1965 Dec.65/271 on the harmonisation of certain provisions affecting competition in transport by rail, road and inland waterway [1965] OJ 88/1500 17–006

1972 Dec.97/242 on State aid in favour of Hilaturas y Tejidos Andaluces SA, now called Mediterraneo Tecnica Textil SA and its buyer [1997] OJ L96/30

1975 Dec.75/327 on the improvement of the situation of railway undertakings and the harmonization of rules governing financial relations between such undertakings and States [1975] OJ L152/3 17–026

1986 Dec.86/561 on an aid to fish producers' organizations granted by the German Government [1986] OJ L327/44 3–037

1986 Dec.2064/86 on Community rules for state aid to the coal industry [1986] OJ L177/1 14–007

1987 Dec.87/14 on the compatibility with the common market of aid under the German Federal/Land Government Joint Regional Aid Programme [1987] OJ L12/17 12–018

1988 Dec.88/167 on aids granted to the Greek industry by the Greek government [1989] OJ L76/18 19–035

1988 Dec.88/283 on French Government aid to Pechiney, a company producing mainly aluminium [1988] OJ L121/57 12–009

1989 Dec.89/58 on aid provided by the United Kingdom Government to the Rover Group, an undertaking producing motor vehicles [1989] OJ L25/92 .. 8–074, 27–006

1989 Dec.89/620 on measures to assist the Belgian inland waterway fleet contained in the plan to restructure the Belgian inland waterway fleet [1989] OJ L356/22 ... 12–009

1989 Dec.89/659 on Ministerial Decision No. E–3789/128 of the Greek Government establishing a special single tax on undertakings [1989] OJ L394/1 11–013

1990 Dec.90/70 on aid provided by France to certain primary processing steel undertakings [1990] OJ L47/28 12–009

1991 Dec.91/175 on aid provided for in Italian law No 120/87 to assist certain areas of the Mezzogiorno affected by natural disasters [1991] OJ L86/23 4–006

1991 Dec.91/306 on the recovery of the Greek national economy 4–025

1991 Dec.91/390 on aid granted by France to Saint-Gobain [1991 OJ L215/11 3–061

1991 Dec.91/555 on aid to be granted by the Belgian Government in favour of the air carrier Sabena [1991] OJ L300/48 8–076

1991 Dec.3010/91 on the information to be furnished by steel undertakings about their investments [1991] OJ L286/20 14–078

1991 Dec.3855/91 establishing Community rules for aid to the steel industry [1991] OJ L362/57 .... 13–052, 14–052

1992 Dec.92/11 on aid provided by the Derbyshire County Council to Toyota Motor Corporation [1992] OJ L6/36 .... 3–004, 3–093

1992 Dec.92/296/EC on aid granted by the Italian Government to Nuova Cartiera di Arbatax [1992] OJ L159/46 12–009

1992 Dec.92/317 on State aid in favour of Hilaturas y Tejidos Andaluces SA, now called Mediterráneo Técnica Textil SA and its buyer [1992] OJ L171/54 27–007

1992 Dec.92/318 on aid granted by Spain to Industrias Mediterraneas de la Piel SA (Impiel), March 25, 1992; [1992] OJ L172/76 8–067

1992 Dec.92/329 on aid granted by the Italian Government to a manufacturer of ophthalmic products (Industrie Ottiche Riunite—IOR) [1992] OJ L183/30 .... 9–008, 26–012

1992 Dec.92/384 concerning the conclusion of an Agreement between the European Economic Community, the Kingdom of Norway and the Kingdom of Sweden on civil aviation [1992] OJ L200/20 17–063

1992 Dec.92/389 on the State aid provided in for in Decree-Laws No 174 of 15 May 1989 and No 254 of 13 July 1989 and in draft Law No 4230 [1992] OJ L207/47 ...10–018, 10–038

1992 Dec.92/465 in repect of land in Wet Berlin made available to Daimler Benz [1992] OJ L263/15 4–008

1992 Dec.92/553 on a proceeding under Council Regulation 4064/89 (Case No.IV/M.190—Nestlé/Perrier) [1992] OJ L356/1 25–034

1993 Dec.93/9 declaring the compatibility of a concentration with the common market (Case No IV/M214—Du Pont/ICI) [1993] OJ L7/13 25–034

1993 Dec.93/412 aid awarded by the German Government to Hibeg and by Hibeg via Krupp GmbH to Bremer Vulkan AG [1993] OJ L185/43 .... 9–024, 25–010

1993 Dec.93/625 on aid granted by the French Government to the Pari mutuel urbain (PMU) and to the racecourse undertakings [1993] OJ L300/15 10–020

1993 Dec.3632/93 establishing Community rules for State Aid to the coal industry [1993] OJ L329/12 .... 14–005, 14–007, 14–008, 14–010, 14–016, 14–022

art.3 14–022

1994 Dec.94/118 on aid to be provided by the Irish Government to the Aer Lingus group [1994] OJ L54/30 ....17–068, 25–035

1994 Dec.341/94 on Community rules for State Aid to the coal industry [1994] OJ L49/1 14–005

1994 Dec.94/449 relating to a proceeding pursuant to Council Regulation (EEC) No 4064/89 (Case No IV/M.308—Kali-Salz/MdK/Treuhand) [1994] OJ L186/38 24–007

1994 Dec.94/653 on the notified capital increase of Air France [1994] OJ L254/73 ....17–065, 25–048, 26–005

1994 Dec.94/662 on the subscription by CDC participations to bonds issued by Air France (93/C 334/04) [1994] OJ L258/26 17–065

1994 Dec.94/696 on the aid granted by Greece to Olympic Airways [1994] OJ L273/22 ... 14–069

1994 Dec.94/698 on increase in capital, credit guarantees and tax exemption in favour of TAP [1994] OJ L279/29 ......8–020, 17–068

1994 Dec.94/996 on the transfer by the Netherlands of a pilot school to KLM 8–020

1994 Dec.94/1068 on aid granted to the Volkswagen Group for investments in the new German Lander [1994] OJ L385/1 4–025

1995 Dec.95/196 on the long-term national aid scheme for agriculture in the northern regions of Finland 13–009

1995 Dec.95/456 Greek aid scheme in the pharmaceutical sector, financed by means of levies on pharmaceutical and other related products [1995] OJ L265/30 3–129

1995 Dec.95/547 giving conditional approval to the aid granted by France to the bank Credit Lyonnais [1995] OJ L308/92 ...19–018, 19–019, 19–020

1996 Dec.96/115 on the aid granted by the Italian State to the company Enichem Agricoltura SpA [1996] OJ L28/18 25–048

1996 Dec.96/228 on a long-term national aid scheme to assist farmers in northern areas of Sweden [1996] OJ L76/29 13–009

1996 Dec.96/278 the recapitalization of the Iberia company [1996] OJ L104/25 ....17–068, 25–060

1996 Dec.96/369 on fiscal aid given to German airlines in the form of a depreciation facility [1996] OJ L146/42 10–023

1996 Dec.96/434 on aid which Italy plans to grant to enterprises in a state of insolvency resulting from the obligation to repay State aid [1996] OJ L180/31 3–006

1996 Dec.96/545 on aid proposed by Germany to Buna GmbH, Sächsische Olefinwerke GmbH, Leuna-Werke GmbH, Leuna-Polyolefine GmbH and BSL Polyolefinverbund GmbH [1996] OJ L239/1 ...12–015, 22–090, 24–005, 25–048

1996 Dec.96/563 on aid from the Land of Lower Saxony to the company JAKO Jadekost GmbH & Co KG [1996] OJ L246/43 9–024

1996 Dec.96/614 on certain measures granted by Italy in favour of Breda Fucine Meridonali SpA [1996] OJ L272/46 ... 3–043

1996 Dec.96/615 on the renewal, for the period 1993 to 1997, of the charge levied on certain oil products for the benefit of the Institut Francais du Petrole (IFP) [1996] OJ L272/53 3–129

1996 Dec.1692/96 on Community guidelines for the development of the trans-European transport network [1996] OJ L228/1 .... 17–054, 22–031

1996 Dec.2496/96 on state aid to for the steel industry [1996] OJ L338/42 14–054

1997 Dec.97/13 on German aid to Mercedes-Benz in Ludwigsfelde (Brandenburg) [1997] OJ L5/30 19–036

1997 Dec.97/81 on aid granted by the Austrian Government to Head Tyrolia Mares in the form of capital injections [1997] OJ L25/26 8–053

1997 Dec.97/239 on aid granted by Belgium under the Maribel bis/ter scheme [1997] OJ L95/25 3–054

1997 Dec.97/242 on State aid in favour of Hilaturas y Tejidos Andaluces SA, now called Mediterráneo Técnica Textil SA and its buyer [1997] OJ L96/30 27–007

1997 Dec.97/257 on guarantees of the Land Brandenburg (Germany) for investment projects in Poland [1997] OJ L102/36 4–047

1997 Dec.97/542 on tax exemptions for biofuels in France [1997] OJ L222/26 .. 3–004, 3–128

1997 Dec.97/789 on the recapitalization of the company Alita-
lia [1997] OJ L322/44 17–065,
17–068, 25–035

1998 Dec.98/204 conditionally approving aid granted by
France to the GAN Group
[1998] OJ L78/1 19–021

1998 Dec.98/212 on the aid granted
by Italy to Enirisorse SpA
[1998] OJ L80/32 12–008

1998 Dec.98/251 on the proposal of
Austria to award aid to the
Hoffmann-La Roche com-
pany for the development
of the drug 'Orlistat', designed for the treatment of
pathological obesity [1998]
OJ L103/28 .... 12–015, 12–017

1998 Dec.98/337 [1998] OJ
L148/36 14–075

1998 Dec.98/365 on alleged State aid
granted by France to SFMI-
Chronopost [1998] OJ
L164/37 8–054
art.1 3–103

1998 Dec.98/384 on aid granted by
the Netherlands to a hydrogen peroxide works in
Delfzijl [1998] OJ
L171/36 ...12–015, 12–020, 12–021

1998 Dec.98/490 on aid granted by
France to the Credit Lyon-
nais Group [1998] OJ
L221/28 ....4–025, 19–020, 19–035

1998 Dec.98/665 on aid awarded by
Germany to HIBEG and by
HIBEG via Krupp GmbH
to Bremer Vulkan AG, fa-
cilitating the sale of Krupp
Atlas Elektronik GmbH
from Krupp GmbH to Bre-
mer Vulkan AG [1998] OJ
L316/25 ...3–101, 25–010, 25–062,
26–011

1998 Dec.98/668/EC Commission decision on State aid granted
by the Republic of Austria
and the Land of Upper Austria to Actual Maschinen-
bau AG [1998] OJ L316/5 3–101,
3–125

1999 Dec.1999/133 on State aid in favour of Cooperative d'ex-
portation du livre français
(CELF) [1999] OJ L44/37 4–034,
25–010, 25–029

1999 Dec.1999/139 on aid granted by
Germany to SHB Stahl–
und Hartguwerke Bösdorf
AG [1999] OJ L45/46 24–038

1999 Dec.1999/148/on State aid
granted by Italy to firms in
the motor vehicle, ship-
building and synthetic fibres industries and to steel
firms covered by the ECSC
Treaty [1999] OJ L47/6 11–011,
14–032

1999 Dec.1999/157 on State aid for
Triptis Porzellan GmbH (in
liquidation), Thuringia
[1999] OJ L52/48 24–039

1999 Dec.1999/262 on aid granted by
France in connection with
the recapitalisation and
transfer of the assets of Societe de Banque Occiden-
tale [1999] OJ L103/19 19–020

1999 Dec.1999/268 on the acquisition
of land under the German
Indemnification and Com-
pensation Act [1999] OJ
L107/21 3–012

1999 Dec.1999/269 authorising, subject to condition, aid granted by Italy to Italstrade
SpA [1999] OJ L109/1 24–003,
24–008, 24–030

1999 Dec.1999/275 on State aid
granted by Germany to
Draiswerke GmbH [1999]
OJ L108/44 24–037

1999 Dec.1999/288 giving conditional approval to the aid granted by Italy to Banco di Napoli [1999] OJ L116/36 19–022,
19–025, 24–039

1999 Dec.1999/332 on aid granted by
Greece to Olympic Air-
ways [1999] OJ L128/1 25–047

1999 Dec.1999/338 authorising subject to conditions, aid
granted by Italy to Societa
Italiana per Condotte d'Acqua SpA [1999] OJ
L129/30 .... 24–003, 24–030

1999 Dec.1999/342 on aid which
Austria plans to grant to
Agrana Stärke GmbH to
build and convert starch
production facilities [1999]
OJ L131/61 24–038

1999 Dec.1999/365 on a proposal by
Austria to grant aid to
LiftgmbH [1999] OJ
142/32 4–047

1999 Dec.1999/374 on aid granted by Germany to Neptun Industrie Rostock GmbH [1999] OJ L144/21 .... 3–134, 24–013

1999 Dec.1999/378 on aid granted by France to Nouvelle Filature Lainière de Roubaix [1999] OJ L145/18 24–028

1999 Dec.1999/380 on State aid granted by Germany to Spindelfabrik Hartha GmbH [1999] OJ L145/32 24–031

1999 Dec.1999/395 on State aid implemented by Spain in favour of SNIACE SA, located in Torrelavega, Cantabria [1999] OJ L149/40 .... 10–015, 24–028

1999 Dec.1999/484 on State aid which the Spanish Government has granted to the company Hijos de Andrés Molina SA (Hamsa) [1999] OJ L193/1 .... 24–010, 24–020, 24–031

1999 Dec.1999/508 conditionally approving aid granted by France to Societe Marselaise de Credit [1999] OJ L198/1 .... 19–022, 19–025

1999 Dec.1999/600 on the state aid granted by Germany to Dieselmotorenwerk Rostock GmbH [1999] OJ L232/24 24–025

1999 Dec.1999/663 on State aid granted by Germany to Maschinenfabrik Sangerhausen (Samag) [1999] OJ L263/19 24–031

1999 Dec.1999/679 on State aid granted by Germany to Dow/Buna SOW Leuna Olefinverbund [1999] OJ L269/36 24–005

1999 Dec.1999/690 on State aid which Germany is planning to introduce for Graphischer Maschinenbau GmbH, Berlin [1999] OJ L272/16 .... 24–035, 24–038

1999 Dec.1999/705 on the state aid implemented by the Netherlands for 633 Dutch service stations located near the German border [1999] OJ L280/87 .... 22–025, 25–029

1999 Dec.1999/720 on State aid granted by Germany to Gröditzer Stahlwerke GmbH and its subsidiary Walzwerk Burg GmbH [1999] OJ L292/27 8–069

1999 Dec.1999/763 on the measures, implemented and proposed, by the Federal State of Bremen, Germany, in favour of Lurssen Maritime Beteiligungen GmbH & Co KG [1999] OJ L301/8 3–134

1999 Dec.1999/840 on State aid granted by the Federal Republic of Germany to Kranbau Eberswalde GmbH [1999] OJ L326/57 ....24–031, 24–042

2000 Dec.2000/21 on state aid granted by the Federal Republic of Germany to Brockhausen Holze GmbH [2000] OJ L7/6 24–028

2000 Dec.2000/39 [2000] OJ L150/1 24–009

2000 Dec.2000/51 Stardust Marine [2000] OJ L206/1 24–009

2000 Dec.2000/75 on State Aid granted by Germany to SKET Maschinen-und Anlagenbau GmbH [2000] OJ L30/25 24–039

2000 Dec.2000/116 on State aid, financed by parafiscal charges, which the Netherlands intends to grant for promoting ornamental plants [2000] OJ L34/20 10–005

2000 Dec.2000/129 on State aid implemented by the Federal Republic of Germany for Lautex [2000] OJ L42/19 ...24–008, 24–030, 24–036, 25–022

2000 Dec.2000/199 on State aid given by Greece to Heracles General Cement Company [2000] OJ L66/1 25–010

2000 Dec.2000/211 on State aid granted by the Federal Republic of Germany to Pittler/Tornos Werkzeugmaschinen GmbH [2000] OJ L65/26 .... 24–016, 24–028

2000 Dec.2000/334 on State aid granted by Italy to Enirisorse SpA [2000] OJ L120/1 12–008

2000 Dec.2000/206 on an aid scheme applied in Greece to cotton by the Greek Cotton Board [2000] OJ L63/27 10–005

2000 Dec.2000/257 on aid granted in Italy by RIBS SpA in accordance with national law on the restructuring of the sugar beet factory [2000] OJ L79/38 13–005

2000 Dec.2000/392 a measure implemented by the Federal Republic of Germany for Westdeutsche Landesbank—Girozentrale (WestLB) [2000] OJ L 150/1 ..... 10–027, 24–009, 24–015, 24–043, 25–009

2000 Dec.2000/393 on aid to be granted by Germany to CBW Chemie GmbH [2000] OJ L150/38 ...24–010, 24–036, 24–039

2000 Dec.2000/395 on State aid implemented by Germany in favour of Entstaubungstechnik Magdeburg GmbH [2000] OJ L150/64 24–039

2000 Dec.2000/410 on the aid scheme which France is planning to implement in favour of the French port sector [2000] OJ L155/52 10–018

2000 Dec.2000/425 on aid granted by France to Gooding Consumer Electronics Ltd [2000] OJ L165/25 24–011

2000 Dec.2000/536 on State aid granted by Italy to Seleco SpA [2000] OJ L227/24 ....24–028, 25–009

2000 Dec.2000/537 on State aid granted by Germany to Elpro AG and its successor companies [2000] OJ L229/44 .... 24–001, 24–011

2000 Dec.2000/567 on the State aid implemented by the Federal Republic of Germany for System Microelectronic Innovation GmbH, Frankfurt/Oder (Brandenburg) [2000] OJ L238/50 .... 24–028, 24–031

2000 Dec.2000/600 conditionally approving the aid granted by Italy to the public banks Banco di Sicilia and Sicilcassa [2000] OJ L256/21 ....19–015, 19–023, 19–025, 24–009, 24–039, 24–041

2000 Dec.2000/620 on State aid to non-residential building tenants in the Customs House Docks Area in Dublin [2000] OJ L260/37 ....10–007, 10–015

2000 Dec.2000/628 on the aid granted by Italy to Centrale del Latte di Roma [2000] OJ L265/15 .... 24–009, 24–043

2000 Dec.2000/648 on State aid which Italy is planning to implement for Siciliana Acque Minerali Srl [2000] OJ L272/36 .... 24–003, 24–028

2000 Dec.2000/668 on State aid granted by Italy to shipbuilders in the form of tax relief under Law No 549/95 [2000] OJ L279/46 10–010

2000 Dec.2000/732 on the State aid implemented by Germany for Korn Fahrzeuge und Technik GmbH (Thuringia) [2000] OJ L295/21 ....24–027, 24–028, 24–038

2000 Dec.2000/735 on the treatment by the Netherlands tax authorities of a technolease agreement between Philips and Rabobank [2000] OJ L297/13 10–014

2000 Dec.2000/797 on State aid granted by the Federal Republic of Germany to Salzgitter AG, Preussag Stahl AG [2000] OJ L323/5 10–011

2000 Dec.2000/808 on the granting of exceptional national aid by the authorities of the Federal Republic of Germany for the distillation of certain wine sector products [2000] OJ L328/49 13–005

2000 Dec.2000/809 on the granting of exceptional national aid by the government of the Italian Republic for the distillation of certain wine sector products [2000] OJ L328/51 13–005

2001 Dec.2001/1 on the State aid implemented by the Federal Republic of Germany for Dessauer Geräteindustrie GmbH [2001] OJ L1/10 ....24–039, 24–042

2001   Dec.2001/43 on State aid imple-
       mented by Spain in favour
       of Snaice SA [2001] OJ
       L11/46 25–010

2001   Dec.2001/89 conditionally ap-
       proving aid granted by
       France to Credit Foncier de
       France [2001] OJ L34/36 ...19–021,
              19–025, 19–030, 24–003,
                                  24–039

2001   Dec.2001/168 on Spain's cor-
       poration tax laws [2001] OJ
       L60/57 10–036

2001   Dec.2001/212 on the aid scheme
       implemented by Italy to as-
       sist large firms in difficulty
       [2001] OJ L79/29 24–047

2001   Dec.2001/224 on reduced rates
       of excise duty and exemp-
       tions from such duty on
       certain mineral oils [2001]
       L84/23 17–045

2001   Dec.2001/274 on the measure
       implemented by EDF for
       certain firms in the paper
       industry   [2001]   OJ
       L95/18 20–091

2001   Dec.2001/354 relating to a pro-
       ceeding under Article 82 of
       the EC Treaty (Case
       COMP/35.141—Deutsche
       Post AG) [2001] OJ
       L125/27 ......8–063, 8–065, 18–011

2001   Dec.2001/685 on the State aid
       implemented by Germany
       for KataLeuna GmbH Cata-
       lysts [2001] OJ L245/26 24–008,
                                  24–038

2001   Dec.2001/695 on State aid
       granted by the Federal Re-
       public of Germany to Phil-
       ipp Holzmann AG [2001]
       OJ L248/46 .... 24–003, 24–028

2001   Dec.2001/825 on State aid C
       67/99 (ex NN 148/98) im-
       plemented by Germany for
       the Dampfkesselbau Ho-
       henturm group, Germany
       [2001] OJ L308/28 24–031

2001   Dec.2001/856 concerning State
       aid to Verlipack, Belgium
       [2001] OJ L320/28 8–021,
                        24–028, 25–041

2002   Dec.2002/14 on the state aid
       granted by France to Scott
       Paper SA Kimberly-Clark
       [2002] OJ L12/1 .. 25–042, 26–013

2002   Dec.2002/15 on State aid imple-
       mented by France in favour
       of Brittany Ferried [2002]
       OJ L12/33 3–084

2002   Dec.2002/52 Soreni le Havre
       [2005] OJ L31/44 24–016

2002   Dec.2002/71 on the State aid im-
       plemented by Germany for
       KHK   Verbindetechnik
       GmbH Brotterode [2002]
       OJ L31/80 24–037

2002   Dec.2002/185 on State aid im-
       plemented by Germany for
       Technische Glaswerke Il-
       menau GmbH, Germany
       [2002] OJ L62/3 24–037

2002   Dec.2002/186 on the State aid
       implemented by Germany
       for Zeitzer Maschinen, An-
       lagen, Geräte ZEMAG
       GmbH [2002] OJ L62/44 ... 24–031

2002   Dec.2002/200 on State aid
       which Spain has imple-
       mented and is planning to
       implement for the restruc-
       turing of Babcock Wilcox
       España SA [2002] OJ
       L67/50 .... 24–003, 24–013

2002   Dec.2002/342   [2002]   OJ
       L126/27 10–030

2002   Dec.2002/404 on the long-term
       national aid scheme for
       agriculture in the northern
       regions of Finland [2002]
       OJ L139/38 13–009

2002   2002/458 on the aid schemes im-
       plemented by Greece in fa-
       vour of the settlement of
       debts by the agricultural co-
       operatives in 1992 and
       1994 [2002] OJ L159/1 13–021

2002   Dec.2002/468 on the State aid
       implemented by Germany
       for Klausner Nordic Tim-
       ber GmbH & Co. KG, Wis-
       mar, Mecklenburg-Western
       Pomerania   [2002]   OJ
       L165/15 25–017

2002   Dec.2002/581 on tax measures
       for banks and banking
       foundations implemented
       by Italy [2002] OJ
       L184/27 19–017

2002   Dec.2002/643 on alleged State
       aid by Germany for Bahn
       Trans GbmH [2002]
       L211/7 3–033

2002 Dec.2002/753 decision on measures implemented by the Federal Republic of Germany for Deutsche Post AG [2002] OJ L247/27 ....3–032, 8–030

2002 Dec.2002/779 on the State aid granted by the Federal Republic of Germany to Zeuro Möbelwerk GmbH, Thuringia [2002] OJ L282/1 ....24–028, 24–031

2002 Dec.2002/783 on State aid implemented by Germany for Neue Erba Lautex GmbH and Erba Lautex GmbH in bankruptcy [2002] OJ L282/48 .... 24–016, 24–020, 24–028, 24–050

2002 Dec.2002/787 on the closure of uncompetitive coal mines OJ L336 ...7–003, 14–001, 14–048

2002 Dec.2002/823 on the State aid granted by the Federal Republic of Germany for ILKA MAFA Kältemaschinenbau GmbH [2002] OJ L296/42 24–025

2002 Dec.2002/865 on the State aid granted by Germany to Graf von Henneberg Porzellan GmbH, Ilmenau [2002] OJ L307/1 ....24–019, 24–042, 24–047

2002 Dec.2002/866 on the State aid implemented by Germany for Hoch-und Ingenieurbau GmbH (HIG) [2002] OJ L307/28 24–037

2002 Dec.2002/871 establishing a joint framework for the communication of information relating to state aid to the coal industry [2002] OJ L300/42

Annex III 14–022

2002 Dec.2002/896 on the State aid implemented by Germany for Gothaer Fahrzeugtechnik GmbH [2002] OJ L314/62 24–039

2002 Dec.2002/898 on the State aid implemented by Germany for SKL Motoren-und Systembautechnik 24–008, 24–037

2002 Dec.2002/901 on State aid implemented by the Netherlands for operations by Dutch tugboats in seaports and on inland waterways in the Community [2002] OJ L314/97 .... 10–021, 25–016

2002 Dec.2002/935 on the State aid granted to Grupo de Empresas Álvarez [2002] OJ L329/1 .... 10–015, 24–024

2002 Dec.2002/937 on the aid scheme implemented by Finland for Åland Islands captive insurance companies [2002] OJ L329/22 .... 10–007, 10–037

2002 Dec.1600/2002 laying down the Sixth Community Environment Action Programme [2002] OJ L242/1

Pt 5 22–011

2003 Dec.2003/81 on the aid scheme implemented by Spain in favour of coordination centres in Vizcaya [2003] OJ L31/26 10–030

2003 Dec.2003/85 on the State aid C 35/2000 (ex NN 81/98) implemented by the Federal Republic of Germany for Saalfelder Hebezeugbau GmbH, Germany [2003] OJ L40/1 24–037

2003 Dec.2003/146 on the tax measures for banking foundations implemented by Italy [2003] OJ L55/56 ....10–027, 19–017

2003 Dec.2003/193 on State aid granted by Italy in the form of tax exemptions and subsidised loans to public utilities with a majority public capital holding [2003] OJ L77/21 .... 10–011, 10–026

2003 Dec.2003/194 on the State aid implemented by Germany for Schmitz-Gotha Fahrzeugwerke GmbH [2003] OJ L77/41 24–035

2003 Dec.2003/216 on State aid granted by France to Credit Mutuel [2003] OJ L88/39

2003 Dec.2003/227 on various measures and the State aid invested by Spain in "Terra Mítica SA", a theme park near Benidorm (Alicante) [2003] OJ L91/23 10–007

2003 Dec.2003/261 on the State aid
      implemented by Germany
      for Ambau Stahl– und An-
      lagenbau GmbH [2003] OJ
      L103/50 ... 24–016, 24–032,24–037

2003 Dec.2003/264 on the State aid
      implemented by Germany
      for Forderanlagen und
      Kranbau Köthen GmbH
      and Kranbau Köthen
      GmbH [2003] OJ L97/73 ...24–003,
      24–031

2003 Dec.2003/281 on State aid im-
      plemented by Germany for
      the Leuna 2000 refiner
      [2003] OJ L108/1 25–046

2003 Dec.2003/282 on the State aid
      implemented by Germany
      for Doppstadt GmbH
      [2003] OJ L108/8 24–008,
      24–036

2003 Dec.2003/284 on the State aid
      implemented by Spain for
      Sniace SA [2003] OJ
      L108/35 24–014

2003 Dec.2003/293 on the measures
      implemented by Spain in
      favour of Refractarios Es-
      peciales SA [2003] OJ
      L108/21 10–016

2003 Dec.2003/372 [2003] OJ
      L132/1 14–070

2003 Dec.2003/383 on State aid im-
      plemented by Germany for
      Technische Glaswerke Il-
      menau GmbH [2003] OJ
      L140/30 ...24–019, 24–028, 25–050

2003 Dec.2003/438 on the aid scheme
      C 50/2001 (ex NN
      47/2000) — Finance com-
      panies — implemented by
      Luxembourg [2003] OJ
      L153/40 .... 10–014, 10–018,
      10–030, 10–037

2003 Dec.2003/442 on the part of the
      scheme adapting the na-
      tional tax system to the spe-
      cific characteristics of the
      Autonomous Region of the
      Azores which concerns re-
      ductions in the rates of in-
      come and corporation tax
      [2003] OJ L150/52 21–002

2003 Dec.2003/469 on the aid scheme
      implemented by Germany:
      "Thuringia working capital
      programme", November
      27, 2002; [2003] OJ
      L157/55 7–007

2003 Dec.2003/501 on the State aid
      scheme—Coordination
      Centres—implemented by
      Luxembourg [2003] OJ
      L170/20

2003 Dec.2003/512 on the aid scheme
      implemented by Germany
      for control and coordina-
      tion centres [2003] OJ
      L177/17 ...10–018, 10–030, 10–037

2003 Dec.2003/515 on the State aid
      implemented by the Neth-
      erlands for international fi-
      nancing activities [2003]
      OJ L180/52 .... 10–005, 10–009,
      10–011, 10–026, 10–036

2003 Dec.2003/530 on the compati-
      bility with the common
      market of an aid that the
      Italian Republic intends to
      grant to its milk producers
      [2003] OJ L184/15 25–035

2003 Dec.2003/531 on the granting of
      aid by the Belgium Govern-
      ment to certain coordina-
      tion centres established in
      Belgium [2003] OJ
      L184/17 25–035

2003 Dec.2003/590 on the State aid
      which the United Kingdom
      is planning to grant to CDC
      Group plc [2003] OJ
      L199/28 10–027

2003 Dec.2003/595 on the aid scheme
      implemented by the Federal
      Republic of Germany in
      connection with the sale
      and export of products from
      the Land of Mecklenburg-
      Western Pomerania [2003]
      OJ L202/20 7–007

2003 Dec.2003/599 on the cash ad-
      vance granted by France to
      Bull [2003] OJ L209 24–026

2003 Dec.2003/601 on aid scheme
      Ireland—Foreign Income
      [2003] OJ L204/51 10–031

2003 Dec.2003/626 on the aid
      scheme implemented by
      Germany—Thuringia loan
      programme for small and
      medium-sized enterprises
      [2003] OJ L223/32 7–007,
      24–015, 24–046

2003 Dec.2003/739 on the aid scheme
      which Italy is planning to
      implement to promote em-
      ployment in the Region of
      Sicily [2003] OJ
      L267/29 10–015

2003 Dec.2003/791 on State aid implemented by Germany for Eisenguss Torgelow GmbH [2003] OJ L300/54 24–028

2003 Dec.2003/875 on State aid implemented by Germany for Klausner Nordic Timber GmbH & Co [2003] OJ L337/1 .... 25–011, 25–017

2003 Dec.2003/879 on State aid which the Netherlands proposes to implement to assist NV Huisvullcentrale Noord-Holland [2003] OJ L327/39 17–016

2003 Dec.2003/883 on State aid scheme—Central corporate treasuries (Centrales de trésorerie) implemented by France [2003] OJ L330/23 .... 10–023, 10–030

2004 Dec.2004/32 on the State aid granted by Spain to Porcelanas del Principado SL [2004] OJ L11/1 .. 24–032, 24–047

2004 Dec.2004/76 on the aid scheme implemented by France for headquarters and logistics centres [2004] OJ L23/1 ....10–009, 10–014, 10–037

2004 Dec.2004/77 on the aid scheme implemented by Belgium—Tax ruling system for United States foreign sales corporations [2004] OJ L23/14 ....10–009, 10–018, 10–030

2004 Dec.2004/165 on the aid scheme implemented by Germany: Thuringia consolidation programme, November 27, 2002; [2004] OJ L61 7–007

2004 Dec.2004/166 on aid which France intends to grant for the restructuring of the Societe Nationale Maritime Corse-Mediterranee (SNCM) [2004] OJ L61/13 .... 24–014, 24–015
art.2 24–041

2004 Dec.2004/167 on State aid implemented by Germany for Space Park Development GmbH & Co, KG [2004] OJ L61/66 3–033

2004 Dec.2004/261 on State aid which Italy is planning to implement in favour of certain heavy goods vehicles designed for the carriage of goods by road [2004] OJ L81/80 10–006

2004 Dec.2004/281 adapting Act of Accession following reform of the common agricultural policy [2004] OJ L93/1 13–010

2004 Dec.2004/291 on a long-term national aid scheme to assist farmers in northern areas of Sweden [2004] OJ L94/61 13–009

2004 Dec.2004/313 on State aid granted by Germany to Graphischer Maschinenbau GmbH (Berlin) [2004] OJ L100/35 24–037

2004 Dec.2004/339 on the measures implemented by Italy for RAI SpA [2004] OJ L119/1 .... 10–011, 18–002

2004 Dec.2004/343 on the aid scheme implemented by France for the takeover of firms in difficulty [2004] L108/38 ......10–037, 24–046

2004 Dec.2004/393 on advantages granted to Ryanair in connection with its establishment at Charleroi [2004] L137/1 .... 3–087, 25–031

2004 Dec.2004/746 association with the Republic of Bulgaria [2004] OJ L328/101 5–022

2004 Dec.2004/838 on State aid implemented by France for France 2 and France 3 [2004] OJ L361/21 ....18–002, 18–003, 18–004

2005 Dec.2005/77 on the aid scheme implemented by the United Kingdom in favour of Gibraltar Qualifying Companies [2005] OJ L29/24 ......10–009, 10–035, 26–020

2005 Dec.2005/145 on State aid granted by France to EDF and the electricity and gas industries [2005] OJ L49/9 9–007

2005 Dec.2005/170 on aid for the construction of a propylene pipeline between Rotterdam, Antwerp and the Ruhr areas notified by Germany [2005] OJ L56/15 3–062

2005 Dec.2005/179 on the declaration that Slovenia is free of brucellosis (B. melitensis) and enzootic bovine leukosis and Slovakia of bovine tuberculosis and bovine brucellosis [2005] OJ L61/37 .... 26–016, 26–016

2005 Dec.2005/217 on measures implemented by Denmark for TV2/Denmark [2005] OJ L85/1 3–022

2005 Dec.2005/238 Aid granted to the fisheries and aquaculture sector in Corsica from 1986 to 1999 [2005] OJ L74/41 13–047

2005 Dec.2005/261 on the aid scheme which the United Kingdom is planning to implement as regards the Government of Gibraltar Corporation Tax Reform [2005] OJ L85/1 ... 21–002

2005 Dec.2005/262 on the aid implemented by France in favour of the Cooperative d'exportation du livre français (CELF) [2004] OJ L85/27 4–034
art.1 4–035

2005 Dec.2005/314 on restructuring aid implemented by France for CMR Marseille [2005] L100/26 24–016

2005 Dec.2005/345 on restructuring aid implemented by Germany for Bankgesellschaft Berlin AG [2005] OJ L116/1 .....4–025, 19–007, 19–024, 24–009, 24–039, 24–041

2005 Dec.2005/346 on the State aid implemented by Germany for MobilCom AG [2005] OJ L116/55 .... 24–040, 24–041, 26–010

2005 Dec.2005/374 on a State aid measure implemented by Germany for Kvaerner Warnow Werft [2005] OJ L120/21 25–046

2005 Dec.2005/378 Commission decision concerning the aid scheme which Belgium is proposing to implement for coordination centres [2005] OJ L125/10 10–030

2005 Dec.2005/406 on ad hoc measures implemented by Portugal for RTP [2005] OJ L142/1 ....18–002, 18–003, 18–004

2005 Dec.2005/407 on the State aid which the nited Kingdom is planning to implement for British Energy Plc [2005] OJ L142/26 20–027

2005 Dec.2005/418 on aid measures implemented by France for Alstrom [2005] OJ L150/24 .... 19–072, 24–003, 24–037, 24–041, 25–031

2005 Dec.2005/468 on the aid scheme implemented by Sweden for an exemption from the tax on energy [2005] OJ L165/21 26–020

2005 Dec.2005/564 on State aid in the form of loans from the Wagnisbeteiligungsgesellschaft and the Landesförderinstitut implemented by Germany for Neue Harzer Werke GmbH [2005] OJ L190/6 .... 24–036, 24–047

2005 Dec/2005/565 on an aid scheme implemented by Austria for a refund from the energy taxes on natural gas and electricity [2005] OJ L190/13 .... 10–038, 26–020

2005 Dec.2005/652 on State aid implemented by Spain (further restructuring aid to the public Spanish shipyards [2005] OJ L240/45 16–020

2005 Dec.2005/655 on the aid scheme implemented by Italy providing for tax credits for investments [2005] OJ L241/59 10–036

2005 Dec.2005/691 on State aid which Austria is planning to implement for Bank Burgenland AG [2005] OJ L263/8 ...24–009, 24–015, 24–035, 24–039

2005 Dec.2005/786 on the State aid implemented by Germany for Chemische Werke Piesteritz [2005] OJ L296/19 .....9–024, 26–010, 26–020

2005 Dec.2005/842 on State aid in the
form of public service compensation granted to certain
undertakings entrusted with
the operation of services of
general economic interest
[2005] OJ L312/67 ...1–017, 8–037,
8–050, 13–012, 17–012,
25–021
Recital 16 8–039
art.2(1)(a) 8–038
(b) 8–038
(c) 8–038
(d) 8–038
(2) 25–021
art.4 .... 8–038, 17–012
art.5 8–039
(1) 17–012
(2) 8–039, 17–012
(b) 8–039
(c) 8–039
(d) 8–039
(3) 8–040

2005 Dec.2005/878 on State aid implemented by Germany for
the Herlitz Group [2005]
OJ L324/64 .... 24–021, 24–023

2005 Dec.2005/920 on a State aid implemented by Germany for
a meat processing compa-
ny, Greuener Salamifabrik
GmbH [2005] OJ L335/48 ...9–024,
26–010

2005 Dec.2005/940 on the State aid
implemented by Germany
for Jahnke Stahlbau GmbH,
Halle [2005] OJ L342/72 24–016,
24–032, 24–039, 24–044,
24–047

2005 Dec.2005/941 on the State aid
which France is planning to
implement for Bull [2005]
OJ L342/81 .... 24–024, 24–026

2006 Dec.2006/39 on the approval of
exceptional national aid by
the Republic of Cyprus to
Cypriot farmers [2006] OJ
L23/78 13–005

2006 Dec.2006/47 on State aid which
France is planning to im-
plement for Euromoteurs
[2006] OJ L307/213 24–016,
24–028

2006 Dec.2006/144 on Community
strategic guidelines for
rural development (2007–
2013) [2006] OJ L55/20 ... 13–006

2006 Dec.2006/145 on the principles,
priorities and conditions
contained in the Accession
Partnership with Croatia
[2006] OJ 55/30 5–025

2006 Dec.2006/161 on aid scheme
implemented by Italy in favour of newly listed com-
panies [2006] OJ L94/42 ... 10–026

2006 Dec.2006/261 on aid scheme
implemented by Italy in favour of newly listed com-
panies [2006] OJ L94/42 ... 10–037

2006 Dec.2006/323 on the exemption
from excise duty on miner-
al oils used as fuel for aluminium production imple-
mented by France, Ireland
and Italy [2006] OJ
L119/12 20–029

2006 Dec.2006/513 on DVB-T in
Berlin-Brandenburg (Ger-
many) [2006] OJ
L200/14 2–039

2006 Dec.2006/515 18–002

2006 Dec.2006/621 on the State aid
implemented by France for
France Telecom [2006] OJ
L257/11 .... 9–009, 20–024

2006 Dec.2006/638 n the aid scheme
implemented by Italy for
certain undertakings for
collective investment in
transferable securities specialised in shares of small-
and medium-capitalisation
companies listed on regu-
lated markets [2006] OJ
L268/1 .... 10–034, 10–037

2006 Dec.2006/643 on State aid
which the United Kingdom
is planning to implement
for the establishment of the
Nuclear Decommissioning
Authority [2006] OJ
L268/37 .... 20–009, 20–010,
20–011, 25–031

2006 Dec.2006/736 on State aid im-
plements by Germany fo
Landesbank Berlin [2006]
OJ L397/58 19–007

2006 Dec.2006/737 on State aid from
Germany for Westdeutsche
Landesbank [2006] OJ
307/22 19–007

2006 Dec.2006/739 on State aid implemented by Germany for
Hamburgische Landesbank
[2006] OJ L307/110 19–007

2006 Dec.2006/741 on State aid implemented by Germany for Landesbank Schleswig-Holstein [2006] OJ L307/134 19–007

2006 Dec.2006/742 on State aid implemented by Germany for Landesbank Hessen-Thuringen [2006] OJ L307/159 19–007

2006 Dec.2006/747 on State aid which France is planning to implement for Euromoteurs [2006] OJ L307/213 24–016

2006 Dec.2006/748 on State Aid implemented by Portugal exempting from corporation tax on capital gains certain operations/transactions by public undertakings [2006] OJ L307/219 .... 10–037, 10–038

2006 Dec.2006/938 on training aid for Ford Genk (Belgium) [2006] OJ L366/32 2–039

2006 Dec.2006/939 on the aid measure notified by the Netherlands for KG Holding NV [2006] OJ L366/40 24–028

2006 Dec.2006/940 on aid scheme implemented by Luxembourg for 1929 holding companies and billionaire holding companies [2006] OJ L366/47 .... 10–031, 10–037

2006 Dec.2006/949 on a measure taken by the Netherlands with regard to VAOP [2006] OJ L383/61 8–014

2007 Dec.2007/74 establishing harmonised efficiency reference values for separate production of electricity and heat [2007] OJ L32/24

2007 Dec.2007/C120 Italy—State aid— rescue and restructuring aid to New Interlin SpA [2007] OJ C120/12 24–020

2007 Dec.2007/175 on broadband network in Appingedam (Netherlands) OJ L86/1 2–039

2007 Dec.2007/204 on State aid implemented by the Slovak Republic for Konas, s.r.o. [2007] OJ L91/37 ....10–017, 24–028

2007 Dec.2007/254 on State aid implemented by the Slovak Republic for Frucona Kosice a.s. [2007] OJ L112/14 24–028

2007 Dec.2007/256 on the aid scheme implemented by France under Article 39 CA of the General Tax Code [2007] OJ L112/41 .... 10–018, 10–023, 10–026, 10–034, 10–038, 25–023, 25–031

2007 Dec.2007/374 on digital decoders (Italy) [2007] OJ L147/1 2–039

2007 Dec.2007/385 on the construction of an ethylene pipeline in Bavaria [2007] OJ L143/16 3–075

2007 Dec.2007/492 on State aid implemented by Germany for the Biria Group [2007] OJ L183/27 .... 24–024, 24–028

2007 Dec.2007/499 on State aid to be implemented by the Region of Sicily for Nuova Mineraria Silius SpA [2007] OJ L185/18 24–028

2007 Dec.2007/509 on State aid which Poland is planning to implement for Daewoo Poland [2007] OJ L187/30 ... 24–028

2007 Dec.2007/612 on training aid to General Motors (Belgium) [2007] OJ L243/71 2–039

2007 Decision of November 6, 2007 on the principles, priorities and conditions contained in the Accession Partnership with Croatia (COM (2007) 658) 5–025

2007 Dec.2007/674 on State aid implemented by France for Ernault [2007] OJ L277/25 24–020

2008 Dec.2008/28 on the aid scheme implemented by Belgium for coordination centres established in Belgium [2007] OJ L90/7 25–051

2008 Dec.2008/119 on the principles, priorities and conditions contained in the Accession Partnership with Croatia [2008] OJ L42/51 5–026

2008 Dec.2008/126 aid to Investbx (United Kingdom) 2–038, 4–061

2008 Dec.2008/145 on State aid planned by Poland for Bison Bial SA [2008] OJ L46/41 24–028

2008 Dec.2008/263 on state aid implemented by Austria for BAWAG-PSK [2008] OJ L83/7 .... 4–025, 19–007

2008 Dec.2008/344 on State aid which Poland has implemented for Technologie Bucsek Group [2008] OJ L116/26 24–042

2008 Dec.2008/406 on State aid which Poland has implemented for Arcelor Huta Warszawa [2008] OJ L143/31 .... 24–042, 25–046

2008 Dec.2008/408 on the State aid C 36/A/06 (ex NN 38/06) implemented by Italy in favour of ThyssenKrupp, Cementir and Nuova Terni Industrie Chimiche [2008] OJ L144/37 20–092
Recital 70 20–092

2008 Dec.2008/711 on State aid implemented by Italy on the tax incentives in favour of certain restructured banks [2008] OJ L237/70 ....10–018, 24–028

2008 Dec.2008/716 on State aid implemented by France for Arbel Fauvet [2008] OJ L238/27 24–020

2008 Dec.2008/717 on State aid implemented by Romania for Daewoo Romania [2008] OJ L239/12 24–028

2008 Dec.2008/746 on State aid implemented by France for building the cruise vessel Le Levant [2008] OJ L252/17 10–034

2008 Dec.2008/854 on State aid which Poland has implemented for Acrcelor Hut Warszawa [2008] OJ L302/9 25–046

2008 Dec.2008/948 on measures by Germany to assist DHL and Leipzig Halle Airport [2008] OJ L346/1 25–031

2010 Decision of September 17, 2008 on State aid—Greece Olympic Airways/Olympic Airlines [2008] L222/2 8–077

2009 Dec.2009/150 concerning a reimbursement mechanism linked to the introduction of a toll system on German motorways [2009] OJ L50/30 25–053

2009 Dec.2009/155 on the loan of EUR 300 million granted by Italy to Alitalia [2009] OJ L52/3 24–024

2009 Dec.2009/174 Postabank Hungary [2009] OJ L62/14 ......24–008, 24–013

2009 Dec.2009/485 on State aid which France is planning to implement for FagorBrandt [2009] OJ L160/11 24–028

2009 Dec.2009/610 on the measure C 16/04 implemented by Greece in favour of Hellenic Shipyards [2009] OJ L225/104 25–042

2009 Dec.2009/809 on the groepsrentebox scheme which the Netherlands is planning to implement 2009] OJ L288/26 .... 10–011, 10–037

2009 Dec.2009/944 on State aid schemes implemented by Italy in favour of glasshouse growers [2009] OJ L327/6 10–018

2009 Dec.2009/972 on aid scheme which Denmark is planning to implement for refunding the CO 2 tax on quota-regulated fuel consumption in industry [2009] OJ L345/18 10–015

2009 Dec.2009/973 on the restructuring aid for Combus A/S [2009] OJ L345/28 24–028

2010 Dec.2010/3 on State aid granted by Poland to Stocznia Szczecinska [2010] OJ L5/1 .... 24–008, 24–020

2010 Dec.2010/13 on aid scheme which Germany intends to grant to modernise the general conditions for capital investments [2010] OJ L6/32 10–037

2010 Dec.2010/38 on State aid concerning a temporary defensive mechanism for shipbuilding (Italy) [2010] OJ L17/50 25–017

2010 Dec.2010/47 on State aid granted by Poland to Stocznia Gdynia [2010] OJ L33/1 ... 24–008

2010 Dec.2010/95 on State aid implemented by Hungary for tax deductions for intra-group interest [2010] OJ L42/3 ...10–011, 10–037

2010 Dec.2010/215 on measures taken by Italy to rescue Sandretto Industrie srl [2010] OJ L92/19 25–046

2010   Dec.2010/359 on adapting and extending the period of application of the measures in Decision 2002/148 concluding consultations with Zimbabwe [2010] OJ L167/39 25–045

2010   Dec.2010/394 on the financing of Hessische Staatswein-guter [2010] OJ L180/30 ... 24–028

2010   Dec.2010/473 on support measures implemented by Spain in the agricultural sector following the increase in fuel prices [2010 OJ L235/1 10–037

2010   Dec.2010/787 on State aid to facilitate the closure of uncompetitive coal mines [2010] OJ L336/24 ....7–003, 14–008, 14–050, 14–051
        exhibit 5 14–011
        art.2(2) 14–051
        art.4 14–051
        (1) 14–051

2010   Dec.2010/C 90/08 [2010] OJ C90/8 10–023

2011   Dec.2011/3 on public transport service contracts between the Danish Ministry of Transport and danske Stats-baner [2011] OJ L7/1 17–016

2011   Dec.2011/5 on the tax amortisation of financial goodwill for foreign shareholding acquisitions implemented by Spain [2011] OJ 7/48 ....10–030, 10–037

2011   Dec.2011/88 on state aid granted by Hungary to MOL Nyrt [2011] OJ L34/55 10–006

2011   Dec.2011/97—State   aid— Olympic   Airways— Restructuring and privatisation [2011] OJ L45/1 ....24–016, 24–028, 25–045

2011   Dec.2011/134 on State aid implemented by Italy for WAM SpA [2011] OJ L57/29 25–023

2011   Dec.2011/179 on State aid implemented by France in favour of Cooperative d'exportation du livre francais [2011] OJ L78/37 ...4–035, 25–009, 25–010, 25–038

2011   Dec.2011/269 on State aid granted by Hungary to Peti Nitrogenmuvek [2011] OJ L118/9 24–028

2011   Dec.2011/363 AS Parex banka [2011] OJ L163/28 24–039

2011   Dec.2011/414 on State aid implemented by Greece in favour of Varvaressos SA [2011] OJ L184/9 ....24–024, 25–041

2011   Decision February 23, 2011 on aid for the Bahnen de Stadt Mohnheim and Rheinische Bahngesellschaft companies in the Verkehrsverbund Rhein Ruhr 17–017

TABLE OF DECISIONS OF THE EFTA

C 182/07 concerning aid to TromsKraft for a wind park (68330) 4–017, 4–050
E 4/97 Norwegian Bankers Association v EFTA Surveillance Authority [1998] 3 C.M.L.R.
   281 25–074
E 9/97 Else Maria Sveinbjornsdottir v Iceland [1999] 1 C.M.L.R. 884 25–073
E 6/98 Norway v EFTA Surveillance Authority [1999] 2 C.M.L.R. 1033 25–074
E 4/01 Karl K Karlsson hf v Ireland [2002] 2 C.M.L.R. 60 25–072
E 2/05 EFTA Surveillance Authority v Iceland, November 24, 2005 25–074
E 6/09 Magasin-og Ukepresseforeningen v EFTA Surveillance Authority, March 30, 2010
   EFTA Court Report 2009–2010 p.4 25–070

TABLE OF EUROPEAN REGULATIONS AND DIRECTIVES

Regulations

1962 Reg.17/62 implementing Articles 85 and 86 of the EC Treaty [1962] OJ 13/204 .....3–120, 25–001
art.14(6) 25–059

1962 Reg.26/62 applying certain rules of competition to production of and trade in agricultural products [1962] OJ L30/993 ....3–123, 13–002
art.4 3–123

1969 Reg.1191/69 on action concerning the obligations inherent in the concept of a public service in transport by rail, road and inland waterway [1969] OJ L156/1 ...3–126, 17–003, 17–006, 17–007, 17–008, 17–009, 17–010, 17–014, 17–015, 17–018, 17–025, 17–028, 17–035
art.1(1) 17–008
(2) 17–008
(4) 17–008
art.2(5) 17–009
art.3 17–010
art.6(2) 17–010
art.7 17–010
section II (arts 3–8) 7–008
art.3 3–126
art.4 17–010
section III (art.9) 7–008
section IV (arts 10–13) 7–008
section V (art.14) 7–008
art.17(2) 17–008

1969 Reg.1192/69 on common rules for the normalisation of the accounts of railway undertakings [1969] OJ L156/8 ...17–003, 17–006, 17–014, 17–015, 17–025, 17–035
art.1(3) 17–025
art.4 17–025

Section II (arts 5–12) 17–026
art.10 17–026
art.13 17–026

1970 Reg.1107/70 on the granting of aid for the transport by rail, road, and inland water [1970] OJ L130/1 ....17–003, 17–006, 17–007, 17–009, 17–014, 17–015, 17–037
art.2(1) 17–009
art.3(1) 17–009
(f) 17–016
(2) 17–009

1971 Reg.1182/71 determining the rules applicable to periods, dates and time limits [1971] OJ L124/1 25–031
art.26(2) 25–031

1973 Reg.706/73 on the Community arrangements applicable to the Channel Islands and the Isle of Man for trade in agricultural products [1973] OJ L68/1
art.2 13–011

1975 Reg.2759/75 [1975] OJ L282/1
art.20(4) 13–004

1976 Reg.1975/76 on the obligations inherent in the concept of a public service in transport by rail, road and inland waterway [1969] OJ L156/1 ... 3–126

1986 Reg.4055/86 applying the principle of freedom to provide services to maritime transport [1986] OJ L378/1 17–052

1989 Reg.1064/89 on the opening of supplementary quotas for imports into the Community of certain textile products originating in certain third countries participating in the 1989 Berlin Trade Fairs [1989] OJ L113/12 27–013

1989 Reg.1101/89 on structural improvements in inland waterway transport [1989] OJ L116/25 17–030

1989 Reg.4064/89 on the control of concentrations between undertakings [1989] OJ L395/1 25–048

    art.6(1)(b) 25–028

1991 Reg.1893/91 on obligations inherent in the concept of public service in transport by road, rail and inland waterway [1991] OJ L169/1 ...17–006, 17–009, 17–010

1991 Reg.3921/91on the conditions under which non-resident carriers may transport goods or passengers by inland waterway within a Member State [1991] OJ L373/1 17–032

1992 Reg.1177/2002 on a temporary defensive mechanism to shipbuilding [2002] OJ L172/1 .... 16–012, 16–013

1992 Reg.2407/92 on licensing of air carriers [1992] OJ L240/1 .... 17–061, 14–084

1992 Reg.2408/92 on access for Community air carriers to intra-Community air routes [1992] OJ L240/8 ....17–061, 17–063

1992 Reg.2409/92 on fares and rates for air services [1992] OJ L240/15 17–061

1992 Reg.3577/92 on the principle of freedom to provide services to maritime transport within Member States (Maritime Cabotage Regulation) [1992] OJ L364/7 ....17–018, 17–052

    art.2 17–052

    art.4(3) 25–016

1993 Reg.2019/93 on specific measures for the smaller Aegean islands concerning certain agricultural products [2002] OJ L68/4 ......13–016 ......

1994 Reg.998/94 on horizontal State aid [1998] OJ L142/1 ...1–017 ...

1994 Reg.3284/94 on protection against subsidized imports from countries not members of the European Community [1994] OJ L349/22 ...6–027, 10–017

    art.2 10–017

1996 Reg.1356/96 on common rules applicable to the transport of goods or passengers by inland waterway between Member States [1996] OJ L175/7 17–031

1996 Reg.2255/96 on granting of aids for transport by rail, road and inland waterway [1996] OJ L304/3 17–016

1997 Reg.543/97 on the granting of aids for transport by rail, road and inland waterway [1997] OJ L84/6 17–006

1997 Reg.1221/97 laying down general rules for the application of measures to improve the production and marketing of honey [1997] OJ L173 13–002

1997 Reg.1310/97 on the control of concentrations between undertakings [1997] OJ L180/1 25–028

1998 Reg.994/98 on horizontal state aid (Enabling Regulation) [1998] OJ L142/1 ... 1–038, 4–001, 7–001, 7–003, 11–001, 11–029, 15–001, 15–002, 22–006, 25–009, 25–021, 25–052, 25–062, 25–062, 27–052

    Recital 9 7–001

    art.1 ......4–001, 7–002, 11–001, 25–006

     (1) 11–001

    art.2 7–002

     (1) 25–021

    art.7 25–009

1998 Reg.1540/98 establishing new rules on aid to shipbuilding 16–003, 16–004, 16–005, 16–006, 16–008, 16–010, 16–012, 16–022

    art.6 16–006

    s.3.3.2 16–008

1999　Reg.659/99 on detailed rules for
　　　　the application of Article
　　　　93 of the EC Treaty (Ar-
　　　　ticle 108 TFEU) [1999] OJ
　　　　L83/1 .... 1–010, 1–022, 1–035,
　　　　　　　　　1–039, 4–001, 5–003,
　　　　　　　　　5–007, 5–009, 8–016,
　　　　　　　　　8–037, 8–071, 9–011,
　　　　　　　　　11–015, 15–001, 17–003,
　　　　　　　　　19–071, 20–086, 24–030,
　　　　　　　　　25–001, 25–002, 25–003,
　　　　　　　　　25–007, 25–008, 25–009,
　　　　　　　　　25–010, 25–012, 25–013,
　　　　　　　　　25–016, 25–020, 25–023,
　　　　　　　　　25–029, 25–031, 25–036,
　　　　　　　　　25–042, 25–045, 25–048,
　　　　　　　　　25–049, 25–060, 25–069,
　　　　　　　　　26–001, 26–009, 27–001,
　　　　　　　　　27–021, 27–026, 27–028,
　　　　　　　　　27–031
　　　preamble para.(4) 25–015
　　　　para.8 25–027
　　　　para.16 25–003
　　　Ch.I 25–013
　　　Ch.II 25–020
　　　Chs II–V 25–013
　　　Ch.III 25–042, 26–001, 26–005
　　　Ch.IV 25–007, 25–013, 25–046
　　　Ch.V 25–013, 25–049
　　　Ch.VI 25–007
　　　Ch.VII 25–008
　　　art.1 .... 8–037, 8–044, 25–037
　　　　(a) 9–026
　　　　(b) 15–002, 25–014
　　　　　(i) 5–004
　　　　　(iv) 25–015
　　　　　(v) 1–031, 8–007, 25–016
　　　　(c)
　　　　(d) 5–010, 25–018
　　　　(f) 25–007, 26–001, 26–003
　　　　(g) 19–071, 25–046
　　　　(h) 1–033, 25–003
　　　art.2 .... 8–041, 25–022
　　　　(1) 25–021, 25–027, 25–037
　　　　(2) 25–043
　　　art.3 .... 25–037, 25–042, 27–053
　　　art.4 ..25–032, 25–040, 27–028, 27–029,
　　　　　　　　　27–029, 27–038
　　　　(2) 25–033, 25–061, 25–062,
　　　　　　　　　27–028, 27–029
　　　　(3) 25–015, 25–028, 25–061,
　　　　　　　25–062, 26–004, 27–027, 27–028
　　　　(4) ...5–005, 25–029, 25–047, 25–061,
　　　　　　　　　26–004, 27–028, 27–030
　　　　(5) 25–022, 25–027, 25–028,
　　　　　　　　　25–064
　　　　(6) 20–056, 25–015, 25–029,
　　　　　　　　　25–037, 25–061
　　　art.5(1) 25–022, 25–043
　　　　(2) 25–022, 25–043

　　　　(3) 25–022
　　　　(4) 8–040, 8–041
　　　　(5) 8–041
　　　art.6 ...5–005, 25–017, 25–031, 25–041,
　　　　　　　　　25–046, 25–051, 26–004
　　　　(1) 1–031, 1–033, 25–003, 25–031
　　　　(2) 25–031
　　　art.7 ..25–028, 25–032, 25–035, 25–040,
　　　　　　25–041, 25–045, 25–051, 25–062,
　　　　　　　　　26–004
　　　　(3) 25–015, 25–028, 25–033,
　　　　　　　　　26–004
　　　　(4) 19–071, 25–015, 25–033,
　　　　　　　　　25–048, 26–004
　　　　(6) 25–036
　　　　(7) 25–036, 25–065
　　　art.8 25–040
　　　art.9 .... 25–041, 25–051, 26–004
　　　art.10 ...1–033, 25–041, 25–043, 26–004
　　　　(1) 25–043, 27–028, 27–029,
　　　　　　　　　27–040
　　　　(3) 25–043, 27–013
　　　art.11 .... 25–006, 25–041, 25–045,
　　　　　　　　25–067, 26–007, 27–003
　　　　(1) 25–039, 25–041, 26–004
　　　　(2) 25–043, 25–045, 26–003,
　　　　　　　　26–003, 26–007, 26–008
　　　　(3) 25–007
　　　art.12 26–004
　　　art.13 .... 25–041, 26–004, 27–028
　　　　(1) 25–045, 27–029
　　　　(2) 25–043, 25–064
　　　art.14 ..8–037, 25–006, 25–035, 25–037,
　　　　　　　　　25–041
　　　　(1) 26–003, 26–005, 26–017
　　　　(2) ...9–024, 25–043, 26–005, 26–006,
　　　　　　　　　26–007
　　　　(3) 26–005, 26–007, 26–012,
　　　　　　　　　26–013
　　　art.15 .... 25–015, 25–041, 26–004,
　　　　　　　　　26–007
　　　　(1) 25–014
　　　art.16 .... 19–071, 25–018, 25–046,
　　　　　　　　26–003, 26–004, 26–008
　　　art.17 .... 25–018, 25–049, 26–003
　　　art.18 .... 25–018, 26–001, 26–003
　　　art.19 .... 1–039, 25–018
　　　　(1) 25–050, 26–020
　　　　(2) 25–051
　　　art.20 .... 25–054, 25–062, 27–029
　　　　(1) 25–053
　　　　(2) 25–003, 25–012, 25–053,
　　　　　　25–054, 27–028, 27–029, 27–039,
　　　　　　　　　27–040
　　　　(3) 25–056
　　　art.21 25–058
　　　　(2) 25–057
　　　art.22 25–058
　　　　(1) 25–058
　　　art.23 .... 19–071, 25–046, 25–047

(1) 26–008
art.24 25–060
art.25 .... 25–008, 27–030
art.26 25–061
(5) 25–061
art.27 .... 25–008, 25–062
art.28 25–062

1999   Reg.718/99 on a Community-
    fleet capacity policy to pro-
    mote inland waterway
    transport [1999] OJ
    L90/1 .... 17–030, 17–031
art.7 17–030

1999   Reg.805/99 implementing
    Council Regulation
    718/1999 on a Community-
    fleet capacity policy to
    promote inland waterway
    transport [1999] OJ
    L102/64 17–030

1999   Reg.1257/1999 on support for
    rural development from
    the European Agricultural
    Guidance and Guarantee
    Fund (EAGGF) [1999] OJ
    L160/80
art.5 13–010
art.7 13–010
(2) 13–010
art.17 13–016
art.26(1) 13–010

1999   Reg.1260/99 laying down gen-
    eral provisions on structural
    funds [1999] OJ L161/1 ... 3–037

2000   Reg.104/2000 on common mar-
    ket organisation in fishery
    and aquaculture products
    (CMO Regulation) [2000]
    OJ L17/22 13–042
art.1 13–042
art.32 13–042
art.11 19–067

2000   Reg.2826/2000 on information
    and promotion actions for
    agricultural products on the
    internal market [2000] OJ
    L328/2 13–032

2001   Reg.68/2001 on the application
    of Articles 87 and 88 of the
    EC Treaty to training aid 3–057,
                        11–002
art.3 3–079

2001   Reg.69/2001 on de minimis aid
    [2001] OJ L10/30 ... 3–079, 7–001,
               7–004, 7–007, 7–010,
                    7–012, 17–033

2001   Reg.70/2001 on State aid to
    small and medium-sized
    enterprises (SME Block
    Exemption Regulation)
    [2001] OJ L10/33 ...4–060, 11–002,
                    11–017, 15–003
Recital 2 15–002
art.3 25–021
art.5(a) 11–022
(b) 11–022
(c) 11–022
Annex 1 9–015

2001   Reg.1049/2001 on access to in-
    formation to State aid con-
    trol proceedings 1–034
art.4(2) 1–034
(3) 1–034

2001   Reg.1448/2001 on specific
    measures in respect of cer-
    tain agricultural products
    for the benefit of the French
    overseas departments
    [2001] OJ L198/3 13–011

2001   Reg.1449/2001 on specific
    measures for the Azores
    and Madeira relating to cer-
    tain agricultural products as
    regards the structural meas-
    ures OJ L198/5 13–011

2001   Reg.1453/2001 on specific
    measures for certain agri-
    cultural products for the
    Azores and Madeira [2001]
    OJ L198/26 13–011

2002   Reg.442/2002 on specific meas-
    ures for the smaller Aegean
    islands concerning certain
    agricultural products
    [2002] OJ L68/4 13–011

2002   Reg.1407/2002 on state aid to
    the coal industry (Coal
    Regulation) [2002] OJ
    L205/1 .....7–003, 14–001, 14–005,
             14–008, 14–009, 14–010,
             14–015, 14–016, 14–019,
             14–021, 14–023, 14–025,
             14–027, 14–031, 14–032,
             14–033, 14–040, 14–048,
                 14–051, 25–021
preface exhibit 2 14–010
exhibit 7 14–038
exhibit 13 14–011
art.1 14–010
art.2(d) 14–021
art.3(1) 14–010
(2) 14–021
art.4 ....14–010, 14–022, 14–026
(c) 14–030
art.5 14–022
(1) 14–022

(2) 14–010, 14–019, 14–020
(a) 14–022
(b) 14–022, 14–023
(3) 14–010, 14–019, 14–024
art.6 14–022
art.7 .... 14–010, 14–029
art.8(2) 14–022
art.10 .... 14–020, 14–022
art.11 14–016
(2) 14–016
art.14 14–016
Annex 14–030
2002 Reg.2204/2002 on state aid for
employment [2002] OJ
L337/3 11–002
2002 Reg.2371/2002 on the conservation and sustainable exploitation of fisheries resources
under the Common Fisher-
ies Policy [2002] OJ
L358/59 13–002
2003 Reg.1/2003 on the implementa-
tion of the rules on com-
petition laid down in Ar-
ticles 81 and 82 of the
Treaty [2003] OJ L1/1 3–120,
25–009, 25–054, 25–059
art.7 27–039
(2) 25–054
2003 Reg.405/2003 on monitoring of
imports of coal originating
in third countries [2003] OJ
L62/1
art.7(c) 14–005
2003 Reg.1059/2003 on the establish-
ment of a common classification of territorial units for
statistics (NUTS) [2003]
OJ L154 21–008
2003 Reg.1782/2003 on common
rules for direct support
schemes under the common
agricultural policy [2003]
OJ L270/1 .... 13–003, 13–016
2003 Reg.1882/2003 adapting provision relating to committees
[2003] OJ L284/1 22–079
2004 Reg.1/2004 to state aid to small
and medium-sized enter-
prises active in the production, processing and mar-
keting of agricultural
products [2004] OJ L1 13–012
2004 Reg.139/2004 on the control of
concentrations between undertakings (EC Merger
Regulation) [2004] OJ
L24/1 ....3–119, 25–028, 25–038
art.10(5) 25–038

2004 Reg.363/2004 amending Regulation 68/2001 on the application of Articles 87 and 88
of the EC Treaty to training
aid [2004] OJ L63/20 11–002,
16–005
2004 Reg.364/2004 on aid for research and development
[2004] OJ L63/22 .. 4–060, 11–002
2004 Reg.386/2004 on nomenclature
codes for certain products
processed form fruit and
vegetables [2004] OJ
L64/25) 13–002
2004 Reg.773/2004 relating to the
conduct of proceedings by
the Commission [2004] OJ
L123/18 .... 3–120, 25–054
art.5 3–120
Reg.794/2004 laying down de-
tailed rules for the application of Article 93 EC Treaty [Article 113 TFEU]
[2004] OJ L140/1 13–008,
17–003, 25–001, 25–007,
25–008, 25–023, 25–031,
25–048, 26–006, 27–001
Recital 10 26–006
art.2 ...24–034, 24–045, 25–023, 25–025
(1) 25–021
art.4 25–024
(1) 25–021
art.7(1) 25–054
arts 8–11 26–006
art.8 .... 25–024, 25–031
art.9 26–006
(3) 26–006
art.10 26–006
art.11(1) 26–006
(2) 26–006
(3) 26–006
Annex I Pt I 25–023
Pt III 25–023
Pt III.7.A 24–034, 24–045
Pt III.8.A 24–034, 24–045
Annex II 25–024
2004 Reg.1595/2004 on aid to small
and medium-sized enter-
prises active in the production, processing and mar-
keting of fisheries products
[2006] OJ C98/5 13–045
2004 Reg.1860/2004 on de minimis
aid in the agriculture and
fisheries sectors [2004] OJ
L325/4 ......7–003, 13–012, 13–015
2005 Reg.1290/2005 on the financing
of the common agricultural
policy [2005] OJ L209/1 13–004

2005 Reg.1698/2005 on support for rural development by the European Agricultural Fund for Rural Development [2005] OJ L277/1 .....13–006, 13–008, 13–010, 13–014, 13–018, 13–019, 13–035
art.2(i) 13–008
art.5 13–006
art.6(2) 13–010
art.10 13–034
art.16(g) 13–008
art.22 13–016
art.26 13–008
art.27 .... 13–008, 13–035
art.28 13–008
art.28 13–007
art.32 .... 13–022, 13–032
art.35(2) 13–021
art.36(a)(i) 13–016
    (ii) 13–016
    (iii) 13–016
arts 43–45 13–035
arts.43–45 13–035
art.52 13–007
art.70(3) 13–006
    (2) 13–008
art.88 13–006
    (1) 13–006, 13–035
art.89 .... 13–006, 13–008
Annex 13–010, 13–020
2005 Reg.1913/2005 on exceptional market support measures caused by restrictions on free movement of poultry meat in order to combat animal disease or severe market disturbances directly linked to the loss of consumer confidence [2005] OJ L307/2 13–004
2006 Reg.318/2006 on common organisation of the markets in the sugar sector [2006] OJ L58/1
recital 36 13–004
art.36 13–004
2006 Reg.320/2006 establishing a temporary scheme for the restructuring of the sugar industry in the Community [2006] OJ L58/1 13–004
2006 Reg.1083/2006 laying down general provisions on the European Regional Development Fund, the European Social Fund and the Cohesion Fund [2006] OJ L210/25 ......3–036, 3–037, 13–042

2006 Reg.1198/2006 on the European Fisheries Fund [2006] OJ L223/1 ....13–042, 13–043, 13–048
art.19 13–042
Annex 13–042
2006 Reg.1628/2006 on national regional investment aid [2006] OJ L302/29 ....15–002, 15–003, 15–008, 21–034 ....
art.2(1)(e) 15–004
    (f) 15–004
    (g) 15–004
    (k)—(m) 15–004
art.7(e) 15–006
art.8(1) 15–005
art.9(2) 15–002
2006 Reg.1692/2006 establishing the second Marco Polo programme for the granting of Community financial assistance to improve the environmental performance of the freight transport system (Marco Polo II) [2006] OJ L328/1 .... 17–048, 17–054
Recital 2 17–004
2006 Reg.1791/06 adapting certain Regulations and Decisions by reason of the accession of Bulgaria and Romania [2006] OJ L363/1 17–006
2006 Reg.1857/2006 on State aid to small and medium-sized enterprises active in the production, processing and marketing of agricultural products [2006] OJ L358/3 ....13–012, 13–016, 22–032
art.4 13–016
art.9 13–021
art.10 13–028
art.11 13–027
art.12 13–029
art.14 13–022
art.15 13–023
art.16 13–024
2006 Reg.1184/2006 applying certain rules of competition to the production of, and trade in, agricultural products [2006] OJ L214/7 ... 3–123, 3–124, 13–002, 13–003
art.3 13–003
2006 Reg.1628/2006 on national regional investment aid [2006] OJ L302/29 15–002

2006   Reg.1791/2006 on the adapting
        of regulations and deci-
        sions, by reason of the ac-
        cession of Bulgaria and Ro-
        mania [2006] OJ L363/1 ... 22–031
2006   Reg.1857/2006 on the applica-
        tion of Articles 87 and 88
        of the EC Treaty to State
        aid to small and mediums-
        sized enterprises active in
        the production of agricul-
        tural products [2001] OJ
        L358 13–029
        art.2(14) 13–024
        art.15 13–016
2006   Reg.1935/2006 on detailed rules
        for the application of Ar-
        ticle 93 EC Treaty [2006]
        OJ L407/1 13–008
2006   Reg.1974/2006 on support for
        rural development by the
        European   Agricultural
        Fund for Rural Develop-
        ment (Implementing Regu-
        lation)   [2006]   OJ
        L368/15 .... 13–008, 13–035
        art.27 13–020
        art.46 13–035
        art.57 13–008
        Annex II point 9 13–008
2006   Reg.1975/2006 on implementa-
        tion of control procedures
        as well as cross compliance
        in respect of rural develop-
        ment support measures
        [2006] OJ L368/74 13–035
2006   Reg.1998/2006 on de minimis
        aid [2006] OJ L379/5 4–044,
                    7–001, 7–003, 7–004,
                    7–007, 7–010, 7–011,
                    7–012, 8–050, 13–002,
                    13–035, 17–033
        Recital 2 7–001
        Recital 3 7–003
        Recital 6 7–003
        Recital 7 7–003
        Recital 10 7–007
        art.1(b) 7–003
        art.2 3–039
        (b) 13–002
        (3) 7–004
        (4) 7–006
        art.3 3–039
        (1) 7–008
        (2) 7–008
        art.6 7–007

2006   Reg.9248/2006   adapting
        Reg.1698/2005 on support
        for rural development by
        the European Agricultural
        Fund   for   Rural
        Development 13–010
2007   Reg.498/2007on the European
        Fisheries Fund [2006] OJ
        L223/1 13–042
2007   Reg.875/2007 on de minimis aid
        in the fisheries sector
        [2007] OJ L193/6 .. 7–003, 13–045
2007   Reg.1182/2007 laying down
        specific rules as regards the
        fruit and vegetable sector
        [2007] OJ L273/1 13–003,
                                            25–024
2007   Reg.1234/2007 establishing a
        common organisation of
        agricultural markets [2007]
        OJ L299/1 13–003
2007   Reg.1370/2007 on public pas-
        senger transport services by
        rail and by road [2007] OJ
        L315/1 .....7–001, 17–002, 17–003,
                    17–006, 17–007, 17–008,
                    17–015, 17–016, 17–017,
                    17–018, 17–019, 17–021,
                    17–023, 17–024, 17–028,
                    17–029, 17–037, 17–039,
                    17–043
        recitals 5–33 17–007
        recital 9 17–020
        recital 10 17–018
        recital 15 17–021
        recital 17 17–019
        recital 18 17–022
        recital 20 17–022
        recital 33 17–023
        recital 37 .... 17–015, 17–028
        art.1(1) 17–018
        (2) 17–018
        art.2(b) 17–017
        (i) 17–020
        art.3(1) 17–021, 17–022
        art.4 .... 17–021, 17–023
        (3) 17–021
        art.5 17–022
        (2) 17–021, 17–022, 17–023
        (b) 17–022
        (4) 17–021, 17–023
        (5) 17–021, 17–023
        (6) 17–021, 17–023
        (7) 17–022
        art.6 .... 17–023, 17–024
        art.7 17–022
        art.9(1) 25–021
        art.10(1) 17–018
        Annex 17–024
        Point 5 17–024

2007 Reg.1535/2007 on de minimis
     aid in the sector of agricul-
     tural production [2007] OJ
     L337 .... 7–003, 7–010, 13–012,
                                    13–013
2008 Reg.479/2008 on the common
     organisation of the market
     in wine [2008] OJ L148 13–003
2008 Reg.736/2008 on state aid to
     small and medium-sized
     enterprises active in the
     production, processing and
     marketing of fisheries prod-
     ucts [2008] OJ L 201/16 ... 13–045,
                                    13–046
2008 Reg.744/2008 on restructuring
     of Community fishing fleets
     affected by the economic
     crisis [2008] L202/1 13–048
2008 Reg.800/2008 declaring certain
     categories of aid compat-
     ible with the common mar-
     ket (General Block Exemp-
     tion Regulation) [2008] OJ
     L214/2008 ... 1–004, 3–038, 4–001,
                 4–002, 4–021, 4–022,
                 4–043, 4–044, 11–003,
                 11–004, 11–006, 11–008,
                 11–010, 11–013, 11–014,
                 11–015, 11–017, 11–018,
                 11–019, 11–021, 11–026,
                 11–027, 11–029, 13–012,
                 13–019, 13–020, 13–023,
                 13–029, 13–035, 13–038,
                 13–046, 15–002, 15–003,
                 15–008, 20–052, 21–034,
                 22–001, 22–006, 22–013,
                 22–014, 22–016, 22–030,
                 22–031, 22–032, 22–033,
                 22–040, 22–044, 22–048,
                 22–049, 22–061, 22–061,
                 22–076, 22–077, 22–079,
                 22–098, 22–099, 23–005,
                 23–012, 23–019, 23–031,
                 23–033, 25–021, 27–052,
                 27–054
     Recital 29 11–013
     art.1 11–006
       (1) 11–006, 22–032
       (3)(b) 13–012
         (c) 13–012
       (5) 11–006
       (6)(a) 11–006
         (c) 11–006
     art.2 11–007
       (2) 11–012
       (4) 11–013
       (12) 15–004
       (10)–(11) 15–004
       (13)–(15) 15–004

       (15)(c) 11–023
       (18) 11–025
       (19) 11–025
       (28) 11–017
     art.3 11–008
     art.4 11–009
     art.5 11–010
     art.6 11–011
       (4) 15–006
     art.7 11–012
     art.8 .... 11–013, 21–034
       (2) 11–013
       (3) 11–013, 22–016
         (e) 15–034
     art.9 11–014
       (1) 21–035
       (4) 11–014, 15–005
     art.10 11–015
     art.11 11–014
     art.12 11–016
       (1) 11–016
     art.13 .... 13–019, 13–038, 21–034
       (9)(b) 13–019
     arts 13–16 11–017
     art.14 .... 11–017, 21–034
       (6) 11–017
     art.15 4–021
     art.16 .... 11–017, 13–038
     Section 3 13–033
     arts 17–25 11–018
     art.18 .... 11–018, 22–044, 22–045,
                             22–076, 22–098
     arts 18–24 11–018
     art.19 .... 11–018, 22–045, 22–048,
                                    22–098
     art.20 .... 11–018, 22–098
     art.21 .... 11–019, 22–098
     art.22 .... 11–019, 22–098
     art.23 .... 11–019, 22–049, 22–061
     art.24 .... 11–019, 22–050, 22–098
     art.25 .... 11–013, 11–018, 22–098
     art.26 11–020
     arts 26–27 .... 11–020, 13–038
     art.27 11–020
     art.28 4–059
     arts 28–29 11–021
     art.28 *et seq* 13–031
     art.29 ... 4–059, 11–010, 11–012, 11–021
     arts 30–37 11–022
     art.34 13–031
     art.35 .... 11–012, 11–022
     art.36(6) 11–022
     arts 38–42 11–023
     arts 40–42 13–038
     Annex I 13–016, 13–034
2009 Reg.74/2009 on support for rural
     development by the Euro-
     pean Agricultural Fund for
     Rural Development [2009]
     OJ L30/100 13–006

2009 Reg.491/2009 on common organisation of agricultural
products [2009] OJ L154 ... 13–003

2009 Reg.597/2009 on protection
against subsidised imports
from countries not mem-
bers of the European Com-
munity [2009] OJ
L188/93 6–027

art.12(1) 6–027

art.15(1) 6–027

art.31 6–027

2009 Reg.1125/2009 on the application of Article 93 of the EC
Treaty [2009] OJ L308/5 ... 25–001

2009 Reg.1225/2009 on protection
against dumped imports
from countries not mem-
bers of the European Com-
munity [2009] OJ
L343/51 6–027

art.21 6–027

2010 Reg.1234/2010 on aid granted in
the framework of the Ger-
man Alcohol Monopoly
[2010] OJ L346/11 13–003

Directives

1973 Dir.73/183 on the abolition of
restrictions on freedom of
establishment and freedom
to provide services in respect of self-employed activities of banks and other
financial institutions [1973]
OJ L45/21 19–001

1975 Dir.75/439 on the disposal of
waste oils [1975] OJ
L194/23 8–026

1977 Dir.77/62 on procedures for the
award of public supply contracts [1977] OJ L13/1

art.26 3–114

1977 Dir.77/388 on harmonization of
laws relating to turnover
taxes (Sixth Directive)
[1977] OJ L145/1

art.17(2)(a) 3–035

1977 Dir.77/780 First Banking Directive [1977] OJ L322/1977 ...19–001

1980 Dir.80/723 on the transparency
of financial relations between Member States and
public undertakings (Transparency Directive) [1980]
OJ L195/35 ...1–017, 8–001, 8–005,
8–015, 8–016, 8–017,
8–041, 8–051, 8–052,
8–057, 13–012, 14–004,
17–012, 17–026, 18–006,
19–006, 19–007, 20–004,
20–087, 24–010
Preamble Recital 11 3–029
art.1 3–041
art.2 ....3–016, 8–014, 20–054
art.2(1)(d) 8–015
art.4(b) 20–013
art.5(2) 8–017

1988 Dir.88/295 on coordination of
procedures on the award of
public supply contracts
[1988] OJ L127/1 3–114

1988 Dir.88/361 Capital Liberalization Directive [1988] OJ
L178/1988 19–001

1989 Dir.89/646 on the coordination
of laws, regulations and administrative provisions relating to credit institutions
(Second Banking Direc-
tive) [1989] OJ
L386/1989 19–001

1990 Dir.90/684 on aid to shipbuilding [1990] OJ L380/27 16–019

1991 Dir.91/440 on the development
of the Community's rail-
ways [1991] OJ L237/25 ...17–026,
17–027, 17–028
art.6 17–027
art.9 17–027

1991 Dir.91/676 on protection of waters against pollution
caused by nitrates from
agricultural sources [1991]
OJ L375/1 13–017

1992 Dir.92/81 on the harmonization
of the structures of excise
duties on mineral oils
[1992] OJ L316/12 3–035,
20–028

1993 Dir.93/76 to limit carbon dioxide
emissions by improving en-
ergy efficiency [1993] OJ
L237/28 22–051

1994 Dir.94/19 on deposit guarantee
schemes [1994] OJ
L135/5 19–015

1996 Dir.96/2 on the liberalisation of
the digital mobile telephone
market [1996] OJ L20/59 ...25–016

1996 Dir.96/75 on the systems of
      chartering and pricing in
      national and international
      inland waterways transport
      [1996] OJ L304/12 17–031
1996 Dir.96/82 on the control of
      major-accident hazards in-
      volving dangerous sub-
      stances [1997] OJ L10/13 22–079
1996 Dir.96/92 on the internal market
      in electricity [1997] OJ
      L27/20 .....3–086, 20–035, 20–036,
                                       20–058
      art.3(2) 20–061, 20–074, 20–076,
                                       20–077
      art.8(4) 20–061, 20–074, 20–076,
                                       20–077
      art.24 ....20–057, 20–058, 20–070
1998 Dir.98/30 on common rules for
      the internal market in natu-
      ral gas [1998] OJ L204/1 ...20–058
1999 Dir.1999/508 conditionally ap-
      proving aid granted by
      France to Societe Marseil-
      laise de Credit [1999] OJ
      L198/1 19–030
2000 Dir.2000/12 on the taking up and
      pursuit of the business of
      credit institutions (Banking
      Consolidated   Directive)
      [2000] OJ L126/1 19–001
2000 Dir.2000/13 on the approxima-
      tion of the laws of the
      Member States relating to
      labelling, presentation and
      advertising of foodstuff
      [2000] OJ L109/29 13–032
2000 Dir.2000/52 on the transparency
      of financial relations be-
      tween Member States and
      public undertakings [2000]
      OJ L193/75 .... 8–001, 8–015
      art.2 20–089
2000 Dir.2000/60 establishing a
      framework for Community
      action in the field of water
      policy [2000] OJ L327/1 13–027
      art.9 13–027
2001 Dir.2001/12 on the development
      of the Community's rail-
      ways [2001] OJ L75/1 17–027,
                                       17–027
2001 Dir.2001/23 on the approxima-
      tion of laws relating to the
      safeguarding or employees'
      rights in the event of under-
      takings, businesses or parts
      of undertakings or busi-
      nesses [2001] OJ L82/16 17–019

2001 Dir.2001/77 on the promotion of
      electricity produced from
      renewable energy sources
      in the internal electricity
      market   [2001]   OJ
      L283/33 22–070
2003 Dir.2003/54 on common rules
      for the internal market in
      electricity (Second Elec-
      tricity Directive) [2003] OJ
      L176/37 .... 20–058, 20–078,
              20–084 ....
      art.3(2) 14–045
      art.11(4) 14–045
      art.19(3) 20–094
2003 Dir.2003/55 on common rules
      for the internal market in
      natural   gas   [2003]   OJ
      L176/57 .... 20–084, 20–094
2003 Dir.2003/87 establishing a
      scheme for greenhouse gas
      emission allowance trading
      within the Community and
      amending   [2003]   OJ
      L275/32 .... 22–045, 22–084,
                               22–085, 22–086
      art.10 22–085
      Annex III criterion 5 22–085
2003 Dir.2003/89 on indication of the
      ingredients present in food-
      stuffs [2003] OJ L308/3 13–032
2003 Dir.2003/93 on mutual assis-
      tance by the competent au-
      thorities in the field of di-
      rect and indirect taxation
      [2003] OJ L264/23 13–033
      art.26(2) 13–033
      Annex I Table b 13–033
2003 Dir.2003/96 on the Community
      framework for the taxation
      of energy products and
      electricity   [2003]   OJ
      L283/51 ...3–035, 11–019, 13–033,
                 20–028, 20–029, 20–031,
                                       22–095
      art.4(2) 3–035, 20–028
      art.17 20–029
2004 Dir.2004/8 on the promotion of
      cogeneration based on a
      useful heat demand in the
      internal energy market
      [2004] OJ L52/50 22–010,
                                       22–072
2004 Dir.2004/35 on environmental
      liability with regard to the
      prevention and remedying
      of environmental damage
      [2004] OJ L143/56 22–077

2004   Dir.2004/109   [2004]   OJ
        L390/38
        art.2(1)(b) 9–014
2005   Dir.2005/81 on the transparency
        of financial relations be-
        tween Member States and
        public undertakings [2005]
        OJ L312/47 .... 8–015, 8–018,
                    13–012, 18–006, 24–010
2006   Dir.2006/32 on energy end use
        efficiency and energy serv-
        ices [[2006] OJ L114/64 ...22–010,
                                    22–051
2006   Dir.2006/111 on the transparen-
        cy of financial relations be-
        tween Member States and
        public undertakings [2006]
        OJ L318/17 ...8–001, 8–014, 8–015,
                        17–012, 19–006
        art.1(b) 8–014
        art.2 8–014
2007   Dir.2007/58 on the development
        of the Community's rail-
        ways [2007] OJ L315/44 17–040
2008   Dir.2008/1 on integrated pollu-
        tion prevention and control
        [2008] OJ L24/8 22–042
2008   Dir.2008/22 [2008] L76/50 9–014
2009   Dir.2009/12 [2009] OJ L70/11 ...14–083
2009   Dir.2009/28 on the promotion of
        the use of energy from re-
        newable sources [2009] OJ
        L40/16 ....20–052, 22–009, 22–047

2009   Dir.2009/29 on improvement
        and extension of the green-
        house gas emission allow-
        ance trading scheme [2009]
        OJ L140/63 ....22–009, 22–089
2009   Dir.2009/31 on the geological
        storage of carbon dioxide
        [2009] OJ L140/114 22–009,
                                    22–028
2009   Dir.2009/72 on common rules
        for the internal market in
        electricity   [2009]   OJ
        L211/55 ...20–058, 20–084, 20–085
        Preamble 20–086
        recital 29 20–086
        art.3 ....20–084, 20–087
        (2) 14–045
        (6) 20–086
        (8) 20–086
        art.15(4) 14–045
        art.19(3) 20–087, 20–095
        art.23(1)(e) 20–094
        art.31(3) 20–094
2009   Dir.2009/73 on common rules
        for the internal market in
        natural   gas   [2009]   OJ
        L211/94 .... 20–084, 20–094
        art.3 ....20–084, 20–087
        art.11 20–086
        art.19(3) 20–087, 20–095

TABLE OF GUIDELINES AND NOTICES

GUIDELINES

1989 Guidelines for the examination of state aids to Community shipping companies SEC (89) 921 final, September 4, 1989 17–049

1992 Guidelines on State aid for SMEs [1992] OJ C213 7–011
para.3.2 7–001

1993 Guidelines on public authorities' holdings in company capital 8–021

1994 Guidelines on rescue and re-structuring State aid 19–018, 19–020, 19–022, 20–054, 24–002, 24–015, 24–031, 24–046

1994 Guidelines on State aid for environmental protection [1994] OJ C72/3 22–003

1994 Guidelines on State aids in the aviation sector [1994] OJ C350/5 ....3–063, 8–020, 17–061, 17–063
para.1.3 24–008
para.43 24–008

1996 Guidelines on State aid for small and medium enterprises [1996] OJ C213/4 24–046

1996 Guidelines on State aid for undertakings in deprived urban areas [1997] OJ C146/6 1–042

1997 Guidelines on State aid to maritime transport [1997] OJ C205/5 .....8–020, 17–049, 17–050, 24–014

1997 Guidelines on State aid for rescue and restructuring firms in difficulty [1997] OJ C283/12 .... 24–016, 24–045
Pt 2.1 24–016
para.4.1 24–045

1998 Guidelines for the calculation of the amount of subsidy in countervailing duty investigations [1998] OJ C394/6 6–027
E(f)(ii) 6–028
pt 4.2 21–027

1998 Guidelines on national regional aid (RAG 1998) [1998] OJ C74/9 .....15–001, 14–032, 15–001, 15–026, 20–044, 21–006, 21–007, 21–008, 21–009, 21–012, 21–013, 21–014, 21–015, 21–019, 21–026, 21–027, 21–028, 21–032, 22–054, 22–055
pt 2 20–046
para.4.4 21–009
para.4.11 21–010
para.4.15 21–010
point 76 22–055

1999 Guidelines on State aid for rescue and restructuring firms in difficulty [1999] OJ C288/2 ...17–037, 19–018, 24–002, 24–013, 24–016, 24–045, 24–046
point 23 .... 19–018, 19–021, 20–054
point 37 19–024

2000 Guidelines for State aid in the agriculture sector [2000] OJ C28, Corrigendum [2000] OJ C232 ... 13–012, 13–017

2001 Guidelines for State aid for advertising of products listed in Annex I to the EC Treaty and of certain non-Annex I products [2001] OJ C252/5 .... 13–012, 13–032

2001 Guidelines for State aid concerning TSE tests, fallen stock and slaughterhouse waste [2002] OJ C324 13–012

2001 Guidelines on risk capital [2001] OJ C235/3 ...4–017, 4–054, 4–055, 4–058, 4–059

para.VI 4–056
para.VI.2 4–017
para.VI.3 4–017
para.VII 4–056
para.VIII 4–056, 4–057

2001   Guidelines on State aid for envi-
     ronmental   protection
     [2001] OJ C37/3 ...13–020, 13–025,
            13–035, 22–003, 22–004,
            22–005, 22–038, 22–046,
            22–054, 22–059, 22–061,
            22–064, 22–079, 22–080,
            22–083, 22–093, 22–095
Ch.F 22–082, 22–083
points 29–30 22–046
point 30 22–064
point 32 .... 22–063, 22–064
point 34–37 22–046
point 36 22–064
point 37 22–064
point 51.1(a) 22–095
  (b) 22–095
point 51.2 22–095
point 61 22–070
point 62 22–070
point 69 22–082
point 70 22–082
point 71 22–082
point 173 13–035

2004   Guidelines on State aid for res-
     cuing   and   restructuring
     firms in difficulty (R & R
     Guidelines)   [2004]   OJ
     C244/2 ....1–038, 4–026, 7–003,
            8–078, 9–032, 11–006,
            13–034, 13–035, 15–008,
            17–040, 17–050, 19–001,
            19–018, 19–025, 19–026,
            19–027, 19–028, 19–029,
            19–030, 19–032, 19–035,
            19–037, 19–039, 19–045,
            19–058, 19–058, 19–062,
            20–051, 20–054, 21–017,
            24–002, 24–013, 24–016
para.5 24–024
para.6 .... 24–001, 24–017
para.7 .... 24–036, 24–038
para.8 24–018
para.10 ....24–015, 24–045, 24–048,
                    24–051
para.11 24–015
para.13 24–016
paras 14–17 24–017
para.18 24–014
paras 19–22 24–019
para.23 24–050
para.25(a) 19–018
  (b) 24–021
paras 25–30 24–020
para.27(a) 24–022

para.26 24–022
para.27 24–022
para.30 24–048
para.31 .... 19–019, 24–038
paras 31–71 24–027
Pt 3.2(ii) 24–038
Pt 3.2.2 24–012
para.34 24–028
paras 38–42 24–038
para.43 24–035
para.52 24–029
paras 52–54 24–029
paras 55–56 24–031
para.57(a) 24–040
paras 57–59 24–032
paras 60–67 24–033
para.62 24–033
paras 68–71 24–034
para.70 19–039
Pt 3.3 13–039
para.72 24–024
paras 72–76 24–024
para.73 20–071
Pt 4 24–045
paras 78–86 24–045
Pt 5 .... 13–039, 24–040
paras 87–98 24–051
para.99–101 24–052

2004   Guidelines on State aid to mar-
     itime transport [2004] OJ
     C13/3 .....17–003, 17–049, 17–050,
           17–051, 17–052, 17–053,
                17–054, 17–056

2005   Guidelines on financing of air-
     ports and start-up aid to air-
     lines deporting from re-
     gional airports [2005] OJ.
     C312/1 .....3–073, 17–003, 17–078,
                  17–081, 17–082
recital 15 17–079
recital 17 17–078
recital 20 17–078
recital 21 17–078
recital 39 17–079
recitals 46–52 17–078
recital 57 17–080
recital 58 17–080
recital 72 17–084
recital 74 17–084
para.4.2 17–080
para.4.3 17–080
para.40 17–079
para.41 17–079
para.76 17–084
para.78(b) 17–084
para.83 17–081

2006 Guidelines on national regional
aid for 2007–2013 (RAG)
[2006] OJ C54/13 ...1–006, 13–019,
13–034, 13–035, 13–049,
15–002, 15–004, 15–007,
15–008, 15–008, 15–009,
15–012, 15–013, 15–015,
15–027, 15–028, 15–029,
15–033, 21–012, 21–013,
21–015, 21–016, 21–017,
21–021, 21–022, 21–028,
21–030, 21–034, 21–035,
22–001, 23–001, 24–014
s.2 15–008
para.8 21–017
para.10 21–021
para.16 21–020
para.19 21–021
para.34 .... 15–008, 21–026
para.35 15–008
para.36 .... 15–004, 15–008, 21–027
para.37 15–008
para.38 15–008
para.39 15–008
para.40 15–008
para.41 21–022
para.44 21–022
para.47 21–025
para.49 21–022
para.51 15–004
para.55 21–028
para.58 21–029
s.4.3 15–002
para.60 15–004
para.63 15–015
para.64 18–034
para.65 .... 15–005, 15–009, 15–025
para.67 15–008
para.68 .... 15–006, 15–009, 15–013,
15–015, 15–028, 15–028, 15–031,
15–033
para.70 15–010
s.4.4 15–008
para.71 21–031
para.76 21–032
para.81 .... 4–053, 21–032
para.86 21–033
para.88 21–033
para.89 21–033
Annex I 14–073
Annex IV 21–023
2006 Guidelines on research and development (R & D) 4–017
2006 Guidelines on State aid to promote risk capital invest-
ments in small and medium
sized enterprises [2006] OJ
C194/2 ....2–038, 4–054, 4–060,
4–061, 4–062, 11–021
s.4.2 point (d) 11–021

s.5 4–061
2007 Guidelines for State aid in the
agriculture and forestry
sector 2007 to 2013 [2006]
OJ C319/01 .... 13–006, 13–012,
13–014, 13–015, 13–016,
13–017
para.21 13–003
Ch.IV.A 13–016
Ch.IV.B 13–019
Ch.IV.C 13–020
para.56 13–020
para.89 13–021
Ch.IV.H 13–021
Ch.IV.J 13–022
Ch.IV.K 13–023
Ch.IV.L 13–024
Ch.V.B.2 13–026
Ch.V.B.3 13–027
para.125(g) 13–027
Ch.V.B.4 13–028
Ch.V.B.5 13–029
Ch.V.C 13–030
Ch.VI.D 13–032
Ch.VI.F 13–033
Ch.VII 13–035
Ch.VIII 13–008
para.194 13–032
para.196 13–017
2008 Guidelines for the examination
of State aid to fisheries and
aquaculture [2008] OJ
C84/10 ....13–047, 13–048, 13–049
2008 Guidelines on State aid for environmental protection
[2008] OJ C82/1 ... 3–115, 11–018,
13–033, 13–034, 13–048,
14–010, 14–061, 20–051,
20–052, 22–001, 22–004,
22–006, 22–008, 22–009,
22–012, 22–013, 20–014,
22–015, 22–017, 22–026,
22–027, 22–029, 22–031,
22–032, 22–033, 22–035,
22–033, 22–040, 22–043,
22–045, 22–047, 22–048,
22–049, 22–050, 22–052,
22–061, 22–065, 22–067,
22–075, 22–076, 22–079,
22–096, 22–098, 22–099
point 4 22–004
point 5 22–011
point 6 .... 22–004, 22–027
point 8 22–004
points 12–16 22–023
point 16 22–014
point 21 22–013
point 22 22–013
point 27 .... 20–056, 22–015
points 30–35 22–015

point 31 .... 22–034, 22–071
point 32 22–063
points 36–37 22–016
points 42–46 22–076
para.1.5.1 22–041
point 45 22–049
points 48–52 22–040
point 51 20–029
point 53 22–077
point 54 22–079
point 55 22–082
point 60 22–031
point 61 22–031
point 63 22–031
point 67 22–029
point 69 22–028
para..2.2 .... 22–003, 22–036
point 70 .... 20–052, 22–043
    (1) 22–079
    (11) 22–072
    (22) 22–036
    (23) 22–036
    (25) 22–003
    (27) 22–078
s.3 24–033
para.3.1.1 .... 22–041, 22–044, 22–050,
                                              22–075
points 74–75 22–041
point 76 22–045
points 76–77 22–042
point 78 .... 22–043, 22–045
point 79 22–044
point 80 22–034
point 81 .... 22–035, 22–052
points 81–83 22–076
point 82 22–038
point 83 22–052
point 84 22–044
point 85 22–047
point 87 22–049
point 88 22–049
point 90 11–018
para.3.1.4 22–050
points 91–93 22–050
para.3.1.5 .... 22–029, 22–050
point 98 22–038
point 100 22–071
para.3.1.6 .... 22–050, 22–074
point 105 22–035
para.3.1.6.2 22–073
point 109(b) 22–067
para.3.1.7 22–074
point 112 22–072
para.3.1.9 .... 22–027, 22–075
points 126–129 22–075
point 130 .... 22–035, 22–076
point 131 .... 22–038, 22–076
points 132–134 22–077
para.3.1.11 22–027
point 135 22–079

point 136 22–079
point 138 22–079
para.3.1.12 22–027
points 140–141 22–025
point 147 20–050
points 147–150 22–029
Ch.5 22–081
points 171–173 22–015
point 174 22–015
para.5.2.2 22–016
2008 Guidelines on State aid for rail-
         way undertakings [2008]
         OJ C184/13 .... 17–004, 17–006,
                          17–027, 17–028, 17–039,
                                                   17–040
recitals 3–4 17–028
recital 15 .... 17–028, 17–029
recital 19 17–029
recital 20 17–029
para.9 17–027
2009 Guidelines for the application of
         State aid rules in relation to
         rapid deployment of broad-
         band networks 1–015, 3–070,
                                                   3–072
para.51 3–070
para.73 3–070
para.75 3–070
para.79 3–070

NOTICES

1983 Notice [1983] OJ C318/03 25–064
1989 Notice (N 340/89) Concerning
         Preliminary Procedure for
         Aid [1990] OJ C103/9 25–029
1992 Notice on aid granted by Italy to
         certain regions in the Mez-
         zogiorno   [1992]   OJ
         C240/7 3–057
1992 Notice on aid which Spain plans
         to grant to Fundix [1992]
         OJ C198/9 3–057
1993 Notice on State aid to the Opel
         Group [1993] OJ C43/14 ... 4–015
1993 Notice concerning aid to SCA
         Aylesford, a manufacturer
         of a newsprint in the UK
         [2993] OJ C46/5 4–032
1995 Notice on cooperation between
         national courts and the
         Commission in the State
         aid field [1995] OJ C312/8 ...1–036,
                                  25–043, 27–052
1996 Notice on the de minimis rule
         for State aid [1996] OJ
         C68/9 ....3–077, 3–079, 7–011
1996 Notice of the procedure provid-
         ed for in Article 88 [1996]
         OJ C311/12 8–053

1997   Notice on the method for setting the reference and discount rates [1997] OJ C273/3 22–057

1998   Notice concerning aid to Everts Erfurt [1998] OJ C97/8 8–080

1998   Notice on the application of the State aid rules to measures relating to direct business taxation [1998] OJ C384/3 ...1–010, 3–045, 3–046, 3–048, 3–049, 3–107, 10–002, 22–094, 23–011
        para.13(2) 3–049
        para.14 3–051
        para.26 3–049
        para.27 3–049

2000   Notice on Guarantees [2000] OJ C71/14) 5–007, 9–001, 26–010

2002   Notice on the determination of applicable rules for the assessment of unlawful state aid [2002] OJ C119/22 ....4–043, 25–042

2005   Notice on a simplified procedure for treatment of certain concentrations [2005] OJ C56/04 11–028

2007   Notice towards an effective implementation of Commission decisions ordering Member States to recover unlawful and incompatible State aid (Recovery Notice) [2007] OJ C272/4 ....26–002, 26–008, 26–012, 26–014
        para.50 26–012
        para.61 26–014
        paras 63–67 26–014
        para.68 26–015

2008   Notice on the application of Articles 87 and 88 of the EC Treaty to State aid in the form of guarantees [2008] OJ C155/02 .... 11–010, 9–001, 9–004, 9–006, 9–010, 9–011, 9–012, 9–013, 9–015, 9–017, 9–018, 9–019, 9–020, 9–021, 9–022, 9–023, 9–025, 9–026, 17–012, 19–004, 19–008

para.1.2 .... 9–006, 19–009
para.2.1 .... 9–010, 9–011
para.2.2 ....9–001, 9–021, 19–004
para.2.3.1 .... 9–003, 19–004
paras 2.3.1–2.3.2 9–021
para.2.3.2 .... 9–026, 19–004
s.3 9–002
para.3.1 .... 9–002, 9.012
para.3.2 .... 9–014, 19–008
    (c) 9–014, 9–019
    (d) 9–014
para.3.3 9–015
para.3.4 9–016
    (f) 9–016
para.3.6 .... 9–013, 9–018
para.4.1 .... 9–004, 9–023
    (c) 9.019
para.4.2 19–008
paras 4.2–4.5 9–023
para.5.2 9–025
para.5.3 9–025

2009   Notice on a Best Practice Code on the conduct of State aid control proceedings [2009] OJ C136/13 .... 1–022, 25–025, 25–026

2009   Notice on a simplified procedure for certain types of aid [2009] OJ C136/3 25–025
        s.2 25–025
        s.3 25–025
        para.1 25–025
        para.15 25–025
        para.16 25–025

2009   Notice on the enforcement of State aid by national courts [2009] OJ C851/22 ....1–036, 25–043, 27–051, 27–053
        s.3 25–043
        para.90 25–043

TABLE OF TREATIES AND CONVENTIONS

Accession Treaty [2003] OJ L236/797 ...5–001,
    5–004, 5–005, 5–006, 5–009,
    5–012, 5–014, 5–015, 5–018,
    5–020, 5–021, 14–065, 14–070,
    13–049, 20–065
  art.22 .... 5–005, 13–011
  art.33h 13–010
  art.36 5–020
  art.37 5–020
  art.38 5–020
  Annex II Ch.6 (26.1) 13–010
  Annex IV 5–005, 5–007, 5–016, 5–018,
    5–019, 13–011, 14–070, 14–072
    Ch.3 .... 5–005, 5–009
    (1) 5–018
      (a) 5–005
      (b) 5–005
      (c) 5–005, 5–006, 5–009, 5–018,
        21–012
    (2) 5–005
    (4) 5–006, 5–018, 5–019
    Ch.4 5–018
    (3) 13–011
    (4) 5–019, 13–011
    Appendix 5–005
  Annex XIV 5–017
    Ch.4(2) 5–017
    (e) 5–017
  Protocol 2 ...5–014, 5–015, 4–017, 14–067,
    14–068
    art.1 5–014
    art.7 5–016
    Annex I 5–015
    Annex II 5–015
  Protocol 8 ....5–014, 5–015, 5–016, 5–017,
    14–067, 14–069, 14–070, 14–071,
    14–072, 14–073
    art.6 5–014
    art.7 .... 5–016, 14–072
    Annex I 5–015
    Annex II 5–015
Accession Treaty with Romania and
  Bulgaria [2005] OJ L157 ... 5–001, 5–020,
    5–021, 5–022, 5–023, 14–075
  art.39 5–020
  Annex V Ch.2 5–021

  (5) 5–021
Annex VII 5–021, 5–023
  Ch.4(B) 5–023
Annex VIII 13–010
  Appendix 5–021
Protocol 2 5–021
  art.9(4) 14–075
  Annex VII 4–076, 14–078
  Appendix A 4–076, 14–078
Act concerning the conditions of acces-
  sion of the Republic of Bulgaria
  and Romania and the adjustments
  to the treaties on which the Euro-
  pean Union is founded 2005 [2005]
  OJ L157/203 13–010
Act concerning the conditions of acces-
  sion of the Czech Republic, the Republic of Estonia, the Republic of
  Cyprus, the Republic of Latvia, the
  Republic of Lithuania, the Republic of Hungary, the Republic of
  Malta, the Republic of Poland, the
  Republic of Slovenia and the Slovak Republic and the adjustments
  to the Treaties on which the European Union is founded 2003[2003]
  OJ L236/369 13–010
Act concerning the conditions of acces-
  sion of the Kingdom of Norway,
  the Republic of Austria, the Republic of Finland and the Kingdom
  of Sweden and the adjustments to
  the Treaties on which the European
  Union is founded 1994 [1994] OJ
  C241/1 ....5–004, 5–007, 13–009
  arts 132–140 13–009
  art.142 13–009
  art.172 .... 13–009, 25–014
  (5) 5–004
Act of Accession 1972
  Protocol No.3 art.1(2) 13–011
Agreement between the EFTA States on
  the Establishment of a Surveillance
  Authority and a Court of Justice
  [1998] OJ C38/6
  art.3 .... 25–070, 25–072

Protocol 3 25–069
  Pt I 25–069
  Pt II 25–069
  art.1(3) 25–073
Agreement establishing an association between the European Economic Community and Malta [1971] OJ L61 5–002
Agreement establishing an Association between the Republic of Cyprus and the European Economic Community [1973] OJ L133 5–002
Agreement on export credits for the ships adopted under the OECD, April 15, 2002 16–009
Agreement on Implementation of Article VII of the General Agreement of Tariffs and Trade 1994 6–013
Agreement on the European Economic Area (EEA Agreement) [1994] OJ L1/3 ....3–136, 4–011, 4–039, 5–004, 5–005, 5–027, 5–028, 25–008, 25–032, 25–071, 25–072, 25–073
  Pt VII 4–039
  art.6 25–072
  art.7 25–071
  art.61 25–073
    (1) 3–137, 5–028, 10–006
    (2) 3–137, 4–011, 5–028
    (3) 3–137
  art.62 ....3–137, 4–011, 25–008
    (d) 4–039
  art.63 .... 3–137, 25–072
  arts 92–94 4–039
  Annex XV 3–137, 25–072
  Protocol 26 .... 25–069, 25–070
  Pt I 25–069
  Pt II 25–069
  Protocol 27 ....25–032, 25–069, 25–073
  Protocol 35 25–072
Basel Accords, July 2005 8–057
Code on aid to the synthetic fibres industry [1996] OJ C94/11 15–001
Declaration of the Fourth Ministerial Conference in Doha 2001 WT/MIN(01)/DEC/1 (2001) 6–021, 6–026
Declaration to the Final Act of the Lisbon Treaty [2007] OJ C306/231 20–003
Doha Work Programme; Ministerial Declaration November 14, 2001 WT/MIN(01)/DEC/1 (2001) 6–026
EC Treaty 1957 ....8–063, 14–006, 14–058, 19–001, 19–009, 20–003, 20–004, 22–065, 26–009
  art.3(1)(g) 12–004
  art.16 8–002
  art.25 (now art.30 TFEU) 3–131
  art.28 (now art.34 TFEU) 10–005, 12–017
  art.31 5–003

art.43 (now art.49 TFEU) 10–005
art.67(1) 19–001
art.69 19–001
art.71 (now art.91 TFEU) 3–126
art.81 (now art.101 TFEU) 3–120
  (1) (now art.101(1) TFEU) 3–120, 5–021
art.82 (now art.102 TFEU) 3–120
art.83(3)(c) (now art.107 TFEU) ... 22–027
art.86(2) 8–037
art.87 (now art.107 TFEU) ...5–013, 4–016, 9–001, 14–004, 20–003
  (1) (now art.107(1) TFEU) 8–029, 10–005, 10–013, 10–020
  (3)(a) (now art.107(3)(a)) 4–020
    (c) (now art.107(3)(c)) 4–020, 22–083
  (d) (now art.107(3)(d) 4–035
art.87 *et seq.* (now art.107 *et seq*) 10–020
arts 87–89 (now arts 107–109) 20–003
art.88 (art.108 TFEU) 5–017, 9–001, 14–004, 17–026, 20–003, 26–001, 26–009
  (1) 22–055
  (2) (now art.108(2) TFEU) 5–008, 12–005, 14–069
  (3) (now art.108(3) TEFU) 22–055, 26–001, 26–003
art.89 (now art.109 TFEU) 3–126
art.90 (now art.110 TFEU) 3–131
art.92(2) (now art.107(2)) 8–080
  (a) 17–064
  (c) (now art.107(2)(c) TFEU) 24–005
  (3) (now art.107(3)) 8–080
  (a) (now art.107(3)(a) TFEU) ...8–080, 24–005
  (c) (now art.107(3)(c) TFEU) 17–065, 24–004, 24–006
art.93(2) (now art.108(2) TFEU) 17–068, 17–069, 24–004, 24–006, 24–007, 25–027, 25–061, 26–008
  (3) (now art.88 TFEU) 17–067
art.94 (now art.109 TFEU) 25–021
art.107(1) 10–005
art.109 (now art.131 TFEU) 4–025
art.175 (now art.232 TFEU) 25–044
art.226 (now art.258 TFEU) 3–112
art.228 .... 1–035, 27–009
art.230 25–062
  (5) (now art.263 TFEU) 25–062
art.295 (now (art.345 TFEU) 24–008
art.299(2) 13–016
art.305(1) 20–003
  (2) 20–003, 20–008
Annex I 5–018, 21–017
Protocol 8–004

Europe Agreement establishing an association between the European Communities and their Member States, of the one part, and the Czech Republic, of the other part [1994] OJ L360 5–002
art.46(2) 5–013
art.64(6) 5–003

Europe Agreement establishing an association between the European Communities and their Member States, of the one part, and the Republic of Bulgaria, of the other part [1994] OJ L358 5–020
Protocol 2 art.9(4) 5–022
Additional Protocol 5–022
art.3 5–023

Europe Agreement establishing an association between the European Communities and their Member States, of the one part, and the Republic of Estonia, of the other part [1998] OJ L68 5–002
art.63(6) 5–003

Europe Agreement establishing an association between the European Communities and their Member States, of the one part, and the Republic of Hungary, of the other part [1993] OJ L347 5–002
art.62(6) 5–003

Europe Agreement establishing an association between the European Communities and their Member States, of the one part, and the Republic of Latvia, of the other part [1998] OJ L26 5–002
art.64 5–002
(6) 5–003

Europe Agreement establishing an association between the European Communities and their Member States, of the one part, and the Republic of Lithuania, of the other part [1998] OJ L51 5–002
art.64(6) 5–003

Europe Agreement establishing an association between the European Communities and their Member States, of the one part, and Romania, of the other part [1994] OJ L357 5–020

Europe Agreement establishing an association between the European Communities and their Member States, of the one part, and the Republic of Poland, of the other part [1993] OJ L348 5–002
art.63(6) 5–003
Protocol 2 art.8(4) 5–014

Europe Agreement establishing an association between the European Communities and their Member States, of the one part, and the Republic of Slovakia, of the other part [1994] OJ L359 5–002
art.64(6) 5–003
Protocol 2 14–074

Europe Agreement establishing an association between the European Communities and their Member States, of the one part, and the Republic of Slovenia, of the other part [1999] OJ L51 5–002
art.65(4)(a) 5–003
(60 5–003

European Atomic Community Treaty (Euratom Treaty) 1957 ..... 3–135, 20–001, 20–002, 20–003, 20–004, 20–008, 20–009, 20–010, 20–012
recital 3 20–005
art.2 20–002
art.4 20–002
art.5 20–004
art.6 20–004
(d) 20–004
art.30 20–004
art.34 20–004
art.37 20–004
Ch.IV (arts 40–44) 20–004
art.67 20–005
art.97 20–002
art.192 20–005
Annex 1 20–002

European Charter of Fundamental Rights [2000] OJ C364/1
art.41 1–023
(2) 1–031
art.42 1–034
art.47 1–021

European Convention on Human Rights 1950
art.6 25–031

EU-Korea Free Trade Agreement 6–032
art.11.11 6–032
art.11.12 6–032
art.11.15(2) 6–032

Final Act Embodying the Result of the Uruguay Round of Multilateral Trade Negotiations 6–013

GATT Subsidies Code 6–010

General Agreement on Tariffs and Trade 1947 (GATT) 3–002, 6–001, 6–011
art.VI 6–002, 6–003
art.VI.5 .... 6–018, 6–019
art.XI 6–007
art.XVI 3–002, 6.002, 6–003, 6–006
s.B.2 6–002
art.XXIII 6–002, 6–003, 6–011

General Agreement on Tariffs and Trade
1994 16–015
General Agreement on Trade in Servic-
es (GATS) 6–003, 6–032
art.I.2 6–026
art.XV 6–026, 6–032
Implementing Rules for candidate
countries 5–003
art.1 5–003
art.4 5–003
Interim Agreement on trade and trade-
related matters between the European Community and the Republic
of Croatia [2001] OJ 330/3 5–024
Inter-institutional Agreement on budgetary discipline and sound financial
management [2006] OJ C139/01 ...13–006
Kyoto Protocol to the UN Framework
Convention on Climate Change
1997 ....22–062, 22–082, 22–084
Marrakech Agreement establishing the
World trade Organisation
Annex 1A 6.003, 6–022
Protocol concerning the conditions and
arrangements for admission of the
republic of Bulgaria and Romania
to the European Union [2005] OJ
L157/29 14–075
Rules of Procedure of the Court of
Justice
art.83 27–042
(2) 27–042
Rules of Procedure of the General
Court
art.104 27–042
Schengen Agreement 1985 5–027
Single European Act 1986 22–002
Small Business Act 2008 11–003
Stabilisation and Association Agree-
ment between the European Com-
munities and their Member States,
of the one part, and the Republic of
Croatia, of the other part [2005] OJ
L26 5–024
Steel Aid Code of the European Coal
and Steel Community 5–014
art.6(5) 14–055
Steel Aid Code of the European Coal
and Steel Community (Second) 14–058
Steel Aid Code of the European Coal
and Steel Community 1985
(Third) 14–052, 14–058
Steel Aid Code of the European Coal
and Steel Community 1989
(Fourth) 14–052
Steel Aid Code of the European Coal
and Steel Community (Fifth) 14–052
Steel Aid Code of the European Coal
and Steel Community (Sixth) 14–055

Treaty between the Kingdom of Belgium, the Kingdom of Denmark,
the Federal Republic of Germany,
the Hellenic Republic, the Kingdom of Spain, the French Republic,
Ireland, the Italian Republic, the
Grand Duchy of Luxembourg, the
Kingdom of the Netherlands, the
Republic of Austria, the Portuguese Republic, the Republic of
Finland, the Kingdom of Sweden,
the United Kingdom of Great Britain and Northern Ireland (Member
States of the European Union) and
the Czech Republic, the Republic
of Estonia, the Republic of Cyprus,
the Republic of Latvia, the Republic of Lithuania, the Republic of
Hungary, the Republic of Malta,
the Republic of Poland, the Republic of Slovenia, the Slovak Republic, concerning the accession of the
Czech Republic, the Republic of
Estonia, the Republic of Cyprus,
the Republic of Latvia, the Republic of Lithuania, the Republic of
Hungary, the Republic of Malta,
the Republic of Poland, the Republic of Slovenia and the Slovak Republic to the European Union
[2003] OJ. L236/1
art.7 13–009
art.9 13–009
Treaty of Amsterdam 1997 .... 8–004, 8–026,
22–002
Protocol 9 .... 18–002, 18–003
Treaty of Paris establishing the European Coal and Steel Community
1952 (ECSC Treaty) 3–002, 3–122,
3–135, 4–001, 4–038, 14–001,
14–003, 14–004, 14–006, 14–008,
14–014, 14–052, 14–054, 14–058,
14–060, 14–062, 20–001, 20–002,
20–003, 20–054, 27–012, 27–043
art.2 14–003
art.3 14–003
art.4 .... 14–003, 14–057
(c) 3–002, 10–013, 14–003, 14–005,
14–054, 20–032
art.39 27–043
art.67 .... 14–003, 14–057
(2) 14–057
(3) 14–003, 20–032
art.95 ....14–053, 14–054, 14–055
(1) 14–003, 14–005
Annex 1 .... 14–004, 14–073
Protocol 2 art.5 5–024
Treaty on European Union 1992 (Maas-
tricht Treaty) ....
art.4(3) 8–007, 26–013

Treaty on the Functioning of the European Union 2008 (Treaty of Lisbon) [2008] OJ C115/47 .... 1–001, 3–002, 3–018, 4–008, 5–001, 5–007, 5–029, 10–004, 10–013, 10–020, 12–004, 14–001, 14–062, 14–073, 14–080, 18–002, 18–003, 18–018, 19–035, 19–060, 20–001, 20–002, 20–004, 20–006, 20–009, 20–032, 22–001, 22–013, 22–014, 22–016, 22–030, 22–032, 22–036, 22–097, 27–009

art.2(c) 17–012

(d) 17–012

art.4(3) 13–004

art.10(3) 27–021

art.11 (ex art. 6 EC) 22–002, 22–012

art.14 .... 8–002, 8–047

art.18 (ex art.12 EC) 3–109

art.28 3–110

art.30 (ex art.25 EC) 3–129, 10–004, 10–005

art.34 ....3–110, 3–111, 3–112, 3–113, 3–114, 10–004, 13–032, 13–041, 26–021

art.35 3–110

art.36 13–008

art.37 .... 3–110, 3–116

Title III (arts 38–44) 13–002

art.39 13–002

art.40 13–004

art.42 .....3–123, 13–002, 13–003, 13–006, 13–008, 13–042

art.43 .....3–117, 13–002, 13–003, 13–004, 13–006, 13–042

art.49 ....3–110, 3–117, 3–118, 10–004

art.56 .... 3–110, 10–004

art.63 10–004

art.66 4–044

art.80 17–062

arts 81–82 3–119

art.87 .... 13–012, 17–023

(1) 17–023

(2)(b) 11–025

(3)(b) 22–086

art.88 ....3–113, 4–038, 13–012

(1) 13–011

(2) 17–045, 17–068, 17–068, 24–030

(b) 17–045

(3) 13–011, 17–068

arts 90–107 17–062

art.92(2)(a) 17–064

art.93 (ex art.73 EC) 3–126, 8–029, 17–001, 17–002, 17–003, 17–006, 17–008, 17–014, 17–015, 17–016, 17–023, 17–029, 17–044, 17–049

art.96 .... 17–001, 17–002

art.100 .... 3–128, 17–003

(2) 17–003

art.101 ....1–008, 1–043, 3–079, 3–120, 5–001, 19–013, 20–039, 25–001, 25–004, 25–038, 25–055, 25–060, 27–021, 27–037

(1) 3–120

(3) 3–120

art.102 ....1–008, 1–043, 3–079, 3–120, 5–001, 8–033, 18–011, 25–001, 25–004, 25–055, 25–060, 27–021

art.106 ....3–127, 8–007, 8–017, 8–026, 8–029, 17–023, 18–003, 18–004

(1) 8–024, 8–033, 20–084

(2) (ex art.86(2) EC) 3–110, 3–126, 3–127, 4–001, 8–015, 8–025, 8–027, 8–028, 8–029, 8–030, 8–033, 8–035, 8–036, 8–037, 8–038, 8–041, 8–042, 8–045, 8–049, 8–062, 8–063, 10–036, 18–002, 18–003, 18–004, 18–006, 18–011, 20–057, 20–061, 20–073, 20–074, 20–076, 20–077, 20–078, 20–084, 20–085, 20–087, 24–043, 25–021, 27–036

(3) (ex art.86(3) EC) 1–017, 4–001, 8–001, 8–037, 8–043, 17–012, 25–021

art.107 ....3–001, 3–002, 3–005, 3–016, 3–021, 3–036, 3–037, 3–039, 3–041, 3–043, 3–054, 3–056, 3–057, 3–067, 3–076, 3–086, 3–106, 3–110, 3–111, 3–112, 3–113, 3–114, 3–119, 3–123, 3–134, 3–127, 3–128, 3–129, 3–135, 4–002, 4–030, 4–038, 4–040, 4–041, 5–003, 5–028, 7–003, 7–012, 8–007, 8–026, 8–027, 8–029, 8–030, 8–040, 8–045, 8–054, 8–067, 8–074, 10–002, 10–002, 10–005, 10–007, 12–014, 12–018, 12–021, 13–002, 13–005, 13–006, 13–014, 13–015, 13–035, 13–045, 14–072, 14–073, 17–001, 17–002, 17–003, 17–011, 17–023, 17–042, 17–063, 18–012, 18–018, 20–057, 20–084, 20–089, 20–090, 22–027, 22–091, 25–001, 25–003, 25–004, 25–035, 25–051, 26–019, 26–021, 27–050, 27–054, 27–057

(1) 1–003, 1–004, 1–024, 1–025,
1–026, 1–039, 3–001, 3–002,
3–004, 3–011, 3–012, 3–013,
3–014, 3–015, 3–017, 3–018,
3–019, 3–020, 3–021, 3–023,
3–027, 3–029, 3–032, 3–034,
3–035, 3–036, 3–037, 3–041,
3–042, 3–046, 3–048, 3–052,
3–057, 3–058, 3–061, 3–063,
3–064, 3–071, 3–073, 3–074,
3–076, 3–082, 3–088, 3–089,
3–098, 3–103, 3–107, 3–116,
3–117, 3–118, 3–120, 4–001,
4–002, 4–003, 4–044, 5–008,
7–001, 7–002, 7–011, 8–003,
8–010, 8–011, 8–013, 8–014,
8–020, 8–025, 8–026, 8–029,
8–030, 8–031, 8–033, 8–034,
8–036, 8–040, 8–053, 8–056,
8–063, 8–064, 9–001, 9–010,
9–011, 9–012, 10–005, 10–006,
10–007, 10–008, 10–010, 10–011,
10–012, 10–013, 10–014, 10–015,
10–016, 10–018, 10–019, 10–022,
10–023, 10–024, 10–025, 10–027,
10–030, 10–031, 10–033, 10–035,
10–036, 10–038, 10–039, 10–040,
10–041, 11–026, 12–001, 13–013,
13–040, 13–044, 17–002, 17–057,
17–064, 14–074, 18–002, 18–012,
19–001, 19–003, 19–005, 19–011,
19–013, 19–014, 19–015, 19–027,
19–041, 19–045, 20–008, 20–012,
20–014, 20–015, 20–019, 20–020,
20–021, 20–021, 20–028, 20–030,
20–032, 20–034, 20–035, 20–043,
20–052, 20–061, , 20–070,
20–075, 20–076, 20–078, 20–088,
20–089, 20–091, 20–094, 20–095,
21–012, 22–003, 22–017, 22–019,
22–023, 22–024, 22–025, 22–056,
22–080, 22–083, 22–088, 22–092,
22–093, 22–094, 23–009, 25–004,
25–005, 25–016, 25–021, 25–021,
25–055, 25–066, 26–022, 27–001,
27–035, 27–054

(2) 1–003, 1–004, 2–033, 3–001,
3–107, 3–110, 4–001, 4–002,
4–003, 4–006, 4–011, 8–021,
8–025, 8–029, 8–041, 10–005,
10–027, 10–041, 13–005, 13–011,
13–044, 14–080, 18–002, 20–041,
20–042, 20–085, 24–044, 25–001,
25–004, 25–021

(a) 4–004, 4–005, 10–005, 17–064,
20–042

(b) 4–006, 4–007, 4–009, 13–026,
17–062, 22–086

(c) 4–008, 4–009, 12–001, 13–027

(3) 1–003, 1–004, 1–026, 1–038,
2–033, 3–001, 3–107, 3–110,
3–114, 3–129, 4–001, 4–002,
4–003, 4–006, 4–008, 4–012,
4–013, 4–014, 4–022, 4–052,
5–028, 8–020, 8–021, 8–024,
8–025, 8–029, 8–036, 8–037,
8–041, 10–005, 10–027, 10–041,
12–002, 12–012, 13–011, 13–044,
14–063, 17–064, 14–086, 18–002,
19–036, 20–041, 20–043, 20–052,
20–076, 20–085, 21–018, 24–019,
25–001, 25–037, 27–001, 27–003,
27–036

(a) 3–074, 4–012, 4–019, 4–020,
4–021, 4–022, 4–030, 4–056,
5–003, 5–020, 11–025, 20–044,
20–046, 21–001, 21–003, 21–003,
21–005, 21–008, 21–009, 21–010,
21–011, 21–014, 21–015, 21–020,
21–021, 21–023, 21–024, 21–025,
21–032, 21–033, 21–034, 24–031,
24–039, 26–019

(b) 1–012, 3–074, 4–012, 4–023,
4–024, 4–025, 4–026, 7–013,
8–024, 9–029, 9–030, 14–080,
18–017, 19–001,19–027, 19–028,
19–029, 19–030, 19–031, 19–033,
19–035, 19–036, 19–039, 19–045,
19–058, 19–068, 19–072, 19–078,
20–050, 22–007, 22–029, 22–096,
23–006

(c) 3–071, 3–074, 3–115, 4–012,
4–015, 4–020, 4–021, 4–022,
4–030, 4–031, 4–033, 4–047,
4–056, 4–062, 8–024, 8–045,
8–076, 12–016, 12–017, 12–018,
12–019, 13–016, 13–035, 14–047,
14–061, 14–080, 15–002, 16–005,
17–014, 17–016, 17–041, 17–044,
17–058, 17–065, 17–068, 14–080,
18–016, 18–017, 18–018, 19–001,
19–018, 19–026, 19–027, 19–030,
19–032, 19–035, 19–078, 20–006,
20–009, 20–011, 20–030, 20–031,
20–044, 20–046, 20–047, 20–050,
20–051, 20–057, 20–061, 20–063,
20–070, 20–074, 20–081, 21–003,
21–004, 21–005, 21–008, 21–009,
21–011, 21–015, 21–021, 21–023,
21–024, 21–025, 21–033, 21–034,
22–004, 22–005, 22–013, 22–026,
22–027, 22–028, 22–029, 22–031,
22–046, 22–047, 22–051, 22–057,
22–059, 22–075, 22–078, 22–079,
22–083, 22–084, 22–086, 22–089,
22–095, 23–004, 24–012, 27–020

(d) 4–012, 4–033, 4–034, 4–035,
4–035, 4–037, 5–028, 25–029

(e) 4–001, 4–012, 4–038, 14–010,
14–021, 14–028, 14–047

art.107 *et seq* 10–001, 10–005, 10–017,
10–018, 10–041

arts 107–109 ....3–108, 3–123, 3–124,
3–128, 13–003, 13–006, 13–042,
13–043

art.108 ....3–001, 3–006, 3–036, 3–039,
3–043, 3–067, 3–076, 3–099,
3–106, 3–110, 3–111, 3–113,
3–119, 3–123, 3–124, 3–125,
3–127, 3–128, 3–133, 3–135,
4–002, 5–003, 5–007, 5–028,
7–003, 8–016, 8–017, 8–025,
8–029, 8–041, 8–044, 10–005,
12–018, 12–021, 13–002, 13–004,
13–006, 13–010, 13–011, 13–035,
13–045, 14–055, 14–072, 14–073,
17–001, 17–008, 17–023, 20–057,
20–084, 20–086, 25–001, 25–003,
25–031, 25–067, 25–069, 25–070,
26–017, 26–018, 26–019, 26–020,
27–050, 27–055, 27–059

(1) 1–017, 1–039, 4–001, 5–004,
5–021, 8–037, 13–003, 13–011,
19–009, 20–012, 24–052, 25–013,
25–018, 25–049, 25–050, 25–052,
25–066, 26–001, 27–025, 27–026,
27–029, 27–054

(2) 1–023, 1–031, 1–033, 1–035,
3–133, 4–001, 4–002, 4–034,
4–040, 4–041, 4–042, 5–015,
5–023, 8–071, 12–008, 12–012,
12–014, 12–016, 12–017, 12–018,
12–019, 13–003, 13–005, 13–005,
13–006, 14–062, 15–012, 19–082,
20–036, 20–056, 20–073, 24–003,
24–010. 24–011, 24–053, 25–002,
25–003, 25–004, 25–005, 25–009,
25–010, 25–011, 25–013, 25–015,
25–017, 25–018, 25–019, 25–028,
25–029, 25–030, 25–031, 25–035,
25–037, 25–038, 25–039, 25–041,
25–042, 25–043, 25–045, 25–045,
25–046, 25–047, 25–049, 25–053,
25–054, 25–063, 25–064, 25–065,
25–066, 25–066, 25–066, 25–067,
26–001, 26–009, 26–009, 26–011,
27–003, 27–004, 27–005, 27–006,
27–006, 27–007, 27–008, 27–013,
27–017, 27–019, 27–020, 27–021,
27–022, 27–023, 27–024, 27–025,
27–027, 27–028, 27–029, 27–031,
27–032, 27–033, 27–037, 27–039,
27–044, 27–048, 27–052, 27–053,
27–058

(b) 17–045

(3) 1–017, 3–015, 3–038, 3–067,
3–079, 3–130, 3–134, 4–011,
4–041, 4–041, 5–005, 5–021,
7–002, 8–029, 8–037, 8–043,
9–026, 9–027, 9–028, 11–001,
13–002, 13–006, 13–033, 15–002,
19–002, 19–004, 20–070, 22–032,
25–004, 25–005, 25–006, 25–007,
25–010, 25–013, 25–015, 25–017,
25–018, 25–021, 25–027, 25–038,
25–039, 25–042, 25–043, 25–055,
25–061, 25–064, 25–067, 26–001,
26–003, 26–009, 26–010, 26–021,
26–022, 27–001, 27–003, 27–015,
27–017, 27–019, 27–024, 27–028,
27–044, 27–050, 27–051, 27–053,
27–054, 27–055, 27–056, 19–036

art.109 ....3–001, 4–040, 7–011, 8–017,
13–006, 25–001, 25–035

art.110 (ex art.90 EC) 3–110, 3–128,
3–129, 3–131, 10–004, 10–005,
10–020, 10–024, 10–039, 13–032,
13–041, 25–004

art.113 10–003

art.114(2) 10–003

art.115 10–003

art.116 (ex art.96 EC) 3–105, 3–106,
10–005, 10–013, 10–029, 10–041

art.117 (ex art.97 EC) 3–105, 3–106,
10–005, 10–013, 10–041

art.121 (ex art.96 EC) 3–105

art.123 (ex art.101 EC) 3–105, 19–013

art.167 ....4–033, 4–035

(4) 4–033

art.174(2) 13–025

art.191 (ex Art.174) 22–002

art.191(2) 22–079

art.206 (ex art.131 EC) 4–045

art.226 .... 3–128, 13–003

art.232 27–039

art.258 ...3–125, 12–017, 27–003, 27–004,
27–005, 27–006, 27–008, 27–037

art.259 27–004

art.260 ....26–013, 27–008, 27–009

(1) 27–008

(2) (ex art.228(3) EC) .. 1–035, 27–008,
27–009, 27–011

art.262 1–027

art.263 ..14–046, 26–017, 27–004, 27–005,
27–005, 27–012, 27–013, 27–017,
27–018, 27–020, 27–021, 27–023,
27–024, 27–025, 27–029, 27–030,
27–031, 27–034, 27–038, 27–037,
27–039, 27–058, 27–059

(1) 8–063

(4) 1–027

art.265 ..25–054, 27–004, 27–005, 27–037,
27–038, 27–037, 27–039, 27–040

art.266 .... 27–007, 27–037

art.267 ..27–001, 27–050, 27–052, 27–058, 27–059, 27–060
art.268 27–048
art.278 .... 27–042, 27–044
art.279 .... 27–003, 27–042
art.297(2) 27–049
art.340 27–048
art.345 .... 8–007, 19–030
art.346 (ex art.296 EC) 3–133, 3–134, 8–073
(1)(b) 3–133
art.348 ......3–133, 3–134, 16–021, 16–027
art.349 ....4–053, 13–006, 13–011
Annex I 13–002, 13–007, 13–007, 13–008, 13–014, 13–032, 13–035
Annex II 3–123, 3–124
Protocol 26 on SGI 8–002
Protocol 27 12–004
UNESCO Convention on the Protection and Promotion of the Diversity of Cultural Expressions 18–002
WTO Agreement on Agriculture 6–003, 6–022, 6–023, 6–025
art.1(a) 6–025
(b) 6–025
(e) 6–023
art.2 6–022
art.3.1 6–002
art.3.2 6–022
art.3.3 6–022
Pt IV 6–022
art.6 .... 6–022, 6–025
art.6.1 6–025
art.6.4 6–025
art.7.1 6–025
art.7.2(a) 6–025
art.8 6–022
art.9 .... 6–022, 6–023
art.9.1 .... 6–022, 6–023
(a)–(f) 6–023
(c) 6–023, 6–024
art.10 6–022
art.10.1 6–023
art.10.2 6–023
art.10.3 6–023
art.10.4 6–023
art.13 6–022
art.21 6–022
Annex 2 6–025
Annex 3 6–025
Annex 4 6–025
WTO Agreement on Implementation of the General Agreement on Tariffs and Trade 1994 (AD Agreement) 6–021

WTO Agreement on Subsidies and Countervailing Measures (SCM Agreement) ...1–004, 6–001, 6.003, 6–004, 6.006, 6–007, 6–009, 6–010, 6–012, 6–013, 6–014, 6–019, 6–020, 6–021, 6–022, 6–025, 6–026, 6–027, 6–029, 6–032, 7–003, 10–017, 11–006, 16–013
art.1 ....6–005, 6–006, 6–007
art.1.1(a)(1) 6–006
(iii) 6–006
(iv) 6–006
(b) 6–007
(2) 6–005
art.1.2 6–008
art.2 .... 6–006, 6–008
(c) 6–008
art.2.3 6–008
art.2.4 6–008
art.3 ....6–010, 6–022, 7–003, 11–006
art.3.1(a) 6–010, 6–024
art.4 ....6–011, 6–012, 6–013
art.4.4 6–012
art.4.6 6–012
art.4.7 6–012
art.4.8 6–012
art.4.9 6–012
Pt III 6–020
art.5 .... 6–011, 6–022
art.6 6–011
art.6.1 ....6–009, 6–011, 6–020
art.6.3(a) 6–011
(b) 6–011
(c) 6–011
(d) 6–011
art.7 ....6–013, 6–020, 6–022
art.7.5 6–012
art.7.7 6–012
art.7.8 6–012
art.8 6–009
Pt V 6–013
art.10 6–013
art.11 6–016
art.12 6–016
art.13 6–016
art.14 ....6–007, 6–010, 6–015
(d) 6–017
art.15.1 6–014
art.15.2 6–014
art.15.4 6–014
art.15.5 6–014
art.18.1 6–015
art.19.2 6–027
art.19.3 6–015
art.19.4 6–015
art.21.3 6–016
art.22 6–016
art.24 6–012
art.25 6–030
art.27.1 6–020

art.27.8 6–020
art.27.9 6–020
arts 27.10–27.11 6–020
art.27.13 6–020
art.31 .... 6–009, 6–011

Annex I 6–010
Annex V 6–010
Annex VII(a) 6–020
   (b) 6–020

Part I

GENERAL

CHAPTER 1

EU STATE AID LAW—NOW A TRULY UGLY SISTER?*

1.	INTRODUCTION	1–001
	The framework of the fourth edition	1–003
2.	AIMS	1–008
3.	MAJOR DEVELOPMENTS AND FUTURE TRENDS	1–010
	The Union Courts	1–024
	Refining the concept of aid	1–025
	The scope of judicial review	1–026
	Locus standi	1–027
	State aid control and good governance	1–031
4.	BENEFICIARIES OF AID	1–033
5.	BLOCK EXEMPTIONS AND GUIDELINES	1–038
6.	CONCLUSION—TOWARDS A REORIENTATION	1–043

1. INTRODUCTION

The fourth edition of this book has been written at a time of considerable **1–001** challenges in European state aid policy and law. The role and impact of the EU state aid regime in the wake of the global financial crisis that followed the collapse of Lehman Brothers has been widely recognised and commented upon. The European Commission's response to the financial crisis is the subject of a new chapter in this fourth edition. But the financial crisis and its aftermath and its implications for the future of state aid control is not the only reason for a thorough updating of the third edition, published in 2006. By mid-2010 the Commission had already delivered on a large number of goals which it set itself in its State Aid Action Plan ("SAAP") of 2005; as a result, a large number of its soft law instruments or guidelines have been overhauled to bring them into line with the so-called "refined economic approach" discussed in greater detail below and in Ch.2 of this volume. In keeping with the aim to decentralise state aid control a new General Block Exemption, replacing the earlier sectoral block exemptions, was adopted in 2008. A separate new chapter of this edition analyses this measure in full. Given the continued flood of case law in the area of state aid

* Leigh Hancher

3

control, the fourth edition provides the reader with a comprehensive update and analysis as well as revised appendices. Although the new Treaty of Lisbon has little impact on the substantive and procedural rules of state aid control, it has brought with it a new system of numbering and a change of terminology, and we have used that new numbering and terminology throughout this volume, except in citations from the pre-Lisbon case law. This introductory chapter sets out the scope of the fourth edition and its aims, and then provides a review of major developments over the last five years, followed by some remarks on future trends in the development of this complex area of European law.

1–002   The scope of the fourth edition. A major difference between the third edition and the previous two editions was that we extended the coverage of the book to include separate chapters addressing a number of topics which are worthy of detailed coverage in their own right. These included a chapter on the economics of granting and controlling state aid, chapters on the various exemption regulations, chapters on different sectors, such as broadcasting, and chapters devoted to particular types of aid, such as state guarantees and aid through taxation, which raise particular problems The same approach is continued in this new fourth edition, which as mentioned, could not be complete without the addition of separate chapters devoted to aid to the financial sector and to the workings of the General Block Exemption mechanism.

  We have again been very fortunate to find a number of willing contributors for these chapters, contributors drawn from the Commission services, writing in a personal capacity, as well as from private practice and universities. The fourth edition is, as a result, a comprehensive treatment of EU state aids law, the primary focus of which is to provide a detailed examination of the substantive and procedural aspects of this complex area of the law.

The framework of the fourth edition

1–003   Part I deals with the general framework of art.107(1) and art.107(2) and (3). Chapter 2 provides a full examination of the application of economic analysis to the assessment of state aids.

  Chapter 3 aims to guide the reader through the complexities of the definition of aid for the purposes of art.107(1). Although the amount of case law on this vexed issue continues to expand, it is still difficult to conclude with any real conviction that this area of the law has stabilised. Although the Court of Justice resolved some past academic debates in its ruling in the *Preussen Elektra*[1] case as to the scope of art.107(1), rulings such as *Stardust Marine*[2] and *Pearle*[3] introduced new elements into the definition, casting some doubt on the value of older precedent. The recent rulings of the General Court in cases such as Case

---

[1] [2001] E.C.R. I–2099.
[2] [2002] E.C.R. I–4397.
[3] [2004] E.C.R. I–7139.

T–156/04 *EDF*[4] and as *France Telecom*[5] continue this well-established tradition. The former case has caused commentators to re-examine the role of the state in the exercise of its public prerogatives including its power to vary tax liabilities and to consider whether there is also room for the application of the market investor test in cases where the state uses taxation measures to restructure companies which it owns or controls. The second case may, if upheld on appeal, put a brake on the Commission's attempt to introduce a wide interpretation of the concept of "economic advantage". The scope of art.107(1) is returned to in various chapters, including the separate chapter on state aid and taxation where the element of selectivity remains a particularly problematic and controversial element in the definition of a state aid (Ch.10).

Chapter 4 deals with the automatic and discretionary exemptions under, **1–004** respectively, art.107(2) and (3). This chapter does not aim to provide an analysis of the various Commission horizontal and sectoral guidelines or the General Block Exemption Regulation. These are all dealt with in separate chapters— reflecting the growing sophistication (if not over-complexity)—of these guidelines and their application in Commission decision-making practice and the case law of the Union Courts.

Chapter 5 deals with the application of the state aid regime to the Member States which joined the European Union on May 1, 2004, and on January 1, 2007, and anticipates the accession of Croatia and Iceland. The fourth edition continues to provide a full analysis of the WTO Subsidies and Countervailing Measures Agreement. Chapter 6 discusses the WTO subsidy regime in detail in the light of the decisions of the WTO Panels and its Appellate Body. Chapter 7 deals with the complexities of the "de minimis" rule and the first amendments to the regulation.

Part II deals with specific issues and covers types of support which may fall **1–005** outside the scope of art.107(1) under certain conditions. Chapter 8 examines public sector aid, including aid to and through public undertakings. The case law of the Courts on compensation for the performance of services of general interest and the Commission's subsequent Decision and accompanying Framework of 2005 are considered in depth in this chapter. Chapter 9 deals with state guarantees, a favoured tool for intervention in the recent financial crisis. Chapter 10 addresses the complex issue of state aids and taxation, while Ch.11 provides a detailed examination of the General Block Exemption Regulation.

Although the Commission is committed to phasing out sectoral aid, and is **1–006** committed to a more horizontal approach which should deliver less and better targeted aid, separate sectoral treatment is required for those sectors which are subject to separate Treaty rules. Part III includes updated chapters on the sectoral aid (Ch.12), on agriculture (Ch.13), and on transport (Ch.17), as well as shipbuilding (Ch.15). The rules adopted for the coal and steel sectors following the

---

[4] [2009] E.C.R. II–4503.
[5] Case T–444/04 [2010] E.C.R. Unreported. See now AG Opinion on appeal, Case C–124/10P, handed down on October 20, 2011.

expiry of the ECSC still remain of relevance and are dealt with in Ch.14. Given the growth of the case law and the large number of Commission decisions, the chapter on broadcasting (Ch.18) first included in the third edition, has been substantially updated.

Even if the policy emphasis has gradually shifted away from special sectoral guidelines for synthetic fibres, automobiles and so on towards a more horizontal approach under the Regional Guidelines and the Framework for Large Investment Guidelines (Ch.15), the case law can only be understood in the light of these older and now extant guidelines and, for that reason, a brief summary of their contents has been included (see Ch.12).

1–007　Part IV is now once again expanded to reflect the growing emphasis on a horizontal approach to aid control in specific sectors. It includes chapters on broadcasting, the financial sector (Ch.9), energy (Ch.20), regional aid (Ch.21), environment (Ch.22), research and development (Ch.23), and rescue and restructuring aid (Ch.24). The last three types of aid are covered by detailed guidelines, whereas the energy sector is only subject to a Commission Communication or Methodology on Aid for so-called "stranded costs". The new chapter on the financial sector completes the sectoral line-up. Part V concentrates, as in the previous editions on the issues of administrative procedures (Ch.25), recovery (Ch.26) and judicial protection (Ch.27)—and all cover subject matter which has become increasingly complex in the wake of recent case law.

2. AIMS

1–008　Our main aim in the early editions of this book was to bring some coherence to bear in an area where it is repeatedly acknowledged by the Union Courts that the Commission must enjoy wide discretionary powers of assessment. State aid control remains beset by political and social considerations. While we predicted in the third edition that the introduction of a more economic-based analysis of national measures in the course of the Commission's assessment of individual aid measures or schemes may eventually militate in favour of a more coherent approach, that presumption still has to be put to empirical testing, and it is too early to draw any firm conclusions here. After all, it has taken almost a decade for economic analysis to permeate the application of arts 101 and 102 of the Treaty, and, even in this area of competition law, it cannot be assumed that the process is by any means complete.

1–009　By focusing on different topics in more detail in the 27 chapters, we are able to provide a more thorough-going analysis of the underlying rules and the ways in which they have been applied and developed by the Commission and, in an increasing number of instances, the courts. Nevertheless the primary target audience is expected to be those who have to deal with state aid issues on a regular basis—practising lawyers, government officials at all levels, regulatory authorities as well as industry—as (potential) beneficiary or complainant. It is with the aim of continuing to provide this audience with a comprehensive guide to the field of state aid law that the fourth edition of this book has also been compiled. Detailed, critical analysis of individual decisions, new guidelines and court rulings is to be found not only in the large number of academic publications on the subject of European state aids, but also in specialised journals, including reviews devoted entirely to the subject of state aids.

3. Major Developments and Future Trends

Less and better targeted aid. The second edition was published shortly after the **1–010** adoption of the Procedural Regulation of 1999 as well as the adoption of a number of key frameworks and guidelines, including the guidelines on rescue and restructuring aid, revised Regional Aid guidelines, revised environmental guidelines and the adoption of measures such as the Notice on Direct Taxation. The single most significant developments heralded in the third edition included the publication of the State Aid Action Plan, the "SAAP", in 2005 and the launching of the great debate on the role of economic analysis in the realm of state aid control.[6] The SAAP is structured around four pillars of reform: less and better targeted aid; a more refined economic approach; more effective procedures; and shared responsibility between the Union and Member States. With the launch of the SAAP, the introduction of the more refined economic approach attracted the most commentary given its innovativeness. There was a less enthusiastic response to the proposals to decentralise more responsibility to national authorities and indeed to allow national courts an enhanced role in assessing the compatibility of particular state measures. The results of the Commission's consultation procedure on the SAAP suggested that the proposal to delegate more powers to independent national authorities had generated the highest level of disapproval from respondents.[7]

The refined economic approach. In the fourth edition we can now assess, if to **1–011** a limited extent, the impact of the Commission's so-called "refined economic approach" to state aid cases over the last five years. As Ch.2 explains, the "refined economic approach" is now more clearly embraced in the numerous sets of guidelines which have been revised in the wake of the adoption of the SAAP. Following the SAAP reforms, the current architecture of state aid control is based on a "three-tiered" system: block exemption, standard assessment and detailed assessment. In respect of the last tier, the Commission must examine whether the aid measure is aimed at a well-defined objective of common interest and must be designed to address market failure, or whether its focus is other, equity-related objectives. The next step is to identify whether the aid measure is the appropriate policy instrument. Does it provide an appropriate incentive effect which modifies the behaviour of the recipient firm to do something it would not otherwise have

[6] COM(107) 2000, June 6, 2005.
[7] See the summary of the consultation exercise, published on February 9, 2006.

done without government intervention? The third and final step is to evaluate the proportionality of the aid measure. This involves considering both the positive and negative effects of the proposed aid measure—the so called "balancing test". All state aid that falls outside the scope of regulations and guidelines is subject to a detailed assessment and balancing test irrespective of the amount of aid or the size of the beneficiaries. Aid falling within the scope of the relevant regulations and guidelines will only be subject to a detailed assessment in cases involving large amounts of aid. The subsequent chapters of this fourth edition evaluate the application of the "refined economic approach" in greater detail in the different sectors of the European economy. It may however be noted here that there is one area of state aid law where the application of the test seems to be notable for its absence: the financial sector.

1–012 **The financial sector.** As discussed in Ch.19, the Commission has approved a massive, and indeed unprecedented, amount of aid to European banks in the period after October 2008, totalling more than 10 per cent of the European GDP, and yet in its detailed decisions on the restructuring plans submitted by the Member States in accordance with the various guidelines adopted by the Commission to shape its policy in this sector, there is no real attempt to apply the "refined economic approach". Indeed no mention is made of it in any of the temporary guidelines. It may be that the specifics of the rescue operations mounted by the Member States to prevent a "systemic" crisis in their banking sectors precluded such an approach, but economic commentators have lamented the Commission's failure to apply the test in its later decisions on restructuring.[8] This may also be partly due to the fact that the Commission has resorted to the rarely used art.107(3)(b), which allows for it to declare aid to be compatible with the Treaty where it remedies a serious disturbance in the economy of a Member State. The shift to a reliance on this article came in response to the call from the European Council of October 15, 2008 that expressly confirmed its support for the Commission's implementation of the state aid regime, but at the same time called for "speedy and flexible action".

1–013 By September 2011, the Commission had taken restructuring decisions on 24 banks. There have been a further 10 cases of orderly liquidation; but only one negative decision with recovery of the aid, in the case of a small Portuguese bank. As of October 2011 there are currently 19 restructuring cases in the pipeline and the Commission is expecting more before the end of 2011. It would appear unlikely that the era of large-scale public support is over. This means that at least for the foreseeable future, the rescue and restructuring of banks will continue to be assessed on the basis of the present crisis-specific rules adopted in 2008–2009. State aid control alone cannot however provide an adequate response to the current malaise, as Commissioner Almunia has stressed in a speech in September 2011:

---

[8] L. Coppi, "The Approach to State Aid in the Restructuring of the Financial Sector", *Competition Policy International*, November 2009.

"Putting the banking system and the financial sector in general, back on a sound footing is a necessary precondition of any recovery. This requires—on top of the urgent need to strengthen economic governance in the eurozone and successfully tackle the sovereign debt problems—that financial regulation and the competition rules work together."

State aid control has undoubtedly helped to contribute to maintaining a level playing field in the European single market during the crisis in the absence of a fully effective regulatory framework. Approval of state support, even under the special regime which has now been in place for three years, is usually subject to far-reaching conditions, such as the remuneration and progressive pay-back of the support received, reduction of balance sheets, including the sale of profitable assets to share the burden of restructuring, and the setting of acquisition and price-leadership bans. This is a regime of "tough love", to echo former Commissioner Kroes, and the sometimes far-reaching conditions for exemption have been necessitated in part by the absence of harmonised and effective financial regulation and supervision. At the time of writing, three appeals against Commission decisions are pending.

As the sovereign debt crisis of 2011 worsens, the Commission has conceded   **1–014**
that more banks may need to be recapitalised, on top of the nine signalled in the July 2011 "stress tests". Even if the Commission's ultimate objective is to come back to a new, post-crisis rescue and restructuring regime for banks, this is unlikely to happen in the near future, given the extent of uncertainty and tensions in the markets. But as Commissioner Almunia has warned, "postponement certainly doesn't mean a blank check for banks and their governments." In the meantime, steps are slowly being taken to set up a common regulatory framework and to create a common reserve of financial resources on which ailing banks and governments can draw. Even if these objectives are realised in the near future this will not remove state aid control from the equation. The number of individual restructuring decisions has in any event placed the Commission in a quasi-regulatory role for the foreseeable future. Most of the restructuring plans will last for five years and the Commission must oversee the implementation of the various commitments contained in the approved plans. Moreover, the creation of a common reserve is primarily a project of the 17 Eurozone countries so that the remaining 10 Member States will continue to be the first port of call for their ailing banks.

Less aid? In the introduction to the third edition we noted that the reforms   **1–015**
introduced by the SAAP are intended to impose a more rigorous approach to state aid control. Has this approach been successful, at least in the other sectors of the economy? The annual State Aid Scoreboards, published prior to the financial crisis, already indicated a mixed result—albeit that certain types of aid and volumes of aid were in decline. We also pondered whether the implementation of the SAAP might lead to a policy reversal, so that the volume of aid (and perhaps even its intensity) becomes a secondary consideration to the potential of the aid

measure or scheme to correct market failures or to prevent distortions of competition.

Indeed, even in areas where the refined economic approach has been taken more seriously, or at least applied with some more conviction, very large sums of money are still being approved. Even if, as required by the SAAP, state aid is better targeted, it is difficult to conclude that this has or could or should lead to a reduction in the volume of state aid disbursed. For example, in 2010 alone, under the EU guidelines for state aid to broadband, the Commission approved the use of over €1.8 billion in public funds for broadband development. Total aid for broadband and "next generation infrastructure" has been estimated at €9 billion. The Europe 2020 Strategy, discussed below, sets ambitious targets for broadband development estimated to require some €330 billion in investment. Public funding should aim to ensure that all citizens have access to high-speed internet in the European Union, including in rural or remote areas. State aid is approved subject to strict conditions in order to avoid distortions of competition: public funds can only be used in areas where private operators are unlikely to invest on commercial terms; and all broadband networks should be open to competition, with subsidised operators offering access to others. The 2011 State Aid Scoreboard, discussed below, indicates that of the 75 decisions adopted in relation to broadband support between 2004 and 2010 the Commission adopted 65 compatible decisions, six no aid decisions and one negative decision. In April 2011 the Commission announced a review of the Broadband guidelines adopted in 2009.[9]

1–016 **The Europe 2020 Strategy.** In June 2011 the Commission produced a report on "State aid contribution to Europe 2020 Strategy" in its Spring State Aid Scoreboard.[10] This report provides an interesting overview of state aid in areas which are of particular relevance to the Europe 2020 Strategy for smart, sustainable and inclusive growth.[11] The report reviews state aid trends in a number of areas, including research and development and innovation, environmental protection, regional development, broadband, small- and medium-sized enterprises and employment training—all of which are key action points in the Europe 2020 strategy. This report raises some interesting questions on the role of state aid policy in the Commission's overall strategy to ensure: smart growth, that is developing an economy based on knowledge and innovation; sustainable growth, that is promoting a more resource efficient, greener and more competitive economy; and inclusive growth, that is fostering a high-employment economy delivering economic, territorial and social cohesion. The Europe 2020 Strategy lays down various priorities for which state aid instruments can be used in a policy mix to contribute to a number of "flagship initiatives". The analysis provided of national levels of support for each of the six areas reviewed reveals

---

[9] Press release IP/11/493 of April 19, 2011. Available on *http://europa.eu/rapid/pressReleases Action.do?reference=IP/11/493&format=HTML&aged=1&language=EN&guiLanguage=en.*
[10] Com (2011) 356 final, June 22, 2011.
[11] Com (2010) 2020.

that by far the largest number of national support measures or schemes fall under the scope of block exemption schemes and can be disbursed without prior Commission authorisation, and confirms that in all these areas the Commission only very rarely takes a negative decision. The number of measures falling outside a block exemption scheme and requiring the so-called detailed assessment is approximately 5 to 9 per cent of the total number of measures notified. The remainder are approved under the standard assessment provided for in the relevant sectoral guidelines. Regional aid continues to account for the highest share of total aid to Europe's industry and services. As the report comments, this type of aid is meant to address the "cohesion disequilibrium" rather than market failures only. Large disparities between the Member States in the volume of aid granted demonstrate different policy approaches however, and the report confirms that it is not the purpose of the state aid rules, or indeed the goal of ensuring "less and better targeted aid", to arrive at a level playing field in terms of public support for any of these six areas across the Member States.

The detailed review of the level of aid to these six areas analysed in the 2011 Spring Scoreboard appears to indicate that the Commission would even welcome more rather than less aid in order to secure the fulfilment of the "flagship initiatives" embraced in the Europe 2020 strategy. In any event, the report confirms the importance of state aid control as an important tool in achieving wider European industrial policy goals.

Public services compensation. In the wake of Case C–280/00 *Altmark*,[12] the **1–017** Commission adopted the so-called "Monti Package" on compensation for public service obligations and used art.106(3) TFEU to adopt an exemption decision on state aid and compensation for services of public interest together with an accompanying set of guidelines. The scope of this package is further discussed in Ch.8. It may, however, be noted here that following the adoption of the first Transparency Directive and its subsequent amendments, this is only the second time that the Commission has made use of its powers under art.106(3) to adopt prescriptive measures in the field of state aids. Individual decisions requiring the suppression of a particular national measure are always taken on the basis of art.108(1) or (3) and, given the procedural requirements with respect to the interests of third parties, it is highly unlikely that art.106(3) could offer the Commission an alternative route to enforce the state aid regime. Nevertheless, the adoption of the Decision 2005/842[13] illustrates its potential for creating a new category of block exemption given that the enabling Council Regulation 998/94[14] restricts the range of Commission Regulations adopted under it to particular types or forms of horizontal aid. The 2005 Decision is in effect a form of sectoral aid block exemption.

---

[12] [2003] E.C.R. I–7747.
[13] [2005] O.J. L312/67.
[14] [1998] O.J. L142/1.

1–018   At the time of writing, the Commission has launched a consultation exercise on a draft package of measures that aims, ambitiously, to introduce both flexibility and legal security into the control of national support for public services. Included in this package are a specific Commission Regulation on de minimis aid for services of general economic interest, a revised exemption decision, and a revised framework for assessing the compatibility of state aid measures for services of general economic interest.[15] If adopted, the new exemption decision should provide a safe harbour for limited amounts of compensation for a larger number of social services, while the revised framework introduces stricter roles on calculating and monitoring state aid for the performance of services of general interest. The new package,[15a] as with its predecessor, necessarily reflects the Commission's limited powers to second-guess a national designation of an activity as being of general interest, as well as its limited powers to require that the performance of such tasks should be conducted efficiently. Both matters are left essentially to the discretion of the Member States, and, as the courts have confirmed, can only be subject to marginal review by the Commission to ensure that no manifest error has occurred.

1–019   Timeframes. The administrative and judicial phases of EU state aid control are not renowned for their speed. If a competitor or other third party wants to contest aid measures which it considers to distort competition, invariably it must have the patience of Job and, inevitably, it must have deep pockets. Furthermore, it must be prepared to confront considerable obstacles to establish that it has standing to challenge a Commission decision. The number of state aid cases reaching the Union courts is still considerable and is almost on a par with competition law cases. Although the General Court has extended the number of its chambers, this does not seem to have resulted in a more rapid turnover of cases.

1–020   Additionally, it cannot go unnoticed that a significant number of rulings by the lower court continue to be appealed to the higher court. The latter court does not of course always follow the General Court and may annul its findings, with the result that the General Court must decide the case anew. This in turn can lead to an eventual (partial) annulment of the original Commission decision so that the latter must in turn adopt a new decision. The entire process is an elaborate one, and a considerable period of time—sometimes extending over more than a decade—can elapse between the initial and ultimate Commission decisions, and of course the second Commission can also be appealed once again to both Courts. The *Ufex* and *Chronopost* cases[16] concerning the French postal sector

---

[15] Available on DG Competition's website.
[15a] The new package was adopted on December 20, 2011.
[16] Joined Cases C–83/01P, C–93/01P and C–94/01P *Chronopost* [2003] E.C.R. I–6993 and Joined Cases C–341/06P and C–342/06P *Chronopost* [2008] E.C.R. I–4777. Case T–613/97 *Ufex v Commission* [2000] E.C.R. II–4055. Case T–613/97 *Ufex II* [2006] E.C.R. II–153. Discussed in Ch.8.

and the SNIACE and *Lenzing* case law on Spanish restructuring aid[17] are just two cases in point. As the CELF saga illustrates,[18] the rights of beneficiaries and competitors before national courts are by no means easy to predict during this elaborate process, which may involve several reversals or modifications of the original positive Commission decision.

The process of judicial review is hardly to be commended for its speed and efficiency. The General Court can take, on average, 48 months to issue judgment in a fully contested case, and further appeal will usually take approximately 18 months.[19] This timeframe has not escaped criticism and question marks are increasingly raised as to whether such delays are not in breach of art.47 of the European Charter of Fundamental Rights. Although the rules of procedure of Courts now make provision for applications for expedited procedures, as well as for the grant of interim measures suspending a Commission decision, applications are very rarely granted in practice.[20]   **1–021**

By the same token it is very rare for the Commission to use its own powers to adopt interim injunctive measures under the Procedural Regulation 659/99 to require an aid measure to be suspended prior to the completion of its formal investigations. Nevertheless the Commission has attempted to streamline its own procedures, and, even if the Commission is bound to adopt first phase decisions within a relatively short period of time (two months), it has endeavoured to speed up the administrative process by introducing a new simplified notification procedure in 2009 for certain types of aid schemes and a "Best Practices" guideline. As announced under the SAAP, a separate recovery unit has been created within DG Competition and in 2007 the Commission published a notice setting out the obligations of Member States in relation to recovery of unlawful aid. If national procedural rules do not enable the enforcement of recovery, the Member State must take steps to put the necessary mechanisms in place, as has been confirmed by the Court in Case C–214/07 *Commission v France*.[21]   **1–022**

Where aid has not been notified and the Commission commences its investigations as a result of a complaint, no deadlines apply, and even where it takes some four or five years for the Commission to complete its preliminary investigations, the Courts have not condemned this forthrightly as a breach of the principle of sound administration now enshrined in art.41 of the European Charter of Fundamental Rights. Rather the courts appear to steer a middle course and may well be prepared to find that the Commission did not conduct the administrative   **1–023**

---

[17] Case T–152/99 *HAMSA* [2002] E.C.R. II–3049, as well as later cases related to Case C–342/96 [1999] E.C.R. I–2459, that is, Case T–36/99 *Lenzing v Commission* [2004] E.C.R. II–3597 and Case C–276/02 *Spain v Commission (GEA)* [2004] E.C.R. I–8091 and Case C–525/04P *Spain v Commission and Lenzing* [2007] E.C.R. I–9947. Discussed in Ch.3.

[18] See further Ch.27 on recovery.

[19] Dumping cases take on average 38 months while competition cases may last up to 56 months. See A.M. Collins, "Building the CFI of tomorrow", paper presented at a conference on the Celebration of 20 years of the CFI, September 25, 2009.

[20] The annual report of the European courts suggests that on average it takes the General Court some four years to process an appeal against a Commission state decision.

[21] [2008] E.C.R. I–8357.

procedures within a reasonable period, for example, in a case where the preliminary investigation lasted for more than 28 months. However, this is of cold comfort to the applicants as the Courts have not accepted unreasonable delay as a ground for declaring a decision unlawful or as evidence, to the requisite legal standard, that the Commission is faced with serious difficulties and should initiate the formal investigation procedure under art.108(2).[22]

The Union Courts

1–024 **The scope of review.** In our third edition we highlighted three major developments in the case law: the Courts' continuing battle to refine the concept of aid and the scope of art.107(1); the scope of judicial review of Commission decisions; and the case law on locus standi and on recovery. In the third edition we suggested that a more tentative development could be discerned in the case law: the gradual extension of the emerging principles of "good governance" or sound administration to the exercise by the Commission of its powers in the field of state aid control. In this fourth edition we revisit these trends.

Refining the concept of aid—a continuing endeavour?

1–025   Despite the rulings in the *Preussen, Stardust* and *Pearle* cases, discussed in detail in Ch.3, which had arguably narrowed down the wide "effects-based" approach to the definition of state aid for the purposes of art.107(1) by narrowing the interpretation of the transfer of the state resources element, and requiring state involvement in how resources at the disposal of a public or private organisation are deployed, it is not easy to predict in many cases whether a particular measure will be deemed to be a form of aid or not. A key goal of the SAAP was to introduce more predictability into state aid control, but of course the SAAP does not bind either the Union or the national courts. Nor did the SAAP purport to deal with the very definition of "state aid", but only with issues of compatibility. The number of cases appealed from the General Court to the European Court of Justice confirms the continuing search for a stable definition of the very concept of aid and its constituent elements. This is particularly, but not exclusively evident in the area of taxation, as the *British Aggregates*[23] and *Dutch Nox*[24] cases illustrate, and as further elaborated upon in Ch.10. Similarly the bounds of the market investor test remain perhaps by their very nature, vague and uncertain. The mere fact that the state has resources at its disposal which no other private actor can deploy has always been an important question mark over the reliability of the test. This is confirmed in the recent *EDF* case, discussed in Ch.3, and is at issue in several of the appeals lodged against Commission decisions relating to recent bank restructuring.[25]

---

[22] See for example, Case T–95/03 *AEESCAM v Commission* [2007] E.C.R. II–4739.
[23] C–487/06 P [2008] E.C.R. I–10515.
[24] Case C–279/08P *Commission v Netherlands* [2011] judgment of September 8, 2011.
[25] Case T–457/09 *Westfalisch-Lippischer Sparkassen v Commission* [2010] O.J. C11/35; T–33/10 *ING v Commission* [2010] O.J. C80/40; Case T–319/11 *ABN-Amro Group* [2011] O.J. C252/35.

The scope of judicial review

It is established law that the Courts exercise a full review in respect of the **1–026** Commission's decisions to classify a state measure as aid within the meaning of art.107(1), unless the case in question involves exceptionally complex economic judgments. Marginal or limited review is confined essentially to the Commission's exercise of its discretion with respect to the application of one of the derogations envisaged in art.107(3). Nevertheless, in the third edition we concluded that the General Court had not shied away from a careful review of the Commission's use of the market investor test or its progeny, such as the private creditor test. An early case in point was the ruling in the *Valmont* case, discussed in Ch.3. Other examples referred to were the application by the Commission of the so-called "private creditor" test, reviewed in Ch.3 and the ruling of the Court in Case C–181/02P *Commissions v Kvaerner Warnow Werft*[26] as well as the ruling in Case T–17/03 *Schmitz-Gotha*.[27]

In the light of *Scott*,[28] it has been suggested that the Courts are moving towards a unified standard of review in competition cases.[29] The Court of Justice relied on *Tetra Laval*,[30] *Spain v Lenzing*,[31] and *GlaxoSmithKline*[32] to spell out the "necessarily limited" scope of review by the Courts of complex economic assessments made by the Commission.[33] In *Scott*, the Court of Justice set aside the decision of the General Court because it exceeded its review jurisdiction in finding that the Commission should have doubted the evidence on which the calculations at issue were based.

Olympic Airways, on the other hand, demonstrates that the Union judge can review the Commission's interpretation of economic data, while respecting the margin of assessment accorded to the Commission in such appraisals.[34] The Court can evaluate the reliability and consistency of the evidence. It can consider whether the facts are accurately stated. It can determine whether the file contains all the information necessary to assess the case. Further, it can determine whether the evidence supports the conclusions drawn. Yet, unless a manifest error of assessment can be established, the Courts remain reluctant to challenge the actual logic of the reasoning on which a decision is based and continue to confine their review of appeals based on failure to provide reasons to the much-repeated, narrow test that the statement of reasons should be sufficient to enable persons concerned to ascertain the reasons for the contested decision and to enable the competent court to exercise its powers of review. As long as this approach is

---

[26] [2004] E.C.R. I–5703.
[27] [2006] E.C.R. II–1139.
[28] C–290/07P *Commission v Scott* [2010] E.C.R. Unreported.
[29] Judge O'Higgins [2011] *EStAL*, Vol.10, nr.1.
[30] Case C–12/03P *Commission v Tetra Laval* [2005] E.C.R. I–987.
[31] Case C–525/04P *Spain v. Lensing* [2007] E.C.R. I–9947, para.57.
[32] Joined Cases C–501/06P, C–513/06P, C–515/06P, C–519/06P *GlaxoSmithKline Services and Ors v Commission and Ors* [2009] E.C.R. I–9291, para.163.
[33] See the Opinion in *Scott* at paras 102–103.
[34] See also, C–290/07P *Commission v Scott* [2008] I–8637, para.64.

applied, a full and detailed review of a Commission decision is excluded unless manifest error or misuse of powers can be established. As noted below at para.1–041, the Courts may take a stricter standpoint in reviewing the exercise of the Commission's discretion when the latter has bound itself by means of guidelines.

Locus standi

1–027   The Commission continues to engage in a ceaseless fight to restrict the admissibility test in arts 263(4) and 262 TFEU to parties who are directly and individually concerned by its decision. Extensive pleadings on the admissibility of the application to annul the Commission decision at issue are now a permanent fixture in the majority of state aid cases. The simple fact of being a potential competitor of the recipient of the contested state measure is not sufficient for the applicant to be regarded as "directly and individually concerned". In this respect the Commission has consistently pleaded that the Union Courts should require the applicant to demonstrate that its market position would be substantially undermined, regardless of the stage that the procedure has reached when the Commission takes the decision which is the subject of an action for annulment.

1–028   At the same time, the Courts have not been tempted to transpose the relatively straightforward approach to standing in the competition and merger law field to state aids control. Instead, a complex set of distinctions has emerged depending on the status of the applicant (actual or potential beneficiary, or actual or potential competitor), the nature of the measure (an aid scheme as opposed to an individual measure), its status as notified or un-notified, the stage of the administrative proceedings to which the annulment action (or action for failure to act) relates and the nature of the pleas raised by the applicant, as well as whether the applicant has had an opportunity (and taken advantage of that opportunity) to become involved during the formal investigation procedure.

1–029   Although several Advocate Generals have called for simplification and a return to *Plaumann* as the basic test to be applied irrespective of the stage reached in the aid investigation procedures, and irrespective of whether the applicant seeks to defend its procedural rights or to challenge the merits of a Commission decision, the ECJ has continued to attach importance to these distinctions.

The result is that the issue of standing has become extremely complex, and as Advocate General Sharpston remarked:

"In particular, under the present approach I find it difficult to see how an applicant can easily avoid being drawn into the merits of a decision when seeking to show that there were still serious difficulties remaining in the Commission's initial assessment of the aid in issue. Through ARE and BAA, the Court has established a veritable tightrope along which applicants and their advocates must gingerly advance. It is all too easy for them to slip and find that they are either trapped by the stricter *Plaumann* test, or that they have not done enough to satisfy the Court that there were indeed procedural errors in the decision they wish to contest" (para 44).[35]

In the subsequent Case C–83/09P *Kronopoly*,[36] the Court of Justice approved the General Court's approach to examine whether certain of the substantive arguments on the merits also supported an express plea to safeguard the applicants' procedural rights under art.108(2). If substantive arguments are linked to a plea alleging disregard for procedural guarantees, then apparently the Courts will not now disregard them. This is surely a welcome improvement.   **1–030**

State aid control and good governance

As the Courts have recognised, since the assessment of the compatibility of state aid with the internal market falls within its exclusive competence, the Commission is bound, in the interests of sound administration of the fundamental rules of the Treaty relating to state aid, to conduct a diligent and impartial examination of a complaint alleging the existence of aid that is incompatible with the internal market. But what do these principles entail in the context of state aid control—a context which is still predominantly one of a privileged dialogue between the Commission and the Member State concerned? Decisions by the Community Ombudsman shed some light on the scope of the application of the principle of good administration in the area of state aid control. By and large the approach is cautious.[37] In Case T–34/03 EUR *Le Levant*, the General Court ruled that the Commission had violated art.108(2) and art.6(1) of the Procedural Regulation as it had not called on the private investors to submit comments. At para.97 of its ruling it pointed out that the irregularity constituted an infringement of a general principle of Community law—the right to be heard. As the recovery decision related directly to them and they were directly affected by the economic consequences of the decision they should have benefited from such a right. The Court recalled in this respect art.41(2) first bullet of the EC Charter of Fundamental Rights.[38] The Commission too has demonstrated that it can successfully rely on art.41(2) of the Chapter in Case C–89/08P.[39]   **1–031**

At para.46 of its earlier ruling, the General Court had stated that it considered it appropriate in the present case to raise of its own motion a plea relating to the defective statement of the reasons on which the state aid decision at issue was based, with regard to the non-application of art.1(b)(v) of Regulation No. 659/1999. It went on to argue that a lack or an insufficiency of reasoning is a matter of public policy which the Community judicature must raise of its own

---

[35] Case C–319/07P [2009] E.C.R. I–5963. The relevant case law is discussed in full in Ch.27.
[36] C–83/09 [2010] E.C.R. Unreported.
[37] See further the website of the European Ombudsman *http://www.ombudsman.europe.eu/ decision/en/aid.htm.*
[38] [2000] O.J. C364/1.
[39] [2009] E.C.R. I–11245.

motion, and then stated at paras 52 and 53 of the judgment that the Commission had, in the decision at issue, examined whether the exemptions at issue constituted new aid or existing aid but, with regard to art.1(b)(v) of Regulation No. 659/1999, merely stated that that provision did not apply in this case, without giving reasons. The Court had held that the particular circumstances of the case were nevertheless such that it was necessary to ascertain whether the tax exemptions at issue could be regarded as existing aid by reason of the fact that at the time they were put into effect they did not constitute aid but that subsequently they became aid due to the evolution of the common market and without having been altered by the Member States concerned. It considered, therefore, that the Commission was required to give adequate reasons for the decision at issue with regard to the applicability of art.1(b)(v) of Regulation No 659/1999.

The ECJ, on appeal, found that the General Court had infringed the Commission's right to be heard and annulled the lower court's decision in Case T–50/06 *Ireland v Commission*.[40] It ruled that:

> "In order to satisfy the requirements associated with the right to a fair hearing, it is important for the parties to be apprised of, and to be able to debate and be heard on, the matters of fact and of law which will determine the outcome of the proceedings. Accordingly, except in particular cases such as, inter alia, those provided for by the rules of procedure of the Community Courts, those Courts cannot base their decisions on a plea raised of their own motion, even one involving a matter of public policy and—as in the present case—based on the absence of a statement of reasons for the decision at issue, without first having invited the parties to submit their observations on that plea" (at paras 56–57).[41]

1–032   Nevertheless, the position of the (potential) beneficiary of a state aid remains weak and they are dependent on the willingness of the Member State concerned to involve them actively in the administrative procedures—the Commission has no separate duties towards such beneficiaries. This is well illustrated by the case of *Fleuren*,[42] discussed in Ch.27. At the same time, however, the General Court has recognised that where a Member State itself does not challenge a decision, the beneficiary may still invoke an infringement of the Member State's right to be heard.[43]

The rights of competitors of aid beneficiaries also remain very limited during the preliminary investigation and especially in circumstances where the Commission considers that the measure in question raises no serious difficulties in respect of its compatibility with the Treaty, as recently confirmed in *M6 and TF1 v*

---

[40] Joined Cases T–50/06, T–56/06, T–60/06, T–62/06 and T–69/06 [2007] E.C.R. II–172.
[41] Ibid. Case C89/08P [2009] E.C.R. I–11245.
[42] Case T–109/01 [2004] E.C.R. II–127.
[43] Joined Cases T–228/99 and T–233/99 *West LB* [2003] E.C.R. II–435.

Commission.[44] In terms of consultation and information during the preliminary examination, the Member State remains the key actor. A competitor will face an uphill struggle in attempting to compile sufficient and convincing evidence to question the financial calculations exchanged between the Commission and the Member State.

4. BENEFICIARIES OF AID

The beneficiaries of aid themselves are not in a much better position, and even **1–033** if a formal investigation under art.108(2) has been opened,[45] their role is "complex and controversial."[46] The administrative procedure involves the Commission and the Member State and no particular role is envisaged for the aid recipient. The recipient merely provides information at the Commission's request. The fact that the Commission used the evidence provided by the applicant to support reasoning which led to the finding that the latter was liable for reimbursement was held to be in keeping with the intention of the formal investigation procedure—which makes "interested parties" a source of information and little more than that.[47]

In the *NOS* case[48] the Netherlands argued that the Commission had violated art.108(2) TFEU and their rights of defence in so far as the contested decision, which ordered recovery of the illegal aid departed substantially from the decision to open the formal examination. NOS argued that its requests to participate in meetings with the Commission had been refused and that it had been denied access to the Commission's file. The General Court held that NOS, the beneficiary of the aid, was an "interested party"[49] and had only the "right to be associated with" the administrative procedure. It is sufficient for the beneficiary of aid to be aware of the *reasoning* for the Commission's decision to open a formal procedure, and for the beneficiary to have the possibility to present its arguments.

As AG Mengozzi observed in his Opinion in *Scott*:

"There is no doubt that that general approach is markedly formalistic, a fact which has attracted considerable criticism in academic writings. Specifically, it is artificial and not always realistic to take as a premise—which seems implicit in this interpretation of the State aid procedure—the idea that the

---

[44] Joined Cases T–568/08 and T–573/08 *M6 and TF1 v Commission* [2010] E.C.R. n.y.r., and now under appeal in Case C–451/10P [2010] O.J. C328/15.

[45] The formal investigation procedure is laid down in art.108(2) TFEU and art.6(1) of Regulation no. 659/1999.

[46] Opinion of February 23, 2010 in C–290/07P *Commission v Scott* [2010] E.C.R. Unreported, para.52.

[47] Case T–354/99 *Kuwait Petroleum v Commission* [2006] E.C.R. II–1475.

[48] Joined Cases T–231/06 and T–237/06 *Kingdom of the Netherlands and Nederlandse Omroep Stichting (NOS) v Commission* [2010] judgment of December 16, 2010.

[49] An "interested party" is defined by art.1(h) of Regulation no. 659/1999.

interests of the State which granted the aid are the same as the interests of the aid recipient. Plainly, the situation cannot be viewed in the same way by the State, which at most can be ordered to recover the aid paid, as by an undertaking, which, if the aid has to be recovered, could risk liquidation. Moreover, aid is not necessarily granted by the national government of the State, it can be granted by some regional or peripheral manifestation of State power : in such cases, it is not necessarily true that the interests of the central government, which alone has the right to participate in the procedure, are the same as those of the local body."

Even if the courts recognise the application of the principle of good administration as set out in art.41 of the Charter, this has not led to any real improvement in the rights of aid beneficiaries or their competitors. It may however be noted that in Joined Cases C–463/10P and C–475/10P *Deutsche Post* and *Germany v Commission*, the ECJ has now recognised the right of an alleged aid beneficiary to challenge the Commission information injunction based on art.10 of the Procedural Regulation 659/99 addressed to the Member State.[50]

1–034 **Access to information.** Although the Courts initially appeared willing to confirm the application of the Council Regulation 1049/2001 on Access to Information to state aid control procedures,[51] albeit that they failed to allow access to the file as an essential pre-condition of any effective right to be heard, recent case law has now reduced the importance of this Regulation in the area of state aid.[52] Despite some cautious early developments in the case law on the application of Regulation 1049/2001 to state aid procedures, the position of competitors in state aid proceedings before the Commission differs materially in many respects from the rights of access to the file established in competition proceedings and this is unlikely to change in the near future. In Case C–139/07 *Technische Glaswerke*[53] the Court of Justice overruled the General Court and interpreted art.4(2) (protection of the purpose of the investigation) of the Regulation to the effect that interested parties except for the Member State responsible for granting aid, do not have any right . . . to consult the documents on the Commission's administrative file", and further that "[a] general presumption exists that disclosure of documents in the administrative file in principle undermines protection of the objectives of investigation activities".

This ruling clearly limits the scope of access to the file while a case is still under investigation, as confirmed by the subsequent *Ryanair* case of December 2010,[54] but as the Ombudsman confirmed in a subsequent decision on a complaint against the Commission for a refusal to supply documents in a state aid

---

[50] [2011] judgment of October 13, 2011.

[51] Case T–76/02 *Mana Messina v Commission* [2003] E.C.R. II–3203.

[52] The right of access to information has now been recognised as a citizen's right in art.42 of the Charter of Fundamental Rights.

[53] [2010] judgment of June 29, 2010.

[54] Cases T–494/08 to T–500/08 and T–509/08 *Ryanair Ltd v Commission* [2010] judgment of December 10, 2010.

investigation, the Courts have concluded that the above general presumption does not exclude an interested party from having a right to demonstrate that a given document is not covered by that presumption.[55]

Following the adoption of an administrative decision, the Commission remains entitled to rely on art.4(3) of the Regulation (protection of the Commission's decision-making process) unless there is an overriding public interest in disclosure. Disclosure must be likely to risk to seriously undermine the decision process, and furthermore that risk must be reasonably foreseeable and not merely hypothetical.[56] The overriding public interest in disclosure must be objective and general in nature and must not be indistinguishable from individual or private interests such as those relating to the pursuit of an action brought against the Union institutions, since such individual or private interests do not constitute an element which is relevant to the balancing of interests provided for in art.4(3) of the Regulation.[57]

Recovery. The Commission's powers to demand recovery of illegal aid were confirmed by the courts at an early stage and are now codified in the Procedural Regulation 659/99. Nevertheless the process of recovery is a complex and lengthy, if not frustrating, process. As underlined in the SAAP, the effectiveness and credibility of state aid control presupposes a proper enforcement of the Commission's decisions. The SAAP announced that the "Commission will pursue a more effective policy and will seek to achieve the immediate execution of all recovery decisions". To this end, the SAAP announced that the Commission, through its newly created recovery unit, would monitor more closely the execution of recovery decisions by the Member States, and will more actively pursue non-compliance under art.108(2), as well seeking to impose fines on Member States who have not carried out recovery orders, (art.260(2) TFEU (ex art.228(3) EC). In Case C–369/07 *Commission v Greece*, the first case concerning the imposition of a fine on a Member State for failing to recover illegal aid, the Court held that art.228 EC confers a wide discretion upon the Court in deciding whether or not to impose such a sanction:

1–035

"The procedure laid down in Article 228(2) EC is aimed at inducing a defaulting Member State to comply with a judgment establishing a failure to fulfil obligations, thereby ensuring that Community law is in fact applied. The measures provided for by that provision, namely a lump sum and a penalty payment, are both intended to achieve this objective. The application of each of those measures depends on their respective ability to meet the objective pursued according to the circumstances of the case. That being so, recourse to both types of penalty provided for is not precluded. It is therefore for the Court, in each case, in the light of the circumstances of the case before it and

---

[55] Case 1735/2010/MHZ, May 3, 2011.
[56] Case C–39/05P and C–52/05P *Sweden and Turco v Council* [2008] E.C.R. I–1429, para.43.
[57] Case T–403/05 *MyTravel v Commission* [2008] E.C.R. II–2027; and on appeal Case C–506/08P [2011] judgment of July 21, 2011.

the degree of persuasion and deterrence which appears to it to be required, to determine the financial penalties appropriate for making sure that the judgment which previously established the breach is complied with as swiftly as possible and preventing similar infringements of Community law from recurring. Therefore, the Court is empowered, in exercising the discretion conferred on it in the field in question, to impose a penalty payment and a lump sum payment cumulatively."[58]

1–036   In 1995, the Commission published a Notice on co-operation between itself and the national courts, drawing attention to the role of the courts and outlining the assistance which the Commission can give, for example in advising on whether aid has been given.[59] This was replaced in 2009 by a new Notice on the enforcement of state aid law by national courts.[60] With only a limited number of DG Competition officials responsible for several hundred cases every year, the Commission is keen to shift the burden of enforcement, to encourage complainants to turn to the courts for redress. Two studies on the enforcement of EU state aid policy at national level of 2006 and 2009, and carried out at the Commission's request, are discussed in greater detail in Chs 26 and 27. These studies confirm that recovery of aid at national level still faces a large number of legal and administrative obstacles. The 2006 study confirmed that national courts play an increasing role in enforcing the Treaty rules. Since 1999, the number of cases had increased from 115 to 357. The largest number of cases were brought in France, Italy and Germany, followed by the Netherlands, Spain, Belgium and the United Kingdom. However, the study found that although private parties are using the rules as a defence against financial burdens imposed by the state, they rarely use the rules to bring challenges before national courts against the distortion of competition caused by the unlawful grant of aid to competitors. The study made a number of recommendations:

- The Commission should adopt a new notice on co-operation between the Commission and national courts in the field of state aid (to replace the existing notice of 1995). As noted, the Commission adopted new guidelines in 2009.[61]

- The Commission should discuss with Member States the ways of achieving minimum standards relating to swift recovery and the grant of interim relief (where breach of art.108(3) is clear) without a competitor of an illegal aid recipient having to show irremediable harm; for example, the adoption of a directive dealing with remedies in state aid cases.

- The Commission should examine the desirability of creating uniform conditions for the award of damages to competitors in the event of an infringement of art.108(3).

[58] [2009] E.C.R. I–5703.
[59] [1995] O.J. C312/8.
[60] [2009] O.J. C85/1.
[61] [2009] O.J. C85/1.

- The Commission should adopt best practice guidelines on recovery. The Commission adopted guidance in October 2007.[62] This Notice sets out guidance on implementing Commission decisions ordering the Member States to recover unlawful aid. The Notice also includes best practice guidance for Commission recovery policy.

Despite the Commission's commitment to improve the record on recovery, its **1–037** powers are limited—national authorities remain responsible. In this respect the Union legal order provides little solace given that national legal procedural rules are primarily a matter for national sovereignty, albeit that the Court has mandated national courts to do their utmost within the boundaries of their own legal orders to ensure the effective and full enforcement of Union law.[63]

At the same time, the Commission is not always clear in its decisions as to how much aid is to be recovered, or from whom, so that the duty of recovery entrusted to the Member State is not always clear. This in turn makes the tasks of national authorities and courts even more complex. The Courts have held that it is sufficient for the Commission to include information and relevant elements enabling the addressee of the decision to work out the amount to be recovered itself without too much difficulty. In *Mediaset*, the applicants claimed that the contested decision did not make it possible to establish a sound recovery methodology for the aid identified as incompatible. The contested decision in fact required the national authorities to carry out a complex market simulation exercise to establish how consumers might have behaved in the absence of the aid measure in question. The General Court held that the Commission had met the requisite test[64] and, on appeal, the ECJ confirmed that the Commission can legitimately declare that there is an obligation to repay the aid in question and leave it to the Member States to calculate the exact amounts to be repaid as part of the more general reciprocal obligation incumbent upon the Commission and the Member States of sincere co-operation.[65]

Another aspect of the case law on recovery that remains unclear is whether the very aim of a recovery decision is to restore the status quo or the previous situation causing the recipient to forfeit the advantage which it had enjoyed over its competitors. It follows that it is not the purpose of a recovery order to penalise the aid recipient. However, if the purpose of recovery is wider, and is to remove the distortion to competition and hence the loss suffered by competitors, then this may not only impact the manner in which recovery is to be quantified, and would not be limited to the monetary value of the aid, but could also determine from whom the aid should be recovered, especially where assets are sold to a third party. This type of approach would align state aid recovery orders more closely with competition law concepts.[66]

---

[62] [2007] O.J. C272/4.

[63] C–526/04 *Labaratoires Boiron SA* [2006] E.C.R. I–7529.

[64] Case T–177/07 [2010] judgment of June 15, 2010.

[65] Case C–403/10P [2011] judgment of July 28, 2011.

[66] G. Monti, "Recovery orders in state aid proceedings: lessons from antitrust?", [2011] *EStal*, vol.10 nr.3, pp.415–424.

5. BLOCK EXEMPTIONS AND GUIDELINES

1–038   The Commission continues to rely heavily on soft law instruments in the field of state aids, including communications, guidelines and frameworks, some of which make express reference to art.107(3) and some which do not. The reasons for choosing guidelines as opposed to other soft law measures are not always clear, nor are the consequences of that choice always evident. Indeed, the Commission continues to prefer to use guidelines in certain fields, such as environment or broadband, even though the Enabling Regulation provides it with a formal legal basis to adopt binding rules, which national courts could enforce, in this area. Following the SAAP reforms, the Block Exemption Regulation allows for automatic exemption of a variety of aids across a number of sectors. Measures which do not satisfy the Block Exemption conditions must be notified and will be assessed under the relevant guidelines. In certain cases the compatibility assessment can be carried out on a "standardised basis", depending on the amount of aid at issue, whereas larger amounts of aid will have to be subject to a detailed assessment. In general, existing guidelines are reviewed and updated at regular intervals, following an extensive public consultation process. However some sets of guidelines are merely prolonged pending a further comprehensive review—a useful tactic to avoid re-opening legal and political controversy. Examples include the cinematic guidelines,[67] the export credit insurance,[68] and, perhaps most importantly, the 2004 Rescue and Restructuring Guidelines, due to expire in December 2011.[69]

The Court had to some extent clarified the relationship between the Block Exemption Regulations (BERs) and guidelines and frameworks in its ruling in Case C–110/03 *Belgium v Commission*.[70] Belgium argued, unsuccessfully, that the BER on employment and training did not comply with the principle of legal certainty and that the Commission had made the system of aid for employment stricter, whereas the Enabling Regulation 994/98 only empowered it to codify existing practice. The Court held that since the Regulation was adopted on the basis of Regulation 994/98 it is binding and of general application. The guidelines and the then applicable multisectoral framework, on the contrary, have no legal basis either in the Treaty or in any legal act adopted under it. It follows that, in the event of any overlap, the provisions of the contested Regulation have precedence over those of the guidelines. Finally the Court rejected the argument that the Regulation was too strict, and recalled the wide discretion which the Commission enjoyed in reconciling different Treaty objectives.

1–039   Nevertheless, the General Court has also held that guidelines bind the Commission, albeit that the Commission retains the power to repeal or amend any guidelines if the circumstances so require. Hence the guidelines themselves must be amended in order to allow the Commission to change its practice. On the other

---

[67] [2001] O.J. C43.
[68] See Ch.4.
[69] [2004] O.J. C244/2.
[70] [2005] E.C.R. I–2801.

hand, the Court has also confirmed that Member States are bound by guidelines in so far as they have agreed to their contents. When the guidelines are based on art.108(1) they constitute one element of the regular co-operation between Member States and the Commission to keep existing aid under review. The Commission is empowered, in accordance with art.108(1) and the Procedural Regulation, to propose appropriate measures, and if these take the form of guidelines which the Member States agree to then they are bound by them. Article 19 of that Regulation also states that the Member State is only bound if it has accepted the proposed guidelines (and subsequent amendments) and has informed the Commission accordingly. So far, however, the Courts do not appear to have given much weight to this latter condition.[71] At the same time, the Courts will examine carefully the compatibility of the provisions of the relevant guidelines with primary law and, in doubtful cases, certain provisions may be reinterpreted in the light of the objective of art.107(1) to ensure undistorted competition.[72] The Court of Justice has repeatedly confirmed that the Commission imposes a limit on the exercise of its discretion when adopting binding guidelines and cannot rely on its wide discretion in the assessment of complex economic and social cases to avoid detailed judicial scrutiny.

In Case T–27/02 *Kronofrance*, the General Court had to interpret a part of the test applied under the former version of the multisectoral framework on regional aid for large investment projects (see Ch.15) and concluded that the Commission had not properly applied the impact on competition test in the light of primary law. On appeal, in Case C–75/05P, the ECJ confirmed that the General Court had not exceeded the limits of powers of review and, furthermore, drew attention to the fact that in view of the ambiguity in the guidelines at issue, the need to appraise the legality of the contested decision with regard to those guidelines was all the more justified (see para.67).[73]

Reliance can be placed on the recitals of the guidelines to justify diverging **1–040** from their main text in order to maintain the objective of undistorted competition.[74] In Case C–91/01 *Solar Tech*, the Court ruled that the Commission's definition of a "small and medium-sized enterprise" should not be interpreted in a formalistic way but must take full account of their purpose (see further, Chs 24 and 25). Where the definitions in question are too vague, this too may result in problems for the Commission, as for example in Case T–137/02 *Pollmeier*, which has led in 2003 to the adoption of a new Commission Recommendation on the definition of micro, small and medium-sized enterprises. In Case T–349/03 *Corsica Ferries*, the General Court annulled the Commission's decision applying the guidelines for rescue and restructuring aid to measures granted by the French government in favour of SNCM. A competitor, Corsica Ferries, claimed that the Commission had not confined the aid to the minimum and claimed that the Commission should have adopted further compensatory measures to ensure

---

[71] See, for example, Case C–382/99 *Netherlands v Commission* [2002] E.C.R. I–5163.
[72] Case T–27/02 *Kronofrance* [2004] E.C.R. II–4177.
[73] [2008] E.C.R. I–6619.
[74] Case C–91/01 *Italy v Commission (Solar Tech)* [2004] E.C.R. I–4355.

competition.[75] The General Court was prepared to take a strict approach to the application of the tests which the Commission had devised for itself in its guidelines.

1–041   Clear reasoning is nonetheless required. In Case T–126/06 *Kronopoly*, the Court found that:

> "It is clear on the face of the Decision . . . . that the Commission did in fact examine the condition concerning the incentive effect of the aid, by explaining why the particular circumstances of the present case enabled the presumption under point 4.2 of the Guidelines to be rebutted and the conclusion to be drawn that there was no incentive effect."

1–042   In still other areas the Commission is reluctant to commit itself to soft-law instruments and has preferred instead to abandon existing guidelines and continue its assessment on an ad hoc basis. If frameworks and guidelines are useful instruments to promote transparency and predictability, they can also prove to be too restrictive and inflexible. A case in point is the fate of the so-called "Regeneration Guidelines"—the Guidelines on state aid for undertakings in deprived urban areas.[76] These guidelines identified deprived urban areas eligible for state aid, but the Commission established that no Member State was able to make use of them, and in 2002 the Commission decided that they should no longer apply.[77] Instead the Commission has attempted to make its practice more transparent by publishing a vademedecum of its decision-making practice in this area.[78]

6. Conclusion—Towards a Reorientation?

1–043   The Treaty state regime has been put to a difficult test during the recent financial crisis. At the outset of the crisis and following the adoption of the various guidelines and emergency procedures, many questioned if things would ever return to normal. At the time of writing this may well be doubted. The Commission's plans to encourage a gradual exit for the banks from exceptional state support appear now to be on the back burner. Nevertheless the Commission's recent staff working paper of October 2011 asserts that its temporary rules were effective in containing the crisis and allowed the state aid discipline enshrined in the Treaty to be maintained. Despite initial protectionist instincts in some Member States, the Commission co-ordinated national action to limit negative spill-over effects, such as untenable subsidy races and distortions of competition that would have fragmented the internal market.[79]

[75] Case T–349/03 [2005] E.C.R. II–2197.
[76] [1997] O.J. C146/6.
[77] [2002] O.J. C119/21.
[78] March 1, 2006.
[79] EU Commission, "The effects of temporary state aid rules adopted in the context of the financial and economic crisis", SEC (2011) 1126 final, October 2011.

This reminds us that the Treaty state aid provisions essentially aim at reducing, if not eliminating, distortions of production and location decisions across Member States—this regime relates to competition between Member States, and not just competition between undertakings. It has been suggested that the Treaty state aid rules share more chromosomes with the internal market rules and the rules on free movement than with its competition or antitrust rules, such as arts 101 and 102. Hence economic analysis should be of a different order and purpose when it is concerned with the actions of Member States as opposed to firms. Thus it follows that the assessment of financial support to firms should not be based solely on its effect on competition in markets or its potential to boost market power, but on other factors involving its eventual impact on trade and also its potentially positive effects, including social and political objectives.[80] The Commission's views on the role of state aid control policy in achieving the Europe 2020 Strategy objectives by supporting smart, sustainable and inclusive initiatives of general common interest confirms this approach.

Continuing divergence between the two systems of competition control should therefore be perhaps welcomed and not criticised, and this is probably also true in respect of the aim of recovery of illegal state aid. Attempts to introduce antitrust concepts should be viewed with some caution. If the amount to be recovered is based on a distortion of competition test this may mean that it is not sufficient to limit recovery to the monetary value of the aid in question.

Nevertheless, irrespective of their genetic make-up, the reach of the Treaty state aid regime into national economies remains extensive, especially as long as the Courts continue to give a generous interpretation to the effect on trade test. At least prior to the financial crisis, the Commission's decisions on swimming pools, zebras and ski-lifts were far better known, and more widely criticised, than its decisions on major bank restructuring packages.[81]

As noted in the third edition, the Commission's approach to applying the state aid regime in the area of direct taxation in its battle against "unfair tax competition" appears to be challenging the limits of Union competence to intervene in matters in which Member States are considered to enjoy continued sovereign powers. The Court's ruling in *Portugal v Commission*, discussed in Chs 3 and 10, has gone some way to reassure the Member States that their constitutional arrangements are immune from the reach of the EU state aid regime. Nevertheless, it is somewhat remarkable to note that the extent of legal uncertainty in the area of the application of the state aid regime to fiscal measures. As Professor Schön notes in his Ch.10, the question of whether a Member State can abolish a sectoral tax without conferring an advantage on those hitherto required to pay this tax is still an open issue.[82]

---

[80] Buendia Sierra, unpublished speech at the Fourth Expert Forum on State Aid, Brussels, May 2006.

[81] See also, W. Bishop, "From Trade to Tutelage: State Aid and Public Choice in the European Union", presentation to the Conference of ACE, December 2, 2005.

[82] See Case T–210/02 *British Aggregates Association v Commission* [2006] E.C.R. II–2789.

An essentially similar criticism is levelled at the Commission's restructuring decisions in relation to Europe's banking sector. Under the guise of state aid control, the Commission is pursuing other ambitions and is imposing regulatory controls in the absence of a harmonised legislative framework. The pending cases before the General Court may throw more light on the scope of the Commission's powers in this particular respect.

1–044   Finally, the developments in the EU state aid regime cannot be considered in total isolation from the global economic context. The desirability of a rigorous approach to state aid control across the 27 Member States has to be considered against a global backdrop. Even if the European Union, in line with its G20 commitments, has publicly resisted the temptations of protectionism and remains committed to minimising any negative impact on trade and investment of the EU's domestic policy actions, the absence of state aid control for support to non-EU companies cannot be entirely ignored. Even before the events of 2008, the impact of Commission decisions restricting proposed national aid packages to persuade global players who can benefit from generous and uncontrolled subsidies elsewhere has always had to be considered. This has always been reflected in the somewhat schizophrenic attitude to export credit insurance and export credit guarantees.[83]

The financial crisis of 2008 provided a sharp reminder that the European Union is the only international economic organisation or quasi-federal arrangement or union which subjects its members to such a rigorous regime. The United States, Canada and Australia do not impose such controls on the ability of states or provinces to attract—or retain—industry. The NAFTA has still to agree on a subsidy control regime. At the same time, in judging the political and economic wisdom of Commission policy and practice, we cannot ignore the eventual impact of legal developments outside the European Union, including the expanding WTO case law on subsidies, as discussed in Ch.6, or tentative steps in the United States to bring state subsidy control within the jurisdiction of the inter-state commerce clause.[84]

---

[83] See further, Ch.4.
[84] *Cuno v Daimler Chrysler*, Supreme Court, 386 F.3d 738 (6th Cir. 2004).

CHAPTER 2

THE ECONOMICS OF STATE AID AND THE BALANCING TEST*

1. INTRODUCTION 2–001
2. SUBSIDIES AS A POLICY INSTRUMENT 2–004
3. WHY SUPRANATIONAL RULES ON SUBSIDIES? 2–008
4. ASSESSING CROSS-BORDER EFFECTS OF STATE AID: BALANCING OF EFFECTS OR COORDINATION OF AID? 2–017
5. THE PROBLEM OF DEFINING OPTIMUM SUBSIDIES 2–024
   Necessity 2–025
   Proportionality 2–026
   Impact on competition in the same and other markets 2–027
   Administrative costs 2–028
   Other costs 2–029
   A case study: Rescue and restructuring aid 2–030
6. THE MAIN FEATURES OF THE COMMISSION'S REFINED ECONOMIC APPROACH 2–033
   Different levels of assessment 2–034
   Positive assessment 2–038
   Negative assessment 2–039
7. CONCLUSIONS 2–041

1. INTRODUCTION

The justification for this chapter is given in the State Aid Action Plan (SAAP) **2–001** of the European Commission[1]:

"Making more use of a refined economic approach is a means to ensure a proper and more transparent evaluation of the distortions to competition and trade associated with state aid measures. This approach can also help investigate the reasons why the market by itself does not deliver the desired objectives of common interest and in consequence evaluate the benefits of state aid measures in reaching these objectives."

* Phedon Nicolaides
[1] European Commission, "State Aid Action Plan: Less and Better Targeted State Aid", COM(2005) 107 final.

Economic analysis of state aid is indispensable. Otherwise, national authorities cannot identify and measure the effects of public assistance they grant to enterprises.

2–002 However, in the formal assessment of state aid by the Commission, economic analysis used to be carried out only in a small number of cases such as rescue and restructuring, risk capital and the assessment of private investor principle.[2] The situation has changed significantly since the publication of the SAAP. The Commission now carries out more frequent and more rigorously thorough economic assessment of state aid.[3]

2–003 This chapter is structured as follows: section 2 examines the economic rationale for state aid; section 3 considers why a system of supranational control of aid may be useful in the context of economic integration; section 4 reviews the possible ways that state aid may be assessed so that it raises joint welfare or promotes the common interest; section 5 identifies typical problems in designing effective and efficient subsidy policies; and finally, section 6 presents the Commission's methodology of economic assessment and considers some landmark cases.

2. SUBSIDIES AS A POLICY INSTRUMENT

2–004 Governments grant state aid or subsidies for many reasons: economic, social, political, strategic.[4] Despite their prevalence, public subsidies are almost always a second-best solution for improving the functioning of markets because they introduce their own distortions and because they can be exploited by special-interest groups.

---

[2] See, for example, the critique in P. Nicolaides, "Markets and Words: The Distortive Effect of Government Pronouncements", *European Competition Law Review*, 2005; 3, pp.119–122; P. Nicolaides and M. Kekelekis, "An Economic Analysis of EC Guidelines on State Aid for the Rescue and Restructuring of Companies in Difficulty", *Intereconomics*, 2004, Vol. 39, nr.4, pp.204–212; P. Nicolaides, "Re-Introducing the Market in the 'Market Economy Investor' Principle", *European State Aid Law Quarterly*, 2003; P. Nicolaides, "Competition and Services of General Economic Interest in the EU: Reconciling Economics and Law", *European State Aid Law Quarterly*, 2003, nr.2.

[3] See M. Dewatripont, "The Economics of State Aid Control: Some Remarks", *Competition Policy International*, 2006 vol. 2; H. Friederiszick, L-H. Röller and V. Verouden, "European State Aid Control: An Economic Framework", in P. Buccirossi (ed.), *Advances in the Economics of Competition*, (Cambridge, MA: MIT Press, 2007).

[4] On the general problem of granting state aid, see S. Lehner, R. Meiklejohn and A. Louw, *Fair Competition in the Internal Market: Community State Aid Policy*, (Luxembourg: OOPEC, 1991); R. Meiklejohn, "The Economics of State Aid", *European Economy*, 1999, no.3, pp.25–31; D. Neven, "The Political Economy of State Aids in the European Community: Some Econometric Evidence", *Cahiers de Recherches Economique*, 1994, no.9402, University of Lausanne; P. Nicolaides and S. Bilal, "An Appraisal of the State Aid Rules of the European Community: Do they Promote Efficiency?", *Journal of World Trade*, 1999, vol.33(2), pp.97–124; *Public Subsidies*, Office of Fair Trading, London, November, 2004; and various speeches by the Chief Economist of DG Competition, European Commission.

There is a large amount of literature on whether, when and how governments **2–005** should aid particular economic activities, industries or regions. By and large, this literature concludes that, on efficiency grounds, aid may be justified when it is intended to correct market failure. The typical reasons cited for market failure are externalities (plus public goods), economies of scale and asymmetric information. Because of these reasons, it is thought necessary for governments to intervene and subsidise activities such as training, research, investment in environmentally friendly processes or backward regions, and supply of important services such as electricity or transport.

The Commission, in the State Aid Action Plan, also acknowledges that:

"One key element in that respect is the analysis of market failures . . . which may be reasons why the markets do not achieve desired objectives of common interest, in particular if they are of an economic nature. In those cases, identifying the market failure at stake will help evaluate better whether state aid could be justified and acceptable, would represent the most appropriate solution, and how it should be implemented to achieve the desired objective without distorting competition and trade to an extent contrary to the common interest."

Market failure is a necessary but not a sufficient condition for providing public support to industry. The "first-best" policy would be to address market failure directly, instead of granting state aid to compensate for it. Only when direct measures are not feasible should aid be considered, as a "second-best" option.

Again, the State Aid Action Plan also accepts that some market failures "may be solved by regulatory or other means." It goes on to add that:

"it is not enough for state aid to target a market failure. Before resorting to State aid, which is in general only the second best option to achieve optimal allocation of resources, it should be verified whether other less distortive measures could remedy the market failure. State aid should be the appropriate policy instrument and should be designed so that it effectively solves the market failure, by creating an incentive effect and being proportionate. In addition, state aid should not distort competition to an extent contrary to the common interest."

The appropriate amount and method of aid may still be too difficult to **2–006** determine. Not only may the government have to rely on incomplete information about the state of the economy, but it may also suffer from asymmetric information. Enterprises seeking to benefit from state aid possess information not directly available to the government which runs the risk of being misled when designing and implementing its aid policy.

The aid-giving agency may be in danger of being "captured" by special **2–007** interest groups. The "politicisation" of state aid is one of the major problems facing aid-granting agencies. Hence, the cost of getting the policy wrong may in reality outweigh the benefits of intervention to correct market failure.

3. WHY SUPRANATIONAL RULES ON SUBSIDIES?

2–008   The State Aid Action Plan justifies control of state aid at the European level in the following terms:

"State aid control comes from the need to maintain a level playing field for all undertakings active in the Single European Market, no matter in which Member State they are established. There is a particular need to be concerned with those state aid measures, which provide unwarranted selective advantages to some firms, preventing or delaying the market forces from rewarding the most competitive firms, thereby decreasing overall European competitiveness. It may also lead to a build-up of market power in the hands of some firms, for instance when companies that do not receive state aid (e.g. non-domestic firms) have to cut down on their market presence, or where state aid is used to erect entry barriers."

2–009   Indeed, subsidies that are not of a general nature have, by definition, an impact on relative prices and therefore on the allocation of resources among sectors. In an open economy, this implies that the terms of trade are affected. If the effect is significant enough it may shift the comparative advantage of the country. While this results in welfare losses when resources are reallocated to inefficient sectors, it may raise national welfare when aid policies are intended to correct market failures so as to shift resources to sectors where the true comparative advantage of a country lies. Note, once more, that for aid to be welfare improving, the efficiency gains derived from aid policies must be larger than the (direct and indirect) costs of state aid.

2–010   Assuming that state aid compensates for market distortions, we can turn to the question of why a group of countries, each of which is presumed (at least initially) to maximise economic efficiency, should need any supranational constraints on their discretion to disburse subsidies? The typical answer is that rational, welfare-maximising behaviour does not preclude subsidy wars in pursuit of "beggar thy neighbour" objectives. Hence, supranational rules may be voluntarily adopted in order to prevent the emergence of predatory or rent-shifting national policies.

2–011   Rent-shifting policies are normally implemented through selection of "national champions" which have, or are expected to acquire, market power (as reflected in large market shares). Because they seek to be selective, they are, as a result, inherently discriminatory (and to a large extent, arbitrary). Given that the process of selection necessarily entails that (i) certain industries must be left out, and (ii) those not favoured are penalised by not having access to public funds, it is not unreasonable to conclude that ultimately the ban on rent-shifting measures, intentionally or unintentionally, prevents governments from discriminating against "unfashionable" economic activities.

Economic policies, especially those that affect traded goods or mobile factors **2–012** of production, generate cross-border spillovers. To the extent that these spillovers are positive (as, in some instances, with subsidies to an industry using imported goods as inputs), there is no need for supranational rules. Countries benefit from the state aid policy of their partners. In contrast, when domestic aid policies generate negative spillover effects (i.e. it reduces the welfare of other countries), supranational rules may protect the interests of partner countries as well. Supranational rules may have the purpose of not only eliminating these negative spillovers, but also of introducing greater transparency and predictability in the partner countries' policy processes. Greater policy transparency and predictability make it easier for companies to plan their investments and for other governments to formulate and implement their own policies.

Supranational rules may also prevent *tit-for-tat* strategies of the type, "since **2–013** you give aid to your industry, I'll help my industry too". Governments often get caught in such "prisoner's dilemma" situations where domestic aid is granted to restore the "level playing field" with subsidised foreign industries. However, all countries would be better off with a cooperative outcome.

The need for supranational rules is further strengthened when the assumption of efficiency maximisation is relaxed. Such rules constrain the decision-making discretion of national governments and make them less vulnerable to domestic lobbying by special interest groups. This is not a farfetched supposition given the fact that external constraints are often sought for internal political reasons. In this context, supranational rules improve the fairness or objectivity of domestic decision-making. Even when supranational rules do not meet efficiency criteria, they may constrain domestic tendencies for interventionist or discriminatory policies (which generally benefit small but organised, politically influential groups as they have to apply to, and accommodate, a larger number of entities). A national specific-interest group is therefore less likely to influence such rules or their application. Besides, supranational rules and institutions help to shield national decision-makers from domestic pressures as they can shift the blame for unpopular or politically difficult decisions not to support specific sectors (generally the so-called "national champions") to international institutions. The prevention of discriminatory measures or discouraging rent-seeking activities is in general welfare improving.

Finally, state aid may also serve non-economic objectives: self-sufficiency, **2–014** protection of national interests (e.g. the defence sector), etc. In the context of the European Union, the integration of the internal market has been the main objective of Community policies and action. It follows that the political objective of market integration may conflict with the economic prescription for efficiency. Supranational rules, however, may serve to clarify and rank these various objectives.

In summary, the case in favour of supranational control does not exclusively **2–015** rest on the presence of cross-border externalities. However, such externalities make supranational overview and assessment necessary. Before concluding this section it is worth identifying the typical market conditions under which aid in one country has a significant negative impact on competition in another.

2–016   The UK Office of Fair Trading undertook a study on the question of cross-border distortion of competition.[5] The study concluded that the magnitude of the competition distortion is determined by:

- the absolute size of the subsidy;

- the relative size of the subsidy in relation to the subsidised costs;

- the degree of selectivity of the subsidy;

- whether the subsidy affects the recipient's costs directly (i.e. whether it is operating aid);

- whether the subsidy is provided on a recurring basis;

- the extent of concentration in the market;

- the level of product differentiation;

- the symmetry (or asymmetry) of firm size in the market;

- the presence of barriers to entry.

For example, the larger the distortion of competition, the bigger the subsidy, the more selective it is, and the higher the degree of market concentration.

The OFT study also found that EU rules allowed state aid that could have a very distortionary effect, because it fell within state aid guidelines, while they prohibited aid with insignificant effects because it fell outside the guidelines. Although this observation was correct, it was not novel.[6] The study further recommended that where the distortion of competition was insignificant, EU rules should have allowed national authorities to implement their policies without much interference by the Commission. Again, this was the right conclusion, but it raised questions as to how EU rules could have been adjusted to offer this flexibility without compromising legal certainty. As we will see in section 5, the Commission's "refined economic approach" and "balancing test" do take into account the presence or absence of risk to competition without compromising too much of legal certainty.

---

[5] "Public Subsidies: A report by the Office of Fair Trading", Office of Fair Trading, London, November, 2004.

[6] See, for example, P. Nicolaides and S. Bilal, "An Appraisal of the State Aid Rules of the European Community: Do they Promote Efficiency?", *Journal of World Trade*, 1999, vol.33(2), pp.97–124.

4. ASSESSING CROSS-BORDER EFFECTS OF STATE AID: BALANCING OF EFFECTS OR COORDINATION OF AID?

If we accept that there is a case to be made both for subsidies to correct market **2–017** failure and for supranational control of such subsidies, the questions that still remain to be answered are how their cross-border effects should be evaluated and whether more extensive coordination of aid may be desirable.

With respect to the first problem, the issue is how the distortion-correction in one country should be weighted against the distortion-creation in another due to the impact on competition. EU state aid policy is based on the premise that "state aid should not distort competition to an extent contrary to the common interest." This is the role of the Commission.

We do not have a general formulation or definition of the meaning of the "common interest" and how the benefits from a market-correcting subsidy in one Member State can be assessed against possible losses in other Member States. Moreover, the SAAP does not explain whether the amount of permissible subsidies can be allowed to vary from Member State to Member State according to the magnitude of market failure in different member states. At present the only allowable variation is the case of regional aid. For all the other kinds of state aid and in all the other guidelines and frameworks, the rates of allowable aid are the same for all Member States. This suggests that it is presumed that market failure is of the same nature and same magnitude across Member States.

We do not know whether state aid which generates larger domestic gains than **2–018** losses abroad should be allowed. In such a situation global welfare increases, even if the welfare of some countries may be negatively affected. In this case, state aid is potentially pareto-efficient, although it hurts some countries. EU rules, as they do not directly address the issue of efficiency, remain ambiguous in relation to such policies.

Therefore, in addition to control of rent-shifting subsidies, supranational supervision of aid must also perform some kind of balancing of positive and negative effects across countries. At present, this is only presumed to happen when EU Member States comply with Commission regulations and guidelines.

In some of the guidelines, in particular those for regional aid, maritime **2–019** transport and broadcasting, the Commission also examines whether aid contributes to the problems of industries with overcapacity (regional guidelines) or whether aid recipients engage in predatory pricing (transport and broadcasting guidelines). Preventing increase in overcapacity or decrease in prices contributes to reducing the distortions of competition.

With respect to the second problem, as is well known from the theory of second-best, intervention to correct one source of distortion in markets with multiple distortions creates its own distortion, which may have the paradoxical effect of actually reducing welfare. For instance, R&D subsidies designed to stimulate technical innovation and productivity, if granted to an industry which operates in a protected sector and which causes environmental pollution, may result, respectively, in a greater misallocation of resources (away from the production of goods where the country has a natural comparative advantage) and to higher national negative externalities in terms of pollution, and thus have a negative welfare impact.

In open economies, internal policies virtually always have a direct or indirect external effect. Even intervention in a non-traded sector may have an indirect effect on a traded sector and thus on a foreign economy.

2–020   An example will help clarify this issue. Firms may choose to invest in a location where other similar firms already maintain production facilities or have an established business presence. They may make that investment in order to obtain access to raw materials, transport networks, factors of production or to benefit from external economies or agglomeration effects. The government may initiate and speed up the process of agglomeration by offering regional invest-ment incentives. In case the government of another country attempts to follow precisely the same policy, the two countries may end up undermining each other's efforts even though both intend to pursue a first-best policy of basically correcting externalities. Both countries are trapped in a prisoner's dilemma situation. Should there be rules on investment incentives of this sort? Not only are there cross-border spillovers, but both countries may be better off by agreeing not to pursue those policies. However, if one country could compensate the other, a better option for both of them would be to agree for one to grant the subsidy while the other refrains from doing the same.

2–021   Consider a different example. A firm that proposes to build a new lean car engine asks the government for research subsidies. The firm wants to carry out research on new component materials, new fuels and new methods of fuel injection. Again there are extensive externalities and at the same time substantial commercial risks. Should the government subsidise this project? Even if sub-sidies are a first-best response to a market failure, should this kind of research still receive public support if governments in other countries intend to support similar projects submitted to them? Should they all subsidise or not? Should they all subsidise a little bit? Should some subsidise, while others refrain from doing so?

2–022   Both examples illustrate typical prisoner's dilemmas. All countries would be worse off without government intervention and yet there is a significant risk that public support could lead to too much intervention, with consequent excessive subsidies and waste of resources. Note that in neither example does the govern-ment explicitly intend to extract rent from other countries. The point is that distortion-correcting aid is not necessarily free of negative cross-border effects, especially when it directly induces a shift in the location of production by influencing investment decisions.

When individual decisions lead to a sub-optimal collective outcome, osten-sibly there is a need for coordination. The problem is how to define and measure this "collective interest" and how to coordinate national policies. In this context a blanket prohibition, as in the case, for example, of export subsidies, would not be appropriate. There is a need for a supranational mechanism or authority to coordinate national aid decisions. That authority needs to have discretion to judge each case on its own merits. Hence, within the context of a regional grouping like the European Union, the pursuit of efficiency necessarily means some form of coordination which, in turn, means the exercise of policy discretion.

It is worth mentioning that the only rules that allow cross-country modulation of the amount of aid that is granted are those concerning regional aid. This means that more aid is allowed in poorer regions because their development handicap is greater than those of richer regions. This is a form of coordination. The question in the context of the EU system of state aid control is whether rules should allow aid intensities to vary according to the degree of market failure experienced in each country.

One way of dealing both with the problem of the balancing of effects felt in **2–023** different countries and with the problem of coordination, which is also consistent with the Commission's more economic approach to state aid, is to modulate permitted subsidies in terms of a percentage in relation to the magnitude of the market failure. This would mean that the amount of subsidies will vary across Member States. It would also mean that the extent of the effect on trade would not matter because, irrespective of how other Member States are affected, it would always be considered to be in the common interest.

5. THE PROBLEM OF DEFINING OPTIMUM SUBSIDIES

In the State Aid Action Plan, the Commission makes the following **2–024** observations:

> "It is important to realise that state aid does not come for free. Nor is state aid a miracle solution that can instantly cure all problems. Tax payers in the end have to finance state aid and there are opportunity costs to it. Giving aid to undertakings means taking funding away from other policy areas."

Therefore, it is important that any subsidy policy is efficient. An authority that wants to offer subsidies has to address the subsequent problems.

Necessity

It needs to be determined whether subsidies are necessary to induce firms to do **2–025** something they would not otherwise do under normal market conditions. This has three aspects. First, the presumed market failure has to be proven. Second, even in the presence of market failure it does not mean that firms will not, for example, invest or hire staff or undertake R&D. They may only do less than what is socially optimum. This means that the subsidy has to be the minimum necessary—which is the issue of proportionality that is examined below. Third, even in the presence of a general market failure it still does not follow that each firm suffers from that failure. For example, a firm may manufacture a very specialised product so that it faces no risk of imitation by competitors. This firm would not need any public incentive to engage in R&D or to retain its technological leadership. For the same reason, in industries where R&D is indispensable for the survival of each firm, subsidies would not be necessary to induce them to undertake research. This is, in essence, the fundamental problem of every subsidy granting authority. It is never clear what the subsidy recipients truly intended to do in where they did not obtain a subsidy.

Proportionality

2–026   Even if the need for subsidies is established in principle, the next problem is to determine the minimum amount necessary. This has two aspects. First, the granting authority has to calculate the amount of subsidy that will induce the recipient firms to carry out the socially optimum investment, training, R&D, etc. Second, the authority has to identify the true costs of the recipients. Every subsidy recipient has a strong incentive to exaggerate its relevant costs. In principle, if each euro of the subsidy fully captures the cost to society for granting that subsidy,[7] then the subsidy is proportional (and, therefore, at its optimum level) when the last euro granted is equal to the extra benefit derived by society (or the marginal cost of the subsidy is equal its marginal benefit).

Impact on competition in the same and other markets

2–027   But subsidies also create costs in terms of the distortions they cause. This is because subsidy recipients obtain an advantage that is not normally available to their competitors. Even if society obtains some benefits from more investment or R&D, it may also experience negative effects by the fact that the recipients capture market share at the expense of potentially more efficient competitors. Not only do national authorities not normally worry about any negative impact on foreign competitors, sometimes they intentionally seek to distort international competition by supporting their national "champions". In any case, consumers lose out from not having access to cheaper or better products. In addition, there is the potential for distortion in adjacent markets. Government subsidies in one market may stimulate demand for inputs from other markets, distorting competition in favour of the suppliers that happen to have access to the subsidy receiving firms.

Administrative costs

2–028   The granting of subsidies is costly for both the authority that provides them and the firms that obtain them. The former have to maintain the necessary administrative infrastructure to process applications and to ensure compliance

---

[7] That is, the subsidy is neither a pure transfer, so it has zero costs, nor does it generate other costs.

with the relevant rules. The latter have to expend resources to apply for subsidies and to report later on how they have used them. It has been estimated that such administrative costs account for about 10 per cent of subsidies granted (5 per cent for the granting authorities and 5 per cent for the recipient firms).[8]

Other costs

Subsidies have to be raised through taxation which is itself an economic distortion. In addition, there is the possibility that subsidies generate spillovers that worsen distortions in other markets or create new distortions in the same market. For example, subsidies to farmers stimulate demand for fertilisers produced through polluting processes in other markets. At the same time, over-production of agricultural products results in excessive use of fertilisers worsening soil degradation of farmland.

Aid that is compatible with EU rules does not mean that is necessary and proportional, causes no other distortions and keeps any other costs to the minimum necessary.

A case study: Rescue and restructuring aid

The purpose of this case study is to show that compliance with existing guidelines does not necessarily guarantee that allowable aid is either necessary or efficient.[9]

Consider the guidelines on state aid for rescue and restructuring which deal with aid to companies in financial trouble. The guidelines impose limits on permissible aid and exempt aid that remedies the social impact of company closure or prevents the emergence of monopoly or oligopoly due to the exit from the market of the company that is in financial trouble.

A requirement of the guidelines is that the aid is capable of bringing the beneficiary company back to long-term viability. For the owners of the company this means that they should be able to make a normal return on their investment. But if that is the condition for granting aid, it immediately raises the question of why aid is needed in the first place? Obviously, the answer is that without the aid, the return to the owners/investors would be lower and would be so low as not to justify any further investment of their own funds. So the question is about the rate of return that the owners of the company should be allowed to make. The guidelines are silent on this point.

Consider the following example. Suppose that the cost of the restructuring plan is 120. With this expenditure, the firm comes back to viability. Also suppose that once the company is restructured, it will generate income whose net present value for the owners is 100. This means that they should invest at maximum not

2–029

2–030

2–031

---

[8] National Audit Office, "Regional Grants in England" (London: Stationery Office, 2003).

[9] For a fuller critique of the rescue and restructuring guidelines and practice of the EU see P. Nicolaides and M. Kekelekis, "When Do Firms in Trouble Escape from State Aid Rules?", *European State Aid Law Quarterly*, 2005; P. Nicolaides and M. Kekelekis, "An Economic Analysis of EC Guidelines on State Aid for the Rescue and Restructuring of Companies in Difficulty", *Intereconomics*, 2004, Vol. 39, nr.4, pp.204–212.

more than 100. If they invest more than 100, the return on their investment will fall below the cost of the new capital (i.e. they could earn a higher return by investing elsewhere). If the government wants to keep this company afloat because its closure will cause significant social upheaval in its area, then it must give aid of at least 20. Indeed, most restructuring cases are based on similar calculations.

Nonetheless, aid may be unnecessary in the following circumstances. Assume that the owners have past obligations towards their workforce. In case of closure they are obliged to pay compensation for laying off workers. In addition, closure may require decommissioning of plants and cleaning up of the sites occupied by the factories of the company. Assume that these closure costs amount to 15. This implies that since the owners would be 15 worse off if the company would close down, their net costs of investing in keeping the company as a going concern is not 100, but 85. Therefore, an aid package of 20 is 15 too much. The owners would be satisfied with aid of just 5. If the closure costs would exceed 20, then no aid would be needed at all to persuade the owners to invest to save the company.

This is just one example that demonstrates that (a) sometimes aid may be unnecessary, and that (b) it is difficult to calculate the truly necessary amount of aid because it requires knowledge of how the recipients would behave without aid.

2–032 In fact, the problem facing the aid granting authority is even more complicated. In the example above it was simply assumed that the purpose of the aid was to encourage the owners of the company to keep it afloat. But the public authority is not just interested in rescuing companies. It is interested in minimising the social impact from company closure. This social impact presumably can be quantified.

Therefore, the amount of state aid that should be granted is not just what is necessary to induce the owners to make further investments. It should also not exceed the value of the social costs it prevents. Otherwise, it would be better to spend the money directly on the workers who are made unemployed. An example will clarify this point.

As before, we assume that the total cost of restructuring is 120 and that the requested aid is 20. If the social costs from the company closure exceed 20, then the public authority should grant the aid. If the social costs are less than 20, then the public authority would save money (which presumably it can invest more productively elsewhere) by not granting the aid and still compensate unemployed workers. In this situation the aid is inefficient.

6. The Main Features of the Commission's Refined Economic Approach

2–033 The Commission applies the refined economic approach to state aid in the form of the so-called "balancing test". As its name indicates, this test examines whether the positive effects of state aid balance out the negative effects.

The balancing test consists of three stages with the following questions:

1. Is the aid measure aimed at a well-defined objective of common interest? For state aid to be exempted it must pursue one of the policy objectives which are defined in art.107(3) [or (2)] TFEU.

2. Is the aid well designed to deliver the objective of common interest; i.e. does the proposed aid address the market failure or other objective? This, in turn, is broken down into three subsidiary questions:

   i. Is state aid an appropriate policy instrument? There may be other instruments that do not involve subsidies and which are equally good or even better at achieving the desired policy objectives.
   ii. Is there an incentive effect; i.e. does the aid change the behaviour of firms? For aid to be exempted it must be capable of inducing firms to do things they would not otherwise do without government intervention.
   iii. Is the aid measure proportional; i.e. could the same change in behaviour be obtained with less aid?

3. Are the distortions of competition and effect on trade limited, so that the overall balance is positive? Even if the aid is appropriate and proportional, it may still generate significant distortions of competition that may harm other member states. These harmful effects have to be taken into account.

Different levels of assessment

The balancing test is not applied to all awards of state aid. Both the practice **2–034** of the Commission and the guidelines that incorporate a balancing test create a process whereby most cases are subject to a simplified assessment. Only a small number of cases are subject to the detailed assessment of the balancing test.

The balancing test is applied to all cases where state aid is granted outside any regulations or guidelines. Once Member States deviate from the provisions of regulations and guidelines they have to justify why aid is necessary and in the common interest and that its negative effects on competition will be limited.

The Court of Justice of the European Union has recognised that, as long as aid **2–035** falls within the exemptions allowed by the Treaty, Member States have the right to design aid measures that are not provided by Commission rules. However, since only the Commission has the power to authorise state aid, Member States still have to persuade the Commission that the aid they propose pursues legitimate goals. The objective of the balancing test in this context is to determine whether such aid is appropriate, necessary and proportional. In other words, the balancing test in this context is a form of general guideline for aid that does not fall within the scope of the specific guidelines. Examples of cases where the balancing test has been applied to measures that were not covered by regulations and guidelines include the broadband schemes mentioned below.

Where state aid falls within regulations or guidelines, its compatibility with the internal market is assessed at three different levels of varying degree of detail. The first and least demanding level applies to aid granted to SMEs and aid that falls below certain thresholds. This kind of aid is presumed to have generally positive effects and limited negative effects, provided it complies with all the requirements laid down in the regulations and guidelines. If the application for aid is made by the requesting undertaking before the project starts, then the Commission also regards the aid to be necessary and to have an incentive effect.

2–036 At the second level, Member States must demonstrate explicitly the necessity of aid. Larger amounts of aid up to certain higher thresholds and aid granted to large enterprises are subject to closer scrutiny by the Commission to determine whether the aid has an incentive effect. If the aid does not induce the recipients to go beyond their normal level of research or environmental protection, then the Commission will conclude that the aid lacks incentive effect and will not authorise it. (Please note that this level is not applicable to risk capital for SMEs simply because aid may not be granted to large enterprises.)

2–037 The third level applies the detailed assessment of the full balancing test. The detailed assessment is performed on aid that exceeds the following thresholds. In the case of R&D&I aid:

- Project aid and feasibility studies (per project/per undertaking):
  - Projects in fundamental research: €20 million;
  - Projects in industrial research: €10 million;
  - For all other projects: €7.5 million;

- Process or organisational innovation in services activities (per project/per undertaking): €5 million;

- Innovation clusters (per cluster): €5 million.

In the case of environmental aid:

- Investment aid (per project/per undertaking): €7.5 million
- Operating aid:
  - Energy saving: €5 million per undertaking for 5 years;
  - Production of renewable electricity and/or combined production of renewable heat: capacity of 125 MW;
  - Production of biofuel: production of 150,000 tons per year;
  - Cogeneration of heat and electricity: capacity of 200 MW.

In the case of risk capital to SMEs:

- Investment: €2.5 million per SME per year;
- Finance for the expansion stage for medium-sized enterprises in non-assisted areas;

- Follow-on investments into companies that already received aid to fund subsequent financing rounds beyond €2.5 million and the companies' early growth financing;

- Participation by private investors below 50 per cent in non-assisted areas or below 30 per cent in assisted areas;

- Seed capital to small enterprises with: (i) less or no private participation by private investors; and/or (ii) predominance of debt investment instruments as opposed to equity and quasi-equity;

- Measures specifically involving an investment vehicle;

- Costs linked to the first screening of companies in view of the conclusion of the investments, up to the due diligence phase ("scouting costs").

Positive assessment

This section reviews cases where the result of the balancing was positive and identifies the reasons that led the Commission to reach that conclusion. **2–038**

I. Broadband networks.[10] In these cases the Commission accepted that aid had an incentive effect for the following reasons:

1. Telecoms companies would not realise any profit by incurring large costs to expand networks and provide services in rural or sparsely populated areas where demand was low.

2. Regulation was not an appropriate instrument because it could not force providers to offer their services at low prices (possibly below cost) so that broadband access would be attractive enough to end users.

3. State aid was an appropriate instrument to remedy market failure and to strengthen territorial cohesion.

At the same time, the assessment of the possible negative effects of state aid did not arouse any significant concerns because of the following:

1. Aid was proportional because public authorities relied on competitive tendering to award contracts.

2. Aid had no disproportionate negative effect because it only aimed to stimulate competition in the regions which were under-provided with broadband services.

3. Aid did not discriminate in favour of any particular technologies.

[10] See, for example, N 57/2005, regional innovative broadband support in Wales (UK); N 284/2005, metropolitan area networks (Ireland).

II. R&D&I.[11] These cases have been assessed or are currently being investigated by the Commission on the basis of the 2006 Framework on state aid to R&D and Innovation.[12] The Commission concluded that aid had an incentive effect and therefore was necessary. The Commission accepted that the aid had an incentive effect primarily because of three factors:

1. The projects had long durations.

2. The risk of failure was high.

3. The envisaged rate of return would have been either too low or negative without aid.

The potential distortive effect of the aid was found not to be excessive because:

1. It was unlikely that state aid would crowd out private investment. The amount of aid was small relative to the normal R&D expenditure in those sectors.

2. There were other strong competitors who were unlikely to be excessively affected by the state aid.

3. The sectors were growing and there were competing technologies so the aid was unlikely to maintain an inefficient market structure.

In the case concerning Peugeot-Citroën, cited in the footnotes, the Commission thought that it was likely that Peugeot-Citroën, the second largest automobile manufacturer in Europe, would have undertaken the project anyway, even in the absence of a state subsidy. The Commission had doubts that there was any market failure. The case was withdrawn.

III. Equity capital for SMEs.[13] The measure in question sought to establish a new investment vehicle to raise equity capital for SMEs. The Commission carried out a detailed assessment on the basis of the Guidelines on Risk Capital for SMEs. According to the Guidelines, aid to investment vehicles is subject to the full balancing test. The positive result of the balancing test was obtained because of the following reasons:

1. There was a well-defined market failure. It was shown that institutional investors would not normally provide finance to SMEs for amounts between £0.5 and 2 million.

---

[11] N 674/2006, aid to Siemens & Lohr for metro trains (France); N 854/2006, aid to Alcatel-Lucent for unlimited mobile TV (France); N 530/2007, opening of formal investigation on R&D aid to Peugeot-Citroën (France).

[12] O.J. C323, 30/12/2006.

[13] Commission Decision 2008/126 on the establishment of Investbx (UK).

2. The returns on investment in the early stages of the development of SMEs were shown to be significantly below average return for investments at later stages of development.

3. The aid had an incentive effect because no investor was willing to establish that vehicle.

4. The aid was also proportional because it was limited in duration (five years) and that the amount (£3 million) was just sufficient to induce the establishment of that vehicle.

The negative effects of the measure were also limited because:

1. Investbx would offer only relatively small amounts of equity capital so the aid would not crowd out other market activities.

2. Investbx would offer its services to SMEs located only in a small geographic area (West Midlands).

3. The distortion of competition was minimal because no other entity offered similar services.

Negative assessment

This section reviews cases where the result of the balancing was negative and identifies the reasons that led the Commission to reach that conclusion.   **2–039**

I. Training.[14]

II. Switch to digital TV and development of broadband networks.[15] The reasons that led the Commission to find that the aid was incompatible with the internal market were the following:

1. Aid was used to support investment for the manufacturing of new products that had to be carried out by the recipient in order to remain in business (e.g. launch of new model, GM and Ford).

2. Aid was used to cover costs of production rationalisation and implementation of changes which were necessary for the recipient to become more

[14] Commission Decision 2007/612 on training aid to General Motors (Belgium); Commission Decision 2006/938 on training aid for Ford Genk (Belgium); Commission Decision C23/2007 on Vauxhall Ellesmere Port (UK); Commission Decision C35/2007 on Volvo Gent (Belgium); Commission Decision C18/2007 on DHL (Germany).
[15] Commission Decision 2006/513 on DVB-T in Berlin-Brandenburg (Germany); Commission Decision 2007/374 on digital decoders (Italy); Commission Decision 2007/175 on broadband network in Appingedam (The Netherlands); Commission Decision C34/2006 on digital terrestrial television in North-Rhine Westphalen (Germany).

efficient (e.g. restructuring and training on new production methods, Ford; new production methods, Volvo and Vauxhall).

3. Aid was used to support the acquisition of legally required permits and/or certificates (e.g. handling new operations, DHL).

4. Aid was used to shift operations or activities from one plant to another or one subsidiary to another, but which would still have to be carried out by the group as a whole. This may be a legitimate consideration for obtaining regional aid but not other kinds of aid (e.g. allocation of operations to a particular plant, GM, Ford and Volvo).

5. Aid was used to support products and/or services which are already provided by the market (e.g. digital TV, Berlin-Brandenburg; digital TV, NRW; Italian decoders; broadband network, Appingedam).

6. Aid was used to support products and/or services without any evidence that the costs of development/production could not be fully borne by companies themselves (e.g. switch to digital TV, Berlin-Brandenburg; digital TV, NRW).

7. Aid was used to reduce the risk associated with new products when the market appeared capable of bearing such risk (e.g. digital TV, Berlin-Brandenburg; digital TV, NRW; Italian decoders).

8. Aid was used to encourage the supply of services which could be made available through imposition of regulatory obligations on the relevant service providers (e.g. switch to digital TV, Berlin-Brandenburg; Italian decoders). So aid was not an appropriate instrument.

9. Aid was used to stimulate competition when there was sufficient competition in the market. Moreover, other policy instruments could be more effective towards that objective (e.g. digital TV, Berlin-Brandenburg; digital TV, NRW; Italian decoders).

10. Aid was used to favour a particular technology when there was no legitimate reason for discriminating against other technologies (e.g. digital TV, Berlin-Brandenburg; digital TV, NRW; Italian decoders).

2–040   In general, aid has been found not to be compatible with the internal market when it is not an appropriate instrument, when it is not necessary and when it discriminates against particular technologies or companies. Then it has an undue distortion of competition which is contrary to the common interest.

7. CONCLUSIONS

2–041   The economic justification for state aid is the correction of market failure. However, a number of qualifications have to be made in this respect. First, market failure is a necessary, but not sufficient, condition. Second, the costs of government intervention to correct market failure may outweigh any benefits. These costs include the cost of distortion to competition, the cost of taxation for raising subsidies, and the cost of administering the disbursement of subsidies. Third, the aid-granting authorities are always at a disadvantage in relation to aid recipients because they do not know the real costs of the latter and, above all, cannot know what the recipients would have done in the absence of aid.

An economic approach to assessing state aid also suggests that supranational control of aid is necessary only when such aid affects cross-border competition. Current state aid rules of the European Union have a wider reach because of the broad interpretation of the concept of effect of trade. This means that EU resources are "wasted" in controlling cases that have little, if any, impact on cross-border competition and on firms in other countries.

But the biggest challenges for supranational control of state aid are, first, to **2–042** balance the effects of aid in one country against the effects in other countries and, second, to determine the extent to which a supranational institution such as the Commission should coordinate national aid. A more economic approach which would modulate the size of permissible aid according to the degree of market failure would significantly address both of these challenges.

Since the publication of the State Aid Action Plan in 2005, the Commission's **2–043** practice has changed significantly. It is now based on the more coherent and economically rational approach which is embodied in the balancing test of the positive and negative effects of state aid. The recent practice of the Commission can be summarised as follows:

1. All state aid that falls outside the scope of regulations and guidelines is subject to the balancing test irrespective of the amount of aid or the size of the beneficiary undertakings.

2. For state aid that falls within the scope of regulations and guidelines, the balancing test is applied only in a small number of cases involving large amounts of aid. The regulations and guidelines define the relevant thresholds.

3. Aid is considered to have positive effects when:

   i. it is an appropriate instrument (i.e. it addresses market failure that cannot be corrected through regulatory measures);
   ii. it is necessary (i.e. it induces beneficiaries to change their behaviour) and;
   iii. it is proportional (i.e. it offers the minimum required level of assistance, which may be ensured by reliance on public procurement and competitive selection of beneficiaries).

4. Aid is considered to have undue negative effects when:

    i. it is granted to inefficient or dominant companies or companies in declining sectors;

    ii. it displaces private investment or research efforts; and

    iii. it discriminates against certain companies or technologies.

CHAPTER 3

THE GENERAL FRAMEWORK*

1. GENERAL 3–001
   The scope of article 107(1): the concept of an aid 3–002
   Intent 3–004
   Advantage 3–005
   Public declarations as an advantage? 3–010
   Indirect advantage 3–011
   Compensation in damages 3–012
2. THE ATTRIBUTES 3–015
   State resources 3–016
   Transfer of state resources 3–020
   Revenue foregone 3–021
   Must the measure impose a cost to the state? 3–022
   *State resources in any form whatsoever: the residual category and the concept of
      public control over private resources* 3–027
   Imputability 3–028
   Subsequent Commission decisions 3–032
   Imputability and harmonised taxation 3–035
   Community resources 3–036
3. THE SELECTIVITY CRITERIA 3–040
   Undertaking 3–041
   General measures 3–042
   Taxation exemptions 3–045
   Direct taxation 3–046
   General or selective tax measures 3–048
   The "logic of the system test" 3–050
   Events versus activities 3–051
   Regional taxation measures and geographical selectivity 3–052
   Material or de facto selectivity 3–053
   Alleviation of social charges 3–054
   Indirect reductions in the costs of certain undertakings 3–055
   Selectivity and support for training 3–057
   Financial support for infrastructure 3–058
   Selectivity and infrastructural aid 3–059
   Selectivity 3–064
   The Broadband Guidelines 2009 3–070
   Conclusion 3–075

* Leigh Hancher

4. EFFECT ON TRADE 3–076
   The de minimis regulation 3–079
   Distortion of competition 3–080
5. STATE PARTICIPATION AND THE MARKET ECONOMY INVESTOR TEST 3–081
   State shareholdings and capital injections for publicly owned or controlled firms 3–082
   Concomitance 3–084
   The MEIT and public undertakings 3–086
   The private creditor test 3–089
   The private seller test 3–093
   Sale of intangible assets 3–099
   The private purchaser test 3–102
   Distortions of competition outside the scope of article 107 3–105
   Forms of prohibited aid 3–107
6. THE RELATIONSHIP BETWEEN ARTICLES 107 TO 109 TFEU AND OTHER PROVISIONS OF
   THE EU TREATY 3–108
   Article 18 TFEU 3–109
   The free movement principles 3–110
   Article 37 3–116
   Free movement of services and establishment 3–117
   The competition rules: articles 101 and 102 3–119
   Articles 101 and 102 3–120
   The EC merger regulation 3–121
   Agriculture 3–123
   Transport 3–126
   Article 106 3–127
   Indirect taxation and para-fiscal charges: article 110 TFEU 3–128
   Article 346 TFEU: derogation for trade in arms and war material 3–133
   The relationship of the EC Treaty rules on state aids to other treaties 3–135

1. GENERAL

3–001   Article 107 TFEU[1] provides:

"1. Save as otherwise provided in this Treaty, any aid granted by a Member State or through State resources in any form whatsoever which distorts or threatens to distort competition by favouring certain undertakings or the production of certain goods shall, in so far as it affects trade between Member States, be incompatible with the common market."

Article 107 permits a declaration of incompatibility with the internal market, but not a directly applicable prohibition of an aid. Article 107(2) and (3) provide for exemptions to this strict prohibition to be applied under certain circumstances. Article 108 regulates the procedural aspects of state aid supervision while art.109 provides that the Council may make appropriate regulations for the application of arts 107 and 108 TFEU.

---

[1] To be found at: *http://europa.eu.int/eur-lex/lex/en/treaties/dat/12002E/htm/C_2002325 EN.003301.html.*

This chapter will provide a detailed examination of what constitutes an "aid". As will become evident, the problematic nature of the definition of "aid" for the purposes of art.107(1) TFEU has been the subject of considerable case law and commentary. The scope of arts 107(2) and (3)—the automatic and discretionary exemptions—will be discussed in Ch.4. Having examined the relevant case law and Commission decisions on the definition of aid, this chapter will then turn to the relationship between art.107(1) and other Treaty provisions.

The scope of article 107(1): the concept of an aid

The concept of an aid is not defined in the Lisbon Treaty (nor was it defined **3–002** in the now expired ECSC Treaty—see Ch.14).

Article 107 refers to aid in any form whatsoever which distorts competition. As with its interpretation of other Treaty articles, the Courts have focused on the purpose of this provision. The Courts have repeatedly ruled that it is *the effect*, not the form, of the aid, which is crucial. As the Court of First Instance (now General Court) recalled in its ruling in Case T–613/97 *Ufex*:

"The aim of Article 92(1) EEC [now Article 107(1)] of the Treaty is to prevent trade between Member states from being affected by advantages granted by public authorities which in various forms, distort or threaten to distort competition by favouring certain undertakings or certain products. The concept of aid thus encompasses not only positive benefits, such as subsidies, but also interventions which, in various forms, mitigate the charges which are normally included in the budget of an undertaking and which, without therefore being subsidies in the strict sense of the word, are of the same character and have the same effect."[2]

This statement is drawn from a long line of case law, originating in the ruling of the Court of Justice on the scope of art.4(c) of the ECSC Treaty and the interpretation of the expression "subsidies or aids granted by States". The Court examined the origins of the expression in the GATT[3] and went on to state that:

"A subsidy is normally defined as a payment in cash or kind made in support of an undertaking other than the payment by the purchaser or consumer of the goods or services which it produces. An aid is a very similar concept which, however, places emphasis on its purpose and seems especially devised for a particular objective which cannot normally be achieved without outside help. The concept of aid is nevertheless wider than that of a subsidy because it embraces not only positive benefits, such as subsidies themselves, but also interventions which, in various forms, mitigate the charges which are normally

---

[2] [2000] E.C.R. II–4055.
[3] GATT 1947 art.16. For a full discussion of WTO-GATT law and subsidies see Ch.6 below.

included in the budget of an undertaking, and which, without, therefore being subsidies in the strict meaning of the word, are similar in character and have the same effect."[4]

3–003 It has been observed that this last sentence has become better known than the antecedent one; the final sentence emphasises the "effect" of a measure while the antecedent one makes further reference to its "purpose" or "objective".[5] In a number of cases in the area of taxation, the European Courts appear to have refined and limited the scope of the "effects" or classic test to some extent. Furthermore, in its early case law the Court established the distortive effects of an aid measure. In Case 173/73 *Italy v Commission* it held that:

"In the application of Article 92(1) [now Article 107(1) TFEU] the point of departure must necessarily be the competitive position existing within the common market before the adoption of the measure at issue. The unilateral modification of a particular factor of the cost of a production in a given sector may have the effect of distorting the existing equilibrium."[6]

In its Consultation Document entitled "Less and better targeted state aid, a roadmap for state aid reform 2005–2009", also known as the State Aid Action Plan,[7] the Commission also observed that:

"State aid control comes from the need to maintain a level playing field for all undertakings active in the Single European Market, no matter in which Member State they are established. There is a particular need to be concerned with those state aid measures, which provide unwarranted selective advantages to some firms, preventing or delaying the market forces from regarding the most competitive firms, thereby decreasing overall European competitiveness. It may also lead to a build-up of market power in the hands of some firms, for instance when companies that do not receive state aid (e.g. non-domestic firms) have to cut down on their market presence or where state aid is used to erect entry barriers. As a result of such distortions of competition, customers may be faced with higher prices, lower quality goods and less innovation" (at para.7).

As discussed in Chs 1 and 2, a competition-based analysis has not been well developed in the field of state aid law, despite the court's reference to the potential anti-competitive effects of state aid measures in Case 173/73. The reform measures introduced in the State Aid Action Plan have to some extent led to a new emphasis on this dimension.

---

[4] Case 30/59 *Steenkolenmijn in Limburg v High Authority* [1961] E.C.R. 1 at 19, and reiterated in Case C–390/98 *Banks v British Coal* [2001] E.C.R. I–6117 at para.30.
[5] R. Plender, "Definition of Aid" in Biondi et al., p.6.
[6] [1974] E.C.R. 709.
[7] COM(107) 2000, June 6, 2005.

Intent

In the Commission's view it is irrelevant that a state body intended to grant an aid, or that a recipient requested an aid, or intended to benefit from an aid:

3–004

"The question of the existence or not of State aid centres on whether the terms and conditions . . . depart from normal commercial practice and criteria to such an extent as to constitute State aid . . . within the meaning of Article 92(1) EEC [now Article 107 (1) TFEU]."[8]

As has been commented elsewhere, in an English court ruling on state aids, the *ICI* case,[9] the Court of Appeal appears to have reasoned erroneously that the inadvertent misapplication of fiscal provisions did not constitute an aid, whereas the knowing misapplication of such a provision would amount to an aid.[10] A Member State does not appear to be required to modify its own fiscal regime to that of another Member State even if the differences between the regimes indirectly benefit certain undertakings.[11] Even if the ultimate beneficiary receives the aid only indirectly, this is not in itself sufficient to remove the scheme from the scope of art.107(1), although the element of indirectness may be a factor in considering whether the recovery of the aid in question should be required[12] (see Ch.26). Further, it makes no difference if the aid scheme is optional and the recipient is under no obligation to take advantage of it.[13]

Advantage

It is also clear that for art.107 to apply, the undertaking must have obtained an advantage or benefit which it would not have received in the normal course of business. A measure cannot be considered state aid within the meaning of art.107 if it has not provided any advantage to the recipient. Case T–471/93 *Tierce Ladbroke*[14] concerned the arrangements made by public authorities in France responsible for horse betting and involved a levy on bets which the PMU takes on behalf of its counterpart in another Member State (Belgium) on races held in that Member State, and the subsequent transfer of a portion of that levy to the counterpart organisation. The arrangements were found not to constitute aid. The transfer of the levy did not exceed the sum that the recipient would have collected

3–005

---

[8] See also Case 61/79 *Denkavit* [1980] E.C.R. 1205, at 1228, see also Commission Decision 92/11 *Toyota* [1992] O.J. L6/36.

[9] *R. v Att-Gen Ex p. ICI* [1987] 1 C.M.L.R. 72.

[10] Lasok, "State Aids and Remedies under the EEC Treaty" [1986] E.C.L.R. 53; Sharpe, "The Role of National Courts in Relation to the Community Law of State Aids", in *State Aid: Community Law and Policy, Band 4 Schriftenreihe der Europaïsche Rechtsakademie* (Trier, 1993), pp.93 et seq. See also Ch.10.

[11] Case C–353/95P *Ladbroke* [1997] E.C.R. I–7007.

[12] See further the Commission Decision 97/542/EC *Biofuels* [1997] O.J. L222/26.

[13] A.G. Darmon, para.44; C–241/94 *France v Commission* [1996] E.C.R. I–4551.

[14] [1995] E.C.R. II–2537.

if it had taken on bets directly for the races it was responsible for organising.[15] On appeal, the Court of Justice confirmed the ruling of the CFI (now the General Court): in order for there to be aid within the meaning of art.107 it is necessary that there is aid favouring certain undertakings or for the production of certain goods and, additionally, for that advantage to come from the state or state resources. These conditions are cumulative. Accordingly, the General Court was right to hold that the failure to prove an advantage to the Belgian PMU was sufficient to justify the Commission's rejection of the complaint. It did not need to examine the argument put forward by Ladbroke that the Belgian PMU's revenue came from a compulsory levy provided for under the rules of French public law.[16]

There must be a gratuitous advantage,[17] in the sense that an undertaking receives a benefit it would not normally have enjoyed from its own commercial endeavours.[18] In this respect it makes no difference that in return for the state support at issue, the undertaking makes certain commitments, phased over time, as for example, where it received support on the condition that it undergoes a phased restructuring programme.[19]

3–006   An aid may still arise where a recipient has been required to pay insufficient consideration for the advantage in question.[20] The test is whether the benefit would not have been received in the normal course of business. Thus a loan at a rate of interest below normal commercial rates, or at rates which were not available to direct competitors,[21] or the provision of capital under normal market conditions but on a scale not normally available in the capital market, could constitute aid.[22] A national law which compensates public firms that had been required to repay previous aid declared illegal is in itself a form of aid.[23]

Similarly, in deciding to open art.108 proceedings against the Portuguese government in relation to aid granted to the national petrochemical company CNP, the Commission concluded that certain elements of a management and leasing contract arrangement concluded between this company and a private consortium constituted state aid. This contract was concluded following a public invitation to tender and related exclusively to the enterprise's plant. The consortium was responsible solely for the direct costs incurred in the operation of the plant, while the CNP remains liable for the old debt. Nevertheless, the annual rent for CNP's plant's existing debts, most of which were owed to the Portuguese

[15] See paras 58 and 59 of *Tierce Ladbroke*. This litigation also raised issues of the application of other Treaty provisions to the levy transfer arrangements in dispute.

[16] Case C–353/95P [1997] E.C.R. I–7007.

[17] Case 61/79 *Denkavit* [1980] E.C.R. 1205.

[18] Case C–387/92 *Banco Exterior* [1994] E.C.R. I–877 at paras 12–13.

[19] C–241/94 [1996] E.C.R. I–4551, A.G. Jacobs at para.54.

[20] Case 78/76 [1977] E.C.R. 595; Case 290/83 [1985] E.C.R. 439. See also T–14/96 *Bretagne, Angleterre, Irelande (BAI) v Commission* [1999] E.C.R. II–139.

[21] Case T–95/94 *Sytraval v Commission* [1995] E.C.R. II–2651; Appeal Case C–367/95P [1998] E.C.R. I–01719.

[22] A.G. Slynn in Case 84/82 *German (BRD) v Commission* [1984] E.C.R. 1451. See also Case 42/93 *Spain v Commission* [1994] E.C.R. I–4175, A.G. Jacobs at para.27.

[23] Case 96/434 *Italy* [1996] O.J. L180/31.

government, was very low. In the Commission's view, where the rent obtained for an enterprise's plant is insufficient not only to obtain a return comparable to that of an investment on the capital market, but even to cover the current servicing costs, a private business would become insolvent. Permission to refrain from paying interest on existing debts merely serves to keep the enterprise artificially alive and therefore constitutes an operating aid.[24]

In a decision concerning the introduction of new financial terms for holders of Digital Replacement Licences (DRLs), the UK authorities had requested the Commission to confirm that the new terms, which amounted to a reduction in licence fees to holders of analogue broadcasting licences did not amount to aid. The reason for the decrease in revenue from fees could be attributed to a decline in the economic value of the licences. No advantage could therefore arise for the broadcasters. The Commission held that the reassessment of the payments due was an intrinsic element of the licensing process, aiming at bringing the fee in line with the market value of the DRLs and is not a discretionary measure aimed at relieving licensees of their normal operating costs and, as a result, did not constitute aid.[25]

3–007

In Case T–475/04 *Bouygues v Commission*[26] the General Court held that the waiver of a significant part of an initial licence fee charged to certain telecommunication operators did not, on the facts of the case, amount to an economic advantage. The licence fee had not been definitively fixed as binding on the operators who were entitled under the terms of the award of the licences in question to withdraw their applications. Hence, the Court held that although the right to use wireless space granted to the operators had an economic value, the amount payable as a fee could constitute a state aid only if there was a difference between the price paid by the various operators concerned. Further, if national authorities had decided to award the licences free of charge, or awarded the licences by means of public auctions or at a standard price, there would have been no aid element, provided these terms were applicable to all operators without distinction. The lower court's ruling was upheld in Case C–431/07P *Bouygues and Bouygues Télécom v Commission.*[27]

3–008

Similarly, in Case C–123/03 and C–129/03 *AEM SPA v AEEG* the Court held that an Italian measure imposing increased charges for a transitional period on access to the national electricity network only on hydroelectricity installations was not considered to entail state aid for other undertakings generating electricity by means of other fuels. The increased charge was intended to offset an earlier advantage enjoyed by the former group of companies in the transition to market liberalisation.[28]

In Case T–233/04 *Netherlands v Commission*[29] however, the General Court upheld a Commission decision to the effect that the transfer of NOx trading

3–009

[24] [1992] O.J. C1/2. On the Commission's approach to operating aid, see generally, Ch.4.
[25] NN 64/2005 [2006] O.J. C218/49.
[26] [2007] E.C.R. II–2097.
[27] Case C–431/07P *Bouygues and Bouygues Télécom v Commission* [2009] E.C.R. I–2665.
[28] [2005] E.C.R. I–2861, para.43.
[29] [2008] E.C.R. II–00591.

emission permits to undertakings free of charge conferred an advantage on those undertakings. By making the allowances tradable, the Dutch state had conferred on them the character of an intangible asset with a market value, which could have been sold or auctioned.[30] Hence the Commission was right to conclude that the state had foregone revenue. On appeal to the ECJ, AG Mengozzi recommended to the ECJ to uphold the General Court's approach that the measure constituted a burden on state resources. The Court ruled that by creating a system of tradable allowances and allocating them free of charge, the Netherlands had conferred an economic advantage on the undertakings in question.[31]

Public declarations as an advantage?

3–010   In Joined Cases T–425/04, T–44/04, T–450/04 and T–456/04 *France Telecom*[32] the General Court held that declarations made by national authorities may result in a financial advantage for an undertaking under certain conditions. The Commission demonstrated in its decision that the French authorities had issued statements in support of France Telecom (FT) which had a positive and stabilising effect in reinforcing FT's investment grading, hence allowing it to borrow on more advantageous terms (paras 234–240). However, the General Court went on to hold that the Commission had failed to show that this advantage resulted in a transfer of state resources given that the public statements were open, imprecise and conditional and therefore not legally binding (see paras 288–289).[33]

Indirect advantage

3–011   An advantage granted directly to certain natural or legal persons who are not necessarily undertakings may constitute an indirect advantage, and therefore state aid, for other natural or legal persons who are undertakings. As the General Court stated in Case T–177/07 *Mediaset*[34]: "aid to consumers is a well-established form of aid . . . the potential recipients of which are indirect (para.177)." The measure in question comprised subsidies to consumers for the purchase of digital decoders in the run-up to digital television switchover in Italy. Mediaset, a digital terrestrial broadcaster, benefitted from this subsidy whereas satellite broadcasters did not as the subsidies were not available to consumers who purchased exclusively for the reception of digital satellite signals. It was irrelevant for the purposes of the categorisation of the subsidy as aid within the meaning of art.107(1) that Mediaset shared this advantage with other broadcasters or that these broadcasters could have financed the acquisition of the

---

[30] Case C–279/08P *Netherlands v Commission* [2011] E.C.R. Unreported September 8, 2011, A.G. Mengozzi.
[31] Judgment of September 8, 2011, at paras 102 to 113.
[32] Judgment of May 21, 2010.
[33] Now subject to appeal, Case C–399/10P [2010] O.J. C317/14.
[34] Judgment of June 15, 2010.

decoders in the absence of aid. On appeal, the ECJ confirmed the ruling of the lower court, in Case C–403/10P.[35]

The determination of the indirect beneficiary is of obvious importance in respect of recovery, as will be further discussed at Ch.26.[36]

Compensation in damages

Where money is paid as a result of compensation in damages owed by the state in accordance with its general legal rules regarding compensation for legal or illegal state acts, this will not amount to state aid. In any event if the compensation due is awarded and calculated according to general rules it is unlikely to meet the selectivity test (see section 3 below).[37] In proceedings concerning claims by a number of Greek firms for compensation in respect of legitimate aid denied them as a result of a technical error held in a previous judgment by the Court to have violated Community rules, the Court ruled that state aid is of a "completely different legal nature from any damages which the national authorities were ordered to pay as compensation".[38]

3–012

In cases where compensation is paid to undertakings in a particular sector who have been required as a result of state policy and/or legislation to cease or fundamentally re-structure and cut back their activities, it is also likely to be the case that financial compensation paid in accordance with the relevant national legal principles is unlikely to amount to aid within the meaning of art.107(1). The Commission's decision-making practice is not entirely consistent on this point, however.

In a decision of January 20, 1999 on the acquisition of land under a German Indemnification and Compensation Act, the Commission concluded that there would be no state aid:

"If the State simply returned to an economic operator something that it had previously expropriated (illegally). This may typically be compensation for losses suffered by the operator as a result of expropriation or similar action (compensation in kind or monetary compensation). In opening the procedure the Commission made it quite clear that, provided that the advantage accorded did not exceed the losses suffered by the operator as a result of such action, no

---

[35] Judgment of July 28, 2011.

[36] For example, in Joined Cases T–415/05, T–416/05 and T–423/05 *Greece v Commission (Olympic Airways)* judgment of September 13, 2010, the General Court held that where state aid assets were transferred from Olympic Airways to a new entity, Olympic Airlines, and some of the aid was granted to the old undertaking after the hiving off in favour of the new undertaking, the mere fact that the new undertaking obtained an indirect benefit is not sufficient to permit recovery of aid from it (at para.105).

[37] See also XXVIIth European Commission Report on Competition Policy (1997), p.247, available at *http://ec.europa.eu/competition/publications/annual_report/1997/broch97_en.pdf*. [Accessed August 24, 2011].

[38] Joined Cases 106 to 120/87 *Asteris v Commission* [1988] E.C.R. 5515.

preferential treatment within the meaning of Article 87(1) of the EC Treaty [107 TFEU] was present. Thus no State aid would be involved."[39]

3–013   The Commission had further observed in its opening decision in this case[40] that the advantage accorded would have been equal to or less than the asset losses referred to, and, relying on the *Asteris* ruling, the Commission held that the compensation merely reflects the legal principles common to all Member States regarding the protection of property rights. It is comparable with the compensation claim that natural persons or legal entities are entitled to make in regard of expropriation or similar action by a higher authority. In Case T–53/08 *Italy v Commission* and the related Case T–62/08 *Terni v Commission*[41] the General Court upheld the Commission's decision that compensation granted to an undertaking for expropriation must be for a limited period and national measures extending that compensation to provide the undertakings in question with additional financial support to compensate for liberalisation of the electricity sector could be evaluated under the state aid regime.

The issue of whether compensation for expropriation as opposed to aid within the meaning of art.107(1) is involved has also arisen in several cases regarding modifications to environmental regulations which have led to the withdrawal of permits or licences to pursue an economic activity. In its decision of June 2004 concerning aid to Akzo Nobel to minimise chlorine transport, the Commission relied first on the fact that the compensation was not selective in nature but awarded in accordance with general legal principles pertaining to the protection of property rights as recognised by the courts, and secondly on its finding that the amount paid only compensated part of the damage assessed, to arrive at the conclusion that no aid was involved.[42]

3–014   At the same time the eventual alteration or withdrawal of a permit to pursue a particular course of business may also be perceived as a normal commercial risk and therefore compensation could amount to a form of aid if the actual level of compensation does not discount that commercial risk.[43]

In several decisions the Commission has considered voluntary as opposed to compulsory schemes instituted by national governments to encourage business operators to terminate or adjust their economic activities. In its decisions concerning the UK government's buy-out schemes relating to salmon net licences, the Commission concluded that the compensation scheme for fishermen who voluntarily surrendered their fishing permits could be characterised as state aid: the schemes created a selective benefit which private undertakings would not have received in their normal course of business. The schemes were, however,

---

[39] 1999/268/EC, Commission Decision of January 20, 1999 on the acquisition of land under the German Indemnification and Compensation Act [1999] O.J. L107/21.

[40] [1998] O.J. C215/7.

[41] Judgment of July 1, 2010 [2010] O.J. C221/3.

[42] N 304/2003, Aid in favour of Akzo Nobel [2005] O.J. C81/48.

[43] N 433/98, Recovery of the economic activities affected by the earthquake in Umbria [1999] O.J. C56; see also N 217/2002, decision on Enschede fireworks disaster [2002] O.J. C164/45.

considered to be compatible with the Commission's guidelines on aid to fisheries and aquaculture sector.[44]

In its decisions on the compensation for the termination of power purchase agreements in Poland[45] and in Hungary,[46] the Commission found that the intended compensation was a prolongation of the advantage which the power producers had obtained under these long-term contracts and therefore had to be considered as state aid within the meaning of art.107(1) (see Ch.20).

2. THE ATTRIBUTES

In principle, in order for a measure to fall within the scope of art.107(1), the **3–015** measure in question must confer a benefit or advantage and all of the following cumulative conditions must be met:

* the aid has been imposed by a public authority;

* the measure results in a transfer of resources from the state or the state receiving less resources;

* the aid distorts competition by favouring certain undertakings or the production of certain goods,

* that the products or services in question are traded within the Union.

In Case C–83/98P *Ladbroke*, the European Court ruled that the concept of aid was an objective one and as such the Court had full powers to review the application of art.107(1) by the Commission.[47] As the Advocate General observed in his Opinion in Case C–290/07P *Scott*, at paras 101 to 103, and confirmed by the Court at para.66 of its subsequent ruling[48]:

"Nevertheless, there are two situations in which the Commission is recognised as enjoying a broader discretion. First of all, for assessing whether the aid is compatible with the common market within the meaning of Article 87(3) EC [107(3) TFEU]. In that context, the review undertaken by the Courts must be confined to determining whether the Commission's decision is vitiated by manifest error or misuse of powers.[49]

---

[44] N 509/2001 as adjusted [2002] O.J. C252/45, N 159/2004 and N 136/2003, Salmon net licences buyout Scheme [2006] O.J. C42/49. See also the letters from the Commission to the UK government, dated June 19, 2002, June 11, 2003 and May 27, 2004.

[45] [2009] O.J. L83/1.

[46] [2009] O.J. L225/53.

[47] [2000] E.C.R. I–3271; Case C–487/06P *British Aggregates v Commission* [2008] E.C.R. I–10515, para.111.

[48] Judgment of September 2, 2010 [2010] O.J. C288/6.

[49] Case C–88/03 *Portugal v Commission* [2006] E.C.R. I–7115, para.99; Case C–66/02 *Italy v Commission* [2005] E.C.R. I–10901, para.135; Case C–456/00 *France v Commission* [2002] E.C.R. I–11949, para.41; and Case C–310/99 *Italy v Commission* [2002] E.C.R. I–2289, para.46.

The Commission is also recognised as enjoying a broader discretion in relation to the existence of aid (and, accordingly, in situations which fall within the scope of Article 107(1)), whenever the decision has necessitated a complex technical or economic assessment. In those cases, the review undertaken by the Courts is generally confined—alongside the need to make sure that there is no manifest error or misuse of powers—to verifying that the Commission has complied with the relevant rules governing procedure and the statement of reasons, and that the facts on which it has based its decision have been accurately stated.[50]

When appraising Commission decisions on state aid which contain complex economic assessments, the Courts of the Union are called upon to perform a delicate balancing act. On the one hand, the Court cannot substitute its own economic assessment for that of the Commission; but, on the other hand, it must check the interpretation that the Commission has placed on economic factors, which means, inter alia, that it must verify that the data used by the Commission for the purposes of assessing a complex situation actually support the conclusions that the Commission then reached."[51]

The various aspects of the definition of an aid within the meaning of art.107(1) will be dealt with in turn. The first two conditions generally determine whether a given measure is a state aid in the sense that it originates from state resources. The remaining two conditions provide further qualifications as to the type of aid which is prima facie incompatible with the common or internal market. As the Court confirmed in Case C–353/95P *Tierce Ladbroke*,[52] where there is no question of a financial advantage to a particular undertaking, the Treaty state aid rules do not apply. The Court has repeatedly stressed that in order to be characterised as a state aid within the meaning of art.107(1) TFEU, all the cumulative conditions of this article must be met.[53] It therefore follows that a national court, in considering whether a measure is aid for the purposes of art.107(1) TFEU and as such should have been notified to the Commission in accordance with art.108(3), must examine whether all four cumulative conditions are met.[54]

State resources

3–016   It is well established that the financial benefit granted to a recipient must have been brought about by the state. Article 107 applies to aid granted by central,

---

[50] Case C–487/06P *British Aggregates v Commission* [2008] E.C.R. I–10515, para.114; Joined Cases C–328/99 and C–399/00 *Italy and SIM 2 Multimedia v Commission* [2003] E.C.R. I–4035, para.39; and Case C–56/93 *Belgium v Commission* [1996] E.C.R. I–723, para.11.

[51] An eloquent illustration of that potential "dilemma" for the Courts of the Union can be seen, by way of example, in Case C–525/04 P *Spain v Lenzing* [2007] E.C.R. I–9947, paras 56 to 58 and the case law cited therein.

[52] [1997] E.C.R. I–7007.

[53] See, for example, Case C–345/02 *Pearle* [2004] E.C.R. I–7139; Case T–136/05 *Salvat v Commission* [2007] E.C.R. II–1933.

[54] Case C–71/04 *Administración del Estado v Xunta de Galicia* [2005] E.C.R. I–7419.

regional or local government bodies and by a private body established or appointed by the state to administer certain resources, even if they originate from private sources.[55] Resources at the disposal of public undertakings, that is undertakings owned or controlled by the state (whether national or regional or local), are also considered to be state resources.[56]

The relationship between the phrases "aid granted by a Member State" and "aid granted through State resources" was the subject of some debate as a number of authors claimed that it was necessary for a financial measure to be funded by a transfer of state resources or through a charge or burden on state resources, in order to be classified as aid. Others maintained that any measure which resulted in the conferral of a selective benefit could come within the definition irrespective of whether that measure actually involved a burden on the state: the key test was whether the measure, whatever its form, had the effect of conferring a selective benefit. The case law of the European Courts was not entirely clear on this matter.

In Case C–379/98 *Preussen Elektra*[57] the scope of art.107(1) TFEU was, however, deemed by the European Court of Justice to be narrower than assumed by many. In that case the Court ruled that a state measure, a federal law which required certain regional electricity distribution undertakings to purchase, at a fixed minimum price, electricity produced from renewable energy sources within the supply area of each distribution undertaking concerned, and, further, required suppliers of electricity from conventional sources partially to compensate the distribution undertakings for the additional costs, did not constitute state aid, because it did not involve the transfer of state resources. The measure in question was a law imposing a minimum price on the regional electricity distributors. In line with earlier case law, including Case 82/77 *Van Tiggele*[58] and Case C–73/91 *Sloman Neptun*,[59] it was apparent that such measures were paid for by private consumers on the one hand, and even if they had the effect of conferring an advantage on a particular beneficiary (in this case the producers of renewable energy) this was inherent in the legislative system. **3–017**

In the subsequent Case C–126/01 *GEMO*, the Court ruled that a measure requiring private undertakings to collect and dispose of animal waste and carcasses amounted to state aid in favour of the beneficiaries of that disposal service—farmers and slaughterhouses. In this case the measure was financed by a tax incentive, which in turn financed by a levy on supermarkets, to act in favour of the intended beneficiaries of the measure. Further, the private undertakings were obliged to provide their services under their public service contracts

---

[55] Case 76/76 *Steinike and Weinlig v Germany* [1977] E.C.R. 595. See N 37/2003, United Kingdom, Digital Curriculum, Commission Decision of October 2, 2003. See also Case C–345/02 *Pearle* [2004] E.C.R. I–7139.

[56] See art.2 of the Transparency Directive, discussed in further detail at Ch.8, section 2.

[57] [2001] E.C.R. I–2099.

[58] [1978] E.C.R. 25.

[59] [1993] E.C.R. I–887.

with the state.[60] As will become apparent the scope of the *Preussen Elektra* ruling has been interpreted narrowly.[61]

3–018   It should be stressed that the *Preussen Elektra* ruling concerned the interpretation of the first part of the definition; it did not deal with the meaning of the second part (or residual category), i.e. the scope of the concept where aid is provided "through State resources in any form whatsoever". It is established case law that aid granted by public or private bodies designated or established by the state, may also be classified as aid within the meaning of art.107(1). Hence the financial resources at the disposal of public undertakings as well as private undertakings controlled by the state could be subject to the EU Treaty discipline on state aids.[62]

In Case T–58/94 *Air France v Commission*, the General Court stated with regard to art.107(1) TFEU:

"that provision therefore covers all financial means by which the public sector may actually support undertakings, irrespective of whether or not those means are permanent assets of the public sector."[63]

3–019   In Case C–83/98P *Ladbroke* the Court confirmed that even if the resources at issue originated from private sources, they could still be deemed to be under public control.[64] *Ladbroke* and the earlier cases (and subsequently *Stardust Marine*—see below) appear to be confined to the scope of this residual category. The concept of public control establishes its outer parameters. This case law does not deal with the first, general category—aid measures granted by the Member State—at all. Although in Case C–83/98P *Ladbroke*, the Court went on to recall the General Court's earlier ruling in Case T–358/94 *Air France*,[65] providing clear confirmation that art.107(1) covers "all financial means by which the public sector may actually support undertakings", it is submitted that this statement can also be seen in the context of its earlier finding that state revenue—in other words, revenue drawn from the broadly defined (residual) category of state resources—was in all events foregone. AG Cosmas made express reference to this element of the definition at para.44 of his Opinion, relying expressly on the *Piaggio*[66] and *Viscido*[67] cases.

Given that the *Preussen Elektra* ruling did not deal with the scope of the residual category, and left aside the potential application of art.107(1) TFEU to private funds under state control, the refusal of the Court to honour the Commission's request to extend the scope of art.107(1) TFEU to include "measures having equivalent effect to a state aid" is probably less problematic than it may

---

[60] Judgment of November 20, 2003 [2003] E.C.R. I–13769.
[61] See Case C–279/08P [2011] Opinion of September 8, 2011 A.G. Mengozzi, at paras 92–94.
[62] See further, Case C–345/02 *Pearle BV and Others* [2004] E.C.R. I–7139.
[63] [1996] E.C.R. II–2019.
[64] [2000] E.C.R. I–3271.
[65] [1996] E.C.R. II–2109.
[66] Case C–295/97 *Piaggo v Ifitalia* [1999] E.C.R. I–3735.
[67] Case C–52/97 *Viscido v Ente Poste Italiane* [1998] E.C.R. I–2629.

at first seem. Many commentators greeted *Preussen Elektra* with the observation that it could create serious holes in the Commission's regulatory net. A Member State could easily devise a scheme which would allow circumvention of the state aid rules. Instead of distributing funds themselves, or via a specially controlled body, they could devise schemes for compulsory direct payments from one individual to another which would have the same effect as a state aid within the meaning of art.107(1). The scope of this "residual category" is discussed in detail below.

Transfer of state resources

It is not necessary that the benefit results in a direct debit to public resources. **3–020** Even if assistance does not come directly from public funds, it becomes a state aid if paid through para-fiscal levies that are obligatory as a result of government action—see Case C–126/01 *GEMO, loc. cit.*[68] In Case C–308/01 *Gil Insurance*, the Court held that:

> "the concept of aid encompasses advantages granted by public authorities which, in various forms, mitigate the charges which are normally included in the budget of an undertaking (see, *inter alia*, Case C–310/99 *Italy v Commission* [2002] E.C.R. I–2289, paragraph 51)."[69]

Revenue foregone

A measure which leads to a reduction in state resources or revenues, whether **3–021** actual or potential—for example in the reduction of the amount of tax or social security or other charges due to be paid to the state—is also characterised as an aid for the purposes of art.107. Even if the application of the measure in question results in a reduction of state revenue from particular firms but at the same time leads to an increase in global revenue earned by that Member State, the measure in question will still fall within the scope of art.107. Thus, for example, where a Member State introduces special tax rules in order to attract inward investment, this type of measure can still be classified as an aid within the meaning of art.107 even if the final result of the measure is to increase the total fiscal revenue earned by that Member State. The application of art.107 to tax and social security charges is examined below, and in further detail in Ch.10.

It may nevertheless be questioned what the scope of the concept of a transfer of resources actually implies in the application of art.107(1) TFEU. There appears to be some support in the case law of the courts for the proposition that art.107 may still apply in certain cases, even though those measures do not entail a transfer of resources from the state, even in the form of revenue foregone. Although this issue has been partly resolved by the *Preussen Elektra* ruling, in

[68] [2003] E.C.R. I–13769.
[69] Case C–308/01 *GIL Insurance Ltd* [2004] E.C.R. I–4777, para.69.

which the Court concluded that the inclusion of the word "or" in the wording of art.107(1) could not imply that the tests were alternatives, subsequent case law still casts doubt on the exact nature of the link between the state measure in question and its financing.

The Court's ruling in Case C–482/99 *France v Commission* (*Stardust Marine*)[70] may be interpreted to mean that it is not necessary to identify a specific transfer of resources—or a specific act leading to the foregoing of revenue—in order for a particular measure to fall within the scope of art.107(1) TFEU. Much depends on the context of the measure in question. In *Stardust*, for example, the Court seemed to imply that it was not necessary to establish that the transaction at issue had been financed by a specific measure; it was sufficient in the first instance that the Member State controlled the resources at issue. In Case T–68/03, the General Court made clear in its ruling on non-payment by Olympic Airlines of airport charges to Athens Airport operated as a private undertaking, that the Commission must state clear reasons as to why it considered the measure in question to be imputable to the state.[71]

Must the measure impose a cost to the state?

3–022   A related issue is whether the measure in question must impose an actual burden in the sense of a net cost to the state or whether the concept of a burden should be conceived more widely as a "charge" or "claim" on state resources. Again the case law is unclear on this point. Given that the Courts have traditionally focused on the effects of the measure in question—as opposed to its form—it is often sufficient that the measure in question results in a selective advantage for a particular undertaking or a particular sector, and, following the ruling in *Preussen Elektra*, that there is a sufficient link between that measure and a charge or claim on state resources. In its decision on *TV2 Denmark*, the Commission examined whether a statutory "must carry obligation" imposed on all owners of common aerial installations to relay the public broadcaster's programmes amounted to a transfer of state resources. It concluded that as the state was neither foregoing any income nor actively transferring funds, the access rule in favour of TV2 did not confer any advantage from state resources on TV2.[72]

In Case C–200/97 *Ecotrade*, where the question of whether a state guarantee was at issue, the Court held that:

"the expression 'aid' . . . necessarily implies advantages granted directly or indirectly through state resources or constituting an additional charge for the State or for organs designated or established by the State for that purpose."[73]

[70] [2002] E.C.R. I–04397.
[71] [2007] E.C.R. II–2911, at para.317.
[72] [2006] O.J. L85/1, p.8, para.68. See also State Aid NN 70/88, *Kinderkanal and Phoenix* [1999] O.J. C238/3.
[73] Case C–200/97 [1998] E.C.R. I–7907, at para.35. See also Case C–295/97 *Piaggo* [1999] E.C.R. I–3735, at para.35.

This may serve to indicate that a transfer of resources in the sense of granting an advantage to an undertaking or a particular sector and an additional burden or charge for the state are two separate or even alternative tests or situations where the government measure in question may be considered to be aid. In *Preussen Elektra*, having established that no transfer of state resources was involved, the Court did not consider it necessary to examine whether the government measure constituted an additional charge for the German state—in the form of tax revenue foregone. This may indicate that the notion that the aid measure must also impose an "additional charge for the State" is neither a decisive independent criterion nor a cumulative one. Much will depend on the nature of the intervention at issue.

In this respect, the Commission's Communication on state guarantees asserts **3–023** that a state aid within the meaning of art.107(1) TFEU can arise at the time at which a state guarantee is made available to a particular undertaking or to a particular sector and not at the later time at which that guarantee is eventually drawn down. Hence the aid arises even if there is no burden on state resources at that point in time. The aid element arises because it confers an advantage on the recipient undertaking who might as a result of the guarantee be able to go on to raise credit on the market on more favourable terms. The Court held that the measure in question "might involve an additional burden for the public authorities, if it were in fact established that the State or public organs were among the principal creditors of the undertaking in difficulty, all the more so because, by definition, that undertaking owes debts of considerable value".[74] In *EPAC*[75] the eventual implementation of the state guarantee was sufficient to entail an additional (potential) burden for the state budget (see further, Ch.9).[76]

At the same time, a transfer of state resources that does not result in a selective advantage will also not amount to an aid—for example, if that transfer of resources represents a form of payment or compensation for specific services rendered or products supplied to the state. In this case the transfer of resources compensates or reimburses the provider of the goods or services in question. In relation to these types of transactions, the Commission and the Courts have developed a number of tests which are designed to verify whether the price paid by the state reflects market prices. These tests are discussed below.

Furthermore, it is not uncommon for the state to finance particular investments **3–024** or to make capital contributions to undertakings in which it holds an interest. Again these types of transactions involve a transfer of state resources but may not necessarily involve a selective advantage or "net cost" to, or a burden on, the state in conferring that advantage if the transfer is made on market terms. In this respect it is necessary to establish whether the state is acting as a private market

---

[74] Case C–200/97 [1998] E.C.R. I–7907, at para.41.

[75] Joined Cases T–204/95 and T–270/97 [2000] E.C.R. II–2267, at para.80.

[76] See also Joined Cases T–228/99 and T–233/99 *Westdeutsche Landesbank Girozentrale en Land Nordrhein-Westfalen v Commission* [2003] E.C.R. II–435, at para.179; Case T–95/03 *Asociación de Estaciones de Servicio de Madrid en Federación Catalana de Estaciones de Servicio v Commission* [2006] E.C.R. II–4739, para.104.

investor—the so-called "private market investor test".[77] It may also be noted here that the intention of the so-called hypothetical market investor appears to be of paramount importance—would such an investor have accepted a rate of return on its investment that was lower than the market rate, taking into account all the circumstances of the particular case? This approach has been criticised for its deviation from the classical "effects-based" approach in as much as the intention behind the grant of an aid is supposedly deemed irrelevant in the classical approach.

3–025   In some cases the General Court seems to stress a third dimension which must be investigated: the effects of the transaction on competitors. From this perspective the question to be clarified is whether the competitor would have been able to obtain on the market the same advantage as the beneficiary. If this question cannot be answered in the affirmative, then an element of state aid may be presumed.[78] In its decision to open formal proceedings in relation to alleged state aid to France Telecom, the Commission provisionally considered that already the announcement of the opening of a substantial credit line (€9 billion) by the French state allowed the beneficiary to improve its financial situation, given that the announcement assisted it in obtaining credit from commercial institutions.[79] This approach has not found favour with the General Court—the Commission's final decision had failed to show that this advantage entailed a transfer of state resources but was more in the nature of an open, conditional and imprecise commitment.[80] This ruling is now under appeal, registered as case C–399/10P.

The contours of what types of measures may fall within the first part of the definition—"an aid granted by the State"—become clearer if one first takes into account the many ways in which the modern state can and does intervene in the market, with the result that a particular undertaking or category of undertakings may enjoy a benefit which would not necessarily have been available under normal market conditions. The modern state assumes at any one time a variety of roles: in the exercise of its prerogative to raise tax revenues; as a shareholder; as the ultimate guarantor that certain public services are provided and at a requisite standard; as a quasi-financial or investment institution; and a regulator of economic and social activity.[81]

---

[77] See in this respect the contribution of V. Kreuschitz, "New Developments in the Application of the Market Economy Investor Principle", *New Developments in European State Aid Law* 2003, pp.29–34, at p.30.

[78] Joined Cases T–228/99 and T–233/99 *WestLB v Commission* [2003] E.C.R. II–435.

[79] Decision C–13/2003 *Measures to support France Telecom* [2003] O.J. C57/69, p.15. and the final decision [2005] O.J. L269/30, subsequently annulled on this point in Joined Cases T–425/04 and T–456/04.

[80] Joined Cases T–425/04, T–444/04, T450/04 and T–456/04 *France v Commission* [2010] E.C.R. II–2099.

[81] It can be argued that it is precisely these different characteristics—the differences of object and general structure—that the Court had in mind when it handed down its ruling in *Sloman Neptun* in 1994, discussed below.

In Case C–280/00 *Altmark*,[82] AG Leger drew a distinction between measures **3–026** adopted by the state in the exercise of its prerogatives and those adopted in its capacity as a provider of, or alternatively a purchaser of, goods and services in the market.[83] In the first category of cases there appears to be little indication that the courts are interested in the underlying economics of the transaction or the "cost" of the measure to the state—it is sufficient that the selectivity test is met. In the second category of cases, however, a greater emphasis appears to be placed on the net financial burden borne by the state or the net financial advantage conferred on the beneficiary of the measure. These different roles and functions may call for differing degrees of emphasis to be placed on the relative importance of the two main constituent elements of a state aid—the nature of the burden on state resources and the nature of the benefit enjoyed—depending on the facts of the case at issue.[84]

State resources in any form whatsoever: the residual category and the concept of public control over private resources

As already noted, the second part of the definition of an aid for the purposes **3–027** of art.107(1)—the so-called residual category—has been held to refer to resources which are not held by the state as such but are at its disposal; in other words, under its permanent control. Hence the nature of the "state resources", which are covered in the second part of the definition, are deemed to be those which are under some form of state or public control even if they are not at the permanent disposal of the government, thus rendering the public or private or mixed public–private legal status of the institution who manages the resources in question to be irrelevant.[85] Furthermore, certain funding arrangements, such as the imposition of a para-fiscal charge on consumers, may also contravene other Treaty rules if, for example, the para-fiscal levy is imposed on imported as well as domestic products, and if only the domestic producers benefit from such a fund (see in particular, Ch.22 (environment), and see further section 6, para.3–128 of this chapter).[86]

Finally, it may be noted that in its judgment in Case C–345/02 *Pearle*,[87] the Court of Justice held that in the circumstances of that case, where a compulsory

---

[82] It can be argued that it is precisely these different characteristics—the differences of object and general structure—that the Court had in mind when it handed down its ruling in *Sloman Neptun* in 1994, discussed below.

[83] See also Case T–156/04 *Electricité de France (EDF)* [2009] E.C.R. II–4503, now under appeal as Case C–124/10P.

[84] See further, L. Hancher "Towards a new definition of a state aid under European law: Is there a new concept of state aid emerging?" in *European State Aids Law Quarterly* 2003, Vol.2, No.3.

[85] In its decision on the legality of the Spanish stranded cost arrangements in July 2001, however, the Commission seemed to imply that if the control was only marginal, this would not be sufficient to bring private resources under the second part of the definition—see below, at Ch.20, section 6.

[86] See C–43/2000 Luxembourg, *loc. cit.*

[87] [2004] E.C.R. I–7139.

levy was paid to a public body, the funds in question were not deemed to be under public control. The initiative to raise the levy and to devote its proceeds to cover the costs of a general advertising campaign was an initiative taken by a private sector organisation. The public body in question merely served as a vehicle for levying and allocating resources collected for a purely commercial purpose which had been determined by the sector itself, and had nothing to do with a policy determined by the Dutch authorities.[88]

Where the fund at issue remains under state control, and the obligation to pay into the fund as well as the right to receive payment from it are subject to state regulation, the measure will be qualified as "state resources"—as was seen in Case T–136/05 *Salvat*, where the General Court examined the regulations relating to the fund in some detail to distinguish it from the *Pearle* case.[89] A similar conclusion was reached by the ECJ in the *Essent*[90] and *Iride*[91] cases, discussed in Ch.20.

In Case C–222/07 *UTECA*, however, the Court held that:

"Article 87 EC [now Article 107 TFEU] must be interpreted as meaning that a measure adopted by a Member State, . . . requiring television operators to earmark 5% of their operating revenue for the pre-funding of European cinematographic films and films made for television and, more specifically, to reserve 60% of that 5% for the production of works of which the original language is one of the official languages of that Member State does not constitute State aid in favour of the cinematographic industry of that Member State".[92]

Imputability

3–028   In Case C–482/99 *France v Commission* (*Stardust Marine*) the Court provided a further clarification of the scope of the second or residual part of the state aid test.[93] It held that even though resources eventually at the disposal of the state may be deemed to be "state resources" it is also necessary to show that the actual deployment of those resources for the benefit of a particular undertaking can be attributed or imputed to some form of government decision. Merely "organic" forms of public control over such resources are not in themselves sufficient. Hence the Court annulled the Commission's decision that capital injections made by two subsidiaries of a publicly owned bank, Credit Lyonnais, to the French charter boat company, Stardust, amounted to aid in that case.

Nevertheless, it is difficult to specify clearly what the actual parameters of the imputability test are likely to be in any one case. Indeed as the Advocate General

[88] See para.37 of its ruling.
[89] Judgement of September 20, 2007 [2007] E.C.R. II–4063.
[90] Case C–206/06 *Essent Netwerk Noord and Others* [2008] E.C.R. I–5497.
[91] Set for appeal as Case C–150/09P.
[92] [2009] E.C.R. I–1407, at para.47.
[93] [2002] E.C.R. I–4397.

himself pointed out in his Opinion in *Stardust*, the Court's previous case law on the matter of the degree of control necessary to establish imputability or attributability was itself unclear. In two cases concerning alleged preferential energy tariffs, the ECJ had no difficulty in reaching the conclusion that the decision by the publicly controlled gas supplier, Gasunie, to award certain preferential tariffs to particular large consumers, could be attributed to the Dutch government. At the relevant time, the Dutch government enjoyed certain rights of veto over Gasunie's commercial decisions and, further, two members of Gasunie were appointed by the government. This type of structure may be sufficient to establish something more than organic control.[94]

Prior to *Stardust*, however, the only relevant authority was the General Court's judgment in *Air France*,[95] where it was held that art.107(1) covered all the financial means by which the public sector may actually support undertakings, irrespective of whether those means are permanent assets of the public sector. This approach was in turn endorsed by the Court of Justice in the *Ladbroke* case.[96] AG Jacobs further concluded in his Opinion in *Stardust* that the reason why in most of the cases concerning aid financed through public undertakings the origin of the resources was not at issue, was that it was accepted law that as long as the resources were under the control of the state and the economic burden of the measures was ultimately borne by the state, then this was sufficient for the purposes of art.107(1). Hence the funds used by the two subsidiaries of the state-owned Credit Lyonnais, SBT and Altus, to finance the measures in favour of *Stardust* were "state resources" within the meaning of art.107(1). **3–029**

The Advocate General was of the view that something more was still required:

"The wording of Article 87(1) EC [now Article 107 TFEU] seems to distinguish between aid granted by a Member State and aid granted through state resources. . . . The second alternative in Article 87(1) EC [now Article 107 TFEU] (aid granted through State resources) thus serves only to preclude circumvention of the State aid rules through decentralised or 'privatised' distribution of aid. This means however, that where aid is granted under the second alternative 'through State resources' the measures must be the result of action of the Member State concerned. That is confirmed by the title of the relevant section 'Aids granted by States' which suggests that in all cases the measure must be ultimately imputable to public authorities" (at para.54).

In its ruling the Court observed that:

" . . . it should first be noted that, according to settled case law, it is not necessary to establish in every case that there has been a transfer of State

[94] Case C–56/93 *Belgium v Commission* [1996] E.C.R. I–723. Case C–181/97 *Van der Kooy* [1999] E.C.R. I–483.
[95] Case T–358/94 *Air France v Commission* [1996] E.C.R. II–2019.
[96] Case C–83/98P *France v Ladbroke Racing and Commission* [2000] E.C.R. I–3271.

resources for the advantage granted to one or more undertakings to be capable of being regarded as a State aid[97] . . . Second it should be recalled that it has already been established in the case law of the Court that Article 87(1) EC [now Article 107 TFEU] covers all the financial means by which the public authorities may actually support undertakings, even whether or not those means are permanent assets of the public sector".

It followed that the Commission did not misinterpret the term "State resources":

in art.107(1) TFEU. "In a context such as that in point here, the position of a public undertaking cannot be compared with that of a private undertaking. Through its public undertakings, the State may pursue objectives other than commercial ones"[98] (at recital 52).

3–030   The Court further reasoned that it cannot be expected for the Commission (or an eventual third party such as a competitor) to establish the actual involvement of the state in a particular decision. At the same time, even if a state is in a position to control a public undertaking and exercise a dominant influence over it:

"actual exercise of that control in a particular case cannot be automatically presumed . . . It is also necessary to examine whether the public authorities must be regarded as having been involved in one way or another, in the adoption of those measures."

The Court suggested that while it would not be necessary to require proof of a specific incitement to take the aid measures in question, it must be accepted that the imputability to the state of an aid measure taken by a public undertaking may be inferred from certain indicators arising from the circumstances in which the measure was taken. Recalling its earlier ruling in Case 67/85 *Van der Kooy* (preferential gas tariffs for Dutch greenhouse growers)[99] the Court suggested that the fact that the body in question could not have taken the contested decision without taking the requirements of the public authorities into account would be indicative of attributability. A further example would be cases in which the public undertaking had to take account of directives issued by the state. Other relevant factors, including the degree of integration of the public undertaking into the structure of the public administration, the extent to which that undertaking participated in the relevant market under normal conditions of competition with private operators, are listed at para.56 of the judgment.[100]

---

[97] The Court relied on Case C–387/92 *Banco Exterior de Espana* [1994] E.C.R. I–877, para.14 and Case C–6/97 *Italy v Commission* [1999] E.C.R. I–2981, para.16.
[98] The Court recalled the eleventh recital in the preamble to the Transparency Directive.
[99] [1988] E.C.R. 219, at paras 36–38.
[100] For a further discussion of *Stardust* see L. Hancher, [2003] C.M.L.Rev., Vol.40, nr.3, pp.739–751.

As a result of cases such as *Preussen Elektra* and *Stardust Marine*, it may be noted that the European Courts are moving away from a formalistic approach to the definition of state resources but at the same time it could also be claimed, as indeed many commentators have done in the wake of the *Preussen Elektra* case, that it is also distancing itself in practice if not in rhetoric, from the classic "effects-based" test discussed above.[101]

The *Stardust* approach was confirmed in Case C–345/02 *Pearle* where the **3–031** Court even appears to go further and to suggest that the decision to confer a particular selective benefit on an undertaking must be attributable to the public authorities: hence an element of control is needed not only to establish that the resources in question are "state resources", but also that the conferral of the specific alleged advantage at issue can be attributed to a state decision. The wording of the judgment is not, however, totally clear on this point. Furthermore, it may well be that the special facts of that case should be borne in mind—the funds in question were levied from the private sector and were deployed by the sectoral organisation for an advertising campaign initiated by it, and not at the direction of the state.[102] In the subsequent *Salvat* case the Court examined the involvement of the state in decisions on how the funds were used.[103]

Subsequent Commission decisions

When the *Stardust* ruling was first handed down by the Court, the Commission **3–032** claimed that it was limited to the facts of the case—the potential for "control" by the state over the activities of the two subsidiaries of the public bank was too indirect—it had to be channelled through Credit Lyonnaise, and thus the attributability test had not been met. In the Commission's view the criteria laid down by the Court in *Stardust* would be easily met where the relationship at issue between the government and the entity in question was a direct one, for example as a result of ownership and/or legislative provisions. In this situation the resources in question appear to already be under "the permanent control" of the state and there is no need to go on and examine imputability: it is presumed. As long as the transactions of the entity met with the "market investor test" or one of its progeny (such as the market debtor test or the market creditor test) they would not fall within the scope of art.107(1) in any event.

The Commission's decision of June 19, 2002[104] requiring the German government to recover some €500 million of illegal aid from Deutsche Post was adopted after the *Stardust* ruling. The Commission applied the attributability test—it considered that the resources involved were at the disposal of the German

---

[101] See further, R. Plender "Definition of an Aid" in Biondi et al. (eds), *The Law of State Aid in the European Union* (Oxford: OUP, 2004) pp.3–41, and L. Hancher "Towards a new definition of a state aid under European law: Is there a new concept of state aid emerging?" in (2003) *European State Aids Law Quarterly*, Vol.2, No.3.

[102] [2004] E.C.R. I–7139. See also Case C–206/06 *Essent Netwerk Noord and Others* [2008] E.C.R. I–5497, discussed in Ch.20.

[103] T–136/05 [2007] E.C.R. II–4063.

[104] [2002] O.J. L247/27.

authorities—even if they were not its permanent assets (see paras 92 and 93 of the decision) and it then went on to state that the transfer payments from the publicly controlled DB-Telekom to Deutsche Post (also publicly owned) were attributable to the state as they were required by law under the Postal Organisation Act (Pt 94). However, it seems that this in itself was not conclusive for a finding that art.107(1) was applicable as the Commission went on to state that even without the provisions of the Act the state would have had recourse to general budget resources to support Deutsche Post (see Pt 95). Although the Commission's decision was subsequently annulled, this particular point was not challenged.[105]

3–033   In its decision of December 17, 2003 concerning state aid implemented by Germany for Space Park Development GmbH & Co,[106] the Commission rejected the argument advanced by the German authorities that the aid in question was granted by a public undertaking—SWG—and could not as such be attributed to the regional authorities who had promoted the Space Park concept. It held that the rules developed in the *Air France* ruling of 1996 were more appropriate "to the situation at stake". The Commission concluded that "it is sufficient that the funds in question constantly remain under public control and are therefore available to the competent national authorities" (para.31 of its decision).

Similarly, in its decision to open formal proceedings against the French state in respect of its re-structuring support to France Telecom (FT), the Commission had little difficulty in imputing the investments of the ERAP—a public entity established as an "EPIC" under French law to meet the *Stardust* criteria—an "EPIC" is a legal structure which allows the state to exercise a dominant influence and direct the use of its resources for particular objectives in favour of other public enterprises. The Commission did not examine any particular state mandate to the ERAP to act in support of FT.[107] In its decision on various measures taken by Greece in favour of Hellenic Shipyards the Commission held that a number of measures of support granted by the then State-owned bank ETVA the Commission examined in some detail the extent of the government's involvement in the privatisation of the shipyards, and concluded that it was impossible for EVTA's management to have developed a lending policy that was not in line with the Greek government's policy of steady support to the shipyards. See paras 3–133—5, below.

3–034   **The Danish TV2 case, the Swedish DVB-T case and the German DVT-B case and other recent Commission decisions in the media sector.** In a series of decisions relating to the media sector, which are further discussed at Ch.18 (broadcasting), the various state measures in question have all been classified as

---

[105] For a further discussion of this case, see Ch.8.
[106] [2004] O.J. L61/66.
[107] See Decision C 13/2003 *Measures to support France Telecom* [2003] O.J. C57/69, p.15. See also its earlier pre-*Stardust* decision on alleged cross-subsidisation in *Deutsche Bahn AG/Bahn Tranis GmbH* of May 7, 2002 [2002] O.J. L211/7.

state aid. These measures have included "ad hoc" payments to television companies, but in some cases the revenues available to public broadcasters which are raised from licence fees from consumers have also been classified as state aid. It has not been a requirement for the applicability of art.107(1) in these decisions that the policy of the recipient (public broadcasting) company to enter into another commercial activity (e.g. advertising, digital curriculum, broadband services or other activities outside the "public service broadcasting" remit) could be attributed to the state as such. Indeed, it has been a condition for the finding of the eventual compatibility of the measures at issue, that the Member State in question has imposed strict controls to prevent cross-subsidisation.

Hence in the German and the *Swedish DVT-B* cases the Commission applied the *Air France* case law—the two companies were economically and legally independent from the state, but the state had a number of means to exercise control of their resources so that these were at the "permanent disposal" of the state. In the German case the entity had been established by the state, and carried out public tasks on behalf of the state.[108] In the Swedish case, the payments made by the public broadcaster SVT to a Swedish telecoms company (Teracom) were deemed to be state resources as SVT was an undertaking entrusted with a public service task over which the state exercises considerable influence through legislation.[109] The Commission's approach was upheld in the General Court's ruling in Case T–21/06,[110] and confirmed by the ECJ on appeal in Case C–544/09P.[111]

Furthermore, Case T–60/03 *Olympic Airways* underlines that the Commission's findings on imputability must be properly reasoned—state involvement cannot merely be assumed.[112]

Imputability and harmonised taxation

Following prolonged negotiations the Community finally agreed on EC Directive 96/03 on the taxation of energy products in late 2003.[113] One problematic aspect in the negotiations leading up to the adoption of this measure was the inter-relationship between certain tax reductions/exemptions and the EU state aid rules. In this respect the compulsory or facultative nature of certain tax exemptions/reductions must be considered. If the tax exemption derives from a Community measure such as a Directive, without leaving any scope for discretionary application at national level, the measure is not imputable to the state and cannot therefore be considered to be a state aid.[114] For example, Council Directive 92/81 provides that mineral oils injected into blast furnaces for the purpose of chemical reduction as an addition to the coke used as a principal fuel is subject to a

3–035

---

[108] See Case T–21/06 *Germany v Commission* [2009] E.C.R. II–197, set for appeal in Case C–544/09P.

[109] See its decisions in Case NN 36/4 C(2004) 2672 and Case NN 3504 Sweden, 2004.

[110] October 6, 2009 [2009] E.C.R. II–197.

[111] Judgment of September 15, 2011.

[112] *loc. cit.* at fn.36.

[113] [2003] O.J. L283.

[114] Case T–351/02 *Deutsche Bahn* [2006] E.C.R. II–1047.

Community wide mandatory exemption. Where, however, the measures concerned result from the national system, they will have to be assessed under the EU state aid rules. A case in point is art.4(2) of the Directive which allows Member States to add all indirect taxes levied on the quantity of energy products[115] (see also Ch.20).

In Case C–460/07 *Puffer*, the Court confirmed that where the right to deduct VAT input tax payable, and the possible related financial advantage for taxable persons carrying out taxable transactions, derives directly from art.17(2)(a) of the Sixth Directive, which the Member States are bound to transpose in their national law, the condition of intervention by the State is not met, so that art.107(1) TFEU cannot apply.[116]

Community resources

3–036   Where a Member State public body (or private body subject to public control) provides a benefit financed not from its own but from Union funds, art.107 probably does not apply insofar as the Member State enjoys no further discretion in the subsequent allocation of those funds. The disbursement of funds that have been received and subsequently allocated in accordance with the relevant rules pertaining to the granting of the Union funds to the Member States are deemed not to require separate notification under art.108. Even though the Member State subsequently receives these Union resources and these are subsequently channelled through national public bodies (i.e. the Managing and Paying Authorities set up under Regulation 1083/2006[117]), this does not appear to mean that they come under national control within the meaning of the residual test of art.107(1) TFEU. The Member States have no discretion in the allocation of the structural funds: funds are only disbursed after a Commission decision has been adopted authorising payment following approval of the requisite single programming documents or operational programmes.

A misallocation by a national authority of a share in a Union tariff quota for meat products to certain traders, allowing those traders to acquire a financial advantage, does not constitute state aid. Any incorrect application of EU law, even if taking the form of an incorrect application of a tariff quota, must be dealt with as a breach of the relevant provisions of EU law.[118] Nevertheless, in the view of AG VerLoren van Themaat:

"in so far as Member States have some discretion in the disbursement of Community resources such as the Social Fund, the Regional Fund, or funds

---

[115] See for the problems this can cause, the Commission's decision on the Swedish eco-tax and energy tax system, NN 3/B/2002, where it concluded that it was necessary to open proceedings as regards the full exemption for the electricity tax for the manufacturing sector. See further, J. Lannering and B. Renner-Loquenz [2003] *Competition Policy Newsletter*, Vol.3 Autumn, pp.75–6.

[116] Judgment of April 23, 2009 [2009] E.C.R. I–3251.

[117] [2006] O.J. L210.

[118] Cases 213–215/81 *Norddeutsches Vieh-und Fleischkontor v BALM* [1982] E.C.R. 3583.

from the European Investment Bank, these could lead to the conferral of pecuniary advantages within the meaning of Article 87".

In Decision 86/561,[119] the Commission held that a German measure convert- **3–037**
ing market stabilisation loans granted under Community Regulation 1975/76 into subsidies to inshore fishermen amounted to a state aid within the meaning of art.107.

The situation is, however, made more complex by the fact that in many instances the Member States are required to co-finance projects or schemes in order to draw down the structural funds provisionally allocated to them. Although there is not yet case law on this issue it would seem that as the Member State has no choice but to match the Community funds, then the financial measure cannot be imputed to it as such—it must be imputed to the Community legal act which mandates co-financing.

At the same time, if the Member State provides additional funds from its own resources, in other words it combines Community funds with national funds, the Member State must also comply with the relevant state aid rules insofar as these are relevant.[120] The Structural Fund Regulation stipulates that a measure is a state aid measure when it satisfies the criteria of art.107(1).[121] This seems to suggest that other funds which fall within the scope of the Regulation are not state aid measures. These can be either Community funds or private funds.

However, even if the funds are state aid in certain situations, a separate **3–038**
notification in accordance with art.108(3) may be dispensed with insofar as the national matching funds are disbursed in strict accordance with the relevant Community structural fund regulations. For example, if the relevant regulation provides that certain forms of support may be granted up to a maximum intensity, then as long the additional financing by the Member State does not exceed the stipulated intensity ceilings, separate notification under the state aid regime is not usually required. This principle is of particular importance in the agricultural sector—see further Ch.13.

Indeed the standard requirement for the compatibility of many forms of national state aid measures, as covered by various specific regulations and guidelines, is that, irrespective of the source of funding, the stipulated maximum intensities have to be honoured; in practice it often makes no real difference at least for the assessment of the compatibility of a measure whether the financial support provided by the structural funds in question is classified as a state aid or not. A similar approach is taken in the General Block Exemption Regulation of 2008[122]—the aid ceilings referred to therein are applied regardless of whether the support is financed entirely from state resources or is partly financed by the Union.

The Commission's guidelines on research and development aid of 1996 made **3–039**
reference to "total official support"—that is Community financing and state aid

---

[119] June 25, 1986 [1986] O.J. L327/44.
[120] See XXXIII Competition Report, 2003, at para.393.
[121] Regulation 1083/2006 [2006] O.J. L210/25.
[122] [2008] O.J. L214/3.

combined.[123] Further, its 2008 environmental guidelines stipulate that the aid ceilings stipulated in the guidelines are applicable irrespective of whether the aid in question is financed wholly or in part from state resources or from Community resources.[124] Furthermore, cumulation of aid authorised under the guidelines with other forms of Union financing is prohibited if "such overlapping" produces an aid intensity higher than that laid down in the guidelines.

It would appear, however, that structural funds receipts need not be included in the calculations necessary to establish whether aid is "de minimis" under arts 2 and 3 of Regulation 1998/2006.[125]

In Case C–321/99P *ARAP v Commission*, the Court held that the Commission must assess the legality of various national measures implementing an aid scheme in the agricultural sector independently of each other in relation to the potential application of each of the relevant Union regulations.[126] In respect of the potential application of arts 107 and 108 to aid eligible for Community co-financing in respect of the relevant agricultural fund Regulations, the Court concluded that this would be incompatible with the precedence over the rules on competition accorded by the Treaty to the common agricultural policy. On those grounds the Court held that such aid was not subject to the application of art.107. National aid granted in derogation from or in addition to the amounts set out in the relevant Union regulations must however be examined separately, case by case, in relation to arts 107 and 108 (see further, Ch.13).

3. THE SELECTIVITY CRITERIA

3–040   If it can be established that the aid in question is granted by the state or through state resources, it is then necessary to consider whether that aid is a prima facie incompatible aid. It must be demonstrated that the aid in question favours certain products or undertakings.

Undertaking

3–041   The concept of an "undertaking" in art.107 is a flexible one, and applies not only to private undertakings, but also public undertakings,[127] even where the latter do not enjoy a separate legal personality.[128] If the undertakings in question do not exercise commercial activities or if their aided non-commercial activities area is accounted for separately, then the measures will not be deemed to fall under art.107(1) TFEU.[129] According to established case law, any activity consisting of offering goods or services in a given market constitutes an economic

---

[123] See further, Ch.23.
[124] See Ch.22.
[125] [2006] O.J. L379/5.
[126] [2002] E.C.R. I–4287.
[127] As defined in art.1 of Directive 80/723, as amended, see Ch.8.
[128] Case 118/85 *Commission v Italy* [1987] E.C.R. 2599.
[129] See for example, N 5/2005—Denmark [2005] O.J. C280/9.

activity.[130] Hence any undertaking, irrespective of its legal status, which is engaging in such activities will be subject, prima facie, to the state aid regime (see further, Ch.8).

In Case C–66/02 *Italy v Commission* the Republic of Italy alleged that art.107 could not apply as the measure in question benefited certain entities which could not be considered as undertakings within the meaning of art.107(1). The Court held that the fact that the aid can benefit undertakings as well as other kinds of beneficiaries who are not undertakings, cannot avoid the application of art.107(1). Nonetheless, it is of course of importance to ensure that the ultimate beneficiaries of the alleged aid are properly identified so that they have an opportunity to participate in the administrative procedures before the Commission.[131]

At the same time it is clear from the case law that the concept of "undertaking" for the purposes of art.107(1) is not the same as for the purposes of the Treaty competition rules. In Case C–480/09P *ACEA-Electrabel*, the Court confirmed that:

"Indeed, as the General Court correctly held at paragraphs 135, 137 and 138 of the judgment under appeal, the concept of an economic unit in State aid matters can differ from that applicable in other areas of competition law. In any event, neither any operational independence on the part of AEP nor the concept of an economic unit applicable in the field of restrictive practices and concentrations is capable of altering the fact that in the light, in particular, of ACEA's power to block decisions for the most important matters concerning the management of AEP, the General Court was entitled, in the circumstances, to confirm the Commission's finding that ACEA exercised joint control over AEP and that the latter formed part of an indivisible whole" (at paras 66–67).

General measures

In order to fall within the scope of art.107(1), the state measure in question **3–042** must have the effect of conferring a selective benefit or advantage. General measures which can benefit the entire economy, such as a lowering of tax rates or interest rates do not create a selective benefit.[132] In order to establish which measure is a "general measure", the benchmark in question must always be the national fiscal system; a comparison of tax rates and tax bases in other Member States is not permissible. In Case T–308/00 *Salzgitter*, the General Court held:

"Consequently, in order to identify what constitutes an advantage as contemplated in the case law on State aid, it is imperative to determine the reference

---

[130] Case C–35/96 *Commission v Italy* [1998] E.C.R. I–3851; Joined Cases C–180/98–184/98 *Pavlov* [2000] E.C.R. I–6451.
[131] Case T–34/02 *Le Levant 001 v Commission* [2006] E.C.R. II–267.
[132] See AG Geelhood in C–308/01 *GIL* [2004] E.C.R. II–4777.

point in the scheme in question against which that advantage is to be compared. In the present case, when a 'normal' tax burden within the meaning of the aforementioned case-law is being determined, comparison of the tax rules applicable in all of the Member States, or even some of them, would inevitably distort the aim and functioning of the provisions on the monitoring of State aid. In the absence of Community-level harmonisation of the tax provisions of the Member States, such an approach would in effect compare different factual and legal situations arising from legislative and regulatory disparities between the Member States. The information provided by the applicant in the present case illustrates, moreover, the disparity which exists between the Member States, particularly as regards tax bases and rates of taxation on capital goods" (at para.81).[133]

The Court has, however, been reluctant to allow general aid schemes, such as export aid schemes applicable to all types of products, to escape prohibition where they could result in the exclusion of a large class of producers.[134] Hence general aid schemes should be distinguished from general economic measures.[135] AG Jacobs in his Opinion in Case C–241/94 recognised the difficulties of distinguishing these two concepts:

"Since Article 92 EEC [now Article 107 TFEU] refers to aid which favours certain undertakings or the production of certain goods, it is usually assumed that the measures which are generally applicable do not fall within its scope. Admittedly there is some force in Advocate General Capotorti's argument in *Commission v Ireland*[136] that 'it is perfectly justifiable to speak of a general principle of public aids to domestic products, if one wishes to avoid the incongruous view that these are sectoral aids which are prohibited and those of wider scope are permitted'; it may, however, be difficult to apply such a principle since the essential distinction between the prohibited aid on the one hand and general social and economic policy on the other becomes blurred."[137]

3–043   In certain cases it has been relatively easy for the Commission to establish that apparently general schemes have a partial effect, in the sense that they operate in favour of certain sectors or regions, from the very structure of the scheme itself, as in Joined Cases 6 and 11/69 *Commission v France* and Case 203/82 *Commission v Italy*.[138] In Case C–241/94 *France v Commission* (*Kimberly Clark*) the Court was asked to consider whether a general scheme which could, at the

---

[133] [2004] E.C.R. II–1933.
[134] Cases 6 and 11/69 *Commission v France* [1969] E.C.R. 523.
[135] Case 57/86 *Greece v Commission* [1988] E.C.R. 2855 and Case T–67/94 *Tierce Ladbroke* [1998] E.C.R. II–1.
[136] Case 249/81 [1982] E.C.R. 4005, at p.4031.
[137] [1996] E.C.R. I–4551, at para.30.
[138] [1969] E.C.R. 523 and [1983] E.C.R. 2525 respectively.

discretion of the authorities, be applied in such a way as to favour certain undertakings, was a state aid. At para.23 of its judgment the Court confirmed that the Commission had been correct to conclude that, on the basis of the wide discretionary powers enjoyed by the body responsible for implementing the scheme, certain undertakings would be put in a more favourable position than others, thus bringing the scheme within the scope of art.107 as well as the notification obligations imposed under art.108 (see further, Ch.25).[139]

In its Decision 96/614[140] the Commission held that an ad hoc derogation from the mandatory rules in the Italian Civil Code regarding winding-up provisions amounted to aid. Where, however, a general support scheme is available, for example for infrastructural development or for site improvement, and such support does not benefit a particular undertaking, this will not amount to aid.[141]

There has been criticism that the Commission has not always been consistent **3–044** in its treatment of certain schemes which appear to be general aid rather than general economic policy measures.[142] Thus, the special rate of corporation tax in Ireland at 10 per cent was generally assumed to be a general economic measure rather than a general aid scheme.[143]

The Courts have generally found the "selectivity criteria" to be easily met. Hence in Case C–143/99 *Adria-Wien Pipeline*[144] a tax measure which distinguished between the manufacturing sector and the rest of the economy, including the service sector, was held to be selective. In its judgment in *Adria* the Court held that an Austrian tax measure awarding a rebate on energy taxes charged on supply of natural gas and electricity to undertakings active (i) in the manufacture of goods, and (ii) insofar as energy taxes exceeded 0.35 per cent of the production value, was in fact a selective measure. The Court observed that "undertakings supplying services may, just like undertakings manufacturing goods, be major consumers of energy" and further that "the ecological considerations underlying the national legislation at issue do not justify treating the consumption of natural gas or electricity by undertakings supplying services differently than the consumption of energy by undertakings manufacturing goods. Energy consumption by each of these sectors is equally damaging to the environment." The Court further held that the criterion applied by the national legislation at issue is not justified by the nature or general scheme of that legislation. Hence the

---

[139] Compare the Court's ruling in Joined Cases C–324 and 342/90 *Germany and Pleuger Worhington v Commission* [1994] E.C.R. I–1173, where the Court rejected the Commission's reasoning justifying the existence of an aid programme as all the aids in question were granted under the same procedure at para.23.

[140] May 29, 1996 [1996] O.J. L272/46.

[141] Clean-up aid to building sites paid before a purchaser was identified was not aid; financing of infrastructures set up by public bodies was not aid. *Matra*-support for infrastructural improvements was not intended to benefit a particular undertaking and hence was not aid.

[142] For a cogent critique, see J. Bourgeois, "State Aids, Taxation Measures and Specificity" in *Liber Amicorum*, M. Waelbroek (Brussels, 1999).

[143] Contrast C–57/97 [1997] O.J. C329/4 re general taxation reductions granted by the Spanish government for export activities.

[144] Case C–143/99 [1999] E.C.R. I–8365.

measure was selective because it was reserved to manufacturing undertakings and not as a result of the limitation expressed in terms of the production value. At para.36 of its ruling the Court seemed to imply that if the rebate of the energy taxes had been applied to all undertakings in the national territory regardless of their activity, and insofar as the energy taxes exceeded 0.35 per cent of the production value, the measure would not have been considered as selective.[145]

However, in a subsequent decision concerning a modification of the same law, the Commission was required to consider whether a tax rebate on gas and electricity paid to all businesses if the taxes together exceeded 0.35 per cent of their net production value would constitute aid. The Commission considered in its preliminary assessment that as only larger companies would benefit from this measure, the tax rebate did not constitute a general measure.[146] The Commission has taken the same approach in its recent decision on the Austrian Green Electricity Act.[147]

Taxation exemptions

3–045   Although increases or decreases in the rates of taxation are usually of general application, tax exemptions which benefit particular sectors or regions or even undertakings can constitute state aid.[148] The Commission has codified its decision-making practice on direct taxation in its Notice of 1998. In this section the general principles on which the Commission has based its approach are briefly summarised. The application of the state aid rules to taxation are dealt with in full in Ch.10.

Direct taxation

3–046   The question of whether particular tax rules may or not give rise to a state aid is a complex one. The application of the "selectivity" test is particularly important in order to establish whether or not a particular tax rule is prima facie a state aid measure within the meaning of art.107(1) TFEU. The Commission has issued a Notice on the application of the state aid rules to measures relating to the direct taxation of business in 1998.[149] Although this Notice provides some guidance, a number of complex issues, most of which are outside the scope of this chapter, remain. These are dealt with in detail at Ch.10.

---

[145] The Commission subsequently approved the energy rebate tax as a state aid compatible with art.107(c) TFEU and with the guidelines for environmental protection. The same law was modified in late 2002—see [2003] O.J. C164/2. See also Case C–368/04 *Transalpine Ölleiting* [2006] E.C.R. I–9957.

[146] [2003] O.J. C164/2 at p.3. Following the Court's ruling in the *Adria Wien* case, the Commission re-examined earlier exemptions it had issued for several national eco-tax exemption schemes. These are discussed further in Ch.20 (energy).

[147] C24/09 [2011] O.J. L235/42. See Ch.20.

[148] Case 70/72 *Commission v Germany* [1973] E.C.R. 813.

[149] [1998] O.J. C384/3.

As explained, a measure will be treated as selective if it favours certain sectors of industry, excluding others.[150] However, a measure which at first sight appears selective, may be justified by the nature or general scheme of the underlying legislation, and thus escape classification as aid within the meaning of art.107(1). Whether a tax measure is justified by the general nature of the scheme of the tax system, or for reasons relating to the logic of the tax system, also remains a highly controversial area. The Commission has, however, incorporated this latter principle into its Notice: accordingly, an exception to the application of the tax system will not involve state aid at all provided that it derives directly from the basic or guiding principles of the tax system in the Member State.[151] A tax measure will be selective if it favours certain undertakings or the production of certain goods or services albeit in comparison with others which, in the light of the objective pursued by the statutory scheme or system in question "are in a comparable legal and factual situation".[152] According to the Notice, the selective advantage may derive from an exception to taxation provisions or from a discretionary practice on the part of the tax authorities. The existence of differentiation within a system will not constitute "state aid" if this can be justified by the "nature or general scheme of the system".[153]

It is then necessary to determine the common system applicable and then seek **3–047** the justification for the exception. This could imply that the complexity of regulatory taxes such as eco-taxes as well as energy saving or efficiency tax measures could justify a more flexible approach. However, as demonstrated by the *Adria-Wien* judgment, it cannot be guaranteed that the Court will be easily convinced. In that case the Court was not impressed by the Austrian government's argument that the Court should consider the introduction of the energy taxes and the rebates, not as isolated measures, but in the broader context of the overall package intended to consolidate the budget, also taking into account the disproportionate impact of the taxes on certain sectors.

Commission practice has been criticised as it does not always allow for a clear indication to be drawn on what may fall within the nature or general system of a scheme. For example, in its assessment of the UK Climate Change Levy's dual-use exemption scheme, the Commission opened a formal investigation because of its doubts about the effects of the "dual-use" exemption. The levy in question was imposed on non-domestic use of energy for fuel purposes but not on energy products used for non-fuel purposes or on energy products that provide fuel as a by-product (dual use). The Commission approved an extended exemption, considering it to be justified by the logic and nature of the system, by reference not only to the environmental aims of the UK legislation, but also taking into account

---

[150] See in this respect the analysis of Case C–143/99 *Adria-Wien* [2001] E.C.R. I–8365, discussed in detail above.

[151] See also in this respect the ruling of the English Court of Appeal in *R. v Commissioners of Customs and Excise Ex p. Lunn Poly* [1999] Eu.L.R. 653.

[152] See in particular the ruling of the Court in Case C–172/03 *Heiser* [2005] E.C.R. I–1627, and Case C–308/01 *GIL* [2004] E.C.R. I–4777, at para.68.

[153] See also, e.g. Case C–143/99 *Adria-Wien* [2001] E.C.R. I–8365, at para.41.

the competitive situation of the affected products on the market.[154] However, in a later decision on an environmental tax imposed by the UK government on the commercial exploitation of rock, sand and gravel when used as an aggregate for construction purposes—the so-called Aggregates Levy—the Commission did not raise objections to a number of exemptions on materials that arise as by-products or waste products from certain processes. The Commission found that these exemptions fell within the general scheme of the levy and thus did not constitute aid.[155] This decision was upheld by the General Court but subsequently annulled by the ECJ.[156]

General or selective tax measures

3–048   The distinction between "general" and "selective" tax measures is not always, however, a clear-cut one. According to the Notice, tax measures which are open to all economic agents in a comparable situation on an equal access basis in a Member State are "general measures". "General measures" may not be reduced in scope through the discretionary power of the state to grant them or "other factors that restrict their practical effect".[157]

The mere fact that there is an exceptionally high number of undertakings benefiting from a scheme may not in and of itself be conclusive for the classification of the measure as general as opposed to selective. In *Kingdom of Belgium v Commission*, the Court held that the fact that the measure in question extended to all Belgian employers of manual workers did not mean that it was a "general measure". According to the ECJ:

"[n]either the high number of benefiting undertakings nor the diversity and importance of the industrial sectors to which those undertakings belong warrant the conclusion that the ... scheme constitutes a general measure of economic policy".[158]

In an opinion delivered on September 18, 2003, in Case C–308/01 *Gil Insurance Ltd*, AG Geelhoed has expressed the view that care should be taken in determining whether a derogation from a standard tax regime imposed a burden or amounted to a grant of aid:

"the notion that a distortion created by an exceptional burden may be viewed as the grant of aid in favour of economic operators who continue to come within the general rule is [in his view] in principle incorrect on both legal and

---

[154] C–18/01, IP/02/491.

[155] N 863/01, C(2002) 1478, of April 24, 2002; this decision was subject to appeal in Case T–210/02 *British Aggregates Association v Commission* [2006] E.C.R. II–2789. See also, for a discussion of the UK litigation on the Aggregates Levy, K. Bacon, "The Concept of State Aid", [2003] E.C.L.R. Vol.24, No.2, pp.54–61.

[156] Case C–487/06P [2008] E.C.R. I–10505.

[157] See also Case C–222/04 *Ministro dell'Economia* [2006] E.C.R. I–289.

[158] Case C–75/97 *Kingdom of Belgium v Commission* [1999] E.C.R. I–3671, at para.32.

economic grounds and on policy grounds . . . . [according to AG Geelhoed] a specific distortion created by an exceptional burden can never be regarded as the grant of aid in favour of the market participants coming under the general measure . . . If the relevant distortion must be eliminated in the interests of the common market the Community will have to eliminate the source of that distortion, namely the exceptional burden, in that connection it must make use of its competences under Articles 96 and 97 EC [now arts 116 and 117 TFEU] and not those under Articles 87 and 88 EC [now arts 107 and 108 TFEU]" (paras 73 et seq.).[159]

As confirmed in Case C–88/03 *Portugal v the Commission*,[160] the simple fact that a state measure can lead to a distortion of competition on the internal market, as the Commission had purported to argue, cannot result in its classification as a state aid for the purposes of art.107(1) TFEU. The Advocate General pointed out (once again) that:

"The Commission's argument that the focus must be solely on whether or not a regional tax reduction has the effect of competitive distortion wrongly conflates the distinction between these conceptually separate instruments (at para.43)."

This distinction, was subsequently confirmed by the Court of Justice in its judgment in Case C–174/02 *Streekgewest Westelijk Noord-Brabant*:

"It must be observed, at the outset, as the Advocate General pointed out . . . . that the Treaty makes a clear distinction between, on the one hand, the regime in Articles 92 of the EC Treaty [now Article 107 TFEU] and Article 93 and 94 of the EC Treaty [now Article 108 and 109 TFEU], concerning State aid and, on the other, that in Articles 96 of the EC Treaty [now Article 116 TFEU] and Article 97 EC [Article 117 TFEU] concerning the distortions which arise from differences between the laws, regulations or administrative provisions of the Member States and, in particular, their tax provisions" (at para. 24).[161]

However, in *Gil* the Court did not directly follow AG Geelhoed's broader **3–049** approach, but ruled that the reasons for applying, exceptionally, a higher rate could be justified in this particular case by the nature and the general scheme of the system.

The question of a possible justification for differentiation between standard rates of tax and derogations is approached on a case-by-case basis and the Notice suggests that the burden of proof lies with the Member State. The Commission

---

[159] [2004] E.C.R. I–4777.
[160] [2006] E.C.R. I–7115.
[161] [2005] E.C.R. I–85.

and the courts will assess whether the relevant measure is consistent with the express purpose and logic of the underlying fiscal system.

With regard to the nature of the objectives that may be relevant to justify differential tax treatment, the Commission takes the view in the Notice that:

"a distinction must be made between, on the one hand, the external objectives assigned to a particular tax scheme (in particular, social or regional objectives) and, on the other hand, the objectives which are inherent in the tax system itself".

Only the latter category may be relied upon to oppose the state aid qualification. Paragraph 13(2) of the Notice recognises that Member States can pursue general policy objectives through their tax systems, and as such, for example, tax certain production costs, including labour, at lower rates. In addition and with regard to differentiation in tax rates the Commission generally considers that the progressive nature of an income tax scale or profit tax scale is justified by the redistributive purpose of the tax (see paras 26 to 27 of the Notice).

The "logic of the system test"

3–050   In Joined Cases C–72 and C–73/91 *Sloman Neptun*, the Court held that the differences between shipping undertakings employing foreign workers on the one hand, and other shipping undertakings on the other, were "inherent in the system and not a means of granting a particular advantage to the undertakings concerned".[162] In Case C–353/95P *Ladbroke v Commission*, the Court also held that there was no state aid where French legislation treated bets on French races differently from bets on Belgian races. Although bets on horse races abroad were subject to the statutory and fiscal retentions in force in the country where the races were organised, this did not amount to the conferral of a specific advantage on organisers of Belgian races: it was justified by the logic of the totalisator system. The so-called "logic of the system test" remains, however, difficult to apply and to a certain extent its very application would seem to contradict the "classic" effects-based approach to the definition of a state aid. This is well illustrated by the *Lunn Poly* saga of taxation cases which was ruled upon by a series of English courts and eventually by the ECJ. The English tax authority, the Commissioners for Customs and Excise, had ruled that an imposition of a higher rate of insurance premium tax (IPT) on insurance provided by suppliers of certain travel services than on insurance provided by others did not constitute state aid because it was justified by the logic of the system. The justification lay in the objective of the system—to counter tax avoidance. This ruling was overturned by the English Divisional Court, which was in turn upheld by the Court of Appeal: the derogation from the higher rate constituted a state aid.

---

[162] [1993] E.C.R. I–887, at para.21.

The Court of Appeal's ruling was subsequently relied upon in hearings before the VAT and Excise Duties Tribunal in *GIL* and *Airtours*. In both cases the applicants had been subject to IPT at the higher rate. They claimed repayment of the difference between the tax paid at the higher rate and the tax which should have been paid at the lower rate. While the applicants in *Airtours* were also travel agents, in *GIL* the appellants were suppliers of insurance relating to domestic appliances (such as televisions and video recorders), who had also been subject to the higher rate of IPT. In *GIL* the VAT Tribunal found, on the basis of *Lunn Poly* and the case law of the European Court, that the differential rate of IPT amounted to an aid, but decided to make a reference to the Court on the questions of whether the higher rate affected trade between Member States, and whether repayment of the difference paid by the appellants was the appropriate remedy. In fact the Court went on to rule that the difference did not amount to a state aid to those taxed at the lower rate. The differential rates were justified by the logic of the system. The Court ruled in Case C–308/01 that:

"in those circumstances, even on the assumption that the introduction of the higher rate of IPT involves an advantage for operators offering contracts subject to the standard rate, the application of the higher rate of IPT to a specific part of the insurance contracts previously subject to the standard rate must be regarded as justified by the nature and the general scheme of the national system of taxation of insurance. The IPT scheme cannot therefore be regarded as constituting an aid measure within the meaning of Article 87(1) EC [107(1) TFEU]" (para.78).[163]

Events versus activities

A measure will amount to an aid if it favours certain undertakings or certain **3–051** products (or sectors), but probably not to measures favouring certain actions or activities which are potentially open to all sectors or types of undertakings. As a rule, fiscal provisions concerning certain "events", such as the acquisition of assets or the accrual of losses, are not directed to "certain undertakings". In this respect the Commission's decision of May 17, 2000 on a Danish statute on tax deducted at source is of interest. The purpose of the amendment to the Danish scheme was to offer highly paid foreign experts, employed for a limited period in a Danish business, taxation at a gross fixed rate. The Commission reasoned that the Danish Act did not benefit certain businesses or activities since it applies to all experts in all areas and its area of application is not restricted to certain regions or sectors. The application is assessed on the basis of objective and non-discriminatory criteria without the tax authorities being given discriminating powers. The information provided to the Commission showed that the scheme would be used in more than 150 sectors, by small and medium-sized as well as by large businesses. The reason for the concentration of the effect of the tax in

---

[163] [2004] E.C.R. I–4777.

certain sectors was that salaries were especially high in these sectors—schemes aimed at the high-paid will have considerably greater effect in sectors with high salaries but this will not constitute state aid.[164]

A similar approach was taken in the Commission's decision on a Belgian fiscal measure in relation to night and team labour (*nacht en ploegenarbeid*)—a measure which allowed a reduction in certain taxes payable by companies organising their production of goods and services with more than two teams of workers employed consecutively between the hours of 20.00 and 6.00. The Commission, relying on para.14 of the Notice, considered that this measure was not selective as every undertaking and every sector that pursued this form of labour organisation could benefit from the derogation. The mere fact that certain economic sectors, e.g. more labour than capital-intensive sectors, were more likely to benefit from the derogation than others did not render the proposed measure to be selective.[165]

Regional taxation measures and geographical selectivity

3–052   The vexed question of whether certain regional tax measures can be deemed selective and thus classified as state aid has come before the Courts in a number of recent cases, challenging the Commission's position that regional state aid in the area of taxation cannot escape the application of art.107(1) just by shifting legislative power to the sub-national level.[166]

In Case C–88/03 *Portugal v Commission*, also referred to as the *Azores* judgment, the fundamental question was whether the tax reductions at issue could be regarded as a measure of general application in the Azores or whether it was, rather, a selective measure that was at issue, conferring an advantage solely on operators established in the Azores, as compared with those operating in Portugal. The Court took the view that in order for a decision to be capable of being regarded as having been adopted in the exercise of sufficiently autonomous powers: first, it must have been taken by a regional or local authority which has, from a constitutional point of view, a political and administrative status separate from that of the central government; second, it must have been adopted without the central government being able to intervene directly as regards its content; and third, the financial consequences of a reduction of the national tax rate for undertakings in the region must not be offset by aid or subsidies from other regions or central government.[167] The Court reiterated those principles in the *UGT-Rioja* case.[168]

The importance of the *Azores* judgment is that it did not concern a federal State having a symmetrical distribution of fiscal power. The Court did not hold that the

---

[164] SG (2000) D/103729.
[165] N603/2003–C(2004) 1375, April 2004.
[166] See Joined Cases T–92/00 and T–103/99 *Territoria Historico de Alava* [2002] E.C.R. II–1385, as confirmed in Case C–186/02 [2006] E.C.R. I–91.
[167] [2006] E.C.R. I–7115.
[168] Cases C–428/06 to C–434/06 [2008] E.C.R. I–6747.

reference framework necessarily had to correspond to the totality of the territory of a Member State.

In *UGT-Rioja*, the Court of Justice rejected the existence of a possible fourth condition as a precondition for application of the three criteria laid down in the *Azores* judgment. The only conditions which must be satisfied in order for the territory falling within the competence of an infra-State body to be the relevant framework in order to assess whether a decision adopted by that body is selective in nature, are the conditions of institutional autonomy, procedural autonomy and economic and financial autonomy as set out in *Portugal v Commission*. This issue is further discussed in Ch.10 at paras 10–007—10–008.

Material or de facto selectivity

As the Advocate General has observed in his Opinion in Cases C–106 and C–107/09 *Commission v Gibraltar*:   **3–053**

"Material selectivity may cover both tax measures limited to undertakings characterised by certain types of activity (sectoral selectivity) and those applicable on the basis of predefined situations in which undertakings are liable to find themselves (horizontal selectivity), for example in the case of tax incentives or measures designed to favour a particular kind of labour force."[169]

This problematic concept has been the subject of various approaches proposed by academic literature as well as by various Advocates General. In *Gibraltar*, the Advocate General has proposed an analysis in three successive stages which would involve, first, seeking to ascertain whether the measure is capable of applying to all undertakings that are in a comparable factual and legal situation, second, verifying whether certain undertakings enjoy more favourable treatment (discrimination) and, finally, ascertaining that the measure can be justified by the nature or structure of the tax regime.[170] Further discussion of the Commission's application of the concept and the relevant case law can be found in Ch.10.

Alleviation of social charges

Similar principles apply to measures relating to social charges. Where a particular industrial sector is exempted from the application of a general social security system without there being any justification for the exemption in the nature or general scheme of the system, then this will constitute an aid.[171] The   **3–054**

---

[169] [2011] E.C.R. Opinion of April 7, 2011.

[170] Opinion of 2011 in Case C–106/09P. The Court has now upheld the Commission's approach in its ruling of November 15, 2011.

[171] Case 310/85 *Deufil v Commission* [1987] E.C.R. 901. Commission Decision 97/239/EC of December 4, 1996 [1997] O.J. L95/25 and further *Maribel Quarter* [1997] O.J. C201/6. See also 26th Report on Competition Policy, 1996 at pt 172 and 27th Report on Competition Policy, 1997 at pt 292.

same reasoning applies to reductions in social charges for firms located in particular regions.[172] Where, in connection with a state policy, social security contributions previously paid by employers are "fiscalised" so that some contributions are taken over completely by the state, the Commission has taken no objection as long as this process does not favour particular sectors or regions. Thus, if the process of fiscalisation proceeds at a faster rate or at a more favourable level for certain sectors or for firms in certain regions, effectively resulting in a selective reduction of costs, this could amount to state aid within the meaning of art.107.[173]

In cases where outstanding social security debts have been cancelled following bankruptcy of the firm involved, but similar debts owed to private creditors have not been waived, then aid could be involved.[174] However, in Case C–200/97 *Ecotrade* the Court considered that the scheme for cancelling social security debts was not selective in nature.[175]

The Commission may concede that there is no element of aid involved, however, where arrangements allow particular enterprises to carry over debts of outstanding charges due to their national social security institutions, provided that repayment is assured and interest is paid. The Commission may also impose reporting requirements in these circumstances to ensure that no element of aid will arise in the future.[176]

Indirect reductions in the costs of certain undertakings

3–055   Undertakings may benefit from indirect reductions in certain costs in a number of ways. A reduction in the charges levied by a public undertaking, such as a utility, may represent an aid under certain conditions. At the same time, a reduction in charges placed upon a certain sector may not be regarded as aid if the reduction is an objective and justifiable response to market forces. In Cases 67, 68 and 70/85 *Van der Kooy v Commission*,[177] the Court ruled that a preferential tariff which was only applicable to a certain sector, and which displayed a downward trend which was not reflected by the tariffs applicable to undertakings in other sectors, would be prima facie evidence for the conclusion that the preferential tariff was an aid. If it could be demonstrated that the preferential tariff was, in the context of the market in question, objectively justified by economic reasons then the preferential tariff would not amount to an aid (see further, Ch.20). The Court has confirmed this approach in its ruling in Case C–56/93 *Commission v Belgium*,[178] which concerned a special tariff also made

---

[172] Case 173/73 *Italy v Commission* [1974] E.C.R. 475.
[173] See, for example, Commission Notice concerning aid granted by Italy to certain regions in the Mezzogiorno [1992] O.J. C240/7.
[174] C–26/97 [1997] O.J. C361/3; Case C–200/97 *Ecotrade v AFS* [1998] E.C.R. I–7907.
[175] See, also 26th Competition Report, 1996, at pt.172 and 27th Report on Competition Policy, 1997, at pt.292.
[176] Commission notice concerning aid which Spain plans to grant to Fundix [1992] O.J. C198/9.
[177] [1988] E.C.R. 219.
[178] [1996] E.C.R. I–723.

available by the Dutch gas company, Gasunie, to producers of fertilisers who used gas as a feedstock, discussed below at Ch.20.

If a state undertaking supplies one of its subsidiaries with goods and services as well as premises at below market rates, there is prima facie an element of state aid involved (Case T–95/94 *Sytraval*[179] at para.36). Similarly, in Case C–39/94,[180] various forms of commercial and logistical support provided by the French Post Office to its wholly owned subsidiaries, SFMI and Chronopost, which are governed by private law and carry on activities open to competition, were considered to be a form of state aid where the remuneration received was less than that which would have been demanded under normal market conditions (para.62). In Case T–613/97 *UFEX v Commission*, ("*Ufex II*") the General Court annulled the Commission's decision finding that it had failed to consider that the transfer by La Poste of the client base of its Postadex product to its subsidiary SFMI-Chronopost constituted an advantage. That finding could not be invalidated by the Commission's assertion that the Postadex client basis had no value in accounting terms.[181] The ECJ however overruled the lower Court, holding that the postal network could not be compared with a market network, which would never have been created by a private undertaking.[182]

The provision of special rates and tariffs through public sector companies is discussed further in Ch.8.

Where the reduction in certain costs is a consequence of a derogation from a **3–056** measure of general economic or social policy, and a justification for that derogation can be established on the basis of the nature or the general scheme of the system, then the selectivity test, discussed above, will not be met. In Case C–189/91 *Petra Kirsammer-Hack v Nurhan Sidal*, the Court was asked to rule on whether the exemption of small and medium-sized firms in Germany from certain national provisions regarding the dismissal of employees. AG Tesauro acknowledged that the measure in question does not involve any direct or indirect debit to state resources, but he urged the Court to adopt a generous interpretation of art.107 and to consider the *ratio legis* of this provision, which in his view is to ensure conditions of equal competition between competing enterprises.[183] He then went on to consider whether the law in question was in fact a general measure or a general aid, and contended that the answer must lie in whether or not the exemption conformed to the general logic of the system of employment protection or whether it did in fact constitute a special, unjustified exemption in favour of a particular sector. The Advocate General supported the Commission's submission that the former was the correct interpretation (at para.65). The Court confirmed this approach and ruled that the indirect reduction in costs borne by the enterprises in question was a result of a general measure of economic policy (at para.17).

---

[179] [1995] E.C.R. II–2651.
[180] [1996] E.C.R. I–3547.
[181] T–613/97 *UFEX and Others v Commission* [2000] E.C.R. II–4055.
[182] Case C–341/6P and C–342/06P [2008] E.C.R. I–4777.
[183] Opinion of November 25, 1992 [1993] E.C.R. I–6185.

In Joined Cases C–72 and 73/91 *Sloman Neptun* the Court reached a similar finding on the question of whether or not a German law excluding from the jurisdiction of the German courts labour law matters affecting seamen working on vessels sailing under a "flag of convenience", and so registered in the international maritime register, amounted to a state aid. In most cases, sailors employed on such vessels received a substantially lower rate of pay than those working on vessels sailing under the German flag. In the light of the general nature and logic of the contested law, it could not be contended that the law had as purpose or effect the conferral of a selective benefit on a particular firm (at para.19).[184]

Selectivity and support for training

3–057   In 1998 the Commission issued a Communication concerning a framework on training aid, stating that:

"being general measures, many training measures are not caught by Article 87(1)[now Article 107(1)] of the Treaty. Most training forms part of the tasks traditionally carried out by the state and by and large benefits people and workers everywhere".[185]

If, however, the training aid is targeted at a particular firm or sector, that form of vocational aid may fall within the scope of art.107. In a 1999 Decision concerning an Italian law concerning fixed-term training and work experience contracts for unemployed persons, the Commission ruled this measure to be a grant of a state aid as the employers received a partial exemption from social security contributions for such employees. In a decision concerning assistance provided to Eli Lilly Ltd, the Commission took the view that it amounted to state aid requiring approval, notwithstanding the fact that it prepared participants for transferable qualifications that were nationally recognised.

The now expired Block Exemption Regulation 68/2001 distinguished between general and specific training. Specific training shall mean training involving tuition directly and principally applicable to the employee's present or future position in the assisted firm and providing qualifications which are not, or are only to a limited extent transferable to other firms or fields of work. General training means training involving tuition which is not applicable only or principally to the employee's present or future position in the assisted firm, but which provides qualifications that are largely transferable to other firms or fields of work and thereby substantially improve the employability of the employees. Training could be considered "general" for the purpose of the Regulation if:

—it is jointly organised by different independent enterprises, or if the employees of different enterprises may avail themselves of the training;

---

[184] See also Joined Cases C–52–54/97 [1998] E.C.R. I–2629.
[185] [1998] O.J. 343/10, at para.13.

—it is recognised, certified or validated by pubic authorities or bodies on which a Member State or the Community has conferred the necessary powers.

Both types of training are deemed to be "aid" for the purposes of art.107(1) but "general" training aid is eligible for higher aid intensities (see further, Ch.11).

Financial support for infrastructure

The general rule is that if the infrastructure is provided for general use as opposed to a dedicated purpose, benefiting no particular user, then there is no selectivity and hence no aid at the level of user. The construction of a road, for example, is usually regarded as general infrastructure. The construction of water or waste treatment facilities may however be regarded as a specific type of infrastructure where selectivity issues may well arise. Nevertheless, if these facilities are also providing services of general economic interest (SGEIs), financial support to the operators of such services may not amount to aid within the meaning of art.107(1) TFEU, if certain conditions are fulfilled. Even if aid to the user can be excluded, it does not necessarily follow that the measure in question would not benefit either the investors in the infrastructure or, if relevant, the operator. It is necessary to consider whether a measure can benefit different categories of recipient.   **3–058**

The following paragraph examines the Commission's approach to infrastructural aid in general, and briefly outlines its policy and related practice in relation to broadband infrastructure and to Regional Airports.

Selectivity and infrastructural aid

The issue of state funding of infrastructure, or other forms of state measures relating to the operation of infrastructure, has become of increasing complexity, given in particular that Member States have resorted to various forms of public-private partnerships (PPPs) or public/private initiatives (PPIs) to operate infrastructure and to distribute public services.   **3–059**

The Market Investor Test and Infrastructural Funding

Infrastructural funding may also be subject to the "market investor test". In Case T–196/04 *Ryanair*, the General Court held that the Commission had applied the private investor test in relation to the airport operator BSCA, but failed to apply it regarding the measures set by the Walloon region. The Court held that it is: **3–060**

"however necessary, when applying the private investor test, to envisage the commercial transaction *as a whole* in order to determine whether the public entity and the entity which is controlled by it, taken together, have acted as rational operators in a market economy".[186]

[186] Case T–196/04 *Ryanair v Commission* [2008] E.C.R. II–3643, para.59.

The argument brought forward by the Commission that the Walloon Region acted only as a regulatory authority was not accepted.[187]

3–061   Certain types of infrastructure are also now referred to as open access infrastructure. In the Commission's view in some of its early decisions, a public infrastructure installation should be required to satisfy a public interest, i.e. a benefit to the economy in general, and furthermore it must be unlikely that the market would finance the infrastructure on the same conditions.[188] Furthermore, if there is no special advantage because the user of the infrastructure contributes to its costs and gains no benefit, again there is no aid.[189] In *Saint-Gobain/ Eurofloat* the Commission also concluded that where a French local body had provided financial support towards infrastructural costs in connection with an industrial site, this was not state aid as long as it was part of a collective work carried out to develop land use for various firms and as such it could not be seen as a selective benefit, and would not constitute aid.[190] Where, however, utility services are installed for the benefit of a single firm, who does not in turn meet the costs of these services, then on the assumption that state resources are involved, this would meet the selectivity test and fall within the scope of art.107(1).[191] In the *Kimberley Clark* case, an industrial park had been situated near a river and thus conferred a specific advantage on paper manufacturers who required water supply and waste treatment facilities.[192]

3–062   If a Member State makes available financial support to provide infrastructure such as road or rail services to improve connections to a new or upgraded site on which certain production facilities are to be sited, it may well be concluded that this could amount to a selective benefit to the end user. Much may depend on the actual circumstances of the case—if for example, the development of road (or rail) infrastructure costs was normally borne by public funds and the benefit of the infrastructural improvements were not solely to be attributed to the owners of the new or upgraded site, but could be seen to be of wider public benefit, then there is at least an arguable case that such a transaction would not constitute aid given the multi-functionality of the infrastructure. In particular, it is of importance that the facility in question is open to all potential users on a non-discriminatory basis. In a case concerning state funding for the construction of a propylene pipeline the Commission concluded that the funding favoured a limited group of users because the pipeline served to transport certain substances only, and hence opened a formal investigation prior to giving its approval.[193]

---

[187] See also *Balfour and Leandro*, "State Aid in the Airline Sector: A change in focus" [2011] EStAL Vol.10, nr.2, p.225.

[188] Commission Non-paper, SGEI and State Aid, November 12, 2002, at pt 60.

[189] [1992] O.J. L293/15.

[190] [1991] O.J. L215/11.

[191] Case C–225/91 *Matra* [1993] E.C.R. I–3203.

[192] [1994] O.J. C170/8.

[193] C–67/2003, and C–2031/2004, decision of June 16, 2004; [2005] O.J. L56/15; see also N 527/2002 Aviation fuel pipeline to Athens Airport [2003] O.J. C148/11. See also, C11/2005 aid for an ethylene pipeline in Bavaria [2007] O.J. L143/16.

In its original "Guidelines on State Aids in the Aviation Sector" of 1994 the **3–063** Commission has stated that "the construction of airport infrastructure projects . . . represents a general measure of economic policy which cannot be controlled by the Commission under the Treaty rules on state aid".[194] The Commission published a new Community framework for the assessment of state aid granted for the financing of airports as well as for start-up aid to airlines departing from regional airports in September 2005, discussed below, which already indicated that the Commission may be taking a stricter approach to this form of support. This was subsequently confirmed in its decision concerning measures of support to the regional airport at Leipzig-Halle,[195] as discussed in Ch.8, where the General Court upheld the Commission's finding that the regional airport in question was an economic activity and even if open access for its users was guaranteed this did not rule out that the support to its operator could fall within the scope of art.107(1).

At the same time, the current Regional Airport Guidelines barely mention the market investor test, and the judgment of the Court in the *Ryan Air* case may cause the Commission to rethink its approach in this respect, following the consultation exercise launched in 2011.

Selectivity

In determining who may enjoy a selective benefit as a result of an infra- **3–064** structure project is of course necessary to examine each of the categories of potential beneficiaries of public assistance—i.e. the end users, the owners/operators as well as the shareholders if a public-private financial construction such as a special purpose company is used. Even if the use of the facility is subject to open and non-discriminatory access, the owners or operators of an infrastructure may still receive a selective benefit if they are not selected by means of an open and non-discriminatory procedure and they receive more than a market price to cover the construction and operation costs of the facility in question.[196] An additional relevant factor may be the issue of who should own the infrastructure on completion. If the relevant transaction or arrangement with private sector parties contemplates transfer of ownership to those parties this may well amount to a selective benefit: much will depend on whether the overall terms of the transaction are market-based.[197]

The Commission's general decision practice confirms that, with respect to **3–065** end-users, funding of educational buildings, sewage treatment facilities and waste deposits or the development of industrial and/or business parks do not fall within the definition of an aid within the meaning of art.107(1). This infrastructure does not aim at specific undertakings but favours any undertaking

---

[194] [1994] O.J. C350, at para.12.

[195] [2008] O.J. L346/1.

[196] For a more detailed application of this approach, see the Commission's decision concerning the London underground (NN 170/2001 UK, C (2002) 438).

[197] See C–21/09 *Port of Pireaus* [2009] O.J. C245/21.

which decides to establish itself there. However, if the construction of an industrial park is intended to favour a specific undertaking, as in the *Kimberly Clark* case, then aid is involved. Even if the infrastructure is specifically designed for the use by one undertaking, a benefit can be excluded if the infrastructure is rented out at market conditions.

Certain types of infrastructure may be considered "multi-functional"—for example a sports stadium, which can be used for concerts or conventions as well as for sports events—and in these cases the Commission will look to see if the project does in fact create a selective benefit.

Even if the infrastructure project is not likely to create a specific or selective advantage for certain categories of end user, it is still necessary to ensure that there are no other categories of potential beneficiaries, in particular, operator/owners or shareholders in special purpose companies or joint ventures.[198]

3–066 **Public-private partnerships.** On the assumption that the infrastructure project may result in a potential selective advantage for, or "favouring of", the operators and/or end users it may then become necessary to examine further whether the public authority commissioning the project or participating in a public-private partnership (PPP) is acting as a prudent market economy investor and paying no more than the market price for the infrastructure; or alternatively, whether the operator of the infrastructure is being required to assume particular obligations which can be classified as public service obligations (PSOs) (also referred to as services of general economic interest (SGEIs)) and that the reward received is commensurate with the net additional costs of providing these services.

The Commission stated its intention, in the context of the State Aid Action Plan, to issue further guidance on aid to or through PPP constructions. In 2008 it published some general guidance in the form of an interpretative communication on the application of Community law to Public procurement and Concessions to Institutionalised Public-Private Partnerships.[199]

3–067 **The market-investor principle and PPPs.** Establishing a "market price" in certain markets, especially where large infrastructure projects are involved, may prove difficult, and all the more so if there is no pre-existing competition on or for the market in question.[200] This may be particularly problematic in PPP constructions where the private partners invariably also become subject to state aid control. The Commission has put increasing emphasis on the procedures for awarding infrastructure projects as a determining factor in establishing whether a market price has been paid to the undertakings constructing and managing an infrastructure facility. Hence a "market price" which excludes aid will be presumed if the private partner is selected through an open, transparent and non-

[198] See for example, Commission Decision N478/2004, *Irish Rail*, of June 7, 2006.
[199] C(2007) 6661, of February 5, 2008.
[200] See further, Case N 356/2002 Network Rail, July 17, 2002.

discriminatory tender procedure.[201] The respect for these principles should probably avoid the need for notification under art.108(3) unless the project involves an element of financial support for the performance of an SGEI. If this element is present, then the question of whether aid is involved at least in respect to operating costs of the infrastructure, and therefore whether prior notification to the Commission is required, must be examined on the basis of the so-called "*Altmark*" criteria (see also Ch.8).[202]

Further guidance on the exact scope of the conditions of openness, transparency and non-discrimination can in part be derived from EU procurement law, even if the application of these principles in the sphere of state aid control is not in all respects identical. It must be emphasised that the three principles apply even if the infrastructure project does not meet the thresholds specified in the various procurement directives. In particular, the principle of openness does not necessarily require that an open tender (one of the four procurement procedures) should be held. If an open tender procedure is not used, the authority commissioning the infrastructure is well advised to obtain expert independent advice in order to establish, insofar as possible, what a "fair" or "economic" price for the project should be.[203]

Infrastructure financing and SGEIs. The criteria developed by the Court in the context of compensation for public services (or SGEIs) in Case C–280/00 *Altmark*[204] may be of some value in assessing at least prima facie whether or not aid has been provided either to the operator or, eventually, to (certain categories of) end users. Some Member States may entrust an operator with the obligation to provide the infrastructure in question as a public service and to compensate the entrusted company for the losses it suffers from providing this service to certain classes of users.   **3–068**

Broadband financing and state aids. This latter premise is also borne out by the Commission's decisions concerning support to broadband infrastructure. Even though the electronic communications sector is fully liberalised and subject to detailed sectoral regulation, the Commission has accepted that market-driven private investment alone would not be sufficient to realise its ambitions for broadband connectivity and that the use of additional public funds may be a necessity. Further, in the context of the financial and economic crisis, broadband infrastructural investment is considered to be effective in bringing about both short-term recovery and longer term advantages. Between 2002 and 2009 the Commission adopted some 55 decisions on broadband financing measures.[205]   **3–069**

---

[201] *Commission v Austria (Teleaustria)* [2003] E.C.R. I–7747.

[202] For a detailed assessment of the application of arts 107 and 108 to PPPs, see Ch.11, "The Respect of State aid rules in Public Private Partnerships" in Mederer et al., *EU Competition Law*, Volume IV: State Aid, Book 1. (Claeys & Casteels: 2008).

[203] See also the Communication of 2008.

[204] [2003] E.C.R I–7747. See para.3–104, below.

[205] A list of Commission decisions is available at *http://ec.europa.eu/competiton/sectors/telecommu nications/broadband_decisions.pdf.*

The Broadband Guidelines 2009

3–070   The Broadband Guidelines of 2009[206] lay down the conditions under which public funding should be granted to broadband development in line with the EU state aid rules, and codify the Commission's extensive decision-making practice (developed in 2003) concerning basic broadband networks, extrapolating the fundamental tenets and applying them to the new area of very high speed, fibre based Next Generation Access ("NGA") networks.[207] The Guidelines distinguish between "white", "grey" and "black" areas, depending on whether there are already adequate private infrastructures in place. Public funding to roll out a broadband network in (mostly rural) white areas, where no adequate infrastructure exists is generally regarded as unproblematic. Conversely, investment in (densely populated) areas where already competing broadband infrastructures exist (black) is prohibited, while a state aid project for grey areas requires a more in-depth analysis. A similar logic is applied in case of aid to NGA networks, distinguishing between "white NGA", "grey NGA", and "black NGA" areas.[208]

Where the Commission authorises state aid, a number of compatibility conditions have to be fulfilled (as detailed in para.51 of the Guidelines). Public authorities must carry out a detailed mapping of the target areas and the use of open tender mechanisms to grant the aid remains crucial. Effective open wholesale access to the subsidised network must be guaranteed, in order to allow alternative operators to compete and avoid re-creation of telecoms monopolies. Moreover, the measures have to be technology neutral, and price benchmarking and claw-back mechanisms need to be put in place to avoid over-compensation. For aid to NGA networks, since the risk of distorting competition could be higher (as basic broadband infrastructures may be already in place in the targeted areas), additional compatibility conditions must be met. The white/black/grey area distinction is adapted to the situation of NGA networks (whose deployment is still at an early stage), by requiring Member States to take into account not only existing NGA infrastructures but also concrete investment plans by telecom operators to deploy such networks in the near future.[209]

3–071   In several early broadband cases the Commission held that the financial support would amount to an aid to both the proposed operator and to end-users, even though the former had been selected by negotiated tender procedures. In two British cases (*Atlas* and *Cumbria*) the operator had been selected in accordance with the restricted, negotiated procedure as opposed to a full open tender, and the Commission viewed this as offering insufficient guarantee that there was

---

[206] [2009] O.J. C235/7.

[207] See also, Commission Recommendation of September 20, 2010 on regulated access to Next Generation Access Networks (NGA), C(2010) 6223.

[208] These terms (white/grey/black) are used to represent different types of market failures in accordance with the State Aid Action Plan ("Less and better targeted state aid: a roadmap for state aid reform 2005–2009". Available at: *http://ec.europa.eu/competition/state_aid/reform/reform.html*.

[209] See paras 73, 75 and 79 of the Guidelines of 2009.

no risk of over-compensation to the operator. It ruled that the measures amounted to aid, albeit that they were exempted under art.107(3)(c). Tenders of this variety have been referred to as a form of "competition for subsidy" which may result in the Member State paying the lowest level of subsidy, but which do not necessarily rule out the existence of a subsidy as such.

In the subsequent *Pyrenees Atlantiques* case of 2004, a broadband infrastructure would be developed and managed by a private entity through a concession contract. The infrastructure would remain in public ownership.[210] The concessionaire was subject to detailed auditing rules and, furthermore, it was allowed a fixed rate of return on its investment (approximately 11 per cent) and if the revenues exceeded a certain amount, the concessionaire was required to repay the surplus to the authorities. Furthermore, although the operator was selected in a final round on the basis of a negotiated procedure, where criteria other than price were used, the Commission concluded that this type of project could not be awarded on the basis of simple price criteria.[211]

It is also interesting to note that this project was seen as potentially benefiting a wide class of end users spread throughout an entire region, whereas in the two British cases the project was deemed to confer an advantage on certain business users located in a particular business park. Finally, it should also be observed that while the British government defended its support for both the Atlas and the Cumbria projects[212] as general infrastructure support that did not fall under art.107(1), the French government based its case on the concept of an SGEI and took rather elaborate steps to meet the four criteria developed by the ECJ in its *Altmark* ruling, discussed below, at para.3–104.

In its decision to approve a fibre deployment project in the French department **3–072** Hauts-de-Seine, the Commission applied the provisions of the Guidelines regarding public service compensation for NGA projects for the first time. In this respect, the Guidelines indicate that building a broadband network can only be qualified as a public service if the network is passive, neutral, open and provides universal coverage in the territory concerned. In addition, the amount of the compensation for building the network cannot go beyond what is necessary to cover the additional costs to deploy the network in non-profitable areas.[213] This decision, which involves some €55 million of public funding to one of France's most densely populated and wealthiest regions, is currently subject to a challenge before the General Court in Case T–79/10 ([2010] O.J. C113/56).

The Commission approved an aid scheme to encourage the deployment of NGA networks in very sparsely populated areas in Finland, that are not covered by private projects.[214] In a German case approved in December 2009, municipalities will invest in and own specific ducts to encourage broadband deployment in

---

[210] In this respect the case can be contrasted with the earlier UK *Cumbria* decision where the operator would eventually become the owner of the infrastructure.

[211] N 381/2004—France, November 18, 2004.

[212] See also the related decision in N 199/2004 *Broadband Business Fund* [2005] O.J. C96.

[213] See Case N331/2008, IP/09/1391.

[214] N388/2009.

underserved areas. If such dedicated ducts are made available to broadband network operators without appropriate payment, this constitutes state aid. In the German case, the aid was found compatible, as it concerned multi-fibre ducts which will allow several broadband operators to deploy their networks, thereby encouraging infrastructure-based competition.[215] In another German case the Commission further clarified that, where a municipal authority is undertaking general civil works (such as digging up public roads), which can be useful also for the deployment of other utility networks (water, electricity, etc.), and allows the placement of ducts and passive infrastructure by broadband network operators at their own expense, this does not constitute state aid (case N383/2009).[216]

In April 2011 the Commission published a detailed questionnaire to invite comments on the proposed revision of the 2009 Guidelines, scheduled for 2012. These include the technological and market development of very high speed broadband infrastructures, the best design of access conditions on subsidised next generation networks, and enhancement of transparency of state aid broadband measures or the role of the national regulatory authorities in such projects. In light of the replies, the Commission will then evaluate whether and to what extent changes are necessary. If appropriate, the Commission will come forward with new draft Guidelines in early 2012.[217]

3-073 **The 2005 Commission Communication on aid to regional airports.** In late 2005 the Commission adopted a Communication on aid to airports and start-up aid to airlines departing from regional airports. This policy guideline gives useful insights into the Commission's policy on various forms of infrastructural aid. In particular, it illustrates the Commission's concern that possible elements of aid may be present in the commercial relationship between the owner and the operator of the infrastructure, i.e. what may be termed the upstream markets for the operation of airports. In this respect the new Communication supplements the Guidelines of 1994 which had been primarily concerned with the downstream market, i.e. the users of the infrastructure. The starting point is that the construction or financing from state resources of an infrastructure project is part of the exercise of public powers and serves the realisation of the Member States' individual transport policy. Hence this type of state measure will not be considered to fall within the scope of art.107(1) unless the operator of the aid enjoys some sort of preferential treatment—for example, where there is an unjustified difference between the price at which the below has been sold and the real market price of the construction of the below project, thus conferring an illegal advantage on the buyer/operator. The enlargement of existing infra projects has to be carried out in such a way that the acquirer of the infra pays a remuneration

[215] N368/2009.
[216] See IP/10/141.
[217] See IP/11/493.

equivalent to market conditions, taking into account the costs of construction, as well as the duration of its use.

It may also be noted that there is no requirement to hold a public or open tender procedure for choosing the operator,[218] the only relevant question is whether remuneration equivalent to market conditions has been paid or not. Similarly, an earlier draft condition—that all possible sources of financial support from the airport itself had been exhausted—has not been included in the final version.

If it is not possible to establish that a market price has been paid, or the remuneration is equivalent to market conditions, then it may still be possible for the measure to obtain exemption, upon notification, under art.107(3)(a), (b) or (c). The Communication sets out a number of criteria which will be used to evaluate the compatibility of the measure.

3–074

The construction of the infrastructure must serve a clearly defined goal of general interest—e.g. regional development or accessibility—and the infra project must be necessary and appropriate for fulfilling these intentions. The mid-term perspectives for the use of the infrastructure must be satisfactory and the compensation from state resources must not go beyond what is necessary to cover the costs of the SGEI, taking into account the relevant receipts and a reasonable profit for discharging these obligations. All potential users must be granted non-discriminatory access. The complete or partial accessibility of an airport for only one user will be critically examined. No distortion of competition contrary to the common interest may arise. However, the Commission states that small and remote regional airports (less than one million passengers per year) do not have any significant influence on trade and competition and their funding is thereby not capable of fulfilling the last two requirements of art.107(1). The guidelines also contain criteria for establishing the compatibility of start-up aid in connection with regional airports.

Conclusion

What is important to stress for the present purposes of examining the Commission's aid to infrastructure projects in general, is that the Commission appears to be pursuing a stricter approach to the application of the state aid rules in sectors where there is competition for the possible operation of the infrastructure. In drafting rules for the financial support of particular infra projects, the Member State must keep this factor in mind. As a result of ongoing liberalisation, airports are now considered to be open to competition as are, for example, harbour infrastructure and toll roads[219] or tunnels,[220] although railway networks may not

3–075

---

[218] An earlier draft of the guidelines had in fact contained such a requirement but this was abandoned in the final version adopted on September 6, 2005.

[219] *Polish motorways*—N462/09.

[220] N420/2005—*Mont Blanc Tunnel*, February 22, 2006.

be.[221] Recent decisions further confirm the application of the refined economic analysis to cases where the infrastructural project is neither a general infrastructure measure, nor an SGEI, as in the *MAN* decision on an Irish broadband project in 2006[222] and the *Irish Ring Road Decision*,[223] also of 2006, and the Bavarian ethylene pipeline decision.[224]

4. EFFECT ON TRADE

3–076   In order to fall within the prohibition of art.107(1) TFEU, the measure in question must have an effect on competition and trade. Given the structure of arts 107 and 108, and the system of prior notification of all planned state aid, it is not incumbent on the Commission to establish that the measure in question can appreciably effect competition or inter-state trade.[225] It is sufficient that the Commission can establish a link between the measure in question and the likely or potential effect on competition and trade, for example if the recipient undertaking(s) compete(s) with other undertakings on markets open to competition. This does not mean that the recipient undertaking has to be active internationally, for example as an exporter of products or services. It is sufficient that the importation of competing products or services from other Member States may be rendered more difficult through the beneficiary's stronger market position. As a general rule, the Commission must at least provide reasons as to why it assumes there is a foreseeable prospect for the measure to affect trade. Where there is over-capacity in the particular sector where the aid is granted, the potential effect on trade will more often be foreseeable, since the probable effect of the grant is to increase or maintain the market share of the recipient, thereby reducing the chances for undertakings established in other Member States to sell their products or services to the market of that Member State.

Accordingly, aid to undertakings operating only locally may affect trade, even if the recipient does not provide services outside its state of origin. In the *Altmark* case the Court held that:

> "the granting of a public subsidy to a (transport) undertaking by a Member State may maintain or increase the supply of transport services by that undertaking, and thus reduce the possibility of other undertakings to provide transport services in that Member State. Thus the condition that the aid must affect trade between Member States, does not depend on the local or regional character of the services supplied, or the scale of the activity covered."[226]

[221] See further, M. Kekelekis "Recent Developments in Infrastructure Funding: When Does It Not Constitute State Aid" [2011] *EStal*, Vol.10, Nr.3, pp.433–444.
[222] N284/2005 of March 3, 2006.
[223] N149/2008 of May 16, 2006
[224] [2007] O.J. L143/16.
[225] Joined Cases C–346/03 and C–529/03 *Atzeni* [2006] E.C.R. I–1875.
[226] Case C–280/00 [2003] E.C.R. I–7747, at paras 78–82.

In Case C–113/00 *Spain v Commission* ([2002] E.C.R. I–7601), the Court held:

"As regards the Spanish Government's first argument that the overall amount of aid in question is small and that it is divided among a large number of farmers, each of whom received a negligible sum in national or Community terms, it is settled case-law of the Court that the relatively small amount of aid or the relatively small size of the undertaking which receives it does not as such exclude the possibility that intra-Community trade may be affected (see, inter alia, Case C–142/87 *Belgium v Commission* [1990] E.C.R. I–959 *(Tube-meuse)*, para.43; Joined Cases C–278/92 to C–280/92 *Spain v Commission* [1994] E.C.R. I–4103, para.42, and Case C–310/99 *Italy v Commission* [2002] E.C.R. I–2289, para.86). Other factors may be decisive when assessing the effect of aid on trade, such as whether the aid is cumulative and whether the undertakings that receive it are operating in a sector that is particularly exposed to competition."

The relevant principles were succinctly summarised by AG Tizzano in Case **3–077** C–172/03 *Heiser*, and the Court went on to reiterate its strict approach to the issue of whether a measure has an effect on trade in Case C–172/03 *Heiser*, which concerned a tax adjustment which it was claimed, amounted to a subsidy to Mr Heiser, a dentist. Mr Heiser and the Austrian government submitted that the measure at issue in the main proceedings was not liable to affect trade between Member States because the amounts involved in the discontinuance of the adjustment of deductions are generally very small: the amount involved is at most €30,000 for the whole of the period covering the years 1997 to 2004, an amount which is far below the de minimis ceiling of €100,000 over a three-year period rule laid down by the (then applicable) Commission Notice on the *de minimis* rule for state aid ([1996] O.J. C68/9) which was applicable on the date of the entry into force of that measure in 1996. Further, the Austrian government argued that the effect of the measure at issue in the main proceedings on trade between Member States was not very marked given the particular nature of medical care which is primarily provided locally.

The Court restated (at ss.32–35) its finding in *Altmark* that there is no threshold or percentage below which it may be considered that trade between Member States is not affected and continued:

"The second condition for the application of Article 92(1) [now Article 107(1) TFEU] of the Treaty, namely that the aid must be capable of affecting trade between Member States, does not therefore depend on the local or regional character of the services supplied or on the scale of the field of activity concerned (see, to that effect, *Altmark Trans and Regierungspräsidium Magdeburg*, para. 82).

As regards the *de minimis* ceiling laid down by the Commission Notice of 6 March 1996, it is not apparent from the case-file put before the Court by the referring court that the amount of the deductions which a medical practitioner may be able to make under a measure such as that at issue in the main proceedings is, in all circumstances, less than the *de minimis* amount, which is set at €100,000 over three years. The national legislation, as the Commission of the European Communities rightly observes, does not lay down any limit on the amount a medical practitioner, as an individual undertaking, may receive as a result of the discontinuance of the adjustment of deductions. Accordingly, it is not established that such a measure can be covered by the *de minimis* rule laid down by that notice."

3–078   It should be noted finally that in early 2004 the Commission issued two draft communications on aid measures considered as having only a limited distortive effect: (a) because of their limited amount (LASA—Limited Amount of State Aid); or (b) because of the sector involved which is characterised by limited trade between the Member States (LET—Limited Effect on Trade).[227] These measures, if adopted, would have provided for a simplified investigation process—they would not have released Member States from the obligation to notify proposed measures.[228] In the final event, and allegedly as a result of objections from its Legal Services that the proposals contradicted established case law, the Commission decided not to adopt these two draft proposals.

The de minimis regulation

3–079   Where the aid concerned is of a very low level, the actual or potential effect on trade may be doubted. Traditionally the European Courts have taken a very strict attitude to so-called de minimis aid, fuelling debate as to the validity of a Communication of 1996 purporting to exempt this type of aid, i.e. of less than €100,000 over a three-year period, completely from notification requirements under art.108(3) TFEU.[229] This Communication was superseded by Reg.69/2001 of January 12, 2001,[230] and subsequently amended in 2006 (see further Ch.7). It should be noted that under the regulation, the de minimis amount is applicable, as under the 1996 Communication, to an undertaking. This term is not defined and as recently confirmed in Case C–480/09P *ACEA Electrabel*, there is no reason to assume that it has the same meaning as that developed by the Courts in the context of arts 101 and 102.

In Case C–382/99 *The Netherlands v the Commission* a Dutch fiscal rule providing a benefit to petrol stations situated near borders was the subject of dispute. The Commission had ruled that it could not be held to apply to a situation in which the aid was cumulated by the owners of several petrol stations nor to cases where the relationship between the owner of the petrol station and an oil company was regulated by particular contract provisions which allowed

---

[227] February 2004, originally available on the website of DG Competition.
[228] February 2004, originally available on the website of DG Competition.
[229] See also Case C–148/04 *Unicredito Italiano* [2005] E.C.R. I–11137.
[230] [2001] O.J. L10/30.

the latter to deduct from contractually agreed price rebates to the latter, the value of the fiscal provision. In both instances the amount of aid in question had to be calculated taking into account who the actual beneficiary of the measure was. The ECJ upheld the Commission decision.[231]

The Regulation introduced further clarifications and now imposes stricter conditions on Member States. Article 3 states that a Member State may only grant a new de minimis aid after having checked that this will not raise the total amount of de minimis aid received during the relevant period of three years to a level above the ceiling. Moreover, the monitoring and reporting obligations are intended to rule out the cumulation of de minimis aids above the ceiling. See further Ch.7 for a detailed discussion of the Regulation.

Distortion of competition

The condition that the state measure must distort or threaten competition is **3–080** usually met with ease. The Courts take the view that aid which is intended to release an undertaking from costs that it would normally have had to bear in its day-to-day management or normal activities, distorts the conditions of competition.[232] Recent case law may indicate the growing importance of this condition as an element of the definition of an aid. Although the impact of a state measure on competition and trade has usually been dealt with together as if they were inextricably linked, a number of cases have emphasised the growing importance of the condition of distortion of competition.[233] In Case C–172/03 *Heiser*, Mr Heiser and the Austrian government argued that this condition was not fulfilled on the ground that the medical practitioners who benefited from such a measure did not face competition based on prices, hence there was no competition to be distorted.

The Court was not impressed by this line of argument:

"Even if, as Mr Heiser and the Austrian Government point out, the choice of a medical practitioner by patients may be influenced by criteria other than the price of the medical treatment, such as its quality and the confidence placed in the medical practitioner, the fact none the less remains that that price is liable to have an influence, or even a substantial influence, on the choice of medical practitioner by the patient."

Of further interest is the Commission's Decision on *Network Rail*[234] where it was argued by the United Kingdom that as the aid beneficiary, Network Rail was a natural monopoly and furthermore there was no developed market in the European Union for railway infrastructure management, and hence that certain

[231] [2002] E.C.R. I–5163.
[232] See Case C–156/98 *Germany v Commission* [2000] E.C.R. I–6857, at para.30.
[233] See Joined Cases T–298, T–312, T–313, T–315 and T–600 to T–607/97, T–1 to T–6/98 and T–23/98 *M. Alzetta v Commission* [2000] E.C.R. II–2319, at para.81.
[234] Case N 356/2002 *Network Rail*, July 17, 2002.

state measures for restructuring the railway infrastructure in the United Kingdom were not to be deemed to be aid as there was no effective competition and no effect on inter-state trade. The Commission accepted that there was no competition on the market for operating and managing the national rail network and, given the current level of sectoral harmonisation, there was also no competition for the market as the UK government had effectively closed the market for competition. The measures in question did not therefore constitute aid.

5. STATE PARTICIPATION AND THE MARKET ECONOMY INVESTOR TEST

3–081   The state may intervene in the economy in many guises: through the exercise of its public prerogative powers (e.g. to levy taxes), or through its ownership or control of certain assets or in its decisions to purchase certain goods and services from the market. It is important to distinguish these two separate roles of the state in understanding the jurisprudence of the European Courts and the decision-making practice of the Commission on the concept of state aid. The active participation of the state in the market economy involves the use of state resources but this does not automatically lead to the conclusion that state aid is involved. This part of Ch.3 is confined to this latter type of state intervention.

State shareholdings and capital injections for publicly owned or controlled firms

3–082   It is established law that not every participation by the state in the capital or operations of a company (private or public) may automatically be classified as aid. Where, for example, the state owns a shareholding in an undertaking it may, under certain conditions, make state resources available in the form of capital injections, for example, to it without falling foul of art.107(1) TFEU. The Treaty takes a neutral position with regard to national property laws and hence state-owned or controlled enterprises must be treated in the same way as private enterprises.[235] It is in this context that the Courts have developed and applied the so-called "private market investor test" or "market economy investor test" (MEIT). In recent years the Courts have extended the logic of this test to embrace a "private purchaser test" and a "private creditor test". Indeed the test is applied to all types of measures, including government capital injections, loans guaranteed by the state, sales of government assets, and privatisations, state guarantees and waivers of debt by the state.

The MEIT does not, however, usually extend to situations where the state is acting in the exercise of its public power, that is using its state prerogatives in areas such as taxation or social security. In respect of the classification of these

---

[235] See also in this context the Commission's decision to open the formal investigation against EdF in 2003, discussed in Chs 9 and 20.

types of measures as state aid or not, the appropriate test is whether the measure is selective, as explained above, in section 3, paras 3–040. Nevertheless, in its recent ruling, and following its earlier ruling in the *Ryanair* case, the General Court in Case T–156/04 *EDF* has applied the market investor test to a state measure which involved a waiver of taxes (see further Ch.8, para.8–023). This ruling is now on appeal.[236]

Although the MEIT test is often criticised as inadequate or as impracticable, **3–083** it has proved difficult to find a more suitable, alternative benchmark. The major limitation in the test is that the state will inevitably be in a different position from any hypothetical private investor. It has theoretically almost unlimited resources, and thus a higher credit rating than most.[237] In the case of very large government investments, particularly in infrastructure, there is often no private investor that could have taken the place of the government. Although the Courts have ruled that the specific interests of the state as such, for example in providing employment or achieving social objectives, cannot be taken into account in applying the MEIT to determine if a measure can be qualified as aid or not,[238] it is recognised that there is a distinction between short-term and long-term investments. The Commission also accepts that minority holdings involve different commercial considerations from those present where an investor is a majority shareholder.

In general, the Commission attempts to examine whether, given all the circumstances, a private investor would have been prepared to shoulder the risk of the investment in question, and on the same commercial terms. In Case T–296/97 *Alitalia* the CFI confirmed that a capital contribution from public funds normally satisfies the test of a private investor operating in the normal conditions of a market economy and does not imply state aid if, inter alia, it was made at the same time as a significant capital contribution on the part of a private investor made in comparable circumstances.[239]

Concomitance

Private participation ("concomitance") may be indicative but not conclusive. **3–084** Participation by employees in the capital of an undertaking does not in itself establish that the contribution from public funds meets the test.[240] According to the ruling of the ECJ in *Seleco*, even a significant participation by private investors is not sufficient in itself to exclude aid.[241] Account must be taken of all relevant economic and legal facts. Where there is no concomitance or an available public benchmark (such as a commercial rating for the borrower), it is

---

[236] Case C–124/10P [2010] O.J. C161/16.
[237] Indeed this is recognised explicitly by the General Court in the *West LB* case at para.272, but that Court failed to suggest a better approach.
[238] Case C–278/92 to C–280/92 *Spain v Commission* [1994] E.C.R. I–4103.
[239] See also its decision of June 7, 2005 on Alitalia's industrial restructuring plan [2006] O.J. L69/1.
[240] Case T–296/97 [2000] E.C.R. II–3871.
[241] Joined Cases C–328/99 and C–399/00 [2003] E.C.R. I–4035.

always difficult to ascertain what terms a private investor would have accepted, as priorities and objective of investors inevitably vary.

The application of the market investor test entails a complex economic assessment, particularly if the beneficiaries are wholly owned by the state. The Courts have consistently held that the Commission in principle enjoys considerable discretion when making such assessments. At the same time the General Court has been prepared to examine the Commission's approach in some detail, as for example in the rulings on *West LB*[242] and *Brittany Ferries*,[243] and in 2003 the President of the Court adopted an order suspending recovery of aid in a case in which the Commission had concluded that the MEIT had not been established.[244]

The application of the market investor test to certain transactions in the public sector may pose particular difficulties if the activities involved are not normally performed under market conditions. In *Ufex I* the General Court had decided that it was not sufficient in itself for the Commission to demonstrate that the public undertaking in a reserved sector (here postal services) was paid the full costs for the provision of logistical and commercial assistance to its subsidiary, acting in a competitive sector.[245] However, the ECJ took a different approach and ruled that La Poste could not be compared to a normal market undertaking as such an undertaking would never have accrued all the costs of developing a postal network that was intended to fulfil a number of public service obligations.[246] (See further Ch.8.)

3–085   It can also be noted that although each case will turn on its own complex facts and economics, as a general rule the Commission tends to consider that any measure which benefits a company in financial difficulties is prima facie aid, regardless of the conditions under which the state decides to act. This reasoning was reportedly applied to the decision of the French government to participate in the rescue of the engineering company, Alstom.[247]

This presumption may be questionable as it disregards the individual circumstances and actually puts the government investor in a different position than a private investor who may well consider that the most rational conduct is to restore lost capital, waive debt or convert debt into equity. In certain cases it would seem that the Commission and the Courts are not prepared to accept the full implications of the so-called "owner effect principle" referred to in the Commission's 1993 Communication, according to which an existing shareholder with a substantial existing, even controlling, investment in an enterprise may act

[242] Joined Cases T–228/99 and T–233/99 *West LB v Commission* [2003] E.C.R. I–435.

[243] [2002] O.J. L12/33.

[244] See Case T–378/02 *Technische Glaswerke Ilmenau v Commission* [2002] E.C.R. II–2921 and T–198/01 of July 8, 2004, suspending the order of recovery. The Commission's decision was eventually upheld by the Court of Justice, however.

[245] Case T–613/97 *Ufex v Commission* [2000] E.C.R. II–4055; Case T–613/97 *Ufex II* [2006] E.C.R. II–1531.

[246] Cases Joined Cases C–83/01 P, C–93/01 P and C–94/01 P *Chronopost* [2003] E.C.R. I–6993 and Joined Cases C341/06P and C–342/06P *Chronopost* [2008] E.C.R. I–4777.

[247] [2003] O.J. C269.

differently from a new investor (see Ch.8). In its opening decision against France Telecom the Commission also appeared to have taken the stance that the principle of concomitance excludes the controlling shareholder taking the first step.[248] In the *West LB* ruling the General Court also appears to have rejected, at least implicitly, the "owner effect principle".[249]

A different situation may arise where a public authority has a pre-existing exposure and attempts to make additional investments to prevent such liability from being asserted. In Case T–98/00 *Linde*, the CFI found that the existing exposure of a public entity to a loss-making contractual obligation justifies the commitment of additional funds in order to reduce future losses.[250]

The MEIT and public undertakings

Capital injections by a state holding company to one of its subsidiaries may fall within the scope of art.107 TFEU. The MEIT also applies to investments made by public undertakings in as much as the resources of these entities can be deemed to be state resources (see further, Ch.8). For example, in its decision concerning the legality of tariff rebates made by EdF to firms in the paper industry, the Commission considered that EdF had acted in accordance with the MEIT. The investigation concerned rebates granted between 1990–1996, i.e. before the adoption of EC Council Directive 96/92 on the internal electricity market, at a time when EdF disposed of overcapacity in nuclear energy. The French authorities demonstrated that EdF covered its variable costs, and at least 35 per cent, and on average 57 per cent, of its fixed costs. In a situation of overcapacity and in the absence of competition, the Commission considered that a private operator would rather sell an additional unit of electricity without covering the total cost for that unit rather than not sell it all. Hence EdF's behaviour was justified on commercial grounds, and the rebates did not constitute state aid. It is of interest to note that the Commission emphasised that the decision should be seen in the context of the prevailing circumstances on the French market in the past, and should not be seen as preventing the Commission from examining the creation of the said overcapacity and its implications in the context of the ongoing liberalisation of the electricity market.[251]

In its ruling in Case C–56/93 *Belgium v Commission*, concerning a special tariff which Gasunie—the Dutch gas supply company which was controlled by the state—had made available to certain large industrial users of gas, the Court held that the special tariff could be explained on market terms.[252]

In its decision to open a formal procedure against the United Kingdom in connection with the aid package to British Energy, the Commission initially formed the view that BNFL, a publicly owned company, was not operating as a

3–086

3–087

---

[248] [2003] O.J. C57/5.
[249] *West LB, op. cit.* at paras 314 and 332–335.
[250] [2002] E.C.R. II–3961.
[251] IP/00/370, April 11, 2000.
[252] [1996] E.C.R. I–723.

private investor in agreeing to re-negotiate a number of nuclear fuel supply contracts with British Energy, but that BNFL's agreement to conclude more favourable contracts could be imputed to the state. Furthermore, BNFL as BE's largest creditor had agreed more favourable standstill conditions than those agreed with private creditors.[253]

It will also be necessary to examine whether in making certain investment decisions a state body is acting in accordance with its state prerogative or whether it is acting as an undertaking, and therefore subject to the MEIT. In its decision concerning the package of various measures which the regional government of Wallonia had offered the Irish company Ryanair in exchange for the latter's agreement to source a large number of flights from the airport of Charleroi, the Commission admitted to having difficulties in applying the private investor principle to BSCA, the company responsible for administering the regional airport, given that the latter's financial structure is closely linked to the Walloon region.[254]

In its ruling annulling this decision, the General Court noted that in applying the private investor test it is necessary to take the commercial transaction as a whole in order to determine whether the public entity, and the entity controlled by it, taken together, acted as rational operators in a market economy. The Commission was, therefore, wrong to find that the financial links binding the Walloon Region to BSCA were irrelevant. It could not be excluded that the Walloon Region not only took part in BSCA's activities but also obtained financial consideration for granting the measures at issue. As such the Walloon Region and BSCA were to be regarded as a single entity for the purposes of the application of the private investor principle.

The Court assessed whether or not the activities of the Walloon Region in relation to levying landing charges constituted economic activities and concluded that the fixing of the amount of landing charges, and the grant of an accompanying indemnity, were activities directly connected with the management of airport infrastructure, which has been held to be an economic activity.[255] The airport charges should have been regarded as remuneration for the provision of services within Charleroi Airport. The fact that airport facilities, and associated management services, are provided by a public authority, did not mean that they are services which are connected with the exercise of powers which are typically those of a public authority. The fact that the Walloon Region is a public authority and that it is the owner of airport facilities does not mean that it cannot be regarded as an entity exercising an economic activity.

3–088 The Court rejected the Commission's argument that the landing charges were themselves laid down by a decree of the Walloon Government. The Court concluded that this did not affect the fact that the activity of setting airport charges is closely connected with the use and operation of Charleroi airport,

[253] [2003] O.J. C180/5 at Pt 119 et seq.
[254] [2004] O.J. L137/1.
[255] Case T–128/98 *Aeroports de Paris v Commission* [2000] E.C.R. II–3929.

which is as an economic activity. Further, the Court rejected an argument that the Walloon Region infringed relevant national regulations by granting a discount to Ryanair. Compliance with national law is not a factor which is relevant to deciding whether the authority acted in accordance with the private investor principle or granted an economic advantage in contravention of art.107(1).

The General Court concluded that the fact that the Walloon Region had regulatory powers in relation to fixing airport charges does not mean that a measure reducing those charges ought not to have been examined by reference to the private investor principle. Such a measure could have been put in place by a private operator, such as the airport concession holder.

The CFI, therefore, concluded that the Commission erred by refusing to examine together the advantages granted by the Walloon Region and by BSCA and failing to apply the private investor principle to the measures adopted by the Walloon Region, despite the economic links between it and BSCA. It was not deemed necessary to examine further whether the Commission erred in its application of the private investor principle to BSCA. The Court also rejected a claim by the Commission that a re-assessment of all the measures at issue by reference to the private investor principle would have led to an even more unfavourable result for Ryanair. The Court can only rule on the legality of the Commission's decision.[256]

The decision-making practice of the Commission also illustrates a modified application of the market investor test in a number of other instances where the state has become involved in market activities. These "tests" have also been considered by the General Court and the ECJ.

The private creditor test

The failure or reticence of a public authority or public undertaking to demand **3–089** money owed to it can also amount to a form of state aid, on the assumption that all the criteria set out in art.107(1) are met. If a pubic undertaking or authority tolerates late payment of amounts due to it by an undertaking, it mitigates their financial burden and confers on them a selective advantage. Public authorities and companies should therefore pursue their debtors with the same vigour as that of a private creditor.[257] The General Court and the ECJ have approached this issue by focusing on whether the public authority concerned pursued all legally possible options and whether it acted promptly. The application of the private creditor "test" was recognised for the first time in Case C–342/96 *Spain v Commission (Tubacex)*[258] and has been further developed in Case T–152/99 *HAMSA*,[259] as well as later cases related to Case C–342/96, that is, Case T–36/99

---

[256] Case T–196/04 *Ryanair Limited v Commission* [2008] E.C.R. II–3643.
[257] Case C–342/96 *Spain v Commission* [1999] E.C.R. I–2459.
[258] [1999] E.C.R. I–2459.
[259] Case T–152/99 [2002] E.C.R. II–3049.

Lenzing v Commission[260] and Case C–276/02 *Spain v Commission (GEA)*[261] and Case C–525/04P *Spain v Commission* and *Lenzing*.[262]

In Case C–342/96 *Spain v Commission (Tubacex)* the Court examined a Commission decision which had found that the Spanish authorities had not acted as a private creditor. The undertaking concerned had not paid taxes and social security for three years before the Spanish authorities had agreed to write off two-thirds of the debts and reschedule repayment of the rest over a 10-year period. The Spanish authorities had in fact attempted to recuperate the debt by seizing property from the undertakings and eventually requiring closure of the company. These measures were sufficient to satisfy the Court that the Spanish state had used all options legally available to it to recover the debt, and it therefore annulled the Commission's decision.

In the *Tubacex* case the Commission had ruled that there was no aid—the measure was general and not selective—and further the Social Security Fund and Fogasa had acted in the same way as a hypothetical private creditor. The General Court, however, held that the authorities had sufficient discretion to set the terms and amount of repayment and concluded that this was sufficient to convert the general measure into a form of state aid. Furthermore, the Court held that the authorities had allowed the debt to accumulate over a 10-year period in the first place, and had then allowed that debt to be rescheduled over a further 10-year period, and had finally permitted the undertaking not to honour the rescheduling agreement (see also Ch.10). After the *Tubacex* ruling the Commission reconsidered and amended its earlier decisions concerning the repayment agreements entered into by Fogasa and several undertakings in financial difficulties, to conclude that the interest rates did not contain elements of state aid.

In its decision concerning *Sniace* SA, which also concerned a rescheduling of debts owed to Fogasa the Commission adopted a decision according to which the arrangements did not constitute aid as the Spanish authorities had acted like a private creditor. In *Lenzing*, one of *Sniace*'s competitors challenged the Commission's decision. In its 2004 ruling the General Court held that the Spanish authorities were bound by law to fix only a statutory rate of interest on outstanding debt, at a rate which was lower than the market rate. A private creditor would not apply the same rate as a private investor who seeks to maximise profits as the former's objective is to minimise losses and may therefore accept a lower rate in order to ensure the company's longer-term survival and thus its ability to repay its debts in full. However, the Commission had not provided any acceptable reasons why a private creditor would have acted like the Spanish authorities and the relevant provisions of the decisions of 1998 and the amended decision of 2000 were annulled.[263]

3–090   In Case C–525/04P Spain then appealed the General Court's judgment to the ECJ, claiming that the General Court had misinterpreted the private creditor test

[260] [2004] E.C.R. II–3597.
[261] [2004] E.C.R. I–8091.
[262] [2007] E.C.R. I–9947.
[263] T–36/99 *Lenzing* [2004] E.C.R. II–3597.

and had incorrectly held that the conclusion of the debt-rescheduling agreements and the non-enforcement of debts following the breach of those agreements could never satisfy that test. The ECJ held that this was an incorrect reading of the General Court's judgment: the Court had not based its assessment of the measures on a presumption that the private creditor would necessarily initiate enforcement procedures to recover debts owed. Rather, the Court had correctly concluded that the Commission had committed a manifest error of assessment in the light of a series of factors particular to the case. The Court had noted a number of contradictions in the Commission's comparison between public and private creditors, and the lack of evidence to substantiate the Commission's conclusions in respect of one of those private creditors and the prospects of Sniace's eventual viability.

The Commission then adopted Decision C(2009) 1479 final of March 10, 2009, holding that the aid granted by the FOGASA and by the Social Security Treasury (TGSS) in favour of SNIACE to be unlawful and incompatible, on the ground that the agreements for debt repayment concluded between SNIACE and FOGASA and the rescheduling agreement concluded between SNIACE and the TGSS did not comply with market conditions as regards the type of interest applicable. This decision was in turn subject to challenge before the General Court.[264]

In Case C–276/02, GEA had failed to repay its tax and social security debts **3–091** and in May 2002 the Commission adopted a recovery decision. This was in turn challenged by Spain. AG Maduro provided an extensive analysis of the private creditor test and concluded that a private creditor with significant assets at its disposal would probably have an interest in maintaining the activity of the debtor company for a certain period if the costs of liquidation would prove higher than the costs of granting aid. As the Court based its decision on the Commission's failure to appreciate the steps taken by the Spanish authorities to recover the sums due, it did not analyse the application of the private creditor test.

The General Court's *HAMSA* ruling indicated possible differences between the private creditor test and the private investor test, where the Court does not attach much importance to the fact that there had been comparable amounts of public and private investment (i.e. concomitance) whereas in *HAMSA* the General Court applied the private creditor test and held that state aid could probably be excluded if liabilities vis-à-vis private creditors exceeded liabilities vis-à-vis public creditors. The existence of a higher amount of public creditors' receivables was not decisive as it would make debt rescheduling very difficult for firms in difficulty.

In Case T–11/2007 the General Court indeed emphasised that the private **3–092** creditor test has to be distinguished from the private investor test.[265] While a

---

[264] T–238/09 *Sniace v Commission* [2009] E.C.R. II–125.

[265] Case T–11/07 *Frucona Kosice v Commission* [2010] E.C.R. judgment of December 7, 2010, para.114. Appeal pending in Case C–73/11P, February 28, 2011.

private investor is pursuing a structural policy guided by the longer-term prospects of profitability of the capital invested, a private creditor is seeking to obtain payment of sums owed to it by a debtor in financial difficulties.[266] An investor must be distinguished from a creditor but the basic question the courts pose is the same: would the beneficiary have obtained such an economic advantage under normal market conditions?[267]

The General Court also made clear that the private creditor test is only satisfied when the state chose the most advantageous procedure, i.e. the procedure that would have generated the highest return. But what kind of assumptions does a private market participant make? Is it not reasonable to suppose that a private creditor will make a cautious assessment of the situation? How optimistic is the state allowed to be under the private creditor test? Although the Court required the state to choose the best procedure, it did not specify what kind of assumptions a state should make to assess which choice is the best. In the meantime, the aid beneficiary has appealed this ruling to the ECJ.[268]

The private seller test

3–093   A further variant on this theme is the "private seller" test which can be applied to decisions of Member States to sell tangible and intangible property, such as land and buildings or equipment or shares or other intangible assets as well as in the context of the privatisation of public entities. Again the predominant criterion is whether the state has concluded the transaction on market terms. The procedures followed in effecting the sale are of key importance.

The Commission issued a Communication concerning aid elements in land sales by public authorities in 1997.[269] Prior to publishing this Communication the Commission had adopted several key decisions concerning the sale of land below market value, in which it held that the behaviour of a public authority, in disposing of an asset to a commercial interest trading in the Community, should correspond to that of a private vendor operating under normal market conditions. A private vendor would examine the possibility of alternative purchase offers and sell the asset to the person making the highest offer. If it is not feasible to establish a reliable reference for market values for the asset, a private vendor would have the asset valued by a professional valuer, taking into account all the prevailing circumstances and non-price conditions of sale, prior to selling it.[270]

---

[266] Case T–11/07 [2010] E.C.R. Unreported, para.114. See also Case T–152/99 *HAMSA v Commission* [2002] E.C.R. II–3049, para.167.

[267] Case C–39/94 *SFEI and Others* [1996] E.C.R. I–3547, para.60; Case C–342/96 *Spain v Commission* [1999] E.C.R. I–2459, para.41.

[268] Case C–73/11P.

[269] [1997] O.J. C209/3. See also the Commission's recent Vademedecum on Aid for Urban Regeneration (2006).

[270] See aid to *Toyota Motor Corporation* [1992] O.J. L6/36.

Land sold at less than market value may constitute a state aid even if the recipient has agreed to undertake certain improvements or other investments in connection with the land in question.[271]

Valuation methods: the ECJ's judgment of September 2, 2010 in C–290/07P **3–094** *Commission v Scott SA* considered a long-running dispute arising out of a public land sale to Scott in France.[272] The Commission had originally found that the sale had occurred at a preferential purchase price and therefore included unlawful aid. This was declared incompatible with the common market in its decision of 2000. The General Court annulled the Commission's decision, holding that the Commission had breached its duty to exercise due diligence by relying on a cost-based method and by applying this method to the facts of the case, and by failing to take into account additional information provided by Scott during the administrative proceedings. The General Court held that costs were not the best proof of the value and even if the method was valid, the Commission had made several mistakes in its calculations, nor did it take into account the price for which Scott sold the land to a third party in 1998.[273]

On appeal, the ECJ annulled the General Court's judgment and referred the case back to the Court. The ECJ emphasised the Commission's broad discretion when performing complex economic assessments and the limits of judicial review in these assessments. In *Scott*, the ECJ held that the Court had exceeded these limits of judicial review by substituting its own economic assessment for that of the Commission and finding that the Commission had acted in breach of its duty to exercise due diligence without demonstrating that the Commission had committed a manifest error of assessment.

In its 1997 Communication, the Commission set out various recommendations **3–095** in order to make its general approach with regard to the problem of state aid through land sales by public authorities transparent, as well as to reduce its own case load. These recommendations describe a simple procedure, which allows Member States to handle land sales in such a way that would by definition exclude state aid, and provides a clear list of cases of land sales that should be notified to the Commission to allow the assessment of whether or not a certain transaction contains aid, and if so whether or not the aid is compatible. Finally, the Communication provides the Commission with a method of treating possible complaints from third parties without extensive proceedings.[274]

Basically, a sale of land following a sufficiently well-publicised, open and unconditional bidding procedure, comparable to an auction, honouring the best or only bid, is by definition at market value and consequently does not contain state aid. An aid is "sufficiently well publicised" if it is repeatedly advertised over a reasonable period (two months or more) in the national press, official gazettes or

---

[271] Case T–155/96R *City of Mainz v Commission* [1996] E.C.R. II–1655.
[272] A summary of the litigation is to be found in the opening paragraphs of the Advocate General's Opinion of February 23, 2010.
[273] Case T–366/00 [2003] E.C.R. II–1763.
[274] [1997] O.J. C209/3.

other appropriate publications, so that it can come to the attention of all potential buyers. If the sale is likely to attract investors on a European or international scale, it should be announced in publications with a regular international circulation.

3–096   An offer is unconditional when any buyer, irrespective of his business, is generally free to acquire the site and use it for his or her own purposes. Restrictions may be imposed for, inter alia, environmental protection or the prevention of public nuisance, as well as to avoid purely speculative bids. General urban and regional planning restrictions imposed on the use of a site do not affect the unconditional nature of the offer. If, however, it is a condition of the sale that the future owner would assume special obligations, the offer can only be regarded as unconditional if all the potential buyers would be required to, and would be able to meet, the obligation.

If no bidding or auction procedure is to take place, an independent valuation should be carried out prior to sale negotiations to establish the market value—that is, the price at which the assets could be sold in an arm's length transaction. The evaluation should be undertaken by an independent asset valuer, which might include a state valuation office or public officers who can act without "undue influence" being exerted on their findings. The primary costs incurred by the public authorities to acquire a site are an indicator of the market value unless a significant period of time has elapsed between the initial purchase and sale of the land. The market value should not be less than the initial purchase price during a period of at least three years after acquisition unless the independent valuer can establish a general decline in the prices for land in the relevant market.

Where special obligations are connected to the land and not to the purchaser or its economic activities, these should apply to every potential buyer. The economic disadvantage of such obligations should be evaluated separately by independent valuers and may be set off against the purchase price. The 1997 Communication only applies to sales of public land, and not to the acquisition of land or the letting or leasing of real estate by public authorities, transactions that may also include aid elements.

3–097   Where the Commission receives a complaint that state aid was involved in a land sales agreement, it will assume that such is not the case if the information provided by Member States shows that the above principles have been observed. However, the Commission is required to exercise some care when considering expert valuations as the Case T–247/01 *Valmont* illustrates. This case concerned a transaction dating back to July 1, 1993, where the Dutch municipality of Maarheeze and Nolte Mastenfabriek BV signed an agreement for the sale of undeveloped land intended for industrial purposes. That agreement fixed a sale price, and it was claimed that Maarheeze had been the recipient of one such subsidy and used it to enable it to sell land below its commercial value. The Commission, relying on its Communication on land sales, held that a Member State which wished to sell a piece of land could have its value estimated beforehand by an expert, and if adhered to then this rules out the existence of state aid; whereas in the present case, the experts' reports were made subsequent to the transaction. The General Court annulled the Commission's decision[275]:

> "Where the Commission carries out an examination for that purpose of the experts' reports drawn up after the transaction in question, it is bound to compare the sale price actually paid to the price suggested in those various reports and to determine whether it deviates sufficiently to justify a finding that there is a benefit. That method makes it possible to take into account the uncertainty of such a determination, which is by nature retrospective, of such market prices" (para.41).

A further complication arose in this transaction from the fact that the Commission classified the car park as "semi-public" by virtue of an agreement concluded with Maarheeze, under which Valmont allowed other parties to make regular and free use thereof. The General Court ruled that the Commission had not established to the requisite legal standard that half of the financing granted to Valmont for it to construct a car park on its premises should be classified as state aid under art.107(1). Consequently the Court annulled that part of the decision also. **3–098**

Sale of intangible assets

Commission practice has clarified situations in which various forms of financial restructuring, often involving a reallocation of shares, can amount to aid. In an early decision, the Commission concluded that certain aspects of the complex financial arrangements between the Dutch state, the Volvo Car Corporation (VCC) and the Mitsubishi Motor Corporation (MMC) involved elements of state aid as a result of the "unduly generous terms" on which the MMC would acquire a holding in the restructured company Nedcar. Article 108 proceedings were therefore initiated in this case,[276] but the Commission eventually concluded that there was no state aid involved. **3–099**

In *Bremer Vulkan*, the Commission held that an element of aid was involved in the transfer of Bremer Vulkan from Krupps because the shares were transferred at a value which was less than their quoted stock price. This decision was subsequently quashed by the Court of Justice in Joined Cases C–329/93, 62/95 and 63/95: *Germany v Commission*; *Hanseatische Industrie-Beteiligungen GmbH v Commission*; and *Bremer Vulkan Verbund AG v Commission*.[277] The transaction involved a series of transactions designed to facilitate the diversification of Krupps out of shipbuilding. The Land Bremen provided a guarantee of DM 126 million to the Hanseatische Industrie-Beteilgungen-Hibeg, with the Land as its sole shareholder. Hibeg and Krupp then formed a special company— **3–100**

---

[275] See, to that effect, Joined Cases T–127/99, T–129/99 and T–148/99 *Diputación Foral de Alava v Commission* [2002] E.C.R. II–1275, at para.73 (a paragraph which was not subject to appeal).

[276] [1992] O.J. C105/16. See further, Ch.8, para.8–048.

[277] [1996] E.C.R. I–5151.

the GbR—into which Krupp brought 2.8 million Bremer Vulkan shares and Hibeg DM 350 million financed by bank credit. The GbR then provided an advance to Krupp, and Hibeg was entitled to sell the shares to third parties at a minimum price of DM 125 each. The Commission reasoned that, as at the time of the transactions made within the context of the GbR the average quoted stock exchange value of the shares was DM 80, and the guarantee covered the exact difference between this value and the DM 350 million stake, aid existed for the benefit of Bremer Vulkan.

3–101   The Court annulled the contested decision in its entirety for lack of reasoning. It held that the Commission's reliance upon the stock market price as the sole determining factor in valuing the shares was too rigid and formal. At para.33 of its judgment the Court listed a series of other factors which should have been taken into account, including the intrinsic worth of Bremer Vulkan, the additional value of which may have been contributed by the block of 2.8 million shares; the synergy effects as a result of the incorporation of the Krupp's subsidiary into Bremer Vulkan's business; as well as forecasts as to how the price would develop. The Court then went on to apply the market investor test, and found that the private investor would have behaved in a similar fashion. The Commission subsequently adopted a second decision condemning the share valuation used, and (hence) the underlying guarantee as aid.[278]

The extent to which financial restructuring operations may represent rescue or restructuring aid is considered in detail in Ch.24.

The private purchaser test

3–102   Where a public authority purchases goods and services on the market, the question may arise as to whether the terms of its purchase could be deemed to be state aid. In these types of cases the application of the EU public procurement rules will be of relevance. In Case T–14/96 *BAI v Commission*[279] the General Court had expressly confirmed for the first time that the state aid rules can be applied to public procurement. The Court adopted as a decisive criterion whether the purchase of travel vouchers by the Spanish authorities represented their actual needs. It follows that a transaction involving the purchase of goods and services for which the State does not have an actual need could be a form of state aid[280] (see further, Ch.8).

3–103 Public Service Obligations—"aid or compensation?" Recent case law has raised issues of whether a financial transfer (including tax revenue foregone) to selected groups of undertakings which nevertheless do not enjoy any specific advantage as a result, constitutes aid. This case law has rapidly become known as the "compensation" category of measures, initiated by the ECJ's analysis of

---

[278] Commission Decision 98/665/EC of February 25, 1998.
[279] [1999] E.C.R. II–139.
[280] Joined Cases T–116/01 and T–118/01 *P&O Ferries* [2003] E.C.R. II–2957 and confirmed on appeal in Joined Cases C–471/03P and C–442/03P [2006] E.C.R. I–4845.

the French tax exemptions in favour of wholesale pharmacies. In its judgment in Case C–53/00 *Ferring*,[281] the Court first established that the tax on direct sales as such—leaving aside the public service obligations (PSOs) imposed on whole-sale distributors—conferred an economic advantage in as much as it only applied to pharmaceutical laboratories and thus de facto constituted the grant of a tax exemption on the wholesale distributors. The Court held that, provided that the tax on direct sales imposed on pharmaceutical laboratories merely corresponds to the additional costs actually incurred by the wholesale distributors in carrying out their PSOs, such a tax measure could be regarded as compensation for the service provided and was not therefore state aid within the meaning of art.107(1). The latter would not enjoy any real advantage as the only effect of the tax exemption would be to put them on an equal competitive footing with other market players.[282]

There is thus a similarity in approach in *Ferring*, which seemed to look at the "net burden" imposed on an undertaking in classifying a measure as state aid, to that taken in the case law concerning the MEIT—in the process of classification it is increasingly relevant to examine not just the impact of the measure on the (intended or potential) beneficiary, but also on its competitors. This in turn may raise a new set of issues including not least whether competitors are operating on the market under the same conditions as the grantor of the aid when the latter is itself a company operating under PSO constraints.[283]

In its later ruling in Case C–280/00 *Altmark*, the ECJ has confirmed in part the "compensation" approach in *Ferring*, albeit under the strict conditions as set out at paras 89–93 of its judgment. Hence the recipient undertaking must actually be entrusted with PSOs which are clearly defined; the parameters on the basis of which compensation is calculated must be established in advance in an objective and transparent manner; the compensation must not exceed that which is neces-sary to cover all or part of the costs incurred in the discharge of the PSOs; and finally, where the undertaking in question is not chosen pursuant to public procurement procedures which would allow for the selection of the tenderer capable of providing those services at least cost to the community, the level of compensation needed must be determined on the basis of an analysis of the costs which a typical undertaking would have incurred in discharging those obligations. **3–104**

The general thrust of these essentially procedural conditions, which will be dealt with in greater detail at Ch.8 below, is to ensure that the state should pay a "market" price for PSO-type services and at the same time to guarantee some

---

[281] [2001] E.C.R. I–9067.

[282] Case C–53/00 [2001] E.C.R. I–9067, at para.27.

[283] Joined Cases C–83/01P, C–93/01P and C–94/01P *Chronopost v Commission* [2003] E.C.R. I–6993, annulling the earlier ruling in Case T–613/97 *Ufex I* [2000] E.C.R. II–4055 in which the General Court in part annulled art.1 of Commission Decision 98/365/EC of October 1, 1997. The General Court subsequently annulled the Commission decision in *Ufex II* in 2006, but the ECJ went on to overturn the General Court's ruling in Joined Cases C341/06P and C–342/06P [2008] E.C.R. I–4777. See further Ch.8, at paras 8–020 et seq and para.8–041.

form of open competition in establishing that price.[284] In this way the interests of competitors can be better secured, and distortions of competition minimised or avoided.

Distortions of competition outside the scope of article 107

3–105   Distortions of competition which may be attributed to general economic factors that result in different competitive conditions in individual Member States should be dealt with in accordance with the procedures laid down in the Treaty on conjunctural policy (art.121 TFEU, ex. art.99 EC) and balance of payments (art.123 TFEU, ex. art.101 EC).

In accordance with art.116 TFEU (ex. art.96 EC), where the Commission finds that a difference between national laws, regulations, etc., distort the conditions of competition on the common market and the resultant distortion must be eliminated, it shall consult the Member State(s) concerned. If this does not lead to the elimination of the distortion then the Council shall on a proposal by the Commission, issue the necessary directive. Article 117 TFEU (ex. art.97 EC) obliges Member States to consult with the Commission on any proposed laws and regulations, etc., or amendments to such provisions, which may cause distortions within the meaning of art.116 TFEU. After consulting the Member States, the Commission shall recommend to the states concerned any measures as may be appropriate to avoid the distortion in question.

3–106   In an early Survey of State Aids in the European Community (1990)[285] the Commission expressed its policy in this area to the effect that aids have a more direct and immediate impact on conditions of competition between Member States than general measures. This prima facie distortive effect of such aids must be contrasted with measures applied generally and in a non-discriminatory way across the whole economy.[286] Although general measures may well distort competition, "it is widely held that the direct effect of most general measures is likely to be diluted across the whole spectrum of economic activity, be compensated or counteracted by other general measures or be neutralised to a large extent by exchange rate changes".

The dividing line between arts 116 and 117 TFEU on the one hand, and arts 107 and 108 on the other, has been dealt with by several Advocate Generals. In Joined Cases 72 and 73/91 *Sloman Neptun*,[287] AG Darmon contended that the key factor in determining whether essentially general measures which distort competition should be dealt with under art.116 TFEU or art.107 TFEU was whether the measure in question constitutes a derogation from generally applicable rules which benefit or otherwise favour a particular sector or enterprise. He

---

[284] See also Case C–451/03 *Servizi Ausilari Dottori Commercialisti* [2006] E.C.R. I–2941.
[285] Second Survey, 1990, European Commission, pp.4 et seq.
[286] The ECJ also touched upon this issue in Case 173/73 *Commission v Italy* [1974] E.C.R. 709, at paras 38 and 39.
[287] [1993] E.C.R. I–887.

questioned the relevance of the concept of "discrimination" in drawing this line of demarcation (at paras 60–67 of his Opinion).

The application of art.96 EC (now art.116 TFEU) et seq has been further considered by AG Geelhoed in his Opinion in Case C–308/01 *Gil Insurance*. He opined as follows:

"In order to redress such global distortions in a common market the Member States must in principle have recourse to their macroeconomic policy instruments and, until the creation of EMU, monetary policy instruments. The Community competences in regard thereto were mainly of a lightly coordinating nature. They were to be found in Articles 103 to 109 of the EEC Treaty. They have now been largely replaced, as regards (financial) economic policy, by Articles 99 and 104 EC [Articles 121 and 126 TFEU respectively] and, for uniform monetary policy within EMU, by Articles 105 to 111 EC [Articles 127 to 133 TFEU]. . . . . Article 100 of the original EEC Treaty [now 114 TFEU] provided for the possibility of harmonisation of legislation. It is not only use of the harmonisation instrument that has led within the common market to an unmistakable convergence in socioeconomic, economic and fiscal legislation. That has also stemmed from independent initiatives by national legislatures. That spontaneous convergence has primarily occurred in the sphere of direct taxation where it has been difficult for the Community to activate its competence.

Finally, between and within national economies imbalances may also occur in parts of sectors: these are referred to as *specific* distortions. They stem from *specific* interventions by the authorities as a result of the imposition of exceptional charges on certain kinds of production or on certain undertakings or as a result of the grant of exceptional benefits. In regard to exceptional burdens those are frequently interventions by the authorities which are known in modern management terms as burdens imposed with a view to regulating conduct. . . . For specific distortions the original EEC Treaty provided for two instruments. In regard to specific distortions as a result of public measures imposing a burden (the term imposing a burden must be more broadly construed than in a purely financial sense since concomitant requirements may also impose burdens), the procedures under Articles 101 and 102 of the EEC Treaty (now Articles 116 and 117 TFEU) were applicable. For distortions as a result of the grant of aid, that is to say for distortions attributable to the specific policy instrument of State aid, Articles 92, 93 and 94 of the EEC Treaty (now Articles 107, 108 and 109 TFEU) provided for a specific Community competence. That specific competence is characterised by more rigorous provisions, more thorough supervisory machinery and wide implementing and monitoring powers for the Commission."[288]

---

[288] [2004] E.C.R. I–4777.

The Court, however, did not examine the potential application of arts 116 and 117 in its ruling but held that the differential tax treatment was justified under the "logic of the system test" discussed above at section 3, and further at Ch.10.

Forms of prohibited aid

3–107   The Treaty does not confine the prohibition of a state aid to any particular form or indeed type of aid. The case law and the decision-making practice of the Commission has confirmed that any state measure which has the effect of conferring a benefit on an undertaking or a particular sector or region is in principle prohibited unless it can be justified under art.107(2) or (3) (see Ch.4). Thus the type of measures which may be prohibited go well beyond straightforward "subsidies" in the form of cash grants or loans.[289]

The Commission has published a number of guidelines and notices on different forms of financial support and the conditions under which they can be deemed to be aid for the purposes of art.107(1). Guidelines falling into the scope of this category include those relating to aid in the form of the sale of real-estate at below market prices, aid through direct taxation measures, and aid in the form of state guarantees. These guidelines set out the circumstances under which particular transactions may not be considered aid at all as well as describing in very general terms the conditions which, if the measure amounts to an aid, it could, following notification, be found to be compatible with the Treaty. These types of guidelines include the Notice on Direct Taxation, the Communication on State Guarantees, for example, and are discussed in Chs 9 and 10 of this book.

A second category of guidelines and notices deal with particular types of aid, both horizontal and sectoral and aim to give guidance to Member States as to when these aids can be considered to be compatible and under what conditions. Guidelines which fall into this second category include, for example, those applicable in the broadcasting sector, the guidelines on state aid for environmental protection, the guidelines on rescue and restructuring aid and the guidelines on regional aid. These various horizontal and sectoral types of aid are considered in full in the subsequent chapters of this book.

6. THE RELATIONSHIP BETWEEN ARTICLES 107 TO 109 TFEU AND OTHER PROVISIONS OF THE EU TREATY

3–108   It is established law that the Commission may not approve an aid measure or scheme if that measure also conflicts with a fundamental principle of Union law, as enshrined in another Treaty article or articles. The relevant case law on discrimination and free movement is also examined in detail in the context of state aid and taxation measures in Ch.10.

---

[289] Case 17/57 *Steenkolenmijnen v High Authority* [1959] E.C.R. 1.

Article 18 TFEU

The General Court in Case T–158/99 *Thermenhotel Stoiser Franz* handed **3–109** down a somewhat unclear ruling on the application of art.18 TFEU (ex art.12 EC) in an appeal by Austrian hotel operators in a region where aid had been granted to an Austrian affiliate of the German Siemens AG for the construction of a hotel in an Austrian tourist region. The hotel operators contended that the Commission's approval, inter alia, contravened art.18. The General Court denied the appeal on the basis of art.18 on the grounds that as:

"the first paragraph of Article 12 [now Article 18 TFEU] applies independently only to situations governed by Community law for which the Treaty lays down no specific rules prohibiting discrimination. . . . it follows that the first paragraph of Article 12 [Article 18 TFEU] of the Treaty is not apt to be applied independently in the context of this action, by reason of the existence of the competition rules of the EC Treaty. They cover discrimination, not in relation to the nationality of the undertakings allegedly affected but by reference to the geography and sector of the market considered."[290]

This ruling has been criticised in that, even if the result is correct, the reasoning is not. Nevertheless, there can be no doubt that aid measures which infringe art.18 of the Treaty may not be approved.

The free movement principles

The Courts have had occasion to rule in the past on the application of arts 34, **3–110** 35 and 37 TFEU (goods), art.49 TFEU (establishment) and art.56 TFEU (services) in relation to state aids, to the effect that any measure infringing these articles cannot be declared compatible under the state aid rules. At the same time the Courts have also made clear that arts 107(2) or (3) could not be used as a justification to derogate from the application of either art.34 or art.110 TFEU. With respect to the former article, once it is established that this article applies, any potential exception to it must be firmly based on the derogations provided in art.36 or under the rule of reason,[291] or under certain circumstances the derogation provided by art.106(2).

The relationship between art.34 and art.107 was first considered by the Court in Case 74/76 *Ianelli & Volpi v Meroni*.[292] In that case the Court ruled that art.34 should not be given so extensive an interpretation as to treat an aid within the meaning of art.107 as a quantitative restriction within the meaning of art.28. This would alter the scope of arts 107 and 108, and "would interfere with the system adopted in the Treaty for the division of powers by means of the procedure for

---

[290] Case T–158/99 [2004] E.C.R. II–1, at paras 146–147.
[291] Case C–21/88 *Pont de Nemours Italiana* [1990] E.C.R. I–889.
[292] [1977] E.C.R. 557.

keeping aids under constant review as described in Article 93 [now Article 108 TFEU]".

3–111   Nevertheless, the Court did not follow the suggestion of the Advocate General that the principle that an aid could not fall under art.34 was unqualified. It went on to qualify its ruling by introducing the so-called "severability test" (at para.14). Thus, those aspects of the aid package contravening with specific provisions of the Treaty other than arts 107 and 108 may be so indissolubly linked to the object of the aid that it is impossible to evaluate them separately so that their effect on the compatibility or incompatibility of the aid viewed as a whole must therefore of necessity be determined in the light of the procedure prescribed in art.108.

Nevertheless, the position would be different if it is possible when a system of aid is being analysed to separate those conditions or factors which, even though they form part of this system, may be regarded as not being necessary for the attainment of its object or its proper functioning. In the latter case there are no reasons based on the division of powers under arts 107 and 108 of the Treaty which permit the conclusion to be drawn that, if other provisions of the Treaty which have direct effect are infringed, those provisions may not be invoked before national courts simply because the factor in question is an aspect of aid.

This severability test has been criticised as easier to state than to apply, and indeed in *Ianelli* the Court seemed to experience some difficulties in applying it to the case in hand.[293]

3–112   It is important to note that the next three cases concerning the relationship between arts 34 and 107 arose in the context of art.226 EC (now art.258 TFEU) proceedings brought by the Commission for infringement of art.34. In Case 249/81 *Commission v Ireland (Buy Irish)*[294] the Irish government contended that the financing of its "Buy Irish" campaign should have been evaluated as a state aid. Similar pleas were made in Case 18/84 *Commission v France*,[295] which concerned tax advantages for newspapers printed in France, and in Case 103/84 *Commission v Italy*,[296] which concerned a subsidy for the purchase of public transport vehicles of national origin.

In all three cases, the art.107 arguments were entered as a defence against the alleged infringement of art.34, and in all three cases the alleged aid had not in fact been notified. Finally, in both the *Italy* and the *France* cases, the contested measure was undoubtedly severable from the aid itself, as was probably also true in *Ireland*.[297] Thus in all three cases the Court held that art.34 applied to the measures at issue. In Case 18/84 the Court observed that the provisions relating

---

[293] A. Dashwood [1977] E.L.Rev. 376 and P. Oliver, *Free Movement of Goods,* at para.6.24; cf. O. Schramme, "Rapport entre les mesures d'effet équivalent à des restrictions quantitatives et les aides nationales" [1985] D.T.D.E. 487.

[294] [1982] E.C.R. 4005.

[295] [1982] E.C.R. 4005.

[296] [1986] E.C.R. 1768.

[297] See the conflicting viewpoints of P. Oliver and E. White, "In Search of the Limits of Article 30" (1989) 26 C.M.L.R. 235, at p.273.

to the free movement of goods, the repeal of discriminatory tax provisions and aid have a common objective, namely to ensure the free movement of goods under normal conditions of competition. The mere fact that a national measure may possibly be defined as an aid within the meaning of art.107 is not an adequate reason for exempting it from the prohibition contained in art.34.[298]

In the last major case to come before the Court involving the relationship **3–113** between these two articles, Case C–21/88 *Du Pont de Nemours*, the contested aid had in fact been notified, albeit belatedly.[299] On a reference from the Regional Administrative Tribunal, the Court was asked whether a national measure reserving a fixed quota (30 per cent) of public contracts to undertakings established in Southern Italy, was an "aid" within the meaning of art.107, and whether it was also in breach of art.34. The Court had no difficulty in finding that the legislation was in conflict with the principles of free movement of goods. It then went on to recall its ruling in Case 103/84 *Commission v Italy*, to the effect that:

> "Article 92 EEC [now Article 107 TFEU] may in no case be used to frustrate the rules of the Treaty on the free movement of goods . . . the fact that a national measure might be regarded as aid within the meaning of Article 92 [107 Article TFEU] is therefore not a sufficient reason to exempt it from the prohibition contained in Article 30 EEC [now Article 34 TFEU]."[300]

The Court declined to consider whether the rules in question were in the nature of aid, but merely reaffirmed that even if they were, this cannot exempt them from the prohibition set out in art.34.

It should be noted that, although the Commission had commenced art.108 proceedings against the Italian government in respect of the law on support for the southern region of Italy, of which the quota rule formed a part, the Commission had reserved its position on this particular matter. Nor had it come to a definite conclusion in the two years following notification.[301]

The Court's judgment has been criticised as adding further confusion to the **3–114** demarcation between the scope of arts 34 and 107,[302] as well as for failing to give due weight to regional disparities.[303] It is perhaps advisable to see the *Du Pont* judgment in its proper context. Preferential quota schemes of the type at issue in *Du Pont* are also incompatible with art.26 of Council Directive 77/62 on procurement, as amended,[304] which is in turn based on the principle that restrictions to

---

[298] At para.5.
[299] [1990] E.C.R. I–889. The plaintiffs contended, however, that art.88 had in fact been breached because not only had notification been late, but, furthermore, the Italian government had put the legislation into effect before the Commission issues its decision on the aid.
[300] At para.20.
[301] It was thus argued at the hearing that, in accordance with Case 120/70 *Lorenz*, the Commission's silence amounted to tacit recognition of the lawfulness of the aid.
[302] J. Winter, "Public Procurement in the EEC" (1991) 28 C.M.L.Rev. 717; [1993] O.J. C43/14 (Opel); [1993] O.J. L127/1 (German pharmaceutical firm).
[303] F. Martin and G. Stehmlann, "Product Market Integration versus Regional Cohesion in the Community" (1991) 16 E.L.Rev. 216.
[304] [1977] O.J. L13/1, as amended by Directive 88/295 [1988] O.J. L127/1.

the free movement of goods in the sphere of public supply contracts are prohibited by art.34. Thus *Du Pont* is in line with the Court's general case law that the scope for national governments to rely upon any derogations from the principle of free movement of goods, including the state aid rules, will be interpreted strictly. The Court ruled that it is not acceptable for aid to include arrangements whose restrictive effects exceed what is necessary to enable the aid to attain the objectives permitted by art.107(3). The fact that the inevitable consequence of aid is some restriction on trade does not mean that all restrictive effects which the aid produces must be regarded as permissible.

It may be noted that in the context of its review of compensation for services of general economic interest, the Commission indicated in its draft framework, published on September 16, 2011, that aid granted through contracts or concessions awarded in breach of the European procurement rules must be considered as incompatible aid.[305]

3–115 In Case T–359/04 *British Aggregates*, the General Court held that in the contested decision, the Commission had only examined the exemption from the tax in question, the AGL, in the light of the Guidelines on Environmental Aid, and the Commission considered that the conditions provided for by the Guidelines were fulfilled. The Commission found the AGL exemption to be compatible with the common market, in accordance with art.107(3)(c) TFEU. However, "the question of the alleged tax discrimination resulting from the alleged infringement of Articles 23 EC and 25 EC or of Article 90 EC [now Articles 28, 30 and 110 TFEU] was not discussed in the contested decision, which makes no reference to any of those provisions." As a result the General Court annulled the decision.[306]

Article 37

3–116 Where a measure is implemented through a state monopoly within the meaning of art.37 TFEU, and this measure may also constitute aid within the meaning of art.107(1), the operations of the state monopoly are not exempted from the application of art.37 by reason of the fact that they may at the same time be classified as aid.[307]

Free movement of services and establishment

3–117 Where the provisions of a national aid scheme infringe arts 43 and 49 of the Treaty, the Commission will require their removal before declaring a scheme to be compatible state aid. It has, however, been confirmed by the ECJ that a state aid scheme cannot be declared unlawful merely because it does not extend to

---

[305] Para.60 of the draft Framework, as discussed in Ch.8, at para.8–050.
[306] Judgement of July 9, 2010.
[307] Case 91/78 *Hansen GmbH v Hauptzolamt Flensburg* [1979] E.C.R. 935.

undertakings established in other Member States. In Case C–351/98 *Spain v Commission* the Court stated that:

"A measure to support investment adopted by a public authority can by definition apply only in respect of the territory for which it is responsible and the authority cannot be criticised for not extending the benefit of the measure to undertakings not established in its territory, since such undertakings are in a wholly different position *vis-à-vis* the authority from undertakings established within the territory. That statement does not, however, mean that such a measure of support cannot be classified as 'aid' within the meaning of Article 107(1) of the Treaty if it fulfils the conditions laid down by that provision."[308]

In its ruling in Case C–451/03 *Servizi Ausiliari Dottori Commercialisti* the Court condemned an Italian measure which provided for the payment of compensation to undertakings assisting tax payers in completing tax declarations as being contrary both to the rules on free movement of services and establishment as well as art.107(1).[309]

In Case C–169/08 the Court held a regional tax imposed on stopovers by **3–118** aircraft or other pleasure craft owned or operated by persons whose domicile was outside the territory of the region to be both a restriction on the free movement of services and contrary to art.49 TFEU as well as state aid within the meaning of art.107(1). The ECJ concluded that, having regard to the characteristics of the regional tax on stopovers, the undertakings with their tax domicile outside the region are, with reference to the legal framework in question, in a comparable factual and legal situation to undertakings established outside the territory. The measure cannot be regarded as general as it does not apply to all operators of aircraft or pleasure boats that make a stopover in Sardinia. The ECJ concluded that the stopover tax amounted to a restriction of the freedom to provide services as it only taxes operators domiciled outside the region and does not impose the same tax on operators within the region. As regards infringement of art.49 TFEU, the ECJ held that the application of that tax legislation makes the services concerned more costly for the persons liable for that tax, who have their tax domicile outside the territory of the region and who are established in other Member States, than they are for operators established in Sardinia. By introducing an additional cost for stopovers made by aircraft or boats operated by persons having their tax domicile outside Sardinia and established in other Member States, the stopover tax creates an advantage for some categories of undertaking established in Sardinia.[310]

The application of the state aid rules and the rules on free movement of services and the right of establishment to the cinematographic industry is further

---

[308] [2002] E.C.R. I–8031, at para.57.
[309] Judgement of March 30, 2006 [2006] E.C.R. I–2941.
[310] November 17, 2009 [2009] E.C.R. I–10821.

considered in the Commission's "Cinema" Communication of September 26, 2001,[311] as amended, and discussed in Ch.4.

The competition rules: articles 101 and 102

3–119   Issues relating to the interaction of the Treaty competition rules (ex. arts 81 to 82 EC) and arts 107 and 108 have arisen in relation to the potential parallel application of these two sets of rules, as well as the EC Merger Regulation.

Articles 101 and 102

3–120   With respect to the possible interaction of art.107(1) with art.101(1) TFEU the leading case—C–225/91 *Matra*—was decided at the time when Council Regulation 17/62 was still in force and which allowed the Commission to grant an individual exemption or negative clearance from the application of what was then art.81(1) EC (now art.101(1) TFEU). The applicants claimed, unsuccessfully, that the Commission had failed to co-ordinate its review of the state aid elements of a proposed package of support granted by the Portuguese government to Ford and VW who had formed a joint venture to produce multi-purpose vehicles, with its assessment for negative clearance of that joint venture under art.101(1) and (3) TFEU. The Court dealt with the procedural aspects of the two sets of rules and stated that although these two procedures were distinct, and they must be carefully followed by the Commission, they must be applied consistently. In the *Matra* case, the state aid decision finding compatibility was taken only three days after the publication of the art.19(3) Notice in which the Commission stated that it intended to grant negative clearance to the joint venture agreement. The Courts concluded that the Commission can take a decision on the compatibility of the planned aid "provided that it has formed the conviction, with sufficient probability that the operation is not in breach of Articles 81 and 82 EC [now Articles 101 and 102 TFEU]".[312] The doctrine of "substantive consistency" has been further strengthened in the *SIDE* case, where the General Court held that the Commission should have shown that it was in a position to arrive at a firm view, based on economic analysis that the recipient of the aid was not in contravention of arts 101 and 102.[313]

Case T–423/07 *Ryanair v Commission* illustrates some of the pitfalls where a company seeks to bring simultaneously a complaint about the infringement of art.107(1) as well as infringement of the antitrust rules. In 2005 Ryanair had complained to the Commission in relation to the exclusive use by Lufthansa and

---

[311] [2001] O.J. C43.
[312] T–17/93 *Matra v Commission* [1994] E.C.R. II–595 and Case C–225/91 *Matra v Commission* [1993] E.C.R. I–3203, at para.45. See also Case T–197/97 [2001] E.C.R. II–303, at paras 76–78.
[313] T–49/93 *SIDE v Commission* [1995] E.C.R. II–2501, at para.72 and C–164/98 *DIR International Film v Commission* [2000] E.C.R. I–1447, at paras 29–30. See also the Commission's opening decision C–43/3005 *Stranded Costs in Poland* [2006] O.J. C52/8.

its Star Alliance partners of Terminal 2 at Munich Airport. It alleged that this arrangement concerned both illegal state aid and abuse of a dominant position. The Commission eventually opened a formal investigation into the state aid issue in 2008,[314] but failed to take a position on the alleged infringement of art.102 TFEU. Ryanair decided to pursue its case for failure to act against the Commission. The General Court considered whether, at the time the Commission was formally called upon to define its position, it was under a duty to act. It ruled that the complaint lodged by Ryanair fell short of the procedural requirements laid down in Reg.1/2003[315] and Reg.773/2004 and hence could not be classified as a complaint in accordance with those Regulations. A complainant wishing to include allegations of an infringement of the Treaty anti-trust rules as well as the state aid rules in a complaint is not necessarily precluded from submitting a single document but it must satisfy all the formal requirements of art.5 of Reg.773/2004.[316] A complainant cannot assume that just because it is an "interested party" for the purpose of the state aid procedures, it will necessarily have a legitimate interest in order to lodge a complaint under the antitrust procedures.[317]

The EC merger regulation

In Case T–156/98 *RJB Mining v Commission*, the Commission approved a **3–121** merger in the German coal sector under the now defunct art.66(2) ECSC while competitors were questioning whether there was a state aid element in the purchase price that benefited the acquiring party—RAG. The Commission did not address the state issue in its decision clearing the merger. The General Court annulled this decision on the grounds that, although the Commission was not required to assess the legality of the supposed aid, namely the aid inherent in the merger in a formal preliminary decision, it could not in its merger analysis ignore the extent to which the financial and thus the commercial strength of the merged entity was strengthened by the financial support provided by that supposed aid.[318] The "RJB doctrine" (that is the inherent link test) was applied in several subsequent decisions.[319]

In Case T–114/02 *BaByliss v Commission*[320] the General Court appears to have imposed limits on the doctrine by narrowing the scope of the "inherent link" test and by finding that while there might be such a link in a privatisation case, there was no such link in a case involving a merger between two private

---

[314] C38/08 (ex. NN 53/07) Germany—Measures in favour of Munich airport Terminal 2.
[315] [2003] O.J. L1/1.
[316] [2004] O.J. L123/18.
[317] Judgment of May 19, 2011.
[318] [2000] E.C.R. I–337, at para.125. See also Case T–175/99 *UPS v Commission* [2002] E.C.R. II–1917.
[319] See COMP/M.2694 *Metronet/Infraco* and COMP/M.2908 *Deutsche Post/DHL* and COMP/M.2621 *SEB/Moulinex*, as well as COMP/ECSC.1350 *Saarbergwerke II*—the decision which followed the annulment of the first decision in *RJB Mining*.
[320] [2003] E.C.R. II–1279.

parties (at para.441). The appeal by the German government (and British Coal) against this ruling to the ECJ was subsequently withdrawn,[321] thus dashing the hope of many commentators that this would have given the higher court the opportunity to limit a flawed doctrine further. It is argued that it is preferable that the Commission should examine the strengthening of the competitive position of the recipient of an aid in the context of a state aid procedure and not as part of the merger decision, in line with the *Matra* doctrine.

3–122 In the *RJB Mining* saga the General Court was indeed required in a separate case brought by RJB to consider the Commission's decision approving operating aid to the merged company Ruhrkohle AG (RAG). The applicant had lodged a formal complaint with the Commission relating to various state aid measures proposed for 1997, 1998 and beyond, and to the alleged aid inherent in the then planned merger, in particular the sale of the publicly owned company Saarberg-werke for DEM 1, despite the fact that the company's non-coal activities had been valued by an independent consultant at DEM 1 billion the year before. It was contended that the Commission had approved the aid without taking into account the merger, which was one of the most fundamental in the history of the coal industry, and that it continued to treat each of the merged undertakings separately, as if each had received the aid separately, even though it was aware of the considerable sums of aid inherent in the merger. The General Court examined this contention in the context of the particular provisions of the ECSC treaty and the then applicable ECSC coal aid code (see Ch.14) and ruled that in the actual circumstances of the investigation, and given the complexity of the case, the Commission had not committed a manifest error in failing to take the alleged aid inherent in the merger into account. Although this ruling was subsequently appealed, this case was withdrawn and removed from the Court register.[322]

Agriculture

3–123 The application of the state aid rules to the agriculture and fisheries sectors is dealt with in full in Ch.13. It may be noted here, however, that the agricultural provisions of the Treaty have precedence over arts 107 to 109 (art.42 TFEU). Article 4 of Regulation 26/62,[323] however, did not apply to the substantive Treaty rules on state aid, but merely makes provision for the application of art.107 and the first sentence of art.108 to the products listed in Annex II to the Treaty. Regulation 26/62 did not apply to either art.107, or to the last sentence of art.108 prohibiting Member States from introducing notified aid until the Commission has reached its decision. Regulation 26/62 has now been replaced by Reg.1184/2006 (O.J. 2006 L214/7).

---

[321] July 17, 2003.
[322] [2002] O.J. C274/24—removal from register of Cases C–427/99P and C–371/00P.
[323] [1959–62] O.J. Spec. Ed, 129; [1962] O.J. 993.

Common market organisations. It is usual to find in the basic regulations **3–124**
setting up such organisations, that provision is made for the full application of
arts 107–109 to the production of and trade in the products in question, "save as
otherwise provided". Thus the rules on state aid remain subordinate to the
provisions on the organisation of the particular sector of the market.[324] Further,
the provisions extending arts 107–109 to production of and trade in the products
covered by the relevant market organisations also lay down that those articles are
applicable only in the absence of provisions to the contrary in the regulations in
question.[325] In the absence of a common organisation, the applicability of arts
107–109 to Annex II products is governed solely by Reg.1184/2006.

The art.107 exceptions do not apply to an aid which is forbidden by the
regulations governing a common market organisation.[326] Thus it is not infre-
quently the case that the Council decides that the aid in question is justified by
"exceptional circumstances" in accordance with the procedures provided for in
art.108, third sub-paragraph (see further, Ch.4).

If the Commission is seeking to enforce the specialised, stricter provisions set **3–125**
out in a regulation, the procedure to be followed is that provided for by art.258
TFEU, and not art.108. Where the alleged aid is in an agricultural sector covered
by a common organisation, the Commission must also indicate the provision of
the agricultural regulation with which the aid is incompatible. Failure to do so
will lead to dismissal of the action.[327] It should, however, be noted that where
aids to agricultural products have been granted illegally, the Commission may
refuse to make EAGGF payments if a link can be established between the
granting of the aid and additional expenditure charged to the EAGGF
budget.[328]

Transport

Article 93 TFEU (ex. art.73 EC) creates an exception in the field of transport **3–126**
to the general rules applicable to state aid by providing that aids that meet the
needs of transport co-ordination or represent requirements for the discharge of
certain obligations inherent in the concept of a public service are compatible with
the Treaty. The second part of the provision is a specific application of art.106(2).
The concept of a public service in the (land) transport sector was further specified
in Reg.1191/69, adopted pursuant to arts 71 and 89 EC (now arts 91 and 109
TFEU) and is now governed by Reg.1370/2007 (O.J. 2007 L315/1).

---

[324] Case 83/78 *Pigs Marketing Board v Redmond* [1978] E.C.R. 2347; Case 177/78 *Pigs and Bacon Commission v Mc Carren* [1979] E.C.R. 2161.
[325] Thus the Court has ruled that the compatibility of national aids for agricultural products is to be assessed in the light of the applicable regulations instituting a common organisation for such products—Case 114/83 *Ste. Initiatives et Co-operation Agricole e.a. v Commission* [1984] E.C.R. 2589.
[326] Case 72/79 *Commission v Italy* [1980] E.C.R. 1411 at 1425. See as an example Commission Decision 98/668/EC [1998] O.J. L316/55.
[327] Case 169/82 *Commission v Italy* [1984] E.C.R. 1603.
[328] For a discussion of this policy, see 18th Report on Competition Policy, 1989 at pt 273.

Regulation 110/70 further specified the scope of art.93 TFEU. Its art.3 provided that Member States may neither take co-ordination measures nor impose obligations inherent in the concept of a public service which involved the granting of aids pursuant to art.93, except in cases or circumstances described in that regulation. It followed that Member States were no longer authorised to rely on art.93 TFEU outside the cases referred to in secondary Community legislation. This was confirmed by the General Court in Case T–157/01 *Danish Buses*.[329]

Article 106

3–127   The application of art.106(2) TFEU (ex. art.86(2) EC) in the context of arts 107 and 108 is dealt with in detail in Ch.8.

Indirect taxation and para-fiscal charges: article 110 TFEU

3–128   In Case 227/83 *Commission v Italy*[330] the Court followed its earlier decisions in Case 47/69 *France v Commission*[331] and Case 73/79 *Commission v Italy*,[332] and ruled that the application of art.110 TFEU (ex. art.90 EC) is not precluded by the provisions on state aids. Article 110 is also directly effective.[333]

The fact that an aid scheme within the scope of arts 107–109 is involved does not prevent the application of art.110 on discriminatory taxation (see also Ch.10). Where a measure is carried out by discriminatory taxation it is irrelevant for the Commission to establish whether such measures of relief may also be considered as aid within the meaning of arts 107–109, since it is clear that such a measure, which may be considered at the same time as forming part of an aid within the meaning of art.107, should in any case be governed by art.100.[334]

From the standpoint of a competitor of the potential recipient of state aid, however, it may be more advantageous to challenge the aid scheme in question on the basis of arts 107 and 108 as opposed to art.110, if the aid in question has not been notified.[335] This will, of course, be otherwise if the aid in question is classified as existing aid.[336]

3–129   In Case 47/69[337] the fact that the aid was financed by a quasi-fiscal charge which was incompatible with art.110, and affected intra-Community trade to such an extent that even though the purpose of the aid itself was acceptable, it

---

[329] March 16, 2004 [2004] E.C.R. II–917.
[330] [1985] E.C.R. 2049.
[331] [1970] E.C.R. 487.
[332] [1980] E.C.R. 1533.
[333] If the Commission chooses to allege breach of art.110 as well as art.107 then it may be obliged to have recourse to art.226—see further, Ch.25, section 2.
[334] Case 17/81 *Pabst und Richarz KG v Hauptzollamt Oldenburg* [1982] E.C.R. 1331. See also *Biofuels* [1997] O.J. L222/26, p.32.
[335] Case C–72/92 [1993] E.C.R. I–5509, at para.19.
[336] Case C–387/92 [1994] E.C.R. I–877.
[337] [1970] E.C.R. 487.

was contrary to the common interest within the meaning of art.107.[338] Recent case law has further clarified the relationship between an aid and a tax financing that aid.

With respect to the application of art.30 TFEU (ex. art.25 EC)—the prohibition on charges having equivalent effect to a customs duty—and art.110 TFEU (ex. art.90 EC)—which prohibits discriminatory forms of indirect taxation—the focus here is not so much on the purpose of the aid and whether it can be declared compatible in relation to its objectives but on the mechanisms for financing the aid. If these mechanisms are contrary to other provisions of the Treaty, including art.30 (and art.110) then the entire measure must be declared incompatible.[339] National courts also have an important role to play here given that art.30 (and art.110) is directly effective.

The *Nygard* judgment concerned a levy imposed by Denmark on the production of live pigs for export. The Danish court was uncertain whether the authorisation granted by the Commission under art.107(3) could preclude it from setting aside a levy used to finance authorised aid and referred the matter to the ECJ. The Court held that the national court must establish whether any directly effective provisions of Community law have been violated in order to protect individual rights. Furthermore, national courts were best placed to carry out an assessment of the manner in which the revenue generated by a domestic parafiscal charge is allocated.[340]

Joined Cases C–261/01 and C–262/01 *Van Calster, Cleeren and Openbaar* **3–130** *Slachthuis NV*[341] concerned the legality of various financial arrangements pertaining to a fund set up to finance services to combat animal diseases and improve animal health and hygiene. In a decision of 1991 the Commission had ruled the 1987 regime to be illegal but in a subsequent decision had held that an amended scheme was compatible with the state aid rules. However, the status of charges paid under the 1987 scheme was unclear. The Belgian government had claimed that the Commission had effectively approved the amended scheme with retroactive effect.

Van Calster, Cleeren and Openbaar Slachthuis sought reimbursement of the contributions they had paid to the fund under the 1987 legislation which they claimed were contrary to Community law.

On referral from the Belgian courts, the Court ruled that even if the Commission had examined the compatibility with the common market of the charges imposed with retroactive effect, it would not have been competent to decide that an aid scheme put into effect contrary to art.108(3) is legal. This would effectively lead to a confusion between the separate and complimentary roles of the Commission and the national courts—the role of the latter being to safeguard the

---

[338] See also Commission Decision 95/456/EC [1995] O.J. L265/30 and Decision 96/615/EC [1996] O.J. L272/53, where the levy in question was not applied to exports.
[339] See also Case C–526/04 *Laboratoires Boiron*, Opinion of the Advocate General, March 30, 2006 E.C.R. I–7529.
[340] Case C–234/99 *Nygard* [2002] E.C.R. I–3657.
[341] [2003] E.C.R. I–12249.

obligation to give prior notification and to order the return of state aid if this has not been duly notified.[342]

3–131   In its ruling in Joined Cases C–34/01 and C–38/01 *Enirisorse* the Court dealt with the obligation to pay a para-fiscal levy or charge and the lawfulness of the levying of the charge, as well as the legality of the allocation of part of the proceeds of the charge to the state-owned "Aziende". The Court recalled its earlier rulings in which it held that:

> "the concept of state aid includes not only certain parafiscal charges, depend-ing on the use to which the revenue from those charges is put (see, inter alia, *Lornoy and Others*, paragraph 28), but also the collection of a contribution constituting a parafiscal charge (see Case C–72/92 *Scharbatke* [1993] E.C.R. I–5509, para. 20). One of the Court's recent decisions also makes it clear that where the method by which aid is financed, particularly by means of compul-sory contributions, forms an integral part of the aid measure, consideration of the latter by the Commission must necessarily also take into account that method of financing the aid (Joined Cases C–261/01 and Case C–262/01 *Van Calster and Others* [2003] E.C.R. I–12249, para. 49)."

The Court then went on to consider whether the charges in question were contrary to arts 25 or 90 EC (now arts 30 and 110 TFEU). It held that:

> "charges, such as the port charges at issue in the main proceedings, constitute internal taxation within the meaning of Article [95] [now Article 110 TFEU] of the Treaty not falling within the ambit of Article [12] [Article 30 TFEU] or Article [30] [Article 34 TFEU] of the Treaty. In the absence of any unequal treatment discriminating against goods from other Member States, the measure by virtue of which a Member State provides for the collection of those charges and the allocation of a significant proportion thereof to a public undertaking, when the sum so allocated corresponds to a service actually provided by that undertaking, does not infringe Article [95] [Article 110 TFEU]."[343]

Hence if the "charge" was actually a fee for a service provided it would not fall within the scope of art.110 as this measure only applies to discriminatory indirect taxation—the fee is not a "tax".[344]

3–132   In its more recent jurisprudence the Court has developed the concept of "hypothecation" in the sense that the revenue from the tax is necessarily allocated for the financing of the aid. In the event of such hypothecation, the revenue from the tax has a direct impact on the amount of aid and, consequently, on the assessment of the compatibility of the aid with the common market.[345]

---

[342] See Case C–39/94 *SFEI* [1996] E.C.R. I–3547, at para.41.

[343] See para.62 of the judgment.

[344] See also the judgment of the Court in Joined Cases C–41/05 and C–393/04 [2006] E.C.R. I–5293, with respect to the interpretation of arts 25 and 90 EC (now arts 30 and 110 TFEU).

[345] Case C–393/04 and C–41/05 *Air Liquide* [2006] E.C.R. I–5293, at para.46.

In Case C–174/02 *Streekgewest Westelijk Noord-Brabant (SWNB)* no such hypothecation existed, since "first it is clear from the order for reference that the provisions of the WBM [the tax in question] do not hypothecate the tax on waste to the financing of the tax exemption. Second, the tax revenue has no impact on the amount of aid. The application of the tax exemption and its extent do not depend on the tax revenue" (at para.25). Consequently, the financial obligations under the WBM could not be regarded as an integral part of the aid measure, and therefore the breach of the obligation to notify the aid measures (i.e. the exemptions to the general levy system) could not lead to the invalidity of the levy system as such.[346]

In a second case, C–175/02 *Pape* (January 13, 2005), the legality of a levy imposed to meet the costs of a so-called "manure bank" was challenged by a farmer on the grounds that he had been required to pay the levy in the financial year preceding the approval of the state aid scheme by the Commission in 1989. Again the Court held that the levy was not hypothecated to the aid for the transport of manure, as the national authorities could exercise a discretion to allocate the revenue from the levy for other purposes. The Court has confirmed this approach in Joined Cases C–266 to C–270/04, C–276/04 and C–231/04 to C–325/04 *Nazairdis SAS* concerning a progressive tax borne by retail stores in France. This tax was not hypothecated to the alleged aid measure as the Minister enjoyed a discretion to allocate revenue to other objectives.[347]

In Joined Cases C–266/04 to C–270/04, C–276/04 and C–321/04 to C–325/04 *Distribution Casino* of 2005 the Court noted that:

"... as regards the allocation of part of the revenue from the TACA [levy] to the financing of basic old-age insurance schemes for self-employed persons in the craft sector and for self-employed persons in manufacturing and trading occupations ... it must be pointed out that the recipient funds (Organic and Cancava) each administer a basic social security scheme founded on a solidarity mechanism. As the activity carried out by the funds concerned does not constitute an economic activity .... the financing of that activity falls outside the scope of Article 87(1) EC." (para.54).

Furthermore, the national legislation at issue in no way established hypothecation of the TACA levy to the old-age insurance schemes for craftsmen and traders. Under the applicable Law No.96–1160, the amount of the TACA allocated for financing the insurance schemes in question was determined each year by joint order of the competent Ministers. In view of the discretion enjoyed by those Ministers, it cannot be accepted that the revenue from the TACA directly affects the amount of the advantage granted to the recipient funds at issue. Finally, the discretion enjoyed by the competent Ministers in respect of the

---

[346] January 13, 2005 [2005] E.C.R. I–85.
[347] [2005] E.C.R. I–19481. See, however, Case C–526/04 *Labatoires Boiron SA* [2006[E.C.R. I–7529.

allocation of funds deriving from the revenue from the TACA precluded the existence of such hypothecation.[348]

In Case C–33/07 *Regie Networks*, the ECJ held that the Commission's decision on a parafiscal levy on advertisements broadcast on radio and television to fund an aid scheme for semi-public broadcasters was invalid. The Commission found the scheme to be compatible with the common market but it had failed to examine the compatibility of the method by which the scheme was financed and was therefore vitiated by an error in law.[349]

Article 346 TFEU: derogation for trade in arms and war material

3–133   The production of and trade in arms, munitions and war materials is subject to special treatment as set down in art.346 TFEU. These provisions do not prevent the Member States from taking such measures as they consider necessary in relation to those particular activities for the protection of essential interests of their security, including state aid measures. The regime established by art.346(1)(b) preserves the Member States' freedom of action in certain matters affecting national defence and security.[350]

This Treaty article has been examined in relation to the state aid rules in Case T–26/01 *Fiocchi Munizioni SpA v Commission*.[351] Where a Member State adopts an aid measure in favour of production or trade in arms on the basis of considerations linked to the need to protect the essential interest of its internal security, the rules of competition do not apply in such cases. The Member State is not required to notify the Commission of the aid measure at the drafting stage and the Commission may not use the art.108 TFEU procedure to examine such aid. However, the Commission must ensure that the measure does not adversely affect the conditions of competition in the common market regarding products which are not intended for specifically military purposes (see last sentence of art.346(1)(b) TFEU). The appropriate procedure is laid down in art.348.

If measures taken in the circumstances referred to in art.346 have the effect of distorting the conditions of competition in the common market, the Commission and the Member State must examine how the measure can be adjusted. Similarly, if the products in question are capable of "dual use"—that is civilian as well as military use—then this must be examined under the joint examination procedure. Following this examination, however, the Commission is not required to adopt a decision on the measure, nor is it empowered to address an appropriate directive or decision to the Member State concerned. However, the Commission can only opt for this special procedure if the Member State's reliance on the art.346

---

[348] [2005] E.C.R. I–9481.
[349] [2008] E.C.R. I–5157.
[350] For a detailed discussion see, B. Heninckx, "Defence Procurement" in 2009, 46 CMLRev, pp.1191–211; and K. van de Casteele in 2007 Revue de Concurrences nr 3, *www.concurrences .com/revue_bib_rdr.php3?id_article.*
[351] [2003] E.C.R. II–3951.

procedure is prima facie credible. If not, the Commission must carry out the standard procedures under art.108(2) and in the course of those procedures, the Member State may rely upon the application of art.346 in its defence.[352] In Case T–26/01 the General Court also appears to have endorsed the power of the Commission to ensure that there are no spill-over effects into markets for dual use products but also effects on military products intended for exports (see para.63).

In Decision C16/04 of July 2, 2008[353] the Commission considered a restructur- **3–134** ing plan submitted by Greece for investments in Hellenic Shipyards SA (HSY), which had originally been put into liquidation in 1992, but after several unsuc- cessful efforts to sell HSY, this process was revoked and instead the Greek government planned to privatise the public shipyards. A package of measures was put in place to facilitate this process and notified on the basis of art.108(3). Greece subsequently claimed that several of the measures investigated by the Commission supported military activities and that they fell under art.346 TFEU (formerly art.296 EC), and so could not be assessed under the state aid rules. The Commission held that it had already identified the measures supporting exclu- sively the military activities of the yard and in an earlier decision it had concluded that these measures fell entirely under art.346 TFEU.[354] However, in its Decision C16/04 it examined various measures of support that were not earmarked to finance a given project so that the Commission was required to determine the extent to which the State support at issue benefitted either civil or military activities. The methodology used to determine the extent of the support for the two different activities is set out at paras 72–75 of the decision. The Commission then went on to consider in some detail the sixteen support meas- ures for HSY that it had identified, and in respect of each measure, to address to what extent the individual measure could be deemed to fall under art.346 TFEU. The Commission accepted that even although HSY did not apply separate accounts for its civil and military activities, it would consider that 75 per cent of the support benefitted the military activities and 25 per cent the civil activities. However, with respect to recovery of the illegal aid for the civil activities, the Commission had to ensure that there was no risk that the reimbursement of aid received by the civil activities would have been financed by funds which should have been earmarked for military activities, as this would be tantamount to indirect support for the civil activities. Greece was therefore required to ensure that the aid would be recovered exclusively from the civil part of the yard. The successor to HSY has challenged the Commission's application of art.346 and its failure to apply art.348.[355]

---

[352] See Commission Decision 1999/763 of March 17, 1999, Germany, [1999] O.J. L301/8 and *Neptun Industrie* [1999] O.J. L144/21. See also IP/05/649 of June 1, 2005.

[353] [2009] O.J. L225/104.

[354] Decision C10/94 and N513/01, referred to at fn.64 of Decision C16/04.

[355] Case T–391/08 *Ellinka Nafigia v Commission*, September 15, 2008, [2008] O.J. 327/29.

The relationship of the EC Treaty rules on state aids to other treaties

3–135   **The ECSC Treaty.** The relationship between arts 107 and 108 and the now defunct Treaty of Paris establishing the European Coal and Steel Community is discussed in detail in Ch.14.

3–136   **The Euratom Treaty.** The application of arts 107 and 108 to matters covered by the Euratom Treaty is examined in Ch.20.

3–137   **The European Economic Area.** Article 61(1) of the EEA Treaty reproduces the terminology of art.107 TFEU. Thus:

> "save as otherwise provided in this Agreement, any aid granted by EU Member States, EFTA States or through State resources in any form whatsoever which distorts or threatens to distort competition by favouring certain undertakings shall, in so far as it affects trade between Contracting Parties, be incompatible with this agreement".

Commission decisions must also take the effect on trade in the EEA into account.

Article 61(2) EEA replicates the types of aid which are automatically compatible with the functioning of the Agreement. Article 61(3) EEA sets out the types of aid which may be compatible with the functioning of the Agreement (see further, Ch.4). Article 62 and art.63/Annex XV EEA deal with procedural aspects (see further, Ch.26). Decisions of the EFTA Surveillance Authority are published separately in the *Official Journal*.

3–138   **The Europe Agreements.** The specific application of the EU Treaty rules on state aids to the 10 new Member States who joined the European Union on May 1, 2004 and the two Member States who joined in 2007 is dealt with in detail in Ch.5.

CHAPTER 4

ARTICLE 107(2) AND ARTICLE 107(3)*

1.	INTRODUCTION	4–001
2.	AUTOMATIC EXEMPTIONS: ARTICLE 107(2)	4–003
	General	4–003
	Article 107(2)(a): aid of a social character	4–004
	Natural disasters and exceptional occurrences	4–006
	Article 107(2)(c) Federal Republic of Germany	4–008
	The EEA Agreement	4–011
3.	ARTICLE 107(3)	4–012
	The Commission's discretion	4–013
	The compensatory justification principle	4–015
	The market failure test	4–017
4.	THE SPECIFIC PROVISIONS	4–018
	Article 107(3)(a)	4–019
	Article 107(3)(b)	4–023
	The Temporary Framework	4–026
	Individual Decisions	4–028
	The automobile sector	4–029
	Article 107(3)(c)	4–030
	Cultural aid	4–033
	Forms of cultural aid	4–036
	Aid to the broadcasting sector	4–037
	Council authorisation in exceptional circumstances	4–038
5.	THE REGULATION OF CERTAIN CATEGORIES AND TYPES OF AID	4–043
	General	4–043
	Export aid	4–044
	Export aid to third countries	4–045
	Export Credit Insurance	4–048
	The Temporary Framework and Export Credit Insurance	4–049
	Operating aid	4–050
	Investment aid measures	4–051
	Investment aid schemes	4–052
	Regional aid and operating aid	4–053
	Risk capital	4–054
	Application of the 2001 Guidelines	4–055
	The revised guidelines of 2006	4–059
	The balancing test	4–060

* Leigh Hancher

The Temporary Framework and Risk Capital 4–062

1. INTRODUCTION

4–001   Even where an aid is prima facie incompatible with art.107(1), it may qualify for exemption if it fulfils the conditions set out in art.107(2) or (3), or where relevant, art.108(2) decisions of the Council. Council Regulation 994/98 gives the Commission power to adopt individual regulations declaring certain types of aid to be compatible with the common market, and exempts them from notification to, and subsequent review by, the Commission. Such aid is then deemed existing aid for the purposes of art.108(1) and Council Regulation 659/99,[1] and the Member States are expected to comply with various reporting requirements in order to allow the Commission to monitor existing aid schemes. Council Regulation 994/98 allows the Commission to adopt further individual regulations for various categories of aid, as enumerated in its art.1. These categories are confined to horizontal forms of aid and currently do not extend to specific sectors. Furthermore, the Commission's State Aid Action Plan of 2005 envisaged a wider use of the "Block Exemption"-type Regulation, as discussed in Ch.1. The individual "Block Exemption" Regulations, now expired and the General Block Exemption Regulation of 2008 are discussed in detail in subsequent chapters.

It may be noted here that in Case C–110/03 *Belgium v Commission*[2] the Court held that the Commission did not exceed its powers by defining compatibility criteria for state aid. The Commission did not have to confine itself to a simple codification of its previous practice, but was allowed to use its experience to lay down new compatibility criteria, including even stricter criteria than those previously used. By means of Council Regulation 994/98 the Commission was entrusted with the power to declare that certain categories of aid were compatible with the common market and were not subject to notification. This Regulation did not, however, confer on the Commission any power to interpret art.107(1) and to impose a general and binding definition of the concept of state aid as laid down in art.107(1) TFEU.

As will be discussed in Ch.8, the Commission has also used art.106(3) as a basis on which to adopt a decision exempting certain types of aid for the compensation of the costs of performing public service obligations or services of general economic interest on the basis of art.106(2) from prior notification and review.[3] Finally, it may be noted that several special sectors, including coal and steel as well as shipbuilding, are governed by separate decisions and regulations (see Chs 14 and 16) which lay down specific criteria with regard to the compatibility of certain types of measures. The decisions adopted with respect to coal

---

[1] Council Regulation (EC) No 659/1999 of March 22, 1999 laying down detailed rules for the application of art.93 of the EC Treaty [art.108 TFEU], [1999] O.J. L83/1.

[2] Case C–110/03 *Belgium v Commission* [2005] E.C.R. I–02801.

[3] State Aid Action Plan, COM (2005) 107 final, June 7, 2005.

and steel take art.107(3)(e) as their legal basis now that the ECSC Treaty has expired (see Ch.14).

Categories of aid, or types of aid or any other individual aid measure which is **4–002** not covered by the General Block Exemption Regulation or a specific decision, must be notified and the Member State must make out a convincing case that the Commission should assess the aid measure as compatible. Numerous frameworks and guidelines issued by the Commission give further guidance to Member States as to when an aid to a particular sector (sectoral aid) or as to when a particular category of aid or type of aid (horizontal aid) may be deemed acceptable. The substantive conditions laid down in these "soft law" measures are discussed in greater detail in subsequent chapters. Despite the fact that many of these instruments are only adopted by the Commission as guidelines or communications, they are not without legal effect. The criteria set down in these types of measures have been held by the courts to be binding on the Commission. The Court held in its judgment in *Belgium and Forum 187 v Commission*,[4] that arts 107 and 108 provide the basis for an appraisal of the scope of the Commission's powers and duties in relation to state aid. Accordingly, although the Commission is bound by the guidelines and notices that it adopts in this area, that applies only in so far as those provisions do not depart from the proper application of the rules in the Treaty. In Case T–369/06 *Holland Malt v Commission*,[5] the General Court held that:

"Where guidelines have been adopted, the Commission is governed by them (*Deufil* v *Commission* and *Regione autonoma della Sardegna* v *Commission*, paragraph 95). It is therefore for the Community judicature to check that the Commission has observed the rules which it adopted (Case T–35/99 *Keller and Keller Meccanica* v *Commission* [2002] E.C.R. II–261, paragraph 77, and *Regione autonoma della Sardegna* v *Commission*, paragraph 96)" (at para. 169).[6]

Further, the Court stipulated that:

"According to the case-law, the Guidelines cannot be understood on the basis of their wording alone. They must be interpreted in the light of Article 107 and of the objective sought by that provision, namely undistorted competition in the common market (see, to that effect, Case T–27/02 *Kronofrance v Commission* [2004] E.C.R. II–4177, paragraph 89). Likewise, although the Commission is bound by the guidelines and notices that it issues in the field of State aid, that is so only to the extent that those texts do not depart from the proper application of the rules in the Treaty, since the texts cannot be interpreted in a way which reduces the scope of Articles 107 and 108 or which contravenes

---

[4] Joined Cases C–182/03R and C–217/03R *Belgium and Forum 187 v Commission* [2003] E.C.R. I–6887.
[5] Case T–369/06 *Holland Malt BV v Commission* [2009] E.C.R. II–3313.
[6] T–171/02 [2005] E.C.R. II–2123.

the aims of those articles (see Joined Cases C–75/05P and C–80/05P *Germany and Others v Kronofrance* [2008] E.C.R. I–00619, paragraph 65 and the case-law cited)" (at paras 138–9).

The General Court's ruling has subsequently been confirmed in Case C–464/09P *Holland Malt v Commission* of December 2, 2010.[7]

Thus the Commission cannot subsequently declare as compatible an individual aid of a type which has been condemned as incompatible by a particular set of guidelines. In determining the compatibility of a particular aid measure or scheme, a Member State may have to have regard to the relevant provisions of a number of guidelines which may have potentially simultaneous application. The absence of coherence between certain guidelines has attracted criticism and it has been one of the aims of the State Aid Action Plan to introduce greater simplification and rationalisation in this respect.

As with any exception from a basic Treaty principle, a derogation from the general prohibition on the grant of aids as laid down in art.107(1) must be interpreted restrictively. In this respect the Commission has traditionally applied the "compensatory justification" principle, as first developed by the Court in Case C–730/79 *Philip Morris*.[8] As discussed in more detail in Ch.2, the economic analysis of state aid is gaining increasing importance as a tool in the assessment of compatibility of particular measures.

This chapter will examine the general principles relating to aid assessment in accordance with art.107(2) and (3) and art.108(2) and the principles applied to the treatment of certain types of aid, such as export aid, operating aid and investment aid as well as risk capital measures. The relevant criteria which have been developed in the context of specific guidelines for sector and horizontal forms of aid are discussed in detail in the relevant chapters in Pts III and IV.

2. Automatic Exemptions: Article 107(2)

General

4–003   Article 107(2) lists the categories of aid which are exempt from the implied prohibition of art.107(1). Exemption is automatic if the Commission considers that the aid falls within one of the three categories listed in the sub-article. Hence, it follows that this type of aid is still subject to Commission control, as the latter is under a duty to keep all systems of aid under review. This raises the question of whether exemption can only be awarded following notification. There is no clear case law on this point with respect to the first category of automatic aid—aid of a social character granted to individual consumers. Article 107(1)

---

[7] Unreported, E.C.R. [2011] O.J. C30/12.
[8] Case C–730/79 *Philip Morris Holland BV v Commission of the European Communities* [1980] E.C.R. 2671.

prohibits aid to undertakings as opposed to individual consumers. It is therefore questionable whether aid measures to individual consumers could be deemed to fall within the definition of an "aid measure" for the purposes of art.107(1) and would therefore require prior notification. The remaining two categories envisage aid to undertakings, however, so notification is still required even though the Commission has a narrower margin of review than that available to it under art.107(3), as discussed below.

Article 107(2)(a): aid of a social character

The exemption can only be relied upon if the aid measure is granted to **4–004** individual consumers and does not result in an indirect benefit to undertakings providing the goods or services in question. In its ruling in Joined Cases C–442/03P and C–471/03P *P&O Ferries (Vizcaya) SV v Commission*[9] the European Court of Justice (ECJ) reviewed the earlier ruling of the Court of First Instance (CFI) (now the General Court),[10] which concerned a Commission decision on various agreements between P&O and the local authority of Bilbao relating to a ferry service.

The Commission, having reviewed the original non-notified measure in 1995, had accepted certain amendments to the original agreement and closed the administrative proceedings on the ground that the aid element had been removed. This decision was subsequently annulled by the General Court in Case T–14/92 *BAI v Commission*,[11] and the Commission commenced the procedures envisaged in art.108(2) and finally adopted a negative decision on the agreements in 2000. The Commission concluded that the amended agreements did not in fact reflect the actual needs of the individual users who were to benefit from a special voucher scheme under which the Bilbao authorities had agreed to purchase a number of vouchers at a fixed price from P&O, irrespective of the actual use made of these vouchers by the ultimate consumers. On appeal against this negative decision, the General Court had rejected the applicants' pleas that art.107(2)(a) was applicable to the scheme in Joined Cases T–116 and 118/01. It upheld the Commission's reasoning that the article could not apply where only one undertaking was benefiting from the aid in dispute and that it had not been established that the social objectives pursued by that aid could only be achieved by purchasing travel vouchers from that undertaking.

P&O appealed the General Court ruling on the grounds that it was the only **4–005** operator who was prepared to offer the social services in question and so there was no question of discrimination in relation to the origin of the products. In such a case, as the social character of the aid as such was not subject to dispute, art.107(2)(a) was applicable. The Court, however, held that the General Court had not erred in law in its interpretation of this article; the original agreement had

[9] [2006] E.C.R. I–4845.
[10] Cases T–116/01 and T–118/01 *P&O v Commission* [2003] E.C.R. II–2957.
[11] [1999] E.C.R. II–139.

not been concluded to satisfy actual needs, but was made with a view to conferring on P&O an advantage which it would not have obtained under normal market conditions. Hence the aid could not be analysed as having been "granted to individual consumers . . . without discrimination related to the origin of the products" (see paras 129–30 of its ruling). It should be noted that the Court attached little importance to the manner by which the operator was selected in establishing whether discrimination was at issue—the fact that the agreements did not reflect the actual needs of consumers was sufficient.[12] (For a further discussion of the "market purchaser test", see Ch.3.)

In a recent decision on a French plan to grant tax aid to insurers for managing certain supplementary sickness insurance policies, although the French authorities had notified the aid under art.107(2)(a),[13] the Commission concluded, following an in-depth investigation, that the measures failed to meet two of the three conditions laid down in that article (whether the benefits were in fact passed on to individual consumers and whether the measures were non-discriminatory). The Commission concluded that the insurers would be the primary beneficiaries. Further, the terms of the measure risked introducing discrimination in favour of certain incumbents.

It should be remembered that the above exemption will not apply where the aid measure is granted to individual consumers but results in an indirect benefit to the undertaking(s) providing the goods or services in question. This was the case in *Mediaset*,[14] where both the General Court and ECJ on appeal found that subsidies granted by the Italian government indirectly favoured the media conglomerate Mediaset over others. The ECJ upheld the ruling of the General Court, reaffirming its view that:

"the provisions of Article 87(2)(a) EC [107(2)(a) TFEU] would be entirely superfluous if, as Mediaset claims, aid granted in the first place to consumers could never be regarded as State aid for the purposes of Article 87(1) EC [107 TFEU]".

Natural disasters and exceptional occurrences

4–006   Article 107(2)(b) exempts aid to make good damage caused by disasters or exceptional occurrences. This provision has proved of importance in relation to measures to compensate damages caused by natural disasters, such as flooding or earthquake damage. The automatic exemption for aid for damage caused by exceptional occurrences has also been invoked in the air transport sector following the disruptions to air travel caused by the attacks on New York and Washington in September 2001.

---

[12] Nevertheless the Court has ruled that, in general, a tender procedure may be necessary in order to ensure respect for the principle of non-discrimination—see Case C–324/98 *Telaustria* [2000] E.C.R. I–10745, at paras 60–63.

[13] Case N 911/2006 France C(2007) 2198, May 30, 2007.

[14] T–177/07 *Mediaset SpA v European Commission* [2010] E.C.R. II–2341, press release 55/10. Also confirmed by the ECJ ruling in C–403/10 P of July 28, 2011, press release 77/11.

The Commission has attempted to ensure that both these categories of exemption are interpreted narrowly. This is especially true in relation to compensation schemes in the agricultural and fisheries sector where it is frequently alleged by national governments that additional support measures are necessary to compensate for loss of income in these sectors as a result of unforeseen events, such as extreme weather conditions.

In past decisions the Commission has also applied a strict proportionality test: the aid should only compensate and make good the loss or damage actually caused by the natural disaster or exceptional occurrence, and it should not be used for the later industrial development of areas affected by natural disasters—this type of aid measure must be assessed under art.107(3). In addition, the Commission will examine to what extent the victims of a disaster could have been expected to, and have in fact been able to, obtain commercial insurance cover. Reconstruction aid granted some time following natural disasters may also fall to be assessed under art.107(3) as opposed to art.107(2).[15]

The Court has, in Case C–278/00,[16] stipulated that any aid provided under this **4–007** provision must be related solely to the economic disadvantages arising directly out of the national disaster in question and the Advocate General in the same case underlined the need for the Member State to demonstrate a clear and direct link between the natural disaster, the resulting damage caused by the disaster and the proposed compensation.[17]

That only economic disadvantages directly caused by natural disasters or other exceptional occurrences qualify for compensation has also been reaffirmed in Case C–73/03 *Spain v Commission*.[18] There must be a direct link between the disadvantages and the state aid—a reduction in VAT on the sale of farmland was not considered to be linked sufficiently directly to losses caused by an exceptional increase in petrol prices (paras 38–39).

In its Report on Competition Policy for 2005, the Commission noted that it had approved aid for flooding damage in Germany and Austria on the basis of art.107(2)(b) on the following guiding principles. In order to avoid a situation where an enterprise would be better off after receiving aid for a natural disaster, overcompensation had to be strictly ruled out, therefore only material damage caused directly by the natural disaster was considered eligible and the maximum compensation of 100 per cent of these costs was not exceeded in any of the cases. To verify that overcompensation was effectively ruled out, a centralised and institutionalised surveillance mechanism needed to be in place to determine to what extent the damage might have been covered by insurance and to guarantee that the maximum possible support was not exceeded. In all cases the concept of damage was based on re-financing costs and/or interruptions in the production

---

[15] See Decision 91/175 of July 25, 1990 [1991] O.J. L86/23. See also the 8th Competition Report, point 164.
[16] *Greece v Commission* [2004] E.C.R. I–3997.
[17] See Commission Decision relating to flood damage in Austria and Germany and several candidate countries, COM(2002) 481 final, August 8, 2002, p.9.
[18] Judgment of November 11, 2004. [2005] O.J. C6/48.

process and the loss of orders, customers or markets was not considered to be eligible (point 574).

Article 107(2)(c) Federal Republic of Germany

4–008   Although this category of exemption appears to have lost its practical significance,[19] especially since re-unification in 1990, proposals to delete it from the Treaty have not been successful. The Lisbon Treaty provides for a mechanism to allow for the removal of this category five years after the entry into force of that Treaty so that, following a proposal from the Commission, a Council Decision supported by a qualified majority will be required. Since political union between the former East and West Germany on October 3, 1990, the rules on state aid have been fully applicable throughout the united Germany.

Initially, aid granted after political union, but in respect of economic advantages accruing before that date, was approved subject to certain conditions by the Commission.[20] In general, however, the Commission has reviewed and assessed aid measures granted post-1990 under art.107(3).[21] This policy was hardly surprising as to have conceded the argument that aid following re-unification could have fallen under the automatic exemption would have meant that the Commission would have to abandon any attempt to scrutinise and evaluate aid proposals amounting to over 30 per cent of the total state aid budget for the entire Community in the mid-1990s.[22]

4–009   In Case C–156/98,[23] the Court confirmed that art.107(2)(c) TFEU must be construed narrowly. Furthermore, although, following the reunification of Germany, art.107(2)(c) of the Treaty falls to be applied to the new *Länder*, such application is conceivable only on the same conditions as those applicable in the old *Länder* during the period preceding the date of that reunification:

> "Therefore, the 'economic disadvantages caused by that division' can only mean the economic disadvantages caused in certain areas of Germany by the isolation which the establishment of that physical frontier entailed, such as the breaking of communication links or the loss of markets as a result of the breaking off of commercial relations between the two parts of German territory. By contrast, the conception advanced by the German government, according to which Article 92(2)(c) of the Treaty [107(2)(c) TFEU] permits full compensation for the undeniable economic backwardness suffered by the

---

[19] The Commission had already stated in its 20th Competition Report in 1991, at point 131, that it considered that there was no longer any economic justification for continuing to subsidise these areas.

[20] For a good example of the Commission's approach see its Decision 92/465 of April 14, 1992, in respect of land in West Berlin made available to Daimler Benz [1992] O.J. L263/15.

[21] See also the judgment in Case C–242/00 *Germany v Commission* [2002] E.C.R. I–5603.

[22] See further, B. Perry, "State Aids in Former East Germany" [1997] E.L.R. 55–91 and the Commission Competition Reports in the years 1995 and 1996.

[23] [2000] E.C.R. I–6851. See also Case C–334/99 *Germany v Commission* [2003] E.C.R. I–1139.

new *Länder*, disregards both the nature of that provision as a derogation and its context and aims.

The economic disadvantages suffered by the new *Länder* as a whole have not been directly caused by the geographical division of Germany within the meaning of Article 92(2)(c) of the Treaty [107(2)(c) TFEU].

It follows that the differences in development between the original and the new *Länder* are explained by causes other than the geographical rift caused by the division of Germany and in particular by the different politico-economic systems set up in each part of Germany."

In Case C–301/96 of 2003,[24] the German government attempted to challenge the Court's interpretation of the scope of art.107(2)(c). It submitted that in the past that provision was not interpreted by the Commission solely as intended to compensate for the disadvantages resulting directly from the frontier between West and East Germany, but also as intended to overcome the economic consequences of the division of Germany into different economic zones. The Court held that, contrary to the German government's claims, that aid was not granted solely for the benefit of the Saarland and, in particular, the legal basis relied on by the Commission in authorising the aid granted to the Saarland was not clearly stated. As the Advocate General observed in para.71 of his Opinion in Joined Cases C–57/00P and C–61/00P *Freistaat Sachsen v Commission*,[25] art.107(2)(b) and art.107(2)(c) TFEU are mentioned as alternatives; since the Saarland decision relates also to aid in favour of the regions adjoining the Soviet zone and of Berlin, it is not possible to deduce from the reference to art.107(2)(c) of the Treaty that that reference was made solely in respect of the Saarland, as it could have been made only in respect of the regions adjoining the Soviet zone and Berlin.

The Court concluded, at para.80 of its ruling, that: **4–010**

"In any event, whatever the interpretation given by the Commission to Art.92(2)(c) of the Treaty [107(2)(c) TFEU] in the past, that cannot affect the correctness of the Commission's interpretation of that provision in the contested decision and hence its validity."

The application of the regional aid framework and the multisectoral frameworks to the former East German *Läender* is discussed in Chs 15 and 21.

The EEA Agreement

Article 61(2) EEA replicates the provisions of art.107(2) and declares that the **4–011** same categories of aid shall be considered compatible with the functioning of the

---

[24] [2003] E.C.R. I–6857.
[25] [2003] E.C.R. I–9975.

EEA agreement. Prior notification requirements are regulated not by the Agreement itself, as art.62 EEA does not contain a provision equivalent to art.108(3), but by implementing regulations. The EFTA surveillance authority (ESA) has adopted a number of procedural and substantive rules in the field of state aid, incorporating most of the principles as well as guidelines and frameworks adopted in the context of the EU state aid regime. The first set of rules was adopted in January 1994 and has been subject to numerous amendments.

3. ARTICLE 107(3) TFEU

4–012   The category of aid covered by this article may be compatible with the common market, on the condition that the Commission has formally given its approval. The first four categories of aid are subject to control by the Commission, whereas, pursuant to art.107(3)(e) the Council has the power to exempt other categories of aid. It must do so on the basis of a qualified majority upon a proposal from the Commission. The four categories of aid subject to Commission approval are:

- aid to certain severely depressed regions (art.107(3)(a));

- aid to promote the execution of an important project of common European interest or to remedy a serious disturbance in the economy of a Member State (art.107(3)(b));

- sectoral and regional aid which does not adversely affect trading conditions to an unacceptable degree contrary to the common interest (art.107(3)(c));

- cultural aid and aid for heritage conservation where such aid does not affect trading conditions and competition in the Union to an extent that is contrary to the common interest (art.107(3)(d)).

The Commission's discretion

4–013   Article 107(3), by using the word "may," confers considerable discretion upon the Commission, the exercise of which is only subject to marginal review by the European Courts. In examining an aid measure or aid scheme the Commission will assess whether each of the four exemptions listed can be applied to the measure or scheme in question and under what criteria, if any, the aid can be authorised. In its 10th Report on Competition Policy in 1981, at point 213, the Commission stated that in view of the increasing number of aid proposals which it had required to review, it would exercise its discretion not to raise an objection to a proposed aid scheme if that aid contained a compensatory justification. Such a justification would have to take the form of a contribution by the beneficiary over and above the effects of the normal play of market forces to the achievement of the Community objectives contained in the derogations of art.107(3). Thus, distortions of competition could be permitted provided that they are necessary to ensure Community objectives. The national interest of the Member State or the benefits obtained by the recipient should not by themselves justify the positive exercise of the Commission's discretionary powers.

The validity of this approach, which has become known as the "compensatory **4–014** justification" principle, was endorsed by the ECJ in the *Philip Morris* case.[26] In this leading case the Court set out guiding criteria upon which the Commission must base its decision on whether or not to exercise its powers to approve an aid. To a certain extent, the principle is a specific expression of the proportionality principle which is applied in all cases involving an exemption from a basic Treaty principle. Is the objective pursued by the measure necessary and, if so, is this the least distortive method of pursuing that objective?

The exercise of the Commission's discretion implies an assessment of economic, technical and policy considerations, and the Commission should take into account not only the necessity of the aid as a means of achieving economic goals but also relevant social objectives. The socio-economic context to which the Commission must refer is the Community or Union one. Subsequently, the Commission indicated that it would take into account the following factors when reviewing proposed aid plans:

- the aid must promote or further a project that is in the Community interest as a whole;

- the aid must be necessary for the achievement of this result, and the objective could not have been obtained otherwise in its absence;

- the duration, intensity and scope of the aid must be proportional to the importance of the intended result.

The compensatory justification principle

Nevertheless the Commission, and indeed the courts, are not always rigorous **4–015** or particularly systematic in their assessment of the necessity of the measure or in questioning the suitability of alternative approaches. Often the Commission is content to establish that, if large amounts of aid are involved, "a serious and substantial quid pro quo is provided". The recipient must make compensatory arrangements—for example by agreeing to divest loss-making assets—proportionate to the exceptional nature and size of the aid granted. The potential recipient's market strength, however, is not viewed as being a significant element of the analysis in most cases. Two notable exceptions are the criteria applied to assessing aid compatibility under the rescue and restructuring guidelines of 1999, as amended in 2004 (see Ch.24) and the criteria developed under the multisectoral framework of 1998 as amended in 2000 (see Ch.15).

[26] Case C–730/39 [1980] E.C.R. 2671. See also 12th Competition Report.

The Commission's failure to take account of the potential benefits of a proposed re-structuring programme can, however, lead to the annulment of a negative decision.[27] Similarly, the Courts have shown themselves willing to enforce the criterion that the aid should be strictly limited to the minimum necessary for the achievement of purposes recognised in art.107(3)(c).[28] Obviously, the concrete application of the "compensatory justification" principle varies depending on the type and form of aid and the extent and indeed the nature of the "contribution" of the beneficiary or recipient will vary considerably. Aid to a firm in difficulty cannot be declared compatible with the common market on the sole ground that restructuring was envisaged, even if the restructuring proves to be successful.[29]

4–016   In accordance with the policy announced in the State Aid Action Plan (SAAP), published in July 2005, state aid control has become more firmly based on economic analysis. The Commission's assessment of the compatibility of an aid measure or scheme should become more firmly grounded on its wider economic impact, its potential to remedy market failures and its impact on competition in a relevant market, as opposed to its impact on rivals' costs. These concepts are discussed in detail in Ch.2.

The SAAP indicates that state aid may contribute to the common interest in two ways. Firstly, it can alleviate market failure, so that state intervention may improve the functioning of markets when competition, if left to its own devices, is unlikely to produce efficient outcomes in terms of prices, output and uses of resources (the efficiency objective). Secondly, it can bring about more acceptable outcomes in terms of social or regional cohesion (the equity objective). Accordingly the SAAP introduces a general balancing test as a conceptual framework for analysing state aid cases. This test requires an examination of the following elements:

- Does the state aid address a market failure or other objective of common interest?

- Is there an incentive effect—i.e. will the aid affect the behaviour of the recipient in a way which meets the objective?[30]

- Will the aid lead to distortions of competition and trade? and

---

[27] Case C–278–280/92 *Spain v Commission (Hytasa)* [1994] E.C.R. I–4103.

[28] Case T–349/03 *Corsica Ferries France v Commission* [2005] E.C.R. II–02197; Case T–35/99 *Keller v Commission* [2002] E.C.R. II–261 and Case T–110/97 *Kneissl Dachstein* [1999] E.C.R. II–2881.

[29] See Case T–20/03 *Kahla Thuringen Porzellan v Commission* [2008] E.C.R. II–2305, upheld on appeal C–537/08P, December 16, 2010.

[30] In any event, aid paid towards an investment or project which had already been commenced without the aid will usually not meet the "incentive effect test"; see T–162/06 *Kronopoly* [2009] E.C.R. II–1, paras 74 and 75, appeal dismissed in Case C–117/09, June 24, 2010. See also T–126/99 *Graphischer Machinenbau GmbH v Commission* [2002] E.C.R. II–2427, paras 37, and 41–44.

● Given the magnitude of the positive and negative effects, is the overall balance positive?

The expiry of a number of important horizontal guidelines in the period after 2005 allowed the Commission to incorporate this new balancing test into revised versions, commencing with the 2006 framework for research and development and innovation,[31] and the risk capital guidelines.[32] In Case T–21/06 *Germany v Commission*,[33] the General Court confirmed that the Commission could rely on the concept of market failure to assess the compatibility of an aid in its Decision of 2006, adopted shortly after the publication of the SAAP, on aid for the introduction of digital terrestrial television broadcasting.

The market failure test

The first case notified under the new 2006 R&D Guidelines, *NeoVal*, gave the **4–017** Commission the opportunity to test its new approach.[34] *NeoVal* concerned a French aid granted to Siemens for the development of a new generation of metro trains. This detailed and extensive decision illustrates how the Commission applies the four stages of the balancing test. Two further cases notified in December 2006, *Projet Bernin 2010*[35] and *TVMSL*,[36] also illustrate the Commission's approach to the "market failure" test.

The question of whether the beneficiary is prepared to contribute a "substantial quid pro quo" or what that contribution might entail would seem to be of, at best, secondary importance in this type of analysis.[37] At the same time the requirement that a potential beneficiary will take on additional obligations—for example environmental improvements beyond those required by national and Community standards—is a relevant factor for assessing a proposed environmental aid scheme in a positive light (see Ch.22)[38] and the revised guidelines on risk capital, discussed below, still seem to reflect the notion of compensatory justification in the context of market failure, even if these particular guidelines depart from the usual approach to calculating eligible costs and linking the level of the aid to be approved to those costs.

---

[31] [2006] O.J. C323/1.

[32] [2006] O.J. C194/2.

[33] T–21/06 *Germany v Commission* [2009] E.C.R. II–00197. See also T–8/06 *FAB Fernsehen aus Berlin GmbH v Commission of the European Communities* [2009] E.C.R. II–00196.

[34] N 674 / 2006, Soutien de l'Agence de l'innovation industrielle en faveur du projet NeoVal [2007] O.J. FFBC120/50.

[35] Commission Decision of July 10, 2007 in case N 887/2006, *Bernin 2010* [2007] O.J. C200/50.

[36] Commission decision N854/2006 Soutien de l'agence de l'innovation industrielle en faveur du programme mobilisateur pour l'innovation industrielle TVMSL [2007] O.J C182/50.

[37] Indeed it is not even considered by the UK's OFT in its proposals of November 2005; see OFT, "European State Aid Control", OFT 821.

[38] See also EFTA case nr 68330, [2011] C182/07 concerning aid to Troms Kraft for a wind park, for a detailed application of the test.

The 2001 version of the Risk Capital Communication had already defined the term market failure as:

"a situation in which economic efficiency is not achieved owing to imperfections in the market mechanisms. A market failure may manifest itself either in the inability of the system to produce goods which are wanted (in this case a risk capital market) or by a miscalculation of resources, which could be improved in such a way that some consumers would be better off and none would be worse off".

Further, the term "market failure" was reserved for cases where it is believed that a "serious misallocation of resources has occurred" (see paras VI.2 and VI.3 of the Risk Capital Communication, 2001).[39] The 2001 Communication was in fact innovative in a number of ways and departed from the then dominant approach to compatibility assessment, based on per se rules and aid intensity tests.[40]

The main thrust behind the introduction of a more refined economic approach in the SAAP has been to make the positive and negative implications of the state aid measure at issue more explicit and to ensure a more systematic assessment of these positive and negative effects. Decision practice following the adoption of the SAAP, as well as the revised horizontal guidelines, indicate that the Commission will examine the incentive effect on the basis of a counterfactual analysis, comparing the levels of intended activity with and without the aid. The Member State may therefore have to provide substantial information which goes beyond an analysis of the aid intensity. It can therefore be seen as a more refined application of the necessity and proportionality tests, which, as already recognised by the Courts, must be applied consistently. Nevertheless, the implementation of a more rigorous economic approach may require access to extensive information and therefore this in turn depends on the willingness of the Member State and the potential beneficiary to co-operate with the Commission.

4. The Specific Provisions

4–018 As already indicated in the introduction to this chapter, the Commission's approach to the regulation of different types of sectoral[41] and horizontal[42] aid schemes are analysed in detail in the following chapters. In this section only the

---

[39] [2001] O.J. C235/3, p.8.

[40] For an overview of the development of the Communication and subsequent Guidelines, see Horacek and Jarosz-Fritz, "Risk Control", Ch.5, in Mederer et al, *EU Competition Law: State Aid* (Claeys and Casteels: 2008).

[41] See for example, C–40/2005 *Ford Genk* [2006] O.J. L366/32; Case C14/2006 *General Motors Antwerp* [2007] O.J. L243/71 and Case N 322/2003, *Fiat Auto* [2003] O.J. C284/36.

[42] T–162/06 *Kronopoly* [2009] E.C.R. II–1, paras 65, 66, 74 and 75; Case C–390/06 *Nuova Agricast Srl v Ministero delle Attività Produttive* [2008] E.C.R I–2577.

general principles are outlined, and certain categories of horizontal aid are discussed.

Article 107(3)(a)

Regions covered by this paragraph are those suffering from abnormally low-living standards or serious underemployment, where the per capita gross domestic product does not exceed 75 per cent of the Community's average in purchasing power. In *Phillip Morris*,[43] the Court stressed that, in assessing regional aid schemes, the local standards of living and unemployment levels must be measured against a Community-wide standard. For the new Member States the position is slightly different—the 10 Member States which acceded in 2004, as well as Bulgaria and Romania, acceding in 2007, were initially all accorded art.107(3)(a) status on accession.   **4–019**

As the Court has recalled:

"the words 'abnormally' and 'serious' in Article 87(3)(a) [now 107(3)(a)] shows that the exemption only concerns areas where the economic situation is extremely unfavourable in relation to the Community [Union] as a whole. The exemption in Article 87(3)(c) [107(3)(c)] on the other hand, is wider in scope inasmuch as it permits the development of certain areas in a Member State which are disadvantaged in relation to the national average without being restricted by the economic conditions laid down in Article 87(3)(a) [107(3)(a)] provided such aid does not adversely affect trading conditions to an extent contrary to the common interest: Conversely the fact that the condition is not mentioned in the exemption under Article 87(3)(a) [107(3)(a)] implies greater latitude in granting aid to undertakings in regions which do not meet the criteria laid down in the exemption. Nevertheless the difference in wording between Article 87(3)(a) [107(3)(a)] and Article 87(3)(c) [107(3)(c)] cannot lead to the conclusion that the Commission should take no account of the Community [Union] interest when applying Article 87(3)(a) [107(3)(a)], and that it must confine itself to verifying the specifically regional impact of the measures involved, without assessing their impact on the relevant market or markets in the Community [Union] as a whole. In such cases the Commission is bound not only to verify that the measures are such as to contribute effectively to the economic development of the regions concerned, but also to evaluate the impact of the aid on trade between member states, and to assess the sectoral repercussions they may have at Community [Union] level."[44]

Regional policy was the first area in which the Commission developed guidelines for the discipline of state aids and by 1988 the Commission had developed   **4–020**

[43] Case 730/39 [1980] E.C.R. 2671.
[44] Case C–113/00 *Spain v Commission* [2002] E.C.R. I–7601, at paras 65–67; Case C–114/00 *Spain v Commission* [2002] E.C.R. I–7657, at paras 78–80; see also Case T–152/99 *Hijos de Molina (HAMSA) v Commission* [2002] E.C.R. II–3049, at para.205.

a separate Communication on the method for the application of art.87(3)(a) and (c) (now art.107(3)(a) and (c)) to national regional aid.[45] The version of the guidelines adopted in 1998 covers the period 1998 to 2006. The most recently amended version, adopted in 2006, applies from 2007 to 2013. The guidelines apply to every sector of the economy, apart from fisheries, the coal industry, transport and shipbuilding. The agricultural sector is still singled out for special treatment, in respect of so-called Annex I products. Regional aid is also totally prohibited for some sectors, including steel and synthetic fibres.

Regions falling under art.107(3)(c) are those with more general development problems in relation to the national as well as the Community situation. With respect to para.(c) the Commission has traditionally applied two alternative primary tests which enable regional problems to be assessed in a Community context. The two alternative tests applied at the national level are income (measured by GNP or gross valued added) and structural unemployment. Thus, in a wealthier Member State the disparities between the region and the state should be considerable to justify the aid. Hence the areas where regional aid is allowed are generally referred to as Assisted Areas (Aas). Tier 1 Aas are considered under art.107(3)(a) and Tier 2 Aas are considered under art.107(3)(c). The application of art.107(3)(a) and (c) to less-developed areas is now dealt with entirely under the relevant regional aid guidelines and is discussed in full in Chs 15 and 21–013, as are the substantial recent revisions to the multi-sectoral framework and the guidelines. One of the main objectives of the last review of the RAG was to attain better coherence between the Commission's regional policy and its competition policy objectives.[46]

4–021 The extent to which certain aid schemes could still benefit from exemption under art.107(3)(a) irrespective of their wider sectoral effects has now been fully clarified, and circumscribed, by the Courts. In Case C–189/91 *Cook*, the Court held that the Commission could not exempt a national aid scheme on the basis of art.107(3)(a) if the aid package in question would have repercussions on a sector already in overcapacity. In Case C–169/95 *Spain v Commission*, the Court confirmed this approach at para.20 of its judgment. In general, however, the weight given to the advantages of aid is likely to vary according to the derogation applied, so that a greater distortion of competition can be accepted in the case of the most disadvantaged regions covered by art.107(3)(a) than in the case of those covered by art.107(3)(c).[47] Case law and relevant Commission practice is discussed further in Chs 15 and 21 on regional aid.

It may also be noted that a key feature of a number of earlier horizontal aid frameworks (e.g., environmental aid, research and development) and the now-expired Block Exemption Regulations is that they allowed higher allowances for projects in designated problem regions—a so-called regional bonus. If special

---

[45] [1988] O.J. C212 of August 12, 1988.

[46] Commission Communication to the Member States on the links between regional and competition policy [1998] O.J. C90/7.

[47] Case T–380/94 *AIUFFASS and AKT* [1996] E.C.R. II–2169, at para.54.

status under art.107(3)(a) or (c) was lost then the entitlement to these additional benefits under the existing horizontal frameworks was also lost. A different approach is now pursued under the General Block Exemption Regulation in so far as regional aid and aid for SMEs are treated separately so that there is no possibility for increasing intensities of SME aid by reference to a regional bonus.[48]

It has been commented that the combined effects of the Lisbon Agenda and **4-022** enlargement could shape EU Cohesion Policy and state aid control policy in ways which have significant implications for those problem regions of Member States who no longer have Assisted Area status under art.107(3). On the one hand the competitiveness agenda—i.e. the Lisbon Agenda—promotes horizontal policies that favour the development of all regions, but using policy instruments where the impact and uptake is likely to be higher in the more prosperous regions; on the other hand, the future of EU Cohesion Policy, and with it regional aid control, targets assistance at the least-prosperous regions. The net effect of this "pincer movement" may be to create a policy vacuum for those regions that are neither well placed to benefit from policies based on innovation or other horizontal priorities, nor yet sufficiently disadvantaged to qualify for regional aid per se.[49] This problem may be exacerbated by the abandonment of earlier Commission policy initiatives to introduce a "significant impact test" which might have introduced some flexibility for regional differentiation. At the same time it should be noted that certain levels of regional investment aid to SMEs can be awarded without prior notification under the General Block Exemption Regulation.

In Case T–184/97 *BP Chemicals*,[50] the General Court upheld the Commission's finding that an aid to a particular enterprise cannot be brought under the derogation provided for in art.107(3)(a)—such aid must be assessed on the basis of art.107(3)(c). In its judgment in Case T–27/02 *Kronofrance v Commission* of December 1, 2004, the Court annulled the Commission's decision approving aid to Glunz AG on the grounds that the Commission had analysed only data on capacity utilisation and not also whether the relevant market was in decline by using data on apparent consumption. Glunz appealed against the ruling, claiming that the General Court infringed art.107(3) TFEU, since it interpreted incorrectly the multi-sectoral regional aid framework for large investment projects, and thereby disregarded the discretion enjoyed by the Commission in drawing up and applying that Community framework. Moreover, it was claimed that the Court's economic assessment, namely that aid in a shrinking market is known to create substantial risks of distortions of competition even if there is no overcapacity in

---

[48] See Commission Regulation (EC) No 800/2008 of August 6, 2008 declaring certain categories of aid compatible with the common market in application of arts 87 and 88 of the Treaty (General Block Exemption Regulation) [2008] O.J. L214/3, art.15.

[49] F. Whislade, European Policies Research Centre Paper, 2006, p.26.

[50] [2000] E.C.R. II–3145.

the sector concerned, was wrong.[51] The General Court's ruling was however upheld in Joined Cases C–75/05P and C–80/05P of September 28, 2008.[52]

Article 107(3)(b)

4–023   Article 107(3)(b) contains two quite distinct derogations: aid to promote the execution of a project of common European interest, and aid to remedy serious disturbances in the economy. This latter derogation has been used as a basis for a series of decisions and guidelines to deal with state aid to the financial sector and to the "real economy" following the global financial crisis of 2008.

4–024   **Projects of common European interest.** This phrase is not defined. It has been suggested that the use of the term "European interest" may also be taken to mean that the project may also be of interest to non-EU European states. The participation of all Member States in the project is not required for an aid to fall within the exception. A project carried out in one single Member State may be deemed to be in the common interest, although aid to a single company in a particular sector is unlikely to qualify.[53] The Commission has a wide discretion in its assessment. It has considered the possible application of art.107(3)(b) to the creation of national emission trading schemes pre-dating the Community scheme,[54] but it has declined to consider aid to promote technological advances leading to greater energy efficiency as qualifying under this provision.[55] In the past, aid to common European projects such as the development of HDTV, the manufacture of aircraft and aircraft parts, as well as projects relating to energy resource diversification, have been considered under this provision and aid under the JESSI programme. Aids awarded by the French government in the framework of the MEDEA +/EUREKA programme were approved under art.107(3)(b). The aid amount was estimated at €76 million and would cover up to 50 per cent of the eligible costs of French companies involved in collaborative research projects with institutions from other Member States.[56]

4–025   **Aid to remedy a serious disturbance.** The disturbance in question must affect the whole of the national economy, and not merely one sector or region. Aids under this derogation are only granted in exceptional circumstances.[57] Aids aimed at dealing with the deterioration in the balance of payments in France in 1968 were authorised under art.109 EC (now art.131 TFEU) and not under this

---

[51] Case T27/02 *Kronofrance v Commission* [2004] E.C.R. II–4177.
[52] Joined Cases C–75/05 P and C–80/05 P *Federal Republic of Germany and Others v Kronofrance SA* [2008] E.C.R. I–06619.
[53] See further, the Commission decision of January 26, 2001 in Case A340–500/600, French repayable advances to the Airbus programme.
[54] UK Emission Trading Scheme 2002. See Ch.20 "State Aid in the Energy Sector".
[55] Joined Cases 62 and 72/87 *Glaverbel v Commission* [1988] E.C.R. 153. See also Case C–148/04 *Unicredito Italiano* [2005] E.C.R. I–1137, at paras 71–72, 74–77, 79 and 82–83.
[56] See B. Allibert, *Competition Policy Newsletter*, No.2, June 2002, pp.67–8.
[57] 2nd Competition Report, 1972, point 120.

exemption. Prior to 2008, the only time the Commission considered that an aid scheme remedied a serious disturbance in the economy of a Member State was in 1991 when aid for a privatisation programme in Greece was approved.[58] In this decision the Commission noted that the privatisation programme was an integral part of the undertakings given under Council Decision 91/306 of March 4, 1991 concerning the recovery of the Greek national economy.[59] The Commission has been reluctant to repeat this exercise,[60] and its decision to extend the exemption granted under Council Decision 91/306 was successfully challenged in Joined Cases T–447, 448 and 449/93.[61]

In Case C–730/79 *Philip Morris* the Court ruled that an aid could not fall within this exception if it leads to the transfer of an investment which could have taken place in another Member State which is in a less favourable situation.[62]

In Case C–301/96 *Germany v Commission*,[63] the German government attempted to rely upon art.107(3)(b) to justify aid to a factory in former East Germany, but the Court ruled that this derogation can only be relied on to deal with serious disturbances which threaten the entire national economy, and not particular regions. In this context, the General Court has also ruled that the disturbance must affect the whole of the economy of the Member State concerned, and not merely that of one of its regions or parts of its territory. This, moreover, is in line with the need to interpret strictly any derogating provision such as art.107(3)(b) TFEU.[64]

The scope of art.107(3)(b) was put to the test in late 2008, as discussed in greater detail in Ch.19 para.19–031. In a series of decisions concerning aid to the financial sector in the early months of the financial crisis, the Commission maintained a strict approach to the interpretation of this provision.[65] The Commission has adopted a series of guidelines based on art.107(3)(b) to address state aid to the financial sector as well as state aid to the "real economy" to facilitate access to finance, also referred to as the "Temporary Framework".[66] Aid to the

---

[58] State Aid NN 11/91,

[59] For an example of a decision refusing to apply art.107(3)(b) to aid argued to be required to remedy the serious disturbances which have arisen as a result of German unification, see the Commission's Notice regarding state aid to the Opel Group [1993] O.J. C43/14.

[60] e.g. Decision 94/1068 [1994] O.J. L385/1.

[61] [1995] E.C.R. II–1971.

[62] At 342.

[63] [2003] E.C.R. I–9919.

[64] Joined Cases T–132/96 and T–143/96 *Freistaat Sachsen, Volkswagen AG and Volkswagen Sachsen GmbH v Commission* [1999] E.C.R. II–3663, para.167.

[65] Commission Decision 98/490/EC in Case C–47/96 *Crédit Lyonnais* [1998] O.J. L221; Commission Decision 2005/345/EC in Case C–28/02 *Bankgesellschaft Berlin* [2005] O.J. L116, points 153 et seq.; and Commission Decision 2008/263/EC in Case C–50/06 *BAWAG* [2008] O.J. L83, point 166. See Commission Decision in Case NN 70/07 *Northern Rock* [2008] O.J. C43/51, Commission Decision in Case NN 25/08 *Rescue aid to Risikoabschirmung WestLB* [2008] O.J. C189 and Commission Decision of June 4, 2008 in state aid C–9/08 *Sachsen LB* [2009] O.J. L104.

[66] Since July 1, 2010, however, the Commission has applied tighter conditions for the compatibility of government guarantees under art.107(3)(b) TFEU. See Directorate General Competition Commission Staff Working Document of April 30, 2010: "The application of State aid rules to Government Guarantee schemes covering bank debt to be issued after 30 June 2010".

financial sector is discussed in detail in Ch.19. The following sections deal with the Temporary Framework and the related Communication on the crisis and the European automobile industry.

The Temporary Framework[67]

4–026   In view of the dimension of the crisis and the difficulties to find credit faced by all types of companies (SMEs and large companies), the Commission adopted the Temporary Community Framework for state aid measures to support access to finance in the current financial and economic crisis (the "Temporary Framework") granting Member States additional ways to deliver finance to enterprises affected by the credit squeeze. As the Temporary Framework states in its opening recitals, these additional possibilities are justified to remedy a serious disturbance in the economy and may be declared compatible with the common market on the basis of art.107(3)(b). The aims of the Temporary Framework are intended to unlock bank lending and facilitate access to finance and to encourage companies to invest in sustainable growth.

The Commission nevertheless remains in favour of a horizontal approach which benefits the whole economy. Consequently, the Commission holds that the proposed aid instruments are the most appropriate ones to achieve the general objectives and that there is no need to single out a sector. Accordingly, apart from the exclusion of fisheries and primary agricultural production, the Framework makes no such distinction. To avoid distortions in the market, the Temporary Framework only applies to companies whose difficulties did not pre-date the crisis and firms with structural difficulties due to their own inefficiencies are expected to restructure in accordance with the standard rules—i.e. the 2004 Rescue and Restructuring Guidelines.[68] In addition, all measures approved under the Temporary Framework must be necessary, appropriate and proportionate to remedy a serious disturbance of the economy as well as respecting in full the various supplementary conditions set out in the Framework itself: see Box 1.

Box 1: The Temporary Framework

The temporary measures as applicable until the end of 2010 were deemed to pursue two objectives:

- to unblock bank lending to companies and thereby guarantee continuity in their access to finance; and

- to encourage companies to continue investing in the future, in particular in a sustainable growth economy, including the development of green products.

[67] [2009] O.J. C16/1.
[68] [2004] O.J. C244/2.

The specific aid instruments to meet those objectives included:

- a lump sum of aid up to €500,000 per company;

- state guarantees for loans at a reduced premium;

- aid in the form of a subsidised interest rate applicable to all type of loans; and

- subsidised loans for the production of green products involving the early adaptation to, or going beyond, future Community product standards.

In addition to the new measures, the Framework provided for a temporary derogation from the Risk Capital Guidelines[69] in order to increase the tranche of finance per target SME (from €1.5 million to €2.5 million) and a reduction of the minimum level of private participation (from 50 per cent to 30 per cent); and a simplification of the requirements of the Export Credit Insurance Communication[70] to use the exemption that allows temporarily non-marketable risks to be covered by the state.

On February 25, 2009, after having gained some experience with the application of the Temporary Framework, the Commission introduced some further technical adjustments.[71] In particular, with respect to the conditions of compatibility for guarantees, the Commission adopted a new grid which adjusts the guarantee safe-harbours according to different levels of collateralisation. Moreover, in addition to the reduction of the annual guarantee premium of two years, the revised safe-harbour premiums contained in the grid could be applied for another eight years without reduction. Finally it should be noted that the Temporary Framework contains additional rules on cumulation. The aid ceilings set out in the Framework are applied regardless of the source of the aid—i.e. whether it is financed by national or Community resources. At the same time the temporary aid measures may be cumulated with other compatible aid or other forms of Community financing providing that the maximum aid intensities indicated in the relevant guidelines or block exemptions are respected.   **4–027**

Individual Decisions

The Commission adopted rapid decisions in cases where the notifications were complete and the conditions of the Temporary Framework respected. By April 2009 the Commission had authorised 24 measures under the Temporary Framework.   **4–028**

An interesting feature of the Temporary Framework is the special provision made for production of green products. Three schemes were approved for France,

---

[69] See below at para.4–054.
[70] See below at para.4–048.
[71] The Consolidated version is published in [2009] O.J. C72/1. A further amendment relating to the agricultural sector was introduced in October 2009.

the United Kingdom and Spain, the latter scheme being aimed specifically at the car sector (see below). The French scheme was notified on January 9, and approved on February 3, while the UK scheme was approved on February 27, some 17 days after notification. The Spanish scheme, notified on March 3, was approved on March 30.

The speed with which such schemes have met with approval, even considering the substantial sums involved—the two UK measures for guarantees and interest rate subsidies for production of green products allowed for a combined risk exposure of €8 billion—has prompted concerns of mere rubber stamping.

In view of the high volatility of financial markets and the uncertainty about the economic outlook, the Commission approved the prolongation of certain measures, with certain adjustments, as set out in the Temporary Framework until December 31, 2011, claiming that this is justified by market conditions. This is also the case for temporary aid for the production of green products as the Commission considers that firms are still finding it difficult to gain access to finance for the production of more environmentally friendly products due to the financial and economic crisis.[72]

The automobile sector

4–029   In a Communication on "responding to the crisis in the European automobile industry" issued on February 25, 2009,[73] the Commission outlined its overall strategy to tackle the specific problems besetting the European car sector. This Communication distinguishes between traditional state aid measures—including environmental aid, aid for R&D and Innovation, regional aid and risk capital, as well as rescue and restructuring measures—and aid that is directly linked to the financial crisis (see Annex 2 of the Communication). The latter type of measures include subsidised interest rates and in particular subsidised loans for the production of green products. The Communication provided a positive framework for subsidies for more environmentally friendly cars and permitted Member States to introduce scrapping schemes. The Commission would not however permit any form of territoriality clause—i.e. that national aid would only be available to car manufacturers committing to invest in the Member State or to source their components from suppliers located in their territory.[74]

Article 107(3)(c)

4–030   This exemption, concerning aid to facilitate the development of certain economic activities or of certain economic areas, is the most important discretionary exemption to the general prohibition on state aids contained in art.107. It is also the most frequently applied exception. Although there is some overlap between

---

[72] [2011] O.J. C15/5.
[73] Com (2009) 104 final.
[74] See IP 09/1929 of December 15, 2009 and MEMO 09/50, MEMO/09/90 and MEMO/09/460 relating to various national measures to limit aid to companies active in a particular territory.

art.107(3)(a) and (c), it should be emphasised that the latter potentially offers more scope to the Member State seeking to justify the aid, even though the recent case law of the ECJ has tended to narrow the distinction between the two subsections (see further, Ch.21 on regional aid).

In Case 248/84 *Germany v Commission*,[75] the Commission stated that para.(a) was not applicable since the region in question enjoyed favourable economic conditions when compared to the rest of the Community. Nor was para.(c) satisfied because unemployment in the particular areas did not vary greatly from the average in Germany as a whole. The Court rejected this approach. It held that para.(c) gave the Commission power to authorise aid intended to promote economic development in areas of a Member State that are disadvantaged in relation to the national average. Paragraph (c) thus offers further possible justifications when compared to para.(a). This places a premium upon the value of the interpretation of "common interest" as expressed in the first sentence of art.107(3)(c) as a safeguard.

Article 107(3)(c) covers sectoral aid as well as regional aid. Two constraints are placed upon the Commission's discretion to approve aid. First, the aid must "facilitate development of certain economic activities or of certain economic areas". Secondly, the regional or sectoral aid must not adversely affect trading conditions to an extent contrary to the common interest.[76] The amount of aid does not constitute a criterion for assessment laid down by art.107(3)(c).[77]   **4–031**

An aid does not facilitate development of an activity if the development would have occurred without the aid. Aid will not be approved where market forces provide a better means of ensuring the development in question, or where it was in an undertaking's own interest to bring about the proposed investment. This results from the application of the compensatory justification principle, discussed above.

The purpose of the aid must be the development of the sector or the regions in   **4–032**
question, and not only of particular undertakings within it.[78] In Case 84/82

---

[75] [1987] E.C.R. 4013.

[76] Despite the slight difference in terminology between the different language versions of art.107(3)(c) the Court has stressed that a qualitative assessment of the effect of an aid on competition is sufficient. In Case 47/69 *France v Commission* [1970] E.C.R. 487, the Advocate General suggested that, while the French and Italian texts supported a "quantitative" interpretation, the German and Dutch versions supported a "qualitative" evaluation, since they require that the measures should not disturb trading conditions to an extent contrary to the common interest. See Case T–214/95 *Het Vlaamse Gewest* [1998] E.C.R. II–0719, at para.88.

[77] See, however, the Commission's decision in State Aid C 5/2004 *Aid in favour of Kronopoly GmbH*, in which the Commission refused to approve an increase in aid as this would not provide any incentives for regional development. See T–162/06 [2009] E.C.R. II–1 and on appeal, Joined Cases C–75/05P and C–80/05P [2008] E.C.R I–06619.

[78] See in this context State Aid N 492/2004 *Regional development aid in favour of SABIC* [2005] O.J. C176—despite its ad hoc nature the Commission found that the aid was compatible as the Dutch authorities had demonstrated that the investment would have a sizeable effect on the whole region, which had been traditionally closely connected with the chemical industry. The fact that the investment concerned headquarters and not production capacity did not alter this assessment.

Germany v Commission[79] the Advocate General was of the opinion that the Commission ought not to have authorised the grants to certain weak undertakings when the market sector as a whole was quite healthy.[80]

Aid must not adversely affect trading conditions to an extent contrary to the common interest.[81] The Commission has stated that this provision requires it to balance the beneficial effects of the aid against the adverse effects on trading conditions and the maintenance of undistorted competition.[82] The Court appeared to follow a different line of reasoning in Case 47/69 *France v Commission*,[83] where it assessed the extent to which trading conditions were liable to be adversely affected independently of the benefits expected to flow from the aid. Even if the objective pursued was worthwhile, at a certain point disruption of the market must be judged contrary to the common interest.

Cultural aid

4–033   Article 107(3)(d) applies to "aid to promote culture and heritage conservation where such aid does not affect trading conditions and competition in the Union to an extent that is contrary to the common interest". It is interesting to note that this provision, unlike art.107(3)(c), makes the eventual grant of an exemption subject to an assessment not only of its effect on trade but also on competition.

The preservation and promotion of cultural diversity are expressed to be among the founding principles of the European models incorporated in art.167 TFEU, which states that:

"The Union shall contribute to the flowering of the cultures of the Member States, while respecting their national and regional diversity and at the same time bringing the common cultural heritage to the fore." Article 167(4) states that: "The Union shall take cultural aspects into account in its action under other provisions of this Treaty, in particular in order to respect and to promote the diversity of its cultures."

In accordance with Commission practice the cultural derogation is interpreted restrictively and is limited to measures for specific projects which are related to the national notion of culture. It is furthermore the rule that the notion of culture

---

[79] [1984] E.C.R. 1451.
[80] ibid. at 1505.
[81] In its notice concerning aid to SCA Aylesford, a manufacturer of newsprint in the UK ([1993] O.J. C46/5), the Commission indicates that it has taken note of certain peculiarities of competition and trade in the newsprint sector, which limit the effect of the proposed aid on trading conditions between Member States. The UK imported three-quarters of its consumption of newsprint, but almost 90 per cent of total imports came from third countries, mainly Sweden, Finland, Norway and Canada. For this and other reasons, the proposed aid was approved.
[82] 14th Report on Competition Policy, 1984, point 202.
[83] [1970] E.C.R. 487.

must be applied to the content and nature of the work or publication, and not the medium or its distribution per se.[84]

The application of this derogation to a French measure concerning aid for **4–034** various schemes to promote the dissemination of books in the French language, including subsidies for the export of small orders of French language books, was considered by the General Court in two separate cases—Case T–49/93 *SIDE v Commission*, and in a second ruling, Case T–155/98 *CELF*.

The original French measure had not been notified but the Commission, having reviewed the measure, declared it to be compatible aid as it satisfied the conditions for derogation under art.107(3)(d) in a decision of 1993. SIDE, a competitor, filed an action for annulment and the Court quashed the first decision on the grounds that the Commission had not based its decision to approve the aid without opening a full investigative procedure on the basis of art.108(2) on adequate grounds. The Commission was therefore obliged to reconsider the matter and adopt a new decision in 1999.[85] The same competitor challenged this decision on a number of grounds, inter alia, on the ground that the Commission had committed a manifest error of assessment in defining the reference market, and hence the effect of the measure on competition. It argued, successfully, that the relevant market was specifically the export agency market, and not that for the export of French language books in general. The Court did not doubt the cultural purpose of the aid measure, but found that the Commission had confused the market for a product—books—with that in issue, the market for a service, namely the service provided by export agencies. Thus the Commission did not carry out a genuine assessment of the effect of that aid on competition, or therefore, any serious assessment as to whether the aid complied with the conditions set out in art.107(3)(d). The Court agreed and held that the Commission should have examined the effects of the contested aid on competition and trade between other operators carrying out the same activity as that for which the aid was granted. Hence it annulled the relevant part of the Commission decision relating to the aid to small orders.[86] The finding of compatibility with regard to the rest of the aid schemes was, however, upheld as the purpose of that aid was to pursue cultural aims.

The Commission was therefore required to adopt a new decision on the aid to **4–035** CELF in respect of small export orders and did so on April 20, 2004.[87] The Commission notes in its second decision that, in addition to the obligations to promote the principles of cultural diversity as enshrined in art.167, the Treaty requires the Union and the Member States to promote cultural diversity in their international relations as a contribution to, inter alia, a dialogue between cultures. The French scheme met the objectives of the Treaty. It then went on to consider

---

[84] See, for example, N 355/05 *Slovak Republic*, aid in favour of a periodical, C(2005) 4457.
[85] Decision 1999/133 of June 10, 1998 [1999] O.J. L44/37.
[86] T–155/98 *Société internationale de diffusion and d'édition (SIDE) v Commission* [2002] E.C.R. II–1179.
[87] Commission Decision 2005/262 EC [2004] O.J. L85/27.

the application of art.107(3)(d) and reasoned, following an extensive examination of the conditions of competition on the relevant market (the export agency business) that the effect on trade and the distortion of competition at Community level are very limited in this particular case.[88] Hence, the measure in question was not contrary to the common interest, and the action taken by the French authorities was proportional to the objective pursued. It simply made it possible for some of the demand, which would not otherwise have been met, to be met by the service provider without worrying about profitability. Interestingly the fact that the main beneficiary of the contested scheme, CELF, had initially enjoyed an exclusive right to profit from it, was not seen as a cause for concern. The Commission reasoned that the scheme had been initiated to remedy the failings of a market abandoned by the industry. Hence it was not surprising that even after the scheme was opened to other participants, the market share held by CELF remained very large. Furthermore, the Commission considered that CELF's position on the market in question had no direct bearing on the granting of aid. In its view it was solely concerned to check the compatibility of the aid on the export agency market under art.107(3)(d).

In its judgment of April 15, 2008 the Court of First Instance (now General Court) in Case T–348/04 annulled the last sentence of art.1 of the aforementioned Commission Decision 2005/262,[89] which had declared the aid to be compatible with the common market under art.107(3)(d). It reasoned that the Commission had committed an error of law with respect to the part of the aid paid to CELF prior to November 1, 1993, the date of entry into force of the Treaty on European Union, by considering that the aid at issue was compatible with the common market by virtue of former art.87(3)(d) (now art.107(3)(d)) when the substantive law in force prior to November 1, 1993 should have been applied. It further concluded that the Commission had failed to take into account the actual costs of processing small orders but estimated these costs on the basis of the total costs borne by CELF and hence had not adequately demonstrated the absence of overcompensation.[90]

Forms of cultural aid

4–036   The Commission's position on the compatibility of state aid to the cinematographic and audio-visual sectors was first set out its 2001 Communication on certain legal aspects relating to these sectors.[91] The general approach is based on

---

[88] The Commission relied on the CFI's ruling in Case T–64/94 *Ladbroke Racing Ltd* [1998] E.C.R. II–1, at paras 152–162.

[89] Case T–348/04 *SIDE v Commission* [2008] E.C.R. II–625.

[90] On December 14, 2010, the Commission issued Decision 2011/179/EU [2011] O.J. L78/37. In its decision it reaffirmed the Court's view that the aid had a cultural purpose for the purposes of art.107(3)(d), but nonetheless found the aid to be incompatible with the internal market because it did not fulfil the criterion of proportionality. In the meantime in Case C–1/09 of March 11, 2010 the ECJ dealt with a number of issues relating to recovery in these complex proceedings. See Ch.26.

[91] [2002] O.J. C43/04.

two criteria: (a) respect of the general legality criterion; and (b) specific compatibility criteria for state aid to cinema and TV programme production. The Communication stated that the specific compatibility criteria would remain valid until June 2004. National aid schemes for the two sectors were authorised until the same deadline.[92]

The so-called "Cinema Communication" makes reference to four compatibility criteria:

- the aid must be directed to a cultural product. Each Member State must ensure that the content of the aided production is cultural according to verifiable national criteria;

- in respect of film production, the producer must be free to spend at least 20 per cent of the film budget in other Member States without suffering any reduction in the aid provided for under the scheme. In other words, the Commission can accept as an eligibility criterion territorialisation in terms of expenditure of up to 80 per cent of the production budget of an aided film or TV work;

- the aid intensity must not exceed 50 per cent of the production budget with a view to stimulating normal commercial initiatives. Difficult and low budget films are excluded from this list. In addition, documentaries or short and animated audiovisual works may be eligible for higher aid intensities; and

- aid supplements for specific film-making activities are not allowed in order to ensure that the aid has a neutral incentive effect and, consequently, the protection/attraction of those specific activities into the Member State granting the aid is to be avoided.[93]

Following a consultation exercise on these specific criteria, the Commission considered whether revision was necessary. While most participants expressed their support for the existing rules, the Commission considered that, although the volume of aid provided did not give rise to concerns, the use of the so-called "territorialisation" clauses in certain schemes was a source of concern. These clauses impose on producers an obligation to spend a certain amount of the film budget in a particular Member State as an eligibility condition for receiving the full aid amount. They therefore constitute a breach of the free movement rules. However, the Commission considered, and indeed continues to maintain, that these clauses could be justified under certain circumstances and within the limits set out in the Communication in order to ensure the continued presence of human

[92] COM(2004) 171, final of March 16, 2004 [2004] O.J. C123.
[93] For an assessment of the application of these four criteria, see N 368/05, Spain, aid for the promotion of audiovisual works in Andalucia, H/2005/1716, September 29, 2005; N692/2006, December 20, 2006, *German Film Fund*; N340/2007, aid for theatre etc., in the Basque country, July 18, 2007.

skills and technical expertise required for cultural creation. The Commission therefore decided to extend the current rules until June 30, 2007, subject to an extensive analysis of the effects of existing aid schemes (particularly in the film sector) that closed in 2008. The rules were again extended for a further period up until December 31, 2012. In preparation for this date the Commission launched a public consultation geared towards reviewing the criteria used to apply EU state aid rules to Member States' financial support for making and distributing films. The Commission has also published an issues paper identifying areas for reflection, such as competing to attract major film productions using state aid, and supporting activities other than production,[94] and invited interested parties to submit their comments by September 30, 2011.

Aid to the broadcasting sector

4–037   The Commission first published a Communication on the application of the state aid rules to public service broadcasting in November 2001. The Communication was revised in 2009. This Communication and the related decision-making practice of the Commission are considered in detail in Ch.18. It may, however, be noted here that the Communication stipulates that in applying art.107(3)(d) the Commission will interpret the notion of culture restrictively. The educational and democratic needs of a Member State have to be regarded as distinct from the promotion of culture, although education may have a cultural aspect. Hence, a restrictive interpretation of art.107(3)(d) in this context means that a Member State should clearly define the extent of the cultural remit when entrusting a public service broadcaster with a cultural mission, and any aid should be clearly linked to cultural component of the public service broadcasting requirement.

Council authorisation in exceptional circumstances

4–038   **Article 107(3)(e).** This article provides for the creation of other "discretionary exceptions" to the general prohibition on aids. Thus, "other categories of aid" may be specified by a decision of the Council acting by a qualified majority on a proposal from the Council. It should be noted that this article only permits the Council to create new categories of exceptions from the basic prohibitions of art.107—the application of the state aid rules to such categories is entrusted to the Commission.[95] Nor is the Council empowered to declare specific aids compatible with the common market.[96]

The Council has now adopted a number of directives under the provisions of this article, including the shipbuilding directives discussed in Ch.16, and the

[94] Available at *http://ec.europa.eu/competition/consultations/2011_state_aid_films/index_en.html* [Accessed August 23, 2011].

[95] Case C–31/94 *Ijseel-Vliet BV* [1996] E.C.R. I–5023, at para.27.

[96] Subject, of course, to its competence under art.88 to intervene prior to the adoption of a negative decision by the Commission, see below.

rules now applicable to the coal sector after the expiry of the ECSC Treaty, discussed in Ch.14.

Article 62(d) EEA. This article contains a similar provision, and provides for discretionary exemption "for other categories of aid as may be specified by the EEA Joint Committee in accordance with Part VII". Part VII deals with the institutional provisions of the EEA. The role and functions of the Joint Committee, which is in charge of the management of the Agreement and settlement of disputes under it, are set out in arts 92–94 EEA.[97] This Committee therefore cannot be equated with the Council, which has the power of decision under art.107.

4–039

Article 108(2). The third sub-paragraph of this article provides that the Council may in exceptional cases decide that aid which the state is granting or intends to grant shall be considered compatible with the common market, in derogation from the provisions of art.107 or any Regulations as provided for in art.109. Where the Commission has already initiated the contentious procedure provided for in art.108, this will have the effect of suspending that procedure until the Council has made its attitude known. If it does not do so within three months, the Commission shall give its decision in the case. It would seem that an application by a Member State is not possible after the Commission has taken a decision refusing authorisation of an aid.[98]

4–040

Case C–110/02 *Commission v Council*[99] concerned aid granted by Portugal to its pig-farming sector. The Commission declared most of the aid to be incompatible with the common market and had ordered recovery in two decisions adopted in 1999 and 2000. The Council, on the application of the Portuguese government, subsequently adopted a decision declaring aid which the Portuguese government intended to pay to the farmers who had been required to repay the illegal aid following the earlier Commission decisions to be compatible with the common market. The Commission challenged the latter measure on the grounds that the Council had exceeded its competence, or alternatively that the Council had committed a manifest error of appreciation in concluding that there were exceptional circumstances as required in the third subparagraph of art.108(2).

The Court held at paras 31 et seq. of its ruling that:

4–041

"It follows that, as the Commission has rightly pointed out, the power conferred upon the Council by the third subparagraph of Article 88(2) EC [now 108(2) TFEU] is clearly exceptional in character.

---

[97] See generally, S. Norberg, "The Agreement on a European Economic Area" (1992) 6 C.M.L. Rev. 1171.

[98] See further, Advocate General Mayras, in Case 70/72 *Commission v Germany* [1973] E.C.R. 813 at 835. A similar procedure is provided for in the application of the EEA state aid rules—see sixth amendment to the procedural and substantive rules in the field of state aid [1996] O.J. L241/41.

[99] Judgment of June 29, 2004 [2004] E.C.R. I–6333.

In such a context, the further provisions in the third and fourth subparagraphs of Article 88(2) [108(2)], whereby, on the one hand, application to the Council by a Member State suspends examination in progress at the Commission for a period of three months, and, on the other, in the absence of a decision by the Council within that period, the Commission is to give a ruling, undeniably indicate that, where that period has expired, the Council is no longer competent to adopt a decision under that third subparagraph in relation to the aid concerned. The taking of decisions the operative parts of which might contradict is thereby avoided.

The enactment of a temporal limitation of that kind on the Council's competence where the Commission has already opened the procedure under the first subparagraph of Article 88(2) EC [108(2)], without, however, yet having adopted a decision declaring the aid incompatible with the common market, and the fact that, at the end of the three-month period laid down by the fourth subparagraph of that provision, the Commission alone retains the competence to rule on the aid concerned, also demonstrate that, if the Member State concerned has made no application to the Council under the third subparagraph of Article 88(2) EC before the Commission declares the aid in question incompatible with the common market and thereby closes the procedure referred to in the first subparagraph of Article 88(2) [108(2)], the Council is no longer authorised to exercise the exceptional power conferred upon it by the third subparagraph in order to declare such aid compatible with the common market."

It may be observed on that latter point that, in Case C–122/94 *Commission v Council* [1996] E.C.R. I–881, the contested decision of the Council did not follow a Commission decision declaring aid incompatible with the common market; the Commission in that case having merely taken the view on the basis of art.108(3) that the aid project in question was not compatible with the common market and opened the procedure laid down by the first subparagraph of art.108(2).[100]

As for the argument of the Portuguese Government that the third subparagraph of art.108(2) TFEU also authorises the Council to rule on aid which a Member State is "granting", whereas in accordance with art.108(3) any "grant" of aid requires precisely that the Commission should have expressed a view on it first, so that the Council has the power to rule on aid which has already been the subject of a previous decision by the Commission, the Court finds that this argument arises from a contradiction in terms. It cannot concomitantly be argued that an aid which a Member State is "granting" within the meaning of the third subparagraph of art.108(2) TFEU is an aid which must necessarily have been

---

[100] The Advocate General, while recognising that the Court had confirmed in Case C–122/94 *Commission v Council* [1996] E.C.R. I–881 that the Council enjoyed a substantial margin of discretion in determining whether and when exceptional circumstances exist which would justify it in authorising a given aid, was of the view that any difficulties encountered by undertakings in reimbursing the aid could not be qualified as exceptional.

previously declared compatible with the common market by the Commission, pursuant to the provisions of art.107 TFEU, and that the Council has the power subsequently to declare such an aid compatible with the common market in derogation from those provisions.

In a series of cases concerning a Council decision on the basis of art.108(2) in respect of a Belgian fiscal scheme it was argued by the Council that the solution upheld in Case C–110/02 could not be applied as the Council had authorised a new aid, distinct from that held to be incompatible with the common market by the Commission. The Court did not accept this line of argument and, recalling its ruling in Case C–110/02, held that the Council was not entitled to adopt the contested act.[101]

4–042

5. THE REGULATION OF CERTAIN CATEGORIES AND TYPES OF AID

General

As state aid control has evolved over the past decades, the Commission's assessment of particular horizontal and sectoral categories of aid has been codified into various frameworks and guidelines as well as Block Exemptions and now the General Block Exemption Regulation. These different measures are discussed in detail in the following chapters in Parts II and III (and IV) of this book. In the remainder of this section we will consider the Commission's approach to various types of aid. Many guidelines have now been revised in the context of the SAAP of 2005. In line with the Commission notice on the determination of the applicable rules for the assessment of unlawful state aid,[102] in the case of non-notified aid, the Commission applies the most recent version of the relevant set of guidelines if the aid was granted after their entry into force and the then prevailing set of guidelines in all other cases. With regard to notified measures, however, the Commission applies the most current set of published guidelines, even if the state measures in question were notified prior to their publication.

4–043

Export aid

Export aid has always been viewed as undesirable and will not be regarded as a candidate for exemption. In exceptional circumstances it may be permitted in the context of safeguard measures under art.66 TFEU. Otherwise, the Commission has maintained a general policy line that export aid can never be permitted, irrespective of its intensity, purpose or form. This tough line has not led to the eradication of this form of aid however.

4–044

---

[101] Case C–399/03 *Commission v Council* [2006] E.C.R. I–5629. See also Case C–182/03 *Belgium v Commission* [2006] E.C.R. I–5479.
[102] [2002] O.J. C119/22.

Export aid may take a number of forms including tax rebates on exports or refunds of levies on exported goods. The promotion of national goods through state supported trade fairs or other forms of publicity campaigns or trade-penetration programmes may also amount to a form of export-related aid for certain undertakings or products within the meaning of art.107(1). Export aids for shipbuilding are covered by the specific regulations applying to that sector (see Ch.16). Neither the General Block Exemption Regulation nor the de minimis Regulation apply to export aid.

Export aid to third countries

4–045   Initially the Commission took a more lenient approach to various forms of export aid for products and services to third countries even though, strictly speaking, such aid could distort competition by placing exporters based in one Member State in a better position to export to a third country than other exporters based in other Member States, as the ECJ had recognised in Case 142/87 *Tubemeuse*.[103] Nevertheless, the approach was to a certain extent justified because trade to third countries is covered by the specific rules of the Treaty relating to external trade policy, i.e. art.206 TFEU (ex art.131 EC), which provides for the harmonisation of the rules on export aid. The Commission was also aware that it would harm the interests of Community exporters when many of their competitors were not subject to similar control by an external body.

4–046   Further progress on limiting export aid has in the meantime been made at both WTO level with the agreement on and adoption of the ASCM as well as a result of the adoption of certain OECD measures, and in particular the OECD Arrangement as well as bilateral free trade agreements which contain so-called "substantive WTO+" rules on subsidies on goods that are enforceable through bilateral dispute settlement procedures with commercial sanctions, as in the case of the EU–Korea FTA[104] (see Ch.6). The Court's ruling in Case C–44/93 *Namur*[105] also called into question the legality of various factors distorting competition between public and private insurers and confirmed that the Commission could take action to secure the withdrawal of existing aid schemes relating to export aid to third countries. In its ruling in Joined Cases T–304/04 and T–306/04 *WAM*[106] the General Court annulled a decision concerning export aid to a large Italian firm in the context of a nationally funded programme for trade penetration into non-EU countries (mainly South-East Asia), on the grounds that the Commission had not sufficiently reasoned its case that the measure had an effect on trade in the European Union.

The ECJ dismissed the Commission's appeal. It held that:

---

[103] [1990] E.C.R. I–959.
[104] See further, A. Jarosz-Friis, N. Pesaresi and C. Kerle in *Competition Policy Newsletter*, no.1, 2010, pp.78–83.
[105] [1994] E.C.R. I–3829.
[106] Joined Cases T–304/04 and T–316/04 *WAM* [2006] E.C.R. II–64, and see also Case T–34/02 *Le Levant 001* [2006] E.C.R. II–267.

"It follows from the above that the Court of First Instance (now General Court), when it held in substance in paragraphs 62 to 76 of the judgment under appeal that the Commission should have carried out a more detailed analysis of the potential consequences of the aid at issue on intra-Community trade and on competition and should have given additional information, in the contested decision, concerning those effects, did not intend to depart from the case-law cited above but to take into account the specific circumstances of the case, and it cannot be accused of erring in law in this respect. Furthermore, that conclusion is not invalidated by the arguments advanced by the Commission with regard to the findings of the Court of First Instance (now General Court) in paragraph 74 of the judgment under appeal. Those findings on the examination of the interdependence between EU and Far Eastern markets relate to the possibility of an indirect effect on trade and intra-Community competition, such as that referred to principally in the *Tubemeuse* judgement. While it is true that the examination of such interdependence cannot be required if it is demonstrated that the State aid directly affects the intra-Community markets, it must however be held that the contested decision, as has been confirmed in the preceding paragraphs of this judgment, does not adequately demonstrate this" (see paras 65–66).[107]

The Commission has, however, consistently condemned aid to promote foreign direct investment in third countries unless the aid is directed at initial productive investments carried out by SMEs. Aid for FDI is likely to strengthen the beneficiary's overall financial and strategic position and affect its relative position vis-à-vis its competitors in the European Union.[108] Aid for trade promotion activities is not considered as productive investment. Aid to large enterprises or their subsidiaries is unlikely to benefit from exemption.[109] The Commission's decisions in the *Cordex*,[110] *Orfama*[111] and *Djebel*[112] cases confirm that this strict policy has been continued in the light of the objectives of the SAAP 2005. In the absence of specific guidelines on aid to FDI projects, the Commission bases its assessment on art.107(3)(c). The Commission has examined in these cases whether the aid was necessary in view of the international competitiveness of the EU sector concerned and/or in view of the risks involved for investment projects in certain third countries, and has then balanced the positive and negative effects. In *Cordex* there was no evidence of any market failures associated with the project, based in Brazil, and the aid could have had a significant impact on the EU market for ropes and twines given that a large proportion of the Brazilian products were imported into the European Union. Oframa, a producer of fashion

4–047

---

[107] Case C–494/06 P *Commission v Italy and WAM* [2009] E.C.R. I–3639.
[108] Case 77/99, *Austrian lifts* [1999] O.J. L142/32. German guarantees for investments in Poland, [1997] O.J. L102/36.
[109] See further, G. Perini, "No export aid to large firms outside the EU", *Competition Policy Newsletter* 2005 No.2, pp.69–70.
[110] C36/2004 [2007] O.J. L156/23.
[111] C41/2004 [2007] O.J. L183/46.
[112] C4/2006 [2007] O.J. L219/30.

knitwear, acquired two companies located in Poland. Portugal notified a fiscal incentive for the benefit of Orfama. As Orfama had concluded the project before applying for the aid, there was no evidence of any incentive effect. The investment was essentially a consolidation of a previously existing commercial relationship and the necessity of the aid had not been demonstrated. The final case concerned an investment for a hotel in Brazil which again had been initiated before the aid had been granted. This decision can be contrasted to an earlier case involving Portuguese aid for hotel investments in Brazil where the recipient had a weak market position.[113]

Export Credit Insurance

4–048   In 1997 the Commission adopted a Communication on Short-term Export Credit Insurance.[114] The Communication draws a distinction between marketable and non-marketable risks. Short-term credit is now frequently provided by both private and public sector insurance companies and is therefore seen as a marketable risk, in comparison to the provision of long-term risk credit insurance. This latter activity is covered by the OECD Arrangement. The Communication recalls that any form of export aid to Member States remains strictly prohibited. Nevertheless, with respect to medium- and long-term export credit insurance the Commission policy was to check that the OECD Arrangements had been complied with—even if they concerned intra-Community trade. This was primarily the responsibility of DG Trade and not DG Competition, however. In the course of 2005, and following two complaints, the Commission was required to consider the legality of various export credit arrangements granted by the French government via the French agency for export credit to the Finnish electricity producer TVO for the purchase of equipment from the French company Areva/Framatome. A formal procedure was opened to investigate, inter alia, the total costs of the loans conformed to market practice. The OECD Arrangement was considered to offer some guidance but was not conclusive in this respect. Hence compliance with the Arrangement is a necessary but not a sufficient condition under the European state aid regime. As the Commission cleared the transaction as market-conform, it did not examine further the interaction between the OECD framework and the European state aid rules.[115]

The 1997 Communication was to apply for a period of five years from January 1, 1998 to December 31, 2002. In 2001, the Commission adopted an amendment to the 1997 Communication (the "2001 amendment") concerning the definition of "marketable risks" which may not be covered by export-credit insurers with the support of the state.[116] The 2001 amendment also extended the validity of the

---

[113] [2004] O.J. L61/76.
[114] [1997] O.J. C281/4.
[115] C45/2006 France, construction of a nuclear power station [2008] O.J. L89/15.
[116] [2001] O.J. C217/2.

1997 Communication until December 31, 2004. The validity of the 1997 Communication was further extended until December 31, 2005 by a Communication adopted by the Commission in 2004.[117]

Although the Commission has indicated that the definition of marketable risks is not immutable and may be reviewed on the expiry of the 1997 Communication, as amended, so far it has not chosen to amend that definition. However, due to the unavailable or insufficient cover in the majority of Member States of export-credit insurance offered by private insurers to small companies with a limited export turnover (which is caused by no or very low profitability reflecting an insufficient spread of foreign countries/buyers and lack of education and knowledge of the complexities of export-credit insurance among such companies, and the related transactional costs) the Commission is prepared to consider their export-related risks as temporarily "non-marketable" in those Member States where there is no adequate cover by the private market.[118] Hungary was the first country to make use of the amended para.2.5.[119] The Commission envisaged to revisit this matter in three years after the entry into force of the latest amendment, i.e. on December 31, 2009. The validity of the 1997 Communication was extended until December 31, 2010,[120] and again until December 31, 2012.[121]

The Commission has also modified its policy on short-term export credit as a result of the current financial and economic crisis, and has concluded that while a lack of insurance or reinsurance capacity does not exist in every Member State, it cannot be excluded that, in certain countries, cover for marketable risks could be temporarily unavailable.

The Temporary Framework and Export Credit Insurance

As discussed at para.4–048, above, exceptional rules for short-term export credit were introduced for both large firms and SMEs at point 4.4 of the above Communication, which states that: **4–049**

" ... In such circumstances, those temporarily non-marketable risks may be taken on to the account of a public or publicly supported export-credit insurer for non-marketable risks insured for the account of or with the guarantee of the State. The insurer should, as far as possible, align its premium rates for such

---

[117] [2004] O.J. C307/12.
[118] See the new, amended point 2.5 of the 1997 Communication which entered into force on January 1, 2006.
[119] See Commission Decision No C 29/2007 [2007] O.J. L239/51.
[120] [2005] O.J. C325.
[121] See Communication of the Commission amending the period of application of Communication of the Commission to the Member States pursuant to art.93(1) of the EC Treaty applying arts 92 and 93 of the Treaty to short-term export-credit insurance, available at *http://eur-lex.europa.eu/LexUriServ/LexUriServ.do?uri=OJ:C:2010:329:0006:0006:EN:PDF* [Accessed August 16, 2011].

risks with the rates charged elsewhere by private export-credit insurers for the type of risk in question.

Any Member State intending to use that escape clause should immediately notify the Commission of its draft decision. That notification should contain a market report demonstrating the unavailability of cover for the risks in the private insurance market by producing evidence thereof from two large, well-known international private export-credit insurers as well as a national credit insurer, thus justifying the use of the escape clause. It should, moreover, contain a description of the conditions which the public or publicly supported export-credit insurer intends to apply in respect of such risks. If the Commission finds that the conditions for the use of the escape clause are fulfilled, its decision on compatibility is limited to two years from the date of the decision, provided that the market conditions justifying the use of the escape clause do not change during that period. Furthermore, the Commission may, in consultation with the other Member States, revise the conditions for the use of the escape clause; it may also decide to discontinue it or replace it with another appropriate system."

In this context, in order to speed up the procedure for Member States, the Commission considers that, until December 31, 2011, Member States may demonstrate the lack of a market by providing sufficient evidence of the unavailability of cover for the risk in the private insurance market. Use of the escape clause will in any case be considered justified if:

(a) a large well-known international private export-credit insurer and a national credit insurer produce evidence of the unavailability of such cover; or

(b) at least four well-established exporters in the Member State produce evidence of refusal of cover from insurers for specific operations.

The Commission, in close cooperation with the Member States concerned, will ensure swift adoption of decisions concerning the application of the escape clause.

Operating aid

4–050   Operating aid usually takes the form, in particular, of tax exemptions or reductions in social security, or other forms of aid which are not linked to eligible investment costs.[122] As such the general rule is that operating aid is prohibited except under very exceptional circumstances as provided for in specific guidelines, such as for example the guidelines on environmental aid of 2001 and 2008

---

[122] For a detailed assessment of what constitutes operating costs as opposed to investment costs see the EFTA decision in Case no.68330 *TromsKraft*, March 16, 2011.

(see Ch.22).[123] If the aid cannot be approved under these guidelines it is likely to be declared incompatible.[124]

In Case T–162/06 *Kronopoly* the General Court recalled that:

"Thus it appears that, in the circumstances, the Commission was right to hold that the aid at issue did not require the beneficiary either to pay consideration or to contribute to an objective in the common interest and that, in consequence, it was operating aid intended to cover the normal running costs that Kronopoly had to bear and, as such, could not be authorised. It should be borne in mind in that regard that, as a rule, operating aid—that is to say, aid which is intended to release an undertaking from costs which it would normally have to bear in its day-to-day management or normal activities—distorts the conditions of competition (see Case C–156/98 *Germany v Commission* [2000] E.C.R. I–6857, para 30)."[125]

Even if it is deemed permissible under exceptional circumstances, this type of aid should always be temporary and reduced over time. Operating aid granted to a Dutch hazardous waste disposal plant to cover the costs associated with early closure of certain installations was approved in Commission Decision C–43/03.[126]

Investment aid measures

Investment aid which is primarily intended to increase production or to enable **4–051** a firm to undertake modernisation or innovation that it would be expected to undertake in the normal course of its business will rarely qualify for exemption and, indeed, is most likely to be viewed as a form of operating aid. Such aid invariably adversely affects trade between Member States and is not in the common interest and cannot usually be justified under the "compensatory justification principle", unless the aid in question is given for a purpose recognised in one of the horizontal guidelines—such as, for example, in connection with restructuring aid or for environmental aid or energy efficiency objectives. Nevertheless, allowable investment aid is still subject to increasingly stringent conditions under the horizontal guidelines. The Regional Aid Guidelines draw a distinction between initial investment and replacement investment and the latter, as a form of operating aid, is only authorised under certain conditions, discussed in detail in Ch.15.

---

[123] See for example, C24/2009 Austrian Green Electricity Act, IP 11/265 of March 8, 2009. A planned exemption from the requirement to purchase green electricity for energy intensive businesses was considered to be operating aid and does not trigger environmental benefits. The aid has subsequently been declared incompatible; IP/11/265 of March 8, 2011, and [2011] O.J. L235/42.

[124] See for example, C1/09, Aid granted by Hungary to MOL Nyrt [2011] O.J. L34/55, at p.69.

[125] [2009] E.C.R. II–1, at paras 74–75.

[126] Aid in favour of AVR [2006] O.J. L84/37.

The dividing line between new and replacement investment is not always easy to discern, certainly in earlier Commission decisions.

Investment aid schemes

4–052   Since the late 1980s the Commission has attempted to ensure the abolition of a large number of general investment schemes—that is, general schemes which empower a national government to intervene to provide financial support in any sector at any time, and provide it with general budgetary powers in this respect. In 1991, for example, the Commission required the abolition of a Dutch aid scheme which allowed the National Investment Bank to provide loans for expansion and investment in companies which could not otherwise obtain such financing from other banks. It was held that this scheme provided general investment aid that does not qualify for any of the exceptions under art.107(3). A French system of industrial policy loans to firms which was not dependent on regional or sectoral criteria, was approved however, on the condition that individual proposed grants were notified in advance and that all aid was restricted to areas eligible for regional aid.

Regional aid and operating aid

4–053   Certain derogations from the more general principles in relation to allowable operating aid are further specified in the guidelines in the case of outermost regions, insofar as it is intended to offset the additional costs arising in pursuit of economic activity from the factors identified in art.349 TFEU, the permanence and combination of which severely restrain the development of such regions and in least-populated regions, insofar as it intended to prevent or reduce the continuing depopulation of those regions. In addition, in both these types of regions, aid which is not both progressively reduced and limited in time and which is intended to partly offset additional transport costs may also be authorised under certain conditions and provided that systematic overcompensation is avoided.[127]

Operating aid should, even if it is to be permitted under exceptional circumstances, only be granted in respect of a predefined set of eligible expenditures or costs—e.g. replacement investments, transport costs or labour costs, and should be limited to a certain proportion of those costs. "Modernisation investment aid" is distinguished from initial investment aid; modernisation aid usually involves replacement aid and is hence deemed to be operating aid. (See further, Ch.15—large investment projects.)

Risk capital

4–054   Risk capital measures are not usually related to specific purposes but are usually forms of capital injections, which are as such difficult to transpose into

---

[127] See, for a further elaboration of these derogations, para.81 of the guidelines on regional aid for 2007–13, discussed in Ch.21.

the jargon of eligible costs and permissible aid intensities. Risk capital is defined as equity financing to companies in their start-up and development phases. The term "venture capital" refers to risk capital provided by specialised investment funds—venture capital funds. These funds usually provide a mix of equity, mezzanine and subordinated loan finance. In response to pleas for more scope to introduce risk capital measures in order to compete with the stronger venture capital market that had emerged in the US in the late '90s, the Commission was required to devise an assessment methodology that was not linked to eligible costs. The first Communication on risk capital of 2001[128] placed strong emphasis on the need to address market failure as a criteria for authorising aid. The provision of risk capital also played an important role in the context of the Lisbon Strategy. A final version of the current guidelines was published on July 19, 2006. In general these guidelines promise a more flexible approach to allow Member States to better target their risk capital measures to the relevant market failure. They also encourage private investors to co-invest with the state. Importantly, the guidelines contain a more refined economic approach to the assessment of risk capital measures, in line with the SAAP of 2005. The current guidelines will cease to be valid on December 31, 2013.

Potential state aid and its eventual compatibility is assessed at three different levels: at the level of the intermediary vehicle or fund; at the level of the investors; and at the level of the enterprises invested in (the investees). If funds are made available on the same terms as those applying to private investors there is no aid.[129]

Application of the 2001 Guidelines

- **Aid at the level of the fund.** If the fund is merely a vehicle for the transfer of aid to investors and/or investees (i.e. target companies), then the fund is not usually viewed as being an aid recipient. If the fund, however, can function as an independent business, and especially in cases involving existing funds with numerous and diverse types of investors, then there may also be aid at the level of the fund.[130]

4–055

- **Aid at the level of the investors.** An aid solely at the level of the investors would not necessarily be treated favourably as it conflicts with the basic goal of the Communication, which is to overcome market failures at the level of the investees. State aid at both the level of the investors and the investees is the most usual constellation; these measures allow investors to participate in the equity of a company on terms more favourable than would have been the case in the absence of state intervention. If the participation

---

[128] [2000] O.J. C235/11.
[129] See N 344/2005, Spain [2006] O.J. C14/12; N 677/2002, Austria [2003] O.J. C148/8; N 403/2002, Austria [2003] O.J. C138/4.
[130] See N 711/2001, UK, Community Investment Tax Credit [2003] O.J. C18/38.

is open to all investors, however, the selectivity criteria may not be met and therefore there is no aid at this level, but only to the investees.[131]

- **Aid at the level of the investees/enterprises.** In a few cases the Commission held that this is the only level at which aid is present, given that the fund is merely a vehicle for the transfer of aid to the investees and the measure is open to all potential investors.[132] Note that the Communication does not apply to debt financing in favour of investees—this has to be assessed on the basis of the Commission notice on the methods for setting the reference and discount rates. This method may also be applied for quasi-equity financing.[133]

4–056　If aid at any or all of these levels is established the Commission assessed the measure in accordance with the criteria set out in ss.VI, VII and VIII of the Communication.

The following criteria were provided for assessing compatibility:

(1) a "safe harbour" for transactions below certain levels (depending on whether the recipient is located in an art.107(3)(a) or (c) region or another area);

(2) above the stipulated levels, there is a need to prove market failure—the aid must be proportionate to the market failure and must minimise distortion; and

(3) additional compatibility criteria are expressed as "positive" and "negative" elements which are to be taken into account.

The Commission presumed the presence of a market failure in the form of an equity gap, without the Member State being required to prove it, where each tranche of finance for an enterprise from risk capital measures, which are in turn wholly or partially financed through state aid, will contain a maximum of €500,000 (€750,000 or €1 million in art.107(3)(a) and (c) regions respectively).[134] The compatibility of the measure must nevertheless be established. If higher tranches are granted the Commission has usually opened a formal investigation.[135] State aid in the form of risk capital cannot be granted to large enterprises, or firms in the shipbuilding, coal and steel sectors. If a potential

---

[131] See N 212/2004, Germany [2005] O.J. C95/8.

[132] See N 306/2004, Ireland [2005] O.J. C37/48.

[133] See German ERDF Venture Capital Funds, N 212/2004 [2005] O.J. C95/8; see also N 698/2002, Germany [2004] O.J. C78/31, debt financing a the level of the fund was assessed under the Communication.

[134] Separate injections of capital within six months of each other are considered to be part of the same tranche, as would different injections over a longer period, if a commitment is made as part of a single transaction; see fn.27 of the Communication and see also N 632/2003, Belgium [2005] O.J. C223/2.

[135] State Aid C 17/2004—UK, Enterprise Capital Funds [2006] O.J. C91.

scheme to encourage risk capital investment does not exclude these undertakings, then the Commission has refused to approve the scheme as notified.[136]

Initially, the Commission took the view that the "safe harbour" had been the **4–057** most important element of the Communication but it must also be observed that this was one of the first Communications to incorporate a concept of "market failure" and to allow a potentially more flexible approach than the traditional guidelines, perhaps at the expense of certainty and predictability.[137] However, the Commission also recalled in the Communication that a departure from the traditional "eligible costs"-based approach, which it still sees as the best guarantee of legal certainty as well as equality of treatment, could also enhance the risk of accepting operating aid, which it continues to view as a highly distortive form of aid.

On the basis of the criteria stipulated at Pt VIII.3 of the 2001 Communication, the Commission took a favourable view of risk capital measures. Seven compatibility criteria are stipulated here—they are not, however, cumulative but are "positive and negative" elements. Not all have equal weight, but the most important are listed first. No single element is essential, however. Indeed, this method gives the Commission substantial flexibility. Aid is assessed favourably if it is targeted to small and medium-sized companies, but to date no Commission decision has approved the provision of risk capital to large enterprises on the basis of the Communication. The decision to invest should be profit-driven. Any element that indicates that the investment decisions will be commercially driven will be regarded as positive. The level of distortion of competition between investors and between investment funds should be kept to a minimum. Sectoral state measures, particularly in sensitive sectors suffering from overcapacity, are judged less positively and national measures must exclude the provision of aid to the shipbuilding and steel and coal sectors. The existence of a business plan and an exit mechanism for the state's direct or indirect involvement will be positively regarded. Finally the possible accumulation of aid measures to a single enterprise should be avoided. This can be problematic in practice as accumulation presupposes the same eligible costs.

The 2001 Communication also set out rules for partnership projects between **4–058** public and private actors. Where a transfer is made by the state and the Commission took the view that the measure provides a minimum incentive to other economy operators, i.e. investors, to make that same transfer, then the aid should be authorised, even if technically an aid to the investors is also involved. Hence, the Commission approved partnership schemes in N 497/2001, Grants for Owner Occupation in Scotland,[138] as well as aid from Saxony-Anhalt in favour of

---

[136] See the Commission Decision C2/2009 on the German Law to Modernise the General Conditions for Capital Investments [2010] O.J. L6/32.
[137] See for the first application of the Communication, the Commission Decision on the UK's Regional Venture Capital Funds in England, CPN 3/2001, pp.72–3; See also Viridian Growth Fund (2001).
[138] [2002] O.J. C32/18.

technology centres that was targeted at the enterprises using the services of the centres.[139]

The revised guidelines of 2006

4–059   Following a consultation in 2006, the Commission made known that it was considering reviewing the safe harbour thresholds and also providing clearer guidance on the definition of "quasi-equity" and rules for mezzanine financing. In general, an important element for positive assessment of risk capital measures is the level of private involvement in order to avoid "crowding out" private resources. Further flexibility on the requisite level of private participation was probably also to be expected. As the 2001 guidelines limited the aid to early financing phases it was contemplated that the new version would take a more lenient view on the provision of capital to certain types of enterprises, such as SMEs, at later stages. At the same time certain forms of state aid in the form of risk capital may fall within the scope of the General Block Exemption Regulation (arts 28 and 29), as discussed in Ch.11.

The balancing test

4–060   The balancing test as outlined in the SAAP is composed of three steps; the first two relate to the positive effects (aim of measure and potential for delivery of objective) and the last (proportionality) to the negative effects. In the 2006 guidelines the Commission indicates that this test is equally relevant for the design of *ex ante* rules. Risk capital measures should be targeted at dealing with the equity gap and are necessary to stimulate private risk capital investment. With regard to the negative effects the Commission proposes to deal with the risk of crowding out and an oversupply of public risk capital. The Commission also proposes to differentiate the thresholds of aid that may be considered necessary depending on the targeted beneficiary, degree of involvement of private investors, the business stage financed, the business sector concerned and the size of the beneficiary. It may be noted that the Commission appears to assume that the provision of risk capital is always in response to a market failure and therefore, at least in the initial assessment of the measure, the market economy test, as discussed at Ch.8, para.8–018 is seldom applied.[140] The Commission appears to have been more willing to apply the test in the second phase if there is information available that private investors have committed equivalent or higher amounts of investment to the funds in question. This was the case in Commission Decision N330/2006 *Berlin Kapital Fonds* and Commission Decision N194/2006 *Screen East Investment Fund (UK)*, June 7, 2006.[141]

---

[139] N 318/2003—Germany [2004] O.J. C67/9.

[140] See for examples where there was no aid involved, Decision N511/2002 *Sardinia*, September 17, 2003. Decision N500/2007 *Technology Sectors Fund*, Berlin, December 12, 2007 (no advantage to the investors in the fund and no advantage to the SMEs).

[141] See more generally, L.S. Morais and M.S. Ferro, "Risk Capital as State Aid" in [2011] EStaL, Vol.10, nr 3, pp.425–432.

The Communication focuses on aid schemes as opposed to ad hoc measures. It is intended to encourage the provision of risk capital to SMEs as defined in the Commission Regulation 70/2001 as last amended by Regulation 364/2004. The risk capital measure must provide at least 70 per cent of its total budget in the form of equity and quasi-equity investment instruments into target SMEs.

The terms "equity" and "quasi-equity" are now defined. The provision of investment tranches beyond the heightened safe harbour threshold of €1.5 million per target SME are now permitted provided the necessary evidence of market failure is submitted and these are proportionate to the size of the target SME.

Further, follow-on investments into target companies that already received aided capital injections to fund subsequent financing rounds beyond the safe harbour thresholds and the companies' early growth financing may also be permitted if this is necessary to avoid dilution of the public participation in these financing rounds while ensuring continuity of financing for the target enterprises so that both public and private investors can fully benefit from the risky investment. Again, account is taken of the specificities of the targeted sector and enterprises and follow-on investment may be authorised provided it is proportionate to the initial investment and to the size of the fund.[142]

In one of its first decisions under the 2006 guidelines, the Commission asked **4–061** and approved aid to Investbx, an innovative regional platform or fund for raising capital for SME's in the UK's West Midlands, and conducted a detailed in-depth assessment on the basis of s.5 of the Guidelines, in which it examined the existence of a market failure that is targeted by the proposed measure. The Commission found that state aid would be provided to Investbx on conditions that would not meet the private investor test, and there would further be state aid to target SMEs. As any investor could use Investbx, the measure was not selective at this level. The primary objective of the aid to Investbx was to address a market failure in financing SMEs due to imperfect or asymmetric information. It further considered that the measure was well targeted and proportional and that the negative effects on competition were limited given that the target SMEs must be located in a particular region, and the aid was granted for a maximum of five years and was subject to a limit of £2 million per SME.[143]

The Temporary Framework and Risk Capital

In the light of the financial crisis, the Commission had relaxed certain of the **4–062** above rules under the Temporary Framework,[144] discussed above at para. 4–026. Following its review of that Framework, the Commission announced that the temporary adaptations of the Risk Capital Guidelines gave a positive signal to

---

[142] See IP/06/1015 and Memo 06/295, July 19, 2006.
[143] Commission Decision 126/2008 of December 20, 2006 on the aid to Investbx C 36/2005 which the United Kingdom is planning to implement [2008] O.J. L45. See further, R. Horacek and Z. Lantos, *Competition Newsletter* nr 2, 2007, pp.70–72.
[144] [2009] O.J. C83/1.

Member States and market participants, but that the financial and economic crisis has left an impact on venture capital markets and that the upper boundary of the SME equity gap has grown. The Commission therefore considered that the increased maximum permitted tranches of finance per SME over a period of twelve months could be applied also outside the context of the financial and economic crisis. Accordingly, the Commission amended the Risk Capital Guidelines based on art.107(3)(c) TFEU.[145]

---

[145] Communication of the Commission—Temporary Union framework for State aid measures to support access to finance in the current financial and economic crisis, [2011] O.J. C6.

CHAPTER 5

STATE AID IN THE ACCESSION COUNTRIES*

1.	INTRODUCTION	5–001
2.	THE STATE AID REGIME UNDER THE EUROPE/ASSOCIATION AGREEMENTS	5–002
3.	THE STATE AID REGIME UNDER THE 2003 ACCESSION TREATY	5–004
4.	AID MEASURE "PUT INTO EFFECT BEFORE ACCESSION"	5–007
5.	AID MEASURE "APPLICABLE AFTER ACCESSION"	5–009
6.	AID MEASURES SUBJECT TO SPECIFIC TRANSITIONAL ARRANGEMENTS IN THE STEEL SECTOR	5–014
7.	AID MEASURES GRANTED IN THE AGRICULTURAL AND TRANSPORT SECTORS	5–018
8.	THE ACCESSION OF BULGARIA AND ROMANIA	5–020
9.	SPECIAL PROVISIONS REGARDING THE STEEL SECTOR IN BULGARIA AND ROMANIA	5–022
10.	ACCESSION NEGOTIATIONS WITH CROATIA AND IRELAND	5–024
11.	CONCLUSION	5–029

1. INTRODUCTION

With the accession of 10 new countries to the European Union on May 1, 2004,[1] and two further countries in 2007,[2] the European Commission was faced with the difficult question of how to apply the rules on state aid to countries which have only recently become market economies and which were under heavy state influence in virtually all sectors of the economy prior to accession. The bilateral association agreements or so-called "Europe Agreements" concluded between the European Union and the twelve accession countries already contained provisions on competition law similar to arts 101 and 102 and the state aid provisions in the TFEU. Similarly, the Accession Treaty of 2003 concerning the accession of the 10 candidate countries to the European Union[3] included a number of provisions regarding the application of competition rules to aid granted in the candidate countries during the pre-accession period. The same system also applied to the accession of Romania and Bulgaria, although, as will

5–001

* Julia Rapp
[1] These countries are: Czech Republic, Cyprus, Estonia, Latvia, Lithuania, Hungary, Malta, Poland, Slovenia, and Slovakia.
[2] Romania and Bulgaria.
[3] O.J. L236, September 23, 2003.

be explained later, a number of safeguard measures had been adopted to take account of the special situation in those countries.

In the following sections, the state aid regime under the Europe and Accession Agreements will be examined before moving on to the rules on state aid included in the 2003 Accession Treaty. Thereafter, some practical issues on the implementation of those rules will be explained with the help of some decision-making practice of the Commission. The chapter will continue with an account of the state aid rules applicable to the last two accession countries, Bulgaria and Romania, under the 2005 Accession Treaty, and conclude with an overview of the accession negotiations with the candidate countries Croatia and Iceland.

2. THE STATE AID REGIME UNDER THE EUROPE/ASSOCIATION AGREEMENTS

5–002   The Europe or Association Agreements (hereafter "Europe Agreements"),[4] concluded with the 10 new Member States,[5] provided a framework for trade and related matters between the European Union and each of the candidate countries to prepare them for accession. In practice, the accession negotiations had been sub-divided into 31 topical chapters of which Ch.6 concerned competition policy. The requirements for the closure of the competition chapter for each candidate country were derived from the conclusions of the Copenhagen European Council which was held in June 1993. This entailed as regards the economic criteria established by the Copenhagen Council, the existence of a functioning market

---

[4] Europe Agreements were concluded for eight acceding countries. They cover the period between the date of their entry into force and the date of accession. There are no Europe Agreements between the Community and either Cyprus or Malta. The only comparable instrument is the Association Agreement. The Maltese Association Agreement does not contain any provision regarding state aid.

[5] Agreement establishing an Association between the Republic of Cyprus and the European Economic Community, O.J. L133, May 21, 1973; Europe Agreement establishing an association between the European Communities and their Member States, of the one part, and the Czech Republic, of the other part, O.J. L360, December 31, 1994; Europe Agreement establishing an association between the European Communities and their Member States, of the one part, and the Republic of Estonia, of the other part, O.J. L68, March 9, 1998; Europe Agreement establishing an association between the European Communities and their Member States, of the one part, and the Republic of Latvia, of the other part, O.J. L26, February 2, 1998; Europe Agreement establishing an association between the European Communities and their Member States, of the one part, and the Republic of Lithuania, of the other part, O.J. L51, February 20, 1998; Europe Agreement establishing an association between the European Communities and their Member States, of the one part, and the Republic of Hungary, of the other part, O.J. L347, December 31, 1993; Agreement establishing an association between the European Economic Community and Malta, O.J. L61, March 14, 1971; Europe Agreement establishing an association between the European Communities and their Member States, of the one part, and the Republic of Poland, of the other part, O.J. L348, December 31, 1993; Europe Agreement establishing an association between the European Communities and their Member States, of the one part, and the Republic of Slovakia, of the other part, O.J. L359, December 31, 1994; Europe Agreement establishing an association between the European Communities and their Member States, of the one part, and the Republic of Slovenia, of the other part, O.J. L51, February 26, 1999.

economy as well as the capacity to cope with competitive pressure and market forces within the European Union.[6] Thus, a candidate country was regarded to be ready for accession only if its companies and public authorities had become accustomed to a competition discipline similar to that of the European Union well before the date of accession. Translated into precise conditions for accession in the competition field, the candidate countries had to put three elements in place before the competition negotiations could be concluded:

(1) they had to dispose of the necessary legislative framework with respect to antitrust and state aid;

(2) they had to have an adequate administrative capacity (in particular, a well-functioning competition authority); and

(3) they had to have a credible enforcement record of the *acquis communautaire* in all areas of competition policy.[7]

In order to implement the conditions in the acceding countries, each of the Europe Agreements contained explicit clauses obliging the candidate countries concerned to apply the same substantive antitrust and state aid rules as in the Union if trade between the European Union and a candidate country was affected. For instance, art.64 of the Europe Agreement concluded with Latvia reads:

"1. The following are incompatible with the proper functioning of this Agreement, insofar as they may affect trade between the Community and Latvia:

(i) all agreements between undertakings and concerted practices between undertakings which have as their object or effect the prevention, restriction or distortion of competition;

(ii) abuse by one or more undertakings of a dominant position in the territories of the Community or of Latvia as a whole or in a substantial part thereof;

(iii) any public aid, which distorts or threatens to distort competition by favouring certain undertakings or the production of certain goods.

2. Any practices contrary to this Article shall be assessed on the basis of criteria arising from the application of the rules of Articles 85, 86 and 92 of the Treaty (now Articles 101, 102 and 107 TFEU) establishing the European Community or, for products covered by the ECSC Treaty, on the basis of corresponding rules of the ECSC Treaty including secondary legislation.

---

[6] The political criteria required that a candidate country disposes of stable institutions guaranteeing democracy, the rule of law, human rights and respect for and protection of minorities.

[7] Y. Devuyst, J. Känkänen, P. Lindberg, I. Orssich and G. Roebling, "EU enlargement and competition policy: where are we now?", *Competition Policy Newsletter*, No. 1, 2002.

3. The Association Council shall, by 31 December 1997, adopt by decision the necessary rules for the implementation of paragraphs 1 and 2."[8]

5–003   The Europe Agreements further stipulate that the candidate countries are qualified as areas where regional aid is permitted according to art.107(3)(a) TFEU, and high maximum aid ceilings apply, since the standard of living is considered to be abnormally low.[9] This concerned all public aid granted during the first years after the entry into force of the Europe Agreement. This period could be extended by further periods of three,[10] four,[11] or five[12] years following a decision of the respective Association Council.[13]

As indicated above, the state aid provisions in the Europe Agreements provided for the adoption of so-called Implementing Rules. These rules have been adopted for almost all candidate countries[14] and contain detailed provisions on, inter alia, the establishment of monitoring authorities, criteria for the compatibility of aid measures, de minimis aid, derogations, and consultation and comity.[15] All in all, it can therefore be said that the state aid provisions in the Europe Agreements and the Implementing Rules follow the same principles as the rules in force in the European Union. This is also of importance when, for instance,

[8] O.J. L26, February 2, 1998, p.18. State aid granted in the agricultural sector and fisheries is assessed pursuant to the respective chapters on agriculture and fisheries. Until the expiry of the ECTS, aid granted in the steel sector fell under Protocol No. 2 of the Europe Agreements. Since July 2002, aid granted in this sector falls, like any other state aid, under the regular provisions on state aid.

[9] This has also been repeated in art.4 of the Implementing Rules for the candidate countries.

[10] Estonia.

[11] Slovenia.

[12] Latvia, Lithuania, Poland, Slovakia, Czech Republic, and Hungary.

[13] See for instance art.65(4)(a) of the Europe Agreement with Slovenia, O.J. L51, 26.2.1999, p.20.

[14]

| | Europe Agreements | | Implementing Rules |
	Entry into force	Reference	Entry into force
Cyprus	(°)	–	(°°)
Czech Rep.	02/1995	Art.64(6)	04/06/1998
Estonia	02/1998	Art.63(6)	01/02/2002
Hungary	02/1994	Art.62(6)	(°°)
Latvia	02/1998	Art.64(6)	01/04/2001
Lithuania	02/1998	Art.64(6)	01/03/2001
Malta	(°)	–	(°°)
Poland	02/1994	Art.63(6)	01/06/2001
Slovakia	02/1995	Art.64(6)	01/12/2001
Slovenia	02/1998	Art.65(6)	02/06/2001

(°) There are no Europe Agreements between the Community and either Cyprus or Malta (see above fn 4).

(°°) There are no Implementing Rules for Cyprus, Malta and Hungary.

[15] It should be noted, however, that the Implementing Rules do not contain any procedural rules like art.108 TFEU or reg.659/1999. Article 1 of the Implementing Rules merely refers to the national procedural rules of the respective accession country. Therefore, all candidate countries adopted procedural rules which closely reflect the EU provisions, e.g. they include a notification obligation and a standstill clause.

discussing the question of the direct effect of the state aid rules in the Europe Agreements.[16]

In the course of the accession negotiations with the acceding countries, it quickly emerged that, whereas the situation in the antitrust field looked satisfactory, progress had been much slower in the state aid field, although the situation varied considerably from country to country. Among the most important issues which remained unsolved before accession were:

(1) The operation of incompatible fiscal aid regimes, such as tax holidays, tax breaks, and tax credits by some candidate countries intended to attract foreign investments. These incompatible fiscal measures were considered a major obstacle for accession and the European Commission was trying to help the candidate countries converting the aid measures into permissible aid arrangements.

(2) The practice in most candidate countries to prop up ailing industries. This problem was particularly acute in the steel sector.[17]

Whilst the European Commission in principle required the candidate countries either to abolish incompatible aid measures or align them with the Community *acquis*, in some rare cases, especially as regards the two areas identified above, consultations resulted in special limited transitory regimes. These were granted in the cases of Cyprus,[18] the Czech Republic,[19] Hungary,[20] Malta,[21] Poland,[22] and

---

[16] As regards the general question of direct effect of provisions in the Europe Agreements, the European Court of Justice stated in the judgment *Sürül v Bundesanstalt für Arbeit*: "it is settled case law that a provision in an agreement concluded by the Community with non-member countries must be regarded as being directly applicable when, regard being had to its wording and to the purpose and nature of the agreement itself, the provision contains a clear and precise obligation which is not subject, in its implementation or effects, to the adoption of any subsequent measure" (Case C–262/96 *Sürül v Bundesanstalt für Arbeit* [1999] ECR I–2685, para.60).

If this statement is applied to the State aid provisions in the Europe Agreements, it seems that since arts 107 and 108 TFEU, to which the Europe Agreements refer, are not directly applicable (except art.108(3) TFEU although whether a direct effect of this provision could be assumed is arguable), it would be difficult to argue that the state aid provisions in the Europe Agreements are sufficiently clear and precise to create direct effect.

[17] Y. Devuyst, J. Känkänen, P. Lindberg, I. Orssich and G. Roebling, "EU enlargement and competition policy: where are we now?", *Competition Policy Newsletter*, No. 1, 2002.

[18] Phase-out of incompatible fiscal aid for off-short companies by the end of 2005 (so-called International Business Enterprises).

[19] Restructuring of the steel industry to be completed by December 31, 2006.

[20] Phase-out of incompatible fiscal aid for SMEs by the end of 2011; modification of incompatible fiscal aid for large companies into regional investment aid; phase-out of incompatible fiscal aid for off-shore companies by the end of 2005; phase-out of incompatible fiscal aid granted by local authorities by the end of 2007.

[21] Phase-out of incompatible fiscal aid for SMEs by the end of 2011; phase-out of operating aid under the Business Promotion Act by the end of 2008; modification of incompatible fiscal aid for large companies into regional investment aid; aid for restructuring of the shipbuilding sector during a restructuring period lasting until the end of 2008; adjustment of the market in the importation, stocking and wholesale marketing of petroleum products under art.31 of the EC Treaty by the end of 2005.

[22] Restructuring of the steel industry to be completed by December 31, 2006.

Slovakia.[23] If the conditions of the transitional arrangements were not fulfilled, aid granted after accession would constitute new aid.[24]

3. THE STATE AID REGIME UNDER THE 2003 ACCESSION TREATY

5–004   Having identified the areas in which transitory regimes had to be implemented and having put in place the conditions of accession as regards the competition chapter, one would assume that the European Union would proceed with the accession of the 10 candidate countries like in the other, previous, enlargement rounds, i.e. on the basis of the "existing aid principle" pursuant to art.1(b)(i) of reg.659/1999.[25]

According to this principle, all aid granted by the enlargement countries before accession to the European Union and continuing beyond accession qualify as existing aid pursuant to art.1(b)(i) of reg.659/1999, with all procedural and substantive consequences. This implies that the Commission can only modify an existing aid measure with effect for the future by proposing "appropriate measures" to the Member State concerned pursuant to art.108(1) TFEU,[26] and, even more importantly, this also implies that the Commission cannot order recovery of aid which has been disbursed in the past under existing aid measures.

However, the state aid provisions in the 1994 Accession Act concerning the accession of Austria, Finland and Sweden already slightly deviated from this approach in that art.172(5) of the Accession Act did not recognise aid measures which had been implemented in contravention of the EEA Agreement or not notified to the EFTA Surveillance Authority as existing aid. Thus, a measure had to be approved by the EFTA Surveillance Authority as a supranational body with powers closely modelled to those of the European Commission to be considered as existing aid upon accession.[27]

> Fiscal aid for special economic zones: phase-out of incompatible fiscal aid for small enterprises by the end of 2011; phase-out of incompatible fiscal aid for medium-sized enterprises by the end of 2010, modification of incompatible fiscal aid for large companies into regional investment aid.
>
> State aid for environmental protection: for investments that relate to standards for which a transitional period has been granted under the negotiations on environment and for the duration of that transitional period; for existing IPPC installations covered by a transitional period under the negotiations on environment; for the IPPC-related investment not covered by a transitional period; for large combustion plants.

[23] Fiscal aid to a beneficiary in the motor vehicle manufacturing sector to be continued by the end of 2008; fiscal aid to one beneficiary in the steel sector to be discontinued at the end of 2009 or when the aid reaches a pre-determined amount. (See for all transitional arrangements: State Aid Scoreboard—Autumn 2004 update—COM(2004)750 final, 16.11.2004, Annex I.)

[24] Estonia, Latvia, Lithuania, and Slovenia did not request any transitional arrangements. (J. Känkänen, "Accession negotiations brought to successful conclusion", *Competition Policy Newsletter*, No. 1, 2003.)

[25] O.J. L83, March 27, 1999.

[26] These could consist of modifications to or the abolition of the aid measure.

[27] Article 172(5) of the Act of Accession concerning the conditions of accession of the Kingdom of Norway, the Republic of Austria, the Republic of Finland and the Kingdom of Sweden, and the adjustments to the Treaties on which the European Union is founded, O.J. C241, August 29, 1994.

To apply this approach to the 2004 accession countries would have pre- **5–005**
supposed that those countries disposed of similar independent state aid review
authorities like the EFTA Surveillance Authority with a state aid regime such as
the EEA Agreement. This was not the case. Although the Commission was in
principle satisfied with the progress achieved in each candidate country as
regards, inter alia, the implementation of state aid control, and therefore closed
the accession negotiations in December 2002, it was nevertheless concerned that
incompatible state aid which had been granted before accession but with continuing effects after accession could be "imported" into the European Union on the
date of accession.[28] It considered that in the absence of any Commission review,
there would be a danger that the continuation of some pre-accession aid measures
that are incompatible with the Internal Market would lead to distortions of
competition. Therefore, the Commission decided to add a second layer to the
filtering process of pre-accession aid and screen the decisions taken by the
national state aid bodies. However, the national authorities would remain the first
instance of review.[29]

This led to the inclusion of Ch.3 of Annex IV in the Accession Treaty,[30] which
determined which measures are considered as existing aid and which measures
constitute new aid: the so-called "existing aid mechanism". Annex IV refers to
the following aid categories:

(1) aid measures which are put into effect before December 10, 1994 are per
se deemed to be existing aid from the date of accession[31];

(2) measures submitted by the acceding countries until November 2002 were
examined by the Commission in the light of the state aid *acquis*. If those
aid measures were considered to be compatible with the EU state aid
rules, they were qualified as existing aid and included in a list of existing
aid measures, which could be found in an Appendix to the Accession
Treaty[32];

(3) for measures not included in the Treaty list and for those submitted
between the finalisation of the Accession Treaty and the actual date of
accession, Annex IV of the Accession Treaty set out the conditions of a
so-called "interim procedure" or "interim mechanism" under which

---

[28] State Aid Scoreboard—Autumn 2004 update—COM(2004)750 final, 16.11.2004, para.2.
[29] Georg Roebling, "Existing Aid and Enlargement", *Competition Policy Newsletter*, No. 1,
2003.
[30] O.J. L236, September 23, 2003, p.797.
[31] Annex IV, Ch.3(1)(a) of the Accession Treaty. December 10, 1994 is the day following the Essen
European Council where the EU had clarified its expectations in the field of state aid. The EU
therefore based the accession negotiations on the assumption that businesses in the new Member
States have been on notice that state funds might become subject to Commission state aid control
since at least the Council of Essen.
[32] Annex IV, Ch.3(1)(b) of the Accession Treaty. The Appendix to Annex IV can be found at O.J.
C227E, September 23, 2003, p.2.

those aid measures could be qualified as existing aid following accession.[33]

The interim procedure consisted of the following steps:

(a) the measure had to be reviewed and approved by the national state aid control authority, which then had to submit the aid measure to the Commission including any other information which was essential for the assessment of the aid measure;

(b) the Commission then assessed the aid measure as to its compatibility with EU state aid rules. In case it did not object to the measure on the ground of serious doubts[34] as to their compatibility with the common market within three months, the aid measure constituted existing aid. A number of those aid measures were included in a subsequent list of existing aid measures published in April 2004.[35]

If, however, the Commission decided to object to a measure under this review procedure, it was regarded as a decision to initiate the formal investigation procedure pursuant to arts 4(4) and 6 of reg.659/1999. This decision would come into effect upon the date of accession.

Consequently, all measures still applicable after the date of accession which constituted state aid and which did not fulfil the conditions of existing aid as set out under Annex IV of the Accession Treaty, or which have not passed the review mechanism, were considered by the Commission as new aid for the purpose of the application of art.108(3) TFEU; i.e. they had to be notified to the Commission upon accession and more crucially, they fell under the standstill clause pursuant to art.108(3) TFEU. Thus, by adopting Annex IV of the Accession Treaty, the Commission reversed the presumption implicit in the existing aid principle and qualified all state aid granted in the new Member States prior to accession as new aid, unless it fell under Annex IV of the Accession Treaty.[36]

In this context, it is important to note that the review procedure of Annex IV does not entail an obligation on the candidate countries to notify aid measures, i.e. they can decide whether and what measures they wish to notify to the

---

[33] Annex IV, Ch.3(1)(c) and (2) of the Accession Treaty. During the first phase of the existing aid mechanism (until November 2002), the 10 candidate countries submitted 320 aid measures out of which 222 measures were approved and included in the list of existing aid measures. During the second phase, between November 2002 and April 2004, the acceding countries notified another 559 aid measures to the Commission pursuant to the interim procedure of which around 175 were withdrawn by the countries themselves. By March 2005 the Commission had approved 329 measures as existing aid. A significant number of measures were submitted right up to the day of accession.

[34] Note that the standard of review pursuant to the interim mechanism is different from the regular state aid provisions: the Commission has to raise *serious* doubts under the interim mechanism instead of *simple* doubts according to art.6 of reg.659/1999.

[35] O.J. C88, April 8, 2004, p.2.

[36] Annex IV applies according to art.22 of the Accession Treaty. The Accession Treaty has been signed by all current EU Member States and the ten accession countries on April 16, 2003.

Commission.[37] But it is evident that, in order to benefit from the classification of a measure as existing aid, it is in the countries' own interest to follow the review procedure of the Accession Treaty. The Commission thus strongly encouraged the candidate countries to follow the interim procedure and notify all pre-accession state aid to the Commission to provide the aid beneficiaries with legal certainty.[38]

Finally, a number of aid categories followed a different regime and fell outside this general approach:

5–006

(1) aid measures subject to specific transitional arrangements as *lex specialis*[39];

(2) aid measures in the agricultural sector[40]; and

(3) aid measures in the transport sector.[41]

When applying the provisions of the Accession Treaty, it became clear that the concept of an aid measure "put into effect before accession" and "applicable after accession" became fundamental for deciding whether the existing aid mechanism of the Accession Treaty applied or not. The following two chapters will explain these concepts with the help of some of the decision-making practice of the Commission.

4. AID MEASURE "PUT INTO EFFECT BEFORE ACCESSION"

The existing aid mechanism pursuant to Annex IV of the 2003 Accession Treaty only applied to measures "put into effect before accession" and "applicable after accession", i.e. measures that were put into effect before accession and not applicable after accession could not be examined by the Commission neither under the interim mechanism procedure nor under the procedures laid down in art.108 TFEU. Thus, neither the Accession Treaty nor the EU Treaty required or empowered the Commission to review these measures and assess their compatibility. They were therefore not subject to any recovery obligation. However, they had to be taken into account for determining the compatibility of aid measures granted or to be granted after accession.

5–007

---

[37] C 27/04 regarding state aid granted by the Czech Republic to Agrobanka Praha, a.s. and GE Capital Bank, a.s. Invitation to submit comments pursuant to art.88(2) of the EC Treaty, O.J. C292, 30.11.2004, and Corrigenda, O.J. C10, 14.1.2005, para.41 ("Agrobanka decision"). The Commission does not consider itself bound by the notification, i.e. the Commission extends its examination beyond the measures notified if it deems them "inextricably linked" to other, not notified aid measures. (Ibid, para.42)

[38] P. Dias, "Existing aid in the acceding countries", *Competition Policy Newsletter*, No. 2, 2004.

[39] See below explanations on the steel sector.

[40] Except fisheries and products derived thereof as specified in Ch.3(1)(c), third paragraph of Annex IV. (See below explanations on the agricultural and transport sector.)

[41] Chapter 3(4) of Annex IV. (See below explanations on the agricultural and transport sector.)

From the perspective of the notifying Member State, it was evidently in its interest to have the measure assessed as being granted before accession since in this case there was a chance that the measure was classified as not being "applicable after accession" and therefore not to be assessed under the EU state aid rules. However, if the Commission concluded that the measure was put into effect after accession, it automatically constituted new aid and the Member State was invited to renotify according to reg.659/1999.

In this context, it is important to note that the Commission usually considers the relevant act of granting an aid measure as consisting in the adoption of the legally binding act by the public authority and not in the subsequent actual payment of the aid.[42] It regards any payment, current or future, under a legal commitment as simply implementing the legally binding act to grant state aid.

5–008   The Commission interpreted the concept of "put into effect before accession" by analogy with the concept of granting of aid. Thus, the relevant criteria for establishing whether a measure is "put into effect before accession" are: (a) the issuance of an act; (b) by a public authority competent in the matter; (c) which legally binds this authority; and (d) that creates legitimate expectations of the beneficiary under national law.[43]

Arguably, the fact of whether an administrative act is issued by an authority entitled to do so and is legally binding is a matter of national law. However, the Commission has to be able to review administrative acts also with respect to national law in order to determine its competence. In its decision regarding state aid granted to the Szczecin Shipyard, it stated:

"the Commission must, especially in borderline cases, be able to review these administrative acts and to assess on the basis of their form and content whether they could have given rise to legitimate expectations on the part of the beneficiaries enforceable before a Polish court of law. This capacity to review national administrative acts is indispensable for the exercise of the Commission's exclusive competence to approve derogations from the general prohibition of State aid with regard to measures put into effect in Poland after 1 May 2004."[44]

---

[42] Case T–109/01, *Fleuren Compost v Commission* [2004] E.C.R. II–129, which reads in paras 73 and 74: "In order to assess whether the aid at issue falls within the scope of application *ratione temporis* of that decision, as defined in the preceding paragraph, it is necessary to examine whether it can be considered as having been granted before 1995. In that regard, the Commission rightly takes the view that the relevant criterion is the legally binding act by which the competent [national] authorities undertake to grant aid." (Case T–109/01, *Fleuren Compost v Commission*, [2004], ECR II–127.) This approach can also be found in the Notice on Guarantees which reads: "The aid is granted at the moment when the guarantee is given, not the moment at which the guarantee is invoked or the moment at which payments are made under the terms of the guarantee. Whether or not the guarantee constitutes State aid and, what the amount of that State aid may be must be assessed at the moment the guarantee is given." (O.J. C71, March 11, 2000, para.2.1.2)

[43] A. Čierna, "Determining Commission's competence: past aid and new aid—application on restructuring aid to Polish shipbuilding", *Competition Policy Newsletter*, No. 3, 2005.

[44] C 19/2005 Commission decision of November 6, 2011 on state aid granted by Poland to Stocnzia Szczecińska, para.205.

In this decision, the Commission had to assess whether the commitment of the relevant public authorities to grant restructuring aid was taken prior to accession. In support of this fact, Poland argued, inter alia, that the Supervisory Board of the company, who approved the restructuring plan, also included members of the State Treasury, the granting authority, which was, at the same time, an important shareholder of the shipyard. Thus, by approving the restructuring plan in the Supervisory Board, the competent authority implicitly committed itself to granting the aid. Therefore, the question raised was whether:

"the decision of a public entity, in its capacity as owner of a public enterprise, to approve the restructuring plan can be considered to be the decision of the same public entity, in its capacity as State authority, to grant the State aid provided for in that restructuring plan."

The Commission concluded that the approval of the restructuring plan that included the aid measures under assessment was not sufficient to "put the measure into effect".[45] In fact, two additional resolutions of the extraordinary shareholders' meeting were necessary to implement the aid measures. In addition, the approval by the President of the Office for Competition and Consumer Protection that was required under national law could also not be considered as creating legitimate expectations that the aid was actually going to be granted.[46] The Commission therefore considered that the aid measures had to be assessed pursuant to art.107(1) TFEU.[47]

---

[45] C 19/2005 regarding restructuring aid granted to Szczecin Shipyard. Invitation to submit comments pursuant to art.88(2) of the EC Treaty, O.J. C222, 9.9.2005, para.45. The Commission raised doubts as to the possibility to exercise this dual function since, firstly, the decision of the Supervisory Board to approve the restructuring plan was not necessarily binding upon the (other) owners of the shipyard. In principle, a Supervisory Board is not empowered, without further acts of the shareholders, to adopt decisions, which would have financial repercussions on the owners and which the owners would be obliged to execute. Secondly, Poland had not proved to the necessary extent that it is possible under national law to assimilate the actions taken by a state body as a market player with actions taken by a state body in pursuance of various public goals, such as employment and regional policy. Thirdly, the approval decision could not be considered to be final since the owner of a company had the possibility to unilaterally change his decision concerning his property. On the other hand, a public authority generally cannot change its own administrative decision since, once issued, it becomes legally binding. And finally, the Commission pointed to the fact that in order to grant aid measures, a certain procedure has to be followed in order to create legitimate expectations under national law for the aid beneficiary. This, however, had not occurred in the case at issue. Therefore, according to the Commission, Poland was not able to provide convincing evidence to demonstrate that the legally binding decision to grant the aid had been taken before accession and consequently instituted proceedings according to art.88(2) EC. See also A. Čierna, "Determining Commission's competence: past aid and new aid—application on restructuring aid to Polish shipbuilding", *Competition Policy Newsletter*, No. 3, 2005.

[46] C 19/2005 Commission decision of November 6, 2011 on state aid granted by Poland to Stocnzia Szczecińska, paras 214, 215.

[47] As regards similar cases where the issue of "put into effect" was disputed, see C 44/2005 regarding restructuring aid in favour of Huta Stalowa Wola S.A., O.J. L81, March 26, 2010, paras 87 et seq.; C 3/2005 as regards restructuring aid granted by Poland to Fabryka Samochodow Osobowych S.A., O.J. L187, July 19, 2007, Corrigendum O.J. L82, February 4, 2010.

5. AID MEASURE "APPLICABLE AFTER ACCESSION"

5–009   When adopting decisions under the interim procedure of the Accession Treaty, it turned out that the notion of "applicable after accession" was a crucial factor in deciding whether or not the Commission should assess a particular measure. The condition under the interim procedure that a measure has to be "applicable after accession" in order to fall within the competence of the Commission was derived from the wording of Annex IV, Ch.3 of the Accession Treaty. Article 1(c), second paragraph reads:

> "All measures *still applicable after the date of accession* which constitute State aid and which do not fulfil the conditions set out above shall be considered as new aid upon accession for the purpose of the application of Article 88(3) of the EC Treaty." [Emphasis added.]

Thus, the Commission limited its review under the interim procedure to aid measures which were still "applicable after accession". However, since the Accession Treaty does not provide any further interpretation of that concept, the Commission developed in its decision-making practice its own interpretation of state aid measures "applicable after accession" and used the Procedural Regulation 659/1999 as guidance. The Commission only considered those measures as "still applicable after accession" that can still give rise, after accession, to the grant of additional aid or to an increase in the amount of aid already granted. Consequently, only those aid measures can be reviewed by the Commission. Furthermore, it emphasised in the decisions that it does not have the competence to review aid measures that have already been finally and unconditionally granted for a given amount before accession.[48] This also indicates that the Commission's finding on lack of competence does not affect the appraisal of the prima facie incompatibility of the state aid measures. The Commission only states that it declines any type of substantive review of the aid measures.

5–010   The Commission argues that for a measure to be considered as "applicable after accession" it must be shown that it is liable to produce an additional benefit that was not known, or not precisely known, when the aid was granted.[49] The following aid measures are therefore considered to be "applicable after accession":

(a) any aid schemes that entered into effect before the date of accession and on the basis of which, without further implementing measures being

---

[48] Para.50 of the Commission decision CZ 14/2003 regarding state aid granted by the Czech Republic to Česká spořitelna, a.s., C(2004)11fin. COR, January 28, 2004, reads:
"[. . .] the Commission considers that either the measures qualify as existing aid on the basis that they were put into effect before 10 December 1994 or they are not applicable after accession. The Commission is thus neither required nor *empowered*, under the interim mechanism, to assess the compatibility of these measures with EC State aid rules." [Emphasis added.]

[49] Commission Decision of July 18, 2007 on state aid C 27/2004, which the Czech Republic has implemented for GE Capital Bank a.s. and GE Capital International Holdings Corporation, USA, O.J. L67, March 11, 2008, para.56.

required, individual aid awards may be made to undertakings defined within the act in a general and abstract manner after accession;

(b) aid that is not linked to a specific project and that is awarded before accession to one or several undertakings for an indefinite period of time and/or an indefinite amount; and

(c) individual aid measures for which the precise economic exposure of the State is not known on the date the aid is granted.

It is worth noting that the first two conditions follow precisely the definition of an "aid scheme" as set out in art.1(d) of the Procedural Regulation 659/1999.[50] Only the last case dealing with individual aid measures is worded differently. The Commission further explained its understanding of individual aid measures "applicable after accession" in a letter to all Member States:

"Individual aid measures as defined in Article 1 (e) of the Procedural Regulation are regarded as 'applicable after accession' if they are likely to increase the liability of the state after the day of accession. DG Competition considers that this condition would in particular apply in the case of exemptions from or reductions of compulsory charges (e.g. exemptions from or reductions of taxes, compulsory social security contributions), where the benefit is still in force after accession, in guarantees or financial constructions like credit lines and 'drawing rights' that extend beyond the date of accession. In all such cases, these measures can be regarded as still applicable after accession: even though the measure has been formally adopted, the total liability for the state is not clearly known at the time the aid was granted."[51]

In addition to the interpretation of the concept "applicable after", which **5–011** applies to all types of aid measures, the Commission has in later decisions specified its approach with respect to certain specific aid measures, namely, indemnities or guarantees granted by the State.

Thus, indemnities or guarantees granted by a Member State covering known litigation, risks and claims, whether ongoing or threatened, fall outside the definition of "applicable after", even if their payment takes place after accession, to the extent that the following conditions are met:

(1) the facts which give rise to the covered risks are precisely defined and included in an exhaustive list closed by the date of accession;

(2) there is an overall cap and a time-limit for the payments that the State can effect; and

---

[50] O.J. L83, March 27, 1999.
[51] See for instance SK 4/2004 regarding state aid granted by the Slovak Republic to OTP Banka Slovensko, a.s., C(2004)2625 fin., para.19.

(3) the guarantee/indemnification relates to events that had already occurred by the date of the granting of this guarantee/indemnification and not for any future events.[52]

5–012   An interesting example illustrating this approach concerned an indemnity granted to the Czech bank Československá obchodní banka, a.s. ("CSOB") in the context of the purchase of another bank.[53] The Commission could only consider the aid measure as not "applicable after accession" because the bank offered to cap the indemnity at a certain sum and introduce an expiry date. Furthermore, CSOB submitted an exhaustive list of claims and waived all its rights for indemnification beyond the claims included in this list. It is worth noting that this waiver was submitted on June 28, 2004, i.e. after the date of accession. Consequently, the Commission indicated in the decision that without the waiver, certain arrangements under the indemnity agreement "might have been applicable after accession". However, with the waiver in place and since no new claims had been submitted since accession, any action under the interim mechanism of the Accession Treaty is "devoid of any purpose" and hence, the measures are "not to be reviewable in accordance with the Interim Mechanism".[54]

The Commission justified this approach by again comparing the granting of an indemnity/guarantee with a "scheme", which is effectively closed by the date of accession and thus preventing the addition of any new claims or modification after accession. However, guarantees for unknown risks will always be considered by the Commission as "applicable after accession" since:

> "the payments made after accession there under would not be linked to a specific legally binding act by the relevant authority stipulating to make payment against a specific, well-defined cost item."[55]

5–013   In another Czech banking case concerning state aid granted to Agrobanka Praha, a.s. ("Agrobanka") and its purchaser GE Capital Bank, a.s. ("GE Capital Bank"),[56] the Commission decided to open the formal investigation procedure because precisely the above conditions did not seem to be fulfilled, i.e. the guarantees and indemnities granted to the Agrobanka to prevent liquiditation did

---

[52] See, for instance, Commission decision C 35/2004 of October 21, 2008 as regards aid granted by Hungary to Postabank and Takarékpénztár Rt./Erste Bank Hungary Nyrt, O.J. L62, March 6, 2009, para.14. See also Commission Decision of July 18, 2007 on state aid C 27/2004, which the Czech Republic has implemented for GE Capital Bank a.s. and GE Capital International Holdings Corporation, USA, O.J. L67, March 11, 2008, para.57.

[53] CZ 46/2003 regarding state aid granted by the Czech Republic to Investiční a poštovní banka, a.s./Československá obchodní banka, a.s., C(2004)2688 fin.

[54] CZ 46/2003 regarding state aid granted by the Czech Republic to Investiční a poštovní banka, a.s./Československá obchodní banka, a.s., C(2004)2688 fin., paras 101 and 102.

[55] CZ 46/2003 regarding state aid granted by the Czech Republic to Investiční a poštovní banka, a.s./Československá obchodní banka, a.s., C(2004)2688 fin., paras 27 and 28.

[56] C 27/2004 regarding state aid granted by the Czech Republic to Agrobanka Praha, a.s. and GE Capital Bank, a.s. Invitation to submit comments pursuant to art.88(2) of the EC Treaty, O.J. C292, November 30, 2004, and Corrigenda, O.J. C10, January 14, 2005.

not fulfil the conditions established by the Commission as the list of claims was not exhaustive, there was no overall cap which would limit the maximum exposure of the State and the risks were not precisely defined. In addition, GE Capital Bank had been granted a "put option", giving GE's parent company the right to sell all its shares in GE Capital Bank to the Czech National Bank under certain circumstances.

In the final decision, the Commission confirmed its assessment of the opening decision on the "applicability after" of the aid measures. It therefore entered into an analysis of the aid measures in question pursuant to art.87 EC (now art.107 TFEU) and the Guidelines on Rescue and Restructuring and concluded that the conditions for applying the Guidelines had been respected, in particular because the bank had been sold via an open, unconditional and transparent tender procedure.[57] In addition, the aid granted in the course of the sale of the bank formed part of several measures taken by the Czech Republic in order to avoid the collapse of the banking sector. This was consistent with art.46(2) of the Europe Agreement with the Czech Republic, which allowed it to adopt measures to ensure the integrity and stability of its financial system. The aid was thus found to be compatible with the state aid rules.[58]

As regards the concept of "applicable after", one of the parties introduced an appeal before the General Court to review the Commission's interpretation. However, as in the meantime, the appellant withdrew his action, such review by the Court will no longer take place.[59]

6. AID MEASURES SUBJECT TO SPECIFIC TRANSITIONAL ARRANGEMENTS IN THE STEEL SECTOR

As already indicated above, the European Union included several transitional arrangements for a number of candidate countries in the Accession Treaty in order to allow them more time to align their national legislation and State aid practice with the *acquis*.[60] One of these transitional arrangements concerns the

5–014

---

[57] Commission Decision of 18.7.2007 on State aid C 27/2004 which the Czech Republic has implemented for GE Capital Bank a.s. and GE Capital International Holdings Corporation, USA, O.J. L67, March 11, 2008.

[58] The Commission also had to decide on aid granted by Hungary to Postabank és Takarékpénztár Rt./Erste Bank Hungary Rt. Similar to the Agrobanka case, Hungary had granted an indemnity for unknown claims which was "not precisely defined and did not involve an exhaustive and binding list finalised by the date of accession. On the contrary, the measure covers indemnities with a wide scope, is not precisely defined and is capped at a high level, which moreover was introduced at a later date" (para.39 of Commission decision C 35/2004 of October 21, 2008 as regards aid granted by Hungary to Postabank and Takarékpénztár Rt./Erste Bank Hungary Nyrt, O.J. L62, March 6, 2009). The Commission therefore concluded that the aid was applicable after accession and continued with the analysis of the aid measure under EU state aid rules.

[59] Commission decision of July 14, 2004 in case CZ 46/2003 Investicní a postovní banka, a.s., OJ 2005 C137/4 appealed in case T–430/2004, *Nomura Principal Investment Plc v Commission*.

[60] The system of transitional arrangements has already been used in the previous enlargement round with Austria, Finland, and Sweden in 1995. An interesting example of the application of a so-called "flexibility clause" in the context of the restructuring of an Austrian sugar and starch company is Case C–321/01P *Agrana Zucker and Stärke AG v Commission* [2002] E.C.R. I–10027.

steel sector which represented an important industrial sector in many of the new Member States.[61]

Over the last decade before accession, significant restructuring in this sector had already been accomplished through privatisations, concentrations or changes in management structures, which was mainly triggered by protocols annexed to the Europe Agreements. These stipulated that candidate countries could exceptionally grant state aid in the steel sector during generally the first five years after entry into force of the Agreement, the so-called "grace period", but only subject to certain conditions.[62] The grace period for granting of the aid was extended in the case of Poland and the Czech Republic until the end of 2003[63] (with restructuring finalised until the end of 2006) if the countries concerned set up a national restructuring programme, which was eventually incorporated into two Protocols[64] attached to the Accession Treaty.[65]

5–015   The protocols essentially provided for a temporary exception of the rule that restructuring aid for the steel sector is prohibited and were also *lex specialis* to the normal transitional rules in the Accession Treaty, provided certain conditions were complied with. Specifically, the provisions in the Steel Protocols authorised certain aid measures granted or to be granted until the end of 2003, the end of the grace period, and requires that the restructuring of the steel sector shall be completed by the end of 2006.[66] The provisions of the Steel Protocols thus extended state aid control under the EU Treaty to any aid granted during the restructuring period of the Czech and Polish steel industries, i.e. between 1997

---

[61] M. Lienemeyer, "State aid for restructuring the steel industry in the new Member States", *Competition Policy Newsletter*, No. 1, 2005.

[62] e.g. art.8(4) of Protocol 2 of the Europe Agreement with Poland (O.J. L348, December 31, 1993). See for more details below.

[63] See art.6 of Protocol No. 8 of the Accession Treaty concerning the Polish steel industry, O.J. L236, September 23, 2003, p.948; and art.1 of Protocol No. 2 of the Accession Treaty concerning the Czech steel industry, O.J. L236, September 23, 2003, p.934.

[64] Protocol No. 2 on the restructuring of the Czech steel industry, O.J. L236, September 23, 2003, p.934. Protocol No. 8 on the restructuring of the Polish steel industry, O.J. L236, September 23, 2003, p.948.

[65] This need for transition has to be seen against the strict state aid regime applicable in the old Member States, which originates from a period of overcapacities in the 1980s and 1990s, the so-called steel crisis. Due to this crisis, the European Commission implemented the 1996 Steel Aid Code of the European Coal and Steel Community (ECSC), which completely prohibited the granting of restructuring and investment aid for companies in the old Member States. This was confirmed and further reinforced in 2002 with the adoption of the Commission Communication on Rescue and Restructuring aid and closure for the steel sector which replaced the normal EC Restructuring Guidelines and which determined that any kind of rescue and restructuring was prohibited in the old Member States. Thus, it is evident that steel producing companies in the new Member States, which, up until accession, had heavily relied on financial support of their governments could not without any transition be able to survive in the EU (M. Lienemeyer, "State aid for restructuring the steel industry in the new Member States", *Competition Policy Newsletter*, No.1, 2005).

[66] As can be seen here, the restructuring period is not necessarily identical with the grace period, i.e. the period in which the granting of State aid is permitted. It is rather logical that the restructuring period is longer, as viability is so to speak the fruit of the state aid. Furthermore, restrictions on capacity should generally last at least throughout the restructuring period (M. Lienemeyer, "State aid for restructuring the steel industry in the new Member States", *Competition Policy Newsletter*, No. 1, 2005).

and 2006, irrespective of whether the aid was still "applicable after accession".[67] In addition, in case the conditions for temporary exemption were not complied with, they allowed the recovery of aid granted before accession and the transitional arrangements ended immediately, i.e. the Commission could open the formal investigation procedure pursuant to art.108(2) TFEU.

As indicated above, the exemption from the state aid rules was subject to certain conditions, i.e. the setting up of a national restructuring programme as well as the fulfilment of certain obligations which were set out in the Protocols attached to the Accession Treaty. The key parameters of the national restructuring programmes were the following:

(1) the overall aim to achieve long term viability of the companies concerned. The restructuring programme must therefore show that viability of the beneficiary companies under normal market conditions will be restored at the end of the restructuring period. In order to do so individual business plans of all beneficiaries of State aid must be presented;

(2) the intensity of aid should be strictly limited to the necessary amount to reach the objective of the restructuring programme, i.e. viability. The "minimum necessary" is determined by two factors: it is the result of the total amount of funds needed to achieve viability minus the amount that the beneficiary himself is able to contribute;

(3) the aid beneficiaries have to offer compensatory measures, mostly in the form of capacity reductions.[68] In this context, the Steel Protocols for Poland and the Czech Republic[69] specify that capacity reductions are only measured on the basis of permanent closure of production facilities by physical destruction.[70] Where no inefficient capacities exist, other compensatory measures may also be feasible.

The companies eligible for restructuring under the national programme were listed in Annex I of the Protocols. They were selected on the basis of viability and proportionality. The length of each restructuring programme followed mainly from the timing for achieving viability, but was generally not shorter than five years.

Additional to the conditions established by the national restructuring programme, the Steel Protocols with Poland and the Czech Republic included a number of obligations and procedural rules. For instance, only the companies included in the protocols were eligible for state aid. The Protocols set up a

[67] E. Szymanska, "Aid in favour of Trinecké Zelezárny, a.s. a steel producer in the Czech Republic", *Competition Policy Newsletter*, No. 1, 2005.
[68] See Annex II of the Protocols.
[69] The Czech and the Polish steel Protocols are in most points identical and are therefore not discussed separately.
[70] Article 7 of the Czech and Polish Steel Protocols.

maximum amount of aid and net capacity reductions for the entire restructuring period. Also, they set out detailed provisions for monitoring and reporting.

5–016   The Commission has adopted a number of decisions regarding the application of the provisions of the Steel Protocols among which one decision is worth mentioning. As regards aid granted to the Polish steel producer Huta Czę-stochowa SA,[71] the Commission examined whether the writing-off of debts by public authorities was consistent with normal market conditions. The Commission was doubtful that a private creditor in the position of the public creditors would have accepted to restructure the company at all. However, after having launched an in-depth probe into the issue, it came to the conclusion that the write-off was compliant with normal market behaviour and therefore did not constitute state aid. However, it also concluded that €4 million of restructuring aid which had been granted prior to the setting up of the national restructuring plan constituted incompatible state aid and had to be recovered by Poland.

This decision was challenged before the Court of First Instance that upheld the Commission's interpretation of Protocol No. 8.[72] Given that at the moment of the publication of Protocol No. 8 in September 2003, the grace period from 1997 to 2003 had almost expired, the General Court did not accept the argument of the applicant ISD Polska that the only meaning of the reference to that period was that calculation of future aid was to be made by taking account retrospectively of the amounts of aid already granted, but not taking the view retroactively that the past aid was unlawful. On the contrary, the purpose of Protocol No. 8 was to establish a comprehensive system for the authorisation of aid intended for the restructuring of the Polish steel industry, and not merely to avoid the aggregation of aid by benefiting companies. It followed that, in relation to Annex IV to the Treaty of Accession and arts 87 and 88 EC (now arts 107 and 108 TFEU), Protocol No. 8 was a *lex specialis*, which extended the review of state aid carried out by the Commission under the Treaty to aid granted in favour of the reorgani-sation of the Polish steel industry during the period from 1997 to 2003.[73]

5–017   As regards Slovakia, the country negotiated a transitional period for one steel mill: Annex XIV, Ch.4(2) of the Accession Treaty allowed the application of a fiscal aid scheme to one beneficiary company, US Steel Košice, in the Slovakian

---

[71] Commission decision of July 5, 2005 in case C 20/2004, O.J. 2006 L366/1.
[72] Joined Cases T–273/06 & T–297/06 *ISD Polska sp z oo v Commission* [2009] E.C.R. II–2181, paras 94 et seq. Appeal to the European Court of Justice (C–369/09, judgment of March 24, 2011) that upheld the General Court's judgment (paras 99 et seq.). See also on the interpretation of the Steel Protocol Case T–288/06 *Regionalny Fundusz Gospodarczy SA (formerly Huta Częstochowa SA) v Commission* [2009] E.C.R. II–2247.
[73] See also restructuring aid granted to the Czech steel producer Trinecké Zelezárny (Commission decision of September 8, 2006 in case C 45/2004). Here, the facts of the case lie different in that the aid was granted for specific purposes, such as environment, R&D, closure and training. The Czech Steel Protocol does not limit the possibility to grant other kinds of aid in accordance with the Community *acquis*. As such, the Commission concluded that aid granted to Trinecké Zelezárny for environmental and R&D projects was compatible with the relevant EC state aid rules. It also concluded that the purchase of shares in Trinecké Zelezárny took place according to normal market conditions.

steel sector.[74] The exemption for Slovakia followed a different regime than the one implemented in favour of Poland and the Czech Republic. Slovakia did not request an extension of the grace period until the date of accession but rather opted for a transitional exemption from the EU State aid rules to continue granting fiscal aid to US Steel Kosice until 2009.[75] In addition, and unlike Protocols 2 and 8, the transitional provisions for Slovakia did not have any clauses allowing the recovery of aid granted prior to accession. However, non-fulfilment of any of the conditions of Annex XIV could lead to the revocation of the transitional provisions.[76]

7. Aid Measures Granted in the Agricultural and Transport Sectors

According to the Accession Treaty, aid measures in the agricultural and transport sectors were excluded from the "existing aid mechanism" of Annex IV.[77] The exception applicable to the agricultural sector reflected the fact that the large majority of acceding countries did not exercise a meaningful monitoring of public support to the agricultural sector. This lacuna was justified by the exemption of agricultural policy from the scope of pre-accession association agreements. The exception for the transport sector can be explained due to the different speeds at which various transport sectors gradually open up to competition.[78]   **5–018**

Thus, state aid granted in the agricultural sector was subject to a special regime under the Accession Treaty as set out in Ch.4 of Annex IV. It provided that aid measures put into effect in a new Member State before the date of accession and still applicable after that date, were regarded as "existing aid" only if the measure was communicated to the Commission as "existing aid" within four months of the date of accession, i.e. by August 31, 2004. These measures enjoyed the protection of "existing aid" until the date of a so-called "sunset clause". In effect, the new Member States had until the end of the third year after the date of accession, i.e. end of April 2007, to bring their measures into line with the requirements of EU state aid rules. However, after December 31, 2007, any

---

[74] O.J. L236, September 23, 2003, p.918.

[75] See for an application of the special exemption regime, the Commission decision SK 5/2004 regarding a reduction of tax concession granted by Slovakia to US Steel Košice, Slovakia, C(2004)3496 fin., September 22, 2004.)

[76] Chapter 4(2)(e) of Annex XIV to the 2003 Accession Treaty.

US Steel Košice has brought an action before the General Court, concerning the scope of application of Annex XIV and especially whether the territorial scope of the sales cap of flat products also includes Bulgaria and Romania. This action was declared as inadmissible by the Court of First Instance (Case T–22/07 *US Steel Košice v Commission* [2009] E.C.R. II–61).

[77] Chapter 3(1)(c) of Annex IV of the Accession Treaty excludes *expressis verbis* its application to activities linked to the production, processing and marketing of agricultural products in Annex I of the EC Treaty. Chapter 3(1)(4) of Annex IV of the Accession Treaty provides for special rules in the transport sector (O.J. L236, September 23, 2003, p.797).

[78] G. Roebling, "Existing Aid and Enlargement", *Competition Policy Newsletter*, No. 1, 2003.

existing state aid that was still incompatible with the *acquis* was considered as new aid.

5–019　Between April and the end of August 2004, the new Member States submitted their "existing aid" measures to the Commission, which was obliged to publish them according to Ch.4(4) of Annex IV.[79] It is important to note, however, that the Commission safeguarded its right to commence procedures regarding these aid measures if they conflict with other parts of Community law such as the rules on the free movement of goods or the common organisations for the markets for agricultural products.

The state aid rules regarding the exemption applicable to the transport sector followed a very similar regime. Chapter 3(4) of Annex IV of the Accession Treaty reads:

"As regards aid to the transport sector, aid schemes and individual aid put into effect in a new Member State before the date of accession, and still applicable after that date, shall be regarded as existing aid within the meaning of Article 88(1) of the EC Treaty until the end of the third year after the date of accession, provided they are communicated to the Commission within four months of the date of accession. This provision shall be without prejudice to the procedures concerning existing aid provided for in Article 88 of the EC Treaty."[80]

It followed from this provision that aid measures in force in the new Member States prior to May 1, 2004 that were communicated to the Commission by August 31, 2004, enjoyed, until the end of April 2007, the protection of "existing aid". According to the Commission, approximately 150 measures relating to the transport sector had been submitted by the new Member States to the Commission under the above mechanism.[81] It is noteworthy, however, that as regards the transport sector, the Commission was not obliged pursuant to Annex IV to publish a list of existing aid measures.

8. THE ACCESSION OF BULGARIA AND ROMANIA

5–020　On December 14, 2004, all 31 policy chapters were closed, and on April 25, 2005, the Accession Treaty with Romania and Bulgaria was signed.[82] This completed the fifth enlargement round of the European Union which already

---

[79] O.J. C147, June 17, 2005, p.2; O.J. C206, August 23, 2005, p.11 (Corrigenda).

[80] O.J. L236, September 23, 2003, p.798.

[81] Most of the aid measures had been notified by Poland and Hungary, which account for more than half of the total number of measures submitted. With regard to the different transport sectors, the information of the Commission shows that the rail sector benefits from most measures while the remaining aid measures are evenly spread among the other transport sectors. (State Aid Scoreboard—Autumn 2004 update—COM(2004)750 final, 16.11.2004, section 1.3.6.3.)

[82] O.J. L157, June 21, 2005 ("2005 Accession Treaty").

started in 2004 with the accession of the 10 new Member States and which foresaw accession of Romania and Bulgaria by January 1, 2007.

As in the previous enlargement rounds, both countries concluded Europe Agreements with the European Union and its Member States, which entered into force in February 1995.[83] Similarly, the countries had to fulfil the political and economic conditions established by the Copenhagen European Council in 1993. As explained earlier, the latter translated as regards the competition chapter into three main elements: (1) the disposal of the necessary legislative framework with respect to antitrust and state aid rules; (2) existence of an adequate administrative capacity, in particular, a well-functioning competition authority; and (3) a credible enforcement record in all areas of competition policy.

Like the 2003 Accession Treaty, the 2005 Accession Treaty signed with Romania and Bulgaria contained a number of safeguard clauses in the event that the acceding countries failed to implement commitments undertaken in the context of the accession negotiations. Thus, both Accession Treaties included a so-called general economic safeguard clause and a specific internal market safeguard clause.[84] However, for Romania and Bulgaria an additional safeguard clause, the postponement clause, was introduced. This clause foresaw that the Council could, on the basis of a Commission proposal, postpone enlargement for one year, i.e. from January 1, 2007 to January 1, 2008. The clause could be triggered if:

"based on the Commission's continuous monitoring of commitments undertaken by Bulgaria and Romania in the context of the accession negotiations and in particular the Commission's monitoring reports, there is clear evidence that the state of preparations for adoption and implementation of the *acquis* in Bulgaria and Romania is such that there is a serious risk of either of those

---

[83] Europe Agreement establishing an association between the European Communities and their Member States, of the one part, and the Republic of Bulgaria, of the other part, O.J. L358, December 31, 1994; Europe Agreement establishing an association between the European Communities and their Member States, of the one part, and Romania, of the other part, O.J. L357, December 31, 1994.

Also in these Europe Agreements, Bulgaria and Romania are defined as areas identical to those areas of the Community qualifying for regional aid under Article 107(3)(a) TFEU, i.e. the least developed regions. In 2000, the Association Councils decided to extend this status for another five years with respect to Bulgaria, Romania, Lithuania and Estonia.

[84] These safeguard clauses can be found in arts 37 and 38 of the 2003 Accession Treaty and arts 36 and 37 of the 2005 Accession Treaty. The general economic safeguard clause allows the new as well as the old Member States to adopt protective measures in the event of difficulties which are "serious and liable to persist in any sector of the economy or which could bring about serious deterioration in the economic situation of a given area." The specific internal market safeguard clause applies in the case of "a serious breach of the functioning of the internal market, including any commitments in all sectoral policies which concern economic activities with cross-border effect [...]." In the event of such imminent risk, the Commission can adopt Regulations or Decisions establishing appropriate measures. Both clauses could be invoked for a period up to three years after accession.

States being manifestly unprepared to meet the requirements of membership in a number of important areas."[85]

The invocation of the postponement clause was made conditional on the findings of the 2006 Monitoring Report.[86] However, based on the positive findings of the report, neither of the clauses were used, and both countries acceded to the European Union as envisaged on January 1, 2007.

5–021   As regards the principle of existing aid, the 2005 Accession Treaty also included an existing aid mechanism, similar to the one of the 2003 Accession Treaty. Chapter 2 of Annex V of the 2005 Accession Treaty[87] defined which aid measures should be considered as existing aid within the meaning of art.108(1) TFEU and described the interim procedure as explained in the context of accession of the ten new Member States. Thus, all measures granted by Bulgaria, which were still applicable after accession and which had been granted after December 10, 1994, or which had not been included in the Appendix to the Accession Treaty or passed the interim procedure were considered as new aid upon accession for the purpose of the application of art.108(3) TFEU.[88]

In contrast, for Romania, the 2005 Accession Treaty contained special provisions that the interim mechanism would only apply once the Commission concluded that Romania's state aid enforcement record had reached a satisfactory

---

[85] Article 39 of the 2005 Accession Treaty. In the case of Romania, the application of the postponement clause was specified and widened in that any serious shortcomings by Romania in its fulfilment of the specific conditions in the competition area, especially as regards the state aid enforcement record, could justify using this safeguard clause at any time before the end of 2006 and acting by qualified majority (whereas normally unanimity is required). The specific conditions in the competition area which have to be fulfilled by Romania were the following: (1) Romania must ensure effective control by its competition authority of any potential state aid, including in relation to state aid foreseen by means of deferral of payments to the state budget of fiscal or social liabilities or deferrals of liabilities related to energy supply; (2) Romania must strengthen its state aid enforcement record without delay. Romania must ensure a satisfactory enforcement record in the areas of both antitrust and state aid; (3) Romania must submit to the Commission by mid-December 2004 a revised steel restructuring plan (including the National Restructuring Programme and the Individual Business Plans) in line with the requirements set out in Protocol 2 on ECSC products to the Europe Agreement and with the conditions set out in the Accession Treaty. In particular, Romania must fully respect its commitments not to grant or pay any state aid to the steel mills covered by the National Restructuring Strategy from January 1, 2005 to December 31, 2008, and to fully respect the state aid amounts and the conditions regarding capacity reductions, decided in the context of Protocol 2 on ECSC products to the Europe Agreement; (4) Romania will continue to devote adequate financial means and sufficient and adequately qualified human resources to the Competition Council; (5) Romania must fulfil the obligations undertaken under the Europe Agreement. (Koen van de Casteele, "Next EU enlargement: Romania and State aid control", *Competition Policy Newsletter*, No.1 2005.)

[86] Commission staff working document, May 16, 2006, SEC (2006) 596, COM (2006) 214 final.

[87] O.J. L157, June 21, 2005, p.268.

[88] Bulgaria submitted two measures that had to be regarded as existing aid upon accession and which were annexed to the Accession Treaty. Appendix to Annex V contains the list of existing aid measures referred to in point 1(b) of the existing aid mechanism provided for in Ch.2 of Annex V, O.J. L157, June 21, 2005, p.277. Publication of a list of measures considered by the Commission as existing aid, within the meaning of art.88(1) of the EC Treaty, upon accession of Bulgaria and Romania to the European Union, O.J. C65, March 11, 2008, p.10.

level,[89] while measures granted before 1994 were also considered as existing aid. In practice, this meant that only cases with a positive assessment by the Romanian competition authority after the date set by the Commission as being the date that Romania's record is satisfactory could be submitted under the existing aid mechanism. However, such a satisfactory level was only considered to have been reached once Romania had demonstrated the consistent application of full and proper state aid control in relation to all aid measures granted in Romania. On the basis of the 2006 Monitoring Report, the Commission eventually chose May 1, 2006 as the starting date for the existing aid mechanism. Furthermore, it was entitled to object to, and in the case of incompatibility, recover state aid granted in the pre-accession period between September 1, 2004 and the starting date of the interim mechanism. Given the little time between the starting date and Romania's accession, Romania made very limited use of the interim mechanism.[90]

As regards agricultural policy and transport, the same rules as with respect to the 10 new Member States applied to Romania and Bulgaria, only with the exception that the sunset clause for these two countries expired on December 31, 2009, i.e. Romania and Bulgaria had until December 31, 2009 to bring their aid measures in compatibility with the state aid rules. After that date, any incompatible aid was considered as new aid. With respect to other transitional arrangements, Bulgaria did not request any exemptions regarding the competition chapter, whereas Romania required a number of them that were included in the Accession Treaty.[91]

9. SPECIAL PROVISIONS REGARDING THE STEEL SECTOR IN BULGARIA AND ROMANIA

As already indicated above, according to the provisions in the Europe Agreements, all countries, including Bulgaria and Romania, had to implement restructuring plans for their steel undertakings within five years from the signature of the Agreements, the so-called "grace period". As Poland and the Czech Republic, also Bulgaria and Romania asked for an extension of the grace period.

5–022

---

[89] Chapter 2(5) of Annex 5 of the 2005 Accession Treaty; State Aid Scoreboard—Spring 2006 update—COM(2006) 130 final, March 27, 2006, p.8.

[90] Publication of a list of measures considered by the Commission as existing aid, within the meaning of art.88(1) of the EC Treaty, upon accession of Bulgaria and Romania to the European Union, O.J. C65, March 11, 2008, p.10, State Aid Scoreboard, Spring 2008 update, COM (2008) 304 final.

[91] Annex VII of the 2005 Accession Treaty, O.J. L157, June 21, 2005, p.138. They concerned the following:
   – Phase-out of incompatible fiscal aid by December 31, 2011 under the Law on Free Trade Areas for undertakings, which signed commercial contracts before July 1, 2002;
   – Phase-out of incompatible fiscal aid by December 31, 2010 under the Government Emergency Ordinance on Deprived Areas for the undertakings, which were given the permanent investor certificate before July 1, 2003.
   As regards the transitional provisions regarding the steel sector, see below.

With respect to Bulgaria, a National Restructuring Programme for the steel industry until 2007 had been adopted and it was agreed that the country would complete its restructuring before accession.[92] It is for this reason that no transitional provisions were included in 2005 Accession Treaty (in contrast to Romania). However, in the context of its regular monitoring, the Commission noticed significant delays in the implementation of various obligations outlined in the Restructuring Programme.[93] It was therefore decided to adopt appropriate measures before accession to ensure the fulfilment of the conditions of the restructuring programme, in return for allowing a longer restructuring period.[94]

5–023   As regards Romania, it had asked for specific transitional provisions regarding the steel sector which were included in Annex VII to the 2005 Accession Treaty. It stipulated that the granting of restructuring aid was compatible with the Internal Market, provided that, inter alia, the terms set out in the National Restructuring Programme and the Individual Business Plans were adhered to throughout the restructuring period of 2002–2008, the aid granted was limited to the companies mentioned in the Annex, no restructuring aid was granted or paid after December 31, 2004, the end of the grace period, and all restructuring was completed no later than December 31, 2008.[95] As in the case of the transitional regimes for Poland and the Czech Republic, if aid was granted in contravention of the conditions of the Accession Treaty, the Commission was entitled to ask for recovery not only of the aid granted in contravention of the conditions after the end of the grace period but also of aid granted before accession. In addition, the transitional arrangements would end immediately, i.e. the Commission could open the formal investigation procedure pursuant to art.108(2) TFEU.

10. ACCESSION NEGOTIATIONS WITH CROATIA AND ICELAND

5–024   Croatia presented its application for EU membership on February 21, 2003, after having signed a Stabilisation and Association Agreement with the EU on October 29, 2001.[96] On October 3, 2005, the EU Member States decided to

---

[92] Council Decision 2004/746/EC of October 18, 2004, O.J. 2004 L328/101.

[93] Bulgaria May 2006 Monitoring Report (Commission staff working document), May 16, 2006, SEC (2006) 594, COM (2006) 214 final, p.30.

[94] Proposal for a Council Decision on a Community Position in the EC-Bulgaria Association Council on the amendment of art.3 of the Additional Protocol to the Europe Agreement establishing an association between the European Communities and their Member States, on the one part, and the Republic of Bulgaria, of the other part, with regard to an extension of the period laid down in art.9(4) of Protocol 2 to the Europe Agreement, COM(2006) 772. Approved by the European Parliament in consultation procedure in legislative resolution on the proposal for a Council decision on the conclusion of an Additional Protocol to the Europe Agreement establishing an association between the European Communities and their Member States, of the one part, and the Republic of Bulgaria, of the other part, with regard to an extension of the period laid down in art.9(4) of Protocol 2 to the Europe Agreement, O.J. C31, February 5, 2004.

[95] Chapter 4(B) of Annex VII, O.J. L157, June 21, 2005.

[96] Stabilisation and Association Agreement between the European Communities and their Member States, of the one part, and the Republic of Croatia, of the other part, O.J. L26, January 28, 2005. An interim agreement, including provisions on competition and State aid entered into force on March 1, 2002 in order to allow the early entry into force of the trade and trade-related

launch accession negotiations with the screening process starting shortly thereafter.[97] The advancement of the negotiations was guided by the candidate country's progress in preparing for accession. As in the previous enlargement rounds, the principles for the negotiations were drawn from the political and economic criteria established by the Copenhagen European Council in 1993.[98]

In its 2005 Monitoring Report on Croatia, the Commission identified a number of shortcomings, especially as regards legislative alignment with European state aid rules and the development of a state aid enforcement record. As regards the latter, the Commission concluded that enforcement needed to be strengthened both in relation to its scope and the carrying out of economic and legal assessment. Also, the notification obligation was not sufficiently respected by aid grantors.[99] Further specific problem areas constituted fiscal aid, the shipbuilding and the steel sector.[100] In these sectors, Croatia had not fulfilled its obligation to establish restructuring programmes and continued to grant state aid.[101]

On February 20, 2006, the Council adopted a Decision as regards the "principles, priorities and conditions contained in the Accession Partnership with Croatia".[102] It identified the following short term priorities in the field of state aid:

    5–025

(1) ensure further alignment of primary and secondary legislation so as to allow effective anti-trust and state aid control with binding decisions applicable to all economic sectors and, as regards state aid, for both aid schemes and individual aid measures;

(2) strengthen the administrative capacity and the independence of the Competition Agency, and ensure the development and training of the judiciary in competition matters;

(3) Strengthen the state aid enforcement record, in particular by ensuring respect of notification obligations and a pro-active assessment of all aid measures;

(4) ensure that existing aid schemes and all fiscal legislation are aligned with the state aid *acquis*;

provisions of the Stabilisation and Association Agreement (O.J. L330, December 14, 2001). (See State Aid Scoreboard—Spring 2006 update—COM(2006) 130 final, March 27, 2006, p.16.)

[97] Screening Report Croatia adopted on 3 May 2006.

[98] State Aid Scoreboard—Spring 2006 update—COM(2006) 130 final, March 27, 2006, p.14.

[99] Croatia 2005 Progress Report, November 9, 2005, SEC (2005) 1424, COM (2005) 561 final, p.59.

[100] Note that pursuant to art.5 of Protocol 2 on steel products to the Stabilisation and Association Agreement, Croatia could exceptionally grant state aid for restructuring purposes for five years after the entry into force of the Agreement, provided that it leads to the viability of the benefiting firms under normal market conditions at the end of the restructuring period, the amount and intensity of such are strictly limited to what is absolutely necessary in order to restore such viability and are linked to global rationalisation and reduction of capacity in Croatia.

[101] State Aid Scoreboard—Spring 2006 update—COM(2006) 130 final, March 27, 2006, p.17.

[102] O.J. L55, February 25, 2006, p.30.

(5) adopt and start implementing viable restructuring programmes in the steel and shipbuilding sectors, in line with EU requirements to ensure, inter alia, that all aid is in line with the *acquis*;

(6) ensure transparency of state aid by establishing a comprehensive inventory and reporting of all aid measures in force at all administrative levels and raise awareness of competition principles.[103]

Already in the 2006 progress report, the Commission noted a considerable progress with the adoption of the new State Aid Act and the new Regulation on state aid, as well as an improved enforcement record of the Competition Agency. Also the alignment with the *acquis* of the fiscal aid showed progress while the adoption of restructuring plans for companies in the shipbuilding sector as well as the adoption of a steel restructuring programme was still lagging behind.[104]

5–026   Further progress in line with the priorities identified in the 2007 Council Decision on the principles, priorities and conditions contained in the Accession Partnership with Croatia was achieved according to the 2007[105] and 2008 progress reports, especially as regards the enforcement record, the fiscal aid measures and the adoption of restructuring plans in the shipbuilding and steel sectors.[106] In its 2009 progress report, the Commission noted that through the launching of the privatisation process for six shipyards, Croatia had made significant progress in its alignment efforts[107] and concluded in the 2010 progress report that while the adoption of a national restructuring plan for the steel sector was still outstanding,[108] legislative alignment was almost completed.[109]

Further progress being achieved in the meantime, President Barroso announced on June 19, 2011 that the European Commission had proposed to the EU Council of Ministers to close the last four chapters in the accession negotiations with Croatia.[110] On June 24, the European Council invited the Council of Ministers to "take all the necessary decisions for the conclusion of the accession

---

[103] These short-term priorities were updated by Council Decision of November 6, 2007 (COM (2007) 658) with the following short-term priorities as regards state aid:
  – adopt a National Restructuring Programme for the steel sector and adopt individual restructuring plans for each of the shipyards in difficulties;
  – complete legislative alignment with EU state aid rules in the area of fiscal aid and align all other remaining aid schemes; adopt the regional aid map.

[104] Croatia 2006 Progress Report, November 8, 2006, SEC (2006) 1385, COM (2006) 649 final, p.32.

[105] Following the 2007 Progress Report, a new Council Decision was adopted on February 12, 2008 (O.J. 2008 L42/51) that reiterated the short-term priorities as already defined in the 2007 Council Decision on the principles, priorities and conditions contained in the Accession Partnership with Croatia.

[106] Croatia 2007 Progress Report, November 6, 2007, SEC (2007) 1431, COM (2007) 663 final, p.31; Croatia 2008 Progress Report, November 5, 2008, SEC (2008) 2694 final, COM (2008) 674, p.34.

[107] Croatia 2009 Progress Report, October 14, 2009, SEC (2009) 1333/2, COM (2009) 533, p.35.

[108] The former restructuring plan had become obsolete due to the economic crisis.

[109] Croatia 2010 Progress Report, November 9, 2010, SEC (2010) 1326, COM (2010) 660, p.33.

[110] MEMO/11/397.

negotiations with Croatia by the end of June 2011 on the basis of the draft common positions recently presented by the Commission with a view to the signing of the Accession Treaty before the end of the year."[111] On June 30, the EU Member States decided to close accession negotiations with Croatia,[112] which should allow for the signature of the Accession Treaty by the end of 2011. Following the ratification procedure in all Member States and Croatia,[113] accession of Croatia as the 28th Member State is foreseen for July 1, 2013.

Iceland presented its application for membership to the European Union on July 17, 2009. Its application for membership has to be seen against the background of the financial crisis and the collapse of the Icelandic banking system in October 2008 which triggered a series of developments. In April 2009, the government changed and in July 2009, on a proposal by the new government of Social Democratic Alliance and Left Green Movement, the Icelandic parliament voted in favour of applying to join the European Union.   **5–027**

When assessing Iceland's application for EU membership, the Commission applies as for all other accession countries the criteria of the 1993 Copenhagen European Council. However, Iceland and the European Union have been cooperating extensively over the last forty years, among others, in the context of the European Free Trade Association, since 1994 in the context of the European Economic Area and since 2001 through the Schengen Agreement, so that the accession negotiations with Iceland will most likely prove to be faster and less contentious in many areas. As such, through the EEA Agreement, Iceland has adopted a significant part of EU Law whose application has been monitored by the EFTA Surveillance Authority, a supranational monitoring authority with similar competences as the European Commission. According to the Commission, the country showed a satisfactory track record in implementing its obligations under the EEA and therefore recommended on February 24, 2010 to open the accession negotiations with Iceland.[114]

As regards the application of the economic criteria of the Copenhagen Council, and in specific the application of state aid rules, the Commission noted in its 2010 screening report that given the almost identical wording of the relevant provisions of the EEA Agreement[115] and arts 107 and 108 of the TFEU and the control of state aid exercised by the EFTA Surveillance Authority, Iceland is largely aligned with the *acquis*. However, the Commission will closely monitor   **5–028**

---

[111] European Council Conclusions of June 23/24, 2011.

[112] IP/11/824.

[113] Croatia voted in favour of accession in a referendum held on January 22, 2012.

[114] Communication from the Commission to the European Parliament and the Council, Commission opinion on Iceland's application for membership of the European Union of February 24, 2010, COM (2010) 62.

[115] Article 61(1) of the EEA Agreement provides that aid granted by the EU Member States and the EFTA States which distorts or threatens to distort competition by favouring certain undertakings or the production of certain goods is incompatible with the Agreement in so far as it affects trade between the contracting parties. Article 61(2) provides that state aid can be compatible with the Agreement, on conditions that are almost identical to those listed in art.107(3) TFEU. The only difference is art.107(3)(d) TFEU concerning the compatibility of state aid to promote culture and heritage conservation, which is not included in the EEA Agreement.

developments in particular as regards measures taken in response to the financial crisis.[116]

11. CONCLUSION

5–029   The enlargement process with the 12 new Member States is generally considered as an economic success, a win-win situation for both new and old Member States and the European Union as a whole.[117] The old Member States win with the increase of the internal market and more trade and investment opportunities. For the new Member States, the adoption of the *acquis communautaire* helped reform the previously centrally planned economies and brought about economic and financial stability. Especially in the field of state aid control, the new Member States had to undergo tough reforms. Here, potentially harsh effects of applying the strict EU state aid rules from the day of accession to countries without any legal tradition in this field could be softened with the introduction of the existing aid mechanism and the interim procedure in the Accession Treaty. From the perspective of the old Member States, these two mechanisms also helped to prevent the "import" of distortive aid into the European Union. Moreover, as can be seen in the context of Romania, the European Union can go even further by introducing additional safeguards which increase the pressure on a country to fully comply with the *acquis* by the date of accession.

The accession of Croatia is foreseen for 2013 and also the accession of Iceland will in all likelihood take place in the near future. Further candidate countries are the Former Yugoslav Republic of Macedonia, Montenegro and Turkey, whereas potential candidate countries include Albania, Bosnia and Herzegovina, Serbia and Kosovo.[118] It is clear that the accession process provides strong encouragement for political and economic reform and that application for accession to the EU is seen as an important step for promoting stability, security and prosperity in the candidate countries. The Treaty of Lisbon introduced the necessary institutional reform to ensure a framework that should allow a smooth adaptation of the Union's institutions once a new Member State joins the European Union.[119] However, major challenges connected, among others, to the severe

---

[116] Screening report Iceland, Ch.8, Competition Policy, March 4, 2011. The next step is the adoption of a draft Common Position by the Commission, proposing the opening of negotiations on Ch.8 to be adopted by the Council.

[117] See, for instance, for an analysis of the effects of accession Commission Communication "Five years of an enlarged EU—Economic achievements and challenges" February 20, 2008, COM (2009) 79/3.

[118] Under UN Security Council Resolution 1244.

[119] Commission Communication of October 14, 2009 on Enlargement Strategy and Main Challenges 2009–2010, COM (2009) 533.

global economic crisis lie ahead, not only as regards the political and economic reform process in the candidate countries but also as regards the "old" Member States. Whereas the European Union is continuously committed to further enlargement,[120] time will tell how and at what pace future enlargement rounds will take place.

---

[120] Commission Communication of October 14, 2009 on Enlargement Strategy and Main Challenges 2009–2010, COM (2009) 533.

CHAPTER 6

WTO REGULATION OF SUBSIDIES*

1. Introduction 6–001
   General 6–001
   Background 6–002
2. The WTO Agreement on Subsidies and Countervailing Measures 6–004
   Definition of a subsidy 6–005
   Specificity 6–008
   Categories of subsidies 6–009
   Remedies 6–012
   Double remedies 6–017
   Special and differential treatment of developing countries (Part VIII, Art.27) 6–020
   Current state of Doha Rules negotiations 6–021
3. The WTO Agreement on Agriculture 6–022
4. The WTO General Agreement on Trade in Services 6–026
5. European Regulation of Countervailing Duties 6–027
6. WTO Subsidy and EU State Aid Control 6–029
   Possible introduction of international disciplines on state aid 6–031

1. INTRODUCTION

General

6–001   Recourse to subsidies as a form of government intervention has traditionally caused a great deal of controversy at international as well as at EU level, owing to the distortions of trade and investment that subsidisation can cause, and the subsequent welfare losses for the international economy as well as for individual countries. The economic impact of subsidies on global competition has become increasingly evident as trade negotiations have succeeded in reducing tariffs and other border measures. Subsidies have therefore always been a natural if complex

---

* Marco Bronckers, Gary Horlick and Ravi Soopramanien

subject matter for international negotiation and regulation.[1] Since its inception, the multilateral trading system has recognised the need to provide some transparency and discipline in this area. In addition, to counter the effects of foreign subsidisation, a number of countries have responded by developing their own countervailing duty procedures. This has led the international regulation of subsidies to become inextricably linked with the multilateral control of unilateral countervailing measures.

International trade law has provided for—albeit limited—regulation of subsidies for over 50 years, to begin with in the General Agreement on Tariffs and Trade (GATT) 1947, with later supplements and amendments. The current regime was established in the World Trade Organization (WTO) Agreement on Subsidies and Countervailing Measures in 1994. The purpose of this short chapter is to outline the current international law on subsidies and countervailing measures.

Background

In the beginning there was art.XVI of the GATT, which in 1947 introduced an **6–002** obligation on parties to notify subsidy schemes which operate directly or indirectly to increase exports or reduce imports of goods. Further, art.XVI provided that in any case in which such subsidisation causes or threatens to cause serious prejudice to any other party, the party granting the subsidy has an obligation to consult with other contracting parties or parties concerned as to the possibility of its limitation. Article XVI also introduced a prohibition, as of January 1, 1958, of export subsidies for products other than primary products, defined as any product of farm, forest or fishery, or any mineral.[2] For primary products, it was provided that the parties should seek to avoid the use of export subsidies and, further, that such subsidies should not be applied in a manner that would result in the subsidising party having more than an equitable share of world export trade in that product. An illustrative list of export subsidies was adopted by the GATT Contracting Parties in 1960. New and unanticipated subsidies, furthermore, could form the basis of a complaint pursuant to art.XXIII of the GATT, to the extent that these subsidies "nullified or impaired" the benefits of tariff concessions.[3]

In addition, from the GATT's inception in 1947, art.VI was included to govern unilateral anti-dumping and countervailing duty actions. Article VI permits a GATT, and now WTO member to apply an extra customs tariff (a "countervailing duty") at its border to offset foreign subsidies. Specifically, a countervailing duty can be imposed to offset a subsidy bestowed, directly or indirectly, upon the

---

[1] For a contrarian perspective on the need for subsidies regulation, see Alan Sykes, "The Questionable Case for Subsidies Regulation: A Comparative Perspective", *Stanford University School of Law—Law and Economics Research Paper Series,* Paper No. 380 (2009).

[2] *Ad* art.XVI, at S.B.2.

[3] See for instance the GATT Panel Reports on: *The Australian Subsidy on Ammonium Sulphate*, adopted on April 3, 1950, 1st Supp. BISD II/188, at para.12ff; and *EEC—Payments and Subsidies Paid to Processors and Producers of Oilseeds and Related Animal-Feed Proteins*, adopted on January 25, 1990, 37th Supp. BISD 37S/86.

manufacture, production or export of any merchandise, in an amount equal to the estimated subsidy determined to have been granted, provided that such a foreign subsidy or subsidies cause material injury to the domestic industry within the country imposing the countervailing duty.

6–003   Article XVI, together with arts VI and XXIII, were subject to subsequent agreements on the interpretation of these articles, notably in 1979. However, art.XVI of the GATT, with its obligations to notify, consult, and limit subsidies was always fairly toothless. Regulation of subsidies was considered ineffective and in need of a drastic overhaul,[4] and this took place in the context of the Uruguay Round (1986–1994). At the same time, one of the major negotiating objectives of the Uruguay Round was to cover agriculture—in particular the use of subsidies for agricultural products.

In April 1994, after lengthy and often acrimonious negotiations, the Agreement on Subsidies and Countervailing Measures (the SCM Agreement) was adopted as part of the Multilateral Agreements on Trade in Goods included in Annex 1A to the Marrakech Agreement Establishing the World Trade Organisation. Similarly, the conclusion of the Agreement on Agriculture, which contains tough regulation and progressive elimination of agricultural export subsidies, was achieved. Cautiously, the topic of subsidies to services was also broached, in the General Agreement on Trade in Services (GATS).

2. THE WTO AGREEMENT ON SUBSIDIES AND COUNTERVAILING MEASURES

6–004   The SCM Agreement first defines the notion of subsidy, as well as the concept of specificity. It then distinguishes two categories of subsidies to which different disciplines are attached: (a) prohibited subsidies; and (b) actionable subsidies.[5]

Definition of a subsidy

6–005   In accordance with SCM art.1, subsidies are deemed to exist when two criteria are fulfilled: firstly, there must be a financial contribution (or price/income support) granted by a government or any public body,[6] including sub-national government entities; secondly, a benefit must be provided.[7]

---

[4] See the "Report of Eminent Persons on Problems Facing the International Trading System", reprinted in 24 I.L.M. 716 (1985) ("Leutwiler Report").

[5] Originally, the SCM Agreement also spoke of non-actionable subsidies. However, that category has expired, see fn.23, below.

[6] The Appellate Body recently defined a "public body" as an "entity that possesses, exercises or is vested with governmental authority", and added a note of caution that "[p]anels or investigating authorities confronted with the question of whether conduct falling within the scope of Article 1.1(a)(1) is that of a public body will be in a position to answer that question only by conducting a proper evaluation of the core features of the entity concerned, and its relationship with government in the narrow sense." See *Appellate Body Report, United States—Definitive Anti-Dumping and Countervailing Duties on Certain Products from China*, WT/DS379/AB/R (2011)("US—AD & CVD from China"), at para.317.

[7] Article 1.1(a)(2) SCM. Such schemes include stabilisation schemes; see GATT Panel Report on Operation of the Provisions of art.XVI, adopted on November 21, 1961, BISD 105/201.

Financial contribution (or price or income support).[8] Article 1.1(a)(1) identifies four categories of financial contribution. It may involve: (i) a direct or potentially direct transfer of funds[9]; (ii) forgone government revenue[10]; (iii) goods or services provided (other than general infrastructure)[11] or purchased by

6–006

[8] The concept of "price or import support" comes from the text of art.XVI GATT 1947. A 1960 GATT Panel Report stated that a system "under which a government, by direct or indirect methods, maintains such a price by purchases and resale at a loss is a subsidy", "Panel Report on Review Pursuant to art.XVI(5)", adopted May 24, 1960, L/1160, BISD 95/188. The Panel also considered that there could be methods by which a government maintained a fixed price above the world price without resort to a subsidy.

[9] A Panel in *US—Aircraft* was asked for the first time to evaluate whether government purchases of services, and government transfers of intellectual property rights, could properly be characterised as "financial contributions" by a government within the scope of SCM art.1.1(a)(1). We will address each in turn. On the issue of government purchases of services, namely NASA R&D projects awarded to Boeing, the Panel concluded, based on the express removal of "purchases" of "services" from prior drafts of the SCM Agreement, that "the drafters could not have removed the express reference to 'purchases' of 'services' in Article 1.1(a)(1)(iii) on the understanding that the reference was superfluous. . . rather, the exclusion of 'purchases' of 'services' from Article 1 can only be seen as a deliberate choice." See Panel Report, *United States—Measures Affecting Trade in Large Civil Aircraft* (Second Complaint), *US—Aircraft*, WT/DS353/R (2011), at para.7.969. The Panel nevertheless evaluated, at para.7.891, that the NASA R&D projects at issue could not properly be characterized as featuring government purchases of services, on account of the fact that "the work that Boeing performed under its aeronautics R&D contracts with NASA was principally for its own benefit or use, rather than for the benefit or use of the US Government." The EU has appealed the Panel's conclusion that government purchases of services fall outside the scope of the SCM Agreement. On the issue of government transfers of IPRs, namely NASA & US Department of Defense (DoD) patent waivers, the Panel declined to make any findings on whether the allocation of IPRs to entities could be characterised as a "financial contribution". The Panel justified its decision on the ground, at para.7.1276, that "it is clear that the allocation of patent rights under NASA and DoD contracts and agreements is not specific to a 'group of enterprises or industries' within the meaning of Article 2 of the SCM Agreement." The Panel—indubitably anticipating an appeal on this point—fleshed out its reasoning on the lack of specificity by assuming, *in arguendo*, that the transfer of IPRs could constitute a "financial contribution." The EU has appealed the Panel's findings on non-specificity.

[10] See Appellate Body Report, *United States—Tax Treatment for 'Foreign Sales Corporations'*, WT/DS108/AB/R (2000) (*US—FSC*), at para.90 ("this cannot, however, be entitlement in the abstract, because governments, in theory, could tax all revenues. There must, therefore, be some defined, normative benchmark against which a comparison can be made between the revenue actually raised and the revenue that would have been raised 'otherwise.' ") See also Appellate Body Report, *Canada—Certain Measures Affecting the Automotive Industry*, WT/DS139/AB/R, WT/DS142/AB/R (2000) (*Canada—Autos*), at paras 90–94.

[11] A Panel in *EC—Aircraft* was asked for the first time to evaluate whether airline infrastructure granted by the EU, France and Germany was specific (i.e. "non-general") for SCM purposes. The Panel noted at the outset that an evaluation of whether infrastructure is a subsidy for the purposes of SCM art.1 will vary on a case-by-case basis. In so doing, the Panel dismissed an argument by the EU that there exists certain categories of infrastructure that are inherently general. See Panel Report, *European Communities and Certain Member States—Measures Affecting Trade in Large Civil Aircraft*, WT/DS316/R (2010) (*EC—Aircraft*), at paras 7.1041–7.1044. See also Panel Report, *US—Aircraft*, supra, note 9, at para.7.431, where the Panel suggested that the main criterion by which to assess whether infrastructure is non-general turned on whether or not the infrastructure in question was "specifically designed" to accommodate the subsidised entity in question. The Appellate Body did not address this issue on appeal but, at para.967. modified the Panel's findings insofar as the Panel had calculated the benefit reaped by Airbus from the use of non-general infrastructure against the "creation" of three infrastructural projects—the Muhlenberger Loch industrial site in Hamburg, the ZAC Aeroconstellation site in Toulouse and a runway extension at Bremen airport. The Appellate Body agreed with the EU

a government[12]; or (iv) payments by or on behalf of a government to a funding mechanism, or government direction to a private body to perform the same functions as outlined above. The last category is probably the most controversial.[13]

6–007   **Benefit to the recipient.** A key feature of the definition of a subsidy under the SCM Agreement is that a benefit must be conferred on the recipient. In sum, a benefit arises if the recipient has received a "financial contribution" on terms more favourable than those available in the market.[14] Accordingly, a benefit for SCM purposes is evaluated against a "market value" standard. Pursuant to this standard, a benefit occurs when a company is placed in a better position financially than it otherwise would have been in absence of the financial contribution

that SCM art.1.1(a)(1)(iii) spoke to the "provision" of infrastructure to a subsidised entity, so that any benefit derived by Airbus stood to be evaluated against Airbus's *exclusive use* of such infrastructure, as opposed to the creation of this infrastructure. The Appellate Body nevertheless cautioned that "we. . . do not view the use of the term 'provision' in Article 1.1(a)(1)(iii) as excluding the possibility that circumstances of the creation of infrastructure may be relevant to a proper characterization of what it is that is provided." See Appellate Body Report, *European Communities and Certain Member States—Measures Affecting Trade in Large Civil Aircraft*, WT/DS316/AB/R (2011)(*EC—Aircraft*), at para.965.

[12] For an analysis of what constitutes a "good", see Panel Report, *United States—Preliminary Determinations with Respect to Certain Softwood Lumber from Canada*, WT/DS236/R (2002).

[13] See Panel and Appellate Body Reports in *United States—Countervailing Duties Investigation on Dynamic Random Access Memory Semiconductors (DRAMS) from Korea*, WT/DS296/R and WT/DS296/AB/R (2005) (*US—Countervailing Duty Investigation on DRAMS*); Panel Reports in *European Communities—Countervailing Measures on Dynamic Random Access Memory Chips from Korea*, WT/DS299/R (2005) (*EC—Countervailing Measures on DRAM Chips*) and *Korea—Measures Affecting Trade in Commercial Vessels*, WT/DS273/R (2005) (*Korea— Commercial Vessels*). See also Panel Report, *United States—Measures Treating Export Restraints as Subsidies*, WT/DS194/R (2001), (*US—Export Restraints*) where the discussion centred on the meaning of "entrusts or directs." The Panel found that the terms encompass (1) an "explicit and affirmative action" of delegation or command, (2) addressed to a particular party, and (3) the "object of which is a particular task or duty" (Panel Report, *US—Export Restraints*, at para.8.29). In *EC—Countervailing Measures on DRAM Chips* (at para.7.57), and *Korea—Commercial Vessels* (at para.7.370), and in *US—Countervailing Duty Investigation on DRAMS* (at para.7.33), the Panels have rejected that a delegation or command should necessarily be "explicit." In the last case, the Appellate Body also stated that an interpretation of the term "entrusts" and "directs" that is limited to acts of "delegation" and "command" was too narrow (at paras 110–111), and left open the possibility, at para.118, that mere governmental "guidance" could in appropriate circumstances inform an instance of "direction" or "entrustment." It also affirmed that the relevant treaty text "is intended to ensure that governments do not evade their obligations under the SCM Agreement by using private bodies to take actions that would otherwise fall within Art.1.1(a)(1) were they to be taken by the government itself. In other words, Art.1.1(a)(1)(iv) is, in essence, an anti-circumvention provision. A finding of entrustment or direction, therefore, requires that the government give responsibility to a private body—or exercise its authority over a private body—in order to effectuate a financial contribution" (at para.113).

[14] See Appellate Body Report, *Canada—Measures Affecting the Export of Civilian Aircraft*, WT/DS70/AB/R (1999) (*Canada—Aircraft*), at para.158. See also the *US—Aircraft* Panel's conclusion that, as Boeing had never made use of specified Washington State sales and use tax exemptions for construction services and equipment, and tax abatements for leasehold excise and property taxes that were otherwise available to Boeing, Boeing could not be said to have received any "financial contributions" in relation to these tax exemptions. See *US—Aircraft*, fn.9, above, at para.7.151. The EU has not appealed the Panel's conclusions on this point.

or price support.[15] Guidelines for calculating benefits are provided in SCM art.14,[16] which is constructed in the negative in that it sets out a number of tests that define circumstances in which a benefit shall not be considered to exist. In other words, it is possible for a government to make a financial contribution that does not confer a benefit—such as a loan at market rates—and thus does not constitute a subsidy. Similarly, a government could also conceivably provide a benefit but not a financial contribution, for example by placing a government restraint on exports,[17] which may benefit users of the product by lowering the price in the domestic market, but is not a financial contribution and thus not a subsidy (such a constraint may contravene art.XI of the GATT 1994).

Export credit guarantees are distinct from other export subsidies regulated by the SCM Agreement, in being defined in terms of a "cost to government".[18] This has led WTO defendants to argue that the relevant benefit should be evaluated against the net costs of a subsidy to the providing authority, so that no benefit exists where the government bears no losses. The Appellate Body in *Canada—Aircraft* rejected this line of argument, determining that SCM art.14, insofar as it sought to calculate the "benefit to the recipient conferred pursuant to paragraph 1 of Art. 1," implied that benefits for the purposes of SCM art.1 may only be calculated under the "benefit to the recipient" standard.[19] WTO Panels must subsequently evaluate the WTO-inconsistency of export credit guarantees against art.14's "market value" standard.[20] A footnote to the SCM Agreement nevertheless considers that measures not constituting export credit guarantees within the meaning of the SCM Agreement, shall not be prohibited under the SCM Agreement.[21] This led Brazil to formulate the argument in *Brazil—Aircraft* that, as their export credit guarantee schemes bore no losses, this by definition precluded a finding that these schemes were export subsidies for SCM Agreement purposes. While a Panel dismissed Brazil's argument, the Appellate Body has yet to react to the so-called "a contrario" argument.[22]

[15] See Appellate Body Report, *United States—Imposition of Countervailing Duties on Certain Hot-Rolled Lead and Bismuth Carbon Steel Products Originating in the United Kingdom*, WT/DS138/AB/R (2000) (*US—Lead and Bismuth II*).

[16] In *Canada—Aircraft*, the Appellate Body stated that "although the opening words of Art.14 state that the guidelines it establishes apply '[f]or the purposes of Part V' of the SCM Agreement, which relates to 'countervailing measures', our view is that Art.14, nonetheless, constitutes relevant context for the interpretation of 'benefit' in Art. 1.1(b)." See, *Canada—Aircraft*, fn.14, above, at para.155.

[17] See, notably, Panel Report, *US—Export Restraints*, fn.13, above.

[18] See Items J and K of the Illustrative List of Export Subsidies contained at SCM Annex I.

[19] See, fn.16, above.

[20] See, fn.14, above.

[21] See SCM fn.5.

[22] Panel Report, *Brazil—Export Financing Programme for Aircraft—Recourse by Canada to Article 21.5 of the DSU (Brazil—Aircraft (Article 21.5—Canada))*, WT/DS46 (2000), at para.6.36. It is suggested in the literature that the Panel did so in order to be mindful of the disparity that such an argument—if accepted—would create between developed and developing WTO Members, to the extent that developed countries would have cheaper access to funds. See Dominic Coppens, "How Much Credit for Export Credit Support under the SCM Agreement?", 12 J. Int'l Econ. L. 63 (2009), at p.112.

Specificity

6–008   Even if there is a financial contribution by a government and a benefit is thereby conferred, a subsidy must also be specific in order to be prohibited or actionable (art.1.2).

A prohibited subsidy is automatically deemed specific (art.2.3) and is per se illegal and countervailable. In order to be actionable, however, a subsidy must be found to be specific. Specific subsidies are defined as those to which access is, formally or in fact, limited to: (a) certain specific *enterprises* or *groups of enterprises*; (b) to *industries* or to *groups of industries*; or (c) to enterprises and/ or industries in a *specific geographical region* (art.2). Non-specific subsidies are those which are generally available according to objective criteria and are broadly distributed to all enterprises or industry in a country. *De jure* non-specificity may be challenged on a number of grounds, including the track record of the granting authority and the actual concentration in the use of a subsidies program (art.2(c)).

As with EU state aid law, the dividing line between specific and general measures may not always be clear. Article 2.4 requires that any determination of specificity "shall be clearly substantiated on the basis of positive evidence"— that is, the investigating authorities of the complaining member bear the burden of proof in demonstrating specificity.

Categories of subsidies

6–009   The SCM Agreement currently distinguishes two categories of subsidies: "prohibited" and "actionable" subsidies.[23]

6–010   **Prohibited subsidies (Part II, Article 3).** Subsidies which are contingent upon export performance in law or in fact (export subsidies) and those contingent upon the use of domestic over imported goods (import-substitution subsidies) are prohibited. The SCM Agreement provides that a member shall neither grant nor maintain them. As to export subsidies, the WTO Appellate Body has said that in considering whether a subsidy is "contingent" upon exportation, one should consider whether the "condition can be demonstrated on the basis of the actual text of the relevant legislation, regulation or other legal instrument."[24] However,

---

[23] There was originally a third category of subsidies: non-actionable subsidies. Even if specific, some research and development, environmental and regional subsidies were immune from action (art.8 SCM). However, this provision had a five-year lifespan, requiring renewal. Members could not reach an agreement as to its extension, so it expired at the end of 1999 along with the presumption of serious prejudice in SCM art.6.1. Thus, all such programs are now actionable. See SCM arts 8 and 31.

[24] See Appellate Body Report, *Canada—Autos*, fn.10, above. See also Panel Report, *Australia— Subsidies Provided to Producers and Exporters of Automotive Leather*, WT/DS126/R (1999) (*Australia—Automotive Leather*), which makes it clear that export contingency requires that there be some explicit or implicit linkage to export in order for a subsidy to be considered contingent in law or fact upon export performance.

even where the granting of a subsidy is not made legally contingent upon export performance, the standard can be met when the facts demonstrate that its granting is in fact tied to actual or anticipated exportation or export earnings. That said, the mere fact that a subsidy is granted to enterprises which export is not enough to deem it an export subsidy.[25] An illustrative list of examples of export subsidies is included in SCM Annex 1.[26] As to import-substitution subsidies, the Appellate Body stated that the same legal standard of "contingency" applies,[27] and that the prohibition extends to subsidies contingent "in fact" upon the use of domestic over imported goods, despite the absence of these words in the relevant text.[28]

Actionable subsidies (Part III, Article 5). This category covers those specific subsidies which, although not prohibited, are actionable because they allegedly cause adverse effects to the interests of other members by injuring their domestic industry, nullifying or impairing their benefits under GATT, or causing them **6–011**

---

[25] See fn.4 to SCM art.3.1(a) SCM. However, see Panel Report, *EC—Aircraft*, fn.11, above, at para.7.678, where the Panel deemed destination-neutral subsidies to be export subsidies, having regard to the "substantial number of exports" required for Airbus to repay loans. In coming to this view, the Panel seemed to hint at the existence of some de minimis exportation threshold that the EU had crossed. Interestingly, the Panel in *US—Aircraft* came to a different conclusion to the Panel in *EC—Aircraft* on this point, despite the EU's reference to the *EC—Aircraft* Panel's conclusions in *US—Aircraft* proceedings, where the EU indicated, at para.7.1487, that it would accept "that there does not need to be a legal obligation to perform, that necessarily involves export sales, in order successfully to argue that that a subsidy is contingent in fact upon anticipated exports. . . on the condition that it be applied consistently in all WTO disputes, which would result in all of the United States' Article 3 claims being rejected in EC—Aircraft." The Panel in *US—Aircraft* held otherwise and determined that, while the EU had adduced sufficient evidence that grantors of the Washington State subsidies at issue had anticipated *some* exports of Boeing aircrafts, the EU had failed to demonstrate that these Washington State subsidies were "tied to," or "contingent" upon export performance. See Panel Report, *US—Aircraft*, fn.9, above, at paras 7.1543 and 7.1589. On appeal, the Appellate Body in *EC—Aircraft* steered closer to the approach of the *US—Aircraft* Panel, and reversed the *EC—Aircraft* Panel's findings that the destination-neutral subsidies at issue were contingent upon export performance. In so doing, the Appellate Body, notably at para.1063, considered that the Panel had ascribed too much importance to the purported motivations of the EU in granting the subsidies at issue: "the standard for finding that the granting of a subsidy is in fact tied to anticipated exportation is not met simply by showing that anticipated exportation is the reason for granting the subsidy. The test is whether the granting of the subsidy is geared to induce the promotion of future export performance by the recipient. The authority's reasons for the granting of the subsidy may provide some evidence to meet the correct standard, but it is not to be equated with that standard. The reason for granting the subsidy is not the same thing as whether the granting of the subsidy is geared to induce the promotion of future export performance by the recipient." The Appellate Body instead suggested that proof that the ratio of anticipated exports to domestic sales of a subsidised product, if tilted towards exportation post-subsidization, could satisfy the "contingency" requirement of SCM art.3.1(a) and fn.4. See Appellate Body Report, *EC—Aircraft*, fn.11, above, at paras 1044–1048.

[26] Note, however, that a subsidy that does not qualify as an export subsidy may still be actionable if it is otherwise specific. SCM Annex I repeats the annex to the 1979 GATT Subsidies Code with a few changes—but not enough changes to avoid possible inconsistencies with the rest of the SCM Agreement. For instance, the "cost to government" standard contained in the definition of export credits in Annex I, Items J and K is not compatible with the "market value" standard codified in art.14 and Annex V. See the discussion above, at text corresponding to fnn.20–22.

[27] See Appellate Body Report, *Canada—Autos*, fn.10, above, at para.123.

[28] See Appellate Body Report, *Canada—Autos*, fn.10, above, at para.143.

serious prejudice.[29] Action can either be through WTO dispute settlement or through the countervailing duty provisions.

The concept of "nullification and impairment" originated in art.XXIII of the GATT, and typically arises when the improved market access offered from a bound tariff reduction is undercut by subsidies. The term "serious prejudice" is undefined.[30] Article 6 indicates only that serious prejudice could exist when the effect of the subsidy is to displace or impede the imports of a like product of another member into the market of the subsidising member; where the effect of the subsidy is to displace or impede the exports of a like product of another member from a third country market; where the effect of the subsidy is a significant price undercutting by the subsidised product as compared with the price of a like product of another member in the same market or significant price suppression, price depression or lost sales in the same market; and/or where the effect of the subsidy is an unusual increase in the world market share of the subsidising member.[31] Causation for the purposes of art.6 must be established on the basis of "genuine and substantial relationship of cause and effect." This requires, notably, recourse to a rigorous non-attribution analysis.[32]

[29] An actionable subsidy is not automatically illegal or countervailable. For example, subsidies whose economic effects are confined to a national industry may not have adverse effects on international trade.

[30] See Panel Report, *United States—Subsidies on Upland Cotton*, WT/DS267/R (2004)(*US—Upland Cotton*), at paras 7.1392–7.1393, where the Panel, while formally declining to define the "outer parameters" of the term "serious prejudice", nevertheless defined "prejudice" as arising upon "a detrimental impact on a complaining Member's production of, and/or trade in, the product concerned", and defined "serious" as "important" and "not slight or negligible" to opine that "the prejudice in terms of the effect on Brazil's production of, and/or trade in, upland cotton must be such as to affect Brazil's production of upland cotton, to a degree that is 'important,' 'not slight or negligible' or 'meaningful.' " On appeal, the Appellate Body observed that neither disputing party took issue with the Panel's deliberations on this point. See Appellate Body Report, *United States—Subsidies on Upland Cotton*, WT/DS267/AB/R (2005), at text corresponding to fn.676.

[31] See SCM art.6, in particular at para.3. For a practical illustration of how WTO Panels address these serious prejudice phenomena, see Panel Report, *EC—Aircraft*, fn.11, above, where the US alleged that it suffered serious prejudice in the form of all six phenomena on account of EU subsidies conferred to the Airbus group of companies, and its affiliates. The Panel in *EC—Aircraft* departed from Appellate Body precedent in *US—Upland Cotton*, by separating its analysis of market phenomena and causation in evaluating whether serious prejudice had arisen in respect of each alleged phenomena. The Appellate Body, while identifying specific methodological errors in respect of the Panel's analysis of displacement pursuant to SCM arts 6.3(a) and (b) and lost sales pursuant to SCM art.6.3(c), upheld the Panel's "two-step" approach, but endorsed the "unitary" approach it advocated in *US—Upland Cotton* as more appropriate towards constructing a counterfactual: "the use of a counterfactual analysis provides an adjudicator with a useful analytical framework to isolate and properly identify the effects of the challenged subsidies. In general terms, the counterfactual analysis entails comparing the actual market situation that is before the adjudicator with the market situation that would have existed in the absence of the challenged subsidies. This requires the adjudicator to undertake a modelling exercise as to what the market would look like in the absence of the subsidies. Such an exercise is a necessary part of the counterfactual approach. As with other factual assessment, panels clearly have a margin of discretion in conducting the counterfactual analysis." See Appellate Body Report, *EC—Aircraft*, fn.11, above, at paras 1109–1110. Note that art.6.1 SCM, which offered a presumption of serious prejudice in some cases, has now expired; see art.31 SCM.

[32] Appellate Body Report, *US—Upland Cotton*, fn.30, above, at para.437. Note that while these findings related specifically to price suppression in art.6.3(c), the Panel in *EC—Aircraft* hinted

Remedies

WTO Dispute Settlement. Prohibited subsidies potentially benefit from **6–012** extremely expedited WTO dispute settlement. Contrary to ordinary procedures, where establishment of a WTO dispute settlement Panel can take more than two months, with prohibited subsidies a Panel is to be immediately established if consultations fail to result in a mutually acceptable solution within 30 days (art.4.4).[33] Article 4 also goes on to specify that, contrary to the general time period for Panel reports of six to nine months, a Panel in a prohibited subsidy case is to issue its decision within 90 days of its composition (art.4.6). The report of the Panel, unless appealed, is to be adopted within 30 days of circulation to all the members (art.4.8). An appeal, which normally takes 60 to 90 days, must be decided within 30 days (art.4.9). Finally, if the measure in question is found to be a prohibited subsidy, the Panel or Appellate Body is to recommend that the subsidising member withdraw the subsidy "without delay," specifying the time period within which the measure must be withdrawn (art.4.7). "Withdrawn" might even mean complete repayment—not just repayment of the benefit remaining at the time of the Panel ruling.[34] This is different from the ordinary rules of the DSU, which do not require that a Panel recommend the withdrawal of the measure, nor does it require the Panel to establish a timetable for implementation. All told, WTO dispute settlement could address an allegation of a prohibited subsidy in six months.

When it comes to actionable subsidies, WTO dispute settlement is also available, provided that the subsidy has "adverse effects" on the trade interests of another member. Here dispute settlement is also expedited—although not quite as expedited as for prohibited subsidies. A dispute settlement proceeding regarding actionable subsidies also begins with consultations, but if consultations fail to result in a mutually satisfactory solution, a party can request the establishment of a Panel within 60 days. The Panel issues its decision within 120 days (art.7.5, as opposed to the regular six to nine months) and an appeal will be decided in 60 to 90 days (art.7.7). Where a Panel or Appellate Body report determines that any subsidy has resulted in adverse effects to the interests of another member, the member granting or maintaining such subsidy must take "appropriate steps" to remove the adverse effects or withdraw the subsidy (art.7.8). All told, WTO dispute settlement regarding an actionable subsidy could

that the same causal requirements also applied to arts 6.3(a), 6.3(b) and 6.3(d). See *EC—Aircraft*, fn.11, above, at para.7.1967. Neither the EU or the US appealed the Panel's findings on this point. Accordingly, the Appellate Body did not address this issue in its report.

[33] A Panel can refer the matter to the permanent group of experts (PGE), established under art.24, with a view to requesting a report on the matter. The group's conclusions on whether the measure in question is a prohibited subsidy must be accepted by the Panel without modification. However, it should be noted that none of the Panels established so far under art.4 have requested the assistance of the PGE.

[34] Panel Report, *Australia—Automotive Leather*, fn.24, above. Note that the Panel refused to require that the repayment include interest—in effect allowing an interest-free loan, contingent on exports, normally a prohibited subsidy!

be over in less than a year. In practice, this has proven to be too short a time period for a Panel to finish. Also, the expedited timeline only applies if the claims are limited to the SCM Agreement.

6–013 **Unilateral countervailing duties.** Members can also resort to "self-help" in the event of prohibited or actionable subsidies, meaning that they can embark upon their own internal procedures with the view to countervailing the alleged subsidy, without needing multilateral authorisation to do so.[35] However, the SCM Agreement includes detailed rules for how members must handle countervailing duty procedures, and challenges to such countervailing measures under the SCM Agreement have proven to be fertile ground for WTO dispute settlement.[36]

Part V of the SCM Agreement sets out the disciplines on the initiation of countervailing cases, investigation by national authorities and rules of evidence. Countervailing duties can only be imposed pursuant to investigations initiated and conducted in accordance with its strictures (art.10). The provisions on countervailing duties procedures follow closely those established for anti-dumping actions.[37]

6–014 A member wishing to impose a countervailing duty must prove the existence of a subsidy, material injury to its domestic industry in its domestic market[38] and causality linking the former to the latter. First of all, the investigating member must prove that there is a subsidy within the meaning of the SCM Agreement: a financial contribution by a government and a benefit thereby conferred. It must also prove that the subsidy is specific.

Further, it must prove that there has been "material injury" to its domestic industry. The determination of injury must be based on an "objective examination" of the volume of the subsidised imports and its effect on prices of like products in the domestic market (art.15.1). The investigating member looks to see whether there has been a significant increase in volume, either in absolute or relative terms, with respect to production or consumption in the importing member. With regard to the effect of the subsidised imports on prices, the member investigates whether there has been significant price undercutting by the subsidised imports as compared with the price of a like product of the importing

---

[35] WTO dispute settlement and countervailing duties procedures can be invoked in parallel, but only one form of relief (either a countervailing duty, if the requirements of Pt V are met, or a countermeasure under SCM arts 4 or 7) shall be available.

[36] *US—Lead and Bismuth II*, fn.15, above; Panel Report, *United States—Countervailing Measures Concerning Certain Products from the European Communities*, WT/DS212//R (2002); Panel Report, *United States—Countervailing Duties on Certain Corrosion-Resistant Carbon Steel Flat Products from Germany*, WT/DS213/R (2002); Panel Report, *United States—Final Countervailing Duty Determination with respect to Certain Softwood Lumber from Canada*, WT/DS257/ R (2003); *US—Countervailing Duty Investigation on DRAMS*, fn.13, above; *EC— Countervailing Measures on DRAM Chips*, fn.13, above.

[37] Final Act Embodying the Result of the Uruguay Round of Multilateral Trade Negotiations, Agreement on Implementation of Article VII of the General Agreement of Tariffs and Trade 1994, April 1994.

[38] Note that countervailing duties actions are limited to injury on the member's domestic market; multilateral measures (i.e. through WTO dispute settlement) can redress injury caused by subsidies to a member's domestic industry on *any* market.

member, or whether the effect of such imports is otherwise to depress prices to a significant degree or to prevent price increases which otherwise would have occurred to a significant degree (art.15.2). In its examination of the impact of the subsidised imports on the domestic industry, a member has to consider all relevant economic factors and indices having a bearing on the state of the industry (art.15.4).

To impose a countervailing duty, the member must prove that subsidisation **6–015** caused material injury to its domestic industry, and in so doing it must not attribute injury caused by other factors to subsidisation (art.15.5). In the words of the WTO Appellate Body, the imposing member must "separate and distinguish" injury caused by other factors, and failure to properly do so can result in invalidation of the countervailing duties in WTO dispute settlement.[39]

At the end of the procedure, a countervailing duty may be imposed, generally expressed as an ad valorem percentage of the import price, intended to compensate for the amount of subsidisation of the imported product. Such a countervailing duty must be levied at "the appropriate amount" (art.19.3) and, in no event may a countervailing duty be imposed on any imported product in excess of the amount of the subsidy found to exist, calculated in terms of subsidisation per unit of the product (art.19.4). The SCM Agreement contains provisions on the calculation of the amount of the subsidy (art.14). On the other hand, rather than imposing countervailing duties, voluntary undertakings may be put in place instead. Undertakings are meant to lead to the elimination or limitation of the subsidy or the removal of its injurious effects through a quota or price increase of the subsidised imports (art.18.1).

Countervailing duties may only remain in force as long as these are necessary, **6–016** and to the extent they are necessary to counteract subsidisation which is causing injury. In accordance with the so-called "sunset clause" (art.21.3), they should in all cases be terminated no later than five years from the imposition (or most recent review) unless the authorities determine that the expiry of the duty would be likely to lead to a continuation of the subsidisation and injury.

Finally, the SCM Agreement provides detailed procedural rules that ensure consultations of the allegedly subsidising member, the transparency of countervailing duty investigations throughout the proceeding, and the ability for interested parties to effectively participate in them and specific time limits (notably, arts 11, 12, 13 and 22).

Double remedies

SCM art.14(d) directs investigating authorities in national countervailing duty **6–017** investigations to impose countervailing duties in respect of government-provided goods or services only where such authorities determine that the provision of a

---

[39] See Appellate Body Report, *United States—Anti-Dumping Measures on Certain Hot-Rolled Steel Products from Japan* WT/DS184/AB/R (2001), at para.223; or Panel Report, *US—Countervailing Duty Investigation on DRAMS*, fn.13, above, at para.7.351ff.

good or service by the government is made for "less than adequate remuneration". This requires an evaluation of "prevailing market conditions" for the good or service in question, through the use of in-country "benchmarks" relating to price, quality, availability, marketability, transportation, and other applicable sale and purchase conditions.

Yet, in a judgment of increasing relevance to China-related trade remedy disputes before the WTO, the Appellate Body strayed from the text of art.14(d) in *US—Softwood Lumber IV* by holding that investigating authorities may resort to out-of-country benchmarks to determine the appropriate private market price (termed "normal value") of a good where the government has intervened in an affected market to such an extent that applicable in-country benchmarks "are distorted, because of the predominant role of the government in the market as a provider of the same or similar goods."[40]

While the Appellate Body contemplated that recourse to out-of-country benchmarks in so-called "analogue" countries would only be possible in rather limited situations, the US Department of Commerce (DOC) has recently applied out-of-country benchmarks to several products under investigation from China.[41] The result is the construction of a normal value for goods or services that can far exceed a constructed in-country equivalent.

6–018   Furthermore, where the goods under investigation are also subject to parallel anti-dumping investigations, there is a risk that investigating authorities may be extracting double remedies from those companies under investigation. This view is premised on the argument that subsidies "pass through" to export prices, which are in turn subject to anti-dumping duties. The use of out-of-country benchmarks in countervailing duty investigations could lead to double-counting in the event that investigating authorities also use an out-of-country benchmark to calculate the anti-dumping margin, as the amount of the subsidy reflected in the export price will not have been deducted from the constructed analogue normal value in the anti-dumping case. Applying anti-dumping duties in addition to countervailing duties on such goods, the argument runs, therefore risks punishing companies twice for the same injury—the imposition of one type of duty should suffice.[42]

---

[40] See Appellate Body Report, *United States—Final Countervailing Duty Determination with respect to Certain Softwood Lumber from Canada*, WT/DS257/AB/R (2004), at paras 102–103. SCM art.14(d), second sentence reads: "the adequacy of remuneration shall be determined in relation to prevailing market conditions for the good or service in question **in the country of provision** or purchase (including price, quality, availability, marketability, transportation and other conditions of purchase or sale)" [emphasis supplied]. Please note that China's Protocol of Accession expressly permits the use of analogue country benchmarks only in antidumping duty investigations until 2013, being 15 years after China's accession to the WTO. See "Report of the Working Party on the Accession of China", WT/ACC/CHN/49 & Corr. 1 (2001), at para.15(d).

[41] See, notably, Appellate Body Report, *US—AD & CVD from China*, fn.6, above.

[42] The Appellate Body in *US—AD & CVD from China* summarised the mechanics of double-remedies as follows: "the dumping margin calculated under an NME methodology 'reflects not only price discrimination by the investigated producer between the domestic and export markets ("dumping")', but also 'economic distortions that affect the producer's costs of production', including specific subsidies to the investigated producer of the relevant product in respect of that

Article VI.5 of the GATT partly recognises the potential for double remedies in such situations, in explicitly prohibiting the double imposition of anti-dumping and countervailing duties on goods benefiting from *export* subsidies. This is because export subsidies are presumed to completely "pass through" (i.e. 100 per cent) to the exported product. Whether or not subsidies other than export subsidies can be said to completely "pass through" to the export price is debatable.[43]

The Appellate Body recently reversed a WTO Panel ruling that ratified DOC's   **6–019**
imposition of dual anti-dumping and countervailing duties on Chinese goods. According to the Panel, the absence of a broader prohibition to that contained in art.VI.5 of the GATT on the imposition of double duties implied that double remedies on (non-export) subsidised goods did not violate any provision of the WTO Agreements.[44] The Appellate Body instead undertook a "systemic" interpretation of the WTO Agreements to opine, on the SCM Agreement's requirement that countervailing duties be calculated at the "appropriate amount," that:

"to us, the requirement that any amounts be 'appropriate' means, at a minimum, that investigating authorities may not, in fixing the appropriate amount of countervailing duties, simply ignore that anti-dumping duties have been imposed to offset the same subsidization."[45]

The Appellate Body considered that it was incumbent on investigating authorities, in setting the "appropriate" amount of a countervailing duty, to determine "whether and to what degree the same subsidies are being offset twice when anti-dumping and countervailing duties are simultaneously imposed on the same imported products."[46] This effectively forces DOC and all other investigating

---

product. An anti-dumping duty calculated based on an NME methodology may, therefore, 'remedy' or 'offset' a domestic subsidy, to the extent that such subsidy has contributed to a lowering of the export price. Put differently, the subsidization is 'counted' within the overall dumping margin. When a countervailing duty is levied against the same imports, the same domestic subsidy is also 'counted' in the calculation of the rate of subsidization and, therefore, the resulting countervailing duty offsets the same subsidy a second time. Accordingly, the concurrent imposition of an anti-dumping duty calculated based on an NME methodology, and a countervailing duty may result in a subsidy being offset more than once, that is, in a double remedy. Double remedies may also arise in the context of domestic subsidies granted within market economies when anti-dumping and countervailing duties are concurrently imposed on the same products and an unsubsidised, constructed, or third country normal value is used in the anti-dumping investigation." See Appellate Body Report, *US—AD & CVD from China*, fn.6, above, at para.542.

[43] In some situations, subsidies may not affect prices at all, so that no "pass through" should arguably be assumed. In other situations, in competitively distorted markets, for instance, subsidies may "pass through" completely to the export price, but have no impact on the normal price (which may be fixed pursuant to a cartel agreement). In this situation, no double-remedies could occur.

[44] See Panel Report, *United States—Definitive Anti-Dumping and Countervailing Duties on Certain Products from China*, WT/DS379/R (2010), at para.14.76.

[45] See Appellate Body Report, *US—AD & CVD* from China, fn.6, above, at para.571.

[46] See Appellate Body Report, *US—AD & CVD* from China, fn.6, above, at para.602.

authorities to find credible ways to calculate the "pass through" percentage of a domestic subsidy, given that any anti-dumping duties imposed on the amount of a subsidy that has not "passed through" will not, by definition, result in double remediation.

Special and differential treatment of developing countries (Part VIII, Article 27)

6–020   Developing countries are treated somewhat differently than developed countries under the SCM Agreement, pursuant to the recognition that "subsidies may play an important role in economic development programs of developing country members" (art.27.1). The SCM Agreement defines three categories of developing country members: (i) least developed country members (LDCs) designated as such by the United Nations (Annex VII(a)); (ii) certain members identified in Annex VII(b) until their GNP per capita has reached US $1,000 per year[47]; and (iii) other developing countries.

The first two categories of developing countries are exempt from the prohibition on export subsidies, while the others initially agreed to give up their export subsidies by January 1, 2003. Regarding subsidies contingent upon the use of domestic over imported goods, LDCs were granted an exemption for eight years from the date of entry in force of the WTO Agreement, while other developing countries were granted an exemption for five years. At the Doha Ministerial Conference, it was however decided to direct the Committee on SCM to extend the transitional periods for certain existing subsidies and regarding certain members.[48] The Committee on SCM decides on the extensions on a program-by-program approach.[49] However, the General Council in July 2007 directed the SCM Committee to comprehensively phase out extensions by December 31, 2015.[50]

Some (additional) special and differential treatment is also accorded regarding actionable subsidies[51] and countervailing duties.[52]

---

[47] Please note that this amount is fixed as the value of $1,000 in 1990.

[48] Doha Ministerial Conference, *Implementation-Related Issues and Concerns*, Decision of November 14, 2001, WT/MIN(01)/17, at para.10.6; see *Procedures for Extensions under Article 27.4 for Certain Developing Country Members*, Committee on SCM, G/SCM/39 (2001), at art.2 regarding eligible programs.

[49] See G/SCM/50 (2002) to G/SCM/102 (2003).

[50] See G/SCM/120 (2007).

[51] Serious prejudice shall be demonstrated by positive evidence, see art.27.8. There is no presumption of serious prejudice under art.6.1 for developing countries. Note, however, that art.6.1 lapsed at the end of 1999. See, fn.31, above. Article 27.9 provides that, regarding actionable subsidies granted by a developing country, other than those described in art.6.1, no action under art.7 (which does not include countervailing duties) may be taken because of harm suffered in third country markets. Finally, the provisions of Pt III (actionable subsidies) do not apply to certain specific types of subsidies, see art.27.13.

[52] Regarding the definition of de minimis subsidies and "negligible" level of imports in countervailing duty investigations, see arts 27.10–27.11.

Current state of Doha Rules negotiations

The November 2001 declaration of the Fourth Ministerial Conference in Doha   **6–021**
provided a broad mandate for negotiations on a wide range of subsidies-related
topics, notably SCM Agreement rules amendments and agricultural reform.[53]
Rules Negotiation Group Chairman Guillermo Valles-Galmés circulated a 2007
document that covered suggested revisions to the WTO Agreement on Implementation of the General Agreement on Tariffs and Trade 1994 (AD Agreement)
and the SCM Agreement. This document has effectively formed the basis of
ongoing rules negotiations.[54] Key suggested revisions to the SCM Agreement
include the harmonisation of investigation principles and practices common to
the AD and SCM Agreements, and the introduction of fisheries subsidisation
disciplines.

Fisheries subsidy disciplines have proven particularly topical in view of
growing concerns relating to overfishing caused by subsidisation. Negotiations
on fisheries rules stalled in 2008, owing to deadlock, before restarting with some
impetus in 2010. This impetus was due in part to a shift in positions from
traditional fisheries subsidisers such as Japan who, after first refusing to discuss
the prospects of any WTO regulation on fisheries, subsequently accepted that
WTO disciplines on overfishing were necessary having regard to a global
shortage of tuna. The appropriate scope of special and differential treatment for
developing countries remains a point of contention,[55] and could prove an obstacle
to the more optimistic calls for an "early harvest" pursuant to which WTO
Members have been encouraged to implement fisheries disciplines ahead of a
final Doha text.[56]

3. THE WTO AGREEMENT ON AGRICULTURE

One of the most notable achievements of the Uruguay Round was the inclusion   **6–022**
of agriculture in the system of multilateral rules, through the conclusion of the
WTO Agreement on Agriculture, part of Annex 1A to the Marrakech Agreement.[57] As to subsidies, while the Agreement on Agriculture allows domestic
support and export subsidies on agricultural products,[58] they are scheduled and

[53] We discuss the Doha implications on agriculture below, at Section 6–022ff.
[54] See "Draft Consolidated Chair Texts of the AD and SCM Agreements", TN/RL/W/213 (2007).
Please note that the bulk of this text is geared towards improving AD Agreement provisions.
Most of the interesting thinking on subsidies in the Doha talks has been in the context of
fisheries, and not the overall SCM Agreement.
[55] See, notably, the text circulated by Brazil, China, India, and Mexico entitled "Fisheries Subsidies: Special and Differential Treatment", TN/RL/GEN/163 (2010).
[56] See ICTSD, "WTO Fisheries Negotiations 'On' Again", 14(35) *Bridges Weekly Trade News
Digest* (2010).
[57] On the WTO Agreement on Agriculture, see Patrick McMahon, "The Agreement on Agriculture", in Macrory, Appleton and Plummer (eds.) *World Trade Organization: Legal, Economic
and Political Analysis* (Springer, 2005), Vol.I.
[58] See Agreement on Agriculture, art.2.

subjected to progressive reduction commitments. Agricultural subsidies not scheduled are not allowed to be introduced.[59] Furthermore, the provisions of all the Multilateral Trade Agreements in Annex 1A to the WTO Agreement apply to agricultural matters, subject only to the provisions of the Agriculture Agreement in case of conflict.[60] With regard to the SCM Agreement, this rule was suspended until January 1, 2004 by the so-called "Peace Clause",[61] but now, any lacunae in the coverage of agricultural subsidies by the Agreement on Agriculture may be caught by the SCM Agreement.[62]

Specific commitments to reduce agricultural subsidies—both domestic support[63] and export subsidies[64]—were calculated on the basis of subsidies granted in the past and enshrined in Pt IV of each member's Schedule of Concessions.[65] According to the Agreement on Agriculture, the scheduled levels of permitted subsidisation are not to be exceeded.[66]

6–023   Export subsidies, defined as subsidies contingent on export performance, including those listed in art.9 of the Agreement on Agriculture,[67] are scheduled and subject to reduction commitments. Article 9.1 lists types of agricultural export subsidies subject to reduction commitments, including direct subsidies by governments, government-facilitated sales for export at less than domestic market price, any other payments financed by virtue of governmental action, government subsidies to reduce the costs of marketing exports (other than widely available export promotion and advisory services), subsidies reducing the costs or providing on more favourable terms international transport and freight, and subsidies contingent on incorporation in exported products.[68] Furthermore, art.10.1 of the Agreement on Agriculture states that export subsidies not listed in art.9.1, for example the export credits, export credit guarantees and insurance programmes mentioned in art.10.2, shall not be applied in a manner which results

---

[59] See Agreement on Agriculture, art.3.3.

[60] See Agreement on Agriculture, art.21.

[61] See Agreement on Agriculture, art.13.

[62] The "Peace Clause" featured in only one dispute, *US—Upland Cotton*. See Appellate Body Report, *US—Upland Cotton*, fn.30, above, at paras 310–394, where the Appellate Body ruled on the non-application of the "Peace Clause" to US domestic support measures challenged by Brazil. See also explicit references to the Agreement on Agriculture in SCM arts 3, 5 and 7.

[63] See Agreement on Agriculture, art.6.

[64] See Agreement on Agriculture, art.9. Note that export subsidies not listed in art.9.1 cannot avail of special treatment under this Agreement, as specified in art.10.

[65] See Agreement on Agriculture, art.3.1.

[66] See Agreement on Agriculture, arts 3.2 and 3.3. It is also clearly set out in art.8 that "[e]ach Member undertakes not to provide *export subsidies* otherwise than in conformity ... the commitments as specified in that Member's Schedule" [emphasis supplied].

[67] See Agreement on Agriculture, art.1(e).

[68] See Agreement on Agriculture, art.9.1(a)–(f). Note that art.9.1(c), in referring to payments "on the export," incorporates a standard lower than the default "contingency" standard otherwise contained at art.1(e). The Appellate Body in *EC—Sugar* interpreted payments "on the export" as payments made "in connection with" exports. See Appellate Body Reports, *European Communities—Export Subsidies on Sugar*, WT/DS265/AB/R (2005) (*EC—Sugar*), at paras 274–275.

in, or which threatens to lead to, circumvention of scheduled export subsidy commitments.[69]

Where a quantity in excess of a reduction commitment is exported, art.10.3 codifies a near presumption that it is subsidised, with the exporting member having to prove that the excess was *not* subsidised. No WTO defendant to date has successfully rebutted this presumption of subsidisation.

Issues of compatibility of member's exports with their subsidy commitments **6–024** under the Agreement on Agriculture have arisen with increasing frequency in WTO dispute settlement, spurred notably by the holdings in the *Canada—Dairy* case, where WTO Panels and the Appellate Body ultimately concluded that Canada had provided illegal export subsidies to products derived from Canadian milk by setting up a system that provided them with access to milk powder at less than its "proper value," determined by comparison to its average total cost of production.[70] More recent cases are the *EC—Sugar Subsidies*[71] and *US—Cotton Subsidies*[72] cases. In the *EC—Sugar Subsidies* case, the Panel and Appellate Body found that the EU's sugar regime, taken as a whole, resulted in illegal export subsidies under art.9.1(c) of the Agreement on Agriculture, which covers payments on export financed by virtue of governmental action. The crux of the *EC—Sugar Subsidies* case was the finding that the EU regime operated to provide EU producers with revenues that cross-subsidised their exports.[73] In the *US—Cotton Subsidies* case, the Appellate Body upheld the Panel's findings that the so-called "Step 2" payments to exporters of US upland cotton were subsidies contingent upon export performance within the meaning of the Agreement on Agriculture. Since the United States had no scheduled export subsidy reduction commitments for upland cotton, it concluded that the United States had acted inconsistently with the Agreement on Agriculture obligation not to provide subsidies in respect of any agricultural product not specified in its Schedule.[74]

In addition, it should not be forgotten that export subsidies not specified in a member's schedule to the Agreement on Agriculture are still covered, and thus potentially prohibited, by art.3.1(a) of the SCM Agreement. This was confirmed

---

[69] However, see the minority view on the Agreement on Agriculture's (non-)regulation of export credit guarantees expressed in Appellate Body Report, *US—Upland Cotton*, fn.30, above, at paras 631–641. Pursuant to the minority view, art.10.2, read in contrast to art.10.4 (setting immediate disciplines on international food aid), suggests that the Agreement on Agriculture does not presently regulate export credit guarantees.

[70] See Appellate Body Report, *Canada—Measures Affecting The Importation of Milk and The Exportation of Dairy Products*, WT/DS103/AB/R and WT/DS113/AB/R (1999) (*Canada—Dairy*).

[71] Panel and Appellate Body Reports, *European Communities—Export Subsidies on Sugar*, WT/DS265/R, WT/DS266/R, WT/DS/283/R (2004), WT/DS265/AB/R, WT/DS266AB/R, WT/DS/283/AB/R (2005) (*EC—Sugar*).

[72] See Appellate Body Report, *US—Upland Cotton*, fn.30, above.

[73] See Panel Report, *EC—Sugar*, at para.7.334 and Appellate Body Report, *EC—Sugar*, at para.270, fn.71, above. For more on cross-subsidisation, see Bernard Hoekman and Robert Howse, "European Community—Sugar: Cross-Subsidization and the World Trade Organization", *World Bank Policy Research Working Paper* 4336 (2007).

[74] See Appellate Body Report, *US—Upland Cotton*, fn.30, above, at para.583.

most recently by the *EC—Sugar Subsidies*,[75] and *US—Cotton Subsidies*[76] cases.

6–025   Secondly, as to domestic support, it is important to note that not all domestic support measures are subject to reduction commitments under the Agreement on Agriculture.[77] In common parlance, domestic support is categorised into three "boxes": "amber", "blue" and "green."[78] What must be reduced under the Agreement on Agriculture are the "amber box" measures of domestic support, which are those considered the most trade-distortive.[79] Such support was called upon to be included in the Aggregate Measure of Support (AMS), from which the reduction commitments were calculated.[80]

Domestic support provided subject to commitments from farmers to limit production (production-limiting measures) falls into the "blue box"[81] and domestic support agreed to have no or minimal trade-distortive effect is classified in the "green box".[82] Blue box and green box measures are not subject to reduction commitments. Furthermore, de minimis support is not required to be reduced.[83]

Due to the sensitivity of the issue, especially for developing countries, agricultural subsidies remain a focus—one might even say a deal-breaker—in the current WTO Doha negotiations.

As things stand, based on the 2008 Revised Draft Modalities for Agriculture document circulated by Committee on Agriculture Chairman Crawford Falconer, developed WTO Members are to eliminate agricultural export subsidies by 2013, while developing Members have until 2016.[84] Additionally, Members must

---

[75] See Panel Report, *EC—Sugar*, fn.71, above, at para.7.381.

[76] See Panel Report, *US—Upland Cotton*, at para.7.751 and Appellate Body Report, *EC— Sugar*, at para.584, fnn.30 and 71, above, respectively.

[77] See "Agreement on Agriculture", art.6 and Annex 2. Please note that pursuant to the Doha Modalities text, which we will discuss in more detail below, "amber" box subsidies will be subject to tiered cuts, while "blue" box subsidies will become bound. "Green" box subsidies will remain unbound, but subject to tighter qualifying criteria.

[78] See *http://www.wto.org/english/tratop_e/agric_e/agboxes_e.htm* [Accessed May 23, 2011]. In comparison, the two categories left in the SCM Agreement (prohibited and actionable subsidies) are no longer referred to in color codes.

[79] For WTO dispute settlement concerning domestic support subsidies, see *Korea—Measures Affecting Imports of Fresh, Chilled and Frozen Beef* (*Korea—Beef*), WT/DS161/R, WT/DS169R (2000) and WT/DS161/AB/R and WT/DS 169/AB/R (2000).

[80] See "Agreement on Agriculture", art.7.2 (a), which identifies what domestic support measures shall be included in the member's calculation of its Current Total AMS (see art.1(a) for the definition of AMS as well as Annex 3 and 4 for the calculation of it). Furthermore, art.6.1 of the same Agreement refers that "the domestic support reduction commitments . . . are expressed in terms of" Total AMS.

[81] See Agreement on Agriculture, art.6.5.

[82] See Agreement on Agriculture, art.6.1. Annex 2 to the Agreement on Agriculture, art.1(a) and (b) defines that "the support in question shall be provided through a publicly-funded government program . . . not involving transfers from consumers; and . . . shall not have the effect of providing price support to producers." Also note art.7.1 of the Agreement.

[83] That is, which does not exceed 5% (10% for developing countries) of the value of production of either the specific product or of total agricultural production: Agreement on Agriculture, art.6.4.

[84] See "Revised Draft Modalities for Agriculture", TN/AG/W/4/Rev.4 (2008), at paras 162 and 163, respectively.

undertake significant cuts (ranging from 45 per cent to 70 per cent) in existing Total AMS.[85]

4. THE WTO GENERAL AGREEMENT ON TRADE IN SERVICES

Subsidies to services as defined in art.I:2 of the GATS are not covered by the **6–026** SCM Agreement. According to art.XV of the GATS members recognise that, in certain circumstances, subsidies may have distortive effects on trade in services. According to this article, members are supposed to enter into negotiations with a view to developing the necessary multilateral disciplines to avoid trade-distortive effects. The GATS called for a future work programme to be drawn up to determine how, and in what time frame, negotiations on such multilateral disciplines will be conducted.

The "Guidelines and Procedures for the Negotiations on Trade in Services", adopted by the Council for Trade in Services on March 28, 2001, provide that members shall aim to complete negotiations under art.XV prior to the conclusion of negotiations on specific commitments.[86] These guidelines were reaffirmed in the Doha Ministerial Declaration,[87] and again in the Hong Kong Ministerial Declaration.[88] However, despite numerous interesting submissions by Members, little (if any) progress has been made in these negotiations.

5. EUROPEAN REGULATION OF COUNTERVAILING DUTIES

In order to implement the WTO SCM Agreement, the EU Council adopted **6–027** Regulation 3284/94 on subsidies, which has most recently been replaced by Regulation 597/2009.[89] The EU Regulation on subsidised imports establishes that in order to apply countervailing duties, the subsidy must be specific and must cause material injury to the Community industry. In accordance with provisions that the SCM called "desirable" but not mandatory,[90] the European Union included two potentially more liberal provisions in its countervailing duty regulation, namely the "Community [now more properly called 'Union'] interest test"[91] and the "lesser duty rule."[92] The Community interest test provides that measures can only be taken if they are not contrary to the overall interest of the Community (domestic industry, users, consumers and intermediaries). This has

---

[85] See "Revised Draft Modalities for Agriculture", TN/AG/W/4/Rev.4 (2008), at paras 13–14.
[86] See "Guidelines and Procedures for the Negotiations on Trade in Services", S/L/93 (2001), at para.7.
[87] See "Doha Ministerial Declaration adopted on 14 November 2001", WT/MIN(01)/DEC/1 (2001), at para.15.
[88] See "Doha Work Program: Ministerial Declaration adopted on 18 December 2005", WT/MIN(05)/DEC (2005), at para.25 and Annex C.4.
[89] [2009] O.J. L188/93.
[90] See SCM art.19.2.
[91] See, fn.89, above, at art.31.
[92] See, fn.89, above, at arts 12(1) and 15(1).

its counterpart in EU Anti-Dumping Regulation 1225/2009.[93] The lesser duty rule requires the measures imposed by the Community to be lower than the subsidy margin, if such lower duty rate is sufficient to remove the injury suffered by the Community industry.

In addition, the European Commission has put out "Guidelines for the calculation of the amount of subsidy in countervailing duty investigations."[94] The Guidelines provide the methodology the European Union uses in calculating the amount of the subsidy (depending on whether it concerns grants, loans, loan guarantees or the provision of goods and services by a government), the investigation period for the calculation of the subsidy and the elements which may be deducted from the subsidy. Examples of subsidy calculations are also provided.

6–028 Regarding government provision of equity capital, the Guidelines explicitly refer to EU state aid law:

" . . . the provision of equity capital does not of itself confer a benefit. The criterion is whether a private investor would have put money into the company in the same situation in which the government provided equity. On the basis of this principle, the matter has to be dealt with on a case-by-case basis, taking account of the Commission's practice as regards state aid policy in this area and the practice of the Community's main trading partners."[95]

A concise summary of the anti-subsidy activities of the European Union is contained in the Commission's Annual Reports on the Communities Anti-dumping and Anti-subsidy Activities. At the end of 2009, the Community had eight definitive anti-subsidy measures in force.[96] While the majority of anti-subsidy measures are in the form of duties, there were 42 undertakings (for anti-dumping and anti-subsidy activities combined) in force at the end of 2009.[97]

6. WTO SUBSIDY AND EU STATE AID CONTROL

6–029 There are several differences between the WTO subsidy and the EU state aid regimes.

To begin with, there is the definition of a subsidy, and notably the issue as to whether or not a subsidy necessarily involves a "cost to government." With the

---

[93] [2009] O.J. L343/51, at art.21.

[94] See "Information from the Commission (Guidelines for the calculation of the amount of subsidy in countervailing duty investigations)" [1998] O.J. C394/6.

[95] See "Information from the Commission (Guidelines for the calculation of the amount of subsidy in countervailing duty investigations)" [1998] O.J. C394/6, at E(f)(ii).

[96] See "28th Annual Report from the Commission to the European Parliament on the European Union's Anti-Dumping, Anti-Subsidy and Safeguard Activities" (2009), COM(2010) 558 final, at para.8.1. According to the interim report for the 29th Annual Report, the Community had 11 definitive anti-subsidy measures in force at the end of 2010. Available at: *http://trade.ec.europa.eu/doclib/docs/2010/january/tradoc_145673.pdf* [Accessed on May 23, 2011].

[97] ibid, at para.9.2. According to the interim report for the 29th Annual Report, the Community accepted 11 undertakings for anti-dumping and anti-subsidy activities combined.

possible exception of export credit guarantees, a financial contribution under the WTO SCM Agreement does not necessarily involve a "cost to government."[98] In this regard, the definition of a subsidy in WTO law could be broader than the notion of state aid in EU law, where "cost to government" (including foregone revenue) is essential to a finding of state aid.[99] In particular, the WTO's definition of a subsidy may be broader to the extent it covers payments made by private entities which are entrusted or directed to do so by a government.[100]

This difference may suggest that WTO law is stricter on subsidies than EU law. However, this does not necessarily follow, as other provisions of substantive EU law (without a counterpart in WTO law) might still catch and prohibit such indirect state support.[101]   **6–030**

Furthermore, the mechanisms available in EU law to enforce the prohibition on trade distorting state aids go much further than WTO remedies. Thus, failure to notify a state aid to the European Commission will lead to its illegality and the obligation on the beneficiary to repay the aid to the subsidising Member State.[102] In contrast, failure to notify subsidies to the WTO Subsidies Committee is not sanctioned.[103] Furthermore, private competitors can seek the enforcement of EU state aid rules before domestic courts in the EU Member States.[104] In contrast, WTO rules on the whole lack direct effect in the European Union, so that EU Member State aid subsidies cannot be easily challenged on the basis of WTO law before EU domestic courts.[105] These WTO rules can only be enforced through government-to-government litigation in the WTO, or through unilateral border remedies (countervailing duties) that protect the domestic market while leaving the effects of the foreign subsidies elsewhere untouched.

Having said that WTO rules lack direct effect, more recent trends in EU case law indicate an increasing receptiveness on the part of EU Courts to WTO pleadings when raised to substantiate violations of EU law.[106]

---

[98] See Appellate Body Report, *Canada—Aircraft*, fn.14, above, at para.160.
[99] See generally Luca Rubini, "The Definition of Subsidy and State Aid: WTO and EC Law in Comparative Perspective" (Oxford 2010); and Marco Slotboom, "A Comparison of WTO and EC Law", (Cameron May 2006), at pp.122–126.
[100] See text at fn.13, above.
[101] See, e.g. Leendert Geelhoed, "The Demarcation of State Aid and Regulatory Charges", *European State Aid Law Quarterly* (2005), at pp.401–405 (on the interrelationship between arts 87, 88 EC and 96, 97 EC, the latter provisions dealing with distortions arising from differences between laws and regulations, and in particular tax provisions, of EU Member States).
[102] See Chs 25, 26 and 27 of this publication.
[103] See SCM art.25. Note that the EU has proposed to strengthen the WTO's notification rules, possibly establishing penalties for defaulting members. See the "WTO Negotiating Group on Rules, WTO Negotiations concerning the WTO Agreement on Subsidies and Countervailing Measures", Proposal by the European Communities, TN/RL/W/30 (2002). So far this proposal does not appear to have met with much enthusiasm from the other WTO members.
[104] See Chs 25 and 26 of this publication.
[105] See Case C–149/96, *Portugal v Council* [1999] E.C.R. I–8395.
[106] See Marco Bronckers, "From 'Direct effect' to 'Muted dialogue': Recent developments in the European Courts' case law on the WTO and beyond", in Bulterman et al (eds) *Views of European Law from the Mountain: Liber Amicorum Piet Jan Slot* (Kluwer, 2009), at pp.403–416.

Possible introduction of international disciplines on state aid

6–031   The European Union has recently signalled its intention to push for international disciplines on antitrust and state aid. As part of its "Europe 2020" growth initiative, the European Commission issued a strategy document on November 9, 2010 that flagged the importance of combating lax competition and state aid rules prevailing in third country markets. The Commission, while expressing a preference for the introduction of competition and state aid disciplines through the WTO, left open the possibility of seeking bilateral alternatives:

> "Absent or ineffective competition and state aid rules in third countries limit market access for EU exporters. The EU therefore has a strategic interest in developing international rules to ensure that European firms do not suffer in third countries from unfair subsidisation of local companies or anti-competitive practices. A multilateral set of rules adopted in the WTO framework would be the best outcome. However, many key issues can also be addressed through bilateral agreements." [107]

6–032   An illustration of the EU's intentions to promote international disciplines on state aid through its bilateral relations with other countries is provided by the recent free trade agreement between the European Union and Korea. This Agreement expressly prohibits two forms of subsidies, where they adversely affect international trade: (i) unlimited guarantees to enterprises; and (ii) support to ailing companies without a credible restructuring plan geared towards ensuring long-term viability.[108] It is of some note that these types of subsidies have not been singled out in the SCM Agreement.

The Agreement between the European Union and Korea otherwise incorporates heightened transparency obligations, pursuant to which the parties must, in addition to exchanging detailed annual reports on subsidies, undertake to provide any further information on subsidies upon request by the other party, subject to "the limitations imposed by the requirements of professional and business secrecy."[109]

Subsidies to services presently fall outside the scope of the subsidies chapter of the Agreement between the European Union and Korea, and are not covered

---

[107] See "Trade, Growth and World Affairs: Trade policy as a core component of the EU's 2020 strategy", COM(2010) 612, at p.13. This document builds upon the Commission's proposal for a "2020 strategy," which the Commission issued on March 3, 2010. See "Europe 2020: a strategy for smart, sustainable and inclusive growth", COM(2010) 2020 final.

[108] See the online text of the EU-Korea Free Trade Agreement, at art.11.11. Available at: *http://trade.ec.europa.eu/doclib/press/index.cfm?id=443&serie=273&langId=en* [Accessed on May 23, 2011]. At the time of writing (May 2011), the FTA has yet to be published in the Official Journal.

[109] ibid, at art.11.12.

by the WTO Agreements either.[110] However, the text of the Agreement between the European Union and Korea commits the parties to use their "best endeavours" to develop rules for subsidies to services, and participate in a first exchange of views on subsidies to services within three years after entry into force of the agreement.[111]

---

[110] See the discussion of art.XV of the GATS above, at Section 6–026.

[111] ibid, at art.11.15(2). A similar commitment in the WTO Services Agreement to discuss possible disciplines on subsidies granted to services has not led to any results after more than fifteen years. It was only recently that a GATS Working Party endorsed a work program relating to the exchange of information on subsidies to services required in order to lay the groundwork for negotiations on disciplines to such subsidies. See "Report by the Chairperson of the Working Party on GATS Rules", S/WPGR/21 (2010), at Pt III.

CHAPTER 7

DE MINIMIS AID*

1. INTRODUCTION 7–001
2. ENABLING REGULATION 7–002
3. DE MINIMIS REGULATION 7–003
   Scope 7–003
   Recipient 7–004
   Calculation 7–005
   Transparent aid 7–006
   Application in time 7–007
   Further conditions 7–008
   Monitoring 7–009
   Cumulation 7–010
4. CONTROVERSY ON THE NATURE OF THE DE MINIMIS RULE 7–011
5. CRISIS MEASURES: TEMPORARY FRAMEWORK—LINK WITH DE MINIMIS 7–013

1. INTRODUCTION

7–001   Article 107(1) of the Treaty on the Functioning of the European Union (TFEU) does not contain any significance test. In principle, as the Court has repeated on many occasions: "[. . .] the relatively small amount of aid or the relatively small size of the undertaking which receives it does not as such exclude the possibility that intra-Community trade might be affected."[1]

Since 1992 the Commission has introduced some more flexibility through the adoption of a de minimis rule.[2] Where the amount of aid to an individual firm, together with any other aid received or receivable for the same purpose over a three-year period, will not exceed ECU[3] 50,000, the amount is considered to be

---

* Koen Van de Casteele
[1] C–142/87, *Belgium/Commission (Tubemeuse)*, [1990] E.C.R. I–959, see also K. Van de Casteele, "Effect on trade", p.395ff, in Mederer, Pesaresi, Van Hoof (eds.), *State Aid*, Claeys and Casteels, 2008.
[2] See para.3.2 of the Community guidelines on state aid for SMEs (O.J. C213, 19.8.1992, p.2), and letter from DG IV to the Member States IV/D/6878 of March 23, 1993.
[3] European Currency Unit, a basket of the currencies of the European Community Member States, used as the unit of account of the European Community, before being replaced by the Euro.

too small to affect trade between Member States and thus to fall within art.107(1) of the Treaty.

In 1996, the Commission adopted the Commission notice on the de minimis rule for state aid and increased the threshold to ECU 100,000.

The Council Regulation No.994/98[4] (so-called "Enabling Regulation") empowers the European Commission "to establish by means of a regulation that certain aid does not fulfil all the criteria of Article [107(1)] of the Treaty and is therefore exempted from the notification procedure laid down in Article [108(3)], provided that aid granted to the same undertaking over a given period of time does not exceed a certain fixed amount."[5]

On this basis, the Commission adopted on January 12, 2001 the Commission Regulation (EC) No.69/2001, which put the de minimis concept on stronger legal footing.[6] The threshold remained fixed at €100,000.

In 2006, in the wake of the State Aid Action Plan,[7] and especially to take account of inflation and GDP growth in the European Union since the ceiling was last increased,[8] a new regulation was adopted: Commission Regulation (EC) No.1998/2006 of December 15, 2006 on the application of arts [107] and [108] of the Treaty to de minimis aid[9] (hereafter "the de minimis Regulation"), which increased the de minimis threshold to €200,000.

2. ENABLING REGULATION

Through the enabling regulation, the Council gives the Commission the power **7–002** to adopt regulations to declare certain categories of aid compatible with the common market or to establish that certain aid does not fulfil all the criteria of art.107(1) TFEU and to exempt them from the notification obligation (art.108(3) TFEU).

Article 1 states that the following categories of aid may be covered by a group exemption regulation:

- aid in favour of small and medium-sized enterprises; research and development; environmental protection; employment and training; and

- aid that complies with the map approved by the Commission for each Member State for the grant of regional aid.

---

[4] Council Regulation (EC) No 994/98 of May 7, 1998 on the application of arts [107] and [108] of the Treaty establishing the European Community to certain categories of horizontal state aid, O.J. L142, May 14, 1998, pp.1–4.
[5] Recital 9 of the Enabling Regulation.
[6] O.J. L10, January 13, 2001, pp.30–32.
[7] "In addition, the threshold under which Member States may grant *de minimis* aid without further specific requirements will be increased to take account of the evolution of the economy."
[8] Recital 2 of the de minimis Regulation.
[9] O.J. L379 of December 28, 2006, pp.5–10.

Article 2 gives the Commission the power to adopt a de minimis regulation in order to establish that certain aid does not fulfil all the criteria of art.107(1) of the Treaty, provided that the aid granted to the same undertaking over a given period of time does not exceed a certain fixed amount.

Procedurally, the Commission is obliged to consult a newly created advisory committee on state aid before adopting regulations pursuant to the enabling regulation. Although the Commission must take the "utmost account of the opinion delivered by the Committee", the latter's role does not seem to go beyond the normal advisory role traditionally played by the "multilateral meetings" with the Member States before the adoption of soft law instruments.

3. DE MINIMIS REGULATION

Scope

7–003   On the basis of the enabling regulation, the Commission adopted Regulation (EC) No.1998/2006 of December 15, 2006 on the application of arts [107] and [108] of the Treaty to de minimis aid.

The de minimis regulation applies to aid granted to enterprises in all sectors, with the exception of:

—the fisheries and aquaculture sectors[10];

—the primary agricultural sector as listed in Annex I to the Treaty;

—the coal sector[11];

—aid for the acquisition of road freight transport vehicles for road transport undertakings[12];

—companies in difficulty[13];

—export aid: in the light of the WTO Agreement on Subsidies and Counter-vailing Measures,[14] the de minimis Regulation does not exempt export aid

---

[10] Covered by Council Regulation (EC) No.104/2000 on the common organisation of the markets in fishery and aquaculture products, O.J. L17, January 21, 2000, p.22.

[11] As defined in the Coal Regulation No.1407/2002, O.J. L205, August 2, 2002, pp.1–8 (which expired on December 31, 2010 and has now been replaced by the Council Decision of December 10, 2010 on state aid to facilitate the closure of uncompetitive coal mines, O.J. L336, December 21, 2010, pp.24–29).

[12] See recital 3 of the de minimis Regulation which justifies the exclusion for the following reasons: "in view of the overcapacity of the sector and of the objectives of transport policy as regards road congestion."

[13] As defined in the Community guidelines on State aid for rescuing and restructuring firms in difficulty, O.J. C244, October 1, 2004, p.2, see recital 7 of the de minimis Regulation.

[14] O.J. L336, December 23, 1994, p.156. Article 3 SCM (Prohibited Export Subsidies): "subsidies contingent, in law or in fact, whether solely or as one of several other conditions, upon export performance", and "subsidies contingent, whether solely or as one of several other conditions, upon the use of domestic over imported goods."

or aid favouring domestic over imported products. Export aid is defined as aid directly linked to the quantities exported, to the establishment and operation of a distribution network or to other current expenditure linked to the export activity.[15] The regulation specifies that aid towards the cost of participating in trade fairs, or aid towards the cost of studies or consultancy services for the launch of a new or existing product on a new market does not normally constitute export aid.[16]

Specific de minimis regulations covering the primary agricultural and fisheries and aquaculture sectors have been adopted.[17] The agriculture de minimis regulation foresees that aid of up to €7,500 per farmer can be granted over a period of three fiscal years, provided that the global amount of such aid does not exceed an amount set by the Commission, calculated as about 0.75 per cent of the value of production in the agricultural sector by the Member State concerned. The de minimis rules for the fisheries sector state that a limited amount of state aid can be given to fisheries companies (€30,000 per company over a period of three fiscal years). As for the primary agriculture sector, there is an overall cap per Member States which is set at 2.5 per cent of the total production value of the fisheries sector.

Recipient

The de minimis Regulation has also moved away from the concept of "enterprise" used in Regulation No.69/2001 and now uses the term "undertaking". This was done in order to take into account case law of the courts which obliges the Commission to look at the real beneficiaries of an aid measure.[18] Thus several legal entities controlled by a same group can no longer each receive de minimis aid if the real beneficiary is the mother undertaking in the group.

7–004

Calculation

The ceiling of €200,000 takes into account all public assistance given as de minimis support over the previous three fiscal years. For undertakings active in the road transport sector, the de minimis ceiling amounts to €100,000. Where the ceiling is exceeded for a given amount, the entire amount can no longer benefit

7–005

---

[15] Article 1(b) of the de minimis Regulation.
[16] Recital 6 of de minimis Regulation.
[17] Originally Commission Regulation (EC) No.1860/2004 of October 6, 2004 on the application of arts 87 and 88 of the EC Treaty to "de minimis" aid in the agricultural and fisheries sectors (O.J. L325, October 28, 2004), then replaced by Commission Regulation (EC) No.1535/2007 of December 20, 2007 on the application of arts [107 and 108 TFEU] to de minimis aid in the sector of agricultural production (O.J. L337, December 21, 2007) and Commission Regulation (EC) No.875/2007 of July 24, 2007 on the application of arts [107 and 108 TFEU] to de minimis aid in the fisheries sector and amending Regulation (EC) No.1860/2004 (O.J. L193, July 25, 2007).
[18] Case C–382/99, *Dutch petrol stations*, [2002] E.C.R. I–05163.

from the de minimis regulation. As such assistance can take various forms (grants, loans, subsidised contracts, etc.), amounts which are not in the form of a cash grant must be converted into their grant equivalent.[19] Furthermore, all figures shall be gross, before any deduction for direct taxation.

The calculations of the grant equivalent of aid payable in several instalments and the calculation of the aid in the form of a soft loan require the use of market interest rates prevailing at the time of the grant.[20] In principle, this should be done on the basis of the reference rate fixed by the European Commission.[21] For countries outside the Euro-zone, the amount will have to be converted into Euros. The calculation should occur at the date on which the de minimis aid is put into effect, i.e. at the date of the legal act or decision awarding the aid.

Transparent aid

7–006   The de minimis regulation only applies to transparent aid, meaning aid for which it is possible to calculate *ex ante* the gross grant equivalent of the aid, without any risk assessment.[22] Thus, a capital injection cannot come under the de minimis regulation unless the total amount of the capital injection remains below the de minimis threshold. The same applies for risk capital measures. For guarantee schemes, a kind of worst-case scenario has been made to calculate how big a guarantee could be, assuming a default rate of 13 per cent, so that it would still stay below the de minimis threshold. Under this scenario, and provided the guarantee does not cover more than 80 per cent of the underlying loan, the guarantee can amount to €1,500,000 (€750,000 in the road transport sector).

Application in time

7–007   The three-year period refers to fiscal years as used for fiscal purposes by the undertaking and is "rolling"—for each new grant of de minimis aid, the total amount of de minimis aid granted during that fiscal year as well as the previous two years needs to be determined. The moment of granting is the moment the legal entitlement to the support arises under national legislation.[23] The new regulation applies from January 1, 2007 until December 31, 2013.[24]

Contrary to the previous de minimis Regulation 69/2001 which did not specify whether it was applicable to aid granted prior to its entry into force (and where

---

[19] Article 2(3) of the de minimis Regulation.
[20] Article 2(3) of the de minimis Regulation.
[21] Published regularly in the O.J. and also available on the website of DG Competition, *http://ec.europa.eu/competition/state_aid/legislation/reference_rates.html*.
[22] Article 2(4) de minimis Regulation.
[23] Recital 10 of de minimis Regulation.
[24] Article 6 de minimis Regulation.

case practice seems to have accepted this[25]), the current de minimis Regulation does contain such rules. The de minimis Regulation can only apply to aid granted before its entry into force for the sectors which were not covered by the earlier de minimis regulation 69/2001, namely the transport sector and the processing and marketing of agricultural products.

Further conditions

The Member State may only grant new de minimis aid after having checked **7–008** that this will not raise the total amount of de minimis aid received during the relevant period of three fiscal years over the €200,000 threshold.[26]

In order to ensure compliance with this rule, a Member State has two options: when granting de minimis aid, Member States must inform the enterprise of the de minimis character of the aid and obtain from the enterprise concerned full information about other de minimis aid received during the previous three years; or, alternatively, the Member State can set up a central register of de minimis aid containing complete information on all de minimis aid granted by any authority within that Member State and the register covers a period of three years.

The requirement to inform the beneficiary of the de minimis character of the aid is a constituent element of de minimis aid.[27] This is important to avoid that de minimis aid would be a form of "franchise", allowing to deduct €200,000 from every grant, whether notified or not, on the grounds that the franchise does not distort competition or affect trade. Hence, in a recovery context, one cannot automatically deduct €200,000 from the amount to be recovered[28] (though Member States could of course decide to grant a new de minimis aid to the company). Otherwise Member States could argue that an enterprise which has not received de minimis aid for the last ten years is eligible for several de minimis aid measures. It must however be recognized that Commission practice under the de minimis rules applicable before 2001 was not always clear.[29]

---

[25] The Commission has examined in much detail the application of the de minimis Regulation No.69/2001 to aid granted prior to its entry into force in its decisions of November 27, 2002 and March 5, 2003, (Commission decision of November 27, 2002 on the aid scheme implemented by Germany–Thuringia working capital programme, O.J. L157, June 26, 2003, p.55; Commission decision of November 27, 2002 on the aid scheme implemented by Germany–Thuringia loan programme for small and medium-sized enterprises, O.J. L223, September 5, 2003, p.32; Commission decision of November 27, 2002 on the aid scheme implemented by Germany–Thuringia consolidation programme, O.J. L61, February 27, 2004; Commission decision on the aid scheme implemented by the Federal Republic of Germany in connection with the sale and export of products from the Land of Mecklenburg–Western Pomerania, O.J. L202, August 9, 2003, p.15) and accepted its retroactive application: "From an economic standpoint, the Commission is of the view that aid measures that, under the Regulation, are not today in an integrated market considered to be aid under Article 87(1) of the EC Treaty could not have constituted aid at an earlier time in a less integrated market."

[26] Article 3(1), second paragraph of the de minimis Regulation.

[27] See R. Repplinger-Hach, "De-minimis-Beihilfen" in M. Heidenhain (ed.), *Handbuch des Europäischen Beihilfensrecht*, (2003: Verlag C.H. Beck) pp.81–82.

[28] See R. Repplinger-Hach, *o.c.*

[29] See J.P. Keppenne, "Guide des aides d'état en droit communautaire", 1999, *Bruylant*, No.167, p.141; A. Sinnaeve, "Block Exemptions for State Aid: More Scope for State Aid Control by Member States and Competitors", CMLR 2001, p.1479.

Monitoring

7–009   Member States must keep records for a period of ten years from the date on which individual de minimis aid was granted and ten years from the last individual aid granted under a de minimis scheme. This information must be provided within 20 working days upon request from the Commission.[30]

Cumulation

7–010   Contrary to the previously existing regulation No.69/2001, the de minimis Regulation now contains a cumulation provision, prohibiting cumulation with state aid in respect of the same eligible costs if it would result in an aid intensity exceeding the one which is applicable. The de minimis Regulation however does not clarify whether undertakings active in different fields (e.g. a farm active in the primary agriculture sector but also offering agro-tourism) can cumulate the different de minimis rules (in this example, Commission Regulation (EC) No. 1535/2007 and the de minimis regulation). It can certainly not have been the intention of the legislator to allow this.[31] On the other hand, it is not certain whether this is adequately monitored, both at the level of the Member States and by the European Commission.

4. CONTROVERSY ON THE NATURE OF THE DE MINIMIS RULE

7–011   The de minimis Regulation is not a block exemption regulation comparable to the other block exemption regulations, since it declares that certain measures do not constitute state aid in the sense of art.107(1) TFEU at all.

The de minimis rule is legally delicate.[32] Indeed, one can question whether the Council could enable the Commission under art.109 TFEU to define in advance the scope of art.107(1). The Commission cannot reinterpret case law on effect on trade, thereby permitting only a limited margin of discretion. Even small aid amounts may have an impact on competition and trade and there is no general threshold below which trade is not affected. The capacity of aid to affect trade does neither depend on the local or regional character, nor on the scale of the activity.

The approach seems nevertheless to have been endorsed by the European Court of Justice:

"In that connection, whilst the Court has held that the relatively small amount of aid or the relatively small size of the undertaking which receives it does not

---

[30] Article 3(3) of the de minimis Regulation.

[31] See in that sense also, H. Nyssens, "De minimis", p.409, in Mederer, Pesaresi, Van Hoof (eds.), *State aid*, (2008: Claeys & Casteels).

[32] See, e.g., M. Berghofer, "The New De Minimis regulation: Enlarging the Sword of Damocles?", EstAL, 2007, p.11.

as such exclude the possibility that intra-Community trade might be affected [. . .], a small amount of aid to an undertaking over a given period does not affect trade between Member States in particular economic sectors. The Commission was therefore entitled to reach the view, in the exercise of its discretion to assess the possible economic effects of aid, that, other than in certain sectors where competitive conditions are of a particular kind and except in respect of export aid, aid in amounts falling below those laid down in the Community guidelines on State aid for SMEs, and subsequently in its Notice on the *de minimis* rule for State aid (OJ 1996 C 68, p. 9), does not affect trade and is therefore not caught by Articles [107] and [108] of the Treaty. The amounts laid down by the Commission have not hitherto been challenged."[33]

The 2006 de minimis regulation raises still further questions: the €200,000 **7–012** threshold is considerably higher than the previously existing threshold of €100,000, by far exceeding any adjustment for inflation since 2001 and even taking into account inflation between 2006 and 2013, the period of validity of the de minimis Regulation. At no point in time does there seem to have been any serious analysis undertaken as to whether the different thresholds chosen indeed implied that there was no affectation of trade or distortion of competition.

The new rules excluding a generalised retro-active application also raise certain questions. As indicated, the Commission took a different view before[34]; the reasoning that aid measures which are not today in an integrated market considered to be aid under art.107 TFEU could not have constituted aid at an earlier time in a less integrated market does prima facie not seem absurd.

Finally under Regulation No.69/2001, €100,000 granted to a company in difficulties would not have constituted state aid, whereas now any amount granted to a similar company must in principle be viewed as state aid (or at least cannot benefit from the de minimis Regulation). In fact, a better legal solution would have been to declare that the measures at stake, if aid at all, have only a limited impact on trade and competition and hence, are exempted from notification and compatible with the common market.[35]

5. Crisis Measures: Temporary Framework—Link with De Minimis

The Temporary Community framework for state aid measures to support **7–013** access to finance in the current financial and economic crisis[36] has also added to

---

[33] Case C–351/98, September 26, 2002, *Spain v Commission ("Renove"),* 2002 E.C.R. I–8031; see also Case C–382/99, June 13, 2002, *Netherlands v Commission ("service stations"),* 2002 E.C.R. I–5163.

[34] See fn.25 above.

[35] See in this context also E. Gambaro, A. Nucara, L. Prete, "Pearle: so much Unsaid!", EstAl 2005, No.1, p.9.

[36] O.J. C16, January 22, 2009, pp.1–9, as amended.

the confusion. Many viewed the possibility to grant a compatible limited amount of aid as a temporary increase of the de minimis threshold. However, that measure is fundamentally different—it requires the prior notification of a scheme to the Commission, which must be approved under art.107(3)(b) TFEU. Prior de minimis aid must be taken into account when granting the compatible limited amount of aid, so that the sum of the aid and the de minimis aid received does not exceed €500,000 between January 1, 2008 and December 31, 2010.

The compatible limited amount of aid has been rolled over.[37] Aid can therefore be granted until December 31, 2011, provided that a scheme existed under the Temporary Community Framework, which has been prolonged and that the application for aid was done before December 31, 2010.

---

[37] Temporary Union framework for state aid measures to support access to finance in the current financial and economic crisis, O.J. C6, January 11, 2011, pp.5–15.

Part II

SPECIFIC ISSUES

CHAPTER 8

PUBLIC SECTOR AID*

1.	GENERAL	8–001
	Introduction to specific issues	8–001
	The concept of a "public undertaking"	8–005
	Procurement principles	8–008
	The concept of an "undertaking"	8–010
	Aid granted by public undertaking	8–013
2.	SURVEILLANCE: RULES CONCERNING TRANSPARENCY	8–015
	The Transparency Directive	8–015
	Challenges to the Directive	8–017
3.	CONCEPT OF STATE AID: THE MARKET ECONOMY INVESTOR PRINCIPLE	8–018
	The market economy investor principle	8–018
	Securitization	8–022
	Regulatory powers, taxation and the MEIP	8–023
4.	COMPATIBILITY OF AID TO PUBLIC UNDERTAKINGS AND UNDERTAKINGS ENTRUSTED WITH	
	THE PERFORMANCE OF AN SGEI	8–024
	Derogations from Article 107	8–024
	The derogations on the basis of Article 106(2)	8–025
	Article 106(2) and exemption from the duty of notification	8–026
	Commission practice following Altmark	8–030
	The Decision on the application of Article 106(2) to public service compensation	8–037
	The Decision thresholds	8–038
	The framework for state aid in the form of public service compensation	8–042
	Appropriate measures for existing aid	8–044
	Assessment	8–045
5.	CROSS-SUBSIDISATION	8–051
	Internal cross-subsidisation as state aid	8–053
	Cost allocation	8–055
6.	PRIVATISATION	8–067
	Conditions for approval of privatisation aid	8–074
	German reunification	8–079

1. GENERAL

Introduction to specific issues

Given the complexity of the economic, financial and political relationships   **8–001**
between the state and its public undertakings, as well as the size and economic

---

* Leigh Hancher

strength of many such companies, and the diversity of their functions, adequate supervision of compliance with the Treaty state aid rules can be difficult to ensure. Consequently, on June 25, 1980 the Commission adopted a Directive on the transparency of Financial Relations between Member States and Public Undertakings (Directive 80/723), using art.106(3) as its legal basis.[1] In its Recitals it is stated that "a fair and effective application of the aid rules in the Treaty to both public and private undertakings will only be possible if these financial relations are made transparent". This so-called "Transparency Directive" has been amended on a number of occasions.[2] The most recent consolidated version, now numbered as Directive 2006/111,[3] is discussed in detail below at para.8–014.

A Member State may make financial provisions towards the public sector in a variety of ways, whether through loans or grants or through the provision of share capital, the acquisition of shares or equity, or through the purchase of specific products or services. In this respect, the so-called "market investor principle" and its many variants, including the "public creditor", the "public debtor" and the "public seller" principles, as discussed earlier at Chs 2 and 3, are equally applicable to transactions between the state and its public sector undertakings. The use of this principle to establish whether a transaction involves state aid and to determine the amount of aid is discussed at section 3 below.

8–002　　In addition, public undertakings are often required to perform special duties, or are entrusted with the performance of particular tasks of general economic interest—also known as services of general economic interest (SGEIs) or public service obligations (PSOs)—which may not always be capable of being executed under normal commercial or market conditions. Further, public undertakings or entities may be required to perform services of general interest (SGIs), for example guaranteeing general security at airports in accordance with the instructions of a state authority, or ensuring the provision of basic schooling. In the Commission's view, services of general interest are market and non-market services that the public authorities classify as being of general interest and may therefore be subject to specific public service obligations. Services of general economic interest are market services that discharge general interest tasks and are therefore subject to specific public service obligations imposed by the Member States.[4] In a Communication of November 2007 the Commission shed some further light on the scope of the concept of an SGI.[5]

---

[1] [1980] O.J. L195/35.

[2] For example, by Commission Directive 2000/52, of July 26, 2000 [2000] O.J. L193/75.

[3] [2006] O.J. L318/17.

[4] Non-Paper, November 12, 2002 and Commission Communication on SGEIs [2001] O.J. C17/4.

[5] Commission Communication (2007) 725 final, Communication from the Commission to the European Parliament, the Council, the European Council, the European Economic and Social Committee and the Committee of the Regions, accompanying the Communication on "A single market for 21st century Europe", "Services of general interest, including social services of general interest: a new European commitment", available at *http://ec.europa.eu/services_general_interest/docs/com_2007_0725_en.pdf*. [Accessed August 15, 2011].

The Lisbon Treaty now contains a Protocol 26 on SGI which introduces the concept of an SGI into primary European law. At the same time art.14 TFEU reproduces art.16 EC, which recognises the fundamental character of such services and the shared competences of the Union and the Member States. Importantly, the article stresses that it is without prejudice to the rules on state aid. Hence the financing of the provision of these services remain subject to the discipline of the state aid rules.

The potential application of the state aid rules to the eventual compensation, remuneration or other financial consideration of other forms of support awarded by the state to ensure that such duties are performed by the undertakings in question has been the subject of considerable controversy in recent years. This complex issue is discussed in detail below at section 4.

Finally, sections 5 and 6 deal with the vexed issue of cross-subsidisation and **8–003** the complex question of privatisation aid. Cross-subsidisation may arise where an undertaking which benefits from an exclusive or special right to provide a certain service, sometimes referred to as a "reserved" service, is able to use the revenue so earned to finance its activities in competitive or de-regulated markets. This issue has been problematic in sectors such as post, telecommunications, energy and transport, where controlled or phased market liberalisation has led to the co-existence of reserved sectors and competitive markets, with national incumbents often active on both. In principle, unfair cross-subsidisation is subject to the state aid rules if the various tests as set out in art.107(1) are met. This is discussed in further detail below at para.8–038.

As to privatisation, Member States may often attempt to make a public undertaking more attractive to the market by granting it a form of "dowry" in advance of privatisation. This may raise state aid issues. The Commission has developed guidelines on certain aspects of privatisation procedures, as discussed below at section 6. For a discussion of the application of the state aid rules to privatisation processes in the Member States which acceded to the European Union in May 2004, see further Ch.5.

With respect to public financial support to the broadcasting sector and the **8–004** financing of public service broadcasting, the Commission has been confronted with a series of difficult test cases, not least because of the adoption at the time of the ratification of the Treaty of Amsterdam of a specific protocol to the EC Treaty. This Protocol recognises the important role of the public broadcasting remit as well as the competence of Member States to define and organise public broadcasting services, and subsequently to provide funds for the fulfilment of the remit. In an attempt to give practical guidelines on the application of the state aid rules to the principles espoused in the Protocol, the Commission adopted a Communication on the application of the state aid rules to public service broadcasting in 2001, which was substantially revised in 2009.[6] The Commission's decision-making practice and the growing body of case law in this area are

---

[6] See also D. Grespan, "A Busy year for State Aid Control in the Field of Public Service Broadcasting", 2010 EStAL Vol.9, nr 1, pp.79–98.

discussed in detail in Ch.18.[7] Finally, Ch.20 on energy deals with the application of the rules on compensation for public service obligations in the energy sector.

State support to national aviation companies—many of which have been traditionally under public ownership or control—has also given rise to complex problems, leading to the adoption of a separate set of guidelines in 1994.[8] State support to Regional Airports, which are often subject to public control or ownership, is dealt with in a separate set of recently revised guidelines, discussed in Ch.17. (See also Ch.3.)

The concept of a "public undertaking"

8–005   Every Member State, to a varying degree, carries out industrial or commercial activities by offering goods and services on the market. The state can enter the market and take part in the economy either through a body that has separate legal personality or through a body that is integrated into the state administration. For the application of the state aid rules of the Treaty this distinction is not relevant. In Joined Cases 188 to 190/80 (*France, Italy and UK v Commission*)[9] and 118/85 (*Commission v Italy*),[10] the Court approved a definition taken from the Transparency Directive (which will be discussed below) according to which a "public undertaking" is "any undertaking over which the public authorities may exercise directly or indirectly a dominant influence by virtue of their ownership of it, their financial participation therein, or the rules which govern it". A "dominant influence" will be presumed where the public authorities "directly or indirectly hold the major part of the undertaking's subscribed capital, control the majority of the votes attaching to shares issued by the undertaking, or can appoint more than half of the members of the undertaking's administrative, managerial or supervisory body".

For example, the Commission considered the "Crédit Foncier de France" (CFF) to be a state-controlled institution.[11] The majority of CFF's capital is controlled by large national and foreign institutional shareholders and investors. However, the government exercises a dominant influence on CFF, appointing its governor and deputy governors and being represented at the annual meeting of shareholders. It also appoints one of three auditors and is represented by a deputy government commissioner. As CFF is state-controlled, the Commission applied the "market economy investor principle" (see below) in assessing whether there is a state aid component in the financial assistance provided to it.

8–006   In another case, the European Court of Justice (ECJ) held that the investment by the "Caisse des Dépôts et Consignations-Participations" (CDC-P) in Air France could properly be regarded by the Commission as arising from conduct

---

[7] [2001] O.J. C320/4.
[8] [1994] O.J. C350/7.
[9] [1982] E.C.R. 2545.
[10] [1987] E.C.R. 2619.
[11] [1996] O.J. C275/2 of September 20, 1996.

imputable to the French state.[12] The CDC-P, a limited company governed by private law, belongs to the public sector, essentially because its majority share-holder is the "Caisse des Dépôts et Consignation" (Caisse). Caisse had placed the funds at the disposal of CDC-P and the tasks of Caisse were governed by statutory rules while its directors are appointed by the government.

In Case C–437/98 *France v Commission (Stardust Marine)*, however, it will be recalled that the Court held that the decision to deploy funds held by a financial institution which was indirectly controlled by the French state had to be attributable to the state (see Ch.3).[13]

Article 345 TFEU provides that the Treaty in no way prejudices the rules in Member States governing the system of property ownership, and allows the Member States freely to decide how to organise their public sector. Member States, therefore, have the right to run a mixed economy and to create and maintain public undertakings, to nationalise whole sectors of the economy, and to acquire or increase a shareholding in companies. At the same time, however, it follows from arts 4(3) TEU, and 106, 107 and 345 TFEU that in principle the state aid rules, as well as all other rules in the Treaty, must apply equally to both private and public undertakings (see, e.g., AG Reischl in Cases 188 to 190/80, referred to above at 8–005). Public undertakings, often used by the authorities as instruments of economic or social policy but at the same time actually or potentially competing with private undertakings, may not be given preferential treatment. This becomes even more important with the completion of the internal market, since Member States may be inclined to favour and thereby protect their public industries. **8–007**

The principles of neutrality and equal treatment are of particular importance in sectors which are subject to market liberalisation, as Member States may be inclined to favour and thereby protect their incumbent, and often public, companies. In this respect the potential application of art.1(b)(v) of Regulation 659/99 should also be borne in mind (see Ch.26).

In accordance with the principles of neutrality and equal treatment, as frequently invoked by the European Courts, the Commission's action must not prejudice or favour public undertakings when it examines a particular operation under art.107. It must establish in each individual case whether a transaction between a Member State and a public undertaking is a normal commercial transaction or whether it contains any elements of aid. Member States should not be granting aid, infringe or distort the mechanisms of fair competition within the common market. In this regard see Case T–156/04 *Électricité de France (EDF) v Commission* discussed at para.8–023, below.

Procurement principles

Where SGEIs (or SGIs or PSOs) are operated on the basis of a contractual arrangement which meets the definition of a public contract under the European **8–008**

---

[12] Case T–358/94 *Air France v Commission* [1996] E.C.R. II–2109.
[13] Case C–482/99 *France v Commission* [2002] E.C.R. I–2009.

Procurement Directives, and if the relevant thresholds are met, the award of that contract should take place in accordance with the procedural rules laid down in these Directives. Where these Directives are not applicable, as for example in the case of the award of public service concessions, there is nevertheless in many cases a duty upon Member States to entrust public services through a transparent and non-discriminatory procedure.[14] If they fail to do this, or if they use a negotiated procedure, this may have an impact on the state aid assessment. Indeed it is one of the "Altmark" conditions, as discussed below, that the SGEI in question should be awarded through an open tender. This does not necessarily mean a full open tender as required by the Directives.[15] Indeed these Directives also allow for a so-called "competitive dialogue procedure". This raises the complex issue of whether the award of such a contract following a tender procedure would exclude a possible aid element altogether.

In its decision on the Welsh Public Sector Network Scheme in May 2007, the Commission provided some useful guidance on this matter. Firstly it verified that a competitive procurement regime would lead to the award corresponding to the objective of achieving best value for money; hence there was no aid to the service provider. The Commission then went on to consider whether there was any potential aid to the users of the network or third parties. The procurement procedure would not necessarily have excluded aid at these two levels. However, any violation of the public procurement rules does not automatically prejudge the compatibility of the financial compensation awarded to the undertaking in question.[16] Failure to respect the state aid rules may affect the application of the procurement rules as contracting entities may, subject to certain conditions, be entitled to exclude from their award procedures, undertakings in receipt of illegal aid.[17]

8–009   It follows from the above that aid granted to public undertakings, whether or not pursuing public duties, is subject to the same rules applying to all forms of aid granted by Member States. Nevertheless, the application of the state aid rules to transactions concerning public undertakings presents particular problems which warrant more detailed examination. These will be discussed in the following paragraphs of this chapter.

For the application of the state aid rules to the export-credit insurance business, which is often state-owned or controlled, reference is made to the 1997 Commission Communication, as amended, that aims at eliminating distortions of

---

[14] Case C–342/98 *Telaustria* [2000] E.C.R. I–10745; see also Commission Communication on the Community rules applicable to contract awards not subject to the Public Procurement Directives, [2006] O.J. C179/2.

[15] See also P. Nicolaides, "State Aid, Advantage and Competitive Selection: What is a Normal Market Transaction?" in 2009 EsTAL. Vol.9, nr 1, pp.65–78.

[16] Case T–17/02 *Fred Olsen* [2005] ECR II–2031, at para.239.

[17] N46/2007. See also, Tossics and Gaal, "Public Procurement and State aid control", Competition Policy Newsletter, No.3, 2007, pp.15–18. See also "Wireless Prague" Case NN24/2007 [2007] O.J. C141/01.

competition between private and public, or publicly supported, export-credit insurers.[18]

The concept of an "undertaking"

The state aid rules only apply to a transfer of resources by a public authority, **8–010** public undertaking or part of the state administration to an "undertaking".[19] Public undertakings should be distinguished from the administration through which the state or any public authority exercises its sovereign or public prerogative powers.[20] Hence, transfers between different parts of the state administration do not constitute a transfer of resources to an "undertaking" within the meaning of art.107(1). In its decision concerning a state guarantee to the Irish Housing Finance Authority (HFA), for example, the Commission held that the HFA was in fact part of the state and hence the state guarantee provided to it for further financing of loans for the construction of social housing was an internal transfer of resources between state authorities.[21]

The concept of an "undertaking" is not defined in art.107(1) (see also Ch.3 at para.3–041) but has been considered in the case law of the European Courts to include any entity performing an economic activity.[22] This case concerned a complaint about the abuse of dominant position (based on systematic late payments to providers of medical goods and equipment by, on average, 300 days) by the management bodies of the Spanish national health system (SNS), which collectively accounted for 80 per cent of purchases of medical goods and equipment in Spain.[23] In the ECJ ruling it was accepted that the provision of healthcare services by SNS was purely of a social nature. The Court held:

> "(. . .) there is no need to dissociate the activity of purchasing goods from the subsequent use to which they are put in order to determine the nature of that purchasing activity, and that the nature of the purchasing activity must be determined according to whether or not the subsequent use of the purchased goods amounts to an economic activity."[24]

Consequently there was no economic activity nor an undertaking involved, and as a result the application of the EU state aid and competition rules could be excluded.

---

[18] Communication 281/03 of the Commission [1997] O.J. C281/4. See also Ch.4 at para.4–038 (export aid to third countries).

[19] See for example the Commission Decision in C9/2009, aid implemented by Belgium, France and Luxembourg in favour of Dexia SA [2010] O.J. L274/53.

[20] A. Deringer, "Equal Treatment of Public and Private Enterprises", General Report prepared for the FIDE Congress in Copenhagen, 1978.

[21] N209/2001 [2002] O.J. C67/33.

[22] Case T–319/99 *FENIN* [2003] E.C.R. II–357. See also Case C–237/04 *Enirsiorse v Sotarbo* [2006] E.C.R. I–2843.

[23] Case C–205/03P *FENIN v Commission* [2006] E.C.R. I–6295.

[24] *FENIN v Commission*, para.26.

In Joined Cases T–231/06 and T–237/06 the Court dismissed the Dutch government's attempts to claim that its public broadcasting foundation, the NOS, which was entrusted with the task of co-ordinating the entire system of public broadcasting, was not an "undertaking" but an organ entrusted with public order functions. The NOS performed economic activities and earned a substantial income in the process (see paras 81–106).[25]

In its ruling in Joined Cases T–443/08 and T–455-08 *Leipzig Halle*,[26] March 24, 2011, the General Court rejected the argument put forward by Germany that a special vehicle established by several regional and local authorities to construct and operate airport facilities was not an undertaking within the meaning of art.107(1) TFEU. The fact that the undertaking was established on a not-for-profit basis was of no relevance (see paras 93–97 and 115–117).[27]

8–011 The "functional" approach developed in the case law is not always easy to apply in practice, as illustrated by the "Italian banking foundation" saga. In its Decision C54/2000 of August 23, 2002, the Commission held that certain fiscal measures introduced in 1998 and 1999 in favour of Italian banking foundations fell outside the scope of state aid control rules because the foundations' activity of managing own assets and using proceeds to donate grants to not-for-profit entities was not an economic activity.[28] The Commission concluded that the obligation to relinquish any controlling shareholdings within a specified time limit, together with the obligations and restrictions imposed by the new legislative regime on the members of the internal bodies and executives of the banking foundations as regards their relationships with assignee banks—in particular the prohibition on performing administrative, managerial or supervisory duties in assignee banks or any other financial or banking undertaking—and the limitations as regards the management of their assets, reinforced the separation between banking foundations and financial institutions, thereby helping "to allay the corresponding concerns expressed in the decision to initiate the procedure". It concluded that the management of their assets was not an economic activity and therefore did not make banking foundations undertakings within the meaning of art.107(1). The Commission also noted that banking foundations were not entitled to own any controlling shareholding in undertakings other than instrumental undertakings. In the latter case, the Commission held that where the activities of instrumental undertakings consisted of providing services in a market where competition exists, the ability of banking foundations "to control undertakings is liable to distort competition and their activities cannot be entirely immune to competition control".

---

[25] Joined Cases T–231/06 and T–237/06 December 16, 2010 [2010] O.J. C38/54; now on appeal, C–104/11P, August 13, 2011.

[26] Joined Cases T–443/08 and T–455/08 *Freistaat Sachsen and Land Sachsen-Anhalt v Commission* [2011] O.J. C145/24. O.J. C252/16.

[27] Now on appeal, C–288/11P, June 8, 2011.

[28] See Commission Press Release, IP/02/1231. See also N 358/2001, C (2001) 3457—Netherlands SIKB—aid to a foundation charged with the task of developing environment norms was not a commercial activity.

The Commission concluded that "the possibility of acquiring control of instrumental undertakings, . . . would not make [banking] foundations undertakings in so far as it did not imply direct involvement in the activity of the controlled undertaking". On that basis, the Commission decided that banking foundations did not qualify as undertakings for the purposes of art.107(1) TFEU unless they carried out an economic activity in the meaning of the case law, that is, by offering goods or services on a market where competition exists, even in one of the "relevant sectors". Nevertheless, the Italian fiscal authorities persisted in treating banking foundations as "undertakings" for taxation purposes, leading to further disputes before the national courts and eventually a reference to the ECJ.

Although the Commission's approach in its Decision C54/2000 was confirmed **8–012** by the Advocate General in Case C–222/04 *Cassa da Risparmio* (at paras 124–125), the Court in its ruling of January 10, 2006 held, at paras 122–125, however, that:

"As regards that activity, a banking foundation acts as a voluntary body or charitable organisation and not as an undertaking. On the other hand, where a banking foundation, acting itself in the fields of public interest and social assistance, uses the authorisation given it by the national legislature to effect the financial, commercial, real estate and asset operations necessary or opportune in order to achieve the aims prescribed for it, it is capable of offering goods or services on the market in competition with other operators, for example in fields like scientific research, education, art or health. On that hypothesis, which is subject to the national court's assessment, the banking foundation must be regarded as an undertaking, in that it engages in an economic activity, notwithstanding the fact that the offer of goods or services is made without profit motive, since that offer will be in competition with that of profit-making operators. Where it is decided that it is to be treated as an undertaking, on account of control of a banking company and involvement in its management or on account of an activity in (inter alia) a social, scientific or cultural field, a banking foundation such as that in question in the main proceedings must, as a result, be subject to the application of the Community rules relating to State aid. The reply to the first and second questions must therefore be that a legal person such as the banking foundation in question in the main proceedings may, after an examination which it is for the national court to conduct taking account of the regime applicable at the material time, be treated as an "undertaking" within the meaning of Art. 87(1) EC [now Art.107(1) TFEU] and, as such, subject at that time to the Community rules relating to State aid."[29]

Aid granted by a public undertaking

This chapter focuses primarily on aid to a public undertaking, as opposed to **8–013** aid by or through a public undertaking to a potential third beneficiary. This latter

[29] [2006] E.C.R. I–289.

subject is dealt with in more detail in Chs 3 and 20. It may, however, be noted here that in general the Courts consider the economic reality of the situation when determining whether a measure constitutes aid—this being inherent in the "effects-based" approach to the definition of a state aid as discussed in Ch.3. Hence, in situations where financial advantages are made available not directly by the state as such, but through public undertakings which it owns or controls, the measure in question may amount to aid within the meaning of art.107(1)—the resources at the disposal of public undertakings are considered to be "state resources" and if they are under the permanent disposal or control of the state, their application in particular transactions may amount to state aid within the meaning of art.107(1).[30]

8–014 The Transparency Directive 2006/111 explicitly covers the flow of public funds to public undertakings from other public undertakings (i.e. undertakings within the meaning of arts 1(b) and 2—i.e. "undertakings which the public authorities may exercise directly or indirectly a dominant influence by virtue of their ownership in it, their financial participation therein, or the rules which govern it"). Furthermore, in Joined Cases 67, 68 and 70/85 *Gebroeders Van der Kooy et al v Commission*, the Court confirmed that:

> "there is no necessity to draw any distinction between cases where the aid is granted by the State and cases where it is granted by public or private bodies established or appointed by the State to administer the aid". The Court therefore found that a special tariff for natural gas supplied by the Dutch state-controlled company Gasunie fell within the scope of art.107(1) as Gasunie "did not enjoy full autonomy in the fixing of gas tariffs, but acted under the control and on the instructions of the public authorities".[31]

In its later ruling in Case C–482/99 *France v Commission* (*Stardust Marine*),[32] the Court suggested that the mere fact that funds supplied by two subsidiaries of the state-controlled bank Credit Lyonnaise could be classified as "state resources" within the meaning of art.2 of the Transparency Directive did not mean that the transaction in question could be classified as aid; the Court accepted the argument put forward by the French Government that the Commission also had to demonstrate that the transaction in question could be attributed or imputed to the state.[33] See further Ch.3 at paras 3–028 et seq. and Ch.20 at section 3. In its opening decision in Case C240/36 *VAOP* of September 30, 2005,[34] the Commission had initially taken the preliminary view that financial measures granted by the Dutch Bank for Local Authorities (BNG) were funded

---

[30] Case T–358/94 *Air France* [1996] E.C.R. II–2109.
[31] [1988] E.C.R. 219. See, however, Case C–53/96 *Belgium v Commission* [1998] E.C.R. I—where the Court held that the granting of a specific tariff to certain gas users was in line with the market investor principle.
[32] [2002] E.C.R. I–2009.
[33] [2002] E.C.R. I–4397.
[34] [2005] O.J. C240/36.

by state resources as the Dutch state appoints representatives to the supervisory board bank in question. However, in its final Decision 2006/949 the Commission concluded that transactions at issue had been concluded on the basis of the market investor principle.[35]

2. SURVEILLANCE: RULES CONCERNING TRANSPARENCY

The Transparency Directive

As explained above, the complexity of the many faceted relationships between the state and the public sector led the Commission to seek first to achieve the necessary degree of transparency on the flows of funds from the state to its public undertakings and from the latter to other public undertakings in order to be in a position to then go on to ensure an effective application of the Treaty state aid rules. The "Transparency Directive" is designed to ensure the discipline of state aids is also applied in an equitable manner to public enterprise. The concept of transparency is closely related to that of equal treatment. The scope of the original Directive 80/723 of 1980 was first extended in 1985 to cover the water, energy, post and telecommunications and transport and public credit institutions. In 1991 the Commission issued a Communication which was designed to reinforce its surveillance system, but following the successful challenge to this "soft law" measure by the French government, the Transparency Directive was further amended in 1993 to incorporate the reporting principles which the Commission had intended to give effect to through its 1991 Communication,[36] and a further Communication was issued in 1993.[37] Note that the annual reporting requirements of the 1994 Communication on the direct or indirect acquisition of holdings by public authorities remain valid for acquisitions in non-public undertakings. The 1991 Communication, as re-adopted in the 1993 Communication, deals in great detail with the application of the market economy investor principle (see below at para.8–018 and also Ch.3).

The Transparency Directive was the subject of further amendment in 2000 to extend its application to public and private undertakings alike, as long as they were provided with special rights or entrusted with services in the general economic interest for which they receive subsidies.[38] A later amendment (Commission Directive 2005/81 adopted in November 2005 and now consolidated as Directive 2006/111) replaced art.2(1)(d) to include not only undertakings enjoying special or exclusive rights but also undertakings entrusted with the operation of a service of general economic interest pursuant to art.106(2) that receive public service compensation in any form whatsoever in relation to such service

8–015

---

[35] Commission Decision 2006/949 EC [2006] O.J. L383/61.
[36] [1993] O.J. L254/16.
[37] [1993] O.J. C307/3.
[38] Directive 2000/52 [2000] O.J. L93/75.

and carry on other activities. This measure should have been implemented into national law by Member States before December 19, 2006.[39]

8–016   The Transparency Directive obliges Member States to supply to the Commission all necessary information in order for the public funds supplied to public undertakings and entrusted undertakings, as well as those undertakings entrusted with an SGEI and receiving compensation therefore, to "emerge" clearly as well as the use to which they were put. The Directive lists a number of financial transactions which could well amount to a form of disguised state aid, including the setting off of operating losses, the provision of grants without requiring repayment, the granting of preferential loans, the foregoing by the state of the normal returns on the funds supplied, and the provision by the state of compensation for the financial burdens imposed by public authorities. The Member State must ensure that this information is kept at the disposal of the Commission for a period of five years. As a result of the 1993 amendments, the Member States are also obliged to file annual reports with the Commission on state intervention for public undertakings in the manufacturing sector having an annual turnover in excess of €250 million. The current Directive also provides for a de minimis rule and does not apply to financial relations between public authorities and public undertakings with an annual turnover of less than €40 million in the two financial years preceding the one in which the relevant funds are made available or used. The Directive does not override the normal procedures and powers of the Commission under art.108 and Regulation 659/99 (see Ch.25).

In accordance with the Transparency Directive, undertakings must keep separate internal accounts. For an application of the requirements of the Directive to accounting techniques, see, for example, the Commission's decision in N531/2005 on measures relating to the setting up and subsequent operation of the banking subsidiary of La Poste, discussed in detail below at para.8–055.[40]

Challenges to the Directive

8–017   The original Transparency Directive 80/723, as well as the 1991 Communication, were the subjects of legal challenges by Member States. With regard to the former measure, the Court upheld the legality of the Directive and found that it was not an attempt to define the concept of aid, a task which falls to the Council on the basis of art.109 (see Ch.25). It is only a statement of the transactions of which the Commission should be informed in order to check whether a Member State has complied with its notification obligations under art.108.[41] The reporting obligations which the Commission purported to impose by means of the 1991 Communication were, however, found to be problematic, given that the Commission had failed to adopt the appropriate legal basis (i.e. art.106) for a measure

---

[39] [2006] O.J. L318/17.
[40] COM(2005) 5412 final, December 21, 2005.
[41] Cases 188 to 190/80, above at para.8–005.

which was capable of producing legal effects separate from those already imposed by art.5(2) of the Transparency Directive.[42]

3. CONCEPT OF STATE AID: THE MARKET ECONOMY INVESTOR PRINCIPLE

The market economy investor principle

This paragraph will only sketch out the principles laid down in relevant **8–018** Commission Communications and related reporting obligations. Further reference should be made to Ch.3 for relevant case law and practice.

In 1981 the Council approved the Commission decision establishing Community rules for aid to the steel industry (see Ch.14) and also approved the fifth shipbuilding directive (see Ch.16). Both measures stated that the concept of aid includes financing measures by the Member States which can not be considered as the provision of equity capital according to standard company practice in a market economy.[43] This same principle was adopted by the Commission in its 1984 Communication to the Member States concerning holdings by public authorities in company capital,[44] as a tool to distinguish "normal" flows of public funds and state aid. This set of guidelines concerns *all* acquisitions of shareholdings by public authorities. Although its principles are of particular importance for the relationship between the state and public undertakings, it is important to emphasise that these principles have a much wider significance.

The 1984 Communication states that there is state aid where fresh capital is **8–019** contributed in circumstances that would not be acceptable to a private investor operating under normal market economy conditions. It specifies situations in which this will be the case: e.g. where the financial position of the company, and particularly the structure and volume of its debt, is such that a normal return (in dividends or capital gains) cannot be expected within a reasonable time from the capital invested; or where the public authority's holding involves the taking over of the non-viable operations of an ailing company. Certain situations will not involve state aid, e.g. where fresh capital is injected into a public enterprise, provided: (a) this fresh capital corresponds to new investment needs and to costs directly linked to them; (b) the industry in which the enterprise operates does not suffer from structural overcapacity; and (c) the enterprise's financial position is sound. For an application of this Communication, see the Commission's decision in N 531/2005 on La Poste, at para.8–055 below.

In its Communication of 1993 concerning public undertakings in the manufacturing sector, the Commission provides a fairly full explanation of how it will

---

[42] Case C–325/91 *France v Commission* [1993] E.C.R. I–3283.
[43] See for example C–133/10 *Commission v Belgium* [2011] Unreported, where the Court held that Belgium had failed to fulfil its obligations under Directive 2005/81.
[44] EC Bulletin 1984, No.9.

apply the private investor principle.[45] Note that there is no reason to limit the approach to aid to public undertakings and to the manufacturing sector. The Commission recognises that where:

"the public authority controls an individual public undertaking or group of undertakings it will normally be less motivated by purely short-term profit considerations . . . and its time horizon will accordingly be longer".

The Commission also recognises that where a call for finance:

"is necessary to protect the value of the whole investment, the public authority like a private investor can be expected to take into account this wider context when examining whether the commitment of new funds is commercially justified".

8–020   Thus, an appreciation of the general economic context will be relevant in assessing how a private investor would act. The Commission recognises that a wide margin of judgment comes into entrepreneurial decisions but that measures will be condemned "when it is beyond reasonable doubt that there is no other plausible explanation for the provision of public funds than considering them as state aid". The Communication proposes extending the market economy investor principle to cover other types of funding for public undertakings in the manufacturing sector. In addition to *capital injections, guarantees* and *loans* will be subject to the test, and the Commission will also assume that an undertaking is being indirectly aided by the state if the return on investment is below that which a market economy investor would expect. For application of the principle to the aviation and maritime sectors see the Commission's communications of 1994 and 1997.[46]

It goes without saying that if the Commission, when comparing the behaviour of the state with that of a private investor, comes to the conclusion that a capital injection, loan or guarantee must be deemed to constitute state aid, such aid may still be compatible with the common market under art.107(3), for example because the measure satisfies the criteria laid down in the guidelines on aid for rescuing and restructuring firms in difficulty, or in frameworks such as those for R&D aid and for aid to the motor vehicle industry.[47] (See also section 6, below.) Recent case law has confirmed that the mere announcement by the State that it intends to inject fresh capital into a state-owned entity may well amount to an

---

[45] See fn.37, above.

[46] Aviation, [1994] O.J. C350/5, and for an example see Commission Decision of July 6, 1994 on aid granted to TAP ([1994] O.J. L279/29) and Decision of October 7, 1994 on aid granted to Olympic Airways ([1994] O.J. L273/22), and Case T–214/95 *Vlaamse Gewest v Commission* [1998] E.C.R. II–0717. Maritime transport: [1997] O.J. L205. See further Ch.16.

[47] See Commission Decision of November 30, 1994 concerning the transfer by the Netherlands of a pilot school to KLM [1994] O.J. L379/13.

"economic advantage" within the meaning of art.107(1), but if this advantage is not funded by state resources then art.107(1) does not apply. (See Joined Cases T–425/04, T–444/04, T–450/04 and T–456/04, *France Telecom,* May 10, 2010, discussed further at Ch.3.)

The application of the Commission's Guidelines on public authorities' hold-   **8–021**
ings in company capital and the Communication of 1993 in its Decision 2001/856 (aid to Verlipack) was further considered by the Court in Case C–457/00 *Belgium v Commission.*[48] According to s.3.2 of the Guidelines, state aid is not involved where fresh capital is contributed under normal market economy conditions. The Belgian public authorities had acquired a holding in the Verlipack group—the largest Belgian producer of hollow container glass—in 1985 but this was transferred to the other major (private) investor, the Beaulieu group, in 1996. In order to deal with continuing financial difficulties the group was restructured, and Beaulieu and a German company, Heye-Glas, set up a holding company, Verlipack I, controlled by Heye. A second holding company, Verlipack II, was set up by the shareholders of Verlipack I and the Walloon Region, which contributed capital of BEF 350 million. In its initial examination of this measure in September 1998 the Commission found the contribution to be consistent with the actions of a provider of risk capital operating under normal market conditions. The simultaneous acquisition of a majority paid up share-holding of BEF 500 million in Verlipack I by a private investor (Heye) indicated there were prospects for future profitability. However, it subsequently transpired that Heye had also received financial assistance from the Walloon region (through two loans for the investment company SRIW) to finance this acquisition for almost 50 per cent. Verlipack II was put into liquidation in 1999. In its subsequent decision of October 2000 the Commission found that the capital injected into Verlipack by the Walloon Region in April 1997 and the two loans granted by SRIW and examined the aid in accordance with the MEIT. It held that a lender of funds would not on the one hand have acquired a shareholding of BEF 350 million and on the other lent risk capital of BEF 500 million covering 50 per cent of the risk in the event of Verlipack's profit outlook proving unfavourable, and hence Belgium had not acted as a private investor. The aid did not fall within the scope of the derogations set out in art.107(2) or (3). As the grant of the first loan was provided under the condition of a write-off in the event of Verlipack's winding up, it could not be regarded as normal behaviour of a private investor. The second loan was pledged without collateral and this too did not conform to the private investor principle. On appeal, the Court confirmed the Commission's findings. In particular, internal company documentation confirmed the substantial risks at stake. As Heye had not been required to provide any guarantee, even though the interest rates on the loans were in line with market rates applying at the relevant time, this did not exclude the aid elements in the loans.

[48] [2003] E.C.R. I–6931.

Securitization

8–022   The first case involving securitisation—that is the conversion of assets into securities in order to raise cash and as such to help reduce the risk of lenders who would be able to share part of that risk with other lenders—concerned the public participation of Austria Wirstschaftsservice GmbH (AWS), a public body that administers the award of grants to Austrian companies in a bond portfolio set up by the private bank Investkredit AG for Austrian enterprises. AWS was not in a position to raise capital from the capital market and did not have sufficient resources and hence it issued a guarantee for the amount of its participation in Investkredit. The latter in turn raised an equivalent amount as liquidity from the capital market at market rates. The guarantee in turn was remunerated by Investkredit as if it were a loan on market conditions. The Commission concluded on the basis of an initial assessment that the participation of AWS was on market conditions, and there was no aid to Investkredit, the investors or the undertakings in the portfolio.[49]

Regulatory powers, taxation and the MEIP

8–023   Case T–156/04 *Commission v France (EDF)*[50] centres on the question of whether a fiscal measure may be subject to the private investor test. The ECJ's earlier ruling in *Spain v Commission*[51] is often taken as a guiding principle, that it was necessary to distinguish between the obligations which the state must assume as owner of the share capital of a company and its obligations as a "public authority". In *EDF*, the General Court held that the mere fact that the state can make use of financial means that are acquired by using public power cannot in itself justify a measure as the expression of its public power. At the same time the Court's case law underlined the importance of the effects of a state measure, as opposed to its objective or aims. Indeed in the *Spain v Commission* case, which was further relied upon in Case C–344/99 *Germany v Commission*,[52] the Court drew a distinction between the obligations which the State must assume as owner of the share capital of a company and its obligations as a public authority, as a criterion to determine which costs should have been taken into account when examining whether a private investor would have chosen the same solution (instead of winding up an undertaking).[53] Hence it can be argued that the ECJ may still apply the private investor test to measures taken in the exercise of public power but uses the test to determine which costs can and cannot be taken into account in the application of that test.

---

[49] N192/2005 [2006] O.J. C79/23.

[50] [2009] E.C.R II–04503, now under appeal in case C–124/10P [2010] O.J. C161/16. See now the Opinion of the Advocate General of October 20, 2011.

[51] Joined Cases C–278/92, C–279/92 and C–280/92 *Spain v Commission* [1994] E.C.R. I–4103, para.22.

[52] C–334/99 *Germany v Commission* [2003] E.C.R. I–1139.

[53] Joined Cases C–278/92, C–279/92 and C–280/92 *Spain v Commission* [1994] E.C.R. I–4103, para.22.

4. COMPATIBILITY OF AID TO PUBLIC UNDERTAKINGS AND UNDERTAKINGS ENTRUSTED WITH THE PERFORMANCE OF AN SGEI

Derogations from Article 107

Once it is established that there is an aid, the Commission may still take into **8–024** account the special characteristics of public enterprises in determining whether or not the aid in question is compatible with the common market, but only where the Treaty entitles it to take account of such considerations, i.e. where they are justified in the Community interest. The Commission quotes examples in its 1993 Communication such as using public companies to provide public services or to act as locomotives for the economy or catalysts for regional development. Aid to public undertakings must also comply with the principles of the relevant guidelines and communications on different forms and types of aid which give further guidance on the application of art.107(3) (see Ch.4). The mere fact that a public undertaking (or an "entrusted undertaking" within the meaning of art.106(1)) performs pubic service obligations does not in itself exempt it from the competition rules.

In its decision on Verlipack, the Commission, having established that the loans and capital injections did not conform to the market investor principle, considered the application of art.107(3)(c) but as the actual investment in Verlipack had been carried out by Heye, the private investor, and not by the Walloon authorities, this derogation could not be applied. Hence the aid was declared to be incompatible with the exception of a portion of one of the loans.[54]

The application of art.107(3)(b) and (c) in the context of the guidelines on rescue and restructuring aid, as well as the temporary frameworks adopted in the wake of the financial crisis of 2008, is further considered at, respectively Ch.24 and at Ch.19.

The derogations on the basis of Article 106(2)

The application of art.106(2) to the state aid regime has been the subject of **8–025** controversy, albeit that this has to some extent been clarified by the Court's ruling in the *Altmark* case.[55] It is of importance to distinguish the implicit application of art.106(2) to the state measure purporting to grant compensation to an undertaking for performing a PSO or SGEI in order to determine whether that measure constitutes aid within the meaning of art.107(1) in the first place, and the potential application of art.106(2) to a measure which is to be classified as aid but which may nevertheless be deemed to be a compatible form of aid (i.e. as a potential derogation in addition to those provided by art.107(2) and (3)). For the sake of clarification we will refer to the former situation as a procedural matter which concerns the eventual obligation to notify the measure in question, while

---

[54] Decision 2001/856 EC of October 4, 2000 [2001] O.J. L320/28, at Pt IV.3.
[55] [2003] E.C.R. I–7247.

the second situation is dealt with as a substantive matter, as it concerns the conditions of assessment of the aid measure which upon notification to it in accordance with art.108, the Commission must apply.

It should also be noted that although art.106(2) is addressed to undertakings, leading to early suggestions in the literature that this article could not be relied upon by Member States to escape their obligations under the state aid rules which are addressed to them, and not to undertakings, it now seems clear that the Commission and the Court consider art.106(2) to apply in full to the state aid regime so that both Member States and undertakings can rely upon the exception.

In order for the derogation in art.106(2) to apply, six conditions must be met.[56] First, the target of the measure must be an undertaking. Second, it must be an entrusted undertaking. Third, the service in question must be a service of general economic interest. Fourth, the performance of the tasks entrusted to that undertaking must be obstructed by the application of the state aid rules. Fifth, the derogation must be proportional to the entrusted tasks. And sixth, trade must not be affected to such an extent as would be contrary to the Community interest.

Given that art.106(2) is a derogation, it must be invoked by the Member State or undertaking in question. The burden of proof that the various conditions are met is on the party claiming the benefit of the exception. In Case T–289/03 *BUPA*, the Court indicated that the lack of proof by the Member State that the criteria are met may constitute a manifest error of assessment (see para.172). Although the Courts have asserted that this article should be applied restrictively given that it is an exception to the Treaty rules, case law would seem to confirm that not all the conditions contained in that article are applied strictly.[57]

Furthermore, it has also been established in the jurisprudence of the Courts that art.106(2) has direct effect, at least in relation to the application of those Treaty articles which have direct effect. Article 107(1), however, is not directly effective: a national court may establish whether a measure is a state aid, but it cannot declare that aid compatible with the common market unless it is covered by an Exemption Regulation. The Courts have yet to confirm that art.106(2) has direct effect in conjunction with art.107(1) TFEU,[58] although the AG in *Ferring* has assumed this to be the case.[59]

---

[56] See AG Leger in Case C–280/00 *Altmark Trans* [2003] E.C.R. I–7247 at para.87.

[57] See, for example, Case T–289/03 *BUPA v Commission* [2008] E.C.R. II–00741.

[58] See also Case C–332/98 *CELF* [2000] E.C.R. I–4833.

[59] AG Tizzano in C–53/00 *Ferring SA v Agence centrale des organismes de sécurité sociale* [2001] E.C.R. I–9067 at para.80: " . . . . there is no reason to constrain national courts to declare illegal aid which it has found to be compatible with the common market in accordance with Article 90(2) simply because the aid was implemented without prior notification being given to the Commission under Article 93(3) of the Treaty. If the conditions for applying the exemption exist, the aid is de jure compatible with the common market without there being any need for Commission authorisation. Furthermore, even if there were a subsequent decision confirming the compatibility of the aid under Article 90(2), that decision would merely have declaratory effect as it would be limited to a statement that the national authorities had not applied the exemption in an abusive manner." Implicitly followed by ECJ at para.41.

Article 106(2) and exemption from the duty of notification

Until 2003 the case law of the ECJ and that of the General Court seemed to **8–026** provide mixed guidance on the issue of whether or not financial support to public or "entrusted undertakings", to compensate them for the performance of obligations imposed upon them in the general economic interest, could be exempt from the state aid rules in the sense that such measures being merely compensation for specific burdens or obligations could not constitute an "advantage" within the meaning of art.107(1). In an early ruling in Case 240/83 *ADBHU*, the ECJ held that the payment for collecting waste oils as required under Council Directive 75/439 constituted payment or indemnity for a service rendered.[60]

Furthermore, in Case 387/92 *Banco de Credito Industrial SAS v Ayuntamiento de Valencia*,[61] a Spanish law conferring a tax exemption on public credit institutions was held in principle to be a form of aid. The Spanish government claimed that if the measure was an aid, it was an existing aid as it related to the period prior to Spain's accession. The Court agreed, and classified the measure as an existing aid. The Court further confirmed that in principle art.106 constituted a valid derogation from art.107, but it did not proceed to consider its application to this particular case given that the aid was an existing aid which had not been further challenged by the Commission.

In the later Case T–106/95 *FFSA*,[62] the General Court confirmed that **8–027** art.106(2) could form an exception to the state aid rules. This latter case involved allegations by competitors to the French La Poste that this institution had received unjustified fiscal benefits, but which the Commission had subsequently judged to be necessary for La Poste to perform various public service duties and hence it could benefit from an exemption under art.106(2). Indeed, the Commission had argued that as the fiscal advantages did not fully offset the costs in providing the PSOs, there was no question of aid at issue, and no need to apply art.107. The General Court did not agree with this approach, but held that the fiscal measures should have been evaluated under art.107, albeit that art.106(2) could be applied if the resulting fiscal benefit could have been equal to or less than the costs incurred in providing the relevant public services. In other words, the Court endorsed the *Banco de Credito* or state aid approach and seemed to suggest that even if the measure only compensated for the performance of the PSOs it still should have been notified in the first place. Obviously failure to respect the notification and related standstill obligations would mean that measure would be illegal at least until the Commission had finally cleared it. As such

---

[60] [1985] E.C.R. 531. See also the 24th Competition Report at Pt.388—environmental charges on the sale of tyres to finance collection and disposal of used tyres in an environmentally friendly way. See also the Commission's Report on Services of General Interest in the Banking Sector, presented to the ECOFIN Council on November 23, 1998, and in the light of the Declaration on Public Credit Institutions in Germany, annexed to the Treaty of Amsterdam.

[61] [1994] E.C.R. I–877.

[62] [1997] E.C.R. II–229.

the measure could be challenged in the national courts. The Court confirmed this same approach in its later ruling in Case T–46/97 *SIC*.[63]

8–028   Subsequently, the ECJ appeared to pursue a different approach to the application of the state aid rules to what may be termed "compensation" measures. In Case C–53/00 *Ferring*, which concerned a fiscal benefit for wholesale distributors of pharmaceutical products who were obliged under French law to hold a full range of products, the Court held that the tax advantage corresponded to the additional costs which the distributors were required to bear in discharging their public service obligations. Although the ECJ did not expressly rule on the notification issue, as noted, the approach seemed to imply that the art.106(2) derogation could be applied directly by the national courts to the granting of new state financing to providers of services of general interest, including any un-notified measure.

The *Ferring* or "net compensation" approach, as it has become known, seemed to indicate a departure from the *FFSA* case, and the Commission subsequently reflected this in its decision making practice.[64] The *Ferring* ruling gave rise to a spate of criticism, as it was claimed that if Member States were released from their duty to notify a measure there could be no independent control as to whether or not the compensation measures at issue did or could lead to overcompensation and hence a disguised form of aid. Furthermore, the Court's position in *Ferring* seemed to be at odds with its earlier ruling in Case C–322/98 *France v Commission ("CELF")* in 2000.[65] The Court was offered an opportunity to revisit *Ferring* in the subsequent cases of *Altmark*[66] and *Gemo*.[67] Although its Advocate Generals issued lengthy opinions on the pros and cons of the "compensation approach" versus "the state aid approach" in both cases, the Court eventually only considered the issue in detail in the *Altmark* case.[68]

8–029   In the *Altmark* case the Court held that compensation for the performance of public service obligations (PSOs) or tasks does not constitute state aid within the meaning of art.107(1) TFEU provided that four cumulative criteria (now often referred to as the *Altmark* criteria or conditions) are fulfilled:

(1) The recipient undertaking must actually have a public service obligation to discharge and the obligations must be clearly defined.[69]

(2) The parameters on the basis of which the compensation is calculated must be established in advance in an objective and transparent manner.

---

[63] [2000] E.C.R. II–2125 at para.84.

[64] See for example *Irish Health Insurance* N 46/2003 [2003] O.J. C186/46.

[65] [2000] E.C.R. I–4833.

[66] C–280/00 [2003] E.C.R. I–7747.

[67] C–126/01 [2003] E.C.R. I–13769.

[68] For a discussion of the different opinions see, inter alia, C. Rizza, "The Financial Assistance Granted by Member States to Undertakings Entrusted with Operation of a Service of General Economic Interest", in Biondi et al. (eds), *The Law of State Aid in the European Union*, 2002, pp.67–84.

[69] It is for the Member State in question to designate a particular service as an SGEI. See in this respect Case T–17/02 *Olsen* [2005] E.C.R. II–2031.

(3) The compensation cannot exceed what is necessary to cover all or part of the costs incurred in the discharge of the public service obligations, taking into account the relevant receipts and a reasonable profit.

(4) When the undertaking which discharges the public service obligations is not chosen pursuant to a public procurement procedure which would allow for the selection of the tenderer capable of providing those services at the least cost to the community, the level of compensation must be determined on the basis of an analysis of the costs which a typical undertaking, well run and adequately with the relevant assets, would have incurred.

Where each of these four criteria are met, public service compensation does not constitute state aid and no prior notification is required for Commission approval under art.108. In all other cases, provided the remaining elements of art.107(1) are satisfied, then public service compensation constitutes state aid that is subject to arts 93, 106, 107 and 108 of the Treaty. In other words, the measure must be notified to the Commission in accordance with art.108(3) and the Commission must assess its compatibility on the basis of art.107(2) or (3). Article 106(2) may also be relied upon as an additional substantive ground for declaring the compatibility of the state aid measure, subject however to the necessity and proportionality tests. In particular, it would appear from the *Ferring* ruling, that any overcompensation for the costs of performing a service of general economic interest could not be justified on the basis of art.106(2). Overcompensation is neither necessary nor proportionate. Subsequent practice indicates, however, that this approach is not always applied.

Finally, it should be mentioned that, following *Altmark*, the Court has gone on to confirm that the four criteria discussed above should be applied in all cases, and also to decisions taken prior to the ruling itself.[70] In Case T–293/03 *BUPA*, the General Court held that: "However, it must be stated that the Court of Justice did not place any temporal limitation on the scope of its findings in Altmark. In the absence of such a limitation *ratione temporis*, those findings resulting from an interpretation of Art. 87(1) EC [now art.107(1) TFEU] are therefore fully applicable to the factual and legal situation of the present case as it presented itself to the Commission when it adopted the contested decision" (at para.158).

The Courts must therefore examine if all four criteria are in fact met, even if the Commission decision actually predates *Altmark*. Furthermore, in assessing whether the Commission has properly analysed and calculated the existence of state aid to one of a number of commercial activities carried out by an enterprise entrusted with an SGEI, the Court requires a full analysis of the compensation provided for the performance of the SGEIs in question in accordance with the

---

[70] See also C–206/06 *Essent* [2008] E.C.R. I–5497 paras 81–85.

Altmark principles, and it will not allow the Commission to "assume" that aid for SGEIs can be a source of subsidy for commercial activities without more.

Commission practice following Altmark

8–030   In a series of decisions adopted concerning aid to the broadcasting service, the Commission held that, as the compensation measure paid to the Italian, Spanish and Portuguese broadcasters did not meet the four *Altmark* criteria, the measure had to be examined under arts 107(1) and 106(2). In these cases the Commission held that the compensation did not exceed the actual net additional costs of providing the services in question, and therefore could be justified under art.106(2). In other words, in this respect art.106(2) is used as a substantive test. This approach was confirmed in a later decision concerning state aid to the French TV stations, France 2 and France 3.[71] These cases are examined in full in Ch.18.

In general the Commission takes a rather less strict approach to the first criteria, that of "entrustment" which has its roots in the case law on art.106(2), but a much stricter approach to the second and fourth criteria.[72] In particular, if the fourth criterion is not met, i.e. there is no open tender procedure, or the Member State has failed to demonstrate that the costs involved are those of a typical, well run undertaking, the Commission assumes that as the *Altmark* test cannot be met, then the measure is to be classified as a state aid and then goes on to assess its compatibility under either art.107 or art.106(2) or both. (See also the postal cases discussed at paras 8–063 et seq below.)

In its decision on aid to Deutsche Post AG, the Commission had made a finding that state aid was present after taking note of the transfers from DB-Telekom and of the net additional costs generated in the open-to-competition sector of door-to-door parcel delivery services, together with the losses recorded by Deutsche Post AG.[73] Thus, the Commission did not attempt to establish the difference between the sums which Deutsche Post AG received and the costs it actually bore in providing a service of general economic interest in order to identify the net additional costs which would thus constitute an advantage. The General Court[74] and the ECJ[75] did not consider this approach to be acceptable (see further below at paras 8–063 et seq).

8–031   Similarly in Case T–388/03 *Deutsche Post and DHL International v Commission*[76] (Belgium), the General Court held that the Commission must respect the fourth *Altmark* condition before concluding that a transaction between the State and a public undertaking does not involve aid within the meaning of art.107(1):

[71] IP/03/1686.
[72] See, for example, *Atlas Broadband and Cumbria Broadband*, discussed in Ch.3.
[73] Commission Decision 2002/753 EC of June 19, 2002, [2002] O.J. L247, p.27.
[74] T–266/02 *Deutsche Post v Commission* [2008] E.C.R. II–1233.
[75] Case C–399/08 P Unreported September 2, 2010.
[76] [2009] E.C.R. II–199.

"It is apparent both from the contested decision and from the exchange of letters and the minutes of the meetings between the Commission and the Belgian authorities that the Commission never verified that the services of general interest which La Poste provided were at a cost which would have been borne by a typical undertaking which was well-run, in accordance with the principle laid down by *Altmark*. The Commission merely relied on the negative balance of all the items of overcompensation and undercompensation in respect of the additional cost of the SGEIs for its finding that the measures examined did not constitute State aid within the meaning of Art. 107(1) EC.

Thus, on the basis of those factors, it must be concluded that the Commission did not carry out an examination of the cost of the services of general interest provided by La Poste compared with the costs which a typical undertaking would have borne, an appraisal which might have enabled it to find that the measures examined did not constitute State aid" (at para.116).

On appeal, the AG advised the ECJ to annul the GC's ruling, but the ECJ has now held that the General Court had rightly ruled that the Commission should have initiated a formal investigation.[77]

In Case T–157/01 *Danish Buses*,[78] and despite the Commission's repeated **8–032** emphasis in its original decision on "exceptional circumstances", the Court took a strict approach to the key question of whether or not the bus company which had allegedly benefited from aid, Combus, was entrusted with PSOs or not. Combus was a sub-contractor who had already been compensated for performing the non-commercial tasks inherent in the bilateral contracts it had concluded with the public transport management undertakings (a part of the Danish local government bodies). There was nothing more exceptional at stake than that the company, Combus, had chosen to bid low to ensure it was awarded the contracts and had suffered substantial losses. The only "special" feature which the Court was prepared to ascribe to Combus arose in connection with its "structural disadvantages" as compared to its private-sector competitors—the costs it had to bear as a result of having been required to employ more costly and privileged ex-public sector officials. This status had nothing to do with its obligations to provide public services, but was part of the history of the restructuring of the state undertaking in preparation for privatisation. The Court correctly confined the *FFSA* case law to situations where the services in question were not provided under conditions of competition. In *FFSA* La Poste had to equip itself with infrastructure in order to perform the services entrusted to it, but could not cover its costs from the tariffs it was allowed to charge, hence the state compensation was justified. The situation that Combus found itself in was completely different. It did not exclusively perform the tasks entrusted to it with the result that it had particular costs to bear: all transport undertakings active in the Danish bus market were in the same situation. Even if Combus still had to perform the contracts to

---

[77] C–148/09P September 22, 2011.
[78] [2004] E.C.R. II–917.

which it was bound, its obligations arose out of the inherent bilateral relationship in the contract itself. Further, Combus had already benefited from the remuneration provided for in its public service contracts. Nor was there any real risk that bus transport services would be disturbed if Combus collapsed financially—other bus operators could move in to take over its responsibilities.

The General Court therefore dismissed the Commission's attempts to rely on *Altmark* as (i) Combus was not actually entrusted with the performance of a PSO obligation, and (ii) the parameters of the compensation had not been established in advance in an objective and transparent manner, and annulled the Commission decision.

8–033   In Joined Cases C–34/01 to C–38/01 *Enirisorse*,[79] the Court considered whether the measure in question distorted competition. The Court first recalled as a broad general principle that any measure which creates a selective benefit that the recipient undertaking would not have obtained in normal market conditions is to be regarded as aid, unless the measure in question was to be regarded as compensation for services provided in order to discharge public service obligations. The Court then examined whether each of the four conditions specified in the *Altmark* case had been met. It appeared that the "Aziende" had not as such been entrusted with public service duties "and still less that such duties had been clearly defined" (para.34).[80] The parameters on the basis of which the compensation was to be calculated were not established in advance. Indeed, in this case neither the services which were to be considered as public services were specified, nor were any details of their costs established. As the Commission and Enirisorse pointed out, the proceeds of the port charges could not reflect the costs actually incurred by the "Aziende" since the amount in question would be linked to the volume of goods transported by all users and shipped to the ports in question. In that way the amount paid varies with the level of activity in the ports concerned (para.38). Hence, as the *Altmark* tests with regard to allocation of duties and calculation of compensation had not been met, the measure was classified as state aid.

As the referring Court had not raised any additional questions with respect to the possible application of art.106(2), it was not necessary for the ECJ to consider any further whether that article nevertheless might have been relied upon as an exception to art.107(1). In any event, as the *Altmark* tests are derived from the existing jurisprudence on art.106(2) it would appear to be difficult to consider that the relevant conditions for an eventual exemption could have been met.[81]

8–034   The *BUPA* case concerned an appeal against the Commission decision finding that the Irish Risk Equalisation Scheme (the RES scheme) for private and public

---

[79] Joined Cases C–34/01 to C–38/01 *Enirisorse* [2003] E.C.R. I–14243.

[80] Referring to earlier case law on the operation of commercial ports, the Court recalled that such activities do not automatically involve the performance of public service duties—Case C–242/95 *GT-Link* [1997] E.C.R. I–449 at para.52.

[81] See also in this respect the detailed discussion of art.106(2) in the context of whether the Italian legislation also constituted an infringement of art.106(1) and art.102 and the potential application of art.106(2) TFEU to this particular issue at paras 92 et seq. of the Opinion of Ms Stix-Hackl in *Enirisorse*, November 7, 2002.

health insurers did not qualify as a state aid within the meaning of art.107(1).[82] The Commission concluded that the compensation provided by the RES nonetheless did not constitute state aid within the meaning of art.107(1), since according to the case law of the Court of Justice[83] it was intended as compensation for the obligations of services in the general economic interest (SGEI obligations) imposed on all insurers active on the Irish PMI market, namely obligations designed to ensure that all persons living in Ireland would receive a minimum level of PMI services at an affordable price and on similar quality conditions. The Commission observed (at recitals 40 and 41 to the contested decision) that this objective would be achieved by establishing solidarity between policy-holders. In particular, the obligation to apply the same premium to all policy-holders for the same type of product irrespective of their health status, age or sex; premiums would therefore be fixed at a higher rate than young persons would have to pay for PMI services priced on the basis of risk assessment and premiums paid by old or sick persons would be much more affordable than if they were fixed by reference to the risk covered. Thus, community rating constituted the very basis of inter-generational solidarity and provided all insured persons with the certainty that the advent of a chronic illness or serious injury would not render the cost of cover unaffordable.

BUPA appealed against this decision to the General Court, which in turn seemed to be prepared to relax somewhat the strict criteria developed in *Altmark*. As regards the *Altmark* criteria, it is noteworthy that the General Court in relation to the first criterion (the existence of a public service obligation) did not demand that the service concerned was available to the entire population of the Member State concerned: instead the obligation to deal with all comers at standard conditions (open enrolment) was considered sufficient to find the existence of a universal service.

As regards competence to determine the nature and scope of an SGEI mission **8–035** within the meaning of the Treaty, and also the degree of control that the Community institutions must exercise in that context, it follows from para.22 of the Communication on SGEIs and from the caselaw of the Court of First Instance that Member States have a wide discretion to define what they regard as SGEIs and that the definition of such services by a Member State can be questioned by the Commission only in the event of manifest error.[84]

The second criterion requires clearly defined parameters for compensation and was not contested. The necessity and proportionality of the compensation were more difficult to establish in the absence of a direct link between the universal service and the need for compensation. Here the General Court accepted that the arrangement was "consistent with the purpose and the spirit of the third Altmark condition in so far as the compensation is calculated on the basis of elements

---

[82] By Decision C (2003) 1322 final of May 13, 2003.
[83] Case C–53/00 *Ferring* [2001] E.C.R. I–9067, para.27.
[84] Case T–17/02 *Olsen v Commission* [2005] E.C.R. II–2031, para.216 and referring to Case T–106/95 *FFSA and Others v Commission* [1997] E.C.R. II–229, para.99.

which are specific, clearly identifiable and capable of being controlled".[85] Likewise, with respect to the fourth *Altmark* condition, the General Court formulated an alternative version because it would not be possible to determine in advance which insurer had a right to compensation and therefore to compare its costs with those of an efficient competitor. Because compensation was based on the average costs in the market (and not on those of the individual competitor) an incentive toward efficiency would be retained. The Court held that the Commission is required to satisfy itself that the compensation does not entail the possibility of offsetting any costs that might result from inefficiency on the part of the insurers (para.249). In the more "classic" cases the SGEI provider is entrusted with the task of providing a given service so that the state is entitled to cover the net costs of the provision of the service. In order to satisfy the proportionality test, which must be applied in order to justify the application of art.106(2) the amount of compensation should not exceed the net costs of the public service mission, taking into account other direct and indirect revenues earned or derived from the public service mission.

8–036   Subsequent case law has generally confirmed the Commission's relatively strict approach to assessing whether the *Altmark* criteria are met, and has primarily turned upon the compatibility assessment under art.106(2) as opposed to the notification requirements. In the subsequent Joined Cases T–309/04 T–329/04 and T–336/04 *TV2/Danmark*, the General Court confirmed the right of the Member State to adopt a broad and qualitative definition of an SGEI.[86] The possibility open to Member States to define broadcasting SGEIs broadly, so as to cover the broadcasting of full-spectrum programming, cannot be called into question by the fact that the public service broadcaster also engages in commercial activities, in particular the sale of advertising space (at para.107).[87] As a result of this case law, and with the exception of the *BUPA* case, there are relatively few examples of decisions and court rulings in which the *Altmark* criteria have been held to have been fulfilled,[88] and the Commission has therefore classified the measure as state aid (subject to the remaining conditions of art.107(1) being met), and gone on to consider whether the state aid can qualify for one of the derogations provided for in art.107(3) or, alternatively, whether the aid can be justified under art.106(2) as a substantive test.

At the same time the Courts have been strict in their insistence that the Commission should adhere to the principle of providing adequate reasons for its decisions on classifying a measure as aid on the basis of the *Altmark* criteria. At para.238 of its ruling in *TV2/Danmark*, the Court held that:

---

[85] *Olsen v Commission*, para.237. This meant applying almost the exact same test as under the second *Altmark* criterion.

[86] [2008] E.C.R. II–2935.

[87] See also Case T–442/03 *SIC v Commission* [2008] E.C.R. II–1161 and Case T–345/05 *TFI* [2009] E.C.R. II–00471.

[88] See its Decision on CADA, discussed in Ch.18 and its Decisions in certain broadband cases, discussed in Ch.3.

" . . . a statement of reasons, which ultimately does no more than reproduce verbatim the wording of the fourth *Altmark* condition, could be sufficient only if it were common ground that the Kingdom of Denmark had put nothing in place that could, in practical terms, ensure compliance with the fourth *Altmark* condition, or if the Commission had established that the analysis carried out by the Kingdom of Denmark was manifestly inadequate or inappropriate for the purposes of ensuring compliance with that condition. However, such circumstances have by no means been established in the present case. On the contrary, given the procedure put in place by the Kingdom of Denmark for determining the amount of licence fee income payable to TV2 between 1995 and 2002, which . . . is not disputed—involved, inter alia, economic analyses drawn up with the help of TV2's competitors, it is conceivable that a serious examination of all the conditions governing the setting of the amount of licence fee income payable to TV2 during the period under investigation—the examination which the Commission should have carried out—would have led to the conclusion that the Kingdom of Denmark ensured that, in essence, the fourth *Altmark* condition was complied with, even before the Court of Justice defined those conditions."

In *SIC*,[89] the Commission's decision was annulled as the Court ruled that the Commission had based its analysis on accounting information that was not sufficiently reliable as it was neither systematically accompanied by an external independent verification or by any other verification system (at para.255). In *Deutsche Post AG v Commission*, the General Court annulled the Commission's decision that state aid had been granted to Deutsche Post since the latter had shown that the amounts of compensation received were insufficient to cover the costs incurred in discharging its public service obligations.[90] The lower Court's ruling was subsequently upheld by the ECJ (see below at paras 8–063 et seq).[91]

The Decision on the application of Article 106(2) to public service compensation

If the compensation paid to a public service provider does not meet the **8–037** *Altmark* criteria, it constitutes state aid and should be notified to the Commission in accordance with art.108(3) and Council Regulation 659/99. The Commission should then assess the compatibility of the aid in question under arts 107(3) and 106(2). One consequence of the *Altmark* ruling has been to cast some doubt on the legality of public service compensation granted prior to July 2003 but which does not meet the four cumulative criteria set out by the Court. Unless that compensation could be classified as "existing aid" within the meaning of

---

[89] See Case T–442/03 *SIC* [2008] E.C.R. II–01161.
[90] Case T–266/02 [2008] E.C.R. II–01233.
[91] Case C–399/08P, Unreported, September 2, 2010.

art.108(1) and art.1 of Regulation 659/99, or unless the 10-year limitation period laid down in art.14 of the Regulation had expired, a risk could arise that such compensation could be declared illegal by national courts for want of observation of the notification and standstill obligations.

To a limited extent these concerns, as well as related concerns on the application of the *Altmark* criteria, are addressed by the Commission's Decision 2005/842/EC on the application of art.86(2) to state aid in the form of public compensation, hereafter the "Decision".[92] This Decision is based on art.106(3) TFEU (ex. art.86(3) EC) which empowers the Commission to adopt both directives and decisions. These measures, often referred to as the "*Altmark* Package", were adopted by the Commission in November 2005.[93] The Decision provides an exemption from notification as measures fulfilling the conditions of the Decision can be deemed to be compatible aid.[94] The SGEI Framework, adopted at the same time, is intended to provide guidelines for the assessment of aid measures which do not meet the *Altmark* criteria and are therefore subject to notification requirements. The SGEI Framework expired in November 2011 and in the course of 2010 the Commission commenced a consultation on the review of the package as part of its wider policy objectives in the area of public services.

In November 2010 the Commission undertook to adopt, by 2011, a Communication and a series of measures on services of general interest, underlining that the European Union and its Member States must ensure that public services are easier to operate at the appropriate level, adhere to clear financing rules and are of the highest quality and are actually accessible to all.[95] In March 2011 the Commission announced that it is considering basing the upcoming reform on two key principles: clarification of a number of key concepts relevant for the application of the state aid rules to SGEIs, and in particular the distinction between economic and non-economic activities; and a diversified and proportionate approach. The Commission aims to make the degree of scrutiny dependent on the nature and scope of the services provided, and to identify those sectors which pose a serious risk to distortion of competition.[96] Subsequently, in December 2011 the Commission published a new Decision revising its earlier Decision of 2005, a new Framework to replace that of 2005 and a further explanatory Communication. These new measures will be discussed at para.8–050.

The 2005 Decision thresholds

8–038   In accordance with art.2(a) of the Decision, if the public service compensation is granted to undertakings in connection with services of general economic

---

[92] [2005] O.J. L312/67.

[93] Commission Decision 842/2005 [2005] O.J. L312/67; Community Framework for state aid in the form of public service compensation, [2005] O.J. C297/4.

[94] See Joined Cases T–231/06 and T–37/06 *The Netherlands and the NOS v Commission*, December 16, 2010, at paras 152 et seq.

[95] Communication from the Commission, "Towards a Single Market Act" Com (2010) 606 final/2 of November 11, 2010, see proposal nr. 25.

[96] Communication from the Commission, "Reform of the EU State Aid Rules on SGEIs", Com (2011) 146 final, March 23, 2011.

interest, and the undertakings have an average annual turnover before tax, all activities included, of less than €100 million[97] during the two financial years preceding that in which the service of general economic interest was assigned and the annual compensation for the service in question is less than €30 million, then no prior notification is required. This threshold of €30 million is determined by taking an annual average representing the value of compensation granted during the contract period or over a period of five years. It should be noted that these thresholds are applicable to undertakings, and not to the units or divisions of those undertakings charged with the performance of SGEIs.

In addition, the Decision exempts public service compensation irrespective of its value, where it is granted to hospitals and social housing undertakings carrying out activities qualified as services of general interest by the Member State concerned (see recital 16 of the Decision).[98] No thresholds are applicable in these two cases (art.2(1)(b)). Compensation for air or maritime transport links to islands may be exempt from notification if average annual traffic in the two financial years prior to the assignment of the service of general economic interest is less than 300,000 passengers (art.2(1)(c)). With regard to airports and ports the thresholds are 1 million passengers for airports and 300,000 for ports (art.2(1)(d)). For credit institutions the threshold is €800 million. The Decision does not apply to land transport.

Article 4 requires that, in order to qualify for exemption from notification, the responsibility for the operation of an SGEI must be entrusted to the undertaking concerned by way of one or more official acts, the form of which may be determined by each Member State. These acts shall specify, in particular:

(a) the nature and duration of the public service obligations;

(b) the undertaking and territory concerned;

(c) the nature of any exclusive or special rights assigned to the undertaking;

(d) the parameters for calculating, controlling and reviewing compensation;

(e) the arrangements for avoiding and repaying any overcompensation.

The fourth *Altmark* criterion is not, however, included in art.4 of the Decision, nor is its application required in the Framework.

Article 5 of the Decision further provides that the amount of compensation **8–039** shall not exceed what is necessary to cover the costs incurred in discharging the SGEI, taking into account the relevant receipts and a reasonable profit on own capital necessary for discharging these obligations. The compensation must

---

[97] For credit institutions the threshold is €800 million in terms of balance sheet total.
[98] In two recent cases the Commission held that the Decision did not apply—E2/2005 *Dutch social housing* [2010] O.J. C31/53 and NN54/2009—*Belgian Hospitals* [2010] O.J. C74/53 and in both cases assessed the compatibility of the measures under the Framework and art.106(2) generally.

actually be used for the provision of the service. The amount of compensation must include all the advantages granted by the state or through state resources in any form whatsoever. Article 5 also offers some further guidance on how the relevant costs and revenue must be calculated.

With regard to costs, art.5(2) provides that all the costs incurred in the operation of the service of general interest should be taken into account. However, given that the recipient undertaking may be involved in various activities, not all of which are classified as SGEIs, then it may only be costs actually associated with the service in question. The compensation to the service may cover all the variable costs, a proportionate contribution to fixed costs common to both SGEIs and other activities, and a return on the capital necessary for fulfilling the public service in line with the normal market return for the sector (art.5(2)(b)). The costs linked with investments "notably concerning infrastructure" may be taken into account when necessary for the functioning of the SGEI. The Decision gives little guidance here on what type of infrastructure falls under art.5(2)(d) and what types of costs are likely to be covered and whether those are different from the fixed costs referred to at art.5(2)(c). Indeed, following on from the Court's ruling in *Altmark*, the Decision is primarily addressed to operating as opposed to investment aid. In its recent proposal for reform of the EU State Aid Rules on SGEIs, the Commission has indicated that it is considering to what extent greater account of both efficiency and quality should be taken when deciding on the approval of state measures in relation to an SGEI. This could include measures aimed at greater transparency as well as measures aimed at taking into account efficiency over the life of an entrustment with the provision of an SGEI.[99]

8–040　　On the revenue side, according to art.5(3) of the Decision, this must include at least the entire revenue earned from the public service, as well as any other revenue generated from a public service operated under special or exclusive rights that generates profit in excess of a reasonable profit on that service, and/or any other benefits derived from the state, irrespective of whether they can be classified as aid for the purposes of art.107. It is for the individual Member State to decide if the profits accruing from other activities outside the scope of the SGEI are to be assigned in whole or in part to the financing of the SGEI in question. Thus, for example, a Member State could specify that revenue earned from activities under competition can be used to finance so-called "reserved" activities. A reasonable profit means a rate of return on own capital that takes account of the risk, or absence of risk incurred by the undertaking by virtue of the intervention by the Member State, particularly if the latter grants special or exclusive rights. This rate should not exceed the average rate for undertakings in the sector concerned in recent years. The Commission has calculated the reasonable profit margin in one case by comparing the rate with that of undertakings

---

[99] See para.4.2.2.2. of Com (2011) 146 final, March 23, 2011.

with comparable activities.[100] Article 5(3) also states that the relevant receipts must include "other advantages granted by the State". These receipts have to be accounted for irrespective of their classification for the purposes of art.107(1), and this means that all revenue derived from special and exclusive rights must be taken into account in assessing whether additional compensation is necessary.

Benchmarking with undertakings in other Member States is permissible providing that the particular characteristics of each sector are taken into account. Member States may also introduce incentive criteria, in particular relating to the quality of service provided and gains in productive efficiency (art.5(4)). In other words, a company which "beats" the initial costs of providing the service as estimated in the initial budgets which were used to establish the parameters of the costs of the service should not be penalised for being efficient.

A company carrying out both SGEIs and activities under competition must **8–041** maintain internal accounts that show the costs and receipts associated with the PSO separately, as well as the parameters for allocating costs and revenues. In respect of activities under competition, the costs shall cover all variable costs, an appropriate contribution to common fixed costs and an adequate return on capital (art.5(5)). The wording of art.5(4) and (5) is based in part on the ECJ's approach in the *Chronopost* case (see below at para.8–055).

If compensation as calculated on the basis of these costs and revenues exceeds the thresholds set out in art.2, or if it relates to non-exempt activities then it must be notified in accordance with art.108 TFEU. The Decision, however, makes it clear that in the Commission's view, overcompensation, subject to the 10 per cent margin (20 per cent for social housing) cannot be justified on the basis of art.106(2). This view seems to be endorsed by the Court's ruling in *Ferring* in which it held that overcompensation could not be justified on the basis of art.106(2). The Commission appears to take the view that small amounts of public service compensation can be justified because the interests of the Union within the meaning of the last part of art.106(2) are not adversely affected. The eventual assessment of measures falling outside the scope of the Decision (and which must therefore be notified as aid measures) on the basis of art.107(2) or (3) or, alternatively, art.106(2), is discussed below.

The exemption from notification of compensation below the stated thresholds is, however, without prejudice to the application of stricter provisions relating to SGEIs contained in sectoral legislation. Member States are further required to carry out regular checks to prevent overcompensation, and must ensure repayment of any overcompensation paid, subject to a margin of 10 per cent (20 per cent for the social housing sector on the condition that the undertaking only operates services of general economic interest) of the amount of annual compensation. Such overcompensation may be carried over and deducted from the amount due in respect of the following period. The Decision also imposes similar but stricter requirements to those contained in the Transparency Directive in

---

[100] Commission Decision 24/2005 [2007] O.J. L95/25 on state aid implemented by France for the Laboratoire Nationale d'Essais.

terms of regular reporting requirements (every three years) and a duty to keep information (for up to 10 years) necessary to determine the compatibility of the compensation with the Decision.

The framework for state aid in the form of public service compensation

8–042   Where public service compensation does not fall within the scope of the decision, given the amounts and sectors involved, and furthermore does not meet the four cumulative *Altmark* criteria, it must be notified to the Commission and the latter can assess it in accordance with the conditions set out in the Community Framework for state aid in the form of public service compensation, also adopted in 2005. This framework is applicable to all sectors with the exception of the transport sector and the public service broadcasting sector. The Framework is intended to give guidance on the substantive assessment which will be applied to the aid measure in question, and is based on the principles of necessity and proportionality. If the state aid is necessary for the operation of the relevant public service, and does not affect the development of trade to an extent contrary to the Community interest, it may be declared compatible with the Treaty under art.106(2) TFEU.

The substantive conditions set out in the 2005 Framework are broadly similar to those developed in the Decision discussed above, and are based on the case law of the Courts. Hence, the recipient undertaking must have been entrusted with the SGEI and the relevant official act should specify the precise nature and duration of the SGEI, the undertaking and the territory concerned, the parameters for calculating, controlling and reviewing the compensation and the arrangements for avoiding and repaying any overcompensation. If any one of these conditions is not met, the measure cannot be held to be compatible with the guidelines. Once again, the fourth *Altmark* criterion is not replicated in the 2005 Framework.

8–043   The amount of compensation to be paid should cover the costs, taking into account the relevant receipts and a reasonable profit for discharging the obligations in question. The methodology for calculating relevant costs and revenues in order to determine the level of compensation to be paid is essentially similar to that set out in the art.106(3) Decision. It should be noted, however, that the Framework also deals with situations where an undertaking is entrusted with the operation of several SGEIs, either because the authority assigning the SGEI is different or because the nature of the SGEI is different. In both cases the undertaking's internal accounts must make it possible to ensure that there is no overcompensation at the level of each SGEI. In its Decision N 531/2005 on the creation and operation of La Poste's postal banking subsidiary, the Commission applied the principles set out in the framework in order to establish that the costs attributed to La Poste's SGEIs had been properly allocated.[101] The General Court

[101] COM (2005) 5412 final.

in Case T–289/03 *BUPA* recognised that Member States had a wide discretion in defining the methodology for the determination of the additional costs incurred in discharging a SGEI, subject to a control of manifest error by the Commission (at paras 214 and 220).

Overcompensation which is not necessary for the operation of the SGEI must therefore be repaid, albeit subject to a 10 per cent margin which can be carried over to the following year; it may be used to finance another SGEI operated by the same undertaking, providing that this transfer is clearly accounted for. However, the 2005 Framework recognises that there may be exceptional cases where overcompensation may be necessary for the operation of the SGEI and this should be explained in the notification and, in any event, should not exceed a period of four years. The amount of overcompensation cannot remain available to an undertaking on the ground that it would rank as aid compatible with the Treaty. If a Member State wants to grant environmental aid, for example, it must notify that aid in accordance with art.108(3) unless it falls within the scope of one of the block exemption regulations.

Appropriate measures for existing aid

The Commission further proposes in the framework that Member States **8–044** should bring their existing schemes regarding public service compensation into line with this framework within 18 months of its publication in the *Official Journal*. Member States will confirm to the Commission that they agree to the proposal of appropriate measure but, in the absence of any reply, the Commission will take it that the relevant Member State does not agree. Aid schemes put into place prior to the *Altmark* ruling would only, however, qualify as existing aid if they fall within one of the definitions of existing aid listed in art.1 of the Procedural Regulation. The Commission Framework does not purport to have retroactive effect. If an existing aid scheme no longer complies with art.108 and appropriate measures are accepted, the Member State will usually be required to modify the existing aid scheme within a stipulated time frame.

Assessment

The 2005 Decision and Framework indicate that the Commission will continue **8–045** to take a strict approach to the application of the four *Altmark* criteria. Particularly if the procedural requirements provided for in the second and fourth *Altmark* criteria are not met as will often be the case, then, unless the compensation is below the €30 million threshold or it represents compensation to an exempted sector, the Commission effectively bases its substantive assessment on the first three criteria, i.e. the undertaking must be entrusted with a specific public service undertaking, the parameters of the compensation must be established in advance and the compensation must not exceed that which is necessary to cover all or part of the costs incurred in discharging the SGEI, taking into account all relevant receipts and a reasonable profit. In addition, the Commission has made it clear that Member States must specify how overcompensation must be avoided and repaid. If the undertaking is not entrusted with an SGEI in accordance with an official act, then art.106(2) cannot be invoked at all: the compatibility of the aid must be considered under art.107.[102]

Similarly, it would seem that if the payment of compensation for the loss incurred by an undertaking in performing public services is made without the parameters of such compensation having been established beforehand, this constitutes a financial measure which falls within the concept of state aid and cannot be exempted from notification on the basis of art.106(2). This would seem to be the case even if the actual compensation received does not exceed what is necessary to cover the actual costs incurred in discharging the SGEI, after deducting relevant receipts and allowing for a reasonable profit level. Indeed, this is the approach taken by the Commission in its decision in relation to the Cumbria Broadband scheme. It may be noted that in this case the service provider who would operate the envisaged broadband infrastructure in Northern England would be selected through a negotiated procedure in accordance with the public procurement rules. Hence, the parameters on which the compensation was calculated were not established beforehand. Furthermore, given that the infrastructure would be owned by that service provider after the termination of the agreement with the Development Agency which initiated the project, the compensation appeared to exceed what was necessary to cover the costs of the service provider for discharging its SGEI obligations. The Commission, however, considered that the aid was compatible under art.107(3)(c).[103]

8–046   It may also be noted that the Framework is in turn a further refinement of the approach to assessment set out in the Commission's Non-Paper of November 12, 2002 on Services of General Interest and state aid, issued prior to the *Altmark* case. At para.100 of the Non-Paper the Commission suggested that where excess compensation benefited a public undertaking, the proceeds of such excess compensation may also be used by the Member State in its capacity as shareholder to inject finance into that undertaking provided that the private investor criterion is met and provided that the transfers were carried out in accordance with the normal procedures of private undertakings, i.e. in the form of a capital increase or a grant of a loan. This possibility was not recognised in the framework, however, and again seemed to confirm the Commission's increasingly strict approach to the issue of public service compensation.

The competitive award of SGEI obligations may be of little relevance if the service in question is only provided by or indeed is legally reserved to a single operator. Furthermore, even if "benchmarking" can be used as an alternative, this approach may have limited use where the entity entrusted with the SGEI has a legal duty to provide a bundle of distinct public services.[104] How is the requisite level of compensation to be assessed if it is efficient in providing some of these

---

[102] Joined Cases C–34/01 to C–38/01 *Enirisorse SpA* [2003] E.C.R. I–14243.
[103] State Aid N 282/2003—United Kingdom.
[104] See for example the Commission's Decision on the Slovenian stranded cost case where the 4th *Altmark* criterion had not been fulfilled, State Aid no. SI 7/2003 of November 7, 2005.

services (e.g. cultural television programmes or basic letter post) as opposed to others (political television programmes or basic small parcel delivery services)? Establishing the actual parameters of the compensation *ex ante* may be difficult if not impossible for complex projects which are designed to run for a considerable period of time. Furthermore, the level of revenue to be earned by an SGEI may also prove difficult to establish in advance, especially if the financial compensation is provided not by way of grant but by way of tax exemption. Given these limitations, more extensive ex post control is often required in order to fulfil the requirements of the Decision and the Framework.

It should be recalled that the Decision and the Framework are primarily concerned with assessing compensation to the provider of the SGEI services and not the recipient of those services. In Case C–126/01 *GEMO*,[105] the companies charged with the obligation to collect infected animal carcasses from farms and slaughter houses were compensated for their additional costs by the proceeds of a levy imposed on the sale of meat products. The beneficiaries of these collection services, the farmers and the slaughter houses were considered to have received state aid as they should have paid for these same services in the normal course of business.

Overcompensation and inefficiencies. Following the adoption of the 2005 Decision and the Framework, and in the light of the fourth *Altmark* criterion, a debate has arisen in the literature as to the extent of the Commission's powers to ensure that SGEI providers are not over-compensated for their tasks. Overcompensation can be a possible source of cross-subsidisation from SGEI to commercial activities, as discussed in section 5. There is however a separate concern that the costs incurred should not produce inefficiencies, otherwise the fourth *Altmark* condition would be deprived of any meaning. Furthermore in the broadcasting sector, as discussed in Ch.18 there is a further concern that there is no overcompensation for competitive media services.[106] The Decision and the Framework seem to allow the state to compensate the actual costs of providing the SGEI in question, irrespective of its level of efficiency. The Commission indicated in its review of these measures that it would consult on the desirability of exercising stricter controls.[107] **8–047**

At the same time it should also be stressed that, just as the Commission may have little power to control inefficiencies in compensating actual costs on the "input" side, it also has no power to determine or rule on the quality of the "outputs" at issue as this would amount to undue interference in the competences of the Member States as recognised by art.14 of the Treaty.[108] That said, the Commission may impose conditions in a positive decision. In the decision on the German TV Case E 3/2005, the Commission did not conclude that too much

---

[105] [2003] E.C.R. I–13769.
[106] See in particular Commission Decision E/2/2008 Austria, October 28, 2008.
[107] See IP/11/347, Commission moves towards reform of state aid rules on Services of General Economic Interest, March 23, 2011.
[108] See Case T–442/03 *SIC III* [2008] E.C.R. II, para.212.

sports on public TV was contrary to the definition of an SGEI, but imposed the condition that sports rights which were unused by the public service broadcasters should be offered to third parties for sub-licensing.[109]

8–048 **Reserves.** The Commission has been prepared to accept that a certain level of overcompensation in the form of reserves may be justifiable in order to deal with fluctuations in SGEI costs and revenues. The 2005 Decision and the Framework make provision for this. Similarly the 2009 Broadcasting Communication allows for the formation of reserves under certain well defined conditions.[110] In Case T–309/04 *TV2*,[111] the Commission had considered that the reserves accumulated by the operator had to be considered as incompatible aid because they had not been constituted for a specific purpose and regularised at fixed intervals. The Court did not accept this analysis and it found that the Commission had failed to properly examine the documents submitted by the Member State in order to justify the reserves. Nor did the Court consider that it should replace the Commission in making this assessment. In the Austrian PSB case the Commission appears to have allowed considerable flexibility with regard to the issue of reserves and has stated that further compensation may be permissible if the performance of the public broadcasting service is threatened due to a drop in the broadcasters' equity capital.[112]

8–049 **The relationship between Article 106(2) and *Altmark*.** Although a strict application of art.106(2) would suggest that no overcompensation is allowed, the Commission can exercise its discretion to consider whether such reserves may be appropriate.

The General Court in the *TF1* case explicitly confirmed the Commission's approach that a measure of compensation which does not satisfy the four *Altmark* criteria can still be justified on the basis of art.106(2).[113] In *Chaine Francasise d'Information Internationale*, the Commission found the benchmarks on which the compensation was calculated were not sufficiently reliable and exhaustive.[114]

In the German PSB Decision C25/2004 *DVB-T Berlin-Brandenburg*[115] it was argued that the fourth condition should have to be interpreted in the light of the *Chronopost* judgement. The Commission could not rely on the costs of commercial broadcasters since they did not bear the same obligations as public service

---

[109] See Case E3/2005, April 24, 2007, discussed by L. Repa and N. Tosics, in *Competition Policy Newsletter*, No.1, 2009, pp.97–99.

[110] [2009] O.J. C257/52.

[111] [2008] E.C.R. II–2935.

[112] Case E2/2008 Financing of the Austrian public service broadcaster ORF [2010] O.J. C309/53.

[113] Case T–354/05 *Télévision Française 1 SA (TF1) v Commission* E.C.R. II–00471. Now under appeal, C–451/10P, September 15, 2010.

[114] Case N 54/2005 France, *Chaîne Française d'Information Internationale*, available at *http://ec.europa.eu/eu_law/state_aids/comp-2005/n054–05.pdf*, C (2005) 1479 Fin, IP/05/689.

[115] C25/2004 [2006] O.J. L200/49.

broadcasters, but should necessarily refer to the costs of the PSB operators. The Commission did not accept this argument. It affirmed that it was for Germany to prove compliance with the fourth condition and not for the Commission to prove that the PSB operators were not efficient. Only the Member State can prove how it has calculated the amount of compensation and whether it has carried out such a comparison with an efficient company.[116]

The Reform of the 2005 "Monti Package". The Commission has now published a draft Regulation which would allow de minimis aid to be granted to undertakings performing SGEIs under certain conditions.[117] In addition, the Commission proposes to amend Decision 2005. Its new Decision of 2011 extends the scope of activities exempted from notification, irrespective of their turnover or size, to include healthcare and social security services, including child care, and access to the labour market and social inclusion of vulnerable groups. For all other sectors, the threshold of aid for which no notification is required is reduced from €30 to €15 million. The period of entrustment is limited to 10 years unless significant investment is required. In addition the new Decision contains rules for calculating net compensation, in particular by providing more detailed guidance on the calculation of reasonable profit levels.

8–50

The new Framework of 2011 will replace the Framework of 2005 and like its predecessor it will provide the framework for assessing the compatibility of compensation for the provision of SGEIs in all cases which do not fall under either the draft de minimis Regulation or the new exemption Decision (or under specific sectoral frameworks or secondary legislation). It is designed to make control of the compensation more predictable for public authorities and providers.

The 2011 Framework pursues the Commission's policy goal to promote the design and delivery of more efficient services, and it focuses on large-scale commercial operations with a clear impact on the internal market, such as transport, telecoms, and energy supply, and will impose stricter scrutiny. This will be done through a variety of measures, including the requirement that the Transparency Directive and the public procurement rules are respected, a requirement for incentives to make efficiency gains over the life of the contract to be included, and a stronger analysis of the effects on competition in the internal market. The Framework includes detailed rules on the calculation of the compensation of both net costs and reasonable profits, and advances a preferred methodology based on net avoided costs for calculating the former. Stricter monitoring and reporting requirements are also introduced.

---

[116] Compare, however, E8/2005; *RTVE* April 20, 2005 annual contributions granted to RTVE were approved only upon the adoption of measures to increase efficiency, forcing RTVE to limit the costs to what was necessary for the fulfilment of its tasks. The Commission concluded that various cost items of the PSB could be benchmarked against the costs incurred by other private competitors, while taking into account the specific PSOs.

[117] The initial draft proposals were published on September 16, 2011. Available at *http://ec.europa.eu/competition/consultations/2011_sgei/index_en.html*.

5. CROSS-SUBSIDISATION

8–051   The 2005 Decision and Framework discussed in section 4 above are intended to avoid overcompensation for public service obligations, and as such are intended to eliminate a potential source of cross-subsidisation from payments or revenue received to perform real tasks to undercut prices or reduce profit levels for activities provided by the same undertakings under conditions of competition. Incumbent providers of special or exclusive rights, whether private or public, may enjoy monopoly revenues which can be deployed in certain cases to lower the costs of providing goods or services under competition. These types of situations give rise to the vexed issue of cross-subsidisation out of reserved markets into competitive markets. Cross-subsidies can be distinguished from other forms of subsidies by the idea that they are financed from internally generated funds, as opposed to being funded from some other, external source, whether these be state provided funds or through some other form of direct or indirect financial benefit. The main problem is to distinguish cases of unlawful aid from lawful intended transfers between profit and loss-making activities, which are part of normal life in the private sector.

The primary origin of cross-subsidies is common costs and non-competitive market structures. There is scope for argument as to how such common costs should be allocated to different activities. Individual sectoral directives (rail, electricity, ground-handling at airports, gas, postal services) require the unbundling of accounts to obtain transparent data on cost allocation and internal cost accounting. However, the relevant directives do not purport to introduce any uniform method of cost accounting and are restricted to individual sectors. The Transparency Directive, as discussed above (para.8–015), only remedies the former problem.

8–052   As will be explained in more detail below, two different forms of cross-subsidisation can be distinguished: (i) where costs are not properly allocated to different services (i.e. some services have to bear a disproportionately high share of costs); and (ii) where costs are properly allocated and lead to profits on some services (reserved activities) and losses on others, which losses are then covered by the profits. Both forms have the same final effects: an activity is performed without covering its real costs by the prices asked for it.

Insofar as the firm is publicly owned or controlled within the meaning of the Transparency Directive, cross-subsidies could be caught by the Treaty state aid rules. If, however, the firm is privately owned but enjoys revenue earned through the exercise of special or exclusive rights the picture is less clear. On the one hand, the private firm supplies the goods or services in question to consumers; the source of its revenue is therefore from non-state sources. On the other hand, if the revenue collected is subject to certain rules and regulations, it may still be deemed to be subject to state control.[118] However, if the private firm is entrusted with the performance of an SGEI and receives both compensation from the state

---

[118] See for example, Case N 37/2003 *BBC Digital Curriculum* [2003] O.J. C271/46.

and revenue for the services it provides, then any overcompensation, whatever its source, would appear to be classified as state aid. In this respect para.20 of the 2005 Framework for public service compensation, discussed above, provides that: "since overcompensation is not necessary for the service of general economic interest, it constitutes incompatible state aid that must be repaid to the State". It is submitted that the same reasoning should be applied to overcompensation in cases where special or exclusive rights have been granted to supply particular products or services. In any event, these latter are usually linked to a service of general economic interest or are granted as a quid pro quo for performance.

Internal cross-subsidisation as state aid

The majority of the Commission statements and decisions, as well as the **8–053** recent case law of the European Courts on the application of the state aid rules to cross-subsidisation, deal with transfers between groups of companies operating under the structure of a public holding company, or between a parent company and its subsidiary, as opposed to purely internal transfers within a single firm. To date the ECJ has only dealt with transfers within groups of companies. In Case C–303/88 *Italy v Commission (ENI-Lanerossi)* and in Case C–305/89 *Italy v Commission (Alfa Romeo)*, both of which involved capital transfers by a public holding company to a subsidiary, the Court held that a private investor may inject capital to ensure the survival of one of its companies and be motivated not only by profit but also for other reasons such as the concern to maintain the trade image of the group or to reorganise its activities. Capital injections by public investors in the absence of any profit, however, even in the long term, must be considered as aid within art.107(1). The same principles were applied concerning investments and losses in *Head Tyrolia Mares*, an Austrian manufacturer of sports articles that were financed by its shareholder Austria Tabakwerke from the proceeds of the tobacco monopoly without any net benefit to the group as a whole.[119]

It should be stressed in this context that the state aid rules do not only apply to purely financial transactions, but also to the provision of services or the supply of goods or personnel or assets on preferential terms between a group of public undertakings which result in a financial benefit for the recipient enterprise. In Case T–95/94 *Sytravel v Commission*, an organisation representing French private courier companies had challenged the Commission's failure to deal with its complaints relating to alleged cross-subsidisation by Sofipost, a subsidiary of the French PTT and Securipost. For example, the Post Office had seconded over 200 staff to Securipost to carry out money transport and other activities previously carried out by the Post Office. Further financial advances and premises were made available on preferential terms. The General Court annulled the Commission's decision not to open a full inquiry in its judgment of September 28,

---

[119] Commission Decision of July 10, 1996, [1996] O.J. L25/26.

1995.[120] The Court ruled that the measures might contain state aid and that the Commission had failed to examine the objections that had been brought forward by the complainants and its decision was furthermore not adequately reasoned. On appeal the ECJ, though criticising the General Court for confusing the requirement to state reasons and the substantive legality of the Commission decision, confirmed that the reasoning of the decision was inadequate.[121]

8–054   An earlier, similar case brought by private courier companies against the French PTT claiming that the latter had conferred various privileges on a member of its group, SFMI—including, for example, personnel and facilities on favourable conditions—was initially rejected by the Commission on the grounds that transactions were conducted at arm's length. The ECJ ruled, however, in Case C–39/94 *SFEI v La Poste*,[122] that the provision of logistical and commercial assistance by a public undertaking to its subsidiaries, which are governed by private law and carry on an activity open to free competition, is capable of constituting state aid if the remuneration received in return is less than that which would have been demanded under normal market conditions. The concept of aid within the meaning of art.107 encompasses not only positive benefits, such as subsidies, but also interventions which, in various forms, mitigate the charges that are normally included in the budget of an undertaking and which, without therefore being subsidies in the strict sense of the word, are of the same character and have the same effect.

While these judgments clarified the application of the state aid rules to transfers of personnel and services between undertakings in the same group, the question of whether such transfers between two different activities or markets— served by one and the same firm—amounts to a state aid appeared to go unanswered. The Commission Framework of 2005 and 2011 on public service compensation indicates that the state aid rules can be applied to internal transfers within one and the same undertaking. Similarly, the Commission's Notice "on the application of the competition rules to the postal sector and on the assessment of certain state measures relating to postal services" also deals with internal transfers between different activities or markets by one and the same firm.[123]

Cost allocation

8–055   As already mentioned, a major difficulty that arises in respect of cross-subsidisation is to determine whether costs have been properly allocated to different activities or markets. If the *Altmark* ruling can be considered to offer guidance on the extent of the revenue a company may legally earn on its reserved

---

[120] [1995] E.C.R. II–2651. See also the Commission notice whereby the Commission announced the initiation of the procedure provided for in art.88 because the measures could indeed include aid [1996] O.J. C311/12.

[121] Judgment of April 2, 1998, Case C–369/95P, [1998] E.C.R. I–1719.

[122] Case C–39/94 (judgment of July 11, 1996) [1996] E.C.R. I–3547. By Decision of October 1, 1997 the Commission decided that the measures do not constitute state aid [1998] O.J. L164/37.

[123] [1998] O.J. C39/2.

activities, or the activities that it is entrusted to perform as SGEIs, then the Court's ruling in *Chronopost* may offer some assistance in considering the other side of the equation—that is, what costs should be allocated where? In Joined Cases C–83/01P, C–93/01P and C–94/01P *Chronopost*, which concerned the question of whether La Poste had provided its subsidiary Chronopost with logistical and commercial assistance at below-market rates, the Commission considered that it was required to examine whether the terms of the transactions between parent and subsidiary were comparable to those of an equivalent transaction between a private parent company, which may well be a monopoly, and its subsidiary. According to the Commission there was no financial advantage if the internal prices at which products and services were provided between companies belonging to the same group were "full-cost prices" (total costs plus a mark-up to remunerate equity capital investment). The General Court annulled this decision on the basis that the Commission should have taken La Poste's legal monopoly over the reserved market expressly into account and should have checked whether the payment received in return by La Poste was comparable to that demanded by a private group of undertakings not operating in a reserved sector, pursuing a structural policy, and guided by long-term prospects (see para.75 of the ruling in Case T–613/97).[124]

Chronopost and the French government in turn appealed against this ruling to the ECJ contending that the General Court had wrongly interpreted the concept of "normal market conditions" used in the *SFEI* judgment. The Court of Justice held that account had to be taken of the costs which La Poste had incurred in creating and maintaining its public service network given that the provision of logistical and commercial services were inextricably linked to that network. The creation and maintenance of this network were thus by definition not in line with a purely commercial approach. Such a network would never have been created by a private undertaking. The ECJ[125] concluded that in the absence of any possibility of comparing the situation of La Poste with that of a private group of undertakings not operating in a reserved sector, in normal market conditions, which are necessarily hypothetical, must be assessed by reference to the objective and verifiable elements which are available. State aid in the form of cross-subsidisation by a parent for logistical and commercial support to its subsidiaries can be excluded if it is established that the price charged properly covers all the additional variable costs incurred in providing that assistance, an appropriate contribution to the fixed costs arising from the use of the network and an adequate return on the capital investment, and further there should be nothing to suggest that these elements have been underestimated or fixed in an arbitrary fashion. Hence, as there was no market operator—even a hypothetical one—to which La Poste could be compared, the "normal market conditions" must be assessed on the basis of objective and verifiable elements. On that basis:

---

[124] [2000] E.C.R. II–4055.
[125] Joined Cases C–83/01P and C–94/01P *Chronopost SA v Commission* [2003] E.C.R. I–6993.

"there is no question of state aid to Chronopost if first, it is established that the price charged properly covers all additional, variable costs incurred in providing the logistical and commercial assistance, an appropriate contribution to the fixed costs arising from use of the postal network and an adequate return on the capital investment in so far as it is used for Chronopost's competitive activity and if, second, there is nothing to suggest that those elements have been underestimated or fixed in an arbitrary fashion" (at para.40).[126], [127], [128]

8–056   Hence, if the revenue that a company earns on its reserved activities exceeds a reasonable level of compensation as calculated on the basis of the *Altmark* criteria, and as further elaborated upon at paras 17 and 18 of the 2005 Commission Framework on public service compensation, and at the same time the company can use this revenue to cover its costs in the competitive sector—or has failed to allocate its costs properly to the reserved sector in accordance with the *Chronopost* criteria,[129] as recalled at para.16 of the Framework—then this could give rise to overcompensation for the services of general interest/reserved services and hence to state aid within the meaning of art.107(1).

The Commission applied the *Chronopost* criteria in its decision concerning the hiving off of La Poste's postal banking activities to a separate subsidiary, Banque Postale.[130] The French government notified its plans to hive off Banque Postale in May 2005 and two months later a formal complaint was lodged claiming that Banque Postale would receive aid on account of the special rights it would enjoy in distributing particular services (the "livret A") and on account of the arrangements made in respect of pension funds and social charges for employees transferred to the new bank, as well as a result of the guarantees it would enjoy from the French state. Finally, it was alleged that La Poste's financial accounts were inadequate. In addition, as subsidiary matters, the complainant raised questions with regard to the bank's inadequate capitalisation, a tax exemption and the advantages it would enjoy as a result of the transfer of certain funds from La Poste. A second complaint was lodged on December 7, 2005, also alleging elements of aid with respect to the exclusive rights for the distribution of livret A services, the fact that La Poste would bear all the costs of setting up the new bank and the advantages which would accrue to the bank given that the barriers to entry for competitors would be substantially raised as a result of the French plans. The Commission limited its examination of the file and chose not to deal with personnel issues or the exclusive rights with respect to livret A. The open-ended guarantee conferred on La Poste was also to be dealt with in a separate procedure. In effect the Commission examined the measures as notified under

---

[126] [2003] E.C.R. I–6993.
[127] [2006] E.C.R. II–1513.
[128] [2008] E.C.R. I–4777.
[129] On the assumption that there are no other applicable benchmarks which could be deemed acceptable.
[130] N 531/2005—France, COM(2005) 5412 final, December 21, 2005.

two headings—the measures linked to the setting up of the Bank and the short-term (one year) state guarantee for regulated savings products to be transferred to it, and the measures linked to the functioning of the new bank. These included employee arrangements as well as various service arrangements ("conventions de prestations de services") regulating the provision of services by La Poste to the bank.

The French authorities claimed that the transaction did not give rise to any new **8–057** injections of capital but simply involved a transfer of accumulated capital derived from the services to be transferred and hence there was no question of aid. The Commission agreed and, relying on point 3.1 of its 1984 Communication on Public Participation, held that no aid could arise as long as there was no injection of fresh capital. As to the issue of whether the amount transferred was sufficient to cover the bank's subsequent activities, the Commission held that this was not for it to decide. The short-term guarantee did not amount to aid either as the conditions on which it had been granted complied with the criteria as set out in the Commission's Communication on Guarantees of 2000 (see further Ch.9) as well as the requirements of the Basel Accords of July 2005.

The Commission's assessment of the measures relating to the subsequent operations of the newly created subsidiary proved more complex, given the absence of a suitable private investor benchmark. The network to be used by the bank was inseparable from that created by La Poste under non-market conditions. In this respect the Commission acknowledged that in its *Chronopost* ruling, the Court had developed a two-fold test in order to establish that a subsidiary of a state entity would not enjoy any special advantages. On the one hand the Commission must verify that La Poste's calculation of its total costs incurred in its economic activities which are to serve as the basis on which to calculate the remuneration to be paid by the subsidiary to the parent have not been under-estimated. It must also ensure that the costs of services provided by the parent to the subsidiary have been properly, objectively and coherently allocated in the parent company's accounts, as required under the Transparency Directive (see section 2). On the other hand, the Commission must ensure that the remuneration paid by the subsidiary covers the costs incurred by the parent in providing the services in question. The techniques deployed in this complex assessment are described in detail in the Commission's decision. It may be noted that the Commission also took into account that the ongoing financial relations between La Poste and the bank would be subject to external supervision by the Court des Comptes in respect of the service conventions, and by the French Postal Regulator in respect of the cost allocation mechanisms for the provision of universal service functions by La Poste. The Commission was able to conclude that the arrangements would not lead to the conferral of an advantage on the bank and therefore that no aid had been granted.

Subsequent decisions in the postal sector confirm that the Commission does **8–058** not apply any single cost allocation methodology but will recognise different methods. In the case of the UK Post Office POL, the Commission analysed a fully distributed cost methodology aiming at identifying the net cost of the public service entrusted to POL, which consisted in the allocation of costs and revenues per post office.[131]

Alternatively, the Commission may examine whether the undertaking in question has been charging prices related to properly allocated costs in the competitive sector, and if it can establish that those costs have not been properly allocated, it may then seek to determine whether this is because costs have been wrongly attributed to reserved activities or that the costs have been reduced by financial transfers from other parts of the group to which the undertaking belongs—transfers which should have been used for the reserved sector. This is the approach that the Commission took in several recent cases, including the *Deutsche Post* case of 2002, which was annulled on appeal by the General Court. The ECJ upheld the lower court's ruling—see below at 8–063.

8–059   **The Danish TV Case.** In its decision of 2004 on *TV2/Denmark* the Commission analysed both the issue of overcompensation for the services it had recognised to fall under TV2's public service remit and the issue of whether there was evidence that TV2 had depressed the prices charged for its commercial activities in the advertising market as two separate prongs of the proportionality test. In other words, if TV2 had been found to have been charging below market prices for its commercial advertising activities, this would have increased its losses and would have resulted in a higher level of overcompensation. In this respect the Commission recalled Pt 58 of the Broadcasting Communication (discussed in detail in Ch.18) and stated that whenever a public service broadcaster undercuts prices in the non-public service activities below what is necessary to recover the standalone costs than an efficient commercial operator in a similar situation would normally have to recover, such practice would indicate the presence of overcompensation of public service obligations. Following a detailed examination of the available data the Commission concluded that there was no clear evidence that TV2 did not attempt to maximise its advertising revenue and that this would have led to an increased need for state funding. In any event, the Commission was of the opinion that any loss of TV2's income from advertising does not exceed the level of overcompensation already established. The Danish government was required to recover €84.3 million (DKK 628.2 million) overcompensation.[132] The Commission did not accept that TV2 needed a capital surplus as a reserve against fluctuations in advertising income as this was not necessary to the performance of its public service remit. In its letter to the German government concerning aid to the German public sector broadcasters,[133] the Commission appears to follow a similar approach and has applied a proportionality test to ensure that state financing for services within the public remit does not result in overcompensation which can in turn be used to cover losses in non-public service

[131] [2006] O.J. C141.
[132] [2006] O.J. L85/13.
[133] E3/2005 of March 3, 2005.

activities such as online activities (online games) and source of cross-subsidisation for the acquisition of sporting rights. If this proves to be the case, then additional losses incurred by these activities can be considered to result in further overcompensation which has to be recovered.

The Commission's decision in *TV2/Denmark* was annulled in Joined Cases T–309/04 and T–317/04, T–329/04, T–336/04 on grounds of insufficient reasoning.[134] The Court concluded that:

"The fact that TV2 did not have to draw on its reserves in 1999 does not support the inference that those reserves had to be regarded as disproportionate to the funding needs of providing the public service. It is in the very nature of a reserve which is built up to deal with an uncertainty that it does not necessarily have to be used. Consequently, for the Commission to conclude, after the event, that the non-use of a reserve is proof that it was unjustified is at odds with its own acknowledgement that such a reserve may be built up and kept for the purposes of guaranteeing the provision of the public service."

In many cases involving allegations of overcompensation and/or cross-sub-   **8–060**
sidisation it is necessary for the Commission to base its eventual decision on clear and unambiguous reasoning. Failure to do so can lead to the annulment of its decision as in the *TV2* case, discussed above, and the *Credit Mutuel* case of January 18, 2005.[135] The Credit Mutuel had been entrusted since 1975 with the exclusive distribution of the Livret bleu, a tax-free savings product for the general public.[136] Originally 50 per cent (and later 65 per cent) of the funds collected via the Livret bleu were allocated to finance public authorities, for which the bank received an intermediary margin. Eventually, all the funds were allocated to various public bodies managing public housing. This product allowed Credit Mutuel to attract and retain a clientele to which it could sell other banking services and products. The economic advantages for the bank were therefore the assets (initially up to 50 per cent of the investments) which it could use freely, the brokerage commission and the intermediary margin paid by the public authorities, and the indirect benefit through attracting and retaining clients.

Several competitors filed a complaint with the Commission in 1991, leading to the opening of a formal procedure in 1998[137] and a final decision declaring the amount of cumulated non-capitalised profit of FRF 1074 million to be overcompensation, which could not be justified on the basis of art.106(2). Credit Mutuel challenged the decision on the grounds, inter alia, that the state measure conferring an advantage on it had not been clearly identified. Although it appeared to have proceeded on the assumption that the granting of the exclusive

---

[134] [2008] E.C.R. II–2935.
[135] T–93/02 *Confederation nationale du Credit Mutuel v Commission* [2005] E.C.R. II–143.
[136] The exclusive distribution rights were subject to separate infringement procedures and eventually in 2009, the system was reformed so that after that date the Livret bleu ceased to exist.
[137] [1998] O.J. C146/6.

rights could be the source of an advantage, the Commission, however, finally determined that the granting of the exclusive rights of distribution was not aid, as this did not result in the transfer of state resources. The tax concession benefited the savers, not the bank, while brokerage commission was identified as state aid and the remaining two advantages, the intermediary margin and the indirect advantages linked to the loss-leader effect, were not clearly analysed in the decision of 2002.[138] The General Court held that, as the Commission had not clearly considered which of the various measures had amounted to aid, and had failed to provide adequate reasons for its findings, the decision had to be annulled.

8–061   Subsequently, in 2006, the Commission extended the scope of the investigation originally opened in 1998 and clarified the terms of its investigation, focussing only on the commission paid to Credit Mutuel for collecting and transferring funds to the public authorities, and adopted a second decision in May 2011, in which it held that Credit Mutuel was not overcompensated for performing what were deemed to be SGEIs. Notably, the Commission deemed it justified for Credit Mutuel to generate a limited profit given the low risk involved and, furthermore, the Commission assessed the level of overcompensation, if any, over a period of time, as opposed to comparing the aid received each year with annual net costs (C88/197 IP 11/634, May 24, 2011).

8–062   **The Dutch TV Case.** In Joined Cases T–231/06 and T–237/06 *Netherlands v Commission*,[139] the General Court ruled that the Commission in order to establish if "ad hoc" overcompensation could be qualified as aid, was not required to establish that the Dutch public broadcaster, NOS, had used the compensation for its public service activities to finance its other, commercial activities and as a result, had actually distorted competition. It was sufficient for the Commission to establish that NOS had been relieved of costs it would normally have borne in the ordinary course of business. The Court went on to consider in the context of art.106(2), and in considerable detail, whether the Commission had properly reasoned its finding that NOS had indeed received a level of aid which was neither necessary or proportionate to its public service tasks (paras 211 et seq.) and furthermore that there were no mechanisms to ensure that eventual overcompensation (taking into account a margin of 10 per cent) could be clawed back (paras 264–268).

8–063   **Deutsche Post.** The Commission condemned as illegal aid, and required recovery of, €572 million from DPAG in its decision of June 19, 2002.[140] This decision, which was based on a "net additional costs approach",[141] was subsequently annulled by the General Court in Case T–266/02, and in 2010 the ECJ

---

[138] [2003] O.J. L88/39.

[139] [2010] Unreported December 16, 2010, now on appeal, C–104/11P [2011] O.J. C28/2.

[140] Commission Decision 2001/354/EC of March 20, 2001 relating to a proceeding under art.82 of the EC Treaty (Case COMP/35.141—Deutsche Post AG), O.J. L125/44.

[141] Bartosch, A., "The 'Net Additional Costs' of Discharging Public Service Obligations: The Commission's Deutsche Post Decision of 19 June 2002", European State Aid Law Quarterly, Vol.1, 2002, No.2, p.189.

upheld the General Court's ruling. In the contested decision the Commission had ruled that the amount of the transfers made—pursuant to art.37(3) of the PostVerfG—by DB Telekom (Deutsche Telekom AG) then a state-controlled entity, in favour of DB Postdienst (Deutsche Post AG) as compensation for the provision of services of general economic interest (SGEI) was higher than that necessary to compensate for the net additional costs attributed to the provision of those services.

The Commission inferred that the amount corresponding to such overcompensation had been used to make good losses in the competitive door-to-door parcel delivery sector which was now open to competition. According to the contested decision, those losses amounted to a total of DEM 1 118.7 million and were the result of DPAG's policy of selling below cost, during the period from 1994 to 1999. The Commission therefore concluded that such overcompensation constituted state aid incompatible with the EC Treaty and ordered Germany to take the necessary steps to recover the aid from Deutsche Post.

In support of its appeal before the ECJ, the Commission raised two grounds: the first alleging breach of arts 107(1) and 106(2) TFEU, in that the General Court held that the method used to conclude that there was state aid was unlawful and the second alleging breach of art.263(1), on the ground that the General Court exceeded its powers by substituting its own method for calculating the additional costs associated with the provision of SGEI for that employed by the Commission.

With regard to undertakings responsible for an SGEI, the Court stressed that **8–064** where a state measure must be regarded as compensation for the services provided by the recipient undertakings in order to discharge public service obligations, so that those undertakings did not enjoy a real financial advantage and the measure thus did not have the effect of putting them in a more favourable competitive position than the undertakings competing with them, that measure was not caught by art.107(1). The ECJ ruled that it follows that, where the Commission must examine the validity of a system of financing an SGEI, it is particularly required to check whether that condition is satisfied:

"45 In that respect ... it must be pointed out that the General Court first of all held, in paragraph 85 of that judgment, that the Commission had failed to check whether the total amount of transfer payments made by DB Telekom exceeded the total amount of the net additional costs in respect of SGEI borne by DPAG.

46 Next, it is clear, in particular from paragraphs 91 and 94 of the judgment under appeal, that the General Court considered that the Commission was not entitled to assume that those transfers constituted an advantage for the purposes of Art. 87(1) EC (now 107(1) TFEU) precisely because it had failed to examine, first, whether the total amount of the transfer payments made by DB Telekom exceeded the total amount of the undisputed additional costs incurred by DPAG and, second, whether DPAG had recorded other net additional costs associated with the provision of an SGEI for which it had the right to claim

compensation out of the total amount of those payments under the conditions stated in the judgment in Altmark . . . "

The Court of Justice found that the General Court could not be accused of having relied upon deficiencies in the method used by the Commission in the contested decision. Indeed, it followed from the foregoing that those deficiencies were noted by the General Court in its examination of the lawfulness of that method in the light of art.107(1).

8–065   It should be noted that the *DPAG* decision, adopted in 2002, pre-dated the *Altmark* ruling by almost a year, but nevertheless the Court has repeatedly stressed that this important ruling is not limited *ratione temporaris* and has continued to apply the *Altmark* test in its review of all Commission decisions, irrespective of the date of their adoption.

An open question following the annulment of the Commission's decision in the *DPAG* case is whether an SGEI provider could offer an SGEI below the tariff imposed by the State in order to prevent market entry into potentially profitable market segments in the expectation that its losses will also be covered by the state. The *DP* case concerned allegations of subsidies from the SGEI into a competitive market segment, but as sectoral liberalisation progresses and the provision of universal services is no longer reserved to one provider, this could become increasingly relevant. In other words, is the SGEI provider able to artificially increase its net SGEI costs for the future by failing to generate sufficient revenue over a particular period? In this respect the Court's ruling in Case T–157/01 *Combus (Danish Buses)* is of interest in that the Court did not accept that the losses accumulated by Combus were directly and exclusively related to the provision of the SGEIs in question but were the result of the submission of tenders with excessively low prices with as part of a strategy to win the tender. Hence compensation could not be justified as an SGEI.[142] The Commission has subsequently opened a further formal investigation into Deutsche Post, in May 2011, and Deutsche Post has appealed the opening decision.[143]

8–066   **Poste Italiane.** Poste Italiane is the universal postal service provider in Italy. Over the period 2000–2005 Poste Italiane received €2.4 billion compensation for discharging the universal postal service obligations entrusted to it.

As the compensation granted by the Italian authorities was not in line with the principles established by the *Altmark* case, notably in that Poste Italiane was not chosen pursuant to a public procurement procedure, this state intervention was ruled to constitute state aid. However, Poste Italiane's net costs for delivering its universal postal service obligations had exceeded the financial support granted by Italy over the period 2000–2005. Thus, the support did not overcompensate the net public service cost of providing the universal postal service ([2006] O.J.

---

[142] T–157/01 [2004] E.C.R. II–917. [2001] C282/33.
[143] Case T–388/11 (2011/C 282/66).

C291/06). In its subsequent decision NN 24/08—Italy, the Commission reached a similar conclusion for the period 2006–2008 (Com (2008) 1606 fin, April 30, 2008).[144]

As to the funds collected from Poste Italiane's customers' current accounts and deposited with the Italian Treasury, the interest paid for these deposits by the Treasury to Poste Italiane constituted state resources. The Commission was concerned that the methodology, based on the Italian budgetary law for 2006, used to define the interest rate paid to Poste Italiane from 2005 onwards resulted in the interest rates being higher than what would have been obtained from a private borrower and opened a formal investigation into the potential state aid to Poste Italiane constituted by more favourable interest rates on the money deposited with the Treasury. The investigation was terminated in November 2006 following a finding that all four *Altmark* criteria were complied with.[145]

6. Privatisation

Privatisation programmes usually involve the sale of all or a majority of the **8–067** shares in public undertakings to private investors. Since it is often necessary to balance the financial situation of the undertakings concerned before they can be sold and since establishing a fair price for the shares may be difficult, many such transactions should be assessed from the perspective of art.107. In order to determine whether a capital injection or the writing off of a debt is necessary to attract buyers constitutes aid, the Commission verifies the reasonableness of the state's behaviour as a market economy investor. The Commission takes the view that a market economy investor intending to maximise the profitability of his investment would have made the capital contribution only if this action will later make him better off in economic terms.

The Court has also confirmed that a tax reduction system essentially designed to strengthen the competitive position in the internal market of certain operators is not a "project of common interest", even if it facilitates the privatisation of public companies. Privatisation cannot in itself be regarded as a project of common interest.[146]

In accordance with the judgment of the Court in Case 234/84,[147] the Commission must determine "whether in similar circumstances a private shareholder, having regard to the foreseeability of obtaining a return and leaving aside all social, regional policy and sectoral considerations, would have subscribed the capital". The state must separate itself as the owner/shareholder in a company

---

[144] See also the Commission decisions on the Greek universal service provider in the post sector, N183/06 [2006] O.J. C141, C21/06 Poland [2005] O.J. C274 and N642/05 Sweden [2007] O.J. C2941.
[145] See D. Boeshertz and P. Icardi, "Poste Italiane: a market fee can fulfil the Altmark criteria", Competition Policy Newsletter 2007 No.1, Spring 2007, pp.121–123.
[146] Case C–184/04 *Unicredito Italiano* [2005] E.C.R. I–11137.
[147] *Belgium v Commission* [1986] E.C.R. 2263.

and as a body responsible for the payment of unemployment/social security benefits, because as owner of the shares of a joint stock company the state is not obliged to cover the balance between the proceeds from a liquidation and the liabilities linked thereto.[148] The Commission further examines whether the price to be paid for the acquisition of the shares, and other possible circumstances, such as the exclusion of financial responsibility for certain existing loss-making activities, warrant the conclusion that the buyer acquires a holding on unduly generous terms.

8–068 The Commission first formulated guidelines for determining when notification of state measures relating to privatisation is considered necessary in 1994 in its 23rd Competition Report at paras 402–404. It may be argued that the Commission at least applies a presumption of aid if the procedures set out in these guidelines have not been followed and it is up to the Member State involved to rebut that presumption. The Courts have not yet, however, endorsed this approach, and in its ruling in Case T–274/01 *Valmont*, the General Court annulled a Commission decision relating to the sale of public land without a prior tender procedure. The General Court found that the Commission must exhaust its own investigative powers before relying on incomplete answers from the defendants.[149] The MEIT test was also considered in Case T–159/99 *Thermenhotel Stoiser Franz*. The General Court held that the Commission, or, as the case may be, the competitors of the undertaking doing business with the state, must prove that the concrete contract terms "exceed the bounds of a normal commercial transaction between two private operators".[150]

The Commission takes the position that there would normally be no state aid concerns if privatisation is carried out by stock exchange flotation or open unconditional tender with the business being sold to the highest bidder. In all other cases, the Commission requires notification of the proposed sale to enable it to check whether aid is being granted. The same rule of thumb applies to the sale of shares on a stock exchange, the sale price is assumed to be the market price and this applies even if debt is written off or reduced prior to the sale, as long as the proceeds exceed the reduction in debt.

8–069 If a sale is not made by way of flotation or open unconditional tender, the Commission has fashioned a set of procedures, largely modelled on the public procurement rules, in order to eliminate a risk of aid. These requirements are as follows:

---

[148] See, e.g. the Decisions of March 25, 1992 concerning privatisation aid by Spain to three manufacturers of textile and shoes: [1992] O.J. L172/76; [1992] O.J. L176/57; [1992] O.J. L175/54. In Appeal (Joined Cases C278–280/92), the Court upheld the Commission Decisions of September 14, 1994, [1994] E.C.R. I–4103. For further developments see Competition Policy Newsletter, 1996, Vol.2, No.3, p.50.

[149] Judgment of September 16, 2004 [2004] E.C.R. II–316, 5, at para.60. See also A. Bartosch, "The Relationship between public procurement and state aid surveillance—the toughest standard applies?" [2002] 39 C.M.L.Rev. 551 at p.575.

[150] [2004] E.C.R. II–0001.

(i) a competitive tender must be held that is open to all comers, transparent, non-discriminatory and non-conditional on the performance of other acts[151];

(ii) the company must be sold to the highest bidder;

(iii) bidders must be given enough time and information to carry out a proper valuation of the assets as the basis for these bids.[152]

It is also acknowledged that independent expert evaluations may be an acceptable alternative for proving the absence of state aid. This evaluation should probably be carried out prior to sale.[153] The Commission has accepted this alternative in several cases.[154] If these procedures are not followed, the Commission is of the view that notification is required.[155] Furthermore, it has stipulated that notification is required if: (a) the sale has followed after negotiation with a single prospective purchaser or a number of selected bidders; (b) if the privatisation involves a sensitive sector, such as synthetic fibres, textiles or the motor industry. All sales should be notified beforehand. The guidelines offer no further guidance on the substantive assessment of a possible aid element—they are limited to the procedures to be followed. Reference to other guidelines, and in particular the guidelines on rescue and restructuring aid, will be necessary in order to establish the eventual compatibility of the proposed aid. These latter guidelines are discussed in full in Ch.24. Furthermore, reliance can be placed on the market economy investor principle, as discussed in detail in Ch.3.

The market price principle will, however, probably fail where only a negative price exceeding the liquidation costs can be achieved on the market. In *Groditizer Stahlwerke* the ECJ stated that in order to establish whether the privatisation for a negative selling price involves elements of state aid, it is necessary to assess whether in similar circumstances a private investor of a dimension comparable to that of the bodies managing the public sector could have been prevailed upon to make capital contributions of the same size in connection with the sale of the undertaking or would instead have chosen to wind it up.[156] In the earlier *Hytasa* cases the Advocate General had taken a similar approach, endorsing a finding of aid where a substantial amount of public finance had been provided in order to make the sale possible in the first place. Hence sale to the highest bidder in such circumstances is not conclusive.[157] Furthermore, in arriving at the market price a distinction should be drawn between the obligations which a state must assume

8–070

---

[151] See for an application of these conditions, Commission Decision on aid granted by Germany to Groditzer Stahlwerke GmbH, [1999] O.J. L292/27.

[152] Similar procedures are applied to the sale of public land and buildings—see the Commission Communication of 1997 [1997] O.J. C209/3.

[153] See on this point, the above guidelines on sale of public land at p.II.2.a.

[154] *Koninklijke Schelde Groep* [2003] O.J. L14/78 and *Saarbergwerke* [2002] O.J. L2003/52. See also *Re-privatisation of TAP ground-handling*, IP/04/1476.

[155] See its approach in relation to the privatisation of Olympic Airways [2004] O.J. C192/2.

[156] Case C–334/99 *Germany v Commission* [2003] E.C.R. I–1139.

[157] Joined Cases C–278/92, C–279/92 and C–280/92 *Spain v Commission* [1994] E.C.R. I–4103.

as owner of the share capital of a company and its obligations as a public company. Losses resulting from not repaying former guarantees, for example, cannot be taken into account when calculating the costs of winding up in cases of liquidation as these arise from a measure taken by a public authority which a private investor could not have taken.

In practice very few privatisations, or partial privatisations, are carried out by means of a full flotation, and government entities resort either to bilateral negotiations or controlled auctions, which are managed by an investment bank or financial adviser. In both types of procedures confidentiality is of optimal importance and a full open tender procedure may interfere with these concerns. Other factors such as timing, the desire to reduce transaction costs, and perhaps also in certain sensitive sectors, a desire to prevent the privatised assets falling into the hands of certain competitors, may make the use of full open tender procedures difficult as well as undesirable. Unsurprisingly, the Commission guidelines have come under fire as being both unnecessary and unworkable as well as inconsistent with the market investor principle. Certainly it may well be the case that the rather heavy handed approach to procedures was primarily designed at the time to prevent privatised assets being transferred at bargain basement prices to existing national champions. The emphasis on open procedures allowed bids from companies based in other Member States and ensured that the state would get a better return on its sales. However, not all privatisations are likely to fall into this category and the majority are likely to be pro-competitive. The more economic-based approach to state aid control has not however rendered these guidelines redundant.

8–071   In Case C46/2007 the Commission adopted a final negative decision on the privatisation of the Romanian state company, Automobile Craiova. In May 2007 the Romanian government had published a tender for the privatisation of the company and the Commission opened the formal investigation procedure under art.108(2) in October 2007 after Romania had signed a sales agreement with the only bidder. At the same time the Commission issued a suspension injunction in accordance with Reg.659/99 ordering Romania to suspend the privatisation procedure pending the Commission's decision. The Commission then investigated the tender award criteria and the conditions attached to the privatisation in order to establish if these were liable to reduce the sales price and provide an advantage to the buyer. In particular the Commission examined the award criteria including a scoring grid for Automobile Craiova. It first concluded that the chosen criteria made it almost impossible for a potential investor intending to follow a different industrial strategy for the plant to win the bid simply by offering a higher price but without meeting the so-called production and integration levels for which higher scores in the grid would be awarded. In fact the grid distorted the competitive conditions for the tender procedure and deterred potential investors as a result of which the State lost privatisation revenue. As these conditions were attached to the privatised entity which resulted in extra costs for the buyer, the Commission concluded that the privatised entity, i.e. Automobile Craiova, was the beneficiary. In Case C41/2007 *Tractorul*, April 2008, the

Commission concluded that the sale of a state-owned tractor producer did not amount to state aid following a formal investigation. The obligations were only formal requirements and did not impose onerous obligations on the potential buyer, but only "best endeavour" clauses.

Case 56/06 of April 2008 concerned the privatisation of the Austrian Land **8–072** Burgenland's bank HYPO Bank Burgenland AG through a tender procedure. The second best bidder was successful although its price was significantly lower than the highest bid. The tender contained a number of conditions but these were not considered to restrict the number of bidders or influence the sale price. However, the Commission had concerns as to why the lower bid had been chosen. Austria had claimed that it had acted consistently with the MEIP and had reduced its own exposure particularly in the light of a state guarantee. The Commission held that the MEIP could only extend to factors which would have been taken into account by a market economy seller. This would exclude the risks stemming from a potential liability to pay out a public guarantee that would never have been incurred by a market investor. In this case the Commission found that the selected bidder had received an advantage as it had paid less for the company than its market value.

In its decision C16/2004 of July 2008 concerning aid to Hellenic Shipyards, **8–073** the Commission examined whether or not a refund guarantee by the State to the purchaser of HSY at the time of privatisation of the yard in 2001–2002 contained an aid. The state had, as seller of HSY, committed to refund the purchaser, HDW/Ferrostaal, any state aid which would be reimbursed by HSY following the potential adoption of a recovery order. The Commission was required to consider if this measure amounted to a state aid and if so who would have benefited from it. As the State owned and subsequently sold only 51 per cent of the shares in HSY the Commission concluded that a well-advised investor would not have accepted to take full responsibility for the very large past liabilities of the firms but would have sought a contribution from the remaining shareholders (in this case the HSY employees). Secondly, when assessing the costs to be supported by the state in the event of liquidation, the costs, supported by the public authority, had to be distinguished from those which would burden the State as a private market operator. Only the latter costs of winding up the firm could be taken into account when assessing whether the State had acted as a market economy seller. The sale had in fact only yielded a very limited amount to the State and yet it had exposed itself to considerable liabilities. Nor was the risk of the guarantee being invoked negligible since HDW itself had insisted on being protected against the repayment of any state aid by HSY and had made its closing agreement conditional on the receipt of the refund guarantee. Hence the Commission concluded that a private investor would have preferred to let the firm go bankrupt rather than sell it. Furthermore, the State had already granted considerable aid to facilitate the transaction in 2001. The guarantee had been concluded between the State and HDW/Ferrostaal which would also have been the formal beneficiary of the indemnification payments. The Commission, on the basis of an expert report, held that no buyer would have been prepared to acquire HSY without the guarantee or assume any additional risk related to potential recovery. Further, the financial situation at HSY was so acute that it would, absent the sale, have gone bankrupt, and so HSY was deemed to be the beneficiary. HDW/Ferrostaal, however, had already factored the guarantee in to its bid, as would all other potential bidders who had been made aware during the award procedure that indemnification was available. As Greece failed to recover this and other aid, the Commission has referred Greece to the Court of Justice for failing to comply with this decision. (See also Ch.3 at para.133, on the art.346 TFEU exception, and Ch.16 on shipbuilding.)

Conditions for approval of privatisation aid

8–074   In giving its consent to privatisation aid on the basis of art.107, the Commission in most cases makes it conditional on the setting up of a detailed and realistic restructuring plan which would enable the long-term profitability of the undertakings to be improved whilst at the same time reducing production capacity.

For example, in 1988 the Commission examined a proposed capital injection by the British government in favour of the Rover Group,[158] which took place within the context of the sale of the remaining car and jeep business of the Rover Group to British Aerospace. The Commission found that the aid was linked to a business plan which foresaw "a substantial reduction in car assembly and component capacities in the order of 30%" and that the plan's central medium-term objective was to transform the Group's production into the niche market for up-market models with higher added value and higher profit margins. This could only contribute to the restructuring of the car industry at the Community level. The Commission nevertheless considered that the proposed aid was excessive in relation to the total cost of restructuring. It could not accept that the total indebtedness of the Group be totally annulled. This would place the company in a far more favourable financial position than most of its Community competitors. The Commission authorised the aid up to a certain maximum, whilst subjecting it to a number of conditions, including the undertaking that, once privatised, the Rover Group would not benefit from any particular guarantees on the part of the state.

8–075   To ensure compliance, the Commission requires the submission of periodic reports giving details of the commercial results of the enterprises concerned, pricing policies and all other information useful for judging the evolution of the enterprise to which the aid is destined. As witnessed in the *Renault* case, the Commission does not hesitate to sanction a breach. In 1989, the Commission noted that the French government had violated two conditions to which the Commission had subordinated the decision of compatibility of the aid. The Commission required Renault to reimburse the state some FF 3,500 million and

---

[158] Decision of July 13, 1988 [1989] O.J. L25/92.

to re-enter on to its debit sheet some FF 2,500 million of supplementary debit.[159]

Another example of the Commission's insistence to improve competition between private and public undertakings by preventing the latter from obtaining advantages derived from the regime under which they operate is the *Sabena* case.[160] The restructuring aid was approved on the basis of art.107(3)(c) under the condition that the role of the State would be restricted to that of a normal shareholder. It is worth noting that, in challenging a Commission decision whereby aid is conditionally authorised, only arguments alleging that the conditions of authorisation are manifestly inappropriate may be capable of calling the legality of the decision in question. In the *Air France* case,[161] the General Court recalled the Commission's broad discretion in this context, the Court's review being a marginal one.

8–076

It is interesting to note that in the decision concerning aid to Compagnie Générale Maritime (CGM) in the context of a restructuring plan, the Commission, as a condition for approval, required that until privatisation has been completed CGM may not expand its business activities and may not apply rates for any of its services which do not fully cover the additional operating costs.[162]

In a decision concerning Olympic Airways, the Commission approved, in September 2008, the launch of a selection procedure for a private investor to purchase various assets from Olympic Airways and Olympic Airways Services. After a prolonged series of investigations and recovery actions, the Greek government had decided to privatise its national flag carrier and therefore went to some lengths to ensure that these companies could be sold off without the risk of giving aid to the Olympic companies or to the private investor purchasing the assets. Care also had to be taken to avoid the transfer of existing state liabilities to an eventual purchaser.[163] Having concluded an unsuccessful open tender procedure in late 2009, the Greek government sought Commission approval for a negotiated sale of the assets in question at market price to a private investor. The failure of the original open tender process was largely to be attributed to the impact of the financial crisis, and the willingness and ability of potential investors to acquire these assets. Hence a direct negotiation was approved as this was still deemed to secure a market price and would therefore satisfy the conditions for the application of the "private investor" test. In its decision of March 2010, the Commission considered that the revised privatisation plan does not give rise

8–077

---

[159] Decision of March 29, 1988; 20th Report of Competition Policy, 1990, Pt 259. Note that in 1991 the Commission raised no objection to the subscription by the French state and Volvo to an increase in the capital of Renault because the state's involvement was in conformity with the "market economy investor" principle. See on the automobile sector, Ch.12.

[160] Decision of July 24, 1991.

[161] [1998] E.C.R. 2405.

[162] [1997] O.J. L5/40. Similar conditions were the subject of the judgment of the General Court in Joined Cases T371 and 394/94 *British Airways* (*"Air France"*) [1998] E.C.R. 2405.

[163] Commission Decision of September 17, 2008 on state aid C 61/07 (ex. NN 71/07) *Greece Olympic Airways Services/Olympic Airlines* [2008] O.J. L222/62. Press Release IP/08/1336.

to state aid concerns. First, under state aid rules the Commission and the Member States must work together in good faith to overcome unforeseen or unforeseeable difficulties encountered in executing recovery decisions. Second, the Greek authorities have so far complied with the Commission decision of September 17, 2008. Third, the direct sale facilitates a faster conclusion of the sale of the privatization of Olympic Airlines' and Olympic Airways Services' assets than re-tendering the assets, while ensuring market prices for the transactions. Finally, the direct sale is expected to ensure the continued provision of routes subject to public service obligations, thereby protecting residents of outlying islands from possible disruptions to air services.[164]

8-078   The recent decision of July 22, 2009 on the Gdansk shipyard in Poland raised novel issues of the application of the state aid rules to a privatisation which occurred during the course of the Commission's investigation.[165] This decision (which is also discussed in Ch.16, Shipbuilding), involved restructuring aid which spanned a period before and after Poland joined the European Union, and involved the application of the Rescue and Restructuring Guidelines and suitable compensatory measures in the light of the privatisation of the shipyard in 2007.[166] The Commission required that privatisation followed an open and transparent procedure and that the State would inform potential investors as to the ongoing state aid investigation. Further the Commission required the State, as seller to impose no conditions on the future owner with regard to the future activity of the company including the planned level of employment, the nature of investments planned, and the business profile. Any such conditions could have deterred certain investors or depressed the sale price, thereby depriving the State of revenue. Potential buyers were requested to prepare a restructuring plan for the Commission's assessment and for final authorisation of the pending aid. The Commission made its intentions known to the State that it would impose strict compensatory measures on the eventual buyer and so it was agreed that these measures should be decided upon before the privatisation process so that potential investors could take an informed decision on the prospects for the shipyard. These conditions are in turn binding upon the private investors who have acquired the shipyard.

German reunification

8-079   Following the reunification of East and West Germany, the management of "East German" companies was entrusted to a private holding company, the Treuhandanstalt, which was charged with the task of restructuring the economy of Eastern Germany by privatising state owned undertakings and financing infrastructure investment with the proceeds of privatisation. In order to enable the transition of these undertakings to a market economy in the best conditions,

---

[164] N 83/2009 [2010] O.J. C25/53.
[165] For a discussion of this decision see Competition Policy Newsletter, nr 3, 2009, pp.68–70.
[166] Opening decision, [2005] O.J. C220/7.

a certain number of aid mechanisms were put in place, for example the partial or total write-off of debts contracted before June 30, 1990 with the banking system of East Germany, the grant of loans at preferential interest rates and the grant of tax exemptions. Without such measures the companies would not survive.

In a decision of September 18, 1991 the Commission announced a special procedure that enabled the Commission to rule on the compatibility of aids granted in order to privatise and modernise the East German economy. It attempted to balance the necessity to transform the economy of the old East Germany to a market economy with the principles of free competition. The key elements are as follows:

- The sale of companies to the highest bidder after an open call for tender is not considered by the Commission to include any aid element. The Commission will be notified of all significant sales and will consider their acceptability under an accelerated procedure.

- The writing off of debts due to the economic and political system which prevailed in the former East Germany as well as exemptions from liability for environmental damage caused before July 1, 1990 will not be considered as aid.

- Guarantees and credits provided by the Treuhandanstalt while companies remain under its ownership or control will generally be considered as a form of aid, although the Commission will generally consider these to be compatible in view of the need to develop the economy of the new Länder.

In a letter to the German government, published in 1993, the Commission **8–080** stated that it suspected that financing by the (former) Treuhandanstalt is used to sell products below market prices or to continue unprofitable operations to the detriment of competitors in other Member States.[167] Such practices are not acceptable. In most cases the Commission based the authorisation of aid on art.92(3) (now 107(3)) rather than on art.92(2) (now 107(2). In a 1994 Decision (464/93) the Commission confirmed that the new German Länder is covered by art.92(3)(a) (now art.107(3)(a)), i.e. that it is an area where the standard of living is abnormally low and where there is serious underemployment.[168]

---

[167] [1993] O.J. C35/3.
[168] See also Notice concerning aid to Everts Erfurt [1998] O.J. C97/8 at para.3.2.2.

CHAPTER 9

GUARANTEES*

1. SUMMARY OF THE COMMISSION'S CURRENT POSITION 9–001
2. TYPES OF GUARANTEES COVERED 9–006
3. GENERAL CONSIDERATIONS IN IDENTIFYING WHETHER A STATE GUARANTEE CONSTITUTES AID 9–011
4. SAFE HARBOURS IN THE NOTICE ON GUARANTEES 9–013
5. PRACTICAL DIFFICULTIES IN APPLYING THE SAFE HARBOURS IN THE NOTICE ON GUARANTEES 9–019
6. AID TO THE LENDER 9–021
7. AMOUNT OF THE AID 9–022
8. ASSESSING THE COMPATIBILITY OF AID IN THE FORM OF GUARANTEES 9–025
9. CONSEQUENCES OF NON-NOTIFICATION 9–026
10. THE TEMPORARY FRAMEWORK 9–029

1. SUMMARY OF THE COMMISSION'S CURRENT POSITION

9–001   The Commission's current position is set out in its Notice on the application of arts 87 and 88 of the EC Treaty (now arts 107 and 108 TFEU) to state aid in the form of guarantees (Notice on Guarantees).[1] The Commission takes the view that state guarantees provided at no premium, or less than market rates, will usually constitute an aid to the borrower, whether or not the guarantee is called upon, because the provision of a guarantee results in a drain on the resources of the state and enables the borrower to obtain better financial terms for a loan than those normally available on financial markets. Typically, the borrower will be able to borrow more cheaply and/or by offering less security. The guarantee may enable the borrower to create new business or raise money to pursue new activities, thereby distorting competition with other firms operating on the market who have to pay a commercial borrowing rate. In the case of a failing firm, a guarantee may enable it to remain on the market instead of being forced to exit

---

* Mark Friend

[1] Commission Notice on the application of arts 87 and 88 of the EC Treaty [now arts 107 and 108 TFEU] to state aid in the form of guarantees [2008] O.J. C155/02. The Notice on Guarantees replaces the previous Notice on the application of arts 87 and 88 of the EC Treaty to state aid in the form of guarantees [2000] O.J. C71/14.

or restructure, again distorting competition. If trade between Member States is affected, then the guarantee will normally fall within the scope of art.107(1).[2]

This is subject to the application of the market economy investor principle. The Notice on Guarantees provides that:

9–002

"State aid is not involved where a new funding source is made available on conditions which would be acceptable for a private operator under the normal conditions of a market economy."[3]

The Notice on Guarantees sets out a number of "safe harbours" within which the Commission will consider the market economy investor principle to be satisfied in relation to an individual guarantee or guarantee scheme.[4] These safe harbours are discussed in more detail in sections 4 and 5 below.

The Commission also takes the view that, in certain circumstances, a state guarantee may confer aid not just on the borrower, but also on the lender.[5] Normally this will not be the case, because the lender will be lending on arm's length commercial terms, so will not be receiving any non-commercial benefit or advantage from the state (i.e. it will be earning a market rate of interest from the borrower reflecting the presence of the guarantee). A similar analysis should logically apply to bondholders who invest in a state guaranteed bond: they are simply getting what they are paying for (a low-risk investment which will typically produce a lower return than one without a state guarantee). However, aid may be present where a guarantee is given after the loan has already been made, or the bond has already been issued, without any adjustment to the terms of the loan or bond to reflect the guarantee. The circumstances in which a state guarantee may be treated as conferring aid on the lender are considered in more detail in section 6 below.

9–003

The Notice on Guarantees provides that the aid element inherent in a state guarantee is: "the difference between the appropriate market price of the guarantee provided individually or through a scheme and the actual price paid for that measure".[6] Establishing the value of the aid element in a guarantee is discussed in more detail in section 7 below.

9–004

Like other types of aid, guarantees that constitute aid are unlawful unless notified to, and approved by, the Commission. The consequences of non-notification for the validity of the guarantee, and potential impact on the lender, are discussed in more detail in section 9 below.

9–005

2. TYPES OF GUARANTEES COVERED

As the Notice on Guarantees makes clear, the state aid rules apply to all forms of guarantees involving a transfer of risk to the guarantor, irrespective of their

9–006

[2] Notice on Guarantees, at para.2.2.
[3] Notice on Guarantees, at para.3.1; see also the references cited at fn.5 of the Notice on Guarantees.
[4] Notice on Guarantees, s.3.
[5] Notice on Guarantees, at para.2.3.1.
[6] Notice on Guarantees, at para.4.1.

legal basis and the transaction covered. The Notice includes a non-exhaustive list of guarantee types covered[7]:

- "general guarantees, i.e. guarantees provided to undertakings as such as opposed to guarantees linked to a specific transaction, which may be a loan, an equity investment, etc.,

- guarantees provided by a specific instrument as opposed to guarantees linked to the status of the undertaking itself,

- guarantees provided directly or counter guarantees provided to a first level guarantor,

- unlimited guarantees as opposed to guarantees limited in amount and/or time. The Commission also regards as aid in the form of a guarantee the more favourable funding terms obtained by enterprises whose legal form rules out bankruptcy or other insolvency procedures or provides an explicit State guarantee or coverage of losses by the State. The same applies to the acquisition by a State of a holding in an enterprise if unlimited liability is accepted instead of the usual limited liability,

- guarantees clearly originating from a contractual source (such as formal contracts, letters of comfort) or other legal source as opposed to guarantees whose form is less visible (such as side letters, oral commitments), possibly with various levels of comfort that can be provided by this guarantee."

9–007   The fourth bullet makes clear that the state aid rules apply to guarantees arising by operation of law, such as the more favourable funding terms obtained by undertakings whose legal status precludes bankruptcy,[8] or those obtained by undertakings whose legal form provides an explicit guarantee or coverage of losses by the state. This was the basis of the Commission's concern about the

---

[7] Notice on Guarantees, at para.1.2. There is an unfortunate ambiguity in the wording of this non-exhaustive list of categories of guarantee, due to the use of the expression "as opposed to" in the first, second, fourth and fifth bullets. Read literally, this might appear to suggest that the types of instrument or measure following the words "as opposed to" are *not* regarded as guarantees. However, that interpretation would represent a major shift in Commission policy, and was clearly not intended.

[8] *EDF* [2005] O.J. L49/9 at para.57: "The Commission takes the view that the fact that EDF cannot be subject to administration or compulsory liquidation proceedings, and therefore cannot be declared bankrupt, is equivalent to a general guarantee covering all its liabilities. Such a guarantee cannot be the subject of any remuneration according to the rules of the market. Such a guarantee, which is unlimited in scope, time and amount, constitutes state aid." The French Government agreed to convert EDF into a limited company, which would result in its becoming subject to the ordinary rules applicable to companies in administration or in compulsory liquidation; the Commission accepted that "making EDF subject to the ordinary law on bankruptcy will have the effect of withdrawing the unlimited State guarantee which it enjoyed" (at para.134).

position of the German Landesbanken, which was resolved by agreement between the Commission and the German government in 2002.[9]

The same principles apply to state acquisitions of shareholdings which result, **9–008** under national law, in the assumption of unlimited liability. This was the reasoning behind the Commission's decision in *IOR*,[10] where the Commission objected to a loan provided to the chronically loss-making IOR by Sofin (an Italian state-owned entity) and the subsequent waiver by Sofin of its right to repayment. On the facts of the case, the Commission concluded that, as IOR had never made a profit during the years covered by its investigation, Sofin had, by becoming the sole shareholder of IOR (thereby incurring liability for its debts), accepted a risk which a private investor would have refused.[11] Similarly, in the *EFIM*[12] case, which concerned the liquidation of the Italian state owned holding company EFIM, the Commission again objected to the operation of the same provisions of the Italian Civil Code, under which a sole shareholder became liable for all the debts of the company concerned. This time, however, the objection related to the lower credit risk inherent in the fact that creditors proving in a liquidation of a state owned company would have access to the "effectively infinite financial resources" of the state.[13] The Commission did *not* regard creditors of EFIM as

---

[9] On March 1, 2002 the Commission announced (see press release IP/02/343) that final agreement had been reached with the German government on the steps to be taken to make the guarantee system of "Anstaltslast" (an unwritten rule of German administrative law requiring the owner of a public law institution or corporation to maintain its solvency to enable it to fulfil its purposes (e.g. by the provision of capital)) and "Gewährträgerhaftung" (a provision contained in the statutes creating certain public law institutions making the owner directly liable to creditors for all liabilities of the institution) compatible with the EU state aid rules. The compromise entailed the following elements: (i) the abolition of Anstaltslast; (ii) a commitment by Germany to repeal the law preventing the Landesbanken from becoming insolvent; (iii) a limited grandfathering of Gewährträgerhaftung so that (a) in respect of liabilities incurred before July 18, 2001 Gewährträgerhaftung would continue to apply without limit of time, and (b) in respect of liabilities incurred up to July 18, 2005 *Gewährträgerhaftung* would continue to apply provided the maturity of the obligation does not extend beyond December 31, 2015.

[10] *IOR* [1992] O.J. L183/30, p.31.

[11] *IOR* [1992] O.J. L183/30, p.31: "[T]he Italian Government claimed that Sofin had acted as any investor in a similar position would have done by covering IOR's losses, because it was the one and only shareholder of IOR until 15 October 1986 and therefore liable under Italian law for all its debts. The liquidation of IOR would consequently have entailed higher costs for Sofin. The Commission cannot subscribe to this point of view. A private investor will normally be reluctant to become the one and only shareholder of a company, if as a consequence he must assume unlimited liability for it; he will make sure that this additional risk is outweighed by additional gains."

[12] *EFIM* [1993] O.J. C349/2.

[13] *EFIM* [1993] O.J. C349/2 p.3, para.5: "Therefore, the creditor of a 100% State owned company will have higher security to receive full repayment in the event of a liquidation. This allows a public undertaking, notwithstanding its increasing debts, to continue trading long after a comparable private undertaking would have been placed in liquidation. When a company wholly owned by a market economy investor goes into liquidation, the creditors' repayment is limited to the amount that can be raised by the sale of the company's and the shareholders' assets. As these are not infinite, the whole of the company's indebtedness will normally not be repaid. It is therefore clear that cases may arise under Article 2362 of the Civil Code, which constitute such discrimination between public and private companies. Moreover, aid is involved even if the company is in liquidation, as in the present case, as the payment enables an operating company to continue in business by the elimination of intra-group indebtedness. The fact that it is the

recipients of aid. This can be justified on the basis that creditors were simply getting what they bargained for when agreeing to lend in the first place (i.e. a low risk loan carrying a rate of interest commensurate with the risk).

9–009   The fifth bullet confirms that "soft" guarantees may also constitute state aid. The "Frequently Asked Questions"[14] published alongside the Notice on Guarantees elaborates further:

> "Letters of comfort or political declarations can contain a transfer of risk when announcing that a company can rely on the support of the state. The same is true for other oral commitments or side letters. Such commitments constitute a guarantee as soon as it becomes obvious that the state intervention lowers the risk to be borne by the lender."[15]

The issue of whether an oral commitment could be viewed as state aid arose for consideration in the *France Télécom* case.[16] During the first half of 2002 France Télécom suffered a series of rating downgrades and by June 2002 was in serious financial difficulties. At that time, the French government was the majority shareholder of the company, with a holding of approximately 56 per cent. On July 12, 2002 *Les Echos* published an interview in which the French Minister for Economic Affairs, Finance and Industry was reported as saying:

> "The State shareholder will behave like a prudent investor and would take appropriate steps if France Télécom were to face any difficulties ... I repeat, if France Télécom were to face any financing problems, which is not the case today, the State would take whatever decisions were necessary to overcome them."

On the same day, the rating agency Standard & Poor's downgraded France Télécom's debt while maintaining its rating at investment grade, based on the French government's stated intentions towards the company.[17] The Commission's decision notes that the announcement of July 12, 2002 led to "an abnormal and not negligible increase in the value of France Télécom's shares and bonds". In addition, the Commission refers to the favourable reaction to the announcement as recorded in an analyst's report published shortly afterwards, noting that:

> "the market was convinced, in light of the Government's declarations, of the state support that would be provided by the Government to France Télécom (even if the market did query the scope and modalities of that support)."[18]

creditors and not the company which receive payment is irrelevant as these operating companies are the final beneficiaries of such aid payments."
[14] MEMO/08/313 May 20, 2008.
[15] MEMO/08/313 May 20, 2008, p.2.
[16] *France Télécom* [2006] O.J. L257/11.
[17] *France Télécom* at paras 36–38.
[18] *France Télécom* at para.221.

In a series of further announcements later in 2002, the French government reiterated its support for France Télécom's plans to strengthen its balance sheet, including on December 4, 2002 its intention to participate in a forthcoming bond issue, and its willingness to make a temporary shareholders loan, at market rates, as an upfront prepayment to enable the company to launch the bond issue at the most opportune moment.[19] In the end, the bond issue was a success and the shareholder loan was never actually made.[20] The December shareholder loan proposal was notified to the Commission as a possible aid, but the Commission's investigation focused not just on the loan proposal but also on whether the prior declarations of support might constitute aid.

This presented a difficulty for the Commission, since although it seemed reasonably clear that the statements (in particular, the July 2002 statement) had reassured the market, and therefore resulted in an advantage to France Télécom, it was less obvious that state resources had been transferred. Arguably, state resources were not committed until the December announcement of the share-holder loan proposal. The Commission had doubts about whether it could establish the existence of an aid on this basis, and ultimately chose not to characterise the July 2002 statement as an aid, instead concluding that the shareholder loan proposal amounted to an aid (albeit the loan was never actually made), which failed the market economy investor test, and was incompatible with the common market[21]:

"(188) The analysis of the present case suggests at first sight the existence of a time lag between the advantages for the Company, which were particularly distinct in July, and the potential commitment of state resources, which seems to be more clearly established in December. Inasmuch as they clearly had an effect on the markets and conferred an advantage on the Company, the declarations by the Minister for Economic Affairs and Finance may be charac-terised as aid. It would not be easy, however, to establish beyond all doubt whether the July 2002 declarations were of such a character as to commit, at least potentially, state resources. In this respect, the Commission has carefully analysed numerous legal arguments seeking to show, firstly, that such public declarations were equivalent from a legal standpoint to a state guarantee and, secondly, that they placed the State's reputation on the line, with economic costs in the event of non-compliance. Taken as a whole, these elements might be thought to actually risk putting state resources in jeopardy (either by making the State liable towards investors, or by increasing the cost of future state transactions). The argument to the effect that the July 2002 declarations are aid is therefore innovative, but probably not without foundation.

(189) The Commission does not, however, have sufficient evidence in the present case to establish irrefutably the existence of aid on the basis of this innovative argument. On the other hand, it does consider that it can establish

[19] *France Télécom* at para.56.
[20] *France Télécom* at para.227.
[21] *France Télécom* at paras 188–189.

the existence of aid elements by following a more traditional approach, taking as a basis the December measures which were the subject-matter of the notification."

It may be observed in passing that, had the Commission taken a different view of the Minister's July 2002 statement, it could potentially have raised significant practical difficulties in terms of a Member State's ability to comply with the obligation to notify aid before it is put into effect. Presumably it would have been necessary to notify the putative aid before publication of the relevant press article. In practice, such a requirement could well be unworkable.

On appeal the Commission's decision was annulled by the General Court.[22] The Court confirmed that in order to qualify as an aid, a measure must not only confer an advantage on the recipient but must also entail a transfer of state resources.[23] On the first point of whether the public declarations since July 2002 conferred an advantage on France Télécom, the Court held that they did. They enabled the company to regain the confidence of financial markets, to access the capital markets on better terms in order to refinance its existing debt, and ultimately contributed to the stabilisation of its fragile financial situation.[24] On the second question, however, the Court disagreed with the Commission. The ministerial statements were open, imprecise and conditional in nature, in particular as regards the nature, scope and conditions of possible state intervention in favour of France Télécom and therefore could not be construed as a state guarantee.[25] It would appear that to constitute a guarantee the statement would have to set out the specific debts guaranteed, or, at the very least, a predefined financial framework such as a credit line up to a certain amount as well as the conditions for granting the assistance envisaged by the statement.

9–010   The Notice on Guarantees also makes clear that art.107(1) applies to guarantees given through state resources by state controlled bodies and which are imputable to public authorities,[26] and therefore leaves open the possibility that one such undertaking could be deemed to confer aid on another; albeit that one would need to establish, on the facts, whether the grantor undertaking was acting on the direction of the state and therefore whether its decision was imputable to the state.[27]

3. GENERAL CONSIDERATIONS IN IDENTIFYING WHETHER A STATE GUARANTEE CONSTITUTES AID

9–011   Notwithstanding the broad language of the Notice on Guarantees, it is clear that not all state guarantees amount to aid: a basic jurisdictional requirement of

---

[22] *France and Others v Commission* (Joined Cases T–425/04, T–444/04, T–450/04 and T–456/04) Unreported May 21, 2010.

[23] *France and Others v Commission* at para.215.

[24] *France and Others v Commission* at para.234.

[25] *France and Others v Commission* at para.279.

[26] Notice on Guarantees (see fn.1, above) at para.2.1.

[27] For the requirement of imputability see Case C–482/99 *France v Commission* [2002] E.C.R. I–4397.

art.107(1) is the need for an effect on trade between Member States; in the absence of such an effect, there is no aid.[28] By implication, the Commission seems to acknowledge that Member States are entitled to form their own judgment on this issue.[29]

Similarly, if a market premium is paid, that will be sufficient to prevent the guarantee being regarded as aid within the meaning of art.107(1). The Notice on Guarantees provides that: "State aid is not involved where a new funding source is made available on conditions which would be acceptable for a private operator under normal conditions of a market economy".[30] In addition, it is submitted that there is no aid where, for example, as frequently happens in state-originated securitisation transactions, the state sells an asset to the issuer and gives the issuer a warranty or similar commitment to underwrite the asset in the event of its non-performance. On the assumption that such a warranty is the kind of obligation which a private sector originator would have been willing to undertake, it seems reasonable to conclude that the warranty is effectively priced into the transaction, so that the issuer is simply getting what it has paid for.

9–012

4. Safe Harbours in the Notice on Guarantees

As noted above, payment of an arm's length fee for a state guarantee is sufficient to rule out the existence of aid. The Notice on Guarantees sets out a number of conditions which, if met, will exclude the existence of aid based on the market economy investor principle. Failure to meet all of these conditions does not necessarily mean that the guarantee will be viewed as aid: however, the Commission counsels notification in cases of doubt.[31]

9–013

In the case of individual guarantees, the conditions are as follows[32]:

9–014

(a) The borrower is not in financial difficulty, assessed in accordance with the Commission's guidelines on state aid for rescue and restructuring firms in difficulty. Small and medium sized enterprises which have been incorporated for less than three years will not be considered to be in difficulty for these purposes.

(b) The guarantee is linked to a specific financial transaction, is for a fixed maximum amount, and is not open-ended.

[28] Notice on Guarantees (see fn.1 above) at para.2.1.
[29] This is also consistent with reg.659/99, which only requires notification of aid fulfilling all the criteria of art.107(1) TFEU.
[30] Notice on Guarantees (see fn.1, above) at para.3.1; see also the references cited at fn.5 of the Notice on Guarantees.
[31] Notice on Guarantees at para.3.6.
[32] Notice on Guarantees at para.3.2.

(c) The guarantee does not cover more than 80 per cent of the outstanding loan or other financial obligation (except for debt securities).[33] The 80 per cent limit must be respected over the lifetime of the loan (e.g. if the loan is repaid over time), and losses must be sustained proportionately and in the same way by lender and guarantor (i.e. there should be no "first loss" provisions protecting the lender).[34]

(d) A "market-oriented" price is paid. This should be assessed by reference to the market price of an equivalent guarantee provided by the private sector. If no such benchmark is available, the total cost of the guaranteed loan should be compared to the market price of a similar non-guaranteed loan. In both cases the borrower should be rated, either by an internationally recognised rating agency or using the internal rating given by the bank providing the underlying loan, and the guarantee/loan benchmarked against guarantees or loans provided to similarly rated companies.[35]

9–015   In the case of individual guarantees provided to small and medium-sized enterprises,[36] the Notice on Guarantees sets out annual premiums applicable to companies in each rating category.[37] Provided the other conditions described at para.9–014(a)–(c) above are satisfied, these premium rates operate as "safe harbours", meaning that a guarantee charged at these rates is deemed not to amount to aid, though guarantees provided at lower premiums are not necessarily classified as constituting state aid.[38]

9–016   In the case of guarantee schemes, the conditions that must be satisfied in order to rule out the existence of aid are as follows[39]:

(a) the scheme is closed to borrowers who are in financial difficulty;

---

[33] As defined by art.2(1)(b) of Directive 2004/109/EC [2004] O.J. L390/38, as amended by Directive 2008/22/EC [2008] O.J. L76/50. See also fn.44 below. The limitation does not apply to a public guarantee provided by the entrusting authority to finance a company whose activity is solely constituted by a properly entrusted Service of General Economic Interest (Notice on Guarantees at para.3.2(c)).

[34] The Notice leaves open the possibility that a guarantee covering more than 80% of a loan may not amount to aid. However, it specifies that if a Member State wishes to provide a guarantee exceeding the 80% threshold on the basis that it does not constitute aid, it should "duly substantiate the claim, for instance on the basis of the arrangement of the whole transaction" and should notify it to the Commission for assessment (para.3.2(c)).

[35] The Commission indicates that it will *not* accept that the guarantee premium is set at a single industry-wide rate (Notice on Guarantees, para.3.2(d)).

[36] As defined in Annex 1 to Regulation (EC) No.70/2001 on the application of arts 107 and 108 of the EC Treaty to state aid to small and medium sized enterprises [2001] O.J. L10/33.

[37] Notice on Guarantees at para.3.3. See revised premiums published in "Corrigendum to Commission notice on the application of Articles 87 and 99 of the EC Treaty (now Articles 107 and 108 TFEU) to state aid in the form of guarantees", [2008] O.J. C244/11.

[38] See the "Frequently Asked Questions" published alongside the Notice on Guarantees, MEMO/08/313 May 20, 2008, which states: "The safe-harbour grid is meant as a simplification tool; Member States may decide not to use it if they believe they can demonstrate that lower premiums are market-conform" (p.4).

[39] Notice on Guarantees at para.3.4.

(b) the extent of the guarantees can be properly measured when granted; this means they must be linked to a specific financial transaction, for a fixed maximum amount and limited in time;

(c) the guarantees do not cover more than 80 per cent of each outstanding loan or other financial obligation (except for debt securities);

(d) the terms of the scheme are based on a realistic assessment of the risk so that the premiums paid by the beneficiary enterprises make it, in all probability, self-financing. This entails that the risk of each new guarantee has to be assessed and a rating applied to the borrower;

(e) the adequacy of the level of premiums must be reviewed at least once a year on the basis of the effective loss rate of the scheme over an economically reasonable time horizon, and premiums adjusted accordingly if there is a risk that the scheme may no longer be self-financing. This adjustment may concern all issued and future guarantees, or only the latter;

(f) the premiums cover the normal risks associated with granting the guarantee, the administrative costs of the scheme, and a yearly remuneration of an adequate capital, even if the latter is not at all or only partially constituted.[40] The administrative costs should include at least the specific initial risk assessment as well as the risk monitoring and risk management costs linked to the granting and administration of the guarantee; and

(g) in order to ensure transparency, the scheme must provide for the terms on which future guarantees will be granted.

In relation to schemes for small and medium-sized enterprises, the Notice on Guarantees provides two derogations from the above conditions: **9–017**

(a) use of the safe harbour premiums established for individual guarantees granted to small and medium sized enterprises. If these premiums are charged, the conditions set out in para.9–016(d), (e) and (f) above are deemed to be satisfied. However, the remaining conditions in para. 9–016(a), (b), (c) and (g) still need to be fulfilled; and

(b) where the scheme is open only to small and medium sized enterprises and the guaranteed amount does not exceed €2.5 million per company, the Commission may accept a single yearly premium for all borrowers in place of the individual risk assessment described in para.9–016(d) above. However, the scheme must remain self-financing and accordingly, all the other conditions mentioned in para.9–016 above still need to be fulfilled.

---

[40] The calculation of the capital remuneration element is covered in detail in the Notice on Guarantees at para.3.4(f).

9–018   As to whether there is an obligation to notify either an individual guarantee or a guarantee scheme if any of the safe-harbour conditions is not satisfied, the Notice on Guarantees states that:

"Failure to comply with any one of the conditions . . . does not mean that the guarantee or guarantee scheme is automatically regarded as State aid. If there is any doubt as to whether a planned guarantee or guarantee scheme constitutes State aid, it should be notified to the Commission."[41]

It should be noted that there is no legal obligation on Member States to notify measures that do not constitute aid. However, the Notice on Guarantees takes the approach of advising Member States to notify in cases of doubt.

5. Practical Difficulties in Applying the Safe Harbours in the Notice on Guarantees

9–019   The Notice on Guarantees has removed one of the more problematic tests for ruling out the existence of aid under the previous Notice, namely the requirement that the borrower would in principle be able to obtain a loan on market conditions from the financial markets without any intervention by the state. Nonetheless, there may still be practical difficulties in applying the conditions in the Notice on Guarantees, which could create uncertainty for lenders and their advisers. The main area of uncertainty arises from the requirement that the guarantee must be limited to 80 per cent of the outstanding loan. The theory behind this is that, by giving the lender some exposure to the risk of borrower default, the lender will have an incentive to assess the creditworthiness of the borrower.[42] Accordingly, the Notice on Guarantees states that the Commission will therefore generally examine more thoroughly any guarantee covering the entirety (or nearly the entirety) of the transaction, unless the Member State duly justifies it, for instance by the specific nature of the transaction.[43] It should be emphasised, however, that the 80 per cent test is an arbitrary limit, which has no firm legal basis. Rather, it may be thought of as an expression of the market economy investor test in one particular situation.

9–020   The 80 per cent limit does not apply to guarantees of debt securities.[44] However, the definition of debt securities is relatively narrow and would not cover swap contracts, types of derivative instruments that are commonly entered into in the context of securitisation transactions. This therefore raises the question of how the 80 per cent limit is to be calculated under a swap contract, where

---

[41] Notice on Guarantees at para.3.6. See also fn.34, above.
[42] Notice on Guarantees at para.3.2(c).
[43] Notice on Guarantees at para.4.1(c).
[44] See fn.33 above. The expression "debt securities" is defined as "bonds or other forms of transferable securitised debts, with the exception of securities which are equivalent to shares in companies or which, if converted or if the rights conferred by them are exercised, give rise to a right to acquire shares or securities equivalent to shares".

the maximum potential liability arising under the contract is likely to be open-ended. In *Channel Tunnel Rail Link*,[45] the Commission concluded that a guarantee covering 100 per cent of the exposure under a swap amounted to state aid but was compatible with the common market, even though it breached the 80 per cent limit in the Notice on Guarantees. It was not necessary, in that case, to consider whether a guarantee covering 100 per cent of the exposure under a swap, given in return for an arm's length fee, could satisfy the market economy investor principle. Logically, however, there seems no reason why it could not do so.

The Commission recognised the difficulties in trying to quantify the potential exposure under a swap. Its analysis focused on the methodology for valuing the guarantee. The United Kingdom argued that the value of the guarantee was the theoretical cost of purchasing a similar guarantee from a private sector institution. This approach was confirmed by the Commission:

"[T]he UK Government has calculated the value of the hedging guarantees at the theoretical cost of purchasing similar guarantees from a private sector institution to £13 million and will guarantee 100% of LCR's potential exposure under the interest swaps it has entered into.

The Commission acknowledges that, for this particular form of financial transactions, it is not possible to calculate in advance the final amount that will be effectively covered by the guarantees and considers, in this particular case, that the method used by the UK government to value the guarantees, i.e. based on a hypothetical purchase price, is justified and represents the most accurate estimation of the value of the guarantees.

Moreover, the Commission takes note of the fact that LCR's counterpart banks under the hedging arrangements, acting commercially, are not prepared to take any risk on the credit of LCR and require collateral for the full amount exposed at any particular time. Therefore, if the guarantees were to cover less than 100%, LCR would still have to provide collateral for the difference, using funds already raised with the result that less financial resources would ultimately be available to fund LCR's cash flow requirements for construction purposes. Under such circumstances, the Commission finds that it can accept that the State guarantees in question covers [*sic*] the underlying transactions in full."[46]

6. Aid to the Lender

The Notice on Guarantees notes that the usual beneficiary of a state guarantee **9–021** will be the borrower,[47] but does not rule out that the lender may also benefit from the aid:

[45] Commission Decision COM(2002) 1446 final of April 24, 2002 on state aid N 706/2001 United Kingdom, *The Channel Tunnel Rail Link*, available on the Commission's web site.
[46] *The Channel Tunnel Rail Link* at paras 78–80.
[47] Notice on Guarantees at para.2.2.

"In particular, for example, if a State guarantee is given *ex post* in respect of a loan or other financial obligation already entered into without the terms of this loan or financial obligation being adjusted, or if one guaranteed loan is used to pay back another, non-guaranteed loan to the same credit institution, then there may also be aid to the lender, in so far as the security of the loans is increased."[48]

In the examples cited by the Commission, the lender's credit position is improved, without the lender having provided any consideration. It is plain that the lender in that situation can be said to derive an advantage, flowing from state resources, which can be treated as aid. Conversely, as indicated at para.9–003 above, there will be no aid to the investors in a state guaranteed bond issue merely by reason of the guarantee, as they are simply getting what they are paying for.

7. AMOUNT OF THE AID

9–022   The Notice on Guarantees provides that the aid element inherent in a state guarantee is: "the difference between the appropriate market price of the guarantee provided individually or through a scheme and the actual price paid for that measure".[49]

9–023   In assessing the amount of aid represented by a guarantee, the Notice on Guarantees states that the Commission will take into account:

(a) whether (in the case of an individual guarantee) the borrower is in financial difficulty (or in the case of a scheme, whether its terms exclude such undertakings);

(b) whether the guarantee is linked to a specific financial transaction, for a fixed maximum amount and limited in time: "In this connection the Commission considers in principle that unlimited guarantees are incompatible with Article [107] of the Treaty";

(c) whether the guarantee covers more than 80 per cent of each outstanding loan or other financial obligation (see para.9–014(c) for further details); and

(d) whether the specific characteristics of the guarantee and loan (or other financial obligation) have been taken into account when determining the premium of the guarantee.[50]

---

[48] Notice on Guarantees at paras 2.3.1–2.3.2.
[49] Notice on Guarantees at para.4.1.
[50] Notice on Guarantees at para.4.1. Further details of the Commission's methodology are provided at paras 4.2–4.5.

In extreme cases, the Commission takes the view that the aid element may **9–024** equal the entire amount of the loan if the borrower could not obtain a loan without a guarantee:

"The Commission notes that for companies in difficulty, a market guarantor, if any, would, at the time the guarantee is granted charge a high premium given the expected rate of default. If the likelihood that the borrower will not be able to repay the loan becomes particularly high, this market rate may not exist and in exceptional circumstances the aid element of the guarantee may turn out to be as high as the amount effectively covered by that guarantee".[51]

No further explanation is provided in the Notice on Guarantees of what is meant by the expression "the amount effectively covered by that guarantee", but in a number of cases where the Commission has ordered recovery of the whole amount of the loan, it appears that only the principal amount of the loan (rather than principal plus interest) has been treated as an aid.[52]

8. ASSESSING THE COMPATIBILITY OF AID IN THE FORM OF GUARANTEES

The Notice on Guarantees does not identify any particular considerations **9–025** relevant to assessing the compatibility of state aid in the form of guarantees (save those described in para.9–023, above). Instead it refers to its guidelines covering horizontal, regional and sectoral aid, noting that "the examination will take into account, in particular, the aid intensity, the characteristics of the beneficiaries and the objectives pursued".[53] There is, however, one important caveat to this: the conditions under which the guarantee may be honoured. The Notice on Guarantees indicates that the Commission will only "accept" state guarantees (i.e.

---

[51] Notice on Guarantees at para.4.1. See also *Chemische Werke Piesteritz* [2005] O.J. L296/19 at paras 107–8, where the Commission noted that, because the aid beneficiary was in severe financial difficulties at the time the guarantees were granted, "the aid element could be as high as 100% of the guarantees". However, the Commission went on to find that the aid element in this particular case was the difference between the reference rate plus 400 basis points and the interest rate payable under the guaranteed loan. In *Greußener Salamifabrik GmbH* [2005] O.J. L335/48, the Commission held (at para.36) that since the guarantees were given to a company that was in financial difficulties, the aid element was equal to "100% of the guaranteed amount".

[52] See, e.g., *JAKO Jadekost* [1996] O.J. L246/43, where the Commission appears to have calculated the "net subsidy equivalent" by reference to the principal amount of the loan. Similarly, in *Bremer Vulkan* [1993] O.J. L185/43 the Commission seems to have calculated the value of the aid as the principal amount covered by the guarantee: "The Commission therefore identifies the following aids: BV received DM126 million aid from Hibeg. This aid operation was made possible by a guarantee on DM126 million plus credit costs and interest . . . ." This is also implicit from the Commission's analysis in *Greußener Salamifabrik GmbH* (fn.51 above). But note that when the Commission orders recovery of an aid it is required also to order payment of interest from the date of receipt until the date of recovery: art.14(2) of Council Regulation (EC) 659/1999, [1999] O.J. L83/1.

[53] Notice on Guarantees at para.5.2.

regard them as compatible with the European Union) "if their mobilisation is contractually linked to specific conditions which may go as far as the compulsory declaration of bankruptcy of the beneficiary undertaking . . . ".[54] Furthermore, the Notice on Guarantees makes clear that these conditions must be agreed when the guarantee is initially granted, and that if the Member State wishes to "mobilise" the guarantee under different conditions from those initially agreed, this will be regarded as new aid, which must be notified.[55]

9. CONSEQUENCES OF NON-NOTIFICATION

9–026   Unless a state guarantee qualifying as state aid has been notified pursuant to art.108(3) before being put into effect, it will be unlawful as a matter of Community law,[56] and may be unenforceable as a matter of national law. The Notice on Guarantees suggests that lenders may be at risk if they accept un-notified guarantees, albeit that questions of enforceability are acknowledged to be a matter for national law.[57] As a matter of Community law, it seems arguable that the state would be allowed, if sued on a guarantee in a national court, to plead its own wrongful act as a defence and thereby to resist payment. This appears to follow from the direct effect of art.108(3) EC and to be supported by the decision of the European Court of Justice (ECJ) in *Alcan (No.2)*:

> "[U]ndertakings to which aid has been granted may not, in principle, entertain a legitimate expectation that the aid is lawful unless it has been granted in compliance with the procedure laid down in [Article 108(3)]. A diligent businessman should normally be able to determine whether that procedure has been followed."[58]

It will be noted that this approach does not sit easily with the case law on repayment of aid, where the rationale for refusing to allow a state to rely on the legitimate expectations of the beneficiary to justify failure to seek repayment is said by the ECJ to be to prevent Member States from relying on their unlawful conduct so as to deprive Commission decisions of their effectiveness.[59]

9–027   It seems to follow from the *EPAC* case[60] that the Commission is entitled to require the immediate cancellation of an un-notified guarantee. The case concerned a guarantee that had been granted by the Portuguese Finance Ministry to

---

[54] Notice on Guarantees at para.5.3.
[55] Notice on Guarantees at para.53. This language dates back to the Commission's earliest communications on state guarantees, beginning with the letter to Member States (SG(89) D/4328 of April 5, 1989) and also appeared in the previous version of the Notice on Guarantees.
[56] "Unlawful aid" is defined in art.1(a) of reg.659/99 as "new aid put into effect in contravention of Article [108(3)] of the Treaty".
[57] Notice on Guarantees at para.2.3.2.
[58] Case C–24/95 *Land Rheinland-Pfalz v Alcan Deutschland (Alcan No.2)* [1997] E.C.R. I–1591 at para.28; see generally Bellamy and Child, *European Community Law of Competition* (6th edn, 2008), at paras 15.103–15.107.
[59] See the cases cited in Bellamy and Child (see fn.58, above), at para.15.105, n.533.
[60] *EPAC* [1997] O.J. L311/25; on appeal Case C–404/97 *Commission v Portugal* [2000] E.C.R. I–4897.

EPAC, the former monopoly cereals marketing organisation, in connection with a loan from a group of private banks. The Commission found the guarantee to be illegal state aid, having been granted in contravention of art.[108(3)], which was incompatible with the common market. Portugal was ordered to "cancel" the aid and take measures to "recover the aid". The Portuguese government argued that the meaning of the Commission's orders to cancel and recover the aid were incomprehensible as the guarantee had not involved any payment or transfer of state resources to EPAC, and that implementation of the decision (i.e. unilateral cancellation of the guarantee) was legally impossible.[61] The Court of Justice was not sympathetic, noting case law that "recovery of unlawful aid is the logical consequence of the finding that it is unlawful and that that consequence cannot depend on the form in which the aid was granted".[62] As the Court of Justice made clear, the only defence available to a Member State is to plead that it is absolutely impossible for it to implement the Commission's decision properly.[63] Where a Member State encounters unforeseen and unforeseeable difficulties in implementing a Commission decision, the Commission and the Member State concerned should "work together in good faith with a view to overcoming difficulties whilst fully observing the Treaty provisions, and in particular the provisions on aid".[64]

A further difficulty stems from the fact that, although the lender will not **9–028** typically be regarded as an aid recipient at the time when the guarantee is issued (the beneficiary of the aid is normally the borrower), it can be argued that if the state makes a payment under an unlawful guarantee (i.e. one that has not been notified pursuant to art.108(3)), it is by definition making a payment which it was not legally obliged to make, which is itself an aid to the lender.[65] This point has yet to be resolved by the Court of Justice.

However, recent guidance on the issue of civil enforceability is to be found in the opinion of Kokott AG in the *Residex* case[66] as well as in the judgment of the Court of Justice in *Residex*.[67] The case concerned the validity under national law

---

[61] Case C–404/97 *Commission v Portugal* [2000] E.C.R. I–4897, at para.29; see also paras 30–32. It was argued that unilateral withdrawal of the guarantee would lead the banks to call in their loan, which would bankrupt EPAC, also putting at issue the government's liability: see para.30.

[62] *Commission v Portugal* at para.38, citing Case C–183/91 *Commission v Greece* [1993] E.C.R. I–3131 at para.16.

[63] *Commission v Portugal* at para.39.

[64] *Commission v Portugal* at para.40.

[65] See Jeremy Lever QC, *Discussion Paper: State Guarantees as State Aid: The effect of European Community Law, a special supplement to Butterworths Journal of International Banking and Financial Law* (January 2002), at para.2.5(b). See also para.2.5(a), where it is argued that where the borrower could not have obtained the loan at all without a state guarantee, the state has "created" business for the lender, and the lender who enters into such a transaction gets an advantage over competitors who are unwilling to participate in the giving of unlawful state aid. Lever acknowledges that this analysis has never yet been advanced by the Commission.

[66] Case C–275/10, *Residex Capital IV CV v Gemeente Rotterdam* Unreported opinion of May 26, 2011.

[67] Case C–275/10, *Residex Capital IV CV v Gemeente Rotterdam* Unreported December 8, 2011.

of a state guarantee, given in breach of art.108(3), and specifically the question of whether a national court had jurisdiction to cancel such a guarantee, and if so, whether it was required under European Union law to exercise that power. The Advocate General discussed the *EPAC* jurisprudence and considered whether the fact that the Commission had in that case required the cancellation of the aid had any bearing on the question of civil enforceability. The Advocate General argued that closer examination of the expression "cancellation" of the guarantee in the Commission's decision showed that it was in reality directed towards recovery of the financial advantage which EPAC had obtained by virtue of the guarantee, in terms of a preferential interest rate, compared to what it would have had to pay without the guarantee.[68] Kokott AG concluded that it was not possible to derive from the previous case law, or from the *EPAC* case more particularly, any obligation on a national court to declare invalid a guarantee which had been granted in breach of art.108(3) and where the only beneficiary was the borrower. By contrast, where the lender was also an aid beneficiary the position was different, as in those circumstances nullity of the guarantee would be an appropriate way of realising the objectives of art.108(3) since it would eliminate the economic advantage obtained by the lender from the public authorities.[69] The Court of Justice gave a more nuanced response to the question referred by the national court, confirming that national courts do have jurisdiction to cancel a guarantee given in breach of art.108(3), but that they also have a certain amount of discretion in deciding how to exercise that power.[70] The Court noted first that it was for the national court "to identify the beneficiary or, as the case may be, the beneficiaries of that guarantee and to effect . . . recovery of the total amount of the aid in question."[71] But that did not necessarily mean the guarantee had to be cancelled:

> "with regard to cancellation of the guarantee, and irrespective of who the beneficiary of the aid may be, European Union law does not impose any specific consequences that the national courts must necessarily draw with regard to the validity of the acts relating to implementation of the aid."[72]

However, given that the objective of the measures which national courts were required to take in the event of an infringement of art.108(3) was "to restore the competitive situation existing prior to the payment of the aid in question", it followed that national courts "must ensure that the measures which they take with regard to the validity of the aforementioned acts make it possible for such

---

[68] fn.66, above at para.41. Note, however, that this does not appear to be supported by the judgment of the Court of Justice in *EPAC*, which refers specifically (at para.47) to the fact that the guarantee was to be cancelled, as well as noting (at para.48) the amount of the aid which was to be recovered (essentially the difference in borrowing costs represented by the guarantee).

[69] fn.66, above at paras 76–77.

[70] fn.67, above at paras 43–49.

[71] fn.67, above at para.43.

[72] fn.67, above at para.44.

an objective to be achieved."[73] The Court then went on to hold that, "when exercising [their jurisdiction to cancel a guarantee]", national courts are:

"required to ensure that the aid is recovered and to that end, they can cancel a guarantee, in particular where, in the absence of less onerous procedural measures, that cancellation is such as to lead to or facilitate the restoration of the competitive situation which existed before that guarantee was provided".[74]

This formulation suggests that cancellation by the national court should be viewed as a measure of last resort, to be used only when no less intrusive remedies are available. Although the Court did not spell out the position clearly, preferring to leave this to the national court, it may well be that in circumstances where the borrower would have been unable to obtain a loan on the capital markets, or from a bank, without a guarantee, and where in addition the guarantee confers an aid on the lender, nothing short of cancellation of the guarantee would meet the Court's twin policy objectives of recovering the aid from the beneficiaries and restoring the *status quo ante*.[75]

10. THE TEMPORARY FRAMEWORK

During 2008 and 2009 the Commission adopted a number of measures to address the global economic and financial crisis, including measures aimed at facilitating companies' access to finance and reducing high risk aversion on the part of banks. The Communication on a temporary framework for state aid measures to support access to finance in the current financial and economic crisis (Temporary Framework), which applies until December 31, 2011 is of particular relevance to guarantees. It details state aid that the Commission will consider compatible with the internal market on the basis of art.107(3)(b), a provision which allows the Commission to declare compatible aid "to remedy a serious disturbance in the economy of a Member State". The Temporary Framework states: "subsidised loan guarantees for a limited period can be an appropriate and well targeted solution to give firms easier access to finance."   **9–029**

Specifically, the Temporary Framework[76] provides that subsidised loan guarantees for small and medium-sized enterprises will be compatible under art.107(3)(b) provided certain conditions are met. Notably, Member States can grant small and medium-sized enterprises a reduction of up to 15 per cent of the annual premium to be paid for new guarantees granted in accordance with safe harbour provisions set out in an annex to the Temporary Framework. However,   **9–030**

---

[73] fn.67, above at para.45.

[74] fn.67, above at para.49.

[75] Communication of the Commission, Temporary Union framework for state aid measures to support access to finance in the current financial and economic crisis [2011] O.J. C6/5.

[76] Temporary Framework (fn.70, above) at para.2.3.

any such guarantee, which may relate to both investment and working capital loans, cannot exceed 80 per cent of the loan for the duration of the loan and can only be granted until December 31, 2011. In addition, the reduction of the guarantee premium can only apply for a specified limited period following the granting of the guarantee.

9–031   Large companies are treated more restrictively. Member States may calculate the annual premium for new guarantees on the basis of the safe harbour provisions set out in the annex to the Temporary Framework, but there is no allowance for a reduction in the guarantee premium and the guarantee may relate to investment loans only.

9–032   Firms in difficulty can no longer benefit from the Temporary Framework and fall to be assessed under the Commission's guidelines on state aid for rescue and restructuring firms in difficulty.

CHAPTER 10

STATE AID IN THE AREA OF TAXATION* [1]

1. INTRODUCTION 10–001
2. GENERAL ASPECTS OF TAX COMPETITION AND STATE AID LAW 10–003
3. THE APPLICATION OF ARTICLE 107(1) TFEU IN TAX MATTERS: THE NOTION OF "AID"
   WITH RESPECT TO TAX 10–006
   General 10–006
   State and infra-state entities 10–007
   The revenue effect of a tax provision 10–009
   Changes of the general legal situation 10–010
   Tax advantage as basic prerequisite for the application of state aid rules 10–011

* Wolfgang Schön
[1] See on this topic in general: Mona Aldestam, *EC State Aid Rules Applied to Taxes—An Analysis
of the Selectivity Criterion* (Uppsala, 2005); Hanno Kube, "Nationales Steuerrecht und europäisches Beihilfenrecht" in: Ulrich Becker, Wolfgang Schön, *Steuer- und Sozialstaat im europäischen Systemwettbewerb* (Tübingen, 2005), pp.99–117 with comment by Wulf-Henning
Roth, pp.119–139; Ennio La Scala, "Il Divieto di Aiuti di Stato e le Misure di Fiscalità di
Vantaggio nel Quadro della Politica Regionale dell'Unione Europea e degli Stati Membri"
[2005] 2 *Diritto e Pratica Tributaria Internazionale*, pp.37–66; Thomas Jaeger, *Beihilfen durch
Steuern und parafiskalische Abgaben* (Vienna, 2006); Corsten Jennert/Benedikt Ellenrieder,
"Unternehmens besteuerung im Lichte des EU-Beihil Ferechts" [2011] EWS pp.305–313;
Raymond Luja, *Assessment and Recovery of Tax Incentives in the EU and the WTO: A View on
State Aids, Trade Subsidies and Direct Taxation* (Antwerp, 2003); Mirko M. Koschyk, *Steuer-
vergünstigungen als Beihilfen nach Artikel 92 EG-Vertrag* (Baden-Baden, 1999); Michael Lang,
*Die Auswirkungen des gemeinschaftsrechtlichen Beihilferechts auf das Steuerrecht, Verhandlun-
gen des 17. Österreichischen Juristentages Wien 2009, Vol.IV/1* (Vienna, 2010); idem, Das
Gibraltar-Urterl des EU 6H: Neue beihilfeacchtliche "Vorgaben für das Steuerrecht" [2011]
Ö512 pp.593–600; Koen Lenaerts, "State Aid and Direct Taxation", in: Heikki Kanninen et al.,
EU Competition Law in Context: Essays in Honour of Virpi Tiili (Oxford and Portland, Oregon,
2009), pp.291–306; Christiana HJI Panayi, "State Aid and Tax: The Third Way?" [2004] 32
Intertax, pp.283–306; Pierpaolo Rossi-Maccanico, "State Aid Review of Member States' Meas-
ures Relating to Direct Business Taxation" [2004] 3 EStAL, pp.229–251; *idem* "State Aid
Review of Business Tax Measures" [2007] 6 EStAL, pp.215–230; Conor Quigley, "General
Taxation and State Aid" in: Andrea Biondi, Piet Eeckhout, James Flynn, *The Law of State Aid
in the European Union* (Oxford, 2003), pp.207–217; *idem* "European State Aid Law and Policy"
(Oxford 2009) Ch.3 "Taxation and State Aid"; Wolfgang Schön, "Taxation and State Aid in the
European Union" [1999] CMLR 911 et seq.; *idem, Die Auswirkungen des gemeinschaftsrechtli-
chen Beihilfenrechts auf das Steuerrecht, Referate und Diskussionsbeiträge, Verhandlungen des
17. Österreichischen Juristentages Wien 2009, Vol.IV/2* (Vienna 2010), pp.21–46; Franz Philipp
Sutter, *Das EG-Beihilfenverbot und sein Durchführungsverbot in Steuersachen* (Vienna,
2005).

"Preferential" and "normal" tax treatment—the national prerogative in tax mat-
ters 10–016
The "nature or general scheme" of a tax 10–019
The "nature and general scheme" of a tax and the selectivity of tax incentives 10–025

4. THE APPLICATION OF ARTICLE 107(1) TFEU IN TAX MATTERS: THE "SELECTIVITY" OR
"SPECIFICITY" OF AN AID 10–032
General 10–032
Recipients and beneficiaries 10–033
"Certain undertakings or the production of certain goods" 10–035
"De facto selectivity" 10–038

5. TAX FINANCING OF STATE AID 10–039
6. STATE AID RULES AND "HARMFUL TAX COMPETITION" 10–041

1. INTRODUCTION

10–001   State aid in the field of taxation and other levies (fees, social security contributions and other charges) plays a major and ever-growing role in the state aid
practice of EU Member States. About 44 per cent of state aid is allocated by
means of tax measures[2]; thus it does not astonish that the *Official Journal* and the
Reports of the European Court of Justice are full of examples of the imaginative
practice of tax aids implemented by all Member States. The Commission[3] and the
Court[4] have scrutinised state aids in forms of tax measures from the beginning of
their work under arts 107 et seq. TFEU. Thus, EU law performs—alongside
WTO law[5]—a major role in disciplining the national legislator's tendency to
regulate economic behaviour by tax incentives.[6]

Nevertheless, it was not until 1998 that the Commission established a systematic approach to the problem of state aids and tax expenditures. This change of
attitude derived from two sources: on the one hand, the Commission's work in
the field of the harmonisation of direct taxation has taken a different course since
the mid-1990s under the auspices of Commissioner (as he then was) Mario
Monti.[7] In 1996, the Commission presented the results of an elaborate investigation on the economic effects of competition between Member States with respect

---

[2] See the Commission's "Scoreboard" on *http://ec.europa.eu/competition/state_aid/studies_
reports/ws5_2.xls*.
[3] Response Burgbacher [1963] O.J. 2235/63.
[4] Case 30/59 *Gezamenlijke Steenkolenmijnen* [1961] E.C.R. 5.
[5] For a comparison of WTO law and EC law in the context of tax subsidies see Hanno E. Kube,
"Competence Conflicts and Solutions: National Tax Exemptions and Transnational Controls"
[2002] 9 *Columbia Journal of European Law*, pp.79–108; Wolfgang Schön, "World Trade
Organization Law and Tax Law" [2004] *IBFD Bulletin* 283 et seq.; Michael Lang, Judith
Herdin, Ines Hofbauer (eds), *WTO and Direct Taxation* (Vienna, 2005). See para.6–025.
[6] For a Comparison with US practice see Deborah H. Schenk, "The Cuno Case: a Comparison of
U.S. Subsidies and European State Aid" [2006] 5 EStAL, pp.3–8; Tracy A. Kaye, "The Gentle
Art of Corporate Seduction: Tax Incentives in the United States and the European Union"
[2008], 57 U. Kan. L. Rev. pp.93 et seq.
[7] See Monti, "Editorial" [1997] *EC Tax Review* 2; Monti, "Editorial" [1998] EC Tax Review
2.

to their tax systems.[8] In 1997, the Commission proposed that the ECOFIN Council adopt a common policy to fight "unfair" instruments of tax competition between them.[9]

It has become common practice that the proceedings against harmful tax competition under this Code of Conduct be supported by an extensive use of arts 107 et seq. TFEU in tax matters.[10]

Parallel to the "unfair tax competition" project, the Commission intensified its general work on tax incentives. This effort resulted in the notice of November 11, 1998,[11] which presented the first fully fledged description of the Commission's approach to tax incentives. This notice not only supplied the relevant public authorities and private enterprises with a reliable basis for their administrative and economic behaviour, it was also intended to boost the Commission's policy in this field. In 2004, the Commission presented an extensive report on the work done on the implementation of the 1998 notice.[12] Nevertheless, it must be recognised that the 1998 notice did not change the relevant legal basis under the Treaty and that tax incentives which were introduced before 1998 are not "grandfathered" with respect to the application of art.107 TFEU in the context of tax law.[13]

    10–002

2. GENERAL ASPECTS OF TAX COMPETITION AND STATE AID LAW

National sovereignty and fiscal federalism. EU law leaves to the Member States plenty of room for manoeuvring in the field of taxation. First of all, the power to tax (and the corresponding budgetary power) is still in the hands of the national governments and parliaments (notwithstanding the budgetary restrictions of EMU). The fundamental decision of whether or not an economic transaction is subject to tax lies within the scope of national sovereignty.[14] The only exemptions are VAT and some major consumption taxes like tobacco tax, petrol tax and alcohol tax: the Member States are bound to levy VAT and those particular consumption taxes within a certain corridor of tax rates in order to

    10–003

---

[8] Commission, "Report on the development of tax systems, Taxation in the European Union" COM(96) 546 final [1997] intertax 23 et seq.

[9] "Towards Tax Coordination in the European Union; a Package to Tackle Harmful Tax Competition" COM(97) 495 final of October 15, 1997.

[10] Commission, fn.8, above, art.6.10.; Code of Conduct, fn.9, above, p.1 and Annex J; Easson "Harmful Tax Competition: The EU and OECD Responses Compared" [1998] *EC Tax Journal* 1, et seq.

[11] [1998] O.J. C384/3.

[12] "Report on the implementation of the Commission notice on the application of the state aid rules to measures relating to direct business taxation", February 9, 2004 Com (2004) 434 (2004 Report), see also: European Commission, Communication "Promoting Good Governance in Tax Matters", 28th April 2009, COM (2009) 201 final at para.2.1.

[13] AG Kokott, Joined Cases C–183/02P and C–187/02P *Daewoo* [2004] E.C.R. I–10609 at para.51.

[14] Quigley, "General Taxation", fn.1, above, p.207.

achieve a "level playing field" for goods and services and to contribute to the Community's budget, part of which is funded by the Member States' revenues from VAT.[15] But for the rest of the indirect taxes (excise duties) and the large bulk of direct taxes (income tax, corporation tax, inheritance tax, wealth tax, etc.) the Member States may exercise discretion regarding the introduction or abolition of tax burdens.[16] Articles 113, 114 (2) and 115 TFEU underscore this national prerogative by prohibiting legislative action of the European Community in tax matters unless there is unanimity amongst all Member States.[17]

Against this background, there can be no doubt that it is for the Member States to decide whether to increase or decrease the overall tax burden within their jurisdiction. This is part of sound "fiscal federalism"[18] which gives the economic subjects the choice to move their activities to a jurisdiction with a high level of taxation (and a high quality of public services) or to move to a country with modest taxes and budgets. EU law also leaves to the Member States the discretion to shift the tax burden from direct taxes to indirect taxes and vice versa (as far as the harmonisation level of VAT is not affected) in order to change the tax conditions of investment and consumption respectively. Moreover, the Member States are not prevented from raising revenue by introducing special consumption taxes which will, by their very nature, function as a tax disincentive with respect to the concerned goods or services.[19]

10–004   Discrimination and restriction of cross-border activities. The legal situation is more stringent when national tax legislation distinguishes between domestic and foreign persons, goods, services or capital. In the case of the free movement of goods, the TFEU itself is clear: art.30 TFEU prohibits the introduction of customs duties or any charges having equivalent effect on import or export of goods, and art.110 TFEU provides that no Member State shall impose, directly or indirectly, on the products of other Member States any internal taxation of any kind in excess of that imposed directly or indirectly on similar domestic products.[20] In the fields of cross-border services, establishment or capital transfer we find no such explicit provisions, but the European Court of Justice (ECJ) has in many decisions established the rule that the sovereignty of the Member States in

---

[15] Farmer and Lyal, *EC Tax Law* (Oxford, 1994), pp.85 et seq., 200 et seq.; Terra and Wattel, *European Tax Law*, 5th edn (Alphen aan den Rijn: 2008) 125 et seq.

[16] Joined Cases 142/80 and 143/80 *Salengo* [1981] E.C.R. 1413 at para.21 (indirect taxation); Case T–67/94 *Ladbroke Racing* [1998] E.C.R. II–1 at para.54 (direct taxation); AG Mischo, Case C–143/99 *Adria-Wien Pipeline* [2001] E.C.R. I–8365 at para.28; Case T–211/04 and T–215/04 *Gibraltar* [2008] E.C.R. II–3745 at para.146; AG Jääskinen, Joined Cases C–106/09P and C–107/09P *Gibraltar* [2011] n.y.r. at paras 137–145.

[17] Schön, "Tax Competition in Europe—The Legal Perspective" [2000] EC Tax Review 90 et seq., at 101 et seq.

[18] Oates, *Fiscal Federalism* (New York, 1972).

[19] Schön, "Der freie Warenverkehr, die Steuerhoheit der Mitgliedstaaten und der Systemgedanke im europäischen Steuerrecht" [2001] *Europarecht*, pp.216–233 and pp.341–362.

[20] Schön, see fn.19, above.

tax matters does not justify national tax rules which result in the discrimination or unjustified restriction of cross-border activities covered by the fundamental freedoms of the TFEU.[21] The same is true where the cross-border trade in goods is restricted by means of direct taxation (which is not covered by arts 30 and 110 TFEU). Thus, any measure which discriminates against or restricts foreign-source capital, goods, services or establishments without justification falls foul of arts 34, 49, 56 and 63 TFEU. These provisions are likewise relevant with respect to general tax measures (e.g. discriminatory rules for foreign branches or subsidiaries irrespective of the trade or business carried out by this branch or subsidiary) and to specific tax measures (e.g. tax deductibility of insurance premiums when paid to domestic insurers).

State aid rules in the context of the EU Treaty. While the fundamental **10–005** freedoms do not distinguish between general and specific tax measures which have discriminating or restrictive effect, this distinction is paramount in the area of state aid law under arts 107 et seq. TFEU.[22] This is due to the fact that art.107(1) TFEU prohibits:

"any aid granted by a Member State or through State resources in any form whatsoever which distorts or threatens to distort competition by favouring certain undertakings or the production of certain goods [. . .], in so far as it affects trade between Member States."

Thus, it is of essential importance to differentiate "selective" tax incentives from general rules which are either not "aids" at all or which apply not only to "certain" undertakings or goods but to the whole economy. These "general measures" cannot be challenged in the context of art.107(1) TFEU.[23] If they lead to major distortions of the competitive situation within the European Union, the Commission and the Council are in the position to act under arts 116 and 117.[24] In order to distinguish cases under art.107(1) TFEU from those under arts 116 and 117 TFEU it suffices to apply the criteria laid down in art.107(1) TFEU.[25]

---

[21] See Case 270/83 *Commission v France* [1986] E.C.R. 273; Case C–279/93 *Schumacker* [1995] E.C.R. I–225; Case C–446/03 *Marks & Spencer* [2005] E.C.R. I–10837; Case C–311/08 *SGI* [2010] Unreported.

[22] Kelyn Bacon, "State Aids and General Measures" [1997] *Yearbook of European Law* 269.

[23] Quigley, "General Taxation", see fn.1, above, pp.207–8; Roth, see fn.1, above, pp.123–30.

[24] Case C–174/02 *Streekgewest Westelijk Noord-Brabant* [2005] E.C.R. I–85 at para.24; AG Geelhoed, Case C–88/03 *Portugal v Commission* [2006] E.C.R. I–7115 at paras 46, 58; AG Geelhoed, Case C–308/01 *GIL Insurance* [2004] E.C.R. I–4777 at paras 58–67; AG Geelhoed, Case C–174/02 *Streekgewest Westelijk Noord-Brabant* [2005] E.C.R. I–85 at paras 28–9; AG Léger, Joined Cases C–182/03 and C–217/03 *Belgium v Commission* [2006] E.C.R. I–5479 at paras 231–3; Terra and Wattel, see fn.15 above, pp.21 et seq.

[25] Decision 2003/515/EC [2003] O.J. L180/52 at para.78; for a close analysis see Sutter (see fn.1 above), pp.31–8.

It is not easy to give a coherent picture of the interdependence between the fundamental freedoms and state aid law in tax matters. In this context we have to distinguish between various situations.

As a starting point, there can be no doubt that a specific tax measure can infringe both the rules on fundamental freedoms and state aid law.[26] In 1985 the Court declared incompatible with both art.28 EC (now art.34 TFEU) and art.87(1) EC (now art.107(1) TFEU) a French tax provision which granted a tax deferment to press undertakings (selective aid) which were supplied by domestic printing companies (discrimination).[27] In 2000, the Court found that a German tax rule which provided specific incentives for the acquisition of small and medium-sized businesses in the *New Länder* infringed both art.43 EC (now art.49 TFEU) and art.87(1) EC (now art.107(1) TFEU).[28] For indirect taxation it has been made clear that taxes on specific goods neither violate art.107(1) EC nor art.30 or 110 TFEU.[29] Another example which has been mentioned in the literature concerns tax provisions which restrict a tax allowance for insurance premiums (selective aid) to premiums paid to domestic insurers[30] (discrimination). Yet an unresolved issue remains: if (selective) state aid is declared compatible with the internal market under art.107(2) and (3) TFEU, it should be accepted that the necessarily inherent discrimination against investments in other regions of the European Union cannot be challenged under the fundamental freedoms—otherwise the sophisticated approach of arts 107 and 108 TFEU would be undermined.[31]

Specific problems are brought about by the relationship between state aid law, fundamental freedoms and the Treaty rules on customs and excise duties in the specific situation of a direct aid for domestic producers financed through the imposition of levies on domestic and foreign-source products. In these cases, we find firstly a violation of art.30 TFEU or art.110 TFEU. In addition, the application of the state aid rules has to take into account that the foreign competitors

---

[26] Case C–169/08 *Regione Sardegna* [2009] E.C.R. I–10821 at paras 19–66; AG Kokott, Case C–169/08 *Regione Sardegna* [2009] E.C.R. I–10821 at paras 26–155; Martha O'Brien, "Company Taxation, State aid and fundamental freedoms: is the next step enhanced co-operation?" [2005] 30 *European Law Review* 218 et seq., at pp.231–3; Pierpaolo Rossi-Maccanico, "Community Review of Direct Business Tax Measures: Selectivity, Discrimination and Restrictions" [2009] EStAL pp.489 et seq. *Michael Lang,* "Seminar J: Steuerrecht, Grundfreiheiten und Beihilfeverbot", *Internationales Steuerrecht* (2010) pp.570–580.

[27] Case 18/84 *Commission v France* [1985] E.C.R. 1339 at para.13.

[28] Case C–156/98 *Germany v Commission* [2000] E.C.R. I–6857 at paras 72–88.

[29] Case T–359/04 *British Aggregates Association* [2010] Unreported at paras 91–102; AG Tizzano, Joined Cases C–393/04 and C–41/05 *Air Liquide* [2006] E.C.R. I–5293 at paras 77–82 and paras 83–93; AG Saggio, Case C–254/97 *Société Baxter* [1999] E.C.R. I–4809 at paras 20–23; AG Alber, Case C–204/97 *Portugal v Commission* [2001] E.C.R. I–3175 at paras 87–8.

[30] Dassesse, "Tax Deductibility of Insurance Premiums: A case of State Aid for Insurance Companies?" [1995/96] *EC Tax Journal* 15 et seq. at 19; Thömmes, "Tax Deductibility for Payments made to Locally Established Industries—A Case of State Aid Prohibited under the EC Treaty?" [1996] intertax 25.

[31] Quigley, "General Taxation", see fn.1 above, pp.216–17; Rossi-Maccanico, fn.26, above, pp.493 et seq.; see also Andreas Bartosch, "EU-Beihilfenrecht" (Munich 2009) "Einleitung" para.5.

contribute to the financing of domestic aid, thus giving rise to a cumulative test.[32] Whether the "financing" side of the aid is also covered by art.107(1) TFEU is dealt with below.[33]

Nevertheless, it must be borne in mind that state aid given to domestic business under arts 107 et seq. TFEU does not fall within the scope of the fundamental freedoms if foreign businesses are not concerned at all by the tax in question and the tax incentive only shifts the tax burden between domestic groups of taxpayers. Thus, a reduction of the corporate tax rate for domestic insurers (including branches and subsidiaries of foreign companies) may constitute state aid with respect to art.107 TFEU, but it does not entail a discrimination or restriction of the activities of companies based in other Member States simply because they are not at all subject to domestic corporation tax.

On the other hand, it seems doubtful whether a tax incentive aimed at the production of certain goods or services but accessible both to domestic and foreign economic agents falls under art.107 TFEU. This may be the case where a Member State grants private persons a tax allowance for building costs in order to boost private house building and to support the building industry but does not restrict this tax allowance to houses built by domestic companies.[34] This measure may be identified as a selective tax incentive but it is questionable whether it does "affect trade between Member States", which would be a prerequisite for the applicability of European state aid law. Nevertheless, art.107(2)(a) TFEU makes it clear that even non-discriminating measures qualify as state aid as well; this paragraph declares compatible with the internal market "aid having social character, granted to individual consumers, provided that such aid is granted without discrimination related to the origin of the products concerned". This exemption would be superfluous if non-discriminating state aid were not covered by art.107(1) TFEU at all. Furthermore, one has to accept the fact that a tax reduction which covers all domestic and foreign undertakings producing certain goods may still distort competition with respect to competing products, e.g. coal with respect to other forms of energy sources.[35] The Court held in *Salengo*[36] and

---

[32] Case 47/69 *France v Commission* [1970] E.C.R. 487, at paras 11–14; Case 77/72 *Capolongo* [1973] E.C.R. 611 at paras 7 et seq.; Case 94/74 *IGAV/ENCC* [1975] E.C.R. 699 at para.18; Case 78/76 *Steinike and Weinlig* [1977] E.C.R. 595 at paras 25 et seq.; Case 105/76 *Interzuccheri* [1977] E.C.R. 1029 at para.10; Case 73/79 *Commission v Italy* [1980] E.C.R. 1533 at paras 6 et seq.; Case C–78/82 *Compagnie commerciale de l'Ouest* [1992] E.C.R. I–1847 at paras 20 et seq.; Case C–17/91 *Lornoy* [1992] E.C.R. I–6523 at paras 16 et seq.; Case C–149,150/91 *Sanders* [1992] E.C.R. I–3899 at para.20; Case C–266/91 *CELBI* [1993] E.C.R. I–4337 paras 8 et seq.; Case C–206/06 *Essent Netwerk* [2008] E.C.R. I–5497 at paras 40–57, 58–96; see also Decision 2000/116/EC [2000] O.J. L34/20 at paras 63–65; Decision 2000/206/EC [2000] O.J. L63/27, 31; above 3–107.

[33] See section 5.

[34] Frick, *Einkommensteuerliche Steuervergünstigungen und Beihilfeverbot nach dem EG-Vertrag* (Sinzheim, 1994), pp.66 et seq.

[35] Evans, *EC Law of State Aid* (Oxford, 1997), p.5.

[36] Joined Cases 142/80 and 143/80 *Salengo* [1981] E.C.R. 1413 at para.28; in Case C–6/97 *Italy v Commission* [1999] E.C.R. I–2981 at paras 28 et seq. The Italian Government had introduced a mineral oil tax reduction for domestic transport enterprises and a compensation mechanism for foreign transport enterprises. As the compensation mechanism was not executed properly, the Court did not accept it as a justification.

France v Commission[37] that state aid by means of taxation is never justifiable if it involves any discrimination of foreign source products. From this, we can draw the conclusion that a non-discriminating tax incentive would still qualify as state aid under art.107(1) TFEU which can be declared compatible with the internal market according to art.107(2) and (3) TFEU.

Finally, the fundamental freedoms are not affected when a Member State gives preferential treatment to foreign-based capital and companies. This is the main feature of the "unfair tax competition"—debate which is focused on tax rules designed to attract foreign capital and other investments by offering conditions which are advantageous in relation to the conditions of the domestic taxpayer.[38] As "reverse discrimination" is—as conventional wisdom has it—not a matter of the fundamental freedoms but of domestic (constitutional) law,[39] one must establish whether arts 107 et seq. TFEU constitute any restriction on this practice. Again, one must distinguish between "general" and "selective" tax measures. If a tax incentive is offered to a single foreign company or to foreign companies engaged in a certain trade, the tax incentive will fall within the scope of arts 107 et seq. TFEU. But it is doubtful whether a tax rule which offers preferential treatment to foreign investors irrespective of their activities must be regarded as a selective state aid within the context of arts 107 et seq.. A tax regime which is organised in order to levy taxes on domestic production factors while leaving cross-border activities out of the picture, might both constitute "harmful tax competition" and can fall foul of art.107(1) TFEU.[40]

3. THE NOTION OF "AID" WITH RESPECT TO TAX

General

10–006   Article 107(1) TFEU declares incompatible with the internal market:

"any aid granted by a Member State or through State resources in any form whatsoever which distorts or threatens to distort competition by favouring certain undertakings or the production of certain goods [. . .], in so far as it affects trade between Member States."[41]

The basic situation covered by this article is one where the state reaches into its pocket and hands out more or less money or other funding to a single enterprise or a certain group of enterprises, thus interfering in a market otherwise

[37] Case 18/84 *Commission v France* [1985] E.C.R. 1339 at para.13.
[38] Code of Conduct, see fn.9, above, Annex B; OECD-Report *Harmful Tax Competition—An Emerging Global Issue* (Paris, 1998) 26; Pinto, "EU and OECD to Fight Harmful Tax Competition: Has the Right Path Been Undertaken?" [1998] intertax 386 et seq., 394 et seq.
[39] Epiney, *Umgekehrte Diskriminierungen* (Cologne, 1994), p.339.
[40] Joined Cases C–106/09P and C–107/09P *Gibraltar* at paras 85–110.
[41] See also art.61(1) EEA and the first judgment of the EFTA-Court on state aid in tax matters: Joined Cases E–5/04 and E–7/04 *Fesil and Finnfjord* at para.76.

not affected by the state. In the area of tax legislation and administration, the situation is quite the opposite in two respects: in this context, the state is present everywhere, as all enterprises have to comply with the rules of a comprehensive tax system covering (nearly) all sorts of economic transactions. In tax matters, free competition is not guaranteed by public non-interference, but on the contrary by a wide-reaching collection of taxes from everyone whose economic situation is comparable to that of other taxpayers. An aid distorting the competitive structure of a market is therefore created by "the absence of a gain for the State in question".[42]

Therefore, it is accepted that the application of the state aid rules to the tax area requires some specific instruments and benchmarks. This specific analysis is not restricted to "taxes" in a narrow sense, meaning public charges levied by the state or sub-national government entities without consideration. It has also to be extended to other public charges like social security contributions,[43] capital duties,[44] road tolls[45] or mining royalties.[46]

State and infra-state entities

Tax incentives falling within the scope of art.107(1) TFEU can result from tax **10–007**
legislation at a different level of domestic legislation. Not only is the "federal" or "central" authority bound by art.107(1) TFEU, but legislative or administrative bodies at a sub-national level are also obliged to comply with this provision.[47] Even traditional guarantees of "fiscal autonomy" which have been granted to sub-national regions are not exempted from the applicability of the state aid rules in tax matters.[48] Moreover, independent public entities in the social security sector are also covered by the rules under art.107(1) TFEU.

Nevertheless, the allocation of legislative power to sub-national levels plays a role since the question of whether a geographically limited advantage granted to a taxpayer is "selective" in nature is determined by the territorial scope of

---

[42] AG Léger, Case C–159/01 *Netherlands v Commission* [2004] E.C.R. I–4461 at para.84.
[43] Case C–378/98 *Commission v Belgium* [2001] E.C.R. I–5107 at paras 2 et seq.; Case C–256/97 *DMT* [1999] E.C.R. I–3913 at para.18; Case C–251/97 *France v Commission* [1999] E.C.R. I–6639 at para.36; Joined Cases C–71/09P, C–73/09P and C–76/09P *Hotel Cipriani* [2011] Unreported at paras 90–102; Joined Cases T–254/00, T–270/00 and T–277/00 *Hotel Cipriani* [2008] E.C.R. II–3269 paras 174–176.
[44] AG Léger, Joined Cases C–182/03 and C–217/03 *Belgium v Commission* [2006] E.C.R. I–5479 at paras 272–6.
[45] Decision 2004/261/EC [2004] O.J. L81/80 at para.28.
[46] Case C–390/98 *Banks* [2001] E.C.R. I–6117 at paras 41–4; Decision 2011/88/EU [2011] O.J. L34/55 at paras 72–88.
[47] Commission, 2004 Report (see fn.12 above) at para.18; Decision 2000/620/EC [2000] O.J. L260/37 at para.57; Decision 2003/227/EC [2003] O.J. L91/23 at para.79; Decision 2002/937/EC [2002] O.J. L329/22 at para.39.
[48] Joined Cases T–92/00 and T–103/00 *Territorio Histórico de Álava* [2002] E.C.R. II–1385 at para.57, Joined Cases T–127/99, T–129/99 and T–148/99 *Territorio Histórico de Álava* [2002] E.C.R. II–1275 at para.142; Joined Cases T–346/99, T–347/99 and T–348/99 *Territorio Histórico de Álava* [2002] E.C.R. II–4259 at para.62; Joined Cases T–227/01 to T–229/01, T–265/01, T–266/01 and T–270/01 *Territorio Histórico de Álava* [2009] E.C.R. II–3029 at para.178.

jurisdiction exercised by the respective legislator.[49] This geographically limited sovereignty in tax matters has to be accepted as being part of traditional "fiscal federalism" at a sub-national level. In Germany, each municipality has the right to set its own tax rate with respect to business tax—this is due to the traditional fiscal autonomy of local communities and it should not be attacked under art.107(1) TFEU.[50]

10–008   In several recent proceedings concerning the Azores, the Basque Country and Gibraltar, the European judges (followed by an abundant wealth of academic writing[51]) have clarified the requirements for this competence of regional or local communities to decide on different tax rates or tax bases within their own budgetary framework.[52] In general, the autonomous power of sub-national units to set their own tax rules does not seem to be controversial.[53] Nevertheless, the Court has made clear that regional state aid in the area of taxation cannot escape

[49] See below, section 4.
[50] Bacon, fn.22, above, p.301.
[51] Christoph Arhold, "Steuerhoheit auf regionaler oder lokaler Ebene und der europäische Bei-hilfenbegriff", *Europäische Zeitschrift für Wirtschaftsrecht* (2006), pp.717 et seq.; Daniel Armesto, "The ECJ's Judgment regarding the Tax Autonomy of the Basque Country", *European Taxation*, 2009, pp.11 et seq.; Andreas Bartosch, "With Greetings from the Azores", [2006] 5 EStAL, pp.667 et seq.; Holger Bielesz, "Judgment of 11 September 2008 in Joined Cases C–428/06 to C–434–06", [2009] 8 EStAL, pp.383 et seq.; Julie Bousin/Jorge Piernas, "Developments in the Notion of Selectivity", [2008] 7 EStAL, pp.634 et seq.; Vittorio di Bucci, "Some Brief Comments on the Court's Judgment in Case C–88/03, Portugal v Commission (Azores)", The European State Aid Law Institute (ed), *New Developments in European State Aid Law 2006* (Berlin, 2006), pp.53 et seq.; José Luís da Cruz Vilaça, "Regional Selectivity and State Aid: The Azores Case", The European State Aid Law Institute (ed), *New Developments in European State Aid Law 2006* (Berlin, 2006), pp.15 et seq.; Bartlomiej Kurcz, "How Selective is Selectivity? A few thoughts on regional selectivity", [2007] 66 Cambridge Law Journal, pp.313 et seq.; William Lindsay-Poulsen, "Regional Autonomy, Geographic Selectivity and Fiscal Aid: Between 'The Rock' and a Hard Place", [2008] E.C.L.R., pp.43 et seq.; Raymond Luja, "Fiscal Autonomy, Investment Funds and State Aid: A Follow-Up", [2009] European Taxation pp.369 et seq.; Phedon Nicolaides, "The Boundaries of Tax Autonomy", [2006] 5 EStAL, pp.119 et seq.; Luís Miguel Romão, "Banco Comercial dos Açores v. Commission (T–75/03)", [2010] 9 EStAL, pp.691 et seq.; Pierpaolo Rossi-Maccanico, "Gibraltar and the unsettled Limits of Selectivity in Fiscal Aids", [2009] 8 EStAL, p.63 et seq.; Michael Sánchez Rydelski, "Geographically limited national tax rate variations and State aid", [2006] European Law Reporter, pp.402 et seq.; Edoardo Traversa, "Is there still room left in EU Law for tax autonomy of Member States' regional and local authorities?", 20 EC Tax Review (2011), pp.4–15 Carlos Urraca Caviedes, "La Sélectivité Régionale", Rodríguez Iglesias et al. (eds), *EC State Aid Law* (Kluwer: 2008), pp.125 et seq.; Carsten Zatschler, "Review of the Judgment in Case C–88/03, Portugal v Commission (Azores Tax Regime)" [2006] 5 EStAL, pp.779 et seq.
[52] Case C–88/03 *Portugal v Commission* [2006] E.C.R. I–7115 at paras 62–84; AG Geelhoed, Case C–88/03 *Portugal v Commission* [2006] E.C.R. I–7115 at paras 51–56; Joined Cases C–428/06 to C–434/06 *UGT–Rioja* [2008] E.C.R. I–6747 at paras 45–144; AG Kokott, Joined Cases C–428/06 to C–434/06 *UGT Rioja* [2008] E.C.R. I–6747 at paras 65–117; Joined Cases T–211/04 and T–215/04 *Gibraltar* [2008] E.C.R. II–3745 at paras 83–116; Case T–75/03 *Banco Comercial dos Açores* [2009] E.C.R. II–143* at paras 69–84; AG Jääskinen, Joined Cases C–106/09P and C–107/09P *Gibraltar* [2011] Unreported at paras 54–62.
[53] Joined Cases T–92/00 and T–103/00 *Territorio Histórico de Álava* [2002] E.C.R. II–1385 at paras 27, 44–5; Joined Cases T–127/99, T–129/99 and T–148/99 *Territorio Histórico de Álava* [2002] E.C.R. II–1275 at para.146; Joined Cases T–346/99, T–347/99 and T–348/99 *Territorio Histórico de Álava* [2002] E.C.R. II–4259 at para.52; Joined Cases T–269/99, T–271/99 and T–272/99 *Territorio Histórico de Guipúzcoa* [2002] E.C.R. II–4217 at para.56; Luja, see fn.1, above, pp.61–3.

control under art.107(1) TFEU just by shifting legislative power to the sub-national level. Therefore the Court requires that the lower-level state entity enjoys full "institutional, procedural and financial autonomy". A beneficial tax rule by a regional or local government must not be procedurally and financially "embedded" in policy measures of the central or federal government which compensate for the loss of revenue; otherwise, this tax reduction will be regarded as state aid in the context of the whole public entity. Moreover, any infra-state tax provision which cannot be attacked from a "regional" point of view constitutes prohibited state aid if it involves other elements of selectivity (e.g. sectoral selectivity).[54]

The revenue effect of a tax provision

Secondly, it should be noted that the overall revenue effect of a specific tax measure is not decisive when the state aid character of a provision has to be ascertained.[55] It may well be that a state allocates tax breaks to outside investors or other groups of taxpayers in order to fuel investment in its territory, thus giving rise to a higher revenue in the broader picture. Nevertheless, the Court has always made clear that such indirect economic and budgetary effects of a specific tax provision do not change the character of the tax incentive as an "aid" granted from "State resources".[56]

10–009

Changes of the general legal situation

The prerequisite that the state has to forego part of its revenue has several consequences for the application of art.107(1) TFEU. First of all, it is now established that any improvement of the general economic and legal "playing field", which does not in itself inflict any cost upon the state is not covered by art.107(1) TFEU. The leading case is *Sloman Neptun*[57] in which the Court dealt with the question of whether a deregulation of labour law which led to a significant reduction of wages in the shipping business could qualify as aid. Although the reduction of wages resulted in a reduction of income tax and social security contributions, this was not regarded as state aid because the prevalent

10–010

---

[54] Case C–169/08 *Regione Sardegna* [2009] E.C.R. I–10821 at paras 59–64; Joined Cases T–211/04 and T–215/04 *Gibraltar* [2008] E.C.R. II–3745 at para.79.

[55] Lenaerts, see fn.1, above, pp.296–297; Luja, see fn.1 above, pp.44–6.

[56] Case C–159/01 *Netherlands v Commission* [2004] E.C.R. I–4461 at para.51; Joined Cases T–92/00 and T–103/00 *Territorio Histórico de Álava* [2002] E.C.R. II–1385 at paras 61–2; Joined Cases T–269/99, T–271/99 and T–272/99 *Territorio Histórico de Guipúzcoa* [2002] E.C.R. II–4217 at para.64; Joined Cases T–227/01 to T–229/01, T–265/01, T–266/01 and T–270/01 *Territorio Histórico de Álava* [2009] E.C.R. II–3029 at para.130; AG Léger, Joined Cases C–182/03 and C–217/03 *Belgium v Commission* [2006] E.C.R. I–5479 at paras 307–9; Commission, 2004 Report, see fn.12, above, at paras 19–20; Decision 2005/77/EC [2005] O.J. L29/24 at paras 58–9; Decision 2004/76/EC [2004] O.J. L23/1 at paras 58–9; Decision 2003/515/EC [2003] O.J. L180/52 at para.84; Decision 2004/77/EC [2004] O.J. L23/14 at paras 51–2.

[57] Joined Cases 72/91 and 73/91 *Sloman Neptun* [1993] E.C.R. I–887.

consequence of the change in labour law was the reduction of the salary which was borne by the seamen and not by the state.[58]

This line of judgments has been reinforced in *PreussenElektra* where the Court did not regard cross-subsidisation in the energy sector as state aid even if the state provided for a mandatory transfer of funds between private entities and suffered a loss of tax revenue as an indirect consequence.[59] The classification changes when these surcharges are to be transferred to a state-run fund which is meant to cover transformation costs for the involved energy companies.[60] In another judgment[61] the Court also made it clear that a change in insolvency law which grants insolvent enterprises protection against its creditors is not in itself state aid even where the collection of taxes is also restricted. Only when the new insolvency law specifically grants relief from tax claims to particular undertakings with large tax debts towards the state, is its qualification as a state aid possible.[62]

Tax advantage as basic prerequisite for the application of state aid rules

10–011   **Exceptional tax benefit.** In tax cases, the prerequisite stated in art.107(1) TFEU that aid must be "granted by a Member State or through State resources" is fulfilled not by direct funding but by the budgetary restraint of the state to levy charges. According to the ECJ, all "measures which, in various forms, mitigate the charges which are normally included in the budget of an undertaking" are recognised as state aid.[63] This includes all tax rules providing relief from the

---

[58] Case 72, 73/91 *Sloman Neptun* [1993] E.C.R. I–887 at para.21; concurring Soltesz, "Die 'Belastung des Staatshaushalts' als Tatbestandsmerkmal einer Beihilfe i.S. des Art. 92 I EGV" [1998] *Europäische Zeitschrift für Wirtschaftsrecht* 747; Conor Quigley, "*European State Aid Law*", see fn.1, above, pp.23–24; dissenting Slotboom, "State Aid in Community Law: A Broad or Narrow Definition?" [1995] *European Law Review* 289.

[59] Case C–379/98 *PreussenElektra* [2001] E.C.R. I–2099 at paras 54–67; see also AG Jacobs Case C–379/98 *PreussenElektra* [2001] E.C.R. I–2099 at paras 114–59, 162; Leigh Hancher, "Towards a New Definition of a State Aid under European Law: Is there a new Concept of State Aid emerging?" [2003] 2 EStAL 365–375 at 368–369.

[60] Case C–206/06 *Essent Netwerk* [2008] E.C.R. I–5497 at para.74; AG Mengozzi, Case C–206/06 *Essent Netwerk* [2008] E.C.R. I–5497 at paras 75–118.

[61] Case C–200/97 *Ecotrade* [1998] E.C.R. I–7907 at para.34.

[62] Case C–200/97 *Ecotrade* [1998] E.C.R. I–7907 at para.38; see also Case C–480/98 *Spain v Commission* [2000] E.C.R. I–8717 at para.18; Case C–295/97 *Piaggio* [1999] E.C.R. I–3735 at para.37.

[63] Case C–75/97 *Belgium v Commission* [1999] E.C.R. I–3671 at para.23; Case C–390/98 *Banks* [2001] E.C.R. I–6117 at para.30; Case C–53/00 *Ferring* [2001] E.C.R. I–9067 at para.15; Case C–308/01 *GIL Insurance* [2004] E.C.R. I–4777 at para.69; Case C–143/99 *Adria-Wien-Pipeline* [2001] E.C.R. I–8365 at para.38; Case C–251/97 *France v Commission* [1999] E.C.R. I–6639 at para.35; Case C–295/97 *Piaggio* [1999] E.C.R. I–3735 at para.34; Case C–5/01 *Belgium v Commission* [2002] E.C.R. I–11991 at para.32; Case C–276/02 *Spain v Commission* [2004] E.C.R. I–8091 at para.24; Case C–66/02 *Italy v Commission* [2005] E.C.R. I–10901 at para.77; Case C–156/98 *Germany v Commission* [2000] E.C.R. I–6857 at para.25; Joined Cases C–128/03 and C–129/03 *AEM SpA* [2005] E.C.R. I–2861 at para.38; Joined Cases C–393/04 and C–41/05 *Air Liquide* [2006] E.C.R. I–5293 at paras 29–30.

"normal" level of taxation for such business. Therefore, it is common ground that this form of advantage qualifies as a state aid in the context of EU law.[64]

State aid in the tax sector can be administered by the legislator itself (even where it provides for binding rules) and by the tax administration where it exercises a discretionary power of its own. It comes in various forms and guises[65]: tax advantages can consist of fully fledged tax exemptions,[66] reduced tax rates, tax holidays, investment allowances, investment credits, accelerated depreciation,[67] tax-free reserves[68] and so on.[69] The tax reductions can be limited[70] or serve transitional purposes.[71] They can consist of specific income measurement rules,[72] the postponement of taxable events by granting "roll-over relief"[73] or a tax relief for reinvested profits.[74] In international matters they can also refer to the application of advantageous rules for international tax allocation ("transfer pricing").[75] When it comes to tax rules applying to corporate groups, the assessment of the "advantageous" character of the tax rule has to be made at the individual level of the taxable company, not at the level of the group as a whole.[76]

It is not necessary that the state aims at financing a specific operation or investment by the taxpayer,[77] but such direct nexus may well support the

[64] Case 70/72 *Commission v Germany* [1973] E.C.R. 813 at para.2; Case C–387/92 *Banco Exterior de Espana* [1994] E.C.R. I–877 at para.13; Case T–106/95 *FFSA* [1997] E.C.R. II–229 at para.168; Case C–200/97 *Ecotrade* [1998] E.C.R. I–7907 at para.34; AG Jääskinen, Joined Cases C–106/09P and C–107/09P *Gibraltar* [2011] Unreported at paras 155–175; Evans, see fn.35 above, 27 et seq.; Craig/de Búrca, *EU Law* 4th edn (Oxford, 2008) 1087; Terra and Wattel, see fn.15, above, p.21; Baudenbacher, *A Brief Guide to European State Aid Law* (London, 1997) pp.6 et seq.; Götz, "Subventionsrecht" in: Dauses (ed), *Handbuch des EU-Wirtschaftsrechts* (Munich, looseleaf, 2011), para.H.III.3; Bacon, see fn.22, above, pp.279 et seq.; Lenaerts, see fn.1, above, pp.295.

[65] For an overview see Koschyk, (see fn.1, above), pp.105–43.

[66] Case C–66/02 *Italy v Commission* [2005] E.C.R. I–10901 at para.78; AG Léger, Joined Cases C–182/03 and C–217/03 *Belgium v Commission* [2006] E.C.R. I–5479 at paras 267–271; Joined Cases T–195/01 and T–207/01 *Government of Gibraltar* [2002] E.C.R. II–2309 at paras 14–21; Case T–189/03 *ASM Brescia SpA* [2009] E.C.R. II–1831 para.71–73; Commission, 2004 Report (see fn.12, above), paras 14–15; Decision 2003/193/EC [2003] O.J. L77/21 at para.48.

[67] Decision 2000/797/ECSC [2000] O.J. L323/5 at paras 15–18, 60–1.

[68] Decision 2003/515/EC [2003] O.J. L180/52 at paras 79–83.

[69] Easson "Tax Competition and Investment Incentives"[1997] EC Tax Journal, pp.63 et seq., pp.78 et seq.

[70] Case T–67/94 *Ladbroke Racing* [1998] E.C.R. II–1 at para.59.

[71] AG Tizzano, Case C–172/03 *Heiser* [2005] E.C.R. I–1627 at para.48.

[72] AG Léger, Joined Cases C–182/03 and C–217/03 *Belgium v Commission* [2006] E.C.R. I–5479 at paras 257–266.

[73] Case C–66/02 *Italy v Commission* [2005] E.C.R. I–10901 at para.78; Case C–156/98 *Germany v Commission* [2000] E.C.R. I–6857 at para.24; Decision 2004/339/EC [2004] O.J. L119/1 at para.64.

[74] Decision 1999/148/EC, ECSC [1999] O.J. L47/6; Decision 2000/668/EC [2000] O.J. L279/46 at paras 8–9.

[75] Commission, 2004 Report (see fn.12, above), paras 9–13; AG Léger, Joined Cases C–182/03 and C–217/03 *Belgium v Commission* [2006] E.C.R. I–5479 at paras 245–66; Joined Cases C–182/03 and C–217/03 *Belgium v Commission* [2006] E.C.R. I–5479 at paras 90–96.

[76] Decision 2009/809/EC [2009] O.J. L288/26 at paras 77–82; Decision 2010/95/EC [2010] O.J. L42/3 at paras 103–105. For a close analysis see Raymond Luja, "Group Taxation, Sectoral Tax Benefits and De Facto Selectivity in State Aid Review" [2009] EStAL, pp.473 et seq.

[77] Case T–67/94 *Ladbroke Racing* [1998] E.C.R. II–1 at para.57.

assumption that a specific tax provision constitutes state aid. Moreover, any broader economic or social purpose behind the tax incentive does not render it immune against the discipline exerted by art.107(1) TFEU.[78] Finally, both optional and mandatory tax breaks fall under the control of art.107(1) TFEU.[79]

10–012 **Discrimination not sufficient.** In recent case law there has been a growing trend towards the assumption that "discriminatory taxation" leads to the application of state aid discipline under art.107(1) TFEU.[80] Contrary to this assumption, the mere fact that there is "selective" different treatment of different groups of taxpayers will not be sufficient to fulfil the requirements of art.107(1) TFEU. Unless there is a specific advantage for a selective group of taxpayers this provision does not apply.[81]

10–013 **Exceptional tax burden.** On the other hand, there is no aid "granted" from the state or its resources when the state distorts competition among undertakings or goods and services by placing an extra tax burden on certain economic agents or activities.[82] Quite the opposite, in the context of the ECSC; art.4c of the (expired) Treaty contained a prohibition which referred to "special charges" as juxtaposed to "aid".[83] Under the TFEU, only arts 116 and 117 TFEU confer upon the Council and the Commission the competence to address distortions resulting from tax rules other than tax incentives—this is extended to "special charges" as well.[84] As this provision has never been applied in the past because it leaves the power to introduce measures against distortions of the competitive situation to the Council of Ministers and not to the Commission alone, this jurisprudence gives virtually full discretion to the Member States to "penalise" certain economic behaviour by tax disincentives.[85]

[78] Case C–75/97 *Belgium v Commission* [1999] E.C.R. I–3671 at para.25; Joined Cases T–92/00 and T–103/00 *Territorio Histórico de Álava* [2002] E.C.R. II–1385 at para.51; Joined Cases T–127/99, T–129/99 and T–148/99 *Territorio Histórico de Álava* [2002] E.C.R. II–1275 at para.169; Joined Cases T–346/99, T–347/99 and T–348/99 *Territorio Histórico de Guipúzcoa* [2002] E.C.R. II–4259 at para.54; Joined Cases T–269/99, T–271/99 and T–272/99 *Territorio Histórico de Guipúzcoa* [2002] E.C.R. II–4217 at para.63; Case C–251/97 *France v Commission* [1999] E.C.R. I–6639 at para.37; Case C–172/03 *Heiser* [2005] E.C.R. I–1627 at para.40.
[79] Decision 2004/339/EC [2004] O.J. L119/1 at para.69.
[80] Case T–210/02 *British Aggregates Association* [2006] E.C.R. II–2789 at paras 104–109; Joined Cases T–211/04 and T–215/04 *Gibraltar* [2008] E.C.R. II–3745 at para.170; Kelyn Bacon, "European Community Law of State Aid" (Oxford, 2009) para.2.86; Lang (2008) (see fn.1, above), pp.23–26; idem fn.1 (2011) 593 et seq. critical Schön (2009) (see fn.1, above), pp.28–31.
[81] AG Jääskinen, Joined Cases C–106/09P and C–107/09P *Gibraltar* [2011] Unreported at paras 150–175, 191–207.
[82] Sutter (see fn.1, above), pp.122–7.
[83] Case C–390/98 *Banks* [2001] E.C.R. I–6117 at paras 29, 34.
[84] AG Geelhoed, Case C–308/01 *GIL Insurance* [2004] E.C.R. I–4777 at para.65; see also Leendert A. Geelhoed, "The Demarcation of State Aid and Regulatory Charges" [2005] 4 EStAL, pp.401–405.
[85] Kim Lundgaard Hansen, "A Taxing Subject" in Baudenbacher et al. (eds), *Liber Amicorum in Honour of Bo Vesterdorf* (Brussels, 2007) pp.673 et seq., at pp.683 et seq.; the only case where the Court took the view that a "special charge" may be qualified as state aid under art.87(1) EC (now art.107(1) TFEU) is Joined Cases C–128/03 and C–129/03 *AEM SpA* [2005] E.C.R. I–2861 at paras 40–3 where an increase of taxation for hydroelectric and geothermal electricity was

Against this background, the introduction of special consumption taxes which qualify as a disincentive with respect to the charged goods or services (tobacco, mineral oil) is (apart from harmonisation) mainly left to the sovereign discretion of the Member State.[86] Even a special tax burden on services and goods delivered by foreign competitors of domestic companies is not prohibited by art.107(1) TFEU but has to be dealt with according to the Treaty provisions on the fundamental freedoms.[87] This makes it necessary to draw an analogy and to establish the notion of "negative aid" within the scope of art.107(1) TFEU.[88]

This makes it necessary to distinguish between a tax incentive, which may qualify as an aid, and a tax disincentive, which does not. This can lead into the apparently aporetic situations where it is difficult to decide whether the higher tax burden or the lower tax burden define the "normal" level of taxation. In the Court, there is no clear line of thinking on this point. While AG Geelhoed[89] seems to favour a dividing line between the "rule" and the "exception" according to the burden for the minority and the majority of taxpayers, AG Fennelly has rejected this delineation.[90] In a Greek case, the Greek government decided to charge an extra levy on business income and allowed a deduction for income earned from export. The Commission regarded this as a prohibited aid favouring export-oriented business and not as a lawful surcharge on domestic-oriented business.[91]

Misapplication of tax law. There is no aid if the state refunds to the taxpayer **10–014** taxes which have been collected without a legal basis. The Court[92] has ruled that these reimbursements do not qualify as state aid because the Member States do not intend to further economic or social aims by this restitution. But this intention is not a legal prerequisite for an aid under art.107(1) TFEU. It is more consistent with the wording of this paragraph to rely on the fact that a state that reimburses funds to which it was not entitled does not transfer "State resources" upon the taxpayer.[93]

---

deemed to constitute state aid for all other energy producers (see also AG Stix-Hackl at para.34). In this case, neither the Court nor the Advocate General addressed the real issue of "negative aid" but simply reached the conclusion that this tax increase was justified by advantages from the liberalisation of the energy market; for a critical analysis see Martina Maier and Philipp Werner, "Review of Judgment AEM SpA v. Autorità per l'Energia Elettrica e per il Gas" [2005] 4 EStAL, pp.657–60.

[86] Joined Cases 142/80 and 143/80 *Salengo* [1981] E.C.R. 1413 at para.21.

[87] Smit and Herzog on the Law of the European Union (Newark, NJ, looseleaf, 2010), at para.107.04.

[88] Wolfgang Schön, "Special Charges: A Gap in European Competition Law", [2006] 5 EStAL, pp.494–503; Bacon (see fn.22, above), p.318; sceptical Bartosch (see fn.31 above), art.87(1) EC para.95.

[89] Case C–308/01 *GIL Insurance* [2004] E.C.R. I–4777 at paras 65 et seq.; Case C–88/03 *Portugal v Commission* [2006] E.C.R. I–7115 at para.49.

[90] Case C–390/98 *Banks* [2001] E.C.R. I–6117 at para.19; see also AG Tizzano, Case C–53/00 *Ferring* [2001] E.C.R. I–9067 at para.39.

[91] Decision 1989/659/EC [1989] O.J. L394/1.

[92] Case 61/79 *Denkavit Italiana* [1980] E.C.R. 1205 at para.31.

[93] AG Reischl, Case 61/79 *Denkavit Italiana* [1980] E.C.R. 1205; Jean-Paul Keppenne, *Guide des aides d'Etat en droit communautaire* (Brussels, 1999) at para.38.

On the other hand, it is not easy to decide whether the misapplication of a tax provision which works to the advantage of the taxpayer constitutes a state aid in breach of art.107(1) TFEU. In the *ICI* case the British High Court held that it was not the Commission's task to investigate the correct application of national tax rules.[94] This has to be dealt with under domestic procedural law. Thus, it was held by the Court of Appeal that only a deliberate misapplication by the tax authorities or the persistence in the misapplication with knowledge of its invalidity can qualify as a state aid.[95] This test has been criticised as it involves an investigation into the individual causes of the misapplication.[96] But in order to relieve the Commission from screening the administration of tax provisions in the whole European Union this approach seems to be a sensible one.[97] In the same vein the Commission made clear in *Technolease* that a "good faith" solution of a disputed question of domestic tax law in favour of the taxpayer which is in line with later general guidelines on the same issue ("sale-and-lease-back") cannot be attacked from a state aid perspective.[98] On the other hand, an administrative practice which systematically applies a favourable standard without checking the economic reality amounts to prohibited state aid.[99]

10–015 **Relevant "consideration" by the taxpayer.** One of the most intensely discussed topics of state aid law concerns the application of art.107(1) TFEU where an advantage transferred to an economic agent is "offset" by the provision of services by this agent, in particular the performance of activities in the public interest. In the tax sector, this topic has been raised by the Court in *Ferring*, where it was accepted in principle that there is no aid if a tax reduction is meant to compensate the taxpayer for services performed.[100] Nevertheless, this recent judgment is not intended to cover a broad range of situations wherever a tax reduction is introduced in order to relieve the taxpayer from an extra burden. The pursuance of general policy objectives is not regarded as constituting a "consideration" in this sense.[101] Both the Court and the Commission have made it clear that a reduction of social security contributions which is implemented to facilitate contractual arrangements between employers and trade unions in favour of the workers constitutes state aid because labour costs have to be borne by the

---

[94] *The Queen v Attorney General ex p. Imperial Chemical Industries Plc*, Tax Cases 60, pp.1 et seq., 22 per Justice Woolf.
[95] *The Queen v Attorney General ex p. Imperial Chemical Industries Plc*, Tax Cases 60, pp.1, 62 per Lord Oliver of Aylmerton.
[96] Lasok, "State Aids and Remedies under the EEC Treaty" [1986] E.C.L.R. 53; Sharpe, "The Role of National Courts in Relation to the Community Law of State Aids" in *State Aids: Community Law and Policy*, Vol.4, pp.93 et seq.; Quigley "General Taxation" (see fn.1, above), pp.209–10; Quigley, "European State Aid Law" (see fn.1, above), pp.70–71; see also para. 3–004, above.
[97] Critical Sutter (see fn.1, above), pp.63–71.
[98] Decision 2000/735/EC [2000] O.J. L297/13 at paras 26–39.
[99] Decision 2003/438/EC [2003] O.J. L153/40 at paras 43–4; Decision 2004/76/EC [2004] O.J. L23/1 at paras 47, 50, 53.
[100] Case C–53/00 *Ferring* [2001] E.C.R. I–9067 at paras 23–7; for an extensive analysis of the foregoing jurisprudence see AG Tizzano at paras 50–63.
[101] Decision 2000/620/EC [2000] O.J. L260/37 at para.58.

employers and those contracts are not concluded in order to perform public services.[102] There is no possible "compromise" regarding labour cost between the state and private business.[103] Moreover, the mere fact that certain enterprises have to participate in ETS trading systems does not justify their exemption from energy taxation.[104]

"Preferential" and "normal" tax treatment—the national prerogative in tax matters

The "private investor test" and the collection of outstanding tax debt.   **10–016**
According to the jurisprudence of the Court, there are two different approaches to "normalcy" in state aid matters which refer to the question of whether the state acts in the exercise of its sovereign or public functions or whether it acts simply as a market participant.[105] Only if the state acts in a private market situation does it make sense to ask whether the beneficiary receives an advantage "below market price".[106] This "private investor test" can be applied with respect to capital injections, guarantees or preferential interest rates from state resources but cannot be applied in the area of taxation where no "market" exists at all.[107] The state does not treat the taxable entities like an "investor". The only situation where the tax authority can be compared to a private person waiving or reducing a claim against an enterprise comes up when there actually exists a tax claim arising from general tax legislation which is not (fully) collected by the tax authorities in order to save the liquidity of the taxpayer. Here, the state behaves like a normal creditor and we can compare it to such a private person.[108] If it can be established that the state does not collect its claims where a private investor would have done so, art.107(1) TFEU can be applied.[109] If the state enjoys a

---

[102] Case C–251/97 *France v Commission* [1999] E.C.R. I–6639 at paras 40–1; Decision 2003/739/EC [2003] O.J. L267/29 at para.24.

[103] AG Fennelly, Case C–251/97 *France v Commission* [1999] E.C.R. I–6639 at paras 18–28.

[104] Decision 2009/972/EC [2009] O.J. L345/18 at paras 36–47.

[105] AG Fennelly, Case C–390/98 *Banks* [2001] E.C.R. I–6117 at paras 19 et seq.

[106] Kapteyn and VerLoren van Themaat, *The Law of the European Union and the European Communities*, 4th edn (Alphen aan den Rijn: 2008), pp.852 et seq.; Müller-Graff, "Die Erscheinungsformen der Leistungssubventionstatbestände aus wirtschaftsrechtlicher Sicht" [1988] 152 *Zeitschrift für das gesamte Handels- und Wirtschaftsrecht*, pp.403 et seq., 418.

[107] AG Jääskinen, Joined Cases C–106/09P and C–107/09P *Gibraltar* [2011] Unreported at para.156; Bartosch (see fn.31, above), art.87(1) EC para.73.

[108] For a waiver of a tax claim resulting in a capital contribution for a company see Case T–156/04 *Electricité de France* [2009] E.C.R. II–4503; Andreas Bartosch, "Case Note on EdF v Commission" [2010] EStAL, pp.679 et seq., at pp.681 et seq.; idem, "The EdF-Ruling—an electrifying Enlightening" [2010] EStAL pp.267 et seq.; Markus Haberkamm/Aline Kühne, "Steuerliche Maßnahmen im Lichte des Europäischen Beihilferechts: Seit EdF ein noch spannungsgeladeneres Feld" [2010] Europäische Zeitschrift für Wirtschaftsrecht, pp.734 et seq.

[109] Case C–256/97 *DMT* [1999] E.C.R. I–3913 at paras 22–5; Case C–480/98 *Spain v Commission* [2000] E.C.R. I–8717 at paras 13–21; Case C–295/97 *Piaggio* [1999] E.C.R. I–3735 at paras 40–1; Case C–276/02 *Spain v Commission* [2004] E.C.R. I–8091 at paras 31–7; see also AG Poiares Maduro, Case C–276/02 *Spain v Commission* [2004] E.C.R. I–8091 at paras 21–6; Decision 2002/935/EC [2002] O.J. L329/1 at para.45; Decision 1999/395/EC [1999] O.J. L149/40 at paras 79–83 (preferential interest rate for rescheduled social security contributions); Philipp Reimer, "Stundung, Erlass und Niederschlagung von Forderungen der öffentlichen

statutory preferential status in insolvency proceedings, the willingness of the state to waive its tax claims like a private creditor may amount to state aid.[110] In practice this leads to complicated factual tests on the behaviour of public entities during the insolvency and restructuring proceedings of ailing enterprises.[111]

10–017 **The comparison between groups of taxpayers.** However, if we consider tax breaks enshrined in the provisions of tax legislation itself we have to return to the simple question of whether the beneficiary is put at an advantage when compared with other taxable persons[112] according to the tax system of the respective Member State.

Since state aid in the form of preferential tax treatment takes place in the artificial world of the tax system and not in a market free of state interference, it is hard to find a reliable instrument in order to identify a "tax incentive". Two diverging approaches are worth considering. On one hand it is possible to take into account the aims and motives of a change in the tax system. This would force the Commission and the Court to take a close look at the genesis of a specific tax rule; the applicability of arts 107 et seq. TFEU would depend on the subjective motives of government and parliament in the respective Member State. On the other hand, one can try to make use of a strictly objective criterion and look at the effects of a tax rule. The Court[113] and the Commission[114] have strongly supported the latter approach and scrutinise the "effects" of a tax rule rather than its aims and causes.

If one puts aside any "subjective" investigation into the aims and causes of a tax measure one has to find "objective" qualities which make it possible to identify a tax incentive. Therefore, the Court[115] and the Commission try to distinguish between a preferential and a "normal" tax regime. In its 1998 notice, the Commission points out that "firstly, the measure must confer on recipients an advantage which relieves them of charges that are normally borne from their budgets".[116] This definition is derived from OECD findings[117] and has also been

---

Hand—sämtlich verbotene Beihilfen?", [2011] Neue Zeitschrift für Verwaltungsrecht, pp.263 et seq.

[110] Case T–11/07 *Frucona Košice* [2010] Unreported at paras 114–115; Decision 2007/204/EC [2007] O.J. L91/37 at paras 49–69. As to the recovery of these waivers see Case C–507/08 *Commission v Slovak Republic* [2010] Unreported at paras 2–6.

[111] For an example see Decision 2003/283/EC [2003] O.J. L108/21 at paras 44–52.

[112] Case C–387/92 *Banco Exterior de Espana* [1994] E.C.R. I–877 at para.14; Case C–6/97 *Italy v Commission* [1999] E.C.R. I–2981 at para.16.

[113] Case 173/73 *Italy v Commission* [1974] E.C.R. 709 at para.26/28; Case C–241/94 *France v Commission* [1996] E.C.R. I–4551 at para.20; Case T–67/94 *Ladbroke Racing* [1998] E.C.R. II–1 at para.52; *Baudenbacher* (see fn.64 above), p.9.

[114] Commission (see fn.11, above) at para.15.

[115] Case 30/59 *Gezamenlijke Steenkolenmijnen* [1961] E.C.R. 5; Case 173/73 *Italy v Commission* [1974] E.C.R. 709 at paras 33–35; Case C–387/92 *Banco Exterior de Espana* [1994] E.C.R. I–877 at para.13; Case C–241/94 *France v Commission* [1996] E.C.R. I–4551 at para.34; see also AG Darmon in Joined Cases 72/91 and 73/91 *Sloman Neptun* [1993] E.C.R. I–887 at paras 50 et seq., Joined Cases C–78/08 to C–80/08 *Paint Graphos* [2011] unreported.

[116] Commission (see fn.11, above) at para.9.

[117] Commission, First Survey on State Aids, 1989, p.39.

introduced in the EU regulation implementing the GATT rules on subsidies.[118] In a similar vein, the WTO Subsidies Agreement refers to the relief of an enterprise from taxes which were "otherwise due" as the benchmark of tax subsidies.[119] Thus, it is decisive for the identification of state aid to fix a normal level of a tax burden from which it can be said that a special tax treatment of certain transactions or enterprises must be labelled advantageous or disadvantageous.

Of course the most effective way of fighting tax incentives from a Union perspective, would be to elaborate on an autonomous general description of a "normal" tax system, regardless of the individual traditions and policies of the Member States, in order to provide the Commission and the Court with a fixed starting point.[120] But this approach is prohibited because it would interfere with the unquestioned sovereignty of the states to generally decide which economic transactions shall be subject to tax. There is, apart from VAT and some consumption taxes, no harmonisation of the tax rates and tax bases at the Union level.[121] Only in rare cases—e.g. when it comes to relief from international double taxation—have global standard setters like the OECD been referred to by the Commission and the Court.[122] Otherwise, there is "no *a priori* conception of what the normal level of charges or benefits should be".[123]

10–018

For these reasons, the only "benchmark", from which a tax measure can be identified as state aid, is the general tax system which has been established by the respective Member State itself. Therefore, the Court[124] and the Commission[125] have stressed the national prerogative in tax matters and accepted that tax measures which arise from the "nature or general scheme" of the national tax system are not deemed to constitute state aid according to art.107(1) TFEU. For the Member State whose tax measures are under investigation according to arts 107 et seq. TFEU this approach is a double-sided one. In principle, it is clear that state aid law cannot call into question the sovereignty of the Member State to shape its own tax system. On the other hand, a Member State is not in the position to defend a preferential tax provision granted to a certain undertaking by pointing to the fact that the same provision exists as a general one in other

---

[118] Article 2, No.1 lit.a)ii) Council Regulation 3284/94 [1994] O.J. L349/22; see also Case 187/85 *Fediol* [1988] E.C.R. 4155 at paras 15 et seq.

[119] Schön (see fn.5, above).

[120] This approach has been proposed by Frick (see fn.34, above), pp.27 et seq.

[121] In harmonised areas of tax law, the European provisions form the "benchmark" for the assessment of a tax advantage (Decision 2009/944/EC [2009] O.J. L327/6 para.62). When European law itself obliges the domestic legislator to introduce a tax benefit, art.107(1) TFEU disapplies as this benefit is not granted by the national "State" (Case T–351/02 *Deutsche Bahn* [2006] E.C.R. II–1047 at paras 99–104).

[122] A.G. Léger, Joined Cases C–182/03 and C–217/03 *Belgium v Commission* [2006] E.C.R. I–5479 at paras 257–9; Commission, 2004 Report, fn.12, above, para.10; Decision 2003/438/EC [2003] O.J. L153/40 at para.42; Decision 2004/76/EC [2004] O.J. L23/1 at paras 45–6, 52; Decision 2004/77/EC [2004] O.J. L23/14 at para.66; Decision 2003/512/EC [2003] O.J. L177/17 at para.26.

[123] A.G. Fennelly, Case C–390/98 *Banks* [2001] E.C.R. I–6117 at para.19; A.G. Jääskinen, Joined Cases C–106/09P and C–107/09P *Gibraltar* [2011] n.y.r. at paras 143–145.

[124] Case 173/73 *Italy v Commission* [1974] E.C.R. 709 at paras 33–5.

[125] Commission, fn.11 above at paras 13 et seq.

Member States or that it is necessary to compensate for preferential treatment in other countries.[126] Thus, the Italian government which had—alongside its own tax system—introduced a tax break for the reconstruction of a single major company could not rely on the fact that similar tax breaks have a long tradition in other Member States[127] and a common system for international reconstructions at the European level was in preparation.[128] Only a change in the general scheme of taxation with respect to company reconstructions in Italy would have served as a justification.

The "nature or general scheme" of a tax

10–019 **Introduction, abolition and reduction of taxes.** As it is clear that the Member State is free to shape the fundamental aspects of its tax system by determining the taxable situations, the tax rate and the tax base, it has to be concluded that art.107(1) TFEU does not prevent the Member State from introducing, reducing or abolishing a tax in order to further its economic aims.[129]

The first conclusion which has to be drawn lies in the fact that the relevant "benchmark" is not defined as the "old law" in comparison with the "new law". It is therefore irrelevant if the situation of the presumed beneficiary of a measure is better or worse in comparison with the situation under the law as it previously stood.[130] Furthermore, it is irrelevant whether a tax reduction forms an integral part of a newly introduced tax so that all taxpayers are confronted with more or less increased financial obligations giving rise to an overall increase in public revenue.[131] The Court only considers whether, under the current law, a taxpayer enjoys an advantageous exception from the rule.

10–020 From this starting point we must also accept that the Member States are free to levy a tax which concerns only a certain group of enterprises, because the state is free to levy taxes on specific goods and services. A tax on beer producers in order to support wine producers is not prohibited; the same holds true for a tax on road hauliers which strengthens the competitiveness of rail freight undertakings.[132] The Member State is free to change its "general tax scheme". The mere fact that there is competition between taxed and non-taxed market participants does not stand in the way of the fiscal sovereignty of the Member States.[133]

---

[126] Case C–172/03 *Heiser* [2005] E.C.R. I–1627 at para.54; Case C–66/02 *Italy v Commission* [2005] E.C.R. I–10901 at para.92; Decision 2000/410/EC [2000] O.J. L155/52 at para.16; Decision 2007/256/EC [2007] O.J. L112/41 para.120; Luja (see fn.1, above), pp.37–8.

[127] Decision 92/389/EC [1992] O.J. L207/47 et seq.; see also Commission, 2004 Report (see fn.12, above) at para.24; Case T–335/08 *BNP Paribas* [2010] Unreported para.164–198; Decision 2008/711/EC [2008] O.J. L237/70 at paras 82–107.

[128] A more lenient approach seems to be taken by Commission, 2004 Report (see fn.12, above) at para.25.

[129] Quigley, "The notion of a State aid in the EEC" [1988] *European Law Review*, pp.242, 245.

[130] Case C–143/99 *Adria-Wien-Pipeline* [2001] E.C.R. I–8365 at para.41; Case T–335/08 *BNP Paribas* [2010] Unreported para.204; Quigley, "General Taxation" (see fn.1, above), p.209.

[131] AG Tizzano, Case C–53/00 *Ferring* [2001] E.C.R. I–9067 at paras 43–5; this was overlooked by AG Mischo, Case C–143/99 *Adria-Wien-Pipeline* [2001] E.C.R. I–8365 at para.62.

[132] AG Tizzano, Case C–53/00 *Ferring* [2001] E.C.R. I–9067 at para.36.

[133] A stricter view seems to be taken by AG Tizzano, Case C–53/00 *Ferring* [2001] E.C.R. I–9067 at paras 40–2.

In its jurisprudence on art.110 TFEU the Court has made clear many times that even specific consumption taxes which put a burden on the production of particular (foreign) goods are not prohibited by the TFEU.[134]

This national prerogative in tax matters was not fully recognised by the Court of First Instance (CFI) (now General Court) in the "Ladbroke Racing" case[135]: the French state had introduced a tax on racing pools which concerned one single enterprise, a racing organiser in Paris. In order to support this ailing enterprise against its British competitors, the French state (among other subsidies) reduced the rate of this specific charge. The Commission held this reduction to be part of a change in the "general tax scheme", which was not subject to art.87(1) EC (now art.107(1) TFEU).[136] The Commission argued that a state that had established a special tax scheme for a single enterprise must be allowed to change this tax scheme for better or worse without falling within the scope of art.87(1) EC (now art.107(1) TFEU). The Commission concluded that this reduction would not constitute a general change of the tax system (and qualify as a prohibited state aid) only if it was a temporary one (or a single deferment of tax arrears) or if it was intended to fund a specific measure or if it would have substantially strengthened a national monopoly. The General Court rejected these distinctions and held that the notion of an "aid" in the context of the European Union covers temporary and permanent tax reductions as well, does not take into account the causes and aims of a reduction and, finally, does not distinguish according to the quantitative aspects of a tax reduction.[137] Surprisingly, the General Court drew the conclusion that, irrespective of the above mentioned distinctions, the tax reduction for the benefit of the racing organiser should be regarded as state aid. This leaves open the question of whether the French state will be able to abolish or reduce this particular tax at all without submitting to the procedures under arts 87 et seq. EC (now arts 107 et seq. TFEU). These topics were not raised again substantially in later proceedings before the Court itself.[138]

The scope of the "General Scheme" of a tax. From the foregoing, it can be concluded that an advantageous tax provision can only be identified as state aid if it favours certain taxpayers who are subject to a broad-based general tax act under the rules of the respective Member State. This has been the case in most decisions or judgments in this field. In a judgment concerning Italian tax incentives, the Court dealt with a typical example of this kind. The Italian government had introduced a tax credit granted only to professional transport undertakings; they were allowed to deduct part of their expenditures for oil from their general obligations in the field of corporation tax, income tax, business tax, payroll tax or VAT. This was declared void[139] as this refund put the transport undertakings

10–021

---

[134] See Schön (see fn.19, above).
[135] Case T–67/94 *Ladbroke Racing* [1998] E.C.R. II–1 et seq.
[136] Decision 93/625/EC [1993] O.J. L300/15 et seq. at para.V.3.
[137] Case T–67/94 *Ladbroke Racing* [1998] E.C.R. II–1 at paras 29, 32 and 68 et seq.
[138] Case C–83/98P *France v Ladbroke Racing* [2000] E.C.R. I–3271.
[139] Case C–6/97 *Commission v Italy* [1999] I–2981.

in a better position than other taxpayers who had to pay these general taxes without any rebate.

The first problem arising from this initial position deals with the extent of this "nature and general scheme" of a tax. In *Gibraltar* the Court clarified that this is not a matter of the regulatory technique but of the substance of the tax regime.[140] In this respect, one has to decide whether a specific tax has to be judged on its own merits or whether it has to be seen as part of a bigger scenario. An example from the United Kingdom: with respect to the British Petroleum Revenue Tax (PRT), a special tax on profits from oil explorations in the North Sea, it has been questioned[141] whether PRT constitutes a tax in its own right, defining its own "nature and general scheme", or whether it forms part of general corporation tax, setting a preferential tax base and tax rate in comparison to other companies. Another example is *GIL Insurance*: the British legislator had raised the insurance tax on particular insurance contracts connected with the rental or sale of domestic appliances to the level of the VAT rate which was applied to these very rentals or sales. Do we have to judge this extra burden in the context of "insurance tax" (where it would form an exception) or in the context of VAT (where it would be in line with the general scheme)? The Court was unclear as it referred to the "particular statutory scheme"[142] (i.e. the Insurance Tax Act) on the one hand but, on the other hand, regarded the higher tax rate for appliance insurance contracts and the VAT rate for appliance sales and rentals to form an "inseparable whole".[143] In *Italy v Commission* the Italian Government sought to defend several tax breaks for banking institutions by referring to the attacked legislation as a "special tax regime" for banks, but this was not accepted by AG Stix-Hackl[144] and the Court as these breaks had to be read in the context of general taxation of corporate profits. To give another example, a "tonnage tax" on shipping profits which is calculated on the (crude) basis of the ship's tonnage was held to constitute a preferential deviation from general corporate income tax and not a tax regime in itself.[145] With respect to the taxation of cooperatives, AG Jääskinen recently pointed out that these legal forms might be subject to a tax system of their own and not comparable to other entities, such as commercial companies, but this was rejected by the Court.[146]

10–022   Therefore, the definition of the "benchmark" should not be decided along the lines of the statutory separation of the tax provisions but with respect to the economic substance of taxation. It is generally accepted amongst the Member

---

[140] Joined Cases C–106/09P and C–107/09P [2011] Unreported at paras 87–104.

[141] Quigley, "The Scope of Article 92 (1) of the EEC Treaty", Harden (ed), *State Aid: Community Law and Policy* (Cologne, 1993), pp.28 et seq., 33; Quigley (see fn.129, above), p.254; Bacon (see fn.22, above), pp.298 et seq.

[142] Case C–308/01 *GIL Insurance* [2004] E.C.R. I–4777 at para.68.

[143] Case C–308/01 *GIL Insurance* [2004] E.C.R. I–4777 at para.74.

[144] AG Stix-Hackl, Case C–66/02 *Italy v Commission* [2005] E.C.R. I–10901 at paras 48–50.

[145] Decision 2002/901/EC [2002] O.J. L314/97 at para.15.

[146] Joined Cases C–78/08 to C–80/08 *Paint Graphos* [2011] Unreported at paras 48–52. AG Jääskinen, Joined Cases C–78/08 to C–80/08 *Paint Graphos* [2010] Unreported at paras 71–78.

States of the European Union that each tax shall raise revenue according to the taxpayers' "ability to pay".[147] This "ability to pay" can be measured by different "indicators", such as "income", "wealth", and "consumption". It is important to consider therefore whether two legally separated taxes tap the same "indicator". As corporation tax is levied on corporate profits and PRT is levied on corporate profits in a certain sector of the economy, one should not hesitate to regard PRT as a specific form of corporate tax which, if it offers preferential treatment as to the tax base or the tax rate, qualifies as state aid. The same holds true for specific rules on bank taxation if they just define exceptions from taxes which are levied generally from all economic agents (corporate income tax and so on). In border-line cases like *GIL Insurance* it can be left to the sovereignty of the Member State as to how to define the "benchmark" for the application of art.107(1) TFEU. Moreover, a selective tax reduction with respect to a local tax (trade tax) may be compensated by a higher tax at the central level, thus leading to no tax advantage at all, if the involved tax benefit and the tax burden form an inseparable "package".[148]

Setting out from the general nature of every tax to raise revenue according to the individual's "ability to pay", one should distinguish the "structural compo-nent" of a tax which is necessary to implement this fundamental structure of a tax, from the "tax expenditure component", which consists of the provisions by which government spending objectives are carried out through the tax system.[149] Obviously, it is easier to describe the "nature and general scheme" in the case of traditional and comprehensive taxes which cover more than a single branch of businesses. Income tax, capital gains tax, wealth tax, inheritance tax or real estate tax are charged with respect to a tax basis which does not in itself involve special advantages or disadvantages for single enterprises or groups of enterprises. Therefore, the Commission is right in stressing the fact that "tax measures of a purely technical nature (for example, setting the rate of taxation, depreciation rules and rules on loss carry-overs; provisions to prevent double taxation or tax avoidance)" do not constitute state aid. They are simply the fine print of the general decision by a Member State to levy an income tax, a wealth tax and so forth.

Nevertheless, one should always bear in mind that among tax theorists and **10–023** practitioners it is highly controversial whether a tax provision contains a techni-cal rule measuring the "ability to pay" of a taxpayer or a tax incentive. Carry-

---

[147] Tipke, *Die Steuerrechtsordnung*, Vol.1 (Cologne, 2000), pp.479 et seq. gives an outline on the international discussion of the "ability to pay" principle; see also Doralt and Ruppe, *Grundriss des österreichischen Steuerrechts*, Vol.1, 9th edn (Wien: 2007), p.17; Fantozzi, *Il Diritto tributario*, 3rd edn (Turin: 2003), pp.37 et seq.; Williams and Morse, *Davies: Principles of Tax Law*, 6th edn (London: 2008) pp.6 et seq.

[148] Joined Cases T–427/04 and T–17/05 *France Télécom* [2009] E.C.R. II–4315 at paras 191–225.

[149] McDaniel, "Personal Income Taxes: the treatment of tax expenditures", Cnossen (ed.), *Tax Coordination in the European Community* (Deventer, 1987), pp.319 et seq., 325; Lang, *System-atisierung der Steuervergünstigungen* (Berlin, 1974), pp.74 et seq.; Frick (see fn.34, above), pp.27 et seq. J. Clifton Fleming/Robert J. Peroni, "Can Tax Expenditure Analysis be divorced form a Normative Tax Base?" 30 *Virginia Tax Review* [2010] pp.135–180.

back and carry-forward of losses are, in theory, considered instruments to measure the ability to pay disregarding the artificial limits of the respective accounting periods; in practice, many tax administrations regard them as instruments to subsidise risk-taking industries. Furthermore, it is not easy to determine whether a depreciation rule takes into account the ordinary life of an asset and "good commercial practice" or whether it goes beyond the objective determination of the financial situation of the taxpayer, thus granting him an incentive to invest in certain assets.[150] In *Stadtwerke Schwäbisch-Hall* the CFI (now General Court) regarded tax accounting rules allowing "clean-up costs provisions" for energy undertakings under German income tax law to constitute "advantageous" treatment,[151] although these can easily be classified as technical expressions of general rules on income measurement. The CFI (now General Court) reached the same result by denying the "selectivity" of these provisions.[152] The decision of a Member State on whether to apply the "realisation principle" to capital gains or to go for a mark-to-market taxation should be left to the domestic legislator.[153] Moreover, the CFI correctly stated that a lower tax rate is not a compensation for business expenditure which influences the tax base anyway.[154]

Another scenario concerns "exceptions from exceptions" to a "general rule". In a French case, the general rule that interest payments are recognised as deductible expenditure had been set aside in the case of intercompany loans, but this special regime had itself suffered a (preferential) exception in the case of central corporate treasuries set up in France by multinationals, thus giving rise to the application of art.107(1) TFEU.[155] In a similar vein, the Commission characterised as state aid a French rule on tax accounting leasing transactions[156] and a German rule on loss carry-forwards[157] where broad-based anti-abuse regimes were partially revoked for specific situations.

10–024   **The "nature and general scheme" of regulatory taxation.** The aforementioned "ability to pay" test does not work in the context of regulatory taxation

---

[150] Decision 96/369/EC [1996] O.J. L146/42, p.46; Case T–86/96 *Arbeitsgemeinschaft Deutscher Luftfahrtunternehmen und Hapag Lloyd* [1998] E.C.R. II–641 at para.61.

[151] Case T–92/02 *Stadtwerke Schwäbisch Hall* [2006] E.C.R. II–11* at para.52.

[152] Case T–92/02 *Stadtwerke Schwäbisch Hall* [2006] E.C.R. II–11* at paras 67–93; the qualification as state aid is supported by Dietmar O. Reich/Marcus Helios, "Do Reserves for the Disposal of Nuclear Waste and Shutdown of Nuclear Power Plants in Germany constitute State Aid?" [2002] 1 EStAL, pp.207–1; Dietmar O. Reich, "No Level Playing Field for Nuclear Power Reserves?" [2006] 5 EStAL, pp.445 et seq.; the ECJ found the action inadmissible for lack of standing (Case C–176/06P *Stadtwerke Schwäbisch Hall* [2007] E.C.R. I–170*).

[153] Peter L. Vesterdorf, "Capital Gains Taxation of Share Profits and EU State Aid Regulation", [2010] 9 EStAL, pp.741 et seq.

[154] Case T–211/05 *Italy v Commission* [2009] E.C.R. II–2777 at paras 130–132.

[155] Decision 2003/887/EC [2003] O.J. L330/23 at paras 22–4, 32–4.

[156] Decision 2007/256/EC [2007] O.J. L112/41 at paras 81–104.

[157] Decision 2010/C 90/08 [2010] O.J. C90/8 at paras 15–17; Christoph Arhold, "The German Scheme on the Fiscal Carry-forward of Losses—a 'Selected' case" [2011] EStAL, pp.71 et seq.; Klaus-Dieter Drüen, "Die Sanierungsklausel des § 8c KStG als europarechtswidrige Beihilfe" [2011] Deutsches Steuerrecht, pp.289 et seq.; Christian Marquart, "Die Möglichkeit der Verlustverrechnung als selektive Beginstigung sanierungsbedürftige Unternehmen", 20 *Internationale Steuerrecht* [2011] pp.445–451.

which is principally meant to further policy goals other than simple budgetary objectives. Well-known examples include environmental taxation ("green taxes") or taxes which aim at health care (tobacco and alcohol taxation). Although these taxes are not principally meant to raise revenue but to further other aims, they are subject to the discipline developed by the court under art.107(1) TFEU.[158]

It should be clear that the "nature and general scheme" of these taxes has to be identified with regard to the non-fiscal objective of the tax as such. Therefore, any environmental taxation has to be measured according to its regulatory objectives.[159] Differences in tax rates have to be justified in the light of the ecological purpose of the law, otherwise they are deemed to contain state aid.[160] But this does neither mean that the "subjective aims" of the legislator are in the foreground nor does it open the door to all sorts of economic policy considerations which might distort competition.[161] Tax reductions which do not follow from this regulatory purpose but which are introduced in order to compensate for competitive disadvantages of a regulatory tax are not expressions of the "nature or general scheme" of a tax and constitute state aid.[162] It goes without saying that a "regulatory tax" which aims specifically at protection of domestic business falls foul of art.110 TFEU or one of the fundamental freedoms of the Treaty and will be disregarded.

To make one thing clear: this specific test only applies where the tax has a truly regulatory nature. This situation must be distinguished from the scenario that some regulatory elements are inserted into a general fiscally oriented tax (like accelerated depreciation for environmentally friendly assets in the context of

---

[158] Case C–159/01 *Netherlands v Commission* [2004] E.C.R. I–4461 at para.51.

[159] Case T–210/02 *British Aggregates Association* [2006] E.C.R. II–2789 at paras 110–146; for an overview on the Commission's practice in this field see Daniel Boeshetz, "Community State Aid Policy and Energy Taxation" [2003] 12 *EC Tax Review*, pp.214–19; Brigitta Renner-Loquenz, "State Aid in Energy Taxation Measures: First Experiences from Applying the Environmental Aid Guidelines 2001" [2003] 2 EStAL, pp.21–27.

[160] Case C–159/01 *Netherlands v Commission* [2004] E.C.R. I–4461 at paras 42–48; Joined Cases E–5/04, E–6/04 and E–7/04 *Fesil and Finnfjord* at paras 83–85; Decision 2002/14/EC [2002] O.J. L12/1 at paras 183–203 (no ecological reasons for a preferential water levy rate); Roth (see fn.1, above), pp.136–139.

[161] The ECJ clarified that this does not mean an assessment of the subjective reasoning of the legislator but an assessment of the underlying principles (e.g. "polluter-pays-principle"); see Case C–487/06P *British Aggregates Association* [2008] E.C.R. I–10515 at paras 82–92, 128–132; Joint Cases C–78/08—C–80/08 *Paint Graphos* [2011] Unreported at paras 66–70; with respect to the highly controversial *British Aggregates Association* jurisprudence see Andreas Bartosch, "Is there a Need for a Rule of Reason in European State Aid Law? Or how to Arrive at a Coherent Concept of Material Selectivity?"[2010] 47 *Common Market Law Review*, pp.729 et seq., at pp.734 et seq.; *idem*, "On Being Selective in Selectivity" [2009] EStAL pp.433 et seq.; Bousin/Piernas (see fn.51, above) pp.642 et seq.; James Flett/Katerina Walkerova, "An Ecotax under the State Aid Spotlight: The UK Aggregates Levy", Rodriguez Iglesias et al. (ed), *EC State Aid Law* (Kluwer: 2008), pp.223 et seq.; Michael Honoré, "Selectivity and Taxation—Reflections in the Light of Case C–487/06 P *British Aggregates Association*" [2009] EStAL, pp.527 et seq., at pp.534 ff.; Lenaerts (see fn.1, above), pp.304–305; Jan Lohrberg, "Clarifications on the Application of the EC State Aid Rules to Fiscal Measures Aimed at Environmental Protection?" [2007] 6 EStAL, pp.538 et seq.

[162] Case C–143/99 *Adria-Wien-Pipeline* [2001] E.C.R. I–8365 at paras 49–54.

general income taxation). Such rules are naturally covered by art.107(1) TFEU but they may constitute non-selective "general measures" or be declared compatible with the internal market.[163]

The "nature and general scheme" of a tax and the selectivity of tax incentives

10–025 **General measures of economic policy.** The Commission regards as "general measures" which do not constitute state aid, "measures pursuing general economic policy objectives through a reduction of the tax burden related to certain production costs (research and development, the environment, training, employment)".[164] From the standpoint of tax law and with respect to the wording of art.107(1) TFEU, this is only half-right. The principal purpose of every tax lies in the collection of money according to the "ability to pay" of the single taxpayer or in the regulatory aim pursued by this legislation. Therefore, the "nature and general scheme" of a tax must be seen in the perspective of the fiscal or regulatory nature of the tax. One must admit that only tax rules which try to describe the parameters of the tax basis according to the "ability to pay" of the taxpayer or to its regulatory purpose belong to its "nature and general scheme".

If the Member State decides to reduce the tax burden with respect to some factors of production (research and development, etc.), it deviates from this general scheme in order to further non-fiscal economic objectives. This deviation must be called aid in the sense of art.107(1) TFEU. The same must be said about advantageous depreciation rules which are open to all economic agents and cause private undertakings to increase investment. Nevertheless, in these cases there is no reason to start proceedings against the Member State, because these aids are not "selective" insofar as they do not favour "certain undertakings or the production of certain goods" as art.107(1) requires.[165]

In order to get a correct picture of the notion of state aid with respect to taxes, one should accept the fundamental distinction between measures in accordance with the "general scheme", which deal with the fiscal aspects of a tax and do not constitute aid at all, and general tax incentives which constitute a non-selective and therefore non-prohibited form of state aid.[166]

10–026 **Specific implementations of the "nature and general scheme" of a tax.** From this distinction we have to draw the conclusion that tax rules exist which do affect certain enterprises, or groups of enterprises, but do not constitute state aid

---

[163] Case C–143/99 *Adria-Wien-Pipeline* [2001] E.C.R. I–8365 at para.31; Case T–210/02 *British Aggregates Association* [2006] E.C.R. II–2789 at paras 116–117.

[164] Commission (see fn.11, above), para.13; Caspari in Mestmäcker et al. (eds), *Eine Ordnungspolitik für Europa. Festschrift für Hans von der Groeben zu seinem 80. Geburtstag* (Baden-Baden: 1987), pp.69 et seq., 79.

[165] Evans (see fn.35, above), p.47.

[166] Bacon (see fn.22, above), p.270; above paras 3–044 et seq.

as they put in concrete terms general fiscal principles of a comprehensive tax system. The Court and the Commission regard these measures as "selective" but afford to the Member States the right to justify these measures as "necessary to the functioning and effectiveness of the tax system".[167] These rules do not discriminate amongst undertakings; they "define the parameters of a system".[168] According to the Court, "there is no advantage where the difference in treatment is justified by reasons relating to the logic of the system".[169] Taking a closer look, in most of these cases there will not even be an "advantage" conferred upon the taxpayer in relation to the system as a whole.[170] Indeed, the prima facie "selectivity" of a tax provision shifts the "burden of proof" to the national legislator which has to show that the rule in question conforms to the underlying domestic tax system.[171] This requires a "relationship" between the selective tax provision and the basic principles of the respective tax framework.[172]

Thus, diverging depreciation rules for different assets are compatible with the "nature and general scheme" of an income or corporation tax as long as they are intended to describe correctly the financial situation of the taxpayer. As a rule, these specific provisions which put in concrete terms general fiscal principles concern certain "events", such as the acquisition of assets, the reconstruction of a company or the accrual of losses, rather than certain "undertakings" as a whole.[173] Tax cuts which bear no relationship to this general scheme (e.g. corporate income reduction for newly listed companies as opposed to other companies[174] or tax-free reserves for international commercial risks which are restricted to multinational companies with subsidiaries in at least four different countries[175]) are not justified in the light of the system. But if only one selective group of taxpayers can be affected by a rule, e.g. when the transformation of municipal undertakings into private stock corporations is accompanied by an

---

[167] Commission (see fn.11, above), paras 23 et seq.
[168] Bacon (see fn.22, above), p.301.
[169] Case C–53/00 *Ferring* [2001] E.C.R. I–9067 at para.17; see also Joined Cases C–128/03 and C–129/03 *AEM SpA* [2005] E.C.R. I–2861 at para.39; Case C–308/01 *GIL Insurance* [2004] E.C.R. I–4777 at para.72; Case C–143/99 *Adria-Wien-Pipeline* [2001] E.C.R. I–8365 at para.42; C–159/01 *Netherlands v Commission* [2004] E.C.R. I–4461 at para.42; Case C–148/04 *Unicredito* [2005] E.C.R. I–11137 at para.51; Case C–66/02 *Italy v Commission* [2005] E.C.R. I–10901 at para.101; Joined Cases T–92/00 and T–103/00 *Territorio Histórico de Álava* [2002] E.C.R. II–1385 at para.60; Joined Cases T–127/99, T–129/99 and T–148/99 *Territorio Histórico de Álava* [2002] E.C.R. II–1275 at para.51; Joined Cases T–346/99, T–347/99 and T–348/99 *Territorio Histórico de Guipúzcoa* [2002] E.C.R. II–4259 at para.59; above para.3–046; Case T–211/05 E.C.R. II–2777 *Italy v Commission* [2009] paras 117–118; Joined Cases T–427/04 and T–17/05 *France Télécom* [2009] E.C.R. II–4315 paras 229–230; AG Jääskinen, Joined Cases C–106/09P and C–107/09P *Gibraltar* [2011] Unreported para.180.
[170] Aldestam (see fn.1, above), pp.85–6; Luja (see fn.1, above), p.51; Rossi-Maccanico (see fn.1, (2007) above), pp.219 et seq.
[171] AG Jääskinen, Joined Cases C–106/09P and C–107/09P *Gibraltar* [2011] Unreported para.217.
[172] Decision 2007/256/EC [2007] O.J. L 112/41 at paras 133–142.
[173] Bacon (see fn.22, above), pp.296 et seq.
[174] Decision 2006/261/EC [2006] O.J. L94/42 paras 26–8.
[175] Decision 2003/515/EC [2003] O.J. L180/52 paras 91–8.

exemption from transfer taxation, this can be justified according to this line of jurisprudence.[176]

10–027 Furthermore, one must agree with the Commission that the corporate tax exemption of charities or other non-profit organisations[177] is justified because they do not strive to earn any profits (foundations and associations) or do not distribute their profits to their members (co-operatives).[178] It is clear that a profit tax runs idle when no profit is earned.[179] But one has to consider the fact that many national tax systems extend this corporate tax exemption to taxes which do not require any income (wealth tax, real estate tax, VAT, inheritance tax) or to corporate taxation of specific profit-making economic activities of non-profit-organisations which do not affect the general character of the organisation (interest and dividend income, capital gains, charitable enterprises like hospitals or homes for the aged). For these cases the Commission has declared that the tax-exempt non-profit activities have to be kept apart from genuine commercial activities in order to prevent cross-subsidisation.[180] With respect to any profit-seeking activity the "nature and general scheme" of the tax does not justify the tax exemption. The mere fact that a company has not been profitable in the past is no justification for an exemption from corporation tax for the future.[181] For cooperatives, AG Jääskinen recently accepted the notion that their commercial structure justified a specific tax regime, but the Court rejected this view.[182]

In the context of non-profit organisations, one has to address the additional issue of whether the respective tax incentives affect any "enterprises" at all in the sense of art.107(1) TFEU. The Commission has been quite generous in accepting that the management of own assets and the use of the proceeds for making grants to not-for-profit bodies operating in the social field does not constitute an economic activity for the purposes of art.107(1) TFEU.[183] But the administration of "controlling shareholdings" may amount to the existence of an "enterprise".[184] Finally, tax incentives for commercial companies who pursue social

---

[176] Decision 2003/193/EC [2003] O.J. L77/21 paras 76–81.

[177] For tax benefits with respect to state-owned enterprises, see Michael Lang, "Die Besteuerung von Körperschaften des öffentlichen Rechts aus dem Blickwinkel des gemeinschaftsrechtlichen Beihilfenrechts", Elisabeth König and Walter Schwarzinger (eds), *Körperschaften im Steuerrecht—Festschrift für Werner Wiesner zum 65. Geburtstag* (Wien: 2004), pp.237–50.

[178] Commission (see fn.11, above) at para.25. For a full coverage of this topic see Marcus Helios, *Steuerliche Gemeinnützigkeit und EG-Beihilfenrecht* (Hamburg, 2005); Josef Isensee, "Gemeinnützigkeit und Europäisches Gemeinschaftsrecht", Monika Jachmann (ed.), *Gemeinnützigkeit* (Cologne, 2003), pp.92 et seq. at pp.113–28; Rainer Hüttemann, "Steuervergünstigungen wegen Gemeinnützigkeit und europäisches Beihilfenverbot" [2006] Der Betrieb, pp.914 et seq.

[179] Case T–67/94 *Ladbroke Racing* [1998] E.C.R. II–1 at para.89.

[180] Decision 2000/392/EC [2000] O.J. L150/1 at para.233.

[181] Letter E3/93 [1993] O.J. C289/2.

[182] Joined Cases C–78/08 to C–80/08 *Paint Graphos* [2011] Unreported at paras 48–52; AG Jääskinen, Joined Cases C–78/08 to C–80/08 *Paint Graphos* [2010] Unreported at paras 79–113.

[183] Decision 2003/146/EC [2003] O.J. L55/56 at para.59.

[184] Case C–222/04 *Cassa di Risparmio di Firenze* [2006] E.C.R. I.–289 at paras 107–118; Andrea Biondi, "Review of Judgment in Case C–222/04" [2006] 5 EStAL, pp.371 et seq.; Helmut Janssen/Klaus Eicker, "Steuerliche Vorteile für gemeinnützige Stiftungen als verbotene Beihilfen", [2006] Zeitschrift für die Steuer- und Erbrechtspraxis, pp.266 et seq.

objectives (e.g. investment in developing countries) can be declared compatible with the internal market according to art.107(2) and (3) TFEU.[185]

The Commission regards a tax levied on a fixed basis in the agriculture or **10–028** fisheries sector as part of the "nature and general scheme" of a tax because it has to take account of "specific accounting requirements or of the importance of land in assets which are specific to certain sectors".[186] This is not at all convincing, bearing in mind that the "nature and general scheme" of a tax refers to certain indicators of "ability to pay". Even if there exists an objective reason to simplify tax bookkeeping in certain economic sectors,[187] this fixed tax basis can only be accepted if the tax burden of the concerned undertakings does not substantially fall short of the average tax burden of comparable enterprises in other sectors of the economy.[188] In addition, an exemption of agricultural business from real estate tax is not self-explanatory as the Commission seems to suggest.[189]

Contrary to the communication of the Commission, one should not assess the progressive nature of income tax as a "selective" measure justified by the social aim of redistribution.[190] Progression as a general feature of a tax system bears no special relationship at all to certain enterprises or the production of certain goods. Furthermore, the progressive system cannot be understood as a "tax incentive" for small earners but rather as a surcharge for high-income taxpayers—it has not only been justified by social aims of economic policy but also by the economic law of diminishing utility.[191] On the other hand, the general progression of a tax rate cannot be compared to provisions which deviate from the general rule on tax rates and tax basis when small and medium enterprises are concerned. These provisions clearly constitute state aid and all one can do is to question their "selectivity".[192]

The problem of the "normal" tax rate. While it is possible to analyse the **10–029** "nature and general scheme" of a tax with regard to the tax base whose task it is to measure the "ability to pay" of a person, things are much more complicated when it comes to the determination of the "normal" tax rate. Naturally, when there is a general tax rate for all undertakings, services or goods, it is easy to identify selective tax rate reductions which deviate in single cases from the tax

---

[185] Decision 2003/590/EC [2003] O.J. L199/28 at paras 28–40; Benicke, "Die Bedeutung des EG-Rechts für gemeinnützige Einrichtungen" [1996] *Europäische Zeitschrift für Wirtschaftsrecht*, pp.165 et seq.

[186] Commission (see fn.11, above) at para.17.

[187] AG Jacobs, Joined Cases C–261/01 and C–262/01 *van Calster* [2003] E.C.R. I–12249 at para.141.

[188] Frick (see fn.34, above), pp.36 et seq.

[189] Commission, 2004 Report (see fn.12, above), para.36.

[190] See also Joined Cases T–92/00 and T–103/00 *Territorio Histórico de Álava* [2002] E.C.R. II–1385 at para.60, Joined Cases T–127/99, T–129/99 and T–148/99 *Territorio Histórico de Álava* [2002] E.C.R. II–1275 at para.164.

[191] Andel, *Finanzwissenschaft*, 4th edn (Tübingen: 1998), pp.294 et seq.

[192] Bacon (see fn.22, above), pp.306 et seq., points to tax thresholds for small enterprises which can be described as de minimis provisions in order to secure the efficiency of taxation. These provisions are features of the "nature and general scheme" of a tax.

burden "normally borne" by the taxpayer (e.g. energy-tax reductions for enterprises with substantially high energy use). But if the state sets two different tax rates for polluting and non-polluting cars, which one complies with the "general scheme" of automobile taxes? This question is not only of academic character, because it makes a difference whether the state introduces an incentive to buy environmentally friendly cars (which would qualify as a state aid) or a disincentive to buy ecologically harmful cars (which belongs to the sovereignty of the state in tax matters and can only be attacked under art.116 TFEU).[193]

In these cases one will only succeed to identify the tax difference as a state aid if the lower tax rate for non-polluting cars deviates from a former higher level or is subject to a time limit or other conditions which restrict the general applicability of this rate. In the case of "purely" regulatory taxes it may also be that the distinction of the tax rates is simply an expression of the "general scheme and nature" of the tax as it follows the environmentally harmful effects of the underlying behaviour.[194]

10–030 **International tax rules.** In the area of international tax law it must be noted that sound fiscal and economic policy traditionally intends to grant relief from juridical or economical double taxation. Therefore, unilateral or bilateral tax reductions or tax exemptions are not in themselves problematic in the light of art.107(1) TFEU. Tax provisions which are advantageous to foreign or domestic investors engaged in cross-border activities are not at all "aids" insofar as they only strive to reduce or compensate for the disadvantageous effects of double taxation.[195] Thus, any exemption or reduction which simply recompenses for taxes the investor has to pay at home or in the source country does not grant the taxpayer a favour but puts him on equal footing with domestic taxpayers or investors. From this it follows that an attractive network of double taxation agreements or a generous waiver of withholding taxes does not necessary constitute "aid" at all.[196] Moreover, the limitation of Treaty benefits by so-called LOB-clauses to companies owned by domestic taxpayers is in line with the general bilateral character of double taxation conventions and does not infringe art.107(1) TFEU.[197]

Therefore, one has to concentrate on tax provisions which give the investor tax breaks which are limited to a selective group of taxpayers. This may be the case where a limit for the deduction of interest paid to shareholders has been lifted in the case of particular treasury subsidiaries of multinational groups[198] or where cross-border loss-compensation was granted only to a selective group of export-

[193] See above, paras 10–011 et seq; Luja (see fn.1, above), pp.35–6.
[194] See para.10–018, above.
[195] Commission (see fn.11 above) at para.26.
[196] Decision 2003/887/EC [2003] O.J. L330/23 at paras 19–21; Decision 2005/378/EC [2005] O.J. L 125/10 at para.33; Easson, fn.69, above, p.80.
[197] See the debate between Christiana HJI Panayi, "Limitation on Benefits and State Aid" [2004] 44 European Taxation, pp.83–98, and Raymond H.C. Luja, "Tax Treaties and State Aid: Some Thoughts"[2004] 44 European Taxation, pp.234–38.
[198] Decision 2003/887/EC [2003] O.J. L330/23 at paras 22–4, 32–4.

oriented companies.[199] The same holds true for a "write-off" of the goodwill of foreign shareholdings which is not available for domestic shareholdings.[200] Favourable deviations from OECD standards on transfer pricing have been attacked regularly in recent years by the Commission.[201]

A borderline scenario is one where there is a choice between the "exemption method" for foreign-source income which lifts the domestic tax burden completely from outbound investment and the "credit method", which avoids double taxation by a tax credit awarded for foreign tax when it comes to the assessment of domestic tax. As a rule, both methods are available under international law (see art.23 of the OECD Model Treaty) and can form the "benchmark" for the international tax rules of a Member State. Most double taxation conventions employ a combination of both methods. Yet the deviation from the chosen benchmark in specific cases can constitute state aid: with respect to Ireland, the Commission declared that a tax exemption for foreign income which was restricted to profit distributions reinvested within Irish territory falls foul of art.107(1) TFEU.[202] In respect of Luxembourg 1929 holding companies, the Commission pointed to the fact that only a restricted group of corporate taxpayers was able to rely on the exemption method.[203]

10–031

In the context of international tax relief, it is clear that any counter-measures taken by other countries in order to compensate for the tax break in a Member State do not change the character of this preferential tax rule as state aid under art.107(1) TFEU.[204]

4. THE "SELECTIVITY" OR "SPECIFICITY" OF AN AID

General

From the foregoing we have drawn the conclusion that the distinction between a tax rule deriving from the "nature and general scheme" of a tax system and a tax measure constituting state aid does not logically coincide with the distinction between "general" and "selective" tax measures. While the first distinction deals with the question of whether there is an "aid" at all, the second one examines whether it favours "certain undertakings or the production of certain goods". In this assessment it is crucial to neatly distinguish the existence of an "advantage"

10–032

---

[199] Decision 2002/342/EC [2002] O.J. L126/27 at para.22.
[200] Decision 2011/5/EC [2011] O.J. L 7/48 at paras 84–119.
[201] Decision 2003/438/EC [2003] O.J. L153/40 at paras 42–44; Decision 2003/81/EC [2003] O.J. L31/26 at paras 26–30; Decision 2004/77/EC [2004] O.J. L23/14 at paras 42–50; Decision 2003/512/EC [2003] O.J. L177/17 at paras 20–28; Luja (see fn.1, above), pp.30–2; Joined Cases C–182/03 and C–217/03 *Belgium v Commission* [2006] E.C.R. I–5479 at paras 90–96.
[202] Commission, 2004 Report (see fn.12, above) at para.16; Decision 2003/601/EC [2003] O.J. L204/51 at para.33.
[203] Commission, 2006 EeC 78/02 [2006] O.J. C78/2 at paras 39–68; Decision 2006/940/EC [2006] O.J. L 366/47 at paras 57–71.
[204] Decision 2003/501/EC [2003] O.J. L170/20 at para.48.

from the "selectivity" of this benefit[205]—a distinction not always clearly drawn by the Commission in its decisions.[206] Again, a Member State's sovereignty can come into play in economic matters. While it is forbidden for the Member States to grant direct or indirect funding to specific enterprises or groups of enterprises, it is part of fiscal federalism that each Member State offers broadly designed economic incentives which are, in principle, available to all agents within the economy and do not distort the internal market in specific areas.[207] Therefore, "a State measure which benefits all undertakings in national territory, without distinction, cannot therefore constitute State aid".[208] State measures which address "certain undertakings"—following geographical, sectoral or horizontal criteria—are subject to state aid discipline.[209]

Recipients and beneficiaries

10–033   Again, this criterion gives rise to special problems in tax matters. While in cases of direct funding it is relatively easy to identify the recipient as the beneficiary of state aid, things are difficult when it comes to the widespread and indirect effects of tax.[210] A tax allowance on mortgage interest payments constitutes an incentive for private persons to invest in housing, but will positively affect the building industry and the banking sector as well.[211] The same is true if a state grants preferential depreciation rules for the acquisition of an aircraft: does this constitute an aid for the buyer (the airlines) or the producer (the aircraft industry)?

It would be too simple to establish a rule stipulating that tax incentives in the

---

[205] This has clearly been laid out by several Advocates-General: AG Léger, Joined Cases C–182/03 and C–217/03 *Belgium v Commission* [2006] E.C.R. I–5479 para.238; AG Tizzano, Joined Cases C–393/04 and C–41/05 *Air Liquide* [2006] E.C.R. I–5293 at paras 40–41; AG Kokott, Case C–169/08 *Regione Sardegna* [2009] E.C.R. I–10821 at paras 125–130; most explicitly AG Jääskinen, Joined Cases C–106/09 P and C–107/09 P *Gibraltar* [2011] Unreported para.158: "I am of the opinion that a measure liable to constitute State aid which is awarded in an indirect form, such as a tax measure, cannot be defined without a reference framework (. . .) The opposite approach would lead to confusion between the concept of selectivity and that of advantage, because in my view the selectivity of a measure involves and unequal distribution of the advantages as between undertakings which are in a comparable situation. Examination of the criterion of selectivity is distinct from examination of the criterion of advantage." For a less analytical view see AG Mengozzi, Case C–487/06 P *British Aggregates Association* [2008] E.C.R. I–10515 paras 80–83; Case T–335/08 *BNP Paribas* [2010] Unreported para.160.

[206] Hugo López López, "General Thought on Selectivity and Consequences of a Broad Concept of State Aid in Tax Matters", [2010] EStAL pp.807 et seq., at 808 et seq.; Raymond Luja, "Revisiting the Balance between Aid, Selectivity and Selective Aid in Respect of Taxes and Special Levies", [2010] EStAL, pp.161 et seq.; Claire Micheau, "Tax Selectivity in State Aid Review: a Debatable Case Practice", [2008] EC Tax Review, pp.276 et seq.

[207] Smit and Herzog (see fn.87, above) at para.107.03; Bellamy and Child, *European Community Law of Competition*, 6th edn (Oxford: 2008) at para.15.023.

[208] Case C–143/99 *Adria-Wien-Pipeline* [2001] E.C.R. I–8365 at paras 34–5; Joined Cases C–106/09P and C–107/09P *Gibraltar* [2011] Unreported at paras 71–75.

[209] AG Jääskinen, Joined Cases C–106/09P and C–107/09P *Gibraltar* [2011] Unreported at paras 176–177.

[210] Pierpaolo Rossi-Maccanico, "The Notion of Indirect Selectivity in Fiscal Aids: A Reasoned Review of the Community Practice", [2009] 8 EStAL, pp.161 et seq.

[211] Frick (see fn.34, above), p.25.

area of "direct taxes" go to the taxpayer and tax incentives in the area of "indirect taxes" go to the customer. The definite beneficiary can only be determined according to the influence of the price mechanism between the involved parties on the allocation of the "tax incentive". In reality, both participants will have a share in the "bounty". Therefore, in order to achieve the "effet utile" of art.107(1) TFEU one should apply the "specificity test" to all involved parties. Thus, a preferential depreciation rule for industry buildings which is not "selective" as to the side of the taxpayer, i.e. the company who commissions the construction of a new building, can be "selective" with regard to the indirectly favoured building industry. The same must be said where the tax incentive is primarily granted to private consumers (who are not "undertakings" or "producers" in the sense of art.107(1) TFEU) but has major effects for their suppliers (e.g. tax allowances for insurance premiums[212] or tax-free interest for savings contracts with a particular banking institution[213]).

The Commission and the Court have quite often dealt with this problem. In **10–034** *Gezamenlijke Steenkolenmijnen*[214] the Court declared that tax-free grants to coal miners constituted state aid favouring the coal industry, and in *3F* the Court accepted the view that tax breaks for seafarers might indirectly benefit the shipowners.[215]

In *Commission v France*[216] the Court held that a tax allowance for private savings in a specific fund which advanced loans to specific undertakings at preferential rates constituted an aid to the benefit of the borrowers. The market mechanism has been specifically addressed by the Court in a German case. According to s.6b, 52 para.8 of the German *Einkommensteuergesetz*, there is a tax break for persons on the acquisition of shares in small and medium-sized companies in Berlin and the *New Länder*. The Court has decided that a tax incentive for potential buyers of particular companies works to the advantage of those target companies which makes it possible to identify the company as a beneficiary of tax incentives given to its shareholders.[217] Tax benefits for investors or investment vehicles are regularly shifted towards the target companies enjoying better capital market conditions.[218] In *Le Levant*, the CFI (now General

---

[212] Mederer "Art.87" in: v.d. Groeben and Schwarze, *Vertrag über die Europäische Union und Vertrag zur Gründung der Europäischen Gemeinschaft—Kommentar*, 6th edn (Baden-Baden, 2003), at para.32; Müller-Graff (see fn.106, above), pp.403 et seq., pp.425 et seq.; Dassesse (see fn.30, above), pp.19 et seq.

[213] Decision 2003/216/EC [2003] O.J. L88/39 at paras 95–97.

[214] Case 30/59 *Gezamenlijke Steenkolenmijnen* [1961] E.C.R. 5; see also Case C–5/01 *Belgium v Commission* [2002] E.C.R. I–11991 at paras 44–47; for an extensive description see AG Stix-Hackl in this case at paras 47–71.

[215] Case C–319/07P *3F* [2009] E.C.R. I–5963 at paras 71–81.

[216] Case 102/87 *France v Commission* [1988] E.C.R. 4067 at para.5.

[217] Case C–156/98 *Germany v Commission* [2000] E.C.R. I–6857 at paras 22–3; see also Case C–382/99 *Netherlands v Commission* [2002] E.C.R. I–5163 at paras 55–67.

[218] Case T–445/05 *Associazione italiana del risparmio gestito* [2009] E.C.R. II–289 at paras 126–132, 159–165; Decision 2006/638/EC [2006] O.J. L268/1 at paras 42–43; Decision 2008/746/EC [2008] O.J. L252/17 at paras 68–91; Decision 2010/13/EC [2010] O.J. L6/32 paras 83–88; Piernas López, "Annotation on Cases T–424/05 and T–445/05: Indirect Advantage and Selectivity Revisited" [2010] EStAL, pp.219 et seq.

Court) addressed the possibility that tax breaks for ship investors are shifted to the enterprise which leases the ship at a reduced price.[219] In *Heiser* the Court did not accept the proposition that VAT reductions for medical services were fully passed on by doctors to insurance companies.[220] Finally, the Commission considered that tax breaks for subsidiaries of an international group can be aid in favour of the particular entity and the whole group at the same time.[221]

"Certain undertakings or the production of certain goods"

10–035 According to art.107(1) TFEU the selectivity of an aid has to be affirmed if "certain undertakings or the production of certain goods" are favoured by a measure. The Court and the Commission have established a very broad understanding of this prerequisite[222]: an aid is selective in this sense if it is not available to all economic agents of an economy. If a measure applies to "all undertakings in national territory, regardless of their activity",[223] there is no reason to apply art.107(1) TFEU. Neither the large number of eligible undertakings nor the diversity and size of the sectors to which those undertakings belong provide any ground for concluding that a state initiative constitutes a general measure of economic policy.[224] Moreover, the selectivity criterion does not require a discretionary power given to the tax authorities. Even if an exception to the benchmark is defined by "objective criteria", there can be selectivity under art.107(1) TFEU.[225]

The selectivity requirement is easily fulfilled if a tax provision leaves it to the discretion of the tax administration to grant the incentive as it sees fit.[226] In these cases the administration has room to subsidise single enterprises or branches or

---

[219] T–34/02 *Le Levant* [2006] E.C.R. II–267 at paras 109–32; Decision 2007/256/EC [2007] O.J. L112/41 para.123.

[220] C–172/03 *Heiser* [2005] E.C.R. I–1627 at para.47.

[221] Commission, 2004 Report (see fn.12, above), para.17.

[222] Aldestam (see fn.1, above).

[223] Case C–143/99 *Adria-Wien-Pipeline* [2001] E.C.R. I–8365 at para.35.

[224] Case C–75/97 *Belgium v Commission* [1999] E.C.R. I–3671 at para.32; Case C–143/99 *Adria-Wien-Pipeline* [2001] E.C.R. I–8365 at para.48; this broad concept was not shared by AG Mischo, paras 42–9.

[225] Joined Cases T–92/00 and T–103/00 *Territorio Histórico de Álava* [2002] E.C.R. II–1385 at para.58; Joined Cases T–127/99, T–129/99 and T–148/99 *Territorio Histórico de Álava* [2002] E.C.R. II–1275 at para.163; Joined Cases T–346/99, T–347/99 and T–348/99 *Territorio Histórico de Álava* [2002] E.C.R. II–4259 at para.61; Joined Cases T–269/99, T–271/99 and T–272/99 *Territorio Histórico de Guipúzcoa* [2002] E.C.R. II–4217 at para.62; Commission, 2004 Report (see fn.12 above), para.38.

[226] Case C–256/97 *DMT* [1999] E.C.R. I–3913 at paras 27–28; Joined Cases T–92/00 and T–103/00 *Territorio Histórico de Álava* [2002] E.C.R. II–1385 at paras 29–35; Joined Cases T–127/99, T–129/99 and T–148/99 *Territorio Histórico de Álava* [2002] E.C.R. II–1275 at paras 148–154; Joined Cases T–227/01 to T–229/01, T–265/01, T–266/01 and T–270/01 *Territorio Histórico de Álava* [2009] E.C.R. II–3029 paras 167–172; Commission (see fn.11, above), para.21; extensively Richard Plender, "Definition of Aid", Andrea Biondi, Piet Eeckhout and James Flynn, *The Law of State Aid in the European Union* (Oxford, 2003) at paras 3–39 at pp.21–4; Sutter (see fn.1, above), pp.52–63.

regions in order to boost their competitive standing. These discretionary powers can have different effects on the position of the taxpayer. State aid can be constituted by rulings on the tax base, the tax rate, the collection of tax arrears, the payment of interest for default or the full or partial abatement of taxes. Thus, an administrative ruling which granted to a single Spanish company the carry-forward of losses was deemed to be selective aid.[227] The same holds true when for "qualifying companies" the corporate tax rate is subject to individual negotiation.[228]

A situation where tax authorities often use their discretionary powers in order to support ailing business arises when they tolerate late payment by struggling enterprises.[229] The application of art.107(1) TFEU in cases of administrative discretion does not require any "arbitrariness" in the tax authority's behaviour.[230]

10–036

If the application of a preferential tax provision is not left to the discretion of the tax authorities, one must ascertain whether the provision itself favours certain undertakings or the production of certain goods (including services of any kind). This does not pose a problem where a provision specifically addresses individual enterprises,[231] certain industries (e.g. tax breaks for the banking sector[232] or special accounting rules for multinational groups[233]) or regions[234] (e.g. depreciation rules for buildings in the New Länder of Germany belonging to the former GDR[235]) or requires certain activities (e.g. holding functions[236]). The Court and the Commission have established far-reaching case law in this respect. Thus, tax advantages for the whole medical sector[237] or for public-owned businesses fall under the selectivity criterion[238] (as long as the benefit is not necessary to ensure that undertakings entrusted with the operation of services of general economic interest fulfil the particular tasks assigned to them[239]), and even a state aid given to all "export-oriented" industries was deemed selective enough to qualify as a

---

[227] Commission [1997] O.J. C 71/2 at para.4.

[228] Decision 2005/77/EC [2005] O.J. L 29/24 at paras 56–58.

[229] Case C–480/98 *Spain v Commission* [2000] E.C.R. I–8717 at paras 19–21; Case C–256/97 *DMT* [1999] E.C.R. I–3913 at paras 19, 27–8.

[230] Joined Cases T–92/00 and T–103/00 *Territorio Histórico de Álava* [2002] E.C.R. II–1385 at paras 29–35; Joined Cases T–127/99, T–129/99 and T–148/99 *Territorio Histórico de Álava* [2002] E.C.R. II–1275 at paras 148–54.

[231] Joined Cases T–427/04 and T–17/05 *France Télécom* [2009] E.C.R. II–4315 at para.231.

[232] Case C–66/02 *Italy v Commission* [2005] E.C.R. I–10901 at para.96; Case C–148/04 *Unicredito* [2005] E.C.R. I–11137 at para.46.

[233] Commission, 2004 Report (see fn.12, above), para.41; Decision 2003/515/EC [2003] O.J. L180/52 at paras 86–90.

[234] The problem of "tax autonomy" of sub-national bodies is discussed under 10–007 and 10–008.

[235] Case C–156/98 *Germany v Commission* [2000] E.C.R. I–6857 at para.23; see also Decision 2005/655/EC [2005] O.J. L241/59 at para.12.

[236] See Commission, 2006/C 78/02 [2006] O.J. C78/2 at paras 69–73.

[237] Case C–172/03 *Heiser* [2005] E.C.R. I–1627 at paras 39–42.

[238] Case C–387/92 *Banco Exterior de Espana* [1994] E.C.R. I–877 at paras 17 et seq.

[239] Article 106(2) TFEU; see Case T–106/95 *FFSA* [1997] E.C.R. II–229 at paras 63 et seq.

forbidden state aid.[240] From this point of view it is possible to declare a relief from energy tax for the whole "manufacturing industry" to be selective if it is not extended to businesses engaged in trade or services.[241] The same holds true for geographically limited tax reductions.[242]

10–037   On the other hand, selectivity cannot be affirmed if there is no relation at all between the tax break and the trade or business carried on by the beneficiary. Thus, a preferential tax treatment for incorporated business (i.e. a reduction of the corporation tax which does not affect partnerships or self-employed traders) does not concern certain undertakings or the production of certain goods but only a legal form of an undertaking which is open to everyone carrying on a trade or business.[243] In recent case-law, AG Jääskinen proposed that the Court accept distinctions between legal forms as non-selective[244] but this does not seem to be the majority view.[245] The Court itself seems to require a clear argument that distinct legal forms derive from different factual or legal situations in order to allow Member States to grant advantageous treatment to one legal form (irrespective of the nature of its commercial activities).[246]

Nevertheless, the Commission has embarked on a concept of "material selectivity" which also includes distinctions which do not refer to specific goods or enterprises.[247] Against this background, the Commission is of the opinion that tax incentives for small and medium enterprises or general tax reliefs for enterprise

---

[240] Decision 2001/168/EC [2001] O.J. L60/57 at para.20.

[241] Case C–143/99 *Adria-Wien-Pipeline* [2001] E.C.R. I–8365 at paras 48–54; Christos Golfinopoulos, "Concept of Selectivity Criterion in State Aid Definition following the Adria-Wien Judgment" [2003] 24 E.C.L.R. 543–549; see also Joined Cases E–5/04, E–6/04 and E–7/04 *Fesil and Finnfjord* at paras 76–81.

[242] AG Geelhoed, Case C–88/03 *Portugal v Commission* [2006] E.C.R. I–7115 at paras 45–47; Commission, 2004 Report (see fn.12, above) at paras 29–33.

[243] Bacon (see fn.22, above), p.302.

[244] AG Jääskinen, Joined Cases C–78/08 to C–80/08 *Paint Graphos* [2011] Unreported, paras 79–113; AG Jääskinen, Joined Cases C–106/09P and C–107/09P *Gibraltar* [2011] Unreported, para.142, fn.76 (for cooperatives); see also Decision 2010/473/EU [2010] O.J. L235/1 paras 155–177.

[245] Joined Cases C–78/08 to C–80/08 *Paint Graphos* [2011] Unreported at paras 48–52; Case C–222/04 *Cassa di Risparmio di Firenze* [2006] E.C.R. I–289 para.136; selectivity was affirmed for "venture capital companies" (Decision 2010/13/EC [2010] O.J. L6/32 paras 70–71, 78–82); for all municipal companies set up under a certain law (Case T–222/04 *Italy v. Commission* [2009] E.C.R. II–1877 at paras 62–66); for public-owned companies (Decision 2006/748/EC [2006] O.J. L307/219 paras 28–39); for 1929 Luxembourg Holding Companies (Decision 2006/940/EC [2006] O.J. L366/47 at paras 72–83); for specialised investment vehicles (Case T–445/05 *Associazione italiana del risparmio gestito* [2009] E.C.R. II–289 paras 147/157; Decision 2006/638/EC [2006] O.J. L268/1 paras 36–41); for REITs see Hein Vermeulen, "Fiscal State Aid and Real Estate Collective Investment Vehicles (CIVs)", 20 EC Tax Review (2011) pp.155–158 with further references to Commission practice.

[246] Joined Cases C–78/08 to C–80/08 *Paint Graphos* [2011] n.y.r. paras 51–61.

[247] Aldestam, fn.1, above, pp.76–80; Bartosch, fn.160 (2010) above, pp.729 et seq.; Bousin/Piernas, fn.51, above, pp.634 et seq.; Bartlomiej Kurcz/Dimitri Vallindas, "Can General Measures be . . . Selective? Some Thoughts on the Interpretation of a State Aid Definition", [2008] 45 *Common Market Law Review* pp.159 et seq.; López López fn.206, above, pp.811 et seq.; Roth, fn.1, above, pp.131–3.

founders or "newly created companies",[248] as well as tax breaks for "undertakings newly listed on a regulated market",[249] concern "certain" undertakings. The same has been said for tax breaks which require a "minimum investment" or the creation of a minimum number of jobs.[250] In the context of "unfair tax competition", the performance of intra-group services for multinationals was several times declared to be "selective" in this sense,[251] and also a tax benefit for the acquisition of foreign shareholdings which was available to all sorts of taxpayers was regarded as selective.[252] This extensive interpretation of the selectivity criterion leads to a major reduction of the power of Member States to shape their tax systems as they see fit.

"De facto selectivity"

On the other hand, tax provisions disguised as "general measures" which seem **10–038** to promote unspecific goals of economic policy, may well aim to give preferential treatment to a single enterprise or a certain branch of enterprises. Therefore, a "substance over form" approach would advocate the application of a "de facto selectivity" criterion. *Easson* cites the case of the Romanian government, which introduced a general tax break for investments exceeding US$50 million, knowing quite well that there was only one (foreign-source) investment of this size in the whole country.[253] In an Italian case, a tax break was introduced concerning the reconstruction of companies whose capital exceeded ITL50 billion provided the reconstruction took place before December 31, 1990. It is doubtful whether one can affirm the "selectivity" of these tax measures bearing in mind that,

---

[248] [1998] O.J. C334/6–8; [1996] O.J. C213/4 at para.2.1.; Joined Cases T–92/00 and T–103/00 *Territorio Histórico de Álava* [2002] E.C.R. II–1385 at para.40; Joined Cases T–127/99, T–129/99 and T–148/99 *Territorio Histórico de Álava* [2002] E.C.R. II–1275 at para.159; Decision 2004/343/EC [2004] L 108/38 at para.25; see also Baudenbacher, fn.64, above, p.21; Lehner, "Die europarechtliche Problematik des §6d EStG und des geplanten §7b EStG, insbesondere in bezug auf das Beihilfeverbot des Art. 92 EWGV"[1983] *Der Betrieb* 1783 et seq.; Luja, fn.1, above, pp.65–6.

[249] Case T–211/05 *Italy v Commission* [2009] E.C.R. II–2777 at paras 119–124; Case C–304/09 *Commission v Italy* [2010] n.y.r.; Decision 2006/261/EC [2006] O.J. L94/42 at paras 26–32.

[250] Joined Cases T–92/00 and T–103/00 *Territorio Histórico de Álava* [2002] E.C.R. II–1385 at paras 37–41, 49–53; Joined Cases T–127/99, T–129/99 and T–148/99 *Territorio Histórico de Álava* [2002] E.C.R. II–1275 at paras 155–7, 159; Joined Cases T–269/99, T–271/99 and T–272/99 *Territorio Histórico de Guipúzcoa* [2002] E.C.R. II–4217 at para.57; Case T–346/99 *Territorio Histórico de Álava* [2002] E.C.R. II–4259 at para.53.

[251] Joined Cases C–182/03 and C–217/03 *Belgium v Commission* [2006] E.C.R. I–5479 at para.122; Commission, 2004 Report, fn.12, above, paras 26–8; Decision 2003/438/EC [2003] O.J. L153/40 at paras 48–50; Decision 2004/76/EC [2004] O.J. L23/1 at paras 63–9; Decision 2002/937/EC [2002] O.J. L329/22 at paras 50–52; Decision 2003/512/EC [2003] O.J. L177/17 at para.32; Rossi-Maccanico (2004) (see fn.1, above), pp.241–2; for specific group interest regimes the Commission distinguishes between rules on interest taxation and deduction which apply to all corporate groups without qualification (Decision 2009/809/EC [2009] O.J. L288/26 at paras 83–128) and tax regimes which exclude specific economic sectors or companies according to size or are simply optional (Decision 2010/95/EC [2010] O.J. L42/3 at paras 106–129).

[252] Decision 2011/5/EC [2011] O.J. L7/48 paras 84–119.

[253] Easson (see fn.69, above), p.83, note 49.

according to the Court, one should not look at the "aims and causes" but strictly at the "effects" of a tax provision. Nevertheless, it was correct of the Commission to classify the Italian tax provision as a prohibited state aid[254] because the tax measure had a time limit and did not change the general tax system. The same holds true for capital gains taxation on restructurings which factually favour banks and insurance companies.[255] Moreover, the Commission has declared a rebate for energy tax in Austria which was dependent on a minimum proportion of energy consumption vis-à-vis the net production value to constitute a "de facto" selective rebate in favour of high-energy undertakings.[256]

Another method of disguised specificity provides preferential treatment for certain production factors, i.e. tax incentives for research and development, reduction in energy expenditure, or employment. The Commission points out that a shift of the tax burden between the factors of production does not constitute state aid, even if the preferential treatment of a certain factor of production benefits certain branches (e.g. high-tech industries or labour intensive services).[257] It is true that the pursuit of general economic goals as employment programmes or high technological standards rests with the sovereignty of the Member States. Even general tax reliefs on investment are not specific enough.[258] But we must accept the fact that a tax relief with application to a certain production factor must be called a selective state aid if it is possible to identify a specific group of "producers" in the sense of art.107(1) TFEU which primarily benefit from the tax break. Thus, a preferential depreciation rule on the acquisition of aircrafts does constitute state aid in favour of airlines, even if it is only one factor of production whose acquisition is facilitated. Even a standard depreciation rate on all sorts of investments assets which effectively works as a specific tax credit for certain groups of undertakings, can qualify as a state aid.[259] Against this background, the Commission has decided that some general rules on leasing taxation might, de facto, work as selective benefits for air and maritime transport industries.[260]

5. Tax Financing of State Aid

10–039   An issue which has been the subject of debate in several recent judgments concerns the interaction of state aid and the way in which this aid is financed. This is especially important in the tax area because the application of state aid rules leads to a recovery of an unlawful aid from the recipient while a challenge

---

[254] Decision 92/389/EC [1992] O.J. L207/47.

[255] Decision 2006/748/EC [2006] O.J. L307/219 para.34.

[256] Decision 2005/565/EC [2005] O.J. L190/13 at paras 45–55; Rossi-Maccanico (2004) (see fn.1, above), p.241.

[257] Commission (see fn.11, above) at para.14.

[258] Michael Lang "Steuervereinfachung und Europarecht" in: Fischer (ed.), *Steuervereinfachung (Jahrbuch No.21) of the Deutsche Steuerjuristische Gesellschaft* (Cologne, 1998), pp.145 et seq., 161.

[259] Easson (see fn.69, above), p.77.

[260] Decision 2007/256/EC [2007] O.J. L112/41 at paras 106–117.

on the financing side would relieve taxpayers from their obligation to contribute to the financing scheme of the aid.[261]

This situation can be addressed from different perspectives. A dimension which has already been mentioned concerns the application of art.110 TFEU to taxes on goods, which are designed to cover both foreign and domestic products but the revenue of which only serves the purposes of the domestic taxpayers, i.e. a parafiscal charge, the revenue of which is used to finance marketing or research efforts for domestic industry. In these cases, both art.110 and art.107(1) TFEU have to be applied.[262]

Another unresolved issue concerns the extension of art.107(1) TFEU to the **10–040** "financing side" of state aid. As far as the means employed by the government to grant state aid is financed from the general budget of a Member State, the state aid aspect and the revenue aspect are disconnected and there is an isolated analysis of the advantage conferred upon a private market participant under art.107(1) TFEU. The picture changes if there is a material nexus between the revenue and the expenditure side of a state aid. In the leading case, *Van Calster*, AG Jacobs proposed that the financing side should be included into the examination under art.107(1) TFEU if a tax or charge is levied "specifically for the purpose of financing an illegally granted aid".[263] The Court itself demanded that the tax forms an "integral part" of the aid measure.[264] In order to fall under this requirement, the tax or charge in question must be "hypothecated" to the aid measures under the relevant national rules.[265] This requires that "the revenue from the tax has a direct impact on the amount of the aid and, consequently, on the assessment of the compatibility of the aid with the common [internal] market".[266] This "automatic" nexus is not given if the amount of the aid is not

---

[261] Case C–390/98 *Banks* [2001] E.C.R. I–6117 at para.90; Joined Cases C–266/04—C–270/04, C–276/04 and C–321/04—C–325/04 *Distribution Casino France SAS* [2005] E.C.R. I–9481 at para.42; AG Jacobs, Joined Cases C–261/01 and C–262/01 *Van Calster* [2003] E.C.R. I–12249 at paras 39–40; AG Geelhoed, Case C–174/02 *Streekgewest Westelijk Noord-Brabant* [2005] E.C.R. I–85 at para.72.

[262] Joined Cases C–261/01 and C–262/01 *Van Calster* [2003] E.C.R. I–12249 at para.48; Case C–204/97 *Portugal v Commission* [2001] E.C.R. I–3175 at paras 40–41; see above, para.10–004.

[263] AG Jacobs, Joined Cases C–261/01 and C–262/01 *Van Calster* [2003] E.C.R. I–12249 at paras 35–37; this is accompanied by an analysis of previous judicature on this topic in paras 29–34; see also the analysis by AG Geelhoed, Case C–174/02 *Streekgewest Westelijk Noord-Brabant* [2005] E.C.R. I–85 at paras 32–36.

[264] Joined Cases C–261/01 and C–262/01 *Van Calster* [2003] E.C.R. I–12249 at para.49.

[265] Case C–175/02 *Pape* [2005] E.C.R. I–127 at para.15; Case C–174/02 *Streekgewest Westelijk Noord-Brabant* [2005] E.C.R. I–85 at para.26; Joined Cases C–266/04—C–270/04, C–276/04 and C–321/04—C–325/04 *Distribution Casino France SAS* [2005] E.C.R. I–9481 at paras 40, 46; Joined Cases C–128/03 and C–129/03 *AEM SpA* [2005] E.C.R. I–2861 at paras 45–46; Joined Cases C–393/04 and C–41/05 *Air Liquide* [2006] E.C.R. I–5293 at paras 39–48; Bartlomiej Kurcz, "Annotation to Judgment in Joined Cases C–393/04 and C–41/05—Air Liquide", [2006] 5 EStAL, pp.597 et seq.

[266] Case C–175/02 *Pape* [2005] E.C.R. I–127 at para.15; Case C–174/02 *Streekgewest Westelijk Noord-Brabant* [2005] E.C.R. I–85 at para.26; Case C–333/07 *Société Régie Networks* [2008] E.C.R. I–10807 at paras 87–90; AG Kokott, Case C–333/07 *Société Régie Networks* [2008] E.C.R. I–10807 at paras 95–115; Mihalis Kekelekis/Ioana Eleonora Rusu, "Régie Networks v Direction de contrôle fiscal Rhône-Alpes Bourgogne" [2009] 8 EStAL, pp.569 et seq.

"logically" dependent on the amount of revenue raised from the tax[267] or if public authorities have discretion in how to allocate the revenue from a tax to recipients.[268]

The most relevant consequence of this restricted view lies in the fact that the Court will not permit those taxpayers not covered by a "tax exemption" or another tax break to challenge their tax bill and claim reimbursement of their tax payments. The mere fact that, from a budgetary standpoint, the high tax burden for "normal" taxpayers serves as compensation for the low tax burden on the beneficiary of the tax incentive does not suffice to make the "normal" tax treatment an "integral part" of the state aid scheme even if it is laid down in the same statutory regime.[269] In order to conclude that the tax financing is unlawful in itself and has to be reimbursed, the revenue from a tax must form a budgetary pool in its own right which is allocated to the beneficiaries of the state aid without any discretionary element in between.

6. STATE AID RULES AND "HARMFUL TAX COMPETITION"

10–041   In 1997, the Council of Ministers established a "High-Level-Group", whose task it was (and is) to identify "unfair competition" between Member States in tax matters. The work of this group resulted in a "Code of Conduct", which gives both abstract definitions and some examples of unfair measures in the field of taxation.[270] In 1999, the group identified a large array of 66 "harmful tax measures".[271] Since then, there has been a growing political consensus to roll back existing instruments of harmful tax competition and to refrain from introducing new ones.[272] This European fight against harmful tax measures finds a parallel movement in the work of the OECD on "Harmful Tax Competition—An Emerging Global Issue".[273]

---

[267] Joined Cases C–266/04—C–270/04, C–276/04 and C–321/04—C–325/04 *Distribution Casino France SAS* [2005] E.C.R. I–9481 at paras 41, 49, 52; the issue was not substantially discussed in Case C–204/97 *Portugal v Commission,* [2001] I–3175 at para.48.

[268] Case C–175/02 *Pape* [2005] E.C.R. I–127 at para.16; in Case C–526/04 *Laboratoires Boiron SA* [2006] E.C.R. I–7529 at paras 31–48 the court decided that a tax has to be reimbursed if the tax and the exemption only concern two competing groups of economic operators; Case C–368/04 *Transalpine Olleitung* [2006] E.C.R. I–9957 paras 50–51; Joined Cases C–393/04 and C–41/05 *Air Liquide* [2006] E.C.R. I–5293 at paras 39–45.

[269] Case C–174/02 *Streekgewest Westelijk Noord-Brabant* [2005] E.C.R. I–85 at para.27; Joined Cases C–266/04—C–270/04, C–276/04 and C–321/04—C–325/04 *Distribution Casino France SAS* [2005] E.C.R. I–9481 at para.41; AG Geelhoed, Case C–174/02 *Streekgewest Westelijk Noord-Brabant* [2005] E.C.R. I–85 at paras 42–45.

[270] [1998] O.J. C2/1. From the abundant literature on the Code of Conduct may be presented: Pinto (see fn.38, above); Easson (see fn.10, above), pp.1 et seq.; Osterweil, "The OECD and The EU: Two Approaches to Harmful Tax" [1999] EC Tax Journal, pp.89 et seq.

[271] Commission press release: Brussels (February 29, 2000)—Nr.4901/99; Helen Nijkamp, "Landmark Agreement on EU tax policy: new guidelines stretch scope of EU Code of Conduct" [2001] 10 EC Tax Review, pp.147–153.

[272] On the legal aspects of tax competition in Europe see: Wolfgang Schön (ed.), *Tax Competition in Europe* (Amsterdam, 2003); Carlo Pinto, *Tax Competition and EU Law* (The Hague, 2003).

[273] Paris, 1998.

In order to grasp the importance of arts 107 et seq. TFEU in the context of unfair tax competition, it has to be borne in mind that while the Code of Conduct has no binding force and cannot be judicially executed among the Member States, the Treaty's articles on state aid confer on the Commission the power to forbid certain measures if they are not covered by the exemptions under art.107(2) and (3) TFEU.[274] Therefore, the Commission has initiated several proceedings against Member States in the context of its fight against "harmful tax competition".[275] These proceedings require that the elements of art.107(1) TFEU are fulfilled, i.e. that the examined tax incentives confer a "tax benefit" upon internationally active business which is "selective" in the above-mentioned sense.[276] Nevertheless, the typical feature of "harmful tax competition", i.e. the "ring-fenced" creation of a beneficial tax environment for foreign investors, does not fully coincide with the definition of state aid under art.107(1) TFEU so that proceedings under art.107(1) TFEU require full examination of the traditional elements of this provision.[277] In this respect, the Court clarified in *Gibraltar* that selective tax benefits are not outside the scope of state aid control due to the regulatory technique employed by the state in question.[278]

While it has been easy in the past to identify special regimes for cross-border investment as "beneficial" in the first place, it is not self-explanatory that these benefits are granted on a "selective" basis. Only an extended interpretation of "certain undertakings and certain goods" in art.107(1) TFEU has put the Commission in the position to attack a whole group of tax provisions which were addressed at multinational groups of companies but did not require a specific economic activity of the beneficiary. This has been criticised as it seems to blur the boundary between arts 116, 117 and art.107(1) TFEU.[279]

---

[274] Schön, fn.17, above, pp.99 et seq.

[275] For an overview see Commission, 2004 Report, fn.12, above; Pierpaolo Rossi-Maccanico, "Commentary of State Aid Review of Multinational Tax Regimes", [2007] EStAL pp.25 et seq.

[276] This point has been extensively laid out by A.G. Jääskinen in the Gibraltar case (see joined Cases C–106/09P and C–107/09P *Gibraltar* [2011] n.y.r. at paras 110–115, 122–134, 141, 220–221); on the application of art.107(1) TFEU in the context of "harmful tax competition" see Martha O'Brien, fn.26, above, pp.218–20; Rossi-Maccanico, fn.1 (2004) above, pp.231–2; Quigley, "General Taxation", fn.1 above, pp.214–6; Schön, fn.17 above, pp.99 et seq.; Augusto Fantozzi, "The Applicability of State Aid Rules to Tax Competition Measures: A Process of 'De Facto' Harmonization in the Tax Field?" in: Wolfgang Schön (ed.), *Tax Competition in Europe* (Amsterdam, 2003) pp.121–32.

[277] Frans Vanistendael, "Fiscal support measures and harmful tax competition" [2000] 9 EC Tax Review, pp.152–60. Court practice so far includes Belgian coordination centres (Joined Cases C–182/03 and C–217/03 *Belgium v Commission* [2006] E.C.R. I–5479 (see Raymond H.C. Luja, "Harmful Tax Policy: When Political Objectives Interfere with State Aid Rules" [2003] 31 *Intertax*, pp.484–88; Jayant Mehta, "Case Report" [2007] EStAL, pp.732 et seq.) and Dutch tax-free reserves for international groups (Case C–519/07 P *Koninklijke Friesland Campina* [2009] E.C.R. I–8495).

[278] Joined Cases C–106/09P and C–107/09P *Gibraltar* [2011] Unreported at paras 87–104.

[279] Francesco Nanetti and Giovanni Mameli, "The creeping normative role of the EC Commission in the twin-track struggle against State aids and harmful tax competition" [2002] 11 *EC Tax Review*, pp.185–90; Gerard Meussen, "The EU-fight against harmful tax competition; future developments" [2002] 11 *EC Tax Review*, pp.157–160.

10–042   The "non-selective" but still "harmful" measure is where the Code of Conduct leads beyond the beaten path.[280] The fight against "harmful" or "unfair" tax competition is aimed not only at a more effective use of state aid law but also at general tax measures which lure foreign capital and other investment away from their source country by offering tax rates or tax bases or an administrative practice which do not reflect the true balance of taxes and public services of the "poaching" Member State. From an economic standpoint, the Code of Conduct attempts to address the situation where a foreign investor is influenced to invest his capital in a country at a preferential low tax charge without having to dispense with public services of high quality at home.[281] As the Code of Conduct has no binding force, in this area it is of crucial importance for the Commission's practice to identify the line between general and selective tax incentives, the latter ones falling under the control of state aid law. Thus, the applicability of state aid law draws a decisive line; it deals with the "crucial and complex issue of the separation of powers within the Community".[282]

---

[280] Code of Conduct (see fn.9, above), Annex B.
[281] OECD (see fn.38, above), p.14.
[282] Bacon (see fn.22, above), p.269.

CHAPTER 11

GENERAL BLOCK EXEMPTION REGULATION*

1. INTRODUCTION 11–001
2. GENERAL BLOCK EXEMPTION REGULATION 11–004
   Articles 13–16: regional investment aid and employment aid 11–017
   Articles 17–25: environmental aid 11–018
   Articles 28–29: risk capital 11–021
   Articles 30–37: aid for research, development and innovation 11–022
   Articles 38–42: "social aid" 11–023
   Final provisions 11–027
3. EXPERIENCE 11–028
4. WHY DOES THE COMMISSION NOT BLOCK EXEMPT MORE MEASURES? 11–029

1. INTRODUCTION

The Council Regulation No.994/98[1] (so-called "Enabling Regulation") **11–001**
empowers the European Commission "to declare that the following categories of
aid should be compatible with the internal market and shall not be subject to the
notification requirements of Article [108(3)] of the Treaty".[2]

Article 1 states that the following categories of aid may be covered by a group
exemption regulation:

- aid in favour of small and medium sized enterprises, research and development, environmental protection, and employment and training; and

- aid that complies with the map approved by the Commission for each
  Member State for the grant of regional aid.

Procedurally, the Commission is obliged to consult a newly created advisory
committee on state aid before adopting regulations pursuant to the enabling

---

* Koen Van de Casteele
[1] Council Regulation (EC) No.994/98 of May 7, 1998 on the application of arts 92 and 93 of the
Treaty establishing the European Community to certain categories of horizontal state aid, O.J.
L142, May 14, 1998, p.1.
[2] art.1(1) of regulation 994/98.

regulation. Although the Commission must take the "utmost account of the opinion delivered by the Committee", the latter's role does not seem to go beyond the normal advisory role traditionally played by the "multilateral meetings" with the Member States before the adoption of soft law instruments.

11–002   A further limitation on the Commission's power to adopt exemption regulations is laid down in point 4 of the preamble of the enabling regulation: the adoption of exemption regulations is only possible where the Commission has gained "considerable experience". That is rather self-evident as the Commission would otherwise not be in a position to define general compatibility criteria.

On this basis, the Commission adopted:

- Commission Regulation (EC) No.68/2001 of January 12, 2001 on the application of arts [107] and [108 TFEU] to training aid,[3] as amended by the Commission Regulation (EC) No.363/2004 of February 25, 2004, amending Regulation (EC) No.68/2001 on the application of arts [107] and [108 TFEU] to training aid[4] (hereafter referred to as "training block exemption regulation").

- Commission Regulation (EC) No.70/2001 of January 12, 2001 on the application of arts [107] and [108 TFEU] to state aid to small and medium sized enterprises,[5] as amended by Commission Regulation (EC) No.364/2004 of February 25, 2004 amending Regulation (EC) No.70/2001 as regards the extension of its scope to include aid for research and development[6] (hereafter referred to as "SME block exemption regulation"). The latter amendment extended the scope of the SME block exemption regulation to include research and development and introduced a new definition for SMEs.

- Commission Regulation (EC) No.2204/2002 of December 12, 2002 on the application of arts [107] and [108 TFEU] to state aid for employment[7] (hereafter "employment block exemption regulation").

- Commission Regulation (EC) No.1628/2006 of October 24, 2006 on the application of arts [107] and [108] of the Treaty to national regional investment aid[8] (hereafter "block exemption regulation for regional aid").

11–003   The introduction of block exemption regulations is a fundamental change in Commission policy—from an *ex ante* control system to an *ex post* control system. The block exemption regulations are also directly applicable by the different administrations and judiciaries of all Member States, whereas the

---

[3] O.J. L10, January 13, 2001, p.20.
[4] O.J. L63, February 28, 2004, p.20.
[5] O.J. L10, January 13, 2001, p.33.
[6] O.J. L63, February 28, 2004, p.22.
[7] O.J. L337, December 13, 2002, p.3; corrigendum O.J. L349, December 24, 2002, p.126.
[8] O.J. L302, November 1, 2006, p.29.

traditional "guidelines" can only be applied by the Commission. Block exemption regulations will also alleviate the burden for the Commission, allowing it to focus more resources on more distortive cases.

The 2005 State Aid Action Plan had put forward the wish to consolidate and extend the scope of the various block exemption regulations into one general regulation. This new General Block Exemption Regulation (hereafter "GBER") which was adopted in 2008,[9] harmonises and consolidates into one text the rules previously existing in five separate Regulations, and enlarges the categories of state aid covered by the exemption. The regulation also has to be seen as contributing to the Small Business Act which was adopted by the Commission on June 25, 2008.[10]

2. GENERAL BLOCK EXEMPTION REGULATION

Benefits of the new GBER. The new GBER will automatically approve whole categories of aid, without the need for notifications. In practice, this implies that Member States can grant aid more quickly. This reduces red tape for the Member State, the beneficiaries and for the Commission. The law both simplifies the existing arrangements for automatic approvals, consolidating them into a single law. It also exempts new types of aid.   **11–004**

Structure. The GBER is divided into three chapters. The first chapter contains a set of common provisions which apply to all aid categories. The second chapter sets out specific provisions for the different categories of aid contained in the GBER. In the third chapter in particular the rules on entry into force and transitional arrangements in relation to the previous block exemption regulations are set out. Finally, there are three annexes, the first containing the definition of small and medium-sized enterprises, and the second and third containing the summary information sheets to be used for reporting purposes.   **11–005**

Scope. Article 1(1) of the GBER list the categories which can come under the GBER. Although 10 measures are listed, 26 measures in fact come under the GBER. The remainder of art.1 defines the scope of application. Although the GBER has a general vocation and limits the number of exclusions compared to the earlier block exemption regulations, there remains a patchwork of (sometimes partially) excluded sectors or activities.   **11–006**

---

[9] Commission regulation (EC) No.800/2008 declaring certain categories of aid compatible with the internal market in application of arts [107] and [108 TFEU], O.J. L214, August 9, 2008, p.3.

[10] Communication from the Commission to the Council, the European Parliament, the European Economic and Social Committee and the Committee of the Regions, "Think Small First—A 'Small Business Act' for Europe" (SEC (2008) 2101, SEC (2008) 2102).

In the light of the international obligations of the European Union,[11] export aid or aid favouring domestic over imported products is excluded. Export aid is defined as aid directly linked to the quantities exported, to the establishment and operation of a distribution network, or to other current expenditure linked to the export activity.

The GBER applies to all sectors, with the exception of:

- the primary agriculture sector, fisheries and aquaculture, except as regards training aid, aid in the form of risk capital, aid in the form of research, development and innovation, and aid for disadvantaged and disabled workers;

- aid for activities in processing and marketing of agricultural products in a limited number of cases (in particular if the aid might be passed on to the primary agriculture sector);

- the coal mining sector, with the exception of training aid, research and development and innovation and environmental aid;

- steel, shipbuilding and synthetic fibres are included, except as regards regional aid.

The GBER does not apply to regional aid schemes which are targeted at specific sectors. The GBER further excludes ad hoc aid to large enterprises.[12]

Finally, the GBER also excludes both undertakings in difficulties[13] and undertakings which are subject to an outstanding recovery decision (so-called "Deggendorf-principle", following the Court judgment in case C–355/95P).[14] Also schemes must contain a clause excluding such companies, otherwise the scheme itself cannot benefit from the block exemption.[15] The exclusion of companies which are subject to a recovery decision must be seen in the light of the desire to enhance enforcement.

To determine whether an undertaking is in difficulty, the Community guidelines on state aid for rescuing and restructuring firms in difficulty[16] provide that a firm is considered as being in difficulty where it is unable, whether through its own resources or with the funds it is able to obtain from its owner/shareholders

---

[11] WTO Agreement on Subsidies and Countervailing Measures, O.J. L336, December 23, 1994, p.156. Article 3 SCM (Prohibited Export Subsidies): "subsidies contingent, in law or in fact, whether solely or as one of several other conditions, upon export performance", and "subsidies contingent, whether solely or as one of several other conditions, upon the use of domestic over imported goods."

[12] art.1(5) GBER.

[13] art.1(6)(c) GBER.

[14] Case C–355/95 P *Textilwerke Deggendorf GmbH (TWD) v Commission of the European Communities and Federal Republic of Germany* [1997] E.C.R. I–2549, paras 25–27; art.1(6)(b) GBER.

[15] art.1(6)(a) GBER.

[16] As defined in the Community guidelines on state aid for rescuing and restructuring firms in difficulty, O.J. C244, October 1, 2004, p.2.

or creditors, to stem losses which, without outside intervention by the public authorities, will almost certainly condemn it to going out of business in the short or medium term. There are two tests to determine whether this is the case. Point 10 gives a series of objective criteria: where more than half of a company's registered capital has been lost and more than one quarter of it was lost over the preceding 12 months or where it fulfils the criteria under its domestic law for being the subject of collective insolvency proceedings. Point 11 contains a list of typical indicators which point at the existence of difficulties. The indicators mentioned are increasing losses, diminishing turnover, growing stock inventories, excess capacity, declining cash flow, mounting debt, rising interest charges and falling or nil net asset value. In order to simplify the administrative burden for Member States, the definition is simplified for SMEs. For them, only the absence of the "hard" criteria in point 10 of the rescue and restructuring guidelines need be verified in order to assess eligibility under the GBER. An SME which has been incorporated less than three years ago is not considered to be a firm in difficulty, unless it meets the conditions for being the subject of collective insolvency proceedings. This should prevent start-ups, which may be loss-making, from being disqualified from support measures which come under the GBER.

Definitions. Article 2 of the GBER contains a long list of definitions which are common for the different parts of the GBER. **11–007**

Exemption. Article 3 provides that aid measures fulfilling all the relevant conditions are exempt from notification. The measure must however contain an express reference to the GBER. Non-respect of this formal condition would lead to losing the benefit of the block exemption, meaning that although measures may be compatible, they could nevertheless be unlawful, since they have not been notified. The Commission cannot sanction such illegality, but competitors could take action before national courts.[17] **11–008**

Calculation. Calculation of aid intensities is explained in art.4 GBER. All calculations should be done before any deduction of tax or charges. The net present value must be calculated for aid paid in instalments. **11–009**

Transparency. Article 5 contains one of the key provisions: the GBER only applies to transparent aid. This provision is similar to what is laid down in the de minimis regulation. Examples of transparent aid listed in the GBER include grants and interest rate subsidies, loans where the gross grant equivalent has been calculated on the basis of the reference rate methodology, guarantees where the methodology has been notified and approved under the GBER or for SMEs **11–010**

---

[17] C–354/90, *Fédération Nationale du Commerce Extérieur des Produits Alimentaires e.a./France* [1991] E.C.R. I–5505, para.12–14. See also C–199/06, *CELF et Ministre de la Culture et de la Communication* [2008] E.C.R. I–469, paras 46–55.

where they respect the safe-harbour premiums laid down in the guarantee notice.[18] Capital injections, repayable advances and risk capital measures are not considered as transparent (with the exception of the risk capital measure permitted under art.29 GBER). Also fiscal measures are not transparent unless there is a cap which ensures that the applicable threshold is respected.

11–011 **Notification obligation.** Above certain thresholds, due to the higher risk of distortion of competition, aid measures must still be notified (art.6 GBER). Although the rules have been simplified and thresholds increased when compared to the previously existing block exemption regulations, there remains nevertheless a wide variation between the different thresholds over different sectors:

- SME investment and employment aid: €7.5 million per undertaking per investment;

- Investment aid for environmental protection: €7.5 million per undertaking per investment;

- Aid for consultancy for SMEs: €2 million per undertaking per project;

- Aid for SME participation in fairs: €2 million per undertaking per project;

- Research and development project aid and feasibility studies: €20 million per undertaking, per project or feasibility study, if predominantly[19] fundamental research; €10 million if mostly industrial research; and €7.5 million for all other projects. The amounts are doubled if it concerns a EUREKA project;

- Aid for industrial property right costs for SMEs: €5 million per undertaking per project;

- Training aid: €2 million per training project;

- Aid for the recruitment of disadvantaged workers: €5 million per undertaking per year;

- Aid for the employment of disabled workers: €10 million per year;

- Aid compensating for additional costs of employing disabled workers: €10 million per undertaking per year.

- Regional aid for large investment projects: 75 per cent of the maximum amount of aid a large undertaking could receive for an investment with eligible costs of €100 million.

---

[18] Commission Notice on the application of arts 87 and 88 of the EC Treaty to state aid in the form of guarantees, O.J. C155, June 20, 2008, p.10.
[19] Meaning that more than 50% of the eligible project costs are incurred through activities which fall in the relevant category of fundamental research or industrial research.

Recently the Commission has adopted specific rules in two Communications, detailing how it will assess measures which exceed the thresholds and thus need to be notified, describing the criteria for the compatibility analysis of state aid to disadvantaged and disabled workers subject to individual notification,[20] and for the compatibility analysis of training state aid cases subject to individual notification.[21]

The fundamental principles are set out in the Commission's State Aid Action Plan. The core element of these principles is the balancing test. The idea behind this test is to disentangle the positive and negative effects resulting from an aid, evaluate them and then balance them. That means first to look at the purpose of state aid: Is there a market failure that needs to be corrected? Furthermore the test looks at the design of the aid measure: Is state aid the appropriate instrument to remedy the problem? Does it induce a change of behaviour in the aid recipient? Is it proportionate? These positive effects have to be balanced against negative effects the aid might bring about. A first example of how the Commission goes about this balancing text in the context of training aid can be found in the *De Tomaso* case.[22]

Cumulation. Article 7 contains some rules on cumulation. First, it requires that **11–012** all public support must be taken into account for determining whether the notification thresholds are met, including, local, regional, national or Community sources. The latter point is in line with the recently clarified position that Community resources can also constitute state aid, as has also been laid down in the de minimis regulation[23] and was already implied by the earlier block exemption regulations.

Cumulation with other aid measures under the block exemption is permitted, as long as it concerns different eligible expenses, or where there is some overlap, as long as the higher applicable threshold is respected. Aid for disabled workers can however be cumulated up to 100 per cent of wage costs. Some more restrictive rules apply for risk capital measures under art.29 GBER and aid for young innovative enterprises (art.35 GBER), although it seems the rule can be easily circumvented by first granting the other exempted aid and only afterwards the risk capital aid or the aid for young innovative firms.

Incentive effect. Another key feature of the GBER is the insistence that the aid **11–013** should have an incentive effect and that it should be instrumental in achieving the

---

[20] O.J. C188 of August 11, 2009, p.6

[21] O.J. C188 of August 11, 2009, p.1

[22] SA31390 (N 344/2010) *Training aid to De Tomaso Automobili SpA*, approved on March 23, 2011 [2011] O.J. C149/54.

[23] See art.2(2) de minimis regulation; the position before was much less clear-cut. For example in the 2003 competition report, it is stated explicitly: "[w]ith respect to competition rules, it should be noted that Community support does not represent State aid within the meaning of Article 87(1), . . . " (para.393). Such reading seems to have been influenced by an old case regarding agricultural export restitutions which confirms that Community resources do not fall under the state aid rules since they do not constitute State resources (cf. para.22 of Cases 213–215/81, *Norddeutsches Vieh- und Fleischkontor*, E.C.R. 1982, p.3583).

desired outcome. If the aid has no incentive effect, it cannot address a market failure and would amount to pure operating aid, which cannot normally be declared compatible with the internal market. The GBER requires for SMEs a rather formal test (in line with previous block exemption regulation) that the beneficiary has made an application for aid before work on the project or activity has started.[24] For larger undertakings, apart from this formal requirement, the Member State must also have verified documentation from the beneficiary showing that there is:

- a material increase in the size of the project/activity;
- a material increase in the scope of the project/activity;
- a material increase in the total amount spent by the beneficiary; or
- a material increase in the speed of completion.

For regional investment aid, the documentation must show that the project would not have been carried out as such in the assisted region concerned in the absence of the aid.

Article 8 GBER should be interpreted in the light of recital 29, which states that the Member State should ensure that the beneficiary has analysed, in an internal document, the viability of the aided project or activity with aid and without aid. This would clearly imply the existence of a company internal document (a business plan or any other analysis or report). The wording used by the GBER indicates that the Member State should "verify" that the internal document "establishes" or "confirms" the criteria mentioned in art.8(3). That seems to suggest that the Member State would, at the very least, have to ensure that there is an internal document, which is prima facie credible and contains indications of the abovementioned analysis. The GBER does not clarify how far this duty to investigate goes for the Member State.

Special provisions apply for fiscal measures and environmental tax reductions, social aid and risk capital. For "automatic" fiscal measures where the aid is granted on the basis of objective criteria and without discretion, no further proof is required. Also for environmental tax reductions under art.25 GBER there is a presumption of incentive effect. Moreover, as the incentive effect of ad hoc aid[25] granted to large enterprises is considered to be difficult to establish, this form of aid should be excluded from the scope of application of this Regulation. As regards aid for disadvantaged or disabled workers, it is accepted that there is incentive effect provided that there is a net increase in the number of dis-advantaged or disabled workers hired by the undertaking concerned or it leads to additional costs in favour of facilities or equipment devoted to disabled workers.

---

[24] art.8(2) GBER.
[25] Defined in art.2(4) as individual aid not awarded on the basis of an aid scheme.

Transparency. Article 9 GBER basically takes over the previously existing **11–014** requirement to submit, within 20 days following the entry into force of an aid scheme or the awarding of an ad hoc aid, a summary information sheet, which shall be published in the Official Journal. Member States are also required to make available on the internet the full text of the aid measure. All measures should also contain an explicit reference to the relevant provision of the GBER. As stated above (see 11–008), absence thereof leads to losing the benefit of the block exemption, meaning that the measure would become unlawful. Specific information obligations apply under art.9(4) for R&D projects above €3 million and for large investment projects.

In addition, Member States must also provide each year a report on the application of the block exemption regulation, in the format foreseen by the Implementing Regulation. Article 11 contains rules about the annual reporting.

Monitoring. Because of the shift away from an *ex ante* control system, the **11–015** Commission foresees more regular monitoring of block exempted measures. To that effect, art.10 provides that Member States must maintain detailed records which must be provided to the Commission within 20 working days upon request.

Member States must keep records for a period of 10 years from the date on which individual aid was granted and 10 years from the last individual aid granted under a scheme. The period of 10 years is based on the limitation period provided for by the Procedural Regulation—the Commission cannot ask for recovery of aid if more than 10 years have elapsed since the unlawful aid was granted. These records must contain all the information necessary to establish that the conditions for exemption are fulfilled. This information must be provided to the Commission within 20 working days upon request from the Commission.

Under the old SME block exemption regulation, Germany tried to give a narrow reading to a similar provision arguing that the provisions relating to monitoring and transparency, which permit the Commission to request all the information which it considers necessary to assess whether the conditions for exemption have been complied with, do not confer on the Commission a general right of review, but limit that right to cases in which there are doubts. The General Court has rejected such a narrow reading.[26] If the information requested by the Commission is not provided, it may eventually withdraw (for the future) the benefit of the block exemption regulation to all or part of the measures.

So far the Commission seems to consider that monitoring functions properly: Ex-post monitoring:

"With the entry into force of the GBER an even higher number of aid measures are no longer subject to the notification obligation. Article 10 of that regulation constitutes the basis for realising ex post monitoring on a sample

---

[26] Case T–376/07, *Germany v Commission* [2009] E.C.R. II–04293.

basis. The result showed that, overall, the part of the existing State aid architecture allowing for the approval of aid schemes and allowing Member States to implement aid measures under the GBER and BERs functions in a satisfactory manner."[27]

No further details are given about the number of measures reviewed or the possible problems encountered.

11–016 **Investment aid.** Article 12 contains a series of common provisions regarding regional investment aid, SME investment aid and environmental investment aid. The article describes what investment aid is for the purpose of the regulation and which conditions apply to be considered as an eligible cost. Nevertheless, one wonders whether art.12(1), which defines an investment as an investment regarding the setting-up of a new investment, the extension of an existing establishment, diversification of output or fundamental change in overall production process, can really apply to environmental investment aid, e.g. where a boiler is replaced with a more energy efficient one, or where an investment is made which reduces water pollution.

Articles 13–16: regional investment aid and employment aid

11–017 This section in the GBER largely takes over the rules which were contained in the regional block exemption regulation. Aid can only be granted in assisted areas and its intensity must comply with the regional aid threshold. Small enterprises benefit from a top-up of 20 per cent and medium-sized enterprises of 10 per cent,[28] except in so-called large investment projects and in the transport sector. An own contribution of 25 per cent is required. Aid can also be calculated on the basis of wage costs. The investment must be maintained for at least five years (three years for SMEs).

Article 14 introduces a new category, namely aid for newly created small enterprises of up to €2 million in (a)-regions and €1 million in (c)-regions, based on a percentage[29] of certain start-up costs (legal, advisory, consultancy and administrative costs etc.) incurred within the first five years. An anti-abuse clause (art.14(6) GBER) prohibits that enterprises controlled by shareholders of undertakings that have closed down in the previous 12 months can benefit if the enterprises are active in the same or adjacent markets.

Another new provision is art.16 which allows for aid schemes in favour of small enterprises created by female entrepreneurs. To qualify, one or more women must hold at least 51 per cent of the capital or be the owners, and a

---

[27] Autumn 2010 Scoreboard, *http://eur-lex.europa.eu/LexUriServ/LexUriServ.do?uri=COM:2010:0701:FIN:EN:PDF* [Accessed August 8, 2011].

[28] This has increased when compared to the SME block exemption regulation where the thresholds were 15% for small enterprises and 7.5% for medium-sized enterprises.

[29] 35% in the first three years in (a)-regions, and 25% in the next two years; 25% in the first three years in (a)-regions, and 15% in the two years thereafter.

woman must be in charge of the management of the small enterprise.[30] The aid amount cannot exceed €1 million. Aid intensity shall not exceed 15 per cent of eligible costs in the first five years after the creation. Eligible costs are similar to those in art.14, with the addition of child care and parent care costs. In contrast to art.14, the newly created enterprise does not need to be established in an assisted area.

Articles 17–25: environmental aid

This is one of the main new fields included in the GBER when compared to the previously existing block exemption regulations. The first part deals with various forms of environmental investment aid as well as environmental studies related to such investments (arts 18–24 GBER), while art.25 deals with aid in the form of environmental tax reductions. **11–018**

Article 18 deals with environmental investment aid, for investments which go beyond Community standards[31] or which increase the level of environmental protection in the absence of Community standards.

Two possibilities exist for calculating the eligible costs:

- Easily identifiable costs basis: where it is easy to identify the total environmental investment cost, e.g. the situation where an extra filter is added to an exhaust, the eligible costs are the cost of that filter, including its installation.

- Counterfactual analysis: this must be done in all cases where the first method is not possible. In such cases, a comparison must be made between the cost of technically comparable investment offering a lower degree of environmental protection that would be realised without aid and the investment realised with state aid.

The calculation method is simpler than in the environmental aid guidelines[32] since no account must be made of the operating benefits or costs.[33] To compensate, aid intensities are lower.

Article 19 GBER constitutes a *lex specialis* clause covering aid for the acquisition of new transport vehicles which go beyond Community standards or which increase the level of environmental protection in the absence of such standards. Block exempted aid is also permitted to allow SMEs to adapt early to future Community standards (art.20 GBER). No such aid is possible to large

[30] See art.2(28) GBER.
[31] There is no list of the environmental Community standards that are referred to in the GBER (or in the environmental aid guidelines for that matter).
[32] Community guidelines on state aid for environmental protection, O.J. C82, April 1, 2008, p.1.
[33] Compare point 90 of the environmental aid guidelines: "Eligible costs must be calculated net of any operating benefits and operating costs related to the extra investment and arising during the first five years of the life of this investment . . . ".

undertakings under the GBER (though it remains possible under the environmental aid guidelines subject to notification and approval by the Commission, see s.3.1.3, points 87ff).

11–019   As regards investment aid for energy saving measures, either one can opt for the simplified calculation methodology, without taking into account operating costs and benefits, in which case the aid intensity may amount to a maximum 20 per cent of eligible costs for large enterprises, 30 per cent for medium-sized enterprises and 40 per cent for small enterprises, or for the same method as in the environmental guidelines, net of operating costs and benefits. In the latter case, the aid intensity can amount up to 60 per cent of eligible costs for large enterprises, 70 per cent for medium-sized enterprises and 80 per cent for small enterprises.[34]

Articles 22 and 23 GBER block exempt respectively investment aid for high-efficiency cogeneration (i.e. simultaneous generation in one process of thermal energy and electrical and/or mechanical energy) and for renewable energy. In both cases, costs shall be calculated without taking account of operating benefits and costs. Aid intensity is 45 per cent with top-ups of 20 per cent for small enterprises and 10 per cent for medium-sized enterprises. Environmental studies can also be supported (art.24 GBER).

Only environmental tax reductions schemes for taxes under the Energy Tax Directive[35] can come under the GBER. In any event, the minimum tax foreseen by the Directive must be paid. The tax reductions can be granted for maximum periods of 10 years, whereafter Member States must evaluate whether such measures are still appropriate.

11–020   Articles 26–27: SME support. Articles 26 and 27 take over the provisions from the SME block exemption regulation, allowing for 50 per cent for consultancy costs and for the first participation in fairs.

Articles 28–29: risk capital

11–021   For the first time, risk capital measures are also block exempted. Article 29 GBER is largely similar[36] to the provisions contained in s.4 of the risk capital guidelines[37] for participations into a profit driven private equity investment fund, which is managed on a commercial basis. The investment tranches cannot exceed

---

[34] Article 21 GBER.

[35] Council Directive 2003/96/EC of October 27, 2003 restructuring the Community framework for the taxation of energy products and electricity, O.J. L283, October 31, 2003, pp.51–70.

[36] At least as it stood before the recent changes whereby the provisions introduced in the context of the Communication from the Commission, "Temporary Community framework for State aid measures to support access to finance in the current financial and economic crisis TF", have now been integrated into the risk capital guidelines, see Communication from the Commission amending the Community guidelines on state aid to promote risk capital investments in small and medium sized enterprises, O.J. C329, December 7, 2010, pp.4–5.

[37] Community guidelines on state aid to promote risk capital investments in small and medium sized enterprises, O.J. C194, August 18, 2006, pp.2–21.

€1.5 million per undertaking over a period of 12 months. The measure must be restricted to providing seed capital and/or start-up capital; for small enterprises (irrespective of location) and for medium-sized enterprises in assisted areas, it can also comprise expansion capital. The investment fund must provide at least 70 per cent of its budget invested into targeted SMEs in the form of equity of quasi-equity. 50 per cent of funding of the investment fund must come from private investors (30 per cent in for funds targeting exclusively SMEs in assisted areas). Fiscal incentives to investment funds and/or their managers, or to investors to undertake risk capital investment are not covered under the GBER.[38]

Articles 30–37: aid for research, development and innovation

The SME block exemption regulation already covered certain forms of R&D **11–022** aid: R&D project aid, aid for technical feasibility studies and aid for patents and other intellectual property rights costs.[39] Under the GBER, project aid and aid for technical feasibility studies can now also be granted to large undertakings. Furthermore, in line with the objective to become a more knowledge-based economy, new provisions have been introduced which provide for aid of maximum €1 million (up to €1.5 million in assisted areas) for young, innovative enterprises (art.35 GBER). This concerns enterprises which have been in existence for less than six years and where the R&D costs represent at least 15 per cent of its total operating costs in at least one of the three years preceding the granting of the aid, or for a start-up without financial history, as certified by an external auditor.

SMEs can also benefit from aid of maximum €200,000 for innovation advisory services and innovation support services. The service providers must be certified. Article 36(6) lists the services which are eligible for support such as management consulting, technological assistance, data banks, market research, quality labelling, etc. Finally, aid can also be given towards the costs of seconding highly qualified personnel from research organisations or large undertakings to SMEs in order to work on R&D&I activities. The aid amounts to maximum 50 per cent of the costs for a maximum of three years per undertaking and per person on loan.

Articles 38–42: "social aid"

These provisions are largely similar to what was already exempted under the **11–023** training and employment block exemption regulations. It covers:

- training aid, with an increased aid intensity for general training;

- aid for the recruitment of (severely) disadvantaged workers with wage subsidies for one or two years;

---

[38] Compare s.4.2, point (d) of the risk capital guidelines.
[39] See arts 5(a), 5(b) and 5(c) of the SME block exemption regulation.

- aid for the employment of disabled workers: life-long wage subsidies with increased aid intensity of 75 per cent.

It should also be noted that wage costs can now also include child care and parent care costs.[40] This should help to ensure a better life-work balance.

11–024   Training aid. As before distinction is made between "general training" and "specific training". Specific training means training involving tuition which is directly and principally applicable to the employee's present or future position in the assisted firm and providing qualifications which are not, or are only to a limited extent, transferable to other firms or fields of work. General training is training involving tuition which is not applicable only or principally to the employee's present or future position in the assisted firm, but which provides qualifications that are largely transferable to other firms or fields of work.

The distinction between "specific training" and "general training" is often difficult to apply in practice. This situation could lead Member States to err on the side of caution. In the case of projects comprising both specific and general training which cannot be separated or projects with respect to which the specific or general character of the training cannot be established, the (lower) intensities for specific training will apply. In case of doubt, Member States can of course also notify the planned aid to the Commission.

Aid granted for specific training is permitted up to 25 per cent. Aid granted for general training is permitted up to 60 per cent (against 50 per cent in the old block exemption regulation). The aid intensity is increased by 10 per cent for training to disadvantaged or disabled workers, and by 10 per cent for medium-sized enterprises and 20 per cent for small enterprises (with an overall maximum of 80 per cent of eligible costs).

11–025   Aid for (severely) disadvantaged workers. A distinction is made between disadvantaged and severely disadvantaged workers. The first category includes, amongst others, persons who have not been in paid employment for the previous six months, which is a considerable simplification compared to the various categories included before, while the second category covers any person who has been unemployed for 24 months or more.[41]

The aid is calculated as a percentage of the wage costs over a period of 12 months (24 months for severely disadvantaged workers) following recruitment, whereby:

- the employment created must in principle represent a net increase in the number of employees, in the establishment and in the enterprise concerned (to avoid shifts from one establishment to another), compared with the average over the past 12 months; and

---

[40] art.2(15)(c) GBER.
[41] art.2(18) and (19) GBER.

- the employment must be maintained for a minimum period consistent with national legislation or applicable collective agreements; if the period of employment is shorter than 12 months (24 months for severely disadvantaged workers), the aid must be reduced pro rata.

These conditions aim at avoiding abuses. Aid must have a positive effect on employment and should not merely enable enterprises to reduce costs which they would otherwise bear. Aid for safeguarding jobs is not eligible under the GBER—normally such aid would constitute operating aid which can only be allowed in very limited circumstances, in particular in areas eligible for aid under art.107(3)(a) TFEU or under the rescue and restructuring guidelines.[42]

Aid for disabled workers. A disabled person must be recognised as such under the national law of Member States, or have a recognised limitation which results from physical, mental or psychological impairment. The aid intensity can amount to a maximum 75 per cent of the wage costs (up from 60 per cent before) and applies throughout the period of employment.   **11–026**

The following conditions apply:

- where the recruitment does not represent a net increase in the number of employees in the establishment concerned, the post or posts must have fallen vacant following voluntary departure, retirement on grounds of age, voluntary reduction of working time or lawful dismissal for misconduct and not as result of redundancy; and
- except in the case of lawful dismissal for misconduct the worker or workers must be entitled to continuous employment in accordance with national legislation or applicable collective agreements. Where the employment is less than 12 months, the aid must be reduced accordingly.

The above-mentioned conditions are aimed at avoiding abuses. For undertakings which already benefitted under the employment block exemption regulation, the condition of a net increase is presumed to be fulfilled for the purpose of the GBER.

Apart from the aid for the recruitment of disabled persons, aid can be granted up to the level needed to compensate for reduced productivity as well as for the costs of adaptation of the premises and equipment and for special assistance. It is questionable whether such support actually constitutes aid in the sense of art.107(1) TFEU, since it is not clear where the advantage for the company lies if it only receives compensation for reduced productivity. The Commission has not specifically clarified the aid character of these measures, but considers that where it constitutes aid, it is compatible and exempt from notification.

---

[42] The employment block exemption regulation also refers to art.87(2)(b), although that seems extremely rare.

Final provisions

11–027   Unlawful aid put into effect prior to the entry into force of the GBER and which meets all the conditions laid down in the regulation (with the exception of the express reference to the regulation) shall be exempt as well.

The GBER entered into force on August 30, 2008 (initially in parallel to the old block exemption regulations). It remains valid until December 31, 2013.

3. EXPERIENCE[43]

11–028   In absolute terms, Member States awarded in 2009 approximately €10.8 billion of aid under block exemptions for industry and services. In relative terms, block exempted aid represented a share of approximately 22 per cent of total horizontal aid to industry and services in 2009.

Looking at the most relevant categories, in 2009 €4.9 billion of aid was awarded for regional investment aid. The second largest category was block exempted aid for SMEs and risk capital. Risk capital accounted for €39 million. Aid for enterprises newly created by female entrepreneurs is also included in this category and amounted to around €0.3 million.

In third position was employment aid which amounted to €1 billion in 2009. Member States earmarked roughly €0.8 billion as training aid under block exempted measures. Block exempted aid earmarked as research, development and innovation aid amounted around €1 billion in 2009. Finally, Member States granted €732 million of environmental protection aid under block exempted measures corresponding to around 6 per cent of total aid for environmental objectives.

4. WHY DOES THE COMMISSION NOT BLOCK EXEMPT MORE MEASURES?

11–029   There would seem to be several measures which hardly raise major competition concerns, where the Commission has already an extensive experience and which nevertheless do not currently under the GBER. One thinks of measures like aid for theatre, dance, heritage conservation, broadband in rural area or for natural disaster compensation.

However, there is currently no legal basis for doing so under the Enabling Regulation. The Commission has tried to cater for these categories by offering a simplified procedure, which generally would lead to an approval decision within one month from notification. If the Enabling Regulation were to be amended, it would seem likely that many of the measures listed in the Notice on a Simplified Procedure would be proposed for inclusion so that they could become block exempted in future.

---

[43] Data taken from Commission Staff Working Document, "Facts and figures on State aid in the Member States", accompanying the Report from the Commission: State Aid Scoreboard— Autumn 2010 Update, COM(2010) 701 final.

Part III

SECTORAL AID

CHAPTER 12

SECTORAL AID INTRODUCTION*

1. GENERAL	12–001
2. THE PERIOD PRIOR TO PUBLICATION OF THE COMMISSION'S COMMUNICATION	12–003
3. THE COMMISSION'S COMMUNICATION ON SECTORAL AID	12–004
4. THE APPLICATION OF THE GENERAL SECTORAL PRINCIPLES	12–008
General	12–008
Chemical and pharmaceutical sector	12–011
5. CONCLUSION	12–021

1. GENERAL

Article 107(3)(c) TFEU provides that aid to facilitate the development of **12–001** certain economic activities may be exempted from the prohibition of art.107(1). Such economic activities may refer to certain sectors of the economy. This type of aid is usually referred to as sectoral aid. There is no single legislative document containing general sectoral aid rules. There are rules for several sectors: agriculture (Ch.13), coal and steel (Ch.14), shipbuilding (Ch.16), transport (Ch.17), broadcasting (Ch.18), the financial sector (Ch.19) and electricity (Ch.20). In addition there are rules for the cinematographic and audio sector,[1] broadband[2] and postal services.[3] Further relevant rules are found in the multi-sectoral framework (Ch.15). The first edition of this framework entered into force in 1998,[4] subsequent editions in 2002 and 2009. Finally, the economic activities referred to in art.107(3)(b) and (c) may concern individual enterprises in difficulty. Occasionally aid schemes for rescue and restructuring for SMEs are approved. The rules for rescue and restructuring aid that have been adopted are

---

* Piet Jan Slot
[1] [2009] O.J. C31/1 Communication from the Commission concerning the state aid assessment criteria of the Commission communication on certain legal aspects relating to cinematographic and other audiovisual works (Cinema Communication).
[2] [2009] O.J. C235/7 Union Guidelines for the application of state aid rules in relation to rapid deployment of broadband networks.
[3] [1998] O.J. C39/2 Notice from the Commission on the application of the competition rules to the postal sector and on the assessment of certain State measures relating to postal services
[4] [1998] O.J. C107/7.

now the most commonly applied horizontal rules. They will therefore be discussed in Ch.24. The first guidelines for rescuing and restructuring firms in difficulty were adopted in 1994.[5]

Before the adoption of these guidelines the Commission applied its policy on sectoral aid. The Commission's policy statements on sectoral aid were basically formulated in the 1970s and were codified in the 1978 communication. Because the Commission's sectoral interventions are still based on these principles, a discussion of these statements, in particular the 1978 communication, is useful.[6]

12–002   This chapter will therefore give a summary of the early policy statements on sectoral aid in general and their application. In Ch.4 the broad context of art.107(3) as well as the rules for certain categories and types of aid, have been dealt with. In addition to a discussion of the 1978 communication on sectoral aid this introductory chapter will look at the application of these general sectoral principles in the 1990s in two specific sectors which did not operate under special rules: the chemical and the pharmaceutical industries. The application of the state aid rules in these sectors since 1999 will be discussed in Ch.24 which will deal with all sectors.

2. THE PERIOD PRIOR TO PUBLICATION OF THE COMMISSION'S COMMUNICATION

12–003   Prior to the publication of its communication in 1978, the Commission had published several general statements on its policy on sectoral aid. Thus the First Report on Competition Policy contains a lengthy paragraph in which the Commission enumerates criteria that should ensure that aid does minimal harm to competition and has a maximum of effectiveness with regard to the balanced development of the Union. Aid must:

- be of a selective nature and only granted to enterprises or to productions, the development and reorganisation of which justifies the presumption that they will be competitive in the long run, having regard to the expected development of the sector concerned;

- be of sufficiently temporary or even digressive nature in order to stimulate the dynamism of beneficiaries. It must foster the necessary adaptations and make it clear to the parties concerned that the artificial situation arising from the granting of aid cannot continue indefinitely. Unless aid is intended to compensate for distortions of competition at Unionlevel, which are created by measures adopted in non-Member countries, purely conservatory aid outside reorganisation programmes and aid for the operation of plants must

---

[5] [1994] O.J. C368/12.
[6] See Case T–20/03, *Kahla/Thuringen Porzellan GmbH v Commission* [2008] E.C.R. II–2305, para.127.

be excluded. Economic and social progress cannot allow, in the long run, unreasonable protection of sectors facing difficulties. Aid systems must therefore avoid preventing the optimum allocation of production factors indefinitely. They must either speed up structural changes or only slow down such changes temporarily, and this only until the necessary reconversion solutions have been found;

- be as transparent as possible, in order that the Union instructions may easily evaluate their incidence and effectiveness with regard to the aims to be attained, in order that the public authorities may be in a position to accurately measure the cost involved, and in order that the enterprises concerned may assess the true situation;

- be of a form well adapted to the objectives in view and, insofar as a choice between various methods is possible, adopt those that have the least effect on intra-Union trade and the common interest.[7]

3. THE COMMISSION'S COMMUNICATION ON SECTORAL AID[8]

The Commission, in describing the general principles, starts with a reference **12–004** to art.3(1)(g) EC (this provision has been deleted from the TFEU. A similar principle is now laid down in Protocol No.27 to the Treaty of Lisbon, on the internal market and competition; the need to ensure that competition in the common market is not distorted). It then sets out three reasons to justify adherence to this principle:

(i) the customs union would founder if Member States could unilaterally circumvent its requirements by granting aid;

(ii) the common market makes little sense unless businesses tackle the market on the strength of their own resources without any aid to distort competition between them; and

(iii) as a corollary, a system which leaves the field open to competition provides for optimum distribution of production factors and ensures the most rapid economic and social progress.

Nevertheless, aid may be justified where it contributes to the achievement of the Union's economic and social aims. This occurs when market forces would:

---

[7] First Report on Competition Policy, point 165.
[8] COM(78) 221 final, May 1978, Competition law in the European Communities, Vol.II: Rules applicable to state aids (Commission of the European Communities, Brussels, 1990), p.39. This communication is no longer included in the new edition of this volume. The summary provided here is largely based on the summary in the 8th Report on Competition Policy.

(i) obstruct progress towards the realisation of these aims;

(ii) permit them to be attained only within unacceptable time limits or unacceptable social costs;

(iii) intensify competition to such an extent that it could destroy itself.

12–005   The Commission considers that sectoral aid should be authorised where it is needed to correct serious regional imbalance, to encourage or accelerate certain activities where this is desirable for social reasons or to neutralise, at least temporarily, certain distortions of competition due to action outside the Union.

The aims, forms and conditions relating to such aids, justifiable in that they facilitate the orderly development of Union structures, must not conflict with the Union's general objectives and must be designed in such a way as to entail a minimum distortion of competition.

On the basis of these general principles the Commission has developed a number of criteria against which it examines the sectoral aid proposals notified to it. The main criteria are the following:

(i) sectoral aid should be limited to cases where it is justified by circumstances in the industry concerned;

(ii) aid should lead to a restoration of long-term viability by resolving problems rather than preserving the status quo and putting off decisions and changes which are inevitable;

(iii) nevertheless, since adjustments take time, a limited use of resources to reduce the social and economic costs of change is admissible in certain circumstances and subject to strict conditions;

(iv) unless granted over relatively short periods, aids should be reduced progressively and clearly linked to the restructuring of the sector concerned;

(v) the intensity of aid should be proportionate to the problem it is designed to resolve so that distortions of competition are kept to a minimum[9];

(vi) industrial problems and unemployment should not be transferred from one Member State to another.

12–006   The Commission does not consider it advisable to define systematically the types of aid to which it is favourably and unfavourably disposed in the case of each industrial sector. To elaborate such guidelines for aid would risk encouraging a more general recourse to aid by Member States even where it is not strictly necessary. It would, moreover, result in some degree of inflexibility, since such

---

[9] Closely related to the proportionality requirement is the anti-cumulation rule. In 1987 the Commission opened the art.88(2) (now 108(2)) procedure against France and Greece because it could not assess what the effects of cumulation might be [1987] O.J. C300/4.

frameworks could not take into account the specific situation of the industry concerned in each Member State. However, in cases where it has become evident that an industry faces a situation of particular difficulty throughout the Union, or is likely to face such difficulty, it is appropriate to develop guidelines which indicate the Commission's policy on aids to this industry. The Commission's approach in the case of such industries has been based on certain common principles. It has recognised that the crisis the specific industry has met, has consequences for employment in general or a series of interventions by Member States designed to protect their industries. In the latter eventuality, aid levels would be uselessly inflated and difficulties transferred from one Member State to another at substantial cost to the Union as a whole. The purpose of the Commission's initiatives in defining guidelines has been to avoid both eventualities and, at the same time, to encourage the restoration of the industries' competitiveness. To these ends it has accepted aids to enable orderly adjustments to market conditions. Such adjustments require both a restoration of competitiveness and either an avoidance of undesirable increases or, in some cases, an actual reduction in production capacity.

In more concrete terms, this has led to the specification of the following principles:

(i) aid should not be granted where the sole effect would be to maintain the status quo. Production aids as such are therefore in principle impermissible unless they are granted for a limited period and are conditional on action by the recipient, which will facilitate adjustment;

(ii) similarly, while rescue measures may be needed in order to provide breathing space during which longer-term solutions to a company's difficulties can be worked out, they should not frustrate any necessary reductions in capacity and should therefore be limited to cases where they are required to cope with acute social problems; and

(iii) since it is a common feature of the industries concerned that capacity is excessive, aid should not be given to investment projects which would result in capacity being increased.

In the case of certain industries, particularly those which are in difficulties, the **12–007** Commission has sought to ensure either that these and other types of aid respect the same criteria or that they are only granted on certain conditions. Thus, where employment aids are given to maintain existing jobs, the Commission has considered that if they are concentrated on industrial sectors which face acute difficulties in all Member States and if they are not associated with appropriate adjustment measures designed to restore a company's viability, the granting of these aids will not resolve the social and industrial difficulties but will rather transfer them to other Member States. Similarly, in sectors suffering from extreme overcapacity, the Commission has required Member States to agree in principle not to grant regional aids for investment projects that would result in increased capacity. A principle not specifically mentioned is the prohibition of operating aid. As discussed in Ch.4, paras 4–050 et seq., the Commission has always opposed such aid.[10]

4. THE APPLICATION OF THE GENERAL SECTORAL PRINCIPLES

General

12–008   The Commission's view on sectoral aid is clearly expressed in its 26th Report on Competition Policy:

"The Commission's negative attitude to sectoral aid schemes has been demonstrated in numerous decisions in the past. This may be the reason why few such schemes were drawn up by Member States in 1994. However, the increased number of *ad hoc* aid cases in favour of individual undertakings, many of them concentrated in certain sectors such as mechanical engineering, paper, foundry products and agricultural, is worrying. In its decisions on the compatibility of such aid cases, the Commission must take into account the sectoral consequences of the aid, particularly in sectors suffering from overcapacity."[11]

The application of the 1978 Communication has been limited because the most depressed sectors have all been the subject of specific Commission frameworks, communications or notices. Most of these will be discussed in the following chapters. The chemical and pharmaceutical sector will be discussed in this chapter as an example of the application of the general principles on sectoral aid to specific sectors.

The application of general principles on sectoral aid has also been limited because important aid proposals increasingly involve large industrial conglomerates. Such aid proposals cannot easily be assessed in the context of one particular sector. The aid granted by Italy to Enirisorse constitutes a good example of such an aid proposal.[12] The non-operating holding company Enirisorse was optimising the economic and financial resources of the ENI group, which in turn consisted of the following industrial activities: mining of non-ferrous metals, coal mining, coke production, metallurgy of non-ferrous metals and, finally, inorganic chemistry. In its decision the Commission followed its guidelines on aid for restructuring when it approved a ITL809 billion recapitalisation plan for the entire conglomerate. A year later the Commission reopened the art.108(2) procedure

[10] See e.g. [1984] O.J. L276/40.
[11] (1995), Pt 363.
[12] Decision 98/212/EC [1998] O.J. L80/32.

because the Italian government had not fulfilled an important condition. In addition it had made fresh capital injections and was planning further injections.[13] On November 26, 1998, the Commission adopted a decision ordering the Italian government recovery due to the fact that the latest recapitalisations by ENI did not offer sufficient financial return since Enirisorse was soon to be wound up.[14]

As this example shows, conglomeration in the industry has the effect that more and more application is given to the guidelines on state aid for rescuing and restructuring rather than to the sectoral guidelines.
12–009

In a number of the Commission's decisions involving sectoral aid, it specifically applied the criteria laid down in its 1978 Communication.

Several Commission decisions analyse whether adequate restructuring plans had been drafted and whether the overcapacity was being tackled.[15] In one instance the Commission also noted that the aid was used to reduce the social and economic costs of change as well as for job creation in areas eligible for regional aid.[16] In one decision the Commission specifically referred to its summary of its Communication in the 8th Report on Competition Policy.[17]

With one exception, the Annual Reports on Competition Policy do not discuss the Commission's Communication. The 13th Report mentions three particular problems in the examination of individual aid cases: aids to rescue firms in difficulties, the problems of defining the degree of restructuring which can be regarded as constituting "a compensatory Union interest" for the granting of aid, and the concept of innovation. The Commission notes that government actions to rescue firms in difficulties may easily lead to the transfer of industrial difficulties and unemployment to other Member States. On the question of defining the necessary degree of restructuring, the Commission expresses the opinion that evidence must be provided that the changes being proposed are sufficient to ensure medium- to long-term viability of the enterprise without aids. The third problem is the growing tendency to present as restructuring what is in fact simple ongoing modernisation and renewal of production facilities. For the control of state aid it is important to recognise the difference between innovation (i.e. the introduction of new products or new production technologies) and the steady development of existing products and production technologies.[18]
12–010

---

[13] [1998] O.J. C70/5. The Commission's action was taken pursuant to the reception of the half-yearly report which was to be submitted as one of the conditions of the previous approval decision.

[14] Decision 2000/334/EC, *Enirisorse* [2000] O.J. L120/1.

[15] Decision 88/283/EEC [1988] O.J. L121/57; Decision 90/70/EEC [1990] L47/28; Decision 89/620/EEC [1998] O.J. L356/22; Decision 92/296/EEC [1992] O.J. L159/46. A more recent example is the Commission's decision approving the aid to Esmaltaciones San Ignacio [1993] O.J. C277/5, where it concluded that the length of the proposed guarantee of seven years appears to be necessary and proportionate.

[16] Decision 88/283/EEC [1988] O.J. L121/57.

[17] Decision 90/70/EEC [1990] O.J. L47/28.

[18] 13th Report on Competition Policy, point 229 and point 230, see also Ch.21.

Chemical and pharmaceutical sector

12–011 **Introduction.** This industrial sector was, and still is, not subject to a specific framework, therefore the Communication on sectoral aid applied at the time.

12–012 **Summary of Commission actions before 1984.** The first time the Commission reported activities to check aid plans in the chemical sector was in the 13th Report on Competition Policy.[19] The United Kingdom was asked to drop aid plans which would have stimulated capacity expansion for polyester and polypropylene foil in the United Kingdom. The Commission considered that other enterprises had similar investment plans which satisfied the market and therefore the UK aid would lead to a distortion of competition.

However, although technological progress was promoted this only served the interest of the undertakings and not the Union as a whole and there could be no justification on the basis of art.107(3). The Commission also opened the art.108(2) procedure against the Netherlands in respect of four aid plans. The Commission did not object to the aid for the conversion of a power plant from coal to gas as this was in line with the Union energy policy. The Commission scrutinised an important aid plan for an Italian chemical enterprise in the light of the overall restructuring of the Italian chemical sector.

12–013 The 14th Report on Competition Policy mentioned that the Commission approved part of the Italian aid plan discussed in its previous report and opened the art.108(2) procedure for the rest of the plan. The partial approval was granted because the Italian chemical sector was making efforts to restructure overcapacity. The Commission's objections concerned aid to a strong enterprise and for investment in capacity that would not be matched by closures in other parts of the industry. Moreover, the Commission did not consider the aid to be justified because, although it was intended for a region with serious unemployment, nevertheless its sectoral effects had to be checked even if this involved investments in the least developed areas. The Italian government finally brought its aid proposals in line with the Commission's views so that the latter could close the procedure.[20]

The Commission refused to approve aid to build a butyl alcohol plant. The Commission was of the opinion that, according to the market investor principle, the aid was not necessary.[21]

The developments since 1984 will be reviewed on the basis of the summaries of the decisions and notices published in the O.J. series and of the cases of the General Court (until 2010 the Court of First Instance (CFI)) and the European Court of Justice (ECJ).

12–014 **Environment.** In a 1991 decision the Commission terminated an art.108(2) procedure against Belgium for investment aid to Solvay.[22] The Commission was

---

[19] Point 263.
[20] 14th Report on Competition Policy, point 247.
[21] [1984] O.J. L276/19.
[22] [1991] O.J. C73/2.

satisfied that the assisted investments were limited to environmental protection and would not lead to an increase in production capacity or an extension or modernisation of production lines in operation for at least two years. The Commission considered that the conditions of the Union framework on state aid in environmental matters had been met.

What is surprising in this case is the contrast between the opinions expressed in the first and second round of discussions. In view of the clear language of the positive decision, it was surprising that the Commission considered it necessary to open the art.108(2) procedure. The Commission noted in the decision to open the art.108(2) procedure,[23] however, that on the bases of the information in its possession, none of the exceptions of art.107 appeared to be applicable.

The Commission tested its guidelines on state aid for environmental protection **12–015** in two decisions. In its decision concerning a hydrogen peroxide plant in Delfzijl in the Netherlands, it observed that the guidelines do not allow aid to be authorised for investment going beyond the standards in force in other Member States, but only for investment going beyond compulsory standards in the Member State concerned.[24] In its decision on aid for Hoffmann-La Roche, the Commission observed that the objective of meeting high safety standards was implemented as part of the company's priorities and could not, therefore, be exempted under the guidelines for environmental aid.[25] In this case the Commission further noted that aid for investment in environmental measures allowing for significantly higher levels of protection to be attained than those required by mandatory standards may be authorised up to a level of 30 per cent gross of the eligible costs.

The Commission's decision concerning the chemical sector in the former GDR also contained an important passage on environmental measures.[26] The aid plan comprised DM 1 billion for the cost of making good the enormous environmental damage afflicted by the industrial sites, such as the chlorine and mercury pollution on the Buna site.

Research and development. In a decision involving aid to Smith-Kline Bio- **12–016** logicals SA, the Commission terminated the art.108(2) procedure because it was satisfied that the conditions of art.107(3)(c) were met. The proposed aid was "intended to contribute to the carrying out of a project in a sector where the Union was significantly lagging behind and which is one of the main focuses of industrial potential". The Union has included biotechnology among the priority areas in its framework programme so as to encourage the investment of human and financial resources in R&D.

In another decision the Commission terminated the art.108(2) procedures involving aid by the Italian government to Sigma-Tau. The project consisted of research on new antihypertensive drugs. The initial project envisaged 38.7 per

[23] [1990] O.J. C280/5.
[24] [1998] O.J. L171/36.
[25] [1998] O.J. L103/28.
[26] [1996] O.J. L239/1 at para.12.

cent intensity, which the Commission considered to be too high. After amendment the Commission concluded that in view of the arrangements for the granting and repayment of the aid and of the fact that the research project included 30 per cent of basic research, the aid has an intensity of 31.56 gross grant equivalent of the real cost of the project which complies with the framework for state aid for R&D.

12–017   In 1986 the Commission started the art.108(2) procedure for aid proposals by the Belgian government to assist research of five pharmaceutical companies. The aid in question helped to reduce total expenditure by a significant extent thus enabling the recipients to lower the prices of their products and/or increase their profits. There was no reference to the R&D framework.

In the same year the Commission opened the art.108(2) procedure against the Belgian government for concluding "programme-agreements" under which the firms involved could increase their prices in return for an undertaking that they would set up laboratory research, investment and employment in Belgium and make a special effort to promote Belgian products abroad. It also found that the aid was not necessary because market forces would have achieved the aims of the project. It also noted that, according to art.107(3)(c), "aid to facilitate the development of certain economic activities" was not applicable because the aid would have had an impact contrary to the common interest on intra-Union trade. It found that, given the intense competition on the Union market, the granting of aid—even indirectly through permission to increase prices with reimbursement of additional sickness insurance costs—had a particularly serious effect on competition. It also opened an art.258 TFEU procedure against Belgium alleging infringement of art.28 (now art.34 TFEU).

In its decision concerning the aid to Hoffmann-La Roche, the Commission found the aid not to be in conformity with its R&D aid guidelines.[27] It did not agree with Austria's claim that the work was eligible for funding as "industrial research" and "precompetitive development activity" as well as "applied research and development".

12–018   **Miscellaneous.** In 1985 the Commission began two art.108(2) procedures against Italy concerning innovation projects.[28] The Commission was of the opinion that the aid would not be used for the benefit of an innovative operation likely to contribute to the attainment of an objective of value to the Union as a whole. A year later the Commission issued a negative decision proscribing the aid.[29] The Commission noted that the innovative aspects of the project were unimportant. Furthermore, it found that the effects of the aid on the competitive position of the firm in the industry would be substantial since the firm was already market leader in Europe. Consequently the exception contained in art.107(3)(c) did not apply.

---

[27] Decision 98/251/EC [1998] O.J. L103/28.
[28] [1985] O.J. C172/3.
[29] Decision 87/14/EEC [1987] O.J. L12/17.

Similar objections were raised by the Commission against Italian aid proposals involving the Innovation Fund.[30] Since no further publications have been found, it may be presumed that in all four cases the Italian government dropped the plans or that it modified them so as to conform to arts 107 and 108. It should be recalled that in the past it was not common for the Commission to publish decisions terminating the art.108(2) procedure. Still, in 1984, the Commission objected to aid for investment in connection with the restructuring of the Italian chemical industry.[31] Again it is difficult to trace the subsequent developments. On the whole, the Commission did not adopt many negative decisions during our reporting period: five in the chemical sector and one in the pharmaceutical sector.

In addition to what has been discussed above, two further decisions call for comment. The proposed aid to Belgian Shell had to be shelved because the Commission noted that, contrary to the assertion of the Belgian government, the aid would not contribute to the development of R&D but only to the purchase of land and the construction of a building.[32] The Commission stressed that, as is shown by the Union framework, it is in favour of R&D. A year later the Commission proscribed an aid plan involving Enimont in Italy. The aid was to be granted in the form of tax relief, structured in such a way as to apply only to a small number of operations, if not just a single operation. Montedison, as the sole recipient of the proposed aid, could improve its cash position appreciably and thus strengthen its financial position and influence competition. Furthermore, the aid would constitute operation aid and not investment aid for which art.107(3)(a) and (c) is designed. Moreover, market conditions in the sector seemed likely to ensure normal development without aid.

12–019

Two additional decisions are worth noting. In a decision published in 1992, the Commission opened the art.108(2) procedure against Greece for its aid plan to public pharmaceutical enterprises.[33] The aid was to be financed out of a 15 per cent flat tax rate on pharmaceutical and beauty products sold in Greece.[34] The Commission noted that the aid did not seem to qualify for the exception of art.107(3)(c) because it did not foster development of activities at Union level without adversely affecting trading conditions to an extent contrary to Union interest. The Commission also noted that repayment of the aid may be ordered and, in particular, interest on arrears started to run on the date on which the unlawful aid was granted.[35]

---

[30] [1984] O.J. C124/13 and 14; [1984] O.J. C269/3.

[31] [1984] O.J. C269/2.

[32] Decision 89/254/EEC [1989] O.J. L106/34.

[33] [1992] O.J. C48/6.

[34] Curiously enough, the Commission does not raise the incompatibly with the provision of the Treaty of such a tax scheme for the financing of aid, see Case 77/72 *Capalongo* [1973] E.C.R. 611.

[35] See Ch.26 section 4. The Commission notes that "This measure is necessary in order to restore the status quo by removing all the financial benefits which the firms receiving unlawful aid have improperly enjoyed since the date on which the aid was paid."

12–020   A last decision concerns the Commission's renewed approval of the preferential gas tariffs granted to the Dutch fertiliser industry.[36] After the ECJ's
annulment of the first Commission decision approving these tariffs, in its judgment of July 12, 1990, the Commission had to give a fresh decision.[37] The gist
of the decision is that, in view of the dire state of nitrate fertilisers producers, the
granting of preferential aid was objectively justified since there was a genuine
concern that without such low tariffs the enterprises involved would have gone
bankrupt. This would have deprived Gasunie, the gas company in question, of an
important commercial outlet. The decision is discussed further in paras 20–025
and 20–089. Similarly, the two cases[38] on the preferential gas tariff in the nitrate
fertiliser sector are discussed in Chs 3 and 20.

Several Commission decisions discuss when the terms of a purchase agreement amount to an aid. In the *Fresenius* case the problem was that, despite
expensive and widespread advertising, only one purchaser was finally interested
in buying the plot of land.[39] In such a case the Commission is prepared to accept
that a slightly lower price may represent the market price. As a result no aid is
involved. The Commission took a similar view in its decision on the aid to the
hydrogen peroxide plant in the Netherlands.[40] State aid elements in sales of land
and buildings by public authorities has also been the subject of a recent Commission communication[41] and is discussed in Ch.3.

5. Conclusion

12–021   The overall picture that emerges from the application of arts 107 and 108 to the
chemical and pharmaceutical sector is that major restructuring operations have
been carried out for which aid was approved by the Commission. The aid to
CDF-Chemie seemed, at the time, particularly massive and one is left wondering
whether all the aid was really necessary and proportionate. In the meantime, that
aid has been dwarfed by the aid operations in the former German Democratic
Republic. But these operations can only be properly understood in their very
specific context. The aid plans for Enichem also stand out for their particular size.
Furthermore, the fact that the approval was subject to the condition of privatisation is a remarkable feature. Such a condition is particularly interesting in view
of the Commission's statement in its guidelines on state aid in the air transport
sector (see Ch.17) that it cannot insist on privatisation. (See further on this issue,
Ch.8, paras 8–067 et seq.)

---

[36] [1992] O.J. C344/4.
[37] Case C–169/84 [1990] E.C.R. I–3083.
[38] Respectively, Joined Cases 67, 68 and 70/85 [1985] E.C.R. 1315; and Case C–169/84 [1990]
E.C.R. I–3083.
[39] [1994] O.J. C21/4.
[40] Decision 98/384/EC [1998] O.J. L171/36.
[41] Commission Communication on state aid elements in sales of land and buildings by public
authorities [1997] O.J. C209/3.

Interesting cases of approval concern aid to improve the environment granted to Solvay and to Hoffmann-La Roche, and the R&D aid to Smith-Kline Belgium. The majority of cases have finally been dropped or adapted to take account of the Commission's objections. In a number of cases the Commission refuted the governments' arguments that the aid would stimulate important innovations. Proposals concerning operating aid will always be opposed by the Commission, as has been demonstrated once again in the decision concerning the aid to the chemical industry in the former GDR. Similarly, aid plans disguised as regional aid will be challenged by the Commission, in particular when they exceed the net grant equivalent of regional aid.[42]

---

[42] e.g. [1991] O.J. C213/3, aid for investment in the alkaline salts industry in Sicily. See further the decision on aid granted to a hydrogen peroxide works in the Netherlands, Decision 98/384/EC [1998] O.J. L171/36. Although the sum of the aid involved was rather small, the Commission noted that the fact that the authorised aid ceiling had been exceeded raised a problem of principle.

CHAPTER 13

AGRICULTURE*

1. INTRODUCTION 13–001
2. COMMON MARKET ORGANISATION 13–003
3. RURAL DEVELOPMENT 13–006
4. ACCESSION TREATIES 13–009
5. MATERIAL STATE AID RULES ON COMPATIBILITY 13–012
   General architecture 13–012
   De minimis rules 13–013
   Compatibility rules applicable to the agricultural sector 13–014
   Investment aid in primary production 13–016
6. FISHERIES AND AQUACULTURE 13–042

1. INTRODUCTION

13–001   Agricultural land and forests cover over 90 per cent of the territory of the European Union. In 2007 there were more than 7.3 million commercial agricultural holdings in EU-27, with a further 6.4 million smallholdings.[1] The total agricultural output amounted to €334 billion in 2009.[2] The average farm size in the European Union in 2007 was 22 hectares, varying from 1.2 hectares in Malta to 134.6 hectares in the Czech Republic.

11.2 million people were employed in agriculture, forestry, hunting or fishing in 2009, representing 5.1 per cent of the total employed population. There are significant differences in agricultural employment between Member States, from 17.1 per cent in Poland to only 1.4 per cent in the United Kingdom. However, the share of agriculture in GDP is proportionally small, representing only 1.3 per cent in 2010 for all the EU Member Stares, ranging from 6.5 in Romania to 0.3 in Luxembourg.[3]

---

* Agnieska Stobiecka-Kuik

[1] Key figures on Europe, Eurostat, 2011 edition, p.100. Please note that the 2007 accession of Romania and Bulgaria added 5 million holdings to the EU-25's existing 10 million.

[2] Agriculture in the EU, Statistical and Economic Information, Report 2010, ISBN 978–92–79–19302–6.

[3] United Nations Economic Commission for Europe, Statistical database for 2010.

The agricultural sector consists of the primary production and processing and marketing of agricultural products. Given its specifics, namely a huge diversity in terms of the size and types of activities involved and the sensitivity of agricultural and rural development policies, agricultural state aids are governed by the Commission's DG Agriculture, rather than by DG Competition. The amount of state aid granted to the agricultural sector totalled €12.7 billion and constituted 15.9 per cent of the total aids (excluding crisis measures) granted in 2010.[4] Needless to say, these figures do not include direct payments or the rural development funds.[5] The largest amounts of state aid in absolute terms were granted by France (€2.4 billion), and in terms of GDP were granted by Finland.

The agricultural products (including fisheries products, see para.13–042, below) listed in Annex I[6] to the TFEU, are subject to the rules stipulated in Part Three, Title III, arts 38 to 44 of the Treaty. According to art.42 TFEU, the rules on competition, including arts 107 and 108 of the Treaty, only apply to production of and trade in agricultural products to the extent determined by the Council and the European Parliament.[7] Agricultural policy objectives take priority over regular competition policy[8]; recourse to state aid measures can therefore only be justified if they respect the objectives stipulated in art.39 TFEU.[9] In contrast to other sectors, the Commission's authority to control and supervise state aids for the production of primary and processed agricultural products[10] does not derive

13–002

---

[4] Total state aid granted by Member States excluding the financial crisis measures amounted to around €73.27 billion in 2010 or 0.6% of EU-27 GDP. Fisheries represented 0.001 of EU–27 GDP.

[5] Expenditure on agriculture and rural development is financed by two funds, which form part of the EU's general budget: the European Agricultural Guarantee Fund (EAGF) finances direct payments to farmers and measures to regulate agricultural markets such as intervention and export refunds, while the European Agricultural Fund for Rural Development (EAFRD) finances the rural development programmes of the Member States. The CAP budget for 2010 is €43.8bn (31% of the EU budget and 6.4% more than in 2009). For 2011 the CAP budget has been reduced by 3%, about 85% being assigned to direct payments. The rural development budget amounts to about €963 million for 2007–2013 and constitutes about 20% of the total CAP budget.

[6] "Agricultural product" means one of the products listed in Annex I of the Treaty, products falling under CN codes 4502, 4503 and 4504 (cork products) and products intended to imitate or substitute milk and milk products, excluding those products covered by Council Regulation (EC) No.2371/2002 of December 20, 2002 on the conservation and sustainable exploitation of fisheries resources under the Common Fisheries Policy, as amended [2002] O.J. L358/59–80. Currently the eight-digit Combined Nomenclature (CN) is used to interpret Annex I, but in practice it is not always easy to determine whether or not it covers a specific product. See M. Erhart, State Aid in the Field of Agriculture, M. Sanchez Rydelski (ed.), *The EC State Aid Regime: Distortive Effects of State Aid on Competition and Trade*, 2006, p.477 (478).

[7] Case C–311/94 *IJssel-Vliet Combinatie v Minister van Economische Zaken* [1996] E.C.R. I–5023, para.31; AG's Opinion in Joined Cases C–346/03 and C–529/03 *Atzeni and others* [2006] E.C.R. I–01875, para.12.

[8] Case 177/78 *Pigs and Bacon Commission v McCarren and Company Ltd* [1979] E.C.R. 2161, para.11; Case C–456/00 *France v Commission* [2002] E.C.R. I–11949, para.33.

[9] Case 177/78 *Pigs and Bacon Commission v McCarren* [1979] E.C.R. 2161.

[10] Art.2(b) of Commission Regulation (EC) No.1998/2006 of December 15, 2006 on the application of arts 87 and 88 of the EC Treaty to de minimis aid,: " 'processing of agricultural products' means an operation on an agricultural product resulting in a product which is also an agricultural product" [2006] O.J. L379; a first-stage processed product is an agricultural product which,

directly from the Treaty, but from legislation adopted by the Council and, as from the Lisbon Treaty, the Parliament, under art.43 TFEU, and is subject to restrictions laid down by the Council. Until the Lisbon Treaty, the Council had wide discretion in the exercise of that power, as it has in the implementation of agricultural policy as a whole.[11] As of the entry into force of the Lisbon Treaty and save a few exceptions,[11a] the Council shares this responsibility with the Parliament, by means of the ordinary legislative procedure. However, application of the special rules in the context of the common agricultural policy is limited to measures relating to Annex I products.

The Council has adopted Regulation (EC) No.1184/2006,[12] art.3 of which lays down a minimum set of state aid rules applicable to products listed in Annex I to the Treaty. According to this provision, only art.108(1) and the first sentence of art.108(3) TFEU apply to aids granted in favour of all products listed in Annex I, meaning that neither art.107 TFEU nor the other provisions of art.108 TFEU are to be applied to state aid in the agricultural sector. As a result, the Commission's control of state aid measures is largely determined by regulations relating to the common markets organisation and structural measures in the rural development field. The compatibility of national state aid measures also has to be assessed in the light of these specific rules.[13]

2. COMMON MARKET ORGANISATION

13–003   Under arts 42 and 43 of the TFEU, it is decided in general terms to what extent the state aid rules apply to a given market organisation.[14] The 2003 CAP reform simplified the common agricultural policy's legislative environment, inter alia, by establishing a horizontal legal framework for all direct payments[15] and

---

following a processing operation, remains such a product, e.g. the extraction of juice from fruit (Commission Regulation (EC) No.386/2004 of March 1, 2004 amending Council Regulation (EC) No.2201/96 and Regulation (EC) No.1535/2003 as regards the combined nomenclature codes for certain products processed from fruit and vegetables [2004] O.J. L64/25) or the slaughter of animals for meat. The processing of Annex I agricultural products into non-Annex I products therefore falls outside the scope of the special rules for agricultural products.

[11] Case 139/79 *Maizena v Council* [1980] E.C.R. 3393, para.23.
[11a] art.43.3 TFEU.
[12] Council Regulation (EC) No.1184/2006 of July 24, 2006 applying certain rules of competition to the production of, and trade in, agricultural products [2006] O.J. L214/7. This Regulation repeals Council Regulation No.26 of April 4, 1962 [1962] O.J. 30.
[13] Case 114/83 *Ste Inititives et Co-opration Agricole v Commission* [1984] E.C.R. 2589.
[14] Joined Cases C–346/03 and C–529/03 *Giuseppe Atzeni and Others* [2006] E.C.R. I–01875, para.40.
[15] Council Regulation (EC) No.1782/2003 of September 29, 2003 establishing common rules for direct support schemes under the common agricultural policy and establishing certain support schemes for farmers and amending Regulations (EEC) No.2019/93, (EC) No.1452/2001, (EC) No.1453/2001, (EC) No.1454/2001, (EC) 1868/94, (EC) No.1251/1999, (EC) No.1254/1999, (EC) No.1673/2000, (EEC) No.2358/71 and (EC) No.2529/2001 [2003] O.J. L270/1.

amalgamating an array of support systems into a single payment scheme. Council Regulation (EC) No.1234/2007 of October 22, 2007 establishing a common organisation of agricultural markets and specific provisions for certain agricultural products (the Single CMO Regulation),[16] replaced 21 existing CMOs at the beginning of 2008. The fruit and vegetable and wine sectors were fully incorporated into the scope of this regulation at a later stage.[17] In practice, art.180 of the Single CMO Regulation provides for the application of the state aid rules of arts 107 to 109 TFEU to all the products concerned.[17a] As a result, only a few agricultural products which are not subject to the CMO are not fully subject to the state aid rules, in particular horsemeat,[18] coffee, vinegars derived from alcohol, and cork.[19] For products for which no market organisation regulation exists,[20] the basic regime of reg.1184/2006[21] applies. This means that the Member States are merely obliged to inform the Commission of such measures, while the Commission's powers with regard to them are limited to providing comments on their compatibility with the state aid rules. It follows that in the case of products which only come within the scope of that regulation, the Commission is not empowered to initiate the procedure provided for by art.108(2) TFEU.[22] However, this is without prejudice to a review under art.108(1) TFEU if a

---

[16] [2007] O.J. L299/1, as amended by Council Regulation (EC) No.491/2009 of May 25, 2009 amending Regulation (EC) No.1234/2007 establishing a common organisation of agricultural markets and on specific provisions for certain agricultural products (Single CMO Regulation) [2009] O.J. L154.

[17] Council Regulation (EC) No.1182/2007 of September 26, 2007 laying down specific rules as regards the fruit and vegetable sector, amending Directives 2001/112/EC and 2001/113/EC and regs (EEC) No.827/68, (EC) No.2200/96, (EC) No.2201/96, (EC) No.2826/2000, (EC) No.1782/2003 and (EC) No.318/2006 and repealing reg.(EC) No.2202/96 [2007] O.J. L273/1. Council Regulation (EC) No.479/2008 of April 29, 2008 on the common organisation of the market in wine, amending regs (EC) No.1493/1999, (EC) No.1782/2003, (EC) No.1290/2005, (EC) No.3/2008 and repealing regs (EEC) No.2392/86 and (EC) No.1493/1999 [2008] O.J. L148.

[17a] At present, the Single CMO Regulation is undergoing a fundamental revision process. See COM(2011) 626 final/2 of October 19, 2011, Proposal for a Regulation of the European Parliament and of the Council establlishing a common organisation of the markets in agricultural products.

[18] Commission Decision N 693/2007 [2008] O.J. C101/7.

[19] See para.21 of the Community Guidelines for State Aid in the Agriculture and Forestry Sector 2007 to 2013 [2006] O.J. C319/1.

[20] There are still some agricultural products and goods which do not benefit from these mechanisms but may benefit from customs protection, production aid or an extension of the rules relating to the markets organisation. They include, e.g., Council Regulation (EC) No.1221/97 of June 25, 1997 laying down general rules for the application of measures to improve the production and marketing of honey [1997] O.J. L173. See Decisions N 671/2001 and 672/2001 France— *OFIVAL, Contrats Plan Etat-régions. Production équine et désaisonnalisation de la production de poulains lourds*; N 693/07 France—*Programme d'aides à la collecte et à l'allotement des poulains lourds.* N278/2005, N281/2004; N9/2010 Italy—*Dispositions régionales en matière de réglementation et de promotion de l'apiculture (Friuli-Venezia-Giulia)*; N 692/2002 Italy— *Honey, project U.N.A.A.P.I.*

[21] See fn.12, above.

[22] Joined Cases C–346/03 and C–529/03 *Atzeni and others* [2005] E.C.R. I–1875, para.39; Case 289/83 *GAARM v Commission* [1984] E.C.R. 4295, para.27.

common market organisation is introduced,[23] as in the case of ethyl alcohol[24] or starch potatoes,[25] or if the Member State does not follow the Commission's recommendations, there is a possibility to apply art.226 TFEU.

These CMO provisions are accompanied by a collateral set of further Council or Commission implementing rules.[26] State aid measures may influence the organisation of the common market by regulating the volume of production or the quality of products.[27] The proper working of the single market based on the common agricultural policy would be jeopardised by uncontrolled granting of national aid, since such aids do not in principle have a lasting effect on the development of the agricultural sector. The Commission's control of state aid should therefore prevent Member States from undermining or creating exceptions to the organisation of the common market.[28] Rules which interfere with the proper functioning of the common organisation of the market are incompatible with that common organisation, even if the matter in question has not been exhaustively regulated by the Council.[29]

13–004   In principle, it is for the Community to seek solutions to problems[30] facing the common agricultural policy; Member States must therefore refrain from taking any unilateral measure, even if that measure is likely to support the common policy of the Community.[31] Such actions are, however, acceptable, if the state aid measure is strictly ancillary to a measure envisaged by the common market organisation.[32] On the other hand, while the establishment of a common organisation of the agricultural markets pursuant to art.40 TFEU does not have the effect of exempting agricultural producers from any national provisions intended to attain objectives other than those covered by the common organisation, it cannot affect the machinery of production or price formation under the common

[23] Case 114/83 *Société d'initiatives et de coopération agricoles v Commission* [1983] E.C.R. 2315, paras 26 and 27.

[24] Although ethyl alcohol is now covered by Council Regulation (EC) No.1234/2007 of October 22, 2007, establishing a common organisation of agricultural markets and on specific provisions for certain agricultural products (Single CMO Regulation). Germany is still authorised to continue to grant this type of aid up to 2017 for a total of €270 million to its Ethyl alcohol monopoly, see Regulation (EU) No.1234/2010 of the European Parliament and of the Council of December 15, 2010 Amending Council Regulation (EC) No.1234/2007 (Single CMO Regulation) as regards the aid granted in the framework of the German Alcohol Monopoly [2010] O.J. L346/11.

[25] N383/2006 CY—*Régime national 2006–2008 pour les producteurs de pommes de terre*; N332/2009 Belgium—*Indemnisation des pertes subies par les producteurs de pommes de terre suite aux mesures prises contre des organismes nuisibles.*

[26] For a list of rules governing common markets organisation see *http://ec.europa.eu/agriculture/ simplification/cmo/index_en.htm.*

[27] Case 51/74 *Van der Hulst v Productschap voor Siergewassen* [1975] E.C.R. 79, para.25.

[28] Case 83/78 *Pigs Marketing Board* [1978] E.C.R. 2347, and Case 177/78 *McCarren* [1979] E.C.R. 2161, para.14, Case C–113/00 *Spain v Commission* [2002] E.C.R. I–7601, para.73.

[29] Case C–1/96 *Compassion in World Farming* [1998] E.C.R. I–1251, para.41, and Case C–428/99 *van den Bor* [2002] E.C.R. I–127, para.35.

[30] Case 90/86 *Criminal Proceedings against Zoni* [1988] E.C.R. 4285, para.26; Case C–86/89 *Italy v Commission* [1990] E.C.R. I–3891, para.19; Case 216/84 *Commission v France* [1988] E.C.R.793, para.18; Case C–173/02 *Spain v Commission* [2004] E.C.R. I–9735, para.19.

[31] Case C–86/89 *Italian Republic v Commission* [1990] E.C.R. I–03891, para.19.

[32] Case C–428/99 *van den Bor* [2002] E.C.R. I–127, para.44.

organisation, whatever its alleged or stated objective may be.[33] When faced with national measures on the quality of products that contained a prohibition of the production of cheese of a quality other than that laid down by the national legislation, the Court of Justice accepted that in the absence of any rule of Community law on the quality of cheese products, the Member States retained the power to apply rules of that kind to cheese producers established within their territory.[34]

The Commission and the Member State must, in accordance with art.4(3) TEU, cooperate in good faith with a view to overcoming difficulties, while fully observing the Treaty and other Community provisions, in particular those regulating the common organisation of the market in the sector concerned and those relating to state aid.[35]

A specific aid scheme may be explicitly provided for in a market organisation regulation.[36] The measure must apply in a non-discriminatory way to all operators concerned, although a particular regulation may allow different treatment of operators if this can be justified by objective circumstances.[37] However once the Council decides that the state aid rules apply in principle to production and trade in a given common market organisation, it may not arbitrarily authorise individual schemes or decide that the state aid rules do not apply to them under the procedure of art.43 TFEU. Such decisions would amount to violations of art.108 TFEU and constitute a clear abuse of powers and procedure.[38]

It is established case law that the Commission has the central role in determining whether aid is compatible with the common market on the basis of art.107 TFEU.[39] However, this competence is subject to an exception stipulated in art.108(2), third indent TFEU, whereby the Council, acting unanimously on an application from a Member State, has a decision-making power in the matter of compatibility, in derogation from art.107 TFEU. This is an extraordinary power

13–005

---

[33] Case C–283/03 *Kuipers* [2005] E.C.R. I–4255, para.44.

[34] Case 237/82 *Jongeneel Kaas and Others* [1984] E.C.R. 483, paras 12–14.

[35] Case C–428/99 *van den Bor* [2002] E.C.R. I–127, paras 40–47.

[36] Following the adoption of Council Regulation (EC) No.1913/2005 of November 23, 2005 amending regs No.2759/75, (EEC) No.2771/75, (EEC) No.2777/75, (EC) No.1254/1999, (EC) No.1255/1999 and (EC) No.2529/2001 as regards exceptional market support measures caused by restrictions on free movement of poultry meat in order to combat animal disease or severe market disturbances directly linked to the loss of consumer confidence [2005] O.J. L307/2; Council Regulation (EEC) No.2759/75 [1975] O.J. L282/1, art.20(4): "Articles 87, 88 and 89 of the Treaty shall not apply to Member States' financial contributions towards the exceptional measures". These measures are co-financed and taken at the request of the Member States.

[37] e.g. see arts 88 and 90 of Regulation EC No. 1234/2007 O.J. L2007, p.1.

[38] Council Regulation (EC) No.318/2006 of February 20, 2006 on the common organisation of the markets in the sugar sector [2006] O.J. L58/1, recital 36 and art.36; see as well Council Regulation (EC) No.320/2006 of February 20, 2006 establishing a temporary scheme for the restructuring of the sugar industry in the Community and amending [2006] O.J. L58/1; reg.(EC) No.1290/2005 on the financing of the common agricultural policy [2005] O.J. L209/1.

[39] Case C–354/90 *Fédération nationale du commerce extérieur des produits alimentaires and Syndicat national des négociants et transformateurs de saumon* [1991] E.C.R. I–5505, paras 9 and 14. See also Council document no.11567/06 of July 12, 2006, last paragraph, concerning the Commission's competence to adopt state aid guidelines for the agricultural sector.

which should be interpreted strictly, so the Council must motivate the exceptional circumstances[40] which justify the adoption of such measures.[41] Decisions based on art.108(2) third indent TFEU may only be challenged if the Council has exceeded the limits of its discretionary power under that provision. The Council has authorised aid on this basis, e.g. in the wine[42] or sugar sectors.[43] The Council may not act on the basis of art.108(2) TFEU once the Commission has taken a negative stance on a particular measure. The Commission has successfully challenged Council decisions authorising state aid to agriculture, precisely in order to reaffirm its exclusive competence in this area.[44] The limits on the Council's powers in this respect have been questioned by the Commission in a recent application against state aid granted for the purchase of agricultural land.[45]

3. RURAL DEVELOPMENT

13–006   As well as the rules concerning state aid in the field of market organisation regulations, a wide range of other state aid rules exist. With regard to socio-structural measures falling within the structural agricultural policy, Member States have considerably more discretion than they have with regard to aid falling within the scope of the common market organisations. Council Regulation (EC)

---

[40] Case C–122/94 *Commission v Council* [1996] I–881, para.12.

[41] See, e.g. Council Decision on the approval of exceptional national aid by the Republic of Cyprus to Cypriot farmers for the purpose of repaying part of agricultural debts created long before the accession of Cyprus to the European Union [2006] O.J. L23/78.

[42] e.g. Council Decision 2000/808/EC of December 19, 2000 on the granting of exceptional national aid by the authorities of the Federal Republic of Germany for the distillation of certain wine sector products [2000] O.J. L328/49; or Council Decision 2000/809/EC of December 19, 2000 on the granting of exceptional national aid by the Government of the Italian Republic for the distillation of certain wine sector products [2000] O.J. L328/51.

[43] Council Decision 2000/257/EC of March 20, 2000 concerning aid granted in Italy by RIBS SpA in accordance with the provisions of national law No.700 of December 19, 1983 on the restructuring of the sugar beet sector [2000] O.J. L79/38.

[44] Case C–110/02 *Commission v Council* [2004] E.C.R. I–6333, paras 33, 44 and 45; Case C–399/03 *Commission v Council* [2006] E.C.R. I–5629, paras 23–29; on a different occasion such challenge was not admitted for procedural reasons see Case C–309/95 *Commission v Council* [1998] E.C.R. I–655.

[45] See Council decisions of December 2009 on the granting of state aid by the authorities of the Republic of Poland, Lithuania, Latvia and Hungary for the purchase of State-owned agricultural land between January 1, 2010 and December 31, 2013, under appeal C–111/10, C–118/10, C–1221/10 *Commission v Council* [2010] O.J. C113. The contested Council decisions concern aid for the purchase of agricultural land in Latvia, Lithuania, Hungary and Poland. As explained in more detail further below, the Commission adopted special prolongation measures in the 2007 Agricultural Guidelines in order to phase out aid for the purchase of land by the end of 2009. It thus specifically addressed the issue of compatibility of aid for the purchase of land in those Guidelines, which were accepted by all Member States under the appropriate measures procedure. Poland notified its acceptance of these appropriate measures on February 26, 2007. The acceptance of the measures in question was published in the Official Journal. The Council, however, considers that the approved aid constituted new aid and it therefore had competence to act on the basis of art.108(2) TFEU.

No.1698/2005 on support for rural development by the European Agricultural Fund for Rural Development (EAFRD)[46] ("the Rural Development Regulation") provides for a wide range of support measures in favour of rural development, which may be co-financed from the Community Funds.[46a] Regulation 1698/2005 is now based on arts 42, 43 and 349 TFEU and establishes the framework for rural development policy for the years 2007–2013, reinforcing the role of rural development as the second pillar of the common agricultural policy.[47] Article 5 of the Rural Development Regulation provides that support measures must be in conformity with the Treaty and any acts adopted on its basis. Articles 88 and 89 of the Rural Development Regulation contain specific provisions in respect of state aid.

Article 88 of the Rural Development Regulation states that save as otherwise provided, arts 107–109 TFEU apply to aid granted by Member States to support rural development, but those articles do not apply to payments made by Member States pursuant to and in accordance with the Regulation within the scope of art.42 of the Treaty. It follows that subject to any specific limitations or derogations provided in the Rural Development Regulation, the provisions of the Treaty are fully applicable to state aid granted in the agricultural sector.

According to the second paragraph of art.88(1) of the Rural Development Regulation, without prejudice to art.89 of the regulation, arts 107, 108 and 109 TFEU do not apply to payments made by Member States pursuant to and in accordance with the Regulation within the scope of art.42 TFEU.[48] As far as the additional national financing[49] is concerned, pursuant to art.89 of the Rural

---

[46] Council Regulation (EC) No.1698/2005 on support for rural development from the European Agricultural Fund for Rural Development (EAFRD) [2005] O.J. L277/1, as amended and consolidated.

[46a] At present, the Community Funds policy is undergoing a revision process. See COM(2011) 615 final of October 6, 2011, Proposal for a Regulation of the European Parliament and of the Council laying down provisions on the European Regional Development Fund, the Regional Development Fund repealing Regulation (EC) No. 1083/2006; see COM(2011) 627 final/2 of 19.10.2011, Proposal for (EAFRD).

[47] According to the Inter-institutional Agreement on budgetary discipline and sound financial management (2006/C 139/01) a minimum of €69.75 billion would be available from EU resources for the Rural Development instrument (see minutes of 2739th Council Meeting Agriculture and Fisheries, Luxembourg, June 19, 2006). According to point 62 of the conclusions of the European Council of December 2005, Member States could transfer additional sums from market-related expenditure and direct payments of the common agricultural policy to rural development, up to a maximum of 20% of the amounts accruing to them from market-related expenditure and direct payments, so the additional resources of up to €40 billion could be transferred to this instrument from market-related expenditure and direct payment budget resources, at the discretion of Member States. See also Council Decision of February 20, 2006 on Community strategic guidelines for rural development (programming period 2007–2013) [2006] O.J. L55/20.

[48] Clarification introduced by Council Regulation (EC) No.74/2009 of January 19, 2009 [2009] O.J. L30/100.

[49] "Additional financing" may be granted either as supplementary aid to measures co-financed by the Community support or as stand-alone financing, e.g. in the case of energy willow in the new Member States.

Development Regulation, the state aid rules apply, except for the first sentence of art.108(3) TFEU.[50]

13–007   The assessment of state aid for the production or processing of products falling outside Annex I to the TFEU is conducted in accordance with the general Treaty rules on state aid, including the notification obligation under the first sentence of art.108(3) TFEU and any horizontal primary and secondary compatibility rules that may be applicable.[51] By way of example, art.28 of the Rural Development Regulation foresees investment aid for the processing or marketing of products covered by Annex I, as well as investment aid for the development of new products, processes and technologies linked to products that may be outside the scope of Annex I TFEU; while art.52 of the Rural Development Regulation allows measures to diversify the rural economy, in particular measures for farms to expand into non-agricultural activities, support for the creation and development of micro-enterprises and encouragement of tourism activities. Such measures are subject to normal state aid compatibility assessment.

13–008   According to art.70(8) of the Rural Development Regulation, public expenditure for the production and trade of Annex I products (including Community money: see the definition in art.2(i) of the Rural Development Regulation) must comply with the limits laid down in respect of state aid, unless the Rural Development Regulation provides otherwise. Articles 26, 27 and 28 of the Regulation provide for maximum aid intensities and the amounts stipulated in the Annex to the Regulation. Since the economic effects of an aid do not change depending on whether it is partly financed by the Community or financed by a Member State alone, the Commission considers[52] that there should be consistency and coherence between its policy in respect of the control of state aid and the support granted under the Community driven common agricultural and rural development policy.

According to the first sentence of art.16(g) of the Rural Development Regulation, each rural development programme will have to include the relevant state aid notification forms as defined by Commission Regulation (EC) No.794/2004 of April 21, 2004 implementing Council Regulation (EC) No.659/1999 laying

---

[50] Under art.89 of the Rural Development Regulation, Member States may make available additional non-mandatory resources, and the minimum co-financing rate for Rural Development funds of 20% defined in art.70(3) of the Council Regulation will not be applicable to additionally transferred funds. Such measures are currently assessed in the course of analysis of the rural development plans if they fall within the scope of art.42 TFEU and no separate state aid decision is taken regarding them. In the course of a review of the Rural Development Regulation, the Commission has suggested a formal change so that the state aid rules would no longer apply directly to the top-ups, although their substance would be mirrored in the control of the rural development programmes, see COM(2011) 627 final/2, fn.47, above, art.88.

[51] AG Romero in Joined Cases C–346/03 and C–529/03 *Francesco Atzori, Giuseppe Atzeni, Giuseppe Ignazio Boi and Marco Scalas Et Renato Lilliu v Regione Autonoma Della Sardegna* [2006] E.C.R. I–1875, para.134.

[52] See Agricultural Guidelines; Title VIII on state aid of Rural Development Regulation only concerns support from Member States. It may therefore be concluded that the general state aid rules apply to Community support for both activities covered by and those falling outside the scope of art.36 TFEU.

down detailed rules for the application of art.93 EC Treaty [113 TFEU],[53] since the scope of this regulation applies to aid in all sectors. The Community may support a number of measures concerning products and activities not related to Annex I products. A rural development measure concerning products not covered by art.42 TFEU must be covered by either one of the applicable state aid block exemption regulations, or a Commission decision already approving it according to the normal state aid notification procedures. Additional financing, including for Annex I products, is subject to compatibility assessment in accordance with the substantive and procedural state aid rules, according to a system reaffirmed in the Commission Implementing Regulation for the Rural Development Regulation 1974/2006[54] (the "Implementing Regulation"), art.57 of which lays down some conditions concerning the application of art.89 of the Rural Development Regulation. Annex II point 9 of the Implementing Regulation provides detailed information on what is required to assess particular measures for compatibility with the state aid rules in the context of approval of rural development programmes.

4. ACCESSION TREATIES

The Accession Treaties may provide for transitional measures modifying the **13–009** application of the common market organisation and structural measures for rural development, and may also define the conditions under which state aid measures will be considered as already existing at the time of accession. Some of these measures are considered as permanent provisions[55] and others as temporary.[56] The former rank as primary law and may not be altered without the consent of all the parties to that particular Treaty, while the latter may be altered according to the same procedures as those applicable to measures amended by virtue of the Treaty of Accession.

[53] Normal notification forms should be used for state aid to non-Annex I products: see Commission Regulation (EC) No.1935/2006 of December 20, 2006 amending Regulation (EC) No.794/2004 implementing Council Regulation (EC) No.659/1999 laying down detailed rules for the application of art.93 of the EC Treaty [2006] O.J. L407/1.

[54] Commission Regulation (EC) No.1974/2006 of December 15, 2006 laying down detailed rules for the application of Council Regulation (EC) No.1698/2005 on support for rural development by the European Agricultural Fund for Rural Development (EAFRD) [2006] O.J. L368/15, as amended several times.

[55] e.g. art.9 of the Treaty between the Kingdom of Belgium, the Kingdom of Denmark, the Federal Republic of Germany, the Hellenic Republic, the Kingdom of Spain, the French Republic, Ireland, the Italian Republic, the Grand Duchy of Luxembourg, the Kingdom of the Netherlands, the Republic of Austria, the Portuguese Republic, the Republic of Finland, the Kingdom of Sweden, the United Kingdom of Great Britain and Northern Ireland (Member States of the European Union) and the Czech Republic, the Republic of Estonia, the Republic of Cyprus, the Republic of Latvia, the Republic of Lithuania, the Republic of Hungary, the Republic of Malta, the Republic of Poland, the Republic of Slovenia, the Slovak Republic, concerning the accession of the Czech Republic, the Republic of Estonia, the Republic of Cyprus, the Republic of Latvia, the Republic of Lithuania, the Republic of Hungary, the Republic of Malta, the Republic of Poland, the Republic of Slovenia and the Slovak Republic to the European Union [2003] O.J. L236/1.

[56] e.g. art.7 of the above Treaty.

With regard to the accession of Austria, Finland and Sweden, the Act of Accession[57] established a specific procedure for state aid existing in each new Member State at the time of accession, and for a specific transitional period. In accordance with art.172 of the Act of Accession, the Commission was informed of all existing agricultural aid schemes in those Member States,[58] and adopted two decisions approving the Austrian and Finnish programmes for the implementation of arts 138–140 of the Act of Accession.[59] Furthermore, art.142 of the Act of Accession stated that the Commission would authorise Finland and Sweden to grant long-term aids to ensure that agricultural activity was maintained in the northern regions, and had determined the regions concerned and the levels of aid in two decisions.[60]

13–010   For the 2004 and 2007 accessions, which extended the common organisation of the markets to total of 12 new Member States, the Acts of Accession[61] introduced a phasing-in mechanism for direct Community payments.[62] They introduced some specific derogations in this respect for the new Member States,

[57] Act concerning the conditions of accession of the Kingdom of Norway, the Republic of Austria, the Republic of Finland and the Kingdom of Sweden and the adjustments to the Treaties on which the European Union is founded [1994] O.J. C241/1.

[58] XXV Competition Report, p.83.

[59] On February 13, 1995 the Commission adopted two decisions approving the Austrian and Finnish programmes for the implementation of arts 138–140 of the Act of Accession, which provided for the granting of transitional, degressive national aid for agricultural products, XXV Competition Report, p.83.

[60] Commission Decision 95/196/EC of June 9, 1995 on the long-term national aid scheme for agriculture in the northern regions of Finland [1995] O.J. L126/35, as last amended by Commission Decision 2002/404/EC of May 24, 2002 [2002] O.J. L139/38 and Commission Decision 96/228/EC of February 28, 1996 on a long-term national aid scheme to assist farmers in northern areas of Sweden [1996] O.J. L76/29, as last amended by Commission Decision 2004/291/EC of March 30, 2004 [2004] O.J. L94/61. It remains to be seen how long the transitional measures will continue to apply; the most recent decisions were taken in 2009, allowing further aids till 2013, so this appears to be a rather long transition period.

[61] Act concerning the conditions of accession of the Czech Republic, the Republic of Estonia, the Republic of Cyprus, the Republic of Latvia, the Republic of Lithuania, the Republic of Hungary, the Republic of Malta, the Republic of Poland, the Republic of Slovenia and the Slovak Republic and the adjustments to the Treaties on which the European Union is founded [2003] O.J. L236/369. Act concerning the conditions of accession of the Republic of Bulgaria and Romania and the adjustments to the treaties on which the European Union is founded [2005] O.J. L157/203; for existing state aid in the agricultural sector, see p.271; for phasing in of direct payments and complementary payments, see p.251; for special temporary additional rural development measures, see Annex VIII to the Act, p.369. The Council adopted a rural development adaptation package with a view to the accession of Bulgaria and Romania to the EU during the 2739th Agriculture and Fisheries Council meeting in Luxembourg on June 19, 2006. The package consists of a Regulation adapting Regulation (EC) No.1698/2005 on support for rural development by the European Agricultural Fund for Rural Development (EAFRD) (9248/06); and two Decisions adapting the Act of Accession of Bulgaria and Romania as regards rural development (9605/06 and 9608/06). Similar steps are expected in the view of Croatia accession.

[62] Council Decision 2004/281/EC of March 22, 2004 adapting the Act concerning the conditions of accession of the Czech Republic, the Republic of Estonia, the Republic of Cyprus, the Republic of Latvia, the Republic of Lithuania, the Republic of Hungary, the Republic of Malta, the Republic of Poland, the Republic of Slovenia and the Slovak Republic and the adjustments to the Treaties on which the European Union is founded, following the reform of the common agricultural policy [2004] O.J. L93/1.

e.g. the possibility to grant complementary national direct payments during the 2004–2006 period,[63] with an exception for Cyprus because it provided such support prior to enlargement.[64] Direct payments, however, are not subject to state aid control under art.108 TFEU.

With regard to rural development, these Acts of Accession established specific measures for the new Member States, which allowed temporary additional support in addition[65] to that resulting from the support envisaged for the 15 Member States in the programming period 2004–2006.[66] Derogations applicable to all the new Member States concerned support for semi-subsistence farms undergoing restructuring, support for compliance with community standards, establishment of producer groups, technical assistance and Leader+ type measures. Subject to these rules, the maximum total amount of support envisaged, expressed as a percentage of the volume of eligible investment, could reach 50 per cent, and in less-favoured areas 60 per cent. The thresholds could be increased by an additional 5 per cent for young farmers. These intensities were 10 per cent higher than the regular allowances for such support for the EU-15.[67] During a transitional period after accession, investment aid could be granted to enterprises to meet minimum standards regarding the environment, hygiene and animal welfare. Beneficiary enterprises had to comply with the relevant standards by the end of the transitional period or the investment period, whichever was earlier.[68] Investment aid was allowed for agricultural holdings which would only attain economic viability at the end of realisation of the investment.[69] This was a more lenient approach in comparison with the normal system, which only allows investment aid to undertakings that are viable and already meet the required Community standards. These special concessions were supposed to help farmers from the new Member States to introduce the necessary adjustments rapidly. Council Regulation (EC) 1698/2005 no longer maintains these derogations, except for a higher aid intensity for investments to comply with the Nitrate Directive.[70]

Annex IV relating to art.22 of the Accession Treaty provides a general **13–011** derogation from the procedures concerning existing state aid provided for by art.108 TFEU (the so-called sunset clause). Pursuant to point 4 of Ch.4, aid schemes and individual aid put into effect in a new Member State before the date

---

[63] art.33h, Act of Accession (see fn.48, above), p.367.

[64] Derogation for direct support for Cyprus up to the level of support existing in 2001, Act of Accession, p.371.

[65] Point 26.1 of Annex II, Ch.6, to the Act of Accession [2003] O.J. L236/365; see also additional support applicable to Malta (SMPPMA), p.367.

[66] art.7 of Council Regulation (EC) No.1257/1999 of May 17, 1999 on support for rural development from the European Agricultural Guidance and Guarantee Fund (EAGGF) and amending and repealing certain Regulations [1999] O.J. L160/80, no longer in force.

[67] Derogation from art.7(2) of Regulation (EC) No.1257/1999.

[68] Derogation from art.26(1) second indent of Regulation (EC) No.1257/1999.

[69] Derogation from art.5 first indent of Regulation (EC) No.1257/1999.

[70] art.6(2) and the Annex to Council Regulation (EC) No.1698/2005 on support for rural development from the European Agricultural Fund for Rural Development (EAFRD) [2005] O.J. L277/1.

of accession and still applicable after that date are regarded as existing aid within the meaning of art.108(1) TFEU, on condition that they were communicated to the Commission four months after the date of accession. Unlike point 3 of Ch.4 to Annex IV to the Accession Treaty concerning competition policy, point 4 of Ch.4 to Annex IV concerning agriculture does not require detailed information concerning the scope, duration, budget or conditions of such measures to be communicated. These elements did not form constitutive criteria for a list of aids to be considered as existing within the meaning of art.108(1) TFEU.[71] When necessary, the new Member States had to amend these aid measures in order to comply with the rules applied by the Commission by the end of the third year from the date of accession at the latest. If they did not comply with the state aid provisions in force at that time, the measures were treated as new aid from May 1, 2007 or January 1, 2010. These measures did not require notification to the Commission if they were adapted to the applicable rules, contrary to cases where substantial changes concerning scope, budget or eligible costs were introduced.

The same sunset clause mechanism for state aid measures in the agricultural sector applies with regard to the accession of Croatia, and there are similar transitional measures to those for the previous enlargements of 2004 and 2007 regarding direct payments and temporary rural development measures.[72] It is expected that negotiations with Iceland will follow the same objectives.

Last but not least, it is also worth noting here that the state aid rules do not apply in their entirety to some EU territories, by virtue of special protocols to the relevant accession treaties. In these cases the Commission may only provide comments on planned state aid measures.[73] The special status of the outermost regions[74] and the Aegean Islands regarding both the common agricultural policy and the state aid rules is also worth noting.[75]

---

[71] Commission's Communication on June 17, 2005 [2005] O.J. C147/2 and on August 23, 2005 [2005] O.J. C206/10.

[72] Screening report, Croatia, Ch.11: Agriculture and Rural Development, July 17, 2006, Treaty concerning the accession of the Republic of Croatia, n.y.p. in O.J., Council of the European Union, Brussels November 7, 2011, 14409/11, ELARG 94 Annex IV, part 3(b), Agriculture, State aids.

[73] Pursuant to art.1(2) of Protocol No.3 on the Channel Islands and the Isle of Man to the Act of Accession of 1972; the Community rules regarding trade in agricultural products applicable to the United Kingdom also apply to the Isle of Man. In accordance with art.2 of Council Regulation (EEC) No.706/73, the Treaty provisions regarding state aid, in particular art.88(1) and the first sentence of art.88(3) apply to the Isle of Man: see Decisions N 338/2002, N 339/2002, N 340/2002.

[74] See art.349 TFEU; Council Regulation (EC) No.1448/2001 of June 28, 2001 amending, as regards structural measures, Regulation (EEC) No.3763/91 introducing specific measures in respect of certain agricultural products for the benefit of the French overseas departments [2001] O.J. L198/3; Council Regulation (EC) No.1453/2001 of June 28, 2001 introducing specific measures for certain agricultural products for the Azores and Madeira and repealing Regulation (EEC) No.1600/92 (Poseima) [2001] O.J. L198/26, Council Regulation (EC) No.1449/2001 of June 28, 2001 amending Regulation (EEC) No.1600/92 concerning specific measures for the Azores and Madeira, relating to certain agricultural products as regards the structural measures [2001] O.J. L198/5; Decision NN 40/2004 *Banana producer groups support (Guadeloupe and Martinique)*.

[75] Council Regulation (EC) No.442/2002 of February 18, 2002 amending Regulation (EEC)

5. MATERIAL STATE AID RULES ON COMPATIBILITY

The Commission assesses state aid in the agricultural sector on the basis of arts 107(2) and (3) TFEU, and as far as agricultural products are concerned, within the limits decided in principle by the Council.[76]

General architecture

The Commission changed the existing rules on state aid compatibility in the **13–012** agriculture sector following the reform of the common market organisations and rural development policies described above, while also taking into account the objectives of "less and better" targeted state aid, in accordance with the Commission's State Aid Action Plan,[77] which aims at a significant reduction of sector-specific state aid rules and a more horizontal approach to granting support. As a result the state aid rules for the primary agriculture sector were simplified by reducing the seven texts in force[78] to three texts: Block Exemption Regulation 1857/2006 on the application of arts 87 and 88 TFEU to state aid to small and medium-sized enterprises active in the production, processing and marketing of agricultural products[79] (the SME Agriculture Regulation); the Community Guidelines for state aid in the agriculture and forestry sector 2007–2013[80] (hereafter the "Agricultural Guidelines"); and Commission Regulation

---

No.2019/93 introducing specific measures for the smaller Aegean islands concerning certain agricultural products [2002] O.J. L68/4.

[76] The Commission adapted the agricultural state aid rules to the rural development reform of 2003. This concerned inter alia the introduction of new state aid possibilities for "animal welfare" (€500 and more per livestock unit and year for voluntarily respecting higher standards); "meeting standards" (€10,000 and more per holding and year for five years to compensate for operating costs from meeting new compulsory standards); and "food quality" (€3,000 per holding and year for five years for joining a quality scheme). Account was also taken of the additional policy changes for rural development agreed by the Council in 2005, notably the proposed abolition of the €250 per hectare and year limit for less favoured area support ("less favoured areas" are those that suffer from a permanent natural disadvantage such as poor soil, an adverse climate or difficult topography, which make it difficult for them to compete on level terms with other areas) and modifications of Natura 2000 payments.

[77] State Aid Action Plan, less and better targeted state aid: a roadmap for state aid reform 2005–2009, SEC(2005) 795, June 7, 2005, COM(2005) 107 final.

[78] Commission Regulation on the application of arts 87 and 88 of the TFEU to state aid to small and medium sized enterprises active in the production, processing and marketing of agricultural products [2004] O.J. L1; Community guidelines for state aid in the agriculture sector [2000] O.J. C28, Corrigendum [2000] O.J. C232; Community Guidelines for state aid for advertising of products listed in Annex I to the TFEU and of certain non-Annex I products [2001] O.J. C252; Community guidelines for state aid concerning TSE tests, fallen stock and slaughterhouse waste [2002] O.J. C324; Commission Regulation (EC) No.1860/2004 of October 6, 2004 on the application of arts 87 and 88 of the TFEU to de minimis aid in the agricultural and fisheries sectors [2004] O.J. L325; Commission communication on state aids: subsidised short-term loans in agriculture [1996] O.J. C44; Commission communication amending the Community framework for state aid for research and development (agriculture part only) [1998] O.J. C48.

[79] Commission Regulation (EC) No.1857/2006 of December 15, 2006 on the application of arts 87 and 88 of the TFEU to state aid to small and medium-sized enterprises active in the production, processing and marketing of agricultural products [2006] O.J. L358/3.

[80] [2006] O.J. C319/1.

No.1535/2007 of December 20, 2007 on the application of arts 87 and 88 of the TFEU to de minimis aid in the sector of agricultural production (hereafter the Agricultural de minimis Regulation).[81] In addition to these sector-specific rules, a number of horizontal rules concerning the definition of aid and compatibility are applicable,[82] especially General Block Exemption Regulation No.800/2008 (hereafter the GBER).[83] In the agricultural sector, in view of the special rules which apply to the primary production of agricultural products, the GBER should exempt only aid in the fields of research and development, aid in the form of risk capital, training aid, environmental aid and aid for disadvantaged and disabled workers insofar as these categories of aid are not covered by the Agricultural SME Regulation. In view of the similarities between the processing and marketing of agricultural products and non-agricultural products, this Regulation should also apply to the processing and marketing of agricultural products provided that certain conditions are met.

De minimis rules

13–013   Due to its specificity, primary production in the agricultural sector is still governed by separate rules, although here too there is an increasing tendency to align them as far as possible with the horizontal rules. The Agricultural de minimis Regulation allows grants of up to €7,500 per holding in any three years in the agricultural sector and within overall limits per Member State. The amounts that each Member State may grant per three-year period have been calculated by the Commission and are set out in the annex to the Regulation.[84] They are based on the average agricultural production output for a given Member

---

[81] Commission Regulation (EC) No.1535/2007 of December 20, 2007 on the application of arts 87 and 88 of the EC to de minimis aid in the sector of agricultural production sectors [2007] O.J. L337.

[82] The following rules concerning the definition of aid and the compatibility of aid with the TFEU are also applicable to the agriculture sector: Commission notice on the application of arts 87 and 88 of the EC to state aid in the form of guarantees [2008] O.J. C155/02, N546/2010; Community Framework for state aid in the form of public service compensation, [2005] O.J. C297/4; Commission Decision 2005/842/EC of November 28, 2005 on the application of art.86(2) of the EC to state aid in the form of public service compensation granted to certain undertakings entrusted with the operation of services of general economic interest [2005] O.J. L312/67; Commission Directive 80/723/EEC of June 25, 1980 on the transparency of financial relations between Member States and public undertakings [2000] O.J. L195/35 as last amended by Commission Directive 2005/81/EC [2005] O.J. L312/47; Commission communication concerning land sales by public authorities [1997] O.J. C209/3; Commission communication on the application of the state aid rules to measures relating to direct business taxation [1998] O.J. C384/3; Application of arts 92 and 93 of the EC to public authorities' holdings, Bulletin EC 9–1984.

[83] Commission Regulation (EC) No.800/2008 of August 6, 2008 declaring certain categories of aid compatible with the common market in application of arts 87 and 88 of the Treaty (GBER) [2008] O.J. L214. It is applicable with some minor exceptions to the processing and marketing of agricultural products with some minor exceptions: see art.1(3)(b) and (c) of the GBER. For further details please refer to Ch.11.

[84] Due to the shift of the processing of agricultural products to a general de minimis, higher global amounts of aid are available for the primary production de minimis, provided the total ceiling of 0.75% of agricultural output allowed per Member State has remained at the same levels.

State. As such, defined aid does not fulfil all the criteria of art.107(1) TFEU; the Member States may grant it without the Commission's prior approval, but the aid must be transparent and accounted for, and Member States must provide information certifying compliance with the two ceilings.[85] Member States may grant de minimis aid for almost any objective they deem appropriate, including operating aid, but the Regulation lays down a few limitations in order to avoid distortion of the common organisations of the markets in agricultural products: no export aid may be granted, and aid may not be linked to the price or quantity of products put on the market or made contingent on the use of domestic products.

It must be borne in mind, however, that beneficiaries active in the processing and marketing of agricultural or non-agricultural products, as well as other non-agricultural activities, are not prevented from profiting from the so-called general de minimis, which currently amounts to €200,000 per fiscal year.[86]

Compatibility rules applicable to the agricultural sector

As described above, the current system consists in principle of two block **13–014** exemption regulations and a set of guidelines. When a specific type of state aid measure is block-exempted, the Agricultural Guidelines refer back to particular provisions of the block exemption regulation for the compatibility assessment. Consequently, some provisions of the block exemption regulation may be considered as effectively exhaustive, i.e. the aid can only be found to be compatible with the common market if it fulfils all the criteria stipulated in the regulation. This structure saves the Commission from having to review large numbers of standard notifications, and leaves it free to concentrate on controlling other aid measures. In addition, only aid for micro, small and medium agricultural holdings may be authorised. Nevertheless, the definition of an SME (no more than 250 employees, a turnover of no more than €40 million or a balance-sheet total of no more than €27 million)[87] means that the vast majority of holdings active in the primary production of agricultural products are covered by these provisions.

It must be underlined that the state aid compatibility rules are very much guided by common market organisation and rural development rules. Nevertheless, the conditions for declaring state aid compatible with art.107 TFEU are not always identical with the conditions required for obtaining co-financing under Regulation (EC) No.1698/2005. The state aid rules are more detailed regarding the eligible costs for particular activities, or may allow different aid

---

[85] This construction seems to allow the Commission to monitor the respect of the WTO obligations imposed by the Agreement on trade in agricultural goods.

[86] There is no cumulation of two de minimis aids for the same undertaking, activity. See Ch.7 on de minimis.

[87] Commission Recommendation of May 6, 2003 concerning the definition of micro, small and medium-sized enterprises (notified under document number C(2003) 1422) [2003] O.J. L124/36.

intensities, especially with regard to activities falling outside the scope of Annex I TFEU, since they are subject to horizontal state aid control measures.

13–015 The Commission has described the compatibility rules in the Agricultural Guidelines, dividing them into types of aid, and then outlining the objectives sought in the "analysis" section and stating the conditions for compatibility in the "policy" section, where eligible costs, aid intensities and other conditions are stipulated.[88] Unless the Guidelines refer to another legislative text or refer specifically to an exception, the whole framework applies to the measures concerned (e.g. concerning incentive effect or eligible costs). A selection of the most relevant compatibility rules are described below.

The state aid compatibility rules contained in the block exemption regulations applicable to primary production and processing and marketing of agricultural products make it simpler for the Member States to grant state aid to this sector. When their conditions are met, a Member State may grant aid immediately, without first notifying it to the Commission. Member States need only inform the Commission of the aid, using a simple information sheet, and only after having granted the aid. According to the latest scoreboard, 2010 aid granted in the agricultural sector on the basis of the block exemption regulations amounted to €1.7 billion, granted by 258 reported measures, in comparison with 146 notified measures. Aid not covered by the regulations must be notified and is assessed in accordance with the conditions stipulated in the Agricultural Guidelines regarding aid intensities, eligible costs and types of aids. Measures pursuing objectives that were not envisaged at all in any of the state aid instruments are assessed directly on the basis of art.107 of the TFEU.[89]

Investment aid in primary production

13–016 Investment in agricultural holdings is governed by art.4 of the Agricultural SME Regulation and Ch.IV.A of the Agricultural Guidelines. The Agriculture SME Regulation requires investment aid to farmers to be "decoupled" and "horizontal", in the sense that it cannot be limited to a given product or animal such as pigs or poultry. In line with the principle established by the 2003 reform

---

[88] The Commission proposed to abolish a number of state aid provisions applicable only to the agriculture sector because they no longer appeared justified, namely short-term loans, land re-parcelling, the administrative costs of the establishment and maintenance of herd books, tests to determine the genetic quality or yield of livestock, aid for the introduction at farm level of innovatory animal breeding techniques or practices and the cost of keeping individual male breeding animals of high genetic quality registered in herd books. Such aid constitutes operating aid. In the Commission's view, the introduction of a de minimis possibility in the agriculture sector via reg.1860/2004 gave Member States some room to continue such support if they wished, without requiring Commission authorisation. Following consultations with the Member States, the Commission decided to keep some of these possibilities, e.g. aid for herd books, and to keep others to a limited extent, such as aid for land purchase.

[89] Indemnisation pour la présence non voulue d'OGM dans les cultures et produits agricoles, SI; N 568/2004—DN; N 679/06—PR.

of the CAP, investment decisions are guided by the market and not by administrative decisions.

The definitions of small and medium-sized enterprises follow the rules in Annex I to GBER, but a new concept for the purpose of intermediary enterprises has been created for the purposes of the Agricultural Guidelines.[90] Investment aid must pursue one of the following objectives: reduction of production costs, improvement and re-deployment of production[91]; improvement in quality, preservation and improvement of the natural environment[92]; or the improvement of hygiene conditions or animal welfare standards.[93] The Commission considers that aid granted retrospectively for activities already undertaken by the beneficiary cannot be viewed as containing the necessary incentive element, and must therefore be considered to constitute operating aid which is only intended to relieve the beneficiary of a financial burden. To maximise the incentive effect of aid and make this effect easier to demonstrate in the case of a notification, the eligibility rules laid down by Member States should ensure that aid in favour of expenditure incurred or services received is only granted after the date of a Commission decision declaring aid or an aid scheme compatible with the Treaty. The only exeption to this rule concerns aid schemes which are compensatory in nature.[94] The maximum gross investment aid intensity must not exceed 50 per cent of eligible costs in less favoured areas ("LFAs")[95] and 40 per cent in other regions. Young farmers[96] may obtain an increase of 10 per cent within five years

[90] Since 2007 the rules for investment aid no longer require the existence of a market outlet test for investment aid, limiting investment aid to capacity increases of 20%, and limitations on the use of second-hand machinery have been abolished. In the past, investment aid might also have been granted to large undertakings subject to the existence of market outlets: see decision C 14/2005 *Holland Malt (Netherlands)*; Case C–464/09 P, judgment of the Court of December 2, 2010, *Holland Malt BV v European Commission* [2011] O.J. C30.

[91] N546/2010—BG, *Aid for investment in agricultural holdings in the form of corporate tax relief.*

[92] N352/2010—ES, *Aides aux investissements non productifs dans les bois privés du réseau Natura 2000 dans la région de Murcia*; N 213/2010—EE, *Measure 2.7 of the Estonian Rural Development Programme 2007–2013 "Natura 2000 support to private forest owners"*; N362/2010—ES, *Aides destinées à la promotion de systèmes de production qui réduisent l'impact environnemental de la culture du petit pois dans la province de Teruel.*

[93] N366/2010, France, *Aide aux investissements réalisés dans les élevages de poules pondeuses en vue de se conformer aux normes de la directive 1999/74/CE*; N341/2010—RO, *Réalisation d'engagements pris en faveur du bien-être et de la protection des porcs.*

[94] Case T–6/06 *Mopro Nord v Commission* [2007] E.C.R. II–72.

[95] The term "less favoured areas" derives from rural development policy. These areas are defined by Member States on the basis of art.17 of reg.(EC) No.1257/1999 of May 17, 1999 on support for rural development from the European Agricultural Guidance and Guarantee Fund (EAGGF) and amending and repealing certain Regulations [1999] O.J. L160/80. From 2010 the LFA concept has been replaced by a reference to areas referred to in art.36(a)(i), (ii) and (iii) of the RD Regulation. It is worth noting that the concept of LFAs applies to primary agricultural production only and that aid to these areas is granted under art.107(3)(c) TFEU.

[96] art.22 of the RD Regulation defines a "young farmer" as aged less than 40 and setting up for the first time on an agricultural holding as head of the holding; SA 32602 Modification to investment aid and young farmer start-up support granted under the Act on the Financing of Rural Industries, FI.

of setting up. The aid level may be up to 75 per cent for investments in the outermost regions[97] of the European Union and the small Aegean islands.[98] Eligible expenses may include the construction, acquisition or improvement of immovable property and the purchase (or lease-purchase) of machinery and equipment, including computer software. General costs linked to those expenditures, such as architects', engineers' and consultancy fees, feasibility studies or the acquisition of patents and licences, are considered eligible as well.[99] Land other than land for construction purposes must be limited to 10 per cent of the investment's eligible expenses.[100]

13–017　　The rules provide a clear definition of what is a "newly introduced" standard for the purpose of allowing additional aid intensities for investment to adapt to new standards. If Member States delay the implementation of compulsory Community standards beyond the date foreseen by Community legislation, this may give farmers in those countries an advantage compared with farmers in Member States which implement the new standards by the dates foreseen in the legislation.

However, when setting up the appropriate aid intensity for investment linked to the meeting of newly introduced standards, the Commission also took into consideration that they often only entail costs for the farmer, without increasing his earning potential. The intensity should therefore reflect the delay involved and be reduced to zero at some point in time. To quantify what it considers as a significant impact on operating, the Commission indicates that standards justifying compensation must lead to an increase in operating costs of at least 5 per cent or a drop in income of at least 10 per cent. The only exception to this rule is expressly envisaged in the Agricultural Guidelines for the implementation of Council Directive 91/676 concerning the protection of waters against pollution caused by nitrates from agricultural sources.[101] A number of Member States were

---

[97] Pursuant to art.299(2) of the EC Treaty, the outermost regions comprise the French overseas departments, the Azores, Madeira and the Canary Islands.

[98] Pursuant to Council Regulation (EEC) No.2019/93 of July 19, 1993 introducing specific measures for the smaller Aegean islands concerning certain agricultural products [1993] O.J. L184/1 (Regulation as last amended by reg.(EC) No.1782/2003 [2003] O.J. L270/1), including any island in the Aegean with a permanent population of 100,000 inhabitants or less.

[99] For eligible expenses in connection with consultancy services or feasibility studies, agricultural undertakings may benefit from more generous aid if granted for "technical support" pursuant to art.15 of the Agricultural BER (see para.13–023, below).

[100] The more restrictive provision concerning land purchase was also introduced as part of the 2006 reform. Under the previous Guidelines (Community Guidelines for State Aid in the Agriculture Sector [2000] O.J. C28/2), 100% of the cost of land purchase was still considered eligible for investment aid. Aid schemes in connection with the purchase of land approved before the entry into force of the 2007–2013 Guidelines could continue as such until December 31, 2009 (see para.196 of the Guidelines). See Council decisions of December 2009 on the granting of state aid by the authorities of the Republic of Poland, Lithuania, Latvia and Hungary for the purchase of State owned agricultural land between January 1, 2010 and December 31, 2013, under appeal C–111/10, C–118/10, C–1221/10 *Commission v Council* [2010] O.J. C113; C9/2010 *Temporary capital tax gains tax relief on sales of cultivated land*, FI.

[101] [1991] O.J. L375/1.

condemned for failing to implement the Nitrates Directive on time,[102] and the Commission has recognised in past practice that the particular difficulties of implementing it justified granting farmers additional aid intensities for investments to comply with its standards.[103] Farmers may also receive up to 100 per cent for investments in traditional landscapes and buildings in the case of non-productive heritage features[104] and the relocation of farm buildings in the public interest.

To ensure that high amounts of support do not increase imbalances in the overall levels of support by Member States, upper limits per hectare for agro-environmental aid, animal welfare and compensatory payments for handicaps in certain areas have been introduced, as well as a possibility to limit compensation for farms of more than 50 hectares (i.e. farms more than twice the average EU size). Such limits already exist when the measures are co-financed. The maximum amounts for state aid intensities were set at a higher level, bearing in mind the express provision in the Rural Development Regulation that state aid may be authorised above the rates for co-financing.[105]

13–018

Processing and marketing of agricultural products. The rules for investment aid in connection with the processing and marketing of agricultural products are defined in the Guidelines, notably Ch.IV.B. Investment aid to companies active in processing and marketing agricultural products must comply with the horizontal state aid rules,[106] with higher aid intensities applicable in specific cases.[107] Large enterprises are only eligible for aid within the limits set by the Guidelines on national regional aid for 2007–2013[108] and GBER.

13–019

---

[102] Case C–258/00 *Commission v France* [2002] E.C.R. I–5959; Case C–69/99 *Commission v United Kingdom* [2000] E.C.R. I–10979; Case C–221/03 *Commission v Kingdom of Belgium* [2005] E.C.R. I–8307; Case C–416/02 *Commission v Kingdom of Spain* [2005] E.C.R. I–7487; Case C–396/01 *Commission v Ireland* [2004] E.C.R. I–2315; Case C–161/00 *Commission v Germany* [2002] E.C.R. I–2753; Case C–127/99 *Commission v Italy* [2001] E.C.R. I–8305; Case C–266/00 *Commission v Luxembourg* [2001] E.C.R. I–2073.

[103] Decision N 486/2005, Ireland; Decision N 103/2005, United Kingdom, *Amendment to the farm Nutrient management*; Decision N 53/2004, United Kingdom, *Farm Waste Management*; Decision N 800/2002, United Kingdom, *Nitrate Vulnerable Zones Grants Scheme*; Decision N 693/2002, United Kindgom, *Changes to the Farm Waste Grant Scheme*; Decision C27/2001, France, *Programme to control pollution of agricultural origin "PMPOA"*. These provisions expired on December 31, 2008.

[104] SA 31518.

[105] For example, if the maximum amount for co-financing is €600 per hectare and year, the maximum state aid would be €720.

[106] Notably art.13 GBER and Guidelines on national regional aid for 2007–2013 [2006] O.J. C54/13.

[107] In setting its policy regarding state aid rules for this aid instrument, the Commission took account of the support possibilities provided by the RD Regulation, while aligning the rules to those applicable to non-agricultural companies. C22/2008 *Aides à El Pozo de Alimentación* [2010] O.J. C217/6. S.A., ES; C23/2008 *Aide à J Garcia Carrion (Castilla la Mancha)*, ES [2010] O.J C217/6.

[108] Large enterprises active in the processing and marketing of agricultural products situated outside assisted regions are therefore no longer eligible for investment aid, unless it is linked to environmental protection. This is a substantial change introduced by the 2006 reform, as such beneficiaries could receive investment aid of up to 40% under the previous agricultural state aid rules.

The similarities between the operation and functioning of enterprises which process and market agricultural products and enterprises producing non-agricultural products have led to harmonisation of the assessment rules governing state aid, in line with the Lisbon agenda.[109] As a result, with the exception of specific rules for "intermediate companies",[110] investment aid of up to 40 per cent of aid intensity for standard projects for large companies in normal areas is no longer allowed. In assisted areas, support was brought into line with the rates applicable to non-agricultural companies, which in many regions reduced the support allowed below the previous level of 50 per cent. Only for the outermost regions does it remain at a level of up to 75 per cent.

13–020   **Environmental and animal welfare aid.** Chapter IV.C of the Guidelines refers to arts 38–40 of the Rural Development Regulation, and the guidelines on state aid for environmental protection (Environmental Aid Guidelines).[111] The GBER also applies to the agriculture sector in relation to environmental aid. The Commission does not authorise aids for combating animal and plant diseases in favour of large undertakings or companies active in the processing and marketing of agricultural products.[112] To benefit from this type of aid, farmers must enter into voluntary commitments lasting five to seven years[113] which go beyond so-called "cross-compliance" with the relevant mandatory standards established in EU and national legislation. Payments under this aid instrument are granted annually, and should cover the additional costs and income foregone as a result of the commitment.[114] The maximum aid amounts are set out in the Annex to the RD Regulation and may be up to 100 per cent intensity for non-productive investments.

13–021   **Setting up of producer groups.** The conditions for granting aid to producer groups are provided in art.9 of Agricultural SME Regulation and Ch.IV.H of the

---

[109] State aid policy was under the Lisbon strategy objectives, notably in the light of the request for less and better aid, and to shift the emphasis away from specific sectors and companies to horizontal support measures such as employment, regional development, environment and training or research: see Presidency Conclusions, Lisbon European Council: March 23 and 24, 2000, point 17, DOC/00/8 of March 24, 2000.

[110] art.13(9)b of GBER.

[111] [2001] O.J. C37/3.

[112] Decision NN 75/200, Germany, *Aid for Bavarian Animal Health Service* [2006] O.J. C244/15.

[113] Unless the farmer can achieve the objective sought in a shorter period of time.

[114] Where necessary, payments may also cover transaction costs, defined in art.27 of the Implementing Regulation as costs related to letting the transaction take place and not directly attributable to the cost of implementing the relevant commitment. Transaction costs must be limited to 20% of the income foregone and additional costs due to the commitment given. Paragraph 56 of the Guidelines requires Member States to provide convincing proof of transaction costs. N79/2010—ES, *Aides à l'application des mesures agroenvironemmentales à la vigne*; N361/2010—ES, *Modernisation et augmentation de l'efficacité énergétique des serres orientés à la production du tomate*; N601/2009—LU, *Régime d'aides pour la sauvegarde de la diversité biologique*.

Agricultural Guidelines. Producer groups[115] may obtain up to €400,000 of aid for starting up their operations. This amount corresponds to the amount set out for co-financed support for such start-up aid in the new Member States in the Rural Development Regulation.[116] This type of aid is limited to SMEs, is of a temporary nature, and targets costs for the establishment of producer groups bringing farmers together with a view to concentrating their supply and adapting their production to market requirements.[117]

Quality of agricultural products. The Commission considers that aid measures for primary production by SMEs which provide an incentive to improve the quality of agricultural products tend to add to the value of agricultural production and help the sector as a whole to adjust to consumer demand, and therefore views such aids favourably. The rules for granting this aid instrument are stipulated in art.14 of the Agricultural SME Regulation[118] and Ch.IV.J of the Guidelines. This type of aid must be granted in kind, e.g. in the form of training, certification or provision of verification services.   **13–022**

Technical support. Aid for technical support such as consultancy or control costs is governed by Article 15 of the Agricultural SME Regulation and Chapter IV.K of the Guidelines. It is limited to small and medium-sized enterprises active in primary production, while other enterprises may profit from training and consultancy support available to other sectors under the GBER or use de minimis aid. Aid in kind of up to 100 per cent of the value of services rendered may be granted in connection with education and training for farmers and farm workers,[119] farm replacement services[120] or consultancy services provided by third parties.[121]   **13–023**

---

[115] SA.32713—The Netherlands, *State aid notification Product board horticulture, vegetables and fruits sector*; C36/2010—Greece, *Aid to cereal producing farmers and cereal collecting cooperatives*; C75/2003—Italy, *Interventions en faveur des coopératives et exploitations agricoles - consolidation des dettes coûteuses (Lazio)*; C46/2003—France, *Cotisations au profit d'INTER-BEV*. For the past practice, see decision N 536/2003—Italy, *Regional intervention for the development of Confidi in the agricultural sector*; Decisions C 9/A/2003 and C B/2003—Germany, *Aid for Bavarian machinery rings*; Decision C 50/2002—Spain, *Aid for producer organisations of olive oil*; Decision C 60/2003—Germany, *Aid which Germany has granted in favour of the acquisition of business shares in winegrowers' co-operatives*; Decision 2002/458/EC of 1 March 2002 *on the aid schemes implemented by Greece in favour of the settlement of debts by the agricultural cooperatives in 1992 and 1994, including aids for the reorganisation of the dairy cooperative AGNO* (notified under document number C(2000) 686) [2002] O.J. L159/1.
[116] art.35(2) of the Rural Development Regulation.
[117] See para.89 of the Guidelines.
[118] With reference to art.32 of the RD Regulation.
[119] The expenses eligible in this context are the costs of organising the training programme, participants' travel and subsistence expenses and the cost of replacement services during the absence of the farmer or farm worker. N323/2010, Amendment of N 577/2006—The Netherlands, *Catalogue Green and Blue Services*.
[120] Farm replacement services may be used when the farmer, the farmer's partner or a farm worker is ill or on holiday.
[121] N 416/2005—DE, *Aid for consultancy services in the potato sector* [2005] O.J. L66/10.

13–024 **Support for the livestock sector.** Article 16 of the Agricultural SME Regulation and Ch.IV.L of the Guidelines envisage aid of up to 100 per cent for the administrative costs of establishing and maintaining herd books and up to 70 per cent for the costs of tests to determine the genetic quality or yield of livestock.[122] All the costs of removing fallen stock[123] may be covered, as well as 75 per cent of the costs of destroying such carcasses.[124] Insurance premiums covering the costs of removal and destruction of fallen stock are also eligible for aid. Compulsory testing of cattle slaughtered for human consumption for bovine spongiform encephalopathies (BSE), may be covered, but it may not exceed €40 per test, including EU payments,[125] provided it is rendered in the form of subsidised services and does not involve direct cash payments to producers, and is consistent with a programme for monitoring and ensuring the safe disposal of all fallen stock in the Member State.

13–025 **Risk and crisis management.** In normal circumstances the "polluter pays" principle[126] establishes the primary responsibility of producers for taking proper care of the removal of fallen stock and financing the associated costs. The state aid rules normally prevent Member States from paying income aid to farmers, because this could distort competition and interfere with the functioning of the common market organisations.[127] Only in exceptional circumstances may such aid be granted to offset the damage caused by such situations.[128]

---

[122] The tests must be carried out by or on behalf of third parties. Checks undertaken by the livestock owners and routine checks of milk quality are not eligible for aid. Commission Decision of October 23, 2007 on Animal Welfare. N 219/2007—IE, *Conservation of Plant and Animal Genetic Resources Scheme.*

[123] C3/2009—PT, *Financement de la collecte, le transport et la destruction des sous-produits obtenus de l'abattage des ruminants et des volailles.* Art.2(14) of the Agricultural BER defines fallen stock as animals killed by euthanasia, with or without a definite diagnosis, or which have died (including stillborn and unborn animals) on a farm or any premises or during transport, but have not been slaughtered for human consumption.

[124] Where the aid is financed through fees or compulsory contributions to finance the destruction of such carcasses (provided the fees or contributions are limited to and directly imposed on the meat sector) up to 100% may be paid for both the removal and destruction of carcasses. Aid of up to 100% in both cases may also be granted when there is an obligation to perform TSE tests on the fallen stock concerned. See also C44/08, *Aides d'Etat en faveur du financement due dépistage des EST chez les bovin, BE.*

[125] This price does not include other costs, e.g. C23/2005, France, *Aides dans le secteur de l'équarrissage en 2003.*

[126] art.174(2) of the TFEU. Concerning state aid, see the Community Guidelines on state aid for environmental protection [2001] O.J. C37/3.

[127] Decision C 49/2002, France, *Aid to finance a public rendering service,* challenged by application in case T–327/04 *Syndicat National de l'Industrie des Viandes (SNIV)* [2008] E.C.R. II–72; N 515/2003, France, *Slaughter tax;* Decision N 515/B/2003, France, *Aides en faveur des bouchers artisans—Taxe d'abattage;* Decision C 23/2005, France, *Disposal of animal waste in 2003 (équarrissage);* see also Case C–126/01 *Ministre de l'economie, des finances et de l'industrie v GEMO SA* [2003] E.C.R. I–13769.

[128] *A contrario* see Decision C 5/2001 (ex N 775/2000), Italy, *Blue tongue compensation;* see also application for annulment rejected in *Regione autonoma della Sardegna v Commission* [2006] E.C.R. 1–1875, para.43.

Natural disasters or exceptional circumstances. The Agricultural Guidelines   **13–026**
specify in Ch.V.B.2 what events the Commission recognises as natural disasters
or exceptional occurrences which allow compensation of up to 100 per cent for
material losses throughout the agricultural sector in accordance with
art.107(2)(b) TFEU. Such aid measures may not be block-exempted and are
subject to notification. The Commission may approve aid schemes to compensate
for damage caused by natural disasters.[129] The Commission recognised the crisis
in the beef market caused by a BSE scare at the end of 2001 and dioxin in 2000
as exceptional occurrences within the meaning of art.107(2)(b) of the
TFEU.[130]

Compensation for adverse weather conditions. Primary producers may obtain   **13–027**
support on the basis of art.107(3)(c) TFEU without prior notification if an
adverse climatic event results in damage to over 30 per cent of normal production,[131] provided they comply with art.11 of the Agricultural SME Regulation or
Ch.V.B.3 of the Agricultural Guidelines. Aid to compensate for damage caused
by such exceptional occurrences must be assessed case by case, and must
therefore be notified individually when an event which could qualify for this type
of aid occurs. It is limited to primary agricultural production,[131a] but includes
large enterprises[132] and over-compensation must be excluded, so insurance premiums are deducted, as are any other proceeds, e.g. from the sale of damaged
products. Since 2010, farmers who are not insured are not entitled to full
compensation. In the case of drought, as from 2011, compensation may only be
paid by Member States which have fully implemented art.9 of the Water Framework Directive in respect of agriculture.[133]

Aid for combating animal and plant diseases. The rules for aid regarding   **13–028**
animal and plant diseases and pest infestations are set out in art.10 of the

---

[129] This possibility was introduced by the 2006 reform. N379/2010—DE, *Guidelines for a national
framework directive on state subsidies for compensation of losses caused by natural disasters in
the agricultural sector*; N209/2010—France, *Ides aux exploitants agricoles de Charente-
Maritime, de Vendée et du nord de la Gironde victimes des inondations marines causées par la
tempête Xynthia du 28 Février 2010*; N131/2010—BG, *Compensation of losses incurred by
agricultural producers for totally devasted areas as a result of natural disasters or adverse
weather conditions.*

[130] More recently, see N 643/08, Special measures relating to meat production of animal origin from
pigs following a dioxin contamination in Ireland.

[131] This may lead to a significant reduction in notifications—309 new measures in this field were
notified by the EU-15 between 2000 and 2005. N649/2009—AT, *Aid for compensation for the
hail damage to wine and fruit growing (Wien)*.

[131a] Decision C29/04—Aid that IT considers granting to the Villasor sugar refinery owned by Sedem
152.

[132] The Commission considers bad weather as a normal business risk for companies that process and
market agricultural products, which may benefit from rescue and restructuring aid if they face
economic difficulties due to bad weather. See para.125(g) of the Guidelines.

[133] Both the insurance requirement and the requirement concerning the implementation of the Water
Framework Directive were introduced by the 2006 reform, and seek to improve risk management by farmers and management of water with a view to the risk of droughts. N414/2009,
France, *Aides de l'Agence de l'eau Artois-Picardie aux engagements agro environnementaux
dans le bassin Artois Picardie (EAEAP)*.

Agricultural SME Regulation and Ch.V.B.4 of the Guidelines.[134] The Commission considers that payment of aid to farmers active in primary production to compensate for losses resulting from animal or plant diseases may only be accepted as part of an appropriate Community, national or regional programme for the prevention, control or eradication of the disease concerned. Accordingly, only diseases which are a matter of concern for the public authorities may be the subject of aid measures, and not measures for which farmers should reasonably take responsibility themselves.[135] Money received under insurance schemes or any costs not incurred because of the disease but which would otherwise have been incurred must be deducted in order to avoid over-compensation. Eligible costs cover health checks, tests and other screening measures, the purchase and administration of vaccines, medicines and plant protection products, and the costs of slaughter and destruction of animals and destruction of crops.[136] The aid must be granted by means of subsidised services.

13–029 **Aid towards the payment of insurance premiums.** According to art.12 of the Agricultural SME Regulation and Ch.V.B.5 of the Guidelines the Commission will declare aid of up to 80 per cent for the payment of insurance premiums compatible with the internal market, provided that this does not constitute a barrier to such services and the measures fulfil all the conditions of the Block Exemption Regulation. Under Ch.V.B.5 of the Guidelines, other aid measures in connection with insurance against natural disasters and exceptional occurrences must be assessed case by case.[137] The Guidelines also foresee the possibility of authorising aid in connection with reinsurance schemes,[138] and other aid measures to support producers in particularly high-risk zones.

13–030 **Aid for closing of capacity.** The Commission authorises aid for early retirement or cessation of farming activities in primary production in accordance with the conditions set out in Ch.V.C,[139] as well as aid for closing production, processing and marketing capacity, provided they are coherent with any Community

---

[134] As in the case of aid for adverse climatic events, the Commission considers animal and plant diseases as normal business risks for companies active in processing and marketing agricultural products.

[135] C31/2006, Italy, *Mesures urgentes pour la prévention de l'influenza aviaire*; N49/2010, N295/2010, Spain, *Aides contre la peste de la mouche d'olivier (Andalucia)*; N300/2010, Spain, *Aid for combating the Mediterranean fruit fly and insect vectors causing viral plant diseases (notification of amendment)*; N107/2010, Italy, *Measure 6.1.14: Containment of animal diseases*; C1/2010, Belgium, *Aide à l'enlèvement et à la destruction des animaux trouvés morts*.

[136] C24/2006, Germany, *Animal Health Service (Bayern)*; C44/2008, Belgium, *Arrêté royal concernant le financement du dépistage des encéphalopathies spongiformes transmissibles chez les animaux*.

[137] By analogy with the rules in the Agricultural BER, aid may be approved at a rate of up to 80% of the cost of insurance premiums when the policy only covers aid against these risk events. C3/2010 *Paiemenents de compensation versés par l'Organisme grec d'assurances (ELGA) pendant l'année 2008 et 2009*.

[138] N 17/2007 *Premium subsidies for insurance of tobacco and partial compensation for damage caused by draught)*, summary notice published in [2007] O.J. C308/07.

[139] N 42/2010, Finland, *Aid for the cessation of agricultural production*.

arrangements to reduce production capacity.[140] Such aid must be available to all operators in the sector concerned, especially if there is over-capacity.[141] The amount of the aid must be strictly limited to compensation for the loss of the value of the assets,[142] plus an incentive payment limited to 20 per cent of their value. The cessation of activity must be irrevocable and aid may not be offered to operators who are merely in financial difficulties.

Aid for research and development. Aid for research and development in the **13–031** agriculture sector is examined in accordance with the criteria set out in the applicable Community framework for state aid for research and development[143] and GBER (arts 28 et seq), including the possibility for additional support for research in favour of the agriculture sector (art.34).

Advertising of agricultural products. According to Ch.VI.D of the Agricultural **13–032** Guidelines, state aid is authorised for advertising campaigns in the European Union devoted to quality products,[144] EU-recognised denominations,[145] or national or regional quality labels. This type of aid is available even to large enterprises which process and market agricultural products.[146] The advertising campaign must not be earmarked for the products of particular companies, and must comply with art.2 of Directive 2000/13/EC[147] and the specific relevant

---

[140] Decision C 6/2003 *Plan Rivesaltes and parafiscal taxes CIVDN* (France) challenged in Case 136/05. Case T–136/05 *EARL Salvat père & fils, Comité interprofessionnel des vins doux naturels et vins de liqueur à appellations contrôlées (CIVDN) and Comité national des inter-professions des vins à appellation d'origine (CNIV) v Commission* [2007] E.C.R. II–04063.

[141] Capacity reduced for animal or human health, sanitary or environmental reasons (e.g. reduction of stocking densities) is also deemed to be in the interest of the sector, even when there is no excess capacity: see Commission Decision of October 1, 2007 on aid for the voluntary or partial suspention of breeding of pigeons following perturbations caused by the avian influenza crisis (Case N 613/2006).

[142] Measured as the current selling value of assets.

[143] Community Framework for state aid on research and development and innovation [2006] O.J. C323/01.

[144] Defined as products fulfilling the criteria to be established pursuant to art.32 of the RD Regulation.

[145] Protected designations of origin (PDO), protected geographical indications (PGI) and other designations of origin protected under Community legislation. SA.32185—SE, *Support for marketing measures of organic products*; NN 7/2007 *Support for the eco-label NT*; SA 32713, Portugal, *Aid for the Product board horticulture, sector vegetables and fruit.*

[146] See, e.g. Commission Decision of January 29, 2007 on Contrat de programme en faveur du Consortium pour la protection de l'ASTI, pour des investissements en matière de publicité (Piemonte) (Case N 725/2006), summary notice in [2007] O.J. C67/6 and Commission Decision on the Agricultural and Horticulture Development Board—Advertising and Promotion Scheme (Case N 529/2007), available under the case number on the DG Competition internet page (not yet published in the O.J.). Community guidelines for state aid for advertising of products listed in Annex I to the Treaty and certain non-Annex I products [2001] O.J. C252/5 have been repealed: see para.194 Guidelines. Member States have to grant aid to non-Annex I products according to the de minimis Regulation.

[147] Directive 2000/13/EC of the European Parliament and of the Council of March 20, 2000 on the approximation of the laws of the Member States relating to labelling, presentation and advertising of foodstuff, [2000] O.J. L109/29. Last amended by Directive 2003/89/EC [2003] O.J. L308/3.

labelling rules. The origin of the products concerned may be stated in the case of EU-recognised denominations and (as a subsidiary message) national or regional quality labels. Direct aid must be limited to 50 per cent intensity, unless the sector contributes at least 50 per cent of the costs. Generic advertising which does not mention origin and benefits all producers of the type of product concerned may obtain up to 100 per cent.[148] In the context of aid for advertising, the Commission monitors closely whether or not aids infringe arts 34 or 110 TFEU.[149]

Public support for advertising in third countries should be limited to support under Council Regulation (EC) No.3/2003 of December 17, 2007 on information and promotion actions for agricultural products on the internal market and in the third countries,[150] which sets up a framework of support measures for advertising that ensures the necessary degree of coherence between Member States, due not least to the consultation process required for setting up such campaigns.[151]

13–033 **Aids linked to energy taxation.** Council Directive 2003/93/EC[152] restructuring the Community Framework for the taxation of energy products and electricity, which gives the Member States the possibility to apply lower excise tax rates for domestic fuel used for agricultural, horticultural, piscicultural and forestry works subject to minimum levels of tariffs. As the Directive does not impose any obligation to grant such reductions,[153] Member States are free to decide whether or not to grant them, and as long as they are sector-selective, they constitute state aid and must be notified to the Commission pursuant to art.108(3) of the Treaty.[154] Chapter VI.F of the Agricultural Guidelines provides that tax reductions on energy products used for the production and marketing of agricultural products will be considered compatible with the common market organisation even though they constitute operating aid,[155] as long as they fulfil certain

---

[148] NN 12a, b, c, d/2006, Belgium, *Promotion of different agricultural products.*

[149] See Case C–325/00 *Commission v Germany* [2002] E.C.R. I–9977; Case C–355/00 *Freskot AE v Elliniko Dimosio* [2003] E.C.R. I–5263; Case C–255/03 *Commission v Belgium* of June 17, 2004, E.C.R [2004] I–09573; Case T–475/10 *Portugal v Commission* [2010] O.J. C328.

[150] O.J. L3,5.1.2008 p.1; see as well Commission Regulation EC 501/2008 of June 2008. In July 2010 the Commission approved 19 programmes to provide information on and promote agricultural products in the EU. The total budget for the programmes, which ran for between one and three years, was €30 million, of which the EU contributed half. The selected programmes covered organic products, agricultural quality products (PDO, PGI, TSG), dairy products, meat, wine, fruit and vegetables, plants, honey and potatoes, IP/10/873. See also for the past policy decision N 195/2003, *AMA Biosiegel and AMA Gütesiegel (Austria)* [2000] O.J. L382/2.

[151] N265/2010, Italy, *Aid scheme for advertising of food and agricultural products in third countries.*

[152] Council Directive 2003/93/EC of October 7, 2003 amending Council Directive 77/799/EEC concerning mutual assistance by the competent authorities of the Member States in the field of direct and indirect taxation, [2003] O.J. L264/23.

[153] Case T–351/02 *Deutsche Bahn AG v Commission* [2006] E.C.R. II–1047, paras 105 and 106.

[154] See art.26(2) of Directive 2003/93/EC; opening decision NN 71/2004, Italy, *Excise duty exemption on fuels in agriculture,* follow-up of the opening decision C 6/2004, ex. NN 70/2001.

[155] C22/2001—ES, *Mesures d'appui au secteur agricole suite de la hausse du coût du carburant.*

conditions.[156] In particular, lower minimum levels of taxation as set out in Table B of Annex I to the Directive may be applied to products used as motor fuel for the purposes of primary agricultural production, provided no differentiation is made within the sector.[157] Again provided there is no differentiation in the sector, a taxation level down to zero may also be applied to energy products and electricity used for primary agricultural production.[158] The Guidelines also foresee the possibility of declaring such tax measures compatible retroactively if they were granted after the Directive entered into force[159] on October 31, 2003 and comply with the provisions set out above. In addition, aid in the form of tax reductions under the Directive may be granted in compliance with s.3 of the GBER (Aid for Environmental Protection) or the Environmental Aid Guidelines.[160]

Production of biomass. Due to its origin as a cultivated or grown resource, bio-energy[161] has a direct relationship with agriculture and forestry. Bio-energy produced from forestry products covered by the scope of Annex I is subject to the state aid compatibility rules applicable to the processing of agricultural products. It therefore has a positive effect on security of energy supply, the environment and employment related to the generation of energy. It also benefits employment in agriculture and forestry sectors, as it can provide new opportunities and outlets for the common agricultural policy through the cultivation of energy crops, afforestation efforts and the proper management of forests, with the extraction of thinnings and fellings.[162]

13–034

If bio-energy falls outside the scope of Annex I, the general state aid rules are applicable. This distinction is not always clear.[163] Aid for investments in the production of biomass may be authorised as operating aid, provided it complies with the conditions in the Environmental Aid Guidelines.[164] The rules in these Guidelines take into account the beneficial effects that energy produced from

[156] C6/2004, Italy, *Exonération d'accises sur les carburants agricoles*; C5/2005, Italy, *Exonération d'accises sur les carburants agricoles*.

[157] The Commission considers that a tax measure applied equally to the whole agricultural sector has a positive impact on its development.

[158] This sub-measure is limited in time and depends on whether the Council repeals the possibility of applying a level of taxation down to zero in Directive 2003/96/EC.

[159] Decision of October 29, 2007 on the refund of energy tax on certain energy products to agricultural producers (Case N 315/2006), summary note in [2007] O.J. C296/2; Commission Decision on Poland's excise tax refund on diesel used in agriculture (Case N 92/2006); Commission Decision of April 4, 2007 on the reduction of excise duty on mineral oils (Case NN 46/A/06 (ex. N 361/A/06)), summary notice in [2007] O.J. C132/1; N 226/2010—LV, *tax exemption for primary producers*; NN 26/2010—CZ, *Partial refund of excise duties*.

[160] N130b/2007, Finland, *Prolongation of N469/2002: Aid for Chipping of Energy Wood*.

[161] Commission Communication on a Biomass Action Plan, COM(2005) 628 final: see also the Commission Communication, An EU Strategy for Biofuels, SEC(2006) 142, February 8, 2006.

[162] Rural Development Regulation, art.X; see also Impact Assessment, Annex to the Commission Communication on a Biomass Action Plan, SEC(2005) 1573 of December 7, 2005, p.16.

[163] e.g. energy willow grown to produce baskets is not an Annex I product, but it is an Annex I product if grown for energy production.

[164] Biomass action plan, especially p.13 and Annex IX, COM(2005) 628 final, December 7, 2005.

biomass may have compared to energy production on the basis of fossil fuels, while aid for investments in assisted areas may be found compatible with the common market under the Guidelines for National Regional Aid.[165]

13–035 **Forestry.** There are 178 million hectares of forests and other wooded land in the European Union, about 42 per cent of its land area. Over the past 20 years, forests have expanded by 5 per cent—approximately 0.3 per cent per year—although the rate varies substantially between Member States.

Forestry products are not in principle covered by Annex I to the TFEU, as the Court confirmed in its judgment in *Atzeni*.[166] Accordingly, aid to forestry holdings is subject in its entirety to the provisions of arts 107 and 108 TFEU.[167]

In 2007[168] the compatibility rules for the application of the state aid rules to forestry were introduced in Ch.VII of the Agricultural Guidelines for the first time. They took into account the objectives stipulated in the EU Forest Action Plan.[169] It is established Commission practice to authorise state aid for the conservation, improvement, development and care of forests, on account of the ecological and recreational functions of the forest environment.[170] To make this practice transparent and avoid overlaps with other rules on state aid for forestry, the Commission found it appropriate to take aid to forestry activities into account in the Rural Development Regulation[171] and its implementing rules,[172] so as to

---

[165] C22/2008—ES, *Aides à El Pozo de Alimentación, S.A.*; C23/2008—ES, *Aide à J Garcia Carrion (Castilla la Mancha)*.

[166] Judgment of February 23, 2006 in joined cases C–346/03 and C–529/03 *Giuseppe Atzeni and Others* [2006] E.C.R. I–01875, para.43; see also *European Parliament v Council* [1999] E.C.R I–1139, para.18. Trees are agricultural products as long as they are sold as living trees. In fact cut trees sold as living trees, whether sold with roots or not, come under the same NACE code as cut flowers. Commission Decision N 362/2007 [2008] O.J. C101/17.

[167] para.43 *Atzeni*; AG Romero, pp.131–134.

[168] Until then the Commission's assessments authorising state aid in favour of growing trees and maintaining forests were based directly on art.107(3)(c) of the Treaty and allowed up to 100% state aid intensity for both investment in forests and damage caused to forests by natural disasters or adverse weather conditions, e.g. Decision N 68/2006, Sweden, *Replanting of trees in storm-felled forest*.

[169] Communication from the Commission to the Council and the European Parliament on an EU Forestry Plan, COM (2006) 302 final, SEC(2006) 748.

[170] Decisions N 660/1996, N 646/1999, N 750/1996, N 752/1996, NN 11/1998, N 286/1998, N 223/1999; N 120/2000; N 369/2000, N 441/2002, N 14/2004, N 233/2004, N 234/2004, N 277/2003, N 283/2005, NN 429/2005.

[171] See art.27 of Council Regulation (EC) No.1698/2005 of September 20, 2005 on support for rural development by the European Agricultural Fund for Rural Development (EAFRD) [2005] O.J. L277 and art.46 of the Implementing Regulation. Aid for forestation measures under arts 43 to 45 RD Regulation that concern Annex I plants (e.g. certain energy crops) benefit from the provisions of art.88(1) RD Regulation, since aid towards the plantation of certain species is comparable to planting multi-annual plants. The measures covered by arts 43–49 RD Regulation in principle concern non-Annex I products.

[172] Regulation (EC) No.1974/2006 of December 15, 2006 laying down detailed rules for the application of Council Regulation (EC) 1698/2005 on support for rural development by the European Agricultural Fund Rural Development (EAFRD) [2006] O.J. L368/15; Commission Regulation (EC) No.1975/2006 of December 7, 2006 laying down detailed rules for the implementation of Council Regulation (EC) No.1698/2005, as regards the implementation of control procedures as well as cross-compliance in respect of rural development support measures [2006] O.J. L368/74.

ensure the consistency of state aid co-financed for forestry activities with EU financing from 2007 to 2013. Special structural rules for the forestry sector are set out in the RD Regulation and its implementing rules, whose provisions aim at improving agricultural policy objectives (e.g. by reducing the agricultural area).[173] It is recognised that forestry and forest-based commercial activities are part of the economy's open sector, and that their commercial functions should be guided primarily by market forces.[174] Moreover, the forestry sector may benefit from aid granted under reg.800/2008 and general de minimis aid,[175] which is not the case for agricultural production. Other EU state aid instruments governing aid granted for industrial production also apply to the forestry sector.[176] All such measures must comply with the general state aid rules,[177] most importantly the GBER and certain Guidelines, in particular the Regional,[178] RDI Framework,[179] Rescue and Restructuring Guidelines,[180] and Environmental Aid Guidelines.[181] They are subject to notification unless exempted by the relevant block exemptions.

Provided an investment concerns tree-growing and the protection of forests, **13–036** the definition of eligible investment costs is very flexible; it includes the purchase or transfer of ownership of forestry lands with the objective of ensuring sustainable forestry, and aid for use of environmentally friendly techniques in the preservation or cultivation of forests, provided commercial exploitation is excluded.[182] Aid intensities may reach up to 100 per cent, but are often restricted by the appropriate Rural Development Regulation ceilings.[183] As well as aids which are typical for the forestry sector due to its natural characteristics, the

---

[173] N434/2010, Italy, *Première installation de systèmes agroforestiers sur des terres agricoles (Mesure 222 du Developement Rural)*, ES; N251/2010 *Mesure 221—Boisement de terres agricoles*; N210/2010—BG, *Measure 223 "First afforestation of non-agricultural land" and measure 226 "Restoring forestry potential and introducing prevention actions" of the Bulgarian Rural Development programme (2007–2013)*.

[174] Point 14 of Council Resolution of December 15, 1998 on a forestry strategy for the European Union [1998] O.J. C56/1.

[175] Commission Regulation (EC) No.1998/2006 of December 15, 2006 on the application of arts 87 and 88 of the EC Treaty to de minimis aid [2006] O.J. C379/5, as amended.

[176] Notably the Guidelines on National Regional Aids and the Community Guidelines on State Aid for Environmental Protection [2001] O.J. C37.

[177] See para.13–012, above.

[178] Guidelines on national regional aid for 2007–2013 [2006] O.J. C54/08.

[179] Community framework for state aid on research and development and innovation [2006] O.J. C323/01, see e.g. Commission Decision of January 27, 2005 on Research and development aid for the vegetative reproduction of the Nordmanns-fir (Nordrhein-Westfalen) (N 440 / 2004) [2005] O.J. C258/04.

[180] Community Guidelines on state aid for rescuing and restructuring firms in difficulty [2004] O.J. C244/2.

[181] See point 173 of the Guidelines [2001] O.J. C37/3. N635/2009—PL, *Aid to the State Forest Holding for recultivation*.

[182] N384/2010, Germany, *Les investissements non productifs dans les terres forestières, ES*. Decision N 277/2003 *Transfer of nature protection land*; N 283/2005, Portugal, *Fonds d'Investissement Immobilier Forestier*. NN 8/2009—GE, *Conservation areas*, under appeal, T–347/09 *Germany v Commission* [2009] O.J. C267/75, where the existence of aid is challenged.

[183] N133/2010, Italy, *Aides dans le domaine des forêts*; N253/2010, Italy, *Mesure 225—Paiements sylvoenvironnementaux*.

Guidelines provide a possibility to grant aid according to the rules for primary agricultural production, for example with regard to adverse weather conditions and natural disasters,[184] technical assistance or the setting up of forestry associations.

13–037 **Direct business taxation.** Also to be mentioned in the context of control of state aid measures in the agricultural sector is the Commission Notice on the application of the state aid rules to measures relating to direct business taxation,[185] which makes it possible to consider that a tax exemption is not selective and therefore does not constitute state aid if its economic rationale makes it "necessary to the functioning and effectiveness of the tax system". However, it is up to the Member State, when notifying the Commission, to provide justification for a derogation by "the nature or general scheme of the system".[186] A number of Commission decisions contain such justifications.[187]

13–038 **Employment and training aid.** Since 2008, aids for the creation of employment in the agriculture sector are covered by reg.800/2008.[188] Although not exempted, aid for employment and training which is limited to the agriculture sector but fulfils all the other conditions of the Regulation may be found to be compatible following notification. Because of the specificities of the agriculture sector, notably primary production, Member States may have an interest in introducing specific aid schemes for the training or employment of disabled workers in the agriculture sector. As long as such aid is open to the whole of the agriculture sector, without limiting support to certain products, the benefits of the support appear to outweigh the risk of distortions resulting from such an approach.

13–039 **Rescue and restructuring firms in difficulty.** Aid for rescuing and restructuring firms in difficulty in the agriculture sector is assessed in accordance with the Commission guidelines on state aid for rescuing and restructuring firms in difficulty.[189] Since 2004 the rules on restructuring aid for companies processing and marketing agricultural products have been the same as for other sectors.[190]

---

[184] N360/2010—DE, *Mecklenburg-Western Pomerania: Forestry aid in the framework of the EAFRD; disaster prevention / construction of a main wet storage area*; N93/2010—PL, *Restoration of forests damaged by adverse weather conditions and prevention measures.*

[185] [1998] O.J. C284.

[186] Case C–159/01 *Netherlands v Commission* [2004] E.C.R. I–4461, paras 45–47.

[187] Decision N 604/b/2004, Denmark, *Fiscal treatment of quotas and payments entitlements*; Decision N 343/2004, Denmark, *Tax on mineral phosphorous in feed phosphates*; N 57/2004, Denmark, *Reduction of land taxes*; Decision N472/2002, Denmark, *Permanent ceiling on land taxes for productive land.*

[188] arts 13, 16, 26–27, 38–39, 40–42.

[189] [2004] O.J. C244/2–17. SA.31855—CY, *Projet de restructuration de l'Abattoir central de Kofinos.*

[190] Decision C 32/1999, Germany, Aid for a meat processing company, Greussener Salamifabriek GmbH.

This enables Member States to have consistent restructuring regimes for SMEs operating in all sectors.[191]

The earlier principle that even small enterprises should offer compensatory measures for receiving restructuring aid has been abandoned. Some special rules have been maintained for farmers only and are stipulated in Ch.V of the Rescue and Restructuring Guidelines. A five-year period instead of the general ten years applies for determining compliance with the "one time, last time" principle.[192] This is simplified by allowing Member States in all cases, not only where restructuring is limited to small agricultural enterprises, to implement capacity reductions at sector level rather than at the level of the farm receiving restructuring aid. Capacity closures must be permanent (not just for five years) and must amount to 5 per cent or 10 per cent, depending on whether the aid is sector-specific or general. Open farmland may be brought back into production after 15 years. Minimum capacity closure requirements are simplified. Capacity closure at sector level must be completed within a year of granting the aid. To ensure that closure is not circumvented, the Member State must undertake not to grant investment aid for increasing capacities for five years. The de minimis threshold below which no capacity closure is required is simplified and reformulated. As long as restructuring aid is not granted for more than 1 per cent of the production capacity of a given sector over any consecutive 12-month period, no capacity closures are required.[193]

Temporary Framework. The Temporary Community Framework for state aid measures to support access to finance in the current financial and economic crisis applied from December 17, 2008 until December 31, 2010.[194] Originally it was not applicable to the agricultural sector. Aid granted under the Temporary Framework constituted state aid pursuant to art.107(1) TFEU, but could be declared compatible on the basis of art.107(3)(b) TFEU; it was a "compatible limited amount of aid". The Temporary Framework required Member States to prove that the measure was necessary, appropriate and proportionate to remedy a serious disturbance in the economy of the Member State concerned. Limited amounts of aid measures for farmers had to be open to the whole agricultural production sector and complement other general crisis measures already put in place by a Member State. They could not be cumulated with de minimis aid. All de minimis aid already received by an undertaking since the beginning of 2008 was to be deducted from the limited amount of aid, so that the total amount per undertaking did not exceed €15,000 between January 1, 2008 and December 31, 2010. It could be cumulated with other compatible aid or other forms of

13–040

---

[191] N83/2010, Italy, Interventions in favour of agriculture enterprises in difficulty. Aid in favour of "Unione pastori società cooperativa agricola" registered in Z.I Taccu, Nurri, Cagliari; C31/2008, France, *Sauvetage de la société "Volailles du Périgord"*; NN 153/03 Aid for enterprises of Kastoria and Eubée departments, opening.

[192] See ch.3.3 of the Rescue and Restructuring Guidelines.

[193] Decision N 75/2004, Italy, Rescue aid in favour of Parmalat suppliers Lombardy.

[194] Temporary Union framework for state aid measures to support access to finance in the current financial and economic crisis [2011] O.J. C6/05, as amended.

Community financing, as long as the maximum aid intensities indicated in the relevant Guidelines or Block Exemption Regulations were respected.[195]

13–041 **Parafiscality.** Although the control of state aid in the agricultural and fisheries sector is heavily influenced by common agricultural and structural development policy measures, a number of issues are of horizontal relevance for state aid control. The specificity of the financing of the sector through parafiscal taxes has led to some interesting questions concerning the assessment of such financing in relation to the existence, compatibility and legality of state aid measures. The Commission must object to aid financed by parafiscal charges in a manner contrary to arts 34[196] or 110 TFEU, as state aid measures may not be incompatible with the other material provisions of EU law.[197] In this context the Court has further developed the criteria for defining state resources and their imputability to the State[198] in cases challenging Commission decisions or through referrals.[199]

6. FISHERIES AND AQUACULTURE

13–042 Due to its social and economic characteristics, the fisheries and aquaculture sector, which is highly sensitive due to the scarcity of fish resources and the difficult working conditions of fishermen, is subject to extensive public intervention, both by the European Union and nationally.

The key goals of Council Regulation 104/2000 on the common organisation of the markets in fishery and aquaculture products[200] (the CMO Regulation) are

---

[195] N396/2010—SI, *Régime temporaire d'aides d'un montant limité dans le secteur agricole, dans le contexte de la crise économique et financière de 2009*; N372/2010—RO, *Aide d'Etat temporaire destinée à assurer l'accès au financement en agriculture*; SA.32173—FR, *Régime temporaire d'aides d'Etat à montant limité adaptées, pour le secteur agricole, au contexte de la crise économique et financière*.

[196] Case C–47/10P Appeal by the Republic of Austria brought on January 28, 2010 against the judgment of the Court of First Instance of November 18, 2009 in Case T–375/04 *Scheucher-Fleisch GmbH and Others v Commission of the European Communities* [2010] O.J. C80/21.

[197] Cases 90–91/63 *Dairy products* [1964] E.C.R. 1277; Case T–315/05 *Adomex v Commission* [2005] O.J. C281/24; Case C–234/99 *Niels Nygard and Svineafgiftsfonden* [2002] E.C.R. I–3657, para.49; Case C–204/97 *Portuguese Republic v Commission* [2001] E.C.R I–3175, paras 48 and 49. See also Decision N 267/2003 *Aides au secteur des produteurs et negociants de vins de liqueur France*. C 43/2004 *Tax parafiscal a la promotion du vin*, PR, under appeal, *Portugal v Commission* [2010] O.J. C328/49.

[198] Case C–261/01 and C–262/01 *Eugene Van Calster and Cleeren* [2003] I–12249, paras 46–49 and 62–63; Case T–136/05 *Earl Salvat v Commission* [2005] E.C.R. II–4063.

[199] Case C–174/02 *Streekgewest Westelijk Noord-Brabant v Staatssecretaris van Financien* [2005] E.C.R. I–85; Case C–175/02 *F.J. Pape v Minister van Lanbouw, Natuurbeheer en Visserij* [2005] E.C.R. I–127, para.15; Case C–517/04 *Visserijbedrijf D.J. Koornstra&Zn.vof v Productschap Vis* [2006] E.C.R. I–5015, para.18; Case T–190/00 *Regione Siciliana v Commission* [2003] E.C.R. II–5015, paras 106–108; Case T–146/03 *Asociación de Estaciones de Servicio de Madrid et Federación Catalana de Estaciones de Servicio v Commission* [2003] E.C.R. II–98; N 561/2008 *Actions conduites par les interprofessions*, FR, under appeal, Case T–302/09 to T–306/09 [2009] O.J C244.

[200] [2000] O.J. L17/22, as amended. At present, the CMO Regulation is undergoing a revision process, see COM(2011) 425 final, Brussels, July 13, 2011, Proposal for a Regulation of the EP and of the Council of the Common Fisheries Policy.

price stability, an appropriate balance between supply and demand, and preference for EU production without damaging the growing demands of the processing industry. Article 1 of the CMO Regulation lists the products covered by its scope. The main difference between the common market organisation in fishery and aquaculture products and the agricultural CMO is that it does not provide for direct payments. The CMO Regulation refers to specific aid measures, including aid for producers' organisations and private storage aid. Article 32 of the CMO Regulation states that, without prejudice to any provisions adopted pursuant to arts 42 and 43 TFEU, arts 107–109 TFEU apply to the production of, and trade in, the fishery and aquaculture products specified in art.1 of the CMO Regulation. Pursuant to Council Regulation 1083/2006 laying down general provisions concerning the European Regional Development Fund, the European Social Fund and the Cohesion Fund,[201] support is granted for structural measures for the primary production, processing and marketing of fishery and aquaculture products. Community participation is provided through the European Fisheries Fund (EFF) established on the basis of reg.1198/2006[202] (the EFF Regulation), which lays down the criteria, procedures and implementing measures regarding Community structural assistance and envisages a budget of €4.96 billion for the period 2007–2013. By comparison, state aid granted to the fisheries and aquaculture sector in 2009 amounted to €0.2 billion or 0.3 per cent of total aid, excluding financial crisis measures, granted by the 27 Member States. The maximum amounts payable under the EFF Regulation and the limits on financial participation by the Member States are listed in the Annex to the Regulation. In accordance with art.42 TFEU, art.19 of the EFF Regulation provides that Member States may introduce supplementary aid measures exceeding the maximum amounts stipulated in the Regulation, provided they comply with arts 107–109 TFEU. Detailed criteria, procedural and implementing measures on such structural assistance are included in reg.498/2007.[203]

The EFF Regulation was tailored to secure a sustainable European fishing and **13–043** aquaculture industry. The Fund is meant both to support the industry in adapting its fleet to make it more competitive and to improve environmental protection. The EFF is also designed to help the fishery communities most affected by the policy changes to diversify their business activities. It especially supports measures that ensure industry access to a skilled labour force. Funding is available for all sectors of the industry—sea and inland fisheries, aquaculture businesses, producer organisations, and the processing and marketing sectors—as well as fishery areas.

[201] Council Regulation (EC) No.1083/2006 of July 11, 2006 laying down general provisions on the European Regional Development Fund, the European Social Fund and the Cohesion Fund and repealing Regulation (EC) No.1260/1999 [2006] O.J. L210/25, see fn.47.

[202] Council Regulation (EC) No.1198/2006 of July 27, 2006 on the European Fisheries Fund [2006] O.J. L223/1. The Commission proposed a new fund for the EU's maritime and fisheries policies for the period 2014–2020, the European Maritime and Fisheries Fund (EMFF). COM(2011) 804 final of December 2, 2011, Proposal for a Regulation on integrated maritime policy.

[203] Regulation (EC) No.498/2007 laying down detailed rules for the implementation of Council Regulation (EC) No.1198/2006 on the European Fisheries Fund [2007] O.J. C120/1.

The EFF has five main priorities: helping the fleet adapt fishing capacity and effort to available fish resources; support for the various industry branches; aid for organisations which represent the sector's collective interests; sustainable development of fishery-dependent areas; and technical assistance to Member States to facilitate the delivery of aid. It is up to Member States to decide how they allocate funds between these different priorities. As well as preserving many measures from the past, the Fund also introduced a range of innovative mechanisms in response to the changing needs of the industry. These include measures to accompany the implementation of recovery plans and encourage more selective fishing methods, and funding for local sustainable development strategies in fishery areas. The fund provides aid for inland fisheries and environmentally-friendly aquaculture. In addition, the Member States benefit from simpler implementation rules and greater flexibility in the application of eligibility criteria, so that they can adjust them more easily to the needs of their national industries.

According to art.7 of the EFF Regulation, to speed up the payment of EU Structural Funds and reduce the administrative burden on both Member States and the Commission resulting from "routine" positive state aid decisions, without relaxing the regime for controlling state aid, arts 107–109 of the TFEU do not apply to payments by Member States, which are the obligatory national co-financing for EU expenditure. However, as already stated above, arts 107–109 of the TFEU remain applicable to any aid which goes beyond what is obligatory under these rules, as provided by art.7(3) of the EFF Regulation. In addition, *ex post* control when Member States are reimbursed under the rules of the Structural Funds remains in place, sometimes requiring to recover state aid as provided by art.99 of the EFF Regulation.

13–044   State aid is only justified if it is in accordance with the objectives of the common fisheries policy (the CFP)[204] stipulated in the Regulations referred to above. The CFP must contribute to efficient fishing activities within an economically viable, competitive and sustainable fisheries and aquaculture industry. It fixes the maximum quantities of fish that may safely be caught every year. These maximum quantities, called "total allowable catches" (TACs), are divided between the Member States.

Based on these objectives, the Commission has established three sets of rules for examining national state aid to fisheries and aquaculture: guidelines, block exemption regulation for small and medium-sized enterprises and the de minimis regulation. Although there are a number of similarities regarding control of state aid measures between the agricultural and fisheries sectors, the system has followed developments in the respective policy areas, and attempts to provide the most appropriate solutions to the particular problems facing those sectors. It is within this framework that the Commission evaluates the notion of state aid in the meaning of art.107(1) of the TFEU and the derogations provided by arts 107(2) and (3) of the TFEU to the principle of prohibition of state aid in the

---

[204] For an application of this principle, see Case C–311/94 *Ijssel-Vliet Combinatie* [1996] E.C.R. I–5023.

fisheries and aquaculture sector.[205] Since state aid in the fisheries sector is only justified if it is in accordance with the objectives of the CFP, both the SME Regulation and the Fisheries Guidelines refer to the Regulations governing the CFP for the compatibility criteria, which correspond to those governing the allocation of EU funds under the EFF.

As explained above, the possibilities for Member States to grant state aid to the fisheries sector have been limited to allow only aids that comply with the conditions laid down for the structural funds for fisheries. It is considered that these aids serve the objectives of the CFP and are unlikely to distort competition. This is why the Commission has considered that a distinction between the primary sector and the processing and marketing sector is not appropriate with regard to fisheries and aquaculture, and the Regulation on the application of arts 107 and 108 TFEU to de minimis aid applies to the whole sector.[206] It provides that transparent aid below €30,000 may be granted over any three-year period to an undertaking active in the production, processing and marketing of fisheries products, without being notified to the Commission, provided that the total amount of such aid does not exceed 2.5 per cent of the annual fisheries output in the Member State concerned. Export aid and aid conditional on the use of domestic over foreign products are not covered by the Regulation, and neither is aid whose amount is fixed on the basis of the price or quantity of products put on the market. The beneficiary must be informed of the de minimis nature of the aid, and Member States are obliged to keep registers and detailed records on such aid for 10 years.

13–045

Member States do not have to notify aid in the fisheries sector which fulfils the conditions laid down in Commission Regulation (EC) No.736/2008 of July 22, 2008 on the application of arts 87 and 88 of the Treaty to state aid to small and medium-sized enterprises active in the production, processing and marketing of

---

[205] It is worth mentioning here two negative decisions without a recovery order concerning UK state aid measures, where a council in northern Scotland in one case (Orkney, Decision C 87/2001 [2002] O.J. C38/2) and a company controlled by a council in the other case (Shetland, Decision on loans for the purchase of fishing quotas in the Shetland Islands (United Kingdom) [2003] O.J. L211/3) purchased fish quotas which were subsequently rented to fishermen belonging to these communities. Recovery of the aid was not required because the Commission considered that in the particular circumstances of the cases, as the funds used for the aid schemes had the same origin as funds considered by the Commission to be private funds in the area of structural funds and the granting authorities could have had the legitimate expectation that those funds could also be considered as private for the purpose of the state aid assessment. A similar approach was taken in a decision concerning an investment made in 1999 and 2000 in a fish processing company, Shetland Leasing and Property Ltd (SLAP). The investigation concluded that the funds used for the investment were derived from two trusts managed by the Shetland Islands Council and had to be considered as state aid. This investment constituted an operating aid incompatible with the common market. However, again, as the same kind of funding was considered to be a private participation in the field of structural funds, recovery of the aid was not required on the grounds of the legitimate expectations of the authorities and granting bodies involved.

[206] Commission Regulation 875/2007 on the application of arts 87 and 88 of the EC Treaty to de minimis aid in the fisheries sector and amending Regulation (EC) No.18960/2004 [2007] O.J. L193/6.

fisheries products (the Fisheries SME Regulation).[207] The Fisheries SME Regulation applies to aid amounts below €1 million or aid designed to finance measures with maximum eligible expenses of €2 million. The categories of aid subject to exemption include aid for promotion[208] or advertising of fishery products, producers' groups, the protection and development of aquatic resources,[209] innovative measures and technical assistance, fishing port facilities, scrapping of fishing vessels, socio-economic measures, investment in processing or marketing of fisheries products, aquaculture and inland fishing. The Regulation exempts some taxes on fuel implemented pursuant to Council Directives on energy taxes and VAT, insofar as these tax exemptions constitute state aid. The main difference from the rules applied before 2008 is the introduction of compatibility rules for the following measures: aid for the temporary cessation of fishing activities; aid for aqua-environmental measures; aid for public health and animal health measures; aid for measures of common interest intended to protect and develop aquatic fauna and flora while enhancing the aquatic environment; aid for investments in public or private fishing ports, landing sites and fishing shelters; aid for measures of common interest intended to implement a policy of quality and value enhancement; aid for pilot projects; and aid for modification for the reassignment of fishing vessels. To ensure that aid is allocated properly, the monitoring is conducted through simplified *ex ante* information to the Commission on the aid to be granted, with publication on the Commission's website and in the Official Journal, and *ex post* reporting obligations.[210]

13–046   Some types of aids covered by Commission Regulation 800/2008 in the fields of research and development, aid in the form of risk capital, training aid and aid for disadvantaged and disabled workers are also applicable to fisheries and aquaculture and exempted from the notification obligation.

Aid exceeding the thresholds set in the SME Fisheries Regulation or granted to enterprises other than small and medium-sized enterprises is not excluded, but the Commission must assess it on a case-by-case basis. Such measures are subject to the notification obligation and are evaluated on the basis of the criteria laid down in the Fisheries SME Regulation.

13–047   The 2008 Guidelines for the examination of state aid to fisheries and aquaculture[211] (the Fisheries Guidelines) were adapted to the EFF objectives and apply to the entire fisheries sector. They concern the exploitation of living aquatic resources and aquaculture, together with the means of production[212] and the

---

[207] [2004] O.J. L201.

[208] N 159/2003, The Netherlands, *Promotion and research for the fishery.*

[209] N 539/2003, Germany, *Aid for conversion of fisheries resources.*

[210] See, e.g. Summary information on state aid granted in conformity with the Commission Regulation (EC) No.1595/2004 of September 8, 2004 on the application of arts 87 and 88 of the TFEU to state aid to small and medium-sized enterprises active in the production, processing and marketing of fisheries products [2006] O.J. C98/5.

[211] [2008] O.J. C84/10. It is worth noting Case C21/2010 *Guidelines for the examination of State Aid to fisheries and aquaculture—Non acceptance of the appropriate measures for the Fisheries Insurance Scheme,* FI.

[212] N 43/2010, Finland, *Investointituki Carelian Caviar Oylle.*

processing and marketing or promotion of the resulting products.[213] The Guidelines cover aid for investment in fleets through the renewal of fishing vessels or for modernisation[214] and in fishing equipment, aid for the permanent withdrawal of fishing vessels through their transfer to third countries, aid for the temporary cessation of fishing activities[215] and aid for compensation for damages due to natural disasters or exceptional circumstances.[216] The Fisheries Guidelines also allow for the possibility to grant socio-economic measures[217] and aid for the outermost regions.[218] It is no longer possible to obtain aid in connection with the purchase of used vessels.[219] The Fisheries Guidelines also introduced measures for relief from company tax in respect of Community fishing vessels operating outside Community waters, and reduced rates of social security contributions and income tax for fishermen employed onboard,[220] with a view to strengthening the competitiveness of the Community fishing fleet operating outside Community waters vis-à-vis third-country fleets operating at lower costs, and to discourage Community operators from registering their fishing vessels in third countries which do not ensure proper control over the activities of their fishing fleets.

The Fisheries Guidelines lay down the rules on procedural matters such as notification, recovery of aid granted unlawfully[221] and the repercussions of expenditure financed by the EFF. They contain two annexes which provide rules for the closer monitoring of approved schemes, one setting out the information to be supplied when aid schemes are notified, and the other specifying the

---

[213] N 632/2007, Italy, *Deliberazione della Giunta regionale n. 80–7203 del 22.10.2007, D.lgs. 143/1997. Misura Campagne di promozione in materia di pesca e acquacoltura. Approvazione bando*; N 284/2009, The Netherlands, *Fonds voor scholpromotie*.

[214] NN 37/2005, Italy, Construction of fishing vessels; N524/2007, The Netherlands, Aid for investments in pulse trawl gear.

[215] N 251/2005, The Netherlands, Aid for reduction of fishing capacities in Ijsselmeer; C 50/03 (ex. NN 163/02) Financial compensation for the temporary cessation of fishing for common spiny lobster in Corsica [2003] O.J. C211/63.

[216] N38b/2006—GR, *Programme ZEUS (mesures en faveur des pisciculteurs dont les exploitations ont été touchées par des calamités naturelles ou des conditions climatiques défavorables)*; N374/2010—DE, *staatliche Beihilfen im Fischerei und Aquakultursektor im Zusammenhang mit Naturkatastrophen*; N191/2010—CZ, *Zmírnění škod způsobených povodněmi na rybách v letních měsících roku 2009*; NN16/2010—FR, *Mesures de soutien accordées aux entreprises conchylicoles et piscicoles touchées par la tempête Klaus du 24 Janvier 2009*; N119/2010—FR, *Plan de soutien exceptionnel aux conchyliculteurs et pisciculteurs des départements touchés par la tempête Xynthia dans le nuit du 27 au 28 Février 2010*.

[217] NN 106/2002, Portugal, *Mesures à caractère socio-économiques- secteur de la pêche (Madère)*.

[218] N354/2007, France, *Aide d'état accordée pour la construction de navires dans le cadre du plan de développement de la flotte de pêche des départements d'Outre-Mer*.

[219] For past practice see decision on aid granted to the fisheries and aquaculture sector in Corsica from 1986 to 1999 [2005] O.J. L74/41; N 592/2003 Determination of the terms and conditions for the granting of contributions for the purchase of used vessels (Italy).

[220] C42/2008, France, *aides aux marins-pecheurs salaries*.

[221] C35/2009, Italy, *Région Sardaigne—mesures urgentes en faveur de l'emploi (loi régionale n. 28/1984)*; C9/2006, France, *Fonds de prévention des aléas à la pêche*; C30/2008, Belgium, *Steunverlening aan de visafslag van Oostende*; C40/2006, UK, Loan assistence schemes; C55/2006—PT, *Bonifications de taux d'intérêt relatifs à des prêts pour des activités dans le secteur de la pêche*; C1/2008, France, *Industries de transformation et de commercialisation du secteur de la pêche et de l'aquaculture*.

information which must appear in the annual report to be submitted to the Commission on all existing aid schemes or individual aid measures granted outside an approved scheme that are not made subject to a specific reporting obligation by a conditional decision.

13–048   Difficulties in the fishing industry were aggravated by the increase in fuel prices.[222] This led to calls by the industry for public intervention to compensate for this sudden increase in costs. Such aid would normally have constituted operating aid which is incompatible with the Treaty.[223] The Commission would not normally approve any aid notified for this purpose, but it should be noted that temporary specific actions to promote the restructuring of EU fishing fleets affected by the economic crisis (adopted in 2008 in response to the sharp rise in fuel prices) are covered by Regulation (EC) No.744/2008 of July 24, 2008 instituting a temporary specific action aiming to promote the restructuring of Community fishing fleets affected by the economic crisis,[224] Ailing companies could therefore obtain aid for rescuing and restructuring firms in difficulty provided they fulfilled the necessary criteria. According to the Regulation, the Commission assesses such schemes on the basis of the Community guidelines on state aid for firms in difficulty,[225] provided that the restructuring is based on realistic economic assumptions in the context at the time, and also taking into account the state and possible evolution of targeted stocks. Rescue aid is to be seen as a short-term aid to keep an ailing enterprise financially afloat for the time necessary to work out a restructuring or liquidation plan, and should be limited to the minimum necessary. The purpose of restructuring must be to ensure the profitability of the enterprise within the meaning of para.37 of the Rescue and Restructuring Guidelines, by reducing operational costs without increasing current overall fishing effort and capacity. Further restructuring of fishing enterprises to restore economic viability often implies investment to adapt fishing vessels, and general rules on aid for such investment are set out in the Fisheries Guidelines, which allow aid for the modernisation and equipment of fishing vessels subject to the rules laid down in the EFF Regulation. The conditions for granting national aid for these purposes are the same as those applicable to Community aid under the EFF Regulation.[226]

---

[222] Between 2003 and 2005 fuel costs rose from approximately 18% to 36% of the value of landings for trawlers, and from approximately 9% to 18% for fleets operating with static gear. This suggests that for most bottom trawlers—by far the biggest segment of the fishing fleet—the net operational profit is negative: see Communication from the Commission to the Council and the European Parliament on improving the economic situation in the fishing industry COM(2006) 103 final of March 9, 2006, p.5.

[223] Decision C3/2001, Belgium, subsidies loans for fishermen, pettily guaranteed by the state, following the rise in fuel prices.

[224] [2008] L202/1.

[225] Decision C 29/2006, Italy, Restructuring of enterprises; NN9/2008, France, *Notification PSR LRP AGRAP 28/08. Plan de sauvetage et de restructuration.*

[226] Communication from the Commission to the Council and the European Parliament on improving the economic situation in the fishing industry COM(2006) 103 final of March 9, 2006, p.7.

State aid for environmental protection is assessed in accordance with the Environmental Aid Guidelines. In addition to the requirements of these Guidelines, aid for environmental protection is not declared compatible if it concerns the capacity of a vessel or serves to increase the effectiveness of its fishing gear. Environmental considerations are taken into account when assessing the compatibility of investment aids.[227]

The Guidelines on National Regional Aid do not apply in the fisheries sector, and regional aid schemes concerning fisheries are examined in the light of the Fisheries Guidelines. Also the Research, Development and Innovation Framework[228] is of application in the sector.[229]   **13–049**

State aid measures existing in the Member States which joined the European Union in 2004 and 2007 were subject to the special interim measures mechanism provided for in the Accession Treaty, described in para.13–011, above. The Member States notified 20 measures for an overall amount of €0.13 billion. Negotiations in Iceland are likely to follow the same pattern subject to similar transitional rules.[230]

In 2010, 14 measures were communicated as exempted under Fisheries SME Regulation.   **13–050**

---

[227] NN 38/2005 and NN 39/2005, Ireland, Aid for development of salmon farming.
[228] Community Framework for State Aid for Research, Development and Innovation [2006] O.J. C323/01.
[229] N419/2007—ES, *développement technologique du secteur de la pêche*.
[230] Screening report, Croatia, Ch.13: Fisheries, July 18, 2006.

CHAPTER 14

STATE AID TO THE COAL AND STEEL SECTORS*

1. INTRODUCTION 14–001
2. THE ECSC TREATY REGIME 14–002
   The state aid provisions to the coal and steel sector 14–003
   The limits of the ECSC Treaty 14–004
   The European coal industry and the need for state aid—an overview 14–005
   Decisions up to the expiry of the ECSC 14–006
3. STATE AID IN THE COAL INDUSTRY 14–008
   EC Council Regulation 1407/2002 ("the Coal Regulation") 14–009
   Decisions taken under Regulation 1407/2002 14–019
   The expiry of Regulation 1407/2002 14–033
   Decision 2010/787 on state aid to facilitate the closure of uncompetitive coal mines   14–050
4. STATE AID IN THE STEEL INDUSTRY 14–052
   State aid to the steel sector before December 31, 2002 14–052
   State aid to the steel sector after December 31, 2002 14–060
   Rescue and Restructuring aid and Closure aid for the Steel Sector 14–062
5. STATE AID FOR COAL AND STEEL IN THE NEW MEMBER STATES 14–065
   Czech Republic 14–068
   Poland 14–069
   Slovakia 14–074
   Romania 14–075
   Turkey 14–079
6. CONCLUDING REMARKS 14–080

1. INTRODUCTION

14–001 The previous edition of this book, published in 2006, dealt largely with the impact of the expiry of the ECSC Treaty in 2002 on the field of state aid to the coal and steel industry. Since then, state aid to this sector has continued to be governed predominantly by sector specific legislation, rather than reverting back to the general provisions of the TFEU, as was anticipated by some. This chapter will discuss the legislative changes made within both the coal and steel industry in turn, with a particular focus on the underlying policy rationale, and follow with

* Tom Ottervanger

a review of how these reforms have been interpreted and applied by the courts and Commission.

The second section of this chapter briefly reviews the mechanics of the legislative framework established by the ECSC regime. Though almost a decade has elapsed since its expiration, the Treaty is not without relevance; its principles and objectives provide the framework for the state aid regime in place today. However, this edition will differ from the last by not detailing in the same depth the material and procedural consequences of the expiry. The third section turns to the effects of the ECSC Treaty cessation before detailing the legislative changes that have been effected in response in the area of coal. In this respect, the section will concentrate principally on the Coal Regulation 1407/2002, but will also look as far as is possible at its successor, Decision 787/2002 on the closure of uncompetitive coal mines, of December 10, 2010. The separate governing regime for steel will be examined in the fourth section. The interpretation and application of these new frameworks by both the Commission and the European courts will also be explored.

The fifth section will deal with the situation in the new Member States and the sixth section will provide some brief conclusions about the future issues which may arise within these industries, and will touch upon their uneasy relationship with the environmental goals of the European Union. This chapter will inevitably overlap, to a certain degree, with the chapter which deals with the Energy Sector. However, best efforts have been made to restrict, as far as possible, the ambit of this chapter to state aid issues applying particularly to the coal and steel sectors. It should also be noted that it does not intend to provide an exhaustive guide; rather to lay the foundations for further research into this fascinating area.

2. THE ECSC TREATY REGIME

As mentioned, the original Treaty remains pertinent to any examination of state aid law to the coal and steel sectors. Its restrictive and prescribed approach towards any such aid is inherent within our modern regime. Further, most of the current regulations expound upon the objectives and considerations originally articulated and as such no chapter on state aid to these sectors would be complete without some explanation of its operation. It also provides the framework upon which the adoption of further legislation has been made, and this will be examined below.   **14–002**

The state aid provisions to the Coal and Steel Sector

Since its inception in 1951 and subsequent expiration in 2002, regulation of state aid granted to the coal and steel industries was achieved primarily through the ECSC Treaty.[1] The general prohibition provided in art.4(c) wholly proscribed   **14–003**

---

[1] Properly called "Treaty establishing the European Coal and Steel Community", it is available for viewing electronically at *http://eur-lex.europa.eu/en/treaties/index.htm*. [Accessed October 26, 2011].

"subsidies or aid granted by States in any form whatsoever", irrespective of any impact on interstate trade. This stark, blanket prohibition was tempered by the more permissive art.67 ECSC which allowed aid to be granted under certain circumstances. Aid would be deemed compatible where, through Member State action, the creation of a serious disequilibrium was likely, such as an increased disparity between production costs (excluding those directly resultant from increased productivity) and which had harmful effects on its own coal and steel industry, or where a change in wages or working conditions had a similarly harmful effect.[2]

The article also provided for a mechanism through which the Commission, following consultation with the Advisory Committee and the Council, could issue recommendations to a Member State that had taken actions having harmful effects on coal or steel undertakings within another Member State, in order that these effects be remedied "by such measures as that State may consider most compatible with its own economic equilibrium". Article 67(3) further provided that the Commission could make recommendations to a Member State where that state's actions reduced differences in production costs by allowing special benefits to, or imposing special charges on, its coal and steel undertakings in comparison with other industries. In addition to these provisions, art.95(1) ECSC provided the Commission with a wide discretion; when it had the unanimous support of the Council it could make "decisions" or "recommendations" in circumstances not specifically provided for in the ECSC Treaty yet necessitating action to ensure the fulfilment of the objectives expressed in arts 2, 3 and 4.[3] The Commission has exercised this authority to create many "Decisions" or "Codes" which have established rules determining the types of aid considered compatible and establishing a notification and monitoring system for state aid to the coal and steel industries.

The limits of the ECSC Treaty

14–004   On occasion, national measures in the sector would not fall under the specific competence of the ECSC, but instead would be dealt with under arts 87 and 88 EC [now 107 and 108 TFEU]. This largely residual competence was affirmed by AG Slynn in *Deutsch Babcock* in his statement that:

"... the EEC Treaty may apply to coal and steel except to the extent that matters are dealt with in the ECSC Treaty or in rules made under it; in so far as the latter has occupied the ground the EEC Treaty provisions are not to have effect."[4]

---

[2] For the precise wording, see art.67 ECSC Treaty.

[3] For example, the mission of the ECSC as articulated in art.2 "to contribute to economic expansion, the development of employment and the improvement of the standard of living in the participating countries through the institution, in harmony with the general economy of the member States, of a common market [internal market] as defined in Article 4."

[4] Opinion of AG Sir Gordon Slynn delivered on April 7, 1987, Case 328/85 *Deutsche Babcock Handel GmbH v Hauptzollamt Lübeck-Ost* [1987] E.C.R. 5119.

This rule was put to the test in the case of *France v Commission*, where it was confirmed that the Transparency Directive of 1980[5] could not be applied to undertakings in the coal sector because the ECSC Treaty alone was authorised to provide the rules in this regard.[6]

It should be noted at this stage that the aid granted under the decisions was available only for mines which produced "coal" within the meaning of Annex I ECSC Treaty, and therefore state aid to lignite mines was excluded. Other types of coal, such as ortho-lignite are covered by the general state aid rules of the European Union and are beyond the ambit of this chapter.

The European coal industry and the need for state aid—an overview

As early as the 1960s it was clear that the majority of the European coal **14–005** mining industry was uncompetitive in the world market for coal. The strict application of art.4(c) ECSC and its categorical prohibition of aid would consequently result in the unavoidable closure of the majority of underground mines in Europe. The position remains the same today; most coal mines simply will not be able to compete without some manner of state aid, a fact which has led to the inevitable decline in production of indigenous coal.[7] This inability to compete largely derives from unfavourable geological conditions, the quality of the extracted coal and labour costs which make the unit production costs in the European States considerably higher than their worldwide counterparts. Both the Commission impact assessment on the expiry of Regulation 1407/2002 on state aid to the coal industry and the "Ecorys Report" examined the feasibility of the coal mining industries across the Member States, when compared with varying world coal price scenarios.[8] To summarise, this analysis painted Poland most auspiciously; it is likely to be able to compete without requiring production aid under each of the scenarios. At the other end of the spectrum, the examination predicts that Spain's public production (HUNOSA), amounting to 9 per cent of its total hard coal production, will not compete without aid under any of the future coal price scenarios.[9] The study further concluded that the current coal

[5] Commission Directive 80/723/EEC of June 25, 1980 on the transparency of financial relations between Member States and public undertakings [1980] O.J. L195/35.

[6] Joined cases 188–190/80 *France Italy and United Kingdom v Commission* [1980] E.C.R. 2545.

[7] For an overview of hard coal production in the EU see the Commission's Second Strategic Energy Review, "The Market for Solid Fuels in the EU in 2004–2006 and Trends in 2007, available at *http://ec.europa.eu/energy/strategies/2008/2008_11_ser2_en.htm*. [Accessed October 22, 2011.] This report fulfils the requirement of art.7(c) Council Regulation No.405/2003 of February 27, 2003 concerning Community monitoring of imports of hard coal originating in third countries, which requires the Commission to regularly publish a report on the market for solid fuels in the European Union with a market outlook.

[8] See Commission Staff Working Document "Aftermath of the expiry of Regulation 1407/2002 on State aid to the coal industry: Impact Assessment" SEC (2009). See also the report produced for the European Commission by Ecorys, "An Evaluation of the Needs for State Aid to the Coal Industry post 2010", December 9, 2008, AE17802: Final Report.

[9] Impact assessment cited above, s.3.1.1, p.9.

subsidising countries, in addition to Spain's private production, would be able to produce competitive coal only were the world coal price to rise to at least €150. At the time of the report in 2009 the price was approximately €50–80.[10]

It is in view of these considerations that the Commission has frequently decided to assist the ailing coal mining industry, responding with a series of temporary framework decisions. These have been adopted since 1965 under the aforementioned art.95(1) ECSC procedure and together establish the conditions under which state aid can be permitted.[11]

The Decisions up to the expiry of the ECSC

14–006   The overarching aims of these decisions were: to overcome the lack of competitiveness of the European coal industry through restructuring; to reduce the dependence on foreign imports of energy and increase the EU's energy security; and to mitigate the often difficult social situation in coal mining areas.[12] The present day relevance of these aims has been called into question and this issue will be specifically examined in section 3. These rules also served to ensure a degree of cohesion between the state aid policies of both the EC and ECSC Treaty.

14–007   The declining coal industry was considerably assisted, the Decisions often ameliorating the social consequences of inevitable mine closure within Europe.[13] There was a strong drive to induce the sector to restructure and shut down expensive pits on the basis of the 1986–93 Decision.[14] That Decision failed in this objective and the heavily subsidised and expensive mines of Germany and Spain remained in operation. A stricter regime was consequently applied under Decision 93/3632 ECSC[15] from 1992 through to the end of the ECSC validity on July 23, 2002. It considered aid to be compatible with the proper functioning of the market if it was given pursuant to the following objectives: "to make, in the light of coal prices in international markets, further progress towards economic

[10] For a more comprehensive and recent examination of coal prices see "The Market for Solid Fuels in the European Union in 2010 and the Outlook for 2011", August 2011, DG ENER/ B3/2011–455. It reported the 2010 prices in Europe to average $104.12, approximately €74 at the time of writing.

[11] See for example Commission Decision No.3632/93/ECSC of December 28, 1993 establishing Community rules for state aid to the coal industry [1993] O.J. L329/12, Commission Decision No.341/94/ECSC of February 8, 1994 implementing Decision No.3632/93/ECSC establishing Community rules for state aid to the coal industry [1994] O.J. L49/1.

[12] Commission Staff Working Document, Impact Assessment cited above, Annex 1 p.51. A summary of the Impact assessment findings is available at *http://eur-lex.europa.eu/LexUriServ/ LexUriServ.do?uri=SEC:2010:0851:FIN:EN:PDF.* [Accessed October 21, 2011.]

[13] The summary cited above points out that, although the jobs which are lost do not have a huge impact on domestic or EU wide unemployment figures, their impact on specific coal mining regions can be significant, for example in Germany, Spain and Romania.

[14] Decision No.2064/86/ECSC of June 30, 1986 establishing Community rules for state aid to the coal industry [1986] O.J. L177/1. The application of this regime was examined in the Report from the Commission on the Application of the Community Rules for State Aid to the Coal Industry in 1993, COM(95) 656 final.

[15] Commission Decision 93/3632/ECSC on rules for state aid to the coal industry [1993] O.J.L329.

viability with the aim of achieving a reduction in aid; to solve the social and regional problems created by the total or partial reduction in the activity of the production units; to help the coal industry to adjust to environmental protection standards."

3. STATE AID IN THE COAL INDUSTRY

The Commission prepared for the expiry of the ECSC Treaty by proposing Regulation 1407/02.[16] This has, until recently,[17] represented the new framework for the regulation of state aid in the coal industry, and ensured that this sector did not revert back to general governance under the EU Treaty provisions. Effective coordination between the two legislative regimes was guaranteed through the establishment of a transitional procedure for the period up to December 31, 2002[18] for those cases which had not been ruled upon prior to July 23, 2002. In effect, three categories of cases were distinguished:

    (i) those cases which had been completed in all factual or legal respects on or before July 23, 2002 within a Member State, which would be subject to the ECSC rules only;

    (ii) those cases in which all relevant factual and legal events occurred after July 23, 2002, which would be subject to the EC [now TFEU] rules only;

    (iii) those cases which had begun prior to the expiry of the ECSC Treaty but which continued after expiry.

The Commission addressed the latter category in its Communication, in which it differentiated between notified and un-notified aid.[19] In short, for notified aid Member States could elect, for aid covering costs for 2002, for the application of the framework laid down in 3623/93/ECSC, with the exception of its procedural rules. For un-notified aid, the EC Council Regulation would apply insofar as the type or form of aid was one which fell within the scope of the Regulation.

Following the expiration of the ECSC Treaty the regimes governing state aid to the coal and steel sectors took completely separate paths. State aid rules and their application to the coal sector will now be examined, with their application to the steel sector being examined in section 4.

14–008

---

[16] Council Regulation (EC) No.1407/2002 of July 23, 2002 on state aid to the coal industry [2002] O.J. L205/1.

[17] Regulation 1407/02 expired on December 31, 2010 but certain subsidies to the coal industry continue to be permissible under Decision 2010/787 on state aid to facilitate the closure of uncompetitive coal mines.

[18] In this regard see Commission Communication concerning certain aspects of the treatment of competition cases arising from the expiry of the ECSC Treaty [2002] O.J. C152/5.

[19] Commission Communication concerning certain aspects of the treatment of competition cases arising from the expiry of the ECSC Treaty para.25.

EC Council Regulation 1407/2002 ("the Coal Regulation")

14–009   The Regulation entered into force on July 23, 2002 and expired on December 31, 2010, again applying only to high, medium and low-grade coal category A and B within the qualification of the international UNECE coal classification system. The next section continues firstly with a general overview of the more salient aspects of the Regulation and its underlying rationale, before studying in greater detail its application by the Commission Union Courts.

14–010   The Coal Regulation was adopted on the basis of art.107(3)(e) TFEU and lays down the general rules for the granting of state aid to the coal industry. Its purpose, as stated in art.1, is to contribute "to the restructuring of the coal industry", taking into consideration both the social and regional effects of this and the necessity to maintain "a minimum quantity of indigenous coal production to guarantee access to reserves."[20] To this end, it provides for three main categories of aid under certain conditions, though these are without prejudice to the other exemptions for aid for research and development, environmental and training aid[21]:

- **Aid for the reduction of mining activity**: permits aid intended to cover the production losses of mines that are part of a closure plan.[22] It should be noted that this provision was only applicable until the end of 2007.

- **Aid for accessing coal reserves**: permits aid for the purpose of ongoing activities (for example, current production aid, and aid for initial investments and accessing reserves on any scale).[23] The granting of such aid is subject to strict conditions detailed in the article and examined more in the next section on the application of Regulation 1407/2002. For example, aid to cover investment costs must be allocated to a production unit which has not previously benefited from aid under art.3 Decision 3632/93/ECSC, or which has already received aid under that provision because it has shown that it is able to reach a competitive position with regards to prices for coal of a similar quantity from third countries. Moreover, production units are required to compose an operating plan and a financing plan which document how the aid to the investment project will guarantee the economic viability of the production unit; and the aid notified and actually paid cannot exceed 30 per cent of the total costs of the relevant investment project for this purpose.

- **Aid to cover exceptional costs**: permits aid to reimburse exceptional costs resulting from the rationalisation and restructuring of the coal industry, not related to current production (inherited liabilities). Specifically mentioned also are costs connected with the environmental rehabilitation of closed mines.[24]

---

[20] art.1 of the Coal Regulation.
[21] art.3(1) of the Coal Regulation.
[22] art.4 of the Coal Regulation.
[23] arts 5(2) and 5(3) of the Coal Regulation.
[24] art.7 of the Coal Regulation.

The policy objectives behind the limited extension of coal subsidies are clearly visible in the preface to the Regulation. Indeed, it captures perfectly the "balancing act" attempted by the Commission, detailing the necessity to ensure access to coal reserves and domestic coal within the Union, whilst at the same time warning that this aim should not undermine the continuing restructuring of the coal industry,[25] a necessity given that the majority of coal will come from outside the Union in the future. This balancing is made even more difficult by other factors such as the environmental impact of coal usage and the drive towards renewable energy and the requirement for a stable and reliable availability of energy. Indeed, this "security of supply" notion is an underlying theme throughout the Regulation, which cites the "diversification of energy sources, both by geographical area and in products" as one of the methods for its attainment. The relevance of this argument will be considered in more detail hereafter. It is acknowledged in the preface that the aid scheme relies on a range of factors, and these, especially the capacity of Union coal to strengthen the Union's energy security, need to be re-evaluated during the course of the scheme in the context of sustainable development by way of a report. On the basis of these reports the Commission will make proposals to the Council, taking into account the development and long-term prospects of the scheme, in particular the social and regional aspects of the restructuring of the coal industry. The Coal Regulation further supports the drive towards more renewable energy sources, since it advocates the reallocation of aid from conventional sources such as coal to renewable energy sources. Aid for renewable energy sources is dealt with under the Community guidelines for environmental protection (see further Ch.22 on Environmental Aid).

The notion that subsidised coal production should be limited to the minimum amount required for effective attainment of energy security is prevalent throughout the Regulation. Under Exhibit 13 "aid to cover initial investment cost allow production units, which are viable, or close to economic viability, to implement the technical investments necessary to maintain their competitive capacity". Such a parameter will inevitably involve the exclusion of units, and these may be granted temporary aid for the alleviation of social and regional consequences of their closure.[26]   **14–011**

Europe is the fourth largest region worldwide for coal consumption, behind China, the USA and India.[27] Roughly a third of power generation within the EU Member States comes from coal[28] and it is thus likely to play a key role in the   **14–012**

[25] Exhibit 2 of the Preface of the Coal Regulation.

[26] On this point see exhibit 5 of Decision 2010/787/EU of December 10, 2010 on state aid to facilitate the closure of uncompetitive coal mines [2010] O.J. L336/24.

[27] The EU fell behind India in terms of coal consumption in 2009. In the European Union approximately 60% of consumption comes from indigenous production, with 130.2 million tonnes of hard coal and 412.5 million tonnes of lignite produced in 2010. For an overview of coal statistics in Europe see "The Market for Solid Fuels in the European Union in 2010 and the Outlook for 2011", August 2011 [DG ENER/B3/2011–455], available at *http://ec.europa.eu/ energy/coal/studies/doc/2011_eu_market_solid_fuels_2010.pdf.* [Accessed October 26, 2011.]

[28] The split in electricity generation for the EU-27 in 2009 was nuclear 27.8%, coal 25.6%, renewables 18.3%, oil and others 5.0%, para.2.3 of the report cited above.

provision of energy over the next decades, though the extent of this will also be dependent on the success of carbon emission reduction technologies. The largest reserves are found in Poland, Czech Republic, with smaller ones present in Spain, Hungary, the United Kingdom and Germany.

14–013   According to the "Ecorys Report" published for the Commission, between 2003 and 2008 over €26 billion of state aid was granted to the hard coal sector.[29] However, the report showed that the total amounts of aid granted to this sector is in decline; it notes that the yearly amounts of subsidies were halved between 2003 and 2008.[30] To 2007, current production aid still amounted to more than 55 per cent of aid going to the coal mining sector. The countries granting the most aid are Germany, France, Spain, Poland and the United Kingdom, though more recently Romania, Slovakia and Hungary are granting aid in this area. In respect of aid for initial investment, the United Kingdom, Poland and Slovenia are most prominent since these Member States contain industries which can still compete and do not require a lot of production aid.

14–014   In assessing the aid granted or envisaged, the Commission starts by examining the purpose of the aid and the criteria to be fulfilled by the granted company to be able to apply for aid. Thereafter, the Commission verifies that the conditions laid down in previous Commission decisions, which have been taken on the basis of the ECSC Treaty, are respected.

14–015   There have been a number of decisions taken by the Commission since the introduction of Regulation 1407/02, mostly authorising aid for the restructuring of Member States' coal industries. Many of the states have grasped the opportunity to phase out their uncompetitive industries mines, whilst, where possible maintaining their own indigenous source and improving their own security of energy supply, in line with the Commission's assessment that, to this end, the diversification of energy sources, both by form and origin is imperative.[31]

14–016   Article 11 of the Regulation required the Commission to report on its application and, more generally, on the restructuring of the coal industry and the effects on the internal market. Moreover, art.11(2) requires that the Commission "evaluate the actual contribution of indigenous coal to long term energy security in the European Union". The findings of this 2007 Communication[32] are detailed below, of course being supplemented with the more recent examples of application of the Regulation. Although the Coal Regulation entered into force on July 24, 2002, art.14 of the Coal Regulation provides that Member States may grant aid between then and December 31, under the rules of Decision No.3632/93 ECSC. Every Member State that granted aid during this period made use of this

---

[29] See 6.1.2, p.25 of the Impact Assessment cited above.

[30] From €6.4 billion in 2003 to €3.2 billion in 2008. A country-by-country break down of the state aid received is available in Annex 1, p.56.

[31] Green Paper of November 29, 2000, "Towards a European strategy for the security of energy supply", COM(2000) 769 final.

[32] Communication from the Commission to the European Parliament, the Council, the European Economic and Social Committee and the Committee of the Regions, Commission Report on the Application of Council Regulation (EC) No.1407/2002 on State Aid to the Coal Industry SEC(2007) 602, COM/2007/0253 final.

possibility, and so the Regulation de facto applied only from January 1, 2003.[33]

14-017 The Communication divides the Member States into three categories: those that have ceased coal subsidies for mines in operation (the Czech Republic, France, Italy), those which grant investment aid (Poland, Slovakia, the United Kingdom), and those granting operating aid (Bulgaria, Germany, Hungary, Romania, Slovenia, Spain).

14-018 **Complete cessation of state aid.** France closed its last coal mine in 2004, but in 2006 permitted a private company to begin mining operations in a new open-cast coal mine, without recourse to subsidies. The Czech Republic privatised its former state-owned mines and no longer offers subsidies. Italy has one operating coal mine in Sardinia but no state aid has yet been notified to the Commission. The report concluded that in these three countries the restructuring process had been completed.

Decisions taken under Regulation 1407/2002

14-019 **Aid for accessing coal reserves.** Aid for accessing coal reserves is the category that consists of the two types of aid examined below: investment aid, and current production aid. Member States may, in accordance with paras 2 and 3 of art.5 of Council Regulation (EC) No.1407/2002, grant aid to an undertaking, intended specifically to production units or to a group of production units, only if the aid contributes to maintaining access to coal reserves.

14-020 **Investment aid (Article 5(2) of the Coal Regulation).** The Commission's approval under art.10 is subject to compliance with the general objectives and criteria and the specific criteria set out in art.5(2) of the Coal Regulation and, more generally, to the aid being compatible with the proper functioning of the internal market. Slovenia, the UK and Poland have now limited their subsidies to investment aid under art.5(2) of the Coal Regulation, with the UK and Slovenia privatising their previously state-controlled industries. This is also in process in Poland. The 2007 Communication concluded that the restructuring process in these countries had been completed, to the extent that all the mines which were not commercially viable have now disappeared from the market.

14-021 In its Decision N 653/2009[34] the Commission considered investment aid granted by Poland to be compatible with art.107(3)(e) TFEU and the Coal Regulation. The measures related to grants for initial investment costs, that is to say fixed capital costs directly related to infrastructure work or to the equipment necessary for the mining of coal resources in existing mines in accordance with art.2(d) of the Coal Regulation. The aid was further restricted insofar as it would only be granted to cover costs associated with hard coal used to produce

[33] Spain C17/2003, France N551/2002, Germany N550/2002 and UK N 740/2002.
[34] N 653/2009, Poland, Investment aid for hard coal mining sector C (2010) 3063.

electricity (including the cogeneration of heat and power), to produce coke and to fuel blast furnaces in the steel industry, where such uses takes places in the European Union. As a result, the aid was therefore deemed to satisfy art.3(2) of the Coal Regulation.

14–022   The Commission regarded the costs covered by the scheme to be compatible with the type of costs listed in Form D of Annex III of the Decision 2002/871/EC[35] (see para.5). Since the measures proposed by the Polish aid scheme excluded aid for purposes other than providing access to coal reserves, and would not be granted in respect of costs related to production itself they fulfilled the conditions of art.5(1) Coal Regulation. The measures also fulfilled the requirements of art.5(2)(a) of the Regulation, which prescribes that:

> "the aid shall be earmarked for existing production units which have not received aid under Article 3 [operating aid] of Decision No.3632/93 ECSC or which have received aid authorised by the Commission under the said Article 3 having demonstrated that they were able to achieve a competitive position vis-à-vis prices for coal of a similar quality from third countries."

Since the ECSC, and its implementing measures such as Decision No.3632/93 expired before Poland's accession to the EU, and since Poland has not, since then, granted operating aid under art.3, the condition was held to be fulfilled. The measures further complied with art.5(2)(b) Coal Regulation, the requirement imposed upon a beneficiary to draw up an operating plan and financial plan showing that the aid will ensure economic viability.

Article 6 plays a fundamental role in reducing the overall aid granted by Member States to their respective coal sectors, providing for the degression of aid. This objective is articulated in the case of the new Member States with a more detailed provision which provides that:

> "the overall amount of aid to the coal industry granted in accordance with Articles 4 and 5 shall not exceed, for any year after 2004, the amount of aid authorised by the Commission in accordance with Article 10 for the year 2004."

In this case of Poland the amount of the aid measure would not exceed the aid accepted by the Commission for the year 2004 so the principle of degression was fulfilled.

Article 8(2) of the Coal Regulation provides that the aid should be the subject of separate accounts. Poland's provision stating that aid for the beneficiary be transferred to a separate account specifically designed for this purpose by the

---

[35] Commission Decision 2002/871/EC of October 17, 2002 establishing a joint framework for the communication of information needed for the application of Council Regulation (EC) No.1407/2002 on state aid to the coal industry [2002] O.J. L300/42.

mining undertaking was one element which went towards satisfying this condition. Further, the Polish state provided that the payment of subsequent instalments would depend on the submission of a report detailing the use of the previous instalment. Under the aid proposal the mining undertakings would be required to submit to the Minister of Economy quarterly reports, annual accounts and a report on the implementation of the initial investment covered by the subsidy during the entire term of the investment.

For other examples of investment aid to coal industries see N 814/2002,[36] which involved a UK Aid scheme to cover initial investment costs to the United Kingdom coal industry. It provides an interesting method of aligning its state aid scheme with the general policy of the European Union to reduce the level of mines, whilst minimising the detrimental impact of their closure. In para.7 it provides that the criteria for eligibility for state aid is the quality of the project, explaining that this will be judged by:

14–023

"considering the number of jobs created or safeguarded, the commercial efficiency of the investment project, the job quality, the wider benefits offered to the local area and the innovation/research and development benefits of the project".

The UK scheme contained a provision which required both the production unit and the concern as owner of the production unit to be viable for the duration of the project, thereby fulfilling art.5(2)(b) of the Coal Regulation.

Current Production aid (Article 5(3) of the Coal Regulation). The 2007 Communication reported the continuance of schemes of operating aid by Bulgaria, Germany, Hungary, Romania and Spain, indicative of the fact that their national mining industries are unlikely to survive without such operating aid. The success of restructuring was deemed to be limited since the production costs were only slightly reduced, or increased, and production costs remained very high when compared with the world market price for coal.

14–024

In Commission Decision NN 20/2009[37] the Commission reviewed measures proposed by the Spanish authorities with regards to a plan for accessing coal reserves and annual state aid for their corresponding coal production. The overall support granted by Spain as current production aid amounts to €1.247 billion. The Commission verified that the aid to the coal sector covered only the difference between the production costs and revenues of the mining units. In addition to this factor, Spain continues to reduce the mining capacity of its coal industry and the relevant state subsidies as demonstrated in Table 2 of the Decision. The procedural requirements of the Regulation were also complied with. Spain had submitted a plan to the Commission for accessing coal reserves

14–025

---

[36] N814/2002 [2004] O.J. C38/4. The Commission found the aid to be compatible with Reg.1407/2002.

[37] NN 20/2009 *Aides à l'industrie charbonnière pour la période 2008–2010* [2009] O.J. C234/5. It should be noted this Decision is so far only available in Spanish.

so that the Commission could identify the set of production units which would constitute beneficiaries of the aid. Therefore the Commission concluded that the proposed aid measures respected the provisions of the Coal Regulation and deemed that they complied with the proper functioning of the internal market.

14–026 **Closure aid (Article 4 of the Coal Regulation).** All Member States have effected some mine closures, with the exception of Italy.[38] Germany, Spain and France have granted closure aid under art.4 of the Coal Regulation in order to cushion the social effects of the mine closure. In the period 2003–2006, France closed two mines, Spain closed eight production units, and committed to closing down a further nine mines by the end of 2007. Hungary also closed two mines within this period, Slovakia one, Poland three, but none of these employed closure aid.

14–027 **Restructuring of the German coal industry.** Germany's restructuring scheme for its coal mines 2006–2010 was approved by the Commission on June 22, 2005,[39] with the Commission considering the plan to be based on the following objectives which were deemed compatible with the Coal Regulation: digression of the financial aid required; reduction of production and slight reduction of production costs; ensuring supplies to customers of appropriate quality and in good time; a socially acceptable reduction in employment; and consideration of the regional impact of the measures.

14–028 In December 2009 Germany notified state aid to implement this scheme for the year 2010 in N592/09.[40] The plan provided for a reduction of the financial aid to the German hard coal mining industry from €2.6 billion in the year 2006 to €2.1 billion in 2010. The aid would cover production losses for hard coal used for the production of electricity and the fuelling of blast furnaces in the steel industry, but also exceptional costs arising or having arisen from the restructuring of the coal industry. The Commission considered the aid to be compatible with art.107(3)(e) of the TFEU.

14–029 **Aid for inherited liabilities (Article 7 of the Coal Regulation).** In the Czech Republic and France, the state continues to pay subsidies for inherited social and environmental liabilities. However, the mining undertakings still in operation do not seem to benefit from these payments. The other Member States, with the exception of Hungary and Italy, have to a certain extent inherited social and environmental costs not only for closed mines but also for mines which are still in operation.

14–030 The Report stated that the Commission had encountered five main problems in applying the state aid rules to the coal industry: the control of the criterion "no

---

[38] Commission Report on the Application of Council Regulation (EC) No.1407/2002 on State Aid to the Coal Industry, cited above.

[39] Commission decision of June 22, 2005 in N 320/2004 [2005] O.J. C228/11.

[40] N592/2009 Financing the completion of the subsidized coal industry for the year 2018 (aid for 2010) [2010] O.J. C94/7.

price distortions" (art.4(c) of the Coal Regulation); the distinction between coal covered by the regulation and coal not covered by the regulation; the reduction of production costs; the control of the categories of aid for inherited liabilities set out in the Annex of the Coal Regulation; and the control of mine closures.

Limits to the application of Regulation 1407/2002. In state aid decision **14–031**
N597/2004[41] the Commission raised no objections to the proposed aid. However, as already discussed, because of its low calorific value and classification as Coal C the product did not fall to be assessed under Regulation 1407/2002. Instead, the aid was assessed under the Guidelines on national regional aid ("the guidelines"). For more on this topic, see the Chapter on Regional Aid.

The General Court's judgment in *Gonzalez y Diez SA v Commission*[42] offered **14–032**
some useful guidance about the limits of the Coal Regulation. The Court ruled that Regulation No 1407/2002 on State aid to the coal industry may not be applied to legal situations which definitively existed before the expiry of the ECSC Treaty. Substantive rules must be interpreted, in order to ensure respect for the principles of legal certainty and protection of legitimate expectations, as applying to situations existing before their entry into force only in so far as it clearly follows from their wording, objectives or general scheme that such an effect must be given to them. The fact that by reason of the expiry of the ESCS Treaty the regulatory framework in question is no longer in force does, according to the Court not alter that situation since the assessment concerns a legal situation which was definitely established at a time when the provisions adopted under the ECSC Treaty were applicable.

The expiry of Regulation 1407/2002

In anticipation of the expiration of the Coal Regulation the Commission **14–033**
conducted a public consultation entitled "The aftermath of the expiry of Regulation (EC) No 1407/2002 on State aid to the coal industry". The stated policy objective was to minimise the possible adverse affects of mine closures that may follow a phasing out of subsidies, especially with regard to their social and environmental aspects. Following this, the Commission produced an Impact Assessment, which summarised the findings of two studies commissioned by the Commission and analysed the potential policy options available following the expiry.

The majority of respondents to the consultation favoured the prolongation of **14–034**
the state aid provisions under the previous regime, citing the necessity to support the coal sector's restructuring goals, to limit the inevitable social and regional impact of mine closures, and to ensure the security of energy by guaranteeing access to coal as an indigenous energy source. Germany spoke out in favour of

---

[41] [2005] O.J. C250/11.
[42] T–25/04 *González y Díez, SA v Commission of the European Communities* [2007] E.C.R. II–03121.

sector-specific rules which would permit state aid along with the process of mine closure until 2018, arguing this would allow all possibility of retraining and retirement options to be exhausted and the avoidance of job losses. The opponents of future coal subsidies largely cited environmental reasons, in particular submitting that the continuation of aid would have a detrimental impact on the production of energy from clean, sustainable and renewable source and disincentivise energy efficiency and savings. Moreover, it was argued that the loss of jobs in the coal mining sector would be more than offset by the resultant increase in jobs in the renewable sector.

14-035   It is clear from the document that the hard coal mines of many Member States remain uncompetitive following the expiry of the ECSC, as was already discussed in para.14–005. The study carried out by Ecorys and the Impact Assessment discussed exemplified this truth, particularly comparing the European coal production costs with the market prices.[43] The analysis showed that some Member States have economically uncompetitive coal production regimes which look set to continue in the future. The results of the analysis have largely already been discussed in para.14–005 so will not be repeated. Suffice to say that unless the price of coal rises considerably the majority of currently coal-subsidising countries will not be able to produce competitive coal.

14-036   There are estimates indicating that the price of coal in 2012 looks set to increase though exact figures vary.[44] However, what remains clear is that with an absence of subsidies some hard coal mines in the other five subsidising countries would have to cease production.

14-037   **Investment aid.** As stated, the Polish and UK governments pointed to the possibility that they might require investment aid after 2010. Respondents from the United Kingdom alluded to the significant initial costs required to access new reserves and the difficulty to obtain bank finance without a state guarantee. They also pointed out that the Regional Aid Guidelines will not always allow investment aid as the coal reserves are not necessarily located in the areas eligible for regional aid. Some respondents further highlighted the significant costs and time which may be required to adapt a coal firing power station before imported coal can be burned. The Industrial Development Agency in Poland estimated that the modernisation of Polish power stations required by a switch to imported coal would take between 15 and 20 years. The Hungarian Power Companies Ltd and Vertesi Power Plant indicated that the cessation of aid for the only Hungarian coal mine would mean its inevitable closure and that even with the modification of the plant's boilers, it would still not reach the efficiency of modern power

---

[43] See p.8 Impact Assessment, cited above.
[44] "Coal Prices to rise in 2011", Reuters, July 25, 2011. See also: *http://community.nasdaq.com/ News/2011–07/coal-prices-to-surge-in-2012.aspx?storyid=86908*; *http://uk.ibtimes.com/ articles/185867/20110724/coal-prices-to-surge-in-2012.htm. http://www.thejakartaglobe.com/ naturalresources/moodys-sees-more-growth-for-indonesian-coal-miners/474017 http://www.worldcoal.org/coal/market-amp-transportation/coal-price/.*

plants. The costs to import coal would be high with rail transport being the only option. The Reports further highlighted the spill over consequences of mine closures onto other industries, suggesting that there would be a reduction in production of mining equipment and the producers of environmental technologies needed for securing the mine and during the clean up of the mine. Furthermore, the closures would have a detrimental effect on companies creating innovations for coal mining such as mining technology, geology and environmental technology. The report also took account of the job losses due to the probable closure of the mines.

Coal subsidies: security of supply. Self sufficiency is thought of as an important   **14–038**
factor in protecting citizens against harmful disturbances, in terms of price increases or physical interruptions of international energy supply. At the forefront of the European Union's energy policy has been a drive to reduce energy dependency. The Commission's Green Paper, "Towards a European Strategy for the security of energy supply" underlined the relevance of diversification of sources of energy supply. To this end, Member States would have also to use their own internal energy sources. Exhibit 7 of the Coal Regulation states that:

> "A minimum level of coal production, together with other measures, in particular to promote renewable energy sources, will help to maintain a proportion of indigenous primary energy sources, which will significantly boost the Union's energy security. Furthermore, a proportion of indigenous primary energy sources will also serve to promote environmental objectives within the framework of sustainable development."

In the sixth Environmental Action Programme 2002–2012 the Commission   **14–039**
cites amongst the objectives "undertaking as soon as possible an inventory and review of subsidies that counteract an efficient and sustainable use of energy with a view to gradually phasing them out" and "encouraging renewable and lower carbon fossil fuel production and consumption by 2010 as set in the Strategy for Sustainable Development".

However, the validity of this factor has been called into question.[45] For   **14–040**
example, in its working document "Aftermath of the expiry of Regulation 1407/2002 on State aid to the coal industry: Impact Assessment",[46] the relevance of the security of supply argument in justifying another coal regulation is questioned. Specifically, the report points out the following in s.3.1.5:

> "Most Member States use a diverse range of fuels in the process of electricity production. Hard coal represents 18% of the EU electricity production (2006 figures), of which 42% is produced in the EU. 68% of the EU hard coal

[45] See M.Frondel, R.Kambeck, C.Schmidt, "Hard Coal Subsidies: A Never Ending Story?" RWI: Discussion Papers, November 2006.
[46] Commission Staff Working Document, "Aftermath of the expiry of Regulation 1407/2002 on State aid to the coal industry: Impact Assessment".

production receives some form of State aid under the Coal Regulation. Hence, subsidised coal serves for only 5.1% of the electricity production in the EU. When taking account only of aid to cover production losses, this figure is reduced to 1.4%. This low percentage raises serious doubts on whether the security of supply still justifies a specific instrument such as the Coal Regulation, at least at a global EU level."

14–041 The probability of disruptions in the supply of imported hard coal seems quite unlikely as the world coal market has shown greater stability than the markets for other energy sources.[47] Hard coal can also be imported from a range of other countries. Energy import dependence of Europe has experienced a fall over the last couple of decades, with the exception of Germany. If the international market consists of a sufficient number of actors and suppliers there is almost always an opportunity to switch suppliers in the case of high prices or no supply. In the same way, a local energy market that is very concentrated may well be a threat to energy security as there are no or few other optional suppliers when prices are too high or the existing suppliers reduce their output. Radetzki concludes that the international coal market is not very risky as far as energy supply is concerned; the market is well developed and competitive, there is little concentration among the suppliers, there are few political risks in the main countries involved, the freight routes are safe from military actions and the supply curve is quite flat.

14–042 Most notably, the report cited studies which suggested that stock-piling imported coal is a more effective method to assure security of supply than subsidising a domestic hard coal production.[48] The IEA does not consider there to be a realistic security of supply justification for financial assistance to indigenous producers to continue. Where member countries justify such aid on social and regional grounds, the IEA believes that there are other, more efficient, methods of targeting scarce financial resources to regions affected by the decline of the indigenous hard coal industry. In Spain and Germany, average production costs are around three times the world market price, and there would be no basis of existence for the coal industry at all, had it not been for the different types of protection and support provided from the respective states.

14–043 The Commission Decision N 178/2010[49] concerned a financial aid system initiated by Spain, which incentivised the production of electricity from domestic coal, and lent support to both Spanish power stations and those Spanish coal mines threatened by closure. Specifically, 10 electricity companies were required to buy Spanish coal and to produce a certain amount of electricity from this indigenous coal. In return for their compliance, the additional costs for implementation were to be paid by the State. The power stations also benefited from

---

[47] For example, the 2006 action taken by Russia when Russia cut off all gas supplies passing through Ukrainian territory.
[48] IEA (2002) Energy Policies of IEA Countries: Germany 2002 Review and Manuel Frondel, Rainer Kambeck, Christopher M. Shmidt (2007), Hard Coal subsisdies: a never-ending story?, Discussion Paper No 53, Rheinisch-Westfalischees Institut fur Wirtschaftsforschung.
[49] [2010] O.J. C312/6.

a "preferential dispatch mechanism". In essence, this represents a failsafe scheme for the sale of this domestically produced electricity on the market. It withdraws certain categories of energy, such as that produced from imported coal and oil, from the market and "fills the gap" with the energy produced by these select power plants. As a result, the higher priced fuel, which can be left unsold on the daily electricity market, will be sold the next day. The system essentially imposed a system consisting of financial compensation in favour of electrical energy consumption from domestic coal.

The system was formally notified to the Commission on May 12, 2010, and, following a lengthy preliminary examination, was authorised on September 29, 2010 until December 31, 2014. The Commission reasoned that the obligation imposed related to the management of a service of general economic interest (see Ch.8) and thus the state aid N178/2010 was compatible with the internal market. Of note was the submission made by the Spanish Government to the Commission in support of the scheme. It claimed that the scheme would avoid the closure of Spanish power stations that produce energy from indigenous coal, and the closure of the national coal mines due to the cessation of coal extraction activities. It also claimed that it would ameliorate some of the energy supply problems that had faced Spain due to three factors: (i) the constant increase of electricity production from renewable sources in detriment of classical sources such as coal or gas; (ii) the intermittent nature of the renewable sources caused by their natural dependence on the weather conditions; and (iii) the lack of adequate interconnection between the Spanish electric system and other European electricity markets. **14–044**

The EU electricity liberalisation directives currently in place allow a Member State, for reasons of security of supply, to impose on electricity producers public service obligations requiring them to produce their electricity from domestic fuel sources, within a limit of 15 per cent of national consumption[50]; in its assessment, the Commission deemed these conditions to be fulfilled. As part of its authorisation it drew commitments from Spain that (i) the coal which can be burned by the indigenous coal power plants under the public service obligations will originate from coal mines subject to all the rules of the future Coal Regulation, and (ii) the quantities of coal concerned will not exceed the declining production targets already set in Spain's National Coal Plan. **14–045**

Public service compensation schemes of a similar nature have been approved in the past in Spain, but also Austria, Ireland and Slovenia. In response to this authorisation, actions under art.263 TFEU were brought before the General Court requesting the annulment of the Commission's decision.[51] They further requested that interim measures be ordered to suspend the application of the Commission's decision pending the final judgment of the General Court. They also filed parallel legal actions directly against Royal Decree 134/2010 before the Spanish Supreme Court with the same purpose, though this will not be dealt with in this chapter. **14–046**

---

[50] arts 3(2) and 11(4) of the Second Electricity Market Directive (Directive 2003/54/EC) and art.3(2) and art.15(4) of the Third Electricity Market Directive (2009/72/EC), the measures of which the Member States have applied since March 2011.

[51] Endesa, Gas Natural, Iberdrola, the Autonomous Community of Galicia.

See also Commission Decision C7/2005,[52] where it endorsed support for green electricity and for security of supply in Slovenia, in line with its practice of authorising state aid aiming to achieve security of electricity supply with the use of domestic fuel.

14–047   **The options after the expiration of 1407/2002.** With these consequences in mind, the Impact Assessment[53] explored several options available to Member States under the general state aid rules for granting aid to the coal mining industry, including the complete cessation of aid, the application of the general state aid rules from 2011, the adoption of specific guidelines based on art.107(3)(c) TFEU, and the adoption by the Commission of a Council Regulation on the basis of art.107(3)(e) TFEU allowing time-limited operating aid (closure aid). These options are succinctly summarised in the summary of the findings of the Impact Assessment already discussed.[54]

14–048   Also produced was an Opinion of the European Economic and Social Committee on the "Proposal for a Council Regulation on State aid to facilitate the closure of uncompetitive coal mines". The Committee recommended the prolongation of the Regulation 1407/2002 and made various suggestions. These included, inter alia, the implementation of a mid-term check on the competitiveness of clean coal compared to the competitiveness of other EU indigenous energy sources in the 2020 perspective, the aid granted to other EU indigenous energy sources and aid supporting the use of coal on the global markets, the volatility of international fossil fuel prices and the added value for Europe of indigenous resources, as well as the costs of converting electric power stations and decommissioning disused mines. The Committee called for a mid-term report to be produced in 2015 on the competitiveness of the European coal industry. It recommended "an effective transition towards a new European sustainable energy model, with a diversified energy mix encompassing all energy sources, technology to cut emission and realistic timeframes for implementing, introducing and maintaining factors lessening its dependence on external resources".

14–049   After considerable debate, on the December 10, 2010 the European Union agreed to allow Member States to extend public aid to the coal mining industry until 2018. The final decision represents a shift from the initial stance of the Commission, which pursued a policy whereby state subsidies to the coal industry were phased out by 2014. The change was brought about through pressure of Member States such as Germany, the Czech Republic and Spain,[55] from the Economic and Monetary Affair Committee of the European Parliament and from the new Commissioner for Competition. It represents the 6th extension since 1965.

---

[52] *http://europa.eu/rapid/pressReleasesAction.do?reference=IP/07/559.*
[53] Commission Staff Working Document, "Aftermath of the expiry of Regulation 1407/2002 on State aid to the coal industry: Impact Assessment".
[54] Available at *http://eur-lex.europa.eu/LexUriServ/LexUriServ.do?uri=SEC:2010:0851:FIN: EN:PDF.* [Accessed October 14, 2011.]
[55] See the stances of Member States on coal subsidies in Annex I Impact Assessment, p.59.

Decision 2010/787 on state aid to facilitate the closure of uncompetitive coal mines

The decision represents a special state aid regime for the hard coal sector that **14–050** provides for the possibility to grant support for the closure of mines until 2018. The new regime aims to facilitate the transition to the general state aid rules applicable to all sectors that do not allow operating aid. At the time of writing, the Commission had rarely applied Decision 2010/787.

In its decision of June 29, 2011 in N175/10,[56] the Commission approved **14–051** Slovenia's plan to grant financial support in relation to the closure of the State-owned coal mine Trbovlje Hrastnik, finding there to be no conflict with European Union law. The scheme was assessed according to Regulation No.1407/2002 for the year 2010 and according to Council Decision 2010/787/EU[57] for the period from January 1, 2011 until December 31, 2015. For the latter period the aid fell within the scope of the Council Decision since the notified aid related to Trbovlje Hrastnik carrying out an activity in connection with coal production and the planned aid covers only costs connected with coal for the production of electricity, the combined production of heat and electricity, the production of coke and the fuelling of blast furnaces in the steel industry, where such use takes place in the Union.[58] The state aid was intended to enable the company to cover the costs arising from, or having arisen from, the closure of the coal production unit and which are not related to current production. Rather, the aid is intended to cover the costs of rationalisation of the mine, in accordance with art.4 of the Decision. More specifically, the aid was to be given in the context of definite closure of Trbovlje Hrastnik mine by the end of 2012 and the amounts did not exceed the relevant costs, as required by art.4(1). The Commission therefore decided to consider the aid to be compatible with the internal market for the period from January 1, 2011 until December 31, 2015 under Council Decision 2010/787/EU.

4. STATE AID IN THE STEEL INDUSTRY

State aid to the steel sector before December 31, 2002

The ECSC Treaty embodied specialist governance for state aid to the steel **14–052** sector and after its expiration the more general provisions under the Treaties apply. As was the case with coal, the steel industry went through a crisis in the 1970s and 80s, as a dramatic fall in demand for steel and structural overcapacity provoked unemployment and severe economic decline. The response was the heavy subsidisation of much of the industry. In an attempt to place more stringent

---

[56] Commission Decision N175/10, Postponement of the closure of mine Trbovlje Hrastnik Ltd [2011] O.J. C294/4.
[57] [2010] O.J. L336/24.
[58] art.2(2) of the Council Decision.

restrictions on this practice, a series of Steel Aid Codes were created. The second of these represented a significant step forward; authorising aid only in return for capacity reduction, to mitigate the structural over-capacity which constituted a major problem in this sector.[59] The third Steel Aid Code of 1985 restricted aid to the steel industry to research and development, environmental protection, closure aid and regional investment aid, and the fourth of 1989 extended these measures until 1991. The fifth[60] prolonged the possibility of aid for research and development, under the same conditions valid for the EC sectors, environmental protection and closure, but limited regional investment aid to Eastern Germany, Greece and SMEs in Portugal up until the end of 1994. These codes represented a method of ensuring fair competition in the steel sector, whilst promoting constant progress in industrial technology and environmental protection. They promoted the closure of unviable capacities under socially acceptable conditions.

14–053   Despite successful reductions in capacity, an economic slow down and remaining over capacity of, at least, 19 million tonnes caused another crisis in the steel industry in the 1990s. The Commission would now only permit the granting of aid in return for significant capacity cuts and as a last resort to render the companies economically viable. To this end, the Council authorised a series of decisions under art.95 ECSC which permitted aid to companies in Eastern Germany, Italy, Spain and Portugal. The Commission was requested to ensure a strict aid discipline based on the provisions of the Steel Aid Code to guarantee that these provisions would not have to be used in the future and to ensure the continuing reduction in capacity. After finding that the capacity reduction was insufficient, the Commission decided in 1995 to withdraw some of the measures to support the restructuring of the EU steel industry. The Commission published two Communications outlining the restructuring: "Fresh Impetus for Restructuring the Steel Industry"[61] and "Restructuring the Community Steel Industry: final assessment and Conclusions".[62]

14–054   We have already seen that art.4(c) of the ECSC Treaty prohibits state aid under normal circumstances. However, the sixth and final Code[63] was created under art.95 ECSC to give aid to the iron and steel industries in severe economic difficulties. Adopted in 1996, for the years 1997–2002, it powerfully restricts the conditions under which state aids are permitted, allowing aid only for research, the promotion of the environment or the closure of companies and, moreover, requires the Commission to draw up annual reports on its implementation.[64] For an interesting reflection on state aid to the Steel industry through the ECSC

---

[59] On this point see A. Shaub, "State aid in the ECSC steel sector", EC Competition Policy Newsletter, Vol.3 No.2, 1997.

[60] Commission Decision No.3855/91/ECSC of November 27, 1991 establishing Community rules for aid to the steel industry [1991] O.J. L362/57.

[61] COM (94) 265.

[62] COM (94) 466.

[63] Commission Decision No.2496/96 ECSC of December 18, 1996 establishing Community rules for state aid to the steel industry [1996] O.J. L338/42.

[64] See, for example, Report from the Commission, Monitoring of art.95 ECSC Steel Aid cases, Fourteenth Report, October 2000, Com (2000) 685 Final.

Treaty, see Humbert Drabbe's speech at European Steel Forum II, on November 10, 2000.[65]

In respect of state aid authorised by the Commission under the Sixth Steel Aid **14–055**
Code or art.95 ECSC Treaty subject to conditions, the Commission has continued to monitor their fulfilment even after July 23, 2002. In case of non-compliance, art.108 TFEU will be applicable. When the aid was notified on or before December 31, 2001 and the Commission in principle initiated the procedure of art.6(5) Steel Aid Code, it would attempt to give a decision by July 23, 2002 on the basis of the information available to it. If this is not possible, for objective reasons, the Commission continues the investigation under Regulation (EC) 659/1999 and adopts a final decision under art.108(2) TFEU.

The Salzgitter case. The Commission, in June 2000, initially approved €19.1 **14–056**
million worth of state aid to be granted by Germany to Salzgitter AG.[66] The aid was designed to allow Salzgitter to produce steel utilising a highly innovative process called Direct Strip casting, which results in less energy consumption than the alternatives. The aid conformed to the EU Environmental Guidelines (see Ch.22) because the positive effects on the environment from its usage largely outweigh potential distortions of competition. In its decision the Commission found that the aid was necessary and proportionate to develop the project. The Commission found that the HSD production would account for less than 1 per cent of Salzgitter's current sales and that the effect on competition would therefore be very limited. At the same time, certain depreciation allowances and tax-free reserves of which Salzgitter had been the recipient were found to be incompatible state aid. The Commission ordered recovery. Salzgitter appealed the decision to the General Court, which partly annulled the decision. The Commission appealed to the Court of Justice.

The ECJ in its judgment considered that the General Court was correct to **14–057**
apply art.4 of the ECSC Treaty in this case[67] as opposed to art.67 of the ECSC Treaty as was submitted. Article 4 provides for the abolition and prohibition of state aid measures that are incompatible with the common market for coal and steel. Article 67 allows Member States to take general, preventative measures in case action by member states in areas other than coal and steel are capable of having significant repercussions on the conditions of competition in those industries. The Court held that action taken under art.67 could not comprise of measures that were prohibited by art.4 and that art.4 would act to prohibit state aid granted to a coal and steel company, even if the aid were granted under a scheme that was not specific to the coal and steel sector. In this respect, assessing a cross-appeal by Salzgitter, the ECJ decided that the General Court was right in finding that the aid did not constitute protective measures under art.67(2) and that

[65] Available at *http://ec.europa.eu/competition/speeches/text/sp2000_020_en.pdf*. [Accessed August 22, 2011.]
[66] N 451/2009, Energy saving by strip casting technology for light steels of Salzgitter Flachstahl GmbH [2010] O.J. C154/2.
[67] C–408/04P *Salzgitter AG* [2008] E.C.R. I–02767.

the Commission was entitled to hold that art.4 and not art.67 applied to the aid.

14–058   The General Court had also held that the adoption of the Second and Third Steel Aid Codes amounted to a partial withdrawal of the 1971 Commission decision not to object to the tax scheme concerned which related to various sectors and had been notified under the EU Treaty. This had created legal uncertainty as to whether the subsequent application of the aid scheme had to be notified as a "plan" under the Third Code. In its judgment, the ECJ reiterates that the ECSC Treaty and the EC Treaty are independent treaties. The EC Treaty cannot produce effects in areas that fall within the scope of the ECSC Treaty and the provisions of the EC Treaty will only apply in the alternative in situations in which there is no specific rule under the ECSC Treaty. As a consequence, given that the Third Steel Aid Code prohibited both aid that was and aid that was not specific to the steel sector, the Commission could not implicitly withdraw the 1971 decision made under the EC Treaty.

14–059   The ECJ, therefore, allowed the Commission's appeal and set aside the General Court's decision, which annulled the Commission's order for recovery of the aid. The case has, therefore, been referred back to the General Court for it to rule on the question of whether the Commission manifestly failed to act and breached its duty of diligence.

State aid to the steel sector after December 31, 2002

14–060   Steel is one of the European Union's largest industries and steel demand is likely to continue over the next decade. According to the EUROFER (the European Confederation of Iron and Steel Industries), the European Union produces approximately 200 million tonnes of steel per year, representing approximately 15–16 per cent of the world's steel output,[68] showing the European Union to be the second largest steel producer in the world.[69] As such it remains a key sector for economic growth and competitiveness in Europe and plays a crucial role in the main industrial sectors. The European Union views it as imperative, therefore, that competition is maintained. Although the steel industry experienced a severe downturn in line with the global recession in 2009, according to data for activity in the EU steel-using industries, Q4–2010 output growth increased 8.3 per cent. EUROFER also declared that business activity within the steel sector has improved in the first quarter of 2011.[70]

14–061   With the expiration of the ECSC Treaty on July 23, 2002, there are three documents which create the framework for state aid to the steel sector: Rescue

---

[68] See also the data available in the Steel Statistical Yearbooks of the World Steel Organisation, available at *http://www.worldsteel.org/statistics/statistics-archive.html*. [Accessed October 18, 2011.]

[69] See *http://www.ec.europa.eu/trade/creating-opportunities/economic-sectors/industrial-goods/steel/*. [Accessed October 18, 2011.]

[70] See *www.eurofer.org/index.php/eng/ . . . /Market%20Report-2011-April.pdf*, see also *http://www.eurofer.org/index.php/eng/Issues-Positions/Economic-Development-Steel-Market*   [Accessed October 13, 2011].

and restructuring aid and Closure aid, Regional aid for large investment projects, Multisectoral frameworks and Commission communication on the modification of the Multisectoral framework. Regional investment aid is prohibited, including the granting of regional aid to SMEs. The Community guidelines on state aid for environmental protection establish the conditions for authorising the granting of state aid for the purposes of environmental protection. These guidelines are applicable until December 31, 2014 and are discussed in more detail in Ch.22. Research and Development aid is permitted in accordance with the provisions of the Community Framework for state aids for research and development.[71] Undertakings in the steel industry may benefit from state aid for training, employment, environmental protection, and research and development as well as from de minimis aid. Small and medium-sized enterprises in the steel industry may benefit from aid for SMEs at aid rates of up to 15 per cent and 7.5 per cent respectively under the Commission "Block Exemption" Regulation for SMEs, but not from the higher rates otherwise available in art.107(3)(a) areas and art.107(3)(c) areas. The Commission will not approve large grants for investment not exempted by that regulation.

Rescue and Restructuring aid and Closure aid for the steel sector

After the expiration of the ECSC Treaty the EC published the Communication **14–062** from the Commission on Rescue and Restructuring aid and closure aid for the steel sector, which codified the desire for stricter rules on state aid to the steel sector. It applied from July 24, 2002 until December 31, 2009, after which the more general Lisbon Treaty rules apply. The Communication pinpoints investment aid and rescue and restructuring aid as two categories producing the most distortive effects on competition in the steel industry. As a consequence, rescue and restructuring aid was categorically prohibited in art.1, whilst closure aid was deemed permissible only under the specific conditions detailed below. The Communication also highlights the prohibition of investment aid to the steel sector as prescribed by the revised multisectoral framework for large investment projects.[72]

In its Communication, the Commission, noting the inefficiencies in and over- **14–063** capacity of the steel industry, states that aid to facilitate structural adjustment can contribute to the development of a healthier steel industry. In this respect it regards certain closure aid as compatible with the internal market and as permitted by art.107(3) TFEU. Article 2.1 permits aid to cover payments payable by

---

[71] The Community Framework for State aids for research and development (R&D) [1996] O.J C45/5.

[72] For more information see Ch.15 on the Multisectoral Framework on regional aid for large investment projects. The Commission began an investigation under art.108(2) TFEU into proposed aid to Dunaferr, a Hungarian steel producer, notified to the Commission on the basis of the Multisectoral Framework on regional aid for large investment projects. However the investigation was closed after Dunaferr decided not to avail itself of the tax relief. Commission press release IP/08/1232.

steel companies to workers made redundant or early retired provided that: the payments are a genuine consequence of the partial or total closure of steel plants which have not already been taken into account for approval of aid; they do not exceed those customarily granted under the rules of the Member States; and the aid does not exceed 50 per cent of those payments.

14–064   Article 2.2 further provides that aid to steel firms that permanently cease the production of steel products may be considered compatible with the internal market where: the steel firms became legal entities before January 1, 2002; they regularly produced steel products before the date of notification of the given aid; they have not reorganised their production or plant structure since January 1, 2002; they close and scrap the installations used to manufacture steel products within six months of the cessation of production or approval of the aid by the Commission, whichever is the later; the closure of their plants has not already been taken into account for approval of aid; and the amount of the aid does not exceed the residual book value of the plants, ignoring that portion of any revaluation since January 1, 2002 which exceeds the national inflation rate.

5. State Aid for Coal and Steel in the New Member States

14–065   One of the most significant changes following the expiry of the ECSC was the accession of new Member States in 2004. In the context of accession, negotiations on the Competition Chapter difficulties arose, especially with regards to the sensitive coal and steel sectors. It was clear that the integration of these new steel industries to market conditions would require restructuring. The European Union therefore negotiated transitional arrangements with three candidate countries: the Czech Republic, Poland and Slovakia. These periods would permit them with a final opportunity to restructure their steel industries, provided that they achieved certain productivity levels after the restructuring and carried out a pre-determined reduction of excess production capacities. The rules are an exception to the rule that restructuring aid for the steel sector is prohibited and are *lex specialis* to the normal transitional rules in the accession Treaty.[73]

14–066   This section will not provide an exhaustive description of the steel state aid issues arising in the context of accession of new Member States to the European Union. Rather, it will briefly explain the relevant state aid provisions before examining some of the case law in this area which relates mostly to the accession of Poland, Romania and the Czech Republic. Following on from that, issues related to the accession of Turkey to the European Union will be examined. More detail can be found in Ch.5.

14–067   The Commission determined in its fourth and final steel monitoring report of 2009 that both the Czech Republic and Poland had met their obligations under

---

[73] Steel restructuring aids were not subject to the "existing aid mechanism" under the Accession Treaty. This was deemed to be the case in the Commission Decision relating to Czech steel producer Trinecke, [2005] O.J. C22/2.

Protocols 2 and 8 to the Treaty of Accession respectively.[74] This final monitoring report supplemented the previous Commission reports and assessed the results achieved in 2006, the last year of the transitional period, taking into account the relevant information made available in 2007 and 2008. In their assessment the monitoring reports focus heavily on capacity reduction, but other restructuring benchmarks such as viability and financial performance, productivity and employment, cost reduction, investments and environmental protection are also considered.

Czech Republic

In short, the Commission found in respect of the Czech Republic that the **14–068** overall amount of state aid granted to beneficiary companies for restructuring purposes was CZK 8.3 billion, so 59 per cent of the Protocol ceiling of CZK 14.15 billion. This aid was granted until the end of 2003. The Commission concluded that, lower than foreseen, the amount of aid actually being granted had no adverse effect on the financial performance of the companies. The Protocol proscribed the granting of restructuring aid to companies not included in the National Restructuring Programme.[75] The Commission initiated an investigation into Trinecke, a Czech steel company not covered by the Protocol, but determined that it had not been awarded any illegal state aid.[76]

Poland

Protocol No.8 provides derogation from the EU state aid rules, which provide **14–069** that restructuring aid may not be granted to the steel industry. It allows for the granting of state aid to eight companies from 1997 to 2003, up to a maximum of about PLN 3.4 billion. In exchange for this, Poland committed to cut more than 1 million tonnes of production capacity. The Commission considers Protocol 8 as the legal basis for the assessment of steel state aid cases between 1997 and 2006, including aid granted before accession.

The grace period for granting restructuring aid to the Polish steel industry **14–070** under the Europe Agreement was extended by the Council until the accession of Poland to the European Union. This arrangement was included in Protocol No.8 to the Treaty of Accession to the European Union. In order to achieve that objective, it covers a time-frame extending before and after accession. More precisely, it authorises the award of a limited amount of restructuring aid from

---

[74] Report from the Commission to the Council and the European Parliament, Fourth monitoring Report on steel restructuring in the Czech Republic and Poland, COM(2009) O141 final available at *http://eur-lex.europa.eu/LexUriServ/LexUriServ.do?uri=COM:2009:0141:FIN: EN:HTML*. [Accessed October 20, 2011].

[75] Three companies were included: Ispat Nova Hut, now Mittal Steel Ostrava (MSO), Valcovny Plechu Fridek-Mystek (VPFM) and Vitkovice Steel (VS), together representing a share of 57% of the Czech crude steel production.

[76] Commission Decision of September 8, 2006 on state aid C 45/04 (ex. NN 62/04) in favour of the Czech steel producer Třinecké železárny a.s. [2007] O.J. L119/37.

1997 to 2003 and forbids any further state aid for restructuring purposes to the Polish steel industry between 1997 and 2006. In that respect, it clearly differs from other provisions of the Accession Treaty such as the interim mechanism set out in Annex IV (the "existing aid procedure"), which only concerns state aid awarded before accession in so far as it is "still applicable after" the date of accession. Protocol No.8 can therefore be regarded as *lex specialis* which, for the matters that it covers, supersedes any other provision of the Act of Accession.

14-071   The beneficiary companies covered by Protocol 8 represented 70 per cent of Poland's crude steel production. The Commission opined that Poland had abided by its Protocol obligations on state aid, by paying PLN 2.73 billion of restructuring aid, 82 per cent of the maximum of PLN 3.38 billion. This aid was also granted before the end of 2003 in accordance with the Protocol. The assessment also showed that the reduced amount had no negative impact on the financial performance of the companies. Similar to the Czech case, state aid provided to Polish steel companies mainly focused on financial restructuring. The net capacity reduction to be achieved by Poland for finished products during the period 1997–2006 was established at 1,231,000 tonnes. On the basis of the information provided, the Commission concluded that all closures were executed in line with the approved plans.

14-072   In Case C–369/09 *ISD Polska*, the ECJ upheld the decision of the General Court[77] when it dismissed an annulment action on state aid in favour of the steel producer Huta. In its judgment it agreed with the reasoning of the General Court; namely that the purpose of Protocol No.8 is to establish a comprehensive system for the authorisation of aid intended for the restructuring of the Polish steel industry and not merely to avoid the aggregation of aid by benefiting companies. As a result the General Court was entitled to dismiss the argument of Poland that Protocol 8 should be interpreted as only covering that period between the date of its publication, in September 2003, and December 31, 2003, an argument which calls into question the retroactive effect of Protocol No.8. The applicants submitted that the element of retroactivity in the protocol was the reference to the period 1997–2003, concerning either the total amount of the state aid which may be granted (point 6 of Protocol No.8) or the net reduction of capacity which the Republic of Poland must achieve (point 7 of the protocol). That meant that the calculation of future aid to be allocated to the beneficiary undertakings up to the end of 2003 was to be done not by retrospectively regarding the aid approved as being, in certain cases, unlawful, but by taking account retrospectively of the amounts of aid already allocated. The ECJ upheld the General Court's ruling; that Protocol No.8 represents a *lex specialis* in relation to Annex IV to the Act of Accession and arts 107 and 108 TFEU, which extended the power of the Commission to monitor aid granted in favour of the Polish steel industry during the period 1997–2003.[78]

---

[77] Joined Cases T–273/06 and T–297/06 *ISD Polska sp. z o.o. and Others v Commission of the European Communities* [2009] E.C.R. II–02181.
[78] Case C–369/09P [2011] judgment of March 24, 2011, at para.10.3.

In its Decision C23/2006[79] the Commission provided further guidance regarding the scope of Protocol 8. It noted that the scope of the Polish NRP and Protocol No.8 is not limited to that of Annex 1 of the ECSC Treaty, instead ruling that it also covers certain steel sectors[80] not covered by the ECSC Treaty,[81] in particular seamless tubes and large welded tubes. This ambit is in accordance with the definition of steel under the EU State Aid rules[82] which applied when Protocol No.8 came into effect. Above all, it follows from the scope of the NRP, which Protocol No.8 implements. Although arts 107 and 108 TFEU would normally not apply to aid awarded before accession and not applicable after accession, Protocol No.8 extends state aid monitoring under the EU Treaty to cover any aid awarded for the restructuring of the Polish steel industry between 1997 and 2006. On May 17, 2011 the General Court[83] upheld an appeal by Buczek Automotive and annulled a decision of the European Commission requiring recovery of state aid granted to the Polish steel producer Technologie Buczek Group. Under the Polish national restructuring programme, Technologie Buczek SA was authorised to receive approximately €4 million of state aid but the Commission had found that restructuring aid of €0.35 million received by Technologie Buczek Group in 2003 had been misused and should be recovered. The General Court decided that the Commission had not provided sufficient reasons or analysis to support its conclusion that the Polish authorities had not acted like a private creditor in the way which it sought to recover public debts from the company. Therefore, the Commission had not demonstrated that the advantage that the company enjoyed (through not being made bankrupt in order to recover public debts) constituted aid. This judgment is currently set for appeal as case number C–405/11P. **14–073**

Slovakia

Protocol 2 of the Europe Agreement with Slovakia is the same as those of Poland and the Czech Republic. It provides that state aid for the restructuring of the steel sector could only be granted during the grace period, which expired in March 1997. Unlike Poland and the Czech Republic, Slovakia did not request an extension. **14–074**

Romania

Transitional arrangements in respect of restructuring aid were made so that Romania could complete the restructuring of its steel industry, in line with the **14–075**

---

[79] Commission Decision on state aid C23/2006, which Poland implemented for steel producer Technologie Buzek Group.

[80] See para.74 of C23/2006 on State Aid C 23/06 (ex. NN 35/06), which Poland has implemented for steel producer Technologie Buczek Group [2008] O.J. L116/26. Decision of July 5, 2005 in case C20/2004 *Huta Czestochowa* [2006] O.J. L366/1.

[81] See [1998] O.J. C320/3.

[82] See Annex B to the Multisectoral Framework (O.J. C70, March 19, 2002, p.8), which was replaced by Annex I to the Guidelines on national regional aid for 2007–2013 [2006] O.J. C54/13.

[83] T–1/08, [2011] judgment of May 17, 2011.

Treaty of Accession.[84] Article 9(4) of Protocol 2 annexed to the Association Agreement allowed the approval of rescue and restructuring aid for the steel sector for five years from the entry into force of the agreement, provided that it complied with the following conditions:

- aid should be given in relation to a feasible restructuring plan, restoring the economic viability of the beneficiary;

- the amount of the aid given should be limited to what is strictly necessary in order to restore the beneficiary's viability;

- the support to any given beneficiary should be progressively reduced;

- the aided restructuring plan should include measures of rationalisation and reduction of excessive production capacities.

14–076 Annex VII of the Protocol to the Treaty of Accession provides for a maximum amount of aid which can be granted to Romanian steel companies and contains an absolute prohibition on aid granted to any steel company which is not listed in Appendix A to Annex VII.

14–077 However, it was only allowed to grant state aid for the purpose of restructuring under the conditions that it would lead to improved viability of the recipient firms under normal market conditions at the end of the restructuring period, the amount and intensity of the aid was strictly limited to what was absolutely necessary in order to achieve such viability, and the total net capacity reduction would be at least 2.05 million tonnes (finished products). The Commission examined the abidance with these conditions in its monitoring reports, referring to years, 2006, 2007 and 2008.

14–078 The aid was granted largely for the purpose of financial restructuring and for certain tax exemptions, with the amounts being determined on the basis of the already approved National Restructuring Programme and the Individual Business Plans, in which investment played a central role in reducing costs and improving the quality of finished products. Most of the amount was granted in 2003 and 2004. No further aid was granted or paid after 2004, either to listed companies or to any other steel producer in Romania. The Commission therefore concluded that Romania had complied with its obligations on state aid. In addition Appendix A of Annex VII to the Treaty of Accession required several production facilities to be closed and these closures were effected in line with the provisions of Decision 3010/91.[85] The last monitoring report concluded that the requirements of Annex VII to the Treaty of Accession had been met.[86]

---

[84] Protocol concerning the conditions and arrangements for admission of the republic of Bulgaria and Romania to the European Union [2005] O.J. L157/29.

[85] Commission Decision No.3010/91/ECSC of October 15, 1991 on the information to be furnished by steel undertakings about their investments [1991] O.J. L286/20.

[86] COM/2010/0476 final Report from the Commission to the European Parliament and the Council, Third Monitoring report on steel restructuring in Romania.

Turkey

The progress of Turkey in joining the European Union is under review by the **14–079** Council, based on the Commission's Progress Reports. The Commission issued its latest Annual Progress Report on November 9, 2010,[87] in which it stated that "little progress was made on State aid to the steel sector". It said that "formal verification of the steel industry restructuring programme by the state aid monitoring authority is called for once that authority is established." State practices in support of this sector made between 2001 and 2006 need to be finally assessed. No further developments can be reported in the national restructuring programme for the Turkish steel industry following the revision made last year. Formal verification of the steel industry restructuring programme by the state aid monitoring authority is called for once that authority is established.

6. CONCLUDING REMARKS

The process of restructuring the coal industry has been going on for decades **14–080** and should finally come to an end in 2018. According to estimates of the International Energy Agency (IEA), coal will have the same importance as oil for the world-wide supply of energy until 2030. State aid is likely to play a much greater role in ensuring cleaner carbon technologies such as Carbon Capture and Storage (CCS). In its Decision N 74/2009[88] the Commission considered that aid used to conduct front end engineering and feasibility studies (FEED-studies) on two industrial-scale CCS demonstration projects was compatible with art.107(3)(c) TFEU, as it was proportionate and contained safeguard minimising potential distortions of competition.[89]

Aid to the steel sector will be scrutinised under the general provisions of the Treaty of the Functioning of the European Union. The categories of state aid permissible to the steel sector were severely curtailed by the Communication from the Commission on rescue and restructuring aid and closure aid for the steel sector. Inefficiencies remain within the sector and it seems unlikely that the granting of state aid in this sector will become commonplace.

---

[87] Turkey 2010 Progress Report accompanying the Communication from the Commission to the European Parliament and the Council-Enlargement Strategy and Main Challenges 2010–2011, COM(2010) 660.

[88] N74/2009 [2009] O.J. C203/2.

[89] See also the Commission's Decision in N381/2010 in which the Commission approves €150 million aid for carbon capture and storage project in The Netherlands [2011] O.J. C149/3.

CHAPTER 15

REGIONAL INVESTMENT AID TO LARGE INVESTMENT PROJECTS: THE RULES UNDER THE STATE AID ARCHITECTURE FOR 2007–2013*

1. INTRODUCTION 15–001
2. THE DEFINITIONS AND PROCEDURAL AND COMPATIBILITY ASSESSMENT RULES APPLICABLE TO REGIONAL AID FOR LARGE INVESTMENT PROJECTS 15–004
   Definition of large investment project 15–004
   Increased transparency requirements for large investment projects 15–005
   Individual notification requirement 15–006
   Compatibility assessment of regional investment aid exceeding the individual notification threshold within the preliminary investigation phase 15–007
   Filters for in-depth assessment 15–009
   Formal investigation and in-depth assessment 15–013
3. THE COMMISSION'S EXPERIENCE IN THE APPLICATION OF THE RULES REGARDING REGIONAL AID TO LARGE INVESTMENT PROJECTS UNDER THE REGIONAL AID GUIDELINES 2007–2013 15–025
   The empirical evidence 15–025
   The experience in applying the rules 15–027
4. CONCLUSIONS AND OUTLOOK 15–033

1. INTRODUCTION

15–001   Regional aid was one of the first fields in which the Commission exerted state aid control, by adopting, until the mid-nineties, a multitude of separate rules.[1] These rules were only codified in 1998 by the Regional Aid Guidelines 1998 (RAG 1998),[2] as part of the first comprehensive reform of state aid rules. This first reform included, in particular, the adoption of the Council 1998 Procedural

---

* Klaus-Otto Junginger-Dittel
[1] For an overview of the evolution of regional state aid control, see P. Olofsson, "L'évolution de la politique des aides à finalité régionale 1956–2004", Competition Policy Newsletter 2005, Nr 3. The key texts adopted were the Council Resolution of October 20, 1971, O.J. C111, p.1, the 1979 Commission communication to the Member States on Coordinating Principles, O.J. C31, p.9, and the 1988 Commission communication to the Member States on the method for the application of art.92(3)(a) and (c) to national regional aid, O.J. C212, p.2.
[2] Guidelines on national regional aid (O.J. C074 , 10/03/1998P 0009–0018).

Regulation,[3] the Council 1998 Enabling Regulation,[4] and the replacement (in principle) of several sector specific texts on regional aid to so called sensitive sectors (e.g. cars,[5] synthetic fibres[6]), with a Multisectoral Framework[7] containing rules applicable to regional investment aid to large investment projects in all sectors.

The 1998 Multisectoral Framework was replaced in 2002 by the 2002 Multisectoral Framework,[8, 9] which was amended in 2003.[10]

In December 2005, the Commission adopted (in principle) the Regional Aid **15–002** Guidelines 2007–2013 (RAG).[11] The RAG entered into force on January 1, 2007, and give an interpretation of arts 107(3)(a) and (c) TFEU. They contain, amongst other things,[12] compatibility criteria for the assessment of the different types of regional aid. The provisions of the 2002 Multisectoral Framework on regional aid to large investment projects were integrated, largely unchanged,[13] into the RAG (s.4.3).

Key rules regarding regional investment laid down in the RAG were also taken over in the 2006 Commission Regional Aid Block Exemption Regulation (RAG BER)[14] which was superseded[15] by the 2008 General Block Exemption Regulation (GBER).[16] These regulations were adopted on the basis of the Council

---

[3] Council Regulation No.659/1999 of March 22, 1999 laying down detailed rules for the application of art.93 (now art.108 TFEU) of the EC Treaty, O.J. L83/1, March 27, 1999, pp.1–9.

[4] Council Regulation (EC) No.994/98 of May 7, 1998 on the application of arts 92 and 93 (now 107 and 108 TFEU) of the Treaty establishing the European Community to certain categories of horizontal state aid, O.J. L142, May 14, 1998, pp.1–4.

[5] Community framework on state aid to the motor vehicle industry (O.J. C279, September 15, 1997, p.1).

[6] Code on aid to the synthetic fibres industry (O.J. C94, March 30, 1996, p.11).

[7] 1998 Multisectoral Framework on regional aid for large investment projects (O.J. C107, April 7, 1998, p.7).

[8] Multisectoral Framework on regional aid for large investment projects (O.J. C70, March 19, 2002, pp.8–20).

[9] For an analysis of the Multisectoral Framework 2002 see S. Cavallo and K. Junginger-Dittel, "The Multisectoral Framework 2002: new rules on regional aid to large investment projects", in Competition Policy Newsletter, No.1 Spring, 2004, p.78.

[10] Commission communication on the modification of the Multisectoral Framework on regional aid for large investment projects (2002) with regard to the establishment of a list of sectors facing structural problems and on a proposal of appropriate measures pursuant to art.88 para.1 of the EC Treaty, concerning the motor vehicle sector and the synthetic fibres sector (O.J. C263, November 1, 2003, pp.3–4).

[11] Guidelines on National Regional Aid For 2007–2013 , O.J. C54, March 4, 2006.

[12] For a full description of the RAG see M.Dittel and K.Junginger-Dittel, Ch.10, "Regional State Aid", in Erika Szyszczak (ed.), *Research Handbook on European State Aid Law*, 2011.

[13] For an overview of the changes made between the 2002 Multisectoral Framework and the rules applicable to large investment projects under the RAG see M. Dittel and K. Junginger-Dittel, L. Hancher, T. Ottervanger and P. Jan Slot (eds), *EC State Aids*, 3rd edn (London, 2006), Ch.14: "The Multisectoral Framework 2002 and its successor rules under the Regional Aid Guidelines 2007–2013: Regional investment aid to (very) large investment projects", p.344.

[14] Commission Regulation (EC) No.1628/2006 of October 24, 2006 on the application of arts 87 and 88 (now 107 and 108) of the Treaty to national regional investment aid, O.J. L302, November 1, 2006, p.29.

[15] Aid schemes that were block exempted under the RAG BER continue to be block exempted pursuant to art.9(2) of the RAG BER until the date of expiry of the approved regional aid maps.

[16] Commission Regulation (EC) No.800/2008 of August 6, 2008 declaring certain categories of aid

Enabling Regulation which introduced the possibility[17] to exempt certain types of aid, including regional aid,[18] under certain conditions from the notification obligation laid down in art.108(3) TFEU.

The compatibility criteria for the assessment of the regional aid to large investment projects laid down in the RAG were complemented in 2009 by the Commission Communication on the in-depth assessment of regional aid to large investment projects (IDAC).[19]

15–003 Today, the general architecture of state aid rules in the area of regional aid is composed of the RAG, the RAG BER, the GBER, and the IDAC. The RAG BER and the GBER exclude regional aid to large investment projects as from a certain threshold of aid from their scope of application; hence only the RAG and the IDAC have a bearing on the assessment of individually notifiable aid to large investment projects. Below the notification threshold, Member States have to respect certain *ex post* information obligations, already laid down in the RAG, and reflected in the BERS, but otherwise aid to large investment can be granted by the Member State concerned on the basis of notified and approved or block exempted aid schemes, within the limits of the approved regional aid map (including regional aid intensity ceilings).

This chapter firstly presents the definitions and rules of relevance for aid to large investment projects. A second section presents the Commission experience in the application of these rules over the last four and a half years. The last section offers an outlook for the period after 2007.

2. The Definitions and Procedural and Compatibility Assessment Rules Applicable to Regional Aid for Large Investment Projects

Definition of large investment project

15–004 Large investment projects are defined by para.60 of the RAG as investment projects with eligible expenditure exceeding €50 million, calculated at prices and exchange rates applicable on the date the aid is granted or notified.[20] The eligible

---

compatible with the common market in application of arts 87 and 88 of the Treaty, L214, August 9, 2008.

[17] This possibility was applied for the first time in 2001 for regional investment aid in the 2001 Commission SME exemption regulation (Commission Regulation No.70/2001 of January 12, 2001 on the application of arts 87 and 88 (107 and 108) of the EC Treaty to state aid to small and medium-sized enterprises) O.J. L10, January 13, 2001, pp.33–42); its recital 2 explicitly refers to regional aid.

[18] Article 1(b) of the Council Enabling Regulation allows the Commission to adopt exemption regulations for, and to declare as compatible "aid that complies with the map approved by the Commission for each Member State for the grant of regional aid".

[19] Communication from the Commission concerning the criteria for the in-depth assessment of regional aid to large investment projects, O.J. C223, September 16, 2009, pp.3–10.

[20] See also arts 2(1)(g) RAG BER and 2(12) GBER (which limits the definition to capital costs).

expenditure to be taken into account in this context is defined either in reference to material and immaterial investment costs resulting from the initial investment project, or with regard to estimated wage costs for jobs directly created by the investment project,[21] whichever is higher.[22]

The RAG specify that, in addition, the "single investment project" (SIP) rule applies, according to which all initial investment projects which consist of fixed assets combined in an economically indivisible way, and which are undertaken by one or more companies in a period of three years are considered to be one single investment project. To verify whether several projects are economically indivisible, account is taken of their technical, functional and strategic links and their immediate geographic proximity.[23]

Increased transparency requirements for large investment projects

Paragraph 65 of the RAG[24] stipulates that Member States have to inform[25] the **15–005** Commission of the granting of any aid to regional investment projects that was not individually notifiable within 20 days of the granting of the aid. The Commission verifies that the aid was granted in line with the provisions of the applied aid scheme and publishes the information on its website.[26]

Individual notification requirement

According to para.68 of the RAG,[27] regional investment aid exceeding a **15–006** certain threshold has to be notified individually, even if it is granted on the basis of an aid scheme. This threshold depends on the standard regional aid ceiling[28] applicable to large undertakings in the region where the investment is to be carried out, and amounts to 75 per cent of the aid amount an investment with

---

[21] See RAG, para.36, and arts 2(1)(e),(f), (k)–(m) RAG BER and 2(10)–(11) and (13)–(15) GBER.

[22] In accordance with para.51 of the RAG, the cost of preparatory studies and consultancy costs linked to an investment by a SME are also eligible, with a maximum aid intensity of 50% of the costs incurred.

[23] In many notified cases the Commission had to establish whether the project for which aid was notified, did constitute a single investment project with an earlier also aided investment project. In several cases the Commission opened the formal investigation to clarify the issue, e.g. in the *Sovello* case (C21/2008, Germany), which was still decided under the slightly different rules of the Multisectoral Framework; and in the *Deutsche Solar* case (C34/2008).

[24] See also arts 8(1) RAG BER and 9(4) GBER.

[25] Standard summary information form.

[26] About 50 to 100 summary information sheets are submitted to the Commission under this transparency mechanism per year. For a more detailed analysis, see Leen de Vreese, "Transparency system for large regional investment projects", in Competition Policy Newsletter 2007–3.

[27] See also arts 7(e) RAG BER and 6(2) GBER.

[28] The standard regional aid ceiling is the aid intensity ceiling defined in a regional aid map for investment projects with eligible expenditure below €50 million. The regional aid maps foresee also adjusted aid intensity ceilings (scaling down) for eligible expenditure exceeding €50 million. The threshold for individual notification corresponds to the maximum aid amount an investment project with eligible expenditure of €100 million could receive if the adjusted aid intensity ceiling was fully applied.

eligible expenditure of €100 million could receive if the standard regional aid ceiling was applicable to the whole amount of €100 million.

Compatibility assessment of regional investment aid exceeding the individual notification threshold within the preliminary investigation phase

15–007 Where aid exceeds the notification threshold, it has to be approved individually by the Commission. It can be approved within the preliminary investigation phase if it meets all the standard compatibility criteria laid down in the RAG, provided it is not filtered out for in-depth assessment by the so-called 68(a) ("market share") and 68(b) ("capacity increase in an underperforming market") tests.

15–008 **Standard compatibility criteria for investment aid.** The standard compatibility criteria as laid down in the RAG[29] apply to all investment aid, whatever the envisaged aid amount. They are summarised in the table below:

Table 1: Summary of standard compatibility criteria

Initial investment (paras 34 and 35 of the RAG)	The aid has to support an initial investment. An initial investment is defined as an investment in material and immaterial assets relating to: — the setting up of a new establishment; — the extension of an existing establishment; — diversification of the output of an establishment into new additional products; — a fundamental change in the overall production process of an existing establishment; and — the acquisition of assets directly linked to an establishment provided the establishment has closed, or would have closed had it not been taken over by a new and independent investor.[30]

---

[29] For individually notifiable aid which is excluded from the scope of application of the RAG BER, respectively the GBER, as well as for ad hoc aid, all compatibility assessment is done on the basis of the RAG.

[30] The notion of establishment is not explicitly defined by the RAG 2007–13, but understood as a production site belonging to an enterprise, and distinct from the legal entity of an enterprise. In the context of a single investment project an establishment may also be operated by several enterprises.

Neither replacement investment, nor the sole acquisition of the shares of the legal entity qualify as "initial investment" (see RAG, fnn.36 and 37). In practice, it is sometimes difficult to define the limits between a fundamental modernisation and replacement investment, since most replacement of equipment involves assets which allow a higher production efficiency, or need less energy, raw materials, etc. In these situations, an assessment on the individual merits of the case becomes necessary. In many situations, investment projects include elements of extension, modernisation, and diversification (see for example N 635/2008, Italy, LIP Fiat Sicily [2009] O.J. C219/52).

Conformity with regional aid map	The project has to be located in an assisted area, as defined by the regional aid map. The aid must have been notified within the period of validity of the map. The total public support[31] must not exceed the applicable adjusted aid intensity ceiling which is defined in the map, pursuant to para.67 of the RAG, taking into account the following **scaling down mechanism for large investment projects:** — for the first €50 million, the standard regional aid ceiling applies; — for the next €50 million, half the standard regional aid ceiling applies; — for eligible expenditure exceeding €100 million, 34% of the standard regional aid ceiling applies.
Eligible expenditure	The aid has to be calculated with respect to elgibile expenditure as prescribed by the RAG. In the case of a Single Investment Project (SIP), the overall expenditure of all sub-projects has be to taken into account. Recognised eligible expenditure is defined either in reference to material and immaterial investment costs resulting from the initial investment project, or with regard to estimated wage costs for jobs directly created by the investment project.

[31] Under the rules on cumulation of aid, laid down in s.4.4 of the RAG, the notion of total public support is broadly defined. To be included under this notion, it is irrelevant: a) in which form the aid is granted; b) whether it comes from local, regional, national or Community sources; c) whether it is granted from one or several regional investment aid schemes or via ad hoc aid (individual aid not covered by an existing aid scheme); or d) whether some of the support qualifies as de minimis aid within the meaning of the applicable de minimis regulation.

Formal incentive effect (para.38 of the RAG)	For discretionary aid,[32] two formal requirements have to be met: first, the aid beneficiary must have applied for aid before the start of works, i.e. the start of the construction work or the first firm commitment to order equipment. The acquisition of land, or prefeasibility studies, are not taken into account to define the "start of works". Second, the authorities in charge of the scheme must have confirmed in writing before the start of the works that, subject to detailed verification, the project in principle meets the eligibility criteria for the scheme. In cases of ad hoc aid, this confirmation is replaced by the requirement of a letter of intent by the competent authority to award aid before the start of works.
Minimum own contribution by the beneficiary (para.39 of the RAG)	Where the aid is calculated on the basis of investment costs, the aid beneficiary has to provide a financial contribution of at least 25% from its own resources, or external financing, in a form which is free of any public support.
Maintenance of the investment/posts created for a minimum period (para.40 of the RAG)	The aid must be made conditional on the maintenance of the investment project in the assisted region for a minimum period of five years (three years for SMEs) after completion of the investment. In addition, where the aid is calculated with regard to wage costs for jobs directly created by the project, the posts have to be filled within three years after completion of the works, and have to be maintained for a minimum period of five years.
Contribution to regional development (s.2 of the RAG)	For ad hoc aid only, the Member State has to give proof that the contribution of the aid to regional development outbalances its sectoral effects.
Viable firm	The aid beneficiary must not be a firm in financial difficulties.[33]

[32] These rules do not apply to aid granted under existing tax aid schemes where a tax exemption or reduction is granted automatically with respect to identified eligible expenditure without any discretion on the part of the authorities.

[33] Regional aid to firms in difficulties within the meaning of the Community Guidelines on state aid for rescuing and restructuring firms in difficulty (RRG), O.J. C244, October 1, 2004, p.2 is prohibited by the RAG, unless it is granted in accordance with the provisions of the RRG .

Sectoral scope (s.2 of the RAG)	The aid must address an activity within the sectoral scope of the RAG. The RAG apply to aid in every sector of the economy apart from the fisheries sector and the coal industry, and the production of agricultural products listed in Annex 1 of the EC Treaty, with the exception of the processing and marketing of such products. In the latter sector, and in several others (transport, shipbuilding) special rules apply. Aid to the steel and synthetic fibers sectors is prohibited.

Filters for in-depth assessment.

Where the notified aid amount exceeds the individual notification threshold mentioned above, the aid can only be approved within the preliminary investigation phase, if the aid project meets two tests defined in para.68 of the RAG 2007–2013, namely: **15–009**

a) the "market share" test (or para.68(a) test);

b) and the "capacity increase in an underperforming market" test (or para. 68(b) test).

However, pursuant to fn.65 of the RAG, these two tests do not need to be carried out if "the Member State demonstrates that the aid beneficiary creates a new product market". In this case, the aid is authorised within the preliminary investigation provided all standard compatibility criteria, including the scaling down of the applicable regional aid intensity ceiling laid down in the individual regional aid map, are respected.

Under the MSF 2002, these two tests had been defined as compatibility criteria. Aid that did not meet the test, had to be prohibited following an opening of the formal investigation. Under the RAG, the failure to meet these tests, now triggers only an in-depth assessment, to be carried out in a formal investigation.

Market share test. Under the "market share" test, the Commission tries to identify situations where a significant market position of the aid beneficiary that could be used for anti-competitive behaviour, could be reinforced by the aid. Under this test, the market share of the aid beneficiary must not exceed 25 per cent of the relevant market which is addressed by the investment project. **15–010**

Product concerned/deemed to be concerned by the investment: To carry out this test, it is first necessary to identify the *product (directly) concerned* by the investment. Normally, this product is the product covered by the investment

471

project, and where the project concerns several products, all products involved. The product concerned may also include products which could, without major additional investment and cost, be produced in the aided production facility. Where the production concerns an intermediate product of which a substantive part is used by the aid beneficiary in captive production, the downstream (final) product may also be a product concerned.

Relevant product market: In a second step, the relevant *product market* has to be identified: the relevant product market includes the product(s) concerned and its (their) substitutes, and/or the downstream product(s) deemed concerned, both from the demand and production side. Substitutes from the demand side are products which are considered, taking into account relative prices, by the consumers (or users of intermediate goods) to be able to replace the product concerned in its intended use. Whereas substitutes from the production site are products which the producer could manufacture instead of the product concerned through flexibility of the production installations.

Geographic market: In a third step, the relevant *geographic market* for the product or products concerned has to be established. The formulation in para.70 of the RAG 2007–2013 seems to suggest that the relevant geographic market should normally be defined at EEA level, but offers some flexibility where another generally accepted market segmentation for which statistical data are readily available seems more relevant. De facto, the Commission assesses markets for the market share test on the basis of the most relevant data and market segmentation, taking into account factors such as trade flows, exports intended by the aid beneficiary, relevant transport costs, and other barriers of trade that might segment markets for the definition of the relevant geographic market.

Result of the 68(a) test: The "market share" test is met if the market share of the beneficiary does not exceed 25 per cent of any of the markets that are considered.

15–011 **Capacity increase in an underperforming market test.** Under the "capacity increase in an underperforming market" test, the Commission tries to identify situations where a major aided investment project addresses a market characterised by overcapacities, since in this situation the risk exists that competitors will be crowded out. The test is carried out in two parts:

Capacity increase: In the first part of the test, the Commission establishes whether the investment project increases the production capacity by more than 5 per cent of the market. The market is measured using apparent consumption data. Apparent consumption is defined for this purpose as production minus exports plus imports of the product concerned. This test is normally carried out at the level of the EEA, even if the product market concerned is defined at a different level.

Underperforming market: In the second part of the test, the Commission tries to establish whether the market concerned is growing slower than the GDP of the European Economic Area. To that end, the average annual growth rate of the market over the last five years is compared to the corresponding growth rate of the EEA. Again the market is measured in terms of apparent consumption at EEA level. The test is normally carried out in volume terms (annual growth in units compared to real GDP growth), and, where available, in value terms (annual growth in value terms, compared to the growth of the EEA nominal GDP). The value terms test is of particular importance in situations that are characterised by growing volumes and sinking prices, whereas an analysis which is solely based on volume terms could hide situations of overcapacities.

Results of the 68(b) test: The "capacity increase in an underperforming market" test is not met if both the capacity increase exceeds 5 per cent of the market, and the markets grows slower than the EEA GDP.

Approval within the preliminary investigation. The Commission can approve the aid on the basis of the preliminary investigation only if all standard compatibility criteria of the RAG 2007–2013 are respected, and both the "market share" and "capacity increase in an underperforming market" tests raise no problems. Otherwise, the Commission has to open the formal investigation pursuant to art.108(2) TFEU. **15–012**

Formal investigation and in-depth assessment

Formal investigation due to doubts regarding the respect of standard compatibility criteria. Where the Commission raises doubts as regards the compatibility of the aid because one or several of the standard compatibility criteria of the RAG does not seem to be met, a standard formal investigation is carried out. A final Commission Decision is taken on the basis of the RAG; the rules under the IDAC play no role. Unless the Member State withdraws or amends its aid project, the aid has to be prohibited, except where the Member State can rebut the Commission's concerns that the standard criterion is not met. Formal investigation to carry out the in-depth assessment is laid down in para.68 of the RAG. **15–013**

Where the Commission has opened its formal investigation because the 68(a) or (b) test has not been passed, it carries it out in two phases:

Phase 1: Confirmation of the results of the 68(a) or (b) tests: Where the Commission has raised doubts in the preliminary investigation that the "market share" or "capacity increase in an underperforming market" tests are not met, it re-examines the issue within the formal investigation on the basis of the comments and observations received. The doubts expressed in the opening decision typically reflect a range of situations:

(a) The preliminary investigation did not allow it to take a definite view on the appropriate definition of the relevant product, and in particular of the geographic market, and the market share of the beneficiary exceeded in one or some of the plausible market definitions applied the 25 per cent threshold.

(b) The preliminary investigation did not allow it to take a definite view on the appropriate definition of the relevant product market, and the Commission had to carry out the 68(b) test on the basis of plausible product markets, and the analysis revealed on one or several of the considered plausible markets defined at EEA level that the test was not met.

(c) There are doubts about the validity and independence of data submitted, and plausibility considerations and further research within the preliminary investigation does not remove these doubts.

(d) There are de facto no doubts that the tests are not met, but the Member State and third party receive a formal possibility to comment since the underlying assessments are also relevant within the in-depth investigation.

15–014   In the first two cases, the Commission tries to establish, on the basis of evidence received and information available, a definite view on the appropriate market definition. Where the Commission is unable to establish such a definite view on the basis of additional information received during the formal investigation, or where the relevant test is not met on the confirmed relevant market, the Commission proceeds to phase 2. The same holds where the formal investigation does not alleviate doubts about the validity and independence of data received, e.g. on the basis of alternative data sources or independent studies and expertise, or, in the last case, where the Member State was unable to prove that the preliminary assessment by the Commission was erroneous.

15–015   *Phase 2: In-depth assessment:* In situations where either the 68(a) or (b) tests are not met, the Commission has to carry out, within the formal investigation, a detailed verification to confirm:

"that the aid is necessary to provide an incentive effect for the investment and that the benefits of the aid measure outweigh the resulting distortions of competition and effect on trade between Member States."[34]

In order to contribute to the transparency and predictability of the Commission's decision making, the Commission announced in the RAG its intention to draw up "further guidance on the criteria it will take into account during this assessment".[35] Details of the way the Commission intends to carry out this in-depth assessment are now laid down in a Commission Communication concerning the criteria for an in-depth assessment of regional aid to large investment

---

[34] Regional Aid Guidelines 2007–2013, para.68.
[35] Regional Aid Guidelines 2007–2013, fn.63.

projects which was published in September 2009 (IDAC).[36] The different elements of this in depth assessment are described below.

Incentive effect[37]: A key element and the point of departure for the in-depth **15–016** assessment is the verification of the incentive effect which takes place at two levels[38]:

(a) At the procedural level, the Commission verifies again that the formal incentive effect requirements, applicable to all regional aid and described above, are met.

(b) At the material level, the Commission analyses the economic incentive effect to determine whether the aid actually contributes to changing the behaviour of the beneficiary and is decisive for the location of the project in the assisted area.

An economic incentive effect can be proven in two scenarios:

(a) In the first scenario, the aid gives an incentive to adopt a positive investment decision in favour of the beneficiary region in a situation where, in absence of the aid, the project would not be profitable for the beneficiary at any location.

(b) In the second scenario, the aid gives an incentive to locate the investment in the beneficiary region rather than elsewhere since it compensates for the region's net handicaps and costs.

The burden of proof that an economic incentive effect exists falls on the **15–017** Member State, which has to give clear evidence that the aid has an impact on the investment choice or location choice, and which has to submit "a comprehensive description of the counterfactual scenario, in which no aid would be granted".[39] To that end, the Member State has to specify which scenario applies and submit relevant proof:

(a) In scenario 1, this proof could be given by submitting company documents[40] that show that in the counterfactual situation (1) the investment would not be profitable without the aid, and that (2) no other location than the target region concerned could be envisaged.

---

[36] Communication from the Commission concerning the criteria for the in-depth assessment of regional aid to large investment projects, O.J. C223, September 16, 2009, pp.3–10.

[37] See IDAC, s.2.3.

[38] The Commission verifies also that state aid is an appropriate instrument to achieve the objective (see IDAC, s.2.2).

[39] IDAC, para.23.

[40] e.g. risk assessments, financial reports, internal business plans, expert opinions, studies, and other documents submitted to an investment committee, and relevant financial market information.

(b) In scenario 2, proof could be given by submitting company documents that show that a realistic comparison has been made between the costs and benefits that arise when locating the investment project in the target region, and those that are expected in an alternative region where the project would be implemented as first choice under the counterfactual situation without any aid.

To demonstrate the lack of profitability under scenario 1, or the respective levels of profitability under scenario 2, standard methodologies as methods to evaluate the net present value of the project (NPV), the internal rate of return (IRR), or the return on capital employed (ROCE), can be used.

Where no incentive effect can be proven, the aid is considered incompatible.

15–018 *Proportionality of the aid*[41]: In a second step, the Commission verifies whether the amount of the aid is proportional, i.e. that its aid amount and aid intensity is "limited to the minimum needed for the investment to take place in the assisted area".[42] Under this proportionality test, the aid will be considered proportionate if:

(a) in scenario 1, the return on investment is in line with the normal rate of return on investment applied by the company in other investment projects, with the cost of capital of the company as a whole, or with returns commonly observed in the sector concerned;

(c) in scenario 2, the aid does not exceed the difference between the net costs for the beneficiary company to invest in the target region and the (lower) net costs to invest in an alternative location, and thus compensates for the lower profitability of the project in the assisted region.

The burden of proof is again on the Member State which should be able to rely on the same documents and calculations already used to establish the incentive effect.

Where the amount or intensity of the notified aid is considered to be disproportionately high, the Commission can declare, in its final decision, the excessive part as incompatible, thus approving only a reduced level of aid.

15–019 **Balancing test.** Where the assessment showed that the aid has an incentive effect and is proportionate, the Commission proceeds to a balancing of the positive and negative effects of the aid.

15–020 *Positive effects:* The key positive effect is the contribution of the aid to regional development.[43] The Member State must:

[41] See IDAC, s.2.4.
[42] IDAC, para.29.
[43] See IDAC, s.2.1.

(a) demonstrate that the aid addresses the equity objective of "furthering economic cohesion by helping to reduce the gaps between the development levels"[44] between the target region and other EU regions;

(b) substantiate the contribution of the investment project to the development of the target region.

To demonstrate the regional contribution of the aid, the IDAC offers a non-exhaustive list of indicative criteria on which Member States can rely, which include:

(a) the number of direct jobs created, their quality, and the required skill level;

(b) the number of indirect jobs created in the local supplier network;

(c) non-aided training activities entered into by the aid beneficiary;

(d) external economies of scale and other benefits from a regional development point of view due to proximity ("clustering effects") which may contribute to better specialisation, improved efficiency and positive spill over effects;

(e) transfer of technology ("knowledge spill over effects");

(f) contribution to regional innovation capability, e.g. on the basis of a cooperation with local higher education institutions; and

(g) indications of a durable engagement of the company in the region.

Negative effects[45]: Key negative effects of aid identified by the IDAC are: **15–021**

(a) the weakening of the competitive situation/crowding out of competitors through the aid, in particular in situations where dominant market players are subsidised and a risk of exclusionary behaviour exists. In this context the Commission takes account of the market shares of the aid beneficiary before and after the investment, the market structure and concentration of the market, possible barriers to entry (in particular where the beneficiary is an incumbent), and the possible presence of (countervailing) buyer power on the market;

(b) the creation, maintenance or reinforcement of inefficient market structures, in particular in situations where the investment induced by the aid reflects a substantial capacity expansion in an underperforming market in absolute or relative decline or one characterised by (the risk of) persistent over-capacities, and which may force competitors out of the market, could

---

[44] IDAC, para.11.
[45] See IDAC, s.3.

reduce incentives for competitors to innovate, or deter low cost firms from entering the market;

    (c) (undesired) negative effects on trade, in particular in situations where the aid permits for the attraction of investments to a target region, which in a counterfactual scenario would have taken place in a region with similar or even higher regional handicaps (i.e. in regions with the same, or a higher regional aid ceiling), where it could result in a substantial loss of jobs.

15–022 *Balancing rules:* The IDAC contains only a limited number of (indicative) balancing rules, and leaves a large margin of discretion to the Commission. The standard situation that the Commission is likely to encounter in in-depth assessments seems to be the situation under scenario 2 whereby a location decision is influenced by the aid. In fact, the probability that a firm invests under scenario 1 into a non-viable investment project purely because of the availability of aid seems rather remote. It is also rather difficult to imagine that a State would grant aid from scarce public resources to support an economic activity which might not be sustainable in the long run, or which, due to its—artificially created—limited viability, is unlikely to lead to major endogenous growth. However, there may be situations where strategic considerations prevail for the firm which are not properly reflected in profitability calculations for an individual project, or where "infant industry" arguments may militate for state support despite a lack of immediate viability of the project.

15–023 *Balancing rules for scenario 2:* Under scenario 2, the counterfactual analysis[46] suggests that the investment would take place in any case, however at a different location. If the aid is proportional, i.e. is limited to the minimum necessary to attract the investment to the target region, and hence does not overcompensate the beneficiary, any possible distortions of competition that might result from high market shares or an increase in capacity in an underperforming market would happen to the same extent without the aid, provided that the two projects address the same geographic markets. In this situation, the aid does not increase the distortion of competition, but merely contributes (as must also be proven under the in-depth assessment[47]) to the achievement of a regional development objective. Paragraph 40 of the IDAC therefore suggests that the aid can normally be approved if its contribution to regional development is proven, unless it has a negative effect on cohesion within the European Union. Such an anti-cohesive effect would exist if the investment project were located, in the absence of any aid, in a region which is poorer, or has the same level of handicaps, as the target region. Paragraph 53 of the IDAC clarifies that if the aid were to prevent an unaided investment in a region with the same, or a higher regional aid ceiling, the outcome of the overall balancing test which is carried out within the in-depth

---

[46] See IDAC, para.40.
[47] para.14 of the IDAC contains a series of elements that might allow the positive effects of the aid to be proven.

assessment would most likely be negative, even in a situation where no other negative effects are present. Such aid would "run counter to the very rationale of regional aid."[48]

Paragraph 54 of the IDAC stipulates that where the aided investment in the target region results in a relocation of activities from another existing location in the European Union and substantial losses of jobs in that location, the social and economic effects in that other location have to be taken into account in the overall balancing. This paragraph seems to address only relocations from a region which is not eligible for regional aid, or which is less disadvantaged than the target region. Unfortunately, the IDAC does not offer any indication of the relative weight of the job loss criterion, compared to the regional contribution criterion in the target region.

Balancing rules for scenario 1: In the less probable case of a scenario 1 project, **15–024** which would not be carried out without aid at any location by the beneficiary, the overall balancing of positive and negative factors is likely to lead to a negative result in particular where the aided (per se non-viable) investment adds capacity to a market in absolute decline (negative growth), and thus contributes to the crowding out of more efficient firms.[49]

A less clear situation arises where the investment leads to a substantial capacity increase on a market in relative decline (positive under-average growth). Here the outcome of the balancing test is likely to depend on the quality of the project in terms of contribution to regional development, and on the relative level of underperformance of the market. A situation where a dominant market player is unable at any location to carry out a viable investment project that addresses the market he dominates is unlikely to arise. The IDAC does not give any explicit indication of what the outcome of a balancing in this situation would be.

3. THE COMMISSION'S EXPERIENCE IN THE APPLICATION OF THE RULES REGARDING REGIONAL AID TO LARGE INVESTMENT PROJECTS UNDER THE REGIONAL AID GUIDELINES 2007–13

The empirical evidence

Cases submitted as ex post information under the transparency mechanism. **15–025** Under the transparency mechanism laid down in para.65 of the RAG (see para.15–005) for non-individually notifiable regional aid to large investment projects, Member States transmitted between January 1, 2007 and May 1, 2011[50] some 250 summary information sheets to inform the Commission *ex post* of aid granting decisions taken under schemes. These cases represent an investment

---

[48] IDAC, para.53.
[49] See IDAC, para.47.
[50] In a limited number of these cases, the aid was already granted before 2006, and was submitted under the (identical) transparency mechanism established under the MSF 2002.

volume of some €20 billion, and an aid amount of roughly €4 billion. They concern a large range of sectors, and originate from a large number of Member States, in particular Germany (55 cases), Spain (37 cases), Hungary (30 cases), Poland (23 cases), and Portugal (21 cases).

The Commission carried out a "light compatibility" check on these cases and on several of them it opened an ex officio investigation since it had doubts as to the correct application of the underlying aid scheme, or the correct application of a block exemption where the underlying scheme proved problematic and had been put into place on the basis of a block exemption. In most cases Member States corrected errors immediately on their own initiative once they had been signalled to them by the Commission services. In one case (C 18/2008, Hungary, *Dunaferr*), which concerned (prohibited) regional investment aid to the steel sector, the Commission opened a formal investigation which became obsolete when Hungary informed the Commission that the aid beneficiary was no longer eligible under the scheme, and that no aid had been granted.[51]

15–026   Individually notified cases. Under the rules applicable for regional aid to large undertakings defined in the RAG, the Commission has so far approved aid in some 30 cases within the preliminary investigation.[52] In three further cases (C34/2008, Germany, *Deutsche Solar AG*,[53] C46/2008, Poland, *Dell*,[54] and C34/2009, *Portugal, Petrogal*), a positive decision was taken following the opening of a formal investigation. In a fourth case, SA.30340 (2011/C) *Poland, Fiat Powertrain*, the Commission closed[54a] the formal investigation[54b] after withdrawal of the notification by the Member State. One positive decision (N 582/2007, Germany, *Propapier*), taken within the preliminary investigation was appealed against by competitors. The ruling of the General Court is outstanding.

In addition to the *Deutsche Solar, Dell* and *Petrogal* and *Fiat Powertrain Poland* cases referred to above, the Commission opened a formal investigation in four further cases, namely C 31/2009,[55] Hungary, *Audi Hungaria*, SA.32169(11)(c), *Germany, Volkswagen*,[55a] SA.32009 (11/C), *Germany, BMW*,[55b] and SA.33152(11)(c), Germany, *Linamar*.[56] The final decisions on these

[51] C18/2008, *Dunaferr*. The public version of the decision is not yet available for confidentiality reasons. Press release IP/08/1232, August 1, 2008.
[52] The Commission also approved in 2007 a very substantial number of cases notified in 2006 under the RAG 1998 and MSF 2002; these cases were assessed pursuant to fn.58 of the RAG on the basis of its predecessor rules.
[53] [2011] C34/2008 O.J. 217/51.
[54] [2010] O.J. L29/53.
[54a] See [2012] O.J. C12/821.
[54b] See [2011] O.J. C151/5.
[55] [2010] O.J. C64/53.
[55a] See [2011] O.J. C361/17.
[55b] See [2011] O.J. C363/20.
[56] See [2011] O.J. C20/10.

cases have not yet been adopted. A series of other cases is in preliminary investigation.

Most cases concern two sectors, namely the photovoltaic and passenger car sectors. More than half of all cases originate from Germany.

The experience in applying the rules

The actual rules on aid to large investment projects largely reflect the rules laid down in the Multisectoral Framework 2002. The underlying provisions were elaborated and discussed with Member States in 2001, and were mainly based on the experience the Commission had had in the 1990s with regards to the Multisectoral Framework 1998 and sectoral rules that existed until 2003 for certain sensitive sectors (e.g. automotive sector, steel, synthetic fibres). These provisions entered into force under the Multisectoral Framework for the generality of sectors only in 2004. When the Commission decided in 2005 to integrate them into the RAG, its experience in applying these provisions was limited to a very small number of cases. **15–027**

Subsequent experience showed that certain provisions integrated into the RAG are highly efficient and non-contested: this applies in particular to the scaling down of aid intensity ceilings for large investment projects (see row 2 of Table 1) and the transparency mechanism, i.e. rules that apply to all large investment projects, and not only to notifiable ones.

Experience in the preliminary investigation. However, the experience in the preliminary investigation also showed that some provisions applicable for the assessment of notified cases are difficult to apply: **15–028**

- The single investment project rule (see para.15–005) is complex. The assessment of whether several projects that took place within the three-year period form part of a single project for the purposes of the RAG is time consuming. If no agreement can be reached with the Member State, a formal investigation becomes necessary. In most cases however, Member States agree to reduce the notified aid intensity sufficiently so as to fall below the SIP aid ceiling. This allowed the Commission to leave the question open. SIP issues have arisen in about half of all cases, particularly complex ones including N 538/2008, Germany, *Ersol Thin Film Erfurt*,[57] and N 539/2008, Germany, *ASI Industries/Ersol Solar Energy*.[58] In two cases, the Commission opened the formal investigation (C34/2008, Germany, *Deutsche Solar AG* and SA.32169 (11/C) Germany, Volkswagen).

- Forecasts of future market shares requested by the 68(a) test are far from straightforward, in particular for markets that have experienced fast growth in the past, but seem to be reaching a situation of growing market saturation.

[57] [2009] O.J. C63/52.
[58] [2010] O.J. C12/53.

In these cases the Commission compares the expected sales of the company with varying growth scenarios (worst case, best case, average growth): N 221/2009, Germany, *Wacker Chemie*,[59] which concerned the production of polysilcon is a typical example.

- The information required to carry out the tests prescribed in para.68 is not always easily available; this is particularly the case for niche or new markets. The case of N 261/2009, Germany, *Liebherr*,[60] which concerned the production of maritime (ship and offshore) cranes, is a good example of a situation in which a study had to be commissioned to collect the necessary data. Of particular interest here is also SA.32009 (11/C) BMW which concerns the production of an electric car, and where the Commission was unable to define the appropriate relevant product market.

- Data sources are not always independent, especially with regard to data on future company sales, which rely heavily on information provided by the beneficiary.

- The appropriate definition of the geographic market frequently raises problems which are difficult to solve on the basis of the investigative powers given to the Commission in the area of state aid and within the legal deadlines foreseen for the preliminary assessment phase. The Commission opened several formal investigations on this issue, e.g. in C31/2009, Hungary, *Audi Hungaria*, C34/2009, Portugal, *Petrogal*, SA 30340 (2011/C), Poland, *Fiat Powertrain* SA.32169 (11/C), Germany, Volkswagen, and SA.32009 (11/C), Germany, BMW.

- The application of the para.68(b) test at EEA level as a filter for in-depth assessment raises methodological problems where the relevant geographic market is worldwide, and large parts of the production are exported out of the EEA: N 261/2009, Germany, *Liebherr*, and SA.30596 (N101/2010), Germany, Globalfoundaries, are interesting examples.[61]

- The reliance on the past performance (compound growth rate over the past five years preceding the investment) of sectors under the para.68(b) test does not always allow for the addressing of foreseeable future problems.

15–029   Overall, the 68(a) and (b) tests have proved rather complex and time consuming. This complexity could certainly be justified in the MSF 2002 environment, where they have served as decisive compatibility criteria both in the preliminary and formal investigation. Under the RAG rules, their importance is much reduced: they serve as filters to identify cases for in-depth assessment, but in the

---

[59] [2010] O.J. C312/53.
[60] Unreported. Press release IP/10/900.
[61] N 810/2006, Germany, *AMD* is another excellent example which was decided under the MSF 2002.

in-depth assessment itself their role appears to be rather limited. There are other criteria which could serve as more efficient filters for an in-depth assessment.

Experience in the formal investigation and with in-depth assessment. The 15–030 table below gives an overview of the reasons which led to the opening of the formal investigation in the eight aforementioned cases, of which only three cases have been finally ruled upon.

Case Product concerned	Reason for opening linked to general compatibility criteria	Reason for opening linked to 68(a) or/and (b) test
C34/2008, Germany: *Deutsche Solar AG* Solar wafers	Single investment project (SIP) issue; the aid beneficiary had received aid for several other investment projects in close proximity within the three-year period	
C46/2008, Poland: *Dell* (1) Desktops (2) Notebooks (3) Servers		(1) Doubts about the appropriate product market definitions (separate v integrated market for desktops and notebooks, respectively segmentation of server market, either by price range or x86/non x86 instruction set architecture). (2) Doubts about the appropriate geographic market definition for servers (EEA or global). (3) Market share in volume terms exceedings 25% on the global x86 server market. (4) Capacity increase by the project exceedings 5% of the apparent consumption of desktops on the EEA markets; in value terms, the desktop segment is in absolute decline.

Case Product concerned	Reason for opening linked to general compatibility criteria	Reason for opening linked to 68(a) or/and (b) test
C31/2009, Hungary: *Audi Hungaria* Engines (diesel and gasoline) for a wide range of passenger car segments		(1) Market share exceeding the 25% threshold for several segments of the car market concerned by the investment on the EEA market, and in one segment at global level. (2) The gross capacity increase by the project[62] exceeds 5% of the apparent consumption on the EEA market on the car market segments concerned; most of these segments were underperforming.
C34/2009, Portugal: *Petrogal* (1) Diesel (2) Naphtha and naphtha derivates	(1) Doubts about the contribution of the aid to regional development,[63] combined with doubts about the necessity of the aid. (2) Doubts about the initial investment character of the project (3) Doubts about the SIP character of the project.	(1) Doubts about the appropriate definition of the geographic market (national, Iberian peninsula, or wider) for diesel and the appropriate level of assessment of the market (ex-refinery, non retail, retail): the market share of the beneficiary at national level exceeds 25%. (2) Insufficient information to carry out tests for second product concerned (naphtha).
SA 30340 (2011/C), Poland: *Fiat Powertrain* Engines (gasoline)	–	(1) The market share of the aid beneficiary exceeds the 25% threshold for a segment of the car market concerned by the investment on the EEA market. (2) Insufficient information to carry out 68(b) test.

[62] Dell offered to limit production in Poland to 5%, to be compensated by increased production elsewhere.
[63] The contribution to regional aid has to be verified since the aid is granted as ad hoc aid.

It seems premature to comment on the three cases on which no decision has been taken thus far.

It is interesting to note that the first of the cases where a decision was adopted, **15–031** C34/2008, Germany, *Deutsche Solar AG*, was never a candidate for the in-depth assessment as laid down in para.68 of the RAG, and clarified by the IDAC. The case concerned an SIP issue, i.e. a disagreement on the allowed maximum aid intensity. The Commission did not have to take a final decision on the SIP issue, since the Member State decided to withdraw some aid for the possible SIP on its own initiative during the formal investigation. Therefore, so far an in-depth assessment has been carried out in only one case, which concerned regional aid to Dell in Poland.[64] The final decision was adopted on September 23, 2009, one week after the adoption of the IDAC, in which it was cited as one of the legal bases for the assessment of the case.[65]

In the verification of the reasons which led to the opening of the formal investigation, the Commission stated that:

"although the information received during the formal investigation has enabled it to achieve a better understanding of the PC sector, it is insufficient for the Commission to conduct a meaningful market investigation which could enable it to define the relevant product market(s) for desktops and notebooks."[66]

In the end the Commission was unable to assuage its doubts that the 68(a) and (b) test were met, and hence proceeded to the in-depth assessment.[67]

The in-depth assessment confirmed the appropriateness of the aid instrument, noted that the case fell under a scenario 2 situation (without aid, the investment would have taken place in Nitra, Slovakia), accepted that the aid had an economic incentive effect on Dell to locate the investment in the target region, found that the notified aid was limited to the amount necessary to compensate for the net additional costs of locating in the target region, and considered that the contribution of the aid to regional development was proven.

The Commission considered at the same time that: **15–032**

"since the aid falls under scenario 2 and . . . the investment project would have been carried out in any event, it is not relevant to consider, as part of the in-depth assessment, the effects that the aid could have in relation to a possible increase in market power as any such market power would exist irrespective

---

[64] C46/2008 [2010] O.J. L29/53.
[65] See paras 111 and 112, including fn.31 of the final decision. The Commission, referring to the judgment in case C–334/07 P *Commission/Freistaat Sachsen*, points 53, 56, and 58, notes that it has to conduct the assessment on the basis of the rules applicable at the time of the decision.
[66] See para.130 of the final decision.
[67] See paras 149 and 150 of the final decision.

of the location of the investment and the level of any such market power would not be affected by the granting of the aid."[68]

Following the same line of argumentation, the Commission rejected doubts regarding the creation or maintenance of inefficient market structures (68(b) test) as irrelevant. Hence, core issues that were discussed at length in the preliminary investigation and in the verification of the doubts that led to the opening decision were therefore found to be completely irrelevant for the outcome of the in-depth assessment. Since the target region (Łódzkie) has a higher regional aid ceiling than the region where Nitra is situated, and since the Commission found that the investment in Poland did not cause job losses in Dell's Irish site Limerick, it concluded that the aid was compatible.

The application of the IDAC and the interpretation of its provisions certainly needs some further testing before definitive conclusions can be drawn. The experience with the *Dell* case, however, constitutes important evidence that the assessment approach outlined in the IDAC is feasible, at least for scenario 2 cases. The fact that the Commission was unable to reach definite market delimitations in the verification of the doubts that led to the opening could possibly be seen as a warning regarding the difficulties the Commission can expect when it is called upon to decide on appropriate definitions of the relevant geographic and product market on the basis of the investigative powers it has under state aid rules, since in the case at hand the question cannot be left open. The IDAC might be substantially more difficult to apply in scenario 1 cases where high market shares and capacity increases in underperforming markets remain important elements in the overall balancing.

4. CONCLUSIONS AND OUTLOOK

15–033   The current Regional Aid Guidelines, block exemption regulations, regional aid maps and schemes all expire at the end of 2013. Work on the review of the Regional Aid Guidelines and the linked block exemption provisions started in 2010. At this stage, it is difficult to predict whether, and in which areas, this review will lead to dramatic changes compared to the present rules. Provided the new Guidelines continue to allow aid for large investment projects, the respective provisions certainly constitute an area where improvements are possible.

Another issue which undoubtedly requires further reflection is the way in which to design the link between the compatibility tests/filters for in-depth assessment under point 68 of the RAG and the IDAC in a meaningful and effective way. On the one hand, the present approach is based on two theories of harm (dominant market player and overcapacities), acting as triggers for in-depth assessment, which under the balancing rules established in the IDAC become irrelevant where the case falls under scenario 2. This seems to reflect the standard

---

[68] para.202 of the final decision.

situation, that the investment and its possible harmful effects through the expansion of the market power of a dominant player, or an increased overcapacity on the market, would at any event have happened (albeit at a different location), and therefore the aid (provided it is proportionate) does not create additional distortion of competition beyond the desired impact on the location choice. The highly time-consuming and work intensive "market share" and "capacity increase" tests could therefore be limited to the assessment of the relatively rare scenario 1 situations, and lose their function as general filters for in-depth assessment.

On the other hand, the present approach verifies both the economic incentive effect of the aid and its contribution to regional development only in the exceptional cases where the Commission has already decided to open the formal investigation and to proceed to an in-depth assessment. Two key conditions for the approval of regional aid are therefore considered to be automatically fulfilled in most cases under the actual rules. However, an assessment of the incentive effect on the basis of purely formalistic criteria, does not necessarily exclude that, after closer examination of an aid measure, it would appear not to be necessary. In particular for larger aid measures a more in-depth assessment might be warranted, whilst for smaller measures with, in principle, a less distortive effect it might be necessary to continue to rely on formal criteria in order to avoid an excessively heavy control system.

It would make sense to maintain the individual notification requirement for aid **15–034** exceeding certain thresholds, to establish the relevant scenario and counterfactual situation already as part of the notification, and to focus the assessment in the preliminary investigation on core aspects of (regional) aid, namely economic incentive effect, proportionality of aid, contribution to regional development and the absence of harmful effects on trade and job losses caused by relocation, whereas the highly time-consuming definition of appropriate product and geographic markets and the subsequent 68(a) and (b) tests should be carried out only in the relatively rare scenario 1 cases.

Such a redesign of the approach should not raise major problems since art.8(3)(e) GBER stipulates already that the Member State, before granting the aid to large undertakings, verifies that documentation prepared by the beneficiary establishes "that the project would not have been carried out as such in the assisted region concerned in the absence of the aid". Therefore, the necessary documentation to prove the economic incentive effect of an aid measure (and the proportionality of the aid), and to identify the counterfactual scenario should in principle be immediately available.

CHAPTER 16

SHIPBUILDING*

1. Introduction 16–001
   The Shipbuilding Regulation 1540/98 16–003
2. New Framework for State Aid for Shipbuilding 16–005
3. The External Aspect 16–011
   Temporary Defensive Mechanism (TDM) 16–011
   OECD negotiations 16–015
   Recent decisions taken by the Commission and/or the Court 16–018

1. Introduction

16–001   The European shipbuilding industry has, over the last 20 years, been transformed from an industry in a form of permanent crisis into an efficient, profitable, high-technology industry. This positive evolution is largely attributable to the efforts of the industry itself, but is to some extent also the result of a successful state aid policy. This transformation of the sector has in turn had a further impact on the state aid rules governing the sector.

Originally one of the sectors receiving most state aid,[1] the rules on state aid to the shipbuilding sector have since become normalised, and more closely aligned with their application to other industrial sectors. It can therefore be argued that the state aid policy of the 1980s and 1990s finally achieved its goals, albeit after considerable expense to the taxpayer.

The specificities of the sector imply, however, that some special rules still apply. There are essentially two aspects that make shipbuilding special in terms of state aid: the first relates to the product itself. In shipbuilding, especially in the European Union, there is very limited serial production and each product is therefore more or less unique (similar to a prototype in most other sectors). In addition, the value of each ship produced often exceeds the value of the entire shipyard.

---

* Michael Schütte
[1] See, e.g. http://eur-lex.europa.eu/LexUriServ/LexUriServ.do?uri=COM:2000:0730:FIN:
en:PDF. [Accessed September 15, 2011.]

As a result of this each order is crucial for a shipyard, and it also means that   **16–002**
a shipyard may encounter serious financial difficulties if a problem arises with
even one single ship. Unfair competition can be particularly detrimental therefore, since the loss of one order may represent the loss of a full year's worth of
work. This may also lead a shipyard to force itself to accept an order for which
it does not have full competence to deliver, simply to keep its workforce
occupied. This may in turn lead to serious consequences if the ship is not built
to the satisfaction of the client.

The other special aspect relates to the use of the product. In contrast with most
other goods, ships are normally not imported, physically or legally, to the
European Union, even when they are bought by EU shipowners. One obvious
reason for this is that they sail on the oceans, and another reason is that ships are
often registered under flags of convenience. The fact that ships are not imported
means that EU shipyards cannot be protected by anti-dumping or countervailing
duties in case there is unfair competition from non-EU Member States. The
traditional trade policy protection is therefore not available to protect EU shipyards and state aid has been used for this purpose.

It is clear then that a strong link exists between trade policy and state aid policy
in the shipbuilding sector, which has had major implications during the last few
years, which will be demonstrated below.

The Shipbuilding Regulation 1540/98

Since the beginning of the 1970s, state aid for shipbuilding has been subject   **16–003**
to specific rules. The aim of these rules was essentially to ensure a socially
acceptable restructuring and downscaling of the industry. Until the end of 2003
the rules were decided by the Council due to their generous aid elements,
although in some respects the rules were also stricter than those governing the
majority of the other industrial sectors. In particular, as a derogation from the
general rules, the rules allowed for operating aid (as a percentage of the contract
value per ship), which was neither degressive nor temporary, as is normally
requested for such aid.

Between 1998 and 2003, the sector was governed by Council Regulation (EC)
1540/98 concerning aid for shipbuilding ("Shipbuilding Regulation"). This regulation expired on December 31, 2003.

To a large extent the Shipbuilding Regulation prolonged the rules of the   **16–004**
previous shipbuilding directives. It did however entail one major change, which
was that contracts signed after December 31, 2000 were no longer eligible for
operating aid, whilst contracts signed before that date were eligible for 9 per cent
aid. Given that in the 1980s the maximum rate of operating aid was around 30
per cent, a dramatic change had already taken place. For contracts signed before
the end of 2000, the ships had to be delivered before the end of 2003 to be
eligible for operating aid, except in certain circumstances. This provision led to
a number of cases being dealt with by the Commission in 2003, as will be
discussed below.

Although the abolition of operating aid had already come into force in 1997 when the regulation was adopted, a major political debate was erupting towards the end of 2000 when this provision was due to come into effect. The reason was that the European shipbuilding industry felt it was facing a major threat in the form of unfair competition from Korean[2] shipyards and that the operating aid was necessary for its survival. Despite intensive lobbying, the Commission and the Council resisted proposals for amendments to the Shipbuilding Regulation, which prohibited operating aid as planned. This led to an order boom for EU shipyards during the last months of 2000. This was followed by a certain boom of orders, but as a consequence of the economic crisis in 2008, many orders were cancelled. The EU shipyards responded to this challenge by restructuring their activity to more specialised vessels, as well as the building of moving off-shore structures. These changes are taken into account by a wider definition of the term "shipbuilding" in the 2012 framework for state aid for shipbuilding.

2. New Framework for State Aid for Shipbuilding

16–005 The 1998 Shipbuilding Regulation was replaced by the Framework on state aid to shipbuilding.[3] First adopted by the Commission on November 26, 2003 ("the 2003 framework") and revised in 2011, leading to the adoption of a new framework in force as of January 1, 2012 ("the 2012 framework").[3a] The 2003 framework was the first time state aid rules for shipbuilding were embodied in the form of Commission guidelines and not in the form of Council-based Community law. The choice of a Commission framework, based on art.107(3)(c) of the TFEU, is in line with the now general use, as regards state aid, of soft law instruments such as frameworks and guidelines. The 2003 framework came into force on January 1, 2004 and the 2012 framework shall apply until December 31, 2013. At that point in time, the exceptions now contained in the 2012 framework are to be integrated into general frameworks and guidelines. In particular, the rules on innovation aid[3b] are to be integrated into the Community framework on state aid for research and development and innovation.[3c] The 2012 framework contains a new definition of shipbuilding,[3d] which better reflects the adapted activities of the shipyards. It now also applies to vessels built for inland waterways as well as to offshore structures.[3e]

The new framework has two principal purposes: firstly it simplifies and standardises the rules concerning aid for shipbuilding. This is in line with the

---

[2] Korea in this article refers to South Korea.
[3] [2003] O.J. C317/11.
[3a] [2011] O.J. C364/09.
[3b] Section 3.2 of the 2012 framework.
[3c] [2006] O.J. C323/1.
[3d] Section 2, para.12 lit. (a) and (d) of the 2012 framework.
[3e] Section 2, para.12 lit. (d) and (e) of the 2012 framework.

general objective of the Community in respect of state aid, which aims at greater transparency and simplification.

As regards substance, the framework shows the aim of aligning rules on shipbuilding with the general rules, frameworks and guidelines on state aid. Normal horizontal state aid rules are extended to the shipbuilding sector as far as possible, and the 2012 framework should be abolished by the end of 2013. To the extent special rules on shipbuilding were then still required, they shall be integrated into other horizontal rules. The shipbuilding sector is eligible to receive aid which it could not under the Shipbuilding Regulation, such as aid based on the Block Exemption Regulations for training, for employment, to SMEs and so called "de-minimis" aid. It should also be noted that the notification obligations have been significantly relaxed when compared with the 1998 Shipbuilding Regulation.

However, the 2012 framework takes into account the fact that the shipbuilding **16–006** industry still exhibits some special characteristics, as explained in the introduction. This motivates the inclusion of some specific measures and specially adapted rules and these are reflected in three categories of aid: (1) aid for innovation; (2) export credits and (3) regional aid. The rules allowing closure aid have been abolished in the 2012 framework, since this exception was never used in practice.

As regards research, development and innovation, the very limited series production, due to the size, complexity and the value of the units produced, implies that "prototypes" generally have to be sold as final products.[4] On the basis of these characteristics, the 1998 Shipbuilding Regulation already introduced a specific provision on innovation aid,[5] making this the only sector to be able to benefit from such support. The application of this provision, however, did not prove entirely satisfactory[6] and was rarely used. In the new framework these difficulties were taken into account when the provision on aid for innovation[7] was revised.

The new text aims at improving and strengthening this provision while main- **16–007** taining the requirement of a technological risk. On the one hand, the framework contains a definition of "innovation" which is more adapted to the specific characteristics of the sector. This should make it easier to use this form of support, in particular by reducing the burden of proof falling on the applicant. Indeed, aid for innovation can now be granted to new products or methods in relation to the "state of the art" in the European Union. There is therefore no longer a need to prove that the innovation was not used commercially by any other operator in the sector within the Community, which was obviously difficult.

---

[4] This would usually exclude them from normal R&D aid, since aid cannot be granted for a prototype which is used commercially.

[5] See art.6 of the Shipbuilding Regulation.

[6] In particular, the requirement according to which it had to be proven that the innovation was not used commercially by any other operator in the EU caused difficulties.

[7] paras 14 et seq. of the 2012 framework.

Furthermore, in order to provide an increased incentive for innovation, the maximum aid intensity was raised from 10 to 20 per cent. Moreover, the aid can now be granted not only for design, engineering and testing, but also exceptionally to validate the innovation. In exceptional circumstances this may imply aid for the construction of a full-scale ship, in case this is necessary to validate the innovation. The Commission has insisted on rather strict provisions for the use of innovation aid, and in particular for the validation part. An example of such an approved aid scheme is the one used in Germany.[8] Similar schemes have been approved also for France and Spain.

16–008   The focus on the promotion of innovation highlights the current desire to support activities which can contribute to greater competitiveness of European industry and therefore have a more long-term positive effect, when compared to more traditional aid.[9]

The 2012 framework abolishes the possibility of granting aid for either partial or total closure of shipyards. Closure can now only be granted under the Community guidelines on state aid for rescuing and restructuring firms in difficulty.[9a]

16–009   As regards export credits the framework refers to the OECD export credit arrangement.[10] This means that ship financing based on the so-called Commercial Interest Reference Rates (CIRR) terms may be compatible with state aid rules, even if this implies that Member States must provide state resources to, e.g. export credit agencies to allow them to provide such financing. The Commission has approved a number of such schemes, such as the one for Spain.[11]

16–010   Lastly, just as in the Shipbuilding Regulation, the 2012 framework contains specific measures on regional aid which are stricter than the normal rules. The rules prescribe for a reduced maximum aid intensity and require that the productivity of existing installations be improved.[12] The aim is to reduce the temptation for Member States to grant aid to increase capacity by enlarging the installations; obviously, an increase in the productivity normally leads to some increase in capacity. There must also not be a link to financial restructuring of the shipyard. Therefore, the objective of regional aid for shipbuilding is only to modernise facilities to be able to provide ships of a higher value, thereby improving the competitive position of the shipyard.

---

[8] *http://ec.europa.eu/eu_law/state_aids/comp-2004/n452-04.pdf*. [Accessed September 15, 2011.]

[9] It is positive to note that industry today seems to share this approach as is shown by the work undertaken within the framework of the initiative *LeaderSHIP 2015*. This initiative, which brought together representatives of all the actors in the sector (manufacturers, suppliers, trade unions, European institutions), dealt with a very broad range of questions concerning the European shipbuilding industry. See Commission press release IP/03/1464, October 28, 2003.

[9a] [2004] O.J. C244/2.

[10] A new sectoral Agreement on export credits for the ships was adopted under the OECD on April 15, 2002. Under the terms of Council Decision 2002/634/EC amending Decision 2001/76/EC with regard to ship export credits, the new sectoral Agreement on export credits for the ships applies in the Community.

[11] *http://ec.europa.eu/competition/state_aid/register/ii/by_case_nr_2008_0390.html#393*. [Accessed September 15, 2011.]

[12] Section 3.1 lit. (a) of the 2012 Framework.

Fair competition is a key element for the competitiveness of any industry. That is true, of course, both inside and outside the European Union. The external aspect of competition policy is all the more important for an industry like shipbuilding, which has perceived that it has experienced serious problems of distortion of competition at world level.

3. THE EXTERNAL ASPECT

Temporary Defensive Mechanism (TDM)

As noted in the introduction, there is a strong link between trade policy and state aid policy in the area of shipbuilding. Due to strong allegations of unfair competition from Korean shipyards the Commission investigated whether these shipyards had been granted aid contrary to WTO rules, and whether the Korean shipyards priced ships at below cost.   **16–011**

The Commission concluded in a report[13] based on the Trade Barrier Regulation (TBR) that EU shipyards indeed had suffered adverse effects and serious prejudices as a result of subsidies and export support. The Commission also found out in other investigations[14] that Korean shipyards in many cases priced its ships below production cost. Based on these reports, the Commission in September 2002 launched a procedure against Korea at the WTO.

This also triggered the so-called Temporary Defensive Mechanism (TDM) into effect, which had been approved by the Council on June 27, 2002, and allowed a form of operating aid for certain types of ships until the WTO procedure had been finalised. The TDM Regulation[15] allowed Member States to provide 6 per cent aid per shipbuilding contract for the ship types identified in the TBR report (container ships, product and chemical tankers), in cases where it could be shown that there was a competing offer from a Korean shipyard offering a lower price. It was at a later stage extended to also include tankers carrying liquefied natural gas. The TDM was originally intended to expire on March 31, 2004, but was subsequently prolonged due to the fact that the WTO proceedings took longer than expected to finalise.   **16–012**

The TDM aid finally expired for contracts signed after March 31, 2005. As was the case for the operating aid under the Shipbuilding Regulation, the ships had to be delivered within three years from this date, unless exceptional circumstances were at hand.

The WTO case *EU v Korea* concerned allegedly unfair competitive practices in the Korean shipbuilding industry. Broadly speaking, two main issues were raised: export subsidies and massive restructuring of Korean yards following the   **16–013**

---

[13] See *http://trade.ec.europa.eu/doclib/cfm/doclib_section.cfm?sec=196&langId=en.*

[14] See reports at *http://trade.ec.europa.eu/doclib/docs/2004/october/tradoc_112208.pdf.* [Accessed September 15, 2011.]

[15] [2002] O.J. L172/1.

Asian financial crisis at the end of 1990s. The final panel report[16] took the view that the export subsidies were illegal, but did not follow the EU's claims concerning the restructuring subsidies (the major part of the contested measures). The WTO accepted the Korean arguments that debt cancellations by public banks were part of normal bankruptcy proceedings. The mixed result of the panel inclined, however, more in favour of Korea.

The TDM was attacked by Korea in the WTO. The WTO panel[17] in this case concluded that the TDM Regulation did not violate the EC's (now EU's) obligations under the GATT 1994 and the Subsidy and Countervailing Measures Agreement. However, the Panel concluded that the TDM was nevertheless an attempt to induce Korea to stop subsidisation of its shipyards and therefore the EC (now EU) did not respect its obligation to use exclusively the WTO dispute settlement system to solve its dispute over Korean subsidisation of shipyards.

16–014   Since WTO rulings do not have retroactive effect, this ruling did not imply that TDM aid had to be recovered. Since the TDM in any case was supposed to end after the WTO ruling, the practical effect of the ruling on the TDM was very limited.

Both Korea and the Commission accepted the rulings by the WTO, which were delivered in 2005. The conflict relating to shipbuilding between these two parties can therefore be considered as closed.

OECD negotiations

16–015   Any account of the international aspects of state aid policy in shipbuilding would not be complete without mentioning negotiations within the framework, the OECD, of an agreement for the re-establishment of normal competition in the shipbuilding industry. The aim of these negotiations is to draw up precise international rules disciplining subsidies in this sector, provide a form of protection against the unfair prices and to set up a specific mechanism for dispute settlement.

Such negotiations started in the early 1990s within the context of the OECD. The background was the problem of subsidies accorded by various countries, and the general feeling that there was an international subsidy race that in the end benefited no country.

16–016   The negotiations ended in an agreement in 1994, but it never entered into force due to the fact that the United States refused to ratify the agreement and its entering into force was dependent upon ratification by all parties. After having waited for several years for the United States to modify its position, in October 2002 the OECD Council mandated a Special Negotiating Group (SNG) to work on a new shipbuilding agreement and finalise a text by the end of 2005. There are 26 countries participating in the SNG (including non-OECD members such as

---

[16] WTO case DS 273. See further: *http://www.worldtradelaw.net/reports/wtopanels/korea-vessels (panel).pdf*. [Accessed August 30, 2011.]

[17] WTO case DS 301. See further: *http://www.worldtradelaw.net/reports/wtopanelsfull/ec-vessels (panel)(full).pdf*. [Accessed August 30, 2011.]

China), with the United States absent due to its insignificant shipbuilding industry and due to the problems in ratifying the previous agreement.

The Commission, acting on behalf of the Member States, strongly supported
the aim of the agreement. The European Union considered that an agreement
should include a discipline on subsidies, an injurious pricing code and an efficient
dispute settlement and remedies.

The negotiations progressed in certain areas, such as stricter prohibition of **16–017**
subsidies than the WTO rules, but by the autumn of 2005 it became evident that
the differences between the parties in other areas were so large that it was decided
to stop the negotiations, and formally take a pause.

One main problem concerned the Special and Differential Treatment requested
by some developing countries, e.g. China. In the view of some delegations these
requests were excessive, given that China is already the third largest shipbuilding
nation in the world.

Another area of major disagreement was the EC's request to include a form of
injurious pricing discipline (basically rules against selling below cost similar to
anti-dumping rules). Several other delegations were strongly against such a
discipline, and it has for the time being been considered impossible to reach a
compromise.

Recent decisions taken by the Commission and/or the Court

Kvaerner Warnow Werft. One long-standing case in shipbuilding is linked to **16–018**
the restructuring of the East German shipyards following German reunification.
Due to the exceptional circumstances in the early 1990s, the Council and the
Commission approved major restructuring aid for six shipyards situated in the
former East Germany. As a counterpart of this aid, the Commission imposed
capacity limitations, which in the view of the Commission, and of the German
authorities, also implied annual production limitations in the form of compensated gross tonnes (cgt).

During one of its inspections, the Commission found out that one of the
shipyards, Kvaerner Warnow Werft, had produced more cgt than its limitation.
Based on this, the Commission ordered the company to repay a certain amount
of the aid it had received. The company challenged the decision, and the Court
of First Instance (CFI) (now General Court) in its judgment[18] annulled the
Commission decision. Its argument was that the Commission decision on which
the Commission argued for a production limitation was not sufficiently clear, and
only foresaw a capacity limitation.

It was, according to the Court, clear that the objective, an actual reduction of **16–019**
capacity, was to be achieved essentially through compliance with a series of
technical restrictions concerning the production plant of the shipyard. It also
stated that if the Commission had really wished to impose an annual ceiling on
actual production, it would have sufficed for it to use the terms production limit

---

[18] Case T–227/99 and T–134/00 *KWW v Commission* [2002] E.C.R. II–1205.

or to specify that the capacity restriction referred, in the present case, to maximum production in optimum conditions. The Court concluded that the Commission committed a manifest error in treating in the contested decisions, contrary to its approach in the authorising decisions, the concept of a capacity restriction as a limit on actual production.

The Commission challenged the judgment in the Court of Justice, which confirmed the judgment of the CFI. The Court noted that, assuming that the Commission was able to take the view that compliance with Directive 90/684 required the authorisations of aid to be subject to the condition that not only the technical capacity of the yard but also its actual production should not exceed 85,000cgt per annum, it should have stated that clearly and unequivocally in its authorising decisions. The Court, however, noted that none of the five authorising decisions mentions specifically that the capacity restriction of 85,000cgt constitutes a yearly ceiling on actual production.

16–020   **IZAR.** On May 12, 2004 the European Commission took a decision[19] concerning aid worth €500 million which the Spanish State holding company, Sociedad Estatal de Participaciones Industriales (SEPI), granted in 1999 and 2000 to the publicly owned civil shipyards, owned at the time by IZAR, a subsidiary of SEPI. The Commission concluded that this amount constituted state aid which could not be approved under the EU rules on aid to shipbuilding. As loans amounting to €192 million had been paid back to SEPI, the sum to be recovered from IZAR amounted to €308 million, plus interest.

On October 20, 2004, the European Commission took another decision[20] with regard to IZAR. The Commission in this decision established that SEPI had granted an additional €556 million to the publicly owned civil shipyards during 2000. This aid, granted in favour of IZAR's civil activities, was not in line with EU state aid rules and the Commission therefore concluded that this amount also had to be recovered from IZAR. These two decisions followed several years of complaints from competitors about the business behaviour of the Spanish public shipyards.

16–021   Following the Commission decisions, Spain has taken several steps in order to reorganise its public shipbuilding sector. The reason is that IZAR had to declare bankruptcy once the recovery claim for the illegal and incompatible aid was introduced in the balance sheet of the company. This was done in January 2005. One aim of the reorganisation was to prevent IZAR's military production from being harmed, which is a legitimate objective in accordance with art.348 TFEU.

This goal is reached by transferring the military production to a new public company ("Navantia"). Since the new company, for viability reasons, will need to have certain civil activities, safeguards have been put in place in agreement with the Commission. Another aim has been to, if possible, rescue employment

---

[19] [2005] O.J. L58/58.
[20] [2005] O.J. L240/45.

in the civil shipyards, while still respecting Community legislation. The objective is to privatise the civil shipyards, through open and transparent market operations. In this way, the Commission may accept that the state aid recovery claim on IZAR will not apply to the privatised shipyards, as it had done in cases in ohter sectors.[21]

Innovation aid. Innovation aid was granted for the improved vessel design and weight in case of the SWATH (small waterplane area twin hull) vessels built by ThyssenNordseewerke for the German customs administration.[22] The challenge consisted of the combination of displacement and speed. Existing SWATH vessels were either heavy and slow, allowing for long range, or rather light but allowing higher speeds. The combination of higher speed with a long operating range required innovative design, requiring additional IT tools. The Commission found these challenges sufficient to constitute an innovation.   16–022

Furthermore, it found that there were substantial risks connected in the project, and found the costs to be eligible. A reimbursement clause that provided for a partial reimbursement in case of success of the innovation—20 per cent of the aid would have to be paid back as of the 5th vessel produced with the new, innovative design—lowered the risk of a negative impact on competition and allowed the approval of the aid.   16–023

Matching. In 2003 the Netherlands notified plans to give aid in support of six shipbuilding contracts in four Dutch shipyards. The purpose of the aid was to match illegal and incompatible aid allegedly offered by another Member State to shipyards in that country which competed for the shipbuilding contracts. As a result of the promised aid, the Dutch shipyards lowered their price and got the contested orders.   16–024

On June 30, 2004 the Commission declared[23] this aid to be incompatible with the Treaty. The Commission underlined in its decision that the principle that a Member State should not act on its own to counter the effects of unlawful aid from another Member State has been clearly established by the Court. Specifically, the Court has held that it is not possible to justify an aid on the ground that other Member States have granted illegal aid. The Commission, furthermore, had doubts concerning the alleged proof that the aid really was available.

The effect of this decision was to reaffirm the need for respect of state aid rules, and that if a Member State suspects that another Member State provides unlawful and incompatible state aid, it should not take unilateral action but inform the Commission about such suspicions. In this way a subsidy race, that in the end would only harm taxpayers, can be avoided.

---

[21] Commission Decision N83/2009 concerning the sale of certain assets by Olympic Airlines/Olympic Airways Services, [2010] O.J. C25/15.
[22] Commission Decision N342/2007, [2008] O.J. C80/2.
[23] [2005] O.J. L39/48.

16–025 **Regional aid.** On July 13, 2009 the Commission decided[24] to authorise regional investment aid to Volkswerft shipyard in Germany. The Commission noted that the investment project mainly consists in making existing equipment more productive, allowing the side-by-side production of different types of vessels.

The Commission underlines that its analysis of regional aid cases is done in three steps: (1) does the investment lead to an improvement or a modernisation of existing installations aiming at an increase in the overall productivity of the yard, and is this aim being achieved, (2) is there an increase in capacity, and (3) can this increase in capacity be accepted. The decision notes that, although there is an increase in capacity expressed in cgt (compensated gross tons), the actual output in numbers of vessels and the actual output of steel will be lower, following the investment. Assessing the effects of the investment on the overall productivity, the Commission concluded that the capacity increase is merely a side effect of the investment and not the main aim of the investment. Consequently, it concluded that the capacity increase can be accepted.

The Commission also noted that the investment related to the actual acquisition of new assets at market prices, and did not lead to a mere replacement of obsolete installations. A mere replacement of obsolete installations would not be considered eligible for state aid.

16–026 **Ship financing.** Financing is a crucial element in shipbuilding, both in terms of financing the construction of a ship and financing its purchase. For this reason several Member States have guaranteed funds aimed at facilitating ship financing. The Commission has had to ensure that these schemes are aid free, and has taken a number of decisions linked to this. The basic principle of the Commission has been that the guarantee fees have to be market-based, and differentiated based on risk factors. This is necessary to ensure that the guarantee schemes will in all probability be self-financing. An example of a Commission decision approving such a scheme concerns the Netherlands.[25] The Commission also took a decision approving a German scheme[26] as being in line with the communication on guarantees.

16–027 **Military/civil production.** Many shipyards and shipbuilding companies mix military and civil production, which can pose problems as regards state aid. Protection of military production, at least for domestic use, is a legitimate interest of a Member State according to arts 346 to 348 TFEU. The Commission had to handle aid provided to mixed military and civil shipyard companies on a few occasions. Besides the cases linked to IZAR, mentioned above, it also took a

---

[24] Commission Decision N227/2009 [2009] O.J. C191/02.
[25] See *Competition Policy Newsletter*, No.2 Summer 2004, p.105, and Commission Decision N197/2007 of September 25, 2007, amended by Commission Decision N541/2007 of November 28, 2007.
[26] See Communication of the Commission on the Application of Articles 87 and 88 EC-Treaty on state aid in the form of guarantees, [2008] O.J. C155/10, corrigendum [2008] O.J. C244/32.

decision related to the Greek Hellenic shipyards. In this case[27] the Commission considered that aid granted to the company did not fall under state aid rules as regards the amount intended for the military section. It estimated this amount as the same proportion of the total aid as the proportion between military and civil production in the company. As regards the rest of the notified aid, attributable to the civil production, the Commission approved part of it as partial closure aid, and in a later final decision[28] deemed the rest of the aid to be incompatible. This aid had to be recovered with interest to the extent that any of the aid had been paid out. In a further decision, the Commission found misuse of state aid and ordered the recovery thereof.[29]

---

[27] [2002] O.J. C186/5.
[28] [2005] O.J. L75/52.
[29] [2009] O.J. L225/104.

CHAPTER 17

TRANSPORT*

1. INTRODUCTION 17–001
2. SECONDARY LEGISLATION ON STATE AID FOR THE INLAND TRANSPORT SECTOR 17–006
    Public service obligations 17–006
    Coordination of transport 17–014
    The PSO Regulation 17–017
    Railways 17–025
    Inland waterways 17–030
    De minimis for transport 17–033
3. THE APPLICATION OF THE RULES 17–034
    General 17–034
    Rail 17–035
    Inland water transport 17–041
    Road transport 17–043
    Combined transport 17–046
    Maritime transport 17–049
    Air transport 17–061
    Airports 17–074
4. CONCLUSION 17–086

1. INTRODUCTION

17–001   State aid policy in the transport sector[1] is more complex than that in other sectors.[2] This is due to the tension between (i) general state aid rules (i.e. the

---

* Tibor Scharf

[1] It is worth noting that the transport sector is an essential component of the European economy. The transport industry as a whole accounts for 7% of GDP and for over 5% of total employment in the EU, 2009 Report on Competition Policy, COM(2010) 282 final, para.375.

[2] 9th Survey on State Aid in the European Union, July 18, 2001 (COM 2001(403) final), para.151, see also Commission decision of 2.3.2005 in case N 384/2004 France, restructuring aid to SNCF, summary notice in [2005] O.J. C172/3.

prohibition of aid), (ii) the aim of creating a Common Transport Policy,[3] as well as (iii) the necessity to take into account other policy considerations such as social, regional and—increasingly—environmental ones, which will often necessitate maintaining services which might not be maintained on purely economic grounds.

The picture is complicated further by the fact the there are special Treaty provisions (art.93[3a]) applicable to inland transport (rail, road including road haulage, inland waterways and intermodal transport)[4] whereas air and maritime transport are covered by arts 107, 108 and sector guidelines.[5] Articles 93 and 96 TFEU contain special rules for state aid to the transport which are applicable in addition to arts 107 and 108.

Article 93 TFEU is a derogation, analogous to those in art.107(2),[6] to the general state aid prohibition in art.107 TFEU.[7] It provides for (i) State aid for the coordination of transport or (ii) aid representing the reimbursement for the discharge of public service obligations, to be compatible with the Treaty. As settled by the Court of Justice in the *Belgian railways* case[8] art.93 TFEU does not, however, exempt transport from the general provisions on state aid, but rather provides an additional basis for allowing state aid.[9] The scope of art.93 TFEU, which therefore applies to measures which constitute state aid as defined by art.107 TFEU,[10] has been specified in secondary legislation which is discussed in the next section.

17–002

Article 96 TFEU on the other hand is a specification of the general aid state aid prohibition contained in art.107 insofar as it prohibits the imposition by Member

---

[3] Cf. Schmidt-Kötters in Haidenhain, "European State Aid Law", München 2010, para.59 who rightly points to the important aim of support for open markets in the sector; more generally on the objectives of the common transport policy, see (for land transport) Regulation (EC) No.1370/2007 of the European Parliament and of the Council of October 23, 2007 on public passenger transport services by rail and by road and repealing Council Regulations (EEC) Nos 1191/69 and 1107/70, paras 4 following.

[3a] Grabitz/Boeing—Maxian Rusche, ECV, art.93, para.23.

[4] Although the terms are not used consistently, see Schmidt-Kötters in Haidenhain, *European State Aid Law*, München 2010, para.54.

[5] Case 156/77 *Commission v Belgium* [1978] E.C.R. 1881, paras 9 and 13 following; 167/73 *Commission v France* [1974] E.C.R. 359, paras 29–32, joined cases 209–213/84 *Ministere Public v Asjes* [1986] E.C.R. 1425 paras 39–42.

[6] See Opinion of AG Léger of March 18, 2002, in Case C–280/00 *Altmark Trans v Nahverkehrsgesellschaft Altmark GmbH* [2003] E.C.R. I–7747, para.84.

[7] art.93 TFEU is one of the articles referred by the words "*Save as otherwise provided in this Treaty.*" in art.107(1) TFEU.

[8] Case 156/77 *Commission v Belgium* [1978] E.C.R. 1881.

[9] Or a lex specialis, see: Regulation (EC) No.1370/2007 of the European Parliament and of the Council of October 23, 2007 on public passenger transport services by rail and by road and repealing Council Regualtions (EEC) Nos 1191/69 and 1107/70, para.3 and "State Aid Policy in the European Community" by P. Nicolaides, M. Kekelekis, M Kleis, 2nd edn, p.68; see more generally Tim Maxian Rusche and Silvia Schmidt, "The post-Altmark era has started: 15 month of application of Regualtion (EC) No. 1370/2007 to public transport services", *ESAL* 2/2011 p.249.

[10] Case 156/77 *Commission v Belgium* [1978] E.C.R. 1881; Erdmenger in von der Groeben/ Schwarze (Hrsg.), "Kommentar zum Vertrag über die Europäische Union und zur Gründung der Europäischen Gemeinschaft", *Nomos-Verlag*, 6. Aufl., 2004, Artikel 73, Rn 3.

States of favourable transport rates and conditions regulated by State authorities for the benefit of particular undertakings or industries.[11] In its second paragraph, this article also contains the relevant procedural rules for its application, essentially subjecting any supporting rates or conditions to Commission approval. The Commission considers any such rates either upon application by a member States or ex officio. It is granted a wide discretion in balancing the effects of such rates, essentially on competition against considerations of regional policy.[12] Article 96 is, however, rarely applied in practice.

17–003   The state aid regime applied in the transport sectors is further characterised by the fact that art.100 TFEU limits the special regime provided for in art.93 TFEU to the inland transport sector, which covers rail, inland waterway and road transport, and does therefore not cover maritime and air transport. Article 100 (2) foresees that it is up to the Council to decide upon the application of state aid rules to the sea and air transport sectors.[13] State aid control in the transport sector is thus effectively split into two groups[14]:

(1) **Inland and combined transport**, subject to extensive secondary legislation[15] which is influenced by the notion of public service obligations and its potential effects on competition in the markets concerned.[16]

(2) **Maritime and air transport** on the other hand are effectively subject to the "normal" state aid regime of art.107. The maritime sector is covered by Union Guidelines.[17] Specific aspects of the aviation sector are also subject to guidelines which govern the financing of airports and start-up aid to airlines departing from regional airports.[18]

---

[11] See Rosa Greaves, *Transport Law of the European Community*, (Athlone, London & Atlantic Highlands, NJ), 1991, p.21; Jung, in Calliess/Ruffert (Hrsg.), EUV/AEUV, (C.H Beck, München) 4th edn 2010, art.96, para.7; Mückenhausen, in Lenz/ Borchardt (Hrsg.), EU Verträge, (Bundesanzeiger Köln, H) 5th edn, 2010, art.96, para.2;

[12] Case 1/69 *Italian Republic v Commission* [1969] E.C.R. 277, para.4.

[13] See Case 167/73 *Commission v France* [1974] E.C.R. 359; and Christopher H. Bovis, "State aid and European Transport: A Reflection on Law, Policy and Practice", *Journal of World Trade* 39(4) [2005], pp.587.

[14] Stefan Tostmann, "Sense and Serendipity—Towards a Coherent Commission State Aid Approach in the Intermodal Transport Sector", *World Competition* [2002] 25 (1), p.103.

[15] Since the judgment by the ECJ in case C–280/00 *Altmark trans* [2003] E.C.R. I–7747 at paras 106–108, the compatibility criteria of art.93 were considered to be exhaustively covered by Council Regulations 1107/70, 1191/69 and 1192/69, and thus now by Regulations (EC) No.1370/2007 of the European Parliament and of the Council of October 23, 2007 on public passenger transport services by rail and by road and repealing Council Regulations (EEC) Nos 1191/69 and 1107/70 and by Regulation 1192/69.

[16] This does not, of course, preclude the general principle, that also aid granted on the basis of this secondary legislation should be suited necessary and proportional to achieving the intended result, see, e.g. Jung, in Calliess/Ruffert (Hrsg.), EUV/AEUV, (C.H Beck, München) 4th edn, 2010, art.93 para.9; Geiger/Khan/Kotzur, "EUV/AEUV", 5th edn, art.93 para.2 (C.H.. Beck, München, 2010).

[17] Commission Communication—Community guidelines on State aid to maritime transport [2004] O.J. C13/3.

[18] Commission Communication—Community guidelines on financing of airports and start-up aid to airlines departing from regional airports [2005] O.J. C312/1.

The state aid control procedure in the transport sector is, however, identical to the one for all other sectors.[19]

The analysis of the application of state aid law to transport in this chapter will follow this dichotomy, focusing firstly on inland transport and considering, secondly, the situation of the maritime and air transport sectors.

Overall, state aid control in the transport sector is heavily influenced by the Union's transport policy, among the main objectives of which are the promotion of environmentally friendly modes of transport in general and the reduction of road transport in particular. Two elements are considered essential to achieve these objectives. First, Member States need to encourage cleaner modes of transport and measures to increase energy efficiency. This has been underlined, for instance, in the Commission's Green Paper on energy efficiency of May 2005.[20] Environmental concerns, including the reduction of greenhouse gases has taken on an additional importance after Kyoto, and so has the need to increase energy efficiency not only on account of environmental concerns, but also—and increasingly importantly—in order to reduce the Union's dependence on energy imports[21] and, in particular, oil.[22] Second, the revitalisation of the railway sector is considered a key element in the Union's common transport policy.[23] In this context, it is seen to be essential to make rail transport competitive enough to remain one of the leading players in the transport system in an enlarged Europe. In 2007, the entire European freight network Union was opened up completely to competition. The arrival of new railway companies make the sector more competitive and encourage the national companies to restructure. In this context, specific guidelines for the railway sector have been adapted in 2008 in order to establish a common approach to public contributions to the railway sector.[24] At the same time, the Union has been pursuing a policy to gradually reduce road freight transport, the (negative) consequences of which are seen as wide ranging:

17–004

---

[19] Hence, Council Regulation (EC) 659/1999 [1999] O.J. L83/1 and Commission Regulation (EC) 794/2004 [2004] O.J. L140/1, are equally applicable to the transport sectors.

[20] COM(2005) 265 final of June 22, 2005, available online at: *http://ec.europa.eu/energy/ efficiency/doc/2005_06_green_paper_book_en.pdf*. See also, Commission Discussion Paper "Services of general economic interest and State aid for instance" of November 12, 2002, available online at: *http://ec.europa.eu/comm/competition/state_aid/others/1759_sieg_en.pdf* the CIVITAS, co-financed by the European Union, initiative aimed at promoting cleaner and efficient urban transport, *http://www.civitas-initiative.org*.

[21] See for instance: White Paper "Roadmap to a Single European Transport Area—Towards a competitive and resource efficient transport system" COM/2011/0144 final, point 6.

[22] It must be mentioned though that whilst an effort is being made via a lenient state aid regime for measures seeking to further the environment, including in the transport sector, far more resources are being spent on measures that are actually harmful to the environment. The German Federal Agency for the Environment (Umweltbundesamt) for instance estimated that in 2008, up to €48 billion were spent on subsidies harmful to the environment in Germany alone (See press release No.72/2008, available online *http://www.umweltdaten.de/publikationen/fpdf-l/3780.pdf* out of which about 23 billion concerned the transport sector.

[23] Communication from the Commission—Community Guidelines on State aid for railway undertakings [2008] O.J. C184/13.

[24] Communication from the Commission—Community Guidelines on State aid for railway undertakings [2008] O.J. C184/13.

additional road infrastructure costs, accidents, congestion, local and global pollution, the reliability of the supply chain and of logistics processes and environmental damage.[25] A prime goal of the Union's transport policy is to increase efficiency by opening up access to transport markets by taking into account the particular characteristics of each transport mode. Union air, ship and road haulage operators now have complete freedom to provide services, cabotage is already free on inland waterways and road haulage and, since January 1999, ferry operators are enjoying steadily increasing rights.[26] As recognised by the Commission, these policy goals lead to a particular tension in the application of state aid control: open and competitive markets do not preclude public intervention, in particular when such intervention can be deemed to be in the general interest[27] or to be aimed at achieving objectives of the Common Transport Policy.[28] This leads to the necessity to be very vigilant about any public intervention which can be abused to protect undertakings from market forces and undermine the goal of better, cheaper services that the liberalisation of transport markets is meant to promote. A strict control of state aid is therefore necessary. It is, on the other hand, also necessary to ensure that such control does not inadvertently frustrate the objectives of the Common Transport Policy.[29]

17–005   Overall aid to the transport sector remains very high: in 2001 it exceeded aid to the manufacturing sector,[30] and in 2006 and 2007 notifications of aid in the transport sector represented the second largest number of notifications for a sector.[31] As rail transport is particularly capital-intensive, aid to this sector can, in countries which dispose of a fine mashed rail network such as the Benelux

---

[25] See Regulation (EC) No.1692/2006 of the European Parliament and of the Council of October 24, 2006 establishing the second Marco Polo programme for the granting of Community financial assistance to improve the environmental performance of the freight transport system (Marco Polo II) and repealing Regulation (EC) No.1382/2003 [2006] O.J. L328/1, recital 2.

[26] Seventh Survey on State aid in the European Union in the Manufacturing and Certain Other Sectors, March 30, 1999, para.49; available online at. *http://ec.europa.eu/comm/competition/ state_aid/survey/rap7_en.pdf.*

[27] As pointed out by Competition Commissioner Almunia, "Competition policy must also help to guarantee accessible and affordable high-quality public services, which are fundamental to citizens' well-being and quality of life and which also contribute to social and territorial cohesion", foreword to the 2009 Report on Competition Policy, COM(2010) 282 final, p.5.

[28] See, for instance: Communication from the Commission—Community Guidelines on state aid for railway undertakings [2008] O.J. C184/13.

[29] Seventh Survey on State aid in the European Union in the Manufacturing and Certain Other Sectors, March 30, 1999, para.50; available online at *http://ec.europa.eu/comm/competition/ state_aid/survey/rap7_en.pdf.*

[30] 31st Report on Competition Policy, para.329, see also State aid Scoreboard—spring 2003 update, Brussels, COM(2003)225 final, of 30.4.2003, Table 3 on p.13, available online at: *http:/ /ec.europa.eu/comm/competition/state_aid/scoreboard/2003/en.pdf* here, the average aid to the transport sector is shown to represent 46% as opposed to 25% for manufacturing on an EU average.

[31] With 8% of total notifications, after agriculture (33%); see Report on Competition Policy 2007 COM (2008)368 final, fn.16, in which somewhat confusingly, all notifications concerning all manufacturing and services sectors are counted together (thus accounting for 53% of notifications) and Report on Competition Policy 2006 COM (2007) 358 final, para.120.

countries, reach up to 60 per cent of total aid.[32] Overall, the Commission estimates that the provision of transport services (including storage, warehousing and other auxiliary activities) account for about 4–5 per cent of Union GDP and for some 4.4 per cent of the total workforce i.e. more than 9.2 million persons (2007 figures).[33]

2. SECONDARY LEGISLATION ON STATE AID FOR THE INLAND TRANSPORT SECTOR

Public Service Obligations

As seen above, one of the two special rules provided by art.93 TFEU for the transport sector concern the reimbursement for the discharge of public service obligations.

17–006

The distortive potential arising from the imposition and any subsequent over-compensation of public service obligations has been recognised early on by the Institutions. In a decision of May 13, 1965, the Council laid down a programme for the harmonisation of national rules that affect competitive conditions in the inland transport sector.[34] This decision dealt also with distortions of competition resulting from the imposition of public service obligations and stipulated that any decision by the competent national authorities to maintain such an obligation entails an obligation to pay compensation. This approach has been implemented through the adoption of Regulations 1191/69[35] and 1192/69[36] and 1107/70,[37] which were—and in the case of Regulation 1192/69 still is—applied to the sector until recently[38] when Regulations 1191/69 and 1107/70 were repealed by Reg-

---

[32] State aid Scoreboard—spring 2003 update, Brussels, COM(2003)225 final, of April 30, 2003, p.5 available online at: *http://ec.europa.eu/comm/competition/state_aid/scoreboard/2003/en.pdf*.

[33] Commission Staff Working Paper accompanying the Report on Competition Policy 2010, COM (2011) final, para.302, available online at *http://ec.europa.eu/competition/publications/annual_report/2010/part2_en.pdf*.

[34] Decision 65/271 [1965] O.J. 1500.

[35] [1969] O.J. L156/1—as last amended by Regulation (EC) No.1893/91 [1991] O.J. L169/1.

[36] [1969] O.J. L156/8—as last amended by Regulation (EC) No.1791/06 [2006] O.J. L363/1.

[37] [1970] O.J. L130/1—as last amended by Regulation (EC) No.543/97 [1997] O.J. L84/6.

[38] The Commission had been seeking to update these Regulations for a long time: an attempt was started in 2000, see 30th Report on Competition Policy, paras 373–375, which reported that the Commission adopted two proposals for Council regulations dealing with public funding in the land transport area, which will transpose into secondary legislation the exemptions laid down in art.93 TFEU. The first instrument, which was to replace Council Regulation (EEC) No.1107/70, was indented to provide a legal basis for the exemption of state aid in the context of the financing of transport infrastructure and the grant of aid in connection with the use of certain types of infrastructure. The second instrument, which was to replace Council Regulation (EEC) No.1191/69, was to provide a framework tailored to ongoing developments that are taking place in the passenger transport market with a view to meeting public needs, laying down rules for non-discriminatory market access and creating transparent conditions for the public financing of such services. See also *Commission Proposal for a regulation of the European Parliament and of the Council concerning the granting of aid for the co-ordination of transport by rail, road and inland waterway,* COM(2000) 5 final, July 26, 2000 [2000] O.J. C/365E/179.

ulation (EC) No 1370/2007[39] (the "PSO Regulation"[40]). The PSO Regulation entered into force on December 3, 2009 and includes four transition periods.[40a] The PSO Regulation lays down the rules applicable to the compensation of public service obligations in inland traffic. Until the entry into force of the new rules, the Commission has continued to apply the existing state aid rules to public service contracts and public service obligations, as clarified in the *Altmark* Judgment.[41]

17–007   As Regulations 1191/69 and 1107/70 have been at the basis of state aid decisions for nearly four decades, and their basic concepts can still be found in the PSO Regulation, they are worthy of a few words. Arguably the most important aspect already reflected in these Regulations is the tension between public service obligations (and the compensation for such obligations) and state aid discipline. The relation between public service obligations and state aid has been further developed by case law, which will also be set out before introducing the recent PSO Regulation which builds on the 1969 Regulations and case law.[42]

17–008   Regulation 1191/69 provided for a regime for action by Member States concerning the obligations inherent in the concept of a public service in transport by rail, road and inland waterways. Such a common regime was important because of the automatic exemption by art.93 TFEU of aid representing reimbursement for the discharge of a public service obligation; in the absence of a regime setting out a legal framework, there could be a temptation for state aid to be granted under the disguise of reimbursements for public service obligation.[43] A public service obligation was defined by Regulation 1191/69 as an obligation to provide a service which a transport undertaking would, if it were considering exclusively its own commercial interests, not assume or would not assume to the same extent and under the same conditions.[44] According to art.1(1), Member States were to terminate all obligations inherent in the concept of a public service (principle of termination of public service contracts). Nevertheless, art.1(2) of Regulation 1191/69 allowed Member States to maintain such obligations insofar as they were essential to ensure the provision of adequate transport services. Article 1(4) provided that financial burdens devolving on transport undertakings as a result of the maintenance of a public service obligation shall be subject to compensation in accordance with the procedure of the regulation.

[39] Regulation (EC) No.1370/2007 of the European Parliament and of the Council of October 23, 2007 on public passenger transport services by rail and by road and repealing Council Regulations (EEC) Nos 1191/69 and 1107/70 [2007] O.J. L315/1.
[40] The same defined term is used here as in the Communication from the Commission— Community Guidelines on state aid for railway undertakings [2008] O.J. C184/13, para.19.
[40a] See arts 8 and 10.
[41] Report on Competition Policy 2009, COM(2010) 282 final, para.379.
[42] The PSO Regulation's recitals contain a chronology of the developments in this area, cf. recitals 5 to 33.
[43] Christopher H. Bovis, "State aid and European Transport: A Reflection on Law, Policy and Practice", *Journal of World Trade* [2005] 39(4), pp.587.
[44] art.2(1).

Section II of Regulation 1191/69 laid down common principles for both terminating and maintaining public service obligations. Section III regulated the application of the rules to passenger transport rates and conditions, while s.IV contained common compensation procedures. Section V allowed Member States to impose new public service obligations.

According to art.17(2) of Regulation 1191/69, Member States were exempted from the notification procedure under art.108 TFEU. They must, however, promptly forward details of compensation payments. In other words, there was an a posteriori obligation to notify, instead of the usual a priori obligation.

Regulation 1107/70 clarified the circumstances in which aid for reimburse- **17–009**
ment of a public service obligation can be granted. According to its art.3(2) such aid could, until the entry into force of relevant Union rules, only be granted where payments are made to rail, road or inland waterway transport undertakings as compensation for public service obligations imposed on them by the State or public authorities and covering either[45] tariff obligations not falling within the definition given in art.2 (5) of Regulation (EEC) No 1191/69; transport under-takings or activities to which that Regulation did not apply. Regulation 1191/69 had been amended by Regulation 1893/91[46] which introduced "*public service contracts*".[47]

The principle of the termination of public service obligations in Council **17–010**
Regulation 1191/69[48] has been the subject of a preliminary ruling by the Court in the case *Kainuun Liikenne*.[49] The Court held that although art.4 of Regulation 1191/69 allows transport undertakings, which are subject to a public service obligation, to apply for the termination of such an obligation in whole or in part, Member States have a discretion as to whether or not to grant such a request. This is so even if the applicant demonstrates that the public service obligation entails economic disadvantages. However, Member States had to respect the rules of arts 3, 6 (2) and 7 of Regulation 1191/69. This implied that a refusal can only be based on the necessity of maintaining the provision of adequate transport serv-ices, having regard to: (i) the public interest; (ii) the possibility of having recourse to other forms of transport and the ability of such forms to meet the transport needs under consideration; and (iii) the transport rates and conditions which can be quoted to users.

Furthermore, the Court held that competent authorities are to select the service that secures the lowest costs for the Union if other services can be offered for equivalent conditions. Hence, the Court recognised, already before the *Altmark*

---

[45] Arguably, this Regulation thus defined the concept of aid meeting the need for coordination of transport in its arts 3(1) and 3(2), A. Collucci in "EU Competition Law, Vol. IV—State Aid" Claeys & Casteels, September 2008, para.4.2103.

[46] [1991] O.J. L169/1.

[47] The notion of public service contract has been specified in the Commission's 21st Report on Competition Policy (para.177) as referring to a contract concluded between the competent authorities of a Member State and a transport undertaking with a view to providing the public with adequate transport services.

[48] As amended by Regulation 1893/91.

[49] Case C–412/96 *Kainuun Liikenne Oy* [1998] E.C.R. I–5141.

case, the necessity of public service obligations whilst framing it so that such obligations disrupt competition as little as possible.

The importance of public services for Member States has also been recognised by the Commission.[50] It is highlighted by the recent public discussion of all aspects of such services,[51] including the way in which they should be provided, as well as by the fact that the draft Constitution explicitly mentioned them.

17–011   The ECJ's ruling in the case *Altmark*[52] further clarified the issue of public service compensation in the context of state aid. It addressed the question of whether and when such compensation constitutes state aid. The Court held first that the existence of an advantage is an essential requirement in order for a measure to constitute state aid. In accordance with its earlier judgment in *Ferring*,[53] the Court held that where the measure merely compensates an undertaking for the discharge of a public service obligation without the undertaking obtaining a real economic benefit as a result, this would not constitute state aid within the meaning of art.107 TFEU. However, the Court held that that the absence of aid is subject to four conditions[54]:

(i) The recipient undertaking must actually have public service obligations to discharge, and the obligations must be clearly defined.

(ii) The parameters on the basis of which the compensation is calculated must be established in advance in an objective and transparent manner, to avoid it conferring an economic advantage which may favour the recipient undertaking over competing undertakings.

(iii) The compensation cannot exceed what is necessary to cover all or part of the costs incurred in the discharge of public service obligations, taking into account the relevant receipts and a reasonable profit.

(iv) Where the undertaking which is to discharge public service obligations, in a specific case, is not chosen pursuant to a public procurement procedure which would allow for the selection of the tenderer capable of providing those services at the least cost to the Union, the level of compensation needed must be determined on the basis of an analysis of the costs which a typical undertaking, well run and adequately provided with means of transport so as to be able to meet the necessary public service requirements, would have incurred in discharging those obligations, taking into account the relevant receipts and a reasonable profit for discharging the obligations.

[50] See, e.g. Report on Competition Policy 2004, para.398 et seq.
[51] See for instance Christian Scharpf "Der Einfluss des Europarechts auf die Daseinsvorsorge" [2005] *EuZW* 295, and the Comité européen de liaison sur les Services d'intérêt général, *www.celsig.org*, and its newsletter *News Europe*, No.146 of February 13, 2004.
[52] Case C–280/2000 *Altmark Trans and Regierungspräsidium Magdeburg* [2003] E.C.R. I–7742.
[53] Case C–53/2000 *Ferring* [2001] E.C.R. I–9067.
[54] Case C–280/2000 *Altmark Trans and Regierungspräsidium Magdeburg* [2003] E.C.R. I–7742, paras 88–93.

Where these conditions are met, the compensation does not constitute state aid and the prior notification obligation is not applicable.

The *Altmark* judgment lead to considerable uncertainty about the state aid law **17–012** situation of a great number of (frequently small and/or local) undertakings in receipt of compensation for public services, often for the provision of local transport. To clarify how the *Altmark* judgment would be applied in practice and to clarify the state aid situation of companies carrying out public service obligation,[55] three pieces of legislation were adopted in 2005 in the so-called "*Monti-Kroes Package*":

(i) **A Commission Decision** based on Article 106(3) of the TFEU Treaty which specified the conditions under which compensation to companies for the provision of public services is compatible with State aid rules and is exempt from the notification requirement.[56]

(ii) **A Union Framework**[56a] which specified the conditions under which compensation not covered by the Commission Decision is compatible with state aid rules.

(iii) An **amendment to the Commission Transparency Directive**[57] clarified that companies receiving compensation and operating on both public service and other markets must have separate accounts for their different activities, so that the absence of over-compensation can be checked.

The *Monti-Kroes Package* has been substantially reviewed in 2011[58] and the Commission Decision and Framework have been replaced as from January 31,

---

[55] See Commission Press release of July 15, 2005, IP/05/937.

[56] Commission Decision of November 28, 2005 on the application of art.86(2) of the EC Treaty to State aid in the form of public service compensation granted to certain undertakings entrusted with the operation of services of general economic interest (2005/842/EC), O.J. L312/67. The decision foresaw essentially that the Decision was applicable to compensation of less than €30 million per year provided its beneficiaries have an annual turnover of less than €100 million. Compensation granted for air and sea transport to islands not exceeding 300,000 passenger in the two years preceding that in which the service of general economic interest was entrusted as well as airports and ports the passenger volume of which does not exceed 1,000,000 (airports) and 300,000 (ports) in the two years preceding the entrustment also benefited from the Decision irrespective of the amounts involved (art.2 (c) and (d)).The conditions for compatibility were that: (1) there is a clearly defined public service mandate (art.4) and; (2) there may not be any over-compensation (art.5(1)).

[56a] Community framework for state aid in the form of public service compensation, published on November 29, 2005, O.J. C297/4.

[57] Commission Directive 2006/111/EC of November 16, 2006 on the transparency of financial relations between Member States and public undertakings as well as on financial transparency within certain undertakings (Codified version) Text with EEA relevance [2006] O.J. L 318/17, and amendment to Commission Directive 80/723/EEC of June 25, 1980 on the transparency of financial relations between Member States and public undertakings, [1980] O.J. L195/35.

[58] Commission Communication on the Reform of the EU State Aid Rules on Services of General Economic Interest of 23.3.2011,COM(2011) 146 final, available online at *http://ec.europa.eu/ competition/state_aid/legislation/sgei.html*.

2012.[59] The 2006 amendment to the Commission Transparency Directive remains valid[59a] and is incorporated into the Communication.[59b]

The new package on SGEI which is relevant to maritime and air transport,[59c] consists of:

(i) A revised **Decision[59d] (the "SGEI Decision")**, which exempts Member States from the obligation to notify public service compensation for certain types of SGEI to the Commission. Whilst the exemption is now granted to a wider range of social services, the notification threshold was lowered to €15 million, which is of pertinence to the transport sector as investments are typically larger in that sector. This decision does **not** apply to the land transport or transport infrastructure sectors.[59e] It does, however, apply to the maritime and air transport sectors,[59f] for which the compensation also has to comply with the sectoral rules contained in Regulations No.1008/2008 and 3577/92[59g] in order to qualify for the exemption from the obligation to notify. In the case of public service compensation for air or maritime links to islands and for airports and ports which constitute services of general economic, interest thresholds are based on the average annual number of passengers as this more accurately reflects the economic reality of these activities and their character of services of general economic interest. These thresholds are of a maximum of 200,000 passengers, in the case of airports, and 300,000 passengers in the case of ports, in both cases during the two financial years preceding that in which the SGEI was assigned.[59h] Other than that the exemption requirements are similar to those in the prior Decision in that they require a clearly defined entrustment (art.4), include a prohibition on overcompensation (art.5) and the necessity for Member States to control the compensation granted. A novel feature is the requirement in art.7 for Member States to publish any entrustment leading to compensation above €15 million to undertakings also having activities outside the scope of the SGEI.

(ii) A new **Communication[59i]** which clarifies basic concepts of State aid which are relevant for the assessment of SGEIs, such as the notions of SGEI, aid, or economic activity.

[59] Point 5 of the Framework, and Article 12 of the Commission Decision.
[59a] Recital 10 (c) of the Communication.
[59b] See para.2.5 of the Communication.
[59c] Inland transport is subject to the PSO Regulation and art.93 TFEU.
[59d] Commission Decision of 20 December on the application of art.106(2) of the Treaty on the Functioning of the European Union to State aid in the form of public service compensation granted to certain undertakings entrusted with the operation of services of general economic interest. O.J. L7/3 of January 11, 2012.
[59e] Recital 24 and art.2(a) of the Decision.
[59f] Recital 24 and art.2(d) of the Decision.
[59g] Recital 24 and art.2(4) of the Decision.
[59h] art.2(e) of the Decision.
[59i] O.J. C8/15 of January 11, 2012.

(iii) A **revised Framework** for assessing compensation not covered by the Commission Decision 2012/21, essentially large compensation amounts granted to operators outside the social services field. Again, this framework applies to the air and maritime sectors, but not to land transport.[59j] Such envisaged compensation for SGEI has to be notified to the Commission and may be declared compatible if it meets certain criteria. The new rules introduce a more precise methodology to determine the amount of compensation, a requirement for Member States to include efficiency incentives in compensation mechanisms, the requirement to comply with Union public procurement rules and equal treatment of providers of the same service when determining compensation. Moreover, the Commission may require Member States to adopt measures to reduce the anticompetitive effects of certain compensations that present a particularly strong potential for distorting competition in the Internal Market.

It should be mentioned that a proposal for a revised de minimis *Regulation*, providing that compensation below a certain threshold does not fall under State aid scrutiny, is expected to be adopted in 2012[59k]

Coming back to the notion of aid as clarified by *Altmark*. As seen above, the fourth *Altmark* condition assumes that a public procurement procedure which would allow for the selection of the tenderer capable of providing those services at the least cost to the Union can assist in establishing that a compensation does not constitute aid. In this context, the Commission has tended to follow the description in *Altmark* literally: therefore, the mere observance of the procedural public procurement rules does not as such rule out the granting of aid. Aid can only be ruled out if it is established that the public procurement procedure has led to the selection of a tenderer capable of providing those services at the least cost to the Union.[60] For instance, in a scenario in which there is only one provider who could provide the service sought by the public authority, or where, in an extreme situation, the public authority tenders out the provisions of goods and services it may not actually need, aid cannot be ruled out.[61] Also, notifications in which the tendering procedure has not taken place at the time of the notification, will arguably have to be viewed with caution. The above nuance is of relevance not only when assessing the remuneration of public service obligations, but the remuneration for goods and services provided to the state more generally and

17–013

[59j] Recital 8 of the Framework.

[59k] See recital 6(b) of the Commission Decision and Commission Press release IP/11/ of 20/12/2011.

[60] See, for instance the case of the London underground Public Private Partnership, Case No.264/02 [2002] O.J. C319/15, which deals with the additional difficulty in assessing the outcome of a negotiated procedure.

[61] See for instance; Sandro Santamato, Nicola Pesaresi, "Compensation for services of general economic interest: some thoughts on the Altmark ruling", [2004] Competition Policy Newsletter, 17; Juan José Martinez, Marleen van Kerckhove, "EC State aid rules and the financing of inland transport infrastructure" [2004] *European Transport Law,* 357.

particularly in the context of infrastructure financing such as combined transport or airport facilities.

Coordination of transport

17–014   The *Altmark* case also had another important implication for the assessment of aid in the inland transport sector: As Regulation 1107/70 specifically refers to Regulations 1192/69 and 1191/69 and complements them, the Court held that Regulation 1107/70 lists exhaustively the circumstances in which Member States may grant aid under art.93 TFEU.[62] Hence, insofar as a measure constituted aid, and Regulation 1107/70 would apply (i.e. aid paid for the discharge of public service obligations or for the coordination of transport), no direct recourse could be had to art.93 TFEU.[63] However, since the PSO Regulation repealed Regulation 1107/70, art.93 can be applied directly again.[63a]

17–015   The other exception provided for in art.93 TFEU is aid meeting the need for the coordination of transport. Whilst Regulation 1191/69 laid down the rules for compensation of public service obligations and other financial burdens, it was felt necessary to specify also the cases and the circumstances in which Member States may take co-ordination measures or impose obligations involving the granting of aid under art.93 TFEU which are not covered by these regulations. Council Regulation 1107/70[64] prohibited Member States from taking co-ordination measures involving the granting of aid pursuant to art.93 TFEU, except in the following circumstances;

(a) where aids granted to railway undertakings not covered by Regulation 1192/69 are intended as compensation for additional financial burdens with those undertakings bear by comparison with other transport undertakings and which fall under one of the heads of normalisation listed in that Regulation;

(b) until the entry into force of common rules on the allocation of infrastructure costs, where aid is granted to undertakings which have to bear expenditure relating to the infrastructure used by them, while other undertakings are not subject to a like burden. In determining the amount of aid thus granted account shall be taken of the infrastructure costs which competing modes of transport do not have to bear;

---

[62] Case C–280/2000 *Altmark Trans and Regierungspräsidium Magdeburg* [2003] E.C.R. I–7742, at para.108.

[63] It has been argued that this is without prejudice to the fact that aid for the inland transport *sector* could be envisaged under art.107(3)(c) TFEU, Stefan Tostmann, "Sense and Serendipity— Towards a Coherent Commission State aid Approach in the Intermodal Transport Sector", *World Competition* [2002] 25(1), p.103. However, the dividing line between a measure aimed at the coordination of transport within the meaning of art.93 TFEU and aid to (a part of) the transport sector will be difficult to find.

[63a] See recital 23 SGEI Decision and Grabitz/Boeing—Maxian Rusche, EGV, art.93 para.38.

[64] Regulation (EEC) No.1107/70 of the Council of June 4, 1970 on the granting of aid for the transport by rail, road and inland water [1970] O.J. L130/1.

(c) where the purpose of the aid is to promote either:

- research into transport systems and technologies more economic for the Union in general; or
- the development of transport systems and technologies more economic for the Union in general. Such aid shall be restricted to the research and development stage and may not cover the commercial exploitation of such transport systems and technologies;

(d) until the entry into force of Union rules on access to the transport market, where aid is granted as an exceptional and temporary measure in order to eliminate, as part of a reorganisation plan, excess capacity causing serious structural problems, and thus to contribute towards meeting more effectively the needs of the transport market.

As mentioned above, the Court in the *Altmark* case held that Regulation 1107/70 lists exhaustively the circumstances in which Member States may grant aid under art.93 TFEU. Precisely for this reason, Regulation 1107/70 was considered obsolete—and thus repealed—by the recent PSO Regulation: it was considered that it limited the application of art.93 without granting an appropriate legal basis for authorising current investment schemes, in particular in relation to investment in transport infrastructure in a public/private partnership. Thus it had to be repealed in order for art.93 of the Treaty to be properly applied to continuing developments in the sector without prejudice to this Regulation or Council Regulation (EEC) No 1192/69. At the same time, Commission State aid guidelines for railway investment, including investment in infrastructure were announced,[65] which will be discussed later.

The previously unclear Commission practice,[66] basing some post-*Altmark*   **17–016** decisions on art.93 TFEU as implemented through secondary legislation,[67] some on art.93 TFEU directly when assessing aid granted that would previously have fallen under art.3(1)(f) of Regulation 1107/70 as inserted by Regulation 2255/96[68] and some on art.107(3)(c) TFEU,[69] even leaving aside the possible consideration that art.107(3)(c) is applied to aid to the sector as a whole, should now be clarified by the adoption of the PSO Regulation.[70]

---

[65] PSO Regulation, recital 37.
[66] See Erdmenger in von der Groeben/Schwarze (Hrsg.), Kommentar zum Vertrag über die Europäische Union und zur Gründung der Europäischen Gemeinschaft, Nomos-Verlag, 6. Aufl., 2004, Aritkel 73, Rn 19.
[67] See for instance Case N249/2004 [2005] O.J. C280/9.
[68] Commission Decision of June 24, 2003 on state aid which the Netherlands proposes to implement to assist NV Huisvuilcentrale Noord-Holland (HVC) (notified under document number C(2003) 1909) [2003] O.J. L327/39.
[69] See for instance N38/2004 [2005] O.J. C136/41.
[70] Though the actual Commission practice remains in the infant stage at the time of writing as the PSO Regulation only entered into force on December 3, 2009, but see Commission Decision 2011/3/EU of February 24, 2010 concerning public transport service contracts between the Danish Ministry of Transport and Danske Statsbaner (Case C41/08 (ex. NN 35/08)) [2011] O.J. L7/1; Commission Decision of February 23, 2011 on Aid for the Bahnen der Stadt Mohnheim (BSM) and Rheinische Bahngesellschaft (RBM) companies in the Verkehrsverbund Rhein Ruhr, not yet published in the O.J.

The PSO Regulation

17–017   The PSO Regulation addresses the situation in which a "competent authority" either compensates public service operators and/ or grants exclusive rights in consideration of the discharge of public service obligations. Public authorities are defined as any public authority or group of public authorities of a Member State or States which has the power to intervene in public passenger transport in a given geographical area, or any body vested with such authority.[71] The main elements of the PSO Regulation are, firstly, the introduction of the obligation to conclude a public service contract when a competent authority decides to grant an exclusive right to an operator and/or compensation, of whatever nature, in return for the discharge of public service obligations and, second, the introduction of rules concerning certain tendering obligations when choosing the transport operator.[72] The purpose of the Regulation is to define how, in accordance with the rules of Union law, competent authorities may act in the field of public passenger transport to guarantee the provision of services of general interest which are among other things more numerous, safer, of a higher quality or provided at lower cost than those that market forces alone would have allowed.

To this end, the Regulation lays down the conditions under which competent authorities, when imposing or contracting for public service obligations, compensate public service operators for costs incurred and/or grant exclusive rights in return for the discharge of public service obligations.[73]

17–018   According to its art.1(2), the PSO Regulation applies to the national and international operation of public passenger transport services by rail and other track-based modes and by road. Services which are operated mainly for their historical interest or their tourist value are excluded. Equally, the PSO Regulation does not cover freight transport services, which should therefore be made compatible with the general Treaty principles (i.e state aid rules) within three years of the entry into force of the PSO Regulation[74] pending which Regulation 1191/69 remains applicable to freight transport.[75]

Member States may apply the Regulation to public passenger transport by inland waterways and, without prejudice to the Maritime Cabotage Regulation,[76] to national sea waters. Indeed it is not intended that the PSO Regulation prevents the integration of services by inland waterway and national sea water into a wider urban, suburban or regional public passenger transport network.[77]

17–019   The PSO Regulation also specifically envisages that competent authorities benefit from the possibility of establishing social and qualitative criteria in order

---

[71] art.2(b) PSO Regulation.
[72] Report on Competition Policy 2007 COM (2008) 368 Final, para.382.
[73] art.1(1) PSO Regulation.
[74] PSO Regulation, paras 11 and 36, art.10(1).
[75] PSO Regulation, art.10(1).
[76] Council Regulation (EEC) No.3577/92 of December 7, 1992 [1992] O.J. L364/7.
[77] PSO Regulation, recital 10.

to maintain and raise quality standards for public service obligations, for instance with regard to minimal working conditions, passenger rights, the needs of persons with reduced mobility, environmental protection, and the security of passengers and employees.[78]

Competent authorities may also establish criteria catering for collective agreement obligations and other rules and agreements concerning workplaces and social protection at the place where the service is provided.[79]

The latter aspect, namely considerations of workers' rights, are further detailed in recital 16 which envisages:

"Where the conclusion of a public service contract may entail a change of public service operator, it should be possible for the competent authorities to ask the chosen public service operator to apply the provisions of Council Directive 2001/23/EC of March 12, 2001 on the approximation of the laws of the Member States relating to the safeguarding of employees' rights in the event of transfer of undertakings, businesses or parts of undertakings or businesses [5]. This Directive does not preclude Member States from safeguarding transfer conditions of employees' rights other than those covered by Directive 2001/23/EC and thereby, if appropriate, taking into account social standards established by national laws, regulations or administrative provisions or collective agreements or agreements concluded between social partners."

It can, therefore, be argued that the PSO Regulation seeks to find the right balance between duly considering more general policy considerations (e.g. environmental, social, general transport policy), whilst still ensuring the enforcement of state aid rules in the rail and road sector. In this respect, the PSO Regulation's approach is in line with the general traditional approach to state aid in the transport sector.

(i) Public service contracts. Public service contracts are seen as a tool to **17–020** guarantee the application of the principles of transparency, equal treatment of competing operators and proportionality, when compensation or exclusive rights are granted. They should define the nature of the public service obligations and the agreed reward.[80]

They are defined comprehensively as: "one or more legally binding acts confirming the agreement between a competent authority and a public service operator to entrust to that public service operator the management and operation of public passenger transport services subject to public service obligations; depending on the law of the Member State, the contract may also consist of a decision adopted by the competent authority:

---

[78] PSO Regulation, recital 17.
[79] PSO Regulation, recital 17.
[80] PSO Regulation, recital 9.

— taking the form of an individual legislative or regulatory act, or

— containing conditions under which the competent authority itself provides the services or entrusts the provision of such services to an internal operator."[81]

17–021 The PSO Regulation makes the grant of public service contracts mandatory when a competent authority decides to grant the operator of its choice an exclusive right and/or compensation, of whatever nature, in return for the discharge of public service obligations.[82]

Such contracts must meet the requirements set out in art.4 of the PSO Regulation, which are partly based on the *Altmark* criteria. Thus public service contracts must:

(a) clearly define the public service obligations with which the public service operator is to comply, and the geographical areas concerned;

(b) establish in advance, in an objective and transparent manner,

(i) the parameters on the basis of which the compensation payment, if any, is to be calculated, and

(ii) the nature and extent of any exclusive rights granted, in a way that prevents overcompensation.

In the case of public service contracts awarded in accordance with arts 5(2), (4), (5) and (6) of the PSO Regulation, these parameters shall be determined in such a way that no compensation payment may exceed the amount required to cover the net financial effect on costs incurred and revenues generated in discharging the public service obligations, taking account of revenue relating thereto kept by the public service operator and a reasonable profit;

(c) determine the arrangements for the allocation of costs connected with the provision of services.

Additionally, art.4 stipulates that public service contracts must the arrangements for the allocation of revenue from the sale of tickets and that such contracts may not run for more than 10 years for coach and bus services and 15 years for passenger transport services by rail or other track-based modes.[83] This limitation is introduced in order to prevent market foreclosure.[84]

The duration may be extended only on the basis of the conditions set out in art.4(4) which essentially caters for situations in which the service operator

---

[81] PSO Regulation, art.2(i).

[82] PSO Regulation, art.3(1).

[83] The duration of public service contracts relating to several modes of transport shall be limited to 15 years if transport by rail or other track-based modes represents more than 50% of the value of the services in question, art.4(3).

[84] PSO Regulation, recital 15.

provides significant assets or exceptional costs are derived from the particular geographic situation in which the services are provided.

Whilst the competent authority can choose to provide the service on its territory[85] itself,[86] subject to control by the Member States to ensure a level playing field for any competitors and in particular, that relevant legal provisions are being adhered to.[87]   **17–022**

In the interest of transparency (and control) art.7 PSO Regulation obliges competent authorities to:

(1) publish an aggregated report on the public service obligations for which it is responsible, the selected public service operators and the compensation payments and exclusive rights granted to the said public service operators by way of reimbursement once a year. This report must distinguish between bus transport and rail transport, allow the performance, quality and financing of the public transport network to be monitored and assessed and, if appropriate, provide information on the nature and extent of any exclusive rights granted.

(2) take the necessary measures to ensure that, at least one year before the launch of the invitation to tender procedure or one year before the direct award, at least some basic information is published in the Official Journal of the European Union.

Finally, the award of public service contracts is—unsurprisingly—subject to the public procurement rules[88] as well as to other relevant Union law.

(ii) Public service compensation. The PSO Regulation's starting point on compensation is that compensation for public service does not constitute an advantage within the meaning of art.87 of the Treaty, provided that four cumulative conditions set out by the Court in the *Altmark* case are satisfied. Where those conditions are not satisfied and the general conditions for the application of art.87(1) of the Treaty are met, public service compensation constitutes state aid and is subject to arts 93, 106, 107 and 108 TFEU.[89]   **17–023**

Hence, art.6 PSO Regulation subjects all compensation to the provisions of art.4 which, as described above, incorporates the *Altmark* criteria. In addition, art.6 PSO Regulation foresees more detailed rules applicable to compensation for cases in which the Regulation allows competent authorities not having recourse to a full tender procedure by direct award (arts 5(2), (4), (5) or (6)).

These rules are set out in the Annex to the PSO Regulation. They aim at avoiding overcompensation for the public service (which would constitute aid)   **17–024**

---

[85] PSO Regulation, recital 18 and art.5(2)(b).
[86] art.5(2)—art.3(1) PSO Regulation only applies to the situation in which the discharge of a public service is granted to an operator of the authority's choice—see also recital 18.
[87] PSO Regulation, recital 18 and art.5(7).
[88] Recital 20 and art.5.
[89] PSO Regulation, recital 33.

and avoiding cross-subsidies where a public service operator not only operates compensated services subject to public transport service obligations, but also engages in other activities by stipulating a separation of accounts in these cases.[90]

Finally, in order to allow the Commission to ensure its duty of enforcing the state aid discipline, art.6 PSO Regulation obliges Member States to communicate within a three-month deadline to the Commission, all information the Commission considers necessary to determine whether the compensation granted is compatible with the PSO Regulation.

Railways

17–025   The development of the railways sector has been a concern for the Union for a long time. Already in 1969, Council Regulation 1192/69[91] laid down common rules for the normalisation of the accounts of railway undertakings. The imposition of financial burdens on railways may cause a distortion of competition vis-à-vis other modes of transport. Such distortion can also occur because of different national rules between railways inter se. Elimination may take place:

(a) by termination of certain classes of financial burdens;

(b) by normalisation of the accounts of railways including the payment of compensation for the effects of financial burdens; and finally

(c) in conjunction with the progressive harmonisation.

In the latter of these cases, Member States retain the right to decide whether normalisation should take place. The regulation defines, in art.4, 15 categories of financial burdens. However, according to art.1(3), normalisation shall not apply to public service obligations covered by Regulation 1191/69. The financial burdens defined in art.4 are, therefore, to be seen in addition to the public service obligation.

17–026   Section II of Regulation 1192/69 provides for common rules for normalisation and compensation. According to art.10, the amount of compensation paid in respect of each category shall be shown in a table annexed to the annual accounts. That table shall also show the compensation for each public service obligation. Article 13 provides that compensation paid pursuant to this regulation shall be exempted from the requirements of art.88 E.C.

---

[90] Point 5 of the Annex to the PSO Regulation. It has been arrgued that these rules are stricter than the ones for SGEIs generally—and certainly than those of the *Monti-Kroes Package*—in exchange of granting member states a large role in ensuring adherence to the annex of the PSO Regulation, see *Grabitz/Boeing—Maxian Rusche*, EGV, art.93 para.47.

[91] This Regulation has been slightly amended by subsequent legislation. A consolidated, albeit not official version compiled by the European communities' office for Official Publications, available at: *http://europa.eu/eur-lex/en/consleg/pdf/1969/en_1969R1192_do_001.pdf*.

In the 1970s, Council adopted Decision 75/327 concerning the improvement of the situation of railway undertakings and the harmonisation of rules governing financial relations between such undertakings and Member States.[92] This Decision may be seen as a quest for transparency pre-dating the Commission's Transparency Directive 80/723, discussed above in Chapter 8. The Decision is a forerunner of Directive 91/440,[93] which was the first major liberalisation legislation. Directive 91/440 required Member States:

(i) to manage railway undertakings in such a way that these understand the need for competitiveness and sound financial management.

(ii) to make railway undertakings independent by giving them a budget and system of accounts which are separate from those of the State.

(iii) to guarantee rights of access for rail transport operators in other Member States to international combined transport services under certain conditions.

(iv) to have separate accounting for railway infrastructure (track and related equipment) and the operation of transport services.

The Directive aimed at achieving greater transparency in the use of public funds and at enabling the measuring of the actual performance of, on the one hand, the management of transport infrastructure, and on the other, the provision of transport services. It is with this requirement in mind that a number of Member States have in recent years set up bodies which manage the railway infrastructure but are separate from the railway companies, which continue to manage the carriage of passengers and freight.

Directive 91/440 has been amended by Directive 2001/12/EC[94] to take account of experience with its implementation and of developments in the railway sector since its adoption. Its art.6 provides that separate accounts are kept for the provision of transport services and the management of railway infrastructure. It specifically prohibits the transfer of funds from one of these activities to the other. This provision seeks to prevent cross-subsidisation between the two activities. A similar provision is included in art.9 to ensure that funds relating to the provision of passenger-transport services as public service are kept separate and are not transferred to/from other activities. Directive 201/12 introduced in art.6 the requirement for Member States to ensure that the functions determining equitable and non-discriminatory access to infrastructure are entrusted to bodies which do not themselves provide any rail transport services.

17–027

[92] [1975] O.J. L152/3.
[93] [1991] O.J. L237/25.
[94] Directive 2001/12/EC of the European Parliament and of the Council of February 26, 2001 amending Council Directive 91/440/EEC on the development of the Community's railways [2003] O.J. L75/1.

As far as the liberalisation of the railway sector is concerned, the Union has issued three "Railway Packages", in 2001, 2004 and 2007, as a result of which the rail freight market was opened to competition on March 15, 2003 on the trans-European rail freight network, then on January 1, 2006 for international freight and finally from January 1, 2007 for rail cabotage. The third railway package set January 1, 2010 as the date for opening up international passenger transport to competition. Some Member States however, such as the United Kingdom, Germany, the Netherlands and Italy, have already (partially) opened up their domestic passenger transport markets before that date.[95]

17–028　**The 2008 Railway Guidelines.**[96] Nevertheless, the railway sector is still the cause of concern from a policy point of view. As explained in the 2008 Railway Guidelines, railways have unique advantages: as a safe and clean mode of transport. Rail transport therefore has great potential for contributing to the development of sustainable transport in Europe, but it suffers from an image problem, having declined steadily from the 1960s to the end of the 20th century. Both goods and passenger traffic volumes have fallen in relative terms compared with the other transport modes. Rail freight has even shown a decline in absolute terms: loads transported by rail were higher in 1970 than in 2000. The traditional railway undertakings were unable to offer the reliability and good timekeeping their customers expected of them, which led to a shift of traffic from rail to the other modes of transport, chiefly road. Although passenger transport by rail might have continued to grow in absolute terms, this increase seems very limited compared with that of road and air transport.[97]

It is in this context, and as announced in the PSO Regulation,[98] that the Commission issued the 2008 Railway Guidelines, the objectives of which is to provide guidance on the compatibility with the Treaty of state aid to railway undertakings as it is defined in Directive 91/440/EEC. They also complement the old Regulation 1192/69. In addition, Ch.3 of the Guidelines applies to urban, suburban and regional passenger transport undertakings.[99]

17–029　The Guidelines are based on the principles established by the Union legislator in the three successive railway packages. Their aim is to improve the transparency of public financing and legal certainty with regard to the Treaty rules in the context of the opening-up of the markets.

However, they do not cover public financing intended for infrastructure managers.[100] Aspects relating to public service compensation are also not covered in the Guidelines as these are already addressed in the PSO Regulation.[101]

---

[95] See para.9 of the Communication from the Commission—Community guidelines on State aid for railway undertakings [2008] O.J. C184/13. This paragraph contains the full list of relevant legislation of the three packages and is therefore a useful summary of the legislative history.

[96] Communication from the Commission—Community guidelines on state aid for railway undertakings [2008] O.J. C184/13.

[97] Railway Guidelines, recitals 3–4.

[98] See recital 37 PSO Regulation.

[99] Railway Guidelines, recital 15.

[100] Railway Guidelines, recital 15.

[101] Railway Guidelines, recital 19.

The Guidelines clarify that after the entry into force of the PSO Regulation, art.93 TFEU will be directly applicable as a legal basis for establishing the compatibility of aid not covered by the PSO Regulation, and in particular aid for the coordination of freight transport. A general interpretation therefore needs to be developed for considering the compatibility of aid for coordination purposes with art.93 TFEU.[102]

In this context, the Guidelines aim at establishing criteria for the examination of compatibility on the basis of art.93 TFEU and for intensity thresholds.[103]

Inland waterways

In 1989, Council adopted Regulation 1101/89 on structural improvements in the inland waterway sector[104] intended to reduce structural overcapacity on the inland waterway market by coordinating the scrapping of vessels at Union level and by introducing a mechanism for regulating capacity called the "old for new" rule which attaches conditions to the placing in service of new capacity.   **17–030**

As this Regulation expired on April 28, 1999 the Council adopted a new regulation on March 29, 1999, Council Regulation No.718/1999,[105] which established a four-year transitional period. In parallel, the Commission adopted Regulation (EC) No.805/1999, which fixed the rate of the special contributions referred to in art.7 of Regulation (EC) No.718/1999, the ratios for the "old-for-new" rule, and the practical arrangements for implementing the Community fleet capacity policy.[106]

Council Regulation No.718/1999 required a gradual reduction of ratios to zero within the four-year period. Accordingly, any company wishing to place new vessels in service or import one from a third country must either scrap an existing vessel in accordance with a certain "ratio", or make a special contribution.[107] At the end of the four-year period on April 29, 2003 the capacity mechanism was converted into a standby mechanism and the "old for new" rule may only be reactivated, whether or not accompanied by structural improvement measures, if it is confirmed that there is a serious crisis in the market.   **17–031**

---

[102] Railway Guidelines, recital 20.

[103] Railway Guidelines, recital 20.

[104] [1989] O.J. L116.

[105] Council Regulation (EC) No.718/1999 of March 29, 1999 on a Community-fleet capacity policy to promote inland waterway transport [1999] O.J. L90/1. N.B. Regulation (EEC) No.1102/89 was repealed by Commission Regulation (EC) No.805/1999 of April 16, 1999 laying down certain measures for implementing Council Regulation (EC) No.718/1999 on a Community-fleet capacity policy to promote inland waterway transport [1999] O.J. L102/64, see art.7 thereof.

[106] Commission Regulation (EC) No.805/1999 of April 16, 1999 laying down certain measures for implementing Council Regulation (EC) No.718/1999 on a Community-fleet capacity policy to promote inland waterway transport [1999] O.J. L102/64.

[107] This regime applies, essentially, only to vessels transporting goods. The way the mechanism works is, in essence, by foreseeing that vessels covered by the regulation which are newly constructed may be brought into service subject to the condition (the "old-for-new" rule) that the owner of the vessel either scraps a certain tonnage of carrying capacity without receiving a scrapping premium or pays a special contribution to the Fund covering his new vessel. See also case T82/01 *VOF Josanne and Others v Commission* [2003] E.C.R. II–2013.

As far as the liberalisation of the sector is concerned, Council Regulation No.1356/96[108] provided the right for all carriers of goods or passengers by inland waterway to carry out transport operations between Member States and in transit through these without discrimination on grounds of nationality or place of business. Council Directive 96/75[109] foresaw that in the field of national and international inland waterway transport in the Community, contracts shall be freely concluded between the parties concerned and prices freely negotiated. As a result, from January 1, 2007, rail transport services for freight were fully opened to competition in the European Union.[110]

17–032   Already in 1991, Council Regulation (EEC) 3921/91[111] essentially opened up the hitherto national inland waterways transport markets. Cabotage was to be allowed on the basis of the following principles:

- All carriers of goods or passengers by inland waterway may perform national transport operations for hire or reward within a Member State that is not their place of business.

- Carriers may perform cabotage on a temporary basis within a Member State without opening a registered office or other place of business there if they are: (a) in compliance with the laws of the country that is their principal place of business and (b) are entitled to perform international goods or passenger transport operations on inland waterways.

- Carriers may only use craft whose owner(s) is/are: natural persons domiciled in a Member State and citizens of a Member State or legal persons who (a) have their principal place of business in a Member State and (b) the majority of whom are citizens of Member States.

- A certificate proving that the carrier has met the above mentioned conditions must be issued either by the Member State in which the craft is registered, or by the Member State in which its owner has his principal place of business.

Cabotage operations are subject to the laws and regulations of the host Member State under the proviso of the application of the Union's rules.

Increasingly the focus in inland waterways has shifted from capacity reduction to a positive stance stemming from the perceived benefits to be derived in terms

---

[108] Council Regulation (EC) No.1356/96 of July 8, 1996 on common rules applicable to the transport of goods or passengers by inland waterway between Member States, with a view to establishing freedom to provide such transport services without restriction [1996] O.J. L175/7.

[109] Council Directive 96/75/EC of November 19, 1996 on the systems of chartering and pricing in national and international inland waterway transport in the Community [1996] O.J. L304/12.

[110] See also Commission working document accompanying the 2008 Competition Report, COM(2009)374 final, paras 265 following.

[111] Council Regulation (EEC) 3921/91 of December 16, 1991 laying down the conditions under which non-resident carriers may transport goods or passengers by inland waterway within a Member State [1991] O.J. L373/1.

of transport and environmental policy from a shift to inland water transport.[112] Hence, the state aid assessment has increasingly become liberal, not to say lenient towards aid in this sector. For instance, it is one of the very few areas in which investment aid has been accepted, subject only to it being directed at achieving an intermodal shift from other transport modes.[113]

De minimis for transport

In June 2005 the Commission published a draft proposal amending the de minimis Regulation by including in its scope the transport sector (except for aid given for the purchase of vehicles by road transport companies) and excluding the coal industry. Observations from all interested parties were received by the Commission as of July 2005[114] and a new Regulation was adopted on December 15, 2006.[115] This new de minimis regulation raised the ceilings for what is recognised as de minimis aid in general from €100,000 to €200,000 per undertaking over each three-year period. It included for the first time also the road transport sector with a lower ceiling of €100,000 over each three-year period to take into account the average small size of undertakings in the road transport sector[116] for which €100,000 can be a substantial. For the same reasons taking into account also the general policy to seek to obtain a shift away from road transport and the overcapacity in the sector aid for aid for the acquisition of road freight transport vehicles is excluded.[117] As mentioned in para.17–012, a new de minimis Regulation for the provisin of SGEI applicable to—among others—the maritime and the transport sector is expected to be adopted in the first half of 2012.

17–033

3. THE APPLICATION OF THE RULES

General

There is no reference to state aid to the transport sector in the reports on competition policy until the 15th Report. The subsequent reports all contain references to the transport sector, which includes rail, inland waterways, air and maritime transport. In recent reports, the Commission notes a substantial increase

17–034

[112] See 2008 Competition Report, para.273; Commission Decision N31/2008 Austria, para.35 available at: *http://ec.europa.eu/eu_law/state_aids/transports-2008/n031-08.pdf*.
[113] Commission Decision N 597/2000 Netherlands [2001] O.J. C102/8; see also A. Colucci in W. Mederer, N. Pesaresi, M. Van Hoof, *EU Competition Law Vol.IV State Aid*, point 4.2148.
[114] 2005 Report on Competition Policy, para.430; IP/04/290.
[115] Commission Regulation (EC) No.1998/2006 of December 15, 2006 on the application of arts 87 and 88 of the Treaty to de minimis aid [2006] O.J. L379/5.
[116] Commission Regulation (EC) No.1998/2006 of December 15, 2006 on the application of arts 87 and 88 of the Treaty to de minimis aid [2006] O.J. L379/5, recital 3.
[117] Commission Regulation (EC) No.1998/2006 of December 15, 2006 on the application of arts 87 and 88 of the Treaty to de minimis aid [2006] O.J. L379/5, recital 3 and art.1(g).

in the number of aid cases in the transport sector, from 52 in 2003 to 77 new cases in 2001, 107 in 2002. In subsequent years, the number of new cases has dropped slightly to 51 in 2003 and 49 in 2004, but has since increased again substantially to 82 in 2006, 62 in 2007. The initial increase was largely attributed to the progressive liberalisation of the inland and air transport sectors. The peak of cases in 2001 and 2002 may be explained partly by the difficulties faced by airlines in the aftermath of September 11, 2001. The subsequent drop in cases may have illustrated a return to lower figures after the 9/11-induced support measures. However, the liberalisation of all rail services by 2007 as well as the increased support for intermodal transport and the revitalisation of the railways, the increased recourse to private financing of transport infrastructure that has also led to a greater focus on transport state aid and the Commission's more active approach to complaints lodged by competitors especially in the field of passenger transport further to the *Altmark*[118] and *Danske Busvoggnmoend* (also known as *"Combus"*)[119] cases[120] all have led to a consistently high number of transport cases. The fact that the number of transport cases is, in percentage terms, generally higher than the contribution of the transport industry to European GDP (7 per cent) and to employment (around 5 per cent),[121] as compared to 7 per cent to 10 per cent of state aid cases[122] may give an indication of the persistent legal complexity of the state aid policy in the area as well as to its increasing competitiveness.

Rail

17–035   Aid to the rail sector has traditionally represented a major proportion of aid paid out in the transport sector.[123] Most aid was given to compensate for the imposition of public service obligations or inherited obligations on railways (regs 1191/69 and 1192/69). This situation has not fundamentally changed. In 2002–2009, the total estimated state aid and other public contributions to rail transport in the Union ranged from €36 to €42.8 billion.[124] However, the high level of aid

---

[118] Case C–280/00 *Altmark* [2003] E.C.R. I–7747.

[119] Case T–157/01 *Danske Busvoggnmoend v Commission* [2004] E.C.R. II–917.

[120] See also Tim Maxian Rusche and Silvia Schmidt, "The post-Altmark era has started: 15 months of application of Regulation (EC) No. 1370/2007 to public transport services", *ESAL* 2/2011 p.249.

[121] Commission working document accompanying the 2008 Competition Report, SEC(2009)1004 final, at para.256; 2009 Competition Report, at para.375.

[122] See 2007 Competition Report, para.21; 2006 Competition Report para.120.

[123] For 1997–1999, for instance , the aid was reported as a percentage of gross value added: Belgium 54.9; Denmark 9.2; Germany 36.39; Greece 21.6; Spain 14.3; France 23.9; Ireland 16.7; Italy 16.7; Luxembourg 43.8 (a very considerable part is for retirements); the Netherlands 19.1; Portugal 2.5; and the United Kingdom 9.7 (EU 15, 25.1, of which Aid on the basis or Regulation 1191/69: 8.8). Ninth Survey on State aid in the European Union in the Manufacturing and Certain Other Sectors, 30 July 18, 2001, COM(2001) 403 final, available online on *http://eur-lex. europa.eu/LexUriServ/site/fr/com/2001/com2001_0403fr01.pdf*, Table 28, p.74.

[124] See DG Competition overview of aid expenditure, subsidies to the railway sector EU-27 (2001–2009), available online at *http://ec.europa.eu/competition/state_aid/studies_reports/ expenditure.html*. For earlier figures see, NERA Study of the financing and public budget contributions to railways, report prepared for the European Commission, January 2004, p.63, available on line at: *http://ec.europa.eu/transport/rail/research/doc/nera2004-final.pdf*.

to the rail sector is increasingly due to the policy of promoting rail as an alternative to road transport.[125] This in turn also leads to aid measures being aimed at achieving an intermodal change in freight transport from road to rail and water.[126]

In its 2001 White Paper on a common transport policy,[127] the Commission stated that rail transport was the strategic sector on which the success of the efforts to shift the balance will depend. One of the main objectives of the Common Transport Policy is the promotion of environmentally friendly modes of transport in order to achieve a reduction in the negative effects of transport. Commission policy is to allow rail transport to be made competitive enough to remain a significant player in the transport system in an enlarged European Union.[128] The Commission has taken a favourable approach to aid in the rail sector, both with regard to rail services and, in particular, to investments in rail infrastructure which, due to heavy investments costs, will in many cases not be viable without public co-financing.[129] Despite all this, the objective of achieving a modal change towards rail has still not been achieved.[130]

The generally favourable assessment of aid in the railway sector[131] has to be considered with this very special policy background in mind. It should, however, also be borne in mind that the assessment of aid to liberalised activities in the rail sector will inevitably be considered with more caution, as the impact on competition of aid to such activities will be more direct.[132]

Following this approach, the Commission authorised a scheme to support the **17–036** movement of intermodal containers by rail in the United Kingdom. The scheme will provide continued support for the deep-sea and short-sea intermodal container business that currently uses rail by granting a fixed rate for each container moved. The aid scheme should contribute to securing growth in this sector and in the domestic intermodal freight business.[133] Similarly the Commission authorised the Land of Saxony–Anhalt (Germany) to grant aid to promote the transfer of freight traffic flows from road to rail. The Land of Saxony–Anhalt was facing

---

[125] See for instance, Commission publication "Revitalising Europe's Railways—Towards an integrated European Railway area", Publications Office 2003, available online at: *http://ec. europa.eu/transport/rail/overview/doc/brochure_en.pdf*. Competition Report 2009, para.390.

[126] See also Commission *White paper—European transport policy for 2010: time to decide* 12.09.2001, COM(2001) 370 final.

[127] White paper—European transport policy for 2010: time to decide, September 12, 2001, COM(2001) 370 final.

[128] 2005 Report on Competition Policy, para.428.

[129] 31st Report on Competition Policy 2001, pt 428.

[130] Commission Communication of September 17, 2010 concerning the development of a Single European Railway Area (COM (2010) 474 final—Not published in the Official Journal, available online at: *http://eur-lex.europa.eu/LexUriServ/LexUriServ.do?uri=COM:2010:0474:FIN: EN:PDF*, see point 1.1.

[131] See also A. Colucci in W. Mederer, N. Pesaresi, M. Van Hoof, "*EU Competition Law Vol IV State Aid*", point 4.2127–4.2129.

[132] See for instance case N323/2004 [2006] O.J. C83/10; see also para.17–039, Fret SNCF Decision.

[133] Commission Decision of N464/2003, UK, Company neutral revenue scheme (CNRS) [2003] O.J. C16/25.

the prospect of an increase of 60 per cent of freight traffic on its territory by 2015 and simultaneously, the cargo subsidiary of Deutsche Bahn (the German Railways) intended to close down 37 fight terminals in Saxony–Anhalt which were not seen to be profitable. Saxony–Anhalt was seeking to promote a sustainable freight transport and to double the amount of freight transported by rail over the next 15 years. It thus notified an aid scheme granting financing to undertakings investing in freight terminals and in rail infrastructure. The scheme intends to safeguard and develop the system of freight traffic centres, as well as handling and loading areas.[134] Equally the Commission has over recent years adopted several decisions to promote rail transport and combined transport.[135] It authorised, for instance, the renewal of a Czech aid measure which guarantees a loan to Czech Railways (Česke drahy)[136] to facilitate the purchase of new passenger rolling stock. In addition, it adopted a final decision, following the opening of the procedure in 2006, concerning aid for the acquisition of certain mobile assets for the use of combined transport operations in the Czech Republic.[137]

An interesting case less directly aimed at the intermodal shift to rail is one in which the Commission approved a German scheme providing for public funding for measures of noise reduction for existing railway freight wagons under the framework of the pilot project 'Silent Rhein'. The retrofitting of railway freight wagons which are mainly used in the Rhine Valley with less noisy brake systems is envisaged in order to enhance noise reduction, and thus increase public acceptance of the[138]

17–037   Rescue and restructuring aid to railway undertakings can serve to illustrate the approach to the railway sector from a different perspective. On February 2, 2005, the Commission approved the restructuring of Fret SNCF,[139] which had been in serious financial difficulties for several years. The restructuring plan provided for reorganising production, improving productivity, reviewing the company's business policy and injecting fresh capital. This capital injection was to serve to modernise Fret SNCF's rolling stock and to overhaul its financial structure. It was foreseen to comprise two parts: a sum of €700 million from SNCF, financed by divestment of assets, and a State contribution not exceeding €800 million. The Commission examined whether the aid to Fret SNCF met the criteria of the Union guidelines on rescue and restructuring aid,[140] which also apply to the rail sector.[141]

---

[134] Case N 308/2002, Promotion of investments for railway infrastructure [2002] O.J. C277.

[135] See, 2009 Competition Report, paras 388–395; 2008 Competition Report, para.267; 2007 Competition Report paras 391–392.

[136] Case N 770/06, State guarantee for the purpose of financing the purchase of railway rolling stock by České Drahy (Czech Railways) [2007] O.J. C227/4.

[137] C12/2006 (ex. N 132/05).

[138] Aid N 324/09 [2009] O.J. C299/5, full text of the decision available online at: *http://ec. europa.eu/eu_law/state_aids/transports-2009/n324-09.pdf*, at para.4.

[139] Case N 389/2004 [2005] O.J. C172/3, Decision available online at: *http://ec.europa.eu/comm/ competition/state_aid/register/ii/by_case_nr_n2004_360.html#386*.

[140] At the time: Community Guidelines on state aid for Rescue and Restructuring firms in difficulty [1999] O.J. C288/2.

[141] Regulation 1107/70 EC used to contain a *lex specialis* for railway undertakings active in the passenger service sector, but this has not been taken over by the PSO regulation.

The Commission took the opportunity of this decision to spell out the general principles on the basis of which it intended to apply state aid control in the rail sector, not only as far as rescue and restructuring aid to rail freight undertakings was concerned.[142] In para.3.2. of the Decision, the Commission stated that generally, rescue and restructuring aid is not admissible if paid out to favour a particular branch of an undertaking only: this inherently carried the risk of cross-subsidisation and/or the weakening of the "one time last time" principle. Nevertheless, the Commission considered that the rail freight sector which, contrary to the rail passenger sector, is in the process of full market opening, was in a very particular situation in which it could be in the common interest to adopt a more favourable approach, albeit on a temporary basis and under certain conditions set out in the decision.[143] The main consideration was that at the time many rail operators had not yet fully unbundled their freight and passenger operations, thus leading to a situation where the freight division had to face a rapidly increasing competition as market opening progresses whilst the passenger services division did not. Bearing in mind the Union aim of ensuring that a revitalised rail freight sector can effectively compete with road transport, the Commission took into account that in the transition period, some railway undertaking had to restructure rapidly to face the competition. In these circumstances, the Commission stipulated that rescue and restructuring aid to rail freight undertakings could be deemed compatible in so far as they:

- Concern the totality of the freight activities of the undertaking in question.

- The freight division is both a separate entity and the restructuring ensures that its autonomy is increased.

- The Commission has ways to control the separation of accounts between the freight and other activities.

- Cross-subsidisation is prohibited.

- The restructuring must result in the definitive transition from protected activity to a market activity. Thus the restructuring plan must in particular contain evidence of a credible approach to ensure that the restructured entity will meet market requirements as regards service quality.

Insofar as the restructuring concerns firms in difficulty, the Commission will **17–038** take into consideration the capacity of the remaining divisions of the undertaking to contribute to the restructuring. And, if the undertaking is public and the decisions taken in it can be attributed to the state, the Commission will assume that any intra-group financing constitutes state aid. In the analysis of distortions of competition resulting from the grant of aid, the Commission will consider the

---

[142] See para.199 of the Decision.
[143] See paras 120–131 of the Decision.

527

state of the freight market opening at the time of the grant of aid, the different economic models of rail as compared to transport and the Union objective to rebalance the different modes of transport. Real commitments in terms of market opening will be requested vis-à-vis competitions from the restructured entity. Finally, the "one time, last time" principle will apply to undertaking as a whole as long as the freight division subject benefiting from restructuring aid is not legally separate from its other activities.

Importantly, as the railway sector was at the time of the decision in the process of being opened up, the Commission announced in its decision that it will propose a framework setting out how it intends to monitor state aid in the railways sector in the future, to be based on the principles of transparency, non-discrimination and proportionality.[144] This has now been done with the publication of the Railway Guidelines (see above).

17–039   In the case of *Fret SNCF*, the Commission concluded that the aid enables Fret SNCF to become viable again by the end of 2006 and that it is strictly limited to its restructuring needs. In addition, the authorised measures were subject to certain conditions concerning a reduction in Fret SNCF's traffic volume during restructuring and an earlier date for opening up the French rail freight market; these provisions were aimed at ensuring that the aid does not constitute a barrier to the development of other operators, which also contribute to developing the carriage of goods by rail. The French authorities undertook to link payment of the aid instalments to the opening up of the market. Payment of the second instalment conditional on the prior opening of the international freight routes. The third instalment was not to be payable before the national market is opened up, this was scheduled to take place before March 31, 2006. This aid was considered sufficient to secure a viable future for Fret SNCF, which will not be eligible for any more restructuring aid for 10 years. This "one time, last time" principle will apply to SNCF as a whole, as long as Fret SNCF is not legally separate from its other activities. Therefore the aid was declared compatible. A recent example is the decision on the restructuring aid to the freight transshipment and logistics firm, *InterFerryBoats*.[145]

In February 2010, the Commission adopted its first decision applying the new PSO Regulation. By this decision,[146] the Commission concluded the formal investigation procedure initiated in 2008 regarding the public-service contracts concluded with the Danish railway company Danske Statsbaner (DSB). The Commission found that the compensation paid by the government every year to DSB for the costs incurred in meeting its public-service obligations was limited to what was strictly necessary to cover those costs.[147]

---

[144] See para.198 of the Decision.
[145] Case C46/05 [2009] O.J. L225/1, see for the application of the "one time last time" criterion, para.352.
[146] Case C41/2008 *Public service contracts between the Danish Government and Dankse Statbaner* [2008] O.J. C309/14. See IP/10/178, February 24, 2010.
[147] Competition Report 2010, para.328.

Finally, purely for the sake of completeness it should be mentioned that the **17–040** Railway Guidelines foresaw a transitional regime under which railway undertakings were allowed to receive restructuring aid in order to assist them in adapting to the new competitive situation, but only up to January 1, 2010.

Only one decision has been adopted on this basis, the *Fret SNCB* decision.[148] The Commission authorised the Belgian State Railway's SNCB's restructuring of its freight activities. The Commission considered that the restructuring plan would address the problems affecting SNCB's freight activities and ensure the viability of those activities without unduly distorting competition in the internal market. In accordance with the 2008 Railway Guidelines, the SNCB's freight division was to be legally separated and transformed into a commercial company under ordinary commercial law. The creation of an independent operator is designed to ensure that there will be no cross-subsidisation between freight and passenger transport activities. The restructuring plan also includes a substantial reduction in the capacity of SNCB's freight activities to contribute to healthy competition in the market concerned. Generally, a division of an undertaking, namely an economic entity without legal personality, is not eligible for restructuring aid on the basis of the 2004 Guidelines on State aid for restructuring.[149]

Considering that the inter-Union passenger rail transport market also started being liberalised as of 2010 with the gradual opening up of Member States' markets planned by 2012,[150] one might expect an increase in state aid cases in this segment of the rail sector in the foreseeable future.

Inland water transport

The inland water transport sector traditionally suffered from overcapacity in **17–041** response to which the above described regulations were adopted. Nevertheless, and increasingly so, this sector is also seen as an alternative to road transport and hence as contributing to the re-balancing of the different transport modes, as recommended by the White Paper on the European transport policy for 2010.[151] With an annual volume of around 130 billion tonne-kilometres of freight, the modal share of river transport accounts for an overall 6 per cent of the total inland transport in the Union,[152] a result switching the transport of goods from roads to inland waterways could be argued to be in the common interest.[153] The European interest in the inland water sector has been further underlined by the adoption in

---

[148] Case N726/2009 *Aide à la restructuration des activités "fret" de la SA de droit public SNCB* [2010] O.J. C327/6. See IP/10/615, May 26, 2010.

[149] [2004] O.J. C244/2.

[150] Directive 2007/58/EC [2007] O.J. L315/44; Competition Report 2010, para.305; see also for Third Package details: *www.http://ec.europa.eu/transport/rail/packages/2007_en.htm*. Schmidt-Kötters in Haidenhain, *European State Aid Law*, München 2010, para.76 on the Third Package.

[151] COM(2001) 370.

[152] Report on Competition Policy 2007 Commission Staff Working Document SEC (2008) 2038, para.375.

[153] 32nd Report on Competition Policy, para.494; cf. Schmidt-Kötters in Haidenhain, *European State Aid Law*, München 2010, para.77.

2006 by the European Commission of a Communication on the promotion of inland waterway transport. The NAIADES Action Programme is intended for the period 2006–2013 and focuses on five strategic areas for a comprehensive Inland Waterway Transport (IWT) policy: market, fleet, jobs and skills, image and infrastructure.[154] In December 2007, the Commission 5 December, the Commission adopted a communication containing a first progress report on NAIADES. The report describes progress in a number of areas, including measures adopted by Member States to promote this environmentally friendly mode of transport,[155] thus again underlining the fundamentally positive view of this mode of transport.

Accordingly, aid schemes to support inland water transport are generally viewed favourably if they aim at achieving an intermodal shift. An example is the scheme notified by the Netherlands aimed at promoting the establishment, extension and bringing into operation of links between industrial plants and inland waterways so as to bring about a modal shift to inland waterway transport. In this case, the Commission took the view that what was involved was in effect public co-financing of infrastructures for which there was no competitive market. Indeed the recipient must fund at least 50 per cent of the total cost of the project and must provide a five-year transport guarantee whereby he undertakes to transship at least the declared quantity of goods by means of the private link to be subsidised.[156] A French scheme intended to encourage the adaptation of the inland waterway fleet to market and security requirements, to maintain a sufficient degree of modernised inland shipping capacity this measure even included a provision to ease the retirement of inland waterway skippers, was approved on the basis of art.107(3)(c), taking into account inland waterway transport's potential to decongest roads.[157]

An equally favourable view is taken of measures promoting not only inland water transport as such, but also its link to road transport. In 2004, for instance, the Commission cleared a Belgian (Walloon) aid scheme aimed at the encouragement of inland water transport thorough the modernisation of the fleet and promotion and renewal of the inland waterway transport profession but also providing for aid to operators of scheduled container combined transport services using inland waterways and operating from a terminal linked to a waterway located in Wallonia. The grant is calculated on the basis of the number of containers transshipped to or from the waterway. The aid was intended to encourage the development of inland waterway combined transport services as opposed to pure road transport, which accounts for nearly all container transport

---

[154] COM(2006) 6 final, available online at: *http://eurlex.europa.eu/LexUriServ/LexUriServ.do ?uri=COM:2006:0006:FIN:EN:PDF.*
[155] COM(2007) 770 final.
[156] Case N 597/2000 [2001] O.J. C102/8 Another example is Case N 550/2001 [2002] O.J. C24/2 in which aid was to be granted for the building of loading and unloading facilities along the Flemish waterways, making inland waterways more accessible.
[157] Case N 299/01 [2001] O.J. C342/7.

in the region.[158] More recent, but similar examples are the approval in 2009 of an amendment to a Dutch regime for the construction of inland transshipment terminals in order to shift more freight traffic from road to inland waterway and rail transport[159] and of state aid designed to shift traffic from road and increasing the efficiency and safety of freight transport by means of establishing a rail-based combined transport between the Port of Naples and the Interporto di Nola.[160]

Until now the Commission has approved state aid schemes for inland water- **17–042**
way transport in accordance with art.107 TFEU on a case-by-case basis. It has ensured that the same rules are applied to comparable state aid given in different Member States and that by this a level playing field has been maintained. In its Communication of January 2006, the Commission had considered the possibility of adopting specific state aid guidelines for the sector but these have not so far materialised.[161]

Road transport

The road transport sector, the share of which keeps rising to the detriment of **17–043**
mainly rail and inland water transport,[162] is not surprisingly one in which aid tends to be viewed with caution. Because this sector keeps growing, it has also not given rise to important aid operations, both in absolute as well as relative terms. Nevertheless, some Member States have notified schemes seeking to redress some of the increases in costs that road hauliers had to face, such as increased fuel costs, the introduction of tolls on motorways or the introduction of environmental legislation.

The Commission has accepted transport investment aid in some cases.[163] However, it should also be stressed that, as confirmed by the General Court,[164] in sectors with overcapacity such as road transport, aid for the purchase of transport vehicles for instance will be seen to distort competition and cannot be

---

[158] Case N 4/2004 [2005] O.J. C125/6. For further examples see 2008 Competition Report, para.273.

[159] Aid N 60/09 [2009] O.J. C125/1.

[160] Aid N 449/08 [2009] O.J. C196/1.

[161] Commission Staff Working Document, Mid-term progress report on the implementation of the NAIADES Action Programme for the promotion of inland waterway transport, SEC(2011) 453 final, 4.4.2011, p.8, available online at: *http://ec.europa.eu/transport/inland/promotion/doc/sec_2011_453.pdf*.

[162] In 2009, it accounted for some 73% of the inland freight transport market, up from 44.3% in 2004; see "Road Freight Transport Vedemecum 2009, available online at: *http://ec.europa.eu/transport/road/doc/2009_road_freight_vademecum.pdf*. And "European Union—Energy & Transport in Figures 2005", see para.3.2.2; available online at: *http://ec.europa.eu/dgs/energy_transport/figures/pocketbook/doc/2005/etif_2005_whole_en.pdf*. Both published by the European Commission.

[163] Case C 11/2002 (ex N 382/01) Italy (Piedmont)—Reduction of tolls for certain heavy goods vehicles in order to divert them from the Lake Maggiore State road 33 to the A/26 motorway [2002] O.J. C87; Case C 14/2002 (ex NN 72/01) Portugal—Reduction of tolls for certain heavy goods vehicles, coaches and buses adopted following the rise in oil prices in summer/autumn 2000 [2002] O.J. C88.

[164] Case T–55/99 *Confederación Española de Transporte de Mercancias v Commission* [2000] E.C.R. II–3207.

granted.[165] Nevertheless, it is possible to grant aid in connection with the purchase of new vehicles, if such an incentive is aimed at environmental protection or safety objectives and actually represents compensation for the costs of higher technical standards than those laid down by national or EU legislation.[166] Equally, public service compensations can be compensated on the basis of the PSO Regulation.

This can be illustrated by recent Commissions as reported in the 2009 Competition report.[167] There the Commission explicitly refers to the wider Community objectives of the common transport policy and environmental protection "*in line with which*" the Commission authorised a regime promoting the purchase of more environmentally friendly heavy goods vehicles in Slovenia.[168] In a similar vein, the authorisation of a German aid scheme aiming at supporting market acceptance of available highly efficient vehicle technologies[169] and an aid scheme supporting the purchase of low-carbon buses in England, is also reported.[170] On the other hand, the limits of aid authorisation comes when support schemes would, for instance, discriminate on the ground of nationality. Hence, in 2006, the Commission took a negative decision on a German scheme providing for the reimbursement of the toll for heavy goods vehicles on German highways. The scheme, meant to partly compensate the costs incurred by German road hauliers by the introduction of the motorway toll was to consist in a one-off toll reimbursement against proof of purchase of excise duties on fuel within Germany. Beneficiaries of the toll reimbursement would be all road hauliers using German motorways, regardless of their nationality, with vehicles of not less than 12 tonnes. One of the main concerns in this case was the potential discrimination of hauliers from other Member States. Whilst in theory the scheme applied regardless of nationality, its link to the requirement to produce a proof of purchase of fuel within Germany ensured that it was less attractive to non-German road hauliers.[171]

17–044   The case of aid for bus operators in the municipality of Wittenberg in Saxony–Anhalt (Germany),[172] is one of the few cases concerning aid for the operation of passenger transport services by road. It concerns a notified measure whereby the municipality of Wittenberg was to tender out the operation of public transport by bus setting a fix price it was willing to pay for the bus service and stipulating a number of specific quality and performance standards including a public service obligation. The municipality set, among other issues, a fixed price which it was willing to pay per passenger, thus providing an incentive for the selected bus

---

[165] Christopher H. Bovis, "State aid and European Transport: A Reflection on Law, Policy and Practice", *Journal of World Trade* 39(4) [2005], pp.587.
[166] 22nd Report on Competition Policy, para.491.
[167] 2009 Competition Report, para.131.
[168] Aid N 395/08 [2009] O.J. C125/1.
[169] Aid N 457/09 [2010] O.J. C25/15.
[170] Aid N 517/09 [2010] O.J. C74/3.
[171] Aid C 54/03 (ex N 194/02) [2009] O.J. L50/30.
[172] Aid N 604/05 [2006] O.J. C207/2.

operator to increase the attraction of public transport by bus. As the compensation system was thus linked not to the actual costs for operating the service , but to the number of passengers, it could not be excluded that the bus operator, should he perform successfully, might actually obtain an overcompensation as compared to the cost of the service. Hence, this could represent state aid. The legal difficulty in this case was that whilst this method of remuneration was seem to be economically efficient, it did not guarantee that an overcompensation of the public service obligation could be excluded for the per passenger payment. Hence, Regulation 1107/70 could no longer be applied and recourse had to be had to art.107(3)(c) TFEU directly on the basis of which the aid was then declared compatible.

A more conventional assessment of public service obligations in the road passenger transport sector can be seen in the UK scheme aimed at offering compensation to the operators of scheduled long-distance coach services, conditional on them offering advantageous ticket fares to elderly and disabled passengers. In this case, there was a mechanism to avoid over-compensation and the aid was declared compatible on the basis of art.93 TFEU.[173]

Further to the *Altmark*[174] judgment the Commission received a number of complaints[175] from competititors active in the provision of local or regional bus services, often complaining about the award of services contracts without a tender. Following these complaints, the Commission started investigations in several Member States. In 2008, it took a final positive decision concerning a public service contract for public passenger transport by bus in the district of Linz in Austria Case C 16/2007 (not yet published in the O.J.).The contract was awarded to Postbus AG without a public procurement procedure. The Commission came to the conclusion that the compensation that was extended to Postbus AG under the terms of the contract constituted state aid, but that such compensation did not exceed the costs incurred in discharging the public service obligations.

In 2002, the Council in an exceedingly rare case of the application of **17–045** art.108(2)(b) unanimously adopted three decisions on the granting of national aid by the Netherlands, Italy and France[176] in favour of road transport undertakings. These decisions ensure that the derogation measures adopted by the Council (2001/224/EC) on March 12, 2001 authorising the Netherlands, Italy and France to apply reduced rates of excise duty for certain mineral oils in favour of road hauliers are considered compatible with the internal market: in 2001 the Council had decided to allow the Netherlands (until October 1, 2002) and Italy and France (until December 31, 2002) to apply reduced rates of excise duty on diesel fuel for road hauliers. However, against the background of the Commission's

---

[173] N 588/02 [2003] O.J. C76/28.
[174] C–280/00 *Altmark* [2003] E.C.R. I–7747.
[175] Competition Report 2008, Staff Working Document: COM (2009) 374 final paras 259 and following.
[176] Netherlands (Doc. 8032/02 + COR1); Italy (Doc. 8033/02 + COR1); France (Doc. 8034/02 + COR1).

decision to launch proceedings against these three countries under art.88(2) of the Treaty (2), the three States in question sought and obtained an acknowledgement from the Council that exceptional circumstances within the meaning of art.88(2)(b) existed, making it possible to consider such aid compatible with the internal market.

Combined transport

17–046   As described above, paras 17–004 and 17–035 the Commission tends to take a favourable view of measures aimed at achieving a modal shift away from road transport to other modes of transport such as rail and inland water or, where applicable, maritime.[177] This can be illustrated by the Commission's approach in the following decisions, which has since been followed on a regular basis.[178]

A favourable approach was taken in 2004 towards an Italian scheme for the Region of Friuli-Venezia-Giulia which is to grant subsidies to firms offering combined transport services by rail to or from the region. These subsidies are limited to offset the differences between the external costs of road and combined transport. The scheme is designed to achieve a reduction in the price of combined transport services in order to compete with road transport under similar market conditions.[179]

Similarly, the Commission approved an Italian regional scheme designed to promote road/sea combined transport services between Sicilian and other Italian and Union ports. The scheme will grant an environmental bonus to small- and medium-sized road transport companies when shipping individual heavy goods vehicles of more than 12 tonnes or semi-trailers. In the light of the specific geographic and economic situation of Sicily, the difficulties in organising the intermodal transport market and the experimental character of the measure, the Commission considered it to be compatible with the Treaty.[180]

17–047   Even schemes designed to counter temporary difficulties faced by inland non-road-transport have been approved, such as a Belgian aid scheme which intends to guarantee access to the port of Antwerp through inland waterway during the reconstruction works on the Antwerp ring road. The scheme will bear the additional costs for the loading and unloading of containers on inland vessels so as not to discourage inland waterway traffic to and from the port of Antwerp during the works.[181]

Equally innovative approach can be the subject matter of (rather long-term) aid: an example is the prolongation for the period 2007–2009 by the Commission

---

[177] In cases where maritime transport can, for geographic reasons, be sent to be a substitute to road transport on a particular route

[178] See for instance more recently: Aid N 415/08 [2009] O.J. C53/1; Aid N 304/08 [2009] O.J. C106/17; Aid N 415/08 [2009] O.J. C53/ 1; Aid N 247/09 [2009] O.J. C255/4; Aid N 316/08 [2009] O.J. C232/2; Aid N 159/2008 [2008] O.J. C202/1; Aid N 195/2008 [2008] O.J. C329/3; Aid N 352/2008 [2008] O.J. C7/1.

[179] Aid N 335/2003 [2004] O.J. C22.

[180] Aid N 551/2003 [2005] O.J. C125/8.

[181] Aid N 88/2004 [2005] O.J. C77/29.

of its approval of financial support by the Italian and French governments for the experimental transalpine railway motorway service previously approved for the period 2003–2006. The project has been developed in parallel with the re-opening of the Mont Blanc road tunnel in order to test an efficient, safe and environmentally friendly way to cross the Alps, one of the biggest bottlenecks for terrestrial traffic in the European Union.[182]

The second "Marco Polo" programme for the granting of Community finan- **17–048**
cial assistance to improve the environmental performance of the freight transport system ("Marco Polo II")[183] further expanded the favourable conditions for State and Union aid to intermodal transport measures aimed at achieving a shift away from road transport. Generally speaking, combined Union and (national) state aid measures of up to 35 per cent intensity can now be granted.[184]

Maritime transport

(i) Introduction. The maritime sector which was traditionally strong, especially **17–049**
in some Member States, suffered a dramatic decline in the since the 1960s, and particularly in the 1980s: between 1980 and 1988 there was an acceleration of the decline, tonnage being practically halved.[185] The main cause has been the difference in Union wage levels and concomitant social charges in comparison with its major competitors, and especially the countries of the so-called "flags of convenience". Another important element is safety and the protection of the environment. It became increasingly difficult for the Union to accept the risks posed by maritime transport taking place in ships registered in jurisdictions which do not, or do not sufficiently, enforce international safety and environmental standards. This is clearly evidenced by the reaction of public opinion every time that a tanker, registered under a flag of convenience, causes a major oil spill. Nevertheless, maritime transport is seen to be of vital importance to the European economy.[186] A two-pronged approach was chosen as a result: on the one hand, major efforts were made in the field of maritime safety in the Union and on the other, a major focus has been to prevent the out-flagging of ships to flags of convenience and to encourage the re-flagging with a Union flag. This last principle has been the main objective of Union state aid policy in the field of

---

[182] Aid cases N 11/2008 and NN 34/2008 [2009] O.J. C38/3; Competition Report Staff Working Document: COM (2009) 379 final 2008 para.266.
[183] Regulation (EC) No.1692/2006 of the European Parliament and of the Council of October 24, 2006 establishing the second Marco Polo programme for the granting of Community financial assistance to improve the environmental performance of the freight transport system (Marco Polo II) and repealing Regulation (EC) No.1382/2003 [2006] O.J. L328/1
[184] Regulation (EC) No.1692/2006 of the European Parliament and of the Council of October 24, 2006 establishing the second Marco Polo programme for the granting of Community financial assistance to improve the environmental performance of the freight transport system (Marco Polo II) and repealing Regulation (EC) No.1382/2003 [2006] O.J. L328/1, art.7.
[185] Select Committee on the European Communities, House of Lords, Community Shipping Measures (HMSO, 1990), p.7.
[186] Jean-François Pons, Eric Fitzgerald, "Competition in the maritime transport sector: a new era" [2002] Competition Policy Newsletter, 1/10.

maritime transport, which as it will be recalled, is not automatically subject to art.93.

A first set of "Guidelines for the examination of State aids to Community shipping companies" was adopted at the end of the 1980s.[187] These were subsequently revised and amended twice: in 1997[188] and in 2004.[189] The 1989 guidelines were already based on the principle that aid should enable the Union shipowners to compete on an equal footing with their main competitors on the world market. To that end, the guidelines allowed aid up to a level where such aid would compensate the calculated hypothetical cost gap between vessels under the cheapest Union flag and a flag of convenience.

The special case of aid to shipbuilding will be discussed in Ch.16.

17–050 **(ii) Legislation: the Guidelines and 2004 Communication.** The 1997 Union Guidelines on State aid to maritime transport had as their general objectives:

- To safeguard EC employment (both on board and on shore);

- To preserve maritime know-how in the Union and develop maritime skills; and

- To improve safety.

Interestingly, these guidelines introduced the notion that operating aid could be granted in the maritime sector, which is a major exception. As it will be recalled, operating aid is generally seen to be highly distortive and therefore not compatible. Here, the following aid measures reducing employment costs were sent to be acceptable, including a maximum reduction of liabilities to zero:

- reduced rates of contributions for the social protection of EC seafarers employed on board ships registered in a Member State; and

- reduced rates of income tax for EC seafarers on board ships registered in a Member State.

However, no aid on net wages of EC seafarers may be granted. In addition to this generous allowance for operating aid, the guidelines also endorsed the fiscal alleviation schemes for ship-owning companies, provided only these companies could show a link with the Union flag and that the fiscal advantages were limited to shipping activities.

---

[187] SEC (89) 921 final, September 4, 1989. *Competition Law in the European Communities.* Vol.IIA: *Rules applicable to State aid.* Situation at December 31, 1994. European Commission (Brussels, 1995), p.437.

[188] [1997] O.J. C205/5. The guidelines provide an extensive description of the development of the shipping sector.

[189] Commission Communication C(2004) 43—Community guidelines on State aid to maritime transport [2004] O.J. C13/3.

A further element in the guidelines is crew relief. The Guidelines indicate that aid in the form of payment or reimbursement of the cost of repatriation of EC seafarers working on board ships registered in the Member States can be accepted up to a limit of 50 per cent of the total cost. In line with the general approach to aid in the maritime sector, investment aid is allowed in certain restricted circumstances, notably when investments increase a ship's safety and environmental performance beyond the mandatory standards in place.

Regional aid will follow the general principles on regional aid, with the proviso that such aid in the shipping sector may only be permitted when it is clear that the benefits will accrue to the region over a reasonable period of time. Keeping in mind the objective of maintaining maritime know-how in the Union, Training aid will be considered to be aid if it is specifically related to maritime activities. R&D aid will be assessed under the framework for aid to R&D, see Chapter 23. Environmental aid will be judged according to the rules of the framework for environmental aid: see Chapter 22. Similarly, the Commission will apply the guidelines on State aid for rescuing and restructuring firms in difficulty, see Chapter 24.

In the penultimate paragraph of the guidelines, the Commission states that **17–051** accumulation of aid can be accepted as long as the total amount (aid consisting of: fiscal privileges for shipowning companies, reduced rates of income tax and social security contributions, crew relief, investment aid and, finally, regional aid) does not exceed a zero reduction of income taxes, social security charges and corporate taxation.

The liberal regime for aid to the maritime sector was seen to be justified in view of the fact that this type of aid causes basically no effect on trade between the Member States, and also bearing in mind the Union objective to re-flag ships under Union flags or prevent them from flagging non-Union flags in the first place. In international shipping the fiscal competition is between Member States and third countries.[190]

These principles have been maintained in the 2004 version of the Guidelines[191] which were intended to strengthen the methods of monitoring the effects of state aid and to give new guidance on tax exemptions, while at the same time ensuring fair competition in the internal market.[192] This follows a survey conducted by the Commission prior to the adoption of the 2004 Guidelines into the effectiveness of Member States' aid measures, which showed that re-registration under the national flag of a significant volume of tonnage had taken place.[193] Considering that one of the main aims is to have ships registered under Union flags, state aid

---

[190] Commission Communication C(2004) 43—Community guidelines on state aid to maritime transport [2004] O.J. C13/3, para.3.1

[191] Commission Communication C(2004) 43—Community guidelines on state aid to maritime transport [2004] O.J. C13/3.

[192] 33rd Report on Competition Policy, para.386.

[193] Commission Communication C(2004) 43—Community guidelines on state aid to maritime transport [2004] O.J. C13/3, p.1.

may as a general rule only be granted in respect of ships entered in a Member States' register.[194]

17–052 One of the other measures covered by the 2004 Guidelines is the so-called "tonnage tax". Under such scheme, the shipowner pays an amount of tax linked directly to the tonnage operated. However, the tonnage tax is then payable irrespective of the company's actual profits or losses.[195]

New also is the inclusion into the Guidelines of the activities of towing and dredging. In principle, the Maritime guidelines cover only maritime transport, as defined in Regulations (EEC) No 4055/86[196] and Regulation (EEC) No 3577/92,[197] according to which maritime transport is essentially[198] the "transport of goods and persons by sea". However, as some Member States considered tugboats and dredgers eligible for aid in their schemes, it has been deemed suitable to clarify their eligibility in the Communication. In both cases, aid can only be granted if the boats in question actually carry out an activity that can be considered maritime transport (i.e. the transport of goods, people, or in the case of dredging, of extracted materials at high seas) for more than 50 per cent of their annual operation time. No derogation from the flag link is possible. The tugging in and into ports and the actual dredging or extraction are explicitly excluded from state aid to maritime transport. This last point is illustrated by the negative decision the Commission took in 2002 in respect of the grant of maritime transport aid to Dutch towage operations carried out inside and around EU ports.[199] As port towage is considered a port service, which does not constitute a maritime transport activity, the grant of maritime transport aid for such port services was considered to be incompatible with the internal market and recovery was ordered.

17–053 Finally, the Communication includes provisions on aid to short-sea shipping. For the purposes of the Communication, this activity refers to the movement of cargo and passenger by sea between ports situated in Member States.[200] The

---

[194] Commission Communication C(2004) 43—Community guidelines on state aid to maritime transport [2004] O.J. C13/3, para.2.2. Some exceptions are, however, foreseen essentially for ships operated from the Community, complying with international standards and by belonging to shipowners established in the Community, when the Member State concerned demonstrated that the non-EU register contributes to the objectives of the Guidelines. Additionally, the shipowners must then commit themselves to increasing or at least maintaining the share of tonnage they will operate under the flag of a Member State.

[195] The Commission approved such schemes in most Member States, see for instance 22nd Report on Competition Policy para.496.

[196] Council Regulation (EEC) No.4055/86 of December 22, 1986 applying the principle of freedom to provide services to maritime transport between Member States and between Member States and third countries [1986] O.J. L378/1.

[197] Council Regulation (EEC) No.3577/92 of December 7, 1992 applying the principle of freedom to provide services to maritime transport within Member States (maritime cabotage) [1992] O.J. L364/7.

[198] Although one could argue that the concept of maritime transport is slightly wider considering that the wording of Regulation (EEC) No.3577/92 suggest a wide interpretation: In its art.2, off-shore supply services are included within the notion of maritime transport.

[199] Case C 56/2001 [2002] O.J. L314/97.

[200] The Communication clarifies that this is not a legal but a "working definition", which although it includes shipping to non-European ports, is restricted to Member States ports for the purposes of the Communication, cf. para.10.

approach concerning aid to short-sea shipping is based on another consideration than aid to maritime transport as such. Short-sea shipping is seen to be beneficial, as it aims to improve the intermodal chain and to decongest roads in the Member States. Akin to its approach to aid for combined transport, the Commission recognises that the launch of short-sea shipping services may by accompanied by substantial financial difficulties which the Member State may wish to attenuate by aid in order to nevertheless promote such services. The conditions imposed on aid to short-sea shipping are:

- The aid must not exceed three years in duration, after which it must be commercially viable.

- The service must be of a kind to allow the transport of essentially cargo that would otherwise be transported by road to be carried wholly or partly by sea, without diverting maritime transport in a way contrary to the common interest.

- The aid must be directed at implementing a detailed project with a pre-established environmental impact, concerning a new route or the upgrading of services on an existing one, with no more than one project financed per line and with no renewal, extension or repetition of the project in question.

- The purpose of the aid must be to cover, either up to a total of 30 per cent (i.e. thus including any other aid received) of the operational costs of the service in question, or to finance the purchase of transshipment equipment to supply the planned service, up to a level of 10 per cent in such investment.

- The aid to implement a project must be granted on the basis of transparent criteria applied in a non-discriminatory way to shipowners established in the Union. The aid should normally be granted for a project selected by the authorities of the Member State through a tender procedure in compliance with applicable Union rules.

- Aid granted to short-sea shipping may not be accumulated with public service compensation.

In December 2008, the Commission issued a Communication providing guid- **17–054** ance on the treatment of state aid measures complementing Community funding for the launching of the "motorways of the sea".[201] It is intended to align the maximum aid intensity and duration provided for in the Community guidelines on state aid to maritime transport[202] to the more favourable conditions allowed for projects covered by the second "*Marco Polo*" programme for the granting of

---

[201] Communication from the Commission providing guidance on State aid complementary to Community funding for the launching of the motorways of the sea [2008] O.J. C317/10.
[202] [2004] O.J. C13/3.

Community financial assistance to improve the environmental performance of the freight transport system (*"Marco Polo II"*)[203] and by the *TEN-T Decision*.[204]

In 2009, a Communication on State aid to ship management companies[205] was adopted. The Communication lays down the criteria for the eligibility of ship management companies to a reduction in corporate tax or the application of the tonnage tax under the 2004 Guidelines.

17–055 **(iii) The Commission's practice.** The Commission's approach to aid to maritime transport, outside the quite standard assessment of tonnage tax schemes,[206] can be illustrated by reference to the following cases.

Approval by the Commission for 10 years of a package of tax measures in favour of the Belgian merchant marine. The package consists of, among other things, a flat-rate tax scheme applicable to maritime transport companies along the lines of that which exists in most Member States with a commercial fleet. The set of tax measures approved by the Commission will help to strengthen the competitiveness of the Belgian fleet in the face of competition from third countries.[207]

A Compatibility decision on a French scheme intended to cover for a period of three years up to 30 per cent of the operating costs of new short-sea shipping services.[208]

An Italian scheme granting an incentive to shipowners for the elimination of single hull tankers over 20 years of age. Whilst the Commission initiated a formal investigation procedure, it concluded it by finding that the aid scheme would provide an important contribution to the protection of the environment and to safer seas.[209]

Further to a the formal investigation procedure in respect of a package of Belgian tax measures in favour of the merchant marine, the Commission refused some of the measures examined. These were a tax reduction for more recent vessels, the transfer of tax credits to within the scope of the company subject to flat-rate taxation and the eligibility of activities not intrinsically related to maritime transport, such as the sale of goods or services not intended for consumption on board and the sale of luxury goods or passenger excursions, and betting and casinos.[210]

---

[203] Established by Regulation (EC) No.1692/2006 of the European Parliament and of the Council of October 24, 2006 [2006] O.J. L328/1.

[204] Decision No.1692/96/EC of the European Parliament and of the Council of July 23, 1996 on Community guidelines for the development of the trans-European transport network [1996] O.J. L228/1.

[205] Communication from the Commission providing guidance on State aid to ship management companies [2009] O.J. C132/6.

[206] See for instance Case N790/99 [2000] O.J. C58/3 or N171/2004 [2005] O.J. C136/42.

[207] Case C 20/2003 (ex-N 433/2002) [2005] O.J. L150/1.

[208] Case C 65/2000 (ex N 679/2000) [2002] O.J. L196.

[209] Case C 97/2001 (ex. N 93/2001) *Maritime transport safety* [2002] O.J. C50/7.

[210] Case C 20/2003 (ex. N 433/2002) [2003] O.J. L150/1.

The Commission concluded a formal procedure regarding the extension to   **17–056**
dredging and cable-laying activities of the regime exempting maritime transport
companies from the payment of income tax and social contributions of seafarers
("DIS regime") in Denmark.[211] The Commission had expressed doubts whether
such activities constituted or could be assimilated to maritime transport. In the
end, the Commission concluded that all dredging activities can be assimilated to
maritime transport except for sailing at the places of extraction. In addition, it
accepted the extension of the DIS regime to cable-laying vessels by applying by
analogy the Maritime Guidelines.[212] This application by analogy was followed
again in 2010 when the Commission authorised the extension of the Dutch
tonnage tax scheme to cable layers, pipeline layers, research vessels and crane
vessels.[213]

In January 2010 the Commission for the first time approved state aid for
launching a "Motorways of the Sea" project on the basis of both the Maritime
Guidelines and the Complementary aid Guidelines.[214] The aid is complementary
to Union financing granted under the Marco Polo II Programme. The project
concerns the establishment of a maritime link operated by GLD Atlantique
between the French port of Nantes/Saint Nazaire and the Spanish port of Gijón.
The aim is to capture between 3 per cent and 5 per cent of the road traffic which
currently passes through the west of the Pyrénées. The overall financing of the
project (state aid and Marco Polo grant) is limited to 35 per cent of the eligible
costs within the first four years of its operation.[215]

(iv) Ports. On a number of occasions, the Commission has assessed aid granted   **17–057**
to ports and port handling facilities. This includes both maritime and inland
waterway ports. In both cases, the assessment has to be seen in the context of the
transport policy goal to achieve a modal shift away from road transport. As more
generally for infrastructure cases, one of the main issues in the case of ports is
whether measures constitute aid: indeed arguably measures will often be partly
aimed at non-commercial activities.[216] This issue has never been clarified successfully in the case of sea ports, as indeed this segment of transport aid is still
characterised by Commission practice only and not by more general guidance.

First, based on a "General study of State aid in the port sector" reviewing
available data and specifying the position of the Commission on the question of

---

[211] Aid C 22/07 [2009] O.J. L119/23.
[212] Competition Report 2009, paras 135 and 401.
[213] Case N714/2009 *Extension of the tonnage tax scheme to cable layers, pipeline layers, research
vesselsand crane vessels* [2010] O.J. C158/2.
[214] Communication from the Commission providing guidance on state aid complementary to
Community funding for the launching of the motorways of the sea [2008] O.J. C317/10.
[215] Cases N573/2009 and N647/2009 *Aide à la mise en oeuvre et à l'exploitation de l'autoroute de
la mer entre le port de Nantes-Saint-Nazaire (France) et le port de Gijón (Espagne) opérée par
GLD Atlantique* [2010] O.J. C74/5. See IP/10/55, January 27, 2010.
[216] M. Kekelekis, "Recent Developments in Infrastructure Funding: When Does It Not Constitute
State Aid?" ESTAL 3/2011 p.933.

public investment in ports,[217] the Commission issued a Green Paper on Sea Ports and Maritime Infrastructure.[218] The purpose of the Paper was to launch a wide-ranging debate on individual port issues and possible future policies, which should help to increase port efficiency and improve port and maritime infrastructure. This should be done by integrating ports into the multimodal trans-European network. So far, no legislative proposal has been published.

One of the first actual cases in which state aid rules were applied to port infrastructure was in 2001 when the Commission approved the Port of Rosyth project.[219] On that occasion, the Commission set out its approach in the 2001 Competition Report in some detail. The Commission normally considers that state financing of infrastructure open to all potential users in a non-discriminatory way and managed by the state does normally not fall under art.107(1) TFEU.[220] From the General Court's judgment in *Aéroports de Paris*,[221] it could be followed that the management and provision of infrastructure facilities can constitute an economic activity for the purposes of art.107(1) TFEU. However, if state support for an infrastructure manager chosen by an open and non-discriminatory procedure for construction and maintenance of transport infrastructure represents a market price it would not normally trigger the application of art.107(1) TFEU. The Port of Rosyth project was authorised under art.107(3)(c) TFEU.

17–058   In a Belgian notification of a Public Private Partnership scheme for the construction of loading and unloading facilities in Flemish Ports to further combined transport,[222] the Commission came to the conclusion that the support scheme constituted aid, as the beneficiary was not selected through a public tender and the infrastructure is not necessarily open to all potential users. Nevertheless, the Commission found the aid to be compatible, based on art.93 TFEU. In assessing the compatibility, the Commission considered the following three criteria, namely:

- Was the contribution of the State necessary to allow the realisation of the project?

- The aid is attributed according to non-discriminatory conditions.

- There is no distortion of competition contrary to the common interest. In that case, the Commission considered the fact that the aid is granted within

---

[217] 19th Report on Competition Policy, pt 211.
[218] COM (97) 678 final, Brussels, December 10, 1997.
[219] Case N 649/2001.
[220] For a more general view of Aid in Infrastructure Funding, see M. Kekelekis, "Recent Developments in Infrastructure Funding: When Does It Not Constitute State Aid?" ESTAL 3/2011, p.933.
[221] Case T–128/98 [2002] E.C.R. II–3929.
[222] N 550/2001 [2002] O.J. C24/2, extended by N 344/2004.

the framework of a public private partnership and that then aid intensity was limited to (50 per cent).

In another Belgian case, this time concerning financial support for infrastructure works in Flemish ports[223] the Commission drew a distinction between the financing of:

(i) maritime access routes and sea locks, which it considers to be State expenditures in the framework of the State's responsibilities in the planning and the development of a maritime transport system in the interest of the general public, which do not benefit a particular undertaking; and

(ii) port infrastructure related to a project, such as harbour basins, docks, access routes and access rails for which it considers that their financing might constitute an advantage for the port authority exploiting these infrastructures.

In the compatibility assessment, the Commission considered that the infrastructure investments notified contribute to a modal shift, and that the notified measure did not exceed the maximum aid intensity for transport infrastructure of 50 per cent. It therefore found the aid to be compatible on the basis of art. 107(3)(c) TFEU.

A 2005 case concerns the notification by the United Kingdom of its intention **17–059** to finance part of the maritime access works (breakwaters and port entrance structures) in the context of the planned development of the outer harbour at Great Yarmouth, to be operated as an extension to the existing river port.[224] Here, the Commission examined aid at two different levels, i.e. at the level of the end-users and at the level of the manager/operator of the infrastructure in question. Since in that case the infrastructure at stake will indeed be open to all potential users on equal and non-discriminatory terms with access prices being charged on commercial terms, the Commission took the view that no state aid to users was involved. Examining the maritime infrastructure, the Commission recalled its practice and policy to consider that public investments in maritime access routes (breakwaters, locks, navigable channels, dredging, etc.), and other maritime infrastructure that benefit the maritime Union as a whole, do not normally give rise to issues of state aid. A distinction is thus made between public or general and user-specific infrastructure.

Nevertheless, even in the case of general infrastructure, the Commission will consider, as it did in the Great Yarmouth case, whether the body in charge of managing the public infrastructure also carries out commercial activities and

---

[223] Case N 520/2003 [2005] O.J. C176/12.
[224] Case N 503/2005 [2006] O.J. C83/10.

hence whether any aid give for the public infrastructure could have a spill-over effect on the body's commercial activities. As this was not the case, the Commission took a no aid decision.

17-060   More recently, the Commission approved a measure to support the construction of a new port in Wilhelmshaven, Germany (*Jade Weser Port project*).[225] The Commission, in its traditional approach, concluded that the public financing of the planned infrastructure does not constitute state aid in favour of the shipping companies using the Jade Weser Port, as long as access to this infrastructure is allowed on equal and non-discriminatory terms. As regards the concession agreement for the construction and operation of the terminal, the Commission found that it did not contain any state aid element, since it had been awarded on the basis of a Europe-wide, open, transparent and non-discriminatory public tender. This decision is in line with previous case practice according to which, in general, no state aid is present at the users' level if transport infrastructure is open to all potential users on equal and non-discriminatory terms. On the other hand, when the construction of public infrastructure is directed at a particular user, giving it an unfair advantage over its competitors, the respective financing normally constitutes state aid.[226]

In the case of aid for the Latvian *Ventssplit* Port, the Commission confirmed that it considered that a port authority will, generally, be exercising an economic activity.[227]

In 2010 the Commission decided to launch a study to collect information to better understand the functioning of ports and the public financing of their infrastructure. On the basis of its results, the Commission will be able to define a reliable approach for moving forward in that field.[228] This could lead to the Commission issuing guidance for the assessment of state aid to ports.

Air transport

17-061   **(i) Introduction.** The Commission's practice in applying state aid to the air transport sector began in earnest in the early 1990s. The explanation for this development can be found partly in the general recession in the early 1990s, which was accentuated by the first Gulf War and which led to serious financial hardship for airlines and hence to state support.[229] Another important feature is the liberalisation of the intra-Union air transport market, the most important steps

---

[225] Case N 110/2008 [2009] O.J. C137/1.
[226] Competition Report 2008 Commission Staff Working Document COM (2009) 37 final, paras 278–279.
[227] See opening decision in Case C39/2009 (ex. N 385/2008) [2010] O.J. C62/7. Public financing of port infrastructure in Ventspils port [2010] O.J. C62/7, paras 62–71.
[228] Competition Report 2010 Commission Staff Working Document COM (2009) 328 final, para.339.
[229] Lübbig/Martin-Ehlers, "Beihilfenrecht der EU", 2nd edn München [2009], p.198, para.515.

towards which were also taken in then early 1990s.[230] This resulted in six major cases of massive aid for the national flag carriers: Aer Lingus, TAP, Air France, Olympic, Iberia and Alitalia, some of which, such as the aid to Olympic, have been running for a number of years now. As a result, the application of state aid rules in the air transport sector is certainly one of the most spectacular areas.[231]

The Commission decisions in these cases have also resulted in four judgments from the General Court. The Commission's experience with the first four decisions has also led to the adoption of sector-specific guidelines on the "Application of Articles 92 and 93 (now 107 and 88) TFEU and Article 61 of the EEA Agreement to State aids in the aviation sector."[232] These arguably restrictive[233] guidelines contained the "one time last time" principle for granting aid.

In the aftermath of the terrorist attacks on September 11, 2001 airlines were, **17–062** again, facing major difficulties. Whilst the sector was already confronted by problems arising out of overcapacity and fuel prices, the attacks led to a dramatic decrease in demand linked with an increase in insurance premiums and costs for security measures. This downturn exacerbated the difficulties.[234] Again, more recently, the Iraq War of 2003 and the SARS outbreak have added to the difficulties, at least for traditional flag carriers.[235] As a result, a number of Member States envisaged to grant their flag carriers state aid.

The Commission reacted by a Communication, issued jointly with the Council and the European Parliament on "the repercussions of the terrorist attacks in the United States on the air transport industry".[236] The Communication acknowledged that some aid could be justified, on the basis of art.107(2) (b) TFEU, as a

---

[230] The air transport sector in the European Union was liberalised in three successive stages. The first "package" of measures adopted in December 1987, started to relax the established rules, for example by limiting the right of governments to object to the introduction of new fares. In 1990 a second "package" of measures opened up the market further, for instance allowing greater flexibility over the setting of fares and capacity-sharing. The last, and arguably most important stage was the subject of a third "package" of measures, which were adopted in July 1992 and applied as from January 1993. This package gradually introduced freedom to provide services within the European Union and led in April 1997 to the freedom to provide cabotage, i.e. the right for an airline of one Member State to operate a route within another Member State. See Council Regulation (EEC) No.2407/92 of July 23, 1992 on licensing of air carriers[1992] O.J. L240/1, which opened the market to all airlines which hold a Community air carrier's licence; Council Regulation (EEC) No.2409/92 of July 23, 1992 on fares and rates for air services [1992] O.J. L 240/15, according to which airlines were no longer required to submit their fares to the national authorities for approval; and Council Regulation (EEC) No.2408/92 of July 23, 1992 on access for Community air carriers to intra-Community air routes [1992] O.J. L240/8.

[231] See also T. Soames and A. Ryan, "State aid and air transport" [1995] ECLR 290–309.

[232] [1994] O.J. C350/5; Lübbig/Martin-Ehlers, "Beihilfenrecht der EU", 2nd edn München [2009], p.199, para.515; Competition Report 1994, paras 374–375.

[233] M. Sànchez-Rydelski, *Handbuch EU Beihilferecht* (Nomos: Baden-Baden, 2003), p.139.

[234] See 31st Report on Competition Policy, para.445: *"The year was divided into two parts, 'before 11 September' and 'after 11 September', with the terrorist attacks in the United States having a major impact on air transport".*

[235] Not necessarily for low-cost carriers though, see Ruwantissa Abeyratne, "The Decision in the Ryanair Case—the Low Cost Carrier Phenomenon" [2004] *European Transport Law*, 585.

[236] Commission Communication of October 10, 2001 on the repercussions of the terrorist attacks in the United States on the air transport industry—COM(2001) 574 final.

reaction to the extraordinary events. Examples were cases where there is no appropriate offer of insurance cover, and aid to offset the losses suffered by airlines following the closure of air space for four days and the high costs involved in increased security measures. Nevertheless, it was also clarified that all these aid measures taken by Member States must be notified to the Commission. A number of state aid measures relating to insurance were authorised by the Commission still in 2001.[237] Nevertheless, the Communication reiterated the Commission policy by stressing:

"that the events of 11 September 2001 must not undermine the Commission's policy on State aid to restructuring based in particular on the 'one-time, last-time' principle. They must not be used as a pretext for bypassing the existing framework for aid to restructuring in order to remedy the serious problems which for months and sometimes years have dogged certain Community airlines attempting to restructure."[238]

A similar issue, albeit of less severity, occurred with the Eyjafjallajökull volcano eruption in Iceland in April 2010: the eruption created a cloud of volcanic ash which covered most of Europe, except the Mediterranean region airspace. In its information note of April 27, 2010, the Commission acknowledged the impact on the air transport industry of the closing of the affected airspace in an information note.[239] The Commission proposed a series of short-term emergency measures and of structural measures to respond to the situation created by the flight restrictions. With regard to possible compensation for the air transport industry, this note indicated that the Commission "could prepare a communication clarifying the requirements to be fulfilled" to provide state aid in the relevant context. In the conclusions on the EU response to the consequences of the volcanic ash cloud on air transport adopted by the Extraordinary TTE (Transport) Council of May 4, 2010[240] where the Council agreed to "recall the existing legal framework applicable to potential support measures by Member States", thereby referring to art.107(2)(b) TFEU which states that "shall be compatible with the internal market (. . .) aid to make good the damage caused by natural disasters or exceptional circumstances". However, as in 2010 no Member State expressed its intention to grant state aid to the air transport industry in the above mentioned context, the adoption of a communication did not appear appropriate.

Like maritime transport, air transport is not automatically subject to the rules of the transport title.[241] As long as the Council has not decided otherwise on the

---

[237] See for instance the cases concerning Belgium and Sweden, Cases NN 139/2001 and NN 141/2001 [2002] O.J. C24/2.

[238] Commission Communication of October 10, 2001 on the repercussions of the terrorist attacks in the United States on the air transport industry—COM(2001) 574 final, para.29.

[239] This information note was presented by Vice-president Kallas in association with Vice-president Almunia and Commissioner Rehn and was endorsed by the Commission on April 27, 2010.

[240] MEMO/10/161.

[241] Case C–49/89 *Corsica Ferries v Direction Générale des Douanes* [1989] E.C.R. 4441.

basis of art.80 TFEU, only the general articles of the Treaty apply to it.[242] Thus, air transport is covered by arts 90 to 107 TFEU.

(ii) The 1994 Guidelines and Commission practice.

The 1994 Guidelines: The Guidelines start with a summary of the liberalisation **17–063** measures for the Union air transport market. It noted that, as of April 1, 1997, the intra-Union market was fully liberalised, including cabotage transport.[243] This has a very important bearing on the compatibility of aid in the sector, because in a fully liberalised market aid will have a direct effect on competition. In the previously existing market, traffic rights, capacity and prices were fully controlled by national governments; therefore, aid would only have an indirect and sometimes marginal effect.

The Guidelines respond to two main concerns:

* To reflect the completion of the internal market for air transport; and

* To increase the transparency, at different levels, of the evaluation process, in relation to, firstly, the data to be provided in the notification by the Member States and, second, to the criteria and procedures applied by the Commission.

The Commission stated that it has a positive approach towards social aid, for it brings economic benefits above and beyond the interests of the firm concerned, facilitates structural changes and reduces hardship.

Operating aid[244] is not normally allowed, except when it is designed to compensate for the operation of public service obligations. There is an extensive section on the establishment of these obligations, detailing the rules laid down in Regulation 2408/92.[245] Aid to compensate for public service obligations will only be approved if the relevant rules of the regulation have been observed. The Commission stated that it will, in the first instance, be for the national authorities, and in particular for the national courts, to ensure the proper application of these rules. Thus, national courts have, on the basis of the directly effective provisions of the regulation, an enhanced role in the process of enforcement of the rules on state aid to compensate for public service obligations. Of course, the application of art.107 TFEU will remain the exclusive domain of the Commission.

---

[242] Case 167/73 *Commission v France* [1974] E.C.R. 359 and Joined Cases 209–213/84 *Ministère Public v Asjes* [1986] E.C.R. 1425.

[243] A special agreement with the EEA Member States has extended the internal market for air transport to these countries. Decision 92/384 [1992] O.J. L200/20.

[244] Defined as aid "which is intended to relieve the recipient undertaking of all or part of the expenses which they would normally have had to bear in their day-to-day management or their usual activities", Case T–55/99, *Confederación Española de Transporte de Mercancias v Commission* [2000] E.C.R. II–3207, para.83.

[245] On access for Community air carriers to intra-Community air routes [1992] O.J. L240/24.

17–064   The Guidelines also recall that the exemption of art.92(2)(a) TFEU, now art.107(2)(a) TFEU, (aid having a social character) had been used only rarely, and that such aid must genuinely be of a social nature and hence in principle can only be granted in favour of certain categories of (socially disadvantaged) passengers. However interestingly, the Commission considered also that such aid might by granted in cases where it is directly linked to an underprivileged region, whereby the Commission means essentially Islands: there the Commission interpreted art.107(2)(a) TFEU widely, considering that such aid might qualify for the exception of art.107(2)(a) TFEU as it would benefit all inhabitants of the disadvantaged region.

There is a long section on the distinction between the state's role as owner of an enterprise and as provider of State aid to that enterprise. The Commission will follow a two-step analysis in order to make such a distinction properly. First, it will determine whether aid is involved according to the market economy investor principle. If it considers that the measure involves aid elements, it will determine whether the aid is compatible with the internal market under art.107(3) TFEU. Capital injections will not involve aid when the public holding to be increased is commensurate with the public shareholding. Furthermore, the market economy investor principle will be satisfied when a normal rate of return can be expected. In this context, the Commission referred to the case law of the ECJ in *ENI-Lanerossi*[246] to argue that it will not normally limit itself to considering short-term profitability only, but will also look to the longer term. It listed several indicators that may be taken into account for assessing the financial performance of the company. It indicated that it may seek the advice of independent experts on the viability of restructuring plans. As the individual decisions to be discussed further below demonstrate, the Commission has indeed made ample use of such external experts. In cases where governments provide loans, the aid element will be relatively easy to establish. Guarantees fall within the scope of art.107(1) TFEU. They will only be accepted if they are contractually linked to specific conditions. An assessment of the aid element in guarantees will involve an analysis of the borrower's financial position.

17–065   **(iii) Restructuring aid.** The Commission will assess restructuring programmes under art.107(3)(c) TFEU as set out in its Guidelines on State aid for rescuing and restructuring. The programme must be self-contained, in the sense that no further aid must be necessary for the duration of the programme. The Commission stressed that restructuring aid can normally only be granted once.[247] The Commission will be particularly vigilant that the restructuring programme do lead to capacity increases. Furthermore, the companies involved must, during the restructuring period, refrain from acquiring shareholdings in other airlines. When governments do decide to privatise they must follow a number of principles set

---

[246] Case C–303/88 *Italy v Commission* [1991] E.C.R. I–1433.
[247] Additionally it should be remembered that, further to case C–355/95P *Textilwerke Deggendorf* [1997] E.C.R. I–2549, paras 25–26, the Commission takes into account any prior aid granted and in particular the failure to repay any prior illegal aid (so-called "Deggendorf Doctrine").

out in the guidelines. The key condition is that a public tender should be organised on a non-discriminatory and transparent basis.

The grant of exclusive rights (such as duty-free shop concessions) should also be organised by transparent bidding procedures. The final sections of the guidelines are devoted to the transparency of financial transactions. In these, the Commission has required Member States to follow the rules laid down in the transparency directives.

As far as restructuring aid is concerned, the approach followed by the Commission is probably best demonstrated by the Air France cases. It should be recalled that in 1991, the Commission considered that a FF 2 billion injection of fresh capital into Air France and in 1992 a total of FF 3.85 billion were regarded as normal financial operations.[248] In 1994, the Commission approved another FF 20 billion capital injection.[249] At the same time, the Commission ruled that a FF 1,497,415,290 subscription by CDC–P to two bond issues of Air France constituted state aid and had to be reimbursed.[250] Applying the market economy investor principle, the Commission found the participation clearly to be an aid, since the projected rate of return was insufficient to satisfy a normal market economy investor. This conclusion was reinforced when the subordinate nature of the loan was taken into account. Since there was no adequate restructuring plan the aid could not be exempted under art.92(3)(c) (now art.107) TFEU. The main capital injection was also considered to be aid, but was approved on the basis of art.92(3)(c) (now art.107) TFEU, albeit subject to a long list of commitments which the French government had to comply with.[251] The aid was to be granted in three instalments. The decision provided that, in order to ensure that the aid remained compatible with the internal market, the payment of the second and the third instalments was subject to the French government respecting all of the conditions imposed and commitments given. It was also subject to the effective implementation of the restructuring plan.

The conditions restricted Air France's commercial freedom drastically: it **17–066** could not acquire new holdings in other carriers, nor increase the number of aircraft, nor increase its capacity on specified routes (although a growth rate of 2.7 per cent per annum was allowed), nor operate more scheduled routes than it did in 1993; it was not to act as price leader, and it had to dispose of its shareholdings in the Meridien Hotel chain. The government was not to grant preferential treatment to Air France as far as traffic rights were concerned, it had

---

[248] See Written Question E–1925/94, Maij-Weggen and Cornelissen [1995] O.J. C36/14–15.
[249] Dec. 94/653/EC [1994] O.J. L254/73.
[250] Dec. 94/662/EC [1994] O.J. L258/26. A year later, the Commission addressed another decision to France, (Dec. 95/367/EC [1995] O.J. L219/34) in order to ensure that effective steps were undertaken for the implementation of its first Decision. It was ordered that France should deposit the illegally implemented aid in a blocked bank account.
[251] It should be noted that the terminology which the Commission uses to denote conditions is not always uniform. In this decision, the term "commitments" is used. The *Alitalia* decision uses the term undertakings (Dec. 97/789/EC [1997] O.J. L322/44).

to modify the traffic distribution system in accordance with the Commission decision on the London–Orly link, and the process of privatisation of Air France had to begin as soon as the company's economic and financial recovery had been achieved. Air France was to continue the implementation of its restructuring plan.[252]

In a communication a year later, the Commission noted that France had submitted a detailed report indicating the steps it had taken to implement its commitments.[253] The Commission appointed an independent expert to verify the implementation of the programme and the commitments. The Commission considered that, taking into account the market conditions, the implementation of the plan was generally proceeding satisfactorily and that France had fulfilled the obligations. Consequently, it had no objections to the payment of the second instalment of the aid. A year later it authorised the payment of the third instalment.[254] Following a similar procedure as it had done the year before, it commissioned an opinion by an independent expert. The overall conclusion was again that the progress of the restructuring was satisfactory, and that most of the conditions were being respected.[255] Coming to its decision, the Commission took into account new undertakings given by France according to which Air France would continue to respect condition 9, the prohibition of price leadership. France would guarantee condition 16, according to which the airport of Orly would be accessible for competitors of Air France. In a new communication in 1997, the Commission noted the further progress exemplified by new restructuring measures.[256] The Commission considered that Air France had succeeded in stabilising its position, and that the company can be expected to consolidate its position on the market.

17–067   Another important milestone in this aid operation was the judgment in *British Airways and Others v Commission* of the General Court of June 25, 1998.[257] The case is quite spectacular since so many competitors chose to challenge the Commission's decision, supported by the governments of the United Kingdom and Denmark and partly by the governments of Norway and Sweden. The applicants put forward numerous arguments relating to the substance of the matter. The Court, ruling some four years later in 1998 found in favour of the

---

[252] The decision stated that the productivity of Air France was much lower when compared with some major private airlines in the Community.

[253] [1995] O.J. C295/2. On two points, Air France had not fully met its obligations. Firstly, it had not yet taken a decision concerning the disposal of its interest in Sabena. Second, it had implemented its plans to sell older aircraft and to acquire new buildings. The Commission deferred the consideration of these points until after the payment of the third instalment.

[254] [1996] O.J. C374/9.

[255] Condition 9, not to apply tariffs below those of its competitors, was breached on two routes; condition 16 to adapt the terminals at Orly in order not to affect competitive conditions to the detriment of the companies operating there suffered some drawbacks as a result of renovation work.

[256] [1997] O.J. C374/6.

[257] Joined cases T–371 and 394/94 [1998] E.C.R. II–2405.

applicants on two points. It ruled that the Commission had failed to give sufficient reasons on two points: one relating to the purchase of new aircraft, and the second concerning the competitive situation of Air France on routes outside the EEA. On the first point, the Court referred to judgments of the Court of Justice *Deufil* and *Executif Regional Wallon*.[258] In these judgments, the Court considered that new investment in modernisation should be carried out using the companies' own resources and not through state aid. In *British Airways*, the contested aid would be used to finance new planes and should therefore have been classified as operating aid. Since the Commission had failed to comment on the relevance of the assertions of the parties and of the judgments cited above, it had failed to specify why it would tolerate the provision of aid in this case. On the second point, the General Court ruled that the Commission had, when the parties concerned had stressed the impact of the contested aid on competition on international routes, not given the slightest indication as to Air France's competitive position on routes outside the EEA. There was no analysis of Air France's international network and the conditions of authorisation relating to the level of supply, its pricing practices and the number of routes operated. In a press release, the Commission announced that it has decided to confirm its decisions as it is of the opinion that the Court has not questioned the substance of the original decision.[259] The Commission took its fresh decision on July 22, 1998[260] without reopening the art.93(3) (now art.88) TFEU procedure.

The Commission's decision declaring the subscription by CDC Participation to bond issues to be incompatible with the internal market was appealed by Air France.[261] Air France's first argument was that CDC-P was not under state control and hence its actions could not be regarded as aid. Its second argument was that the Commission had improperly applied the market economy investor principle. The third and the fourth arguments contested the finding of the date on which CDC-P took its investment decision as well as the context in which CDC-P had made its decision. Air France also complained that the Commission had failed to adopt the least restrictive measure, as it could have required the aid only to be altered instead of reimbursed. The General Court rejected all of these arguments, as well as some additional objections, and dismissed the appeal. On the argument about recovery it ruled that the Commission was entitled to order repayment of the capital injected, since the case involved a very complex issue of securities. The securities had already been subscribed and its inherent characteristics could not be altered. Its judgment provides a careful and detailed analysis of the full context of the aid operation as well as the different elements of the plan.

---

[258] Respectively Case 310/85 [1987] E.C.R. 901; and Joined Cases 62 & 72/87 [1988] E.C.R. 1573.
[259] IP/98/682, July 22, 1998.
[260] [1999] O.J. L63/66.
[261] Case T–358/94 [1996] E.C.R. II–2109.

17–068   The Commission's decision in the *Aer Lingus*[262] case followed a similar pattern to that in the Air France case, as did the cases of the Tap Air Portugal[263] and Alitalia[264] restructuring.[265] This decision was appealed by Ryanair, a competitor of Aer Lingus. In its judgment of September 15, 1998, the General Court dismissed the appeal.[266] The interest of the case is in the fact that the Court commented extensively on a situation in which in the context of Rescue and Restructuring aid, the Commission approves the grant of aid in several tranches, and the conditions for granting these tranches are varied subsequent to the decision. The Court started with the presumption that failure to comply with the conditions set in the Commission decision will make the aid incompatible with the internal market. It followed that the subsequent tranches could not be released without a new Commission decision granting a formal derogation from the condition in question. For that purpose, the Commission would have to examine the case, and if such examination led it to conclude that the subsequent tranches of the aid were no longer compatible with the internal market, or if it did not enable it to overcome all the difficulties involved in determining whether the subsequent tranches could be approved, it would have to reopen the art.93(2) (now art.108) TFEU procedure. However, this requirement could be waived in the event of relatively minor deviations from the original condition, which leave no doubt as to whether the aid is still compatible with the internal market. The Court added that in respect of successive tranches paid over a number of years, the Commission must have the power to manage and monitor such implementation. In particular, it must be able to deal with developments, which could not have been foreseen when the initial decision was adopted. The Commission may, therefore, vary the conditions without opening the art.108 TFEU procedure, provided that such variation does not give rise to doubts as to the compatibility of the aid.

The Court went on to ascertain whether, in the circumstances, the Commission should have reopened the art.88(2) TFEU procedure. Referring to settled case law, it considered that the Commission enjoys a wide discretion in the application of arts 88(3) and 107 (3)(c) TFEU. The Court also stated, that, by analogy with art.88(3) TFEU, payment of the aid must be suspended when the Commission reopens, or initiates,[267] the art.88(2) TFEU procedure, until the Commission adopts its final decision.[268] On the facts, the Court dismissed Ryanair's application.

---

[262] Dec. 94/118/EC [1994] O.J. L54/30.

[263] Dec. 94/698/EC [1994] O.J. L279/29.

[264] Dec. 97/789/EC [1997] O.J. L322/44.

[265] The last major restructuring case, Iberia, went another way as the Commission took a non-aid decision in application of the market investor principle, Dec. 96/278/EC [1996] O.J. L104/25, see also written question E–430/96 by Mr Malone [1996] O.J. C173/58.

[266] Case T–140/95 *Ryanair v Commission* [1998] E.C.R. I–3327.

[267] Such may be the case when the original aid plan was approved without opening the art.93(2) (now art.108 TFEU) procedure. However, in cases such as the present ones which led to the imposition of important conditions, this is not likely.

[268] para.87.

The saga of *Olympic Airways*[269] began in 1994 with the restructuring of **17–069**
Olympic Airways, when the Commission approved a 1.564 million ECU aid plan
for Olympic Airways.[270] It was still running in 2010 and must be one of the most
work-intensive-complex but also rich state aid series of all. It goes some way to
illustrate the economic and political importance accorded by some Member
States to their flag carriers.

The art.93(2) (now art.108) communication in 1994 on the original plan
incited reactions from four governments and several airlines. The decision also
revealed that the Commission had experienced serious difficulty in obtaining all
of the necessary information. The list of conditions was very extensive and
comprised, apart from the usual conditions to avert an effect on competition,
several conditions relating to the implementation of the third liberalisation
package. Notwithstanding a clear condition that the Greek government should
not grant any further aid, it gave the airline further aid. The Commission
responded within order that the third instalment of the earlier approved aid be
suspended, and it also reopened the art.93(2) (now art.108) procedure.[271] On July
28, 1998, it approved the new restructuring plan although it reduced the amount
proposed from DRA 54 to 48 billion[272] to take account of the DRA 13.2 billion
that had been paid out illegally.[273]

The Commission decided in March 2002 to launch a formal investigation
under art.88(2) of the Treaty into possible misuse of aid granted by Greece and
authorised in 1994 and 1998 and the grant of further aid to Olympic Airways and
its subsidiaries. On December 11, 2002, the Commission established that some
of the aid previously granted by Greece and further aid that was illegal because
it had not been notified were incompatible with the Treaty.[274] It therefore called
on Greece to recover aid paid after August 14, 1998.

The saga continued when in 2004 the Commission decided to open a state aid
investigation in respect of Greece, expressing doubts about the establishment and
privatisation of a company called Olympic Airlines (NOA)—which took over the
aviation activities of Olympic Airways, purportedly in an attempt to evade the
recovery obligation imposed upon Olympic Airways—as well as a number of
other measures.[275] The Commission also called into question the non-recovery
by the Greek State of illegal and incompatible aid after the December 2002
decision, the non-payment by the company of tax debt in 2003, the provision of
an advance (over €130 million) by the Greek State to fund the restructuring and
privatisation of the company, and the non-payment by the company of the airport
modernisation tax charged to passengers.[276]

---

[269] See also: Lübbig/Martin-Ehlers, *"Beihilfenrecht der EU"*, 2nd edn, München [2009],
pp.200–202, paras 519–525.

[270] Decision 94/696/EC [1994] O.J. L273/22.

[271] [1996] O.J. C176/5. See also Written Question 96/c 305/143, by Alexandros Alavanos [1996]
O.J. C305/102.

[272] About 340,750 drachma = 1€.

[273] Agence Europe No. 7273, July 30, 1998.

[274] See 2002 Report on Competition Policy, para.507.

[275] [2004] O.J. C192/2.

[276] 2004 Report on Competition Policy, para.591.

17–070   In 2005, the Commission concluded its investigation into allegations surrounding the granting by Greece of illegal and incompatible aid to Olympic Airways.[277] The Commission concluded that since December 11, 2002 (the date of its previous decision concerning the Greek flag carrier) Olympic Airways and NOA had continued to receive unlawful state aid. In opening the investigation procedure the Commission had expressed doubts about the continuing non-payment by Olympic Airways of tax and social security liabilities, as well as about the way in which NOA was established in late 2003. In December 2003 all flight activities that were previously carried on within the Olympic Airways Group by Olympic Airways, Olympic Aviation and Olympic Macedonian were concentrated in a new entity renamed NOA. In May 2005, the Court ruled that the creation of the (new) company NOA was structured in such a way as to make it impossible, under national Greek law, to recover the debts of the former company Olympic Airways from the new company NOA and that accordingly this operation created an obstacle to the effective implementation of the 2002 Decision, the obligation of which Greece had thus failed to fulfil.[278] Having carried out an in-depth study of the finances of Olympic Airways and of NOA, the Commission found in September 2005 that Greece had granted illegal and incompatible state aid through a number of measures including the non-payment of tax and social security liabilities, the overvaluation of the assets transferred by Olympic Airways to NOA, cash grants made by the State to Olympic Airways and the lease of aircraft to NOA at below cost.[279] This decision[280] is currently subject to a challenge brought by Greece.[281]

In 2007 the Commission had to refer Greece to the European Court of Justice for its failure to recover illegal state aid, estimated to amount to over €100 million, granted to Olympic Airways between 1998 and 2002.[282] Also in 2007, the Commission opened a further investigative procedure into alleged state aid granted to this company since 2005.[283] In addition, in the Olympic Airways dossier, the General Court partly confirmed one of the Olympic Decisions of the Commission[284] because it did not contain an adequate statement of reasons with regard to toleration of non-payment of charges due to Athens airport and VAT on fuel and spare parts.[285]

17–071   In 2008, the Commission found that a privatisation plan submitted by the Greek authorities involving the sale of certain assets of the two companies in bundled form did not involve state aid, provided that the undertakings given by the Greek authorities were fully met.[286] The privatisation process must be

---

[277] 2005 Report on Competition Policy paras 619–621.
[278] Case C–415/03 *Commission v Hellenic Republic* [2005] E.C.R. I–3875, paras 33–36.
[279] Case C 11/2004 [2004] O.J. C192/2.
[280] C(2005) 2706 final, of September 14, 2005.
[281] Case T–415/05 [2010] E.C.R. Unreported. See [2006] O.J. C22/19.
[282] Case C–369/07 [2009] E.C.R. I–5703.
[283] Case C–61/07 [2010] O.J. L222/62.
[284] Commission Decision 2003/372/EC [2003] O.J. L132/1.
[285] Case T–68/03 [2007] E.C.R. II–2911.
[286] Cases N 321/2008, N 322/2008 and N 323/2008 [2010] O.J. C18/9.

overseen by an independent monitoring trustee who will ensure compliance with the decision and the commitments made. In a separate but related decision,[287] after having carried out an in-depth study of the finances of Olympic Airways Services and of NOA, the Commission found that, since its last decision in 2005, Greece had granted further state aid to the flagship carrier. This aid was considered to be illegal and incompatible with the Treaty, and the Commission ordered the recovery thereof. Since part of the investigation into the payment by the State to Olympic Airways Services of "damages" following a series of arbitration panel awards required further detailed investigation, this part of the investigation remains open. In addition, the Court of Justice declared that Greece had failed to fulfil its obligation to recover the aid which the Commission had deemed incompatible in 2005, from NOA.

In 2009 the Commission issued yet two more Olympic Airways decisions: subject to conditions, the Commission decided on certain changes that the Greek authorities intended to introduce in the sales processes of NOA.[288] In addition, the Commission approved the intention of the Greek authorities to cover part of the costs of the voluntary redundancy scheme to be implemented by Olympic Catering SA in respect of certain of its staff.[289]

In 2010, in the case *Hellenic Republic, Olympic Airways and Olympic Airlines v European Commission*[290] the General Court partially annulled the Commission decision finding that certain measures granted to Olympic Airways and NOA, the new airline formed by the Greek State and which had taken over the flying activities of Olympic Airways, constituted incompatible state aid. The General Court recalled that, if there is economic continuity, NOA could be considered as the beneficiary of the aid granted to Olympic Airways before NOA took over its flying activities. The Court confirmed that the economic continuity was sufficiently demonstrated in this case and that aid granted to Olympic Airways before the creation of NOA could thus be recovered from NOA. However, the Court found that the unlawful aid granted to Olympic Airways after NOA took over its flying activities, could not be recovered from the latter on the mere ground that it derived an indirect benefit. This factor does not suffice to conclude that NOA was the effective recipient of that aid, as the finding of economic continuity is irrelevant for the measures granted after the takeover. The Commission should have identified the alleged advantage granted by Olympic Airways to NOA and assessed separately whether, having regard to the market economy investor principle, it constituted state aid. Furthermore, as regards the application of the market economy investor principle, the Court recalled the Commission's obligation to examine the difference between the rents for the sub-leasing of aircraft paid by NOA and those available in normal competitive conditions on the market. From a procedural perspective, the Court recalled that the Commission

17–072

---

[287] Case C–61/2007 [2010] O.J. L222/62.
[288] Aid N 83/09 [2010] O.J. C25/15.
[289] Aid N 487/09 [2010] O.J. C29/2.
[290] Joined cases T–415/05, T–416/05 and T–423/05 *Hellenic Republic, Olympic Airways and Olympic Airlines v European Commission* [2010] E.C.R. As yet Unreported.

had to prove that the rents were not in line with market conditions and that it can only adopt a decision based on the information available if the Member State does not provide the required information in spite of an information injunction.[291]

17–073 **(iv) Application of the Communication on the repercussions of the terrorist attacks in the United States on the air transport industry.** This communication has been a feature of State aid control to the air transport sector, especially in the years 2001–2003,[292] and in fact is mentioned in every one of the Commission's Annual Reports on Competition Policy since 2001.

The Commission authorised not only aid linked to the increase in insurance premiums, (as mentioned above in para.17–062), but also schemes set up by several Member States to compensate airlines for the losses caused by the closure of certain parts of the airspace between September 11 and 14, 2001, provided the criteria set out in the communication were fulfilled.[293] On the other hand, the Commission took a more cautious approach to aid granted to cover insurance costs after September 14 and initiated a formal investigation into the extension, notified by France, of the French aid scheme in order to cover such costs incurred after September 14, 2001, followed by a final negative decision.[294] A similar approach was taken in a Greek scheme also pertaining to costs incurred after September 14 and for zones not actually closed to traffic.[295]

Airports

17–074 **(i) Introduction.** One of the main issues in assessing measures for airports is whether they constitute aid in the first place. *Aéroports de Paris*,[296] found that the management and provision of infrastructure facilities may constitute an economic activity for the purposes of art.107(1) TFEU. For airports, this question arises broadly speaking from two angles: (i) support for the infrastructure and (ii) support for its management. Insofar as the state finances infrastructure managed by the State and open to all potential users in a non-discriminatory way, it does normally not fall under art.107(1) of the TFEU.[297] If however, infrastructure

---

[291] Competition Report 2010, paras 136 and following.

[292] It is mentioned in each of the Reports for 2001 to 2003, but no longer in the ones for 2004 and 2005.

[293] France: Case N 806/2001 [2002] O.J. C59; United Kingdom: Case N 854/2001 [2002] O.J. C98/5; Germany: Case N 269/2002 [2003] O.J. C23/5.

[294] Case C 42/2002 (ex. N 286/2002) [2003] O.J. L77/61.

[295] Opening Decision: C 39/2003 (ex. NN 119/2002) [2003] O.J. C199/3, closing partly negative decision taken on April 26, 2006.

[296] T–128/98 *Aéroports de Paris v Commission of the European Communities* [1998] E.C.R. II–3929.

[297] Therefore, the mere transfer of an airport infrastructure from one public body to another will be seen to be neutral from a state aid point of view, see case NN86/2001 [2004] O.J. C38/6.

investment results in the preferential treatment of some carriers over others, state aid could be involved.[298]

From 2000, the Commission also began looking into airport financing.[299] The **17–075** Commission decided that the exemption from Dutch corporation tax granted to the Dutch Schiphol Group, i.e. the company which owns and operates Amsterdam Schiphol airport as well as other airports in the Netherlands, constituted state aid and that it should therefore be discontinued by January 1, 2002.[300]

In 2001 the Commission decided that the public financing by the region of Piedmont (Italy) of improvements to, and further development of, the infrastructure of the airports of Turin, Cuneo and Biella could not be considered to be state aid. It was considered that the location of the airports in question and their predominantly local importance as far as their economic and competition impact was concerned amply justified this conclusion.[301]

(ii) The *Ryanair/Charleroi* decision. On February 12, 2004, the Commission **17–076** took a decision concerning aid granted by the Walloon Region and the publicly owned Brussels South Charleroi Airport (BSCA) to the low-cost airline Ryanair in relation to its establishment at Charleroi.[302] The decision followed a two-year investigation into Charleroi airport's agreement with Ryanair for the establishment of its first base of operation on the European continent. The deal involved a whole range of measures such as one-off incentives for the opening of new routes, discounts off the published airport charges, contributions to training and start-up costs for establishing the base. The Commission concluded that no private market operator in the same situation as BSCA would have granted the same advantages to Ryanair as BSCA did. Therefore, since the private market investor principle had not been adhered to in this case, the advantages granted to Ryanair constituted state aid which was found to potentially distort competition. However, the Commission considered that some of the aid granted to Ryanair at Charleroi could be compatible with the internal market in the context of transport policy, as it permits the development and improved use of a secondary airport infrastructure which is currently underused and represents a cost to the Union as a whole. In particular, aid which permits genuine development of new routes

---

[298] See NN109/98, Manchester Airport, decision available online at: *http://ec.europa.eu/comm/ secretariat_general/sgb/state_aids/transports-1998/nn109-98.pdf*. Andreas Bartosch, "Wettbewerbsverzerrungen auf den Märkten für den Betrieb und die Nutzung von Flughafeninfrastrukturen", *WuW* 11/2005, 1122.

[299] 31st Report on Competition Policy, para.448. There had been some cases which could also be related to airport financing before then, such as the one on Oostenede Airport, Dec. 98/337/EC [1998] O.J. L148/36. In that case the regional government had granted aid calculated as a function of the number of passengers and intended to confer a competitive advantage on the use of Oostende airport, as well as aid for the financing of a flight-advertising programme and a subsidy intended to compensate for the additional costs of using Oostende airport. The Commission accepted the subsidy for the financing of the advertising campaign but considered that the other measures constituted aid and were incompatible with the internal market.

[300] E 45/2000 [2004] O.J. C37/13. See also IP/01/934.

[301] N 58/2000 [2004] O.J. C64/12.

[302] Case C76/2002 [2004] O.J. L137/1.

was, under clearly defined conditions, considered to be compatible. The Commission pointed out that it is not opposed to the granting of reductions to airlines to encourage them to launch new routes of increase flight frequency as such, provided such discounts are granted without discrimination.[303] It was also recognised that small airports may require public finance to survive and have an important economic role and significant social impact.[304]

17–077   As far as the case of Ryanair at Charleroi is concerned, some of the aid granted was not considered to be compatible and the Belgian authorities agreed in 2004 with Ryanair to put part of the incompatible aid, around €4 million, on an escrow account, while awaiting a judgment by the General Court[305] on the action for annulment of the Commission decision brought by the airline. Belgium had to sue Ryanair before an Irish court to obtain repayment of the additional amount of around €2.3 million.

As the Commission recognised in the *Ryanair* decision, there was no overall Union vision on how some airport charges can be financed by the public, nor was there a common framework for charging for the use of airport infrastructure.[306] The decision set out the Commission's approach to aid measures granted at regional or secondary airports, but the Commission announced in its decision a framework on the financing of airports.

However in 2008, the General Court annulled the Commission's Ryanair decision of 2004. The Court considered that the Commission should have examined the measures granted by the Walloon Region and by BSCA together and should have applied the private investor principle to the measures adopted by the Walloon Region, since there are close economic links binding these two entities.[307]

17–078   **(iii) The Guidelines.** The Commission followed up on this announcement by adopting, on December 9, 2005, the "Community guidelines on financing of airports and start-up aid to airlines departing from regional airports".[308] In those Guidelines, the Commission also responded more generally to developments in the air transport sector, namely the emergence of low-cost airlines and increased competition between airports, and in particular between regional airports, which has been particularly active in recent years in a drive to attract new air links. These Guidelines seek to enhance the transparency of the applicable rules by establishing what the Commission will or will not allow.

The Guidelines specifically recognise the benefits brought about by low-cost airlines and regional airports, whilst also acknowledging that regional airports

---

[303] See Ryanair decision, C76/2002 [2004] O.J. L137/1, paras 265–266.
[304] See Ryanair decision, C76/2002 [2004] O.J. L137/1, paras 285 and 295.
[305] Case T–196/04 *Ryanair v Commission* [2007] E.C.R. II–4523.
[306] See Ryanair decision, C76/2002 [2004] O.J. L137/1, para.353.
[307] Case T–196/04 *Ryanair v Commission* [2007] E.C.R. II–4523.
[308] Commission Communication—Community guidelines on financing of airports and start-up aid to airlines departing from regional airports [2005] O.J. C312/1.

often face a competitive disadvantage as compared to established hubs.[309] Guide-lines thus take a positive approach to developing regional airports, however ensuring compliance with the principles of transparency, non-discrimination and proportionality in order to prevent distortions of competition which would not be justified by the common interest in terms of public funding to regional airports and state aid to airlines.[310]

The Guidelines recall that the starting point for establishing the presence of state aid is whether the airport or the airline in question is engaged in an economic activity, irrespective of whether the airport or airlines is privately or publicly owned. The private market economy investor principle is described in order to clarify when public funding constitutes aid, namely when a private shareholder would not, in similar circumstances, "having regard to the foresee-ability of obtaining a return and leaving aside all social, regional policy and sectoral considerations", have subscribed to the capital in question.[311] However, it also warned that the private market investor principle is very difficult to apply to airport operators which do not finance their own investments, pay correspond-ing fees or whose operating costs are partly covered by public founds over and above a task undertaken in the general interest.

As far as public service obligations are concerned, the Guidelines refer to the **17–079** four cumulative criteria established by the Court of Justice in *Altmark*[312]: if the four Altmark criteria are met, then compensation for public service obligation does not constitute state aid.

It is considered that aid to smaller regional airports[313] is less likely to distort competition or affect trade to an extent contrary to the common interest, but it is also specifically stated that this is a matter of a case-by-case analysis and that therefore any measure which may constitute state aid to an airport must be notified.[314] Indeed the number of passengers using an airport as such does not necessarily provide proper guidance as to the possible distortions of competition

---

[309] See Guidelines, recitals 17 and 20.

[310] See Guidelines, recital 21.

[311] See Guidelines, recitals 46–52.

[312] Case C–280/00 *Altmark Trans und Regierungspräsidium Magdeburg v Nahverkehrsgesellschaft Altmark* [2003] E.C.R. I 7747; See above para.17–011.

[313] The Guidelines classify airports into four categories, A to D (see recital 15): category A being "large community airports" with more than 10 million passengers a year; category B national airports with annual passenger volume of between 5 and 10 million; category C large regional airports with an annual passenger volume of between 1 and 5 million; and category D small regional airports with less than 1 million passengers annually. The Guidelines generally assume that aid category C and D airports are less likely to distort competition or affect trade to an extent contrary to the common interest (see recital 39).

[314] Guidelines, para.40; the only exception being provided in para.41 for airports in category D which are entrusted with a mission of general economic interest and which meet certain conditions. It is therefore not the case that the Guidelines exclude category D airports per se as is sometimes claimed; see for instance Andreas Bartosch, "Wettbewerbsverzerrungen auf den Märkten für den Betrieb und die Nutzung von Flughafeninfrastrukturen", *WuW* 11/2005, pp.1122 and 1128.

that aid to such an airport might cause. The geographic catchment area of the airport and its vicinity to other airports may be equally relevant.[315]

Having thus set out the general parameters, the Guidelines consider in more detail two types of aid:

> (i) Financing of airports: this type of aid being subdivided into, financing of airport infrastructure, aid for the operation of airport infrastructure, and aid for airport services; and
>
> (ii) Start-up aid.

17–080   *(a) Financing of airports:* As far as the financing of airports is concerned, the Guidelines assume that airport services, including ground handling services, as well as the operation of airport infrastructure are commercial activities, which should in principle be financed without State resources.[316] An exception is made for services up to the threshold of two million passengers: the airport operator acting as service provider may offset its various sources of revenue and losses between purely commercial activities. However, in the absence of competition in the provision of ground handling services, airport operators are warned to take particular care not to infringe competition rules.

Whilst the provision of airport infrastructure should in principle also be financed by the airport operator from its own resources,[317] any benefit conferred to an airport operator by a public authority not acting as a private market investor should be notified as state aid. The sale of land or the privatisation of an undertaking, does generally not constitute state aid where these operations are made at market prices, particularly following a sufficiently well publicised open, unconditional and non-discriminatory bidding procedure which ensures that potential applicants are treated equally.[318]

Aid granted for airport infrastructure can be declared compatible pursuant to arts 107, (3)(a), (b) or (c) or 106(2), depending on the circumstances. The Commission will, in particular, examine whether:

- the construction or operation of the infrastructure meets a clearly defined objective of general interest;

- this infrastructure is necessary and proportional to the objective;

- it has satisfactory medium-term prospects for use, taking into account the existing infrastructure;

---

[315] Andreas Bartosch, "Wettbewerbsverzerrungen auf den Märkten für den Betrieb und die Nutzung von Flughafeninfrastrukturen", *WuW* 11/2005, pp.1122 and 1128.

[316] Guidelines, paras 4.2 and 4.3; See also Jim Callaghan, "Implications of the Charleroi case for the Competitiveness of EU Air Transport" [2005] *E.C.L.R.* Issue 8, p.439, who argues that "only relatively remote regional airports that have little to offer in terms of tourist attractions or business opportunities will require sustained intervention by government".

[317] Guidelines, recital 57.

[318] Guidelines, recital 58.

- all potential users have access to it in an equal and non-discriminatory manner; and

- the development of trade is not affected to an extent contrary to the Union interest.

In 2005, the Commission adopted two decisions relating to the financing of airport infrastructure,[319] which however, predate the Guidelines. In the first decision, the Commission decided that a German aid scheme for the construction and development of regional airports in structurally weak regions is compatible with EU state aid rules. The scheme allows for grants which are used only for investment costs in airport infrastructure that are open to all potential users on equal terms. However, no cost for the daily operational activity of the airport is eligible for financial support, nor may any specific investments by an air carrier that uses the airport in question be funded under the scheme.[320] The second decision concerned the creation of a public-private partnership to develop and operate Antwerp International Airport at Deurne. The Commission considered, in particular, that the amount of public contributions and the choice of a commercial partner were finally determined by means of an open and non-discriminatory public tendering procedure, which respected the principle of equal treatment between competitors and ensured that the level of public participation is limited to the minimum necessary, and hence found the aid to be compatible.[321]

17–081

In 2006, the Commission had also begun a dialogue with Member States aimed at taking stock of existing aviation support measures throughout the European Union so that all such financing can be brought into line with the 2005 Aviation State aid guidelines by June 2007 as provided for by point 83 of the Guidelines.[322] The Commission scrutiny was intensified in 2007, when it widened the scope of its inquiry relating to matters covered by the 2005 Aviation State aid guidelines and opened a number of formal investigation procedures in respect of a number of airports. These cases involved the financing of the airports and business relationships with various airlines.[323]

In 2008 the Commission closed the formal investigation procedure concerning State measures involving the DHL Group and the Leipzig-Halle Airport[324] in application of the 2005 guidelines.[325] The three measures under investigation were: capital contributions to Leipzig Airport for financing the construction of the new southern runway; an agreement between Leipzig Airport, its parent company and DHL, which provides several assurances to DHL; and a comfort letter issued by the Land Sachsen in favour of Leipzig Airport and DHL which guarantees that Land Sachsen will compensate DHL for damages in the event

17–082

---

[319] 2005 Report on Competition Policy, paras 623–624.
[320] Case N 644i/2002—*Germany* [2005] O.J. C126/12.
[321] Case N 355/2004—*Belgium* [2005] O.J. C176/11.
[322] Competition Report 2006 COM (2007) 358 final, para.293.
[323] Competition Report 2007 COM (2008) 368 final, para.418.
[324] Case C48/2006 [2008] O.J. L346/1.
[325] Case C48/2006 [2008] O.J. L346/1, see para.256.

that DHL is no longer able to operate as planned at the airport, for example if night flights are banned by the regulatory authorities. The Commission concluded that the capital injections into Leipzig Airport were compatible with the Treaty rules. On the other hand, the Commission found that the assurances granted to DHL under the terms of the agreement and the comfort letter in favour of DHL chanelled through Leipzig Airport were incompatible. The Commission consequently ordered recovery of the incompatible aid linked to the assurances and prohibited the granting of the comfort letter.[326]

17–083   More recently, in 2010 the Commission closed a formal investigation procedure into the agreement concluded until 2016 between Bratislava Airport and Ryanair concerning Ryanair's operations at this airport. Having carried out a cost-benefit-analysis of this agreement, the Commission concluded that in similar circumstances a private investor operating under normal market conditions would have entered into the same or similar commercial arrangement as the operator of Bratislava Airport. Therefore, no advantage was being granted to Ryanair.[327]

Finally, and for the sake of completeness, it should be mentioned that a new Directive on airport charges entered into force in 2009.[328] It applies, more from a competition angle, to EU airports that are above a minimum size and establishes a common framework of airport charging, thereby setting common principles to be observed by EU airports when determining the level of the charges in order to ensure that airport charges do not discriminate among airport users. The Directive sets forth a compulsory procedure for regular consultation between airport managing bodies and airport users, with the possibility for either party to have recourse to an independent supervisory authority whenever a decision on airport charges or the modification of the charging system is contested by airport users.

17–084   *(b) Start-up aid:* The Guidelines recognise that airlines are not always prepared to run the risk of opening new routes from unknown and untested airports without incentives.[329] Equally, it is recognised that airports need a sufficient number of passengers per year to operate successfully.[330] Therefore, the Commission accepts that public aid can be paid temporarily to airlines to provide them with the necessary incentives to create new routes or new schedules form

---

[326] Competition Report 2008 Staff Working Paper accompanying the Report, COM (2009) 374 final, para.289.

[327] Case C12/2008 *Agreement between Bratislava Airport and Ryanair*. See IP/10/56, 27.1.2010, Competition Report 2010, para.319.

[328] Directive 2009/12/EC of the European Parliament and of the Council of March 11, 2009 [2009] O.J. L70/11.

[329] The Commission's cautious approach is supported by the considerations that whilst airlines might be reluctant to commit themselves to untested airports, such airports may also offer considerably commercial advantages such as lower congestion resulting in better facilitation of passengers and cargo by reducing circling time or in-air waiting and faster turn-around; Ruwantissa Abeyratne, "The Decision in the Ryanair Case—the Low Cost Carrier Phenomenon" [2004] *European Transport Law*, 585.

[330] Although no clear threshold for break-even is set; Guidelines, recital 72.

regional airports with a view to attract a sufficient number of passengers to break even within a limited period of time.[331] Nevertheless, the Commission also considers that start-up aid can be distortive as between airlines and between airports insofar as they are in competition with one another. Hence start up aid can only[332] be declared compatible subject to conditions designed to prevent undue distortions:

- The Recipient's air carriers must dispose of a valid operating licence issued by a Member State.[333]

- The aid is aimed at Regional airports. Accordingly, the aid is paid for routes linking a regional airport in category C or D[334] to another EU airport.

- Only in duly substantiated exceptional cases can aid for routes between national airports category B be considered.[335] This could be the case, for instance, where one of the airports is located in a disadvantaged region.[336] However, these conditions are not applicable in the case of routes departing from airports located in outermost regions and bound for neighbouring third countries, which are subject to a case-by-case assessment.

- Only new routes or new schedules not leading to a mere transferring of traffic from an existing route or high-speed train can benefit from the aid. Start-up aid granted for a new air route corresponding to a high-speed train link is therefore specifically excluded, as this would counteract the Commission's policy on intermodality.

- The aid must lead to an increase in the net volume of passengers. Clearly the Commission will have to be satisfied that the route is a genuinely new route in order to avoid aid getting paid in respect of routes that are not actually newly started ones. Therefore, aid will not be able to be granted to an airline which, having used up all the aid for a given route, applies for aid for a competing route departing from another airport in the same city or conurbation or the same airport system and serving the same or a similar destination. However, the mere substitution, during the aid period, of one route for another leaving from the same airport and expected to generate at least an equivalent number of passengers, will not call into question the continuation of payment of aid for the complete period, as long as this substitution does not affect the other criteria under which the aid was initially granted. Hence, the public body proposing to grant start-up aid should carry out an analysis

---

[331] Guidelines, para.74.
[332] The Commission is, however, not bound to actually declare such aid compatible even in the case is meets all the criteria: the Guidelines stipulate that the Commission "may" (as opposed to "shall" or such wording) approve aid meeting these criteria, see recital 79.
[333] Council Regulation (EEC) No.2407/92 on licensing of air carriers.
[334] Guidelines, para.79.
[335] Guidelines, para.78(b).
[336] Guidelines, para.76.

of the impact of the new route on competing routes prior to granting the aid.

- The route must be viable long-term without aid and degressive aid and of limited duration limited to three years. Therefore, when submitting its application, any airline applying for a grant of start-up aid must provide a business plan showing, over a substantial period, the viability of the route after the aid has expired.

- The amount of aid in any one year may not exceed 50 per cent of total eligible costs for that year and total aid may not exceed an average of 30 per cent of eligible costs. For routes from disadvantaged regions, i.e. the outermost regions, the regions referred to in art.107(3)(a), and sparsely populated regions, degressive aid may be granted for a maximum period of five years. For such routes, the amount of aid per year may equally not exceed 50 per cent of total eligible costs but total aid may go up to an average of 40 per cent of eligible costs. If the aid is granted for five years, it may be maintained at 50 per cent of total eligible costs for the initial three years. In any event, the period during which start-up aid is granted to an airline must be substantially less than the period during which the airline undertakes to operate from the airport in question, as indicated in the business plan also required by the Guidelines. Furthermore, the aid must be stopped as soon as the objectives in terms of passengers have been reached or when the route breaks even irrespective of whether this takes place at the end of the period initially foreseen.

- Compensation for additional start-up costs: the amount of aid must be strictly linked to the additional start-up as opposed to running costs incurred in launching the new route. Therefore, costs which air operators would have to bear once the route is up and running are not eligible. Examples of eligible start-up costs mentioned in the guidelines are the marketing and advertising costs incurred at the outset for publicising the new link.

- Any aid payments must be linked to the net development of the number of passengers transported. The amount per passenger must, for example, decrease with the net increase in traffic for the aid to remain an incentive and to avoid adjusting ceilings.

- As always, aid may not be granted on discriminatory terms. Therefore, any public body which plans to grant start-up aid to an airline for a new route must adequately publicise its plan in good time to enable all interested airlines to offer their services. Such publication must include the description of the route as well as the objective criteria in terms of the amount and the duration of the aid. The rules and principles relating to public procurement and concessions must be respected where applicable. Linked with this requirement, and for added transparency, Member States must ensure that the list of routes receiving aid is published annually for each airport, in each instance indicating the source of public funding, the recipient company, the amount of aid paid and the number of passengers concerned. Furthermore appeal procedures must be provided for at Member State level to ensure that there is no discrimination in the granting of aid.

● In order to ensure that the aid beneficiaries respect any undertakings they make to an airport when the aid is paid, penalty mechanisms must be implemented.

● Finally, start-up aid cannot be combined with other types of aid granted for the operation of a route even if paid out by another Member State, and cannot be paid out in cases in which a route has been reserved for a single carrier.

An especially lenient approach is foreseen for outermost or peripheral regions **17–085** (such as the DOM/TOM) in which case the need to ensure accessibility and to bolster their integration into their regional markets to reduce their disadvantage from the European economy is taken into account: here, the Commission will not raise any objection to aid for services to neighbouring non-member countries, thus enshrining Commission practice. A similar approach is taken to regions referred to in arts 107(3) and for sparsely populated regions.

Finally, it should be mentioned that the Commission launched a public consultation on the application of the 2005 Guidelines in April 2001,[337] but at the time of writing no conclusion were yet available.

4. Conclusion

The combination of the specific Treaty provisions, secondary legislation and **17–086** sector-specific guidelines, as well as the very diverse conditions of the different transport markets render state aid control in the transport sector is more complicated than in other sectors. At the same time, aid granted in the transport sector tends to be particularly large in terms of amount, especially in the rail sector. In view of the increasing liberalisation of the transport sectors and most recently the passenger rail sector, effective state aid control become all the more important if (the nascent, depending on the sector) competition is to grow effectively. Interestingly, aid to the road transport sector is almost conspicuously absent from the Commission's state aid control practice. Some argue, of course, that subsidies are hidden in the low contributions made by the sector to the cost of infrastructure. It is also economically incoherent to seek to achieve on the one hand a shift away from road transport and at the same time, for instance, grant tax relief to company cars or to exempt flight kerosene from taxes as is the case in some Member States.

As state aid control is at least partly complaint driven, and considering the increased focus on the intermodal shift away from road transport and increasing environmental awareness, one can speculate whether this might change.

[337] See *http://ec.europa.eu/competition/consultations/2011_aviation_guidelines/index_en.html*.

The application of the aid rules in the air transport sector has been going through a turbulent period for some time now. Massive aid operations have provided a lifeline for national carriers in an environment of liberalising markets. The establishment of the guidelines, the Commission's insistence on the acceptance of stringent conditions by the Member States granting aid, and finally the active participation and scrutiny of the Commission's actions and the observance of the conditions by competitor airlines supported by their national governments, may have brought about a change in government attitudes. The fact that competitors are actively challenging the Commission's decisions in court will not only continue to force the Commission to do a thorough job, but should also serve as a warning to national authorities which might be inclined to adopt a liberal attitude to state aid.

CHAPTER 18

BROADCASTING*

1. INTRODUCTION 18–001
2. PUBLIC SERVICE BROADCASTING 18–002
   Public service remit 18–003
   Entrustment and supervision 18–004
   Choice of funding of public service broadcasting 18–005
   Transparency requirements for the state aid assessment 18–006
   Net cost principle and overcompensation 18–007
   Financial control mechanisms 18–008
   Diversification of public broadcasting services 18–009
   Proportionality and market behaviour 18–010
3. FINANCING DIGITAL SWITCHOVER 18–012

1. INTRODUCTION

State aid enforcement in this sector affects both public service and commercial **18–001** broadcasting. Public service broadcasting ("PSB") has attracted most of the Commission's enforcement activity. The application of state aid rules to PSB implies a complex balancing act on two levels. On the one hand, due to the role of broadcasting (and more specifically PSB) in the functioning of a democratic society and in the development of social and cultural values, state aid enforcement requires a delicate handling of the interface between EU-centred state aid control and national policies. On the other hand, the converging nature of the communications markets (to which broadcasting belongs) makes it difficult to draw a line between any identifiable market failures (which may require or justify state intervention) and adjacent commercial activities that are increasingly inextricably linked to the traditional notion of TV or radio broadcasting but are not subject to the same market failures or public policy considerations. This double challenge makes state aid enforcement in PSB one of the areas in which the reconciliation of potentially conflicting interests (European v national and public

* Antonio Bravasso

v private) is most arduous.[1] In 2009, the Commission published a Communication from the Commission on the application of State aid rules to public service broadcasting ("PSB Communication")[2] which supersedes the 2001 Communication on the application of State aid rules to public service broadcasting (the "2001 PSB Communication").[3]

In addition, broadcasting is currently subject to one of the most important technological changes since its introduction: digitalisation (i.e. the process of gradual transition from use of analogue transmission technology to digital technology). Digitalisation affects the type and scope of services that may be offered by broadcasting operators. It has changed the traditional role of broadcasting in modern society, as well as its relationship with other commercial activities such as the provision of online services. The adoption of new digital technologies requires an investment by both users and broadcasters and therefore is an area that can be relevant for the application of state aid rules when state resources are used to facilitate this process.

This chapter is divided into two main parts. The first will be devoted to PSB and the application of state aid rules to public service broadcasters that are also operating in economic areas adjacent to traditional forms of broadcasting within the communications sector. The second will look at the application of state aid rules to commercial broadcasting, with particular reference to the digital switchover process.

2. PUBLIC SERVICE BROADCASTING

18–002   The issue of PSB is sensitive due to its strong national and political dimension.[4] Within the EU legal system, PSB was the subject of the ninth Protocol to the Amsterdam Treaty, which stresses the link between the system of public broadcasting in the Member States and the "democratic, social and cultural needs of each society." The Amsterdam Protocol states that the provisions of the Treaty on the Functioning of the European Union (TFEU) shall be:

"without prejudice to the competence of Member States to provide for the funding of public service broadcasting insofar as such funding is granted to

---

[1] A. Bavasso, "Public service broadcasting and State aid rules: between a rock and a hard place" (2002) *European Law Review*, p.340; S. Coppieters, "The Financing of Public Service Broadcasting" in *Law of State aid in the European Union* (OUP, 2003), p.265; N. Sumrada and N. Nohlen "Control of State Aid for Public Service Broadcasting Analysis for the European Commission's Recent Policy" (2005) *European State Aid Law Quarterly*, p.1. See also Commission MEMO/05/73 "Public service broadcasting and state aid—frequently asked questions" available on-line at: *http://www.ebu.ch/CMSimages/en/BRUDOC_INFO_EN%20169_tcm6-36027.pdf* [Accessed August 22, 2011.]

[2] Communication from the Commission on the application of State aid rules to public service broadcasting (2009/C 257/01).

[3] [2001] O.J. C320/04, Annex I, s.3.

[4] For example the role of public service broadcasting in promoting cultural diversity has been recognised by the 2005 UNESCO Convention on the Protection and Promotion of the Diversity of Cultural Expressions; approved by Council Decision 2006/515/EC of May 18, 2006.

broadcasting organisations for the fulfilment of the public service remit as conferred, defined and organised by each Member State, and insofar as such funding does not affect trading conditions and competition in the Community to an extent which would be contrary to the common interest."

PSB entails what, in EU law terms, is a service of general economic interest (SGEI) (see further Ch.8). Under the terminology adopted by the Commission, "general interest" is defined as covering both "market and non-market services." The Commission's Communication on services of general interest in Europe recognised that "the broadcast media play a central role in the functioning of modern democratic societies, in particular in the development and transmission of social values".[5] The Commission also recognises that PSB can be financed, at least in part, by revenue derived from commercial activities outside the scope of the SGEI, such as the sale of advertising spots or programmes, that benefit indirectly from the resources made available to the SGEI.[6] However, PSB remains subject to the TFEU rules, including those on state aid. State aid can take any form, ranging from a direct financial subsidy (e.g. the receipt of funds from the licence fees) to any form of intervention or assistance which has the same effect (such as forfeiting the payment of fees for frequency allocation, or capital injections).[7]

The PSB Communication states that measures of state financing of public service broadcasters are normally to be regarded as state aid if they meet the three conditions of art.107(1) (i.e. when: (i) they are an advantage granted by a Member State or through state resources; (ii) they distort or threaten to distort competition by favouring certain undertakings (or the production of certain goods); and (iii) they affect trade between Member States). This is confirmed by the Commission's decisional practice.[8] Typical forms of state support include

---

[5] COM(2000) 580 final, p.35 [2001] O.J. C17/04.

[6] Communication from the Commission to the European Parliament, the Council, the European Economic and Social Committee and the Committee of the Regions accompanying the Communication on a single market for 21st century Europe"—Services of general interest, including social services of general interest: a new European commitment at art.2.1.

[7] See generally Ch.3.

[8] Interestingly, in the case of PSB, when art.107(1) is found to apply, the assessment of compatibility in Commission decisions is carried out exclusively under art.106(2), a provision that—as described below—implies derogation from TFEU rules (see, for example, Commission Decision of December 2, 2009 on State Aid No C38/2009 (ex NN 58/2009) on the new tax-based funding system for public broadcasting in Spain), [2009] O.J. L/1/11 at para.17; Commission Decision of June 22, 2006 on State Aid C 2/2004/ (ex NN 170/2003) on the ad hoc financing of Dutch public service broadcasters [2004] O.J. L/49/2008 at para.61; Commission Decision of October 15, 2003 on the measures implemented by Italy for RAI SpA [2004] O.J. L119/1 (*RAI*) at para.99; Commission Decision of December 10, 2003 on State aid implemented by France for France 2 and France 3 [2004] O.J. L361/21 (*France 2–3*) at para.6; and Commission Decision of May 22, 2002 on State Aid N 631/2001—United Kingdom, *BBC Licence fee* at [2003] O.J. C23/03 (*BBC Licence fee*) at para.18) rather than compatibility based on TFEU rules, namely under art.107(2) and (3) EC which identify various types of aid which either must be (art.107(2)) or may be (art.107(3)) considered compatible with the common market.

direct financing by budget or levy, and also capital injections or debt cancellations. In *RAI*,[9] the Commission determined that both the 1992 transfer by the state to RAI of ITL100 billion, and a tax exemption granted to RAI on the revaluation of its assets, constituted state aid. Annual capital injections granted by the state over a four-year period were also found to constitute state aid in the *RTP*[10] case, as were both the grant to RTP of a loan by a fund managed by the institute responsible for managing the debt of the Portuguese state, and the rescheduling of debt due to the social security scheme. In *France 2–3* capital injections by the state to France 2 over a six-year period, as well as state investment grants to both channels, were similarly determined to be state aid. In *TV2/Danmark(I)*[11] a package of financial measures granted by the State authorities to TV2 were held to constitute state aid. These included licence fee resources allocated to TV2; exemption from corporation tax; state guarantees for operating loans; and an exemption from interest and service charges on state loans covering the establishment and initial operating period of the channel. In *TV2/Danmark(II)*[12] the Commission examined a capital injection provided to TV2 by the state, and the conversion of state loans into equity in TV2, as part of a package of measures designed to allow for the recovery of the aforementioned state aid by the authorities, and for the company's subsequent recapitalisation. These measures were also held to constitute state aid.

Normally, the support measures described above are attributable to public authorities and involve the transfer of public resources. In addition, to the extent that they fail the market economy investor principle,[13] they satisfy the selectivity criteria by favouring only certain broadcasters, thereby distorting competition. For example, in *TV2/Danmark(II)* the Commission considered that the method employed by the Danish authorities in determining the value of TV2 was acceptable. The analysis was based on future cash flows of the company, incorporating a sensitivity and risk analysis and discounted against the weighted average cost of capital (WACC), which was in turn derived from the cost of the debt of the company, its gearing and its equity costs. The cost of the debt was calculated as the sum of the risk-free rate and the credit spread pertaining, given the overall credit rating of TV2; the cost of equity (i.e. the required rate of return) was derived using the Capital Asset Pricing Model, a widely used market-based methodology; and the optimal gearing of the company, i.e. the proportion of debt and equity which maximises its value, as determined by Danske Bank. As this valuation method was considered to be reasonable, both the capital injection necessary for the recapitalisation and the debt-for-equity swap could be seen as

[9] Commission Decision (2004/339/EC) of October 15, 2003 on the measures implemented by Italy for RAI SpA [2003] O.J. L119/47.
[10] See Commission Decision of October 15, 2003 on ad hoc measures implemented by Portugal for RTP [2005] O.J. L142/1 (*RTP*).
[11] See Commission Decision of May 19, 2004 on State Aid C 2/2003 (ex NN 22/02)—Denmark, *State funding of TV2/Danmark* [2005] O.J. C69/42 (*TV2/Danmark(I)*).
[12] See Commission Decision of October 6, 2004 on State Aid N 313/2004—Denmark, *Recapitalisation of TV2/Danmark A/S* [2005] O.J. C172/03 (*TV2/Danmark(II)*).
[13] PSB Communication at para.21.

a reasonable investment by a long-term investor. However, the Danish authorities had indicated that they were not long-term investors, but rather intended to privatise the company in the near future. Consequently, they had not behaved as a market economy investor would have done, and had favoured TV2 over other undertakings.

Generally, state support to PSB affects trade between Member States, given that the acquisition and sale of programmes often takes place at an international level; advertising also has cross-border effect and ownership of broadcasters may extend to more than one Member State.[14] For example, in *M6 v Commission*,[15] the Court of First Instance (CFI) (now General Court) examined the licensing system of the European Broadcasting Union, whose members, drawn from across the European Union, participate in a television programmes exchange system (Eurovision) which allows for the joint acquisition and exploitation of television rights to international sporting events.

The PSB Communication incorporates both the *Ferring*[16] judgment and the *Altmark*[17] judgment which now form part of the acquis communautaire in this area. In *Altmark*, the European Court of Justice (ECJ) considered that state funding for an entity discharging a public service obligation does not confer an economic advantage if four cumulative conditions are met[18]:

(a) the recipient must have public service obligations which require compensation and must be clearly defined;

(b) parameters on the basis of which compensation is calculated must be established in advance in an objective and transparent manner;

(c) the compensation cannot exceed what is necessary to cover all or part of the costs incurred in the discharge of the public service obligations, taking into account reasonable profit; and

(d) when the company is not chosen through public procurement, a comparison is made with the costs that a typical company in the sector would incur (including reasonable profit).

[14] PSB Communication at para.22; see also Commission Decision of December 2, 2009 on state aid No.C38/2009 (ex. NN 58/2009) New tax-based funding system for public broadcasting in Spain, [2009] O.J. L/1/11at para.20; Commission Decision of August 4, 2008 on state aid No.C(2008)4224 *Rescue aid to TV2 Danmark* [2008] O.J. C/9/2009, para.30; State Aid N 622/03, C(2005) 586 final, para.19; [2004] O.J. C216/03 of August 28, 2004 at para.46; letter to be addressed to Sweden in case NN/04 published on the Commission's website on August 19, 2004 at para.56; *RAI* at paras 91–94; *France 2–3* at paras 59–63; *BBC Licence Fee* at paras 22–23; RTP at paras 149–50; TV2/Danmark at paras 73–76; TV2/Danmark II at paras 35–37; Commission Decision of September 29, 1999 on State Aid NN 88/98; *BBC News 24* [2000] O.J. C78/6 (BBC News 24) at paras 27–32; and Commission Decision of October 1, 2003 on state aid N 37/2003–United Kingdom, *BBC Digital Curriculum* [2003] O.J. C271/06 (*BBC Digital Curriculum*) at para.25.

[15] See Joined Cases T–185/00, T–216-00, T–299/00 and T–300/00 *M6 v Commission* [2002] E.C.R. II–3805.

[16] See Case C–53/00 *Ferring v ACOSS,* [2001] E.C.R. I–9067 (*Ferring*).

[17] See Case C–280/00 *Altmark Trans GmbH and Regierungspräsidium Magdeburg v Nahverkehrsgesellschaft Altmark GmbH* (*Altmark*) [2003] E.C.R. I–17747.

[18] *Altmark* at para.88.

The main focus of the PSB Communication is on whether state funding of public services broadcasting can be exempted from the application of the EU competition rules (including those on state aid) under the general derogation for services of general economic interest (art.106(2)) (see further Ch.8).[19] In this respect, the PSB Communication, echoing the case law of the ECJ, reaffirms that the art.106(2) derogation is to be interpreted narrowly,[20] and considers that three conditions must be fulfilled[21]:

(a) the service in question must be a service of general economic interest and clearly defined as such by a Member State (the public service remit condition);

(b) the undertaking in question must be explicitly entrusted by the Member State with the provision of that service (the entrustment condition); and

(c) the application of the competition rules of the TFEU (in particular, the ban on state aid) must obstruct the performance of the particular task assigned to the undertaking and the exemption from such rules must not affect the development of trade to an extent that would be contrary to the interests of the Community (the proportionality test).

Each of these will be considered below.

Public service remit

18–003   The definition of public service remit falls within the competence of Member States, which can take such decisions at national, regional or local level. The PSB Communication recognises in para.47 that, given the specific nature of the broadcasting sector, and the need to safeguard the editorial independence of the public service broadcasters:

> "a qualitative definition entrusting a given broadcaster with the obligation to provide a wide range of programming and a balanced and varied broadcasting offer is generally considered, in view of the interpretative provision of the [Amsterdam] Protocol, legitimate under Article 106(2)."[22]

The Commission's policy is to make its assessment under art.106(2), taking into account the "democratic, social and cultural needs of each society". The

---

[19] art.106(2) provides that undertakings entrusted with the operation of services of general economic interest are subject to the TFEU rules (in particular those on competition) only insofar as the application of such rules does not obstruct the performance, in law or in fact, of the particular tasks assigned to them. However, pursuant to art.106(2), the development of trade must not be affected to such an extent as would be contrary to the interests of the Union.

[20] See generally Bellamy and Child, *European Community Law of Competition*, 6th edn (OUP: 2008), pp.1061–69 and Buendia Serra, *Exclusive Rights and State Monopolies* (OUP: 1999).

[21] PSB Communication para.37.

[22] PSB Communication para.47.

PSB Communication goes on to state that "it is not for the Commission which programmes are to be provided and financed as a service of general economic interest, nor to question the nature or the quality of a certain product."[23] However, the Commission would intervene in cases of "manifest error"; in other words when the public service remit as defined by the Member States includes activities that could not reasonably be considered to meet the democratic, social and cultural needs of each society.

The challenging question in this sector is to determine to what extent it can be accepted that activities in adjacent markets within the communications sector can form part of the PSB remit. This is not an easy question in an area where digitalisation creates new commercial opportunities and blurs boundaries between different forms of communications. The PSB Communication gives the example of e-commerce as an activity that clearly does not meet that test. Other services which may not be considered programmes in a traditional sense (such as online information services) may nevertheless be considered to fall within the public service remit. This is the Commission's attempt to square the circle of preserving non-commercial values at a national level with the residual power of the Commission (and ultimately the European Courts) as a guardian of all values and principles (including the economic ones) expressed in the TFEU.

The *Kinderkanal* and the *BBC News 24* cases pre-date the PSB Communication but are in line with the Commission's subsequent position. In those two cases, the Commission looked at the financing of, respectively, a children's channel and a 24-hour advertising-free news channel and accepted that these activities fell within the exception of art.106(2).[24] The Commission Decision in *BBC News 24* is very interesting in many respects. First, the Commission, despite acknowledging that art.106, as a derogatory provision, has to be interpreted restrictively,[25] also recognised that its assessment has to take into account the ninth Protocol of the Amsterdam Treaty on the system of public service broadcasting which underlines Member States' competence to define the public service broadcasting remit. In *BBC News 24*, this competence was not contested as a matter of principle, rather insofar as it extended its public service status to the provision of a special interest channel dedicated to news. Part of the question revolved around deciding whether the service in question was a "public service" or an "ancillary service" as defined in the Royal Charter for the continuance of the BBC (the "Charter"). The Commission limited its assessment as to whether the services of BBC News 24 were services of general economic interest under art.106(2) in the light of the Broadcasting Protocol (rather than whether they fell into one category rather than another, as provided by the Charter). On this basis, the Commission concluded that the provision of news can be considered a public service mission in broadcasting and in particular that "a 24-hour service would help to meet the democratic and social need of a society, as referred to in the

[23] PSB Communication para.48.
[24] See Commission Decision of February 24, 1999 on state aid NN 70/98, *Kinderkanal and Phoenix* [1999] O.J. C238/3 (*Kinderkanal*) and *BBC News 24* NN88/98 [2000] O.J. C78.
[25] *BBC News 24* at para.39.

Protocol, by allowing coverage of a wider range of events and a more in-depth analysis of the events."[26] It appears clear from this statement that the subject matter of the dedicated channel is essential to the Commission's assessment. Even if the Commission denies an intrusion in Member State competence to decide what fulfils a public service function within broadcasting, a value judgment on the merits implies an indirect shift of competence at EU level.

In *TV2/Danmark(I)* the Commission states that despite the fact that TV2's obligation "was of a qualitative nature and rather widely defined," it was in line with the 2001 PSB Communication. In Denmark, TV2 was entrusted with the obligation to provide to the Danish public a wide range of programmes and services comprising news coverage, general information, education, art and entertainment, through "television, radio, Internet and the like". TV2's internet site informed users about TV2's television programmes and had other commercial operations such as games and chat rooms. The information service was found to be part of the PSB service. TV2's commercial service was found to be a "purely commercial activity."[27] In *BBC Digital Curriculum*, the Commission examined the BBC's plans to develop a "Digital Curriculum", an online service providing interactive learning materials free to homes and schools and accessible through the BBC's existing website and a dedicated portal. Following concerns raised by the Commission regarding the definition of the public service mission of the Curriculum, the UK Authorities outlined a "commissioning plan,"[28] to be published 15 months before the launch of the service, which would set out the subjects the Curriculum would cover, accompanied by explicit criteria for exclusion.

The Commission viewed the public service mission of the Curriculum as having then been adequately defined. In *RTP*, the Commission considered the public service remit of the Portuguese broadcasting channel. A general definition of the channel's public service remit as being to provide two television channels of national coverage, one more general and the other focused more on specific audiences, was considered to be "qualitative and rather broad",[29] but legitimate. Legal obligations imposed on RTP regarding Portuguese film finance and promotion were considered to be a legitimate specific obligation, instrumental in fulfilling RTP's general public service broadcasting obligations, as any such films would subsequently be broadcast as public service television programmes. In *France 2 and 3*, the Commission considered the definition of the public service tasks of the two channels to be legitimate. The public service remit of the two channels was specified in a schedule of obligations as "providing all sections of the public with information, cultural enrichment and entertainment" (France 2) and "facilitating in particular the expression of and provision of information to the different cultural, social and professional communities and philosophical

---

[26] *BBC News 24* at para.49.
[27] *TV2(I)* at para.92.
[28] *BBC Digital Curriculum* at para.43.
[29] *RTP* at para.164.

groupings."[30] In *RAI* the Commission dealt briefly with the definition of the public service remit and entrustment conditions under the same heading, concluding that the general obligations of the channel, including education and protection of national and regional cultures, with no explicit inclusion of any commercial activities, ensured that the entire range of the channel's programming could be identified with PSB, entrusted exclusively to RAI under two statutes. PSB remit and entrustment were again reviewed together in *TV2/Danmark(II)*, reflecting the fact that both had been previously considered in detail in the *TV2/Danmark(I)* decision, while in both the Flemish[31] and Irish[32] public service broadcasters cases the Commission agreed with the complaints of private broadcasters who believed the PSB remits were not defined in accordance with the PSB Communication. In order to comply with the TFEU the Flemish authorities redefined the PSB remit to:

"introduce a provision which clarifies that the broadcasters may not launch new services or activities which are not covered by the on-going five-year management contract without a prior evaluation and an explicit entrustment by the Flemish government."[33]

The PSB Communication realises that broadcasters must find new sources of funding to fulfil their public service remit, such as online advertising or the provision of services against payment,[34] and has decided that in providing these services it will not necessarily:

"mean that they are manifestly not part of the public service remit provided that the pay element does not compromise the distinctive character of the public service in terms of serving the social, democratic and cultural needs of citizens, which distinguishes public services from purely commercial activities."[35]

For example in *Dutch PSB*[36] the Commission found that the public service remit was "in particular for new types of audiovisual services, not sufficiently precise."[37] Therefore the Dutch PSB amended their public service remit definition, and in doing so excluded online merchandising and sale of TV guides.[38]

---

[30] *France 2 and 3* at para.71.

[31] See Commission decision of February 27, 2008 on State Aid E 8/2006, State funding for Flemish public broadcaster *VRT* [2008] O.J. C143.

[32] See Commission decision of February 27, 2008 on State Aid E 4/2005, Ireland—State aid financing of RTE and TNAG *(TG4)* [2005] O.J. C121.

[33] N. Tosics, R. Van de Den and A. Riedl "Funding of public service broadcasting and State aid rules—two recent cases in Belgium and Ireland" (2008) *Competition Policy Newsletter*, p.82.

[34] PSB Communication para.82.

[35] *ibid*, para.83.

[36] See Commission decision of January 26, 2010 State Aid:E/2005, The Netherlands on annual financing of the Dutch public service broadcasters [2005] O.J C/74/2010.

[37] *ibid*, para.159.

[38] *ibid*, para.218.

Entrustment and supervision

18–004 On the question of entrustment, the ECJ case law on art.106 used to be somewhat hesitant,[39] particularly in the early stages of liberalisation, when the ECJ seemed to rely on the interpretation by national courts of their applicable legislation to interpret art.106(2).[40] In time, when a wider consensus emerged around the notion of liberalisation, one can trace in the Court's case law a tendency to be less reliant on the national legal framework. This became blatantly clear in *Italy v Commission*[41] when the Court stated that the purpose of art.106(2) is to "safeguard the tasks which a Member State sees fit to entrust to a specific body".[42] However, when dealing with locus standi, the Court stated that:

"It must be further observed that the application of art.90(2) [now art.106(2)] of the TFEU is not left to the discretion of the Member State, which has entrusted an undertaking with the operation of a service of general economic interest."[43]

As a result of this approach the definition of services of general economic interest is increasingly influenced by the Community dimension. The ECJ also gradually moved towards a more factual approach in its analysis of services of general economic interest, which enabled it to preserve the flexible character of the provision entrenched in the drafting of art.106.[44]

---

[39] Case 155/73 *Sacchi*, [1974] E.C.R. 409, at para.14.
[40] See Case 127/73 *BRT v SABAM and NV Fonoir*, [1974] E.C.R. 313 at para.22 which stated "it is the duty of the national court to investigate whether an undertaking which invokes the provisions of art.90(2) [now art.106(2)] for the purposes of claiming derogation from the rules of the TFEU has in fact been entrusted by Member States with the operation of a service of general economic interest". In this case the Court concluded anyway that an undertaking to which the state has not assigned any task and which manages private interests, cannot invoke art.106(2).
[41] Case 41/83 *Italy v Commission*, [1984] E.C.R. 873 at para.30.
[42] *ibid.* at para.29.
[43] *ibid.* at para.30.
[44] In *Corbeau* (Case C–320/91 *Criminal Proceedings against Paul Corbeau* [1993] E.C.R. I–2533), with regard to postal services, it stated that "it cannot be disputed that the Régie des Postes is entrusted with a service of general economic interest consisting in the obligation to collect, carry and distribute mail on behalf of all users throughout the territory of the Member States concerned, at uniform tariffs and on similar quality conditions, irrespective of the degree of economic profitability of each individual operation" (para.15) and in *Almelo*, (Case C–393/92 *Municipality of AlmeloEnergiebedrijf Ijsselmij NV* [1994] E.C.R. I–1477) the Court noted that "as regards the question whether an undertaking such as IJM has been entrusted with the operation of services of general interest, it should be borne in mind that it has been given the task, through the grant of a non-exclusive concession governed by public law of ensuring the supply of electricity in part of the national territory. Such an undertaking must ensure that throughout the territory in respect of which the concession is granted, all customers, whether local distributors or end users receive uninterrupted supply of electricity in sufficient quantities to meet demand at any given time, at uniform tariff rates and on terms which may not vary save in accordance with objective criteria applicable to all customers" (paras 48 and 49).

In the PSB Communication, the Commission takes the view that it is in the interests of Member States to be as precise as possible in the definition of the obligations imposed upon public service broadcasters; otherwise the Commission would not be able to grant any exemption under art.106(2). The PSB Communication states[45] that it is "desirable" that an appropriate authority or body monitors the application of an agreement between the State and the undertaking entrusted with the public service remit. This requirement is in line with the second condition under the *Altmark* judgment.

In *TV2/Danmark(I)*, the Commission found that the public service remit had been properly entrusted to TV2, before going on to examine the mechanisms by which the delivery of such remit was supervised. In this case, compliance with public service obligations had been monitored by the National Audit Office and the Public Service Council, and later by the preparation of an annual report for approval by the Radio and Television Board. Financial control had been monitored by the National Audit Office. In *RTP*, the Commission verified that the public service remit had been entrusted to RTP under various laws and contracts, as well as confirming that control mechanisms had been put in place to ensure that RTP's fulfilment of its public service obligations was adequately monitored. Such verification was undertaken by means of internal, government and external audits, both of the performance and of the finances of the channel. Similarly, in *France 2 and 3*, the Commission examined first the statutory basis for the entrustment of the two channels with public service broadcasting, then the means by which this was monitored by the French authorities—by ensuring external parties were represented at board level; maintaining Parliamentary power over the channels' budgets; and obliging the channels to report annually, both to the minister responsible for communications and to the Broadcasting Authority. Comparably, in *RTVE/Spanish* the public service remit was seen to be sufficiently entrusted to RTVE by the Spanish authorities implementing control mechanisms which included ex ante control on new services and introducing a binding definition of what constitutes a "significant new service".[46]

Choice of funding of public service broadcasting

The PSB Communication clearly identifies[47] that two different funding categories can be used in public service broadcasting: "single-funding" (i.e. only through public funds) and "dual-funding" (a combination of public funds and commercial activities). In *RTVE/Spain* there was concern from the Commission that as RTVE moved from "dual" to "single funding" they would be overcompensated by the Spanish authorities as proper budgetary planning could not be calculated as commercial income varies on a yearly basis. However, the Spanish authorities explained that with the elimination of advertisements there was now

18–005

---

[45] PSB Communication para.53.
[46] See Commission Decision of December 2, 2009 on state aid No C38/2009 (exNN 58/2009) on new tax-based funding system for public broadcasting in Spain [2009] O.J. L/1/11 at para.39.
[47] PSB Communication para.57.

more air time to be financed, therefore setting a budgetary ceiling of €1,200 million was "cautious and close to the reasonably foreseeable net cost of the public service compensation".[48]

Transparency requirements for the state aid assessment

18–006   The PSB Communication promotes greater transparency in PSB including: (i) separation of accounts "as only on the basis of proper cost and revenue allocation can it be determined whether the public financing is actually limited to the net costs of the public service remit and thus acceptable under art.106(2)"[49]; (ii) assigning costs and revenues correctly; and (iii) establishing clear cost-accounting principles.

Already prior to the PSB Communication the *BBC News 24* case indicated the importance of accounts separation, and costs allocation and recovery, in determining whether the proportionality condition is met. The PSB Communication recognises that in order to carry out the assessment necessary to confirm that the art.106(2) derogation applies, a "clear and appropriate separation between public service activities and non-public service activities" is required with proper cost and revenue allocation. The PSB Communication builds on the existing requirements of the Transparency Directive.[50] The Commission acknowledges that separation of accounts may be difficult or indeed unfeasible in relation to costs. Different activities carried out by public service broadcasters, within or outside their public service remit, may share the same input. Member States—the Commission remarks—may consider the whole of the programming of the broadcasters, as covered by the public service remit, while at the same time allowing for its commercial exploitation. However, the Commission will expect that, on the revenue side, broadcasters give a detailed account of the sources and amount of all income accruing from the performance of non-public service activities. This implies that, in cases of resources used in connection with both public service and non-public service tasks, their costs should be allocated on the basis of the difference in the broadcasters' total costs with or without non-public service activities (i.e. by reference to the hypothetical situation in which the non-public service activities were to be discontinued).

The Commission considers that, unlike in other utility sectors, costs that are entirely attributable to public service activities, while also benefiting commercial activities, need not be apportioned between the two, and can be entirely allocated to public service.[51] This lowers the burden of share up compatibility for public service broadcasters. The Commission seems to envisage, for instance, that the

---

[48] Commission Decision on July 20, 2010 on state aid No.C38/2009 (exNN 58/2009) on new tax-based funding system for public broadcasting in Spain [2009] O.J. L/1/11 at para.43.
[49] PSB Communication para.61.
[50] Directive 80/723 on the transparency of financial relations between Member State and public undertaking [1980] O.J. L195/35 as amended lastly by Directive 2005/81/EC [2005] O.J. L312/47.
[51] PSB Communication para.67.

production costs of a programme which is shown as part of the public service remit but is also sold to other broadcasters does not need to be apportioned separately as cost distribution risks "being arbitrary and not meaningful."

In *RTVE/Spain* greater transparency was introduced to the PSB including greater controls on the auditing of the PSB with effective ex post budgetary control due to internal auditing, followed by a final external audit by a private auditing firm.[52]

Net cost principle and overcompensation

Provision of public service that have a "dual" nature public/commercial often   **18–007** give rise to a risk of overcompensation in PSB as calculating the cost of carrying out public service tasks can be difficult to correctly identify. The PSB Communication provides that the amount of public compensation must "not exceed the net costs of the public service mission, taking also into account other direct or indirect revenues derived from the public service mission."[53] It also establishes the rule of thumb that in general an amount of up to 10 per cent of the annual budgeted expenses of the public service mission "may be deemed" necessary to "withstand cost and revenue fluctuations". Overcompensation above this limit "must be recovered without undue delay".[54] As an exception public service broadcasters may be allowed to keep an amount in excess of 10 per cent in case of expenses specifically earmarked in advance and for the purposes of a non-recurring major expense necessary for the fulfilment of the public service mission (e.g. cost of major technological investment such as digitalisation).[55]

In *France III*,[56] France prevented overcompensation by enshrining the rule for calculating PSB state aid in law while also specifying that separate accounts[57] must be used to take account of different revenue, direct and indirect, derived from the public funding. Even prior to the PSB Communication, overcompensation was still an important issue to the Commission; their enquiry into Portuguese public broadcasting was only closed after Portugal agreed to introduce safeguards which would avoid overcompensation.[58]

Financial control mechanisms

The methods by which overcompensation is calculated are demonstrated in   **18–008** *TV2/Danmark(I)*. In examining the issue of overcompensation of TV2 by the

---

[52] See Commission Decision of December 2, 2009 on state aid No C38/2009 (ex NN 58/2009) on new tax-based funding system for public broadcasting in Spain [2009] O.J. L/1/11 para.38.

[53] PSB Communication 71.

[54] PSB Communication 73.

[55] PSB Communication 74.

[56] See Commission Decision of July 20, 2010 on State Aid C27/09 (ex N 34/B/09) France on budgetary grant for France Télévisions which the French Republic plans to implement in favour of France Télévisions [2009] O.J. L/59/2011.

[57] *ibid* para.106.

[58] See also press release IP/06/349 of March 22, 2006 "Commission closes inquiry into financing of Portuguese public broadcaster following commitments."

Danish authorities, the Commission first calculated the cost of the general economic interest part of the TV2 service, i.e. the gross public service cost (TV2 was legally obliged to keep the accounts of its public service and commercial activities separate), and then deducted from this figure the net benefits accruing to TV2 from the commercial exploitation of those public service activities. This provided the Commission with a figure for net public service cost, from which could then be deducted the cash input provided by the Danish State. On this rationale, the Commission found that the State had overcompensated TV2 for its public service broadcasting. In *TV2/Danmark(II)*, the Commission examined the methods used by the Danish authorities to determine the value of the channel,[59] prior to its incorporation, recapitalisation and a capital injection by the state. The valuation was determined to be valid, and so no overcompensation was found.[60]

Thus, States must take measures to ensure that their public sector broadcasters are not overcompensated; different states take varying courses of action. France, as referred to above in 2.5, enshrined the rule for calculating PSB state aid in law while Spain and the Netherlands introduced the PSB Communication rule that introduced a limit on funding to 10 per cent over net costs, this 10 per cent can then be maintained in a reserve fund by the PSB in order to compensate for possible losses in previous years but anything over this 10 per cent will flow back into the state budget.

Diversification of public broadcasting services

18–009 Digitalisation has created new opportunities in PSB which the Commission believes should be used "to benefit society."[61] To do this the public sector broadcasters are allowed to diversify their distribution platforms using state aid and distribute audiovisual services on all platforms, providing that their actions still maintain their public service remit and do not disproportionally effect the market. As referred to above, in para.18–003, new sources of funding are being found that also fulfil the broadcaster's public service remit, such as online advertising or the provision of services against payment, and as long as these

---

[59] This was based on the future cash flows of the company, incorporating a sensitivity and risk analysis and discounted against the weighted average cost of capital (WACC).

[60] It would appear that the quantification would be obtained by comparing the pricing policy adopted by the public service broadcaster against the pricing policy that would have been adopted by an "efficient" commercial operator to recover stand-alone costs. This implies the adoption of a number of analytical assumptions on the commercial strategy of broadcasters, which may be difficult to make. In addition, a number of those costs are shared between the public service activities and the commercial ones. Their quantification in order to determine the amount to be recovered may be difficult and debatable. The PSB Communication itself recognises the difficulty of apportioning those costs to the extent that the same document states that their allocation is not required for accounting purposes. Whilst, in the Commission's view, cost recovery is different from cost apportionment for accounting purposes, the quantification of cost will remain an open issue to determine whether overcompensation has occurred.

[61] PSB Communication para.81.

sources "do not compromise the distinctive character of the public service in terms of serving the social, democratic and cultural needs of citizens",[62] they fall within the public service remit.

Proportionality and market behaviour

The PSB Communication devotes great attention to the choice of *funding*   **18–010** *transparency* and *proportionality*. In performing the proportionality test, the Commission will start from the premise that "State funding is normally necessary for the undertaking to carry out its public service task." As stated above, Member States are free to choose the means of financing public service broadcasting, including single funding or dual funding and state aid must not exceed the net costs of the public service mission. The Commission will scrutinise the proportionality of the measures adopted against the aim of not distorting competition in the common market. The proportionality test,[63] which is widely applied in the EU case law, is at the core of the delicate balancing act between national and EU competence and between social, cultural and democratic values on the one hand, and antitrust and internal market policies on the other.

The Commission's approach to the proportionality test presupposes an analysis of cost allocation between PSB activities and other commercial activities and an evaluation of the PSB funding requirement in light of possible overcompensation. In addition, the test is based on a qualitative balancing act between the attainment of the PSB objectives and restriction and distortions of competition. This test is therefore the centrepiece of the Commission's analysis. The proportionality condition presupposes transparency in cost allocation and it therefore cuts across the second and third condition in *Altmark*.

The PSB Communication also considers the issue of proportionality from the point of view of distortions which may occur as consequence of (or which are simply facilitated by) the existence of state funding and which are not necessary for the attainment of the public service mission. As an example, the Commission envisages the possibility that a public service broadcaster, on the strength of state funding, might depress the prices of advertising or other non-public service activities on the market with a consequent reduction in the revenue of competitors. The Commission will evaluate these pricing policies to determine whether public service broadcasters undercut prices "below what can reasonably be considered to be market-conform, so as to reduce the revenue of competitors."[64]

---

[62] PSB Communication para.83.

[63] See generally T. Tridimas, *The General Principles of EC Law* 2nd edn (OUP: 2006), pp.136–241; G. Schermers and D. Waelbroeck, *Judicial Protection in the European Communities* (6th edn) (Kluwer: 2001) pp.100–103; and J. Schwarze, *European Administrative Law Revised* 1st edn (Sweet & Maxwell: 2006).

[64] PSB Communication at para.94.

18–011   In *BBC News 24* the Commission's approach in relation to the evaluation of whether the services of general economic interest distort competition "to an extent that would be contrary to the public interest" highlights the discretional (and ultimately political) character of the provision. The Commission stated that "the formulation of art.[106](2) indicates that a certain effect on trade and its development can be tolerated because of the general-interest nature of the service provided."[65] The Commission implies that art.106(2) is to be interpreted as allowing "a certain amount of damage to competitors" and that "some distorting effect has to be taken into account and tolerated, whilst it must neither be made impossible for competitors to continue to do business nor must potential competitors be precluded from entering the market."[66] This seems to introduce a sort of de minimis rule which cannot be read other than as an attempt to preserve flexibility and discretion in a delicate area of EU law. The PSB Communication acknowledges that the characteristics and competitive structure of each market are unique, and for this reason states that circumstances where conditions in a given market are distorted beyond the degree necessary for the fulfilment of the public service mission cannot be defined and must be determined on a case-by-case basis. The PSB Communication specifies, however, that this should not be taken as an indication that state aid can be justified as a method of increasing supply and competition in a given market, as this would produce a major distortion of competition in that market and ultimately have a negative effect on consumers.

In *TV2/Danmark(I)*, the Commission attempted to examine whether the fact that TV/Danmark, a competitor of TV2, was unable to cover the stand-alone costs of its TV operations by the prices charged by TV2 indicated a depression of the Danish television advertising market, caused by TV2 and distorting competition in that market. The Commission was not able to establish whether TV2 had behaved in this way, although it considered that such behaviour would have been quite possible given the channel's strong market position. It was able to establish, however, that over the previous five years, TV2 had decreased its prices in real terms, something for which it could compensate using its capacity reserve, although its competitors, forced to follow suit to survive, lacked such a reserve. Ultimately, the Commission concluded that there was no clear evidence that TV2's pricing behaviour had systematically depressed the Danish television advertising market.[67]

Going forward, particularly in the context of an enforcement policy that is sensitive to the relationship between state aid, liberalisation and general antitrust considerations, one would expect greater interface between this area and antitrust principles. In particular, one would expect the principles developed in the context of the Commission's decisional practice on cross-subsidisation and predatory

---

[65] *BBC News 24* at para.87.
[66] *BBC News 24* at para.93.
[67] See also press release IP/06/349 of March 22, 2006, "Commission closes inquiry into financing of Portuguese public broadcaster following commitments".

behaviour by (former) legal monopolists operating in both reserved and non-reserved areas of business to gain greater importance.[68]

3. FINANCING DIGITAL SWITCHOVER

Broadcasting in the European Union is still going through one of the most **18–012** important technological changes since its introduction: digitalisation—the transition from analogue to digital broadcasting. The adoption of new digital technologies by operators and users requires investment. Given the support for digitalisation at national and EU level[69] this process can be relevant for the application of state aid rules. One of the industrial policy themes that overlap with the state aid analysis concerns the issue of choice of technology that benefits from any form of state support. The issue of discrimination of state support in favour of a particular broadcasting technology therefore features frequently in the Commission's state aid decisions, creating an important point of contact with industrial policies looked after by DG Information Society. In its Communication on the transition from analogue to digital broadcasting ("Switchover Communication") the Commission took the position that:

"[the technology neutral approach] encourages facilities-based competition and investment, thus contributing to the multi-platform approach of Europe. This implies a regulatory playing field. In principle, each network should compete on its own strengths."[70]

The Communication on interoperability of digital interactive television services ("Interoperability Communication") reiterates that technological neutrality is a fundamental principle.[71]

Both the Switchover and the Interoperability Communications stress the importance of network competition in contributing to the roll-out of digital services[72] and the importance of a competition-based market-led approach.[73]

---

[68] In this sense see Case COMP/35.141 *Deutsche Post AG* [2001] O.J. L125/27 in which the Commission stated that "to avoid subsidising mail-order parcel services by using revenue from the reserved area, DPAG must earn revenue on this parcel service which at least covers the costs attributable to or incremental to producing that specific service" (para.10); on the use of a Long-Run Average Incremental Cost benchmark in predatory pricing cases involving activities protected by a legal monopoly, see also DG Competition discussion paper on application of art.102 of the TFEU to exclusionary abuses of December 2005 at paras 124–26.

[69] Digital Switchover was explicitly mentioned as a key element of the eEurope 2005 Action Plan, which was launched at the Seville European Council meeting in June 2002.

[70] Communication from the Commission to the Council, the European Parliament, the European Economic and Social Committee and the Committee of Regions on the transition from analogue to digital broadcasting, COM(2003) 541 final of September 17, 2003, s.2.1.

[71] COM(2004) 541 final; and Communication from the Commission to the Council, the European Parliament, the European Economic and Social Committee and the Committee of Regions on reviewing the interoperability of digital interactive television services pursuant to Communication COM(2004) 541, COM(2006) 541 final of February 2, 2006.

[72] See Switchover Communication at para.2.1.

[73] *ibid.* and para.2.2.

Therefore, in principle, any Member State intervention must avoid any distortion of competition, allowing each network to compete "on its own strengths" on a "regulatory level playing field."[74]

The Commission has applied art.107 to a number of situations that relate to the digital switchover.[75] In determining whether any of the measures in question gives rise to state aid under art.107(1) the Commission will adopt its standard four-step analysis: (i) is there any intervention by the State or through State resources; (ii) does the measure in question confer an economic advantage to the recipient; (iii) does it distort or threaten to distort competition; and (iv) is the state measure capable of affecting trade between Member States?

18–013   The first criterion is usually easily met as the state authorities typically involved usually grant state subsidies. The German DVB-T Decision (now set for appeal as C–544/09P *Germany v Commission*) found that a non-notified subsidy granted by the Berlin-Brandenburg media authority to commercial broadcasters to meet their transmission costs via the DVB-T network constituted unlawful state aid. The Swedish DVB-T Decision concerned direct payments by the Government treasury to the Swedish public service broadcasters and payments made by the public service broadcasters, under the influence of the State, to the DVB-T network operator (also state-owned). In addition, in the letters sent to Sweden opening the proceedings[76] the Commission characterised payments by the Swedish National Debt Office to a national Swedish public broadcaster to cover a deficit on the licence fee account set aside specifically to cover the broadcaster's transmission costs as aid granted by the State or through State resources. The Commission considered the finances used by the broadcaster to make payments to Teracom, the state-owned operator of the only television network in Sweden, for rolling out the DVB-T network, to be State resources, and that any advantages derived from it were advantages conferred by the State. The Commission suspected that the broadcaster was overpaying Teracom for its service, and that such overpayment would provide Teracom with an economic advantage. In considering other advantages accruing to Teracom, the Commission expressed doubts as to whether a credit guarantee made available to it, proposed by the Swedish government and approved by the Parliament, fulfilled

---

[74] *ibid.*

[75] See Commission Decision C25/04 (ex NN 36/04), now set for appeal as Case-C–544/09 P *Germany v Commission,* with the judgment scheduled for September 15, 2011. The pending case is an appeal against judgment T–21/06 concerning state aid for the introduction of digital terrestrial television in Berlin—Com decision C(2005) 3903 of November 9, 2005.; Commission's letter to the Swedish Foreign Affairs Minister in Case C 24/04 (ex NN 35/04) [2004] O.J. C238/04 *(Swedish DVB-T)*; State Aid N 662/03—Austria, *Digitalisierungfonds (Austrian Digital)* [2005] O.J. C228, Commission press release IP/07/960 of December 21, 2005, and the recent ECJ judgment in C–403/10 n.y.r. DVB-T stands for digital video broadcasting over a terrestrial network. See also C–104/11 P *NOS v Commission* and C–105/11 P *Netherlands v Commission,* appeal brought against the judgments of the General Court of December 16, 2010 in case T–231/06 *Netherlands v Commission* and T–237/06 *NOS v Commission* (state aid; annulment of Commission Decision C(2006) final of June 22, 2006 concerning the ad hoc measures implemented by the Netherlands for the purpose of financing public broadcasters in the Netherlands in relation to the state aid case No C 2/2004 (ex NN 170/2003)).

[76] State Aid C 24/04, [2004] O.J. C238/04 of September 25, 2004.

the conditions necessary to prevent such a guarantee from being regarded as state aid, and also whether the risk-related fee provided for in the proposal was adequate.

The Commission also questioned whether capital injections from the State to Teracom, again approved by the Parliament, were in accordance with the private investor principle. The Commission considered it to be unlikely that external creditors would have injected cash into the operator, considering its solvability ratio at the time of the transaction and that it had been making substantial losses for the previous three years. In the Austrian Decision the aid which was notified and eventually approved consisted of a scheme of five measures concerning: (i) pilot projects and research activities regarding digital transmission; (ii) the development of programmes and innovative services; (iii) financial interventions to reduce the additional costs faced by broadcasters whilst broadcasting both analogue and digital TV in parallel ("simulcast phase"); (iv) financial incentives for consumers to switch to digital reception at an early stage; and (v) subsidies for low-income consumers purchasing terminal equipment. Finally, in the Italian case, the measure concerned a direct subsidy financed by the State for the purchase of DTT decoders.

Under established ECJ case law, the concept of state aid is defined by reference **18–014** to its effects,[77] regardless of such effects being created directly or indirectly by the measure in question.[78] In the German DVB-T Decision, the commercial broadcasters which were the direct beneficiaries of the subsidy undertook to use the DVB-T network of T-Systems (a subsidiary of Deutsche Telekom AG) which held one of the two licences to operate a digital terrestrial network in Berlin Brandenburg and on that basis were found to be the recipient of an economic advantage. In its initial letter, the Commission found that the subsidy was not based on any specific cost and in fact was decided (and granted) after the switchover had been agreed. In addition, T-System was initially found to be an indirect beneficiary of the state aid (irrespective of whether the compensation granted to the private broadcasters constituted state aid) because the fact that private broadcasters receive a subsidy when distributing over DVB-T means that they will be more inclined to use DVB-T.[79]

A similar approach was also confirmed in the Italian case on financing of DTT decoders. The immediate beneficiaries of the state aid were manufacturers and dealers of the decoders that can receive a T-DVB or C-DVB signal, as the subsidies incentivise the consumption of such goods. However, in opening an investigation on the legality of the subsidies, the Commission relied on the consideration that the real beneficiaries were terrestrial television broadcasters and network operators.

[77] See amongst others Case 173/73 *Italy v Commission* [1974] E.C.R. 709 at para.13; Case 310/85 *Deufil v Commission* [1987] E.C.R. 901 at para.8; Case T–67/94 *Ladbroke Racing v Commission* [1987] E.C.R. II–1 at para.52.
[78] See Case C–156/98 *Federal Republic of Germany v Commission* [2000] E.C.R. I–6857 at para.26.
[79] *German DVB-T* at paras 31–37.

The issue of technological neutrality is at the heart of the Commission's analysis on distortion of competition and, ultimately, influences its views on compatibility. In opening its investigation on digital television subsidies in Germany and Sweden, the Commission treated T-DVB and S-DVB television broadcasting as substitutable in terms of demand for the provision of broadcasting services and in terms of "acquisition" and "distribution" of content using different platforms:

"On the downstream market, it seems that cable, DTH and even DVB-T, although some technical and commercial differences exist between the different distribution methods, are substitutable. First of all, it seems that the price and the contents of the packages offered are very similar. With the introduction of digital services, offerings by DTH, DVB-T and cable could become less homogeneous, thereby increasing the incentive for consumers to switch. Secondly, the aforementioned development of digital services will make the different distribution systems even more substitutable. Finally, consumers will assess the offering by a cable, DVB-T or satellite operator by the ability to supply an attractive and broad range of services at an attractive price. They will most likely have no preference for any technical means of delivering the new digital services, whether by DTH, broadband cable or any other platform in combination with a back channel for interactive services. In the upstream market, the distributors acquire the rights to distribute content. Although broadcasters wish to be as widely distributed as possible (and therefore could see distribution systems as complementary rather than alternative) they have indicated that they regard cable and DTH as competing distribution channels. Given the technical and commercial features of DVB-T, it can be assumed that DVB-T is also to be considered as a competing infrastructure. Therefore, it can be concluded that a certain degree of substitutability between cable, DVB-T and DTH exists."[80]

18–015   The Commission's decision (due for appeal in the ECJ) was that subsidies granted to commercial broadcasters for using the Berlin-Brandenburg DVB-T network were liable to distort competition. The subsidies were decided post-switchover; they were not based on specific switchover costs and differed between broadcasters with no objective justification for such differentiation. Furthermore, the subsidies were found to indirectly favour the DVB-T network over competing TV platforms, such as cable and satellite, and so were not technologically neutral. The issue of technological neutrality is also at the centrepiece of the Commission decision to open an investigation into the granting of subsidies paid out in Italy to consumers in order to buy or rent digital decoders, without notifying the measure to the Commission. The subsidy was provided for interactive decoders capable of receiving programmes in digital terrestrial technology or the same programmes retransmitted via cable but not

---

[80] *German DVB-T* at paras 42, 43; see also *Swedish DVB-T* at paras 52, 53.

satellite. The subsidies were not notified and the Commission found that the subsidies granted between 2004 and 2005, for the purchase of certain digital terrestrial decoders constituted unlawful state aid.[81] However, the Commission also stated that where the decoders were technology neutral and proportionate to the objective of promoting the transition to digital television and interoperability then they were compatible with state aid rules.[82] The General Court and the EU Court of Justice respectively dismissed as unfounded appeals by Mediaset SpA against the European Commission's decision[83] and the General Court's decision.[84]

The question of effect on trade has been consistently treated by the Commission. It has acknowledged that when state aid strengthens the position of an undertaking compared with other undertakings competing in intra-community trade, the trade between Member States must be regarded as affected by the aid. In the broadcasting sector, state aid recipients and aggrieved competitors are often internationally active and, at a minimum, the acquisition of broadcasting rights takes place internationally. Also advertising markets can have a cross-border nature, particularly for homogenous linguistic areas.[85]

In ruling on the illegality of this German DVB-T aid the Commission recognised that in the case of digital switchover public intervention can be beneficial through regulation, financial support to customers, information campaigns or subsidies to overcome a specific market failure or to ensure social cohesion. In the press release announcing the ruling on the illegality of the aid in question[86] the Commission stated that it views favourably the following types of aid:

(a) funding for the roll-out of a transmission network in areas where otherwise there would be insufficient TV coverage;

(b) financial compensation to public service broadcasters for the cost of broadcasting via all transmission platforms in order to reach the entire population, provided this forms part of the public service mandate;

(c) subsidies to consumers for the purchase of digital decoders as long as they are technologically neutral, especially if they encourage the use of open standards for interactivity;

(d) financial compensation to broadcasters which are required to discontinue analogue transmission before the expiry of their licences, provided this takes account of granted digital transmission capacity.

---

[81] See Commission Decision of January 24, 2007 on state aid C 52/2005 (ex. NN 88/2005, ex. CP 101/2004), Italy, *Subsidy to digital decoders* [2005] O.J. L/147/2007.
[82] *Subsidy to digital decoders* (Italy).
[83] Case T–177/07 *Mediaset SpA v Commission*, judgment of June 15, 2010, Unreported.
[84] Case C–403/10 P *Mediaset SpA v Commission*, judgment of July 21, 2011, Unreported.
[85] *German DVB-T* at para.46, *Swedish DVB-T* at para.56.
[86] Commission press release IP/05/1394 of November 9, 2005.

18–016   These indications were based on a scheme designed to promote and develop digital television in Austria which had previously been approved by the Commission. In the Austrian case, subsidies to low income consumers purchasing equipment were found to be compatible as aid having a social character and being granted to individual consumers without discrimination.[87] In addition, the measures in question were not selective as to the broadcasting technology, thereby promoting the development of the whole sector.[88] In fact, the Austrian subsidy had only qualified for art.107(3)(c) approval after the Austrian authorities had abandoned their original plan to only subsidise terrestrial and not cable and satellite TV. The Commission decision states:

> "Whereas the original measure initially favoured digital terrestrial television, the Austrian authorities have, during the notification process, modified the measure subsequently in order to promote the digitisation of all broadcasting transmission networks (terrestrial, cable and satellite). Notably, during the notification procedure, the authorities decided to remove an envisaged measure on the specific funding of the roll-out of DVB-T (Digital Terrestrial Television) infrastructure from the notified scheme."[89]

18–017   In the Austrian case the Commission rejected the argument by the national authorities that the other measures be evaluated under art.107(3)(b) as projects of Common European Interest on the basis that these did not form part of a transnational programme supported by a number of Member States, and the project was not one of common interest. However, in the context of its art.107(3)(c) analysis the Commission noted specifically that the measures in question were in line with the Switchover Communication, and that the digitalisation of TV transmission can be viewed as "a policy objective which can be seen in line with Community interest and priorities."[90] Unlike the measures scrutinised in the German and Swedish DVB-T cases[91] (and the subsequent Italian one), the Austrian measures favoured no given technology or transmission platform, and so were technologically neutral.

Furthermore, in Austria the beneficiaries were to be selected in open calls for proposals, based on pre-defined criteria: the funding was temporary, as recommended by the Switchover Communication; potential beneficiaries would need to demonstrate the necessity of funding; applicants were required to justify all

---

[87] This approach was also subsequently confirmed in the *German DVB-T* case in which the Commission did not object to subsidies to 6,000 households satisfying such criteria.

[88] State Aid N 622/03, C [2005] 586 final, para.35.

[89] para.11.

[90] para.34.

[91] *German DVB-T* at para.43. Along similar lines the Commission has previously objected to a Swedish subsidy scheme which did not provide for technological neutrality: "The [Swedish] government has nevertheless, contrary to the Commission Communication on the Switchover opted for state funding of the specific technology DVB-T, rather than DVB-S, DVB-C or even DVB-H33. Cable and satellite providers are able to deliver the same or a very similar service to the broadcasters and the consumers, but do not receive funding. Consequently, there is a distortion of competition." *Swedish DVB-T* at para.54.

funding requirements; the results of the financed projects would be made available to the public, save in certain specified circumstances; applications by non-Austrians would be possible; and the scheme would be reported on annually, with the Commission receiving copies of such reports. The Commission accepted that all these safeguards ensured that competition would not be distorted to an extent contrary to the common interest and on that basis it decided that the measures were compatible with art.107(3)(c).

The above decisions indicate that the Commission is strongly in favour of digital switchover, and when the Switchover Communication is adhered to, accepts the use of public subsidies that aid digitalisation. In 2006 a public subsidy whose primary objective was "to ensure the availability of affordable advanced broadband services for businesses located in 14 business parks in rural areas of North Wales"[92] was approved on the basis that it was compatible with art.107(3)(c) i.e. aid to facilitate the development of certain economic activities or certain economic areas, and the overall effect of the measure on competition and supply of broadband connectivity in North Wales was deemed to be positive.[93] However, the Commission is also willing to declare measures incompatible with art.107 even where the innovation is purely designed to aid digitalisation, for example, again in 2006 the Commission declared that public funding for fibre to the home broadband in a small village in the Netherlands was incompatible with the TFEU.[94]

18–018

---

[92] Commission letter of February 22, 2006, state aid N 131/2005, United Kingdom, *FibreSpeed Broadband Project Wales*.

[93] *FibreSpeed Broadband Project Wales*, para.54.

[94] See Commission Decision of July 19, 2006 on the measure C 35/2005 (ex N 59/2005) on Netherlands plans to implement concerning broadband infrastructure in Appingedam [2005] O.J. L/86/2007.

PART IV

HORIZONTAL AID

CHAPTER 19

FINANCIAL SECTOR*

1. INTRODUCTION 19–001
2. BANKS AND THEIR POSITION AS GRANTORS OR TRANSMITTERS OF STATE AID 19–002
   Public subsidy banks as grantors of state aid 19–003
   Private banks as transmitters of state aid—triangular situations 19–004
3. ARTICLE 107(1) TFEU—STATE AID MEASURES IN FAVOUR OF BANKS 19–005
   State investments in banks ([re]capitalisation) 19–006
   Liquidity guarantees 19–008
   Liquidity facilities 19–010
   Liquidity support by central banks 19–011
   Support by Deposit Guarantee Funds 19–014
   Bad banks and other asset relief measures 19–016
   Tax incentives for market restructuring 19–017
4. APPROVAL OF RESCUE AND RESTRUCTURING UNDER ARTICLE 107(3)(C) TFEU 19–018
5. RESCUE (EMERGENCY) AND RESTRUCTURING CASES DURING THE FINANCIAL CRISIS
   UNDER ARTICLE 107(3)(B) TFEU 19–031
   Overview of the financial crisis 19–032
   General principles 19–035
   Emergency aid 19–045
   Restructuring aid 19–058
   Winding-up aid 19–077
6. FORESIGHTS: STATE AID TO FINANCIAL INSTITUTIONS—CURRENT AND FUTURE CHAL-
   LENGES 19–078
   *Short-term: the consequences of the European Council's summit on October 26–27,
   2011* 19–079
   *Implications of prolonged economic crisis for the restructuring plans of financial
   institutions* 19–082

1. INTRODUCTION

The legal rules of the international financial architecture constructed after the **19–001**
Second World War were non-liberal and remained so for decades. Although the
EEC Treaty had laid down the foundations of an integrated lending market in the
European Union by laying down the fundamental right of establishment, freedom

* Christoph Arhold

to provide services and free movement of capital across the Internal Market, the First Banking Directive[1] had granted only (limited) freedom for the establishment of branches while envisaging future liberalisation through mutual recognition and home country control.[2] These only partially liberal rules of the EEC were revised in 1989,[3] when first steps to abolish discriminatory barriers to provide financial services were set by the Capital Liberalization Directive.[4] The Second Banking Directive[5] then provided the legal instruments for minimum harmonisation, especially the mutual recognition of home country rules with respect to cross-border provision of financial services and bank branching: credit institutions authorised in a Member State may open branches in another Member State by simply complying with a notification requirement.[6] The Own Funds Directive; the Solvency Ratio Directive; the Large Exposures Directive; the Capital Adequacy Directive; the Deposit-Guarantee Directive; the Post-BCCI Directive; the Reorganisation and Compulsory Winding up of Credit Institutions; and the Consolidated Supervision Directive further complemented the prudential safeguards of the Second Banking Directive.[7] The implementation of these banking directives and the subsequent coordination of national legislation permitted the progressive liberalisation of the EU financial services market which was the necessary precondition for developing competition between banking institutions. At the same time, the harmonisation of the regulatory framework and thus the establishment of a level playing field put enormous pressure on business models of incumbent public banks, making necessary and/or partly revealing the already existing state support of these institutions.

Against this background, it is not surprising that the Commission started effectively controlling state aid in favour of the financial sector relatively late (only in the 1990s) after the sector had been subject to liberalisation, privatisation

---

[1] Council Directive 77/780 of December 12, 1977 [1977] O.J. L322/1977.

[2] Despite the direct effect of freedom of establishment and freedom to provide services, capital movement restrictions could still constitute barriers to trade of financial services, as art.67(1) EC had no direct effect. Abolition of capital movement restrictions was therefore only possible through directives enacted on the basis of art.69 EC, see Rossi/Sansonetti, "Survey of State aid in the lending sector—A Comprehensive Review of Main State Aid Cases", European Business Law Review, Vol.18, No.6, 2007, pages 2–6, also available under *http://www.side-isle.it/ocs/ viewpaper.php?id=75&cf=1*, p.3 [Accessed November 15, 2011].

[3] Buch / Heinrich, Financial Integration in Europe and Banking Sector Performance, Kiel January 2002, pp.2–3, downloadable under *http://iep-berlin.net/fileadmin/website/09_Publikationen/ Sonstige/EU_Market/buch.pdf.* [Accessed November 15, 2011].

[4] Council Directive 88/361 of June 24, 1988 [1988] O.J. L178/1988.

[5] Second Council Directive 89/646 of December 15, 1989 on the coordination of laws, regulations and administrative provisions relating to the taking up and pursuit of the business of credit institutions amending the Directive 77/780 [1989] O.J. L386/1989.

[6] France accepted complete capital liberalisation as a quid pro quo with Germany for the promise of monetary union, see Abdelal, Writing the rules of global finance: France, Europe, and capital liberalization Review of International Political Economy 13: February 1, 2006: 1–27, p.7.

[7] The Second Banking Directive, as subsequently amended, was codified and combined along with the 73/183 Directive, the First Banking Directive, the Own Funds Directive, the Solvency Ratio Directive, the Large Exposure Directive and the Consolidated Supervision Directive in a single Directive: the European Parliament and Council Directive 2000/12/EC [2000] O.J. L126/2000 as amended by the European Parliament and Council Directive 2000/28/EC [2000] O.J. L257/2000 the Banking Consolidation Directive.

and the breaking-up of national monopolies together with increasing harmonisation at European level. Until then, the Commission had focused on the role of the banks as transmitters of state aid (aid granted to national undertakings via the national banking system, see below under point 219), which still plays an important role. In the middle of the 90s, a number of public banks in France and Italy needed state aid, since increasing competition meant that they could not cope with the solvency requirements any longer. These were the first big state aid cases in the financial sector, and all were assessed under art.107(3)(c) TFEU and the R & R Guidelines (see below under point 4). Member States took and continue to take a variety of measures to protect their public banks from increasing competition, to provide incentives for market restructuring or to ensure financial market stability, not all of these partly very sector specific measures being state aid within the meaning of art.107(1) TFEU (see below under point 3). The ongoing dramatic financial markets crisis, started in 2008 by the US subprime crisis, and currently continuing in the form of the sovereign bonds crisis, has provoked a huge amount of rescue and restructuring aid: altogether EUR 1,240 billion. Most of the aid used—EUR 757 billion, or 61 per cent of the total—was in the form of liquidity guarantees. Other forms of aid were capital injections (EUR 303 billion), impaired asset reliefs measures (EUR 104 billion), and liquidity assistance (EUR 77 billion). The aid was concentrated in few Member States. At national level, the top three banking markets—the United Kingdom, Germany and France—received 60 per cent of the total amount of aid. The aid was also concentrated on a limited number of banks. The ten largest beneficiaries in the European Union received more than half of the total aid; the next 20 received one quarter; and all the other beneficiaries—about 190 banks—shared the remaining quarter among themselves.[8] Almost all of it was approved as aid to remedy a serious disturbance in the economy of a Member State (art.107(3)(b) TFEU), by around 250 Commission decisions based on five related Commission Communications (see below under point 5). As market conditions continue to worsen, Member States and Commission are pondering about new support rules for tarnished systemic banks, and even discussing the possibility of direct community aid (see below under point 6).

2. Banks and Their Position as Grantors or Transmitters of State Aid

For a long time, the Commission's state aid control units have dealt with banks **19–002** only as grantors or transmitters of state aid, not as beneficiaries of state aid. Public subsidy banks may act as grantors of state aid by directly providing grants, low interest loans or low premium guarantees covering private bank loans for the

[8] See speech of Commissioner Almunia of October 4, 2011, The impact of the crisis state aid regime for banks, downloadable under *http://europa.eu/rapid/pressReleasesAction.do?reference =SPEECH/11/632&format=HTML&aged=0&language=EN&guiLanguage=en* [Accessed November 20, 2011.]

real economy (see below under para.19–003), while private banks may act as transmitters of state aid, if they assign state guaranteed, low-interest loans to beneficiary undertakings. In the latter case, the private bank may not (only) be the transmitter, but (also) the beneficiary of the state guarantee. In addition, it is a long-disputed question whether an infringement of the standstill clause (art.108(3) TFEU) renders the state guarantee void *erga omnes*, so that the bank cannot invoke the guarantee in case of default, even if it acted only as transmitter, because it has offered interest rates fully transferring the economic advantage of the state guarantee to the borrower (see below under para.19–004).

Public subsidy banks as grantors of state aids

19–003   Public subsidy banks act as direct grantors of state aid by, for instance, providing grants, low-interest loans or guarantees to the real economy. Trying to keep the costs of their subsidy policy as low as possible, Member States often provide their subsidy banks with far-reaching public guarantees, in order to enable them to get the same funding and refinancing conditions as the State itself. Whether such guarantees constitute state aid depends on whether public subsidy banks may be considered undertakings within the meaning of EU competition law. This could be disputed for banks whose sole purpose is to grant subsidies. It may be argued that granting subsidies is per se a purely sovereign and thus non-economic activity. To that extent the state support to the subsidy bank concerned should not be considered to fall within the definition of state aid. In the so-called Understanding II between the Commission and Germany relating to "institutional liability" (*Anstaltslast*) and "guarantor liability" (*Gewährträger-haftung*) for the benefit of the German specialised credit institutions (including the KfW and the subsidy branches of the German Landesbanks) the Commission has agreed that both types of liability (*Anstaltslast* and *Gewährträgerhaftung*[9]) can be retained for the benefit of legally independent subsidy banks, to the extent that their activities are limited to a very precisely defined catalogue of public subsidy tasks. All commercial activities had to be either abandoned or else isolated from state liability by separating them out into legally independent undertakings free from state support. In a 2004 decision concerning the *Finnish Municipality Finance Plc* (MFL) the Commission confirmed—for the first time explicitly that such specialised credit institutions[10] are not undertakings within

---

[9] For Anstaltslast and Gewährträgerhaftung, see in more detail below under point 3.2.2.

[10] Defined in the Report of the European Commission to the Council of Ministers: Services of general economic interest in the banking sector, adopted by the Commission on June 17, 1998 and presented to the ECOFIN Council on November 23, 1998, point 3.2. Downloadable at *http://ec.europa.eu/competition/state_aid/studies_reports/archive/report_bank_en.html*. [Accessed: 15 November, 2011]. In that report the Commission expressed the opinion that state aid problems can only be dispelled if all the banks compete on the same conditions for the provision of services of general economic interest. The only situation recognized to be a clearly non-commercial activity was the raising of funds for the public sector (point 3.3).

the meaning of art.107(1) TFEU.[11] MFL may benefit from state guarantees only with respect to its public tasks. Such public tasks include the financing of municipalities and municipal federations ("in-house" or "closed-cycle"-approach) as well as the distribution of subsidies (financing at preferential terms) at the request of the public authorities; in particular, financial support of environment-friendly investments, infrastructure, housing and services of general interest. MFL is not allowed to provide financing to other companies at market terms as such financing is an economic activity that can also be provided by any other commercial financial institution not benefiting from public support. These principles have subsequently been confirmed in the decision on the recapitalisation of the *Mortgage and Land Bank of Latvia* (LHZB).[12] The assessment of state-supported programmes in relation to their real economic beneficiaries under state aid rules of course remains a task for the Commission.[13]

Private banks as transmitters of state aid—triangular situations

Usually, the beneficiary of a state guarantee is the borrower, not the lending bank, because the bank is transferring the economic advantage of the loan to the borrower. Compared to a situation without a guarantee, the state guarantee enables the borrower to obtain better financial terms for a loan than those normally available on the financial markets. Typically, with the benefit of the state guarantee, the borrower can obtain lower rates and/or offer less security. In some cases, the borrower would not, without a state guarantee, find a financial institution prepared to lend on any terms. It is therefore normally the borrower who should provide remuneration for risk-carrying by an appropriate premium. When the borrower does not need to pay the premium, or pays a low premium, it obtains an advantage. Any potential economic advantages in favour of the lending bank have normally been neutralised by the lower interest rate.[14] There are exemptions from this general principle. Point 2.3.1 of the Guarantee Notice mentions the following two examples:

19–004

—if a state guarantee is given ex post in respect of a loan or other financial obligation already entered into without the terms of this loan or financial obligation being adjusted, or

---

[11] State aid N179/2004—Finnish municipal guarantees.

[12] State aid NN 60/2009, paras 30–38, Latvia: Recapitalization of "The Mortgage and Land Bank of Latvia". See also state aid N715/2006, para.22, Finland: Tax exemption to Finnvera Oyj.

[13] State aid NN 60/2009, para.40, Latvia: Recapitalization of "The Mortgage and Land Bank of Latvia"; State aid N 715/2006, para.29, Finland: Tax exemption to Finnvera Oyj; state aid No.E 10/2000, point 2, Germany: Anstaltslast and Gewährträgerhaftung. For more details on the implementation in practice at KfW see Weber, *Zeitschrift für das gesamte Kreditwesen*, [2006] 882.

[14] Point 2.2 Commission Notice on the application of arts 87 and 88 of the EC Treaty to State aid in the form of guarantees [2008] O.J. C155/10 ("Guarantee Notice").

—if one guaranteed loan is used to pay back another, non-guaranteed loan to the same credit institution, then there may also be aid to the lender, in so far as the security of the loans is increased.[15]

The Guarantee Notice refers to the constellations mentioned above merely as examples for situations in which the lender (partially) retains the economic advantage resulting from the state guarantee. They should therefore not be interpreted strictly: state aid cannot be excluded if the state guarantee improves the position of the lender, due to a reduction in its risk exposure without a corresponding adjustment to the loan conditions.

If a state guarantee backing up a joint loan facility is unlawfully[16] benefitting only one bank of the consortium granting the *joint facility*, the question arises of whether the guarantee is void only as far as the actually advantaged bank is concerned or whether the nullity extends to apply to the guarantee as a whole *erga omnes*.[17] From the perspective of the purpose of state aid law—to prevent distortions of competition—the first scenario should be preferable. However, given the lack of case law and guidance by the Commission with respect to this question it may be argued that the principle of *effet utile* requires that the guarantee does not cover the joint facility anymore at all.

The risk of voidness due to an infringement of the standstill clause of art.108(3) TFEU arises not just in situations involving state aid for the benefit of the financing bank, but also in cases where an unlawful guarantee confers an advantage only to the borrower. Guarantees differ from other state aid measures, such as grants or tax exemptions, since in the case of a guarantee, the State also enters into a legal relationship with the lender. The question whether the unlawfulness of the aid affects the legal relations between the State and third parties is a matter which has to be examined under national law. Whether the effect of nullity is limited to the relationship between the state body and the aid recipient (or the aid recipient and the credit institution) or whether the guarantee contracts between the credit institution and the state body are also affected, is highly disputed:

—In its Guarantee Notice the Commission explicitly points out the risks which banks can potentially face as a result of an infringement of the standstill clause, indicating that it would prefer it if banks were obliged to assess compatibility with the standstill clause.[18]

---

[15] Where the guarantee contains aid to the lender, attention should be drawn to the fact that such aid might, in principle, constitute operating aid which is only approvable in very rare circumstances.

[16] Because it was not notified to the European Commission beforehand according to art.108(3) TFEU.

[17] In its rulings the ECJ has consistently emphasized that the validity of legal acts to implement state aid measures will be impaired if the authorities of the Member State fail to observe the prohibition on putting measures into effect set out by art.108(3) TFEU. Settled case law of the ECJ since the judgment C–354/90 [1991] E.C.R. I–5505; RdNr. 12, Fédération nationale du commerce extérieur des produits alimentaires (FNCP).

[18] Point 2.3.2 Guarantee Notice. See also Soltész [2005] WM 265.

—On the other hand, it may be argued that in situations where the bank providing the loan does not profit from the guarantee it should not bear the risk of voidness. Therefore, it should only be the promise under the guarantee, i.e. the legal relationship between the state body and the borrower, which ought be covered by the nullity.[19]

In *Residex Capital*, the ECJ had to decide upon the question of whether a State can actually rely on the nullity of the guarantee in its relations with the financing bank. In her Opinion issued on May 26, 2011 Advocate General Kokott took a differentiated view:

—To the extent that the lender is not itself a beneficiary of the aid, a state guarantee must not be considered void on the grounds of an infringement of the standstill clause of art.108(3) TFEU.[20]

—A state guarantee for a private loan issued contrary to art.108(3) TFEU and not subsequently approved by the European Commission must nonetheless be considered to be void if the lender is itself the beneficiary of the aid, i.e. especially in circumstances as described by point 2.3.1 of the Guarantee Notice.[21]

The approach of the Advocate General would have been a major step for the banking sector towards more legal certainty in connection with state guarantees. Unfortunately, the ECJ did not follow the clear-cut rule suggested by the Advocate General.

While the Court denied an obligation of the national courts to declare unlawfully granted state guarantee null and void in order to prevent the infringement from continuing,[22] it accepted the national courts' freedom to do so in compliance with their domestic law, at least if in the case at stake cancellation of the guarantee is the most "effective" remedy, and there are no less onerous procedural measures to restore the competitive situation which existed before the aid was granted. It is not excluded that in a concrete case the cancellation of the loan contract may be a better way to achieve this objective, so the bank can still invoke the state guarantee.[23] Although the Court here seems to accept some proportionality arguments, which may be invoked before the national courts, lenders still risk having unlawful state declared null and void by national courts, even where they can not be considered the state aid recipient. It remains to be

---

[19] Cf. Hadding [2005] WM 485, 486 ff.; Koenig/Haratsch [2005] Z.H.R. 169, 77, 86 ff.; cf. also Cranshaw [2008] W.M. 338.

[20] Opinion, in Case C–275/10, *Residex Capital IV CV* [2011] E.C.R. Unreported, paras 66–68.

[21] Opinion, in Case C–275/10, *Residex Capital IV CV* [2011] E.C.R. Unreported, para.88.

[22] See ECJ, C–275/10, *Residex Capital IV CV* [2011] E.C.R. Unreported, para.44: "[. . .] with regard to cancellation of the guarantee, and irrespective of who the beneficiary may be, European Union law does not impose any specific consequence . . . with regard to the validity of the acts."

[23] Ibid., paras 46–47.

seen whether in applying the proportionality test required by the *Residex* ruling, national courts will draw on the arguments set out in AG Kokott's opinion.

3. ARTICLE 107(1) TFEU—STATE AID MEASURES IN FAVOUR OF BANKS

19–005   In order to be considered as state aid within the meaning of art.107(1) TFEU, a measure must fulfil the following six constituent elements: (i) There must be a transfer of State resources; that (ii) is imputable to the State (imputability); (iii) grants an economic advantage; (iv) to certain undertakings or the production of certain goods (selectivity); (v) thus threatening to distort competition (distortion of competition); and (vi) affecting trade between Member States" (effect on trade). If any of these constituent elements is not fulfilled, the measure does not fall within the scope of art.107(1) TFEU and thus EU state aid control does not apply. Since the liberalisation of the European financial market, the elements of effect on trade and distortion of competition are regularly met, since—unlike in antitrust law—in state aid law the distortive effects do not have to be appreciable. More often, the criteria of imputability or transfer of state resources may be questionable, for instance with respect to measures taken by deposit guarantee funds (see below under paras 19–014—19–015) or national central banks (see below under paras 19–011—19–013). The selectivity criterion may be at stake in taxation cases (see below under para.19–017). Nonetheless, like in other sectors, the economic advantage of a measure is the most problematic part of the state aid assessment.

For the existence of an economic advantage, it must be established that the bank receives an economic advantage which it would not have obtained under normal market conditions.[24] This has to be considered from the State perspective by asking whether a private undertaking of comparable size to the public entity in question would have granted the advantage to the same extent and on the same terms. If, according to this test, the arrangement at stake represents a normal commercial transaction in the course of which the State behaved as a rational operator in a market economy and did not mainly have regard to any economic or social policy objectives,[25] it may be assumed that there is no state aid present (so-called Market Economy Operator Test ("MEOT")). It is irrelevant if the Member State was also pursuing political objectives.[26] The first Commission decisions and court rulings which established these principles dealt with state capital holdings, and therefore the applicable test was called Private Investor Test (for the application of this test on the financial markets see below under paras 19–006 and 19–007). Since then, the courts have developed further tests to match other instruments used by Member States, such as the Private Creditor Test in

---

[24] See for example Case C–39/94 [1996] E.C.R. I–3547, para.60—Case C–342/96 *Spain/Commission* [1999] E.C.R. I–2459, para.41.
[25] Case T–98/00 *Linde/Commission* [2002] E.C.R. II–3961, para.49.
[26] See for example Case C–56/93 *Belgium/Commission* [1996] E.C.R. I–723, paras 78–79.

cases of debt remissions and rescheduling, or the Private Vendor Test for privatisations. Other sub-categories can be developed, such as a Private Guarantor Test for cases concerning state guarantees either guaranteeing the bank's debt service (liquidity side, see below under paras 19–008 and 19–009) or the performance of its assets (asset side, see below under para.19–016). Ultimately however, all these various tests are no more than variants on the one underlying MEOT: did the Member State act in the same way as a market economy operator in the same situation would have?

State investments in banks ([re]capitalisation)

If (re-)capitalisation of a (public or private) bank is (partly) made by state **19–006** funds, i.e. if the State becomes a new investor in the bank or extends its existing investment, the Private Investor Test applies for the assessment of whether this investment contains state aid.[27] The test dates back to the Commission's position on public authorities' holdings ("the Commission's Position").[28] According to point 3.2 of the Commission's Position, state aid is not involved where fresh capital is contributed in circumstances that would be acceptable to a private investor operating under normal market economy conditions.[29] On the other hand, aid is assumed to be present where the financial position of the company, and particularly the structure and volume of its debt, is such that a normal return (in dividends or capital gains) cannot be expected within a reasonable time. Capital injections to profitable companies can constitute aid as well, if the expected return is not sufficiently high.[30] An informed private investor, i.e. an investor who wishes to maximise his profits but without running excessive risks in comparison with other participants in the market, would, when calculating the appropriate return to be expected for his investment, in principle require a minimum return equivalent to the average return for the sector concerned. This has been confirmed by the General Court in the ground breaking WestLB judgement.[31] According to the view taken by the court, the requirement to take the behaviour of an informed private investor into account cannot be regarded as discriminating against the public investor, as a public investor is not in the same

[27] For more details to the Private Investor Test in general see Arhold [2011] MünchKomm-BeihVgR, art.107, pts 143 and following.
[28] Government Capital Injections, Application of arts 92 and 93 of the EEC Treaty to public authorities' holdings [1984] Bull. EC 9, p.28–29. As early as 1980, the so-called Transparency Directive (Directive 80/723 [1980] O.J. L195/35, most recently amended by Directive 2005/81 [2005] O.J. L312/47, consolidated version in Directive 2006/111 [2006] O.J. L318/17) obligated the Member States to report in detail each year on the subsidies granted to public undertakings.
[29] Confirmed by Case 40/85 *Belgium/Commission* [1986] E.C.R. 2321, para.13.
[30] Commission communication to the Member States—Application of arts 92 and 93 of the EEC Treaty and of art.5 of Commission Directive 80/723/EEC to public undertakings in the manufacturing sector [1993] O.J. C307/3.
[31] Case T–228/99 and T–233/99 *Westdeutsche Landesbank Girozentrale and Land Nordrhein-Westfalen/Commission* [2003] E.C.R. II–435, para.255; see also Stöckl [2003] *European Law Reporter*, 156, and Prieto [2003] Journal du droit international, p.649–650.

situation as a private investor. The private investor can only count on his own resources in order to finance his investments and is liable, up to the limits of those resources, for the consequences of his decisions. The public investor, on the other hand, has access to resources flowing from the exercise of public power, in particular from taxation.[32] The average return is, however, merely one of several analytical tools that can potentially be used. It is not an automatic criterion for determining the existence and amount of state aid. It does not relieve the Commission of its obligation to make a complete analysis of all factors that are relevant to the transaction at issue and its context, including the situation of the beneficiary undertaking and of the relevant market.[33]

19–007   In times of economic crisis, it is particularly difficult for the Member State to demonstrate that its participation in a capital increase was in compliance with the Private Investor Test, for the following reasons:

—If private shareholders make a disproportionately low contribution to a capital injection to an undertaking, there is a prima facie suspicion that aid is present, especially if the disproportionate contribution is largely attributable to the undertaking's poor profit outlook.[34]

—On the other hand, according to the Communication, state aid is taken not to be present where the public holding in a company is increased, provided the capital injected is proportionate to the number of shares held by the authorities and is accompanied by an injection of capital by private shareholders, and the private investor's participation has real economic significance.[35] However, particularly strict criteria have to apply when assessing a capital contribution made to an undertaking in difficulty. In such a situation it is not enough for the private shareholders (particularly the minority shareholders) to make a proportionate contribution, unless certain minimum conditions are fulfilled, namely those which a prudent private investor would have required, such as the presentation of a credible and realistic restructuring plan.[36]

[32] Case T–228/99 and T–233/99 *Westdeutsche Landesbank Girozentrale and Land Nordrhein-Westfalen/Commission* [2003] E.C.R. II–435, paras 271 and following.

[33] Case T–228/99 and T–233/99 *Westdeutsche Landesbank Girozentrale and Land Nordrhein-Westfalen/Commission* [2003] E.C.R. II–435, paras 250 and following.

[34] Case T–358/94 *Air France/Commission* [1996] E.C.R. II–2109, paras 148, 149.

[35] Case T–358/94 Air France/Commission [1996] E.C.R. II–2109, paras 148 and following. During the financial crisis, the participation in the recapitalisation of Dexia by shareholders whose behaviour was not imputable to the State, limited to 12.4 per cent of the total capital increase, was considered insufficient to conclude that the public shareholders acted as private investors in a market economy, see Commission Decision of February 26, 2010 on state aid C9/09 (ex NN 49/08, NN 50/08 and NN 45/08) implemented by the Kingdom of Belgium, the French Republic and the Grand Duchy of Luxembourg for *Dexia SA* [2010] O.J. L274/54, pt.126.

[36] Case C–328/99 and C–399/00 *Italian Republic and SIM 2 Multimedia SpA/Commission* [2003] E.C.R. I–4035, paras 44, 48. For a case where there was both considerable private capital and a restructuring plan, meaning that State aid could be ruled out, see *Citynet Amsterdam* [2008] O.J. L247/27; in that respect see Gaal/Papadias/Riedl [2008] CPN, p.82. During the financial crisis, the principle was confirmed by Commission Decision of February 26, 2010 on state aid C9/09 (ex NN 49/08, NN 50/08 and NN 45/08) implemented by the Kingdom of Belgium, the

—Even if there is a restructuring or turnaround plan, the inherent element of risk means that the returns expected in the event that restructuring proves successful must be significantly higher than the average market return.[37] In such situations, the minimum rate of return must include the risk premium which a private investor requires in order to give a certain financial commitment. It must therefore be directly proportionate to the risk inherent in the investment. The Commission has to establish the minimum rate and the expected rate of return using the most recent version of the restructuring plan available.[38]

—Moreover, the presence of aid cannot be ruled out where private investments in the same undertaking occur only after the allocation of public funds,[39] or only after the State has announced that it will participate in a capital increase or support the undertaking by other means.[40]

—Most importantly, the Commission will in general presume that there is aid, if the capital increase is combined with other types of aid.[41] That presumption does not apply if a capital injection follows directly after the repayment of unlawfully received aid. If the business case and the definite prospects for earnings of a public sector undertaking justifies a capital injection then it will not matter whether it was the repayment of aid that caused the need for a capital injection. In addition, the capital injection is not automatically to be considered a circumvention of the aid's recovery. This has been confirmed in several Landesbanks cases: there had been seven cases in which

French Republic and the Grand Duchy of Luxembourg for *Dexia SA* [2010] O.J. L274/54, pt 126.

[37] Case T–296/97 *Alitalia/Commission* [2000] E.C.R. II–3871, paras 113 and following; as well as Case T–301/01 *Alitalia/Commission* [2008] E.C.R. II–1753, paras 236 and following.

[38] Case T–296/97 *Alitalia/Commission* [2000] E.C.R. II–3871, paras 165–169

[39] Case T–20/03 *Kahla Porzellan/Commission* [2008] E.C.R. II–2305, para.254; Case C–301/87 *France/Commission* [1990] E.C.R. I–307, para.40.

[40] France Telecom [2006] O.J. L257/11, para.227.

[41] Government Capital Injections, Application of arts 92 and 93 of the EEC Treaty to public authorities' holdings [1984] Bulletin EC 9, pp.28–29, pt 3.4. For an example during the financial crisis see state aid NN 42/2008—Belgium, NN 46/2008—Luxembourg NN 53/A/2008—Netherlands Restructuring aid to Fortis Bank and Fortis Bank Luxembourg, O.J. 2009 C80/7, pt.62. This principle also applies to other measures than capital increases, see Commission Decision of April 5, 2011 on the measures No.C 11/2009 (ex NN 53b/2008, NN 2/2010 and N 19/2010) implemented by Dutch State for ABN AMRO Group NV (created following the merger between Fortis Bank) Nederland and ABN AMRO N), not published yet, points 219–242, especially pt 235:

> "based on the chronology of the measures (I), the common purpose of the measures (II) and the situation of the companies at the time of each measure (III), the Commission concludes that they are not sufficiently distinct to be judged against the MEIP independently. The Commission considers all measures to be part of one lengthy restructuring process."

Confirmed also by Commission Decision of February 26, 2010 on state aid C 9/09 (ex NN 49/08, NN 50/08 and NN 45/08) implemented by the Kingdom of Belgium, the French Republic and the Grand Duchy of Luxembourg for *Dexia SA* [2010] O.J. L274/54, pt 26; as well as Commission Decision of June 29, 2011 on the state aids Nos SA.32504 (2011/N) and C11/2010 (ex N 667/2009) implemented by Ireland for *Anglo Irish Bank and Irish Nationwide Building Society*, Unreported, pt 103.

assets of public housing companies had been transferred to German Land-esbanks as core capital for insufficient consideration. The Commission ordered the repayment of the state aid.[42] In three cases,[43] the owners of Landesbanks informed the Commission that they planned capital increases to (partly) outweigh the consequences of the aid repayment. For the Com-mission, the key question in examining these cases was again only whether the expected total return on the investment was in line with the return a market-economy investor would expect for comparable investments in share capital and preference shares. This question was answered in the affirmative.

—The Commission recognises the differences between minority holdings and majority holdings and their significance for the investment time horizon, which will normally tend to be motivated by purely short-term profit considerations if there is no possibility to exercise control.[44] In the case of majority holdings, long-term strategic considerations may under certain circumstances justify a rate of return that is lower than the market rate (so-called "owner effect"). The burden of proof is incumbent on the Mem-ber State.[45] However, the scope of the owner effect is limited. Without concrete prospects of profitability a private owner would opt for the liquida-tion of the undertaking, if that would entail less costs than a new capital injection.[46] In that respect the costs of liquidation must be compared with the costs for maintaining business operations. When considering liquidation

---

[42] *Federal Republic of Germany for Westdeutsche Landesbanken Girozentrale* (WestLB) [2000] O.J. L150/1; Commission Decision 2006/737/EC of October 20, 2004 on aid from Germany for Westdeutsche Landesbank—*Girozentrale* (WestLB), now WestLB AG [2006] O.J. L307/22; Commission Decision 2006/736/EC of October 20, 2004 on state aid implemented by Germany for *Landesbank Berlin* [2006] O.J. L307/1; Commission Decision 2006/738/EC of October 20, 2004 on state aid implemented by Germany for *Norddeutsche Landesbank—Girozentrale* [2006] O.J. L307/58; Commission Decision 2006/739/EC of October 20, 2004 on state aid implemented by Germany for *Bayerische Landesbank—Girozentrale* [2006] O.J. L307/81; Commission Decision 2006/740/EC of October 20, 2004 on state aid implemented by Germany for *Hambur-gische Landesbank—Girozentrale, now HSH Nordbank AG* [2006] O.J. L307/110; Commission Decision 2006/741/EC of October 20, 2004 on state aid implemented by Germany for *Land-esbank Schleswig-Holstein—Girozentrale, now HSH Nordbank AG* [2006] O.J. L307/134; Com-mission Decision 2006/742/EC of October 20, 2004 on state aid implemented by Germany for *Landesbank Hessen-Thüringen—Girozentrale* [2006] O.J. L307/159.

[43] State aid NN 71/2005—*HSH Nordbank*; state aid NN 72/2005, *BayernLB*; state aid NN 34/2007—*Nord/LB*. For details on these decisions, see: Simon [2007] EStAL 499, and Friede-riszick/Tröge [2006] CPN 1, 105.

[44] Commission communication to the Member States—Application of arts 92 and 93 of the EEC Treaty and of art.5 of Commission Directive 80/723/EEC to public undertakings in the manu-facturing sector [1993] O.J. C307/3 para.30.

[45] Case T–228 and 233/99 *Westdeutsche Landesbank Girozentrale* and *Land Nordrhein-Westfalen/ Commission* [2003] E.C.R. II–435, para.270.

[46] This test is in line with the Commission's constant practice. See Joined Cases T–129/95, T–2/96 and T–97/96 *Neue Maxhütte Stahlwerke* [1999] E.C.R. II–17, para.124. However, winding up costs are normally difficult to calculate and estimates are faced with uncertainties, see for example Commission Decision 2005/345/EC in Case C–28/02 *Bankgesellschaft Berlin* [2005] O.J. L116/1, pts 163 and following. Also Commission Decision 2008/263/EC in Case C–50/06 *BAWAG* [2008], pt 166.

costs a distinction has to be drawn between the obligations which the State must assume as owner of the share capital of a company and its obligations as a public authority. It follows that the costs arising from redundancies, the payment of unemployment benefits and other social security benefits must not be taken into consideration for the purpose of applying the Private Investor Test.[47] The Commission takes the view that costs related to (even lawful and compatible) state aid, for instance resulting from global defi- ciency guarantees in favour of public banks such as the German *Gewähr- trägerhaftung* or the Austrian *Ausfallhaftung* cannot be taken into account when calculating the liquidation costs, since private investors would not grant such aids.[48] The same applies for losses which the State would have to bear in consequence of a systemic crisis caused by the fall of a systemic bank. This is true even with respect to indirect losses which will probably be borne by the beneficiary bank itself as a consequence of such general banking crisis. These are not costs which can be taken into account when applying the Private Investor Test, at least if the public bank's involvement in a risk shield is disproportionate in relation to the involvement of other private banks and bank associations.[49] However, losses arising from share- holder loans may be taken into consideration.[50]

In light of these principles, it cannot come as a surprise that almost all capital increases by public funds during the financial crisis have been considered state aid.[51] Only in the decision in *Hypo Steiermarkt* did the Commission accept that the State's participation in a capital increase was in line with the Private Investor Test. The Commission exclusively referred to the fact that the capital increase was executed by the public owner Land Steiermark and the private owner Raiffeisen Steiermark pro rata according to the pre-existing ownership structure and was subject to identical conditions. Furthermore, the private owner's share, which amounted to 75 per cent minus one share, had a real economic sig- nificance.[52] The capital increase was part of a strategic reorientation, which had

---

[47] Case T–129/95, T–2/96 and T–97/96 *Maxhütte/Commission* [1999] E.C.R. II–17, paras. 118–119.

[48] For Austrian Ausfallhaftung, see Commission Decision of May 7, 2004 on state aid C–44/03 (ex NN 158/01) which Austria is planning to implement for *Bank Burgenland AG* [2005] O.J. L263/8, pt.65. For German Gewährträgerhaftung see Commission Decision of June 4, 2008 on state aid C–9/08 (ex NN 8/08, CP 244/07) implemented by Germany for *Sachsen LB* [2009] O.J. L104/34, pt.82. and Commission Decision of September 20, 2011 on state aid SA 29338 (C29/2009, ex N 264/2009), granted by Germany to HSH Nordbank, not published yet, points 147–151.

[49] Commission Decision of October 21, 2008 on state aid measure C–10/08 (ex NN 7/08) implemented by Germany for the restructuring of *IKB Deutsche Industriebank AG* [2009] O.J. L278/32, pt 70 and following.

[50] Case T–323/99 *INMA and Itainvest/Commission* [2002] E.C.R. II–545, para.100.

[51] See also Restructuring Communication, pt 14: "In the current crisis governments have recapi- talised banks on terms chosen primarily for reasons of financial stability rather than for a return which would have been acceptable to a private investor."

[52] Commission Decision of July 22, 2009, state aid NN 40/2009 *Hypo Steiermarkt* [2009], O.J. C206/02, pt 15.

been presented to the owners.[53] The case demonstrates that in general the Private Investor Test is applicable also in extraordinary circumstances like the financial crisis, even though the chances to pass it will be considerably reduced.[54]

Liquidity guarantees

19–008 **General principles.** The core of a bank's business is borrowing money at low interest rates and lending at high interest rates. Borrowing, i.e. funding its lending and investment business, is thus the fundament of each banking business. Difficulties may occur, for instance, if a bank's business model is based on long-term lending and short-term funding, and the interest rate for the refinancing of the short term funding suddenly increases at a not predicted rate. In such a situation the bank may risk suffering losses. Depending on the bank's business model, the losses may become existential. The problem gets worse in times of a financial crisis where confidence between banks is reduced or even totally destroyed, as was the case after the Lehman collapse in autumn 2008. Banks are no longer able to generate their funding from other banks on the so called interbank market. If this market dries out, short-term lending collapses, and banks—even if their fundamental business concept is sound—may find it difficult to service their debts; they get liquidity problems. The problem may be more evident for wholesale banks than for retail banks, which benefit from continuous money transfers by their private clients. However, even these banks may be hit existentially, in particular when a systemic crisis causes panic amongst private clients, who then try to save their money by a run on the bank. In all these cases, State guarantees are a means of last resort lending. In principle, the Commission's Guarantee Notice also applies to banks and describes the circumstances under which a state liquidity guarantee would not have to be considered state aid, because it is in line with market conditions and that it would thus have been made available on those conditions by a private guarantor too[55]:

—The borrower is not in financial difficulty.

—The extent of the guarantee can be properly measured when it is granted. This means that the guarantee must be linked to a specific financial transaction, for a fixed maximum amount and limited in time.

---

[53] Commission Decision of July 22, 2009, state aid NN 40/2009 *Hypo Steiermarkt* [2009], O.J. C206/02, pt 3.

[54] The Commission's view taken in the Dexia case that "the principle of the private investor in a market economy applies only under normal market conditions", and that measures taken "at the height of the financial crisis under entirely abnormal market conditions" could therefore not be assessed under the Private investor Test, is too far-reaching, Commission Decision of February 26, 2010 on state aid C–9/09 (ex NN 49/08, NN 50/08 and NN 45/08) implemented by the Kingdom of Belgium, the French Republic and the Grand Duchy of Luxembourg for *Dexia SA* [2010] O.J. L274/54, pt.126.

[55] Guarantee Notice, pt 3.2. See further Arhold [2011] *MünchKommBeihVgR*, pts 183 and following.

—The guarantee does not cover more than 80 per cent of the outstanding loan or other financial obligation.

—A market-oriented price is paid for the guarantee.

According to the MEOT, there is no state aid if it can be shown that a usual market premium was paid. However, the calculation of what is a usual amount for a market premium is by its nature subject to uncertainties. In that respect the 80 per cent rule and its implementation can be seen as an economic litmus test. For if the financial obligation is not wholly covered by a state guarantee, the lender has a greater incentive to properly assess, secure and minimise the risk arising from the lending operation, and in particular to properly assess the borrower's creditworthiness. It is evident that in the circumstances of a financial crisis, in most cases already the first criterion (the bank not being in economic difficulties) will not be met, much less the 80 per cent and market price requirements. For an individual guarantee, the cash grant equivalent of a guarantee should normally be calculated as the difference between the market price of the guarantee and the price actually paid.[56] In its Impaired Assets Communication the Commission has clarified that the amount of state aid is set at the maximum net liability for the State, if the beneficiary bank "cannot find any independent private operator on the market willing to provide a similar guarantee."[57] In this case, no market price can be established, because the guarantee is not offered on the market at all. During severe financial crisis like in 2008/09, this is the typical scenario.[58]

In particular: unlimited global State guarantees for public banks. The 19–009 Commission also regards as state aid in the form of a guarantee the more favourable funding terms obtained by enterprises, incl. banks, whose legal form rules out bankruptcy or other insolvency procedures or provides an explicit state guarantee or coverage of losses by the State.[59] Such general guarantees covering all business debts of the financial institutions normally have the consequence that the banks have at least the same rating as their respective state owners/guarantors and therefore a funding advantage. Such guarantees traditionally applied to certain German and Austrian banks and the French CDC.

In Germany, such general guarantees in favour of savings banks and Landesbanks were called *Anstaltslast* (institutional liability) and *Gewährträgerhaftung* ("GTH", guarantor liability). They already existed before the EEC Treaty came into force and therefore constituted existing state aid within the meaning of

---

[56] Point 4.2 Guarantee Notice.

[57] Point 15, fn.2 IAC.

[58] See for instance Commission Decision in case C 9/2008 of July 4, 2008 *SachsenLB* [2009] O.J. L104/34; Commission Decision of May 29, 2009 in case N 264/2009; *Rescue aid to HSH Nordbank AG* [2009] O.J. C179, pt 1, Commission Decision of May 7, 2009 in case N 244/2009 *Commerzbank* [2009] O.J. C147, pt 4; Commission Decision of February 26, 2010 on state aid C–9/09 (ex NN 49/08, NN 50/08 and NN 45/08) implemented by the Kingdom of Belgium, the French Republic and the Grand Duchy of Luxembourg for *Dexia SA* [2010] O.J. L274/54, pt 145.

[59] Point 1.2 Guarantee Notice.

art.108(1) TFEU, to which the so-called appropriate measures procedure applies. Within this specific procedure, the Commission and Germany concluded several understandings about how to change the legal situation. According to the first agreement dated July 17, 2001 (*"Verständigung I"*), *"Anstaltslast"* and *"Gewährträgerhaftung"* had to be abolished within a transitional period lasting until July 18, 2005. However, within this transitional period new liabilities could still be covered by *Gewährträgerhaftung* provided their maturity would not go beyond December 31, 2015 (so-called grandfathering).[60] *Verständigung I* had an unintentional side effect. In view of the higher funding costs, which would arise without the state guarantee, some Landesbanks took on a large amount of cheap liquidity, mostly in the form of ten year term bonds issued until July 18, 2005. They then had to invest the liquidity quickly. Part of it obviously found its way to the US subprime market and other poisonous assets, later causing the Landesbanks' need for financial support during the financial crisis.

In Austria, public regional mortgage banks ("Landeshypothekenbanks") and saving banks used to benefit from the so-called *Ausfallhaftung*, very similar to the German *Gewährtragerhaftung*. In the event of liquidation or insolvency of the bank, the guarantor, i.e. Austria and its regional or local authorities, had the obligation to meet all the liabilities of the bank which could not be satisfied from its assets. Since the Ausfallhaftung already existed prior to Austria's accession to the European Union, it was—as the German Gewährträgerhaftung—considered existing aid. In 2003, an agreement was reached between the Commission and Austria, according to which the Ausfallhaftung would be phased out progressively. The phase-out schedule provided for a transitional period, which lasted until April 1, 2007. During this period, the existing guarantees were allowed to remain in place for operations, which mature before September 30, 2017. After April 1, 2007, no new instruments covered by the Ausfallhaftung were to be initiated. However, the guarantees will be "grandfathered" for all liabilities existing at April 2, 2003 until they mature. All liabilities entered into during the transitional period until April 1, 2007 are covered by the guarantees if they mature before September 30, 2017. For those maturing after September 30, 2017, the guarantees will not be maintained.[61]

In France, State support is often provided through Caisse des Dépôts et Consignations ("CDC"). CDC was founded by the law of April 28, 1816, and is based on art.L518–2 of the French Finance Code. The French Parliament exercises control over its activities and guarantees its autonomy through the Supervisory Board.[62] The role of the Supervisory Board is to monitor CDC's major and

---

[60] See E 10/2000 for details [2002] O.J. C146, p.6 and [2002] O.J. C150, p.7) and *http://ec.europa.eu/comm/competition/state_aid/register/ii/by_case_nr_e2000_0000.html#10*. [Accessed: November 15, 2011].

[61] Commission Decision C(2003) 1329 final [2003] O.J. C175.

[62] The board has thirteen members: three deputies, three qualified figures, including two nominated by the President of the Chamber of deputies and one by the President of the Senate; a representative from the Highest Administrative Court; two representatives from the Court of State Auditors; the governor of the Bank of France; the Treasury and Economic Policy general manager.

strategic decisions, shareholding initiatives, savings fund management and audit accounts. The imputability of CDC decisions to the State has been confirmed by the ECJ in the Air France judgement in 1996.[63] In a 2003 decision, the Commission stated that CDC's commercial activities must be distinguishable from its public services (such as granting state aid, this is comparable to Verständigung II with respect to German Landesbanks[64]) and that CDC may not grant unlimited guarantees to its commercial funds.[65] France agreed to abolish the general guarantee CDC had given to its commercial subsidiary IXIS by January 24, 2007 at the latest. In that context, the Commission established that CDC's measures were imputable to the State within the meaning of the *Stardust Marine* judgment.[65a] CDC was considered to be a public bank sui generis operating and funded through State resources. Important strategic and business actions of CDC were under the control of the State whose representatives made up the highest management body. For these reasons amongst others, the Commission concluded that CDC could not act without taking account of the requirements of the public authorities and it was extremely unlikely that such a decision could be taken without its knowledge. Therefore, despite CDC's special autonomy, the Commission takes the view that its measures are imputable to the State.[66] This has been confirmed in the recent *Dexia* decision, where the Commission took the view that imputability can be established at least in such cases where CDC's measures occur concomitantly with other measures taken by the State.[67]

In addition, it is not possible to take the potential exposure of the State under the unlimited state guarantees into account when assessing whether a support measure by the public shareholders may be in line with the private investor test: while the Commission recognises that state support might exceptionally be accepted by a market economy investor if the liquidation costs for the seller would be higher, for the calculation of the liquidation cost only those liabilities can be considered which would have been entered into by a market economy investor. This shall exclude liabilities stemming from state aid (such as the

---

[63] Case T–358/94 *Air France v Commission* [1996] E.C.R. II–2109, paras 58ff.: "58 The Caisse was established by the Finance Law of 1816 as an 'etablissement spécial' placed 'under the supervision and guarantee of the legislature'. Its tasks—including in particular the administration of public and private funds composed of compulsory deposits—are governed by statutory and regulatory rules and its Director-General is appointed by the President of the Republic, the appointment of its other directors being a matter for the government. 59 Those factors are sufficient for it to be held that the Caisse belongs to the public sector. Although it is subject only to the 'legislature', the legislative power is one of the constitutional powers of a State, and thus conduct of the legislature is necessarily imputable to the State."

[64] See below at para.19–060.

[65] State aid Case E50/2001, *France, CDC IXIS*. See also COM aid measures implemented by France for Alstom [2005] O.J. L150/24, point 116.

[65a] Case C–482/99 *France v Commission ("Stardust Marine")* [2002] E.C.R. I–4397.

[66] See Bufton [2003] CPN 2, p.26.

[67] State aid Case C–9/2009 (ex. NN 45/2008, NN 49/2008 and NN 50/2008), state aid implemented by the Kingdom of Belgium, the French Republic and the Grand Duchy of Luxembourg for Dexia SA, point 125. See also opening decision in state aid, Case C–4/10, France, Suspected aid to the company Trèves [2010] O.J. C133, p.12, points 56–59.

unlimited guarantees) as these would have not been taken over by a market economy investor.[68]

Liquidity facilities

19–010   Besides granting state guarantees, the State may also support banks directly with liquidity, for instance through framework liquidity facilities granted by subsidy banks. In order to exclude the existence of state aid, the risk margins applied in such a case must be in line with the Communication from the Commission on the revision of the method for setting the reference and discount rates ("Communication on reference and discount rates"),[69] which provides for specific high margins for companies in difficulty.[70]

Liquidity support by central banks

19–011   Under normal circumstances, central banks control money supply through the central interest rate on credit for the banking sector. Banks always need liquidity from central banks. This relates to the demand for banknotes and coins in the economy but also to the fact that banks are required to keep a certain amount of reserves in their current accounts with the central bank. The Eurosystem through its refinancing operations supplies liquidity in the form of loans to banks against collateral. These operations take place at least once a week. As banks can always deposit in ECB's standing deposit facility and, conversely, borrow (against collateral) in the marginal lending facility, interest rates on these facilities form the floor and ceiling for very short term money market interest rates. In normal times, the ECB can quite precisely steer the interest rates in the short end of the money market by offering sufficient liquidity and setting the minimum bid rate in the credit operations with its counterparties. This sets the marginal funding cost for banks. Before the Lehman collapse in September 2008, the ECB relied mostly on the structural features of this operational framework to absorb the money market shocks coming from the financial crisis in place since 2007. After the collapse, there was a need for more significant measures to safeguard the liquidity of the financial market. Inter alia, the ECB took the following measures:

- First, the Eurosystem provided unlimited central bank liquidity to Euro area banks at a fixed rate (i.e. the main refinancing rate) and against adequate collateral in all refinancing operations.

---

[68] Commission Decision of April 30, 2008 on state aid C56/06 (ex. NN 77/06) implemented by Austria for the privatisation of Bank Burgenland [2008] O.J. L239/32, point 134; Commission Decision in case C–9/2008 of July 4, 2008 *SachsenLB* [2009] O.J. L104/34, point 82; Commission Decision of September 20, 2011 on state aid SA 29338 (C–29/2009, ex. N 264/2009), granted by Germany to HSH Nordbank, Unreported, points 147–151.

[69] [2008] O.J. C14/6.

[70] Commission Decision of October 21, 2008 on state aid measure C–10/08 (ex. NN 7/08) implemented by Germany for the restructuring of IKB Deutsche Industriebank AG [2009] O.J. L278/32, points 78–81.

- Second, the list of assets eligible for use as collateral was extended.

- Third, the Eurosystem provided liquidity for longer periods, up to one year (longer-term refinancing operations (LTROs)).

- Fourth, in order to address Euro area banks' needs to fund their US dollar assets, the Eurosystem provided liquidity in this and other foreign currencies.

- Finally, in order to support the long-term refinancing operations of the financial sector, the ECB initiated a significant programme to purchase Euro-denominated covered bonds issued in the Euro area.[71]

All these measures might be considered as economic advantages for the whole financial sector (sector related selectivity within the definition of state aid in art.107(1) TFEU[72]). They do not qualify as state aid, however, because they are taken by the ECB, so that there is no transfer of state but of supranational resources.

These considerations do not automatically apply to actions taken by the national central banks ("NCB"). Already in 1988, in the Greek Export Credit Case, the ECJ pointed out that the funds of NCBs may constitute state resources whose transfer may be imputable to the State if the NCB "acted under direct State control."[73] During the financial crisis, the Commission was asked to decide on liquidity measures taken by NCBs, as Member States wished to accompany guarantees or recapitalisation schemes with complementary forms of liquidity support, with the provisions of public funds (including funds from the NCBs). The Commission differentiated between the following: **19–012**

Where a NCB reacts to a banking crisis not with selective measures in favour of individual banks, but with general measures open to all comparable market players in the market (e.g. lending to the whole market on equal terms), such general measures, for instance activities of NCBs related to monetary policy, such as open market operations and standing facilities, should not constitute state aid.[74] The reasoning in its Banking Communication does not fully disclose whether the Commission takes the view that such measures are not selective,[75] do not constitute the transfer of state resources or are at least not imputable to the State. In any case, it would probably be politically unacceptable to prohibit NCBs from taking measures which the ECB can adopt without taking state aid control

---

[71] Compare in more detail, *González-Páramo*, Member of the Executive Board of the ECB The European Central Bank and the policy of enhanced credit support, speech at the University of Málaga, Málaga, June 18, 2010, downloadable from *http://www.ecb.int/press/key/date/2010/html/sp100618_2.en.html*. [Accessed November 15, 2011].

[72] See Arhold [2011] MünchKommBeihVgR, art.107(1) TFEU, points 386–387.

[73] Case 57/86, *Greece v Commission* [1988] E.C.R. 2855, para.13.

[74] Banking Communication, point 51.

[75] They should be considered sector related selective, since they support only the financial sector.

law into account. Thus, the easing of state aid control with respect to NCBs also serves the equal treatment of States which are not members of the Eurozone.

19–013   As the Commission has established in the Northern Rock case,[76] dedicated support to a specific financial institution may also be found not to constitute state aid, but only if the following four cumulative criteria, which have been also laid down in the Banking Communication,[77] are met:

- the financial institution is **solvent** at the moment of the liquidity provision and the latter is not part of a larger aid package[78];

- the facility is **fully secured by collateral** to which haircuts are applied, in accordance with its quality and market value;

- the central bank charges a **penal interest rate** to the beneficiary;

- the measure is taken at the **central bank's own initiative**, and in particular is not backed by any counter-guarantee of the State.

These conditions shall ensure that the NCB has acted within its independent central bank task to safeguard the stability of the financial system, and not as a vehicle for the transmission of state aid because the measure either does not constitute transfer of state resources or is at least not imputable to the Member State. Only if these cumulative conditions are met will the NCB's action fall outside the scope of art.107(1) TFEU. The Commission applied these criteria, for instance, in its decision concerning the liquidity assistance granted to Fortis Bank by the Belgian National Bank ("BNB") in September 2008 in the scope of Fortis Bank's rescue through sale to Belgium, the Netherlands and Luxemburg. During the state aid investigation, Belgium argued that the measure did not constitute state aid, since it was provided at the discretion of BNB, acting in the context of its ordinary monetary remit.[79] The Commission denied this by observing that the liquidity assistance was part of a larger aid package[80] and that the credits granted

---

[76] Commission Decision of December 5, 2007, state aid NN 70/2007 (ex. CP 269/07, United Kingdom, Rescue aid to Northern Rock [2008] O.J. C43/1, paras 32–33.

[77] Banking Communication, point 51.

[78] As the ECB has repeatedly stressed, the provision of emergency liquidity assistance is a central bank function, which consists in giving support in exceptional circumstances and on a case-by-case basis to temporarily illiquid but solvent credit institutions. However, supporting insolvent financial institutions is incompatible with the monetary financing prohibition as laid down in art.123 TFEU. Any national central bank measure has to respect art.123 TFEU and the EU state aid rules. While for the latter, the European Commission is responsible, the ECB controls compliance with the monetary financing prohibition. The monetary financing prohibition, as defined in art.101 of the Treaty, is essential to ensure that the primary objective of monetary policy, namely to maintain price stability, is not impeded. For more details on art.123 TFEU, see for instance the ECB's Convergence Report May 2006, p.68; the Convergence Report December 2006, p.30; the Convergence Report May 2007, p.22 and the Convergence Report May 2008, p.24, all of which are available on the ECB's website.

[79] Decision of December 3, 2008 in state aid NN 42/2008, Belgium, NN 46/2008, Luxembourg NN 53/A/2008, Netherlands Restructuring aid to Fortis Bank and Fortis Bank Luxembourg, point 26.

[80] Above Decision, point 44.

by BNB were backed by a guarantee from the Belgian State (with retroactive effect),[81] so that at least two of the above-mentioned criteria were not met. In addition, BNB accepted sureties which were ineligible in respect of monetary policy operations.[82]

Support by Deposit Guarantee Funds

Since the first important case in the banking sector, Banco Español de Crédito SA (Banesto)[83] in 1994, it has been accepted that under certain circumstances, support measures by deposit guarantee funds, even if organised in public legal form, are not to be considered state aid. Banesto was one of the largest Spanish banks when it encountered serious difficulties in the early nineties. The Spanish central bank decided to intervene with an emergency plan to rescue and restructure the bank. The state-owned Fondo de Garantía de Depósitos (Deposit Guarantee Fund, FGD), in which private banks participated freely, unanimously approved the plan that included: (i) making up for losses by application of all the reserves and share premiums, and reduction of the bank's capital; (ii) a capital increase by the fund in the amount of Ptas 180 billion; (iii) the purchase and immediate resale to Banesto of impaired assets by the fund, with a loss of around Ptas 285 billion at their nominal value; as well as (iv) an interest-subsidy loan provided by the fund for an amount of Ptas 315 billion over four years, carrying an estimated cost for the fund of Ptas 41 billion for foregone interest. In addition, Banesto's president and management board were to be replaced. The FGD recovered parts of its costs by selling its stake in Banesto to Banco de Santander by means of a public tender. The Commission considered the measures not to be state aid in terms of art.107(1) TFEU, given:

19–014

- that private banks participate freely in the FGD;

- private banks' majority contribution to the FGD's resources;

- their unreserved participation in the Banesto restructuring plan;

- the one-shot solution of the support;

- the rapid return of Banesto to the private market; and

---

[81] Above Decision, point 45. The State's counter guarantee was also the decisive reason why the Commission considered the BNB's liquidity assistance in favour of Dexia to be state aid; see Commission Decision of February 26, 2010 on state aid C 9/09 (ex. NN 49/08, NN 50/08 and NN 45/08) implemented by the Kingdom of Belgium, the French Republic and the Grand Duchy of Luxembourg for Dexia SA [2010] O.J. L274/54, point 134.

[82] Above Decision, point 46.

[83] See Press Release from December 15, 1994, "Commission approves Banesto's rescue", IP/94/1226, available at: *http://europa.eu/rapid/pressReleasesAction.do?reference=IP/94/1226&format=HTML&aged=1&language=EN&guiLanguage=en.* [Accessed November 15, 2011]. The decision has never been published. Actions against it by a minority shareholder have been dismissed as inadmissible, see Case T–41/01 *Rafael Pérez Escolar v Commission* [2003] E.C.R. II–2157. Confirmed by ECJ in Case C–379/03 P, see [2005] O.J. C19/10.

- the particular responsibilities of the National Supervision and Monetary authorities, here represented by the Central Bank, for the stability of the financial market.

19–015   Even though the publicly available reasoning of the Commission's decision is a cryptic conglomeration, it seems that the contribution by FGD was probably considered state aid free mainly because the fund was financed voluntarily by the banks (private and public) and thus did not qualify as state resources.[84] However, since the entry into force of European Parliament and Council Directive 94/19/EC on deposit guarantee schemes,[85] no bank may accept deposits unless it is a member of an officially recognised deposit guarantee scheme. The aim of this directive is to reinforce the stability of the banking system and the protection of depositors in a Union context from which all restrictions on freedom of establishment and freedom to provide services have been removed. The Directive does not specify how the systems are to be set up and organised, but fixes a minimum threshold of €100,000 to cover unavailability of deposits and establishes the principle that the systems must have the necessary means to that end, chiefly through recourse to the contributions of their associate members. Nor does the Directive specify how the systems could or should come into play. It can thus not be ruled out that a guarantee system could opt for solutions other than the refunding of depositors, provided they meet the aims of the directive. In particular, it is possible that a system may come into operation by granting resources that allow a bank to remain in business although its position would normally trigger the procedure for the refunding of depositors. Because of the combination of the two factors, i.e. the compulsory nature of the contributions and the possibility of using those contributions to allow the financial survival of a bank in difficulty, it cannot be excluded that support by such deposit guarantee schemes may contain state aid. In the Banco di Sicilia case,[86] the Commission had to decide under which circumstances the support by a deposit guarantee fund financed by compulsory contributions could be considered state aid free. At stake was the contribution of ITL 1,000 billion from Fondo Interbancario di Tutela dei Depositi (FITD) to the liquidation of Sicilcassa in order to cover part of the deficit resulting from the transfer of Sicilcassa's assets and liabilities to Banco di Sicilia. The Commission developed a two-fold state aid test, in order to exclude the existence of state aid that could be involved by not directly refunding the

---

[84] See Commission Decision to open the formal investigation procedure in state aid case C–16/98 (NN 10/98), Italy, *Banco di Sicilia and Sicilcassa* [1998] O.J. C297/3, fn.3. A different view take Rossi/Sansonetti, "Survey of State aid in the lending sector—A Comprehensive Review of Main State Aid Cases", available under *http://www.side-isle.it/ocs/viewpaper.php?id=75&cf=1.* [Accessed November 15, 2011]. Section 2 lit. f, p.9: "The Commission eventually considered that the transaction did not constitute State aid because the private investor principle had been followed."

[85] O.J. L135, 31.5.1994, p.5.

[86] Final Commission Decision of November 10, 1999 conditionally approving the aid granted by Italy to the public banks Banco di Sicilia and Sicilcassa [2000] O.J. 2000 L256/21.

depositors but by backing up the transfers of the related assets to a different bank:

- taking account of the constraints imposed by the deposit guarantee schemes directive, the measures must comply with the least cost principle; and

- must not be imputable to the Member State concerned.[87]

During the preliminary investigation procedure, the Commission first thoroughly examined whether the support of the sale and transfer of the assets were actually the least costly approach. Then, it examined the FITD's legal form and composition, as well as its bylaws and voting procedures. All Italian banks were represented in FITDs. The Commission took the view that there had been no public influence on the FITD's decision after having thoroughly analysed its decision-making structure, so that the measure was not imputable to the Member State. The significance of the "least cost principle" for the purpose of the state aid assessment is not totally clear.[88]

Decisions taken during the financial crisis with respect to the Danish winding-up scheme[89] have confirmed that imputability to the state is the decisive criterion for the assessment of whether support measures of such funds constitute state aid. The Fund operating the Danish scheme was originally an ordinary Deposit Guarantee Fund set up solely to compensate depositors in case of liquidation of a bank, and intervening only once a bank was bankrupt. All Danish financial institutions were obliged to contribute to the Fund. During the financial crisis, the Danish authorities proposed to introduce a legislative amendment under which the Fund may decide to contribute to the bailing out of a failing bank, by providing to an acquiring bank funds or a guarantee on senior liabilities of a failing bank. The objective of the proposed amendment was to facilitate a marketbased solution for bailing out the failing bank by allowing for a reduction of the negative price, i.e. the difference between the inherent value of assets of a bank and its senior liabilities, to a potential acquirer (so-called "compensation scheme"). Under the compensation scheme, the Fund would thus pay a cash contribution or provide a guarantee to the acquiring bank. The mechanism of the

---

[87] Commission Decision to open the formal investigation procedure in state aid case C–16/98 (NN 10/98), Italy, *Banco di Sicilia and Sicilcassa* [1998] O.J. C297/3, point 3.1.

[88] Some take the view that the Commission has followed the absence of state aid, because the FITD had acted like a private creditor to avoid a more expensive default, since the State was the controlling shareholder and subordinated creditor of Sicilcassa; see Rossi/Sansonetti, "Survey of State aid in the lending sector—A Comprehensive Review of Main State Aid Cases", available at *http://www.side-isle.it/ocs/viewpaper.php?id=75&cf=1.* [Accessed November 15, 2011], s.2 lit. f, pp.13–14. It is, however, unlikely that the Commission could have come to a different solution if Sicilcassa had been a private bank, in which the State had no share. Nor could the Commission had come to a different decision if the FITD's approach had not complied with the least cost principle, but had never the less not been imputable to the public authorities. Point 39 of the final Commission Decision of November 10, 1999 [2000] O.J. L256/21, Italy, Banco di Sicilia and Sicilcassa seems to focus solely on the imputability criterion.

[89] Com, decision of August 1, 2008 in State aid decision SA. 33001 (2011/N)—Denmark—Part B; Amendment of the Danish Winding up Scheme for credit institutions.

"compensation scheme" would only be activated if it was less costly for the Fund to provide the needed compensation than handling the distressed bank through the winding-up scheme, where the Fund has to compensate the depositors. Under the compensation scheme, all depositors and simple creditors were taken over by the financial institution (acquirer) subject to the payment of compensation and on condition that the resulting entity would be viable. In particular, after the takeover, the acquiring bank had to be profitable, including in the long term, and had to have the financial, managerial and other capacities to take over the distressed bank in order to create a possibly lasting solution to the distressed bank's situation. The Fund could intervene only if the intervention through the "compensation scheme" was the least costly option, i.e. even less costly than a controlled winding-up of the failing bank. The decision to intervene is taken by a measurement committee nominated by the Minister for Economic and Business Affairs and evaluates the cost of the various options for the Fund (compensation of depositors in case of winding-up as against provision of funds or guarantees to an acquiring bank).

The Commission accepted that for advantages to be capable of being categorised as aid within the meaning of art.107(1) TFEU, they must, first, be granted directly or indirectly through State resources and, second, be imputable to the State.[90] Both conditions were considered to be met:

- State resources are involved where funds come from contributions made compulsory by State legislation and are managed and apportioned in accordance with that legislation, even if they are administered by institutions separate from the State.[91] This was the case here, since all Danish financial institutions were obliged to contribute to the Fund based on national legislation.

- Even though Denmark submitted that the Fund's decision is taken independently of the State and that the Fund is a private independent institution, the Commission took the view that the decisions taken by the Fund under the compensation scheme were also imputable to the State. In application of the criteria laid down by the ECJ in the Stardust Marine judgement.[92] the Commission observed that several elements indicated that the intervention in a distressed bank under the compensation scheme is managed and monitored by the Danish authorities, in particular[93]:

  - The decision of the Fund to provide compensation to an acquiring bank in the form of funds or guarantees is guided very precisely by the legislation, describing in detail the conditions under which the Fund may

---

[90] See Case C–345/02 *Pearle and others* [2004] E.C.R. I–7139, at paras 34 and 35 and the judgments referred to therein.
[91] See Case 173/73 *Italy v Commission* [1974] E.C.R. 709, at para.16.
[92] Case C-482/99 *France v Commission* ("Stardust Marine") [2002] E.C.R. I–4397, at para.55.
[93] Com, decision of August 1, 2008 in State aid decision SA. 33001 (2011/N)—Denmark—Part B; Amendment of the Danish Winding up Scheme for credit institutions, points 44–49.

decide to contribute to bailing out a distressed bank (for instance only if the intervention is the least costly option).
– The measurement committee, which evaluates the cost of the various options for the Fund (compensation of depositors in case of winding-up as against provision of funds or guarantees to an acquiring bank), and which assesses whether the acquiring bank will also be able to handle the distressed bank in the long-term and whether the solution is viable from a business perspective, is nominated by the Minister for Economic and Business Affairs. It is on the basis of the assessment and recommendation from the measurement committee that the Fund then decides to intervene or not.
– The Board of Directors of the Fund is appointed by the Minister for Economic and Business Affairs, and the agreement between the acquiring bank and the Fund regarding the provision of compensation (whether in the form of funds or guarantees) is conditional on the permission of the Minister for Economic and Business Affairs.
– In addition, the FSC, set up by the Danish authorities to organise the winding-up of failing banks, will execute the Fund's decision to provide compensation to an acquiring bank.

Even though on the basis of the information provided by Denmark on the sales process, the price to be achieved for the sale under the compensation scheme was the maximum possible market price, and therefore there would be no advantage to the acquirer of the failing bank,[94] state aid was involved, since the compensation paid by the Fund constitutes an advantage to the economic activity of the failing bank,[95] since it could continue to exist on the market thanks to the Fund's support.[96] With respect to the MOET, the Commission considered that the conduct of the Fund could not be compared to the conduct of a market economy operator trying to minimise its losses by investing in a company whose failure might generate those losses. In particular, the Fund acts in the context of obligations imposed on it by the State, namely that of compensating depositors. A market economy operator would never have such an obligation in case of a wind-down of a failing bank. The obligation of the Fund to compensate depositors in case of a wind-down of a failing bank is an obligation which the State bears as a public authority, pursuant to an EU Directive. The obligation to compensate depositors in no way derives from an earlier market transaction into which the State entered. The cost for the State and the Fund resulting from the bankruptcy of a financial institution cannot therefore be taken into consideration

---

[94] Com, decision of August 1, 2011 in State aid decision SA. 33001 (2011/N)—Denmark—Part B; Amendment of the Danish Winding up Scheme for credit institutions, point 53.
[95] Com, decision of August 1, 2011 in State aid decision SA. 33001 (2011/N)—Denmark—Part B; Amendment of the Danish Winding up Scheme for credit institutions, point 54.
[96] In the sales transaction, the economic activity is continued and not dissolved, since the assets and liabilities of the failing bank remain as a whole and are not likely to be fully and immediately integrated into the structure of the respective buyer.

for the purpose of applying the market economy creditor test. Hence, the Commission concluded that in the event of bankruptcy of a financial institution the State would not bear costs as a market operator. Accordingly, compensating the buyer of (part of) a distressed institution cannot trigger the market economy investor test, since bankruptcy would not result in any cost for the State as a market operator.[97] As the Commission also found the other constituent elements to be fulfilled, it concluded that the scheme involved State aid, but, in light of the financial crisis, approved it under art.107(3)(b) TFEU.[98]

During the financial crisis, the Commission had also to deal with an extension of the Belgian State deposit guarantee scheme to Branch 21 products of insurance companies. The protection of insurance products is not covered by Community legislation. Directive 94/19/EC does not apply. In its decision concerning Emergency aid in favour of Ethias, the Commission took the view that, despite being open to any insurance company, the extension had been subscribed to only by Ethias. The measure therefore seemed de facto to be selective in favour of Ethias. It was also considered to be imputable to the State, financed by state resources and giving an economic advantage to Ethias.[99] Later, in its decision concerning the restructuring of Ethias, the Commission changed its opinion, since according to the information provided by the Belgian authorities after the Emergency aid decision, "that scheme is open to all insurance companies established in Belgium or branches of insurance companies established in another Member State under the same conditions."[100] Therefore, the Commission considered that "the advantage conferred by the measure is not selective and therefore does not constitute State aid in the meaning of Article 107(1) TFEU."[101] The decision does not address the question whether extending the coverage of the deposit guarantee may be sector-related, selective in favour of the insurance industry.[102]

Bad banks and other asset relief measures

19–016 It is the normal duty of banks to assess the risk of the assets they acquire and to make sure they can cover any associated losses. Asset relief measures are state

---

[97] Com, decision of August 1, 2011 in State aid decision SA. 33001 (2011/N)—Denmark—Part B; Amendment of the Danish Winding up Scheme for credit institutions, point 56, with reference to Joined Cases C–278/92, C–279/92 and C–280/92 *Spain v Commission* [1994] E.C.R. I–4103, para.22, where the ECJ stated that a distinction must be drawn between the obligations which the State must assume as owner of the share capital of a company and its obligations as a public authority, and therefore costs arising from the obligations of the State as a public authority, including the aid for restructuring, must not be taken into consideration for the purpose of applying the Private Investor Test.

[98] Confirmed, for instance in decision of October 7, 2011 in State aid Case No. SA 33639 (2011/N)—Denmark Rescue Aid for Max Bank, points 37–43.

[99] Commission Decision of February 12, 2009 in state aid Case NN 57/2008, Belgium, Emergency aid for Ethias [2009] O.J. C176/1, point 49.

[100] Commission Decision of May 20, 2010 in state aid Case N 256/2009 Restructuring aid to Ethias, Belgium [2010] O.J. C252/5, point 98.

[101] Commission Decision of May 20, 2010 in state aid Case N 256/2009 Restructuring aid to Ethias, Belgium [2010] O.J. C252/5, point 99.

[102] See with respect to de facto selectivity for certain industrial sectors ECJ C–126/01 [2003] O.J. I–13769, para.38, GEMO; see also MünchKommBeihVgR/Arhold art.107(1) TFEU, points 388–392.

aid in as much as they free the beneficiary bank from (or compensate for) the need to register either a loss or a reserve for a possible loss on its impaired assets and/or free regulatory capital for other uses.[103] This would notably be the case where impaired assets are purchased or insured at a value above the market price, or where the price of the guarantee does not compensate the State for its possible maximum liability under the guarantee. In its IAC, the Commission has observed that under the circumstances of the financial crisis, there was no asset relief measure available on the market, so that measures taken by the State were normally to be considered state aid.[104] Asset relief measures may help safeguard the stability of individual banks and whole financial sectors. In principle, two broad approaches to managing assets subject to relief measures can be considered:

- the segregation of impaired assets from good assets within a bank or in the banking sector as a whole:

  - An asset management company (bad bank or risk shield) for each bank, whereby the impaired assets are transferred to a separate legal entity, with the assets still being managed by the ailing bank or a separate entity[105] and possible losses shared between the good bank and the State.
  - Alternatively, the State could establish an independent/autonomous institution (often called an "aggregator bank") to purchase the impaired assets of either an individual bank or of the banking sector as a whole.[106] This approach could also involve prior nationalisation;

- an asset insurance scheme whereby banks retain impaired assets on their balance sheets but are indemnified against losses by the State.[107]

Tax incentives for market restructuring

Not all Member States were prepared for the liberalisation of the European financial markets sector in the early 1990s. The incumbent public banks in Italy

19–017

---

[103] Communication from the Commission on the treatment of impaired assets in the Community banking sector [JAC] [2009] O.J. C72/1, point 15.

[104] Point 15, fn.2 IAC. For the calculation of the state aid amount see further below under point 5.4.4.

[105] Such separate vehicle was set up in the cases of West LB, Crédit Lyonnais, and Banco di Napoli and SachsenLB (see point 4 below).

[106] This approach has been followed in the restructuring of the Czech banking sector in the late 1990s, early 2000, where the Czech consolidation bank Konsolidační banka ("KOB") acquired bad assets from various Czech banks, at the beginning (191 onwards) mostly related to bad loans from trading within the former Soviet bloc. In September 2001, the KOB turned into an agency ("CKA") that also had to absorb other impaired assets, in particular privatisation and other nonperforming loans. Public impaired corporations were also set up in Sweden to manage the non-performing loans of financial institutions as part of the resolution policy for the financial crisis in 1992/1993.

[107] An insurance model was chosen in case of Commission Decision of September 20, 2011 on state aid SA 29338 (C–29/2009, ex. N 264/2009), granted by Germany to HSH Nordbank, Unreported.

and France soon came into a state of financial crisis and some of them had to be supported by rescue and restructuring state aids.[108] Besides this individual aid, Italy also took general measures in order to make its banks fit for the liberalised market. By Law No.218 of July 30, 1990 containing provisions on the privatisation, capital restructuring and consolidation of credit institutions governed by public law (so called "Legge Amato"), Italy undertook a reform of the banking system. That law made it possible to convert credit institutions governed by public law into public limited companies. To that end, a public bank was authorised to hand over the banking institution to a public limited company, so as to separate the transferring legal entity, known in practice as "the banking foundation", which owned the shareholdings, from the assignee public limited company, which was the sole proprietor of the banking business. The banking foundations were non-profit institutions created to temporarily control the newly privatised banks.[109] Law No.461 of December 23, 1998 (so called "Legge Ciampi") empowered the Italian government to introduce specific tax rules to favour restructuring of the national banking system by way of consolidation. These were introduced in 1999 by legislative decrees, which introduced, in particular, a tax advantage in the form of a reduction from 37 to 12.5 per cent of the rate of income tax for banks which merge or engage in similar restructuring, for five consecutive tax years, provided that the profits are placed in a special reserve which may not be distributed for a period of three years. The tax advantages were aimed at strengthening the corporate dimension of the newly privatised banks, in order to ensure "that the achievement of monetary union did not in fact result in the erosion of the Italian banking system to the benefit of the most solid European banks owing to the fact that the Italian banking system was significantly behind in relation to its European competitors".[110] Following a Parliamentary question, the Commission assessed the scheme and decided that the tax advantages constituted incompatible state aid. The fact that the banking sector in Italy was in need of restructuring could not justify the grant of state aid.[111] The ECJ upheld the Commission's decision by confirming in particular that the tax reduction was selective, because it applied solely to the banking sector (sector-related selectivity). It did not benefit undertakings in any other

---

[108] For more details see further at para.24–004.
[109] Implementation of the "Amato Law" in 1990 (separation of banking operations and social mandate) resulted in the public sector banks being split into public limited companies (banks) and private-law foundations for the social security activities, which, however, owned the banks. The State's influence remained intact for the time being. It was not until the "Ciampi Law" of 1998 that the groundwork was laid for material privatisation. Following numerous mergers and acquisitions across all institutional groups, the shareholdings of the foundations were reduced to less than 50%. Nevertheless, owing to formal and informal agreements between the owners, the influence of the public sector has remained—albeit to a lesser degree (e.g. via shareholder agreements among foundations, major investors etc.). Later, consolidation in the banking sector led to the formation of fewer universal banks (banking groups), see *Polster*, Deutsche Bank research, EU Monitor Financial Market Special, November 25, 2004, p.1.
[110] Case C–148/04 *Unicredito Italiano SpA* [2005] E.C.R. I–11137, para.61.
[111] Commission Decision 2002/581/EC of December 11, 2001 on the tax measures for banks and banking foundations implemented by Italy [2002] O.J. L184/27.

economic sectors.[112] In addition, within the banking sector it benefitted only undertakings which merged or restructured, and was therefore also selective within the banking sector itself.[113] The ECJ further confirmed that the tax reduction was not justified by the nature and overall structure of the tax system in question, since it was not an adaptation of the general tax scheme to the particular characteristics of banking undertakings. Rather, it was "put forward expressly by the national authorities as a means of improving the competitiveness of certain undertakings at a certain stage in the development of the sector."[114] Other general measures in support of the Italian banking sector have also been found incompatible.[115]

4. APPROVAL OF RESCUE AND RESTRUCTURING UNDER ARTICLE 107(3)(C) TFEU

Before the current financial crisis erupted, the European state aid rules did not **19–018** contain specific rules for rescue and restructuring state aid for financial institutions. Rather, the general Community Guidelines on rescuing and restructuring firms in economic difficulty ("R&R Guidelines"[116]) were applied. Therefore, in principle, banks were treated in the same way as undertakings from other sectors. However, even without sector-specific soft law, the Commission had already acknowledged at an early stage that state aid control in the financial sector must take into account the specific features of the banking sector and the sensitivity of financial markets.[117] In its 25th Report on competition policy from 1995,[118] the Commission clearly pointed out the peculiarities of the banking sector in comparison to other economic sectors: it bears social and statutory traits such as the protection of depositors, macroeconomic and financial concerns such as the stability of the sector and the smooth operation of the payments system, as well as political and international issues such as possible repercussions in the form of panic in other financial institutions in the same country or other countries due to

---

[112] Case C–148/04 *Unicredito Italiano SpA* [2005] E.C.R. I–11137, paras 45–46, with reference to Case C–75/97 *Belgium v Commission* [1999] E.C.R. I–3671, para.33.

[113] Case C–148/04 *Unicredito Italiano SpA* [2005] E.C.R. I–11137, paras 47–48.

[114] Case C–148/04 *Unicredito Italiano SpA* [2005] E.C.R. I–11137, para.51.

[115] See for instance Commission Decision 2003/146/EC of August 22, 2002 on the tax measures for banking foundations implemented by Italy [2003] O.J. L55/56. For further details see See Rossi/ Sansonetti, "Survey of State aid in the lending sector—A Comprehensive Review of Main State Aid Cases", available at *http://www.side-isle.it/ocs/viewpaper.php?id=75&cf=1*. [Accessed November 15, 2011], s.2 lit. f, p.32 ff.

[116] The first Community Guidelines on Rescue and Restructuring state aid date back to 1994, "R&R Guidelines (1994)" [1994] O.J. 1994 C368/12. The next version was the "R&R Guidelines (1999)" [1999] O.J. C288/2; the last version was published in [2004] O.J. C244/2, the "R&R Guidelines (2004)".

[117] See for instance Commission Decision of July 26, 1995 giving conditional approval to the aid granted by France to the bank Crédit Lyonnais [1995] O.J. L308/92, s.3.1, point 1.

[118] XXV Report on Competition Policy (1995), COM (96) 126 final.

the considerable interdependence existing in this sector, particularly in the case of the failure of a major institution.[119]

However, before the financial crisis, state aid to banks in economic difficulty could, in principle, only be approved under the sector neutral R&R Guidelines. The Commission assessed a series of rescue and restructuring cases on this basis, all of which were approved. In return for the approval, the Commission usually required substantial restructuring of the banks, including divestment of branches and business activities and, in the case of public banks, the banks' privatisation.

Under the R&R Guidelines, in general, rescue aid can be granted to support a bank in difficulties under the condition that:

> it is temporary (not more than six months), it takes the form of loan guarantees or loans and the interest rate for the loan is at least comparable to those used for loans to healthy firms—such as the reference rates adopted by the Commission.[120]

Concerning the second condition, the experience with the first French and Italian rescue measures in the 1990s banking sector as described below apparently led the Commission to introduce an exemption in the (1999) R&R Guidelines. According to this exemption rescue aid for banks could be granted in a form other than loan guarantees or loans, such as capital injections or subordinated loans, which would enable the beneficiary bank to temporarily continue carrying on its banking business in accordance with the legislation on solvency ratios for credit institutions. This state aid then had to be taken into account for the assessment of the restructuring plan and the necessary compensatory measures.[121] In 2004, this exemption was narrowed: the rescue aid must not be a structural financial measure related to the bank's own funds. While the exemption still provides more leeway for banks than for companies from other sectors, it appears to set stricter conditions for rescue aid than the R&R Guidelines (1999), since capital injections appear not to be allowed anymore.[122] Under certain circumstances, risk shields can be considered as a temporary lending of necessary capital to back up mark-to-market losses related to certain investment portfolios, and thus enabling the bank concerned to continue its business in accordance with the prudential legislation in force.[123] Such risk shields have a structural element as they go beyond the mere provision of liquidity. If they are structured in a way that means they can in principle be abolished after a period of six months, i.e. designed in a reversible manner, these risk shields seem to be

---

[119] XXV Report on Competition Policy (1995), COM (96) 126 final, point 197.
[120] Point 25(a) R&R Guidelines (2004).
[121] Point 23, fn.17 R&R Guidelines (1999).
[122] Point 25(a), fn.3 R&R Guidelines (2004). Commission Decision of April 30, 2008 in state aid Case NN 25/2008 (ex. CP 15/08) *WestLB riskshield*, Germany, point 46. See also state aid NN 70/2007 (ex. CP 269/07), United Kingdom, *Rescue aid to Northern Rock*, point 43.
[123] Commission Decision of April 30, 2008 in state aid Case NN 25/2008 (ex. CP 15/08) *WestLB riskshield*, Germany, point 47.

the least structural measure possible in order to settle regulatory problems of a bank in economic difficulties in line with the banking legislation[124] in cases where the only alternative would be a capital injection or similar measures qualifying as Tier 1 capital.

Restructuring aid can be granted only if: **19–019**

- the aid is granted in the context of a coherent and realistic restructuring plan enabling the bank to return to full viability within a reasonable period;

- it does not exceed what is strictly necessary; and

- if undue distortion of competition due to the aid is avoided by appropriate compensatory measures from the aid beneficiary.

- Furthermore, the measure has to comply with the one time-last time principle.

In the 1990s, the Commission applied these principles to rescue and restructuring aid in favour of a couple of French and Italian public banks that got into economic difficulties shortly after the liberalisation of the European financial market. The first and groundbreaking case concerned the French group Crédit Lyonnais ("CL").[125] At the end of 1993, CL was the leading European banking group in terms of total assets. The bank's main shareholder was the French government. When the French real estate market collapsed in the first half of the 1990s, CL recorded heavy losses (all in all FRF 8.7 billion in 1992 and 1993). In order to prevent the bank's solvency ratio from falling below the 8 per cent minimum required by EU legislation, the French Government decided to perform a capital increase of nearly FRF 5 billion, and took over 44 per cent of the bank's impaired assets. The latter was carried out by a hiving-off operation: out of a total of outstanding loans of more than FRF 100 billion in the real estate sector, FRF 42 billion of doubtful claims insufficiently backed by provisions were transferred to an ad hoc company specifically set up for this purpose (called "OIG"). Despite this intervention, CL recorded further losses in 1995. The French Government therefore initiated a new rescue mechanism by creating another special hive-off vehicle, called Consortium de Réalisations (CDR), which was to take over almost FRF 190 billion of the bank's assets, including the non-performing or questionable assets covered by the first rescue measure.[126] In order to finance the purchase of the assets, CDR received a participating loan of FRF 135 billion (corresponding to the net value of the hived-off assets) from SPBI (Société de

---

[124] Cf. Commission Decision of April 30, 2008 in state aid Case NN 25/2008 (ex. CP 15/08) *WestLB riskshield*, Germany, point 49, Commission Decision of December 5, 2007 in case NN 70/2007, *Rescue aid to Northern Rock* [2008] O.J. C43/1, point 46.

[125] Commission Decision of July 26, 1995 giving conditional approval to the aid granted by France to the bank Crédit Lyonnais (*Crédit Lyonnais I*), [1995] O.J. L308/92.

[126] As concerns the legal structure, CDR was a wholly owned, non-consolidated subsidiary of Crédit Lyonnais.

Participation Banque-Industrie, later transformed into EPFR[127]), a holding company specifically set up for the financing of the hiving-off and controlled by the main shareholders in CL (i.e. the Government, Thomson-CSF and CDC). The arrangement also provided the possibility of increasing the loan by an additional tranche of FRF 10 billion.[128] This operation limited the bank's accounting loss for 1994 to FRF 12.1 billion. As a quid pro quo for the participation loan, EPFR would receive income from a " better fortunes clause" in respect of CL.[129]

19–020   The restructuring plan submitted by the French authorities in 1995 contained a number of measures concerning strategy redefinition, the sale of subsidiaries, cost reduction and risk management and control. According to the plan, CL would be able to generate a profit from 1995 on and by the end of 1999 would have recorded a return on its equity of 12.4 per cent. Due to the better fortunes clause, it would also contribute to the cost of the hive-off operation until 1999. In July 1995 the Commission conditionally approved the financial transactions described above on the basis of the R&R Guidelines (1994), according to which it set a number of strict conditions,[129a] inter alia:

- reduction of the bank's commercial presence outside France by 35 per cent in balance sheet terms until the end of 1998;

- clear division between CL and the CDR regarding their managers, their administration and the system of controlling and supervising the management of the hiving-off vehicle;

- prohibition on repurchasing the hived-off industrial and commercial assets for a price lower than the price at which the assets were initially transferred to the CDR;

- introduction of the EPFR loan allowing for the setting up of the zero-coupon bond[129b];

---

[127] At the end of 1995, SPBI was transformed into a public administrative institution, the "Etablissement Public de Financement et de Restructuration" (EPFR), which enabled it to qualify for an unlimited state guarantee in respect of all the risks and costs associated with the commitments transferred to CDR, including carrying costs.

[128] To provide SPBI/EPFR (see preceding footnote) with the necessary funds, Crédit Lyonnais would grant it a non-participating loan up to a maximum of FRF 145 billion. With this, EPFR was to grant the participating loan of FRF 135 billion to CDR and, over and beyond, buy long-term zero-coupon bonds amounting to FRF 10 billion. The bond transaction was intended to enable EPFR to earn an income which would allow it to absorb the balance of the losses the CDR would record between 1995 and 2014 (the maturity date for both of the loans). The annual rate of interest applicable was initially fixed at 7% in 1995 and at 85% of the money market rate (MMR) from 1996. The participating loan granted to CDR was to be partly amortised at the end of each financial year.

[129] This included (i) a contribution of 34% of Crédit Lyonnais' net consolidated result, (ii) group share (prior to the entry in the accounts of the contribution and the appropriation from the financial year to the fund for general banking risks and prior to French corporation tax) plus (iii) 26% of the fraction of that result exceeding 4% of the consolidated capital and reserves.

[129a] Commission Decision, *Crédit Lyonnais I*, s.7.1.

[129b] See fn.128 for further details.

- obligation to use the proceeds of sales for restructuring purposes;
- full implementation of the restructuring plan submitted to the Commission.

Moreover, it was provided that the EPFR would receive not only the proceeds of the privatisation of CL but also a substantial share of the bank's profits (in accordance with the better fortunes clause). Despite the State's intervention in both 1994 and 1995, CL's financial situation continued to deteriorate. Only one year after the first rescue measures, the French authorities decided to set up a third refinancing package, submitting to the Commission a plan to grant a rescue aid in form of a capital increase of nearly FRF 4 billion and other additional state aid measures. On September 25, 1996, the Commission decided to approve the rescue aid and to initiate the formal investigation procedure concerning these restructuring aid elements which it approved under the R&R Guidelines (1994), although the exact amount of aid granted could not be established.[129c] A far-reaching divestment program would ensure that the bank would assume a substantial proportion of the financing of the restructuring plan. Main compensatory measures were:

- the obligation to privatise CL by October 1998 at the latest;
- CL's obligation to distribute 58 per cent of its net profits as dividends up to and including 2003;
- the limitation of the bank's annual growth to 3.2 per cent per annum in the three years to come;
- the maintenance of its solvency ratio at the 2001 level until at least 2014;
- the implementation of a far-reaching program of sales and closures reducing CL's commercial presence (i.e. a balance sheet reduction by one third compared to the end of 1994, further closures and sales of assets worth FRF 310 billion, and the reduction of its French domestic network from 2,200 branches to 1,850 until the year 2000).

In parallel, the French authorities tried to further support CL in rather sophisticated ways, for instance by the recapitalisation of Société de Banque Occidentale (SDBO), a CL subsidiary, and the subsequent contribution of some of its assets to CL. The Commission considered this complex transaction (partly) as state aid granted by France to CL in the form of recapitalisation of SDBO before contributing its profitable branch to CL incompatible with the R&R Guidelines (1994), because the aid had not allowed SDBO to return to viability, and thus had to be

---

[129c] Especially due to the unclear costs of the asset relief measure, see Commission Decision of May 20, 1998 concerning aid granted by France to the Crédit Lyonnais group [notified under document number C(1998) 1454] [1998] O.J. L221/28 (as follows *Crédit Lyonnais II*), ss.7.1 and 7.2.

regarded as operating aid in favour of CL. The Commission accordingly ordered France to recover the aid of FRF 240.5 million.[129d]

19–021   Similarly to the CL case, the intervention of the French Government in favour of Crédit Foncier de France (CFF) was motivated by the sudden deterioration of the bank's solvency ratio (in this case to 0.5 per cent).[130] The French government therefore guaranteed CFF's debts and—via the Caisse des Dépôts et Consignations—increased the capital by FRF 1.85 billion. The Commission approved these state aid measures as compatible with the R&R Guidelines (1999) subject to the full implementation of the restructuring plan and the following compensatory measures and conditions:

- substantial reduction in the balance sheet (from FRF 392 billion at December 31, 1995 to FRF 296 billion at December 31, 1998, i.e. a 25 per cent reduction)[131];

- sale of international network[132];

- privatisation of CFF: the Commission considered that the privatisation ought to ensure that, in future, CFF turns to its private shareholders and to the market for any additional resources it may need.[133]

In September 1996, the Commission approved an aid measure granted by France to restructure the ailing GAN group, the fifth largest insurance company in France in terms of turnover with wide operations abroad and controlling 93 per cent of the Crédit Industriel et Commercial (CIC) banking group, the fifth largest bank in the French Association of Banks. While the banking business had been affected by the crisis of the French real estate sector, the insurance business suffered from the economic decline of its main customers, French SMEs.[134] The French Government intended to support the restructuring of the group, which included a privatisation of CIC[135] with a prior recapitalisation by public funds in the amount of FRF 2.86 billion. The Commission approved the aid subject to full implementation of the restructuring plan. In early 1997, the French authorities recognised that this aid was insufficient, as the group's financial situation had worsened and the CIC privatisation failed. They notified some FRF 20 billion of additional aid, namely a FRF 11 billion capital increase and a Government

---

[129d] Commission Decision of July 22, 1998 on aid granted by France in connection with recapitalisation and transfer of the assets of Société de Banque Occidentale [1999] O.J. L103/19.

[130] Commission Decision 2001/89/EC of June 23, 1999 conditionally approving aid granted by France to Crédit Foncier de France [2001] O.J. L34/36.

[131] Commission Decision 2001/89/EC (see fn.130 above), point 97.

[132] Commission Decision 2001/89/EC (see fn.130 above), point 98.

[133] Commission Decision 2001/89/EC (see fn.130 above), point 104.

[134] See Rossi/Sansonetti, "Survey of State aid in the lending sector—A Comprehensive Review of Main State Aid Cases", available at: *http://www.side-isle.it/ocs/viewpaper.php?id=75&cf=1*. [Accessed November 15, 2011], s.2 lit. f, p.12.

[135] The main concession/compensatory measure in return for this old decision, see Commission Decision 98/204/EC of July 30, 1997 conditionally approving aid granted by *France to the GAN group* [1998] O.J. L78/ 1, point 5.2.

commitment to cover GAN's estimated losses of FRF 9 billion (through hive-off vehicles). The Commission opened a formal investigation with regard to the new and old measures, and finally decided to approve the aid to GAN subject to several conditions, inter alia:

- reduction of GAN's international insurance operations;

- privatisation of GAN's insurance business, of its banking group CIC and of other subsidiaries.[136]

Another important French banking case concerned Société Marseillaise de **19–022** Credit (SMC),[137] a publicly owned deposit bank which mainly operated in the south of France. As of 1991 the bank had registered substantial losses which added up to over FRF 6 billion in the course of the following years. In light of the European solvency requirements, France initiated a number of capital injections. The first set of measures provided until 1996 involved capital injections of over FRF 2 billion, with respect to which the Commission opened a formal investigation procedure in September 1996. In order to cover further losses SMC had incurred in 1997 and to allow for the bank's privatisation, the French authorities initiated a second aid package involving another capital injection of nearly FRF 3 billion and a maximum guarantee of around FRF 400 million to cover any guarantees necessary in the course of SMC's privatisation. In July 1998, the Commission extended the formal investigation proceedings to these additional aid measures. At this point the privatisation of SMC had successfully been launched: in April 1998, SMC was about to be sold to a French private-sector bank and the acquirer had agreed to implement a restructuring plan. In its final decision of mid-October 1998, the Commission came to the conclusion that the aid measures were compatible with the Internal Market.[138] The restructuring plan was found to provide for sufficient compensatory measures, since SMC's balance sheet total had dropped by 16 per cent from 1992 to 1997. The following conditions had to be met[139]:

- Further limitation of SMC's business activities, including the immediate and definitive abandonment of five business divisions, the closure of its real estate loan operations and the divestment of its main international business branch, as well as the cessation of its venture capital business. These commitments would lead to a further reduction of almost FRF 3 billion in

---

[136] Commission Decision 98/204/EC of July 30, 1997 conditionally approving aid granted by *France to the GAN group* [1998] O.J. L78/1, point 5.3.

[137] Commission Decision of October 14, 1998 conditionally approving aid granted by France to Société Marseillaise de Crédit (notified under document number C(1998) 3210) [1999] O.J. L 198/1.

[138] Commission Decision of October 14, 1998 conditionally approving aid granted by France to Société Marseillaise de Crédit (notified under document number C(1998) 3210) [1999] O.J. L198/1, s.5.3.1.

[139] Above Decision s.5.3.2.

balance sheet terms, which was equal to 12.6 per cent of the 1997 balance sheet and 10 per cent of net receipts from banking in 1997.

- Reduction of retail banking business: SMC's net receipts from banking were to fall by 25 per cent in comparison with 1997. The same would apply to exposures on customer business and on securities portfolios.

- Outsourcing of specialised financial and administrative skills activities within the retail banking business, such as the safekeeping of securities or management on behalf of third parties.

For the Italian financial sector, the Commission had to decide two important banking cases in the second half of the 1990s. They concerned two former public banks, Banco di Napoli and Banco di Sicilia. Both State aid cases were approved on the basis of the R&R Guidelines. Banco di Napoli[140] was a former public monetary institution which, at that time, ranked seventh in the Italian market in terms of balance sheet total. It was active in various areas of the financial market, including merchant banking, management of trust funds, and social security insurance, with a large presence not only throughout the national territory but also abroad. Due to a first restructuring implemented via the "Legge Amato" in 1990, which had aimed at partial privatisation of the public banks, the bank's banking activities were entrusted to a joint stock company separate from the former public body. Its social security activities in turn were entrusted to a "banking foundation" which held the capital of the banking company.[141] Before the initiation of the aid measures in question, the Foundation held 48.1 per cent of the bank's equity and 71.2 per cent of its voting rights. The bank ran into financial difficulties in the mid-nineties, which virtually wiped out its assets and made it impossible for the bank to comply with the solvency ratios. The liquidity crisis was temporarily resolved by means of a loan jointly provided by the Cassa Depositi e Prestiti (the state financing division) and other banks. Three months later, the Italian Government approved a recapitalisation of ITL 2,000 billion by the Treasury, a backing of the bank's bad assets and several tax reductions totalling over ITL 17 billion. The overall net cost to the Italian State was estimated in a range from ITL 2,217 billion to 11,895 billion. The bank's restructuring included its privatisation via the sale of 60 per cent of the bank's equity, which was achieved in early 1997. In this context, provision was made for the possibility of setting up a hive-off vehicle which had the task to manage, liquidate and deconsolidate some ITL 12,400 billion of the bank's poor performing assets. The Commission approved the aid in July 1998. The absorption of the distressed credit by the State, the covering of the bank's losses conferred to the hive-off vehicle, and certain advance payments made by the Central bank were

---

[140] Commission Decision of July 29, 1998 giving conditional approval to the aid granted by Italy to Banco di Napoli (notified under document number C(1998) 2495) [1999] O.J. L116/36.
[141] See above for further details on the Legge Amato at para.19–017.

considered compatible with the Internal Market in the light of the R&R Guidelines (1994).[142] Again, the Commission set a number of conditions for its approval. It acknowledged that the measures which had already been adopted by the Italian authorities had produced a considerable reduction in the size of the bank, but given the high amount of aid, further compensatory measures had to be taken: an additional 18 branches in northern and central Italy should be sold or transferred by the end of 1998 (in addition to the sale and transfer of more than 60 branches in Italy and abroad which had already been carried out, altogether around 10 per cent of its branches). Banco di Napoli had to refrain from repurchasing any assets stemming from the liquidation of one of its subsidiaries, and the bank had to implement the restructuring plan.[143]

The Banco di Sicilia case[144] had a similar background to Banco di Napoli, **19–023** since Banco di Sicilia was also a former public credit institution which had been transformed into a joint stock company pursuant to the "Legge Amato". Its business activity extended to different areas of financial intermediation and credit business, with branches throughout Italy and a number of subsidiaries abroad. It also ran into serious financial difficulties in the mid-nineties. When it was just about to emerge from this period of crisis, Banco di Sicilia decided to acquire the assets and liabilities of Sicilcassa, a small regional bank which had been put into compulsory liquidation in September 1997. Owing to its own weak position, however, the transaction necessitated substantial financial support from the State. This involved: (i) a capital contribution of ITL 3,400 billion from the Italian Central Bank to cover the losses caused by the compulsory liquidation of Sicilcassa as part of the transfer of its business activities to Banco di Sicilia; (ii) another capital injection of ITL 1000 billion into Banco di Sicilia by Mediocredito centrale, a state-owned holding company controlling Banco di Sicilia; and (iii) the transfer to Banco di Sicilia of the stake held by the State treasury in the bank Irfis (52 per cent).[145] The Commission approved the aid granted by Italy to both banks with an estimated total of €2.4 billion (ITL 4,600 billion). The approval was given on condition that Banco di Sicilia would continue the restructuring already under way and sell or close 55 branches in Sicily before the end of 2000 (altogether around 10 per cent of its branches). The bank was prohibited from opening new branches in the region for three years. These requirements had become necessary to reduce the bank's market share in southern Italy because, following the integration of Sicilcassa, Banco di Sicilia almost doubled the number of its branches.[146] The Commission also welcomed that

---

[142] Commission Decision of October 14, 1998 conditionally approving aid granted by France to Société Marseillaise de Crédit (notified under document number C(1998) 3210) [1999] O.J. L198/1, s.5.2.

[143] Above Decision, section 5.4.

[144] Commission Decision of November 10, 1999 conditionally approving the aid granted by Italy to the public banks Banco di Sicilia and Sicilcassa (notified under document number C(1999) 3865) [2000] O.J. 2000 L256/21.

[145] Irfis Mediocredito della Sicilia SpA was a small public sector financial institution specialising in the management of regional aid for Sicilian firms.

[146] Commission Decision *Banco di Sicilia and Sicilcassa*, points 110–111.

Banco di Sicilia's parent, Mediocredito Centrale, was to be privatised by June 2000 under an open and non-discriminatory procedure and that in the future any additional financing would be obtained at market conditions.

19–024   Bankgesellschaft Berlin (BGB)[147] concerned restructuring aid granted to the leading credit institution in the Berlin area at that time. Bankgesellschaft Berlin (BGB) was mainly active in the retail banking, real estate financing and capital markets sectors. It had been founded in 1994 by bringing together several credit institutions formerly controlled by the Land Berlin. This included inter alia the Landesbank Berlin ("LBB"), which in the retail banking business traded under the two successful brands of Berliner Sparkasse and Berliner Bank, as well as the Berliner Bank AG and the BerlinHyp AG. In 2001 the group's balance sheet total was about €189 billion, and in 2002 about €175 billion. In 2001, BGB ran into serious difficulties; as a result of high-risk real estate transactions, BGB incurred heavy losses. To avoid immediate action by the German banking supervisory authorities, the Land Berlin, BGB's majority shareholder, provided a capital injection of almost €1.8 billion. The Commission provisionally approved this intervention as rescue aid in the summer of 2001, pending the submission and approval of a restructuring plan. During the following months, further risks were identified, stemming in particular from ongoing real estate transactions carried out by some of BGB's subsidiaries, so that the Land, at the end of 2001, intervened again by providing BGB with comprehensive risk guarantees ("risk shield"), covering risks up to a theoretical maximum of €21.6 billion.[148] The real risk was estimated between €2.7 billion in a best-case and €6.1 billion in a worst-case scenario. At the end of January 2002, Germany submitted a restructuring plan.

The Commission decided to initiate a formal investigation procedure,[149] inter alia because of the risks arising from a possible recovery decision in a parallel state aid procedure concerning the transfer of a public housing company's (Wohnungsbau Kreditanstalt) assets to BGB's subsidiary LBB.[150] In order to tackle that risk, the Land Berlin in the meantime had undertaken to provide BGB and the relevant subsidiary with financial support in case the Commission issued a recovery order forcing their capital ratios to fall below a certain minimum ("the Recovery Agreement").[151] This agreement was valued up to €1.8 billion. The key components of the revised restructuring plan were a substantial reduction in

---

[147] Commission Decision of February 18, 2004 on restructuring aid implemented by Germany for Bankgesellschaft Berlin AG (notified under document number C(2004) 327) [2005] O.J. L116/1.

[148] Above Decision, points 28–31.

[149] [2002] O.J. C141/11.

[150] See Commission Decision *Bankgesellschaft Berlin AG*, point 32. There have been seven cases in which assets of public housing companies had been transferred to German Landesbanks as core capital for insufficient consideration. The Commission took recovery decision with respect to all of them, see references in point 42.

[151] For further details see Commission Decision *Bankgesellschaft Berlin AG*, points 32–33. The minimum ratios were specified as follows: a total capital ratio of 9.7% and a corecapital ratio of 6%. The agreement was also subject to the suspensory condition that the Commission would approve such aid; see point 35 of the decision.

BGB group's business and a concentration on private and corporate customers in the Berlin area. Some operations, such as the capital market business and real estate financing were to be reduced, whereas others would be wound up completely.[152] Germany eventually undertook to hive off the real estate service, which was the primary cause of the crisis. Other key commitments involved the privatisation of well-performing Berliner Bank, which accounted for BGB's very large share of the Berlin retail market,[153] the sale of the Land's shares in BGB (including its other retail brand, Berliner Sparkasse) by the end of 2007, the divestment of Berlin-based Weberbank, as well as the sale or closure of other domestic and foreign branches and subsidiaries. In the context of the viability assessment, the Commission had to take account of the potential recovery risk for the group stemming from an open state aid procedure as well as of the forthcoming abolishment of the existing state guarantees (*Anstaltslast* and *Gewährträgerhaftung*),[154] both with regard to Landesbank Berlin (LBB). Owing to the comprehensive divestment commitments which had been undertaken by Germany and BGB, the Commission took the view that there had been enough measures to compensate for the distortion of competition. The divestments, closures and additional measures to slim down BGB's business volume would reduce the group's balance sheet to 65 per cent of its 2001 size by the end of the restructuring period. The Commission found the Recovery Agreement between the Land Berlin and BGB an appropriate but exceptional measure, admissible only to the extent the recovery would inevitably undermine the viability of the company. It was considered as additional restructuring aid, which created the need for additional compensatory measures to which Germany had finally committed, in particular with the divestment of Berliner Bank.[155]

In 2004, the Commission had just to take another decision on bank restructuring, this time concerning the Austrian Bank Burgenland ("BB").[156] BB is a regional mortgage bank; its business is confined largely to the territory of the Federal Province of Burgenland, which was also the main shareholder in BB holding—before the aid measures took place—50.63 per cent of BB's equity. Other important shareholders were Bank Austria (40.34 per cent) and Bausparkasse Wüstenrot (7 per cent). Under the Austrian concept of Ausfallhaftung[157] the Province of Burgenland was liable as deficiency guarantor for all the bank's liabilities. In the course of the audit of BB's annual accounts for 1999 a fraud involving the loss of some €189 million was discovered in connection with a certain credit management scheme, giving rise to a valuation adjustment of €171 million, which exceeded the Bank's core capital of €80 million and would,

19–025

---

[152] Commission Decision *Bankgesellschaft Berlin AG*, point 24.

[153] This had been a contested issue throughout the entire investigation procedure, see Graeper/ Moser, "Enforcement of State Aid control in the banking sector" Bankgesellschaft Berlin AG, EC CPN, No.2, Summer 2004, p.95.

[154] For more details on Anstaltslast and Gewährträgerhaftung, see above at para.19–009.

[155] See point 308 of Commission Decision *Bankgesellschaft Berlin AG*.

[156] Commission Decision of May 7, 2004 on state aid C–44/03 (ex. NN 158/01) which Austria is planning to implement for Bank Burgenland AG [2005] O.J. L263/8.

[157] For more details on the concept of Ausfallhaftung see above at para.19–009.

therefore, have led directly to BB's insolvency, meaning that the Province of Burgenland's Ausfallhaftung would have come into effect in the amount of €247 million. In order to avoid these consequences, the Province of Burgenland concluded a guarantee agreement for an amount of €171 million to cover BB's bad debts, which would have represented excessive balance sheet debt. The guarantee was combined with better-fortune agreements providing that the bank should use all receipts to reduce the guaranteed amounts. This better fortune clause should apply until BB was actually privatised. In parallel, Bank Austria AG sold almost all of its shares in BB at €0.07 per share to the Province of Burgenland, as a first step for the intended entire privatisation of BB.

Austria's argument that, through the guarantee agreement, the Province of Burgenland avoided greater financial loss, since otherwise it had had to pay more under the Ausfallhaftung, was rejected by the Commission, since under the MEOT[158] costs following from previous state aid measures could not be taken into account.[159] However, the Commission approved the measures in the light of the R&R Guidelines (2004) as restructuring aid. The compensatory measures required were relatively soft, taking into account BB's small size and its location in an assisted area:

- Disposal of holdings amounting to €3.5 million that were not necessary for its operations in the period from 2001 to July 2003 (reduction of its holdings by around one third).

- Closing of one of its existing 17 branches (in Parndorf) as part of its restructuring. Closure of the Parndorf branch was equivalent to a reduction in market presence of just under 6 per cent.

- Restricting its activities by desisting from granting Federal loans.[160]

Given the small size of the bank and its tiny market presence, the Commission recognised that further compensatory measures would jeopardise its viability. In addition, it observed that in past decisions on bank restructuring, it had regarded a reduction in market presence of 10 per cent as sufficient in cases where the banks concerned had pursued an expansionary business policy in the years preceding their economic difficulties.[161] In the case of smaller banks which were still much bigger than BB, the Commission did not require any reduction in the

---

[158] With respect to the Market Economy Operator Test, see more details above at paras 19–005—19–007.

[159] Decision *Bank Burgenland*, point 65.

[160] Decision *Bank Burgenland*, points 96–100. Confirmed in Commission Decision of April 30, 2008 on state aid C 56/06 (ex. NN 77/06) implemented by Austria for the privatisation of *Bank Burgenland* [2008] O.J. L239/32.

[161] Commission Decision 99/288/EC of July 29, 1998 giving conditional approval to the aid granted by Italy to Banco di Napoli [1999] O.J. L 116/36 and Commission Decision 2000/600/EC of November 10, 1999 conditionally approving the aid granted by Italy to the public banks Banco di Sicilia and Sicilcassa [2000] O.J. L256/21; see also summaries above.

branch network.[162] Therefore, the Commission did not require any additional compensatory measures.[163]

The decision concerning the first restructuring of another Austrian bank, **19–026** BAWAG-PSK,[164] in 2007 was the last elaborate banking case the Commission had to deal with before the outbreak of the financial crisis. BWAG was the fourth largest bank in Austria. As an unlisted banking and financing corporate group, active in all areas of financial services in Austria and abroad, it operated the largest centrally managed distribution network in the country (about 157 "BAWAG" and 1,300 post-office "PSK" outlets), had 1.2 million private customers and more than 60,000 business customers. Following speculative financial investments during the period 1995–2004, BAWAG lost money and was not able to close its 2005 balance sheet. Alerted by the press, depositors withdrew large amounts of money from saving accounts in spring 2006. To avoid a severe liquidity crisis, the Austrian Parliament adopted the "BAWAG P.S.K Sicherungsgesetz", a law providing for a financial guarantee worth €900 million to BAWAG-PSK. Despite BAWAG's significance for the Austrian market, the Commission still took the view that BAWAG-PSK's insolvency/bankruptcy would not have had systemic implications on the Austrian financial system, let alone on the whole Austrian economy.[165] In this context, the Commission was of the view that at least 95 per cent of the depositors' accounts would have had a deposit of less than €20,000 and would therefore have been guaranteed against BAWAG-PSK insolvency by means of the legally minimum guaranteed deposit fund. The fact that other banks could have been called upon for the purpose of securing deposits in the event of insolvency was not enough in itself to justify a finding that all operators in the Austrian banking sector would have been endangered.[166] The Commission therefore assessed the guarantee still under art.107(3)(c) TFEU and the R&R Guidelines (2004) and not yet under art.101(3)(b) TFEU. Until 2006, BAWAG-PSK was indirectly wholly owned by the Austrian federation of trade unions (Österreichischer Gewerkschaftsbund, "ÖGB"). ÖGB sold BAWAG-PSK to a consortium led by the US private equity group Cerberus Capital Management L.P. The deal was completed on May 15, 2007. In addition to the purchase price, the consortium agreed to implement a capital injection of €600 million. The Commission considered this transfer to a private investor to be a central element towards solving the difficulties of the past and enabling positive economic development for the bank, since it could be assumed that a company will more likely be sustainably viable if it is under the

---

[162] Commission Decision 1999/508/EC of October 14, 1998 conditionally approving aid granted by France to Société Marseillaise de Crédit [1999] O.J. L198/1 and Commission Decision 2001/89/EC of June 23, 1999 conditionally approving aid granted by France to Crédit Foncier de France [2001] O.J. L 34/36, see also summaries above.

[163] Decision *Bank Burgenland*, points 101–102.

[164] Commission Decision of June 27, 2007 state aid C–50/2006 (ex. NN 68/2006, CP 102/2006) implemented by Austria for BAWAG-PSK [2008] O.J. L83/7.

[165] Commission Decision of June 27, 2007 state aid C–50/2006 (ex. NN 68/2006, CP 102/2006) implemented by Austria for BAWAG-PSK [2008] O.J. L83/7, point 164.

[166] BAWAG-PSK Decision, point 166.

control of a new, private owner and that this ensures that the company will not have to rely on state aid again (sale as key aspect of the restructuring).[167] Nevertheless, in 2009 BAWAG needed additional state aid in the form of recapitalisation and asset guarantees in connection with the "structured credit book", which contained a variety of asset-backed securities (ABS). This additional state aid has been approved under art.107(3)(b) TFEU.[168]

19–027   In 2007, the first banks fell victim to the approaching financial crisis and had to be rescued, as they had aggressively invested in US sub-prime securities. This involved three German banks—the Landesbank of Saxony, Sachsen LB,[169] the Landesbank of North Rhine-Westphalia, West LB,[170] and the Deutsche Industriebank AG, IKB[171]—as well as UK bank Northern Rock.[172] These first state aid cases during the financial crisis were, at least with respect to their initial rescue measures, still assessed under art.107(3)(c) TFEU in conjunction with the R&R Guidelines (2004). In all of these early decisions, the Commission still took the view that the crisis was not of such scope as to cause a disturbance in the entire economy of a Member State, and that serious economic disruption cannot be remedied by an aid that resolves the problems of a single recipient only, as opposed to the acute problems facing all operators in the industry. The Commission was not convinced yet, that the systemic effects that might result from the bankruptcy of one of the beneficiary banks could reach a size constituting "a serious disturbance in the economy" of the Member State concerned within the meaning of art.107(3)(b) TFEU.[173] This approach was history after the fall of Lehman Brothers.

Sachsen LB was the central institution for savings banks in Saxony, based in Leipzig, with a group balance-sheet total of €67.8 billion. Because of investments in US sub-prime markets, Sachsen LB, like other European banks, ran into financial difficulties. In January 2008 Germany notified two measures in favour of Sachsen LB to the Commission: a liquidity facility of €17.1 billion granted by other Landesbanks and a guarantee by the Land of Saxony in the context of the sale of Sachsen LB to LBBW, the Landesbank of Baden-Württemberg; in the course of the sale an agreement was signed, identifying the structural investments of Sachsen LB as two portfolios. One portfolio with a nominal value of €11.8 billion was sold with it to LBBW. A second portfolio with a nominal value of €17.5 billion remained in a special investment vehicle. To this end, the Free State

---

[167] BAWAG-PSK Decision, point 175.

[168] See Commission Decision of June 30, 2010 state aid N 261/2010 (ex. PN 9/2010), Austria Second restructuring aid for BAWAG PSK [2010] O.J. C250/5.

[169] Commission Decision of June 4, 2008 state aid C 9/08 (ex. NN 8/08, CP 244/07) implemented by Germany for Sachsen LB [2009] O.J. L104/34.

[170] Commission Decision of April 30, 2008 in state aid Case NN 25/2008 (ex. CP 15/08) *WestLB riskshield*, Germany.

[171] Commission Decision of October 21, 2008 on state aid measure C–10/08 (ex. NN 7/08) implemented by Germany for the restructuring of IKB Deutsche Industriebank AG [2009] O.J. L278/32.

[172] State aid NN 70/2007 (ex. CP 269/07), United Kingdom, Rescue aid to Northern Rock.

[173] Commission Decision of April 30, 2008 in state aid case NN 25/2008 (ex. CP 15/08) *WestLB riskshield*, Germany, points 41–42.

of Saxony granted a guarantee for the amount of €2.75 billion which was to cover potential losses of the portfolio in the vehicle. The net sales price of Sachsen LB was finally fixed at €328 million. Germany claimed that the measures complied with the private investor test and therefore did not constitute state aid. As to the liquidity facility, the Commission concluded that no market economy investor would have granted such a facility to Sachsen LB, but that the measure was compatible with the Internal Market as rescue aid (liquidity support and limited to six months). The state guarantee in the context of the sale had the effect that the sales price was negative for the Land of Saxony, as the potential losses stemming from the coverage under the guarantee were higher than the proceeds from the sale. Therefore a private vendor in the position of the owners of Sachsen LB would have not sold the bank but opted for its liquidation.[174] However, the measure was approved as restructuring aid under the R&R Guidelines (2004): Sachsen LB had been sold to a new investor and contributed more than 50 per cent to the restructuring costs. As compensatory measures, a clear reduction in Sachsen LB's financial market activities had taken place, in particular by closure or divestiture of important subsidiaries.[175]

In July 2007, IKB, a German medium-sized bank, whose main shareholder **19–028** was the German public bank Kreditanstalt für Wiederaufbau (KfW), ran into difficulties due to huge portfolio investments related to US-subprime mortgages. It received state aid with a total amount of €9 billion. The measures in favour of IKB included capital injections and risk shields provided jointly by public subsidy bank KfW and three German banking associations, as well as liquidity facilities provided by KfW. In line with the restructuring plan, IKB was sold to the US investment fund Lone Star in an open, non-discriminatory and unconditional tender completed in August 2008. The Commission's approval decision was based on the R&R Guidelines (2004), accepting that the own contribution to the restructuring plan reached 50 per cent, if the proceeds from divestments implemented as compensatory measures were taken into consideration.[176] With respect to compensatory measures the Commission took into account the overall reduction in IKB's balance-sheet of 47.2 per cent and the limitation of the balance-sheet total to €33.5 billion by the end of the restructuring period, i.e. September 30, 2011, which should ensure that the closures and divestitures are not circumvented by rebuilding the business in other parts of the bank or simply transferring it.[177] Furthermore, the Commission welcomed the replacement of the

---

[174] For more information on the Private Vendor Test, see Arhold [2011] MünchKommBeihVgR, art.107(1) TFEU, points 158 and following.

[175] Commission Decision of June 4, 2008 on state aid C–9/08 (ex. NN 8/08, CP 244/07) implemented by Germany for Sachsen LB [2009] O.J. L104/34, points 122–128.

[176] Commission Decision of October 21, 2008 on state aid measure C–10/08 (ex. NN 7/08) implemented by Germany for the restructuring of IKB Deutsche Industriebank AG [2009] O.J. L278/32, point 105.

[177] Commission Decision of October 21, 2008 on state aid measure C–10/08 (ex. NN 7/08) implemented by Germany for the restructuring of IKB Deutsche Industriebank AG [2009] O.J. L278/32, points 110–111.

former top management, which sent a valuable signal against moral hazard.[178] In addition, the bank has been sold in an open and non-discriminatory manner which gave competitors an opportunity to acquire the bank. In the Commission's view, this in itself also constituted a kind of compensation for the competitive harm which the aid caused to them.[179] As the state of the financial markets deteriorated drastically after September 2008 and more and more state-backed securities were issued by competing credit institutions, IKB found it increasingly difficult to obtain in the financial markets the liquidity it needed to implement the restructuring plan. As the bank has only small deposits it relies on refinancing in the interbank and capital markets to maintain its business activities. Given the widespread malfunctioning of the interbank and capital markets at that time, it appeared impossible for the bank to obtain liquidity on acceptable terms. It therefore had to be supported twice by guarantees under the general German aid scheme Financial Market Stabilisation Fund Act (Finanzmarktstabilisierungs-fondsgesetz, "FMStFG"), once for liabilities up to €5 billion,[180] the other time for liabilities up to a volume of €7 billion.[181] Both liquidity supports have been approved under art.107(3)(b) TFEU in connection with the Banking Communication.

19–029   With respect to Northern Rock, there was an actual run on the bank when depositors started to fear that the bank was about to fail. Northern Rock Plc was the UK's 5th largest mortgage bank with a balance-sheet total of £101 billion (€150 billion) as of December 31, 2006. Northern Rock's core activity was residential mortgage lending, which represented more than 90 per cent of all outstanding loans made by the bank. In August and September 2007, a significant rationing of funds in the sterling money markets occurred and the mortgage securitisation market virtually closed down. This created severe liquidity difficulties for Northern Rock whose business model was particularly reliant on frequent short term funding in these markets. When Northern Rock was unable to meet its funding needs it requested the support of the Bank of England for emergency liquidity assistance pending a longer-term solution for its current difficulties. On September 14, 2007, the Bank of England granted emergency liquidity assistance to Northern Rock against sufficient collateral and a penal interest rate. However, the assistance did not calm the situation and news of the Bank of England's support caused a bank run. In order to stop the bank run and to avoid contagious effects leading to a wider banking crisis, the UK Treasury announced guarantee arrangements for all existing accounts in Northern Rock on September 17, 2007. Further, the UK's Treasury clarified the assumed liability guarantee backed by State resources via a publication on its website on September 20, 2007. On

---

[178] See in more detail with respect to the principle of moral hazard below at para.19–042.
[179] Commission Decision of October 21, 2008 on state aid measure C–10/08 (ex. NN 7/08) implemented by Germany for the restructuring of IKB Deutsche Industriebank AG [2009] O.J. L278/32, point 113.
[180] Commission Decision of December 22, 2008 in state aid Case, N 639/2008 on a liquidity guarantee to IKB.
[181] Commission Decision of August 17, 2009 in state aid Case N 400/2009, Germany, Liquidity guarantee for IKB.

October 9, 2007, the Treasury extended the guarantee to new retail deposits and, together with the Bank of England, modified the terms and conditions of the emergency liquidity assistance, losses from which were from that date also covered by a Treasury indemnity. In its decision, the Commission concluded that the emergency liquidity assistance provided by the Bank of England on September 14, 2007, which was secured by sufficient collateral and was interest-bearing, did not constitute state aid.[182] However the guarantee on deposits granted by the Treasury on September 17, as well as the measures granted on October 9, which provided further liquidity and guarantees to Northern Rock and were secured by a Treasury indemnity, did constitute state aid, which the Commission authorised as rescue aid in line with the R&R Guidelines (2004).[183] In line with these guidelines, the UK authorities had given a commitment to deliver a restructuring plan to the Commission by March 17, 2008. Meanwhile the Commission had acknowledged that the global financial crisis created serious disturbances in the economy of the Member States. For the United Kingdom this was confirmed in the Commission's various approvals of the measures under-taken by the United Kingdom to combat the financial crisis.[184] Therefore, the restructuring aid measures were finally approved under art.107(3)(b) TFEU.[185]

Since the end of 2007 the ongoing turmoil in the financial markets hit another **19–029a** Landesbank, WestLB, a commercial bank based in North Rhine-Westphalia, Germany's largest federal state. With total assets of €285.3 billion as at December 31, 2006, it was a major German financial services provider. Especially affected were its structured portfolio investments of about €23 billion, which included exposures to US sub-prime real estate loans. WestLB was unable to refinance the structured portfolio by selling notes on the market and the mark-to-market loss that had to be accounted for in the balance sheet was so significant that it would have pushed WestLB's capital ratios towards the required minimum level. The public owners (the State of North Rhine-Westphalia, NRW Bank, two regional savings banks associations and two municipal associations) therefore announced on February 8, 2008 the transfer of the crisis-ridden assets from WestLB to a special purpose vehicle and to provide a risk shield of €5 billion. The Commission approved the measure as rescue aid under the R&R Guidelines (2004).[186] Germany had committed to submit a restructuring plan by August 8, 2008. In the meantime the Commission has acknowledged in its first three

---

[182] For the rules applying to liquidity support by national central banks see above at para.19–011.

[183] State aid NN 70/2007 (ex. CP 269/07)—United Kingdom, Rescue aid to Northern Rock.

[184] See amongst others Commission Decisions in Case N507/2008, Financial support measures to banking sector in the UK [2008] O.J. C290/1, Commission Decision in Case N650/2008, Notification of modifications to the financial support measures to the banking industry in the UK [2009] O.J. C054/3 and Commission Decision in Case N193/2009, Extension of credit guarantee scheme (CGS) [2009] O.J. C145/3.

[185] Commission Decision of October 28, 2009 on the state aid C 14/2008 (ex. NN 1/2008) implemented by the United Kingdom for Northern Rock [2010] O.J. L112/38.

[186] Commission Decision of April 30, 2008 in state aid case NN 25/2008 (ex. CP 15/08) *WestLB riskshield*, Germany.

Banking Communications and in its approval of the German Rescue package[187] that there is a threat of serious disturbance in the German economy and that measures supporting banks are apt to remedy serious disturbance in the German economy. Therefore the legal basis for the Commission's assessment was art.107(3)(b) TFEU, under which the restructuring plan was approved subject to certain conditions.[188] One of the conditions was the privatisation of the bank. The plan was, however, never implemented, since WestLB was in need of even more state support. The formal investigation with respect to further state aid measures is still pending.[189]

19–030   Besides the typical issues laid down under the R&R Guidelines with respect to the limitation of eligible forms of rescue aid or the requirement of the 50 per cent own contribution to the restructuring, the decisions taken under the R&R Guidelines are characterised by two specific features:

- Except for Northern Rock, all the decisions concerned public banks, and in all the decisions the Commission either requested privatisation of the bank or took the intention of the Member State to that effect positively into account. There was a clear pressure on the Member States to offer privatisation as a quid pro quo. The rationale lying behind this pressure by the European Commission may be traced back to the liberalisation of the financial markets in the 90s. As described above, the liberalisation revealed the existence and necessity of financial support of the incumbent public banks, especially on the French and Italian financial markets. Member States tried to support their banks with various forms of state aid, including special taxation rules. Against this background, it is understandable that the Commission tried to connect the approval of state aid to the promise of privatisation, which should further the integration of one European financial market. Although this approach is not fully in line with the Treaty's neutrality with respect to public or private company ownership according to art.345 TFEU, under Commissioner Kroes it has been maintained even in the scope of assessments under art.107(3)(b) TFEU. As the financial crisis developed, there was less and less political acceptance of fire sales of public propriety. The approach was eventually abandoned by Commissioner Almunia in 2010.

- Under art.107(3)(c) TFEU, the Commission's main task was to make sure that competition was distorted as little as possible. It tried to reach this goal

---

[187] Commission Decision of December 12, 2008, N 625/2008 *Rettungspaket für Finanzinstitute in Deutschland* [2009] O.J. C143/1.

[188] Commission Decision of May 12, 2009 on state aid which Germany proposes to grant towards the restructuring of WestLB AG (C 43/08 (ex. N 390/08), [2009] O.J. L345/1.

[189] State aid, Germany, C–40/09 (ex. N 555/09), *Additional aid for WestLB AG related to spin-off of assets*, Invitation to submit comments pursuant to art.108(2) TFEU [2010] O.J. C66/15, and state aid, Germany, C–40/09 (ex. N 555/09), Extension of formal investigation procedure, WestLB AG, Invitation to submit comments pursuant to art.108(2) TFEU [2011] O.J. 2011 C23/9.

by inter alia introducing a rule according to which the beneficiary bank's own funds should not to be increased beyond what was strictly necessary, i.e. to meet its regulatory obligations on minimum own funds.[190] A credit institution that only narrowly satisfies the solvency requirement does not have any room for growth until it can attract fresh capital or increase its own capital and reserves by achieving a high rate of profit. The growth of an inefficient institution is consequently held back, while a bank that is generating sizeable profits has potential for growth linked to its profitability.[191] Under normal market conditions, this approach may be efficient in order to limit the bank's future growth and thus the distortive effects of the aid.[192] In times of financial crisis, however, the focus of the Commission's investigation is on restoring stability of the financial institution concerned as well as the whole sector. In order to reach this aim, banks must have a capital buffer strong enough to absorb possible further systemic shocks. Therefore, under art.107(3)(b) TFEU the Commission often requires more than the regulatory minimum own capital ratios, and instead limits the amount of accepted risk weighted assets or takes other measures to ensure that the beneficiary bank does not engage in distortive growth strategies, but recapitalises itself appropriately.[193]

---

[190] Commission Decision of October 14, 1998 conditionally approving aid granted by France to Société Marseillaise de Crédit (notified under document number C(1998) 3210) [1999] O.J. L198/1, s.5.3.3.

[191] Commission Decision 2001/89/EC of June 23, 1999 conditionally approving aid granted by France to Crédit Foncier de France [2001] O.J. L34/36, point 94.

[192] See Commission Decision 2001/89/EC of June 23, 1999 conditionally approving aid granted by France to Crédit Foncier de France [2001] O.J. L34/36, point 95: "One result of the solvency requirement is that in the case of credit institutions it is possible to arrive at a hypothetical estimate of the distortion of competition caused by State aid. If the aid can be equated with a capital injection, the distortion of competition can be assessed in terms of weighted assets. A capital injection of EUR 1 million, or any measure with equivalent effect, would allow a bank to increase the weighted assets in its balance sheet (given the compulsory solvency ratio of 8%) and thus to expand its activities. Such an operation would create a potential distortion of competition equivalent in terms of activity to around EUR 12.5 million (since, without the aid, the bank would not have been able to increase its risk weighted assets by EUR 12.5 million). This relationship also means that if State aid to a credit institution exceeds the latter's own funds, the distortion of competition caused would be greater than the whole of the weighted assets. In such a situation the role of the compensatory measures is to limit the distortion estimated very roughly in this manner."

[193] See for instance point 27, fn.4 Banking Communication. However, the logic behind this principle is still valid and was also used during the financial crisis, see Commission Decision of April 5, 2011 on the measures No.C 11/2009 (ex. NN 53b/2008, NN 2/2010 and N 19/2010) implemented by Dutch State for *ABN AMRO Group NV* (created following the merger between Fortis Bank Nederland and ABN AMRO N), Unreported, point 315, fn.123: "The Commission is aware of the fact that dividends paid by ABN AMRO Group to the State—its sole shareholder—could trigger hybrid coupons. The Commission wants to avoid a situation in which ABN AMRO Group would pay marginal dividends to the State in order to circumvent the hybrid coupon ban. The Commission does not object to the payment of a sizeable dividend to the State of at least EUR 100 million even if that payment has certain consequences on hybrid coupons because a large dividend hints at restored viability and also helps to keep potential excess capital in check, which helps to limit undue distortions of competition."

5. Rescue (Emergency) and Restructuring Cases During the Financial Crisis under Article 107(3)(b) TFEU

19–031   The cases discussed in point 4 were the only reference cases when the financial crisis hit. The existing soft law quickly proved to be insufficient.

Overview of the financial crisis

19–032   In the new millennium, banks increasingly started to trade in highly complex products such as derivatives, swaps and other risk management products. They grew their businesses by grouping loans and packages of loans (for instance in Collateralized Debt Obligations (CDOs)[194]) to third parties, including other banks. This gave the selling banks more leeway because the loans were taken off their balance sheets, so that the regulatory requirements on core capital ratios were more easily met. This also led to more relaxed lending practices, which in certain countries like the United States were additionally fuelled by artificially low interest rates, leading to an investment bubble in the housing sector.[195] Many financial institutions, investment banks in particular, issued large amounts of debt during 2004–2007, and invested the proceeds in mortgage-backed securities (MBS), essentially betting that house prices would continue to rise, and that households would continue to make their mortgage payments. Some banks' business strategies were similar to and based on the concept of individuals taking out a second mortgage on his residence to buy another house or invest in the stock market. This strategy proved profitable during the housing boom, but problems started to surface when overstretched borrowers in the United States started to default on their loans, triggering the US sub-prime crisis. As a result, the prices of asset-backed securities (ABS) collapsed, and banks which had invested directly in asset-backed securities, or whose commercial strategies were reliant on aggressive growth in sales, started to encounter difficulties.[196] The crisis was further aggravated by massive usage of credit default swaps (CDS). CDSs are financial instruments used as a hedge and protection for debt holders, in particular MBS investors, from the risk of default. As the net worth of banks

---

[194] CDOs are a type of structured asset-backed security (ABS) with multiple "tranches" that are issued by special purpose entities and collateralised by debt obligations, including bonds and loans. Each tranche offers a varying degree of risk and return so as to meet investor demand. CDOs' value and payments are derived from a portfolio of fixed-income underlying assets. CDO securities are split into different risk classes, or tranches, whereby "senior" tranches are considered the safest securities. Interest and principal payments are made in order of seniority, so that junior tranches offer higher coupon payments (and interest rates) or lower prices to compensate for additional default risk. In other words, a CDO is a promise to pay out cash flows to investors in a prescribed sequence, based on how much cash flow the CDO collects from pooling its bonds and other assets. If cash collected by the CDO is insufficient to pay all of its investors, those in the lower layers (tranches) suffer losses first.

[195] From 2000 to 2003, the Federal Reserve lowered the federal funds rate target from 6.5% to 1.0% in order to soften the effects of the collapse of the dot-com bubble and of the September 2001 terrorist attacks, and to combat the perceived risk of deflation. The Fed believed that interest rates could safely be lowered because the rate of inflation was low.

[196] Lowe, "State Aid Policy in the context of the financial crisis" [2009] CNP 1, pp.3 ff.

and other financial institutions deteriorated because of losses related to subprime mortgages, the likelihood increased that those providing the protection would have to pay their counterparties. This created uncertainty across the financial system, as it was unclear to investors which companies would be required to bear the ultimate cost of mortgage defaults. Like all swaps and other financial derivatives, CDSs may either be used to hedge risks (specifically, to insure creditors against default) or to profit from speculation. The latter usage increased considerably during the last decade. In the United States alone, the volume of outstanding CDSs increased 100-fold from 1998 to 2008.

In 2007 a first wave of state aid was necessary to rescue Landesbank Sachsen LB, IKB, WestLB and the UK bank Northern Rock, for the last of which there was an actual run on the bank. These first rescue measures were still being assessed under art.107(3)(c) TFEU in conjunction with the R&R Guidelines (2004).[197]

The price to be paid for letting systemic banks fail could be observed when US **19–033** bank Lehman Brothers failed in September 2008. The Lehman Brothers experience confirmed that financial markets are subject to significant systemic risks of instability, due to the negative externalities that a bank failure generates on its competitors. While the failure of a company normally tends to favour its competitors and potentially even strengthens the economy as a whole by removing an inefficient player, a bank failure may weaken its competitors and negatively affects the financial markets in which they interact:

- First, as banks have extensive exposures to one another, losses of one bank will be borne by other banks. The position of these banks may in turn be weakened and entail losses for their own creditor banks. Losses can spread directly through interbank exposures or indirectly through guarantees, credit lines, or insurance against credit risks (CDS) that are being drawn and called.

- Second, the failure of one bank leads to an adjustment in the expectations regarding the viability of other banks with similar business strategies.

- Third, the development of negative externalities across banks is also subject to amplifying dynamics. For instance: following the realisation of losses on its assets, a bank may attempt (or even be obliged by the regulatory provisions) to reduce its leverage by selling securities, which might trigger a fall in price of these securities, thereby inflicting a new round of losses on the securities portfolios of other banks, which generates the need to deleverage further. Alternatively, the bank can reduce its leverage by restricting its credit to the real economy, which increases the probability of default of all other borrowers in the economy, again inflicting a new round of losses on their credit portfolio and a similar downward spiral.[198]

---

[197] See above at paras 19–027—19–030.
[198] See Maes/Kijanski, "Competition and the financial markets: Financial sector conditions and competition policy" [2009] CPN 1, p.12.

The failure of Lehman Brothers initiated exactly this development. It caused severe shocks to confidence across the whole banking system, so that banks were reluctant to lend money to each other and the whole inter-bank market virtually collapsed. As a consequence, banks were not in a position to access sufficient liquidity to lend money to their customers. For a couple of weeks, it was simply not possible to get a bank loan, whatever the project. In the period that followed, markets have recuperated only slowly and remain vulnerable to further shocks to this day.

In autumn 2008, Member States' governments reacted by introducing support schemes for the financial sector, initially by guaranteeing the security of the bank accounts at financial institutions, in order to restore confidence in the financial sector and to avoid further runs on banks in Europe. Later, the liquidity and own core capital problems of the banks were addressed by liquidity guarantees and recapitalisation measures, both on an ad hoc basis and via general schemes.

In reaction to these measures, and under severe pressure from the Member States,[199] between October 2008 and July 2009 the Commission adopted four Communications setting out how it would apply state aid rules during the financial crisis,[200] and in December 2010 added a fifth communication prolongating and slightly adapting the other four with a view to preparing the transition to the post-crisis regime. As the financial crisis had meanwhile been aggrivated by the sovereign debts crisis, the Commissioin abandoned the objective of a quick exit, but on December 1, 2011 published a Prolongation Communication, which also should encourage banks to apply for state capital in order to reach the own capital rations deemed necessary in light of the state bonds crisis.

—The first guidance paper was adopted on October 13, 2008: the Banking Communication.[201] The Banking Communication was put together in a rush to provide a level playing field for the Member States' initial rescue actions, laying down general requirements and principles for a variety of state aid

---

[199] On October 7, 2008, the ECOFIN Council adopted Conclusions committing to take all necessary measures to guarantee the stability of the banking system. Financial support to systemically relevant financial institutions was recognized as one necessary means. It was agreed that public intervention had to be decided on at national level but within a coordinated framework and on the basis of a number of EU common principles. In consequence, the Commission offered to shortly issue guidance as to the broad framework within which the compatibility of these state aid measures could be rapidly assessed; see also point 3 of the Banking Communication.

[200] In view of the exceptional crisis, there have even been calls for the Commission to suspend state aid control policy temporarily. Then Commissioner for Competition, Neely Kroes refused this by stressing that "State aid control law is not part of the problem but part of the solution", a statement that became the slogan of Ms Kroes' state aid control policy; see for instance Commissioner Kroes briefing of the Economics and Finance Ministers on financial crisis measures on December 2, 2008, MEMO 08/757, or her speech "EU state aid rules—part of the solution" on EStALI conference in Luxembourg on December 5, 2008. See also Föcking/Ohrlander/Ferdinause, "Competition and the financial markets: The role of competition policy in financial sector rescue and restructuring" [2009] CPN 1, p.7.

[201] Communication from the Commission, The application of state aid rules to measures taken in relation to financial institutions in the context of the current global financial crisis [2008] O.J. C270/8 (the Banking Communication).

measures, especially with respect to liquidity schemes, but also recapitalisation measures. As a general rule, emergency aids were only approved temporarily and under certain circumstances individual beneficiaries had to submit restructuring plans to the Commission for further approval.

—In the meantime, the financial crisis had more and more impact on the real economy, as even sound banks restricted their loan policies in order to keep liquidity and core capital ratios at a high level. Therefore, Member States also aimed to provide extra capital to banks which were not in economic difficulties, but which were prevented from applying for additional capital by the severe conditions linked to recapitalisations under the Banking Communication. Therefore, after extensive discussions with the European Central Bank ("ECB")[202] and the Member States,[203] on December 5, 2008, the Commission adopted additional detailed guidance especially for recap measures: the Recapitalisation Communication.[204] The Recapitalisation Communication distinguished between banks that were fundamentally sound and received temporary support to enhance the stability of financial markets and restore lending to businesses and consumers, and distressed banks whose business models have brought about a risk of insolvency and which therefore pose a greater risk of distortions to competition. Only the latter were subject to in-depth restructuring and severe compensatory measures.

—Although the rescue measures adopted by the Member States from October 2008 stopped the total collapse of the financial sector, in early 2009 it became apparent that further measures were needed in order to restore trust and to return the financial sector to normal functioning. One reason for the remaining credit squeeze was the uncertainty about the amount and value of impaired assets on the European banks' balance sheets (especially in the form of CDOs, ABSs and CDSs); several Member States announced their intention to complement their existing support measures by providing some form of relief for impaired bank assets. Those announcements, in parallel with a similar initiative in the United States, triggered a wider debate within the Community on the merits of asset relief as a government support measure for banks. In the context of that debate, the Impaired Assets Communication ["IAC"][205] was prepared by the Commission, in consultation with the ECB, and builds on the recommendations issued on February

---

[202] See ECB, "Recommendations of the Governing Council of the European Central Bank on government guarantees for bank debt, 20 October 2008." Available at: *http://www.ecb.int/pub/pdf/other/recommendations_on_guaranteesen.pdf.* [Accessed November 15, 2011].

[203] The ECOFIN Council of December 2, 2008 recognised the need for further guidance for precautionary recapitalisations to sustain credit, and called for its urgent adoption by the Commission.

[204] Communication from the Commission, The recapitalization of financial institutions in the current financial crisis: limitation of aid to the minimum necessary and safeguards against undue distortions of competition [2009] O.J. C10/2 (the Recapitalisation Communication).

[205] Communication from the Commission on the treatment of impaired assets in the Community banking sector [2009] O.J. C72/1.

5, 2009 by the Eurosystem.[206] The IAC focuses on issues to be addressed by Member States in considering, designing and implementing asset relief measures, such as: (i) transparency and disclosure requirements; (ii) burden sharing between the state, shareholders and creditors; (iii) aligning incentives for beneficiaries with public policy objectives; (iv) eligibility, valuation and management of impaired assets; and (v) the relationship between asset relief, other government support measures and the restructuring of banks.[207]

—The first three communications laid out the principles of how emergency aid measures for banks had to be assessed, in which forms they could be granted, for which banks a viability plan was acceptable, and for which a more serious restructuring plan had to be provided in order to approve these measures beyond the six-month period to which emergency aid was normally limited. When it was time to submit the restructuring plans in 2009, the Commission published the Restructuring Communication[208] for financial institutions. The Restructuring Communication sets out the conditions for the approval of a restructuring plan, with a view to ensuring that the banks return to long-term viability without State support, contribute to the restructuring costs (burden-sharing) and adopt measures to limit competition distortions. Together with the three previous Communications on Banking, Recapitalization and Impaired Assets, these rules form a body of guidance for assessing various support measures during the systemic crisis.

—On December 2, 2009 the ECOFIN Council established the necessity to design a strategy for the phasing-out of support measures which would be transparent and duly coordinated among Member States in order to avoid negative spill-over effects but also to take into account the specific circumstances varying across Member States.[209] In reaction, since July 1, 2010 the Commission has applied tighter conditions for the compatibility of government guarantees with art.107(3)(b) TFEU.[210] A second exit step was put forward by the so called Exit Communication[211] with the requirement that, as of January 1, 2011, every bank in the European Union having recourse to

[206] Point 3 IAC.

[207] Point 4 IAC.

[208] Commission communication on the return to viability and the assessment of restructuring measures in the financial sector in the current crisis under the state aid rules [2009] O.J. C195/9 (Restructuring Communication).

[209] In the same vein, the European Parliament insisted in its Resolution of March 9, 2010 on the Report on Competition Policy 2008 (*http://www.europarl.europa.eu/sides/getDoc.do?type=TA &language=EN&reference=P7-TA-2010-0050*. [Accessed November 15, 2011]) that state support to financial institutions should not be unduly prolonged and that exit strategies should be elaborated as soon as possible.

[210] See Commission Staff Working Document of April 30, 2010: *http://ec.europa.eu/competition/ state_aid/studies_reports/phase_out_bank_guarantees.pdf*. [Accessed November 15, 2011].

[211] Communication from the Commission on the application, from January 1, 2011, of state aid rules to support measures in favour of banks in the context of the financial crisis [2010] O.J. C329/7.

state support in the form of capital or impaired asset measures will have to submit a restructuring plan, thereby removing the previously applied distinction between fundamentally sound and distressed banks.

In its Exit Communication, the Commission extended the applicability of the communication package until December 31, 2011, and adapted them with a view to preparing the transition to the post-crisis regime, where new, permanent State aid rules for bank rescue and restructuring in normal market conditions should apply. This should be the case, market conditions permitting, as of January 1, 2012. However, due to the sovereign debts crisis market conditions did not permit it, and so the Commission had to further extent the crisis rules for banks. It did so until further notice in the Prolongation Communication[212] of December 1, 2011. The main provisions consist in explaining how to ensure that the State is adequately remunerated if Member States decide to recapitalise their banks. Recap measures were considered increasingly likely in the future, since the European Council's Banking Package of October 2011,[213] which stipulated, inter alia, that banks should be required to demonstrate by June 20, 2012, a common equity quote of 9 per cent after accounting for market valuation of sovereign debt exposures. The Banking Package also requested the possibility of guarantees on bank liabilities to limit deleveraging actions caused by the 9 per cent requirement. Both issues were addressed in the Prolongation Communication: (i) a revised methodology was agreed concerning the remuneration of guarantees for banks' funding needs. The revised methodology establishes the minimum fees that should apply where the guarantees are granted on a national basis. The new rules apply for guarantees covering debt with a maturity between one and five years (seven in case of covered bonds). The rules for shorter maturities remain the same; (ii) With respect to recapitalisation measures, guidance is given on the use of market-based valuations to give a reasonable assurance of an adequate remuneration for the State. Member States are still obliged to submit a restructuring plan (or an update of a previously approved plan) for all banks which receive public recapitalisation, be it from national or EU sources, even if this recapitalisation is only due to the new 9 per cent rule.[214] However, the Commission will determine the need for restructuring through a proportionate assessment of the long-term viability of banks, taking particular account of whether the capital shortage is essentially linked to the sovereign debts crisis, the public capital injection is limited to the amount necessary to offset losses stemming from marking sovereign bonds of the EEA Member States to market in banks which are otherwise viable, and the analysis shows that the bank in question did not take excessive risk in acquiring sovereign debt.

---

[212] Communication from the Commission on the application, from January 2012, of State aid rules to support, measures in favour of banks in the context of the financial crisis [2011] O.J. C356/7.

[213] With respect to the Council's Banking Package see in more detail in s.6 (Foresights), paras 19–079 to 19–083.

[214] The necessity to submit viability, restructuring or liquidation plans, differs from one state aid measure to the other, see in detail below at para.19–037.

19–034   Safeguarding the Internal Market and creating a level playing field among the banks were the main objectives of the Commission's reaction to the financial crisis. This should be achieved in two phases: first, by setting the parameters for access to so-called emergency aid in a coordinated manner, and then through a more thorough and forward-looking assessment of the banks' restructuring needs to ensure their return to viability without state support, and the return of the financial sector to normal market functioning through mechanisms that minimise competition distortions.[215] Hence, the rules aimed to strike a balance between short-term financial stability and long-term concerns for the preservation of normal market functioning, and focused on undistorted competition. This balance reflects the evolution of the crisis: at its beginning, safeguarding financial stability was the overriding objective. Therefore a wide array of rescue measures, including loans, guarantees and recapitalisations, were temporarily allowed. Ad hoc individual emergency aids and even general emergency aid schemes were approved at record speed, sometimes over the weekend.[216] The extraordinary action and amount of money put into the banking system in the first months of the crisis[217] was effective in halting the panic and restoring trust. While this first phase of speedy approval of emergency aid and general guarantee schemes continued at a slower pace from mid-2009 on, the second step phase began: the Commission began to review the banks' restructuring plans (submitted to it in order to demonstrate their long-term viability), while providing sufficient compensatory measures to allow the approval of state aid beyond the initial six-month period for emergency aid. In the end, of the large banks, only a few relatively unaffected by the crisis opted not to benefit from these schemes, including the Santander group, Barclays and Deutsche Bank.[218]

In parallel, Member States and EU institutions have since been discussing on a national, European and global level new regulatory provisions[219] and other measures to prevent any future systemic financial crisis (phase 3). While phase 2 has not been terminated, and phase 3 has only just begun, the European and US

---

[215] Philip Lowe, "State Aid Policy in the context of the financial crisis" [2009] CNP 1, pp.3 ff.; see also Arhold, "Globale Finanzkrise und europäisches Beihilfenrecht—Die (neuen) Spielregeln für Beihilfen an Finanzinstitute und ihre praktische Anwendung" [2008] EuZW, pp.713 ff.

[216] Decision to approve emergency aids were delivered in as little as 24 hours in the case of Bradford and Bingley, Commission Decision of October 1, 2008, Rescue aid to Bradford and Bingley [2008] C290/2.

[217] "In the period from October 2008 until mid-July 2009 the [. . .] total volume of the approved guarantee measures amounts to €2.9 trillion and the recapitalisation measures amount to €313 billion. (DG Comp's Review of guarantee and recapitalisation schemes in the financial sector in the current crisis, August 7, 2009, p.2.

[218] However, Deutsche Bank benefitted indirectly by the state aid for Postbank AG, the majority stake in which has been bought gradually by Deutsch Bank AG in 2009 and 2010.

[219] Especially by the new rules of the Basel Committee on Banking Supervision (BCBS) the new rules of the so called "Basel III" package, a comprehensive set of reform measures, developed to strengthen the regulation, supervision and risk management of the banking sector. These measures aim to improve the banking sector's ability to absorb shocks arising from financial and economic stress, whatever the source, to improve risk management and governance, and to strengthen banks' transparency and disclosures. Because of the sovereign debts crisis, the European Council has taken even stricter measures to stabilise the European banks, see in detail below, paras 19–079—19–083.

debt crisis, and its likely impact on banks with government bonds on their balance sheet from Member States with acute debt problems (such as Portugal, Ireland, Italy, Greece and Spain[220]), might lead to a new systemic crisis[221] and another round of phase 1 measures.

This development is also affecting the reform of the rules for banking restructuring. All six Communications highlight the temporary nature of the admissibility of such aid measures, according to which such aid can only be justified as an emergency response to the unprecedented stress in financial markets and only as long as those exceptional circumstances prevail. The Restructuring Communication was originally to apply for aid notified until December 31, 2010, but its application was prolonged by one year, until December 31, 2011, by the Exit Communication. The other Communications do not have an expiry date. The ultimate goal was a return to the normal state aid regime for the rescue and restructuring of banks, based on art.107(3)(c) TFEU (see above at paras 19–018—19–030). The Commission wanted to draw up new, permanent state aid rules for bank rescue and restructuring in normal market conditions, taking into account the experience gained during the crisis and to be applied from January 1, 2012.[222] A first draft of these new or updated R&R Guidelines was scheduled for July 2011 but as of February 2012 had not been published yet. Instead, Competition Commissioner Almunia announced that the Commission will extend the application period of the communication package for at least one year in order to address the new turmoil in the financial sector.[223] In parallel, on October 12, 2010, the Commission presented a new communication to the European Parliament: "A roadmap to stability and growth",[223a] which addresses the current sovereign debt and Euro crisis. In this Communication, the Commission observes that the ongoing uncertainty in the sovereign debt markets has led to increasing volatility and is putting the banking sector under mounting pressure. The banks' access to liquidity must be facilitated and the long-term liquidity in the sector must be restored. For this reason, a coordinated recapitalisation effort shall restore confidence in and within the financial market. The Council discussed these proposals at its summit on October 26–27, 2011 against the background of a proposed haircut of the Greek state bonds, which will lead to further deterioration of the banks' own capital rations. In order to be able to absorb the necessary revaluation of State bonds, banks shall increase their own

---

[220] So called PIIGS States for States who have (contrary to the TFEU provisions governing the European Monetary Union) been supported by the other Member States and the European Central Bank in order to overcome their debt crises. However, in October 2011, it was likely that the debt crisis was going to hit other Member States, too.

[221] Or is it still the same crisis coming in again through the backdoor?

[222] Point 8 Exit Communication.

[223] See speech "The impact of the crisis State aid regime for banks" in front of the European Economic and Social Committee on October 4, 2011, downloadable under *http://europa.eu/ rapid/pressReleasesAction.do?reference=SPEECH/11/632&type=HTML*. [Accessed November 15, 2011].

[223a] Communication form the Commission COM(2011)669, "A roadmap to stability and growth", downloadable at *http://ec.europa.eu/commission_2010–2014/president/news/speeches-state ments/pdf/20111012communication_roadmap_en.pdf*. [Accessed November 15, 2011].

capital up to 9 per cent Common Equity quote. It will, however, be quite difficult for the banks, especially for those still in restructuring, to find the required capital on the market. It is likely that another round of recapitalisation state aid will have to be assessed under the Commission's crisis Communications, even if financed by the EFSF. Therefore, the Commission has further extended the applicability of the financial crisis rule in its Prolongation Communication of December 1, 2011, this time even without explicit deadline, see para.19–033, above.

General principles

19–035 **Legal basis.** All six Banking Communications are based on art.107(3)(b) TFEU. While state aid to individual undertakings in difficulties is normally assessed under art.107(3)(c) TFEU and the R&R Guidelines (see above at paras 19–018—19–030), the Commission understood that the R&R Guidelines would not be flexible enough for the aid measures necessary to address the financial crisis. The Commission therefore "reactivated" art.107(3)(b) TFEU, a provision under which the Commission may approve state aid "to remedy a serious disturbance in the economy of a Member State". The economic disturbance must affect the entire Member State and not just be of a regional dimension.[224] The Commission's practice in applying art.107(3)(b) TFEU has been very restrictive. The last time this article was applied before the financial crisiswas in the 1980s, when the Greek economy faced serious economic imbalances following accession and when the European Union (then European Communities) had authorised specific exceptional measures aiming at correcting the situation.[225] Article 107(3)(b) TFEU has been interpreted very narrowly. Even with respect to state aid to banks, the Commission had always taken the view that invoking this provision was possible only in genuinely exceptional circumstances where the entire functioning of financial markets was jeopardised.[226] In the Commission's view, aid benefiting one operator only could not address the kind of situation targeted by the second part of art.107(3)(b) TFEU.[227] The Commission applied this principle even to the rescue and restructuring of banks with obvious systemic relevance to their financial markets, such as Crédit Lyonnais case[228] and BAWAG[229] (see above at para.19–031). After the fall of Lehman Brothers, however, there could no longer be any doubt that the financial crisis was a serious disturbance in the economy not only of a single Member State but of the whole

[224] See Joined Cases T–132/96 and T–143/96 *Freistaat Sachsen and Volkswagen AG v Commission* [1999] E.C.R. II–3663, para.167.
[225] Commission Decision 88/167/EEC of October 7, 1987 concerning Law 1386/1983 by which the Greek Government grants aid to Greek industry, [1989] O.J. L76/18.
[226] Point 11 Banking Communication.
[227] Commission Decision of June 27, 2007 state aid C–50/2006 (ex. NN 68/2006, CP 102/2006) implemented by Austria for BAWAG-PSK [2008] O.J. L83/7, point 169.
[228] Commission Decision of May 20, 1998 concerning aid granted by France to the Crédit Lyonnais group [1998] O.J. L221/28.
[229] Commission Decision of June 27, 2007 state aid C–50/2006 (ex. NN 68/2006, CP 102/2006) implemented by Austria for BAWAG-PSK [2008] O.J. L83/7.

Internal Market; in conjunction with this exceptional context prevailing since mid-September 2008, the fall of an European systemic bank could, significantly worsen the disturbance and finally result in the collapse of the entire financial market, with severe collateral damage in other economic sectors.[230]

Recourse to art.107(3)(b) TFEU is possible only as long as the crisis situation justifies its application,[231] and only to the extent that the solution of the systemic crisis justifies the aid measures, while distortions of competition have to be avoided or minimised as far as possible. In line with the refined economic approach, introduced as the main point of the State Aid Action Plan shortly before the financial crisis,[232] any state aid compatible under art.107(3) TFEU has to be:

19–036

—well-targeted, in order to be able to achieve effectively the objective of remedying a serious disturbance in the economy. This requires that the financial support of the beneficiary bank is necessary to either remedy a serious disturbance, which has already occurred or to prevent the occurrence or aggravation of such disturbance. This in turn means that the beneficiary bank must be of relevance for the financial system, i.e. the bank must have systemic relevance. This relevance may result from its leading position in certain market segments, from the significance of its lending activities for the real economy, or its intense financial relationships with other banks,[233] especially the significance of its integration and interconnection with other banks in the Member State concerned or even Europe wide.[234] As a principle, the bank's collapse would have to entail a serious disturbance for the financial sector and thus the economy of (at least) the Member State concerned. Regularly, the national central banks have to confirm the systemic importance of the beneficiary bank[235];

---

[230] State aid NN 42/2008, Belgium; NN 46/2008, Luxembourg; NN 53/A/2008, Netherlands Restructuring aid to Fortis Bank and Fortis Bank Luxembourg [2009] O.J. C80/7, points 72–73.

[231] Point 12 Banking Communication.

[232] See State Aid Action Plan, "Less and better targeted state aid: a roadmap for state aid reform 2005–2009" COM/2005/0107 final. See also staff working paper "Common principles for an economic assessment of the compatibility of State aid under Article 87.3 EC-Treaty", downloadable at *http://ec.europa.eu/competition/state_aid/reform/economic_assessment_en.pdf.* [Accessed November 15, 2011].

[233] See for instance Commission Decision of December 14, 2009, state aid N 422/2009, *RBS* [2010] O.J. C119/1, point 129; Commission Decision of April 5, 2011 on the measures No.C 11/2009 (ex. NN 53b/2008, NN 2/2010 and N 19/2010) implemented by Dutch State for ABN AMRO Group NV (created following the merger between Fortis Bank) Nederland and ABN AMRO N), point 282.

[234] Commission Decision of December 22, 2009 in the State aid Case N 640/2009 (ex-PN 119/2009)—Austria Rescue aid (capital injection and asset guarantee) to *BAWAG-PSK* [2009] O.J. C55/3, point 48.

[235] See for instance, state aid NN 42/2008, Belgium, NN 46/2008, Luxembourg NN 53/A/2008, Netherlands, Restructuring aid to Fortis Bank and Fortis Bank Luxembourg [2009] O.J. C80/7, point 71.

—proportionate to the challenge faced, not going beyond what is required to attain this effect; and

—designed in such a way as to minimise negative spill-over effects on competitors, other sectors and other Member States.[236]

The last criterion is explained in the Recapitalisation Communication as three levels of competition which risk being disturbed. First, distortion of competition between Member States: state aid measures by one Member State to its own banks should not give those banks an undue competitive advantage over banks in other Member States. This type of distortion of competition may materialise even if the aid scheme applies to all financial institutes in the Member State in the same way, i.e. to a scheme which is only of sectoral selectivity. Such aid may also prompt a subsidy race among Member States and create difficulties for the economies of Member States which have not introduced excessive state aid schemes. A coherent and coordinated approach to state aid is therefore indispensable to the preservation of a level playing field (ensuring fair competition between Member States). Second, distortion of competition between distressed and sound banks: aid schemes, which are open to all banks within a Member State without an appropriate degree of differentiation between beneficiary banks according to their risk profiles, may give an undue advantage to distressed or less-performing banks compared to banks which are fundamentally sound and better-performing. This will distort competition on the market, distort incentives, increase moral hazard and weaken the overall competitiveness of European banks (ensuring fair competition between banks). Third, distortion of competition between those banks which receive state aid and those which do not: state aid, in particular its remuneration, should not have the effect of putting banks that do not have recourse to the aid in a significantly less competitive position. The aid measures should therefore be adequately remunerated in order to facilitate the return to normal market functioning (ensuring a return to normal market functioning). The Commission's Communications address all three kinds of distortion of competition by the following general principles, which are also mirrored in the specific rules described in detail at paras 19–031 et seq.

19–037 **The differentiation between emergency aid and restructuring aid.** The Banking, Recapitalisation and Impaired Asset Communications, all differentiate between emergency and restructuring aid. In order to overcome the liquidity squeeze, the Commission has allowed emergency aids under relatively soft conditions,[237] and has been ready to ensure the swift adoption of decisions upon complete notification, if necessary within 24 hours and over a weekend,[238] and indeed did so in a couple of cases. Emergency aids under the Financial Crisis Communications differ from rescue aids under the R&R Guidelines both in form

---

[236] Point 15 Banking Communication.
[237] See below at para.19–031.
[238] Point 53 Banking Communication.

and also in their legal consequences: they can take the form of measures, which change the financial and even corporate structure of the beneficiaries, for instance recapitalisations, nationalisations or asset reliefs; and unlike in cases of rescue aids, the submission of a restructuring plan is not always necessary where the emergency aid applies in excess of six months.

Under the conditions laid down in these Communications, Member States must submit viability, restructuring or liquidation plans for the individual beneficiary banks within a deadline of between three and six months. The real balancing between stabilisation of the financial sector and distortion of competition takes place when assessing these plans. The Banking Communication already contains certain principles with respect to restructuring, in general referring to the principles laid down in the R&R Guidelines.[239] It was, however, quickly established that the R&R Guidelines were on the one hand too strict and on the other hand too one-dimensional to properly address the problems of the financial crisis, so that the Commission published a Restructuring Communication, tailor-made for the restructuring of financial institutions during the financial crisis.[240] The necessity to submit viability, restructuring or liquidation plans differs from one state aid measure to the other:

—With liquidity guarantees, the emergency measure has to be followed by adequate steps leading to a restructuring of the beneficiary, or, if no such restructuring is feasible, its liquidation, if the liquidity guarantee has to be called upon for the benefit of an individual financial institution because the bank defaults on a covered liability,[241] a situation that is tantamount to technical insolvency. However, as the financial crisis weakened in 2010, the Commission understood that "a persistent failure to obtain a considerable proportion of the funding needed without government guarantees may indicate a lack of confidence in the viability of a bank's business model".[242] Therefore, the Commission considers it appropriate that guarantee schemes to be prolonged beyond June 30, 2010 should include a threshold which, if exceeded, triggers the requirement of a viability review, i.e. submitting a viability plan within three months of the granting of the guarantees exceeding the following thresholds:

- 5 per cent of outstanding guaranteed liabilities over total liabilities; and
- total amount of guaranteed debt of €500 million.

Other than a viability plan, a restructuring plan is to be submitted within six months after the payment under the guarantee. According to the Banking

[239] Point 35, fn.2 Banking Communication.
[240] For details of the assessment of restructuring plans, see below at para.19–018.
[241] Point 30 Banking Communication.
[242] DG Competition staff working document, "The application of state aid rules to government guarantee schemes covering bank debt to be issued after 30 June 2010", downloadable at *http:/ /ec.europa.eu/competition/state_aid/studies_reports/phase_out_bank_guarantees.pdf*. [Accessed November 15, 2011].

Communication, a liquidation plan need only be notified where liquidation is accompanied by additional state aid.[243]

—For recapitalisation measures, the Banking Communication requested restructuring plans for all beneficiary banks, even though the Communication established that a distinction between fundamentally sound institutions and financial institutions suffering from more structural solvency problems linked, for instance, to their particular business model or investment strategy should be made when assessing the restructuring plans of the individual banks concerned, and especially the extent of the necessary restructuring.[244] The Recapitalisation Communication changed this approach: fundamentally sound banks had only to provide a viability plan demonstrating that there is no need for further state aid,[245] while state capital for distressed banks could only be accepted on the condition of either a bank's winding-up or a thorough and far-reaching restructuring, including a change in management and corporate governance where appropriate, and severe compensatory measures.[246] Therefore, either a comprehensive restructuring plan or a liquidation plan will have to be presented for these banks within six months of recapitalisation.[247] This distinction between sound and distressed banks for the purposes of submitting a restructuring plan was removed by the Exit Communication. As of January 1, 2011, a restructuring plan will be required from every beneficiary of a new recapitalisation measure (irrespective of whether they are designed as individual measures or granted in the context of a scheme).[248]

—The Impaired Assets Communication (IAC) initially also differentiated between restructuring and viability plans, while it differs from the strict good bank/bad bank or black and white approach, categorising the cases in various shades of grey, which may trigger the necessity for in-depth restructuring. In all cases, Commission approval of asset relief measures would be granted only for a period of six months, and conditional on the commitment to present either a restructuring plan or, initially, a viability review for each beneficiary institution within three months of its accession to the asset relief programme or of the grant of ad hoc emergency asset relief. The distinction between restructuring plan and viability review has been abolished by the Exit Communication. As of January 1, 2011, a restructuring plan is required from every beneficiary of an impaired asset measure.[249]

---

[243] Point 30, fn.1 Banking Communication.
[244] Point 35 Banking Communication.
[245] For viability plan decisions see Decision of August 17, 2010 on state aid N 372/2009, The Netherlands, Restructuring Aid to AEGON [2010] O.J. C290/1, and Commission Decision of January 28, 2010 on state aid N 371/2009, the Netherlands, Viability plan SNS REAAL [2010] O.J. C93/2.
[246] See below at para.19–063.
[247] Point 44 Recapitalisation Communication.
[248] Point 13 Exit Communication.
[249] Point 13 Exit Communication.

Currently,[250] there is a requirement to notify viability, restructuring of liquidation plans in the following situations:

	Viability Plan	Restructuring Plan	Liquidation Plan
Liquidity guarantee	5% of outstanding guaranteed liabilities over total liabilities; and total amount of guaranteed debt of EUR 500 million	If the guarantee is called upon because the bank defaults on a covered liability and bank is not liquidated	Only if liquidation is accompanied with additional State aid
Recapitalisation	No	Yes, if bank is not liquidated	Only if liquidation is accompanied with additional State aid
Asset Relief	No	Yes, if bank is not liquidated	Only if liquidation is accompanied with additional State aid

The differentiation between fundamentally sound and distressed banks. The **19–038** differentiation between fundamentally sound and distressed banks was already mentioned in the Banking Communication. Distressed banks were defined as banks with problems that are a result of their particular business model or business practices whose weaknesses are exposed and exacerbated by the crisis in the financial markets (endogenous problems[251]). If such institutions were to be returned to long-term viability rather than liquidated, a far-reaching restructuring of their operations would be required.[252] In contrast, fundamentally sound banks were those whose difficulties stemmed exclusively from the general market conditions which had severely restricted access to liquidity (exogenous problems[253]). Long-term viability of these institutions may require less substantial restructuring.[254] A more precise definition of fundamentally sound banks can be found in the Annex to the Recapitalisation Communication, where the indicators for the assessment of a bank's risk profile are listed, according to which fundamentally sound banks should have:

---

[250] As of October 23, 2011.
[251] Point 14 Banking Communication. Characterised by losses resulting form, for instance inefficiencies, poor asset-liability management or risky investment strategies.
[252] Point 2 Banking Communication.
[253] Point 14 Banking Communication.
[254] Point 2 Banking Communication.

—sound capital adequacy. The Commission will value positively the assessment of the bank's solvency and its prospective capital adequacy as a result of a review by the national supervisory authority; such a review will evaluate the bank's exposure to various risks (such as credit risk, liquidity risk, market risk, interest rate and exchange rate risks), the quality of the asset portfolio (within the national market and in comparison with available international standards), the sustainability of its business model in the long term and other pertinent elements;

—a size-limit for the recapitalisation. No more than 2 per cent of the bank's risk-weighted assets,[255] or, in the case of insurance companies, 25 per cent of the minimum solvency margin requirements[256];

—current CDS spreads equal or inferior to the average;

—current rating of A or above and a stable or positive outlook.

In the evaluation of these indicators, the situation of banks which face difficulties due to the current exceptional circumstances must be taken into account, although they would have been regarded as fundamentally sound before the crisis, as shown, for instance, by the evolution of market indicators such as CDS spreads and share prices. Where a bank that was initially considered fundamentally sound fell into difficulties after recapitalisation took place, a restructuring plan for that bank has to be notified.[257]

The original rationale for establishing a distinction between sound and distressed banks and for setting the above-mentioned range of indicators was the fear that capital needs resulting from impairments, higher expectations of the markets as to the capital levels of banks and temporary difficulties in raising capital on markets would otherwise lead to sound banks diminishing their lending to the real economy in order to avoid having to submit a restructuring plan when having recourse to state resources.[258] At the end of 2010, however, the banking sector faced fewer difficulties in raising capital, so that the distinction

---

[255] In practice, the Commission has regularly established that the beneficiary bank had to undergo in-depth restructuring if its asset related state aid exceeded 2% of the total bank's RWA, referring to point 4 Restructuring Communication and point 55 IAC; see for instance Commission Decision of November 18, 2009 on state aid C 10/09 (ex. N 138/09) implemented by the Netherlands for ING's Illiquid Assets Back Facility and Restructuring Plan [2010] O.J. L274/139, point 119.

[256] In the case of insurance companies, regulatory capital is not defined in terms of RWA. Their minimum capital requirements are defined in terms of minimum solvency margin requirements, where the available capital defined as the available solvency margin must be at least equal to the minimum solvency margin requirements. However, as 2% of RWA represents a quarter of the minimum capital requirements for banks, the Commission has taken the view that this provision of the Restructuring Communication can be applied also to insurance companies, taking 25% of the minimum solvency margin requirements as a relevant proxy for the 2% RWA benchmark, see Commission Decision of May 20, 2010 in state aid Case N 256/2009 Restructuring aid to Ethias, Belgium [2010] O.J. C252/5, point 103.

[257] Point 42 Restructuring Communication

[258] Point 13 Exit Communication.

between sound and distressed banks no longer seemed relevant in order to determine which banks should submit a restructuring plan, and thus every bank benefitting from a recapitalisation or asset relief measure from January 2011 on must go through restructuring.[259] As the distinction has never applied for liquidity guarantees anyway, it is of less importance. At most, the indicators may still be used as parameters for assessing the extent of the necessary restructuring, although the (relative and absolute) amount of state aid has meanwhile become the most important parameter.[260]

Admissibility of general aid schemes. In contrast to the R&R Guidelines,[261]   **19–039** from the very beginning of the crisis the Commission has recognised that due to the particular nature of the current problems in the financial sector, state aid may have to extend beyond the stabilisation of individual financial institutions and include general schemes[262]; not only for liquidity measures, but also for structural measures like recapitalisations and asset reliefs. However, pursuant to point 70 of the R&R Guidelines (2004):

> "any aid actually granted [. . .] during the restructuring period, including aid granted in accordance with an approved scheme, must be notified individually to the Commission to the extent that the latter was not informed thereof at the time of its decision on the restructuring aid."

The Commission takes the view that this principle applies also to restructuring aid approved under the Banking Communication, although the Banking Communication does not address this issue. The Commission does not regard the Banking Communication as a special regulation that might override this procedural rule.[263] Moreover, under certain circumstances, state aid granted under the approved scheme even has to be followed up by the individual notification of a viability or restructuring plan to the Commission. As the necessity of restructuring plan submission has been extended more and more, the relevance of general schemes has become almost entirely limited to emergency aid. These schemes may have a maximum term of two years.[264] Since under art.107(3)(b) TFEU, only aid to remedy a serious disturbance in the economy of a Member State can be approved, the Commission must regularly assess whether the financial crisis still exists to an extent justifying the approved schemes. Therefore, the compatibility of any such general national aid scheme must be reviewed at least every six

---

[259] Point 14 Exit Communication.
[260] See below at para.19–063.
[261] According to the R&R Guidelines, rescue and restructuring schemes are only admissible for SMEs. All R&R state aid for large companies must be individually notified with the European Commission.
[262] Point 2 Banking Communication.
[263] Commission Decision of December 22, 2008 in state aid N 639/2008, Germany, Guarantee for IKB, point 24.
[264] Point 52 Banking Communication.

months.[265] In practice, not all Member States took the opportunity to notify general aid schemes:

[266]

Member State	Liquidity guarantee/ assistance	Recapitalisa- tion	Asset relief measures	Other
Austria	X	X	X	
Cyprus	X			
Denmark	X	X		Winding-up aid scheme
Finland	X	X		
France	X	X		
Germany	X	X	X	
Greece	X	X		
Hungary	X	X		Support for home buyers
Ireland	X	X	X	
Latvia	X			
Lithuania	X	X	X	
The Nether- lands	X			
Poland	X	X		
Portugal	X	X		
Slovakia	X	X		
Slovenia	X			
Spain	X	X	X	
Sweden	X			
United Kingdom	X	X		Support for home buyers

19–040 **Non-discrimination.** The aid schemes have to be non-discriminatory, i.e. the eligibility criteria of financial institutions for coverage by aid measures such as liquidity guarantees[267] or recapitalisations[268] must be objective, taking due account of their role in the relevant banking system and the overall economy, and non-discriminatory so as to avoid undue distortive effects on neighbouring markets and the internal market as a whole, and especially large-scale subsidy races: "The risk was not hypothetical; in the early days of the crisis we did see

---

[265] For emergency liquidity guarantee schemes, see point 24 the Banking Communication, for recapitalisation schemes see point 34 Banking Communication and points 40ff. Recapitalisation Communication.
[266] As of September 20, 2011.
[267] Point 18 Banking Communication.
[268] Point 18 Banking Communication.

large movements of capital between Member States in search of highest level of protection."[269]

Adequate remuneration. The term "adequate remuneration" used in the Commission Communications does not mean the same as "at market rate". Otherwise, the absurd consequence would be that the only measures approvable under the Communications would be those which fall outside the scope of art.107(1) TFEU because they meet the Market Economy Operator Test.[270] "Adequate remuneration" therefore means something which comes as close as possible to what could be considered a market price, thereby minimising the amount of the aid but remaining below the actual market rate.[271] Such a price is then "market oriented". Sometimes this term is also used for situations in which the real market value cannot be determined because the relevant markets have crashed. A remuneration rate not too far removed from current market prices is essential to avoid crowding out recapitalisation via the private sector and facilitating the return to normal market conditions.[272]

19–041

Moral hazard and burden sharing. In economic theory, moral hazard is a situation in which a party insulated from risk behaves differently from the way in which it would behave if it were fully exposed to the risk, i.e. it has a tendency to act less carefully and takes more risks. Financial bail-outs of financial institutions by state support can encourage risky lending in the future, if those that take the risks come to believe that they will not have to carry the full burden of potential losses. There are two main issues with moral hazard in the current financial crisis:

19–042

—First, the financial support for banks in difficulty might have the effect of protecting those responsible for the difficulties of the bank, i.e. the providers of funds (owners and creditors of the beneficiary bank) and the bank managers from the consequences of their past (excessive) risk taking.[273] Inter alia, owners and managers are responsible for one of the most harmful moral hazard problems, the bonus systems for traders: Most traders have a bonus or incentive element to their remuneration that includes an option-like element. In other words, they share in the profits they make (above a given threshold), but not in the losses. To maximise their expected remuneration, therefore, they should take on as much risk as possible. This incentive will

---

[269] With respect to the first global guarantee in Ireland, Commissoner Almunia, Developments in state aid policy State Aid Round Table, BDI Berlin, November 11, 2011, downloadable at *http://europa.eu/rapid/pressReleasesAction.do?reference=SPEECH/11/748&format=HTML&aged=0&language=EN&guiLanguage=en* [Accessed November 20, 2011].

[270] With respect to the MEOT see above at paras 19–005 et seq.

[271] Point 26, first bullet point Banking Communication, point 24 Recapitalisation Communication.

[272] Point 25 Recapitalisation Communication.

[273] See Maes/Kijanski, "Competition and the financial markets: Financial sector conditions and competition policy" [2009] CPN 1, p.12(14).

become progressively stronger as their trading position deteriorates below the level required to earn a bonus.[274]

—Second, the rescue measures might strengthen the expectation that insurance will be provided in future cases of distress, because the bank is too big to fail. In fact, supporting banks too big to fail may give smaller banks a strong incentive to become themselves too big to fail, in order to benefit from an implicit free insolvency insurance. This may create renewed incentives for excessive risk taking, also for banks which had not taken excessive risks in the past but which now find themselves forced to observe that their competitors are being bailed out without any negative consequences.[275]

These issues must be addressed in the scope of mandatory financial and corporate restructuring of the banks concerned. Conditions to the approval decision may provide for a number of restrictions that may ensure that incumbent owners and creditors do not (fully) profit from the state aid, for instance by ban on payment of dividends or coupons on hybrid capital, high remuneration of the state aid measures and even forced exit of the incumbent owners, for instance by way of nationalisation. During the crisis, (partial) nationalisations took place with respect to several banks, often in consequence of the dilution of existing shareholders in the scope of capital increase with public funds. While these nationalisations have not been requested by the European Commission, they were positively taken into account when assessing burden sharing and moral hazard.[276] Nationalisation in the form of the mere take-over of existing shares constitutes state aid neither in favour of the bank, nor in favour of the former shareholders, as long as they are only indemnified at the amount of the bank's value without state aid.[277] Most of these conditions would at the same time serve the principle of burden sharing, which is closely linked to the moral hazard problem: the more burden the bank, its owners and creditors actually have to bear, the less moral hazard problems occur. For the management, different provisions must apply, for instance limits on salary, including the prohibition of

---

[274] See further Dow, "What Is Systemic Risk? Moral Hazard, Initial Shocks, and Propagation", London Business School, Monetary and Economic Studies, December 2000, p.1.

[275] See Maes/Kijanski, "Competition and the financial markets: Financial sector conditions and competition policy" [2009] CPN 1, p.12(14).

[276] See for instance state aid SA 32745 (2011/NN), Austria Restructuring of *Kommunalkredit Austria AG* [2011] O.J. C239/2; Commission Decision of July 18, 2011 on state aid C15/2009 (ex. N196/2009), which Germany has granted or intends to grant to Hypo Real Estate, unreported, point 121.

[277] See for instance Commission Decision of July 18, 2011 on state aid C15/2009 (ex. N196/2009), which Germany has granted or intends to grant to *Hypo Real Estate*, Unreported, point 121, fn.35; Commission Decision of February 16, 2009 in Case N 61/2009, Change of ownership of Anglo-Irish Bank, [2009] O.J. C 177/2; and Commission Decision of October 28, 2009 state aid C–14/08 (ex. NN 1/08) implemented by the United Kingdom for Northern Rock [2010] O.J. L112/38, points 105–111.

bonuses or the introduction of bilateral risk sharing contracts,[278] imposition of good cooperative governance rules and even the exchange of the management.[279] While the burden sharing rules may diminish the incentive to become or remain too big to fail, since the "insurance is not for free", this will depend on how consistently such conditions will be used. A different and additional way to reduce moral hazard in financial markets is to downsize the beneficiary banks to a level considerably below systemic importance. This is one reason why balance sheet reductions have been ordered in almost all restructuring cases during the financial crisis. Balance sheet reductions are, however, limited: they must not put the bank's viability at risk.

Clawback/better fortunes clause. The Commission's awareness that during the   **19–043** financial crisis short-term stabilisation of the financial market has top priority, and will initially be more important than preventing or minimising distortion of competition, is mirrored by the clawback and/or better fortune clauses that can be found in all of the first four Commission Communications. These clauses are door openers that allow the Commission (and in application of general schemes, the national authorities) to approve state aid measures if they are temporarily not in line with other principles, but will be compliant once the additional burden sharing has been realised, additional compensatory measures have been taken, or part of the state aid has been repaid at a later stage.[280]

Prevention of undue distortions of competition. The Banking Communications   **19–044** stress the need for safeguards against possible abuses and distortions of competition.[281] Most of the statements made in the Communications can be generalised, i.e. can be applied to all forms of financial crisis aid. The most important principle is that state aid must be limited to the minimum necessary and may not allow the beneficiary to engage in aggressive commercial strategies. As a general rule, the higher the level of remuneration of the state aid in question, i.e. the lower the relative state aid amount, the less need there is for safeguards, as the price level will limit distortions of competition.[282] In order to minimise distortions of competition general schemes must provide for an adequate combination of some or all of the following elements and provisions, effectively enabling the Member State concerned to enforce these elements[283]:

---

[278] The optimal contracts in the literature involve payments from the trader or the manager to the firm (in the case of bad performance) as well as payments from the firm to the trader (in the case of good performance). However, such contracts are rarely seen in practice. Some firms have tried to force traders' bonuses to be retained within the firm for some years—effectively allowing part of the bonus to be reclaimed later in case of poor performance—but these efforts have met with resistance in the labour market.

[279] For an overview about the conditions and commitments, which have been used in the Commission's decisions during the financial crisis, see below at para.19–071.

[280] For capitalisation measures see points 34, 38, fn.1, and 39 Banking Communication; for liquidity guarantees see point 26, third bullet point Banking Communication.

[281] See for instance points 27 ff. and 35 ff. Banking Communication, points 35 ff. Recapitalisation Communication.

[282] Point 35 Recapitalisation Communication.

[283] Point 27 Banking Communication.

—behavioural constraints, ensuring that beneficiary financial institutions do not engage in aggressive expansion against the background of the guarantee, for instance by restrictions on:

- commercial conduct;
- pricing;
- advertising the state aid for commercial purposes[284];
- business expansion, e.g. through the introduction of a market share ceiling or the retention of profits in order to ensure adequate recapitalisation[285];
- external commercial expansion by mergers or acquisitions: while mergers and acquisitions can constitute a valuable contribution to the consolidation of the banking industry with a view to achieving the objectives of stabilising financial markets and ensuring a steady flow of credit to the real economy, restrictions may be necessary, in order not to privilege those institutions with public support to the detriment of competitors without such support.[286]

—limitations to the size of the balance sheet of the beneficiary institutions in relation to an appropriate benchmark (e.g. gross domestic product or money market growth) while safeguarding the availability to grant credits to the economy.[287]

—the prohibition of other conduct irreconcilable with the purpose of the aid such as, for example, share repurchases by beneficiary financial institutions or the issuance of new stock options for management.

In individual ad hoc state aid cases or when assessing restructuring plans, the Member State may be required to commit to or, if the aid is approved after the formal investigation procedure, the Commission will impose as conditions additional constraints and obligations.[288]

Identification of certain measures falling outside the scope of Article 107(1) TFEU

19–045   In its communications, the Commission has not only dealt with the question under which conditions certain measures will probably be approved under art.107(3)(b) TFEU, but also when they are not likely to constitute state aid at all. Even if ultimately it is the Union Courts' task to define the term "state aid" within the meaning of art.107(1) TFEU, the Communications of the Commission

---

[284] Point 27, fn.4 Banking Communication, point 36 Recapitalisation Communication.
[285] Point 27, fn.4 Banking Communication.
[286] Point 37 Recapitalisation Communication.
[287] Point 27, fn.5 Banking Communication. For the definition of banks in distress, see above at paras 19–031 et seq.
[288] See for more information on these commitments and conditions below at paras 19–031 et seq.

give useful guidance on how the Commission interprets the case law with respect to the financial sector. As this guidance does not depend on whether the sector is currently in a crisis situation or not, it is dealt with above under point 3.

Emergency aid. The general concept of emergency aid is relatively similar to the concept of rescue aid under the R&R Guidelines: it is normally only approved for a certain period of time and will often be followed by a restructuring plan. However, there are differences, which have prompted the Commission to treat this kind of aid differently:

—Member States may set up general emergency aid schemes, even for large companies.

—Emergency interventions may take the form of structural measures.

—In certain circumstances, emergency measures may go beyond six months without the requirement to notify a restructuring plan.

—To be eligible, the beneficiary bank does not have necessarily to be in economic difficulties within the meaning of the R&R Guidelines.[289]

—No "one time last time" principle during the financial crisis.[290]

The conditions for the approval of emergency state aid vary between the different forms of state aid.

Liquidity guarantees and other liquidity support. Liquidity guarantees are **19–046** guarantees covering the liabilities of a financial institution. General liquidity

---

[289] Unclear: Commission Decision of December 14, 2009, state aid N 422/2009, *RBS* [2010] O.J. C119/1, point 180, which states under the heading of the compatibility of the liquidity assistance with the Banking Communication: "The Commission recalls that, as set out in the Banking Communication, the liquidity support for financial institutions from public resources (including the central bank) when constituting aid, can be found compatible, according to the principles of the Rescue and Restructuring Guidelines. First in order to be eligible for rescue aid the beneficiary must be in difficulty. In this case given its tight liquidity position, RBS was in difficulty." However, the Banking Communication does not stipulate such condition. In fact, during the crisis many banks were supported by recapitalisation and liquidity assistance, nor because they were in difficulty within the definition of the R&R Guidelines, but in order to prevent them to further restrict their lending exposure to the real economy. The statement of the Commission may have been caused by the fact that the liquidity assistance has been granted already on October 13, 2008, i.e. two weeks before the Banking Communication has been published.

[290] There have been a couple of cases where the Commission had to temporarily approve a second emergency state aid, see for instance: Commission Decision of July 11, 2011 on state aid SA 33216 (2011/N), Ireland, Second rescue of Bank of Ireland [2011] O.J. C274/2; Decision of October 17, 2011 on state aid Case SA 33751 *Dexia Banque Belgique*. Anglo-Irish received no fewer than four emergency recapitalisations: Commission Decision of June 26, 2009 on state aid Case N 356/2009, *Recapitalisation of Anglo Irish Bank* by the Irish State [2009] O.J. C235/3; Commission Decision of March 31, 2010 on state aid Case NN 12/2010 and C11/2010 (ex. N 667/2009), Second rescue measure in favour of Anglo Irish Bank [2010] O.J. C214/3; Commission Decision of August 10, 2010 on state aid Case NN 35/2010 (ex. N 279/2010), Ireland, Temporary approval of the third recapitalisation in favour of Anglo Irish Bank [2010] O.J. C290/4.); Commission Decision of December 21, 2010 in Case SA 32057 (2010/NN), Ireland, Temporary approval of the fourth recapitalisation and guarantee in respect of certain liabilities in favour of Anglo Irish Bank [2011] O.J. C76/4.

guarantee schemes are to be considered temporary emergency measures to address the acute symptoms of the financial crisis. If the guarantee is drawn upon with respect to an individual beneficiary, this beneficiary must go through restructuring.[291] Beyond the general principles set out above, the following conditions apply to general emergency liquidity guarantee schemes, whether established by way of a declaration, legislation or contractual regime. These provisions apply by analogy to individual ad hoc guarantees.[292]

The selection of the types of debt and liabilities covered by the guarantee must be targeted, to the extent practicable, to the specific source of difficulties and restricted to what can be considered necessary to confront the relevant aspects of the current financial crisis.[293] Because of the drying-up of interbank lending, guaranteeing certain types of wholesale deposits and even short and medium-term debt instruments may also be justified.[294] The limitation of the amount of the guarantee available, possibly in relation to the size of the beneficiary's balance sheet may also be an element safeguarding the proportionality of the scheme.[295] The extension of the coverage of any guarantee to further types of debt beyond this relatively broad scope would require a closer scrutiny as to its justification.[296]

In application of the general state aid principle that the amount and intensity of the aid must be limited to the strict minimum, Member States have to take appropriate steps to ensure a significant contribution from the beneficiaries and/or the sector to the cost of the guarantee and, where the need arises, the cost of state intervention if the guarantee has to be drawn upon.[297] This may be done by an adequate combination of some or all of the following elements:

—the guarantee scheme must be based on adequate remuneration by the beneficiary financial institutions individually and/or the financial sector at large, e.g. through an association of private banks. In practice, most of the Member States' liquidity guarantee schemes were of the first category, while the costs were borne by the financial sector at large in only exceptional cases.[298]

---

[291] See above at para.19–018.
[292] Commission Decision of November 19, 2008 in state aid Case N 574/2008, Belgium State guarantees for Fortis Bank [2008] O.J. C38/2, point 39.
[293] Point 20, Banking Communication.
[294] Point 21, Banking Communication.
[295] Point 21, fn.2 Banking Communication.
[296] Point 22, Banking Communication.
[297] Point 25–26, Banking Communication.
[298] For instance in Denmark, where the liquidity and winding-up aid measures were financed by private contributions through Det Private Beredskap (DPB), the Danish Contingency Association. DPB would pay an annual premium over two years of DKK 15 billion (around €2 billion). In addition it has to put up DKK 10 billion (around €1.3 billion) to cover losses in the winding-up company in any event, and would cover additional losses of up to DKK 10 billion, once the first DKK 25 billion have been spent. Any losses exceeding these contributions would be taken over by the State, see Commission Decision of October 10, 2008 on state aid NN 51/08, Guarantee scheme for banks in Denmark [2008] C273/2, several times prolonged and extended.

—Adequate remuneration reflecting the varying degree of risks and the beneficiaries' different credit profiles and needs.[299] The adequate remuneration was initially determined following general ECB Recommendations of October 2008. In the case of a bond with maturity over one year, the applicable fee comprised a flat charge of 50 basis points augmented by each bank's median five-year senior debt CDS spread observed in the period January 1, 2007 to August 31, 2008.[300] For banks without CDS data, but with a credit rating, an equivalent CDS spread should be derived from the median value of five year CDS spreads during the same sample period for the rating category of the bank concerned, based on a representative sample of euro area large banks, to be defined by the Eurosystem.[301] The credit risk elements in that pricing model were based upon data that predated the most acute phase of the crisis which followed the bankruptcy of Lehman Brothers in September 2008, while CDS spread differentials across banks are actually significantly higher than pre-Lehman and are likely to remain so. Up to March 2010, this has been considered necessary to facilitate banks' access to external funding and thereby safeguard financial stability. However, in March 2010, the Commission took the view that market financing had improved to such an extent that the pricing of government support should be brought closer to market conditions, thus better reflecting individual banks' current creditworthiness. The Commission introduced a minimum increase in the fee for guarantees, to be differentiated according to the beneficiary bank's creditworthiness. The approval of the extension of a guarantee scheme beyond June 30, 2010 would therefore require the fee for a government guarantee to be higher than under the pricing formula recommended by the ECB, by at least:

- 20 basis points for banks with a rating of A+ or A[302];
- 30 basis points for banks rated A–[303]; and
- 40 basis points for banks rated below A–, banks without a rating will be considered to belong to the category of banks with a BBB rating.[304]

Member States would have the possibility to go beyond these minimum requirements in defining the top-ups for the guarantee fee. As a further element of flexibility allowing Member States to adjust the conditions to the specific circumstances prevailing in their financial sectors, the Commission

---

[299] Point 26, first bullet point Banking Communication.

[300] See *http://www.ecb.int/pub/pdf/other/recommendations_on_guaranteesen.pdf.* Last accessed November 15, 2011.

[301] For an example see Commission Decision of August 17, 2009 in state aid Case N 400/2009, Germany, Liquidity guarantee for IKB, point 37.

[302] Or A1 and A2 depending on the rating system employed.

[303] Or A3 depending on the rating system employed.

[304] In the case of divergent assessments by different rating agencies the relevant rating for the calculation of the fee increase should be the higher rating. The material time for the rating in the determination of the guarantee fee is the day on which the guarantee is granted in relation to a specific bond issuance by the beneficiary.

would accept a different model for the calculation of a fee increase provided that it can be unequivocally demonstrated that this formula leads at least to the minimum rise set out above for the banks concerned.[305]

—In its Banking Communication, the Commission takes the view that the beneficiary undertaking or the sector should also contribute by covering at least a considerable part of the outstanding liabilities if the guarantee has to be activated, so that the Member State must bear only the amounts exceeding this private sector contribution.[306] This rule can only be implemented by a kind of internal recovery provision between the public guarantor and the beneficiary, since otherwise the state guarantee cannot sufficiently solve the liquidity problems.

—Furthermore, the Commission recognises that beneficiaries may have problems paying an appropriate remuneration immediately. Member States can therefore consider a claw-back/better fortunes clause that would require beneficiaries to pay either additional remuneration for the provision of the guarantee as such (in case it does not have to be activated) or to reimburse at least a part of any amounts paid by the Member State under the guarantee (in case it needs to be drawn upon) as soon as they are in a position to do so.[307]

In addition, the aid schemes or measures have to reduce the distortion of competition to the minimum possible.[308] In individual ad hoc cases, different commitments had been made to achieve this goal, for instance by refraining from taking unfair advantage of the favourable situation created by the public guarantee (especially with regard to advertising) or by limiting the growth of the balance sheet any by refraining from occupying a leading position on particularly relevant markets.[309] If the guarantee is called upon, the submission of a restructuring or liquidation plan within six months is mandatory.[310]

Schemes which directly support the liquidity situation of a bank by public liquidity funding (including sources from the central bank where it constitutes aid[311]) can also be found compatible under similar conditions.[312]

19–047 **Recapitalisations.** The Recapitalisation Communication strictly distinguishes between fundamentally sound banks on the one hand and distressed banks on the

---

[305] See DG competition staff working document, The application of state aid rules to government guarantee schemes covering bank debt to be issued after June 30, 2010, April 30, 2010, downloadable at *http://ec.europa.eu/competition/state_aid/studies_reports/phase_out_bank_ guarantees.pdf.* [Accessed November 15, 2011].

[306] Point 26, second bullet point, Banking Communication.

[307] Point 26, third bullet point, Banking Communication.

[308] See above at para.19–035.

[309] See for instance Commission Decision of November 19, 2008 in state aid Case N 574/2008, Belgium state guarantees for Fortis Bank [2008] O.J. C38/2, point 18a.

[310] See above at para.19–034.

[311] To the circumstances under which central bank support does not constitute state aid, see above at para.19–011.

[312] Point 52, Banking Communication.

other.[313] The recapitalisation of distressed banks is subject to much stricter requirements than the recapitalisation of fundamentally sound banks: besides the fact that the use of state capital for distressed banks can only be accepted if the Member State submits either a comprehensive restructuring plan or a liquidation plan within six months of recapitalisation,[314] whereas for fundamentally sound banks only a viability plan needs to be presented[315] until the redemption of the State, behavioural safeguards for distressed banks in the rescue and restructuring phases should, in principle, also include:

—a restrictive policy on dividends (including a ban on dividends, at least during the restructuring period);

—limitation of executive remuneration or the distribution of bonuses;

—an obligation to restore and maintain an increased level of the solvency ratio compatible with the objective of financial stability; and

—a timetable for redemption of state participation.[316]

Notwithstanding these stricter rules for distressed banks, the following principles apply to the recapitalisation of all banks.

Eligibility under national schemes must be based on objective criteria, such as the need to ensure a sufficient level of capitalisation with respect to the solvency requirements. The Commission looks favourably on national schemes in which the financial supervisory authorities must evaluate the need for recapitalisation in each individual case.[317] The capital injection must not allow the beneficiary to engage in aggressive commercial strategies or expansion of its activities or other purposes that would imply undue distortions of competition. The means to achieve this objective may include:

19–048

—the obligation to maintain an enhanced minimum solvency requirement level; and/or

—the limitation of the total size of the balance sheet.

According to the instrument chosen (e.g. shares, warrants, subordinated capital, etc.) the Member State concerned shall receive rights corresponding to its contribution to the recapitalisation. The issue price of new shares must be fixed on the basis of a market-oriented valuation,[318] so that the shares of the other

---

[313] Point 12–13, Recapitalisation Communication.
[314] Point 44, Recapitalisation Communication.
[315] For further details, see above at para.19–011.
[316] Point 45, Recapitalisation Communication.
[317] Point 37, Banking Communication.
[318] It is clear to the Commission that an exact evaluation of (especially distressed) banks under the circumstances of the financial crisis is impossible.

shareholders will be sufficiently diluted. This corresponds to the general principles of burden sharing and moral hazard as laid down above, and also prevents
that the other shareholders—in case they are undertakings—receive indirect state
aid. In emergency cases, there is sometimes not sufficient time for the Commission to assess whether the share price has been fixed at an appropriate level. In
some cases, the Commission has made this assessment during the restructuring
plan investigation and insisted that the advantage stemming from the share price
fixed at too low a rate was outbalanced by other claw-back and burden sharing
commitments.

In order to reduce the state aid in favour of the financial institution to a
minimum, the aid measures must also ensure that public support is only given in
return for an adequate remuneration. The best way to ensure this is to use
instruments such as preferred or preferential shares: preferred shares not only
increase the probability that the State receives appropriate remuneration, but also
function as a burden sharing tool in relation to the old shareholders, since they
can receive dividends only after the new capital has been served.[319]

In any case, it is mandatory that in principle, adequate remuneration has to take
into account the risk profile of the bank concerned: banks with a higher risk
profile must pay more. In designing recapitalisation schemes open to a set of
different banks, Member States should carefully consider the entry criteria and
the treatment of banks with different risk profiles and differentiate their treatment
accordingly.[320] The main indicators for the risk profile are:

—compliance with regulatory solvency requirements;

—prospective capital adequacy as certified by the national supervisory
   authorities;

—pre-crisis and current CDS spreads and ratings.[321]

In the Recommendations of its Governing Council of November 20, 2008, the
European Central Bank proposed a methodology for benchmarking the pricing of
State recapitalization measures for fundamentally sound institutions in the Euro
area.[322] The Commission has translated this into the following parameters:

—First, as a general rule, the Commission accepts the remuneration set in a
   deal where state capital injections are on equal terms with significant
   participation (30 per cent or more) of private investors.[323]

---

[319] Commission Decision of May 20, 2010 in state aid Case N 256/2009 Restructuring aid to Ethias,
Belgium [2010] O.J. C252/5, points 129–130.
[320] Point 13, Recapitalisation Communication.
[321] Point 14, Recapitalisation Communication.
[322] Point 15, Recapitalisation Communication.
[323] Point 21, Recapitalisation Communication, with reference to Decision of October 27, 2008 in
Case N 512/08 Support measures for financial institutions in Germany, point 54. As to the
question of under which circumstances, and in light of the Private Investor Test, the participation
of private investors will lead to a presumption that there is no aid involved, see above at
para.19–006.

—Second, in any other cases, adequate remuneration will be set individually on the basis of a price corridor (entry level) or the required nominal rate of return between an average of 7 per cent on preferred shares with features similar to those of subordinated debt and an average of 9.3 per cent on ordinary shares.[324] This remuneration will be differentiated at the level of the individual bank on the basis of the following parameters:

- the type of capital chosen (ordinary shares, non-core Tier 1 capital, or Tier 2 capital)—the lower the subordination, the lower the required remuneration in the price corridor;
- an appropriate benchmark risk-free interest rate;
- the individual risk profile at national level of all eligible financial institutions (including both financially sound and distressed[325] banks).[326]

Alternative pricing methodologies remain possible, provided they lead to higher remunerations.[327] Member States may, for instance, choose a pricing formula that in addition includes step-up or payback clauses, claw-back mechanisms or better fortunes clauses.[328] Such features should be chosen appropriately so that, while encouraging an early end to the State's capital support of banks, they should not result in an excessive increase in the cost of capital.[329] In the HSH Nordbank case, a different route has been followed, which combined the issue price and the counterpart question in a joint answer: as preferred shares were not available, the allegedly market-oriented issue price was reduced by 10 per cent, which worked as an ex ante dividend for the new shares.[330] In ad hoc individual recapitalisation cases, in principle the correct remuneration has to be assessed individually. However, if the remuneration complies with one of the remuneration mechanisms provided for by a national recapitalisation aid scheme already approved by the Commission, the scheme's mechanism could be used as a benchmark for the assessment of whether the recapitalisation at least in the context of the emergency aid decision was adequately remunerated.[331]

—Third, the Commission accepts recapitalisation schemes open to all or almost all banks in a given Member State on a less differentiated basis, where pricing mechanisms lead to a level of total expected annualised return

---

[324] Point 27, Recapitalisation Communication.
[325] However, fn.2 to point 46, Recapitalisation Communication indicates that a return in excess of 10% is adequate for distressed banks.
[326] Point 28, Recapitalisation Communication. Distressed banks may not be able to bear prices corresponding to their risk profiles. In such cases, it is nevertheless required that the prices come as close as possible to the required level, point 44, Recapitalisation Communication.
[327] Point 30, Recapitalisation Communication.
[328] Point 39, Banking Communication.
[329] Point 29, Recapitalisation Communication.
[330] Commission Decision of September 20, 2011 on state aid SA 29338 (C 29/2009, ex. N 264/2009), granted by Germany to HSH Nordbank, Unreported.
[331] Commission Decision of December 22, 2009 in state aid Case N 640/2009 (ex. PN 119/2009), Austria Rescue aid (capital injection and asset guarantee) to BAWAG PSK [2009] O.J. C55/3, points 67–72.

for all banks participating in a scheme which is sufficiently high to cater for the variety of banks and the incentive to exit. This level should normally be set above the upper bounds of the price corridor, and can include a lower entry price and an appropriate step-up, as well as other differentiation elements and safeguards as described above.[332] The Commission has so far accepted recapitalisation measures with a total expected annualised return of at least 10 per cent for Tier 1 instruments for all banks participating in a scheme. As an example of a combination of a low entry price with such differentiation elements, the Commission Decision of November 12, 2008 in Case N 528/08 the Netherlands, Aid to ING Groep NV may be mentioned. In this case, for the remuneration of a sui generis capital instrument categorised as core Tier 1 capital, a fixed coupon (8.5 per cent) was coupled with over-proportionate and increasing coupon payments and a possible upside, which resulted in an expected annualised return in excess of 10 per cent.[333] For Member States with risk-free rates of return significantly divergent from the Eurozone average, such a level may need to be adapted accordingly. Adjustments are also necessary in accordance with developments of the risk-free rates.

19–049   Except for cases where state capital injections are on equal terms with significant participation (30 per cent or more) from private investors,[334] recapitalisation measures also need to contain appropriate incentives for state capital redemption (as soon as the financial markets allow this). The Member States are free to propose exit mechanisms to the Commission, which will assess them on a case-by-case basis. In general, the higher the size of the recapitalisation and the higher the risk profile of the beneficiary bank, the more necessary it becomes to set out a clear exit mechanism.[335] The Recapitalisation Communication lists the following incentives, which may be combined:

—High remuneration for the state recapitalisation, so that banks automatically look for alternative capital once the markets function normally again, to be implemented by an add-on to the entry price determined according to the above parameters[336]; in the RBS Case, for instance, UK had committed itself not to accept any buy back (of shares) offer from RBS unless the price for such buy back is the greater of (i) 100 per cent of the original issue price in the first three years, 110 per cent in year 4, 120 per cent in year 5 and 130

---

[332] Point 36, Recapitalisation Communication.
[333] Commission Decision of November 18, 2009 on state aid C 10/09 (ex. N 138/09) implemented by the Netherlands for ING's Illiquid Assets Back Facility and Restructuring Plan [2010] O.J. L274/139.
[334] Point 21, Recapitalisation Communication, unless the terms of the deal are such as to significantly alter the incentives of private investors.
[335] Point 34, Recapitalisation Communication.
[336] Point 31, Recapitalisation Communication.

per cent in year 6 and beyond, and (ii) the stock market price as it would be if the B share were converted into ordinary shares.[337]

—Price mechanisms, which increase over time, for instance via step-up clauses[338]; in the second BAWG restructuring, for instance, the Austrian participation capital has a step-up clause starting in 2014, increasing the initial coupon of 9.3 per cent post tax per year.[339]

—Increasing global rates of remuneration instead of the nominal, for instance through call options or other redemption clauses, or mechanisms that encourage private capital raising, for instance by linking the payment of dividends to an obligatory remuneration of the State which increases over time.[340]

—Restrictions on dividends, strengthening at the same time the capital basis of the bank and its capability to lend to the real economy, but allowing for dividend payment where this represents an incentive to provide new private equity to fundamentally sound banks, for example by limitations in time or to a percentage of the profits generated, or linked to the contribution of new capital (for example by paying out dividends in the form of new shares). Where the redemption of the State is likely to occur in several steps, the gradual relaxation of any restriction on dividends, in tune with the progress of redemption, could be envisaged.[341]

The combination of the level and type of remuneration and—where and to the **19–050** extent appropriate—a restrictive dividend policy needs to represent a sufficient exit incentive for the beneficiary banks.[342] The Commission considers, in particular, that restrictions on payment of dividends are not needed where the level of pricing correctly reflects the banks' risk profile, and step-up clauses or comparable elements provide sufficient incentives for exit and the recapitalisation is limited in size.[343]

Again, except for cases with sufficient private contribution,[344] recapitalisation measures, as other state aid measures, must be limited to the minimum necessary and entail other provisions to reduce distortions of competition as much as

---

[337] Commission Decision of December 14, 2009, state aid N 422/2009, *RBS* [2010] O.J. C119/1, point 139.

[338] Point 31, Recapitalisation Communication.

[339] Commission Decision of June 30, 2010 in the state aid Case N 261/2010 (ex. PN 9/2010), Austria, Second restructuring aid for BAWAG PSK [2010] O.J. C250/5, point 93.

[340] Point 32, Recapitalisation Communication.

[341] Point 33, Recapitalisation Communication.

[342] For such a package see the BAWAG case: besides the step-up clause, BAWAG committed on a dividend ban applicable until the end of 2011 and a dividend restriction limiting the dividend to 17.5% of distributable profit until the participation capital had been repaid, thus providing further strong incentives to repay the State as soon as possible; see Commission Decision of June 30, 2010 in state aid Case N 261/2010 (ex. PN 9/2010), Austria, Second restructuring aid for BAWAG PSK [2010] O.J. C250/5, point 93.

[343] Point 34, Recapitalisation Communication.

[344] Point 21, Recapitalisation Communication.

possible.[345] These provisions may consist of a combination of the behavioural safeguards described above at paras 19–047 and 19–048, the extent of which will be based on a proportionality assessment taking into account all relevant factors and, in particular, the risk profile of the beneficiary bank, the relative size of the capital injection and the level of capital endowment reached.[346]

Furthermore, when Member States use recapitalisation with the objective of financing the real economy, they have to ensure that the aid effectively contributes to this. To that end, in accordance with national regulation, they should attach effective and enforceable national safeguards to recapitalisation which ensure that the injected capital is used to sustain lending to the real economy.[347]

19–051   **Asset relief measures.** Banks typically hold a variety of assets, including: cash, financial assets (treasury bills, debt securities, equity securities, traded loans, and commodities), derivatives (swaps, options), loans, financial investments, intangible assets, property, plants and equipment. Losses may be incurred when assets are sold below their book value, when their value decreases and reserves are created on possible loss, or ex post when the revenue streams at maturity are lower than the book value. It is the normal duty of banks to assess the risk of the assets they acquire and to make sure they can cover any associated losses. During the financial crisis, the Commission accepted that asset relief measures could contribute to the strengthening of the institutions' capital requirements. To these measures similar considerations should apply as those applicable to recapitalisations.[348] Asset relief measures became even more important as a tool to enforce transparency and thus to rebuild confidence in and among the financial institutions. The Impaired Assets Communication (IAC) offers more specific guidance on the application of state aid rules to such measures. It covers a broad variety of differently designed asset measures.[349] Although Member States should design and implement them in the most effective manner,[350] they can also take other issues into account, in particular their budgetary situation,[351] and can thus choose

---

[345] Point 35, Recapitalisation Communication.

[346] Point 38, Recapitalisation Communication.

[347] Point 39 Recapitalisation Communication. See for instance Commission Decision of 14 December 2009, State aid N 422/2009, *RBS* [2010] O.J. C119/1 RBS, footnote 95: Commitment *"to increase its lending to homeowners and businesses (meeting RBS's normal commercial terms) by £25 billion for the period until March 2010."*

[348] Point 40f Banking Communication.

[349] Annex II IAC presents examples of possible approaches and describes examples from the past. A broad distinction may be made between relief measures, where impaired assets will be segregated from the good assets within a bank or in the banking sector as a whole (for instance via the creation of a bad bank of the beneficiary involved or via a self-standing public institution, which purchases the impaired assets), and asset insurance or guarantee schemes whereby the beneficiaries keep their impaired assets on the balance sheets but are indemnified against losses by the State.

[350] Point 8 IAC.

[351] Point 10 IAC.

between different forms of asset relief, for instance asset purchase, asset insurance, asset swap or a hybrid of such arrangements.[352]

The main conditions to be met by national asset relief measures or schemes are:

- any asset relief measure must be based on a clear identification of the magnitude of the bank's asset-related problems and its intrinsic solvency prior to the support. Thus applications for asset relief should be subject to:
  - —full ex ante transparency and disclosure of impairments by eligible banks on the assets which will be covered by the relief measures, based on adequate valuation, certified by recognised independent experts and validated by the relevant supervisory authority, in line with the principles of valuation described further below[353];
  - —an application for aid by an individual bank should be followed by a full review of that bank's activities and balance sheet, with a view to assessing the bank's capital adequacy and its prospects for future viability (viability review). Given its scale, the review could be finalised after the bank enters into the asset relief programme. In practice, during the financial crisis, almost all relief measures were granted as emergency measures before the asset valuation or the viability review could have been finalised.[354] The results of the valuation and the viability review could be established only later during the investigation procedure and taken into account in the assessment of necessary restructuring.[355]

In light of the objective of restoring confidence within the financial sector, point 5.3 IAC tries to put pressure on the financial institutions to make use of the national asset relief schemes including their transparency requirements by limiting the enrolment window of national schemes to six months from the launch of scheme. In practice, however, this incentive did not work, since Member States did not adopt relief schemes but solely granted ad hoc individual asset relief measures.

When determining the range of eligible assets for relief, a balance needs to be **19–052** found between meeting the objective of immediate financial stability and the need to ensure the return to normal market functioning over the medium term. It is not only classic "toxic assets" (for example, US mortgage backed securities and associated hedges and derivatives), which triggered the financial crisis, that are eligible. The Commission has instead taken a pragmatic approach including

---

[352] Point 11 IAC. These different arrangements are discussed in detail in Annex II to the IAC.

[353] As an example, see Commission Decision of December 14, 2009, state aid N 422/2009, *RBS* [2010] O.J. C119/1, points 149–152.

[354] See for instance Commission Decision of December 22, 2009 in state aid Case N 640/2009 (ex. PN 119/2009), Austria, Rescue aid (capital injection and asset guarantee) to BAWAG PSK [2009] O.J. C55/3, points 66.

[355] Wisely accepted as admissible alternative in point 20, IAC.

elements of flexibility, which would ensure that other assets also benefit from relief measures to an appropriate extent[356]:

—Annex III of the IAC lays down categories of assets ("baskets") of impaired assets.

—In addition, the IAC allows Member States whose banking sectors are additionally affected by other factors of such magnitude as to jeopardise financial stability (such as the burst of a bubble in their own real estate market) to extend eligibility to other well-defined national categories of assets corresponding to the systemic threat upon due justification, without quantitative restrictions.[357] This clause initially only covered the impaired assets after the bursting of the Spanish real estate bubble, and thus is also known as the "Spanish Clause". In light of the flexible approach the clause is meanwhile interpreted more largely, for instance for assets of segments like shipping, aviation or real estate, which have been particularily affected by spillover effects of the financial crisis.[358] The Commission has even accepted the transfer of assets, which—without being impaired assets within the meaning of Annex III IAC—are not of strategic significance any more for the profoundly changed business model of the restructured financial institute.[359]

—In addition, of the overall assets covered by a relief mechanism banks may be relieved of a maximum of 10–20 per cent of impaired assets outside this scope of eligibility without the necessity of a specific justification.[360]

—On the other hand, assets which have entered the balance sheet of the beneficiary bank after a specified cut-off date prior to the announcement of the relief programme or measure are not eligible since otherwise this could result in asset arbitrage and would give rise to inadmissible moral hazard. Initially, a uniform and objective cut-off date, such as the end of 2008, was to ensure a level playing field among banks and Member States.[361] But since Member States did not set up general impaired asset schemes, and as time went by, this cut-off date was abandoned. In practice, it was sufficient that the relief measure would apply solely to impaired assets already existing on the beneficiary bank's balance sheet at the time the aid was granted.

—Furthermore, assets that cannot be considered impaired at all should not be covered by a relief programme, since asset relief should not provide an

[356] Point 32, IAC.
[357] Point 34, IAC.
[358] Decision of September 20, 2011 on state aid SA 29338 (C 29/2009, ex. N 264/2009), granted by Germany to HSH Nordbank, Unreported, point 166.
[359] Commission Decision of July 18, 2011 on state aid C15/2009 (ex. N196/2009), which Germany has granted or intends to grant to Hypo Real Estate, Unreported, point 80.
[360] Point 35, IAC.
[361] Point 36, fn.1 IAC.

open-ended insurance against future consequences of recession.[362] Nevertheless, in practice the Commission has also applied the IAC to relief measures which not only covered impaired assets, but went far beyond that,[363] sometimes covering almost the entire asset portfolio of the bank concerned,[364] sometimes covering only a specific portfolio of assets not qualifying as impaired under the IAC, for instance the traditional Dutch mortgage portfolio in the ABN AMRO case, of which even external experts did not expect the performance to deteriorate to a significant extent. The asset guarantee was implemented for the sole purpose of capital relief, since traditional recapitalisation was not opportune for the Dutch State.[365] The Commission accepted that this "capital relief instrument"[366] was an alternative to a traditional capital increase rather than a protection against toxic assets. When justifiying the this broad interprwetation of impaired assets, the Commission also refers to point 65 of IAC, according to which he wider the eligibility criteria, and the greater the proportion which the assets concerned represent in the portfolio of the bank, the more thorough the restructuring and the compensatory measures must be. In the Commission's view, an in depth restructuring can thus justify quite bvroad "impaired" assets portfolios,[367] to which, however, the general principles behind the IAC apply, even if they are solely capital relief instruments.[368]

Valuation of the impaired assets and pricing and burden sharing concepts are **19–053** described in point 5.5 of the IAC. Three values must be differentiated: the current market value of an asset, its real economic value and its book value:

—As a first stage, assets should be valued on the basis of their current market value, whenever possible. In general, any transfer of assets covered by a

---

[362] Point 36, IAC.

[363] In the *RBS* case, the Commission has accepted a portfolio covering a large pool of assets beyond those commonly referred to as toxic assets, including residential mortgages, consumer finance, corporate bonds, corporate loans, lease finance, project finance, leveraged finance, commercial real estate loans, structured credit assets and derivatives. The Commission observed that RBS's problems stemmed "from the accumulation of risky loans in different entities of the group. This accumulation of risky loans is the result of the less than prudent originating and risk management policies applied across the board to the group's entities. They are also symptomatic of the group's aggressive expansion policy in the years preceding the current crisis. Therefore, to achieve the objective of shoring up RBS's balance sheet by providing certainty on the level of future impairments, the measure had to be wide ranging"; see for instance Commission Decision of December 14, 2009, state aid N 422/2009, *RBS* [2010] O.J. C119/1, points 167–170.

[364] See Decision of September 20, 2011 on state aid SA 29338 (C 29/2009, ex. N 264/2009), granted by Germany to HSH Nordbank, Unreported.

[365] Commission Decision of April 5, 2011 on the measures No.C 11/2009 (ex. NN 53b/2008, NN 2/2010 and N 19/2010) implemented by Dutch State for ABN AMRO Group NV (created following the merger between Fortis Bank Nederland and ABN AMRO N), Unreported, point 295.

[366] ABN AMRO Group NV Decision, point 284.

[367] Commission Decision of September 20, 2011 on state aid SA 29338 (C 29/2009, ex. N 264/2009), granted by Germany to HSH Nordbank, Unreported, point 167.

[368] HSH Nordbank Decision, points 284 and 297.

scheme at a value in excess of the market price will constitute state aid. The current market value may, however, be quite far removed from the book value of those assets or even non-existent in the absence of a market during the financial crisis, in which case an asset's market value may effectively be as low as zero.[369]

—As a second stage, the value attributed to impaired assets in the context of an asset relief program (the "transfer value") will inevitably be above current market prices in order to achieve the relief effect.[370] To ensure consistency in the assessment of the compatibility of aid, the Commission considers a transfer value reflecting *the underlying long-term economic value* (the "real economic value") of the assets, on the basis of underlying cash flows and broader time horizons, an acceptable benchmark indicating the compatibility of the aid amount as the minimum necessary.

—Consequently, in principle the financial institutes must bear any losses resulting from the difference between the assets' book value and their real economic value (as evaluated *ex ante*)[371] when the asset purchase or the asset insurance[372] takes place.

Book value 100	Difference of 50 to be borne by the bank	
	Real economic Value 50	Difference of 25 maximum state aid
	(transfer value or insured value)	Market value 25

19–054   In order to prevent undue distortions of competition and to avoid subsidy races between Member States,[373] the valuation process both with regard to the market value and the real economic value has to follow the same guiding principles and processes listed in the IAC and its Annex IV.[374] In practice, the calculation of the real economic value is of more importance than the calculation of the market value. This follows from the fact that the former is decisive for the bank's own

---

[369] Point 39, IAC.

[370] The aid amount corresponds to the difference between the transfer value of the assets (normally based on their real economic value) and the market price, point 20, fn.2, IAC.

[371] Point 22, fn.2, IAC.

[372] In the case of an insurance measure, the transfer value is understood as insured amount, see point 41, fn.1, IAC.

[373] Point 37, IAC.

[374] Point 42, IAC.

contribution and the calculation of the state aid amount involved, the latter only for the amount of state aid, which in asset relief guarantee or insurance models can sometimes be established without knowing the exact market value of the assets, since the guaranteed amount serves as a cap.[375] In a couple of cases, the Commission has expressed the view that it is difficult to determine the aid amount if the aid is granted by way of a risk shield. The aid element involved in a guarantee to a company in difficulty can be as high as the amount potentially covered by the guarantee, but can, on a case-by-case analysis, also be lower.[376] If there is no market price in the absence of a market, because the market for the assets in the portfolio concerned has mostly dried up, the aid amount is likely to be the same as the transfer value or the insured value, i.e. the nominal value of the asset guarantee.[377] The amount of state aid may influence the extent of the restructuring measures, but this is less precise (and thus more negotiable) than the extent of own contribution. The valuation of the real economic value is, however, often as difficult as the valuation of the market price.

The principles laid down in the IAC remain relatively high level and abstract, and do not go much beyond the statement that the valuation must be based on observable market inputs and realistic and prudent assumptions about future cash flows. The Commission accepts that there may be assets so complex that a reliable forecast of developments in the foreseeable future is almost impracticable. At least for such assets, uniform hair-cut methods shall be applied in order to at least approximate the real economic value,[378] although this logically results in less accurate pricing. More important is that all methods must be based on rigorous stress-testing against a scenario of protracted global recession.[379]

In practice, the Commission has used Moody's CDOROMs to rate synthetic CDOs and CDOs of CDOs, using severe stress factors and hair cuts.[380] This method was even applied in cases where the asset relief did not solely cover impaired but also other assets, sometimes even the whole portfolio of the beneficiary bank.[381] Certainly, in such cases the results of the CDOROM are less accurate. In any case, it might be questioned whether the utilisation of a standardised simulation model for the calculation of synthetic CDOs may be considered sufficient to establish the value of a certain state aid measure or whether the

---

[375] Decision of September 20, 2011 on state aid SA 29338 (C–29/2009, ex. N 264/2009), granted by Germany to HSH Nordbank, Unreported, point 157.

[376] Commission Decision of October 21, 2008 on state aid measure C–10/08 (ex. NN 7/08) implemented by Germany for the restructuring of IKB Deutsche Industriebank AG [2009] O.J. L278/32, point 77; Commission Decision of June 4, 2008 on state aid C–9/08 (ex. NN 8/08, CP 244/07) implemented by Germany for Sachsen LB [2009] O.J. L104/34, point 71.

[377] Commission Decision of May 12, 2009 on state aid which Germany proposes to grant towards the restructuring of WestLB AG (C 43/08 (ex. N 390/08) [2009] O.J. L345/1, points 57–58.

[378] Point 40, IAC.

[379] Annex IV.1, IAC.

[380] Moody's assumptions are already embedded in the model, but can be easily modified by the user, allowing maximum flexibility. In order to run the model, users simply input the collateral portfolio characteristics, such as amount, industry, ratings and country, as well as the tranche attachment and size.

[381] For instance in Commission Decision of September 20, 2011 on state aid SA 29338 (C–29/2009, ex. N 264/2009), granted by Germany to HSH Nordbank, Unreported.

Commission and its experts must carry out an in-depth valuation of the whole portfolio instead. In light of the urgency and the number of cases the Commission had to deal with, this method may have been appropriate to receive approximate indications to be used in establishing the extent of the necessary own contribution and compensatory measures. It could probably be successfully challenged when used for the purpose of a recovery decision.[382]

Where the valuation of assets still appears too complex, alternative approaches may be taken, such as the creation of a "good bank" whereby the State purchases the good assets rather than the impaired assets. Nationalisation is a further alternative, with a view to carrying out the valuation over time in a restructuring or orderly winding-up context, thus eliminating any uncertainty about the proper value of the assets concerned.[383]

19–055 As mentioned above, in compliance with the general principle of burden sharing, banks must bear the losses associated with impaired assets to the maximum extent. Once assets have been properly evaluated, the losses, i.e. the difference between market value and real economic value, must be borne by the bank:

—In the case of transfer of assets, the bank receives state bonds only up to the real economic value of the assets transferred to the State.

—In the case of asset guarantees or insurances, the bank accepts a non-guaranteed first loss piece in the amount of the difference between book and real economic value of the covered asset portfolio. For this purpose, the first-loss piece has to be sufficiently large so that it covers at least the long-term expected losses on the covered assets.[384]

If bearing these losses would lead to a situation of technical insolvency, the bank normally must either be put into compulsory administration or be wound-

---

[382] The Commission argues that while a portfolio approach necessarily implies a greater use of assumptions, extrapolation and other approximation compared to approaches which value assets individually, therefore inherently embed a greater degree of imprecision, this "is not necessarily synonymous of a lower valuation. In some instances, when valuing portfolios experts have a tendency to air on the side of caution and use more conservative assumptions", Commission Decision of December 14, 2009, state aid N 422/2009, *RBS* [2010] O.J. C119/1, footnote 101.

[383] Point 38, IAC. As an example for nationalisation and the "good bank" concept, see Commission Decision of October 28, 2009 on state aid C–14/08 (ex. NN 1/08) implemented by the United Kingdom for Northern Rock [2010] O.J. L112/38, points 105–111. See also Commission Decision of February 16, 2009 in Case N 61/2009, Change of ownership of Anglo-Irish Bank, [2009] O.J. C177/2. After nationalisation, Anglo-Irish received further state aid in form of massive recapitalisation, in order to permit orderly winding up; see Commission Decision of June 29, 2011 on the state aids Nos SA 32504 (2011/N) and C–11/2010 (ex. N 667/2009) implemented by Ireland for Anglo Irish Bank and Irish Nationwide Building Society, Unreported.

[384] Commission Decision of December 14, 2009, state aid N 422/2009, *RBS* [2010] O.J. C119/1, point 153. See also Commission Decision of February 26, 2010 on state aid C 9/09 (ex. NN 49/08, NN 50/08 and NN 45/08) implemented by the Kingdom of Belgium, the French Republic and the Grand Duchy of Luxembourg for Dexia SA [2010] O.J. L274/54, point 159.

up.[385] In such a situation, with a view to preserving financial stability and confidence, protection or guarantees to bondholders may be appropriate. Shareholder protection is, however, normally excluded.[386] Where putting a bank into administration or its orderly winding up appears unadvisable for reasons of financial stability, for instance because the bank's size or type of activity would be unmanageable in an administrative or judiciary procedure or via an orderly winding-up without having dangerous systemic implications on other financial institutions or on lending to the real economy,[387] it may be possible to grant additional aid. This would entail applying a transfer value above the real economic value, for instance by accepting a lower first loss piece in guarantee schemes, as emergency aid for the period necessary to devise either a restructuring or a liquidation plan. The restructuring must be far-reaching and conditions must be introduced allowing the recovery of this additional aid at a later stage, for example through claw-back mechanisms,[388] e.g.:

—in the case of an insurance scheme, by a clause of "first loss", to be borne by the bank (typically with a minimum of 10 per cent) and a clause of "residual loss sharing", through which the bank participates to a percentage (typically with a minimum of 10 per cent) of any additional losses[389];

—higher remuneration[390];

—conversion of state losses into bank shares[391];

—skimming off of profits to the state aid grantor[392];

—nationalisation and subsequent re-privatisation.

With a claw-back mechanism the beneficiary bank normally repays the advantage arising from the higher assumption of risk at a later stage, i.e. it would have to repay the entire amount secured by the guarantee which exceeds the real economic value. If no full recovery (claw-back) is possible, far-reaching compensatory measures must be provided for.[393] In fixing the necessary claw-back it

19–056

---

[385] Point 22, IAC.

[386] See Commission Decision of November 5, 2008 on state aid NN 39/08, which Denmark grants to Roskilde Bank [2009] O.J. C12/3; and Decision of October 1, 2008 on state aid NN 41/08, wich United Kingdom grants to Bradford & Bingley [2008] O.J. C290/2.

[387] A justification by the monetary and/or supervisory authority would be necessary in this respect, see point 23, fn.4, IAC.

[388] Point 41, IAC.

[389] Point 24, IAC.

[390] Point 24, fn.5, IAC. Point 25, IAC. In such cases, nationalisation should always be considered see point 23, IAC. See, for instance, Commission Decision of November 18, 2009 on state aid C 10/09 (ex. N 138/09) implemented by the Netherlands for ING's Illiquid Assets Back Facility and Restructuring Plan [2010] O.J. L274/139, point 115.

[391] Point 25, IAC. In such cases, nationalisation options may always be considered an option, see point 23, IAC.

[392] Commission Decision of July 18, 2011 on state aid C15/2009 (ex. N196/2009), which Germany has granted or intends to grant to Hypo Real Estate, Unreported, point 85.

[393] Commission Decision of December 15, 2009 on state aid C 17/09 (ex. N 265/09) by Germany for the restructuring of Landesbank Baden-Württemberg [2010] O.J. L188/1, point 60.

can be taken into account whether it is unlikely that the guarantee will be taken up before the guarantor of the state aid has formed substantial reserves for such payments from the claw back fees.[394] As a general rule, the lower the contribution upfront the higher the need for a shareholder contribution at a later stage, either in the form of a claw-back and/or in the form of additional compensatory measures to limit the distortion of competition when assessing the necessary in-depth restructuring.[395] The deviation from the result of valuation should be more restricted for assets of which the value can be established on the basis of reliable market input than for those for which markets are illiquid. Non-compliance with this principle has to lead to more far reaching restructuring and more severe compensatory measures or even to an orderly winding-up.

The burden sharing based on the valuation of the assets must be distinguished from the pricing of the relief measure. The remuneration for the state must adequately take account of the risks of future losses exceeding those that are projected in the determination of the "real economic value" and any additional risk stemming from a transfer value above the real economic value. Such remuneration may be provided:

—in the case of asset transfers by setting the transfer price at below the "real economic value" to a sufficient extent so as to provide for adequate compensation for the risk in the form of a commensurate upside[396];

—in form of warrants for shares in the banks equal in value to the assets (implying that a higher price paid will result in a higher potential equity stake). Where the guarantee needs to be drawn upon, the Member State could use the warrants to acquire shares corresponding to the amounts that had to be covered by the guarantee; and

—in case of asset guarantees or insurances by an appropriate guarantee fee accordingly; the guarantee fee may be paid in the form of shares with a fixed cumulative interest representing the target return.

19–057   The calculation of the necessary target return is based on the remuneration, which would have been required for recapitalisation measures achieving the same capital effect as the proposed asset relief measure, in compliance with the Commission's Recapitalisation Communication, while taking into account the specific features of asset relief measures and particularly the fact that they may involve higher exposure than capital injections, since the State incurs a larger risk, related to a specific portfolio of impaired assets, with no direct contribution

---

[394] Commission Decision of December 15, 2009 on state aid C 17/09 (ex. N 265/09) by Germany for the restructuring of Landesbank Baden-Württemberg [2010] O.J. L188/1, points 65.

[395] Point 25, IAC. See for more details with regard to restructuring below at paras 19–062 and 19–063.

[396] See for instance state aid N 255/2009, Belgium, and N 274/2009, Luxembourg, Additional aid for Fortis Banque, Fortis Banque Luxembourg and Fortis holding [2009] O.J. C178/2, points 114–115.

by the bank's other income generating activities and funds, and beyond its possible stake in the bank.[397] On the other hand, in asset guarantee cases, it may also be taken into consideration that in contrast to recapitalisation measures, no liquidity is provided.[398] In practice the Commission has held that an interest rate of 6.25 per cent is to be considered sufficient to outweigh the advantage arising from the capital relief percentage.[399] According to the Recapitalisation Communication, 7 per cent can be regarded as appropriate compensation for Tier 1 capital without the supply of liquidity. In view of the equity capital relief effect the compensation should however be reduced by 0.75 per cent to 6.25 per cent p.a.: equity capital can consist of up to 50 per cent of Tier 1 capital and up to 50 per cent of Tier 2 capital in order to meet the regulatory requirements. As according to the Recommendation of the European Central Bank of November 20, 2008, on recapitalisation measures a difference of 1.5 per cent exists between the price of Tier 1 capital and Tier 2 capital; a reduction of 150 basis points is appropriate,[400] and the Tier 2 capital should then be compensated for at a rate of 5.5 per cent. The average of both rates is 6.25 per cent.[401] If the asset relief measure does not free any regulatory capital, lower remuneration is possible.[402]

In the case of a transfer of the impaired assets to a legally separated restructuring unit, the unit continuing an economic activity on the market ("the good bank") is the actual beneficiary of the measure, even if the measure directly favours the restructuring unit.[403] Therefore, the good bank has to remunerate the state guarantee for the impaired assets.[404] In case of prior nationalisation, the benefit which the good bank may enjoy as a result of the asset relief measure will be at least partially recuperated through a higher sale price when the good bank is re-privatised. In such exceptional conditions, it is acceptable that the proceeds

---

[397] Footnote 11, IAC.

[398] Annex IV.2, IAC.

[399] Commission Decision of December 15, 2009 on state aid C 17/09 (ex N 265/09) by Germany for the restructuring of Landesbank Baden-Württemberg [2010] O.J. L188/1, point 61. See also Commission Decision of June 30, 2010 in state aid Case N 261/2010 (ex. PN 9/2010), Austria, Second restructuring aid for BAWAG PSK [2010] O.J. C250/5, fn.18.

[400] See Commission Decision of July 31, 2009 in state aid case N 314/09, German asset relief scheme [2009] O.J. C199/3.

[401] Commission Decision of December 15, 2009 on state aid C–17/09 (ex. N 265/09) by Germany for the restructuring of Landesbank Baden-Württemberg [2010] O.J. L188/1, point 65.

[402] Commission Decision of February 26, 2010 on state aid C–9/09 (ex. NN 49/08, NN 50/08 and NN 45/08) implemented by the Kingdom of Belgium, the French Republic and the Grand Duchy of Luxembourg for Dexia SA [2010] O.J. L274/54, point 158. See also Commission Decision of July 18, 2011 on state aid C15/2009 (ex. N196/2009), which Germany has granted or intends to grant to Hypo Real Estate, Unreported, point 84.

[403] Commission Decision of October 28, 2009 on the state aid C–14/08 (ex. NN 1/08) implemented by the United Kingdom for Northern Rock [2010] O.J. L112/38, point 94. As a result of the aid to the restructuring unit, the "good bank" is able to continue the economic activity, being freed from the burden of the impaired assets transferred to the restructuring unit.

[404] See state aid SA 32745 (2011/NN), Austria, Restructuring of Kommunalkredit Austria AG [2011] O.J. C239/2, point 86. In this case, the Commission accepted that the KA Finance (restructuring unit) paid the remuneration only because both KA Finance and KA New were fully nationalized and KA New was to be privatised again, and because of certain other measures such as a skimming off clause.

of the sale of the bank is a form of remuneration for the State to the extent that it diminishes the total rescue costs (and thus no further remuneration is necessary).[405]

Whatever the model, in order to facilitate the bank's focus on the restoration of viability and to prevent possible conflicts of interest, it is necessary to ensure clear functional and organisational separation between the beneficiary bank and its impaired assets, notably as to their management, staff and clientele.[406] In practice, this is not always immediately possible[407] to achieve, especially with respect to asset relief measures covering almost all of the bank's asset portfolio.[408] In such cases, a complete segregation of the covered assets and of the staff managing them would be difficult and potentially damaging to the objective of minimising the expected losses. Therefore, there is no requirement for portfolio managers to be dedicated to the management of covered assets or to otherwise keep covered assets separate from the bank's other assets.[409] However, the beneficiary bank must put in place adequate safeguards to prevent conflicts of interest and ensure losses on the covered assets are reduced to the minimum. Such safeguards may include, in particular, adequate independent oversight and supervision rules. Additionally, a 10 per cent vertical slice of losses in excess of the first-loss kept by the beneficiary bank may work as an appropriate incentive to maximise recoveries on defaulted assets and hence minimise losses.[410]

Restructuring aid

19–058 **General remarks.** Where a financial institution has received emergency state aid, under certain circumstances the Member State must submit a viability plan, a restructuring plan or a liquidation plan, in order to confirm or re-establish individual banks' long-term viability without reliance on state support. The criteria under which such plans have to be submitted have been described above at para.19–037. The Restructuring Communication does not alter those criteria. It complements them by explaining how the Commission will assess the compatibility of restructuring aid granted by Member States under art.107(3)(b)

---

[405] Commission Decision of October 28, 2009 on state aid C–14/08 (ex. NN 1/08) implemented by the United Kingdom for Northern Rock [2010] O.J. L112/38, point 116.

[406] Points 45–46, IAC. A possible solution is the transfer of the structured assets to indirect subsidiaries of the bank. As long as the subsidiaries have the only objective to manage the structured assets and run them off, the assets may be still present on the bank's balance sheet at consolidated group level; see Commission Decision of June 30, 2010 in state aid Case N 261/2010 (ex. PN 9/2010), Austria, Second restructuring aid for BAWAG PSK [2010] O.J. C250/5, point 65.

[407] See Commission Decision of July 18, 2011 on state aid C15/2009 (ex. N196/2009), which Germany has granted or intends to grant to Hypo Real Estate, Unreported, point 81, where the Commission accepted that the separation will take place by September 30, 2013 at the latest.

[408] Commission Decision of September 20, 2011 on state aid SA 29338 (C 29/2009, ex. N 264/2009), granted by Germany to HSH Nordbank, Unreported, point 169.

[409] Commission Decision of December 14, 2009, state aid N 422/2009, *RBS* [2010] O.J. C119/1, point 178.

[410] Commission Decision of December 14, 2009, state aid N 422/2009, *RBS* [2010] O.J. C119/1, point 178.

TFEU.[411] Restructuring aid within this meaning is emergency aid, which has been temporarily authorised under art.107(3)(b) TFEU upon the condition that a viability or restructuring plan is submitted, as well as any new aid that may be notified as needed for restructuring. Moreover, the Restructuring Communication will also apply to aid which was temporarily authorised by the Commission as rescue aid under the R&R Guidelines during the financial crisis.[412] The Restructuring Communication consists of six sections: (1) introduction, (2) restoring long-term viability, (3) own contribution by the beneficiary (burden sharing), (4) limiting distortions of competition, (5) monitoring and procedural issues, and (6) temporary scope of the Communication. Sections 2 (restoring long-term viability) and 6 (temporary scope) apply to both, viability as well as restructuring plans. The Commission will normally request less detailed information for viability plans. In case of doubts as to the viability of the bank, the Commission will, in particular, seek evidence of adequate stress testing and of validation of the results of the stress testing by the competent national authority. Sections 3, 4 and 5 only apply to cases where the Member State is under an obligation to notify a restructuring plan.[413] The Restructuring Communication does not address liquidation plans[414] in detail, which are explained further below at para.19–077. By and large, the Restructuring Communication confirms the main principles established by the R&R Guidelines for the compatibility of restructuring aid: restoration of long-term viability without state support; minimisation of the aid/ adequate burden-sharing; and measures to limit competition distortion. However, the financial crisis made it necessary to adapt these principles:

—The most important objective of the Restructuring Communication is the restoration of financial stability and market confidence. As the return to long-term viability is superior to other aims, the Restructuring Communication provides for thorough viability assessments under severe stress assumptions.

—It grants more time for the restructuring, at the end of which return to long term viability must be achieved (up to five years, compared to the usual practice of two to three years under the R&R Guidelines).

[411] Point 4, Restructuring Communication.

[412] Point 4, fn.1, Restructuring Communication. This clarification was necessary for a couple of cases, the investigation of which had started still under the R&R Guidelines, namely the WestLB and Northern Rock Cases, see above at para.19–029. See also Commission Decision of September 29, 2010 on state aid C–32/09 (ex. NN 50/09) implemented by Germany for the restructuring of Sparkasse KölnBonn [2011] O.J. L235/1, point 69.

[413] In the assessment of a restructuring plan, the Commission will be guided by the requirements (i) to ensure the restoration of long-term viability of the financial institution in question, (ii) to ensure that aid is kept to the minimum and that there is substantial private participation to the costs of the restructuring, and (iii) to safeguard that there is no undue distortion of competition and no unjustified benefits deriving from the activation of the guarantee. See point 31 of the Banking Communication.

[414] Points 9 and 21, Restructuring Communication mention that in the event that the bank cannot be restored to viability, the restructuring plan must indicate how it can be wound up in an orderly fashion within an appropriate time frame that preserves financial stability.

—There is no fixed 50 per cent threshold of own contribution as required by the R&R Guidelines. Adequate burden-sharing is instead achieved through the appropriate price for state intervention, and through temporary restrictions on coupon and dividend payments.

—There is no strict need for *ex ante* appropriate burden sharing, as long as longer-term damage to the level playing field for banks and to competitive financial markets can be prevented by claw-back clauses.

—There is no "one time last time" principle during the financial crisis.[415]

19–059 **Restoring long-term viability.** The viability or restructuring plan must be comprehensive, detailed and based on a coherent concept. It should demonstrate how the bank will restore long-term viability without state aid as soon as possible, and in any case within a restructuring period of not more than five years.[416]

Long-term viability is achieved when:

"a bank is able to cover all its costs including depreciation and financial charges and provide an appropriate return on equity, taking into account the risk profile of the bank. The restructured bank should be able to compete in the marketplace for capital on its own merits in compliance with relevant regulatory requirements."[417]

Should further aid not initially be foreseen in the notified restructuring plan become necessary during the restructuring period, this will be subject to individual *ex ante* notification and any such further aid will be taken into account in the Commission's final decision.[418] This will normally make further compensatory measures and a new restructuring plan necessary.[419] A model restructuring plan is reproduced in the Annex to the Restructuring Communication, listing the information, which normally has to be presented in the plan, including:

---

[415] As examples for repeated restructuring aids, see Commission Decision of June 30, 2010 in state aid Case N 261/2010 (ex. PN 9/2010), Austria, Second restructuring aid for BAWAG PSK [2010] O.J. C250/5. Sometimes, a second or third restructuring aid became necessary before the Commission had closed the investigation procedure with respect to the first measure. In these cases, the Commission simply extends the current investigation, see for instance Decision on November 5, 2010 on state aid C–40/09 (ex. N 555/09), Extension of formal investigation procedure, *WestLB AG* [2011] O.J. C23/9.

[416] Point 15, Restructuring Communication.

[417] Point 12, Restructuring Communication.

[418] Point 16, Restructuring Communication.

[419] For Anglo Irish Bank, four different restructuring plans (November 30, 2009, May 31, 2010, October 26, 2010, January 31, 2011) were necessary before the Commission could come to a final decision. The different restructuring plans, which cumulated into the proposal of a merger with the also nationalised INBS, had become necessary as the sentiment towards the Irish State, since the nationalisation of Anglo Irish its only shareholder, had worsened due to the Sovereign debt crisis, see Commission Decision of June 29, 2011 on state aids Nos SA 32504 (2011/N) and C–11/2010 (ex N 667/2009) implemented by Ireland for Anglo Irish Bank and Irish Nationwide Building Society, Unreported, points 37–50.

—comparison with alternative options, including a break-up, or absorption by another bank, in order to demonstrate that no less costly or less distortive solutions are available to maintain financial stability[420];

—identification of the causes of the bank's difficulties and weaknesses and an outline of how the proposed restructuring measures remedy these problems,[421] including, for example, focussing on core business, reorientation of business models, closure or divestment of business divisions/subsidiaries, changes in the asset-liability management and other changes[422];

—information on the business model of the beneficiary, including in particular its organisational structure, funding (demonstrating viability of the short and long-term funding structure), corporate governance (demonstrating prevention of conflicts of interest as well as necessary management changes), risk management (including disclosure of impaired assets and prudent provisioning for expected non-performing assets), asset-liability management, cash-flow generation, off-balance sheet commitments (demonstrating their sustainability and consolidation), leveraging, current and prospective capital adequacy in line with applicable supervisory regulation (based on prudent valuation and adequate provisioning), remuneration incentive structure (demonstrating how it promotes the beneficiary's long-term profitability)[423];

—as long-term viability requires that the bank is able to survive without any state support clear plans for redeeming any state capital received and renouncing state guarantees. The more significant the reliance on state aid, the stronger the indication of a need to undergo in-depth restructuring in order to ensure long-term viability.[424] According to the Prolongation Communication, there may be no need for significant restructuring if public recapitalisation was only needed because of the confidence crisis on sovereign debt, and if the public capital injection is limited to the amount necessary to offset losses stemming from marking sovereign bonds of the Contracting Parties to the EEA Agreement to market in banks which are otherwise viable, and if the analysis shows that the banks in question did not take excessive risk in acquiring sovereign debt.[425] This shall encourage banks to apply for State recapitalisation in order to fulfil the 9 per cent Common Equty ratio by June 2012 as requsted by the European Council's banking package.[425a] However, the Prolongation Communication does not lift the obligation to notify a restructuring plan; and the Commission

---

[420] Point 9, Restructuring Communication.
[421] Point 10, Restructuring Communication.
[422] Point 55, IAC.
[423] Point 11, Restructuring Communication.
[424] Point 15, of the Exit Communication.
[425] Point 14, prolongation Communication.
[425a] See para.19–079, below.

probably enjoys large discretion in determining what "excessive risk" taking and "no significant restructuring" shall mean.

The viability of each business activity and centre of profit should be analysed, with the necessary breakdown. The return to viability of the bank should mainly derive from internal measures. It may be based on external factors such as variations in prices and demand over which the undertaking has no great influence, only if the market assumptions made are generally acknowledged. Restructuring requires a withdrawal from activities which would remain structurally loss making in the medium term.[426] This withdrawal is necessary to achieve viability and therefore does not count as a compensatory measure.

19–060 The expected results of the planned restructuring need to be demonstrated under a base case scenario as well as under "stress" case scenarios. For this, restructuring plans need to take account, inter alia, the current and future prospects of the financial markets, reflecting base-case and worst-case assumptions. The stress testing should, to the extent possible, be based on common parameters agreed at the Community level, and, where appropriate, adapted to cater for country- and bank-specific circumstances. There are no strict thresholds for the appropriate return on equity, since the return depends on the risk profile of the bank concerned.[427] Focussing on overcoming the financial crisis, the Commission regularly requests relatively low risk profiles. In addition, the necessary compensatory measures further mitigate the profitability of the banks concerned. Therefore, the appropriate return on equity will probably be lower than it was before the crisis.[428] In some cases, the Commission has required that the bank does only grant new loans with a minimum RAROC,[429] in order to

---

[426] Point 11, Restructuring Communication. See for instance Commission Decision of April 5, 2011 on the measures No.C 11/2009 (ex. NN 53b/2008, NN 2/2010 and N 19/2010) implemented by Dutch State for ABN AMRO Group NV (created following the merger between Fortis Bank Nederland and ABN AMRO N), Unreported, point 308. As this applies only to restructuring cases, it is no mandatory for viability review cases, as long as the bank can demonstrate that the whole business is viable on the long term.

[427] See for instance state aid SA 32745 (2011/NN), Austria, Restructuring of Kommunalkredit Austria AG [2011] O.J. C239/2, point 80.

[428] The following ROEs have been considered sufficient: 15% (state aid N 422/2009, *RBS* [2010] O.J. C119/1, point 194); 10–12% (Commission Decision of December 15, 2009 on state aid C–17/09 (ex. N 265/09) by Germany for the restructuring of Landesbank Baden-Württemberg [2010] O.J. L188/1, point 72); 9–10% in 2014 for a retail bank in normal market conditions (Commission Decision of September 29, 2010 on state aid C–32/09 (ex. NN 50/09) implemented by Germany for the restructuring of Sparkasse KölnBonn [2011] O.J. L235/1, point 69); 8–11% after tax; for German pfandbrief and public project financing bank HRE considered sufficient for viability and even for the purpose of re-privatisation, see German Commission Decision of July 18, 2011 on state aid C15/2009 (ex. N196/2009), which Germany has granted or intends to grant to Hypo Real Estate, Unreported, point 101. In most of the other decisions, the ROE to be achieved at the end of the restructuring period was blackened as business secret. It may be presumed that the average ROE accepted by the Commission was even lower.

[429] Risk adjusted return on capital (RAROC = Expected Return/Capital) is a risk-based profitability measurement framework for analysing risk-adjusted financial performance and providing a consistent view of profitability across businesses.

ensure that the bank's margins remain sufficiently high.[430] Long-term viability also requires that any state aid received is either redeemed over time, for instance by the Member State selling the shares to other shareholders or new investors, or is remunerated according to normal market conditions, meaning that the appropriate return condition also applies to capital injected by the State.[431]

As the TFEU is neutral as to the ownership of property, state aid rules apply equally to private and public banks.[432] In particular, this means that the privatisation of public banks cannot be per se considered as positive from a state aid control law perspective, even though changing the market structure via certain privatisations may have been on the Commission's agenda during the first decade of the new millennium. The German Landesbanks cases may serve as an example. The Landesbanks performed particularly badly during the crisis, since before 2005—the end of the transition period during which new 10-year loans benefitting from the banks' shareholder guarantees ("Gewährträgerhaftung") could still be raised—they had taken on large amounts of cheap liquidity and had then invested this money in CDOs and ABS with high interests, inter alia also with respect to US subprime items. Under Commissioner Kroes, it was a political objective to privatise these banks so that the same problems could not occur again in the future. The public owners were forced to propose exit scenarios, because the Commission argued that the viability of the Landesbanks could only be demonstrated by an abstract market test, i.e. the sale of the public shares to new private investors: privatisation as litmus test for long-term viability.[433] Under Commissioner Almunia, there was a paradigm shift: the abstract litmus test was abandoned. Instead, the business plans of the Landesbanks were scrutinized individually in even more detail, which led to quite different consequences for the public banks concerned.[434]

The paradigm shift may have been caused by the Restructuring Communication itself, which clearly provides that while the sale of an ailing bank to another financial institution can contribute to the restoration of long-term viability,[435]

---

[430] See for instance Commission Decision of July 18, 2011 on state aid C–15/2009 (ex. N196/2009), which Germany has granted or intends to grant to Hypo Real Estate, Unreported, point 106: minimum of 10% RAROC on individual transaction basis.

[431] See further for the so called Private Investor Test above at para.19–006.

[432] Point 14, Restructuring Communication.

[433] See Arhold [2011] MünchKommBeihVgR, Pt 2, D.III. privatisations. One of the conditions to Commission Decision of May 12, 2009 on state aid which Germany proposes to grant towards the restructuring of WestLB AG (C 43/08 (ex. N 390/08)) [2009] O.J. L345/1 was actually the exit of the public owners. The bank had to be privatised in whole or in parts. This condition has been challenged before the General Court in Case T–457/09 *Westfälisch-Lippischer Sparkassen- und Giroverband v Commission* [2010] O.J. C11/35. The application for interim suspension of the decision was dismissed by order of the president of the General Court of March 18, 2011, 9 *Westfälisch-Lippischer Sparkassen- und Giroverband v Commission* [2011] O.J. C160/22.

[434] LBBW and HSH Nordbank are considered to have got off lightly. WestLBb is likely to be broken down to a small service bank for its regional savings banks. In January 2012 BayernLB was still pending without any clear indication of the Commission's future decision

[435] As an example see the merger between Fortis Netherlands and ABN AMRO N, Commission Decision of April 5, 2011 on the measures No.C 11/2009 (ex. NN 53b/2008, NN 2/2010 and N 19/2010) implemented by Dutch State for ABN AMRO Group NV (created following the merger between Fortis Bank Nederland and *ABN AMRO N*), point 305.

may help to restore market confidence, and may also contribute to the consolidation of the financial sector, this does not mean that the requirements of viability, own contribution and limitations of distortions of competition do not have to be respected.[436] This also makes privatisations or mergers between Landesbanks (consolidation of Landesbanks sector[437]) much more difficult. The failed merger between WestLB and BayernLB is a good example.[438] If a bank cannot credibly return to long-term viability, not even by selling or merging it, the bank has to be wound-up or liquidated.

It depends on the business plan concerned, what level of own capital ratio is required to ensure long term viability. The riskier the business model, the higher the bank's tier 1 capital ratio should be, so that the bank may overcome the next market recession or other financial turmoil without new state aid.[439] An increase of the own capital ratio over the restructuring period may be achieved by different measures, for instance by a reduction of the RWAs (reduction of balance sheets), or by ploughing back profits (the ban on dividends or other disbursements may ensure this).

19–061   As the aid's objective is to restore the stability of the financial markets, the Commission's goal is always that after restructuring the bank concerned has a less risky business model than before. In order to achieve this, the Commission may request the banks to abandon certain business activities. This interacts with the requests for higher own capital ratios. The Commission has therefore a clear preference for conservative and risk averse business models, which do not

---

[436] Points 17 and 19, Restructuring Communication.

[437] Initially a joint objective of the Kroes Commission and of the German Federal Government, which has been mirrored in the condition catalogues, see for instance Commission Decision of December 15, 2009 on state aid C 17/09 (ex. N 265/09) by Germany for the restructuring of Landesbank Baden-Württemberg [2010] O.J. L188/1, Annex, point 12:

"LBBW will assist in a general consolidation of Landesbanks in accordance with economic principles and LBBW's business model. If mergers of individual Landesbanks come up for consideration by LBBW, LBBW will be guided by the need to ensure the long-term viability of the merged institution ands its sustainable ability to make appropriate loands to the real economy. Any purchases/mergers as part of a possible consolidation of Landesbanks will require the prior approval of the European Commission."

[438] In press release MEMO/10/433 of September 21, 2010, Commissoner Almunia made the following statement: "Given that both banks are under restructuring process, a merger itself may not automatically result in restoration of their long-term viability", adding: "The Commission would need to assess whether the merged entity would be viable in the long-term and whether the measures to ensure burden sharing and to limit competition distortions are adequate".

[439] See for instance Commission Decision of December 15, 2009 on state aid C 17/09 (ex. N 265/09) by Germany for the restructuring of Landesbank Baden-Württemberg [2010] O.J. L188/1, point 72: a Tier 1 capital ratio of 9–11%—even under extreme stress conditions—would lie far above the regulatory level and would correspond to the market's expectations of a bank with the risk profile of LBBW. See also Commission Decision of September 29, 2010 on state aid C 32/09 (ex. NN 50/09) implemented by Germany for the restructuring of Sparkasse KölnBonn [2011] O.J. 2011 L235/1, point 69: Tier-1 ratio improving from 6.1% in 2009 to 8–9% in 2014 considered sufficient for a retail bank in normal market conditions. For the German pfandbrief and public project financing bank HRE, the Commission considered a core capital ratio of 12.4 (base case) sufficient, see Commission Decision of July 18, 2011 on state aid C15/2009 (ex. N196/2009), which Germany has granted or intends to grant to Hypo Real Estate, Unreported, point 101. Against the background of Basel 3 and the sovereign debts crisis, market expectations may have meanwhile been increased.

expose the bank to excessive risk, for instance classic retail and corporate activities.[440]

Viability problems may also be connected to the bank's difficulties in receiving appropriate funding, often with respect to foreign currencies (US$).[441] In these cases, either the reduction of the business activities requiring funding in that currency and/or specific commitments as to future funding policy may be requested.[442]

Viability assessments of undertakings in difficulty are always associated with a relatively high degree of uncertainty, all the more so in an environment of a deep financial crisis with permanently changing parameters. In addition, often the banks concerned complicate this task by detaining or colouring relevant information. In some cases, the Commission's viability stamp had a half-life of just a few months, for instance in the *WestLB* decision.[443] Here, the Commission was informed only four months later that the initial forecasts were obsolete and additional aid was required. The negotiations of a new, much harsher restructuring are still ongoing today.[444] The Commission's main task is therefore to make sure on a reliable and comprehensive data basis that there is at least a sufficient likelihood of long term viability.

Aid limited to the minimum and own contribution by the beneficiary (burden sharing). In order to limit distortions of competition and address moral hazard, aid must be limited to the minimum necessary and an appropriate own contribution to restructuring costs must be provided by the aid beneficiary, including its owners[445]:   **19–062**

—Restructuring aid must be limited to covering restructuring costs, i.e. costs, which are necessary for the restoration of viability. The beneficiary should not be able to use the aid to finance market-distorting activities not linked to the restructuring process, for example acquisitions of shares in other undertakings or new investments, unless they are essential for restoring its viability.[446] Such prohibitions of external growth can be found in almost all decisions.[447] A prohibition to take over competing companies is also a

---

[440] Commission Decision of June 30, 2010 in state aid Case N 261/2010 (ex. PN 9/2010), Austria, Second restructuring aid for BAWAG PSK [2010] O.J. C250/5, point 88.

[441] Commission Decision of September 20, 2011 on state aid SA 29338 (C 29/2009, ex. N 264/2009), granted by Germany to HSH Nordbank, Unreported, point 221.

[442] See in particular Commission Decision of February 26, 2010 on state aid C 9/09 (ex. NN 49/08, NN 50/08 and NN 45/08) implemented by the Kingdom of Belgium, the French Republic and the Grand Duchy of Luxembourg for Dexia SA [2010] O.J. L274/54, points 166–198.

[443] Commission Decision of May 12, 2009 on state Aid C 43/2008, *WestLB* [2009] O.J. L345/1, point 75.

[444] See also Laprévote, "Selected issues raised by bank and restructuring plans", ESTAL 2012, p.93.

[445] Point 22, Restructuring Communication.

[446] Point 23, Restructuring Communication.

[447] See below at para.19–075.

mandatory compensatory behavioural measure (see below at para.19–073).

—In order to limit the aid amount to the minimum necessary, banks should first use their own resources to finance restructuring. This may involve, for instance, the sale of assets. State support should be granted on terms which represent an adequate burden-sharing of the costs. This means that the costs associated with the restructuring are not only borne by the State but also by those who invested in the bank, by absorbing losses with available capital and by paying an adequate remuneration for state interventions.[448] As discussed at paras 19–031, above, the other Communications provide detailed guidance regarding the pricing of state guarantees, recapitalisations and asset relief measures. To the extent that such a price is being paid, the shareholders of the bank see their position diluted in a financial sense.[449] It is always considered positively if in exchange for its recapitalisation, the State received shares issued at a discount compared to the stock market price at the time of the announcement, so that the aid does not wholly protect the existent shareholders against the consequences of the group's past losses, but that they are strongly diluted by the state recapitalisations.[450] Since December 1, 2012, such discount has become mandatory.[450a] However, in contrast to the R&R Guidelines, which fix thresholds of 50 per cent own contribution to the restructuring costs of large companies, in the Restructuring Communication there are no fix *ex ante* thresholds. During the financial crisis, it would be impossible to let a systemic bank to fail simply because it cannot sufficiently contribute to the restructuring costs. In such cases, a relatively low *ex ante* own contribution must be compensated by a further contribution at a later stage of the restructuring, for example in the form of claw-back clauses and/or by farther-reaching restructuring including more severe compensatory measures.[451]

—Unless dividend bans are necessary because amortisation of profits is necessary to reach sufficient own capital ratios (return to viability) or because of insufficient *ex ante* own contribution (burden sharing), even during the restructuring phase banks normally shall remain able to remunerate capital, including in the form of dividends and coupons on outstanding subordinated debt, out of profits generated by their activities. However, banks may not use state aid to remunerate own funds (equity and subordinated debt) when those activities do not generate sufficient profits. Therefore, during the restructuring phase, the discretionary offset of losses (for example by

---

[448] Point 24, Restructuring Communication.
[449] Point 24, fn.4, Restructuring Communication.
[450] Commission Decision of December 14, 2009, state aid N 422/2009, *RBS* [2010] O.J. C119/1, point 216.
[450a] Points 7–8, Prolongation Communication.
[451] Point 25, Restructuring Communication. See also points 24–25 IAC.

releasing reserves or reducing equity)[452] in order to guarantee the payment of dividends and coupons on outstanding subordinated debt, is in principle prohibited and can only exceptionally be allowed if it is necessary to ensure refinancing of the bank or as an exit incentive.[453] If a beneficiary bank has not complied with the Commission's policy on Tier 1 and Tier 2 capital instruments, this infringement of burden sharing has to be compensated by additional compensatory measures.[454] If the bank repays early (parts of) the state aid received, this may prompt the Commission to ease the restrictions: "If a bank is able to raise [. . .] a significant amount of capital from the market and has a clear strategy in the medium term, it should no longer be restricted in the use of its capital if and where this does not threaten the implementation of its restructuring plan."[455] In the interest of promoting refinancing by the beneficiary bank, the Commission may favourably regard the payment of coupons on newly issued hybrid capital instruments with greater seniority over existing subordinated debt. Transactions such as buy-backs and the exercise of call-options of Tier 1 and Tier 2 capital instruments may also infringe the principle of burden-sharing in so far as they protect the Tier 1 and Tier 2 capital holders from their exposure to the inherent risk of their investment. Banks subject to a state aid investigation must therefore consult the Commission before making announcements to the market concerning Tier 1 and Tier 2 capital transactions. This is to enable the Commission to balance, considering the concrete circumstances at hand, the interest in the bank's return to viability with the interest in ensuring burden-sharing and thus of limiting competition distortion.[456] During the restructuring phase, banks should normally not be allowed to purchase their own shares.[457]

Limiting distortions of competition and ensuring a competitive banking sector—compensatory measures. Financial stability remains the overriding objective of aid to the financial sector during a systemic crisis, but safeguarding systemic stability in the short-term should not result in longer-term damage to the level playing field and competitive markets. In this context, measures to limit 19–063

---

[452] This does not prevent the bank from making coupon payments when it is under a binding legal obligation to do so, see point 26, fn.6, Restructuring Communication.

[453] Point 24, fn.4, Restructuring Communication, with further references to points 31 IAC and points 33, 34 and 45 of the Recapitalisation Communication.

[454] Commission Decision of November 18, 2009 on state aid C 10/09 (ex. N 138/09) implemented by the Netherlands for ING's Illiquid Assets Back Facility and Restructuring Plan [2010] O.J. L274/139, point 138.

[455] Commission Decision of November 18, 2009 on state aid C 10/09 (ex. N 138/09) implemented by the Netherlands for ING's Illiquid Assets Back Facility and Restructuring Plan [2010] O.J. L274/139, point 139.

[456] EMO/09/441 of October 8, 2009, Commission recalls rules concerning Tier 1 and Tier 2 capital transactions for banks subject to a restructuring aid investigation.

[457] See Commission Decision of December 18, 2008 in case N 615/2008 *Bayern LB* [2009] O.J. C 80/4.

distortions of competition (so-called "compensatory measures") play an important role.[458] They should be tailor-made to address the distortions identified on
the markets where the beneficiary bank operates following its return to viability
post restructuring, while at the same time adhering to a common policy and
principles.[459] The nature and form of the compensatory measures depend on the
following two criteria, while restoring the stability of the financial sector must
always be kept in view, so that compensatory measures must not compromise the
above-mentioned top priority, the bank's return to viability.[460]

First, the amount of state aid (including the conditions and circumstances
under which it was granted), including any kind of rescue aid, will be assessed
both in absolute terms (amount of capital received, aid element in guarantees and
asset relief measures) and in relation to the bank's risk-weighted assets. This
approach is also in line with the principle that the more significant the reliance
on state aid is, the stronger the indication of a need to undergo in-depth
restructuring in order to ensure long-term viability.[461] In practice, the Commission has tried to combine the need for in-depth restructuring and compensatory
measures by calculating the extent of the necessary balance sheet reduction on
the basis of the overall aid amount. The question is whether the Commission has
sufficiently differentiated between the amount of aid in the form of liquidity
assistance and structural aid, such as recapitalisations. Equal accounting of both
would counter the Commission's initial distinction between sound banks suffering mainly from contagious liquidity problems and banks having real solvency
issues resulting, for instance, from hazardous investments in toxic assets. As the
nominal aid amount of liquidity assistances is normally higher than the one of
asset relief measures, this would cause a tendency that would put "sound banks"
under more severe restructuring than distressed banks.[462] However, it seems that
the Commission has recognised this problem and has differentiated between
these two state aid classes. For instance, in the *Dexia* Decision, it has acknowledged that "aid amounts corresponding to recapitalizations should not be added
to funding guarantees, since the two categories of measures do not have the same
distortive effects on competition."[463] During the negotiations, the Commission
has often used a graph similar to the following,[464] in order to explain what the
peer group of the beneficiary bank concerned was in terms of liquidity and recap/
asset relief state aid, the vertical y-axis showing the liquidity guarantee/balance
sheet ratio, the horizontal x-axis the recap and asset relief/RWA ratio. The further

---

[458] Point 29, Restructuring Communication.
[459] Point 30, Restructuring Communication.
[460] Point 32, Restructuring Communication.
[461] Point 15, Exit Communication.
[462] See Laprévote, "Selected issues by bank restructuring plans under EU State aid rules" [2011], EStAL 2012, p.93.
[463] Commission Decision of February 26, 2010, state aid C 9/2009, *Dexia* [2010] O.J. L274/54, para.150.
[464] The graphic is neither complete nor exact. It is used for illustration purposes, only. Certain banks like Northern Rock have not been used in the sample, since their structural aid/RWA ratio would have gone beyond the scope of this graph.

left and the lower the position of the bank, the less the state aid it received. In general, the Commission has taken the view that an in-depth restructuring is necessary if the beneficiary bank has received state aid in excess of 2 per cent of the bank's total RWA.[465]

Pictogram 1:

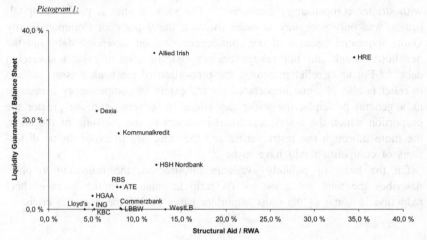

The Commission intended to treat banks with a comparable overall aid amount equally, taking into account that structural aid normally weighs more heavily than liquidity support, and taking into account all further aggregating and mitigating parameters, especially the conditions and circumstances under which the aid was granted. They may have an impact on the balance sheet reduction, and can trigger other additional compensatory measures, such as claw-back payments. For instance, if aid departing from the principles laid down in the other three Communications—especially as to the adequate remuneration—has been exceptionally approved, the resulting additional distortion of competition will require additional structural or behavioural safeguards.[466] Where for reasons of financial stability the entry price has been set at a level significantly below the market price, it should be ensured that the terms of the financial support are revised in the restructuring plan so as to reduce the distortive effect of the subsidy.[467] On the other hand, again, the greater the burden sharing and the higher the own contribution, the less moral hazard and thus the less need for further compensatory measures exists.[468] In addition, the Commission may also distinguish between aid measures necessitated exclusively by the current bottleneck in access to liquidity in relation to an otherwise fundamentally sound financial institution, as opposed to assistance provided to beneficiaries that are additionally suffering from structural

19–064

---

[465] Commission Decision of November 18, 2009 on state aid C 18/09 (ex. N 360/09) implemented by Belgium for KBC [2010] O.J. L188/24, point 140.
[466] Point 31, fn.2, Restructuring Communication, with further references to point 58, IAC.
[467] Point 34, Restructuring Communication.
[468] Point 31, Restructuring Communication.

solvency problems linked for instance to their particular business model or investment strategy (that's why the y-axis in the above graph is less important than the x-axis).[469] In principle, assistance to the latter category of beneficiaries is likely to raise greater concerns and will therefore have to be addressed with stricter compensatory measures.[470] The same applies if public recapitalisation was only necessary in order to reach the 9 per cent Common Equity Quote requested because of the confidence crisis on sovereign debt and the beneficiary bank did not take excessive risk in acquiring such sovereign debt.[470a] For asset relief measures, the proportion of the bank's assets subject to relief is also of some importance for the extent of compensatory measures: as a general principle, the wider the eligibility criteria, and the greater the proportion which the assets concerned represent in the portfolio of the bank, the more thorough the restructuring and the remedies to avoid undue distortions of competition will have to be.[471]

On the basis of publicly available information, the following graph[472] describes the total aid amount/RWA ratio in relation to the balance sheet reduction in some of the most important cases during the financial crisis:

Pictogram 2:

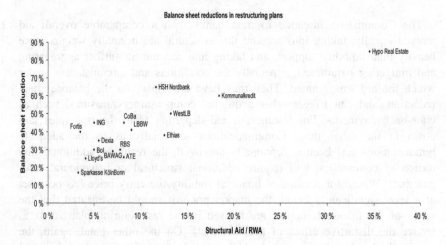

Balance sheet reductions in restructuring plans

---

[469] As an example for "sound banks" see Commission Decision of April 5, 2011 on the measures No.C 11/2009 (ex. NN 53b/2008, NN 2/2010 and N 19/2010) implemented by Dutch State for ABN AMRO Group NV (created following the merger between Fortis Bank) Nederland and ABN AMRO N), points 305 and 320.

[470] Point 33, Banking Communication. See also Commission Decision of June 30, 2010 in state aid Case N 261/2010 (ex. PN 9/2010), Austria, Second restructuring aid for BAWAG PSK [2010] O.J. C250/5, point 103; state aid NN 42/2008, Belgium, NN 46/2008, Luxembourg NN 53/A/2008, Netherlands, Restructuring aid to Fortis Bank and Fortis Bank Luxembourg [2009] O.J. C80/7, point 92.

[470a] Point 14, Prolongation Communication.

[471] Point 35, IAC.

[472] The graphic is neither complete nor exact. It is used for illustration purposes only. Certain banks like Northern Rock have not been used in this sample, since their structural aid/RWA ratio would have gone beyond the scope of this graph.

Not surprisingly, the graph does not demonstrate full consistency between **19–065** the state aid/RWA ratio and the required balance sheet reduction, as (i) it only shows the relation between the structural aid/RWA ratio and the balance sheet reduction,[473] and (ii) it does not mirror all additional parameters which the Commission had to take into account. If it was only for the structural aid/RWA ratio, the graph would probably describe a perfect curve rising steeply at the beginning somewhere in the region of Lloyd's, Dexia, Commerzbank and then levelling slightly just between HSH Nordbank and Kommunalkredit and finally to Hypo Real Estate. For the banks above this ideal curve, other (aggravating) parameters must have been applied (like relatively high liquidity guarantees[474]), while probably less aggravating or more mitigating factors applied in the case of banks below the curve. In this context, it must be kept in mind that the size of the reduction does not always reflect the quality of the structural measures undertaken: distinctions must be made between run-offs of activities, deleveraging and divestitures of existing businesses,[475] between measures undertaken in the interest of restoration of viability and those implemented to address a concrete competition concern and, finally, between structural measures put in place in core markets and ancillary markets of the beneficiary bank.

Furthermore, the Commission should make a distinction between state aid categories. An example: due to the severe stress tests applied for the calculation of the real economic value of the assets covered, the state aid amount of an asset guarantee may relatively easily reach the nominal amount of the guarantee. In this case, the state aid value of the asset guarantee would be the same as the state aid amount of a recapitalisation of the same nominal amount, although the guarantee is less favourable for the bank, because unlike in the recapitalisation scenario no liquidity is granted. Furthermore, in a guarantee case, it is still unclear whether the Member State will actually have to pay the State aid amount calculated by the Commission. Nevertheless, it seems that Royal Bank of Scotland (RBS) (a multiplier of 2.5 between state aid/RWA ratio and balance sheet reduction) and Sparkasse KölnBonn (multiplier of 1.5) got off relatively lightly, while Fortis (multiplier of more than 11) did not. The latter may be explained by the break-up of the Dutch activities which took place before the acquisition by BNP Paribas, which the Commission considered as equivalent to a balance sheet reduction.[476]

The second criteria is the characteristics of the market(s) on which the bank **19–066** will operate.[477] The Commission will analyse the likely effects of the aid on the

---

[473] The exact amount of liquidity guarantees is not always publicly available, while the structural aid/RWA ratio is normally published in the Commission Decision.

[474] Like for HSH Nordbank, compare pictogram 1.

[475] See for instance Commission Decision of November 18, 2009 on state aid C 10/09 (ex. N 138/09) implemented by the Netherlands for ING's Illiquid Assets Back Facility and Restructuring Plan [2010] O.J. L274/139, point 143.

[476] See Laprévote, "Selected issues by bank restructuring plans under EU State aid rules" [2012] EStAL, p.93.

[477] See to this extent also point 59 IAC, which, however, focuses more on distortive nature of the measure itself: "The Commission will assess the scope of the compensatory measures required, depending on its assessment of competition distortions resulting from the aid, and notably on the

markets where the bank operates after the restructuring. If the restructured bank has limited remaining market presence, additional constraints, in the form of divestments or behavioural commitments, are less likely to be necessary. The measures will be tailored to market characteristics (concentration levels, capacity constraints, the level of profitability, barriers to entry and to expansion)[478] to make sure that effective competition is preserved.[479] In some areas, divestments may generate adverse consequences and may not be necessary in order to achieve the desired outcomes, in which case the limitation of organic growth may be preferred to divestments. In other areas, especially those involving national markets with high entry barriers, divestments may be needed to enable entry or expansion of competitors.[480]

There are in general three kinds of compensatory measures: financial charges, structural measures and (other) behavioural commitments, which interact and affect each other. For instance, where structural measures and/or behavioural restraints are not appropriate, the Commission may accept the imposition of a claw-back mechanism, for example in the form of a levy on the aid recipients.[481] Financial charges, which limit the distortion of competition may include remuneration of the State aid and claw-back mechanisms in different forms.[482]

Structural measures are mainly divestitures and the reduction of business activities. Banks may be required to divest subsidiaries or branches, portfolios of customers or business units, or similar measures. In order for such measures to increase competition and contribute to the internal market, they should favour the entry of competitors and cross-border activity, ideally without discrimination between businesses in different Member States (preservation of an internal market in financial services).[483] While limiting any disadvantages for other European banks, these structural conditions have to respect the primary objective of restoring the long-term viability of the banking sector: Where the immediate implementation of structural measures is not possible due to market circumstances, for instance because finding buyers for divested assets at appropriate prices is currently impossible—most conditions provide for an

---

basis of the following factors: total amount of aid, including from guarantee and recapitalisation measures, volume of impaired assets benefiting from the measure, proportion of losses resulting from the asset, general soundness of the bank, risk profile of the relieved assets, quality of risk management of the bank, level of solvency ratios in the absence of aid, market position of the beneficiary bank and distortions of competition from the bank's continued market activities, and impact of the aid on the structure of the banking sector."

[478] Point 32, fn.1, Restructuring Communication.

[479] In highly concentrated markets, for instance, where all main players have benefited from state aid, it might be disproportionate to impose limitations on price leadership on all the aided players.

[480] Point 32, Restructuring Communication. See for instance the divestment of RBS's Rainbow Business, which addressed the group's leadership on the UK retail banking market (Commission Decision of December 14, 2009, state aid N 422/2009, *RBS* [2010] O.J. C119/1, point 244).

[481] Point 42, Restructuring Communication.

[482] See in more detail the table below at para.19–073.

[483] Point 35, Restructuring Communication.

extension of the time period for the implementation of these measures, especially if it can be shown that the proceeds that can be obtained would be lower than the book value of the respective holding at the time of the sale or would produce losses in the group accounts in accordance with the IFRS accounting standards.[484]

In addition, the Communication also pays more attention to overall national market structures and market opening measures, in order to prevent a situation in which the large number of simultaneous restructuring cases closes down national market structures, and to preserve cross border activities of banks. The sheer number of approval decisions under divestment commitments and conditions in combination with this Communication's approach actually grants the Commission a considerable market structuring power. If banks are obliged to divest businesses, either by selling their shares in subsidiaries or their assets belonging to certain activities, the Commission normally requires that the buyer of these businesses fulfils certain criteria, the standard ones being as follows:

19–067

—the purchaser must be independent of and unconnected to the divesting financial institute,[485] within the meaning of art.11 of Commission Regulation (EC) No.2790/1999 on the application of art.101(3) TFEU[486];

—the purchaser is in a reasonable position to satisfy all the necessary conditions imposed by the relevant competition authorities as part of any merger control process and by any other competent authorities[487];

—the purchaser does not held more than a certain share in specific markets or business segments[488];

—the purchaser must satisfy the national regulatory authority as to the adequacy of its financial resources (both in respect of liquidity and capital), the competency and experience of the leadership, the adequacy of its risk and control standards, the adequacy of its attitude to customers in terms of fair customer treatment, adequate service and fair pricing, and the long-term

---

[484] See for instance Commission Decision of June 30, 2010 in state aid Case N 261/2010 (ex. PN 9/2010), Austria, Second restructuring aid for BAWAG PSK [2010] O.J. C250/5, point 43.

[485] See already Commission Decision of May 12, 2009 on state aid which Germany proposes to grant towards the restructuring of WestLB AG (C 43/08 (ex. N 390/08)) [2009] O.J. L 345/1, Annex, point 6.4. See also Commission Decision of May 20, 2010 in state aid Case N 256/2009, Restructuring aid to Ethias, Belgium, [2010] O.J. C252/5, annex, point 2.5.

[486] See for instance Commission Decision of December 14, 2009, state aid N 422/2009, *RBS*, OJ 2010 C119/1, point 99.

[487] See already Commission Decision of May 12, 2009 on state aid which Germany proposes to grant towards the restructuring of WestLB AG (C 43/08 (ex. N 390/08)) [2009] O.J. L 345/1, Annex, point 6.4. See also Commission Decision of December 14, 2009, state aid N 422/2009, *RBS*, [2010] O.J. C119/1, point 99. Also Commission Decision of May 20, 2010 in state aid Case N 256/2009 Restructuring aid to Ethias, Belgium, [2010] O.J. C252/5, annex, point 2.5.

[488] See for instance Commission Decision of December 14, 2009, state aid N 422/2009, *RBS*, [2010] O.J. C119/1, point 99.

viability, success and sustainability of the entity, assessed by reference to (amongst other things) its business plan[489];

—the purchaser has sufficient resources, proven expertise and incentive to maintain and develop the business as viable and active competitive forces in competition with the seller and other competitors.[490]

19–068   Certain eligibility criteria shall ensure that the divestment takes places smoothly and efficiently, for instance the obligation that the buyer will satisfy all the necessary conditions imposed by the relevant competition authorities as part of any merger control process. Other criteria do not (mainly) serve the fast implementation of the compensatory measures but focus instead on market structuring through the divestments in order to ensure more stability and/or more competition on the relevant market by requiring, for instance, that the buyer satisfies the national financial control agency as to its ability and willingness to maintain and develop the acquired business. Other criteria are not directly buyer related but concern only the way the business has to be offered, in parts and/or in whole:

—The requirement to offer the activities on the market as parts and as a whole makes sure that all interested competitors may be able to bid for parts of the business, and therefore helps to make the divestment procedure efficient and competitive.[491]

—The obligation to offer a certain business as a whole only or to require certain sizes or packaging of the businesses to be divested does not mainly serve the efficiency of the implementation of the compensatory measures but the improvement of the competitive structure on and/or the stability of the relevant market.[492]

Conditions, which focus on the competitive structure of the market after the implementation of the restructuring plan—either buyer or process related—

---

[489] See for instance Commission Decision of December 14, 2009, state aid N 422/2009, *RBS*, O.J. 2010 C119/1, point 99.

[490] See for instance Commission Decision of December 14, 2009, state aid N 422/2009, *RBS*, [2010] O.J. C119/1, point 99; Commission Decision of May 20, 2010 in state aid Case N 256/2009 Restructuring aid to Ethias, Belgium, [2010] O.J. C 252/5, annex, point 2.5; Commission Decision of September 29, 2010 on state aid C 32/09 (ex. NN 50/09) implemented by Germany for the restructuring of Sparkasse KölnBonn, [2011] O.J. L235/1, Annex II, point 25(b).

[491] See for instance Commission Decision of May 12, 2009 on state aid which Germany proposes to grant towards the restructuring of WestLB AG (C 43/08 (ex. N 390/08)) [2009] O.J. L345/1, Annex, points 4.1 and 4.2.

[492] In the beginning, this condition was related to stability of the financial market rather than to effective competition; see Commission Decision of May 12, 2009 on state aid which Germany proposes to grant towards the restructuring of WestLB AG (C 43/08 (ex. N 390/08)) [2009] O.J. L345/1, Annex, point 6.4.: "on the basis of its financial resources and in particular its rating, must be able to ensure the solvency of the bank." Later during the crisis, the Commission focused more on competition, see for instance Commission Decision of December 14, 2009, state aid N 422/2009, *RBS*, [2010] O.J. C119/1, point 99.

should only be admissible for as long as the financial stability of the market would otherwise be jeopardised. Conditions (and even commitments when rendered during the formal investigation period[492a]), which are not necessary when seen in the light of the objective of art.107(3)(b) TFEU can be challenged before the Union Courts. The danger that the divestment may worsen the competitive structure on the relevant market, for instance by creating a monopoly or a tight oligopoly, has to be assessed by the competent merger control authorities in the scope of the merger control procedures. The Commission's state aid units are neither competent for nor in charge of this assessment.

Another form of structural measure is the limitation of the bank's expansion in **19–069** certain product or geographic market areas, for instance via market-oriented remedies such as specific capital requirements, annual growth caps or by limiting the admissible market share or market position (for instance: not to be one of the three leading companies).[493] However, the Commission must pay particular attention to the need to avoid retrenchment within national borders and a fragmentation of the single market.[494]

Banks cannot be allowed to use state aid to offer their customers terms (rates in particular) which cannot be matched by their un-aided competitors. This may take the form of limitations on the bank's position in league tables or of various types of price-leadership clauses, for instance prohibition of proposing the highest interest rates offered on the market to retail depositors[495] or minimum pricing on new loans.[496] In several decisions[497] the Commission considered it appropriate to limit the price leadership ban to markets where the bank has a significant presence, defined for the purpose of the price leadership ban as having a market share of at least 5 per cent. According to the leadership ban in the ING Case, the beneficiary bank should not offer more favourable prices than its three best priced competitors in the relevant markets.[498] This clause has been explicitly challenged by *ING* before the General Court.[499] In any case, such a clause

---

[492a] Case T–301/01 *Alitalia/Commission* [2008] E.C.R. II–1753, paras 378–381.

[493] Commission Decision of September 20, 2011 on state aid SA 29338 (C 29/2009, ex. N 264/2009), granted by Germany to HSH Nordbank, Unreported, annex I, point 4.9.

[494] Point 36, Restructuring Communication.

[495] Point 39, fn.1, Restructuring Communication, and point 44, Restructuring Communication.

[496] For instance in the form of net interest revenue obligation in support of the price leadership ban in the private banking segment, where the price leadership ban is not sufficiently effective, see Commission Decision of April 5, 2011 on the measures No.C 11/2009 (ex. NN 53b/2008, NN 2/2010 and N 19/2010) implemented by Dutch State for ABN AMRO Group NV (created following the merger between Fortis Bank) Nederland and ABN AMRO N), Unreported, point 326.

[497] See for instance Commission Decision of May 7, 2009 in Case N 244/09 *Commerzbank* [2009] O.J. C147/4; Commission Decision of November 18, 2009 on state aid C 10/09 (ex. N 138/09) implemented by the Netherlands for ING's Illiquid Assets Back Facility and Restructuring Plan [2010] O.J. L274/139, point 150; and Commission Decision of November 18, 2009 on state aid C 18/09 (ex. N 360/09) implemented by Belgium for KBC [2010] O.J. L188/24.

[498] Commission Decision of November 18, 2009 on state aid C 10/09 (ex. N 138/09) implemented by the Netherlands for ING's Illiquid Assets Back Facility and Restructuring Plan [2010] O.J. L274/139, point 150.

[499] Action brought on January 28, 2010, *ING Groep v Commission* (Case T–33/10) [2010] O.J. C80/40.

depending on the price policy of the bank's competitors is very difficult to monitor. In recent decisions the Commission has therefore voluntarily abstained from that clause. In segments where a price leadership ban is less efficient, the Commission may also request the compatibility with other parameters such as net interest revenue or the bank's obligation to cover its own administrative costs and transfer and transaction costs for its private banking customers who wish to change financial institute,[500] or, in the case of insurance companies, by fixing a specific level of combined ratios for certain insurance products.[501]

19–070   Prohibition of the acquisition of competing businesses ("acquisition ban"). This prohibition of external growth is mandatory and must apply for at least three years (it may apply longer).[502] When banks are faced with bad loans in their loan portfolio, the restructuring of those loans sometimes requires solutions such as converting debt into equity. Those situations are considered to be normal banking practice and are not covered by the acquisition ban.[503] In exceptional circumstances and upon notification, acquisitions may be authorised by the Commission where they are part of a consolidation process necessary to restore financial stability or to ensure effective competition.[504] The exemption clauses were considered to be especially important for the German Landesbanks cases and the politically supported consolidation of the Landesbanks sector. All Ländesbanks decisions have an explicit exemption from the merger prohibition as long as the merger takes place between two or more Landesbanks, subject to the Commission's approval. In practice, except for the very early take-over of SachsenLB by LBBW, the consolidation did not take place. Quite apart from the Landesbanks consolidation, these clauses are also important as most of the Commission decisions impose requirements with regard to the divestiture of businesses and subsidiaries of the beneficiary banks during the restructuring period, meaning that a lot of competing businesses and entities are put up for sale during a limited period of time. Whether all this business can be sold to banks, which have not benefitted from state aid (and are therefore not under a prohibition of external

---

[500] See Commission Decision of April 5, 2011 on the measures No.C 11/2009 (ex. NN 53b/2008, NN 2/2010 and N 19/2010) implemented by Dutch State for ABN AMRO Group NV (created following the merger between Fortis Bank Nederland and ABN AMRO N), Unreported, point 326–327.

[501] See Commission Decision of May 20, 2010 in state aid Case N 256/2009 Restructuring aid to Ethias, Belgium [2010] O.J. C252/5, point 144: insurance products are standardised only to a limited extent. Besides price, the attractiveness of an insurance policy depends to a large extent on other factors such as the extent of the cover and quality of services. Therefore, an outright price leadership ban could give rise to some problems of implementation in the insurance market.

[502] Point 40, Restructuring Communication. Commission Decision of April 5, 2011 on the measures No.C 11/2009 (ex. NN 53b/2008, NN 2/2010 and N 19/2010) implemented by Dutch State for ABN AMRO Group NV (created following the merger between Fortis Bank Nederland and ABN AMRO N), Unreported, point 312.

[503] Commission Decision of April 5, 2011 on the measures No.C 11/2009 (ex. NN 53b/2008, NN 2/2010 and N 19/2010) implemented by Dutch State for ABN AMRO Group NV (created following the merger between Fortis Bank Nederland and ABN AMRO N), Unreported, point 312, fn.102.

[504] Point 41, Restructuring Communication.

growth), is doubtful. Even though the Commission is prepared to extend binding deadlines of up to five years in cases where finding a buyer for subsidiaries or other activities or assets appears objectively difficult,[505] the Commission may nevertheless receive numerous applications for sales to other beneficiary banks. This may put the Commission in a position to further influence the structure of the financial market(s).

The Commission has also considered the Member State's commitment to privatise the bank as an acceptable compensatory measure, since "the sale of the bank to a competitor constitutes in itself a type of compensation."[506]

(Other) behavioural commitments, which shall be accepted as compensatory measures, must serve to prevent the beneficiary from using state aid to the detriment of competitors which do not enjoy similar public support. Examples are the prohibition of advertising with state aid,[507] a cap on marketing, advertising and sponsorship costs as well as customer mobility commitments.[508]

Overview of standard conditions and commitments and their potential motives. According to art.7(4) of the Procedural Regulation,[509] after the formal investigation procedure the Commission may attach to a positive decision conditions subject to which an aid may be considered compatible with the Internal Market and may lay down obligations to enable compliance with the decision to be monitored (a so-called "conditional decision"). This possibility does only exist for decisions terminating the formal investigation procedure, not for decisions at the end of the preliminary investigation procedure. During both procedures, the Member State may address any doubts of the Commission as to the compatibility with the Internal Market by modifying its state aid project. In practice, these modifications often take the form of certain commitments how the Member State, the aid grantor or the beneficiary will act in future, and thus how the state aid project will be executed. Even though both commitments and conditions may have the same contents and objective, they differ in some points:

19–071

---

[505] Point 37, Restructuring Communication.

[506] See state aid NN 42/2008, Belgium, NN 46/2008, Luxembourg, NN 53/A/2008, Netherlands, Restructuring aid to Fortis Bank and Fortis Bank Luxembourg [2009] O.J. C80/7, point 95. See also Commission Decision of October 21, 2008 on state aid measure C 10/08 (ex. NN 7/08) implemented by Germany for the restructuring of IKB Deutsche Industriebank AG [2009] O.J. L278/32, point 113.

[507] Point 44, Restructuring Communication, with reference to Commission Decision of November 12, 2008 in Case N 528/2008 *ING* [2008] O.J. C328/10, point 35. This prohibition was already laid down in the Banking Communication and can be found in almost all decisions since. See for example Commission Decision of November 19, 2008 in Case NN 49/2008, NN 50/2008 and NN 45/2008 Guarantees to Dexia Unreported, point 73; Commission Decision of November 19, 2008 in Case N 574/2008 Guarantees to Fortis Bank [2009] O.J. C38/2, point 58 and Commission Decision of December 3, 2008 in Case NN 42/2008, NN 46/2008 and NN 53/A/2008 Restructuring aid to Fortis Bank and Fortis Bank Luxembourg [2009] O.J. C80/7), point 94.

[508] Commission Decision of July 15, 2010 on Case N546/2009, Recapitalisation of Bank of Ireland [2011] O.J. C40/9, Annex I, points 10.g et seq.

[509] Council Regulation No.659/1999 of March 22, 1999 laying down detailed rules for the application of art.93 (now art.88) of the EC Treaty [1999] O.J. L83/1, March 27, 1999, pp.1–9.

	Conditions	**Commitments**
Admissibility	Only at the end of the formal investigation procedure	Any time
Possible Contents	Only conditions, which are necessary to make the State aid compatible with the Internal Market	Any kind
Judicial review	Separately challengeable before the Union Courts.	Commitments given during the preliminary investigation procedure can not be challenged (no legal interest, since the project as notified is approved)[510] Commitments given during the formal investigation procedure may be challenged under certain circumstances[511]
Consequences of failure to comply	Reopening of the formal investigation procedure (misuse of aid)[512] and/or Treaty infringement action before the Union Courts[513]	Opening of investigation procedure, since the aid is not covered by the Commission's approval

19–072   Conditions and commitments normally remain in place, depending on the scope, size and duration of the aid, for a period ranging between three years and the entire duration of the restructuring period, in rare cases even beyond it.[514] They also serve as a clear incentive to repay the aid as soon as possible.[515] In exceptional cases, the Commission has requested a certain commitment going beyond the restructuring period, for instance commitments to pay no or only limited amounts of dividends even in the first years after the restructuring

[510] Case T–6/06 *wheyco GmbH/Commission* [2007] E.C.R. II–72, para.101.
[511] Case T–301/01 *Alitalia Linee aeree italiane SpA/Commission* [2008] E.C.R. II–1753, paras 373–381.
[512] art.16, art.1(g) and art.7(4) of the Procedural Regulation.
[513] art.23 of the Procedural Regulation.
[514] Commission Decision of June 30, 2010 in state aid Case N 261/2010 (ex. PN 9/2010), Austria, Second restructuring aid for BAWAG PSK [2010] O.J. C250/5, point 48. Or with respect to HRE: until complete repayment of the silent participations of the State, see Commission Decision of July 18, 2011 on state aid C15/2009 (ex. N196/2009), which Germany has granted or intends to grant to Hypo Real Estate, Unreported, Annex I, point 9.1(ii)(d).
[515] Point 44, Restructuring Communication.

period.[516] An applicability beyond the restructuring period is in the very nature of claw-back commitments, which depend on the bank's return to profitability. The same applies to remunerations of impaired asset measures guaranteeing assets with long maturities.

As seen above, financial, structural, behavioural commitments and conditions may be necessary to safeguard return to viability, limit the aid to the absolute minimum and ensure burden sharing, as well as to compensate for the distortion of competition caused by the state aid. Other commitments remain possible, when dealing with bank failures in accordance with the aim of art.107(3)(b) TFEU, i.e. the restoration of the proper functioning of the financial sector. In its overall assessment the Commission may positively consider such commitments (by the beneficiary or the Member State concerned), which may accompany the other structural or behavioural measures normally required of the beneficiary in order to limit the distortion of competition.[517] Examples for such commitments are:

—lending to the real economy—where this condition also contains certain lending targets in Member States other than the state which grants the aid, this may be regarded as an important additional positive effect of the aid[518];

—prohibition on originating CDOs;

—certain eligibility criteria for buyers of divested businesses.[519]

These commitments/conditions serve the stability of the financial market as a whole and (partly) shall minimise the financial crisis's negative impact on the real economy. All conditions/commitments may serve different aims at the same time, for instance a ban on dividends may be necessary to reach a certain own capital ratio necessary for long time viability and at the same time ensures effective burden-sharing. The ban on external growth is normally required in order to make sure that aid is only spent for the restructuring (aid limited to the minimum), and also as a behavioural compensatory measure. This has to be kept in mind when negotiating with the Commission the concrete list of conditions/commitments. As a general principle and in the light of the aim of art.107(3)(b) TFEU, compensatory measures may not compromise the prospects of the bank's return to viability. Similarly, these measures should not decrease competition but, instead ensure that effective competition is preserved.[520] Below is an overview of a wide range of typical conditions/commitments and their possible objectives.

---

[516] Commission Decision of September 20, 2011 on state aid SA 29338 (C 29/2009, ex. N 264/2009), granted by Germany to HSH Nordbank, Unreported, Annex II, point 4.

[517] Point 44, Restructuring Communication, with reference to Commission Decision 2005/418/EC of July 7, 2004 on the aid measures implemented by France for Alstom [2005] O.J. L150/24, point 204.

[518] Point 33, Restructuring Communication.

[519] See in more detail above at paras 19–067 and 19–068.

[520] Point 32, Banking Communication.

19–073

Commitment/ Condition	Target						
	Viability	Own contri- bution/aid limited to the mini- mum	Burden Sharing/ moral hazard	Compen- satory Measures	Claw back	Exit from State aid	Financial market stability[521]
Financial							
Remuneration		X	X	X			
Price mechanisms, which increase over time[522]						X	
Skimming off of profits to the State aid grantor		X	X[523]	X			
Minimum return on securities							
Additional compen- sation on asset relief guarantee				X	X		
Structural							
(Re-)Privatisation/ Exit	X			X[524]	X[525]	X[526]	X[527]

[521] Conditions and commitments, which serve the stability of the financial market as a whole.

[522] See for instance Commission Decision of December 14, 2009, state aid N 422/2009, *RBS* [2010] O.J. C119/1, point 139.

[523] Such commitments/conditions may ensure that shareholders (other than the public aid grantors) and hybrid capital creditors will not receive any payments during the restructuring phase and/or until the State aid has been paid back. This contributes to their burden sharing. If profits will be distributed to the aid grantor instead of being ploughed back by the bank, this will also increase the bank's own contribution and limit the aid to the minimum. In order to make sure that this is not at the expense of viability, such clauses are normally applicable only above a certain minimum core capital quote, for instance 8% in the case of Kommunalkredit, see state aid SA 32745 (2011/NN), Austria, Restructuring of Kommunalkredit Austria AG [2011] O.J. C239/2, point 34.

[524] State aid NN 42/2008, Belgium, NN 46/2008, Luxembourg, NN 53/A/2008, Netherlands, Restructuring aid to Fortis Bank and Fortis Bank Luxembourg [2009] O.J. C80/7, point 95.

[525] Commission decision of October 21, 2008 on state aid measure C 10/08 (ex. NN 7/08) implemented by Germany for the restructuring of IKB Deutsche Industriebank AG [2009] O.J. L278/32, point 113. See also state aid NN 42/2008, Belgium, NN 46/2008, Luxembourg, NN 53/A/2008, Netherlands, Restructuring aid to Fortis Bank and Fortis Bank Luxembourg [2009] O.J. C80/7, point 95.

[526] Commission Decision of July 18, 2011 on state aid C15/2009 (ex. N196/2009), which Germany has granted or intends to grant to Hypo Real Estate, Unreported, point 85, if in combination with prior (partial) nationalisation.

[527] While nationalisation has been considered positively for the purpose of burden sharing and the avoidance of moral hazard, nationalised banks should be re-privatised as soon as possible (privatisation as exit strategy), see state aid SA 32745 (2011/NN), Austria, Restructuring of Kommunalkredit Austria AG [2011] O.J. C239/2, point 34. See also state aid NN 42/2008, Belgium, NN 46/2008, Luxembourg NN, 53/A/2008, Netherlands, Restructuring aid to Fortis Bank and Fortis Bank Luxembourg [2009] O.J. C80/7, point 96: "measures should be taken to ensure that that period of public ownership of the bank is minimised."

Commitment/ Condition	Target						
	Viability	Own contribution/aid limited to the minimum	Burden Sharing/ moral hazard	Compensatory Measures	Claw back	Exit from State aid	Financial market stability
Cessation of (some) commitments if sale to private investors	X			X[528]		X	
(Partial) nationalisation[529]			X[530]		X		
Reduction of balance sheet amount/ RWA				X			
Annual growth cap				X			
Divestment of shareholdings/ business units	X	X		X	X		
Value preservation of divestments[531]				X			
Possible Extension of divesture divestment[532]	X						X
Contingent divestment clause[533]				X			

[528] Commission decision of February 26, 2010 on state aid C 9/09 (ex. NN 49/08, NN 50/08 and NN 45/08) implemented by the Kingdom of Belgium, the French Republic and the Grand Duchy of Luxembourg for Dexia SA [2010] O.J. L274/54, Annex I, point 16.

[529] During the crisis, (partial) nationalisations took place with respect to several banks, often in consequence of the dilution of existing shareholders in the scope of capital increase with public funds. While these privatisations have not been requested by the European Commission, they were positively taken into account when assessing burden sharing and moral hazard.

[530] See Commission decision of October 28, 2009 on state aid C 14/08 (ex. NN 1/08) implemented by the United Kingdom for Northern Rock [2010] O.J. L112/38, point 149: The bank was nationalised and its former shareholders will only be compensated on the basis of the value of the company without any state support. As a consequence, this compensation is likely to be close to zero. This means that the former shareholders have been wiped out and thus can be considered as having sufficiently supported the consequences of the failure of the bank.

[531] See for instance Commission Decision of December 14, 2009, state aid N 422/2009, *RBS* [2010] O.J. C119/1, points 101–103. Far reaching: Commission Decision of November 18, 2009 on state aid C 18/09 (ex. N 360/09) implemented by Belgium for KBC [2010] O.J. L188/24, Annex, points (xix)–(xxiv).

[532] Many decisions provide for an extension of the divestment deadline if the beneficiary bank can demonstrate that it was not possible to sell the business at book value. This possibility is in line with the general concept that the compensatory measures shall not put at risk the viability of the beneficiary bank, see for instance Commission decision of September 20, 2011, state aid SA 29338 (C 29/2009, ex N 264/2009), HSH Nordbank, Unreported, Annex I, point 7.2.

[533] This clause requires the bank to further reduce its RWA or balance sheet (or take other painful measures) in case it falls short of its existing divestment or funded balance sheet reduction targets, see for instance Commission decision of December 14, 2009, state aid N 422/2009, *RBS* [2010] O.J. C119/1, point 95.

Commitment/ Condition	Target						
	Viability	Own contri-bution/aid limited to the mini-mum	Burden Sharing/ moral hazard	Compen-satory Measures	Claw back	Exit from State aid	Financial market stability
Divestiture Trustee[534]				X			
Eligibility criteria for buyers of divested business[535]				X[536]			X[537]
Business to offer in whole or in parts				X[538]			X[539]
Business restric-tions/termina-tions[540]	X			X			
Prohibition of pro-prietary trading ac-tivities	X			X			X

[534] Normally, the obligation to appoint a divestiture trustee arises only if the disposals of the operating businesses have not been completed by the deadlines. The divestiture trustee will then dispose of the businesses at no minimum price, see for instance Commission decision of December 14, 2009, state aid N 422/2009, *RBS* [2010] O.J. C119/1, point 96; Commission Decision of June 30, 2010 in the state aid Case N 261/2010 (ex. PN 9/2010), Austria, Second restructuring aid for BAWAG PSK [2010] O.J. C250/5, points 52–54; Commission decision of November 18, 2009 on state aid C 18/09 (ex. N 360/09) implemented by Belgium for KBC [2010] O.J. L188/24, Annex, point (xxix); Commission decision of September 29, 2010 on state aid C 32/09 (ex. NN 50/09) implemented by Germany for the restructuring of Sparkasse KölnBonn [2011] O.J. L235/1, point 95.

[535] See for instance Commission Decision of December 14, 2009, state aid N 422/2009, *RBS* [2010] O.J. C119/1, point 96.

[536] Certain eligibility criteria shall ensure that the divestment takes places smoothly and efficiently, for instance the obligation that the buyer will satisfy all the necessary conditions imposed by the relevant competition authorities as part of any merger control process.

[537] Certain criteria do not (mainly) serve the fast implementation of the compensatory measures but focus on structuring the market through the divestments in order to ensure more stability and/or more competition on the relevant market by requiring, for instance, that the buyer satisfies the national financial control agency as to its ability and willingness to maintain and develop the acquired business, see for instance Commission Decision of December 14, 2009, state aid N 422/2009, *RBS* [2010] O.J. C119/1, point 96.

[538] The requirement to offer the activities as parts and as a whole on the market ensures that all interested competitors may be able to bid for parts of the business, and therefore helps making the divestment procedure efficient and competitive, see for instance Commission decision of May 12, 2009 on state aid which Germany proposes to grant towards the restructuring of WestLB AG (C 43/08 (ex. N 390/08)) [2009] O.J. L345/1.

[539] The obligation to offer a certain business as a whole only or to require certain sizes or packaging of the businesses to divest does not mainly serve the efficiency of the implementation of the compensatory measures but the improvement of the competitive structure on the relevant market, see for instance Commission Decision of December 14, 2009, state aid N 422/2009, *RBS* [2010] O.J. C119/1, point 99.

[540] This may have the form of a simple run-down of business portfolios as in Commission Decision of November 18, 2009 on state aid C 18/09 (ex. N 360/09) implemented by Belgium for KBC [2010] O.J. L188/24, Annex, point (xxxiii), or the form of the closure of bank locations, see for instance Commission decision of May 12, 2009 on state aid which Germany proposes to grant towards the restructuring of WestLB AG (C 43/08 (ex. N 390/08)) [2009] O.J. L345/1, point 71, on the form of termination of activity in certain banking segments like, for instance, the financing of aircraft, see Commission decision of September 20, 2011 on state aid SA 29338 (C 29/2009, ex. N 264/2009), granted by Germany to HSH Nordbank, Unreported, Annex I, point 4.5.

Commitment/ Condition	Target						
	Viability	Own contri-bution/aid limited to the mini-mum	Burden Sharing/ moral hazard	Compen-satory Measures	Claw back	Exit from State aid	Financial market stability
Prohibition on orig-inating CDOs				X			X
Acquisition ban		X[541]		X			
Debt level obliga-tions[542]	X			X			
Funding and liquid-ity Commitments	X						
Price leadership ban				X			
Minimum pricing on loans	X[543]			X[544]			
Maximum retail in-terest rates	X			X			
Minimum Core Capital ratios	X						X
Job cuts[545]	X						
(Other) behavioural							
Exchange of the former top manage-ment			X[546]				
Imposition of cor-poration govern-ance[547]	X		X				

[541] The prohibition of external growth shall ensure that state aid is not used for acquisition of competitors, see, for instance, Commission decision of November 18, 2009 on state aid C 10/09 (ex. N 138/09) implemented by the Netherlands for ING's Illiquid Assets Back Facility and Restructuring Plan [2010] O.J. L274/139, point 137. The scope of this prohibition varies in the different decisions, see in more detail below.

[542] The Commission has accepted different benchmarks and thresholds. For instance "not higher than fifth in the Global All Debt League Table", see state aid N 422/2009, *RBS* [2010] O.J. C119/1, point 107.

[543] See state aid SA 32745 (2011/NN), Austria Restructuring of Kommunalkredit Austria AG [2011] O.J. C239/2, point 82: "Given the importance of securing decent margins, the commit-ment consisting of granting new loans only if a minimum level of RAROC (risk adjusted return on capital) of 10% can be achieved, on a loan by loan basis, is appropriate and necessary."

[544] Commission Decision of April 5, 2011 on the measures No.C 11/2009 (ex. NN 53b/2008, NN 2/2010 and N 19/2010) implemented by Dutch State for ABN AMRO Group NV (created following the merger between Fortis Bank Nederland and ABN AMRO N), Unreported, point 326; Commission Decision of July 18, 2011 on state aid C15/2009 (ex. N196/2009), which Germany has granted or intends to grant to Hypo Real Estate, Unreported, point 129.

[545] See Commission decision of May 7, 2009 on state aid N 244/2009, *Commerzbank*, Germany [2009] O.J. C147/4. point 77.

[546] Commission decision of October 21, 2008 on state aid measure C 10/08 (ex. NN 7/08) implemented by Germany for the restructuring of IKB Deutsche Industriebank AG [2009] O.J. L278/32, point 113. Positively noted in state aid SA 32745 (2011/NN), Austria, Restructuring of Kommunalkredit Austria AG [2011] O.J. C239/2, point 89.

[547] A good example of a far reaching change in the corporate governance structure is the LBBW Case, where the Commission obliged Germany to make the bank less subject to "improper influence by its public shareholders", see Commission decision of December 15, 2009 on state aid C 17/09 (ex. N 265/09) by Germany for the restructuring of Landesbank Baden-Württemberg [2010] O.J. L188/1, points 84–87.

Commitment/ Condition	Target						
	Viability	Own contribution/aid limited to the minimum	Burden Sharing/ moral hazard	Compensatory Measures	Claw back	Exit from State aid	Financial market stability
Sustainable remuneration policy[548]			X				X
Ban on dividends	X[549]		X[550]			X[551]	
Restriction on dividends beyond the restructuring period	X		X[552]			X[553]	
Ban on coupons on hybrid capital[554]	X		X				
Creation of a RU	X						X
Internal separation of credit substitute business	X						X
Liability Management commitments[555]							
Lending to the real economy							X
Reduction of operating cost	X						
Cap on Marketing, Advertising and Sponsorship costs[556]	X			X			

[548] Most banks were already under such obligation, since they befitted from liquidity assistance under national liquidity guarantee schemes, which have to set such conditions. The conditions in the Commission Decisions concerning the restructuring plans are therefore normally only relevant fort the time after the liquidity guarantees will have been terminated.

[549] A ban on dividends may lead to higher core capital ratios and thus enhances the viability of the bank.

[550] A ban on dividends counteracts moral hazard, since the owners realise that in case of state support of their financial institute, there will be a financial burden. However, this reasoning applies only to existing shareholders and hybrid capital creditors. A prohibition of payments to new providers of capital can therefore not be justified by the principle of burden sharing and moral hazard. In some decisions, the Commission has explicitly accepted that new hybrid capital instruments shall not be subject to the ban on dividend or coupon payments as long as the payment of dividends or coupons on new securities will not create a legal obligation to make any dividend or coupon payments on the existing hybrid capital instruments or shares, see state aid N 422/2009, *RBS* [2010] O.J. C119/1, point 104.

[551] Commission Decision of June 30, 2010 in state aid Case N 261/2010 (ex. PN 9/2010), Austria, Second restructuring aid for BAWAG PSK [2010] O.J. C250/5, point 93.

[552] Commission Decision of June 30, 2010 in state aid Case N 261/2010 (ex. PN 9/2010), Austria, Second restructuring aid for BAWAG PSK [2010] O.J. C250/5, point 101.

[553] Commission Decision of June 30, 2010 in state aid Case N 261/2010 (ex. PN 9/2010), Austria, Second restructuring aid for BAWAG PSK [2010] O.J. C250/5, point 93.

[554] In all decisions, the Commission has accepted that the ban does apply, unless there is a legal or an existing binding contractual obligation to pay.

[555] Such as debt for equity offers, see Commission Decision of 15 July 2010 on Case N546/2009, Recapitalisation of *Bank of Ireland* [2011] O.J. 2011 C40/9, Annex I, point 6.

[556] Commission Decision of 15 July 2010 on Case N546/2009, Recapitalisation of *Bank of Ireland* [2011] O.J. C40/9, Annex I, point 7.

Commitment/ Condition	Target						
	Viability	Own contri-bution/aid limited to the mini-mum	Burden Sharing/ moral hazard	Compen-satory Measures	Claw back	Exit from State aid	Financial market stability
Ban on advertising with State aid[557]			X	X			
Customer Mobility commitments[558]				X			
Monitoring Trustee[559]	X	X	X	X	X	X	X

The frequency of occurrence of these commitments/conditions vary. Their **19–074** usage depends on the concrete circumstances of the case. However, as can be seen from the table below covering most of the main bank restructuring cases of the past two years, certain commitments/conditions are meanwhile standard. This includes:

—appointment of a monitoring trustee[560];

—ban on advertising with state aid;

—ban on coupons on hybrid capital;

—business restrictions/termination;

—divestment of shareholdings/business units;

—reduction of balance sheet amount;

—acquisition ban.

While the monitoring trustee and advertising ban clauses are relatively identical in the Commission Decisions, the design of the other commitments/conditions varies considerably from case to case. There is, for instance, no standard acquisition ban clause. They vary in terms of scope, for instance: "acquisitions whose purpose is to expand RBS's activities outside of its business model"[561]; "any financial institutions or other businesses in actual or potential competition with BAWAG"[562]; "any purchases of financial institutions in competition with LBBW"[563]; "any share in both financial and non-financial institutions. Participation business, related to the original client business of KA Neu's business model,

---

[557] This condition exists in almost all Commission decisions.
[558] For detailed clauses see Commission Decision of 15 July 2010 on Case N546/2009, Recapitalisation of *Bank of Ireland* [2011] O.J. C40/9, Annex I, point 10.
[559] This condition serves the sound implementation of all other conditions and/or commitments.
[560] See in more detail below under para.19–076.
[561] Commission Decision of 14 December 2009, State aid N 422/2009, *RBS*, [2010] O.J. C119/1, point 108.
[562] Commission Decision of 30 June 2010 in the State aid Case N 261/2010 (ex PN 9/2010)—Austria Second restructuring aid for *BAWAG* P.S.K., [2010] O.J. 2010 C250/5, point 46
[563] Commission Decision of 15 December 2009 on State aid C 17/09 (ex N 265/09) by Germany for the restructuring of *Landesbank Baden-Württemberg* [2010] O.J. L188/1, Annex, point 11.

remains possible if not exceeding a total cumulative amount of [X]"[564]; "any acquisition of more than 5 % of the share capital of other credit institutions or investment firms [. . .] or insurance companies"[565]; "take control of other credit institutions or investment companies that have their registered office or a subsidiary or branch in Belgium or Luxembourg and have substantial operations there"[566]; "With regard to a ban on acquisitions, the Belgian authorities commit that KBC will refrain from acquiring control,[. . .] of financial institutions. KBC will moreover refrain from acquiring control of businesses other than financial institutions if such an acquisition would slow down the repayment of the amount of EUR 7 billion of core Tier-1 Yield Enhanced securities to the Belgian authorities . . . "[567]; "not to acquire more than 20 % of the shares in other financial institutions"[568]; "acquiring any finance institutions or other businesses in potential competition with Commerzbank"[569]; "any acquisition of any Financial Institution"[570]; and possible exemptions: sometimes, acquisitions are admissible if the costs remain below a certain level,[571] in other cases, an exemption can only be granted by the Commission, in particular if this is essential in order to safeguard financial stability or competition in the relevant markets.[572]

---

[564] State aid SA.32745 (2011/NN)—Austria Restructuring of *Kommunalkredit Austria AG* [2011] O.J. C239/2, point 34.

[565] Commission Decision of 26 February 2010 on State aid C 9/09 (ex NN 49/08, NN 50/08 and NN 45/08) implemented by the Kingdom of Belgium, the French Republic and the Grand Duchy of Luxembourg for *Dexia SA* [2010] O.J. L274/54, Annex I, point 2

[566] State aid N 255/2009, Belgium, and N 274/2009, Luxembourg, Additional aid for Fortis Banque, Fortis Banque Luxembourg and Fortis holding [2009] O.J. C178/2, point 128.

[567] Commission Decision of November 18, 2009 on state aid C 18/09 (ex. N 360/09) implemented by Belgium for KBC [2010] O.J. L188/24, point 66. Similar: Commission Decision of November 18, 2009 on state aid C 10/09 (ex. N 138/09) implemented by the Netherlands for ING's Illiquid Assets Back Facility and Restructuring Plan [2010] O.J. L274/139, Annex II, point (b).

[568] Commission Decision of September 29, 2010 on state aid C 32/09 (ex. NN 50/09) implemented by Germany for the restructuring of Sparkasse KölnBonn [2011] O.J. L235/1, Annex I, point 8.

[569] Commission Decision of May 7, 2009 on state aid N 244/2009, *Commerzbank*, Germany [2009] O.J. C147/4, point 70.

[570] Commission Decision of July 15, 2010 on Case N546/2009, Recapitalisation of Bank of Ireland [2011] O.J. C40/9, Annex I, point 8.

[571] Commission Decision of December 14, 2009, state aid N 422/2009, *RBS*, [2010] O.J. C119/1, point 108; state aid SA 32745 (2011/NN), Austria, Restructuring of Kommunalkredit Austria AG [2011] O.J. C239/2, point 34; Commission Decision of April 5, 2011 on the measures No.C 11/2009 (ex. NN 53b/2008, NN 2/2010 and N 19/2010) implemented by Dutch State for ABN AMRO Group NV (created following the merger between Fortis Bank Nederland and ABN AMRO N), Unreported, art.5; Commission Decision of July 15, 2010 on Case N546/2009, Recapitalisation of Bank of Ireland [2011] O.J. C40/9, Annex I, point 8.

[572] Commission Decision of May 7, 2009 on State aid N 244/2009, *Commerzbank*, Germany [2009] O.J. C147/4, point 70; Commission Decision of November 18, 2009 on state aid C 10/09 (ex. N 138/09) implemented by the Netherlands for ING's Illiquid Assets Back Facility and Restructuring Plan [2010] O.J. L274/139, Annex II, point (b); Commission Decision of November 18, 2009 on state aid C 18/09 (ex. N 360/09) implemented by Belgium for KBC [2010] O.J. L188/24, point 66; state aid SA 32745 (2011/NN), Austria, Restructuring of Kommunalkredit Austria AG [2011] O.J. C239/2, point 34.

Commitment/Condition	Banks																
	CoBa[573]	WestLB (2009)[574]	NR[575]	ING[576]	KBC[577]	RBS[578]	LBBW[579]	Dexia[580]	Ethias[581]	BAWAG[582]	BOI[583]	Sp. Köln[584]	KK[585]	Fortis (B)[586]	ABN AMRO[587]	HRE[588]	HSH[589]
Financial Commitments																	
Price mechanisms, which increase over time						X				X							
Skimming off of profits to the State aid grantor									X				X			X	
Minimum return on securities					X												
Additional compensation on asset relief guarantee							X										X
Structural Commitments																	
(Re)Privatisation/Exit		X	X						X				X	X		X	X
Cessation of (certain) commitments if sale to private investors			X					X	X		X					X	
(Partial) nationalisation			X			X							X	X		X	

709

Commitment/Condition	CoBa	WestLB (2009)	NR	ING	KBC	RBS	LLBW	Dexia	Ethias	BAWAG	BOI	Sp. Köln	KK	Fortis (B)	ABN AMRO	HRE	HSH
Structural Commitments																	
Reduction of balance sheet amount	45%	50%	75%[590]	45%[591]	17%[592]	30%	41%	35%	38%[593]	29%[594]	30%	17%	60%	40%[595]		85%	65%
Reduction of impaired assets							X										
Annual growth cap													X			X	
Divestment of shareholdings/business units	X	X		X	X	X	X	X	X	X	X	X				X	X
Value preservation of divestments				X	X	X	X	X	X		X	X					
Extension of divesture deadline	X	X			X		X	X	X		X	X				X	X
Contingent divestment clause		X[596]				X[597]											
Divestiture Trustee							X	X		X	X	X				X[598]	
Eligibility criteria for buyers of divested businesses		X				X			X			X					

710

Commitment/Condition	Structural Commitments																
	CoBa	WestLB (2009)	NR	ING	KBC	RBS	LLBW	Dexia	Ethias	BAWAG	BOI	Sp. Köln	KK	Fortis (B)	ABN AMRO	HRE	HSH
Obligation to offer business in whole and/or or in parts		X				X											
Business restrictions/terminations	X	X	X		X			X	X	X	X	X	X			X	X
Prohibition of proprietary trading activities		X						X				X	X				X
Prohibition on originating CDOs					X[599]												
Acquisition ban	X		X	X	X	X	X	X	X	X	X	X	X	X	X	X	X
Debt level obligations						X											
Funding and liquidity commitments				X				X					X				
Price leadership ban	X		X	X	X		X		X[600]			X			X		
Minimum pricing on loans								X					X			X	
Maximum retail interest rates														X			

711

Commitment/Condition	CoBa	WestLB (2009)	NR	ING	KBC	RBS	LLBW	Dexia	Ethias	BAWAG	BOI	Sp. Köln	KK	Fortis (B)	ABN AMRO	HRE	HSH
Structural Commitments																	
Minimum Core Capital quote					X												
Job cuts	X																
Other (behavioural) Commitments																	
Exchange of the former top management														X[601]			
Imposition of corporate governance							X		X[602]			X					X
Sustainable remuneration policy	X				X			X								X	X
Ban on dividends	X					X		X[603]		X	X	X	X			X	X
Restriction on dividends beyond restructuring period										X[604]						X	X
Ban on coupons on hybrid capital	X	X	X[605]	X		X	X	X		X	X	X	X		X	X	X
Creation of RU			X					X								X	X

Commitment/Condition								Other (behavioural) Commitments									
	CoBa	WestLB (2009)	NR	ING	KBC	RBS	LLBW	Dexia	Ethias	BAWAG	BOI	Sp. Köln	KK	Fortis (B)	ABN AMRO	HRE	HSH
Internal separation of credit substitute business							X										
Liability Management commitment											X					X[606]	
Lending to the real economy	X				X	X[607]	X					X				X	X
Reduction of operating costs	X							X									
Cap on Marketing, Advertising and Sponsorship costs											X						
Ban on advertising with State aid	X		X	X	X	X	X	X	X	X		X	X		X	X	X
Customer Mobility commitments			X[608]														
Monitoring Trustee	X	X		X	X	X	X	X	X	X	X	X	X			X	X

713

573 Commission Decision of May 7, 2009 on state aid N 244/2009, *Commerzbank*, Germany [2009] O.J. C147/4.

574 Commission Decision of May 12, 2009 on state aid which Germany proposes to grant towards the restructuring of WestLB AG (C 43/08 (ex. N 390/08)) [2009] O.J. L345/1. In this decision, the Commission approved the subsidies granted that far on the condition of a restructuring of the bank involving the refocusing of its core activities. Subsequently, and as part of the restructuring plan, Germany set up a bad bank, the Erste Abwicklungsanstalt (EAA), to which WestLB hived off a portfolio of toxic and non-strategic assets representing approximately 30% of the bank's total assets with a view of their progressive liquidation. As the bad bank was expected to make losses, it received €3 billion in capital from State agency SoFFin. This aid was not foreseen in the original restructuring plan but as Germany argued financial stability grounds, the operation was granted temporary approval. A new investigation was opened. At the time of the deadline of this publication, this investigation was still pending. It is obvious, however that WestLB will have to be downsized much more than initially proposed.

575 Commission Decision of October 28, 2009 on state aid C 14/08 (ex. NN 1/08) implemented by the United Kingdom for Northern Rock [2010] O.J. L112/38.

576 Commission Decision of November 18, 2009 on state aid C 10/09 (ex. N 138/09) implemented by the Netherlands for ING's Illiquid Assets Back Facility and Restructuring Plan [2010] O.J. L274/139.

577 Commission Decision of November 18, 2009 on state aid C 18/09 (ex. N 360/09) implemented by Belgium for KBC [2010] O.J. L188/24, point 70.

578 Commission Decision of December 14, 2009, state aid N 422/2009, *RBS* [2010] O.J. C119/1.

579 Commission Decision of December 15, 2009 on state aid C 17/09 (ex. N 265/09) by Germany for the restructuring of Landesbank Baden-Württemberg [2010] O.J. L188/1.

580 Commission Decision of February 26, 2010 on state aid C 9/09 (ex. NN 49/08, NN 50/08 and NN 45/08) implemented by the Kingdom of Belgium, the French Republic and the Grand Duchy of Luxembourg for Dexia SA [2010] O.J. L274/54. The restructuring approved by this decision eventually failed. On October 17, 2011, the Commission has temporarily approved as Emergency aid the nationalisation of Dexia Bank Belgium (DBB) through its acquisition by the Belgian State for €4 billion to be paid to Dexia SA (State aid Case SA 33751 *Dexia Banque Belgique*). The Commission acknowledges that this measure is necessary to preserve financial stability. The acquisition by the Belgian State of DBB is an integral part of the restructuring package for Dexia SA. Belgium has six months to notify a new restructuring plan for the bank.

581 Commission Decision of May 20, 2010 in state aid Case N 256/2009 Restructuring aid to *Ethias—Belgium* [2010] O.J. C252/5. Ethias is mainly an insurance company.

582 Commission Decision of June 30, 2010 in state aid Case N 261/2010 (ex. PN 9/2010), Austria, Second restructuring aid for BAWAG PSK [2010] O.J. C250/5.

583 Commission Decision of July 15, 2010 on Case N 546/2009, Recapitalisation of Bank of Ireland [2011] O.J. C 40/9. With this decision, the Commission authorised the restructuring package for BOI. However, the performance of an in-depth and comprehensive Prudential Capital Adequacy Review ("PCAR") and a Prudential Liquidity Assessment Review ("PLAR") (together the "PCAR/PLAR exercise"), carried out in liaison with the European Commission, the International Monetary Fund ("IMF") and the ECB, showed that BOI needed a capital injection of €5.2 billion, of which €4.2 billion should be Core Tier 1 capital and €1 billion in the form of contingent capital. This additional capitalization was notified to the Commission, which approved it temporarily as Emergency aid with decision of July 11, 2011 on state aid SA 33216 (2011/N), Ireland, Second rescue of Bank of Ireland [2011] O.J. C 274/2. Ireland has six months to submit a revised restructuring plan.

584 Commission Decision of September 29, 2010 on state aid C 32/09 (ex. NN 50/09) implemented by Germany for the restructuring of Sparkasse KölnBonn [2011] O.J. L 235/1.

585 State aid SA 32745 (2011/NN), Austria, Restructuring of Kommunalkredit Austria AG [2011] O.J. C239/2.

[586] State aid NN 42/2008, Belgium, NN 46/2008, Luxembourg, NN 53/A/2008, Netherlands, Restructuring aid to Fortis Bank and Fortis Bank Luxembourg [2009] O.J. C80/7 and state aid N 255/2009, Belgium, and N 274/2009, Luxembourg, Additional aid for Fortis Banque, Fortis Banque Luxembourg and Fortis holding [2009] O.J. C178/2. In autumn 2008, Belgium, Luxembourg and The Netherlands took a series of aid measures in favour of Fortis and Fortis Luxemburg. Afterwards, the Dutch operations of Fortis Bank, including ABN AMRO, were sold to the Dutch State. The remainder was bought by the Belgian State, which sold 75% to the French bank BNP Paribas. As a result of this sale, BNP Paribas also controlled Fortis Bank Luxembourg. In spring 2009, further state aid was granted in the scope of the sale to BNP Paribas after a Belgian court had declared void the initial sale to BNP. The decisions only address state aid to Belgian/Luxemburgish Fortis, not state aid to Dutch Fortis and ABN AMRO, which has been approved by on April 5, 2011 in the *ABN AMRO* decision.

[587] Commission Decision of April 5, 2011 on the measures No.C 11/2009 (ex. NN 53b/2008, NN 2/2010 and N 19/2010) implemented by Dutch State for ABN AMRO Group NV (created following the merger between Fortis Bank) Nederland and *ABN AMRO N*), Unreported.

[588] Commission Decision of July 18, 2011 on state aid C15/2009 (ex. N 196/2009), which Germany has granted or intends to grant to Hypo Real Estate, Unreported. By this decision, the Commission approved restructuring aid consisting of capital injections of €10 billion, an asset relief measure with an aid element of about €20 billion, as well as liquidity guarantees amounting to €145 billion for the banking group Hypo Real Estate ("HRE"). HRE was in existential difficulties since the fail of Lehman brothers in autumn 2008 and had to be financially supported several times before and after its nationalization in 2009, with several emergency aids approved by and several restructuring plans submitted to the Commission. For an overview see Arhold/Kovacs, "Hypo Real Estate Group—the longest Chain of German State Aid Measures" [2011] EStAL 1, p.9.

[589] Commission Decision of September 20, 2011 on state aid SA 29338 (C 29/2009, ex. N 264/2009), granted by Germany to HSH Nordbank, Unreported.

[590] Commission Decision of October 28, 2009 on state aid C 14/08 (ex. NN 1/08) implemented by the United Kingdom for Northern Rock [2010] O.J. L112/38, points 114 and 156.

[591] Commission Decision of November 18, 2009 on state aid C 10/09 (ex. N 138/09) implemented by the Netherlands for ING's Illiquid Assets Back Facility and Restructuring Plan [2010] O.J. L274/139, point 143.

[592] As part of the restructuring plan, see Commission Decision of November 18, 2009 on state aid C 18/09 (ex. N 360/09) implemented by Belgium for *KBC* [2010] O.J. L188/24, points 40 and 172.

[593] Commission Decision of May 20, 2010 in state aid Case N 256/2009 Restructuring aid to Ethias, Belgium [2010] O.J. C252/5, before point 3.

[594] In consequence of the divestments, partly already committed in the first restructuring, see Commission Decision of June 30, 2010 in state aid Case N 261/2010 (ex. PN 9/2010), Austria, Second restructuring aid for BAWAG PSK [2010] O.J. C250/5, points 19 and 39.

[595] Via sale of the Dutch business to the Netherlands, which accounted for 25% of Fortis Bank's income in the first six months of 2008, half its net profits, 35% of the retail branches and 47% of the workforce, see state aid NN 42/2008, Belgium, NN 53/A/2008, Netherlands, Restructuring aid to Fortis Bank and Fortis Bank Luxembourg [2009] O.J. C80/7, points 93–96.

[596] If not sold by the deadline, the business has to expire. No new business can be accepted, Commission Decision of May 12, 2009 on state aid which Germany proposes to grant towards the restructuring of WestLB AG (C 43/08 (ex. N 390/08)) [2009] O.J. L345/1, Annex, points 5.7 and 6.7.

[597] RBS has also committed to the sale of additional businesses and assets amounting to £60 billion of RBS's RWA in case this targeted balance sheet reduction is not achieved by the end of the restructuring period (compulsory divestment), see Commission Decision of December 14, 2009, state aid N 422/2009, *RBS* [2010] O.J. C119/1, points 59, 74, 95, 217 and 250 [20–30%].

[598] In particular with respect to (re)privatisation, see Commission Decision of July 18, 2011 on state aid C15/2009 (ex. N196/2009), which Germany has granted or intends to grant to Hypo Real Estate, Unreported, Annex I, point 3(ii).

[599] Securitisation transactions for purposes of management of regulatory capital or credit risk or to raise liquidity are not covered by this prohibition, see Commission Decision of November 18, 2009 on state aid C 18/09 (ex. N 360/09) implemented by Belgium for KBC [2010] O.J. L188/24, Annex, point (xiii).

[600] Commission Decision of May 20, 2010 in state aid Case N 256/2009 Restructuring aid to Ethias, Belgium [2010] O.J. C252/5, point 1.14. For the insurance company, the price leadership prohibition was translated into fixed levels of combined ratios.

[601] No condition but taken positively into account.

[602] Far reaching and detailed commitments in point 1 of the Annex to Commission Decision of May 20, 2010 in state aid Case N 256/2009 Restructuring aid to Ethias, Belgium [2010] O.J. C252/5.

[603] Until the end of 2011. Afterwards, the extent of restrictions depends on certain parameters, such as Core Tier 1 capital ratio, see Commission Decision of February 26, 2010 on state aid C 9/09 (ex. NN 49/08, NN 50/08 and NN 45/08) implemented by the Kingdom of Belgium, the French Republic and the Grand Duchy of Luxembourg for Dexia SA [2010] O.J. L274/54, Annex I, points 8–9.

[604] Commission Decision of June 30, 2010 in state aid Case N 261/2010 (ex. PN 9/2010), Austria, Second restructuring aid for BAWAG PSK [2010] O.J. C250/5, point 93.

[605] See Commission Decision of October 28, 2009 on state aid C 14/08 (ex. NN 1/08) implemented by the United Kingdom for Northern Rock [2010] O.J. L112/38, points 29 and 150.

[606] In the form of commitments re new IT systems, see Commission Decision of July 18, 2011 on state aid C15/2009 (ex. N196/2009), which Germany has granted or intends to grant to Hypo Real Estate, Unreported, Annex I, point 10.4.

[607] Commission Decision of December 14, 2009, state aid N 422/2009, *RBS* [2010] O.J. C119/1, fn.95.

[608] Commission Decision of July 15, 2010 on Case N546/2009, Recapitalisation of Bank of Ireland [2011] O.J. C40/9, Annex I, points 10.g et seq.

Monitoring. The Commission normally requests the appointment of a trustee to   **19–076**
monitor the implementation of the restructuring plan, including all conditions
and commitments of the bank and the Member State concerned. The monitoring
trustee must be independent of the bank, possess the necessary qualifications to
carry out its mandate, for example as an investment bank or consultant or auditor,
and shall neither have nor become exposed to a conflict of interest. The Trustee
shall be remunerated by the bank in a way that does not impede the independent
and effective fulfilment of its mandate.[609] The trustee is either appointed by the
Member State, the state grantor or the bank[610] after the Commission's approval.
The Commission's approval is necessary, since the trustee will have to work for
and act upon the instructions of the European Commission. There is a differentiated appointment procedure, if the Commission does not accept the first
proposal of the bank/aid grantor.[611]

The monitoring trustee must regularly (either every three or every six
months[612]) submit to the Commission detailed reports on the proper implementation of the restructuring plan, the first report normally due no later than six
months after the decision.[613] In this first report, the trustee has to propose a
detailed work plan to the Commission describing how it intends to monitor
compliance with the obligations and conditions attached to the decision.[614]
Normally the bank must provide and cause its advisors to provide the trustee with
all such cooperation, assistance and information as the trustee may reasonably
require to perform its tasks. Therefore, the trustee will normally have full and
complete access to any of the banks, records, documents, management or other
personnel, facilities, sites and technical information. In addition, the trustee may
even appoint advisors (in particular for corporate finance or legal advice) at the
bank's expense.[615] The trustee can only be discharged or replaced with the
approval of the European Commission.[616]

Winding-up aid

In all Financial Crisis Communications the liquidation or orderly winding-up   **19–077**
of a distressed bank is explicitly mentioned as a valuable option for the Member

---

[609] Commission Decision of May 20, 2010 in state aid Case N 256/2009 Restructuring aid to Ethias,
Belgium [2010] O.J. C252/5, Annex I, point 60.

[610] Commission Decision of May 20, 2010 in state aid Case N 256/2009 Restructuring aid to Ethias,
Belgium [2010] O.J. C252/5, Annex I, point 59.

[611] See for instance Commission Decision of May 20, 2010 in state aid Case N 256/2009 Restructuring aid to Ethias, Belgium [2010] O.J. C252/5, Annex I, points 61–64.

[612] According to Annex V IAC. Where the Member State is already subject to a reporting
requirement for other forms of aid to its banks, such a report must be complemented with the
necessary information concerning the asset relief measures and the banks' restructuring plans.

[613] Point 46, Restructuring Communication

[614] Commission Decision of May 20, 2010 in state aid Case N 256/2009 Restructuring aid to Ethias,
Belgium [2010] O.J. C252/5, Annex I, point 66.

[615] See, for instance, Commission Decision of May 20, 2010 in state aid Case N 256/2009
Restructuring aid to Ethias, Belgium [2010] O.J. C252/5, Annex I, points 69–73.

[616] See, for instance, Commission Decision of May 20, 2010 in state aid Case N 256/2009
Restructuring aid to Ethias, Belgium [2010] O.J. C252/5, Annex I, points 74–735.

States. Such a controlled liquidation, possibly carried out in conjunction with a contribution of public funds, may be applied in individual cases, either as a second step, after rescue aid to an individual financial institution when it becomes clear that the latter cannot be restructured successfully, or in one single action. If a restructuring plan aims at the resolution of a financial institution, the Commission does not have to assess its viability.[617] However, the other elements of the restructuring Communication apply. The Commission has therefore to assess the following parameters:

—**Limitation of restructuring costs and of the amount of aid:** The Member State has to demonstrate that the chosen winding-up scenario is the less costly option, in particular that an immediate liquidation would be more costly and would present more systemic risks.[618] In ensuring that the aid amount is kept to the minimum necessary in view of the objective pursued, it needs to be taken into account that the protection of financial stability within the current financial turmoil may imply the necessity to reimburse certain creditors of the liquidated bank through aid measures. The choice of criteria for the selection of the types of liabilities for this purpose should follow the same rules as apply in relation to the liabilities covered by a guarantee scheme.[619]

—**Own contribution of the institutions concerned:** Normally, the own contribution of institutions to their winding-up is maximised through the sale of their assets.

—**Burden-sharing by shareholders and subordinated creditors:** Moral hazard has to be minimised, notably by excluding shareholders and possibly certain types of creditors from receiving the benefit of any aid in the context of the controlled winding-up procedure.[620] Shareholders may be best excluded by full nationalisation of the financial institute before winding-up.[621] If the nationalised institute is to be wound up softly so as to save State resources (in contrast to a rapid liquidation scenario), it may, however be

[617] Commission Decision of June 29, 2011 on state aids Nos SA 32504 (2011/N) and C 11/2010 (ex. N 667/2009) implemented by Ireland for Anglo Irish Bank and Irish Nationwide Building Society, Unreported, point 142.

[618] Commission Decision of June 29, 2011 on state aids Nos SA 32504 (2011/N) and C 11/2010 (ex. N 667/2009) implemented by Ireland for Anglo Irish Bank and Irish Nationwide Building Society, Unreported, points 143 and 151–159.

[619] Point 48, Banking Communication.

[620] Point 46, Banking Communication.

[621] A good example is the *Anglo Irish* case. During the financial crisis, Anglo Irish Bank was nationalised received at least €32 billion in recap and IA relief state aid, which corresponds to 43.9% of its RWA value. INBS received a total of €6.2 structural state aid, i.e. 59% of the value of its RWA. Both financial institutes were nationalised, then several restructuring plans were communicated to the European Commission, and still their cases were hopeless. Ireland eventually decided to merge the two entities and submit a plan for a orderly winding-up to the Commission, see Commission Decision of June 29, 2011 on state aids Nos SA 32504 (2011/N) and C 11/2010 (ex. N 667/2009) implemented by Ireland for Anglo Irish Bank and Irish Nationwide Building Society, Unreported.

difficult to prevent creditors from indirectly benefitting from the State support. This can be accepted if the creditors' participation in the burden-sharing is not feasible without increasing the cost of the resolution for the State.[622]

—**Measures limiting the distortion of competition:** In a winding-up scenario, the distortion of competition is limited as the institutions will almost completely exit all the markets where they were present. However, it must be ensured that during the time of winding-up, competition is distorted as little as possible. Therefore, the commercial activities of the financial institute have to be limited to the maximum extent possible.[623] As long as the beneficiary financial institution continues to operate it should not pursue any new activities, but merely continue the ongoing ones. The banking licence should be withdrawn as soon as possible.[624] To avoid undue distortions of competition, the liquidation phase should be limited to the period strictly necessary for the orderly winding-up.[625] In the *Anglo Irish* case, a winding-up period of ten years has been accepted. All related commitments taken by the Member State concerned must remain valid and applicable until all assets of the beneficiary bank are fully worked out.

—**No aid to purchasers:** In order to ensure that no aid is granted to the buyers of parts of the financial institution to be wound-up, certain sales conditions have to be respected: the sales process should be open and non-discriminatory, the sale should take place on market terms, the financial institution or the government, depending on the structure chosen, should maximise the sales price for the assets and liabilities involved, Where the application of these criteria leads to the finding of aid to buyers or to sold economic entities, the compatibility of that aid will have to be assessed separately.[626]

6. FORESIGHTS: STATE AID TO FINANCIAL INSTITUTIONS—CURRENT AND FUTURE CHALLENGES

Short, medium and long-term foresights have to deal with different issues. In the short term, banks have to comply with the recapitalisation requirements established by the European Council (see below at para.19–079). In the medium term, the question arises whether the stress tested restructuring plans are actually

19–078

---

[622] See Commission Decision of June 29, 2011 on state aids Nos SA 32504 (2011/N) and C 11/2010 (ex. N 667/2009) implemented by Ireland for Anglo Irish Bank and Irish Nationwide Building Society, Unreported, point 170.

[623] Commission Decision of June 29, 2011 on state aids Nos SA 32504 (2011/N) and C 11/2010 (ex. N 667/2009) implemented by Ireland for Anglo Irish Bank and Irish Nationwide Building Society, Unreported, point 142.

[624] Point 48, Banking Communication.

[625] Point 47, Banking Communication.

[626] Points 49–50, Banking Communication.

robust enough to cope with the new financial turmoil and economic downturn caused by the sovereign debts crisis, and especially whether any necessary adjustments of the restructuring plans will trigger new investigation procedures (see below at para.19–082). Finally, the Commission had announced that it will publish new Banking Communications for the time after the financial crisis, i.e. communications based on art.107(3)(c) TFEU, which will, however, take into account the experience made during the last three years. As the draft of this new banking package has not been published, it is too early to speculate about its content. Nevertheless, it would not come as a surprise if the Commission were to stress some of the principles applied under art.107(3)(b) TFEU, especially the ones concerning burden sharing and moral hazard, and that therefore winding-up and liquidation of financial institutes would be a realistic option in the future.

Short-term: the consequences of the European Council's summit on October 26–27, 2011

19–079   The European sovereign debt crisis which began in the so called PIIGS States (Portugal, Italy, Ireland, Greece and Spain) hit especially hard Greece but spread even further and led to an overall confidence crisis on sovereign debts and bonds.[627] On October 26/27, 2011, European leaders at the Euro Summit agreed to a number of measures aimed at relieving the stress in Europe's financial system. These measures include:

—the development of a voluntary bond exchange with banks (accepted by the Institute of International Finance (IIF)) and other private creditors at a discount of 50 percent on the nominal amount of outstanding Greek sovereign debt[628];

—an agreement to leverage the European Financial Stability Facility (EFSF) rescue fund by four to five times through credit enhancement and possible SPV structures; and

—a recapitalisation of the European banks and an improvement of their access to medium-term funding.

19–080   At first, rather general parameters were established, which have to be developed over the next months. With respect to the banks, the Council has agreed

---

[627] For an overview see *http://en.wikipedia.org/wiki/European_sovereign_debt_crisis*. [Accessed November 15, 2011].

[628] On October 27, 2011, the Heads of State or Government of the Eurozone agreed upon the establishment of a new program for Greece of €100 billion funded by the EU and the IMF. An agreement was reached with the private sector to bring Greek debt on to a sustainable path, which provides for a discount of 50% of the debt held by private creditors, or a write-off in the order of €100 billion. The Member States of the Eurozone are willing to contribute to all the measures relating to the private sector to the tune of €30 billion. These measures, together with an ambitious Greek reform programme, would be instrumental to reach a debt level of 120% by 2020.

upon the Consensus on Banking Package,[629] based on the two principles mentioned:

—the need to ensure the medium-term funding of banks, in order to avoid a credit crunch and to safeguard the flow of credit to the real economy, and to coordinate measures to achieve this; and

—the need to enhance the quality and quantity of capital of banks to withstand shocks and to demonstrate this enhancement in a reliable and harmonised way.

With respect to the medium-term funding, the Council has concluded:

—**Guarantees on bank liabilities** would be required to provide more direct support for banks in accessing term funding (short-term funding being available at the ECB and relevant national central banks), where appropriate. This is also an essential part of the strategy to limit deleveraging actions.[630]

—A truly **coordinated approach** at EU-level regarding entry criteria, pricing and conditions (Commission shall explore this together with EBA, EIB, and ECB).

With respect to recapitalisation, the principal rules shall be:

—**Capital target**: a capital ratio of 9 per cent of the highest quality capital and after accounting for market valuation of sovereign debt exposures,[631] both as of September 30, 2011, is needed to create a temporary buffer. This quantitative capital target will have to be attained by June 30, 2012, based on plans agreed with national supervisors and coordinated by EBA.[632] Consequently, all potentially systemic banks across all Member States—i.e.

---

[629] *http://www.consilium.europa.eu/uedocs/cms_data/docs/pressdata/en/ec/125621.pdf*. [Accessed November 15, 2011].

[630] The way in which deleveraging is to be avoided remains vague. Given the 9% Core Tier 1 ratio target by mid-2012, banks with difficulties in receiving or maintaining this ratio will have very incentive to preserve capital through deleveraging. The question can only be whether banks with rather comfortable common equity ratios can outweigh this.

[631] Accounting for all exposures to EU sovereign debt of the banks concerned (prudent valuation of all sovereign debt, whether in the banking book or the trading book) to ensure full transparency on asset quality, see Communication form the Commission COM(2011) 669, "A roadmap to stability and growth", downloadable under *http://ec.europa.eu/commission_2010–2014/president/news/speeches-statements/pdf/20111012communication_roadmap_en.pdf*. [Accessed November 15, 2011}.

[632] EBA= European Banking Authority. European Banking Authority was established by Council and EP Regulation (EC) No.1093/2010, has officially come into being as of January 1, 2011 and has taken over all existing and ongoing tasks and responsibilities from the Committee of European Banking Supervisors (CEBS). It acts as a hub and spoke network of EU and national bodies safeguarding public values such as the stability of the financial system, the transparency of markets and financial products and the protection of depositors and investors.

the banks that were covered by the EBA's July 2011 stress tests—must be covered by the recapitalisation effort. This prudent valuation would not affect the relevant financial reporting rules. National supervisory authorities, under the auspices of the EBA, must ensure that banks' plans to strengthen capital do not lead to excessive deleveraging, including maintaining the credit flow to the real economy and taking into account current exposure levels of the group including their subsidiaries in all Member States, cognisant of the need to avoid undue pressure on credit extension in host countries or on sovereign debt markets.

—**Financing of capital increase:** Banks should first use private sources of capital, including through restructuring and conversion of debt to equity instruments. Banks should be subject to constraints regarding the distribution of dividends and bonus payments until the target has been attained. If necessary, national governments should provide support , and if this support is not available, recapitalisation should be funded via a loan from the EFSF in the case of Eurozone countries.

The Consensus accepts that EU state aid rules remain fully applicable, even in the event that European resources (EFSF)[633] are involved.[634] Any form of public support, whether at a national or EU-level, will be subject to the conditionality of the current special state aid crisis framework, which the Commission has indicated will be applied with the necessary proportionality in view of the systemic character of the crisis.

19–081   A preliminary and indicative aggregated capital target at the EU level, based on June's figures and end-September sovereign bond yields, amounted to €106 billion. The EBA has disclosed the final capital shortfall on December 8, 2011 (see table below). Banks were required to submit to their respective national authorities by the end of 2011 their plans detailing the actions they intend to take to reach the set targets. These plans will have to be agreed with National Supervisory Authorities and discussed with the EBA. Banks will be expected to withhold dividends and bonuses.

---

[633] The European Financial Stability Facility (EFSF) is a Luxembourg-registered company owned by Euro Area Member States. It was created by the Euro Area Member States ("EAMS") following the decisions taken May 9, 2010 within the framework of the Ecofin Council. As part of the overall rescue package of €750 billion, EFSF is able to issue bonds guaranteed by EAMS for up to €440 billion for on-lending to EAMS in difficulty, subject to conditions negotiated with the European Commission in liaison with the European Central Bank and International Monetary Fund and to be approved by the Eurogroup.

[634] Subject to further implementation of these rules, it seems that national governments unable to provide the necessary state aid, will be funded via a loan from the EFSF, which they will then use to recapitalise the beneficiary banks.

Table: Breakdown by country and individual banks[635]

Banks individual results			
Country	Bank	Bank code	Shortfall millions Euro
Austria FMA OENB	ERSTE GROUP BANK AG	AT001	743
	RAIFFEISEN ZENTRALBANK ÖSTERREICH AG	AT002	2,127
	ÖESTERREICHISCHE VOLKSBANK AG[(1)]	AT003	1,053
Belgium	DEXIA[(2)]	BE004	6,313
	KBC BANK	BE005	0
Cyprus	MARFIN POPULAR BANK PUBLIC CO LTD	CY006	1,971
	BANK OF CYPRUS PUBLIC CO LTD	CY007	1,560
Denmark Danish FSA (Finanstilsy- net)	DANSKE BANK	DK008	0
	JYSKE BANK	DK009	0
	SYDBANK	DK010	0
	NYKREDIT	DK011	0
Finland	OP-POHJOLA GROUP	FI012	0
France	BNP PARIBAS	FR013	1,476
	CREDIT AGRICOLE	FR014	0
	BPCE	FR015	3,717
	SOCIETE GENERALE	FR016	2,131
Germany BuBa BaFin	DEUTSCHE BANK AG	DE017	3,239
	COMMERZBANK AG	DE018	5,305
	LANDESBANK BADEN-WÜRTTEMBERG	DE019	0
	DZ BANK AG DT. ZENTRAL-GENOSSEN- SCHAFTSBANK	DE020	353
	BAYERISCHE LANDESBANK	DE021	0
	NORDDEUTSCHE LANDESBANK -GZ-	DE022	2,489
	HYPO REAL ESTATE HOLDING AG, MÜNCHEN	DE023	0
	WESTLB AG, DÜSSELDORF	DE024	224
	HSH NORDBANK AG, HAMBURG	DE025	0
	LANDESBANK HESSEN-THÜRINGEN GZ, FRANKFURT		
	LANDESBANK BERLIN AG	DE026	1,497
	DEKABANK DEUTSCHE GIROZENTRALE, FRANKFURT	DE027	0
	WGZ BANK AG WESTDT. GENO. ZEN- TRALBK, DDF	DE028	0
		DE029	0

[635] *http://www.eba.europa.eu/capitalexercise/2011/2011-EU-Capital-Exercise.aspx* [Accessed February 15, 2012].

Banks individual results

Country	Bank	Bank code	Shortfall millions Euro
Hungary	OTP BANK NYRT.	HU036	0
Ireland	ALLIED IRISH BANKS PLC	IE037	0
	BANK OF IRELAND	IE038	0
	IRISH LIFE AND PERMANENT	IE039	0
Italy	INTESA SANPAOLO S.p.A	IT040	0
	UNICREDIT S.p.A	IT041	7,974
	BANCA MONTE DEI PASCHI DI SIENA S.p.A	IT042	3,267
	BANCO POPOLARE - S.C.	IT043	2,731
	UNIONE DI BANCHE ITALIANE SCPA (UBI BANCA)	IT044	1,393
Luxembourg	BANQUE ET CAISSE D'EPARGNE DE L'ETAT	LU045	0
Malta	BANK OF VALLETTA (BOV)	MT046	0
Netherlands	ING BANK NV	NL047	0
	RABOBANK NEDERLAND	NL048	0
	ABN AMRO BANK NV	NL049	0
	SNS BANK NV	NL050	159
Norway	DNB NOR BANK ASA	NO051	1,520
Poland	POWSZECHNA KASA OSZCZĘDNOŚCI BANK POLSKI S.A. (PKO BANK POLSKI)	PL052	0
Portugal	CAIXA GERAL DE DEPÓSITOS, SA	PT053	1,834
	BANCO COMERCIAL PORTUGUÊS, SA (BCP OR MILLENNIUM BCP)	PT054	2,130
	ESPÍRITO SANTO FINANCIAL GROUP, SA (ESFG)	PT055	1,597
	BANCO BPI, SA	PT056	1,389
Slovenia	NOVA LJUBLJANSKA BANKA D.D. (NLB d.d.)	SI057	320
	NOVA KREDITNA BANKA MARIBOR D.D. (NKBM d.d.)	SI058	0
Spain	BANCO SANTANDER S.A.	ES059	15,302
	BANCO BILBAO VIZCAYA ARGENTARIA S.A. (BBVA)	ES060	6,329
	BFA-BANKIA	ES061	1,329
	CAJA DE AHORROS Y PENSIONES DE BARCELONA	ES062	630
	BANCO POPULAR ESPAÑOL, S.A.	ES064	2,581

Banks individual results			
Country	Bank	Bank code	Shortfall millions Euro
Sweden	NORDEA BANK AB (PUBL)	SE084	0
	SKANDINAVISKA ENSKILDA BANKEN AB (PUBL) (SEB)	SE085	0
	SVENSKA HANDELSBANKEN AB (PUBL)	SE086	0
	SWEDBANK AB (PUBL)	SE087	0
UK	ROYAL BANK OF SCOTLAND GROUP plc	GB088	0
	HSBC HOLDINGS plc	GB089	0
	BARCLAYS plc	GB090	0
	LLOYDS BANKING GROUP plc	GB091	0

It is likely that we will see a second round of State aid investigations by the European Commission concerning banks that could not provide sufficient capital.

On December 1, 2012, the Commission has published its Prolongation Communication, with which it has prolonged and adjusted the extraordinary crisis rules, in order to facilitate the implementation of the European Council's "Banking package". In view of regulatory changes (9 per cent Common Equity quote by end of June 2012) and the changing market environment, the Commission anticipated that State capital injections may in the future more commonly take the form of shares bearing a variable remuneration, and has given guidance on the use of market-based valuations to give a reasonable assurance of an adequate remuneration. In future shares must be subscribed by the State at an appropriate discount to the latest share price. The Commission has also reviewed guidance on the fees that banks must pay for guarantees to ensure the aid is limited to the minimum necessary and to reflect the risk for public finances.

The Commission will continue to require Member States to submit a restructuring plan (or an update of a previously approved plan) for all banks which receive public support in the form of recapitalisation or impaired asset measures, be it from national or EU sources, regardless of the size or the reason for support. However, by assessing to what extent the bank will have to be restructured in order to reach long-term viability, the Commission will take full account of whether:

- the capital shortage is essentially linked to the confidence crisis on sovereign debt (i.e. to the obligation to achieve a minimum Common Equity Quote of 9 per sent at the end of June 2012);
- the public capital injection is limited to the amount necessary to offset losses stemming from marking sovereign bonds of the Contracting Parties to the EEA Agreement to market;
- the bank would otherwise be viable,

- the analysis shows that the bank in question did not take excessive risk in acquiring sovereign debt.

If these four conditions are fulfilled, there is no need for a *significant* restructuring.[636] Whether this means that there is also no need for significant compensatory measures remains to be seen.

Implications of prolonged economic crisis for the restructuring plans of financial institutions

19–082   The recrudescence of the financial and economic crisis (as caused by the sovereign bonds crisis) may hit the restructured banks considerably. It is likely that at least some of them will get into difficulties to fully implement their restructuring plans. The correct implementation of the restructuring plan is, however, normally an important condition to the approval condition, or—in decisions taken after the preliminary investigation procedure—a decisive commitment.

The question is, what kind of action is required if such conditions or commitments are not (fully) complied with. There is only one judgement of the General Court dealing with this question, taking a rather strict approach, according to which in case of the failure to fulfil a condition, the Commission must take a formal derogation from the condition in question.[637] The Court then establishes, under which circumstances the Commission must open the formal investigation procedure before it can take such a derogation decision. This can be avoided only under the following conditions:

—Even with the derogation, the aid remains compatible with the Internal Market. If it can not overcome all the difficulties involved in determining whether the aid remains compatible, the Commission is under a duty to carry out all the requisite consultations and, for that purpose, to initiate or, where appropriate, to re-open, the procedure under art.108(2) TFEU.[638]

—It must be a relatively minor deviation from the initial condition, which leave it with no doubt as to whether the aid at issue is still compatible with the Internal Market.[639]

19–083   The Court accepts that in case of conditions with respect to a restructuring plan, the results of which will be achieved only after a number of years, the Commission must enjoy a power to manage and monitor the implementation of the restructuring plan in order, in particular, to enable it to deal with developments which could not have been foreseen when the initial decision was adopted.

---

[636] Point 14, Prolongation Communication.
[637] Case T–140/95 *Ryanair Limited v Commission* [1998] E.C.R. II–3327, para.83.
[638] *Ryanair Limited v Commission*, para.87.
[639] *Ryanair Limited v Commission*, para.88.

It is therefore possible that, in the light of a change in external circumstances which occurs after the initial decision, the Commission might, inter alia, vary the conditions governing the implementation of the restructuring plan or of its monitoring, without re-opening the formal investigation procedure, providing none the less that such variations do not give rise to doubts as to the compatibility of the aid at issue with the Internal Market.[640] Nevertheless, even in such circumstances, a formal decision has to be taken (if the deviation is not significantly minor). In practice, the Commission has started to take so called "Monitoring decisions", with an MC Number.[641] So far, they have been related to the extension of a divestiture deadline, exchanging the companies to be divested, or exemptions from coupon bans.[642]

---

[640] *Ryanair Limited v Commission*, para.89.
[641] The Commission also calls them decisions sui generis, stressing that they are not explicitly provided for in the Procedural Regulation.
[642] See State aid SA.29832 — The Netherlands — State aid MC 10/09 — GHT1 hybrids call of ING, [2011] O.J. C46/29, Commission decision of 21 December 2010 in SA.29510 € — MC8/2009 — Monitoring of WestLB, unreported; State aid SA.29833 97 Belgium — State aid MC 11/09 — Extension of the target date of certain divestments by KBC, [2011] O.J. C346/9; SA.29833 (MC 11/09) — Monitoring of KBC — replacement own contribution measures, winddown of Romstal and extension deadline divestment KBL, [2012] O.J. C38/1; State SA.30062 — Germany Monitoring of LBBW aid — State aid MC 15/09 — LBBW Deka divestment, [2011] O.J. C245/21; Commission decision of 2 May 2010 in SA.30962 € — $ — Monitoring of Ethias, unreported; SA.31189 (MC 7/10) Monitoring of BAWAG P.S.K., new commitments regarding investment limits, [2012] O.J. C29/3; State aid MC 12/10 — Sparkasse KölnBonn divestments to the City of Cologne, [2011] O.J. C 271/20

CHAPTER 20

THE ENERGY SECTOR*

1.	GENERAL INTRODUCTION	20–001
2.	THE EURATOM TREATY	20–002
	General	20–002
	Commission Decisions	20–006
	EdF	20–012
	Transparency	20–013
3.	THE EU TREATY FRAMEWORK	20–014
	The definition of a state aid	20–015
	Selectivity	20–030
	State participation and the market economy investor test	20–035
	Effect on trade	20–039
4.	ARTICLE 107(2) AND (3)—THE EXEMPTIONS	20–041
	The automatic exceptions—Article 107(2) TFEU	20–042
	The discretionary exceptions—Article 107(3) TFEU	20–043
5.	RESCUE AND RESTRUCTURING AID	20–054
	Conditions for approval of rescue aid	20–055
	Restructuring aid	20–056
6.	THE METHODOLOGY ON STRANDED COSTS	20–057
	The individual decisions	20–060
7.	THE ENERGY SECTOR AND ARTICLE 106(2) TFEU	20–076
	The Commission's guidance notes on Directives 2003/54 and 2003/55	20–084
8.	AID THROUGH ENERGY COMPANIES	20–088
	Preferential tariffs	20–089
	Recent tariff cases	20–091
	Cross-subsidisation	20–094

1. GENERAL INTRODUCTION

20–001   The European Treaties' rules on state aid are of considerable importance to the energy sector given the traditionally high level of involvement of governments in energy production and supply. This has been equally true in the past, due in part to the traditional role of the state as owner or part-owner of major companies within the sector, as in the present. Governments continue to play an important

* Leigh Hancher

728

role with respect to ensuring an orderly transition from closed to open markets under competition and, more recently, with respect to ensuring long-term investments in the interests of security of supply and in securing the realisation of large-scale investment projects. The rules on state aid may also be of relevance to the restructuring of public utilities including their eventual privatisation. Furthermore, many of the activities of energy sector companies, whether private or public, may be eligible for subsidisation, for example in the form of aids to promote environmentally friendly energy technologies, to promote the production and use of renewable energy as well as to stimulate the transition away from carbon-intensive fuels. Para-fiscal levies or taxes may be a preferred instrument in this respect. Finally, the energy sector may in itself provide a source of aid to other sectors of the economy, for example through the provision of special or preferential tariffs for certain energy users.

The application of the state aid rules under the EU and ECSC Treaties to the energy sector, as well as the absence of specific rules under the Euratom Treaty to deal with national financial support to the Community's nuclear sector, present a large number of conceptual as well as practical problems. The first set of issues may in part be attributed to the continuing difficulties in defining with any degree of real certainty the actual scope of the concept of an "aid". The second issue is to be attributed to the lack of transparency which has traditionally characterised the relationship between state intervention in publicly owned or controlled firms.

This chapter will focus on the principal European state aid control mechanisms—those contained in the EU Treaty—but will also touch on the relation between the EU state aid rules and the Euratom Treaty which governs most aspects of the nuclear sector. The application of the EU state aid rules to the coal sector, following the expiry of the ECSC Treaty is dealt with in Ch.14.

2. THE EURATOM TREATY

General

The Euratom Treaty, unlike the EU and ECSC Treaties does not contain any specific provisions on state aid control. At the same time, the Euratom Treaty is a "lex specialis". Nuclear energy may remain a special case in that the EU Treaty rules cannot be straightforwardly and directly applied to evaluate aid to this sector.

20–002

The Euratom Treaty entrusts the Commission with a duty to promote the development and use of nuclear energy (arts 2 and 4 Euratom).[1] This duty of promotion does not appear to be open-ended nor, given that the Euratom Treaty

---

[1] art.197 Euratom which defines such terms as special fissile materials, source materials and ores, does not appear to apply to waste materials. Furthermore, the activities covered in Annex 1 to the Treaty would not seem to apply to decommissioning or storage as such—but only to certain forms of research.

unlike the ECSC Treaty is unlimited in its duration, should it be seen as indefinite. To exclude a sector—which is, after all, now a "mature" sector of the economy of a number of Member States—from any form of state aid discipline whatsoever would seem to furnish that sector with a considerable advantage over and above other competing fuel forms which are subject to the full discipline of the EU Treaty rules. Moreover, to accord a completely separate or privileged status to the state funding of nuclear energy would seem to make something of a nonsense of the concept of a single European electricity market, a concept which is predicated on competition between all forms of electricity, irrespective of the source of their generation.

20–003   Article 305(2) EC (now repealed) stated that the provisions of the EC Treaty should not derogate from the rules establishing the Euratom Treaty. This provision was worded slightly differently from art.305(1) EC (also repealed) which stated that the EC Treaty shall not affect the provisions of the ECSC Treaty. As the ECSC Treaty contained specific provisions on state aid to the coal and steel sectors, there was no doubt that the relevant provisions applied to the exclusion of arts 87 and 88 EC (now arts 107 and 108 TFEU).

With regard to nuclear energy, the relationship between the EC Treaty and the Euratom Treaty proved a source of controversy during the IGC leading up to the drafting of the Convention, and the Lisbon Treaty failed to resolve this. Although some Member States called for the abolition of the Euratom Treaty and the consolidation of certain of its provisions into the new Union Treaty, the Euratom Treaty now forms part of the new constitutional arrangements, albeit in essentially unamended form. Protocol 36 governs the relationship between the new Treaty and the Euratom Treaty Some Member States supported the idea of revising and updating the Euratom Treaty, and confirmed their willingness to do so in a Declaration to the Final Act of Lisbon Treaty.[2]

The legal relationship between the Euratom Treaty and the EU state aid rules has not yet been fully clarified by the courts however, and this has led to considerable debate as to whether the EU state aid regime may also apply to the nuclear sector. In his Opinion in Joined Cases 188–190/88 Advocate General Reischl was of the opinion that arts 87 to 89 EC (now arts 107–109 TFEU) should be applied to regulate state aid to the nuclear sector. This was not precluded by the application of art.305(2) EC. The Court did not address the issue directly. The Court did not accept the submission of the French government that the so-called Transparency Directive derogated from the provisions of the Euratom Treaty as the French government had not established this point.[3]

20–004   Thus, the starting point should be that the EU Treaty rules apply to the nuclear sector provided that those rules are not at variance with those of the Euratom Treaty. Further, even where for certain matters the provisions of the Euratom Treaty as a lex specialis can take precedence over the provisions of the EU Treaty

---

[2] [2007] O.J. C306/231, at p.268.
[3] See para.29 of Joined Cases 188–190/80 *France and the UK v Commission (Transparency Directive)* [1982] E.C.R. 2545.

as a lex generalis, in the interpretation of the lex specialis the Court may call on the lex generalis. In Ruling 1/78 the Court held that, in the light of the EC Treaty, the provisions of the Euratom Treaty on the nuclear internal market "appear to be nothing other than the application, in a highly specialised field, of the legal conceptions which form the basis of the structure of the general common market".[4]

Although the Commission has adopted a number of decisions relating to state aid to the nuclear sector, it has tended to avoid arriving at a definitive position on the application of the EU state aid rules to the sector, and has usually found a means to declare the measure in question not to be aid, or if in the alternative that it might be aid, this aid has in any event been found to be justified (see below 20–006). As a result of this practice, no direct challenges against a Commission decision have been lodged before the courts. In the meantime and pending definitive guidance from the European Courts, it may be observed that the Euratom Treaty, even if it does not contain a specific state aid regime, does not appear to immunise all national measures from Commission supervision. Article 5, for example, gives the Commission considerable powers to co-ordinate the nuclear research undertaken by Member States. The Commission may issue a specific or general request to Member States, persons or undertakings to communicate to it their programmes relating to the research which it specifies in the request. After giving those concerned a full opportunity to comment, the Commission may deliver a reasoned opinion on each of the programmes communicated to it. These opinions enable the Commission to discourage unnecessary duplication and to direct research towards sectors which are insufficiently explored. Article 6 provides that to encourage the carrying out of research programmes communicated to it the Commission may, inter alia, promote the joint financing by the Member States, persons or undertakings concerned (art.6(d)). Similar duties of notification of various aspects of investment in nuclear power facilities are imposed on Member States by way of arts 34, 37 and in Ch.IV (arts 40–44) Euratom. Furthermore, the promotion of nuclear safety is a Union competence which must be linked to the protection against the dangers arising from radiation, laid down in art.30, Ch.3, relating to health and safety.[5]

In addition, the rules governing supplies and the operation of the Euratom **20–005** Supply Agency can be taken to support the conclusion that it was the intention of the framers of the Treaty that various forms of unfair competitive practices, including "all practices designed to secure a privileged position for certain users (of ores, source materials and special fissile materials) shall be prohibited". In this context art.67 stipulates that

"[p]rices shall be determined as a result of balancing supply against demand . . . the national regulations of the Member States shall not contravene such practices. Pricing practices designed to secure a privileged position for

---

[4] [1978] E.C.R. 2151, at 2172.
[5] This is confirmed in Case C–29/99 [2002] E.C.R. I–1121.

certain users in violation of the principle of equal access ... shall be prohibited".

Finally, Member States are, in accordance with art.192 Euratom, under a general duty to ensure the fulfilment of the Treaty objectives and abstain from any measure which could jeopardise the attainment of those objectives. Recital 3 of the Euratom Treaty also confirms as one of those objectives, the guarantee of security of supply.

Commission Decisions

20–006   To date the Commission has assessed a number of proposed national aid measures to the nuclear sector under the EU Treaty state aid rules, although it is cautious of the manner in which it frames its decisions. It tends to phrase its decisions in such a way that it does not take a definitive position on the application of art.107(1) and further adds that, even if it would be applied, the aid in question would be compatible with art.107(3)(c). In C 31/2002—Transitional regime for the Belgian electricity market—it concluded that the proposed compensation of €377,033 million to Electrabel and SPE to meet the costs of dismantling experimental nuclear sites would be compatible with art.107(3)(c), but provided no further reasons for this finding.[6]

In 1989 the UK authorities notified a package of state aid measures destined for the nuclear industry in England and Wales and in Scotland just prior to privatisation of the sector in 1989. The Commission authorised:

a   a guarantee of up to GBP 2.5 billion to cover present and future liabilities in the nuclear sector, including decommissioning of existing power stations at the end of their lives;

b   use of the proceeds of a levy (the non-fossil fuel levy) on consumers to bring down the higher costs of nuclear produced power and to promote renewable energy sources;

c   the debt write-off provision of up to GBP 1.4 billion for Scottish nuclear production.

The UK authorities undertook to provide to the Commission by June 30, 1991 a detailed plan outlining the future of the aided nuclear sector. The debt writedown was planned for Scotland to ensure that the new company was viable and did not run the risk of going bankrupt. A total of GBP 1.4 billion was written off on the assumption that remaining debt would be serviced from cash flow.

20–007   Further details of the approved aid are only scantly described in the press notice issued on the decision.[7] It is noteworthy that the Commission approved the

---

[6] [2002] O.J. C222/2.
[7] IP/90/267, March 28, 1990.

non-fossil fuel levy as a state aid which was expected to average GBP 1.150 million per year (1.55 bn ECU) over eight years, and would be used, inter alia, to cover the difference between the price negotiated in the contracts between distribution companies and nuclear suppliers and the market price of electricity from other suppliers. The levy was to be phased out in 1998. The Commission reasoned that the plants had to be kept in operation for a certain time in order to earn sufficient profits to meet liability for decommissioning.

With regard to the provision of up to GBP 2.5 billion (GBP 700 million was allocated to Scotland) the Commission reasoned that this would be used for storage and reprocessing of nuclear fuel, treatment or storage for disposal of waste and decommissioning of nuclear installations. It places the costs accruing from the past directly on the government rather than the consumer—a cost which would have to have been borne by the government in any event if the present system of supply (i.e. public sector) had been continued.

In a reply to a question from H. Breyer in 2000,[8] the Commissioner for Energy   **20–008**
stated that the provisions of the Euratom Treaty, as provided for by art.305(2)EC apply to the nuclear industry. "There is thus no systematic method of identifying state assistance to the nuclear industry".[9] In the same reply she also reported that the Commission was dealing with a complaint concerning the sums set aside by nuclear undertakings for their future decommissioning costs and was investigating that complaint "in accordance with Community law".[10] A reply to a written question in June 2000 concerning the special tax treatment for decommissioning obligations enjoyed on German nuclear producers by Competition Commissioner Monti was based on the assumption that art.107(1) could apply to such a measure if all the conditions for the application of that article were met (WQ P–1873/00).

In its decision of December 11, 2001 concerning the application of the EU state aid rules to German tax treatment of reserves for the decommissioning of nuclear power plants and the safe disposal of nuclear waste, the Commission ruled that on the basis of a complaint by a number of regional energy supply companies, the rules in question did not constitute state aid because the tax treatment in question was apparently equally applicable to all undertakings that have to constitute similar reserves. It did not therefore confer a "selective benefit" on a particular sector and hence could not be caught by art.107(1).[11] It was noted in conclusion that "the Commission's decision does not affect the application of the Euratom Treaty and is only valid to the extent that the EC Treaty is applicable".[12] The Commission's decision was upheld on appeal: the

---

[8] Written question E–1286/00 of April 19, 2000.
[9] Written answer to E–1286/00, June 16, 2000.
[10] See also Commissioner De Palacio's reply to WQ P–2422/99, December 13, 1999 where she claims that the Euratom Treaty has no provisions concerning competition and state aid and that complaints about state aid being awarded for electricity production using nuclear energy have never been substantiated.
[11] COM (2001) 3967 final, December 11, 2001.
[12] IP01/1799, December 11, 2001. For earlier parliamentary questions on this issue, see WQ E–2472/97, P/K/1998 C 76/114 and WQ P–1873/00 [2001] O.J. C53/195.

General Court confirmed that the measures in question were general taxation rules, and therefore not aid within the meaning of art.107(1).[13]

20–009 **British Energy.** An attempt to resolve the interplay between the Euratom Treaty and the EU Treaty state aid is evident in the Commission's Decision C52/03 to open procedures against the restructuring aid granted by the UK government to British Energy (BE) in 2003.[14] This important case, which is also discussed below at section 5, concerned a package of seven measures. The Commission observed that several of the measures in question concerned issues covered by the Euratom Treaty,

"and therefore have to be assessed accordingly. However, to the extent that they are not necessary for or go beyond the objectives of the Euratom Treaty or distort or threaten to distort competition in the internal market, they have to be assessed under the EC Treaty".[15]

More specifically, the Commission considered that two sets of measures had to be assessed in the light of the objectives of the Euratom Treaty. These included measures to cover the reprocessing, storage and ultimate disposal of spent fuel and for decommissioning nuclear power stations which would be assumed by the UK government, and measures concerning the renegotiation of nuclear fuel supply agreements concluded by BE with BNFL, a publicly owned company. BNFL would reduce its prices to BE by some GBP 1000 million. The Commission took the view that a normal private creditor would not have acted in this manner and therefore the measure had to be imputed to the state. The UK government, on the other hand, contended that all the measures should be assessed under the Euratom Treaty, as the aims of the measures were to preserve the safety of nuclear power stations, to ensure the safe management of nuclear liabilities and to enhance security of supply by maintaining diversity of fuel sources in Great Britain as well as to avoid carbon dioxide emissions. On September 22, 2004 the Commission adopted a decision approving the restructuring plan for British Energy. In its final decision[16] the Commission approved the re-structuring plan subject to important conditions. BE agreed to cap its production capacity and not to extend its fossil fuel activities outside the United Kingdom and would also refrain from acquiring hydro capacity from its UK competitors. The funds received under the approved plan would be ring-fenced and BE would create three separate businesses, each with separate accounts. Adherence to the further condition that BE would not be allowed to undercut prices charged by its non-aided competitors on the market for supply to large users is monitored by an independent trustee.

[13] Case T–92/02 *Stadtwerke Schwäbisch Hall ao v Commission* [2006] E.C.R. II–11.
[14] [2003] O.J. C180/5.
[15] See Pt III of the Decision, at p.6.
[16] Commission press release, September 22, 2004, IP/04/1125.

Subsequently, in December 2004 the Commission launched a formal inves- **20–010** tigation into the UK government's plans to transfer BNFL's nuclear assets to a state-backed Nuclear Decommissioning Authority (NDA).[17] In its final decision 2006/643/EC of April 2006[18] the Commission authorised transfer of nuclear assets from BNFL to NDA subject to conditions. The Commission assessed the measures in the view of the objectives of Euratom Treaty and came to a conclusion that the measures were appropriate to address the combination of objectives pursued and thus were fully in line with the objectives of Euratom Treaty. Next the Commission assessed the existence of aid to the NDA and the BNFL. In the case of presumed aid to the NDA the Commission observed that the measure would provide an unlimited guarantee to the NDA as the State would cover all the NDA's expenses if these could not be covered by the NDA's revenues from commercial activities or by financial assets transferred to it. Therefore, the unlimited guarantee was considered to be an advantage granted by the State to the NDA. However, the Commission authorised the measure on the grounds that the aid in question was in line with the objectives of the Euratom Treaty and did not affect competition to an extent contrary to the common interest, which meant that both the necessity and proportionality test for a measure to be deemed compatible with the internal market under art.107(3)(c) TFEU were fulfilled. The Commission noted that the NDA would continue to operate some of the assets and thus would not comply with the "polluter pays" principle. However, because the NDA would operate the power plants for a residual time, the Commission gave an authorisation to the measure imposing similar conditions on the NDA to the ones imposed on British Energy.

The Commission also assessed whether BNFL was a recipient of aid. The **20–011** Commission found that since BNFL complied with the "polluter pays" principle the measure did not include aid to the BNFL.

In these decisions the Commission seems to take account of the objectives of the Euratom Treaty when assessing the necessity of a measure found to constitute state aid. Where the impact on competition and trading conditions is likely to be negative, the Commission authorises the measure imposing a number of condition to ensure that the negative impact is minimised.

EdF

In its decision to require the French Government to put an end to the unlimited **20–012** state guarantee[19] to EdF under art.108(1) the Commission considered that its

---

[17] IP/04/1430.

[18] [2006] O.J. L268/37.

[19] A number of entities who had the status of an "EPIC" under French law were entitled to unlimited guarantees and the Commission has concluded in a number of cases that this is contrary to art.107(1)—see most recently the decision on IFP where the Commission concluded that the guarantee is compatible with the state aid rules provided that IFP's economic activities are conducted solely on an ancillary basis and are connected with its main activity of public research, IP/11/802 of June 29, 2011.

decision was without prejudice to the application of or respect for the provisions of the Euratom Treaty.[20]

Transparency

20–013   The nuclear sector was originally exempted from the rules on financial reporting under the regime concerning the transparency of financial relations between Member States and public undertakings. Commission Directive 80/723 (the "Transparency Directive"), art.4(b) excluded the energy sector in general and the nuclear sector in particular, but this exemption was subsequently dropped when the Directive was amended in 1985[21] and has not re-surfaced in any subsequent amendment. The latest, consolidated version of the Directive dates from November 2006[22] and covers all public undertakings in the manufacturing sector[23] (see further, Ch.2, section 2).

3. THE EU TREATY FRAMEWORK

20–014   This section will provide a brief examination of what constitutes an "aid" in the energy sector. As will become evident, the problematic nature of the definition of "aid" for the purposes of art.107(1) TFEU is of particular importance in the energy sector.

The definition of a state aid

20–015   In principle, and as explained in detail in Ch.3, in order for a measure to fall within the scope of art.107(1) TFEU, the measure in question must fulfil all of the four cumulative conditions set out in that article.

20–016   **The concept of advantage.** The core of the concept of state aid is that it confers an economic advantage on the (potential) recipient—that is an advantage that the recipient would not enjoy under normal market conditions. Combined with the courts' insistence that the form of the measure is irrelevant and that it is the effect of the measure that is of key importance, this means that a wide variety of state action can potentially fall within the scope of the treaty state aid regime, provided of course that the cumulative criteria as set out above are met.

The three examples below are illustrative of the Commission's approach to this issue in the energy sector.

---

[20] E 3/02—EdF [2003] O.J. C164/7, at pt.60.
[21] [1985] O.J. L229/20.
[22] [2006] O.J. L318/17.
[23] Manufacturing being subsection DA up to and including subsection DN of the NACE (Rev.1) classification [1993] O.J. L83/1. This amendment was introduced in the revision to the Directive in 1993.

The Concept of Advantage in the Hungarian and Polish PPAs. In the Hungarian and Polish decisions on long-term power purchase agreements (PPAs), in order to determine whether these contracts as a generic system provided an economic advantage to power generators, the Commission had to assess whether, via the PPAs, generators obtain economic advantages that they would not obtain from the market. PPAs could provide eligible generators with an advantage if the parties to these agreements are placed in a better economic position than other companies. Even though the details of individual PPAs may vary, in the Commission's view, all PPAs are structured around a core, invariable principle: the mandatory purchase of most (sometimes all) of the electricity generated by the companies concerned, at a price reviewed periodically in accordance with the principle that the total costs (fixed and variable) of generating electricity, plus a profit margin, are passed on to the consumer.[24]

    20–017

This meant that, for the duration of the contracts, the commercial risk associated with operating the power plants was borne by the buyer of the electricity, i.e. PSE in Poland and MVM in Hungary. This included the risk associated with fluctuations in electricity generation costs and, in particular, fuel costs; the risk associated with fluctuations in end-user electricity prices; and the risk associated with fluctuation in end-user electricity demand. These are the typical risks that any power generator without a PPA would bear itself. The longer the period is, the greater the value of the guarantee, since it protects against a risk whose occurrence is increasingly unpredictable. Given that, unusually, it has limited its assessment to the period after May 2004, i.e. the date of Accession, the Commission did not consider it necessary to establish whether the business case for the PPAs might have been different in the mid 1990s and whether the PPAs would have indeed met the commercial objectives of MVM and PSE at the time they were concluded. Surprisingly, even taking 2004 as the starting point, the Commission failed to consider the disadvantages for buyers relying on spot markets and short term contracts—that is the exposure to volatility and liquidity risk.

Tariff cases. In the 2007 Sector Inquiry,[25] the Commission took issue with regulated supply tariffs because "such supply tariffs have adverse effects for competition and thus for consumers in the longer run", mentioning that it had received a complaint concerning Spanish tariffs and that it was investigating whether "any violations of state aid or antitrust rules have taken place".[26] In January 2007 the Commission started a state aid investigation on the Spanish regulated tariffs,[27] and in June of the same year it also started a state aid

    20–018

---

[24] The Polish electricity regulator, URE, indirectly retained the right to check whether the costs charged to PSE are justified and reasonable, but the Commission held that in practice URE used this power only to check that the costs were actually linked to electricity generation. See Poland: Commission Decision of September 25, 2007 [2009] O.J. L83/1. Hungary: Commission Decision of June 4, 2008, [2009] O.J. L225/53.

[25] See DG Competition report on energy sector inquiry (SEC (2006) 1724, January 10, 2007).

[26] See Sector Inquiry, paras 610–612.

[27] See Case C 3/2007 [2007] O.J. C43/9.

investigation on regulated supply tariffs in France.[28] While these investigations were still pending, in 2009 the Commission adopted a final decision[29] relating to tariffs for certain energy-intensive users in Italy (the *Alcoa* case), discussed below at para.20–091.[30]

20–019 **Licensing.** In its decision C1/2009 on MOL, the Commission found that a prolongation agreement between MOL and the Hungarian State which allowed the company to enjoy a limited exemption from increased mining fees on hydrocarbon extraction while MOL's competitors had to pay full concession fees, constituted aid within the meaning of art.107(1) TFEU.[31]

20–020 **State resources.** In Case C–379/98 *PreussenElektra*[32] the Court ruled that a state measure, a federal law which required certain regional electricity distribution undertakings to purchase at a fixed minimum price electricity produced from renewable energy sources within the supply area of each distribution undertaking concerned, and further required suppliers of electricity from conventional sources partially to compensate the distribution undertakings for the additional costs, did not constitute state aid, because it did not involve the transfer of state resources. The measure in question was a law imposing a minimum price on the regional electricity distributors. Such measures were paid for by private consumers on the one hand, and even if they had the effect of conferring an advantage on a particular beneficiary (in this case the producers of renewable energy) this was inherent in the legislative system. Following this ruling the Commission decided in May 2002 that German laws on the promotion of electricity from renewable energy sources and from combined heat and power (CHP) did not constitute state aid within the meaning of art.107(1) TFEU as state resources were not involved. The Commission noted that the measures were applicable without distinction to public and private operators and suppliers.[33]

It should be stressed that the *PreussenElektra* ruling concerned the interpretation of the first part of the definition of a state aid measure; it did not deal with the meaning of the second part, i.e. the scope of the concept where aid is provided "through State resources in any form whatsoever". It is established case law that aid granted by public or private bodies designated or established by the state, may also be classified as aid within the meaning of art.107(1) TFEU. Hence the financial resources at the disposal of public undertakings as well as private undertakings controlled by the state could be subject to the EU Treaty discipline on state aids.[34]

---

[28] See Case C 17/2007 [2007] O.J. C164/9. In 2009, the Commission took note of a change in the original measure under investigation and adopted a decision extending the scope of the investigation (see [2009] O.J. C96/18).

[29] Case C 36/06 [2010] O.J. L227/62.

[30] See Case C 36/B/2006, [2010] O.J. L227/62. See also case T–332/06 *Alcoa Trasformazioni v Commission* [2009] E.C.R. II–29, and upheld on appeal in Case C–194/09P, July 21, 2011.

[31] C (2010) 3553 final, June 9, 2010.

[32] [2001] E.C.R. I–2099.

[33] See Press Release IP/02/739.

[34] See further Case C–345/02 *Pearle* [2004] E.C.R. I–7139.

Given that the *PreussenElektra* ruling did not deal with the scope of the   **20–021**
residual category, but left the potential application of art.107(1) TFEU to private
funds under state control open, the refusal of the Court to honour the Commission's request to extend the scope of art.107(1) TFEU to measures having
equivalent effect to a state aid is probably less problematic than it may first seem.
Many commentators greeted *PreussenElektra* with the observation that it could
create serious holes in the Commission's regulatory net. A Member State could
easily devise a scheme which would allow circumvention of the state aid rules.
Instead of distributing funds themselves, or via a specially controlled body, they
can devise schemes for compulsory direct payments from one individual to
another which would have the same effect as a state aid within the meaning of
art.107(1).

Indeed, this "result" has been apparent in the energy sector. Certain Member
States have imposed obligations on, for example, energy supply companies to
pay a surcharge to electricity producers to compensate the latter for so-called
"stranded costs"—that is past investments which can no longer be exploited
commercially due to energy market liberalisation.[35] (See below at section 6.) If,
however, the state aid legislation designates that a component of the end users'
purchase price must be paid to an intermediary over which it exercises some
control, and then in turn paid to a particular group of beneficiaries, the measure
has been classified as state aid.[36] In its decision on the UK's Renewables
Obligation and Capital Grants for Renewable Technologies, which obliges all
licensed electricity suppliers in Scotland, England and Wales to ensure that a
proportion of electricity supplied to customers in Great Britain comes from a
renewable source of energy, the Commission found that one aspect of the scheme
(a redistribution fund) did constitute state aid, although it was compatible with
the environmental aid guidelines.[37] (See further Ch.22.)

Furthermore, certain funding arrangements, such as the imposition of a para-
fiscal charge on energy consumers, may also contravene other Treaty rules if, for
example, the para-fiscal levy is imposed on imported electricity as well as
domestic energy and if only the domestic producers benefit from such a fund (see
Ch.3).[38]

In its ruling in Case C–206/06 *Essent Netwerk*,[39] the Court of Justice shed
some further light on the definition of state resources. The Dutch measure at issue
in this case provided for the payment to the designated company, SEP, of a stated

---

[35] See IP/02/322 UK: Compensation to NIE for stranded costs constitutes no state aid. A levy
imposed on final consumers was collected by distributors or the network operator and was
transferred to NIE. This did not include a transfer of state resources.

[36] See for example the Commission's Decision on green certificate systems in Belgium
(N4155A/01) [2002] O.J. C30/14 and in Sweden—N 789/2002 of February 5, 2003 [2003] O.J.
C120/8. In its opening Decision in C 43/2002 concerning a compensation fund in Luxembourg,
however, the Commission formed the preliminary view that the measures in question were aid
[2002] O.J. C255/15.

[37] Commission Decision of November 28, 2001 on N 504/2000 [2002] O.J. C30/15.

[38] See C 43/2000 *Luxembourg, loc cit* [2009] O.J. L159/11. See also State aid for Green Electricity
in Austria, IP/06/953.

[39] [2008] E.C.R. I–5497.

sum levied by way of a surcharge on electricity consumers for the defrayal of stranded costs and for the payment of the excess levied through the surcharge to be paid to the Minister. The charge had to be paid to the network operator who was required to transfer a fixed sum to SEP and to pay the excess to the Minister. The network operator was at the relevant time, owned by the Dutch local authorities and provinces. The SEP was owned by the generators—who were both under public as well as private control. The Court held that the surcharge proceeds remained under public control and were available to the national authorities. This distinguished the measure at issue here from the situation in Case C–345/02 *Pearle and Others*[40] (see Ch.3) where the advertising campaign had been organised for a purely commercial purpose and had nothing to do with a policy determined by the state. In the present case, the payment of the fixed sum to the SEP had been the subject of a decision of the legislature. Likewise, the measure differed from that referred to in *PreussenElektra*, as the SEP had been appointed to manage a State resource.

20–022   In a subsequent case in 2009, Case T–25/07 *Iride*,[41] the applicants claimed that the measure at issue, a system for covering stranded costs, did not involve state resources but rather entailed transfers between economic actors—i.e. final consumers of electricity and electricity distributors—even though it was channelled through a separate fund.[42] It therefore claimed that following PreussenElektra, the contested measure did not amount to state aid. The General Court held that the sums in question were indeed state resources, not only because they are under constant state control, but also because they are state property. In this respect, the Court distinguished the case at hand from *PreussenElektra* by arguing that in the latter case:

> "apart from the creation of the legal obligation to purchase at a minimum price, the State had not played any role in the collection and/or redistribution of the funds in question."

By contrast, in *Iride*, the funds were collected and managed by a fund, which was a public body, before being redistributed to the recipient.

20–023   **Austrian Green Electricity Fund.** The Commission has also maintained a strict approach to the definition of state resources, and has interpreted the *Pearle* case very narrowly. Thus, in a recent decision concerning an Austrian law to support production of electricity from renewable energy sources,[43] the Commission held that the system at hand differed significantly from the *PreussenElektra* scheme to the extent that, the body in charge of administering the funds, which was a

---

[40] [2004] E.C.R. I–7139.
[41] [2009] E.C.R. II–245.
[42] See also for a similar approach, the CFI's ruling in Case T–332/06 *Alcoa* [2009] E.C.R. II–29.
[43] See Case C 24/2009 [2009] O.J. C217/12 and the final decision of March 2011 [2011] O.J. L235/42.

private law entity appointed by concession to act as a settlement centre, was and should remain subject to strict monitoring and financial support from the State. Moreover, even if the entity administering the funds was private, thus did not provide a sufficient basis to consider that the financial resources channelled through it were of private nature and not imputable to the State. The sesttlemetn centre had to use the funds collected from customers for a purpose designated by law. Similarly, in the case of support for renewable energy in Luxembourg,[44] the role played by a compensation fund, acting under the control of the State, was enough to conclude that state resources were present.

Finally, the approach of the Commission to the notion of "State resources"   **20–024** developed in a number of its decisions on state action in favour of public companies deserves mention. In January 2003, the Commission opened a formal investigation procedure in respect of the financial measures introduced by the French authorities for France Télécom. The measures included inter alia the shareholder loan granted by France to France Télécom in December 2002 in the form of a 9 billion Euro credit line. The investigation concluded with the decision of August 2, 2004[45] where the Commission ruled that in the context of the declarations made by the government from July to December 2002, the shareholder loan constituted state aid incompatible with the internal market. The Commission claimed that if considered alone, the loan would probably have been considered not to constitute state aid. However, the Commission viewed the declarations as having the effect of restoring confidence to the market and ruled out the application of prudent private investor principle in that case. It was the first time the Commission has examined this type of aid and therefore it decided not to order recovery of this aid. Both France Télécom[46] and the French Republic[47] brought separate actions against the Commission's decision claiming to annul it in its entirety. In its subsequent ruling the General Court held that although the companies in question had benefitted from an advantage, this had not been financed with state resources.[48]

In its ruling in the *SIC* case,[49] the Court indicated that:

"only objective findings leading to the conclusion that the State legally had to repay that issue in the event of default by RTP [the potential beneficiary] would permit a finding of the existence of a State guarantee."

Thus, it is necessary to show that the potential beneficiary has a legal entitlement to the particular measure—a mere promise is not sufficient.

Imputability. In Case C–482/99 *France v Commission (Stardust Marine)*, the   **20–025** Court provided a further clarification of the scope of the second or residual part

---

[44] Case C 43/2002 [2002] O.J. C255/15.
[45] Commission Decision No.C(2004) 3060 [2006] O.J. L257/11.
[46] Case T–444/04 [2005] O.J. C19/30.
[47] Case T–425/04 [2005] O.J. C31/26.
[48] Joined Cases T–444/04 and T–425/04, ruling of March 2011.
[49] Case T–442/03 [2008] E.C.R. II–1161.

of the state aid test.[50] It held that even though resources which may eventually be at the disposal of the state may be deemed to be "state resources" it is also necessary to show that the actual deployment of those resources for the benefit of a particular undertaking can be attributed to some form of government decision. Merely "organic" forms of public control over such resources are not in themselves sufficient. Hence the Court annulled the Commission's decision that capital injections made by two subsidiaries of a publicly owned bank, Credit Lyonnais, to the French charter boat company, Stardust, amounted to aid in that case. Nevertheless, it is difficult to specify clearly what the actual parameters of the imputability test are likely to be in any one case. The Court's previous case law on the matter of the degree of control necessary to establish imputability or attributability was itself unclear. In two cases concerning alleged preferential energy tariffs, discussed below, the European Court of Justice had no difficulty in reaching the conclusion that the decision by the publicly controlled gas supplier, Gasunie, to award certain preferential tariffs to particular large consumers, could be attributed to the Dutch government. At the relevant time, the Dutch government enjoyed certain rights of veto over Gasunie's commercial decisions and, further, two members of Gasunie were appointed by the government. This type of structure may be sufficient to establish something more than organic control.[51] In the *Olympic Airways* case the Court made clear in its ruling on non-payment by Olympic of airport charges to Athens Airport—operated as a private undertaking—that the Commission must state clear reasons as to why it considers a measure to be imputable to the State.[52]

20–026   The implications for the energy sector of the "Stardust" ruling are of some importance given that several Member States still own or control parts of their countries' energy enterprises. Should a government (whether national or local) seek to exert control or influence over, for example, the tariffs charged to certain groups of users or to ensure that capacity in pipelines, electricity networks, storage facilities or interconnectors is reserved to particular undertakings, or for the dispatch of renewable forms of energy, state aid issues may well arise. The case of the French regulated tariff, mentioned above, provides a good illustration, as the Commission, following the *Stardust Marine* jurisprudence, imputed to the State a tariff adopted by EDF.[53] In its final decision on the Polish and on the Hungarian PPAs the Commission confirmed that the PPAs were attributable to the state as they pursued general policy objectives of the state, formulated at privatisation.[54]

20–027   In its decision on the package of rescue and restructuring measures adopted in relation to the UK's British Energy (see para 20–009, above) the Commission concluded that certain contractual agreements between BE and BNFL could not

[50] [2002] E.C.R. I–4397.
[51] Case C–56/93 *Belgium v Commission* [1996] E.C.R. I–723; Joined Cases 67, 68 and 70/85 *Van der Kooy* [1988] E.C.R. 219.
[52] T–68/03 *Olympiaki Aeroporia v Commission* [2007] E.C.R. II–2911.
[53] See Case C 17/2007 [2007] O.J. C164/9.
[54] Case C 43/2005 [2008] O.J. C58/8.

be attributed to the UK government for two reasons; the contracts had been concluded prior to the intervention of the UK government in the affairs of BE, and secondly the companies had acted under a fiduciary duty in accordance with British company law in revising the contracts at issue in order to maximise value and minimise financial exposure on the basis of the information available to them at the relevant time. This was substantiated by the relevant extracts of Board meetings which were made available to the Commission.[55]

Imputability and Taxation on Energy Products. Following prolonged negotia-   **20–028**
tions the Community finally agreed on Directive 2003/96 on the taxation of energy products in late 2003.[56] One problematic aspect in the negotiations leading up to the adoption of this measure was the inter-relationship between certain tax reductions/exemptions and the EU state aid rules. In this respect the compulsory or facultative nature of certain tax exemptions/reductions must be considered. If the tax exemption derives from a Community measure such as a Directive, without leaving any scope for discretionary application at national level, the measure is not imputable to the state and cannot therefore be considered to be a state aid. For example, Council Directive 92/81 provides that mineral oils injected into blast furnaces for the purpose of chemical reduction as an addition to the coke used as a principal fuel is subject to a Community wide mandatory exemption. In Case T–351/02 *Deutsche Bahn*, the German railway company had complained to the Commission that the exemption granted under this Directive for aviation fuel, as implemented into German law, was distorting competition between rail and air services. The Commission replied that the exemption was as a result of the implementation of the EU Directive and was not a grant of aid by Germany. The General Court confirmed the Commission's standpoint. It recalled that it was not sufficient for the purposes of art.107(1) that the aid had been granted through state resources—it must also be imputable to the state. These are separate and cumulative conditions.[57] Where, however, the measures concerned result from the national system, they will have to be assessed under the EU state aid rules. A case in point is art.4(2) of the Directive 2003/96 which allows Member States to add all indirect taxes levied on the quantity of energy products.[58]

Mineral Oils used as a fuel for aluminium production. This case concerned an   **20–029**
appeal brought by the Commission against the judgment of the General Court of

---

[55] Commission Decision 2005/407/EC of September 22, 2004 on the state aid which the United Kingdom is planning to implement for British Energy Plc [2005] O.J. L142/26.
[56] [2003] O.J. L 283.
[57] Case T–351/02 *Deutsche Bahn v Commission* [2006] O.J. C 131/37.
[58] See for the problems this can cause, the Commission's Decision on the Swedish eco-tax and energy tax system, NN 3/B/2002 where it concluded that it was necessary to open proceedings as regards the full exemption for the electricity tax for the manufacturing sector. See further, J. Lannering and B. Renner-Loquenz, "State aid and eco-taxes: bundling of eco-taxes for State aid assessment", *Competition Policy Newsletter*, No.3 Autumn, 2003, pp.75–6.

December 12, 2007 in *Ireland and Others v Commission*,[59] in which that court annulled Commission Decision 2006/323/EC of December 7, 2005 concerning the exemption from excise duty on mineral oils used as fuel for aluminium production in Gardanne, in the Shannon-region and in Sardinia respectively implemented by France, Ireland and Italy. The Commission classified as state aid incompatible with the common market exemptions from excise duties on mineral oils which had been granted by the Council of the European Union on a proposal from the Commission several years earlier in accordance with the relevant directives concerning excise duty. It considered that those exemptions constituted new aid, which should therefore be recovered from the recipients. The Commission conceded, however, that the Council decisions authorising them had given rise to a legitimate expectation that they conformed with the rules of the common market. It therefore ordered recovery of the aid only as from the date of publication in the *Official Journal* of the notice of commencement of the formal procedure for examination of those exemptions in the light of the state aid rules. Actions for annulment of the contested decision were brought by Ireland, the French Republic and the Italian Republic, and by two companies, Eurallumina SpA and Aughinish Alumina Ltd. The ECJ held that the Commission did not have to provide any detailed reasons as to why it considered the earlier Council exemptions to be irrelevant to the substance of its assessment. The Court held that:

"Furthermore, it also follows clearly... that, while the Commission had taken the view, when the decisions authorising the exemptions at issue were adopted by the Council, that those exemptions did not give rise to distortions in competition or interfere with the working of the internal market, the fact remains that they had never been analysed or authorised under the State aid rules, on the basis of which the Commission came to the opposite conclusion."[60]

The conditions under which Member States can grant tax reductions or exemptions from a harmonised environmental or energy tax, such as those foreseen in the Energy Taxation Directive 2003/96, are defined in pt. 51 of the Environmental Guidelines of 2008 and art.17 of the Energy Taxation Directive. This latter article makes provision for tax reduction on the consumption of energy products for energy-intensive business.[61] (and is further discussed in Ch.22 environmental aid).

Selectivity

20–030 In order to fall within the scope of art.107(1) TFEU the state measure in question must have the effect of conferring a selective benefit or advantage.

[59] Joined Cases T–50/06, T–56/06, T–60/06, T–62/06 and T–69/06 *Ireland and Others v Commission* [2007] E.C.R. II–172.
[60] Case C–89/08P [2009] E.C.R. I–11245.
[61] See N 190A/2005—United Kingdom, *Modification of the Climate Change Levy* [2006] O.J. C 146/05.

General measures which can benefit the entire economy, such as a lowering of tax rates or interest rates do not create a selective benefit. In order to determine whether a measure is selective, the applicable system of reference must be defined.[62]

The courts have generally found the "selectivity criteria" to be easily met. Hence in Case C–143/99 *Adria-Wien Pipeline*,[63] a tax measure which distinguished between the manufacturing sector and the rest of the economy, including the service sector, was held to be selective. In its judgment in *Adria-Wien*, the court held that an Austrian tax measure awarding a rebate on energy taxes charged on supply of natural gas and electricity to undertakings active (i) in the manufacture of goods; (ii) in so far as energy taxes exceeded 0.35 per cent of the production value, was in fact a selective measure. The Court observed that "undertakings supplying services may, just like undertakings manufacturing goods, be major consumers of energy" and further that:

> "the ecological considerations underlying the national legislation at issue do not justify treating the consumption of natural gas or electricity by undertakings supplying services differently than the consumption of energy by undertakings manufacturing goods. Energy consumption by each of these sectors is equally damaging to the environment."

The Court further held that the criterion applied by the national legislation at issue is not justified by the nature or general scheme of that legislation. Hence the measure was selective because it was reserved to manufacturing undertakings and not as a result of the limitation expressed in terms of the production value. At para.36 of its ruling, the Court seemed to imply that if the rebate of the energy taxes had been applied to all undertakings in the national territory regardless of their activity, and insofar as the energy taxes exceeded 0.35 per cent of the production value, the measure would not have been considered as selective.[64] However, in a subsequent decision concerning a modification of the same law, the Commission was required to consider whether a tax rebate on gas and electricity paid to all businesses if the taxes together exceeded 0.35 per cent of their net production value would constitute aid. The Commission considered in its preliminary assessment that as only larger companies would benefit from this measure, the tax rebate did not constitute a general measure.[65]

---

[62] For an interesting application of the selectivity test to the choice of a Member State to award a concession or an authorisation, see C1/2009 Aid in favour of Mol, discussed above.

[63] Case C–143/99 [1999] E.C.R. I–8365.

[64] The Commission subsequently approved the energy rebate tax as a state aid compatible with art.107(3)(c) TFEU and with the guidelines for environmental protection. The same law was modified in late 2002, see [2003] O.J. C164/2. The question of whether those companies who had been required to pay the tax prior to the modification of the law have standing to claim a rebate was before the Court in Case C–368/04 *Transalpine Olletung GmbH* [2006] E.C.R. I–9957.

[65] [2003] O.J. C164/2, at pt.3.

Following the Court's ruling in the *Adria-Wien* case, the Commission re-examined earlier exemptions it had issued for several national eco-tax exemption schemes. In the case of the Danish 10 per cent CO_2 tax exemption, the Commission had considered this to be a general measure as it was available for all VAT-registered companies. On review it established that the VAT-criterion did not preclude certain categories of company, for example in the service sector. The objective of the Danish government when applying the VAT-criterion was to make a distinction between domestic consumers and others. In order to ensure the underlying objectives a further adjustment was made so that certain types of VAT-registered companies were not eligible for relief if their energy consumption corresponded only to that of a domestic user. That resulted in the exclusion of certain service activities but the Commission held that this was justified under "the nature or general scheme of the system" and did not render the measure selective.[66]

20–031   In the Finnish and Swedish decisions, the Commission examined so-called two tier systems where higher targeted tax reductions for energy intensive consumers were available alongside a general tax reduction for most types of companies. The latter types of exemption were considered selective and in the Finnish case and the Swedish case the Commission granted an exemption on the basis of art.107(3)(c) TFEU as it considered the regimes to comply with its guidelines on state aid for environmental protection.[67] These guidelines are discussed in detail in Ch.22. In a decision[68] of September 26, 2006, the European Commission opened a formal investigation to examine whether Danish plans to grant CO_2 tax exemptions to companies covered by the EU's Emissions Trading Scheme (EU ETS) were compatible with EU Treaty state aid rules. The Danish government claimed that it intends to eliminate double regulation of CO_2 emissions, by taxes and emission quotas imposed by the EU ETS. The government argued that double regulation will not reduce the emissions, but will increase costs companies have to bear and create a double burden for them. According to the Commission, the measure might distort competition by increasing tax differentiation in an area where the European Union has harmonised taxes. Furthermore, with the tax exemptions, the energy tax rate paid by the companies concerned would be below the minimum rates set out in the Energy Tax Directive. Additionally, companies participating in the EU ETS have received most of the emission allowances for free. The Commission did not rule out that this measure might run contrary to the 'polluter-pays' principle. In its opening decision[69] of November 11, 2006, concerning Swedish CO_2 tax reductions, the Commission raises similar arguments

20–032   Exemptions for certain categories of consumers, such as large consumers, to pay a form of stranded costs levy into a compulsory fund, are considered a form

[66] N 841/A/2000 [2002] O.J. C238/13.
[67] Finland, NN 75/2002 [2002] O.J. C309/17, NN 3/A/2001 and NN 4/A/2001. See also M. Infeldt, "Eco-Tax Reliefs", *Competition Policy Newsletter*, No.1 Spring, 2003, pp.103–4.
[68] C 41/2006 [2006] O.J. C274/25.
[69] C 46/2006 [2006] O.J. C297/27.

of selective benefit.[70] The Commission's final negative decision on the Austrian Green Electricity Act of March 2011 found that an exemption to purchase renewable electricity for undertakings whose costs increased by 0.5 per cent of their net production value was selective even although the measure was open to all sectors.[71]

It may also be noted that the EU Treaty does not deal with the issue of whether a specific tax system imposing a surcharge tax on a certain economic sector constitutes a selective advantage in favour of those undertakings that are excluded from the tax. In accordance with arts 4(c) and 67(3) of the ECSC Treaty special charges on steel and coal producers were prohibited. Although there is little case law on this issue, the Commission has dealt with the matter in the area of energy taxes, where it recognises that specific or special charges are solely concerned with a Member State's discretion in forming its tax system and do not constitute aid within the meaning of art.107(1).[72] At para.13 of its Notice on aid through direct taxation the Commission observes that Member States maintain their power to spread their tax burden as they see fit across the different factors of production. Nevertheless in Joined Cases C–128/03 and C–129/03 *AEM SpA*,[73] an increase in taxation for certain types of electricity was deemed to constitute aid for all other energy producers. The Court considered the aid measure justified by advantages arising from the liberalisation of the energy market. In 2009, the General Court upheld a Commission decision, which had, inter alia, found that a tax exemption applicable to certain undertakings active in the supply of energy but which was not applicable to other undertakings, was nevertheless justified by the nature or general scheme of the system.[74]

The need to distinguish between the object of the measure (relevant for the **20–033** compatibility assessment) and its effects (relevant for the qualification of the measure as aid) underpinned the decision by the Court of Justice to set aside a judgment by the General Court. In the *British Aggregates* case, the General Court had accepted that the Commission was right in holding that the pursuance of environmental protection rendered a dedicated levy non-selective. However, the Court of Justice found a fault in this reasoning, by re-stating that:

"Article 87(1) EC [Article 107(1) TFEU] does not distinguish between the causes or the objectives of State aid, but defines them in relation to their effects . . . In the light of that case-law, the unavoidable conclusion is that the Court of First Instance disregarded Article 87(1)EC [Article 107(1) TFEU], as

---

[70] C 43/2002, Luxembourg [2002] O.J. C255/15.
[71] Commission Decision of March 8, 2011 on State aid measure No.C 24/2009 (ex N 446/2008) State aid for energy-intensive businesses under the Green Electricity Act in Austria, Brussels, March 8, 2011 C(2011) 1363 final. [2011] O.J. L235/42.
[72] Commission Decision of April 24, 2002 on State Aid N 863—UK, *Aggregates Levy*; Case T–210/02 [2003] E.C.R. II–2789 and on appeal, Case C–487/06P [2008] E.C.R. I–10505, paras 84–92. See also the opinion of the A.G. Geelhoed of September 18, 2003 in Case C–308/01 *GIL Insurance Ltd* [2004] E.C.R. I–4777.
[73] Judgment of April 14, 2005 [2005] E.C.R. I–02861.
[74] Case T–189/03 *AEM Brescia SpA v Commission* [2009] E.C.R. II–1831.

interpreted by the Court of Justice, by holding . . . that Member States are free, in balancing the various interests involved, to set their priorities as regards the protection of the environment and, as a result, to determine which goods or services they decide to subject to an environmental levy, with the result that the fact that such a levy does not apply to all similar activities which have a comparable impact on the environment does not mean that similar activities, which are not subject to the levy, benefit from a selective advantage".

20–034 **Green Certificates and Emission Trading Schemes.** Systems where a tradable emission or pollution document is considered as authorised proof of a certain production that can not however be sold or auctioned to the recipient do not involve State resources and hence do not fall within the scope of art.107(1) TFEU. The Commission's decision in the Dutch Nox emission trading scheme is illustrative of the problems of determining whether such a scheme is a state aid or not. The Dutch scheme was based on tradable emission credits which were neither direct permits nor mere forms of authorised proof or certification. This system is a form of dynamic cap system—new companies or companies wishing to expand do not have to acquire allowances but they must comply with the relative emission system. The annual allowed absolute emission per facility was calculated inter alia on the energy use of that facility. If the producer exceeded this absolute emission ceiling, it would have to buy Nox credits or borrow the credits of its obligation in the following year, or ultimately, pay a fine. The tradable Nox credits thus contributed directly to the absolute emission standard imposed by the state. Hence the Commission considered the scheme to be comparable to a direct Nox emission allowance allocation. As the producer has an incentive to pay for the tradable emission documents these will represent a value to it. Furthermore, the Dutch government had an option to sell or auction[75] the emission standards and receive revenue. The credits were provided free of charge, so state revenues were foregone. Finally, the scheme was selective as it benefited a selected group of large industrial undertakings. The scheme was therefore considered to constitute state aid and was considered for exemption under the Guidelines on environmental protection.

On appeal, however, the General Court quashed the Commission decision because of the measure's lack of selectivity.[76] In particular, the Court found that the criterion for application of the measure in question was therefore an objective one, without any geographic or sectoral connotation. Moreover, since the measure in question was aimed at the undertakings which are the biggest polluters, that objective criterion was furthermore in conformity with the goal of the measure, that is the protection of the environment, and with the internal logic of the system.[77] The Commission appealed this ruling and the ECJ, concluding that

[75] See further M. Konings, "Emission Trading—Why state aid is Involved" *Competition Policy Newsletter*, No.3, autumn 2003, pp.77–79.
[76] Case T–233/04 *Netherlands v Commission* [2008] E.C.R. II–591, and on appeal Case C–279/08P judgment of September 8, 2011.
[77] Case T–233/04 [2008] E.C.R. II–591, paras 84–100.

the measure was indeed correctly classified by the Commission as selective, quashed the General Court's ruling.[78]

State participation and the market economy investor test[79]

It is established law that not every participation by the state in the capital or operations of a company (private or public) may automatically be classified as aid. Where, for example, the state owns a shareholding in an undertaking it may under certain conditions make state resources available to it (e.g. in the form of capital injections) without falling foul of art.107(1) TFEU. The EU Treaty takes a neutral position with regard to national property laws and hence state-owned or controlled enterprises must be treated in the same way as private enterprises.[80] It is in this context that the courts have developed and applied the so-called "private market investor test or market economy investor test" (MEIT). The application of the market investor test entails a complex economic assessment, particularly if the beneficiaries are wholly owned by the state (see Ch.8, section 1).

20–035

As explained in Ch.3, the courts draw a distinction between state participation through acts of public prerogative and intervention through other means in their national economy. Several recent cases have thrown some light on how the courts will deal with measures which take the form of fiscal measures but which nevertheless can be deemed, for various reasons to have the same effect as the intervention of a normal private investor. Hence in Case T–196/04, *Ryan Air*, the court held that:

"When examining the measures at issue, the Commission should have differentiated between the economic activities and those activities which fell strictly under public authority powers. In addition, whether the conduct of an authority granting aid complies with national law is not a factor which should be taken into account in order to decide whether that authority acted in accordance with the private investor principle or granted an economic advantage in contravention of Article 107(1) TFEU. It does not follow from the fact that an activity represents in legal terms an exemption from a tariff scale laid down in a regulation that that activity must be described as non-economic".[81]

In Case T–156/04 *EDF v Commission*, the Court was requested to examine the legality of a Commission decision condemning various fiscal measures adopted in the context of the restructuring of EDF in order to remedy the company's under-capitalisation in relation to its transmission network. The French government had, inter alia, waived payment of certain taxes due by EDF following a

---

[78] Case C–279/08P *Netherlands v Commission*, September 8, 2011.
[79] See Ch.8 at s.3.
[80] See also in this context the Commission's Decision to open the formal investigation against EdF, 2003.
[81] [2008] E.C.R. II–3143.

revision of its accounting system as part of its 'contrat d'entreprise' with the French state for the period 1997–2000, and in preparation for the liberalisation of the electricity market as required by EC Directive 96/92. The Commission had considered certain of these measures to constitute aid and had opened a formal investigation under art.108(2) TFEU.[82] In December 2003 the Commission adopted a final decision in which it held that the non-payment of company tax by EDF amounted to aid and directed the French State to recover some 14 billion FFr from EDF. The French authorities claimed that these various measures did not amount to aid but should have been seen as a normal investment. The Commission rejected this argument on the grounds that the private investor principle did not apply in the context of the operation of the exercise of state prerogative powers—including fiscal powers. A state could not combine both roles or functions. The General Court upheld the French government's plea that it has acted as a prudent market investor irrespective of the form chosen for the capital injection. The fact that the state had access to financial resources accrued through the exercise of state authority was not in itself sufficient justification to regard the state's actions as attributable to an exercise of state authority.[83]

20–036 **The MEIT and Energy Undertakings.** As mentioned, the MEIT also applies to investments made by public undertakings in as much as the resources of these entities can be deemed to be state resources. In its decision concerning the legality of rebates made by EdF to firms in the paper industry, the Commission considered that EdF had acted in accordance with the MEIT. EdF had granted certain advances to paper mills for the purpose of installing electrical infra-red paper drying equipment. These advances corresponded to a reduction in the price for electricity normally consumed by the dryer for the duration of the six-year supply contract. The investigation concerned rebates granted between 1990 and 1996, i.e. before the adoption of EC Council Directive 96/92 on the internal electricity market, at a time when EdF disposed of overcapacity in nuclear energy. The French authorities demonstrated that EdF covered its variable costs, and at least 35 per cent and on average 57 per cent of its fixed costs. In a situation of overcapacity and in the absence of competition, the Commission considered that a private operator would rather sell an additional unit of electricity without covering the total cost for that unit than not sell it all. Hence EdF's behaviour was justified on commercial grounds, and the rebates did not constitute state aid. It is of interest to note that the Commission emphasised that the decision should be seen in the context of the prevailing circumstances on the French market in the past, and should not be seen as preventing the Commission from examining the creation of the said overcapacity and its implications in the context of the ongoing liberalisation of the electricity market.[84]

---

[82] [2002] O.J. C280/8.
[83] December 15, 2009. On appeal in Case C–124/10P, the Advocate General has recommended in his Opinion that the General Court's ruling should be annulled.
[84] IP/00/370, April 11, 2000.

More recently the Commission approved a guarantee provided by the French   **20–037**
government to the Finish electricity producer TVO to cover a loan to purchase
part of its nuclear plant from the French company AREVA NP. The Commission
had opened a formal investigation following two complaints to verify whether
the guarantee had been given on market terms. The Commission found that TVO
would have been able to finance the entire operation without state intervention as
TVO had a good credit rating and was not in difficulty. TVO had also already
raised substantial capital on the international markets without the guarantee and
finally, the fee paid was not below than the costs of the loans concluded at the
same time without state guarantees. Finally, the measure did not confer a benefit
on AREVA NP as it had been selected by TVO before the guarantee was
granted.[85]

The Commission reached a similar conclusion in N419/2009 Malta—
Investments on electricity and interconnector infrastructure.[86] The construction
of an interconnector between Malta and Italy was to be financed in part from
funds under the Economic Recovery Fund as well as equity contributions from
the electricity company and guaranteed loans. The Commission found the terms
of the guarantee to comply with the Notice on Guarantees and deemed the
measure not to constitute aid. The Commission's approach to state guarantees is
further discussed in Ch.9

The market investor test and PPAs. Buyers have an interest in concluding   **20–038**
long-term contracts, in the view of the Commission in the Polish and Hungarian
PPA cases, only if these contracts provide them some hedging against fluctuations in the electricity market, and in particular against changes linked to
fluctuations in fuel costs. For this reason a buyer would have an economic
interest in a long-term contract of this type only if the seller offered to take part
of the risk associated with fluctuations in fuel costs or if the generating technology ensured stable fuel costs, as is the case with hydropower plants, and, in
certain conditions, nuclear plants. Hence the Commission considered that in both
cases the conclusion of the PPAs was attributable to the state and further, given
the policy objectives pursued by the PPAs when assessed against market conditions prevailing at Accession, that the market investor test did not apply.[87]

Effect on trade

In *Scottish Nuclear*, in a decision concerning the application of art.101 TFEU   **20–039**
to the Scottish electricity sector, the Commission noted that although the geographical location of Scotland on the fringe of the Community and the resultant
physical constrains of the system did not make electricity exchanges with other
Member States very likely, there was a sufficient effect on inter-state trade for the

---

[85] IP/07/1400 September 26, 2007.
[86] [2010] O.J. C57.
[87] Poland C 43/2005 [2009] O.J. L83/1; Hungary C 41/2005 [2009] O.J. L225/53.

purposes of art.101 TFEU to apply that article and to issue a comfort letter.[88] Similarly, in relation to the various packages of aid to the Scottish electricity industry the Commission appears to have assumed that there was a potential effect on trade in taking its approval decision.[89] This approach can be contrasted with a recent decision concerning aid to the renewable sector in Ireland where the absence of international interconnection was deemed to preclude an effect on trade.[90] The General Court has confirmed in Case T–303/05 *ACEA Electrabel v Commission*, that an aid measure to support the construction of a district heating network in the Rome area can affect trade given that aid to the recipient will strengthen its position vis-à-vis other energy suppliers.[91]

20–040 **Infrastructural aid.** The question of state funding of infrastructure or other forms of state measures relating to the operation of infrastructure has become of increasing complexity, given in particular that Member States have resorted to various forms of public-private partnerships to operate infrastructure, including energy infrastructure, and to distribute private services. (See further Ch.3.)

If a public authority undertakes to provide infrastructure such as road or rail services to improve connections to a new or upgraded site on which energy production facilities are to be sited, it may well be concluded that this could amount to a selective benefit. Much may depend on the actual circumstances of the case—if, for example, the development of road (or rail) infrastructure costs was normally borne by public funds and the benefit of the infrastructural improvements were not solely to be attributed to the owners of the new or upgraded site, but could be seen to be of wider public benefit, then there is at least an arguable case that such a transaction would not constitute aid given the multi-functionality of the infrastructure.[92] In particular, it will be of importance that the facility in question is open to all potential users on a non-discriminatory basis. In a case concerning state funding for the construction of a propylene pipeline the Commission concluded that the funding favoured a limited group of users because the pipeline served to transport certain substances only, and hence opened a formal investigation prior to giving its approval.[93]

In determining who may enjoy a selective benefit of an infrastructure project it is of course necessary to examine the potential beneficiaries of public assistance, i.e. the end users, the owners/operators as well as a the shareholders if a public-private financial construction is used. Even if the use of the facility is subject to open and non-discriminatory access the owners or operators of an infrastructure may still receive a selective benefit if they are not selected by means of an open and non-discriminatory procedure and they receive more than

---

[88] [1990] O.J. L245/8.
[89] See IP/90/267, March 28, 1990.
[90] [2002] O.J. C222/2.
[91] [2009] ECR II–137, upheld on appeal Case C–480/09P.
[92] See also Commission Decision on State Aid N 503/2005 United Kingdom—*Great Yarmouth Outer Harbour* COM (2005) 5440 final, December 21, N 503/2005 [2009] O.J. L83/1.
[93] C 67/2003, C 69/2003, Decision of June 16, 2004; see also N 527/2002 *Aviation fuel pipeline to Athens Airport* [2003] O.J. C148/11.

a market price to cover the construction and operation costs of the facility in question (see Ch.3). Establishing a "market price" in certain markets may prove difficult—especially if there is no competition on or for the market in question.[94] In this respect the criteria developed by the Court in the *Altmark* case (see Ch.8, section 4), albeit in a different context, may be of value in assessing whether or not aid has been provided.

4. ARTICLE 107(2) AND (3)—THE EXEMPTIONS

As discussed in Ch.4, the Treaty provides for so-called automatic and discretionary exemptions. **20–041**

The automatic exceptions—Article 107(2) TFEU

With regard to the exceptions listed in art.107(2) TFEU it is well established **20–042** that the Commission has no discretion in their application. Its primary task is to ensure that the conditions for exemption are met.

Article 107(2)(a) TFEU provides that aid having a social character and granted to individual consumers is compatible with the internal market provided that the aid in question is granted without discrimination in regard to the origin of the products or service concerned. To determine if this is in fact the case, it must be ascertained whether consumers benefit from the aid in question irrespective of the economic operator supplying the product or service capable of fulfilling the social objective relied on by the Member State concerned. If, for example, a social form of aid was provided to consumers to install smart meters in their homes allowing them to switch easily between energy suppliers but the aid in question would only be disbursed if the consumers either purchased meters from locally based companies or had such meters installed by a local company, then art.107(2)(a) TFEU could not apply.[95] In a decision on aid to private persons to encourage installation of facilities using renewable energy resources, the Commission concluded that there was no aid involved as the scheme did not confer an advantage on certain undertakings or the production of certain goods.[96]

The discretionary exceptions—Article 107 (3) TFEU

Article 107(3) TFEU lists the conditions under which the Commission may **20–043** exempt aid covered by art.107(1) TFEU. It is settled case law that the Commission enjoys wide discretionary power in applying this article.

---

[94] See further State Aid N 356/2002 *Network Rail*, July 17, 2002 [2002] O.J. C232.
[95] See, in particular Joined Cases T–116/01 and T–118/01 *P&O Ferries (Vizcaya) v Commission* [2003] E.C.R. II–2957, at para.163.
[96] N 241/04—Austria, *Viennese Aid Programme*, September 9, 2004.

20–044 **Article 107(3)(a)—Regional Aid.** Article 107(3)(a) TFEU provides that aid to promote the economic development of areas where the standard of living is abnormally low or where there is serious underemployment may be considered compatible with the internal market. The criteria applied by the Commission in assessing the compatibility of regional aid with the internal market were reviewed and simplified in 1998 with the publication of Guidelines on Regional Aid,[97] updated in 2006, apply to every sector, with some limited exceptions (see Chs 15 and 21). They apply to the energy sector. For a useful illustration of their recent application to various energy-related subsidies for renewables and for gas distribution networks in Poland, see the Commission's decision in N434, N435 and N436.[98]

It is now established Commission practice, and endorsed by the courts, only to grant an exemption on the basis of either of these sub-articles to multi-sectoral general aid schemes open in a given region to all firms in the sector concerned, as opposed to individual ad hoc subsidies to a single firm, or aid confined to one area of activity.[99] As a result of this sector-wide approach, an ad hoc payment for example to a power producer to locate a new generation plant in a particular region would not be compatible with art.107(3)(a) or (c) TFEU as a form of regional aid. This would not preclude the Commission exempting it on the basis of art.107(3)(c) TFEU on other grounds, for example in the interests of environmental protection or energy security, and from applying the ceilings specified in the now revised guidelines and the multi-sectoral framework accordingly (see Ch.15).

20–045 An example of such an aid arose in relation to a project initiated by the Basque authorities for the construction of a CCT power station and a re-gasification plant to be built near the port of Bilbao. The proposal was not part of any current regional aid scheme authorised by the Commission. The projects were owned by consortia comprising large energy producers. The aid for the CCT plant was to take the form of a non-repayable grant with an aid intensity of approximately 7.5 per cent while the aid to the re-gasification plant would also be in the form of a non-repayable grant, representing an aid intensity of 9.5 per cent. The Commission had doubts about the compatibility of these aid measures as they were not only ad hoc, but also the relevant product market—the electricity market in Spain—did not appear to be in decline. It further doubted the eligibility of certain costs, and in particular the classification of intangible assets as eligible expenditure. The Spanish Government defended the aid as the project was of strategic importance with regard to the energy policy of the Basque country, since it will help guarantee electricity and natural gas supplies in the region. The project would further help reduce the cost of transport of electricity and gas to the region, where only 20 per cent of total demand is satisfied by local production. They

---

[97] [1998] O.J. C74/9, as amended [2000] O.J. C258/5.
[98] [2009] O.J. C234/1.
[99] Case T–152/99 *HAMSA v Commission* [2002] E.C.R. II–3409, at paras 201–9.

further argued that the Spanish market was suffering from under-investment in new capacity.

The Commission took the view that the projects fell within the scope of the **20–046** multisectoral framework but as it was an ad hoc aid it was bound to examine it in accordance it with pt 2, second paragraph of the Guidelines on National Regional Aid of 1998 to ensure that the advantages for the region offset the distortions of competition which ad hoc can cause.[100] The entire Basque region is an assisted area, in accordance with art.107(3)(c) TFEU as well as with pt 3.1 of the multisectoral framework. Self-sufficiency in electricity in a particular region while a legitimate aim, was not one of the listed objectives in the guidelines. However, as the project would improve production and distribution of energy in areas which are currently lacking in this respect, the gasification project would have a compensatory effect. Subsequent power cuts in Spain in the winter of 2001 demonstrated the need for new investment in electricity plants.

Nevertheless, the demand for electricity was growing only marginally in Spain and hence the Commission could only conclude that this was a market in decline, based on the criteria provided in pt 7.8 of the multisectoral framework. After some adjustments to the amounts and categories of eligible expenditure to bring the package into line with both the regional guidelines and the multisectoral framework, the Commission approved the aid. This decision is illustrative of the technical complexities imposed by the detailed rules in the framework as well as the need to consider the interaction of different guidelines and frameworks which may be applicable to the same set of measures. Furthermore, the interaction of the regional aid guidelines and those relating to restructuring aid may also need to be examined.[101]

In its decision C1/2009 on MOL, it was recalled that Hungary's entire territory could be regarded as such an art.107(3)(a) TFEU at the date of accession and most of its regions could still benefit from such aid.[102] However as state aid can in principle be authorised only for investment costs, the aid at stake could not be regarded as investment aid. As far as operating aid was concerned, the measure did not facilitate the development of any activities or economic areas and it is not limited in time, degressive or proportionate to what is necessary to remedy specific economic handicaps.

In practice, in regard to the energy sector, the Commission has relied most **20–047** heavily on art.107(3)(c). Where appropriate regional considerations may still be examined in its assessment even if the regional aid guidelines as such are not at issue.

The Commission took account of the special regional situation in Northern Ireland in its decision in N 660/A/2000—*exemption from climate change levy for*

---

[100] [1998] O.J. C74/9.
[101] Case T–152/99 *Molina v Commission* [2002] E.C.R. II–3049, at 199–209.
[102] Commission Decision of June 9, 2010 on state aid C 1/09 (ex NN 69/08) granted by Hungary to MOL Nyrt [2011] O.J. L34/55. This decision is currently under challenge: Case T–499/10 [2010] O.J. C346/52.

natural gas in Northern Ireland.[103] The UK authorities had proposed a five-year exemption from the CCL for natural gas consumption by all businesses (irrespective of size and activity) located in Northern Ireland with the aim of encouraging the substitution of coal and oil for natural gas to reduce CO_2 emissions. This exemption was considered selective in that it favoured undertakings located in a specific region. The Commission assessed the scheme on the basis of art.107(3)(c) TFEU and on the basis of the Community guidelines on state aid for environmental protection. It noted the special geographical and political circumstances which had delayed the arrival of natural gas in Northern Ireland until 1996, the low levels of consumption (only 2.4 per cent in 1999) and the resultant high gas prices in that region. Adding the CCL to gas would hinder further penetration of this fuel and would act as a real barrier to the development of a market demand for gas and would also obstruct the further extension of gas infrastructure in Northern Ireland. An exemption was therefore granted.

20–048   The Commission opened a full investigation into an Italian measure to grant ad hoc regional aid allowing the takeover of a closed traditional power plant for its conversion from conventional fuel to palm oil. As the works on the project had started before the aid was granted, the Commission doubts whether the measure could have a real incentive effect. Second, the Commission doubts whether the transactions in the framework of the takeover of the closed power plant were based on market conditions. Finally, the impact on the region where the plant is situated has to be fully investigated.[104] On September 15, 2010 the Commission found that the aid measure was incompatible with the internal market. The decision has been appealed by the beneficiary.[105]

20–049   The Commission has authorised the provision of state grants amounting to €390 million for the construction or capacity increase of four underground gas storage sites in Poland. Gas storage enhances security supply and enables a country to deal with supply disruptions or seasonal variations in consumption. The projects are open to all operators at regulated conditions. The Commission focused its competitive assessment on the positive contribution of the projects to an improved security supply in Poland and in the European Union. The aid amount corresponds to the financial needs and the low financial attractiveness of the projects. The projects will increase the overall storage capacity available in Poland, thereby enabling all market players, not only the beneficiary of the aid, to better meet mandatory reserves.[106]

20–050   **Article 107(3)(b).** Article 107(3)(b) provides that aid may be compatible with the internal market if it promotes the execution of an important project of common European interest. Point 147 of the 2008 Guidelines on Environmental

[103] July 18, 2001.
[104] Case C 8/09 *Fri-El Acerra* [2009] O.J. C95/20.
[105] Pending Case T–551/10 *Fri-El Acerra Srl v Commission* [2011] O.J. C30/52.
[106] Commission Decision N 660/2009 Aid to PGNiG for underground gas storage in Poland [2010] O.J. C213/9.

Aid,[107] provides that aid to promote the execution of important projects of common European interest which are an environmental priority and will often have beneficial effects beyond the frontiers of the Member States concerned can be authorised under this provision.

In its decision on the UK Emission Trading Scheme, the Commission considered the application of art.107(3)(b) TFEU to the scheme, acknowledging that such schemes could well be considered as projects of common European interest. However, it went on to conclude that many of the key elements of the design of the UK scheme would not necessarily be reflected in a European scheme—in particular because the British scheme was not mandatory—and therefore based its assessment on art.107(3)(c).

Article 107(3)(c). Article 107(3(c) provides that aid to facilitate the development   **20–051** of certain economic activities or of certain economic areas, where such aid does not adversely affect trading conditions to an extent contrary to the common interest may be considered compatible with the internal market. The Commission has adopted various guidelines on the application of art.107(3)(c) to particular forms of aid and for aid to particular sectors. Although there is no specific guideline or notice dealing with aid to the energy sector as such, in July 2001 the Commission adopted a Methodology on Stranded Costs in the Energy Sector. Furthermore, a number of the guidelines may be of particular relevance to the sector generally, including the guidelines on environmental aid which deals with aid for renewable energy sources and energy efficiency.[108] (see Ch.22). The guidelines on rescue and restructuring aid are also of relevance (see further Ch.24).[109]

Investment and operating aid for the promotion of energy from renewable   **20–052** **energy sources.** As part of the Commission's new energy and climate change policy, the Commission proposed a revised framework for the development of renewable energy, which included new binding targets for the share of energy that Member States must derive from renewable energy sources by 2020. The new Renewable Energy Directive was adopted in parallel and without prejudice to the 2008 Guidelines and the General Block Exemption Regulation (GBER). As such, national support measures covered by the Renewable Energy Directive which constitute state aid within the meaning of art.107(1) TFEU must be compatible with the State Aid rules.[110] Aid granted for the investment in and/or operations of the promotion of energy from renewable energy sources may be

---

[107] [2008] O.J. C82/24.

[108] Given the increasing importance of bio-fuels, the guidelines on state aid to the agricultural sector may also be of some relevance to the energy sector. An example of the application of these guidelines is the Commission decision N 295/03 on the *British Bio-Energy Infrastructure Scheme* COM (2004) 2282, June 18, 2004.

[109] For a recent example see the Commission's approval of a state guarantee for the French IFP, IP/11/802, June 29, 2011.

[110] See Commission staff working document: "The Renewable Energy Progress Report", Commission Report in accordance with art.3 of Directive 2001/77/EC, art.4(2) of Directive 2003/30/EC and on the implementation of the EU Biomass Action Plan, SEC/2009/0503 FINAL, s.1.

justified where it meets the criteria set out in the 2008 Guidelines, and where there are no mandatory Community or Union standards governing the share of energy that an individual undertaking must generate from renewable energy sources. The 2008 Guidelines identify the following as renewable energy sources: wind, solar, geothermal, wave, tidal, hydropower installations, biomass,[111] landfill gas, sewage treatment plant gas, and biogases.[112] The adoption of the 2008 Guidelines has provided greater clarity and predictability as to the application of the exemption provisions set out in art.107(3) TFEU, in addition to providing detailed rules relating to renewable energy, the promotion of energy efficiency, and emission trading.[113]

The German 'top gas recycling' project related to a €30 million investment aid for the implementation of a processor recycling the gas emitted in the steel making process.[114] The Commission took into account in a number of factors, in particular the fact that even with the doubling of the present CO_2 price, the project will remain unprofitable for the firm. The know-how of the project would be shared collectively by the large majority of EU steel producers.[115]

20–053 **Carbon capture and storage (CCS).** Aid for CCS projects is discussed in detail in Ch.22. By way of example, the Commission approved aid for a CCS demonstration project in Rotterdam, the Netherlands, which covers the whole cycle. CO_2 from power generation is captured and stored in a depleted gas field. The grant reached 55 per cent aid intensity. The cost estimate for the capture plant was based on global field study for a full scale capture plants and was done on the basis of a tender. Economic evidence demonstrated that the investment would not have been viable without the aid and the beneficiary committed to share information on the result of the project[116]

5. RESCUE AND RESTRUCTURING AID

20–054 In principle this form of aid is typically granted in a situation of acute financial distress where state funding is often the last resort to keep the beneficiary from

---

[111] The 2008 Guidelines note with respect to biomass that only aid for investment in or the operation of aid for the production of sustainable biofuels will be authorised under the provisions of the 2008 Guidelines relating to the promotion of energy from renewable energy sources.

[112] 2008 Guidelines, para.70. The Commission's list of renewable energy sources is exhaustive, perhaps a regrettable absence of flexibility, given the fast rate of technological development in the renewables sector. See response of the Dutch authorities to the 2nd consultation document of the European Commission relating to: Community Guidelines on State Aid for environmental protection", p.3.

[113] See for example, the Austrian co-generation case N 295/2008 [2010] O.J. C154/1 which concerned only a modest aid amount of 16 million and a 35% aid intensity. The effects on the market were particularly limited on this case, as the aid amount accounts for a minor share of the beneficiary production costs.

[114] C(2010) 1245/2, March 9, 2010.

[115] In the French biomass boiler case C (2010) 7684 final the assessment was based on the balancing test and the Commission concluded that without the aid the investment would not take place N 295/2003 [2005] O.J. C316/22.

[116] This project was also eligible for support under the European energy program for recovery of up to €180 million.

going into administration. The UK government's rescue of the bankrupt British Energy is a case in point. In the *British Energy* case, the United Kingdom put the rescue package into place in September 2002 and the Commission took a decision not to raise objection on the case on November 27, 2003.[117] At the same time, rescue and restructuring aid is probably one of the most distortive forms of state aid as it covers the ongoing operating expenses of a company. This type of aid is usually strictly forbidden as it will always have a severe impact on competitors and intra-Community trade. The source of the aid may be any level of government and any public undertaking as defined by art.2 of the Transparency Directive.[118]

In order to try to balance these different issues, the Commission published detailed rules on rescue and restructuring aid, first in 1994[119] and later in 1999.[120] The 1999 guidelines expired in 2004 and a new version was adopted in July 2004. The number of cases involving challenges to the application of the 1999 and 2004 rescue and restructuring guidelines illustrate the difficulties involved in these cases.[121] (see further Ch.24).

Conditions for approval of rescue aid

According to the guidelines rescue aid must be: (i) in the form of remunerated **20–055** guarantees and loans; (ii) limited to the amount necessary to keep the enterprise in business; (iii) restricted in duration; and (iv) to alleviate a social crisis without adverse spill-over effects on other Member States.

The first two conditions are usually the most controversial. To restrict a rescue package to loans and guarantees may prove over-simplistic. In *British Energy*, the Commission approved loan and deposits by the government (which served as collateral for British Energy's trading and non-trading (regulatory) counter-parties). The guidelines provide that the rescue aid should not be in effect for more than six to 12 months, unless there are exceptional circumstances.

Restructuring aid

In accordance with the 2004 guidelines, the basic conditions for approving **20–056** restructuring aid are: (i) a restructuring aid can only be granted once within a 10-year period (the one last shot principle); (ii) that a coherent restructuring plan is in place which ensures the return to viability in the foreseeable future; and (iii)

---

[117] [2003] O.J. C39/15.

[118] [2002] O.J. L193/75; see also Case C–482/99 *Stardust Marine* [2002] E.C.R. I–4397.

[119] [1994] O.J. C368/12.

[120] [1999] O.J. C288. Separate guidelines applied to the coal sector under the ECSC Treaty, and a transitional period is provided in accordance with the Communication from the Commission concerning the expiry of the ECSC Treaty [2002] O.J. C152/5, and Annex B of the Multisectoral Framework on Regional Aid for Large Investment Projects [2003] O.J. C70.

[121] See, for example, T–73/98 *Prayon-Rupel v Commission* [2001] E.C.R. II–86; T–35/99 *Keller v Commission* [2002] E.C.R. II–261; T–126/99 *Graphischer Maschinenbau GmbH v Commission* [2002] E.C.R. II–2427.

that the aid must be limited to the absolute minimum, requiring own investment from private sources and that the aid recipient must reduce capacity or take other compensatory measures. Restructuring plans require complex financial and business plans which if prepared by the beneficiary should also be reviewed by the Member State with the assistance of external experts. In *British Energy* the Commission retained its own experts to review the restructuring plan. Complex cases raise issues of when the information provided by the Member State can be considered complete. The UK Government submitted its plan to restructure British Energy six months after the rescue package had been put in place and, following an exchange of letters, the UK authorities informed the Commission that they considered the notification as complete, and gave notice to the Commission that they would implement the measures unless the Commission would take a decision within a period of 15 days, in application of art.4(6) of Regulation 659/99 (see Ch.26 on procedures). The Commission took a decision to open the formal procedure pursuant to art.108(2) on July 23.[122] It is apparent that the Commission was forced to work under pressure, especially given the complexity of the matters involved.

A recent example of the application of these guidelines was in the case of the Ottana rescue and restructuring in Sardinia, Italy. As a result of shortages of funds to pay for fuel oil, Ottana got into financial difficulties and was given a guarantee for a loan of €5 million. Almost a year later that guarantee was prolonged on the basis of a restructuring plan to prepare for its conversion to coal and to vegetable oil, and to allow Ottana to shift its power from the day-ahead market to the more profitable balancing market. Ottana Energia subsequently formed a joint venture with a private partner who injected some €15 million of equity—approximately 25 per cent of the project's total costs—into the new joint venture. As the Italian government had illegally prolonged the rescue aid for a period of 12 years, and the Commission doubted that the plan could restore the company to long-term viability, it considered it was obliged to open proceedings under point 27 of the Guidelines. In its final decision, the Commission accepted Italy's arguments that the company would make significant profits as of 2010 and that its return on equity should match those of its competitors. Hence the Commission concluded that the plan was capable of restoring long-term viability. Although the first phase of the plan was financed by regular cash flows, which could not be accepted as own contribution as it is seen as being at least induced by state aid, the second phase is entirely financed through shareholder equity or by external finance or the production assets (and not by the state guarantee). Finally Ottana would pay back the rescue aid loan between 2009 and 2014. As for the compensatory measures, divestiture of certain assets was acceptable as this was not a sacrifice, but given Ottana's small size, only production limitations were considered to be feasible. Moreover, as Ottana was the only alternative supplier to the two dominant suppliers, Enel and Endesa with a 95 per cent share

---

[122] [2003] O.J. C180/5.

of the market, its very survival contributes to stabilising competition on the Sardinian energy market.[123]

6. THE METHODOLOGY ON STRANDED COSTS

Article 24 of EC Directive 96/92 provided that Member States could apply to the Commission for a derogation from certain provisions of the Directive if this was necessary in the light of long-term commitments or guarantees that could no longer be honoured on account of the entry into force of Directive 96/92 EC. The Directive provided a strict timetable for the notification of the request for derogation.[124]

20–057

Although this provision indicated that Member States were entitled to apply to the Commission for permission to derogate from certain provisions of the Directives, this did not in turn allow the Commission to grant a derogation from the EU Treaty state aid rules. Hence in a series of decisions in mid-1999 the Commission rejected a number of national submissions based on art.24 on the grounds that they envisaged potential state aid measures which had to be notified, and if appropriate approved in accordance with arts 107 and 108 TFEU. After considerable internal preparation the Commission finally issued a Methodology on state aid linked to stranded costs in the energy sector in July 2001 and, on the same day, adopted three decisions on applications from Spain, Austria and the Netherlands. The Methodology indicates how the Commission intends to apply art.107(3)(c) and art.106(2) to allow certain types of aids, under certain conditions.[125]

Commitments or guarantees of the type referred to in the Methodology and art.24 of the Directive are referred to as "stranded costs" or non-market conform costs. They may in practice take a variety of forms, including long-term contracts, investments undertaken with an implicit or explicit guarantee of sale or investments undertaken outside the scope of normal activity. In order to qualify as stranded costs, commitments or guarantees must become uneconomical on account of the effect of Directive 96/92 on energy prices, and must significantly affect the competitiveness of the undertaking (para.3). It should be noted that Directive 98/30 on the internal gas market did not contain an equivalent provision given that a separate procedure was provided in that Directive for dealing with long-term take-or-pay contracts entered into before the adoption of that Directive.

20–058

There is, however, no equivalent to art.24 of Directive 96/92 in EC Directive 2003/54,[126] or EC Directive 2009/72 which has repealed the 2003 directive in

---

[123] Case C11/2007 [2009] O.J. L259/22.

[124] [1997] O.J. L27/20. See also Case C–17/03 *VEMW* [2005] E.C.R. I–4983, in which the Court held that art.24 was the only possible derogation procedure for long-term contracts reserving priority access to certain companies.

[125] Communication of July 25, 2001; see also Thirty-First Report on Competition Policy (2001), pts 346–53. See also IP/01/1077.

[126] [2003] O.J. L176/37.

full.[127] Hence it would appear that the Methodology does not apply to state aid measures which might be aimed at commitments or guarantees which become uneconomic after July 1, 2004—the date on which the electricity market for smaller industrial and commercial customers should have been opened up to competition. Obviously, this will not preclude the Commission from examining any individual notifications on their own merits, as in its decision on "Hungarian Stranded Costs legislation" in 2010.[128] Nevertheless, the point of departure for the Methodology is that state aid which is designed to facilitate the transition to a liberalised electricity market may be viewed favourably to the extent that any distortion of competition is counterbalanced by the contribution made to the achievement of a Community objective which market forces could not achieve. Furthermore, the Commission has reasoned that if there was no compensation for stranded costs, there would be a greater risk that costs might be passed on to captive customers. Stranded cost aid would also encourage electricity undertakings to reduce the risks relating to their historic commitments or investments and thus encourages them to maintain their investments in the long term (see para.4). Although this "transition period" would appear to have now expired, even after the implementation of Directive 2003/54 security of supply considerations remain valid, as perhaps does the concern that costs should not be passed on to the albeit smaller group of captive customers.

20–059   The basic principle of the Methodology is that compensation for stranded costs should be limited in time and extent. They should not exceed the costs actually borne by the undertakings, directly caused by the liberalisation of the market, and resulting in losses. Hence no compensation could be permitted if it only contributed towards falling profitability. The compensation must be fixed *ex ante* and should also include an *ex post* adaptation mechanism which would take into account the real evolution of the market, and in particular the actual evolution of electricity market prices.

The Methodology attempts to preserve the interests of new entrants; financing arrangements for the aid must not have the effect of deterring outside undertakings or new players from entering national or regional electricity markets. In particular, aid must not be financed from levies on electricity in transit between Member States or from levies linked to the distance between the producer and the customer (para.5).

The individual decisions

20–060   At the same time as it published its Methodology on state aid linked to stranded costs, the Commission adopted three individual decisions applying the Methodology and closed its procedures following a preliminary investigation.

20–061 **Austria.** In the Austrian case, compensation of €456 million was envisaged for three hydropower projects and a further €132 million for a lignite-fired plant. The

---

[127] [2009] O.J. L211/55.
[128] C (2010) 2532 of April 27, 2010, [2010] O.J. C213.

sums would be paid out annually for costs incurred in the preceding business year and would be financed by contributions from both regional network operators and other customers who historically consumed the electricity produced in the plants which had become stranded. The scheme would be phased out at the end of 2009, at the latest. Given, however, that the payments were made by consumers the Commission noted that it had doubts as to whether the system actually fell within the scope of art.107(1) TFEU as it did not appear that state resources were involved. However, the funds raised were transferred via a fund to the beneficiaries and it appeared that the state had some marginal control over this fund. Although it did not reach a definite conclusion on this issue, the Commission concluded that even if state aid was involved the planned compensation was in line with the Methodology and could be eligible for authorisation on the basis of art.107(3)(c) TFEU. The compensation to be paid to the lignite plant was authorised on the basis of art.106(2) TFEU (and arts 3(2) and 8(4) of Directive 96/92) as contributing to security of supply and thus a service of general economic interest.

Belgium. In the Belgian case, the envisaged state aid contained three elements. **20–062** First, the dismantling of nuclear plants throughout Belgium; secondly, financing the costs of a new pension regime in the electricity sector; and thirdly, promoting renewable energy sources. After the initial filing with the Commission, Belgium subsequently withdrew from the overall filing of its financing scheme of the contemplated scheme. For its final assessment the Commission still awaits to this date additional information from Belgium on this subject. Although the Commission was therefore not in a position to assess whether the scheme qualified as state aid, it nevertheless comments on the applicability of the Methodology on the respective elements.

The Commission found that the compensation of the costs related to the dismantling of nuclear plants, insofar as it would qualify as state aid, was in compliance with the Methodology. The scheme provided for compensatory funds being paid to Electrabel and SPE, for the costs that these companies would incur in dismantling nuclear plants, pursuant to an agreement between these companies and the Belgian state that was entered into prior to February 19, 1997, the date set in the Methodology. In its extensive assessment of this element of the scheme, the Commission concluded, inter alia, that the size of these stranded costs would significantly weaken these companies' competitive positions. Furthermore, the agreement with the Belgian state did not contain provisions to amend the agreements. The dismantling of the plants would not result in profits for the companies and the assets involved were not owned by these companies. Also the amount of the stranded costs would not result from a decreased power price or loss of market share but was an amount fixed beforehand corresponding to the amount of the compensation. The Commission also took into consideration the high environmental risks.

With respect to the pension issues for which a subsidy of €758 million would **20–063** be granted to the two companies, the Commission had considerable doubts whether the Methodology could apply. The reason for Belgium to grant the subsidy was (it was argued) that prior to liberalisation the power prices in Belgium were maintained at a low level (compared with power prices in other Member States) and that as a result of these low prices, the companies had not been able to create sufficient means to finance the pension rights. However, based on an engagement between the state and the electricity sector, employees in the sector that were hired after January 1, 1993 are entitled to pensions. The Commission considered that this would probably not qualify as a stranded cost under the Methodology because the pension obligation was set by law and would effect the entire electricity sector and not only on the two companies involved (Electrabel and SPE), that were the sole actors on the market prior to the liberalisation. As a consequence no disparity would result in this respect between newcomers and these two existing actors. The Commission furthermore indicated that the impossibility to quantify the amount of the subsidies and the long term of the contemplated scheme, would lead it to conclude that this part of the Belgian scheme would not qualify as stranded costs under the Methodology. Last but not least, the Commission doubted whether the regime would be in compliance with the conditions stated under 4.2 and 4.5 of the Methodology and therefore in compliance with art.107(3)(c) of the Treaty. The Commission stated that in order to qualify as stranded costs, it is required to explicitly indicate the existence of the commitment of the Belgian state to set the prices in the future at a level high enough to create reserves necessary to finance the pensions. It therefore opened formal proceedings and invited the submission of further comments.[129]

The Commission ruled that the third element of the Belgian subsidy, a financing scheme for the promotion of energy from renewable sources, should not be regarded as state aid. Reference was made to the ruling of ECJ in the *PreussenElektra* case as the amounts levied by both Electrabel and SPE on electricity tariffs would not pass through a state-controlled or state-designated fund. (See para.20–018, above.)

20–064   **Greece.** The Greek stranded costs decision is comprised of three components. The first component involved compensation for the costs for the Greek Public Power Corporation (PPC) in relation to power stations that are unprofitable in a liberalised market, as they were built at a time when inflation was very high. Until liberalisation the costs were recovered in a system under which the prices were fixed on an ad hoc basis by the state. The compensation will be paid until 2015 and adjusted annually to the actual amount of the costs incurred by PPC with a cap of €929 million.

The second component involved compensation paid by the state to PPC for water resource management and irrigation work in conjunction with the construction of the power plants, imposed on PPC by the state, up to an amount of €324

---

[129] [2002] O.J. C222/2.

million. Both elements were concluded by the Commission to be in compliance with the Methodology.

The third component, compensation by the state for losses resulting from a low-priced, long-term power sales agreement with Aluminium of Greece, was not regarded as state aid to PPC as PPC was not the ultimate beneficiary of the compensation.

Hungary. The Commission opened a formal investigation into Hungary's long-term power purchase agreements (PPAs) concluded between the state-owned electricity network operator MVM Rt. and the power generators in 2005.[130] The Commission took the view that those agreements constituted state aid and expressed doubts about the compatibility of the PPAs with the criteria of the Methodology for analysing state aid linked to stranded costs. First, the Commission questioned whether the very principles of long-term PPAs foreclosing a significant part of the market could be compatible with the objectives of the Methodology, which is to increase the pace of the liberalisation of the energy sector by granting fair compensations to incumbent companies which are faced with unequal competition. Second, the Commission had doubts whether the Methodology criteria as regards computation of eligible stranded costs and attribution of actual compensations are fulfilled.

20–065

Given that the contracts were concluded before accession, but that they were not notified in full compliance with the special procedure as annexed to the Accession Treaty, the Commission treated the aid as new aid, as opposed to past or existing aid. This classification has been challenged before the General Court by one of the Hungarian electricity generators, BERT.[131] In its final decision on Case C45/2005[132] the Commission held that the PPAs could not be deemed compatible under the Methodology. The Commission examined whether the contracts themselves were compatible with the Stranded Cost Methodology and concluded that several elements of the main principles constituting the PPAs do not met the conditions laid down in s.4 of the Methodology. Instead of helping transition to a competitive market the PPAs had rather created an obstacle to the development of substantial competition. As a consequence they also contradicted the principles laid down in s.5 of that Methodology. Subsequently, the Commission approved a separate stranded costs compensation scheme for those generators whose PPA contracts had been terminated following decision C45/2005. The compensation related to justified investment costs up to December 31, 2009 (i.e., the initial investment costs incurred before May 1, 2004) and the discounted cash flows expected to be generated in the future until the originally foreseen expiry date of the PPAs, as calculated on the basis of a simulation model used by the Hungarian authorities in the context of the implementation of the decision C45/2005. The Hungarian authorities had in fact decided not to compensate all

[130] [2005] O.J. C324/12.
[131] Case T–80/06 [2006] O.J. C108/25.
[132] [2009] O.J. L225/53, at paras 417–432.

eligible stranded costs: in cases where they exceed the amounts to be recovered pursuant to the PPA decision, the authorities would not pay the company the differences between the two amounts.[133]

20–066 **Ireland.** Ireland planned to introduce and notified to the Commission a programme where the state would impose on the state-owned Electricity Supply Board (ESB) a public service obligation to purchase the electricity generated by new green electricity plants (RES-E) under 15-year contracts at a guaranteed price. Only two plants were to be selected under the scheme, in accordance with public procurement rules. The national energy regulator (CER) would certify the excess costs arising out of this obligation, being the difference between the net costs of operation of ESB without the obligation and the net cost including the operation. The latter would be calculated by taking the price of RES-E and deducting the Best New Entrants price (in the absence of real market prices) which would be based on the costs of CCGT electricity generation. The excess costs would be covered by funds collected by the TSO through different levies on domestic and professional connections to be determined by CER and passed on to ESB. ESB would not be allowed any profit on this activity.

In its assessment, the Commission noted that CER would exert significant control over the payments, but at the same time concluded that ESB would derive no competitive advantage from the scheme and that therefore the scheme included no state aid to ESB.

20–067   A considerable and specific economic advantage which would distort competition was, however, conferred on the two producers that will supply ESB. The Commission concluded that the scheme would include elements of state aid as far as the two selected producers were concerned. Because the financing of ESB's obligations was controlled and collected by CER and the state-owned TSO, the funds were deemed to be state sources.

As the scheme was notified one day prior to the Methodology being adopted—July 25, 2001—the Methodology was not applied as such. Nevertheless, the scheme was approved by the Commission as it complied with the Community Guidelines on environmental aid, as the Member State concerned could show that the support: (i) is essential to ensure the viability of the renewable energy sources concerned; (ii) does not overall result in overcompensation; and (iii) does not dissuade renewable energy producers from becoming more competitive.

20–068 **Italy.**[134] This decision covers in particular the grant of aid to cover stranded costs concerning, on the one hand, the construction costs for generation plants built prior to 1997 and, on the other hand, the costs linked to a "take-or-pay" contract for Nigerian gas to be used in electricity production, signed by ENEL in 1992. The first set of measures were paid out for the period 2002–03 and totalled €850 million. There will be no further entitlement to compensation by either ENEL or

---

[133] State aid N 691/2009, C (2010) 2532, April 27, 2010.
[134] IP/04/1429, December 1, 2004.

those companies which have inherited its stranded assets. The costs related to the adjustment of the gas contract are calculated to be €1,465 million and are linked to the transfer of the management of the gas outside Italy until 2009. The aid is limited to compensation for the gas as a fuel for electricity generation.

In April 2006[135] the Commission opened a formal investigation into an alleged €16 million subsidy which Italy intended to grant to local utility companies as these had not been covered by the earlier notification. The Italian authorities had notified the intended grant of aid in March 2005, but three years prior to this, the Commission had taken a negative decision on fiscal aid to the local utility companies,[136] including AEM Torino, and Italy had still failed to recover the amounts of illegal aid granted at that time. In accordance with Case C–355/95P *Deggendorf*, when assessing the compatibility of new aid the Commission must take into account the fact that the beneficiaries may not have complied with earlier Commission decisions requiring recovery of illegal aid.[137]

Luxembourg. The scheme proposed by the Luxembourg government related to a long-term agreement for the supply of electricity by RWE to the incumbent distribution company and TSO Cegedel. It is one of the few measures where the Commission has refused to accept the aid in question to be justified. Cedegel provided for 70 per cent of the national electricity usage and 93 per cent of its demand was sourced by this long-term agreement with RWE. This agreement would terminate on December 31, 2000. The Luxembourg government requested approval of a transitional regime until this date. This request was denied by the Commission based on the assessment that the agreement did not contain any "take-or-pay" obligations for Cedegel as the electricity actually taken (MWh) was calculated afterwards, and the power capacity (MW) could be adjusted regularly. Therefore, if eligible consumers were to decide to switch suppliers, Cedegel could adjust its off-take from RWE, resulting in a normal and acceptable commercial risk only.

20–069

The Netherlands. Two types of assets considered as "stranded" were notified— long-term city heating contracts and a coal-gasification plant.[138] In its earlier notification under the art.24 procedure, the Dutch Government had envisaged a more extensive range of assets which would become stranded but, following negotiations with the sector itself and on the advice of an independent committee, the Dutch Government restricted its application under art.108(3) TFEU to those investments which had been executed at the direct request of the government at the relevant time. The compensation for the city heating contracts was to be based on an annual calculation of the related fuel price risk which producers had to bear. In the Netherlands, city heating is based on a link to gas prices. With

20–070

---

[135] IP/06/451, April 5, 2006.
[136] IP/02/817, June 5, 2002.
[137] See also Case T–303/05 *ACEA Electrabel* [2009] ECR II–137, upheld on appeal, Case C–480/09P. See further Ch.22 on Recovery.
[138] [2001] O.J. C7.

regard to the coal-gasification plant, this was to be auctioned and compensation would be restricted to the estimated value as determined by an independent valuation and the actual proceeds of the auction. The estimated total budget was €600 million. Initially, the Dutch government had proposed to fund this compensation by way of a levy imposed on all customers connected to the network system, the proceeds of which would be transferred to the beneficiaries. However, following discussions, this financing mechanism was withdrawn and the government provided in later legislation that the funding would be provided by a charge on the general state budget.

The Commission concluded that state aid within the meaning of art.107(1) TFEU was involved but declared the aid to be compatible with art.107(3)(c) TFEU and the Methodology.

20–071 **Poland.** The Commission initiated a formal investigation into long-term power purchase agreements (PPAs) in Poland in 2005.[139] The Polish authorities had drafted legislation that would allow generators to cancel their PPAs in exchange of compensation. The Commission found that both measures, PPAs as well as the draft law, could constitute state aid but had doubts whether the measures were compatible with the conditions of the Methodology for analysing state aid linked to stranded costs. The stranded costs referred to in the Act were closely linked to investments in power plants that cannot be recouped as a result of liberalisation of the internal market in electricity. In its final decision, the Commission took the view, as it did in previous files concerning Greece and Portugal, that footnote 5 of the Methodology applied to these specific stranded costs and justified the award of compensation after 2006 and until the end of the original PPAs. In the light of the above, the Commission concluded that the Act complied with the criterion laid down in pts 3.1 to 3.12 Methodology. The maximum stranded costs compensation did not exceed the permissible level and could therefore be regarded as eligible within the meaning of the Methodology. The Commission then analysed whether the aid fulfilled the conditions laid down in points 4.1 to 4.6 of the Methodology.

In accordance with point 4.1, the maximum amounts of compensation were calculated on the basis of clearly defined, individual power plants and take or pay contracts. The compensation actually paid would not exceed these maximum amounts and would take account of actual trends in underlying economic data, in particular electricity prices and volumes of gas purchased under take or pay contracts. For instance, should actual electricity prices differ from the base market price, the amount of actual compensation would be amended accordingly. The actual amounts of compensation for take or pay contracts would also take account of the actual conditions in which the power generators concerned purchase their gas and sell their electricity on the market. In accordance with point 4.4, the base market price increased significantly over time, as a result of which the amount of compensation payable would decrease to a certain extent,

[139] [2006] O.J. C52/8.

which the Commission viewed favourably. Under point 4.5 the maximum amount of compensation to be paid to a given company is to be fixed in advance. This takes account of beneficiaries' future profits resulting from productivity gains. The notification of the aid specified in particular how stranded cost calculations will take account of changes in various economic factors (including prices, market shares or other relevant factors indicated by the Member States and listed in the Methodology).

In accordance with point 4.6, the Polish authorities had undertaken not to grant any rescue or restructuring aid to beneficiary companies under the Act for a period of ten years after the last payment to the companies concerned. This period, which extends until 2037 for certain companies, is compatible with the "one time last time" principle as interpreted by the Commission in point 73 of the Guidelines on state aid for rescuing and restructuring firms in difficulty. This provided sufficient assurance that undue cumulation of aid would not occur within the framework of the Stranded Costs Methodology. Eligible power generators were authorised to receive aid in accordance with the Stranded Costs Methodology as of May 1, 2004.[140]

Portugal. After prolonged negotiations, the Commission decided not to raise **20–072** objections to various plans by the Portuguese government to compensate three energy providers for the cancellation of long-term power purchase agreements (PPA), concluded with the publicly owned network operator REN prior to market liberalisation. The PPAs had assured the producers a guaranteed off-take at a fixed price which covered their investment costs. The investments in question were considered to be of fundamental importance and would generate heavy losses in the future. If the losses were not compensated in any manner, they would jeopardise the viability of the undertakings concerned. Furthermore, the investments were irrevocable—they could not be recovered except through operation or through a sale at a very reduced price. The Commission had been provided with a list of costs to be covered when the income from the power plant would prove insufficient. These costs were identified in the PPAs. The computation of the maximum value of the compensation is based on a series of economic assumptions, taking as base price that which would be offered by a new entrant using a combined cycle gas turbine. Only if the actual market price would be lower than this price would it be taken into account for the calculation of the compensation. The Commission considered this approach to be consistent with the one taken in past cases and it would guarantee that the compensation would match the actual sums invested. In addition, as in earlier cases, the computation model would take the actual evolution of electricity prices into account.[141]

Slovenia. The Commission authorised compensation for stranded costs for three **20–073** Slovenian electricity generators: TE Šoštanj, NE Krško and TE Trbovlje.[142] The

---

[140] [2009] O.J. L83/1.
[141] IP/04/1123, September 22, 2004.
[142] [2007] O.J. L219/9.

measure aims at mitigating the difficulties faced by a number of power plants during the process of liberalisation of the electricity sector in Slovenia. The Commission found the measure to be state aid, but concluded that scheme was in line with the Methodology. In particular, the Commission decided that since the state guarantee for Krško nuclear plant has been awarded before accession, it cannot any longer be subject to the assessment under state aid rules. Moreover, the Commission found the aid for closing the gas fired part of Trbovlje plant compatible with the criteria of the Methodology and lastly the Commission decided that the aid for Šoštanj plant can be authorised under art.106(2) TFEU because although it does not meet the Methodology criteria, it still qualifies for the exemption from state aid rules as compensation for a service of general economic interest as regards security of electricity supply.[143] The Commission also decided to open a formal investigation into the so-called system of preferential dispatching of electricity to assess the compatibility of the measure with the state aid rules. Under the scheme network operators are obliged to purchase energy at fixed price, above market price, from producers of renewable energy and therefore the scheme provides an advantage to those producers. The Commission had doubts whether this measure was in accordance with its environmental guidelines, Stranded Costs Methodology and the rules linked to a compensation for services of general economic interest. Therefore, the Commission decided to initiate the formal procedure under art.108(2) TFEU.[144] Following agreement to revise the financing mechanisms of the scheme, the Commission approved the measures.[145]

20–074 **Spain.**[146] Similar issues of initial classification of the compensation payment system as aid arose in the Commission's assessment of the Spanish measures, known as the CTC system (Costes de Transicion a la Competencia) which provided for payments to cover the cost of electricity generated from indigenous coal and for so-called technological payments. The beneficiaries—the electricity production companies—would be compensated for the investments that had become non-economic after liberalisation of the Spanish market which had, prior to liberalisation, been subject to a state-imposed tariff system (Marco Legal Estable) introduced in 1987. The CTCs were incorporated by means of a levy modifying the tariff system. The coal-fired plant operators would receive approximately €1,774 million and a further €8,644 million was allocated to the technological CTCs. The compensation was linked to the evolution of the market price and if the price rose above a fixed ceiling the compensation would be reduced accordingly. The scheme was scheduled to expire in December 2010. Further modifications were introduced in 1998 allowing for the securitisation of the receipts due under the scheme so that the beneficiaries could sell the right to receive the revenues to third parties.

[143] IP/05/126.
[144] IP/05/126.
[145] IP/07/549 [2007] O.J. L219/9.
[146] Case BB 49/99 *Spain* [2001] O.J. C7.

As consumers appeared to pay the levy and it was unclear whether the state had more than marginal control over its distribution, the Commission did not definitively determine whether aid was involved. However, on the preliminary assumption that the scheme could be classified as aid, the Commission declared it to be compatible with art.107(3)(c) TFEU as interpreted in the Methodology. The technological CTCs would be reduced in line with foreseeable future revenues for each of the assets concerned. This was verified by an independent expert. With regard to the compensation for indigenous coal-fired electricity generation, the Commission concluded that although it did not comply with the Methodology it would nevertheless benefit from an authorisation as compensation for the provision of a service of general economic interest (security of supply) in accordance with art.106(2) TFEU and arts 3(2) and 8(4) of the Directive 96/92.

United Kingdom. The Commission also ruled in February 2002 that a series of **20–075** measures adopted by the United Kingdom in favour of Northern Ireland Electricity (NIE) in compensation for stranded costs related to PPAs which were based on fixed prices between it and four electricity generators did not fall within the scope of art.107(1) TFEU. The compensation would be met by a levy imposed on all final consumers which would be collected by distributors and/or the network operator and transferred to NIE. Hence the levy did not constitute "state resources" within the meaning of art.107(1) TFEU.[147]

It should be noted that the sums involved in many of these decisions are considerable and the aid involved would appear to allow the incumbent major energy providers to maintain a position of competitive strength for some time after market opening. It remains to be seen whether this will in fact deter new market entrants.

7. THE ENERGY SECTOR AND ART.106(2) TFEU

The application of art.106(2) TFEU to state support in the energy sector has **20–076** arisen in a number of cases. Given that the Commission's own approach to the application of art.106(2) TFEU has had to take into account the conflicting interpretations of that article as handed down by the General Court on the one hand, and the ECJ on the other, it is important to bear in mind that its own decision-making practice may not always seem consistent. (See also Ch.8.)

Two of the "stranded costs" decisions handed down in July 2001 relied in part on the possible application of art.106(2) TFEU as a possible additional exemption to art.107(3) TFEU In the Austrian case, the sum of €132 was paid as stranded costs compensation to the lignite-fired plant at Voitsberg. Insofar as state resources were involved and the measure fell within the scope of art.107(1) TFEU, the Commission concluded that this might fall under art.106(2) TFEU in

---

[147] IP/02/322 of February 27, 2002.

the light of arts 3(2) and 8(4) of EC Directive 96/92 on the internal electricity market. Similarly in the Spanish case, the Commission considered that planned compensations for costly electricity production plants on the one hand, and a premium for the generation of electricity out of indigenous coal on the other hand, might amount to state aid. The premium for the use of indigenous coal did not appear to comply with the requirements of the Methodology but the Commission considered that it might benefit from an authorisation as a compensation for a service of general economic interest as regards security of supply according to art.106(2) and in the light of arts 3(2) and 8(4) of Directive 96/902.

20–077   In several cases decided after the ECJ's ruling in *Ferring* in 2002 but before the *Altmark* ruling of July 2003, the Commission took the view that as long as the state measure in question would not result in over-compensation to the beneficiary, the state aid rules would not apply (see Ch.8). Thus it approved an Irish measure requiring the Electricity Supply Board (ESB) to have at its disposal a specific quantity of electricity from generating stations which use peat as their primary energy source. This quantity would not exceed 15 per cent of the overall primary energy necessary to produce the electricity consumed in Ireland on an annual basis. The ESB had a number of options open to it to meet this quota. The most economical option appeared to be to accelerate the closure of six existing peat-powered plants and replace them by two new and more efficient ones. Although the new plants would be more efficient, the cost of the electricity which they generated would be in excess of the average electricity market prices, resulting in losses for ESB. The aid measure as notified aimed to compensate the ESB for the difference between the generation costs for electricity produced from peat and the average electricity price on the production market, the compensation scheme would be financed by a levy on consumers connected to the grid network. The Commission decided that in the event that the system constituted a state aid, it could be authorised as a compensation for a service of general economic interest as regards security of supply in accordance with art.106(2) TFEU and in the light of arts 3(2) and 8(4) of Directive 96/92.[148]

In its decision to open proceedings in the context of an existing aid scheme, to require the French government to withdraw the unlimited state guarantee to EdF, the Commission considered briefly whether art.106(2) TFEU could be relied upon as a justification for the measure. While it recognised that EdF did indeed perform public service functions and was entitled to receive compensation to cover the net costs for the performance of these tasks, it was still necessary to ensure that the compensation was both necessary and proportionate. A guarantee which was unlimited in duration and in amount could not be deemed proportionate. Furthermore, the French authorities had not invoked any evidence to justify the application of art.106(2) TFEU.[149]

20–078   In its decision concerning the Irish CADA scheme, which concerned a scheme for "capacity payments" to generators who undertook the construction of new

---

[148] B. Allibert, "Ireland", *Competition Policy Newsletter*, No.1, February 2002, p.95.
[149] See pts 46–8 of its decision to open proceedings [2003] O.J. C164/7.

capacity, it was held that this scheme was designed to ensure the security of the electricity supply in Ireland. Qualifying generators were selected on the basis of a competitive process. The Commission concluded that all four of the *Altmark* conditions had been met and ruled that art.107(1) TFEU did not apply.[150] In the recent decisions concerning the Polish and Hungarian PPAs the generators who were parties to the respective PPAs argued that these contracts conferred SGEIs upon them and that therefore the PPAs fell outside the scope of art.107(1) TFEU. The generators argued in both cases that the PPAs should be regarded as implementing SGEIs for the purpose of securing electricity supplies and environmental protection and should be held to fulfill the criteria laid down in the *Altmark* judgment, which means that they did not constitute aid within the meaning of art.107(1) TFEU. They also invoked security of supply as one of the SGEIs that the PPAs can fulfill. The Commission countered that security of supply could be an SGEI, subject to the restrictions provided for in Directive 2003/54/EC, that is, provided that the generators concerned use indigenous primary energy fuel sources, and that the total volume of energy does not exceed in any calendar year 15 per cent of the total primary energy necessary to produce the electricity consumed in the Member State concerned.[151] In both cases the PPAs concerned quantities of energy that were largely in excess of the 15 per cent. Furthermore, they did not solely concern generators using indigenous primary energy fuel sources. Finally, the Commission noted that the power plants concerned by the PPAs did not exhibit any special characteristics that would make them particularly well adapted to meet security of supply objectives. In fact, they were just normal plants connected to the network, and therefore contributed to overall security of supply in Poland and in Hungary, just like any other power plant in the sector.

The generators also argued that art.106(2) TFEU might apply to the PPAs even where they did not fulfill the criteria of the Altmark judgment. The Commission ruled that art.106(2) TFEU can apply only to companies which have been entrusted with providing genuine SGEIs, and that SGEIs must be entrusted to specific companies, which was not the case. Finally, compensation for providing the SGEI must be proportionate to the costs incurred; in other words, it must be possible to carry out an assessment of the scope of the SGEIs in order to calculate the associated costs.[152]

Spanish Coal. The Spanish authorities introduced a scheme to compensate **20–079** electricity generators for using indigenous coal, on the grounds that the country is poorly interconnected with other major European electricity markets and in view of the country's share of renewable energy, production is highly intermittent with insufficient available capacity at peak times. Without the aid a number of plants would have closed, increasing dependence on imports and threatening

[150] State Aid N 475/2003, December 16, 2003 [2004] O.J. C34/7.
[151] See Commission decisions in cases N 34/99 [2002] O.J. C5/2; NN 49/99 [2001] O.J. C268/5; N 6/A/2001 [2002] O.J. C77/25; and C 7/2005 [2007] O.J. L219/9.
[152] Poland [2007] O.J. L83/1; Hungary [2007] O.J. L225/53.

security of supply. Therefore, taking into consideration that the scheme was transitory in nature, and that the volume of electricity concerned was limited (less than 10 per cent of national consumption), the Commission decided to allow this measure.[153]

20–080 **Latvia.** In a decision[154] concerning the construction of a new thermal power plant in Latvia, the Commission took account of the specificity of the Latvian market and its effective isolation from neighbouring energy markets. Latvia is particularly dependent on gas and the closure of the Lithuanian nuclear power plant at the end of 2009 put at risk the ability of Latvia to ensure security of supply in the long term. The project will also be made available through a competitive selection process

20–081 **The Netherlands.** The stimulation of the extension of the production of offshore gas fields in the Netherlands is a project based on a tax deduction to encourage investment in the exploration and exploitation of small marginal gas fields on the Dutch continental shelf in the North Sea. The Commission, applying the balancing test described in Ch.4, held that the measure was justified on the basis of art.107(3)(c) TFEU because it increases the supply of natural gas and as such enhances security of supply in the Netherlands, and for a number of countries in the EU.[155]

20–082 **Poland.** The Commission approved almost €400 million of aid,[156] more than 50 per cent aid intensity for the construction and capacity increase for four underground gas storage sites in Poland. The projects all have a common European interest and the Commission recognised that gas storage enhances security of supply and enables a country to deal with supply disruptions or seasonal variations in consumption. The storage capacity will be in this case open to all operators and access is regulated.

20–083 **Estonia.** The Commission had opened an in-depth investigation[157] into an Estonian project to grant up to €1.5 billion over 20 years to the operators of two newly constructed 300MW plants using oil-shale. Estonia had claimed that the aid was necessary to increase security of supply but the Commission was concerned that as no competitive tender was foreseen the beneficiary would be the publicly owned incumbent that controlled significant activity along the value chain from mining to distribution. The Estonian government subsequently withdrew its notification.

---

[153] Case N 178/2010 [2010] O.J. C312.
[154] N 675/2009 [2010] O.J. C213/9.
[155] N 718/2009, February 20, 2010.
[156] N 660/2009 [2010] O.J. C213/53.
[157] IP/11/349, 23 March 2011.

The Commission's guidance notes on EC Directives 2003/54 and 2003/55

The Commission published on January 16, 2004 a series of non-binding **20–084** "guidance notes" on various issues relating to Directives 2003/54 (electricity) and 2003/55[158] (gas) with a view to clarifying the interpretation of certain of their provisions. These notes are available on DG Energy's website. A separate note deals with public service obligations (PSOs). Directives 2003/54 and 2003/55 make an number of references to arts 106(1) and (2), 107 and 108 TFEU. However, this note has not been updated in the light of the adoption and entry into force of the latest Directives 2009/72 (electricity) and 2009/73 (gas[159]).

Article 3 of each of the 2009 Directive recognises that Member States may impose pubic service obligations relating to securing, including security of supply, regularity, quality and price of supplies and environmental protection on electricity and gas undertakings.

In its guidance notes, the Commission observes that only services which **20–085** cannot be provided by the market can be deemed to be PSOs. It therefore follows that supply of gas or electricity to eligible (i.e. non-captive) customers cannot be deemed a PSO and that as of 2007—the date for full liberalisation of both markets—supply to all classes of customers falls outside the scope of art.106(2). Any support to an entity providing services to a particular category of customers (e.g. in an underdeveloped region) would have to be assessed under art.107(2) or (3). Although the Electricity Directive requires that all household consumers enjoy universal service, this right does not entail a right to uniform tariffs irrespective of location. It only entails a right to reasonable, easily and clearly comparable and transparent prices.[160] However, as the directives recognise other objectives as candidates for PSO status, including security and reliability of supply and consumer and environmental protection objectives, the application of art.106(2) cannot be ruled out as an eventual justification for financial support in relation to such objectives.

Of particular interest to the application of the EU Treaty state aid rules in the **20–086** light of the Directives is art.3(6) (2009/72) which stipulates that

"where financial compensation, other forms of compensation and exclusive rights which a Member State grants for the fulfilment of the obligations set out in paragraphs 2 and 3 are provided, this shall be done in a non-discriminatory and transparent way".[161]

---

[158] [2003] O.J. L176.
[159] [2009] O.J. L211/94.
[160] Case C–265/08 *Federutility and Others v Autorità per l'energia elettrica e il gas* [2010] E.C.R. I–03377.
[161] See also in this respect recital 28 of the Preamble which recognises the right of Member States to provide adequate economic incentives using all existing national and Community tools. These tools "may include liability mechanisms to guarantee the necessary investment".

As to whether such financial measures can be characterised as state aid, the Commission's guidance notes defer to the courts' case-law and the Commission's decisions as well as paras 83–101 of the Commission's "non-paper" of 2002 (see further Ch.8). The Directives themselves cannot therefore be interpreted as affecting in any way the initial question of whether a particular measure is an aid or not. In this respect the Commission's guidance notes also make clear reference to the *Altmark* ruling. In addition, a separate duty of notification to the Commission is imposed by virtue of art.3(8) (2009/72) and (11) (2009/73) with respect to all measures and changes to such measures, whether these may involve a derogation from the Directive or not, to carry out universal service (electricity) and public service obligations. This general duty of notification is without prejudice to the duty to notify financial support measures in accordance with art.108 and Council Regulation 659/99.[162]

20–087   The provisions of art.3 of the Directives may, however, be of some importance in evaluating the compatibility of certain national state aid measure in accordance with art.106(2). As the Directives explicitly recognise—albeit in global terms—a number of objectives as legitimate PSOs, it will be for a Member State seeking to rely on art.106(2) as a justification for a state aid measure to demonstrate that it is necessary, appropriate and proportionate and is the least distortive mechanism available to it.[163] In the Spanish coal case, the Spanish Government successfully invoked art.106(2). The method of support at issue here comprised a preferential dispatch mechanism, called in the modified Royal Decree:

> "whereby every day, the outcome of the clearing of the Spanish organised day-ahead electricity market will be modified to the extent necessary to ensure that the above-mentioned coal-fired power plants can place pre-defined volumes of electricity generated out of indigenous coal on that market".

On the basis that Spain committed to ending the applicability of the modified Royal Decree and the state aid measures that it contains by December 31, 2014 at the very latest and that this measure is transitory because the justifications provided by Spain indicate that it serves the purpose of mitigating certain concrete risks hanging over Spain's security of supply over a period of four years, the Commission concluded that the notified aid is compatible with the internal market on the basis of art.106(2).[164]

The Commission opened a formal investigation into various measures of support to the Maltese electricity sector in 2011, measures which the Maltese government defends as being necessary to ensure security and reliability of supply and thus justifiable under art.106(2).[165]

---

[162] See in this respect recital 29 of the Preamble.

[163] Furthermore, the guidance notes indicate that the Commission will apply the provisions of the Transparency Directive and art.19(3) of the Directives strictly, to ensure that there is no abusive cross-subsidisation between different services or products.

[164] Case C 178/2010 [2010] O.J. C312.

[165] Case C 32/10 [2011] O.J. C52/3.

8. AID THROUGH ENERGY COMPANIES

Aid may be provided to certain groups of final consumers through energy **20–088** companies owned or controlled by the state insofar as the resources of such companies can be considered to be state resources. In this respect alleged aid through an energy company may take a number of forms. In the first place, two inter-related situations can be considered: preferential tariffs for energy supply or network system use and cross-subsidisation between different classes of consumers. In the second place, a state-owned or controlled company may be required to purchase energy (such as domestically produced coal or renewable energy) at a higher price or on more advantageous terms than a normal market purchaser might have done so. In both cases, it is possible that these actions could amount to the conferral of a selective benefit, and providing all the remaining elements of art.107(1) are present, this could constitute, prima facie, state aid.

Preferential tariffs

In principle, the resources at the disposal of any undertaking which is either **20–089** owned or controlled by the state or to which it grants special or exclusive rights within the meaning of art.2 of the Transparency Directive 2000/52, as amended, may be considered to be state resources. Following the ruling of the ECJ in Case C–482/99 *France v Commission ("Stardust Marine")*[166] it is now also necessary for the purposes of establishing the applicability of art.107(1) TFEU to attribute or impute a decision or policy to deploy these resources in a particular way, to the state itself in order to bring either preferential tariffs or cross-subsidisation practices within the scope of art.107(1). As the Commission had adopted as the sole criterion, the "organic criterion"—that is that the banks in question as public undertakings were under the control of the state—its interpretation of the criterion of "imputability" was erroneous. (See para.20–024, above.)

The potential applicability of the market economy investor principle must also be examined see para.20–034, above. In certain circumstances, the Commission as well as the Courts have recognised that an undertaking may be acting as a market investor by offering special tariffs to certain sectors in order to meet commercial pressures, and to protect its market position, for example, if faced with competition from other fuels or means of producing the same end product.[167] In Case C–56/93 *Belgium v Commission*, the court upheld a Commission decision rejecting complaints against the Dutch Gasunie for allegedly having granted aid to certain categories of large users. The special tariff which applied to Dutch ammonia producers was found to be justified on commercial grounds. The fact that it also furthered a political aim of the national government did not mean that it constituted aid within the meaning of art.107. (see para.79)

---

[166] [2002] E.C.R. I–4397.
[167] Joined Cases C–67, 68 and 70/85 *Van der Kooy* [1988] E.C.R. 219.

20–090   In the light of the *Stardust Marine* ruling the court's rulings in several earlier cases concerning special gas tariffs available for users in the horticulture and fertiliser sectors, although handed down some time ago, and before energy market liberalisation,[168] may now provide only limited guidance as to when a form of preferential tariff or cross-subsidisation policy or indeed preferential purchase arrangements can be held to be attributable to the state. The various "elements" outlined by the Court at para.56 of its ruling in *Stardust* will have to be considered. Thus if an energy supplier chooses to grant a particular tariff to a certain group of users on the basis of its own commercial policies and this policy cannot be attributed to the state, then it is likely that tariff would not qualify as a form of state aid. If, however, the company was mandated by law or as a result of indirect pressure from its government owners had to grant preferential tariffs, the situation may be different.

At the same time, although the Commission was prepared to adopt a lenient attitude to various contracts between state-owned or controlled energy producers and large consumers in the past which allowed off-take by the latter at preferential rates, the logic of those decisions essentially rested on the fact that the incumbent was best served if it could get rid of its surplus on the home market. As exports of surplus capacity were hardly possible before market liberalisation, the Commission found that sale at prices which just covered variable costs to be acceptable commercial practice and therefore not contrary to art.107. Now that the internal markets for energy have been progressed, it is unlikely that the Commission will accept that this is the only possible market outlet.[169] Cancellation of large volumes of outstanding debt for energy supplies has not been considered normal commercial behaviour and has been condemned as aid by the Commission.[170]

Recent Tariff Cases

20–091   **Alcoa.** The conditions under which Alcoa, a major energy consumer, purchased electricity from ENEL, the then Italian electricity monopolist, had first been assessed by the Commission in 1996.[171] At that time, the Commission examined the electricity tariff, which ENEL charged the plants in question. The Commission took the view the tariffs did not constitute state aid because ENEL was behaving like an operator acting under normal market conditions. This decision was in line with earlier case-law and decision practice on electricity tariffs, notably the 1988 *Van der Kooy* judgment and the 2000 *EDF* decision.[172] Under

---

[168] Joined Cases C–67, 68 and 70/85 *Van der Kooy* [1988] E.C.R. 219; Case C–56/93 *Belgium v Commission* [1996] E.C.R. I–723.

[169] See, in particular, the Commission's informal decisions on the special tariffs accorded by EdF to various large industrial users; 19th Competition Report, pt 168 and 20th Competition Report, pt.186.

[170] See Aid to BUNA [1996] O.J. L239/1.

[171] [1996] O.J. C288/4.

[172] See Case 67/85 *Van der Kooy v Commission* [1988] E.C.R. 219; and Commission decision of April 11, 2000 on the measure implemented by EDF for certain firms in the paper industry [2001] O.J. L95/18.

this line of cases, it was established that preferential electricity tariffs, i.e. tariffs made available only to certain consumers, did not confer an advantage, and hence fell outside art.107(1) TFEU, where they were justified on commercial grounds.

In the 1996 *Alcoa* decision, the Commission was satisfied that this requirement was met because the tariff covered the marginal cost and at least a proportion of the fixed costs of the supplier, in circumstances where there was overcapacity and Alcoa was amongst the largest consumers. Although the economic circumstances of supply and demand had not changed since its prior assessment, in 2009 the Commission took issue with a change in the mechanism of the tariff. This is because the measure no longer consisted in ENEL applying a tariff for the supply to Alcoa, which was equivalent to a market price, but in the grant of a reimbursement by a public fund, financed through state resources (in order to offset the difference between the price paid to the supplier and the tariff approved by the Commission in 1996). Contrary to its 1996 *Alcoa* decision and the earlier 2000 EDF decision, discussed above at para.20–035, in the 2009 Alcoa decision the Commission was no longer concerned about the level of the tariff. According to the Commission, the mere existence of a component designed to mitigate the price paid by the consumer was in and of itself conferring an advantage on the latter, regardless of (i) the price actually charged by the supplier; and/or (ii) the level of support provided by the State.

Alcoa challenged this decision unsuccessfully before the General Court in Case T–332/06, and the ECJ has upheld the lower Court's approach.[173]

Terni. The aid in this case consisted in a preferential tariff for the supply of **20–092** electricity, the aim of which was to compensate for expropriation of Terni in 1962. Terni was operating in the steel, cement and chemicals sectors. It owned and operated an hydroelectric power plant mainly for its own needs. The Italian government decided then that "[g]iven its strategic importance for the country's energy supply, Terni's hydroelectricity assets should be nationalised by the way of transferring its assets to ENEL". The Terni tariff was first applied from 1963 to 1992. The disputed measure in the case consists in its renewed temporal extension by Law No. 80/05 as from January 1, 2005. The measure had been extended once, from 1992 to December 31, 2001. This renewal included a provision on the progressive decrease of the level of the aid granted to Terni (by way of lower electricity tariff). The measure was notified to the European Union, and the European Commission decided "not to raise objections" to the application of Law No.9/91.

A progressive phase-out of the measure was also meant to follow the liberalisation of the electricity market. However, Terni argued here that the liberalisation process did not deliver the expected result, which was to enable the Terni companies to purchase electricity directly on the liberalised power market at competitive rates, "similar to the production costs they would have had if they

---

[173] [2000] E.C.R. II–29; Case C–194/09P, July 21, 2011.

had retained possession of the expropriated plants The Commission assessed the tariff as a state aid in Decision 2008/408/EC of November 20, 2007.[174] In its decision, the Commission held that "the compensation granted by the State for an expropriation of assets does not normally qualify as State aid.".[175] Indeed, the "true compensatory nature" of the measure was the core question examined in Case T–62/08. The General Court held that it is:

"completely unambiguous that the Terni tariff was granted by way of compensation for a very specific period, with no possibility of postponing the expiry date,"

which was fixed to December 31, 1992 and extended by Law No. 80/05 until 2010 (under tariffs and quantities agreed upon in 2004). The extension in time of the measures did not however have a compensatory purpose.[176]

20–093 **Portovesme, ILA and Eurallumnia.** In February 2011, the Commission held that operating aid granted by Italy in the form of subsidized electricity prices was incompatible with EU state aid rules and should be recovered. Following in-depth investigations,[177] the Commission concluded that two preferential electricity tariff schemes introduced in the Italian Region of Sardinia in favor of three energy-intensive companies constituted incompatible operating aid. The companies are Portovesme, a zinc and lead producer, Eurallumina, which produces aluminum, and ILA, a manufacturer of processed aluminum products. After an in-depth investigation, the Commission concluded that the preferential tariffs offered to these companies merely reduced the operating costs of the beneficiaries and improved their competitive position without furthering any goal of common interest. The Commission also prohibited the project to grant identical tariffs as of 2005 to the same beneficiaries, as well as chlorine producer Syndial.

Italy claimed that it had to subsidise the energy-intensive companies because electricity was more expensive in Sardinia. The scheme was financed by all electricity users in Italy, both companies and end consumers. The first scheme was implemented by Italy in 2004 without prior notification to the Commission. Following complaints, the Commission opened an in-depth investigation on both measures. As a consequence, Italy discontinued the scheme that year. However, the following year Italy had notified virtually identical subsidies in favor of the same beneficiaries The Commission opened an in-depth investigation in April 2006.[178]

---

[174] Commission Decision 2008/408/EC of November 20, 2007 on the State aid C 36/A/06 (ex NN 38/06) implemented by Italy in favour of ThyssenKrupp, Cementir and Nuova Terni Industrie Chimiche [2008] O.J. L144/37.

[175] Recital 70 of the contested decision.

[176] See paras 74 and 119, Case T–62/08, July 1, 2010. Now under appeal, Case C–488/10P, September 2010 O.J. C346/33.

[177] C 36/b/2006 and C 38/a/2004, IP/11/215.

[178] IP/06/541, April 27, 2006.

Cross-subsidisation

On the assumption that the decision to grant a particular tariff is attributable to **20–094** the state, a further relevant issue is on what basis a tariff could be deemed to be a form of unfair cross-subsidisation. This is a complex issue and one on which the Directives on the internal electricity and gas markets as well as the general case law of the Court do not provide definitive guidance. If one takes the example of a company which owns both network assets and a supply company, and that company uses its profits on its network activities to finance the construction of a new generating plant or the installation of new metering systems, is this a form of cross-subsidisation that can be prohibited under art.107(1). Is such a situation different from that in which an energy supply company charges its captive customers a higher price per kilowatt hour for the energy supplied than that which it supplies to its large industrial users? The answers to these questions are by no means straightforward.

Article 19(3) of the Electricity Directive 2003/54 and now art.31(3) of Directive 2009/72,[179] provides that electricity undertakings shall keep separate accounts for each of their transmission and distribution activities in order to avoid discrimination, cross-subsidisation and distortion of competition. Their annual audit process should verify that there has been no discrimination or cross-subsidisation. In accordance with art.23(1)(e) the national regulatory authorities must ensure that accounts are effectively unbundled and must ensure that there are no cross-subsidies between generation, transmission, distribution and supply activities.

These provisions do not indicate, however, what is meant by the term "cross-subsidisation". Internal transfers from profit-making to loss-making activities are, after all, a fact of normal commercial life in all sectors, whether public or private. The main issue, however, is that often energy companies are not "normal" companies; they have traditionally enjoyed certain exclusive or special rights to supply certain services or types of customers or areas. It is the risk that they can generate additional or surplus revenue from these "reserved" activities (e.g. supply to captive customers) to finance activities under competition (e.g. supply to eligible customers) that creates regulatory and competition concerns. Similarly, if reserved activities bear a disproportionate share of common costs this will have the same end result: the activity under competition can be performed without covering its real costs by the prices charged for it.

In general, the Commission's concern has been limited to the cross-subsidisation of services under competition through unfair revenue or cost allocation methods; the subsidisation of the reserved sector by revenues generated in the competitive sector is not problematic. This approach was upheld by the General Court in Case T–106/95 *FFSA*.[180]

---

[179] See the identical provisions for gas in Directive 2004/55, now repealed and replaced by Directive 2009/73.
[180] [1997] E.C.R. II–229.

20–095   To date, the case law of the courts has generally concerned the provision of logistical assistance and commercial services by a public undertaking to a subsidiary where the remuneration received in return is alleged to be less than that which would have been demanded under normal market conditions.[181]

Furthermore, although separate or unbundled accounts are required in accordance with art.19(3), the Directives do not prescribe any particular method of cost accounting, and in particular do not require any specific treatment of "common costs" and their proper allocation to different services or activities. It will be up to national regulators to monitor cross-subsidisation but whether this will also entitle the regulators to develop their own cost-allocation methodologies will remain a question of national law.

The tests laid down in Case C–280/00 and Case C–94/01P *Chronopost*, as discussed in Ch.8, section 4, may help to give some further, albeit limited, guidance in this area. In addition, the Commission's Communication and Decision on compensation for the provision of services of general economic interest may be of some, limited significance (see also Ch.8 paras 8–037 to 8–050). Hence if the revenue which a company earns on its reserved activities exceeds a reasonable level of compensation as calculated on the basis of the *Altmark* criteria and at the same time the company can use this revenue to cover its costs in the competitive sector—having failed to allocate these costs in accordance with the Chronopost criteria[182]—then this could give rise to a state aid within the meaning of art.107(1) TFEU.

---

[181] Case C–39/94 *SFEI* [1996] E.C.R. I–3547.

[182] On the assumption that there are no other applicable benchmarks which could be deemed acceptable.

CHAPTER 21

REGIONAL AID*

1. INTRODUCTION 21–001
   Definition 21–001
   Regional selectivity 21–002
   Compatibility: Treaty provisions 21–003
2. FIRST STEPS TO CO-ORDINATE NATIONAL REGIONAL AID SYSTEMS IN THE 1970S AND
   1980S 21–005
3. THE 1998 REGIONAL AID GUIDELINES 21–006
   Scope 21–007
   Demarcation of regions 21–008
   Permissible forms of aid 21–009
   Regional aid maps and notification of aid schemes 21–011
4. RULES APPLICABLE TO NEW MEMBER STATES PRIOR TO ADOPTION OF THE REGIONAL AID
   GUIDELINES 2007–2013 21–012
5. MULTISECTORAL FRAMEWORKS 1997 AND 2002 21–013
6. THE REGIONAL AID GUIDELINES 2007–2013 21–014
   Background and legislative history 21–014
   Scope of application 21–017
   Aid schemes versus ad hoc aid 21–018
   Demarcation of regions 21–019
   Article 107(3)(a) regions 21–020
   Statistical effect regions 21–021
   Aid intensity for Article 107(3)(a) regions 21–022
   Article 107(3)(c) 21–023
   Aid intensities for Article 107(3)(c) regions 21–025
   Regional investment aid 21–026
   Eligible costs when determined on the basis of investment costs 21–028
   Eligible costs when determined on the basis of wage costs 21–029
   Aid for large investment projects 21–030
   Cumulation of aid 21–031
   Operating aid 21–032
   Enterprise aid 21–033
   *Procedure: regional aid maps, notifications, General Block Exemption Regulation,
     simplified notification procedure* 21–034
   Application of guidelines, transparency and review 21–035

* Thomas Jestaedt

783

1. Introduction

Definition

21–001   Regional aid is the most important form of aid by volume.[1] Regional aid is horizontal aid that is geared towards all undertakings located in a particular region; the purpose of regional aid is to promote investment and the creation of jobs, as well as to remove structural disadvantages for undertakings operating in under-developed regions.

Regional selectivity

21–002   Under the "specificity" test, an economic benefit granted by a Member State to certain undertakings constitutes state aid if it is not available to all other undertakings within the Member State's territory. Thus, where a Member State grants benefits to undertakings located in a particular region which are not available elsewhere, the grant will normally meet the specificity test and qualify as state aid.

The qualification of measures adopted by regions based on autonomous constitutional powers is more complex: in particular, the issue has arisen to what extent tax benefits that regions grant by relying on autonomous legislative powers that they have vis-à-vis the central government of a Member State can be qualified as state aid. On March 30, 2004, the European Commission decided that the planned reform of Gibraltar's company taxation laws which would have consisted of abolishing the current 35 per cent corporate tax rate and replacing it with a payroll tax kept at 15 per cent of profits constituted state aid.[2] The Commission took the view that Gibraltar's taxation of corporations had to be compared to that generally applicable in the United Kingdom. Since the tax rate in Gibraltar was more favorable than the general UK corporate tax rate, the Commission found aid to be present. Similarly, in its decision of December 11, 2002,[3] the Commission declared the tax reductions for residents of the autonomous region of the Azores as state aid since they deviated from the general taxation applicable in Portugal. The Portuguese Republic challenged that decision on the basis that the Commission had misapplied the selectivity criterion. In his opinion of October 22, 2005,[4] AG Geelhoed suggested that, in assessing the selectivity of tax measures adopted by regional governments, three scenarios must be distinguished:

(a) Where the central government unilaterally decides that the general tax rate should be reduced within the defined geographic area, such a measure is selective.

[1] In 2004, Member Sates granted a total of €12.3 billion of aid to art.107(3)(a) regions, which corresponds to 27% of total aid. Commission State Aid Scoreboard—Autumn 2005 update at 1.9, p.23.
[2] Decision 2005/261 [2005] O.J. L85/1.
[3] Decision 2003/442 [2003] O.J. L150/52.
[4] Opinion of AG Geelhoed, Case C–88/03 *Portuguese Republic v Commission* Unreported.

(b) Where all local authorities at a particular level (regions, districts or others) have the autonomous power to set the tax rate for the geographical jurisdiction, whether or not, without reference to a national tax rate, a tax rate that is more favourable in one region than in another does not fulfil the selectivity criterion.

(c) Where a local authority can decide that a particular tax rate should be lower than the national tax rate and should be applicable only within the territory of that local authority, Advocate General Geelhoed suggests that the tax advantage should not be regarded as aid if the local authority decides on it fully autonomously in the following respects:

- institutionally: within the local authority's own constitutional, political and administrative status;
- procedurally: without interference from the central government; and
- economically: without cross-subsidisation from the central government.

In its judgment of September 6, 2006, the ECJ followed the Advocate General's proposal. It rejected the Portuguese government's assertion that the benefits conferred by the Azores tax scheme were not selective. It pointed to the fact that the Portuguese government was offsetting the adverse economic effects of the reduction and tax revenue for the Azores by a centrally managed financing mechanism (*Portuguese Republic v Commission* Case C–88/03, at Pt 75). Thus the local authority when deciding on the scheme was not economically independent.

Compatibility: Treaty provisions

The Treaty distinguishes between aid to promote the development of under- **21–003** developed areas (art.107(3)(a)) and aid designed to facilitate the development of other areas (art.107(3)(c)). Aid under art.107(3)(a) can be declared compatible with the Treaty without specific requirements, whereas the aid under art.107(3)(c) can be declared compatible only if it does "not adversely affect trading conditions to an extent contrary to the common interest". This limitation does not apply to state aid designed to develop underdeveloped areas[5]; in those areas, the Commission must only take into account the sectoral effects that an aid may have in order to avoid distortions in a particular sector with overcapacities.[6]

Underdeveloped regions are regions with development problems as compared to the Community as a whole or to the individual Member State. Article 107(3)(a) TFEU provides that aid to promote the economic development of areas

---

[5] Case C–198/91 *Cook v Commission* [1993] E.C.R. I–2487; Case C–42/93 *Spain v Commission* [1994] E.C.R. I–4175.
[6] Case T–380/94 *Aiufass and AKT v Commission* [1994] E.C.R. II–2169 at para.58.

where the standard of living is abnormally low or where there is a serious underemployment can be considered compatible with the common market. According to the European Court of Justice (ECJ), the use of the terms "abnormally" and "serious" in art.107(3)(a) suggests that the economic situation in the relevant area must be extremely unfavourable in relation to the Community as a whole.[7]

21–004   By contrast, art.107(3)(c) allows greater flexibility in assessing the degree of underdevelopment. The relevant indicators do not necessarily relate to the standards of living and underemployment.

In general, regional aid is granted in the form of investment aid with the aim to create jobs by allowing investments in new, or the extension or modernisation of existing, production sites. There is a strong bias against operating aid as a means of remedying structural disadvantages from which companies in underdeveloped areas suffer.

2. First Steps to Co-ordinate National Regional Aid Systems in the 1970s and 1980s

21–005   The first steps undertaken by the Community to address regional state aid issues aim at the co-ordination of national regional aid systems. A First Resolution on general regional aid systems was adopted in October 1971,[8] and amended and supplemented by further communications in 1975[9] and 1978.[10] The 1978 Communication also suggested that the Commission would publish further guidelines on the accumulation of aid for different purposes. A Communication setting out these guidelines was released in 1985.[11]

In 1988, the Commission adopted a Communication in which it made explicit use of the derogations in art.107(3)(a) and (c).[12] At the time of the adoption of the 1988 Guidelines, the Commission was reviewing the regional policy as a cornerstone of the Community cohesion policy following the accession of Portugal, Spain, and Greece. The Community's cohesion policy aims at reducing disparities between levels of development of the richer and poorer regions in Europe. The control of regional aid takes into account that this aid can both contribute to, and, where it is granted without observing the rules of the Treaty,

---

[7] Case C–248/84 *Germany v Commission* [1987] E.C.R. I–4013.
[8] [1971] O.J. C111/7.
[9] Commission Communication of February 26, 1975, and 5th Report on Competition Policy, 1975, points 85–87.
[10] Commission Communication of December 21, 1978 [1979] O.J. C31/9.
[11] [1986] O.J. C3/3.
[12] Commission Communication on the methods for the application of EEC Treaty art.92(3)(a) and (c) (now 87) to regional aid [1988] O.J. C212/2, as updated by the Communication of March 13, 1990 [1990] O.J. C163/5. The publication of this Communication in part resulted from the Court's ruling in Case C–248/84 *Germany v Commission* [1987] E.C.R. I–4013 where the Court annulled the Commission's decision for lack of reasoning.

undermine cohesion. A further amendment to Pt II of the 1988 Communication was published in late 1994.[13]

3. THE 1998 REGIONAL AID GUIDELINES

The next round of enlargement in 1995 as well as the approaching accession **21–006** of Member States with a GDP well below the Community average made it necessary to develop new guidelines. In 1998, the Commission replaced the 1988 Communication with Guidelines on national regional aid[14] (the "regional aid guidelines 1998"). The regional aid guidelines 1998, for the first time, consolidated all Commission communications on regional aid, in particular as they applied in different sectors. At the same time, they were designed to prepare the enlargement of the European Union.

Scope

The regional aid guidelines 1998 applied to all regional aid granted in every **21–007** sector of the economy except the production, processing and marketing of agricultural production, fisheries and the coal industry which were covered by a specific rule. Specific rules also continued to exist for transport, steel, shipbuilding, synthetic fibres and motor vehicles and for ad hoc aid for undertakings in difficulty.

Demarcation of regions

In the regional aid guidelines 1998, the Commission determines the regions **21–008** that are eligible for regional aid pursuant to a three-step approach: first, the Commission determines which overall percentage of the Community population should be eligible for aid. In order for the aid to be exceptional, the overall percentage has to be below 50 per cent. For the years 2000–2006 which are addressed in the regional aid guidelines 1998, the ceiling was set at 42.7 per cent of the Community population.[15] Secondly, the Commission looks at all regions that come within the derogations of art.107(3)(a) TFEU. These regions are determined by NUTS Level II Geographical Units.[16] In an art.107(3)(a) region, the per capita gross domestic product must be less than 75 per cent of the Community average.

---

[13] [1994] O.J. C364/8.

[14] Guidelines on national regional aid [1998] O.J. C74/9.

[15] For the individual Member States, the relevant percentages were Greece, Ireland and Portugal: 100%; Spain: 79.2%; Italy: 43.6%; Finland: 42.2%; France: 36.7%; Germany: 34.9%; Luxembourg: 32%; Belgium: 30.9%; United Kingdom: 28.7%; Austria: 27.5%; Denmark: 17.1%; Sweden: 15.9%; the Netherlands: 15%.

[16] NUTS stands for *Nomenclature des unités territoriales statistiques* which is defined in Regulation (EC) 1059/2003 [2003] O.J. L154.

The art.107(3)(c) ceiling is obtained by deducting from the overall ceiling (of 42.7 per cent) the population of the regions eligible under the art.107(3)(a) derogation. Thus, while the regions eligible under art.107(3)(a) TFEU are determined by reference to an objective factor (GDP below 75 per cent of Community average), the regions eligible under art.107(3)(c) are determined by reference to the overall ceiling which was determined based essentially on political considerations. Finally, the art.107(3)(c) Community ceiling is distributed among the different Member States according to a distribution key which refers to the unemployment and the standard of living in the Member States. As a rule, the more favourable a Member State's situation as regards unemployment or the standard of living is, the more selective are the thresholds used for the distribution of the ceiling on art.107(3)(c) coverage.

Member States must notify to the Commission the list of regions they propose for an art.107(3)(c) derogation. In principle, these regions must be NUTS Level III areas with a population of at least 100,000 inhabitants.

Permissible forms of aid

21–009 The regional aid guidelines 1998 permit three forms of aid: investment aid; aid for job creation; and operating aid, which is limited to art.107(3)(a) areas and to exceptional cases.

Aid for initial investment is available for investments in fixed capital, which is maintained for at least five years, to either set up a new establishment, as part of an existing establishment, or to start up an activity involving a fundamental change in the product or production process of an existing establishment.[17] The acquisition of an establishment previously closed can qualify as an initial investment; however, replacement investments are not covered.

The aid intensity is calculated as a percentage of the overall investment. The overall investment is measured on the basis of the so-called "standard base" which includes land, buildings and machinery. The aid notified by the Member States is expressed in gross terms as a percentage of the overall investment, the so-called "Net Grant Equivalent" (NGE). The Commission issued a table with the permissible aid intensities ranging from 65 per cent of the net grant equivalents for the outermost regions of the Community,[18] to 40 per cent of NGE for regions with a per capita GDP of more than 60 per cent of the Community average under art.107(3)(a) and 50 per cent as a general rule and with 20 per cent as the general rule for art.107(3)(c) derogation.

21–010 Regional aid for job creation must be linked to the implementation of an initial investment project.[19] Jobs must have been created within three years of the completion of the investment and must exclusively concern the activity to which the investment relates. The jobs must be maintained for at least five years. The

---

[17] Regional aid guidelines 1998 at para.4.4.
[18] The Azores, Madeira, the Canary Islands, and the four French overseas departments.
[19] Regional aid guidelines 1998 at para.4.11.

amount of the aid must not exceed a certain percentage of the wage cost of the person hired (gross wage before tax plus the compulsory social security contributions) calculated over a period of two years. The percentage corresponds to the intensity allowed for investment aid in the area concerned.

Operating aid is normally prohibited. However, under exceptional circumstances, it can be allowed in art.107(3)(a) regions.[20] It must take the form of tax exemptions or reductions of social contributions and must be limited in, and decrease progressively, over time.

Regional aid maps and notification of aid schemes

The demarcation of regions is enforced by means of regional aid maps, which the Commission adopts pursuant to a notification by the relevant Member State. The regional aid map shows the art.107(3)(a) and (c) regions as well as the permissible aid intensities. Following the adoption of aid maps, Member States notified their regional aid schemes. **21–011**

4. RULES APPLICABLE TO NEW MEMBER STATES PRIOR TO ADOPTION OF THE REGIONAL AID GUIDELINES 2007–2013

The method applied, vis-à-vis the new Member States, was laid down in Annex IV, Ch.3, para.(1)(c) (under art.22) of the Accession Treaty. Under that provision, accession states had to submit lists of measures which they wished to be considered as existing aid within the meaning of art.108(1) TFEU. These lists included the regional aid maps and the regional aid schemes which the accession candidates submitted in 2003 and 2004. Between December 2003 and December 2004, the Commission sent letters to each of the new Member States[21] confirming that it regarded the notified measures as existing measures within the meaning of art.108(1). This exercise was facilitated by the fact that the accession states were under an obligation to bring their national law in line with the *Acquis Communautaire* prior to their accession becoming effective. **21–012**

The method of bringing the regional aid schemes of accession states under the umbrella of the existing regional aid guidelines 1998 led to an increase of the overall ceiling of the EU population benefiting from regional aid by more than 10 per cent.

5. MULTISECTORAL FRAMEWORKS 1997 AND 2002

At the same time as it adopted the regional aid guidelines 1998, the Commission, for the first time, issued the so called "Multisectoral Framework for large **21–013**

---

[20] Regional aid guidelines 1998 at para.4.15.
[21] Published on the Commission's website.

investment projects".[22] The Multisectoral Framework established a notification obligation for regional investment aid projects with total investment costs of at least €50 million and an aid intensity of at least 50 per cent of the permissible ceiling, as well as a contribution of at least €40,000 per job created, or in case the total aid amount was at least €50 million. The purpose was to submit large investment projects to a special state aid scrutiny in order to prevent an unhealthy subsidisation competition of Member States for these projects. The permissible aid ceiling was determined by reference to a formula consisting of a competition factor determined by the capital invested per job created and a factor that took into account the regional effects.

The Commission applied the Multisectoral Framework 1998 in a number of cases which it started to review in 2000. The result was that, despite the sophistication of the formula for determining the ceiling, in almost every case the framework did not lead to a reduction of the aid intensity. This led the Commission to adopt a new Multisectoral Framework in 2002, which provides for a linear reduction of the permissible aid intensity depending on the amount of eligible expenses: where they are below €50 million, the beneficiaries are entitled to 100 per cent of the regional ceiling; for eligible costs between €50 million and €100 million, 50 per cent of the regional ceiling apply; and for eligible expenses above €100 million, 34 per cent of the regional ceiling can be granted.[23] The notification requirement was abolished for all investments below €100 million. Where it is proposed that an investment entails eligible costs of €100 million or more, the aid must be notified.

Details of the multisectoral frameworks 1998 and 2002, as well as their successor incorporated in the regional aid guidelines 2007–13, are described in Ch.15.

6. The Regional Aid Guidelines 2007–2013

Background and legislative history[24]

21–014 The regional aid maps approved under the regional aid guidelines 1998 expired on December 31, 2006. Thus, there was a need to at least revise the maps. In addition, the Commission had to take into account the conclusions of several European Councils, which decided that aid in the European Union should be concentrated on "less and better-targeted state aid". The third cohesion report of the European Union set three main objectives: (i) the promotion of conversion by supporting growth and job creation in the least developed Member States and regions; (ii) the strengthening of regional competitiveness and employment by

[22] Multisectoral Framework for large investment projects [1998] O.J. 107/7.
[23] Multisectoral Framework for large investment projects [2002] O.J. C70/8.
[24] Discussed in detail in the European Policy Research Paper, No.58 (November 2005) published by the European Research Centre.

supporting a limited number of areas of intervention—innovation and the knowledge economy, environment and risk prevention, accessibility and service of general economic interest; and (iii) European territorial co-operation.[25]

The main driving factor for the reform of the regional aid guidelines 1998 was enlargement: since the regional aid policies of the new Member States had simply been brought under the existing umbrella of the regional aid guidelines 1998, the population ceiling had increased from 42.7 per cent (for the EU-15) to 52.2 per cent (for the EU-25), and the art.107(3)(a) regions from 22 per cent to 34.2 per cent. Without reform, the population coverage would rise to 55.1 per cent (for the EU-27).

In May 2004, the Commission made available a working paper in which it **21–015** defined the art.107(3)(a) areas by reference to the EU-25 GDP and limited the art.107(3)(c) coverage to so-called "ear marked" regions rather than regions determined by reference to national population quarters.[26] Another key element of the working paper was the reduction of award ceilings across the board. The working paper was followed by a non-paper in December 2004 in which DG Competition took into account the main conclusions that it had drawn from the consultation process. In essence, however, the non-paper followed the basic approach proposed in the working paper.

The most controversial part of the papers submitted in 2004 was the concentration of eligible art.107(3)(c) regions to regions ear-marked by the Community rather than the Member States. After a further round of consultations with the Member States in July 2005, the Commission issued a new draft Communication in which it retreated from the position that art.107(3)(c) regions should be determined by the Commission and reverted to the system of the regional aid guidelines 1998 where those areas are selected by the Member States. The draft Communication has become the basis for the Guidelines on national regional aid for 2007–2013 (the "regional aid guidelines 2007–13"), which the Commission adopted on December 21, 2005.[27]

The regional aid guidelines 2007–13 constitute a compromise between the **21–016** original approach of the Commission on concentrating regional aid on the most under-developed areas and Member State expectations, in particular as to the phasing out of regions that, under the new approach, will no longer be eligible.

Under the regional aid guidelines 2007–13, the overall population coverage is set at 43.1 per cent of the EU-25 population, down from a level of 52.2 per cent. The level of 43.1 per cent was chosen so as to avoid that any given Member State would lose more than 50 per cent of its entitlement.

---

[25] Third Progress Report on Cohesion: Towards a new partnership for growth, jobs and cohesion, Communication from the Commission, Brussels, May 17, 2005, COM(2005) 192.

[26] Review of the Regional Aid Guidelines—a first consultation paper for the experts in the Member States, available at: *http://ec.europa.eu/comm/competition/state_aid/regional/*.

[27] Guidelines on national regional aid for 2007–13 [2006] O.J. C54/13.

Scope of application

21–017   The regional aid guidelines 2007–13 are applicable to all sectors of the economy, with the exception of the fisheries and the coal industry. In the agricultural sector, they do not apply to the production of agricultural products listed in Annex I of the EC Treaty; they do, however, apply to the processing and marketing of such products. There are also special rules for the transport and shipbuilding sectors.[28]

The Commission considers that regional aid to the steel industry is incompatible with the common market. The same applies to regional investment aid in the synthetic fibres sector. Finally, when aid is granted to a firm in difficulties within the meaning of the Community guidelines on state aid for rescuing and restructuring firms in difficulties, the provisions of those guidelines must be observed, in particular those regarding notification.[29]

Aid schemes versus ad hoc aid

21–018   The Commission takes the position that regional aid should as a rule be granted as part of the regional aid policy of the Member States. Thus, the aid will normally be granted as part of an aid scheme. However, the Commission is willing to look at ad hoc aid and to assess it in individual cases.[30] In those cases, the Member State bears the burden of proving that the aid in question contributes to a coherent regional development strategy. However, the fact that aid is granted on an ad hoc basis only does not prevent it from being qualified as regional aid and from being eligible to be declared compatible under art.107(3).[31]

Demarcation of regions

21–019   The demarcation of regions is the core of the regional aid guidelines 2007–13. As in the regional aid guidelines 1998, the Commission has set a limit for the overall population coverage. The Commission started out with the percentage adopted for 1998, i.e. 42 per cent, and applied an additional safety net to ensure that no Member State loses more than 50 per cent of the coverage of its population under the old guidelines; this resulted in an overall population coverage of about 43.1 per cent on an EU-25 basis, which will rise to 46.6 per cent once Bulgaria and Romania have joined the European Union.

Article 107(3)(a) regions

21–020   The demarcation of the art.107(3)(a) regions follows the principle laid down in the regional aid guidelines 1998: all regions that have less than 75 per cent of

---

[28] Regional aid guidelines 2007–13 at para.8.

[29] Community guidelines on state aid for rescuing and restructuring firms in difficulty [2004] O.J. C244/2.

[30] Regional aid guidelines 2007–13, at para.10.

[31] Case C–278/92 *Spain v Commission* [1994] E.C.R. I–4103, p.49.

the Community average per capita gross domestic product (GDP), measured in purchasing power standards, are eligible.[32] In addition, the so-called "outermost regions", i.e. territories belonging to the European Union located outside the European continent, are considered art.107(3)(a) regions regardless of the GDP that is achieved in them.

Statistical effect regions

The Commission further recognises that there are regions that qualify for **21–021** art.107(3)(a) status if the EU-15 average GDP is applied and which no longer qualify if the standard is EU-25 GDP. Thus, the non-eligibility of these regions is due only to the statistical effect of enlargement. Under the regional aid guidelines 2007–13, these regions continue to benefit from the art.107(3)(a) status until December 31, 2010.[33] In 2010, the Commission will review the position of these regions. If the GDP per capita has declined below 75 per cent of the EU-25 average, the regions will continue to be eligible under art.107(3)(a); otherwise they will revert to an art.107(3)(c) status.

Aid intensity for Article 107(3)(a) regions

The permissible aid intensities are determined by reference to the GDP. In the **21–022** regional aid guidelines 2007–13 the Commission assesses the aid intensity by looking at the Gross Grant Equivalent rather than NGE.[34] This is due to a decision of the Court of First Instance (CFI) which prohibited the Commission from taking into account tax effects when assessing the amount of aid.[35] Where the GDP is below 45 per cent of the EU-25 average, the aid intensity can be 50 per cent gross, where the GDP is below 60 per cent, the relevant figure is 40 per cent gross, and where it is below 75 per cent, the threshold for the aid intensity is 30 per cent gross.[36] In statistical effect regions, the maximum intensity can be 20 per cent.

The guidelines provide for bonuses for small companies of 20 per cent and for medium-sized companies of 10 per cent.[37]

Article 107(3)(c)

After intense consultation with the Member States, the Commission has **21–023** maintained the principle whereby Member States themselves determine which

---

[32] Regional aid guidelines 2007–13 at para.16.
[33] Regional aid guidelines 2007–13 at para.19.
[34] Regional aid guidelines 2007–13 at para.41.
[35] Joined cases T–298/97, T–312/97, T–313/97, T–315/97, T–600/97 to 607/97, T–1/98, T–3/98 to T–6/98 and T–23/98 *Alzetta Mauro v Commission* [2000] E.C.R. II–2319.
[36] Regional aid guidelines 2007–13 at para.44.
[37] Regional aid guidelines 2007–13 at para.49.

regions within their territory should be eligible under art.107(3)(c). The Commission has also recognised the necessity to provide for some transitional rules so as to avoid too drastic effects on regions that were eligible under the regional aid guidelines 1998.

The Commission has maintained the principle that art.107(3)(c) regions are determined by deducting the populations of all those regions that qualify by applying the objective 75 per cent of average GDP test throughout the European Union from the overall population ceiling of 43.1 per cent. The remaining balance is then distributed between the Member States using a distribution key that takes account of variations in GDP per capita and unemployment between the regions, both in a national and a community contact. The detailed key is set out in Annex IV to the guidelines. The resulting regional aid coverage is as follows:

	B (%)	DK (%)	D (%)	Gr (%)	Esp (%)	F (%)	Irl (%)	I (%)	Lux (%)	NI (%)	Ös (%)	Port (%)	SF (%)	S (%)	UK (%)
Disadvantaged Areas (Art.107(3)(a))	0	0	12.5	36.6	36.2	2.9	0	29.2	0	0	0	70.1	0	0	4.0
"Statistical effect" areas	12.4	0	6.1	55.5	5.8	0	0	1.0	0	0	3.4	3.8	0	0	0.6
Other areas (Art.107(3)(c))	13.5	8.6	11.0	7.9	17.7	15.5	50.0	3.9	16	7.5	19.1	2.8	33.0	15.3	19.3
Total	25.9	8.6	29.6	100	59.6	18.4	50.0	34.1	16	7.5	22.5	76.7	33.0	15.3	23.9

The three Baltic states, Malta, Poland and Slovenia have 100 per cent coverage under art.107(3)(a).

21–024   Based on the allocations of total eligible population percentages for art.107(3)(c), Member States determine which regions they want to make eligible on their territory. While Member States have some discretion, the Commission sets out certain factors that Member States must take into account when designating areas. These include:

- the economic development regions;

- regions with GDP per capita of less than the EU-25 average or an unemployment rate higher than 115 per cent of the national average;

- islands and other regions categorised by similar geographical isolation with low GDP per capita or high unemployment;

- regions adjacent to art.107(3)(a) regions.

Aid intensities for Article 107(3)(c) regions

21–025   The normal aid intensity for an art.107(3)(c) region will be 15 per cent of the gross grant equivalent. The aid intensity is reduced to 10 per cent where the GDP of the region in question is above, and the unemployment rate is below, that of the EU-25 average.[38]

Finally, in regions that are adjacent to art.107(3)(a) regions or third countries where the aid intensity can be higher, the aid intensity can be increased so as to ensure that the difference between the two aid intensities does not exceed 20 per cent.

Regional investment aid

Investment aid is the normal form of regional aid. Its purpose is to enhance **21–026** initial investment and to create jobs. During the process leading up to the adoption of the regional aid guidelines 2007–13, there was some discussion as to whether investment aid is the best means of promoting cohesion.

The regional aid guidelines 1998 distinguished between "aid for initial investment" and "aid for job creation". The regional aid guidelines 2007–13 combine both forms of aid in the definition of regional investment aid which must be tied to an "initial investment". An initial investment means an investment in material and immaterial assets relating to:

- the setting up of a new establishment;

- the extension of an existing establishment;

- the diversification of the output of an establishment into a new, additional product (the regional aid guidelines 1998 referred to a possible "fundamental change in the product or production process for an existing establishment"—this is no longer sufficient; the investment must relate to "new" products); or

- a fundamental change in the overall production process of an existing establishment.[39]

As was the case under the regional aid guidelines 1998, replacement investments are not covered.

Regional investment aid is calculated by reference either to the material and **21–027** immaterial investment costs from an initial investment project or by reference to the estimated wage costs for jobs directly created by the investment project.[40]

Where the aid is calculated by reference to the initial investment cost, these costs are computed by aggregating the costs for the acquisition of material assets relating to land, buildings and plant/machinery. In the case of an acquisition of an establishment, only the costs of purchasing assets from third parties can be taken into consideration. Further, immaterial assets such as costs caused by the

---

[38] Regional aid guidelines 2007–13 at para.47.
[39] Regional aid guidelines 2007–13 at para.34.
[40] Regional aid guidelines 2007–13 at para.36.

transfer of technology through the acquisition of patent rights, licences, know-how or unpatented technical know-how can be included.

Where the aid is calculated by reference to investment costs, the Commission requires that the aid beneficiary provides a financial contribution of at least 25 per cent either through its own resources or by external financing free of any public support. This was also a requirement under the regional aid guidelines 1998.[41]

The investment that is to be subsidised must be maintained in the region for a minimum period of five years. Where the aid is calculated on the basis of wage costs, the relevant jobs must be filled within three years of the completion of the works and must be maintained for at least five years.

Eligible costs when determined on the basis of investment costs

21–028   The regional aid guidelines 2007–13 incorporate detailed rules on eligible expenses which to a large extent mirror those of the regional aid guidelines 1998: acquisition costs of land, buildings and plants/machinery are fully eligible. SMEs can also benefit from a subsidisation of 50 per cent of the consultancy cost and preparatory studies linked to the investment.

The regional aid guidelines 2007–13 deviate from their predecessors in that they allow the inclusion of the acquisition costs for intangible assets (e.g. acquisition of intellectual property rights) of up to 50 per cent for large companies and 100 per cent for SMEs.[42]

Eligible costs when determined on the basis of wage costs

21–029   Aid calculated on the basis of wage costs must refer to the expected costs arising from job creation as a result of an initial investment project. The jobs created are determined by the number of employees directly employed in a particular establishment as compared with the average of the previous 12 months.[43] Any job losses must therefore be deducted.

Aid for large investment projects

21–030   The regional aid guidelines 2007–13 have incorporated the rules of the multi-sectoral framework 2002. These are discussed in Ch.14.

Cumulation of aid

21–031   As was the case under the regional aid guidelines 1998, the regional aid guidelines 2007–13 provide that the aid ceilings under the guidelines apply regardless of whether the aid is granted from different programmes or different

---

[41] Regional aid guidelines 1998, at 4.2.
[42] Regional aid guidelines 2007–13 at para.55.
[43] Regional aid guidelines 2007–13 at para.58.

sources.[44] The same applies where the aid intensity is partly based on investment costs for material or immaterial investments and partly on wage costs. In each of those instances the maximum intensity allowed must be observed.

Operating aid

There is a strong bias in the rules on regional aid, and state aid law in general, **21–032** against operating aid. Operating aid is permissible only in art.107(3)(a) regions, provided that the Member State demonstrates the existence and importance of handicaps in the regions for which operating aid is envisaged.[45] In principle, operating aid must always be temporary and reduced over time.

There is an exception that applies for the outermost regions and the least populated regions. In these regions, operating aid may be granted over a longer period of time; however, it is subject to strict limitations.[46] Operating aid to the financial services sector is excluded altogether.

Enterprise aid

Aid for newly created small enterprises is a new form of aid that the Commis- **21–033** sion created to encourage business start-ups. The background is the perceived low levels of entrepreneurial activity and even lower than average rates of business start-ups in assisted regions.

The aid is limited to small enterprises. The Commission will approve aid schemes that provide for up to a total of €2 million per enterprise in art.107(3)(a) regions and up to €1 million for small enterprises in art.107(3)(c) regions.[47] The eligible costs include all advisory, consultancy and administrative costs related to the setting up of the enterprises as well as operating costs such as interests on external finance, rental fees, energy, water, heating, taxes and depreciation.

The aid intensity is limited to 35 per cent for the first three years and 25 per cent for the following two years in art.107(3)(a) regions and to 25 per cent for the first three years and 15 per cent in the following two years for art.107(3)(c) regions.[48] These aid intensities can be increased by 5 per cent where the GDP per capita is less than 60 per cent of the EU-25 average and in regions with a population density of less than 12.5 per cent inhabitants per square kilometre.[49]

The Commission cautions that Member States should put in place means to prevent small enterprises from closing down and subsequently reopening only to be entitled to this type of aid.

[44] Regional aid guidelines 2007–13 at para.71.
[45] Regional aid guidelines 2007–13 at para.76.
[46] Regional aid guidelines 2007–13 at para.81.
[47] Regional aid guidelines 2007–13 at para.86.
[48] Regional aid guidelines 2007–13 at para.88.
[49] Regional aid guidelines 2007–13 at para.89.

Procedure: regional aid maps, notifications, General Block Exemption Regulation, simplified notification procedure

21–034   Just as under the regional aid guidelines 1998, the Commission has adopted regional aid maps under the regional aid guidelines 2007. These maps form an integral part of the guidelines and have the same binding force to the extent that they have been accepted by the Member States. The regional aid maps show the art.107(3)(a) regions as well as the statistical effect regions and the art.107(3)(c) regions for each Member State.

On October 24, 2006, the Commission adopted Block Exemption Regulation 1628/2006 on national regional investment aid[50] which abolished the notification requirement for all regional investment aid schemes that comply with the regional aid guidelines and the regional aid maps. The exemption is limited to "transparent aid", i.e. aid whose intensity can be determined as a percentage of the investment costs *ex ante* without the need for a risk assessment; therefore, aid schemes involving public shareholdings, risk capital and state guarantee are excluded. The exemption also does not apply to aid in favour of large investment projects where the total amount of aid exceeds 75 percent of the maximum amount of aid an investment with a legible expenditure of €100 million could receive (i.e. a maximum aid of €37 million in those regions where the aid ceiling would be 50 percent). Thus, major large investment projects with high aid amounts remain subject to a notification requirement.

On July 7, 2008, the European Commission adopted the General Block Exemption Regulation 800/2008,[51] which in arts 13 and 14 incorporates the provisions of reg.1628/2006 (which it repealed simultaneously) and expands the scope of application of the exemption by raising the basic aid intensities for investment and employment aid for SMEs. In addition, the General Block Exemption exempts aid for newly created small enterprises and assist in regions in line with the regional aid guidelines 2007–13.

The General Block Exemption Regulation subjects the exempted aid to a number of conditions that the Commission regards as common to all horizontal aid but which, in part, go beyond the conditions as set by the regional aid guidelines 2007–13. The most prominent condition in this respect is the finding of a specific "incentive effect" of the aid as required by art.8 of the General Block Exemption Regulation.

While notifications are no longer required for aid qualifying under the General Block Exemption Regulation, Member States are still obliged to inform the Commission of an aid scheme or individual measure[52] within 20 days of putting it into effect.

Regional aid that does not qualify for an automatic exemption under the General Block Exemption Regulation requires to be notified individually. Ad hoc

[50] O.J. L302 of November 1, 2006, p.29.
[51] O.J. L214 of August 9, 2008, p.3.
[52] Art.9(1) General Block Exemption Regulation.

regional aid below the individual notification thresholds laid down in point 64 of the regional aid guidelines for a large investment project can benefit from the notice on a simplified procedure for treatment of certain types of aid.[53]

Application of guidelines, transparency and review

The regional aid guidelines 2007–13 apply to all regional aid to be granted **21–035** after December 31, 2006. For all aid to be awarded or to be granted before 2007, the regional aid guidelines 1998 will continue to apply.[54]

In order to further increase transparency, the Commission has announced that it will, when reviewing regional aid schemes, systematically seek an undertaking from a Member State that it will publish the full text of the final aid scheme on the internet and that the internet address of the publication will be communicated to the Commission.

[53] O.J. C136 of June 16, 2009, p.3.
[54] Regional aid guidelines 2007–13 at para.105.

CHAPTER 22

ENVIRONMENTAL AID*

1. SUMMARY 22–001
2. THE EU ENVIRONMENTAL POLICY AND STATE AID LAW 22–002
   Environmental Guidelines 2008 22–004
   General Block Exemption Regulation 22–006
   Crisis measures 22–007
3. KEY PRIORITIES IN EU ENVIRONMENTAL POLICY 22–008
   Energy and climate-change policy 22–009
   Environmental protection 22–011
4. MARKET FAILURE AND JUSTIFICATION OF ENVIRONMENTAL STATE AID 22–012
   The balancing test 22–014
   Incentive effect and proportionality 22–015
5. ENVIRONMENTAL MEASURES—WHEN DO THEY CONSTITUTE STATE AID? 22–017
   Transfer of state resources 22–018
   Advantage for the undertaking 22–021
   Selectivity 22–023
   Distortion to competition and effect on trade between Member States 22–025
6. COMPATIBILITY OF ENVIRONMENTAL AID WITH THE TFEU 22–026
7. APPLICATION OF THE ENVIRONMENTAL GUIDELINES AND THE GBER 2008 22–030
   The scope of the environmental guidelines 2008 and the GBER 22–031
   Three levels of assessment 22–033
8. CALCULATING ELIGIBLE INVESTMENT COSTS—THE METHOD 22–034
   Reference investment 22–035
   Operating benefits and costs 22–037
9. AID TO GO BEYOND COMMUNITY STANDARDS OR IN ABSENCE OF SUCH STANDARDS ... 22–041
10. AID FOR THE ACQUISITION OF NEW TRANSPORT VEHICLES 22–047
11. AID FOR EARLY ADAPTATION TO FUTURE COMMUNITY STANDARDS 22–049
12. AID FOR ENVIRONMENTAL STUDIES 22–050
13. AID FOR ENERGY SAVING (INVESTMENT/OPERATING AID) 22–051
14. AID FOR RENEWABLE ENERGY SOURCES (INVESTMENT/OPERATING AID) 22–053
    Investment aid for renewable energy sources 22–054
    Operating aid for renewable energy sources 22–062
15. AID FOR COGENERATION (INVESTMENT/OPERATING AID) 22–072
16. AID FOR ENERGY-EFFICIENT DISTRICT HEATING (INVESTMENT/OPERATING AID) 22–074
17. AID FOR WASTE MANAGEMENT 22–075
18. AID FOR THE REMEDIATION OF CONTAMINATED SITES 22–077
19. AID FOR THE RELOCATION OF UNDERTAKINGS 22–079

* Melvin Könings and Ilze Jozepa

Absence of state aid in indemnification measures in line with the general system . 22–080
20. AID INVOLVED IN TRADABLE PERMIT SCHEMES/EMISSION TRADING SYSTEMS 22–081
21. AID IN THE FORM OF ENVIRONMENTAL TAX EXEMPTIONS OR REDUCTIONS 22–090
22. COMPATIBILITY OF AID UNDER ARTICLE 107(3)(B) TFEU 22–096
23. STATE AID EXPENDITURE ON ENVIRONMENTAL AID 22–097
24. OUTLOOK TO FURTHER DEVELOPMENT 22–099

1. SUMMARY

In this chapter we describe the origin and characteristics of state aid with **22–001** respect to environmental protection and provide examples of its application in practice. The principal rules are laid down in the Community guidelines on state aid for environmental protection,[1] (hereafter the environmental guidelines 2008). These guidelines are an important instrument for the implementation of the EU climate change and energy related targets. This chapter will describe the provisions of the environmental guidelines 2008 and the practical application.

We also touch upon the General Block Exemption Regulation, hereafter the GBER, which provides conditions under which environmental aid in Member States is exempted from the obligation to obtain prior approval from the European Commission.[2] Usually there are no major differences with regard to the substantive conditions under which aid may be granted under Community frameworks and guidelines (such as the environmental guidelines 2008) and the GBER. These state aid rules should impose similar conditions in order to ensure the compatibility of the aid with the TFEU; they define eligible beneficiaries, set maximum aid intensities, define eligible expenses and may include additional conditions for certain aid measures. However, the rules of the environmental guidelines 2008 do differ quite substantially from the GBER in practice. Therefore, careful examination and comparison is needed to understand the differences.

The environmental guidelines 2008 are divided into a standard assessment and a detailed assessment. A detailed assessment method for large aid amounts provided to individual enterprises has been introduced in order to allow for a deeper scrutiny of the individual cases which have the greatest potential to distort competition and trade. Schemes involving tax exemptions and reductions will only be assessed at the level of the scheme, i.e. individual enterprises will not be subject to a detailed assessment. High aid amounts have a greater risk of distorting competition and trade, and will therefore be subject to a detailed assessment. Thus, high aid amounts to individual beneficiaries must be notified individually to the Commission, even if they are granted under a scheme already approved by the Commission. The detailed assessment does not mean of course, that the envisaged state aid will be prohibited. It only means that the Commission

---

[1] Community guidelines on state aid for environmental protection [2008] O.J. C82/1.
[2] Commission Regulation (EC) No.800/2008 of August 6, 2008 declaring certain categories of aid compatible with the common market in application of arts 87 and 88 of the Treaty (General Block Exemption Regulation) [2008] O.J. L214/3.

will carefully check whether the aid is necessary and actually contributes to environmental protection without creating undue distortions of competition.

In practice, a considerable portion of environmental state aid is further provided through other state aid rules, and in particular through regional aid.[3] In such cases, it is not so much the environmental effect of the envisaged measure that leads to compatibility with the TFEU, but the regional location. Herewith, a substantial amount of environmental aid is provided through support mechanisms that fall outside the scope of the environmental guidelines 2008.

Finally, we see many support measures that fall even outside the scope of state aid law and also fall out of the scope of the State Aid Scoreboard, the monitoring instrument of the Commission. The support of green electricity in one Member State is provided through state aid instruments, whilst in others non-state aid instruments are applied. The policy effect and the effect on competition can be quite similar, yet from a state aid (monitoring) point of view there may be significant differences. Herewith, state aid statistics are rather limited for drawing firm conclusions on the effect of public policies.

In sum, there are roughly five ways of providing support—through (1) the GBER, (2) standard assessment, (3) detailed assessment under the environmental guidelines, (4) other state aid rules, and (5) non-state aid instruments.[4]

2. THE EU ENVIRONMENTAL POLICY AND STATE AID LAW

22–002   In the early years of the European Economic Community, environmental protection was not among the original common goals of peace and economic growth by free trade. However, environmental aspects were gradually taken into account and it is now recognised that environmental protection can also increase the competitive advantage of Europe by stimulating efficient use of natural resources and innovation in industry. Environmental action by the European Community began in 1972 with four successive Environmental Action Programmes.

With the Single European Act 1986, environmental protection became a recognised policy of the European Union. Furthermore, the Treaty of Amsterdam (which entered into force in 1999) recognised the principle of sustainable development as one of the particular EU aims. Under art.11 of the TFEU (ex. art.6 EC), environmental protection requirements must be integrated into the definition and implementation of the Union policies and activities, in particular with a view to promoting sustainable development. Article 191 TFEU (ex. art.174 EC) establishes the objectives and the guiding principles of the common environmental policy. Union policy on the environment shall contribute to pursuit of the following objectives:

---

[3] Guidelines on national regional aid for 2007–2013 [2006] O.J. C54/13.

[4] The authors of this chapter would like to thank Brigitta Renner-Loquenz for her valuable contribution to the previous edition.

- preserving, protecting and improving the quality of the environment;
- protecting human health;
- prudent and rational utilisation of natural resources;
- promoting measures at international level to deal with regional or world-wide environmental problems, and in particular combating climate change.

The Treaty establishes that Union policy on the environment has to aim at a high level of protection, taking into account the diversity of situations in the various regions of the Union. It has to be based on the precautionary principle and on the principles that preventive action should be taken, that environmental damage should, as a priority, be rectified at source and that the polluter should pay. It follows that competition policy and environmental policy should not be seen as contradicting, and the requirements of environmental protection need to be integrated into the definition and implementation of competition policy.

Environmental measures implemented by national, regional and local author-   **22–003**
ities can favour certain companies or the production of certain goods. Such selective measures may distort competition between companies. It is therefore important that the benefits of environmental protection measures be well balanced with the distortion of competition that they cause. EU state aid policy is aimed at avoiding disproportionate state support measures which unduly distort competition. Member States are required to notify to the Commission of all state aid measures before putting them into effect. The Commission analyses state support measures in two steps: (1) whether the measure constitutes state aid within the meaning of art.107(1) TFEU; and if so, (2) whether the positive impact of the aid measure in leading to increased environmental protection outbalances its potentially negative effects on trade and competition. If the overall balance is positive the Commission approves the aid measure.

Competition policy recognised the importance of environmental policy in the early 1970s. The first rules on granting state aid for environmental purposes were established in 1974.[5] From 1974 onwards, the Commission issued a series of policy guidelines in the form of Communications to Member States on environmental aid. Although the "polluter pays"[6] principle was internationally gaining recognition, environmental aid could be authorised mainly to help undertakings to make necessary investments to achieve certain mandatory minimum standards. However, the evolution of environmental state aid policy has limited this kind of aid substantially. In the 1990s the "polluter pays" principle was also introduced with regard to rules governing state aid. In 1994 the Commission adopted the

---

[5] Commission Memorandum on state aid in Environmental Matters [1974] SEC(74) 4264.
[6] This principle means that the costs of measures to deal with pollution should be borne by the polluter who causes the pollution. All costs associated with the protection of the environment should be included in the firm's production costs and in principle no state aid should be granted for such costs. See para.2.2, point 70(25) of the Environmental Guidelines 2008 [2008] O.J. C82/1.

Community guidelines on state aid for environmental protection, which were valid until December 31, 2000.[7] The Commission admitted, however, that full cost internalisation was not yet possible and that state support might be necessary on a temporary basis, to encourage firms to adapt to mandatory standards. The following environmental guidelines, which stressed the need to further internalise the environmental costs, entered into force on February 3, 2001 and were applicable until December 31, 2007. These former guidelines are still applicable to non-notified environmental aid which was granted during their duration.

Environmental Guidelines 2008

22–004   The current Community Guidelines on State Aid for Environmental Protection entered into force on April 2, 2008, replacing the 2001 Guidelines, and will be applicable till December 31, 2014. The guidelines clarify how the Commission intends to apply its discretion in the context of art.107(3)(c) TFEU and establish the conditions under which the Commission considers state aid for environmental protection compatible with the internal market. The aim of the guidelines is to stimulate aid measures which lead to a higher level of environmental protection than would be possible without the aid. At the same time, the Commission has envisaged that the guidelines have to contribute to effective implementation of the environmental aspects of the ambitious energy and climate change-related targets of the European Union. The "polluter pays" principle remains central.[8]

In line with the objectives set out in the State Aid Action Plan,[9] the environmental guidelines aim to ensure better targeted aid. Further, the analysis of the economic effects of environmental aid has become more relevant. The general rule is that the greater the amount and complexity of an aid measure, the greater the risk that competition can be distorted. In line with its refined economic approach, the Commission applies gradually more thorough assessment procedures on aid measures, which have a greater potential effect on trade and competition.

22–005   Compared to the previous guidelines, the current rules contain a number of new provisions, e.g. for aid for early adaptation to mandatory EU environmental standards or in the absence of such standards, aid for the acquisition of new transport vehicles which exceed mandatory standards, aid for environmental studies, aid for district heating, aid for waste management and aid involved in tradable permit schemes. Previously no guidelines were available and such measures had to be assessed directly pursuant to art.107(3)(c) TFEU.[10] Following the pattern of the environmental guidelines 2001, measures for energy saving,

---

[7] [1994] O.J. C72/3; [2000] O.J. C14/8; [2000] O.J. C184/25.

[8] Point 6 of the Environmental Guidelines 2008 [2008] O.J. C82/1.

[9] "State Aid Action Plan—Less and better targeted State aid: A roadmap for State aid reform 2005–2009" [2005] COM(2005) 107 final, points 4 and 8 of the Environmental Guidelines 2008 [2008] O.J. C82/1.

[10] See for example state aid C 61/2002, United Kingdom, *Newsprint reprocessing WRAP program* (investments undertaken by recycling firms) [2002] O.J. C283/7; state aid N 304/2003, The Netherlands, *AKZO Nobel* (relocation aid for the matters of external safety) [2005] O.J. C81/5.

renewable energy sources, including aid relating to the production of sustainable biofuels, cogeneration, the remediation of contaminated sites and the relocation of undertakings, are, with some modifications, covered by the current guidelines.

A novelty influencing the amount of aid is that aid intensities for large enterprises have gone from a range of 30 per cent–40 per cent to 50 per cent–60 per cent, whilst for small enterprises the intensities have increased from 50 per cent–60 per cent to 70 per cent–80 per cent. Furthermore, where an investment to improve on community standards or improve the level of environmental protection in the absence of standards involves eco-innovation, a further 10 per cent aid bonus may be granted. In addition, a possibility to grant 100 per cent following a competitive procedure has been introduced. Contrary to the 2001 guidelines there is no longer a bonus for aid to assisted regions or for renewable energy installations "serving all the needs in an entire community". The permissible aid is limited to a certain percentage of the eligible extra costs which are necessary to reach a higher level of environmental protection compared to a situation without any state aid.

As far as tax reductions are concerned, the guidelines maintain the possibility of long-term reductions and exemptions from environmental taxes without conditions as long as after reduction, the companies concerned pay at least the minimum valid in the EU for harmonised taxes. Where the companies do not pay at least the minimum tax level, long-term derogations remain possible but Member States must demonstrate that these derogations are necessary and proportionate.[11]

General Block Exemption Regulation

In 2008, the Commission used the possibility granted by reg.994/1998[12] to declare certain environmental aid measures compatible with the internal market for the first time. The GBER provides certain forms of environmental aid with an exemption from the obligation to notify the aid to the Commission prior to granting it.[13] In general, the GBER follows the substantive rules set out in the environmental guidelines 2008, although smaller aid intensities are permitted. As opposed to investment aid, the GBER does not cover any forms of operating aid, i.e. operating aid for the benefit of energy saving measures, renewable energy and high efficiency cogeneration. Aid to district heating, waste management, remediation of contaminated sites, relocation of undertakings and tradable emission permit schemes is excluded from the scope of the GBER.

A novelty is that with the adoption of the GBER and the environmental guidelines, the Commission has created a three-band assessment procedure for

22–006

---

[11] MEMO/08/31, January 23, 2008.

[12] Council Regulation (EC) 994/1998 of May 7, 1998 [1998] O.J. L142/1.

[13] Commission Regulation (EC) No.800/2008 of August 6, 2008 declaring certain categories of aid compatible with the common market in application of arts 87 and 88 of the Treaty (General Block Exemption Regulation) [2008] O.J. L214/3.

environmental aid measures, depending on their size and complexity. Below a certain threshold, straightforward investment aid measures can be compatible under the GBER while less straightforward and operating aid measures are subject to standard assessment under the environmental guidelines 2008. Above the threshold, the investment or operating aid measure will be subject to a detailed assessment. Fiscal aid is treated as a separate group of measures, to which specific rules apply. Exemptions or reductions from environmental taxes can either be subject to the GBER or have to be compatible with the tax-related provisions of the environmental guidelines.[14] In section 7 of this chapter, the three-band assessment model is discussed in more detail.

Crisis measures

22–007   In 2009, in response to the economic and financial crisis, the Commission introduced a Temporary Framework for state aid, which gave Member States additional possibilities for providing businesses with improved access to financing.[15] The Framework also contained measures benefiting companies that would face difficulties gaining access to finance for production of more environmentally friendly and energy efficient products, i.e. green products. The Commission stated that, under certain conditions, interest rate subsidies for investment loans could be compatible with art.107(3)(b) TFEU, which declares aid "to remedy a serious disturbance in the economy of a Member State" compatible with the internal market. The subsidised loans can be granted until December 31, 2011. The Commission has approved many schemes under this provision for most Member States.[16] Most of these schemes had a rather general character and were not specifically targeted at environmental policies. However, many of these measures will also have an important environmental effect, such as the construction of new buildings (energy saving) and investments in new machinery (cleaner technology).

3. KEY PRIORITIES IN EU ENVIRONMENTAL POLICY

22–008   The environmental guidelines 2008 are one of the instruments in order to implement the priorities of the EU policies on energy and environmental protection. Several key priorities can be identified in these two fields. They explain the logic behind certain support measures covered by the environmental guidelines

---

[14] Alexander Winterstein, Bente Tranholm, "Helping to combat climate change: new State aid guidelines for environmental protection", Competition Policy Newsletter (2008) 2, p.12.

[15] Temporary Framework for state aid measures to support access to finance in the current financial and economic crisis [2009] O.J. C83/1.

[16] See for example state aid N 11/09, France; N 72/09, United Kingdom; N 140/09, Spain; N 426/09, Germany; and N 542/09, Italy.

2008 and justify the compatibility of certain measures with the internal market.

Energy and climate-change policy

The objective of the EU energy policy is to ensure a supply of energy to all **22–009** consumers at affordable prices while respecting the environment and promoting healthy competition on the European energy market. The policy has to contribute to the targets that the European Union has set itself regarding the reduction of greenhouse gasses and tackling climate change. The European Union has committed itself to at least a 20 per cent reduction of greenhouse gas emissions by 2020 compared to 1990, a binding target of a 20 per cent share of renewable energy in the total EU Energy consumption by 2020, and a 20 per cent reduction in primary energy use compared with projected levels, to be achieved by improving energy efficiency. These form the so called "20–20–20" targets.

In the spring of 2008, the European Parliament and the Council adopted the energy and climate change legislative package proposed by the Commission, which contained instruments to implement the 20–20–20 targets. Among others, the package includes a directive which promotes renewable energy and establishes sustainability criteria for biofuels and bioliquids.[17] Also, a directive on a revised EU Emissions Trading System (ETS) for greenhouse gases[18] and a directive to promote the development and safe use of carbon capture and storage (CCS)[19] have been adopted. The role of the environmental guidelines 2008 in this package is to ensure that national aid measures intended to boost climate objectives are well targeted and that unnecessary distortion of competition is avoided.

The environmental aid legislation also has to be seen in the context of earlier **22–010** steps that the European Union has taken to reach its energy-efficiency objectives. The 2006 Commission Action Plan for energy efficiency set out measures to improve the energy performance of products, buildings and services, to improve the yield of energy production and distribution, to reduce the impact of transport on energy consumption, to facilitate financing and investments in the sector, to encourage and consolidate rational energy consumption behaviour and to step up international action on energy efficiency.[20] Besides this, the Member States have to adopt and aim to achieve an overall national indicative energy savings target

---

[17] Directive 2009/28/EC of the European Parliament and of the Council of April 23, 2009 on the promotion of the use of energy from renewable sources and amending and subsequently repealing Directives 2001/77/EC and 2003/30/EC [2009] O.J. L140/16.

[18] Directive 2009/29/EC of the European Parliament and of the Council of April 23, 2009 amending Directive 2003/87/EC so as to improve and extend the greenhouse gas emission allowance trading scheme of the Community [2009] O.J. L140/63.

[19] Directive 2009/31/EC of the European Parliament and of the Council of April 23, 2009 on the geological storage of carbon dioxide [2009] O.J. L140/114.

[20] Communication from the Commission of October 19, 2006 entitled "Action Plan for Energy Efficiency: Realising the Potential" [2006] COM(2006) 545 def.

of 9 per cent over nine years, to be reached by way of energy services and energy efficiency improvement measures.[21] The Cogeneration Directive aims at facilitating the installation and operation of electrical cogeneration plants.[22] In its Biomass Action Plan dating from 2005 the Commission set out a series of actions aimed at increasing the demand for biomass, improving supply, overcoming technical barriers and developing research.[23] Other legislative acts are already contributing to reduced energy consumption by imposing energy efficiency standards, e.g. for buildings, cars and electronic appliances.

In the spring of 2011, the Commission presented a proposal to amend the rules on taxation of energy products. The new proposal aims at restructuring the way energy products are taxed to remove current imbalances and take into account both their CO_2 emissions and energy content. The aim is to promote energy efficiency and the consumption of more environmentally friendly products.[24]

Environmental protection

22–011 EU environmental legislation has already improved the quality of the European environment significantly. However, there is still need and room for improvement. The European Commission closely monitors the main areas of environmental protection: waste, water, air, nature protection and environmental impact assessment. Regarding the targets of environmental protection, the environmental aid guidelines 2008 follow the priorities of the Sixth Environmental Action Programme, *Environment 2010: Our Future, Our Choice,* which covers the period from July 2002 to July 2012. The Action Programme represents the environmental dimension of the EU's Sustainable Development Strategy and identifies four priority areas for action: climate change, nature and biodiversity, health and the quality of life, and natural resources and waste.[25] Besides the environmental policy objectives, environmental state aid cases often coincide with fiscal policy, industry policy ("national champions"), public ownership and the introduction of new market instruments, such as green certificates and emission trading.

---

[21] Directive 2006/32/EC of the European Parliament and of the Council of April 5, 2006 on energy end-use efficiency and energy services and repealing Council Directive 93/76/EEC [2006] O.J. L114/64.

[22] Directive 2004/8/EC of the European Parliament and of the Council of February 11, 2004 on the promotion of cogeneration based on a useful heat demand in the internal energy market and amending Directive 92/42/EEC 2004/8/EC [2004] O.J. L52/50.

[23] Biomass action plan (COM(2005) 628 final) [2005] O.J. C49.

[24] Proposal for a Council Directive amending Directive 2003/96/EC restructuring the Community Framework for the taxation of energy products and electricity (COM(2011) 169/3), IP/11/468, April 13, 2011.

[25] Point 5 of the environmental guidelines 2008. See Decision 1600/2002/EC of the European Parliament and of the Council of July 22, 2002 laying down the Sixth Community Environment Action Programme [2002] O.J. L242/1. It should be noted that health is not covered by the Environmental Aid Guidelines 2008 [2008] O.J. C82/1.

4. MARKET FAILURE AND JUSTIFICATION OF ENVIRONMENTAL STATE AID

In this section, we look at the reasoning behind state aid for environmental **22–012** protection. Why is it permissible and under what conditions? According to art.11 TFEU, environmental protection requirements must be integrated into EU policies, including the internal market policy. However, internal market regulations and state aid rules in particular are sometimes seen as a hindrance to rapid deployment of government measures to improve the quality of Europe's environment. Likewise, environmental standards are often perceived as barriers to market access. The environmental guidelines 2008 aim at tackling this seeming antagonism and integrating both policy areas. The key factor is to find the right balance between the safeguarding of competition and a level playing field in the internal market on the one hand and the need to stimulate environmental protection and sustainable energy policy on the other hand.

It is common knowledge that markets do not always lead to an efficient solution and the best outcome for society. Negative (external) effects of production such as pollution arise when undertakings do not take into account the full cost of their action in their production decisions. If undertakings have no incentive to reduce their pollution or take steps to protect the environment, the costs of environmental damage which might be caused by the production are in effect borne by the society as a whole. Hence, from society's point of view, it is desirable that the price of goods reflects the real production costs, including the external costs (negative externalities). Such market failures can be tackled by ensuring that the polluter pays the full cost of the pollution. Classical examples of measures which governments can take to internalise externalities are environmental standards or environmental taxes. If the price of goods is increased due to such measures, then most probably the production and consumption of environmentally unfriendly goods and also pollution would decrease.

If the "polluter pays" principle could be fully implemented, there would be no need for further government intervention. However, it is not always the most feasible solution. Firstly, it can be technically difficult to calculate the exact cost of pollution. Secondly, the rising price of products as a result of the full implementation of the polluter pays principle may cause disturbances in the economy or run counter to, e.g. social policy objectives. Therefore, a gradual inclusion of full pollution costs in the price of products might be preferable. Furthermore, in the absence of community standards, the regulatory requirements and taxation levels may differ amongst Member States. Higher environmental standards in a Member State will lead to higher additional costs to undertakings. These cost differences for individual firms will have an effect on their investment decisions. In such situations state aid may be a solution.

In order to correct the cost disadvantage for undertakings active in their **22–013** territory, and make higher regulatory standards possible, Member States may use state aid as an instrument which will stimulate undertakings to take actions that are not mandatory. State aid can be an incentive for an undertaking in order to reduce pollution and other negative impacts on the environment, as well as reach higher level of environmental protection than required by Community standards.[26] In this way, state aid can contribute to a common objective of environmental protection. It can be a useful complementary tool in cases where the polluter pays principle cannot be applied in full, but it should not be seen as a means to relieve a polluter of the costs of its pollution, thereby countering the objective of better environmental protection.[27]

The Commission has traditionally adopted a rather favourable approach to aid for environmental protection. These kinds of environmental measures are normally granted in the form of schemes, not as individual aid. Certain types of environmental measures are considered to be less distortive of competition since they are undertaken in an area of Community interest. The objective of such schemes could include support for renewable energy, energy efficiency or waste management. A peculiar part of environmental aid is the acceptance of operating aid. The environmental guidelines 2008 allow operating aid for specific purposes. If a Member State has introduced a high level of environmental taxes in the absence of Community harmonised tax, or of a level higher than the tax envisaged by the Community legislation, then, under certain conditions ensuring an environmental counterpart, the guidelines justify the awarding of environmental tax exemptions for companies. Also for state aid to renewable energy sources, operating aid is allowed, even at large scale. This is quite rare in general state aid policy, as operating aid is generally forbidden in, for instance, regional aid to R&D projects or aid to SMEs.

In the environmental guidelines 2008 and the GBER, the Commission has identified a series of measures in respect of which it considers a priori that state aid will address a market failure hampering environmental protection or improve on the level of environmental protection. It is then up to the Member States to demonstrate that concrete measures comply with the conditions of the environmental aid rules and do not distort competition unnecessarily. Measures which fall neither under the environmental guidelines 2008 nor the GBER can still be compatible with the TFEU, but in such cases the Commission will base the assessment directly upon art.107(3)(c) TFEU.

The balancing test

22–014   In assessing whether an aid measure can be deemed compatible with the internal market, the Commission balances the positive impact of the aid measure in reaching an objective of common interest against its potentially negative side effects, such as distortion of trade and competition. The Commission has developed this "balancing test" over the years. With respect to environmental aid the test was for the first time formalised in the environmental guidelines. It follows

---

[26] Points 21 and 22 of the environmental aid guidelines 2008 [2008] O.J. C82/1.
[27] Winterstein, "Helping to combat climate change: new State aid guidelines for environmental protection", Competition Policy Newsletter (2008) 2, p.14.

the general pattern set out in the State Aid Action Plan, putting an important emphasis on the analysis of the economic effects of aid.[28] This balancing test has been applied to the design of both the environmental guidelines and the GBER, and it forms a framework for the assessment of individual cases.

The balancing test is structured as follows:

(1) Is the aid measure aimed at a well-defined objective of common interest?

(2) Is the aid well designed to deliver the objective of common interest that is to say, does the proposed aid address the market failure or other objective?

    (a) is state aid an appropriate policy instrument?

    (b) is there an incentive effect, namely does the aid change the behaviour of undertakings?

    (c) is the aid measure proportional, namely could the same change in behaviour be obtained with less aid?

(3) Are the distortions of competition and effect on trade limited, so that the overall balance is positive? If the overall balance of an aid measure is positive, it can be deemed compatible with the TFEU.[29]

Incentive effect and proportionality

In their analyses of environmental aid, Member States must examine the notions of incentive effect and proportionality of the envisaged measure. First of all it must be verified that the investment or action would not have been undertaken without any state aid. One should not forget that, for a company, investment in environmental protection can be interesting in its own right. Investment in environmentally friendly production can lead to, for example, reduced input prices and energy savings as well as increased revenues due to an environmentally friendly image. The incentive effect is identified through counterfactual analyses, comparing a situation without aid and a situation with aid. The authority which provides aid must collect supporting evidence for, e.g. a more environmentally friendly production process, or products, expected environmental effects, such as reduced pollution or faster implementation of future standards. State aid in order to meet mandatory community standards has no incentive effect, as a company would have to meet these standards in any case.[30] Possible advantages of environmental aid, like production advantages in terms of quantity and quality, have to be taken into account and will reduce the incentive effect. If the aid contributes to behaviour which goes beyond the norm on the

22–015

---

[28] State Aid Action Plan, "Less and better targeted State aid: A roadmap for State aid reform 2005–2009" [2005] COM(2005) 107 final, paras 11, 20.

[29] Point 16 of the environmental aid guidelines 2008 [2008] O.J. C82/1.

[30] Points 27–27, 171–173 of the environmental guidelines 2008 [2008] O.J. C82/1.

given market or the risks associated with the investment are higher, an incentive effect is more evident.

State aid is considered to be proportional only if the same result could not be achieved with less aid. The aid must be limited to the minimum amount necessary to achieve a certain environmental objective. The underlying principle of the guidelines is therefore to limit the eligible costs for investment aid based on the notion of the extra (net) cost necessary to meet the environmental objectives. This concept implies that, in order to establish the amount of aid, a realistic counterfactual scenario must be examined and all the economic benefits which the company gains by investing in an environmental measure, must in principle be subtracted from the additional investment costs. The calculation of eligible costs is discussed in further detail in section 8 of this chapter.

As indicated, certain economic benefits of environmental aid, such as, a green image, are difficult to quantify. Moreover, it is required under the environmental guidelines 2008 that eligible costs are reduced to the extent the operating benefits get higher. However, this effect has to be limited to generally five years after the investment has been made. Therefore the Commission limits permissible aid to a certain percentage of the eligible extra costs. An exception has been made for situations where aid has been granted after "a genuinely competitive bidding process on the basis of clear, transparent and non-discriminatory criteria." In that case the aid to the selected companies may reach 100 per cent of the eligible costs, as it is expected that the biddings will reflect all potential benefits derived from the additional investment.[31] Aid in the form of tax reductions is limited to a period of 10 years followed by a re-evaluation.

22–016   Within the framework of the guidelines, the Commission assesses the overall potential of state aid to distort competition as rather limited. The Commission pays particular attention to the possibility that an aid measure may help maintain inefficiency of companies, distort dynamic incentives (crowd out competing innovations in other Member States), create market power or exclusionary practices, artificially alter trade flows or the location of production. The lower the expected effect of aid on the environment, the more important it becomes to verify its effect on market shares and profits of competing, less environmentally friendly producers.[32] At the end of the balancing test the positive effects (enhanced environmental protection) of state aid must outweigh the negative ones (distortion of competition), in order for the measure to be justified and compatible with the TFEU.

For measures falling under the GBER, the Commission has figuratively speaking taken most of the steps of the balancing test on behalf of the authorities and included them in the design of the guidelines. Therefore, with respect to limited amounts of aid given to SME's, the analysis is straightforward: measures which comply with the criteria of the GBER are deemed to have an incentive effect, if the aided project has not started before the submission of the aid application. Aid

---

[31] Points 30–35, 174 of the environmental guidelines 2008 [2008] O.J. C82/1.
[32] Points 36–37 and para.5.2.2. of the environmental guidelines 2008 [2008] O.J. C82/1.

awarded to large enterprises, however, requires more thorough, individual scrutiny of the incentive effect.[33]

5. Environmental Measures—When do they Constitute State Aid?

Member States have introduced a wide range of national, regional and local **22–017** environmental policy measures to protect the environment. As with any measure imputable to public authorities, an environmental support measure is considered to be a state aid measure as defined under art.107(1) TFEU if it fulfils all the following four criteria:

● transfer of state resources;

● advantage for the undertaking;

● selectivity; and

● distortion to competition and effect on trade between Member States.

In some instances, the interpretation as to whether all criteria are fulfilled and thus whether or not the measure constitutes state aid is complex. The guidelines apply to state aid but do not discuss the concept of state aid, which derives from art.107(1) TFEU and from the case law of the Union Courts.[34] In recent years several rulings have had a significant impact on the application of the notion of state aid in environmental measures. Also, the decision practice of the Commission demonstrates that important national measures do not fall under the notion of state aid in the meaning of art.107(1) TFEU and thereby remain outside the competition control of the European Commission. Some examples relevant for environmental measures and the state aid criteria are given below.

Transfer of state resources

Transfer of state resources includes grants from the central, regional or local **22–018** government's budget, revenue foregone, i.e. environmental tax relief or government authorities selling (buying) environment-related goods and services or land below (above) market price. According to the case law of the Union Courts, the yield of a levy which is obligatory under national law and transits through a body established by law (which may be either public or private) constitutes state resources within the meaning of art.107 (1) TFEU when the resources remain under constant state control and therefore available to the national authorities.[35] The transfer of state resources criterion is also fulfilled in the case of a fund which is set up and managed by the state and which is financed through

---

[33] art.8.3 of the GBER.
[34] See also fn.24 of the environmental guidelines 2008 [2008] O.J. C82/1.
[35] Case C–206/06 *Essent Netwerk Noord v Aluminium Delfzijl* [2008] E.C.R. I–05497, para.70.

compulsory contributions imposed upon the electricity consumers by legislation. For example, the Netherlands set up two measures called MEP (Milieukwaliteit van de Electriciteits Productie) to support Dutch producers of renewable electricity[36] and of combined heat and power (CHP).[37] The measures were financed through a compulsory contribution by all electricity consumers in the form of an increased connection fee and the contributions were collected to the state-established fund. The Commission decided that the measures constitute state resources in the light of the Treaty and therefore the measures were considered to be state aid for Dutch energy producers.[38]

In the *PreussenElektra* case,[39] the Court of Justice decided that no transfer of state resources is involved where private electricity distributors have to pay a higher feed-in price for electricity generated from renewable sources. This landmark decision by the Court opened the door for the establishment of advantageous financial systems to support the local green electricity production, without the restraints of state aid control and procedures. The *PreussenElektra* case concerned an obligation imposed on electricity distributors in Germany to pay a higher feed-in price for electricity generated from renewable sources. The Court ruled that the measure incontestably constituted an advantage for the producers of electricity from renewable sources as they received guaranteed higher prices than would otherwise be the case. However, for a measure to rank as state aid, it was not enough that the advantage was conferred by the state. According to the Court, the advantage has to be provided directly or indirectly through state resources. Having regard to the facts of the case, the Court found that insofar as the system of electricity pricing in Germany required one private company to pay another a higher price than would otherwise have been the case, it did not involve the use of state resources and therefore could not be deemed to be state aid. The simplified model below shows how it works:

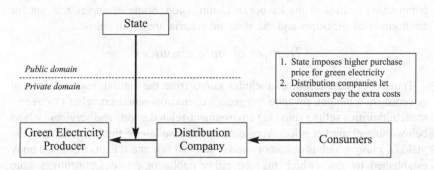

---

[36] State aid N 707/2002, The Netherlands, MEP (Stimulating renewable energy) [2003] O.J. C148/11.

[37] State aid N 708/2002, The Netherlands, MEP (Stimulating combined heat and power production (CHP)) [2003] O.J. C148/11.

[38] Meanwhile the connection fee is abolished and the scheme is financed through general budget. See state aid N 478/07, The Netherlands, Stimulating renewable energy, modification and prolongation of the MEP (N 707/02) and MEP stimulating CHP (N 543/05) [2008] O.J. C39/3.

[39] Case C–379/98 *PreussenElektra AG v Schleswag AG* [2001] E.C.R. I–2099.

The crucial element for the Court was that the German electricity pricing system required private companies to pay other companies a higher price for renewable electricity, so the resources involved were coming from private companies. There was no state body or fund established by the state to collect and redistribute the benefits as it was in the aforementioned Dutch case promoting renewable electricity and combined heat and power measures.

A negative side of the judgment was that there did not seem to be a solid **22–019** economic logic to the judgment, as the case was based upon a rather formalistic, legal distinction. Moreover, the judgment had also raised several complicated questions. For instance, what if Member States impose a purchase obligation on public enterprises? Or what if private resources in a situation similar to the *PreussenElektra* case transit through a fund that is to some extent under the control of the public authorities, e.g. for practical purposes?[40] The General Court has answered the last question in its *Iride* judgment: if the revenue from a tariff supplement is collected and managed in a special account by a public fund, the sums in question must be categorised as state resources. That is not only because they are under constant state control, but also because they are state property.[41]

Following the *PreussenElektra* ruling, the Commission decided in the course of 2002 that two non-notified German cases, which were very similar to the *PreussenElektra* case, did not constitute state aid within the meaning of art.107(1) TFEU.[42] In order to promote sustainable energy supply, Germany introduced two laws to support electricity from renewable energy sources and from combined heat and power (CHP) production. The two laws—the *Erneuerbare Energien Gesetz (EEG),* in force since April 2000, and the *Kraft Wärme Kopplungsgesetz (KWKG),* in force since May 2000—oblige operators to connect green electricity generation installations to the electricity grid, to purchase green electricity as a priority and to pay a minimum price for green electricity which is above the market price for electricity. These laws clearly give an economic advantage to operators of green electricity installations and have the potential to distort competition in a liberalised electricity market. Still, the Commission decided that these measures do not fall under the definition of state aid within the meaning of art.107(1) TFEU, based on the *PreussenElektra* judgment. Moreover, the Commission considered that since the obligations apply both to numerous private and some public net operators, the German laws could not be considered to involve any state subsidies. This seems justified as the laws treat the public and private companies in exactly the same way, and as there is no indication that state resources are transferred via the public companies to the

---

[40] In general when parafiscal levies are collected by a state fund and redistributed by the fund, the money involved becomes state property before being redistributed.

[41] Case T–25/07 *Iride SpA and Iride Energia SpA v Commission of the European Communities* [2009] E.C.R. II–00245, paras 24–28.

[42] State aid NN 27/2000, Germany, Act on granting priority to renewable energy sources [2002] O.J. C164/3 and State aid NN 68/2000, Germany, Law on the protection of electricity generated from combined heat and power [2002] O.J. C164/3.

beneficiaries. The Commission had received numerous comments on the economic and ecological effects of the laws. The question was particularly raised on the EEG's potential to overcompensate beneficiaries, in particular wind power generation. But as the Commission had decided that these German laws do not constitute state aid within the meaning of art.107(1) TFEU, it was not within the Commission's competence to take position on this question.

The two laws relevant in the case favour electricity from renewable energy sources and from CHP installations by obliging operators to purchase green electricity at minimum prices. The Commission had received several complaints alleging that the green power producers were being unfairly subsidised, but since the two laws did not amount to state aid the issues raised were regarding the competence of Germany as regards competition law.

22–020 In another application of the *PreussenElektra* ruling, the Commission decided that the issuing of green certificates for electricity from renewable sources to the electricity producers did not involve state resources and thus did not constitute state aid. By issuing the certificates, the State only certified proof of the production of green electricity. The state could not have sold these certificates to the producers and therefore did not forego revenue by granting the certificates for free.[43] Several years later, Flemish authorities introduced an obligation for the distribution grid operators to purchase the green certificates—which represent the production of 1000 kWh photovoltaic energy—when offered to them, at a certain minimum price. According to the Commission, such a purchase obligation at fixed minimum price which is directly paid between the market participants from their own resources and without any transmission via a fund or account managed by the State does not constitute state aid, as it represents a mechanism similar to the *PreussenElektra case*.[44] Where, however, the state at the same time created a fund to collect revenues from penalties raised in a green certificate system and re-distributed them under state control, the mechanism was considered to involve state resources.[45]

Other Member States have introduced parafiscal levy systems in order to finance the costs of the purchase obligation and channel these resources through a body controlled by the public authorities. Due to the nature of the finance mechanism and the public control involved, such feed-in tariff systems have been considered by the Commission to constitute state aid.[46]

Advantage for the undertaking

22–021 Most environmental support measures also constitute an advantage for the undertaking. In some cases the Commission found that there was no selective

---

[43] State aid N 550/2000, Belgium, Green electricity certificates [2001] O.J. C330/2.
[44] State aid N 254/06, Belgium, *Panneaux photovoltaïques* [2006] O.J. C314/80.
[45] State aid N 504/2000, United Kingdom, Renewables obligation and capital grants for renewables technologies [2002] O.J. C30/12.
[46] State aid NN162/a/2003, Austria, Support of electricity production from renewable sources under the Green Electricity Act (Feed-in tariffs) [2006] O.J. C221/8.

advantage. For instance, in the Dutch case concerning a waste disposal system for car wrecks, the Commission found that there is no economic advantage for the companies and therefore no state aid.[47] The aim of this waste management system is to ensure that the companies that produce and sell cars also take responsibility for a high degree of recycling of car wrecks. This measure corresponds to the "polluter pays" principle. The Dutch government has declared that all car producers and importers have to pay a charge for each car which is registered in the Netherlands. The resources are paid to car dismantling companies. As the charge for car producers and importers and premiums to the dismantling companies corresponds to the cost of recycling, the Commission found that there is no advantage and thus no state aid for car producers nor for car dismantling companies. Furthermore, indemnifications do not normally entail a selective advantage to the company insofar as they merely compensate for damage resulting from an official act, where the indemnification is the direct result of this official act. A general system for indemnifications is a necessary means to safeguard the constitutional rights of property. This was accepted by the Commission in the Dutch measure which was deigned to compensate for the relocation of car dismantling company Steenbergen because of the nuisance it caused to the surroundings.[48]

A landmark Court ruling on the existence of state aid and the advantage criterion is the *Altmark* ruling. In the case of *Altmark Trans GmbH* the Court of Justice established criteria to determine when compensation paid for a service of general economic interest does not constitute an advantage for the firm involved.[49] Following the Court ruling, the Commission published several documents on the application of the new doctrine by the *Altmark* ruling, including a Framework, a Decision and a draft Directive. After the Court ruling, some Member States tried to apply the *Altmark* criteria to environmental cases, e.g. in the Belgian case on second circuit water.[50] However, usually a compensation for a service of general economic interest should be aimed at large groups in society. Examples include citizens taking the bus in rural areas or receiving postal mail in remote areas. Of course, it is good for society when companies receive a subsidy or compensation to improve their own environmental performance. However, such aid cannot be characterised as a public service obligation. If that was to be the case, it would lead to the end of state aid control on environmental measures.

22–022

Selectivity

Where environmental measures favour a generally applicable technology rather than specific companies or sectors, the measure fails to be selective and

22–023

[47] State aid C 11/2001 (ex. N 629/2000), The Netherlands, Waste disposal system for car wrecks [2002] O.J. L68/18.
[48] State aid N575/2005, The Netherlands, Relocation car dismantling company Steenbergen [2007] O.J. C80. See para.20–019 of this chapter for a more detailed description of the case.
[49] Case C–280/00 *Altmark Trans GmbH and Regierungspräsidium Magdeburg v Nahverkehrsgesellschaft Altmark GmbH* [2003] E.C.R. I–7747.
[50] State aid N 443/2003, Belgium, Second circuit water [2006] O.J. C21/4.

therefore does not constitute state aid. The Commission considered this to be the case for a national measure supporting electricity from Combined Heat and Power production,[51] but assumed existence of aid for lack of evidence supplied by the Member State for a similar German measure.[52]

Another interesting example of a large aid scheme that was deemed to be a general measure is the Energy Investment Rebate system in the Netherlands (EIA). This tax-relief programme gives a direct financial advantage to companies that invest in energy saving equipment and sustainable energy. In the Commission decision on the off-shore wind park Q7, the Commission laid out the criteria for considering fiscal systems as general measures.[53] The Commission indicated that this measure is a general measure in accordance with points 12–16 of the Commission Notice on the application of the state aid rules to measures relating to direct business taxation,[54] hereafter business taxation notice. The measure must be open to all firms on an equal basis, in accordance with point 13 of the business taxation notice. The minimum level of eligible costs should be relatively low in order to make the measure accessible to both small and large firms. The aid should be granted without any discretionary power of the State on the basis of objective criteria, in accordance with point 13 of the business taxation notice. The scope of the measure or the practical effect should not be restricted on an individual basis. The measure should pursue a general economic policy objective (energy saving), in accordance with point 13, second indent of the business taxation notice. In such a case the Commission considers a scheme as a general measure which does not constitute state aid within the meaning of art.107(1) TFEU.

22–024   The exemption of green electricity from an energy tax was considered to be in the general nature and logic of the tax system. The energy tax was considered as an environmental tax aiming to reduce CO_2 emissions. As green electricity does not contribute to long-term CO_2, taxation of green electricity would have run counter to the environmental objective of the tax system. However, the Commission did not take a clear stance on the issue, but nevertheless also tested the compatibility of the measures.[55]

As for the selectivity criterion in state support measures, another interesting example is the *Adria-Wien Pipeline GmbH* case[56] concerning an Austrian legislative measure. The Austrian authorities provided tax exemptions from energy taxes on natural gas and electricity. Although the measure was established in the

---

[51] State aid C 18/2001 (ex. N 123/2001), United Kingdom, Climate change levy [2002] O.J. C185/2 and state aid NN 30/B/2000 and N 678/2001, The Netherlands, Zero tariff for the green electricity [2002] O.J. C30.

[52] State aid N 449/2001, Germany, Continuation of the ecological tax reform after 2002 [2002] O.J. C137/24.

[53] State aid N 266/2003, The Netherlands, Q7 offshore windpark [2003] O.J. C266.

[54] [1998] O.J. C384/3.

[55] State aid C 18/2001 (ex. N 123/2001), United Kingdom, Climate change levy [2002] O.J. C185/22. It should be noted that the measure was aimed at industrial CHPs in a large number of sectors and benefiting companies independent of their size, location or economic activity, opposite to measures which target electricity production for the grid.

[56] Case C–143/99 *Adria-Wien Pipeline GmbH* [2001] E.C.R. I–8365.

context of an overall package of measures to consolidate the budget, and exemptions were based on objective automatic criteria without the administrative authorities having any discretionary power in selecting the beneficiaries, and the measure gave benefits for a very large number of undertakings, the Court of Justice found that the measure was selective. One of the main reasons for this conclusion was that the tax exemption was applied only for undertakings whose activity was mainly in the manufacturing sector.

The Court of Justice found that the ecological considerations underlying the national legislation did not justify treating the consumption of natural gas or electricity by undertakings supplying services differently than the consumption of such energy by undertakings manufacturing goods, the damage to the environment being similar. The Court stated that undertakings in the services sector may, just like undertakings in the manufacturing sector, be major consumers of energy and incur high levels of energy taxes and therefore they are in a disadvantaged position. Based on these arguments the Court of Justice regarded these measures to be selective and to constitute state aid within the meaning of art.107(1) TFEU.

Distortion to competition and effect on trade between Member States

The General Court has confirmed that aid in a sector which is subject to **22–025** liberalisation at EU level can lead by itself to a real or potential impact on competition and trade. The General Court thereby rejected the argument that aid concerning heating through a municipal heating network is not in competition with any other products.[57] In contrast to the above, if a market is not open to competition, a state support measure does not involve state aid within the meaning of art.107(1) TFEU. For example, in the Netherlands the supply of drinking water is governed by official concession rules: within an area designated by the government, a water supply company is required to ensure the supply of drinking water. If the sole beneficiaries of an aid measure are drinking water companies, it is not considered state aid pursuant to art.107(1) TFEU.[58]

Interestingly, the Commission ruled out an effect on trade in an Italian measure in the province of Bolzano to support the creation of a network of service stations for the sale of natural gas used as motor fuel, with a view to reducing air pollution.[59] According to the Commission, in the case at hand, the geography of the area in conjunction with the intrinsically local nature of the fuel supply activity enabled the Commission to rule out the existence of competition between Italian and non-Italian service stations and the impact on intra-Union trade of the measure. The measure was not caught by art.107(1) TFEU. The Commission noted that in its decision on a Dutch state aid concerning service stations located

---

[57] Case T–303/05 *AceaElectrabel v Commission* [2009] E.C.R. II–00137, paras 70–71.
[58] State aid N 588/06, The Netherlands, *Subsidy measure vital Gelderland* [2007] O.J. C107/1.
[59] State aid N 275/08, Italy, Refuelling infrastructure for natural gas-powered vehicles (Bolzano) [2008] O.J. C256/1.

near the German border,[60] the Commission had stated that a reduction in excise duty on fuel, granted to the dealers of service stations, could involve the pass-through of state aid to oil companies linked with the dealers by exclusive purchase agreements containing a PMS clause (an obligation on the part of the oil company to compensate the dealer for unforeseen losses). The Commission argued that, by granting aid to dealers, the authorities would be in fact relieving the oil company from the obligation to compensate the dealer under the PMS clause. However, in the case at hand, the grant was designed to subsidise investment costs, not to prevent losses to dealers arising from differences in excise duties across Member States. Therefore, the PMS clause did not play any role and an impact on intra-Union trade was ruled out. This case forms an interesting precedent for local initiatives designed to stimulate a roll-out of networks of re-fuelling points for unconventional motor fuel.

6. COMPATIBILITY OF ENVIRONMENTAL AID WITH THE TFEU

22–026   State aid for environmental purposes that complies with the limits and conditions of the environmental aid guidelines can be authorised under art.107(3)(c) TFEU. Where a state aid does not fall within the scope of the environmental aid guidelines, but where it contributes to environmental protection without hampering competition to an unacceptable degree, it can be approved directly under art.107(3)(c). Several types of aid were deliberately not included in the environmental guidelines 2008, because, according to the Commission, there was not sufficient experience to set out a comprehensive guidance for the assessment of such cases. The Commission has approved a number of such national initiatives, which contributed to environmental objectives and did not distort competition to an extent contrary to the interests of the Union.

Aid involved in tradable permit schemes can be authorised under the 2008 guidelines.[61] However, the Commission endorsed a purely national scheme of the United Kingdom which fell outside the scope of the above provisions because of its innovative character and the specific objective. The United Kingdom introduced a trading system for CO_2 emissions related to energy consumption. The system, called "the Carbon Reduction Commitment" (CRC), applies to non-energy intensive sectors of economy, for example hospitals, hotels, banks, not covered by the EU Emissions Trading System. In these sectors, energy costs are so minor that the additional costs related to the introduction of the system would not be enough to trigger a change in behaviour of the companies. Therefore, in addition to all allowances in the CRC system being sold by auction, participants' environmental performance would be ranked in a performance league table and the auction revenue would be paid back to participants as a subsidy. Participants

---

[60] Decision 1999/705/EC of July 20, 1999 on the state aid implemented by the Netherlands for 633 Dutch service stations located near the German border [1999] O.J. L280/87.
[61] Points 140–141 of the environmental guidelines 2008 [2008] O.J. C82/1.

ranked on the top of the performance League Table would benefit the most from the recycling mechanism. The Commission found the measure to be in line with art.107(3)(c) TFEU because it pursued an objective of common interest in a necessary and proportionate way.[62]

The guidelines allow investment aid to firms improving on Community stan-   **22–027**
dards. This has been interpreted by the Commission as referring to standards which apply directly to firms by limiting their emission levels or waste. Aid can therefore only be granted to companies reducing their own pollution. However, where Community legislation imposes standards directly on Member States, e.g. in the packaging waste directive, it is often incumbent upon companies to take measures to allow the State to meet its obligation. Consistent with its decision-making practice,[63] the Commission included a new provision in the environmental guidelines 2008. The s.3.1.9 provides a framework for waste management, as the beneficiaries of this aid are investing in reducing pollution generated by other undertakings.

Several other types of aid measures which were formerly assessed directly under art.107(3)(c), are now included in the scope of the environmental guidelines 2008, thus codifying the decision-making practice of the Commission. In the past, the Commission authorised aid to reduce the risks of chlorine transport.[64] The aid was found to be outside the scope of the guidelines, which exclude aid for matters of safety.[65] The Commission authorised the aid based directly on art.87(3)(c) (now art.107) as it was a matter of safety for the public in general for which the justification was very similar to an environmental reasoning. The criteria established for investment aid were applied by analogy. Under the current guidelines, aid for preventive action in order to reduce the risk of environmental damage is considered an incremental part of actions designed for environmental protection. For example, relocation of firms with a view on external risk prevention is now eligible under s.3.1.11. Also, national emission trading schemes, which the Commission formerly authorised directly under art.107 TFEU,[66] are now subject to specific provisions under s.3.1.12 of the environmental guidelines 2008.

A growing group of measures assessed directly under art.107(3)(c) concerns   **22–028**
state aid for CO_2 capture, transport, storage facilities or individual elements of the Carbon Capture Storage (CCS) chain. Given the strategic importance of carbon capture technologies for the long-term goals to limit climate change, and as part of the 2008 climate and energy package for reaching the EU 2020 environmental objectives, the Commission generally encourages such projects.[67]

---

[62] State aid N 629/08, United Kingdom, Carbon Reduction Commitment (CRC) [2009] O.J. C238/1.
[63] State aid C 61/2002, United Kingdom, Newsprint reprocessing WRAP program [2002] O.J. C283/7; and N 443/2003, Belgium, Second Circuit Water [2006] O.J. C21/4.
[64] State aid N 304/2003, The Netherlands, *AKZO Nobel* [2005] O.J. C81/5.
[65] Point 6 of the environmental guidelines [2001] O.J. C37/3.
[66] State aid N 416/2001, United Kingdom [2002] O.J. C88/16; State aid N 35/2003, The Netherlands [2003] O.J. C227/8.
[67] Point 69 of the environmental guidelines [2008] O.J. C82/1.

A directive promoting the development and safe use of CCS has been adopted.[68] The Commission has set up and financially supported the world's first project network for early large-scale CO_2 capture and storage in 2010. Pilots are carried out in the Netherlands, Poland, Spain, United Kingdom, Germany and Italy.[69] Several projects are benefitting from authorised state aid measures. The Commission approved a scheme for a tender to conduct two front-end engineering and feasibility studies (FEED studies) on two industrial-scale CCS demonstration projects in the United Kingdom. The aim of the FEED studies was to reduce the technical, environmental and financial risks of the construction of a commercial-scale coal-fired power plant equipped with post-combustion CCS technology.[70] The Commission also approved €150 million aid for CCS in the Netherlands to a joint venture between E.ON and GDF Suez. The joint venture would construct a CO_2 capture plant in the Rotterdam port area with the aim to capture part of the CO_2 emitted by E.ON's coal-fired power plant and transport it to a depleted gas field in the North Sea for storage.[71]

The Commission has also approved aid to two other Dutch CCS projects. A demonstration project at Nuon's power plant in Buggenum aims at optimising the energy efficiency of CO_2 capture (pre-combustion technology) for large-scale applications in the electricity sector.[72] Another authorisation concerns a €5 million investment aid for a pipeline infrastructure to transport waste CO_2 from a bioethanol plant in Rotterdam to greenhouses in the "Zuidplaspolder". The waste CO_2 would be used to enhance crop growth, thereby reducing the current use of CO_2 in flue gases obtained through the burning of natural gas in boilers and cogeneration installations. The environmental effect of this aid measure would be realised by the change in behaviour of the greenhouses using waste CO_2 instead of the use of natural gas to produce their own CO_2. This would lead to primary energy savings on the part of the end consumers, which should in turn reduce CO_2 emissions, thus contributing to environmental protection. However, the beneficiary of the aid was a network company, which in this case does not carry out any activities of environmental protection. As the environmental guidelines apply to an action designed to prevent environmental damage by a beneficiary's own activities, the measure was deemed to be compatible directly on the basis of art.107(3)(c).[73]

22–029   The Commission has also assessed state aid for other types of infrastructure on the basis of art.107(3)(c) TFEU before. These cases concerned pipelines, transport infrastructure, and the transmission of a waste product, notably waste heat

---

[68] Directive 2009/31/EC of the European Parliament and of the Council of April 23, 2009 on the geological storage of carbon dioxide [2009] O.J. L140/114.
[69] IP/10/1140, September 17, 2010.
[70] State aid N 74/09, United Kingdom, CCS Demonstration Competition, FEED [2009] O.J. C203/2.
[71] State aid N 381/2010, The Netherlands, Aid for a CCS-project in the Rotterdam harbour area.
[72] State aid N190/2009, The Netherlands, CO_2 Catch-up pilot project at Nuon Buggenum plant [2010] O.J. C238.
[73] State aid N208/2010, The Netherlands, Aid for CO_2 delivery to Zuidplaspolder, points 39–45.

from local industry in a district heating and cooling network.[74] These previous infrastructure cases were assessed under the Treaty directly together with criteria of the Environmental Aid Guidelines which were applied by analogy.[75] As regards aid for electricity connection networks for renewable energies, aid measures for such projects do not qualify for assessment under the environmental guidelines but may be compatible with art.107(3)(c) TFEU.[76] It should be noted that aid for district heating infrastructure is explicitly excluded from the scope of the Environmental Aid Guidelines.[77] For example, the Commission authorised three Polish schemes on heating distribution networks,[78] a €26 million French aid for a district heating network in Paris[79] and an aid scheme for district heating installations and infrastructures in Veneto, Italy[80] directly under art.107(3)(c) TFEU.

Finally, a measure can be approved under art.107(3)(b) TFEU where it promotes the execution of important projects of common European interest, which are an environmental priority and have beneficial effects beyond the frontiers of the Member States concerned. However, the aid must be necessary for the project to proceed, the project must be specific, well defined and qualitatively important, and must make a clear, exemplary and clearly identifiable contribution to the common European interest. The project must be substantial in size and produce substantial environmental effects. In such cases, the Commission may authorise aid at higher rates than otherwise laid down in the environmental guidelines.[81] For example, major CCS projects could be eligible under this article. However, during the lifetime of the current guidelines, no national environmental measure has been authorised under art.107(3)(b).

7. APPLICATION OF THE ENVIRONMENTAL GUIDELINES AND THE GBER

As indicated in the introduction to this chapter, there are five ways of providing lawful support to environmental measures. We already touched upon the measures not constituting state aid and measures that were approved directly on

22–030

---

[74] State aid cases N485/2008, Austria, Aid Scheme for District Heating and Cooling Infrastructure and Cooling Installations [2009] O.J. C191/1; N584/2008, France, ADEME Aid scheme for renewables 2009/2013 [2009] O.J. C195.

[75] State aid N208/2010, The Netherlands, Aid for CO_2 delivery to Zuidplaspolder, point 46.

[76] State aid N 55/09, Poland, Constructing and modernisation of electricity connection networks for renewable energies in Poland [2006] O.J. C206/3.

[77] Point 67, fn.44 of the environmental guidelines [2008] O.J. C82/1. The exclusion applies in so far as the aid for district heating infrastructure cannot be considered compatible with the provisions related to energy saving measures of para.3.1.5 of the guidelines.

[78] State aid N 54/09, Poland, Modernisation of heating distribution networks in Poland [2009] O.J. C204/2.

[79] State aid N630/2009, France, Project T3 East Paris. Construction of a district heating network in the North-East of Paris.

[80] State aid N 494/2010, Italy, Aid scheme for district heating installations and infrastructures in Veneto [2011] C(2011) 1619.

[81] Points 147–150 of the environmental guidelines [2008] O.J. C82/1.

the basis of the TFEU. In this chapter we take a closer look at the scope of the environmental guidelines 2008 and the GBER.

The scope of the environmental guidelines 2008 and the GBER

22–031   The environmental guidelines 2008 apply to state aid for actions to protect the environment. This has to be understood as any action designed to remedy or prevent damage to physical surroundings or natural resources by a beneficiary's own activities, to reduce the risk of such damage or to lead to more efficient use of natural resources. This includes energy saving measures and the use of renewable sources of energy. The design and manufacture of environmentally friendly products, machines or means of transport which can be operated with fewer natural resources are not covered by the guidelines.[82] The guidelines also exclude actions taken with a view to improving safety or hygiene.[83]

Environmental research, development and innovation activities are covered by the state aid rules for R&D and innovation.[84] However, the market introduction (diffusion) stage of eco-innovation (acquisition of eco-innovative assets) is subject to the environmental guidelines 2008.[85] Environmental protection measures relating to air, road, railway, inland waterway and maritime transport infrastructure, including any Trans-European Transport Network projects,[86] are also excluded from the application of the environmental guidelines. State aid to environmental training activities and aid to SMEs for advisory and consultancy services in the environmental field can be granted under the GBER.[87]

The environmental guidelines 2008 apply to aid to protect the environment in all sectors governed by the Treaty, including those subject to specific Union rules on state aid (steel processing, shipbuilding, motor vehicles, synthetic fibres, transport, coal, agriculture and fisheries) unless such specific rules provide otherwise. For agriculture and fisheries, these Guidelines apply to aid for environmental protection in favour of undertakings active in the processing and marketing of products. In the field of agricultural primary production, these guidelines apply only to measures which are not already covered by the Community guidelines for state aid in the agriculture and forestry sector 2007–2013, and

---

[82] Point 60 of the environmental guidelines [2008] O.J. C82/1.

[83] This does not, however, exclude approval of such measures directly under art.107(3)(c) TFEU.

[84] Community Framework for state aid for research and development and innovation [2006] O.J. C323/1 and Commission Regulation (EC) No.800/2008 of August 6, 2008 declaring certain categories of aid compatible with the common market in application of arts 87 and 88 of the Treaty (General Block Exemption Regulation) [2008] O.J. L214/3.

[85] Point 63 of the environmental guidelines [2008] O.J. C82/1.

[86] Decision No.1692/96/EC of the European Parliament and of the Council of July 23, 1996 on Community guidelines for the development of the trans-European transport network [1996] O.J. L228/1. Decision as last amended by Council Regulation (EC) No.1791/2006 [2006] O.J. L363/1.

[87] General Block Exemption Regulation [2008] O.J. L214/3.

in the field of fisheries and aquaculture primary production they apply only where no specific provisions dealing with environmental aid exist.[88]

The environmental guidelines do not apply to stranded costs, for which the **22–032** Commission developed a separate methodology.[89] At the time the European electricity market was not liberalised, recovery of all investments by electricity undertakings was achieved through adequate tariff fixation by the states. In these circumstances, many of these undertakings invested in relatively costly electricity production plants (like green electricity plants) or for instance long-term take or pay contracts. The decrease of electricity prices following the liberalisation of the sector may compromise the recovery of many of these investments or long-term contract costs, and thus generate non-recoverable costs. Such costs are generally known as "stranded costs", which have led to several particular stranded costs cases. On July 26, 2001, the Commission adopted the "Methodology for analysing State aid linked to stranded costs" that sets out the criteria to examine whether a stranded costs compensation mechanism that constitutes state aid can be authorised under the TFEU. So far, the Commission has assessed stranded costs compensation measures in various Member States.[90] Some of the authorised measures were directly related to the policy of renewable energy, like the Dutch coal-gasification plant Demkolec[91] and the Austrian hydropower projects Freudenau, Mittlere Salzach and Obere Drau.[92] See further Ch.20 of this book.

The Commission has exempted several categories of environmental aid from the notification requirement of art.108(3) TFEU by bringing them under the GBER. The authorities must, however, follow the requirements of the GBER regarding transparency, monitoring and reporting. The exempted types of aid are open to companies operating in all sectors governed by the Treaty, including the primary production of agricultural products, as long as the aid measure in question is not covered by the agriculture block exemption regulation.[93] The GBER is in principle not applicable to fisheries and aquaculture. Both aid

[88] Point 61 of the environmental guidelines [2008] O.J. C82/1.
[89] The Methodology for stranded costs was never published on paper. It was communicated by letter to the Member States: Commission letter SG (2001) D/290869 of August 6, 2001. The Methodology is available on the website of the European Commission, DG COMP, *http://ec.europa.eu/competition/state_aid/legislation/stranded_costs_en.pdf*. [Accessed May 14, 2011].
[90] See in particular cases State aid NN 49/99, Spain, Competition transition costs scheme [2001] O.J. C268/7; State aid N 133/2001, Greece, Stranded costs [2003] O.J. C9/6; State aid N 161/2004, Portugal, Portuguese stranded costs [2005] O.J. C250/9; State aid C 43/2005, Poland, State aid awarded by Poland as part of Power Purchase Agreements and the State aid which Poland is planning to award concerning compensation for the voluntary termination of Power Purchase Agreement [2009] O.J. L83/1; State aid N 691/2009, Hungary, Hungarian stranded costs compensation scheme [2010] O.J. C213.
[91] State Aid N 597/1998—The Netherlands, *Stranded costs* [2006] O.J. C178.
[92] State Aid N 34/1999—Austria, *Compensation for stranded costs* [2002] O.J. C5.
[93] Commission Regulation on the application of Articles 87 and 88 of the EC Treaty to State aid to small and medium-sized enterprises active in the production of agricultural products and amending Regulation (EC) No.70/2001 [2006] O.J. L358/3, which covers, e.g. environmental investment aid in agricultural holdings.

schemes and ad hoc aid are eligible under the GBER, the only exception being aid in the form of environmental tax exemptions or reductions which is open only to schemes. The GBER does not apply to ad hoc individual environmental aid granted to large enterprises.[94] Such aid must be notified under the environmental guidelines 2008. Concerning the types of aid which are found to be compatible with the internal market, the GBER follows the assumptions set out in the guidelines. However, the permissible aid intensities are reduced, due to the simplified method used to calculate eligible extra investment costs. This method does not take various operational benefits into account. Operating aid is excluded from the GBER and still has to be notified. See also section 8 of this chapter.

Three levels of assessment

22–033   With the adoption of the GBER and the environmental guidelines, the Commission has created a three-band assessment procedure for environmental aid measures. The environmental guidelines are split into a standard assessment and a detailed assessment, which are applied depending on the size and complexity of the aid measures. Individual cases which have the greatest potential to distort competition and trade are subject to deeper scrutiny. Several assumptions are made: aid to SMEs is deemed to have a less distortive effect on trade than aid to large enterprises. Aid measures which favour SMEs are more likely to have an incentive effect, while this is less likely for individual ad hoc aid to large enterprises (also within approved schemes) for which the incentive effect has to be demonstrated explicitly. The bands are applied as follows:

1. The GBER covers straightforward investment aid measures below €7.5 million per company per project. Aid to SME's is deemed a priori to have an incentive effect when the aided project has not started before the aid application. For large enterprises receiving aid within the framework of a scheme, an additional analysis of the incentive effect must be submitted. Ad hoc individual environmental aid granted to large enterprises is excluded.

2. A standard assessment procedure covers aid measures which presumably can address a certain market failure or improve the level of environmental protection, which are proportionate and have a limited negative impact on competition and trade. This applies to investment and operating aid measures which comply with the requirements of s.3 of the environmental guidelines 2008 and remain under the thresholds of detailed assessment or are granted to installations of a production capacity below a certain threshold. Aid to SMEs is deemed a priori to have an incentive effect when the aided project has not started before the submission of an aid application. The incentive effect has to be demonstrated for all other

---

[94] art.1.1 of the General block exemption Regulation [2008] O.J. L214/3.

projects, for instance aid to large enterprises of less than €7.5 million per company per project or operating aid for energy saving measures of less than €5 million over a five year period.

3. Due to a higher risk of distortion of competition, a detailed assessment is applied to the following aid measures:

- measures covered by the GBER but subject to individual notification requirements;
- investment aid exceeding €7.5 million for one undertaking (including aid within approved schemes);
- operating aid for energy saving exceeding €5 million per company in 5 years;
- operating aid for the production of renewable electricity and/or combined production of renewable heat if resulting renewable electricity generation capacity exceeds 125 MW;
- operating aid for biofuel production if resulting production exceeds 150 000 tonnes per year;
- operating aid for cogeneration if resulting production from cogeneration exceeds 200 MW;
- operating aid to new plants producing renewable energy, regardless of the above mentioned thresholds, when the amount is calculated on the basis of the external costs avoided. The external costs avoided represent a monetary quantification of the additional socio-environmental damage, for example air pollution with CO_2 or other pollutants, that society would experience if the same quantity of energy were produced by a production plant operating with conventional forms of energy.

Tax exemptions and reductions of environmental taxes are subject to an independent set of rules described in Ch.4 of the environmental guidelines 2008 and are not subject to detailed assessment. However, other types of environmental aid provided in the form of fiscal aid and exceeding the above thresholds are assessed according to the requirements of a detailed assessment.[95]

8. CALCULATING ELIGIBLE INVESTMENT COSTS—THE METHOD

In order to be compatible, environmental aid must be limited to the minimum amount needed to achieve the level of environmental protection sought. Therefore, eligible costs for investment aid are based on the notion of the extra (net) cost necessary to meet the environmental objectives. This concept implies that, in order to establish how much aid can be granted, all the economic benefits which a company gains from an investment must, in principle, be subtracted from

22–034

---

[95] Fn.59 of the environmental guidelines [2008] O.J. C82/1.

the additional investment costs.[96] Hence, eligible costs must be limited to the extra investment costs necessary to achieve a higher level of environmental protection than required by the mandatory EU standards and are calculated in two steps. First, the extra costs directly related to environmental protection have to be defined by reference to the counterfactual situation, where appropriate. Second, operating benefits have to be deducted and operating costs have to be added.[97]

Reference investment

22–035   In some cases, the extra costs can easily be established. For example, when an existing production process is upgraded for the benefit of improved environmental performance and necessary parts or machinery, e.g. a particulate filter, can clearly be identified in the total investment. The installation of a filter presumably does not lead to more production or direct economic benefits except that of less emissions. Where such clear distinction is not possible, the investment costs have to be compared with the costs of a reference investment in the absence of state aid, the so called "counterfactual". The correct counterfactual is the cost of a technically comparable investment that provides a lower degree of environmental protection (corresponding to mandatory Union standards, if they exist) and that would credibly be realised without aid ("reference investment"). Technically comparable investment means an investment with the same production capacity and all other technical characteristics (except those directly related to the extra investment for environmental protection) in, for example, a conventional plant or an upgrade to a state-of-the-art technology.

Concerning aid for renewable energy sources, the guidelines specify further that the reference investment is a conventional power plant or a conventional heating system with the same capacity in terms of effective production of energy.[98] Investment in waste management has to be compared to a conventional production, which does not involve the same capacity.[99] The environmental guidelines 2008 contain an important addition, which clarifies that such a reference investment must, from a business point of view, be a credible alternative to the investment.[100] Obviously, the choice of a reference investment has a direct effect on the amount of permissible state aid and can be a subject of a discussion.[101] Correct identification of the counterfactual scenario is also key to determining to what extent a state aid measure has an incentive effect in changing the behaviour of a firm and improving its environmental performance.

[96] Point 31 of the environmental guidelines [2008] O.J. C82/1.
[97] Point 80 of the environmental guidelines [2008] O.J. C82/1.
[98] Point 105 of the environmental guidelines [2008] O.J. C82/1.
[99] Point 130 of the environmental guidelines [2008] O.J. C82/1.
[100] Point 81 of the environmental guidelines [2008] O.J. C82/1.
[101] For example, see correspondence between the European Renewable Energy Council (EREC) and the European Commission on reference plants for renewable energy projects, May/June 2010, *http://www.ner300.com/?p=75*. [Accessed April 20, 2011].

In some cases, the Commission has accepted a national measure without the   **22–036**
comparison with a reference investment.[102] To allow the Commission to take into
account the "no investment" scenario, a Member State would have to demonstrate that this is a credible alternative with consistent information and evidence.
For the analysis of aid to off-shore wind park Borkum, "Alpha Ventus", Germany did provide information regarding the internal decision-making process
which demonstrated that the beneficiary company and its shareholders would
have not carried out the project jointly and in the same timeframe without the aid.
This non-investment would have corresponded to a slower off-shore wind technology development and exploitation and subsequently a lower level of environmental protection, and accordingly would less serve the common interests of the
European Union. The Commission considered that the project would have a
strategic value for both the beneficiary and the European Union, and found it
compatible with the TFEU.[103]

The investment may take the form of a tangible asset, e.g. land, buildings,
plant, equipment, strictly where necessary to meet environmental objectives and
investments in production methods with a view to protecting the environment.
Also investment in intangible assets, e.g. technology transfer through the acquisition of operation licences or know-how purchased on market terms, is
permissible.[104]

Operating benefits and costs

Generally eligible costs must be calculated net of any operating benefits and   **22–037**
operating costs related to the extra investment for environmental protection and
arising during the *first five* years of the life of the investment concerned. This
means that operating benefits must be deducted and operating costs may be added
to the extra investment costs. Slight variations on this calculation method apply
to investment aid for energy savings and aid for waste management.[105]

Operating benefits cover cost savings or additional ancillary production
directly linked to the extra investment for environmental protection. Benefits of
additional ancillary production can arise from, for instance, the sale of residual
products, e.g. ashes, or extra heat production, when the production via the
renewable technology is carried out at a relatively higher temperature. Also
benefits accruing from other support measures whether or not they constitute
state aid (operating aid granted for the same eligible costs, feed-in tariffs or other
support measures) are counted. By contrast, proceeds flowing from the sale by

---

[102] State aid N 56/2003, Germany, Environment aid for Villeroy & Boch [2005] O.J. C305/18; State
aid N 72/2004, Italy, Environmental aid Caffaro [2005] O.J. C100/27; State aid N 455/06, Italy,
Promotion of District Heating [2007] O.J. C152/2; State aid N 234/2008, Sweden, Investment
aid to solar heating [2009] O.J. C2; State aid N 66/2009, Sweden, State aid scheme for solar cells
[2009] O.J. C160.
[103] State aid N 521/2008, Germany, Aid to Offshore Wind Park Borkum, "Alpha Ventus", October
27, 2010, points 111–116.
[104] para.2.2, point 70 (22) and (23) of the environmental guidelines [2008] O.J. C82/1.
[105] Points 82, 98 and 131 of the environmental guidelines [2008] O.J. C82/1.

the undertaking of tradable permits issued under the European Trading System are not included. Operating costs refer to additional production costs flowing from the extra investment for environmental protection.

22–038   A good example of the calculation of the eligible costs and the influence of the operating benefits and costs is the *Q7 offshore windpark* case.[106] In June 2003, the Dutch authorities notified an individual state aid measure to the European Commission for an off-shore wind park called Q7. For this particular project, the Commission had to apply, for the first time since the adoption of the environmental guidelines 2001, a detailed calculation method in order to calculate the eligible costs of the project. The same method applies to state aid covered by the current 2008 guidelines. The objective of the notified individual aid measure was to facilitate the creation of the project Offshore Wind Park Q7 in the North Sea at some 23 kilometres out of the coast, west of the city of IJmuiden in the Netherlands. In order to calculate the eligible investment costs of the project the Commission had to take a lot of different cost factors into account, including a reference investment. In this case the reference investment for renewable energy plants or any other electricity generation investment is a Steam and Gas facility (better known as STAG). Next was the variable "benefits of capacity increase". This variable does not apply to a newly created off-shore wind park project.

As far as the variable "costs savings" is concerned, the Commission first took into account the fact that wind is free. The wind park will therefore benefit from fuel savings as compared to the reference investment, i.e. the value of the natural gas that would have to be purchased to produce the same amount of energy in a STAG facility during the first five years of the investment. Another important cost saving engendered in the first five years was the net present value of the operating aid to the wind park. The Dutch authorities provided operating aid to cover extra costs of green electricity production, which are usually related to higher investment costs.

When calculating eligible costs of the investment, the operating aid must be taken into account as well, in order to prevent double support. Next, the Dutch authorities showed that extra operating costs related to the construction and maintenance of the Q7 wind park compared with a STAG largely outweigh the benefits that are obtained from the cost savings (fuel savings and operating aid). The Commission identified the following extra operating costs:

- maintenance and inspection costs, based on several preventive visits per wind turbine per year and unscheduled repairs as required;

- non-maintenance repairs, which cover the deductibles under the insurance policy, which have to be paid by the owners. That means a deductible for each loss or damage to property above sea level and for loss of or damage to property below sea level;

---

[106] State aid N 266/2003, The Netherlands, Q7 off-shore windpark [2003] O.J. C266.

- insurance costs, covering machine breakdown and damage by external causes ("property damage") as well as business interruption[107];

- administration and management;

- decommissioning costs, which is a reservation the investor has to put aside in order to pay for the removal of all the windmills after 20 years and the cleaning of the site;

- environmental monitoring during the operation of the wind park. The monitoring programme will last five years and includes research into the effects on bird life, sea mammals, benthos and fishes, geomorphology of the seabed, visual impact and monitoring of drifters and near accidents.

Furthermore, the Dutch authorities provided evidence that, contrary to a STAG reference facility, an off-shore wind park has to be phased into production gradually. Herewith, there is a foregoing of electricity market revenue. The financial costs of the project, i.e. depreciation and interest, were excluded from the assessment of the additional operating costs. The reasoning was that the investment aid to the project aims to reduce the additional need for capital for the investor at the start of the project. If the additional financial costs during the project were included in the calculation of the maximum amount of investment aid at the start of the project, the assessment would result in double counting additional investment costs.   **22–039**

The additional operating costs were calculated by taking the net present value of the annual operating costs of the reference investment in the first five years as a starting point, then adding the net present value of the fuel costs of the reference investment in the first five years, deducting the net present value of the aforementioned operating costs for the off-shore wind park Q7 in the first five years and the net present value of the foregone revenues to Dutch authorities to phased production in the first five years. This calculation resulted in the net present value of the balance of cost savings in the first five years. The net present value of the balance of cost savings in the first five years of the operating of the off-shore wind park Q7 turned out negative. In other words, both the investment costs of the project and the gross operating costs were higher than the reference investment The Q7 project also benefited from another investment support scheme, the aforementioned EIA scheme. The Commission considers this measure as a general measure. The EIA support will, however, diminish the financing needs by the investor of this project. Therefore, the Dutch authorities had to deduct this support from the initial investment when calculating the eligible costs of the project.

---

[107] As far as business interruption is concerned, only the part of the insurance premium that concerns the lost market revenue of electricity is taken into account. The part that covers the loss of possible operating aid, i.e. green certificates related to a tax reduction and direct operating aid, is excluded from this calculation.

Other examples of eligible costs calculations can be found in more recent Decisions of the Commission, for instance, on German aid to Top Gas Recycling project,[108] Austrian support for co-generation of electricity and heat,[109] a Dutch guarantee facility for geothermal energy,[110] or Italian incentives for investments in solar energy on decommissioned landfills.[111]

22–040   In order to calculate eligible costs of environmental investment aid under the GBER the same extra cost approach of the guidelines must be followed. However, given the complexity of the calculation method, the Commission allows for a simplified approach under the GBER. The extra investment costs can be calculated without taking into account operating benefits, cost savings or additional ancillary production and without taking into account operating costs engendered during the life of the investment. The aid intensities are accordingly lower than the ones provided by the guidelines. No operating aid is allowed under the GBER.[112] Operating aid is restricted under the environmental guidelines 2008 to energy-saving measures, support for renewable energy, including production of bio-fuels, and cogeneration. The conditions prescribing the limits of such aid are described in sections 13, 14, 15 and 16 of this chapter.

9. Aid to go Beyond Community Standards or in Absence of Such Standards

22–041   An important part of state support measures concerns individual incentives to companies to achieve higher level of environmental protection. Often undertakings lack incentives to invest in activities and production which go beyond mandatory standards if the cost of doing so exceeds the benefit for the undertaking. In such cases state aid may be granted. Aid for undertakings which goes beyond Community standards or which increases the level of environmental protection in the absence of community standards, is hence compatible under the environmental guidelines 2008.[113]

Aid for undertakings which goes beyond Community standards or which increases the level of environmental protection in the absence of Community standards should provide individual incentives to companies to achieve higher environmental protection. Normally, an undertaking does not have an incentive to go beyond mandatory standards if the cost of doing so exceeds the benefit for the undertaking. In such cases state aid may be granted to give an incentive to

---

[108] State aid N 450/2009, Germany, Top Gas Recycling (TGR) Project—Aid to ArcelorMittal Eisenhüttenstadt GmbH [2010] O.J. C94.

[109] State aid N 295/2008, Austria, Investment aid for co-generation of electricity and heat (CHP)— Mellach of Verbund Austrian Thermal Power GmbH and Co KG [2010] O.J. C154.

[110] State aid N 442/2009, The Netherlands, Guarantee facility for geothermal energy [2009] O.J. C284.

[111] State aid N 6/09, Italy, Incentives for investments in solar energy on decommissioned landfills (Piedmont Region), May 29, 2009.

[112] Points 48–52 of the environmental guidelines [2008] O.J. C82/1.

[113] ss.1.5.1. and 3.1.1 of the environmental guidelines [2008] O.J. C82/1.

undertakings to improve environmental protection. In accordance with the Community objective to support eco-innovation, more favourable treatment can be accepted for eco-innovation projects that address the double market failure linked to the higher risks of innovation, coupled with the environmental aspect of the project. Aid for eco-innovation thus aims to accelerate the market diffusion of eco-innovations.

In order to be compatible, the investment aid measures have to meet several conditions regarding their target, aid intensity and eligible costs. Moreover, such aid must have an incentive effect. The aid must target two situations:

- the investment has to enable the beneficiary to increase the level of environmental protection resulting from its activities by going beyond the applicable Community standards, irrespective of the presence of mandatory national standards that are more stringent than the Community standard; or

- the investment has to enable the beneficiary to increase the level of environmental protection resulting from its activities in the absence of Community standards.

Aid may not be granted where improvements bring undertakings into compliance with Community standards already adopted and not yet in force. However, this exception does not concern aid for early adaptation to future standards and for the acquisition of new transport vehicles, which are discussed in the following paragraphs.[114]

A community standard is defined as a mandatory Community standard setting **22–042** the levels to be attained in environmental terms by individual undertakings. Also the obligation under Directive 2008/1/EC (the so called IPPC Directive) to use the best available techniques are considered as a Community standard.[115] Norms or targets set at EU level which are binding for Member States but not for individual undertakings are not deemed to be "Community standards" within the meaning of environmental state aid.

The intensity of investment aid to go beyond Community standards or in the absence of such standards must not exceed 50 per cent of the eligible investment cost, except when the investment aid is granted in a genuinely competitive bidding process on the basis of clear, transparent and non-discriminatory criteria. Such a tender must effectively ensure that the aid is limited to the minimum necessary for achieving the environmental gain. Such a bidding process must be non-discriminatory and provide for the participation of a sufficient number of undertakings. In addition, the budget related to the bidding process must be a binding constraint in the sense that not all participants can receive aid. Finally, the aid must be granted on the basis of the initial bid submitted by the bidder, thus

[114] Points 74–75 of the environmental guidelines [2008] O.J. C82/1.
[115] Directive 2008/1/EC of the European Parliament and of the Council of January 15, 2008 concerning integrated pollution prevention and control [2008] O.J. L24/8.

excluding subsequent negotiations. Under such conditions, the aid intensity may amount to up to 100 per cent of the eligible investment cost.[116]

22–043   The guidelines allow several bonuses. Where the investment concerns the acquisition of an eco-innovation asset or the launching of an eco-innovation project, the aid intensity may be increased by 10 percentage points. Eco-innovation means all forms of innovation activities aimed at significantly improving environmental protection. Eco-innovation includes new production processes, new products or services, and new management and business methods, whose use or implementation is likely to prevent or reduce the risks for the environment, pollution and other negative impacts of resources use, throughout the life cycle of related activities. Minor changes or improvements, an increase in production or service capabilities through the addition of manufacturing or logistical systems, changes in business practices, workplace organisation etc., which are very similar to those already in use are not considered eco-innovation. Also, ceasing to use a process, capital replacement or extension and various cyclical changes fall outside the definition of the environmental guidelines 2008, alongside trading of new or significantly improved products.[117]

The bonus for eco-innovation applies provided that the following conditions are fulfilled:

a)   the eco-innovation asset or project must be new or substantially improved compared to the state-of-the-art in its industry in the Community. The novelty could, for example, be demonstrated by the Member State on the basis of a precise description of the innovation and of market conditions for its introduction or diffusion, comparing it with state-of-the-art processes or organisational techniques generally used by other undertakings in the same industry;

b)   the expected environmental benefit must be significantly higher than the improvement resulting from the general evolution of the state-of-the-art in comparable activities. It can be demonstrated using quantitative parameters comparing eco-innovative activities with non-innovative activities; and

c)   the innovative character of these assets or projects involves a clear degree of risk, in technological, market or financial terms, which is higher than the risk generally associated with comparable non-innovative assets or projects. This risk could be demonstrated by the Member State, for instance, in terms of costs in relation to the undertaking's turnover, time required for the development, expected gains from the eco-innovation in comparison with the costs, or probability of failure.[118]

---

[116] Points 76–77 of the environmental guidelines [2008] O.J. C82/1.
[117] Point 70 of the environmental guidelines [2008] O.J. C82/1.
[118] Point 78 of the environmental guidelines [2008] O.J. C82/1.

Another group profiting from bonuses is the SMEs. The aid intensity may be increased by 10 percentage points for medium-sized enterprises and by 20 percentage points for small enterprises. The bonuses for eco-innovation and SME's are complementary. For example, a small enterprise which sets up an environmental investment project involving eco-innovation could be entitled to a maximum of 20 per cent plus 10 per cent bonus in addition to the basic 50 per cent, thus adding up to 80 per cent aid for the extra environmental costs of the investment.[119]

In line with the general principles of environmental aid, the eligible costs are **22–044** restricted to the extra investment costs necessary to achieve a higher level of environmental protection, as discussed in section 8 of this chapter. In the case of investments aiming at obtaining a level of environmental protection higher than Community standards the counterfactual situation in order to determine the part of the investment directly related to environmental protection should be chosen as follows:

- where the undertaking is adapting to national standards adopted in the absence of Community standards, the eligible costs consist of the additional investment costs necessary to achieve the level required by the national standards;

- where the undertaking is adapting to, or goes beyond, national standards which are more stringent than the relevant Community standards or goes beyond Community standards, the eligible costs consist of the additional investment costs necessary to achieve a level of environmental protection higher than the level required by the Community standards. The cost of investments needed to reach the level of protection required by the Community standards is not eligible; and

- where no standards exist, eligible costs consist of the investment costs necessary to achieve a higher level of environmental protection than that which the beneficiary would achieve in the absence of any environmental aid.[120]

The GBER provides an exemption from the prior notification obligation for lesser amounts of environmental investment aid which goes beyond Community standards. The two main differences between art.18 GBER as opposed and Ch.3.1.1 of the environmental guidelines 2008 are the aid intensity and the way eligible costs are calculated. The amount of aid is restricted to 35 per cent of the eligible costs plus 10 per cent for medium-sized companies or plus 20 per cent for small undertakings. No bonus is provided for eco-innovative measures. The eligible costs can be determined without taking operating benefits into account.[121]

[119] Point 79 of the environmental guidelines [2008] O.J. C82/1.
[120] Point 84 of the environmental guidelines [2008] O.J. C82/1.
[121] art.18 of the GBER.

22–045   In 2010, the European Commission authorised an investment aid of €30 million granted by Germany towards ArcelorMittal Eisenhuettenstadt GmBH's "Top Gas Recycling" (TGR) project. TGR is an innovative process that enables the separation of CO_2 from other emission gases as they come out of the furnace and recycles the CO_2-free emissions for the production of steel. The project notified by Germany concerned only the separation of CO_2 without transport and storage. The use of TGR would reduce CO_2 emissions by 16 per cent as compared to existing state-of-the-art technology, as steel makers use less coke. This was the first ever application of TGR technology on an industrial scale.[122] The case was treated as an aid in the absence of environmental standards. Although the blast furnace of the beneficiary was an installation subject to the EU Emission Trading Scheme (ETS), i.e. the ETS Directive, the ETS imposes on companies an obligation to present to the authorities a certificate on each ton CO_2 emitted.[123] The Commission considered that this requirement was not equal to a Community standard because ETS does not oblige individual companies to reduce their emissions to a certain level, but only requires them to cover actual emissions with tradable permits. Companies may choose how they satisfy the obligation.

The Commission's investigation found that the aid was necessary as without the aid ArcelorMittal Eisenhueteenstadt would not translate the technology into an industrial-scale application. The assessment took into account that even if the CO_2 price, currently around €14/t, would double, it would still be too low to trigger an investment in TGR technology. It was envisaged that companies participating in a ULCOS consortium, representing in total approximately 90 per cent of steel production within the European Union, would share among them the technological know-how from the TGR project for free. Therefore the know-how of the project could be seen as a public good benefiting the ULCOS partners collectively. The Commission concluded that the environmental benefits triggered by the aid would largely outweigh potential distortions of competition and approved it. Because of the amount of aid, the measure fell under the detailed assessment of the environmental guidelines 2008. The foreseen aid amount of €30.18 million equalled 55.2 per cent of the net extra costs of €54.7 million, and in line with the environmental guidelines 2008, did not include the CO_2 costs savings. As the investment concerned the launching of an eco-innovation project, the aid intensity could be increased by 10 per cent above the 50 per cent which is normally allowed for aid for going beyond applicable EU standards according to points 76 and 78 of the guidelines.

In 2010, the Commission authorised a Dutch subsidy scheme on air quality improvement in the province of Noord-Holland.[124] In this scheme local authorities and private investors can receive grants for activities that lead to an

[122] State aid N 450/2009, Germany, Top Gas Recycling (TGR) Project—Aid to ArcelorMittal Eisenhüttenstadt GmbH [2010] O.J. C94.

[123] Directive 2003/87/EC of the European Parliament and of the Council of October 13, 2003 establishing a scheme for greenhouse gas emission allowance trading within the Community and amending Council Directive 96/61/EC [2003] O.J. 275/32.

[124] X 411/09 [2010] O.J. C20/02.

improvement beyond the standards on the emissions of fine dust (PM10) and nitrogen dioxide (NOx). Projects are assessed on the impact of a project expressed in kilogrammes reduction of substances PM10 and NOx, cost effectiveness, degree of innovation, economic perspective and broad application of the project, with a maximum grant per project of €250,000. The scheme fulfilled the conditions for investment aid for undertakings to go beyond environmental standards (arts 18 and 19 GBER).

In the past, the Commission also took a hybrid approach to environmental aid. **22–046** In 2001, the Commission decided that the French measure concerning a fund for environmental investments and sustainable energy called FIDEME,[125] was in line with the provisions of the environmental guidelines, but also with the Community guidelines on state aid for small and medium-sized enterprises (SMEs)[126] and the Commission communication on state aid and risk capital.[127] This measure was, in particular, aimed at providing risk capital for small and medium-sized green electricity production companies.

In Germany, a measure promoting investments to create new methods of production which have special environmental relevance was introduced in 2003.[128] The measure aims at resource preservation and creation of more efficient production processes as well as production with less environment-impairing consequences. The scheme focuses on: (1) the introduction of innovative production processes and an efficient use of natural resources and the reduction of emissions and waste; (2) the substitution and avoidance of environment-impairing materials used in the production process; (3) limiting volatile organic compounds in the production process; (4) pilot projects aiming at reducing the energy consumption in the production process; and (5) innovative plants for the treatment and use of waste. The aid is granted in the form of grants or soft loans and is limited to investments aiming to achieve significantly higher levels of environmental protection than is required by current standards. The loans run over a period of 13 years at an interest of three per cent per year. Taking into account the present reference rate of Germany of 5.06 per cent, results in an aid intensity of a loan of 13.4 per cent gross. If the market interest changes considerably, the interest rate may be raised up to a maximum 10 per cent per year. The maximum aid intensity is 30 per cent gross of the eligible costs. If the investment is carried out by SMEs, an extra 10 percentage points gross of aid is allowed which will then amount to a maximum of 40 per cent. Furthermore, in regions which are eligible under art.107(3)(c) TFEU, firms may receive additional aid of five per cent gross. The eligible costs concern tangible investments and spending on technology transfer. Eligible costs are only the extra investment costs which are necessary to meet environmental objectives in order to exceed existing mandatory standards. To achieve this, the beneficiaries are obliged to calculate

---

[125] State aid N 354/2001, France, FIDEME (Fonds d'investissement de l'environnement et de la maîtrise de l'énergie) [2002] O.J. C59.
[126] [1996] O.J. C213.
[127] [2001] O.J. C235/3–11.
[128] N 559/2002 [2003] O.J. C76/27.

separately, according to an objective and transparent method, those extra invest-ment costs necessary to meet the environmental objectives. Excluded from support are costs not attributable to environmental protection as for example costs for the basic investment. The conditions of the programme were in accor-dance with the environmental guidelines 2001 (in particular points 29–30 and 34–37).

10. Aid for the Acquisition of New Transport Vehicles

22–047 Transport is a major source of overall greenhouse gas emissions (about 30 per cent) as well as local pollution by particulates, NOx and SOx, and a major contributor to poor air quality in urban areas. Environmental aid for the use of cleaner modes of transport is therefore encouraged. The general rules set out for environmental investment aid apply to aid for undertakings improving on Com-munity standards or increasing the level of environmental protection in the absence of Community standards in the transport sector. However, state aid provided for the acquisition of new transport vehicles for road, railway, inland waterway and maritime transport, can also be provided in order to comply with Community standards already adopted. Such aid is permissible when vehicles are acquired before the entry into force of the standards.[129]

For vehicles already in use, operations with an environmental objective in the transport sector are eligible as far as the extra net cost approach is observed alike the investment aid to go beyond Community standards. State aid may be given in order to upgrade existing means of transport to meet higher standards if these standards entered into force after such vehicles were procured and put to use or if no environmental standards apply to the particular means of transport.

One has to bear in mind that community standards refer to norms for individ-ual undertakings. For example, there is currently no obligation under EU law for individual undertakings to use a certain share of electric or zero emission cars. The obligations under the Renewable Energy Directive 2009/28/EC of 10 per cent renewable energy in transport is directed at Member States and contains no binding rules as to what share individual undertakings have to attain. Conse-quently, the aid for the acquisition of electric vehicles is not bound by Commu-nity standards.[130] It should be noted that (indirect) aid to dealers and manufacturers of environmentally "more friendly" cars, must be assessed directly under art.107(3)(c) TFEU since the scope of the environmental guide-lines 2008 excludes the production or manufacturing of environmentally friendly means of transport.

22–048 The GBER allows for state aid for purchases of transport vehicles under the same conditions as those which apply to this type of aid under the environmental

---

[129] Point 85 of the environmental guidelines [2008] O.J. C82/1.
[130] State aid N 386/2010, Denmark, Pilot scheme for purchase of electric vehicles, March 8, 2011.

guidelines 2008. However, due to the absence of a notification obligation, the maximum aid intensity is restricted to 35 per cent of the extra investment cost necessary to reach environmental standards which go beyond the level required by the Community standards. An additional 20 per cent and 10 per cent can be added to aid for small and medium-sized enterprises respectively.[131]

The Commission has authorised several aid schemes for the acquisition of new, environmentally friendly transport vehicles pursuant to the environmental guidelines 2008. In 2009 the Commission authorised a British state aid scheme for purchasing low-carbon buses. The main objective of the scheme is to reduce the CO_2 emissions produced by public buses through the introduction of a "Green Bus Fund". Buses capable of achieving at least a 30 per cent reduction in CO_2 emissions compared to standard buses are eligible to apply for the aid scheme. The scheme does not provide for any particular technology however. The grants will be awarded on the basis of a bidding procedure. Priority will be given to bids requiring the lowest grant per vehicle. The beneficiaries will be bus operators. A budget of £30 million was made available from 2009 to 2011 under the scheme. The Commission found the scheme compatible with EU state aid rules, and in particular with its Communication on environmental protection. In 2009, the Commission also approved a German aid scheme to promote use of hybrid buses in public transport of €20 million (N 457/09, November 19, 2009). Finally, the Commission authorised a similar Danish scheme for DKK 15 million (approximately €2 million) of public funding for a pilot program incentivising the purchase of electric cars. The scheme supports projects aimed at testing and test-running electric vehicles under realistic conditions and is expected to increase the number of wholly electrically propelled cars in Denmark, thereby decreasing the dependency on fossil fuel and reducing carbon dioxide emissions. The Commission concluded that the aid is unlikely to lead to significant distortions of competition in the internal market and is therefore compatible with the EU Treaty rules in view of the environmental benefits it will bring about.

11. Aid for Early Adaptation to Future Community Standards

Environmental aid legislation does not authorise aid to assist undertakings to comply with existing Community standards, because such aid would not lead to a higher level of environmental protection. However, state aid may significantly speed up the implementation of newly adopted Community standards which are not yet in force. State aid for this purpose is compatible under the environmental guidelines 2008, provided that the investment is implemented and finalised at least one year before the entry into force of the standard.[132] **22–049**

---

[131] art.19 of the GBER.
[132] Points 45 and 87 of the environmental guidelines [2008] O.J. C82/1.

It is important to distinguish between the adoption of new compulsory standards and the date of entry into force of such standards. The environmental guidelines 2008 specifically refer to the entry into force of such standards. Two counting periods are distinguished: higher aid intensities are permitted for aid when the implementation and finalisation takes place more than three years before the entry into force of a new standard. The maximum aid intensities are 25 per cent for small enterprises, 20 per cent for medium-sized enterprises and 15 per cent for large enterprises. The aid intensity is 20 per cent for small enterprises, 15 per cent for medium-sized enterprises and 10 per cent for large enterprises if the implementation and finalisation take place between one and three years before the mandatory date of entry into force. The eligible costs for this type of aid must be limited to the extra investment costs necessary to achieve the level of environmental protection required by the Community standard compared to the existing level of environmental protection required prior to the entry into force of this standard.[133]

The GBER limits the beneficiaries of aid for early adaptation to future Community standards to SMEs which implement the investment at least one year before the entry into force of such standards. The aid intensity is limited to 15 per cent of the eligible costs for small enterprises and 10 per cent for medium-sized enterprises if the implementation and finalisation take place more than three years before the date of entry into force of the standard and 10 per cent for small enterprises if the implementation and finalisation take place between one and three years before the date of entry into force of the standard. The eligible costs are determined in the same manner as the extra investment costs under the environmental guidelines 2008.[134]

12. AID FOR ENVIRONMENTAL STUDIES

22–050 Companies tend to underestimate the possibilities and benefits related to energy saving and renewable energy, which leads to under-investment. Therefore the Commission is in favour of state aid which stimulates studies into investments aimed at achieving a level of environmental protection going beyond Community standards, as well as studies on energy saving and production of renewable energy, which illuminate the potential of environmental investment.

Aid to companies for studies directly linked to investments for the purposes of achieving standards under the conditions set out in s.3.1.1, of achieving energy saving under the conditions set out in s.3.1.5, and of producing renewable energy under the conditions set out in s.3.1.6 of the environmental guidelines 2008 is considered compatible with the internal market if the conditions set out in Ch.3.1.4 of the guidelines are fulfilled. This also applies in cases where, following the findings of a preparatory study, the investment under investigation is not

---

[133] Points 45 and 88 of the environmental guidelines [2008] O.J. C82/1.
[134] art.23 of the GBER.

undertaken. The aid intensity for environmental studies is restricted to 50 per cent of the costs of the study. Where the study is undertaken on behalf of an SME, the aid intensity may be increased by 10 per cent for medium-sized enterprises and by 20 per cent for small enterprises.[135] Remarkably, state aid for the purpose of environmental studies exempted under the GBER, art.24, is subject to similar conditions and aid intensities as the aid permitted under the environmental guidelines 2008. Schemes awarding aid to environmental studies are often incorporated in general (environmental) aid schemes. For example, the umbrella English Environmental Aid Scheme contains a sub-scheme dedicated to environmental studies which contribute towards the implementation of European and British energy-efficiency and emission reduction targets as well as studies in the field of promotion of energy from renewable energy sources. The scheme relates to the provisions of GBER art.24 allowing up to the maximum available thresholds.[136]

13. AID FOR ENERGY SAVING (INVESTMENT/OPERATING AID)

This type of aid addresses the market failure linked to negative externalities by creating individual incentives to attain environmental targets for energy saving and for the reduction of greenhouse gas emissions. At Community level the aim has been set to achieve at least a 20 per cent reduction in greenhouse gas emissions by 2020 compared to 1990. Furthermore, Member States are obliged to adopt and aim to achieve an overall national indicative energy savings target of 9 per cent over nine years in accordance with Directive 2006/32/EC of the European Parliament and of the Council of April 5, 2006 on energy end-use efficiency and energy services and repealing Council Directive 93/76/EEC. State aid may be appropriate where the investments resulting in energy savings are not compulsory pursuant to applicable Community standards and where they are not profitable, that is to say where the cost of energy saving is higher than the related private economic benefit. In the case of small and medium-sized enterprises, more favourable support may be needed to take into account the fact that these enterprises often underestimate the benefits related to energy savings over long periods, which leads to their under-investment in energy saving measures.

Investment and/or operating aid enabling undertakings to achieve energy savings will be considered compatible with the common market within the meaning of art.107(3)(c) of the TFEU, if the following conditions are fulfilled. For investment aid, the aid intensity must not exceed 60 per cent of the eligible investment costs. Where the investment aid for energy saving is to be given to SMEs, the aid intensity may be increased by 10 percentage points for medium-

22–051

---

[135] Points 91–93 of the environmental guidelines [2008] O.J. C82/1.
[136] For example, State aid X491/2009, United Kingdom, *One North East and Yorkshire Forward Environmental Action Scheme 2009—2013*; State aid X760/2009, *Welsh Assembly Government Environmental Protection Scheme*; and State aid X97/2010—South East England Development Agency, General Block Exemption Scheme 2010–2013.

sized enterprises and by 20 percentage points for small enterprises. Where the investment aid is granted in a genuinely competitive bidding process on the basis of clear, transparent and non-discriminatory criteria, effectively ensuring that the aid is limited to the minimum necessary for achieving the maximum energy saving, the aid intensity may amount to up to 100 per cent of the eligible investment cost. Such a bidding process must be non-discriminatory and must provide for the participation of a sufficient number of undertakings. In addition, the budget related to the bidding process must be a binding constraint in the sense that not all participants can receive aid. Finally, the aid must be granted on the basis of the initial bid submitted by the bidder, thus excluding subsequent negotiations.

22–052 The eligible costs must be limited to the extra investment costs necessary to achieve energy savings beyond the level required by the Community standards. The calculation of extra costs must respect the following rules:

(a) the part of the investment directly related to energy saving must be identified in accordance with the general rules laid down in points 81 and 83 of the environmental guidelines 2008;

(b) a level of energy saving higher than Community standards must be identified;

(c) identifying operating benefits/costs: eligible costs must be calculated net of any operating benefits and operating costs related to the extra investment for energy saving and arising during the first three years of the life of this investment in the case of SMEs, the first four years in the case of large undertakings that are not part of the EU CO_2 Emission Trading System and the first five years in the case of large undertakings that are part of the EU CO_2 Emission Trading System. For large undertakings this period can be reduced to the first three years of the life of this investment where the depreciation time of the investment can be demonstrated not to exceed three years.

Also operating aid for energy saving is allowed under the environmental guidelines 2008, but only if the following conditions are met:

(a) the aid is limited to compensating for net extra production costs resulting from the investment, taking account of benefits resulting from energy saving. In determining the amount of operating aid, any investment aid granted to the undertaking in question in respect of the new plant must be deducted from production costs;

(b) the aid is subject to a limited duration of five years.

In the case of aid which is gradually reduced, the aid intensity must not exceed 100 per cent of the extra costs in the first year but must have fallen in a linear fashion to zero by the end of the fifth year. In the case of aid which does not decrease gradually, the aid intensity must not exceed 50 per cent of the extra costs.

14. AID FOR RENEWABLE ENERGY SOURCES (INVESTMENT/ OPERATING AID)

This type of aid addresses the market failure linked to negative externalities by creating individual incentives to increase the share of renewable sources of energy in total energy production. Increased use of renewable energy sources is one of the Community's environmental priorities as well as an economic and energy related priority. It is expected to play an important role in meeting the targets for the reduction of greenhouse gas emissions. At Community level, in the Communication from the Commission to the European Council and the European Parliament—an energy policy for Europe—the target has been set for renewable energy to account for 20 per cent of overall EU energy consumption by 2020.   **22–053**

State aid may be justified if the cost of production of renewable energy is higher than the cost of production based on less environmentally friendly sources and if there is no mandatory Community standard concerning the share of energy from renewable sources for individual undertakings. The high cost of production of some types of renewable energy does not allow undertakings to charge competitive prices on the market and thus creates a market-access barrier for renewable energy. However, due to technological developments in the field of renewable energy and to gradually increasing internalisation of environmental externalities, the cost difference has shown a decreasing trend over the past years, thus reducing the need for aid.

Investment aid for renewable energy sources

For investment aid the aid intensity must not exceed 60 per cent of the eligible investment costs. Where the investment aid for renewable energy sources is to be given to SMEs, the aid intensity may be increased by 10 percentage points for medium-sized enterprises and by 20 percentage points for small enterprises. Where the investment aid is granted in a genuinely competitive bidding process on the basis of clear, transparent and non-discriminatory criteria, effectively ensuring that the aid is limited to the minimum necessary for delivering maximum renewable energy, the aid intensity may amount to up to 100 per cent of the eligible investment cost. Such a bidding process must be non-discriminatory and must provide for the participation of a sufficient number of undertakings. In addition, the budget related to the bidding process must be a binding constraint in the sense that not all participants can receive aid. Finally, the aid must be granted on the basis of the initial bid submitted by the bidder, thus excluding subsequent negotiations.   **22–054**

For renewable energy, eligible investment costs must be limited to the extra investment costs borne by the beneficiary compared with a conventional power plant or with a conventional heating system with the same capacity in terms of the effective production of energy. The eligible costs must be calculated net any operating benefits and operating costs related to the extra investment for renewable sources of energy and arising during the first five years of the life of this investment.

The Commission has decided upon several investment aid measures for renewable energy sources under the 2001 environmental guidelines. In 2000 the British authorities introduced a scheme called "Renewable Obligation and Capital Grants for Renewable Technologies."[137] In this scheme, amongst others, capital grants were introduced with an aid intensity of 40 per cent for off-shore wind projects, biomass and energy crop power projects and small-scale biomass heat and CHP projects. The Commission assessed these grants using the criteria of the environmental guidelines. As all criteria were met, this measure was approved by the Commission in November 2001.

In December 2001 the Commission decided that a Greek scheme for investments in sustainable energy was compatible with the EC Treaty.[138] The objectives of this scheme are: (1) to contribute to the security of energy supply and the reduction of the dependence of Greece and the European Union on imported forms of primary energy through the diversification of energy supply sources; (2) to enhance the economic activity and regional development of Greece; and (3) to protect the environment, especially by reducing greenhouse gases. The instrument of this aid measure is to provide grants through a tender procedure. The approval of this scheme by the Commission was based on a mixture between the Guidelines on National Regional Aid[139] and the environmental guidelines. Most projects in this scheme are to be expected to be eligible under the criteria of the aforementioned regional aid guidelines. These criteria are often wider than the criteria of the environmental guidelines. However, some of the Greek energy investment projects may not satisfy all the conditions set out in regional aid guidelines. In these cases, the aid granted will respect the conditions set out in the environmental guidelines; hence the measure was approved by the Commission.

22–055   In state aid case N 234/2008, the Swedish authorities notified an investment aid project for heating installations and solar panels. The Commission stated that the solar heating installation must always coexist with an alternative heating installation capable of supplying virtually all the heat needed during some periods of the year. The Commission thus found that the entire investment cost of the solar heating system constitutes an extra investment cost for the investor, whose cost for investing in a conventional heating system will remain unchanged and can thus not be deducted from the eligible costs. Another practical example was another Swedish state aid case, N 66/2009, state aid scheme for solar cells. According to the Swedish authorities, the most credible alternative would, in this

---

[137] State aid N 504/2000, United Kingdom, Renewable Obligation And Capital Grants For Renewable Technologies [2002] O.J. C30/15.
[138] State aid N 323/2001, Greece, Aid For Investment In Sustainable Energy [2002] O.J. C98/32.
[139] [1998] O.J. C74/9.

case, be to instead buy electricity from the grid. This is because the aid supports small-scale electricity production in housings or buildings for other individual purposes, which are connected to the grid (the connection is a requirement for receiving aid under this scheme and cannot be included in the eligible costs). Electricity production is normally not carried out in such buildings. Thus, in this particular case all investment costs minus the operational net benefits during the first five years following the investment are eligible for aid. Also in this case no reference investment was brought into the calculation of eligible costs.

In June 2003, the Dutch authorities notified the Commission, pursuant to art.88(3) ECT, of their intention to grant aid to the project Offshore Wind Park Q7 under an approved state aid scheme called VAMIL.[140] Under the appropriate measures under art.88(1) ECT, proposed at the moment of the introduction of the aforementioned Community guidelines on state aid for environmental protection (see also point 76 of these guidelines), Member States are obliged to notify in advance any individual case of investment aid granted under an authorised scheme where the eligible costs exceed €25 million and where the aid exceeds the gross grant equivalent of €5 million. This was the case for the present notification.

The objective of the notified individual aid measure was to facilitate the creation of the project Offshore Wind Park Q7 in the North Sea at some 23 kilometres out of the coast, west of the city of IJmuiden in the Netherlands. The off-shore wind park will consist of 60 windmills with an individual capacity of two Megawatts each and an estimated total yearly electricity production of approximately 438,000 MWh. Until now, most off-shore wind parks in Europe have been installed in near-shore areas with a water depth of 5 to 15 metres. The biggest potential for off-shore wind energy in the North Sea, however, lies at distances of more than 20 kilometres from the coastline with water depths of 20–30 metres. Q7 is one of the first off-shore wind parks that will be situated at 23 kilometres from the coastline in water depths of 20–25 metres.

The estimated total initial investment costs of this project are €275 million at **22–056** 2002 prices. The aid will be provided through the aforementioned VAMIL scheme, a fiscal free (accelerated) depreciation mechanism. Each year a ministerial decision adopts the list of environmental investments that will be eligible for VAMIL that year.[141] This aid scheme foresees the possibility for the investments on the list to apply for free depreciation. This means that the investor is allowed to depreciate the full investment in the first year, which leads to interest savings and liquidity advantages for the investor. The notified state aid through this VAMIL free deprecation is €16.5 million. Apart from the investment aid through the free fiscal depreciation (VAMIL), the off-shore wind park Q7 will also benefit from other support instruments. The public support (not necessarily state aid within the meaning of art.107(1) TFEU) will be taken into account when

---

[140] The VAMIL regime was approved Commission decision July 6, 1994, state aid N 262/94 [1994] O.J. C267.

[141] *Aanwijzingsregeling willekeurige afschrijving milieu investeringen 2002*, published in the Staatscourant December 21, 2001, No.248, p.51.

calculating the eligible costs for the envisaged VAMIL aid. The off-shore wind park Q7 will also benefit from a fiscal measure stimulating environmental investments called EIA (*energie investeringsaftrek*). This tax-relief programme gives a direct financial advantage to companies that invest in energy-saving equipment and sustainable energy.[142] For the off-shore wind park Q7 this benefit is appreciated at €49.8 million. The Dutch authorities indicated that this measure is a general measure in accordance with points 12–16 of the Commission Notice on the application of the state aid rules to measures relating to direct business taxation,[143] hereafter business taxation notice. Therefore the Dutch authorities did not notify the EIA measure under the state aid rules and procedures. The EIA measure is open to all firms on an equal basis, in accordance with point 13 of the business taxation notice. The minimum level of eligible costs is relatively low (€450 per energy saving investment and €2000 per year), which makes the measure very accessible to both small and large firms. The EIA aid is granted without any discretionary power of the State on the basis of objective criteria, in accordance with point 13 of the business taxation notice. Therefore, the scope of the measure or the practical effect cannot be restricted on an individual basis. The EIA measure applies without distinction to all energy saving goods; at least some of these goods may be largely used by undertakings in all sectors of the economy. The EIA measure pursues a general economic policy objective (energy saving), in accordance with point 13, second indent of the business taxation notice. On the basis of this information the Commission agreed that the EIA measure is a general measure which does not constitute state aid within the meaning of art.107(1) TFEU.

At the time the case was notified, the primary support mechanism for green electricity in The Netherlands was an operating aid scheme called MEP. Previous Dutch support instruments were aimed at stimulating *demand* through a reduced tariff in the energy tax for renewable electricity for consumers, a feed-in tariff rebate for producers of renewable energy and a provision in the energy tax for CHP electricity producers. The MEP subsidy scheme aims at stimulating *supply*, through operating aid for a fixed period of a maximum of 10 years, with a total budget of €2.503 million. On March 19, 2003 the Commission authorised this support mechanism.[144] The MEP decision is an interesting example of the application of the provisions of the environmental guidelines on operating aid to renewable energy. For the first time, the Commission took a detailed decision on this kind of operating aid. The Commission's decisions on MEP confirmed that operating support systems that are financed through a fund, constitute state aid within the meaning of art.107(1) TFEU. In this respect, the Court jurisprudence has established three cumulative criteria in order to assess the involvement of

---

[142] 55% of the annual investment costs of energy saving equipment (purchase costs and production costs) are deductible from the fiscal profit over the calendar year in which the equipment was procured. After tax assessment the measure usually results in approximately 19% of the total investment costs (depending on the level of income or corporate tax).

[143] [1998] O.J. C384/3.

[144] State aid N 707/2002, MEP, Stimulating Renewable Energy [2003] O.J. C148/11.

state resources where money is transferred by a fund.[145] The fund must be established by the State, it must be fed by contributions imposed or managed by the State and it must be used to favour specific enterprises. The MEP fund is ordered by the State and managed by the State company TenneT. The fund is financed through a compulsory contribution by all Dutch electricity consumers, imposed by the State, in the form of an increased connection fee. This increase in the connection fee is equal for all consumers, thus irrespective of whether it is a large consumer or a small one, it amounts to €34 in 2003.[146] The scheme will only favour the producers of renewable electricity and producers of CHP electricity in The Netherlands who are feeding that electricity into the Dutch electricity grid. The MEP operating aid for wind at sea consists of a MEP subsidy of €0.068 per kilowatt-hour produced. The off-shore wind park Q7 will benefit from this operating aid for a guaranteed period of 10 years. Thirdly, green electricity was also supported in the Netherlands through a tax reduction in the regulatory energy tax (REB). The operating aid for producers of green electricity under the fiscal regime of 2003 is €0.029 per kilowatt-hour of green electricity produced.

The Commission examined the proposed aid measure in the light of **22–057** art.107(3)(c) TFEU and, in particular, in the light of the aforementioned environmental guidelines. Hereto, the Commission had to calculate whether the aid provided under the VAMIL state aid scheme respects the maximal aid intensities possible under the environmental guidelines. The aid intensity is a typical state aid monitoring and assessment instrument, i.e. the notified amount of aid divided by the eligible costs of the project.

In order to calculate the eligible investment costs of the off-shore wind project at hand, several cost factors have to be taken into account. First of all, a reference investment. According to the Dutch authorities, the reference investment in the Netherlands for renewable energy plants or any other electricity generation investment is a Steam And Gas facility (STAG). The investment cost of this type of installation is approximately €64,294 per yearly produced GWh. For a capacity in terms of effective production of energy of 438 GWh (capacity of Q7), the reference cost is thus €28,160,772.

Next is the variable "benefits of capacity increase". This variable does not apply to this new created off-shore wind park project. As far as the variable "costs savings" are concerned, the Dutch authorities first take account of the fact that wind is free. The wind park will therefore benefit fuel savings. The value of the natural gas that would have to be purchased to produce the same amount of

---

[145] See Case C–173/73 *Italy v Commission* [1974] E.C.R. 709; and Case C–78/76 *Steinike v Germany* [1977] E.C.R. 595.

[146] The increased connection fee, although set at a fixed price, could be viewed as a parafiscal levy on the whole electricity consumption of a consumer, hence including a part of which is imported. However, the Commission argued that the deduction, even for large consumers, of the proportion of the corresponding fee to the percentage of imported electricity, would remain minimal, considering the amount of the fee (€34), and disproportionate to the administrative burden imposed.

energy in a STAG facility during the first five years of the investment is calculated at €7,778,784 per year, which leads to a net present value of €35,490,599 in the first five years.[147]

Another important cost saving engendered in the first five years is the net present value of the operating aid to the wind park. The aforementioned operating aid (MEP subsidy and the tax reduction) is provided by the Dutch authorities to cover extra costs of green electricity production, which are usually related to higher investment costs (in this project nearly tenfold). When calculating eligible costs of the investment, the operating aid must be taken into account as well, in order to prevent double support. The net present value of the MEP subsidy and the tax reduction engendered in the first five years is €163,871,513. Apart from the regular fuel costs, i.e. natural gas, the reference investment (STAG plant) has annual operating costs of €844,823, which corresponds to a net present value of €3,854,494 in the first five years. In order to calculate the additional operating costs of the off-shore wind park Q7, these costs will be deducted from the envisaged operating costs of Q7.

22–058   The Dutch authorities have shown that extra operating costs related to the construction and maintenance of the Q7 wind park compared with a STAG largely outweigh the benefits that are obtained from the cost savings (fuel savings and operating aid). The following operating costs for Q7 were identified as:

- maintenance and inspection costs, based on several preventive visits per wind turbine per year and unscheduled repairs as required;

- non-maintenance repairs, which covers the deductibles under the insurance policy, which have to be paid by the owners of Offshore Wind Park Q7. That means a deductible for each loss or damage to property above sea level and for loss of or damage to property below sea level;

---

[147] In the case of the off-shore wind park Q7 all net present value calculations are based on the date December 31, 2003 (last day of the first year of the investment) and a reference and discount rate of 4.8%, in accordance with Commission notice on the method for setting the reference and discount rates [1997] O.J. C273/3.

The latest rates are available at *http://europa.eu.int/comm/competition/state_aid/others/refer ence_rates.html.*

The net present value of the fuel savings is calculated as follows:

Year:	X = Fuel costs conventional plant
1	X / (1,0480)
2	X / (1,0480)^2
3	X / (1,0480)^3
4	X / (1,0480)^4
5	X / (1,0480)^5
	Total fuel savings in the first 5 years

- insurance costs, covering machine breakdown and damage by external causes ("property damage") as well as business interruption[148];

- administration and management;

- decommissioning costs, which is a reservation the investor has to put aside in order to pay for the removal of all the windmills after 20 years and the cleaning of the site;

- environmental monitoring during the operation of the wind park. The monitoring program will last five years and includes research into the effects on bird life, sea mammals, benthos & fishes, geomorphology of the seabed, visual impact and monitoring of drifters and near accidents.

Furthermore, the Dutch authorities have provided evidence that, contrary to a STAG reference facility, an off-shore wind park has to be phased into production gradually. Herewith, there is a foregoing of electricity market value.

It should be noted that the financial costs of the project (i.e. depreciation and interest) are excluded from the assessment of the additional operating costs. The reason is as follows: the investment aid to the project aims to reduce the additional need for capital for the investor at the start of the project. When the additional financial costs during the project would be included in the calculation of the maximum amount of investment aid at the start of the project, the assessment will result in double counting additional investment costs.

The additional operating costs are calculated by taking the net present value of **22–059** the annual operating costs of the reference investment in the first five years as a starting point, then adding the net present value of the fuel costs of the reference investment in the first five years, deducting the net present value of the afore-mentioned operating costs for Q7 in the first five years and the net present value of the foregone revenues Dutch authorities to phased production in the first five years. This calculation will result in the net present value of the balance of cost savings in the first five years. The net present value of the balance of cost savings in the first five years of the operating of Q7 turned out negative.[149] In other words, both the investment costs and the gross operating costs of the project are higher than the reference investment. This outcome sits uneasily with point 60 of the environmental guidelines, and its statement that "unlike most other renewable sources of energy, biomass requires relatively less investment but brings higher operating costs". The environmental guidelines seem to indicate that usually renewable energy sources, like wind energy, require higher investment, but lower operating costs, although this is not specifically required. As the calculation of the eligible costs of this wind park contains commercially sensitive

---

[148] As far as business interruption is concerned, only the part of the insurance premium that concerns the lost market revenue of electricity is taken into account. The part that covers the loss of green certificates (related to the tax reduction) and MEP subsidy is excluded from this calculation.

[149] Please note that this is without taking into account the operating aid (MEP and the tax reduction) yet.

information, we will use a fictional amount for the balance of cost savings: €30 million.

As regards the variable "benefits of ancillary production", the Commission notes that there are no other products produced than electricity and that there is thus no ancillary production in this case. As indicated before, the Q7 project will also benefit from another investment support scheme, the aforementioned EIA scheme, which results in a direct benefit of €49,791,269. In order to calculate the eligible costs of the Q7 project, the Commission applied the following calculation method:

Initial investment costs[150]	€285.193.670	
Reference investment	€ 28.160.772	(−)
Operating aid (MEP and REB tax)	€163.871.513	(−)
Balance of costs savings	€ 30.000.000[151]	(−)
Other investment support (EIA)	€ 49.791.269	(−)
Eligible costs	€ 73.370.116[152]	

Therefore, the notified aid of €16,552,831 would represent 22.5 per cent[153] of the eligible investment costs, which remains under the maximum aid intensity of 40 per cent that can be allowed for investments in renewable energy projects under point 32 of the environmental guidelines 2001. In July 2003 the Commission decided that the notified VAMIL aid to Offshore Wind Park Q7 respects the provisions of the Community Guidelines on state aid for environmental protection.[154] Therefore the Commission considered that the aid measure falls under the derogation provided for in art.107(3)(c) TFEU and authorised the aid.

22–060 This calculation method of eligible costs has been applied by the Commission mutatis mutandis in similar projects on electricity production from renewable energy sources. The calculation of the eligible costs of the project at hand has shown that many cost variables and other state aid and support measures have to be taken into account. The assessment has also shown the complicated relationship between investment aid assessment and operating aid assessment, which are clearly interdependent. The Dutch public support to this specific project in the first five years of more than €230 million shows a vigorous commitment by the Dutch authorities to stimulate investments in electricity production from renewable energy sources. Nevertheless, it should be noted that the reference investment of this project is valued under €30 million. On top of that, the net operating costs of this project are higher than the net operating costs of the reference investment.[155] Finally, the operating aid will continue after five years for (at least) another five years, herewith increasing the total public support to this

---

[150] i.e. the aforementioned total investment costs, namely €275,000,000 (prices of 2002), increased by 3.7% (discount rate used by the investor), which results in €285,193,670.
[151] NB: this is a fictional variable.
[152] NB: this is a fictional variable.
[153] NB: this is a fictional aid intensity.
[154] State aid N 266/2003 [2003] O.J. C266.
[155] Net meaning here without taking into account financing costs (depreciation and interest).

specific project to more than €300 million. Is it therefore fair to conclude that the case at hand has shown that the off-shore wind power industry still has quite a number of hurdles to jump before being a competitive player on the electricity market? As far as the constraints of EU state aid law is concerned, the provisions of the EC Treaty and the environmental guidelines seem to be wide enough to grant considerable amounts of public support.

Another interesting approach would be to calculate the eligible costs under the method of the General Block Exemption Regulation. This calculation is rather theoretical, as the wind park concerned is very large and would not fit under the GBER, notification under the environmental guidelines is compulsory. An important feature under the GBER is that the extra costs and benefits in the first five years will not have to be taken into account. Article 23 of the GBER explains the calculation method for renewable energy. Environmental investment aid for the promotion of energy from renewable energy sources is allowed under the GBER under lower aid intensities than the environmental guidelines 2008 (45 per cent instead of 60 per cent), but the eligible costs shall be only the extra costs borne by the beneficiary compared with a conventional power plant or with a conventional heating system with the same capacity in terms of the effective production of energy, without taking account of operating benefits and operating costs. This is a small text with a huge implication. For the Q7 wind park, this would mean that the eligible costs would be:

22–061

Initial investment costs[156]	€285,193,670	
Reference investment	€ 28,160,772	(–)
Other investment support (EIA)	€ 49,791,269	(–)
Eligible costs	€207,241,629	

This would (theoretically) result in three times more eligible costs than the calculation under the environmental guidelines 2001 (similar to environmental guidelines 2008). The reduction of the maximum aid intensity from 60 per cent (environmental guidelines 2008) to 45 per cent (GBER) is easily compensated. Again, this calculation is rather theoretical, as the Q7 case is quite large and must be notified under the environmental guidelines. But it is not so complicated to cut a wind park into various parts or single wind mills, herewith opening up the possibility to apply the GBER.

Operating aid for renewable energy sources

Following the adoption of the Kyoto Protocol to the UN Framework Convention on Climate Change, adopted in December 1997, many Member States have introduced support measures in order to stimulate the production and use of renewable energy sources. The instruments that Member States use for this

22–062

---

[156] i.e. the aforementioned total investment costs, namely €275,000,000 (prices of 2002), increased by 3.7% (discount rate used by the investor), which results in €285,193,670.

support are very different and range from familiar investment subsidies to more novel forms of operating aid, for instance tax reductions and exemptions, and green certificate and emission trading schemes.

Most support measures are aimed at the electricity market. Essentially, the electricity market can be divided into various parts. First, there is electricity production, where electricity producers are active, but also owners or traders in renewable energy sources. The next part is electricity distribution. High voltage grid operators (often public companies) are usually connected to the producers of electricity. Distribution companies bring the electricity from the high voltage grid to the consumers and often these distributors also levy environmental and consumer taxes before selling the electricity to the consumers. Finally, there is the demand side, i.e. the energy consumers like households and companies.

The European Commission has encountered various measures by the Member States to support the production and use of green electricity. These measures are with regard to various parts of the electricity market as described above. As far as production is concerned, direct grants[157] are given to producers. In some Member States producers can sell green certificates in order to (partially) cover their extra production costs.[158] In Germany producers of green electricity get a fixed higher price from the distributor for their electricity produced.[159] The Dutch authorities introduced a measure that allows distributors to put a rebate on their energy tax payments, which they then have to fully transfer to a producer of green electricity.[160] As far as distribution is concerned, the Netherlands intro-duced in 2000 tax exemptions in the national energy tax for green electricity.[161] The Dutch energy tax is levied by the distributor. Thus, a Dutch distributor can decide to pass on the financial benefit of the tax exemptions fully to the consumer, or to keep some benefit for his/her own extra costs to sell green electricity (marketing) or profits. The United Kingdom introduced a similar climate change levy on the non-domestic use of energy. Included in the measure were reduced rates and even total exemption from the levy for a period of 10 years for various beneficiaries.[162] When a part or all of the financial benefit of such an energy tax exemption is passed on to the consumer, the latter will also be beneficiary of the support measure.

---

[157] State aid N 304/2000, The Netherlands, CO_2 Reduction Plan [2000] O.J. C328/32.

[158] State aid N 550/2000, Belgium, Green Electricity Certificates (Flanders) [2001] O.J. C330/3; and State aid N 415/A/2001, Belgium, Green Certificate Mechanism (Wallonia) [2002] O.J. C30/14.

[159] State aid NN 27/2000, Germany, Act On Granting Priority To Renewable Energy Sources [2002] O.J. C164/5; and State aid NN 68/2000, Germany, Law On The Protection Of Electricity Generated From Combined Heat And Power [2002] O.J. C164/3.

[160] State aid N 651/2001, The Netherlands, Special Provision In The Energy Tax For Producers Of Sustainable Heat [2002] O.J. C77.

[161] State aid NN 30b/2000, The Netherlands, Tax Rate Increase In Relation To The Green Electricity Zero Tariff [2002] O.J. C30.

[162] State aid C 18/2001 (ex. N 123/2000), United Kingdom, Climate Change Levy [2001] O.J. C185/22.

Finally, the Commission has also approved various measures on renewable energy sources that are not related to the electricity market. In the Netherlands, for instance, the use of renewable gas[163] is supported by a tax exemption in the energy tax.[164] The Dutch authorities also have a fiscal provision in the energy tax for producers of sustainable heat, i.e. heat generated by renewable energy sources.[165]

Operating aid for the production of renewable energy may be justified in order **22–063** to cover the difference between the cost of producing energy from renewable energy sources and the market price of the form of energy concerned. That applies to the production of renewable energy for the purposes of subsequently selling it on the market as well as for the purposes of the undertaking's own consumption. Member States may choose to grant operating aid for renewable energy sources under three options.

Member States have as of yet made little use of the third paragraph of point 32 of the environmental guidelines (support up to 100 per cent of the eligible costs of the investment) for green electricity in particular. This option was applied in the Austrian investment scheme for renewable heat production called Grants for Biomass.[166] This scheme provides for assistance towards investment in the installation of wood-fired solid biomass heating systems. The Austrian authorities argued that there is no technical reason for installing such plants, because heating is already being provided by conventional heating systems. Heat produced using biomass is considerably more expensive than heat produced from fossil fuels and only if there is substantial relief at the investment stage can heat produced from biomass be offered at a reasonable market price. Thus, unless the Austrian authorities were prepared to bear up to 100 per cent of the extra cost, biomass plants would not be built. The Commission agreed to this analysis and approved the notified measure in June 2001.

Solar cell systems are increasingly used in order to secure the energy supply within the European Union and because of its environmental advantages, especially the reduction of greenhouse gas emissions. In the Commission Decision on case N 524/04 (Sweden),[167] the Commission argued that even if the costs for solar cell systems are expected to decrease until 2010, investments in such systems are foreseen to be considerably more expensive than investments in other types of energy. Depreciation of solar systems at current price levels of electricity run up to 70 years, which is technically unfeasible. The Swedish support scheme brings depreciation down to 21 years. The Swedish scheme was approved under point 32, third paragraph, of the environmental guidelines 2001.

---

[163] Renewable gas is defined as landfill gas, sewage treatment plant gas and biogas. This kind of natural gas does not contribute to long-cycle CO_2 emissions, hence it qualifies as renewable energy source.
[164] State aid N 168/A/2001, The Netherlands, Modifications Energy Tax 2001 [2002] O.J. C30.
[165] State aid N 651/2001, The Netherlands, Modifications Energy Tax 2000 Sustainable Heat [2002] O.J. C77.
[166] State aid N 645/2000, Austria, Grants for Biomass [2001] O.J. C234/12.
[167] March 16, 2005, [2005] O.J. C226/6.

For solar installations, the Commission has approved aid intensities which are even up to 100 per cent.[168]

22–064   In Spain, support to promote investments in renewable energy and energy efficiency has been provided since 2001.[169] An objective of the support is, among others, to achieve a contribution from renewable energy sources of 12 per cent of the demand of primary energy in 2010 and a reduction of the energy intensity by 7.2 per cent in 2012. As a consequence of the scheme, a reduction of 300 000 tonnes per year of CO_2 emissions is expected. Aid is provided in the form of a direct grant. Under the scheme, investments in renewable energy can receive support of between 10 and 30 per cent of the reference costs, while investments in energy efficiency can receive support of 40 per cent of the reference costs. The maximum gross aid intensity is in all cases limited to 40 per cent of the eligible costs (plus a regional bonus of 5 or 10 per cent in certain eligible regions and a bonus of 10 per cent for SMEs). Eligible investments in energy efficiency can, for example, be investments in better energy saving and substitution of energy in the industry, investments in energy efficiency in buildings, energy efficiency in the public sector and public transport, non-industrial cogeneration and reuse of residuals as energy. The Commission found that the measure constitutes state aid which is compatible with the common market since it is in line with the environmental guidelines 2001 (in particular points 30, 32, 36 and 37).

In addition biofuel promotion should benefit both security of supply and climate change policy in a sustainable way. Therefore, state aid may be an appropriate instrument only for those uses of renewable energy sources where the environmental benefit and sustainability is evident. More particularly, biofuels not fulfilling the sustainability criteria set out in art.15 of the proposal for a Directive of the European Parliament and the Council on the promotion of the use of energy from renewable sources [17] will not be considered eligible for state aid. When designing their support systems, Member States may encourage the use of biofuels which give additional benefits—including the benefits of diversification offered by biofuels made from wastes, residues, cellulosic and ligno-cellulosic material—by taking due account of the different costs of producing energy from traditional biofuels, on the one hand, and of those biofuels which give additional benefits, on the other hand. With regard to hydropower installations it should be noted that their environmental impact can be twofold. In terms of low greenhouse gas emissions they certainly provide potential. Therefore, they can play an important part in the overall energy mix. On the other hand, such installations might also have a negative impact, for example on water systems and biodiversity.

---

[168] In C 60/2002, Italy, Reduction of the greenhouse gases emissions [2004] O.J. L81/72, an aid intensity of 75% was approved; and in N 158/2002, United Kingdom, First Phase Major Photovoltaic Demonstration Programme [2002] O.J. C238/12, an aid intensity of 100% was authorised.

[169] State aid N 188/2005, Spain, Modification of aid schemes for renewable energy and energy efficiency [2005] O.J. C307/4. That measure replaces, modifies and prolongs state aid N 459/2001, not yet published in the O.J. N 460/2001, not yet published in the O.J., and N 198/2002 [2003] O.J. C/23.

Option 1: extra cost approach. Member States may grant operating aid to **22–065** compensate for the difference between the cost of producing energy from renewable sources, including depreciation of extra investments for environmental protection, and the market price of the form of energy concerned. Operating aid may then be granted until the plant has been fully depreciated according to normal accounting rules. Any further energy produced by the plant will not qualify for any assistance. However, the aid may also cover a normal return on capital. Any investment aid granted to the undertaking in question in respect of the new plant must be deducted from production costs when determining the amount of operating aid. When notifying aid schemes to the Commission, Member States must state the precise support mechanisms and in particular the methods of calculating the amount of aid. Unlike most other renewable sources of energy, biomass requires relatively low investment costs, but higher operating costs. The Commission will, therefore, be amenable to operating aid for the production of renewable energy from biomass exceeding the amount of investment where Member States can show that the aggregate costs borne by the undertakings after plant depreciation are still higher than the market prices of the energy.

In June 2001 the Commission decided not to raise objections against a Danish scheme in favour of power plants using renewable energy sources and set up in the period 2000–2003.[170] In this measure the Danish authorities ensure a comparable income level through fixed consumer prices over a period of 10 or 12 years. Once the planned green certificate system is implemented, part of the guaranteed income will emanate from the sale of such certificates on the market. The aid element is determined as the difference between the guaranteed income and the market price of electricity at each point in time. The present value of the aid will not exceed the present value of the investment costs for each type of RE-based power plant. Therefore, as the measure was in line with option 1 of the environmental guidelines, the Commission decided that the measure was compatible with the EC Treaty.

In October 2001 the Commission approved a Luxembourg scheme that aims at encouraging the development of green electricity.[171] The scheme provides operating aid to photovoltaic plants and wind power, biomass and small hydropower plants, in line with option 1 of the environmental guidelines. In December 2001 the Commission decided upon a Dutch fiscal provision in the energy tax for producers of sustainable heat.[172] In this case the Commission took note that the production costs of heat produced by industrial biomass/CHP installations exceed the market price of conventional heat. The aid intensity of 17.5 per cent of the extra costs is acceptable and can even be considered low, given the

---

[170] State aid N 278/2001, Denmark, Electricity Reforms, New RE-based Power Plants [2001] O.J. C263/6.

[171] State aid N 842/2000, Luxembourg, Electricity Reforms, New RE-based Power Plants (*Prime d'encouragement écologique*) [2002] O.J. C5/5.

[172] State aid N 651/2001, The Netherlands, Modifications Energy Tax 2000 Sustainable Heat [2002] O.J. C77.

uneconomic status of biomass/CHP installations. As the other conditions set out in the environmental guidelines were also met the Commission approved the measure.

Another Dutch measure following option 1 for operating aid, called partial exemption energy tax for waste incineration units, was approved in December 2001.[173] Electricity produced from biomass in waste incineration plants was already exempted from the regulatory energy tax. Biomass accounts for between 50 per cent and 60 per cent of the combustible waste in the Netherlands. Compared with traditional electricity plants waste incineration plants are faced with extra costs when generating electricity from waste. The tax exemption only offsets part of the extra production costs. Therefore, 50 per cent of the energy tax on total electricity produced by incineration of waste was already eligible for an exemption from the energy tax.[174] On January 1, 2000 the Dutch energy tax was increased, therefore the amount of the tax exemption also changed, as well as the aid intensity. The Commission approved this increase as a state aid measure under the "old" environmental guidelines in 2000.[175]

22–066   In 2001 the Dutch authorities notified another increase of the partial tax exemption for waste incineration plants, as the energy tax was to increase again. This time, the Commission used the provisions of the new environmental guidelines, in particular option 1 for operating aid. While assessing this case for waste incineration plants, the Commission decided that the exemption in the Dutch energy tax for green electricity was justified by the nature or general scheme of the tax system (NN30/b/2000[176]). The use of the biodegradable fraction of waste as a fuel for electricity production does not contribute negatively to long-cycle CO_2 emissions, hence it is not a fuel for which a penalisation in the form of the energy tax is intended. However, in this case for waste incineration the Dutch authorities chose not to give a direct exemption on the energy tax to consumers. Instead the Dutch authorities proposed a partial rebate to be given by the energy distributors to the operators of the waste incineration units. This different approach had mainly practical reasons, as (1) a specific tariff in the regulatory energy tax for partial tax exemption is prevented, (2) consumers, distributors and producers are not obliged to set up an enormous amount of specific contracts on (partially) tax exempted electricity and (3) there are only a limited number of operators of waste incineration units, hence a limited amount of rebate transactions are needed. The consequence of this approach is that consumers have to pay the energy tax on electricity of the operators of the waste incineration units. Instead of transferring this levied tax to the tax authorities the distribution

---

[173] State aid N 239/2001, The Netherlands, Partial Exemption Energy Tax For Waste Incineration Units [2002] O.J. C32.

[174] This aid measure was approved by the Commission by letter dated July 22, 1998 for a period of three years from the date the measure entered into force (N 753/97).

[175] State aid NN 30/A/2000, The Netherlands, Tax Rate Increases In Relation To The Rinse Water Exemption, The Exemption For De-Inking Residue, The Green Electricity Zero Tariff And The Exemption For Waste Incineration Plants [2001] O.J. C117/14.

[176] By letter dated November 28, 2001 on state aids NN 30/B/2001 and N 678/2001 [2002] O.J. C30/16.

companies are allowed to pass on the levied tax to the aforementioned operators. Thus, an explicit difference is established as regards the Dutch green electricity tax exemption (NN30/b/2000), where no tax is levied at all in the first place. Therefore the Commission did not consider the Dutch partial rebate for waste incineration units justified by the nature or general scheme of the tax system. Therefore the notified measure constitutes state aid.

In their notification the Dutch authorities illustrated the extra costs, borne by the operators of the waste incineration plants to produce electricity, by comparing the production costs of the electricity of two different waste incineration plants, a large one (471 GWh) and a small one (147 GWh) to the market price of regular electricity.[177] According to this information the notified aid only partially covered the extra costs, resulting in an aid intensity ranging from 27 per cent to 69 per cent, with an average aid intensity of 49 per cent. As the other criteria of the environmental guidelines were also met, the Commission considered the partial exemption in the energy tax for waste incineration units, which corresponds to a total exemption for the biodegradable fraction of the waste, compatible with the internal market.

The Commission decision on the aforementioned state aid measure MEP **22–067**
(N707/2002) has set limits to the total aid amount that can be obtained in the form of operating aid (MEP). Previous Dutch support instruments were aimed aid stimulating *demand* through a reduced tariff in the energy tax for renewable electricity for consumers, a feed-in tariff rebate for producers of renewable energy and a provision in the energy tax for CHP electricity producers. The MEP subsidy scheme aims at stimulating *supply*, through operating aid for a fixed period of maximum 10 years, with a total budget of €2,503 million. On March 19, 2003 the Commission authorised this support mechanism.[178] The MEP decision is an interesting example of the application of the provisions of the environmental guidelines on operating aid to renewable energy. For the first time, the Commission took a detailed decision on this kind of operating aid. The Commission's decisions on MEP confirmed that operating support systems that are financed through a fund constitute state aid within the meaning of the Treaty. In this respect, the Court jurisprudence has established three cumulative criteria in order to assess the involvement of state resources where money is transferred by a fund.[179] The fund must be established by the state, it must be fed by contributions imposed or managed by the state and it must be used to favour specific enterprises. The MEP fund is ordered by the state and managed by the state company TenneT. The fund is financed through a compulsory contribution by all Dutch electricity consumers, imposed by the state, in the form of an increased connection fee. This increase in the connection fee is equal for all

---

[177] Please note, when an electricity production unit is installed in a plant, the costs of a cooling system are prevented. Hence in order to calculate the extra costs, the costs of a cooling system are deducted from the investment costs of the electricity unit.

[178] State aid N 707/2002 MEP—Stimulating Renewable Energy [2003] O.J. C148/11.

[179] Case C–173/73 *Italy v Commission* [1974] E.C.R. 709; Case C–78/76 *Steinike v Germany* [1977] E.C.R. 595.

consumers, thus irrespective of whether it is a large consumer or a small one, it amounts to €34 in 2003.[180] It should be noted that, in terms of energy and environmental policies, this set up is not in line with the "polluter pays" principle (small consumers that pollute less pay proportionally much more than large consumers that pollute more). Moreover, it could run contrary to the "universal service" principle, as the price to pay for good quality electricity might appear to be disproportionately high for small consumers. Nevertheless, in the present state of Community law the Member States remain free as regards the design of their fiscal and parafiscal regimes. The scheme will only favour the producers of renewable electricity and producers of CHP electricity in the Netherlands who are feeding that electricity into the Dutch electricity grid.

According to the environmental guidelines (option 1), Member States may grant state aid to compensate for the difference between the production cost of renewable energy and the market price of the form of power concerned. According to the aforementioned decision on MEP:

" . . . the aid of € 0.068 per kWh only partially covers the extra costs. Taking into account the existing fiscal stimulation in the form of a reduced energy tax and assuming that the entire energy tax rebate is passed on to the producers, the aid intensities of the total operating aid vary from 16% to 100%. Thus, the total operating aid does not exceed the difference between the production costs of the renewable electricity and the market price for regular energy."

According to point 109(b) of the environmental guidelines 2008 operating aid for renewable energy is only allowed until the plant has been fully depreciated according to normal accounting rules. Any further energy produced by the plant will not qualify for any assistance. However, the aid may also cover a normal return on capital. When any investment aid granted to the undertaking in question in respect of the new plant must be deducted from production costs when determining the amount of operating aid. When notifying aid schemes to the Commission, Member States must state the precise support mechanisms and in particular the methods of calculating the amount of aid. These criteria sometimes seem to be overlooked in state aid cases. It is imperative that these criteria constitute a kind of claw back clause in the aid instrument.

22–068   **Option 2: market mechanisms.** The second option is aimed at new instruments linked to market mechanism, in particular green certificates and tender-procedures. There are various ways of organising these new instruments. By introducing green certificates, Member States try to cover the extra costs of green

---

[180] The increased connection fee, although set at a fixed price could be viewed as a parafiscal levy on the whole electricity consumption of a consumer, hence including a part of which is imported. However, the Commission argued that the deduction, even for large consumers, of the proportion of the corresponding fee to the percentage of imported electricity, would remain minimal, considering the amount of the fee (€34) and disproportionate to the administrative burden imposed.

electricity production by adding the proceeds of the regular electricity market and the proceeds of producing green electricity. In practice that means that the producer of green electricity sells his green electricity on the regular electricity market as regular electricity. He thus gets a standard market price for his electricity, which usually does not cover his extra costs. However, for the green character of the electricity produced the producer can receive a certificate. In practice this green certificate is often an administrative number or electronic key, handed out by executive bodies of the authorities. The producer usually gets the certificate(s) for free from the authorities, as long as he can show that he has produced a certain amount of green electricity, which was sold as regular electricity. On a separate certificate market the producer can then sell the green certificates. The following section takes a closer look at the Belgian green certificate system that was approved by the Commission in July 2001.

Member States may also grant support for renewable energy sources by using market mechanisms such as green certificates or tenders. These market mechanisms allow all renewable energy producers to benefit indirectly from guaranteed demand for their energy, at a price above the market price for conventional power. The price of these green certificates is not fixed in advance but depends on supply and demand. Where the market mechanisms constitute state aid, they may be authorised by the Commission if Member States can show that support is essential to ensure the viability of the renewable energy sources concerned, does not in the aggregate result in overcompensation and does not dissuade renewable energy producers from becoming more competitive. The Commission will authorise such aid systems for a period of 10 years.

In 2001, Belgium introduced a green certificate system including a purchase obligation at the level of electricity distributors.[181] An obligatory minimum number of green certificates corresponds to a percentage of their total electricity delivery to electricity consumers. When distributors do not have a sufficient amount of green certificates (to be determined annually by a specified calculation method) the distributors have to pay a fine. The purpose of the system of fines is twofold: it creates an obligatory incentive for the distributors to buy green certificates, and it offers distributors a way out when the prices of the green certificates are rising too high. The Belgian authorities want to introduce a market for green electricity, but as supply and demand are not yet well developed the system of fines acts as a safety net for distributors in order not to pay too much for the development of green electricity production. The revenues of the fine will flow to a public fund, which will be used to support individual projects on sustainable energy. The mechanism of this fund and the conditions of these projects were to be elaborated at a later stage. The obligation imposed on all Belgian distributors to possess a certain number of green certificates at the end of each year will result in an additional income for producers of green electricity to cover a part of their (higher) production costs. It is therefore an economic

---

[181] State aid N 550/2000, Belgium, Green Electricity Certificates (Flanders) [2001] O.J. C330/3; and State aid N 415/A/2001, Belgium, Green Certificate Mechanism (Wallonia) [2002] O.J. C30.

advantage granted to the producers of green electricity. The producers of green electricity are a specific group of electricity producers, who are active in trade between Member States. The position of these green electricity producers will be strengthened by this scheme, which may lead to a change in market conditions for their competitors. This strengthening must be regarded as affecting that trade. In order to decide that the notified measure on green certificates constitutes state aid within the meaning of the Treaty, the Commission had to determine whether state resources are at stake.

22–069   In the following (simplified) figure, various cash flows and obligations in the notified green certificates measure are summarised:

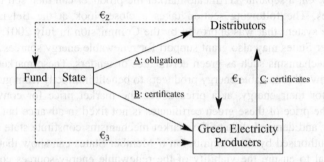

The Belgian system starts with the obligation by the state for distributors to purchase a certain amount of green certificates (obligation A). The *PreussenElektra* case has shown that an obligation imposed on private electricity supply undertakings to purchase electricity produced from renewable energy sources at fixed minimum prices does not involve any direct or indirect transfer of state resources to undertakings which produce that type of electricity. The obligation to purchase a specific amount of green certificates appears comparable to the obligation to purchase electricity produced from renewable energy sources at fixed minimum prices. Hence the Commission decided that no state resources within the meaning of the Treaty are present in this obligation.

The State offers the producers of green electricity the green certificates for free (B). The green electricity producers have to prove that they have produced a certain amount of green electricity and they will get a corresponding number of green certificates in return. They can sell these certificates to the distributors on the (future) green certificate market. Herewith, the state offers the producers intangible assets. However, the Belgian authorities only provide an authorised proof that the green electricity is actually produced. Hence, with regard to the provision of green certificates by the state to producers, state resources within the meaning of the Treaty are not at stake.

When distributors buy green certificates from producers of green electricity or traders (cash flow $€_1$ and certificates sales C), no state resources in the meaning of the Treaty are at stake, as these actions take place in the electricity market. When distributors do not have a sufficient number of green electricity certificates they have to pay a fine to the Belgian authorities, in the figure cash flow $€_2$. The revenues of these fines will be collected in a fund, which will be specifically established and controlled by the Belgian authorities in the near future to support Belgian projects on increasing the production of green electricity (this support is cash flow €3 in the figure). The Belgian authorities indicated that the specifications of this fund would be notified at a later stage after implementation of the green certificate system. The Commission can only decide on the possible state aid aspects of this fund when it is notified. Therefore the Commission concludes that, in principle, the notified measure at hand does not constitute state aid within the meaning of the Treaty.

Although the Commission found that the issuing of green certificates by the **22–070** Belgian authorities did not involve state resources, it continued assessing the notified measure on the basis of the environmental guidelines. In points 61 and 62 of the environmental guidelines 2001 specific criteria were set for the introduction of green certificate systems. The environmental guidelines allow green electricity producers to benefit indirectly from guaranteed demand for their energy, at a price above the market price for conventional power. These systems may be authorised by the Commission if Member States can show that (1) the support is essential to ensure the viability of the renewable energy sources concerned, (2) the support does not in the aggregate result in overcompensation for renewable energy, (3) the support does not dissuade renewable energy producers from becoming more competitive and (4) that the support is limited to a duration of 10 years.[182] As the Belgian measure met these conditions the Commission declared it compatible with the internal market.

In the Netherlands a system on green certificates was introduced in order for distributors to apply a tax relief on green electricity. The Commission approved the Dutch tax relief on green electricity in 2001.[183] When distributors want to apply the tax relief, they are able to use green certificates, in order to prove that their electricity sold is green. The certificate system as such has not been notified, as the Dutch authorities are of the opinion that the measure is voluntary for all participants and that the measure is only an administrative facility. As more and more Member States introduce green certificates, it becomes important to ensure that the internal market rules are respected, and that consumers or distributors in one Member State can also fulfil their purchase obligation by buying certificates issued in another Member State in due time. Green certificates have already been implemented in Denmark, Belgium, the Netherlands and the United Kingdom.[184]

---

[182] It should be noted that the condition on overcompensation in point 62 of the environmental guidelines 2001 requires an assessment *in the aggregate*. In practice some types of green electricity production are almost competitive in the regular electricity market (especially wind power), whilst other forms are far from being competitive (photovoltaic power). As green certificates do not make a distinction between the various types of green electricity, assessment on overcompensation was only carried out at a general level in order to prevent overcompensation for the green electricity sector as a whole (instead of an assessment at company level or per type of green electricity).

[183] State aid NN 30b/2000, The Netherlands, Tax Rate Increase In Relation To The Green Electricity Zero Tariff [2002] O.J. C30.

[184] State aid N 504/2000, United Kingdom, Renewable Obligation And Capital Grants For Renewable Technologies [2002] O.J. C30.

One of the problems arising now is that the definition of green electricity is not fully harmonised in the European Union. There is only harmonisation for a minimal definition, which is based on the definition of renewable energy sources in Directive 2001/77/EC on electricity from renewable energy sources.[185] However, Member States are allowed to limit the definition of green electricity in their aid measures. The Dutch authorities for instance have excluded all hydropower from the Dutch zero tariff for green electricity from January 1, 2002 onwards.[186] The Dutch authorities will therefore not accept a green certificate issued in respect of Belgium hydropower for instance.

The Member State can also introduce a call for tenders. In 2001 the Irish authorities notified two measures in accordance with this option for operating aid.[187] Via these measures suppliers of green electricity are invited to offer the best price for a specified type and amount of green electricity during a period of 15 years. The winner of the tender procedure gets a 15-year contract to deliver an amount of specific green electricity at a guaranteed price. Thus, these measures account for the difference in cost price of the different types of green electricity production. The Commission approved these measures in January 2002.

22–071 **Option 3: regular rules on operating aid.** Member States may also grant operating aid in accordance with the general provisions set out in point 100 of the environmental guidelines 2008.

Finally, the third option refers to the more general rule of operating aid, offered for aid to waste management and energy saving (duration limited to five years and the aid intensity limited to 50 per cent for non-degressive aid and to 100 per cent in the first year for degressive aid). This fourth option was used in two measures of a Dutch fiscal case in 2001 called "tax relief for good quality CHP-power and the stimulation of heat produced by geothermal energy."[188] The CHP

---

[185] Directive 2001/77/EC of the European Parliament and the Council on the promotion of electricity produced from renewable energy sources in the internal electricity market of September 27, 2001 [2001] O.J. L283/33.

[186] Hydropower is power produced from the energy of falling water using turbines. It is a non-fossil, non-nuclear source of energy and production leads to virtually no CO_2 emissions. Because it makes use of energy flows that are eternal in human perspective (being part of the global water cycle), hydropower is usually deemed as a renewable energy source. Nevertheless, the production of hydropower is associated with several impacts that pose an impediment to the sustainability criteria of hydropower. Reservoirs are for instance also used for pumped storage, where they function as a "battery" for the conventional electricity power plants. When pumping, CO_2 is emitted. Storage of water leads to the deposition of biomass, which, when entering the decomposition stage, leads to the production of methane, one of the greenhouse gases. Hydropower installations can divert water from rivers or divert the flow of water from one river to another, which has an impact on the ecosystems of rivers, on fish populations, alteration of sediment regimes, and sinking ground water levels. Finally, hydropower plants are also a source of local disturbance like landscape deterioration, cultural and historic losses, loss of tourism potential and economic losses resulting from the obstruction to circulation on the river.

[187] State aid N 826/2001, Ireland, Alternative Energy Requirements I to IV [2002] O.J. C59; and state aid N 553/2001, Ireland, Alternative Energy Requirements V [2002] O.J. C54.

[188] State aid N 168/A/2001, Netherlands, Modifications Energy Tax 2001 [2002] O.J. C30.

measure aimed at providing support for small and medium-sized CHP installations. The market conditions in the Netherlands for CHP installations had worsened in recent years. While the price of natural gas had gradually increased, the price of electricity in the Netherlands had decreased. Thus, as regards the CHP installations the fuel got more expensive, while the revenues (electricity) decreased. The Dutch authorities expected that these market conditions would continue in the years to come. To stimulate the use of CHP, the Dutch authorities proposed a tax rebate on the energy tax for all consumers of all electricity generated by Dutch CHP installations that meet a minimum conversion efficiency, in accordance with point 31 of the environmental guidelines. Dutch electricity distribution companies are obliged to include the energy tax in their price of electricity to consumers and to pay the revenues of the energy tax to the Dutch tax authorities. The proposed measure allows the energy companies to deduct a rebate from their payments to the tax authority, on the condition that the electricity delivered was generated by a Dutch CHP-installation and that the revenues of this deduction will be paid to the owner of the CHP-installation where the electricity was produced. The Dutch authorities were aiming specifically at stimulating small and medium-sized CHP-installations. As a result an annual fixed maximum of 1000 GWh per operating company of a CHP-installation was included in the measure. The maximum aid intensity of the measure was calculated at 46 per cent (based on detailed comparison with various alternative power production methods).

The measure on geothermal energy was an unusual case, as there were no operators of CHP installations using geothermal energy in the Netherlands when the measure was notified. The measure aimed to encourage undertakings to start business in this technology. This technology refers to energy in the soil being used in the production of heat, especially for application in city heating projects. City heating projects usually make of combined heat and power (CHP) installations, as the output of these installations is heat and electricity. In the Netherlands, consumers and industry have to pay energy tax on electricity and gas, but not on heat.[189] The energy distribution companies are obliged to include the energy tax in their prices for gas and electricity. The energy companies, which are subject to payment of the levied energy tax on natural gas and electricity to the tax authorities, may apply a deduction on their payment, to the extent that heat produced by geothermal energy has been delivered and sold. The rebate on the energy tax on gas and electricity will contribute to the extra costs of a geothermal installation. In order to calculate the extra costs of these installations, the Dutch authorities compared the estimated costs of heat produced by geothermal installations to heat produced by regular heat installations, which are fuelled with natural gas. Based on this calculation the rebate resulted in an aid intensity between 21 per cent and 46 per cent. Thus, both cases had a maximum

---

[189] According to the Dutch authorities the use of heat as a source of energy should not be discouraged by a tax, as heat is usually produced by environmentally friendly CHP installations.

aid intensity below 50 per cent and the duration of the non-degressive measures was limited to five years. The Commission decided that the conditions set out in the environmental guidelines were met and the measures were compatible with the internal market in accordance with the Treaty.

15. AID FOR COGENERATION (INVESTMENT/OPERATING AID)

22–072   Cogeneration of heat and electricity (hereafter "CHP") is the most efficient way of producing electricity and heat simultaneously. By producing both electricity and heat together, less energy is wasted in production. The Community strategy outlined in the Commission's cogeneration strategy of 1997 sets an overall indicative target of doubling the share of electricity production from cogeneration to 18 per cent by 2010. Since then the importance of CHP for the EU energy strategy has been underlined by the adoption of Directive 2004/8/EC of the European Parliament and of the Council of February 11, 2004 on the promotion of cogeneration based on a useful heat demand in the internal energy market and amending Directive 92/42/EEC [19] and by a chapter on cogeneration in the Commission Action Plan for Energy Efficiency: Realising the Potential [20]. The latter document also points to the potential of waste heat, for example from industry or utilities and for useful applications, such as in district heating (hereafter "DH"). Further, DH may be more energy efficient than individual heating and may provide a significant improvement in urban air quality. Therefore, provided that DH is shown to be less polluting and more energy efficient in the generation process and the distribution of the heat, but more costly than individual heating, state aid can be granted with a view to giving incentives to attain environmental targets. However, as in the case of renewable energies, the progressive internalisation of environmental externalities in the costs of other technologies can be expected to reduce the need for aid by bringing about a gradual convergence of these costs with those of CHP and DH.

In accordance with point 112 of the environmental guidelines 2008 investment and operating aid for cogeneration will be considered compatible with the internal market, provided that the cogeneration unit satisfies the definition of high-efficiency cogeneration set out in point 70(11), and provided that for investment aid a new cogeneration unit will overall make primary energy savings compared to separate production as defined by Directive 2004/8/EC and Decision 2007/74/EC or improvement of an existing cogeneration unit or conversion of an existing power generation unit into a cogeneration unit will result in primary energy savings compared to the original situation. For operating aid, an existing cogeneration must satisfy both the definition of high-efficiency cogeneration and the requirement that there are overall primary energy savings compared to separate production as defined by Directive 2004/8/EC and Decision 2007/74/EC.

22–073   The aid intensity for investment aid must not exceed 60 per cent of the eligible investment costs. Where the investment aid for cogeneration is to be given to

SMEs, the aid intensity may be increased by 10 percentage points for medium-sized enterprises and by 20 percentage points for small enterprises, as set out in the table. Where the investment aid is granted in a genuinely competitive bidding process on the basis of clear, transparent and non-discriminatory criteria, effectively ensuring that the aid is limited to the minimum necessary for achieving the maximum energy saving, the aid intensity may amount to up to 100 per cent of the eligible investment cost. Such a bidding process must be non-discriminatory and must provide for the participation of a sufficient number of companies. In addition, the budget related to the bidding process must be a binding constraint in a sense that not all participants can receive aid. Finally, the aid must be granted on the basis of the initial bid submitted by the bidder, thus excluding subsequent negotiations. Eligible costs must be limited to the extra investment costs necessary to realise a high-efficiency cogeneration plant as compared to the reference investment. Eligible costs must be calculated net of any operating benefits and operating costs related to the extra investment and arising during the first five years of the life of this investment.

Operating aid for high-efficiency cogeneration may be granted in accordance with the rules for operating aid for renewable energy laid down in s.3.1.6.2 of the environmental guidelines 2008. Aid can be granted to undertakings distributing electric power and heat to the public where the costs of producing such electric power or heat exceed its market price. The decision as to whether the aid is necessary will take account of the costs and revenue resulting from the production and sale of the electric power or heat. Aid can also be granted for the industrial use of the combined production of electric power and heat where it can be shown that the production cost of one unit of energy using that technique exceeds the market price of one unit of conventional energy. The production cost may include the plant's normal return on capital, but any gains by the undertaking in terms of heat production must be deducted from production costs.

16. Aid for Energy Efficient District Heating (Investment/Operating Aid)

As concerns aid for energy efficient district heating, investment aid will be **22–074** considered compatible with the internal market, provided that it leads to primary energy savings and that the beneficiary district heating installation satisfies the definition of energy efficient district heating and that the combined operation of the generation of heat (as well as electricity in the case of cogeneration) and the distribution of heat will result in primary energy savings, or the investment is meant for the use and distribution of waste heat for district heating purposes. The aid intensity for district heating installations must not exceed 50 per cent of the eligible investment costs. If the aid is intended solely for the generation part of a district heating installation, energy efficient district heating installations using renewable sources of energy or cogeneration will be covered by the rules set out in ss.3.1.6 and 3.1.7 respectively. Where the investment aid for energy efficient district heating is to be given to SMEs, the aid intensity may be increased by 10 percentage points for medium-sized enterprises and by 20 percentage points for small enterprises. Where the investment aid is granted in a genuinely competitive bidding process on the basis of clear, transparent and non-discriminatory criteria, effectively ensuring that the aid is limited to the minimum necessary for achieving the maximum energy saving, the aid intensity may constitute up to 100 per cent of the eligible investment cost. Eligible costs must be limited to the extra investment costs necessary to realise an investment leading to energy efficient district heating as compared to the reference investment. Eligible costs must be calculated net any operating benefits and operating costs related to the extra investment and arising during the first five years of the life of this investment.

A regular example of a district heating investment case is an Italian state aid case N 364/09. In this case state aid was provided for the creation of a cogeneration power plant and for the recovery and use of waste heat from industrial processes to be connected to a district heating network in the area of Aosta, Italy (Valle d'Aosta), with a state aid budget of €5.6 million.[190]

17. AID FOR WASTE MANAGEMENT

22–075   The Sixth Environment Action Programme identifies waste prevention and management as one of the four top priorities. Its primary objective is to separate waste generation from economic activity, so that economic growth will not lead to increased waste production. In this context, state aid may be granted to the producer of the waste under s.3.1.1 of the environmental guidelines 2008 as investment aid to go beyond Community standards or aid to improve on environmental protection in absence of such standards. Investment aid to firms improving on Community standards has been interpreted by the Commission as referring to standards which apply directly to firms by limiting their emission levels or waste. Aid can therefore only be granted to companies reducing their own pollution. However, where Community legislation imposes standards directly on Member States, e.g. in the packaging waste directive, it is often on companies to take measures to allow the state to meet its obligation. Following up its decision on the WRAP case on support for investments undertaken by recycling firms,[191] the Commission included a new provision in the environmental guidelines 2008. Currently, s.3.1.9 provides a framework for waste management, when the beneficiaries are investing in managing or recycling waste generated by other undertakings.[192] Current compatibility conditions to a large extent formally codify the previous decision making practice of the Commission.

[190] *http://ec.europa.eu/competition/state_aid/cases/232008/232008_1033893_23_1.pdf.*
[191] See state aid C 61/2002, United Kingdom, Newsprint reprocessing WRAP program [2002] O.J. C283; and state aid N 443/2003, Belgium, Second Circuit Water [2006] O.J. C21.
[192] S.3.1.9 of the environmental guidelines [2008] O.J. C82/1.

Environmental investment aid for the management of waste of other under-takings, including activities of re-utilisation, recycling and recovery, can be compatible with the internal market within the meaning of art.107(3)(c) of the TFEU, provided that such management is in accordance with the hierarchical classification of the principles of waste management.[193] However, the aid ele-ments must ensure that the polluter pays principle is not circumvented and the normal functioning of secondary materials markets is not distorted. Therefore such aid must be restricted to the investment aimed at reducing pollution generated by other undertakings ("polluters") and not extend to pollution gen-erated by the beneficiary itself. The aid may not indirectly relieve the polluters from a burden that should be borne by them under Union law, or from a burden that should be considered a normal company cost for the polluters. Furthermore, the investment must go beyond what is called the "state-of-the-art" or use conventional technologies in an innovative manner, the materials treated would otherwise be disposed of, or be treated in a less environmentally friendly manner and finally, the investment may not simply increase demand for the materials to be recycled without increasing collection of those materials. Aid intensity for this type of aid is restricted to 50 per cent of the eligible investment costs. Where the investment aid for waste management is to be given to SMEs, the aid intensity may be increased by 10 per cent for medium-sized enterprises and by 20 per cent for small enterprises.[194]

According to the environmental guidelines 2008, eligible costs must be limited **22–076** to the extra investment costs necessary to realise an investment leading to waste management and borne by the beneficiary compared to the reference investment, that is to say, a conventional production not involving waste management with the same capacity. The cost of such reference investment must be deducted from the eligible cost. For the calculation of eligible costs one is referred back to points 81–83 of the guidelines. If the investment is solely aimed at environmental protection without generating any other economic benefits, no extra operating benefits are deducted from the eligible costs.[195] State aid for investment by undertakings managing or recycling waste created by other undertakings is explicitly excluded from the GBER. This type of aid falls within the scope of the environmental guidelines 2008 and can be approved by the Commission under the conditions described above.[196] Aid to companies for the reduction of their own waste or emissions is eligible under art.18 of the GBER (investment aid).

The costs of treating industrial waste should normally be borne by the com-panies in accordance with the "polluter pays" principle. Aid may nevertheless be granted where national standards are introduced which are more stringent than the applicable Community rules, or where national standards are introduced in

---

[193] Communication from the Commission on the review of the Community Strategy for Waste Management [1996] (COM(96) 399 final), as re-iterated by the Commission in its Thematic Strategy for the prevention and recycling waste [2005] (COM(2005) 666 final).

[194] Points 126–129 of the environmental guidelines [2008] O.J. C82/1.

[195] Points 130 and 131 of the environmental guidelines [2008] O.J. C82/1.

[196] art.18 of the GBER.

the absence of Community rules. The Commission accepts the necessity of aid in these cases in order to compensate firms for the temporary loss of competitiveness at international level. In 2002, the French government introduced an aid scheme for the elimination of dangerous waste for the water.[197] The objective of the scheme is to preserve the water resources by promoting the elimination of waste that can pollute the subsurface and surface water or disturb the functioning of municipal purification plants. In order to achieve that objective, the scheme aims at orienting the waste pollutants, which are normally put in a disposal, in the relevant elimination procedures, successful at the technical level and optimal at the environmental level. The aid is provided to enterprises that produce the waste, when these enterprises treat the waste in appropriate procedures in order to significantly reduce the potential pollutant. It is granted in the form of grants which are calculated on the basis of the difference between the cost of the treatment of the waste in the dedicated procedure and the cost of elimination of the same waste by disposal. Each beneficiary can benefit from the aid for a maximum of five years, either as a fixed level of 50 per cent during that period or at an aid level which is degressive in a linear manner from 100 per cent to 0 per cent during the five year period. The scheme was found to be in line with the environmental guidelines 2001 (particularly points 42–46).

18. AID FOR THE REMEDIATION OF CONTAMINATED SITES

22–077   Member States are allowed to provide investment aid for remediation of contaminated sites. However, aid for remediation purposes is not covered by the GBER and all aid measures must be notified to the Commission. This type of aid is intended to create an individual incentive to counterbalance the effects of negative externalities, where it is not possible to identify the polluter and make it pay for repairing the environmental damage it has caused. The environmental damage concerned covers pollution of the soil or of surface water or groundwater. The aid can be given to the person responsible for the remediation work only in cases where the polluter cannot be identified or cannot be made to bear the costs. The aid may amount to up to 100 per cent of the eligible costs, less the increase in the value of the land, and may not exceed the actual costs of a remediation. All expenditure incurred by an undertaking in remediating its site is considered eligible investment.[198] Remediation work carried out by public authorities on their own land is not considered state aid. In case the land is sold after remediation, its price must represent its market value in accordance with the Commission Communication on state aid elements in sales of land and buildings by public authorities.[199]

---

[197] State aid N 496/2002 [2003] O.J. C108/5.
[198] Points 53 and 132–134 of the environmental guidelines [2008] O.J. C82/1.
[199] [1997] O.J. C209/3.

There are currently no mandatory EU standards which would force a benefici-ary to carry out remediation measures in contaminated sites. It should be mentioned though that Union rules have been adopted in the field of environ-mental responsibility but they apply to pollution originating after April 1, 2007.[200] In 2006, the European Commission introduced a draft EU Soil Frame-work Directive after being proposed in an EU Thematic Strategy for Soil Protection.[201] The directive sought to harmonise and raise the level of soil protection across the European Union. The proposal would inter alia require Member States to identify and remediate contaminated land. Due to lack of political agreement between the Member States the negotiations on the directive have been stalled since 2010.

The "polluter" within the meaning of the environmental guidelines refers **22–078** therefore to the person liable under the law applicable in each member state. In the Netherlands for example, the Supreme Court ruled that an undertaking could not be held liable for the cost of rehabilitation of industrial sites polluted before 1975, because at the time of the pollution, the detrimental effect of the activity on the environment was not clear. That decision was considered as being national law.[202] Another example is found in Austria where a liability for environmental damages was introduced for the first time by the Water Protection Law of 1959. As a result no one can be made liable for damages dating from before that time. The Commission has accepted this reasoning in the assessment of several Austrian remediation measures.[203] In the aforementioned cases, the Commission accepted the application of *pro rata temporis* principle. It means here that liability is attributed to a polluter in proportion to the moment the pollution was caused. Accordingly, a beneficiary can receive state aid only for that proportion of the total remediation costs, which is caused by pollution before the national legal "cut-off date".[204]

The definition of a "contaminated site" in the meaning of point 70(27) of the guidelines covers sites with a confirmed presence, caused by man, of dangerous substances of such a level that they pose significant risk to human health or the environment taking into account current and approved future use of the land. As

---

[200] Directive 2004/35/EC of the European Parliament and of the Council of April 21, 2004 on environmental liability with regard to the prevention and remedying of environmental damage [2004] O.J. L143/56.

[201] Proposal for a Directive of the European Parliament and of the Council establishing a framework for the protection of soil and amending Directive 2004/35/EC, COM(2006) 232 final and Thematic Strategy for Soil Protection, COM(2006) 231 final.

[202] State aid N 520/2001, The Netherlands, Soil protection agreement [2002] O.J. C146; state aid C 187/2003, The Netherlands, Rehabilitation of polluted gas works sites; state aid N 501/05, The Netherlands, Financial strength support soil rehabilitation [2006] O.J. C313/13; state aid N 85/2005, The Netherlands, Soil rehabilitation of polluted industrial sites [2005] O.J. C228.

[203] State aid N 9/2002, Austria, Guidelines 2002 for the rehabilitation of inherited waste [2002] O.J. C164; state aid N 383/2008, Austria, 2008 Guidelines for Remediation of Inherited Waste [2009] O.J. C50; state aid N 135/2010, Austria, Aid for the Remediation of a Contaminated Site in Linz [2010] C312; state aid 197/2010, Austria, Individual Aid for the Remediation of the Contami-nated Site in Unterkärnten [2010] O.J. C265.

[204] See also Saskia Dirkzwager, De Rijk, "Two Dutch cases on State aid and soil rehabilitation", Competition Policy Newsletter (2007) 1.

a consequence, measures regarding remediation of land damaged from or suffering the risk of subsidence are excluded. The same applies to remediation of land on which there are buildings or structures that are derelict or otherwise unsuitable for any new use. In the past, the Commission has authorised aid for such purposes based directly on art.107(3)(c) TFEU. The Commission considered that the aid was the minimum needed; applicants participated in an open competition ensuring *value for money* outcomes of the measure; the "polluter pays" principle was respected; the eligible costs were those allowed also by the guidelines at that time and the costs of the work undertaken were verified independently.[205]

19. AID FOR THE RELOCATION OF UNDERTAKINGS

22–079   Another type of investment aid can be awarded to major polluters for the purpose of their relocation to areas where such pollution will have a less damaging effect, which will reduce external costs. Aid for relocation purposes falls outside the scope of the GBER and all aid measures must be notified to the Commission. The beneficiary of relocation aid can be an undertaking located in an urban area, or a Natura 2000 designated conservation area and lawfully carries out an activity that creates major pollution and must, on account of that location, move from its place of establishment to a more suitable area.[206] In line with the precautionary principle, the current guidelines extend the scope of relocation aid to undertakings which pose a potentially high risk to people and the environment in case of an accident involving dangerous substances in accordance with the Seveso II Directive. This Directive is aimed at prevention and control of such industrial accidents.[207] Herewith the 2008 guidelines go further than the 2001 guidelines which recognised only actual polluters as beneficiaries of relocation aid and excluded aid to prevent risk of pollution.

In 2004, the Commission authorised aid to reduce the risks associated with chlorine transport.[208] The aid of €31.68 million was used for the relocation of Akzo-Nobel production facilities of chlorine and mono-chlorine acetic acid with a view to minimise chlorine transport in the Netherlands. The measure was found to be outside the scope of the 2001 guidelines, which excluded environmental aid for matters of external safety.[209] The aim of the measure was primarily to increase external security of people and surroundings in the vicinity of the transportation routes rather than environmental protection. The aim of relocation was not prevention of damage to the environment but rather reduction of the *risk*

---

[205] State aid N 385/2002, United Kingdom, prolonged by state aid N 221/2006, United Kingdom, Support for Land Remediation [2006] O.J. C222.

[206] Point 136 of the environmental guidelines [2008] O.J. C82/1.

[207] Council Directive 96/82/EC of December 9, 1996 on the control of major-accident hazards involving dangerous substances [1997] O.J. L10/13 as last amended by Regulation (EC) No.1882/2003 of the European Parliament and of the Council [2003] O.J. L284/1.

[208] State aid N 304/2003, The Netherlands, *AKZO Nobel* [2005] O.J. C81.

[209] See Community guidelines on state aid for environmental protection [2001] O.J. C37/3, point 6.

of such damage. The Commission noted however that the preventive approach was directly related to the notion of environmental protection. Under art.191(2), Union policy on the environment is inter alia based on the precautionary principle and on the principles that preventive action should be taken.[210] The Commission considered it appropriate at that time to assess whether the aid measure was directly compatible with art.107(3)(c) and with the environmental guidelines 2001 at the same time. Obviously, based on the experience of this and several other cases in the past, the Commission included aid measures designed to prevent risk of damage to the environment in the new environmental guidelines 2008. Also the concept of environmental protection for the purpose of the environmental guidelines has been extended to include any action *to reduce risk* of damage to physical surroundings or natural resources by beneficiary's own activity.[211]

The guidelines establish several restrictive criteria which must be met cumulatively. State aid may be justified if the relocation is directed by environmental or risk prevention reasons and must have been ordered by an administrative or judicial decision of a competent public authority or an agreement between the competent public authority and the undertaking. The beneficiary must comply with the strictest environmental standards applicable to the new site.[212] The aid intensity may not exceed 50 per cent of the eligible investment costs, increased by a 10 per cent bonus for medium-sized enterprises and 20 per cent for small enterprises. Yields from the sale or renting of the plant or land abandoned, the compensation paid in the event of expropriation, any other gains related to the relocation, such as gains from improvement in the technology used and accounting gains resulting form a better use of the plant and capacity increase, are taken into account. Regarding the costs, the expenses connected with the purchase of land or the construction or purchases of new plant of the same capacity as the plant abandoned, as well as any penalties imposed on the undertaking for early termination of the contract for renting of land or buildings, are taken into account.[213]

Absence of state aid in indemnification measures in line with the general system

The possibility of grant relocation aid under the environmental aid guidelines has until now been rarely used by the Member States. One of the scarce examples is a "Relocation Aid Grants" measure designed by the United Kingdom, which has been approved under the relevant provision of the environmental guidelines 2001.[214] This is explained by the accepted principle that indemnifications or **22–080**

---

[210] The Commission addresses this issue in the Communication on the precautionary principle (COM(2000)1 def), February 2, 2000.

[211] Point 70(1) of the environmental guidelines [2008] O.J. C82/1.

[212] Points 54 and 135 of the environmental guidelines [2008] O.J. C82/1.

[213] Point 138 of the environmental guidelines [2008] O.J. C82/1.

[214] As part of state aid N 385/2002, prolonged by state aid N221/2006, United Kingdom, *Support for Land Remediation* [2006] O.J. C222.

compensations normally do not entail a selective advantage to the company in so far as they merely compensate for damage resulting from an official act, where the indemnification is the direct result of this official act. It has to be noted that this official act should not itself be aimed at cancelling a previous state aid measure that would be incompatible with the Union law. A general system for indemnifications derives directly from constitutional rights of property as recognized by the judicial system.

The Commission has accepted the absence of state aid in a compensation of €821,600 for the relocation of car dismantling company Steenbergen. The noise nuisance and smell originated by the activities of Steenbergen were causing complaints by neighbouring households and relocation of this small firm was generally desirable from the environmental point of view. The Commission took into account that the activities of Steenbergen at that time were in line with all national environmental standards. The company possessed a licence with an unlimited duration and the authorities had no legal reason to terminate it thus avoiding compensation. Expropriation of Steenbergen was not a suitable alternative. Moreover, before the authorities could decide on an expropriation, they were legally obliged to try to reach an agreed solution with the owner concerned. In line with the general system, the indemnification in this case compensated only partially the estimated damage. The Commission admitted that the indemnification to Steenbergen did not constitute state aid within the meaning of art.107(1) TFEU.[215]

20. AID INVOLVED IN TRADABLE PERMIT SCHEMES/EMISSION TRADING SYSTEMS

22–081   Tradable permit schemes may involve state aid in various ways, for example when permits and allowances are granted for less than their market value and such granting is imputable to Member States. The Commission will assess the necessity and the proportionality of state aid involved in a tradable permit scheme according to the following criteria:

(a) the choice of beneficiaries must be based on objective and transparent criteria, and the aid must be granted in principle in the same way for all competitors in the same sector/relevant market if they are in a similar factual situation;

(b) full auctioning must lead to a substantial increase in production costs for each sector or category of individual beneficiaries;

(c) the substantial increase in production costs cannot be passed on to customers without leading to important sales reductions. This analysis may be

---

[215] State aid N575/2005, The Netherlands, Relocation car dismantling company Steenbergen [2007] O.J. C80.

conducted on the basis of estimations of inter alia the product price elasticity of the sector concerned. These estimations will be made in the relevant geographic market. To evaluate whether the cost increase from the tradable permit scheme cannot be passed on to customers, estimates of lost sales as well as their impact on the profitability of the company may be used; and

(d) it is not possible for individual undertakings in the sector to reduce emission levels in order to make the price of the certificates bearable. Irreducible consumption may be demonstrated by providing the emission levels derived from best performing technique in the European Economic Area (hereafter "EEA") and using it as a benchmark. Any undertaking reaching the best performing technique can benefit at most from an allowance corresponding to the increase in production cost from the tradable permit scheme using the best performing technique, and which cannot be passed on to customers. Any undertaking having a worse environmental performance shall benefit from a lower allowance, proportionate to its environmental performance.

The state aid must have an incentive effect. State aid for environmental protection must result in the aid recipient changing its behaviour so that the level of environmental protection is increased. The Commission considers that aid does not present an incentive effect for the beneficiary in all cases in which the project has already started prior to the aid application by the beneficiary to the national authorities. If the aided project has not started before the aid application, the requirement of incentive effect is presumed to be automatically met for all categories of aid granted to an SME, except in cases where the aid must be assessed in accordance with the detailed assessment in Ch.5 of the environmental guidelines 2008. For all other aided projects, the Commission will require that the incentive effect is demonstrated by the notifying Member State. To demonstrate the incentive effect, the Member State concerned must prove that without the aid, that is to say, in the counterfactual situation, the more environmentally friendly alternative would not have been retained. For this purpose, the Member State concerned must provide information demonstrating that:

(a) the counterfactual situation is credible;

(b) the eligible costs have been calculated in accordance with the methodology set out in points 81, 82 and 83; and

(c) the investment would not be sufficiently profitable without aid, due account being taken of the benefits associated with the investment without aid, including the value of tradable permits which may become available to the undertaking concerned following the environmentally friendly investment.

According to point 55 of the environmental guidelines 2008, tradable permit **22–082** schemes may involve state aid in various ways, for example, when Member

States grant permits and allowances below their market value and this is imputable to Member States. This type of aid may be used to target negative externalities by allowing market-based instruments targeting environmental objectives to be introduced. If the global amount of permits granted by the Member State is lower than the global expected needs of undertakings, the overall effect on the level of environmental protection will be positive. At the individual level of each undertaking, if the allowances granted do not cover the totality of expected needs of the undertaking, the undertaking must either reduce its pollution, thus contributing to the improvement of the level of environmental protection, or buy supplementary allowances on the market, thus paying a compensation for its pollution. To limit the distortion of competition, no over-allocation of allowances can be justified and provision must be made to avoid undue barriers to entry.

The criteria set out in point 55 form the basis for the Commission's assessment of situations arising during the trading period ending on December 31, 2012. With respect to situations arising during the trading period after that date, the Commission will assess the measures according to whether they are both necessary and proportional. Finally, this will inform the revision of these Guidelines taking into account, in particular, the new Directive on the EU CO_2 Emission Trading System, for the trading period after December 31, 2012.

Chapter F of the environmental guidelines 2001 also made reference to the obligation of the Member States and the Community as parties to the Kyoto Protocol to achieve the greenhouse gas reductions agreed to by means of internal and coordinated policies and measures, including economic instruments and also by means of the instruments established by the Kyoto Protocol itself.[216] The Commission also considered the emission trading instruments such as quotas, allowances, certificates and credits to be intangible assets for recipients if they are tradable in the market. When the state on its own initiative allocates such assets free of charge, the allocation can constitute state aid. At the time of the adoption of the environmental guidelines 2001 no Community provisions in this area existed. The Commission therefore considered it to be, without prejudice to the Commission's right of initiative in proposing such provisions, up to each Member State to formulate the policies, measures and instruments it wishes to adopt in order to comply with the targets set under the Kyoto protocol.[217] The Commission took the view that some of the means adopted by Member States could constitute state aid, but that it was still too early to lay down the conditions for authorising any such aid.[218]

22–083   Prior to the entry into force of the environmental guidelines 2001, the Commission adopted a decision on the Danish national CO_2 emission-trading scheme for electricity producers.[219] It considered that granting of emission allowances

---

[216] Point 69 of the environmental guidelines [2001] O.J. C37/3. The instruments under the Kyoto Protocol are namely international emissions trading, joint implementation (JI) and the clean development mechanism (CDM).

[217] Point 70 of the environmental guidelines [2001] O.J. C37/3.

[218] Point 71 of the environmental guidelines [2001] O.J. C37/3.

[219] State aid N 653/1999, Denmark [2000] O.J. C322/9.

for free constituted state aid but approved the aid based on art.87(3)(c) EC (now 107(3)(c) TFEU). After entering into force of the environmental guidelines 2001 the Commission approved the UK national CO_2 emission trading scheme[220] and the Dutch NOx emission trading scheme,[221] in both cases considering the measure to constitute state aid. A Danish emission-trading scheme in CO_2 quotas was approved by the Commission in March 2000.[222] The Danish authorities allocate emission permits for free to electricity producers established in Denmark based on their historical emissions during the period 1994–1998. The Commission determined that giving producers emission permits for free (intangible assets) constitutes state aid under art.107(1) of the Treaty and approved the state aid directly using art.107(3)(c), without reference to the "old" environmental guidelines.[223]

In November 2001 the Commission approved a British measure called Emission Trading Scheme.[224] In the same period the Commission adopted a proposal for an emission-trading Directive.[225] This Commission proposal foresees the obligatory implementation of greenhouse gas emission trading in all Member States of the Community as of January 1, 2005 and a mandatory inclusion of a number of activities giving rise to greenhouse gas emissions. The British scheme clearly differed from the Commission proposal, as it had a much more voluntary set up. The UK scheme was notified for a period of five years. The scheme grants an incentive to companies in return for absolute emission reductions for which they bid in an auction. The incentive will not be used by the business sector to achieve Community standards. It will be used to go beyond those standards or to deliver these standards sooner than would otherwise be required, or both. Since the UK trading scheme is to be established on a voluntary basis, the availability of a financial incentive is necessary to attract participants to join the scheme. The scheme also establishes an emission trading system which allows target holders from different mechanisms to trade emission allowances amongst themselves and with other participants (entering via an emission reduction project or participants simply opening a trading account), provided they reduce emissions further below their target. Emission allowances are allocated to participants for free.

---

[220] State aid N 416/2001, United Kingdom [2002] O.J. C88/16. The approval was based on Ch.F of the environmental aid guidelines. Considering the explicit lack of criteria for approval established by the guidelines, this needs to be read rather as making reference to Ch.F which refers to the possibility for direct approval under art.87(3)(c) EC.

[221] State aid N 35/2003, The Netherlands [2003] O.J. C227/8. The Netherlands have appealed against this decision before the European Court of Justice, claiming that the measure does not constitute state aid.

[222] State aid N 416/1999, Denmark, CO_2 Quotas [2000] O.J. C354.

[223] State aid measures pursuing environmental objectives are normally assessed in the light of the environmental guidelines. However, the "old" guidelines ([1994] O.J. C72/3) did not take into account this form of state intervention. Therefore the system was assessed on the basis of art.87(3)(c) EC directly.

[224] State aid N 416/2001, United Kingdom, Emission Trading Scheme [2002] O.J. C88.

[225] Proposal for a Directive of the European Parliament and of the Council establishing a scheme for greenhouse gas emission allowance trading within the Community and amending Council Directive 96/61/EC [2001] COM 581, adopted on October 23, 2001 [2002] O.J. C075E/33–44.

22–084   As far as the existence of state aid is concerned the UK government provides on a discretionary basis, out of state resources, a grant to companies which undertake to achieve emission reduction targets in return and participate in the trading scheme. This grant confers an advantage to those companies, which distorts competition between those companies and their competitors and could potentially affect trade between Member States. The incentive money therefore constitutes state aid within the meaning of the Treaty. As regards the trading mechanism the UK authorities allocate a limited number of transferable emission permits free of charge to the participants. The state thus provides these companies with an intangible asset for free, which can be sold on a market to be created. The fact that there will be a market is a sign of the value of the asset being allocated. This has to be considered to be an advantage to the recipient companies. The fact that companies will have to incur expenses in order to realise the value of the allowances does not change the existence of an advantage, but can be considered a positive element in the assessment of the compatibility of the measure. The advantage distorts competition between companies. Companies that are able to make a profit from the allowances can use this profit when competing with other companies not having access to such a scheme. This can affect trade between Member States. The value of the permits is predicted to be considerable. By the envisaged arrangements, the British authorities forego revenue, which could derive from auctioning the emission permits. One could argue that the voluntary nature of the scheme would hinder a different allocation of allowances than free allocation, as companies would not be likely to participate in such an auction. However, the British authorities opted deliberately for a voluntary approach and by taking this option forewent the other option to gain revenue from an auction in the context of a mandatory scheme. The Commission therefore concluded that also the trading mechanism constitutes state aid within the meaning of the Treaty.[226]

There were no specific provisions in the environmental guidelines 2001 for emission trading schemes. The Commission considered some important elements in the British notified measure. The scheme was an additional effort before rules at the Community level are established. It had to provide valuable insight in the functioning of an emission trading market for the benefit of any later initiatives, as it was the first multisectoral trading scheme in the European Union. The scheme rewards companies going beyond existing standards and achieves a net environmental benefit. In order to capitalise the potential aid from the free allocation of allowances, companies have to reduce emissions further than their target levels. This can be considered as a counterpart, in line with the spirit of the environmental aid guidelines. The scheme is limited in time. The UK authorities shall comply with any EU instrument on emission trading when it comes into force, foreseen in 2005, and adapt this scheme to the extent necessary for

---

[226] See also State aid N 653/1999, Denmark, CO_2 Quotas [2000] O.J. C322; and state aid C 18/2001 (ex. N 123/2000), United Kingdom, Climate Change Levy [2001] O.J. C185, for the free allocation of allowances for companies entering into Climate Change Agreements.

compliance with such a directive. The Commission accordingly decided to consider the aid to be compatible with art.107(3)(c) of the TFEU.

The Emissions Trading Directive (ETS directive)[227] introduced for the first time an EU-wide, multi-sector CO_2 trading system and is a major instrument in the Commission's Climate Change Policy. This emissions trading scheme (ETS) started on January 1, 2005 and aims at helping EU Member States to achieve compliance with their commitments under the Kyoto Protocol by using a market based instrument.

Cornerstones of the implementation of the ETS are the so-called National Allocation Plans (NAPs). These plans establish the total number of emission allowances Member States plan to allocate for the trading period and the methods of allocating them to different installations in the economic activities involved. The ETS directive requires the Commission to assess compliance of these plans with the ETS directive. Criterion 5 of Annex III of this directive requires that a National Allocation Plan "shall not discriminate between companies or sectors in such a way as to unduly favour certain undertakings or activities in accordance with the requirements of the Treaty, in particular Articles 87 and 88[107 and 108] thereof".

22–085

In its guidance document, the Commission confirmed that "the normal state aid rules will apply".[228] By letter of March 17, 2004 to the Member States, the two director generals of DG Environment and DG Competition described under what circumstances state aid may be involved in National Allocation Plans. They also described what they considered as potentially most distortive practices in the context of allowance allocation, potentially leading to incompatible state aid. The letter indicated that the assessment of the NAPs would primarily aim to ensure the environmental effectiveness of the overall scheme and to prevent significant distortions of competition, which could arise in particular in case of over-allocation of allowances.

The Commission considered that the allocation of emission allowances confers a selective advantage to certain undertakings, which has the potential to distort competition and to affect intra-Community trade unless the allowances were sold to the recipients at market price. As regards the use of state resources and their imputability to Member States, the specificity of the ETS directive led to a differentiated assessment. Article 10 of the ETS directive obliges Member States for the first trading period from 2005 until 2007 to allocate at least 95 per cent of the allowances free of charge. This allows Member States to sell up to a maximum of 5 per cent of the allowances. To the extent that a Member State does not use its possibility to sell allowances at market price, the measure appears to be imputable to the Member State and to entail the use of state resources.[229]

---

[227] Directive 2003/87/EC of the European Parliament and of the Council of October 13, 2003 [2003] O.J. L275/32.

[228] COM(2003) 830, January 7, 2004.

[229] Another potential element of state resources was seen in the possibility to "bank" allowances from the first to the second trading period. Member States have so far not made much use of this possibility, which is in any case not foreseen for the second trading period.

22–086   The existence of aid in the context of issuing emission allowances under the ETS is not undisputed. It is indeed questionable if the Commission is right in assuming that every National Allocation Plan confers a selective advantage to the entire trading population by comparing the situation of trading companies with the non-trading population. It could be argued more restrictively that a NAP grants a selective advantage only in case it treats different groups of the trading population in a different manner which is not justified by the nature and internal logic of the emission trading system.

When the NAPS were submitted to the Commission, it assessed further if any potential aid was consistent with and seemed to be necessary to achieve the overall environmental objective of the ETS directive. It should be noted that the Commission until now screened all NAPs in the context of the ETS directive in order to identify obvious problems of probably incompatible state aid. Until now, the Commission did not take any formal state aid decision on a NAP. It has therefore also not yet taken an opinion on whether state aid approval would be based on art.107(3)(c) or on art.107(2)(b).[230] Instead of launching formal state aid procedures, the Commission sought contact with the Member State concerned in particular where a NAP seemed to contain one of the following features:

- Any potential aid does not contribute to achieve the environmental objective of the measure (this appears to be the case where a Member State allocates a total number of allowances which is not consistent with projected emissions or where it is inconsistent with its path to Kyoto).

- Beneficiaries do not deliver a sufficient environmental counterpart for any potential aid (this will be the case where they receive more than realistically projected emissions, as the aid would then not have an incentive effect to change behaviour).

- A plan leads to discrimination between trading sectors or installations, e.g. by using unjustified different allocation methods for different sectors or applying an allocation method differently to certain undertakings; also with regard to unjustified different treatment of new entrants vis-à-vis incumbents.

The criteria which the Commission applied to assess compliance of potential state aid involved are also described, if somewhat vague, in the Commission

---

[230] At first sight art.87(3)(b) is the less likely option. While the implementation of an EU-wide emission trading system may be perceived as an important project of common European interest, the specific requirements established in point 72 of the environmental aid guidelines are not necessarily met. First and foremost, an emission trading system may well be established on the basis of all allowances being sold to participants at market price and thus without the need to grant aid. It may be argued though that the directive itself apparently sees a need for free allocation as it prevents Member States from selling most of the allowances.

Decisions taken on the National Allocation Plans and in the accompanying Commission communications.[231]

Another example of environmental aid through emission trading is a Dutch **22–087** scheme on the atmospheric pollutant NOx. The Netherlands have a national emission ceiling for NOx at 260 kilotons in 2010. On the basis of this national target, the Dutch authorities have set a target of 55 kilotons of NOx emission by 2010 for its large industrial facilities. Regular instruments, like emission permit requirements and legislation on emission limits, were not sufficient to meet this target for 2010 or could incur excessive compliance costs. Therefore the Dutch authorities developed a NOx credit trading regime for large industrial facilities, which entered into force in 2004. The system covers all industrial facilities with installed total thermal capacity above 20 MWth (approximately 250 large companies). In 2000, these companies emitted 90 kilotons of NOx. The Dutch trading regime is laid down in national legislation, which will include a uniform NOx emission standard for each industrial facility. The NOx emission standard for 2010 for large industrial facilities is defined by their absolute emission target of 55 kilotons in 2010 divided by their total estimated absolute energy consumption in 2010 (1100 PJ). Herewith, the NOx emission standard reflects the maximum allowable gram of NOx per unit of energy (50g/GJ). This is a relative emission standard, instead of an absolute emission standard like an annual allowance or permit. The relative emission standard (called Performance Standard Rate) is flexible, so if economic growth would lead to an increase in absolute emissions above expected calculation, the authorities can tighten the PSR, ensuring that the 2010 target can be achieved.

The key feature of the system is that it offers a choice to facilities subject to the mandatory legislation. They can comply with the NOx emissions standard set for them either by taking measures to reduce NOx in their own facility, or by buying emission reductions (kilograms of NOx) that have been or will be achieved elsewhere, or by a combination of both. This emission trading system differs from the "cap and trade" system, whereby an absolute ceiling is set for each facility. New companies or companies wishing to expand do not have to acquire allowances. They just need to comply with the relative emission standard. This feature ensures that new companies, among which are also non-Dutch companies operating within the geographical limits of the Netherlands, are able to participate in the scheme. In the absence of Community provisions in the area of NOx emission trading, and without prejudice to the Commission's right of initiative in proposing such provisions, it is for each Member State to formulate the policies, measures and instruments on the reduction of NOx emission. The system is not voluntary; each facility must comply with the emission standard. Trading however, is optional. Emission reductions in the form of NOx credits will be offered in the "emission market" by facilities whose emissions are below the emission standard. A facility's total NOx emission in a year, adjusted for any

---

[231] These documents are accessible at *http://www.europa.eu.int/comm/environment/climat/emission_plans.htm.*

NOx credits bought or sold, must be compatible with the allowed emission, which is based on the uniform emission standard set for that year and the amount of energy used by that facility. Thus, the absolute allowed annual emission is calculated using the relative emission standard and the amount of energy used by the facility. The Dutch authorities check at the end of each year whether the facility has met the required absolute emission. In the course of each year NOx credits can be bought, sold, saved or lent for future periods. Each facility decides for itself whether, and to what extent, it is worthwhile exchanging emission reductions for the given year or a future year. When a facility would fail to meet its obligation, the Dutch authorities will put a penalty on the facility.

22–088   In these systems a variety of tradable emission or pollution documents are used, like quotas, allowances, certificates and credits. The Commission considers the tradable emission documents as intangible assets provided by the authorities to the recipients. As regards state aid assessment, there are two kinds of trade systems:

1. systems where a tradable emission or pollution document is considered as an intangible asset representing a market value which the authorities could have sold or auctioned as well, leading to foregone revenues (or a loss of state resources), hence state aid within the meaning of art.107(1) of the TFEU[232];

2. systems where a tradable emission or pollution document is considered as authorised proof of a certain production that can not be sold or auctioned to the recipient, hence no foregone revenues, therefore no state resources and no state aid within the meaning of art.107(1) of the TFEU.[233]

The difference between the two systems is whether the public authorities have an alternative option to sell or auction the intangible asset to the recipient. In the first kind of system there is a rationale for the public authorities to sell or auction the emission or pollution document to the producer of that emission or pollution, as the tradable emission or pollution document will give him the right to emit or pollute (directly or indirectly). In the second kind of system the tradable emission or pollution document has no value to the recipient in relationship to the state and it will merely serve as an authorised proof of certain production or emission. Hence, there is no rationale for the public authorities to sell or auction it to the producer of that emission or pollution document.[234]

---

[232] See for instance state aid N 653/1999, Denmark, CO_2-quota system [2000] O.J. C322/9 and state aid N 416/2001, United Kingdom, Emission trading scheme [2002] O.J. C88.
[233] See for instance state aid N 550/2000, Belgium, Green Electricity Certificates [2001] O.J. C330/3.
[234] The fact that a tradable emission or pollution document has a value to the recipient in relationship to third parties (like the distributors or consumers in green electricity certificates) is of other importance in this respect.

The fact that there will be a market for trading emission or pollution documents is a sign of the value of the asset being allocated. The fact that undertakings will have to have expenses in order to realise the value of the tradable emission or pollution documents does not change the existence of an advantage, but can be considered a positive element in the assessment of the compatibility of the scheme concerned. The NOx emission scheme was based on tradable emission credits. These credits do not represent direct permits (or allowances) as in other emission schemes, nor do they solely represent an authorised proof. The annual allowed absolute emission per facility will be calculated on the basis of the general PSR and the energy use of that facility in the year at hand. When the producer would exceed this absolute emission ceiling, he has the obligation to buy NOx credits, to borrow the credits of his obligation in the following year or, ultimately, he is fined.

The tradable NOx credits will thus contribute directly to the absolute emission standard imposed by the state. Therefore, the Commission considers the notified NOx emission trade system comparable to a direct NOx emission allowance allocation. Secondly, it is the producer himself who is obliged to meet his emission standard. The producer has an incentive to pay for the tradable emission documents, as long as the price of that tradable emission document is lower than the costs of reducing his own emission or when the price of that tradable emission document is lower than the penalty. In the notified scheme the producer emitting NOx is penalised when he does not meet his emission standard. The same producer will also be a recipient of tradable emission documents (NOx credits). The issued tradable emission document to the recipient will therefore represent a value as regards his obligation to meet his absolute emission ceiling imposed by the state. Thirdly, the Dutch authorities do have an option to sell or auction the emission standards. As the emission of NOx is an environmentally harmful activity (pollution) it would be possible for the state to receive revenues through a permit system or for instance through an auction of emission allowances. The Dutch authorities provide the NOx credits as free intangible assets, thus suffering foregone revenues. Therefore, the Commission decided that these private systems do constitute state resources within the meaning of art.107(1) of the TFEU.

The Commission had to assess the NOx emission trading scheme directly **22–089** under art.107(3)(c) TFEU, as the environmental guidelines 2001 do not provide clear criteria for emission trading of air pollutants. The Commission acknowledges that the reduction of emission of atmospheric pollutants is a priority of environmental policy of the European Union and the Dutch initiative is an additional effort before rules at the Community level are established. This scheme is the first multisectoral emission trading scheme in the European Union concerning conventional air pollution and it will provide valuable insight in the functioning of a NOx emission trading market for the benefit of any later initiatives at EU or at national level. The notified scheme rewards undertakings going beyond existing standards and achieves a net environmental benefit. In order to capitalise the potential aid from the free allocation of NOx credits, undertakings concerned have to reduce emissions further than their target levels. This can be considered as a counterpart, in line with the spirit of the environmental guidelines 2001. Therefore the Commission decided to authorise the scheme directly under art.107(3)(c) TFEU.

The Dutch authorities however did not accept this outcome. As a principle matter, the Dutch authorities held on to their conclusion that the scheme does not constitute aid. Consequently, the Dutch authorities went to Court with this case, arguing that the state aid classification of the scheme results in bureaucratic obligations (like annual reports) and possible harmful consequences like cumulation with other aid instruments.[235]

In 2010, the European Commission launched a public consultation to prepare Guidelines on how Member States can support sectors exposed to certain additional costs in the context of the 2013 EU Emission Trading System (ETS–3). The EU ETS was introduced in 2005 to promote the reduction of CO_2 emissions and prevent climate change. For the 3rd trading period 2013–2020, the amended ETS Directive 2009/29/EC foresees that Member States may grant state aid in favour of sectors exposed to a significant risk of "carbon leakage". "Carbon leakage" is the result of the increase in the CO_2 component of electricity prices (indirect emission costs) which firms may not be able to pass on or to bear. It occurs when global greenhouse gas emissions increase because companies, that cannot pass on to their customers this increased electricity costs generated by the CO_2 costs, move their production outside the European Union to countries where no CO_2 constraints exist and reduce their EU-based share in world production. State aid for indirect emission would thus aim at mitigating this potential perverse effect of the ETS system. The deadline for replies is May 11, 2011.

21. AID IN THE FORM OF ENVIRONMENTAL TAX EXEMPTIONS OR REDUCTIONS

22–090   Reductions of and exemptions from environmental taxes concerning certain sectors or categories of undertakings may make it feasible to adopt higher taxes for other undertakings, thus resulting in an overall improvement of cost internalisation, and to create further incentives to improve on environmental protection. Accordingly, this type of aid may be necessary to target negative externalities indirectly by facilitating the introduction or maintenance of relatively high national environmental taxation. For aid to be compatible, it must be shown that the exemptions or reductions are necessary for all the suggested categories of beneficiaries and that they are proportional in size. This is assumed to be the case if beneficiaries pay at least the Community minimum tax level set by the applicable Directive, if any. Otherwise, the necessity will depend on the extent to which the national tax impacts on production costs as well as on the possibility

---

[235] An action against the Commission was brought before the Court of Justice of the European Communities on September 5, 2003.

to pass on the tax to consumers and reduce profit margins. Proportionality will depend on the extent to which the beneficiaries can further reduce their consumption or emission, pay a part of the national tax or enter into environmental agreements to reduce pollution.

Aid in the form of reductions of or exemptions from environmental taxes must be necessary and proportional. The Commission will consider the aid to be necessary if the following cumulative conditions are met:

(a) the choice of beneficiaries must be based on objective and transparent criteria, and the aid must be granted in principle in the same way for all competitors in the same sector/relevant market if they are in a similar factual situation;

(b) the environmental tax without reduction must lead to a substantial increase in production costs for each sector or category of individual beneficiaries; and

(c) the substantial increase in production costs cannot be passed on to customers without leading to important sales reductions. In this respect, Member States may provide estimations of inter alia the product price elasticity of the sector concerned in the relevant geographic market as well as estimates of lost sales and/or reduced profits for the companies in the sector/category concerned.

The Commission will consider the aid to be proportional if one of the following conditions is met:

(a) the scheme lays down criteria ensuring that each individual beneficiary pays a proportion of the national tax level which is broadly equivalent to the environmental performance of each individual beneficiary compared to the performance related to the best performing technique within the EEA. Under the aid scheme any undertaking reaching the best performing technique can benefit, at most, from a reduction corresponding to the increase in production costs from the tax, using the best performing technique, and which cannot be passed on to customers. Any undertaking having a worse environmental performance shall benefit from a lower reduction, proportionate to its environmental performance;

(b) aid beneficiaries pay at least 20 per cent of the national tax, unless a lower rate can be justified in view of a limited distortion of competition; or

(c) the reductions or exemptions are conditional on the conclusion of agreements between the Member State and the recipient undertakings or associations of undertakings whereby the undertakings or associations of undertakings commit themselves to achieve environmental protection objectives which have the same effect as if point (a) or (b) or the

Community minimum tax level were applied. Such agreements or commitments may relate, among other things, to a reduction in energy consumption, a reduction in emissions or any other environmental measure and must satisfy the following conditions:

  i. the substance of the agreements must be negotiated by each Member State and must specify in particular the targets and fix a time schedule for reaching the targets;

  ii. Member States must ensure independent and timely monitoring of the commitments concluded in these agreements;

  iii. these agreements must be revised periodically in the light of technological and other developments and stipulate effective penalty arrangements applicable if the commitments are not met.

22–091   In June 2008, Denmark notified to the Commission two environmental tax reliefs from environmental taxes for the cement industry: one from the newly introduced tax on nitrogen oxide (NOx) and a full exemption from the existing waste tax on certain waste from cement production. According to the environmental guidelines, aid in the form of reductions of or exemptions from environmental taxes will be considered compatible with the internal market provided that it contributes at least indirectly to an improvement in the level of environmental protection and that the tax reductions and exemptions do not undermine the general objective pursued. As regards the NOx tax reduction, there is an indirect environmental benefit stemming from the fact that the general tax level can be higher than it would be without the reduction. As regards the risk of undermining the general objective pursued, Denmark tried to keep the reduction to a minimum by limiting the number of beneficiaries and requiring that the beneficiary still pays 53 per cent of the full tax. The Commission considered that the measure was necessary and proportionate and approved the proposed NOx tax reduction on October 28, 2009. However, with respect to the full exemption from the waste tax, the Commission had doubts about the necessity and proportionality of the tax exemption, in particular since the full exemption would leave the company with no incentive to contribute to the environmental objective of the waste tax. The Commission opened a formal investigation procedure on October 28, 2009 (now case C 30/2009) and invited third parties to provide comments. A final decision has not yet been adopted.

Member States have sometimes argued that a reduction from an environmental tax, which does not even exist in other Member States, cannot be regarded as an advantage for its firms, even more where despite of the reduction the beneficiaries pay a higher tax than before the introduction of the tax. Article 107 TFEU however becomes relevant where the state measure has the potential to benefit certain undertakings compared to other undertakings, which are in a comparable factual and legal situation.[236] Neither a comparison with the previous legal situation of the beneficiaries nor a comparison with their competitors in

---

[236] Case C–143/99 *Adria-Wien Pipeline and Wietersdorfer & Peggauer* [2001] E.C.R. I–8365, point 41.

other Member States can therefore be successfully used to demonstrate the non-aid character of a national measure. Exemptions from environmental taxes themselves have by their very nature usually a negative environmental impact. However, the Commission acknowledges that these exemptions may be necessary in order to enable a Member State to introduce a new environmental tax, despite its, at first negative, impact on the competitiveness of the national economy. This holds true in particular where a tax has not been harmonised at European level. The guidelines therefore allow certain tax exemptions, provided that the overall net effect of the environmental tax, including the effects of the exemptions, is positive for the environment.

In the judgment by the European Court of Justice on November 8, 2001 in the **22–092** *Adria-Wien Pipeline* case[237] the question was raised as to whether the Austrian national measures which provided for exemptions from energy taxes on natural gas and electricity only in the case of manufacturing companies should be regarded as state aid or not within the meaning of art.107(1) TFEU. The Austrian government argued that the tax exemptions in question did not constitute state aid as the tax measures were part of a wider package of measures intended to consolidate the budget, affecting a much wider range of companies and other socio-economic groups. The package should therefore be considered as a whole. Secondly, the Austrian government argued that the tax exemptions were only for the implementation period of the package to facilitate the implementation of the measures for those most affected by them, in this case, manufacturing companies. Finally, the Austrian government argued that the tax exemptions had no selective nature, because they were granted on the basis of objective criteria, laid down by law. Moreover, the authorities had no discretion in selecting the companies eligible for the tax exemption.

The Court of Justice found these arguments unfounded. The Court argued that a large number of companies affected per se does not automatically mean that the measure is a general measure. Secondly, it found no proof that manufacturing companies were in any way more affected by energy taxes than companies in other sectors, like the service sector, which can also be a major consumer of energy. Furthermore, the legislation did not contain any provisions that would suggest that the tax exemptions were temporary measures. Therefore, the ecological considerations that were mentioned in support of the system were not convincing, as energy consumption is damaging to the environment regardless of the sector in which the consumer operates. The Court therefore concluded that unless the energy tax rebates apply to all companies within the national territory, the measures in question do constitute state aid within the meaning of art.107(1) of the Treaty.

In the Commission Decision for the UK Climate Change Levy[238] the Commission decided amongst other things that a tax exemption for industrial combined

---

[237] Case C–143/99 *Adria-Wien Pipeline and Wietersdorfer & Peggauer* [2001] E.C.R. I–8365.
[238] State aid C 18/2001 (ex. N 123/2001), United Kingdom, Climate Change Levy [2001] O.J. C185/22. This UK notification raised an array of different state aid questions, one of which (exemption for dual-use fuels) also led to the initiation of formal investigation proceedings.

heat and power (CHP) plants was not selective and therefore did not constitute state aid within the meaning of art.107(1) of the TFEU, as industrial CHP plants were widely used in most sectors of the UK economy. Nevertheless, as opposed to the *Adria-Wien Pipeline* case, there have been several recent cases where the Commission has decided that tax exemptions from energy taxes are justified by the nature of the tax system. In the Commission decision for the aforementioned UK Climate Change Levy[239] the Commission decided that the production of green electricity by its nature does not add to climate change problems. As the production of green electricity does not contribute to long-cycle CO_2 emissions, it is logical that the CO_2 tax does not apply. The objective of the tax measure is to address the CO_2 problem, so it is inherent in the nature of the tax measure that green electricity producers are not penalised. Therefore, the Commission was of the opinion that the tax exemption falls outside the scope of application of art.107(1) of the Treaty.

22–093   The same reasoning was applied in the decision on a Dutch tax measure in November 2001 called "Tax Rate Increase In Relation To The Green Electricity Zero Tariff", which provided similar tax exemptions for green electricity in the Dutch energy tax legislation.[240] The same reasoning was also used in another Dutch tax measure called "Zero Rate In The Energy Tax For Renewable Gas",[241] also approved by the Commission in November 2001. This measure aims at the Dutch gas market. Renewable gas is defined as landfill gas, sewage treatment plant gas and biogas. As these kinds of natural gases do not contribute to long-cycle CO_2 emissions, it is inherent in the nature of the tax that producers of renewable gas are not penalised. However, the Commission continued to examine the aforementioned UK and Dutch fiscal measures applying the guidelines on environmental aid. For the UK levy, compatibility was assessed, for the first time, on the basis of "operating aid in the form of tax reductions or exemptions and based on the conclusion of agreements between the Member State and the aid recipients". In the Dutch green electricity case,[242] compatibility was assessed on the basis of the rules applicable to existing taxes. As all conditions set out in the environmental guidelines were fully met in both cases, the Commission did not raise any objections to these types of exemptions. Thus the Commission decided that even if, contrary to the assumption of no state aid within the meaning of art.107(1) TFEU, the measure would constitute state aid, the measures were compatible with the environmental guidelines. This kind of decision gives a go-ahead for the measure(s) concerned, but the Member States are not given full clarity whether the measures do or do not constitute state aid within the meaning of art.107(1) TFEU.

---

[239] State aid C 18/2001 (ex. N 123/2001), United Kingdom, Climate Change Levy [2002] O.J. C185/22.

[240] State aid NN 30b/2000, The Netherlands, Tax Rate Increase In Relation To The Green Electricity Zero Tariff [2002] O.J. C30.

[241] State aid N 168/A/2001, The Netherlands, Modifications energy tax 2001 [2002] O.J. C30.

[242] State aid NN 30b/2000, The Netherlands, Tax Rate Increase In Relation To The Green Electricity Zero Tariff [2002] O.J. C30.

The Dutch zero tariff for green electricity resulted in an interesting economic and political paradox. In 2001, the Commission came to the conclusion that the measure in principle did not constitute state aid, see above. Only one year later, the Dutch authorities notified an update of their energy tax.[243] Instead of applying a zero rate tariff, the Dutch authorities introduced minimum rates for green electricity. The minimum rates were still lower than the regular energy tax rates, but no longer a zero rate was applied. Thus, the Dutch authorities introduced a partial taxation on green electricity. The Commission came to the conclusion that the new measure included taxation on green electricity. Accordingly, the tax base of the levy was not only on the output of CO_2, but on the use of energy as such. Therefore, the Commission decided that the tax reduction was no longer inherent in the nature of the tax measure. Accordingly, the measure was earmarked as a state aid measure, and approved under the environmental guidelines 2001. From a legal point of view, the assessment was correct. From a political point of view, a no-aid measure turned into an aid measure, whilst the advantage of the measure to the beneficiaries was decreased. Statistically, the Dutch authorities lowered their expenditure on green electricity by having less foregone tax revenues, but they increased their state aid expenditure enormously by €2.8 billion. In the state aid scoreboard that year expenditure on green electricity was suddenly booming, whilst practical expenditure was actually going down.

Another example of a tax measure that does not constitute state aid according **22–094** to art.107(1) of the TFEU is the following case. In 2000 the UK authorities notified a measure called "Enhanced Capital Allowances for energy efficient investments".[244] The measure is intended to provide a tax-incentive to encourage businesses to invest in energy saving technologies. The measure covers equipment in several technology classes provided it meets strict energy saving criteria. This measure will enable businesses to take tax relief that they would be entitled to under existing law earlier than permitted under the current rules. A business will be able to write off immediately its expenditure on qualifying equipment against its taxable profits. In line with the Commission notice on the application of the state aid rules to measures relating to direct business taxation,[245] all businesses will be able to claim the enhanced capital allowances, regardless of size, industrial or commercial sector, or location and no restrictions are imposed on the source of the equipment in the qualifying technology classes. Therefore the Commission decided in March 2001 that the measure does not constitute state aid according to art.107(1) of the Treaty.

There was also a fiscal case in which the Commission decided that the measure does constitute state aid according to art.107(1) TFEU. In December 2001 the Commission decided upon a Dutch fiscal case called "provision in the energy tax

---

[243] State aid N 652 /2002, Fiscal reforms energy tax 2003 [2003] O.J. C104.
[244] State aid N 797/2000, United Kingdom, Enhanced Capital Allowances for energy efficient investments [2001] O.J. C160.
[245] [1998] O.J. C384/3.

for producers of sustainable heat".[246] This measure within the Dutch energy tax legislation aims at promoting combined heat and power-installations (CHP) fired with biomass. The measure is a fiscal incentive for production of heat by CHP installations that use biomass. The measure works as follows. The energy distribution company, which collects the energy tax on regular electricity and natural gas from consumers, may apply a deduction on the total energy tax to be paid to the tax authorities, when sustainable heat has been delivered from the producer to the relevant distribution company. In this respect it should be noted that there is no energy tax levied on heat in the Netherlands. The Dutch authorities are of the opinion that the use of heat as a source of energy should not be discouraged by a tax, as it is usually produced by environmental friendly CHP installations. As there is no tax levied on heat, the aforementioned deduction by the distribution companies is financed by foregone revenues on the levied tax on regular electricity and/or natural gas. The aid intensity of this measure is calculated at 17.5 per cent of the extra costs. As far as the question "state aid or not" is concerned the Commission noticed that the measure gives an advantage to the companies concerned (producers of sustainable heat) as the deduction of the tax is passed on to the producers of sustainable heat by the energy distribution companies. As the state will suffer foregone revenues, this measure is financed by state resources. Furthermore, the use of biomass/CHP installations in the Netherlands is limited to two companies. For the short and possibly medium term only very specific industrial CHP installations will produce heat from biomass. In addition, non-industrial CHP's are not excluded,[247] hence a selective amount of power stations are supported by this measure. Therefore this measure is selective. Finally, heat deliverance is limited to the near surroundings of the location of production, due to high costs of transport of heat. In practice there is no cross border trade in heat in the Netherlands. However, the recipient operators do not only produce heat, but also electricity. The financial assistance provided to the recipient biomass CHP undertakings therefore distorts or threatens to distort competition on the electricity market. The Commission therefore decided that art.107(1) of the TFEU is applicable to this measure.

22–095   In Sweden, there is a relatively high tax on energy, the objective of which is to increase energy saving and energy efficiency. In order, for environmental reasons, to have relatively high energy tax levels and at the same time maintain the competitiveness of the manufacturing sector, tax relief is allowed for the manufacturing industry. A lower tax rate applies for electricity used in the

---

[246] State aid N 651/2001, The Netherlands, Modifications Energy Tax 2000 Sustainable Heat [2002] O.J. C77.

[247] In the British Climate Change Levy case (state aid C 18/2001 (ex. N 123/2001), United Kingdom, Climate Change Levy [2001] O.J. C185/22) the power of non-industrial CHP, i.e. power stations, was explicitly excluded from tax exemption. For power stations, the production of electricity is core business, and the electricity produced is in direct competition with the same product from conventional electricity producers. Electricity from CHP systems is therefore not exempted from energy tax in the United Kingdom if it is sold via the grid. Only CHP electricity that is used on the site of the power station is exempted, as these CHP power stations are in the same situation as any other auto-generator in any other sector of the economy.

production of companies in the manufacturing sector.[248] The Commission has approved the relief as it was in line with the environmental guidelines as well as with the "Energy Tax Directive".[249] According to the guidelines, non-degressive tax exemptions covering a 10-year period from environmental taxes can in certain cases be justified when a Member State introduces a new tax in the absence of a harmonised Community tax or when the tax in a Member State exceeds that laid down by Community legislation. In the Swedish case, the lower tax rate remains higher than the applicable minimum level. Therefore, the Commission considered the notified aid scheme to be compliant with the Energy Tax Directive and with the environmental guidelines (particularly points 51.1(b) and 51.2) and it was thus approved on the basis of art.107(3)(c). In addition to this general energy tax relief for electricity consumed during the production process, the Swedish authorities introduced in 2004 a system with voluntary agreements on energy saving with energy-intensive companies.[250] For these companies, a zero-tax rate on electricity used in their production processes will be applied under the condition that they participate in a five year programme for increased energy. The programme imposes certain obligations to be fulfilled by the companies during the programme and penalty provisions in case these obligations are not fulfilled. The obligations are considered to replace the steering effect of the energy tax on electricity used in the production processes of the undertakings. The fact that energy costs constitute an important part of these companies' total costs is an additional incentive for the companies to implement energy saving measures. Since the scheme was found to be in line with the conditions of the environmental guidelines (in particular point 51.1(a)) and with the Energy Taxation Directive, the Commission authorised the scheme on the basis of art.107(3)(c).

22. COMPATIBILITY OF AID UNDER ARTICLE 107(3)(B) TFEU

Aid to promote the execution of important projects of common European interest which are an environmental priority may be considered compatible with the internal market according to art.107(3)(b) TFEU provided that the following conditions are fulfilled:

22-096

a) the aid proposal concerns a project which is specific and clearly defined in respect of the terms of its implementation including its participants, its objectives and effects and the means to achieve the objectives. The Commission may also consider a group of projects as together constituting a project;

---

[248] State aid N 156/2004 [2005] O.J. C137/5.
[249] Council Directive 2003/96/EC of October 27, 2003 restructuring the Community Framework for the taxation of energy products and electricity [2003] O.J. L283/51.
[250] State aid N 253/2004 [2005] O.J. C136/43.

b) the project must be in the common European interest: the project must contribute in a concrete, exemplary and identifiable manner to the Community interest in the field of environmental protection, such as by being of great importance for the environmental strategy of the European Union. The advantage achieved by the objective of the project must not be limited to the Member State or the Member States implementing it, but must extend to the Community as a whole. The project must present a substantive contribution to the Community objectives. The fact that the project is carried out by undertakings in different Member States is not sufficient;

c) the aid is necessary and presents an incentive for the execution of the project, which must involve a high level of risk; and

d) the project is of great importance with regard to its volume: it must be substantial in size and produce substantial environmental effects.

In order to allow the Commission to properly assess such projects, the common European interest must be demonstrated in practical terms: for example, it must be demonstrated that the project enables significant progress to be made towards achieving specific environmental objectives of the Community. The Commission will consider notified projects more favourably if they include a significant own contribution of the beneficiary to the project. It will equally consider more favourably notified projects involving undertakings from a significant number of Member States. When the aid is considered to be compatible with the internal market in accordance with art.107(3)(b) TFEU, the Commission may authorise aid at higher rates than otherwise laid down in the environmental guidelines 2008.

23. State Aid Expenditure on Environmental Aid

22–097   Before mentioning statistics on environmental state aid, it should be noted that many environmental and energy saving support measures are not considered to be state aid measures within the meaning of the TFEU and are not covered by the data on state aid expenditure. Examples of such aid measures are discussed in section 5 of this chapter. As indicated by the data of the European Commission, the total aid expenditure earmarked for environmental protection amounted to €13.2 billion in 2009, (excluding aid to agriculture, fisheries, transport as well as crisis measures).[251] In relative terms, aid amount spent on environmental protection represented 22.6 per cent of total aid or 0.11 per cent of EU-27 GDP in 2009. Several Member States spent a substantial part of its total amount of aid for

---

[251] The source of these data is the Commission staff working document "Facts and figures on State aid in the Member States Accompanying the State Aid Scoreboard", Autumn 2010 Update of December 1, 2010 (SEC (2010) 1462 final).

environmental protection and energy savings: Sweden (82%), the Netherlands (62%), Latvia (51%), Finland (41%), Germany (37%), the United Kingdom (36%), and Austria (35%). Of the total amount of environmental aid in 2009, just €732 million was granted on the basis of the GBER, which could be due to the novelty of the exemptions in 2009. Almost half of this aid was granted by Germany. This country together with Spain and Belgium contributed to around 91 per cent of total environmental aid granted using block exempted measures in 2009.

For the European Union as a whole, the trend of aid for environmental protection decreased from 25.5 per cent to 23.3 per cent of total aid to industry and services between 2004–2006 and 2007–2009. In absolute terms, it however increased by €0.8 billion. Over the last six years Member States granted on average 75 per cent of aid through indirect forms, such as tax exemptions and allowances, while direct aid instruments, e.g. grants or subsidies, represented on average 25 per cent of total environmental aid.

The overall level of expenditure in environmental aid in the European Union is strongly influenced by the largest aid grantors, Germany, Sweden, the United Kingdom and the Netherlands. In Germany and Sweden, tax exemptions account for a large share of total environmental aid. A tax exemption from the energy tax on electricity for industry has been the most significant aid expenditure for Sweden from 2005 onwards and represents more than half of the environmental aid in Sweden. In Germany, expenditure rose steadily up to 2006 following the approval in 2002 of measures that prolonged several tax exemptions from the German energy taxation on electricity and mineral oils. Following modifications to these tax exemptions in Germany, aid granted under environmental tax exemption schemes fell significantly, by €3.2 billion between 2006 and 2009.

In the period 2004–2010, the Commission took 347 final decisions on state aid for environmental protection, i.e. energy saving or other environmental protection objectives. This included 320 compatible aid decisions, 21 no-aid decisions and 6 negative decisions. The large majority of the decisions taken (slightly above 82%) concerned schemes, 6 per cent concerned the individual application of a scheme and 11 per cent related to ad hoc measures. Five Member States accounted for half of the decisions taken: Italy (44), Germany (38), the Netherlands (36), the United Kingdom (33) and the Czech Republic (26). Almost 140 decisions were taken in the years 2006–2007, prior to the entry into force of the environmental aid guidelines and the GBER. The detailed economic assessment was introduced in April 2008 in the environmental aid guidelines, and 10 positive detailed assessment decisions have been taken by the Commission in the period until the end of 2010. Member States introduced 219 block exempted measures, of which 194 were schemes. The highest numbers of schemes were introduced by Germany (40), Italy (39), Spain (38) and the United Kingdom (21). As to the detailed objectives pursued by these aids, the most popular one was the promotion of energy from renewable energy sources (art. 21 of the General Block Exemption Regulation), that existed (as a single objective or one of the objectives) in 120 block exempted measures. It was followed by investments in energy

22–098

saving measures (art.21 GBER, 101 measures), investment aid enabling under-takings to go beyond EU standards for environmental protection (art.18 GBER, 71 measures), aid for environmental studies (art.24, 61 measures) and investment aid for high efficiency cogeneration (art.22 GBER, 58 measures). The other GBER objectives played less important roles (art.19, 42 measures; art.20, 25 measures; art.25, 7 measures).[252]

In light of the Europe 2020 Strategy, the European Commission is of the opinion that state aid may be necessary to achieve the EU environmental objectives that cannot be achieved through market-based incentives or through regulation. The role of state aid control is to ensure that aid for an environmental objective does not unduly distort competition. State aid control can also accompany further the harmonisation of support schemes across Member States towards a European internal market for energy. State aid control may play a role in particular to increase harmonisation of support to renewables to limit competition distortions between renewables produced in different Member States and avoid overcompensation in the coming years.

24. OUTLOOK TO FURTHER DEVELOPMENT

22–099   The current environmental guidelines are applicable until the end of 2014. The Commission will probably review the current guidelines in the course of 2014, in order to prepare new guidelines for environmental aid. It is also common practice that the Commission publishes a questionnaire and invites all Member States and other interested parties to share their experiences with the current guidelines.

The scope of the environmental guidelines is quite limited to environmental aid. There are several areas that are connected to or similar to environmental aid with strong parallels in the argumentation for aid grants. Examples are safety of civilians and employees and health of consumers and employees. State aid in order to stimulate the reduction of the use of raw materials does not to fall within the scope of the guidelines. Also state aid to district heating infrastructure and for instance grey water systems falls outside the scope of the environmental guide-lines. The 2008 environmental guidelines introduced new rules for eco-efficient innovative research and development, market introduction and investments in order to promote the take-up of environmental technologies. Until 2008, these kinds of project fell in between the environmental guidelines and the R&D framework.[253] R&D of new innovative environmentally friendly technologies was not valued extra within the scope of the aid guidelines for R&D, nor in the guidelines on state aid for environmental protection when investments are made

---

[252] State aid Scoreboard; Report on State aid contribution to Europe 2020 Strategy, Spring 2011 Update of June 22, 2011 (COM(2011) 356 final).

[253] See also the Consultation Document on State Aid for Innovation, see: *http://europa.eu.int/comm/ competition/state_aid/others/action_plan/*. Press Release IP/05/1169.

in such technologies. In the meantime we have seen a certain eco-innovation bonus, although not many Member States have actually used this provision.

The 2005 State Aid Action Plan introduced a general balancing test that should be used in state aid policy. The environmental guidelines 2008 were adapted to this economic approach, introducing a large number of economic indicators and criteria for large environmental cases. In practice this brings forward an enormous administrative burden in the notification process, both for Member States and the Commission. This increase in the assessment criteria can also bring forward an increase in potential risk that the cases are contested for the national and European courts. This is an interesting paradox: the more rules and criteria we try to put on environmental state aid measures in order to increase transparency and limit possible distortion of competition, the more complicated the assessment gets, with also a risk of an increase in legal uncertainty. And this legal uncertainty often leads to less environmental investments. If there is only a simple definition of eligible costs (like the initial investment costs) and a simple aid intensity, it is quite hard to contest the aid. But if we add a lot of economic parameters to the assessment and a lot of qualitative judgement, opinions will differ more and more and legal uncertainty will increase. In many Member States this has actually happened. Instead of simplification of the rules in order to increase environmental investments, the top priority seems to be focussed on strict competition policy and limiting public expenditure, herewith limiting environmental investments.

The general block exemption regulation (GBER) has brought significant relief in the administrative burden of the notification procedure for some types of environmental aid. Herewith, the GBER has probably accelerated the introduction of new environmental state aid measures. However, the GBER did not change the criteria for granting significantly, nor did it relieve part of the complicated calculation methods. The environmental guidelines are still in need of a further simplification of the definition of eligible cost. The Dutch case N 266/2003 (Offshore Windpark Q7, investment in renewable energy sources) showed the complexity of the calculation method. For every single large investment case, Member States need to compare the costs of an environmentally friendly investment with the cost of an investment using the best available technique. This case-by-case assessment is quite costly and time consuming. Therefore, a simplified method should be considered, also for the larger cases. If investments in renewable energy is really that important to European policy makers, the state aid rules should not hinder green developments in the European economy.

CHAPTER 23

RESEARCH, DEVELOPMENT AND INNOVATION AID*

1. INTRODUCTION 23–001
   Policy background RDI 23–002
   SAAP and the innovation communication 23–003
   Balancing test 23–004
   New architecture: GBER, detailed assessment and effects-based approach 23–005
   Important projects of common European interest 23–006
   Matching clause 23–007
2. NOTION OF AID FOR R & D 23–008
   Public funding of research organisations 23–009
   Indirect aid from the public funding of research organisations 23–010
   Fiscal aid 23–011
3. STANDARD ASSESSMENT 23–012
   Incentive effect 23–013
   R & D projects 23–014
   Innovation aid 23–015
4. DETAILED ASSESSMENT 23–022
   Effects-based analysis 23–023
   Assessment criteria 23–024
   Balancing: a stricter approach than in the past 23–029
5. CONCLUSION 23–030
   Reporting obligations 23–031
   Some statistics 23–032
   Mid-term review 23–034

1. INTRODUCTION

23–001   The R & D & I Framework[1] has been in force since the beginning of 2007. It is the successor of two previous frameworks of 1986 and 1996 whose scope was however largely limited to R & D projects. To that extent, the 2006 Framework for R & D & I constituted a break-through for state aid policy, as it was the first

---

* Thibaut Kleiner
[1] Framework for State aid for Research and Development and Innovation [2006] O.J. C 323/1.

real deliverable of the State Aid Action Plan (SAAP)[2] in terms of implementing a refined economic approach.[3]

The novelties of the R & D & I Framework included, in the first place, clear provisions on funding of research organisations and on aid to R & D projects. Second, the R & D & I Framework included a set of innovation measures. Third, the R & D & I Framework included a section explaining how the Commission will carry out a detailed assessment of large R & D cases. The R & D & I Framework was the first application of the new economic approach to state aid, as reflected especially in its architecture, the way it justifies the granting of aid for the measures covered, including innovation, and in the provisions governing the assessment of large individual aid.

Policy background RDI

Research, development and innovation (R & D & I) is one of the European Union's top priorities, and has been at the core of its strategic economic agenda for a number of years. This was already set out in the 14th Report on Competition Policy (1984, at pts 255 and following). R & D & I was promoted in the Lisbon Strategy in 2000 and 2005[4] and most recently in the Europe 2020 strategy.   **23–002**

The Europe 2020 strategy[5] puts R & D & I at its heart with the objective of achieving an overall R & D spending of 3 per cent of the GDP. In particular, the Commission indicates that there is a clear need to improve the conditions for private R & D in the European Union. The R & D spending in Europe is below 2 per cent, compared to 2.6 per cent in the US and 3.4 per cent in Japan, mainly as a result of lower levels of private investment. The Europe 2020 Communication makes an explicit reference to the role of State aid:

"State aid policy can also actively and positively contribute to the Europe 2020 objectives by prompting and supporting initiatives for more innovative, efficient and greener technologies, while facilitating access to public support for investment, risk capital and funding for research and development".

An important way to stimulate innovation is by fostering effective competition. Competition in free and open markets pushes firms to innovate, as this is a way for them to improve and differentiate their products, increase their appeal to customers and thereby survive competitive pressures. However, there are situations where markets on their own fail to ensure optimum levels of R & D & I and

---

[2] State Aid Action Plan: Less and better targeted state aid: a roadmap for state aid reform 2005–2009 (Consultation document COM (2005)107).

[3] The 2005 Regional Aid Guidelines and Framework for Services of General Economic Interest, while introducing some improvements in the analysis of distortions of competition, did not explicitly refer to the balancing test, for instance.

[4] Communication to the Spring European Council—Working together for growth and jobs—A new start for the Lisbon Strategy—Communication from President Barroso in agreement with Vice-President Verheugen; SEC (2005) 192.

[5] Europe2020: A strategy for smart, sustainable and inclusive growth; COM (2010) 2020.

where state aid may be needed. On that basis, the primary objective of the new Framework for R & D & I is twofold[6]:

- to help Member States to channel a larger share of their total state aid budgets towards R & D and innovation; and

- to help Member States target R & D & I state aid towards the best projects, on the basis of economic analysis, so that distortions of competition and trade are minimised and public spending efficiency is maximised.

SAAP and the innovation communication

23–003   The SAAP launched a state aid reform to support less and better targeted aid. It made, however, very clear that better targeted aid may also mean more aid for R & D, and also more aid to innovation. Before 2005, aid for innovation was regarded rather suspiciously by the Commission, as it resembles, to some extent, operating aid, which is normally only very exceptionally authorised. As it is a normal activity of firms to innovate, and as innovation is inherently difficult to define, and rather close to the market, the Commission was not very keen to offer specific provisions for state aid to innovation. However, this taboo was broken by SAAP and even more by the Communication on state aid for innovation.[7]

The Communication outlined the parameters for possible measures that could deserve state aid support, on the basis of an application of the balancing test broadly defined in the SAAP and applied to innovation. It explained that state aid could only be a moderate solution to the many problems of lack of innovation in the Union. It also recognised that there was scope for state aid for innovation, and launched a consultation in that respect.

> "A series of concrete and targeted innovation-related activities, subject to this consultation, were identified, which clearly address the market failures that are hampering innovation and for which the benefits of State aid are likely to outweigh any possible harm to competition and trade. In doing so, the Commission used a methodology in line with the economic approach defined in the State Aid Action Plan."

On that basis, the Communication provided for consultation a series of possible measures to be included in a future framework for R & D & I. These measures were also inspired from case practice, as recorded in the Vade Mecum for Innovation.[8]

The consultation on state aid for innovation raised considerable interest.[9] This provided a good platform to then make concrete proposals to Member States as

---

[6] European Commission, Press Release IP/06/1600 of November 22, 2006.

[7] Consultation document on state aid for innovation; COM (2005) 436 final.

[8] Commission Staff Working Document; Community rules on state aid for Innovation; vade mecum; SEC (2004) 1453.

[9] The Commission received 124 contributions from 25 countries, of which 2 non-Member States; in addition 24 respondents represent EU-wide interests. In particular, 20 replies come from France, 13 from the UK and 10 from Germany.

regards new measures for innovation. In particular, the Commission decided not to grant aid on the basis of a generic definition of innovation, but rather to specific measures, targeting well-defined market failures.

As a result, the 2006 R & D & I Framework contains eight types of aid measures:

—aid for R & D projects

—aid for technical feasibility studies

—aid for industrial property right costs for SMEs

—aid for young innovative enterprises

—aid for process and organisational innovation in services

—aid for innovation advisory services and for innovation support services

—aid for the loan of highly qualified personnel for SMEs

—aid for innovation clusters.

Member States can tailor this package to support R & D & I according to their national preferences, needs and specificities. The Framework indicates to Member States how they can use the following types of measures in conformity with the state aid rules.

Balancing test

The new framework for R & D & I embraced the refined economic approach **23–004** to more specifically justify the aid measures considered as compatible, and the criteria for the analysis. In assessing whether an aid measure can be deemed compatible with the common market, the Commission balances the positive impact of the aid measure in reaching an objective of common interest against its potentially negative side effects by distortion of trade and competition. The State Aid Action Plan, building on existing practice, has formalised this balancing exercise in what has been termed a 'balancing test'. It operates in three steps to decide upon the approval of a State aid measure; the first two steps are addressing the positive effects of State aid and the third is addressing the negative effects and resulting balancing of the positive and negative effects. The Framework explained that a state aid measure for R & D & I will be authorised on the basis of a three-part test:

1. the aid must address a well-defined market failure;
2. the aid must be well targeted: state aid must be an appropriate instrument, the aid measure must have an incentive effect and must be proportionate to the problem tackled;
3. the distortions to competition and trade resulting from the aid measure must be limited enough so that, on balance, it can be declared compatible.

The Framework outlines the main market failures hampering R & D and innovation: knowledge spill-overs, imperfect and asymmetric information, coordination and network failures. It then gives guidance on a series of types of state aid measures that can address these market failures without excessively distorting competition and trade.

All notified aid has to be assessed first under the provisions in Ch.5 of the Framework. In that chapter, the Commission has identified a series of measures for which it considers a priori that State aid targeting these measures will address a specific market failure hampering R & D & I. The Commission has furthermore elaborated a series of conditions and parameters, which aim at ensuring that State aid targeting these measures actually presents an incentive effect, is proportionate and has a limited negative impact on competition and trade. Chapter 5 thus contains parameters in respect of the aided activity, aid intensities and conditions attached to compatibility. In principle, only measures which fulfill the criteria specified in Ch.5 are eligible for compatibility under art.107(3)(c) TFEU on the basis of this framework. In Ch.6, the Commission presents more specifically how it will assess the necessity and incentive effect of the aid. In Ch.7, the Commission presents more specifically in which cases and how it will conduct a detailed assessment.

New architecture: GBER, detailed assessment and effects-based approach

23–005   One of the objectives of State aid reform was to focus the Commission's resources better, and to reduce the bureaucratic burden for Member States, so that an increasing proportion of non-problematic state aid can be approved rapidly, while the most distortive measures would be subject to greater investigation. This is precisely what the rules governing state aid for R & D & I tried to achieve.

Before 2006, only measures concerning R & D aid for SMEs could be exempted. This limited to a great extent the possibility for Member States to use the block exemption, as most of their R & D state aid schemes were also targeting large companies. With the new R & D & I Framework and the GBER, things were greatly improved. First of all, large companies were also included in the GBER (but for ad hoc aid). Second, the GBER reproduced identically the provisions of the Framework, which made it possible to avoid complexities and duplications. Third, a number of innovation measures were included, thus largely enlarging the scope of the previous block exemption. Only aid for process and organisational innovation in services and aid for innovation clusters were considered too novel to be included in the GBER.

As a result, the overall architecture of SA rules for R & D & I is based on several levels. The first level includes non aid measures, which are influenced by state aid rules, for instance on research organisations and fiscal incentives. The second level includes exempted schemes as per the General Block Exemption Regulation. The third level includes schemes that are still subject to notification. Finally, the fourth level concerns the detailed assessment of the large R & D cases, where the Commission focuses its scrutiny.

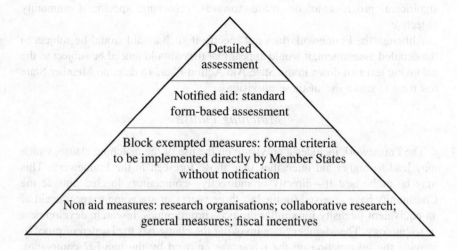

The R & D & I Framework explains how its scrutiny is based on the same balancing test, but varies according to the presumed intensity of the distortions of competition.

Important projects of common European interest

The R & D & I Framework clarifies the cumulative conditions under which a **23–006** project can be considered as falling within the scope of art.107(3)(b) and be supported as a project of common European interest. The conditions are the following:

—Project must be clearly defined;

—Project must be in common European interest;

—Aid must be necessary to carry out the project and present an incentive effect;

—Project must be very risky;

—Project is of great importance in terms of character and volume, objective and size.

No specific proportionality requirements are foreseen beyond the mere indication that a significant own contribution is expected. The Commission will consider notified projects more favourably if they include a significant own contribution of the beneficiary to the project. It will equally consider more favourably notified projects involving undertakings or research entities from a significant number of Member States. In order to allow for the Commission to properly assess the case, the common European interest must be demonstrated in practical terms: for example, it must be demonstrated that the project enables significant progress to be made towards achieving specific Community objective.

Although the Framework does not specify if such an aid would be subject to the detailed assessment, it would appear that they should indeed be subject to the balancing test laid down in the State Aid Action Plan. To date, no Member State has tried to make use of these provisions

Matching clause

23–007 The Framework includes a provision on the use of the matching clause, which may lead to higher aid intensities than those foreseen in the Framework. This may be authorised if—directly or indirectly—competitors located outside the Community have received (in the last three years), or are going to receive aid of an equivalent intensity for similar projects, programmes, research, development or technology. The Member State invoking the clause has the burden of proof to provide the information on the advantage enjoyed by the non-EU competitor. However, the Framework appears relatively flexible as regards the type of evidence the Commission may accept. Although a similar clause was already included in the 1996 Framework, it has never been used so far.

2. NOTION OF AID FOR R & D

23–008 The Commission's State aid guidelines typically focus on compatibility, especially since the notion of aid is objective and there is normally very little margin of discretion for the Commission to consider whether a measure is, or is not state aid. However, the RDI Framework took the rather unprecedented step of trying to clarify the notion of aid for a number of situations involving R & D & I state financing. One of the reasons for this was the perceived legal uncertainty about certain interactions between public and private actors, and about the possibility for universities to increasingly engage into commercial activities.

Public funding of research organisations

23–009 A first area covered by the R & D & I framework is that of situation of universities and research organisations.[10] First of all, it makes clear that the research organisation must first qualify as an undertaking within the meaning of art.107(1) TFEU to be considered recipient of aid. This does not depend upon its legal status (organised under public or private law) or economic nature (i.e. profit

---

[10] The Commission provides quite a precise definition of research organisations: "'research organisation' means an entity, such as university or research institute, irrespective of its legal status (organised under public or private law) or way of financing, whose primary goal is to conduct fundamental research, industrial research or experimental development and to disseminate their results by way of teaching, publication or technology transfer; all profits are reinvested in these activities, the dissemination of their results or teaching".

making or not). What is decisive for its qualification as an undertaking is whether the research organisation carries out an economic activity, which is an activity consisting of offering goods and/or services on a given market.

In that respect, the Commission explained what it considered to constitute non-economic activities in the field of research. The Framework clarifies that the core activities of universities and research organisations, like teaching, independent research and dissemination of research results, do not fall under state aid rules, because they are considered non-economic activities. The Commission furthermore considers that technology transfer activities (licensing, spin-off creation or other forms of management of knowledge created by the research organisation) are of non-economic character if these activities are of an internal nature and all income from these activities is reinvested in the primary activities of the research organisations. Therefore, a substantive part of their funding does not need to be notified to the Commission.

However, where universities rent out research or innovation infrastructure to business or carry out research under contract to companies, they may be competing with other (commercial) economic actors. A number of complaints have been made (before 2007) that universities distort competition if they do not operate on market terms, but rather use the support they get for their non-economic activities to predate on commercial competitors. The R & D & I Framework clarifies the State aid rules which apply in such situations. In particular, accounting separation and correct cost allocation is a solution to secure a level playing field.

Indirect aid from the public funding of research organisations

In the case of contract research, the Framework clarifies that the research **23–010** organisation should deliver its services at market price to avoid indirect aid to the contractor. The Framework also makes clear that in some instances, aid can be provided to the users of the university infrastructures, e.g. through subsidised prices, without this leading to a finding of aid at the intermediary level of the university, on the condition that there is equality of treatment with private providers, and the choice is left to the users to use the state aid to buy services from public universities or from private commercial providers. Admittedly, this provision should only apply in a situation where the commercial activity of the university is limited and residual to its non-economic research activities.

Finally, the Framework covers also the situation where there is collaboration between a research organisation and businesses. In general, the Commission promotes the view that research organisations should behave like private undertakings when they collaborate on a research project, and should try to maximise their benefits from the venture. On the one hand the Framework defines the conditions to avoid support to the research organisation being passed on to companies, and on the other it takes a favourable view on collaborative research between research organisations and enterprise partners and allows them a 15 per cent bonus on top of the basic aid intensity.

Fiscal aid

23–011 The R & D & I Framework does not provide guidance as to when a fiscal measure in favour of R & D & I may not be considered state aid. This is, however, explained in the 1998 notice on direct business taxation.[11] R & D tax incentives are considered not to involve aid if they are available to all enterprises and constitute general measures. Provided that they apply without distinction to all firms and to the production of all goods, the following measures pursuing general economic policy objectives through a reduction of the tax burden related to research and development costs do not constitute state aid. This rationale has been applied consistently in the Commission's decision practice.[12]

3. STANDARD ASSESSMENT

23–012 The R & D & I Framework contains a series of rules for R & D & I measures that are to be deemed compatible. It provides some explanation as to why some measures are covered and why certain parameters are retained. A series of additional conditions are also introduced, in particular as regards the incentive effect of the aid. With the exception of aid for process and organisational innovation in services and for innovation clusters, all innovation measures have been included in the GBER.

Incentive effect

23–013 A major development in the 2006 R & D & I Framework compared to the previous rules is the more precise definition and categorisation of the concept of incentive effect, which now appears as the central parameter of the assessment of the Commission. The Framework makes it clear that State aid must have an incentive effect, i.e. result in the recipient changing its behaviour so that it increases its level of R & D & I activity. As a result of the aid, the R & D & I activity should be increased in size, scope, amount spent or speed. Interestingly, this condition is not limited to the detailed assessment but is considered a prerequisite for any aid. However, the burden of proof varies according to the aid amount, type of measure and type of beneficiary.

The incentive effect is presumed to be automatically met in a series of cases:

—project aid and feasibility studies where the aid beneficiary is an SME and where the aid amount is below EUR 7.5 million for a project per SME;

[11] Commission notice on the application of the State aid rules to measures relating to direct business taxation; [1998] O.J. C384/3.
[12] See e.g. decision of February 13, 2008, Spain, The reduction of tax from intangible assets N 480/07 [2008] O.J. C80/1.

—aid for industrial property rights costs for SMEs;

—aid for young innovative enterprises;

—aid for innovation advisory services and innovation support services;

—aid for the loan of highly qualified personnel.

For all other measures, the Member State must demonstrate that a change of behaviour results from the aid compared with a situation without aid, leading to more R & D & I. When assessing an aid scheme, the conditions relating to the incentive effect shall be deemed to be satisfied if the Member State has committed itself to granting individual aid under the approved aid scheme only after it has verified that an incentive effect is present and to submitting annual reports on the implementation of the approved aid scheme.

R & D projects

The provisions on aid to R & D projects (including technical feasibility **23–014** studies) represent the more stable part of the Framework as they substantially maintain the approach in place since 1986. This being said, some modifications were introduced in the 2006 Framework to modernise the various stages of research and to restructure the bonus system.

Aid to R & D projects is linked to the definition of the eligible activities and costs, the aid intensities and bonuses. The classification of R & D activities—fundamental research, industrial research and experimental development—is based on the internationally used definitions contained in the OECD Frascati Manual. In 2006 the old category of pre-competitive development was expanded to cover research closer to market activities, such as prototypes which can be used commercially. In order to highlight this change, this category was then renamed "experimental development". More specifically, the Framework makes it clear that the various stages of research (fundamental research, industrial research, pre-competitive research) should not be seen as linear model. This means that a project could well start with experimental development before embracing some fundamental research. Such a change was considered important to better fit with the way modern R & D is organised.

Eligible costs are also consistent with the international practice, including for accounting purposes. The scope is wide as it concerns all expenditures related to R & D projects. It is important however to stress that costs are eligible only to the extent they refer to the project: if for instance equipment is also used in production, it will be eligible for R & D aid only in proportion to its use for the research. Aid intensities are differentiated according to the activity: 100 per cent is allowed for fundamental research (where companies are not able to appropriate results); 50 per cent is allowed for industrial research; and 25 per cent is allowed for experimental development, which includes prototyping.

Another noticeable change in the 2006 R & D & I Framework is the restructuring of the bonus system and, in particular, the disappearing of the regional bonuses, which were present in the previous framework. This is justified by the need to focus on excellence in R & D and by the lack of effectiveness of these bonuses, given the already high levels.[13] The new R & D & I framework tries to focus state aid towards the most valuable projects, no matter where they are located. This is in line with EU Research Policy, which is supporting excellence in research. In addition, the permissible aid intensities of the R & D & I Framework are already very high and have not been used to their limit by many Member States.

As a result, the bonus structure was on the whole considerably simplified by the Framework: according to the aid beneficiary or type of project, justified on the basis of increased externalities from the aid. In addition to these basic aid intensities, there is the possibility to add bonuses when projects are carried out by small (+20 per cent) or medium-sized enterprises (+10 per cent), or when they involve cross-border co-operation or collaboration with a research organisation (+15 per cent).

Innovation aid

23–015   The most noticeable change in the standard assessment of the R & D & I Framework is the introduction of a number of new aid possibilities, in favour of innovation. Most of these new possibilities are limited to SMEs; whilst they can also benefit large companies, there is a requirement that large companies collaborate with SMEs. The new possibilities are precisely justified on the basis of market failures and benefited from past experience in Member States and from the consultation organised around the Communication on State aid for Innovation. Here is a brief account of the measures.

23–016   **Aid for IPR costs for SMEs.** Eligible costs are those relating to the application and its renewal, to translation and to other legal costs, including defending the validity of the right in front of the opposition. Aid intensity is the up to the same level of the R & D project which first led to the IPR concerned.

23–017   **Aid to Young Innovative Enterprises** (YIE) was introduced in order to facilitate funding of start-ups. YIE are defined as enterprises with less than six years of activities and either R & D intensive (greater than 15 per cent of turnover spent on R & D) or with a very innovative product or service (to be demonstrated by an expert). Aid is allowed up to 1 million cash equivalent (and up to 1.5 million in assisted regions), in whatever form, with also the possibility to cumulate it

---

[13] However, the new Framework takes regional considerations into account in three areas, where economic analysis shows that a differentiated treatment is desirable to better target state aid. First, differentiated funding possibilities are offered for young innovative enterprises, according to the location of the region, to account for higher risk factors for creating a research intensive company in a poor region. Second, higher aid possibilities are offered to support the creation of innovation clusters in assisted areas. Third, the detailed assessment procedure, which relates to large amounts of aid, takes regional specificities into account for the analyses of both the market failures and the incentive effect.

with R & D and risk capital aid. The large flexibility in the form of aid was purposely introduced to avoid red tape and to facilitate the bridging of finance at the early stage of their creation.

Aid for process and organisational innovation in services was introduced in order to allow support activities which do not fall easily within the traditional categorisation of R & D but which are nevertheless an important driver of innovation, notably through the adoption of Information and Communication Technology (ICT). This is in particular the case for services, where innovation is not necessarily defined as R & D and is more closely linked to process and organisational change. In order to limit abuse of this provision,[14] which applies outside any sectoral scope (i.e. also for manufacturing companies), several cumulative conditions were introduced, including eligibility for large enterprises only if projects involve collaboration with an SME. Given the novelty and arguable complexity of this measure, it was not included in the GBER.

23–018

Aid for innovation advisory services and for innovation support services covers the very diverse range of activities performed by technology centres and incubators in favour of SMEs. In practice, it covers aid for consultancy related to innovation services. The very wide definition of permissible advisory and support services was conceived to allow a large degree of flexibility to granting agencies. Some conditions are nevertheless introduced to avoid abuses, in particular the need for providers to be certified. One interesting provision is also that if services are provided by public entities free of charge or below cost, the difference must be recorded as aid and the design of the scheme must secure equal access of private operators, so that beneficiaries can choose to use the aid with public or private providers, without discrimination. This provision was introduced to cope with the specificities of, e.g. chambers of commerce and other public or para-public entities, which provide such advisory services and sometimes do not realise that they may distort competition by crowding out private operators. The Framework makes it clear that services should therefore be provided at market price.

23–019

Aid for the loan of highly qualified personnel was included to promote the transfer of knowledge from research organisations and large enterprises to SMEs. Qualified personnel include researchers, engineers, designers and marketing managers with solid background. Seconded personnel must work on R & D & I projects in the SME and can be supported at 50 per cent of costs which include salaries and agency costs. This measure was introduced in particular to foster collaboration across the value chain between large enterprises and SMEs. A series of conditions are present to avoid windfall profits for large companies.

23–020

---

[14] For instance, calling innovation a mere change in the organisational chart. The R & D & I Framework provides a series of definition and guidance to explain what is *not* innovation in that context.

23–021 **Aid for innovation clusters** was designed for the setting up, expansion and animation of innovation clusters, as a measure in support of the entity operating the cluster itself. The measure actually covers both clusters created by large enterprises (e.g. Philips) and those situations where firms in an area group together (e.g. the Italian industrial clusters or the French "pôles de compétitivité"). Aid is allowed both for investment in research and innovation infrastructures (e.g. laboratories, testing platforms but also offices and conference centres) and for cluster animation (support, training and networking support). The combination of both investment and operating aid is meant to be digressive, to provide incentives to clusters to become self-sustainable over time.

4. Detailed Assessment

23–022   The introduction of a detailed assessment for individual aid notified above a certain threshold was one of the most important novelties of the 2006 R & D & I Framework. As explained above, this corresponds to the goal set in the State Aid Action Plan, namely that the Commission's scrutiny should focus on most distortive aids, and it counterbalances the expansion of the GBER's coverage of R & D & I aid measures. Interestingly, the detailed assessment part of the Framework also provides some more general guidance and description of the positive and negative effects of aid, and also makes it possible to well understand the Commission's reasoning as regards compatibility.

Effects-based analysis

23–023   The Framework clarifies that even if R & D & I aid is generally well regarded by the Commission, it can have also distortive effects, which makes it important to carefully verify that large individual aid amounts are nevertheless acceptable. Aid for R & D & I can have very negative effects on competition, as well as benefits. It can be abused to protect national players, keep inefficient firms afloat, distort competition and artificially maintain costly, fragmented markets. It can lead to less investment in R & D & I because it discourages private companies from intervening alongside their subsidised competitors. Furthermore, state aid is not a "magic wand" to solve Europe's innovation problems. State aid cannot replace structural reforms and it should certainly not delay them. It is only one tool in a much bigger tool-box needed to spur R & D and innovation.[15]

Contrary to the standard assessment, which is based on a form-based compatibility test, the detailed assessment is an effects-based analysis. It tries to establish if an aid measure should be declared compatible, because overall its positive effects outweigh its negative impact on competition and trade. The detailed

---

[15] Including: first class universities and higher education; cutting-edge fundamental public research; research and innovation infrastructures; well-performing financial markets; efficient policies for protecting and managing intellectual property rights; general business environment supporting entrepreneurship.

assessment thus clearly sets a higher burden of proof on Member States, in particular to demonstrate the positive effects of the aid.

However, the R & D & I framework is also explicit that the criteria described in the detailed assessment are indicative and that it is not necessary to obtain all the information listed in the Framework for the Commission to be able to conclude its analysis. It says:

"The detailed assessment is a proportionate assessment, depending on the distortion potential of the case. Accordingly, the fact that a detailed assessment will be carried out does not necessarily imply the need to open a formal investigation procedure, although this may be the case for certain measures. Provided Member States ensure full co-operation and provide adequate information in a timely manner, the Commission will use its best endeavours to conduct the investigation in a timely manner."

In addition, the Framework makes it clear that it will take into account some "strategic" considerations in its assessment, notably the international competitiveness of the European R & D & I as a result of the aid. This illustrates that the Commission did not completely overlook industrial policy considerations in the design of its R & D & I state aid rules.

However, as the framework provides a list of factors that the Commission will take into account, there may have been a temptation to apply a check-list approach, in verifying that for most elements mentioned by the guidelines, some information would be asked by the Commission and in checking their conformity, even for cases raising limited risks for competition.[16]

Assessment criteria

When looking more specifically at the criteria provided by the detailed analysis section, it is clear that the degree of detail varies in terms of what type of information should be provided by Member States, and how prescriptive the Framework is. **23–024**

As regards market failure, the Framework provides useful descriptions of them, but is not very explicit as to what kind of evidence can be regarded as sufficient to demonstrate that a market failure is demonstrated. A series of market failures are identified, which hamper R & D and innovation and which can justify granting state aid to improve the market outcome: **23–025**

- Positive externalities: R & D & I activities generate new knowledge, which is beneficial to society because it can be used by many companies to invent or improve products and services. However, from the perspective of a single

---

[16] Example: N 185/2007—France—NanoSmart SOITEC, where the beneficiary was a small competitor of Intel [2007] O.J. C284/3 or N 5/2009—France—CARMAT where the beneficiaries were SMEs or spin-off from a research center, competing with large multinationals like Siemens or GE [2009] O.J. C176/1.

company, only the private benefits from investing in R & D & I are accounted for. As a result, R & D & I activities are sometimes not undertaken by private companies, because they consider the resulting private benefits too limited, whereas the benefits for society, due to the knowledge spill-overs of R & D & I, could be important.

- Public goods: R & D & I activities generate new knowledge, which can not always be protected (e.g. through patents). Private companies may thus refrain from investing in R & D & I because they are afraid that the results of their investments may be used by competitors and they consequently cannot generate any profit from their investments.

- Imperfect and asymmetric information: R & D & I activities are particularly risky and uncertain. This means that they are affected by imperfect and asymmetric information. As a result, too few human and financial resources may be invested in R & D & I projects, which would however be highly valuable for society.

- Coordination and network failures: R & D & I activities are often unsure and complex and it is not easy for private companies to work together, identify suitable partners and coordinate R & D & I projects. As a result of these coordination and network failures, R & D & I projects that could have been conducted in common between a group of firms are sometimes not undertaken at all, whereas society as a whole would have benefited.

In practice, it seems that Member States did not really use studies to demonstrate a market failure, but resorted to more circumstantial evidence. In particular, funding problems were demonstrated in some cases, on the basis of some letters from banks stating they were not ready to finance a given R & D project.[17] Besides, the Commission was not very explicit as to the referential for analysing the presence of a market failure. It appeared ready to accept not only EU-level, but also National level. Interestingly, it also seems that the Commission was more ready to accept a market failure in a case where it had already found one in the same sector, as shown from the many cases dealing with aeronautics.

As regards the criterion of whether state aid is an appropriate instrument, the Framework did not provide very detailed guidance and only mentioned that the Commission would look at any impact assessment that the Member State may have made. It does not seem that the Commission's decision paid extensive attention to this criterion, even though it was routinely mentioned in decisions.

23–026   The analysis of incentive effect, by contrast, is fairly developed in the Framework and has led to substantive analysis by the Commission in its decision practice. An important feature is the need for the Member State to explain the counterfactual scenario, i.e. what would have happened in the absence of aid. In the Commission's decision practice, it seems that very often the counterfactual

---

[17] See, e.g. N 296&297/2009—Germany—Diehl Air cabin [2010] O.J. C70/21.

scenario is that no project would be conducted.[18] In a minority of cases, a different project would have been undertaken.[19] The Commission used a series of financial indicators to examine the presence of incentive effect, and in particular the Net Present Value of the project, with and without aid. This was then compared to the necessary corporate return for the company in the determined sector, to find out whether in the absence of aid, the project would be conducted, and whether the aid would subsequently change the behaviour of the company and conduce it to undertake the research project.[20]

As regards proportionality of the aid, the Framework was not very expansive **23–027** as to the criteria it would use, only mentioning the selection of the project/beneficiary and the aid amount. In practice, the Commission seems to have used the result of the incentive effect analysis to possibly question the design of the aid measure. This led to possibly amendments in the design of the aid.

As regards distortions of competition, the Framework contains an important **23–028** list of criteria to assess the negative effects of the measure. It goes to great lengths to outline the nature of the distortions:

- R & D & I aid can distort the dynamic incentives of market players to invest (crowding out effect);

- R & D & I aid can create or maintain positions of market power;

- R & D & I aid can maintain an inefficient market structure;

- State aid may also have a negative effect on trade in the common market.

It then provides a set of criteria that may indicate a more substantial distortion (or conversely less of a distortion). These criteria can be used by Member States when they design their measures and can help minimise distortions. To that extent the Framework can be useful in guiding them towards better targeting their state aid.

Maybe thanks to this, it seems that the Commission's decision practice has not needed to focus too much on distortions of competition, possibly because in many instances, R & D & I projects did not appear to have substantial negative effects, either because of the position of the beneficiary (SME or small market share[21]) and remaining competition in (or for) the market,[22] or because of the

---

[18] See e.g. N 349/2007—France—OSIRIS—Soufflet for a new industrial process for the production of enzymes [2007] O.J. C304/5.

[19] See e.g. N 854/2006—France—TVMSL—Alcatel Lucent for the developing of a satellite based solution for TV broadcasting on 3G mobile phones [2007] O.J. C182/5.

[20] See e.g. N 674/2006—France—R&D NeoVal for the development of a new automatic metro system on rubber tyres [2007] O.J. C120/1.

[21] See e.g. SA.31083 (N 240/2010)—Sweden—Aid for the Domsjö project [2011] O.J. C180/1.

[22] See e.g. N 854/2006—France—TVMSL—Alcatel Lucent for the developing of a satellite based solution for TV broadcasting on 3G mobile phones [2007] O.J. C182/5.

form of aid (repayable advances[23]) or distance from the market and uncertainty about the commercial impact.[24]

Balancing: a stricter approach than in the past

23–029   In the light of these positive and negative elements, the Commission balances the effects of the measure and determines whether the resulting distortions adversely affect trading conditions to an extent contrary to the common interest. The Framework makes it clear that the Commission would not apply a mechanical approach but would rather have an overall proportionality approach.

In general, the application of the detailed assessment has led to a stricter approach than in the past. In some cases, the Commission's scrutiny led to materially different results, as compared to their original design. In particular, an opening of the investigation procedure due to doubts on the necessity and incentive effect of the aid resulted in the withdrawal of the notification in one case,[25] and in the modification of the aid instrument and/or reduction of the envisaged aid amount in two others.[26]

Moreover, important changes have also been achieved during the preliminary investigation, including reductions of aid amounts and of eligible costs,[27] application of more stringent conditions for reimbursable advances, and introduction of clear commitments on dissemination of knowledge and access to IPR.[28]

5. CONCLUSION

23–030   The R & D & I Framework has been in force for a number of years by now. While it was very advanced compared to other guidelines at the time of its adoption, other guidelines and frameworks have followed in the same direction in the meantime. It nevertheless can be seen as a breakthrough in the Commission's approach to compatibility analysis, in particular through a new architecture of rules and the implementation of a refined economic analysis. A few additional elements and statistics allow concluding this chapter.

Reporting obligations

23–031   Member States must submit a report each year illustrating a correct application of the state aid rules. In particular, information is required as regards the

---

[23] See e.g. N 597/2007—France—Aid to LowCO$_2$motion [2008] O.J. C299/6.

[24] See e.g. N 1/2008—France—H2E for the development of hydrogen-powered batteries and applications [2009] O.J. C38/5.

[25] N 530/07—France—VHD for the development of hybrid diesel cars; interestingly the technology was developed without state aid and is today available on the market on Peugeot's cars (decision not yet available).

[26] Following opening of the detailed investigation for C 33/2008—Sweden—State loan for R & D to Volvo Aero/Genx [2008] O.J. C253/31 and C9/2007—Spain—R&D aid to ITP for the Trent 1000 project (IP/07/395) [2007] O.J. C108/18.

[27] See e.g. N 597/2007—France—Aid to LowCO$_2$motion [2008] O.J. C299/6.

[28] See e.g. N 493/09—France—Aid to the Project GAYA [2010] O.J. C213/9.

beneficiaries of the measure. The Commission may request additional information regarding the aid granted, to check whether the conditions of the Commission's decision approving the aid measure have been respected. For all aid granted under an approved scheme to large undertakings, Member States must also explain in the annual report how the incentive effect has been respected

In addition to the annual report, the R & D & I Framework contains specific transparency obligations. Member States are required to inform the Commission about any individual aid granted above EUR 3 million. This novelty was introduced as a way to control the correct application of the GBER, in a situation where a number of measures covered by the Framework are also covered by the GBER. It follows the example of the regional aid guidelines, where a similar approach has been adopted. In general, the transparency provisions proved very useful in supporting a correct implementation of the rules by Member States.

Some statistics

The state aid scoreboard provides some interesting statistics as regards the use **23–032** of the R & D & I Framework, which are worth mentioning here. Admittedly state aid is only one complementary element in the much larger tool-box needed to boost R & D & I, and it cannot replace the reforms needed to tackle structural weaknesses in this specific area. State aid represented a relatively small share of total public spending for R & D & I (€10.6 billion, equal to 0.09 per cent of GDP in 2009). In 2009, EU spending on R & D stood at 2.01 per cent of GDP (around €236.5 billion), the highest level ever, but still well below the 3 per cent target. The public sector was the source of funds for around one third of total R & D & I expenditure in the European Union (0.65 per cent of GDP). There are also huge differences between Member States.

What is striking is the increased number of decisions and amounts in the field of R & D & I, and at the same time the increased scrutiny of aid involving large amounts, showing that the objectives of SAAP have been achieved to a great extent in that respect. The average expenditure in State aid for R & D & I increased during the period 2007–2009 (€8,758 million) by almost 40 per cent in comparison with the period 2004–2006 (€6,277 million).[29] Over the long-term, the trend shows a steady increase of R & D & I aid both in relative and in nominal terms. It increased between 2004 and 2009 from 0.05 per cent (€5.7 billion) of EU GDP to 0.09 per cent in 2009.

Since the entry into force of the R & D & I Framework on January 1, 2007 and until the end of 2010, the Commission has approved 195 state aid schemes, of which 143 pure R & D schemes, 14 innovation-oriented schemes and 38 mixed measures, pursuing both R & D and innovation objectives. At the same time, the Commission has approved an additional 44 individual applications of a scheme or ad hoc R & D aid measures, of which 39 after detailed assessment (including

---

[29] DG COMP 2010 State aid Autumn Scoreboard. State of play Dec 31, 2009. Data for EUR 27.

two measures for which formal investigation procedures were conducted). Two individual cases were withdrawn. Moreover, the Commission has monitored a total of 192 individual measures granted on the basis of approved aid schemes which exceed €3 million but are not individually notifiable.

23–033   The effects of the GBER were also largely positive in terms of progressive in-take. In 2009, there were 99 schemes providing aid for fundamental research, 299 for industrial research and 290 for experimental development. The GBER was also used for measures relating to innovation, 107 of which referred to industrial property rights for SMEs, 54 to young innovative enterprises, 78 to innovation advisory and support services and 39 to the loan of highly qualified personnel. Nevertheless, the total amount of R & D & I aid granted through block exempted measures is still relatively low—€977 million granted in 2009—when compared with the total amount of aid awarded under the GBER for industry and services in 2009—€10 831 million.[30]

From a geographical point of view, the Member States with the highest average expenditure on R & D & I during the period 2007–2009 were Germany (€2,240 million), France (€1,919 million), Spain (€994 million) and Italy (€802 million).[31] On the contrary, the Member States with the lowest expenditure were Cyprus, Latvia and Malta with €1 million.

Mid-term review

23–034   The Commission is expected to publish a mid-term review of the R & D & I Framework end 2011. One issue is whether the notification thresholds estab-lished in the Framework have been high enough to avoid excessive scrutiny. Until now, there have been less than 45 notifications in about 5 years, which is less than 9 per year. The mid-term review will be the occasion to review if the situation is adequate or if changes would appear necessary, e.g. to diminish the number of notifications further.

As regards the design of the state aid measures themselves, a comprehensive overhaul is unlikely at this stage before a more thorough review is conducted, since many Member States have only a recent and limited experience with the new elements in the Framework. In the medium term, however, it is likely that a more thorough review of the R & D & I framework will be necessary, to address the challenges of the innovation agenda set by the Commission.[32] In that context, it will be interesting to examine whether the relatively strict stance of the current framework will be maintained.

[30] DG COMP 2010 Autumn State aid Scoreboard.
[31] DG COMP 2010 State aid Autumn Scoreboard.
[32] See, e.g. Europe 2020 Flagship Initiative: Innovation Union SEC (2010) 1161.

CHAPTER 24

RESCUING AND RESTRUCTURING AID*

1. GENERAL COMMENTS 24–001
   Introduction 24–001
   Nature of the Commission decisions on rescue and restructuring 24–003
   Examples of some typical decisions on rescue and restructuring aid in the 1990s 24–004
   Privatisation 24–008
   The position of the undertaking 24–011
   Principles for interpreting the guidelines 24–012
2. THE MAIN ELEMENTS OF THE GUIDELINES 24–013
   Introduction 24–013
   Scope 24–014
   Meaning of "firm in difficulty" 24–015
   Definition of "r&r aid" 24–017
   Only certain reasons for giving r&r aid are acceptable 24–018
   Compatibility with the internal market 24–019
3. CONDITIONS FOR AUTHORISATION FOR INDIVIDUAL AID: RESCUE AID 24–020
   Aid must consist of liquidity support in the form of loan guarantees or loans 24–020
   Aid warranted on grounds of serious social difficulties 24–021
   Restructuring or liquidation plan 24–022
   Aid restricted to the amount needed to keep the firm in business, i.e. the proportion-
      ality criterion 24–023
   One time last time 24–024
4. CONDITIONS FOR AUTHORISATION FOR INDIVIDUAL AID: RESTRUCTURING AID 24–027
   Restoration of long-term viability 24–027
   Restructuring 24–028
   Aid limited to the minimum/aid in proportion to the restructuring costs and benefits . 24–035
   A substantial contribution from the beneficiary 24–036
   Compensatory measures 24–038
   Specific conditions 24–041
   Full implementation of restructuring plan and observance of conditions 24–042
   Applicability of Article 106(2) TFEU 24–043
   Applicability of Article 107(2) TFEU 24–044
5. AID SCHEMES FOR SMEs 24–045
6. MISCELLANEOUS 24–048
   The simplified procedure 24–048
   Monitoring and annual reporting 24–049
   Recipients of previous unlawful aid 24–050

* Piet Jan Slot

Restructuring aid for the agricultural sector 24–051
Appropriate measures under Article 108(1) 24–052
7. CONCLUSION 24–053

1. GENERAL COMMENTS

Introduction

24–001 Rescue aid is granted to firms in difficulty, that is to firms in a situation of acute financial distress where state funding is often the last resort to keep the company from going into administration. Rescue aid has a potentially very distortive effect on competition because normally inefficient firms should quit the market. However, the demise of large firms causing serious unemployment may have undesirable social consequences. This was happening particularly in the former GDR where in Berlin between 1991 and 1997 140,000 jobs were lost (54 per cent of all industrial jobs).[1] The granting of aid may help the transition to normal market conditions. The Commission's policy has been to accommodate the transition of firms in difficulty while at the same time limiting the effects of such aid on competition. The rescue of firms in difficulty will often involve urgent measures of a structural nature. Firms on the verge of bankruptcy can only be rescued if they are restructured. Consequently, the Community state aid policy addresses both rescue and restructuring aid simultaneously.[2] Rescue and restructuring operations are a common feature of a market economy. Recently, the financial crises have aggravated the difficulties in the real sector. This is reflected in the 21 decisions for firms in the industrial sector which the Commission adopted in 2010.[3]

24–002 In 1979 the Commission articulated its policy on aid for rescuing and restructuring for the first time.[4] In 1994 the Commission adopted its first guidelines on state aid for rescuing and restructuring.[5] A new versions of these guidelines were adopted in 1999[6] and in 2004.[7] The 2004 guidelines have been prolonged until October 2012.[8] This chapter will analyse and discuss the main elements of these 2004 guidelines, henceforth referred to as the 2004 guidelines. It will do so on the basis of the Commission's practice as laid down in its decisions and communications adopted since 1999 and the judgments of the Community Courts. The majority of these decisions have been adopted on the basis of the 1994 and 1999 guidelines but since the main principles of the guidelines have been kept they

---

[1] Decision 2000/537 (EC) *Elpro* [2000] O.J. L229/44, at para.39.

[2] This is stressed in the 2004 Community guidelines on state aid for rescuing and restructuring, at para.6.

[3] Commission staff working document SEC(2011) 690, June 10, 2011, point 112.

[4] 8th Report on Competition Policy 1979, at paras 177, 227 and 228.

[5] [1994] O.J. C368/12.

[6] [1999] O.J. C288/2.

[7] [2004] O.J. C244/2.

[8] Communication from the Commission concerning the prolongation of Community Guidelines on state aid for rescuing and trestructuring firms in difficulty [2009] O.J. C156/3.

remain relevant for the interpretation of the 2004 guidelines. There are two other chapters in this book that deal with rescue and restructuring. The first is Ch.16 on shipbuilding. This sector has been the subject of intense state aid supervision since the beginning of the 1970s therefore a separate chapter has been devoted to it. As is well known the financial crisis has resulted in massive state aid support starting in 2008. The state aid supervision initially followed the principles of the rescue and restructuring guidelines. Gradually, the special features of this sector were addressed with the help of additional guidelines.[9] For this reason a separate Ch.19 is devoted to this sector. This general chapter will, where appropriate, refer to and discuss the application of the general principles in the two other sectors. The first and second editions of this book contained a separate chapter on motor vehicles because at the time this sector was covered in a special framework. This sector is now part of the overall R&R policy.[10]

We start this chapter with some general remarks about the nature of the Commission decisions on rescue and restructuring aid. The principles laid down in these decisions have been developed over the years by the Commission. This will be demonstrated by a summary of some of the major Commission decisions in the 1990s most of which were adopted on the basis of the 1994 guidelines. Even though the 2004 guidelines are silent on the question of whether privatisation is a condition for approval of rescue and restructuring aid, the question is very important. Therefore, the next section will discuss this question and the following section will look at the position of the beneficiary undertaking. The final section of the introductory part of this chapter will discuss general principles for the interpretation of the rescue and restructuring guidelines as they have evinced from the case law of the Community courts.

Nature of the Commission decisions on rescue and restructuring

Commission decisions concerning rescue and restructuring aid are normally not standard or run-of-the-mill decisions. Given the nature of this type of aid it will usually take the Commission quite some time and effort before it can take a final decision; therefore many decisions are taken on the basis of art.108(2) TFEU. The decision to open the art.108(2) TFEU procedure may give various reasons for pursuing the assessment of the proposed aid. Sometimes there is no restructuring plan.[11] Often the Commission will note that important elements of the restructuring plan need to be clarified by the authorities of the Member State[12] or that it has doubts whether the conditions for approving the aid are met.[13] During the formal procedure the authorities of the Member State will

24–003

---

[9] See Annual Report 2008, point 33 and Annual Report 2010, points 34–41.

[10] See for recent developments in this sector, F.M. Salerno, "The Restructuring of the Automobile Industry: A European Solution for a European Problem?", EStAL 1/2010, pp.99–105.

[11] See, e.g. Decision C 1/2006 *Chupa Chups* [2006] O.J. C97/2.

[12] See, e.g. Decision C 1/2000 *Holzmann* [2000] O.J. C110/2. In this case the German authorities only provided a restructuring plan in broad terms that had to be fleshed out.

[13] See, e.g. Decision C 10/04 *Bull* [2004] O.J. C102/12; Decision C 10/2006 *Cyprus Airways* [2006] O.J. C113/2.

usually provide further clarifications. Furthermore, interested parties may submit comments. The absence of such comments may be a sign that there is little or no risk that competition will be distorted. Comments from interested parties are normally useful for the Commission to understand the particular characteristics of the industry and help it to reach a well-founded decision.[14] Overall, the clarifications from the governments and the comments from the industry may or may not convince the Commission that planned aid is compatible with the internal market. The Commission will take its final decision accordingly. The decision will provide a summary of the Commission's assessment of whether the aid meets the conditions of the guidelines. A positive decision will typically state that all or part of the aid measures are compatible with the internal market.[15] It may require that the restructuring plan must be fully implemented and that the Member State concerned shall submit an annual report to the Commission.[16] If need be, a bi-annual reporting obligation is imposed.[17] In addition, the positive decision may contain conditions specific to the case at hand.[18] A good example of a major restructuring operation is the *Alstom* decision.[19] Although the €3.03 billion[20] aid plan has in the end been declared compatible with the internal market, the long list of conditions reflect the hard-fought nature of the Commission's approval. The decision contains major divestiture obligations supervised by a trustee, conditions requiring France to implement measures to open up the French rolling stock market including "unbundling obligations". For some, quarterly reporting obligations have been imposed. During the formal investigation procedure a large number of comments were received, among which 20 sets from the electricity industry, 19 from the rail transport sector, five from employees' organisations as well as comments from Alstom's main competitors Siemens, GE and two others who did not want their identity to be revealed. A negative decision will normally be accompanied by a recovery order when the aid has already been implemented.[21]

Examples of some typical decisions on rescue and restructuring aid in the 1990s

24–004   In a decision of 1990 the Commission accepted the aid to Quimigal[22] in Portugal. It took the opinion that "with the financial streamlining, the shedding

---

[14] See, e.g. Decision C (2001)403 *Kataleuna* [2001] O.J. L245/26. In this case a 100% capacity expansion was considered acceptable due the peculiar characteristics of the industry and the fact that there was no structural overcapacity.

[15] See, e.g. Decision 2001/695 (EC) *Holzmann* [2001] O.J. L24/46.

[16] See, e.g. Decision 2003/264 (EC) *Kranbau* [2003] O.J. L9773.

[17] See, Decision 1999/269 (EC) *Italstrada* [1999] O.J. L109/1; Decision 1999/338 (EC) *Societa Italiana* [1999] O.J. L129/30.

[18] See, e.g. Decision 2002/200 (EC) *Babcock Wilcox* [2002] O.J. L67/50; Decision 2001/89 (EC) *Crédit Foncier de France* [2001] O.J. L34/36.

[19] Decision 2005/418 (EC) *Alstom* [2005] O.J. L150/24.

[20] The Commission's estimate is €3.03–3.08 billion, see table 7 at para.144. The amount of the restructuring is estimated to be between 10.3 and 10.4 billion.

[21] See, e.g. Decision 2000/648 (EC) *Siciliana Acque Minerali* [2000] O.J. L272/36.

[22] Decision C 25/89 *Quimigal* [1990] O.J. C188/3.

of major loss makers and a radical reorganisation allowing the injection of private capital, were necessary for the strengthening of the Portuguese and Community chemicals market". The aid was approved under art.92(3)(c) (now 107). The Commission further noted that there were closures and a reduction of capacity and a serious reduction of the workforce. A month later the Commission closed the art.93(2) (now 108) procedure against France involving aid to CDF Chimie.[23] The Commission had originally challenged the granting of FF 4,366, 2,000 and 3,100 million of aid, and argued that the Community petrochemical market was experiencing a certain amount of instability reflected in large cyclical fluctuations in supply and demand. Moreover, the undertaking was extremely active in intra-Community trade in 1988. A 44 per cent turnover was achieved outside France, a large proportion of which was achieved on the Community market. The Commission considered that the aid contributed to "large reductions and the total closure of capacity for low added-value products in sectors that are extremely vulnerable to market conditions and increasing competition from non-Community manufacturers". According to the Commission, CDF was making a major contribution to the rationalisation of these chemical sectors at Community level. Thus FF 9,466 million of aid was approved.

In 1992 the Commission partly acquiesced, in a Portuguese plan, to aid CNP and EPSI, public enterprises in the chemical sector.[24] The part accepted concerned restructuring aid for investment in plant modernisation, a training programme and financial restructuring. According to the Commission, the aid was not disproportionate in view of the seriousness of the situation and did not place the undertaking in a more favourable position than that of its Community competitors. EPSI is the only Portuguese producer of polymers and plays a central role in the Portuguese economy. The aid was therefore exempted under art.92(3)(c) (now 107). It is interesting to note that the Commission does not substantiate its conclusion that the restructuring aid is proportionate. There is no indication of what percentage of restructuring costs may be contributed in the form of aid. The part of the aid plan which consisted of operating aid was not accepted by the Commission and formed the subject of an art.93(2) (now 108) procedure.

In two of the above cases the Commission also pointed to the fact that the **24–005** recovery of the undertakings Quimigal and EPSI was vital to the development of certain regions in Portugal. In the period after the publication of the first edition of this book, a number of important decisions concerning the restructuring of the chemical industry have been taken. Probably the most spectacular decision concerned almost the entire chemical industry in the former German Democratic Republic. The operation involved a total of some DM 9.5 billion.[25] The bulk of the aid concerned aid for investment, cash-flow compensation, a waiver of debt and environmental indemnification. The Commission stressed that the whole

---

[23] Decision C 26/86 and C 43/87 *CdF Chimie* [1990] O.J. C198/2.
[24] Decision C 47/91 *CNP and EPSI* [1992] O.J. C1/5.
[25] Decision 96/545 (EC) *Leuna-Werke* [1996] O.J. L239/1. See also the follow up Decision 1999/679 (EC) [1999] O.J. L269/36, concerning the third and fourth amending agreements.

operation was without precedent in the history of the Community and gave due consideration to the grave social and economic problems in the new Bundesländer and East Berlin. It declared the aid compatible with the internal market pursuant to art.92(3)(a) and (c) (now 107). It was of the opinion:

"that the derogation provided for in Art.92(2)(c) [107(2)(c)]must be interpreted strictly, notably as regards the need for such aid, which must therefore be limited to the minimum necessary to compensate those specific remaining disadvantages that are caused by the former division. Difficulties companies in the former German Democratic Republic are facing, which result from the fact that these companies need to stand up to competitors in the Community and the EEA after unification, cannot be interpreted as disadvantages caused by the former division of Germany."

24–006   The operation was further complicated by the fact that Dow Chemical was the only interested party willing to carry out the privatisation and restructuring plan. Even so the Commission did check whether the compensatory justification principle was met (see para.4–015). The Commission also accepted a planned capacity increase for the sector of derivatives as an unavoidable consequence of the integrated concept that Dow was proposing. It concluded that the expansion would not lead to overcapacity on the Community market. It was thus able to conclude that the aid proposal would be in conformity with its guidelines for rescuing and restructuring firms in difficulties. In that context it observed that investment aid leading to a profitable exploitation and operating aid serving to compensate operating costs for a longer period, should be clearly distinguished and that only the former aid was acceptable.

In two Commission decisions, in 1994 and 1995, separate aid proposals concerning the Italian chemical company Enichem were approved.[26] The 1994 decision noted that the Commission had examined the plan in the light of the corresponding state aid rules and concluded that the remarkable reduction of the workforce would have a beneficial effect both on the results of Enichem and the chemical sector as a whole. It was approved pursuant to art.92(3)(c) (now 107)(3)(c). The Commission's decision was appealed by BP Chemicals.[27] The Court of First Instance (now General Court) took the view that the case presented serious difficulties, which should have led the Commission to open the art.92(2) (now 108 TFEU) procedure. The Court noted that the third capital injection had to be considered in the context and in relation with the first two injections. The

---

[26] Decision C 12/94 *Enichem Agricultura* [1994] O.J. C330/7; this involved ITL 1,794 billion capital injections serving a comprehensive restructuring plan which was considered exemptible aid. Another capital injection of ITL 3,000 billion would, according to the Commission, have been undertaken by a private investor in a market economy. The second decision [1996] O.J. L28/18, involved another ITL 1,918 billion capital injection.

[27] Case T–11/95 *BP Chemicals v Commission* [1998] E.C.R. II–3235. It is interesting to note that BP's appeal was supported by the UK government.

Court also expressed doubts as to whether the third injection satisfied the market economy investor principle.

The 1995 decision assessed the plan for the restructuring of Enichem Agri-   **24–007**
cultura's fertiliser activities closely following the Commission's guidelines on aid for rescuing and restructuring firms in difficulties. In the accompanying conditions the Commission stipulated that Italy should comply with its commitment to privatise part of Enichem. The Commission opened further procedures in the chemical industry in the former German Democratic Republic.[28] The length of these art.93(2) (now 108) notices in the *Everts* and *Kali und Salz* cases clearly demonstrates the Commission's concerns. On November 30, 1998, the Commission authorised €534 million to InfraLeuna.[29]

Privatisation

Ever since state aid has been doled out to undertakings that are owned or   **24–008**
controlled by governments, the question has arisen whether the objective of restructuring leading to economic and commercial viability should not ultimately lead to privatisation. The Commission's 23rd Report on Competition Policy discussed this issue.[30] The question has been discussed extensively in the context of the air transport sector because that sector is characterised by the presence of many government-owned national flag carriers. The Commission did not follow the recommendation of the Comité des Sages, the committee that was advising it on the application of the state aid in the aviation sector, that restructuring accompanied by aid should ultimately lead to privatisation.[31] Its main argument was that such a requirement would be contrary to the principle of art.295 EC (now 345 TFEU), namely that the Treaty does respect public ownership of undertakings. Nevertheless, para.43 of the guidelines for the application of state aid rules in the aviation sector[32] provides the following principles that are applicable in case of privatisation:

(1) Aid is excluded and therefore notification is not required, if, upon privatisation, the following conditions are fulfilled:

- the disposal is made by way of an unconditional public invitation to tender on the basis of transparent and non-discriminatory terms;

---

[28] Decision C 47/97 *Leuna 2000 refinery* [1997] O.J. C394/14; Decision C 42/97 *Everts Erfurt* [1998] O.J. C37/8. This is an unusually long art.93(2) (now 88) notice, expressing grave doubts about the compatibility of the proposed aid to the manufacturer of natural latex products. The last decision, C 74/97 *Kali und Salz* [1998] O.J. C197/7, concerns the aid proposal for the Kali und Salz company which is part of the restructuring effort which also involved the merger with the THA company. The latter was conditionally approved by the Commission, 94/449 (EC) *Kali und Salz* [1994] O.J. L186/38. This decision was subsequently annulled by the ECJ in Case C–68/94 and C–30/95 [1998] E.C.R. I–1453.
[29] Agence Europe, November 30, 1998.
[30] 1993, points 402 et seq. These conditions are similar to those mentioned below.
[31] See the summary of the 1994 report of the Comité de Sages at para.1.3 of the 1994 guidelines for the application of arts 92 and 93 in the aviation sector [1994] O.J. C350/5.
[32] [1994] O.J. C350/5.

- the undertaking is sold to the highest bidder;
- the interested parties have a sufficient period in which to prepare their offer and receive all the necessary information to enable them to undertake a proper evaluation.

(2) The following sales are subject to notification because there is a presumption that they contain aid:

- all sales by way of restricted methods or where sales take the form of a direct trade sale[33];
- all sales which are preceded by a cancellation of debts by the state, public undertakings or any other public body;
- all sales preceded by a conversion of debt into capital or by "recapitalisation";
- all sales that are realised in conditions that would not be acceptable for a transaction between market economy investors.

All such sales must be valued by an independent expert. The sales must be effected on the basis of non-discriminatory procedures respecting the rules on freedom of establishment and the freedom to provide services.

The above principles have also been applied in the case of rescue and restructuring aid in general even though the guidelines on rescue and restructuring are silent on the question of public or private ownership as well as the question of privatisation. The latter is not mentioned as a condition for approval of the aid in the guidelines. Nevertheless, in the cases for restructuring of firms in difficulty in former East Germany, privatisation as well as other cases whereby state-owned firms were privatised is normally a necessary condition of adapting the firm to competitive markets. In such cases the Commission has followed the above-summarised rules that privatisation should be carried out by a public tender.[34] In the *Lautex* decision the Commission considered that withdrawal from the privatisation contract gave rise to serious doubts about the full implementation of the restructuring plan.[35]

24–009   The decision in *Stardust Marine* gives an extensive discussion of the rules that should be followed according to the Commission when a state-owned firm is privatised.[36] Two important elements evince from this decision. First, the invitation to tender should cover the full range of potential bidders. Secondly, conflict

---

[33] See, e.g. Decision 1999/269 (EC) *Italstrada* [1999] O.J. L109/1, p.10.
[34] See, e.g. Decision 2001/685 (EC) C(2001)403, *Kataleuna* [2001] O.J. L245/26, at para.61; Decision 2002/898 (EC) *SKL Motoren* [2002] O.J. L314/75, at para.77; Decision 2003/282, *Doppstadt* [2003] O.J. L108/8, at para.9; Decision 2009/71 *Posta Bank Hungary* [2009] O.J. L 62/14, para.64; Decision 2010/3 *New Szcecin Shipyard* [2010] O.J. L5/1, at para.349; Decision 2010/47 *Gdynia Shipyard* [2010] O.J. L33/1, at para.403.
[35] Decision 2000/129 (EC) *Lautex* [2000] O.J. L42/19, at para.100.
[36] Decision 2000/51 (EC) *Stardust Marine* [2000] O.J. L206/1, at paras 10, 59–82, 116. It is important to note that the annulment of the decision in Case C–482/99 *France v Commission* [2002] E.C.R. I–4397 did not relate to this element of the decision.

of interests should be avoided. The Commission found that some of the buyer's shareholders were part of the Stardust's management. It concluded that the bid had benefited from discriminatory conditions. The *Centrale del Latte di Roma*[37] decision provides an example of a privatisation operation that did not involve state aid.

In the *Banco di Sicilia* case the Commission notes that privatisation should provide the definitive solution to the problems of the proportionality of the aid and the own contribution. Privatisation will ensure that in the future the firm will turn to private shareholders or the market if it requires financing.[38] In *Bank-gesellschaft Berlin*, the Commission considered that after the restructuring, the privatisation of the bank would have sufficient prospects of success.[39] In the *Bank Burgenland* case the Commission assumed that there was a good chance that the bank privatisation would be successful.[40]

In 2004 the Commission concluded a lengthy investigation into the transfer of public assets to seven German regional public banks. The procedure lasted some 10 years and resulted in an order to recover €3 billion plus interest.[41]

The above-mentioned rules may be inapplicable when a firm takes over the **24–010** assets of a company in receivership provided that the terms of the acquisition are such as to exclude any suggestion that the operation was mounted in order to make incompatible aid look compatible and escape from a possible future recovery.[42] There will be a presumption of state aid in the absence of a tender.[43] The above-outlined principles are also relevant in the context of the restructuring of firms in the new Member States.

Privatisation of public undertakings is not always required but a level playing field has to be secured. This neutrality between public and private undertaking is

---

[37] Decision 2000/628 (EC) *Centrale del Latte di Roma* [2000] O.J. L265/15, at paras 59–68 and 81–93.

[38] Decision 2000/600 (EC) *Banco di Sicilia* [2000] O.J. L256/21, at para.119.

[39] Decision 2005/345 (EC) *Bankgesellschaft Berlin* [2005] O.J. L116/1, at para.256. In para.174 the Commission noted that the failure of the privatisation process raised doubts about the soundness of the remaining real estate business.

[40] Decision 2005/691 (EC) *Bank Burgenland* [2005] O.J. L263/8, at para.87.

[41] IP/04/1261, October 20, 2004. The following banks were the subject of the investigation: WestLB, €979 million plus interest, Landes Berlin, €810 million plus interest, Norddeutsche Landesbank, €472 million plus interest, Landesbank Schleswig-Holstein €432 million plus interest, Bayrische Landesbank, €260 million plus interest, Hamburgische Landesbank €90 million plus interest, Landesbank Hessen-Thüringen €6 million plus interest. WestLB has been the subject of an earlier decision 2000/39 (EC) [2000] O.J. L150/1 which had been annulled by the CFI in 2003 case. The 2004 WestLB decision is the Commission's reaction to the judgment of the CFI. Joined cases T–228/99 and T–233/99 *Westdeutsche Landesbank Girozentrale and Land Nordrhein-Westfalen v Commission of the European Communities* [2003] E.C.R. II–435.

[42] See C 67/99 *Dampfkessel* [2000] O.J. C379/4. See, for a case where the sale of assets was not preceded by a tendering procedure and therefore raised state aid concerns, Decision 1999/484 (EC) *Hamsa* [1999] O.J. L193/1, at para.119.

[43] Decision 2000/393 (EC) *CBW Chemie* [2000] O.J. L150/38. In this case the Commission opened the art.108(2) procedure because it had doubts about the tender procedure. Its doubts were dispelled during the art.108(2) procedure.

the subject of the rules of the so-called transparency directive.[44] The directive has the objective of securing a fair and effective application of the aid rules to both public and private undertakings. This will be possible only if the financial relations between the government and the undertaking are made transparent. The transparency rules for public undertakings should enable a clear distinction to be made between the role of the state as public authority and its role as proprietor. The transparency directive has been amended several times. The last time was in November 2005 to reflect the Commission's policy implementing the *Altmark* principles.[45]

The position of the undertaking

24–011   State aid always creates an intricate triangular relationship between the Commission as the guardian of the rules, the Member State as grantor of aid with the purpose of implementing national policy objectives of such social policy,[46] and the intended beneficiary. Even though the role of the latter is always important, it is absolutely vital in the case of rescue and restructuring aid. It is the firm that has to draw up and implement the restructuring plan. The government can only do so much to prepare a good plan and to assist with the implementation. This is up to the firm and this vital role is acknowledged in the procedural rules. In most of the decisions that form the basis for this chapter the intended beneficiary played an active role, in particular, of course, during the art.108(2) TFEU procedure. The decisions normally contain a summary of the comments submitted by other parties. It is also customary that the intended beneficiary assists the government in preparing its answer to the comments raised by other parties and, of course, the Commission. If, however, at the end of the day the firm and/or its shareholders do not fulfil their obligations that they have assumed under the restructuring plan, the rescue and restructuring operation fails.[47] The Commission is aware of this risk and therefore often imposes reporting obligations sometimes as often as twice a year.[48] But basically the responsibility for the proper implementation of the restructuring plan lies largely with the government, in close co-operation with the firm in difficulty. Nevertheless, one might wonder whether there are more effective ways of ensuring that the objectives of the rescue and restructuring operation are safeguarded. In this context, the experience with positive conditional merger decisions imposing important obligations may be referred to. It is not uncommon in such cases to appoint trustees to oversee the successful implementation of the conditions attached to the approval of the merger.

---

[44] Directive 80/723 [1980] O.J. L195/35.
[45] Directive 2005/81 [2005] O.J. L312/47. See further Ch.8.
[46] This was expressed clearly by the ECJ in the *Boussac* case, Case C–301/87 *France v Commission* [1990] E.C.R. I–307.
[47] See, e.g. Decision 2000/245 (EC) *Gooding Consumer Electronics* [2000] O.J. L165/25.
[48] Decision 2000/537 (EC) *Elpro* [2000] O.J. L229/44.

Principles for interpreting the guidelines

The judgment of the CFI (now General Court) in the *Schmitz-Gotha* case[49]   **24–012**
provides a useful summary of the general principles applicable for the interpretation of the guidelines. The CFI (now General Court) reiterates the well-
established approach of the Community Courts that in the application of the state
aid rules the Commission has a wide discretion involving economic and social
assessments that must be made in a Community context. Judicial review of the
manner in which that discretion is exercised is confined to establishing that the
rules of procedure and the rules relating to the duty to give reasons have been
complied with. It also relates to verifying the accuracy of the facts relied on, that
there has been no error of law, manifest error of assessment in regard to the facts
or misuse of powers. The CFI (now General Court) reminds us that the Commission may lay down for itself guidelines for the exercise of its discretionary
powers. They contain directions on the approach to be followed by the Commission and they may not depart from the Treaty rules. Restructuring aid can only
be declared compatible with the internal market according to art.107(3)(c) if
there is a restructuring plan designed to reduce or redirect its activities. Point
3.2.2. of the guidelines stipulate that the restructuring plan must fulfil three
material conditions. First, it is essential that it restores the viability of the
beneficiary firm within a reasonable timescale and on the basis of realistic
assumptions. Secondly, that it avoids undue distortions of competition. Thirdly,
that it be in proportion to the restructuring costs and benefits. These conditions
are cumulative, the Commission must therefore declare a restructuring aid plan
incompatible if one of the conditions are not met. According to the guidelines,
aid must be strictly necessary to restore the viability of the beneficiary. This
means that it must not only meet the objective pursued of restructuring the firm
but it must also be proportionate to that objective. According to the latter
principle any aid in excess of the strict return to viability of the beneficiary
cannot in principle be eligible under the guidelines. Furthermore, in order to fulfil
its duty to co-operate with the Commission, the Member State concerned must
provide all the necessary information to enable the Commission to verify that the
conditions for the derogation from which it seeks to benefit are satisfied.

2. THE MAIN ELEMENTS OF THE GUIDELINES

Introduction

In the 2004 Report on Competition Policy the Commission noted the following   **24–013**
characteristics of these guidelines:

"The new guidelines therefore introduce somewhat stricter rules as regards
rescue and restructuring aid, since this category is considered the most critical

---

[49] Case T–17/03 [2006] E.C.R. II–1139. Even though the judgment concerns restructuring aid the
principles apply also to rescue aid.

one. The Commission is well aware, though, of the social implications of situations where companies, whether through their own fault or not, get into difficulties which might result in this kind of aid.

The 'one time, last time' principle has been reinforced, and the question has been addressed of the circumstances in which aid granted to an ailing firm has to be taken into account when the company becomes bankrupt and is taken over by another company.

A newly created company is not eligible for rescue and restructuring aid and is regarded as such for three years following the start of operations in the relevant field of activity. This ban was introduced in the 1999 guidelines. The Commission considers that the ban does not apply in cases where the State measures and restructuring constitute elements of a single operation.[50]

Contrary to the previous guidelines, which made a strict and problematic[51] distinction between rescue aid and restructuring aid, the new guidelines allow aid for urgent structural measures to be included in the amount to keep the firm in business during the period for which rescue aid is granted.[52] Member States are given the opportunity to opt for a simplified procedure for the approval of rescue aid. The passage from rescue to restructuring aid is thus easier to determine: once a restructuring plan has been established and is being implemented, all further aid will be considered restructuring aid.

The requirement of a substantial contribution to the restructuring process from the recipient has been reinforced and clarified. The two-fold purpose of this own contribution is to demonstrate that the markets believe in the feasibility of a return to viability of the restructuring company within a reasonable time and to guarantee that the aid is limited to the minimum required to restore viability, while limiting the distortion of competition. To this end the Commission will also request compensatory measures to minimise the effect on competitors.

The Commission guidelines on State aid for rescuing and restructuring firms in difficulty are applicable from 10 October 2004 until October 2012."[53]

Scope

24–014   According to para.18 the guidelines apply to all firms in all sectors except the coal and steel sector.[54] The guidelines apply without prejudice to the specific rules of the guidelines for the air transport sector.[55] The guidelines for state aid

---

[50] Commission Decision C(2001) 1780, 2002/200 (EC) *Babcock* [2002] O.J. L67/50, at paras 85 et seq.

[51] Under the 1999 guidelines, simultaneous grants of rescue and restructuring aid were impossible, although such a possibility is desirable in some cases in order to introduce certain restructuring measures early on in the process.

[52] See, e.g. Decision 1999/374 (EC) *Neptune* [1999] O.J. L144/21, dealing with rescue as well as restructuring aid at para.3.

[53] Communication from the Commission concerning the prolongation of Community Guidelines on state aid for rescuing and restructuring firms in difficulty [2009] O.J. C156/3

[54] See Ch.14.

[55] [1994] O.J. C350/5, see Ch.16.

to maritime transport refer to the guidelines for rescue and restructuring aid.[56] It should be noted that sectors facing structural problems are subject to the Communication on the multisectoral framework on regional aid for large investment projects (2002) and the regional aid guidelines 2007–13, which are discussed in Ch.15. Furthermore, aid that does not fall within the definition of specific codes or guidelines, falls within the scope of general rescue and restructuring aid guidelines. Thus in the *Sniace* decision the Commission noted that aid not in direct support of the industrial process as described in the synthetic fibres code cannot be deemed to fall within the scope of that code.[57]

Meaning of "firm in difficulty"

The guidelines state that there is no Community definition of what constitutes **24–015** "a firm in difficulty." The Commission gave an explanation in the 1994 guidelines. The key characteristic seems to be that the firm without the help of the public authorities is no longer able to raise sufficient finance for its continuity.[58] A firm in difficulty is defined as a firm which is:

> "unable to recover through its own resources or by raising the funds it needs from shareholders or borrowing. The typical symptoms are deteriorating profitability or increasing size of losses, diminishing turnover, growing inventories, excess capacity, declining cash flow, increasing debt, rising interest charges and low net asset value. In acute cases the company may already have become insolvent or gone into liquidation."

Paragraph 10 of the guidelines refers to the disappearance of the registered capital of a limited liable company, where more than half of the capital has disappeared, where a company fulfils the criteria under domestic law for being the subject of collective insolvency proceedings. Paragraph 11 refers to additional situations such as growing losses and declining cash flow. An extensive discussion of the concept firm in difficulty is found in the Commission's decision *Société Nationale Maritime Corse-Méditerranée (SNCM)*.[59] In the *Freistaat Sachsen* judgment the General Court rejected the argument that there should be a specific definition for firms in difficulties for regional aid.[60]

[56] [2004] O.J. C13/3, in point 8. The 1997 guidelines [1997] O.J. C205/5 for maritime transport made the same reference. See also Decision 2004/166 (EC) *Société National Maritime Corse-Méditerranée* [2004] O.J. L61/13, at para.262.

[57] Decision 2003/284 (EC) *Sniace* [2003] O.J. L108/35, at para.50.

[58] In Decision 2003/626 (EC) *Thuringia loan programme* [2003] O.J. L223/32, at para.75.

[59] Decision 2004/166 (EC) *Société Nationale Maritime Corse-Méditerranée (SNCM)* [2004] O.J. L61/13, at paras 288–97. Although this decision has been adopted under the guidelines on state aid for rescuing and restructuring for maritime companies, the definition of the concepts is the same as that under the general R&R guidelines. See also Decision 2005/691 (EC) *Bank Burgenland* [2005] O.J. L263/8, at paras 74–76.

[60] Case T–102/07 and T–120/07 *Freistaat Sachsen v Commission* March 3, 2010, Unreported, para.76. Further elements of the concept of firms in difficulty are discussed in paras 103–112. In case C–459/10 P, of July 21, 2011, the ECJ dismissed the appeal. No grounds relating to concept of firms in difficulty were raised. See also joined cases T–267/08 and T–279/08, *Region Nor-Pas-de-Calais v Commission*, May 12, 2011, Unreported, paras 133 et seq.

In the *Westdeutsche Landesbank* case the Commission decision stated that the bank was not an undertaking in difficulty whose viability must be restored with the support of state aid.[61] In the *Hungarian Posta Bank* case the Commission refused to approve further restructuring aid because the bank was already viable.[62]

24–016   In the *Sardegna* judgment the CFI (now General Court) held that the first paragraph of Pt 2.1 of the 1997 guidelines indicates the importance which the Commission attaches to trend indicators but this does not make other indicators unsuitable.[63] Such indicators will only be suitable if it is thereby possible to identify the genuine and demonstrable difficulties which the eligible firms have encountered.

A newly created firm is not eligible for rescue and restructuring aid for the first three years following the start of its operations.[64] However, exceptions have been made in the case of firms in the new Länder in Germany since the transition from a planned to a market economy poses special problems. In the *Pittler/Tornos* decision the Commission gave a nuanced interpretation of this requirement.[65] It noted that this rule is usually not applied to newly established firms that take over or rent the assets of a firm in respect of which liquidation proceedings have been initiated. The new company that has evolved out of bankruptcy proceedings benefits from this rule as long as the activity of the bankrupt company is continued. It does not apply when there is just a sale of individual assets.[66] This approach was mentioned in fn.10 of the 1999 version of the guidelines, which notes that this approach applies to companies emerging from liquidation or a take-over of assets occurring before January 1, 2000.[67] Consequently, in the 2004 guidelines this note has been dropped.

According to para.13 of the guidelines, a firm belonging to or being taken over by a larger business group is not normally eligible for r&r aid. This may be different if the firm difficulties are intrinsic and not the result of arbitrary cost allocation in the group and the difficulties are too serious to be dealt with by the

---

[61] Decision 2000/392 (EC) *Westdeutsche Landesbank* [2000] O.J. L150/1, at para.245. In this case the Commission ordered the recovery of €807.7 million.

[62] Decision *Posta Bank* 2009/174 [2009] O.J. L62/14, para.91.

[63] Case T–171/02 *Regione autonoma della Sardegna v Commission* [2005] E.C.R. II–2123, at para.111. Even though the CFI was interpreting the 1997 guidelines it can, in view of the fact the text of the 2004 does not basically differ on this point, be assumed that the same interpretation will apply in the context of the 2004 guidelines. See also case T–20/03 *Kahla/Thuringen Porzellan v Commission* [2008] E.C.R. II–2305.

[64] Decision 2011/97 *Olympic Airways* [2011] O.J. L45/1, In Decision 2006/47 *Euromoteurs* [2006] O.J. L307/213, point 41 the Commission stated that a firm set up two years and a month prior to the notification cannot be considered to be newly created.

[65] Decision 2000/211 (EC) *Pittler/Tornos* [2000] O.J. L65/26, at para.24.

[66] Decision 2003/261 (EC) *Ambau Stahl* [2004] O.J. L103/50.

[67] In Decision 2002/783 (EC) *Neue Erba Lautex* [2002] O.J. L282/48, at paras 44–48, Germany claimed the benefit of the exception of fn.10. The Commission rejected this view and considered that the group constituted by the bankrupt Erba Lautex and its 100% subsidiary NEL should be regarded as the relevant recipient. In Decision 2005/940 (EC) *Jahnke Stahlbau* [2005] O.J. L342/72, at para.78, the Commission noted that the application was limited to cases brought before December 31, 1999. Moreover, it noted that this case differed from previous cases because the ailing firm was not taken over on a long-term basis.

group. The Commission applied the principle that newly established companies are barred from receiving rescue and restructuring aid in two negative decisions in 2004.[68]

Definition of "r&r aid"[69]

Rescue aid is by nature temporary and reversible. The objective of rescue aid is to keep the firm in business while working out a restructuring or liquidation plan. That is why rescue aid may include restructuring aid.[70] The aid must be temporary and limited to the minimum necessary. It must not exceed six months. It must be in the form of loans or loan guarantees with an interest rate at least comparable to those observed to healthy firms. Once the restructuring or liquidation plan has been adopted and is being implemented, further aid will be considered restructuring aid.   **24–017**

Restructuring aid is designed to allow reorganisation and rationalisation of the firm. The financial restructuring will involve capital injections and debt reduction. It should not be limited to compensation for past losses.

Only certain reasons for giving r&r aid are acceptable

According to para.8 of the guidelines only certain reasons can be accepted for r&r aid. The guidelines mention social or regional policy considerations and the promotion of SMEs. They also mention, as an exception, the desirability of maintaining a competitive market structure when the demise of firms could lead to an oligopolistic structure.   **24–018**

Compatibility with the internal market[71]

Rescue and restructuring aid can only be exempted under art.107(3) TFEU if it is compatible with the internal market. An important element in this respect is that the aid must be proportionate in view of the objectives it is to achieve. This follows from the general principle of proportionality that underlies all exceptions in Community law. Aid must be commensurate with objectives which the measure is designed to achieve[72] and must be limited to the strict minimum needed to enable restructuring.[73] This is largely secured by requiring a substantial contribution from the beneficiary and compensatory measures. This is further discussed below in paras 24–035 and 24–036. The Commission has also taken   **24–019**

---

[68] Decision 2002/52 (EC) *Soreni le Havre* [2005] O.J. L31/44 and Decision 2003/34 (EC) *CMR Marseille* [2005] O.J. L100/26.
[69] paras 14–17 of the guidelines.
[70] para.6 of the guidelines.
[71] paras 19–22 of the guidelines, this is largely secured by requiring a substantial contribution from the beneficiary and compensatory measures such as capacity reduction.
[72] Joined Cases 67, 68 and 70/85 *Kwekerij Gebroeders Van der Kooy* [1988] E.C.R. 219.
[73] See e.g. Decision 2002/865 (EC) *Graf von Henneberg Porzellan* [2002] O.J. L307/1, at paras 131–135.

the view that existing aid should be taken into account for the calculation of the proportionality of the aid.[74]

3. Conditions for Authorisation for Individual Aid: Rescue Aid[75]

Aid must consist of liquidity support in the form of loan guarantees or loans

24–020   In a situation where firms are in acute financial difficulties, Member States may bail them out for a short period, usually six months, with liquidity help in the form of loan guarantees or loans bearing normal interest rates.[76] In the latter case there is aid involved because commercial financial institutions would in that situation not be willing to provide loans on the normal commercial interest rates. The aid element of the measure consists therefore of the surcharge that would have to be paid on top of the normal commercial rate in order to induce a bank to provide a loan at all. In the *MobilCom* case the Commission approved €50 million rescue aid to provide immediate liquidity for the ailing firm.[77]

In the *Hamsa* decision the Commission noted that the interest rate on the loans was not the applicable market rate, hence it did not meet the criteria for rescue aid.[78] It also noted that the firm had already received aid of the same type and for the same reason. This finding was upheld by the CFI (now General Court) upon appeal.[79] In the *Neue Erba Lautex* decision the Commission found that the capital increase was not liquidity support and was not granted on market conditions. Moreover, the period of six months was substantially exceeded.[80] Finally, the Commission concluded that the aid had been granted when a restructuring plan had already been prepared. Thus the aid was assessed as restructuring aid.

Aid warranted on grounds of serious social difficulties

24–021   According to para.25(b) of the guidelines, the aid must be warranted on grounds of serious social difficulties and have no unduly adverse spill-over effects on other Member States. In the *Herlitz* case the Commission took into account that the company was a large employer in the assisted area of Berlin and

---

[74] Decision 2003/383 (EC) *Technische Glaswerke Ilmenau* [2003] O.J. L140/30 at para.96; Decision 2002/865 (EC) *Graf von Henneberg Porzellan* [2002] O.J. L307/1, at para.109.
[75] paras 25–30 of the guidelines.
[76] In Decision 2010/3 *New Szczecin Shipyard* [2010] O.J. L5/1, para.255, the Commission found that the rescue aid went well beyond the six months. See also Decision 2007/C120 [2007] O.J. C120/12; Decision 2007/674 *Ernault* [2007] O.J. L277/25, para.11; Decision 2008/716 *Arbel Fauvet Rail* [2008] O.J. L238/27, para.44.
[77] [2003] O.J. C80/5; see also Report on Competition Policy 2004 at para.422.
[78] Decision 1999/484 (EC) *Hamsa* [1999] O.J. L193/1, at paras 108–109.
[79] Case T–152/99 *Hijos de Andres Molina (Hamsa) v Commission* [2002] E.C.R. II–3049, at paras 50 et seq.
[80] Decision 2002/783 (EC) *Neue Erba Lautex* [2002] O.J. L282/48, at paras 50–51.

Brandenburg.[81] An immediate disorderly insolvency would have led to serious social difficulties.

Restructuring or liquidation plan[82]

Paragraph 27(a) of the guidelines requires that the granting of the rescue aid **24–022** will be followed by the submission of a credible and substantiated restructuring plan or a liquidation plan. The requirements for such a plan correspond to similar requirements for the approval of the restructuring aid. These are discussed below in paras 24–027 et seq.

Aid restricted to the amount needed to keep the firm in business, i.e. the proportionality criterion

In the *Herlitz* case the rescue loan was only used when the liquidity loan could **24–023** no longer cover the increased liquidity needs.[83]

One time last time[84]

According to para.72 of the guidelines, rescue aid should be a one-off opera- **24–024** tion. This has also been stressed by the Comité des Sages which was to make recommendations for aid to the air transport industry. In the same paragraph the Commission states that the principle is also applicable to restructuring aid. In *Grupo de Empresas Alvarez* the Commission noted that it was less than 10 years ago that the firm had received aid and thus declared the aid incompatible.[85] In the *Varvaressos* decision the Commission concluded that the measures were tranches of the same restructuring operation and therefore that the principle was not infringed.[86] The Commission allows a number of exceptions to this rule in exceptional and unforeseeable circumstances for which the firm is not responsible. In *Everts* it allowed new aid measures because the parent company could not meet its obligation which it had assumed under the previous restructuring plan. In the 2008 *Alitalia* decision the Commission noted that the conditions for exceptions from this rule had not been met.[87]

In this context mention should also be made of the so-called *Deggendorf* rule according to which no fresh aid may be implemented as long as previously incompatible aid has not been recovered.[88] This principle was applied by the Commission in the 2004 *Bull* decision.[89]

[81] Decision 2005/878 (EC) *Herlitz* [2005] O.J. L324/64, at para.111.
[82] paras 26, 27 of the guidelines, including reduction in production capacity T–152/99, at paras 77 et seq.
[83] Decision 2005/878 (EC) *Herlitz* [2005] O.J. L324/64, at para.113.
[84] paras 5, 72–76 of the guidelines, see Case T–152/99, at paras 50 et seq.
[85] Decision 2002/935 (EC) *Grupo de Empresas Alvarez* [2002] O.J. L329/1, at para.72.
[86] Decision 2011/414 *Varvaressos* [2011] O.J. L184/9, at para.100.
[87] Decision 2009/155 *Alitalia* [2009] O.J. L52/3, at para.99. See also decision 2007/492 *Biria Group* [2007] O.J. L183/27, paras 106–108.
[88] Joined Cases T–244/93 and T–486/93 *Textilwerke Deggendorf* [1995] E.C.R. II–2265.
[89] Decision 2005/941 (EC) *Bull* [2005] O.J. L342/81, at para.76.

24–025   In the *Dieselmotorenwerk Rostock* decision the Commission found that all the conditions for granting rescue aid had been satisfied.[90] In this case the restructuring aid replaced the rescue aid since all the measures were prolonged on more favourable terms. The rescue aid measures were approved by the Commission, the restructuring aid measures were not.

In *ILKA MAFA* the Commission accepted that the original restructuring period was extended and that this did not lead to any increase of the aid.[91] In this case the investor contribution had been increased to a degree that is significant within the meaning of the guidelines.

24–026   In the 2002 *Bull* decision the Commission accepted the explanations of the French government.[92] The Commission's summary of these explanations is quite unintelligible, especially in the light of an earlier Commission decision approving aid to Bull.[93] In 2004 the Commission took a fresh decision in this case approving €517 million subject to the implementation of the restructuring plan.[94] The decision explains at length that the "one time last time" principle cannot be applied absolutely. According to the Commission, indiscriminate application of this principle would excessively restrict the category of aid being regarded as necessary. It would not allow the Commission to examine in each particular case whether a project was necessary in order to attain the objectives of the Treaty.

4. CONDITIONS FOR AUTHORISATION FOR INDIVIDUAL AID: RESTRUCTURING AID

Restoration of long-term viability[95]

24–027   The purpose of restructuring aid is to allow the firm in difficulty to restore its long-term viability with financial help not available on the market. The Commission, basing itself on the *Breda Fucine* judgment,[96] takes the view that extraordinary income should not be taken into account in assessing the return to viability.[97] The main instrument for securing the viability of the restructuring is the restructuring plan. When aid has already been unlawfully implemented but nevertheless according to a restructuring plan this may help the Commission to assess the first phases of the plan.

Restructuring

24–028   The grant of the aid must be conditional on implementation of a restructuring plan which must be endorsed by the Commission.[98] The restructuring plan must

---

[90] Decision 1999/600 (EC) *Dieselmotorenwerk Rostock* [1999] O.J. L232/24, p.30.
[91] Decision 2002/823 (EC) *ILKA MAFA* [2002] O.J. L296/42, at para.51.
[92] Decision 2003/599 (EC) *Bull* [2003] O.J. L209/1, at para.62.
[93] This aid is summarised in para.9 of the Decision.
[94] Decision 2005/941 (EC) *Bull* [2005] O.J. L342/81.
[95] paras 31–71 of the guidelines.
[96] Cases T–126–127/96 *Breda Fucine* [1998] E.C.R. II–3437.
[97] Decision 2000/732 (EC) *Korn Fahrzeuge* [2000] O.J. L295/21, at para.59.
[98] para.34 of the guidelines.

lead to the restoration of long-term viability.[99] When this condition is not met the Commission will declare the aid incompatible.[100] This approach has been endorsed by the CFI (now General Court) in the *Hamsa* judgment.[101]

In the absence of a restructuring plan the Commission will not approve the aid.[102] Moreover, the restructuring plan must be credible.[103] In the *Zeuro* case the Commission refused to approve the aid because the restructuring plan was not well founded.[104] In the *Ilmenau* case the Commission found that the restructuring plan was not realistic and therefore asked the German government to recover the aid.[105] In several other cases the Commission had to conclude that the restructuring plan did not provide it with sufficient information even after an information injunction.[106]

The assessment of the restructuring plan will depend on the specific conditions of the relevant industry. In *Holzmann* the Commission accepted that the rather poor prospects of the industry justified extensive financial support.[107] The restructuring plan must be based on realistic assumptions about the development of the particular market in which the beneficiary operates.

Amendments of the restructuring plan.[108] According to para.52 of the guidelines, a Member State may, during the restructuring period, ask the Commission to agree to changes to the restructuring plan and the amount of the aid. The Commission may allow such changes where they meet the following conditions: 24–029

[99] Examples of credible restructuring plans are found in the following decisions 2007/204 *Konas* [2007] O.J. L91/37, para.84; 2007/509 *Daewoo Poland* [2007] O.J. L187/30, paras 71 et seq.; 2008/145 *Bison Bial* [2008] O.J. L46/41, para.55; 2009/485 *FagorBrandt* [2009] O.J. L160/11, para.66; 2010/394 *Hessische Staatsweingueter* [2010] O.J. L180/30, para.128.

[100] Decision 2000/21 (EC) *Brockhausen Holze* [2000] O.J. L7/6, at para.60; Decision 2000/211 *Pittler/Tornos* [2000] O.J. L65/26; Decision 2000/536 (EC) *Seleco* [2000] O.J. L227/24, at para.103. Decision 2006/47 *Euromoteurs* [2006] O.J. L307/213, at paras 46 et seq. Decision 2006/939 *KG Holding* [2006] O.J. L366/40, para.38; Decision 2007/254 *Frucona* [2007] O.J. L112/14, para.124; Decision 2008/711 *Italian Banks* [2008] O.J. L237/70, para.115; Decision 2009/973 *Combus* [2009] O.J. L345/28, para.355; Decision C38/2007 *Arbel Fauvet Rail* [2010] C(20100 4112 final; Decision 211/97 *Olympic Airways* [2011] O.J. L45/1, para.231.

[101] Case T–152/99 *Hijos de Andres Molina (Hamsa) v Commission* [2002] E.C.R. II–3049, at para.77.

[102] Decision 1999/395 (EC) *SNIACE* [1999] O.J. L149/40; Decision 2000/648 *Siciliana Acque* [2000] O.J. L272/36; Decision 2000/567 (EC) *System Microelectronic Innovation* [2000] O.J. L238/50, at para.32. Case T–20/03 *Kahla/Thuringen Porzellan v Commission* [2008] E.C.R. II–2305, para.274. See also the following decisions 2007/492 *Biria Group* [2007] O.J. L183/27, para.99; 2007/499 *Nuova Mineraria* [2007] O.J. L185/18, para.33; 2008/71 *Daewoo Romania* [2008] O.J. L239/12, para.99; 2011/269 *Peti Nitrogenmuvek* [2011] O.J. L118/9, para.65.

[103] Decision 1999/378 (EC) *Nouvelle Filature* [1999] O.J. L145/18, p.24; Decision 2003/791 (EC) *Eisenguss Torgelow* [2003] O.J. L300/54, at para.47; Decision 2001/856 (EC) *Verlipack* [2001] O.J. L320/28, at para.144.

[104] Decision 2002/779 (EC) *Zeuro* [2002] O.J. L282/1, at para.81. See also Decision 2002/783 (EC) *Neue Erba Lautex* [2002] O.J. L282/48, at para.48.

[105] Decision 2003/383 (EC) *Technische Glaswerke Ilmenau* [2003] O.J. L140/30, at paras 154–156.

[106] Decision 2000/732 (EC) *Korn Fahrzeuge* [2000] O.J. L295/21, at para.66.

[107] Decision 2001/695 (EC) *Holzmann* [2001] O.J. L248/46, at paras 92 et seq.

[108] paras 52–54 of the guidelines.

(a) the revised plan must still show a return to viability within a reasonable time scale;

(b) if the amount of the aid is increased, any requisite compensatory measures must be more extensive than those initially imposed;

(c) if the proposed compensatory measures are smaller than those initially planned, the amount of the aid must be correspondingly reduced;

(d) the new timetable for implementation of the compensatory measures may be delayed with respect to the timetable initially adopted only for reasons outside the company's or the Member State's control. If that is not the case, the amount of the aid must be correspondingly reduced.

If the conditions imposed by the Commission or the commitments given by the Member State are relaxed, the amount of aid must be correspondingly reduced or other conditions may be imposed.

24–030   Should the Member State introduce changes to an approved restructuring plan without duly informing the Commission, the Commission will initiate proceedings under art.88(2) of the Treaty, as provided for by art.16 of reg.659/1999 (misuse of aid).

In the *Italstrada* and *Societa Italiana* decisions the Commission acknowledged that the original restructuring plan had not been successfully implemented as a result of a very serious crisis. It accepted the need for additional restructuring measures.[109] Such fresh measures also have to satisfy the conditions of the guidelines. In the *Lautex* case the Commission observed that the constant amendments to the restructuring plan made it seem unreliable.[110]

24–031   **Restructuring in assisted areas.**[111] Rescue and restructuring aid may be intended for firms in assisted areas for which art.107(3)(a) provides an exception. This type of aid may therefore cumulate with regional aid.[112] The guidelines state that the fact that a firm is located in an assisted area does not justify a permissive approach to aid for restructuring.[113] Moreover, the Commission follows the principles laid down in the guidelines for rescue and restructuring aid rather than the regional aid rules when the main purpose of the aid is to restore a firm in difficulty.[114] However, para.56 of the guidelines states that the conditions for authorising aid may be less stringent as regards the implementation of compensatory measures and the size of the beneficiary's contribution. In several decisions

[109] Decision 1999/269 (EC) *Italstrada* [1999] O.J. L109/1, p.11; Decision 1999/338 (EC) *Societa Italiana* [1999] O.J. L129/30, p.40.

[110] Decision 2000/129 (EC) *Lautex* [2000] O.J. L42/19, at para.77.

[111] paras 55–56 of the guidelines.

[112] See also Ch.21.

[113] Decision 2000/567 (EC) *System Microelectronic Innovation* [2000] O.J. L238/50, at para.30 contains an elaborate discussion of this issue.

[114] Decision 2002/779 (EC) *Zeuro* [2002] O.J. L779/1, at para.59; Decision 2002/186 (EC) *Zeitzer Maschinen* [2002] O.J. L62/44, at para.36; Decision 2003/264 (EC) *Kranbau* [2003] O.J. L97/73, at para.40.

under the 1994 guidelines the Commission expressed the view that a more flexible approach is permissible for the reduction of capacity in cases of aid to restructuring in assisted areas.[115] There are, of course, also cases where neither the conditions for the application of art.107(3)(a) nor the guidelines are present.[116]

Aid for restructuring SMEs.[117] According to the Commission, aid to SMEs **24–032** tends to affect trade between the Member States less than that granted to medium-sized and large firms. This also applies to restructuring aid. Therefore the normal conditions are applied less strictly in that no compensatory measures will normally be required[118] and the reporting obligation will be less stringent. Moreover, the restructuring plan does not have to be approved by the Commission. However, it must meet the requirements set by the guidelines and be approved by the Member State concerned. The granting of the aid must be conditional on full implementation of the restructuring aid plan. The Member State has the obligation to verify that the conditions are fulfilled. There are several decisions in the East German Länder that concern such aid.[119]

Aid to cover the social costs of restructuring.[120] Restructuring often involves **24–033** a reduction of the company's workforce. Such costs may be covered by general social security schemes which may include redundancy benefits and early retirement pensions. There may also be general social support schemes which go beyond statutory or contractual obligations. When such schemes are available generally without sectoral limitations they are deemed to involve aid. If such schemes are used to support restructuring of particular industries they may be considered aid because of their selective nature.[121]

Need to inform the Commission of any aid granted.[122] According to para.69 **24–034** of the guidelines, notification of aid for restructuring a large or medium-sized enterprise must indicate all other aid of any kind which is planned to be granted to the recipient firm during the restructuring period. According to art.2, second paragraph of reg.794/2004, supplementary information is needed. Part III.8.A of

---

[115] Decision 2001/825 (EC) *Dampfkesselbau Hohenturm* [2001] O.J. L308/28, at para.67; Decision 1999/380 (EC) *Spindelfabrik Hartha* [1999] O.J. L142/32, p.36; Decision 1999/484 (EC) *Hamsa* [1999] O.J. L193/1, at paras 133, 141; Decision 1999/840 (EC) *Kranbau Eberswalde* [1999] O.J. L326/57, at para.41.
[116] Decision 1999/663 (EC) *Maschinenfabrik Sangerhausen* [1999] O.J. L263/19.
[117] paras 57–59 of the guidelines.
[118] Decision 2004/32 (EC) *Porcelanas del Principado* [2004] O.J. L11/1, at para.113.
[119] e.g. Decision 2005/940 (EC) *Jahnke Stahlbau* [2005] O.J. L/72; Decision 2003/261 (EC) *Ambau Stahl- und Anlagenbau* [2003] O.J. L103/50.
[120] paras 60–67 of the guidelines.
[121] para.62 of the guidelines. The Commission refers to the judgment in Case C–241/94 *France v Commission (Kimberly Clark)* [1996] E.C.R. I–4551.
[122] paras 68–71 of the guidelines.

Annex 1 contains the supplementary information sheet.[123] Normally the notification must precede the granting of the aid. However, in the *Grafischer Maschinenbau* judgment the CFI (now General Court) ruled that the Commission cannot infer from the mere fact that the development was commenced before the date of notification, that the aid does not satisfy the criterion concerning inducement.[124]

Aid limited to the minimum/aid in proportion to the restructuring costs and benefits

24–035   Like rescue aid, restructuring aid has to be proportional. According to para.43 of the guidelines:

> "the amount and the intensity of the aid must be limited to the strict minimum of the restructuring costs necessary to enable restructuring to be undertaken in the light of the existing financial resources of the company, its shareholders or the business to which it belongs."

In *Graphischer Maschinenbau* the Commission deducted the development costs of DM 4.875 million because these did not provide any additional incentive.[125] In the *Schmitz-Gotha* decision the Commission found that the aid was in excess of the minimum and therefore ordered recovery of the full amount.[126] In the *Bank Burgenland* case the Commission was of the view that because of the bank's own efforts, which involved running down all its hidden reserves and a reduction of the staff and material costs of 10 per cent, the aid was limited to the minimum.[127]

A substantial contribution from the beneficiary[128]

24–036   According to the guidelines, the Commission will normally require at least 25 per cent contributions to the restructuring in the case of small enterprises, 40 per cent for medium-sized enterprises and 50 per cent for large enterprises. In the *Wagnisbeteiligungsgesellschaft* decision the Commission considered that 3 per cent was too low.[129] In the *Lautex* decision 7.8 per cent was considered to be too low.[130] In the *CBW* decision the Commission accepted 19 per cent because the case concerned a management buy-out.[131] The Commission has also accepted

---

[123] part III.7.A. provides a similar supplementary information sheet for rescue aid.
[124] Case T–126/99 *Grafischer Maschinenbau v Commission* [2002] E.C.R. II–2427.
[125] Decision 1999/690 (EC) *Graphischer Maschinenbau* [1999] O.J. L272/16, p.24.
[126] Decision 2003/194 (EC) *Schmitz-Gotha* [2003] O.J. L77/41, at para.66. This decision was upheld by the CFI in Case T–17/03 *Schmitz-Gotha v Commission* [2006] E.C.R. II–1139.
[127] Decision 2005/691 (EC) *Bank Burgenland* [2005] O.J. L263/8, at para.108.
[128] paras 7, 43–45 of the guidelines.
[129] Decision 2005/564 (EC) *Grafischer Maschinenbau* [2005] O.J. L190/6, at para.38.
[130] Decision 2000/129 (EC) *Lautex* [2000] O.J. L42/19, at para.94.
[131] Decision 2000/393 (EC) *CBW Chemie* [2000] O.J. L150/32, p.48.

workers' contribution to the restructuring without, however, considering it as an investor contribution.[132] Presumably this means that such a workers' contribution cannot replace the investor contribution.

The Commission has accepted even lower percentage own contributions, in **24–037** particular when it concerns aid to an SME in an assisted area.[133] The absence of a private investor contribution is a ground for not approving the aid.[134]

In the *SKL Motoren* decision the Commission accepted the offering of licences to the ailing firm by the investor as a significant contribution.[135] In the *Alstom* decision[136] the Commission considered €700 million on a total of €3.03 billion aid to be significant. It noted that the divestiture of several activities will allow parts of the capital requirements to be covered. In the *Grafischer Maschinenbau* judgment the CFI (now General Court) has ruled that the Commission cannot infer from the mere fact that the development was commenced before the date of notification, that the aid does not satisfy the criterion concerning inducement.[137] In the follow-up decision the Commission accepted that under certain circumstances, the political decision taken by the regional authority could be considered a sufficient inducement.[138]

Compensatory measures[139]

Compensatory measures often take the form of reductions in capacity, in **24–038** particular if the restructuring aid is granted in a market characterised by structural overcapacity. Consequently, aid measures for firms in such sectors cannot be approved under the guidelines.[140] The Commission will also withhold its approval if, despite an information injunction addressing this aspect the Member State fails to provide the necessary information.[141] This may be different in other circumstances. In the *Kataleuna* decision the Commission noted that the relevant market was not characterised by overcapacity, in fact it was one with very good growth perspectives. It also noted that the industry was characterised by a very

---

[132] Decision 2003/282 (EC) *Doppstadt* [2003] O.J. L108/8, at para.91. In this case the Commission considered a 30% contribution as significant.

[133] Decision 2002/71 (EC) *KHK Verbindetechnik* [2002] O.J. L31/80, at para.61 (11.5%); Decision 2003/85 (EC) *Saalfelder Hebezeugbau* [2003] O.J. L40/1, at para.89 (18.7%); Decision 2003/261 (EC) *Ambau Stahl* [2003] O.J. L103/50, at para.73 (12.41%); Decision 2002/866 (EC) *Hoch- und Ingenieurbau* [2002] O.J. L307/28, at para.47 (13.45%); fn.17 of this decision mentions further decisions, *GMB Magnete Bitterfeld* [1998] O.J. C50/6 (12%); *Stahl- und Maschinenbau Rostock* [1999] O.J. C365/9 (12%); *Draiswerke* [1999] O.J. L108/44 (11%).

[134] Decision 2002/185 (EC) *Technische Glaswerke Ilmenau* [2002] O.J. L62/30, at para.107.

[135] Decision 2002/898 (EC) *SKL Motoren* [2002] O.J. L314/75, at para.61.

[136] Decision 2005/418 (EC) *Alstom* [2005] O.J. L150/24, at para.215.

[137] Case T–126/99 *Grafischer Maschinenbau v Commission* [2002] E.C.R. II–2427.

[138] Decision 2004/313 (EC) *Grafischer Maschinenbau* [2004] O.J. L100/35, at para.30.

[139] paras 7, 31, 38–42 of the guidelines.

[140] Decision 1999/342 (EC) *Agrana* [1999] O.J. L131/61; Decision 1999/139 (EC) *Stahl- und Hartgutwerke* [1999] O.J. L45/46, p.49.

[141] Decision 2000/732 (EC) *Korn Fahrzeuge* [2000] O.J. L295/21, at para.62.

large minimum efficient scale so that the expansion of the production capacity was crucial to the success of the restructuring plan.[142]

The Commission's approach is well illustrated in the following passage:

"The Commission takes note that no structural excess of production capacities exists on the relevant market. Moreover, the Commission notes that GMB has abandoned certain activities and has reduced its product range. In addition, the forecast turnover for the improved products will grow at the same rate as the world market sales prospects. The Commission also takes into account that GMB is the smallest supplier of roller bearers and that other suppliers belong to international and financially strong groups. In accordance with point 3.2(ii) of the Community guidelines, where there is no structural excess of production capacity in a relevant market in the Community served by the recipient, the Commission does not normally require a reduction of capacity in return for the aid. Accordingly, since there is no evidence of excess capacity, since GMB's market shares are relatively small and since the production of the products is redistributed within the KBA group and therefore does not increase the capacity, the Commission does not see any need for measures to be adopted to offset adverse effects of the aid on competitors."[143]

24–039   The Commission has taken several other decisions in which it noted that there was no evidence that the sector was suffering from overcapacity and hence it did not require capacity reductions.[144] In some decisions the question whether capacity reductions are required is also linked to the fact that the firm is located in a region eligible for assistance under art.107(3)(a) as well as the fact that it is an SME.[145]

In several decisions in the banking sector the Commission has taken the view that a substantial reduction of the balance sheet represents a contribution to the distortion of competition.[146] In the *Bankgesellschaft Berlin* case the Commission made it clear that the aid could not be approved on the basis of compensatory measures which would leave the bank's market share basically intact.[147] After intensive negotiations the *Berliner Bank* was to be sold thereby reducing the

---

[142] Decision 2001/685 (EC) *Kataleuna* [2001] O.J. L245/26, pp.34 and 35.

[143] Decision 1999/690 (EC) *Graphischer Maschinenbau* [1999] O.J. L272/16, p.22.

[144] Decision 2000/75 (EC) *Sket Maschinenbau* [2000] O.J. L30/25, at para.48; Decision 2000/395 (EC) *Entstaubungungstechnik Magdeburg* [2000] O.J. L150/64; Decision 2002/896 (EC) *Gothaer Fahrzeugtechnik* [2002] O.J. L314/62, at para.50; Decision 2005/940 (EC) *Jahnke Stahlbau* [2005] O.J. L342/72, at para.89.

[145] Decision 2000/393 (EC) *CBW Chemiewerke* [2000] O.J. L150/38, p.47. See also B.a.3. above; Decision 2001/1 (EC) *Dessauer Geräteindustrie* [2001] O.J. L1/10; Decision 1999/157 (EC) *Triptis Porzellan* [1999] O.J. L52/48, p.52.

[146] Decision 2001/89 (EC) *Crédit Foncier de France* [2001] O.J. L34/36, at para.97. In Decision 2000/600 (EC) *Banco de Sicilia* [2000] O.J. L256/21, the Commission accepted the closure of 55 branches and a commitment not to open any new ones as a sufficient offsetting measure at para.110.

[147] Decision 2005/345 (EC) *Bankgesellschaft Berlin* [2005] L116/1, at para.300.

market share of the parent company by one-third.[148] In the *Banco di Sicilia* case the Commission notes that privatisation should provide the definitive solution to the problems of the proportionality of the aid and the own contribution. Privatisation will ensure that in the future the firm will turn to private shareholders or the market if it requires financing.[149] In the *Banco di Napoli* case the bank reduced its total balance sheet with 43 per cent and closed down 77 branches, which accounted for 10 per cent of its establishments.[150] In the *Bank Burgenland* case the Commission accepted a reduction of 6 per cent market presence, in particular in view of the fact that a further reduction of branches would jeopardise the viability of the bank.[151] As discussed in Ch.19, measures to mitigate the effect on competition are a common feature of the Commission decisions in the financial sector since its crisis in 2008. At the time of writing this fourth edition most decisions are not yet in the public domain.[152]

In the *MobilCom* case the aid had a particularly serious effect on competitors.[153] Consequently, the approval of the aid was subjected to specific conditions in the field of the marketability of services. Mobil was obliged to suspend the internet offer of some services during a certain period. According to para.57(a) the grant of restructuring aid to SMEs will not usually be linked to compensatory measures. Even though Ch.5 of the guidelines does not reiterate this point it can be assumed that this exemption applies also in case of SME aid schemes.

24–040

Specific conditions

When aid measures for publicly owned firms are proposed, privatisation may often be necessary to eliminate distortions. This has been discussed above in the paragraph on privatisation. Several major decisions contain conditions specific to the case at hand. A good example is the *Alstom* decision,[154] which imposed an obligation on France to withdraw from Alstom's capital the obligation for intended beneficiary to divest itself from major assets, as well as the obligation to conclude one or more industrial partnerships. Another example is the *SNCM* case.[155] The decision obliges SNCM to sell all its direct and indirect holdings in five companies and to refrain from offering lower prices than its competitors.

Several banking decisions contain obligations to hive off important subsidiaries or branches.[156] As noted above, the Commission also imposed specific

24–041

---

[148] *Bankgesellschaft Berlin* at para.302.
[149] Decision 2000/600 (EC) *Banco di Sicilia* [2000] O.J. L256/21, at para.119.
[150] Decision 1999/288 (EC) *Banco di Napoli* [1999] L116/36, p.53.
[151] Decision 2005/691 (EC) *Bank Burgenland* [2005] O.J. L263/8, at paras 98–102.
[152] Decision 2011/363 *AS Parex banka* [2011] O.J. L163/28 is an exception.
[153] Decision 2005/346 (EC) *MobilCom* [2005] O.J. L116/55, at paras 195–199.
[154] Decision 2005/418 (EC) *Alstom* [2005] O.J. L250/24.
[155] Decision 2004/166 (EC) *Société Nationale Maritime Corse-Méditerranée (SNCM)* [2004] O.J. L61/13, art.2.
[156] Decision 2005/345 (EC) *Bankgesellschaft Berlin* [2005] O.J. L116/1; Decision 2000/600 (EC) *Banco di Sicilia* [2000] O.J. L256/21. See Ch.19.

conditions upon *MobilCom*, prohibiting it for a period of seven months from offering online contracts for mobile telephony.[157]

Full implementation of restructuring plan and observance of conditions

24–042   In its decisions approving restructuring aid the Commission normally notes that the company must fully implement the restructuring plan. Otherwise, the Commission will declare the aid incompatible and order recovery of the aid.[158] As was noted above in para.24–011, the implementation of the restructuring plan is crucially dependent on the firm and its shareholders. Member States have limited influence on the firms. In some major restructuring operations, Member States have appointed members on the board of the firm to see to it that the company duly implements the restructuring plan.[159] On the whole the impression is that governments are normally ill-prepared to handle major rescue and restructuring operations.[160]

In the *Graf von Henneberg Porzellan* case the Commission noted that most of the plans had failed and thus the restructuring plan had not been fully implemented.[161] Failure to implement restructuring plan may also imply that the aid has been misused. In the *Arcelor Huta Warszawa* case the Commission concluded that the aid had been misused.[162]

Applicability of Article 106(2) TFEU

24–043   In the past Member States have claimed the benefit of the exemption of art.106(2) TFEU. In the *Centrale del Latte di Roma* the Commission held that this article does not apply to a company that produces and markets dairy products.[163] In the *Westdeutsche Landesbank* case the Commission found that this provision was not applicable.[164] Claims for art.106(2) exemptions are now less likely to occur after the *Altmark* judgment.[165]

Applicability of Article 107(2) TFEU

24–044   Even though many Commission decisions concern the former GDR territories, the German government has not claimed that the aid should be authorised under

---

[157] Decision 2005/346 (EC) *MobilCom* [2005] O.J. L116/55, at paras 195–199.

[158] e.g. Decision 1999/840 (EC) *Kranbau Eberswalde* [1999] O.J. L326/57, at para.47; Decision 2001/1 (EC) *Dessauer Geräteindustrie* [2001] O.J. L1/10. See also case T–68/03 *Olympiaki Aeroporia Yperies* [2007] E.C.R. II–2911, para.130.

[159] This was the action taken by the Dutch government in the RSV case, see NJB, 1985, pp.273 et seq.

[160] See reports of national accounting offices. See also case T–68/03 *Olympiaki Aeroporia Yperies* [2007] E.C.R. II–2911, para.264.

[161] Decision 2002/865 (EC) *Graf von Henneberg Porzellan* [2002] O.J. L307/1, at para.136.

[162] Decision 2008/406 *Arcelor Huta Warszawa* [2008] O.J. L143/31, paras 73 et seq. See also Decision 2008/344 *Technologie Buczek Group* [2008] O.J. L116/26, para.100.

[163] Decision 2000/628 (EC) *Centrale del Latte di Roma* [2000] O.J. L265/15 at para.113.

[164] Decision 2000/392 (EC) *Westdeutsche Landesbank* [2000] O.J. L150/1 at para.246.

[165] Case C–280/00 *Altmark* [2003] E.C.R. I–7747. See Ch.8.

art.107(2).[166] Of course, this exemption has been rendered largely inoperative ever since the confirmation by the ECJ of the Commission's position that this article only refers to economic disadvantages caused in certain areas as a result of the isolation caused by the physical frontier.[167]

5. Aid Schemes for SMEs[168]

The guidelines contain special rules for schemes for providing rescue and/or restructuring aid for SMEs in Ch.4. The 1999[169] and 1997[170] guidelines had similar rules. The firms concerned must fulfil the Community definition of SME. The Commission will authorise such schemes only if the grant of aid is conditional on full implementation of a restructuring plan. The usual other conditions apply as well. The benefit of these special rules for SMEs is that no notification is required if one of the three conditions enumerated in para.10 of the guidelines is met.[171] The aid must be notified if none of these criteria are met. The notification, according to reg.794/2004, Pt III.7.A. and Pt III.8.A of Annex 1, requires the use of the supplementary information sheet.[172]

24–045

There is also no obligation to monitor and report annually on individual cases. Instead there is an obligation to provide annual reports on the operation of the scheme. Furthermore, there is no requirement for compensatory measures.[173] Extensions of approved aid schemes do not normally benefit from the approval and have to be notified.[174]

In the *Thuringia* loan programme[175] case the Commission found that the terms of the programme did not fulfil the conditions laid down in the 1994 guidelines because the rules did not require notification of individual cases in sensitive

24–046

---

[166] Decision 2005/940 (EC) *Jahnke Stahlbau* [2005] O.J. L342/72, at para.49.
[167] Case C–156/98 *Germany v Commission* [2000] E.C.R. I–6857.
[168] paras 78–86 of the guidelines.
[169] [1999] O.J. C288/2, at paras 64–70.
[170] [1997] O.J. C283/12, at para.4.1.
[171] para.10 of the 2004 guidelines states: "In particular, a firm is, in principle and irrespective of its size, regarded as being in difficulty for the purposes of these Guidelines in the following circumstances:
   (a) in the case of a limited liability company (1), where more than half of its registered capital has disappeared and more than one quarter of that capital has been lost over the preceding 12 months;
   (b) in the case of a company where at least some members have unlimited liability for the debt of the company (3), where more than half of its capital shown in the company accounts has disappeared and more than one quarter of that capital has been lost over the preceding 12 months;
   (c) whatever the type of company concerned, where it fulfils the criteria under its domestic law for being the subject of collective insolvency proceedings."
[172] According to art.2, second paragraph, the information sheets must be used in addition to the general notification sheet.
[173] See above para.24–039.
[174] Case T–152/99 *Hijos de Andres Molina* [2002] E.C.R. II–3049, at paras 30–34.
[175] Decision 2003/626 (EC) *Thuringia loan programme* [2003] O.J. L223/32, at paras 111 and 112.

sectors, nor did they require notification in case of repeated restructuring aid. In the case of the French aid scheme for the take-over of firms in difficulties the Commission considered that art.44 *septies* of the French General tax code constituted aid. The Commission found that several elements of the restructuring aid did not meet the conditions of the 1999 guidelines and could therefore not be justified.[176] The aid was, inter alia, not in the form of a loan guarantee or a loan bearing normal interest rates. Furthermore, there was no sound restructuring programme.

24–047   The Commission also found several cases of state aid in Italy not to be covered by a scheme on special measures for large firms in crisis incompatible with the internal market.[177] The Commission had stipulated that for large firms notification of aid was required. In the *Porcelanas del Principado* case the Commission found that an aid measure did not fulfil the condition of the previously approved aid scheme.[178] The scheme excluded aid to companies in difficulty. Hence the aid was regarded as new aid. In the *Graf von Henneberg Porzellan* case the Commission found several measures not be covered by the previously approved aid scheme.[179]

6. MISCELLANEOUS

The simplified procedure[180]

24–048   The Commission will try to take a decision within a period of one month for rescue aid when the aid is limited to €10 million and at least one of the three conditions of Pt 10 of the guidelines is satisfied.[181]

Monitoring and annual reporting

24–049   As was noted above, almost all positive decisions require the Member States to provide periodic reports, usually annual reports, although bi-annual reports are imposed in case of particularly sensitive aid measures.[182] Paragraph 86 of the guidelines provide for standardised reports in case of approval of aid schemes.

---

[176] Decision 2004/343 (EC) *France aid scheme for take over of firms in difficulty* [2004] O.J. L108/30, at para.48.
[177] Decision 2001/212 (EC) [2001] O.J. L79/29.
[178] Decision 2004/32 (EC) *Porcelanas del Principado* [2004] O.J. L11/1, at para.96; see also Decision 2005/940 (EC) *Jahnke Stahlbau* [2005] O.J. L342/72, at para.58.
[179] Decision 2002/865 (EC) *Graf von Henneberg Porzellan* [2002] O.J. L307/1, at paras 96 et seq. The Commission reached a similar conclusion in Decision 2005/564 (EC) *Wagnisbeteiligungsgesellschaft* [2005] O.J. L190/6, at para.22.
[180] para.30 of the guidelines.
[181] See fn.58 above.
[182] In case T–68/03 *Olympiaki Aeroporia Ypiresies v. Commission* [2007] E.C.R. II–2911, the Court found that the reporting obligation had not been observed.

Recipients of previous unlawful aid[183]

In cases where rescue or restructuring aid that was declared incompatible by **24–050** the Commission was granted previously, fresh aid cannot be approved without looking at the effect of the old aid as well. The Commission refers to the *Deggendorf* case law according to which unlawful aid has to be recovered before fresh aid can approved.[184] When assessing new aid the cumulative effect of the old and the new aid shall be taken into account, as well as the fact that the old aid has not been repaid. The Commission applied this principle in the *Neue Erba Lautex* decision.[185]

Restructuring aid for the agricultural sector[186]

In view of the common agricultural policy, separate rules are included for **24–051** restructuring in the agricultural sector. Structural excess capacity in the sector will be defined by the Commission on a case-by-case basis taking into account in particular the extent and trend for the relevant product category over the past three years, market stabilisation measures, the development of world market prices and the presence of sectoral limits in Community legislation. The Commission may also exempt aid to SMEs from individual notification even if the SME does not meet at least one of the three criteria enumerated in Pt 10 of the guidelines.[187] This part of the guidelines is discussed in Ch.13.

Appropriate measures under Article 108(1)[188]

The Commission notes that it will propose that Member States will adopt **24–052** appropriate measures to adapt their existing aid schemes if it feels the need to do so. It will make authorisation of any future aid scheme conditional on compliance with the obligations following from art.108(1). In practice, the adjustment of existing aid schemes usually takes place in the context of concrete cases where Member States claim that the proposed aid forms part of an approved aid scheme. This has been discussed above in section 5.

7. CONCLUSION

As has been noted above, this chapter is largely based on the guidelines on **24–053** rescue and restructuring of the Commission and its application of the principles contained therein based on some 120 decisions published in the Official Journal

---

[183] para.23 of the guidelines.
[184] Case C–355/95P *Textilwerke Deggendorf v Commission* [1997] E.C.R. I–2549.
[185] Decision 2002/783 (EC) *Neue Erba Lautex* [2002] O.J. L282/48, at paras 57–9.
[186] paras 87–98 of the guidelines.
[187] See fn.55 above.
[188] paras 99–101 of the guidelines.

L-series since 1999 until July 2011. The decisions opening art.108(2) have not been studied separately because their content is normally incorporated in the final decision published in the Official Journal series. Other positive decisions have been published in the C-series in "cartouche" form, i.e. a publication in the form of a very brief summary together with several other decisions. These documents do not provide insight in the substance of the case. It is not possible on the basis of the material presented in this chapter to assess the effectiveness of the Commission's policy in this area. Any such assessment would have to define appropriate standards for the measurement of the effect on competition. The reader is referred to the discussion of the economic analysis of the state aid in Ch.2.

PART V

PROCEDURE AND REMEDIES

CHAPTER 25

ADMINISTRATIVE PROCEDURE*

1. Introduction 25–001
2. Direct Effect 25–004
3. The System of Procedural Rules 25–007
4. The Procedural Regime 25–013
   Introduction: the structure of Regulation 659/99 25–013
   Existing aid and new aid 25–014
   Notified new aid 25–020
   The simplified procedure 25–025
   The preliminary procedure of Article 108(3) TFEU and Article 2(1) Regulation
      659/99 25–027
   The formal procedure of Article 108(2) TFEU and Article 6(1) Regulation 659/99 ... 25–031
   The standstill clause 25–037
   Withdrawal of notification 25–040
   Unlawful aid 25–042
   Misuse of aid 25–046
   Existing aid schemes 25–049
5. Rights of Interested Parties 25–053
6. Monitoring 25–057
7. Common Provisions 25–060
   Professional secrecy 25–060
   Publication of decisions 25–061
8. Handling of State Aid Cases Within the Commission 25–063
9. Interim Orders and Final Decisions 25–067
10. Procedures Under the EEA Agreement 25–068
    Introduction 25–068
    Does the law of the EEA Agreement have supremacy over national law of the EFTA
       Member States? 25–073

1. Introduction

Council Regulation 659/99 lays down rules for the application of art.108 **25–001** TFEU.[1] The Regulation provides a comprehensive and solid basis for the supervision of the prohibition on state aid. Commission Regulation 794/2004,[2] imple-

---

* Piet Jan Slot

[1] Council Regulation (EC) 659/99, March 22, 1999 [1999] O.J. L83/1.

[2] Commission Regulation (EC) 794/2004, April 21, 2004 [2004] O.J. L140/1. Last amended by Commission Regulation 1125/2009 [2009] O.J. L308/5.

menting reg.659/99 lays down detailed rules for the application of art.108 TFEU. Unlike the implementation of arts 101 and 102 TFEU, which was detailed in reg.17/62 and subsequent rules, arts 107 and 108 had, until 1999, not been properly implemented by means of a regulation adopted by the Council on the basis of art.109. The European Court of Justice (ECJ) repeatedly pointed to this gap and provided the rules to cover it where this proved necessary.[3]

By virtue of art.108, the Commission is responsible for enforcing art.107, which sets forth the conditions which render state aid incompatible with the common market. In certain circumstances an exemption will (art.107(2)) or may (art.107(3)) be granted by the Commission (see Ch.4). The mechanism for applying arts 107 and 108 has been developed over the years by decisions of the Commission and, more importantly, the European Court of Justice (ECJ) and the General Court (GC) (formerly the Court of First Instance (CFI)), Block Exemptions and Communications and letters from the Commission to the Member States.

25–002   Regulation 659/99 provided to a large extent a codification of the then existing case law of the Community Courts and the Commission's practice. The regulation is not fully comprehensive in the sense that not all previous case law of the Community Courts has been incorporated. Thus, the regulation does not indicate to what extent the final Commission decisions have to address issues raised by complainants.[4] The regulation is also not comprehensive in that it does not cover all relevant issues. The regulation does not deal with the powers of the Council provided for in art.108(2), third paragraph, which are discussed in para. 25–035. The regulation does not address whether or not interested parties may have access to the files. This topic has, among writers on competition policy, been the subject of an extensive debate.[5]

The purpose of this chapter is to explain the procedural rules applying to state aid as contained in the two regulations and the additional rules derived from the case law of the Community Courts and from the Commission's communications and practice. This involves, first of all, an overview of the main provisions of the regulations. The provisions will be discussed against the background of the case law of the Community Courts. This chapter will also focus on the central role and

---

[3] e.g. in Case 84/82 *Germany v Commission* [1984] E.C.R. 1451, at para.10 and Case 301/87 *France v Commission* [1990] E.C.R. I–307, at para.14.

[4] This requirement can be inferred from Case C–367/95P *Commission v Sytraval* [1998] E.C.R. I–1719.

[5] See e.g. C. D. Ehlermann and B. J. Drijber, "Legal Protection of Enterprises: Administrative Procedure, in Particular Access to Files and Confidentiality" [1996] E.C.L.R. 375; and M. Levitt, "Access to the File: the Commission's Administrative Procedures in Cases under Arts 85 and 86" (1997) 34 C.M.L.Rev. 1413. Both articles comment on the Commission's notice on this topic [1997] O.J. C23/3. The debate was stimulated by the CFI in its judgment in Case T–95/94 *Sytraval v Commission* [1995] E.C.R. II–2651. In this judgment the Court noted that it was particularly difficult for complainants to obtain the necessary information to substantiate their complaints. The CFI held that therefore the Commission is under a duty to investigate matters of its own motion and examine objections that the complainant would have raised if it had been able to collect the relevant information. On appeal the ECJ overruled this part of the judgment, Case C–367/95P [1998] E.C.R. I–1719.

powers of the Commission in the assessment of the compatibility of state aid with the common market and in ensuring that the Member States respect their Treaty obligations. The important but subsidiary role of the national courts, which have no jurisdiction to rule on the compatibility of aid with the common market, will be discussed in section 2 of this chapter and, in more detail, in Ch.26, section 6 and Ch.27, section 4. This chapter will also outline the procedure that the Commission follows for the supervision of the rules on state aid.

Although arts 107 and 108 TFEU do not mention third parties, para.16 of the   **25–003** preamble to reg.659/99 notes that it is appropriate to define all the possibilities which third parties have to defend their interests in state aid procedures. Regulation 659/99 provides a definition of interested parties and gives them certain rights during the procedures. Interested parties comprise, according to art.1(h) of reg.659/1999, beneficiaries, competing undertakings and trade associations. Article 20(2) of the same regulation provides that any interested party can bring a complaint. Until the entry into force of reg.659/99, the Commission examined complaints,[6] especially from those directly concerned such as competitors, as a general administrative practice but without accepting any specific legal obligation to do so. It also recognised that complainants were entitled to a response. Complaining parties, and other parties affected by the grant of aid, may, according to art.6(1) of reg.659/99, comment on a case in response to the notice which the Commission is required to publish if it decides to open the proceedings referred to in art.108(2) TFEU.[7] The rights of third parties are further dealt with in para.25–053 of this chapter, and also in Ch.26, section 6 and Ch.27, section 3.

2. Direct Effect

The task of assessing whether state aid is compatible with the common market   **25–004** is reserved for the Commission. Natural or legal persons cannot contest this compatibility on the basis of art.107.[8] Unlike arts 101 and 102, art.107 has no direct effect. In Case 77/72,[9] the ECJ held that the provisions of art.107(1) may have direct effect only if they are implemented by acts based on art.110 or, as the case may be, on art.108(2) paras 3 and 4. The regime for state aid clearly differs from the competition rules of arts 101 and 102 as far as the question of direct effect of the substantive norm (i.e. art.107(1)) is concerned. Article 101(2) gives

---

[6] At the time there was no specific form for lodging a complaint but there was a general form for complaints addressed against Member States for failure to comply with their Treaty obligations which could be lodged with the Commission. The use of this form does not give the complainant any special rights or status. There is a form for the submission of complaints in state aid cases [2003] O.J. C116/3. The form is also published on the website of DG COMP.

[7] Case 323/82 *Intermills v Commission* [1984] E.C.R. 3809.

[8] Case 78/76 *Steinike & Weinlig v Germany* [1977] E.C.R. 987.

[9] Case 77/72 *Capolongo v Maya* [1973] E.C.R. 611.

national courts the power to declare anti-competitive arrangements void. National courts enjoy no such powers in the area of state aid.

By contrast, national courts do have the power to enforce the direct effect of art.108(3), last sentence. This sentence contains the so-called "standstill provision". It reads: "the Member State concerned shall not put its proposed measure into effect until this procedure has resulted in a final Decision". The proper enforcement of this provision is crucial for the effective control of state aid. In the *Lorenz* case,[10] and many cases since, the ECJ decided that art.108(3) also applied to aid that had not been notified at all, and that the standstill provision had direct effect and thus could be relied on by individuals before national courts. The immediately applicable nature of this provision extends to the whole period during which it applies. Thus, the direct effect extends to all unlawful aid which has been implemented without being notified and, in the event of notification, operates during the preliminary period and, where the Commission sets in motion the contentious procedure, up to the final decision (these procedures are dealt with in section 3 below).

25–005   As to the nature of the direct effect, the Court held in the fourth point of its ruling in the *Lorenz* case that:

> "While the direct effect of the last sentence of Article 93 [now 108] compels national courts to apply this provision without it being possible to object on the grounds of rules of national law, whatever they may be, it is for the internal legal system of every Member State to determine the legal procedure leading to this result."

The direct effect of art.108(3) has been clarified by the judgment of the ECJ in the *Fédération Nationale* and the *Italy v Commission (Tirrenia di Navigazione)* judgments.[11] In the former judgment, the Court held that the validity of acts putting aid into effect is affected by the failure of the Member State concerned to notify the aid. It further specified that national courts must enforce art.108(3) even if the Commission subsequently finds that the aid, although introduced unlawfully, is nevertheless compatible in substance with the common market. Both the Commission and the Advocate General pointed to the fact that the decision taken on the basis of art.108(2) does not have retroactive effect and cannot, therefore, cure procedural defects. In its judgment in the *SFEI* case, the ECJ added that national courts are competent to adjudicate state aid cases pending before them even though the Commission is seized of the matter.[12] Following the two successive *CELF* judgments[13] it is now clear that national

---

[10] Case 120/70 *Lorenz v Germany* [1973] E.C.R. 1471.
[11] Case C–354/90 *Fédération Nationale v France* [1991] E.C.R. I–5523; Case C–400/99 *Italy v Commission* [2001] E.C.R. I–7303.
[12] Case C–39/94 *SFEI v La Poste* [1996] E.C.R. I–3577.
[13] Case C–199/06 *Centre déxportation du Livre Francais (CELF)* [2008] E.C.R. I–469 and case C–1/09 *Centre d'éxportation du Livre Francais (CELF)* [2010] E.C.R. I–2099, para.37.

courts must, if they are satisfied that the conditions of art.107(1) are met, suspend the aid if it has been granted illegally. They must also order the payment of interest over the period that the aid was granted illegally. They may, within the framework of its domestic law, if appropriate, also order the recovery of the unlawful aid already granted.[14] Where national courts find that aid has been granted in breach of art.108(3) this must in principle lead to its repayment in accordance with the procedural rules of domestic law. In the judgment *Italy v Commission* the Court clarified that also in a situation where the Member State contests the qualification of certain aid as new aid, the decision to open the art.108(2) procedure must lead the Member State to suspend the aid.[15] Such a decision may also be invoked before a national court called upon to enforce the standstill clause of art.108(3).

Following these judgments, it is clear that there is a penalty for Member States **25–006** not observing art.108(3) in a situation where the aid is nevertheless subsequently approved. National courts must, in principle, order them to pay damages and may issue injunctions, as will be further dealt with in Ch.26, section 6. Where aid has been financed by charges imposed on undertakings, national courts must in principle order refunding of the amounts levied.[16] Furthermore, as will be discussed in section 4, below, art.11 of reg.659/99 empowers the Commission to issue suspension as well as recovery injunctions. According to art.14 of the regulation, the Commission is also entitled, in its final negative Decision in which it orders recovery, to order the Member States to require the beneficiary to pay interest from the period during which the aid was unlawful until it was declared compatible with the common market (see also section 4, below). National courts can also apply group exemptions enacted pursuant to art.1 of reg.994/98.[17]

3. THE SYSTEM OF PROCEDURAL RULES

This section will provide a brief overview of the general provisions of reg.659/ **25–007** 99.[18] Regulation 659/99 starts by defining the different concepts of aid. The

---

[14] Case C–199/06 [2008] E.C.R. I–469, para.53; Case C–1109 [2010] E.C.R. I–2099, para.3.
[15] Case C–400/99 *Italy v Commission* [2001] E.C.R. I–7303, at para.59. See also Joined Cases T–269/99, T–271/99 and T–272/99 *Territorio Historico Guipuzcoa et al v Commission* [2002] E.C.R. II–4217, at para.38.
[16] Case C–261/01 and C–262/01 *Van Calster* [2003] E.C.R. I–12249, at para.54. This follows when the method of financing is an integral part of the unlawful aid measure. See also Case C–393/04 *Air Liquide Industries Belgium* [2006] E.C.R. I–5293 and Case C–526/04 *Laboratoires Boiron* [2006] E.C.R. I–7529.
[17] [1998] O.J. L142/1.
[18] See for a discussion of the background of reg.659/99, Sinnaeve and Slot, "The new Regulation on State aid procedures" [1999] C.M.L.Rev. 36, pp.1153–1194; A. Sinnaeve in M. Heidenhain, *Handbuch des Europäischen Beihilferechts* (Beck: 2003) Ch.8, pp.659–662.

regulation provides an extensive procedure for notified aid. In addition, Commission Regulation 794/2004 sets out detailed provisions for notification and provides for a mandatory notification form. Regulation 659/99 specifies the different decisions that the Commission can take to close the preliminary and the formal procedures. It is to be noted that the regulation does not enable the Commission to close the preliminary procedure with a negative decision, nor does it empower the Commission to impose conditions and obligations when taking a positive decision at the end of the preliminary procedure.

Regulation 659/1999 lays down rules for unlawful aid, which, according to art.1(f), is defined as new aid put into effect in contravention of art.108(3) of the Treaty. This includes non-notified aid and aid that is notified but subsequently implemented without the Commission's approval. The Regulation includes rules on recovery and injunctions to suspend or provisionally to recover the aid. In this context, an interesting feature but hitherto little used is art.11(2) of reg.659/99, allowing the Commission to authorise the Member State to couple refunding of the aid with the payment of rescue aid to the firm concerned. Chapter IV of reg.659/99 provides rules for the procedure regarding misuse, while Ch.V gives detailed rules for the existing aid schemes.

Chapter VI of reg.659/99 deals with the rights of interested parties. It gives interested parties the right to inform the Commission of any alleged unlawful aid and any alleged misuse of aid. As will be discussed below in section 5 and in Ch.27, section 3, these provisions have to be supplemented with the case law of the Community Courts.

25–008   Chapter VII contains rules on the monitoring of aid. These rules cover all existing aid schemes as well as cases for which the Commission has imposed specific reporting obligations. They also provide for on-site monitoring.

The final chapter of reg.659/99 contains common provisions on confidentiality of information, and of the addressee of the decisions as well as the publication of decisions. Article 25 of the regulation states that decisions concluding the preliminary and formal procedure shall be addressed to the Member State concerned. It may be recalled that the CFI (now General Court) in its *Sytraval* judgment had assumed that such decisions may be addressed to the complainant.[19] The ECJ, on appeal, reversed this finding and held that such a decision is addressed to the Member State concerned.[20] This issue is further discussed in Ch.27, section 3. Article 27 of reg.659/99 gives the Commission the power to adopt further, implementing, provisions, which it did by enacting reg.794/2004.

25–009   Finally, the regulation confirms the establishment of an Advisory Committee on State Aid: "confirms", because this Committee had already been established according to art.7 of reg.994/98 on group exemptions.[21] According to art.29 of reg.659/99, the Committee shall be consulted on drafts for further implementing

---

[19] Case T–95/94 *Sytraval v Commission* [1995] E.C.R. II–2651.

[20] Case C–367/95P *Commission v Sytraval* [1998] E.C.R. I–1719.

[21] Council Regulation 994/98 on the application of arts 92 and 93 EC Treaty (now arts 107 and 108 TFEU) to certain categories of horizontal state aid [1998] O.J. L142/1.

provisions. When the position of this Committee is compared with the somewhat similar Advisory Committee under reg.1/2003, it is worth observing that the State Aid Committee, unlike the Competition Committee, will not be consulted on individual decisions. This is not really surprising in view of the subject matter; indeed, it would create an awkward situation if Member States were able to advise on their own aid proposals.

Regulation 659/99 has by and large created a coherent legal regime for the enforcement of the EC state aid rules. This regime was long overdue. In the period before the adoption of the regulation, procedures sometimes dragged on for years even after the ECJ's judgment in the *Boussac* case.[22] For example, in the *Westdeutsche Landesbank* case, 16 meetings between the Commission and the German authorities took place over a period of more than four years before the Commission opened the art.108(2) procedure.[23] Nevertheless, as the *CELF* saga demonstrates, the interaction of the procedural rules with the judicial protection rules of EU law can lead to a protracted legal dispute that has, even after 20 years, not ended.[24] After three positive decisions which were all annulled by the CFI (General Court), the Commission adopted a negative decision ordering recovery of the aid. This decision has been appealed. It is also likely that the national recovery procedures will be challenged in French courts. This is further discussed in Chapter 27, below.

Regulation 659/99 does not say what the Commission should do when its **25-010** decision has been in whole or partly annulled or otherwise affected by decisions of Community Courts. As evinces from the case law the answer to this question depends on the grounds of annulment.

The ECJ ruled in its judgment in *Spain v Commission*[25] that the Commission may resume the procedure at the very point at which the illegality occurred. In this case, this meant that the Commission was entitled to take the completed investigation measures of the formal procedure as its starting point and thus could dispense with the need to start a new procedure. If, however, the Commission's decision is annulled on substance, it would have to reconsider whether or not the reopening of the art.108(2) procedure is necessary. Thus, in the *Brittany Ferries* case, the CFI (now General Court) annulled the Commission's decision, holding that, contrary to the view of the Commission, the measure in question constituted aid.[26] Such a ruling obliges the Commission to reopen the case and consider the possibility of an exemption. It seems unlikely that this could be achieved by opening the art.108(3) procedure. A reopening of the formal procedure would seem to be necessary. The Commission reopened the art.108(2)

---

[22] Case C–301/87 *France v Commission* [1990] E.C.R. I–307.
[23] Decision 2000/392 (EC) *Westdeutsche Landesbank* [2000] O.J. L150/1. In the *Seleco* decision 2000/536 [2000] O.J. L227/24, it took the Commission also almost four years to open the art.108(2) procedure.
[24] See the latest Commission Decision 2011/179 *CELF* [2011] O.J. L78/37.
[25] Case C–415/96 *Spain v Commission* [1998] E.C.R. I–6993.
[26] Case T–14/96 *Bretagne Angleterre Irlande (BAI) v Commission* [1999] E.C.R. II–139.

procedure after the Court annulled its Decision 93/412 on aid to *Bremer Vulcan*.[27] The Commission did not, however, reopen the art.108(2) procedure in its decision on aid to *Air France* after its original decision was annulled by the CFI (now General Court) on two grounds, since the annulment was essentially on grounds of reasoning, which the Commission considered could be remedied without reopening the art.108(2) procedure.[28] In the *CELF* case the Commission noted in 2011 that procedure initiated by its decision of July 30, 1996 remained open.[29] The Commission adopted a decision extending the procedure and inviting comments making it clear that this was the art.108(2) TFEU procedure.[30]

25–011 In one instance the Commission withdrew its negative decision pending an appeal against it before the CFI (now General Court) and reopened the art.108(2) procedure.[31] The Commission seemed to have been convinced by the arguments of the beneficiary and the German government. It also noted that no legitimate expectations or acquired rights stood in the way of reassessment of the case.

The Commission's decision may also be affected by a preliminary ruling of the ECJ. This happened in the *Piaggio* case.[32] The ECJ found that the Commission had erroneously qualified the measure as existing aid.[33] The ECJ also ruled that

---

[27] The first Commission decision was published in [1993] O.J. L185/43. This decision was annulled in Joined Cases C–329/93, 62 and 63/95 *Germany v Commission* [1996] E.C.R. I–5151. The fresh Decision 98/665 is published in [1998] O.J. L316/25. The Commission reopened the art.108(2) procedure after its decision concerning state aid in favour of the Coopérative d'exportation du livre français (Celf) had been partly annulled. It took a new decision declaring the aid compatible, 1999/133 [1999] O.J. L44/37. It reopened the art.108(2) procedure in the *Sniace* case, C–342/96 *Spain v Commission* (the *Tubacex* judgment) [1999] E.C.R. I–2459. The Commission adopted a new decision amending the previous decision, 2001/43 [2001] O.J. L11/46. It reopened the art.108(2) procedure after the General Court annulled its decision in Joined Cases T–447, 448 and 449/93 *AITEC v Commission* [1995] E.C.R. II–1971, concluding with Decision 2000/199 [2000] O.J. L66/1. In the latter case the General Court annulled the decision to close the art.108(2) procedure. The Commission therefore enlarged the art.108(2) procedure. The Commission reopened the art.108(2) procedure following the judgment of the General Court in Case T–184/97 *BP Chemicals v Commission* September 27, 2000 [2001] O.J. C60/4. See further the Commission Decision to reopen the art.108(2) procedure in *Radio and Television Portugal* [2002] O.J. C85/9; the *Chemische Werke Piesteritz*, following the judgment of the General Court in Case T–73/98 *Société chimique Prayon v Commission* [2001] E.C.R. II–867; Commission Decision to reopen the art.108(2) procedure in the *Glunz* case following the judgment of the General Court in Case T–27/02 *Kronofrance v Commission* [2004] E.C.R. II–4177. Commission Decision to reopen the art.108(2) procedure pursuant to the annulment of its previous decision by the General Court in Case T–157/01 *Danske Busvognmaend* [2004] E.C.R. II–917 [2005] O.J. C233/28. It should be noted that in this case the Commission took more than a year to initiate the procedure.

[28] [1999] O.J. L63/66, at para.11.

[29] Decision 2011/179 *CELF* [2011] O.J. L78/37.

[30] [2009] O.J. C142/6.

[31] Decision 2003/875 [2003] O.J. L337/1.

[32] Case C–295/97 *Piagio v International Factors* [1999] E.C.R. I–3725.

[33] The ECJ ruled in paras 54 and 46 that: "The Commission has, however, classified the system under Law No 95/79 as an 'existing State aid', whilst recognising that that Law, although promulgated after the entry into force of the Treaty, was not notified to it in accordance with Art.93(3) of the Treaty. Its position is based on reasons of practical expediency, including, in particular, its own doubts, which extended over 14 years, concerning the classification of Law No 95/79 as State aid, the expectations of traders subject to that system, the infrequent application of the system, and the impossibility in practice of obtaining repayment of the sums which might be recoverable. That position cannot be accepted."

national laws which derogate from the ordinary bankruptcy law must be regarded as granting state aid. The Commission reacted to this judgment by opening the art.108(2) procedure.[34]

Regulation 659/99 provides the complainant limited rights. Article 20(2) does not give interested parties an unambiguous right to lodge a complaint nor does it provide for rights of complainants and other interested parties during the procedure. The Commission has made life a little easier for complainants by publishing a form for the submission of complaints.[35] Nevertheless, the position of the complainant during the preliminary procedure is unsatisfactory. The regulation obliges the Commission to send a copy of a decision terminating the formal procedure to complainants, but there is no such obligation at the end of the preliminary procedure. It should be remembered that the ECJ in its *Cook* judgment[36] noted that complainants should have the possibility of lodging an appeal against decisions terminating the preliminary procedure. However, without information it will be difficult for complainants to protect their rights. It would not be surprising if future judgments of the Community Courts were to rule that the Commission must properly inform complainants at the end of the preliminary procedure and thus supplement the regulation. The Commission, for its part, remains reluctant to give too much room to third parties in the preliminary procedure, as is evidenced in its reply to a written question by Ms Carlsson.[37] It is of the opinion that inviting comments from third parties during the preliminary procedure would be disproportionate in that this would cause delay. It also points to the fact that it needs to protect the confidentiality of notifications and correspondence with Member States.

The Commission is also reluctant to allow the intervention of key players in the state aid procedures in the financial sector. In the *ING* case it objected to the intervention of the Dutch Central bank in the proceeding before the General Court.[38] In a clearly worded order the GC gave the Central Bank leave to intervene.

4. THE PROCEDURAL REGIME

Introduction: the structure of Regulation 659/99

The regulation provides for four different procedures (Chs II–V of the regulation) according to the type of state aid involved: a procedure for notified aid, for unlawful aid, for misuse of aid and for existing aid schemes. A definition of these

25–012

25–013

[34] [1999] O.J. C245/27. The Commission also referred to the judgment of the ECJ in Case C–200/97 *Ecotrade v AFS* [1998] E.C.R. I–7907.
[35] [2003] O.J. C116/3. This form is also published on the website of DG COMP. Part VII of the form draws the attention of complainants to the fact that they may wish to not have their identity disclosed.
[36] Case C–198/91 *Cook v Commission* [1993] E.C.R. I–2487.
[37] E–2532/97 [1998] O.J. C82/103.
[38] Case T–33/10 [2010] O.J. C80/40, pending.

concepts can be found in Ch.I of the regulation. The qualification of aid as notified, unlawful, misused or existing is of utmost importance, since it determines which chapter of the regulation applies. Each procedure is only subject to the rules of the relevant chapter, except where cross-references to other chapters are made. The number of cross-references increases the complexity of the regulation, but it avoids unnecessary repetitions and ensures coherence. In view of the basic obligation to notify every new aid to the Commission, the main procedure is that regarding notified aid. It sets out a two-phase procedure for the examination of notified aid, based on art.108(2) and (3) TFEU as developed by the Court and reinforced by the rules of the Regulation. The procedure for unlawful aid only defines those rules which differ from the rules for notified aid and adds a cross-reference to the applicable articles contained in the chapter on notified aid. The content of most of the provisions in this chapter is derived from the case law of the Courts. Some new provisions are designed to increase the efficiency of state aid control. Chapter IV of the regulation on misuse of aid is limited to one article since it is largely based on the chapter regarding unlawful aid. Chapter V mainly codifies the procedure for existing aid as it is foreseen by art.108(1) TFEU and has been applied by the Commission for a long time.

Existing aid and new aid

25–014   Aid granted by Member States has to be distinguished according to whether it is new aid or existing aid. Furthermore, a clear distinction should be made between existing aid and existing aid schemes as will be discussed below. The distinction between new or existing aid is crucial. Article 1(b) of the regulation defines "existing aid" as follows:

"(i) without prejudice to Articles 144 and 172 of the Act of Accession of Austria, Finland and Sweden, all aid which existed prior to the entry into force of the Treaty in the respective Member State, that is to say, aid schemes and individual aid which were put into effect before, and are still applicable after the entry into force of the Treaty;

(ii) authorised aid, that is to say, aid schemes and individual aid which have been authorised by the Commission or by the Council;

(iii) aid which is deemed to have been authorised pursuant to Article 4(6) of this regulation or prior to this Regulation but in accordance with this procedure;

(iv) aid which is deemed to be existing aid pursuant to Article 15[39];

(v) aid which is deemed to be an existing aid because it can be established that at the time it was put into effect it did not constitute an aid, and

---

[39] According to art.15(3), any aid with regard to which the time limitation period has expired, shall be deemed to be existing aid.

subsequently became an aid due to the evolution of the Common Market and without having been altered by the Member State. Where certain measures become aid following the liberalisation of an activity by Community law, such measures shall not be considered as existing aid after the date fixed for liberalisation."

The first element of the definition has not given rise to difficulties in the content of the Regulation, although the expression "still applicable after" in the context of accession has been the source of dispute.[40] In the *AEM* case[41] the applicant, relying on the *Namur-Les Assurances*[42] judgment, sought to argue that measures introduced in Italy before the entry into force of the EEC Treaty would qualify as measures under this provision. The CFI [General Court] dismissed the argument noting that the measures were substantially different from the original ones.

The second category of existing aid refers to the most common form, i.e. aid 25–015 approved by the Commission under the procedure of art.108(3) or (2) which is now laid down in art.4(3) and art.7(3) or (4) of the Regulation.[43] Existing aid does not include substantial alterations of previously approved aid.[44] It also refers to the far less usual procedure of art.108(2), third paragraph, whereby the Council may decide that aid is compatible with the common market. The third category refers to aid that the Commission has approved by default. Under the case law of the ECJ, Member States were entitled to implement new aid if the Commission failed to adopt a decision within a period of two months following its notification.[45] Article 4(6) of the Regulation largely codifies this case law and allows Member States to implement the aid if the Commission fails to act, and notify the Commission thereof. It adds that the Commission has a period of 15 working days from receipt of the Member State's notice to adopt a decision which will then bar the Member State from implementing the aid. This procedure is useful because it clarifies that the Commission can no longer prolong the period by asking additional information, a practice that was disapproved by the ECJ in Case C–99/98 *Austria v Commission* [2001] E.C.R. I–1101.

The fourth category refers to aid that cannot be recovered as a result of the limitation period of 10 years to which art.15 subjects the Commission's powers. Even though art.15 is primarily intended to limit the powers of the Commission

---

[40] See Ch.5, paras 5–015 and 5–016. The rules defining the distinction between existing aid and new aid in the 2004 accessions are discussed above in Ch.5.

[41] Case T–301/02 *AEM v Commission* [2009] E.C.R. II–01757, para.126. In the same vein, Case T–292/02 *ACEA v Commission* [2009] E.C.R. II–01659, para.123; and Case T–222/04 *Italy v Commission* [2009] E.C.R. II–01877, para.99.

[42] Case C–44/93 *Namur-Les Assurances* [1994] E.C.R. I–3829.

[43] Joined Cases T–239 and 323/04 *Italy v Commission* [2007] E.C.R. II–3265, para.79.

[44] Joined Cases T–227–229/01, 265–266/01 and 270/01 *Teritorio Historico de Alava v Commission* [2009] E.C.R. II–3029, para.233; Case T–332/06 *Alcoa Trasformazioni v Commission* [2009] E.C.R. II–29, para.128; Joined Cases T–231 and 237/06 *Netherlands v Commission* [2010] E.C.R. Unreported, para.197.

[45] Case 120/70 *Lorenz v Germany* [1973] E.C.R. 1471. The ECJ specified that Member States could implement such aid after giving the Commission notice.

to recover aid, the combination of this provision with the terms of art.1(b)(iv) has the result that the Commission is also time-barred from assessing the compatibility of the aid with the common market. It should be noted, however, that in Joined Cases T–195/01 and T–207/01 *Gibraltar v Commission* [2002] E.C.R. II–2309 at para.130, the CFI appeared to doubt that art.15 went any further than precluding recovery of aid granted more than 10 years previously.

25–016   The fifth category embodies a dynamic concept of state aid.[46] In the *Forum 187* judgment the ECJ[47] noted that the concept of "evolution of the common market" is not defined in reg.659/99. "That concept, which may be understood as a change in the economic and legal framework of the sector concerned, does not apply in a situation where . . . the Commission alters its appraisal on the basis of a more rigorous application of the Treaty rules on State aid."[48] In the *Territorio* judgment the CFI (General Court) applied this interpretation.[49] Thus it held that the Commission may apply the Treaty rules more rigorously without having to follow the rules for existing aid in a situation where the measure was not previously subject of a Commission investigation. Had it been investigated previously it would have been considered state existing aid.

The idea is that a state measure, which at the time that it was enacted did not have an anti-competitive effect because the relevant market was not liberalised or only partially opened up, may subsequently take on the character of a state aid. It is possible that subsequent liberalisation may create a situation where the earlier state measure may subsequently have the effect of a state aid. This provision seems to take its cue from the general principle of Community law that prohibition provisions can only be applied once they have been sufficiently clarified by the Commission or the Community Courts.[50] Therefore, such measures are, according to this provision, deemed to be existing aid. This implies that for such measures, according to the present case law,[51] no recovery can be ordered. An example may illustrate this. Prior to the liberalisation of the telecom

---

[46] para.(4) of the preamble states: "whereas the completion and deepening of the internal market is a gradual process, reflected in the permanent development of state aid policy; whereas following these evolutions certain measures, which at the moment they were put into effect did not constitute state aid, may have become state aid." In case T–50, 56, 60, 62 and 69/06 *Ireland and others v Commission* [2007] E.C.R. II–172, the General Court considered it appropriate to raise of its own motion a plea relating to the defective statement of reasons with regard to the application of art.1(b)(v) of reg.659/99, para.46. The General Court annulled the decision for want of sufficient reasoning. In case C–89/08P *Commission v Ireland* [2009] E.C.R. I–11245, the ECJ set the judgment of the General Court aside stating in para.84: "that decision did not necessarily need to contain specific explanations concerning the inapplicability in the present case of Art. 1(b)(v) of reg. 659/99."

[47] Joined cases C–182 and 217/03, *Belgium v Commission* [2006] E.C.R. I–5479, paras 71 et seq.

[48] In this judgment the ECJ did not have to apply this interpretation because it was addressing the argument that the Commission's decision lacked a legal basis.

[49] Cases T–230–232/01, 267–269/01 *Territorio Historico v Commission* [2009] E.C.R. II–00139, para.249.

[50] Joined Cases 209–213/84 *Ministère Public v Lucas Asjes (Nouvelles Frontières)* [1986] E.C.R. 1425, at paras 67 et seq.

[51] As will be discussed in Ch.26, the ECJ's case law on recovery has been developed in the context of unlawful aid.

market prescribed by Directive 96/2 on the liberalisation of the digital mobile telephone market,[52] the incumbent telephone operators, usually the national monopolies such as Deutsche Telecom and France Telecom, were given licences free of charge. The opening of the market led several governments to organise the distribution of additional licences through an auction. This created a situation where new entrants had to pay substantial fees for their licences whereas the incumbents had already obtained theirs without charge. In such a situation, the new entrants may want to seek ways to redress the financial imbalances through the rules on state aid. However, the definition given in art.1(b)(v), first sentence, seems to deny the new entrants a remedy to redress this financial imbalance. Nor does the second sentence of this provision help them because the licences were given before the date fixed for liberalisation by Community law. The *Gibraltar* case provides an illustration of a situation where the argument was made that a measure did not constitute aid at the time it was put into effect but subsequently became aid due to the evolution of the common market.[53] The Gibraltar government argued that the Companies (Taxation and Concessions) Ordinance should be regarded existing aid because it was only when the Commission started to apply the relatively refined state aid criteria in 2001 that it could be considered state aid. In the *Alzetta* case the CFI (General Court) held that part of the system of aid in question did not at the time of its introduction come within the scope of art.107(1) and thus had to be classified as existing aid.[54] The fact that the concept of state aid evolved by virtue of decisions of the Commission and of the Community Courts is recognised in art.1(b)(v) of reg.659/99.[55]

The second sentence of this provision limits the general principle outlined above. According to this provision, measures which become aid after liberalisation of an activity by Community law shall not be considered existing aid after the date fixed for liberalisation. Such measures shall be considered new aid. This presumably means such measures that became aid as a result of liberalisation, and not as the text reads "following the liberalisation".[56] Measures cannot be

25–017

---

[52] [1996] O.J. L20/59.

[53] Joined Cases T–195/01 and T–207/01 *Government of Gibraltar v Commission* [2002] E.C.R. II–2309, at para.113.

[54] Joined Cases T–298/97, 312/97, 313/97, 315/97, 600/97 to 607/97, 1/98, 3/98 to 6/98 and 23/98 *Alzetta v Commission* [2000] E.C.R. II–2319, at para.40. This point was not appealed in Case C–298/00P *Italy v Commission* [2004] E.C.R. I–4087. A similar dispute about aid granted in conformity with art.4(3) of reg.3577/92 (maritime cabotage) was at issue in Case C–400/99 *Italy v Commission* [2005] E.C.R. I–3657 and Case T–246/99 *Tirrenia di Navigazione v Commission* [2007] E.C.R. II–65. In Joined Cases T–346/99, 347/99 and 348/99 *Territorio Historico de Alava v Commission* [2002] E.C.R. II–4259, the applicant's argument that the tax measure had to be considered existing aid because of the evolution of the internal market, was rejected at paras 80–84.

[55] See Commission Decision 2002/901 [2002] O.J. L314/97, at para.73 where the Commission noted that the aid did not become aid due to the evolution of the common market or following the liberalisation of the sector.

[56] Since such measures have been put into effect before the liberalisation they can, logically, not have been enacted after liberalisation.

challenged in cases where the liberalisation has not been required by Community law.

The distinction between existing and new aid has often been a source of dispute. Several judgments of the Community courts provide examples of such disputes.[57] Member States often take the position that the aid is covered by a previously approved aid whereas the Commission takes the view that it is not.[58] The Member State's position that measures have to be qualified as existing aid will not bar the Commission from treating aid as new aid, although a decision to initiate art.108(2) procedure in such circumstances will be a reviewable act.[59] Its decision to open the art.6 of reg.659/99 procedure, the art.108(2) TFEU procedure for new aid, has independent legal effects.[60] Such a decision might also be invoked before a national court in the context of a dispute about an infringement of the stand-still clause of art.108(3) TFEU. It also has the effect that the intended beneficiaries should be aware that payments will be unlawful. Aid alleged to have been made on the basis of a previously authorised scheme of aid but that does not comply with the conditions laid down in the Commission decision approving the scheme must be regarded as new aid.[61]

25–018   In the *British Aerospace* case,[62] the applicants denied that the Commission Decision concerning additional aid to British Aerospace was dependent on an earlier Commission decision on the matter. In other words, they claimed that the additional aid was new aid. The Commission maintained that its second decision was merely implementing its earlier decision. The Court held that the Commission was not entitled to adopt a new decision stating that the Member State had not complied with an earlier decision without bringing infringement proceedings under art.108(2), second sub-paragraph, or opening proceedings under art.108(2), first sub-paragraph.[63] In the cases of *Spain v Commission* and *Italy v*

---

[57] See Case C–44/93 *Namur Les Assurances du Credit v Nationale Delcrederedienst and Belgium* [1993] E.C.R. I–3829; Case C–313/90 *CIRFS v Commission* [1993] E.C.R. I–1125, at para.25; Case C–295/97 *Piaggio v International Factors* [1999] E.C.R. I–3735; T–190/00, *Regione Siciliana v Commission* [2003] E.C.R. II–5015. See also Case T–50/06 *Ireland v Commission* and Case C–89/08 P discussed in fn.46 above; Joined Cases T–265, 292 and 504/04, *Tirrenia de Navigazione* [2009] E.C.R. II–21, para.134. Commission Decision 2003/875 of December 23, 2002 [2003] O.J. L337/1 et seq. provides an extraordinary example of a procedure where the Commission decided to withdraw a decision in which it had declared a measure incompatible with the common market. In the new decision the Commission stated that it had based its earlier Decision 2002/468 [2002] O.J. L165/15 et seq. on incorrect information. The new decision states that the aid constitutes existing aid.

[58] See, e.g. the Commission Decision to open the art.108(2) procedure in the case of aid for *Combined transport Rotterdam-Prague* [1999] O.J. C213/23, at para.4; Decision in the *Landesbank Berlin* case [2002] O.J. C239/12; Commission Decision 2010/38 *Shipbuilding Italy* [2010] O.J. L17/50, paras 18–19.

[59] See Case C–400/99 *Italy v Commission (Tirrenia)* [2001] E.C.R. I–7303; Case T–176/01 *Ferriere Nord v Commission* [2004] E.C.R. II–3931 and Case T–354/05 *Télévision Française v Commission* [2009] E.C.R. II–471, para.81.

[60] Case C–400/99 *Italy v Commission* [2001] E.C.R. I–7303 at paras 57–59.

[61] Case C–36/00 *Spain v Commission* [2002] E.C.R. I–3243, at para.42.

[62] Case C–294/90 *British Aerospace and Rover Group v Commission* [1992] E.C.R. I–493.

[63] See also Case C–261/89 *Italy v Commission* [1991] E.C.R. I–4437, discussed by J.A. Winter, "Supervision of State Aid: Art.93 and the Court of Justice" (1993) C.M.L.Rev. 311.

Commission,[64] the governments claimed that the disputed aid had become exist-ing aid after the Commission had failed to observe the two-month period provided for in art.108(3).

According to art.108(1) TFEU existing aid schemes in Member States shall be kept under constant review by the Commission. According to art.17 of reg.659/99 the Commission shall obtain the necessary information from the Member States for such review. Aid schemes are defined in art.1(d) as an act on the basis of which, without further implementing measures, individual aid may be granted. It is important to distinguish clearly between existing aid on the one hand and existing aid schemes on the other hand.[65] Existing aid can as a rule not be challenged by the Commission except when the conditions attached to its approval have not been observed. In the latter case, art.16 of reg.659/99 empow-ers the Commission to open the formal investigation procedure. By contrast, existing aid schemes can be challenged albeit only with prospective effects as regards their abolition or amendment.[66] According to art.18 of reg.659/99 the Commission shall propose to the Member States any appropriate measures required by recent developments, or by the functioning of the common market. Article 108(2) TFEU provides that if the Commission finds that the aid scheme is not compatible with the common market or that the aid is being misused, the Member States concerned must abolish or alter such aid. This is spelt out in more detail in arts 18 and 19 of reg.659/99 and discussed in paras 25–049 et seq., below.

Even though existing aid schemes can be challenged by the Commission, the qualification of an aid as falling under an existing aid scheme exempts it from the standstill obligation or any risk of a recovery order and therefore provides it important protection. Thus it is not surprising that similar disputes as to the classification of aid, i.e. whether it is new aid or aid awarded on the basis of an approved aid scheme, have arisen.[67] In the *Fleuren* judgment the CFI (General

25–019

---

[64] Cases C–312/90 [1992] E.C.R. I–4117 (Spain); C–47/91 [1992] E.C.R. I–4145 (Italy), see para.25–008.

[65] This distinction is not always properly made. See in particular the ECJ in its judgment in Case C–44/93 *Namur Les Assurances du Credit v Nationale Delcrederedienst and Belgium* [1993] E.C.R. I–3829 where the Court stated: "11. As far as existing aid is concerned at para.(1) of Art.93 gives the Commission the power, in cooperation with the Member States, to keep aid under constant review. As part of that review, the Commission proposes to the Member States any appropriate measures required by the progressive development or by the functioning of the common market. Paragraph (2) of the same article provides that, if, after giving notice to the parties concerned to submit their comments, the Commission finds that aid is not compatible with the common market having regard to Article 92, or that such aid is being misused, it is to decide that the State concerned shall abolish or alter such aid within a period of time to be determined by the Commission (judgment in Case C–47/91 *Italy v Commission* [1992] E.C.R. I–4145, at para.23). As far as existing aid is concerned, therefore, the initiative lies with the Commission."

[66] See A. Sinnaeve in M. Heidenhain, *Handbuch des Europäischen Beihilfenrechts* (Beck Mün-chen: 2003), pp.735 et seq.

[67] See, e.g. the Commission's decision to open the art.108(2) procedure in the *Hirschfelder Leinen* case [2000] O.J. C272/2. The decision to open the art.108(2) procedure in *Thüringer Indus-triebeteiligungsfonds* [2001] O.J. C166/14. The decision to open the art.108(2) procedure in the *Kahla Porzellan* case [2002] O.J. C26/19. See also case T–354/05 *Télévisons Française* [2009] E.C.R. II–471, paras 187 et seq.

Court) ruled that a Member State cannot by amending a previously approved aid scheme unilaterally extend the scope of that approval.[68] In *Gibraltar v Commission* the CFI ruled that the Commission cannot classify the entire legislation as new aid when amendments should be regarded as severable elements to an original 1967 tax scheme.[69]

Notified new aid

25–020 Regulation 659/99 codifies the rules for notified new aid as they have been developed in the case law of the ECJ. Chapter II of the Regulation lays down the procedural rules regarding notified aid.

25–021 **Notification.** According to art.2(1) of reg.659/99, new aid shall be notified to the Commission. This provision reiterates the rule of art.108(3), last sentence of the Treaty. According to art.1(c) alterations to existing aid are also considered new aid. Article 4(1) of the implementing Regulation 794/2004 defines an alteration of an existing aid as any change other than modifications of a purely formal or administrative nature which cannot affect the evaluation of the compatibility of the aid measure. The scope of the notification obligation is identical to that of art.107(1) TFEU.[70] Article 2(1) notes that provisions provided for in regulations pursuant to art.94 of the Treaty (now art.109 TFEU) may contain exemptions to the notification obligation. This refers in particular to group exemptions and the de minimis exemption provided for in art.2(1) of reg.994/98.[71] The most important among those is reg.800/2008 the General Block Exemption discussed in Ch.11, above. The Commission has adopted further regulations.[72] Another exemption is provided for in art.9(1) of reg.1370/2007 (see further Ch.17 on transport). Yet another exemption from the obligation to notify is the individual award of aid pursuant to a previously approved general aid scheme.[73] There are special notification rules for aid in the coal sector.[74]

A further exemption follows from the case law of the ECJ. Measures compensating for public service obligations satisfying the conditions laid down in the *Altmark* judgment are not considered to be state aid and hence do not have to be

---

[68] Case T–109/01 *Fleuren Compost BV v Commission* [2004] E.C.R. II–127.
[69] Joined Cases T–195/01 and T–207/01 *Government of Gibraltar v Commission* [2002] E.C.R. II–2309, at para.113.
[70] A. Sinnaeve, "State Aid Procedures: Developments since the entry into force of the Procedural Regulation," (2007) 44 CML Rev. 965–1033, at p.967.
[71] Council Regulation (EC) 994/98 of May 7, 1998 on the application of arts 92 and 93 (now 107 and 108 TFEU) of the Treaty establishing the European Community to certain categories of horizontal state aid [1998] O.J. L142/1.
[72] See e.g. art.3 of reg.70/2001, on state aid to small and medium-sized enterprises [2001] O.J. L10/33.
[73] A. Sinnaeve, "The Present and Future State Aid Procedures", in *Understanding State Aid Policy in the European Community*, Bilal/Nicolaides (eds) (Kluwer: 1999).
[74] Art.9 of Council Regulation (EC) 1407/2002 on state aid to the coal industry [2002] O.J. L205/1. See further Ch.14.

notified.[75] The Commission has issued a Decision specifying that certain types of public service compensation are compatible with art.106(2) of the TFEU.[76] The Decision does not apply to land transport and only applies to compensation for public service obligations in the air and maritime transport sector that are defined in secondary legislation.[77] Article 2(1) of the decision limits its scope to:

- public service compensation granted to undertakings with an average annual turnover of less than €100 million which receive annual compensation of less than €30 million;

- public service compensation granted to hospitals and social housing undertakings carrying out activities qualified as services of general economic interest by the Member State concerned;

- public service compensation for air or maritime links to islands on which average annual traffic during the two financial years preceding that in which the service of general economic interest was assigned does not exceed 300,000 passengers; and

- public service compensation for airports and ports for which average annual traffic during the two financial years preceding that in which the service of general economic interest was assigned does not exceed 1,000,000 passengers, in the case of airports, and 300,000 passengers, in the case of ports.

The Commission Decision is based on the application of art.106(3) TFEU, and although it gives some helpful illustrations of the criteria of art.106(2) it does not of course preempt the *Altmark* case law. The *Altmark* judgment is based on the interpretation of art.107(1) TFEU.[78] Therefore, compensation in line with the *Altmark* criteria above the thresholds laid down under the first indent or above the thresholds of the third and fourth indent is nevertheless not caught by the prohibition of Art.107(1) TFEU and thus does not have to be notified.

In addition, the Commission has adopted a Framework for the assessment of measures that do not satisfy the conditions of the decision but can be found

---

[75] Case C–280/00 *Altmark Trans v Nahverkehrsgesellschaft* [2003] E.C.R. I–7747.

[76] Decision of November 28, 2005 on the application of art.106(2) of the TFEU to state aid in the form of public service compensation granted to certain undertakings entrusted with the operation of services of general economic interest [2005] O.J. L312/67.

[77] art.2(2) of the Decision states: "In the field of air and maritime transport, this Decision compensation granted to undertakings in connection with services of general economic interest as referred to in Art.86(2) [106(2)] of the Treaty which complies with Regulation (EEC) No 2408/92 and Regulation (EEC) No 3577/92, when applicable."

[78] See paras 86 and 87 of the judgment. As explained in the Opinion of AG Jacobs in Case C–126/01 *Ministre de l'écoonomie v Gemo* [2003] E.C.R. I–13769, at paras 97 et seq., the question of whether compensation should be considered state aid has been approached from two different lines. First, the compensation approach where such compensation is assessed under art.107(1). Secondly, the state aid approach which considers such compensation state aid but then proceeds to examine whether it can be exempted under art.107(2). See J.A. Winter, "Re(de)fining the notion of State aid in Art.87(1) [107(1)]of the EC Treaty" (2004) C.M.L.Rev. 41, pp.495–502. See also Ch.3.

compatible with the common market pursuant to art.106(2).[79] Such measures should, however, be notified. In the view of the Commission, measures that do not formally satisfy the conditions of its decision and the *Altmark* judgment may still qualify for the exemption of art.106(2) TFEU if they satisfy the substantive criteria.

25–022   Article 2(2) of reg.659/99 obliges Member States to provide all necessary information to enable the Commission to take a decision. Regulation 794/04 provides detailed procedures and prescribes the use of notification forms. Article 5(1) of reg.659/99 empowers the Commission to request additional information when it considers that the information received is incomplete. The Commission shall acknowledge the receipt of such information from the Member State concerned. Article 5(2) of reg.659/99 states that if the Member State does not respond to the Commission's request or provides incomplete information, the Commission shall send a reminder allowing for an appropriate additional period within which the information shall be provided. Member States do not always provide the information requested by the Commission. Moreover, the information may also be misleading and contradictory.[80] Article 5(3) of reg.659/99 goes on to state that:

"The notification shall be deemed to be withdrawn if the requested information is not provided within the prescribed period, unless before the expiry of that period either the period has been extended with the consent of both the Commission and the Member State concerned, or the Member State concerned, in a duly reasoned statement, informs the Commission that it considers the notification to be complete because the additional information requested is not available or has already been provided. In that case, the period referred to in Article 4(5) [i.e. the two month period] shall begin on the day following the receipt of the statement. If the notification is deemed to be withdrawn, the Commission shall inform the Member State thereof."

25–023   These extensive provisions on notification end a long-running dispute between the Commission and the Member States.[81] It is now clear that the two-month

---

[79] Community Framework for state aid in the form of public service compensation [2005] O.J. C297/4.

[80] See, e.g. Commission Decision 2000/129 [2000] O.J. L42/19, at para.60.

[81] In Case 84/82 *Germany v Commission* [1984] E.C.R. 1451, the Commission took the view that the beginning of the period would start only from the time when it was in a position to form a view on the plan notified, that is to say after it has obtained necessary supplementary information and established appropriate contacts with the Member State concerned, capable, perhaps, of leading to the preparation of an amended aid scheme. The ECJ stated that: "the Commission should proceed with due expedition in order to take account of the interest of the Member States in obtaining clarification in cases in which there may be an urgent need to take action; otherwise, after the expiry of an appropriate period, which the Court set at two months, the Member State concerned may implement the measures in question after giving the Commission prior notice thereof." Following the judgments of the ECJ in Cases C–301/87 *France v Commission (Boussac)* [1990] E.C.R. I–307 and C–142/87 *Belgium v Commission (Tubemeuse)* [1990] E.C.R. I–959, it was clear that the Commission may issue an interim order requiring the Member States to supply the necessary information.

period will start from the receipt of a complete notification or from the receipt of a duly reasoned statement of the Member State concerned that it considers the notification complete.[82] If the Member State does not comply with the request the notification is deemed to be withdrawn thus discharging the Commission of any obligation to adopt a decision thereon. However, if the Member State insists on a decision the Commission will adopt a decision on the basis of the information received. The Commission may not use the interim order for other purposes.[83]

Notification has to be made by the Member State, it cannot be made by the recipient.[84] Notification has to be done in a proper way, simple letters or communications are not appropriate.[85] The rules on notification contained in the regulations are quite comprehensive and apt to avoid the resurgence of disputes between the Commission, playing for time, and notifying Member States.[86] Commission Regulation 794/2004 prescribing the use of a notification form further reduces the chance of disputes between the Commission and the Member States. Article 2 of the Regulation provides that, except for simplified notifications, all notifications shall be made on the notification form set out in Pt I of Annex I to the regulation. Supplementary information needed for the assessment of the measures in accordance with regulations, guidelines, frameworks and other texts shall be provided on the supplementary information sheets set out in Pt III of Annex I. This Annex contains supplementary information sheets for all types of aid that are subject to specific regulations, guidelines and the multisectoral framework. These notification forms will be discussed in the respective chapters of this book. Notifications shall be transmitted by the Permanent Representative of the Member State concerned and be addressed to the Secretary-General of the Commission. Notifications shall be transmitted electronically.

The notification form is quite comprehensive. It requires, inter alia, information on the amount of the aid, the form of the aid and the means of funding,[87] as well as the nature of the aid. Member States should also indicate whether there are outstanding recovery orders. According to art.4 small alterations to existing aid shall be notified on the simplified notification form of Annex II of reg.794/

25–024

---

[82] See Case C–99/98 *Austria v Commission* [2001] E.C.R. I–1101 for an extensive discussion of this point. In its judgment the ECJ made a clear distinction between questions that the Commission was allowed to ask for clarification and those that were asked with the purpose of gaining time.

[83] Case C–17/99 *France v Commission* [2001] E.C.R. I–2481 at para.28: "It is not appropriate for the Commission, when it is in a position make a definitive assessment of the aid, to issue an interim decision to require the Member State to provide further information which might establish the existence of an adequate restructuring plan."

[84] Case C–442 and 471/03P *P&O European Ferries* [2006] E.C.R. I–4845, para.103.

[85] Decision 2011/134 *WAM SpA* [2011] O.J. L57/29, paras 101–104. See also Decision 2007/256 *French General Tax Code* [2007] O.J. L112/41, paras 154–155.

[86] Such rules were indeed highly necessary as was evidenced in several cases before the entry into force of reg.659/99. See in particular Case C–99/98 *Austria v Commission* [2001] E.C.R. I–1101 where the preliminary procedure lasted for more than 17 months. In this period the Commission sent four letters asking further questions.

[87] This is in accordance with the ECJ judgment in Joined Cases C–261/01 and 262/01 *Van Calster* [2003] E.C.R. I–12249, at para.51; see also Case C–345/02 *Pearle v Hoofdbedrijfschap Ambachten* [2004] E.C.R. I–7139.

2004. Article 8 of the regulation provides that the time limits of state aid procedures shall be calculated in accordance with reg.1182/1971.[88] The rules on non-notified new aid will be discussed below.

The simplified procedure

25–025 In 2009 the Commission, in a Notice, introduced a simplified procedure in an effort to streamline the notification process.[89] This procedure is intended "for measures which only require the Commission to verify that the measure is in accordance with existing rules and practices without exercising any discretionary powers.[90] . . . Other aid measures will be subject to the appropriate procedures and normally to the Code of Best Practice."[91] According to s.2 of the Notice, the procedure can be used for three categories of aid:

(i) Category 1: Aid measures falling under the "standard assessment" sections of existing frameworks or guidelines.

(ii) Category 2: Aid measures corresponding to well-established Commission decision-making practice.

(iii) Category 3: Prolongation or extension of existing schemes.

Section 2 of the Notice contains a long and very detailed list of measures and should be consulted carefully. Section 3 outlines the elements of the procedure. According to the Commission, pre-notification contacts with the notifying Member State are beneficial. Such contacts allow identification at an early stage of the relevant Commission instruments or precedent decisions, the degree of complexity which the Commission's assessment is likely to involve and the scope and depth of the information required for the Commission to make a full assessment of the case.

The Member State is invited to submit a draft notification form with the necessary supplementary information sheets provided for in art.2 of reg.(EC) No.794/2004, and the relevant precedent decisions if appropriate, via the Commission's established IT application. In simple cases a draft notification is not necessary. The Notice describes the timeframe for the procedure.[92]

---

[88] [1971] O.J. L124/1.

[89] [2009] O.J. C136/3, Commission Notice on a Simplified Procedure for Certain Types of Aid.

[90] para.1 of the Notice.

[91] para.1 of the Notice. Commission Notice on a Best Practices Code on the conduct of state aid control proceedings [2009] O.J. C136/13.

[92] paras 15 and 16 provide: " Within two weeks from the receipt of the draft notification form, the Commission services will organise a first pre-notification contact. The Commission will promote the holding of contacts via email or conference calls or, at the specific request of the Member State concerned, organise meetings. Within 5 working days after the last pre-notification contact, the Commission services will inform the Member State concerned whether it considers that the case qualifies prima facie for treatment under the simplified procedure, which information still needs to be provided for the measure to qualify for treatment under that procedure, or whether the case will remain subject to the normal procedure.

16. The indication by the Commission services that the case concerned can be treated under the simplified procedure implies that the Member State and the Commission services agree prima facie that the information provided in the pre-notification context would, if submitted as

In addition, the Commission has published a Best Practices Code in order to **25–026** explain and further facilitate the procedure.[93] The Code also stresses the importance of pre-notification meetings. According to the Commission: "the results of the Code are encouraging: in particular, it had a significant impact on complaints-handling, with an increasing number of Complainants informed of the status of their complaints."[94] The Best Practices Code provides details on how the procedures should be carried out in practice. It contains voluntary arrangements between the Commission and the Member States with the aim of providing more streamlined and predictable procedures. The Commission wants to ensure, with the help of the Simplified Procedure, that clearly compatible aid measures are approved within a month from a complete notification. A transparency provision allows third parties to provide their input.

The preliminary procedure of Article 108(3) TFEU and Article 2(1) Regulation 659/99

Following notification the Commission has, according to art.4(5) of the regula- **25–027** tion, a period of two months to terminate the preliminary examination of art.108(3) of the Treaty. The preliminary procedure is intended merely to enable the Commission to form a prima facie opinion on the partial or complete compatibility of the aid in question.[95] It must be distinguished from the formal procedure which is designed to enable the Commission to be more fully informed of all facts of the case where the Commission has serious doubts about the compatibility of the aid. This procedure gives Member States and the parties concerned the possibility to express their views.

There are, according to the regulation, three ways in which the Commission may conclude the preliminary examination.[96]

The first is a decision that the notified government measure does not constitute **25–028** aid. This procedure is laid down in art.4(2) of the Regulation. The obvious

a formal notification, constitute a complete notification. The Commission would thus, in principle, be in a position to approve the measure, once formally notified on the basis of a notification form embodying the result of the pre-notification contacts, without a further request for information."

[93] Commission Notice on a Best Practices Code on the conduct of state aid control proceedings [2009] O.J. C136/13.

[94] Commission Staff Working Paper Accompanying the Report from the Commission on Competition Policy 2010, COM(2011) 328 final, Brussels, June 10, 2011 paras 98–100.

[95] Case C–204/97 *Portugal v Commission* [2001] E.C.R. I–3175, at para.32 citing other judgments; Case C–198/91 *Cook v Commission* [1993] E.C.R. I–2487, at para.22; Case C–225/91 *Matra v Commission* [1993] E.C.R. I–3203, at para.16; Case C–367/95P *Sytraval and Brinks's France* [1998] E.C.R. I–1719, at para.38.

[96] para.8 of the preamble notes that in all cases where the Commission cannot find the aid to be compatible with the common market, it should open the art.93(2) (now 108) of the Treaty procedure. According to the preamble, this provides the best protection for the rights of interested parties. Consequently, the regulation does not mention the possibility that the Commission may already after the preliminary procedure come to the conclusion that the aid is not compatible with the common market. In the past there was doubt whether it was possible for the Commission to conclude the preliminary procedure with a negative decision: see, e.g. Case C–313/90 *CIRFS v Commission* [1993] E.C.R. I–1125.

advantage of such a decision for the Member State concerned, as well as for the enterprises involved, is that it allows them to proceed without further ado.

The second way of concluding the preliminary procedure is a positive decision provided for in art.4(3) of the Regulation. A positive decision implies that the notified measure constitutes aid but can be exempted under one of the exemptions. In cases where a positive decision is taken, the Commission shall specify which exemption under the Treaty has been applied. From a comparison with art.7(3) of the regulation, it appears that the Commission has no power to impose conditions or obligations under this procedure.[97] In the past, the Commission sometimes imposed conditions under the preliminary procedure.[98] Now it can only do so pursuant to the formal procedure of art.108(2) of the Treaty, and henceforth only under art.7 of the regulation.

25–029   The third way of terminating the preliminary procedure is to initiate the procedure of art.108(2) of the Treaty. According to art.4(4), the Commission is under an obligation to initiate the proceedings under art.108(2) of the Treaty where it finds that doubts are raised as to the compatibility with the common market of the notified aid. It was not clear that the Commission was under such an obligation.[99] Until the entry into force of this regulation, there were instances where Member States did not supply information.[100] It was also not uncommon for the Member State concerned and the Commission to engage in informal discussions.[101] Long and tedious negotiations could weaken the credibility of the Commission; thus it is fortunate that such disputes are now much less likely to occur. The Regulation makes it clear that such Commission action shall take the form of a Decision,[102] although whether such a decision is an appealable decision depends on the circumstances. The Commission also initiates the art.108(2)

---

[97] A comparison may be drawn with the situation existing under the Merger Control Regulation prior to its amendment in 1997. According to art.6(1)(b) of reg.4064/89, the Commission could not impose conditions and obligations. This was amended by reg.1310/97 [1997] O.J. L180/1 and is now incorporated in reg.139/2004 [2004] O.J. L24/1. It is somewhat surprising that the Commission has not incorporated its experience in the field of merger control into the new regulation on procedures for state aid. Just as in the field of merger control it is conceivable that, even in the preliminary procedure, the imposition of obligations and conditions may be necessary.

[98] See, e.g. [1993] O.J. C256/6–11 and [1998] O.J. C384/20.

[99] See Case C–313/90 *CIRFS v Commission* [1993] E.C.R. I–1125 and Case T–49/93 *SIDE v Commission* [1995] E.C.R. II–2501. The *SIDE* judgment led to a fresh Commission Decision 1999/133 [1999] O.J. L44/37 finding that the exemption of art.107(3)(d) TFEU applied. The obligation to open the art.108(2) procedure in case the Commission harbours doubts has now also been confirmed by the judgment in Case C–204/97 *Portugal v Commission* [2001] E.C.R. I–3175, at para.51. In Case T–73/98 *Prayon* [2001] E.C.R. II–867, the CFI used the term "serious difficulties", it also held that this criterion may not be approached subjectively at para.48. The CFI carefully reviewed whether the Commission possessed sufficient information to enable it to reach an informed decision. It found that the Commission did not. See also Case T–388/03 *Deutsche Post* [2009] E.C.R. II–199, para.99.

[100] See, e.g. the Commission's Notice in [1999] O.J. C92/5. See Case T–30/01 *Territorio Histórico de Álava* [2009] E.C.R. II–2919, paras 259 et seq.

[101] See, e.g. the Commission's Notice N340/89 [1990] O.J. C103/9; this sometimes coincided with disputes about the date from which the two-month period was to start.

[102] Case C–47/91 *Italy v Commission (Italgrani)* [1992] E.C.R. I–4145 and Case C–400/99 *Italy v Commission (Tirrenia)* [2001] E.C.R. I–7303, see paras 25–017, above.

procedure if it considers that the requirements of the block exemptions are not met.[103]

The preliminary procedure may also be concluded by default of the Commission. Article 4(6) provides that where the Commission has not taken a decision within the prescribed time limits, the aid shall be deemed to have been authorised. Member States may then implement the aid after giving the Commission prior notice.[104] The Commission has 15 working days following the receipt of the notice to take a decision. In *Spain v Commission* the ECJ ruled that this time limit has to be calculated on the basis of the date of notification of the Member State concerned.[105] For obvious reasons, the Commission tries to avoid the approval of aid by default. A default approval is also of less comfort to a beneficiary than a reasoned decision, since a default approval is susceptible to annulment for lack of reasoning.

The Regulation does not contain any further rules on the procedure to be observed by the Commission during the preliminary procedure. Nor does it provide any rights for interested parties other than the right to inform the Commission of any alleged unlawful aid or any alleged misuse of power (see further section 5, below). Thus, the regulation seems to take its cue from the judgment in the *Sytraval* appeal,[106] and not the judgment of the CFI (now General Court)[107] in the same case, which imposed the burden of proof on the Commission and gave the complainant considerable rights. In this way, the regulation clearly preserves the distinction between the preliminary and the formal procedures. In the *Nuova Agricast* judgment the ECJ ruled that the validity of a Commission decision not to open the art.108(2) procedure cannot be

25–030

---

[103] Decision 1999/705 [1999] O.J. L280/87. In this Decision the Commission took the view that the requirements of the de minimis block exemption had not been met because the aid had an effect on trade between the Member States. The decision was upheld by the ECJ in Case C–382/99 *Netherlands v Commission* [2002] E.C.R. I–5163.

[104] See the Commission Decision in the case of restructuring aid in favour of British Energy [2003] O.J. C180/5 where the UK government informed the Commission that it considered the information complete and consequently it would proceed with the implementation of the aid. In Case T–187/99 *Agrana Zucker v Commission* [2001] E.C.R. II–1587, Austria had failed to give notice that the two-month period had expired. The aid concerned could therefore not be regarded as existing aid. In Case T–176/01 *Ferriere Nord SpA v Commission* [2004] E.C.R. II–3931, Italy did not inform the Commission but claimed that it had not given the Commission an "extension" of the 15-day period. The CFI (now General Court) noted that reg.659/99 does not provide for such an extension, at para.63.

[105] Case C–398/00 *Spain v Commission* [2002] E.C.R. I–5643. The judgment also held that the notification by the Member State may be made by fax. The fact that the Commission's officials were not available when the fax was received cannot put into question the date of the receipt.

[106] Case C–367/95P *Commission v Sytraval* [1998] E.C.R. I–1719.

[107] Case T–95/94 *Sytraval v Commission* [1995] E.C.R. II–2651, which imposed an obligation on the Commission to address a reasoned decision to the complainant. It also imposed on the Commission a duty to examine objections that the complainant would have raised if he had been able to collect the relevant information. The CFI (now General Court) also reversed the burden of proof, ruling that the Commission cannot impose the burden of proof on the complainant since in most cases he would not be able to collect the information in support of his allegation.

assessed by reference to information which was not available when it was closing the preliminary procedure.[108]

The formal procedure of Article 108(2) TFEU and Article 6(1) Regulation 659/99

25-031   Article 6 of the Regulation gives detailed rules for the "formal investigation procedure", as it is called. According to art.6(1), the Commission's decision to initiate the procedure shall summarise the relevant issues of fact and law. It shall include a preliminary assessment of the proposed aid and indicate any doubts as to its compatibility with the common market.[109] Member States and interested parties shall be invited to submit comments within a prescribed period, normally not exceeding one month.[110] The Commission is entitled to send the decision to identified third parties.[111] The notice shall indicate the interested parties so as to allow them to present observations.[112] The Commission is not obliged to solicit comments from specifically interested parties.[113] Furthermore, Commission notices request the authorities of the Member States to forward a copy of the letter announcing the opening of the procedure of art.108(2) immediately to the intended beneficiary.[114] According to art.8 of reg.794/2004, the time limits provided for in reg.659/99, reg.794/2004 or fixed by the Commission pursuant to art.108 TFEU shall be calculated in accordance with reg.1182/71.[115] The Commission may extend that period. According to art.26(2) of the Regulation, such a decision shall be published in the Official Journal. The Commission publishes these decisions in the C-series.

---

[108] Case C–390/06 *Nuova Agricast* [2008] E.C.R. I–2577, para.60. The English text of this paragraph does not seem to be accurate, the French text is more precise.

[109] Joined Cases T–127/99, T–129/99 and T–148/99 *Territorio Historio et al v Commission* [2002] E.C.R. II–1275, at para.136 seems to suggest that the Commission should clearly indicate which elements of the measure concerned it contests. In Joined Cases T–111/01 and T–133/01 *Saxonia Edelmetalle GmbH v Commission* [2005] E.C.R. II–1579, the CFI (now General Court) ruled that the decision to open the formal procedure must be sufficiently precise in order to allow interested parties to assess whether they want to submit observations at para.50. See also Case T–34/02 *EURL Le Levant v Commission* [2006] E.C.R. II–267, paras 77–83.

[110] In Cases T–126 and 127/96 *Breda Fucine and EFIM v Commission* [1998] E.C.R. II–3437, the complainants argued that the notice did not contain sufficient information and thus were of the opinion that the final decision should be annulled. A similar argument was rejected in Joined Cases T–30/01 and 86–88/02 *Territorio Historico v Commission* [2009] E.C.R. II–2919, para.328. In Case C–319/07P *3F v Commission* [2009] E.C.R. I–5963, para.57, the Court held that a trade union should have the possibility to show that it is a party concerned. The Court noted that the Community does not only have an economic but also a social purpose.

[111] Case T–198/01 *Technische Glaswerke Ilmenau v Commission* [2004] E.C.R. II–2717; Joined Cases C–74 and 75/00P *Falck Spa and others v Commission* [2002] E.C.R. I–7869, para.83.

[112] Case T–34/02 *EURL Le Levant 001 v Commission* [2006] E.C.R. II–267, at para.91. It is interesting to note that as a result of the CFI decision to annul the decision, the CFI did not have to address the argument that the Commission's failure to properly indicate the interested parties amounted to a violation of art.6 ECHR.

[113] Joined cases T–267/08 and T–279/08 *Région Nord-Pas-de-Calais v Commission* [2011] E.C.R. Unreported, para.75.

[114] e.g. [1999] O.J. C113/6.

[115] [1971] O.J. L124/1.

Article 6(2) prescribes that the comments received shall be communicated to the Member States. Interested parties may request that their names be withheld from such communication. The Member State concerned may reply to the comments submitted, and must normally do so within one month, although there is a possibility for an extension of that period. Member States regularly make use of this right.[116] Interested parties who have submitted comments are not informed about comments from other parties. The formal procedure is not contentious as far as they are concerned. Nevertheless, the Commission is obliged to examine comments from third parties.[117] A failure to do so results in annulment of the decision for failure to state sufficient reasons. Sinnaeve comments that pleas to give third parties a right to be informed and heard would not seem warranted in view of the fact that in only 50 per cent of the cases are comments received from them.[118] It may equally be argued that the other half of the cases were comments are given may be the really important cases where such rights contribute to the quality of the decision-making process.

The comments by third parties constitute an important element in the art.108(2) procedure, they are a valuable source of information for the Commission allowing it to assess potential distortions of competition as in the area of the merger control regulation, it is an important element in the protection of the interests of competitors. In the *Alstom* decision the Commission received a large number of comments.[119] In the *Charleroi Airport* case a total of 11 interested parties, including seven competitors and the potential beneficiary Ryanair, provided the Commission with extensive comments.[120]

According to the ECJ, the art.108(2) procedure is adversarial.[121] Accordingly, the Commission is obliged to ensure the right to a fair hearing.[122] The Commission is also obliged to communicate to the Member State concerned its opinion on the observations presented by third parties and on which the Commission intends to base its decision. The Court has also ruled that the Commission cannot base its decisions on information on which the Member State concerned has not been in a position to express its opinion.[123] However, such irregularity will only entail the annulment of the Commission's decision if it is established that, had it

---

[116] e.g. Decision 2006/643 [2006] O.J. 268/37, paras 72 et seq. where the UK responds to comments by Greenpeace in the case of the Nuclear Decommissioning Authority; Decision 2007/256 [2007] O.J. L112/41, paras 71 et seq.; Decision 2008/948 [2008] O.J. L346/1, para.162.

[117] Case T–366/00 *Scott SA v Commission* [2007] E.C.R. II–797, para.141. A useful summary of the rights of interested parties is found in Joined Cases T–427/04 and T–17/05 *French Republic v Commission* [2009] E.C.R. II–4315, paras 147–149. See also Case T–156/04 *Electricité de France v Commission* [2009] E.C.R. II–4503, paras 101 et seq.

[118] Sinnaeve, "Present and Future of State Aid Procedures".

[119] Decision 2005/418 [2005] O.J. L150/24. There were 20 sets of comments from the electricity sector, customers, suppliers, subcontractors, competitors and employees' representatives, 19 for the rail transport sector and five from employees' organisations covering the two sectors.

[120] Decision of February 12, 2004, 2004/393 [2004] O.J. L137/1. The summary of the comments cover 10 pages in the Decision.

[121] Case 84/82 *Germany v Commission* [1984] E.C.R. 1451.

[122] See also Joined Cases T–228/99 and T–233/99 *Westdeutsche Landesbank Girozentrale v Commission* [2003] E.C.R. II–435, at para.147.

[123] Case C–400/99 *Italy v Commission* [2005] E.C.R. I–3657, at para.31.

not been for that irregularity, the outcome of the procedure might have been different.[124] Even if this last test seems to leave the Commission quite a bit of leeway, it should, of course, be remembered that the Court administers such a test *ex post*. For the Commission, which must necessarily make an *ex ante* evaluation, the requirement may be stringent enough to secure fair proceedings. The Commission normally organises meetings with the national authorities.

25–032   Beneficiaries, complainants and other interested parties do not have such a right,[125] nor do they have a right of access to documents[126]; nevertheless, the Commission organises meetings with them.[127]

As can be inferred from our review of the Commission's decisions, Member States often avail themselves of the opportunity to submit comments.[128] Trade federations or associations do so as well. Interested parties are also represented.[129] In general, comments from other governments, the government concerned and competitors, strengthen the hand of the Commission in dealing with difficult and delicate state aid cases considerably. The Commission is obliged to reopen the procedure when it is presented with additional information if it considers that this information is sufficiently reliable.[130] Article 7 gives detailed rules for the taking of decisions to close the formal investigation procedure and lists the different categories of decisions that may be taken.[131] The structure of this article is similar to that of art.4 concerning decisions taken pursuant to the preliminary procedure.

25–033   The first category is a decision finding that the notified measure does not constitute aid. This may be the result of amendments proposed by the Member State concerned to the measure originally notified. It has been observed that the formal, and not the preliminary, procedure is the proper context for negotiations between Member States and the Commission.[132] Thus, the comparable provision in art.4(2) does not contain the words "where appropriate following modification by the Member State concerned". Limiting negotiations to the formal procedure enhances the transparency and effectiveness of the procedure.

The second category is the positive decision. Such a decision shall specify which Treaty exception has been applied. Article 7(3) also contains a reference to the possibility that the proposed aid has been modified. Article 7(4) empowers

---

[124] Case C–301/87 *France v Commission* [1990] E.C.R. I–307, at para.24. See also Case C–288/96 *Germany v Commission* [2000] E.C.R. I–8237.
[125] Joined Cases T–228/99 and T–233/99 *Westdeutsche Landesbank Girozentrale v Commission* [2003] E.C.R. II–435, at para.21.
[126] Case C–139/07P *Commission v Technische Glaswerke Ilmenau* [2010] E.C.R. Unreported, para.61.
[127] Joined Cases T–228/99 and T–233/99 *Westdeutsche Landesbank Girozentrale v Commission* [2003] E.C.R. II–435, at para.21.
[128] It is submitted that after entry into force of the EEA Treaty, EFTA countries can also submit their comments (see below, section 10, Protocol 27).
[129] See in this context case C–319/07P *3F v Commission* [2009] E.C.R. I–5963, para.57.
[130] Case C–290/7P *Commission v Scott SA* [2010] E.C.R. Unreported, para.96.
[131] The website of the DG for Competition of the Commission gives one list of the decisions according the legal basis.
[132] Case 84/82 *Germany v Commission* [1984] E.C.R. 1451.

the Commission to attach conditions and obligations to the positive decision. The practice of imposing conditions and obligations is well known in the area of the supervision of state aid, but it is the first time that this power has been spelled out in legislation. Several regulations in the field of competition law provide such a power. Conditions are designed to make the aid compatible with the common market, and their non-fulfilment will cause the aid to be incompatible with the common market. In its judgment in the *Aer Lingus* case,[133] the CFI considered:

"that the effect of failure to comply with a condition imposed in a Decision approving aid under Art.92(3)(c) [now 107] of the Treaty is to raise a presumption that subsequent tranches of the aid are incompatible with the Common Market."

In several important Decisions the Commission has imposed the obligation that the aid could only be implemented in tranches after the relevant obligations had been met (cf. Ch.17 on transport).   **25–034**

Obligations are often imposed to enable the Commission to monitor the implementation of the aid.[134] They usually oblige Member States to submit regular reports. Obligations may, however, also relate to other duties to be performed. It should be noted that the Commission's terminology is not always consistent. Some decisions refer to undertakings instead of obligations.[135] Other decisions do not refer to a specific term but use language stating that the aid is accepted provided that the government fulfils certain commitments.[136]

Article 7 of reg.659/99 does not mention another form of positive decision.   **25–035**
The formal procedure may also be concluded by a positive decision of the Council considering the aid compatible with the common market in derogation from the provisions of art.107 or from regulations enacted on the basis of art.109. Article 108(2), third paragraph, empowers the Council, acting unanimously, on application of the Member State to take such a decision. If the Commission has already initiated the formal procedure, the application by a Member State shall suspend the procedure until the Council has taken a decision. The Council has three months to take a decision. Failing such a decision the Commission shall

---

[133] Case T–140/95 *Ryanair v Commission* [1998] E.C.R. II–3327, at para.86.
[134] Bellamy and Child, *European Community Law of Competition*, 6th edn (London, 2008), p.724, fn.477 notes that in competition law, the Commission makes a distinction between these two concepts: "If a condition is not met, the exemption is of no effect. If an obligation is not met the Commission's recourse is to revoke the exemption under Art.8(3)(b) of Reg. 17." In the *Nestlé-Perrier* case [1992] O.J. L356/1, the merger was approved subject to the condition that one source of mineral water was to be sold. In the *ICI* case [1993] O.J. L7/13, the merger was approved subject to the obligation that a sufficient production capacity would be put at the disposal of competitors.
[135] e.g. Commission Decision concerning the recapitalisation of the company Alitalia [1997] O.J. L322/44.
[136] e.g. Commission Decision concerning aid for Aer Lingus [1994] O.J. L54/30.

give its decision. There have been a number of such positive Council decisions.[137] In its important judgment *Commission v Council* the ECJ ruled that the Council can no longer take such decisions once the three-month period is over or whenever the Commission has declared the aid incompatible with the common market.[138] Thus the power of the Council is limited to take decisions while the formal procedure is still pending and is subject to the requirement that exceptional circumstances can be invoked. Furthermore, the Council has to pay due regard to previous decisions finding the aid originally granted incompatible.[139] The text of art.108(2), third paragraph, does not seem to exclude the possibility that the Council exercises its powers even before the opening of the formal procedure, although the fact that the Council has three months to take a decision sits uncomfortably with the two-month time limit for the preliminary period. The judgment of the Court confirms the leading role of the Commission for the enforcement of the prohibition on state aid. In the second judgment, *Commission v Council*, the ECJ rejected the view of the Council that it was entitled to adopt a decision authorising new aid distinct from that declared incompatible by the Commission.[140]

The third category is the negative decision. In practice, several Commission decisions contain both a positive and a negative decision.[141] That is to say, part of the proposed aid is approved and part declared incompatible with the common market. It should be noted that the rules on recovery are laid down in art.14 of the Regulation (see further, Ch.26 on recovery).

25–036   Article 7(6) provides for a time limit for the completion of the formal procedure.[142] According to this provision, the Commission shall endeavour to adopt a decision within a period of 18 months from the opening of the procedure. Presumably, this is to be read as the opening of the formal procedure. This time limit may be extended by common agreement between the Commission and the Member State concerned.[143] The Commission cannot be required to extend the procedure when the Member State concerned modifies the aid.[144] After the

---

[137] See, e.g. Council Decision of July 16, 2003 on the granting of aid by the Belgian government to certain co-ordination centers established in Belgium [2003] O.J. L184/17 discussed by J-M Huez, "Décision finale positive dans le dossier des centers de coordination belges", Competition Policy Newsletter, No. 1, Spring 2005; Council Decision of July 16, 2003 on the compatibility with the common market of an aid that the Italian Republic intends to grant to its milk producers [2003] O.J. L184/15. See in general W. Mederer, Groeben-Schwarze and M. Heidenhain, *Handbuch des Europäischen Beihilferechts* (Beck: 2003), pp.464–8.

[138] Case C–110/02 *Commission v Council* [2004] E.C.R. I–6333, at paras 32 and 43.

[139] Case C–110/02 [2004] E.C.R. I–6333, at para.38.

[140] Case C–399/03 *Commission v Council* [2006] E.C.R. I–5629.

[141] e.g. Commission Decision concerning *German aid to Mercedes-Benz in Ludwigsfelde (Brandenburg)* [1997] O.J. L5/30.

[142] It may be recalled that in its judgment in Case 223/85 *RSV v Commission* [1987] E.C.R. 4617, the ECJ held that where the Commission did not take a decision declaring the aid incompatible after a period of 26 months, it was prevented from ordering recovery.

[143] In case C–49/05P *Ferriere Nord SpA v Commission* [2008] E.C.R. I–68, paras 48–50, the ECJ observed that the time limit is not imperative and may be extended by mutual agreement. See also Case T–301/01 *Alitalia v Commission* [2008] E.C.R. II–1753, para.160.

[144] Joined Cases C–15/98 and C–105/99 *Italy v Commission* [2000] E.C.R. I–8855, at para.43.

expiry of the time limit, the Member State concerned may request the Commission to take a decision within two months. Article 7(7) states that the Commission decision shall be taken on the basis of the information available to it. If the Commission does not have sufficient information to establish compatibility, it shall take a negative decision. In such a case the General Court shall review whether the Commission has respected the procedural requirements of reg.659/99 and stated sufficient reasons for the decision.[145]

The standstill clause

According to art.3 of reg.659/99, aid that has to be notified under art.2(1) shall not be put into effect before the Commission has taken or is deemed to have taken a decision authorising such aid. This article is a copy of art.108(3) TFEU. Aid which is exempted from notification, may be implemented. Such aid, in fact, is then to be considered as existing aid. This is consistent with the wording of art.1(1) of the Regulation on certain categories of horizontal state aid (group exemptions) which declares such aid to be compatible with the common market. Like art.108(3) TFEU, art.3 has direct effect. As explained in section 4 of Ch.27, the direct effect of the standstill clause empowers the national courts to freeze the aid and order the payment of interest and/or recovery. The Commission's power to order recovery is based on art.14 of reg.659/1999.   **25–037**

It may be useful to review the status of the standstill clause throughout the different procedures. First, the standstill clause will, of course, apply throughout the preliminary procedure. It will, according to art.4(6), lapse if the Commission fails to take a decision under the preliminary procedure. This rule was first formulated by the ECJ in the *Lorenz* case, which ruled that the Member State may implement the proposed state aid after the expiry of the two-month period on the condition that the Commission is given prior notice.[146] The latter condition is now specified in art.4(6) in the sense that after the Commission has received such notice it has 15 working days to formulate a reaction. In the absence of such a reaction, the Member State concerned may implement the aid.[147] This specification is useful. It was always clear that the notice should serve to give the Commission a chance to make good its own ineptness. The 15 working days "terme de grace" will spur it into action. Secondly, the standstill clause continues to apply after the Commission initiates the art.108(2) procedure. Thirdly, the standstill clause lapses when the Commission takes a positive decision under this procedure. If it takes a negative decision the standstill clause will also cease to be applicable, although it will be replaced by the prohibition contained in the decision. Interestingly, there is no provision comparable to

---

[145] Case T–318/00 *Freistaat Thüringen v Commission* [2005] E.C.R. II–4179, paras 89–90.

[146] Case 120/70 *Lorenz v Germany* [1973] E.C.R. 1471.

[147] According to case C–99/98 *Austria v Commission* [2001] E.C.R. I–1101, at para.43, implementation has to be understood as "as promising the aid unconditionally." The Commission cannot rely on press articles to establish that the authorities gave an unconditional and legally binding promise.

art.4(6) of the regulation addressing the situation where the Commission fails to adopt a decision. In the system of the regulation it is then for the Member State concerned to request the Commission to take a decision. If the Commission should, notwithstanding such a request, fail to adopt a decision it is logical to assume that the Member State may then implement the measure. It would not be logical to assume that the Member State has to observe a similar duty to notify, as it has under art.4(6) of the Regulation, since the Commission has already been invited to take a decision.

25–038   The question may be raised as to what will happen to the standstill clause when the Community Courts annul a negative Commission decision. It seems logical to assume that the standstill clause will continue to apply. Only a fresh, positive decision by the Commission can declare the aid compatible with the common market.[148]

What if a positive Commission decision is annulled? In its *Cofaz II* judgment the ECJ declared the Commission's positive decision void.[149] The ECJ did not address the legal consequences for the validity of the aid measures, i.e. the question of whether the standstill clause revived. In its latest decision in the *CELF* case, the Commission notes that following the Court's judgment the formal investigation procedure initiated by its Decision of July 30, 1996 remains open.[150] On the April 8, 2009 the Commission adopted a Decision extending the 1996 procedure that was based on art.108(2) TFEU and inviting comments from interested parties.[151] The Commission does not explicitly indicate whether the standstill clause covers the entire period or only the periods after the positive Commission decisions were annulled. Judging from the fact that it orders recovery for the period from 1982 to 2001, the date when the Small Orders Programme was terminated, it is clear that the Commission holds the view that the standstill obligation extends over the entire period.[152] In other words, the Commission does not take the view that there were periods during which the aid was lawful, i.e. after the positive decisions until their annulment.[153] The Commission also finds

---

[148] See already Case C–301/87 *France v Commission (Boussac)* [1990] E.C.R. I–307, where the Court ruled that the Commission cannot rely on the absence of notification to declare the aid incompatible. It has a duty to examine such aid.

[149] Case C–169/84 *Cofaz II* [1990] E.C.R. I–3083.

[150] Decision 2011/179 [2011] O.J. L78/37, para.33 of the Decision refers to Judgment T–348/04 *SIDE v Commission* [2008] E.C.R. II–625.

[151] [2009] O.J. C142/6. The first decision was based on art.108(3) TFEU but the CFI (now General Court) in case T–49/93 *SIDE v Commission* [1995] E.C.R. II–2501 (the first CFI judgment annulling the Commission decisions) annulled that decision holding that the Commission should have opened the art.108(2) procedure. Hence all subsequent Commission decisions were based on art.108(2) TFEU.

[152] See para.168 of the Decision.

[153] See (my annotation) of the first *CELF* judgment of the ECJ C–199/06 [2008] E.C.R. I–469 in 46 CML Rev. (2009) pp.623–639; and C. Vadja and P. Stuart "Effects of the Standstill Obligation in National Courts—all said after CELF? An English Perspective" (2010) EStAL 3, pp.629–637. See also the second judgment of the ECJ C–1/09 of March 11, 2010 Unreported.

that there are no exceptional circumstances giving rise to a legitimate expectation.[154] Drawing on parallel situations in the field of art.101 TFEU, we would assume that the standstill clause will revive from the date of the Court's judgment annulling a positive decision. The CFI (now General Court) ruled in Case T–51/89[155] that the withdrawal of an exemption under a block exemption is non-retroactive. Another parallel is contained in art.10(5) of the Merger Control Regulation:

"Where the Court of Justice gives a judgment which annuls the whole or part of a Commission Decision taken under this Regulation, the periods laid down in the Regulation start again from the date of the judgment."[156]

Alterations of notified aid must also be notified. The Commission may be **25–039** informed during the consultations, which take place following the initial notification. The standstill clause also applies to alterations. If alterations are substantial, so as to amount to a new aid plan, the new aid will be examined separately on its own merits.[157]

According to art.11(1) the Commission may take a decision to suspend any unlawful aid (suspension injunction). Thus, if a measure is implemented without awaiting the outcome of the procedure of art.108(2) and (3), the Commission may issue an interim order suspending the payment of the aid.[158] The order has the effect of confirming the standstill clause. If the Member State does not suspend payment, the Commission may bring the matter before the Court.

Withdrawal of notification

Article 8 of reg.659/99 allows Member States to withdraw a notification in due **25–040** time before the Commission has taken a decision to art.4 or art.7. When the Commission has initiated the formal investigation it shall close that procedure.[159]

Revocation of a decision. Article 9 of reg.659/99 provides that the Commission **25–041** may revoke its decisions referred to above if these were based on incorrect information if such information was a determining factor for the decision.[160]

---

[154] paras 151–167 of the Decision. Although the two questions are closely linked, it is possible to argue that eventhough the standstill clause applied during the entire period, the very special circumstances of the case call for application of the legitimate expectations principle.

[155] Case T–51/89 *Tetrapak* [1990] E.C.R. II–309. See AG van Gerven in his conclusion of October 11, 1990 in Case C–234/89 *Delimitis* [1991] E.C.R. 935, at para.6.

[156] Reg.139/2004 [2004] O.J. L24/22.

[157] Cases 91 and 127/83 *Heineken* [1984] E.C.R. 3435, at para.21.

[158] Case C–301/87 *France v Commission* [1990] E.C.R. I–307; Case C–142/87 *Belgium v Commission* [1990] E.C.R. I–959.

[159] See Commission Communication regarding aid for a barge controlling centre in the port of Rotterdam [2001] O.J. C27/43.

[160] In Case T–25/04 *Gonzalez y Diez v Commission* [2007] E.C.R. II–3121, para.97, the CFI held that the Commission's right to revoke a decision is not restricted solely to the situation referred to in art.9 of reg.659/99. In Decision 2011/414 [2011] O.J. L184/9, paras 126–128, the Commission explained that in its first it was unaware of the fact that the beneficiary already received aid. Therefore, the "one time last time" principle was examined.

Before doing so, it must give the Member State concerned the opportunity to submit comments. The Commission shall in such cases open the formal procedure, and arts 6, 7, 10, 11(1), 13, 14 and 15 shall apply mutatis mutandis. The reference to arts 10, 11, 13, 14 and 15 implies that such aid is considered to constitute unlawful aid.[161] These provisions are discussed below at paras 25–042 et seq. It is interesting to observe that art.9 incorporates the principles enunciated by the ECJ in the *British Aerospace* judgment by analogy.[162] The Commission has opened the art.108(2) TFEU procedure several times because it considered that its previous decision was based on incorrect information. It did so in the *Verlipack*[163] and the *Varvaressos* cases.[164]

Unlawful aid

25–042   Despite many years of active policing of the Commission supported by complaints there still is a substantial amount of unlawful aid in the EC. In the period from 2000 to June 30, 2010, the Commission took 910 decisions on unlawful aid.[165] In 21.6 per cent of the cases (197 cases) it took a negative decision. There are also some egregious cases of unlawful aid. In December 1996 the Commission received a complaint about state aid unlawfully granted in 1987.[166] Some of the cases concerning misused aid are very complex. In the *Hellenic Shipyards* Decision the Commission investigated some 16 measures, 12 of which concerned unlawful aid.[167]

Regulation 659/99 provides for comprehensive rules on non-notified aid. Chapter III concerns the procedure regarding unlawful aid. The Commission has the same powers vis-à-vis unlawful aid as it has for notified aid. The Commission will assess the compatibility of unlawful aid with the common market in accordance with the substantive criteria set out in any instrument in force at the time when the aid was granted.[168] However, as was noted above in para.25–006, there is a penalty for Member States not observing the notification obligation of

---

[161] See Commission Decision on aid for *E-Glass AG* [2005] O.J. C220/3.

[162] Case C–294/90 *British Aerospace and Rover v Commission* [1992] E.C.R. I–493. In this case the Commission had failed to reopen the formal procedure after it received information that the UK government had not properly implemented its previous conditional decision. As a result, the ECJ annulled the decision. The opinion of AG van Gerven in this case is particularly illuminating on the issues involved in instances where inappropriate implementation takes place. It should be noted that the powers of the Commission to revoke a decision provided for in art.9 relate only to a situation where incorrect information was provided during the preliminary or formal procedures. Thus the *British Aerospace* judgment provides only analogous guidance.

[163] Commission Decision 2001/856 [2001] O.J. L320/28.

[164] Commission Decision 2011/414 [2011] O.J. L184/9.

[165] COM(2010) 701 December 2, 2010, p.64.

[166] See Decision C(2000) 2183 [2002] O.J. L12/1. The Commission ordered recovery of the original amount of €6.03 million with interest amounting to 12.3 million. Appeals against the Decision were dismissed by the CFI in Case T–366/00 *Scott v Commission* [2003] E.C.R. II–1763 and the ECJ in Case C–276/03P [2005] E.C.R. I–8437, see further Ch.26 at paras 26–003.

[167] Decision 2009/610 [2009] O.J. L225/104.

[168] Commission Notice on the determination of the applicable rules for the assessment of unlawful state aid [2002] O.J. C119/22.

art.108(3). In a situation where the aid is nevertheless subsequently approved, the Commission does not have the competence to decide that aid implemented contrary to art.108(3) TFEU or the standstill clause of art.3 of reg.659/99 is lawful.[169] Consequently, even if the Commission will, at the end of the procedure of art.108(2), decide that the aid is compatible with the common market, the implementation of the aid will be suspended during the procedure and interest will have to be paid over the period that the aid was unlawfully implemented. The fact that the Commission does not for a long period open an investigation cannot confer on it the nature of existing aid.[170]

Article 10 of reg.659/99 starts with the situation where the Commission has in **25–043** its possession information from any source regarding alleged unlawful aid. Such information may reach the Commission ex officio, by way of a complaint or as a result of co-operation between national courts and the Commission.[171] According to art.10(1), the Commission shall examine such information without delay. It shall, if necessary, request the information according to the rules applicable to notified aid, arts 2(2) and 5(1) and (2) respectively. Article 10(3) provides:

"Where, despite a reminder pursuant to Art.5(2), the Member State concerned does not provide the information requested within the period prescribed by the Commission, or where it provides incomplete information, the Commission shall by Decision require the information to be provided ('information injunction'). The Decision shall specify what information is required and prescribe an appropriate period within which it is to be supplied."

It is important to note that in case of unlawful aid the Commission is not, according to art.13(2) of reg.659/99, bound by the time limits of the art.108(3) and (2) procedures of 2 and 18 months respectively. This provision confirms the position that the Commission has adopted so far in its practice.[172] There is one exception to this rule. Article 11(2), second paragraph, of the Regulation provides that after the aid has been effectively recovered the Commission shall take a decision within the time limit applicable to notified aid. It may be assumed that a similar duty to take a timely decision will apply when the Member State concerned induces, upon its own initiative, recovery satisfying the requirements of art.14(2).

The Community Courts have not entertained the question of whether a time **25–044** limit applies in cases of non-notified aid. In its judgment in the *Gestevision* case,

---

[169] Joined Cases C–261/01 and C–262/01 *Van Calster* [2003] E.C.R. I–12249, at para.73.
[170] Joined Cases T–195/01 and T–207/01 *Gibraltar v Commission* [2002] E.C.R. II–2309.
[171] On April 9, 2009, the Commission published a notice on the enforcement of state aid by national courts [2009] O.J. C851/22. The notice replaced the 1995 Co-operation Notice. Section 3 of this notice outlines the Commission support for national courts. In para.90 of the notice the Commission observes that national courts may also request assistance from it by asking it for "legal and economic" information. See also Case C–39/94 *SFEI v La Poste* [1996] E.C.R. I–3547.
[172] Notwithstanding this position, the Commission tries to complete the procedure within two months after having received satisfactory information, as in cases of notification.

the CFI (now General Court) held that the *Lorenz* period is not the appropriate time limit for concluding the investigation of complaints by the Commission in a case where the aid was not notified.[173] This statement gives rise to two questions. First, is the time limit for concluding the investigation of a complaint different in the case of a notified aid? Since, in the case of a notified aid the Commission is under a duty to conclude the preliminary procedure within two months, the answer may well be yes. In such a situation, it would seem logical to apply the same term as the *Lorenz* term. The second question is: which term should be applied for concluding the procedures for non-notified aid as regards the Member State concerned? This question should be distinguished from the time limit which has to be observed vis-à-vis the complainant. The interests of the complainant in an expeditious handling of the complaint have to be balanced against the burden on the limited administrative capacity of the Commission for handling state aid cases and the interests of the other parties involved: the Member State concerned, the beneficiaries and other possible competitors. The complainant can always bring an action in a national court to prevent the aid being implemented.[174] As far as Member States are concerned, it can be argued that their failure to notify puts them in a position where they can no longer claim the benefit of the application of the general principle that the Commission must act within a reasonable time limit.[175] Of course, this argument does not apply to other interested parties who have an interest in obtaining certainty as to the compatibility of the aid. The intended beneficiary may be in a particularly delicate position. In line with the *Gestevision* judgment, it could be argued that he might also bring an art.175 (now 232) action to have the aid declared compatible with the common market. Prolonged discussions under the preliminary procedure do not foster transparency, and weaken the position of third parties that are unable, under this procedure, to submit comments.

25–045   Notwithstanding the exceptions from the time limits for the normal procedural rules for notified aid, the examination of unlawful aid will subsequently take place according to these procedures, as is stated in art.13(1) of the Regulation.[176]

---

[173] In its judgment in Case T–95/96 *Gestevision Telecinco v Commission* [1998] E.C.R. II–3407, the CFI ruled that the two-month time limit of the *Lorenz* case did not apply to the time-limit which the Commission has to observe for concluding the investigation upon a complaint. In para.79 of the judgment, the CFI (General Court) noted: "that the two-month period referred to in *Lorenz* cannot apply as it stands in a case such as this, where the aid in dispute has not been notified to the Commission".

[174] cf. Case C–39/94 *SFEI v Commission* [1996] E.C.R. I–3547.

[175] For this principle, see para.73 of the *Gestevision* judgment.

[176] In Case C–372/97 *Italy v Commission* [2004] E.C.R. I–3679, the ECJ noted in para.45, that if the Commission were required to demonstrate the real effect of aid which has already been granted, that would ultimately favour those Member States which grant aid in breach of the notification duty. See also Case C–298/00 *Italy v Commission* [2004] E.C.R. I–4087, at para.49. In case T–210/02 *British Aggregates Association* [2006] E.C.R. II–2789, paras 165–167 the CFI held that the Commission has an obligation to open the art.108(2) procedure when it experiences serious doubts also when it investigates unlawful aid. In Case T–196/02 *MTU Friedrichshafen* [2007] E.C.R. II–2889, para.46, the CFI (General Court) held that "art.13(1) of reg. 659/99 does not allow the Commission to impose on a particular undertaking an obligation to repay aid where the transfer of state resources from which that undertaking benefitted is hypothetical."

It will be able to take the same decisions as provided for in art.7 of the Regulation. The chapter on unlawful aid in the Regulation contains further rules on injunctions for the suspension or provisional recovery of such aid, as well as further rules for recovery. The explicit recognition of the Commission's powers in art.11 of the Regulation puts to rest a dispute over the question of whether the Commission had such powers prior to the enactment of reg.659/99.[177] As early as 1995, the Commission addressed a Communication to the Member States in which it stated that it had the power to issue recovery injunctions.[178] So far, the Commission has never used this power. In the *Olympic Airways* case it intended to issue a suspension decision.[179] Greece argued that this would disproportionate and unjustified and would seriously jeopardise the efforts it was making to find a solution to the companies' difficulties. The Commission reneged. According to art.11(2), third paragraph, the Commission may authorise a Member State to couple the refunding with the payment of rescue aid.[180] A Commission injunction to suspend the aid should be distinguished from a Commission decision to qualify certain measures as new aid and hence open the procedure of art.108(2) TFEU even though the latter will normally lead the Member States to suspend payment of the aid.[181] The difference between the two is that the former has a binding nature and the Commission may refer the matter directly to the ECJ if the Member State does not comply with the order. A decision to open the art.108(2) TFEU procedure does not as such have a binding nature.

Misuse of aid

Article 1(g) of reg.659/99 defines misuse as use by the beneficiary contrary to **25–046** a decision finding that the aid is compatible with the common market or a decision imposing conditions. Chapter IV of reg.659/99, art.16 provides that the Commission may in case of misuse of aid open the formal procedure of art.108(2) c.q. art.6 of reg.659/99. It also provides that the usual rules for this procedure apply mutatis mutandis. This includes the power to order recovery.[182] Article 23 of reg.659/99 empowers the Commission to refer infringements of conditional or negative decisions directly to the ECJ. The Commission has the burden of proof that aid is misused.[183]

---

[177] Sinnaeve, "Present and Future of State Aid Procedures", who points to the judgment in Case T–107/96R *Pantochim v Commission* [1998] E.C.R. II–0311. In Case C–400/99 *Italy v Commission* [2001] E.C.R. I–7303, the ECJ observed that the Commission already had that power prior to the enactment of Regulation 659/99, at para.46.

[178] [1995] O.J. C156/5.

[179] Decision 2011/97 [2011] O.J. L45/3, paras 99–100.

[180] This was discussed in Decision 2010/359 [2010] O.J. L167/39, para.54.

[181] Case C–400/99 *Italy v Commission* [2001] E.C.R. I–7303.

[182] Joined Cases T–111 and 133/01 *Saxonia Edelmetalle v Commission* [2005] E.C.R. II–2335, para.111.

[183] Joined Cases T–111 and 133/01, *Saxonia Edelmetalle v Commission* [2005] E.C.R. II–2335, paras 86 and 93.

The *Bremer Vulcan* decision on the misuse of restructuring aid is a case in point.[184] In this case the Commission found that DEM 788.7 million aid was misused and ordered recovery.[185] In the *Leuna* case the Commission appointed a consultant to examine whether the aid had been used in conformity with the Commission's approval decisions.[186] In the end the Commission found that the aid was compatible with the common market.

25-047   The question of what to do if the conditions attached to a positive decision are not fulfilled arose in the *Aer Lingus* case, where the Commission had subjected its approval of the aid to conditions before the second and third tranches of aid could be released.[187] The CFI (now General Court) held that the Commission must reopen the procedure of art.108(2) (i.e. art.4(4) of the Regulation) when the conditions for releasing the additional tranche of the aid are not met. The Commission may only derogate from this procedure in the event of relatively minor deviations from the initial condition, which leave it in no doubt as to whether the aid is still compatible with the common market. The Court subsequently found that the Commission was justified in authorising the second tranche without opening the procedure of art.108(2) TFEU, but the carefully worded paragraphs of the judgment suggest that the Commission does not have a wide margin of discretion in such cases. The Court noted that, on the whole, the conditions had been met and that the Commission had merely rebalanced the conditions. In doing so it had also strengthened certain conditions.

Combining the power of the Commission provided for in art.23 of reg.659/99 and the judgment of CFI in the *Aer Lingus* case, the following rules may be formulated. When the Commission has no doubts that the conditions have not been observed it may refer the case directly to the ECJ. The Commission will probably do so when it considers the damage done by the disregard of the conditions is such that the aid has to be stopped and recovered. If the Commission is of the opinion that the failure can be remedied or is not a serious failure or only a minor failure to observe the conditions, it will reopen the formal investigation procedure.[188] In the *Olympic Airways* case the Commission opened the art.108(2) procedure because it found a breach of several conditions set out in its previous decision approving the aid. In addition it found that new and non-notified aid had been granted.[189]

---

[184] [1990] O.J. L108/34.

[185] Another example of misuse of aid concerned Commission Decision 2005/374 [2005] O.J. L12021, see in particular paras 78–79. See also Decision 2008/406 [2008] O.J. L143/41, para.73; Decision 2008/854 [2008] O.J. L302/9, para.69; Decision 2010/215 [2010] O.J. L92/19, para.31.

[186] Commission Decision 2003/281 [2003] O.J. L108/1.

[187] Case T–140/95 *Ryanair v Commission* [1998] E.C.R. II–3327.

[188] A good example of this "second chance" approach is found in the decision of the Commission to reopen the art.108(2) procedure in the case of aid to Pertusola Sud [2001] O.J. C149/13. The procedure was eventually closed and the Commission found that the conditions had been met [2003] O.J. L264/28. Another example is the Commission's decision on aid granted to Gonzalez y Diez [2003] O.J. C87/17.

[189] Commission Decision 1999/332 [1999] O.J. L128/1. In 2002 the Commission took another decision for alleged non-compliance with the conditions of the decision approving the aid [2002] O.J. C98/8.

Regulation 659/99 does not provide rules on how the Commission should **25–048** handle conditions and obligations, whether or not they relate to the conditional approval of aid in tranches.[190] There may also be a question as to how far the Commission's powers, referred to in art.7(4) of reg.659/99 to impose conditions when it approves aid, actually stretch. There is no equivalent to the Commission's notice on remedies acceptable under reg.139/2004, the old merger control regulation.[191] In its guidelines for the application of state aid in the aviation sector,[192] it took the view that it could not impose privatisation as a condition for approval. Nevertheless, it has in several decisions approved the aid plan on the assumption that the company concerned was to be privatised.[193] Thus, it will not actually impose the condition that the enterprise concerned has to be privatised, yet the very promise by the Member State concerned that it will privatise will often soften the Commission's attitude.

Existing aid schemes

As has been discussed in para.25–014, above, reg.659/99 provides an exten- **25–049** sive definition of the notion of existing aid as well as existing aid schemes. It should also be recalled that only existing aid schemes can be challenged by the Commission and existing aid cannot. Chapter V of reg.659/99 lays down procedural rules for reviewing existing aid schemes. These rules provide an elaborate version of art.108(1) of the Treaty. As was discussed in para.25–017 the Commission's view will, subject to review by the Community courts, prevail in a dispute between a Member State and the Commission about the qualification of aid as existing aid or new aid. In view of the text of art.17 of reg.659/99 it may be assumed that this assumption also applies for existing aid schemes.

According to art.108(1) the Commission shall, in co-operation with the Member States, keep under constant review all systems of existing aid. The review of existing aid schemes is important as part of the effort to create a "level playing field" in the internal market.[194] When the Commission is of the opinion that an existing aid scheme is incompatible with the common market it will start a procedure asking for information. This procedure is outlined in art.17 of the Regulation. According to the first paragraph the Commission shall, in co-operation with the Member States, obtain all necessary information for a review of existing aid schemes. Interested parties may forward to the Commission information alleging the incompatibility of the aid. This does not confer any right of

---

[190] Commission Regulation 794/2004 [2004] O.J. L140/1, gives rules for the annual reports that the Member States have to submit. This information is intended to enable the Commission to monitor overall aid levels. It does not cover information which may be necessary in order to verify that particular aid measures respect Community law.

[191] [2008] O.J. C267/1.

[192] [1994] O.J. C350/5; see further Ch.16.

[193] See, e.g. Decision 94/653 concerning the notified capital increase of Air France [1994] O.J. L254/73; Decision 96/115 *Enichem Agricola* [1996] O.J. L28/18; and Decision 96/545 *Aid by Germany to Buna* [1996] O.J. L239/1.

[194] 21st Report on Competition Policy, 1991, p.154.

defence on that party.[195] Where the Commission finds that the existing aid scheme is no longer compatible with the common market, it shall inform the Member State of its preliminary view and give the Member State the opportunity to submit its comments within a period of one month.[196] The Commission may extend this period.[197] Where the Commission is investigating a case which has allegedly been made pursuant to a previously approved state aid scheme, it must first examine whether the aid is covered by that scheme and satisfies the conditions laid down in the decision approving it.[198]

25–050   Where the Commission, in the light of the information submitted, concludes that the aid scheme is not, or is no longer, compatible with the common market, it shall issue a recommendation. The recommendation may propose a substantive amendment to the aid scheme,[199] or the introduction of procedural requirements or the abolition of the aid scheme.

If, according to art.19(1) of reg.659/99, the Member State accepts the proposals, it shall inform the Commission. The latter shall confirm such acceptance whereupon the Member State concerned shall be bound by its acceptance to implement the appropriate measures.[200] Where the Commission finds that the aid was effectively covered by an existing aid scheme it will close the art.108(1) TFEU procedure.[201]

25–051   Article 19(2) of reg.659/99 addresses the situation where the Member State does not accept the Commission's proposals for amendment of the existing aid scheme. In that case, the Commission shall, if it is of the opinion that the proposed measures are necessary, initiate the formal proceedings.[202] The relevant articles (6, 7 and 9) shall apply mutatis mutandis. This will mean that all the procedural rules for new aid apply, except the standstill clause. Moreover, in the case of an existing aid scheme, the rules of the chapter on unlawful aid are not applicable. Consequently, there can be no recovery or suspension orders. An illustrative example of the procedure for existing aid is found in the procedure against Belgium for the coordination centres. In this case the Commission's approach was endorsed by the Community courts except that the Court held that

---

[195] Case T–354/05 *Télévision Française v Commission* [2009] E.C.R. II–471, para.101.
[196] A good example of such a procedure is the Commission's decision to open the art.108(2) procedure against Belgium in the case of the co-ordination centres [2002] O.J. C147/2.
[197] In the case of the Investment Allowance Law of 1991 the Commission gave the German government two months to present its comments [1999] O.J. C76/2, at para.15.
[198] Case C–47/91 *Italy v Commission* [1994] E.C.R. I–4635; Case C–278/95 *Siemens SA v Commission* [1997] E.C.R. I–2507. In the *Ramondin* case the Commission came, after an extensive review, to the conclusion that the aid was not covered by the previously approved aid scheme and opened the art.108(2) procedure [1999] O.J. C194/18. The case was concluded with a decision finding some measures compatible and others incompatible. The latter had to be recovered [2000] O.J. L318/36.
[199] See for examples of such an opinion [1993] O.J. C289/2 and C341/14.
[200] See, for an example, Decision 89/93, where the Commission considered that Germany had taken the appropriate measures proposed by it under art.93(1) (now 108) [1993] O.J. C256/9.
[201] Commission Decision 2003/383 [2003] O.J. L140/30, at paras 95–96.
[202] See the Commission Decision concerning state aid for the German producers of Kornbranntwein [2002] O.J. C308/6. See also Commission Decision on the aid scheme implemented by Belgium for coordination centres established in Belgium [2007] O.J. L90/7.

the Commission should have provided for appropriate transitional measures.[203] The Commission's decision to open the art.108(2) procedure for an existing aid scheme is an act that produces legal effect and hence can be challenged.[204]

When the Commission is reviewing a specific aid alleged to have been made on the basis of a previously authorised scheme, it must first examine whether the aid is covered by that scheme.[205] It cannot examine it directly on the basis of art.107 TFEU.

The rules discussed so far all relate to individual aid schemes. Article 108(1) TFEU has also been used by the Commission as the basis for the adoption of Community frameworks or guidelines, such as the framework for state aid to the motor vehicle industry. Neither the regulation on procedures nor reg.994/98 on group exemptions provides rules for such Commission frameworks. It is therefore useful to summarise the relevant case law. In its judgment *Spain v Commission* the ECJ held that:

25–052

"by making application of the framework subject to its acceptance by the Member States and by providing for it to be valid for two years, at the end of which the Commission was to review its utility and scope, the original framework fully complied with the obligation of regular, periodic co-operation imposed on the Commission and the Member States by Art.88(1) [108(1)] of the Treaty."[206]

In a second judgment involving the same parties, the Court ruled that, after the expiry of the original Framework, a new framework must be adopted by the same procedure.[207] In another judgment, the Court confirmed the power of the Commission to adopt such frameworks. It also held that Member States which are subject to the obligation of co-operation under art.108(1) and which have accepted rules laid down in guidelines by the Commission must apply those guidelines when deciding on an application for individual aid[208]:

"Where the Commission finds that aid alleged to have been made in pursuance of a previously authorised scheme of aid does not comply with the conditions laid down in its decision approving the scheme and is therefore not covered by it, that aid must be regarded as new aid."[209]

[203] Commission Decision 2008/28 on the aid scheme implemented by Belgium for coordination centres established in Belgium [2007] O.J. L90/7. Case T–189/08 *Forum 187 ASBL v Commission* [2010] E.C.R. Unreported.
[204] Case C–400/99 *Italy v Commission* [2005] E.C.R. I–3657, para.9.
[205] Case C–321/99P *Associacao dos Refinadores (ARAP) v Commission* [2002] E.C.R. I–4287.
[206] Case C–135/93 *Spain v Commission* [1995] E.C.R. I–1651.
[207] Case C–292/95 [1997] E.C.R. I–1931.
[208] Case C–311/94 *IJssel-Vliet v Minister van Economische Zaken* [1996] E.C.R. I–5023.
[209] Case C–36/00 *Spain v Commission* [2002] E.C.R. I–3243, at para.26.

5. RIGHTS OF INTERESTED PARTIES

25–053   The first paragraph of art.20 of reg.659/99 reiterates and extends the right for interested parties to submit comments during the formal investigation procedure.[210] This right is already provided for in art.108(2) TFEU but art.20(1) extends these rights insofar as it does not, as art.108(2) does, limit them to the parties concerned. Article 20(1) provides that parties who have submitted comments, and the aid beneficiaries, shall be sent a copy of the decision concluding the formal procedure. The provision does not set a time limit within which the Commission shall send a copy of the decision. That would have been helpful in order to avoid a situation where, due to the very late publication of the decision, interested parties cannot observe the two-month deadline for an appeal.

Article 20(2) of reg.659/99 gives an interested party the right to inform the Commission of any alleged unlawful aid or any alleged misuse of aid. The Commission has published a form for the submission of complaints.[211] The form asks the complainant to give the main elements of the alleged aid, grounds for the complaint and the effect on the complainant's interest. Complainants may request that their identity will not be disclosed. The Commission subsequently informs the interested party if it does not proceed upon the given information. The Commission will send a copy of the decision if it does take action.

25–054   The question has been raised whether interested parties have a right similar to that of a complainant in competition law cases under art.7(2) of reg.1/2003 and art.7(1) of reg.773/2004.[212] The text of art.20(2) shows considerable differences with the text of art.7(2) of reg.1/2003 but the actual position of the interested party may nevertheless be substantially the same. Avoiding the word complaint or application (as in art.7(2) of reg.1/2003) does not necessarily have legal consequences. The essential part of the provision seems to be that the Commission has a duty to inform the interested party that it will not proceed with the case (in the terminology of the regulation, "taking a view on the case"). As shall be argued in Ch.27, section 3, we are of the opinion that the complainant has a right to a decision addressed to him and therefore has a corresponding right to bring an art.265 TFEU action.

Article 20 of reg.659/99 is silent on the rights of complainants and other interested parties during the formal procedure.[213] Drawing on the comparison with such rights under reg.1/2003 and reg.773/2004, parties have argued that they should have been heard or should have had access to the files. These arguments have not been accepted by the Community Courts. In the *Ilmenau* case the applicant (the beneficiary) argued that although it was not a direct party to the

---

[210] In Decision 2009/150 concerning a reimbursement mechanism linked to the introduction of a toll system on German motorways [2009] O.J. L50/30, para.20, 10 third parties submitted comments.

[211] [2003] O.J. C116/3. The form is also published on the website of DG COMP.

[212] Commission Regulation (EC) 773/2004 of April 7, 2004 relating to the conduct of proceedings by the Commission pursuant to arts 81 and 82 of the EC Treaty [2004] O.J. L123/18–24.

[213] As the ECJ held in Case C–367/95P *Commission v Sytraval* [1998] E.C.R. I–1719, interested parties do not have rights during the preliminary procedure.

procedure the fact that its existence may be threatened by the final decision justified the conferment of further rights.[214] The CFI (now General Court) ruled that the provisions on procedure for reviewing state aid do not give a special role to interested parties. In the *Fleuren* case the CFI (General Court) held that when the beneficiary of the aid has failed to submit comments the Commission is under no obligation to communicate with the beneficiary.[215] In the *Ufex* judgment the CFI (General Court) held that complainants do not have a right of access to the files and documents.[216]

The parallel with the position of the complainant in competition law cases also raises the question about the Commission's discretion or the applicability of the so-called "*Automec* doctrine".[217] It will be recalled that in this judgment the CFI (General Court) recognised the Commission's right to set its priorities and hence to refuse to pursue complaints beyond a preliminary stage of forming an opinion on the case. The question is whether the Commission will have a similar discretion in the area of state aid.

25–055

At first sight, the answer may be negative since, contrary to the position in competition cases, the complainant in state aid cases does not have equally far-reaching opportunities for recourse to national courts.[218] National courts do not have jurisdiction to rule on the compatibility of aid with the common market. Thus the legal protection by national courts, discussed in Ch.27, section 4, differs fundamentally from the position in competition law cases because, contrary to arts 101 and 102, art.107(1) does not have direct effect. This is only partially compensated for by the remedies based on the direct effect of art.108(3). Another important argument would be that in state aid cases the Commission must necessarily judge the compatibility of state aid with the common market. This seems to be the corollary of the reasoning of the ECJ in its *Boussac* judgment.[219] In that judgment the ECJ rejected the Commission's thesis that aid implemented without observing the obligations of art.108(3) would automatically be incompatible with the common market. The Court held that state aid constitutes an important instrument of national economic policy and, consequently, the Commission was under a duty to examine its compatibility.

On the other hand, the Commission's policy of soliciting complaints necessarily brings with it an increasing number of complaints. As recent practice has shown, not all of these complaints merit a thorough investigation. A more robust Commission policy would therefore seem to need some form of setting priorities.

25–056

---

[214] Case T–198/01 *Ilmenau* [2004] E.C.R. II–2717, at para.193; see also Case T–109/01 *Fleuren Compost v Commission* [2004] E.C.R. II–127, at paras 41–43.

[215] Case T–109/01 *Fleuren Compost v Commission* [2004] E.C.R. II–127, at para.47. The CFI added that the Commission cannot be held responsible for the failure of the Member State to send the recipient of the aid a copy of the letter to initiate the procedure of art.108(2).

[216] Case T–613/97 *Union Française de L'Express (Ufex) v Commission* [2000] E.C.R. II–4055, at para.90.

[217] Case T–24/90 *Automec Srl v Commission (Automec II)* [1992] E.C.R. II–2223.

[218] As will be remembered this was one of the main arguments for allowing the Commission a discretionary margin.

[219] Case C–301/87 *France v Commission* [1990] E.C.R. I–307. In Joined Cases C–261/01 and C–262/01 *Van Calster* [2003] E.C.R. I–12249, reiterated this rule.

The Commission may do this by raising the threshold of the *de limitis* block exemption but it could also seek the discretion to set its priorities especially in cases where the effect on trade between the Member States is small.[220]

Article 20(3) of reg.659/99 provides that interested parties shall have the right to obtain copies of decisions concluding the preliminary and formal procedure, as well as decisions concerning unlawful aid and suspension or recovery injunctions.

6. MONITORING

25–057   The rules contained in the regulation are designed to give the Commission the necessary powers to supervise the enforcement of state aid. This relates in particular to compliance with the Commission's decisions and the conditions laid down in positive decisions.[221] Rules on monitoring will also be important for the supervision of state aid implemented without notification pursuant to group exemptions. Without a proper mechanism of supervision it may be very difficult for the Commission to follow what is going on in the Member States. At the same time, the group exemption regulations will greatly enhance the possibilities for control of state aid by interested third parties through national courts because they will lay down precise and transparent criteria.[222]

Article 21 of reg.659/99 obliges the Member States to submit annual reports on all existing aid schemes. As there are many aid schemes operating in the respective Member States, this amounts to a very substantial obligation. According to art.21(2), the Commission may commence the procedure for existing aid if Member States fail, despite a reminder, to submit the report.

25–058   Article 22 lays down rules for on-site inspection. These powers may be used where the Commission entertains serious doubts whether its decisions are being complied with.[223] The Commission may only undertake inspections after it has given the Member State concerned the opportunity to submit comments. The inspections relate to the premises and land of the undertakings concerned. The officials authorised by the Commission are empowered to ask for oral explanations on the spot, to examine books and other business records, presumably computer files, and take or demand copies.

The Commission shall inform the Member State concerned in good time and in writing. The latter may object to the Commission's choice of experts. In such

---

[220] See, e.g. Case T–274/01 *Valmont* [2004] E.C.R. II–3145.

[221] In Case T–140/95 *Ryan Air v Commission* [1998] E.C.R. II–3327, the CFI held that the Commission enjoyed the power to manage and monitor, vary the conditions governing the implementation of state aid without opening the formal procedure. See also Case T–73/98 *Prayon v Commission* [2001] E.C.R. II–867, at para.46.

[222] Sinnaeve, "Present and Future of State Aid Procedure" in *Understanding State Aid Policy in the European Community*, Bilal/Nicolaides (eds) (Kluwer: 1999).

[223] It is not clear from the text of art.22(1) whether or not the Commission has a discretionary power in this respect. According to this provision: "Member States shall allow the Commission to undertake on-site monitoring visits".

a case, the experts shall be appointed by common agreement. The officials shall produce an authorisation in writing specifying the subject-matter and the purpose of the visit. Officials authorised by the Member State concerned may be present at the visit. The Commission shall provide the Member State with a copy of any report.

A comparison with the earlier draft for the Regulation[224] shows that a provision for rules, designed to offer the Commission's officials assistance in cases where the enterprise concerned opposes the monitoring visit, has been deleted. This provision was modelled after art.14(6) of reg.17/62, the predecessor of reg.1/2003. A second provision that has not made it into the final version is a provision on co-operation with national independent supervisory bodies. This provision would have established a co-operation procedure between the Commission and the national bodies, presumably the Courts of Auditors, in cases where the Commission had serious doubts about compliance with its decisions. The Member States may have opposed inclusion of these provisions because they would have intruded too much on their domestic wheeling and dealing.

25–059

7. COMMON PROVISIONS

Professional secrecy

Article 24 of reg.659/99 requires that the Commission, Member States, their officials and other servants, including independent experts appointed by the Commission,[225] shall not disclose information which they have acquired through the application of the Regulation and which is covered by the obligation of professional secrecy. The Commission has issued a communication on professional secrecy in state aid decisions.[226] This Communication sets out how the Commission will deal with requests by Member States to consider parts of decisions confidential. The Communication indicates which criteria the Commission will apply when determining whether information can be deemed to constitute business secrets. It also outlines the general principles which the Commission follows in deciding on requests for confidential treatment. Finally, it outlines the procedure. The rules also apply to information submitted by complainants, other Member States and the beneficiary.[227]

25–060

---

[224] [1998] O.J. C116/13.

[225] The Commission often appoints such experts see, e.g. its Decision (96/278) on the *Iberia* case [1996] O.J. L104/25; and see further Ch.16.

[226] [2003] O.J. C297/6.

[227] para.37 of the Communication. In para.23 the Commission states: "If there is a complainant involved, the Commission will take into account the complainant's interest in ascertaining the reasons why the Commission adopted a certain decision, without the need to have recourse to Court proceedings (1). Hence, requests by Member States for parts of the decision which address concerns of complainants to be covered by the obligation of professional secrecy will need to be particularly well reasoned and persuasive. On the other hand, the Commission will not normally be inclined to disclose information alleged to be of the kind covered by the obligation of professional secrecy where there is a suspicion that the complaint has been lodged primarily to obtain access to the information."

On the other hand, the Commission has a duty to respect the rights of defence of interested parties. If the Commission wishes to argue the confidentiality of technological information it must state reasons so that the Community Courts may review them. The Commission may not rely on its duty to preserve professional secrecy to such an extent as to deprive the rules relating to the burden of proof of their substance.[228]

As has been observed above in section 1, reg.659/99 does not include rules on access to files. Parties have tried to draw on the analogy with the case law of the Community Courts on similar issues in the context of the application of competition policy. These efforts have not been met with success. The CFI (now General Court) has ruled that it is inappropriate to refer to the case law on arts 101 and 102 TFEU when issues such as due process and procedural rights are concerned.[229]

Publication of decisions

25–061   Article 26 of reg.659/99 lays down rules for the publication of the decisions of the Commission. It should be noted that these rules do not indicate whether the publication takes place in the L- or C-series of the Official Journal; the practice now is to publish decisions concluding the formal investigation in the L-series and all other decisions in the C-series.

The decisions pursuant to art.4(2) and (3), under the preliminary procedure finding that the measure does not constitute aid or a decision that the aid can be exempted, shall be published in the form of a summary notice in the Official Journal. Decisions to open the formal procedure pursuant to art.4(4) of the regulation shall be published in their authentic language version in the Official Journal.[230] In the Official Journal published in languages other than the authentic language version, the authentic language version shall be accompanied by a meaningful summary in the language of that Official Journal. Obviously, this provision is designed to strike a balance between the language requirements and the desire to save time in the often protracted procedures. Decisions concluding the formal procedure shall be published in full in all languages in the Official Journal. Decisions prolonging the preliminary procedure pursuant to art.4(6) of the Regulation and decisions acknowledging the closure of a procedure after the withdrawal of an aid proposal, shall, in the form of a short notice, be published in the Official Journal. The Council, acting pursuant to art.108(3) TFEU, may decide to publish its decisions.[231]

---

[228] T–73/98 *Prayon* [2001] E.C.R. II–867, at para.84.

[229] T–198/01 *Ilmenau* [2004] E.C.R. II–2717, at paras 192 et seq. See also T–613/97 *Ufex* [2000] E.C.R. II–4055, at paras 89–90.

[230] This will be the Official Journal of the language of the case.

[231] It is not clear why the text of art.26(5) of the regulation has reiterated the requirement that the Council shall act unanimously since this is already stated in the text of art.93(2) of the EC Treaty (now 108 TFEU). It now looks as if the Council has to take another decision, unanimously, on the question of publication.

The rules on publication largely codify the existing Commission practice. The **25–062** Commission did publish positive decisions but not always in a consistent manner. The practice of publishing positive decisions in the Official Journal L-series started in 1987. These are decisions taken at the end of the formal procedure. The Commission has great practical difficulties in arranging the timely publication of its decisions. Of course, the language regime of the Community imposes a formidable burden on the translation services. In this respect, the possibility of publishing summaries in languages other than the language of the Member State concerned may bring some relief. Yet it is usually the publication of lengthy decisions at the end of the formal procedure that causes the Commission serious time problems. It is not uncommon that such decisions are published nine months after the actual date of the decision.[232] This practice affected the possibilities of interested parties who would have wanted to lodge an appeal.[233]

Article 20 of reg.659/99 now addresses this point and obliges the Commission to send a copy of the decision pursuant to art.7, that is the formal procedure, to interested parties who have submitted comments and to any beneficiary of individual aid. There is no such obligation for the Commission in the case of decisions which are taken pursuant to the preliminary procedure, this may leave, in particular, complainants without adequate information on which to base their appeal.[234] Positive decisions at the end of the preliminary procedure are published in summary form in the C-series. Usually such summaries are very brief indeed, but sometimes they can be rather extensive.[235] Such publications are not made on the date of adoption of the decision so that similar problems as discussed above for publication in the L-series may arise.[236] The judgment of the CFI (now General Court) in the *Olsen v Commission* case has now solved this issue.[237] The publication of the summary notice in the Official Journal combined with the fact that this publication gives a reference to the text of the decision on

---

[232] e.g. Commission Decision 98/665 of February 25, 1998, concerning aid to HIBEG via Krupp to Bremer Vulcan, was published in [1998] O.J. L316/25, dated November 25, 1998.

[233] This problem is very well illustrated in the judgment in case T–14/96 *Bretagne Angleterre Irlande (BAI) v Commission* [1999] E.C.R. II–139. In the proceedings the Commission argued that the application was inadmissible since it was submitted outside the time-limit of the fifth paragraph of art.230 of the Treaty. According to the Commission, the applicant had been given a press release, which gave sufficient details for the applicant to be able to mount an appeal. Since the date of the appeal (February 1, 1996) was more than two months after the date of communication of the press release to the complainant, the Commission considered that the appeal was inadmissible. The Court noted that the decision was only published in the Official Journal on December 8, 1995, six months afterwards, and hence it considered the appeal admissible. See also Case T–123/97 *Salomon v Commission* [1999] E.C.R. II–2925.

[234] It may be assumed that the beneficiaries of individual aid will usually be informed by the Member State concerned. Moreover, the interests of the beneficiaries in preliminary state aid procedures will also be defended by the governments concerned.

[235] See, e.g. [1993] O.J. C281/7, a positive decision on aid to Leyland DAF Vans Ltd; and [1993] O.J. C310/7, aid to SEAT in Spain.

[236] e.g. on March 9, 2006 Commission Decisions pursuant to art.4(2) and (3) taken on December 7, 2005 were published in the [2006] O.J. C57/4.

[237] Case T–17/02 *Fred Olsen SA v Commission* [2005] E.C.R. Unreported June 15, 2005.

the Commission's website must be considered as a publication for the purpose of art.230(5) EC (now 263 TFEU).[238]

Article 27 of reg.659/99 empowers the Commission to adopt implementing provisions. Such provisions can only be adopted after the Advisory Committee, established in art.28 of the Regulation, has been consulted. The Advisory Committee shall also be consulted on the adoption of regulations on group exemptions, according to art.8 of reg.994/98 on group exemptions.[239]

8. HANDLING OF STATE AID CASES WITHIN THE COMMISSION

25–063   The Commission registers all pending state aid cases. The Secretariat General keeps a central register. Cases decided prior to November 23, 2010 are classified into notified ("N"), unnotified ("NN"), existing aid ("E"), employment block exemption case ("XE"), SME block exemption case ("XS"), training block exemption case ("XT") and cases in which formal proceedings have been opened ("C"). The case number consists of the appropriate letters followed by the serial number and year of registration in the relevant part of the register, e.g. "N 1/91" or "NN 16/88".[240] Cases decided after November 23, 2010 are numbered according to a new system: cases are indentified by one single number, prefixed by "SA", e.g. SA.12345. Individual procedures are indicated in the details of the case where relevant.

The Directorate General for Competition (DG Comp) is responsible for the majority of the state aid cases. The Directorate General for Agriculture handles cases in the agricultural sector; the Directorates General for Transport and Energy and Fisheries and Maritime Affairs handle the cases within their respective fields of competence.

25–064   Nowadays,[241] the Commission concludes the art.108(3) review either with a positive decision addressed to the Member States and published in the Official Journal (C-series), or with a decision to open the art.108(2) procedure.[242] This applies both to notified and non-notified aid. In the case of notified aid the Commission is, according to art.4(5) of reg.659/99, bound by the two-month

---

[238] At para.80 of the judgment. Paras 72–87 of this judgment give a helpful overview of the issues involved.

[239] Council Regulation 994/98 of May 7, 1998, on the application of arts 92 and 93 of the Treaty (now 107 and 108 TFEU) establishing the European Community to certain categories of horizontal state aid [1998] O.J. L142/1.

[240] When the Commission closes the preliminary procedure without opening the art.108(2) TFEU procedure this number N or NN is indicated in the cartouche, i.e. the summary publication in the C-series of the O.J. It can also be found under this number in the register on the website. When the Commission closes the preliminary procedure with a decision to open the art.108(2) procedure the number of the case is changed to a C number while the old N or NN number will be indicated in parentheses. When the Commission closes the case of the formal procedure with a final decision this decision will also get a number first indicating the year and the number of the legislative act.

[241] For a long time the Commission did not publish such decisions: see, e.g. the decision that gave rise to Case C–169/84 *Cofaz* [1986] E.C.R. 408.

[242] It may, of course, also happen that the Commission does not give any reaction.

period of the *Lorenz* judgment. Article 13(2) of the Regulation provides that for non-notified aid the time limits of the preliminary and the formal procedure shall not apply. As has been observed above in section 7, the Regulation now specifies the obligations of the Commission to publish decisions.

When the Commission opens the art.108(2) TFEU procedure, it transfers the case from the part of the register in which it was originally registered (e.g. as "N", "NN", "E", "XE", "XS" and "XT") to the "C" section. The Member State is informed by letter and an announcement is made in the Official Journal (C-series). Since the Commission's notice of 1983,[243] it has included a paragraph stating that the aid plan may not be implemented unless and until the Commission approves it.

The Commission points out that any aid granted before the procedure has **25–065** resulted in a final decision is unlawful and may have to be repaid. In the case of non-notified aid it includes a paragraph pointing out that, failing a reply from the government or in the event of an inadequate reply, it is entitled pursuant to the *Boussac* judgment to take a final decision under art.108(2), now confirmed by art.7(7) of reg.659/99. The Commission started this practice following a letter it wrote to the Member States on the consequences of that case.[244] The purpose of such notices is to give interested parties the possibility to defend their interests: thus, information should be adequate for this purpose.

In the *Breda Fucine* case, the parties challenged the final Commission decision arguing that the notice failed to give them sufficient information.[245] The CFI (now General Court) rejected the pleas noting that in this case it was difficult for the Commission to provide more information since this concerned non-notified aid.

The art.108(2) procedure is concluded either by issuing a negative decision **25–066** prohibiting the aid, a conditional decision allowing the aid under certain conditions, or by a positive decision. The first and the second types of decision are published in the Official Journal, L-series, and the third in the Official Journal, C-series.[246] The Commission also issues a press notice of all cases on the day the decision is taken, except for minor cases.

Apart from the Official Journal, the Annual Reports on Competition Policy provide in Vol.I, an overview of the most important cases by category and by Member State. This is a description of the main cases for which the formal procedure of art.108(2) of the Treaty has been initiated. Volume II of the Annual Report on Competition Policy provides a list of all cases handled in that

---

[243] [1983] O.J. C318/03.
[244] Case C–301/87 [1990] E.C.R. I–307. The letter (ref. SG (91) D/4577) is from March 4, 1991 and is published in *Competition Law in the European Communities*, Vol.IIA, Rules Applicable to State Aid (Brussels, 1995), p.91.
[245] Cases T–126 and 127/96 *Breda Fucine and EFIM v Commission* [1998] E.C.R. II–3437.
[246] In case T–327/04 *Syndicat national de l'industrie des viandes v Commission* [2008] E.C.R. II–72, the CFI (now General Court) ruled that the publication of a succinct summary is sufficient. Moreover the Commission advises of the possibility to consult the full text on internet.

particular year.[247] The 2010 Annual Report is accompanied by an annex listing all the measures adopted as a response to the economic and financial crisis.

List of cases in sectors other than agriculture, fisheries, transport and the coal industry:

(1) Cases in which the Commission found, without opening a formal investigation, that there was no aid element within the meaning of art.107(1) TFEU.

(2) Measures which the Commission considered compatible with the common market without opening a formal investigation under art.108(2) TFEU.

(3) Aid cases in which the Commission initiated proceedings under art.108(2) TFEU in respect of all or part of the measure.

(4) Aid cases in which the Commission extended proceedings under art.108(2) TFEU in respect of all or part of the measure.

(5) Interim decisions requiring the Member State to supply the information needed by the Commission.

(6) Measures in which the Commission found no aid element (art.108(2) TFEU).

(7) Cases in which the Commission considered that the aid was compatible with the common market and terminated proceedings under art.108(2) TFEU by way of a positive final decision.

(8) Cases in which the Commission considered that the aid was compatible with the common market under certain reservations and terminated proceedings under art.108(2) TFEU by way of a conditional final decision.

(9) Cases in which the Commission considered that the aid was incompatible with the common market and terminated proceedings under art.108(2) TFEU by way of a negative or partly negative decision.

(10) Aid cases in which the Commission terminated proceedings under art.108(2) TFEU after the Member State withdrew the proposed measure.

(11) Cases in which the Commission noted the Member State's agreement to ensuring the compliance of existing aid awards following the proposal of appropriate measures under art.108(1) TFEU.

(12) Decisions to seize the Court under the second indent of art.108(2) TFEU.

---

[247] This is the enumeration followed in the Annual Report 2004.

(13) Other Commission decisions.

Next there is a list of state aid cases in other sectors: agriculture, fisheries and transport. The list for aid cases in the agricultural sector is particularly long.

List of State aid cases in other sectors:

(1) In the agricultural sector.

(2) In the fisheries sector.

(3) In the transport sector.

Finally, there is also a list of judgments of the Community Courts.

Another source of useful information is the Scoreboard, an annual publication of the Commission. According to the Commission's website:

"The Scoreboard is the Commission's benchmarking instrument for State aid, measuring progress towards the goals of the Lisbon agenda of March 2000 which called on the Commission, the Council and Member States to 'further their efforts to . . . reduce the general level of State aid, shifting the emphasis from supporting individual companies or sectors towards tackling horizontal objectives of Community interest, such as employment, regional development, environment and training or research'. The Scoreboard was launched by the Commission in July 2001 to provide a transparent and publicly accessible source of information on the overall State aid situation in each of the EU Member States and on the Commission's current State aid control activities. It is published twice a year, one in the spring, the other in the autumn. Since 2005, the autumn update includes state aid expenditure figures for the previous calendar year while the spring update focuses on selected state aid topics."

9. Interim Orders and Final Decisions

If the interim orders issued by the Commission referred to in art.11 of the **25–067** Regulation are not complied with by the Member State within the time period fixed by the Commission, it may bring the matter directly before the ECJ for a declaration of infringement. Such a procedure is justified, given the urgent nature of the matter, because the Member State concerned has been given the opportunity to present its observations. It is thus the outcome of a pre-contentious adversarial procedure just as it is with the procedure foreseen in art.108(2).[248]

Commission decisions under art.108 do not have to demonstrate the actual effect of aid already implemented when making a finding of incompatibility.

---

[248] Case C–301/87 *France v Commission* [1990] E.C.R. I–307, at para.23, and Case C–142/87 *Belgium v Commission* [1990] E.C.R. I–959.

Such a requirement would, according to the ECJ in its judgment in the *Boussac* case,[249] be tantamount to putting Member States who disregard art.108(3) TFEU in a favourable position.

10. PROCEDURES UNDER THE EEA AGREEMENT

Introduction[250]

25–068   The relevant provision of the EEA Agreement is the following:

Article 62

"1. All existing systems of State aid in the territory of the Contracting Parties, as well as any plans to grant or alter State aid, shall be subject to constant review as to their compatibility with Art.61. The review shall be carried out:

    (a) as regards the E.C. Member States, by the E.C.[EU] Commission according to the rules laid down in Article 93 [now 108] of the Treaty establishing the European Economic Community;

    (b) as regards the EFTA State, by the EFTA Surveillance Authority according to the rules set out in an agreement between the EFTA States establishing the EFTA Surveillance Authority which is entrusted with the powers and function laid down in Protocol 26.

2. With a view to ensuring a uniform surveillance in the field of State aid throughout the territory covered by this Agreement, the E.C. Commission and the EFTA Surveillance Authority shall co-operate in accordance with the provisions set out in Protocol 27."

This means that both the Commission and the EFTA Surveillance Authority ensure compliance with the state aid rules of the EEA Agreement. Each institution is responsible for their territories, i.e. the EFTA Surveillance Authority is responsible for the EFTA states and the Commission for the EU Member States.

25–069   The procedures governing the EFTA Surveillance Authority are identical to those of the Commission.[251] The basic rules for enforcement are contained in Protocol 26 of the EEA Agreement. Protocol 26 states:

---

[249] Case C–301/87 *France v Commission*, at para.33.

[250] The author is indebted to Bjørnar Alterskjær, Kaja Breivik Furuseth and Marianne Clayton, for their helpful comments on this part. A complete overview of the EFTA state aid rules can be found at the website *www.eftasurv.int*, "The EFTA Surveillance Authority's State Aid Guidelines".

[251] Protocol 3 to the Agreement between the EFTA States on the Establishment of a Surveillance Authority and an ECJ (ESA/Court Agreement). Part I of this protocol is the equivalent of art.108 TFEU and Pt II is equivalent to reg.659/1999.

"The EFTA Surveillance Authority shall, in an agreement between the EFTA States, be entrusted with equivalent powers and similar functions to those of the E.C. Commission, at the time of the signature of the Agreement, for the application of the competition rules applicable to State aid of the Treaty establishing the European Economic Community, enabling the EFTA Surveillance Authority to give effect to the principles expressed in Articles 1(2)(e), 49 and 61 to 63 of the Agreement. The EFTA Surveillance Authority shall also have such powers to give effect to the competition rules applicable to State aid relating to products falling under the Treaty establishing the European Coal and Steel Community as referred to in Protocol 14."

Protocol 27 provides for the alignment of state aid policies of the EC and the EFTA States. Protocol 27 states:

"In order to ensure a uniform implementation, application and interpretation of the rules on State aid throughout the territory of the Contracting Parties as well as to guarantee their harmonious development, the E.C. Commission and the EFTA Surveillance Authority shall observe the following rules:

(a) exchange of information and views on general policy issues such as the implementation, application and interpretation of the rules on State aid set out in the Agreement shall be held periodically or at the request of either surveillance authority;

(b) the E.C. [EU] Commission and the EFTA Surveillance Authority shall periodically prepare surveys on State aid in their respective States. These surveys shall be made available to the other surveillance authority;

(c) if the procedure referred to in the first and second subparagraphs of Art.88(2)[108(2)] of the Treaty establishing the European Economic Community or the corresponding procedure set out in an agreement between the EFTA States establishing the EFTA Surveillance Authority is opened for State aid programmes and cases, the EC [EU] Commission or the EFTA Surveillance Authority shall give notice to the other surveillance authority as well as to the parties concerned to submit their comments;

(d) the surveillance authorities shall inform each other of all Decisions as soon as they are taken;

(e) the opening of the procedure referred to in paragraph (c) and the Decisions referred to in paragraph (d) shall be published by the competent surveillance authorities;

(f) notwithstanding the provisions of this Protocol, the E.C. [EU] Commission and the EFTA Surveillance Authority shall, at the request of the other surveillance authority, provide on a case-by-case basis information and exchange views on individual State aid programmes and cases;

995

(g) information obtained in accordance with paragraph (f) shall be treated as confidential."

25–070   Read literally, Protocol 26 suggests that the Surveillance and Court Agreement shall have a provision with equivalent powers and similar functions as the EU Commission: this would seem to mean the equivalent of art.108 TFEU. These powers are laid down in Pt I of Protocol 3 to the Surveillance and Court Agreement which corresponds to art.108 TFEU. It is important in this context to remember that the relevant rulings of the ECJ will govern the interpretation of the EEA state aid rules. This follows from art.3 of the Surveillance and Court Agreement, a treaty between Norway, Iceland and Liechtenstein.[252]

Article 3 of the Surveillance and Court Agreement provides:

"1. Without prejudice to future developments of case law, the provisions of Protocols 1 to 4 and the provisions of the acts corresponding to those listed in Annexes I and II to this Agreement, in so far as they are identical in substance to corresponding rules of the Treaty establishing the European Economic Community and the Treaty establishing the European Coal and Steel Community and to acts adopted in application of these two Treaties, shall in their implementation and application be interpreted in conformity with the relevant rulings of the Court of Justice of the European Communities given prior to the date of signature of the EEA Agreement.

2. In the interpretation and application of the EEA Agreement and this Agreement, the EFTA Surveillance Authority and the EFTA Court shall pay due account to the principles laid down by the relevant rulings by the Court of Justice of the European Communities given after the date of signature of the EEA Agreement and which concern the interpretation of that Agreement or of such rules of the Treaty establishing the European Economic Community and the Treaty establishing the European Coal and Steel Community in so far as they are identical in substance to the provisions of the EEA Agreement or to the provisions of Protocols 1 to 4 and the provisions of the acts corresponding to those listed in Annexes I and II to the present Agreement."

The EFTA Court and the EFTA Surveillance Authority will interpret Pt I of Protocol 3 of the Surveillance and Court Agreement in the same way as the ECJ and the General Court interpret art.108 TFEU. The obligation to follow the ECJ's interpretation prior to the entry into force of the EEA Agreement, and to pay due account to later case law from the ECJ follows from art.3 of the Surveillance and Court Agreement. In practice, the EFTA Surveillance Authority and the EFTA Court follow the case law of the ECJ regardless of whether this is case law prior

---

[252] *http://secretariat.efta.int/Web/legaldocuments/ESAAndEFTACourtAgreement/Documents/ Surveillance_and_Court_Agreement_-_SCA_consolidated.pdf.*

to or after the entry into force of the Agreement. The *Magasin-og Ukepressefor-eningen v EFTA Surveillance Authority* judgment provides a good example of this principle.[253] In that judgment the EFTA court denied a competitor standing to bring a case against the Authority for failure to act. The EFTA court applied similar conditions as the EU judiciary.

A crucial question concerning the EEA Agreement is whether its provisions will have direct effect. Article 7 of the Agreement provides:

25–071

> "Acts referred to or contained in the Annexes to this Agreement or in Decisions of the EEA Joint Committee shall be binding upon the Contracting Parties and be, or be made, part of their internal legal order as follows:
>
> (a) an act corresponding to an E.C. (EU) Regulation shall as such be made part of the internal legal order of the Contracting Parties;
>
> (b) an act corresponding to an E.C. (EU) directive shall leave to the authorities of the Contracting Parties the choice of form and method of implementation."

As we can see from the wording, the EEA Agreement as such does not demand that its provisions shall have direct effect or have supremacy over national law.

In the European Union, the question on the effect of the EEA Agreement has to be resolved by recourse to the general principles of EU law. The CFI (now General Court) was confronted with the question on direct effect of the EEA Agreement in Case T–115/94 *Opel Austria*.[254] The Court concluded that the Agreement forms an integral part of the Community legal order and that the provisions of such an agreement may have direct effect if they are unconditional and sufficiently precise (para.101). Since the EEA Agreement is part of community law, it also has primacy over national law and secondary community legislation.

25–072

In EFTA, the effect of the EEA Agreement has to be resolved by EEA law and national law. Protocol 35 of the EEA Agreement demands that, if necessary, the EFTA States shall introduce a rule in their internal legal order which ensures that implemented EEA law prevails. This obligation does, however, only apply to implemented EEA law. If a directive is not implemented, nationals cannot invoke the rules directly. This view is confirmed by the EFTA Court in the *Karlsson* judgment.[255] The Norwegian Supreme Court has ruled in a similar vein.[256]

---

[253] Case E–6/09 March 30, 2010, EFTA Court Report 2009–2010, p.144.

[254] Case T–115/94 *Opel Austria* [1997] E.C.R. II–39.

[255] Case E–4/01 *Karl K. Karlsson hf. v The Icelandic State*, Decision of May 30, 2002. The case may be viewed at *http://www.dinesider.no/customer/770660/archive/files/Decided%20Cases/2002/04-01advisoryopinion-e.pdf.*

[256] Finanger (Supreme Court Report 2000, p.1811), but the court ruled that there is an obligation of harmonious interpretation. In Finanger, interpretation in line with EEA law was not possible due to a clear wording of the Norwegian legislation. However, in Finanger II (Supreme Court Report 2005, p.1690), the Norwegian government was held liable for incorrect transformation of the contested directive. See Graver, "The Effects of EFTA Court Jurisprudence on the Legal Orders of the EFTA States", ARENA Working Papers WP 04/18, at *http://www.arena.uio.no/publications/wp04_18.pdf.*

Does the law of the EEA Agreement have supremacy over national law of the EFTA Member States?

25–073 When discussing the effective implementation of the state aid rules in the EEA the question arises whether the law of the Agreement has supremacy over national law. In practice, all implemented EEA law will normally have the same effect as if supremacy existed, given the obligation to make implemented EEA law prevail in the national legal order. Furthermore, the EFTA Court has ruled that the state can be liable for breaches of EEA law such as the failure to implement or the wrong implementation of EEA law.[257] So even if an individual cannot rely directly on the non-implemented measure, compensation can be claimed from the state if the conditions for liability are fulfilled.

The Commission's practices are followed by the Authority on the basis of Protocol 27 of the EEA Agreement.

25–074 Article 63 of the EEA Agreement reads as follows: "Annex XV contains specific provisions on State aid". Annex XV provides, inter alia, that the EC Commission and the EFTA Surveillance Authority shall take due account of the principles and rules contained in various communications and letters from the Commission to the Member States on prior notification, procedures and recovery. The EFTA Surveillance Authority is also under an obligation to adopt similar guidelines as the Commission and to publish them in the EEA Section of, and in the EEA Supplement to, the Official Journal.

The EFTA Court follows the case law of the ECJ and the General Court closely, in line with its obligations under art.6 of the EEA Agreement and art.3 of the Surveillance and Court Agreement.[258]

In accordance with point (e) in Protocol 27 of the EEA Agreement, all state aid decisions of the EFTA Surveillance Authority are published. The decisions are published in the EEA Section of, and in the EEA Supplement to, the Official Journal in the same format as that used by the Commission.[259]

---

[257] Case E–9/97 *Else Maria Sveinbjörnsdóttir v The Icelandic State*, Decision of December 10, 1998, as confirmed in *Karlsson*, Sveinbjörnsdóttir may be viewed at *http://www.dinesider.no/ customer/770660/archive/files/Decided%20Cases/1998/9–97%20advisory%20opinion.pdf*.

[258] See Case E–6/98 *Norwegian Government v EFTA Surveillance Authority*, Decision of May 21, 1999, *http://www.dinesider.no/customer/770660/archive/files/Decided%20Cases/1999/98% 2006%20judgment.pdf*; Case E–4/97 *Norwegian Bankers' Association v EFTA Surveillance Authority*, Decision of June 12, 1998, *http://www.dinesider.no/customer/770660/archive/files/ Decided%20Cases/1998/4–97%20decision.pdf*; Case E–2/05 *EFTA Surveillance Authority v The Republic of Iceland*, Decision of November 24, 2005 at para.38, *http://www.dinesider.no/cus tomer/770660/archive/files/Decided%20Cases/2005/e.%202%2005_judgment_final.pdf*.

[259] See, e.g. Authorisation of state aid pursuant to art.61 of the EEA Agreement and art.1(3) of Protocol 3 to the Surveillance and Court Agreement [1994] O.J. C366/4; EFTA Surveillance Authority decision not to raise objections and [1998] O.J. C337/6.

CHAPTER 26

RECOVERY OF UNLAWFUL AID*

1. INTRODUCTION 26–001
2. THE CONCEPT OF UNLAWFUL AID 26–003
3. THE RULES ON RECOVERY OF UNLAWFUL AID 26–005
4. COMMISSION'S POWER TO DEMAND RECOVERY 26–009
   Source of power 26–009
   Use of power 26–010
5. POSITIONS OF MEMBER STATES AND RECIPIENTS CONCERNED 26–013
   General principles 26–013
   Insolvency proceedings; transfer of shares or assets 26–014
   Legitimate expectations 26–017
6. ACTIONS BY THIRD PARTIES BEFORE THE NATIONAL COURTS 26–021

1. INTRODUCTION

This chapter deals with the recovery of unlawful aid. Lawful aid cannot be recovered.[1] It is therefore vital to know what constitutes unlawful aid. Regulation 659/99 laying down detailed rules for the application of art.88 EC (now art.108 TFEU),[2] contains a chapter on the procedure regarding unlawful aid. Ch.III. Article 1(f) of this Regulation defines "unlawful aid" as new aid put into effect in contravention of art.88(3) (now art.108(3) TFEU). Notwithstanding this definition, it must be assumed that the following aid measures can be said to be unlawful: aid implemented without being notified before or during the preliminary procedure, or during the formal procedure of art.108(2) TFEU. The regulation's definition of unlawful aid is not very illuminating; therefore, we shall analyse this concept further in section 2, below. Section 3 will discuss the rules contained in the regulation on the recovery of unlawful aid. Section 4 will review

26–001

---

* Paul Adriaanse and Tom Ottervanger
[1] With regard to lawful aid, the Commission can, according to art.108(1) TFEU, only propose appropriate measures required by the progressive development or by the functioning of the internal market. The Commission may propose, in particular (a) substantive amendment of the aid scheme, or (b) introduction of procedural requirements, or (c) abolition of the aid scheme. See art.18 of reg.659/1999, March 22, 1999 [1999] O.J. L83/1.
[2] March 22, 1999 [1999] O.J. L83/1 (Procedural Regulation).

the circumstances in which the Commission can require repayment to be made. In the fifth section, the positions of Member States and recipients concerned will be considered while the final section will discuss actions by third parties before national courts. In sections 5 and 6 the emphasis will be on the possibilities for recovery by the Member States, rather than on recovery as part of private enforcement, i.e. actions for recovery based on art.108(3) by competitors against Member States. The "private enforcement" and more general aspects of judicial protection will be discussed in Ch.28.

26–002   Over the years the Commission has launched several studies on the enforcement of EU state aid policy at national level. A first study was carried out in 1999, followed by a comprehensive study consisting of two parts, which became available in early 2006.[3] The purpose of the latter study was, amongst other things, to identify the strengths and weaknesses of national recovery procedures. In 2009 an update of the data on the application of state aid rules by national courts and their extension to the 27 Member States was presented.[4]

While recovery has somewhat improved, it appears from these studies that recovery of unlawful aid still faces a number of obstacles: lack of clarity as to the identity of the national body responsible for issuing a recovery decision, and of the beneficiary required to repay the aid, and as to the exact amount of the aid to be repaid; absence of a clear predetermined procedure to recover aid in some Member States; no availability or no use of interim relief to recover aid; stay of the recovery proceedings while an appeal is pending; difficulties experienced by the governmental authorities of a Member State when recovering aid at local level; and the particular consequences for the enforcement of recovery decisions of insolvency of the beneficiary of unlawful aid. All this results, generally, in an excessive length of the recovery proceedings.[5]

Experience shows that recovery is a time-consuming and cumbersome exercise. Nevertheless, progress has been made towards the execution of pending recovery decisions. The Autumn 2010 Update of the State Aid Scoreboard states: "The amount of illegal and incompatible aid recovered since 2000 has further increased and amounted to €12 billion on 30 June 2010. That means that the percentage of illegal and incompatible aid still to be recovered has fallen from 75% at the end of 2004 to around 11% on 30 June 2010."[6]

---

[3] "Study of the Enforcement of State Aid law at the national level", reports coordinated by Jestaedt, Derenne, Ottervanger (to be downloaded from: *http://bookshop.europa.eu/is-bin/ INTERSHOP.enfinity/WFS/EU-Bookshop-Site/en_GB/-/EUR/ViewPublication-Start? PublicationKey=KD7506493*). See also Ch.28, section 4.

[4] "2009 update of the 2006 Study on the enforcement of state aid rules at national level—FINAL REPORT", coordinated by Derenne, Kaczmarek and Clovin (*http://ec.europa.eu/competition/ state_aid/studies_reports/enforcement_study_2009.pdf*).

[5] For more extensive analysis of national State aid practice, see P.F. Nemitz (Ed.), *The Effective Application of EU State Aid Procedures. The Role of National Law and Practice*, International Competition Law Series 29 (Alphen a/d Rijn: Kluwer Law International, 2007).

[6] Autumn 2010 Update of the State Aid Scoreboard, p.15. (*http://eur-lex.europa.eu/LexUriServ/ LexUriServ.do?uri=COM:2010:0701:FIN:EN:PDF*).

In 2003 the Competition DG set up a new unit within State Aid Directorate H. The new unit is specifically charged with ensuring the enforcement of state aid decisions. The fact that Commission decisions are enforced not by Commission departments, but by Member States under their national procedures, constitutes a weak point in the enforcement system. Member States do not always give sufficient priority to the implementation of recovery decisions. The new unit has three main tasks: the effective enforcement of recovery decisions; ensuring a more coherent approach to the monitoring and control of implementation by Member States of other state aid decisions (especially conditional decisions); and procedural reform. In 2007 the Commission issued a Notice which gives guidance to Member States as to how to achieve a more immediate and effective execution of recovery decisions.[7] Further guidance was provided in 2009 in a Notice on the enforcement of State aid law by national courts,[8] followed by a specific website to provide practical information to national courts and other parties involved[9] and a Handbook on Enforcement of EU State aid law by national courts, which was issued in 2010.[10]

2. THE CONCEPT OF UNLAWFUL AID

The definition of unlawful aid is the key concept relevant for recovery. As **26–003** transpires from arts 11(2), 14(1) and 16 of the Procedural Regulation, the Commission's power to order recovery is restricted to unlawful aid and cases of misuse of aid. As was noted above, the concept of unlawful aid is defined in art.1(f) of the Regulation as "new aid" put into effect in contravention of art.88(3) EC (now art.108(3) TFEU). Which forms of new aid are covered by this definition?

First, this definition covers situations where aid is implemented without notification. At first sight this looks like a clear-cut case; there are, however, instances where Member States and the Commission may hold a different view on the notion of state aid. This difference of opinion will usually translate into a refusal or failure to notify. It should further be noted that situations may also arise where a Member State is of the opinion that a certain aid does not have to be notified because it has already been approved as part of a general aid scheme.[11] According to consistent case-law of the European Court of Justice (ECJ) a positive decision of the Commission on the compatibility of the aid does not have

---

[7] Notice from the Commission—Towards an effective implementation of Commission decisions ordering Member States to recover unlawful and incompatible state aid [2007] O.J. C272/4 ("Recovery Notice").

[8] Commission notice on the enforcement of State aid law by national courts [2009] O.J. C85/1.

[9] See also B. Brandtner, T. Beranger and C. Lessenich, "Private State Aid Enforcement" (2010) *EStAL* (1), p.23–32 on p.31.

[10] *http://ec.europa.eu/competition/publications/state_aid/national_courts_booklet_en.pdf.*

[11] In Case C–313/90 *CIRFS v Commission* [1993] E.C.R. I–1125, both the Commission and France were of the opinion that there was no obligation to notify the measure concerned. The ECJ held otherwise and annulled the Commission's Decision not to open the formal procedure.

the effect of regularising, retrospectively, implementing measures which were invalid because they had been taken in disregard of the prohibition laid down by art.108(3) TFEU. Any other interpretation would have the effect of according a favourable outcome to the non-observance, by the Member State concerned, of the last sentence of art.108(3) TFEU and would deprive it of its effectiveness.[12] The Commission itself may not order the repayment of unlawful aid which has been declared compatible in a positive decision. However, one should be aware of a procedure followed in a case where the original Commission decision approving the aid has been annulled by the European Courts. For example, in the *CIRFS* judgment the ECJ ruled that the Commission should not have authorised the aid under the preliminary procedure while doubts persisted as to the compatibility of the aid with the common market.[13] In order to comply with the judgment, the Commission opened the formal procedure. In its decision concluding this procedure, the Commission found a substantial part of the aid to be incompatible with the common market and ordered recovery thereof.[14]

Secondly, the term unlawful aid will cover notified aid which is, notwithstanding the standstill obligation, implemented before the Commission has given its approval. This may take place during the preliminary or the formal procedure. Such situations will, however, not occur very often. Once Member States bother to notify they will normally await the Commission's decision. Thirdly, aid can be considered to be unlawful when the aid is granted in breach of a negative Commission decision. This applies to new aid, but also to cases of existing aid. Once the Commission has, pursuant to the procedures of arts 17 and 18 of the Procedural Regulation, clearly articulated its view that the aid is no longer compatible with the internal market, the original lawful implementation of the aid can no longer constitute a basis for its continuation. If the Commission subsequently closes the formal procedure, which it has engaged to assess the compatibility of an existing aid, with a negative decision, it would seem logical that it can order the Member State concerned to stop disbursing any additional payments. Without such a power the Commission would not be in a position to restore competitive conditions. The principle of legitimate expectations will require that such an order can only take effect ex nunc. The same principle may also necessitate a certain period of grace.[15] But if the Member State concerned should fail to give effect to the Commission's order, a second order to recover the monies disbursed after the first order took effect would be an appropriate remedy. The same reasons that led the ECJ to rule that the Commission had the power to recover unlawful aid would seem to apply here.

---

[12] Case C–199/06 *CELF v SIDE* [2008] E.C.R. I–469 at para.40. Case C–354/90 *Fédération Nationale v France* [1991] E.C.R. I–5505 at para.16.
[13] Case C–313/90 *CIRFS* [1993] E.C.R. I–1125.
[14] [1995] O.J. L159/21.
[15] In this respect it is relevant to point out that according to art.11(2) of the Procedural Regulation the Commission may, in cases where it issues a recovery injunction, authorise the Member State to couple the refunding of the aid with the payment of rescue aid to the firm concerned.

Recovery can also take place when lawfully implemented aid is subsequently *misused* by the beneficiary in contravention of a decision of the Commission not to raise objections,[16] or a positive decision[17] or a conditional decision.[18] Article 16 of the Procedural Regulation empowers the Commission to open the formal procedure pursuant to art.4(4) of the regulation. The second sentence of art.16 provides that arts 6, 7, 9 and 10, 11(1), 12, 13, 14 and 15 shall apply mutatis mutandis. The result is that the powers to recover and to issue recovery injunctions are also applicable in cases of misuse of aid.

26–004

3. THE RULES ON RECOVERY OF UNLAWFUL AID

The rules on the procedures to be followed in case of non-notified new aid contained in Ch.III of the Procedural Regulation have been dealt with in Ch.26. Here the rules on recovery of alleged unlawful aid shall be discussed. The Commission's power to recover aid where it takes a negative decision is laid down in the regulation.[19] Article 14(1) provides that the Commission *shall* decide that the Member State concerned shall take all necessary measures to recover the aid. Recovery shall not be required when this would be contrary to a general principle of EU law. According to art.14(2), the Commission shall also require interest to be paid from the date on which the unlawful aid was at the disposal of the beneficiary until the moment of recovery. It is important to note that the Commission is under an obligation to order both recovery and the payment of interest (prior case law seemed to point in the direction of the Commission having a discretionary power). However, following the ruling in the *AITEC* case,[20] it would appear that a competitor has no power to require the Commission to bring such an action against a Member State. Moreover, it is settled case law that private individuals are not entitled to bring proceedings before the European Courts against a Member State for failure to fulfil its obligations in this field.

26–005

According to art.14(3), Member States shall effect recovery without delay and in accordance with the procedures under national law, provided that they allow the immediate and effective execution of the Commission's decision. Member States shall take all necessary steps, including provisional measures. These rules, echoing an underlying political compromise existing at the time of the adoption of the regulation, nevertheless contain a powerful potential development in the light of the interpretation of the principle of supremacy of EU law over national laws (notably the words "provided that . . . .").

[16] art.4(3) of the Procedural Regulation.
[17] art.7(3) of the Procedural Regulation.
[18] art.7(4) of the Procedural Regulation.
[19] It should be noted that some Commission decisions constitute a combination of approving a part of the aid and disapproving the other part, see, e.g. Dec. 94/653 [1994] O.J. L254/73, on Air France and Dec. 94/662 [1994] O.J. 258/26, concerning the subscription by CDC Participation to bonds issued by Air France.
[20] Case T–277/94 *AITEC v Commission* [1996] E.C.R. II–351. See also Ch.27, section 2.

26–006   Pursuant to art.14(2) of the Procedural Regulation, Regulation 794/2004[21] (the "Implementing Regulation") among other things deals with "interest" in recovery cases. Recital 10 specifies that the purpose of recovery is to re-establish the situation existing before the aid was unlawfully granted. Therefore, in order to ensure equal treatment, the advantage should be measured objectively from the moment when the aid was made available to the beneficiary. In order to achieve this objective, arts 8 to 11 lay down the methods for fixing the interest rate and of applying interest. Article 9 specifies that, unless otherwise provided for in a specific decision, the interest rate to be used for recovering aid shall be an annual percentage rate fixed for each calendar year (calculated on the basis of the interbank swap rate and, where no such rate or similar reference point exists in a Member State, the Commission will fix the applicable rate in close co-operation with the Member State concerned (art.9(4)). The Commission publishes current and relevant historical interest rates in the *Official Journal* (art.10). The Implementing Regulation further provides that the interest rate to be applied shall be the rate applicable on the date on which the unlawful aid was first at the disposal of the beneficiary (art.11(1)). Compound interest will be applied in order to ensure full neutralisation of the financial advantages resulting from the unlawfully paid aid (art.11(2)). Furthermore, the interest rate shall be recalculated at five-yearly intervals (art.11(3)). This approach is in line with the Commission communication of May 8, 2003, which makes clear that the effect of unlawful aid is to provide the recipient with funding on conditions similar to those of a medium-term non-interest-bearing loan.[22]

Interest to be recovered on the sums unlawfully granted is aimed at eliminating any financial advantages incidental to such aid, that, in itself, would constitute aid which could distort, or threaten to distort, competition; the General Court did, however, observe that interest may only be recovered in order to offset financial advantages that actually result from the allocation of the aid to the recipient, and must be in proportion to the aid.[23] In case of unlawfully granted state aid that is declared compatible with the internal market, according to the ECJ, the undue advantage will have consisted, first, in the non-payment of the interest which the aid recipient would have paid on the amount in question of the compatible aid, had it had to borrow that amount on the market pending the Commission's decision, and, second, in the improvement of its competitive position as against the other operators in the market while the unlawfulness lasts.[24]

Such interest is not "default interest", i.e. interest payable by reason of the delayed performance of the obligation to repay the aid; the interest must, instead, be equivalent to the financial advantage arising from the availability of the funds

---

[21] Commission Regulation 794/2004 of April 21, 2004 implementing Council Regulation 659/1999 [2004] O.J. L140/1.
[22] Commission communication on the interest rates to be applied when aid granted unlawfully is being recovered [2003] O.J. C110/21.
[23] Case T–459/93 *Siemens v Commission* [1995] E.C.R. II–1675 at paras 97–99.
[24] Case C–199/06 *CELF v SIDE* [2008] E.C.R. I–469 at para.51.

in question, free of charge, over a given period.[25] The interest period cannot start to run before the date (a date which, in principle, must be fixed by the Commission and not the national authorities) on which the recipient of the aid actually had those funds at its disposal.[26] As will be discussed in para.26–013, below, provisions of national law may not render recovery practically impossible. This is not the case if national legislation in a non-discriminatory manner provides that the debts of insolvent companies cease to produce interest from the date of the declaration of insolvency[27]—in such a case, according to the ECJ, the Commission should exclude from the recovery order interest falling due after the recipients were declared insolvent. It is not clear what the precise impact of this judgment is but it would seem unlikely that the Commission in each and every recovery order would have to take into account the possibility of insolvency proceedings (on "insolvency" see further para.26–014, below).

Article 15 of the Procedural Regulation limits the Commission's powers to recover to a period of 10 years. The limitation period begins on the day on which the unlawful aid is awarded. The limitation period shall be interrupted if a measure is taken by the Commission (or a Member State) with regard to the unlawful aid; each interruption shall start time running afresh. The General Court, supported by the ECJ, has decided that not only a formal act is capable of constituting a measure of such a kind as to interrupt the limitation period. A single request for information is an act which has the effect of interrupting the limitation period. Moreover, the fact that the beneficiary was not aware of the letter does not deprive this request of the effect of interrupting the 10-year limitation period. The ECJ has recognised that the wording of art.15 does not give guidance as to whether there is a requirement to notify the action to the beneficiary of the aid if the limitation period is to be interrupted. The ECJ further found that art.15 is designed to protect interested parties such as the Member State and the beneficiary which would therefore have a "practical interest" in being informed by the Commission of any action which is capable of interrupting the limitation period. However, that "practical interest" cannot have the effect of making the interruption subject to the requirement that such action be notified to the beneficiary of the aid measure concerned.[28] It is noteworthy that the "practical interest" of the beneficiary does not translate into any procedural right (other then the right to put forward arguments, as any other interested party, in the formal review procedure). At the same time, however, as also pointed out by Advocate General Jacobs, nothing in the wording of the Procedural Regulation suggests the existence of a duty on the Commission to inform the beneficiary of any action that would interrupt the limitation period. The period is also suspended as long as the Commission's decision is subject to proceedings before the ECJ, which presumably should include proceedings before the General Court.

26–007

---

[25] Case T–459/93 *Siemens v Commission* [1995] E.C.R. II–1675 at para.101.

[26] Case T–459/93 *Siemens v Commission* [1995] E.C.R. II–1675 at para.103.

[27] Case C–480/98 *Spain v Commission* [2000] E.C.R. I–8717 at paras 37 and 38.

[28] Case T–369/00 *Département du Loiset v Commission* [2003] E.C.R. II–1789 and to the same effect: Case T–366/00 *Scott v Commission* [2003] E.C.R. II–1763, upheld in Appeal, Case C–276/03P [2005] E.C.R. I–8437.

Article 11 gives the Commission the power to issue injunctions for the suspension or provisional recovery of the aid. The adoption of the first type of injunction, the "suspension injunction", is only subject to the requirement that the Member State concerned must be given the opportunity to submit its comments. The "recovery injunction" can only be adopted if the following strict criteria are fulfilled: according to an established practice, there are no doubts about the aid character of the measure concerned; there is an urgent need to act; and there is a serious risk of substantial and irreparable damage to a competitor. Recovery is to be effected in accordance with the procedure of art.14(2) and (3). The Commission has not yet used this possibility. Contrary to the Commission's power to order recovery, the use of the recovery injunction is subject to the Commission's discretion: art.11(2) clearly states that the Commission may issue such a decision.

26–008 Article 11(2) also gives the Commission the power to authorise the Member State concerned to couple the refunding of the aid with the payment of rescue aid to the firm concerned. This provision may seem at variance with earlier case law. In Case 52/84 *Commission v Belgium*,[29] the Commission argued before the ECJ that the Belgian government had failed to fulfil its obligations under the Treaty by not complying with the Commission's decision ordering it to withdraw aid from Bloch. According to the ECJ, the fact that full recovery of the sum paid out was impossible did not discharge the government from its duty to recover the amount, "because the Commission's objective was to withdraw the aid, and that objective could be attained by proceedings for winding up the company, which the Belgian authorities, in their capacity as shareholder or creditor, could institute". So even an ensuing *bankruptcy* of the recipient does not absolve the grantor state from its duty to recover aids. In Case 63/87 *Commission v Greece* the ECJ observed that any financial difficulties which exporters might face following abolition of the illegal aid did not constitute absolute impossibility.[30] This case law can only be reconciled with the new power for the Commission if it will secure that the objectives of the aid rules—i.e. the restoration of equal competitive conditions—are upheld. In any case, as a general principle, Member States cannot grant beneficiaries of unlawful aid, which has been declared incompatible with the internal market, new aid intended to neutralise the effect of repayment.[31] The last sentence of art.11(2) states that the provisions of this paragraph shall be applicable only to unlawful aid implemented after the entry into force of the regulation. It should be noted that, according to art.16, the same rule will apply to misused aid. This provision should not, it is submitted, be read as meaning that the power to issue recovery injunctions cannot be used for misused aid.

In cases of non-compliance with recovery decisions of the Commission, art.23(1) of the Procedural Regulation provides that the Commission may refer

---

[29] [1986] E.C.R. 89.
[30] [1988] E.C.R. 2875.
[31] Case C–110/02 *Commission v Council* [2004] E.C.R. I–6333 at paras 42 and 43.

the matter to the ECJ directly in accordance with art.93(2) EC (now art.108(2) TFEU). In addition, as explained in the Recovery Notice of the Commission,[32] if certain conditions are met, the Commission may require the Member State to suspend the payment of a new compatible aid to the beneficiary or beneficiaries concerned in application of the Deggendorf principle.[33]

4. COMMISSION'S POWER TO DEMAND RECOVERY

Source of power

Even though the Commission's power to require recovery of unlawful aid is now firmly established in the Procedural Regulation, it may nevertheless be useful to provide the background in the case law. In its *Kohlengesetz* judgment,[34] the ECJ held as early as 1973 that the Commission was competent under art.108(2) (at that time art.93 EEC) to decide that a State must alter or abolish a state aid that is incompatible with the internal market. "To be of practical effect", it stated, "this abolition or modification may include an obligation to require repayment of aid granted in breach of the Treaty, so that, in the absence of measures for recovery, the Commission may bring the matter before the Court." This right to order recovery has been confirmed, implicitly or explicitly, in a great number of judgments since 1985,[35] such as the *Alcan* and *Siemens* cases.[36] Recovery is the logical consequence of the illegality of aid. The objective of recovery is to re-establish the previously existing situation. By repaying the aid the recipient forfeits the advantage which it enjoyed over its competitors on the market, and the situation prior to the payment is considered to be restored. Therefore, according to the ECJ, "the recovery of State aid unlawfully granted for the purpose of re-establishing the previously existing situation cannot in principle be regarded as disproportionate to the objectives of the Treaty in regard to State aids."[37]

26-009

The 1973 judgment in *Kohlengesetz* formed the basis for the Commission's announcement in 1983 that recipients of illegal aid would be liable to repay it. The Commission had already published a communication in the *Official Journal* of 1980,[38] in which it stated that "the Commission has decided to use all measures at its disposal to ensure that Member States' obligations under art.88 (now art.108 TFEU) are respected". Three years later the Commission published another communication[39] in which it observed:

---

[32] [2007] O.J. C272/4 at para.71.
[33] Case C–355/95P *Textilwerke Deggendorf GmbH (TWD) v Commission* [1997] E.C.R. I–2549.
[34] Case 70/72 *Commission v Germany (Kohlengesetz)* [1973] E.C.R. 813.
[35] e.g. Case 52/84 *Commission v Belgium* [1986] E.C.R. 89; Case 310/85 *Deufil v Commission* [1987] E.C.R. 901.
[36] Case C–24/95 *Land Rheinland Pfalz v Alcan* [1997] E.C.R. I–1591; Case T–459/93 *Siemens v Commission* [1995] E.C.R. II–1675.
[37] Case C–142/87 *Tubemeuse* [1990] E.C.R. I–959.
[38] [1980] O.J. C252/2.
[39] [1983] O.J. C318/3.

"In spite of this formal reminder and the numerous other reminders it has had occasion to deliver in connection with aids under examination, the Commission is obliged to note that illegal aid grants are becoming increasingly common, i.e. aid incompatible with the Common Market granted without the obligations laid down in art.88 (now art.108 TFEU) having been fulfilled."

As a result, the Commission informed potential recipients of the risk attaching to any aid granted to them illegally, "in that any recipient of the aid granted illegally, i.e. without the Commission having reached a final Decision, may have to refund the aid". Since then the Commission, in its notice to other Member States and interested parties, which is published in the *Official Journal* soon after the opening of formal proceedings under art.108(2) TFEU, usually included a warning to potential aid recipients of the risks of aid measures adopted contrary to art.108(3). In line with the Opinion of Advocate General Van Gerven in Case C–303/88, the ECJ followed the view of the Commission that if the decision substantiates the incompatibility of the aid with the EC Treaty (now TFEU), the Commission can require recovery without further motivation; the argument sometimes raised by Member States that recovery is disproportionate is usually rejected as " . . . recovery is the logical consequence of a decision of illegality and cannot therefore be disproportionate".[40] The ECJ accepted that the recovery of the total amount of aid was ordered "because of the seriousness and scale of the breach". The justification may seem, according to the Court, "excessively laconic", but had to be read in the context of a decision which explained in detail the impact of the aid on a sector in crisis.

Use of power

26–010   Following the 1983 communication, the Commission has made increasing use of orders for repayment. The Commission started to order recovery in earnest in 1984. Since that year this has been standard practice. Of course, such a negative decision only has effect if it clearly specifies exactly what is required from the Member State concerned.[41] In its Recovery Notice the Commission states that it "will continue its present practice of identifying in its recovery decisions, where possible, the identity of the undertaking(s) from whom the aid must be recovered."[42] It will also endeavour, when it has the necessary data at its disposal, to quantify the precise amount of aid to be recovered.[43] However, when ordering

---

[40] Case C–303/88 *Italy v Commission* [1991] E.C.R. I–1433; Case C–419/06, *Commission v Hellenic Republic* [2008] E.C.R. I–00027.

[41] Case 213/85 *Commission v Netherlands* [1988] E.C.R. 281.

[42] [2007] O.J. C272/4 at para.32.

[43] *ibid* at para.37. In case C–441/06 the Court confirmed that it is sufficient for the Commission's decision to include information enabling the recipient to work out itself without too much difficulty the amount to be recovered. The member state must provide the Commission the information necessary to determine the final amount of aid to be repaid, *Commission v French Republic,* [2007] E.C.R. I–08887.

recovery the Commission is not required to fix the exact amount to be recovered, as long as the recipient and the Member State are able without too much difficulty to calculate the amount to be repaid.[44] In this respect it is worth noting that although recovery by way of a cash payment is the method preferred by the Commission (because it is easy to supervise), alternative methods are allowed provided the Member State ensures that the measure chosen is transparent and eliminates the distortion of competition caused by the unlawful aid (re-establishing the normal conditions of competition being the purpose of the recovery order, even though it is, to say the least, doubtful whether recovery indeed necessarily always achieves that purpose). Measures that relate to uncertain future events rather than being unconditional and immediately applicable are not acceptable alternatives.[45]

The order may, for example, relate to the difference between the value, as established by the Commission, of *land* owned by a government authority and sold to a company and the price paid by this company. In the case of *interest subsidies*, the Commission will quantify the difference between the market rate at the time the loan was granted and the preferential rate attaching to the loan. Particular issues may arise in the case of state aid in the form of *state guarantees*. Normally, the aid element is the difference between the interest rate that the beneficiary would have had to pay for a loan on market terms, i.e. without a guarantee, and the rate at which a guaranteed loan was actually provided. However, if the beneficiary was in severe financial difficulties at the time the guarantees were granted and the loans made available, the aid element could be as high as 100 per cent of the guarantees as nobody would have granted the loans without any guarantee.[46] Even in cases where a loan on which a state guarantee is granted does not in itself contain any aid element because it is secured in line with market requirements (in the sense that the interest rate is comparable to interest rates charged for healthy firms), the premium paid for the guarantee may be held not to be a market premium. In the *MobilCom* case, the Commission decided that given the company's difficult economic situation and the fact that it was on the brink of insolvency, the premium (respectively 0.8 per cent and 1 per cent plus application fee of €25 million for a loan of €112 million) did not reflect the risk that the State was running; no private investor would have granted a guarantee on those terms.[47] Note that according to the Commission the question whether the illegality of the aid in the form of a guarantee affects the legal relationship between the State and third parties (such as the lending banks) is a

---

[44] Case C–480/98 *Spain v Commission* [2000] E.C.R. I–8717 at paras 25 and 26.

[45] Case C–209/90 *Commission v Germany* [1992] E.C.R. I–2613.

[46] See Commission Decision 2005/786 [2005] O.J. L296/19 at para.107, in which case the Commission ordered discontinuation of the loan (i.e. full repayment) as well as payment of the difference in interest rates; see also the Commission Notice on the application of arts 87 (now 107) and 88 (now 108) to state aid in the form of guarantees [2000] O.J. C71/14 and Ch.9 on Guarantees.

[47] Decision 2005/346 [2005] L116/55 at para.125.

matter which has to be examined under national law whereby the national courts should take into account the breach of EU law.[48]

26–011 Where an *equity injection* is involved, the Commission is entitled to take the view that abolition of the advantage granted must require the repayment of the capital contributed.[49] In its decision concerning aid by the Greek government to Halkis Cement Company by allowing public enterprises not to collect claims on Halkis, the Commission stated that it was unable to quantify the aid so the government must itself determine the amount of aid to be recovered. Sometimes the Commission leaves the Member States the choice between various alternatives as long as they abolish the aid with effect from the time it was originally granted. The Commission had a particularly hard time in the *Bremer Vulkan* case.[50] The aid was given through a complicated scheme involving an exchange of shares and a guarantee. The ECJ held that the Commission was not required to base its assessment of the value of the shares on the stock exchange price alone. Hence it annulled the Commission's decision. In the meantime the Commission has adopted a fresh decision, again ordering recovery.[51]

In July 1990 the Commission had ordered the recovery by the UK government of £44.4 million of aid illegally granted to British Aerospace in connection with the purchase of BAe by the Rover Group. The Commission stated that the British government had incorrectly executed an earlier decision whereby aid was authorised subject to a number of conditions. The 1990 decision was annulled by the ECJ on procedural grounds, but the Commission reopened a procedure under art.108(2) and demanded recovery.[52] In its ruling on the *TWD Textielwerke Deggendorf* cases,[53] the General Court distinguished *British Aerospace* from the situation in *Deggendorf* on the grounds that the first aid to Deggendorf had been declared illegal following a full inquiry based on art.108(2), whereas the aid granted to British Aerospace had been discovered subsequent to the Commission's original decision and therefore had to be analysed separately under a full art.108(2) procedure so that all of the parties concerned could exercise their rights in full.

26–012 An unreasonable delay in giving a negative decision could prevent the Commission from requiring recovery.[54] In another decision published two years later,[55] the Commission decided that although the aid was unlawful (not having been notified) and incompatible with the common market, repayment should not

---

[48] Notice on the application of arts 87 (now 107) and 88 (now 108) to State aid in the form of guarantees [2000] O.J. C71/14. See Decision 2005/920 [2005] O.J. L335/48 at para.79; Joined Cases T–204/97 and T–270/97 *EPAC v Commission* [2000] E.C.R. II–2267; and Ch.9 on Guarantees. See also Case C–275/10 *Residex Capital* [2011] E.C.R. n.y.r. (December 8, 2011) on the consequences of breach of art.108(3) TFEU in relation to guarantees.

[49] Case T–55/99 *CETM v Commission* [2000] E.C.R. II–3207.

[50] Joined Cases C–329/93 and 62 and 63/95 *Germany v Commission* [1997] E.C.R. I–5151.

[51] Decision 98/665 [1998] O.J. L316/25.

[52] Case C–294/90 *British Aerospace and Rover v Commission* [1992] E.C.R. I–493.

[53] Joined Cases T–244 and 486/93 *TWD Deggendorf v Commission* [1995] E.C.R. II–2265; Case C–355/95P *TWD Deggendorf v Commission* [1997] E.C.R. I–2549.

[54] Case 223/85 *Rijn-Schelde-Verolme v Commission* [1998] E.C.R. 4716.

[55] Decision 92/329/EEC of July 25, 1990 [1992] O.J. L183/30.

be demanded. This was based on the long interval between the date the aid became known to the Commission, probably in the autumn of 1987, and the date of the decision. It is remarkable, however, that according to the decision the Italian government had not been very co-operative, which may at least partly explain the delay.

In accordance with art.14(3) of the Procedural Regulation, the Commission requires recovery in accordance with the procedures and provisions of national law. The question as to whether the Commission, when ordering repayment, must take into account that the recipient paid corporate income tax on the amounts received came before the General Court in the *Siemens* case. The General Court ruled that this is a matter for the national authorities, who should take this into account, "provided that the application of those rules does not make such recovery impossible in practice or discriminate in relation to comparable cases governed by national law".[56] In its Recovery Notice the Commission "considers that in such cases, the national authorities will need to ensure that the beneficiary will not be able to enjoy a further tax deduction by claiming that the reimbursement has reduced his taxable income, since this would mean that the net amount of the recovery was lower than the net amount initially received."[57]

Where an aid granted in the form of a tax exemption has been declared unlawful, it is not correct to assume that recovery of the aid in question must necessarily take the form of a retroactive tax, which would as such be absolutely impossible to enforce; instead, the Member State must merely take measures ordering the undertakings which have received the aid to repay sums equivalent in amount to the tax exemption unlawfully granted to them.[58]

5. POSITIONS OF MEMBER STATES AND RECIPIENTS CONCERNED

General principles

The ECJ has reaffirmed on several occasions the principle that, although **26–013** recovery has to be effected by applying the relevant national legal provisions, a Member State cannot invoke a rule of domestic law to oppose the reimbursement of aid. In *Commission v Belgium*,[59] the Belgian government had not recovered an aid which had been declared illegal by the Commission on the grounds that following regionalisation, competence in this area had passed from the State to the regions. The ECJ nevertheless considered that it was established jurisprudence that a Member State cannot cite procedural provisions or domestic rules of order to justify the failure to respect obligations arising from EU law. In the *ENI-Lanerossi* case,[60] the Italian government also tried to oppose the restitution of

[56] Case T–459/93 *Siemens v Commission* [1995] E.C.R. II–1675, para.83.
[57] Recovery Notice at para.50.
[58] Case C–193/91 *Commission v Greece* [1991] E.C.R. I–3131 at para.17.
[59] Case C–74/89 *Commission v Belgium* [1990] E.C.R. I–492.
[60] Case C–303/88 *Italy v Commission* [1991] E.C.R. I–1433.

aids that had already been granted, on the basis that Italian law prohibited restitution of aid that had been illegally granted to ENI (the public holding company). The ECJ considered that this fact could not prevent the full application of EU law and therefore had no effect on the obligation to proceed with the recovery of the aid in question. In *Commission v France*, the French authorities argued that the delay in implementing the recovery decision, due to the application of a rule providing for the suspensory effect of actions brought against demands for payment laid down by French law, was expressly authorised by art.14(3) of Regulation No 659/1999. The Court ruled: "By providing for the suspensory effect of actions brought against demands for payment issued for the recovery of aid granted, the procedure laid down by French law and applied in the present case cannot be considered to allow the 'immediate and effective' execution of Decision 2002/14. On the contrary, by granting such suspensory effect, the procedure can considerably delay the recovery of the aid. Thus, by failing to have regard to the objectives pursued by the Community (Union) rules on State aid, that national procedure has prevented the immediate restoration of the previously existing situation and prolonged the unfair competitive advantage resulting from the aid at issue. It follows that the procedure provided for by national law in the present case does not fulfil the conditions laid down in art.14(3) of the Procedural Regulation. The French rule providing for the suspensory effect of actions brought against demands for payment should therefore have been left unapplied."[61] In the *Lucchini* case the Court ruled that Community law also "precludes the application of a provision of national law, such as art.2909 of the Italian Civil Code, which seeks to lay down the principle of res judicata in so far as the application of that provision prevents the recovery of State aid granted in breach of Community law which has been found to be incompatible with the common market in a decision of the Commission which has become final."[62]

If unforeseen or unforeseeable difficulties would arise in recovering aid, the ECJ has consistently held that the Commission and Member States should "work together in good faith to overcome the difficulties in full compliance with the provisions of the Treaty, and in particular those on aid", in keeping with art.4(3) TEU.[63] This principle was also followed in the case *Commission v Germany* in which the German government argued that the obligation to recover the aid was not legally binding, because recovery was to be effected under national law. The ECJ rejected the argument, stating that there was a definitive obligation to recover the aid. The German government's only defence would be to plead that it was *absolutely impossible* to implement the decision properly. It is for the Member State concerned to present a proposal on how the difficulties relating to the recovery of the aid should be overcome, including those difficulties relating to the calculation of the aid.[64] The only defence available to a Member State being that it is absolutely impossible for it to properly implement the decision, a

---

[61] Case C–232/05 *Commission v France* [2006] E.C.R. I–10071 at paras 51–53.
[62] Case C–119/05 *Lucchini* [2007] E.C.R. I–6199 at para.63.
[63] Case 94/87 *Commission v Germany* [1989] E.C.R. 175.
[64] Case 94/87 *Commission v Germany* [1989] E.C.R. 175.

Member State cannot justify the non-application of a recovery decision if its difficulties are of a merely technical and administrative nature; moreover, an absolute impossibility to execute the decision does not exist if there are indirect ways of calculating the amount of the aid to be recovered.[65]

If the ECJ finds that a Member State has failed to fulfil its obligation, the State shall, according to art.260 TFEU, be required to take the necessary measures to comply with the judgment of the ECJ. If the Commission then considers that the Member State concerned has not taken the necessary measures to comply with the judgment of the ECJ, it may bring the case before the ECJ after giving that State the opportunity to submit its observations. If the Court finds that the Member State concerned has not complied with its judgment it may ultimately impose a lump sum or penalty payment on it. See further Ch.27 at para.27–008.

Insolvency proceedings; transfer of shares or assets

Particular enforcement problems arise in the many cases where the beneficiary **26–014** is insolvent and/or has gone bankrupt. Recovery must then take place under a large variety of national insolvency procedures that often tend to protect the economic activities against creditors, including the Member State, in an attempt to achieve continuation of the business. Insolvency proceedings tend to take several years while in the meantime the activities of the insolvent company, and thereby the distortion of competition, continues. The fact that a company is insolvent or bankrupt does not affect the obligation of repayment; removal of this obligation in the event of liquidation would render meaningless the state aid rules.[66] However, the ultimate objective of the law is the abolishment of the unlawful aid; therefore liquidation of the company, even though preventing repayment, brings the distortion of competition to an end, at least for the future. The Commission therefore states in its Recovery Notice "that a decision ordering the Member State to recover unlawful and incompatible aid from an insolvent beneficiary may be considered to be properly executed either when full recovery is completed or, in case of partial recovery, when the company is liquidated and its assets are sold under market conditions."[67] Where possible, the Member State, as creditor of the recovery claim, is obliged to register the claim in the insolvency proceedings.[68] The ECJ has consistently held that "the restoration of the previous situation and the elimination of the distortion of competition resulting from the unlawfully paid aid may, in principle, be achieved by registration of the liability relating to the repayment of the aid in question in the schedule of liabilities."[69] However, the sole registration might not always be sufficient to ensure the

---

[65] See, e.g. Case C–378/98 *Commission v Belgium* [2001] E.C.R. I–5107 at para.41.
[66] Case C–42/93 *Spain v Commission* [1990] E.C.R. I–4175.
[67] Recovery Notice at para.61.
[68] Case C–499/99 *Commission v Spain* [2002] E.C.R. I–603.
[69] Case C–331/09 *Commission v Poland* [2011] E.C.R. n.y.r. (April 14, 2011).

immediate and effective implementation of the recovery decision. The Commission, therefore, requires that the Member State concerned should immediately register its claims in the bankruptcy proceedings and, if necessary, dispute the refusal by the insolvency administrator to register its claims. The Commission takes the view that the authorities responsible for the execution of the recovery decision should also appeal any decision by the insolvency administrator or the insolvency court to allow a continuation of the insolvent beneficiary's activity beyond the time limits set in the recovery decision. In such cases, national courts should, according to the Commission, not allow for a continuation of an insolvent beneficiary's activity in the absence of full recovery. In the case where a continuation plan is proposed to the creditors' committee implying a continuation of the activity of the beneficiary, the national authorities responsible for the execution of the recovery decision should only support this plan if it ensures that the aid is repaid in full within the time limits foreseen in the Commission's recovery decision.[70]

Insolvency proceedings often bring about a transfer of assets or shares of the insolvent company by the administrator to a third party. But also outside the sphere of insolvency it is possible that the assets of the beneficiary, or its shares, are sold. From a state aid discipline perspective this raises various issues: does the obligation of repayment follow the assets (which, if all goes well, are replaced by cash)?; is there a case of circumvention of the recovery order?; or is perhaps the buyer benefiting from (new) state aid?

26–015   The Commission enjoys a relatively wide discretion in the application and enforcement of the state aid provisions and, as a matter of policy, it takes a strict approach to any attempts to evade the effect of an adverse state aid decision. The purpose of the recovery of unlawful state aid is to re-establish the previously existing situation. The unlawful aid must be recovered from the undertaking which actually benefited from it. In principle, the beneficiary is the recipient, i.e. the undertaking which received the aid. However, the aid might also be recovered from other undertakings if it is established that they benefited from it.[71] Such a situation can arise when the recipient is bought by another company or when the assets of the recipient are transferred to another undertaking at a price that is lower than their market value or to a successor company set up in order to circumvent the recovery order.[72]

With regard to the acquisition of the recipient by another company through a *share deal* the ECJ has ruled in 2004 in Case C–277/00 that when the recipient is bought at a market price "that is to say at the highest price which a private investor acting under normal market conditions was ready to pay for that company in the situation it was in, in particular after having enjoyed State aid", the aid element is assessed at the market price and included in the purchase price.[73] If the state aid element is correctly reflected in the market price, the buyer

---

[70] Recovery Notice at paras 63–67.
[71] Case C–277/00 *Germany v Commission* [2004] E.C.R. I–3925 at para.75.
[72] Recovery Notice at para.68.
[73] Case C–277/00 *Germany v Commission* [2004] E.C.R. I–3925 at para.80.

cannot be regarded as having benefited from an advantage. In the same case, the ECJ held that when the recipient retains its legal personality and continues to carry out its activities, it is considered that this company retains the competitive advantage connected with the aid and it is therefore this same company, and not the purchaser of the shares, that is required to repay an amount equal to the aid. In his opinion in case C–277/00, Advocate General Tizzano favoured such an approach, because it removes the advantage which causes the distortions of competition. Moreover, he pointed out that "the seller's opportunities for speculation would be considerably reduced (and in practice would become part of the normal risks of business) since any possible loss caused by the recovery of aid would normally have to be taken into consideration in determining the conditions of sale".[74] In the *CDA Datenträger Albrechts* case decided by the General Court,[75] the Commission stated that normally in the case of a share deal it is the target and not the purchaser that remains liable for repayment of the illegal state aid, regardless of whether the repayment is taken into account in determining the conditions of sale.

The above principles were applied by the Commission in a decision concern- **26–016**
ing aid to Spanish shipyards.[76] The Commission held that the change of ownership of the yards does not mean that the recovery of the aid could fall on the previous owner of the companies. The reason is that the companies were transferred, not on market terms in open and transparent tendering procedures, but in the form of a reorganisation of companies within the same group, with the use of a symbolic price. Insofar as companies are bought under non-discriminatory competitive conditions and at the market price (that is the highest price which a private investor acting under normal competitive conditions was ready to pay), the aid element was assessed at the market price and included in the purchase price. Only in such circumstances, the buyers cannot be regarded as having benefited from an advantage. They could not therefore be asked to repay the aid element in question. However, in the present case these conditions were not met. The buyer acquired the shares of companies belonging to the same group as the buyer and eliminated them as legal entities after the acquisition of the shares. As successor to the previously legally independent share companies, the buyer is now the beneficiary and has to repay the aid granted to those yards.

With respect to the *sale of assets*, according to the ECJ, a transfer of the advantage created by the aid may occur when the assets of the beneficiary are transferred to a third party at a price that is lower than their market value, or to a successor company that is set up to circumvent the recovery order; in such a case, the recovery order can be extended to that third party.[77] In the *Olympic Airways* decision, the ECJ endorsed the view of the Advocate General that the

---

[74] Opinion of AG Tizzano delivered on June 19, 2003 in Case C–277/00 *Germany v Commission* at para.84.

[75] Case T–324/00 *CDA Datenträger Albrechts* [2005] E.C.R. II–4309.

[76] Decision 2005/179 [2005] O.J. L58/42 at para.120.

[77] Case C–277/00 *Germany v Commission* [2004] E.C.R. I–3925.

Commission may be compelled to require that recovery is not restricted to the original undertaking, but is extended to the undertaking which continues the activity of the original undertaking in cases where certain elements of the transfer point to economic continuity between the two undertakings; indeed, the ECJ considered that, where a transfer of assets form the beneficiary to a new company was structured in such a way that it would be impossible to recover the debts of the beneficiary from the new company, that operation created an obstacle to the effective implementation of the recovery decision.[78]

Legitimate expectations

26–017   Many Commission decisions and European Courts' cases deal with the principle of protection of legitimate expectations. The rule that this principle may preclude the Commission from ordering recovery has been established by the ECJ and is also stipulated in art.14(1) of the Procedural Regulation which provides in the second sentence that "the Commission shall not require recovery of the aid if this would be contrary to a general principle of Community law". However, it is only the beneficiary, and not the Member State concerned, that may entertain a legitimate expectation and only in exceptional circumstances. Basically, as will be shown by cases discussed in the following paragraphs, legitimate expectations can only be invoked successfully if they are the result of conduct by the Commission, or other EU institutions, and if the aid is granted in compliance with the procedure laid down in art.108. A "diligent businessman" should normally be able to determine whether that procedure has been followed.

It is important to note that even when the Member State or beneficiary concerned has not presented the Commission with any argument based on the existence of legitimate expectations, the Commission is, pursuant to art.14(1), required ex officio to take into consideration the exceptional circumstances that provide justification. When the Commission has failed to take into account legitimate expectations allegedly entertained by the recipient of unlawful aid, the decision can be challenged before the General Court under art.263 TFEU and/or, indirectly, in national enforcement proceedings (see para.28–009 of Ch.28). The General Court has ruled that recipients " . . . can rely on such exceptional circumstances, on the basis of the relevant provisions of national law, only in the framework of the recovery procedure before the national courts, and it is for them alone to assess the circumstances of the case, if necessary after obtaining a preliminary ruling on interpretation from the Court of Justice".[79] This wording may suggest that recipients of unlawful aid can only rely on the defence of legitimate expectations in litigation before the national courts and not in appeal proceedings before the European Courts, nor perhaps even in the administrative

---

[78] Judgment of May 12, 2005, Case C–415/03 *Commission v Greece*, not yet published at paras 33 and 34, and Opinion of AG Geelhoed of February 1, 2005, also at paras 33 and 34.
[79] Case T–109/01 *Fleuren Compost v Commission* at para.137; [2004] E.C.R. II–127.

procedure before the Commission. Such a far-reaching conclusion would be contrary to the jurisprudence of the European Courts and to the practice of the Commission (see below) as well as the language of art.14(1) of the Procedural Regulation. What the General Court may have had in mind, however, is that it is only for the national courts to examine those exceptional circumstances that follow from provisions of national law. Such an interpretation would assume that these arguments can still be raised before the national court even if the recipient could have challenged the negative Commission decision under art.263 TFEU, but did not do so as a result of which the decision has become final.

In Case 94/87 *Commission v Germany*,[80] the German government argued that **26–018** the principle of legitimate expectations under German law obliged the national authority to give the protection of the legitimate expectations of the undertaking that received aid, greater weight than the public interest of the Community in having the aid recovered. The ECJ rejected the argument. As the ECJ has consistently ruled, in principle the recovery of aid unlawfully paid must take place in accordance with the relevant procedural provisions of national law, as long as these provisions are to be applied in such a way that the recovery of the aid is not rendered impossible in practice. Where a provision, such as that contained in the German Code, requires the various interests involved to be weighed before a defective administrative measure is withdrawn, the interests of the Community must be taken fully into consideration.

This principle was taken further in Case 5/89 *Commission v Germany*.[81] The German government argued again that the protection of the legitimate expectations of the undertaking which received the aid must prevail over the public interest of the Community in having the aid recovered. In addition, a German law prohibited the revocation of an administrative measure granting a benefit more than one year after the administrative authority became aware of the circumstances constituting grounds for revocation. The ECJ was unsympathetic to these arguments and held that a Member State may not plead provisions, practices or circumstances in its own internal legal system as a reason for not complying with EC law obligations. In this case, the one-year time limit would clearly render the application of art.108 impossible in practice. It was held that the principle of legitimate expectations also formed part of the EU legal order. However, the ECJ ruled that undertakings which received aid should not have any legitimate expectation unless the aid has been granted in accordance with art.108. A diligent businessman would normally be able to determine whether that procedure had been followed, even if the State in question was responsible for the illegality.[82] Only in exceptional circumstances, a recipient might have legitimately assumed that an aid was lawful and so might decline to refund the aid.

The ECJ was clear that a Member State could not itself rely on the recipient's **26–019** legitimate expectations, since this would in practice nullify the effectiveness of

---

[80] [1989] E.C.R. 175.
[81] Case C–5/89 [1990] E.C.R. I–3437; Case C–24/95 *Alcan Deutschland v Commission* [1997] E.C.R. I–1591.
[82] See also Case T–109/01 *Fleuren Compost* [2004] E.C.R. II–127 at para.144.

arts 107 and 108, in that Member States could rely on their own unlawful conduct to escape the provisions of the Treaty. In the *RSV* case,[83] the ECJ accepted that there were exceptional circumstances due to the extraordinary delay by the Commission in deciding that the aid must be recovered. The same would have been true, in all probability, in the *Cofaz* case,[84] if the Commission had ordered repayment and the recipients (rather than the State, which cannot rely on the principle of the protection of legitimate expectations) had appealed the decision. In a case, concerning an aid scheme for Sardinian farmers, an initial two-year stage was held necessary to gather relevant facts while a second stage of two years and nine months was held necessary to seek clarifications; in both stages the Italian Government was considered to be responsible for the delay and, according to the ECJ, the slowness of the procedure could not have given rise to a legitimate expectation that the unnotified aid to the farmers was lawful.[85]

In the *Deufil* case[86] the ECJ ruled that the fact that polypropylene yarns were not covered by the aid code could not give rise to legitimate expectations because the code merely gives guidelines of the Commission's policy but does not, and cannot, grant exceptions from arts 107 and 108. In another case, the ECJ rejected Spain's argument that the Commission had always interpreted art.107(3)(a) in such a way that it was not directly concerned with the effect of regional aids on sectoral considerations, as not conferring upon a Member State a legitimate expectation that the Commission's interpretation was the correct one.[87] In the *Alcan* case,[88] the recipient of the aid argued that in its earlier jurisprudence the ECJ had been concerned with the obligations of the offending Member States— the judgments say nothing about the rights of the recipients of the aid. It argued that a recipient was entitled to rely on this principle and therefore it imposed no further restriction on the recipients of an aid in relying on national rules precluding recovery. Neither the ECJ nor the Advocate General shared this view: the obligation on a Member State to recover unlawful aid and the rights of the recipient are plainly two sides of the same coin. Alcan could not rely on the principle of legitimate expectations where the aid was illegally granted: a diligent businessman can be expected to verify that the procedure laid down in the Treaty has been followed. In Case C–298/00P[89] the ECJ confirmed the conclusion of the General Court that the fact that the recipients are small undertakings cannot justify a legitimate expectation on their part as to the lawfulness of the aid. In the *CETM* case[90] the General Court held that the fact that loans were made by private

---

[83] Case 223/85 *Rijn-Schelde-Verolme v Commission* [1987] E.C.R. 901. See Case C–298/00 *Italy v Commission* [2004] E.C.R. I–4087, where a delay of almost two years was not considered exceptional; also: Case T–55/99 *CETM v Commission* [2000] E.C.R. II–3207 at paras 137–154.

[84] Case C–169/84 *Cofaz v Commission* [1986] E.C.R. 408.

[85] Cases C–346/03 and C–529/03 *G. Atzani v Regione autonoma della Sardegna* [2006] E.C.R. I–1875.

[86] Case 310/85 *Deufil v Commission* [1987] E.C.R. 901.

[87] Case C–169/95 *Spain v Commission* [1997] E.C.R. I–0135.

[88] Case C–24/95 *Land Rheinland Pfalz v Alcan* [1997] E.C.R. I–1591.

[89] Case C–298/00P *Italy v Commission, (Alzetta et al.)* [2004] E.C.R. I–4087.

[90] Case T–55/99 [2000] E.C.R. II–3207 at paras 119–31.

banks, without involvement by the public authorities, cannot give rise to a legitimate expectation that the reductions in interest rates were of state origin. Ignorance cannot be regarded an exceptional circumstance.

In some cases it was argued by the beneficiary of aid that a Commission decision approving the measure at issue causes "legitimate expectations", and would therefore preclude recovery even if the decision is annulled at a later stage. However, the Courts have held that so long as the period for bringing an action against such a positive decision has not expired, and so long as the appeal procedure is pending, the beneficiary cannot be certain as to the lawfulness of the aid and, therefore, cannot entertain legitimate expectations (assuming, of course, the aid is granted contrary to the art.108 procedure).[91] The public interest in preventing market distortions requires repayment of illegal aid and encompasses the right of competitors to challenge positive decisions. Balancing the public interest against the private interest of the beneficiary, the ECJ concluded that where the Commission issues a (second) negative (recovery) decision after a (first) positive but not final decision (because subject to judicial review) has been annulled, the beneficiary cannot rely on legitimate expectations.[92]

26–020

There are various examples of cases where the Commission in its decision took into consideration exceptional circumstances and refrained from ordering the recovery of unlawfully granted aid because such recovery would be contrary to the respect for the legitimate expectation of beneficiaries. One example concerned selective tax exemptions and tax reductions in Austria for energy intensive undertakings, which had also been subject of the *Adria-Wien* judgment of the ECJ.[93] In its decision the Commission held that " . . . the wording of the Court's answer to the second question in Adria-Wien may have led some beneficiaries to believe in good faith that the national measures would cease to be selective.; . . . the Commission comes to the conclusion that in the present case recovery would be contrary to the principle of legitimate expectations".[94] In another case, concerning Gibraltar tax regimes, the Commission decided that:

> " . . . it is reasonable to assume that a conscientious businessman, acting in good faith, could legitimately have believed that by opting for the less generous Qualifying Companies regime rather than the manifestly legal (in state aid terms, existing) Exempt Companies regime, he would also enter a regime whose legality was not in doubt. Accordingly, the Commission concludes that an order for recovery would, in the exceptional circumstances of this case, be contrary to a general principle of Community law".[95]

---

[91] Cases T–116/01 and T–118/01 *P&O European Ferries v Commission* [2003] E.C.R. II–2957; Case C–91/01 *Italy v Commission (Solar Tech)* [2004] E.C.R. I–4355.
[92] See for example Decision 2005/786 [2005] L296/19 at para.137. See also Case C–199/06 *CELF v SIDE* [2008] E.C.R. I–469.
[93] Case C–143/99 [2001] E.C.R. I–8365.
[94] Decision 2005/565 [2005] O.J. L190/13 at para.66.
[95] Decision 2005/77 [2005] O.J. L29/24 at para.100.

A final example is the case where the Commission had, contrary to art.19(1) of the Procedural Regulation, not published what came down to the change of a Swedish measure from existing to new aid; here too, the Commission refrained from recovery, this time because it was difficult to show that beneficiaries were informed—some may in good faith have believed that the new, unlawful measures were still to be regarded as "existing aid".[96]

6. ACTIONS BY THIRD PARTIES BEFORE THE NATIONAL COURTS

26–021   As will be discussed in more detail in Ch.28, the last sentence of art.108(3), providing the so-called standstill obligation, has direct effect. It may be relied upon by individuals before the national courts. A national court has no jurisdiction to rule on the compatibility of aid with the internal market but may have cause to interpret and apply the concept of aid contained in art.107 in order to determine, for example, whether state aid introduced without observance of the preliminary examination procedure provided for in art.108(3) ought to have been subject to this procedure. It may also have to decide whether a contested measure falls under the provisions on state aids or under another provision, such as art.34 TFEU. In the *salmon exporters* case,[97] the ECJ held that the validity of acts implementing aid is affected by the failure of a Member State to notify the aid. The national courts must guarantee the rights of those affected and draw the necessary conclusions according to national law, as regards both the validity of acts granting aid and the recovery of financial support granted in infringement of art.108(3). The role of the national courts in safeguarding plaintiffs' rights is fundamentally different from the Commission's role of assessing the compatibility of aids and in no way conflicts with that latter role. A decision by the Commission that an aid is compatible with the internal market does not regularise a posteriori the acts granting aid in infringement of art.108(3), which remain invalid. As the ECJ stated, any other interpretation would encourage non-observance by the Member States of the last sentence of art.108(3) and would deprive it of its useful effect.[98]

It follows, first, that third parties, such as competitors who may be injured by illegal aid (i.e. aid implemented prior to notification, during the contentious procedure, or after a negative decision) should be able to obtain an injunction from national courts, thus preventing the actual granting of the aid. If a rule of national law would preclude a national court from granting interim relief, such a rule must be set aside.[99] Second, third parties who can prove that they have suffered losses caused by the unlawful implementation of aid may have an action for damages in the national courts. This is so not only for damages caused by aid granted contrary to a negative decision but also, as a result of the *Fédération*

---

[96] Decision 2005/468 [2005] O.J. L165/21 at paras 58–63.
[97] Case C–354/90 *Fédération Nationale v France* [1991] E.C.R. I–5505.
[98] As confirmed in Case C–199/06 *CELF v SIDE* [2008] E.C.R. I–469 at para.40.
[99] Case C–213/89 *R. v Secretary of State for Transport Ex p. Factortame* [1990] E.C.R. I–2433.

Nationale case,[100] if paid prematurely and found compatible with the Treaty. The view that, in all Member States, an action for damages must be available, despite what the national rules say, is supported by the judgment of the ECJ in *Francovich*.[101] The ECJ made it clear that the full effectiveness of Community law and the protection of individual rights would be endangered unless individuals had a right to claim reparation of damages resulting from a breach of such a right by a Member State. Member States have a duty to eliminate all illegal consequences resulting from a breach of a EU law obligation. It seems that not only competitors, but also creditors of the beneficiary who suffer as a result of repayment, may have an action for damages.

Where a national court finds that a Member State has granted aid, as defined **26–022** in art.107(1), in breach of the prohibition in art.108(3), it is in principle obliged to order its recovery—as the ECJ determined in its *SFEI* judgment. However, there can be exceptional circumstances in which the recovery of unlawful state aid would not be appropriate.[102] The principles of this judgment, as confirmed and elaborated in later case law, have been detailed and expanded by the Commission in its Notice on the enforcement of state aid law by national courts. As is explained in this notice, recovery is not the only means of guaranteeing the prohibition. The State may also, and independently of any obligation to recover the aid, be subject to claims for damages brought in the national courts on the basis of EU law by competitors who incur loss or damage as a result of unlawfully implementing the aid. Other remedies include preventing the payment of unlawful aid, recovery of illegality interest and interim measures against unlawful aid.[103] In the *CELF* case the ECJ ruled that after a final positive Commission decision the national court is no longer under an EU law obligation to order full recovery. However, in such circumstances the national court must order the aid recipient to pay interest in respect of the period of unlawfulness.[104]

---

[100] Case C–354/90 *Fédération Nationale v France* [1991] E.C.R. I–5505.
[101] Joined Cases C–6 and 9/90 *Francovich and Bonifaci v Italy* [1991] E.C.R. I–5357.
[102] Case C–39/94 *SFEI v La Poste* [1996] E.C.R. I–3547 at para.67. It is noteworthy that in his Opinion in this case, AG Jacobs considered that there may well be exceptional circumstances in which recovery could not be required by the national courts, even if the aid was not notified.
[103] [2009] O.J. C85/1 at para.26.
[104] Case C–199/06 *CELF v SIDE* [2008] E.C.R. I–469 at para.52.

CHAPTER 27

JUDICIAL PROTECTION*

1. INTRODUCTION 27–001
2. ENFORCEMENT BY THE COMMISSION BEFORE THE ECJ 27–003
   Articles 258 and 108(2) (second subparagraph) TFEU 27–003
   Powers of the Commission in special cases 27–006
   Article 260 TFEU 27–008
3. ACTION AGAINST THE COMMISSION 27–012
   Action for annulment (Article 263 TFEU) 27–012
   Action by complainants for failure to act (Article 265 TFEU) 27–037
   Interim measures (Articles 278/279 TFEU) 27–042
   Action for damages (Article 288 TFEU) 27–048
4. THE ROLE OF NATIONAL COURTS 27–050
   General 27–050
   Direct effect of Article 108(3) TFEU 27–053
   The enforcement of negative Commission decisions 27–057
   The implementation of positive Commission decisions 27–060

1. INTRODUCTION

27–001   The Commission, the Union Courts and the national courts have separate but
complementary roles in the application of the state aid rules. The Commission is
the administrative authority that has the exclusive power, under the supervision
of the General Court and the Court of Justice (ECJ), to decide whether aid is
compatible with the internal market. It enjoys to a varying degree (depending on
the issues concerned) discretion where it involves difficult economic appraisals,
in determining whether a particular measure contains an element of state aid
within the meaning of art.107(1) TFEU and even more so in deciding whether
any of the exemptions, as laid down in art.107(3), apply to the measure in
question. Judicial control, as described below, by the Union Courts is a complex
matter, not least because of the Commission's discretion. The procedural requirements to be followed in state aid decisions are, to a certain extent, specified in
legislation (see Ch.26 describing the Council Regulation 659/1999, as well as the

* Leo Flynn and Tom Ottervanger

1022

implementing Commission Regulation 794/2004, laying down detailed rules for the application of art.108, partly codifying existing procedures and partly introducing new instruments to strengthen the control of aid).

National courts are responsible for the protection of rights and the enforcement of the duties of the Member States, usually at the behest of private parties. Where the Commission has not issued group exemptions (as discussed in para.27–037) their role is limited to the enforcement of the prohibition laid down in the last sentence of art.108(3). National courts must draw the appropriate conclusion from an infringement of the prohibition on implementation of planned aid in accordance with national law (as regards the validity of aid measures, the recovery of aid and interim measures). Only the Commission can decide that state aid is compatible with the internal market, but national courts can consider whether a measure constitutes state aid within the meaning of art.107(1). In applying art.107(1), they may, and sometimes must, refer preliminary questions to the ECJ pursuant to art.267 TFEU; in the meantime, interim measures may be ordered if necessary to safeguard the interests of the parties pending final judgment.

The following sections shall first examine the role of the ECJ in enforcement **27–002** actions by the Commission and, secondly, the role of both Union Courts in supervising the activities of the Commission as the authority responsible for the implementation of the state aid rules, with special emphasis on the position of complainants. Finally, this chapter shall cover the role of the national courts. This chapter shall not deal in great detail with actions before the national courts by Member States against the beneficiary, or by competitors against the Member State or the beneficiary, to obtain *recovery* of illegal aid, as these issues are dealt with separately in Ch.27. For the administrative procedure to be followed by the Commission, and the position of interested parties (beneficiaries, competitors, trade associations) during that procedure, reference is made to Ch.26. Inevitably there is some overlap between chapters.

2. ENFORCEMENT BY THE COMMISSION BEFORE THE ECJ

Articles 258 and 108(2) (second subparagraph) TFEU

If a Member State refuses to notify aid, it fails to fulfil an obligation under the **27–003** Treaty. The Commission may then commence an action under art.258 against the defaulting Member State. If the state does not settle the matter in the first phase of the procedure, the Commission may bring the matter before the Court.[1] Note that the Commission does not have the choice between the art.258 and the art.108(2) procedures in assessing whether or not aid is compatible with the internal market. The Commission must use the formal investigation procedure of art.108(2), rather than the procedure of art.258, if it wishes to prohibit aid

[1] Case C–61/90 *Commission v Greece* [1992] E.C.R. I–2407.

(because that procedure provides all parties concerned with more guarantees than the preliminary phase of the art.258 procedure).[2]

As has been outlined above (see Ch.26 as well as art.11 of Regulation 659/1999), when finding that aid is granted or altered without having been notified or during the procedure under art.108(2) and (3), the Commission may issue an interim order requiring the Member State to suspend the aid, after enabling the State to express its views. If the State does not comply, the Commission may bring the matter before the Court. The instrument of interim orders or injunctions is not a novelty. As Advocate General Jacobs pointed out in *Boussac*,[3] the Court had already accepted that the Commission can obtain such orders brought under art.279, in connection with art.107(3) or art.258. For example, in Joined Cases 31/77R and 53/77R—*Commission v UK*,[4] the UK government had implemented a subsidy for pig producers without awaiting a Commission decision. Thereupon the Commission required the United Kingdom to terminate the subsidy and, when the Member State did not comply, began an enforcement action under art.108(2), second subparagraph. It also requested the Court to make an interim order under art.279. The action was upheld by the Court. The whole procedure, from introduction of the aid to the Court's injunction, took only a few months.[5]

27–004   If the Member State concerned fails to conform with a negative decision within the term prescribed by the Commission, the latter (as well as other Member States) may refer the matter directly to the ECJ in accordance with art.108(2), second subparagraph. The special procedure derogates from the general procedure under art.258. In such infringement procedures the Member State may raise, in its defence, issues relating to the interpretation of the decision or the execution thereof, e.g. whether the state has taken sufficient steps to order recovery.[6] The State cannot challenge the validity of the decision after the expiry of the two-month period of art.263. Such a "defensive challenge" is not permitted because the system of remedies set up by the Treaty distinguishes between the actions under arts 258 and 259 TFEU and those under arts 263 and 265 TFEU. They have different objectives. A Member State cannot argue the unlawfulness of a negative decision in an action for a declaration that it has failed to implement that decision. This could only be different if the decision "contained particularly serious and manifest defects such that it could be deemed non-

---

[2] Case 290/83 *Commission v France* [1985] E.C.R. 439.
[3] [1990] E.C.R. I–307.
[4] [1977] E.C.R. 921.
[5] Other "pre-*Boussac*" examples: Case 70/72 *Commission v Germany (Kohlgesetz)* [1973] E.C.R. 813 at para.20, where the Court stated that "Article [108(3)] involves the power of the Commission to take immediate interim measures"; and Case 171/83 R *Commission v France* [1983] E.C.R. 2621.
[6] See, for example Case C–280/95 *Commission v Italy* [1998] E.C.R. I–259. In that procedure under art.108(2), second subparagraph, the Court examined whether recovery was absolutely impossible.

existent".[7] The only defence available to a Member State opposing an application by the Commission under art.108(2) TFEU is to plead that it was absolutely impossible for it to implement the decision.[8] The condition that it be absolutely impossible to implement a decision is not fulfilled where the Member State merely informs the Commission of the difficulties it faces, without taking any real steps to recover the aid from the undertakings concerned, and without proposing to the Commission any alternative arrangements for implementing the decision which could have enabled those difficulties to be overcome.[9] Thus, where Italian courts had interrupted recovery proceedings launched by that Member State against beneficiaries to give effect to a negative decision, the Court found the national interim suspension decisions were not taken in compliance with the criteria in *Zuckerfabrik*[10] and *Atlanta*[11] and therefore ruled that Italy was in breach of its obligation to ensure immediate and effective recovery[12] (see further para.26–013).

It is settled case law that private parties are not entitled to bring proceedings **27–005** pursuant to art.263 or art.265 TFEU against the refusal by the Commission to institute proceedings before the ECJ under art.258 against a Member State to fulfil its Treaty obligations. The Commission enjoys a discretionary power in deciding whether to bring such proceedings. In the 1990 *Boussac* case the Court decided that the means of redress provided under art.108(2), second subparagraph, is no more than a variant of the art.258 action for a declaration of failure to fulfil Treaty obligations.

Therefore, in *AITEC*[13] the General Court found that the Commission is not bound to commence proceedings provided for in art.108(2), second subparagraph, but "has a wide discretion which excludes the right of any individual to require it to adopt a specific position" (para.66). In that case, the action for annulment under art.263 of the refusal of the Commission to bring an action before the ECJ under art.108(2), second subparagraph, on account of Greece's failure to comply with a negative decision, was held to be inadmissible. The claim for a declaration of failure to act under art.265 was also held to be inadmissible. The Court left open the possibility that, in certain cases, the Commission may be bound, in the interests of sound administration and transparency, to inform a complainant of the steps taken in consequence of a negative decision. However, the Court found that in the present case the Commission undertook an adequate exchange of information with the applicant.

[7] Case C–404/97 *Commission v Portuguese Republic* [2000] E.C.R. I–4897.
[8] Case C–214/07 *Commission v France* [2008] E.C.R. I–8357, para.44.
[9] Joined Cases C–485/03 to C–490/03 *Commission v Spain* [2006] E.C.R. I–11887, para.74.
[10] Joined Cases C–143/88 and C–92/89 *Zuckerfabrik Süderdithmarschen and Zuckerfabrik Soest* [1991] E.C.R. I–415.
[11] Case C–465/93 *Atlanta Fruchthandelsgesellschaft and Others(I)* [1995] E.C.R. I–3761.
[12] See Case C–304/09 *Commission v Italy* [2010] E.C.R. I–0000, judgment of December 22, 2010, paras 44–55; and Case C–302/09 *Commission v Italy* [2011] E.C.R. I–0000, judgment of October 6, 2011, paras 46–55.
[13] Case T–277/94 [1996] E.C.R. II–351.

Powers of the Commission in special cases

27–006   *British Aerospace and Rover*[14] dealt with the question whether the Commission has the power, without opening the procedure of art.108(2), to adopt a decision in which it establishes that the conditions laid down in an earlier decision have not been observed. In 1988 the Commission had approved aid subject to certain conditions.[15] In 1990 the Commission found that benefits were granted that were incompatible with the internal market since they did not respect the terms of the 1988 decision and by letter of July 17, 1990[16] ordered recovery. The Commission had not reopened the procedure of art.108(2) and considered the letter not as an independent decision but as an extension of its previous decision. The Court, in annulment proceedings against the 1990 "decision", held that the Commission should have brought proceedings before the Court against the Member State concerned directly under art.108(2), second subparagraph, without first being required to initiate the procedure under the first subparagraph of art.108(2) or under art.258. If, however, the Commission considered that new aid had been paid that was not previously notified or examined in an earlier investigation, it was obliged to open a new inquiry pursuant to art.108(2), first subparagraph, and give notice to allow the parties concerned and third parties to submit their comments. Failure to open that procedure will result in the annulment of the decision.[17]

The Commission took the lessons learned from the *Rover* case at heart, as can be seen from Case C–36/00 *Kingdom of Spain v Commission*. The Commission, after having opened the procedure under art.108(2) TFEU, had found that certain special tax credits for Spanish shipyards were not in accordance with the conditions of an earlier decision authorising aid and were incompatible with the internal market, and therefore were to be recovered. The Court did not accept the plea by the Spanish Government that the Commission had to review the measures as existing aid rather than as new aid. The aid at issue, according to the Court, was not covered by the authorising decision so the Commission was right to institute the second phase procedure.[18]

27–007   That situation must be distinguished from one in which, because the Court has annulled a negative decision, the Commission prepares a new decision. In Case C–415/96[19] the Court held, in annulment proceedings brought by Spain against such a "new" decision,[20] that the consequence of the Court's earlier annulment of the previous decision[21] is that the Commission must comply with that judgment when it seeks to replace the previous decision. In doing so, the Commission

[14] Case C–294/90 *British Aerospace and Rover v Commission* [1992] E.C.R. 493.
[15] Dec. 89/58/EEC [1989] O.J. L25/92.
[16] [1991] O.J. C21/2.
[17] See also the *Air France* case: Joined Cases T–371 and T–394/94 *British Airways v Commission* [1998] E.C.R. II–2405.
[18] Case C–36/00 *Kingdom of Spain v Commission* [2002] E.C.R. I–3243.
[19] *Spain v Commission* [1998] E.C.R. I–6993. See also Ch.25, s.3.
[20] Dec. 97/242/EC [1997] O.J. L96/30.
[21] Dec. 92/317/EEC [1992] O.J. L171/54.

is entitled to resume the procedure at the very point where the illegality had occurred. The Commission, therefore, is not necessarily required to open a new inquiry and go through the whole art.108(2) procedure. In the case at hand, the Court had in the earlier judgment annulled the previous decision because the Commission had not given adequate reasons for its view that a restructuring plan would not ensure the viability of the beneficiary of the aid concerned. The requirements of the first paragraph of art.266 are then satisfied if, in the new decision, the reasons for that view are adequately spelled out, without it being necessary to repeat the whole procedure. Of course, the Member State and the beneficiary are entitled to challenge again the adequacy of the reasons in the "new" decision.

In one of the *TWD Deggendorf* cases, the question was raised whether the Commission has the power to approve payment of lawful and compatible aid but to make authorisation of payment conditional on repayment of old aid that was prohibited.[22] The General Court and the ECJ upheld the Commission's decision. New aid cannot be compatible with the internal market as long as old aid is not repaid, since the failure to repay the unlawful aid constituted an essential factor when examining the compatibility of new aid.

Article 260 TFEU

Article 260 requires Member States to take the necessary measures to comply with judgments of the Court. If a State does not comply with a judgment in an enforcement action under art.108(2), second subparagraph, or art.258, the Commission may bring a second action.[23] Under the procedure of art.260(2) TFEU for infringement of art.260(1) TFEU the Commission may, in the event of continued non-compliance with the original Court ruling, request the Court to impose a lump sum or penalty payment on the Member State concerned. The Court's jurisdiction is unlimited. In some cases[24] the Commission has started the administrative procedure in accordance with art.260(2) TFEU that could lead to a request to the Court to impose financial penalties.   **27–008**

The Court gave its first ruling under art.260(2) TFEU in the field of state aid against Greece in Case C–369/07.[25] The Court ruled that the Member State had failed to comply with the earlier ruling in Case C–415/03 that it had not executed the recovery obligation laid down in a Commission decision finding three aid measures implemented in favour of Olympic Airways to be incompatible with the internal market. In Case C–369/07 while Greece accepted that the aid had not been recovered from Olympic Airways at the date of the Commission's reasoned   **27–009**

---

[22] Joined Cases T–244/93 and 486/93 [1995] E.C.R. II–2265; upheld on appeal in Case 355/95P [1997] E.C.R. I–2549.

[23] For an example in the area of state aids: Case C–375/89 *Commission v Belgium* [1991] E.C.R. I–367, Summ. pub.

[24] See Report on Competition Policy 2001 at para.486; Report on Competition Policy 2002 at para.568; Report on Competition Policy 2004 at para.615.

[25] Case C–369/07 *Commission v Greece* [2009] E.C.R. I–5703.

opinion,[26] it claimed to have recovered the aid prior to the hearing of the case before the Court, by means of a set-off of the amounts to be recovered against amounts Greece claimed to owe to the airline as a result of arbitration proceedings. The Court held that where the Commission had shown that there had been a breach of EU law by the Member State, the burden of proof was on the Member State to demonstrate that breach had been brought to an end. In that context, the Court recalled that where reimbursement of illegal state aid takes a form other than that of a cash payment, the Member State must show that the means of repayment chosen are sufficiently transparent to allow the Commission to satisfy itself that the distortion of competition caused by the aid has been eliminated. The Court considered that Greece had shown that such repayment had been made in respect of an incompatible capital injection to be recovered but had not done so in respect of aid arising from persistent non-payment of a national tax and from non-payment of airport rental fees.

27–010　　In Case C–369/07 the Commission sought the imposition of a penalty payment of €53,611 for each day from the Court's judgment that its earlier ruling had not been executed. Penalty payments will be ordered by the Court only if the failure to implement the earlier ruling persists up to the date on which the Court examines the facts. Since the aid arising from two measures had not been recovered by Greece when the Court examined the facts, the Court imposed a penalty payment of €16,000 for each day of delay in executing the judgment in Case C–415/03. It fixed that amount in light of the duration of the infringement (more than four years), the seriousness of the infringement (based on the vital nature of the Treaty rules on State aid; the inherently cross-border nature of the air transport market; and relatively small proportion of the aid that had been repaid) and the ability of the Member State to pay. The Court's description of the seriousness of the infringement seems applicable to almost all cases where a Member State is previously found to have infringed its obligations to execute a state aid decision, since its analysis relies heavily on the importance of the state aid rules ensuring undistorted competition in the internal market.

27–011　　Under art.260(2) TFEU the Court is free to impose a lump sum payment in addition to or instead of a penalty payment. The Commission sought both remedies against Greece in Case C–369/07. The Court agreed that the effective prevention of future repetition of similar infringements of EU law required the adoption of a dissuasive measure, such as a lump sum payment. The Court has a broad discretion in setting the amount of the lump sum, and in Case C–369/07 it ordered Greece to pay €2 million to the Commission, approximately one-seventh of the amount which the Commission had sought.

---

[26] Prior to the entry into force of the Lisbon Treaty, as in Case C–369/07, art.228 EC (the predecessor to art.260 TFEU) required the Commission to send the Member State a reasoned opinion fixing a deadline for compliance with the earlier judgment before it could lodge an action for failure to execute that previous ruling at the Court. That requirement no longer exists as of December 1, 2009.

3. ACTION AGAINST THE COMMISSION

Action for annulment (Article 263 TFEU)

Admissibility (general). The conditions of admissibility of an action under art.263 are a matter of public policy and the Court may examine them on its own motion.[27]   **27–012**

In order to be a challengeable act, the contested measure must not be purely preparatory or merely confirmatory but must bring about a distinct change in the legal position of the applicant. Those measures which definitively determine the position of the Commission upon the conclusion of an administrative procedure, and which are intended to have binding legal effects capable of affecting the interests of the complainant, are open to challenge. By contrast, it is not possible to challenge intermediate measures whose purpose is to prepare for the final decision, which do not have those effects.

A decision of the Commission to open the art.108(2) procedure may be challenged on the basis of art.263 under certain conditions.[28] The Court ruled that such a decision amounts to a prohibition to grant aid before the art.108(2) procedure is completed. Citing its judgment in Case C–354/90,[29] the Court ruled that the decision to open the art.108(2) procedure may indeed have legal effects on the Member State, since the Commission, as opposed to the national governments, had identified the aid measures as "new" aid. Therefore, the opening of the art.108(2) procedure would block the (further) granting of aid by a Member State that considers it is entitled to do so. The validity of such a decision may be challenged in proceedings before the Court if challenge of the final decision would not offer adequate legal protection. The Court found that to be the case since the effects of the opening of the procedure were irreversible. The findings in those cases apply mutatis mutandis to (potential) aid recipients. Given that aid could not be legally disbursed to them until the Commission adopts a final decision, they too satisfy the test applied by the Court in those two cases.   **27–013**

The *review* by the Court of the legality of such an opening decision may only concern the qualification of the measure as "new" or "existing" aid where the status of the measure is disputed by the Member State and not the compatibility with the Treaty.[30] In *Alcoa v Commission* (Case C–194/09P, July 21, 2011) the Court held that where the applicant in an appeal against a decision to initiate the investigation procedure challenges the assessment by the Commission classifying the disputed measure as state aid, review by the court is limited to ascertaining whether or not the Commission has made a manifest error of assessment. A

---

[27] Case T–55/99 *CETM v Commission* [2000] E.C.R. II–3207.

[28] Case C–312/90 *Spain v Commission* [1992] E.C.R. I–4117, and Case C–47/91 *Italy v Commission* [1992] E.C.R. I–4145. Also, for example, Case T–123/97 *Salomon v Commission* [1999] E.C.R. II–2925 at para.54.

[29] Case C–354/90 *Fédération nationale du commerce extérieur des produits alimentaires and others v France* [1991] E.C.R. 5523.

[30] Joined Cases T–126/96 and 127/96 *BFM v Commission* [1998] E.C.R. II–3437. See more recently, Case T–332/06 *Alcoa Transformazioni v Commission* [2009] E.C.R. II–29* Summ.pub, paras 35 and 36.

decision to initiate a formal investigation procedure can also be the object of an application for interim measures.[31]

On the other hand, where the Commission decides to open the formal investigation procedure in regard to compatibility only and that decision is disputed by a competitor who alleges that the Commission erred when it found that a precondition for compatibility was met, the opening decision does not have such legal effects independent of the final decision. Such a finding must be considered as a provisional one, on which the competitor can make observations during the art.108(2) procedure. As a result the opening decision is merely preparatory and so is not a challengeable act.[32]

Where the Commission addresses an information injunction to a Member State under art.10(3) of Regulation 659/1999, that act, although it may be considered to be a step in the internal procedure leading to a decision and not a final measure in its own right, is nevertheless an attackable act. According to the ECJ, such a decision is intended to produce legal effects independent from the final decision terminating the state aid investigation and therefore constitutes an act open to challenge under art.263 TFEU.[33]

By contrast, where the Commission writes to a Member State in the context of monitoring the enforcement of a negative decision requiring recovery, informing that Member State that full execution of the recovery decision requires reimbursement of illegal aid from a given beneficiary, that letter is not an attackable act which the beneficiary in question can challenge.[34] The letter does no more than recall the obligations flowing from the earlier recovery decision.

27–014   Even if the contested measure is a challengeable act, an action for annulment is admissible only insofar as the applicant (if it is not a Member State) has an interest in the annulment of the contested measure. Such an interest presupposes that the annulment of the measure must of itself be capable of having legal consequences so that the action must be likely, if successful, to procure a benefit for the party who brought it. That requirement to have a demonstrable interest does not apply to actions brought by Member States.[35]

27–015   As a result, if aid has been declared *compatible* with the internal market, an action brought by the beneficiary will normally be inadmissible because the applicant does not have a vested and present interest in bringing the procedures. In Case T–141/03 *Sniace v Commission*,[36] the applicant asserted that the Commission had erred by classifying a loan as state aid, even though the measure was

---

[31] Joined Cases T–195/01R and T–207/01R *Government of Gibraltar v Commission* [2001] E.C.R. II–3915.

[32] Case T–87/09 *Andersen v Commission* [2009] E.C.R. II–225* Summ.pub, paras 52–62.

[33] Joined Cases C–463/10P and C–475/10P *Deutsche Post and Germany v Commission* [2010] E.C.R. II–0000, judgment of October 13, 2011, paras 41–45.

[34] Case T–44/05 *SP Entertainment Development v Commission* [2007] E.C.R. II–19*, Summ. pub., paras 21–23.

[35] Case T–233/04 *Netherlands v Commission* [2008] E.C.R. II–591, para.37; Joined Cases T–309/04, T–317/04, T–329/04 and T–336/04 *TV2/Danmark and others v Commission* [2008] E.C.R. II–2935, paras 63 and 64; Joined Cases T–425/04, T–444/04, T–450/04, Case T–456/04 *France and others v Commission* [2010] E.C.R. II–2099, para.120.

[36] [2005] E.C.R. II–1197.

unconditionally approved. The Court dismissed the action as inadmissible since the applicant had not shown that there was a concrete risk that competitors would start litigation before the national courts based on the last sentence of art.108(3); and even if they did, all defences would be available and the national court could make a reference for a preliminary ruling concerning the validity of the Commission decision. Since, according to the Court, the action was inadmissible, the "Deggendorf-doctrine" (see paras 27–007 and 27–043 et seq.) would not apply. Equally, there is an absence of an interest where applicants are not entitled to benefit from any aid declared incompatible by the Commission's final decision.[37] There is also a lack of interest for applicants who grant the aid in question (i.e. public authorities which are not the Member State) to challenge the finding that aid is present, if that aid is declared compatible with the internal market.[38] The General Court has additionally ruled that the applicant has no interest where it challenges a commitment offered by a Member State in light of which the Commission decides not to open the formal investigation procedure.[39]

Conversely, an applicant who is the beneficiary of an allegedly existing aid has an interest in bringing proceedings to challenge the qualification of assistance as aid or as new aid, even if it does not challenge the Commission's decision that the assistance in question is aid compatible with the internal market.[40] Equally, an applicant who is the beneficiary of an aid found to be incompatible but for which no recovery is required has an interest in bringing proceedings to challenge the qualification of assistance as aid, as well as of challenging the Commission's decision that the aid in question is not compatible with the internal market.[41] In the same way, where an applicant challenges a Commission decision requiring recovery of aid for which it is jointly and severally liable, it retains an interest even where the entirety of the aid has been recovered from other named beneficiaries in circumstances where the latter can still challenge the national recovery measures.[42] Similarly, a complainant has an interest in challenging the commitments accepted by the Commission as a basis for finding aid to be compatible; following annulment, the Commission would have to assess whether it will be appropriate to seek additional commitments.[43]

If the applicant is challenging a decision finding aid partially compatible and partially incompatible, it seems to have an interest to challenge the decision as a whole.[44] In order for the Commission to show that an applicant (potential

27–016

---

[37] Case T–189/08 *Forum 187 ASBL v Commission* [2010] E.C.R. II–1039, para.79; Case T–94/08 *Centre de coordination Carrefour SNC v Commission* [2010] E.C.R. II–1015, para.58.

[38] Joined Cases C–443/08 and T–455/08 *Freistaat Sachsen v Commission* [2011] E.C.R. II–0000, judgment of March 24, 2011, paras 47–68.

[39] Case T–6/06 *wheyco v Commission*, Order of July 9, 2007, unpublished, paras 95 and 96.

[40] Joined Cases T–265/04, T–292/04 and T–504/04 *Tirrenia di Navigazione v Commission* [2009] E.C.R. II–21*, Summ.pub., paras 63–82.

[41] Joined Cases T–425/04, T–444/04, T–450/04, Case T–456/04 *France and others v Commission* [2010] E.C.R. II–2099, paras 121–124.

[42] Case T–291/06 *Operator ARP v Commission* [2009] E.C.R. II–2275, para.27.

[43] Case T–354/05 *TF 1 v Commission* [2009] E.C.R. II–471, paras 89–91.

[44] Joined Cases T–309/04, T–317/04, T–329/04 and T–336/04 *TV2/Danmark and others v Commission* [2008] E.C.R. II–2935, para.71.

beneficiary challenging a negative decision) has no interest, it must adduce proof that annulment will not procure a benefit.[45]

27–017   Commission decisions on the basis of art.108(2) declaring aid *incompatible* with the internal market may be challenged by a Member State, and by natural and legal persons who are the beneficiaries of the aid where they will be able to show that the contested decision is of direct and individual concern to them.[46] Natural and legal persons (i.e., applicants other than the Member State to whom the contested decision is addressed) will only have standing if they meet the requirements of art.263, fourth paragraph, i.e. if the Commission decision prohibiting a national measure, usually addressed to a Member State, is of direct and individual concern to the applicant.

The standing of *third parties*, usually competitors, to bring proceedings against a state aid decision raises complex issues. The case law has introduced distinctions between applicants seeking annulment on the ground that the Commission breached the obligation to initiate the formal art.108(2) ("second phase") procedure or has infringed the procedural safeguards of art.108(2), or on the ground that the decision whereby aid is approved (under art.108(3) or following the art.108(2) procedure) infringes Union law (i.e. calling into question the merits of the decision). That area of law is further complicated by the distinction between individual aid measures and general aid measures; in addition, the position of associations representing third parties also raises special issues of admissibility. Paragraph 27–021 will deal specifically with the admissibility of third-party applicants that have been complaining about aid to (a) competitor(s).

27–018   The Union Courts take a somewhat restrictive view where (potential) aid beneficiaries challenge negative decisions declaring *general aid measures* incompatible with the internal market (and, where appropriate, requiring recovery). The Court in *Gebroeders van der Kooy*[47] held that a Dutch measure granting aid to horticulturists was of a general nature. Consequently, the Court denied that Van der Kooy, one of the recipients of the alleged aid, was directly and individually concerned in the meaning of art.263. Some two decades after that original judgment, the Court continues to confirm in its rulings that an undertaking cannot, in principle, contest a Commission decision prohibiting a sectoral aid scheme if it is concerned by that decision solely by virtue of belonging to the sector in question and being a potential beneficiary of the scheme.[48]

---

[45] Case C–519/07P *Commission v Koninklijke FrieslandCampina* [2009] E.C.R. I–8495, paras 66 and 67.

[46] The Commission accepted that point without dispute in Case 730/79 *Philip Morris* [1980] E.C.R. 2671. Note that an action against a decision that is purely confirmatory of an earlier decision is inadmissible only if the decision confirmed has become final in relation to the person concerned through not having been challenged before the Court within the required period. Where the confirmed decision has not become final, the person concerned is entitled to challenge the original decision, the confirmatory decision or both: Case T–188/95 *Noord-West Brabant* [1998] E.C.R. II–3713 at para.108.

[47] Joined Cases 67, 68 and 70/85 *Kwekerij Gebroeders van der Kooy* [1988] E.C.R. 219.

[48] Case C–519/07P *Commission v Koninklijke FrieslandCampina* [2009] E.C.R. I–8495, para.53; Case T–309/02 *Acegas-APS v Commission* [2009] E.C.R. II–1809, paras 50–54; Case T–300/02 *AMGA v Commission* [2009] E.C.R. II–1737, para.50.

At the same time, however, the Courts have held, explicitly or implicitly, that the actions by the actual beneficiaries (or their representative organisations, see below) of general aid schemes against recovery orders are admissible where recovery has been ordered by the Commission.[49] Admittedly, the Court has also held that it was "not self-evident" that an action against a decision addressed to Italy concerning aid schemes intended for categories of persons defined in a general manner would have been admissible.[50] The Court was concerned in that case with the issue of whether a national court could refer an issue of validity of a Commission decision where the applicant before the national court had brought proceedings before the General Court (which were dismissed as being out of time, without the question of standing being resolved). Since it took a narrow view of the "*Deggendorf*-doctrine" (see paras 28–007 and 28–043 et seq.), there was no need for the Court to investigate the issue of standing before the General Court in any great detail.

The General Court also accepts, with the approval of the Court, that the applicant is individually concerned if it had already applied for the aid which was prohibited and had taken all measures needed to qualify for the aid in relation to which the national authorities had no discretion.[51]

As to *professional associations*, the Union Courts have in a series of cases **27–019** established that actions brought by an association (which, as is usually the case in state aid matters that are normally addressed to a Member State, is not the addressee of the Commission Decision) are admissible where the association has a particular interest in acting (especially because its negotiating position may be affected by the decision). In *Gebroeders van der Kooy*[52] the Court recognised the standing of the Landbouwschap, an organisation of general interest, because it was negotiating gas tariffs (that were held to be incompatible with the internal market) on behalf of horticulturists. The Court reached the same conclusion with respect to the Comité International de la rayonne et des fibres synthetiques (CIRFS), an association of the main producers of synthetic fibres, because it had been in close contact with the Commission, both in setting up the aid discipline and during the administrative procedure preceding the Court case.[53]

However, in *Aktiongemeischaft Recht und Eigentum*, concerning a decision authorising aid without initiating the second phase following a negative decision based on art.108(2) EC, the Court made clear that even the active participation of an association representing third-party competitors in the previous art.108(2)

---

[49] Case T–55/99 *CETM v Commission* [2000] E.C.R. II–3207; Joined Cases C–15/98 and C–105/99 *Italy and Sardegna Lines v Commission* [2000] E.C.R. I–8855; Joined Cases C–71/09P, C–73/09P and C–76/09P *Comitato "Venezia vuole vivere" v Commission* [2011] E.C.R. I–0000, judgment of June 9, 2011, paras 51–66; Joined Cases T–227/01 to T–229/01, T–265/01, T–266/01 and T–270/01 *Diputación Foral de Alava and Gobierno Vasco v Commission* [2009] E.C.R. II–3029, paras 113–115; Case T–335/08 *BNP Paribas v Commission* [2010] E.C.R. II–0000, judgment of July 1, 2010, para.67.
[50] Joined Cases C–346/03 and C–529/03 *Atzeni and others* [2006] E.C.R. I–1875.
[51] Case C–519/07 P *Commission v Koninklijke FrieslandCampina* [2009] E.C.R. I–8495, paras 55 to 58.
[52] Joined Cases 67, 68 and 70/85 *Kwekerij Gebroeders van der Kooy* [1988] E.C.R. 219 at 268.
[53] Case C–313/90 *CIRFS v Commission* [1993] E.C.R. I–1125.

procedure and in discussions concerning implementation of the decision, playing an important role as interlocutor, is insufficient to render it an individually concerned negotiator of the same kind as the Landbouwschap and CIRFS. The mere exercise of those procedural rights does not give the association, as such, standing to attack a decision adopted by the Commission under art.108(2) or art.108(3) and addressed to a person other than that association.[54] According to the Court, actions are also admissible where the association has substituted itself for one or more of the members whom it represents on condition that those members were themselves in a position to bring an admissible action.[55] There-fore, as a general rule, an association responsible for protecting the collective interests of companies is, as such, entitled to bring an action for the annulment of a state aid decision only: (i) where the members would have been entitled to do so individually (which means, in the case of third parties, either that they are seeking to safeguard their rights under art.108(2) or, alternatively, that if they call into question the merits of a decision appraising the aid as such, that their position is substantially affected (see further below)); or (ii) where the associa-tion is able to rely on a particular interest in acting, especially because its negotiating position is affected by the measure concerned.[56] The Court confirmed in *3F* that for an association to claim that it was individually concerned by a decision independently of the standing of its members that association would have to show that it was involved in the adoption of the national measure examined in the contested Commission decision or was closely involved in the process by which the Commission adopted the guidelines or other measures on which the Commission based its assessment of compatibility.[57]

27–020   *Regional and local authorities* may also have standing in an action for annulment.[58] For example, in Case T–214/95, the General Court held that the Flemish region was directly and individually concerned since the negative decision prevented it from exercising its own powers which consist of granting the aid in question.[59] In a case where the Commission had decided that aid by Germany for various investment projects of Volkswagen in Saxony was incom-patible with art.107(3)(c) TFEU, the question arose whether a challenge to the validity of that decision by the Freistaat Sachsen (Free State of Saxony) was

[54] Case C–78/03P *Commission v Germany and Aktiongemeischaft Recht und Eigentum* [2005] E.C.R. I–10737.
[55] Case T–380/94 *Aiuffas and AKT v Commission* [1996] E.C.R. II–2170; Joined Cases T–447, 448 and 449/93 *AITEC v Commission* [1995] E.C.R. II–1971; Case T–455/05 *Associazione italiana del risparmio gestito and Fineco Asset Management v Commission* [2009] E.C.R. II–289.
[56] Case T–55/99 *CETM v Commission* [2000] E.C.R. II–3207; Case T–292/02 *Confservizi v Commission* [2009] E.C.R. II–1659.
[57] Case C–319/07P *3F v Commission* [2009] E.C.R. I–5963, paras 91–95.
[58] Cases 62/87 and 72/87 *Executif Regional Wallon and Glaverbel v Commission* [1988] E.C.R. 1573.
[59] [1998] E.C.R. II–717. See also: Case T–155/96 R *Stadt Mainz v Commission* [1996] E.C.R. II–1655; and Case T–238/97 *Comunidad Autonoma de Cantabria v Council* [1998] E.C.R. II–2271.

admissible. The General Court[60] concluded that Saxony was "individually concerned" by the Decision, because Saxony (like the other Länder) has its own regional aid programmes and is the body that must initiate recovery procedures; the Decision therefore affects not only the socio-economic situation in its territory but also the exercise of its autonomous powers. Since the German national authorities did not exercise any discretion when communicating the Decision to Saxony, it is also "directly concerned". Conversely, there is no such individual concern for public law entities whose rights derive from the State or from an autonomous territorial entity and which do not enjoy financial autonomy.[61]

It is interesting to note that in matters of state aid, liability always lies with the Member State concerned, irrespective of the public authority that granted the aid. Regional and local authorities do not play an independent role in the administrative proceedings. However, compromise deals between the Commission and the Member State concerned become vulnerable where a regional or local authority can challenge a Commission decision before the Union Courts. Under the ECSC Treaty, regional and local authorities were not entitled to bring an action seeking annulment of a state aid decision adopted under that Treaty.[62]

As to *employees organisations* and similar bodies, the General Court, in a case brought by an association formed to protect the rights of the members of a Spanish mutual social welfare association established by Telefonica de España for the benefit of its (former) employees, held as follows: "since the applicant is in fact an association of employees of the undertaking which allegedly benefited from a state aid, it in no way competes with that undertaking and cannot establish an interest in bringing proceedings on account of competitive effects". Therefore, the applicant was not admissible.[63] The same conclusion was reached in 1998 by the General Court concerning an annulment action brought by several associations representing the interests of the employees of an aid recipient.[64] The mere fact that trade unions and similar organisations might be considered as "parties concerned" in the contentious procedure under art.108(2) and might be entitled to submit arguments of a social nature, was considered insufficient to hold that they are individually concerned. Similarly, in *Comité d'éntreprises de la Société francaise de productions*,[65] the Court rejected an appeal by the works council of SFP, a French broadcaster, and a trade union representing the broadcasting sector in France against a judgment of the General Court which had found them not to have standing to challenge a Commission decision ordering recovery

---

[60] Joined Cases T–132/96 and T–143/96 *Freistaat Sachsen v Commission* [1999] E.C.R. II–3663.

[61] Case T–2/08 *Landesanstalt für Medien Nordrhein-Westfalen v Commission* [2009] E.C.R. II–195*, Summ.pub.; Case T–24/06 *MABB v Commission* [2009] E.C.R. II–198*, Summ.pub.

[62] Case T–70/97 *Région Wallone v Commission* [1997] E.C.R. II–1513.

[63] Case T–178/94 *Asociación Telefónica de Mutualistas v Commission* [1997] E.C.R. II–2529.

[64] Case T–189/97 *Comité d'entreprise de la Société française de production v Commission* [1998] E.C.R. II–335. In contrast to Regulation 1064/89 on merger control there are no legislative provisions as regards state aid which expressly grant procedural prerogatives to the recognised representatives of the employees.

[65] Case C–106/98P [2000] E.C.R. I–3659.

of aid from SFP. The Court confirmed that, being persons other than those to whom the decision was addressed, those applicants were not individually concerned within the meaning of the fourth paragraph of art.263. The status of negotiators with regard to the social aspects within the company constituted only a tenuous link with the actual subject-matter.

Whether the Union courts still take such a robust view of trades unions' entitlements when they seek to challenge a state aid decision has been called into question by the judgment on appeal of 2009 in *3F*.[66] There, the Court considered that a trade union might be regarded as 'concerned' within the meaning of art.108(2) TFEU if it shows that there is likely to be a real effect on its situation or on that of its members by the granting of aid.[67] The Court indicated that there could be such a real effect on the situation of a trade union if its competitive situation vis-à-vis other trade unions were to be affected by the aid considered in the contested decision.

27–021 **The position of complainants.** Competitors may become involved in state aid proceedings by lodging a complaint and/or by expressing their views in response to the publication by the Commission of its decision to initiate an investigation pursuant to art.108(2). They may also take action once the art.108(2) procedure has been concluded. Their degree of involvement may have a bearing on the possibilities to challenge a Commission decision. Usually, competitors want to act against positive decisions, i.e. decisions declaring an aid measure compatible with the internal market after the art.108(2) procedure has been brought to an end. They may also specifically wish to challenge the legality of the conditions of authorisation imposed on a Member State.[68] Competitors may not only want to bring proceedings against final decisions but may also want to act against decisions whereby the Commission has decided, for whatever reason, not to open the procedure of art.108(2) ("first phase decisions").

It should be noted at the outset that, as opposed to the regime of arts 101 and 102 TFEU, there were until 1999 no rules in the Treaty or in secondary legislation dealing with the protection of the interests of third parties. The Procedural Regulation, laying down detailed rules for the application of art.108 and discussed above and in Ch.26, deals with the rights of interested parties but has in our view only little effect on this judge-made area of law. The following paragraphs shall discuss the complex case law about the access to the Union judicature for complainants on the basis of the fourth paragraph of art.263. It usually concerns actions against Commission decisions addressed to a Member State. The law distinguishes between, on the one hand, first phase decisions on the basis of art.108(3), finding that aid is compatible with the internal market without initiating the formal review procedure and, on the other hand, second phase decisions on the basis of art.108(2).

[66] Case C–319/07P *3F v Commission* [2009] E.C.R. I–5963.
[67] Case C–319/07P *3F v Commission* [2009] E.C.R. I–5963, paras 33 and 59.
[68] See Joined Cases T–371/94 and T–394/94 *British Airways and others and British Midland v Commission* [1998] E.C.R. II–2405.

As a final general remark, it should be borne in mind that "complainant" in the present context is a synonym for competitors who submit a complaint to the relevant services of the Commission. The mere fact that a natural person, such as an individual taxpayer, or a legal person, such as a non-governmental organisation, lodges a complaint with the Commission does not mean that they may be able to acquire standing since the bare fact of being a complainant does not mean that they can automatically be considered as "parties concerned" within the meaning of art.108(2). Indeed in Case T–188/95 the General Court expressly rejected the proposition that individual taxpayers who object to the manner in which national tax revenue is spent on an alleged illegal aid would be parties concerned for the purposes of the Treaty if they were to send a complaint to the Commission, noting that such an approach would be inconsistent with the case-law on the notion of "parties concerned" and would undermine the requirement of individual concern laid down in the fourth paragraph of art.263.[69]

The position of complainants: first phase decisions. In a series of cases the Union Courts have upheld the rights of third-party complainants to challenge the Commission's decision not to open the adversarial art.108(2) procedure with respect to individual aid measures.[70] Usually the complainant is informed by the Commission in a letter that the Commission has decided, by decision addressed to the Member State concerned, that the measure complained of does not constitute state aid, or is deemed to be compatible with the internal market. **27–022**

In *Cook* and *Matra* the ECJ confirmed that it is only in the contentious phase, when the Commission requires a more complete picture of the affair, that third parties are entitled to put their views forward in writing. The Commission's ruling of compatibility following the preliminary investigation was held to be a reviewable act, since that offered the only procedural guarantee available to third parties. As repeatedly stated by the Union courts, the failure to open the procedure provided for in art.108(2) deprives the parties concerned, within the meaning of that provision, of their rights. Therefore, the "parties concerned" within the meaning of art.108(2) are also considered to be "individually concerned", within the meaning of art.263, by the decision at the end of the preliminary phase not to open the contentious phase, to the extent that they seek to protect their procedural rights under the former provision.[71]

The law has been further clarified by the Court's ruling in *Aktionsgemeinschaft Recht und Eigentum*[72] concerning an appeal by the Commission to set aside the judgment of the General Court at first instance.[73] As to the admissibility of an **27–023**

---

[69] *"Noord-West Brabant"* [1998] E.C.R. II–3713, para.68.

[70] e.g. Case C–181/91 *Cook* [1993] E.C.R. I–2478; Case C–225/91 *Matra* [1993] E.C.R. I–3203; Case T–11/95 *BP Chemicals v Commission* [1998] E.C.R. II–3235.

[71] e.g. Case C–367/95P *Commission v Sytraval* [1998] E.C.R. I–1719 at para.41; Case T–11/95 at para.89; Case T–188/95 at paras 57 and 58.

[72] Case C–78/03P *Commission v Germany and Aktiongemeischaft Recht und Eigentum* [2005] E.C.R. I–10737.

[73] Case T–114/00 *Aktionsgemeinschaft Recht und Eigentum v Commission* [2002] E.C.R. II–5121.

action by a complainant against a first phase decision the Court distinguished the following situations. First, the persons entitled under the fourth paragraph of art.263 to bring proceedings are those persons who seek to safeguard their procedural rights under art.108(2), i.e. the right to receive notice and participate in the procedure by submitting comments on the measure reviewed by the Commission; that procedure is obligatory if the Commission experiences serious difficulties in establishing whether or not there is state aid and whether or not it is compatible with the internal market.[74] Second, however, if the applicant only calls into question the *merits* of the decision as such, the mere fact that the party may be "concerned" for the purposes of art.108(2) cannot suffice to render the action admissible.[75] Therefore, if a complainant challenges a first phase decision on other grounds than the procedural grounds of the *Cook* and *Matra* case law, the traditional test for admissibly of *Plaumann*[76] under the fourth paragraph of art.263 applies. The complainant must then demonstrate a particular status, i.e. that its market position is substantially affected by the aid.[77] The test for a complainant to challenge a first phase decision on its merits is in fact the same test as that which applies for the admissibility of actions against a second phase decision, as will be discussed below.

Thus standing requirements in relation to decisions not to open the contentious phase, if the challenge is based on procedural grounds, are more liberal than in relation to final decisions. A difference in approach can indeed be justified. Protection of third-party interests is otherwise very limited at the initial stage. They do not have the choice about whether or not to co-operate with the Commission which they do have in art.108(2) proceedings. If, in the second phase, they do actively co-operate but do not like the result, they will usually be entitled to challenge the final decision on the basis of art.263. Also, as Advocate General Tesauro pointed out in his Opinion in the *Cook* case, competitors will normally only have a very limited amount of information at their disposal when they seek to challenge a Commission decision not to open art.108(2) proceedings. In those circumstances, it would be difficult for a competitor to show precisely how an aid scheme of which he has only scant details would substantially and adversely affect him under the doctrine.

27–024   It is worth noting that Advocate General Jacobs in his Opinion in *Aktionsgemeinschaft Recht und Eigentum*, discussed above, took a somewhat different position. In his view the *Cook* and *Matra* doctrine confers standing on competitors as "parties concerned" in the meaning of art.108(2), thus departing from the terms of the fourth paragraph of art.263. That lighter test has in his view opened the door too wide under art.108(3). He therefore advocated a return by

[74] Joined Cases C–75/05P and C–80/05P *Germany v Kronofrance and Commission* [2008] E.C.R. I–6619, paras 35–44.
[75] Case T–481/07 *Deltalinqs and SVW v Commission*, Order of December 9, 2009, not published, paras 40–42; Case T–193/06 *TFI v Commission* [2010] E.C.R. II–0000, judgment of September 13, 2010, paras 74–76.
[76] Case 25/62 *Plaumann v Commission* [1963] E.C.R. 95.
[77] T–266/94 *Skibsvaerftsforeningen and others v Commission* [1996] E.C.R. II–1399, paras 45–48.

the Court to the requirement of individual concern (but taking a somewhat broader view, similar as in competition and anti-dumping cases) rather than relying on the different notion of "party concerned". In its ruling the Court, however, did not adopt the solution proposed by the Advocate General and has, so it seems, refused to reconsider *Cook* and *Matra*.

The issue was more recently put to the Court in *Kronoply and Kronotex*, (a case concerning third parties that were not competitors of the aid recipient on the market for the goods which they manufacture but were rival purchasers of the same raw materials as the aid recipient) and it reaffirmed *Cook* and *Matra* once again.[78]

Generally, there shall be no individual concern where a competitor challenges   **27–025** a Commission decision refusing to open the contentious phase with respect to *general aid schemes*. In *Kahn Scheepvaart* the General Court found that in respect of a general aid scheme whose beneficiaries are defined only in general and abstract manner there could not be any competing undertakings who would be a "party concerned" within the meaning of art.108(2), since the existence of an actual beneficiary (and thus an actual competitor, who can be distinguished individually from all other persons and so have standing) presupposes an actual award of individual aid.[79]

However, in *Noord-West Brabant*[80] the General Court held that it was necessary to examine whether "despite the general nature of the aid" the applicant (complainant), who was not a competitor of the beneficiaries of the aid measure concerned, nevertheless has the status of a "party concerned" within the meaning of art.108(2), in which case the action would be admissible. Thus, it was necessary to examine whether the applicant's competitive position was affected. The Court came to the conclusion that, as a result of the aid measure concerned, customers of the applicant, a water distribution company, would be encouraged to switch to self-supply to meet their water needs. The aid directly affected the structure of the market in which the applicant operates and, therefore, its competitive position. Despite the general nature of the aid measure, the applicant was held to be a "party concerned" within the meaning of art.108(2) and, therefore, "directly and individually concerned" by the contested "first phase" decision insofar as the measures affecting its competitive position were concerned.

A refusal by the Commission to propose pursuant to art.108(1) to a Member State, following a complaint by a third party, appropriate measures in respect of an *approved* general aid scheme does not constitute an attackable act for the purposes of art.263. However, it is open to competitors to contest before the national court the decision of the national authorities to grant aid and to call into

---

[78] Case C–83/09P *Commission v Kronoply and Kronotex* [2011] E.C.R. I–0000, judgment of May 24, 2011. That position was also confirmed in Case C–148/09P *Belgium v Deutsche Post* [2011] E.C.R. I–0000, judgment of September 22, 2011.
[79] Case T–398/94 *Kahn Scheepvaart v Commission* [1996] E.C.R. II–477.
[80] Case T–188/95 *"Noord-West Brabant"* [1998] E.C.R. II–3713.

question the validity of the Commission's decision to approve the general aid scheme of which the aid forms part.[81]

27–026 **Standard of review, second phase decisions.** As to the *scope of the Commission's powers* in refusing to open the contentious procedure, the Union Courts and Regulation 659/99 have developed the following principles. The Commission, when finding in favour of a measure, may restrict itself to the preliminary examination only if it is able to satisfy itself in the course of the initial examination that the measure does not constitute aid within the meaning of art.108(1) or, if it does, would in any event be compatible with the internal market.[82] If, on the other hand, the initial examination leads the Commission to the opposite conclusion, or if it does not enable it to overcome all the difficulties involved in determining whether the aid is compatible with the internal market, the Commission, as reiterated by the ECJ in the *Sytraval* judgment,[83] "is under a duty to carry out all the requisite consultations and for that purpose to initiate the procedure under art.108(2)". The Commission may not decline to open the procedure because of other reasons "such as third party interests, considerations of economy of procedure or any other ground of administrative convenience".

27–027 The lawfulness of a decision not to raise objections therefore depends on whether there are doubts as to the compatibility of the aid with the internal market. The Commission has no discretion in that respect but it does have some margin to identify and evaluate all the relevant circumstances in order to determine whether or not they project doubts. The concept of doubts is an objective one. For example, the length and circumstances of the preliminary examination may in certain cases constitute evidence that the Commission may have had doubts regarding the compatibility of a measure with the internal market.[84] If the time spent by the Commission on the preliminary examination under art.108(2) considerably exceeds the time usually taken, that factor alone may lead to the conclusion that the Commission encountered serious difficulties. Such was the case, for example, in *SIC v Commission*[85] where the Commission took about three years to conclude the preliminary investigation by deciding that the measures concerned did not constitute state aid. According to the General Court such a period far exceeds the normal time required to form an initial opinion. Therefore, apparently, the Commission was not able to resolve all the issues raised in due time and the Court annulled the decision. However, while the Commission cannot delay its treatment of complaints from interested parties indefinitely, it is entitled to give different degrees of priority to the complaints

---

[81] Case T–330/94 *Salt Union v Commission* [1996] E.C.R. II–1475. See also para.4.4.
[82] e.g. Case T–11/95 *BP Chemicals v Commission*; Case C–367/95P *Commission v Sytraval* [1998] E.C.R. I–1719.
[83] Case C–367/95P *Commission v Sytraval* [1998] E.C.R. I–1719.
[84] art.4(3) Reg.659/1999; Case T–73/98 *Société Chimique Prayon-Rempel v Commission* [2001] E.C.R. II–867 at paras 44 and 45; Case C–148/09 P *Belgium v Deutsche Post* [2011] E.C.R. I–0000, judgment of September 22, 2011.
[85] Case T–46/97 [2000] E.C.R. I–5719.

brought before it.[86] Moreover, the passage of an even longer period of time (more than four years) in pursuing a preliminary examination was found by the General Court in *3F* to be justified by the circumstances and context of the procedure, explaining that "while the length of the preliminary examination can constitute an indication of the existence of serious difficulties, it does not of itself suffice to show the existence of such difficulties".[87]

The Union Courts must therefore ascertain whether the assessments made by the Commission involved serious difficulties justifying the opening of the contentious procedure. In annulment proceedings the applicant bears the burden of proving the existence of serious difficulties or doubts.[88]

Regulation 659/99 clarifies the procedural mechanism. It provides that, upon **27–028** receiving a complaint regarding allegedly unlawful aid, the Commission *must* examine the information without delay (art.10(1)). According to art.13, a preliminary examination of possible unlawful aid *must* result in a decision pursuant to art.4(2), (3) or (4), i.e. that the measure does not constitute state aid, or that the measure is compatible with the internal market, or that a formal investigation shall be initiated. As has been pointed out by the General Court in the *Deutsche Bahn* judgment, aside from the possibility of taking a decision under art.4, the Commission can also inform the complainant that "there are insufficient grounds for taking a view on the case" pursuant to art.20(2).[89] According to the General Court the Commission is not entitled to close cases in ways outside the procedural framework provided for in the Regulation.

The *Sytraval* judgment of the ECJ also deals, in more detail than the Regulation and the *Deutsche Bahn* judgment, with the extent of the obligations of the Commission towards the complainant as far as the statement of reasons and the investigation of the complaint are concerned. The General Court had formulated stringent requirements in that respect. It put the burden of collecting the relevant evidence upon the shoulders of the Commission once the complainant had sufficiently established there was good reason to assume that aid was involved. It also imposed an obligation on the Commission to conduct a contradictory debate in the preliminary procedure of art.108(3), very much along the lines of the procedure of art.108(2). The ECJ rejected that view and held that the Commission is not under an obligation to conduct an exchange of views with the complainant at the stage of the initial review provided for by art.108(3). However, the Commission is required, in the interest of sound administration of the fundamental rules of the Treaty relating to state aid, to conduct a diligent and impartial examination of the complaint, which may make it necessary for it to examine matters not expressly raised by the complainant. Thus, while the complainant may have no further say in the preliminary art.108(3) procedure, the

---

[86] Case C–119/97 *Ufex and Others v Commission* [1999] E.C.R. I–1341, para.88; Case T–475/04 *Bouygues and Bouygues Télécom v Commission* [2007] E.C.R. II–2097, paras 158 and 159.
[87] Case T–30/03 RENV *3F v Commission* [2011] E.C.R. II–0000, judgment of September 27, 2011, para.70.
[88] Case T–73/98; Case C–83/09P.
[89] Case T–351/02 [2006] E.C.R. II–1047.

Commission is under at least some duty to depart from the contents of the complaint should it be necessary to do so in the interests of diligence. Of course, should the Commission decide to open the formal investigation procedure of art.108(2), the complainant will have the opportunity of expressing its views in response to the call for comments included in the publication of the notice in the Official Journal.

27–029   As is shown by the *Deutsche Bahn* case, there may often be a thin line between a formal Commission decision under art.4(2) of the Regulation, holding that the measure at issue does not constitute aid, and an informal position taken by the Commission under art.20(2) of the Regulation, stating that there are insufficient grounds for taking a view on the case.

In recent years the Union Courts have made clear that where a letter from the services of the Commission definitively rejects a complaint regarding alleged illegal aid (and so implicitly refuses to open the formal investigation procedure), that letter constitutes an attackable act which the complainant has standing to challenge. In a major ruling in 2008, in Case C–521/06 *Athinaïki Techniki* v *Commission*,[90] the Court held that to determine whether an act in matters of State aid constitutes a decision within the meaning of art.4 of the Regulation, it is necessary to ascertain whether the Commission has, at the end of the preliminary examination stage, definitively established its position in the act under considera-tion on the measure under review (i.e. whether that measure constituted aid or not, that the Commission had no doubts about its compatibility with the internal market, or that it did have such doubts). In that analysis, it is irrelevant how the Commission labels the act in question, whether it is sufficiently reasoned, whether it refers to the legal basis used and whether the act in question was notified to the Member State concerned.

Athinaïki Techniki arose when the Commission's services wrote to a complain-ant who had drawn the attention of the Commission to a procedure by which Greece had disposed of 49 per cent of the capital of a firm, alleging that state aid had been granted to the successful bidder. DG COMP had indicated that there was no state aid involved if the relevant rules on public procurement were respected. When the service of the Commission responsible for those rules informed the complainant that it did not intend to continue examining the public procurement complaint, DG COMP then wrote to the complainant informing it that "there are insufficient grounds for continuing to examine that case" and "in the absence of additional information to justify continuing the investigation, the Commission has [. . .] closed the file on the case". The Court considered, based on the substance of the decision by DG COMP to take no further action on the State aid complaint and on the intention of the Commission disclosed in the letter, that the Commission had decided to end the preliminary examination procedure initiated by the complainant. The Commission had thus, in line with the analysis of the Court in its *Sytraval* judgment, implicitly refused to initiate the procedure in art.108(2), which was an attackable act that could be challenged by

[90] Case C–521/06 *Athinaïki Techniki v Commission* [2008] E.C.R. I–5829.

persons intended to benefit from procedural guarantees during the formal investigation procedure. The Court also indicated that its qualification of the contested act was unaffected by the possibility that the complainant might supply the Commission with additional information.

The approach in *Athinaïki Techniki* was endorsed and developed by the Court in 2010 when it ruled in *NDSHT*.[91] The services of DG COMP had written to a complainant who had objected to the alleged provision of state aid to a competitor carrying out a range of tourism-related activities. In a first reply DG COMP stated that it had "reached the conclusion that there are not sufficient reasons for continuing the investigation of your complaint" because some of the activities were carried out on market conditions, others either did not affect trade between Member States or were existing aid, while others were either not aid since they were permissible compensation for the provision of SGEI or were existing aid. In a second reply, DG COMP stated that the information it held did not indicate that those measures constituted unlawful state aid and that no decision under art.20 of the Regulation could be addressed to the complainant.

The General Court considered that the letters were a finding that the measures were existing aid and were therefore not a decision under art.4 of the Regulation and were not open to attack. On appeal, the Court rejected the analysis of the General Court. It ruled that the examination of a complaint, on the basis of art.10(1) of the Regulation, initiates a preliminary examination stage, and that art.13(1) of the Regulation obliges the Commission to close that preliminary examination stage by adopting a decision pursuant to art.4 of the Regulation (no-aid decision, compatible aid decision or opening decision). Where the examination of a complaint leads the Commission to find no grounds for concluding that there is state aid, it refuses by implication to open the procedure in art.108(2). Equally, according to the Court, where the Commission classifies the measures complained of as existing aid subject to the constant review procedure in art.108(1), that classification is also a decision refusing by implication to open the procedure in art.108(2). Therefore, an action for annulment of a decision not to initiate the procedure under art.108(2) in either of those forms which is brought by a party concerned within the meaning of art.108(2) is admissible where that party seeks thereby to safeguard its procedural rights under art.108(2). In the case in hand, the Court held that since the Commission had concluded that there were not sufficient reasons for continuing its investigation of the complaint, in the contested letters the Commission had expressed its wish to terminate its preliminary examination and was refusing by implication to open a formal investigation procedure under art.108(2). The letters were therefore an act open to challenge for the purposes of art.263.

The ECJ held in *Sytraval* that it was the decision addressed to the Member State which forms the subject-matter of any action for annulment which the complainant may bring, and not the letter to that complainant informing him of

27–030

---

[91] Case C–322/09P *NDSHT v Commission* [2010] E.C.R. I–0000, judgment of November 18, 2010.

the decision (such a letter must be distinguished from the "Article 20 letter" discussed in the previous paragraph). Thus, one would assume that the statement of reasons for the decision should be also couched in terms relevant to the addressee, namely the Member State. However, the Court held that as regards a Commission decision finding that no state aid as alleged by a complainant exists, the Commission must at least provide the complainant with an adequate explanation of the reasons for which the facts and points of law put forward in the complaint have failed to demonstrate the existence of state aid (the Commission is not required, however, to define its position on matters which are manifestly irrelevant or insignificant, or plainly of secondary importance). Article 25 of Regulation 659/99 confirms that decisions must be addressed to the Member State concerned. However, in a case where the Commission did not address a decision under art.4(4) of the Regulation to the Member State, but rather to the complainant, it cannot rely on its non-compliance with art.25 of the Regulation in order to deny the complainant its procedural rights under art.263 TFEU. In such a case, the complainant may institute proceedings against the decision which is addressed to him.[92]

27–031 **The position of complainants: second phase decisions.** The first judgment of the ECJ in the *Cofaz* case shows that in the case of competitors, natural or legal persons whose market position is substantially affected by proposed or implemented aid and who have asserted themselves clearly in the administrative procedure under art.108(2) may have standing.[93]

The General Court, in a case concerning aid to Italgrani brought by competing starch producers, has indicated that the test for the admissibility of competitors in actions against positive decisions closing the art.108(2) procedure as formulated by the ECJ in the *Cofaz* case should not be interpreted narrowly.[94] In *Cofaz* the Court stated that companies in a position to establish the existence of the two cumulative criteria—substantial effect on their position and active involvement in the procedure—are "concerned" within the meaning of art.263. However, according to the General Court, there may be other specific circumstances distinguishing the third party individually as in the case of the addressee.

27–032 In annulment proceedings brought by BP Chemicals against a Commission decision closing a proceeding under art.108(2) by declaring aid, in the form of three consecutive capital injections, to BP's competitor EniChem compatible with the internal market, the General Court examined whether BP was in a distinct competitive position notwithstanding the fact that it had not exercised its

---

[92] Case T–351/02 *Deutsche Bahn v Commission* [2006] E.C.R. II–1047, para.55; Case C–521/06 *Athinaïki Techniki v Commission* [2008] E.C.R. I–5829, para.44; Case C–322/09P *NDSHT v Commission* [2010] E.C.R. I–0000, para.47.

[93] Case C–169/84 [1986] E.C.R. 391, para.25. Four years later the Court annulled the Commission decision because the Commission had drawn incorrect findings from the evidence before it and hereby committed "a manifest error of appraisal": Case C–169/84, [1990] E.C.R. 3083. As to the requirement of being "substantially affected", it was confirmed by the Court in Case C–78/03P *Commission v Germany* [2005] E.C.R. I–10737 at para.72.

[94] Case T–442/93 [1995] E.C.R. II–1329, para.49.

right to submit comments in the course of the art.108(2) procedure concerning the two first injections.[95] The General Court concluded that with respect to the first two capital injections BP's situation as one of many competitors was quite different from that of the applicants in *Italgrani*, discussed above, whose market shares accounted for all the relevant markets and where the aid was specifically designed to increase Italgrani's production capacity in markets already characterised by excess capacity. It seems that the General Court was of the opinion that there were indeed special circumstances in *Italgrani* that justified an extension of the *Cofaz* rule. Such circumstances were, according to the General Court, not present in the *BP* case, as a result of which that part of BP's action was dismissed as inadmissible.[96]

The crucial issue for competitors who seek to show that they have standing to **27–033** challenge a final decision taken after the procedure in art.108(2) or to challenge the merits of a decision (express or implicit) not to open the procedure in art.108(2) is therefore that their market position was (or would be) substantially affected by the aid measure. According to the General Court in Case *TF 1*, the applicant must demonstrate the magnitude of the prejudice to its market position.[97] That test must be conducted by reference to beneficiaries of the aid measures in issue.[98] The Court ruled in *Aktionsgemeinschaft Recht und Eigentum* that, in the case of an association bringing annulment proceedings, even if some of the applicant's members are direct competitors of the aid beneficiaries whose competitive position is necessarily affected by the contested decision, it does not follow that their position in the market could be substantially affected by the disputed aid since all undertaking in the sector in the European Union may be regarded as competitors of beneficiaries of the disputed aid scheme.[99] Subsequently, the Court confirmed in *Deutsche Post and DHL Express (formerly DHL International)* that the simple fact of being present in the same market as the beneficiary does not make a competitor individually concerned.[100]

It seems from *Deutsche Post and DHL International* that identification by name in the decision is not sufficient, nor is the production of market share

---

[95] Case T–11/95 [1998] E.C.R. II–3235.

[96] As to the third capital injection, BP had no opportunity to submit its observations in the absence of a notice on the opening of a procedure under art.108(2). Therefore, that part of the action was declared admissible. See also Case C–106/98P *Comité d'enterprise de la Société française de production (et alia) v Commission* [2000] E.C.R. I–3659 where the Court held that to be recognised as individually concerned the applicant cannot rely on its status as a competitor of the beneficiary but must show that the circumstances distinguish it in a similar way as the beneficiary.

[97] Case T–193/06 *TF1 v Commission* [2010] E.C.R. II–0000, judgment of September 13, 2010, para.77. That approach can also be seen in Case T–117/04 *Werkgroep Commerciële Jachtshaven Zuidelijke Randmeren and Others v Commission* [2006] E.C.R. II–3861, para.53; and the test is fully confirmed and applied in Case T–54/07 *Vtesse Networks v Commission* [2011] E.C.R. II–0000, Order of January 21, 2011.

[98] Case T–193/06 *TF1 v Commission* [2010] E.C.R. II–0000, judgment of September 13, 2010, paras 78 and 91.

[99] Case C–78/03P *Commission v ARE* [2005] E.C.R. I–10737 at para.72.

[100] Case C–367/04P *Deutsche Post and DHL Express (formerly DHL International) v Commission* [2006] E.C.R. I–26*, Summ.pub., paras 40 and 41.

figures, for an applicant to show it is individually concerned.[101] Equally, in *Scheucher-Fleisch* the General Court held that the mere fact that there is over-capacity on the market where the applicant is active does not suffice to show that the applicant is substantially affected in its position on the market.[102] On the other hand, the Court ruled in *British Aggregates* that to be substantially affected does not require demonstration of significant decline in turnover, appreciable financial losses or significant reduction in market share following the grant of the aid in question. It can arise from loss of an opportunity to make a profit or less favourable development than would have been the case without the aid.[103]

Some disappointed applicants have objected to the requirement to show how their position in the market is affected by pointing out that when the Commission determines if aid is present, the Union Courts do not require it to engage in a full market analysis. However, in *Deutsche Post and DHL Express (formerly DHL International)* the Court noted that the two tests fulfil quite distinct and separate functions.[104]

27–034   The general conditions for admissibility regarding all actions before the Union Courts apply in state aid-related proceedings. As such, an application for annulment will be dismissed as inadmissible if the applicant is not represented by an independent lawyer,[105] or if the application is lodged out of time.[106] Equally, if the applicant ceases to be represented by a lawyer in the course of the proceedings, the Union Court might declare of its own motion that the action has become devoid of object.[107] As to the starting point for the time limit for instituting proceedings under the fifth paragraph of art.263 TFEU, the General Court has held that where the complete text of decisions is published in the *Official Journal*, the date of publication is the date which starts the period running for competitors.[108] Where the Commission publishes a summary notice of the decision in the *Official Journal* combined with placing the full text of that decision on the Commission's website (which is the case for decisions reached at the end of the preliminary examination), it constitutes publication for the purposes of art.263 TFEU.[109]

---

[101] Case T–388/03 *Deutsche Post and DHL International v Commission* [2009] E.C.R. II–199, paras 49 to 51.

[102] Case T–375/04 *Scheucher-Fleisch v Commission* [2009] E.C.R. II–4155, para.59.

[103] Case C–487/06P *British Aggregates v Commission* [2008] E.C.R. I–10505, para.53.

[104] Case C–367/04P *Deutsche Post and DHL Express (formerly DHL International) v Commission* [2006] E.C.R. I–26*, Summ.pub., para.47.

[105] Case T–94/07 *EREF v Commission* [2009] E.C.R. II–220*, Summ. pub.; Case T–40/08 *EREF v Commission* [2009] E.C.R. II–222*, Summ. pub.; both orders were confirmed on appeal in Joined Cases C–74/10 and C–75/10P *EREF v Commission* [2010] E.C.R. I–0000, Order of September 29, 2010.

[106] Case T–327/04 *SNIV v Commission* [2008] E.C.R. II–72*, Summ. pub.; T–392/05 *MMT v Commission* [2006] E.C.R. II–97*, Summ. pub.

[107] Case T–210/99 *Gankema v Commission* [2004] E.C.R. II–781; Case T–216/99 *Ter Huurne's handelsmaatschappij v Commission*, Order of March 23, 2004; Case T–128/09 *Meridiana and Meridiana fly v Commission*, Order of October 3, 2011.

[108] Case T–123/97 *Salomon v Commission* [1999] E.C.R. II–2925.

[109] Case T–354/05 *TF1 v Commission* [2009] E.C.R. II–471, para.35.

Standard of review: second phase decisions. The scope of the powers of the   **27–035**
Commission to refuse to open the formal investigation procedure has been dealt
with above when discussing first phase decisions.

As to the action for annulment of a final ("second phase") decision, Union
Courts have held that art.107(1), dealing with state intervention "in any form
whatsoever" that distorts competition, does not distinguish between state measures by reference to their causes or aims but defines them in relation to their
effects. The characterisation of a measure as "state aid" is the responsibility of
the Commission (and the national courts) and cannot justify the attribution of a
broad discretion to the Commission, save for particular circumstances owing to
the complex nature of the intervention in question.[110] Such circumstances can,
for example, be present when it concerns the application of the "private market
investor" principle, which may require a complex economic assessment.[111]
Judicial review of such a measure is limited to compliance with procedural rules
and the requirement to state reasons, and whether an error in law has been made,
whether the facts have been accurately stated and whether there has been any
manifest error of assessment or a misuse of powers; the Court is not entitled to
substitute its own economic assessment but in many instances does scrutinise the
facts in great detail. In *Scott*, the Court of Justice reaffirmed the limited scope of
review by the Union Courts of complex economic assessments in competition
cases including state aid cases.[112] It is worth noting that where aid is granted
unlawfully, the Court takes the view that the Commission is not required to
demonstrate the *actual* effect of the aid measure on competition and on
trade.[113]

It has consistently been held by the Union Courts that in the application of   **27–036**
art.107(3) the Commission enjoys a broad discretion (irrespective of whether the
action has been brought by the Member State or beneficiary concerned or by a
complainant).[114] Since that discretion involves complex economic and social
appraisals, the Court must confine itself to verifying whether the Commission
complied with the rules governing procedure and the statement of reasons,
whether the facts have been accurately stated and whether there has been any
manifest error of assessment or misuse of powers.[115] It is not for the Court to
substitute its own economic assessment for that of the Commission although in
many instances the Court does analyse the facts and effects in rather great

[110] Case T–67/94 *Ladbroke Racing v Commission* [1998] E.C.R. II–1.
[111] Joined Cases T–126/96 and 127/96 *BFM v Commission* [1998] E.C.R. II–3437.
[112] See Case T–198/01 *Technische Glaswerke Ilmenau v Commission* [2004] E.C.R. II–2717; and
Case C–290/07P *Commission v Scott* [2010] E.C.R. I–0000, judgment of September 2, 2010.
[113] e.g. Joined Cases T–116/01 and T–118/01 *P&O Ferries (Vizcaya) v Commission* [2003] E.C.R.
II–2957.
[114] e.g. Joined Cases T–371/94 and 394/94 *British Airways and Others and British Midland v
Commission* [1998] E.C.R. II–2405; Case T–67/94 *Ladbroke Racing v Commission* [1998]
E.C.R. II–1.
[115] See Case C–399/08 P *Commission v Deutsche Post* [2010] E.C.R. I–0000, judgment of September 2, 2010, para.97; Case C–290/07P *Commission v Scott* [2010] E.C.R. I–0000, judgment
of September 2, 2010, paras 66, 68 and 84.

detail.[116] Moreover, the legality of the decision must be assessed on the basis of the factual and legal elements existing at the time when the decision was adopted. The same principles apply to the review by the Court of the legality of conditions of authorisation imposed on a Member State[117] and of the legality of the application of art.106(2).[118] However, the Commission is bound by provisions of Union law other than those relating to state aid (such as, for example, directives in the area of the free movement of goods or of environmental protection)[119] as well as by the guidelines and notices that it issues in the area of supervision of state aid where they do not depart from the rules in the Treaty and are accepted by the Member States.[120]

In order for the Union courts to exercise their supervisory jurisdiction, the statement of reasons must in a clear and unequivocal fashion disclose the reasoning followed by the Commission. Where the Commission has approved aid and where complainants are involved, that requirement cannot be determined solely on the basis of the interests of the Member State to which that decision is addressed. The requirement to provide reasons must in such a case also be determined by the interests of the competitors of the beneficiary of the aid.[121]

Action by complainants for failure to act (Article 265 TFEU)

27–037   Article 265 provides for a remedy against an institution's failure to act, where such failure is contrary to Union law. Such an action is only admissible if the institution in question has first been called upon to act. If, within two months, it has not defined its position, the action may be brought before the General Court. The Court action is inadmissible once the Commission has defined its position, because at that point in time the applicant has no further interest in obtaining a declaration for failure to act. Whether the "position" that the Commission has taken as such is lawful, is a different matter. The legality is irrelevant for the purpose of deciding whether the Commission has defined a position, and whether measures referred to in the first paragraph of art.266 should be taken.[122]

When a natural or legal person brings the action, the literal terms of the Treaty require the applicant to show that the failure concerns an act that would have

---

[116] Case T–349/03 *Corsica Ferries France v Commission* [2005] E.C.R. II–2197.

[117] In Joined Cases T–371/94 and 394/94 *British Airways and Others and British Midland v Commission* [1998] E.C.R. II–2405, the General Court held that "only those arguments alleging that the conditions of authorisation were inherently and manifestly inappropriate, and in particular legally inadequate in scope, may be capable of calling in question the legality of the contested decision" (para.393). Arguments alleging that control of the implementation of the conditions is ineffective cannot be examined (para.292).

[118] Case T–106/95 *FFSA v Commission* [1997] E.C.R. II–229; Case T–67/94 *Ladbroke Racing v Commission* [1998] E.C.R. II–1.

[119] Case T–184/97 *BP Chemicals v Commission* [2000] E.C.R. II–3145 at paras 54 et seq.

[120] Case T–198/01 *Technische Glaswerke Ilmenau v Commission* [2004] E.C.R. II–2717, paras 148 et seq.; Case C–91/01 *Italy v Commission* [2004] E.C.R. I–4355, para.45; Case C–464/09P *Holland Malt v Commission* [2010] E.C.R. I–0000, judgment of December 2, 2010, paras 46 and 47.

[121] e.g Case C–367/95P, *Commission v Sytraval* [1998] E.C.R. I–1719

[122] Case T–26/01 *Fiocchi Munizioni v Commission* [2003] E.C.R. II–3951.

been addressed to him (art.265, third paragraph). In state aid cases, competitors of a beneficiary of aid most often complain that the Commission is not taking action under art.108(2) against a third party, namely a Member State.[123] The question, therefore, is whether the Commission is under an obligation to address a decision to a complainant whereby the Commission rejects the complaint (i.e. decides not to initiate the formal investigation procedure). That question must be distinguished from the question as to whether the Commission can be forced to bring a case before the ECJ. In that respect, it has been established by the Court that the Commission has no obligation to commence proceedings before the ECJ against Member States under art.258 (or under art.108(2), second subparagraph).[124]

However, notwithstanding the literal terms of the third paragraph of art.265, **27–038** the Union Courts have repeatedly recalled that arts 263 and 265 TFEU merely prescribe one and the same method of recourse. On that basis, they have reasoned that the third paragraph of art.265 entitles individuals both to bring an action for failure to act against an institution which has failed to adopt an act which otherwise would be addressed to them and against an institution which they claim has failed to adopt a measure which would have concerned them directly and individually.[125] Since it is evident that complainants are not potential addressees of any of the decisions which the Commission might adopt pursuant to art.4 of the Regulation following the preliminary examination stage, their standing under art.265 depends on whether they would be directly and individually concerned by those withheld measures.[126]

In the context of state aid, that reasoning was first developed in *Gestevisión* **27–039** *Telecinco*,[127] which concerned an action pursuant to art.265 brought by a complainant, a Spanish commercial television company, against the Commission for failure to take any decision following its initiation of the preliminary examination stage in relation to a grant made by government bodies to public television companies. The General Court recalled the case-law of the Court based on the comparison between arts 263 and 265, so that the third paragraph of art.232 must be interpreted as also entitling applicants to bring an action for failure to act against an institution which they claim has failed to adopt a measure that would have concerned them in the same way. Accordingly, the General Court found that the Commission was wrong to consider that the claim for a declaration of failure

---

[123] In Case 246/81 *Bethel v Commission* [1982] E.C.R. 2277, concerning the application of art.101, the applicant was asking the Commission not to take a decision in respect of him but to open an inquiry with regard to third parties (airlines) and to take decisions in respect of them. On that basis the Court denied the applicant recourse under art.265.

[124] Case C–87/89 *Sonito v Commission* [1990] E.C.R. I–2005; Case 247/87 *Star Fruit v Commission* [1989] E.C.R. 291. See further on the relationship between art.263 and art.108(2), second subparagraph at paras 27–003 et seq. of this chapter.

[125] See, e.g. Case C–68/95 *T. Port* [1996] E.C.R. I–6065, para.59; Case T–17/96 *TF1 v Commission* [1999] E.C.R. II–1757, para.27; Case T–395/04 *Air One v Commission* [2006] E.C.R. II–1343, para.25.

[126] See Case T–41/01 *Pérez Escolar v Commission* [2003] E.C.R. II–2157, confirmed on appeal in Case C–379/03P *Pérez Escolar v Commission*, Order of October 1, 2004, not published.

[127] Case T–95/96 [1998] E.C.R. II–3407.

to act was inadmissible on the sole ground that the applicant was not the person to whom any measures the Commission might adopt in the case at hand would be potentially addressed. If the complainant could prove itself to be directly and individually affected by a decision that the Commission might adopt vis-à-vis the Member State concerned at the end of the first phase, then it was entitled to bring an art.265 action for failure to act. Those conditions were indeed fulfilled in *Gestevisión Telecinco*, the complainant being a "party concerned" within the meaning of art.108(2), since it is a direct competitor of the beneficiary of the aid in question and since its complaints prompted the preliminary investigation.[128]

Thus the position of the complainant in state aid cases is comparable to that enjoyed by complainants in competition cases by virtue of art.7 of Regulation 1/2003, which states that natural or legal persons who can claim an interest have the right to complain and therefore the corresponding right to bring an art.265 action should the Commission fail to take a position. Although the wording is different, it also follows from art.20(2) of Regulation 659/99 that the Commission must inform the complainant that it will not proceed with the case. It is arguable in light of *Athinaïki Techniki* and *NDSHT* that in state aid cases that right to an action by the Commission means that such an action will constitute a "decision" addressed to the complainant or to the Member State which can be challenged by the complainant insofar as the challenge seeks to protect any procedural rights the complainant may enjoy under art.108(2) (see paras 27–022 et seq.).

Finally, it should be noted that, as held by the General Court in the *Kahn Scheepvaart* case,[129] the possible existence of a remedy at domestic level, whereby the complainant could challenge the grant of aid, cannot affect the admissibility of a claim for a declaration of failure to act.

27–040   If an action for failure to act is admissible because the applicant has standing to challenge the withheld act, the Union courts must determine if the Commission was under a duty to act at the time when it was formally called on to define its position.[130] The applicant must therefore show the Commission was under an obligation to act on or before the date of receipt of the letter of formal notice, that has not been fulfilled. Because the Commission has exclusive competence to assess the compatibility of state aid with the internal market, the Commission must conduct a diligent and impartial examination of a complaint alleging aid to be incompatible with the internal market.[131] In order for the Commission to be in breach of art.265 as regards measures complained of, the applicant must show that it had pointed to alleged unlawful aid in respect of those matters before sending its letter of formal notice. Simply because a complainant announces that a certain document is allegedly a State aid complaint, it does not follow that the

---

[128] Case T–167/04 *Asklepios Kliniken v Commission* [2007] E.C.R. II–2379, para.52.
[129] Case T–398/94 [1996] E.C.R. II–477 at para.50.
[130] Case T–95/96 *Gestevisión Telecinco v Commission* [1998] E.C.R. II–3407, para.71.
[131] Case T–95/96 *Gestevisión Telecinco v Commission* [1998] E.C.R. II–3407, para.72.

Commission automatically falls under an obligation to adopt a State aid decision in relation to that document.

In *Ryanair* the General Court rejected the Commission's argument that the Commission is only under a duty to act if the interested party has used the standard form for complaints.[132] Based on arts 10(1) and 20(2) of Regulation 659/1999 it has to be determined in a given case whether the Commission was seised of a complaint or put in possession of information regarding alleged unlawful aid. The interested party is, in that respect, not required that the Commission is provided with detailed information. However, the interested party must at the very least specify that the measure concerned constitutes unlawful aid.

If the Commission is under a duty to act, the Commission cannot prolong indefinitely its preliminary investigation into measures which are the subject of that complaint.[133] Whether the duration of the procedure is excessive will be judged by the Union courts on a case-by-case basis, in light of the particular circumstances of each case and, especially, its context, the various procedural steps followed by the Commission, the complexity of the case and its importance for the various parties involved. However, where the complaint concerns illegal aid the Commission is not required to complete the preliminary investigation within the same period of time applicable to measures notified to the Commission by the Member State.[134]   **27–041**

In *Gestevisión Telecinco* the Commission had not defined its position in respect of two complaints, one received 47 months before the letter of formal notice, the other 26 months beforehand. The General Court held that those periods were so long that they had to be considered sufficient to allow the Commission to be able to close the preliminary investigation unless the Commission could point to exceptional circumstances. Finding that no such circumstances had been shown by the Commission, the General Court granted the declaration of failure to act sought. A similar declaration was granted in *TF1* where the applicant, a French commercial television company, showed that the Commission had wrongfully failed to close the preliminary examination into financing of public television broadcasting channels in France 31 months after TF1 had complained to the Commission.[135] On the other hand, the General Court has held that a period lasting nearly six months to deal with a relatively complex case concerning several Italian airports did not exceed the limits of a reasonable time frame,[136] while a period of 12 months was not considered too long to deal with a complicated case concerning all public sector hospitals in Germany.[137]

---

[132] T–442/07 *Ryanair v Commission* [2011] E.C.R. II–0000, judgment of September 29, 2011, paras 33 and 34.
[133] Case T–95/96 *Gestevisión Telecinco v Commission* [1998] E.C.R. II–3407, para.74.
[134] Case T–95/96 *Gestevisión Telecinco v Commission* [1998] E.C.R. II–3407, para.79.
[135] Case T–17/96 *TF1 v Commission* [1999] E.C.R. II–1757.
[136] Case T–395/04 *Air One v Commission* [2006] E.C.R. II–1343.
[137] Case T–167/04 *Asklepios Kliniken v Commission* [2007] E.C.R. II–2379.

Interim measures (Articles 278/279 TFEU)

27–042   Actions brought before the Court do not have, according to art.278 TFEU, any suspensory effect. Nevertheless, the Treaty declares in the same article that the Union Courts may, if they consider that circumstances so require, order the suspension of the application of a contested act. Furthermore, art.279 TFEU declares that the courts may prescribe "any necessary interim measures" in "any cases before it".

Article 83 of the Rules of Procedure of the Court of Justice (RP)[138] lays down additional conditions which have to be fulfilled. Paragraph 1 provides that an application for suspension of the operation of a measure adopted by an institution shall be admissible only if the applicant is challenging that measure in proceedings before the Court. According to the second sentence of para.1, an application for any other interim measure shall only be admissible if it is put forward by a party to a case before the Court and relates to that case. Pursuant to art.83(2) RP, a decision ordering the suspension of the operation of a measure adopted by an institution is conditional upon the existence of circumstances giving rise to urgency and of pleas of fact and law establishing a prima facie case for the grant of a suspension. The interim measures "must be provisional in the sense that they must not prejudge the decision on the substance of the case".[139] In addition to the criteria of urgency and of a prima facie case (also referred to as *fumus boni juris*), the Union Courts must have regard to the balance of convenience where they decide to grant interim measures.

27–043   Recourse in state aid cases to interim measures has traditionally not been widespread but it has grown noticeably in recent years. The Union Courts have generally take a sceptical approach to requests to suspend any recovery obligation laid down in a decision finding illegal and incompatible aid. In *Federal Republic of Germany v Commission*[140] that Member State requested a suspension of the operation of a Commission decision ordering recovery of aid granted to a steel undertaking, until the ECJ had ruled on the merits of the case requesting annulment of the same decision. The President of the Court dismissed the Commission's argument that suspension was not possible. He found that art.39 ECSC imposes no such restriction on the Court's power to grant interim measures, referring to the *Plaumann* case[141] in which it was held that the provisions of the ECSC Treaty regarding the right of interested parties to bring an action must not be interpreted restrictively. Moreover, the unavailability of interim measures in such a case would not be compatible with the general principle of Union law which gives individuals a right to complete and effective judicial protection. That principle requires that interim protection be available to individuals, if it is necessary for the full effectiveness of the future decision, in order to ensure that there is no lacuna in the legal protection provided by the Court.

---

[138] Article 104 RP of the General Court is identical to art.83 RP of the ECJ.
[139] See Case T–84/96R *Cipeke v Commission* [1996] E.C.R. II–1313.
[140] Case C–399/95R [1996] E.C.R. I–2441 (pursuant to art.39 ECSC).
[141] Case C–25/62 [1963] E.C.R. 107.

Nevertheless, in light of the exclusive power of the Commission to authorise measures involving aid elements, the President stated that "any suspension of a Commission decision declaring unlawful aid to be incompatible with the [internal] market and requiring its repayment should be contemplated with circumspection" (para.56) and went on to state that the applicant must show exceptionally serious grounds to justify the continuation of a situation that contravenes the recovery measures ordered by the contested decision. The President came to the conclusion that the fact that the immediate implementation of a Commission decision may lead to the winding up or liquidation of the undertaking concerned is not sufficient, in the absence of evidence giving rise to doubts as to the validity of the decision, to justify a suspension order. The harm that such suspension would seek to prevent would be merely the unavoidable consequence of the application of the strict rules concerning aid in the steel sector.

In *Pantochim*[142] an undertaking established in one Member State, which was **27-044** refused by the authorities in another Member State the benefit of aid given to its competitors, applied for an interim measure under art.278, ordering the Commission to require the authorities of the latter State to grant it the aid in question. The Court, after assessing settled case-law,[143] dismissed the application on the grounds that the Commission, in a procedure under art.108(2) regarding non-notified aid, can only require the Member State concerned to suspend payment of aid and to provide it with information necessary for examination. Hence, the scope of interim measures is limited where relief is sought against a decision opening the art.108(2) procedure. Any Commission measure not having the purpose of counteracting any breach of the rules of art.108(3) (and, in particular, breach of the prohibition of payment of aid until the Commission adopts a final decision) has no foundation within the system and must be regarded as unlawful. Moreover, asking the Court to assume the role of the Commission would be contrary to the inter-institutional division of powers.

In general, the criterion of urgency tends to be the most important in decisions to grant or reject applications for interim measures. In *Stadt Mainz*[144] the applicant applied, pursuant to art.278, for the suspension of the operation of a decision finding that it had sold land at an undervalue to Fort Malakoff, a distribution firm, and ordering the recovery of that aid. The President recalled well-established case-law that "urgency" is apparent if implementation of the contested measures gives rise to serious and irreparable damage which could not be put right if the contested decision were annulled or which would be disproportionate to the defendant's interest in having the measures implemented, even when they are the subject of legal proceedings. It is for the applicant to prove that those conditions are satisfied.[145] The President dismissed the application on the

---

[142] Case T–107/96R [1996] E.C.R. II–1361.
[143] Case C–39/94 *SFEI v Commission* [1996] E.C.R. I–3547 at para.45.
[144] Case T–155/96R [1996] E.C.R. II–1655.
[145] Case T–237/99R *BP Nederland and others v Commission* [2000] E.C.R. II–3849, para.49.

grounds that the applicant had failed to submit sufficient evidence[146] that an urgency would arise out of the implementation of the decision that would allegedly lead to an obligation to institute legal proceedings to recover the alleged state aid or from the possibility of annulment of the land sale contract. In a similar case[147] the President of the General Court stated that the possibility of future and uncertain events, which could lead to damage, is not sufficient to justify the urgency of an order for interim measures especially since the public interest had to be counterbalanced against the interest of third parties who were not parties to these proceedings, in particular the beneficiaries of the aid.

27–045 In *Société Chimique Prayon-Rupel*[148] the President of the General Court held that the applicant, a third-party competitor of the beneficiary, has to prove that it cannot wait for a decision or judgment on the merits without suffering serious and irreparable damage. The occurrence of the damage has to be foreseeable to a reasonable extent. In that case, there were no reasons to assume that damages would indeed occur as a result of the granting of aid since the German Government had agreed to supervise the restructuring plan.

The Union Courts have consistently held that damage of a purely pecuniary nature cannot be considered as irreparable, save in exceptional circumstances, since it can ultimately be the subject of financial compensation.[149] However, an interim measure will be justified if, without it, the applicant would be in a position that could imperil its existence before final judgment in the main action. It is therefore for the applicant to show that implementation of the contested decision (or a specific provision of that decision) would inevitably cause it to go into liquidation and disappear from the market before a ruling in the main action. That analysis must take account of the material situation of the applicant; when considering whether to grant interim measures the Union Courts will take into consideration the resources of any corporate group to which the applicant belongs.[150] Where the applicant has a well-resourced parent company, it is not enough that there is a unilateral refusal by the parent to grant financial support in order to show urgency, since the Union Courts consider their interests to be objectively merged.[151] There is no requirement that the applicant is a wholly owned subsidiary for the parent's resources to be taken into account; the Union Courts will look to see if the parent firm is the principal owner.[152] That case-law applies to natural persons as well as legal persons.[153]

---

[146] See also Case T–86/96R *Arbeitsgemeinschaft Deutscher Luftfahrt-Unternehmen v Commission* [1998] E.C.R. II–641, where the President of the General Court demanded "hard evidence allowing him to determine the precise consequences which the absence of the measures applied for would in all probability entail".

[147] Case T–239/94R *EISA v Commission* [1994] E.C.R. II–703 at para.22.

[148] Case T–73/98R [1998] E.C.R. II–2769.

[149] Case T–181/02R *Neue Erba Lautex v Commission* [2002] E.C.R. II–5081, para.84.

[150] Case T–1/08R *Buczek Automotive v Commission* [2008] E.C.R. II–42*, Summ.pub., para.34.

[151] Case T–468/08R *AES Tisza v Commission* [2008] E.C.R. II–346*, Summ.pub., para.45.

[152] Case T–352/08R *Pannon Hőerőmű v Commission* [2009] E.C.R. II–9*, Summ.pub., para.47.

[153] Case T–120/07R *MB Immobilien Verwaltungs v Commission* [2007] E.C.R. II–130*, Summ. pub., paras 38–41.

In cases where a beneficiary seeks to suspend the recovery obligation set down by the Commission in a decision finding that there is illegal and incompatible aid, the Union Courts have held that to prove the urgency of the application, the beneficiary must show not only that recovery would menace its continued existence but also that national law does not offer it remedies to prevent immediate recovery.[154]

Government of Gibraltar[155] concerns, amongst other things, the relationship **27-046** between, on the one hand, the concept of "urgency" as a condition for an expedited procedure and, on the other hand, the concept of "urgency" as a condition for suspension. The President of the General Court found that the criteria for the existence of a "particular urgency" that need to be satisfied if the Court is to decide under an expedited procedure are "only partly the same" as those that apply in an application for interim measures. The President did not discuss the differences and overlaps but instead emphasised that the prevention of serious and irreparable harm is crucial for an order granting interim relief. In that case the application was dismissed.

In exceptional and very particular circumstances, interim measures can indeed **27-047** by justified, as was the case in *Technische Glaswerke Ilmenau*,[156] albeit partially and temporarily, and subject to several conditions. In *Belgium v Commission*,[157] a complex case where the Commission had ordered the Member State to abolish a tax scheme that qualified as existing aid, the President of the Court accepted the presence of a *fumus boni juris* and granted interim relief in the form of transitory measures. There have also been a number of cases in which interim measures were granted to applicants on a provisional basis, before the Commission was given an opportunity to make observations on the relief sought,[158] but such orders are no guarantee that the interim measures will be granted once the Union court has heard both parties.[159]

Action for damages (Article 340 TFEU)

An action for damages in state aid cases against the Commission (and, in **27-048** exceptional aid cases, against the Council) must be based on art.340, second

---

[154] Case T–440/07R *Huta Buczek v Commission* [2008] E.C.R. II–39*, Summ.pub., para. 68; Case T–238/09R *Sniace v Commission* [2009] E.C.R. II–125*, Summ.pub., para.27.

[155] Joined Cases T–195/01R and T–207/01R [2001] E.C.R. II–3915.

[156] Case T–198/01R [2004] E.C.R. II–2717.

[157] Joined Cases C–182/03R and C–217/03R [2003] E.C.R. I–6887.

[158] T–490/10R *Endesa and Endesa Generación v Commission*, Order of the President of the General Court of November 3, 2010, not published. That provisional suspension order was set aside by Order of the President of the General Court of February 17, 2011.

[159] See Case T–457/09R *Westfälisch-Lippischer Sparkassen- und Giroverband v Commission* in which the President of the General Court granted provisional interim measures (suspension of a deadline by which a subsidiary of a bank of which the applicant was a part-owner had to cease writing new business) but subsequently dismissed the application for interim measures without holding a hearing: Order of the President of the General Court of January 31, 2011 and Order of the President of the General Court of March 18, 2011.

paragraph. Article 268 confers exclusive jurisdiction on the ECJ in such situations. Liability is governed by Union law and must be determined on the basis of general principles common to the laws of the Member States, such as the requirement that there be a sufficiently serious breach of a norm intended to confer rights on individuals and that there be a direct causal link between the violation of EU law and the loss suffered by the applicant.

At least in theory the Commission could, for example, be held liable by competitors of the recipient of aid if the Commission wrongfully approves certain aid, or if it neglects the implementation of illegal aid. In *Société des Products Bertrand* an action for damages was dismissed because the applicant was not able to prove a causal link between the aid to its (Italian) competitors and a decline in its own sales (in France).[160] In *BAI* the applicant claimed damages for "moral prejudice" and for loss suffered due to the Commission's delay in communicating to BAI the decision which closed the art.108(2) procedure concerning aid to another company. No casual link was established between the delay and the material prejudice. Also, no "real and certain" moral prejudice was established. Therefore, the action was dismissed.[161]

Actions for damages have also been brought against the Commission: (i) by applicants connected with the beneficiaries of aid measures which the Commission had found to be incompatible aid in a decision that was subsequently annulled, as well as (ii) by potential beneficiaries unhappy with the Commission decision which prevented them from obtaining aid.

27–049   The first category can be seen in *Boychou*[162] and *FG Marine*.[163] Both cases arose from the Commission's decision that France had granted illegal and incompatible state aid to Stardust Marine, a decision that was annulled because the Commission did not establish that the measure in favour of the firm was attributable to the Member State. The alleged aid arose when Crédit Lyonnais, a State-owned bank, had through CDR, its wholly owned subsidiary, carried out capital injections into Stardust; once the firm was recapitalised CDR sold it to FG Marine. The negative decision was adopted by the Commission on September 8, 1999; on September 13, 1999 FG Marine exercised an option to return its ownership of Stardust to CDR; on September 24, 1999 Stardust started receivership proceedings; and on October 13, 1999 the Commission notified the negative decision to the French authorities. In *Boychou* the administrator of Stardust Marine, which had been placed in liquidation following the receivership proceedings, sought damages for the losses resulting to Stardust from the annulled decision, while *FG Marine* was an attempt to obtain compensation for the lost profits on the investments which the applicant had made into Stardust which it had surrendered by exercising the option in September 1999. The General Court

---

[160] [1976] E.C.R. 1. See also Case 114/83 *Société d'Initiatives et de Cooperation Agricoles v Commission* [1984] E.C.R. 2589, discussed by P. Lasok, "State Aids and Remedies under the EEC Treaty" [1986] E.C.L.R. 81.
[161] [1999] E.C.R. II–0123.
[162] Case T–344/04 *Boychou v Commission* [2007] E.C.R. II–92*, Summ.pub.
[163] Case T–360/04 *FG Marine v Commission* [2007] E.C.R. II–91*, Summ.pub.

dismissed both actions on the basis that no causal link had been established between any breaches by the Commission and the losses invoked by the applicants. The General Court emphasised that, as laid down in the last sentence of art.297(2) TFEU, the Commission decision took effect only when it was notified on October 13, 1999 so that when the sell option was exercised and the receivership proceedings were begun, that decision could have had no legal effects.

The second category can be seen in *Nuova Agricast and Cofra*,[164] in which two Italian firms sought compensation for losses they claimed were caused by a Commission decision to authorise an Italian regional aid scheme which contained what they argued was an excessively restrictive transitional mechanism for firms (such as themselves) which had unsuccessfully sought aid under an earlier version of that scheme. The applicants had challenged the validity of the Commission's decision before the General Court but their action was dismissed as being out of time.[165] They had also persuaded a national court to refer questions on the validity of the decision to Court, which ruled that the decision did not breach the principle of equal treatment or contain an inadequate statement of reasons.[166] Their claim of non-contractual liability was dismissed because the General Court found that the Commission was under no obligation to ensure that a more liberal transitional mechanism was put in place by the Italian authorities, which would have covered the applicants' situations, so the Commission had not acted unlawfully. The General Court also noted that insofar as the applicants alleged a failure to supply adequate reasoning, those claims were without effect since a breach of the duty to give reasons cannot be a ground for the Commission's non-contractual liability.[167]

4. THE ROLE OF NATIONAL COURTS

General

In disputes before national courts (including administrative tribunals) questions of Union law may arise. Under art.267, national courts are entitled, and sometimes obliged, to refer such questions to the ECJ. The rulings of the Court concern, as far as relevant here, the interpretation of Treaty provisions, and in particular arts 107 and 108, and the validity and interpretation of acts of the Union institutions, especially Commission decisions. National courts have no

27–050

---

[164] Joined Cases T–362/05 and T–363/05 *Nuova Agricast and Cofra v Commission* [2008] E.C.R. II–297*, Summ.pub.
[165] Case T–98/04 *Nuova Agricast and Others v Commission*, Order of June 15, 2005, not published in the E.C.R.
[166] Case C–390/06 *Nuova Agricast* [2008] E.C.R. I–2577.
[167] That ruling was unsuccessfully appealed in Case C–67/09P *Nuova Agricast and Cofra v Commission* [2010] E.C.R. II–0000, judgment of October 14, 2010.

jurisdiction to rule on the compatibility of aid with the internal market. Assessment of the compatibility of aid falls within the exclusive competence of the Commission. Therefore a national court may not, in a request for a preliminary ruling, ask the ECJ for guidance on the compatibility with the internal market of a given grant of aid or an aid scheme.[168] The essential role of the national courts in the area of state aid is to preserve the right of individuals confronted with a (potential) breach by a Member State of the prohibition of art.108(3), as will be discussed below; additionally, they play a crucial role in the enforcement of negative decisions, as is discussed in Ch.26.

National courts may not themselves declare Commission decisions invalid. Where the challenge to the national act implementing a negative Commission decision raises issues of the validity of the latter, the national court would be required to refer the matter to the ECJ.[169] In urgent cases, however, where the national court has serious doubts as to the validity of a Union act on which a national measure is based and where a private party would suffer irreparable damage from the application of the decision, it may suspend the enforcement of the national measure.[170] In *Department of Trade and Industry v British Aerospace*,[171] the British government had been required by the Commission to seek recovery of illegal aid to British Aerospace. The recipients had brought annulment proceedings against the Commission decision[172] and therefore applied to the national court for a stay of the UK government's recovery proceedings, pending the outcome of their challenge in the ECJ. The English High Court granted the stay.

27–051   Aid cases before national courts usually concern disputes between a private party and a national authority. The private party is either, as defendant or plaintiff in civil or administrative proceedings, the now reluctant beneficiary of aid with respect to which recovery is ordered, or a company harmed by the aid suing a Member State for an injunction to prevent payment of aid, or for recovery and/or damages. In addition to those actions, relatively frequently re-active actions are brought for the annulment of the imposition of a financial burden from which another company is exempted. Standing and remedies in such cases are determined by national law and may differ from one Member State to another. National courts may be faced with a variety of issues when dealing with state aid. This section shall deal with some general topics such as the doctrine of "direct effect" (the "standstill" provision of art.108(3)) and its implications for the powers of the national courts, the application by the national courts of "block exemptions", and their role in the implementation of (negative and positive) Commission decisions. The intervention of the national courts in the recovery of

---

[168] Case C–297/01 *Sicilcassa* [2003] E.C.R. I–7849.
[169] Case 314/85 *Foto Frost* [1987] E.C.R. 4599.
[170] Joined Cases C–143/88 and C–92/89 *Zuckerfabrik Süderdithmarschen and Zuckerfabrik Soest* [1991] E.C.R. I–415.
[171] [1991] 1 CMLR 165.
[172] See Case C–294/90 *British Aerospace and Rover v Commission* [1992] E.C.R. I–493.

illegal state aid is the subject, among other things, of Ch.26 that specifically deals with various issues of "recovery".

In 2009 the Commission adopted a Notice on the enforcement of state aid law by national courts. The 2009 Enforcement Notice replaces the 1995 Cooperation Notice[173] in light of a study on the enforcement of state aid law at national level commissioned by the Commission in 2006[174] that was in turn updated in 2009.[175] The 2006 Enforcement Study updated the findings of a report which had been prepared in 1999 for the 15 "old" Member States,[176] while broadening the coverage to the 12 Member States which joined on or after May 1, 2004 and also expanding considerably the sections on recovery.

One of the noteworthy findings of the 2006 Enforcement Study was that the **27–052** majority of cases initiated by a private party are cases where state aid arguments are raised to escape the imposition of taxes or levies from which competitors are exempted or which are used to finance unlawful aid. The number of cases where private parties sued competitors or, more often, Member States is still rather limited. According to the study that lack of litigation is probably due to the diversity between and within each Member State of procedural and substantive rules, and the lack of transparency of state aid measures and the costs and uncertain outcome of litigation. As a result the 2009 Enforcement Notice seeks to encourage private litigation by making the powers and responsibilities of national courts clearer as well as by providing a mechanism by which national courts can obtain information and opinions on state aid matters from the Commission.

Council Regulation 994/98[177] empowers the Commission to declare by means of block exemption regulations that certain categories of aid should be compatible with the internal market and shall not be subject to the notification requirement of art.108(2). It concerns aid in favour of small and medium-sized enterprises, R&D, environmental protection and employment, subject to certain thresholds and other conditions. Such block exemptions can, as stated in the preamble of the regulation, be directly applied by the national courts, without prejudice to art.267 TFEU. They should therefore increase the involvement of national courts in state aid cases. On the basis of the "Enabling Regulation" 994/98 the Commission has adopted several block exemptions, the most important of which in terms of scope is the General Block Exemption Regulation,

---

[173] Commission notice on co-operation between national courts and the Commission in the State aid field, [1995] O.J. C312/8.
[174] "Enforcement of EC State Aid Law at the national level", reports co-ordinated by Jestaedt, Derenne, Ottervanger, *http://bookshop.europa.eu/is-bin/INTERSHOP.enfinity/WFS/EU-Book shop-Site/en_GB/-/EUR/ViewPublication-Start?PublicationKey=KD7506493.*
[175] *http://ec.europa.eu/competition/court/state_aid_judgments.html.*
[176] "Application of EC State Aid Law by the Member State Courts", report co-ordinated by Jestaedt, Ottervanger and Van Cutsem, published by the Commission in April 1999 and available on the internet at: *http://ec.europa.eu/competition/state_aid/studies_reports/application_ ms/index.html.*
[177] [1998] O.J. L142/1.

Commission Regulation (EC) No.800/2008. For detailed discussion of that regulation and the others, reference is made to the relevant chapters in this book.

Direct effect of Article 108(3) TFEU

27–053   National courts can enforce the directly applicable provision of art.108(3), last
sentence, reading as follows: "the Member State concerned shall not put its
proposed measures into effect until this procedure has resulted in a final decision". As stated in various cases by the Union Courts and codified by art.3 of
Regulation 659/99 that obligation has direct effect in relation to all unnotified aid
and, if notified, operates during the preliminary period and the formal investigation period. For a detailed discussion of art.108(3) TFEU and art.3 of the
regulation, see Ch.25.

In its 2009 Enforcement Notice, the Commission pointed out that national
courts must, until the final decision of the Commission, preserve the rights of
individuals confronted with the (potential) breach by state authorities of the
prohibition in art.108(3). National courts are encouraged to use all national
remedies to freeze payments or order the return of sums illegally paid. They must
safeguard rights that individuals enjoy due to the direct effect of the prohibition
in the last sentence of art.108(3), applying all relevant provisions of national law
to implement the direct effect of that obligation. The initiation of a procedure by
the Commission under either art.108(3) or (2) does not relieve national courts of
their duty to safeguard rights of individuals in the event of a breach of the
requirement to give prior notification.[178] The following issues may arise.

27–054   First, a national court may have cause to interpret and apply the concept of aid
in art.107 to determine whether state aid introduced without observance of the
preliminary examination procedure in art.108(3) ought to have been subject to
that procedure.[179] Having determined whether a measure constitutes state aid, the
court must consider whether the aid is subject to the standstill obligation in the
last sentence of art.108(3). Aid can be lawfully implemented without Commission approval if it is block exempted or if it is "existing" aid. National courts
may therefore be called on to determine if a Block Exemption Regulation is
applicable or whether the aid is existing. New aid that is not block exempted falls
within art.108(3), while existing aid falls within art.108(1). In the latter case, the
court will have to verify that there have not been any modifications; if there have,
art.108(3) will come into play. From the wording of art.108(3) and the case-law
of the Court, the classification of a measure as "state aid", to which the
"standstill obligation" applies, includes the determination by the national court
of the effect on competition and on trade, i.e. fulfils all the criteria of
art.107(1).[180]

---

[178] Case C–39/94 *Syndicat français de l'Express international (SFEI) v La Poste* [1996] E.C.R.
I–3547.
[179] Case C–354/90 *Fédération nationale du commerce extérieur des produits alimentaires and
others v France* [1991] E.C.R. I–5505.
[180] Case C–345/02 *Pearle and others* [2004] E.C.R. I–7139 at paras 32 and 33; Joined Cases
C–393/04 and 41/05 *Air Liquide Industries Belgium* [2006] E.C.R. I–5293, paras 33–36.

Second, third parties, such as competitors who stand to suffer loss due to the grant of illegal aid (i.e. aid implemented prior to notification or during the contentious procedure) can obtain an injunction from a national court, thus preventing the actual granting of the aid. Moreover, a court may be required to declare prematurely granted aid unlawful and order recovery without ruling on its compatibility with the internal market. The national court should declare measures adopted before a compatibility decision by the Commission unlawful and order the State to recover the aid. Unlike the national courts, the Commission cannot order the return of aid on the sole ground that it was not notified in accordance with art.108(3).

Remedies available from the national court in that context also include recovery of illegality interest. In its *CELF* judgment the Court made clear that the need to recover the financial advantage resulting from premature implementation of the aid is part of the national courts' obligations under art.108(3).[181] Illegality interest may be sought whenever the national court is ordering full recovery of unlawful aid under art.108(3) or where there is no obligation to recover the aid itself, in the wake of a positive decision by the Commission.

Third, it has been questioned which parties have locus standi to invoke **27–055** art.108(3). Any remaining doubts as to the locus standi of private parties in national proceedings on state aid questions were removed by the preliminary rulings of the ECJ in the *Streekgewest Brabant*, *Pape* and *Nazairdis* cases.[182] Those cases concerned national proceedings brought against levies imposed on the claimants; the purpose of these levies was to finance aid granted to another company. That company, however, was not a competitor of the claimants. The actions were based on a breach of art.108(3) TFEU. The key question was whether persons subject to a levy that finances aid granted to other parties can also rely on art.108(3) irrespective of whether or not they are affected as competitors. The Court answered in the affirmative holding that such an aid could not be considered separately from the effects of its method of financing; therefore, the notification obligation under art.108(3) also covered the method of financing and the consequences of a failure to notify also apply to that aspect of the aid. As a result, Member States are in principle required to repay charges levied in breach of Union law (i.e. the last sentence of art.108(3)) where the charges form an integral part of the unlawful state aid measure. It follows from *Streekgewest* and *Pape* that, in the future, the locus standi question will have to be limited to a finding of whether or not the claimant is indeed affected by the measure since national rules cannot limit standing only to competitors of the beneficiary. That will probably require a showing of either that the claimant is a (direct) competitor of the aid recipient or that the claimant will suffer an economic loss as a consequence of the aid being granted.

---

[181] Case C–199/06 *CELF and Ministre de la Culture et de la Communication* [2008] E.C.R. I–469, paras 52 and 55.

[182] Case C–174/02 *Streekgewest Westelijk Noord-Brabant v Staatssecretaris van Financiën* [2005] E.C.R. I–85; Case C–175/02 *F.J. Pape v Minister van Landbouw, Natuurbeheer en Visserij* [2005] E.C.R. I–127; Cases C–266/04 *Casino France* [2005] E.C.R. I–9481.

Fourth, third parties who can prove that they have suffered loss caused by the unlawful implementation of aid may have an action for damages in a national court against the Member State that granted the aid. Such action against the Member State may be based on national law but even if there is no such legal base for a damages action in a given Member State, breaches of the standstill obligation may trigger State liability as a matter of Union law where the criteria laid down in *Brasserie du Pêcheur and Factortame* are fulfilled. Such liability exists where the rule of Union law infringed is intended to confer rights on individuals (which is the case for art.108(3)), where the breach of Union law is sufficiently serious, and where that breach has caused an actual and certain financial damage to the claimant.

In *SFEI v La Poste*,[183] the ECJ addressed the question of whether the recipient of aid who does not verify that the aid has been notified to the Commission in accordance with art.108(3) may incur liability on the basis of Union law. The Court held that art.108 does not impose any specific obligation on the recipient of aid, and that Union law does not provide a sufficient basis for the recipient to incur liability in such a case. Nevertheless, that does not prejudice the possible application of national law to the grant of aid in breach of art.108(3), where the acceptance by an economic operator of unlawful assistance causing damage to other economic operators creates a cause of action under the national law.

27–056   In the *SFEI* case the national court also asked whether a national court, examining a case under the last sentence of art.108(3), is obliged to decline jurisdiction or, at least, to stay proceedings if a complaint has been submitted to the Commission, until the Commission decides whether or not the measures constitute state aid. The Court held that, as noted above, a (preliminary) examination by the Commission does not release national courts from their duty to enforce art.108(3); when the national court has doubts as to whether the measure at issue should be categorised as state aid, it may seek clarification on factual or legal issues from the Commission, by requesting information or an opinion (in accordance with the 2009 Enforcement Notice), who must then respond as quickly as possible. Of course, the national court can (or must) also request a preliminary ruling on legal issues from the ECJ.

Finally, there remains a risk of conflicting decisions on the question of whether state aid is involved if the national court does not suspend the proceedings pending a Commission investigation. Abbamonte suggests that national courts should normally suspend proceedings until the Commission has classified the measure as state aid or not.[184] It is submitted that such a solution would only be acceptable if at the same time they blocked the alleged aid by ordering interim measures, unless they are convinced that the measure concerned does not qualify

---

[183] Case C–39/94 *SFEI v La Poste* [1996] E.C.R. I–3547.
[184] "Competitor's Rights to Challenge Illegally Granted Aid and the Problem of Conflicting Decisions in the Field of Competition Law" (1997) 2 E.C.L.R., p.87.

as state aid.[185] If national courts had to wait for a Commission decision while the beneficiary receives, or continues to enjoy the aid, they would not be able to perform their role as guardians of the rights of third parties under art.108(3).

The enforcement of negative Commission decisions

A national court can enforce a Commission decision made under art.108(2) **27–057** which holds that a particular aid is contrary to art.107. In *Capolongo v Maya*,[186] the ECJ clarified that, for aid declared incompatible with the internal market, "the provisions of art.[107(1)] are intended to take effect in the legal systems of Member States, so that they may be invoked before national courts, where they have been put in concrete form by acts having general application provided for by art.[109] or by decisions in particular cases envisaged by art.[108(2)]".

Where recovery of aid is sought following a negative decision of the Commission, the recovery must take place in accordance with the relevant procedural provisions of national law. The provisions are not to be applied in such a way that the immediate and effective recovery required by Union law is prevented.[187] Following a negative decision, an action to obtain an injunction to prevent the actual granting of the aid, or an action for damages by a third party (e.g. a competitor, or a beneficiary who suffers as a result of recovery) may be initiated in a national court. See further, Ch.27.

Case C–188/92 *TWD Textilwerke Deggendorf v Bundesminister für Wirt-* **27–058** *schaft*[188] raises the issue of whether a recipient of a state aid that the Commission has declared unlawful, may, when called upon to repay the aid in accordance with the Commission's decision, challenge the latter's validity before the ECJ on a reference from the national court under art.267 even although it failed to challenge directly the Commission's original decision under art.263. In that case, the Commission declared aid to TWD illegal in a decision addressed to Germany in September 1986. The national ministry concerned subsequently informed TWD of the Commission's decision, and had pointed out the availability of art.263 proceedings. The ministry then revoked the legal basis on which the aid had been granted to TWD, thus obliging it to repay the aid. In April 1987 TWD commenced proceedings for the annulment of the minister's decision. The Oberverwaltungsgericht of Nordrhein-Westfalen took the view that the question of whether TWD's action was well founded depended on the validity of the 1986 Commission decision, but that national court was in doubt as to whether TWD

---

[185] That was the case in a matter decided by the Dutch Supreme Court on October 7, 2005 (discussed in the Dutch Report of Pt I of the 2006 study for the Commission on the enforcement of state aid policy at the national level, see above section 4.4). That manner of proceeding is specifically advocated at point 62 of the 2009 Enforcement Notice, recommending that the unlawful aid and the illegality interest be put on a blocked account until the substance of the matter is resolved.

[186] Case 77/72 [1973] E.C.R. 611.

[187] Case C–232/05 *Commission v France* [2006] E.C.R. I–10071, paras 49–53; Case C–210/09 *Scott and Kimberly Clark* [2010] E.C.R. I–4613, paras 26–32.

[188] [1994] E.C.R. I–833.

was entitled to question the validity of that decision before the national courts, since it had failed to utilise the art.263 procedure.

The national court referred two questions to the Court. First, is a national court bound by a Commission decision pursuant to art.108(2) when examining the implementation of that decision by the national authorities at the suit of the recipient of the aid when the latter has not instituted proceedings under art.263, second paragraph? Second, if the answer to the first question is negative, is the national court entitled to rule on the validity of the original Commission decision? The Court decided to deal with the first question only. TWD, relying on the Court's judgment in *University of Hamburg*,[189] contended that the remedies established by arts 263 and 267 are autonomous. The Commission on the other hand, relying on the Court's judgment in Case 156/77 *Commission v Belgium*,[190] claimed that art.263 is the only appropriate remedy if the principle of legal certainty and the coherence of the system of remedies established by the Treaty is to be properly safeguarded.

27–059   The Court decided that, based on the requirements of legal certainty, it is not possible for a recipient of aid, forming the subject-matter of a Commission decision adopted on the basis of art.108, who could have challenged that decision and who allowed the mandatory time limit laid down by the third paragraph of art.263 to expire, to call in question the lawfulness of that decision before the national courts in an action brought against the measures taken by the national authorities for implementing that decision. It would now seem that the possibility of challenging a Commission decision by way of art.267 proceedings would remain open to aid recipients belonging to a general class or category of undertakings who would not meet the test of "directly and individually concerned" as laid down in art.263, fourth paragraph.

An example of the application of the "*Deggendorf*-doctrine" is to be found in Case T–141/03.[191] The General Court dismissed an action under art.263 against a Commission decision as inadmissible; it added that, the action being declared inadmissible, nothing would prevent the applicant from requesting a national court, in case national proceedings would be brought, e.g. by a third party, to make a reference under art.267 as to the validity of the Commission decision. Another example concerns a 2006 preliminary ruling in *Atzeni and others*, a reference by an Italian court.[192] The case before the national court concerned a dispute between farmers and a regional authority with respect to the validity of a negative Commission decision, prohibiting various aid measures and ordering recovery, in the agricultural sector. The aid recipients had already brought before the General Court an action for annulment of that decision which action had been dismissed as inadmissible because it had been brought out of time.[193] The General Court had not ruled on the standing of the applicants. If they had had

[189] [1983] E.C.R. 2771.
[190] [1978] E.C.R. 1881.
[191] *Sniace v Commission* [2005] E.C.R. II–1197.
[192] Joined Cases C–346/03 and C–529/03 *Atzeni and others* [2006] E.C.R. I–1875.
[193] Case T–21/02 *Atzeni and others v Commission*, Order of May 29, 2002, unpublished.

standing, but had been too late, the art.267 reference for a preliminary ruling relating to the same decision as the art.263 proceedings would be inadmissible in light of the *Deggendorf*-jurisprudence described above. The ECJ therefore examined whether, as in *Deggendorf*, the decision addressed, as usual, to the Member State made explicit reference to, and had been communicated to the individual recipient(s). It concluded that the case at issue concerns a general aid measure and that the decision was not addressed to the recipients; therefore, an action under art.263 would probably not have been admissible and, accordingly, the reference for a preliminary ruling was admissible. Thus, where it is not clear that the claimant before a national court can bring an annulment action under art.263 (for example where the measure was an aid scheme with a wide coverage for which the claimant may not be able to demonstrate an individual concern), the national court must, in principle, offer legal protection.[194] However, even in those circumstances, the national court must request a preliminary ruling under art.267 where it has serious doubts about the decision's validity.

The implementation of positive Commission decisions

A competitor of a beneficiary of aid cleared by the Commission may want to challenge the Commission decision concerning the aid. In *Salt Union*, which involved a challenge by a competitor of the granting of aid to a specific company under a general aid scheme approved by the Commission, the General Court stated that it is open to competitors to contest, before the national courts, the decision of national authorities to grant state aid to an undertaking competing with them.[195] If the aid forms a part of the general aid scheme, undertakings may call into question in such national proceedings the validity of the Commission's decision to approve that scheme. The Court further stated that if such an action were brought in a national court, the latter might (and, indeed, in certain circumstances must) refer a question to the ECJ for a preliminary ruling under art.267 TFEU.

27–060

---

[194] Case C–119/05 *Luchini* [2007] E.C.R. I–6199, para.53.
[195] Case T–330/94 *Salt Union Ltd v Commission* [1996] E.C.R. II–1475.

APPENDIX 1

EU COMPETITION LAW RULES APPLICABLE TO STATE AID

Situation as at March 1, 2011

Adopted from the European Commission Handbook © European Union, 2011

The online version of this handbook is available on the Competition website: *http://ec.europa.eu/competition/state_aid/legislation/compilation/index_en.html*

A. TREATY PROVISIONS ON STATE AID

1. Core provisions of the Treaty on the Functioning of the European Union (TFEU), formerly called "Treaty establishing the European Community" (TEC)

Article 107
Article 108
Article 109

Other relevant provisions

Article 3 of the Treaty of the European Union (TEU)
Article 3 of the TFEU
Article 4 of the TFEU
Article 5 of the TFEU
Article 6 of the TFEU
Article 14 of the TFEU
Article 42 of the TFEU
Article 50 (1) and 50 (2) (h) of the TFEU
Article 93 of the TFEU
Article 106 of the TFEU
Article 119 of the TFEU
Article 346 of the TFEU

Annexes

Protocol (no.26) on Services of General Interest
Protocol (no.27) on the Internal Market and Competition

Appendix 1

B. GENERAL PROCEDURAL RULES

B.1 Procedural Regulation

B.1.1 Council Regulation (EC) No 659/1999 of 22 March 1999 laying down detailed rules for the application of Article 93 of the EC Treaty, OJ L 83, 27.03.1999, p. 1

B.1.1.1 Amendment of Article 1(b)(i) of Council Regulation no 659/99 by Act of accession of Czech Republic, Estonia, Cyprus, Latvia, Lithuania, Hungary, Malta, Poland, Slovenia and Slovakia, OJ L 236, 23.09.2003, p. 345

B.1.1.2 Amendment of Article 1(b)(i) of Council Regulation no 659/99 by Council Regulation (EC) No 1791/2006 of 20 November 2006, by reason of the accession of Bulgaria and Romania, OJ L 363, 20.12.2006, p. 27

B.2 Implementing Regulation (IR)

B.2.1 Commission Regulation (EC) No 794/2004 of 21 April 2004 implementing Council Regulation (EC) No 659/1999 laying down detailed rules for the application of Article 93 of the EC Treaty, OJ L 140, 30.04.2004, p. 1.

B.2.1.1 Commission Regulation (EC) No 1125/2009 of 23 November 2009 amending Regulation (EC) No 794/2004 implementing Council Regulation (EC) No 659/1999 laying down detailed rules for the application of Article 93 of the EC Treaty, as regards Part III.2, Part III.3 and Part III.7 of its Annex I, OJ L 308, 24.11.2009, p. 5–13

B.2.2 General information sheet (Annex I, Part I of the IR, as modified on 30.01.2008) 1.11.2008

B.2.3 Table of supplementary information sheets (Annex I, Part III of the IR of 21.04.2004).

The supplementary information sheets are included in the corresponding section in Chapters E and F.

B.2.4 Simplified notification form (Annex II of the IR, as modified on 30.01.2008) 1.11.2008

B.2.5 Standardised reporting format for existing aid (This format covers all sectors except agriculture). (Annex III A of the IR of 21.04.2004)

B.2.6 Information to be contained in the annual report to be provided to the Commission (Annex III C of the IR of 21.04.2004)

B.3 Simplified procedure

B.3.1 Commission Notice on Simplified procedure for the treatment of certain types of State aid OJ C 136 of 16.06.2009, p. 3

B.4 Best Practices Code

B.4.1 Commission Notice on a Best Practices Code on the conduct of State aid control proceedings OJ C 136 of 16.06.2009, p. 13

B.5 Recovery notice

B.5.1 Notice from the Commission—Towards an effective implementation of Commission decisions ordering Member States to recover unlawful and incompatible State aid, OJ C 272, 15.11.2007, p. 4

B.6 Rules for unlawful State aid

B.6.1 Commission notice on the determination of the applicable rules for the assessment of unlawful State aid (notified under document number C (2002) 458), OJ C 119, 22.05.2002, p. 22

B.7 Enforcement of State aid law by national courts

B.7.1 Commission notice on the enforcement of State aid law by national courts, OJ C 85 of 09.04.2009, p. 1

B.8 Professional secrecy

B.8.1 Commission communication C(2003) 4582 of 1 December 2003 on professional secrecy in State aid decisions,, OJ C 297, 09.12.2003, p. 6

B.9 Obsolescence of certain documents

B.9.1 Commission communication concerning the obsolescence of certain State aid policy documents, OJ C 115, 30.04.2004, p. 1

C. ENABLING REGULATION AND GENERAL BLOCK EXEMPTION REGULATION

C.1 Enabling Regulation

C.1.1 Council Regulation (EC) No 994/98 of 7 May 1998 on the application of Articles 92 and 93 (now 87 and 88 respectively) of the Treaty establishing the European Community to certain categories of horizontal State aid, OJ L 142, 14.05.1998, p. 1

C.2 *De minimis* aid

C.2.1 Commission Regulation (EC) No 1998/2006 of 15 December 2006 on the application of Articles 87 and 88 of the EC Treaty to *de minimis* aid, OJ L 379, 28.12.2006, p. 5

C.3 General block exemption Regulation

C.3.1 Commission Regulation (EC) No 800/2008 of 6 August 2008 declaring certain categories of aid compatible with the common market in application of Article 87 and 88 of the Treaty (General block exemption Regulation) OJ L 214, 9.8.2008, p. 3–47

C.4 Definition of SME

C.4.1 Commission Recommendation of 6 May 2003 concerning the definition of micro, small and medium-sized enterprises (notified under document number C (2003) 1422), OJ L 124, 20.05.2003, p. 36
C.4.2 Commission communication—Model declaration on the information relating to the qualification of an enterprise as an SME, OJ C 118, 20.05.2003, p. 5
C.4.2.1 Corrigendum to the Commission Communication—Model Declaration on the information relating to the qualification of an enterprise as an SME, OJ C 156, 04.07.2003, p. 14

D. TEMPORARY RULES ESTABLISHED IN RESPONSE TO THE ECONOMIC AND FINANCIAL CRISIS

D.1 Horizontal rules

D.1.1 Communication from the Commission—Temporary framework for State aid measures to support access to finance in the current financial and economic crisis, (consolidated version of the Temporary Framework adopted on 17 December 2008, as amended on 25 February 2009), OJ C 83 of 07.04.2009, p. 1
D.1.2 Communication from the Commission amending the Temporary Community framework for State aid measures to support access to finance in the current financial and economic crisis, OJ C 261 of 31.10.2009, p. 2
D.1.3 Communication from the Commission amending the Temporary Community framework for State aid measures to support access to finance in the current financial and economic crisis, OJ C 303 of 15.12.2009, p. 6
D.1.4 Communication from the Commission—Temporary Union framework for State aid measures to support access to finance in the current financial and economic crisis, OJ C 6 of 11.01.2011, p. 5

D.2 Financial sector

D.2.1 Communication from the Commission—The application of State aid rules to measures taken in relation to financial institutions in the context of the current global financial crisis, OJ 2008 C 270, 25.10.2008, p. 8

D.2.2 Commission Communication Recapitalisation of financial institutions in the current financial crisis: limitation of the aid to the minimum necessary and safeguards against undue distortions of competition. OJ C 10, 15.1.2009, p. 2–10

D.2.3 Communication from the Commission on the treatment of impaired assets in the Community banking sector, OJ C 72, 26.3.2009, p. 1–22

D.2.4 Commission communication on the return to viability and the assessment of restructuring measures in the financial sector in the current crisis under the State aid rules, OJ C 195, 19.8.2009, p. 9

D.2.5 Communication from the Commission on the application, from 1 January 2011, of State aid rules to support measures in favour of banks in the context of the financial crisis, OJ C 329, 7.1.2011, p. 7

E. HORIZONTAL RULES

E.1 SME aid

E.1.1 Supplementary information sheet on SME aid (Annex I, Part III.1 of the IR of 21.04.2004)
* *See also:* Rules on General Block Exemption Regulation (see Chapter C)

E.2 Training aid

E.2.1 Communication from the Commission—Criteria for the compatibility analysis of training state aid cases subject to individual notification OJ C 188, 11.8.2009, p. 1

E.2.2. Supplementary information sheet on training aid (Annex I, Part III.2 of the IR of 21.04.2004)
* *See also:* Rules on General Block Exemption Regulation (see Chapter C)

E.3 Employment aid

E. 3.1 Communication from the Commission—Criteria for the compatibility analysis of state aid to disadvantaged and disabled workers subject to individual notification OJ C188, 11.8.2009, p. 6

E.3.2 Supplementary information sheet on employment aid (Annex I, Part III.3 of the IR of 21.04.2004)
* *See also:* Rules on General Block Exemption Regulation (see Chapter C)

E.4 Regional aid

E.4.1 Guidelines on national regional aid for 2007–2013, OJ C 54, 04.03.2006, p. 13
* Please note that pursuant to paragraph 101 of RAG 2007–2013 all approved **regional aid maps** of the Member States (effective as from 1. January 2007) were published in the *Official Journal of the European Union* and are considered as an integral part of present guidelines.

E.4.2 Communication from the Commission concerning the criteria for an in-depth assessment of regional aid to large investment projects, OJ C 223, 16.09.2009, p.3.

E.4.3 Communication of the Commission on the review of the state aid status and the aid ceiling of the statistical effect regions for the period 1.1.2011–31.12.2013, OJ C 222, 17.08.2010, p.2

E.4.4 Supplementary information sheet on regional aid (Annex I, Part III.4 of the IR as modified on 24.10.2006)

E.4.5 Supplementary information sheet on regional aid for large investment projects (Annex I, Part III.5 of the IR as modified on 24.10.2006))

E.5 Research and Development and Innovation aid

E.5.1 Community Framework for State aid for Research and Development and Innovation, OJ C 323, 30.12.2006, p. 1
E.5.2 Supplementary information sheet for research and development and innovation aid: aid schemes (Annex I, Part III.6 a of the IR as modified on 30.01.2008)
E.5.3 Supplementary information sheet for research and development and innovation aid: individual aid (Annex I, Part III.6 b of the IR as modified on 30.01.2008)
* *See also:* Rules on General Block Exemption Regulation (see Chapter C)

E.6 Environmental aid

E.6.1 Community guidelines on State aid for environmental protection, OJ C 82, 01.04.2008, p. 1
E.6.2 Supplementary information sheet on environmental protection aid (Annex I, Part III. 10 of the IR as modified on 31.10.2008)
* *See also:* Rules on General Block Exemption Regulation (see Chapter C)

E.7 Risk capital aid

E.7.1 Community guidelines on State aid to promote risk capital investments in small and medium-sized enterprises, OJ C 194, 18.08.2006, p. 2
E.7.1.1 Communication from the Commission amending the Community guidelines on State aid to promote risk capital, OJ C 329, 7.12.2010, p. 4
E.7.2 Supplementary information sheet on risk capital aid (Annex I, Part III. 11 of the IR as modified on 30.01.2008)
* *See also:* Rules on General Block Exemption Regulation (see Chapter C)

E.8 Rescue and Restructuring aid

E.8.1 Communication from the Commission—Community guidelines on State aid for rescuing and restructuring firms in difficulty, OJ C 244, 01.10.2004, p. 2
* See also: Communication from the Commission—Rescue and restructuring aid and closure aid for the steel sector (notified under document No C(2002) 315), OJ C 70, 19.03.2002, p. 21 (see Chapter F)
E.8.2 Commission Communication concerning the prolongation of the Community Guidelines on State Aid for Rescuing and Restructuring Firms in Difficulty, OJ C 156, 09.07.2009, p. 3
E. 8.2.1 Corrigendum to the Commission communication concerning the prolongation of the Community guidelines on State aid for rescuing and restructuring firms in difficulty, OJ C 174, 28.07.2009, p.17
E.8.3 Supplementary information sheet on aid for rescuing firms in difficulty: aid schemes (Annex I, Part III.7 A of the IR of 21.04.2004)
E.8.4 Supplementary information sheet on aid for rescuing firms in difficulty: individual aid (Annex I, Part III.7 B of the IR of 21.04.2004)
E.8.5 Supplementary information sheet on aid for restructuring firms in difficulty: aid scheme (Annex I, Part III.8 A of the IR of 21.04.2004)
E.8.6 Supplementary information sheet on aid for restructuring firms in difficulty: individual aid (Annex I, Part III.8 B of the IR of 21.04.2004)

F. SECTOR—SPECIFIC RULES

F.1 Audiovisual production

F.1.1 Communication from the Commission to the Council, the European Parliament, the Economic and Social Committee and the Committee of the Regions on certain legal aspects relating to cinematographic and other audiovisual works, OJ C 43, 16.02.2002, p. 6

F.1.2 Communication from the Commission to the Council, the European Parliament, the Economic and Social Committee and the Committee of the Regions on the follow-up to the Commission communication on certain legal aspects relating to cinematographic and other audiovisual works (Cinema communication) of 26.09.2001(published in OJ C 43 on 16.02.2002), COM(2004) 171 final, OJ C 123, 30.04.2004, p. 1

F.1.3 Commission communication concerning the prolongation of the application of the Communication on the follow-up to the Commission communication on certain legal aspects relating to cinematographic and other audiovisual works (cinema communication) of 26 September 2001, OJ C 134, 16.06.2007, p. 5

F.1.4 Communication from the Commission concerning the State aid assessment criteria of the Commission communication on certain legal aspects relating to cinematographic and other audiovisual works (cinema communication) of 26 September 2001, OJ C 31 of 07.02.2009, p. 1

F.1 5 Supplementary information sheet on aid for audiovisual production (Annex I, Part III.9 of the IR of 21.04.2004)

F.2 Broadcasting

F.2.1 Communication from the Commission on the application of State aid rules to public service broadcasting (Text with EEA relevance), OJ C 257, 27.10.2009, p.1

F. 3 Electricity (stranded costs)

F.3.1 Commission Communication relating to the methodology for analysis State aid linked to stranded cost, Adopted by the Commission on 26.07.2001.

F.4 Postal services

F.4.1 Notice from the Commission on the application of the competition rules to the postal sector and on the assessment of certain State measures relating to postal services, OJ C 39, 06.02.1998, p. 2

F.5 Shipbuilding

F.5.1 Framework on State aid to shipbuilding, OJ C 317, 30.12.2003, p. 11 1.11.2008

F.5.2 Communication Commission on the submission to individual notification of the application of all regional investment aid schemes to the shipbuilding sector and proposal of appropriate measures pursuant to Article 88 paragraph 1 of the EC Treaty, OJ C 263, 01.11.2003, p. 2

F.5.3 Commission communication concerning the prolongation of the Framework on State aid to shipbuilding—adopted by Commission on 24 October 2006, OJ C 260, 28.10.2006, p. 7

F.5.4 Communication from the Commission concerning the prolongation of the Framework on State aid to shipbuilding—adopted by the Commission on 3 July 2008 Official Journal C 173 of 8.7.2008, p. 3

F.6 Steel

F.6.1 Communication from the Commission: Rescue and restructuring aid closure aid for the steel sector, OJ C 70, 19.03.2002, p. 21

F.6.2 Communication from the Commission: Multisectoral framework on regional aid for large investment projects OJ C 70, 19.03.2002, p. 8

F.6.3 Communication from the Commission concerning certain aspects of the treatments of competition cases resulting from the expiry of the ECSC Treaty (Text with EEA relevance), OJ C 152, 26.06.2002, p. 5

F.7 Broadband

F.7.1 Communication from the Commission: Community Guidelines for the application of State aid rules in relation to rapid deployment of broadband networks, OJ C 235, 30.09.2009, p.7

F. 8 Transport

F.8.1 Regulation (EC) No 1370/2007 of the European Parliament and of the Council of 23 October 2007 on public passenger transport services by rail and by road and repealing Council Regulations (EEC) Nos 1191/69 and 1107/70, OJ L 315, 03.12.2007, p.1

F.8.2 Communication from the Commission—Community guidelines on State aid for railway undertakings, OJ C184 of 22.07.2008, p. 13

F.8.3 Community guidelines on State aid to maritime transport, OJ C 013, 14.01.2004, p.3 1.3.2011

F.8.4 Communication from the Commission providing guidance on State aid complementary to Community funding for the launching of the motorways of the sea, OJ C 317, 12.12.2008, p. 10

F.8.5 Communication from the Commission providing guidance on State aid to shipmanagement companies, OJ C 132, 11.6.2009, p. 6

F.8.6 Communication from the Commission—Community guidelines on financing of airports and start-up aid to airlines departing from regional airports, OJ C 312, 09.12.2005, p. 1

F.8.7 Application of Articles 92 and 93 of the EC Treaty and Article 61 of the EEA agreement to State aids in the aviation sector, OJ C 350, 10. 12. 1994, p. 5

F. 9 Coal

F.9.1 Council Decision of 10 December 2010 on State aid to facilitate the closure of uncompetitive coal mines, OJ L 336, 21.12.2010, p.24

G. SPECIFIC AID INSTRUMENTS

G.1 State Guarantees

G.1.1 Commission Notice on the application of Articles 87 and 88 of the EC Treaty to State aid in the form of guarantees, OJ C 155, 20.06.2008, p10

G.1.1.1 Corrigendum to Commission notice on the application of Articles 87 and 88 of the EC Treaty to State aid in the form of guarantees, OJ C 244, 25.9.2008, p 32.

G.2 Public Land Sales

G.2.1 Commission Communication on State aid elements in sales of land and buildings by public authorities, OJ C 209, 10.7.1997, p. 3

G.3 Export Credit Insurance

G.3.1 Communication of the Commission to the Members States pursuant to Article 93 (1) of the EC Treaty applying Articles 92 and 93 of the Treaty to short-term export—credit insurance (Text with EEA relevance), OJ C 281, 17.09.1997, p. 4

G.3.2 Communication of the Commission to Member States amending the communication pursuant to Article 93(1) of the EC Treaty applying Articles 92 and 93 of the Treaty to shortterm export-credit insurance (Text with EEA relevance), OJ C 217, 02.08.2001, p. 2

G.3.3 Commission communication concerning the prolongation of the Communication of the Commission to the Member State pursuant to Article 93(1) of the EC Treaty applying Articles 92 and 93 of the Treaty to short-term export-credit insurance (Text with EEA relevance), OJ C 307, 11.12.2004, p. 12

G.3.4 Communication of the Commission to Member State amending the communication pursuant to Article 93(1) of the EC Treaty applying Articles 92 and 93 of the Treaty to shortterm export-credit insurance, OJ C 325, 22.12.2005, p. 22

G.3.5 Communication of the Commission amending the period of application of Communication of the Commission to the Member States pursuant to Article 93(1) of the EC Treaty applying Articles 92 and 93 of the Treaty to short-term export-credit insurance, OJ C 329, 7.12.2010, p. 6

G.4 Fiscal aid—Direct Business Taxation

G.4.1 Commission Notice on the application of the State aid rules to measures relating to direct business taxation, OJ C 384, 10.12.1998, p. 3

H. REFERENCE/DISCOUNT RATES AND RECOVERY INTEREST RATES

H.1.1 New Communication from Commission on the revision of the method for setting the reference and discount rates, OJ C 14, 19.01.2008, p.6
* See also: Commission Regulation (EC) No 794/2004 of 21 April 2004—implementing Council Regulation (EC) No 659/1999 laying detailed rules for the application of Article 93 of the EC Treaty: Chapter V—Interest rate for the recovery of unlawful aid (see Chapter B, consolidated version)

I. TRANSPARENCY OF FINANCIAL RELATIONS BETWEEN MEMBER STATES AND PUBLIC UNDERTAKINGS

I.1. The Commission's position: Application of Articles 92 and 93 (now 87 and 88) of the EEC Treaty to public authorities' holdings, Bulletin EC 9–1984
I.2 Commission communication to the Member States: Application of Articles 92 and 93 [now 87 and 88] of the EEC Treaty and of Article 5 of the Commission Directive 80/723/EEC to public undertakings in the manufacturing sector, OJ C 307, 13.11.1993, p. 3
I.3 Commission Directive 2006/111/EC of 16 November 2006 on the transparency of financial relations between Member State and public undertakings as well as on financial transparency within certain undertakings, OJ L 318, 17.11.2006 , p. 17, (Codified version)

J. SERVICES OF GENERAL ECONOMIC INTEREST (SGEI)

J.1 Community framework for State aid in the form of public service compensation, OJ C 297, 29.11.2005, p. 4
J.2 Commission Decision of 28 November 2005 on the application of Article 86(2) of the EC Treaty to State aid in the form of public service compensation granted to certain undertakings entrusted with the operation of services of general economic interest (notified under document number C(2005)2673), OJ L 312, 29.11.2005, p. 67
* See also: Rules on Transparency of financial relations between Members states and public enterprises (see Chapter I)

APPENDIX 2

EUROPEAN COURT OF JUSTICE JUDGMENTS AND ORDERS

This appendix has been updated to September 22, 2011

C–148/09 *Belgium v Deutsche Post* [2011] judgment of September 22, 2011.

Type of procedure: Appeal against the judgment of the CFI in case T–388/03 *Deutsche Post and DHL International v Commission* annulling the Commission's decision of July 23, 2003 not to raise objections, following the preliminary examination procedure provided for in art.108(3) TFEU, to several measures taken by the Belgian authorities in favour of La Poste SA.

Highlights: The CFI rightly found that it is not for the European Union judicature to interpret an action brought by an applicant as a challenge of the substance of a decision where the applicant sought to protect its procedural rights pursuant to art.88(2) EC [now art.108(3) TFEU] and art.6(1) of Regulation No.659/1999, if the applicant has not expressly raised a plea to that effect. The ECJ reaffirmed that under art.4(4) of Regulation 659/1999 the Commission must adopt a decision initiating the formal investigation procedure under art.108(2) TFEU and art.6(1) of that regulation if the measure raises doubts. The concept of "doubts" referred to in art.4(4) of Regulation No.659/1999 is an objective one and their existence must be sought not only in the circumstances in which the contested measure was adopted but also in the assessments upon which the Commission relied. The length and circumstances of the preliminary procedure may constitute evidence that the Commission may have had doubts regarding the compatibility of the aid at issue with the common market. The CFI's analysis of the circumstances of the adoption and the content of the contested decision highlighted the doubts that the Commission should have had as to the compatibility of the notified measure with the common market, doubts which were adequate to support the conclusion that it should have initiated the formal investigation procedure under art.108(2) TFEU and art.6(1) of Regulation No.659/1999. The appeal was dismissed.

Case C–544/09 P *Federal Republic of Germany v European Commission* [2011] judgment of September 15, 2011.

Type of procedure: Appeal against the judgment of the CFI of October 6, 2009 in Case T–21/06 *Germany v Commission*, seeking annulment of Commission Decision C(2005)3903 of November 9, 2005 on the state aid which the Federal Republic of Germany implemented for the introduction of digital terrestrial television (DVB-T) in Berlin-Brandenburg.

Highlights: The ECJ confirmed that the German support for the costs incurred by private broadcasters due to the switchover from analogous to digital television on the terrestrial platform constituted state aid. The Court found that the CFI correctly held that such state aid may only be granted if the Member State proves that it is a necessary and proportionate instrument to correct a market failure. Similarly the ECJ held that the CFI was correct to hold that Germany failed to demonstrate that because the broadcasters had already agreed to the switchover before state aid was envisaged. The ECJ also sided with the CFI finding that the principle of technology neutrality should play a role in its state aid analysis; as well as its finding that this was a general principle enshrined in the Commission's communication of 2003 on the digital switchover and does not permit state support to discriminate between different platforms. State support given exclusively to a terrestrial platform infringes this principle, unless the Member State documents that there are structural competition problems from the existing offers from other platforms. Germany did not demonstrate that its state aid was aimed at correcting such problem.

Joined Cases C–89/10 and C–96/10 *Beef NV (C–89/10) v Belgische Staat and Frans Bosschaert (C–96/10) v Belgische Staat, Vleesgroothandel Georges Goossens en Zonen NV and Slachthuizen Goossens NV* [2011] judgment of September 8, 2011.

Type of procedure: Reference for a preliminary ruling from the Rechtbank van Eerste Aanleg te Brussel (Belgium) under art.267 TFEU.

Highlights: This judgment discusses whether EU law lays down rules for the reimbursement of charges paid in breach of EU law. EU law does not preclude the application of a limitation period of five years for claims in respect of debts owed by the State, to claims for the reimbursement of charges paid in breach of that law. EU law does also not preclude national legislation which grants an individual a longer limitation period to recover charges from an individual acting as an intermediary, to whom he unwarrantedly paid the charges and who paid them on behalf of that first individual for the benefit of the State, whereas, if that first individual had paid those charges directly to the State, the action of that individual would have been restricted by a shorter time limit. Derogation from the ordinary rules governing actions between private individuals for the recovery of sums paid but not due, on condition that the individuals acting as intermediaries may effectively bring actions against the State for sums which may have been paid on behalf of other individuals.

Case C–279/08 P *European Commission v Kingdom of the Netherlands* [2011] judgment of September 8, 2011.

Type of procedure: Appeal against the judgment of the CFI of April 10, 2008 in Case T–233/04 *Netherlands v Commission* by which the Court annulled Commission Decision C(2003) 1761 final of June 24, 2003 on state aid N 35/2003 concerning the emission trading scheme for nitrogen oxides notified by the Kingdom of the Netherlands.

Highlights: According to the ECJ the CFI did not hold that the measure was not selective on the sole ground that it was governed by an objective criterion. The ECJ held that the CFI was wrong to conclude that the Commission had not sufficiently established that the selectivity criterion was met. The CFI also erred in law concerning the burden of proof for the Commission. The CFI considered that "the beneficiary undertakings are determined in accordance with the nature and general scheme of the system, on the basis of their significant emissions of NOx and of the specific reduction standard to which they are subject" and that "ecological considerations justify distinguishing undertakings which emit large quantities of NOx from other undertakings". The General Court held that "that objective criterion is furthermore in conformity with the goal of the measure, that is, the protection of the environment and with the internal logic of the system". The ECJ disagreed and found for the Commission. The ECJ dismissed the cross-appeal by the Netherlands confirming the CFI's conclusion that the emission allowances having the character of tradable intangible assets constitute state resources. According to the ECJ the *Preussen Elektra* judgment cannot be applied to the present case. The ECJ observed that the Commission is not required to establish the existence of a real impact of the aid on trade between the Member States but only to examine whether that aid is capable of affecting such trade.

Joined Cases C–78/08 to C–80/08 *Ministero dell'Economia e delle Finanze and Agenzia delle Entrate v Paint Graphos Soc. coop. arl (C–78/08); Adige Carni Soc. coop. arl, in liquidation v*

Agenzia delle Entrate and Ministero dell'Economia e delle Finanze (C–79/08) *and Ministero delle Finanze v Michele Franchetto* (C–80/08) [2011] judgment of September 8, 2011.

Type of procedure: Reference for a preliminary ruling concerning the interpretation of art.107 TFEU and the principle prohibiting the abuse of rights in tax matters.

Highlights: The definition of aid is more general than that of a subsidy because it includes not only positive benefits but also measures which, in various forms, mitigate the charges which are normally included in the budget of an undertaking and which thus are similar in character and have the same effect. For the purpose of calculating corporation tax, the basis of assessment of the producers' and workers' cooperative societies concerned is determined in the same way as that of other types of undertaking, namely on the basis of the amount of net profit earned as a result of the undertaking's activities at the end of the tax year. Corporation tax must therefore be regarded as the legal regime of reference for the purpose of determining whether the measure at issue may be selective. Second, it should be noted that, by way of derogation from the rule generally applicable to legal persons, the taxable income of the producers' and workers' cooperative societies concerned is exempt from corporation tax. Those cooperative societies therefore enjoy a tax benefit to which profit-making companies are not entitled. Article 107(1) TFEU does not distinguish between the causes or the objectives of State aid, but defines them in relation to their effects. Tax exemptions which are the result of an objective that is unrelated to the tax system of which they form part are subject to the rule of art.107(1) TFEU. It is therefore for the Member State concerned to introduce and apply appropriate control and monitoring procedures in order to ensure that specific tax measures introduced for the benefit of cooperative societies are consistent with the logic and general scheme of the tax system and to prevent economic entities from choosing that particular legal form for the sole purpose of taking advantage of the tax benefits provided for that kind of undertaking.

Case C–403/10 P *Mediaset SpA v European Commission* [2011] judgment of July 28, 2011.

Type of procedure: Appeal against the judgment of the CFI in Case T–177/7 in which the Court dismissed the application by Mediaset for annulment of Commission Decision 2007/374 EC of January 24, 2007 on state aid C52/2005 implemented by the Italian Republic for the subsidised purchase of digital decoders.

Highlights: The CFI was correct to reject the plea raised before it as inadmissible on the ground that Mediaset had not explained how the fact that aid is applied in a discriminatory manner does not permit the inference that it is selective for the purposes of art.87(1) EC [now art.107(1) TFEU]. The Commission is always obliged to order the recovery of aid which it declares to be incompatible with the common market, unless such recovery would be contrary to a general principle of EU law. The Commission can legitimately confine itself to declaring that there is an obligation to repay the aid in question and leave it to the national authorities to calculate the exact amounts to be repaid. The CFI committed no error in law in holding that it is for the national court, if a case is brought before it, to rule on the amount of aid to be recovered, thereby rejecting Mediaset's argument alleging an infringement of the principle of legal certainty. The appeal was dismissed in its entirety.

Joined Cases C–474/09 P–C–476/09 P and C–471/09 P–C–473/09 P *Territorio Histórico de Vizcaya—Diputación Foral de Vizcaya* (C–474/09 P), *Territorio Histórico de Álava—Diputación Foral de Álava* (C–475/09 P) *and Territorio Histórico de Guipúzcoa—Diputación Foral de Guipúzcoa* (C–476/09 P) *v European Commission* [2011] judgment of July 28, 2011.

Type of procedure: Appeal against the judgment of the CFI of September 9, 2009 in Joined Cases T–227/01–T–229/01 and T–265/01, T–266/01 and T–270/01 *Diputación Foral de Álava and Gobierno Vasco and Others v Commission.*

Highlights: The ECJ dismissed the appeal. First, it considered that the conduct of the Commission in relation to the 1988 and 1993 tax schemes could not enable the appellants to have a legitimate expectation that the measures at issue providing for 45% tax credits and reductions in the tax base were lawful. Secondly, the ECJ considered that the CFI did not disregard the right to a fair hearing and the procedural rules relating to the taking of evidence. Thirdly, with regard to the 45% tax credits on investments, the Court confirmed, as did the CFI, that the Commission did not infringe the principle of proportionality when it found, in its decision, that the Spanish authorities' obligation of recovery was to apply to the entirety of the aid granted and was not to be restricted to amounts exceeding the ceilings fixed for regional aid. Fourthly, the Commission is not bound by the two month term for concluding the preliminary procedure in case of unlawful aid.

Case C–459/10 P *Freistaat Sachsen and Land Sachsen-Anhalt v European Commission* [2011] judgment of July 21, 2011.

Type of procedure: Appeal against the judgment of the CFI in Case T–396/08 *Freistaat Sachsen and Land Sachsen-Anhalt v European Commission*, concerning the partial annulment of Commission Decision 2008/878/EC of July 2, 2008 on state aid which Germany is planning to implement for DHL, and seeking annulment of the first paragraph of art.1 of Commission Decision 2008/878/EC of July 2, 2008.

Highlights: The ECJ dismissed the appeal. The CFI was right to hold that the Commission could base its assessment of the aid not only on the criteria of Regulation 68/2001 (training aid) but also on art.107(3)(c) TFEU, in particular on the criterion of necessity.

Case C–194/09 P *Alcoa Trasformazioni Srl v European Commission* [2011] judgment of July 21, 2011.

Type of procedure: Appeal against the judgment of the CFI in Case T–332/06 *Alcoa Trasformazioni v Commission*, by which that court dismissed Alcoa's action for the partial annulment of Commission Decision 2006/C 214/03.

Highlights: The CFI was entitled to find that the Commission's assessment of the electricity tariff at issue for the period from 1996 to 2005 had been carried out by taking into consideration the market conditions as foreseeable by the Commission for that period. The CFI was also entitled to endorse the Commission's point of view to the effect that its approval of that tariff in the Alumix decision was of limited duration precisely because it was based on an economic assessment of the circumstances prevailing at a given time. The statement of reasons required by art.253 EC [now 296 TFEU] must be appropriate to the measure at issue and must disclose in a clear and unequivocal fashion the reasoning followed by the institution which adopted the measure in question in such a way as to enable the persons concerned to ascertain the reasons for the measure and to enable the competent Court to exercise its power of review. The CFI correctly held that it is permissible for the Commission merely to summarise the relevant issues of fact and law, include a preliminary assessment as to the aid character of the state measure in question and set out its doubts as to the measure's compatibility with the common market. Consequently, the CFI did not err in law in finding that the Commission had given adequate reasons for the contested decision by explaining clearly the grounds which led it to conclude provisionally that the measure at issue constituted aid and stating that it had serious doubts as to whether it was compatible with the common market.

Case C–303/09 *European Commission v Italian Republic* [2011] judgment of July 14, 2011.

Type of procedure: Action under art.108(2) TFEU for failure to fulfil obligations by the Italian Republic.

Highlights: By failing to adopt, within the period prescribed, the measures necessary to recover from the beneficiaries all the aid granted under the aid scheme declared incompatible with the common market by Commission Decision 2005/315/EC of October 20, 2004 on the aid scheme implemented by Italy for firms investing in municipalities seriously affected by natural disasters in 2002, the Italian Republic has failed to fulfil its obligations under art.5 of that decision. The only condition which may relieve a Member State from its obligations is an absolute impossibility to recover. Italy has not invoked such an impossibility.

Joined cases C–465/09 P to C–470/09 P *Territorio Histórico de Vizcaya—Diputación Foral de Vizcaya, Territorio Histórico de Álava—Diputación Foral de Alava and Territorio Histórico de Guipúzcoa—Diputación Foral de Guipúzcoa v European Commission* [2011] judgment of June 9, 2011.

Type of procedure: Appeal against the judgment of the CFI which held that Basque tax exemptions were state aid incompatible with the common market.

Highlights: It can, in the case of non-notified aid, not be presumed from the the the fact that the Commission remained silent that aid is approved under art.108(3) TFEU. The ECJ sided with the CFI upholding the Commission's decisions finding that the Basque tax exemptions granted to newly-established undertakings are state aid incompatible with the common market. The regional authorities involved may not rely on the length of the procedure conducted by the Commission, as they contributed to the situation themselves by failing to cooperate and notify the aid.

Joined Cases C–71/09, C–73/09 and C–76/09 *Comitato "Venezia vuole vivere", Hotel Cipriani Srl and Società Italiana per il gas SpA (Italgas) v European Commission* [2011] judgment of June 9, 2011.

Type of procedure: Appeal against the judgment of the CFI concerning an aid scheme for social security contributions granted to undertakings in Venice and Chioggia.

Highlights: The CFI rightly held that the alleged compensatory character of the advantages granted under the scheme in question does not allow them to cease to be classified as aid within the meaning of art.87 EC [now art.107 TFEU]. The Commission may confine itself to studying the general characteristics of an aid scheme, without being required to examine each particular case of its application. Specifically, the Commission is required only to examine whether the aid is capable of affecting trade between Member States and distorting competition and not to establish the existence of an actual impact of the aid on such trade and an actual distortion of competition. For those reasons, the ECJ dismissed the appeals against the judgment of the CFI and confirmed the order for recovery of the unlawful aid. Reductions in social security contributions granted to Venice and Chioggia undertakings constitute unlawful aid which must be repaid.

Case C–451/10 P *Télévision française 1 SA (TF1)* [2011] judgment of June 9, 2011.

Type of procedure: Appeal against a judgment of the CFI concerning state aid for radiotelevision.

Highlights: The CFI has not failed to apply the correct rules for establishing the burden of proof.

Case C–83/09 *European Commission v Kronoply GmbH & Co KG and Kronotex GmbH & Co KG* [2011] judgment of May 24, 2011.

Type of procedure: Appeal against a judgment of the CFI which declared admissible an action brought for the annulment of a Commission Decision to raise no objections to the State aid granted by Germany to Zellstoff Stendal GmbH.

Highlights: In an action for annulment an applicant can invoke any plea to show that the assessment of the information and evidence which the Commission had at its disposal during the preliminary examination phase of the measure notified should have raised doubts as to the compatibility of that measure with the common market. Under art.1(h) of Regulation No.659/1999, "interested party" means, inter alia, any person, undertaking or association of undertakings whose interests might be affected by the granting of aid. This term covers an indeterminate group of persons, which is not restricted to direct competitors of the beneficiary of the aid. The ECJ held that the CFI had correctly held that this term does not rule out the possibility that an undertaking which is not a direct competitor of the beneficiary of the aid, but which requires the same raw material for its production process, can be categorised as an interested party, provided that that undertaking demonstrates that its interests could be adversely affected by the grant of the aid. For that purpose, it is necessary for that undertaking to establish, to the requisite legal standard, that the aid is likely to have a specific effect on its situation.

Case C–305/09 *European Commission v Italian Republic* [2011] judgment of May 8, 2011.

Type of procedure: Action under art.108(2) TFEU for failure to fulfil obligations by the Italian Republic.

Highlights: The only condition which may relieve a Member State from its obligations is an absolute impossibility to recover. Italy has not invoked such an impossibility. Under art.14(3) of Regulation 659/1999, national courts must ensure that the decision ordering the recovery of the unlawful aid is fully effective and achieves an outcome consistent with the objective pursued by the that decision. Therefore an annulment of national measures implementing a Commission Decision ordering recovery of unlawful aid is irreconcilable with the requirements arising from art.14(3) of Regulation 659/1999.

The fact that the majority of state aid was recovered before the time limit will not alter a finding that a state has failed in its obligation to take all measures to recover unlawful state aid by not ensuring complete recovery of all sums owed. Where legislative steps intended to ensure the implementation by national courts of a Commission Decision requiring a Member State to recover unlawful aid are taken too late or prove ineffective, they will not meet the required standard of "all measures necessary".

Case C–331/09 *European Commission v Republic of Poland* [2011] judgment of April 14, 2011.

Type of procedure: Action under art.108(2) TFEU for failure to fulfil obligations by the Polish Republic.

Highlights: A Member State to which a decision requiring recovery of illegal aid is addressed is obliged under art.288 TFEU [ex. 249 EC] to take all measures necessary to ensure implementation of that decision. It must also be pointed out that apprehension of internal difficulties in the course of implementing a decision on state aid cannot justify a failure by a Member State to comply with its obligations under Community law.

Case C–369/09 P *ISD Polska sp. z o.o. and Others v European Commission* [2011] judgment of March 24, 2011.

Type of procedure: Appeal against a judgment of the CFI which dismissed the annulment action against a Commission decision in favour of a steel producer.

Highlights: In an appeal the jurisdiction of the ECJ is confined to a review of the findings of law on the pleas argued before the CFI. The right to rely on the principle of the protection of legitimate expectations extends to any person in a situation where the Community authority has, by giving him precise assurances, caused him to entertain expectations which are justified. A proposal for a decision from the Commission submitted to the Council cannot provide the foundation for any legitimate expectation that the aid in question will comply with the legal rules of the European Union.

Case C–254/10 P *Centre de coordination Carrefour* [2011] judgment of March 3, 2011.

Type of procedure: Appeal against a judgment of the CFI dismissing an action for annulment.

Highlights: The appeal is manifestly unfounded and some of the arguments are inadmissible.

Case C–304/09 *Commission v Italian Republic* [2010] judgment of December 22, 2010.

Type of procedure: Action under art.108(2) TFEU for failure to fulfil obligations by the Italian Republic

Highlights: The condition that it be absolutely impossible to implement a decision is not fulfilled where the Member State merely informs the Commission of the legal, political or practical difficulties involved in implementing the decision, without taking any real steps to recover the aid from the undertakings concerned, and without proposing to the Commission any alternative arrangements for implementing the decision which could have enabled those difficulties to be overcome.

Case C–507/08 *Commission v Slovak Republic* [2010] judgment of December 22, 2010.

Type of procedure: Action under art.108(2) TFEU for alleged failure to fulfil obligations by the Slovak Republic.

Highlights: European Union law requires Member States to take all appropriate measures to ensure the execution of Commission decisions on the recovery of unlawful aid but respects the specific features of the various procedures provided by Member States for that purpose. In this regard the Member State to which a decision addressed is required actually to obtain, without delay, repayment of the wrongful State aid. In the event of difficulties the Commission and the Member State will work together in good faith with a view to overcoming those difficulties.

Case C–480/09 P *AceaElectrabel Produzione SpA v European Commission* [2010] judgment of December 16, 2010.

Type of procedure: Appeal against a judgment of the CFI dismissing an application for annulment of a Commission Decision concerning state aid that Italy intended to grant for the reduction of greenhouse gas emissions.

Highlights: The ECJ held that the CFI was entitled to form the view that the Commission, did not commit a manifest error of assessment in concluding that ACEA and AEP formed an economic unit in so far as the earlier aid and the aid at issue are concerned.

Case C–362/09 P *Athinaïki Techniki AE v European Commission* [2010] judgment of December 16, 2010.

Type of procedure: Appeal against a judgment of the CFI holding that there was no longer any need to adjudicate on the action seeking annulment of the Commission's decision to take no further action, since that decision had become devoid of purpose.

Highlights: The Commission may only withdraw a decision to take no further action on a complaint regarding alleged unlawful aid in order to remedy illegality affecting that decision. The Commission, after such withdrawal, cannot resume the procedure again at a stage earlier than the exact point at which the illegality found had occurred. The General Court erred in finding that the Commission was entitled to withdraw the contest act in the circumstances of the case.

Case C–239/09 *Seydaland Vereinigte Agrarbetriebe GmbH & Co KG v BVVG Bodenverwertungs-und-verwaltungs GmbH* [2010] judgment of December 16, 2010.

Type of procedure: Reference for a preliminary ruling.

Highlights: National Courts must ensure the full effectiveness of EU law and so it is for them to consider national law as a whole in order to assess to what extent it may be applied so as not to produce a result contrary to that sought by EU law. Article 107 TFEU must be interpreted as not precluding a provision of national law laying down calculation methods for determining the value of land, offered for sale by public authorities in the context of a privatisation plan, so that the price actually paid by the purchaser reflects, in so far as is possible, the market value of that land. Where the provision leads to a result far removed from the market value, and thereby contrary to EU law, those courts or administrative authorities responsible for the application of that rule are required to disapply the provision of national law in question.

Case C–537/08 P *Kahla Thüringen Porzellan GmbH v European Commission* [2010] judgment of December 16, 2010.

Type of procedure: Appeal against a judgment of the CFI which dismissed an application for annulment of a Commission decision on the state aid granted by Germany to a company which produced porcelain dishes and china.

Highlights: The CFI did not breach the principle of legal certainty and was correct in its assessment that the letter from the German authorities, which excluded failing firms from benefits, constituted part of the authorised aid scheme. The appellant was therefore fully aware of the specific restriction. The letter of the German authorities was part of the notified aid programme and that it was precisely on the basis of the information contained therein that the Commission decided not to raise any objection to the notified aid scheme. It follows that the CFI was entitled to form the view that that scheme did not allow the grant of subsidies to private undertakings, such as the appellant, and, therefore, that the aid which the appellant had received did not meet the conditions laid down under that scheme. The principle of legitimate expectations could not be relied upon. The absence of any explicit restriction detailed could not be deemed to constitute precise, unconditional in and consistent expectation information leading to a belief that the category of failing firms was not excluded from receiving the benefits.

Case C–464/09 P *Holland Malt BV v Commission* [2010] judgment of December 2, 2010.

Type of procedure: Appeal against a judgment of the CFI in Case T–369/06 *Holland Malt v Commission*, dismissing its application for annulment of Commission Decision 2007/59/EC of September 26, 2006 concerning the state aid granted by the Netherlands to Holland Malt BV.

Highlights: The Commission enjoys a wide discretion in the application of art.107(3) TFEU. However, when it adopts rules of conduct and announces by publishing them that they will apply to the cases to which they relate, it restricts this discretion. To do otherwise would expose it to the risk of being found in breach of general principles of law such as equal treatment or the protection of legitimate expectations. The Commission is therefore bound in the specific area of state aid, by the guidelines and notices that it issues, to the extent that they do not depart from the rules in the Treaty. The CFI was correct to hold that the Commission correctly applied both point 4.2.5 of the Community Guidelines for state aid in the agriculture sector and art.107(3) TFEU. The ECJ dismissed the appellants submission that the CFI had not responded to its argument that, by relying on the Guidelines, the Commission had not correctly applied that Treaty provision. The appeal was dismissed in its entirety.

Case C–322/09 P *NDSHT Nya Destination Stockholm Hotell & Teaterpaket AB v European Commission* [2010] judgment of November 18, 2010.

Type of Procedure: Appeal against a judgment of the CFI which declared inadmissible NDSHT's action for annulment of a decision relating to a complaint concerning allegedly unlawful state aid granted by the City of Stockholm to Stockholm Visitors Board.

Highlights: The ECJ ruled that the CFI had erred in law in holding that the act in question did not have the characteristics of a decision producing binding legal effects such as to affect the appellant's interests and, in particular, that it did not constitute a decision pursuant to art.4 of Regulation No.659/1999. Consequently it was to be regarded as open to challenge for the purposes of art.263 TFEU. Since the Commission concluded that there were not sufficient reasons for continuing the investigation of the complaint, it follows from the substance of the act in question that that institution formed a definitive opinion on the measures examined, thus expressing its wish to terminate its preliminary examination. With that finding it refused by implication to initiate the formal investigation procedure under art.108(2) TFEU. The ECJ reiterated that those measures which definitively determine the position of the Commission upon the conclusion of an administrative procedure, and which are intended to have legal effects capable of affecting the interests of the complainant constitute acts open to challenge for the purposes of art.263 TFEU. The judgment under appeal was set aside and the case was referred back to the CFI.

Case C–67/09 P *Nuova Agricast Srl and Cofra Srl v European Commission* [2010] judgment of October 14, 2010.

Type of procedure: Appeal against a judgment of the CFI dismissing actions for damages in respect of losses allegedly suffered as a result of the adoption by the Commission decision not to raise objections to an aid scheme for investment in the less favoured regions of Italy.

Highlights: Where state aid infringes general principles of European Union law, such as legal certainty it cannot be declared by the Commission to be compatible with the internal market. The ECJ reiterated the requirement for relying on legitimate expectation, namely that the precise assurances must have been given by the relevant institution. Further, if a prudent and alert economic operator could have foreseen the adoption of a measure likely to affect his interests, the party cannot plead that principle if the measure was adopted. The ECJ reiterated that the principle of legal certainty required that European Union legislation must be certain and its application foreseeable by those subject to it. The ECJ held because since the 1997 decision indicated an expiry date, it was foreseeable for the undertakings likely to avail themselves of the 1997–1999 aid scheme that, after that date, no further invitation to apply for aid could be launched under that scheme. The appeal was therefore unfounded.

Case C–399/08 P *European Commission v Deutsche Post AG* [2010] judgment of September 2, 2010.

Type of procedure: Appeal against the judgment of the CFI in Case T–266/02 *Deutsche Post v Commission*, annulling the Commission Decision on measures implemented by the Federal Republic of Germany for Deutsche Post.

Highlights: Where a state measure is regarded as compensation for services provided by the recipient undertakings in order to discharge public service obligations, that measure is not caught by art.107(1) TFEU since the services qualify as services of general economic interest. For such compensation to actually escape classification as state aid, a number of conditions must be satisfied. In particular, the compensation should not exceed what is necessary to cover all or part of the costs incurred in the discharge of public service obligations, taking into account the relevant receipts and a reasonable profit for discharging those obligations.

The CFI noting the deficiencies in the Commission's examination of lawfulness under art.107 TFEU, did not substitute its own method for that of the Commission but confined its examination to the judicial review of the contested decision's legality. In particular, it restricted itself to verifying whether there had been any manifest error of assessment, misuse of powers and whether the rules on procedure and on the statement of reasons had been complied with. It was under no obligation to examine the application of the all the *Altmark* criteria once it was clear that one of the criteria had not been met. It did not exceed its powers.

Appendix 2

Case C–290/07 P *European Commission v Scott SA* [2010] judgment of September 2, 2010.

Type of procedure: Appeal against a judgment of the CFI annulling art.2 of Commission Decision 2002/14/EC of July 12, 2000 on the state aid granted by France to Scott Paper SA/Kimberly-Clark insofar as it related to aid granted in the form of a preferential price for developed land.

Highlights: In the area of state aid, the Commission enjoys a broad discretion which involves economic assessments which must be made in a European Union context, but this does not imply that the European Union judicature must refrain from reviewing the Commission's interpretation of economic data. The review by the EU judicature of the complex economic assessments made by the Commission is however necessarily limited and confined to verifying whether the rules on procedure and on the statement of reasons had been complied with, whether the facts had been accurately stated and whether there had been any manifest error of assessment or misuse of power. The Commission is required, in the interest of sound administration and fundamental rules of the TFEU relating to state aid, to conduct a diligent and impartial examination of the contested measures, so that it has the most complete and reliable information possible. The lawfulness of a decision concerning state aid falls to be assessed by the European Union judicature in the light of the information available to the Commission at the time when the decision was adopted. The ECJ held that the CFI had exceeded its jurisdiction by holding that the Commission had acted in breach of of its duty to exercise due dilligence. Likewise the CFI failed to identify any manifest error of assessment.

Case C–139/07 P *European Commission v Technische Glaswerke Ilmenau GmbH* [2010] E.C.R. I–05885 (June 29, 2010).

Type of Procedure: Appeal against a judgment of the CFI annulling the Commission's decision of May 28, 2002 in so far as it refused access to documents concerning procedures for reviewing state aid granted to Technische Glaswerke Ilmenau GmbH.

Highlights: Article 4(2), third indent, Regulation No.1049/2001 regarding public access to European Parliament, Council and Commission documents entails the exception of the right of access if disclosure of documents would be likely to undermine the protection of the purpose of inspections and investigations. The purposes of interpreting the exception laid down in this Article is explained. The CFI should have taken into account that interested parties other than the Member State concerned in the procedures for reviewing state aid do not have the right to consult the documents in the Commission's administrative file, and, therefore, have acknowledged the existence of a general presumption that disclosure of documents in the administrative file in principle undermines protection of the objectives of investigation activities. That general presumption does not exclude the right of those interested party to demonstrate that a given document disclosure of which has been requested is not covered by that presumption, or that there is a higher public interest justifying the disclosure of the document concerned by virtue of art.4(2) of Regulation No.1049/2001. The judgment of the CFI was annulled and the ECJ dismissed the action brought against the Commission Decision.

Case C–140/09 *Fallimento Traghetti del Mediterraneo SpA v Presidenza del Consiglio dei Ministri* [2010] E.C.R. I–05243 (June 10, 2010).

Type of procedure: Reference for a preliminary ruling by the Tribunale di Genova (Italy). In its reference the Court asked whether national legislation of the kind laid down in Law No.684, which provides for the possibility of the payment of state aid, in the absence of agreements and without the prior establishment of precise and stringent criteria capable of ensuring that payment of the aid cannot give rise to distortion of competition, is compatible with the principles of Community law and, in particular, with the provisions laid down in arts 86 EC, 87 EC and 88 EC [now arts 106, 107 and 108 TFEU] and in Title V [formerly Title IV] of the Treaty. Furthermore, in that regard, may importance be attached to the fact that the beneficiary is required to apply tariffs imposed by the administrative authority?

Highlights: The subsidies at issue in the main proceedings were paid during the entire period without the public service obligations imposed on the recipient undertakings being clearly defined, without the parameters on the basis of which the compensation for those obligations is calculated being established in advance in an objective and transparent manner, and without ensuring that that compensation did not exceed what was necessary to cover the costs arising from the discharge of those obligations. Since the fourth *Altmark* condition is not satisfied either, those subsidies do not therefore fulfil any of the *Altmark* conditions. Under European Union law subsidies paid pursuant to national legislation providing for payments on account prior to the approval of an agreement, constitute state aid if those subsidies are liable to affect trade between Member States and distort or threaten to distort competition, which it is for the national court to determine.

Case C–210/09 *Scott SA and Kimberly Clark SAS v Ville d'Orléans* [2010] E.C.R. I–04613 (May 20, 2010).

Type of procedure: Reference for a preliminary ruling asking whether a possible annulment by the French administrative court of assessments issued for the recovery of aid by the Commission of the European Communities is incompatible with the common market, on the ground that those assessments infringe legislative provisions relating to the physical presentation of those assessments, given the ability of the competent administrative authority to remedy the vitiating defect in those decisions.

Highlights: Article 14(3) of Council Regulation (EC) No.659/1999 of March 22, 1999 is to be interpreted as not precluding, in circumstances in which amounts corresponding to the aid in question have already been recovered, annulment by the national court of assessments issued in order to recover the unlawful state aid on grounds of there being a procedural defect, where it is possible to rectify that procedural defect under national law. That provision does, however, preclude those amounts being paid once again, even provisionally, to the beneficiary of that aid.

C–138/09 *Todaro Nunziatina & C. Snc v Assessorato del Lavoro, della Previdenza Sociale, della Formazione Professionale e dell'Emigrazione della regione Sicilia* [2010] E.C.R. I–04561 (May 20, 2010).

Type of procedure: Reference for a preliminary ruling concerning the interpretation of the Commission 1995 Decision concerning measures to promote employment and of the Commission Decision 2003/195 on the scheme by which Italy plans to aid employment in the Region of Sicily, and the validity of those decisions.

Highlights: In order to interpret the 1995 Decision, it is appropriate not only to examine the actual text thereof, of which only a summary was published in the Official Journal, but also to refer to the Italian Government's notification of May 18, 1995 of the measures adopted. Any late payment of the aid can give rise to the calculation of interest only in respect of amounts of aid due after the date of the Commission decision authorizing the aid. The right to obtain payment of interest in the event of late payment of the aid and the detailed arrangements and rates applicable to that interest fall within the scope of national law.

Case C–1/09 *Centre d'exportation du livre français (CELF) and Ministre de la Culture et de la Communication v Société internationale de diffusion et d'édition (SIDE)* [2010] E.C.R. I–02099 (March 11, 2010).

Type of procedure: Reference for a preliminary ruling from the Conseil d'Etat (France). It asked firstly whether a national court may stay proceedings concerning the obligation to recover state aid until the Commission has ruled, by way of a final decision, on the compatibility of the aid where a first decision of the Commission declaring that aid to be compatible has been annulled by the Community judicature. It asked secondly, could a situation where the Commission has on three occasions declared the aid to be compatible before those decisions were annulled by the CFI constitute an exceptional circumstance which may lead the national court to limit the obligation to recover the aid?

Highlights: A national court before which an application has been brought, on the basis of art.108(3) TFEU, for repayment of unlawful state aid may not stay the adoption of its decision on that application until the Commission has ruled on the compatibility of the aid with the common market following the annulment of a previous positive decision. The adoption by the Commission of three successive decisions declaring aid to be compatible which were subsequently annulled by the Community judicature, is not, in itself, capable of constituting an exceptional circumstance such as to justify a limitation of the recipient's obligation to repay that aid, in the case where that aid was implemented contrary to art.108(3) TFEU.

Case C–150/09 P *Iride SpA v Commission* [2010] E.C.R. I–00005 (January 21, 2010).

Type of procedure: Appeal against a judgment of the CFI.

Highlights: The ECJ held that the CFI had correctly interpreted the TWD/Commission principle, according to which no aid can be authorized when incompatible aid has not been recovered.

Case C–89/08 P *European Commission v Ireland and Others* [2009] E.C.R. I–11245 (December 2, 2009).

Type of procedure: Appeal against a judgment of the CFI annulling the Commission Decision concerning the exemption from excise duty on mineral oils used as fuel for alumina production in Gardanne, in the Shannon region and in Sardinia respectively implemented by France, Ireland and Italy.

Highlights: The ECJ held that the CFI failed to observe the rule that the parties should be heard, in particular, when it decides a dispute on a ground it has identified of its own motion. The CFI erred in law in holding that the Commission failed to fulfil the obligation to state reasons imposed on it by art.253 EC with regard to the non-application in the present case of art.1(b)(v) of Regulation No.659/1999.

Case C–169/08 *Presidente del Consiglio dei Ministri v Regione Sardegna* [2009] E.C.R. I–10821 (November 17, 2009).

Type of procedure: Reference for a preliminary ruling from the Corte costituzionale (Italy). The questions concerned the interpretation of arts 49 EC and 87 EC [now arts 56 and 107 TFEU].

Highlights: The concept of "aid" encompasses not only directly positive benefits but also interventions which, in various forms, mitigate the charges which are normally included in the budget of an undertaking and which therefore, without being subsidies in the strict sense of the word, are of the same character and have the same effect. Tax legislation which grants certain undertakings exclusion from the obligation to pay a tax, constitutes state aid, even if it does not involve the transfer of state resources. With regard to the selectivity nature of the tax legislation at issue, it must be established whether, having regard to the characteristics of the regional tax on stopovers, the undertakings having their tax domicile outside the territory of the region are in a factual and legal situation comparable with that of undertakings which are established in that territory. Consequently, tax legislation, adopted by a regional authority, which establishes a tax on stopovers to be imposed only on natural and legal persons whose tax domicile is outside the territory of the region, constitutes a state aid measure in favour of undertakings established in that territory.

Case C–520/07 P *Commission of the European Communities v MTU Friedrichshafen GmbH* [2009] E.C.R. I–08555 (September 17, 2009).

Type of procedure: Appeal against a judgment of the CFI annulling art.3(2) of the Commission Decision on the state aid implemented by Germany for SKL Motoren und Systembautechnik GmbH in so far as it orders the recovery jointly and severally from MTU Friedrichshafen GmbH of the amount of €2.71 million.

Highlights: Article 13(1) of Regulation No.659/1999 empowers the Commission, once it finds that aid has been granted or altered without notification, to adopt a decision on whether the aid is compatible or not with the common market on the basis of the information available, when it is faced with a Member State which does not fulfil its duty to cooperate and has not provided the Commission with the information requested. Furthermore, if appropriate, such a decision may, according to art.14, call for the recovery of the amount of aid that has already been paid. However, the Commission is at least required to ensure that the information at its disposal, even if incomplete and fragmented, constitutes a sufficient basis on which to conclude that an undertaking has benefited from an advantage amounting to state aid. That is even more relevant when the Commission orders recovery of the aid. Therefore, the Commission cannot assume that an undertaking has benefited from an advantage constituting state aid solely on the basis of a negative presumption, based on a lack of information enabling the contrary to be found, if there is no other evidence capable of positively establishing the actual existence of such an advantage. The ECJ held that the CFI did not err in law.

Case C–519/07 P *Commission of the European Communities v Koninklijke FrieslandCampina NV* [2009] E.C.R. I–08495 (September 17, 2009).

Type of Procedure: Appeal against the judgment of the CFI annulling the Commission Decision on the state aid implemented by the Netherlands for international financing activities.

Highlights: Where a contested measure affects a group of persons who were identified or identifiable when that measure was adopted by reason of criteria specific to the members of the group, those persons might be individually concerned by that measure inasmuch as they form part of a limited class of traders. Accordingly, the CFI was right to find that KFC had standing. With regard to legitimate expectations it was decided that even if the EU had first created a situation capable of giving rise to legitimate expectations, an overriding public interest may preclude transitional measures from being adopted in respect of situations which arose before the new rules came into force but which are still subject to change. In the absence of an overriding public interest, the Commission will have infringed a superior rule of law if it fails to couple the repeal of a set of rules with transitional measures for the protection of the expectations which a trader might legitimately have derived from the EU rules. Furthermore, it was common ground that the Commission treated differently, in the contested decision, those undertakings benefiting from a scheme and those undertakings whose requests for first authorisation were pending on the date of that decision, by granting a transitional scheme to the former and not to the latter. The CFI erred in law by holding that the difference of treatment was not justified. The CFI erred in law holding that the Commission breached the principles of protection of legitimate expectations and of equal treatment respectively, by restricting the benefits of a transitional scheme to the beneficiaries of that tax scheme alone.

Case C–319/07 P *3F v Commission of the European Communities* [2009] E.C.R. I–05963 (July 9, 2009).

Type of procedure: Appeal against a judgment of the CFI dismissing its application for annulment of the Commission Decision not to raise objections to the Danish fiscal measures applicable to seafarers employed on board vessels registered in the Danish International Register.

Highlights: When assessing the compatibility of state aid in the maritime transport sector, the social aspects of the Community guidelines may be taken into account by the Commission as part of an overall assessment which includes a large number of considerations of various kinds, linked in particular to the protection of competition, the Community's maritime policy, the promotion of

Community maritime transport, or the promotion of employment. It cannot be ruled out that organisations representing the workers of the undertakings benefiting from aid may, as parties concerned within the meaning of art.108(2) TFEU, submit observations to the Commission on considerations of a social nature which it can take into account if appropriate. Therefore, the Community judicature must, in order to assess whether the applicant's arguments based on the Community guidelines suffice to establish its status of a party concerned within the meaning of art.88(2) EC [now art.108(2) TFEU], examine the social aspects of the measure at issue with regard to those guidelines, which contain the legal conditions for assessing the compatibility of the state aid in question. The CFI failed to address the appellant's argument relating to its competitive positive nor did it address the appellant's argument relating to the social aspects of the fiscal measure. The CFI did not err in law by considering that the appellant's situation was not comparable to that of Landbouwschap or CIRFS, situations which it rightly described as altogether special or indeed exceptional. The appellant, which is only one of the many trade unions in the European Union representing seafarers, and only one of the many trade unions operating in Denmark, and is not the only representative of seafarers, did not occupy a clearly circumscribed position as negotiator which was intimately linked to the actual subject-matter of the contested decision. It was not directly involved in the adoption by the Danish legislature of the fiscal measures at issue to which the Commission decided not to raise objections, its opposition to those measures not being enough for it to be classified as a negotiator within the meaning of Van der Kooy and CIRFS.

Case C–369/07 *Commission of the European Communities v Hellenic Republic* [2009] E.C.R. I–05703 (July 7, 2009).

Type of procedure: Action under art.260 TFEU for failure to fulfill obligations.

Highlights: The Commission was entitled to confine itself to insisting on compliance with the obligation to recover the amounts of aid in question and to leave to the competent national authorities the task of calculating the precise amount of the sums to be recovered, including interest payable on those sums due. In the context of proceedings under art.260 TFEU, it is for the Commission to provide the Court with the information necessary to determine the extent to which a Member State has complied with a judgment declaring it to be in breach of its obligations. Where, in such proceedings, the Commission has provided sufficient evidence to suggest that the breach of obligations complained of has persisted, it is for the Member State concerned to challenge, in a detailed manner, the substantive content of that evidence and to prove that the breach has ceased. Since there are no Community provisions on the procedure for recovery of wrongly paid amounts of aid, such financial assistance must, in principle, be recovered in accordance with the relevant procedural provisions of national law. A Member State which, pursuant to a decision of the Commission, is obliged to recover unlawful aid is thus free to choose the means of fulfilling that obligation, provided that the measures chosen do not adversely affect the scope and effectiveness of Community law. It follows that, in principle, so long as it is provided for under the national legal system as a mechanism for extinguishing debts, a set-off operation can constitute an appropriate means by which state aid may be recovered. The ECJ held that Greece had failed to demonstrate to the requisite standard that the total amount of aid was reimbursed. It imposed a periodic penalty payment and the payment of a lump sum.

Case C–129/08 *Carlos Cloet and Jacqueline Cloet v West-Vlaamse Intercommunale voor Economische Expansie, Huisvestingsbeleid en Technische Bijstand CVBA (WVI)* [2009] E.C.R. I–00096 (June 4, 2009).

Type of procedure: Reference for a preliminary ruling. Sale of a plot of land by an intercommunal organisation to an undertaking active in Benelux on preferential terms, following a compulsory purchase order. Question of whether or not obligation to notify exists.

Highlights: There was no need to reply to the reference since the referring court was unable to provide the ECJ with the required explanations.

Case C504/07 *Associação Nacional de Transportadores Rodoviários de Pesados de Passageiros (Antrop) and Others v Conselho de Ministros, Companhia Carris de Ferro de Lisboa SA (Carris) and Sociedade de Transportes Colectivos do Porto SA (STCP)* [2009] E.C.R. I–03867 (May 7, 2009).

Type of procedure: Reference for a preliminary ruling concerning the interpretation of arts 93 and 107 TFEU and Regulation (EEC) No.1191/69.

Highlights: Where aid measures fall within the scope of Regulation No.1191/69 on action by Member States concerning the obligations inherent in the concept of a public service in transport by rail, road and inland waterway their compatibility with Community law must be assessed in accordance with the provisions laid down by that regulation and not in the light of the Treaty provisions relating to state aid. Since the obligation to pay compensation is, under Regulation No.1191/69, necessarily linked to the performance of public service obligations, an undertaking which is regarded as offering a public passenger transport service in a municipality without being subject to any public service obligations, is not entitled to such compensation. Where a national court finds certain aid measures to be incompatible with that regulation, it is a matter for that court, having regard to the fact that that regulation is directly applicable, to establish all the consequences, under national law, as regards the validity of the acts giving effect to those measures.

Case C–494/06 P *Commission of the European Communities v Italian Republic and Wam SpA* [2009] E.C.R. I–03639 (April 30, 2009).

Type of procedure: Appeal against a judgment of the CFI in Joined Cases T–304/04 and T–316/04 *Italy and Wam v Commission* by which it annulled the Commission Decision C 4/2003 on state aid implemented by Italy for Wam SpA.

Highlights: The statement of reasons prescribed in art.296 TFEU must be appropriate to the measure at issue and must disclose in a clear and unequivocal fashion the reasoning followed by the institution which adopted that measure in such a way as to enable the persons concerned to ascertain the reasons for it and to enable the Court to carry out its review. For qualification as state aid, it is not necessary to demonstrate that the aid has a real effect on trade between Member States and that competition is actually being distorted, but only to examine whether that aid is liable to affect such trade and distort competition. The ECJ upheld the approach of the CFI judging that the Commission had not sufficiently stated its reasons relating to the existence of an effect on trade and a distortion of competition resulting from an export state aid.

Case C–431/07 P *Bouygues SA and Bouygues Télécom SA v Commission of the European Communities* [2009] E.C.R. I–02665 (April 2, 2009).

Type of procedure: Appeal against a judgment of the CFI dismissing an action for annulment of Commission decision regarding the modification of payments due from Orange and SFR for Universal Mobile Telecommunications System (UMTS) licences.

Highlights: The CFI indicated the reasons why it considered that, by reason of the general scheme of the system of Community telecommunications law, the waiver of the claims at issue was not covered by the concept of state aid incompatible with Community law. The grounds stated in the judgment under appeal make it possible, to the requisite legal standard, to understand the reasons for which the CFI held that, by reason of the general scheme of the system, the reduction in the fees due from Orange and SFR and, accordingly, the waiver of the claims against them could not be regarded as state aid. The procedure under art.108(2) TFEU is essential whenever the Commission has serious difficulties in determining whether aid is compatible with the common market. The concept of serious difficulties is an objective one and their existence must be sought not only in the circumstances in which the contested measure was adopted but also in the assessments upon which the Commission relied.

The CFI carried out precisely such an examination when it analysed the reasons for which the Commission had considered that the measure aligning fees did not constitute a selective advantage and that it did not infringe the principle of non-discrimination. It did not err in law when it examined the Commission's assessments in order to evaluate whether they had been established on the basis of sufficient information and whether they were such as to enable the existence of any serious difficulty to be ruled out. With regard to a national measure reducing the fees to be paid by the first two operators to have obtained UMTS licences so as to align the conditions under which all licences were granted, such a procedure excludes the possibility that those operators might suffer discrimination, where the very purpose of that alignment is to take account of the fact that, at the time that the licence was awarded to a new operator, none of the three operators had entered the market—for reasons not of their own choosing, with the result that their situation was, for that reason, comparable.

Case C–415/07 *Lodato Gennaro & C. SpA v Istituto nazionale della previdenza sociale (INPS) and SCCI* [2009] E.C.R. I–02599 (April 2, 2009).

Type of procedure: Reference for a preliminary ruling from the Tribunale ordinario di Nocera Inferiore (Italy), concerning the interpretation of the guidelines on aid and to and also Commission Regulation 2204/2002 on the application of arts 107 and 108 of the TFEU to state aid for employment.

Highlights: In order to determine whether there has been an increase in employment, the guidelines on aid to employment, should be interpreted as meaning that the average number of annual working units for the year preceding recruitment should be compared with the average number of annual working units for the year following such recruitment. Those guidelines should be interpreted in close conjunction with the guidelines on national regional aid. It follows that, according to the guidelines on national regional aid, job creation means the net increase in the number of persons employed full-time in one year (part-time and seasonal work being annual labour unit fractions) in an establishment compared with the average over a period of time.

Case C–222/07 *Unión de Televisiones Comerciales Asociadas (UTECA) v Administración General del Estado* [2009] E.C.R. I–01407 (March 5, 2009).

Type of procedure: Reference for a preliminary ruling from the Tribunal Supremo (Spain) concerning the interpretation of arts 12 and 87 EC [now arts 18 and 107 TFEU], and art.3 of Council Directive 89/552/EEC of October 3, 1989 on the coordination of certain provisions laid down by law, regulation or administrative action in Member States concerning the pursuit of television broadcasting activities.

Highlights: Article 3 of Council Directive 89/552/EEC and art.18 TFEU must be interpreted as meaning that they do not preclude a measure adopted by a Member State such as the measure at issue in the main proceedings which requires television operators to earmark 5% of their operating revenue for the pre-funding of European cinematographic films and films made for television and, more specifically, to reserve 60% of that 5% for the production of works of which the original language is one of the official languages of that Member State. Article 107 TFEU must be interpreted as meaning that a measure adopted by a Member State, such as the measure at issue in the main proceedings, requiring television operators to earmark 5% of their operating revenue for the pre-funding of European cinematographic films and films made for television and, more specifically, to reserve 60% of that 5% for the production of works of which the original language is one of the official languages of that Member State does not constitute state aid in favour of the cinematographic industry of that Member State.

Case C–333/07 *Société Régie Networks v Direction de contrôle fiscal Rhône-Alpes Bourgogne* [2008] E.C.R. I–10807 (December 22, 2008).

Type of procedure: Reference for a preliminary ruling from the Cour administrative d'appel de Lyon (France) concerning the validity of the decision of the Commission November 10, 1997 not to raise any objections to the new version of an aid scheme to support local radio stations.

Highlights: A decision adopted at the end of the preliminary investigation under art.108(3) TFEU must simply state the reasons why the Commission faces no serious difficulties in assessing the compatibility of the state aid in question with the common market. This may be inferred not only from the wording but also from the context. It is not obligatory for the Commission to expressly state which of the exceptions set out in art.107(3) TFEU is pertinent. In its assessment of the legality of a state aid measure, the Commission must only take into account information at its disposal at the time the decision is adopted, especially when the measure is considered compatible with the common market. Whilst analysing a measure, the Commission must also take the method of financing the aid into account when it constitutes an integral part of that measure. Since the Commission failed to take account of the method by which that aid was financed its assessment is vitiated by an error. Therefore the contested decision is invalid. The question of whether a relationship of competition between the persons liable to pay a charge and the recipients of aid financed by that charge exists may be of interest for the Commission's assessment; however it cannot constitute an additional criterion to determine the obligation to notify aid. A tax must be considered an integral part of an aid measure when it is used to finance and has a direct impact on the amount of that aid. The Court may decide in each specific case which effects of a measure should be considered definitive.

Case C–487/06 P *British Aggregates Association v Commission of the European Communities and United Kingdom* [2008] E.C.R. I–10505 (December 22, 2008).

Type of procedure: Appeal against the judgment of the CFI in Case T–210/02 *British Aggregates v Commission* dismissing BAA's application for partial annulment of Commission Decision on state aid file N 863/01.

Highlights: A Member State's freedom to define their environmental policy does not exclude the application of state aid rule to an environmental levy. The CFI did not err in law in its examination of the condition requiring that the appellant must have been individually concerned. This condition does not come automatically with the status of being a competitor of the undertaking receiving aid. The CFI disregarded art.87(1) EC [now art.107(1) TFEU], as interpreted by the ECJ by holding, in para.115 of the judgment under appeal, that Member States are free, in balancing the various interests involved, to set their priorities as regards the protection of the environment and, as a result, to determine which goods or services they decide to subject to an environmental levy, with the result that the fact that such a levy does not apply to all similar activities which have a comparable impact on the environment does not mean that similar activities, which are not subject to the levy, benefit from a selective advantage. That approach, which is based solely on a regard for the environmental objective being pursued, excludes a priori the possibility that the non-imposition of the AGL on operators in comparable situations in the light of the objective being pursued might constitute a "selective advantage", independently of the effects of the fiscal measure in question, even though art.87(1) EC [now art.107(1) TFEU] does not make any distinction according to the causes or objectives of state interventions, but defines them on the basis of their effects. That conclusion is all the more cogent in the light of para.128 of the judgment under appeal, to the effect that potential inconsistencies in the definition of the scope of the AGL in relation to the environmental objectives pursued may be justified, even if they are based on objectives unrelated to environmental protection, such as the desire to maintain the international competitiveness of certain sectors. Consequently, the distinction made as between undertakings also cannot be justified by the nature or general scheme of the system of which it forms part. The CFI also erred in distinguishing the present case from the facts which gave rise to the judgment in *Adria-Wien Pipeline and Wietersdorfer & Peggauer Zementwerke.*

Case C–384/07 *Wienstrom GmbH v Bundesminister für Wirtschaft und Arbeit* [2008] E.C.R. I–10393 (December 18, 2008).

Type of procedure: Reference for a preliminary ruling from the Verwaltungsgerichtshof (Austria), concerning the interpretation of the last sentence of art.108(3)TFEU.

Type of Highlights: Where the unlawful implementation of aid is followed by a positive Commission decision, Community law does not preclude the recipient from, on the one hand, demanding the disbursement of aid payable for the future and, on the other hand, keeping aid received that was granted prior to the positive decision, subject always to the consequences arising from unlawfulness of aid disbursed prematurely. The criterion that determines whether aid can be disbursed to a recipient in relation to a period predating a positive decision, or whether that recipient can keep aid already disbursed is therefore the finding, by the Commission, that the aid is compatible with the common market. Thus, the prohibition on putting state aid into effect laid down in the last sentence of art.108(3) TFEU does not require a national court to dismiss an action brought by an aid recipient concerning the amount of that aid allegedly due in respect of a period predating a decision of the Commission finding that aid to be compatible with the common market.

Case C–344/07 P *Commission of the European Communities v Freistaat Sachsen* [2008] E.C.R. I–109465 (December 11, 2008).

Type of procedure: Appeal against a judgment of the CFI annulling in part a Commission Decision on an aid scheme which the Federal Republic of Germany was planning to implement.

Highlights: Although the notification of proposed aid is an essential requirement of the control of that aid, it is only a procedural obligation, intended to allow the Commission to ensure both preventive and effective control of the aid which Member States intend to grant to undertakings. It is for the Commission to apply the rules in force at the time when it gives its decision, the only rules on the basis of which the lawfulness of the decision it takes in that regard falls to be assessed. Where the legal rules under which a Member State notified proposed aid change before the Commission takes its decision, the Commission must, on the basis of the new rules, ask the interested parties to express their views on the compatibility of that aid with those rules. The situation is different only if the new legal rules do not contain any substantial amendments in relation to those previously in force. The CFI made an error of law in holding that the contested decision infringes the principle of non-retroactivity

Case C–295/07 P *Commission of the European Communities v Département du Loiret and Scott SA* [2008] E.C.R. I–09363 (December 11, 2008).

Type of procedure: Appeal against a judgment of the CFI annulling a Commission Decision on the state aid granted by France to Scott Paper SA/Kimberly-Clark in so far as that decision concerns the aid granted in the form of the preferential land price referred to in art.1 thereof.

Highlights: A decision of the Commission which fits into a well-established line of decisions may be reasoned in a summary manner, for example by a reference to those decisions. If, however it goes appreciably further than the previous decisions, the Commission must give an account of its reasoning. The CFI was fully entitled to find that the imposition of compound interest was the first manifestation of a new and important policy of the Commission which it ought to have justified. The CFI may not, merely because it considers a plea relied on by the applicant in support of its action for annulment to be well-founded, automatically annul the challenged act in its entirety. It errs in law when it annuls in its entirety a decision ordering the recovery of state aid on the basis of conclusions restricted to the reasons for the calculation of the present-day value of the initial amount of the aid by applying a compound rate of interest. The issue of whether the present-day value of that amount must be calculated by applying a simple interest rate or a compound interest rate does not affect the finding, in the contested decision, that the aid is incompatible with the common market and that it must be recovered. The CFI cannot be criticised for having failed to separate the question of compound interest from that of simple interest, as it cannot replace the calculation of the present-day value of the initial amount of aid using a compound interest rate with one using a simple interest rate without altering the substance of the contested decision.

Case C–501/07 P *SABAR SpA v Commission of the European Communities* [2008] E.C.R. I–00163 (November 25, 2008).

Type of procedure: Appeal against an order of the CFI dismissing the application for annulment of the Commission decision declaring incompatible with the common market the aid scheme provided for under Italian legislation in the form of tax exemptions and subsidised loans to public utilities with a majority public capital holding.

Highlights: The Court dismissed the appeal as manifestly unfounded.

Case C–500/07 P *Territorio Energia Ambiente SpA (TEA) tegen Commissie van de Europese Gemeenschappen* [2008] E.C.R. I–00161 (November 25, 2008).

Type of procedure: Appeal against an order of the CFI dismissing an application for a ruling that Commission on state aid granted by Italy in the form of tax exemptions and subsidised loans to public utilities with a majority public capital holding, did not apply to the appellant and, in the alternative, that the appellant did not benefit from any unlawful aid, and for the consequential annulment, in so far as necessary, of that decision.

Highlights: The appeal was dismissed as manifestly unfounded.

Case C–214/07 *Commission of the European Communities v French Republic* [2008] E.C.R. I–08357 (November 13, 2008).

Type of procedure: By its action, the Commission of the European Communities asked the Court to declare that, by failing to implement within the prescribed period Commission Decision on the aid scheme implemented by France for the takeover of firms in difficulty, the French Republic failed to fulfil its obligations under arts 5 and 6 of that Decision, the fourth paragraph of art.249 EC and art.10 EC [now art.288 TFEU].

Highlights: Court reaffirmed the criteria of absolute impossibility of giving effect to decision. In the event of difficulties, the Commission and the Member State must, pursuant to the principle of genuine cooperation as laid down in art.4 TFEU, work together in good faith with a view to overcoming those difficulties whilst fully observing the Treaty provisions and, in particular, the provisions on state aid. The condition that it be absolutely impossible to implement a decision was not fulfilled where the defendant Member State merely informed the Commission of the legal, political or practical difficulties involved in implementing the decision, without taking any real steps to recover the aid from the undertakings concerned, and without proposing to the Commission any alternative arrangements for implementing the decision which could have enabled those difficulties to be overcome.

Joined Cases C–428/06–C–434/06 *Unión General de Trabajadores de La Rioja (UGT-Rioja) and Others v Juntas Generales del Territorio Histórico de Vizcaya and Others* [2008] E.C.R. I–06747 (September 11, 2008).

Type of procedure: Reference for a preliminary ruling.

Highlights: This judgment basically applies the criteria established by the ECJ in its judgment *Portugal v Commission* (the *Azores* judgment) Case C–88/03. For satisfaction of the "selectivity criterion" as required by art.107(1) TFEU, it is appropriate to examine whether, within the context of a particular legal system, that measure constituted an advantage for certain undertakings in comparison with others which were in a comparable legal and factual situation. The reference framework need not necessarily be defined within the limits of the Member State concerned, so that a measure conferring an advantage in only one part of the national territory is not selective on that ground alone for the purposes of art.107(1) TFEU. In order that a decision taken by a regional or local authority could be regarded as having been adopted in the exercise of sufficiently autonomous powers, that authority must first have, from a constitutional point of view, a political and administrative status which was distinct from that of the central government. Next, the decision must have been adopted without the central government being able to intervene directly as regards its content. Finally, the financial consequences of a reduction of the national tax rate for undertakings in the region must not be offset by aid or subsidies from other regions or central government. These three conditions are commonly considered to be the criteria of institutional, procedural, and economic and financial autonomy.

Joined Cases C–75/05 and C–80/05 P *Federal Republic of Germany (C–75/05 P), Glunz AG and OSB Deutschland GmbH (C–80/05 P) v Kronofrance SA* [2008] E.C.R. I–06619 (September 11, 2008).

Type of procedure: Action for annulment of a judgment of the CFI annulling a Commission Decision not to raise objections against the state aid granted by the German authorities to Glunz.

Highlights: In the context of supervision of state aid under art.108 TFEU, where, without initiating the procedure under art.108(2) TFEU, the Commission finds on the basis of art.88(3) EC [now art.108(3) TFEU] that an aid is compatible with the common market, the persons intended to benefit from the procedural guarantees provided for in art.108(2) TFEU may secure compliance therewith only if they are able to challenge that decision before the Community judicature. Therefore, where, by an action for annulment of a Commission decision taken at the end of a preliminary examination, an applicant seeks to secure compliance with the procedural guarantees provided for in art.108(2) TFEU, the mere fact that it has the status of a "party concerned" within the meaning of that provision is sufficient for it to be regarded as directly and individually concerned for the purposes of the fourth paragraph of art.263 TFEU. In adopting rules of conduct and announcing their application, the Commission imposes a limit on the exercise of its discretion under art.107(3) TFEU and cannot depart from those rules under pain of being found to be in breach of general principles of law, such as equal treatment or the protection of legitimate expectations. It is for the CFI to verify whether the Commission has observed those rules. In determining whether aid within the Multi-sectoral Framework and regional aid for large investment projects is compatible with the common market, the CFI does not disregard the Commission's broad discretion if it reviews whether the Commission complied with that framework, and if it ascertains whether the Commission took account, when determining the applicable adjustment factor, of whether that aid was intended for a declining market. The CFI is also justified in holding that the multisectoral framework should be interpreted in the light of art.107 TFEU and of the principle of incompatibility of public aid set out therein, in order to attain the objective sought by that provision, namely undistorted competition in the common market.

Case C–521/06 P *Athinaïki Techniki AE v Commission of the European Communities* [2008] E.C.R. I–05829 (July 17, 2008).

Type of procedure: Action for annulment the order of the CFI in Case T–94/05 *Athinaïki Techniki v Commission* dismissing as inadmissible Athinaïki Techniki's action.

Highlights: A letter by which the Commission informs a complainant seeking a declaration of infringement of arts 107 and 108 TFEU, that "in the absence of additional information to justify continuing the investigation, the Commission has, for the purposes of administrative action, closed the file . . . " indicates that the Commission actually closed the file for the purposes of administrative action. It is apparent from the substance of that act and from the intention of the Commission that it has thus decided to bring to an end the preliminary examination procedure initiated by the complainant. By that act, the Commission has stated that the review initiated had not enabled it to establish the existence of state aid within the meaning of art.107 TFEU and it has implicitly refused to initiate the formal investigation procedure provided for in art.108(2) TFEU. The CFI erred in law holding that the contested act did not have legal effect and cannot therefore be the subject of an action for annulment.

Case C–206/06 *Essent Netwerk Noord BV supported by Nederlands Elektriciteit Administratie-kantoor BV v Aluminium Delfzijl BV, and in the indemnification proceedings Aluminium Delfzijl BV* *v Staat der Nederlanden and in the indemnification proceedings Essent Netwerk Noord BV v Nederlands Elektriciteit Administratiekantoor BV and Saranne BV* [2008] E.C.R. I–05497 (July 17, 2008).

Type of procedure: Reference for a preliminary ruling from the Rechtbank Groningen (Netherlands), concerning the interpretation of arts 25 EC, 87(1) EC and 90 EC [now arts 30, 107(1) and 110 TFEU].

Highlights: The Court reiterated the *Altmark* conditions for exemption of a measure from art.107(1) TFEU when a public service obligation is being discharged by the undertaking receiving aid, namely that the undertaking must have a clear public service obligation to discharge; the parameters for calculation of compensation must be established in advance in a clear and transparent manner; there should be no over compensation of the undertaking taking into account the relevant receipts and a reasonable profit; and the compensation must be determined on the basis of an analysis of the costs which a typical undertaking, well run and adequately provided with the requisite means so as to be able to meet the necessary public service requirements, would have incurred in discharging those obligations, taking into account the relevant receipts and a reasonable profit for discharging the obligations.

Joined Cases C–341/06 and C–342/06 P *Chronopost SA and La Poste v Union française de l'express (UFEX) and Others* [2008] E.C.R. I–04777 (July 1, 2008).

Type of procedure: Appeals against a judgment of the CFI partly annulling a Commission Decision concerning alleged state aid granted by France to SFMI-Chronopost.

Highlights: Contrary to the CFI, the ECJ found that providing logistical and financial assistance to a subsidiary active in the express courier market did not constitute any aid within the meaning of art.107(1) TFEU. Moreover, the ECJ ruled, first, that the Commission decision was not insufficiently reasoned in the light of the standard established by the *Chronopost I* ruling. Again disagreeing with the CFI, the ECJ held that this Commission decision contained all the relevant elements to conclude that this test was indeed fulfilled and, consequently, could justifiably deny the existence of any advantage within the meaning of art.107(1) TFEU. Secondly, the ECJ found that the transfer of La Poste's client base, an intangible asset with economic value, to Chronopost did not involve any transfer of state resources as long as La Poste retained the economic value of the activities transferred by virtue of maintaining a majority shareholding in its subsidiary.

Case C–39/06 *Commission of the European Communities v Federal Republic of Germany* [2008] E.C.R. I–00093 (June 19, 2008).

Type of procedure: Action under art.108(2) TFEU for failure to fulfil obligations concerning the state aid implemented for Kahla Porzellan GmbH and Kahla/Thüringen Porzellan GmbH.

Highlights: The Court declares that, in failing to take all the measures necessary to recover certain aid declared incompatible with the common market the Federal Republic of Germany failed to fulfil its obligations. The Court stated that in an infringement action, the illegality of the decision cannot serve as a defense, except if the act is non-existent. Therefore, Member States cannot rely on the general principle of legitimate expectations as a defense for failure to recover illegal aid. It must be raised in an action for annulment against the recovery order.

Case C–49/05 P *Ferriere Nord SpA v Commission of the European Communities* [2008] E.C.R. I–00068 (May 8, 2008).

Type of procedure: Appeal against the judgment of the CFI, dismissing an action for annulment of Commission Decision 2001/829/EC, ECSC of March 28, 2001 on the state aid which Italy is planning to grant to Ferriere Nord SpA.

Appendix 2

Highlights: The ECJ clarified the right of the parties concerned to participate in the formal state aid investigation procedure. The CFI held that when third parties have already submitted their comments during the formal investigation procedure and the Commission is to base its Decision on new principles and criteria for assessment which would alter its analysis of the notified aid, it must invite the parties concerned to submit their comments in that regard. However, most importantly, the CFI considered that in the case at issue the new Guidelines had not changed the relevant criteria. The ECJ upheld this judgment of the CFI. The ECJ found it unnecessary to examine the issue of the law applicable in time, since in any event the contents of the old and the new framework were identical in substance.

Case C–408/04 P *Commission of the European Communities v Salzgitter AG* [2008] E.C.R. I–02767 (April 22, 2008).

Type of procedure: Action for annulment the judgment of the CFI partly annulling a Commission Decision on state aid granted to the Federal Republic of Germany to Salzgitter AG, Preussag Stahl AG and the group's steel-industry subsidiaries, now known as Salzgitter AG—Stahl und Technologie (SAG).

Highlights: The CFI committed an error of law in holding, first, that the adoption of the Third Steel Aid Code led, implicitly, to a partial withdrawal of the authorisation of the ZRFG granted by the 1971 Decision and, second, that art.6 of that code did not make it possible to determine clearly whether application of the ZRFG after adoption of that code was covered by the obligation to notify "plans" laid down in that Article. Even though the CFI was entitled to hold that a beneficiary of state aid can rely on the principle of legal certainty to support an action for annulment of a decision ordering recovery of that aid, it wrongly applied this principle in the case before it when it failed to examine whether the Commission had manifestly failed to act and clearly breached its duty of diligence in the exercise of its supervisory powers, the sole grounds which, in exceptional cases, can render illegal a Commission decision ordering recovery, under the ECSC Treaty, of non-notified aid.

Case C–390/06 *Nuova Agricast Srl v Ministero delle Attività Produttive* [2008] E.C.R. I–02577 (April 15, 2008).

Type of procedure: Reference for a preliminary ruling from the Tribunale ordinario di Roma (Italy), concerning the validity of the Decision of the Commission of July 12, 2000 not to raise objections against an aid scheme for investment in the less-favoured regions of Italy until December 31, 2006.

Highlights: State aid cannot be declared by the Commission to be compatible with the common market if it entails provisions which contravene general principles of Community law, such as the principle of equal treatment. The preliminary stage of the procedure for reviewing aids under art.108(3) TFEU is intended merely to allow the Commission to form a prima facie opinion on the partial or complete conformity of an aid measure or an aid scheme. If this is not the case, the Commission would be encouraged systematically to initiate the investigation procedure under art.108(2) TFEU and to give the parties concerned notice to submit their comments, in order to prevent information which could not be available to it leading to the annulment of its decision to authorise the aid measure or the aid scheme in question. Since the number of categories excluded from the benefit of a measure is potentially unlimited, the Community institutions cannot be under a duty to provide specific reasoning in relation to each of them. Nonetheless, where the beneficiaries of the measure, on the one hand, and other excluded operators, on the other, are in a comparable situation, the Community institution which is the author of the act is under a duty to explain in what way the difference in treatment thus introduced is objectively justified and to give specific reasons in that regard.

Case C–305/07 *Radiotelevisione italiana SpA (RAI) v PTV Programmazioni Televisive SpA* [2008] E.C.R. I–00055 (April 9, 2008).

Type of procedure: Reference for a preliminary ruling from the Tribunale ordinario di Genova (Italy).

Highlights: The reference was dismissed as manifestly inadmissible.

Case C–419/06 *Commission of the European Communities v Hellenic Republic* [2008] E.C.R. I–00027 (February 14, 2008).

Type of procedure: Failure of a Member State to fulfill obligations and to take measures to comply with Commission Decision C(2005) 2706 of September 14, 2005 on the recovery of aid granted to Olympic Airlines.

Highlights: The Court finds that Greece had not fulfilled its obligations, either by the end of the time period laid down by the Commission or by the date on which the present action was brought. In addition, Greece has not relied on any absolute impossibility to implement the decision. In the context of an action for failure to fulfil obligations, a Member State to which a state aid decision has been addressed cannot validly justify failure to implement that decision on the basis of its alleged illegality. The argument of Greece that the solution would be disproportionate was rejected as recovery of aid is the logical consequence of a decision of illegality and cannot therefore be disproportionate.

Case C–199/06 *Centre d'exportation du livre français (CELF) and Ministre de la Culture et de la Communication v Société internationale de diffusion et d'édition (SIDE)* [2008] E.C.R. I–00469 (February 12, 2008).

Type of procedure: Reference for a preliminary ruling from the Conseil d'État (France) concerning the interpretation of art.88(3) EC [now art.108(3) TFEU].

Highlights: National courts are under an obligation to remedy the consequences of an aid being unlawfully implemented. Whilst the Commission has to examine the compatibility of the aid, the national courts must preserve the rights of the individuals faced with a possible breach of the notification requirement. If a recipient has obtained an aid unlawfully, even if it is declared compatible with the Common market, the national Court must order interest to be paid on the amount between the time of the unlawful granting and the compatibility decision. The Court added that where a Commission decision declaring compatible with the common market aid implemented in breach of the last sentence of art.108(3) TFEU is annulled by the Community Court, the obligation arising from that provision to remedy the consequences of the aid's unlawfulness extends also, for the purposes of calculating the sums to be paid by the recipient, and save for exceptional circumstances, to the period between that adoption of the Commission's positive decision and its annulment by the Community court. Furthermore, recipients of unlawful aid cannot rely on the principle of legitimate expectations to preclude the reimbursement of that aid, provided that the Commission decision is challenged within the time limits for appeals.

Case C–280/05 *Commission of the European Communities v Italian Republic* [2007] E.C.R. I–00181 (December 6, 2007).

Type of procedure: Actions for failure to fulfill obligations.

Highlights: The Court declared that, by failing to adopt the measures necessary to recover from the beneficiaries the aid declared unlawful and incompatible with the common market within the prescribed period, the Italian Republic failed to fulfill its obligations. The Court repeated its case-law that the only defence for failure to recover an aid declared incompatible is total impossibility. When faced with difficulties Member States must respect the duty of cooperation (art.4 TFEU) and contact the Commission. An action for annulment as such is not a defence in the infringement proceedings.

Appendix 2

Case C–107/07 *Friedrich Weber v Commission of the European Communities* [2007] E.C.R. I–00177 (November 29, 2007).

Type of procedure: Appeal against the order of the CFI dismissing as inadmissible an action brought against the decision of the Secretary-General of the Commission of May 27, 2005 rejecting the applicant's request for access to a letter sent by the Directorate-General for Competition to the German Federal Government concerning state aid proceedings in relation to the financing of public-law broadcasting bodies in Germany.

Highlights: Appeal was dismissed as manifestly inadmissible.

Case C–176/06 *Stadtwerke Schwäbisch Hall GmbH, Stadtwerke Tübingen GmbH and Stadtwerke Uelzen GmbH v Commission of the European Communities* [2007] E.C.R. I–00170 (November 29, 2007).

Type of procedure: Appeal against the judgment of the CFI dismissing the action seeking annulment of Commission Decision C(2001) 3967 final of December 11, 2001 declaring that the German tax exemption scheme applied to the reserves established by nuclear power stations for the purpose of disposal of their radioactive waste and the permanent closure of their plants does not constitute state aid as referred to in art.107(1) TFEU.

Highlights: The ECJ annulled the CFI judgment because it changed the legal qualification the object of the appeal. The ECJ held that the applicants sought a decision on the substance of the case and did not seek the protection of their procedural rights.

Case C–296/07 P *Commission of the European Communities v Scott SA* [2007] E.C.R. I–00166 (November 22, 2007).

Type of procedure: Appeal against the order of the President of the CFI in Case T–366/00 *R Scott v Commission*, not published in the ECR ("the order under appeal"), ruling that there was no longer any need to take a decision in that case.

Highlights: Under the first subparagraph of art.104(1) of the Rules of Procedure of the CFI, an application to suspend the operation of any measure adopted by an institution, made pursuant to art.278 TFEU, is admissible only if the applicant is challenging that measure in proceedings before the General Court.

Case C–260/05 P *Sniace SA v Commission of the European Communities* [2007] E.C.R. I–10005 (November 22, 2007).

Type of procedure: Appeal against the judgment of the CFI Case T–88/01 *Sniace v Commission* dismissing as inadmissible its action for the annulment of Commission Decision 2001/102/EC of July 19, 2000 on state aid granted by Austria to Lenzing Lyocell GmbH & Co. KG.

Highlights: It is clear from the case law that the appellant ought, on any view of the matter, to have demonstrated that the contested decision was likely to substantially affect its position on the market. In the course of its unappealable assessment of the facts, the CFI concluded that in this case the appellant had not demonstrated that the contested decision was likely to harm its legitimate interests by substantially affecting its position on the market. For the reasons set out in paras 34–40 of this judgment, none of the arguments advanced by the appellant in support of the first ground of appeal can call into question that conclusion.

Case C–525/04 P *Kingdom of Spain v Commission of the European Communities* [2007] E.C.R. I–09947 (November 22, 2007).

Type of procedure: Appeal against the judgment of the CFI Case T–36/99 *Lenzing v Commission* partly annulling Commission Decision 1999/395/EC of October 28, 1998 on state aid implemented by Spain in favour of Sniace SA, located in Torrelavega, Cantabria as amended by Commission Decision 2001/43/EC of September 20, 2000.

Highlights: The ECJ reiterated the point that when attempting to establish individual concern in the field of state aid, an undertaking cannot rely solely on its status as a competitor of the recipient undertaking but must also demonstrate that its circumstances distinguish it in a similar way to the undertaking in receipt of the aid. The CFI did not merely note in general terms that Lenzing and Sniace were in competition with each other, but based its findings as to the adverse effect on Lenzing's position on the market on a number of factors adduced by the latter to show in essence the distinctiveness of the competitive situation of the viscose fibres market, which was characterised by a very small number of producers and by serious production overcapacity, the significance of the distortion created by the grant of aid to an undertaking operating in such a market, and the effect of that aid on the prices applied by Sniace. The CFI was entitled to conclude that keeping an operator in business in a market displaying the characteristics of the viscose market, characteristics which the Spanish Government did not dispute, might have appreciable effects on the position of its competitors. The CFI did not base its assessment of the measures in question on any illegality per se of the debt-rescheduling and debt-repayment agreements or on the presumption that, if those agreements were not honoured, any private creditor would necessarily initiate enforcement procedures in order to recover the debts owed to him. On the contrary, the CFI concluded that the Commission made a manifest error of assessment, in the light of a series of factors and circumstances peculiar to the case in point.

Case C–12/07 *Autostrada dei Fiori SpA and Associazione Nazionale dei Gestori delle Autostrade (AISCAT) v Governo della Repubblica italiana and Others* [2007] E.C.R. I–00162 (November 16, 2007).

Type of procedure: Reference for a preliminary ruling by the Tribunale di Gevova (Italy).

Highlights: Questions referred without sufficient explanation of the factual and legislative context. The reference for a preliminary ruling, was manifestly inadmissible.

Case C–441/06 *Commission of the European Communities v French Republic* [2007] E.C.R. I–08887 (October 18, 2007).

Type of procedure: Action under art.108(2) TFEU for failure of a Member State to fulfil obligations by failing to execute within the prescribed period Commission Decision 2005/709/EC on the state aid implemented by France for France Télécom.

Highlights: When ordering the recovery of incompatible aid, the Commission is not required to fix the exact amount be recovered. It is sufficient for the Commission's decision to include information enabling the recipient to work out itself, without too much difficulty, the amount. Where a Member State fails to provide the Commission with the information requested and necessary for calculation of the amount of aid to be recovered it fails to fulfill its obligations under art.4(3) TFEU.

Case C–320/05 P *Fred Olsen SA v Commission of the European Communities* [2007] E.C.R. I–00131 (October 4, 2007).

Type of procedure: Appeal against the judgment of the CFI in Case T–17/02 *Olsen v Commission*, dismissing the action for annulment of the Commission's Decision of July 25, 2001 relating to state aid file NN 48/2001, aid for the Transmediterránea shipping company.

Highlights: Appeal was dismissed because the arguments raised by applicant were manifestly unfounded.

Case C–177/06 *Commission of the European Communities v Kingdom of Spain* [2007] E.C.R. I–07689 (September 20, 2007).

Type of procedure: Action under art.108(2) TFEU for failure to fulfill obligations, brought on April 4, 2006.

Highlights: In an action for failure to fulfil obligations, except in the case of the non-existence of the act, a Member State is not entitled to raise the defence of the unlawfulness of a negative decision of the Commission when a direct action against that decision is pending before the Community Courts. The only defence available in opposing an application by the Commission under art.108(2) TFEU for a declaration of failure to fulfill Treaty obligations is to plead that it was absolutely impossible for it properly to implement the decision. In an action for failure to fulfill obligations brought by the Commission under art.108(2) TFEU, the Court does not need to examine the form of order sought against a Member State for failing to notify the Commission of the measures implementing a decision declaring a system of aid incompatible with the common market and requiring it to be withdrawn, with suspension of aid not yet paid and recovery of aid already paid, where that Member State did not in fact implement the decision within the prescribed period.

Case C–191/07 P *Jean-Yves Sellier v Commission of the European Communities* [2007] E.C.R. I–00113 (September 18, 2007).

Type of procedure: Appeal against the order of the CFI dismissing as inadmissible the action by the applicant for annulment of the Commission's Decision of July 14, 2006 to take no action on his complaint alleging that French legislation concerning the deposit of funds held by notaries with certain banking establishments was contrary to Community law.

Highlights: The Court dismissed the appeal as manifestly inadmissible.

Case C–119/05 *Ministeri dell'Industria, del Commercio e dell'Artigianato v Lucchini SpA* [2007] E.C.R. I–06199 (July 18, 2007).

Type of procedure: Reference for a preliminary ruling by the Consiglio di Stato (Italy).

Highlights: A national court which is called upon to apply provisions of Community law is under a duty to give full effect to those provisions, if necessary refusing of its own motion to apply any conflicting provision of national legislation. The primacy of Community law means requires that the assessment of the compatibility of aid measures with the common market falls within the exclusive competence of the Commission. The ECJ ruled that national courts are under an obligation to give full effect to Community law, if necessary by refusing to apply any conflicting provision of national legislation, including the principle of res judicata.

Case C–404/04 P *Technische Glaswerke Ilmenau GmbH v Commission of the European Communities* [2007] E.C.R. I–00001 (January 11, 2007).

Type of procedure: Appeal against the judgment of the CFI in Case T–198/01 *Technische Glaswerke Ilmenau v Commission* dismissing the action for annulment of Commission Decision 2002/185/EC of June 12, 2001 on state aid implemented by Germany for Technische Glaswerke Ilmenau GmbH.

Highlights: The appeal consists largely of a reiteration of the pleas and arguments put forward before the General Court the other arguments are ill-founded.

Joined Cases C–485/03 to C–490/03 *Commission of the European Communities v Kingdom of Spain* [2006] E.C.R. I–11887 (December 14, 2006).

Type of procedure: Actions for failure to fulfill obligations pursuant to art.108(2) TFEU, brought on November 19, 2003.

Highlights: When negative decisions are taken in cases of unlawful aid, the recovery thereof ordered by the Commission takes place under the conditions set out in art.14(3) of Council Regulation (EC) No.659/1999. The only defence available to a Member State in opposing an application by the Commission under art.108(2) TFEU for a declaration that it has failed to fulfill its Treaty obligations is to plead that it was absolutely impossible for it properly to implement the decision ordering recovery. The condition that it be absolutely impossible to implement a decision is not fulfilled where the defendant government merely informs the Commission of the legal, political or practical difficulties involved in implementing the decision, without taking any real step to recover the aid from the undertakings concerned, and without proposing to the Commission any alternative arrangements for implementing the decision which could have enabled those difficulties to be overcome.

Case C–232/05 *Commission of the European Communities v French Republic* [2006] E.C.R. I–10071 (October 5, 2006).

Type of procedure: Action for failure to fulfill obligations pursuant to art.108(2) TFEU.

Highlights: The application of national procedures should not impede the restoration of effective competition by preventing the immediate and effective execution of the Commission's decision for the recovery of incompatible state aid under art.14(3) Regulation 659/1999. The legality of the Commission decision must be challenged in the CFI and cannot be invoked in the national court procedure, at least not when the decision was not challenged in the CFI in time.

Case C–368/04 *Transalpine Ölleitung in Österreich GmbH and Others v Finanzlandesdirektion für Tirol and Others* [2006] E.C.R. I–09957 (October 5, 2006).

Type of procedure: Reference for a preliminary ruling from the Verwaltungsgerichtshof (Austria) concerning the interpretation of the last sentence of art.108(3) TFEU.

Highlights: Whilst assessment of the compatibility of aid measures with the common market falls within the exclusive competence of the Commission, subject to review by the Community Courts, it is for the national courts to ensure that the rights of individuals are safeguarded where the obligation to give prior notification of state aid to the Commission pursuant to art.108(3) is infringed. A Commission decision finding aid which was not notified compatible with the common market does not have the effect of regularizing ex post facto implementing measures which were invalid because they were taken in disregard of the prohibition laid down by the last sentence of art.108(3) TFEU, since otherwise the direct effect of that provision would be impaired and the interests of individuals, which are to be protected by national courts, would be disregarded. The last sentence of art.108(3) TFEU must be interpreted as meaning that it is for the national courts to safeguard the rights of individuals against possible disregard, by the national authorities, of the prohibition on putting aid into effect before the Commission has adopted a decision authorising that aid. In doing so, the national court must take the Community interest fully into consideration and must not adopt a measure which would have the sole effect of extending the circle of recipients of the aid.

Case C–336/04 *Banca Popolare FriulAdria SpA v Agenzia delle Entrate, Ufficio Pordenone* [2006] E.C.R. I–00091 (September 14, 2006).

Type of procedure: Reference for a preliminary ruling from the Commissione tributaria provinciale di Pordenone (Italy) on the validity of Commission Decision 2002/581/EC relating to tax measures for banks and banking foundations implemented by Italy.

Highlights: Article 107 TFEU et seq., art.14 of Council Regulation (EC) No.659/1999, and the principles of the protection of legitimate expectations, legal certainty and proportionality cannot preclude a national measure ordering the recovery of aid pursuant to a Commission decision which has classified that aid as incompatible with the common market and consideration of which in the light of those same provisions and general principles has disclosed no factor of such a kind as to affect its validity.

Case C–186/02 P *Comunidad Autónoma de la Rioja v Ramondín SA and Ramondín Cápsulas SA* [2006] E.C.R. I–00091 (September 14, 2006).

Type of procedure: Appeal against the judgment of the CFI in Joined Cases T–92/00 and T–103/00 *Diputación Foral de Álava and Others v Commission* dismissing their applications for annulment of Commission Decision 2000/795/EC of December 22, 1999 on the state aid implemented by Spain for Ramondín SA and Ramondín Cápsulas SA.

Highlights: The CFI rightly observed that a measure is only vitiated by misuse of powers if it appears, on the basis of objective, relevant and consistent evidence, to have been taken with the exclusive or main purpose of achieving an end other than that stated. The appeals were dismissed.

Case C–526/04 *Laboratoires Boiron SA v Union de recouvrement des cotisations de sécurité sociale et d'allocations familiales (Urssaf) de Lyon* [2006] E.C.R. I–07529 (September 7, 2006).

Type of procedure: Reference for a preliminary reference from the Cour de Cassation (France) state aid concerning the interpretation of various provisions of the EC Treaty relating to state aid, but particularly arts 107 TFEU and 108(3) TFEU.

Highlights: Community law must be interpreted as meaning that a pharmaceutical laboratory liable to pay a contribution such as that provided for by art.12 of Law No.97–1164 is entitled to plead that the fact that wholesale distributors are not liable for that contribution constitutes state aid, in order to obtain reimbursement of the part of the sums paid which corresponds to the economic advantage unfairly obtained by wholesale distributors. Community law does not preclude the application of rules of national law which make reimbursement of an obligatory contribution, such as that provided for in art.12 of Law No.97–1164, subject to proof by the claimant seeking reimbursement that the advantage derived by wholesale distributors from their not being liable to pay that contribution exceeds the costs which they bear in discharging the public service obligations imposed on them by the national rules and, in particular, that at least one of the so-called *Altmark* conditions is not satisfied. In order to ensure compliance with the principle of effectiveness, if the national court finds that the fact of requiring a pharmaceutical laboratory such as Boiron to prove that wholesale distributors are overcompensated, and thus that the tax on direct sales amounts to state aid, is likely to make it impossible or excessively difficult for such evidence to be produced, since inter alia that evidence relates to data which such a laboratory will not have, the national court is required to use all procedures available to it under national law, including that of ordering the necessary measures of inquiry, in particular the production by one of the parties or a third party of a particular document.

Case C–88/03 *Portuguese Republic v Commission of the European Communities* [2006] E.C.R. I–07115 (September 6, 2006).

Type of procedure: Action for annulment of Commission Decision 2003/442/EC on the part of the scheme adapting the national tax system to the specific characteristics of the Autonomous Region of the Azores which concerned reductions in the rates of income and corporation tax.

Highlights: In order to determine whether a measure was selective and consequently likely to constitute state aid, it was necessary to examine the reference framework which was not necessarily that of the territory of the Member State concerned. In the case of a measure adopted by an infra-state entity which establishes a lower tax rate in part of the territory of a Member State, the framework could therefore be limited to the geographical area concerned where the entity, notably by virtue of its status and powers, occupied a fundamental role in the definition of the political and economic environment in which the undertakings present on the territory under its competence operated. This question could arise only if three conditions were met: the decision must have been taken by a regional or local authority which had, from a constitutional point of view, a political and administrative status separate from that of the central government; it must have been adopted without the central government being able to directly intervene as regards its content; and finally, the financial consequences of a reduction of the rate for undertakings in the region must not be offset by aid or subsidies from other regions or central government, the regional or local authority assuming the political and financial consequences of such a measure.

Case C–399/03 *Commission of the European Communities v Council of the European Union* [2006] E.C.R. I–05629 (June 22, 2006).

Type of procedure: By its application, the Commission sought annulment of Council Decision 2003/531/EC on the granting of aid by the Belgian Government to certain coordination centres established in Belgium.

Highlights: If the Member State has made no application to the Council under the third paragraph of art.108(2) TFEU before the Commission declares the aid incompatible with the common market, the Council is no longer authorized to exercise the exceptional power conferred upon to declare such aid compatible with the common market. The Council can neither counter such a Commission decision by itself declaring that aid compatible with the market, nor undermine the effectiveness of that decision by declaring compatible with the common market, in accordance with the third subparagraph of art.108(2) TFEU, an aid designed to compensate the beneficiaries of the unlawful aid declared incompatible with the common market for the repayments they are required to make pursuant to that decision.

Joined Cases C–182/03 and C–217/03 *Kingdom of Belgium (C–182/03) and Forum 187 ASBL (C–217/03) v Commission of the European Communities* [2006] E.C.R. I–05479 (June 22, 2006).

Type of procedure: Action for annulment of Commission Decision 2003/757/EC on the aid scheme implemented by Belgium for coordination centers established in Belgium in so far as it does not authorise it to grant, even temporarily, renewal of coordination centre status to the coordination centers which benefited from that scheme as at December 31, 2000.

Highlights: Forum 187 has not established that the regime in question is justified by the nature or the general scheme of the Belgian tax system of which it forms part and it must therefore be held that the selective nature of the scheme has been established. It is sufficient to find that the shortfall of tax and social security revenue on that State's part resulting from the exemptions considered above means that the advantages which they gave rise to are granted through state resources. Where the Community had first created a situation capable of giving rise to legitimate expectations, an overriding public interest may preclude transitional measures from being adopted in respect of situations which arose before the new rules came into force but which are still subject to change. The ECJ reiterates that the general principle of equal treatment requires that comparable situations must not be treated differently and that different situations must not be treated in the same way unless such treatment is objectively justified. By failing to adopt transitional measures for those coordination centres with an authorisation which expired at the same time as or shortly after the notification of the contested decision, the Commission infringed the general principle of equal treatment and so the decision was annulled.

Case C–399/03 *Commission of the European Communities v Council of the European Union* [2006] E.C.R. I–5629 (September 23, 2006).

Type of procedure: Action for annulment of Council Decision 2003/531/EC on the granting of aid by Belgium to certain coordination centres established in Belgium.

Highlights: The ECJ annulled the unanimous Council decision adopted under the third paragraph of art.108(2) TFEU setting aside the Commission Decision and declaring the aid scheme compatible. It recalled its judgment in Case C–110/02 *Commission v Council* of June 29, 2004, in which it held that the right conferred on the Council to take a unanimous decision on a state aid scheme can never be exercised where the Commission has already taken a decision on the same scheme.

Case C–466/04 *Manuel Acereda Herrera v Servicio Cántabro de Salud* [2006] E.C.R. I–05341 (June 15, 2006).

Type of procedure: Reference for a preliminary ruling from the Tribunal Superior de Justicia de Cantabria (Spain) on the interpretation of arts 22 and 36 of Council Regulation (EEC) No.1408/71 of June 14, 1971 on the application of social security schemes to employed persons, to self-employed persons and to members of their families moving within the Community, and the interpretation of arts 10 EC, 12 EC, 49 EC, 81 EC, 82 EC, 87 EC and 249 EC [now arts 18, 56, 101, 102, 107 and 288 TFEU].

Highlights: The Court cannot give a preliminary ruling on a question submitted by a national court where it is quite obvious that the ruling sought by that court on the interpretation or validity of Community law bears no relation to the actual facts of the main action or its purpose, where the problem is hypothetical. The justification for a reference for a preliminary ruling is not that it enables advisory opinions on general or hypothetical questions to be delivered but rather that it is necessary for the effective resolution of a dispute.

Joined Cases C–393 and C–41/05 *Air Liquide Industries Belgium SA v Ville de Seraing and Province de Liège* [2006] E.C.R. I–05293 (June 15, 2006).

Type of procedure: Reference for a preliminary ruling from the Cour d'appel de Liège (Belgium) and Tribunal de première instance de Liège concerning the interpretation of the concept of state aid and the legal consequences which may arise at national level because of such aid. It also concerned the interpretation of the concepts of charge having equivalent effect and internal taxation.

Highlights: The exemption from a municipal or provincial tax on motive force granted solely in respect of motors used in natural gas stations, to the exclusion of motors used for other industrial gases, may be regarded as state aid within the meaning of art.87 EC [now art.107 TFEU]. It is for the referring courts to establish whether the conditions relating to the existence of state aid are met. Those liable to pay a tax cannot rely on the argument that the exemption enjoyed by other businesses constitutes state aid in order to avoid payment of that tax or to obtain reimbursement of it, since even if the exemption at issue constitutes aid within the meaning of art.107 TFEU, the fact that the aid may be unlawful does not affect the tax itself.

Case C–207/05 *Commission of the European Communities v Italian Republic* [2006] E.C.R. I–00070 (June 1, 2006).

Type of procedure: Action under art.108(2) TFEU for failure to fulfill obligations by the Italian Republic.

Highlights: The Court declares that by failing to adopt, within the prescribed period, the necessary measures to recover from the recipients aid declared unlawful and incompatible with the common market by Commission Decision 2003/193/EC, the Italian Republic failed to fulfill its obligations under arts 3 and 4 of that Decision.

Case C–442/03 P and C–471/03 P *P & O European Ferries (Vizcaya) SA (C–442/03 P) and Diputación Foral de Vizcaya (C–471/03 P) v Commission of the European Communities* E.C.R. I–04845 (June 1, 2006).

Type of procedure: Appeal against the judgment of the CFI in Joined Cases T–116/01 and T–118/01 *P&O European Ferries (Vizcaya) and Diputación Foral de Vizcaya v Commission* dismissing an application seeking the annulment of art.2 of Commission Decision 2001/247/EC of November 29, 2000 on the aid scheme implemented by Spain in favour of the shipping company Ferries Golfo de Vizcaya SA, now P&O European Ferries (Vizcaya) SA, and ordering the repayment of the aid held to be incompatible with the common market.

Highlights: Under art.108(3) TFEU only the Member States are required to notify any plans to grant or alter state aid. That obligation will not be satisfied through notification by the undertaking receiving the aid. There are no specific obligations on the recipient of aid under art.108 TFEU. Therefore, the fact that on the date on which a proposal for an agreement was sent to the Commission, it is irrelevant that no legislation provided that notification had to be made by the government concerned in order to be lawful. The CFI found that the aid at issue was unlawful and consequently rejected the complaints set out in the preceding paragraph of this judgment. The CFI wrongly held that the parties concerned and the Commission themselves considered the aid in dispute to be un-notified aid.

Case C–451/03 *Servizi Ausiliari Dottori Commercialisti Srl v Giuseppe Calafiori* [2006] E.C.R. I–02941 (March 30, 2006).

Type of procedure: Reference for a preliminary ruling from the Corte d'appello di Milano (Italy) concerning the interpretation of arts 4 EC, 10 EC, 82 EC, 86 EC and 98 EC [now arts 119, 102, 106 and 120 TFEU] on competition, arts 43 EC, 48 EC and 49 EC [now arts 49, 54, and 56 TFEU] relating to freedom of establishment and freedom to provide services, and art.87 EC [now art.107 TFEU] on state aid.

Highlights: A measure by which a Member State provides for the payment of compensation from state funds to certain undertakings responsible for helping taxpayers in connection with the completion of tax declarations and filing them with the tax authorities must be classified as state aid within the meaning of art.107(1) TFEU, where:

- the level of the compensation exceeds what is necessary to cover all or part of the costs incurred in the discharge of public service obligations, taking into account the relevant receipts and a reasonable profit for discharging those obligations; and

- the compensation is not determined on the basis of an analysis of the costs which a typical undertaking, well run and adequately provided with the means required so as to be able to meet the necessary public service requirements, would have incurred in discharging those obligations, taking into account the relevant receipts and a reasonable profit for discharging the obligations.

APPENDIX 3

GENERAL COURT JUDGMENTS AND ORDERS

Joined Cases T–109/05 and 444/05 *Navigazione Libera del Golfo Srl (NLG) v European Commission* [2011] judgment of May 24, 2011.

Type of procedure: Application for annulment of Commission Decisions D(2005) 997 of February 3, 2005 and D(2005) 9766 of October 12, 2005 refusing the applicant access to certain information which was not reproduced in the published version of Commission Decision 2005/163/EC of March 16, 2004 on the state aid paid by Italy to the Adriatica, Caremar, Siremar, Saremar and Toremar shipping companies.

Highlights: The Court annuled Commission Decision D(2005) 997 of February 3, 2005 in so far as it concerned refusal of access to detailed elements of the extra costs borne annually by Caremar SpA relating to passenger transport services on the Naples-Beverello/Capri line both by ferries and by high-speed craft.

Case T–423/07 *Ryanair Ltd v Commission* [2011] judgment of May 19, 2011.

Type of procedure: Application for a declaration that the Commission failed to act in unlawfully failing to adopt a position on the applicant's complaint concerning, first, aid allegedly granted by the Federal Republic of Germany to Lufthansa and its Star Alliance partners in the form of the exclusive use of Terminal 2 at Munich Airport (Germany) and, second, alleged abuse of a dominant position by Munich Airport.

Highlights: The Court affirmed the general duty of the Commission under Regulations 1/2003 and 773/2004, when seised of a complaint, to examine carefully the factual and legal considerations brought to its notice by the complainant, before it makes a decision, within a reasonable time, about whether to investigate further. Where it adjudges that investigation of a complaint under art.102 TFEU is not necessary it must inform the applicant of its decision.

The Court considered that the applicant did not satisfy the requirements prescribed in those Regulations. The applicant alleged only that the exclusive use by Lufthansa and its Star Alliance partners of Terminal 2 at Munich Airport constituted abuse of a dominant position. The applicant's complaint did not contain any statement of facts which explained in what way Munich Airport occupied a dominant position, or why the fact of reserving Terminal 2 for Lufthansa and its Star Alliance partners constituted abuse of a dominant position by Munich Airport. For this reason the complaint lodged could not be classified as a complaint brought in accordance with Regulations 1/2003 and 773/2004. Therefore, at the time when the Commission was formally called upon to define its position within the meaning of art.232 EC [now art.265 TFEU], it was not under a duty to act.

As to the state aid part of the complaint, the Court held that by adopting one of the decisions referred to in the letter of formal notice, the Commission had properly defined its position and the letter has become devoid of purpose.

Case T–1/08 *Buczek Automotive sp z o.o. v European Commission* [2011] judgment of May 17, 2011.

Type of procedure: Action for partial annulment of Commission negative decision.

Highlights: The General Court partially annulled the Commission's decision in Case C23/06 *Technologie Buczek*, on the grounds that: i) the Commission did not prove that the method chosen by the Polish authorities for ensuring recovery of public debt from the company did not meet the market economy creditor test; and ii) the Commission did not substantiate its reasoning that the measures would have an effect on competition and intra-community trade.

The Court reaffirmed the established jurisprudence on the application of the market economy creditor test to measures taken to ensure recovery of public debt from a company in difficulty. The test is whether a market creditor in a similar situation, taking into account all relevant factors, would have chosen to recover outright through bankruptcy proceedings, or would have accepted a (collective) debt reorganisation agreement allowing the company to continue its activity. The Court confirmed the Commission's conclusion that, by not asking for an insolvency procedure, the authorities had granted an advantage to the beneficiary. However, the Commission did not adequately demonstrate that this advantage would not have been granted under normal market circumstances, in accordance with the criterion of the hypothetical private creditor. The Commission ought to have demonstrated that the bankruptcy scenario would have been more advantageous for a market creditor than recovery through a debt reorganisation agreement.

The judgment confirms the jurisprudence on the duty to state reasons for finding effect on competition and intra-community trade according to which the Commission does not have to provide an extensive market analysis, but must nevertheless indicate the reasons which led it to conclude that the measure(s) in question have an effect on competition and intra-community trade. It is not sufficient simply to state that the measures had an effect on competition and intra-community trade.

Joined Cases T–443/08 and T–455/08 *Freistaat Sachsen and Land Sachsen-Anhalt and Mitteldeutsche Flughafen AG and Flughafen Leipzig-Halle GmbH v European Commission* [2011] judgment of March 24, 2011.

Type of procedure: Application seeking annulment of a Commission decision approving as compatible aid a capital injection of €350 million granted in 2004 for the purpose of construction of a new southern runway at Leipzig-Halle airport.

Highlights: The operation of an airport is an economic activity. The public financing of the construction of airport infrastructure constitutes state aid. The only exception is with regards to certain activities that form part of the exercise of public powers. For qualification of an activity as economic, it is of no relevance that it is not carried out by private operators or would not be profitable.

Case T–3/09 *Italian Republic v European Commission* [2011] judgment of February 3, 2011.

Type of procedure: Application for annulment of Commission Decision 2010/38/EC of October 21, 2008 on state aid C 20/08 which Italy was planning to implement through a modification of scheme N 59/04 concerning a temporary defensive mechanism for shipbuilding.

Highlights: Where state aid has been notified but not yet paid, in its review the Commission adopts its decision on the compatibility with the common market on the basis of the date on which the effects of the planned aid become established. Where the aid has been paid unlawfully with no prior notification, the relevant rules are those in force at the time when the aid was paid. It was held by the Court that Regulation No.1177/2002 does not contain provisions exempting the Member States of their obligation to notify under art.108(3) TFEU [ex. 88(3)].

Case T–584/08 *Cantiere navale De Poli SpA v European Commission* [2011] judgment of February 3, 2011.

Type of procedure: Action for annulment of Commission Decision 2010/38/EC of October 21, 2008 on state aid concerning a temporary defensive mechanism for shipbuilding.

Highlights: The Commission cannot be criticised for not taking into account comments submitted by the applicant more than three months after the expiry of a period clearly stated in the Official Journal and has not failed in any procedural obligation by not doing so. Where aid has been granted unlawfully without prior notification, the relevant substantive rules are those in force at the time when the aid was paid. Regulation No.1177/2002 does not contain any provisions which alter the fundamental obligation to notify under art.108(3) (ex. 88(3) EC).

Joined Cases T–231/06 and T–237/06 *Kingdom of the Netherlands and Nederlandse Omroep Stichting v European Commission* [2010] E.C.R. (December 16, 2010).

Type of procedure: Application for the annulment of Commission Decision 2008/136/EC of June 22, 2006 concerning subsidies to the public broadcasting.

Highlights: The Commission cannot use in its decision facts with respect to which the Member State did not have an opportunity to be heard. The beneficiaries are involved in the administrative procedure as interested parties and do not have the same rights of defence as the Member States. There is no violation of the rights of defense or the more limited rights of the beneficiaries, if the final decision differs from the opening decision as a result of the evolution of the file.

The NOS (the public broadcasting organization) is an "undertaking", albeit one charged with a public task. As to the four *Altmark* criteria, the Court concludes that the Commission in its decision has sufficiently explained why the criteria are not satisfied in this case. Therefore, the compensation in question qualifies as state aid. Furthermore, the Court has established that the Commission was right in finding that certain ad hoc payments, all things considered, qualify as new aid rather than existing aid.

Joined Cases T–494/08 and 500/08 and 509/08 *Ryanair Ltd v European Commission* [2010] E.C.R. (December 10, 2010).

Type of procedure: Application for annulment of the Commission's implied decisions refusing to grant to the applicant access to certain documents relating to procedures for reviewing state aid allegedly granted to the applicant by the operators of various airports. In addition it sought annulment of the subsequent express decisions refusing access to those documents.

Highlights: The Court restated the principle that an applicant's interest in bringing proceedings must, in the light of the purpose of the action, exist at the stage of lodging the action, failing which the action will be inadmissible. If this interest disappears in the course of proceedings, a decision of the Court on the merits will not bring him any benefit.

Interested parties are entitled to rebut the general presumption that documents, disclosure of which has been requested, would, in principle, undermine the purpose of the investigation or further adduce evidence that there is a higher public interest justifying the disclosure of the document concerned by virtue of art.4(2) of reg. No.1049/2001 The applicant did not adduce evidence capable of rebutting the general presumption and so the application for annulment was rejected.

Case T–11/07 *Frucona Košice a.s. v European Commission* [2010] E.C.R. (December 7, 2010).

Type of procedure: Action for annulment of Decision 2007/254/EC of June 7, 2006 on state aid C 25/05 (ex. NN 21/2005) implemented by the Slovak Republic for Frucona Košice a.s.

Highlights: The Court recalls that the legality of a decision regarding state aid is to be assessed in the light of the information available to the Commission when the decision was adopted. An applicant cannot rely on matters of fact which were not put forward in the course of the pre litigation procedure laid down in art.108 TFEU [ex. 88 EC]. In deciding that DG Comp was the appropriate Directorate-General to carry out the investigation, the Court had regard to the high proportion of the undertaking's turnover generated by its activities related to the production of alcohol and spirits.

The Court reiterated that, when reviewing the Commission's application of the test of a private creditor in a market economy, the Court must restrict itself to verifying whether the Commission complied with the relevant rules governing procedure and the statement of reasons, whether the facts have been accurately stated and whether there has been any manifest error of assessment of those facts or a misuse of powers.

According to the case law, under the procedure for reviewing state aid, the role of interested parties other than the Member State concerned is confined to providing the Commission with all the information needed to guide it with regard to its future action. The action was dismissed in its entirety.

Case T–452/08 *DHL Aviation SA/NV and DHL Hub Leipzig GmbH v European Commission* [2010] judgment of October 7, 2010.

Type of procedure: Application for the partial annulment of Commission Decision 2008/948/EC of July 23, 2008 on measures by Germany to assist DHL and Leipzig-Halle Airport.

Highlights: The recovery of unlawful aid will not depend on the consequences under national law of failure to comply with art.108(3) TFEU. Thus, the fact that the benefits received might be regarded as void under German law did not alter the fact that DHL actually received the aid in question and it would seriously compromise the aims of EU state aid rules if such aid could not be recovered on this basis. Consequently, the Court dismissed the action.

Case T–193/06 *Télévision française 1 SA (TF1) v European Commission* [2010] judgment of September 13, 2010.

Type of procedure: Application for annulment of Commission Decision C(2006) 832 final of March 22, 2006 relating to support measures for the cinema and audiovisual industry in France.

Highlights: The General Court dismissed the action brought by TF1 seeking annulment of the Commission decision of 2006 approving French aid in support of cinematographic and audiovisual production because TF1 did not demonstrate that it was individually concerned by that decision. Specifically, it did not demonstrate that its competitive position was substantially affected in relation to its competitors, television service providers and large audiovisual communications groups which are beneficiaries of the measures at issue.

Case T–415/05, T–416/05 and T–423/05 *Hellenic Republic (T–415/05), Olympiakes Aerogrammes AE (T–416/05) and Olympiaki Aeroporia Ypiresies AE (T–423/05) v European Commission* [2010] judgment of September 13, 2010.

Type of procedure: Application for annulment of Commission Decision C(2005) 2706 final of September 14, 2005 on state aid for Olympiaki Aeroporia Ypiresies AE.

Highlights: The General Court annuled, in part, the Commission's decision relating to state aid granted to Olympic Airways and Olympic Airlines. The Commission did not examine the relationship between the rents paid by Olympic Airlines for the sub-leasing of aircraft and market rents and further failed to examine individually the value of various intangible assets transferred to that company as part of the restructuring of Olympic Airways.

Case T–359/04 *British Aggregates Association and Others v European Commission* [2010] judgment of September 9, 2010.

Type of procedure: Application for annulment of Commission Decision C(2004) 1614 final of May 7, 2004 not to raise objections to the modified exemption for Northern Ireland in the context of the scheme of levies on aggregates in the United Kingdom.

Highlights: State aid cannot be approved if found to be discriminatory. Despite its margin of discretion, the Commission cannot declare as compatible aid that violates specific obligations arising from other Treaty provisions. The Treaty does not allow for the approval of aid in the form of tax discrimination in respect of products originating from another EU Member State. The Commission did not examine the issue of tax discrimination and the possible violation of arts 28, 29, and 110 TFEU and so the Court found that the Commission was not entitled to adopt a decision of no objection. Therefore, the Court annulled Commission Decision C(2004) 1614 final not to raise objections to the change in the exemption, in Northern Ireland, from the levy on aggregates in the United Kingdom.

Case T–369/08 *Freistaat Sachsen and Land Sachsen-Anhalt v European Commission* [2010] E.C.R. (July 8, 2010).

Type of procedure: Application for the partial annulment of Commission Decision 2008/878/EC of July 2, 2008 on state aid which Germany was planning to implement for DHL.

Highlights: The General Court dismissed the appeal which held that the proposed grant of training aid to the express courier services company, DHL, was incompatible with the internal market.

Case T–304/08 *Smurfit Kappa Group v Commission* [2010] E.C.R. (July 5, 2010).

Type of procedure: Action for the annulment of Commission Decision C(2008) 1107 of April 2, 2008, declaring compatible with the common market national regional aid which the German authorities intend to grant to Propapier PM2 for the construction of a paper mill at Eisenhüttenstadt.

Highlights: The term "business secrets" relates to particular information of a commercial, competition-related, financial or accounting nature, where that information is not normally available to third parties outside the undertaking and which, because it is recent, cannot be considered to be historic. Information can lose its confidential nature where the public at large or specialist circles can have access to it. Unless there is evidence of a special interest in protecting its confidentiality, information that is five or more years old is generally historic.

Joined Cases T–568/08 and T–573/08 *Métropole télévision (M6) and Télévision française 1 SA (TF1) v European Commission* [2010] E.C.R. (July 1, 2010).

Type of procedure: Applications for annulment of Commission Decision C (2008) 3506 final of July 16, 2008 relating to the proposed grant, by the French Republic, of capital funding of €150 million to France Télévisions SA, and applications for an order that the Commission open a formal investigation procedure.

Highlights: Where a state measure for financing a public service constitutes state aid within the meaning of the Treaty, that measure can nevertheless be declared compatible with the common market if it meets the conditions laid down in the Treaty. The Court dismissed the action, ruling that the Commission had no basis for suspicion that the funding would be used for purposes other than for financing public service broadcasting.

Case T–335/08 *BNP Paribas and Banca Nazionale del Lavoro SpA (BNL) v European Commission* [2010] E.C.R. (July 1, 2010).

Type of procedure: Application for annulment of Commission Decision 2008/711/EC of March 11, 2008 on state aid C 15/07 (ex. NN 20/07) implemented by Italy on the tax incentives in favour of certain restructured banks.

Highlights: In this case, a favourable tax regime was in place for profits realised upon the transfer of banking assets as part of a realignment. While it was argued by the applicant that the special tax treatment under this regime should not be compared with the normal tax system because companies would not have disposed of the assets in the absence of the special regime, the Court pointed out that the situation to be assessed must be based on a company's actual conduct. Hence, the correct comparison was that of using the normal regime as it is to be assumed that the company would also have disposed its assets in the absence of the special regime.

Judgments in Cases T–53/08, T–62/08, T–63/08 and T–64/08 *Italian Republic, ThyssenKrupp Acciai Speciali Terni SpA, Cementir Italia and Nuova Terni Industrie Chimiche v European Commission* [2010] judgment of July 1, 2010.

Type of procedure: Application for annulment of Commission Decision 2008/408/EC of November 20, 2007 on state aid C 36/A/06 (ex. NN 38/06) implemented by Italy in favour of ThyssenKrupp, Cementir and Nuova Terni Industrie Chimiche.

Highlights: Measures which, in various forms, mitigate the burdens normally included in the budget of an undertaking, such as the supply of goods or services on preferential terms, constitute benefits. With regards to the review of state aid, the principle of observance of the rights of the defence requires that the Member State concerned be able to effectively make known its views on the observations submitted by interested third parties. However, the Commission is not required to hear the views of the recipient of state resources or to inform the Member State and/or the aid recipient concerned, before adopting its decision, where the interested parties and the Member State concerned have been given notice to submit their comments. Undertakings to which aid has been granted may not entertain a legitimate expectation that the aid is lawful unless it has been granted in compliance with procedural requirements, that is, following prior notification. For these reasons, the Court dismissed the actions.

Case T–177/07 *Mediaset SpA v European Commission* [2010] judgment of June 15, 2010.

Type of procedure: Application for the annulment of Commission Decision 2007/374/EC of January 24, 2007 on state aid C 52/2005 (ex. NN 88/2005, ex. CP 101/2004) implemented by the Italian Republic for the subsidised purchase of digital decoders.

Highlights: A plea based on infringement of art.253 EC (now 296 TFEU) is a separate plea from one based on a manifest error of assessment. While the former, which alleges absence of reasons or inadequacy of the reasons stated, goes to an issue of infringement of essential procedural requirements and, involving a matter of public policy, must be raised by the Court of its own motion, the latter, which goes to the substantive legality of a decision, is concerned with the infringement of a rule of law relating to the application of the Treaty.

The statement of reasons must disclose in a clear and unequivocal fashion the reasoning followed by the institution which adopted the measure, so as to enable the persons concerned to ascertain the reasons for it so that they can defend their rights and ascertain whether or not the measure is well-founded, and to enable the Court to exercise its power of review. In the absence of pertinent provisions of Community law, the recovery of aid which has been declared incompatible with the common market is to be carried out in accordance with the rules and procedures laid down by national law. Disputes arising in connection with the enforcement of recovery are a matter for the national court alone.

Joined Cases T–425/04, 444/04, 450/04, 456/04 *French Republic, France Télécom SA, Bouygues SA and Bouygues Télécom SA and Association Française des opérateurs de réseaux et services de télécommunications (AFORS Télécom) v European Commission* [2010] E.C.R. II–02099 (May 21, 2010).

Type of procedure: Actions for annulment of Commission Decision 2006/621/EC of August 2, 2004 on the state aid implemented by France for France Télécom.

1111

Highlights: The General Court reiterated the requirements of state aid, namely a financial advantage, and the fact that it comes directly or indirectly from state resources. Although the Commission is allowed to take note of all events leading up to the December 2002 Decision of the French State to offer support to FT, the Commission did not manage to establish the link between state resources (in the December measures) and the advantage resulting from the July declarations.

Case T–189/08 *Forum 187 ASBL v European Commission* [2010] E.C.R. (March 18, 2010).

Type of procedure: Action for the annulment of Commission Decision 2008/283/EC of November 13, 2007 amending Decision 2003/757/EC on the aid scheme implemented by Belgium for coordination centres established in Belgium, in so far as it does not provide reasonable prospective transitional periods for the coordination centres concerned by the judgment of the Court of Justice in Joined Cases C 182/03 and C 217/03 *Belgium and Forum 187 v Commission.*

Highlights: Associations may bring actions when they represent the interests of undertakings that have standing in the proceedings, when their own interests as associations are individually concerned or when a legal provision confers them procedural rights. Article 48(1) of the Rules of Procedure must be read in the light of art.66(2), according to which the submission of evidence in rebuttal and the amplification of previous evidence are permitted.

There is no interest in bringing proceedings when the annulment of a decision that allegedly does not provide for a reasonable transitional period is sought. Such an annulment would lack any benefit for the applicant, as the applicant is already in a new situation, rendering the transitional period (meant to enable adaptation) devoid of purpose. Future uncertain circumstances, in casu the declaration of a new transitional period, cannot be relied upon to establish an interest in seeking annulment.

Case T–94/08 *Centre de coordination Carrefour SNC v European Commission* [2010] E.C.R. (March 18, 2010).

Type of procedure: Action for the annulment of Commission Decision 2008/283/EC of November 13, 2007 amending Decision 2003/757/EC on the aid scheme implemented by Belgium for coordination centres established in Belgium, in so far as it does not provide an adequate transitional period.

Highlights: For an action to be admissible, the applicant must have an interest in the annulment of the contested measure. This is not the case when the annulment of a decision that allegedly does not provide for a reasonable transitional period is sought. Such an annulment would lack any benefit for the applicant, as the applicant is already in a new situation, rendering the transitional period, meant to enable adaptation, devoid of purpose. Future uncertain circumstances, in casu the declaration of a new transitional period, cannot be relied upon to establish an interest in seeking annulment.

Case T–190/07 *KEK Diavlos v European Commission* [2010] E.C.R. (March 18, 2010).

Type of procedure: Application for annulment of Commission Decision C(2006) 465 final of February 23, 2006 ordering the reimbursement of the advance, together with interest, paid under a contract for financial assistance, concluded under the Prince programme, for an operation entitled "The EURO".

Highlights: The Court dismissed the action for annulment.

Joined Cases T–102/07 and T–120/07 *Freistaat Sachsen (Germany) (T–102/07), MB Immobilien Verwaltungs GmbH and MB System GmbH & Co KG (T–120/07) v European Commission* [2010] E.C.R. (March 3, 2010).

Type of procedure: Application for annulment of Commission Decision 2007/492/EC of January 24, 2007 on the state aid C 38/2005 (ex. NN 52/2004) implemented by Germany for the Biria Group.

Highlights: To determine the aid element in a loan to a company in difficulty, a reference to the Commission notice on the method for setting the reference rate and discount rates is not sufficient to motivate the calculation of the risk premiums. The 1997 Reference rate Notice will not be not sufficient to justify the determination of a risk premium in a particular case. Moreover, the Notice does not clarify if different risk premiums can be cumulated taking into account different risks. While cumulation is not excluded, the Commission has to motivate in its decision the applied methodology for cumulating different risk premiums by referring to the practice of the financial markets in this respect or a study. Although the General Court to a large extent confirmed the Commission's assessment, it annulled the decision (C–38/2005) for lack of motivation on one particular point.

Case T–36/06 *Bundesverband deutscher Banken eV v European Commission* [2010] E.C.R. II–00537 (March 3, 2010).

Type of procedure: Application for annulment of Commission Decision C(2005) 3232 final of September 6, 2005 relating to the transfer of the Hessischer Investitionsfonds (Hessian Investment Fund) as a silent partnership contribution to Landesbank Hessen-Thüringen Girozentrale.

Highlights: The obligation to state reasons is a procedural requirement which must be differentiated from the notion of whether the reasons are correct, which goes to the substantive legality of the contested measure. Whether the Commission can classify a funding contribution simply based on the description given by the parties is a question that goes to the substance of the reasoning, not to its adequacy.

A contested decision that fits into a well-established line of decisions known to the applicant may be reasoned summarily. When a confidential version of a decision is produced and communicated to the applicant before the hearing, it must be considered that the applicant was in a position to defend its rights. Whether the remuneration agreed upon between the public authority and the undertaking is in line with market conditions due to the impossibility of eliminating the concentration of risk in that undertaking is not a question of adequacy but rather of substance of the reasoning.

Case T–163/05 *Bundesverband deutscher Banken eV v European Commission* [2010] E.C.R. II–00387 (March 3, 2010).

Type of procedure: Application for annulment of Commission Decision 2006/742/EC of October 20, 2004 on aid granted by Germany to Landesbank Hessen-Thüringen Girozentrale.

Highlights: The point of view of a single investor is not to be used when assessing whether a transaction is in line with market conditions; rather it is necessary to take into account the interaction between the various economic operators and the context of the said transaction. The comparison of a special fund with other hybrid instruments is economically complex and as such, the Commission enjoys wide discretion of assessment. However, since the purpose of state aid control is to determine whether the recipient undertaking receives an economic advantage which it would not have obtained under normal market conditions, it is not sufficient to only take the private investors' point of view into account. As it is the existence of an advantage for the undertaking that is decisive for state aid law, it cannot be concluded that state aid arises from a transaction between an investing public authority and an undertaking when the latter accepts a remuneration that is lower than that agreed on the market for cash investments, provided that the lower remuneration is consistent with the disadvantages for the recipient of the transaction in question. In other words, insofar as the overall terms of the transaction are not more advantageous for the undertaking than those which it could have obtained if the transaction related, as would normally be the case, to liquid capital, it does not gain an advantage, and as such the transaction cannot be deemed to give rise to state aid.

Case T–156/04 *Electricité de France (EDF) v European Commission* [2010] E.C.R. II–04503 (December 15, 2009).

Type of procedure: Application for annulment of Commission Decision C(2003) 4637 dated December 16, 2003 concerning state aid granted by France to Electricité de France (EDF).

Highlights: The Commission failed to examine whether a fiscal relief granted by France to EDF, as its sole shareholder, could have been analysed as a capital injection which a market investor would have carried out under normal market conditions. The Court refers to the distinction between public intervention in the capital of an undertaking with an economic objective that might also be pursued by a private investor and intervention which is justified by the pursuit of a public interest objective which must be regarded as action taken by the State in the exercise of its public authority. The fact that the state has access to financial resources accrued through the exercise of state authority is not in itself sufficient justification for regarding the State's actions as attributable to the exercise of state authority.

The Court underlined that the application of the private investor principle cannot be refused simply on the basis of the form of the state intervention (in this case waving of a fiscal debt was qualified by the Commission as within the remit of public authority and therefore outside of the private investor principle). The form is irrelevant for the question whether a private investor could have made a similar capital increase, be it in a different form.

Joined Cases T–427/04 and T–17/05 *French Republic (T–427/04) and France Télécom SA (T–17/05) v Commission of the European Communities* [2009] E.C.R. (November 13, 2009).

Type of procedure: Action for annulment of Commission Decision 2005/709/EC of August 2, 2004 concerning state aid paid by France to France Télécom.

Highlights: The Court confirms that the state aid consists in the annual difference between the business tax actually paid by France Telecom (FT) and the amount which would have been due if FT had followed the taxation rules which should have been applicable by ordinary law. Secondly, the Court reiterates that aid given to a company cannot be offset by a specific charge imposed on the same company on another source not related to the aid. The Court also confirmed that during the periods under examination, the French authorities established two different taxation schemes (a temporary and a final one) and that any over-taxation resulting from the earlier taxation scheme cannot be used to offset any under-taxation in the later period.

The Court also points out that at the point of the introduction of the tax scheme, it was not clear that this would not entail any aid and France should therefore have notified the measure to the Commission. In the absence of such a notification, the Member State cannot rely on legitimate expectations. The fact that the Commission remained silent in its decision of 1995 regarding French La Poste on the same article of the national law at stake, does not mean that it has taken a position on the acceptability of that exemption. As to the recovery of the aid, the Court held that it is sufficient if the Commission decision identifies the aid and contains indications allowing the national author-ities to calculate the aid amount to be recovered without excessive difficulty.

Case T–376/07 *Federal Republic of Germany v Commission of the European Communities* [2009] E.C.R. (November 25, 2009).

Type of procedure: Application for annulment of Commission Decision C(2007) 3226 of July 18, 2007 requiring information to be provided concerning two state aid schemes coming under Commis-sion Regulation (EC) No.70/2001 of January 12, 2001 on the application of arts [107 TFEU] and [108 TFEU] to state aid to small and medium-sized enterprises.

Highlights: The Court confirmed that under art.9(2) of the Commission Regulation (EC) No.70/2001 the Commission is empowered to request information from the Member State which it considers necessary to assess if the conditions of the BER have been complied with in all circumstances. It thus rejected Germany's argument that information could only be requested where the Commission had evidence raising doubts about compliance. Moreover, the Court stated that the interpretation of art.9(2) of the Commission Regulation (EC) No.70/2001 was unambiguous and that there was therefore no need to interpret it in the light of art.3(3) of Council Regulation (EC) No.994/98.

Case T–375/04 *Scheucher-Fleisch GmbH and Others v Commission of the European Communities* [2009] E.C.R. (November 18, 2009).

Type of procedure: Application for annulment of Commission Decision C(2004) 2037 final of June 30, 2004 on state aid NN 34A/2000 concerning the quality programmes and labels AMA Biozeichen and AMA Gütesiegel in Austria.

Highlights: There is direct concern when, in case of a decision granting aid, the possibility that the national authorities will not grant the aid authorised by the contested Commission decision is purely theoretical. An applicant who contests a decision establishing a measure as State aid must have a "special status" within the meaning of *Plaumann v Commission*. For this purpose it is irrelevant whether the measure is individual or general in nature. A "special status" is given when the applicant's market position is substantially affected by the measure. A "special status" is not achieved simply by being a competitor of the undertaking receiving aid. The measure must distinguish the undertaking in a similar way as to the addressee itself. The possibility of putting forward arguments during the preliminary procedure does not preclude the right to make use of the procedural guarantee contained in art.108(2) TFEU.

The Commission may only decide that aid is compatible with the common market when no serious difficulties result from the preliminary examination. When serious difficulties do arise, the Commission has no discretion on deciding to open the formal procedure. The concept of "serious difficulties" is objective. It is thus necessary to investigate the circumstances under which the contested measure was adopted and also its content as well as to compare the grounds of the decision with the information available to the Commission.

The Guidelines for state aid for advertising (certain agricultural products) prohibit national quality control schemes restricted to products of a particular origin. A restriction of aid to national products is thus unlawful. The Commission can therefore not authorise a national aid scheme without ascertaining in an in-depth assessment whether it incorporates such prohibited provisions.

Case T–24/06 *Medienanstalt Berlin-Brandenburg (MABB) v Commission of the European Communities* [2009] E.C.R. II–00198 (October 6, 2009) (see also Case T–8/06 and Case T–21/06).

Type of procedure: Application for annulment of Commission Decision 2006/513/EC of November 9, 2005 on the state aid which the Federal Republic of Germany has implemented for the introduction of digital terrestrial television (DVB-T) in Berlin-Brandenburg.

Highlights: The Court clarifies in this case that the application of the Media Authority (MABB, the public body granting the aid) is not admissible. The Court points out the following aspects: (1) the tasks of the MABB are defined by the State (*in casu* the Länder) and its alleged autonomy only concerns implementing modalities of the aid scheme; (2) its resources are state resources because they come from charges imposed by the public authorities and non-used resources go back to the Länder; (3) the MABB is under state control by the Court of Auditors and the Parliament, so that it can be seen as belonging to the public administration; (4) it is not "independent" because it is under budgetary and legal supervision; and (5) its interests are not different from those of the public authorities.

Case T–21/06 (in conjunction with Case T–8/06) *Federal Republic of Germany v Commission of the European Communities* [2009] E.C.R. II–00197 (October 6, 2009).

Type of procedure: Application for annulment of Commission Decision 2006/513/EC of November 9, 2005 on the state aid which the Federal Republic of Germany had implemented for the introduction of digital terrestrial television (DVB-T) in Berlin-Brandenburg.

Highlights: Mere indirect beneficiaries of state aid are also covered by art.107 TFEU and may indeed be subject to recovery, even when the quantification of the amounts to be recovered may not be precisely straightforward. The notion of market failure is included in the 2003 Communication on the transition from analogue to digital broadcasting. The Commission did not exceed its discretion under art.107(3)(c) TFEU in finding the aid measure incompatible, given that Germany had not been able to demonstrate that the financial support granted for terrestrial digital television was an appropriate and necessary means to enable the switch-over from analogue to digital broadcasting. Regarding the question of technological neutrality, the Court confirmed that the aid measure was not granted in a technologically neutral manner but noted that it might be justifiable to support digital terrestrial broadcasting to the detriment of cable and satellite if the latter are dominant in the region as this may have a positive effect on the competitive structure of the market.

The Court confirmed the Commission's finding of distortion of competition given that, on the one hand, most licences for digital terrestrial TV were distributed without open and non-discriminatory tender, which could have compensated for the selective advantage, on the other hand, the decisive criterion for granting the new frequencies was that the beneficiary was already present on the geographic market concerned for analogue broadcasting.

Case T–8/06 (in conjunction with Case T21/06) *FAB Fernsehen aus Berlin GmbH v Commission of the European Communities* [2009] E.C.R. (October 6, 2009).

Type of procedure: See above.

Highlights: See above.

Case T–75/03 *Banco Comercial dos Açores, SA v Commission of the European Communities* [2009] E.C.R. (September 10, 2009).

Type of procedure: Annulment of the final part of art.1 and arts 2, 3 and 4 of Commission Decision 2003/442/EC of December 11, 2002, concerning the part of the scheme adapting the system of national tax on the specificities of the autonomous Region of the Azores which concerns the part on reductions of tax rates on income.

Highlights: To bring an action for annulment, the applicant must have benefited individually from an aid granted under an aid scheme (tax regime) and recovery of the said aid must have been ordered by the Commission. When an infra-state entity has the power to define the political and economic context in which undertakings under its jurisdiction operate, it is sufficient to analyse the area in which the said entity has jurisdictional powers in order to determine whether a measure is selective. The fact that a regional fiscal system strives to correct disadvantages and inequalities does not justify, in light of the national fiscal system, every fiscal benefit granted by the infra-state entity. A measure is not justified merely due to the fact of it being adopted based on a regional development or social cohesion policy.

Even when aid or the benefited undertakings are of minor economic importance, it cannot be excluded a priori that trade between Member States is affected. When analysing an aid regime the Commission is not obliged to examine every concrete case that did not surpass the de minimis amount of aid established in reg. No.69/2001. Based on the facts known when the measure in question was adopted, it is up to the Member State to prove not only the importance of the additional costs resultant of the said measure but also the proportional relation between such costs and the advantages created by the measure.

The order for recovery of illegally granted state aid is the logical consequence of the declaration of its illegality and does not depend on how the aid was granted. It is thus irrelevant if the aid was conceded as a general measure. The fact that the state administration applied the measure in question does not create a legitimate expectancy for its beneficiaries in the legitimacy of the measure.

Case T–369/06 *Holland Malt BV v Commission of the European Communities* [2009] E.C.R. (September 9, 2009).

Type of procedure: Application for annulment of Commission Decision 2007/59/EC of September 26, 2006 concerning the state aid granted by the Netherlands to Holland Malt BV.

Highlights: It is sufficient for the Commission to establish that a state aid measure is liable to affect intra-Community trade. It does not have to establish a real effect. The degree to which the position of an undertaking is strengthened is irrelevant since there is no limit below which Community trade is not affected. Guidelines must be interpreted in accordance to art.107 TFEU and its objective, namely undistorted competition in the common market. Exceptions to the rule that state aid is incompatible with the common market must be strictly interpreted. A Member State must provide the Commission with all necessary information, even that which is in the public domain, as the Commission is not obligated to seek information on its own motion.

Cases T–230/01–T–232/01 and T–267/01–T–269/01 *Territorio Histórico de Álava—Diputación Foral de Álava and Comunidad autónoma del País Vasco—Gobierno Vasco and Others v Commission of the European Communities* [2009] E.C.R. II–00139 (September 9, 2009).

Type of procedure: Application in Cases T–230/01 and T–267/01 for annulment of Commission Decision 2002/892/EC of July 11, 2001 on the state aid scheme applied by Spain to certain newly established firms in Álava; application in Cases T–231/01 and T–268/01 for annulment of Commission Decision 2002/806/EC of July 11, 2001 on the state aid scheme applied by Spain to certain newly established firms in Vizcaya; and application in Cases T–232/01 and T–269/01 for annulment of the Commission decision 2002/894/EC of July 11, 2001 on the state aid scheme applied by Spain to certain newly established firms in Guipúzcoa.

Highlights: The Court dismissed the appeals and clarified its approach on the selectivity criteria in the context of fiscal measures adopted by the Basque countries.

Cases T–227/01–T–229/01, T–265/01, T–266/01 and T–270/01 *Territorio Histórico de Álava—Diputación Foral de Álava and Comunidad autónoma del País Vasco—Gobierno Vasco and Others v Commission of the European Communities* [2009] E.C.R. II–03029 (September 9, 2009).

Type of procedure: Applications in Cases T–227/01 and T–265/01 for annulment of Commission Decision 2002/820/EC of July 11, 2001 on the state aid scheme implemented by Spain for firms in Álava in the form of a tax credit amounting to 45% of investments; applications in Cases T–228/01 and T–266/01 for annulment of Commission Decision 2003/27/EC of July 11, 2001 on the state aid scheme implemented by Spain for firms in Vizcaya in the form of a tax credit amounting to 45% of investments; and applications in Cases T–229/01 and T–270/01 for annulment of Commission Decision 2002/894/EC of July 11, 2001 on the state aid scheme implemented by Spain for firms in Guipúzcoa in the form of a tax credit amounting to 45% of investments.

Highlights: The Court upheld the Commission's assessment of selectivity, holding that the tax credit only applied to investments in new fixed assets exceeding a certain threshold, whilst the possible reduction in the tax base was limited to newly established firms and, among them, to those with significant financial resources at their disposal, capable of making significant investments and generating a substantial numbers of jobs. The Court rejected the submission that the tax measures were justified by the nature and internal logic of the tax system. The applicants had only referred to general objectives of economic policy which are extraneous to the tax measures concerned and cannot prevent their classification as state aid.

Article 14 Reg.659/1999 makes no distinction according to whether the aid measure is a subsidy or a tax relief, and the recovery of illegal aid through the repayment of the sums in question is the most appropriate means of cancelling out the effects of the distortion of competition and of restoring the previously existing competitive situation.

Cases T–30/01–T–32/01, T–86/02–T–88/02 *Territorio Histórico de Álava—Diputación Foral de Álava and Others v Commission of the European Communities* [2009] E.C.R. II–02919 (September 9, 2009).

Type of procedure: Applications in Cases T–30/01 to T–32/01 for annulment of the Commission Decision of November 28, 2000 to initiate the procedure under art.88(2) EC [now art.108(2) TFEU] in relation to the tax advantages in the form of corporation tax exemption for certain newly established firms granted by provisions adopted by the the Álava, Guipúzcoa and Vizcaya provincial councils. Applications in Cases T–86/02 to T–88/02 for annulment of Commission Decisions 2003/28/EC, 2003/86/EC and 2003/192/EC of December 20, 2001 on a state aid scheme in the form of corporation tax exemption implemented by Spain in 1993 for certain newly established firms in Álava (T–86/02), Vizcaya (T–87/02) and Guipúzcoa (T–88/02).

Highlights: In order to fall under art.1(b)(v) of reg.659/1999, a measure should fulfil two conditions: 1) it does not constitute aid at the time it was put into effect—this must be demonstrated by a Commission Decision and cannot be tacit or implied from the Commission's silence over a period of time; 2) it becomes aid due to the evolution of the common market—this does not cover a change in the Commission's appraisal or policy. Neither the Code of Conduct nor the 1998 Fiscal Communication indicate a change in the assessment criteria for the notion of aid.

The Court confirms that the tax measures constitute operating aid, notwithstanding the entry conditions. Quantification of the tax exemptions is based on the profits made by the companies, without any correspondence to the size of the investment or the number of jobs created. Only the Member State itself can raise a claim regarding the rights of defence since this is a subjective irregularity. Furthermore, the irregularity would in any event only lead to annulment if it is established that, had it not been for that irregularity, the outcome of the procedure might have been different.

Regarding the principles of legal certainty and good administration the Court finds that a period of 6.5 years between the time the Commission became aware of the schemes and the initiation of the formal investigation procedure was not unreasonable for the following reasons: 1) taking in account the complexity of the examination; 2) the responsibility for the length of the procedure lied in large part with the Spanish authorities; and 3) in the same period the Commission examined other tax systems adopted on which the Commission might have taken the view that they should be dealt with more quickly. The length of the preliminary examination cannot give rise to legitimate expectations that the aid was lawful unless there are exceptional circumstances, which was not demonstrated here. The Court also rejects the claim that there was a change in the Commission's policy which would justify legitimate expectations.

Finally, the Court finds that, since it upheld the final decisions, the applicants no longer have any interest in obtaining the annulment of the opening decisions, so that those actions for annulment became devoid of purpose.

Case T–303/05 *AceaElectrabel Produzione SpA v Commission of the European Communities* [2009] E.C.R. (September 8, 2009).

Type of procedure: Annulment of Commission Decision 2006/598/EC of March 16, 2005 concerning state aid that Italy (Regione Lazio) intends to grant for the reduction of greenhouse gas emissions; i.e. environmental aid for construction of urban heating system.

Highlights: The Court ruled that the Commission is not required to determine the market concerned nor to carry out an economic analysis of the actual situation. Subsequently, it confirmed the Commission's argumentation based on the substitution effect of the municipal heating system and on the fact that the aided project of energy production is part of the energy sector, which is liberalised and competitive. The Court confirmed the conclusion of the Commission that ACEA (beneficiary of the old incompatible aid to be recovered) and the applicant (beneficiary of the new aid) are for the purposes of the assessment of the aid at hand considered as a single economic entity given; its ownership structure, blocking powers of ACEA as regards strategic decisions concerning the applicant, transfer of branch of ACEA concerned by the new aid to the applicant, absence of functional autonomy of the applicant and also the fact that the company marketing the energy produced by the applicant is controlled by ACEA. The Court thus clarified that, for an undertaking to belong to a group, the group does not need to have a majority participation in that undertaking. It also confirmed that the stronger controlling powers of Electrabel did not exclude that ACEA also had control over the beneficiary.

As regards the interpretation of the *Deggendorf* case law, and, more specifically its application in case of aid schemes, the Court first recalled that the Commission when examining compatibility of state aid with the common market should take into consideration all relevant elements including the context already assessed in the previous decision as well as the obligations which this previous decision imposed on Member States. Furthermore the Court refers to the *Deggendorf* case which already concluded that the Commission did not go beyond its discretionary powers by imposing the suspension of payments of new aid until old incompatible aid is reimbursed based on the cumulative effects of both aid grants. The Court continues that this applies both for individual aid and for aid granted on the basis of an aid scheme. On the claim that the Commission should have determined the amounts to be recovered from individual beneficiaries under the scheme in order to assess their cumulative effect with the new aid, the Court finds that such determination shall be done by the Italian authorities. To admit that the *Deggendorf* case law would not apply when this was not done would incentivise the authorities not to comply with their obligation in order to allow the beneficiaries to circumvent the principles of the *Deggendorf* case law. The fact that the exact amounts to be reimbursed are not known, does not prevent the Commission from finding that the new aid will be added to the old non-reimbursed aid and that such cumulation within the same group causes on its own distortion of competition.

Case T–211/05 *Italian Republic v Commission of the European Communities* [2009] E.C.R. II–02777 (September 9, 2009).

Type of procedure: Application for annulment of Commission Decision 2006/261/EC of March 16, 2005 on aid scheme C 8/2004 [ex. NN 164/2003] implemented by Italy in favour of newly listed companies.

Highlights: The General Court confirmed that the tax advantages granted by the Italian authorities to newly listed companies were selective. The advantages were only available to undertakings newly listed on a regulated market and having obtained the listing during the brief period for which the aid scheme was applicable. Furthermore, the measure was not justified by the nature and the overall scheme of the Italian tax system since Italy had not demonstrated that it was justified by the alleged objective, i.e. to encourage listing on the stock exchange. Indeed, the tax relief applied to future profits of the beneficiaries, which are unrelated to the listing; the short duration of the measures excluded many potential beneficiaries, thus contradicting the alleged objective; Italy had not demonstrated that listed companies had specific characteristics (disadvantages) as compared to other companies, and even if this were the case, the tax relief had no connection to those alleged characteristics.

Joined Cases T–81/07, T–82/07 and T–83/07 *Jan Rudolf Maas and Others v Commission of the European Communities* [2009] E.C.R. II–02411 (July 1, 2009).

Type of procedure: Application for annulment of Commission Decision 2006/939/EC of July 19, 2006 on the aid measure notified by the Netherlands for KG Holding NV.

Highlights: Under art.6 of Regulation No.659/1999 the decision to initiate the procedure must give the interested parties the opportunity effectively to participate in the formal investigation procedure, during which they will have the opportunity to put forward their arguments. The sole purpose of the procedure provided for in art.88(2) EC [now art.108(2) TFEU] is to oblige the Commission to take steps to ensure that all persons who may be concerned are notified and given an opportunity of putting forward their arguments.

The mere fact that the undertaking has gone bankrupt does not therefore call into question the principle that unlawful aid must be recovered. Bankruptcy does not mean that recovery of the aid has become impossible. The Member State concerned may register its claim as one of those undertakings' liabilities. In the event of difficulties, the Commission and the Member State concerned must respect the principle underlying art.10 EC [now art.4(3) TFEU], which imposes a duty of genuine cooperation on the Member States and the Community institutions, and must work together in good faith with a view to overcoming difficulties whilst fully observing the Treaty provisions, and in particular the provisions on state aid.

Finally, the right of a person to bring proceedings cannot be restricted simply because, although that person could, in the course of the administrative procedure, have submitted observations on an assessment communicated when the art.88(2) EC procedure was opened and then repeated in the contested decision, he did not do so.

Case T–291/06 *Operator ARP sp. z o.o. v Commission of the European Communities* [2009] E.C.R. II–02275 (July 1, 2009).

Type of procedure: ECSC—Application for the partial annulment of Commission Decision 2006/937/EC of July 5, 2005.

Highlights: As is apparent from the wording of art.6(1) of reg. No.659/1999, the Commission's analysis is necessarily preliminary in nature. It follows that the Commission cannot be required to present a complete analysis of the aid in question in its notice of intention to initiate that procedure. The Commission must, however, define sufficiently the framework of its investigation so as not to render meaningless the right of interested parties to put forward their comments. Considering the obligation to state reasons, the Court cannot examine the substantive legality of the reasons relied on by the Commission to justify its decision. In a plea based on a failure to state reasons or a lack of adequate reasons, objections and arguments which seek to challenge the merits of the contested decision are therefore misplaced and irrelevant. Finally, the widening of the group of entities required to repay the aid can be justified only if the transfer of assets leads to the risk of circumvention of the effects of the recovery order and if, as a result of the takeover of assets, the original beneficiary of the aid is left like an "empty shell" from which it is not possible to secure repayment of the unlawful aid. Moreover, that widening may be justified by the fact that the person or entity acquiring the assets retains the actual benefit of the competitive advantage connected with the receipt of the aid granted. In that regard, the Court of Justice has held that, where an undertaking that has benefited from unlawful State aid is bought at the market price, the purchaser cannot be regarded as having benefited from an advantage in relation to other market operators.

Case T–288/06 *Regionalny Fundusz Gospodarczy SA v Commission of the European Communities* [2009] E.C.R. II–02247 (July 1, 2009).

Type of procedure: Application for the partial annulment of Commission Decision 2006/937/EC of July 5, 2005 on state aid C 20/04 (ex. NN 25/04) in favour of Huta Częstochowa SA inasmuch as it declares certain aid to be incompatible with the common market and orders the Republic of Poland to recover it.

Highlights: If an application initiating proceedings sets out the grounds for annulment with sufficient clarity and precision to enable the defendant to defend itself effectively and for the Courts to exercise their judicial review, it satisfies the minimum requirements laid down by the first paragraph of art.21 of the Statute of the Court of Justice and by art.44(1)(c) of the Rules of Procedure of the General Court.

Furthermore, it follows from the actual wording of Protocol No.8 that it applies to aid granted before accession. The purpose was to establish a comprehensive system for the authorization of aid intended for the restructuring of the Polish steel industry and not merely to avoid the aggregation of aid by benefiting companies. It follows that Protocol No.8 is a *lex specialis* in relation to arts 107 and 108 TFEU [ex. 87 EC and 88 EC] which extends the review of state aid carried out by the Commission pursuant to the EC Treaty to aid granted in favour of the reorganization of the Polish steel industry during the period from 1997 to 2003.

Article 9(4) of reg. No.794/2004 provides only that the fixing of the applicable recovery interest rate must be effected in "close cooperation" with the Member State concerned, but does not require an "agreement". In determining the rate applicable in accordance with art.9(4) of reg. No.794/2004, the Commission enjoys a measure of discretion. However, art.11(2) of that Regulation states expressly that the interest rate is to be applied on a compound basis until the date of the recovery of the aid and that the interest accruing in the previous year is to be subject to interest in each subsequent year. Lastly, the Commission was not under any obligation to indicate in the Decision the interest rate for recovery of the aid in question, given that it was not even required to identify precisely the principal amount of the recoverable aid and that it was entitled to limit itself to indicating merely the methods permitting the Member State to calculate the aid.

Joined Cases T–273/06 and T–297/06 *ISD Polska sp. z o.o. and Industrial Union of Donbass Corp v Commission of the European Communities* [2009] E.C.R. II–02181 (July 1, 2009).

Type of procedure: Applications for the partial annulment of Commission Decision 2006/937/EC of July 5, 2005 on state aid C 20/04 (ex. NN 25/04) in favour of Huta Częstochowa SA inasmuch as it declares certain aid to be incompatible with the common market and orders the Republic of Poland to recover it.

Highlights: An entity is individually affected, having thus a right of action, when a Commission decision negatively affects it due to a differentiating factual situation which distinguishes the entity in the same way as the addressee of the decision. A right of action cannot be questioned merely in the name of procedural economy. The consistent practice of the Commission to publish in the Official Journal its decisions closing an investigation procedure creates a legitimate expectation that all such decisions will be published.

An entity is directly concerned by a decision when it affects the entity's legal situation, leaving no discretion in its implementation and resulting automatically from the direct application of Community rules. Due to the lack of legal basis in the Treaty, the Court has no jurisdiction to declare the Republic of Poland's obligation to recover aid as non-existent. Protocol No.8 of the Annex IV to the Treaty of Accession is a *lex specialis*. Protocol No.8 of the Annex IV to the Treaty of Accession applies to the Polish steel industry as a whole and not only to the companies listed in its Annex 1. Events that have occurred after the adoption of a decision cannot retroactively render it unlawful. In its decision to initiate the formal investigation, the Commission must sufficiently define its investigation, in order to enable the right of interested parties to present comments. In a decision to initiate a formal investigation, the lack of an express mention of the aid does not enable the applicants to invoke an infringement of the principle of legitimate expectations. A Commission proposal for a Council decision does not give rise to a legitimate expectation.

Case T–222/04 *Italian Republic v Commission of the European Communities* [2009] E.C.R. II–01877 (June 11, 2009).

Type of procedure: Application for annulment of art.2 of Commission Decision 2003/193/EC of June 5, 2002 on state aid granted by Italy in the form of tax exemptions and subsidised loans to public utilities with a majority public capital holding.

Highlights: Any grant of aid to an undertaking pursuing its activities in the Community market is liable to cause distortion of competition and affect trade between Member States. As regards the condition relating to the effect on inter-state trade, this is also affected by the measure in question when undertakings established in other Member States have less chance of providing their services in the market of the Member State concerned. In the grounds of its decision on state aid, the Commission is bound to refer at least to the circumstances which show that the aid is such as to affect trade between Member States. On the other hand, it is not bound to demonstrate the actual effect of aid already granted.

Aid which existed before the entry into force of the EC Treaty and which could be properly put into effect in accordance with the conditions laid down in art.108(3) TFEU is to be regarded as existing aid within the meaning of art.108(1) TFEU. On the other hand, measures to grant or alter aid, where the alterations may relate to existing aid or initial plans notified to the Commission, must be regarded as new aid subject to the obligation of notification laid down by art.108(3) TFEU. Finally, compensation for services to discharge public service obligations do as a general rule not constitute state aid according to art.107(1) TFEU if they meet the cumulative conditions set out by the *Altmark* judgment.

Case T–189/03 *ASM Brescia SpA v Commission of the European Communities* [2009] E.C.R. II–01831 (June 11, 2009).

Type of procedure: Application for annulment of arts 2 and 3 of Commission Decision 2003/193/EC of June 5, 2002 on state aid granted by Italy in the form of tax exemptions and subsidised loans to public utilities with a majority public capital holding.

Highlights: In order to be individually concerned, an undertaking cannot only rely on the fact that it is an undertaking within the sector in question and is a potential beneficiary of the aid scheme, but it must also be an actual recipient of individual aid granted under that scheme of which recovery has been ordered. As regards the condition relating to the effect on inter-state trade, this is also affected by the measure in question when undertakings established in other Member States have less chance of providing their services in the market of the Member State concerned. Measures to grant or alter aid, where the alterations may relate to existing aid or initial plans notified to the Commission, must be regarded as new aid subject to the obligation of notification laid down by art.108(3) TFEU. Finally, compensation for services to discharge public service obligations do as a general rule not constitute state aid according to 107(1) TFEU if they meet the cumulative conditions set out by the *Altmark* judgment.

Case T–309/02 *Acegas-APS SpA v Commission of the European Communities* [2009] E.C.R. II–01809 (June 11, 2009).

Type of procedure: Application for annulment of arts 2 and 3 of Commission Decision 2003/193/EC of June 5, 2002 on state aid granted by Italy in the form of tax exemptions and subsidised loans to public utilities with a majority public capital holding.

Highlights: An undertaking which declared a loss for tax purposes for the relevant period and whose assessment to tax was thus effectively nil and which fails to adduce any convincing evidence to establish that it nevertheless benefited from the scheme in question is not individually concerned by a Commission decision prohibiting a sectoral aid scheme consisting in a three-year income tax exemption. An action brought by such an undertaking for the annulment of such a decision is inadmissible. Moreover, the fact that it is possible for the Commission to determine more or less precisely the number, or even the identity, of the persons to whom a measure applies by no means implies that the measure must be regarded as being of individual concern to those persons.

Case T–301/02 *AEM SpA v Commission of the European Communities* [2009] E.C.R. II–01757 (June 11, 2009).

Type of procedure: Application for annulment of arts 2 and 3 of Commission Decision 2003/193/EC of June 5, 2002 on state aid granted by Italy in the form of tax exemptions and subsidised loans to public utilities with a majority public capital holding.

Highlights: In order to be individually concerned, an undertaking cannot only rely on the fact that it is an undertaking within the sector in question and is a potential beneficiary of the aid scheme, but is must also be an actual recipient of individual aid granted under that scheme of which recovery has been ordered. The Commission is required only to examine whether that aid is liable to affect such trade and to distort competition. In the case of an aid scheme the Commission may confine itself to examining the characteristics of the scheme and to determine whether it is likely to benefit in particular undertakings engaged in trade between Member States. Furthermore, any grant of aid to an undertaking pursuing its activities in the Community market is liable to cause distortion of competition and affect trade between Member States. As regards the condition relating to the effect on interstate trade, this is also affected by the measure in question when undertakings established in other Member States have less chance of providing their services in the market of the Member State concerned.

Aid which existed before the entry into force of the EC Treaty and which could be properly put into effect in accordance with the conditions laid down in art.108(3) TFEU is to be regarded as existing aid within the meaning of art.108(1) TFEU. On the other hand, measures to grant or alter aid, where the alterations may relate to existing aid or initial plans notified to the Commission, must be regarded as new aid subject to the obligation of notification laid down by art.108(3) TFEU. Where an aid scheme has been analysed in a general and abstract manner, the possibility cannot be ruled out that, in an individual case, the amount granted under the scheme escapes the prohibition laid down in art.107(1) TFEU.

Finally, when the Commission takes a decision declaring aid incompatible with the common market, the role of the national authorities is confined to implementing that decision and they do not enjoy any discretion in that regard, those authorities may, when implementing that decision, take such reservations into account.

Case T–300/02 *Azienda Mediterranea Gas e Acqua SpA (AMGA) v Commission of the European Communities* [2009] E.C.R. II–01737 (June 11, 2009).

Type of procedure: Application for annulment of arts 2 and 3 of Commission Decision 2003/193/EC of June 5, 2002 on state aid granted by Italy in the form of tax exemptions and subsidised loans to public utilities with a majority public capital holding.

Highlights: Natural or legal persons other than the addressee may claim that a decision is of individual concern to them only if that decision affects them by reason of certain attributes which are peculiar to them, or by reason of factual circumstances which differentiate them from all other persons and thereby distinguish them individually in the same way as the person addressed. An undertaking cannot, as a general rule, bring an action for the annulment of a Commission decision prohibiting a sectoral aid scheme if it is concerned by that decision solely by virtue of the fact that it belongs to the sector in question and is a potential beneficiary of the scheme. Such a decision is, vis-à-vis such an undertaking, a measure of general application covering situations which are determined objectively and entails legal effects for a class of persons envisaged in a general and abstract manner. However, an undertaking which is concerned by the decision at issue not only as an undertaking in the sector in question and a potential beneficiary of the aid scheme concerned but also as an actual recipient of individual aid granted under that scheme, recovery of which had been ordered by the Commission, is individually concerned by the decision and the action which it brings against it is admissible. An undertaking which made only losses and did not therefore benefit from a three-year income tax exemption is not individually concerned by a Commission decision prohibiting a sectoral aid scheme consisting in such an exemption. An action brought by such an undertaking against such a decision is inadmissible.

Case T–297/02 *ACEA SpA v Commission of the European Communities* E.C.R. II–01683 (June 11, 2009).

Type of procedure: Application for annulment of arts 2 and 3 of Commission Decision 2003/193/EC of June 5, 2002 on state aid granted by Italy in the form of tax exemptions and subsidised loans to public utilities with a majority public capital holding.

Highlights: Being a potential beneficiary of a sectoral aid measure is insufficient to bring an action for annulment of a Commission decision prohibiting that aid. Rather it is necessary to be an actual recipient of individual aid under the sectoral aid scheme. When examining an aid scheme, the Commission is not obliged to examine the individual cases to which the scheme applies. It is hence not obliged to request any information regarding specific cases to which the scheme applies. The fact that a scheme is applicable to several companies operating in different sectors, some of which are open to competition, is sufficient to conclude that the scheme is liable to influence competition and trade between Member States. The fact that the contested measure is directly awarded to companies does not mean that there is no competition and that trade between Member States is not affected. A scheme only favouring companies solely active on a national market is nevertheless liable to affect trade between Member States, as the scheme creates an obstacle for foreign undertakings wishing to establish themselves on that market.

When the substance of a scheme is altered, new aid arises. There is, however, no substantial alteration when the new element is severable from the initial scheme. The extension of aid to a new class of beneficiaries constitutes such an alteration that is severable from the initial scheme. When a scheme applies to several sectors, the Commission is not obliged to examine all individual sectors. Aid granted to undertakings in difficulty must be linked to a comprehensive restructuring plan, in order for it to be considered compatible with the common market. The Commission is solely obliged to order the recovery of aid under the meaning of art.107 TFEU and not of amounts which, either, do not constitute aid, are existing aid, or are compatible with the common market. The concept of aid is a legal one to be interpreted based on objective factors and national courts have jurisdiction to interpret the concepts of aid and existing aid.

Case T–292/02 *Confederazione Nazionale dei Servizi (Confservizi) v Commission of the European Communities* [2009] E.C.R. II–01659.

Type of procedure: Application for annulment of arts 2 and 3 of Commission Decision 2003/193/EC of June 5, 2002 on state aid granted by Italy in the form of tax exemptions and subsidised loans to public utilities with a majority public capital holding.

Highlights: Actions brought by associations are admissible in certain situations: where the association represents the interests of undertakings which themselves have locus standi; where the association is differentiated by reason of the impact on its own interests as an association, in particular because its position as a negotiator has been affected by the measure of which annulment is sought; and where a legal provision expressly confers on it a number of rights of a procedural nature.

As regards an action brought by an association of undertakings against a Commission decision declaring an aid scheme incompatible with the common market, concerning the first situation referred to above, the possibility of determining more or less precisely the number or even the identity of the persons to whom a measure applies does not mean that that measure must be regarded as being of individual concern to them, as long as it is established that that application takes effect by virtue of an objective legal or factual situation defined by the measure in question.

Concerning the second situation, the fact that the association participated at the administrative stage by virtue of art.1(h) and art.20 of Regulation No.659/1999, concerning the application of art.88 EC [now art.108 TFEU], cannot lead to the conclusion that it was affected in its position as negotiator by the measure of which annulment is sought. Those provisions do not confer any special status on representative associations by comparison with that conferred on any other interested party.

With regard to the third situation, while art.1(h) and art.20 of Regulation No.659/1999 confer procedural rights on interested parties, the mere fact that an association was able to submit its comments in the procedure under art.108(2) [ex. 88(2) EC] and may be regarded as being concerned cannot suffice to render its action admissible.

Case T–152/06 *NDSHT Nya Destination Stockholm Hotell & Teaterpaket AB v Commission of the European Communities* [2009] E.C.R. II–01517 (June 9, 2009).

Type of procedure: Application for the annulment of the decision contained in the Commission's letters to NDSHT of March 24, and April 28, 2006, relating to a complaint concerning allegedly unlawful state aid granted by the City of Stockholm to Stockholm Visitors Board AB.

Highlights: The Court held that the appeal was inadmissible because the Commission's letters informing the complainant of its decision not to pursue the complaint were not actionable measures for the purposes of art.263 TFEU. With respect to existing aid, the initiative to propose to a Member State to review any such aid lies with the Commission alone. Furthermore, the applicable procedure as regards existing aid, set out in arts 17–19 of reg.659/1999, does not contemplate the possibility of a decision addressed to the Member State concerned being adopted by the Commission at the end of the preliminary examination stage.

The Court further noted that, if, following an initial assessment, the Commission finds that the complaint relates not to unlawful aid, but to existing aid, it cannot do more than inform the applicant pursuant to the second sentence of art.20(2) of reg.659/1999, that there are insufficient grounds for taking a view on the case. The Court concluded that, to the extent it does not constitute a decision on the compatibility of the measures at stake with the EC state aid rules, it does not have any impact on the applicants' legal position, such informal communication does not constitute an actionable measure and that the applicant's action was therefore inadmissible.

Case T–332/06 *Alcoa Trasformazioni Srl v Commission of the European Communities* [2009] E.C.R. II–00029 (March 25, 2009).

Type of procedure: Application for annulment of Commission Decision 2006/C 214/03, initiating the procedure laid down in art.88(2) EC, concerning state aid C 36/06 (ex. NN 38/06)—Preferential electricity tariff to energy intensive industries in Italy, in so far as that decision relates to the electricity tariffs applicable to the two primary aluminium plants owned by Alcoa Trasformazioni.

Highlights: The Court dismissed the action.

Case T–354/05 *Télévision française 1 SA (TF1) v Commission of the European Communities* [2009] E.C.R. II–00471.

Type of procedure: Application for the annulment of Commission Decision C(2005) 1166 final of April 20, 2005 on aid granted to France Télévision.

Highlights: The *Altmark* test, which seeks to determine the existence of state aid within the meaning of art.107(1) TFEU, should not be confused with the art.106(2) TFEU test, which is used to determine whether a measure constituting state aid may be regarded as compatible with the common market. The Court held that the Commission correctly found that the French audiovisual license system constituted state aid because it did not meet all the conditions set out by the *Altmark* case. The Court also concluded that such a system, as amended to take into account the Commission's recommendations, was in itself correct, and compatible with the common market.

Case T–68/05 *ASA v Commission of the European Communities* [2009] E.C.R. II–00355 (March 10, 2009).

Type of procedure: Application for annulment of Commission Decision 2005/374/EC of October 20, 2004 on a state aid measure implemented by Germany for Kvaerner Warnow Werft.

Highlights: Article 4(1) of Directive 90/684 on aid to shipbuilding provides that "production aid in favour of [shipyards] may be considered compatible with the common market provided that the total amount of aid granted in support of a [shipbuilding or ship conversion] contract does not exceed, in grant equivalent, a common maximum ceiling expressed as a percentage of the contract value before aid". Therefore, aid paid to cover losses from shipbuilding contracts and competition aid both come within the category of operating aid provided for in this Article. A decision of the Commission which finds that competition aid has to be accounted under aid granted to a beneficiary to cover shipbuilding contract losses alone is vitiated by a manifest error of assessment where the Commission has, in an initial decision, differentiated between those two types of aid, by taking the view that they are to have different uses, that is to say, on the one hand, to compensate for the beneficiary's lack of competitivity, and on the other, to cover those contract losses.

Case T–445/05 *Associazione italiana del risparmio gestito and Fineco Asset Management SpA v Commission of the European Communities* [2009] E.C.R. II–00289 (March 4, 2009).

Type of procedure: Application for annulment of Commission Decision 2006/638/EC of September 6, 2005 on the aid scheme implemented by Italy for certain undertakings for collective investment in transferable securities specialised in shares of small and medium-capitalisation companies listed on regulated markets.

Highlights: A recipient of aid obligated by a Commission Decision to return the said aid is individually concerned by that decision, even if the aid measure is of general application. An association which protects collective interests of undertakings is only entitled to bring an action for annulment of a Commission decision when its represented undertakings are also entitled to do so or when the association has a particular interest in acting. Regarding the statement of objections, the Commission is not obligated to examine each particular case of an aid scheme, it is sufficient to examine its general characteristics. When an aid scheme has not been notified, the Commission is not required to demonstrate the actual effect of aid granted but only to show that the aid can affect trade between Member States.

An advantage granted directly to natural or legal persons who are not undertakings may constitute an indirect advantage to others who are undertakings. State aid also exists in this case, as it is not required that the undertaking be a direct beneficiary.

Not only subsidies but also measures which mitigate charges normally borne are considered state aid. An advantage may be justified by the nature or general scheme of the system of which it is part. An advantage that benefits any investment vehicle fulfilling the conditions established does not make the measure at issue general and hence not selective. Aid may be selective in light of art.107(1) TFEU even if it concerns a whole economic sector. A mere increase in liquidity constitutes an advantage in light of art.107(1) TFEU. The objective of a measure cannot lead to that measure not being considered state aid.

Case T–424/05 *Italian Republic v Commission of the European Communities* [2009] E.C.R. II–00023 (March 4, 2009).

Type of procedure: Action for annulment of Commission Decision 2006/638/EC of September 6, 2005 on the aid scheme implemented by Italy for certain undertakings for collective investment in transferable securities specialised in shares of small and medium-capitalisation companies listed on regulated markets.

Highlights: If the Commission transiently qualifies measures as being new aid, it may contact the Member State in question to discuss the qualification. The fact that the Commission's initial qualification varies from its final decision does not lead to a contradiction that may invalidate the final decision. In its obligation to state reasons, the Commission is not requested to adopt a position regarding all arguments presented, being it sufficient to state the facts and legal considerations which are essentially important for the decision. In this light, the Commission is not obligated to examine each particular case of an aid scheme, it is sufficient to examine its general characteristics. An advantage granted directly to natural or legal persons who are not undertakings may constitute an indirect advantage to others who are undertakings. State aid also exists in this case, as it is not required that the undertaking be a direct beneficiary.

Not only subsidies but also measures which mitigate charges normally borne are considered state aid, for example a tax reduction. An independent decision taken by investors does not eliminate the effects that the advantage resulting from favorable tax conditions have on the normal functioning of the market. In order to decide whether an advantage exists, the Commission is not to take into account the position of the investors but of undertakings in similar conditions.

Aid may be selective in light of art.107(1) TFEU even if it concerns a whole economic sector. Even aid of minor importance may affect trade between Member States. The distinction between structural and functional aid is irrelevant, as any type of aid may lead to competition distortions and may affect trade between Member States. The legality of a Commission's decision stating that new aid does not fall under the derogatory conditions of art.107(3) TFEU is only to be analysed in light of the referred article and not in accordance to the Commission's previous decisional practice.

Joined Cases T–265/04, T–292/04 and T–504/04 *Tirrenia di Navigazione SpA (T–265/04), Caremar SpA and Others (T–292/04) and Navigazione Libera del Golfo SpA (T–504/04) v Commission of the European Communities* [2009] E.C.R. II–00021 (March 4, 2009).

Type of procedure: Applications for annulment in part of Commission Decision 2005/163/EC of March 16, 2004 on the state aid paid by Italy to the Adriatica, Caremar, Siremar, Saremar and Toremar shipping companies.

Highlights: On appeal, the Court annulled the Commission's decision to the extent that it qualified the measures as new aid holding, inter alia, that the decision was vitiated by a lack of reasoning because it did not provide any explanation for the Commission's rejection of the applicants' argument that the key aspects of the aid scheme at stake, and its funding, had been established by laws adopted already in 1936 and 1953 and thus constituted existing aid.

Case T–25/07 *Iride SpA and Iride Energia SpA v Commission of the European Communities* [2009] E.C.R. II–00245 (February 11, 2009).

Type of procedure: Application for annulment of Commission Decision 2006/941/EC of November 8, 2006 on state aid C 11/06 (ex. N 127/05) which Italy is planning to implement for AEM Torino in the form of grants to reimburse the stranded costs in the energy sector, in so far as (i) it contains a finding of state aid and (ii) it makes compatibility of that aid with the common market conditional upon repayment by AEM Torino of earlier unlawful aid granted under the scheme for "municipalised" undertakings.

Highlights: Only advantages granted directly or indirectly through state resources are to be treated as aid within the meaning of art.107(1) TFEU. Concerning compensation granted to energy distributors or producers from a special account administered by a public body and funded by the revenue from the application of a specified component of the electricity tariff, charged to all final customers, the sums redistributed to the recipient must be categorised as state resources, not only because they are under constant state control, but also because they are state property before being redistributed to the recipient.

The opening-up of a previously partitioned market cannot be regarded as anomalous in relation to normal market conditions. The alteration of the legislative framework in the electricity sector which occurred as a result of Directive 96/92 concerning common rules for the internal market in electricity is therefore part of normal market conditions. Concerning a state aid decision in which the Commission restricts itself to stating only that "the measure under assessment should be considered state aid", the Commission complies with the requirements for the statement of reasons where the legal and factual context of that decision includes a decision concerning similar measures, which does contain a detailed statement of the reasons.

With regard to a state aid scheme, the lack of precise information from the Commission, as regards the undertakings which benefit from an unlawful scheme and the precise sums they have received, does not affect the validity of an order for recovery or constitute an obstacle to its execution since, on the one hand, the Member State concerned is the entity best placed to obtain that information and, on the other hand, the Commission is entitled, in the absence of cooperation from the Member State concerned, to take a decision on the basis of the information available to it.

Furthermore, the Commission does not exceed the limits of its discretion under art.107(3) TFEU when it takes a decision declaring that aid to be compatible with the common market, but subject to the condition of prior repayment by the undertaking of unlawful aid received earlier, by reason of the cumulative effect of the aid in question. The criterion that there must be no cumulative effect of the new aid under consideration and earlier unlawful and incompatible aid that has not been repaid falls within the scope of the general examination of the compatibility of aid which the Commission must undertake, and is therefore merely one of the factors to be taken into consideration by the Commission when it applies art.107(3) TFEU.

Case T–388/03 *Deutsche Post AG and DHL International v Commission of the European Communities* [2009] E.C.R. II–00199 (February 10, 2009).

Type of procedure: Application for annulment of Commission Decision C(2003) 2508 final of July 23, 2003 raising no objections, following the preliminary examination procedure provided for in art.88(3) EC [now art.108(3) TFEU], to various measures adopted by the Belgian authorities in favour of La Poste SA, the Belgian public postal undertaking.

Highlights: When an applicant seeks to safeguard his procedural rights pursuant to art.108(2) TFEU, he may rely on any of the grounds set out in the second paragraph of art.263 TFEU, provided that they are directed at the annulment of the contested decision and, in any event, the initiation by the Commission of the procedure referred to in art.108(2) TFEU.

It is not for the Court to rule at that stage of the Commission's procedure whether aid exists or whether it is compatible with the common market. The formal investigation procedure under art.108(2) TFEU is obligatory if the Commission experiences serious difficulties in establishing whether or not aid is compatible with the common market. The notion of serious difficulties is an objective one. The fact that the time spent considerably exceeded the time usually required for a preliminary examination under art.108(3) TFEU may thus, with other factors, justify the conclusion that the Commission encountered serious difficulties of assessment necessitating initiation of the procedure under art.108(2) TFEU.

Case T–162/06 *Kronoply GmbH & Co KG v Commission of the European Communities* [2009] E.C.R. II–00001 (January 14, 2009).

Type of procedure: Application for annulment of Commission Decision 2006/262/EC of September 21, 2005 on state aid No. C 5/2004 (ex. N 609/2003) which Germany was planning to implement for Kronoply.

Highlights: The Commission, in a decision finding a state measure to be incompatible operating aid which cannot be authorised due to the lack of incentive effect and necessity, must explicitly state the reasons for that finding. Member States must not be permitted to make payments which, although they would improve the financial situation of the recipient undertaking, are not necessary for the attainment of the objectives specified in art.107(3) TFEU. It is not acceptable for aid to include arrangements, in particular as regards its amount, whose restrictive effects exceed what is necessary to enable the aid to attain the objectives permitted by the Treaty.

After a notification by a Member State of an aid project and its authorisation by the Commission, that State may notify a plan to introduce new aid in favor of an undertaking or to alter aid already granted to it. The new notification is subject to review by the Commission, which may declare the aid compatible with the common market. The fact that national legislation provides that a project must be completed within a certain period does not automatically lead to the loss of the possibility of applying for and obtaining authorisation, after the expiry of that period, for an increase in the aid already granted for that project.

Case T–455/05 *Componenta Oyj v Commission of the European Communities* [2008] E.C.R. II–00336 (December 18, 2008).

Type of procedure: Application for annulment of Commission Decision 2006/900/EC of October 20, 2005 on the state aid implemented by Finland for investment aid to Componenta Corporation.

Highlights: The Court annuled Commission Decision 2006/900/EC of October 20, 2005 on the state aid implemented by Finland for investment aid to Componenta Corporation for insufficient reasoning as to the method for determining the amount of aid concerning the valuation of real estate.

Cases T–211/04 and T–215/04 *Government of Gibraltar (T–211/04) and United Kingdom of Great Britain and Northern Ireland (T–215/04) v Commission of the European Communities* [2008] E.C.R. II–03745 (December 18, 2008).

Type of procedure: Applications for annulment of Commission Decision 2005/261/EC of March 30, 2004 on the aid scheme which the United Kingdom is planning to implement as regards the Government of Gibraltar Corporation Tax Reform.

Highlights: In order to assess the selectivity of a measure adopted by an infra-state body and designed to determine a reduced tax rate in relation to that applying in the rest of that Member State, it must be examined, first, whether that measure has been devised by a regional or local authority which has a political and administrative status separate from that of the central government; secondly, it must be examined whether it has been devised without the central government being able to intervene directly as regards its content; and third, whether the financial consequences of that infra-state body introducing the measure are offset by aid or subsidies from other regions or from the central government of the Member State concerned. Then, in order for the Commission to classify a tax measure as selective, it must begin by identifying and examining the common or "normal" regime under the tax system applicable in the geographical area constituting the relevant reference framework. It is in relation to this common or "normal" tax regime that the Commission must, secondly, assess and determine whether any advantage granted by the tax measure at issue may be selective by demonstrating that the measure derogates from that common regime inasmuch as the measure differentiates between economic operators who, in light of the objective assigned to the tax system of the Member State concerned, are in a comparable factual and legal situation. If the Commission has demonstrated that such a differentiation is none the less not selective when it arises from the nature or general scheme of the system of charges of which it forms part, it is for the Member State to show in a third stage that those differentiations are justified by the nature and general scheme of its tax system in that they derive directly from the basic or guiding principles of that system. If the Commission has failed to carry out the first two stages of the review of a measure's selectivity, it cannot embark upon the third and final stage of its assessment, as otherwise it will go beyond the limits of that review.

Case T–196/04 *Ryanair Ltd v Commission of the European Communities* [2008] E.C.R. II–03643 (December 17, 2008).

Type of procedure: Application for annulment of Commission Decision 2004/393/EC of February 12, 2004 concerning advantages granted by the Walloon Region and Brussels South Charleroi Airport to the airline Ryanair in connection with its establishment at Charleroi.

Highlights: When applying the private investor test, it is necessary to envisage the commercial transaction as a whole in order to determine whether the public entity and the entity which is controlled by it, taken together, have acted as rational operators in a market economy. The Commission must examine all the relevant features of the measures and their context, including those relating to the situation of the authorities responsible for granting those measures.

For the purposes of determining whether a measure of state aid constitutes an advantage within the meaning of art.107(1) TFEU, a distinction must be drawn between the obligations which the State must assume as an undertaking exercising an economic activity and its obligations as a public authority. Whilst it is clearly necessary, when the State acts as an undertaking operating as a private investor, to analyse its conduct by reference to the principle of the private investor in a market economy, application of that principle must be excluded in the event that the State acts as a public authority. In the latter event, the conduct of the State can never be compared to that of an operator or private investor in a market economy. The provision of airport facilities by a public authority to airlines, and the management of those facilities, in return for payment of a fee the amount of which is freely fixed by that authority, can be described as economic activities; although such activities are carried out in the public sector, they cannot, for that reason alone, be categorised as the exercise of public authority powers.

Case T–388/02 *Kronoply GmbH & Co KG and Kronotex GmbH & Co KG v Commission of the European Communities* [2008] E.C.R. II–00305 (December 10, 2008).

Type of procedure: Annulment of the Commission's Decision of June 19, 2002 to raise no objections to aid granted by the German authorities to Zellstoff Stendal for the construction of a production plant for pulp.

Highlights: The Court dismisses the action. The Court holds that companies competing against beneficiaries of state aid face restrictive locus standi and judicial review criteria.

Cases T–362/05 and T–363/05 *Nuova Agricast Srl and Cofra Srl v Commission of the European Communities* [2008] E.C.R. II–00297 (December 2, 2008).

Type of procedure: Action for damages for the loss allegedly suffered by the applicants as a result of the adoption by the Commission of the Decision of July 12, 2000 declaring compatible with the common market an aid scheme for investment in the less-favoured regions of Italy and as a result of the Commission's conduct during the procedure which preceded the adoption of that decision.

Highlights: The Court dismissed the actions (on appeal see: Case C 67/09 P of October 14, 2010).

Joined Cases T–254/00, T–270/00 and T–277/00 *Hotel Cipriani SpA and Others v Commission of the European Communities* [2008] E.C.R. II–03269 (November 28, 2008).

Type of procedure: Action for annulment of Commission Decision 2000/394/EC of November 25, 1999 on aid to firms in Venice and Chioggia by way of relief from social security contributions under Laws Nos 30/1997 and 206/1995.

Highlights: Where the Commission finds that an aid scheme is incompatible with the common market and requires that the aid paid out be recovered, all the actual beneficiaries of the scheme are individually concerned by the Commission's decision. The Court thus recognizes standing of beneficiaries of a state aid scheme to bring an action against a Commission decision declaring aid incompatible and ordering its recovery.

Like all the rules of Community competition law, the Treaty rules on aid are intended to ensure, not perfect competition, but effective or efficient competition. Under those circumstances, compensation for structural disadvantages makes it possible to avoid categorisation as aid only in certain specific situations. In the case of a multisectoral aid scheme, the Commission is merely required to ascertain whether the measure under consideration fulfils the two conditions for the application of art.107(1) TFEU, namely, that it is likely to affect trade between the Member States or competition, where sufficient relevant information for that purpose has been communicated to it during the administrative procedure.

The Commission has a wide discretion when applying art.107(3)(c) TFEU, the exercise of which involves complex economic and social assessments which must be made in a Community context. It is for the Community judicature to verify whether those rules have been observed by the Commission. Measures to grant or alter state aid must be regarded as new aid. In particular, where the alteration affects the actual substance of the original scheme, the latter is transformed into a new aid scheme. On the other hand, if the alteration is not substantive, only the alteration as such is liable to be classified as new aid, which is subject to the obligation to notify. After having categorised the geographical extension of an existing and authorised state aid regime as new aid, the General Court recalls that the burden of proof concerning the alleged overcharges borne by the beneficiaries of state aid falls upon the national authorities or the interested third parties and not upon the Commission. Furthermore, in the absence of sufficient evidence, the General Court rules that the Commission sufficiently motivated its decision to require the recovery of the aid granted.

Case T–70/07 *Cantieri Navali Termoli SpA v Commission of the European Communities* [2008] E.C.R. II–00250 (November 12, 2008).

Type of procedure: Action for annulment of Commission Decision 2006/948/EC of July 4, 2006 on state aid which Italy plans to implement for Cantieri Navali Termoli SpA.

Highlights: The Court dismisses the action.

Joined Cases T–309/04, T–317/04, T–329/04 and T–336/04 *TV 2/Danmark A/S and Others v Commission of the European Communities* [2008] E.C.R. II–02935 (October 22, 2008).

Type of procedure: Application, in Cases T–309/04 and T–317/04, for annulment of Commission Decision 2006/217/EC of May 19, 2004 on measures implemented by Denmark for TV 2/Danmark and, in the alternative, of art.2 of that decision or of paras 3 and 4 of that Article, and, in Cases T–329/04 and T–336/04, for annulment of that decision in so far as it establishes the existence of state aid which is partly compatible with the common market.

Highlights: The possibility open to Member States to define broadcasting services of general economic interest broadly, so as to cover the broadcasting of full-spectrum programming, cannot be called into question by the fact that the public service broadcaster also engages in commercial activities, in particular the sale of advertising space. Calling such activities into question would be tantamount to making the very definition of the broadcasting service of general economic interest dependent on its method of financing. A service of general economic interest is defined in relation to the general interest which it is designed to satisfy and not in relation to the means of ensuring its provision.

A decision to initiate the procedure must give interested parties the opportunity effectively to participate in the formal investigation procedure. For that purpose, it is sufficient for the parties concerned to be aware of the reasoning which has led the Commission to conclude provisionally that the measure in issue might constitute new aid incompatible with the common market.

Irrespective even of whether, in state aid matters, the private investor test is relevant for the assessment of state funding for public services, the Court finds that the decision initiating the procedure cannot be interpreted as capable of leading the applicants to believe that the over-compensation would pose problems in the light of the prohibition on state aid only if there was cross-subsidiation and, in consequence, not to elaborate any further their arguments based on the private investor test.

The Court stated that by not examining information that nevertheless had a direct bearing on the question whether the measures at issue constituted state aid within the meaning of art.107(1) TFEU, the Commission failed to fulfil its obligation to examine, a failure which in turn explains its failure to provide an adequate statement of reasons.

Case T–20/03 *Kahla/Thüringen Porzellan GmbH v Commission of the European Communities* [2008] E.C.R. II–02305 (September 24, 2008).

Type of procedure: Application for annulment of Commission Decision 2003/643/EC on the state aid implemented by Germany for Kahla Porzellan GmbH and Kahla/Thüringen Porzellan GmbH, in so far as that decision concerns the financial assistance granted to Kahla/Thüringen Porzellan GmbH.

Highlights: A Commission decision ruling on whether an aid measure is consistent with an approved general aid scheme falls within the scope of the Commission's obligation to ensure the application of arts 107 TFEU and 108 TFEU. The Commission may adopt a policy as to how it will exercise its discretion in the form of measures such as the Community guidelines on state aid for rescuing and restructuring firms in difficulty, in so far as those measures contain rules indicating the approach which the institution is to take and do not depart from the rules of the Treaty.

Therefore, aid granted to a firm in difficulty cannot be declared compatible with the common market on the sole ground that restructuring was envisaged, even if the restructuring ends up being successful. In order for the Commission to be in a position to assess whether the aid granted can encourage the beneficiary undertakings to act in a way that contributes to achieving the aim set out in art.107(3)(c) TFEU, it must first check whether the restructuring plan fulfils all the substantive conditions laid down in the said guidelines on aid for rescuing and restructuring firms in difficulty.

Case T–301/01 *Alitalia—Linee aeree italiane SpA v Commission of the European Communities* [2008] E.C.R. II–01753 (July 9, 2008).

Type of procedure: Action for annulment of Commission Decision 2001/723/EC concerning the recapitalisation of the company Alitalia.

Highlights: With regard to the admissibility of the action, the Court considers that Alitalia still had a legal interest in pursuing its action, even though its recapitalisation has been fully authorised and achieved since the Commission did not raise any objections to the payment of the third and final instalment of the aid and in spite of the fact that Alitalia received all the aid and is no longer subject to the obligations and conditions that were to be complied with during the period in which the plan was being implemented.

The obligation upon a Community institution to give effect to an annulment judgment delivered by the Community judicature derives from art.266 TFEU. Compliance calls for the adoption of a number of administrative measures and is not normally possible immediately. The institution concerned is allowed a reasonable period within which to comply with a judgment annulling one of its decisions. The question whether or not the period is reasonable depends on the nature of the measures to be taken and the attendant circumstances.

Furthermore, there is no provision in reg. No.659/1999 requiring the Commission to make available again to the third parties concerned the same opportunity in the investigation which led to the second decision, since the Commission was required to base its new analysis solely on information which was available to it when it took its initial decision on which the third parties had already defined their position. In this case, the Court finds that the decision contains sufficient reasoning, in particular as regards the determination of the minimum rate and the internal rate (for the purpose of applying the criterion of the private investor operating on market principles). It is not for the Court to substitute its economic assessment for that made by the Commission. Moreover, a plea directed against the conditions to which the compatibility of the aid with the common market was made subject, cannot be regarded as inadmissible on the ground that those conditions are not attributable to the Commission, which has exclusive jurisdiction to find that aid is incompatible with the common market. The Court finds that the Commission's decision is not vitiated by any procedural defect and confirms the validity of each of the conditions imposed on Alitalia.

Case T–266/02 *Deutsche Post AG v Commission of the European Communities* [2008] E.C.R. II–01233 (July 1, 2008).

Type of procedure: Action for annulment of Commission Decision 2002/753/EC on measures implemented by the Federal Republic of Germany for DPAG.

Highlights: Where state resources were granted to an undertaking as compensation for additional costs associated with the provision of a service of general economic interest under the conditions laid down in Case C–280/00 *Altmark*, the Commission, if it is not to render art.106(2) TFEU entirely ineffective, cannot classify as State aid all or part of the public resources granted, as long as the total amount of those resources remains below the additional costs generated by carrying out the public service mission. The Commission is required to conduct a diligent and impartial examination of a complaint, which may make it necessary for it to examine matters not expressly raised by the complainant.

Where state resources are transferred to an undertaking entrusted with providing a service of general economic interest, the Commission cannot overlook the information provided to it by the Member State in an attempt to show that the applicant had not enjoyed any advantage through public resources; it cannot conclude that state aid had been granted without having first checked whether the public resources bestowed an advantage on the recipient. It is only where the Member State, notwithstanding the Commission's order, fails to provide the information requested that the Commission is empowered to terminate the procedure and make its decision, on the basis of the information available to it, on the question of whether or not the aid is compatible with the common market.

Case T–442/03 *SIC Sociedade Independente de Comunicação, SA v Commission of the European Communities* [2008] E.C.R. (June 26, 2008).

Type of procedure: Commission Decision 2005/406/EC of October 15, 2003 on ad hoc measures implemented by Portugal for RTP, the Commission decided that certain of the ad hoc measures constituted state aid compatible with the common market (art.1), whilst the other ad hoc measures did not constitute state aid.

Highlights: Member States have the power to define broadcasting Services of General Economic Interest (SGEI). In addition, the Court concluded that the derogation laid down in art.106(2) TFEU does not entail the requirement to organise a competitive tendering prior to the award of the public (television) service to RTP.

Secondly, the Court held that public service broadcasters have to comply with the quality standards defined in their public service remit. However, it pointed out that only Member States—not the Commission—are able to assess the PSB's compliance with their remit. Moreover, the Court called the Commission to a diligent and impartial investigation concerning the verification of the proportionality of the costs of the public service. Finally, the judgment emphasised the importance of SGEI in the public broadcasting service, under the light of the Amsterdam Protocol on the system of public broadcasting in the Member States and the Resolution of the Council and of the Member States of January 25, 1999 concerning public service broadcasting.

Case T–348/04 *Société internationale de diffusion et d'édition SA (SIDE) v Commission of the European Communities* [2008] E.C.R. II–00625 (April 15, 2008).

Type of procedure: Action for annulment concerning Commission Decision 2005/262/EC on the aid implemented by France in favour of CELF.

Highlights: The analysis as to unnotified whether aid is compatible with the common market does not only require an assessment of whether, at the time when the relevant decision was adopted, the Community interest demanded that the aid be repaid. The Commission must also ascertain whether, during the period in which the aid in question was paid, that aid was likely to distort competition. Community legislation on state aid would be neither clear not predictable for those who are subject to it if aid which could not be regarded as compatible during a particular period, in the absence of a derogation which was applicable in that period, could subsequently be regarded as compatible if such a derogation were made available. Moreover, to consider that aid which has not been notified can be declared compatible with the common market by virtue of a derogation which was not in force when that aid was paid would result in conferring an advantage on the Member State which granted it in relation to any other Member State which might have intended to grant similar aid but refrained from doing so since there was no derogation authorising this.

In the application of art.107(3) TFEU, the Commission has a wide discretion the exercise of which involves complex economic and social assessments which must be made in a Community context. It is not for the General Court, therefore, to substitute its economic assessment for that made by the institution which adopted the decision. With regard to the examination of export aid in the book sector granted to a book agency, the purpose of which is to offset the extra costs of handling small orders, it would in the absence of tele-transmission only be acceptable to apply a multiplying factor to the costs incurred in processing small orders if tele-transmission was clearly less widely used in processing small orders than in other orders.

Case T–233/04 *Kingdom of the Netherlands v Commission of the European Communities* [2008] E.C.R. II–00591 (April 10, 2008) (see also case C–279/08P).

Type of procedure: Application for annulment concerning Commission adopted Decision C(2003) 1761 final relating to state aid N 35/2003 concerning the NOx emission trading scheme ("the measure in question").

Highlights: According to settled case law, classification as aid requires that all the conditions set out in art.107(1) TFEU are fulfilled. For advantages to be capable of being classified as aid within the meaning of art.107(1) TFEU, they must, first, be granted directly or indirectly through state resources and, second, be imputable to the state. In this case, the tradability of the emission allowances provided for by the measure in question constitutes an advantage for the enterprises subject to the prescribed NOx emission standard.

Furthermore, an economic benefit granted by a Member State constitutes state aid only if, by displaying a degree of selectivity, it is such as to favour certain undertakings or the production of certain goods. In the present case, the beneficiary undertakings are determined in accordance with the nature and general scheme of the system, on the basis of their significant emissions of NOx and of the specific reduction standard to which they are subject. Ecological considerations justify distinguishing undertakings which emit large quantities of NOx from other undertakings. Thus, differentiation arose from the nature or overall structure of the scheme of which it is part. The measure in question cannot therefore be classified as state aid.

Case T–289/03 *British United Provident Association Ltd (BUPA), BUPA Insurance Ltd and BUPA Ireland Ltd v Commission of the European Communities* [2008] E.C.R. II–0008 (February 12, 2008).

Type of procedure: Action for annulment concerning decision C(2003) 1322 final of May 13, 2003 of the Commission, where it decided not to raise objections concerning the establishment of the RES (Risk Equalisation Scheme) Ireland.

Highlights: Member States have a wide discretion to define what they regard as services of general economic interest. The Member State's power to define services of general economic interest is not, however, unlimited and cannot be exercised arbitrarily for the sole purpose of removing a particular sector from the application of the competition rules. The control which the Community institutions are authorised to exercise concerns whether or not there is a manifest error of assessment. In the context of the necessarily restricted control, by both the Commission and the Court, of the necessity and the proportionality of the compensation for discharging a mission involving the provision of a service of general economic interest, there is no scope for calling in question either the validity of the objectives pursued or the lawfulness of the rules governing the functioning of a risk equalisation system on the private medical insurance system of a Member State. The Commission must ensure that a mission satisfies certain minimum criteria of a service of general economic interest within the meaning of the Treaty, and to demonstrate that those criteria are indeed satisfied in the particular case. These are, notably, the presence of an act of the public authority entrusting the operators in question with such a mission and the universal and compulsory nature of that mission (public service obligation). Furthermore, the Member State must indicate its reasons and why it to be distinguished from other economic activities.

It does not follow either from the relevant legislation or from the case-law that the formulation of the operative part of decisions adopted pursuant to art.107 TFEU in conjunction with art.106(2) TFEU must of necessity meet specific requirements. Although it might appear desirable, in the interest of clarity and legal certainty, that the Commission should expressly mention in the operative part of the act the Treaty provisions which it is applying, the failure to do so does not constitute an error of law provided that it is quite clear upon reading the statement of reasons in conjunction with the operative part of the act precisely what those provisions are.

In the context of an action for annulment of a Commission decision on state aid, the applicant has no standing to raise pleas alleging infringement of provisions of Community law distinct from those coming under arts 107 TFEU and 108 TFEU, read together, where appropriate, with art.106 TFEU.

Joined Cases T–50/06, T–56/06, T–60/06, T–62/06 and T–69/06 *Ireland (T–50/06), French Republic (T–56/06), Italian Republic (T–60/06), Eurallumina SpA (T–62/06) and Aughinish Alumina Ltd (T–69/06) v Commission of the European Communities* [2007] E.C.R. II–00172 (December 12, 2007).

Type of procedure: Actions for annulment of Commission Decision 2006/323/EC of December 7, 2005 on the exemption from excise duty on mineral oils used as fuel for alumina production in the Gardanne region, the Shannon region and Sardinia, implemented by France, Ireland and Italy respectively.

Highlights: The Commission was required, in the present case, to ascertain whether the contested exemptions could be regarded as existing aid by reason of the fact that at the time they were put into effect they did not constitute aid but that subsequently they became aid due to the evolution of the common market and without having been altered by the Member States concerned, in accordance with art.1(b)(v) of Regulation No.659/1999. It follows that the Commission was required to give adequate reasons for the contested decision with regard to the applicability in the present case of that article and therefore could not merely make the statement in the preamble to that decision, according to which "[it] does not apply in this case". The Commission has infringed the duty to give reasons imposed on it by art.296 TFEU with regard to the non-application in the present case of art.1(b)(v) of Regulation No.659/1999. Consequently, the contested decision must be annulled.

Case T–254/05 (related to T–375/03) *Fachvereinigung Mineralfaserindustrie eV Deutsche Gruppe der Eurima—European Insulation Manufacturers Association v Commission of the European Communities* [2007] E.C.R. II–00124 (September 20, 2007).

Type of procedure: Action for annulment of Commission Decision C(2005) 379 of February 11, 2005 relating to state aid N 260b/2004, Germany, Prolongation of the scheme to promote the use of insulation material from renewable raw materials.

Highlights: The Court dismisses the action as inadmissible.

Case T–136/05 *EARL Salvat père & fils, Comité interprofessionnel des vins doux naturels et vins de liqueur à appellations contrôlées (CIVDN) and Comité national des interprofessions des vins à appellation d'origine (CNIV) v Commission of the European Communities* [2007] E.C.R. II–04063 (September 20, 2007).

Type of procedure: Action for annulment of art.1(1) and (3) of Commission Decision 2007/253/EC of January 19, 2005 on the Rivesaltes plan and CIVDN parafiscal charges operated by France.

Highlights: Only a measure the legal effects of which are binding on the applicant and are capable of affecting his interests by bringing about a distinct change in his legal position is an act or decision which may be the subject of an action for annulment under art.263 TFEU. However, this does not dispense the Community judicature from examining whether the Commission's finding contained in the decision has binding legal effects such as to affect the applicant's interests. Persons other than those to whom a decision is addressed can claim to be individually concerned only if that decision affects them by reason of certain attributes which are peculiar to them, or by reason of factual circumstances which differentiate them from all other persons and thereby distinguish them individually in the same way as the person addressed. The two criteria of direct concern are, first, the fact that the measure in question must directly produce effects on the individual's legal situation and, secondly, the fact that the measure must not allow any discretion to the addresses of the measure, who must implement it. For the applicant undertaking to be directly concerned both the above criteria must be satisfied, whether or not it challenges the order for recovery issued to the Member State. Concerning a decision finding aid incompatible with the common market the Commission must state the reasons why the measures in question came within the scope of art.107(1) TFEU. The fact that the Commission does so in a global fashion, cannot in itself be regarded as an infringement of the duty to state reasons, especially where the measures in question are all part of the same course of action. Lastly, only advantages granted directly or indirectly through state resources are held to be aid within the meaning of art.107(1) TFEU. In that context, inter-branch contributions, created by a decision of an inter-branch committee in order to finance aid to be paid to certain producers in the sector concerned must be classified as state resources in so far as the State is perfectly capable, by exercising its dominant influence over that committee, of directing the use of its resources in order, as occasion arises, to finance specific advantages in favour of certain undertakings.

Case T–375/03 *Fachvereinigung Mineralfaserindustrie eV Deutsche Gruppe der Eurima—European Insulation Manufacturers Association v Commission of the European Communities* [2007] E.C.R. II–00121 (September 20, 2007).

Type of procedure: Application for annulment of Commission Decision C(2003) 1473 final of July 9, 2003 declaring the measures which the German authorities propose to take to promote the use of insulating materials produced from renewable raw materials compatible with the common market (state aid No.694/2002).

Highlights: The Court dismisses the action; the Court rules that, by adopting the guidelines on state aid for environmental protection, the Commission did not deprive itself of the possibility to adopt a decision on the basis of art.107(3) TFEU. The Court rejected the applicant's claim that the Commission had erred in not opening an in-depth investigation under art.108(2) TFEU and that it had committed errors of fact and reasoning in assessing the aid and in determining that it would have environmental benefits. Contrary to what was claimed, the Commission did not encounter serious difficulties in assessing the aid measure and had not erred in finding the aid to be compatible with the common market. Further, the Commission's decision did not breach the principles of proportionality and non-discrimination.

Joined Cases T–239/04 and T–323/04 *Italian Republic (T–239/04) and Brandt Italia SpA (T–323/04) v Commission of the European Communities* [2007] E.C.R. 03265 (September 12, 2007).

Type of procedure: Action for annulment of Commission Decision 2004/800/EC on the state aid scheme put into effect by Italy providing for urgent measures to assist employment, which was notified to the Italian Republic on April 1, 2004.

Highlights: The fact that a state measure providing for an employment aid scheme is designed to safeguard employment has no bearing on its classification as state aid, since art.107(1) TFEU does not distinguish between measures of state intervention by reference to their causes or their aims but defines them in relation to their effects. In order for an aid scheme to be considered compatible with the common market in the light of reg. No.2204/2002 (state aid for employment) it is not enough for the conditions which it sets to be fulfilled only in certain cases where the scheme could, potentially, be applied.

It is necessary for the aid granted on the basis of that scheme to fulfil those conditions in all such cases. The obligation to state reasons is an essential procedural requirement, as distinct from the question whether the reasons given are correct, which goes to the substantive legality of the contested measure. The Commission is required to demonstrate that a measure constitutes state aid and that it is incompatible with the common market. However, the Commission is not required to demonstrate the actual effect of unlawful aid on competition and trade between Member States.

In the case of an aid scheme, the Commission may confine itself to examining the general characteristics of the scheme at issue without being required to examine each particular case in which it applies, in order to determine whether that scheme contains aid elements. In view of the mandatory nature of the review of state aid by the Commission under art.108 TFEU, undertakings to which aid has been granted may not, in principle, entertain a legitimate expectation that the aid is lawful unless it has been granted in compliance with the procedure provided for by that article. If the beneficiary of the aid considers that exceptional circumstances exist on which it was entitled to base a legitimate expectation that the aid was lawful, and such a case is brought before a national court, it is for that court to assess the aid, if necessary after obtaining a preliminary ruling on interpretation from the Court of Justice.

Case T–25/04 *González y Díez, SA v Commission of the European Communities* [2007] E.C.R. II–03121 (September 12, 2007).

Type of procedure: Action for the annulment of arts 1, 3 and 4 of Commission Decision 2004/340/EC of November 5, 2003 concerning aid to the company González y Díez SA to cover exceptional costs (aid for 2001 and incorrect use of the aid for 1998 and 2000).

Highlights: Article 108(2) TFEU must be interpreted as enabling the Commission to review, after July 23, 2002, the compatibility with the common market of state aid granted in the fields falling with the scope of the ECSC Treaty ratione materiae and ratione temporis, and the application by the Member States of decisions authorising state aid adopted pursuant to the ECSC Treaty, in respect of situations existing prior to the expiry of that Treaty.

Although procedural rules are generally held to apply to all disputes pending at the time when they enter into force, this is not the case with substantive rules. The latter must be interpreted, in order to ensure respect for the principles of legal certainty and the protection of legitimate expectations, as applying to situations existing before their entry into force only in so far as it clearly follows from their wording, objectives or general scheme that such an effect must be given to them.

The right to contest a decision to initiate the formal procedure may not diminish the procedural rights of interested parties by preventing them from challenging the final decision and relying in support of their action on defects at any stage of the procedure leading to that decision. The examination carried out by the Commission in the context of the new formal procedure, opened with a view to revoking its earlier decision finding that part of the aid had been used incorrectly and to adopt a new decision in that regard, must relate to all the amounts of aid covered by the first examination in the context of the procedure which led to the adoption of that earlier decision. In carrying out the procedure involving review of state aid the Commission must take account of the legitimate expectations which the parties concerned may entertain as a result of what was said in the decision to initiate the procedure and, subsequently, that it will not base its final decision on the absence of information which, in the light of what was said in that decision, the parties concerned could not have formed the view that they were under a duty to make available to it.

Case T–348/03 *Koninklijke Friesland Foods NV v Commission of the European Communities* [2007] E.C.R. II–00101 (September 12, 2007).

Type of procedure: Action for annulment of art.2 of Commission Decision 2003/515/EC of February 17, 2003 on the state aid implemented by the Netherlands for international financing activities in so far as it excludes from the transitional scheme those operators who, as at July 11, 2001, had lodged a request with the Netherlands tax authority for application of the aid scheme in question but whose request had not yet been determined by that date.

Highlights: The Court annuls art.2 of Commission Decision 2003/515/EC. The Court considered that the Friesland Foods had a legitimate expectation that a reasonable transitional period would be granted. Therefore the European Commission infringed the principle of protection of legitimate expectations. In addition the principle of equal treatment was not respected either as companies which lodged their requests before July 11, 2001 and whose requests had not been determined were treated differently than companies which lodged it on that date.

Case T–68/03 *Olympiaki Aeroporia Ypiresies AE v Commission of the European Communities* [2007] E.C.R. II–02911 (September 12, 2007).

Type of procedure: Action for annulment of Commission Decision 2003/372/EC on aid granted by Greece to Olympic Airways. It finds therein that most of the objectives of the 1998 restructuring plan had not been attained, that the conditions imposed by the 1998 approval decision had not been fully met and that the restructuring aid had therefore been wrongly implemented.

Highlights: It is, in principle, for the Commission to provide proof, in a decision finding misapplication of previously approved aid and referring to the existence of new non-notified aid, both of the misapplication of the aid and the grant of new aid. It follows from the provisions of art.108(2) and (3) TFEU that if that is not established, the existing aid is covered by the earlier decision approving it and the new measures cannot be regarded as state aid within the meaning of art.107(1) TFEU. On the other hand, the burden of proof of the compatibility of aid with the common market is borne principally by the Member State concerned, which must show that the conditions for that derogation are satisfied. Any significant amendment to a restructuring plan accepted by the Commission in a decision approving restructuring aid requires, in principle, that the Member State concerned submit a revised plan in all relevant detail so as to permit the Commission to assess its compatibility with the common market.

The mere fact that payment facilities are accorded in a discretionary manner by a public creditor is not sufficient to characterise such facilities as state aid. They must also be clearly greater than those which would have been accorded by a private creditor in a comparable situation. No provision of Community law requires the Commission to fix the exact amount of the aid to be recovered. It is sufficient for the Commission's decision to include information enabling the recipient to work out that amount himself, without overmuch difficulty. The Commission may confine itself to declaring that there is an obligation to repay the aid in question and leave it to the national authorities to calculate the exact amounts to be repaid. The advantage to the debtor of tolerance, of non-payment or delayed payment of his debt is constituted precisely by the exemption from, or delay in, payment of the debt from the time at which it fell due. That advantage does not necessarily coincide with the amount which a private creditor could have recovered if he had ceased to tolerate the default or delay in payment. The failure to pay value added tax is not, in principle, sufficient to raise a presumption that an undertaking has enjoyed an advantage within the meaning of art.107(1) TFEU. It is the Commission's duty to verify whether, in the circumstances of the case, non-payment confers a cash-flow advantage on the person concerned.

Case T–196/02 *MTU Friedrichshafen GmbH v Commission of the European Communities* [2007] E.C.R. II–02889 (September 12, 2007).

Type of procedure: Action for annulment of Commission Decision 2002/898/EC on the state aid implemented by Germany for SKL Motoren- und Systembautechnik.

Highlights: Article 13(1) of Regulation No.659/1999 empowers the Commission to adopt a decision on the basis of the information available when it is faced with a Member State which fails to comply with its obligation of cooperation and refuses to provide information requested from it for the purpose of assessing the compatibility of aid with the common market. However, given the Commission's very wide discretion, before taking such a decision, it must comply with certain procedural requirements. In particular where despite a reminder the Member State concerned does not provide the information requested within the period prescribed by the Commission, or where it provides incomplete information, the Commission must issue a decision requiring the information to be provided. That decision must specify what information is required and set an appropriate deadline for it to be provided. Finally, it is only if a Member State fails to comply with such an injunction that the Commission has the power to terminate the procedure and take a decision as to whether or not the aid is compatible with the common market on the basis of the information available.

Article 13 does not allow the Commission to impose on a particular undertaking an obligation to repay, even jointly and severally, a fixed part of the amount of the aid declared to be incompatible, where the transfer of state resources from which that undertaking benefited is hypothetical. A Commission's decision imposing on an undertaking the obligation to repay part of the aid jointly and severally, is not in any way a logical consequence of the implementation of the procedure laid down by the TFEU in relation to state aid, since the Member State providing the aid which is ordered to be recovered is under an obligation to require recovery from the actual beneficiaries under the Commission's supervision, without it being necessary to name those beneficiaries expressly in the recovery decision and to specify the amount of the sums which must be repaid by each beneficiary.

Case T–360/04 *FG Marine SA v Commission of the European Communities* [2007] E.C.R. II–00092 (July 19, 2007).

Type of procedure: Claim for compensation for loss allegedly caused by Commission Decision 2000/513/EC of September 8, 1999 on aid granted by France to the company Stardust Marine.

Highlights: Dismisses the action as unfounded. There is no direct causal effect between the conduct complained of and the alleged damage.

Case T–344/04 (related to T–360/04) *Denis Bouychou v Commission of the European Communities* [2007] E.C.R. II–00091 (July 19, 2007).

Type of procedure: Claim for compensation for loss allegedly caused by Commission Decision 2000/513/EC of September 8, 1999 on aid granted by France to the company Stardust Marine, represented by Denis Bouychou, as insolvency administrator.

Highlights: Dismisses the claim as unfounded. There is no direct causal effect between the conduct complained of and the alleged damage.

"[. . .] [T]out ce qui précède qu'il n'existe pas de lien de causalité direct entre le comportement reproché à la Commission et le préjudice allégué. Dès lors, le recours doit être rejeté, sans qu'il soit nécessaire d'examiner, d'une part, la question de savoir si les vices entachant la Décision constituent une violation suffisamment caractérisée du droit communautaire et, d'autre part, celle relative à la réalité du préjudice."

Case T–167/04 *Asklepios Kliniken GmbH v Commission of the European Communities* [2007] E.C.R. II–02379 (July 11, 2007).

Type of procedure: Application for a declaration under art.232 EC that, by failing to take a decision under art.4(2), (3) or (4) of Council Regulation EC No.659/1999 of March 22, 1999 laying down detailed rules for the application of art.88 EC on the complaint lodged by the applicant concerning the award of allegedly unlawful aid to publicly-owned hospitals in Germany, the Commission has failed to fulfil its obligations under art.88 EC and arts 10(1) and 13(1) of reg. No.659/1999.

Highlights: Since arts 263 and 265 TFEU prescribe one and the same remedy, it follows that beneficiaries may in order to safeguard procedural rights as an interested party derived from art.108(2) TFEU, also admissibly bring an action for a declaration that the Commission failed to act by not adopting a decision under art.108(3) TFEU following his complaint, provided the aid was in fact granted and does not constitute a general aid scheme. The adoption by the Commission of a decision of general scope does not by itself constitute a definition of position by the Commission on that complaint. Only the actual application of those criteria to the situations complained of can constitute a definition of position for the purposes of the second paragraph of art.265 TFEU. Similarly, the opportunity to comment on the content of the draft of a general decision cannot be assimilated to the initiation of the formal investigation procedure under art.108(2) TFEU. Furthermore, the fact that the Commission itself prepared a general decision on the category of aid which includes the measure complained of does not release it from that task to conduct a diligent and impartial examination of a complaint. However, the reasonableness of the duration of the investigation of a complaint of allegedly unlawful state aid must be determined in relation to the particular circumstances of each case. Where a Community legal case important for the assessment of the aid complained of is ongoing, the Commission may legitimately postpone its examination pending clarification of the legal framework within which the examination of the complaint has to be conducted.

Case T–475/04 *Bouygues SA and Bouygues Télécom SA v Commission of the European Communities* [2007] E.C.R. II–02097 (July 4, 2007).

Type of procedure: Annulment of decision state aid NN 42/2004, France, which was notified to the French Republic, relating to the amendment of the fees payable by Orange and SFR for the UMTS licences.

Highlights: A Commission decision is sufficiently reasoned if it dismisses a complaint against a national measure equalising fees due from operators for the granting of Universal Mobile Telecommunications System (UMTS) licences for lack of one of the cumulative factors defining the concept of state aid within the meaning of art.107(1) TFEU, namely the granting of an advantage to the beneficiary, without giving reasons for that dismissal by reference to the other factors defining that concept, and by reason of the fact that the measure in question implements a Community directive and, in particular, the principle of non-discrimination laid down by that directive.

A decision raising no objections may be adopted by the Commission at the preliminary examination stage under art.108(3) TFEU, without opening the formal investigation stage under art.108(2) TFEU, only if the Commission is able to satisfy itself at the end of that preliminary examination, without serious difficulties, that the planned aid is compatible with the common market.

UMTS licences, have an economic value that the manager of that domain is bound to take into account when he determines the amount of fees to be paid by the operators involved, and therefore constitute a state resource. Hence, the exercise of state functions does not preclude the taking into account of economic facts in connection with the management of a scarce public resource such as the radio frequencies constituting the public airwaves, to which a right of access or a right of usage may be granted. The Member States simultaneously perform the roles of telecommunications regulator and manager of the public assets that constitute the wireless airwaves.

Case T–246/99 *Tirrenia di Navigazione SpA and Others v Commission of the European Communities* [2007] E.C.R. II–00065 (June 20, 2007).

Type of procedure: Action for annulment of the Commission's decision of August 6, 1999 to initiate the procedure under art.88(2) EC [now art.108(2) TFEU] concerning the state aid granted by the Italian Republic to undertakings in the Tirrenia di Navigazione group.

Highlights: The Court dismisses the action.

Case T–357/02 *Freistaat Sachsen v Commission of the European Communities* [2007] E.C.R. II–01261 (May 3, 2007).

Type of procedure: Action for annulment of Commission Decision 2003/226/EC on an aid scheme which the Federal Republic of Germany is planning to implement, "Guidelines on assistance for SMEs—Improving business efficiency in Saxony", Subprogrammes 1 (Coaching), 4 (Participation in fairs), 5 (Cooperation) and 7 (Design promotion).

Highlights: Even where a planned aid scheme satisfies all the conditions under the Commission's communication on accelerated clearance in order for an examination period of 20 working days from the date of notification to apply, it is only "in principle" that the Commission undertakes not to object after that period has expired, thus reserving its full powers "to decide".

To apply a new rule on the compatibility of state aids to aid notified before it entered into force is permissible only if it clearly follows from the terms, objectives or general scheme of the new rules concerned that they are intended to apply retroactively and if the legitimate expectations of those concerned are duly respected. Commission Regulation No.70/2001 on the application of arts 87 and 88 of the EC Treaty (now 107 and 108 TFEU) to state aid to small and medium-sized enterprises could not be used before its entry into force. There is nothing in its wording which authorizes such an application, nor were the Member States in a position to predict either its definitive content or the date of its entry into force. Furthermore, such an application would go against the foreseeability which is designed to ensure the publication by the Commission of the texts concerning the criteria which it intends to implement when assessing the compatibility of aid. Finally, as the assessment concerning aid implemented without complying with the obligation to notify is made by reference to the rules in force at the time the aid was paid, this could have the effect of encouraging Member States to free themselves from the obligation to notify, since, by doing so, they would incur no greater risks and penalties than by notifying.

The possibility of bringing an action for annulment against the Commission's decision to open the formal investigation procedure in respect of planned aid may not diminish the procedural rights of interested parties by preventing them from seeking the annulment of the final decision and relying in support of their action on defects at any stage of the procedure leading to that decision. In order for the notification of planned state aid to be regarded as complete, for the purposes of the preliminary examination phase, it is sufficient for it to contain such information as will enable the Commission to form a prima facie to initiate the formal investigation procedure.

Case T–369/00 *Département du Loiret (France) v Commission of the European Communities* [2007] E.C.R. II–00851 (March 29, 2007).

Type of procedure: Action for annulment against Commission Decision 2002/14/EC on the state aid granted by France to Scott Paper SA/Kimberly-Clark. After the present action was lodged, the Commission served a corrigendum to the contested decision on the French Republic on March 2, 2001. Article 1 and recitals 172, 217 and 239(b)(a) to the contested decision were amended accordingly.

Highlights: A Commission decision on the repayment of state aid which the decision declares to be unlawful, does not satisfy the requirement to state reasons laid down by art.296 TFEU if it renders review by the addressee of the decision and by the court impossible by failing to include sufficient information as to the manner in which the Commission calculated the amount to be repaid, such failure consisting in: (1) not stating that the Commission used a compound rate of interest for which no provision was made in legislation and which did not correspond to the Commission's previous practice, even though in the case in point the choice of compound interest had important consequences for the amout to be repaid; (2) not giving any explanation as to the choice of the rate applied; (3) not giving any explanation as to the link between the advantage retained by the beneficiary and the amount it was required to repay; and (4) an apparent inconsistency between the choice of compound interest in respect of the calculation as at the decision date of the amount to be repaid and simple interest in respect of the interest to be charged for the period between the decision and actual repayment.

Case T–366/00 *Scott SA v Commission of the European Communities* [2007] E.C.R. II–00797 (March 29, 2007).

Type of procedure: Action of annulment of Commission Decision 2002/14/EC on the state aid granted by France to Scott Paper SA/Kimberly-Clark. After the present action was lodged, the Commission served a corrigendum to the contested decision on France on March 2, 2001. Article 1 and recitals 172, 217 and 239(b)(a) of the contested decision were corrected accordingly.

Highlights: Although the procedure for review of state aid governed by art.108 TFEU accords no special role to the recipient of the aid as compared with all interested parties, and even though the recipient of aid does not have the status of a party to the procedure, the Commission, in the light of its obligation to conduct a diligent and impartial examination of the case, might be obliged in certain circumstances to take into account the observations of the recipient of aid submitted after the expiry of the time laid down to do so by the decision to open the procedure.

Although particular circumstances which allowed for only a partial assessment of the exact value of the aid may be taken into consideration in the assessment of the legality of the Commission's decision, nevertheless, the essential issue as to the determination of the value of the aid is a point of fact upon which the Community Court must carry out a comprehensive review, and the mere fact that the Commission may have to resort to an approximate evaluation does not mean that it has a margin of appreciation with regard to the determination of the amount to be recovered. During the art.108(2) TFEU investigation procedure, the Commission is bound to use the most reliable method to determine the value of the property and to conduct a diligent and impartial examination. The sale price of the property is not necessarily determined by the costs incurred by the vendor because it is in fact influenced by various factors, including supply and demand on the market at the time of the sale.

In the area of state aid, in accordance with the principles laid down in the case-law and by Regulation No.659/1999, where there is no information to the contrary from interested parties, the Commission is empowered to base itself on the facts it has available at the time it adopts its final decision, even if they are incorrect, provided that the factual elements in question were the subject of an information injunction issued by the Commission to the Member State to provide it with the necessary information. When the Commission bases a decision on the information available as to certain facts, without having complied with the procedural requirements established by the case-law and laid down in Regulation No.659/1999, the Court is entitled to review the issue as to whether taking those facts into account was likely to give rise to an error of assessment vitiating the legality of the contested decision. The failure of the Member State to cooperate does not mean that the Commission's conduct is thereby exempt from all judicial review by the Community courts. The Commission must use all of its powers in order to obtain, so far as possible, the relevant information and must act with due care. The Commission must also use all of the powers available to it to avoid the possibility that the failure of a Member State to cooperate could have negative and unwarranted consequences for such third parties.

Case T–237/02 *Technische Glaswerke Ilmenau GmbH v Commission of the European Communities* [2006] E.C.R. II–05131 (December 14, 2006).

Type of procedure: Application for annulment of the Commission's Decision of May 28, 2002 refusing the applicant access to documents relating to procedures for controlling state aid.

Highlights: Although it is not prohibited for an intervener to use arguments different from those used by the party it is supporting, that is nevertheless on the condition that they do not alter the framework of the dispute and that the intervention is still intended to support the form of order sought by that party. The mere fact that a document referred to in an application for access under Regulation No.1049/2001 regarding public access to European Parliament, Council and Commission documents concerns an interest protected by an exception cannot justify application of that exception. Such application may, in principle, be justified only if the institution has previously assessed, firstly, whether access to the document would specifically and actually undermine the protected interest and, secondly, in the circumstances referred to in art.4(2) and (3) of that Regulation, whether there was no overriding public interest in disclosure. In addition, the risk of a protected interest being undermined must be reasonably foreseeable and not purely hypothetical. Consequently, the examination which the institution must undertake in order to apply an exception must be carried out in a concrete individual manner and must be apparent from the reasons for the decision. Furthermore, it follows from that regulation that all the exceptions in paras 1 to 3 of art.4 thereof are stated as having to apply "to a document". That concrete examination must, therefore, be carried out in respect of each document covered by the application. Moreover, only a concrete individual examination, as opposed to an abstract overall examination, can enable the institution to assess the possibility of granting the applicant partial access under art.4(6) of that Regulation and, as regards the application on a temporal basis of the exceptions to the right of access, art.4(7) of that Regulation provides that the exceptions as laid down by paras 1 to 3 of that article are to apply only for the period during which protection is justified on the basis "of the content of the document". The obligation for an institution to undertake a concrete individual assessment of the content of the documents covered in the application for access is thus an approach to be adopted as a matter of principle, which applies to all the exceptions in paras 1 to 3 of art.4 of that Regulation, whatever may be the field to which the documents sought relate, and which concerns, in particular, that of cartels or the control of public subsidies. Only in exceptional cases and only where the administrative burden entailed by a concrete, individual examination of the documents proves to be particularly heavy, thereby exceeding the limits of what may reasonably be required, may a derogation from the obligation to examine the documents be permissible.

Case T–146/03 *Asociación de Empresarios de Estaciones de Servicio de la Comunidad Autónoma de Madrid and Federación Catalana de Estaciones de Servicio v Commission of the European Communities* [2006] E.C.R. II–00098 (December 12, 2006).

Type of procedure: Application for partial annulment of Commission Decision 2003/293/EC of December 11, 2002 on the measures implemented by Spain in the agricultural sector following the increase in fuel prices.

Highlights: Article 1 of Commission Decision 2003/293/EC is annulled in so far that it finds that the measures to support agricultural cooperatives provided for by Royal Decree Law 10/2000 on emergency support for agriculture, fisheries and transport do not constitute aid within the meaning of art.107(1) TFEU.

Case T–95/03 *Asociación de Empresarios de Estaciones de Servicio de la Comunidad Autónoma de Madrid and Federación Catalana de Estaciones de Servicio v Commission of the European Communities* [2006] E.C.R. II–04739 (December 12, 2006).

Type of procedure: Application for annulment of Commission Decision C(2002) 4355 final of November 13, 2002 concerning Spanish legislation on the opening of service stations by hypermarkets.

Highlights: The Community judicature will declare to be admissible an action for the annulment of a Decision based on art.108(3) TFEU, brought by a person who is concerned within the meaning of art.108(2) TFEU, where he seeks to safeguard the procedural rights available to him under the latter provision. By contrast, if the applicant calls into question the merits of the decision appraising the aid as such, it must then demonstrate that it has a particular status within the meaning of Case 25/62 *Plaumann v Commission*. That applies in particular where the applicant's market position is substantially affected by the aid to which the decision at issue relates.

A state measure which does not involve a direct or indirect transfer of state resources cannot be regarded as state aid for the purposes of art.107(1) TFEU, even if it satisfies the other conditions laid down in that provision.

Where interested third parties submit complaints to the Commission relating to state measures which have not been notified the Commission is bound, in the context of the preliminary stage laid down in art.108(3) TFEU, to conduct a diligent and impartial examination of the complaints in the interests of sound administration of the fundamental rules of the EC Treaty relating to state aid. The purpose of that examination is simply to allow the Commission to form an initial opinion on the classification of the measures submitted for its assessment and their compatibility with the common market. Although the need to conduct administrative procedures within a reasonable period is a general principle of Community law, the mere adoption of a decision after the expiry of such a period is not in itself sufficient to render unlawful a decision taken by the Commission at the conclusion of an initial examination conducted under art.108(3) TFEU. The fact that the time spent considerably exceeds the time usually required for a preliminary examination under art.108(3) TFEU may, with other factors, justify the conclusion that the Commission encountered serious difficulties of assessment necessitating initiation of the procedure under art.108(2) TFEU. The fact that the Commission expresses doubts on the basis of the information at its disposal, as to whether a state measure constitutes state aid, and no longer expresses such doubts after receiving supplementary information from the complainants, does not lead to the conclusion that the Commission encountered serious difficulties.

However, where it finds that such difficulties exist, the Commission enjoys a certain margin of discretion in identifying and evaluating the circumstances of the case in order to determine whether or not they present serious difficulties. In accordance with the objective of art.108(3) TFEU and its duty of sound administration, the Commission may, amongst other things, engage in talks with the complainants in an endeavor to overcome, during the preliminary procedure, any difficulties encountered. That power presupposes that the Commission may bring its position in line with the results of the talks it engaged in, without that alignment having to be interpreted, a priori, as establishing the existence of serious difficulties.

Case T–217/02 *Ter Lembeek International NV v Commission of the European Communities* [2006] E.C.R. II–04483 (November 23, 2006).

Type of procedure: Action for annulment.

Highlights: In an action for annulment brought under art.263 TFEU, the legality of a Community measure must be assessed on the basis of the information existing at the time when the measure was adopted. On the other hand, there is nothing to prevent the interested party from raising a plea in law against the final decision not raised at the stage of the administrative procedure. This also applies to an applicant which, although perfectly aware of the initiation of a formal investigation procedure concerning in particular a debt waiver from which it benefited and of the need and importance for it to supply certain information because of the doubts already expressed by the Commission as regards that debt waiver, decided not to participate in the formal investigation procedure and did not even claim that the reasons given in the decision to initiate the formal investigation procedure were insufficient to allow it properly to exercise its rights.

Where a public authority favours an undertaking operating in a sector characterised by intense competition by granting it a benefit, there is a distortion of competition or a risk of such distortion. That is the case, for example, where a public body waives without genuine consideration a debt which it held against an undertaking which pursues its activity in a sector which is entirely open to competition. When financial aid granted by a Member State strengthens the position of an undertaking compared with other undertakings competing in intra-Community trade, that trade must be regarded as affected by that aid. The Commission cannot be accused of discrimination arising from different treatment applied to comparable situations by reason of the fact that it assessed by different methods the value to be taken for securities which a company successively acquired and transferred, since that assessment referred to values at different dates and in different contexts.

The obligation to provide a statement of reasons is laid down in art.296 TFEU. When applied to decisions finding that measures constitute state aid, this principle requires that the reasons for which the Commission considers that the aid measure in question falls within the scope of art.107(1) TFEU should be indicated. Assuming that aid was granted, the Commission must also set out sufficiently clearly the facts and legal considerations of essential importance in the scheme of the decision, such as, for example, those allowing the applicants and the Court to ascertain the reasons for the Commission's view that the transaction at issue led to a distortion of competition and affected trade within the Union.

Case T–117/04 *Vereniging Werkgroep Commerciële Jachthavens Zuidelijke Randmeren and Others v Commission of the European Communities* [2006] E.C.R. II–03861 (September 27, 2006).

Type of procedure: Action for annulment.

Highlights: A decision adopted at the end of the formal investigation procedure provided for in art.108(2) TFEU is of individual concern to any undertaking which was at the origin of the complaint which led to the opening of that procedure, and whose views were heard during that procedure and determined the conduct of that procedure provided that its position on the market was significantly affected by the measure which is the subject of the decision. The mere fact that the decision at issue may have some influence on competitive relationships on the relevant market and that the undertaking concerned is in some sort of competitive relationship with the beneficiary of the decision does not satisfy that test of significant effect. As regards the extent to which the applicant's position on the market was affected, it is not for the Community Court, when considering whether an application is admissible, to make a definitive finding on the competitive relationship between the applicant and the undertaking in receipt of the aid. In that context, it is for the applicant alone to adduce pertinent evidence to show that the Commission's decision may adversely affect its legitimate interests by seriously jeopardising its position on the market in question.

Furthermore, an action for annulment brought by an association of undertakings which is not the addressee of the contested measure is admissible only in two cases. The first is where the association, in bringing its action, has substituted itself for one or more of the members whom it represents, on condition that those members were themselves in a position to bring an admissible action. The second is where there are special circumstances, such as the role which it might have played in the procedure leading to the adoption of the measure of which annulment is requested. The fact that an association intervenes with the Commission during the procedure under the state aid provisions of the Treaty for the purpose of defending the collective interests of its members, where its role does not go beyond the exercise of the procedural rights granted to interested parties under art.108(2) TFEU, is not sufficient in itself to establish locus standi.

Case T–166/01 *Lucnichi SpA v Commission of the European Communities* [2006] E.C.R. II–02875 (September 19, 2006).

Type of procedure: Action for annulment.

Highlights: Article 3 of the Sixth Steel Aid Code provides that aid for environmental protection granted to the steel industry may be deemed compatible with the common market and it provides for the Annex to the Code and the Community guidelines on state aid for environmental protection to apply cumulatively, without making any distinction at that stage between different types of investment. In order to be eligible for environmental aid, it is not necessary for the notified investments to serve purposes that relate only to environmental protection, to the exclusion of all others, nor is it necessary for the investments to have no impact on production capacity. Investment made for environmental purposes cannot be declared ineligible by reason only of the fact that it may have an impact on production. Since the second part of the Annex to the Code excludes investment made for economic reasons from aid to encourage firms to contribute to significantly improved environmental protection, and since, in order for investment made in an undertaking's plant to be eligible as aid for environmental protection, the onus is on the authorities of the Member State concerned to establish that it was made for reasons of environmental protection and was the consequence of the voluntary decision of the undertaking to improve on environmental protection, the Commission will, in the absence of evidence put forward by those authorities in that regard, satisfy its duty to state reasons if it merely records that there has been a failure to provide such evidence.

Case T–210/02 *British Aggregates Association v Commission of the European Communities* [2006] E.C.R. II–02789 (September 13, 2006).

Type of procedure: Admissibility associations, action for annulment, preliminary procedure.

Highlights: Proceedings brought by an association of undertakings challenging the validity of a Commission decision not to raise objections at the end of the preliminary investigation procedure relating to state aid are admissible where that measure is liable substantially to affect the position of at least one of its members on the market. In such a case, the association is entitled to raise any of the pleas of illegality listed in the second paragraph of art.263 TFEU, and not only the duty to initiate the formal investigation procedure of art.108(2).

An environmental levy can be distinguished precisely by its particular scope and purpose, and thus cannot in principle be related to any overall system. It is for the Commission, when assessing an environmental levy for the purposes of the Community rules on state aid, to take account of the environmental protection requirements referred to in art.6 TFEU. That article provides that those requirements are to be integrated into the definition and implementation of, inter alia, arrangements which ensure that competition is not distorted within the internal market. In particular, the decision to impose an environmental levy only in the aggregates sector, and not generally in all the sectors involving the operation of quarries and mines having the same impact on the environment, falls within the power of the Member State in question to set its priorities in the economic, fiscal and environmental fields.

A Commission decision not to raise objections against a sectoral environmental levy, taken at the end of the preliminary investigation procedure and which briefly sets out the essential grounds on which it is based, cannot be considered to be affected by a failure to state adequate reasons as regards an association representing well-informed economic operators, having regard to the freedom of the Member States to determine their fiscal and environmental policy by imposing an environmental levy. Since an environmental levy on the commercial exploitation of aggregates which is charged against products and not on the income of producers constitutes an indirect tax governed by the principle of taxation in the country of destination laid down under art.111 TFEU, the exemption which is available to exporters is justified by the internal logic of the tax system so that it cannot be considered as conferring a selective advantage on exporters and is not subject to the application of art.107(1) TFEU.

The procedure under art.108(2) TFEU is obligatory where the Commission experiences serious difficulties in establishing whether or not aid is compatible with the common market. On the other hand, if the initial analysis results in the Commission taking the contrary view of the aid's compatibility with the common market, the Commission has a duty to gather all necessary views and to that end to initiate the procedure under art.108(2) TFEU. Where interested third parties submit complaints to the Commission relating to state measures which have not been notified under art.108(3) TFEU, the Commission is bound, in the context of the preliminary procedure referred to in that provision, to conduct, in the interests of the proper application of the fundamental rules of the Treaty relating to state aid, a diligent and impartial examination of those complaints.

Joined Cases T–304/04 and T–316/04 *Italian Republic (T–304/04) and Wam SpA (T–316/04) v Commission of the European Communities* [2006] E.C.R. II–00064 (September 6, 2006).

Type of procedure: Application for annulment of Commission Decision 2006/177/EC of May 19, 2004 on state aid C 4/2003 (ex. NN 102/2002) implemented by Italy for WAM SpA.

Highlights: Annuls Commission Decision on State aid implemented by Italy for WAM SpA. The fact that the undertaking operated in the common market and took part in trading was condered by the Court not to be sufficient to determine a "distortion of competition" or "an effect on trade". The Court called for an analysis of the potential effects of funding in this case. Furthermore, a plea based on infringement of art.296 TFEU is a separate plea from one pased on a manifest error of assessment; the obligation to state reasons is a separate question from that of the merits of those reasons. The former is an issue of infringement of essential procedural requirements which must be reaised by the courts on their own motion, the latter goes to the substantive legality and concerns the infringment of a rule of law relating to the application of the treaty, and can be examined by the courts only if it is raised by the applicant.

Case T–613/97 *Union française de l'express (UFEX), DHL International SA, Federal express international (France) SNC and CRIE SA v Commission of the European Communities* [2006] E.C.R. II–01531 (June 7, 2006).

Type of procedure: Action for annulment, this judgment is given following referral of the case back to the Court of First Instance by judgment of the Court of Justice in Joined Cases C 83/01 P, C 93/01

P and C 94/01 P *Chronopost and Others v UFEX and Others* setting aside the judgment of the Court of First Instance in Case T–613/97 *UFEX and Others v Commission.*

Highlights: The requirements to be satisfied by the statement of reasons depend on the circumstances of each case, in particular the content of the measure in question, the nature of the reasons given and the interest which the addressees of the measure, or other parties to whom it is of direct and individual concern, may have in obtaining explanations. In the case of a Commission decision finding that no state aid as alleged by a complainant exists, the Commission must at least provide the complainant with an adequate explanation of the reasons for which the facts and points of law put forward in the complaint have failed to demonstrate the existence of state aid. The Commission is not required, however, to define its position on matters which are manifestly irrelevant or insignificant or plainly of secondary importance. Other than in exceptional circumstances, the statement of reasons must be contained in the decision itself, and it is not sufficient for it to be explained subsequently for the first time before the Court. A failure to state the reasons cannot be remedied by the fact that the person concerned learns the reasons for the decision during the proceedings before the Community judicature.

For the purposes of art.107 TFEU, the concept of aid covers not only positive benefits, such as subsidies, but also interventions which mitigate the charges which are normally included in the budget of an undertaking and which are similar in character and have the same effect. The supply of goods or services on preferential terms is one of the indirect advantages which have the same effects as subsidies. The transfer, for no consideration, to a subsidiary governed by private law, of the client base of a service which does not belong to the reserved sector, created by its parent company operating in a reserved market with the resources of its legal monopoly therefore constitutes state aid. In this respect, the creation and marketing of address lists for certain activities constitute, in themselves, economic activities.

Case T–354/99 *Kuwait Petroleum (Nederland) BV v Commission of the European Communities* [2006] E.C.R. II–01475 (May 31, 2006).

Type of procedure: Action for annulment.

Highlights: An action for annulment brought by a natural or legal person is not admissible unless the applicant has an interest in seeing the contested measure annulled. The applicant must retain a personal interest in the annulment of the contested decision. That is not the case for an undertaking which is no longer subject to any obligation to repay. Where the validity of the same decision is at issue in cases pending before both the ECJ and the General Court and the latter has found it necessary to stay the proceedings pending judgment by the ECJ, the pleas in law and arguments which have been rejected previously by the ECJ will not necessarily be rejected automatically as inadmissible before the General Court, on two grounds. First, the staying of the proceedings before the General Court pursuant to the third paragraph of art.54 of the Statute of the ECJ does not remove the General Court's jurisdiction over the case and it retains full and exclusive jurisdiction to recommence hearing the case when the stay of proceedings is ended. Second, the principle of upholding the rights of the defence does not permit pleas in law validly put forward before one court to be rejected by another court before which the applicant in that action has not had the opportunity to appear and present argument. It remains for the General Court, which judges the merits of the case, to ascertain whether the solution given by the ECJ may be applied to the case before it in the light of any differences of fact or of law.

Furthermore, the case concerned two pleas, first disregard of the concept of state aid and, second, infringement of the principle of sound administration. Firstly, the Commission is entitled to find that a Member State, by granting aid to service station dealers as compensation for losses of income resulting from increases in excise duty on light oil, assumes all or part of the obligations assumed by the oil company supplying those stations under an exclusive purchasing agreement including a "price management system clause". This aid must thus be recovered from the oil company, even though that price management system clause is not necessarily overriding and/or automatic in nature, since the clause is intended to be applied and the company did in fact apply it in the circumstances described by the Commission. Furthermore, the Commission, when it is faced with an aid scheme such as that in the present case, is generally not in a position—nor is it required—to identify exactly the amount of aid received by individual recipients. Secondly, the administrative procedure regarding state aid is opened only against the Member State and the undertaking which received the state aid only have the right to be involved to the extent appropriate in the light of the circumstances of the case. Under art.108(2) TFEU the Commission has a duty to put the interested parties on formal notice to put forward their comments during the formal investigation phase. Although that obligation does not require the Commission, when it merely has serious doubts, to present a complete analysis on the aid in question, it must define sufficiently the framework of its investigation so as not to render meaningless the right of interested parties to put forward their comments.

Case T–395/04 *Air One SpA v Commission of the European Communities* [2006] E.C.R. II–01343 (May 10 2006).

Type of procedure: Action for failure to act.

Highlights: Articles 263 and 265 TFEU merely prescribe one and the same legal remedy. It follows that, just as the fourth paragraph of art.263 TFEU allows individuals to bring an action for annulment against a measure of an institution not addressed to them provided that the measure is of direct and individual concern to them, the third paragraph of art.265 TFEU must be interpreted as also entitling them to bring an action for failure to act.

Where, without initiating the formal review procedure under art.108(2) TFEU, the Commission finds, by decision adopted on the basis of art.108(3) TFEU, that aid is compatible with the common market, the persons intended to benefit from the procedural guarantees provided for by art.108(2) TFEU may secure compliance therewith only if they are able to challenge that decision before the Community judicature. For those reasons, an action for the annulment is admissible when it seeks to safeguard the procedural rights available to it under the latter provision. On the other hand, if the applicant calls in question the merits of the decision appraising the aid as such or a decision taken at the end of the formal investigation procedure, the mere fact that it may be regarded as concerned within the meaning of art.108(2) TFEU cannot suffice to render the action admissible. It must then demonstrate that the decision affects it by reason of certain attributes which are peculiar to it or by reason of circumstances in which it is differentiated from all other persons and by virtue of those factors distinguishes it individually as in the case of the person addressed. That applies in particular where the applicant's market position is substantially affected by the aid to which the decision at issue relates. The parties concerned, within the meaning of art.108(2) TFEU, are those persons, undertakings or associations whose interests might be affected by the grant of the aid, in particular undertakings competing with the recipients of that aid, and trade associations. This interpretation was given expression in art.1(h) of Regulation No.659/1999, setting out detailed rules for the application of art.108 TFEU, which states that "interested party" is to mean "any Member State and any person, undertaking or association of undertakings whose interests might be affected by the granting of aid, in particular the beneficiary of the aid, competing undertakings and trade associations". The status of "interested party" is not therefore restricted to undertakings that are substantially affected by the grant of aid. The Commission cannot indefinitely prolong its preliminary investigation into state aid. Whether or not the duration of the investigation of a complaint is reasonable must be determined in relation to the particular circumstances of each case and, especially, its context, the various procedural stages to be followed by the Commission and the complexity of the case.

Case T–17/03 *Schmitz-Gotha Fahrzeugwerke GmbH v Commission of the European Communities* [2006] E.C.R. II–01139 (April 6, 2006).

Type of procedure: Action for annulment.

Highlights: In order to be declared compatible with the common market in application of art.107(3)(c) TFEU, a restructuring aid plan for a firm in difficulty must be linked to a restructuring programme designed to reduce or redirect its activities. Point 3.2.2 of the Community Guidelines on state aid for rescuing and restructuring firms in difficulty, which lays down that requirement, stipulates that the restructuring plan must fulfil three material conditions. It is essential, first, that it restore the viability of the beneficiary firm within a reasonable timescale and on the basis of realistic assumptions; second, that it avoid undue distortions of competition; and, third, that it be in proportion to the restructuring costs and benefits. As those conditions are cumulative, the Commission must declare a restructuring aid plan to be incompatible if even one of those conditions has not been satisfied. It follows from the third point that any aid in excess of the strict return to viability of the beneficiary cannot in principle be eligible under the Guidelines. In order to fulfil its duty to co-operate with the Commission, the Member State concerned must provide all the information necessary to enable the Commission to verify that the conditions for the derogation from which it seeks to benefit are satisfied. Finally, once the Commission has given the interested parties the opportunity to submit their comments on planned aid of which it has been notified, it cannot be criticised for having failed to take account of any elements of fact which could have been submitted to it during the administrative procedure but which were not, as the Commission is under no obligation to consider, of its own motion and on the basis of prediction, what elements might have been submitted to it.

Case T–351/02 *Deutsche Bahn AG v Commission of the European Communities* [2006] E.C.R. II–01047 (April 5, 2006).

Type of procedure: Action for annulment.

Highlights: Only measures which produce binding legal effects such as to affect the interests of an applicant by bringing about a distinct change in his legal position may be the subject of an action for annulment under art.263 TFEU. That applies to a letter sent to a complainant undertaking by the Commission where the Commission takes a clear, reasoned and definitive position by stating that the measure at issue does not constitute aid. For advantages to be capable of being categorised as aid within the meaning of art.107(1) TFEU, they must, inter alia, be imputable to the State. That does not apply to a tax exemption provided for by national legislation which only implements a provision which imposes on Member States a clear and precise obligation not to levy the harmonised excise duty on certain fuel. In transposing the exemption into national law, Member States are only implementing Community provisions in accordance with their obligations stemming from the Treaty. Therefore, the national provision at issue is not imputable to the Member State, but in actual fact stems from an act of the Community legislature. It is of little significance in that regard that the exemption was granted through state resources as the imputability of aid to a state is separate from the question whether aid was granted through state resources. It is a matter of separate and cumulative conditions. As some of the conditions which are fundamental to the application of art.107 TFEU are not satisfied, such an exemption does not fall within the scope of that article.

The requirements of a statement of reasons must be appraised by reference to the circumstances of each case, in particular the content of the measure in question, the nature of the reasons given and the interest which the addressees of the measure, or other parties to whom it is of direct and individual concern, may have in obtaining explanations. It is therefore not necessary for the reasoning to go into all the relevant facts and points of law to meet the requirements of art.296 TFEU for the statement of objections.

The principle of equal treatment prohibits comparable cases from being treated differently, thereby subjecting some to disadvantages as opposed to others, unless such treatment can be objectively justified. The tax exemption for aviation fuel in this case does not infringe the principle of equal treatment because the situation of air transport undertakings is clearly different from that of rail transport undertakings.

INDEX

Access to information
state aid, 1–034
Accession states
Accession Treaty 2003,
    5–004—5–006
agriculture, 5–018—5–019,
    13–009—13–011
aid measure put into effect before
    accession, 5–007—5–008
Bulgaria, 5–020—5–023
coal industry, 14–065—14–079
conclusion, 5–029
Croatia, 5–024—5–028
Europe Agreements
    aid measure applicable after
        accession, 5–009—5–013
    generally, 5–002—5–003
Iceland, 5–024—5–028
introduction, 5–001
regional aid, 21–012
Romania
    existing aid, 5–021
    generally, 5–020—5–021
    interim measures, 5–021
    introduction, 5–020—5–021
    postponement clause, 5–020
steel industry, 5–014—5–017,
    5–022, 5–023,
    14–065—14–079
transport, 5–018—5–019
Actions
see also **Actions for annulment**
failure to act, 27–037—27–041
interim measures, 27–042—27–047

Actions for annulment
admissibility, 27–012—27–020
complainants' position,
    27–022—27–036
first phase decisions,
    27–022—27–025
second phase decisions,
    27–026—27–036
standard of review,
    27–026—27–030
Administrative procedure
see **Procedure**
Advertising
agriculture, 13–032
Advisory bodies
Advisory Committee on State Aid,
    25–009
Agriculture
accession states, 5–018—5–019,
    13–009—13–011
adverse weather conditions,
    13–027
advertising, 13–032
animal diseases, 13–028
Art.107(1) TFEU
    common market organisations,
        3–124, 3–125
    introduction, 3–123
biomass production, 13–034
closing capacity, 13–030
Common Agricultural Policy,
    13–001—13–002
common market organisations
    Accession Treaties,
        13–009—13–011

Agriculture—*cont.*
common market
organisations—*cont.*
generally, 13–003—13–006
compatibility rules, 13–014,
13–015
Council Regulation, 13–001
de minimis
fisheries, 13–044—13–045
rules, 13–013—13–015
direct taxation, 13–037
disasters, 13–026
employment creation, 13–038
energy taxation, 13–033
environmental aid, 13–020
European Agricultural Fund for
Rural Development
Accession Treaties,
13–009—13–011
generally, 13–006—13–008
European Fisheries Fund,
13–042—13–043
fisheries
de minimis, 13–044—13–045
generally, 13–042—13–043
guidelines, 13–047
regional aid, 13–049
small and medium-sized
enterprises,
13–045—13–046
temporary measures, 13–048
forestry, 13–035—13–036
indirect taxes, 13–041
insurance premiums, 13–029
introduction, 13–001
investment aid in primary
production, 13–016—13–018
livestock, 13–024
marketing agricultural products,
13–019
plant diseases, 13–028
processing agricultural products,
13–019
producer groups, 13–021

Agriculture—*cont.*
quality of agricultural products,
13–022
research and development, 13–031
restructuring aid, 24–051
risk management, 13–025
rural development,
13–006—13–008
sectoral aid
Accession Treaties,
13–009—13–011
common market organisation,
13–003—13–006
fisheries, 13–042—13–049
introduction, 13–001
rural development,
13–006—13–008
state aid compatibility,
13–012—13–041
small and medium-sized
enterprises
fisheries, 13–045—13–046
state aid compatibility,
13–012—13–041
statistics, 13–001
technical support, 13–023
Air transport
see **Airports; Carriage by air**
Airports
financing, 17–080—17–083
guidelines, 17–078—17–084
infrastructure, 3–061—3–062
introduction, 17–074, 17–075
Ryanair/Charleroi decision,
17–076—17–077
start-up aid, 17–084, 17–085
Animal diseases
agriculture, 13–028
Animal welfare
agriculture, 13–020
Annulment actions
see **Actions for annulment**
Anti-competitive practices
effect on trade, 3–080

Approvals
broadcasting, 4–037
compensatory justification
   principle, 4–014—4–016
cultural aid, 4–033—4–036
extent of discretion, 4–013
generally, 4–012
introduction, 4–001—4–002
overview, 3–001
projects of common European
   interest, 4–022—4–024
remedying a serious economic
   disturbance, 4–025
severely depressed regions,
   4–019—4–022
Temporary Framework,
   4–026—4–062

Arms trade
Art.107(1) TFEU, 3–133

Article 106(2) TFEU
energy
   Commission's guidance,
      20–084—20–087
   Estonia, 20–083
   introduction, 20–076—20–078
   Latvia, 20–080
   Netherlands, 20–081
   Poland, 20–082
   Spanish coal, 20–079
generally, 8–025
notification exemption,
   8–026—8–030
post-*Altmark* practice,
   8–030—8–036
public services
   compensation, 8–037

Article 107 TFEU
advantage, 3–005—3–011
agriculture
   common market organisations,
      3–125, 3–1245
   introduction, 3–123
aid of a social character,
   4–004—4–005
airports, 3–073—3–074

Article 107 TFEU—*cont.*
alleviation of social charges, 3–054
approvals
   broadcasting, 4–037
   compensatory justification
      principle, 4–014—4–016
   cultural aid, 4–033—4–036
   extent of discretion, 4–013
   facilitation of development of
      certain economic activities
      or areas, 4–030—4–032
   generally, 4–012
   introduction, 4–001—4–002
   market failure test, 4–017
   overview, 3–001
   projects of common European
      interest, 4–024
   remedying a serious economic
      disturbance, 4–025
   severely-depressed regions,
      4–019—4–022
   Temporary Framework,
      4–026—4–029, 4–049
arms trade, 3–133
attributes of an "aid"
   community resources,
      3–036—3–039
   imposition of a cost to the state,
      3–022—3–026
   imputation, 3–028—3–035
   introduction, 3–015
   public control over private
      resources, 3–027
   revenue foregone, 3–021
   state resources, 3–016—3–027
   transfer of state resources, 3–020
automatic exemptions
   aid of a social character,
      4–004—4–005
   EEA Agreement, 4–011
   exceptional circumstances,
      4–006—4–007
   general, 4–003
   German reunification,
      4–008—4–010

Article 107 TFEU—*cont.*
automatic exemptions—*cont.*
  introduction, 4–001—4–002
  natural disasters, 4–006—4–007
  overview, 3–001
balancing test, 4–060—4–061
banks
  asset relief measures, 19–016
  capitalisation, 19–006, 19–007
  deposit guarantee schemes,
    19–014, 19–015
  liquidity, 19–008—19–013
  market restructuring, 19–017
  measures in favour of banks,
    19–005—19–017
  rescue aid, 19–018
  restructuring aid,
    19–019—19–030
broadcasting sector, 4–037
capital injections for publicly
    owned firms, 3–082—3–083
certain categories of aid
  balancing test, 4–060—4–061
  export aid, 4–044—4–047
  export credit insurance,
    4–048—4–049
  general, 4–043
  guidelines, 4–055—4–059
  investment aid, 4–051—4–052
  operating aid, 4–050
  regional aid, 4–053
  risk capital, 4–054—4–062
community resources,
    3–036—3–039
compensation in damages,
    3–012—3–014
compensatory justification
    principle, 4–014—4–016
concept of an "aid"
  advantage, 3–005—3–011
  compensation in damages,
    3–012—3–014
  gratuitous advantage, 3–005
  indirect advantage, 3–011
  intent, 3–004

Article 107 TFEU—*cont.*
concept of an "aid"—*cont.*
  introduction, 3–002—3–003
  public declarations, 3–010
concomitance, 3–084—3–085
cultural aid, 4–033—4–036
de minimis Regulation, 3–079
direct taxes, 3–046—3–047
discretionary exemptions
  broadcasting sector, 4–037
  compensatory justification
    principle, 4–014—4–016
  cultural aid, 4–033—4–036
  extent of discretion, 4–013
  generally, 4–012
  introduction, 4–001—4–002
  market failure test, 4–017
  overview, 3–001
  projects of common European
    interest, 4–024
  remedying a serious economic
    disturbance, 4–025
  severely-depressed regions,
    4–019—4–022
  Temporary Framework,
    4–026—4–029, 4–049
distortion of competition, 3–080
ECSC Treaty, 3–135
EEA Agreement, 4–011
effect on trade
  de minimis Regulation, 3–079
  distortion of competition, 3–080
  generally, 3–076—3–077
energy
  advantage, 20–016, 20–017
  effect on trade, 20–039—20–040
  emissions trading, 20–034
  green certificates, 20–034
  imputation, 20–025—20–028
  infrastructure, 20–040
  introduction, 20–014
  market economy investor test,
    20–035—20–039
  meaning of "aid",
    20–015—20–029

Article 107 TFEU—*cont.*
energy—*cont.*
  mineral oils used for aluminium
    production, 20–029
  selectivity, 20–030—20–039
  state participation, 20–035
  state resources, 20–020—20–024
  tariff cases, 20–018, 20–019
  tax, 20–028
Euratom Treaty, 3–136
Europe Agreements, 3–138
European Economic Area, 3–137
exceptional circumstances
  art.62(d) EEA, 4–039
  art.107(3)(e) TFEU, 4–038
  art.108(2) TFEU, 4–040—4–042
exceptional occurrences,
  4–006—4–007
exemptions
  automatic exemptions,
    4–003—4–011
  discretionary exemptions,
    4–012—4–038
  introduction, 4–001—4–002
  overview, 3–001
export aid
  credit insurance, 4–048, 4–049
  generally, 4–044
  third countries, 4–045—4–047
facilitation of development of
  certain economic activities or
  areas, 4–030—4–032
fisheries, 3–123—3–125
free movement principles,
  3–110—3–118
free movement of services, 3–117,
  3–118
general economic factors,
  3–109—3–110
German reunification
  exemptions, 4–008—4–010
gratuitous advantage, 3–005
imposition of a cost to the state,
  3–022—3–026

Article 107 TFEU—*cont.*
imputation
  harmonised tax, 3–035
  imputation generally,
    3–028—3–035
indirect reductions in costs of
  undertaking, 3–055—3–056
indirect taxes, 3–128—3–132
infrastructure
  airports, 3–073—3–074
  financial support, 3–058
  introduction, 3–058
  market-investor principle, 3–067
  public-private partnerships,
    3–066
  services of general interests,
    3–068
  training support, 3–057
intangible asset sales,
  3–099—3–101
intent, 3–004
introduction, 3–001
investment aid
  measures, 4–051
  schemes, 4–052
"logic of the system" test, 3–050
market economy investor test
  capital injections for publicly
    owned firms,
    3–082—3–083
  concomitance, 3–084—3–085
  introduction, 3–081
  private participation,
    3–084—3–085
  public undertakings,
    3–086—3–088
  state shareholdings,
    3–082—3–083
market failure test, 4–017
market-investor principle, 3–067
Merger Regulation, 3–121—3–122
motor industry, 4–029
natural disasters, 4–006—4–007
operating aid
  generally, 4–050

Article 107 TFEU—*cont.*
operating aid—*cont.*
regional aid, 4–053
private creditor test, 3–089—3–092
private participation,
3–084—3–085
private purchaser test,
3–102—3–104
private seller test, 3–093—3–098
projects of common European
interest, 4–024
public control over private
resources, 3–027
public services, 3–102—3–104
public undertakings, 3–086—3–088
public-private partnerships, 3–066
regional aid, 4–053
regional tax measures, 3–052
relationship with other provisions
arms trade, 3–133
art.101, 3–120
art.106(2), 3–127
art.110, 3–128—3–132
competition law, 3–119
free movement principles,
3–110—3–118
free movement of services,
3–117, 3–118
indirect taxes, 3–128—3–132
introduction, 3–109
Merger Regulation,
3–121—3–122
war materials, 3–133
remedying a serious economic
disturbance, 4–025
revenue foregone, 3–021
risk capital, 4–054—4–062
scope of Art. 107(1),
3–002—3–010
selectivity criteria
activities, 3–051
alleviation of social charges,
3–054
de facto selectivity, 3–053
direct taxes, 3–046—3–047

Article 107 TFEU—*cont.*
selectivity criteria—*cont.*
events, 3–051
general measures, 3–042—3–044
indirect reductions in costs of
undertaking, 3–055—3–056
introduction, 3–040
"logic of the system" test,
3–050
material selectivity, 3–053
regional tax measures, 3–052
selective tax measures,
3–048—3–049
social charges, 3–054
tax, 3–045—3–047
undertaking, 3–041
services of general interests, 3–068
severely-depressed regions,
4–019—4–022
social charges, 3–054
source of the "aid"
community resources,
3–036—3–039
imposition of a cost to the state,
3–022—3–026
imputation, 3–028—3–035
introduction, 3–015
public control over private
resources, 3–027
revenue foregone, 3–021
state resources, 3–016—3–027
transfer of state resources, 3–020
state resources, 3–016—3–027
state shareholdings, 3–082—3–083
tax
activities, 3–051
direct taxes, 3–046—3–047
events, 3–051
general, 10–006
infra-state entities,
10–007—10–008
introduction, 3–045
legal changes, 10–010
"logic of the system" test,
3–050

Article 107 TFEU—*cont.*
  tax—*cont.*
    regional measures, 3–052
    revenue effect of tax provision,
      10–009
    selective measures,
      3–048—3–049
    state entities, 10–007, 10–008
    tax advantage, 10–011—10–015
  Temporary Framework
    generally, 4–026
    individual decisions, 4–028
    motor industry, 4–029
    objectives, 4–026
    risk capital, 4–062
    technical adjustments, 4–027
  training support, 3–057
  transfer of state resources, 3–020
  transport, 3–126
  undertakings, 3–041
  war materials, 3–133
"Automatic exemptions"
  aid of a social character,
    4–004—4–005
  EEA Agreement, 4–011
  energy, 20–042
  exceptional circumstances,
    4–006—4–007
  general, 4–003
  German reunification,
    4–008—4–010
  introduction, 4–001—4–002
  natural disasters, 4–006—4–007
  overview, 3–001
"Balancing test"
  overview, 1–011
Banks
  see also **Financial institutions**
  art.107 TFEU
    asset relief measures, 19–016
    capitalisation, 19–006, 19–007
    deposit guarantee schemes,
      19–014, 19–015
    liquidity, 19–008—19–013
    market restructuring, 19–017

Banks—*cont.*
  art.107 TFEU—*cont.*
    measures in favour of banks,
      19–005—19–017
    rescue aid, 19–018
    restructuring aid,
      19–019—19–030
    asset relief measures, 19–016
    background, 19–001
    bad banks, 19–016
    capitalisation, 19–006, 19–007,
      19–047—19–050
    deposit guarantee schemes,
      19–014, 19–015
    emergency aid, 19–037, 19–045
    general aid schemes, 19–039
    grantors of state aid, 19–002,
      19–003
    liquidity, 19–008—19–013
    market restructuring, 19–017
    measures in favour of banks,
      19–005—19–017
    private banks, 19–004
    public subsidy banks, 19–002
    recapitalisation, 1–014
    rescue aid, 19–018
    restructuring aid, 19–019—19–030
    state aid, 1–013, 1–014
    stress tests, 1–014
    transmitters of state aid, 19–002,
      19–004
Block exemptions
  see **General Block Exemption
    Regulation**
Broadband networks
  infrastructure, 3–069, 3–070
Broadcasting
  digital replacement licences, 3–007
  discretionary exemptions, 4–037
  financing digital switchover,
    18–012—18–018
  introduction, 18–001
  public service broadcasting
    diversification, 18–009
    entrustment, 18–004

Broadcasting—*cont.*
  public service broadcasting—*cont.*
    financial control, 18–008
    net cost principle, 18–007
    overcompensation, 18–007
    proportionality, 18–010
    public services, 18–003
    supervision, 18–004
  sectoral aid
    financing digital switchover,
      18–012—18–018
    introduction, 18–001
    public service broadcasting,
      18–002—18–011
Bulgaria
  generally, 5–020—5–023
  introduction, 5–001, 5–020—5–021
  steel industry, 5–022, 5–023
Capital
  art.107(1) TFEU, 4–054
Capital duty
  taxation as an aid, 10–006
Capitalisation
  banks, 19–006, 19–007,
    19–047—19–050
  financial institutions, 19–006,
    19–007, 19–047—19–050
  market economy investor test,
    3–082—3–083
Carriage by air
  introduction, 17–061—17–062
  legislation, 17–063—17–064
  restructuring aid, 17–065—17–072
  terrorism, 17–073
Carriage by road
  application of rules,
    17–043—17–045
Case management
  procedure, 25–063—25–066
Chemical industry
  conclusion, 12–021
  environmental protection,
    12–014—12–015
  generally, 12–011—12–012
  introduction, 12–008—12–009

Chemical industry—*cont.*
  miscellaneous, 12–018—12–020
  research and development,
    12–016—12–017
Climate change
  environmental aid, 22–009, 22–010
Coal industry
  Accession States, 14–065—14–079
  Coal Regulation
    accessing coal reserves, 14–019
    closure aid, 14–026
    complete cessation of aid,
      14–018
    current production aid, 14–024,
      14–025
    expiry, 14–033—14–049
    Germany, 14–027, 104–028
    inherited liabilities, 14–029,
      14–030
    investment aid, 14–020—14–023
    limits, 14–031, 14–032
    policy, 14–010—14–017
    provisions, 14–009—14–032
  Czech Republic, 14–068
  ECSC Treaty
    generally, 14–005—14–007
    introduction, 14–001
    limits of treaty, 14–004
    pre-expiry decisions,
      14–006—14–007
  generally, 14–005
  Germany, 14–027, 104–028
  introduction, 14–001
  Poland, 14–069—14–073
  restructuring, 14–080
  Romania, 14–075—14–078
  sectoral aid
    ECSC Treaty regime,
      14–004—14–008
    introduction, 14–001
  Slovakia, 14–074
  Turkey, 14–079
  uncompetitive coal mines, 14–050,
    14–051

Combined transport
see **Multimodal transport**
Comfort letters
guarantees, 9–009
Common agricultural policy
generally, 13–001—13–002
Common market organisations
see **Internal market**
Compatibility
research and development aid,
23–008
Compensation
compensatory justification principle
discretionary exemptions,
4–014—4–016
concept of an "aid",
3–012—3–014
restructuring aid, 24–038—24–040
Confidentiality
procedure, 25–060
Contaminated land
environmental aid, 22–077, 22–078
Contributions
restructuring aid, 24–036—24–037
Court of Justice of the European
Union
role, 1–024
Croatia
accession negotiations,
5–024—5–028
Cross-subsidisation
see **Subsidies**
Culture
discretionary exemptions,
4–033—4–036
Cumulation
de minimis, 7–010
General Block Exemption
Regulation, 11–012
Customs duty
taxation as an aid, 10–004
Czech Republic
coal industry, 14–068
steel industry, 14–068

De minimis
agriculture, 13–013—13–015
background, 7–001
calculation, 7–005
cumulation, 7–010
EC Regulation
application in time, 7–007
calculation, 7–005
cumulation, 7–010
entry into force, 7–012
further conditions, 7–008
introduction, 7–003
monitoring, 7–009
recipient, 7–004
scope, 7–006
time limits, 7–007
transparent aid, 7–006
effect on trade, 3–079
enabling Regulation, 7–002
entry into force, 7–012
fisheries, 13–044—13–045
further conditions, 7–008
introduction, 7–001
monitoring, 7–009
nature of rule, 7–011, 7–012
Temporary Framework, 7–013
threshold, 7–002
time limits, 7–007
transport, 17–033
Declarations of incompatibility
art. 107(1) TFEU, 3–001
Defence industry
shipbuilding, 16–027
Deposit guarantee schemes
banks, 19–014, 19–015
Derogations
culture, 4–033—4–036
Digital switchover
broadcasting, 18–012—18–018
Direct effect
procedure, 25–004—25–006
Direct taxes
selectivity criteria, 3–046—3–047
Disabled persons
social aid, 11–026

Disasters
agriculture, 13–026
automatic exemptions,
    4–006—4–007
"Discretionary exemptions"
see also **Temporary Framework**
broadcasting, 4–037
common European interest projects
    energy, 20–050
    generally, 4–024
compensatory justification
    principle, 4–014—4–016
cultural aid, 4–033—4–036
energy
    art.107(3)(a) aid,
        20–044—20–050
    art.107(3)(b) aid, 20–050
    art.107(3)(c) aid, 20–051
    carbon and capture storage,
        20–053
    introduction, 20–043
    renewable energy sources,
        20–052
extent of discretion, 4–013
facilitation of development of
    certain economic activities or
    areas
    aid intensity, 21–025
    energy, 20–051
    generally, 21–004
    regions, 21–023—21–024
generally, 4–012
introduction, 4–001—4–002
market failure test, 4–017
overview, 3–001
projects of common European
    interest
    energy, 20–050
    generally, 4–024
regional aid under art.107(3)(a)
    aid intensity, 21–022
    energy, 20–044—20–050
    generally, 21–003
    overview, 4–019—4–022
    regions, 21–020

"Discretionary exemptions"—*cont.*
regional aid under Art.107(3)(c)
    aid intensity, 21–025
    energy, 20–051
    generally, 21–004
    regions, 21–023—21–024
remedying a serious economic
    disturbance, 4–025
severely-depressed regions
    aid intensity, 21–022
    energy, 20–051
    generally, 21–003
    overview, 4–09—4–22
    regions, 21–020
shipbuilding, 16–005
transport, 17–001
Discrimination
financial institutions, 19–040
Dual use goods
military goods, 3–133
Economic development
aid intensity, 21–025
energy, 20–051
regions, 21–023—21–024
Economic resources
attributes of an "aid", 3–010
energy, 20–020—20–024
environmental aid,
    22–012—22–016
generally, 3–016—3–027
transfer, 3–020
Economics
assessment of cross-border effects,
    2–017—2–023
balancing of effects,
    2–017—2–023
case study, 2–030—2–032
co-ordination of aid,
    2–017—2–023
conclusions, 2–041—2–043
design of effective and efficient
    policies
    administrative costs, 2–028
    competition impact, 2–027
    introduction, 2–024

Economics—*cont.*
 design of effective and efficient
  policies—*cont.*
  necessity, 2–025
  other costs, 2–029
  proportionality, 2–026
 generally, 2–001—2–003
 rationale, 2–004—2–007
 supranational rules, 2–008—2–016
 use of system of supranational
  control, 2–008—2–016
ECSC Treaty
 see also **Coal industry; Steel
  industry**
 art.107(1) TFEU, 3–135
 energy, 20–001
 generally, 14–004—14–008
 introduction, 14–001
EEA Agreement
 automatic exemptions, 4–011
 procedure
  introduction, 25–068—25–072
  supremacy of law,
   25–073—25–074
Effect on trade
 see **Inter-state effect**
Emissions trading
 Art.107 TFEU, 20–034
 environmental aid,
  22–081—22–089
Employment aid
 agriculture, 13–038
 General Block Exemption
  Regulation, 11–017
Energy
 aid having a social character,
  20–042
 aid through energy companies
  cross-subsidisation,
   20–094—20–095
  introduction, 20–088
  preferential tariffs,
   20–089—20–093

Energy—*cont.*
 art.106(2) TFEU
  Commission's guidance,
   20–084—20–087
  Estonia, 20–083
  introduction, 20–076—20–078
  Latvia, 20–080
  Netherlands, 20–081
  Poland, 20–082
  Spanish coal, 20–079
 art.107 TFEU
  advantage, 20–016, 20–017
  effect on trade, 20–039—20–040
  emissions trading, 20–034
  green certificates, 20–034
  imputation, 20–025—20–028
  infrastructure, 20–040
  introduction, 20–015
  market economy investor test,
   20–036—20–038
  meaning of "aid",
   20–015—20–029
  mineral oils used for aluminium
   production, 20–029
  selectivity, 20–030—20–033
  state participation,
   20–036—20–038
  state resources, 20–020—20–024
  tariff cases, 20–018, 20–019
  tax, 20–028
 art.107(2) TFEU, 20–042
 art.107(3) TFEU, 20–044—20–051
 automatic exemptions, 20–042
 British Energy decision,
  20–009—20–011
 carbon capture and storage, 20–053
 Commission Decisions
  British Energy, 20–009—20–011
  EdF, 20–012
  generally, 20–006—20–008
 common European interest
  projects, 20–050
 cross-subsidisation,
  20–094—20–095

Energy—*cont.*
  discretionary exemptions
    art.107(3)(a) aid,
      20–044—20–050
    art.107(3)(b) aid, 20–050
    art.107(3)(c) aid, 20–051
    carbon capture and storage,
      20–053
    introduction, 20–043
    renewable sources, 20–052
  ECSC Treaty, 20–001
  emissions trading, 20–034
  Euratom Treaty
    Commission Decisions,
      20–006—20–013
    general, 20–002—20–005
    transparency, 20–013
  exemptions, 20–041—20–053
  indirect taxes, 20–001
  introduction, 20–001
  preferential tariffs,
    20–089—20–093
  privatisation, 20–001
  regional aid
    art.107(3)(a), 20–044—20–050
    art.107(3)(c), 20–051
  renewable energy, 20–001, 20–052
  rescue aid
    conditions for approval, 20–055
    introduction, 20–054
  restructuring aid
    conditions for approval, 20–056
    introduction, 20–054
  stranded costs
    Commission decisions,
      20–060—20–075
    Greece, 20–064, 20–065
    introduction, 20–057—20–059
    Ireland, 20–066, 20–067
    Italy, 20–068
    Luxembourg, 20–069
    Netherlands, 20–070, 20–071
    Portugal, 20–072
    Slovenia, 20–073
    Spain, 20–074

Energy—*cont.*
  stranded costs—*cont.*
    UK, 20–075
    transparency, 20–013
Energy policy
  Action Plan, 22–011
  environmental aid, 22–009, 22–010
  tax, 22–010
Enforcement
  action against Commission
    annulment, 27–012—27–036
    failure to act, 27–037—27–041
    interim measures,
      27–042—27–047
  action for failure to act,
    27–037—27–041
  actions for annulment
    admissibility, 27–012—27–020
    complainants' position,
      27–022—27–036
    first phase decisions,
      27–022—27–025
    second phase decisions,
      27–026—27–036
    standard of review,
      27–026—27–030
  Court of Justice of the European
    Union
    art.108(2) TFEU,
      27–003—27–005
    art.258 TFEU, 27–003—27–005
    art.260 TFEU, 27–008—27–011
    special cases, 27–006—27–007
  failure to act, 27–037—27–041
  interim measures, 27–042—27–047
  introduction, 27–001—27–002
  national courts
    direct effect of art.108(3) TFEU,
      27–053—27–056
    enforcement of negative
      decisions, 27–057—27–059
    general, 27–050—27–051
    implementation of positive
      decisions, 27–060
  procedure, 27–002

Enforcement—*cont.*
recovery of aid, 27–002
refusal to notify aid,
    27–003—27–005
Environmental aid
absence of Community standards,
    22–041—22–046
advantage for the undertaking,
    22–021, 22–022
agriculture, 13–020
aid to go beyond Community
    standards, 22–041—22–046
amount of aid, 22–005
animal welfare, 13–020
art.107(3)(b) TFEU, 22–096
climate change, 22–009, 22–010
cogeneration, 22–072, 22–073
Community standards,
    22–041—22–046, 22–049
compatibility, 22–026—22–029
contaminated land, 22–077,
    22–078
crisis measures, 22–007
distortion of competition, 22–003
distortion to competition, 22–025
district heating, 22–074
early adaption to Community
    Standards, 22–049
early adaption to standards, 22–005
effect on trade, 22–025
emissions trading,
    22–081—22–089
energy policy, 22–009, 22–010
energy saving, 22–051, 22–052
energy-efficient district heating,
    22–074
environmental measures
    advantage for the undertaking,
        22–021, 22–022
    balancing test, 22–014
    incentive effect, 22–015
    introduction, 22–012
    proportionality, 22–015, 22–016
    selectivity, 22–023, 22–024
    state aid, 22–017—22–025

Environmental aid—*cont.*
environmental measures—*cont.*
    transfer of state resources,
        22–018—22–020
environmental protection
    generally, 22–011
    introduction, 22–002
environmental studies, 22–050
further developments, 22–099
General Block Exemption
    Regulation, 11–018, 11–019
    application, 22–030—22–033
    assessment procedure, 22–006
    exemption, 22–006
    generally, 22–001
    operating aid, 22–006
Guidelines (2001), 22–004
Guidelines (2008)
    application, 22–030—22–033
    background, 22–004
    introduction, 22–001
    purpose, 22–004
investment aid, 22–034—22–040
justification for aid,
    22–012—22–016
key policy priorities,
    22–008—22–011
levels of assessment, 22–033
market failure, 22–012—22–016
new transport vehicles, 22–047,
    22–048
operating aid, 22–051, 22–052
policy, 22–002—22–007
"polluter pays" principle, 22–003
relocation of undertakings, 22–079,
    22–080
renewable energy,
    22–053—22–071
selectivity, 22–023—22–024
State Aid Action Plan, 22–004
state aid expenditure, 22–097,
    22–098
state resources, 22–018—22–020
summary, 22–001
sustainable development, 22–002

Environmental aid—*cont.*
  tax, 22–005, 22–090—22–095
  Temporary Framework, 22–007
  transfer of state resources,
    22–018—22–020
  transport, 22–047—22–048
  waste management, 22–075,
    22–076
Environmental protection
  introduction, 22–002
  justification, 22–012—22–016
  market failure, 22–012—22–016
  strategies, 22–011
Environmental taxation
  taxation as an aid, 10–024
Euratom Treaty
  art.107(1) TFEU, 3–136
  Commission Decisions,
    20–006—20–013
  general, 20–002—20–005
  transparency, 20–013
Europe 2020 Strategy
  generally, 6–031, 6–032
  overview of state aid, 1–016
Europe agreements
  aid in accession states
    aid measure applicable after
      accession, 5–009—5–013
    aid measure put into effect
      before accession,
      5–007—5–008
    generally, 5–002—5–003
  art.107(1) TFEU, 3–138
  generally, 5–001
**European Agricultural Fund for
  Rural Development**
  Accession Treaties,
    13–009—13–011
  generally, 13–006—13–008
European Economic Area
  art.107(1) TFEU, 3–137
European Fisheries Fund
  generally, 13–042—13–043

Exemptions
  see also **Regional aid**; **Sectoral
    aid**
  art.62(d) EEA, 4–039
  art.107(1) TFEU, 4–006—4–007
  art.107(3)(e) TFEU, 4–038
  art.108(2) TFEU, 4–040—4–042
  automatic exemptions
    aid of a social character,
      4–004—4–005
    EEA Agreement, 4–011
    exceptional circumstances,
      4–006—4–007
    general, 4–003
    German reunification,
      4–008—4–010
    introduction, 4–001—4–002
    natural disasters, 4–006—4–007
    overview, 3–001
  discretionary exemptions
    broadcasting, 4–037
    compensatory justification
      principle, 4–014—4–016
    cultural aid, 4–033—4–036
    extent of discretion, 4–013
    generally, 4–012
    introduction, 4–001—4–002
    motor industry, 4–029
    overview, 3–001
    projects of common European
      interest, 4–024
    remedying a serious economic
      disturbance, 4–025
    severely-depressed regions,
      4–019—4–022
  introduction, 4–001—4–002
  motor industry, 4–029
  overview, 3–001
  remedying a serious economic
    disturbance
    discretionary exemptions, 4–025
  sectoral aid
    agriculture, 13–001—13–049
    broadcasting, 18–001—18–018
    coal and steel, 14–001—14–080

Exemptions—*cont.*
  sectoral aid—*cont.*
    introduction, 12–001—12–021
    large investment projects,
      15–001—15–034
    shipbuilding, 16–001—16–027
    transport, 17–001—17–086
  serious economic disturbance,
    4–025
Exports
  export credit insurance,
    4–048—4–049
  generally, 4–044
  third countries, 4–045—4–047
Financial institutions
  see also **Banks**
  asset relief measures,
    19–051—19–057
  background, 19–001
  capitalisation, 19–006,
    19–047—19–050
  challenges facing state aid
    decisions, 19–078
  discrimination, 19–040
  emergency aid, 19–037, 19–045
  financial crisis, 19–032—19–034
  generally, 1–012—1–014
  impact of economic crisis, 19–082,
    19–083
  liquidity, 19–046
  moral hazard, 19–042
  restructuring aid
    adequate remuneration, 19–041
    better fortunes clause, 19–043
    burden sharing, 19–042, 19–062
    clawback, 19–043
    discrimination, 19–040
    distortion of competition,
      19–044, 19–063—19–070
    distressed banks, 19–038
    emergency aid, 19–037
    financial crisis, 19–032—19–034
    fundamentally sound banks,
      19–038
    general aid schemes, 19–039

Financial institutions—*cont.*
  restructuring aid—*cont.*
    generally, 19–058
    legal basis, 19–035, 19–036
    long-term viability,
      19–059—19–061
    measures falling outside
      Art.107(1) TFEU, 19–045
    moral hazard, 19–042
    standard conditions,
      19–071—19–075
    supervision, 19–076
  sovereign debt crisis,
    19–079—19–081
  supervision, 19–076
  winding-up, 19–077
Fisheries
  art.107(1) TFEU, 3–123—3–125
  de minimis, 13–044—13–045
  generally, 13–042—13–049
  guidelines, 13–047
  regional aid, 13–049
  small and medium-sized
    enterprises, 13–045—13–046
  temporary measures, 13–048
Forestry
  generally, 13–035—13–036
Freedom of movement
  art.107(1) TFEU, 3–110—3–118
  taxation as an aid, 10–004
Freedom to provide services
  art.107(1) TFEU, 3–117, 3–118
GEBR
  see **General Block Exemption
    Regulation**
**General agreement on tariffs and
    trade**
  see **International trade**
**General Block Exemption
    Regulation**
  application, 11–003
  benefits, 111–004
  calculation, 11–009
  categories of aid, 11–001
  commencement, 11–027

General Block Exemption Regulation—*cont.*
considerable experience, 11–002
consultation, 11–001
cumulation, 11–012
definitions, 11–007
disadvantaged workers, 11–025
employment aid, 11–017
environmental aid, 11–018, 11–019
  application, 22–030—22–033
  assessment procedure, 22–006
  exemption, 22–006
  generally, 22–001
  operating aid, 22–006
ex post control, 11–003
exclusions, 11–006
exemptions, 11–008
incentive effect, 11–013
investment aid, 11–016
limitations, 11–002
limitations on powers, 11–002
notification, 11–011
policy, 11–003
potential areas for block
  exemption, 11–029
regional aid, 11–017
research and development, 11–022
research and development aid,
  23–005
risk capital, 11–021
scope, 11–006
small and medium-sized
  enterprises, 11–020
social aid
  disabled workers, 11–026
  disadvantaged workers, 11–025
  meaning, 11–023
  training aid, 11–024
State Aid Action Plan 2005,
  11–003
statistics, 11–028
structure, 11–005
supervision, 11–015
training, 11–024
transparency, 11–010, 11–014

General Block Exemption Regulation—*cont.*
use of regulation, 11–028
Germany
coal industry, 14–027, 14–028
reunification, 4–008—4–010,
  8–079—8–080
Guarantees
amount of aid, 9–022—9–024
assessment of compatibility, 9–025
comfort letters, 9–009
current position, 9–001—9–005
express contractual guarantees,
  9–006
lenders, 9–021
market economy investor principle,
  9–001
non-notification, 9–005,
  9–026—9–028
Notice on Guarantees,
  9–001—9–004, 9–010
notification, 9–026—9–028
operation of law, 9–007
safe harbour, 9–013—9–020
state resources, 9–009
state shareholdings, 9–009
swap agreements, 9–006
Temporary Framework,
  9–029—9–032
types covered, 9–006—9–010
Harmonisation
tax
  imputation, 3–035
Health
taxation as an aid, 10–024
Iceland
accession negotiations,
  5–024—5–028
Imputation
energy, 20–025—20–028
generally, 3–028—3–035
harmonised tax, 3–035
Indirect taxes
art.107(1) TFEU, 3–128—3–132
energy, 20–001

Infrastructure
airports, 3–073—3–074
broadband, 3–069, 3–070
financial support
airports, 3–073—3–074
generally, 3–058
market-investor principle, 3–067
public-private partnerships,
3–066
services of general interests,
3–068
introduction, 3–058
market-investor principle, 3–067
public-private partnerships, 3–066
services of general interests, 3–068
training support, 3–057
Inland waterways
application of rules,
17–041—17–042
Insolvency proceedings
recovery of aid, 26–014
Insurance premiums
agriculture, 13–029
Intangible assets
market economy investor test,
3–099—3–101
Inter-state effect
de minimis Regulation, 3–079
distortion of competition, 3–080
energy, 20–040
generally, 3–076—3–077
Interested parties
introduction, 25–007
rights, 25–053—25–056
Interim measures
actions, 27–042—27–047
procedure, 25–067
Internal market
agriculture
Accession Treaties,
13–009—13–011
generally, 13–003—13–006

International trade
General Agreement on Tariffs and
Trade
generally, 6–001—6–003
WTO Agreement on Agriculture,
6–022—6–025
WTO Agreement on Subsidies and
Countervailing Measures 1994
categories of subsidy,
6–009—6–011
definition of subsidy,
6–05—6–07
definition of a subsidy,
6–005—6–007
developing countries, 6–020
Doha Rules, 6–021
double remedies, 6–017
EC implementing regulation,
6–027—6–028
generally, 6–004
remedies, 6–012—6–016
specificity, 6–008
TFEU state aid control
compared, 6–029, 6–030
WTO General Agreement on Trade
in Services, 6–026
Investment aid
General Block Exemption
Regulation, 11–016
measures, 4–051
overview
generally, 21–013
Guidelines (2007–2013), 21–030
regional aid, 21–026—21–027
schemes, 4–052
Judicial protection
see **Enforcement**
Judicial review
locus standi, 1–027—1–030
scope, 1–026
Legitimate expectations
recovery of aid, 26–017—26–020
Liquidation
rescue aid, 24–022

Liquidity
banks, 19–008—19–013
financial institutions, 19–046
rescue aid, 24–020
Loans
rescue aid, 24–020
Locus standi
judicial review, 1–027—1–030
Maritime transport
see **Shipping**
Market economy investor test
capital injections for publicly
owned firms, 3–082—3–083
concomitance, 3–084—3–085
energy, 20–036—20–038
guarantees, 9–001
introduction, 3–081
private creditor test, 3–089—3–092
private participation,
3–084—3–085
private purchaser test
introduction, 3–102
private seller test, 3–093—3–098
public sector
generally, 8–018—8–021
securitisation, 8–022
public undertakings, 3–086—3–088
regulatory powers, 8–023
sale of intangible assets,
3–099—3–101
state shareholdings, 3–082—3–083
Measures having equivalent effect
taxation as an aid, 10–004
Mergers
art.107(1) TFEU, 3–121—3–122
Military goods
art.107(1) TFEU, 3–133
Mining
taxation as an aid, 10–006
Monitoring
see **Supervision**
Motor industry
Temporary Framework, 4–029

Multimodal transport
application of rules,
17–046—17–048
National insurance contributions
selectivity criteria, 3–054
taxation as an aid, 10–006
**"Nature or general scheme of a
tax"**
abolition of tax, 10–019, 10–20
general measures of economic
policy, 10–025
international tax rules,
10–030—10–031
introduction of taxes,
10–019—10–020
normal tax rate, 10–029
reduction of tax, 10–019, 10–020
regulatory taxation, 10–024
scope of general scheme,
10–021—10–023
selectivity of tax incentives,
10–025—10–031
specific implementation,
10–026—10–028
Notification
formal procedure, 25–031—25–036
General Block Exemption
Regulation, 11–011
guarantees, 9–026—9–028
introduction, 25–020
large investment projects, 15–006
new aid, 25–021—25–024
preliminary procedure,
25–027—25–030
public sector, 8–026—8–030
regional aid
Guidelines (1998), 21–011
Guidelines (2007–2013), 21–034
restructuring aid, 24–034
simplified procedure, 25–025,
25–026
withdrawal, 25–040—25–041
OECD
shipbuilding, 16–015—16–017

Operating aid
environmental aid, 22–051, 22–052
generally, 4–050
regional aid, 21–032
Para-fiscal charges
see **Indirect taxes**
Pharmaceutical industry
conclusion, 12–021
environmental protection,
12–014—12–015
generally, 12–011—12–012
introduction, 12–008—12–009
research and development,
12–016—12–017
Plant diseases
agriculture, 13–028
Polluter pays
environmental aid, 22–003
Ports
generally, 17–057—17–060
Privatisation
see also **Public sector**
conditions for approval,
8–074—8–078
energy, 20–001
generally, 8–067—8–073
German reunification,
8–079—8–080
rescue aid, 24–008—24–010
restructuring aid, 24–008—24–010
Procedure
application of Art.108 TFEU,
25–001
case management,
25–063—25–066
common provisions
case handling within
Commission,
25–063—25–066
professional secrecy, 25–060
publication of decisions,
25–061—25–062
compatibility, 25–004
confidentiality, 25–060
definitions, 25–013

Procedure—*cont.*
direct effect, 25–004—25–006
EEA Agreement
introduction, 25–068—25–072
supremacy of law,
25–073—25–074
existing aid
definition, 25–014
generally, 25–014—25–019
schemes, 25–049—25–052
final decisions, 25–067
formal procedure, 25–031—25–036
interested parties
introduction, 25–007
rights, 25–053—25–056
interim orders, 25–067
introduction, 25–001—25–003
misuse of aid, 25–046—25–048
monitoring, 25–057—25–059
new aid, 25–014—25–019
notification
withdrawal, 25–040—25–041
notified new aid, 25–021—25–024
formal procedure,
25–031—25–036
introduction, 25–020
preliminary procedure,
25–027—25–030
procedural regime
existing aid, 25–014—25–019
introduction, 25–013
new aid, 25–014—25–019
notified new aid,
25–020—25–024
publication of decisions,
25–061—25–062
revocation of decision, 25–041
standstill clause
generally, 25–037—25–039
introduction, 25–004
supervision
introduction, 25–008
system of rules, 25–007—25–012
unlawful aid, 25–042—25–045

Proportionality
rescue aid, 24–023
research and development aid,
    23–027
restructuring aid, 24–035
Public private partnerships
infrastructure, 3–066
Public procurement
principles, 8–008, 8–009
Public sector
art.106(2)
    generally, 8–025
    notification exemption,
        8–026—8–030
    post-*Altmark practice*,
        8–030—8–036
    public services, 8–037
art.107 TFEU, 8–024
assessment, 8–045, 8–046
cross-subsidisation
    cost allocation, 8–055—8–066
    generally, 8–051—8–052
    internal subsidisation,
        8–053—8–054
framework for aid, 8–042—8–044
generally, 8–001—8–004, 8–037
inefficiencies, 8–047
market economy investor test
    generally, 8–018—8–021
    regulatory powers, 8–023
    securitisation, 8–022
overcompensation, 8–047
privatisation
    conditions for approval,
        8–074—8–078
    generally, 8–067—8–073
    German reunification,
        8–079—8–080
public procurement, 8–008, 8–009
public service obligations, 8–008
public services
    assessment, 8–045, 8–046
    framework for aid,
        8–042—8–044
    generally, 8–037

Public sector—*cont.*
public services—*cont.*
    inefficiencies, 8–047
    overcompensation, 8–047
    reform of Monti Package, 8–050
    relationship between Art.106(2)
        and Altmark, 8–049
    reserves, 8–048
    threshold, 8–038—8–041
public undertaking, 8–005—8–007
services of general economic
    interest, 8–008
services of general interest, 8–008
surveillance, 8–015—8–017
threshold, 8–038—8–041
transparency, 8–015—8–017
Public sector aid
Commission consultation, 1–018
Monti package, 1–017
Public service broadcasting
diversification, 18–009
entrustment, 18–004
financial control, 18–008
financing, 18–002
funding, 18–005
introduction, 18–002
overcompensation, 18–007
proportionality, 18–010
public service remit, 18–003
supervision, 18–004
transparency, 18–006
Public services
public sector, 8–008
transport, 17–004—17–011
Public undertakings
aid granted by undertaking, 8–013,
    8–014
concept, 8–005—8–007
generally, 8–001—8–004
market economy investor test,
    3–086—3–088
public sector, 8–005—8–007
undertaking, 8–010—8–012

Publication
Commission decisions
procedure, 25–061—25–062
Railways
application of rules,
17–035—17–040
development of sector, 17–025
Recovery of aid
Commission's power,
26–009—26–012
general principles, 26–013
insolvency proceedings, 26–014
introduction, 26–001—26–002
judicial protection, 27–002
legitimate expectations,
26–017—26–020
member states, 26–013—26–020
overview, 1–035—1–037
recoverable aid, 26–003—26–004
rules, 26–005—26–008
third party actions,
26–021—26–022
transfer of shares or assets,
26–014—26–016
Recovery of tax
taxation as an aid, 10–016
"Refined economic approach"
balancing test, 2–033—2–040
generally, 1–011
levels of assessment,
2–034—2–037
main features, 2–033—2–040
negative assessment, 2–039
positive assessment, 2–038
Regional aid
accession states, 21–012
ad hoc aid, 21–018
aid schemes, 21–018
art.107(1) TFEU, 4–053
art.107(3)(a) TFEU
aid intensity, 21–022
generally, 21–003
regions, 21–020
art.107(3)(c) TFEU
aid intensity, 21–025

Regional aid—*cont.*
art.107(3)(c) TFEU—*cont.*
generally, 21–004
regions, 21–023—21–024
co-ordination of systems, 21–005
compatibility, 21–003—21–004
definition, 21–001
demarcation of regions
Guidelines (1998), 21–008
Guidelines (2007–2013), 21–019
eligible expenses
investment costs, 21–028
wage costs, 21–029
energy
art.107(3)(a), 20–044—20–050
art.107(3)(c), 20–051
enterprise aid, 21–033
General Block Exemption
Regulation, 11–017
generally, 15–001—15–003
Guidelines (1998)
aid maps, 21–011
demarcation of regions, 21–008
introduction, 21–006
notification of schemes, 21–011
permissible forms of aid,
21–009—21–010
scope, 21–007
Guidelines (2007–2013)
ad hoc aid, 21–018
aid schemes, 21–018
application, 21–035
art.107(3)(a) regions,
21–020—21–022
art.107(3)(c) regions,
21–023—21–025
background, 21–014—21–016
cumulation, 21–031
demarcation of regions, 21–019
eligible expenses,
21–028—21–029
enterprise aid, 21–033
general, 21–023—21–024
investment aid, 21–026—21–027

Regional aid—*cont.*
Guidelines (2007–2013)—*cont.*
large investment projects aid,
21–030
notification, 21–034
operating aid, 21–032
procedure, 21–034
regional aid maps, 21–034
review, 21–035
scope of application, 21–017
statistical effect regions, 21–021
transparency, 21–035
intensity
art.107(3)(a), 21–022
discretionary exemptions
facilitation of development of
certain economic
activities or areas,
21–025
regional aid
art.107(3)(c), 21–025
severely-depressed regions,
21–022
introduction
compatibility, 21–003—21–004
definition, 21–001
regional selectivity, 21–002
investment aid, 21–026—21–027
large investment projects
application of rules,
15–025—15–034
approval, 15–012
capacity increase, 15–011
definition, 15–004
empirical evidence,
15–025—15–034
formal investigation,
15–013—15–024
Guidelines (2007–2013), 21–030
in-depth assessment, 15–009,
15–013—15–024
market share test, 15–010,
15–011
notification, 15–006

Regional aid—*cont.*
large investment projects—*cont.*
preliminary investigation phase,
15–007, 15–008
standard compatibility criteria,
15–008
transparency, 15–005
multisectoral frameworks 1998 and
2002, 21–013
notification
Guidelines (1998), 21–011
Guidelines (2007–2013), 21–034
operating aid, 21–032
other areas, 21–004
procedure, 21–034
regional aid maps, 21–034
regional selectivity, 21–002
severely-depressed regions
aid intensity, 21–022
energy, 20–044—20–050
generally, 21–003
overview, 4–019—4–022
regions, 21–020
shipbuilding, 16–025
specificity test, 21–002
statistical effect regions, 21–021
transparency, 21–035
underdeveloped areas
generally, 21–003

Regions
see also **Regional aid**
demarcations
Guidelines (1998), 21–008
Guidelines (2007–2013), 21–019

Reinvestment relief
taxation as an aid, 10–011

Renewable energy
energy, 20–001
environmental aid,
22–053—22–071

Rescue aid
acceptable reasons for grant,
24–018
appropriate measures, 24–052
background, 24–002

Rescue aid—*cont.*
  banks, 19–018
  Commission decisions
    examples, 24–004—24–007
    generally, 24–003
  compatibility, 24–019
  conclusion, 24–053
  conditions for authorisation
    liquidation plan, 24–022
    liquidity support, 24–020
    loan guarantees or loans, 24–020
    "one time last time",
      24–024—24–026
    proportionality, 24–023
    restructuring plan, 24–022
    serious social difficulties,
      24–021
  elements
    acceptable reasons for grant,
      24–018
    compatibility, 24–019
    "firm in difficulty",
      24–015—24–016
    introduction, 24–013
    "r&r aid", 24–017
  energy
    conditions for approval, 20–055
    introduction, 20–054
    "firm in difficulty",
      24–015—24–016
  guidelines (2004)
    acceptable reasons for grant,
      24–018
    background, 24–002
    compatibility, 24–019
    elements, 24–013—24–019
    "firm in difficulty",
      24–015—24–016
    interpretation, 24–012
    introduction, 24–013
    "r&r aid", 24–017
    scope, 24–014
  introduction, 24–001—24–002
  liquidation plan, 24–022
  liquidity support, 24–020

Rescue aid—*cont.*
  loan guarantees or loans, 24–020
  "one time last time",
    24–024—24–026
  privatisation, 24–008—24–010
  proportionality, 24–023
  "r&r aid", 24–017
  recipients of previously unlawful
    aid, 24–050
  reporting, 24–049
  restructuring plan, 24–022
  serious social difficulties, 24–021
  simplified procedure, 24–048
  small and medium-sized
    enterprises, 24–045—24–047
  steel industry, 14–062—14–064
  supervision, 24–049
  undertakings, 24–011
Research and development aid
  agriculture, 13–031
  balancing test, 23–004, 23–029
  block exemption, 23–005
  compatibility, 23–008
  conclusions, 23–030
  detailed assessment
    criteria, 23–024, 23–025
    distortion of competition,
      23–028
    effects-based analysis, 23–023
    generally, 23–005, 23–022
    incentive effect, 23–026
    proportionality, 23–027
  distortion of competition, 23–028
  effects-based approach, 23–005
  Europe 2020 strategy, 23–002
  fiscal aid, 23–011
  Framework
    balancing test, 23–004
    detailed assessment,
      23–022—23–029
    generally, 23–001
    matching clause, 23–007
    measures, 23–003
    mid-term review, 23–034

Research and development aid—*cont.*
Framework—*cont.*
standard assessment,
23–012—23–021
General Block Exemption
Regulation, 11–022, 23–005
incentives, 23–013
indirect aid, 23–010
innovation advisory services,
23–019
innovation aid, 23–015—23–021
innovation clusters, 23–021
innovation support services,
23–019
loan of highly qualified personnel,
23–020
matching clause, 23–007
policy background, 23–002
process and organisational
innovation in services, 23–018
projects of common European
interest, 23–006
proportionality, 23–027
public funding of research
organisations, 23–009
reporting obligations, 23–031
small and medium-sized
enterprises, 23–016
standard assessment
generally, 23–012
incentives, 23–013
innovation aid, 23–015—23–021
projects, 23–014
statistics, 23–032
three-part test, 23–004
young innovative enterprises,
23–017

Restructuring aid
acceptable reasons for grant,
24–018
agriculture, 24–051
air transport, 17–065—17–072
appropriate measures, 24–052
art.106(2) TFEU, 24–043

Restructuring aid—*cont.*
art.107(2) TFEU, 24–044
art.108(1) TFEU, 24–052
assisted areas, 24–031
background, 24–002
banks, 19–019—19–030
Commission decisions
banks, 19–019—19–030
examples, 24–004—24–007
generally, 24–003
compatibility, 24–019
compensatory measures,
24–038—24–040
conclusion, 24–053
conditions for authorisation
art.106(2) TFEU, 24–043
art.107(2) TFEU, 24–044
assisted areas, 24–031
compensatory measures,
24–038—24–040
contribution from beneficiary,
24–036—24–037
financial institutions,
19–071—19–075
implementation of plan, 24–042
notification, 24–034
proportionality, 24–035
restoration of long-term viability,
24–027
restructuring plan,
24–028—24–030
small and medium-sized
enterprises, 24–032
social costs, 24–033
specific conditions, 24–041
contribution from beneficiary,
24–036—24–037
elements
acceptable reasons for grant,
24–018
compatibility, 24–019
"firm in difficulty",
24–015—24–016
introduction, 24–013
"r&r aid", 24–017

Restructuring aid—*cont.*

energy
  conditions for approval, 20–056
  introduction, 20–054
financial institutions
  adequate remuneration, 19–041
  better fortunes clause, 19–043
  burden sharing, 19–042, 19–062
  clawback, 19–043
  discrimination, 19–040
  distortion of competition,
    19–044, 19–063—19–070
  distressed banks, 19–038
  emergency aid, 19–037
  financial crisis, 19–032—19–034
  fundamentally sound banks,
    19–038
  general aid schemes, 19–039
  generally, 19–058
  legal basis, 19–035, 19–036
  long-term viability,
    19–059—19–061
  measures falling outside
    Art.107(1) TFEU, 19–045
  moral hazard, 19–042
  standard conditions,
    19–071—19–075
  supervision, 19–076
"firm in difficulty",
  24–015—24–016
guidelines (2004)
  acceptable reasons for grant,
    24–018
  background, 24–002
  compatibility, 24–019
  elements, 24–013—24–019
  "firm in difficulty",
    24–015—24–016
  interpretation, 24–012
  introduction, 24–013
  "r&r aid", 24–017
  scope, 24–014
introduction, 24–001—24–002
notification, 24–034
privatisation, 24–008—24–010

Restructuring aid—*cont.*

proportionality, 24–035
"r&r aid", 24–017
recipients of previously unlawful
  aid, 24–050
reporting, 24–049
restoration of long-term viability,
  24–027
restructuring plan
  amendments, 24–029—24–030
  generally, 24–028
  implementation, 24–042
simplified procedure, 24–048
small and medium-sized
  enterprises
  conditions for authorisation,
    24–032
  generally, 24–045—24–047
  social costs, 24–033
specific conditions, 24–041
steel industry, 14–062—14–064
supervision, 24–049
undertakings, 24–011
Reunification
exemptions, 4–008—4–010
privatisation, 8–079—8–080
Revocation
procedure, 25–041
Risk management
agriculture, 13–025
Road transport
see **Carriage by road**
Roll-over relief
taxation as an aid, 10–011
Romania
coal industry, 14–075—14–078
existing aid, 5–021
generally, 5–020—5–021
interim measures, 5–021
introduction, 5–001, 5–020—5–021
postponement clause, 5–020
steel industry, 14–075—14–078
steel sector, 5–022, 5–023
Rural areas
agriculture, 13–006—13–008

Safe harbour
guarantees, 9–013—9–020
Sectoral aid
see also **Coal industry**; **Steel industry**; **Transport**
agricultural products
Accession Treaties,
13–009—13–011
common market organisation,
13–003—13–006
fisheries, 13–042—13–049
forestry, 13–035—13–036
introduction, 13–001
rural development,
13–006—13–008
state aid compatibility,
13–012—13–041
broadcasting
financing digital switchover,
18–012—18–018
introduction, 18–001
public service broadcasting,
18–002—18–011
chemical industry
conclusion, 12–021
environmental protection,
12–014—12–015
generally, 12–011—12–012
introduction, 12–008—12–009
miscellaneous, 12–018—12–020
research and development,
12–016—12–017
Commission Communication
(1978)
application, 12–008—12–010
chemical industry,
12–011—12–021
criteria, 12–003
generally, 12–004—12–007
overview, 12–001—12–002
pharmaceutical industry,
12–011—12–021
criteria, 12–003
financing digital switchover,
18–012—18–018

Sectoral aid—*cont.*
introduction, 12–001—12–002
operating aid, 12–007
pharmaceutical industry
conclusion, 12–021
environmental protection,
12–014—12–015
miscellaneous, 12–018—12–020
research and development,
12–016—12–017
public service broadcasting
diversification, 18–009
entrustment, 18–004
funding, 18–005
introduction, 18–002
net cost principle, 18–007
overcompensation, 18–007
proportionality, 18–010
public service remit, 18–003
transparency, 18–006
shipbuilding
EC Regulation, 16–003—16–004
external aspect,
16–011—16–027
introduction, 16–001—16–002
new framework,
16–005—16–010
OECD negotiations,
16–015—16–017
recent decisions,
16–018—16–027
temporary defence mechanism,
16–011—16–014
steel
ECSC Treaty regime,
14–002—14–004
introduction, 14–001
Services of general economic interest
infrastructure, 3–068
public sector, 8–008
Shares
guarantees, 9–008
market economy investor test,
3–082—3–083

Shipbuilding
background, 16–001
discretionary exemption, 16–005
EC Regulation, 16–003—16–004
external aspect
OECD negotiations,
16–015—16–017
recent decisions,
16–018—16–027
temporary defence mechanism,
16–011—16–014
introduction, 16–001—16–002
new framework, 16–005—16–010
OECD negotiations,
16–015—16–017
recent decisions
civil production, 16–027
IZAR, 16–020—16–021
Kvaerner Warnow Werft,
16–018—16–019
matching, 16–024
military production, 16–027
regional aid, 16–025
ship financing, 16–026
three-year delivery limits,
16–022—16–023
sectoral aid
EC Regulation, 16–003—16–004
external aspect,
16–011—16–027
introduction, 16–001—16–002
new framework,
16–005—16–010
temporary defence mechanism,
16–011—16–014
Shipping
Commission's practice,
17–055—17–056
introduction, 17–049
legislation, 17–050—17–054
Slovakia
coal industry, 14–074

**Small and medium-sized
enterprises**
agriculture
fisheries, 13–045—13–046
General Block Exemption
Regulation, 11–020
rescue aid, 24–045—24–047
research and development aid,
23–016
restructuring aid
conditions for authorisation,
24–032
generally, 24–045—24–047
SMEs
See **Small and medium-sized
enterprises**
"Social aid"
General Block Exemption
Regulation
disabled workers, 11–026
disadvantaged workers, 11–025
meaning of social aid, 11–023
training aid, 11–024
Social impact
restructuring aid, 24–033
"Soft law measures"
introduction, 1–038—1–042
State aid
access to information, 1–034
accession states
Accession Treaty 2003,
5–004—5–006
agriculture, 5–018—5–019
Bulgaria, 5–020—5–023
Croatia, 5–024—5–028
Europe Agreements,
5–002—5–003
Iceland, 5–024—5–028
introduction, 5–001
Romania, 5–020—5–023
steel industry, 5–014—5–017,
5–022, 5–023
transport, 5–018—5–019
art.107 framework
attributes, 3–015—3–039

State aid—*cont.*
  art.107 framework—*cont.*
    effect on trade, 3–076—3–077
    general, 3–001—3–010
    infrastructure, 3–058—3–069
    selectivity criteria,
      3–040—3–069
    state participation,
      3–081—3–107
  attributes of an aid
    community resources,
      3–036—3–039
    imposition of a cost to the state,
      3–022—3–026
    imputation, 3–028—3–035
    introduction, 3–015
    public control over private
      resources, 3–027
    revenue foregone, 3–021
    state resources, 3–016—3–027
    transfer of state resources, 3–020
  balancing test
    overview, 1–011
  banks, 1–013, 1–014
  detailed assessment
    overview, 1–011
  economics
    assessment of effects,
      2–017—2–023
    conclusions, 2–041—2–043
    design of effective and efficient
      policies, 2–024—2–032
    introduction, 2–001—2–003
    rationale, 2–004—2–007
    supranational control,
      2–008—2–016
  Europe 2020 Strategy, 1–016
  financial institutions,
    1–012—1–014
  governance, 1–031—1–032
  introduction, 1–001—1–009
  major developments,
    1–009—1–032
  procedure
    definition, 25–014

State aid—*cont.*
  procedure—*cont.*
    generally, 25–014—25–019
    schemes, 25–049—25–052
  public policy, 2–004—2–007
  rationale, 2–004—2–007
  refined economic approach, 1–011
  refining concept of aid, 1–025
  reorientation of provisions,
    1–043—1–044
  standard assessment, 1–011
  three-tiered system, 1–011
  timeframes, 1–019—1–023
  unlawful aid
    general concept,
      26–003—26–004
    introduction, 26–001—26–002
    procedure, 25–042—25–045
    types, 26–001
State Aid Action Plan 2005
  adoption, 1–009, 1–010
  economics
    generally, 2–002
  General Block Exemption
    Regulation, 11–003
  introduction, 1–001
  less aid, 1–015
  procedural reforms, 1–035
  scope of art.107(1), 3–003
"State participation"
  capital injections for publicly
    owned firms, 3–082—3–083
  concomitance, 3–084—3–085
  energy, 20–036—20–038
  introduction, 3–081
  private creditor test, 3–089—3–092
  private participation,
    3–084—3–085
  private purchaser test
    introduction, 3–102
  private seller test, 3–093—3–098
  public undertakings, 3–086—3–088
  sale of intangible assets,
    3–099—3–101
  state shareholdings, 3–082—3–083

Steel industry
Accession States, 14–065—14–079
Bulgaria, 5–022, 5–023
closure aid, 14–062, 14–063
conclusions, 14–080
Czech Republic, 14–068
ECSC Treaty, 14–001—14–008
introduction, 14–001
Poland, 14–069—14–073
post-December 31st 2002, 14–060,
  14–061
pre-December 31st 2002,
  14–052—14–059
rescue aid, 14–062—14–064
restructuring aid, 14–062—14–064
Romania, 14–075—14–078
Salzgitter case, 14–056—14–059
Slovakia, 14–074
Turkey, 14–079
Stranded costs
Commission decisions,
  20–060—20–075
Greece, 20–064, 20–065
introduction, 20–057—20–059
Ireland, 20–066, 20–067
Italy, 20–068
Luxembourg, 20–069
Netherlands, 20–070, 20–071
Portugal, 20–072
Slovenia, 20–073
Spain, 20–074
UK, 20–075
Subsidies
cost allocation, 8–055—8–066
energy, 20–094—20–095
generally, 8–051—8–052
internal subsidisation,
  8–053—8–054
**Subsidies and Countervailing
  Measures Agreement 1994**
categories of subsidies,
  6–009—6–011
definition of subsidy,
  6–005—6–007
developing countries, 6–021

**Subsidies and Countervailing
  Measures Agreement
  1994**—*cont.*
Doha Rules, 6–021
double remedies, 6–017—6–019
EC implementing regulation,
  6–027—6–028
generally, 6–004
specificity, 6–008
TFEU state aid control compared,
  6–029, 6–030
Supervision
de minimis, 7–009
financial institutions, 19–076
General Block Exemption
  Regulation, 11–015
generally, 25–008
procedure, 25–057—25–059
public service broadcasting,
  18–004
rescue aid, 24–049
restructuring aid, 24–049
Sustainable development
environmental aid, 22–002
Swap agreements
guarantees, 9–006
Tariffs
preferential tariffs
  energy, 20–089—20–093
Tax
abolition of taxes,
  10–019—10–020
application of Art.107(1) TFEU
  general, 10–006
  infra-state entities,
    10–007—10–008
  legal changes, 10–010
  revenue effect of tax provision,
    10–009
  state entities, 10–007
  tax advantage, 10–011—10–015
capital duty, 10–006
collection of outstanding tax debt,
  10–016
consumption taxes, 10–003

Tax—*cont.*
customs duties, 10–004
discrimination, 10–012
energy policy, 22–010
energy products, 20–028
environmental aid, 22–005,
    22–090—22–095
environmental taxes, 10–024
exceptional tax benefit, 10–011
exceptional tax burden, 10–013
free movement principles, 10–004
general measures of economic
    policy, 10–005, 10–025
generally, 10–001—10–002
green taxes, 10–024
harmful tax competition,
    10–041—10–042
health-related taxes, 10–024
infra-state entities,
    10–007—10–008
international tax rules,
    10–030—10–031
introduction of taxes,
    10–019—10–020
investment allowances or credits,
    10–011
legal changes, 10–010
legal framework
    cross-border trade, 10–004
    discrimination, 10–004
    fiscal federalism, 10–003
    national sovereignty, 10–003
measures having equivalent effect,
    10–004
mining royalties, 10–006
misapplication of tax law, 10–014
"nature or general scheme of a
    tax"
    general measures of economic
        policy, 10–025
    international tax rules,
        10–030—10–031
    introduction of taxes,
        10–019—10–020
    normal tax rate, 10–029

Tax—*cont.*
"nature or general scheme of a
    tax"—*cont.*
    regulatory taxation, 10–024
    scope of general scheme,
        10–021—10–023
    selectivity of tax incentives,
        10–025—10–031
    specific implementation,
        10–026—10–028
negative aid, 10–013
normal tax rate, 10–029
overview
    direct taxes, 3–046—3–047
    introduction, 3–045
    "logic of the system" test,
        3–050
    regional measures, 3–052
    selective measures,
        3–048—3–049
preferential tax treatment,
    10–016—10–018
private investor test, 10–016
reduced rates, 10–011
reduction of taxes,
    10–019—10–020
regional tax
    de facto selectivity, 3–053
    geographical selectivity, 3–052
    material selectivity, 3–053
    selectivity criteria, 3–052
regulatory taxation, 10–024
reinvestment relief, 10–011
revenue effect of tax provision,
    10–009
road tolls, 10–006
roll-over relief, 10–011
selective incentives, 10–005
selectivity criteria, 3–048—3–049
selectivity or specificity of an aid
    beneficiaries, 10–033—10–034
    "certain undertakings or the
        production of certain
        goods", 10–035—10–037
    de facto selectivity, 10–038

Tax—*cont.*
 selectivity or specificity of an
  aid—*cont.*
  general, 10–032
 selectivity of tax incentives,
  10–025—10–031
 social security contributions,
  10–006
 state entities, 10–007
 tax advantage
  consideration by taxpayer,
   10–015
  exceptional tax benefit, 10–011
  exceptional tax burden, 10–013
  misapplication of tax law,
   10–014
  "nature or general scheme" of a
   tax, 10–019—10–031
  preferential tax treatment,
   10–016—10–018
 tax financing, 10–039—10–040
 tax holidays, 10–011
 tax incentives, 10–002
 tax-free reserves, 10–011
 taxation as an aid,
  10–019—10–020
 tobacco duty, 10–024
 transfer pricing, 10–011
 unfair instruments of tax
  competition, 10–001
 value added tax, 10–003
Tax competition
 taxation as an aid,
  10–041—10–042
Tax credits
 taxation as an aid, 10–011
"Temporary Framework"
 approvals, 4–026—4–062
 art.107 TFEU
  generally, 4–026
  individual decisions, 4–028
  motor industry, 4–029
  objectives, 4–026
  risk capital, 4–062
  technical adjustments, 4–027

"Temporary Framework"—*cont.*
 de minimis, 7–013
 environmental aid, 22–007
 guarantees, 9–029—9–032
 motor industry, 4–029
Terrorism
 air transport, 17–073
TFEU
 see **Treaty on the Functioning of
  the European Union**
Time limits
 de minimis, 7–007
Tobacco products
 taxation as an aid, 10–024
Tolls
 taxation as an aid, 10–006
Training
 General Block Exemption
  Regulation, 11–024
 infrastructure, 3–057
Transfer pricing
 taxation as an aid, 10–011
Transparency
 energy, 20–013
 General Block Exemption
  Regulation, 11–010
 large investment projects, 15–005
 public sector, 8–015—8–017
 regional aid, 21–035
Transport
 aid in accession states,
  5–018—5–019
 air transport, 17–061—17–085
  introduction, 17–061, 17–062
  legislation, 17–063—17–064
  restructuring aid,
   17–065—17–072
  rules, 17–061—17–085
  terrorism, 17–073
 airports
  application of rules,
   17–076—17–084
  financing, 17–080—17–083
  guidelines, 17–078—17–084
  introduction, 17–074—17–075

Transport—*cont.*
  airports—*cont.*
    Ryanair/Charleroi decision,
      17–076—17–077
    start-up aid, 17–084, 17–085
  application of rules
    air transport, 17–061—17–085
    airports, 17–076—17–084
    generally, 17–034
    inland waterways,
      17–041—17–042
    multimodal transport,
      17–046—17–048
    ports, 17–057—17–060
    railways, 17–035—17–040
    road transport, 17–043—17–045
    shipping, 17–049—17–073
  art.93 TFEU, 17–001
  art.96 TFEU, 17–001
  art.107(1) TFEU, 3–126
  conclusion, 17–086
  coordination, 17–014—17–016
  de minimis, 17–033
  discretionary exemption, 17–001
  inland transport
    secondary legislation,
      17–006—17–016
  inland waterways,
    17–030—17–032,
    17–041—17–042
  application of rules,
    17–041—17–042
  introduction, 17–001—17–005
  marine transport, 17–049—17–073
  multimodal transport,
    17–046—17–048
    application of rules,
      17–046—17–048
  overview, 17–002—17–005
  ports, 17–057—17–060
  PSO Regulation
    compensation, 17–023, 17–024
    overview, 17–017—17–019
    public service contracts,
      17–020—17–022

Transport—*cont.*
  public service obligations,
    17–004—17–011
  railways, 17–025—17–029,
    17–035—17–040
    application of rules,
      17–035—17–040
  road transport, 17–043—17–045
  secondary legislation,
    17–004—17–019
  public service obligations,
    17–004—17–011
  shipping
    Commission's practice,
      17–055—17–056
    introduction, 17–049
    legislation, 17–050—17–054
Treaties
  see also **Treaty on the
    Functioning of the European
    Union**
  World Trade Organisation
    Agriculture, 6–022—6–025
    background, 6–002—6–003
    general, 6–001
    General Agreement on Trade in
      Services, 6–026
    Subsidies and Countervailing
      Measures 1994,
      6–004—6–021, 6–029,
      6–030
    Trade in Services, 6–026
**Treaty on the Functioning of the
  European Union**
  art.11, 22–002
  art.101, 3–120
  art.106(2)
    generally, 8–025
    notification exemption,
      8–026—8–030
    post-*Altmark practice*,
      8–030—8–036
    public service compensation,
      8–037—8–050

Treaty on the Functioning of the European Union—*cont.*
art.107
  see also **Article 107 TFEU**
  exemptions, 4–001—4–062
  generally, 3–001—3–116
art.108, 3–001, 25–001
art.108(1), 24–052
art.108(2), 4–040—4–042,
    27–003—27–005
art.109, 3–001
art.191, 22–002
art.258, 27–003—27–005
art.263
  admissibility, 27–012—27–020
  complainants' position,
    27–022—27–036
  first phase decisions,
    27–022—27–025
  second phase decisions,
    27–026—27–036
  standard of review,
    27–026—27–030
art.265, 27–037—27–041
art.346, 3–133
arts 278/279, 27–042—27–047

Turkey
  coal industry, 14–079
  steel industry, 14–079
Undertakings
  selectivity criteria, 3–041
Value added tax
  taxation as an aid, 10–003
Waste management
  environmental aid, 22–075, 22–076
Weather
  agriculture, 13–027
Winding-up
  financial institutions, 19–077
Withdrawal
  notification
    procedure, 25–040—25–041
World Trade Organisation
  background, 6–002—6–003,
    6–022—6–025
  general, 6–001
  General Agreement on Trade in
    Services, 6–026
  Subsidies and Countervailing
    Measures 1994,
    6–004—6–021, 6–029, 6–030